D0458125

BURT FRANKLIN: BIBLIOGRAPHY & REFERENCE SERIES 374
Theatre & Drama Series 13

"THE STAGE" CYCLOPÆDIA

"THE STAGE" CYCLOPÆDIA

A Bibliography of Plays

An Alphabetical List of Plays and other Stage Pieces of which any record can be found since the commencement of the English Stage, together with Descriptions, Authors' Names, Dates and Places of Production, and other Useful Information, comprising in all nearly 50,000 Plays, and Extending Over a Period of Upwards of 500 Years

COMPILED BY

REGINALD CLARENCE

BURT FRANKLIN
NEW YORK

Published by LENOX HILL Pub. & Dist. Co. (Burt Franklin)
235 East 44th St., New York, N.Y. 10017
Originally Published: 1909
Reprinted: 1970
Printed in the U.S.A.

S.B.N.: 8337-05814
Library of Congress Card Catalog No.: 74-135176
Burt Franklin: Bibliography and Reference Series 374
Theatre and Drama Series 13

PREFACE

The object of the present work has been to compile an alphabetical list of plays, operas, oratorios, sketches, and other stage pieces of which any record can be found since the commencement of the English Stage, giving authors' names, dates of production, and recording important revivals. The entries have been corrected up to October 1, 1909.

It is nearly 100 years since the last book of the present kind was published, and it is obvious that the very large number of plays, operas, oratorios, sketches, etc., which have been produced during that period have made the work of compilation exceedingly heavy. The book referred to is "The Drama Recorded; or, Barker's List of Plays," a small volume of about 200 pages, published in 1814, and giving title, author's name, and date of publication of the plays referred to within its covers. Altogether, some 6.500 plays are mentioned, the particulars in all cases being of the briefest description. The present volume contains references to about 50,000 plays.

In order to make the Cyclopædia as comprehensive as possible, reference has been made to the works of the great Roman and Grecian authors, for it is to such masters as Plautus, Terence, Seneca, Aristophanes, Æschylus, Sophocles, Euripides, and others that the plots of some important plays can be traced. The works of these classic writers will be found in collective forms under the headings Greek Plays, Latin Plays, etc. References have also been made under the headings French Classical Plays, German Classical Plays, etc., to the works of Molière, Corneille, Gœthe, Schiller, Tasso, and other more modern geniuses, and our own Shakespeare has received serious attention.

Tragedy and Comedy both originated in Greece some 500 years B.C. The early Roman dramatic writers belonged to a little later period.

England was late in receiving the art. Geoffrey, a Frenchman by birth, an Abbot of St. Albans, introduced religious tragedies to his scholars about 1110 A.D. The first piece they acted was called "The Miracles of St. Catherine." After that date Mysteries and Miracle Plays were performed from time to time.

These representations were given in churches or on wooden moveable platforms raised in the market-places.

The most important of the Miracle Plays are the Chester Plays, the Coventry Plays, the Wakefield (Towneley) Plays, and the York Plays. Full particulars of these and other similar representations will be found under the heading Miracle Plays. In the year 1378 the scholars of St. Paul's School presented a petition to King Richard II. praying His Majesty to prohibit some persons from representing publicly the history of the Old Testament.

On July 18, 19, and 20, 1390, Interludes were played at Skinner's Well. The Chester Plays were performed between 1328 and 1577, and we again hear of their performance in 1600.

In 1535 a comedy called "Piscator; or, The Fisher Caught," was written by one John Hoker, but the first English comedy proper is generally acknowledged to have been "Ralph Roister Doister," by Nicholas Udall, in 1551. Another early comedy was "Gammer Gurton's Needle," written by Bishop Still about 1566, and printed in 1575.

The first English tragedy worthy of consideration was by Thomas Sackville, Lord Buckhurst, and called "Gorboduc" (although it is said that the first two acts were from the pen of Thomas Norton and the remaining two only were by Sackville). It was acted before Queen Elizabeth on January 18, 1562, and printed in 1565.

The first Italian comedy was Bajardo's "Timone," produced before 1494, but a pastoral drama by Agnolo Poliziano, entitled "Orfeo," had appeared in 1472. In that year also the first Spanish comedy was written. The first Italian opera is regarded by Sismondi to have been "Daphne," which dates from about 1594.

It may be mentioned that the first patent to act plays was granted by Queen Elizabeth, in 1574, to James Burbage, the father of the great tragedian, Richard Burbage, an actor in the Earl of Leicester's company.

The first theatre built was erected on the site of what is now Holywell Lane, Shoreditch. A lease was granted to James Burbage on April 13, 1576, and the building, costing between £600 and £700, was erected and opened a few months later. It was known as The Theatre, and it had but a short life. The ground landlord, in 1597, stated that he required the ground for other purposes, and the building was pulled down. The materials were removed to Bankside, Southwark, and there was erected The Globe.

But in the meantime other theatres had been built. The Curtain was erected in the same neighbourhood as The Theatre in 1577; The Hope, on Bankside, was built in 1585, but this was indeed a poor structure; The Rose, in the same district of Bankside, was opened in 1592, and The Blackfriars—the site of which is now covered by the office of the *Times* and Playhouse Yard—was built in 1596. It was at The Globe and The Blackfriars that the works of Shakespeare were first produced.

After that time theatres sprung up in different directions. The Theatre Royal, Drury Lane, was built in 1663, and the noted Lincoln's Inn Theatre was erected in 1672.

At the present time there are no fewer than fifty-nine theatres in London alone, and sixty-four variety theatres. In addition to these there are many other halls licensed for dramatic performances.

For the purposes of easy reference and research, care has been taken in the present work to give references and cross-references in cases where plays have been derived from novels or from other plays, and in other ways the Cyclopædia has been made as complete as possible.

In compiling this work, a task which has covered a period of upwards of twenty years, I have received valuable assistance from many sources, and I wish specially to acknowledge the information kindly supplied by Dr. Gow, the headmaster of Westminster School, and by Dr. Gray, of Bradfield College, Berkshire, where notable representations of Latin and Greek plays respectively are periodically given; also the services kindly rendered by the Librarians at the British Museum, Guildhall, and other libraries; the continuous and helpful work of my wife; the very valuable assistance rendered by Mr. L. Carson, Editor of The Stage; Mr. George Grahame, and Mr. Fred Grove, all of whom have contributed much useful information and practical help.

It may not be generally known that the library of the British Museum contains upwards of 600,000 playbills, carefully arranged and bound in 340 volumes. There are 170 volumes of London playbills, 167 volumes of provincial playbills, and three volumes containing foreign playbills. Liberal reference has been made to these and to many other smaller collections.

The lives of noted theatrical personages, the histories of our theatres, the numerous collections of plays and other dramatic works, have all received careful scrutiny, and it is from such sources that the information within these pages has been derived.

In dealing with such an enormous number of dates it is too much to expect the absence of errors, but every care has been taken to attain that accuracy and completeness which are necessary to ensure the usefulness and reliability of the information contained in a work of this description.

December 6, 1909. REGINALD CLARENCE.

SUBSCRIBERS.

A list of the subscribers to this work will be found on page 500.

ABBREVIATIONS

A=acts
Ac=acted
Adap.=adapted, adaptation
Add.=added, additional
Alt.=altered, alteration
Amat.=amateur
Arr.=arranged
Ascr.=ascribed
B.O.=ballad opera
Borr.=borrowed
Burl.=burlesque
Burla.=burletta
C.=comedy
C.D.=comic drama
C.G.=Covent Garden
C.O.=comic opera
(C.P.)=copyright performance
Ca.=comedietta
Cant.=cantata
Comp.=composed
D.=drama
D.L.=Drury Lane
Div.=divertissement
Dom.=domestic
Dr.=dramatic
Dram.=dramatised
Duol.=duologue
Eng.=English
Ent.=entertainment
Epi.=epilogue
Eq.=equestrian
Extrav.=extravaganza
F.=farce, farcical
f.=founded
Fr.=French
fr.=from
H.=hall
Hay.=Haymarket
H.M.=His Majesty's
Her M.=Her Majesty's
Hist.=historical, history
Hum.=humorous
Inc.=incident
Inst.=institute
Int.=interlude
K.=king
L.I.F.=Lincoln's Inn Fields
Lib.=libretto
Lic.=licensed
M.=music
M.C.=mu ical comedy
M.D.=musical drama
M.E.=musical ent.
M.F.=musical farce
M.H.=Music Hall
M.I.=musical interlude
M.P.=musical play
MS.=manuscript
Mat.=matinée
Melo-d.=melo-drama
Monol.=monologue
Mus.=musical
N.ac.=not acted
N.p.=not printed
N.publ.=not published
O.=opera
O.H.=Opera House
Oa.=operetta
Occ.=occasional
Op. bo.=Opera-Bouffe
Op. C.=Opera Comiqu
Orat.=oratorio
Orig.=original
P.=play
P.H.=public hall
P.O.W.=Prince of Wales
Pant.=pantomime
Pav.=pavilion
Perf.=performance, performed
Pl.=played
Pr.=printed
Prel.=prelude
Pro.=prologue
Prod.=produced
Publ.=published
Ps.=pseudonym
Q.=Queen
R.=rooms
Rev.=revival, revised
Rom.=romance, romantic
S.C.=serio-comic
Sacr.=sacred
Sat.=satirical
Sk.=sketch
Spec.=spectacle, spectacular
T.=tragedy
T.C.=tragi-comedy
T.H.=Town Hall
T.R.=Theatre Royal
Tab.=tableau
Tr.=transformed
Transl.=translated, translation
Trfd.=transferred
Unf.=unfinished
Unk.=unknown
V.=vaudeville
Ver.=version
Wr.=written

"THE STAGE" CYCLOPÆDIA

A Bibliography of Plays

A

A.B.C.; OR, FLOSSIE THE FRIVOLOUS, THE. M.P. 2 a. H. C. Newton. M. by Grabau, Gustave Chandon, and others. Wolverhampton Grand, March 21, 1898; Stratford Borough, May 2, 1898.

A BASSO PORTO. O. Spinelli. See *At the Harbour Side.*

A.D. 5005. M.C. Pro. 2 a. Tom Heffernon. M. by C. W. Nightingale. Ryde R., August 18, 1905.

A LA FRANCAISE. Piece. 1 a. A. O'D. Bartholeyne. Avenue, July 8, 1893.

A.S.S. F. 1 a. J. M. Maddox. Lyceum, April 23, 1853; Criterion, August 13, 1887.

ABAELLINO, THE GREAT BANDIT. P. fr. the German by Wm. Dunlap. New York, February 11, 1801. Pr. 1802.

ABANDONDINO THE BLOODLESS. D. H. J. Byron. Pub. by S. French, Ltd.

ABANDONED WOMAN, AN. D. 5 a. Miles Wallerton and Francis Gilbert. Newcastle-on-Tyne Palace, March 6, 1905.

ABBE CONSTANTIN, L'. C. 3 a. Hector Cremieux and Pierre Decourcelle. New York, 1888; Royalty, October 15, 1888; Shaftesbury, June 7, 1905.

ABBE DE L'EPEE; OR, DEAF AND DUMB, THE. P. Adap. by W. Dunlap fr. Fr. of Bouilly. New York, 1801.

ABBE VANDREUIL. D. Col. Addison. Lyceum, March 18, 1860.

ABDALLA. T. J. Delap. Pr. 1803. N. ac.

ABDALLAH. Spec. cant. by Alfred Gilbert. St. George's Hall, July 14, 1887.

ABDEKAN. O. Boieldieu. St. Petersburg, 1806.

ABDELAZER; OR, THE MOOR'S REVENGE. T. Mrs. Aphra Behn from Marlow's *Lust's Dominion.* Duke of York's, 1671. Pr. 1677. Dr. Young's *The Revenge* founded on this piece.

ABDICATED PRINCE; OR, THE ADVENTURES OF FOUR YEARS, THE. T.C. Anon. Pr. 1690. Whitehall, 1690.

ABDICATION OF FERDINAND; OR, NAPOLEON AT BAYONNE, THE. Hist. P. 5 a. Anon. Pr. 1809.

ABDUCTION OF BIANCA; OR, THE BRIGAND'S DOOM, THE. Absurdity. W. Sapte, jun., and Cecil M. York. Silver Fête, Kensington, July 11, 1888.

ABEL. Orat. Alfièri. C.G., 1755. Trans. by C. Lloyd, 1815.

ABEL. Orat. Dr. Arne. 1710-78.

ABEL, DEATH OF. See *Death of Abel.*

ABEL DRAKE. D. 5 a. Tom Taylor and John Saunders. Leeds T.R., October 9, 1874; Princess's, May 20, 1876.

ABEL DRAKE'S WIFE. D. Richmond H.M., January 25, 1872.

ABEL DRUGGER. Before 1776 Garrick played in this piece.

ABELARD AND HELOISE. D. 3 a. J. B. Buckstone, Surrey.

ABELAZOR. O. Purcell. London, 1677.

ABENCERAGES (LES). O. Cherubini. Paris, 1813.

ABIDING POWER OF LOVE, THE. Sk. Shoreditch Empire, Dec. 5, 1908.

ABIMELECH. Orat. Anon. Hay. Pr. 1760.

ABIMELECH. Orat. Arnold. 1739-1802.

ABODE OF LOVE, THE. Sk. 1 a. Dor Deane and Fred C. Brooke. Albert M.H., Canning Town, September 11, 1905.

ABON; OR, THE SLEEPER AWAKENED. Burl. by Joseph Tabrar. Coventry T.R., August 3, 1885.

ABON HASSAN. Mus. D. 2 a. M. by Von Weber. Darmstadt, 1810. Adap. to Eng. stage by Cooke. D.L., April 22, 1825.

ABON HASSAN; OR, AN ARABIAN KNIGHT'S ENTERTAINMENT. Burl. 1 a. Arthur O'Neil. Charing Cross. December 11, 1869.

ABON HASSAN; OR, THE HUNT AFTER HAPPINESS. Fairy Extrav. in rhyme. 1 a. Francis Talfourd. St. James's, December 26, 1854.

ABOUKIR BAY; OR, THE GLORIOUS FIRST OF AUGUST. Mus. D. Richard Sicklemore. Brighton. Pr. 1799.

ABOUT TOWN. C. 3 a. Arthur à Becket. Court, May 12, 1873.

ABOVE AND BELOW. C.D. 2 a. Edwd. Stirling. Lyceum, July 6, 1846.

ABOVE SUSPICION. D. 3 a. Geo. Capel. York T.R., May 19, 1882; Sadler's Wells, March 24, 1884.

ABRADATES AND PANTHEA. T. Roberts. Act. by Scholars of St. Paul's School, 1770, N.p. Taken from Xenophon.

ABRADATES AND PANTHEA. T. John Edward. Pr. 1808. Founded on story in Xenophon's Cyropædia.

ABRAHAM AND ISAAC. See "Miracle Plays."

ABRAHAM PARKER. P. Capt. Addison. Adelphi, July 20, 1846.

ABRAHAM'S FAITH. A "Divine Dialogue." Geo. Lesley. Pr. 1675.

ABRAHAM'S SACRIFICE. P. Trans. fr. Fr. of Theodore Beza by Arthur Golding. Pr. 1577.

ABRAHAM'S SACRIFICE. Cant. J. J. Haite. Hackney Manor R., December 8, 1868.

ABRAME AND LOT. In Henslowe's List of Plays acted by the Earl of Sussex's Servants, Jan. 9, 1593.

ABRA-MULE; OR, LOVE AND EMPIRE. T. Rev. Joseph Trapp. L.I.F. Pr. 1704.

ABREISE DIE. O. D'Albert. Modern German.

ABROAD AND AT HOME. C.O. 3 a. J. G. Holman. Music by Shield. C.G., November 10, 1796; D.L., May 28, 1822. Originally called *The King's Bench.*

ABSALOM. Orat. By C. R. 1764.

ABSALOM AND ACHITOPHEL. In 2 parts. Dryden.

ABSALON. T. Peele. 1590.

ABSALON. Latin T. John Watson; before 1598.

ABSCHIED VON REGIMENT. P. 1 a. Otto Eric Hartleben. Gt. Queen Street, December 12, 1904.

ABSENCE OF MIND; OR, WANTED £5. Ca. 1 a. Adap. fr. one of Kotzebue's German farces by Wm. Poel. Victoria T.; Olympic, July 11, 1884.

ABSENT APOTHECARY, THE. F. Smith. D.L., November 10, 1813. N.p.

ABSENT MAN, THE. F. 2 a. Isaac Bickerstaff. D.L., March 21, 1763. A hint of this piece taken from *La Bruyere.*

ABSENT MAN, THE. F. Thos. Hull. C.G., April 28, 1764. N.p.

ABSENT MAN, THE. F. Ca. 1 a. Geo. Roberts. Adap. fr. Fr. V., *Les Absences de Monsieur.* Holborn T., June 18, 1870.

ABSENT-MINDED BEGGAR; OR, FOR QUEEN AND COUNTRY, THE. M.D. 4 a. G. Arthur Shirley. Princess's, November 25, 1899.

ABSENT NYMPH; OR, THE DOATING SWAIN, THE. Mus. Int. Daniel Bellamy, sen. and jun. Pr. 1739.

ABSENT SON, THE. Burl. Adelphi. October 29, 1828.

ABSENT WITHOUT LEAVE. F. Strand, August 28, 1837.

ABSENTEE, THE. Court, July 3, 1908.

ABSOLUTION. Dr. inc. 1 a. Henry Murray. Glasgow T.R., April 8, 1892.

ABSURDITIES OF A DAY, THE. Skit on *Follies of a Night.* G. à Beckett.

ABU HASSAN. O. 1 a. Weber. Comp. 1810. D.L., May 12, 1870. See *Abon Hassan.*

ABUDAH; OR, THE TALISMAN OF OROMANES. Oriental Fairy Tale. 2 a. F. on one of "Tales of Genii." M. by Kelly and Cooke. D.L., April 13, 1819.

ABUSES. Contains C. and T. Ac. before Kings of Gt. Britain and Denmark in England July 30, 1606

ABYSSINIAN WAR, THE. D. 2 a. W. Travers, Britannia, June 1, 1868.

ACADEMIA DI MUSIA. 1 Act of. D.L., May 12, 1817.

ACADEMIE; OR, THE CAMBRIDGE DUNS, THE. C. J. Barnes. 1675.

ACANTE ET CEPHISE. O. 3 a. Rameau, Nov. 18, 1751.

ACCEPTED BY PROXY. Duol. Ellis Kingsley. Steinway Hall, June 8, 1893.

ACCOLASTUS.—See *Acolastus.*

ACCOMPLICES, THE. C. Goethe. About 1790.

ACCOMPLISHED MAID, THE. C.O. Edwd. Toms. Transl. of *La Buona Figliuola.* Pr. C.G., December 3, 1766.

ACCOMPLISHED RAKE, THE. C. Mentioned for sale in Mr. Barker's Catalogue. J. Shearman, 1799.

ACCOUNT RENDERED. Duol. W. B. D. Harrison and Beta Harrison. Collard's Rooms, London, July 6, 1894.

ACCUSATION; OR, THE FAMILY OF AUGLADE. P. 3 a. F. on hist. facts. J. Howard Payne. D.L., February 1, 1816.

ACCUSING SPIRIT; OR, THE THREE TRAVELLERS OF THE TYROL, THE. D. 3 a. W. E. Suter. Grecian, March 5, 1860.

ACE OF CLUBS. D. 5 a. Adap. by Arthur Shirley fr. Pierre Decourcelle's D., *L'As de Trèfle.* Pr. at Paris Ambigu, March 15, 1883; Darlington T.R., March 22, 1889.

ACE SOIR. Royalty, May 17, 1897.

ACHADEMIOS. C. John Skelton. Circ., 1523.

ACHARNIANS. C. (Greek.) B.C. 425 Aristophanes. Transl. by Mitchell, 1820-2; Hickie, 1853; Rudd. 1867. See "Greek Plays."

ACHILLE ET POLYZENE. O. Colasse. (An act by Lulli.) 1687.

ACHILLE IN SCIRO. O. Metastasio. 1736. M. by Leo. See "Italian Plays."

ACHILLES. O. 2 a. John Gay. C.G., February 10, 1733. Pr. 1733.

ACHILLES; OR, IPHIGENIA IN AULIS. T. Transl. fr. Racine's *Iphigénie* by Abel Boyer. Ac. Dec., 1699. D.L., 1702. Pr. 1700. Republ. under the title of *The Victim; or, Achilles and Iphigenia in Aulis,* 1714. Rev. at C.G., March 23, 1778, under title of *Iphigenia.*

ACHILLES IN PETTICOATS. O. Alt. fr. Gay by Geo. Colman. C.G., 1774.

ACHILLES IN SCYROS. O. Transl. from Metastasio by John Hoole. Pr. 1800.

ACHILLES IN SCYROS. O. Cherubini. Paris, 1804.

ACHILLES IN SCYROS. Greek masque. Alfred Austin. Leighton House, Holland Park Road, July 19, 1909.

ACI, GALATEA E POLIFEMO. Serenata. Handel. 1708.

ACIS AND GALATEA. O. Camistron. M. by Lulli. 1683.

ACIS AND GALATEA. O. Masque. Peter Motteux, from Ovid's *Metam.,* with the Mus. Ent. in an O., called *The Mad Lover.* D.L. and L.I.F. Pr. 1701.

ACIS AND GALATEA. An Ent. of Dancing. D.L., 1728.

ACIS AND GALATEA. Pastoral O. Handel. Perf. at Cannons, 1721. Words by Gay and additions by Pope, Hughes and Dryden. Rescored for Van Swieten November, 1788. D.L., June 20, 1838. O. 3 a. John Gay. Taken fr. Ovid's *Metamorphoses.* M. by Handel. King's T., June 10, 1732; pl. 1732; D.L., February 5, 1842.

ACIS AND GALATEA. A Dance. D.L., 1749. First appearance of Sig. Campioni.

ACIS AND GALATEA. O. Haydn. Vienna. C 1780.

ACIS AND GALATEA. Paraphrase. Oxberry. Pub. by S. French, Ltd.

ACIS AND GALATEA; OR, THE BEAU, THE BELLE, AND THE BLACKSMITH. Extrav. Thos. F. Plowman. Wr. for annual dram. Pfce. at Victoria T., Oxford, December, 1869.

ACIS AND GALATEA; OR, THE NIMBLE NYMPH AND THE TERRIBLE TROGLODYTE. Extrav. F. C. Burnand. Olympic, April 6, 1863.

ACOLASTUS. C. Dr. Palsgrave, probably the first dr. writer. Pr. 1540. Transl. fr. Wm. Fullonius' C., 1529.

ACROBAT, THE. D. 4 a. Adap. by Wilson Barrett from *Le Paillasse* of MM. D'Ennery and Marc Fournier—a ver. of *Belphegor*. New Olympic, April 21, 1891.

ACROBAT, THE. See *The Battle of Life*.

ACROSS HER PATH. P. 4 a. F. on Annie Swan's novel of same name, by Annie Irish. Terry's, January 21, 1890.

ACROSS THE CONTINENT. D. Pro. and 3 a. Jas. M'Closkey. Alfred, July 8, 1871.

ACROSTATION; OR, THE TEMPLAR'S STRATAGEM. F. Mr. Pilon. C.G., 1784.

ACT AT OXFORD, AN. C. Thos. Baker. 1704. N.ac. Afterwards called *Hampstead Heath.* and ac.

ACT OF FOLLY, AN. D. 4 a. Lewis B. Goldman. Basingstoke Drill Hall, June 7, 1887.

ACT OF PIRACY. F. 1 a. L. Montague. Publ. by S. French, Ltd.

ACTAEON AND DIANA. Int. R. Cox. Taken with the pastoral story of the Nymph Œnone fr. Ovid's *Metamorphoses*. Publ. 1656. 2 edit. ac. at The Red Bull.

ACTEON. O. Auber. Paris, 1836.

ACTING RUN MAD; OR, THE DUNSTABLE ACTOR. 1 a. Rev. Lyceum, December 26, 1835.

ACTING THE LAW. D. 5 a. Frank Harvey. Brentford T.R., September 29, 1890.

ACTION FOR BREACH, AN. P. 1 a. M. E. Francis (Prod. by the Argonauts). Rehearsal, November 13, 1908 (mat.).

ACTOR. See *Step-Brothers*.

ACTOR, THE. C. 3 a. T. Edgar Pemberton. Birmingham P.O.W., May 14, 1886.

ACTOR OF ALL WORK; OR, FIRST AND SECOND FLOOR, THE. Ca. G. Colman. Taken fr. the F. Hay, August 13, 1817.

ACTOR'S AL FRESCO. Mus. P. J. Blewett, T. Cooke, and C. E. Horn. 1823.

ACTOR'S ART, AN. C.Sk. J. L. Shine. Camberwell Empire, January 7, 1907.

ACTOR'S FROLIC, AN. M.C. 2 a. Guy Logan. M. by Dr. Storer. Clacton-on-Sea O.H., September 30, 1895.

ACTOR'S HONOUR, AN. C. 1 a. Harry Leader. Dublin T.R., July 20, 1903; Crouch End O.H., August 31, 1903.

ACTOR'S RETREAT, THE. F. 1 a. A. Halliday and W. Brough. Adelphi, August 11, 1864.

ACTOR'S ROMANCE. P. Theodore Kremer. Camden, February 8, 1904; Fulham Grand, August 8, 1904.

ACTORS' TERRITORIAL, THE. Sk. Sydney Blow and Douglas Hoare. Holloway Empire, August 2, 1909.

ACTOR'S WIFE, THE. Dom. D. 4 a. Adap. fr. his novel of the same title by Edmund Leathes. Manchester St. James's T., October 24, 1884.

ACTORS, THE. Sk. Hastings Hipp., October 26, 1908.

ACTRESS AT HOME, AN. P. 1 a. Kennington P.O.W., April 22, 1901.

ACTRESS BY DAYLIGHT, AN. P. St. James's, April, 1871.

ACTRESS OF ALL WORK, THE. P. 1 a. Strand, 1819; Lyceum, August 31, 1821; rev., D.L., October 17, 1823.

ACTRESS OF PADUA, THE. P. John Brougham. Taken fr. the "Angelo" of Victor Hugo. Hay., 1855.

ACTRESS'S HONOUR, AN. P. 1 a. J. P. Gore and A. Bell. Britannia, July 21, 1907. C.P., December 16, 1907.

ADAM. See "Miracle Plays."

ADAM; OR, THE FATAL DISOBEDIENCE. O. Richd. Jago. Fr. Milton's "Paradise Lost." Pr. 1784.

ADAM BEDE. D. 3 a. Adap. from Geo. Eliot's novel by J. E. Carpenter. Surrey, February 28, 1862.

ADAM BEDE. D. 4 a. Adap. by Howell Poole. Holborn T., The International, June 2, 1884.

ADAM BUFF; OR, THE MAN WITHOUT A SHIRT. F. 1 a. E. L. Blanchard. Surrey, March 4, 1850.

ADAMLESS EDEN, AN. C.O. M by Walter Slaughter. Lib. by H. Savile Clarke. Op. C., December 13, 1882.

ADDER IN THE PATH, AN. D. Glasgow P.O.W., July 3, 1871.

ADELA. T. Mrs. West. Pr. 1799. N.ac.

ADELA. O. 3 a. Wr. and comp. by J. H. Brown and T. L. Selby. Nottingham Mechanics', February 8, 1888.

ADELA. T.O. 3 a. Fredk. Tolkien. Wigan Court T., April 14, 1897.

ADELAIDA DI BORGOGNA. O. Rossini. Rome, 1818.

ADELAIDA E COMINGIO. O. Fioravante. Milan, 1810.

ADELAIDE. O. G. Cocchi, Rome, 1743.

ADELAIDE. T. Miss Alderson. Ac. at Private Theatre at Norwich, January 4, 1791.

ADELAIDE. T. Henry James Pye. D.L. Pr 1800.

ADELAIDE. T. 5 a. R. Shiel. 1814.

ADELAIDE. Dr. fragment. 1 a. Wm. Poel. Adap. fr. Dr. Hugo Muller's German P. of same name. V., July 5, 1887.

ADELAIDE. P. 1 a. Adap. fr. the German by Gustav Hein and David Bispham. Matinée T., June 20, 1898.

ADELAIDE DE BRABANT; OR, THE TRIUMPH OF VIRTUE. Dr. P. Probably only a ballet. C.G., 1784.

ADELAIDE DE PONTHIEU. C.G., 1794.

ADELAIDE DU GUESCLIN. T. Voltaire. 1734.

ADELAIDE OF WULFINGEN. T. 4 a. Fr. German of Thompson. Pr. 1801. N.ac.

ADELAZAR. C. Mrs. Behn. 1677.

ADELE ED EMERICO. O. Mercadante. Milan, 1822.

ADELFRID. Hist. Dr. Joseph Moser. Wr. in 1807. N.p.

ADELGITHA; OR, THE FRUITS OF A SINGLE ERROR. T. 5 a. M. G. Lewis. D.L., May 19, 1801; D.L., 1828. Pr. 1806.

ADELINA. C. Miss Hannah Brand. N.ac. Pr. 1798. An alt. of *La Force du Naturel* by Des Fouches.

ADELINE. M.D 3 a Alt. fr. the French of R. C. G. de Pixerécourt by Howard Payne. D.L., February 9, 1822.

ADELMORN THE OUTLAW. Rom. D. 3 a. M. E. Lewis. Prod. 1801. D.L., May 4, 1801.

ADELPHI. English transl. of Terence's C. (B.C. 160). Also called *Adelphi; or, the Brothers*. By Richard Bernard, 1598; Charles Hoole, 1663; Laurence Echard, 1694; Bentley, 1726; T. Cook, 1734; S. Patrick, 1745; Gordon, 1752; G. Colman, 1765; into blank verse, 1774; Barry, 1857. See "Latin Plays."

ADELPHI OF TERENCE, THE. Pl. by Westminster Scholars, St. Peter's College, Westminster. See Westminster Plays.

ADELSON E. SALVINA. O. Bellina. Naples, 1824.

ADHERBAL. T. Legrange. 1687.

ADINA, O IL CALIFFO DI BAGDAD. O. Rossini, Lisbon, 1818.

ADINA; OR, THE ELIXIR OF LOVE. English ver. of Donizetti's O., *L'Elisir d'Amore*. Liverpool R. Court, February 24, 1892.

ADMIRABLE BASHVILLE; OR, CONSTANCY UNREWARDED, THE. D. 2 tabl. G. Bernard Shaw. F. on his novel, "Cashel Byron's Profession." Imperial, June 8, 1903. Rev. H.M.T., January 26, 1909.

ADMIRABLE CRICHTON. T. G. Galloway. Prod. 1802.

ADMIRABLE CRICHTON, THE. F. D.L., June 12, 1820.

ADMIRABLE CRICHTON. Fantasy. 4 a. J. M. Barrie. D. of York's, November 4, 1902. Rev. Duke of York's March 2, 1908.

ADMIRAL, THE. Sk. Adap. fr. the French of Octave Feuillet. Notting Hill Coronet, February 10, 1899.

ADMIRAL BENBOW. D. Surrey, April 16, 1838.

ADMIRAL GUINEA. P. 4 a. Wm. Ernest Henley and Robt. Louis Stevenson. Avenue, November 29, 1897. Rev. H.M., June 4, 1909 (mat.).

ADMIRAL JACK; OR, H.M.S. SKYLARK. Nautical M. Extrav. 2 a. Buckstone Clair and W. Snell Robinson. Walthamstow King's, July 21, 1902.

ADMIRAL PETERS. C. 1 a. W. W. Jacobs and Horace Mills. Adapt. fr. Jacob's story of the same name. Eastbourne Pier, August 3, 1908. Garrick, May 25, 1909.

ADMIRAL TOM, KING OF THE BUCCANNEERS. Nautical D. W. Travers. Britannia, September 21, 1868.

ADMIRAL'S LADY, THE. Rom. C. Prol. 3 a. Arthur Shirley. Brixton, February 22, 1905.

ADMIRAL'S LADY, THE. Sk. Holborn Empire, June 29, 1908.

ADOLPHUS AND CLARA; OR, THE TWO PRISONERS. C. 1 a. Eleanor H——. Transl. fr. the French of J. B. Marsollier. Prod. 1804. A transl. of the D. fr. which Kenney took his O. of *Matrimony*.

ADONE. O. B. Ferrari. M. by Monteverde. Venice, 1639.

ADONE, L'. O. Monteverde. 1568-1643.

ADONIS. Burl. 3 a. Orig. prod. in Amer. Gaiety, May 31, 1886.

ADONIS VANQUISHED. C. 2 a. Vincent Amcott's adap. from *Le Dégel*. St. James's.

ADOPTED CHILD, THE. O. Attwood. London, 1793

ADOPTED CHILD, THE. M.D. 2 a. Saml. Birch Prod. 1795. D.L., April 21, 1815; Lyceum, 1817.

ADOPTED SON, AN. P. 1 a. Cecil Newton. Athenæum H., Tot. Ct. Rd., May 9, 1894.

ADOPTED SON, THE. T. Wm. Preston. Song fr. this piece pr. in his poetical works. 1793.

ADOPTION F 1 a. Richd. Henry. Toole's, May 26, 1890.

ADOPTION OF ARCHIBALD, THE. C. 3 a. Edgar Selwyn. Worthing T.R., February 2, 1903; Avenue, February 6, 1903.

ADORATION OF THE EASTERN SAGES, THE. Mentioned by Hawkins in "Origin of the English Drama," 1773.

ADRASTA; OR, THE WOMAN'S SPLEEN AND LOVE'S CONQUEST. T.C. John Jones. Prod. 1635. N. ac. Partly from *Boccace*.

ADRASTUS PARENTANS. Latin T. Peter Mease. Dedicated to Launcelot Andrews, Bishop of Winchester. MS. in British Museum.

ADRIAN AND ORRILA; OR, A MOTHER'S VENGEANCE. P. 5 a. Wm. Dimond. C.G., November 15, 1806.

ADRIAN IN SIRIA. O. Pergolesi. Naples, 1734.

ADRIAN IN SYRIA. O. Fr. Metastasio. By John Hoole. Prod. 1800.

ADRIAN IN SIRIA. Metastasio. M. by Caldara. 1731.

ADRIANO, L'. O. G. Albos. Rome, 1750.

ADRIANO IN SIRIA. O. G. Colla. Milan, 1763.

ADRIENNE; OR, THE SECRET OF A LIFE D. 3 a. H. T. Leslie. Lyceum, November 12, 1860.

ADRIENNE LECOUVREUR. P. 5 a. Scribe and Legouvé. 1849. Adap. by H. Herman. Court, December 11, 1880; Her M., July 4, 1890.

ADRIENNE LECOUVREUR. D. Adelphi, August 25, 1862.

ADRIENNE LECOUVREUR. O. 4 a. In Italian. Francesco Cileà. Lib. by A. Colantti, based on Scribe and Legouvé's play. C.G., November 8, 1904.

ADRIENNE LECOUVREUR. P. 5 a and 6 tabl. Sarah Bernhardt Coronet, June 27, 1905.

ADRIENNE LECOUVREUR. New ver. 5 a. Olga Nethersole, of Scribe and Legouve's French. P. Bradford Royal, November 2, 1906.

ADRIFT. D. 4 a. Aldershot T.R., January 24, 1887.

ADRIFT ON THE WORLD. D. Marylebone, November 28, 1874

ADRIFT ON THE WORLD. D. 3 a. J.C. Twist. Southend Pier Pav., January 23, 1894.

ADRIFT ON THE WORLD; OR, EVERY CLOUD HAS A SILVER LINING. D. 3 a. F. Bousfield. Oriental, April 13, 1868.

ADRONICUS (also called *Adronicus's Impiety's Long Success; or, Heaven's Late Revenge*). T. Plot fr. Fuller's "Life of Adronicus" in "Holy State." Pr. 1661. (An attack on the Cromwell Party.)

ADRONICUS COMNENIUS. C. J. Wilson. Pr. 1663.

ADVENTURE, AN. Sk. T. W. Atherstone. Strand, June 25, 1901.

ADVENTURE IN THE LIFE OF SHERLOCK HOLMES, AN. Episode. 3 scenes. John Lawson. Paragon M.H., January 6, 1902. Garston T.R., May 8, 1902.

ADVENTURE OF LADY URSULA, THE. C. 4 a. Anthony Hope. Duke of York's, October 11, 1898, and February 18, 1901. Rev. Criterion, January 5, 1909.

ADVENTURER, THE. F. D.L., 1790.

ADVENTURER, THE. Rom. C. 3 a. F. Kinsey Peile. Hastings, Gaiety, July 6, 1905.

ADVENTURER, THE. See *Amana; The Lady of Lyons.*

ADVENTURER; OR, PLOTS IN SPAIN, THE. D. Surrey, April 1, 1856.

ADVENTURER; OR, THE FIEND'S MOUNTAIN, THE. D. 5 tabl. D.L., October 13, 1856.

ADVENTURERS, THE. Dr. piece. 2 a. Pr. 1777.

ADVENTURERS, THE. F. E. Morris. D.L., March 18, 1790.

ADVENTURERS, THE. C. 3 a. F. on Emile Augier's *L'Aventurière* (Comédie Française, March 23, 1848, the original of Tom Robertson's *Home*, January 14, 1869). Strand, June 24, 1892.

ADVENTURES IN MADRID. C. Mrs. Pix. Queen's T., Hay. Pr. circ. 1709.

ADVENTURES OF A BILLET DOUX. C. J. Mathews. See *Adventures of a Love Letter.*

ADVENTURES OF A LOVE LETTER, THE. C. 2 a. Ch. Mathews. D.L., November 19, 1860.

ADVENTURES OF A NIGHT, THE. F. Wm Hodson. D.L., March 24, 1783.

ADVENTURES OF A NIGHT, THE. Rom. C. 3 a. Fr. Calderon's C., *Los Empeños de Seis Horas*, by Meyrick Milton. Edinburgh Lyceum, June 19, 1893; Strand, July 21, 1893.

ADVENTURES OF A NIGHT, etc. See *Los Empeños de Seis Horos.*

ADVENTURES OF A VENTRILOQUIST; OR, THE ROGUERIES OF NICHOLAS, THE. F. 3 a. Moncrieff. Adelphi, 1823.

ADVENTURES OF DICK TURPIN AND TOM KING, THE. S.C. D. 2 a. W. E. Suter. Sadler's Wells.

ADVENTURES OF FIVE HOURS, THE. C. Adapt. by Geo. Digby and Sir Saml. Tuke of Calderon's *Los Empeños de Seis Horos.* Ac. 1662. Pr. 1663.

ADVENTURES OF FRANCOIS, THE. P. 5 a. Langdon Mitchell. Halifax Grand, October 25, 1900 (C.P.).

ADVENTURES OF HALF AN HOUR, THE. F. Christopher Bullock. Pr. 1716. Ac. at L.I.F., March 19, 1716.

ADVENTURES OF 101, THE. Sk. Camberwell Empire, June 1, 1908.

ADVENTURES OF MOLL, THE. M.C. 3 a. Frank Barrett, Percy French, and J. A. Robertson. Manchester, Princes, June 14, 1905.

ADVENTURES OF THE COUNT DE MONTE CRISTO, THE. D. Pro. and 3 a. H. Smith. Lyric, March 6, 1899.

ADVENTURES OF TOM TRIP; OR, THE WOUNDED SAILOR. Naval F. Henry Siddons. Newcastle, 1798. N.p.

ADVENTURES OF ULYSSES; OR, RETURN TO ITHACA. Mendham. 1811.

ADVENTURESS, THE. C.D. B. H. Hilton. Liverpool Alexandra, February 28, 1871.

ADVENTURESS, THE. P. Pro. and 4 a. Adapt. fr. the French by T. S. Amory. Newcastle-on-Tyne T.R., May 15, 1882.

ADVERSITY OF ADVERTISEMENT, THE. Triviality. 2 a. Nugent Monck. Yeovil O.H., January 26, 1903.

ADVERTISEMENT. F. Fennell. 1791. N.p.

ADVERTISEMENT; OR, A BOLD STROKE FOR A HUSBAND, THE. C. Mrs. Gardner. Hay., August 9, 1777. N.p.

ADVICE GRATIS. F. 1 a. C. Dance. Olympic, September 29, 1837.

ADVICE TO HUSBANDS. Ca. 1 a. C. S. Lancaster. Princess's, October 6, 1846.

ADVOCATE, THE. C.D. 4 a. Adapt. fr. the French by Chas. Lander. Kilburn T.H., December 3, 1886.

ADVOCATE AND HIS DAUGHTER, THE. J. Ebsworth. Olympic, February 26, 1852.

ADVOCATE OF DURANGO. D. 4 a. John Wynne. Publ. by T. Benwith, 215, Regent Street, 1853.

ADVOCATE'S DAUGHTER, THE. P. Edinburgh, 1856.

ÆLLA. Tragical interlude. Chatterton. Pl. before "Master Canynge" at his house, Rodde Lodge, and before the Duke of Norfolk. Pr. 1777.

ÆMILIA. Latin C. by Cecill. Pl. at St. John's, Cambridge, 1615.

ÆNEAS; OR, DIDO DONE. Burl. H. S. Granville. Cork T.R., March 2, 1868.

ÆNEAS'S REVENGE. With the T. of Polyphemus. Henry Chettle. Ac. 1598.

ÆNEID. See *Epic Poems*

ÆOLOSICON. Aristophanes. See "Greek Plays."

ÆREOSTATION; OR, THE TEMPLAR'S STRATAGEM. F. 2 a. Fredk. Pilon. C.G., October 29, 1784.

ÆSOP. C. 2 parts. Sir John Vanbrugh. Taken fr. C. *Esope* of Boursault. D.L., 1697.

ÆSOP. F. D.L., 1778 (1 night). N.p.

ÆSOP; OR, THE GOLDEN BUBBLE. B. 2 a. A. R. Slous. Birmingham P. of W., March 3, 1879.

ÆSOP'S CROW. P. Perf. in the 16th century before the Court. (Most of the actors were dressed as birds.) It is mentioned in a tract called *Beware the Cat.* 1584.

ÆSOP'S FABLES. F.C. 3 a. J. P. Hurst. Strand, June 19, 1889.

ÆTHIOP; OR, CHILD OF THE DESERT. P. W. Dimond. C.G., October 6, 1812.

ÆTIUS. Op. trans. fr. Metastasio by John Hoole. Pr. 1800.

AFFAIR OF HONOUR, AN. F. 1 a. W. Leman Rede. Queen's, March 12, 1835. Pl. in New York, 1838.

AFFAIRE DES POISONS L'. P. Prol. and 5 a. Victorien Sardou. (Orig. prod. at Porte St. Martin, December 7, 1907.) His Majesty's, June 15, 1908.

AFFAIRES SONT LES AFFAIRES, LES. C. 3 a. Octave Mirbeau. Royalty, January 19, 1906. See *Business is Business.*

AFFAIRS AT THE SHRUBBERY. F. C. 2 a. J. P. Hatherleigh and P. M. Roberts. Paisley T., March 9, 1908 (amat.).

AFFECTED LADIES, THE. C. Trans. fr. *Les Précieuses Ridicules* of Molière by John Ozell.

AFFECTIONATE FATHER, THE. C. Jas. Nelson. Pr. 1786.

AFFINITIES. D. 5 a. Adapt. by Mrs. Campbell Praed and Mrs. Jopling fr. former's novel. Pl 1885

AFFLICTED FATHER, THE. D. Hayley, 1745-1820.

AFRANCESADO. D. 2 a. T. J. Serle. C.G., October 19, 1837.

AFRICAINE, L'. O. Meyerbeer. Pr. Académie, Paris, April 28, 1865. In Italian, C.G., July 22, 1865. In English, C.G., October 21, 1865.

AFRICAINE, L'. Burl. F. C. Burnand and Montagu Williams. Strand, November 18, 1865.

AFRICAINE, L'; OR, THE BELLE OF MADAGASCAR. Burl. 1 a. Capt. Arbuthnot. First extrav. on the subject.

AFRICAN GRATITUDE. Another title for *The Slave*. Tottenham Street New T., 1830.

AFRICAN MILLIONAIRE, THE. Melod. Cape Town, S. Africa, June 18, 1904.

AFRICANDER MAID, THE. Sk. Middlesex, November 16, 1908.

AFRICANS; OR, WAR, LOVE, AND DUTY, THE. P. 3 a. Geo. Coleman the Younger. Hay. and C.G., July 29, 1808. Plot fr. *Les Nouvelles du Florian*.

AFTER. P. 1 a. J. Scott Battams. Vaudeville, May 27, 1887.

AFTER A STORM COMES A CALM. Ca. 1 a. J. M Morton.

AFTER ALL. C 3 a. Wm. Duckworth. Liverpool P.O.W., October 13, 1873.

AFTER ALL. V. lib. by Frank Desprez. M. by Alfred Cellier. Op. Comique, December 16, 1878.

AFTER ALL. P. Prol. 3 a. Freeman Wills and Fredk. Langbridge. Fr. Lord Lytton's novel, "Eugene Aram." Dublin T.R., October 7, 1901; Avenue, January 15, 1902.

AFTER BALACLAVA. Sk. Empress, June 24, 1908.

AFTER DARK; A TALE OF LONDON LIFE. D. 4 a. Dion Boucicault. Princess's, August 12, 1868, and rev. November 9, 1891.

AFTER DARKNESS, DAWN. Dom. D. 1 a. A A. Dowty. Toole's, May 27, 1882.

AFTER DINNER. F. 1 a. Herbert Gardner.

AFTER DINNER. F. F. Helmore, Uxbridge T.R., May 18, 1871.

AFTER LONG YEARS. D 1 a. S. Grundy. Taken fr. Scribe and Camille's *Le Mauvais Sujet*. Folly, December 6, 1879.

AFTER LONG YEARS. C.D. 3 a. Arthur Law. Fr. story by Mrs. Herbert Purvis. Torquay T.R., October 20, 1886; Criterion, February 2, 1887.

AFTER LONG YEARS. Ca. Gerald Godfrey 1 a. Dewsbury T.R., December 22, 1888; Pavilion, December 16, 1889.

AFTER MANY DAYS. Ca. 1 a. Arthur Elwood. Globe, March 14, 1887.

AFTER MANY DAYS. P. 1 a. Robert Hickings. Eastbourne New Pier Pavilion, December 2, 1901.

AFTER MANY YEARS. C. A. R. Eyres. St. Geo. H., February 5, 1880.

AFTER MANY YEARS. P. 1 a. Annie Hughes. Douglas, Gaiety, September 16, 1907.

AFTER MARRIAGE. Ca. 1 a. J. W. Jones. Leeds T.R., April 30, 1875.

AFTER SEVEN YEARS. Dr. Sk. Marie Muggeridge. Belfast, Royal, April 26, 1907.

AFTER TEN YEARS. P. 1 a. Percy H. Vernon on Victor Hugo's *Les Misérables*. Birkenhead, T. Metropole, October 21, 1892.

AFTER THE BALL. Edw. Yates. Gallery of Illustration, 1859.

AFTER THE BALL. Ca. F. Kinsey Peile. St. James's T., July 16, 1895; Queen's H. (small), June 24, 1898.

AFTER THE BALL. F.C. Edward Ferris, B. Matthews, and Neville Doone. Globe, March 27, 1901 (C.P.); Margate Grand, October 29, 1903.

AFTER THE PARTY. C. 1 a. T. H. Lacy. Publ. by S. French, Ltd. Plot similar to *Forty Winks*.

AFTER THE RACES. Co. episode. 1 sc. Walter Howard. Collins' M.H., August 18, 1905.

AFTER THE REHEARSAL. Ca. Charles Osborne. Wolverhampton T.R., September 9, 1888.

AFTER THE STORM. P. 1 a. Cyril Austen-Lee. Dumbarton Burgh H., December 11, 1895.

AFTER TWENTY YEARS. P. 1 a. Maurice H. Hoffman. Mechanics' Inst., Stockport, January 23, 1896.

AFTERGLOW, THE. C. 3 a. C. Fraser Wood. Llandudno Grand, September 11, 1903.

AFTERMATH. P. 1 a. Bayswater Bijou, June 22, 1893.

AFTERNOON. See *Princess Carlo's Plot*.

AFTERTHOUGHTS. Epis. 1 a. Albert E. Drinkwater. Bayswater Bijou, June 12, 1899; Coronet, November 22, 1905; Garrick, June 5, 1908.

AGAINST MOMUS' AND ZOILUS'S. Dr. Piece. John Bale, Bishop of Ossory. Probably written between 1530 and 1540.

AGAINST THE TIDE. D. C. H. Hazlewood. Britannia, June 2, 1879.

AGAINST THE TIDE. D. 4 a. F. A. Scudamore. Surrey, August 3, 1896.

AGAINST THOSE WHO ADULTERATE THE WORD OF GOD. Dr. piece. John Bale. Probably written between 1530 and 1540.

AGAMEMNON. T. Trans. from Seneca (B.C. 58-32) by J. Studley. Pr. 1563; Newton T., 1581.

AGAMEMNON. P. Ascribed to Henry Chettle and Thos. Dekker. Ac. 1599.

AGAMEMNON. T. J. Thompson. D.L. 1734. Pr. 1738.

AGAMEMNON. T. Trans. from Æschylus (B.C. 458) by R. Potter. Pr. 1777. Symons, 1824; Boyd, 1824; Buckley, 1849; Davies, 1868; Plumptre, 1869.

AGAMEMNON. T. Alfièri, 1783. Trans. by C. Lloyd. 1815.

AGAMEMNON. See "Greek Plays."

AGAMEMNON AND CASSANDRA; or, THE PROFIT AND LOSS OF TROY. Burl. R. Reece. Liverpool Prince of Wales's, April 13, 1868.

AGAMEMNON AND ULYSSES. P. Acted before the Court, 1584.

AGAMEMNON CHŒPHORI AND EUMENIDES. See *The Story of Orestes*.

AGATHA. P. 3 a. Isaac Henderson. Criterion, May 24, 1892. Afterwards called The *Silent Battle*.

AGATHA. P. 3 a Mrs. Humphry Ward and Louis N. Parker. His Majesty's, March 7, 1905.

AGATHA; OR, THE LAWFUL WIFE. D. Pro. and 3 a. Oswald Brand. Sadler's Wells, August 15, 1892.

AGATHA; OR, THE LOST CHILD OF THE MANOR. Oa. Maurice Johnstone. Co-operative Hall, Morley, April 30, 1894.

AGATHA TYLDEN, MERCHANT AND SHIPOWNER. P. 4 a. Edward Rose. Haymarket, October 17, 1892.

AGATHOCLES; or, THE SICILIAN TYRANT. T. P. Perrinchief. 1676.

AGE D'AMOUR, L'. P. 4 a Pierre Wolff. Terry's, June 5, 1905.

AGE OF INNOCENCE, THE. Ca. Fredk. Ferm. Royalty, December 5, 1904. C.p.

AGE OF LOVE, THE. P. 1 a. W. Waite Sanderson. Art Gallery, Newcastle-on-Tyne, November 8, 1895.

AGE WE LIVE IN, THE. D. 5 a. Birmingham Grand, May 22, 1893.

AGED FORTY. C. 1 a. John Courtney. Princess's, February 2, 1844.

AGENT, THE. F. Francis Raphael. Parkhurst, March 21, 1892.

AGENT, THE. M.F. E. N. O'Connor and F. Warden Reed. Oldham Colosseum, January 6, 1902.

AGES AGO. E. W. S. Gilbert. M. by F. Clay. Gallery of Illustration, November 22, 1869.

AGESILAS. T. Corneille. 1666. See "French Classical Plays."

AGGRAVATING SAM. C.D. 2 a. C. J. Mathews and Co. Lyceum, December 6, 1854.

AGGRESSION; OR, THE HEROINE OF YUCATAN. Ballet of Action. ? by Mr. Farley. C.G. April, 1805.

AGIS. T. John Home. Founded on story in Spartan History. D.L. February 21, 1758.

AGIS (Agide). T. Alfieri, 1783. Trans. by C. Lloyd. 1815.

AGITATOR, THE. Orig. P. 1 a. Mrs. Oscar Beringer. Hicks. December 9, 1907.

AGLAURA. T.C. Sir John Suckling, Bart. Acted at private house in Blackfryars, 1646. Pr. 1638.

AGLAVAINE AND SELYSETTE. D. 5 a. Alfred Sutro, Transl. fr. Maurice Maeterlinck. Court, November 15, 1904.

AGMUNDA. T. Hannah Brand. Hay. This is her play, *Huniades*, revised.

AGNES. C. 2 a. Adap. fr. Molière's *L'Ecole des Femmes*. By Robert Buchanan. Comedy, March 21, 1885.

AGNES. See *Jealousy, Andrea, The Countess and the Dancer.*

AGNES BERNAUER. P. 2 a. T. J. Serle. C.G., April 20, 1839.

AGNES BERNAUER. O. F. Mottl (Weimar, 1880).

AGNES DE CASTRO. T. Mrs. Cockburn. F. on French novel of same name. Transl. by Mrs. Behn. T.R., 1696.

AGNES DE HOHENSTAUFEN. O. Spontini. 1838.

AGNES DE VERE; OR, THE BROKEN HEART (or, The Wife's Revenge). D. 3 a. Adap. fr. the French by J. B. Buckstone. Adelphi, November 10, 1834.

AGNES OF BAVARIA. P. 5 a. Fredk. Hawley. Gaiety, October 31, 1883.

AGNES OF BAVARIA; OR, LOVE AND LOVE'S VISION. D. F. Haywell. Nottingham T.R., November 9, 1868.

AGNES ST. AUBYN. Do. D. Miss Pardoe. Adelphi, January, 1841.

AGNES SOREL. O. G. A Beckett. St. James's, December, 1835.

AGNESE. O. Paer. 1820.

AGNESE. O. Guindani, Piacenza. 1878.

AGONY COLUMN, THE. Afterwards called *The Morning Post.* F. Aubrey Fitzgerald. T.H., Kilburn, July 10, 1894.

AGONY COLUMN, THE. F.P. 1 a. Tom Terriss. Gaiety, February 6, 1901

AGONY COLUMN, THE. See *A Bold Advertisement.*

AGRA-MA-CHREE. D. 5 a. Edmund Falconer. Manchester T.R., March 8, 1875.

AGREEABLE RE-UNION, L'. Divertissement. Ac. at King's, December 30, 1806.

AGREEABLE SEPARATION, THE. C.E. Dr. Collingwood. Pr. (n.d.) N.ac.

AGREEABLE SURPRISE, THE. C. Anon. Ac. at Mr. Rule's Academy. Pr. 1766. Transl. from "Marivaux."

AGREEABLE SURPRISE. THE. C.O. 2 a. John O' Keefe. Hay., 1781, 1796, 1806, 1823, 1832. Originally prod. at Dublin as *The Secret Enlarged.*

AGRIPPA, KING OF ALBA, OR THE FALSE TIBERINUS. T.C. Tr. fr. the French of Quinault (1637-88) by J. Dancer. T.R., Dublin, Pr. 1675.

AGRIPPINA. T. Bergerac Containing thoughts and phrases fr. Shakespeare.

AGRIPPINA. O. Handel. Venice, 1708.

AGRIPPINA. T. Thos. Gray (died 1772). Pr. 1775.

AGRIPPINA. T. in rhyme. John, Lord Hervey (died 1743). N.p. N.ac.

AGRIPPINA. See *Julia Agrippina.*

AGRIPPINA, EMPRESS OF ROME. T. Thos. May. Ac. 1628. Pr. 1639 and 1654. See *Julia Agrippina.*

AH! QUE L'AMOUR EST AGREABLE. C. Delaporte. 1862.

AH! WHAT A PITY!! OR, THE DARK KNIGHT AND THE FAIR LADY. M.D. Lyceum, September 28, 1818.

AHASUERUS. See *King Ahasuerus.*

AIDA. Ital. O. 4 a. Verdi. Cairo, December 24, 1871. C.G., June 22, 1876.

AIDA. O. 4 a. Verdi. Trans. into Eng. by Henry Hersee. H.M.T., February 19, 1880.

AIDA, L'. C.D. Croydon T.R., June 19, 1876.

AIDAN; OR, THE WARFARE OF LOVE Hist. D. 4 a. James J. Blood. Birmingham, St. Aidan's Ass. R. November 20, 1905.

AIEULE, L'. O. Boieldieu. Paris, 1841.

AIGLON, L'. D. 6 a. Edmond Rosland. T. Sarah Bernhardt November 15, 1900; Her M., June 3, 1901.

AILEEN; OR, FOILED AT LAST. D. 2 a. J. P. Collins. Grecian, April 15, 1872.

AILEEN ASTHORE; OR, IRISH FIDELITY. D. 4 a. C. H. Hazlewood. Portsmouth, R. Albert, February 20, 1871.

AINE, L'. Royalty, October 26, 1887.

AIR-BALLOON, THE. Mus. D. Pr. 1784.

AIREY ANNIE. A travestie of *Ariane.* 4 a. (1 scene). F. C. Burnand. Strand, April 4, 1888.

AIRSHIP, THE. F. 1 a. R. Hastings, with "suggestions" by G. Lane. Canterbury, April 5, 1909.

AIRSHIP, THE. Sk. Roland Hastings. Tottenham Palace, August 9, 1909.

AJAX. T. Tr. fr. Greek of Sophocles (B.C. 420) by W. Jackson, rev. by Rowe 1714-6; L. Theobald, 1714; Geo. Adams, 1729; Thos. Franklin, 1759; R. Potter, 1788; Dale, 1824; G. Burges, 1849; Plumptre, 1865. See "Greek Plays."

AJAX AND ULYSSES. P. Ac. at Court in the winter of 1571-2.

AJAX FLAGELLIFER. Latin P. Supposed to have been ac. before Queen Elizabeth at Cambridge, 1564. Ac. at Oxford, 1605.

ALABAMA, THE. Altered fr. *H.M. Sloop "Spitfire."* E. J. M. Morton D.L., March 7, 1864.

ALABAMA, THE. P. 4 a. Augustus Thomas. Originally prod. in America. Garrick, September 2, 1895.

ALABAMA, PRIVATEER; OR, THE SCOURGE OF THE NORTH, THE. D. Liverpool Colosseum, September 23, 1872.

ALABASTER STAIRCASE, THE. C. 3 a. Robert Marshall. Comedy, February 21, 1906.

ALADDIN. O. M. by Bishop. D.L., April 29, 1826.

ALADDIN. 2 a. Lyceum, August 5, 1844.

ALADDIN. Burl. D. R. Reece. Gaiety, December 24, 1881.

ALADDIN; OR, THE LAMP AND THE SCAMP. Burl. 3 scenes. E. R. Ratton. Bayswater Bijou, December 4, 1897.

ALADDIN; OR, THE MAGIC LAMP. M. Extrav. A. E. Pike. Birkenhead, St. Cath. Inst., January 30, 1896.

ALADDIN; OR, THE SCAMP, THE TRAMP, AND THE LAMP. Burl. Lloyd Clarance. Blackpool New Grand T., May 14, 1883.

ALADDIN; OR, THE WONDERFUL LAMP. Pant. M. by Shield. C.G., 1788

ALADDIN; OR, THE WONDERFUL LAMP. M.D. Farley, 1813.

ALADDIN; OR, THE WONDERFUL LAMP. Rom. Spec. 2 a. C.G., 1826.

ALADDIN; OR, THE WONDERFUL LAMP. Extrav. 1 a. J. R O'Neill. Originally pl. by Marionette Co. at Adelaide Gallery.

ALADDIN; OR, THE WONDERFUL LAMP. Burl. Extrav 1 a. H J Byron. Strand, April 1, 1861.

ALADDIN; OR, THE WONDERFUL LAMP. Burl. Frank W. Green. Charing Cross, December 23, 1874.

ALADDIN; OR, THE WONDERFUL LAMP IN A NEW LIGHT. Burl. G. à Beckett. Princess's, July 4, 1844.

ALADDIN AND THE FLYING GENIUS. Burl. Extrav Philharmonic, December 26, 1881

A-LADD IN AND WELL OUT OF IT. Burl. Extrav. Folkestone Town Hall, January 15, 1889. See *A-Lad-In.*

ALADDIN AT SEA. M. Extrav. 1 a. I. Zangwill. Camborne Public Rooms, January 25, 1893.

ALADDIN THE SECOND. Op. Extrav. Alf. Thompson. Gaiety, December 24, 1870.

ALADDIN'S LAMP. W. Best. St. Geo. H., March 3, 1883.

A-LAD-IN AND WELL OUT OF IT. Pant. Bruce Smith. M. arr. by J. Halliday, Junr. Perf. by Drury Lane Theatre children, Albert H., March 22, 1909.

ALAHAM. T. Fulke Greville, Lord Brooke. Written after the manner of the ancients, with a chorus between the acts. The prol. was spoken by a Ghost, who gave an account of each character in the piece. 1633.

ALAN'S WIFE. Study. 3 sc. F. on story by Elin Ameen. Terry's, April 28, 1893. (Independent T.)

ALARBAS. Dram. O. By "A Gentleman of Quality." Prod. 1709.

ALARCOS. T. 5 a. Rt. Hon. Benjamin Disraeli, M.P. 1839. Astley's, August 1, 1868.

ALARKAS. T. F. C. Schlegel. 1802.

ALARM, THE J. M. Swiney. Pr. at Cork. (Before 1812.)

ALARMING SACRIFICE, AN. D. J. B. Buckstone. Hay., July 12, 1849.

ALARMIST; OR, CHEERFUL OPINIONS, THE. Int by J. P. Roberdean. Ac 1800. Pr. 1803.

ALARUM FOR LONDON; OR, THE SIEGE OF ANTWERP, WITH THE VENTUROUS ACTS AND VALIANT DEEDS OF A LAME SOLDIER, AN. T.C. Probably by Marston, assisted by Marlowe and Shakespeare. Plot taken from the *Tragical History of the City of Antwerp.* Ac. by Lord Chamberlain's servants, 1602.

ALASCO. T. Shee. 1824.

ALASKA. D. 4 a. Adap. by Albert Rogers from American ver. of W. L. Lockwood, Stockton Royal, August 6, 1906.

ALBA. Ac. at Oxford before Albertus de Alaxo, a Polish Prince. 1583.

ALBEKE GALLAS. P. Thos. Heywood and Wentworth Smith. Ac 1602. N. pl.

ALBERT AND ADELAIDE; OR, THE VICTIM OF CONSTANCY. Rom. Probably by Saml. Birch. C.G., 1798. N. pl.

ALBERT AND ADELAIDE. See *Captain of Spilsbury.*

ALBERT AND ROSALIE. 1808. See *Dramatic Appellant.*

ALBERT ARNALL; OR, THE DEATH SPELL. Burl. D.P.H. Victoria, March 27, 1837.

ALBERT DE ROSEN. D. 4 a. Mrs. S. Lane. Britannia, August 30, 1875.

ALBERTA. T. J. Carter. Prod. 1787. N. a.

ALBERTUS WALLENSTEIN, LATE DUKE OF FRIDLAND AND GENERAL TO THE EMPEROR FERDINAND II. T. Henry Glapthorne. Globe, Bankside, 1634. Prod. 1639.

ALBIN O. Flotou. Vienna, 1856.

ALBINA, COUNTESS RAIMOND. T. Mrs. Cowley. Prod. Hay., 1779.

ALBION. Interlude. Probably same as *Albyon Knight.*

ALBION; OR, THE COURT OF NEPTUNE. Masque. T. Cooke. Prod. 1724.

ALBION AND ALBANIUS. O. J. Dryden. M. by Charles II.'s French bandmaster, Lewis Grabue. Ac. at T. in Dorset Gardens. Prod. 1685.

ALBION QUEENS; OR, THE DEATH OF MARY QUEEN OF SCOTS, THE. T. John Banks. D.L., March 6, 1704.

ALBION QUEENS. See *Island Queens.*

ALBION RESTORED; OR, TIME TURN'D OCULIST. Masque N. ac. Prod. 1757.

ALBION'S TRIUMPH. Masque. By Aurelian Townsend. Perf. at Court by King, Queen, and several noblemen, 1631.

ALBOVINE, KING OF THE LOMBARDS. T Sir Wm Davenant. Prod. and perf. 1629.

ALBUM, THE. F. T. Haynes Bayly. St. James's, April 16, 1838.

ALBUMAZAR. See *The Astrologer.*

ALBUMAZAR. C. David Garrick. D.L., 1773. Alteration of Tomkis' *Albumazar.*

ALBUMAZAR, THE ASTRONOMER. C. Thos. Tomkis, of Trin. Coll., Cam. An imitation of an Italian C. by Porta called *L'Astrologo* Ac. before King at Cambridge by gentlemen of Trin. Coll., March 9, 1614. Afterwards rev. at D.L., with prol. by Dryden.

ALBYON KNIGHT, THE. P. Anon. 1565. Mentioned by Kirkman.

ALCAID; OR, THE SECRETS OF OFFICE, THE. C.O. 3 a. Jas. Kenney. Hay., August 10, 1824.

ALCAMENES AND MENALIPPA. T. W. Philips. (Died December 12, 1732.)

ALCANTARA. C O. 2 a. E. B. Woolf. M. by Julius Eichberg. Connaught, November 1, 1879.

ALCESTE. O. 5 a. Lulli. January 19, 1674.

ALCESTE. T. Lagrange, 1690.

ALCESTE. O Smollett, 1747.

ALCESTE. O. Calzabigi. M. by Glück. Vienna, 1775, Paris, 1776.

ALCESTIS. T. Transl. fr. Euripides (B.C. 438). R. Potter, 1781; M. Wodhull, 1782; Edwards, 1824; Nevins, 1870; Williams, 1871; and with Buckley's prose transl. See "Greek Plays."

ALCESTIS, THE ORIGINAL STRONG-MINDED WOMAN. Classical Burl. 1 a. Francis Talfourd. Strand, July 4, 1850.

ALCHEMIST, THE. Mediæval p. 3 a. Osmond Shillingford. Birmingham T.R., March 25, 1897.

ALCHEMIST, THE. Sk. Wm. Warden and Fredk. Lloyd. Bedford, August 17, 1908.

ALCHEMIST, THE. See *The Empiric.*

ALCHEMIST OF MODENA; OR, THE WRONGS OF A LIFE, THE. D. F. Charlton. Britannia, November 10, 1868.

ALCHYMIST, DER. R.O. 3 a. Fr. Washington Irving's novel. M. by Spohr. July 28, 1830. D.L., March 20, 1832.

ALCHYMIST, THE. C. Ben Jonson. Ac. by His Maj. servants, 1610. Prod. 1610. Tr. August 3, 1664. Alt. into *The Tobacconist* by F. Gentleman, 1870. Alt. ver. perf. D.L. Rev. by Elizab. Stage Soc. and pl. at Apothecaries' H., Blackfriars, February 24, 1899, and at the Imperial, July 11, 1902.

ALCIABIADES; OR, ALCIBIADES. T. Th. Otway. Story fr. Nepos and Plutarch. This was Otway's first play, and dedicated to the Earl of Middlesex. Duke of York's, 1675. T.R., 1687.

ALCIBIADE. T. Campistron, 1688.

ALCIBIADES. T. Wm. Shirley. About 1776.

ALCIBIADES. See *Nepos.*

ALCIDA. Greene, 1588.

ALCIDES LES. Tours de Force displayed by MM. Manche and Daras. First time in this country. D.L., April 20, 1829.

ALCINA. O. Handel. 1685-1759.

ALCINE. O. A. Campra. 1705.

ALDERMAN, THE. C. 3 a. Adap. fr. the French *L'Heritage de M. Plumet* of Barrière and Capendu by Jas. Mortimer. Criterion, April 29, 1887.

ALDERMAN'S GOWN; OR, A TRIP TO PARIS, THE. F. 1 a. H. Abrahams. Strand, October 6, 1851.

ALDGATE PUMP. J. F. Saville. Strand, June 7, 1841.

ALEMÆON. P. Ac. before the Court at Whitehall, December, 1573.

ALERAME, THE KNIGHT OF THE LION. Melo-d. Denvil. Pavilion, February 4, 1833.

ALESSANDRO. O. Sacchini. 1734-86.

ALESSANDRO NELL' INDIE. O. Metastasio, 1729. See *Alexandro, etc.*

ALESSANDRO AND STRADELLA. See *Stradella.*

ALESSANDRO STRADELLA. O. Flotow. Hamburg, 1844.

ALEXANDER. O. Anthony Henley (died 1711). M. by Purcell.

ALEXANDER AND DIOGENES. See *Lilly's Court Comedies.*

ALEXANDER AND LODOWYKE. P. Martin Slaughter. Ac. 1598. N.p.

ALEXANDER AND STATIRA; OR, THE DEATH OF BUCEPHALUS. Burl. Prob. by Dr. Geo. Wallis. Ac. at York, Leeds, and Edinburgh. Before 1812.

ALEXANDER AND THE KING OF EGYPT. Mock P. Ac. Pr. 1788.

ALEXANDER BALUS. O. Dr. Thos. Morell. C.G., 1748.

ALEXANDER, CAMPASPE, AND DIOGENES. T.C. John Lyly. Pl. before Q. Eliz. by Children of St. Paul's 1584, and at Blackfriars. Pr. 1584 Pl. taken from Pliny's Nat. History.

ALEXANDER THE GREAT. T. Fr. Racine by John Ozell. 1714. See "French Classical Plays."

ALEXANDER THE GREAT. O. L.I.F 1715.

ALEXANDER THE GREAT. F. Joseph Dilley and W. Albery.

ALEXANDER THE GREAT. T. Alt. fr. Lee's *Rival Queens.* D.L. C.G. Pr. 1770.

ALEXANDER THE GREAT. See *The Rival Queens.*

ALEXANDER THE GREAT; OR, THE CONQUEST OF PERSIA. Pant. J. D'Egville. D.L. Pr. 1795. M. by Krazinski Miller.

ALEXANDER THE GREAT; OR, THE RIVAL QUEENS. T. 5 a. Nat. Lee, 1678. D.L. C.G., 1807.

ALEXANDER THE GREAT; OR, THE RIVAL QUEENS. Burl. Colley Cibber. N.p.

ALEXANDER THE GREAT IN LITTLE. Burl. T. Dibdin Strand, August 7, 1837.

ALEXANDER THE SIXTH. T. Ac. before His Majesty. Entered at Stationers' Co., October 16, 1607.

ALEXANDER'S FEAST. Concerto. Handel. 1685-1759.

ALEXANDER'S FEAST. O. Anon. 1751.

ALEXANDRA. P. 4 a. Adap. fr. the German of Dr. Richard Voss. Royalty March 4, 1893.

ALEXANDRAEAN TRAGEDY; OR, THE ALEXANDRIANS, THE. T. Rt. Hon. Wm. Alexander, Earl Stirling. Plot fr. Quintus Curtius. Pr. 1605. See *The Monarchic Tragedies.*

ALEXANDRE. T. Racine. 1665.

ALEXANDRO NELL' INDIE. O. Piccini, Rome, 1758; Naples, 1774.

ALEXAS; OR, THE CHASTE GALLANT. Philip Massinger. Ac. by Kings Co. September 25, 1639.

ALEXINA. P. Knowles. Strand May 21, 1866.

ALEXIS. D. 4 a. Harold Vallings. Cryst. Pal., November 26, 1885.

ALEXIS AND DORINDA. M. piece. L.I.F. 1725. N.p.

ALEXIS'S PARADISE. O. Anon. 1680.

ALEXIS'S PARADISE; OR, A TRIP TO THE GARDEN OF LOVE AT VAUXHALL. C. Jas. Newton. Pr. 1722 and 1732.

ALEXIUS; OR, THE CHASTE LOVER. See *Alexas.*

ALFONSO AND CLAUDINA, THE FAITHFUL SPOUSE; OR, THE HATED RACE. 1 a. Cry. Palace, 1862.

ALFONSO AND ESTRELLA. O. 3 a. Schubert, Weimar. 1854.

ALFONSO, KING OF CASTILE. T. M. G. Lewis. C.G., January 15, 1802. Pr. 1801.

ALFONSO THE NOBLE. Hist. O. in Yiddish. J. Gordin. Pav., April 1, 1907.

ALFRED. T.C. (Dedicated to Lady Blount by her brother, R.K.) 1659.

ALFRED. Masque. Jas. Thomson and David Mallet. Ac. at Cliefdon, August 1, 1740. Pr. 1740.

ALFRED. O. Alt. fr. masque of same name by Arne or his pupil, Burney. C.G., 1745.

ALFRED. T. John Home. C.G. (3 nights). Pr. 1778.

ALFRED. T. Mallet, by David Garrick. D.L. Pr. 1773.

ALFRED. Hist. T. Ac. at Sheffield 1789.

ALFRED. P. Lady Clarke Jervoise. New, June 28, 1904.

ALFRED. See *The Magic Banner.*

ALFRED. See *Rule, Britannia.*

ALFRED; OR, THE MAGIC BANNER. D. 3 a. J. O'Keefe Hay., 1796. Pr. 1798.

ALFRED; OR, THE ROAST BEEF OF OLD ENGLAND. Masque. J. Thomson and Mallet. Converted into pl. by Mallet 1751. It contains the famous song, "Rule Britannia."

ALFRED AND EMMA. P. F. on Kotzebue's *Red Cross Knights.* 1806.

ALFRED LE GRAND. Hist. ballet. Lyceum (rev.), June 9, 1823.

ALFRED THE GREAT. Mus. D. Anon. D.L., 1745.

ALFRED THE GREAT. D. H. M. Milner. Coburg, February 9, 1824.

ALFRED THE GREAT; OR, THE MINSTREL KING. Hist. Extrav. Robt. B. Brough. Olympia, December 26, 1859.

ALFRED THE GREAT; OR, THE PATRIOT-KING. Hist. P. 5 a. J. Sheridan Knowles. D.L., 1831.

ALFRED THE GREAT AT ATHELNEY. T. Stratford de Redcliffe. 1876.

ALFRED THE GREAT, DELIVERER OF HIS COUNTRY. T. Anon. Pr. 1753.

ALFRED THE GREAT INGRATE. Burl. Wentworth V. Bayley. Portsmouth T.R., May 8, 1871.

ALGERIAN, THE. O. vaud. 3 a. Glen M'Donough. M. by Reginald de Koven. Parkhurst, September 25, 1893 (C.P.).

ALGERINE SLAVES, THE. M.E. James Cobb. Ac. at the O.H. in the Hay. 1792. An abridgement of *The Strangers at Home.*

ALGONAH. C.O. James Cobb. D.L., April 30, 1802. An alt. fr. *The Cherokee.* Songs pr. 1802.

ALHAMBRA; OR, THE THREE BEAUTIFUL PRINCESSES. Burl. extrav. Albert Smith. Princess's, April 21, 1851.

ALI BABA. O. Cherubini. Paris, 1833.

ALI BABA. Fairy tale. 4 scenes. Mrs. Hugh Bell. Adelphi, May 18, 1903.

ALI BABA; OR, THE FORTY NAUGHTY THIEVES. Burl. Birkenhead T.R., May 14, 1883.

ALI BABA; OR, THE FORTY THIEVES. C.O. 4 a. Lib. by Sig. Emilio Taddei. M. by Sig. Bottesini. Lyceum, January 17, 1871.

ALI BABA; OR, THE THIRTY-NINE THIEVES. Burl. extrav. 1 a. H. J. Byron. Strand, April 6, 1863.

ALI BABA A LA MODE. O. Extrav. Robt. Reece. Gaiety, September 14, 1872.

ALI BABA, M.P. F Wynne Scarlett. Aberdeen, H.M.T., April 3, 1893; Southend Empire, June 4, 1894. (2nd edition.)

ALI D'AMORE, LE. O. Rauzzini. London, February 27, 1776.

ALI PACHA; OR, THE SIGNET RING. M.D. 2 a. John Howard Payne. C.G., October 19, 1822.

ALICE. P. Nigel Playfair and Rosina Filippi. Fr. Lewis Carroll's two books. Court, May 29, 1905.

ALICE GREY, THE SUSPECTED ONE; OR, THE MORAL BRAND. Dom. D. 3 a. J. T. Haines. Surrey, April 1, 1839

ALICE IN WONDERLAND. Children's p., being a dramatised version of incidents in Lewis Carroll's book By H. Savile Clarke. M. by Walter Slaughter. P. of W.'s, December 23, 1886; Globe, December 26, 1888; Op. C., December 22, 1898; V., December 19, 1900, and February 4, 1901; Apollo, December 23, 1907.

ALICE MAY. D. Edw. Fitzball. Surrey, 1852.

ALICE PIERCE. See *All's Perce.*

ALICE SIT-BY-THE-FIRE. P. 3 a. J. M. Barrie. Duke of York's, April 5, 1905.

ALICE THE MYSTERY. Burl. 1 a. J. Smith. Publ. by S. French, Ltd.

ALICE THROUGH THE LOOKING-GLASS. Fairy P. Y. Knott. F. on Lewis Carroll's book. M. by W. Tilbury. New, December 1, 1903. C.p., New, December 22, 1903.

ALICE WESTON. D. 4 a. Pub. by S. French, Ltd.

ALICE, WHERE ART THOU? Rom. D. 4 a. Louie Neville Banwell. Weymouth Jubilee H., March 2, 1905. (C.P.) Oxford Empire, June 18, 1906.

ALICE WINGOLD. Astley's, May 5, 1862.

ALIEN STAR, AN. P. 1 a. Bertha N. Graham, 92, Victoria St., S.W. February 5, 1908.

ALIENATED MANOR, THE. C. 5 a. Joanna Baillie. Ptd. in 1800.

ALIENS. P. 1 a. By "Bedford Row." Lyric, June 3, 1889. (C.P.)

ALINE, REINE DE GOLCONDE. O. 3 a. Sedaine. M. by Monsigny. April 15, 1767.

ALINE, THE ROSE OF KILLARNEY. D. 3 a. Edwd. Stirling. Strand, July 10, 1843.

ALIVE AND MERRY. F. D.L., May 17, 1796. N.p.

ALIVE AND MERRY. F. 2 a. C. Dance. C.G., September 30, 1839.

ALIVE OR DEAD. D. 4 a. Robt. W. Hall. St. George's, May 25, 1876; Park, May 3, 1880.

ALL A MISTAKE. F. C.G., July 2, 1825.

ALL A MISTAKE. Ca. 1 a. Mrs. Newton Phillips. Ladbroke H., January 28, 1890.

ALL ABOUT A BONNET. Mus. Ca. Herbert Harraden. Terry's April 30, 1891.

ALL ABOUT A BOUT. Sk. 3 scs. Irving B. Lee, under direction of Frank Beal. New Cross Empire, November 9, 1908.

ALL ABOUT THE BATTLE OF DORKING; OR, MY GRANDMOTHER. Ex. F. C. Burnand and Arthur Sketchley. M. by Theodore Hermann. Alhambra, August 7, 1871.

ALL ABROAD. O. 1 a. Arthur Law. M. by A. J. Caldicott. P. of Ws., February 21, 1890.

ALL ABROAD. F.C. 3 a. W. Burnside. Parkhurst, December 10, 1892.

ALL ABROAD. Mus. F. 2 a. Owen Hall and J. T. Tanner. M. by Fredk. Rosse, lyrics by W. H. Risque. Portsmouth T.R., April 1, 1895; Criterion August 8, 1895; Court, January 2, 1896.

ALL ALIVE AND MERRY. C. S. Johnson. L.I.F., 1738. N.p.

ALL ALIVE, OH! F. 3 a. Adap. fr. Alexandre Bisson and André Sylvane's *Disparu* (Gymnase, Paris, March 19, 1896). Strand, June 16, 1897.

ALL AT C; OR, THE CAPTIVE, THE COFFER, AND THE COCOATINA. M.D. 1 a. Major Millett, R.W.F., and Lieut. Wilcox, R.N. Ac. on board H.M.S. Tamar, December 29, 1873.

ALL AT COVENTRY; OR, LOVE AND LAUGH. F. 2 a. W. T. Moncrieffe. Olympic, January 8, 1816; Adelphi, Victoria T., 1842.

ALL AT HOME; OR, THE IRISH NIECES. Pr. at Dublin, 1804. N. ac.

ALL AT SEA. Ca. Sydney Grundy. Man. T.R., August 8, 1873.

ALL AT SEA. Mus. sketch. Lib. by Arthur Law. M. by Corney Grain. St. George's H., February 28, 1881.

ALL AT SEA. M.C. 2 a. Edward Paulton. Llandudno Prince's, May 21, 1903; Kingston County, June 15, 1903; Peckham Crown, September 7, 1903.

ALL AT SIXES AND SEVENS. F. M. by Whitaker. D.L., March 21, 1829.

ALL BEDEVILLED; OR, THE HOUSE IN AN UPROAR. F. Moses Browne. Pr. 1723. See *Polidus*.

ALL BUT LOST; OR, THE TOTEM OF THE TORTOISE. D. F. Warrington. Dundee T.R., October 11, 1869.

ALL BUT ONE. D. W. Travers. Britannia, February 15, 1868.

ALL BY CHANCE. Ca. J. T. Belverstone. Leicester T.R., June 9, 1879.

ALL CHANGE HERE. Ca. Royston Keith. Eastbourne T.R., August 8, 1898.

ALL FLETCHER'S FAULT. P 3 a. Mostyn T. Piggott. Suggested by Charles Reade's story, "Christie Johnstone." Avenue, December 19, 1903.

ALL FOOLES. C. Geo. Chapman. Plot f. on Terence's Heautontimorumenos. Blackfriars, before His Majesty, 1606. Pr. 1605.

ALL FOR FAME; OR, A PEEP AT THE TIMES. C. Sk. Andrew Cherry. D.L., May 15, 1805.

ALL FOR GOLD. D. 3 a. Cherry Griffiths. Britannia, September 9, 1878.

ALL FOR GOLD; OR, FIFTY MILLIONS OF MONEY. D. 4 a. F. upon *Le Juif Errant* of Eugène Sue by Francis Hopkins. Birmingham T.R., July 15, 1878; Surrey, February 21, 1881.

ALL FOR HER. D. 3 a. Palgrave Simpson and Herman C. Merivale. Mirror, October 18, 1875; rev. Grand, May 17, 1897.

ALL FOR HER; OR, THE LOST PLEAID. See *All for Love*, etc.

ALL FOR HIMSELF. C.D. 3 a. C. Wills. Liverpool Alexandra, June 5, 1874.

ALL FOR LOVE; OR, THE LOST PLEIAD. P. J. S. Coyne. Adelphi, January 16, 1838.

ALL FOR LOVE; OR, THE WORLD WELL LOST. T. John Dryden. Based on Shakespeare's *Antony and Cleopatra.* D.L., 1678. Entered at Stationers' Hall, January 31, 1677-8.

ALL FOR MONEY. C. Thos. Lupton. Pr. 1578.

ALL FOR MONEY. C. 3 a. Mlle. Guillon Le Thierre. Hay., July 12, 1869.

ALL FOR NOTHING. Queen Anne's Gate, July 17, 1880.

ALL FOR THE BETTER; OR, THE INFALLIBLE CURE. C. F. Manning. D.L., 1703. Pr. 1703.

ALL FOR THEM. Ca. Henry P. Lyste. Folly, April 17, 1876.

ALL HALLOWS EVE. Hay., July 11, 1859.

ALL HALLOWS EVE. Irish C.D. 4 a. Hon. Mrs. Forbes and J. W. Whitbread. Dublin, Queen's T., April 20, 1891.

ALL IN A BUSTLE. C. Probably by Francis Lathom Pr. 1795 N. ac.

ALL IN A FOG. F. T. J. Williams. Surrey, October 16, 1869.

ALL IN GOOD HUMOUR. Dr. piece. 1 a. W. C. Oulton. Hay. Pr. 1792.

ALL IN HOT WATER. F. 1 a. James Bruton. 1858.

ALL IN THE DARK. 2 a. J. R. Planché. New Royalty, November 21, 1861.

ALL IN THE DARK; OR, THE BANKS OF THE ELBE. C.D. 2 a. M. by Barham Livius. Lyceum, July 11, 1822. Ac. but once before.

ALL IN THE DOWNS; OR, BLACK-EYED SUSAN. O. F. on Douglas Jerrold's D. Lyrics by Tom Jerrold. M. by W. Meyer Lutz. Gaiety, November 5, 1881.

ALL IN THE RIGHT. F. Thos. Hull. Transl. fr. Destouches. C.G., April 26, 1766.

ALL IN THE RIGHT; OR, THE CUCKOLD IN GOOD EARNEST. F. Pr. 1762.

ALL IN THE WRONG. C. 5 a. Arthur Murphy. Fr. Molière's *Cocu Imaginaire.* D.L., 1761. Rev. December 2, 1814. Pr. 1761.

ALL IS NOT GOLD THAT GLITTERS. P. Henry Chettle and Sam Rowley. Ac. 1600.

ALL IS TRUE. Play. T. at Bankside, June, 1613.

ALL IS VANITY; OR, A CYNIC'S DEFEAT. Ca. Alfred Thompson. Liverpool, P. of Ws., August 19, 1878; Hay., April 9, 1879.

ALL JACKSON'S FAULT. F. Alice O'Connell. Athenæum H., Tottenham Court Road, November 27, 1889.

ALL LOST. D. 1 a. Tom Craven. Sadler's Wells, July 21, 1883.

ALL MISTAKEN. C. Wm. Shirley. C. 1760. N.p. N.ac. An alt. of Shakespeare's *Comedy of Errors*.

ALL MISTAKEN; OR, THE MAD COUPLE. C. Hon. Jas. Howard. T.R., 1672. Pr. 1672.

ALL-MY-EYE VANHOE. Burl. Ph. Hayman. Trafalgar, October 31, 1894.

ALL-OF-A-SUDDEN-PEGGY. C. 3 a. Ernest Denny. Duke of York's, February 27, 1906.

ALL ON A SUMMER'S DAY. Eliz. Inchbald. C.G., December 15, 1787. N.p.

ALL ON ACCOUNT OF ELIZA. C. 3 a. Leo Dietrichstein. Shaftesbury, April 3, 1902.

ALL OR NOTHING. A proverb. By Hamilton Aide. Garden Mansion, Queen Anne's Gate, July 17, 1880.

ALL PLEAS'D AT LAST. C. Anon. Ac. Dublin. Pr. 1783.

ALL PLOT; OR, THE DISGUISES. C. Stroude. Duke's T., between 1662 and 1671.

ALL PUZZLED. F. Anon. 1702.

ALL SORTS AND CONDITIONS OF MEN. P. 3 a. Jan Van Wetherelt. Version of Besant's novel. Camberwell Metropole, December 1, 1902.

ALL THAT GLITTERS IS NOT GOLD. C.D. 2 a. Thos. and J. M. Morton. Olympic, January 13, 1851; rev. Adelphi, December 23, 1896.

ALL THE COMFORTS OF HOME. F.C. 3 a. Adap. fr. *Ein Toller Einfall* by W. Gillette and H. Duckworth. Globe, January 24, 1891.

ALL THE DIFFERENCE. D. 1 a. Ronald McDonald St. Geo. H., January 9, 1896.

ALL THE FUN OF THE FAIR. A dr. mélange. 1 a. Duse Mohamed. Gloucester Palace, September 30, 1907.

ALL THE WORLD'S A STAGE. F. 2 a. I Jackman. D.L., April 7, 1777. Prod. 1777. Edinburgh, 1782; rev. D.L., May 31, 1819, and April 1, 1824.

ALL THE YEAR ROUND. Ballet. Alhambra, January 21, 1904.

ALL THROUGH A WIRE. F. Sk. Frank Herbert. St. Alban's H., June 12, 1894.

ALL THROUGH ARABELLA. P. 3 a. Adap. fr. the German. A. M. Dittini. Mr. and Mrs. Calvert Routledge. Scarboro' Lond., June 25, 1902; Blackpool O.H., November 8, 1902; Govan Lyceum, November 26, 1902; St. Leonard's Pier Pav., January 5, 1903; C. Palace, April 24, 1903.

ALL THROUGH YOU. Sk. B. Daly. Shepherd's Bush Empire, March 27, 1907.

ALL UP AT STOCKWELL; OR, THE GHOST NO CONJUROR. Int. D.L., April, 1772. N.p.

ALL VOWS KEPT. C. Capt. Downes. Ac. at Dublin, Snock Alley. Pr. 1733.

ALL WELL AT NATCHITOCHES. Monol. Mathews. Lyceum, March 25, 1824.

ALL WITHOUT MONEY. C. See *The Novelty*.

ALL'S FAIR IN LOVE. Charade. H. Hersee.

ALL'S FAIR IN LOVE; OR, A MATCH FOR THE LAWYERS. F. J. Tobin. C.G., April 29, 1803. N.p.

ALL'S LOST BY LUST. T. Wm. Rowley. Plot taken fr. Novel 3 of "Unfortunate Lovers." Ac. by Lady Elizabeth's servants at the Phœnix, 1633. Prod. 1633.

ALL'S ONE; OR, ONE OF THE FOURE PLAIES IN ONE CALLED "A YORKSHIRE TRAGEDY." Pl. by King's Players, 1608. Spurious play ascribed to Shakespeare.

ALL'S PERCE (Alice Pierce). Mentioned in Henslowe's list as belonging to the Rose T.

ALL'S RIGHT. Burla. Olympic, January 21, 1833.

ALL'S WELL THAT ENDS WELL. C. 3 a. Shakespeare. Wr. circa 1604. 1st folio 1623. F. on Boccaccio's novel, "Giglietta di Nerbona," which was in Painter's "Palace of Pleasure," Ptd. 1566. Possibly a later version of the lost play, *Love's Labour's Won*, given by Meres in his "Palladis Tamia. Ptd. 1598.

ALL'S WELL THAT ENDS WELL. C. Alt. fr. Shakespeare by Fredk. Pilon. H.M., 1785; with alt. by J. P. Kemble, D.L. Pr. 1793.

ALLEGORICAL, MORAL, DRAMATIC, MUSICAL ENTERTAINMENT, by way of Epithalamium. Pr. 1770 in a novel entitled "Constantia; or, the Distressed Friend."

ALLEGRO, IL PENSEROSO, IL MODERATO, L'. O. Handel. London. 1740.

ALLENDALE. F.C. 3 a. Eden Phillpotts and G. B. Burgin. Strand, February 14, 1893.

ALLOW ME TO APOLOGISE. F. 1 a. J. P. Wooler. Olympic, October 28, 1850.

ALLOW ME TO EXPLAIN. F. W. S. Gilbert. P. of W.'s, November 4, 1867.

ALMA; OR, THE DAUGHTER OF FIRE. D. Grecian, October 20, 1851.

ALMA L'INCANTATRICE. Ital. O. M. Flotow. Paris and C.G., July 9, 1878.

ALMA MATER; OR, A CURE FOR COQUETTES. Dion Boucicault. Hay., September 19, 1842.

ALMADIS DE GRECE. O. Lamotte. 1704.

ALMAHIDE; OR, THE CAPTIVE. J. Phillips (Milton's nephew). Being a transl. of *Almahide*, a French play by Mlle. de Scudéry. 1677.

ALMAHIDE; OR, THE CONQUEST OF GRANADA BY THE SPANIARDS. T. 2 parts. Dryden. 1669-70. See *Almanzor*.

ALMAHIDE AND HAMET. T. Benj. Heath Malkin. F. on Dryden's *Conquest of Granada*. Pr. 1804. N. ac

ALMANAC, THE. P. Ac. by the Prince's players before the Court in the winter of 1611-12.

ALMANZOR AND ALMAHIDE; OR, THE CONQUEST OF GRANADA. Being 2nd part of Almahide. John Dryden. T.R. Pr. 1672.

ALMAVIVA. O. See *Barbière di Siviglia*.

ALMEDA; OR, THE NEOPOLITAN REVENGE. Tragic D. Pr. 1801. Said to be written by a Lady. Taken fr. *The Life of Rozelli*.

ALMENA. O. Richd. Rolt. D.L. Pr. 1764.

ALMEYDA; OR, THE RIVAL KINGS. T. Geo. Edmund Howard. Story fr. Almoran and Hamet by Dr. Hawkesworth. Pr. 1769.

ALMEYDA, QUEEN OF GRANADA. T. 5 a. Sophia Lee. D.L., April 20, 1796. Pr. 1796.

ALMIDA. T. Mrs. Celisia. D.L., January 12, 1771. Pr. 1771. Fr. Voltaire's *Tancrede*.

ALMIGHTY DOLLAR, THE. Melo D. 5 a. W. Wood. Barnsley T.R., December 13, 1888.

ALMIGHTY GOLD. Sk. Brixton Empress, June 29, 1908.

ALMINA. Her M., April 26, 1860.

ALMIRA. O. Handel. Hamburg, 1705. Rev. at opening of new O.H., Hamburg, 1874.

ALMIRINA. T. Isaac Jackman. Royalty, September 10, 1787. Ac. by one person with the aid of wooden figures.

ALMORA AND NERINE. Ballet. Victoria T.

ALMORAN AND HAMET. See *Almeyda*.

ALMORAN AND HAMET. Eastern tale of enchantment. M. by Cooke. D.L., April 8, 1822.

ALMOST A LIFE D. 6 tableaux. Adap. fr the French by Miss Ettie Henderson. Liverpool, Court T., November 6, 1882.

ALMOST A QUEEN. P. 1 a H. A. Saintsbury. Liverpool, Shakespeare, September 11, 1905.

ALMOST HIS BRIDE. P. Stephen Pritt. Preston R., September 13, 1909.

ALMOST HUMAN. S. Metcalfe Wood. M. by Edwd. Sillward. Canterbury M.H., November 3, 1902.

ALMSHOUSE, THE. F.C. 3 a. Wm. Lockhart and Loring Fernie. Parkhurst, December 6, 1892.

ALMYNA. See *Arabian Nights, Is Marriage a Failure?*

ALMYNA; OR, THE ARABIAN VOW. T. Mrs. Delarivier Manley. Fr. Life of Caliph Valid Amanzor and Arabian Nights. Hay., 1707. Pr. 1707.

ALONE. C.D. 3 a. J. Palgrave Simpson and Herman C. Merivale. Court T., October 25, 1873.

ALONE IN CHINA. D. 4 a. Henry Johnson. Birmingham, Alex., June 13. 1904; Brixton, June 20, 1904.

ALONE IN LONDON. D. Prol. and 4 a. Robt. Buchanan and Harriet Jay. Olympic, November 2, 1885; Princess's, December 21, 1891; September 30, 1899.

ALONE IN THE PIRATE'S LAIR. Nautical D. C. H. Hazlewood. Britannia, September 23, 1867.

ALONE IN THE WORLD. Grecian. September 14, 1863.

ALONE IN THE WORLD. D. 4 a. Eliot Galer. Reading T.R., November 13, 1871.

ALONE IN THE WORLD. D. 4 a. Prentiss Ingram. Princess's, April 23, 1892.

ALONE IN THE WORLD; OR, WITHOUT A HOME. D. F. Fuller. Dewsbury T.R., April 14, 1871.

ALONZO. T. 5 a. John Home. D.L., 1773. Prod. 1773.

ALONZO AND IMOGENE; OR, THE DAD, THE LAD, THE LORD, AND THE LASS. Burl. W. W. Bird. Richmond, April 17, 1869.

ALONZO AND LEONORA. T. Dr. Young.

ALONZO ET CORA. O. 4 a. Méhul, February 15, 1791.

ALONZO THE BRAVE. H. M. Milner, author of *Frankenstein.*

ALONZO THE BRAVE; OR, FAUST AND THE FAIR IMOGENE. Burl F. C. Burnand. Strand, February 5, 1855; Cambridge A.D.C. Rooms, 1857.

ALONZO YE BRAVE AND YE FAYRE IMOGENE. Burl. Sam M. Harrison. Liverpool Alexandra, April 2, 1876.

ALP, THE BRIGAND. D. Strand, March, 1832.

ALPHONSO, KING OF NAPLES. T. Geo. Powell. T.R., 1691. Taken from *The Young Admiral of Shirley.*

ALPHONSUS, EMPEROR OF GERMANY. T. Geo. Chapman. Blackfriars, 1654. Pr. 1654.

ALPHONSUS, KING OF ARRAGON. Hist. P. By Robert Greene. Pr. and ac., 1599.

ALPINE HOLD, THE. D. J. T. Haines. Victoria, June 3, 1839.

ALPINE TOURISTS. Ca. 1 a. Newton Phillips. Ladbroke Hall, January 24, 1888.

ALPS, THE. F.C. 3a. Rev. ver. of *Loyal Lovers.* Adap. fr. *Le Voyage de M. Perrichon.* Cambridge, June 2, 1886.

ALSATIA. See *The Squire of*——and *The Gentleman of* ——.

ALT-HEIDELBERG. P 5 a. By Wilhelm Meyer-Forster. Great Queen Street, November 22, 1902. (German Season.)

ALTA; OR, RIGHT AGAINST MIGHT. D. 4 a. Una. New Cross Hall, September 4, 1884.

ALTAMIRA. T. Benjamin Victor. D.L., 1776. Written fifty years previously.

ALTAR OF FRIENDSHIP, THE. C. 4 a. Madeleine Lucette Ryley. Criterion, March 24, 1903.

ALTEMIRA. T. in rhyme. Roger Boyle, Earl of Orrery. L.I.F., 1702. Pr. 1739.

ALTERNATIVE, THE. C. Ac. at Dublin, 1796.

ALTOGETHER. F. Edwd. Dowsett. Edmonton T.H., February 17, 1894.

ALTOGETHER MORAL TRILBY, AN. Extrav. 1 a. C. B. Kay. Newton Abbot Alexandra H., February 11, 1896.

ALUCIUS. P. Ac. before the Court at Whitehall late in the year 1579.

ALUMNI PLAY, THE. F. 1 a. Clara Harriet Sherwood. Copyrighted 1891.

ALUREDUS. T.C. "Gulielmo Drureo." Pr. 1628.

ALWAYS INTENDED. C. 1 a. Horace Wigan. Olympic, April 3, 1865.

ALWAYS READY. D. 3 a. E. Romaine Callender. Newcastle-on-Tyne T.R., July 28, 1873; East London, October 31, 1874.

ALWAYS SIT UP FOR YOUR HUSBAND. F. W. F. Sorrell. Hastings M.H., November 24, 1873.

ALWYN AND BERTHOLDY. Dom. d. Surrey, April 11, 1831.

ALZIRA. T. Wm. Somerville. (Died 1743.) Transl. from Voltaire. N. pl. (n. ac.).

ALZIRA. T. Thos. Franklin. About 1765.

ALZIRA; OR, THE SPANISH INSULT REPENTED. T. Aaron Hill. Transl. from Voltaire's *Alziré.* D.L., 1735; also at L.I.F. and C.G. Pr. 1736.

ALZUMA. T. Arthur Murphy. C.G., 1773. Prod. 1778.

AMADAN, THE. D. 3 a. Dion Boucicault. Richmond, January 29, 1883.

AMADIS. O. Also called *Amadis of Gaul.* King's T. Pr. 1715. Possibly transl. of It. O. by Heidegger

AMADIS; OR, THE LOVES OF HARLEQUIN AND COLUMBINE. Pant. Rich. L.I.F., 1718.

AMADIS DE GAULL. O. 5 a. Lulli. January 18, 1684.

AMAKOSA. D. E. Fitzball. Astley's, March 28, 1853.

AMALASONT, QUEEN OF THE GOTHS. T. John Hughes. Wr. 1693; finished by Wm. Duncombe in MS.

AMALDERAC, THE BLACK PIRATE. D. Pavilion, January 13, 1840.

AMANA. Dr. Poem. Mrs. Eliz. Griffith. Taken fr. *The Adventurer.* Prod. 1764 or 1765. N. ac.

AMANT DIFFICILE, L' C. Lamotte. 1672-1731.

AMANT ET LE MARI, L' O. F. J. Fétis. Paris, 1820.

AMANT JALOUX, L' O. Grétry. 1778.

AMANTS DE VERONA, LES. It. O. 5 a. Marquis d'Ivry (under the ps. of Richard Yevid). Wr. in 1864. Perf. privately in 1867 and publicly at the Salle Ventadour, October 12, 1878. C.G., May 24, 1879.

AMANTS MAGNIFIQUES C Molière. 1670. See "French Classical Plays."

AMASIS. T. Legrange. 1677-1758.

AMASIS, AN EGYPTIAN PRINCESS. C.O. 2 a. Book by Fredk. Fenn; music by P. M. Faraday. New, August 9, 1906.

AMASIS, KING OF EGYPT. T. Ch. Marsh. Ac. one night at Little T. in Haymarket. Prod. 1738.

AMATEUR DETECTIVE, AN. F. and M.P. Arthur Lloyd. Pier Pav., Hastings, May 23, 1868.

AMATEUR FIRE BRIGADE; OR, THE FIRE FIGHTERS OF FRIZZLINGTON, THE. Sk. By A. Jefferson. Glasgow Metropole, February 2, 1907 (C.P.).

AMATEUR MODEL, AN. Sk. E J. Malyon and H. H. Morell. Cambridge M H., February 22, 1902.

AMATEUR RAFFLES. AN. Mus. duol. Wr. by H. Clayton; lyrics by A. Anderson; music by R. Nairn. London Pavilion, March 2, 1908.

AMATEUR SOCIALIST, THE. C. 3 a. W. Kingsley Tarpey Criterion, October 13, 1906.

AMATEUR WIFE, AN F.C. 3 a. Mrs. Lancaster Wallis. Criterion, April 27, 1897.

AMATEURS AND ACTORS. M.F. 2 a. R. Brinsley Sheridan. M. selected by David Dulcet. Lyceum, August 29, 1818.

AMATEURS AND ACTORS. 2 a. Peake.

AMAZON QUEEN; OR, THE AMOURS OF THALESTRIS TO ALEXANDER THE GREAT, THE. T.C. John Weston. 1667. Pr. (n. ac.).

AMAZON'S MASKE, THE. Ac. at Court before the Queen and the French Ambassador in the winter of 1578-9.

AMAZONS, THE. F. Rom. 3 a. A. W. Pinero. Court, March 7, 1893.

AMBASSADOR, THE. C. 4 a. John Oliver Hobbes. St. James's, June 2, 1898.

AMBASSADOR'S LADY, THE. Rom. D. T. E. Wilks. Strand, August 3, 1843.

AMBASSADRESS, THE. O. Auber. Paris, 1836. St. George's O.H., February 15, 1868 (rev.).

AMBASSADRICE Op. C. Scribe. 1837.

AMBER BOX, THE. C.O. Prod. at Dublin, 1800.

AMBER GIRL, THE. E. and H. Gordon-Clifford. Kew Prince's H., September 12, 1894.

AMBER HEART, THE P. Alf. C. Calmour. Lyceum, June 7, 1887; Evening bill, May 23, 1888.

AMBER WITCH, THE D. City of Lon., 1851.

AMBER WITCH, THE. O. By Vincent Wallace. H.M.T., February 28, 1861. By Moody-Manners Co., Southport O.H., January 12, 1899; Shakespeare, Clapham, March 22, 1899.

AMBER WITCH, THE. D. H. Saville. Victoria T., 1862.

AMBIGUOUS LOVER, THE. F. Miss Sheridan. Dublin, 1781. N.p.

AMBITION. Surrey, September 28, 1857.

AMBITION. P. Standard, March 14, 1870.

AMBITION. C. 3 a. Leslie Fomm. Globe, April 27, 1899.

AMBITION. D. H. L. Walford. Gall. of Illus., December 14, 1870.

AMBITION. See *A Farmer's Story*.

AMBITION; OR, MARIE MIGNOT. D. 3 a. Thomas Mayhew. Hay., September 13, 1830.

AMBITION'S SLAVE; OR, A GAME OF CHESS. D. 3 a. Joseph Fox. Leicester O.H., January 15, 1883; Standard, March 24, 1883.

AMBITIOUS MRS. MORESBY, THE. Dom.D. 1 a. Miss E. White. Comedy, April 22, 1898.

AMBITIOUS SLAVE; OR, A GENEROUS REVENGE, THE. T. Elkanah Settle. T.R., 1694. Pr. 1694.

AMBITIOUS STATESMAN; OR, THE LOYAL FAVOURITE, THE. T., in blank verse. John Crowne. T.R., 1679. Pr. 1679.

AMBITIOUS STEPMOTHER, THE. T. Nicholas Rowe. D.L. and L.I.F. Pr. 1700, and with add. scene 1702. Rev. by Garrick at D.L. 1758.

AMBITIOUS VENGEANCE. Tragic D. 3 a. By Bella Crusca (Mr. Robert Merry). Pr. 1790. N.ac.

AMBITIOUS WIDOW, THE. C.Ent. William Woty. Pr. 1789.

AMBOYNA; OR, THE CRUELTIES OF THE DUTCH TO THE ENGLISH MERCHANTS. T. J. Dryden. "Founded on history." T.R., 1673. Pr. same year.

AMBROSE GWINETT; OR, A SEASIDE STORY. Melo-d. 3 a. Douglas Jerrold. Coburg T., 1828; City T., January, 1832.

AME EN PEINE. O. Flotow. Paris, 1846.

AMELIA; O. Henry Carey. M. by J. F. Lampe. Perf. at French T. in Hay., 1732.

AMELIA. M.Ent. Richd. Cumberland. Taken from *The Summer's Tale*. C.G. Pr. 1768. Alt. and ac. at D.L. Pr. 1771.

AMELIA. Do. Ep. Nigel Playfair. Garrick, January 22, 1903.

AMELIA; OR, THE DUKE OF FOIX. P. Franklin. Trans. fr. Voltaire. Ac. December, 1752.

AMENDS FOR LADIES; WITH THE MERRY PRANKS OF MOLL CUT-PURSE OR THE HUMOURS OF ROARING. C. Nath. Field. Ac. at Blackfriars, 1618. Pr. 1618. Whitefryars, 1639. The second part of his *Woman's a Weathercock*.

AMERGAN. O. Pro. 2 a. Paul M'Swiney. Cork O.H., February 23, 1881.

AMERICA. F. 1 a. J. H. Barber. 1805. N. ac.

AMERICAN, THE. P. 3 a. Jos. Derrick. Alex. Pal., June 19, 1882.

AMERICAN, THE. P 3 a. Geo. Murray Wood. Glasgow, Gaiety, April 16, 1883.

AMERICAN, THE. P. 4 a. F. by Henry James upon his novel of same name. Southport, Winter Gardens, January 3, 1891; Op. Comique, September 26, 1891.

AMERICAN AMBASSADRESS, AN. M.P. 2 a. Glen Macdonough. M. by Victor Herbert. Bayswater, Victoria H., November 21, 1904. (C.P.)

AMERICAN ASSURANCE. M.C. F. W. Sidney. Eastbourne, Dev. Park, September 3, 1894.

AMERICAN BEAUTY, AN. M.C. Hugh Morton and Gustave Kerker. Shaftesbury, April 25, 1900.

AMERICAN BELLE, THE. M.C. 2 a. Hugh Seton and S. Ward. Cheltenham O.H., April 19, 1897; Camberwell Metropole, May 17, 1897.

AMERICAN BRIDE, AN. D. 4 a. By "Lawrence Olde" (Sir Wm. Young) and Maurice Noel. Lyric, May 5, 1892; Terry's, October 11, 1893.

AMERICAN CITIZEN, AN. C. 4 a. Madeline Lucette Ryley. Duke of York's, June 19, 1899.

AMERICAN HEIRESS, THE. M.P. 2 a. A. Branscombe and Geo. Day. M. by Herbert Simpson, Guy Jones, Ed. Dean, and Frank Lambert. Birmingham T.R., April 3, 1899; Fulham Grand, May 1, 1899; rev. ed. Newcastle, Tyne T., August 7, 1899.

AMERICAN HEROINE; OR, INGRATITUDE PUNISHED, THE. Pant. Hay., March 19, 1792. F. on *Incle and Yarico*.

AMERICAN INDIAN; OR, VIRTUES OF NATURE, THE. P. 3 a. Jas. Bacon. Pr. 1795.

AMERICAN LADY, THE. C. 3 a. H. J. Byron. Cri., March 21, 1874.

AMERICAN PROFESSOR, THE. Sk. Ardwick Green Empire, July 18, 1904.

AMERICAN SINGER DOWNSTAIRS, THE. Sk. Teesdale Locke and J. F. Downes. Queen's Gate H., December 18, 1899.

AMERICAN SLAVES; OR, LOVE AND LIBERTY. C.O. Ac. at Dumfries, 1792.

AMERICAN WIDOW, THE. Ca. Rosina Filippi. Camberwell Metropole, August 24, 1903.

AMERICANS, THE. C.O. Arnold. M. by M. P. King and Mr. Braham. 1811. Rev. Lyceum, July 30, 1818.

AMERICANS ABROAD. F.C. 2 a. Peake. Lyceum, September 3, 1824.

AMI DE LA MAISON. O. Marmontel. M. by Grétry. Paris, 1771.

AMICI DI SIRACUSA. Gli. O. Mercadante. Rome, 1824.

AMICO FRITZ, L'. O. 3 a. P. Mascagni. F. on Erckmann's Chatrian's novel, "L'Ami Fritz." First time in Eng. C.G., May 23, 1892; Manchester, Prince's, September 24, 1892.

AMID NORTHERN LIGHTS. Sk. Bedford, November 30, 1908.

AMILIE; OR, THE LOVE TEST. O. J. T. Haines. Rooke. C.G., December 2, 1837.

AMINA. P. 1 a. Affleck Scott. (Prod. by the Play Actors.) King's H., W.C., March 22, 1908.

AMINTA. Ital. pastoral D. Transl. fr. Torquato Tasso by J. Reynolds. Pr. 1628. J. Dancer. Pr. 1660.

AMINTA. Past. C. By Tasso in Ital. and Eng. Transl. by P. B. Du Bois. Pr. 1726. See "Italian Classical Plays"

AMINTA; OR, THE COQUETTE. Oa. Howard Glover. J. Greenford. Hay., January 26, 1852.

AMINTAS. P. J. Oldmixon. T.R. Pr. 1698. Transl. fr. *The Aminta of Tasso.*

AMINTAS. Dr. Past. Transl. fr. Tasso by Wm. Ayre. Pr. 1737.

AMINTAS. Eng. O. Compiled fr. Ital. of Metastasio and Eng. O. of Rolt's "Royal Shepherd or Royal Shepherdess" by Tenducci. C.G., 1769.

AMINTAS. See *Amyntas.*

AMLETO. O. F. Faccio. Lib. by Boito. Genoa, May 30, 1865.

AMONG THE AMALEKITES. C. 3 a. Emelie Bennett. Portsmouth T.R., June 22, 1889.

AMONG THE BREAKERS. C. 2 a. John Brougham. P.O.W., Liverpool, June 6, 1868; Strand, July 26, 1869.

AMONG THE BRIGANDS. Dr. f. 4 a. Weedon Grossmith. Birmingham Royal, October 25, 1907. See *Billy Rotterford's Descent.*

AMONG THE MORMONS. Artemus Ward. Egyptian H., November 13, 1866.

AMONG THE RELICS. C.D. 3 a. F. A. Palmer. Plymouth T.R., November 22, 1869.

AMONG THE STARS. Travesty. Arthur Shirley. Hippodrome, November 20, 1905.

AMONG THIEVES. Dram. Epis. 1 sc. William Gillette. Palace, September 6, 1909.

AMOR AM BORD. Sir A. Sullivan and W. S. Gilbert. Berlin. Publ. in 1882.

AMOR TIRRANICO, L'. O. F. Feo, 1713. (MS. at Naples Real Collegio di Musica.)

AMOR TRA NEMICI. O. A. Ariosti. Venice, 1708.

AMORE SEGRETO, L'. O. Spontini. Naples. 1799.

AMORELLE (CUVEE RESERVEE, 1798) C.O. Barton White. Lyrics by Ernest Boyd-Jones. M. by Gaston Serpette. Kennington T., June 8, 1903; Comedy, February 18, 1904.

AMORES. Ovid. See "Latin Plays."

AMORES PERINTHI ET TYANTES. Latin C. Wm. Burton. Wr. in 1596. (N. ac. and n.p.)

AMOROSO, KING OF LITTLE BRITAIN. S.C. Int. J. R. Planché. M. by Cooke. D.L., April 21, 1818; Lyceum, October 25, 1820.

AMOROUS ADVENTURE; OR, THE PLAGUE OF A WANTON WIFE, THE. Pant Hay., 1730.

AMOROUS BIGOT, WITH THE SECOND PART OF TEAGUE O'DIVELLY, THE. C. Thos. Shadwell. Ac. by Their Majesties' servants, 1690. See *The Lancashire Witches.*

AMOROUS COLONEL, THE. F. 1 a. Eric Stanley. Wisbech, Selwyn H., January 20, 1904.

AMOROUS FANTASME. T.C. Sir Wm. Lower. Transl. from *The Fantome Amoreux* of Quinhault. Pr. 1660.

AMOROUS GALLANT; OR, LOVE IN FASHION. C. Transl. fr. Corneille by J. Bulteel. Sometimes called *The Amorous Orontus.* Pr. 1665 or 1675.

AMOROUS GODDESS; OR, HARLEQUIN MARRIED. Pant. D.L., 1744.

AMOROUS JILT, THE. Thomas Rud. 1698. Given as the first title of Mrs. Behn's c., *The Younger Brother.* Pr. 1696.

AMOROUS MISER; OR, THE YOUNGER THE WISER, THE. C. Peter Anthony Motteux. Pr. 1705. Repr. 1707, and called *Farewell Folly; or,* etc.

AMOROUS OLD WOMAN. C. By Thos. Duffet. D.L. 1684. Pr. 1764; afterwards republ. as *The Fond Lady.*

AMOROUS ORONTUS. See *The Amorous Gallant.*

AMOROUS PHANTASM, THE. See *The Amorous Fantasme.*

AMOROUS PRINCE, THE. Mus. pot-pourri. Richmond, April 8, 1907.

AMOROUS PRINCE; OR, THE CURIOUS HUSBAND, THE. C. Mrs. Aphra Behn. Plot built on novel of "Curious Impertinent" and Davenport's *The City Night Cap.* D. of Yks. T., 1671. Pr. 1671.

AMOROUS QUARREL, THE. C. J. Ozell. Transl. fr. Molière's play, *Despit Amoureux.*

AMOROUS WAR, THE. C.T. Rev. Dr Jasper Maine. Prod. 1648.

AMOROUS WIDOW; OR, THE WANTON WIFE, THE. C. Thomas Betterton, f. on Molière's *George Dandin ou Le Mari Confondu.* T.R., 1670. Pr. 1706. *Barnaby Brittle* taken fr. this.

AMOS CLARK. D. Prol. 4 a. Watts Phillips. Q., October 19, 1872.

AMOSIS. Fr. P. 1 a. St. James's, July 3, 1905.

AMOUR A LA MODE, L'; OR, LOVE A LA MODE. F. 3 a. Hugh Kelly, Transl. fr. the Fr. Prod. 1760.

AMOUR ET L'OPINION, L'. C. Brifant, 1781-1857.

AMOUR ET SON CARQUOIS, L'. O. 2 a. C. Lococq. 1868.

AMOUR MEDECIN, L'. C. Molière. 1665. See "French Classical Plays."

AMOUR MOUILLE, L'; OR, CUPID AND THE PRINCESS. C.O. 3 a. Eng. ver. by W. Yardley and H. Byatt. Fr. the French of Preval and Liorat. Add. lyrics and M. by Paul Rubens and Landon Ronald. Lyric, April 5, 1899.

AMOUR VAINQUEUR, L'. Mytho. Div. D.L., November 9, 1839.

AMOURETTES, LES. C.O. M. by D. F. R. G. Josè. Lib. J. Percival, adap. fr. Planché's V., *Somebody Else*. Dublin, Auc. Concert R., April 14, 1885.

AMOUREUX DE BOULOTTE, LES. Oa. M. Lacompte. Charing Cross, March 7, 1871.

AMOURS DE CATHERINE, LES. O. 1 a. C. Maréchal. Paris, 1876.

AMOURS DE DIABLE. O.C. St. George's, 1852

AMPHITRUO. B.C. 254-184 Plautus. Transl. into blank verse by Thornton, Rich, Warner, and Colman. 1769-74. See "Latin Plays."

AMPHITRUS. See *Westminster Plays*.

AMPHITRYON. C. Transl. fr. Molière (1668) by John Ozell. Rev. Lawrence Echard, pr. 1694. Thos. Cooke, pr. 1746. Bonnel Thornton, pr. 1767. O. Sedaine, 1781 (see *Jack Juggler*). C. Adrieux, 1782. See "French Classical Plays."

AMPHITRYON; OR, THE TWO SOCIAS. C. J. Dryden. F. on the two *Amphitryons* of Plautus and Molière. Ac. T.R., 1691. Pr. 1691. D.L., November 18, 1826. Alt. fr. Dryden by Dr. J. Hawkesworth. Ac. D.L. Pr. 1756.

AMPHRISA; OR, THE FORSAKEN SHEPHERDESS. Pant. D. Thos. Heywood. Pr. 1637.

AMPLE APOLOGY. F. 1 a. Geo. Roberts. Princess's T., March 13, 1865.

AMPLE SECURITY. F. C. H. Stephenson. Southampton T.R., September 5, 1872.

AMSTERDAM; OR, BY THE SIDE OF THE ZUYDER ZEE. Ballet. 3 sc. Geo. R. Sims and Charles Fletcher. M. by Herman Finck. Blackpool Winter Gardens, July 12, 1909.

AMY ARLINGTON. Grecian. May 11, 1863.

AMY ROBSART. D. 4 a. Andrew Halliday. D.L., September 24, 1870.

AMY ROBSART. Burl. Mark Kingthorne. Norwich T.R., May 10, 1880.

AMY ROBSART. O. 3 a. Fr. novel of Sir Walter Scott by Sir Augustus Harris. French ver. by Paul Milliet. English adap. by Frederic Weatherly. M. by Isidore de Lara. C.G., July 20, 1893.

AMY'S BURGLAR. Ca. L. C. White. Cripplegate Inst., April 3, 1907; Croydon P.H., June 11, 1907.

AMYNTA. Past. Transl. fr. Italian of Torquato Tasso by John Dancer. Pr. 1660. See *Aminta*.

AMYNTAS. D. Past. Transl. fr. the Italian of Tasso into Hexameter verse by Abraham Fraunce. Pr. 1591.

AMYNTAS. See *Amintas*.

AMYNTAS; OR, THE IMPOSSIBLE DOWRY. Past. Thos. Randolph. Ac. at Whitehall before the King and Queen. Pr. 1638.

AMYNTAS OF TASSO. Transl. fr. original Italian by Percival Stockdale. Pr. 1770.

ANACONDA, THE TERRIFIC SERPENT OF CEYLON. West London, November 1, 1822; Bath, 1826.

ANACREON. Ballet. Rameau. 1754.

ANACREON. C.O. Sedaine. 1766.

ANACREON. Orat. Cherubini. D.L., March 25, 1825.

ANACREONTE IN SAMO. O. Mercadante, Naples, 1820.

ANACREONTICS REVIVED. List of Songs. C.G., 1800.

ANARCHIST, THE. P. 4 a. Ed. Gieve. Widnes Alexandra T., September 3, 1894.

ANARCHIST TERROR, THE. D. 4 a. West London, October 21, 1901.

ANARCHISTS, THE. T. 1 a. Rowan Orme. Court, July 7, 1908. (Mat.)

ANARCHY. See *Paul Kauvar*.

ANARCHY; OR, PAUL KAUVAR. D. 5 a. Adap. fr. the French by Steele Mackaye. Elephant and Castle, April 27, 1887.

ANATO, KING OF ASSYRIA. P. F. on Verdi's O., *Nabucco*. City of London, 1850.

ANATOMIST; OR, THE SHAM DOCTOR, THE. C. 1 a. Edwd. Ravenscroft. Ac. at T. in Little L.I.F., 1697. Pr. 1697. M. Masque inserted herein, called *The Loves of Mars and Venus*. Edinburgh, 1781. Alt. ver. Pr. 1763.

ANAXIMANDRE. C. Andrieux. 1782.

ANCESTORS OF THE CROWN. D. Prol. and 4 a. Max Goldberg. Glasgow G.T., June 23, 1902; Manchester Q., September 19, 1904.

ANCESTRESS; OR, THE DOOM OF BAROSTEIN, THE. Melo-d. 2 a. M. Lemon. City of London, May 27, 1837.

ANCHOR OF HOPE; OR, THE SEAMAN'S STAR, THE. D. 2 a. Ed. Stirling. Surrey T., April 19, 1847.

ANCHOR'S WEIGHED, THE. Nautl. D. 3 a. T. R. Taylor. Standard, May 14, 1883.

ANCHORA MACHREE. D. Sunderland Lyceum, March 13, 1871.

ANCIENT BRITONS. Sk. H. C. Sargent. Liverpool Empire, May 13, 1907.

ANCIENT LIGHTS. Ca. Fredk. Bingham. Richmond P.O.W., December 19, 1903.

ANCIENT MARINER, THE. Cant. J. F. Barnett. Birmingham M. Festival, 1867; St. James's H., February 11, 1868.

ANCIENT TIMES. D. Joseph Strutt. Pr. 1808. N.ac.

ANDERSON HEIRLOOMS, THE. C. 1 a. E. A. Thurlow. Duke of York's, June 7, 1904.

ANDRE. T. Ac. at New York. Probably by W. Dunlap. Pr. 1798.

ANDRE. O. M. Bayard, G. Lemoyne. St. James's April 16, 1853.

ANDRE CHENIER; OR, A ROMANCE OF THE REVOLUTION. O. 4 a. Lib. by Luigi Illica; music by Umberto Giordano. Manchester Q.T., April 2, 1903; Camden, April 16, 1903; C.G. (first time in original Ital.), November 11, 1905.

ANDREA (or ANDRIA). English transl. of Terence's C. (B.C. 166). 1520. Pr. (probably by Rastell) 1530; Maurice Kyffin, 1588; Richd. Bernard, 1598; T. Newman, 1627; after the method of Dr. Webbe, 1629; L. Echard, 1694; Ch. Hoole, 1663; Bentley, 1726; T. Cooke, 1734; S. Patrick, 1745; Gordon, 1752; Geo. Coleman, 1765; Goodluck, 1810; Sir H. Englefield, 1814; Dr. W. Gardiner, 1821; J. A. Phillips, 1836; Barry, 1857. Acted at Westminster School, December, 1904. See "Latin Plays."

ANDREA. French C. 4 a. Sardou. Op. C., May 20, 1875.

ANDREA. See *Jealousy*, *Agnes*, *The Countess and the Dancer*, *Conscious Lovers*.

ANDREAN (or ANDRIAN) OF TERENCE, THE. Latin and English. At Sherbourne. N.d.

ANDREAS HOFER. P. Surrey, June 11, 1832.

ANDREW. Melo-d. 3 a. Mohamed and Marlen. Bournemouth T.R., February 25, 1895.

ANDREW MILLS. D. Spennymoor Cambridge T., October 16, 1876.

ANDREW OF HUNGARY. T. Landor. 1839.

ANDREW PATERSON. D. 1 a Nora Vynne and St. John Hankin. Bayswater Bijou T., June 22, 1893.

ANDRIA. See *Andrea.*

ANDRIA. See *Westminster Plays.*

ANDROBOROS. Biographical F. 3 a—viz., The Senate, The Consistory, and the Apotheosis. Governor Hunter. Pr. at Meropolis after 1700.

ANDROCLES AND THE LION. Panto. S. King Alexander (S. Planche). Bristol T.R., 1893.

ANDROMACHE. T. J. Crowne. Trans. fr. *Andromaque* of Racine. Ac. at D.K.'s T. in Dorset Gardens, 1675.

ANDROMACHE. Trans. of Euripides B.C. 417 by Michl. Wodhull. Pr. 1782. R. Potter 1783, Edwards and Hawkins 1868, with Buckley's prose. Transl. in Bohn's series. See "Greek Plays."

ANDROMACHE. O. Gretry. Paris, 1780.

ANDROMACHE. P. 3 a. Gilbert Murray. Garrick, February 25, 1901.

ANDROMANA; OR, THE MERCHANT'S WIFE (sometimes called *Andromana; or, The Fatal and Deserved End of Disloyalty and Ambition*). T. F. on story of Plangus in Sir Philip Sidney's *Arcadia*, by Jas. Shirley. Pr. 1660. See *Cupid's Revenge.*

ANDROMAQUE. T. Campistron, 1683.

ANDROMAQUE. Sarah Bernhardt's season. Adelphi, June 17, 1903.

ANDROMAQUE OF RACINE. A ver. by Ambrose Philips. See *The Distres't Mother.* See "French Classical Plays."

ANDROMEDA. O. B. Ferrari. M. by Manelli. Venice, 1637

ANDROMEDA. O. G. Colla. 1772.

ANDROMEDA. Greek T. 1 a. Rose Seaton. Vaudeville, March 24, 1890.

ANDROMEDE Corneille. See "French Classical Plays."

ANDRONIC. T. Campistron, 1686.

ANDRONICO. O. Mercadante (Venice), 1822.

ANDRONICUS COMNENIUS. T. J. Wilson. 1664. See *The Unfortunate Usurper.*

ANDY BLAKE; OR, THE IRISH DIAMOND. C.D. 2 a. Boucicault. Played in America 1856 or earlier. Adelphi, February 10, 1862.

ANGEL. P. 1 a. Bertha Moore. Court, June 24, 1909 (mat.).

ANGEL, THE. 3 a. R. Walters and W. Gordon.

ANGEL BOY, THE. Ca. Walter Monck. Orig. Prod. by Royal Acad. Mus. March 28, 1900. St. George's Hall, June 29, 1900.

ANGEL KING, THE. P. 5 a. Ross Neil. Sydenham. Westwood House, July 17, 1884.

ANGEL OF DEATH, THE. D. 5 a. Geo. Conquest. Grecian T., May 20, 1861; Surrey, September 19, 1898. See *The Angel of Midnight.*

ANGEL OF HIS DREAMS, THE. Do. d. 4 a. Geo. A. de Gray. Castleford Royal, April 26, 1909.

ANGEL OF ISLINGTON, THE. F. E. L. Blanchard. 1838.

ANGEL OF MIDNIGHT, THE: A "Legend of Terror." 3 a. Fr. French of T. Barriere and E. Plouvier. Adapt. by W. E. Suter and T. H. Lacy. First perf. at T. de Ambigu, Paris, March 5, 1861. Perf. at Grecian T. as *The Angel of Death*, May 20, 1861.

ANGEL OF MIDNIGHT, THE. D. J. Brougham. Princess's, February 15, 1862.

ANGEL OF THE ATTIC, THE. C.D. 1 a. T. Morton. Princess's, May 27, 1843. See *Louison.*

ANGEL OF THE SWAMP, THE. Ca. H. A. Saintsbury and Gene Stratton Porter. Lincoln Royal, August 9, 1907.

ANGEL OF UNREST, THE. N. 4 a. R. A. Green. Brighton R.T., March 4, 1907; Stratford Boro', March 25, 1907.

ANGEL ON EARTH, AN. Do. D., Alfred M. Dalor, founded on Dickens's "The Old Curiosity Shop." St. Helen's T.R., February 12, 1902. September 1, 1902.

ANGEL OR DEVIL. D. 1 a. J. Stirling Coyne. Lyceum, March 2, 1857.

ANGEL UNAWARES, AN. C. 3 a. Robert Vernon Harcourt. Bournemouth R., July 31, 1905. Terry's, September 12, 1905.

ANGEL'S VISIT; OR, THE TRIALS OF LOVE, AN. D Prol and 2 a. W. H. Abel. East London, September 21, 1870.

ANGEL'S WHISPER; OR, THE SPIRIT OF PEACE, THE. D. 3 a. H. N. King. Bath T.R., February 20, 1869.

ANGELA. Far. C. 3 a. G. Duval and Cosmo G. Lennox. Comedy, December 4, 1907.

ANGELA; OR, A WOMAN'S WIT. Oa. Lecocq. D.L., September 28, 1878.

ANGELA; OR, FAITHFUL AND TRUE. D. 4 a. Matthew Wordhaugh. Barnsley, January 23 1871.

ANGELA TERESA. P. 3 a. Geo. Bancroft. Comedy, July 30, 1897 (C.P.).

ANGELICA. O. Metastasio. M. by Porpora. 1722

ANGELICA; OR, QUIXOTE IN PETTICOATS. C. 2 a. Pr. 1758. Taken from Mrs. Lenox's *Female Quixote.*

ANGELINA. C.O Mary Goldsmith. Ac. at a provincial theatre, 1804. N.p.

ANGELINA. P. 3 a. Adap. by W. Cooper from Alexandre Bisson's *Une Mission Délicate* Vaudeville, May 9, 1889.

ANGELINA'S LOVER. C. 1 a. Frank Stayton. Wyndham's, September 24, 1903.

ANGELINE DE LIS. J. T. Haines. St. James's, September 29, 1837.

ANGELIQUE ET MEDOR. O. Thomas. Paris, 1843.

ANGELO. T. 4 a. Adap. to English stage by author of "Peregrine Pickle." Olympic, August 11, 1851.

ANGELO. D. 5 a. Victor Hugo. (Mdme. Sarah Bernhardt's season.) Coronet, June 19, 1905

ANGELO AND THE ACTRESS OF PADUA. D. 4 a. Fr. French of Victor Hugo, by G. H. Davidson. Haymarket, 1855. See *Actress of Padua.*

ANGELO, THE TYRANT OF PADUA. Victoria T., 1835.

ANGELS AND LUCIFERS. F. Ed. L. Blanchard. R. Manor House, Chelsea, 1838. Olympic, October 25, 1841.

ANGELS OF PARIS, THE. D. 4 a. Frank Rogers and Matt. Wilkinson. Scarborough T.R., May 17, 1894.

ANGELUS, THE. O. Prol, and 4 a. (in Eng.). M. by E. W. Naylor, M.Doc., lib. by Wilfred Thornley. C.G., January 27, 1909.

ANGLAIS A BORDEAUX, L'. Op. C. Favart, 1763-72.

ANGLER; A SPORT AFTER RAIN, THE. Ballet Div. M. by M. Solly. Lyceum, June 21, 1817 (third time).

ANGLING IN TROUBLED WATERS. D. 4 a. Ed. Towers. Pavilion, October 14, 1872.

ANGLOISE, L'. Piece. 1 a. Pierre Mille and C. de Vylars. Shaftesbury, March 21, 1908.

ANGLOMANE. C. Saurin, 1752.

ANIMA E CORPO, L'. The first work approaching to Modern Oratorio. Emilio del Cavaliere. 1600.

ANIMAL MAGNETISM. C. 3 a. Mrs. Inchbald. Taken from the French. C.G., April 26, 1788. N.p.

ANIMATED PORTRAIT, THE. Ballet Div. Lyceum, July 30, 1816.

ANNA. C. Ascribed to Miss Cuthbertson. Ac. by D.L. Co. at the O.H. in the Haymarket, February 25, 1793.

ANNA. P. 4 a. Berte Thomas. Bayswater Bijou, October 30, 1903 (C.P.).

ANNA BOLENA. O. Donizetti. Milan, 1822.

ANNA BOLEYN. Banks. See *Anna Bullen.*

ANNA BOLEYN. Hist P. Miss Dickenson, 1877.

ANNA BULLEN; OR, VIRTUE BETRAY'D (sometimes called *Anne Bullen*). T. Mr. Banks. D.L., 1682.

ANNA MARIA'S PIANO. F. 1 a. Nugent Robinson. Dublin T.R., May 13, 1872.

ANNA MICHAELOONA. P. 1 a. Raymond Needham. Rehearsal T., July 4, 1909.

ANNA OF NORWAY; OR, THE DEATH OF BOTHWELL. D. 3 a. Wybert Reeve, Sheffield, T.R., March 8, 1869.

ANNA OF THE PLAINS. Dr. ver. of Alice and Claude Askew's novel, by H. A. Saintsbury (C.P.). Court, December 22, 1906; Worthing R.T., January 28, 1907; Crystal Pal., March 4, 1907.

ANNE BLAKE. P. 5 a. Westland Marston. Princess's, October 28, 1852. Standard, May 27, 1861.

ANNE BOLEYN. D. Poem. Milman. 1826.

ANNE BOLEYN. T. G. H. Boker, 1850.

ANNE BOLEYN. Burl. Extrav. Conway Edwardes. Royalty, September 7, 1872.

ANNE BOLEYN. D. 5 a. Tom Taylor. Haymarket, February 5, 1876.

ANNE BOLEYN; OR, THE JESTER'S OATH. P. 4 a. R. Dodson. Victoria, March 22, 1873.

ANNE MIE. D. Herr Rosier Faasseu. Imperial, June 7, 1880. Adap. by Clement Scott. P O.W., November 1, 1880.

ANNETTE AND LUBIN. C.O. 1 a. C. Dibdin C.G., October 2, 1778. Pr. 1778. Taken from Fr. piece of same title.

ANNETTA E. LUCINDA. O. G. Pacini (His 1st O.) Milan, 1813.

ANNETTE ET LUBIN. Op.C. Favart, 1763-72.

ANNETTE ET LUBIN. O. Martini, 1789.

ANNIE LAURIE. P. 1 a. Graham Moffat. Glasgow Athenæum, March 26, 1908.

ANNIE MONKSWORTH. Britannia, July 18, 1859.

ANNIE OF EDENSIDE; OR, THE COQUETTE CURED. D. Charles Vynne. Carlisle, Bijou T., February 27, 1868.

ANNIE OF THARAU. O. 3 a. Transl. by Mdme. Zoblinsky. M. by Heinrich Hoffman. Edinburgh, Princess's, April 12, 1880.

ANNIE TYRRELL. Surrey. January 26, 1852

ANNIVERSARY, THE. F. C.G., 1758.

ANO DESPUES DE LA BODA. Gil y Zarate, 1825.

ANOMALY, THE. Do. P. L. Cyril Penson. Royalty, December 12 1903.

ANONYMOUS LETTER, THE. C. 3 a. Mark Ambient and Frank Latimer. Lyric. May 5, 1891

ANONYMOUS LETTER, THE. Ca. 1 a. G. S. Street. Vaudeville, June 18, 1907.

ANONYMOUS LETTERS. F. Frederic Jacques. Camden Town R. Park H. October 17, 1888 (amat.).

ANOTHER. F.C. 3 a. Miss Emily Hodson. Vaudeville, December 14, 1885.

ANOTHER DRINK. Burl. Saville Clarke and Lewis Clifton. Folly, July 12, 1879.

ANOTHER ELOPEMENT. Vaud. C. 2 a. Frederic de Lara, Ladbroke Hall, December 6, 1888.

ANOTHER GIRL. M.C. 2 a. Harry Nicholls. M. by Cecil Cook. Bedford Park Club. January 13, 1904.

ANOTHER GUY; A DREAM OF THE FIFTH OF NOVEMBER. Sk. Fred Conquest. Surrey, October 2, 1905.

ANOTHER JOLT. Duol. Horace Bedwell. Queen's Gate H., South Kensington, May 11, 1896.

ANOTHER MAN'S MONEY D. Wilton B. Payne. T.R., Dewsbury, September 4, 1884.

ANOTHER MAN'S MONEY. P. 2 a. Walter Mallett. Bayswater Bijou, November 27, 1901. (Amateurs.)

ANOTHER MAN'S WIFE. C.D. 4 a. W. J. Vaughan and Fenton Mackay. Blackburn, Prince's T., August 7, 1893; Croydon Grand, May 28, 1900; Clapham, Shakespeare, June 4, 1900.

ANOTHER MAN'S WIFE. Do. D. 4 a. Miles Wallerton. L'pool Queen's, February 8, 1909; Pavilion, October 11, 1909.

ANOTHER MATINEE. Ca. F. Castris. Ladbroke H., May 17, 1887; Vaudeville, June 19, 1888.

ANOTHER MATINEE. See *A Stage Coach.*

ANOTHER PAIR OF SHOES. F. Frederick Hay. Globe, September 13, 1875.

ANSTER FAIR; OR, MICHAEL SCOTT THE WIZARD. An Easter Folly. M. by Cooke Hughes. D.L., March 31, 1834.

ANSWER PAID. F. C. Burnand and W. Austin. St. George's H.

ANTARCTIC. "Bouffonerie Musicale." H. B. Farnie. Strand, December 27, 1875.

ANTELOPE, THE. M.C. Adrian Ross. (Adapt. fr. the F.). M. by Hugo Felix; lyrics by Adrian Ross. Waldorf, November 28, 1908.

ANTEMIRE. T. Voltaire. 1720.

ANTHONY AND CLEOPATRA. See *Antony and Cleopatra, All for Love.*

ANTHONY DEAN'S DOUBLE. Ca. 3 scenes Adap. by Paul Sylvester from the story by W. S. Grogan. Haymarket, June 11, 1906.

ANTHONY'S LEGACY. Ca. A. G. Charleson. Wigan T.R., April 18, 1891; Parkhurst T., December 11. 1893.

ANTI-CHRISTIAN OPERA; OR, MASS UNMASK'D, THE. Geo. Paul. Pr. 1755.

ANTI-GAVOTTE. Strand, February 2, 1857.

ANTI-MATRIMONIAL SOCIETY, THE. Ca. Miss Beauchamp. Dublin Gaiety, March 9, 1876; Gravesend Pavilion, February 20, 1884.

ANTIDOTE, THE. C Alfieri, 1805. Transl. by C. Lloyd, 1815.

ANTIGALLICAN, THE. F Mr. Mozeen. Pr. 1762. See *The Heiress.*

ANTIGONE. T. Trans. fr. Sophocles (B.C. 441). D. by Rotron, 1633; Geo. Adams. Pr. 1729; T. Franklin, 1759; R. Potter, pr. 1788; Dale, 1824; W. Bartholomew, 1844; Plumtre, 1865. See "Greek Plays."

ANTIGONE. O. Glück. Rome. 1756.

ANTIGONE. T. Alfieri. 1783. Trans. by G. Lloyd, 1815.

ANTIGONE. Burl. E. L. Blanchard. Strand, 1845.

ANTIGONE. T. (Sophocles.) M. by Mendelssohn. C.G., January 2, 1845; D.L., May 1, 1850; Hampstead Conservatoire, November 4, 1895.

ANTIGONE, THE THEBAN PRINCESS. T. Thomas May. Pr. 1631.

ANTIGONE OF SOPHOCLES, THE. In 2 parts. Transl. by Robert Whitelaw. Crystal Pal., November 6, 1890.

ANTIOCHUS. T. John Mottley. Ac. at L.I.F. April 13, 1721. Pr. 1721.

ANTIOCHUS. T. By a Gentleman of Gloucester. Pr. 1733. N. ac.

ANTIOCHUS. T. Chas. Shuckborough. Pr. 1740. N.ac.

ANTIOCHUS ET CLEOPATRE. T. Deschamps, 1717.

ANTIOCHUS THE GREAT; OR, THE FATAL RELAPSE. T. Mrs. Jane Wiseman. L.I.F. Pr. 1702.

ANTIPODES, THE. C. Richd. Brome. Ac. by Queen's Servants at Salisbury Court, 1638. Pr. 1640.

ANTIPODES, THE. D. 3 a. Tom Taylor. Holborn, June 8, 1867.

ANTIPODES, THE. D. Jefferys Allen-Jefferys. Prince's Street Assembly Rooms, Yeovil, July 2, 1896.

ANTIQUARIAN, THE. F. F. on *The Virginian Mummy*. G. Stead. R. Artillery T., Woolwich, November 15, 1889.

ANTIQUARY, THE. C. Shakerly Marmion. Cockpit, 1641. Ac. by Their Majesties' Servants. Pr. 1641.

ANTIQUARY. M.P. 3 a. Fr. Sir Walter Scott. C.G., January 25, 1820.

ANTIQUARY AND THE BLUEGOWN BEGGAR, THE. Coburg, July 2, 1832.

ANTIQUITY. F. 2 a. Pr. 1808. N.ac.

ANTOINE, TRAGEDY OF. See *Antony*.

ANTOINETTE RIGAUD. C. 3 a. Fr. M. Raymond Deslandee's French piece of the same name, by Ernest Warren. St. James's, February 13, 1886.

ANTOINETTE SABRIER. Fr. P. 3 a. Romain Coolus. Avenue, June 18, 1904.

ANTONIO. See *Don Antonio*.

ANTONIO; OR, THE SOLDIER'S RETURN. T William Godwin. D.L., December 13, 1800. Pr. 1800.

ANTONIO AND MELLIDA. Hist. P. John Marston. Ac. by children of St. Paul's School, 1601. Pr. 1602. Part II. is called *Antonio's Revenge*.

ANTONIO AND VALLIA. C. Massinger. Entd. on Stationers' Co. books, June 29, 1660. N.p. Destd. by Warburton's servant.

ANTONIO'S REVENGE; OR, THE SECOND PART OF ANTONIO AND MELLIDA. T. John Marston. Ac. by children of St. Paul's School, 1601. Pr. 1602.

ANTONIUS; OR, THE TRAGEDY OF MARC ANTHONY. See *Antony*, by Countess of Pembroke.

ANTONY. T. By Samuel Daniel (?). Taken fr. the French of Garnier, and prod. by Mary Countess of Pembroke. Date at end of play, November 26, 1590. Pr. 1595.

ANTONY. T. Dumas. 1831.

ANTONY AND CLEOPATRA. T. Shakespeare, 1608. Ent. Stationers' H., May 20, 1608; first folio, 1623. Founded on Plutarch's "Life of Marcus Antonius." Ac. by Capell and Garrick. Pr. 1758. Ac. D.L. Arr. by Lewis Wingfield for Mrs. Langtry. M. by Ed. Jakobowsky. Ballets by John d'Auban. Princess's, November 18, 1890. Version rev. Olympic, May 24, 1897. Rev. by Mr. Tree, H.M., December 27, 1906; rev. by Mr. R. Flanagan, Manchester Queen's, December 26, 1908.

ANTONY AND CLEOPATRA. T. Sir Chas Sedley, Bart. Ac. Duke of York's T., 1677. See *Beauty the Conqueror*.

ANTONY AND CLEOPATRA. T. Henry Brooke. Pr. 1778. N. ac.

ANTONY AND CLEOPATRA. Burla. Ta. Selby. Adelphi, November 7, 1842.

ANTONY AND CLEOPATRA. Burl. J. F. Draper. Royal Hall, Jersey, December 16, 1870.

ANTONY AND CLEOPATRA. Italian ver. of Shakespeare's T. Lyric, June 19, 1893. Eleonora Duse season.

ANTONY AND CLEOPATRA. Burl. Arthur Miller. M. by A. D.Adamson and W. R. Cazenove. Sutton Pub H., December 2, 1896 (amat).

ANTONY AND CLEOPATRA. See *Cleopatra*.

ANTONY AND CLEOPATRA; OR, HIS TORY AND HER STORY. F. C. Burnand. Haymarket, November 21, 1866.

ANTONY AND CLEOPATRA MARRIED AND SETTLED. Burl. 1 a. C. Selby. Adelphi, December 4, 1843.

ANTY BLIGH. P. 1 a. G. Hamilton Moore. Fr. story by John Wakefield. Gt. Queen St., April 24, 1905.

ANXIOUS TIME, AN. F. Ellis Reynolds. St. George's Hall, January 29, 1889.

ANY ORDERS? Sk. Mrs. A. Wallis. Acton Central H., May 2, 1900.

ANY PORT IN A STORM. Hay., December 5, 1853.

ANYTHING ELSE? M.C. 1 a. Ladbroke H., April 8, 1892.

ANYTHING FOR A CHANGE. C. 1 a. Shirley Brooks. Lyceum, June 7, 1848.

ANYTHING FOR A QUIET LIFE. C. Thos. Middleton. Ac. Globe and Blackfryars. Pr. 1662.

ANYTHING NEW? M.F. 2 a. Pocock. M. by C. Smith. Lyceum, July 1, 1811.

APARTMENTS: VISITORS TO THE EXHIBITION MAY BE ACCOMMODATED. Extrav. 1 a. Wm. Brough. Princess's, May 14, 1851.

APHRODITE AGAINST ARTEMIS. T. in verse. T. Sturge Moore. King's C. G., April 1, 1906.

APHRODYSIAL; OR, SEA FEAST, THE. P. William Percy, 1602. This is an unpub. MS. preserved in a private library.

APIUS AND VIRGINIA. See *Appius and Virginia*.

APOCRYPHAL LADIES. C. Margaret Duchess of Newcastle. Divided into 23 scenes, but not into acts. Pr. 1662.

APOLLO AND DAPHNE. D. Thos. Heywood. Pr. 1637.

APOLLO AND DAPHNE. Masque. John J. Hughes. M. by Pepusch. D.L. Pr. 1716.

APOLLO AND DAPHNE. O. Pr. 1734.

APOLLO AND DAPHNE; OR, HARLEQUIN'S METAMORPHOSES. Pant. John Thurmond. D.L., 1725. Pr. 1727.

APOLLO AND DAPHNE; OR, THE BURGOMASTER TRICKED. Lewis Theobald. Pr. 1726. This is vocal parts of pant. played two years before. M. by Mr. Rich.

APOLLO ET HYACINTHUS. Latin C. Mozart, May 13, 1767.

APOLLO, M.D. F. Sir Randall Roberts, Bart. Jodrell (Novelty), December 26, 1888.

APOLLO SHROVING. C. Wm. Hawkins. Ac. by his Scholars. Hadleigh School, Suffolk, June 2, 1626. Pr. 1627.

APOLLO TRA LE MUSE. O. B. Aliprandi. Munich, 1737.

APOLLO TURN'D STROLLER; OR, THEREBY HANGS A TALE. Sir John Oldmixon. Royalty T. Pr. 1787.

APOLLO'S CHOICE; OR, THE CONTEST OF THE AONIDES. M. Burl. 2 a. Pr. 1815. ? N.ac.

APOLLO'S FESTIVAL. D.L., May 18, 1814.

APOLLO'S HOLIDAY; OR, A PETITION TO THE MUSES. A prel. for the opening of a new theatre at Durham, 1792, by James Cawdell. Probably same as *An Appeal to the Muses.*

APOLOGY FOR ACTORS, AN. Thos. Heywood. 1612.

APOLONIUS AND SILLA. See *Twelfth Night.*

APOSTATE; OR, ATLANTIS DESTROYED, THE. T. 5 a. John Galt. Pr. 1814. ? N.ac.

APOSTATE MOOR, THE. T.P. Coburg, December 31, 1832.

APOSTLES, THE. Orat. Edw. Elgar. Birmingham, October 14, 1903; C.G., March 15, 1904

APOSTOLATE, THE. T. 5 a. R. Shiel. C.G., May 3, 1817.

APOTEOSI D'ERCORE, L'. O. Mercadante (Naples), 1819.

APOTHEOSIS OF PUNCH, THE. Masque to ridicule Sheridan's Monody on Garrick's Death. Patagonian T., Exeter 'Change. Pr. 1779, probably by Leonard M'Nally.

APOTHICAIRE ET PERRUQUIER. O. 1 a. M. by Offenbach. 1861.

APPARITION, THE. C. Trans. fr. Plautius by Richd. Warner Originally called *Mostellaria* On this play *The Intriguing Chambermaid* f. Pr. 1773.

APPARITION, THE. M.D. Rom. J. C. Cross. Hay., September 3, 1794. Pr. 1794.

APPARITION; OR, THE SHAM WEDDING, THE. C. D.L., November 25, 1713. Pr. 1714.

APPEAL TO THE AUDIENCE, AN. Albany Brown. St. James's, December 6, 1852.

APPEAL TO THE FEELINGS, AN. F. 1 a. T. A. Palmer. Nottingham, T.R., March 15, 1875.

APPEAL TO THE MUSES; OR, APOLLO'S DECREE, AN. See *Apollo's Holiday.*

APPEAL TO THE PUBLIC, AN. 1 a. J. Oxenford. Ac. at New York, 1849.

APPEARANCE IS AGAINST THEM. F. Mrs. Inchbald. C.G., October, 1785. Pr. 1785. Revived in 1804 as *Mistake Upon Mistake; or, etc.*

APPEARANCE OF THE ANGELS TO THE SHEPHERDS, THE. Mentioned in Hawkins' "Origin of the English Drama." 1773.

APPEARANCES. C. 2 a. J. Palgrave Simpson. Strand, May 28, 1860.

APPIUS. T. John Moncrieff. C.G. Pr. 1755.

APPIUS AND VIRGINIA. One of the earliest tragedies by an unknown author, under the initials R. P. Not divided into acts. Lessing's *Emilia Galotti* is a modern ver. Ac. 1563. Pr. 1575.

APPIUS AND VIRGINIA. T. John Webster. Story taken from Livy, Florus, etc. Pr. 1654. Ac. 1659. Rev. and alt. by Betterton, and ac. at Duke's T. as *The Roman Virgin; or, The Unjust Judge,* 1679.

APPIUS AND VIRGINIA. T. J. Dennis. 1705. D.L., 1709. Pr. 1709.

APPIUS AND VIRGINIA. See *Virginia.*

APPLE, THE. P. 1 a. Inez Bensusan. Prod. by the Play Actors. Court, March 14, 1909.

APPLE BLOSSOMS C. 3 a. Albery. Vaudeville, September 9, 1871.

APPLE PIE. Surrey, December 26. 1866.

APPLES. C. 1 a. Julian Sturgis. Ladbroke H., November 28, 1887.

APPRENTICE, THE. F. 2 a. Arthur Murphy. D.L. and Edinburgh. Pr. 1756.

APPRENTICE'S PRIZE, THE. Rich. Brome and Thos. Heywood (died 1652). Entered at Stationers' Co., April 8, 1654. N.p.

'APPY 'AMPSTEAD. Sk. Wal Pink. M. by Geo. Le Brunn. Oxford Music H., February 3, 1902.

APRIL DAY. Burl. 3 a. O'Hara. Hay., August 22, 1777. Pr. 1777. Afterwards reduced to 2 a.

APRIL FOLLY. Ca. 1 a. Adap. from Beauchamp's story, "Vengeance," by J. P. Hurst. Olympic, April 6, 1885.

APRIL FOOL, AN. F. 1 a. A. Halliday and Wm. Brough. D.L., April 11, 1864.

APRIL FOOL, AN. Ca. Marguerite Adamson. Rehearsal, W.C., June 26, 1908 (amat.).

APRIL FOOL; OR, THE FOLLIES OF A NIGHT. F. Leonard M'Nally. C.G., April 1, 1786. N.p. The plot was used in *Mad World, my Masters, Country Lasses, The Slip,* and *The Spendthrift.*

APRIL JEST, AN. Sk. Terry's, July 26, 1893.

APRIL RAIN. C. Prol. and 2 a. Leonard S. Outram. Reading T.R., May 10, 1886.

APRIL SHOWERS. C. 3 a. Bellamy and Romer. Terry's, January 24, 1889.

APRON STRINGS. Duol. Basil Hood. Terry's, June 9, 1897.

AR-RIVALS; OR, A TRIP TO MARGATE, THE. Travestie by "J. M. Banero and A. D. Pincroft." Avenue, June 24, 1884.

ARAB, THE, T. Rd., Cumberland; D.L., March 8, 1875. N.p.

ARAB BOY, THE. D.

ARAB GARDENER, THE. P. 1 a. Gladys Unger (adap. fr. the Fr.). Vaudeville, November 12, 1908.

ARAB OF THE DESERT. Pavilion, January 2, 1832. Astley's, February 18, 1856.

ARABELLA; OR, THE BANKS OF THE LEVEN, with the interlude of *The Caledonian Witches.* Ro. D. 3 a. Joseph Moser. Wr. 1808. N. ac., n.p.

ARABI NELLE GALLIE (GLI). O. Pacini. Milan, 1827.

ARABIA SITIENS; OR, A DREAME OF A DRYE YEARE. T.C. Wm. Percy, 1601. An unpubl. MS. in private hands.

ARABIAN NIGHT, AN. C. Adap. by Augustin Daly. New York, 1879.

ARABIAN NIGHTS, THE. F.C. 3 a. Sydney Grundy. Founded on Von Moser's *Harouñ Alraschid*. Globe, November 5, 1887; transf. to Comedy, December 5, 1887; rev. Comedy, November 5, 1892. See *Poor Arthur*.

ARABIAN NIGHTS, THE. See *Almyna, Is Marriage a Failure?, Ali Baba.*

ARAJOON; OR, THE CONQUEST OF MYSORE. J. S. Coyne. Adelphi, October 22, 1838.

ARBANES; OR, THE ENAMOURED PRINCE. Past. Mentioned in catalogue of library of Macklin.

ARBITRATION; OR, FREE AND EASY. F. 2 a. Probably by Reynolds. C.G., December 11, 1806.

ARBRE ENCHANTE, L'. O. Glück. Vienna, 1759.

ARCADES. Masque. John Milton. M. by Henry Lawes. Pl. at Harefield House. Circ. 1634.

ARCADIA. Past. Jas. Shirley. F. on Sir Philip Sidney's *Arcadia*. Ac. at Phœnix by Her Majesty's servants, 1640. Pr. 1640. *Philoclea* founded on this.

ARCADIA. See *Andromana, Argalus and Parthenia, Cupid's Revenge.*

ARCADIA; OR, THE SHEPHERD'S WEDDING. Past. Words by Robt. Lloyd. M. by Stanley. D.L., 1761. Pr. 1761.

ARCADIA REFORMED. P. Mr. Daniel and drawn out of *Fidus Pastor*. 1605. This was supposed to be *Queen's Arcadia of Daniel.* Pr. 1606.

ARCADIAN BROTHERS, THE. J. R. O'Neil. Marionette T., May 3, 1852.

ARCADIAN LOVERS, THE; OR, METAMORPHOSIS OF PRINCES. D. Probably by Moore. M. in the Bodleian Library.

ARCADIAN NUPTIALS, THE. Masque introduced into *Perseus and Andromeda*. C.G., 1764.

ARCADIAN PASTORAL, THE. M.P. 5 a. Lady Craven. Ac. at Burlington Gardens, 1782

ARCADIAN VIRGIN, THE. P. Wm. Haughton and Henry Chettle. Ac. in 1599.

ARCADIANS, THE. Fantl. and Musl P. 3 a. Mark Ambient and A. M. Thompson. Lyrics by Arthur Wimperis. M. by Lionel Monckton and Howard Talbot. Shaftesbury, April 28, 1909.

ARCADIE. Oa. John Burton. M. by Francis Willoughby. Margate T.R., September 17, 1888.

ARCHERS; OR, MOUNTAINEERS OF SWITZERLAND, THE. O. 3 a. Ac. in New York. Founded on *Helvetic Liberty*. Pr. 1796.

ARCHIBALD DANVERS, M.D. Ca. Gertrude and Ethel Armitage Southam. Southport Pavilion T., October 20, 1893.

ARCHIE LOVELL. D. 4 a. F. C. Burnand. Royalty, May 16, 1874.

ARCHIPROPHETS. T. Grimald. 1547. Latin—John the Baptist.

ARCHITECT, THE. Dr. sk. 2 a. Nicholas Gypsum. Pr. 1807.

ARCHITOPIA, UNLIMITED: A LYRICAL LAY OF LADYE LAND. Extrav. Arthur W. Earle and E. Howley Sim. Holborn T.H. May 4, 1894.

ARDEN OF FEVERSHAM. T. Pr. 1592. Ascribed by some to Shakespeare. Ac. by Elizabethan Stage Society at St. George's H., July 9, 1897.

ARDEN OF FEVERSHAM. T. Geo. Lillo. D.L., July 19, 1759. Pr. 1762. Left imperfect by Lillo and finished by Dr. J. Hoadly. Alt. ver. at C.G., April 14, 1790. Sadler's Wells, 1852.

ARDEN OF FEVERSHAM. See *Murderous Michael.*

ARE YOU A MASON? F.C. 3 a. Adap. from German. C. Logenbrüder. Residenz T., Berlin, December 4, 1897; Worthing T.R., September 9, 1901; Shaftesbury, September 12, 1901.

ARE YOU A SMOKER? OR, A NICOTINE NIGHTMARE. F.C. W. Stephens and H. Chance Newton. Waldorf, December 27, 1906.

ARE YOU A SOCIALIST? Sk. Bedford, August 17, 1908.

ARE YOU THE MAN? P. 4 a. Frank Price. Reading County, March 13, 1909; C.P. Burton O.H., May 13, 1909.

AREA BELLE, THE. F. 1 a. Wm. Brough and A. Halliday. Adelphi, March 7, 1864. See *Penelope.*

AREA SYLPH. O. 1 a. B. Fry. Pub. by S. French, Ltd.

ARETHUSA. F. 3 a. Alfred Sutro. King's, Hammersmith, May 25, 1903.

ARETHUSE. O. A. Campra. 1701.

ARETOEUS; OR, THE ROMANCE OF A PATENT. M.D. 2 a. Lib. by Gunners C. F. Fuller and Fred Cape. M. by Gunner Campbell Williams. H.M.S. Rainbow, April 7, 1881.

ARGALUS AND PARTHENIA. T.C. Henry Glapthorne. Plot on Sidney's *Arcadia*. Ac. at Court and at D.L., 1639. Pr. 1639.

ARGENTINA STREGA PER AMORE; OR, HARLEQUIN MULTIPLIED BY ARGENTINA'S WITCHCRAFT FOR LOVE. Pant. 3 a. Ac. at King's T. in Hay. Pr. 1726.

ARIADNE. Olympic, January 28, 1850.

ARIADNE; OR, THE BULL, THE BULLY, AND THE BULLION. Burl. Vincent Arncotts. No date.

ARIADNE. O. Benda. 1721-95.

ARIADNE; OR, THE MARRIAGE OF BACCHUS. O. By "P.P." Trans. fr. the Fr. Presented by the Academy of Music at C.G., 1674. Dedicated to Charles II.

ARIADNE; OR THE TRIUMPH OF BACCHUS. O. Thos. D'Urfey. Pr. 1721. (N. ac.)

ARIANA A NAXOS. Orat. Hadyn. 1791.

ARIANE. T. Corneille. 1672.

ARIANE. D. 4 a. Adap. fr. Mrs. Campbell Praed's novel *Wedlock*, by herself and Mr. Richard Lee. Op. C., February 2, 1888.

ARIANE. See *Airey Annie.*

ARIANNA. O. Monteverde. 1607. Lost except for a few quotations.

ARIEL. Burl. fairy D. 3 a. F. C. Burnand. Gaiety, October 8, 1883.

ARIODANT. O. 3 a. Méhul. October 11, 1798.

ARIODANTE AND GINEVRA. P. Anon. 1582. F. on a story in *Orlando Furioso*, by Ariosto.

ARION; OR, THE STORY OF A LYRE. Burl. F. C. Burnand. Strand, December 20, 1871.

ARISTIPPUS; OR, THE JOVIAL PHILOSOPHER. T.C. Thos. Randolph. (To which is added *The Conceited Pedlar.*) Pr. 1635.

ARISTOCRATIC ALLIANCE, AN. C. 3 a. Adap. by Lady Violet Greville fr. MM. Emilie Augier and Jules Sanden's *Le Gendre de M. Poirier*. Criterion, March 31, 1894.

ARISTOCRATIC ASSASSIN, AN. F. Harry Siddons. T.R., Dumfries, August 10, 1875.

ARISTOCRATIC BURGLAR, AN. "Nocturne." 1 a. Charles Dering. Glasgow Royalty T., June 14, 1897.

ARISTOCRATIC NOODLE, AN. Ventriloquial P. 1 a. Kennerley Sidney. Saltley, Carlton, April 18, 1905.

ARISTOCRATS, THE. M. absurdity. 2 scs. James and Thos. Passmore. M. by Peter Conroy. Poplar, Queen's, October 10, 1904.

ARISTODEMUS. Monodrama. Pr. 1802.

ARISTOMENE. T. Marmontel. 1749.

ARISTOMENES ; OR, THE ROYAL SHEPHERD. T. Anne, Countess of Winchelsea. Story on Lacedaemonian hist. Pr. 1713. N. ac.

ARIZONA. D. 4 a. Augustus Thomas. Adelphi, February 3, 1902.

ARK ON THE SANDS, THE. D. C. Rennell. Brighton, T.R., October 19, 1870.

ARKWRIGHT'S WIFE. D. 3 a. Tom Taylor and John Saunders. Leeds, T.R., July 7, 1873. Globe, November 6, 1873.

ARLEQUIN BARBIER. Pant. 1 a. M. by Offenbach, 1855.

ARLESIENNE, L'. D. 3 a. Alphonse Daudet. Royalty, June 4, 1906.

ARLINE ; OR, THE FORTUNES OF A BOHEMIAN GIRL. Brother Brough.

ARLING LODGE. D. L. C. Turner. Bath, T.R., May, 1872.

ARM OF THE LAW, THE. P. 3 a. Eugène Brieux. Adap. fr. *La Robe Rouge*. Garrick, February 16, 1904; rev. Garrick, May 25, 1909 (mat.).

ARMADA ; A ROMANCE OF 1588, THE. Spec. D. 5 a. Henry Hamilton and Augustus Harris. D.L., October 22, 1888.

ARMADALE. See *Miss Gwilt*.

ARMAND ; OR, THE PEER AND THE PEASANT. P. 5 a. Mrs. Mowatt. Marylebone, June 18, 1849; D.L., February 28, 1853.

ARMED BRITON ; OR, THE INVADERS VANQUISHED, THE. P. 4 a. W. Burke. 1805. (N. ac.)

ARMENIAN GIRL, AN. M.C. 2 a. Hildyard Marris. Manchester C.T., August 2, 1897.

ARMGART. D. poem. George Eliot (Mrs. Evans). 1874.

ARMIDA. O. B. Ferrari. 1639.

ARMIDA. O. Jomelli. 1714-74.

ARMIDA. O. Rossini. Naples, 1817.

ARMIDE. O. 5 a. Glück. Lib by Calzabigi. Paris, 1777. C.G., July 6, 1906.

ARMIDE ET RENAUD. O. Lulli. Paris, 1686.

ARMINIUS. T. Campistron. 1684.

ARMINIUS. T. Wm. Paterson. Refused a license. Pr. 1740. N. ac.

ARMINIUS. T. Murphy. 1798.

ARMINIUS ; OR, THE COMPANION OF LIBERTY. T. Arthur Murphy. Pr. 1798. (N. ac.)

ARMISTICE, THE. J. Howard Payne. Surrey, July, 1822.

ARMOREL OF LYONESSE ; OR, THE CLEVEREST MAN IN TOWN. Adap. fr. Besant's novel by W. Heron Browne and S. Boyle Lawrence. Op. C., December 30, 1890.

ARMOURER, THE. C.O. Richard Cumberland. C.G., April 4, 1793. Songs only pr., 1793. M. probably by Capt. Warner.

ARMOURER, THE. Hist. D. R. Dodson. Britannia, March 27, 1876.

ARMOURER, THE. P. 4 a. Naomi Hope. Whitehaven Royal T., September 20, 1894.

ARMOURER OF NANTES. O. Balfe. C.G., February 12, 1863.

ARMOURER'S DAUGHTER, THE. Extrav. H. T. Arden. Cremorne, August 11, 1866.

ARMOURER'S DAUGHTER, THE. P. Terence Norrey. Eccles Lyceum, October 14, 1901.

ARMS AND THE MAN. Rom. C. 3 a. Bernard Shaw. Avenue, April 21, 1894; rev. Savoy, December 30, 1907.

ARMY OF THE NORTH, THE. Melo-d. J. R. Planché. C.G., October 29, 1831.

ARMY, THE NAVY, AND THE VOLUNTEERS, THE. Ent. Metro. M.H., July 18, 1870.

ARNOLD OF WINKELRIED. D. 5 a. Mark Lemon. Surrey, July 25, 1836.

AROLDO. O. Verdi. Rimini, 1857.

ARRAH-MA-BEG. City of London, October 15, 1866.

ARRAH-NA-BROGUE. Sadler's Wells, October 25, 1865.

ARRAH-NA-POGUE ; OR, THE WICKLOW WEDDING. D. 4 a. Dion Boucicault. Dublin T.R., November 5, 1864. Princess's, March 22, 1865, and August 29, 1891 (rev.).

ARRAH NIEL ; OR, THE VALE OF KNOCKFIERNA. D. Liverpool Adelphi, April 1, 1872.

ARRAIGNMENT. Oa. Don Trueba. Adelphi, August 15, 1831.

ARRAIGNMENT OF LONDON, THE. P. R. Daborne and C. Tourneur. 1613.

ARRAIGNMENT OF PARIS, THE. D. Past. George Peele. At Court, before Q. Eliz., by the children of Chapel Royal, 1584. Pr. 1584

ARRIVALS. See *Ar-Rivals*.

ARRIVED AT CROW STREET; OR, THESPIAN FROM TANDERAGEE. D. 1 a. Dublin, 1796.

ARRIVED AT PORTSMOUTH. M. Ent. W. Pearce. C.G., October 30, 1794.

ARROGANT BOY, THE. D. Pr. 1802. An afterpiece for children.

ARSASES. T. Wm. Hodson. Pr. 1775 (N. ac.).

ARSENE LUPIN. P. 4 a. Francis de Croisset and Maurice Leblanc. Paris Athénée, October 28, 1908; Duke of York's, August 30, 1909.

ARSINOE ; OR, THE INCESTUOUS MARRIAGE. T. A. Henderson. Story is Egyptian. Pr. 1752. N.ac.

ARSINOE, QUEEN OF CYPRUS. O. Peter Motteux. D.L., 1705. Pr. 1707.

ART. D. C. Reade. St. James's, February, 1855.

ART. C.D. Cunningham Bridgeman. Paignton Bijou T., August 24, 1874.

ART AND ARTIFICE; OR, WOMAN'S LOVE. D. 5 a. J. Brougham. Ac. at New York, 1859.

ART AND LOVE. D. sk. 1 a. A. W. Dubourg. Op. C., February 17, 1877.

ART AND NATURE. C. Rev. James Miller. D.L., 1738. F. on *Arlequin Sauvage* of De l'Isle and *Le Flateur* of Rousseau.

ART OF MANAGEMENT ; OR, TRAGEDY EXPELLED, THE. D. piece. Mrs. Charlotte Clarke. Ac. at Concert Room in York Buildings. Pr. 1735.

ARTAMENE. O. Glück. Crema. 1743.

ARTASERS, L'. O. G. Abos. Venice, 1746.

ARTASERSE. O. A. Ariosti. 1724.

ARTASERSE. O. Metastasio. Before 1730.

ARTASERSE. O. Glück (his 1st o.). Milan, 1741.

ARTASERSE. O. L. Caruso. Perf. in London, 1774.

ARTAXERXES. O. Glück. 1741.

ARTAXERXES. O. 2 a. M. by T. A. Arne. Fr. the *Artaserse* of Metastasio. C.G., February 2, 1762. Pr. 1761.

ARTAXERXES. O. Trans. fr. Metastasio by John Hoole. Pr. 1767. D.L., June 6, 1815. Lyceum, July 13, 1816.

ARTAXERXES. O. Dorn. 1831.

ARTE AMANDI, DE OVID. See "Latin Plays."

ARTECHINO FORTUNATO. Marionette T., February 3, 1852.

ARTEMISIA. O. Cimarosa. Venice, 1801.

ARTFUL. Sk. 1 a. Geo. Bellamy and Sydney Blow. Lon. Col., January 25, 1909.

ARTFUL AUTOMATON. A. Law and King Hall. St. George's H., 1865.

ARTFUL CARDS. F.C. 3 a. F. C. Burnand. Gaiety, February 24, 1877.

ARTFUL DODGE, THE. F. 1 a. E. L. Blanchard. Olympic, February 2, 1842.

ARTFUL GIRL, AN. Ca. W. Pett Ridge and Joseph E. Pearce. Birkbeck Inst., June 29, 1892.

ARTFUL HUSBAND, THE. C. Wm. Taverner. L.I.F. 1716. Pr. 1716.

ARTFUL LITTLE SPOUSER. F. 1 a. L. Robertson and M. Comerford. Ptd. 1878.

ARTFUL MISS DEARING. C. 3 a. Arthur Law. Eastbourne D.P., April 5, 1909; Terry's, April 10, 1909.

ARTFUL WIFE, THE. C. Wm. Taverner. L.I.F., 1717. Pr. 1718.

ARTHUR. T. Nicholas Trot. Pr. (n.d.) See *The Misfortunes of Arthur.*

ARTHUR. See *King Arthur.*

ARTHUR AND EMMELINE. D. Ent. D.L., November 22, 1784. Pr. 1784.

ARTHUR, KING OF ENGLAND, THE LIFE OF. P. Richard Hathwaye. Ac. by the Lord Admiral's Servants. 1598.

ARTHUR, MONARCH OF THE BRITONS. T. Wm. Hilton. Pr. 1776. N.ac.

ARTHUR ORTON. D. W. Stephens. Warrington P.O.W., December 11, 1874.

ARTHUR'S BAKERY CO.; OR, THE ORIGINAL A.B.C. Burl. Pro. and 2 a. Words by Frank Silvester. M. by Ellen Gwenydd Elwes. *Matinée* T., November 22, 1898.

ARTHUR'S SHOW. Int. or Masque very popular in Shakespeare's time; probably compiled fr. Mallory's *Morte Arthur.* Mentioned by Justice Shallow in the 2nd part of King Henry IV.

ARTIFICE, THE. C. Mrs. Centlivre. D.L., 1721. Pr. 1721.

ARTIFICE, THE. C.O. 2 a. Wm. Augustus Miles. D.L., April 14, 1780. Pr. 1780.

ARTIFICIAL FLOWER-MAKERS; OR, THE LAST NEW YEAR'S GIFT, THE. D. 2 a. C. H. Hazlewood. Britannia, December 18, 1871.

ARTISAN, L'. O. Halévy. Paris, 1827.

ARTIST, THE. Ca. G. V. Wibrow. Eastbourne T.R., August 6, 1894.

ARTIST AND HIS FAMILY, THE. Surrey, February 28, 1859.

ARTIST'S DILEMMA, AN. Sk. Greenwich Palace, June 3, 1907.

ARTIST'S MODEL, AN. M.C. 2 a. Owen Hall. Lyrics by Harry Greenbank. M. by Sidney Jones. Daly's, February 2, 1895; transf. to Lyric, May 28, 1895.

ARTIST'S MODEL, THE. F. Neville Lynn. Park Town H., Battersea, March 5, 1892.

ARTIST'S REVENGE, THE. Piece. 1 a. Partly f. on Ouida's novel "Puck," and converted into 1 a. by H. Austin. Brixton H., June 16, 1903.

ARTIST'S WIFE, THE. C. 2 a. G. A. Beckett. Hay., July 28, 1838.

ARTISTE DE TERRACINA, L'. Ballet. D.L., March 28, 1853.

ARTISTIC DILEMMA, AN. Ca. C. Fenton. Surrey Masonic H., Camberwell, December 13, 1893.

ARTLESS CINDERELLA. M. fairy tale. 3 scenes. Wr. and composed by H. K. Hamilton Field. St. Andrew's Inst., Carlyle Place, May 9, 1895.

ARTS AND CRAFTS. Piece. 1 a. Ada and Dudley James. Ladbroke H., March 9, 1897.

ARVIRAGUS; OR, THE ROMAN INVASION. Hist. T. Rev. Wm. Tasker. Ac. at Exeter. Pr. 1796.

ARVIRAGUS AND PHILICIA. T.C. in 2 parts. Lodowick Cartell. F. on British Hist. Blackfriars, 1639. Pr. 1639.

AS A MAN SOWETH. P. W. J. T. Collins. Newport (Mon.) Lyceum, April 2, 1904.

AS A MAN SOWS. P. 4 a. Alicia Ramsey and Rudolph de Cordova. Grand, August 22, 1898.

AS A MAN SOWS. P. 1 a. Nellson Morris. Islington, Myddleton H., December 12, 1907.

AS COOL AS A CUCUMBER. F. W. B. Jerrold. See *Cool as a Cucumber.*

AS DE TREFIE, L'. See *Ace of Clubs.*

AS GOLD THROUGH FIRE. D. 4 a. Edinburgh R. Princess's, June 23, 1873.

AS GOOD AS GOLD. Ca. Chas. Coghlan. Lyceum, December 18, 1869.

AS GOOD AS GOLD. D. 4 a. F. S. Jennings. Hammersmith Lyric, May 14, 1906.

AS IN A GLASS; OR, HIS DOUBLE. F.C. 2 ac. and 3 sc. Adap. fr. *The Ourang-Outang; or His Double.* By Geo. Herbert Rodwell and Charles Lauri, jun. Op. C., October 17, 1887.

AS IN A LOOKING-GLASS. P. 4 a. Adap. by F. C. Grove fr. the novel of the same name, by F. C. Philips. Op. C., May 16, 1887.

AS IN A LOOKING-GLASS. See *Lena, Miragè.*

AS IT SHOULD BE. Ent. 1 a. W. C. Oulton. Hay., June 3, 1789. Pr. 1789.

AS LARGE AS LIFE. F. piece. 3 a. A. Shirley. Terry's, May 13, 1890.

AS LIKE AS TWO PEAS. F. 1 a. Hubert Lille. Hay., June 30, 1854.

AS MERRY AS MAY BE. P. Richard Hathwaye. Ac. at Court, 1602.

AS MIDNIGHT CHIMES. D. 4 a. Edwd. Marris. Hull Alexandra. July 11, 1904; Dalston, October 31, 1904.

AS NIGHT COMETH. P. 1 a. Walter E. Crogan. Wolverhampton G.T., January 23, 1899.

AS ONCE IN MAY. C. 1 a. J. Hartley Manners. Shaftesbury, January 23, 1902.

AS PLAIN AS CAN BE. P. Ac. before Q. Elizabeth, July 14, 1567.

AS PLAYED BEFORE HIS HIGHNESS. C. 1 a. Alistair N. Taylor. Adap. fr. story in *The Smart Set.* Manchester Prince's, May 4, 1904.

AS THE WORLD GOES. Thos. Horde, jun.

AS YOU FIND IT. C. Chs. Boyle, third Earl of Orrery. Ac. at L.I.F. Pr. 1703.

AS YOU LIKE IT. C. 5 a. Shakespeare, 1600. Ent. Stationers' Co., August 4, 1600. Fol. 1623. Shakespeare played Adam in this play. Plot taken fr. Lodge's *Rosalynd; or, Euphue's Golden Legacye*. Pr. 1590. An additional scene writ. by Moser. Pr. 1809. P. revised by J. P. Kemble and ac. at C.G., 1810; Royalty, 1872. Rev. on opening of Shaftesbury T. under J. Lancaster, October 20, 1888; Mrs. Langtry at St. James's, February 24, 1890; Daly's company at Lyceum, July 15, 1890; Daly's, April 30, 1894; St. James's, December 2, 1896; Comedy, February 27, 1901; St. James's, January 9, 1906; and rev. by John Hart, Manchester, Prince's, August 12, 1907; arr. in 3 a., H.M., October 7, 1907; rev. Manchester, Queen's, January 11, 1908.

AS YOU LIKE IT. See *Rosalynde*.

AS YOU MAKE YOUR BED SO YOU MUST LIE IN IT. Sk. 1 a. Publ. by S. French, Ltd. Same plot as *The Value of Truth*.

AS YOUR HAIR GROWS WHITER. P. 4 a. Herbert Fuller. St. Helen's O.H., May 28, 1907; Pavilion, October 4, 1909.

ASCANIO. O. Saint-Saëns. 1890.

ASCHENBROEDEL (Cinderella). Gt. Queen Street, December 23, 1905.

ASCOT. F.C. 2 a. Percy Fendall. Oldham Adelphi, October 13, 1879; Folies Dramatiques (Novelty), March 29, 1883.

ASDRUBAL. T. Jacob Montfleury, 1647.

ASHANTEE WAR, THE. D. Wm. Lowe. Greenock T.R., February 27, 1874.

ASHANTEE WAR, THE. Burl. Jas. Sandford. Sheffield Alex. O.H., May 25, 1874.

ASHBY MANOR. P. 2 a. W. Allingham. Pr. 1883

ASHES. P. 3 a. Edwd. Collins and R. Saunders. P.O.W., November 30, 1894.

ASHES. Episode. 1 a. J. F. Stansfield and M E. Ward. Coatbridge T.R., March 9, 1906.

ASHES OF THE PAST. P. 1 a. W. Chapman Huston. Tavistock Place, Passmore Edwards' Settlement, June 4, 1904.

ASHORE AND AFLOAT. Naut. D. 3 a. C. H. Hazlewood. Surrey, February 15, 1864.

ASIATIC, THE. C. by "— YEO." Ac. at Portsmouth 1790.

ASINARIA; OR, THE ASS COMEDY (B.C. 254-184). C. Plautus. Transl. into bl. verse by Thornton, Rich, Warner and Colman, 1769-74. See "Latin Plays."

ASK NO QUESTIONS. Burla. 2 a. C. Selby. Olympic, October 24, 1838.

ASLAM, THE LION. D. W. Barrymore. Surrey, February 16, 1824.

ASMODEUS, THE DEVIL ON TWO STICKS. Adelphi, April 27, 1859.

ASMODEUS, THE LITTLE DEMON; OR, THE ——'S SHARE. C.D. 2 a. Adapt. fr. Scribe's *Part du Diable* by Thos. Archer. Surrey, June 12, 1843.

ASPACIA. T. 3 a. Mrs. Hughes. Pr. 1790.

ASPARAGUS GARDEN. C. Richard Brome. 1634.

ASPARAGUS GARDEN. See *'Sparagus Garden*.

ASPIRATIONS OF ARCHIBALD, THE. Int. E. Ion Swindley. Eastbourne D.P., June 28, 1909.

ASPRAND. T. Salisbury T., March 20, 1805.

ASRAEL. O. Franchetti. Italy.

ASS-ASS-INATION. Extrav. Theodore Ed. Hook. Orange H., nr. Windsor, January 30, 1810. N.pr.

ASS DEALER, THE. C. Trans. fr. Plantus by Richard Warner. Pr. 1774. Taken fr. Greek play *Onacos*.

ASSASSIN, THE. D. 4 a. E. Hill Mitchelson. Wigan T.R., December 23, 1901; Stratford T.R., February 24, 1902.

ASSAULT AND BATTERY. Ca. 1 a. Eille Norwood. Harwich Public H., July 14, 1887.

ASSEDIO DI CALAIS, L'. O. Donizetti. Naples, 1828.

ASSEDIO DI CORINTO, L'. O. Rossini. Milan, December 26, 1828; King's T., June 5, 1834.

ASSEDIO DI FIRENZE, L'. O. Bottesini. Paris, 1856.

ASSEMBLY, THE. C. By a Scots gentleman (possibly Dr. Arch Pitcairne). Pr. 1722.

ASSEMBLY, THE. F. Jas. Worsdale. Dublin, 1740. N.p.

ASSEMBLY; OR, SCOTS REFORMATION, THE. C. Pr. 1766.

ASSIGNATION, THE. C. Probably by Sophia Lee. D.L., 1807. N.p.

ASSIGNATION, THE. Sat. 3 a. Hamilton Aïde. New T., December 7, 1905.

ASSIGNATION; OR, LOVE IN A NUNNERY, THE. C. J. Dryden. Ac. at T.R., 1672. Pr. 1673.

ASSIGNATION; OR, WHAT WILL MY WIFE SAY? THE. D. 2 a. Gilbert à Beckett. Prod. September 29, 1837.

ASSOMMOIR, L'. D. Zola. 1878. See *Drink, D.T., Destroyed by Drink, The Curse of Drink, Gin and the Use and Abuse of Drink*.

ASSOMMOIR, L'. P. 5 a. and 8 tab. taken fr. the book of Emile Zola by MM. W. W. Busnacn and Gastineau (opening piece of M. Guitry's season); rev. Adelphi, June 21, 1909.

ASSOMMOIR, L'; OR, THE CURSE OF DRINK. D. W. Sydney's ver. of Zola's novel. Glasgow P.O.W., August 16, 1879.

ASSOMMOIR, L'; OR, THE CURSE OF DRINK. D. 6 a. John Foote. Dewsbury R., September 27, 1879.

ASSUMPTION OF THE VIRGIN, THE. "A mystery." Perf. by the citizens of Lincoln, June 7, 1483.

ASSURANCE COMPANY, THE. P. E. Fitzball. C.G., April 23, 1836.

ASTOUNDING PHENOMENA. 1 a. C. J. Mathews.

ASTRÆA APPEARED. Olivari. 1797. Trans. fr. Metastasio.

ASTREA; OR, TRUE LOVE'S MIRROUR. Pastl. Leonard Willan. Plot fr. romance of same name. Pr. 1651.

ASTROLOGER, THE. C. Jas. Ralph. Taken fr. *Albumazar*. Ac. 1 night at D.L., 1744.

ASTRONOMER, THE. F. Amphlett. Wolverhampton T., 1802.

ASTUZIE FEMMINILI, LE. O. Cimarosa. Naples, 1793.

AT A HEALTH RESORT. P. 1 a. H. M. Paull. Comedy, June 2, 1893.

AT A JUNCTION. Duol. Margaret Young. Caxton H., April 15, 1909.

AT BAY. D. Pro. and 4 a. Ina Leon Cassilis and Chas. Lander. Ladbroke H., April 9, 1888; Novelty, April 20, 1896.

AT BREAK OF DAY. P. 1 a. F. Thorpe Tracey. Shoreham Swiss Gdns., December 12, 1894.

AT BREAK OF DAY. D. 4 a. W. Bailey, jun., and Chas. Berte. W. London, August 24, 1903.

AT CRIPPLE CREEK. Amer. P. 4 a. Hal Reid. Dover R., January 5, 1905 ; Stratford Borough, March 13, 1905.

AT CROSS PURPOSES. Ca. 1 a. Ada M. Rose. Steinway H., November 8, 1902.

AT DEAD OF NIGHT. Melo-d. 5 a. Harold Whyte. Novelty, April 26, 1897.

AT DUTY'S CALL. Milit. P. Rewritten by John Gerant. Folkestone Pleasure Gardens T., January 31, 1898. See *Khartoum*.

AT ENGLAND'S COMMAND. "Revolutionary Episode," in 1 sc. Wr. by Edward Thane. Queen's Poplar, August 24, 1908.

AT EVENSONG. P. 1 a. Fewlass Llewllyn. Hastings Gaiety, February 22, 1905.

AT HOME. Ent. C. Mathews. 1818.

AT HOME. Mus. epis. Max Roger. Alhambra, May 10, 1909.

AT HOME SUNDAYS. C. 1 a. Sir W. L. Young. Publ. by S. French, Ltd.

AT LAST. Ca. Herbert Gough and A. Morris Edwards. Bristol Prince's, March 19, 1886.

AT LAST; OR, A NEW LIFE. D. Lloyd Clarance. Gt. Grimsby T.R., September 17, 1883.

AT MAMMON'S SHRINE. C.D. 1 a. Benj. Landeck. Leicester R.O.H., May 30, 1887.

AT SANTA LUCIA. O. 2 a. Transl. by Wm. Grist. M. by Pierantonio Tasca. Manchester T.R., October 1, 1894.

AT SIXES AND SEVENS. Ca. 1 a. J. M. Morton. Publ. by S. French, Ltd.

AT STAKE. C. 3 a. J. M. Killick. St. Geo. H., October 26, 1870.

AT THE CROSS ROADS. D. 1 a. J. J. Dilley. Kew, Prince's H., October 20, 1894.

AT THE FERRY. P. 1 a. Mrs. Fawcett. Kilburn, April 26, 1897.

AT THE FOOT OF THE ALTAR. D. 4 a. Fredk. Jarman. Londonderry O.H., September 20, 1897, Stratford T.R., October 25, 1897; W. London, November 1, 1897.

AT THE FOOT OF THE LADDER. D. Prol. and 3 a. W. Travers. E. London, October 16, 1860.

AT THE HARBOUR SIDE. C. 3 a. Niccola Spinnelli, Eugene Checchi. Eng. adap., Percy Pinkerton. Ac., 1st time, Cologne, 1894; Brighton T.R., March 17, 1900; Coronet, November 14, 1900. See *A Basso Porto*.

AT THE KIRK ARMS. C. 1 a. E. J. Malyon and C. James. Brighton Aquar., November 29, 1897.

AT THE PANTOMIME. M. Sk. Corney Grain. St. Geo. H., December 18, 1890.

AT THE POINT OF THE SWORD. Fencing Sk. Egerton Castle. D.L., November 21, 1901.

AT THE RACES. F. Sk. Lincoln Royal, March 24, 1884.

AT THE RISING OF THE MOON. Irish rom. 1 a. A. Demain Grange. Coronet, April 1, 1901.

AT THE STAGE DOOR. Sk. Chas. Wilson and Geo. Bull. M. by Geo. W. Byng. Walham Green Granville, January 11, 1904; Metropolitan M.H., August 31, 1905.

AT THE SWORD'S POINT. Military D. 4 a. Horace Lashbrooke and Richd. Davis Perry. Norwich T.R., June 9, 1884.

AT THE WORLD'S MERCY. M.C.D. 4 a. Carr Loates. Stratford R., September 14, 1908.

AT WAR WITH THE WORLD. C. melo-d. 4 a. G. Lyttleton. Greenwich Carlton, May 9, 1904.

AT WAR WITH WOMEN. D. 4 a. Frank Bateman. Manchester Metropole, July 28, 1902; Stratford T.R., June 1, 1903.

AT ZERO. M. rom. 3 a. Lester Teale. Lyrics by Talbot Hughes. M. by Fredk. Rosse. Reading County T., July 4, 1898.

ATALANTA. C., in Latin. Phillip Parsons. 1612.

ATALANTA. Burl. Geo. P. Hawtrey. M. arr. and composed by Arthur E. Dyer. Strand, November 17, 1888.

ATALANTA; OR, THE GOLDEN APPLES. Extrav. 1 a. Francis Talfourd. Hay., April 13, 1857; rev. with song imitated fr. Fr. *Clic Clac*, by W. H. C. Nation. Astley's, October 27, 1866; Hay., July 28, 1870.

ATALANTA IN CALYDON. D. Poem. Swinburne, 1864.

ATAR GULL. P. G. Almer. Royalty, November 12, 1861.

ATCHI. Ca. J. Maddison Morton. P.O.W., September 21, 1868.

ATHALIA. O. Handel. 1733.

ATHALIA. O. Mendelssohn. 1844.

ATHALIAH. T. Wm. Duncombe. Transl. of Racine's *Athalie*. Pr. 1724.

ATHALIAH. T. Thos. Brereton. Left unfinished.

ATHALIE. T. Racine. 1690. Transl. by J. C. Knight, 1822. D.L., August 9, 1855. See "French Classical Plays."

ATHEIST; OR, THE SECOND PART OF THE SOLDIER'S FORTUNE, THE. C. Thos. Otway. Ac. at Duke's T., 1684. Pr. same year.

ATHEIST'S TRAGEDY; OR, THE HONEST MAN'S REVENGE, THE. Cyril Tourneur. Pr. 1612.

ATHELSTAN. T. Dr. Browne. Founded on British history. Ac. at D.L. Pr. 1756.

ATHELSTANE. C. of London, June 12, 1854.

ATHELWOLD. T. Aaron Hill. An alteration of his *Elfrid; or, The Fair Inconstant*. D.L., 1730. Pr. 1731.

ATHELWOLD. Hist. T. 5 a. Wm. Smith. D.L., May 18, 1843.

ATHENAIS. T. Legrange. 1677-1758.

ATHENIAN CAPTIVE, THE. T. S. Talfourd. C.G. Hay., 1838.

ATHENIAN COFFEE HOUSE, THE. C. Anon.

ATLANTIS; OR, THE LOST LAND. Extrav. 3 a. Maurice Dalton and Ernest Genet. M. by T. Maltby Haddon. Gaiety, March 17, 1886; Op.C., June 17, 1893.

ATOMS IN THE FRENCH REVOLUTION. D. episode. Edwd. H. Cooper. D. of York's, June 7, 1904.

ATONEMENT, THE. D., pro., and 3 a. Founded on Hugo's *Les Miserables*. Wm. Muskerry. Victoria Theatre, August 31, 1872; 4 a. and 10 tableaux, Sadler's Wells, September 14, 1872; Manchester Queen's Theatre, January 25, 1877.

ATONEMENT, THE. D. 1 a. C. Allen Fisher. Aberystwith Bijou, June 11, 1894.

ATONEMENT. D. 1 a. Albert Chevalier. Eastbourne, Devonshire Park, April 8, 1907.

ATONEMENT; OR, THE GOD DAUGHTER, THE. D. 2 a. J. Poole. Hay., May 24, 1836.

ATROCIOUS CRIMINAL, THE. F. 1 a. Palgrave Simpson. Olympic, February 18, 1867.

ATTAQUE DU MOULIN, L'. O. Louis Gallet. F. on Zola's novel. M. by A. Bruneau. C.G., July 4, 1894.

ATTAR GULL; OR, THE SERPENT OF THE JUNGLE. P. Geo. Almar. Surrey, June 11, 1832.

ATTIC DRAMA, AN. Fred James. Garrick, April 18, 1898.

ATTIC STORY, THE. F. 1 a. J. M. Morton. D.L., May 19, 1842.

ATTILA. T. Corneille. 1667. See "French Classical Plays."

ATTILA. O. Verdi. Venice, 1846.

ATTILA. Poetl. P. 4 a. L. Binyon. H.M., August 15, 1907 (C.P.); September 4, 1907.

ATTILIO REGOLO. O. Metastasio. 1740.

ATYS. O. 5 a. Lulli. Paris. January 10, 1676.

ATYS. O. Ariosti. 1700.

ATYS. O. Piccini. 1780.

AU JAPON. Pant. 1 a. St. George's H., May 20, 1896.

AU TRAVERS DU MER. Oa. Prince Poniatowski. St. George's H., June 6, 1873.

AUBREY CLOSES THE DOOR. P. 1 a. Cosmo Hamilton. Blackheath Concert H., January 28, 1904.

AUBREY'S SISTER. F. c. 3 a. Royston Keith. Ealing, June 22, 1903.

AUCASSIN ET NICOLETTE. O. Gétry. Versailles, 1779. Ver. by Andrew Lang. Perf. by amat. Tunbridge P.H., February, 1903.

AUCHINDRANE. See *Ayrshire Tragedy.*

AUCTION, THE. F. Theophilus Cibber. Ac. at Hay. Pr. 1757.

AUCTION OF PICTURES, THE. Samuel Foote. Hay., 1748. N.p.

AUCTIONEER, THE. C. 3 a. J. M. Morton and Robert Reece. Bournemouth T.R., May 30, 1898.

AUGUSTA; OR, THE BLIND GIRL. D. 3 a. D.L., January 14, 1823.

AUGUSTALES, LES. O. F. Rebel and F. Francœur. 1744.

AUGUSTO, L'. T. Amore. 1665.

AUGUSTUS. T. Edwd. Biddle. Pl. 1717.

AUGUSTUS AND GULIELMUS; OR, THE VILLAGERS. Melo-d. W. A. Holland. Hay., March, 1806. N.p.

AUGUSTUS CÆSAS. A play under this title is mentioned in a list of bks. pr. for R. Bentley about 1691 (prob. not publ.).

AULD ACQUAINTANCE. C.D. 1 a. (or 2 a.). Joseph J. Dilley. St. George's H., March 23, 1878.

AULD LANG SYNE. C.D. 3 a. George Lash Gordon. Edinburgh Princess's, November 9, 1877; Park T., May 26, 1878.

AULD LANG SYNE. P. 1 a. Lorma Leigh. Ladbroke H., June 19, 1891.

AULD LANG SYNE. Ca. Basil Hood. P.O.W., November 5, 1892.

AULD MAN AND HIS WIFE, THE. One of the eight ints. by Sir David Lindesay. Pr. 1792.

AULD ROBIN GREY. M.E. Saml. James Arnold. Hay. Pr. 1794.

AULD ROBIN GRAY. Ballet. By Byrne. D.L., June 3, 1814.

AULD ROBIN GRAY. D.L. April 19, 1858.

AULD ROBIN GRAY. D. 1 a. Adap. fr. Jean Marie by George Roy. See *Marie.* Imperial, September 22, 1883.

AULD ROBIN GRAY. See *The Wanderer*

AULULARIA. C. B.C. 254-184. Plautus. Transl. into blank verse by Thornton, Rich, Warner, and Colman, 1769-74. See "Latin Plays."

AULULARIA. See *Westminster Plays.*

AUNT AGATHA'S DOCTOR. M. Ca. Herbert Harraden. Terry's, April 30, 1891.

AUNT CHARLOTTE'S MAID. F. 1 a. J. M. Morton. Adelphi, 1858; Windsor T. and Hay.

AUNT CHIMPANZEE. M.F. 1 a. Robert A. P. Williams. Wrexham St. James's T., October 30, 1897 (C.P.).

AUNT DINAH'S PLEDGE. D. 2 a. H. Seymour. Publ. by S. French, Ltd.

AUNT GABRIELLE. C. 3 a. J. C. New. St. John's Hill, Strathblaine Hall, June 5, 1908.

AUNT JACK. F. 3 a. Ralph R. Lumley. Court, July 13, 1889.

AUNT JANE'S FLAT. Ca. Bertha Moore. Queen's Gate H., June 14, 1901.

AUNT MARGARET. F.C. 3 a. Sydney T. Pease. Croydon T.R., June 11, 1897.

AUNT MARIA'S WILL. F. 3 a. R. H. Curtis. Dover T.R., June 23, 1904.

AUNT MINERVA. Ca. By C. Tudor. Guildhall School of M., March 15, 1902.

AUNT OR UNCLE. F. 3 a. Rev. A. J. Wilson, D.D. Church Inst. H., Wandsworth, May 21, 1885.

AUNT REBECCA. F. Allan Atwood and Russell Vaun. Cheltenham O.H., December 19, '1895; Kilburn, February 3, 1896.

AUNT TABATHA. F. Frank H. Morland. Lowestoft P.H., June 3, 1894.

AUNT'S ADVICE. Ca. E. G. Southern. Hay., December 3, 1861.

AUNTIE. F. 3 a. H. J. Byron. Toole's, March 13, 1882.

AUNTIE OF THE FINGER-POST. Monol. Bertha N. Graham. Cripplegate Inst., April 4, 1907.

AUNTIE'S MOTOR. C. 3 a. Godfrey John and Carlo War. Hackney Manor T., February 21, 1899.

AURAMANIA; OR, DIAMOND'S DAUGHTER. D. P. and 4 a. Miss Johana Pritchard. Alfred, September 4, 1871.

AURELIANA IN PALMIRA. O. Rossini. Milan, December 26, 1813; King's, June 22, 1826.

AURELIO AND MIRANDA. D. 5 a. Jas. Boaden. D.L., December 29, 1798. Pr. 1799. F. on Mr. Lewis' novel "The Monk."

AURENG-ZEBE; OR, THE GREAT MONGUL. T. 5 a. J. Dryden. Ac. at T.R. Pr. 1676, 4to. 1692.

AURORA FLOYD. Adap. fr. Miss Braddon's novel by B. Webster. Adelphi, March 11, 1863.

AURORA FLOYD. D. 3 a. Fr. Miss Braddon by Wm. Suter. Queen's T., April 4, 1863.

AURORA FLOYD. 3 a. Fr. Miss Braddon by J. B. Ashley and Cyril Melton. Imperial, August 24, 1885.

AURORA FLOYD; OR, THE DARK DUEL IN THE WOOD. D. 3 a. C. H. Hazlewood. Britannia T., April 21, 1863.

AURORA'S CAPTIVE. P. 1 a. Tom Gallon. Ladbroke H., December 13, 1904 (C.P.).

AURORA'S NUPTIALS. Dr. Perf. D.L. Pr. 1734.

AUS DER SCHWEIZ. O. Fantasy. Bachmann. M. by Raff.

AUSTERLITZ; OR, THE SOLDIER'S BRIDE. Melo-d. 3 a. J. T. Haines. Queen's T., and at New York, 1845.

AUSTRALIA; OR, THE BUSHRANGERS. D. 5 a. W. A. and A. G. Stanley. Grecian, April 16, 1881.

AUTHOR, THE. C. 2 a. Saml. Foote. D.L. Pr. 1757. Edinburgh, 1781.

AUTHOR AND THE BOOKSELLER, THE. Dr. piece. Charlotte M'Carthy. Pr. circa 1765.

AUTHOR'S FARCE; OR, THE PLEASURES OF THE TOWN, THE. C. 3 a. H. Fielding. Perf. at little theatre in Haymarket, 1730. Pr. 1730.

AUTHOR'S TRIUMPH; OR, THE MANAGERS MANAGED, THE. F. Anonym. Intended to have been ac. at L.I.F., April 14, 1737.

AUTHORS, THE. Dr. satire. 2 a. Lindesius Jones. Ac. and Pr. 1755.

AUTOGRAPHE, L'. St. James's, November 3, 1890.

AUTRE MOTIF, L'. C. 1 a. Edouard Pailleron. Royalty, April 17, 1902.

AUTUMN MANŒUVRES. Ca. W. R. Stow. Vaudeville, October 14, 1871.

AVALANCHE, THE. Sens. Epis. F. Neville. Inc. and vocal M. by Carl Kiefert. London Hipp., September 23, 1907.

AVALANCHE; OR, THE TRIALS OF THE HEART, THE. Rom. D. 3 a. A. Harris. Surrey, October 3, 1854.

AVANT, PENDANT ET APRES. V. Scribe. Before 1822.

AVARE, L'. C. Molière. 1667. Fr. the Aulularia of Plautus. See "French Classical Plays."

AVENGER, THE. P. G. W. Lovell. Surrey, 1835.

AVENGER; OR, SLAVES OF PASSION, THE. M.D. 4 a. Fred Moule. Queen's T., Leeds, September 29, 1899.

AVENGING HAND, THE. M.D. Hubert Bartlett. Prince's T., Blackburn, July 31, 1899.

AVENTURIER, L'. O. Poniatowski. Paris, 1865.

AVENTURIÈRE, L'. C. Augier. Princess's, May 23, 1870.

AVENTURIERE, L'. Princess's, May 2[illegible] 1870. See *The Adventurers' Home.*

AVERAGE MAN; OR, HOW THE AVERAGE BECAME THE ABNORMAL, AN. C.D. 4 a. S. X. Courte. Folkestone Pleasure Gdns., March 6, 1895; Op.C., June 13, 1895.

AVOCAT PATELIN, L'. F. D. Brueys. 1706. Reproduction of a C. attributed to Blanchet, who died 1519. Bouillet says still more ancient.

AVVISO AI MARITATI, L'. O. L. Caruso (his last O.). Rome, 1810.

AWAKENING, THE. C. 3 a. Arthur Benham. Garrick, October 1, 1892.

AWAKENING, THE. P. 4 a. C. Haddon Chambers. St. James's, February 6, 1901.

AWAKENING, THE. P. 1 a. Lyddell Sawyer (produced by the English Play Society). Terry's, May 16, 1909.

AWAKENING OF PAN, THE. Sk. Camberwell Empire, June 21, 1909.

AWAKING. D. 1 a. Campbell Clarke. Alt. and adapt. fr. French of Sandeau and Decourcelle. Gaiety, December 14, 1872.

AWAKING. See *Marcel.* Second adap. of *Awaking,* by C. Clarke.

AWAY WITH MELANCHOLY. F. 1 a. J. M. Morton. Princess's, March 13, 1854.

AWFUL EXPERIENCE, AN. Duo. Mrs. Christina Dening. Somerville Club, 231, Oxford Street, February 21, 1893.

AWFUL RISE IN SPIRITS, AN. Extrav. T. Taylor. Olympic, September 7, 1863.

AWKWARD. Ca. Manchester Comedy T., September 28, 1885.

AWKWARD AFFAIR, AN. F. Fredk. Hay. Duke's, October 19, 1878.

AWKWARD ARRIVAL. C. 2 a. Publ. by S. French, Ltd.

AWKWARD DILEMMA, AN. F. Wynne Scarlett. T.R., Consett, April 24, 1893.

AXIS, THE. C. 3 a. Cyril Harcourt. Worthing R., September 12, 1904; Criterion, July 5, 1905.

AYLMER'S SECRET. P. 1 a. Stephen Phillips. Adelphi, July 4, 1905.

AYRSHIRE TRAGEDY. T. Sir W. Scott. 1830.

AYRSHIRE TRAGEDY. See *Auchindrane.*

AZAEL, THE PRODIGAL. D. 3 a. F. on Scribe and Auber's *L'Enfant Prodigue,* by Edward Fitzball. D.L., February 19, 1851.

AZOR AND ZEMIRA; OR, THE MAGIC ROSE. O. 3 a. Spohr. C.G., April, 1831.

B

B. B. F. 1 a. F. C. Burnand and Montagu Williams. Olympic, March 22, 1860.

BA KAU; OR, THE PRINCE'S NAP AND THE SNIP'S SNAP, LA. Burl. J. E. Roe. Shcreham, Swiss Gardens, June 7, 1869.

BAB; OR, SAVED BY A CHILD. D. Burnley, T.R., September 11, 1882.

BAB-BALLAD-MONGER; OR, THE MYSTERIOUS MUSICIAN AND THE DUKE OF DIS-GUISEBURY, THE. Travestie. Frank Lindo. Op. C., July 30, 1892.

BABBAGE'S PUPPETS. F. Bolton T.R., September 22, 1884.

BABBEO L'INTRIGANTE. O. Sarria. Naples, 1872.

BABBLE SHOP, THE. Travesty on *The Bauble Shop.* E. Rose. Trafalgar, March 30, 1893.

BABEL AND BIJOU. See *Babil and Bijou.*

BABES; OR, WHINES FROM THE WOOD, THE. Burl. 2 a. Harry Paulton. M. by W. C. Levey. Birmingham T.R., June 9, 1884; Toole's, September 9, 1884. Wr. up to date, A. C. Shelley, Strand, February 4, 1895.

BABES IN THE WOOD. This title was registered at Stationers' Hall in 1595.

BABES IN THE WOOD. Rob Yarrington in 1601 wrote *Two Lamentable Tragedies,* one of which was about a young child murdered in a wood by two ruffians by command of its uncle.

BABES IN THE WOOD. Burl. F. Robson.

BABES IN THE WOOD. Burl. T. A. Palmer.

BABES IN THE WOOD. Burl. C. W. McCabe and Geo. Belmore. M. by W. C. Vernon. Battersea Park Town T., A[illegible] 3, 1893.

BABES IN THE WOOD, THE. C. 3 a. Tom Taylor. Hay., November 10, 1860.

BABES IN THE WOOD, THE. Burl. G. L. Gordon and G. W. Anson. Liverpool P.O.W., April 16, 1877.

BABES IN THE WOOD, THE. Burl. Geo. Capel. Gaiety T.; Douglas, Isle of Man, July 26, 1884.

BABES IN THE WOOD, THE. Burl. 2 a. J. G. Grahame and Bert Arlett. M. by J. G. Grahame. Willenhall T.R., April 27, 1895.

BABES IN THE WOOD, AND THE GOOD LITTLE FAIRY BIRDS, THE. Burl. D. 1 a. H. J. Byron. Adelphi, July 18, 1859.

BABETTE. C.O. 3 a. Lib. adap. from Ordonneau and Verneuil's *La Grappe D'Amour*. M. by Gustav Michiels. Strand, January 26, 1888.

BABETTE. C.O. 3 a. Harry B. Smith. M. by Victor Herbert. Bayswater, Vict. H., November 5, 1903.

BABIL AND BIJOU. Fantastic M.D. 18 tab. and prol. and 5 a. Dion Boucicault and J R. Planché. C.G., August 29, 1872.

BABIOLE. O. 3 a. MM. Clairville and Gastineau. M. by Laurent de Rille. Adap. into English by Robert Reece. Manchester, Prince's T., March 10, 1879.

BABLER, THE. C. Transl. from Voltaire, and pr. in Dr. Franklin's Edition.

BABOO OR PRINCE. F.C. 3 a. F. C. Daly. Neville Dramatic Studio, April 5, 1897.

BABTISM AND TEMPTATION. C. Bishop Bale. Mentioned by author in list of his own works.

BABTISTES. T. in Latin. George Buchanan, 1578. Another edition was pub. in London the same year.

BABTISTES. Scriptl. D. 5 short a. Ascr. by Peck to Milton, 1642.

BABY. F.C. 3 a. Robert Soutar and F. Herbert. Southend, Alexandra T., July 17, 1890.

BABY. F. J. E. Cowell. Eastbourne, Pier Pav., December 24, 1892.

BABY, THE, f. by Lady Violet Greville on one of Max Adler's "Elbow Room" Stories. Originally produced as *Baby: A Warning to Mesmerists*, at Brighton T.R., October 31, 1890. Terry's, April 9, 1891.

BABY; OR, A MIDNIGHT TRUST. Dom. Dr. 4 a R. Waldron and Lionel Ellis. Preston, Prince's, March 23, 1896.

BABY; OR, A SLIGHT MISTAKE. F.C. 3 a. Walton Hook. T.R., Ipswich, June 4, 1888; Vaudeville, June 7, 1888.

BABY'S BIRTHDAY. A. Bucklaw.

BABY'S ENGAGEMENT. Ca. Robt. Rogers. Wolverhampton T.R., December 19, 1892.

BABY'S SHOE, A. Sk. Ada Roscoe. Manchester Palace, October 23, 1907; Bedford, July 6, 1908.

BABYLONIANS, THE. Aristophanes. See "Greek Plays."

BACCARAT; OR, THE KNAVE OF HEARTS. P. W. E. Suter. Sadler's Wells, March 4, 1865.

BACCHAE, THE. P. Transl. from Euripides, B.C. 480-407, by R. Potter. Pr. 1781.

BACCHÆ OF EURIPEDES, THE. Transl. into Eng. rhyming verse by Gilbert Murray. Court, November 10, 1908 (mat.).

BACCHANALIANS, THE. T. Transl. from Euripides by Michael Wodhull. Pr. 1782. O. Buckley, in Bohn's Library. See "Greek Plays."

BACCHIDES. C. B.C. 254-184. Plautus. Latin, based on Greek C. by Menander. Transl. into blank verse by Thornton, Rich, Warner and Colman, 1769-74. See "Latin Plays."

BACCHUS AND ARIADNE. Ballet. D.L., May 9, 1798.

BACHELOR OF ARTS, A. C.D. 2 a. Pelham Hardwick. Lyceum, November 23, 1853; D.L., December 19, 1855

BACHELOR QUARTERS. See *The Bungalow.*

BACHELOR'S BUTTONS. F. 1 a. E. Stirling. Strand, May 29, 1837.

BACHELOR'S DREAM, A. Sk. Eastbourne Hipp., April 5, 1909.

BACHELOR'S ROMANCE, A. C. 4 a. Miss Martha Morton. Edinburgh T.R., September 10, 1897; Gaiety, September 11, 1897; Globe, January 8, 1898.

BACHELOR'S WIDOW, THE. C. 3a. F. J. O'Hare. Lyrics by Mostyn T. Piggott. M. by Edwin Boggetti. Royalty T., Glasgow, June 1', 1897; Terry's, June 14, 1898; Brighton Eden, August 4, 1899.

BACHELOR'S WIFE, A. C. F. Watson. New York, January 11, 1858; D.L., October 29, 1860.

BACHELORS. F.C. Prol. and 3 a. A. A. Aldred. New Cross H., June 18, 1884.

BACHELORS. C. Adap. from the German by Robt. Buchanan and Hermann Vezin. Hay., September 1, 1884.

BACHELORS, THE. C.O. M. by Alfred Taylor, lib. by C. H. M. Wharton. Prince's T., Manchester, June 8, 1885.

BACHELORS, THE. See *The Batchelors.*

BACHELORS' HALL. F. G. L. Gordan. Liverpool P.O.W., January 13, 1877; Op. C., April 21, 1887.

BACHELORS' WIVES. F. 3 a. F. Bousfield. Strand, December 15, 1886. See *Batchelors' Wives.*

BACK FROM INDIA. Pottinger Stevens and Cotsford Dick. St. George's H.

BACK IN FIVE MINUTES. F. H. T. Johnson. Parkhurst T., February 16, 1891; Strand, April 22, 1891.

BACK IN TOWN. M.Sk. Corney Grain. St. Geo. H., October 29, 1894.

BACK TO THE LAND. P. 1 a. Andrew Wicks. Savoy. October 30, 1905.

BACK TO THE STONE AGE. M.P. 2 a. George Jervis. Peckham Crown, August 5, 1904 (C.P.).

BACKING THE FAVOURITE. F. G. L. Gordon. Op.C., August 7, 1875.

BACKING THE VARMINTS. F. G. L. Gordon. Op. C., August 7, 1875.

BACKSHEESH. M.Sk. Corney Grain. St. Geo. H., December 26, 1884.

BACKSLIDER, THE. Duol. 1 a. Osmond Shillingford. Strand, April 15, 1895.

BACKWARD CHILD. P. 1 a. H. L. Childe Pemberton. Pub. by S. French, Ltd.

BAD BARGAIN, A. Ca. Sydney Grundy. 1879.

BAD BEGINNING MAKES A BAD ENDING, A. P. Ac. before the English Court, May, 1613. (This play is not known to exist.)

BAD BOYS. C. 3 a. Adapted from the French piece, *Clara Soleil*, by Clement Scott. Comedy, April 29, 1885.

BAD CHARACTER, A. P. 4 a. F. A. Scudamore. Fulham Grand, April 8, 1901.

BAD LOT, A. F.C. 3 a. Adap. from the French by Harry Paulton and "Mostyn Tedde." Northampton O.H., June 24, 1887; Camberwell Metropole, May 23, 1898.

BAD LOVERS. C. Coyne. 1836.

BAD PENNY, A. F. 1 a. W. Lestocq. Vaudeville, June 13, 1882.

BAD QUARTER OF AN HOUR, A. Ca. 1 a. Miss Costello. Dublin, Queen's Royal, August 31, 1896

BADEN-BADEN; OR, THE PRETTY HUNCHBACK. C. 3 a. Richd. Bateman. Barnstaple T.R., January 12, 1872.

BAFFLED; OR, PARMA VIOLETS. American D. 4 a. Standard, September 19, 1881.

BAFFLED CRIME, A. D. 4 a. C. W. McCabe. Novelty, November 23, 1896.

BAFFLED SPINSTER. C. 1a. Publ. by S. French, Ltd.

BAG OF GOLD, THE. Hillyard. Olympic, June 27, 1852.

BAG OF TRICKS, A. Duol. Mary Potter. Brighton T.R., May 18, 1896.

BAGATELLE. O. 1 a. M. by Offenbach. 1874.

BAGGING A BARRISTER. Duol. Reginald Stockton. West London, August 10, 1896.

BAGPIPE MAD. Sk. Holloway Empire, July 12, 1909.

BAGUE DE THERESE. C. Carmouche. 1861.

BAIGNEUSE, LA. G. R. Sims. M. by Ivan Caryll. Palace, November 11, 1901.

BAIL UP. Australian D. 4 a. Julian Hughes. F. on Hume Nisbet's novel. Kidderminster T.R., May 19, 1893 (C.P.).

BAILIFF, THE. Ca. 1 a. F. W. Broughton. Bath T.R., April 5, 1890; Royalty, May 17, 1890; Toole's, July 3, 1890.

BAILIFF, THE. Sk. Messrs. Karno, Kitchen and Durell. Wigan Hipp., April 19, 1907.

BAIRN, THE. Scotch D. 3 a. Geo. Duncan. Aberdeen, H.M.O.H., June 17, 1878.

BAJASETTE. O. G. Coochi. Romo, 1716.

BAJAZET. T. Racine. 1672. See "French Classical Plays."

BAJAZET. See *Barbarossa.*

BAL D'ETE. Div. 1 tab. D.L., October 2, 1852

BAL MASQUE, LE. C.O. 3 a. Arthur H. Ward. M. by Henry Vernon. Parkhurst, May 16, 1898.

BALACLAVA. D. 3 a. J. B. Johnstone. Standard, June 10, 1878.

BALACLAVA DAY. D.L., March 17, 1856.

BALACLAVA JOE; OR, SAVED FROM THE JAWS OF DEATH. D. C. P. Emery. Entd. at Stationers' H. April 20, 1893.

BALAMIRA; OR, THE FALL OF TUNIS. T. R. Shiel. C.G., 1818.

BALANCE OF COMFORT, THE. C. 2 a. R. J. Raymond. Adelphi, 1835.

BALANCE OF COMFORT, THE. C. 1 a. W. Bayle Bernard. Hay., November 23, 1854.

BALDER'S DOD. D. Evald or Ewald. 1773.

BALISHAM BUDDHISTS, THE. Magical Epis. Nevil Maskelyne. St. George's H., August 2, 1909.

BALL, THE. C. James Shirley and Chapman. Lic. 1632. D.L., 1639. Pr. 1639.

BALLA-GO-FAUGH. Irish D. 3 a Edward Towers. Pavilion, November 13, 1880.

BALLAD GIRL, THE. Pavilion, December 3, 1866.

BALLAD-MONGER, THE. Rom.P. 1 a. Adap. by Besant and Pollock from Theodore de Banville's *Gringoire.* Hay., Sepember 15, 1887; H.M., June 20, 1903.

BALLAD-SINGER, THE. M.P. 3 a. Tom Craven. Hastings, Gaiety T., July 16; 1891; Eleph. and Ca., March 13, 1893.

BALLERINA AMANTE, LA. D. Cimarosa. Venice, 1785

BALLET DE LA PAIX. O. F. Rebel and F. Francœur. Academie, 1738.

BALLET GIRL, THE. M.C. 2 a. Jas. T. Tanner. Lyrics by Adrian Ross. M. by Karl Kiefert. Wolverhampton, Grand T., March 15, 1897; Brixton, August 2, 1897.

BALLINASLOE BOY, THE. D. 2 a. C. H. Hazlewood. Britannia, June 24, 1867.

BALLO DELLE INGRATE, IL. O. Monteverde. 1568-1643.

BALLO IN MASCHERA, UN. O. Verdi. Rome, 1859; Lyceum, June 15, 1861.

BALLOON, THE. F.C. 3 a. J. H. Darnley and G. Manville Fenn. Terry's, November 13, 1888; Strand, February 6, 1889.

BALLOONACY; OR, A FLIGHT OF FANCY. Extrav. F. C. Burnand and H. P. Stephens. Royalty, December 1, 1878.

BALLY VOGAN. D. 4 a. Arthur Lloyd. Newcastle Tyne T., July 25, 1887.

BALLYHOOLEY; OR, A NIGHT ON THE BIG WHEEL. F.C. 3 a. J. Russel Bogue. Doncaster O.H., May 5, 1898 (c.p.); Workington T.R., October 14, 1901.

BAMBOOZLING. F. 1 a. Thos. Egerton Wilks. Olympic, May 16, 1842.

BAND, RUFF AND CUFF. Int. See *Exchange Ware.*

BANDIT, THE. O. 3 a. Pr. 1814. N.ac.

BANDIT KING, THE. D. 5 a. and 3 tabx. Orig. prod. in America; Manchester Queen's, September 16, 1895; Pavilion, December 2, 1895.

BANDIT'S BLUNDER THE. Burl. Sk. Ward Barry. West London, March 8, 1909

BANDIT'S DAUGHTER, THE. Sk. Bedford, November 11, 1907.

BANDIT'S DEATH, THE. See *The Spirit of Poetry.*

BANDITO, IL. O. Ferrari. Casale, 1880.

BANDITS, THE. Hippodrome sensation. Alicia Ramsay and Rudolph de Cordova. Hippodrome, June 16, 1902.

BANDITTI; OR, A LADY'S DISTRESS, THE. C. T. D'Urfey. Plot fr. Shirley's *Sisters.* T.R., 1686. Pr. 1686.

BANDITTI; OR, LOVE'S LABYRINTH, THE. O. O'Keefe. M. by Dr. Arnold. C.G., 1781. See *Castle of Andalusia.*

BANISHED DUKE; OR, THE TRAGEDY OF INFORTUNATUS, THE. T.R., 1690. Pr. 1690.

BANISHED FROM HOME. D. 3 a. J. Cherry Griffiths. Britannia, May 3, 1875.

BANISHED STAR, THE. C. J. B. Buckstone. Prod. in New York, 1840.

BANISHMENT OF CICERO, THE. T. Richd. Cumberland. Pr. 1760. N. ac.

BANK HOLIDAY. C.D. 2 a. Herbt. B. Cooper. Liverpool P.O.W., July 14, 1886.

BANK NOTE; OR, LESSONS FOR LADIES, THE. C. Wm. Macready. C.G., 1795. Fd. on *Artful Husband.*

BANK OF ENGLAND, THE. P. 4 a. Max Goldberg. Clapham Shakespeare, November 26, 1900.

BANK ROBBERY, THE. Melo-d. Forbes Dawson. Strand, January 24, 1896. (C.P.)

BANK ROBBERY, THE. Sk. Edwd. Ranier. Sadler's Wells, December 14, 1903.

BANKER'S CLERK, THE. Sk. Ch. A. Stephenson. Waterloo Bridge Road, Victoria H., November 2, 1903.

BANKER'S DAUGHTER, THE. D. W. C. Foster. N. Shields T.R., May 24, 1876.

BANKER'S DAUGHTER, THE. C. Bronson Howard. Adap. by J. Albery, and ac. as *The Old Love and the New.*

BANKRUPT, THE. C. Saml. Foote. Hay., 1773. Pr. 1776.

BANKS AND BREAKS. D. O'Bryne and M'Ardle. Liverpool R. Amphi., May 17, 1869.

BANKS OF THE BOYNE WATER. D. Bishop Auckland T.R., March 3, 1884.

BANKS OF THE HUDSON, THE. D. 3 a. Victoria, December, 1829.

BANNIAN DAY. M. Ent. Geo. Brewer. Hay., June 11, 1796. Pr. 1796.

BANNISTER'S BUDGET WITH THE SHIPWRECK; OR, 2 WAYS OF TELLING A STORY. Ent. D.L., May 30, 1814.

BANQUET, THE. F.C. 3 a. F. Freeth, B.A. Kilburn Town H., May 26, 1888.

BANQUETERS, THE. Aristophanes. See "Greek Plays."

BANSHEE; OR, THE SPIRIT OF THE BOREEN, THE. Irish D. 5 a. John Levy. Eleph. and C., February 28, 1876; Manchester Queen's, July 24, 1876.

BANSHEE'S SPELL, THE. C.D. Dr. J. S. W. Watson. Torquay T.R. and O.H., May 22, 1882.

BANTRY BAY. M. Int. 1 a. Probably by Mr. Reynolds. C.G., February 18, 1797. Pr. 1797.

BANTRY BAY. P. 1 a. Stephen Bond. Surrey, December 17, 1897.

BAPTISM AND TEMPTATION. See *Of Baptism*, etc.

BAPTISTES. T. G. Buchanan. 1506-1582.

BAPTISTES. See *Tyrannical Government.*

BARARK JOHNSON; OR, THE BLIND WITNESS. D. 1 a. W. Reeve. Surrey, April 8, 1844.

BARATARIA; OR, SANCHO TURNED GOVERNOR. F. Alt. fr. D'Urfey by Fredk. Pilon. C.G., 1785.

BARBARA. P. 1 a. Jerome K. Jerome. Globe, June 19, 1886.

BARBARA ALLEN. Spec. Chas. Dibdin, jun. Songs only Pr. N.d.

BARBARA GROWS UP. C. 3 a. Geo. J. Hamlen. Glasgow Royalty, September 6, 1909.

BARBARES, LES O. Saint Saëns. 1901.

BARBAROSSA. T. 5 a. John Brown, D.D. 1755. C.G., December 1, 1802. Plot derived fr. *Merope, Bajazet,* and *Mourning Bride.* Language bor. from *Paradise Lost* and *Annus Mirabilis.* Pr. 1755.

BARBAZON; OR, THE FATAL PEAS. O. 1 a. Lib. by Arthur Matthison and Ferd. Wallerstein. D.L., September 22, 1877.

BARBE-BLEUE. Op. bo. 3 a. and 4 tab. M. by Jacques Offenbach. Lib. by Meilhac and Halévy. First perf. in this country at St. James's T. in French, 1869. Avenue, June 16, 1883.

BARBER AND HIS BROTHERS, THE. M. burla. Adelphi, 1826.

BARBER AND THE BRAVO; OR, THE PRINCESS WITH THE RAVEN LOCKS, THE. F.D. Isabella Vernier. Surrey, Oct., 1846.

BARBER BARON; OR, THE FRANKFORT LOTTERY, THE. F. T. J. Thackeray. Hay., September 8, 1828.

BARBER BRAVO, THE. Princess's, 1846.

BARBER OF BAGDAD, THE. F. E. Fitzball. Surrey, November 20, 1826.

BARBER OF BAGDAD, THE. O. Peter Cornelius. Eng. lib. by Rev. Marmaduke E. Browne. Pl. by students of R. Coll. Mus. Savoy, December 9, 1891.

BARBER OF BATH, THE. Oa. Lib. by H. B. Farnie. M. by Offenbach. Olympic, December 18, 1879.

BARBER OF PERA, THE. Melo-d. 2 a. Joseph Moser. Wr. 1806. N.p. N. ac.

BARBER OF SEVILLE, THE. C.O. 2 a. Prose by Mr. Fawcett. Poetry by Mr. Terry. C.G., 1824. Pl. in 3 a. Lyceum, July 3, 1824. See *Barbiere di Seviglia.*

BARBER OF SEVILLE; OR, THE USELESS PRECAUTION, THE. C. 4 a. A transl. by Mrs. Griffiths of Beaumarchais' piece. Pr. 1776. N. ac.

BARBER'S TRIP TO PARIS, THE. Burl. Wolverhampton P.O.W., February 28, 1876.

BARBERS OF BASSORA, THE. C.O. 2 a. J. M. Morton. C.G., November 11, 1837.

BARBIER DE SEVILLE, LE. C. Beaumarchais. 1775.

BARBIER DE SEVILLE, LE. O. Rossini. Paris, May 6, 1824.

BARBIER DE TROUVILLE, LE. O. 1 a. Lecocq. 1871.

BARBIERE DI SIVIGLIA. Paisiello. St. Petersburg, 1780.

BARBIERE DI SIVIGLIA, IL. Op. bo. Music by Morlacchi. 1814.

BARBIERE DI SIVIGLIA. O. Rossini. Rome, February 5, 1816. Sir H. Bishop alt. this, King's T., January 27, 1818. D.L., July 27, 1835. Pr. orig. in Rome under the title of *Almaviva.*

BARBIER VON BAGDAD, DER. O. Cornelius. 1824-1874.

BARCAROLLE. O. Auber. Paris, 1845.

BARD AND HIS BIRTHDAY, THE. W. Brough. Gallery of Illustration, April 20, 1864.

BARDELL *V.* PICKWICK. Sk. John Hollingshead. Gaiety, January 24, 1871.

BARDELL *V.* PICKWICK. Oa. 2 a. T. H. Gem. M. by F. Spinney. Pr. 1881.

BARDES, LES. O. Lesueur. 1763-1837.

BAREFACED IMPOSTORS. F. 1 a. J. Doe, Richard Roe, and J. Noakes. Canterbury T.R., August 15, 1854.

BARENHAUTER, DER. O. S. Wagner. 1899.

BARGEMAN OF THE THAMES. Grecian. January 24, 1871.

BARKOUF. Op. bo. 3 a. M. by Offenbach. 1861.

BARLEY MOW, THE. W. Frith and Corney Grain. St. Geo. H., 1884.

BARMAID, THE. C. 3 a. Geo. Dance. Manchester Comedy T., August 31, 1891.

BARMECIDE; OR, THE FATAL OFFSPRING. Dr. rom. 3 a. Action by Johnson. M. by Cooke. D.L., November 3, 1818.

BARMECIDE, LES. T. Laharpe, 1778.

BARMECIDE FEAST, A. C. 1 a. A. J. Dearden. Ealing New, February 22, 1904.

BARN AT BECCLES, THE. C. 1 a. Geo. Hughes and A. Bickley. Hackney Manor R., December 8, 1891.

BARNABY BRITTLE; OR, A WIFE AT HER WIT'S END. F. 2 a. Alt. fr. Betterton's *Amorous Widow.* C.G., April 18, 1781. Edinburgh, 1788. Pr. 1782. See ***George Dandin.***

BARNABY RUDGE. Dom. D. 3 a. Chas. Selby and Chas. Melville. English O.H., June 28, 1841.

BARNABY RUDGE. Ver. Adelphi. January, 1842

BARNABY RUDGE. Ver. Watts, Phillips, and Vining Princess's, November 12, 1866.

BARNABY RUDGE. D. 4 a. Ver. Marylebone, November 4, 1876.

BARNABY RUDGE. See *Dolly Varden.*

BARNADO AND FIAMATA (? PHEAMETA) Mentioned by Henslow as having been ac. at Rose T., October 29, 1595.

BARNAVELT. The T. of Sir John Van Olden Barnavelt. A MS. in British Museum. Ms. addit., 18,653 (apparently the author's autograph.)

BARNES OF NEW YORK. D. Hal Collier-Edwards. Marylebone, June 23, 1888.

BARNES OF NEW YORK. See *Mr. Barnes of New York, Marina, Good Old Barnes of New York.*

BARNEY THE BARON. F. 1 a. Lover.

BARNWELL. See *George Barnwell.*

BARON, THE. C. See "Theatrical Recorder." F. Holcroft.

BARON DE TRENCK, THE. Operatic D. 3 a. M. by Mr. Reeve. Founded on a Hist. Anecdote. Lyceum, September 4, 1820.

BARON ET LA DANSEUSE, LE. Comic Pant. 1 a. Giovanni Pratesi. M. by Iginio Corsi, Cry. Pal., August 4, 1898.

BARON GOLOSH. C.O. 2 a. M. by Audran. Add. numbers by Leslie Stuart and Meyer Lutz. Adap. from Maurice Ordonneau and Edmund Audran's *L'Oncle Celestin.* Swansea New T. and Star O.H., April 15, 1895; Trafalgar T., April 25, 1895.

BARON KINKVERVANKOTFDORSPRAKENGATCHDERN, THE. M. Comp. Miles Peter Andrews. Hay. Pr. 1781.

BARON OF CORVELLE, THE. C.O. John Green and Ernest Hanson. Halifax, Grand T., March 3, 1892.

BARON RUDOLPH. American Serio-Comic D. 4 a. Bronson Howard. Hull T.R., August 1, 1881.

BARON'S DAUGHTER; OR, MINE HOST OF THE FLAGON, THE. Burl. 2 a. E. W. Bowles and G. R. Phillips. West T., Albert H., February 7, 1893.

BARON'S WAGER, THE. Ca. 1 a. Sir C. Young. Scarborough Londesborough T., February 7, 1881; Avenue, October 2, 1897.

BARONE DI TROCCHIA, IL. O. L. Caruso. (His. first O.) Naples, 1773.

BARONESS, THE. C.O. 3 a. Cotsford Dick. Royalty, October 5, 1892.

BARONET, THE. C.D. E. Howard Vincent. Bury T.R. and O.H., July 3, 1885.

BARONET, THE. D.Sk. Henry Sinclair. St. Geo. H., June 6, 1893 (amat.).

BARONET ABROAD, AND THE RUSTIC PRIMA DONNA, THE. M.D. 1 a. Lennox Horne. St. James's T., November 9, 1864.

BARONET'S WAGER, THE. Ca. Mrs. Keeble, Peterboro' Drill H., June 25, 1869.

BARONS OF ELLENBERG, THE. P. See *Dramatic Appellant.*

BARRACK ROOM. Ca. T. H. Bayly. Ac. in New York, 1836.

BARREN LAND. P. 4 a. Henry Byatt and Wm. Magnay. Olympic, April 11, 1888 (in 3 a), and Wolverhampton T.R., February 16, 1889.

BARREN TITLE, A. See ***His Lordship.***

BARRICADE, THE. D. Prol. and 4 a. Adap. by Clarance Holt of Victor Hugo's ***Les Miserables.*** Croydon T.R., October 11, 1869; Duke's T., September 7, 1878.

BARRIER, THE. P. 4 a. A. Sutro. Comedy, October 10, 1907.

BARRIER BETWEEN, THE. D. 4 a. H. C. M. Hardinge. Windsor T.R., July 22, 1901.

BARRIER OF PARNASSUS. C. Dibdin.

BARRINGTON'S BUSBY; OR, WEATHERING THE ADMIRAL. Ca. 1 a. Julia Agnes Fraser. Devonport T.R., October 4, 1883.

BARRINGTONS, THE. D. 4 a. S. J. Adair Fitzgerald and J. H. Merrifield. Novelty, March 6, 1884.

BARRISTER, THE. P. 2 a. Surrey, March 1, 1852

BARRISTER, THE. F.C. 3 a. Geo. Manville Fenn and J. H Darnley. Leeds, Grand T., March 19, 1837; Comedy, September 6, 1887; Royalty, May 17, 1890.

BARRY, MDME. DU. V. Ancelot. 1836.

BARRY DOYLE'S REST CURE. P. 3 a. W. Gayer Mackay and Robert Ord. Court, September 25, 1907.

BARS OF GOLD. Dr. Sk. 1 a. Josephine Rae and Thos. Sidney. St. Leonards-on-Sea, June 6, 1892.

BARTHOLOMEW FAIR. C. Ben Jonson. Ac. by the Lady Elizabeth's servants. Hope T., Bankside, October 31, 1614. Pr. 1614.

BARTHOLOMEW FAIRING, A. 5 short acts. Pr. 1649. N. ac

BARTONMERE TOWERS. C. 3 a. Rutland Barrington. Savoy, February 1, 1893.

BARWISE'S BOOK. C. 2 a. H. T. Craven. Edinburgh T.R., April 13, 1870; Hay., April 25, 1870.

BASCULE, LA. C. 4 a. Maurice Donnay. Royalty, July 9, 1906.

BASE IMPOSTOR, A. P. Horace Wigan.

BASHFUL LOVER, THE. T.C. Philip Massinger. Ac. by King's Co. May 9, 1636, and by His Majesty's Servants at Blackfryars, 1655. Pr. 1655.

BASHFUL MAN, THE. M.F. 2 a. F. on Humphrey Repton's story, by W. T. Moncrieff. Lyceum, September 20, 1824.

BASIL'S FAITH. C. Hull T.R., June 6, 1874.

BASILEIA. T.C. Ac. by the scholars of Cranbrook School, 1666.

BASILISKA. D. Hull, Jarrow Street Rooms, July 22, 1870.

BASKET GIRLS OF LIVERPOOL, THE. D. C. H. Hazlewood. Liverpool Colosseum, January 11, 1875.

BASKET-MAKER, THE. Mus. Ent. J. O'Keefe. Hay., September 4, 1790. Pr. 1798.

BASOCHE, THE. C.O. 3 a. Albert Carré. M. by André Messager. Eng. ver. by Sir Aug. Harris and Eugene Oudin. Prod. orig. at Paris Op.C., May 30, 1890. R. English O.H., November 3, 1891; rev., Guildhall Sch. of M. T., March 15, 1901.

BASSET TABLE, THE. C. Mrs. Centlivre. D.L. Pr. 1706.

BASSO PORTO. See *A Basso Porto.*

BASTARD, THE. T. Attributed to Cosmo Manuche. Pr. 1652.

BASTARD, THE. T. Robert Lovett. Mentioned in 1724. N.p.

BASTARD CHILD; OR, A FEAST FOR THE CHURCHWARDENS, THE. Dram. satire. 2 a. Daniel Downright. Pr. 1768.

BASTIEN AND BASTIENNE. O. L. Mozart. Leipsic, 1770; Daly's, December 26, 1894.

BASTILLE, THE. Ent. John Dent. Royal Circus. Pr. circa, 1789.

BA-TA-CLAN. Op. bo. 1 a. M. by Offenbach.

BAT AND BALL. M. Absurdity. Frank Russell. Richmond, September 15, 1881.

BATCHELORS, THE. P. Transl. fr. the German of Imand. Pr. 1799. N.ac

BATCHELOR'S WIVES. See *Bachelor's Wives.*

BATCHELOR'S WIVES; OR, THE BRITISH AT BRUSSELS. Oa. M. by M. Kearns. Lyceum, July 14, 1817.

BATEMAN'S MASQUE. A masque of the seventeenth century. MS.

BATH; OR, THE WESTERN LASS, THE. C. T. D'Urfey. D.L., 1697. Pr. 1701.

BATH ROAD, THE. Int. D.L., October 14 1830.

BATH ROLL, A. Oa. C. J. Knight and Arthur W. Youens. Seal H., Kent, April 26, 1894.

BATH UNMASKED, THE. C. Odingsells L.I.F., February 27, 1725. Pr. 1725.

BATHING. F. 1 a. Jas. Bruton. Olympic, January 31, 1842.

BATHING MACHINE; OR, THE FISHERMEN CAUGHT, THE. M. Int. Ac. at Brighton 1790.

BATTAGLIA DI LEGRANO, LA. O. Verdi. Rome, January 27, 1849.

BATTAILE DE DANES. C. Scribe and Legouvé. 1851.

BATTERED BATAVIANS; OR, DOWN WITH THE DUTCH. Ent. Jas. Cawdell. Scarborough, 1798.

BATTLE OF ALCAZAR, THE. T. Peele. Ac. by Lord High Admiral's servants, 1594. Pr. 1594. Plot fr. Heywood's *Cosmography* in History of Spain.

BATTLE OF AUGRIM; OR, THE FALL OF ST. RUTH, THE. T. Robert Ashton. Pr. 1777.

BATTLE OF BOTHWELL BRIGG, THE. P. Adap. by Farley. C.G., May 22, 1800.

BATTLE OF CHEVY CHASE, THE. D. Newcastle Tyne T., March 29, 1875.

BATTLE OF EDDINGTON; OR, BRITISH LIBERTY, THE. T. Probably by John Penn. Pr. 1792. Hay. and prov. theatres.

BATTLE OF HASTINGS. T. Richard Cumberland. D.L., January 24, 1778. Pr. 1778.

BATTLE OF HERMANN. D. 1776-1811. Kleist.

BATTLE OF HEXHAM; OR, DAYS OF OLD, THE. M. play. 3 a. Geo. Colman, the younger. M. by Dr. Arnold. Hay., August 11, 1789; D.L., 1820. Pr. 1808.

BATTLE OF JERSEY, THE. Rom. D. 3 a. Jersey T.R., January 6, 1881.

BATTLE OF LIFE, THE. D. 3 a. Dramatised by Albert Smith fr. Charles Dickens' story. Lyceum, December 21, 1846.

BATTLE OF LIFE, THE. D. 3 a. E. Stirling. Surrey, January, 1847.

BATTLE OF LIFE, THE. D. 3 a. Dr. Ver. of Dickens' story, arr. by C. Dickens, jun. Gaiety, December 26, 1873.

BATTLE OF LIFE, THE. New ver. of *Le Paillasse* (the original of *Belphegor, the Mountebank,* Surrey, 1851, and *The Acrobat,* Olympic, April 21, 1891). Standard, May 22, 1893.

BATTLE OF LIFE, THE. D. 4 a. A. W. Parry and Thos. Dobb. Liverpool Adelphi, August 6, 1894.

BATTLE OF LIFE, The. P. 4 a. Alan Grey. Bayswater, Bijou (c.p.), March 30, 1901.

BATTLE OF LIFE, THE. Dom Sk. Prod. by J. Wright Aitken. Hoxton Variety, December 9, 1907.

BATTLE OF LIFE; OR, THE OTHER WOMAN, THE. Dom. D. 4 a. Gus. C. Livesey and G. H. Turner. West London, June 17, 1904 (C.P.).

BATTLE OF LUNCARTY, THE. Hist. P. Geo. Galloway. Pr. 1806. N.ac.

BATTLE OF POICTIERS; OR, THE ENGLISH PRINCE, THE. See *Edward the Black Prince,* by Mrs. Hoper.

BATTLE OF PULTAWA; OR, THE KING AND THE CZAR, THE. D. 2 a. C.G., February 23, 1829.

BATTLE OF SEDGMOOR, THE. F. 1 a. Said to be by the then Duke of Buckingham. Pr. 1707. N. ac.

BATTLE OF SEDGMOOR, THE. D. 3 a. G. Almar. Pavilion T., February, 1837.

BATTLE OF THE ALMA, THE Astley's, 1859.

BATTLE OF THE HEART, THE. D. 4 a. J. Wilkins. Duke's, March 13, 1880.

BATTLE OF THE NILE, THE. Dram. Poem. Pr. 1799. The idea taken fr. the *Persæ* of Æschylus. See "Greek Plays."

BATTLE OF THE NILE, THE. Sadler's Wells, 1807.

BATTLE OF THE POETS; OR, THE CONTENTION FOR THE LAUREL, THE. Scriblerus Tertius. Some say by Thos. Cooke. Ac. at Little T. in Hay., 1730. Pr. 1731.

BATTLE OF THE SEXES, THE. Melo-d. P. Prol. and 4 a. John D. Sanders. Clapham Shakespeare, July 18, 1898.

BATTLE OF THE VICES AGAINST THE VIRTUES. Moral P. MS. of the time of Charles I.

BATTLE OF WATERLOO, THE. Military melo-d. 3 a. J. H. Amherst. Astley's, May 17, 1869.

BATTLE ROYAL, A. C. 3 a. Arthur Matthison. Liverpool Alexandra, November 25, 1878.

BATTLE ROYAL, THE. F. Alt. fr. Sir John Vanbrugh. Hay., 1785.

BATTLE THROUGH LIFE, THE. C.D. 4 a. W. H. Mitchell. Barnsley T.R., February 25, 1890 (c.p.). Alt. to 5 a. and pl. at same T., March 28, 1890.

BAUBLE SHOP, THE. P. of modern London life. 4 a. H. A. Jones. Criterion, January 26, 1893.

BAUER EIN SCHELM, DER. O. Dvorák, b. 1841, Bohemia.

BAVARDS, LES. O. 2 a. Offenbach. 1863.

BAVARIAN GIRLS; OR, THE BLACK HELMET, THE. D. 4 a. W. E. Suter. Sadler's Wells, November 13, 1869.

BAWDYHOUSE SCHOOL; OR, THE RAKE DEMOLISHED. F. Pr. 1744.

BAXTER'S TRAGEDY. Ac. 1602. N.p.

BAYADERE, LA. Div. D.L., February 20, 1845.

BAYES IN PETTICOATS. See *The Rehearsal.*

BAYES' OPERA. By Gab. Odingsells. F. on *The Beggar's Opera.* D.L., 1731. Pr. 1730.

BAZILETTE. Oa. Justin F. Fitzsimon. Philharmonic, February 21, 1881.

BEACON, THE. M.D. 2 a. Joanna Baillie. Pr. 1812.

BEACON BELL, THE. Sk. Wal Pink. Shepherd's Bush Empire, September 9, 1907.

BEACON LIGHT; OR, THE WRECKER'S DOOM, THE. D. 1 a. Lloyd Clarance. Stockton-on-Tees T.R., June 1, 1891.

BEACON OF LIBERTY, THE. D. C.G., October 8, 1823.

BEAR A BRAIN. P. Thos. Dekker. Ac 1599. N.pr.

BEAR AND FORBEAR. P. 1 a. Geo. Bell. Adap. fr. the German. Publ. by S. French, Ltd.

BEAR HUNTERS; OR, THE FATAL RAVINE, THE. Melo-d. 2 a. J. B. Buckstone. Victoria T.

BEARD'S NIGHT. Pr. 1760. Consisting of Dryden's Secular Masque, set by Royce, and other pieces. At the Long Room in Hampstead.

BEARDING THE LION. Ca. 1 a. Ch. S. Fawcett. Manchester Prince's, February 25, 1884.

BEARNAISE, LA. C.O. 3 a. Alfred Murray. M. by Audré Messager. Adap. fr. the French of Letterrier and Vanloo. Birmingham Grand, September 27, 1886; P.O.W., October 4, 1886.

BEARS NOT BEASTS. F. H. M. Milner. Coburg, 1822.

BEARS NOT BEASTS. C.O. 1 a. Lib. by Geo. Capel. M. by H. Round. Ashton-under-Lyne Booth's T, November 22, 1880.

BEAST AND THE BEAUTY. Mrs. E. S. Ratton. S. George's H., January 29, 1900 (amat.).

BEAST AND THE BEAUTY. Arthur Milton. York T.R., March 23, 1901.

BEAST AND THE BEAUTY. P. 4 a. Fredk. Melville. Standard, October 9, 1905.

BEAST AND THE BEAUTY; OR, NO ROSE WITHOUT A THORN, THE. Burl. F. C. Burnand. Royalty, October 4, 1869.

BEATA. Do. D. 3 a. Adap. from *Rosmer of Rosmersholm* by Austin Fryers. Globe, April 19, 1892.

BEATRICE. P. 3 a. Rosina Filippi. Court, May 29, 1905.

BEATRICE DI TENDA. O. Bellini. Venice, 1833.

BEATRICE ET BENEDICT. O. Berlioz. 1803-1869. Fd. on Shakespeare's *Much Ado About Nothing.*

BEATRIX. P. 4 a. A. Crocker. Adap. fr. Thackeray's novel, "Esmond." Margate R.T., April 13, 1908.

BEAU AUSTIN. C. 4 a. W. E. Henley and R. L. Stevenson. Hay., November 3, 1890.

BEAU BROCADE. Rom. P. 4 a. Baroness Orczy and Montague Barstow. Originally prod. at Eastbourne D.P., May 4, 1908; June 1, 1908.

BEAU BRUMMELL, THE KING OF CALAIS. D 2 a. Blanchard Jerrold. Lyceum, April 11, 1859.

BEAU DEFEATED; OR, THE LUCKY YOUNGER BROTHER, THE. C. Mr. Barker. L.I.F. Pr. circa 1700.

BEAU LAVENDER; OR, THE BUTTERFLY OF FASHION. Oa. 1 a. Geo. Glennie. M. by Reg. Clarke. Bayswater Bijou, July 21, 1896.

BEAU MERCHANT, THE. C. By "Mr. S., Gentleman of Gloucester" (according to Coxeter, Mr. Blanch). Pr. 1714. N. ac.

BEAU NASH. C. 3 a. D. Jerrold. Hay., July 16, 1834.

BEAU'S ADVENTURES, THE. F. Phil Bennet. Pr. 1733. ?N. ac.

BEAU'S DUEL; OR, A SOLDIER FOR THE LADIES, THE. C. Mrs. Centlivre. L.I.F., October 21, 1702. Pr. 1702.

BEAU'S STRATAGEM, THE. C. 5 a. Geo. Farquhar. Hay., March 8, 1707; D.L., 1710; rev. Hay., January 5, 1856. Pr. 1707. See *Beaux*, etc.

BEAUTIES, THE. P. James Shirley. January 21, 1632-3. N. p.

BEAUTIFUL ARMENIA; OR, THE ENERGY AND FORCE OF LOVE, THE. C. Edmund Ball. Pr. 1778. Taken from *The Eunuch of Terence.* N. ac.

BEAUTIFUL AVENGER, THE. D. 4 a. F. A. Scudamore. Stratford R., April 4, 1904.

BEAUTIFUL FIEND, A. Melo-d. 4 a. Geo. Wybrow, Frank M. Thorne. Hyde T.R., December 22, 1900; Peckham, Crown, August 12, 1901.

BEAUTIFUL FOR EVER. F. 1 a. Fredk. Hay. Liverpool, P.O.W. T., September 14, 1868.

BEAUTIFUL FOR EVER. F. G. F. Hodgson. Surrey, October 5, 1868.

BEAUTIFUL HAIDEE; OR, THE SEA NYMPH AND THE SALLEE ROVERS. Extrav. F. on *Don Juan.* Ballad of Lord Bateman and Legend of Lurlim. H. J. Byron. Princess's, April 6, 1863.

BEAUTIFUL TEMPTRESS, THE. Sk. Wm. P. Sheen. Brit., April 3, 1905.

BEAUTY. Masque. Ben Jonson. Presented before the Court at Whitehall, January 14, 1607-8. Pr. 1608.

BEAUTY. C. Jonson, 1616.

BEAUTY AND GOOD PROPERTIES OF WOMEN. See *The Craft of Rhetoric.*

BEAUTY AND HOUSEWIFERY. C. Ac before the Court at Windsor by the Lord of Hundesdon's servants, 1582.

BEAUTY AND THE BARGE. F. 3a. W. W. Jacobs and Louis N. Parker. New, August 30, 1904; transf. to Hay., January 2, 1905.

BEAUTY AND THE BEAST. Extrav. 2 a. J. R. Planchè. C.G., April 12, 1841.

BEAUTY AND THE BEAST. Burl. A. W. Stratford. M. by L. E. Goddard. Buckingham T.H., January 25, 1894.

BEAUTY AND THE BEAST. Ballet. Alhambra, January, 1898.

BEAUTY AND THE BEAST. Lib., P. Milton and H. Lowther. Belfast T.R., March 28, 1902.

BEAUTY AND THE MONSTER. C. Transf. fr. Fr. of Countess of Genlis. Pr. 1781.

BEAUTY AND VIRTUE. Serenata. D.L., 1762.

BEAUTY DOCTOR, THE. Farc. sk. Gertrude Jarman. Pass. Edwards' Settlement, May 6, 1909.

BEAUTY IN A TRANCE. T. John Ford. Ent. at Stationers' H. September 9, 1653. N.p. Destroyed by Warburton's servant.

BEAUTY IN DISTRESS. T. Peter Motteux. L.I.F., 1698. Pr. 1698.

BEAUTY OF BATH, THE. M.P. 2 a. Seymour Hicks and Cosmo Hamilton. Lyrics, C. H. Taylor; music, H. E. Haines. Aldwych, March 19, 1906.

BEAUTY OF GHENT, THE. Ballet by Albert. M. by Adolphe Adam. First time in Eng. D.L., February 11, 1844.

BEAUTY OF WOMEN. C. Pr. by Rastel about 1530.

BEAUTY OR THE BEAST. F. 1 a. J. Oxenford. D.L., November 2, 1863.

BEAUTY SHOP, THE. M.C. 3 scenes. W. H. Kirby. Music by Geo. Gee; lyrics by D. B. Watson. Ayr Gaiety, November 15, 1906.

BEAUTY SHOW, THE. C.O. 2 a. Lib. by Herbert Manley. M. by Gwilym Morgans. St. Leonard's Pier Pav., June 26, 1899.

BEAUTY STONE, THE. Rom. D. 3 a. A. W. Pinero, J. Comyns Carr, and A. Sullivan. Savoy, May 28, 1898.

BEAUTY THE BEST ADVOCATE. A re-written ver. of *Measure for Measure*, by D'Avenant or Gildon. L.I.F., 1700.

BEAUTY THE CONQUEROR; OR, THE DEATH OF MARK ANTONY. T. Sir Chas. Sedley. Pr. 1702. N. ac. See *Antony and Cleopatra*.

BEAUTY'S FOILS. F.C. 3 a. C. S. Fawcett. Strand, December 21, 1893.

BEAUTY'S TRIUMPH. Masque. T. Duffett. Pres. by scholars of Mr. Banister and Mr. Hart at Boarding School at Chelsea. Pr. 1676.

BEAUX' STRATAGEM. Burla. Surrey, 1810.

BEBE. M.C. 3 a. Kinsey Peile. Southend Empire, October 21, 1901; Camberwell Metro., October 28, 1901.

BECAUSE I LOVE YOU. D. 4 a. F. A. Scudamore. Fulham Grand, August 4, 1902.

BECAUSE OF BILLY RUDD. Piece. 1 a. Cosmo Hamilton. Strand, December 19, 1898.

BECAUSE SHE LOVED HIM. P. 4 a. Fred Brock. St. Geo. H., February 11, 1901. (C.P.)

BECKET. Hist. P. Blank verse. Prol. and 4 a. Tennyson. Arr. by Henry Irving. Lyc., February 6, 1893; D.L., February 29, 1905.

BECKET. See *Fair Rosamund, Thomas à Becket*.

BECKY. C.D. Adap. Thackeray's "Vanity Fair." Flora Haytor. Torquay T.R., August 22, 1901.

BECKY SHARP. P. 4 a. Adap. Thackeray's "Vanity Fair." David Balsille. Croydon Grand, June 24, 1901.

BECKY SHARP. P. 5 a. Fr. same. Robt. Hichens. Cosmo Gordon Lennox. P.O.W., August 27, 1901.

BECKY SHARP. P. 1 a. A scene from Thackeray, arr. by J. M. Barrie. Terry's, June 3, 1893.

BED OF ROSES, A. Ca. 1 a. H. A. Jones. Globe, January 26, 1882.

BEDOUINS; OR, ARABS OF THE DESERT, THE. C.O. 3 a. Dublin. Pr. 1802.

BEDROOM WINDOW, THE. F. 1 a. E. Stirling. Olympic, March 18, 1847.

BEE AND THE ORANGE TREE, THE. Fy. Spec. 1 a. Planché. Hay., December 26, 1845.

BEECHBOROUGH MYSTERY, THE. C.D. 4 a. Eliot Galer and Jas. Drew. Birmingham G., June 17, 1889.

BEECH'S TRAGEDY. P. Mentioned in Henslowe's Diary, 1599.

BEEF TEA. Oa. Harry Greenbank. M. by Wilfred Bendall Lyric, October 27, 1892.

BEEHIVE, THE. M.F. 2 a. J. V. Millingen. Lyceum, January 19, 1811, and rev. July 18, 1815.

BEEN HAD. Pleon. Publ. by J. Dicks.

BEETHOVEN. D. 1 a. Gustav Hein. Aberdeen O.H., October 17, 1879.

BEETHOVEN'S ROMANCE. P. 4 a. S. A. Raphael. Royalty, December 1, 1894.

BEETLE, THE. P. 1 a. Court, June 21, 1909 (mat.).

BEFORE BREAKFAST. F. M. by Mr. Barnett. Lyceum, August 31, 1826.

BEFORE THE DAWN. P. 1 a. Hen. Byatt. Op. C. April 15, 1895; transferred to Strand April 22, 1895.

BEFORE THE DAWN. Sk. Oxford, May 10, 1909.

BEFORE THE MAST. D. 4 a. F. W. Broughton. Olympic, March 8, 1884.

BEFORE THE SUN GOES DOWN. P. 1 a. Cosmo Hamilton. Terry's, December 26, 1899.

BEGGAR, THE. C. 1 a. F. W. Broughton. Strand, July 8, 1889.

BEGGAR BOY OF BRUSSELS. J. B. Buckstone.

BEGGAR GIRL'S WEDDING, THE. D. 4 a. Walter Melville. Elephant and Castle, October 19, 1908.

BEGGAR MY NEIGHBOUR; OR, A ROGUE'S A FOOL. C. 3 a. Hay., October 10, 1802. Ascribed to Mr. Morton. N.pr. Part of plot taken from *The Nephews* of Iffland.

BEGGAR OF BETHNAL GREEN, THE. J. Sheridan Knowles. 3 a. D.L., 1831; Victoria Mch., 1834. See *Blind Beggar and Beggar's Daughter*.

BEGGAR ON HORSEBACK. A. P. 5 a. E. Ferriss and B. P. Matthews. Kingston R.C., August 6, 1906.

BEGGAR ON HORSEBACK, THE. F. O'Keefe. Hay., 1785 Pr. 1798.

BEGGAR ON HORSEBACK, THE. C. Sullivan. Hay., March 21, 1846.

BEGGAR STUDENT, THE. C.O. 4 a. M. by Millöcker. Lib. adap. fr. the German by W. Beatty Kingston. Alhambra, April 12, 1884.

BEGGAR WENCH, THE. O. in MS. Sold as part of the library of Mr. Anthony Murphy.

BEGGAR'S BUSH, THE. T.C. Beaumont and Fletcher. Ac. 1622. Pr. 1647. See *The Merchant of Bruges, The Lame Commonwealth*.

BEGGAR'S DAUGHTER OF BETHNAL GREEN, THE. C. D.L., November 22, 1828.

BEGGAR'S HOTEL, THE. Sk. G. R. Sims. Sadler's Wells, June 15, 1908.

BEGGAR'S OPERA, THE. C.O. 2 a. John Gay. M. by Linley. L.I.F., 1727; January 29, 1728. Pr. 1728. C.G., December 16, 1732. An alteration of this piece by Capt. Thompson. C.G., October, 1777. A transl. in Fr., called *L'Opera du Gueux*, by A. Hallam, Representée sur le Petit Theatre François dans le Marché au Foin. Pr. 1750. Lyceum, July 7, 1821. Dr. Pepusch adap. M. to this.

BEGGAR'S PANTOMIME; OR, THE CONTENDING COLUMBINE, THE. F. L.I.F. Pr. 1736. D.L.

BEGGAR'S PETITION; OR, A FATHER'S LOVE AND A MOTHER'S CARE, THE. D. 3 a. Geo. Dibdin Pitt. City T., October 18, 1841.

BEGGAR'S UPROAR, THE. Extrav. Hubert Jay Morice. Surrey, May 7, 1870.

BEGGAR'S WEDDING, THE. Ballad O. 3 a. Chs. Coffey. First ac. at Dublin in 1 a. at little T. in Hay. under title of *Phœbe*, 1729. Rev. 1763. Part seems borrowed fr. *The Jovial Crew*.

BEGGING LETTER, THE. D. 3 a. Mark Lemon. D.L., December 31, 1853.

BEGINNING AND THE END, THE. Dom. D. 4 a. Mrs. Lovell (Miss Lacy). Hay., October 27, 1855.

BEGINNING AND THE END OF THE SOUTH WALES STRIKE, THE. D. Cardiff T.R., May 24, 1875.

BEGONE DULL CARE; OR, HOW WILL IT END? C. Fred Reynolds, C.G. Pr. 1808. Partly taken fr. *The Heir at Law*.

BEGUM'S DIAMONDS, THE. C.D. 3 a. J. P. Hurst. Avenue, January 22, 1889.

BEHIND A CURTAIN. Monol. Mrs. Burton Harrison. Madison Sq. T., January 13, 1887.

BEHIND A MASK. C. 3 a. Bernard H. Dixon and Arthur Wood. Royalty, March 8, 1871.

BEHIND A MASK. Duo. Mrs. Bradshaw. Steinway H., June 20, 1902.

BEHIND THE CURTAIN. D. 4 a. Geo. Roberts. Holborn T., April 18, 1870.

BEHIND THE SCENES. C. 3 a. Adap. by G. P. Hawtrey and Felix Morris fr. *The First Night*. Transl. p. *Le Père de la Debutante*. Comedy. July 4, 1896.

BEHIND THE SCENES. Sk. London Coliseum, August 10, 1908.

BEHIND THE SCENES; OR, ACTORS BY LAMPLIGHT. Burla. 1 a. Ch. Selby. Strand, September 12, 1839.

BEHIND TIME. F. 1 a. B. Webster, jun. Adelphi, December 26, 1865.

BEIDEN LEONOREN DIE. C. 4 a. Paul Linden. Royalty, January 25, 1904.

BEIDEN NEFFEN DIE. O. 3 a. Mendelssohn. February 3, 1824.

BEIDEN PADAGOGEN DIE. O. 1 a. Mendelssohn. Berlin, 1821.

BEL DELMONIO. D. 4 a. By John Brougham. F. on *L'Abbaye de Castro*. Lyceum, October 31, 1863. See *Broken Vow*.

BELA. Rom. D. 4 a. Gerald Godfrey. Adap. fr. the French. Belfast T.R., January 8, 1886.

BELFORD CASTLE. Lunn. Publ. by J. Dicks.

BELFREY DREAM, A. Sk. Camberwell Palace, May 15, 1908.

BELGRAVIA; OR, NORTH AND SOUTH. F. Leamington Victoria Pav., August 28, 1882.

BELIEVE AS YOU LIST. C. Philip Massinger. Ac. May 7, 1631. Ent. Stationers' Co., September 9, 1653, and June 29, 1660. N.p. Destroyed by Warburton's servant.

BELINDA. M.C. 2 a. B. C. Stephenson and Basil Hood. M. by Walter Slaughter. Manchester Prince's, October 5, 1896.

BELINDA. P. 4 a. Rosina Filippi. Adap. fr. Rhoda Broughton's novel. Court, May 15, 1905.

BELINDA AND THE BURGLAR. F.Sk. H. C. Sargent. Bloombury H., November 9, 1906.

BELISAIRE. T. Rotrov. 1645.

BELISARIO. O. Donizetti. Venice, 1836.

BELISARIUS. T. W. Philips. L.I.F. Pr. 1725.

BELISARIUS. T. John Philip Kemble. Hull, 1778. N.p.

BELISARIUS. T. Hugh Downman. Exeter. Pr. 1786.

BELISARIUS. T. Scene fr. an MS. Play. Pr. October 17, 1795. Possibly by Miss Brooke.

BELISARIUS. See *The Chelsea Pensioner*.

BELL IN CAMPO. T. 2 parts. Margaret Duchess of Newcastle. Pr. 1662 (n.ac.).

BELL OF BELLE HAWKE. D. Exeter T.R., April 2, 1873.

BELL RINGER; OR, THE SPIRIT OF THE CHIMES, THE. D. 4 a. Sutton Vane and Arthur Shirley. Plymouth T.R., May 27 1897 (C.P.); Manchester Queen's, March 21, 1898; Grand, July 25, 1898.

BELL-RINGER OF NOTRE DAME; OR. THE HUNCHBACK'S LOVE, THE. D. 3 a W. H. Abel. East London, July 8, 1871.

BELL-RINGER OF ST. PAUL'S; OR THE HUNTSMAN AND THE SPY, THE. M.D. 3 a. Thompson Townsend. Sadler's Wells, March 4, 1839.

BELLA'S BIRTHDAY. F. C. H. Stephenson. Princess's, January 9, 1873.

BELLA'S INTENDED. Ca. Edward Rose. Liverpool Alexandra, October 15, 1883.

BELLADONNA; OR, THE BEAUTY AND THE GREAT BEAST. O. 3 a. M. by A. Cellier. Lib. by Alfred Thompson. Manchester Prince's, April 27, 1878.

BELLAMERE, EARL OF CARLISLE. T. 1807.

BELLAMIRA. C. Sheil. 1818.

BELLAMIRA; OR, THE MISTRESS. C. Sir Chas. Sedley, Bart. F. on *The Eunuch* of Terence. Ac. by H. Mai. servants, 1687. Pr. 1687.

BELLAMIRA, HER DREAM; OR, THE LOVE OF SHADOWS. T.C. 2 pts. Thos Killegrew. Pr. 1664.

BELLAMONDE; OR, THE KING'S AVENGER. D. Pro. and 3 a. Edward Towers. Pavilion, November 15, 1879.

BELLAMY, THE MAGNIFICENT. Social extrav. in 5 a. Adapt. fr. Roy Horniman's novel of same name. New, October 6, 1908.

BELLE ARSENE, LA. O.C. Favart, M. by Monsigny.

BELLE AU BOIS DORMANT, LA. Ballet. 3 a. F. on *The Sleeping Beauty*. Invented by Aumer. M. by Herold 1st time in Eng. D.L., February 13, 1833.

BELLE BELAIR. P. 4 a. Ralph Lumley. Avenue, May 19, 1897.

BELLE CLARISSE, LA. D. Prol. and 4 a. Ladbroke H., March 9, 1891.

BELLE HELENE, LA. O. 3 a. M. by Offenbach. 1865.

BELLE HELENE, LA. C.O. Eng. ver. by Charles Lamb Kenney. Gaiety, October 23, 1871.

BELLE HELENE, LA. Extrav. F. C. Burnand. Alhambra, August 16, 1873.

BELLE LURETTE. Op. bo. E. Blum Blau, Toche, and Offenbach. Gaiety, July 6, 1881.

BELLE NORMANDE, LA. Bouffonniere Musicale. 3 a. A. Maltby and R. Mansell. M. by Vasseur and Grevé. Globe, January 26, 1881.

BELLE OF ANDULASIA, THE. Spectacular bal. extrav. in 3 sc. Lib. and lyrics by G. R. Sims and Chs. Fletcher. M. by Herman Finck. Invented and arr. by J. R. Huddlestone and John Tiller. Blackpool Winter Gardens, July 6, 1908.

BELLE OF BLACKPOOL. M.P. 3 a. Wilfred Davis. Goole T.R., November 27, 1902.

BELLE OF BOHEMIA, THE. M.C. Harry B. Smith. M. by Ludwig Englander. St. Geo. H.. September 17, 1900 (C.P.).

BELLE OF BONN, THE. Mus. Epis., with m. by F. Knowles and S. Brook. Richmond, April 29, 1907.

BELLE OF BRITTANY, THE. M.P. Leedham Bantock and P. J. Barrow. Lyrics by P. Greenbank. M. by Howard Talbot. Additional numbers by Marie Horne. Queen's, October 24, 1908.

BELLE OF CAIRO, THE. M.P. 2 a. Cecil Raleigh and Kinsey Peile. M. and lyrics by Kinsey Peile. Court, October 10, 1896. Rev. by H. C. Newton, Hammersmith Lyric, December 2, 1901.

BELLE OF INDIA, THE. C.O. Lib., lyrics, and m. by Rajah Rann Singh. Collins's M.H., December 26, 1905.

BELLE OF MADRID, THE. Burl. O. 2 a. Fritz Ivie. M. by W. C. Pike. Rhyl Grand Pav., September 19, 1898.

BELLE OF MAYFAIR, THE. M.C. 2 a. C. H. E. Brookfield and Cosmo Hamilton. M. by Leslie Stuart. Vaudeville, April 11, 1906.

BELLE OF NEW YORK, THE. M.P. 2 a. Hugh Morton. M. by Gustave Kerker. Originally prod. in America. Shaftesbury, April 12, 1898; Adelphi, November 27, 1901.

BELLE OF ST. CRISPIN, THE; OR, THE LADY COBBLER. M.C. 2 a. Alfred A. Ellis. M. by Percival Knight and Denham Harrison. Eleph. and C., October 25, 1900.

BELLE OF THE BALL, THE. Bal. divert. C. Wilhelm. M. comp. and selected by C. Clarke. Dances and action arr. by F. Farren. Empire, September 30, 1907.

BELLE OF THE BALL, THE. M.P. 3 a. A. Norden. M. by E. T. De Banzie and Michael Dwyer. Southport O.H., July 7, 1908; Peckham Crown, October 19, 1908.

BELLE OF THE BARLEY MOW; OR, THE WOVER, THE WAITRESS, AND THE WILLAN. Burl. H. T. Arden. Cremorne Gdns., September 23, 1867.

BELLE OF THE BATH; OR, HIS HYDROPATHIC HIGHNESS, THE. M.F. 2 a. Arthur Eliot. M. by F. Sydney Ward. Bayswater Bijou, June 17, 1898.

BELLE OF THE HOTEL, THE. P. Niblo's Gdn., N.Y., 1842.

BELLE OF THE SEASON. Effingham T., April 16, 1866.

BELLE OF THE WEST, THE. M.C. 3 a. Harry B. Smith. M. by Karl L. Hoschna. Bayswater Vict. H., August 28, 1905 (C.P.).

BELLE RUSSE, LA. D. 4 a. David Belascoe. Orig. prod. at New York, Wallack's T. Edinburgh Princess's, June 26, 1882; Pavilion, April 17, 1886.

BELLE SAUVAGE, LA. Burl. Adap. fr. J. Brougham's *Pocohontas.* S. James's, November 27, 1869.

BELLE VUE. D. 3 a. R. Quittenton. Victoria, April 2, 1877.

BELLE VUE; OR, HARD TIMES IN MANCHESTER. D. John Price. Salford P.O.W., September 17, 1883.

BELLE'S STRATAGEM, THE. C. 3 a. Hannah Cowley. C.G., February 22, 1780. Pr. 1782.

BELLE'S STRATAGEM, THE. C. By —. Ac. by His Maj. servants. Pr. 1781. Imitation of Mrs. Cowley's play.

BELLENDON. Ac. Rose T., June 8, 1594, by Lord Admiral's men. N.p.

BELLEROFONTE, IL. O. Mysliweczek. 1764.

BELLEROPHON. O. 5 a. Lulli. Paris. January 31, 1679.

BELLES OF THE KITCHEN, THE. F. Ac. in New York, 1874; Adelphi, 1875.

BELLES OF THE VILLAGE. Rustic B.O. 2 a. Hugh Foster. M. by John Fitzgerald. Avenue, November 18, 1889. (Pl. by children.)

BELLES WITHOUT BEAUX; OR, THE LADIES AMONG THEMSELVES. Oa. M. by G. Ware. Characters by 7 ladies. Lyceum, August 6, 1819.

BELLING THE CAT. Ca. 1 a. Martin Becher. St. George's H., November 6, 1886.

BELLISARIUS. See *Belisarius.*

BELLMAN OF LONDON, THE. P. R. Daborne (died 1628).

BELLOWS-MENDERS, THE. See *The Lady of Lyons.*

BELLS, THE. D. 3 a. Leopold Lewis. Adap. fr. *The Polish Jew* (Le Juif Polonais) by Erckmann Chatrian. Lyceum, November 25, 1871, rev. November 25, 1896; rev. by H. B. Irving, Queen's, September 22, 1909.

BELLS, THE. See *The Bells of the Sledge.*

BELLS ACROSS THE SNOW. Rom. D. 4 a. W. Bevan Robinson. Greenwich, January 2, 1905.

BELLS BELL-ESQUED AND THE POLISH JEW POLISHED OFF; OR, MATHIAS, THE MUFFIN, THE MYSTERY, THE MAIDEN, AND THE MASHER, THE. Burl. Norwich T.R., March 13, 1883.

BELLS IN THE STORM, THE. D. C. H. Hazlewood. Sadler's Wells, February 14, 1874.

BELLS OF FATE. D. 5 a. Edward Darbey. Keighley Queen's, September 21, 1891; Sadler's Wells, November 9, 1891.

BELLS OF HASLEMERE, THE. D. 4 a. Henry Pettitt and Sydney Grundy. Adelphi, July 28, 1887.

BELLS OF OLD YORK, THE. D. 5 a. Rass Challis. Deal Globe, September 17, 1908.

BELLS OF SHANDON; OR, THE LADY OF MUNSTER, A TALE OF THE RIVER LEE, THE. D. 4 a. Dundee T.R., September 21, 1868.

BELLS OF THE SLEDGE, THE. D. Pro. and 3 a. Adap. by Horace Allen fr. *Le Juif Polonais.* Leigh (Lancs.) T.R., December 26, 1891.

BELLUM GRAMMATICALE. T.C. Ac. before Q. Elizabeth in Christ Church, Oxford, September 24, 1592.

BELMAN OF LONDON, THE. P. Robert Daborne. Wr about 1612. Mentioned in Henslowe's papers. (N.p.)

BELMAN OF PARIS, THE. Fr. T. Wr. by Thos. Dekkins and John Day. July 30, 1623.

BELMONT AND CONSTANCE; OR, THE ELOPEMENT FROM THE SERAGLIO. O. M. by Mozart. 1st time in England, D.L., June 23, 1841.

BELOVED OF HATHOR, THE. P. 1 a. Florence Farr and O. Shakespear. Bayswater Bijou, January 20, 1902.

BELOVED VAGABOND, THE. P. 3 a. Based on the novel of the same name. W. J. Locke. Dublin Royal, October 10, 1907; H.M., February 4, 1908.

BELOW LONDON BRIDGE. D. 4 a. Richard Dowling. Novelty, April 6, 1896.

BELPHEGER. Burl. L. Buckingham.

BELPHEGOR B. Webster's ver. of *Le Paillasse.* Adelphi, January, 1851

BELPHEGOR. Rom. C.O. 3 a. Lib by Wilton Jones. M by Alfred Christensen. South Shields T.R., October 26, 1889.

BELPHEGOR; OR, THE MARRIAGE OF THE DEVIL. T.C. J. Wilson. Dorset Grdn., 1690. Pr. 1691.

BELPHEGOR; OR, THE MOUNTEBANK AND HIS WIFE. D. 4 a. Adap. fr. the French by J. Courtney. Surrey, January 20, 1851

BELPHEGOR; OR, THE MOUNTEBANK AND HIS WIFE. D. 3 a. T. Higgie and T. H. Lacy. Victoria, January 27, 1851.

BELPHEGOR: OR, THE WISHES. C.O. 2 a. Miles Peter Andrews. D.L., 1778.

BELPHEGOR THE MOUNTEBANK. See *The Battle of Life.*

BELPHEGOR THE MOUNTEBANK; OR, WOMAN'S CONSTANCY. D. 3 a. Transl. and adap. fr. French of Dennery and Marc Fournier by Chs. Webb. Lyceum, 1856; Rev. Sadler's Wells, April, 1866.

BELSHAZZAR. D. Poem. Milman, 1822.

BELSHAZZAR. Orat. Handel. 1747.

BELSHAZZER. Sacred D. Miss H. Moore. Pr. 1782.

BELTESHAZZAR; OR, THE HEROINE JEW. Dr. Poem. Thos. Harrison. Pr. 1727. N. ac.

BEN. P. 1 a. Arthur Shirley. Croydon R., December 10, 1904.

BEN. P. 1 a. Blanche Eardley. St. James's, June 29, 1905 (C.P.).

BEN BOLT. D. 2 a. J. B. Johnstone. Surrey, March 28, 1854.

BEN HUR. D. 6 a. Adap. by W. Young fr. Lew Wallace's novel. D.L., April 3, 1902.

BEN LIEL. C. of London. May 4, 1857.

BEN-MY-CHREE, THE. Rom. D. 5 a. Hall Caine and Wilson Barrett. F. on Caine's "The Deemster." Princess's, May 17, 1888.

BEN NAZIR THE SARACEN. T. Grattan. D.L., May 21, 1827.

BEN THE BOATSWAIN. Naut. D. 3 a. T. E. Wilks. Surrey, August, 1839; in 2 a., D.L., August 23, 1858.

BENDING OF THE BOUGH, THE. C. 5 a. G. Moore. Dublin Gaiety, February 21, 1900.

BENDO (OR BYNDO) AND RICHARDS. Ac. at Rose T., March 4, 1591. N.p.

BENEATH THE SHADOW OF BIG BEN. See *'Neath the Shadow*, etc.

BENEATH THE STARS. D. 5 a. By Brandon Ellis. Newcastle-on-Tyne Palace, April 21, 1899 (C.P.); Manchester, Q's. T., June 25, 1900; Surrey, October 8, 1900.

BENEATH THE SURFACE. Sk. 1 a., 4 Sc. Chas. Norman. Manchester Metro.; July 18, 1904.

BENEATH THE SURFACE; OR, THE LOSS OF THE EURYDICE. D. 4 a. Mortimer Murdoch. Grecian, June 2, 1873; Marylebone, June 8, 1878.

BENEDICK AND BEATRICE. P. of Shakespeare's *Much Ado About Nothing.* Ac. at Court, May, 1613.

BENEFICE, THE. C. Dr. Robt. Wild. Pr. 1689. Plot taken fr. *The Return from Parnassus.*

BENEFIT OF THE DOUBT, THE. C. 3 a. A. W. Pinero. Comedy, October 16, 1895.

BENEVOLENT CUT-THROAT, THE. P. 7 a. Transf. fr. German D. of Klotzboggenhaggen by Fabins Pictor. Pr. 1800.

BENEVOLENT MAN; OR, MEDLEY LOVERS, THE. C. Maynard Chamberlain Walker. Dublin, 1771. N.pr.

BENEVOLENT PLANTERS, THE. See *The Friends.*

BENGAL TIGER, THE. F. 1 a. C. Dance. Olympic, December 18, 1837; Princesses, June 21, 1870.

BENIOWSKI. O. Boieldieu. Paris, 1800.

BENJAMIN FRANKLIN. P. John Brougham. (Died 1880.)

BENLIEL, THE SON OF THE NIGHT. D. Dundee, People's T., December, 1884.

BENNETS, THE. P. 4 a. Rosina Filippi. Adap. fr. Jane Austen's "Pride and Prejudice." Court, March 29, 1901.

BENVENUTO CELLINI. O. 2 a. M. by Berlioz. Wds. by Wailby and Barbier. Prod. at Académie Royale de Musique, September 3, 1838. Perf. at C.G. in 3 a. June 25, 1853.

BENYOWSKI. Kotzebue, 1811. English ver. called *The Virgin of the Sun.*

BENYOWSKY; OR, THE EXILES OF KAMSCHATKA. O. P. 3 a. M. by Sir J. Stevenson, Cooke, Horn, Livius, and Kelly. D.L., March 16, 1826.

BEQUEATHED HEART. Peake. Publ. by J. Dicks.

BERENICE. T. Racine, 1670. Hero and heroine meant for Louis XIV. and Henrietta of England. See "French Classical Plays."

BERGERE CHATELAINE, LA. O. Auber. Paris, 1820.

BERGERS, LES. O. 3 a. Offenbach. 1866.

BERGERS DE WATTEAU, LES. O. 1 a. M. by Offenbach. 1856.

BEROWNE. See *Borbonne.*

BERTA; OR, THE GNOME OF THE HARTZBERG. O. H. Smart. Hay., May 26, 1855.

BERTHA BRENDA. P. 1 a. Leslie Thomas. Prod. by "The Curtain Raisers." Rehearsal, March 11, 1909.

BERTHOLDI AT THE COURT OF KING ALBOINO. C.O. C.G. Pr. 1754.

BERTRAM; OR, THE CASTLE OF ST. ALDOBRAND. T. 5 a. Rev. R. C. Maturin. M. by Cooke. D.L., May 9, 1816. D.L., 1861.

BERTRAND ET RATON. C. Scribe, 1833.

BERYL. P. 3 a. L. M. Baker. Lincoln T.R. (C.P.), October 31, 1906.

BESIDE A CRADLE. Monol. Grace Latham. Willis's Rooms, April 18, 1888.

BESIDE THE BONNIE BRIER BUSH. P. 4 a. Jas. McArthur and Augustus Thomas. Adap. fr. the novel by Ian Maclaren. Liverpool, Shakespeare, April 3, 1905; St. James's, December 27, 1905.

BESS. P. 3 a. Mrs. Oscar Beringer. Cape Town T.R., December 1891; Peterborough T.R., November 11, 1872; St. James's, June 12, 1893.

BESSIE. D. 1 a. E. H. Brooke. Royalty, May 1, 1878.

BESSIE BELL AND MARY GRAY. M.D. A. Maclaren. 1808.

BEST BIDDER, THE. F. Miles Peter Andrews. D.L., 1782.

BEST HEART IN THE WORLD. Dr. sk. 2 a. Jos. Moser. Pr. 1807. N. ac.

BEST INTENTIONS. P. 1 a. Percy F. Marshall and Richard Purdon. Northampton O.H., December 11, 1890.

BEST MAN, THE. F. 3 a. Ralph R. Lumley. Toole's, March 6, 1894.

BEST MAN, THE. Oa. G. M. H. Playfair. M. by W. F. Winckworth. Brighton, St. Barthol.'s Parish H., February 21, 1898.

BEST MAN WINS, THE. F. Mark Melford. Novelty, January 27, 1890.

BEST OF FRIENDS, THE. D. of modern life. 4 a. Cecil Raleigh. D.L., September 18, 1902.

BEST OF HER SEX, THE. Dom. D. 4 a. Wm. A. Armour and Robert Cheval. Bedford, County, September 14, 1905. (C.P.); Bedford Colosseum, May 13, 1907; Stratford Royal, August 31, 1908.

BEST MUST WIN, THE. D. 4 a. W. Wallerton and F. Gilbert. Stockton R., October 23, 1902 (C.P.); Shakespeare, December 15, 1902.

BEST PEOPLE, THE. C. 4 a. Mrs. Fairfax. Globe, July 14, 1890.

BEST PEOPLE, THE. C. 3 a. Frederick Lonsdale. Wyndham's, August 5, 1909.

BEST WAY, THE. C. 1 a. Horace Wigan. Olympic, September 27, 1866.

BETHELEM GABOR. P. John Burk.

BETRAYED. D. W. G. Wills. Edinburgh T.R., August 18, 1873.

BETRAYED; OR, THE VICAR'S DAUGHTER. D. 5 a. Adap. fr. Oliver Goldsmith's *The Vicar of Wakefield*, by R. Mansell. Manchester, Queen's, June 28, 1886.

BETRAYED; OR, WHAT MEN CALL LOVE. Melo-d. 4 a. Cecil du Guè. Dalston, June 12, 1905. See *What Men Call Love.*

BETRAYED BY A KISS. C. 1 a. "Jay Nibb" (Mr. Saintsbury). Op. C. May 5, 1891.

BETRAYER OF HIS COUNTRY, THE. T. Hy. Brooke. 1741. N.p See *The Earl of Westmorland.*

BETROTHAL, THE. P. 5 a. By G. H. Boker. D.L., September 19, 1853.

BETSY. C. 3 a. F. C. Burnand. Taken fr. the French. Criterion, August 6, 1879. Rev. December 29, 1896; Wyndham's, July 17, 1902.

BETSY BAKER. See *The Laundry Belle.*

BETSY BAKER. M. Ver. of J. M. Morton's F. of same name. Lawrence Hanray. Bayswater Bijou, February 26, 1895.

BETSY BAKER; OR, TOO ATTENTIVE BY HALF. F. 1 a. John Maddison Morton. Princess's, November 13, 1850; D.L., March 16, 1857.

BETSY'S BAILIFF. Ca. Ed. Arnold Shute. Nuneaton Drill H., October 10, 1893.

BETTA THE GIPSY. O. 5 a. Prest. by Mme. Mellor. Wds. by E. Waltyen. M. by Emelio Pizzi. Collins's, June 10, 1907.

BETTER ANGEL; OR, THE LEGACY OF WRONG, THE. D 2 a. Wybert Reeve. South Shields T.R., February 24, 1868. Pl. in 4 a. Newcastle, Tyne T., December 5, 1870.

BETTER-HALF, THE. Ca. 1 a. T. J. Williams. Strand, June 26, 1865.

BETTER LAND, THE. D. 4 a. Dorothy Granville. Liverpool Queen's, June 22, 1908.

BETTER LATE THAN NEVER. P. Decker. Supposed to have been ac. 1599.

BETTER LATE THAN NEVER. C. Wm. Davies. (For a private theatre.) Pr. 1786.

BETTER LATE THAN NEVER. C. Miles Peter Andrews D.L., 1790.

BETTER LATE THAN NEVER. D. Edwin Palmer. Middlesbrough T.R., September 5, 1870.

BETTER LATE THAN NEVER. C. 2 a. F. C. Burnand. Royalty, June 27, 1874.

BETTER LATE THAN NEVER. Ca. M. Seaton. Liverpool P.O.W., May 7, 1900.

BETTER LIFE, THE. D. 4 a. Ar. Shirley and Sutton Vane. Adelphi, February 5, 1900.

BETTER LIFE, THE. P. 4 a. G. Carlton Wallace. Leeds R., November 10, 1904.

BETTER LUCK NEXT TIME. C.D. 3 a. Reginald Moore. York T.R., May 20, 1870.

BETTER POLICY, THE. Ca. Henry Here. Coronet, July 16, 1900.

BETTER SELF; OR, THREE TEMPTATIONS. D. Prol. and 3 a. Lincoln T.R., April 13, 1882.

BETTER THAN GOLD. D. Sk. 3 sc. J. M. East and Ernest Dodson. Hammersmith Lyric, May 28, 1894.

BETTING BOOK, THE. D 4 a. Sutton Vane. Brighton R., February 26, 1902; Pavilion, April 14, 1902.

BETTING BOY'S CAREER. Victoria, August 16, 1852.

BETTY. O. Donizetti. Naples, 1836; Gaiety, September 26, 1870.

BETTY; OR, THE COUNTRY BUMPKINS. Ballad F. Henry Carey. D.L., 1738. Pr. 1743.

BETTY MARTIN. F. A. Harris. Fr. the French vaudeville, *Le Chapeau de l'Horloger*. Mme. Girardin. Adelphi, March 8, 1855.

BETTY MARTIN. See *The Clockmaker's Hat.*

BETWEEN THE ACTS. Duol. G. Templeman Norman. Comedy, March 22, 1898.

BETWEEN THE DANCES. P. 1 a. H. T. Johnson. Avenue, October 1, 1901.

BETWEEN THE LIGHTS. D. 4 a. Edwin J. Lampard Bootle, December 17, 1894.

BETWEEEN THE POSTS. Duol. 1 a. Adap. by Mrs. Hugh Bell of her "L'Indécis." Newcastle-on-Tyne T.R., September 9, 1887. See *The Man that Hesitates.*

BETWEEN TWO STOOLS. C.Oa. Louisa Gray. Glendower Mansions, South Kensington, July 30, 1886.

BETWEEN TWO WOMEN. D. 4 a. Fredk. Melville. Rotherhithe, Terriss, October 27, 1902.

BETWIXT THE CUP AND THE LIP. Ca. Mrs. E. Argent Lonergan. Hackney, Morley H., November 28, 1896.

BEULAH SPA; OR, TWO OF THE B'HOYS. F. Dance. Olympic, November 18, 1833.

BEVERLEY D. Saurin, 1748.

BEVERLEY BOGEY, THE. P. 2 a. Mary Hingeston Randolph and Aveton Giffard. Bayswater Bijou, December 11, 1897.

BEVERLEY'S DAUGHTERS. C.O. 2 a. Windsor T.R, November 17, 1902. C.P.

BEVIS. C. 3 a. H. H. Davies. Hay., April 1, 1909.

BEWARE OF THE CENTENIER. F. Jersey T.R., February 25, 1877.

BEY OF BAGHDAD, THE. Burl. Ch. Carlton. Whittlesea Pub. H. Pr. August 30, 1897.

BEYOND. D. 3 a. Leigh R., September 29, 1904. C.P.

BEYOND; A STUDY OF A WOMAN BY A WOMAN. Suggested by a character of Renè Maizeroy. Criterion, February 1, 1894.

BEYOND HUMAN POWER. D. 2 a. Jessie Muir. Transl. fr. Norwegian of B. Björnson. Royalty, November 7, 1901.

BEYOND THE BREAKERS. D. 4 a. Sutton Vane. Grand, October 9, 1893.

BEZSEMENOVS, THE. P. 4 a. Maxim Gorky. Terry's, April 23, 1906.

BIANCA. T. R. Shepherd. Pr. at Oxford, 1772. N. ac.

BIANCA. T. Ingemann. 1817.

BIANCA. O. Balfe. C.G., December 6, 1860.

BIANCA CAPELLO. D. Trans fr. the German of Meissner by A. Thompson. Pr. 1796

BIANCO CAPELLO. T.O. 4 a. A. Randegger. Brescia, 1854.

BIANCA E FALIERO. O. Rossini. Milan, December 26, 1819.

BIANCA E FERNANDO. O. Bellini. Naples, 1826.

BIANCA ORSINI. O. Petrella. Naples, 1874.

BIANCA VISCONTI. T. Willis. 1843.

BIARRITZ. M.F. Jerome K. Jerome and Adrian Ross. M. by F. Osmond Carr. P.O.W., April 11, 1896.

BIB AND TUCKER. C. 2 a. Gaiety, August 14, 1873.

BIBERPETZ, DIE. C. 4 a. G. Hauptman. Pr. at the Court under the title of *The Thieves*, March 21, 1905; St. Geo. H., February 13, 1900; Gt. Queen St., April 15, 1907.

BIBLIOTHEKER, DER. O.C. October 20, 1894.

BICKERSTAFF'S BURIAL; OR, WORK FOR THE UPHOLDERS (sometimes called *Bickerstaff's Burying*). F. 3 a. Mrs. Centlivre. Ac. D.L., 1717; also at Hay. Pr. Afterwards rev. under title of *The Custom of the Country*.

BICKERSTAFF'S UNBURIED DEAD. Moral D. L.I.F., 1743. Rev. as a prel. under the title of *Live Lumber; or, The Unburied Dead* at C.G., 1796.

BICYCLE, THE. D. Sk. Mrs. Hugh Bell. Comedy, March 12, 1896.

BICYCLE GIRL, THE. M.C. 3 a. Chas. Osborne and E. M. Stuart. Add. lyrics by Hugh Seton. M. by Orlando Powell. Add. numbers by Edgar Ward and Arnold Cooke. Nottingham Grand, March 29, 1897.

BID FOR FORTUNE, A. D. 4 a. Barry Williams. Croydon T.R., June 21, 1901; Liverpool Rotunda, December 8, 1902; Greenwich Carlton, September 14, 1903.

BIDDY O'NEIL; OR, THE DAUGHTER OF ERIN. D. 2 a. W. H. Pitt. Britannia, March 29, 1869.

BIG BANDIT, A. M. piece. 1 a. Malcolm Watson. M. by Walter Slaughter. St. George's H., April 30, 1894.

BIG BLUE BOWL, THE. Jap M. fantasy. Frank Castles. St. George's Hall, May 29, 1888.

BIG CLAUS AND LITTLE CLAUS, THE PRINCESS AND THE SWINEHERD, AND THE SOLDIER AND THE TINDER-BOX. Fairy Tales for the Stage by Basil Hood. M. by Walter Slaughter. Terry's, December 23, 1897.

BIG FORTUNE, A. D. 4 a. Wm. Bourne. Blyth T.R., May 14, 1891; Surrey, July 6, 1891.

BIGAMY. P. 4 a. Fred Moule. Croydon R., Feb. 8, 1904.

BIGGEST SCAMP ON EARTH, THE. Melo-d. 4 a. F. A. Scudamore. Surrey, August 3, 1903.

BIGOT, THE. P. F. C. Grove. Ealing Lyric H., November 19, 1890 (C.P.).

BIJOU PERDU. Little piece. Adam. Lib. by Deforges. 1855.

BIJOU RESIDENCE TO LET, A. Ca. Adap. fr. the French by Mdme. Van de Velde. Nottingham T.R., September 18, 1889.

BILBERRY OF TILBURY. M.F.P. 3 a. Silvanus Dauncey and Geo. D. Day. M. by Guy Jones. Northampton O.H., April 18, 1898; Brixton T., July 18, 1898; Criterion, August 8, 1898.

BILIOUS ATTACK, A. F. 1 a. Arthur Wood. Holborn T., April 18, 1870; Sadler's Wells, April 1, 1872.

BILKER BILK'D, THE. See *Stroller's Packet*.

BILL ADAMS, THE HERO OF WATERLOO. M.P. 2 a. Herbert Shelley and Reginald Bacchus. M. by Stephen Philpot. Add. numbers by Mark Mason and Hermann Finck. Eastbourne T.R., February 26, 1903; Stoke Newington Alexandra, March 30, 1903.

BILL BAILEY Sk. Palace T. of V. December 13, 1904.

BILL JONES. G. A. Amherst. (Died 1851.)

BILL JONES. Kerr. Publ. by J. Dicks.

BILL OF EXCHANGE. C. David Fisher. Brighton, September 18, 1879.

BILL OF FARE; OR, FOR FURTHER PARTICULARS ENQUIRE WITHIN, THE. F.Sk. 1 a. Hay., June 15, 1822.

BILL-STICKER, THE Douglas Jerrold. Strand.

BILL-STICKERS BEWARE. F. P.O.W., Birmingham, September 20, 1875.

BILLEE TAYLOR. Nautical C.O. 2 a. Lib. by H. P. Stephens. M. by Edward Solomon. Imperial, October 30, 1880. See *Billy Taylor*.

BILLET MASTER; OR, THE FORGERY, THE. Pr. 1787. Ascr. to W. Ward.

BILLIARDS. Sk. Pr. by Harry Tate, Manchester Royal, December 23, 1907 (C.P.); Oxford, June 22, 1908.

BILLING AND COOING. C. 2 a. John Oxenford. Royalty, January 16, 1855.

BILLY. M.C. 2 a. G. Cooper and Adrian Ross. M. by Osmond Carr. Newcastle Tyne T., April 11, 1898; Stoke Newington, August 22, 1898.

BILLY BANTER. P. Valentine V. Fenn. Cardiff R., December 14, 1904.

BILLY DOO. F. 1 a. C. Marsham Rae. Globe, April 20, 1874.

BILLY ROTTERFORD'S DESCENT. Rev. and renamed ver. of the sensational f. entitled *Among the Brigands*, by R. Lascelles. Pr. Birmingham R.T., October 25, 1907; rev., March 23, 1908; Hammersmith King's, May 11, 1908.

BILLY TAYLOR. Burl. Buckstone. Adelphi, November 9, 1829.

BILLY'S LITTLE LOVE AFFAIR. C. 3 a. H. V. Esmond. Criterion, September 2, 1903.

BINBIAN MINE, THE. Rom. d. 3 a. Adap. fr. Mrs. Campbell Praed's novel, "The Ladies' Gallery," by the authoress and Mr. Justin M'Carthy. Margate T.R., October 6, 1888; Bristol, Prince's, November 23, 1888; under title of *Two Friends*.

BINKS THE BAGMAN. F. 1 a. J. Stirling Coyne. Adelphi, February 13, 1843.

BINKS, THE DOWNY PHOTOGRAPHER. M. absurdity. 1 a. Strand, October 17, 1893.

BIORN. O. 5 a. Lib. by Frank Marshall. M. by Lauro Rossi. Queen's, January 17, 1877.

BIRD AT THE NECK, THE. P. 1 a. "X. L." Portsmouth R., March 9, 1905; Hammersmith, King's, March 22, 1905.

BIRD IN A CAGE, THE. C. James Shirley. Ac. at Phœnix, D.L., 1633. Pr. 1633.

BIRD IN THE BUSH. P. 1 a. May C. Henry. Publ. by S. French, Ltd.

BIRD IN THE HAND WORTH TWO IN THE BUSH, A. P. 3 a. Fredk. Phillips. Surrey, January 19, 1857; Globe, September, 1878.

BIRD OF PARADISE. F. Adap. fr. the French by Alfred Thompson. Gaiety, June 26, 1869.

BIRD OF PASSAGE. B. Webster. F. 1 a Hay., September 10, 1849.

BIRD'S NEST, THE. P. 1 a. Frank Lindo. Fulham Grand, July 11, 1898.

BIRDCAGE WALK. F. H. Leigh Bennett and A. B. Tapping. Hove Town H., April 20, 1892.

BIRDS, THE. C. B.C. 409. Aristophanes. Transl. by Mitchell, 1820-22; Carey, 1824; Hickie, 1853; Rudd, 1867; rev. at Cambridge, November 24, 1903. See "Greek Plays."

BIRDS IN THEIR LITTLE NESTS AGREE. F. 1 a. Marsham Rae. Hay., November 13, 1876.

BIRDS OF A FEATHER. M. by J. Morehead. 1796.

BIRDS OF ARISTOPHANES, THE. Piece. 1 a. J. R. Planché Hay., April 13, 1846.

BIRDS OF PREY. Oa. M. by — Cross. Lib. by — Hawkins. Huddersfield, Victoria H., April 8, 1884.

BIRDS OF PREY; OR, A DUEL IN THE DARK. D. 3 a. T. W. Robertson.

BIRDS OF PREY. See *The Mouth of the Pit.*

BIRON'S CONSPIRACIE. T. Chapman. 1604.

BIRON'S TRAGEDY. T. Chapman. 1605.

BIRTH. C. 3 a. T. W. Robertson. Bristol, New T.R., October 5, 1870.

BIRTH AND BREEDING. C. Adap. fr. the German by Jerome K. Jerome. Edinburgh T.R., September 18, 1890 (c.p.).

BIRTH OF BEAUTY; OR, HARLEQUIN WILLIAM THE CONQUEROR. Extrav. Wm. Akhurst. Sanger's, December 26, 1872.

BIRTH OF HERCULES, THE. Masque. Wm. Shirley. M. by Dr. Arne. Intended for representation at C.G., 1763. Pr. 1765.

BIRTH OF JUPITER. Olivari, 1797. Transl. fr. Metastasio.

BIRTH OF MERLIN; OR, THE CHILD HAS LOST A FATHER (or, *The Child Hath Found His Father*). T.C. Wm. Rowley and Wm. Shakespeare. Publ. 1662.

BIRTHDAY, THE. Ent. 3 a. Mrs. Penny. Pr. 1771.

BIRTHDAY, THE. C. 3 a. T. Dibdin. C.G. Pr. 1799. An alt. fr. a D. of Kotzebue's called *Fraternal Enmity*. D.L., January 17, 1815.

BIRTHDAY, THE. Div. November 17, 1828.

BIRTHDAY, THE. C. 1 a. Geo. Bancroft. Court, December 8, 1894.

BIRTHDAY; OR, ARCADIAN CONTEST, THE. M. past. Royalty. Songs pr. 1787.

BIRTHDAY; OR, THE PRINCE OF ARRAGON, THE. Dr. piece with songs, by J. O'Keefe. Hay., August 12, 1783. Pr. 1783.

BIRTHDAY TRIBUTE, A. Int. Richard Sickelmore. Brighton, August 12, 1805. N.p.

BIRTHDAYS, THE. C.D. 3 a. Geo. Roberts. Newcastle T.R., February 20, 1883.

BIRTHPLACE OF PODGERS, THE. Dom. sk. 1 a. John Hollingshead. Lyceum, March 10, 1858.

BIRTH-NIGHT; OR, MODERN FRENCH REFORMATION, THE. C.O. 3 a. Pr. 1796.

BIRTHRIGHT; OR, THE BRIGAND'S RANSOM. D. 4 a. John Douglass. Huddersfield T.R., June 1, 1894. Hammersmith, Lyric, May 31, 1897.

BISHOP, THE. Afterwards called *Martha.* F.C. 3 a. Wilford F. Field. Tottenham. October 25, 1894.

BISHOP OF THE FLEET, THE. Rom. D. Prol. and 3 a. C. A. Clarke and Fredk. Mouillot. Scarboro' Londesboro' T., December 26, 1889.

BISHOP'S CANDLESTICKS, THE. P. 1 a. Norman McKinnell. F. on well-known incident in Victor Hugo's *Les Miserables*. D. of York's, August 24, 1901; rev. Kingsway, December 20, 1907.

BISHOP'S EYE, THE. P. 3 a. Clo Graves. Vaudeville, February 22, 1900.

BISHOP'S MOVE, THE. C. 3 a. J. Ol. Hobbes and Murray Carson. Garrick, June 7, 1902, and July 13, 1903.

BIT OF DRAPERY, A. Ca. Preston Hope. Camberwell Metro., August 30, 1897.

BIT OF FUN, A. Sk. Argyll Saxby. Finsbury Pk. H., March 14, 1898.

BIT OF HUMAN NATURE, A. D. 1 a. Mrs. Geo. Corbett. Terry's, June 27, 1899.

BIT OF OLD CHELSEA, A. P. 1 a. Mrs. Oscar Beringer. Court, February 8, 1897; Royalty, October 5, 1897; Avenue, January 6, 1898.

BIT OF OLD WORCESTER, A. C. 1 a. John Porter. Friern Barnet Parish Room. April 24, 1900.

BITER, THE. C. 3 a. Nichs Rowe. L.I.F. Pr. 1705.

BITTER COLD. D. 2 a. W. S. Foote. Ac.

BITTER COLD. Alfred Coates.

BITTER COLD. D. 2 a. Marylebone, January 25, 1868.

BITTER FRUIT. D. 3 a. A. W. Dubourg. Liverpool Alex., October 6, 1873.

BITTER LESSON, A. P. 1 a. J. R. Harris Burnland and Alec Weatherly. Lyric, May 15, 1896; Brighton T.R., June 1, 1896.

BITTER LOVE, A. D. 3 a. Ellen Lancaster Wallis and J. W. Boulding. Edinboro' Lyceum. October 19, 1883, (under title *For Wife and State*), Belfast T.R., October 21, 1884.

BITTER RECKONING, THE; OR, A ROVER FROM MANY LANDS. D. 3 a. C. H. Hazlewood. Britannia, June 19, 1871.

BITTER SEA, THE. Rom. P. 2 a. Herbert T. Rainger. Cheltenham Vict. Rooms, April 21, 1904.

BITTER SWEET. Rom. 1 a. C. S. Kitts. Bristol T.R., October 29, 1895. C.P.

BITTER SWEETS: A STORY OF THE FOOTLIGHTS. C.D. Alfred Parry. Cambridge T.R., August 8, 1878; Oxford T.R., January 13, 1880.

BITTER WRONG; OR, A WIFE IN ENGLAND NO WIFE IN FRANCE. Dom. D. 5 a. and 7 tab. Geo. Lander and John Douglass. Standard, April 14, 1884.

BIZZARRIE D' AMORE, LE. O. Raimondi. Genoa, 1907.

BLACK AGAINST WHITE. "Sporting and dr. sk." 1 scene. Worland S. Wheeler. Paragon, January 27, 1908.

BLACK AND WHITE. D. 3 a. Wilkie Collins and Mr. Fechter. Adelphi, March 29, 1869. Exeter T R., September 24, 1877.

BLACK AND WHITE. M.F.C. 3a. Mark Melford and W. Sapte, jun.; H. Cottesmore and H. Trevor. M. by John Crook. Southampton, P.O.W., December 27, 1897. Kingston, R. County, February 21, 1898; Clapham, Shakespeare, August 1, 1898.

BLACK BALL, THE. C.D. 4 a. Fred D'Arcy. Bristol T.R., October 26, 1895. (C.P.)

BLACK BATMAN OF THE NORTH. P. Ac. 1598. Ascribed to Henry Chettle. Second Part of same piece acted 1598, when Chettle was assisted by Robert Wilson.

BLACK BEARD; OR, THE CAPTIVE PRINCESS, THE. B.P. by J. C. Cross. Royal Circus. Published 1809.

BLACK BISHOP, THE. Dom. D. 4 a. Barry Williams. T.R., Kidderminster, April 14, 1898; Bilston T.R., October 7, 1898; Stratford T.R., June 18, 1900.

BLACK BOARDER, THE. F. Horace Johnstone. Kilburn T.R., May 17, 1897.

BLACK BOOK, THE. D. 3 a. J. P. Simpson. D.L., February 2, 1857.

BLACK BUSINESS, A. Melo-d. Arthur Matthison. Huddersfield T.R., August 19, 1878; Newark T.R., February 6, 1879.

BLACK BUT COMELY. D., f. on Whyte-Melville's story, by Miss Stephanie Forrester. Gaiety, September 16, 1882.

BLACK CÆSAR. D. Queen's T., 1832.

BLACK CAT, THE. (See *Eastward Ho!*) Oriental burl. Lib. by C. M. Rodney. M. by C E. Howells. Walsall, St. George's T., July 31, 1893; Eleph and C., August 14, 1893.

BLACK CAT, THE. P 3 a. John Todhunter. Op. C., December 8, 1893. (Independent T. repres.)

BLACK COTTAGE, THE. P. 1 a. David Kimball. Dr. ver. of Wilkie Collins's story of same name. Court, March 3, 1909. (Amat.)

BLACK COTTAGE, THE. P. 1 a. Fd. on Wilkie Collins's novel. Terry's, May 23, 1909.

BLACK CROOK, THE. Op. bo. 4 a. J. and H. Paulton. Alhambra, December 23, 1872; Liverpool Amphitheatre, May, 1875.

BLACK DEVIL, THE. Sk. Transl. by Lauderdale Maitland fr. the Italian. Hammersmith Palace, August 31, 1908.

BLACK DEVIL, THE. T. epis. Carlo Broggi. Transl. by Herbert Dansey. Pr. by the Argonauts. Rehearsal W.C., November 13, 1908 (mat.).

BLACK DIAMONDS; OR, THE LIGHTS AND SHADOWS OF PIT LIFE. D. 5 a. Louis S. Denbigh and Fenton Mackay. Southend Alexandra, September 30, 1890; West Hartlepool Gaiety, January 15, 1891; Surrey, July 11, 1892.

BLACK DOCTOR, THE. D. 5 a. Transl. from *Le Docteur Noir* of Anicet-Bourgeois and Dumanoir by T. V. Bridgeman. Porte Sainte Martin T., July 30, 1846; City of Lon., November 9, 1846.

BLACK DOG OF NEWGATE, THE. P. Richd. Hathwaye, assisted by John Day and W. Smith. Ac. 1602. Second part prod. same year, when a fourth author (unknown) assisted.

BLACK DOMINO. Burla. 1 a. C. Mathews. January 18, 1838.

BLACK DOMINO. Op. C. An English ver. of Scribe's *Le Domino Noir* (1837). 1841.

BLACK DOMINO. C.O. 3 a. H. F. Chorley. M. by Auber. C.G., February 20, 1861.

BLACK DOMINO, THE. D. 5 a. Geo. R. Sims and Robert Buchanan. Adelphi, April 1, 1893

BLACK DOMINO; OR, THE MASKED BALL, THE. C.D. 3 a. Adapted fr. the French by T. E. Wilks. Sadler's Wells, February 6, 1838.

BLACK DOVE, A. Study. 1 a. E. and H. Gordon-Clifford. Kew, Prince's H., September 12, 1894.

BLACK DWARF, THE. Rom. Melo-d. See *The Wizard*.

BLACK EDITOR, THE. F. O. J. Wendlant.

BLACK-EYED SUSAN; OR, ALL IN THE DOWNS. D. 2 a. Douglas Jerrold. Surrey, June 8, 1829; City T., 1831; rev. Sadler's Wells, 1866; rev. Adelphi, December 23, 1896; rev. ver. by Oswald Brand, in 3 a., Grand, September 19, 1904

BLACK-EY'D SUSAN. New ver. of D. Jerrold's P. by Roy Redgrave. Dover Tivoli, May 7, 1898.

BLACK-EY'D SUSAN. See *All in the Downs, Blue-Eyed Susan.*

BLACK-EY'D SUSAN; OR, THE LITTLE BILL THAT WAS TAKEN UP. Burl. F. C. Burnand. New Royalty, November 29, 1866; rev. March 3, 1870.

BLACK FLAG; OR, ESCAPED FROM PORTLAND. D. 4 a. Henry Pettitt. Grecian, May 9, 1879; Olympic, March 7. 1892.

BLACK HAND; OR, THE DERVISE AND THE PERI, THE. D. spec. Adelphi, October 10, 1834.

BLACK HAWKS; OR, THE WILD CAULIFLOWER OF THE SAUSOMONE. Birmingham Queen's, October 30, 1893.

BLACK HEART; OR, THE HYPNOTIST, A. D. 3 a. Bernard Copping. Hastings Pav. Pier, November 24, 1902.

BLACK HEARTS; OR, THE KING OF DARKNESS. D. 3 a. E. Towers. New East London, May 30, 1868.

BLACK HORSE, THE. P. Fletcher. Before 1620. See Palaemon and Arcyte.

BLACK HUGH, THE OUTLAW. D. 2 a. W. Rogers. New York, 1836. Surrey.

BLACK JOUNE. P. Mentioned by Henslowe as belonging to the stock of the Rose T. Circa March, 1598.

BLACK KNIGHT OF ASHTON, THE. D. Butler Stanhope. Stalybridge People's H., March 30, 1874.

BLACK LADY, THE. P. Ac. by Lady Elizabeth's servants, May 10, 1622.

BLACK MAIL. D. 4 a. Watts Phillips. Grecian, October 16, 1880.

BLACK MAIL. C.D. 4 a. Alt. to 3 a. G. H. Roque and Dr. G. H. R. Dabbs. Shanklin. Lit. Inst., September 3, 1887; Criterion, October 17, 1888.

BLACK MAIL. See *Blackmail.*

BLACK MAN, THE. Int. attrib. to Cox. Pr. 1659.

BLACK MARK, A. P. 1 a. G. Gugglsberg. Worthing Royal, December 9, 1907.

BLACK MASK, THE. D. Prol. and 3 a. F. Marriot Watson. Manchester St. James's T., July 31, 1899; Stratford T.R., December 29, 1902.

BLACK PRINCE, THE. T. Roger Boyle, Earl of Orrery. Duke of York's T., October 19, 1667. Pr. 1669.

BLACK PRINCE, THE. Op. bo. 3 a. H. B. Farnie. M. by Lecocq. St. James's, October 24, 1874.

BLACK PRINCE, THE. M.P. 3 a. Norman Bernard Page. Nottingham Mechanics' H., June 29, 1903.

BLACK ROVER, THE. Melo-d. O. 3 a. Wr. and comp. by Luscombe Searelle. Globe, September 23, 1890.

BLACK SHEEP. C. 3 a. J. Stirling Coyne. Hay., April 22, 1861.

BLACK SHEEP. D. 3 a., f. on Edmund Yates' novel and arr. by J. Palgrave Simpson and the author. Olympic, April 25, 1868.

BLACK SHEEP, THE. Panto. pastoral. André Raffalovich. M. by Cotsford Dick. Albert H. West T., April 17, 1894.

BLACK SHEEP, THE. Sk. Brixton Empress, May 10, 1909.

BLACK SPIRITS AND WHITE. P. T. Dibdin. Sadler's Wells, 1826.

BLACK SQUIRE, THE. C.O. 3 a. H. Pottinger Stephens. M. by Florian Pascal. Torquay T.R. and O.H., November 5, 1896.

BLACK TOWER OF LONDON; OR, A FOSTER-BROTHER'S REVENGE, THE. D. Cecil Pitt. Britannia, September 22, 1869.

BLACK TULIP, THE. P. 5 a. Drawn by Sydney Grundy. P. Alex. Dumas' *La Tulipe Noire.* Hay., October 28, 1899.

BLACK VAMPIRE, THE. D. 5 a. C. A. Clarke and Harry Spiers. Manchester St. James's, April 9, 1900; Britannia, September 10, 1900.

BLACK VULTURE, THE. D. G. H. B. Rodwell. Adelphi, October, 1830.

BLACK WEDDING, THE. Entered at Stationers' Co., November 29, 1653.

BLACKAMOOR WASH'D WHITE, THE. C.O. Henry Bate. D.L., 1776. Songs only pr.

BLACKAMOOR'S HEAD. F. D.L., May 16, 1818.

BLACKBERRIES. M.C. 1 a. Mark Melford. Liverpool P.O.W., June 14, 1886; Comedy, July 31, 1886.

BLACKBIRDING. D. C. H. Hazlewood. Britannia, September 3, 1873.

BLACKFRIARS' MASQUE, THE. A masque of the seventeenth century.

BLACKLEG, THE. D. 5 a. Butler Stanhope. Birkenhead T.R., October 18, 1886.

BLACKMAIL. D. 3 a. Herbert J. Stanley. Adelphi, Liverpool, April 27, 1896. See *Black Mail.*

BLACKMAILER, THE. Irish-American d. Nellie Whitbread. Dublin Queen's, January 9, 1905.

BLACKMAILERS, THE. P. 4 a. John Gray and André Raffalovich. P.O.W., June 7, 1894.

BLACKMAILERS, THE. C.D. 3 a. Forbes Dawson. Wigan T.R., May 15, 1901 (C.P.).

BLACKMAILERS, THE. D. 3 a. Mrs. T. P. O'Connor and H. Henderson Bland. Kingston R.C., October 19, 1908.

BLACKNESS. C. Jonson. 1616.

BLACKSMITH, THE. M.F. 1 a. W. Collier. Victoria, January, 1834.

BLACKSMITH, THE. Irish d. Fred Maeder. H.M.T., Carlisle, January 30, 1892.

BLACKSMITH OF ANTWERP, THE. F. O'Keefe. C.G., 1785. Pr. 1789.

BLACKSMITH'S DAUGHTER, THE. An old p. mentioned in Gosson's *School of Abuse.* 1579. N.p.

BLACKSMITH'S DAUGHTER, THE. Dom. c. 1 a. Arnold Goldsworthy and E. B. Norman. Op.C., October 16, 1888.

BLACKSMITH'S DAUGHTER, THE. Melo-d. 4 a. Thos. Naden. Bilston T.R., September 8, 1893.

BLACKSMITH'S DREAM. THE. Scena. Norwich R., January 7, 1905 (C.P.).

BLADE BONE, THE. Int. Haymarket, August 20, 1788. Not repeated. N.p.

BLADUD; OR, THE SWELL AND THE SWINEHEAD. C.O. 2 a. E. Fogg and S. Pool. M. by D. L. C. Thomas and C. Wright. Bath R.T., April 11, 1908.

BLAISE LE SAVETIER. C.O. F. A. Philidor. (His first co.) 1759.

BLANCHARD DIAMONDS, THE. P. 4 a. G. Harcard Pierson and Robert P. Oglesby. Sunderland Avenue, November 8, 1904; Hull, Grand, February 13, 1905.

BLANCHE. C. 3 a. Arthur Sketchley. Liverpool Alexandra, March 14, 1870.

BLANCHE DE MALETROIT. P. 1 a. A. E. W. Mason. F. on story by R. S. Stevenson. Ladbroke H., June 30, 1894.

BLANCHE DE VALMY. D. W. B. Bernard. Princess's, 1845.

BLANCHE FARREAU. D. W. Calvert. Adap. fr. Charles Gibbon's novel, "For the King." Afterwards known as "Life and Honour." Liverpool T.R., October 6, 1890.

BLANCHE HERIOT; OR, THE CHERTSEY CURFEW. Dom. and hist. d. 2 a. Albert Smith. Surrey, September 26, 1842.

BLANCHE OF JERSEY. D. 2 a. R. B. Peake. Lyceum, August 9, 1837.

BLANCHE OF NAVARRE. P. 5 a. G. P. R. James. New York, 1839.

BLANCHE OF NEVERS. O. Balfe. C.G., November 21, 1863.

BLANCHE WESTGARTH; OR, THE NEMESIS OF CRIME. D. 3 a. Templeton Lucas. Grecian, March 6, 1871.

BLANCHETTE P. 3 a. M. Brieux, transl. by J. T. Grein and M. L. Churchill and Miss Martia Leonard. Albert H., West T., December 8, 1898; Court, May 24, 1901; Royalty, March 1, 1907.

BLANK CHEQUE, A. Sk. W. J. Locke. Empire, December 16, 1908.

BLARNEY. D. Auguste Creamer. Newcastle under-Lyne T.R., March 1, 1875.

BLARNEY. F. J. D. Logue. Norwich T.R., March 12, 1875.

BLAZING BURGEE. Burl. 1 a. T. G. Bowles. Publ. by S. French, Ltd.

BLAZING COMET; THE MAD LOVERS; OR, THE BEAUTIES OF THE POETS, THE. P. Samuel Johnson. Hay. Pr. 1732.

BLAZING WORLD, THE. C. in two parts (unfinished). Margaret, Duchess of Newcastle. 1668, 1674.

BLEAK HOUSE. D 3 a. J. P. Burnett. Liverpool P.O.W., November 8, 1875.

BLEAK HOUSE. Adap. of Dickens's story, by J. Stillwell and W. Benson. Margate T.R., November 26, 1903.

BLEAK HOUSE. D. Geo. Lander. Pavilion, March 25, 1876.

BLEAK HOUSE. See *Jo, Lady Deadlock's Secret, Move On.*

BLEAK HOUSE; OR, EVENTS IN THE LIFE OF JO. P. 5 a. Oswald Brand. Adap. fr. Dickens. Islington Grand, June 1, 1903.

BLEAK HOUSE; OR, POOR JO. D. Eliza Thorne. Sheffield, Alexandra O.H., April 28, 1876.

BLEEDING AND DYING JESU, THE. Orat. Keiser. 1673-1739.

BLESSINGS OF BALAAM, THE. P. 1 a. Mrs. St. Clair Stobart. St. James's, June 4, 1909. Mat.

BLESSINGS OF P*** AND A SCOTCH EXCISE; OR, THE HUMBUG RESIGNATION, THE. F. Ac. at the New T. in S—A—y Street. Pr. 1763.

BLETCHINGTON HOUSE. Hist. d. 3a. H. T. Craven. C. of Lon., April 20, 1846.

BLIGHTED BACHELORS. F.C. and Burl. Llewellyn Williams. Derby Corn Exchange T., August 29, 1881.

BLIGHTED BACHELORS, THE. Extrav. Nelson Lee. Liverpool T.R., March 29, 1875.

BLIGHTED BEING, A. F. 1 a. Adap. fr. the French vaudeville, *Une Existence Décolorée*, by Tom Taylor. Olympic, October 16, 1854.

BLIND. D. 1 a. Mr. Edmund Maurice. Adap. fr. the Fr. *Aveugle* of Messrs. Chas Hellem and Pol d'Estoc. New Cross Empire, April 27, 1908.

BLIND BARGAIN; OR, HEAR IT OUT, THE. C. 5a. Fredk. Reynolds. C.G., October 24, 1804.

BLIND BEGGAR OF ALEXANDRIA, THE. C. Neither divided into acts or scenes. Geo. Chapman. Ac. circ. 1596. Pr. 1598.

BLIND BEGGAR OF BETHNAL GREEN; THE. Ballad F. Robt. Dodesley. D.L., 1739. Pr. 1741.

BLIND BEGGAR OF BETHNAL GREEN, WITH THE MERRY HUMOUR OF TOM STRAND, THE NORFOLK YEOMAN, THE. C. John Day. Ac. by Prince's servants. Prod. 1600. Second Part by Haughton and Day. Ac. 1601. A Third Part by same authors in 1601.

BLIND BEGGAR OF BETHNAL GREEN, THE. H M. Milner, author of *Frankenstein*.

BLIND BEGGAR OF BETHNAL GREEN. See *Beggar of Bethnal Green*.

BLIND BEGGARS, THE. Mus. D. Possibly by W. B. Hewitson. C.G. Pr. 1808.

BLIND BEGGARS, THE. See *The Two Blinds*.

BLIND BEGGARS OF BURLINGTON BRIDGE. Arthur Clements and J. Malone. Liverpool, 186-.

BLIND BOY, THE. Melo-d. 2 a. Jas. Kenney. M. by Davy. C.G., December 1, 1807, Lyceum, August 17, 1818.

BLIND EAT MANY A FLY, THE. P. Thos Heywood. Ac. 1602. N.p.

BLIND FOUNDLING, THE. D. C. H. Phelps. Birkenhead T.R., December 18, 1899; Greenwich Carlton, April 15, 1901.

BLIND GIRL; OR, A RECEIPT FOR BEAUTY, THE. C.O. Thos. Morton. C.G., April 22, 1801. Songs pr. 1801.

BLIND GIRL'S FORTUNE, THE. D. A version of *The Two Orphans*. East London, November 21, 1874.

BLIND HEARTS. D. 4 a. Charles Collins. Birmingham T.R., December 17, 1877.

BLIND JEALOUSY. P. 1 a. W. O. Waud. Ladbroke H., January 21, 1904.

BLIND JUSTICE. D. Prol. and 3 a. E. C. Bertrand. Wolverhampton T.R., September 23, 1886; Standard, April 11, 1887.

BLIND JUSTICE. Dr. Epis. R. Cullum and H. E. Garden. Met., May 3, 1909.

BLIND LADY, THE. C. Sir Robert Howard. Plot taken from *Cosmography*. Pr. 1661.

BLIND LOVE, Ca. 1 a. Geo. Roberts.

BLIND LOVE. Sk. W. A. Tremayne and W. S. Hartford. Middlesex, June 28, 1909.

BLIND MARRIAGE, A. P. 4 a. Francis Francis. Criterion, August 20, 1896.

BLIND MUSICIAN, THE. Sk. John Jackson. Brixton Empress, December 28, 1908.

BLIND SINGER, THE. D. 3 a. Dr. Geo. H. R. DABBS. Comedy, April 22, 1898.

BLIND SISTER, THE. D. 4 a. Paul Meritt and Geo. Conquest. Grecian, October 26, 1874.

BLIND SPINSTER, A. F. 1 a. Fred Lloyd. Belfast Empire, May 16, 1903.

BLIND WITNESS, THE. D. 4 a. J. S. Blythe. Margate Grand, March 6, 1899; Clapham Shakespeare, March 13, 1899.

BLIND WITNESS OF ABERDARE, THE. D. Merthyr Tydfil Cambrian T., February 5, 1872.

BLIND WOMAN OF SPA, THE. C. Transl. from the French of Mdme. Genlis. Pr. 1781.

BLINDFOLD. Ca. R. Soutar. Gaiety, May 4, 1882.

BLINDNESS AMONGST ENEMIES. D. T.R., Paisley. February 25, 1878.

BLOBB'S HOLIDAY. F. Charles Crozier. Marylebone, April 18, 1892.

BLOCKHEADS; OR, THE FORTUNATE CONTRACTOR, THE. Op. as performed at New York. Pr. 1783.

BLODWIN. O. Dr. Joseph Parry. Swansea Music Hall, June 20, 1878.

BLONDIN ON THE TIGHT-ROPE. F. Aberdeen, H.M.O.H., February 5, 1873.

BLOODHOUND OF THE LAW, A. Melo-d. 4 a Thomas Raceward. Peckham Crown, March 24, 1902.

BLOODY BANQUET, THE. T. Ascribed to Thos. Barker. Ac. T.R. Pr. 1620. Some say by Robt. Davenport.

BLOODY BROTHER; OR, ROLLO DUKE OF NORMANDY, THE. T. Beaumont and Fletcher. See *The Three Merry Boys*. Ac. after 1624, and at Hampton Court, January 24, 1637. See *Rollo Duke*, etc.

BLOODY DUKE; OR, THE ADVENTURES FOR A CROWN, THE. T.C. Ac. at Court of Alba Regalis by persons of great quality. Pr. 1690.

BLOODY PLOT DISCOVERED, A. T. Ascribed to a Mr. Ball, probably the author of *The Beautiful Armenia*. Pr. 1780.

BLOOMER COSTUME; OR, THE FIGURE OF FUN, THE. F. E. Stirling Strand, September, 1851.

BLOOMERISM; OR, THE FOLLIES OF THE DAY. F. J. H. Nightingale and C. Milward. Adelphi, October, 1851.

BLOSSOM OF CHURNINGTON GREEN; OR, LOVE, RIVALRY, AND REVENGE, THE. Burl. d. 1 a. Francis Radcliffe Hoskins.

BLOT ON THE 'SCUTCHEON, A. D. 3 a. Robert Browning. D.L., February 11, 1843. Rev. by Browning Society, Olympic, March 15, 1888.

BLOTTED OUT. C.D. 3 a. David James, jun. Wigan T.R., August 11, 1884.

BLOW FOR BLOW. D. Pro. and 3 a. H. J. Byron. Holborn, September 5, 1868.

BLOW IN THE DARK, THE. Ca. 1 a. Thompson Townsend. Surrey, 1855.

BLOWER JONES. F. 1 a. Sadler's Wells, February 28, 1881.

BLOWER JONES. See *£100 A-Side*.

BLUE AND BUFF; OR, THE GREAT MUDDLEBOROUGH ELECTION. C.O. Lib. by E. V. Ward. M. by Wm. L. Frost. Liverpool Bijou O.H., January 24, 1880; Hay., September 5, 1881.

BLUE BEARD. First dramatised at Paris in 1746.

BLUE BEARD. M. spec. Colman. M. by Kelly. 1798.

BLUE BEARD. Burl. 1 a. J. R. Planche and Charles Dance. Olympic, January 1, 1839.

BLUE BEARD. C.O. Sedaine, 1797; M. by Grétry. 1866.

BLUE BEARD. Op. bo. Offenbach. 1868.

BLUE BEARD. O. 4 a. W. S. North. M. by J. M'Cullum. Dublin, Nat. Childr. Hosp., January 13, 1894.

BLUE BEARD; OR, FEMALE CURIOSITY. Dr. rom. Geo. Colman, jun. D.L. Pr. 1798. D.L., May 27, 1831.

BLUE BEARD; OR, THE FLIGHT OF HARLEQUIN. Pant. C.G., 1791.

BLUE BEARD; OR, THE HAZARD OF THE DYE. Burl. D. 3 a. F. C. Burnand. Gaiety, March 12, 1883.

BLUE BEARD; OR, THE LOVES OF SELIM AND FATIMA. Burl. H. J. Arden. Crystal Palace, March 29, 1869. Under the title of *Blue Beard, the Great Bashaw; or, The Loves of Selim and Fatima*, Crystal Palace, April 14, 1873.

BLUE BEARD AND FAT EMMA; OR, THE OLD MAN WHO CRIED HEADS. Burl. Frank Green. North Woolwich Gdns., June 18, 1877.

BLUE BEARD AND SON. Burl. Bath T.R., March, 1883.

BLUE BEARD FROM A NEW POINT OF HUE. H. J. Byron. Adelphi, December 26, 1860.

BLUE BEARD IN A BLACK SKIN. Operatic absurdity. Morton Williams. Norwich T.R., June 7, 1875.

BLUE BEARD RE-PAIRED. O. extrav. 1 a. Adap. fr. the French of Henri Meilhac and Ludovic Halévy. H. Bellingham. Olympic, June 2, 1866.

BLUE BEARD RE-TRIMMED. Burl. Park, July 9, 1877.

BLUE BELLS OF SCOTLAND, THE. C.D. 5 a. Robert Buchanan; partly taken fr. the same author's prose romance, "A Child of Nature." Novelty, September 12, 1887.

BLUE BOAR, THE. F. 3 a. Louis N. Parker and Murray Carson. Liverpool Court, August 31, 1894; Terry's, March 23, 1895.

BLUE BONNETS. 3 a. T. A. Palmer.

BLUE DAHLIA, THE. Ca. 1 a. Adap. by Hallewell Suttcliff and Hubert Bartlett fr. the former's story, "The Descent of Reginald Hampton." Devonport Metropole, October 27, 1898.

BLUE DEVILS. F. 1 a. Geo. Colman the younger, fr. the French of M. Patrat. C.G., April 24, 1798. Pr. 1808. Lyceum, June 4, 1819.

BLUE-EYED SUSAN. C.O. 3 a. F. on Douglas Jerrold's drama, *Black-Eyed Susan.* Lib. by Geo. R. Sims and Henry Pettitt. M. by F. Osmond Carr. P.O.W., February 6, 1892.

BLUE-EYED WITCH; OR, NOT A FRIEND IN THE WORLD, THE. D. 3 a. C. H. Hazlewood. Britannia, June 16, 1869.

BLUE-FACED BABOON, THE. Addison. Pub. by J. Dicks.

BLUE GERANIUM, THE. C. 3 a. Wilfrid Thorneley and Coryton Day. Winchmore Hill H., November 15, 1905.

BLUE JEANS. American d. 4 a. Joseph Arthur. Northampton O.H., February 14, 1898; Clapham Shakespeare, February 28, 1898.

BLUE-LEGGED LADY, THE. F. W. J. Hill. Court, March 4, 1874.

BLUE MONKEY, THE. M.F. 2 a. Bk. by Walter R. Flint. M. by H. Wilkinson, A. Taggart and others. Brighton Pal. Pier, July 22, 1907.

BLUE MOON, THE. M.P. 2 a. Harold Ellis and Percy Greenbank. M. by Howard Talbot and Paul Rubens. Northampton O.H., February 29, 1904; Kingston-on-Thames, County, March 14, 1904; Lyric, August 28, 1905.

BLUE OR GREEN. Ca. Mrs. Hugh Bell. Comedy, March 12, 1896.

BLUE RIBBONS. F. 3 a. Walter Browne and J. E. Soden. Gaiety, May 11, 1887.

BLUE RIVER VALLEY. Sk. Greenwich Barnard's M.H., December 19, 1904.

BLUEBELL-IN-FAIRYLAND. M.D.P. 2 a. Seymour Hicks. M. by Walter Slaughter. Vaudeville, December 18, 1901. Rev. ver. Aldwych, December 23, 1905.

BLUEBOTTLE, THE. Exmouth Pub. H., January 18, 1909.

BLUEJACKETS; OR, HER MAJESTY'S SERVICE, THE. F. 1 a. Edward Stirling. Adelphi, October 15, 1838.

BLUFF. F.Sk. St. Albans County Hall, April 6, 1899.

BLUFF AND BUNKUM. Sk. P. Martin. Bedford, March 7, 1907.

BLUFF KING HAL. Op. bo. 3 a. Lib. C. O'Neil. M. by G. Richardson. Cheltenham T.R., April 10, 1877.

BLUFF KING HAL. Pant. Frank Hall. Sadler's Wells, December 26, 1887.

BLUFF KING HAL; OR, THE FIELD OF THE CLOTH OF GOLD. Pant. Henry Spry. Sanger's Amphitheatre, December 26, 1882.

BLUFF KING HAL; OR, THE MAIDEN, THE MASHER, AND THE MONARCH. Burl. Alexandra O.H., Sheffield, March 12, 1883.

BLUFFING ONE'S WAY. C. 3 a. Eugene Scribe. Adap. and modernised fr. *Le Puff; Ou Mensonge et Verite.* Royalty, February 22, 1909.

BLUNDERER, THE. C. Transl. fr. Molière. Pr 1762.

BLUNDERS. Ca. Op.C. April 11, 1898.

BLURT MASTER CONSTABLE; OR, THE SPANIARD'S NIGHT WALK. C. Thomas Middleton. Ac. by the Children of St. Paul's, 1602. Pr. 1602.

BLUSH ROSE. Op. bo. M. by Offenbach, Lib. by G. D'Arcy. Plymouth T.R., May 22, 1876.

BOABDIL EL CHICO; OR, THE MOOR THE MERRIER. Burl. F. C. Burnand. Astley's.

BOADICEA. T. Fletcher. 1611.

BOADICEA. T. Richard Glover. D.L. Pr. 1753.

BOADICEA. Story. Same as *Bonduca.*

BOADICEA, QUEEN OF BRITAIN. T. Charles Hopkins. L.I.F. 1697. Pr. 1697.

BOADICEA UNEARTHED. Burl. 1 a. W. J. Rix and F. J. Gillett. Kilburn T.H., January 29, 1895.

BOARD AND RESIDENCE. F. 1 a. Conway Edwards. Globe, October 8, 1870.

BOARD OF CONVIVIALITY; OR, FUN AND HARMONY, THE. Int. C.G., May 13, 1806. N.p.

BOARDING HOUSE; OR, FIVE HOURS AT BRIGHTON, THE. M.F. 2 a. Sam. Beazley. Lyceum, July 15, 1815.

BOARDING SCHOOL, THE. W. B. Bernard. Hay., 1841.

BOARDING SCHOOL; OR, BREAKING UP, THE. Dibdin.

BOARDING SCHOOL; OR, THE SHAM CAPTAIN, THE. O. C. Coffey. Taken fr. Durfey's *Love for Money.* D.L. and Pr. 1733.

BOARDING SCHOOL MISS, THE. C. Ascribed to Dr. Paul Joddrell. Pr. 1787. N. ac.

BOARDING SCHOOL ROMPS. See *The Boarding School*, by C. Coffey. An alt. of Durfey's *Love for Money; or, The Boarding School.*

BOAST OF BILLINGSGATE, THE. P. Richard Hathwaye, assisted by John Day. Ac. 1602. N.p.

BOATMAN OF THE SHANNON, THE. Irish d. 3 a. by Edward Towers. Pavilion, February 24, 1877.

BOATSWAIN'S MATE, A. P. 1 a. W. W. Jacobs and H. C. Sargent Adap. fr. W. W. Jacobs's story of same title. Wyndham's, April 15, 1907. See *Bo'sun's Mate.*

BOB. C.D. 3 a. Fred Marsden. First prod. in America. Liverpool Alexandra, September 3, 1888; Jodrell (Novelty), December 26, 1888; Strand, February, 1889.

BOB. O. 1 a. C. Bridgman. M. by F. Cellier. Walsall H.M.T., April 8, 1903; Adelphi, June 6, 1903.

BOB BRADSHAW'S DREAM. P. 1 a. B. W. Thomas. Strand, May 29, 1899.

BOB BRAGSHAWE. C. 3 a. Wm. Brown. Southport O.H., August 17, 1876.

BOB BRETTON; OR, THE DEAD SHOT OF THE WOODS. D Victoria, July 6, 1877.

BOB LUMLEY'S SECRET; OR, THE DARK DEEDS OF BLUEGATE FIELDS. D. 2 a. C. and W. Pitt. Britannia, December 20, 1869.

BOB SHORT. F. 1 a. Mark Lemon. Hay.

BOB THE OUTCAST. D. W. F. Lyon. Richmond, September 19, 1881.

BOB'S MRS. KENNINGHAM. P. 1 a. Beatrix M. De Burgh. Liverpool, P.O.W., November 20, 1902.

BOBADIL; OR, SULTAN FOR A DAY. C.O. 3 a. Walter Parke. M. by Luscombe Searelle. Teddington Bijou, January 5, 1903 (C.P.).

BOBBIE'S BABY: A DOMESTIC DIFFICULTY. Sk. 1 a. Ridgewood Barrie. St. Leonards Pier Pav., February 8, 1902.

BOBBO. Oa. 1 a. J. T. Tanner and Adr. Ross. M. by Osmd. Carr. Manchester Prince's, September 12, 1895.

BOBBY A1; OR, A WARM RECEPTION. F. 1 a. G. S. HODGSON. Surrey, October 7, 1872.

BOBETTE. C.O. 1 a. Alfred Delila Edouard Messa. Nott. Hill Coronet, October 22, 1900.

BOBINET THE BANDIT; OR, THE FOREST OF MONTESCARPINI. M.F. C.G., December 4, 1815.

BOCCACE. See *Adrasta.*

BOCCACCIO. Op.C. 3 a. M. by Suppé. Eng. lib. by R. Reece and H. B. Farnie. Comedy, April 22, 1882.

BOCCAGH, THE. D. 3 a. W. Gomersall. Worcester T.R., August 4, 1884.

BOER MEISJE, A. P. 1 a. H. T. Johnson. Gt. Queen St. T., July 10, 1900.

BOER OR BRITON. See *Briton and Boer.*

BOGIE. P. 3 a. H. V. Esmond. St. James's, September 10, 1895.

BOGUS AGENT, THE. Robt. Batho. Balham Assembly Rooms, October 1, 1895.

BOGUS BANDIT, A. C.D. 1 a. Leopold Montague. Crediton T.H., February 5, 1896.

BOHEME, LA. Rom.O. 4 a. G. Giacosa and L. Illica. M. by Puccini. F. on H. Murger's *Scenes de la Vie de Bohême.* C.G., October 2, 1897, and June 24, 1899. See *The Bohemians.*

BOHEME, LA. O. Leoncavallo.

BOHEMIA AND BELGRAVIA. C. 3 a. Arthur O'Neill. Royalty, June 8, 1872.

BOHEMIAN, A. P. 4 a. Louis N. Parker. Globe, February 18, 1892.

BOHEMIAN CARNIVAL, ETC. Perf. by Brousil family. D.L., July 16, 1856.

BOHEMIAN GIRL, THE. O. 3 a. A. Bunn. M. by Balfe. D.L., November 27, 1843; June 16, 1856; November 28, 1862; Alex. Pal., July 29, 1876; D.L., May, 1884. Ac. at Her M. February, 1858, as *La Zingara.*

BOHEMIAN GIRL. See *Arline, The Merry Zingara.*

BOHEMIAN G'YURL AND THE UNAPPROACHABLE POLE, THE. Burl. H. J. Byron. Op.C., January 31, 1877. Transfd. to Gaiety, July, 1877.

BOHEMIANS, THE. O. 3 a. Offenbach. Adap. by H. B. Farnie. Op.C., February 24, 1873.

BOHEMIANS, THE. O. 4 a. Puccini. F. on Henri Murger's novel, "La Vie de Bohême." Manchester R., April 22, 1897.

BOHEMIANS; OR, THE ROGUES OF PARIS, THE. D. 3 a. Edwd. Stirling. Adap. fr. Sue's *Mysteres de Paris.* Adelphi, November 6, 1843.

BOHEMIANS; OR, THE THIEVES OF PARIS, THE. Adap. fr. Sue's play. City of London, November 20, 1843. Another ver. at Queen's, December 4, 1843.

BOHEMIANS OF PARIS; OR, THE MYSTERIES OF CRIME, THE. D. 3 a. C. Z. Barnett. Surrey, November 27, 1843.

BOHEMIANS. See *La Boheme, The Cross Roads of Life.*

BOHEMIENNE. O.C. St. George's, 1862.

BOHEMOS. F. 1 a. J. Davidson. Adap. fr. the Fr. of Miguel Zamacois. (Sarah Bernhardt season.) Adelphi, June 17, 1903; Court, January 9, 1904.

BOILING WATER. F.C. 3 a. Ju. Cross. Comedy, July 22, 1885.

BOITE AU LAIT, LA. O. 4 a. Offenbach. 1877.

BOITE D'ARGENT. C. Dumas fils. 1858.

BOLD ADVERTISEMENT, A. Prod. as *The Agony Column.* Duol. Louis N. Parker, Steinway H. (Misses Cowen and Marriott's *mat.*), November 19, 1895.

BOLD BEAUCHAMPS, THE. An ancient p. mentioned in "The Knight of the Burning Pestle," 1613.

BOLD DICK TURPIN. Oa. M. by Henry Leslie. Lib. by J. Palgrave Simpson. St. James's, May 17, 1878.

BOLD DRAGOONS, THE. C.D. 2 a. Morris Barnett. Adelphi.

BOLD RECRUIT, THE. Oa. Words by B. C. Stephenson. M. by F. Clay. Canterbury T.R., August 8, 1868; Gall. of Illus., July 19, 1870.

BOLD STROKE FOR A HUSBAND, A. C. 5 a. Mrs. Cowley. C.G., February 25, 1783; D.L., May 27, 1815. Rev. after twenty-one years. See *The Advertisement.*

BOLD STROKE FOR A WIFE, A. C. Mrs. Centlivre. L.I.F., February 3, 1718. Pr. 1717. D.L.

BOLIVAR; OR, LIFE FOR LOVE. D. 3 a. W. G. Wills. Dublin T.R., November 3, 1879.

BOLT FROM THE BLUE, A. Oa. 1 a. S. Nuttall and R. Rayne. M. by F. Blunt. St. Albans County H., May 20, 1903.

BOMBASTES FURIOSO. Burl. T.O. 1 a. Wm. Barnes Rhodes. Hay., August 7, 1810.

BOMBAY CAPTAIN. 1 a. L. Horne.

BOMBAY TO HENLEY. M.C. Walter Parke. M. by P. and E. Bucalossi. Ladbroke H., March 14, 1895 (C.P.).

BOMBO THE DWARF. American D. 3 a. J. Holmes Grover. Dublin Q.T., May 10, 1880.

BON-BON BOX. 1 a. F. Bowyer.

BON FILS. C. Florian, 1785.

BON MENAGE. C. Florian, 1782.

BON PERE. C. Florian. 1783.

BON SOIR, MONSIEUR PANTALON. Oa. Adelphi, August, 1852. See *Twice Killed.*

BON TON. C. 3 a. General Burgoyne. D.L., March 18, 1775.

BON TON; OR, HIGH LIFE ABOVE STAIRS. F. 2 a. David Garrick. D.L. Pr. 1776. Edinburgh, 1783.

BONA FIDE TRAVELLERS. F. 1 a. Wm. Brough. Adelphi, October 30, 1854.

BONBOUROUCHE. C. 2 a. Georges Courteline. Royalty, July 23, 1906.

BOND OF LIFE, THE. D. 3 a. H. F. Saville. Reading Assembly R., May 14, 1870.

BOND OF MARRIAGE, THE. P. 4 a. Walter Nixey. Llanelly Royalty, January 7, 1909 (C.P.), and May 5, 1909. See *The Derelict.*

BOND OF NINON, THE. P. 3 a. Clotilde Graves. Savoy, April 19, 1906.

BOND STREET, 4 P.M. M. sk. Corney Grain. St. Geo. H., June 4, 1894.

BONDAGE. P. 4 a. Adap. fr. the Fr. of Pierre d'Abry. Op.C., March 31, 1883.

BONDMAN, THE. T.C. Philip Massinger. Cockpit, D.L., December 3, 1623. Pr. 1624. See *The Noble Bondman.*

BONDMAN, THE. T.C. Alt. fr. Massinger by Richd. Cumberland. C.G., October 13, 1779. N.p.

BONDMAN, THE. O. 3 a. M. by Balfe. Lib. by Bunn. D.L., December 11, 1846.

BONDMAN, THE. D. 5 a. Hall Caine. Bolton T.R., November 19, 1892; D.L., September 20, 1906; Adelphi, January 5, 1907.

BONDMAN; OR, LOVE AND LIBERTY, THE. T.C. D.L., June 8, 1719. Pr. 1719. Revl. by Betterton of Massinger's play.

BONDOCANI; OR, THE CALIPH ROBBER, IL. C.O. T. Dibdin. C.G., November, 1800. Pr. 1801.

BONDS WITHOUT JUDGMENT; OR, LOVE'S OF BENGAL. F. Probably by Edwd. Topham. C.G., May, 1787. N.p.

BONDUCA. T. Beaumont and Fletcher (probably Fletcher alone). Prod. before March, 1619. Pr. 1647. Converted by Thos. Sheridan into a spectacle.

BONDUCA. T. Alt fr. Beaumont and Fletcher by Geo. Coleman (the elder). Hay., 1778; pr. 1778. Alt., add. to, and ac., C.G. Pr. 1808.

BONDUCA. An alt. ver. called *Caractacus* by J. R. Planché. D.L., 1837.

BONDUCA; OR, THE BRITISH HEROINE. T. Alt. fr. Beaumont and Fletcher. Ac. at T.R., 1696. Publ. by Geo. Powell, 1696.

BONDUCA. See *Boadicea.*

BONDWOMAN, THE. Entd. Stationers' Co. September 23, 1653. N.p.

BONE OF CONTENTION, A. Ca. 1 a. C. Harding. St. Geo. H., November 23, 1870 (amateurs).

BONE SQUASH DIABLO. Nigger O. Rice. Surrey, 1836; Adelphi, October, 1839.

BONES OF MEN, THE. D. Pro., 4 a. Cyril M. Church, adap. fr Martin H. Potter's novel. Surrey, April 6, 1903.

BONHOMME JADIS, LE. C. 1 a. Henri Murger. Comédié Française, 1852; Royalty, January 31, 1889.

BONIFACIO AND BRIDGETINA; OR, THE KNIGHT OF THE HERMITAGE; OR, THE WINDMILL TURRET; OR, THE SPECTRE OF THE NORTH-EAST GALLERY. Burl. melo-d. Adap. fr the French of Martainville and adap. to the English stage by T. Dibden. C.G., March 31, 1808 Pr. 1808.

BONIFAZIO. O. Poniatowski. Rome, 1844.

BONNE D'ENFANTS, LA. O. 1 a. Offenbach. 1856.

BONNE MERE. C. Florian, 1784.

BONNET BUILDER'S TEA PARTY, THE. F. C. H. Hazlewood. Strand.

BONNET CONSPIRATORS, THE. Rom. c. 4 a. Violet A. Simpson. Court, July 13, 1909.

BONNIE ANNIE LAURIE. P. 4 a. C. Daly. Edinboro' Lyceum, August 1, 1898.

BONNIE BOY BLUE. Burl. Vic. Stevens. Chatham O.H., April 18, 1892; Parkhurst, May 20, 1892.

BONNIE DUNDEE. D. E. Falconer. D.L., February 23, 1863.

BONNIE DUNDEE. Hist D. 5 a. Malcolm E. Boyd, Torquay R., February 24, 1881.

BONNIE DUNDEE. Rom. Hist. P. 5 a Laurence Irving. Adelphi, March 10, 1900.

BONNIE DUNDEE. See *The Lost Cause.*

BONNIE FISH WIFE, THE. M.I. 1 a. Chas. Selby. Strand, September 20, 1858.

BONNIE PRINCE CHARLIE. D. J. B. Johnstone. E. London, July 18, 1868.

BONNIE PRINCE CHARLIE. D. Wm. Lowe. Dumfries T.R., March 13, 1876.

BONNIE PRINCE CHARLIE. Spec. Chas. Exley. Hengler's, December 21, 1878.

BONNIE PRINCE CHARLIE. Moncrieff.

BONNIE PRINCE CHARLIE. D. 2 a. T. Herbert Terriss. Chiswick, Bedford Pk. Club, June 8, 1889.

BONNY BOY. F. 3 a. T. G. Warren. Criterion (under title of *My Bonny Boy*), December 2, 1886; Novelty, April 19, 1888.

BONNY LASS OF LEITH; OR, THE HUMOURS OF DUGALD M'BICKAR, THE. M.Int. by a gentleman of Edinburgh. Edinburg, 1793.

BONOS NOCHIOS. Int. Entd. at Stationers' Co. by Jeffery Charlton, January 27, 1608.

BOODLES. Ca. Adap. fr. the French by Herbert Lee-Bennett. Richmond T.R., May 5, 1894.

BOOK THE THIRD, CHAPTER THE FIRST. Ca. 1 a. Transl. and adap. fr. the French of Eugéne Pierron and Adolphe Laferrière. First perf. at the Odéon, September 19, 1851, and at Hay. as *The Novel Expedient,* June 30, 1852; Court, June 12, 1875.

BOOKMAKER, THE. C. 3 a. J. W. Pigott. Terry's, March 19, 1889; Gaiety, August 9, 1890.

BOOKMAKER, THE. Sk. Rotherhithe Hippodrome, September 20, 1909.

BOOKSELLER, THE. Transl. fr. "The Theatre of Education" of Mdme. Genlis. Pr. 1781.

BOOKWORM, THE. D. 1 a. Alec Nelson (Dr. Edward Aveling). Tottenham Court Road Athenæum H., April 18, 1888.

BOOM OF BIG BEN, THE. D. 4 a. Adap. by A. Shirley fr. *Le Porteur aux Halles* of A. Fontanes. Pavilion, November 18, 1901; Princess's, December 16, 1901

BOOMERANG THE. C. 3 a. G. W. Boyle and F. Robertson. Streatham H., December 12, 1906 (prod. by amateurs).

BOOT ON THE RIGHT LEG, THE. F. Olympic, October 9, 1871.

BOOTBLACK, THE. D. Pro. and 4 a. Arthur Jefferson. North Shields T.R., January 11, 1897 (C.P.); Sheffield Alexandra, July 26, 1897; West London, July 18, 1898; renamed *London by Day and Night* in 1898.

BOOTLE'S BABY. P. 4 a. Hugh Moss, adap. fr. John Strange Winter's story of the same name. Stratford T.R., February 16, 1888 (C.P.); Globe, May 8, 1888; Garrick, February 20, 1900.

BOOTS AT THE HOLLY TREE INN; OR, THE INFANT ELOPEMENT TO GRETNA GREEN. 1 a. B. Webster. F. on Dickens. Adelphi, February 4, 1856.

BOOTS AT THE SWAN, THE. F. 1 a. Chas. Selby. Strand, July 6, 1842.

BORBONNE, P. Mentioned by Henslowe as amongst the stock of the Rose T., 1598.

BORDER HEROINE, A. D. Clarence Burnette. Blyth T.R., June 29, 1896.

BORDER MARRIAGE, A. C.D. 1 a. W. J. Sorrell. Adap. fr. *Un Mariage à l'Arquebuse*. Adelphi, November 3, 1856. Adap. by H. T. Craven. St. James's, January, 1860.

BORDERERS, THE. T. Wordsworth. 1795-6. Pr. 1842.

BORGIA KING, THE. A. R. Slous. Adelphi, 1858.

BORN OF HILDA. D. Pro. and 3 a. Edwin France. Windsor T.R., May 13, 1878.

BORN TO BE LOVED. F. 3 a. Miss Jessica Solomon. Albert H., January 19, 1909 (amat.).

BORN TO GOOD LUCK: OR, THE IRISHMAN'S FORTUNE F. 2 a. Tyrone Power, C.G., March 17, 1832; D.L., September 27, 1832; rev. at Princess's T., 1864

BORN TO SAVE. D. 4 a. C. H. Clarke. Adap. for representation by Lionel Douglas. Wolverhampton T.R., December 3, 1883.

BORN WITH A CAUL. See *David Copperfield*.

BOROUGH POLITICS. C.D. 2 a. Westland Marston. Hay., June 27, 1846.

BORROWED. F.P. 3 a. Adap. from Maurice Desvallière's C., *Prêtemoi la Femme*, by Ernest Warren. New Cross H., September 17, 1885.

BORROWED FEATHERS. Millingen. Queen's T., February 27, 1856.

BORROWED PLUMAGE. Sk. Bedford, May 10, 1909.

BORROWED PLUMES. F. 1 a. G. A. Maltby. D.L., 1868.

BORROWED UNCLE, THE. Ca. Tom Gallon and Leon M. Lion. Stratford Borough, February 13, 1905.

BORROWING A HUSBAND. C. 1 a. W. T. Moncrieff. Princess's, 1843.

BORROWING BOOTS. Chinese p. Transl. by Archibald Little, F.R.G.S. St. Geo. H., February 21, 1899.

BOSCABEL; OR, THE ROYAL OAK. Hist D. 4 a. H. S. Springate. Wolverhampton P.O.W., March 8, 1880.

BOSOM FRIENDS. C. 1 a. Horace Wigan. Bradford T.R., September 1, 1871.

BOSSU, LE. English ver. of this d. ac. at City of London, July, 1866. See *The Black Dwarf*, *The Duke's Device*, *The Duke's Motto*, *The Motto on the Duke's Crest*.

BO'SUN'S MATE, THE. M.C. 1 a. Walter Browne. M. by Alfred J. Caldicott. St. Geo. H., November 26, 1888. See *Boatswain's*, etc.

BOTH OF THEM. Ca. Glasgow Royalty, May 18, 1889.

BOTH SIDES OF THE QUESTION. Duol. Malcolm C. Salaman. Steinway H., July 14, 1891.

BOTH SIDES OF THE WORLD. D. Pro. 3 a Bailey. Eleph. and C., May 29, 1882; Halifax Gaiety, May 28, 1883.

BOTHERATION; OR, A TEN YEARS' BLUNDER. F. Walley, Chamberlain Oulton. C.G., May 8, 1798. Pr. 1798.

BOTHWELL. T. Ware.

BOTHWELL. T. Swinburne, 1874.

BOTTLE, THE. D. 2 a. T. P. Taylor. City of London T., October 1, 1847.

BOTTLE IMP. THE. Melo-d. 2 a. Peake. F. on a German legend. M. by G. H. Rodwell. Lyceum, July 7, 1828.

BOTTLE OF SMOKE. Adelphi, May 22, 1856.

BOTTLED REQUEST, A. Sk. Brixton Empress, December 7, 1908.

BOTTLES. F. Chas. Squier. Richmond H.M.T., October 17, 1881.

BOTTOM THE WEAVER, THE MERRY CONCEITED HUMOURS OF. Int. Taken fr. *A Midsummer Night's Dream*. Ascribed to Robert Cox. Pr. 1660.

BOUGHT. C.D. 3 a. Frank Harvey. Sunderland T.R., December 18, 1873; Brighton T.R., April 15, 1874

BOULANGERE, LA. C.O. 3 a. 4 tab. H. B. Farnie. Fr. Meilhac and Halévy. M. by Offenbach. Globe, April 16, 1881.

BOULD SOGER BOY, THE. F. 1 a. Edwd. Stirling. Strand, November, 1851.

BOULE DE NEIGE. O. 3 a. M. by Offenbach. 1872.

BOULOGNE. C. 3 a. F. C. Burnand. Gaiety, April 30, 1879.

BOUNCE. F.P. 3 a. Alfd. Maltby. Liverpool P.O.W., August 7, 1876; Op. C., October 30, 1876.

BOUNCING A BURGLAR. Sk. Greenwich Barnard's, October 16, 1908.

BOUNCING KNIGHT, THE. A Droll by Kirkman fr. Shakespeare's P. of *Henry IV*. 1672.

BOUND 'PRENTICE TO WATERMAN. D. 3 a. Pub. by S. French, Ltd.

BOUND TO SUCCEED; OR, A LEAF FROM THE CAPTAIN'S LOG-BOOK. D. G. Conquest and H. Pettitt Grecian, October 29, 1877.

BOUND TO THE WHEEL. Pavilion, April 2, 1866.

BOUND TO WIN. Sport.D. 4 a. Mrs. F. G. Kimberley. Accrington Prince's, December 18, 1901 (C.P.); Elephant and Castle, August 4, 1902.

BOUNDERS, THE. F.C. 3 a. C. A. Clarke. North Shields T.R., March 8, 1894.

BOUQUET; OR, THE LANGUAGE OF FLOWERS, THE. D. 3 a. Edwd. Towers. E. London, October 24, 1870; Gloucester T.R., April 16, 1883; Bath T.R., February 16, 1885.

BOUQUETIERE, LA. O. Adam. Paris, 1847.

BOURBON. Rose T., November 2, 1597. N.p.

BOURGEOIS A LA MODE, THE. C. Dancourt, 1654. See *The Confederacy*.

BOURGEOIS GENTILHOMME. C. Molière. 1670. Royalty, June 6, 1906. See "French Classical Plays."

BOURSE, LA. F. Ponsard. 1856.

BOURSE OU LA VIE, LA. C. 4 a. 5 scenes. Alfd. Capus. Avenue, June 27, 1904.

BOW BELLS. P. City of London, May 25, 1863.

BOW BELLS. C.D. 3 a. Henry J. Byron. Royalty, October 4, 1880.

BOW OF ORANGE RIBBON, THE. P. 4 a. Frank Cooper and Henry Jardine. Daly's (C.P.), August 3, 1897.

BOW STREET OPERA, THE. 3 a. Pr. 1773.

BOWERY GIRL; OR, BEAUX AND BELLS OF NEW YORK, THE. M. Conception. Wr. and comp. by Leo Dryden. Clapham Avondale H., January 22, 1902; Pimlico Standard, March 31, 1902.

BOWL'D OUT; OR, A BIT OF BRUMMAGEM. F. 1 a. H. T. Craven. Princess's, July 9, 1860.

BOX B. M. Trifle. Corney Grain. St. George's H., May 22, 1893.

BOX AND COX. F. 1 a. J. Mad. Morton. Lyceum, November 1, 1847. See *Cox and Box.*

BOX AND COX, MARRIED AND SETTLED. F. 1 a. J. Stirling Coyne. Hay., October 15, 1852.

BOX LOBBY CHALLENGE, THE. C. 5 a. Richd. Cumberland. Hay., Feb. 22, 1794. Pr. (n.d.), circ., 1794. Royalty, June 22, 1894.

BOX LOBBY LOUNGERS, THE. Prel. Chas. Stuart. D.L., May 16, 1787. N.p.

BOX OF MISCHIEF. F. 1 a. S. Peake.

BOY, THE. See *The New Boy.* Arthur Law. D.T. Eastbourne, February 1, 1894.

BOY BOB. Military P. 3 a. Camberwell Metropole, September 25, 1899.

BOY DETECTIVE, THE. D. 3 a. W. Travers. Effingham, June 10, 1867.

BOY FROM DOWN THERE. F. 3 a. Harry Pleon. Ramsgate Marina T., May 23, 1901. (C.P.)

BOY KING, THE. Adap. fr. the French. Adelphi, 1845.

BOY O'CARROLL. C. 4 a. B. M. Dix and E. G. Sutherland. Newcastle T.R., April 27; London. prod. Imperial, May 19, 1906.

BOY OF SANTILLANE; OR, GIL BLAS AND THE ROBBERS OF ASTURIA, THE. Rom. D. 3 a. M. by Cooke and Blewitt. D.L., April 16, 1827.

BOY WANTED, A. M.P. Geraldine Verner. M. and lyrics by Wallace Pringle. Southampton P.O.W., June 9, 1902.

BOY'S BEST FRIEND, A. Dom. D. 4 a. G. Roydon Duff and Walter Edwin. New T., April 7, 1908 (C.P.); Lowestoft Marina, May 10, 1909.

BOY'S PROPOSAL, A. P. 1 a. Arthur Eckersley. Birmingham Empire, February 15, 1909; Adelphi, March 29, 1909.

BOYCOTTED. M.Ca. M. C. Salaman. M. by Eugene Barnett. St. George's Hall, July 5, 1884.

BOYHOOD OF BACCHUS, THE. Extrav. by S. Rede. Olympic, October 6, 1845.

BOYNE WATER. Buckstone.

BOYS, THE. F.C. 3 a. Henry Seton. Croydon G.T., May 11, 1908; Court, July 9, 1908 (mat.).

BOYS AND GIRLS. Sk. by Corney Grain. St. George's H., December 24, 1892.

BOYS OF WEXFORD, THE. Irish Dom.D. 3 a. E. C. Matthews. Glasgow Metropole, June 26, 1899; Liverpool Grand, September 22, 1899.

BOYS TOGETHER. F.C 4 a. W. Howell Poole. Adap. fr. novel by Mountney Jephson. Liverpool P.O.W., March 28, 1887.

BOYS TOGETHER. D. 4 a. Haddon Chambers and Comyns Carr. Adelphi, August 26, 1896.

BOYS WILL BE BOYS. Ca. Jos. Mackay. Op. C., July 29, 1889.

BRACE OF GAOL BIRDS, A. D. 1 a. Mark Welford. Sheffield T.R., September 14, 1889.

BRACE OF HUMBUGS, A. Ca. J. Cutler. K.C. Brixton, July 1, 1907.

BRACE OF PARTRIDGES, A. F.C. 3 a. Robert Ganthony. Kingston Royal County, November 15, 1897; Strand, February 10, 1898.

BRACEWELL'S ADVENTURES WITH A RUSSIAN PRINCESS. F. Manchester Q., February 15, 1878.

BRACKEN HOLLOW. D. 2 a. Mrs. Augustus Bright. Sheffield Alex., November 27, 1878.

BRACONNIERS, LES. O. 3 a. M. by Offenbach. 1873.

BRADAMANTE. T. Garnier. 1580.

BRADFIELD COLLEGE, BERKS, PLAYS AT. Performances of Greek Plays are given here triennally from Æschylus, Sophocles, and Euripides in the order named:—

1883. *The Alcestius of Euripides.*
1890. *The Antigone of Sophocles.*
1892. *The Agamemnon of Æschylus.*
1895. *The Alcestis of Euripides.*
1898. *The Antigone of Sophocles.*
1900. *The Agamemnon of Æschylus.*
1904. *The Alcestis of Euripides.*
1907. *The Antigone of Sophocles.*

See "Greek Plays."

BRAG. C. 3 a. W. G. Wills. A reconstructed vers. of *Ellen; or, Love's Cunning.* Hay., June 12, 1879.

BRAGANZA. T. 5 a. Robt. Jephson. D.L., February 17, 1775. Pr. 1775. Plot resembles *Venice Preserved.*

BRAGANZIO, THE BRIGAND. Burl. 1 a. Famar Hall. Pub. by S. French, Ltd.

BRAGGADOCHIO, THE. See *Stroller's Packet.*

BRAGGADOCIO; OR, THE BAWD TURN'D PURITAN, THE. C. by a person of quality. Pr. 1691.

BRAGGARD CAPTAIN, THE. C. Transl. fr. Plautus by Bonnell Thornton. Pr. 1767.

BRAIN REVIVER, THE. F. 1 a. Percy J. Barrow. Portsmouth Prince's, January 27, 1898.

BRAND. Fourth a. of H. Ibsen's P. transl. by C. H. Hereford. Op. C., June 2, 1893.

BRAND FROM THE BURNING, A. D. 4 a. Geo. S. King. Liverpool Rotunda, December 23, 1907; Croydon R.T., February 3, 1908; Hammersmith Lyric, March 23, 1908.

BRAND IN DE JONGE JAN. D. 1 a. Herman Heyermans. Albert H., July 1, 1904.

BRAND OF CAIN, THE. D. G. L. Gordon. Birkenhead T.R., July 16, 1875.

BRAND OF CAIN; OR, BRANDED AS CAIN, THE. Melo-d. 4 a. Miss Violet Sims. Windsor R., July 4, 1904; Greenwich Carlton, September 5, 1904.

BRAND OF SHAME. D. 4 a. F. Cooke. Pentre Lyceum, February 26, 1904. C.p.

BRANDED. Spec. D. 5 a. Richd. Lee. Princess's, April 2, 1881.

BRANDED RACE, Surrey, September 27, 1858.

BRANDED WOMAN, THE. D. 4 a. F. W. Clive. Burnley Gaiety, August 7, 1905; Stratford R., July 15, 1907.

BRANDYMER. Rose T., April 6, 1591. N.p.

BRANHOWLTE. P. Ment. in Henslowe's Diary, 1597.

BRANTINGHAME HALL. D. 4 a. W. S. Gilbert. St. James's, November 29, 1888.

BRAS DE FER. D. 2 a. E. Manuel. Britannia, May 17, 1875.

BRASS. C.D. 5 a. Geo. Faucett Rowe. Liverpool Alexandra, May 11, 1877; Hay., August 13, 1877.

BRASS BOTTLE, THE. F. 4 a. F. Anstey, fr. one of his stories. Hay., March 13, 1907 (C.P.); Vaudeville, September 16, 1909.

BRAVADO. Ca. Adap. fr. the French by Mrs. T. E. Smale. Strand, July 3, 1889.

BRAVE AND THE FAIR, THE. Ballet of Action. Lyceum, July 11, 1816.

BRAVE AS A LION. Ca. John T. Douglass. Standard, March 11, 1872.

BRAVE COWARD, A. P. 3 a. J. S. Blythe. Strand, December 3, 1886.

BRAVE HARRY THORN. D. H. Stanley. Longton Victoria, August 31, 1874.

BRAVE HEARTS. Dom. Story. 2 a. Arthur Matthison. Another vers. of *The Poor Nobleman*, an adap. of *Le Gentilhomme Pauvre*, by Dumanoir and Lafargue. Criterion, January 24, 1881.

BRAVE HEARTS. Rom.D. Geo. Comer and Fred Benton. Middleton T.R., November 3, 1898 (C.P.); Darwen T.R., March 6, 1899; Stratford T.R., June 24, 1901.

BRAVE IRISHMAN, THE. F. 1 a. Thos. Sheridan. Edinburgh.

BRAVE IRISHMAN, THE. See *Captain O'Blunder*.

BRAVE SCOTTISH HEARTS. D. K. E. Hall. Coatbridge Prince's, June 9, 1873.

BRAVIN'S BROW. Marylebone, June 20, 1863.

BRAVING THE STORM. F. 1 a. Miss Adelaide Woodruffe. D.L., February 24, 1871; Sadler's Wells, October 21, 1871.

BRAVING THE STORM. D. 4 a. W. P. Sheen. Rugby T.R., March 24, 1890.

BRAVO, IL. O. Mercadante. Milan, 1839.

BRAVO, LE. O. Salvayre. Paris, 1877.

BRAVO, THE. Melo-d. 3 a. F. on Cooper's novel, "The Bravo," by J. B. Buckstone. Adelphi, 1833.

BRAVO; OR, THE BRIDGE OF SIGHS, THE. Melo-d. 2 a. C. Z. Barnett.

BRAVO TURN'D BULLY; OR, THE DEPREDATORS. Dr. Ent. Pr. 1740.

BRAZEN AGE, THE. Hist. D. 5 a. Thos. Heywood. Pr. 1613. Taken from Ovid's *Metamorphoses*.

BRAZEN BUST, THE. Melo-d. 2 a. C. Kemble. M. by Bishop. C.G., May 29, 1813.

BRAZEN MASK; OR, ALBERTO AND ROSABELLA. Bal. Panto. by John Fawcett. Poetry by T Dibdin. M. by Davy and Mountain. C.G., April 5, 1802. Pr. 1802.

BRAZILIAN, THE. C.O. 3 a. M. by Chassaigne. Words by Max Pemberton and W. Lestocq. Newcastle-on-Tyne T.R., April 19, 1890. (C.P.)

BREACH OF PROMISE, A. C.D. 2 a. T. W. Robertson. Globe, April 10, 1869.

BREACH OF PROMISE, A. F.C. 3 a. Adap. fr. the French by Alfred Durny and St. Agnan Choler. Walsall T.R., April 7, 1884.

BREACH OF PROMISE, A. Ca. 1 a. Mabel Freund-Lloyd. Op. C., December 1, 1891.

BREACH OF PROMISE, A. Sk. 1 scene. Middlesex M.H., February 12, 1900.

BREACH OF PROMISE OF MARRIAGE, THE. C. Adap. fr. Scribe's *La Chaine*. Adelphi, February, 1842. See *Silken Fetters*.

BREAD OF OTHERS, THE. P. 2 a. Turgeney. Transl. by J. Nightingale Duddington. Prod. by the Incorp. Stage Society, Kingsway, February 21, 1909.

BREAD-WINNER, THE. P. 3 a. Alfred C. Calmour. Avenue, March 26, 1892.

BREAK BUT NOT BEND. D. 3 a. C. H. Hazlewood. Britannia, October 2, 1867.

BREAKERS AHEAD; OR, A SEAMAN'S LOG. D. 3 a. J. T. Haines. Victoria, April 10. 1837.

BREAKING A BUTTERFLY. P. 3 a. F. on Ibsen's D. *Norah* by H. A. Jones and H. Hermann. Prince's T., March 3, 1884.

BREAKING IT GENTLY. Ca. 1 a. Richard Warren. River Parish H. D. (prod. by amateurs), May 9, 1906.

BREAKING IT GENTLY. P. 1 a. Affeck Scott. Prod. by the Play Actors, King's H., W.C., March 22, 1908; Vaudeville, May 20, 1908 (mat.).

BREAKING IT OFF. M.Ca. By Neville Doone. M. by John Crook. Southend-on-Sea Empire, March 21, 1898.

BREAKING IT OFF. F.C. 3 a. F. C. Phillips and Walter Parke. Hastings Pier Pav., May 4, 1903.

BREAKING POINT, THE. P. 3 a. Edward Garnett (refused a license by the Lord Chamberlain). Prod. by the Stage Society privately before members and friends. Hay., April 5, 1908.

BREAKING THE ICE. Oa. 1 a. Lib. by Chas. Thomas. M. by Miss Harriet Young. Brighton R. Pavilion, November 25, 1878; Court, November 9, 1885.

BREAKING THE ICE. See *The Holly Branch*.

BREAKING THE NEWS. Ca. 1 a. Arthur M. Heathcote. Brompton Hosp., March 14, 1893.

BREAKING THE SPELL. English ver. of Offenbach's Oa. *Le Conscrit*, adap. by H. B. Farnie. Lyceum, May 2, 1870; Garrick, April 26, 1904.

BREBIS DE PANURGE, LES. C. 1 a. Meilhac and Halévy. P.O.W., May 24, 1886.

BRED IN THE BONE. D. Prol. and 4 a. F Teale Lingham. Edmonton T.R., May 24, 1890. (C.P.)

BREED OF THE TRESHAMS, THE. P. 4 a. John Rutherford. Newcastle-on-Tyne T.R., September 28, 1903; Kennington, December 7, 1903; Lyric, June 3, 1905; Adelphi, June 3, 1907.

BREEZE FIRST, THE. F.C. 1 a. W. R. Denny. West Hartlepool T.R., March 6, 1891.

BREEZE FROM NEW YORK, A. Ca. 1 a. Francis Raphael. Kew Prince's H., November 20, 1893.

BREEZE IN THE BALTIC; OR, THE DANES IN THE DUMPS, A. Piece. 1 a. By a gentleman of Edinburgh. Ac. at Edinburgh, 1801.

BREEZY MORNING, A. Ca. 1 a. Eden Phillpotts. Lyric Club. Leeds Grand, April 27, 1891; Comedy, December 8, 1891; also Oa. ver.

BRENNORALT; OR, THE DISCONTENTED COLONEL. T. Sir John Suckling. Ac. in Blackfriars. Pr. 1646.

BRER RABBIT AND BRER FOX. One of Uncle Remus's stories. Adap. by Philip Carr. 1 a. Court, December 26, 1903.

BRER RABBIT AND UNCLE REMUS. C.Oa. Walter Parke. M. by Florian Pascal. Ladbroke H., December 17, 1903. (C.P.)

BREWER OF PRESTON. M.F. Preston T.R., January 24, 1876.

BREWER OF PRESTON; OR, MALT AND HOPS, THE. C.D. 1 a. T. H. Reynoldson. Surrey T.

BREWER OF TADCASTER, THE. Local D. Arthur Rodgers. Tadcaster Empire, August 5, 1897.

BREWING A BRUIN. F. Louis Gee. Britannia, June 2, 1873.

BREWSTER'S MILLIONS. C. 4 a. Fr. story of same name by George Barr McCutcheon, Winchell Smith, and Byron Ongley. Hicks, May 1, 1907; tfd. to Duke of York's, August 26, 1907; tfd. to Hicks, October 14, 1907; rev. Wyndham's, June 22, 1909.

BRIAN BOROIHME; OR, THE MAID OF ERIN. 3 a. Poetical ver. of D. O'Mara's D. by Jas. Sheridan Knowles. Pl. in Ireland circ. 1810. C.G., April 20, 1837. N.p.

BRIARS AND BLOSSOMS. D. 3 a. C. H. Hazlewood. Britannia, December 3, 1873.

BRIBERY ON BOTH SIDES. F. C.G., May 4, 1784. N.p.

BRIC-A-BRAC. Ca. 1 a. Adap. fr. D'Hervilly's *La Soupière*, otherwise *Le Bibelot*, by Sir J. J. Coghill, Bart. Ladbroke H., October 20, 1888. See *Under Cover*, *Cups and Saucers*.

BRIC-A-BRAC WILL, THE. C.O. S. Adair Fitzgerald and Hugh Moss. M. by Emilio Pizzi. Lyric, October 28, 1895.

BRICHANTEAU. P. 4 a. Adap. by M. de Férandy fr. the novel of Jules Claretie. Royalty, January 22, 1906.

BRIDAL, THE. Adap. of Beaumont and Fletcher's *The Maid's Tragedy* by J. Sheridan Knowles. Prod. at Hay., 1837, by Macready.

BRIDAL, THE. Monol. W. E. Grogan. Wyndham's, June 30, 1900.

BRIDAL OF FLORA, THE. Ballet by Byrne. D.L., November 9, 1816.

BRIDAL PHANTOM. Grecian, May 24, 1863.

BRIDAL RING, THE. D. Rom. 2 a. Fredk. Reynolds. M. by Condell. C.G., October 16, 1810.

BRIDAL TOUR, A. C. 3 a. Dion Boucicault. Hay., August 2, 1880.

BRIDAL TRIP, A. F. 1 a. Jas. Mortimer. Brighton T.R., March 6, 1876.

BRIDAL WREATH, THE. Rom.D. 2 a. C. H. Hazlewood. City of London T., 1861.

BRIDALS, THE. C. Margaret Duchess of Newcastle. Publ. among her works, 1668.

BRIDE, THE. C. Thos. Nabbs. D.L., 1638. Pr. 1640.

BRIDE, THE. C. Korner, 1808.

BRIDE AND BRIDEGROOM, THE. C. 4 a Arthur Law. New, May 5, 1904.

BRIDE OF ABYDOS, THE. Rom.D. 3 a From Byron's poem by Wm. Dimond. M. by Kelly. D.L., February 5, 1818.

BRIDE OF ABYDOS; OR, THE PRINCE, THE PIRATE, AND THE PEARL, THE. Burl. Extrav. H. J. Byron. Strand, May 31, 1858.

BRIDE OF DUNKERRON, THE. Cant. H. Smart. St. James's H., March 28, 1865.

BRIDE OF LAMMERMOOR, THE. D. 4 a. (afterwards 3 a.). Adap. fr. Scott's Romance by John Wm. Calcraft. Edinburgh T.R., May 1, 1822; Marylebone T., 1848.

BRIDE OF LAMMERMOOR, THE. O. 3 a by Donizetti. D.L., April 14, 1845.

BRIDE OF LAMMERMOOR, THE. D. 3 a. and tab. Stephen Phillips. Glasgow King's, March 23, 1908.

BRIDE OF LAMMERMOOR. See *The Last Heir*.

BRIDE OF LOVE. Poetical P. 4 a. Robt. Buchanan. F. on the Greek legend of *Eros and Psyche*. Adelphi, May 21, 1890.

BRIDE OF LUDGATE, THE. C.D. 2 a. Douglas Jerrold. D.L., December 8, 1831.

BRIDE OF MESSINA, THE. T. Schiller. 1803.

BRIDE OF MESSINA, THE. O. 3 a. Lib. adap. fr. Schiller by H. Müller, composed by J. H. Bonawitz. Portman Rooms, April 23, 1887.

BRIDE OF NEATH VALLEY, THE. M. composition by John Thomas. St. James's H., June 19, 1867.

BRIDE OF SONG, THE. Oa. 1 a. H. B. Farnie. M. by Sir Julius Benedict. C.G., December 3, 1864.

BRIDE OF THE WAVE, THE. D. 3 a. W. Travers. New East London, October 12, 1867.

BRIDE'S DEATH SLEEP, THE. D. 3 a. C. H. Hazlewood. City of London, July 4, 1868.

BRIDE'S TRAGEDY, THE. T. Beddoes, 1822.

BRIDEGROOM, THE. P. 1 a. Rehearsed by Mr. E. Lyall Swete. Adap. fr. the Ger. of Frau Viebig by Nigel Playfair. Playhouse, May 4, 1908.

BRIDES OF ARAGON, THE. T. Beer, 1823.

BRIDES OF VENICE, THE. O. M. by Julius Benedict. D.L., April 22, 1844.

BRIDGE. Arthur Clements and J. Malone. Liverpool, 186-.

BRIDGE. P. 1 a. Graham Hill. Canterbury T.R., February 13, 1906.

BRIDGE. P. 4 a. Alicia Ramsey. Garrick, October 14, 1907. (C.P.).

BRIDGE OF NOTRE DAME; OR, THE PARRICIDE'S CURSE, THE. D. 3 a. E. N. Hudson. Surrey, April, 1847.

BRIDGE OF SIGHS, THE. Op. bo. 3 a. H. S. Leigh. M. by Offenbach. St. James's, November 18, 1872.

BRIDGE OF SIGHS, THE. Dr. Study in 2 ep. Edgar Martin Seymour. Lyric Club, June 2, 1901.

BRIDGE OF SIGHS; OR, A POOR GIRL'S LOVE STORY, THE. Melo-d. 4 a. Oswald Brand. Grand, April 4, 1904.

BRIDGE TANGLE, A. Society C. 4 a. Mrs. Frank White and Mrs. Caleb Porter. Court, November 12, 1908 (mat.).

BRIDGE THAT CARRIES US SAFE OVER, THE. Dr. sk. 1 a. By R. B. Peake. Lyceum (third time), June 20, 1817.

BRIDGET O'BRIEN, ESQUIRE. F.C. 2 a. Fred Lyster and John F. Sheridan. Op. C., October 29, 1887.

BRIDGET'S BLUNDERS. F. 1 a. Lita Smith. Eastbourne Dev. Pk. T., August 5, 1892

BRIER CLIFF. D. Geo. Morris. 1842.

BRIER ROSE, A. C. 3 a. H. Little. Cripplegate Inst., May 7, 1907.

BRIGADIER GERARD. C. 4 a. A. Conan Doyle. Imperial, March 3, 1906.

BRIGAND, THE. Rom. d. 2 a. J. R. Planché. Fr. the French. D.L., November 18, 1829; Rev. at Surrey, February 2, 1867.—See *Massaroni.*

BRIGAND, THE. M.Sc. M. comp. and arr. by F. Allwood. Standard, October 14, 1907.

BRIGAND; OR, NEW LINES TO AN OLD BAN DITTY, THE. Burl. Gilbert à Beckett. Hay., December 24, 1867.

BRIGAND AND HIS BANKER, THE. P. T. Taylor. F. on *Le Roi des Montagnes* of Edmond About. Lyceum, October 1, 1860.

BRIGAND AND HIS SON, THE. Melo-d. 1 a. Publ. by S. French, Ltd.

BRIGAND'S SECRET. Britannia, October 8, 1858.

BRIGANDS, THE. Op. bo. 3 a. Lib. transl. by W. S Gilbert from *Les Brigands* by Meilhac and Halévy (Variétés, December 10, 1869). M. by Offenbach. Plymouth T.R., September 2, 1889; Avenue, September 16, 1889.

BRIGANDS, LES. See *Falsacappa.*

BRIGANDS OF CALABRIA, THE. Rom. d. 1 a.

BRIGANDS OF TARRAGONNA, THE. Sk. Shepherd's Bush Empire, August 10, 1908.

BRIGANTI, I. O. Marcadante. Milan, 1836.

BRIGGATE; OR, THE OUTCAST. Local sk. By Cyrus Bell. Leeds Grand, March 3, 1884.

BRIGHT BEAM AT LAST, A. D. G. H. Macdermott. Britannia, September 9, 1872.

BRIGHT DAYS; OR, THE PRIDE OF TWO ISLES. Irish M.D. 4 a. Horace Wheatley and C. A. Aldin. Liverpool Rotunda, April 1, 1889; Eleph. and C., July 1, 1889.

BRIGHT FUTURE, THE. Dom. D. 4 a. Sefton Parry. Grand, August 4, 1883.

BRIGHT IDEA, A. M. sk. Lib. by Arthur Law. M. by Arthur Cecil. St. George's H., May 30, 1881.

BRIGHTER DAYS IN STORE. D. 2 a. E. Towers. City of London, November 23, 1867.

BRIGHTON. F.C. 4 a. Bronson Howard. Orig. in America as *Saratoga.* N.Y. 5th Av. T., December, 1870; Court T., May 25, 1874; Hay., June, 1875; Olympic, January, 1880; Criterion, October, 1881; Criterion, April, 1884; Criterion, December 1, 1891.

BRILLIANTS, THE. Int. C.G., June 7, 1799. N.p.

BRINE OGE, THE. D. 4 a. W. J. Patmore. Dewsbury T.R., May 6, 1896. (C.P.)

BRINGING HOME THE BRIDE. Vaud. 2 a. Moncrieff. Prod. 1838.

BRINGING IT HOME. P. 1 a. H. M. Richardson. Manchester Gaiety, October 5, 1908.

BRISTOL DIAMONDS. F. 1 a. John Oxenford. St. James's, August 11, 1862.

BRISTOL TRAGEDY, THE. John Day. Ac. by the Lord Admiral's servants, 1602. N.p.

BRISTOWE MERCHANT, THE. Ford and Decker.

BRITAIN'S AWAKENING. D. 1 a. Norman Wrighton. West London. February 8, 1908.

BRITAIN'S BRAVE TARS; OR, ALL FOR ST. PAUL'S. Dr. sk. ent. D.L., 1797.

BRITAIN'S DEFENDERS; OR, A FIG FOR AN INVASION. S.C. sk. Sadler's Wells, April 17, 1797.

BRITAIN'S GLORY; OR, A TRIP TO PORTSMOUTH. M.E. Mr. Benson. Hay. Pr. 1794.

BRITAIN'S HAPPINESS. M. Int. P. Motteux. Ac. at "both the theatres." Pr. 1704. Previously intended for an introduction to an O., which was to have been called *The Loves of Europe.*

BRITAIN'S JUBILEE. M. piece. J. S. Arnold. Ac. by the D.L. Co. at the Lyceum, October 25, 1809.

BRITANNIA. Eng. O. Mr. Lidiard. Hay. Pr. 1732.

BRITANNIA. Masque. by David Mallett. M. by Dr. Arne. D.L., 1755. Pr. 1755.

BRITANNIA Sk. Arthur Shirley. M. by Geo. Le Brunn. Paragon M.H., February 16, 1903

BRITANNIA; OR, THE GODS IN COUNCIL. Dr. Poem. Robert Averay. Pr. 1756.

BRITANNIA; OR, THE ROYAL LOVERS. With a comic int. called "The Beggar's Pantomime; or, The Contending Columbines." L.I.F. Pr. 1736.

BRITANNIA AND BATAVIA. Masque. Geo. Lillo. Pr. 1740.

BRITANNIA REDIVIVA; OR, COURAGE AND LIBERTY. Allegorical masque. M. by John Dunn Perf. at the New Wells, Clerkenwell. Pr. 1746.

BRITANNIA TRIUMPHANS. Masque. Sir W. Davenant and Inigo Jones. Presented at Whitehall by Charles I. and his Lords on the Sunday after Twelfth Night, 1637. Pr. 1637.

BRITANNIA'S REALM. Spec. Ballet. Prol. 4 scenes. Chas. Wilson. M. by Landon Ronald. Alhambra, June 16, 1902.

BRITANNICUS. T. Racine. See "French Classical Plays."

BRITANNICUS. T by J. Ozell. Transl. fr. Racine. Pr. 1714.

BRITANNICUS. T. Sir Brooke Boothby. Transl. fr. Racine. Pr. 1803.

BRITISH AMBASSADOR, THE. C. 3 a. R. Ganthony. Richmond P.O.W., November 5, 1903.

BRITISH BORN. D. Prol. and 3 a. Paul Meritt and Hy. Pettitt. Grecian, October 17, 1872.

BRITISH ENCHANTERS; OR, NO MAGIC LIKE LOVE, THE. Tragic O. Rt. Hon. Geo. Granville (Lord Lansdowne). Q.T., Hay., 1707. Pr. 1706.

BRITISH FORTITUDE AND HIBERNIAN FRIENDSHIP; OR, AN ESCAPE FROM FRANCE. M.D. 1 a. J. C. Cross. C.G. Pr. 1794.

BRITISH HERO, A. Military D. 5 a. Norman Henry. Worthing Assem. R., July 12, 1894.

BRITISH HEROINE, THE. T. J. Jackson. C.G., May 5, 1778. N.p. Ac. in Dublin the preceding year under the title of *Giralda; or, The Siege of Harlech.*

BRITISH KINGS. T. James Mylne. Pr. 1790. N. ac.

BRITISH LEGION. T. H. Bayly. St. James's. May 7, 1838.

BRITISH LOYALTY; OR, LONG LIVE THE KING. Dr. Effusion. 2 a, with songs. Jos. Moser. Pr. 1809.

BRITISH ORPHAN, THE. T. Mariana Starke. Ac. at Mrs. Crespigny's private theatre at Camberwell, April 7, 1790, by amateurs.

BRITISH RECRUIT; OR, WHO'S AFRAID? THE. Int. C.G. Pr. 1795.

BRITISH SAILOR; OR, THE FOURTH OF JUNE, THE. Mus. Int. C.G., 1789. N.p.

BRITISH SLAVE. D. J. B. Howe.

BRITISH SOLDIER, A. D. 4 a. Perth. Condie and Collier. Manchester, St. James's, December 11, 1899.

BRITISH SOLDIER; OR, LIFE'S CAMPAIGN, THE Norwich T., March 16, 1805.

BRITISH STAGE; OR, THE EXPLOITS OF HARLEQUIN, THE. F. perf. at "both theatres." Pr. 1724. Designed as an after-piece to *Harlequin Dr. Faustus* and *The Necromancer*.

BRITOMARTE, THE MAN-HATER. Effingham, July 2, 1866.

BRITON, THE. T. Ambrose Philips. D.L., February 19, 1722. Pr. 1721.

BRITON AND BOER. D. 4 a. Fred Cooke. Liverpool Star T., January 1, 1900; Greenwich, Morton's, August 20, 1900.

BRITONS ROUSED. Int. with songs. C.G., May 16, 1798.

BRITONS, STRIKE HOME; OR, THE SAILORS' REHEARSAL. Bal. F. Edwd. Philips. Pr. 1739. D.L., 1742.

BRITONS, TO ARMS; OR, THE CONSUL IN ENGLAND. M.D. Archd. Maclaren. Pr. 1803.

BRITTANY FOLK V. 1 a. Lib. Walter Frith. M. by Alfred J. Caldicott. St. Geo. H., March 20, 1889.

BRIXTON BURGLARY, THE. F. 3 a. Fred W. Sidney. Terry's, December 6, 1898; Strand, June 23, 1900.

BROAD ARROW, THE. D. 5 a. Gerald Holcroft. Standard, September 7, 1885.

BROAD BUT NOT LONG. Extrav. C.G., June, 1814.

BROAD PATH AND THE NARROW WAY, THE. D. Eccleshill Mechanics' Inst., March 18. 1899.

BROAD ROAD, THE. P. 3 a. Robt. Marshall. Terry's, November 5, 1898.

BROADWAY BELLES, THE. M.F. 2 a. John Lacklands. Kingston County. June 5, 1905.

BROKEN AT THE FOUNTAIN. P. 1 a. R. Hope. Ladywell Parish H., May 25, 1905.

BROKEN BAIL. D. 3 a. G. L. Gordon. Edinboro' Princess's, June 14, 1878.

BROKEN BARRIER, THE. P. 4 a. H. C. M. Hardinge. Camberwell Metropole, March 2, 1903.

BROKEN BONDS. D. 5 a. A. C. Calmour. Brighton T.R., November 14, 1883.

BROKEN BRANCH. Op. bo. 3 a. H. F. du Terreaux. Op. C., August 15, 1874.

BROKEN BUTTERFLY, A. Dr. epis. Fred. Moule. Battersea Pal., April 5, 1909.

BROKEN CHAIN; OR, THE LADY OF NUREMBERG, THE. P. Surrey, October, 1838.

BROKEN COUPLING, THE. "M. Raillery of the Rails." 1 a. M. by J. A. Moonie. Edinburgh Waterloo R., February 21, 1890.

BROKEN FETTERS. P. 1 a. Chas. Thursby. Mat. T. (late St. George's H.). July 22, 1897.

BROKEN GOLD, THE. Bal. O. Chas. Dibdin. C.G., February 8, 1806.

BROKEN HALO, A. P. 1 a. Charles Thursby. Globe, March 17, 1900.

BROKEN HEART, THE. T. 5 a. John Ford. Blackfriars, 1633. Pr. 1633. Rev. by Elizabethan Stage Society at Matinée T. (late St. George's H.), June 11, 1898; Royalty, November 21, 1904.

BROKEN HEART; OR, THE FARMER'S DAUGHTER OF THE SEVERN SIDE, THE. Melo-d. D. Jerrold. City T., 1832.

BROKEN-HEARTED CLUB, THE. Ca. 1 a. Stirling Coyne. Hay., January 16, 1868.

BROKEN HEARTS. Fairy P. 3 a. W. S. Gilbert. Court, December 9, 1875; Savoy, June 4, 1888.

BROKEN HEARTS. P. Z. Lubin. Pavilion (Jewish season). August 24, 1908.

BROKEN HOME. City of London, July 4, 1859.

BROKEN IDOL. Sk. Collins's M.H., January 2, 1905.

BROKEN IDYLLS. Ca. 1 a. Mabel S. Medd.

BROKEN LIFE, A. P. 3 a. Louis N. Parker. Vaudeville, March 28, 1892, under title of *Chris*. Grand, May 2, 1892.

BROKEN LILY, THE. D. Pro. and 3 a. E. Towers. East London, December 24, 1878.

BROKEN LINKS. C.D. 4 a. Henry Holmes. Richmond H.M.T., March 20, 1882; Stratford T.R., February 6, 1888.

BROKEN MELODY, THE. P. 3 a. Herbert Keene. James Leader, and J. T. Tanner. P.O.W., July 28, 1892; Princess's, January 14, 1902.

BROKEN OFF. Ca. 1 a. Mrs. Newton Phillips. Ladbroke H., May 24, 1892; Ryde T.R., February 2, 1894 (amat.).

BROKEN PEARLS. D. 4 a. W. J. Archer. City of London, June 10, 1867

BROKEN PROMISES; OR, THE COLONEL, THE CAPTAIN, AND THE CORPORAL. Ballad O. 3 a. Lyceum July 5, 1825.

BROKEN SEAL, THE. See *Village Priest*.

BROKEN SIXPENCE, A. P. 1 a. Mrs. G. Thompson and Miss Kate Sinclair. Ladbroke H., April 11, 1889; Toole's, June 15, 1889.

BROKEN SOIL. P. 3 a. Padraic M'Cormac. Colne Royalty, March 26, 1904.

BROKEN SPELLS. D. 3 a. Westland Marston and W. G. Wills. Court, March 27, 1872.

BROKEN STOCK-JOBBERS; OR, WORK FOR THE BAILIFFS, THE. F. Ac. in Exchange Alley. Pr. 1720.

BROKEN STRING, THE. M.Ep. A. C. Calmour. Kingston T.R., December 14, 1896. Mat. T. (late St. George's H.), June 16, 1897.

BROKEN SWORD; OR, THE TORRENT OF THE VALLEY, THE. Melo-d. 2 a. Adap. fr. the French, *La Valée du Torrent*, by Wm. Dimond. C.G., October 7, 1816.

BROKEN TIES. Dom. D. 2 a. J. Palgrave Simpson. Olympic, June 8, 1872.

BROKEN TO HARNESS. D. F. on Edmund Yates's novel by Mervyn Dallas. Brighton T.R., June 30, 1883.

BROKEN TOYS. D. 2 a. John Daly. Sadler's Wells, November 4, 1850.

BROKEN VOW, THE. Adap. fr. the French, *L'Abbé de Castro*, by Dion Boucicault. Olympic, February, 1851.

BROKEN VOW: A ROMANCE OF THE TIMES OF SIXTUS THE FIFTH, THE. D. 5 a. Taken from *L'Abbé de Castro* by John Brougham. Lyceum, October 31, 1863. See *Bel Demonio*.

BROKEN VOWS; OR, LOVE'S CONFLICTS. D. 4 a. Edwd. Towers. East London, February 18, 1871.

BROKER BEWITCHED, THE. F. 2 a. Pr. (N.D.)

BROKER OF BOGOTA, THE. T. Bird. 1803-1854.

BROKERS AHEAD. Sk. Paragon, April 6, 1908.

BRONZE HORSE, THE. Fairy O. Auber. M. adap. by Cooke. D.L., January 5, 1836.

BRONZE HORSE, THE. M. Spec. Howard Paul. F. on Scribe and Auber's *Le Cheval de Bronze*. Alhambra, July 4, 1881.

BROOK, THE. M. Extrav. 2 a. N. Salsbury. Liverpool Alexandra T., July 12, 1880; Alexandra Pal., September 13, 1880.

BROOKE OF BRAZENOSE. P. 3 a. Neville Doone and T. R. F. Coales. Criterion, June 8, 1905.

BROTHER AGAINST BROTHER. D. 4 a. Frank Harvey. Ipswich Lyceum, August 10, 1895; Hammersmith Lyric (5 a.), March 23, 1896.

BROTHER AND SISTER. T. Ford, 1633.

BROTHER AND SISTER. C.O. 1 a. Wm. Dimond. C.G., February 1, 1815; Lyceum, October 1, 1824.

BROTHER BEN. F. 1 a. J. Maddison Morton. C.G.

BROTHER BILL. F.C. 3 a. Carlton Dawe. Kennington P.O.W., May 26, 1902.

BROTHER BILL. Far. Dom. C. Sk. 1 a. J. F. Watson. Broughton Victoria, July 20, 1907.

BROTHER BILL AND ME. F. 1 a. W. E. Suter. August, 1858.

BROTHER BOB. J. B. Johnstone. Surrey T.

BROTHER FOR BROTHER. D. 3 a. F. on Dumas' romance, "Les Frères Corses." Arthur Shirley. Pavilion, August 7, 1899.

BROTHER GEORGE. C.O. 3 a. Frank Desprez. M. by P. Bucalossi. Portsmouth T.R., May 16, 1892.

BROTHER OFFICERS. C. 3 a. Leo Trevor. Garrick, October 20, 1898.

BROTHER PELICAN; OR, FALKA'S BABY. Burl. 2 a. Words and lyrics by Alfd. Rae and W. H. Dragnil. M. by G. Operti, Ernest Allen, and W. C. Levey. Belfast T.R., February 8, 1894.

BROTHER SAM. C. John Oxenford, Sothern, and Buckstone. Hay., May 24, 1865.

BROTHER TOM. Buckstone.

BROTHER'S CRIME, A. D. 4 a. Vivian Edmonds. Warrington T.R., March 27, 1893.

BROTHER'S LIFE, A. D. W. Gordon. Paignton R. Bijou, July 16, 1874.

BROTHER'S PORTRAIT, A. P. 1 a. Ern. E. Norris and Fewlass Llewellyn. Eleph. and C., April 3, 1905.

BROTHER'S REVENGE, A. Victoria, March 6, 1854.

BROTHER'S REVENGE, A. Sk. Bedford M.H., March 26, 1900.

BROTHERHOOD OF THE SEVEN KINGS. D. 5 a. Mrs. L. T. Meade, R. Eustace, and Max Elgin. Taken fr. stories of same title in *Strand Magazine*. S. Shields R., April 30, 1900.

BROTHERS. C. 3 a. Chas. Coghlan. Court, November 4, 1876.

BROTHERS. D. 4 a. R. T. Sager. Baroldswick Mechanics' Inst., July 17, 1897.

BROTHERS. Sk. C. H. Williams, Britannia, March 13, 1907.

BROTHERS, THE. C. fr. Terence. Plot fr. History of Macedonia.

BROTHERS, THE. C. Jas. Shirley. Licensed 1626. Blackfriars 1652. Pr. 1652.

BROTHERS, THE. T. Dr. E. Young. D.L., March 3, 1753. Written and rehearsed 30 years previously, and pr. 1752.

BROTHERS, THE. C. 5 a. Richd. Cumberland. D.L.; C.G., December 2, 1759. Pr. 1769. Based on *The Little French Lawyer*. See *Adelphi*.

BROTHERS, THE. C. in MS. In library of Mr. Murphy.

BROTHERS, THE. *School for Scandal* played under this title at Tottenham St. New T., 1830.

BROTHERS, THE. Burla. 1 a. T. E. Wilks. St. James's.

BROTHERS, THE. C. 3 a. John Brockbank. Cambridge T.R., August 7, 1875.

BROTHERS, THE. P. 1 a. Henry Byatt. Vaudeville, March 10, 1887; Olympic (rev.), February 20, 1888; Vaudeville, May 28, 1888.

BROTHERS; OR, A PLUNGE IN THE DARK. D. 4 a. A. Olive Lipthwaite. Marylebone, November 25, 1885.

BROTHERS AND CHUMS. M. Ep. 2 a. Oscar Mills. Ferndale Tudor H., August 6, 1900.

BROTHERS IN ARMS. D. Stalybridge Grand, September 3, 1894.

BROTHERS OF EDEN, THE. C.D. R. Ernest Rist. St. Helen's T.R. and O.H., May 1, 1885.

BROUGHT TO BOOK. Ca. 1 a. Fredk. Hay. Charing Cross, August 28, 1875.

BROUGHT TO BOOK. C.D. G. H. McDermott and Henry Pettitt. Britannia, May 8, 1876.

BROUGHT TO JUSTICE. D. Henry Pettitt and Paul Merritt. Surrey, March 27, 1880.

BROUGHT TO LIGHT. D. J. Percival. Aberdeen T.R., March 27, 1872.

BROUGHT TO LIGHT. D. 4 a. Edwd. Darbey. Rotherham T.R., August [illegible], 1889; Greenwich Morton's, July 28, 1890.

BROUGHT TO LIGHT; OR, WATCHING AND WINNING. D. Prol. and 4 a. T. A. Palmer. Plymouth R., 1868.

BROUGHT TOGETHER. C. 1 a. Fred Mouillot. Eleph. and C., October 29, 1894.

BROWN AND THE BRAHMINS; OR, CAPTAIN POP AND THE PRINCESS PRETTY-EYES. Burl. f. on *The Illustrious Stranger*, by R. Reece. Globe, January 23, 1869.

BROWN AT BRIGHTON. F.C. 3 a. Fenton McKay and Walter Stephens. Avenue, December 20, 1902.

BROWN BEAR. Sk. Paragon M.H., December 25, 1904.

BROWN MAN, THE. M.D. M. by Mr. Reeve. Lyceum, August 19, 1819.

BROWN OF B. CO. M. Ca. 1 a. Duncan Tovey. Cripplegate Inst., October 26, 1901.

BROWN PAPER PARCEL. C. 1 a. Pub. by S. French, Ltd.

BROWNE THE MARTYR. F. 1 a. Templeton Lucas. Court, January 20, 1872. See *The Martyr*.

BROWNE, WITH AN "E." 1 or 2 a. Leopold Montague. Pub. by S. French, Ltd.

BROWNIE AND THE PIANO-TUNER; OR, THE PIANO-TUNER AND THE BROWNIE. P. 4 sc. Wr. and with incid. m. com. by L. E. Lomax. Roy. Coll. of M., May 6, 1907.

BRUDER VON ST. BERNHARD DIE. D. 5 a. Anton Ohorn. Great Queen Street, April 6, 1906.

BRUM. F. Frank Deprez. Leeds T.R., March 15, 1880.

BRUMMAGEM JIM; A TRAVELLER'S TALE. "Arthurian Romance." Basil Hood. The Palace M.H., November 7, 1904.

BRUNHOWELE. Mentioned by Henslowe as belonging to the Rose T.

BRUSCHINI I DUE. O. Rossini. Venice, 1819.

BRUSCHINO. O. Rossini. Paris, December 28, 1857.

BRUTUS. T. Miss Bernard. 1690.

BRUTUS. T. Voltaire. 1730.

BRUTUS (JUNIUS). T. Alfieri. 1783. Transl. by C. Lloyd, 1815.

BRUTUS (JUNIUS). T. Andrieux. 1828.

BRUTUS (LUCIUS JUNIUS). T. Lee. 1679.

BRUTUS (LUCIUS JUNIUS). T. Duncombe. 1784.

BRUTUS (MARCUS). T. Alfieri. 1783. Transl. by C. Lloyd, 1815.

BRUTUS; OR, THE FALL OF TARQUIN. T. 5 a. J. Howard Payne. M. by Hayward. D.L., December 3, 1818.

BRUTUS AND CASSIUS. T. Chénier. 1764-1811. See *Conspiracy of Brutus.*

BRUTUS OF ALBA; OR, AUGUSTA'S TRIUMPH. O. Geo. Powell. Dorset Gdns., 1690. Pr. 1697.

BRUTUS OF ALBA; OR, THE ENCHANTED LOVERS. Tragic O. by Nahum Tate. Duke's T., 1678. Pr. 1678. Taken fr. the IV. Book of Virgil's Æneid.

BRUTUS ULTOR. T. 5 a. Michael Field. Pr. 1886.

BRUYERE, LA. See *The Absent Man.*

BUBBLE, THE. A Droll by Kirkman fr. the p. of Greene's *Tu Quoque*, by Cook, 1672.

BUBBLE AND SQUEAK. F. Fredk. Hay. Vaudeville, May 12, 1871.

BUBBLE REPUTATION, A. F.C. 3 a. James Willing and John Douglass. Standard, April 6, 1885.

BUBBLES. Dom. Ca 1 a. Chas. S. Fawcett Gaiety, October 8, 1881.

BUBBLES; OR, THE MATRIMONIAL OFFICE, THE. C. 3 a. Joseph Moser. Pr. 1808. N. ac.

BUBBLES IN THE SUDS; OR, A VILLAGE WASHERWOMAN. M.V. 1 a. Elephant and C., April 11, 1887.

BUBBLES OF THE DAY. C. 5 a. D. Jerrold. C.G., February 25, 1842.

BUBBLES OF THE DAY. See *Humbugs of the Hour.*

BUCCANEERS, THE. C.O. 2 a. Loughman St. L. Pendred. M. by Berthon F. Pendred and Miss Glazier. Organ part arr. by Arnold Russell, M.B. Streatham Town H., April 9, 1894.

BUCK IS A THIEF, THE. Whitehall, by the King's Co., 1623.

BUCK'S LODGE, THE. Int. D.L., 1790.

BUCKINGHAM. Ac. at Rose T. by the Earl of Sussex's servants, December 30, 1593. N.p.

BUCKINGHAM. D. 4 a. W. G. Wills. Olympic, November 29, 1875.

BUCKINGHAM. C. Oa. Julian Edwards. Northampton Town H., December 28, 1877.

BUCKRAM IN ARMOUR. See *The Disappointed Gallant.*

BUCKSTONE AT HOME; OR, THE MANAGER AND HIS FRIENDS. D.Sk. by J. Stirling Coyne. Hay., April 6, 1863.

BUCKSTONE'S ADVENTURE WITH A POLISH PRINCESS. F. 1 a. Slingsby Lawrence. Hay., July 4, 1855.

BUCKSTONE'S ASCENT OF MOUNT PARNASSUS. Extrav. Planché. Hay., Easter Monday, 1853.

BUCKSTONE'S VOYAGE ROUND THE GLOBE J. R. Planché, Hay., April 17, 1850.

BUD AND BLOSSOM. P. 1 a. Lady Colin Campbell. Terry's, June 3, 1893.

BUDGET OF BLUNDERS, A. F. By Greffulche. C.G., February, 1810. N.p. Possibly by the author of *Is He a Prince?* and *The Portrait of Cervantes.*

BUFFALO BILL. D. 4 a. George Roberts. Elephant and C., May 30, 1887.

BUFFALO BILL; OR, A LIFE IN THE WILD WEST. D. 4 a. By Col. Stanley and Charles Hermann. Sanger's, May 28, 1887 (first time in London).

BUFFALO GIRLS; OR, THE FEMALE SERENADERS, THE. F. Edward Stirling. Surrey, April 17, 1847.

BUFFO; OR, THE STORY OF A BROKEN HEART. P. 1 a. Ralph Roberts. Dundee H.M.T., September 5, 1904.

BUFFOON (SIR HERCULES). C. Lacy. 1622-1681.

BUGBEARS, THE. C. John Geffrey. In MS. in Marquis of Lansdowne's Library.

BUGLE CALL, THE. P. 1 a. L. N. Parker and A. Addison Bright. Hay., November 23, 1899.

BUGLE CALL, THE. Div. C. Wilhelm. M. by Sidney Jones. London Empire, October 9, 1905.

BUGLER BOB. Sk. Dora Langlois. Portsmouth People's Palace, October 28, 1901.

BUILDER OF BRIDGES, THE. P. 4 a. Alfred Sutro. St. James's, November 11, 1908.

BUILDERS, THE. P. 3 a. Norah Keith. Criterion, November 10, 1908 (mat.).

BUILDING FUND, THE. C. 3 a. Wm. Boyle Abbey. Dublin, April 25, 1905; St. Geo. H., November 28, 1905.

BUILT ON SAND. D. 5 a. Frank Harvey. Sheffield Alexandra O.H., May 3, 1886.

BUKOVIN. O. Z. Fibich (influenced by Mozart and Weber). 1874.

BULL. See *John Bull.*

BULL BY THE HORNS, THE. F. d. 3 a. H. J. Byron. Gaiety, August 28, 1876.

BULL IN A CHINA SHOP. C. 2 a. C. Mathews. Boston, U.S.A., 1864; also in England.

BULL'S HEAD, THE. Oa. Lyceum, July 14, 1818.

BULL-FIGHTER, THE. Rom. d. G. Almar. About 1835.

BULLDOGS AHOY! Dr. sk. 3 scs. Brien Daly and Algernon Syms. Sadler's Wells, December 30, 1899.

BULLS AND THE BEARS, THE. F. Colley Cibber. D.L., December, 1715.

BULMER'S THREAT. D. 1 a. Alex. M. Lee. Bayswater Bijou, June 18, 1908 (amat.).

BULSE, THE. Dr. piece. 1 a. Ascribed to Dr. Joddrell. Pr. 1787. N. ac.

BUMBLE. Oa. Lib. F. by Frank A. Clement on an incident in "Oliver Twist." M. by Oliver Notcutt. Ladbroke H., July 7, 1891.

BUMBLE'S COURTSHIP. Comic int. 1 a. Frank E. Emson

BUMBRUSHER, THE. F. Intended to be transl. into Latin and ac. before Fellows of University of Cambridge. Pr. 1786.

BUMP OF BENEVOLENCE, THE. Saville.

BUNCH OF BERRIES, THE. F. E. L. Blanchard. Adelphi, May 8, 1875.

BUNCH OF KEYS, A. M.C. 3 a. Chas. Hoyt and Geo. Lash Gordon. Avenue, August 25, 1883.

BUNCH OF SHAMROCKS, A. D. Frank Bateman and John Douglass. Edinburgh Royalty T., June 2, 1896. (C.p.)

BUNCH OF VIOLETS, A. P. 4 a. F. on Octave Feuillet's *Montjoye* by Sydney Grundy. Hay., April 25, 1894.

BUNCH OF VIOLETS. Sk. Prod. by A. Estcourt. Empress, March 8, 1907.

BUNDLE OF PROLOGUES, A. Prel. supposed by David Garrick. D.L., April 28, 1777.

BUNGALOW, THE. F.C. 3 a. F. by Fred Horner on Eugène Medina's *La Garconnière*. T. Déjazet, October 22, 1888. Prod. as *Bachelor's Quarters* (c.p.), P.O.W., January 21, 1889; Toole's, October 7, 1889.

BUNGLES. C. 3 a. De Svertchkoff and Harry Morphew. Ealing Lyric H., December 16, 1892.

BUNKERED; OR, TOO MANY COOKS SPOIL THE BROTH. Amer. Comedy D. 4 a. Gerald Ransley. Liverpool Balfour Inst., April 11, 1908 (amat.).

BUNKERING OF BETTY, THE. P. 1 a. Jean du Rocher. D.L., May 11, 1909 (mat.).

BUNKUM MULLER. Hay., February 24, 1864.

BUONA FIGLIUOLA MARITATA, LA. O. Piccini, Rome. 1769. See *The Accomplished Maid*.

BUONAPARTE; OR, THE FREEBOOTER. D. 3 a. John Scott Ripon. Pr. 1803.

BURCH AND HIS DETRACTORS. F. Preston T.R., February 3, 1875.

BURGLAR, THE. M.P. 1 a. Percy F. Parry. Brockley St. Peter's H., April 11, 1901.

BURGLAR ALARM AND THE DETECTIVE CAMERA; OR, DICK CLYDE'S INVENTION, THE. D. John Gannon. Liverpool Adelphi, January 30, 1893.

BURGLAR AND THE BISHOP, THE. M. V. Sir J. Jocelyn Coghill, Bart. M. by Wellesley Batson. Folkestone Pier, May 22, 1893.

BURGLAR AND THE JUDGE, THE. F. 1 a. F. C. Philips and C. H. E. Brookfield. Hay., November 5, 1892; rev. Court, January 20, 1893.

BURGLAR WHO FAILED, THE. C. 1 a. St John Hankin. Criterion, October 27, 1908.

BURGLAR'S BABY, THE. C.D. 3 a. John Douglass and Ch. Williams. Ealing Lyric, October 27, 1897.

BURGLAR'S DARLING, A. Scena. Herbert Fuller. Manchester Grand, November 26, 1904.

BURGLAR'S DILEMMA, THE. Sk. Francis Gilbert. Liverpool Westr. M.H., February 16, 1903.

BURGLAR'S EXTRA TURN, THE. M. Sca. Will Lennox. West London, June 5, 1907.

BURGLARS. Farcl. T. 3 a. Mark Melford. Brighton T.R., March 2, 1885; Avenue, April 9, 1885; Norwich T.R., February 28, 1887 (title changed from *A Reign of Terror* to *Burglars*).

BURGLARS. F. 2 a. Patrick Wharncliff. Wandsworth Town H. (amateurs), January 19, 1903. (C.p.)

BURGLARS. P. 1 a. Sivori Levey. Bayswater Bijou, April 29, 1909.

BURGLARY. F. 1 a. C. J. Mead Allen.

BURGOMASTER OF SAARDAM; OR, THE TWO PETERS, THE. C. F. Reynolds. C.G., September, 1818. Rev. at Hay., September, 1824, as *'Twould Puzzle a Conjurer*.

BURGOMASTER'S DAUGHTER. Marylebone, May 25, 1863.

BURIAL OF CHRIST. See "Miracle Plays."

BURIED ALIVE. Melo-d. Adap. fr. the French by H. M'Pherson. Newcastle-on-Tyne Amphi., May 1, 1899.

BURIED TALENT, A. P. 3 a. L. N. Parker. Sherborne Assembly Ro., December 3, 1886; afterwards pl. in 1 a, Glasgow Royalty, May 23, 1890; Vaudeville, June 5, 1890; Comedy, May 19, 1892.

BURMESE IDOL, A. D. 1 a. M. wr. and comp. by L. Stiles. Kingston County, May 20, 1907.

BURNING OF JOHN HUSS, THE. T. Ralph Radcliff. N.p

BURNING OF SODOM, THE. T. Ralph Radcliff. N.p.

BURNSIDE AND CO.: A HOUSE OF CARDS. P. 3 a. Georges Mitchell. Adap. by L. N. Parker. Dublin T.R., October 1, 1903.

BURNT OFFERING, A. D. 1 a. Austin Fryers and John M. Fisher. Gray's Inn. Rd. St. Alban's H., July 17, 1894.

BURY FAIR. C. Thos. Shadwell. F. partly on Molière's *Les Précieuses Ridicules* and on Duke of Newcastle's *Triumphant Widow*. Ac. and pr. 1689.

BUSH KING, THE. D. 4 a. W. J. Lincoln. Surrey, November 6, 1893.

BUSHMAN AND SOLDIER. Sk. Nat Gould. Eastern Empire, February 4, 1901.

BUSHRANGERS, THE. Melo-d. Bernard Espinasse and Harry Leader. Grand, May 30, 1904.

BUSHWIFE, THE. P. 1 a. Mrs. St. Clair Stobart. St. James's. June 4, 1909 (mat.).

BUSINESS IS BUSINESS. C. 3 a. By Horace Wigan. Brighton T.R., June 22, 1874.

BUSINESS IS BUSINESS. P. 3 a. Sydney Grundy. Adap. fr. "Les Affaires Sont les Affaires" of Octave Mirbeau. H.M., May 13, 1905.

BUSIRIS, KING OF EGYPT. T. Rev. Ed. Edwd. Young, LL.B. D.L., March 7, 1718. Pr. 1719.

BUSSY D'AMBOIS. T. Geo. Chapman. Ac. and pr. 1607. Plot taken fr. French historians in reign of Henry III. of France.

BUSSY D'AMBOIS: HIS REVENGE. T. Geo. Chapman. Ac. Whitefriars and pr. 1613.

BUSSY D'AMBOIS; OR, THE HUSBAND'S REVENGE. T. T. D'Urfey. Ac. T.R., 1691. Pr. 1691.

BUSTLE'S BRIDE. M.F. Bernard Capes. M. by J. Parry Cole. Avenue, November 12, 1884.

BUSTOWN BY THE SEA. C.Sk. E. C. Matthews and Wal. Pink. M. by J. E. Baker. Brixton Empress, October 21, 1907.

BUSY BODY, THE. C. 3 a. Mrs. Susannah Centlivre. Based on Dryden's "Sir Martin Marall," 1667. D.L., May 12, 1709. Pr. 1709. Hay., 1828, and July, 1855.

BUSY BODY, THE. C. Transl. fr. "The Theatre of Education" of Mdme. de Genlis. Pr. 1781.

BUSY BODY, THE. See *Too Curious by Half*.

BUSY DAY, A. C. 3 a. Lib. W. A. Brabner and C. H. Taylor. M. by H. E. Baker. Blackburn T.R., April 22, 1901.

BUT, HOWEVER. F. 1 a. H. Mayhew and H. Baylis. Hay., October 30, 1830; T.R., Belfast, January 31, 1876.

BUTHRED. T. Anonymous. Called in Scotland *Blue-thread* and in Ireland *Butter-head*. Said to have been by Mr. Johnstone, author of *The Reverie, Chrysal*, and other pieces, but not substantiated. C.G., December 8, 1778. Pr. 1778.

BUTLER, THE. Dom.C. 3 a. Mr. and Mrs. Herman Merivale. Manchester T.R., November 24, 1886; Toole's, December 6, 1886.

BUTTE DES MOULIN, LA. O. Boieldieu. Paris, 1852.

BUTTERCUP AND DAISY. M.C. 3 a. Geo. Dance. M. by Arthur Richards and others. Liverpool Court, June 17, 1895; Kilburn T., September 9, 1895.

BUTTERFLIES. M.p. 3 a. F. on the fantastic C. *The Palace of Puck*. W. J. Locke. Hay., April 2, 1907. Re-written by same author. J. A. Robertson. Newcastle, Tyne, April 20, 1908. Apollo, May 12, 1908.

BUTTERFLIES IN FAIRYLAND. Sk. Hipp., December 23. 1904

BUTTERFLY. C. Mrs. Comyns Carr. An adap. of *Frou-Frou*. Glasgow Gaiety, September 12. 1879.

BUTTERFLY, THE. P. 1 a. Walter Rhoades. Bloomsbury Drill H., May 4, 1887 (amat.).

BUTTERFLY FEVER. C. 3 a. Re-adap. fr. *La Papillone* by Jas. Mortimer. Criterion, May 17, 1881.

BUTTERFLY KISSES. P. 1 a. Carmel Goldsmid. Ryde Pier Pavilion, August 30. 1909.

BUTTERMILK VOLUNTEERS. Adelphi, M[illegible] 6, 1850.

BUXOM JOAN. Burl. Mr. Willett. Taken fr. original song, "A Soldier and a Sailor," in *Love for Love*. Hay., June, 1778. Pr. 1778.

BY AND BY. Rom. C. 4 a. St. George's H., February 3, 1896.

BY COMMAND OF THE CZAR. D. R. Glover and Chas. M. Hermann. Victoria, November 5, 1877.

BY COMMAND OF THE KING. D. Edwd. Towers. New Pavilion, November 25, 1871.

BY LAND AND SEA. D. 4 a. J. A. Campbell and J. L. Shine. Birmingham T.R., June 8, 1886.

BY MUTUAL CONSENT. Ca. 1 a. Charles Windermere. Greenock T.R., April 15, 1901; Avenue, February 6, 1903.

BY ORDER OF THE CZAR. See *Under the Canopy*.

BY ROAD AND RAIL. M. Sk. Corney Grain. St. George's Hall, November 20, 1893.

BY ROYAL COMMAND. C.D. 3 a. Edwd. Stirling. Lyceum, August, 1856.

BY SHEER PLUCK. D. 4 a. Bertram Damer. Irving T., Seacombe, February 14, 1903; Liverpool Rotunda, June 16, 1903; Surrey, June 29, 1903.

BY SPECIAL LICENCE. D. Prol. and 4 a. Frank Marryat. Longton T.R., May 16, 1887.

BY SPECIAL REQUEST. Ca. 1 a. J. Malcolm Watson. Strand, February 7, 1887.

BY STILL WATERS. Ep. in Arcady. A. F. Cross. Rugby T.R., November 6, 1901.

BY THE HAND OF A WOMAN. D. 4 a. W. A. Brabner. Greenwich Carlton, April 28, 1902.

BY THE LIGHT OF A CANDLE. P. 1 a. Oscar Rose. Notting Hill Ladbroke H., April 12, 1902.

BY THE MIDLAND SEA. Ep. Justin Huntly McCarthy. Criterion, June 21, 1892.

BY THE SEA. F. Strand, April 1, 1872.

BY THE SEA. D. 1 a. Adap. by Alec Nelson fr. Theuriet's *Jean-Marie*. Ladbroke H., November 28, 1887.

BY THIS TOKEN. Ca. 1 a. J. Keith Angus. Sadler's Wells, May 6, 1884.

BY WHOSE HAND? P. 4 a. Eugene Gotere. Harrogate O.H., December 2, 1905; Liverpool Rotunda, March 23. 1906.

BYE-ELECTION, THE. Sk. Canterbury, January 11, 1909.

BYEWAYS. C. 1 a. Geo. S. Payne. Comedy. March 10. 1897.

BYGONE DAYS. C.D. Prol. and 3 a. Cyril Harrison. St. Leonard's Pier Pav., January 23, 1899.

BYGONES. Ca. 1 a. A. W. Pinero. Lyceum, September 18, 1880; rev. May 4, 1895.

BYRON. See *Borbonne*.

BYRON'S CONSPIRACY. Geo. Chapman. Circa 1608. See *Conspiracy*.

C

CABAL, THE. As ac. in George Street. Pr. 1763.

CABAL AND LOVE. T. Transl. fr. the German of Schiller. Pr. 1795. N. ac. See *Harper's Daughter*.

CABARET DE LUSTUCRU; LE. See *Follies of a Night*.

CABDRIVER. Buckstone.

CABIN BOY, THE. M. Ent. 1 a. D.L., June 28, 1836.

CABIN BOY, THE. D. 2 a. Edwd. Stirling. Adelphi, March 9, 1846.

CABINET, THE. C.O. 3 a. Thos. Dibdin. F on an ancient ballad, "The Golden Bull." M. by Reeve, Moorhead, Davy, Corri, and Braham. C.G., February 9, 1802, and July 25, 1804.

CABINET AND CUPID, THE. P. 1 a. Edwd. Ferris and B. P. Matthews. Sheffield T.R., September 12, 1902.

CABINET MINISTER, THE. F. 4 a. A. W. Pinero, Court, April 23, 1890; rev. Hay., June 1, 1905.

CABINET QUESTION, A. C.D. 1 a. J. R. Planché. Hay., September 23, 1845.

CABINET. SECRET, A. C. 2 a. L. H. F. Du Terreaux. Philharmonic, October 19, 1872.

CABLE CAR, THE. Howellian Burl. 2 a. Clara Harriet Sherwood. C.P. 1891.

CABMAN No. 93. F. T. J. Williams. Lyceum, December 26, 1867.

CABOTINS. P. 4 a. Edouard Pailleron. Royalty, January 17, 1906.

CADI, THE. O.C. Adap. of *Le Caid* by Arthur Matthison. Manchester Prince's, December 8, 1880.

CADI OF BAGDAD, THE. C.O. 3 a. Abraham Portal. D.L., February 19, 1778. Songs only published.

CADI'S DAUGHTER, THE. Oa. 1 a. E. Fitzball. M. by Nelson. D.L., January 27, 1851.

CADMUS ET HERMIONE. O. Lulli, Paris, 1852.

CADUTA DE GIGANTI, LA. O. Gluck. Hay., January 7, 1746.

CADUTA DE GIGANTI, LA. Orat. Rossi. (In MS.)

CAEDMAR. O. 1 a. Granville Bantock. Crystal Palace, October 18, 1892.

CAELIA; OR, THE PERJURED LOVER. T. Chas. Johnson. Ep. by H. Fielding. D.L., December 11, 1732. Pr. 1733.

CAELINA; OR, A TALE OF MYSTERY. D. 2 a. John Wallace. Pr. 1802. Taken fr. a Fr. play, *Cœlina ou L'Enfant du Mystère*, by Guilbert de Pixérécourt.

CAERNARVON; OR, THE BIRTH OF THE PRINCE OF WALES. M. Ent. John Rose. M. by Attwood. Hay., August 12, 1793. Pr. 1793.

CAESAR. See *King Caesar*.

CAESAR AND CLEOPATRA. P. 5 a. G. Bernard Shaw. Newcastle-on-Tyne T.R., March 15, 1899; Leeds G.T., September 16, 1907; Savoy, November 25, 1907.

CAESAR AND POMPEY. Rom. T. Geo. Chapman. Ac. Blackfriars, 1607. Pr. 1607.

CAESAR AND POMPEY. See Warres of *Pompey and Caesar*.

CAESAR AND POMPEY; OR, CAESAR'S REVENGE, THE TRAGEDY OF. Ac. by students at Oxford. Pr. 1607.

CAESAR AND POMPEY, THE HISTORY OF. Ac. before 1580

CAESAR BORGIA. P. 4 a. J. H. McCarthy. Edinburgh Royal, October 21, 1907.

CAESAR BORGIA, SON TO POPE ALEXANDRA VI. T. in blank verse. Nath. Lee. Duke's T., 1680. Pr. 1680. Plot built on histories of Guicciardini and Marina and Ricant's *Lives of the Popes*. Rev. Hay., August 19, 1707; D.L., January 3, 1719.

CAESAR IN EGYPT. T. An adap. by Colley Cibber of *The False One*, and taken fr. Pompée of Corneille. D.L., December 9, 1724. Pr. 1725.

CAESAR, THE WATCH DOG OF THE CASTLE. Rom. D. 2 a. Adap. fr. the Fr. Moncrieff. Victoria, April 29, 1844.

CAESAR'S FALL. John Webster, Drayton, Middleton and Munday. 1602.

CAESAR'S REVENGE. T.

CAESAR'S TRAGEDY. Ac. before the Court at Whitehall, May, 1613. Sup. to be the T. of Julius Caesar.

CAESAR'S WIFE. P. 2 a. Transl. of "L'Enigme." Paul Hervien. Wyndham's, March 1, 1902.

CAFE CONCERT, THE. M.Sk. Chas. Parsons and Will Ashworth. M. comp. by C. B. Yearsley in 2 sc. Empress, June 17, 1907.

CAFFRES; OR, BURIED ALIVE, THE. Mus. Ent. 2 a. Ascr. to Mr. Eyre. M. by J. Davy and others. C.G., June 2, 1802. N.p.

CAGLIOSTRO, THE MAGACIAN. D. C. A. Clarke. Park, June 12, 1875.

CAGNOTTE, LA. F. E. Labiche and A. Delacour. Gaiety, June, 1880; Royalty, March 4, 1907.

CAGOT; OR, HEART FOR HEART, THE. P 5 a. Edmund Falconer. Lyceum, December 6, 1856.

CAID, LE. O. A. Thomas. Paris, 1849. See *The Cadi*.

CAIN. 3 a. Mystery. Byron. Pr. 1821

CAIN: OR, A YEAR AND A DAY. D. Stockton-on-Tees T.R., August 26, 1878.

CAIO GRACCO. O. Leo. 1720. See *Gracchus*.

CAITIFF OF CORSICA; OR, THE UNIVERSAL BANDITTS, THE. Hist. D. 5 a. Pr. 1807. N. ac.

CAIUS GRACCHUS. T. John Joshua. Earl of Carysfort. Pr. 1810

CAIUS GRACCHUS. T. 5 a. J. Sheridan Knowles. 1815. D.L., November 18, 1823.

CAIUS GRACCHUS. T. Monti. 1825. Rend. into Fr. by Duplissis, 1854, and into Eng. by Lord J. Russell, 1830.

CAIUS MARIUS, HISTORY AND FALL OF. T. T. Otway. An adap. of Shakespeare's *Romeo and Juliet*. The plot may be found in Plutarch's "Life of Caius Marius" and in Lucan's "Pharsalia." Duke's T., 1680. Pr. 1680. Hay., March 18, 1707; D.L., February 21, 1715, and May 10, 1717.

CALANDRIA, LA. C. Bibbi. 1490. The first Italian C.

CALAYNOS. T. 5 a. Geo. H. Baker. Sadler's Wells, May 10, 1848.

CALDRON, THE Pant. D.L., 1785

CALEB: OR, THE CURSE. C.D. 3 a. Miss S. A. Johnson. Terry's, June 6, 1893.

CALEB QUOTEM AND HIS WIFE; OR, PAINT, POETRY, AND PRETTY. O. 3 a. Henry Lee. Pr. 1809. Orig. prod. as F., 2 a, Hay., July 6, 1798, as *Throw Physic to the Dogs*.

CALEB WILLIAMS. See *The Iron Chest*.

CALEDON'S TEARS; OR, WALLACE. T. G. Nesbit. Pr. 1733.

CALEDONIA; OR, THE PEDLAR TURNED MERCHANT. T.C. Pr. 1700.

CALEDONIAN LAURELS; OR, THE HIGHLANDER'S RETURN. Ballet by Byrne. D.L., November 3, 1815.

CALIFE DE BAGDAD, LE. O. Boieldieu. Paris, 1800.

CALIFFO DI BAGDAD. See *Adina*.

CALIFORNIA JOE. D. J. G. Rainbow. Rotherham T.R., January 21, 1878.

CALIFORNIAN GIRL, A. D. H. E. Fielding. Tonypandy T.R., August 15, 1902. C.P.

CALIGULA, EMPEROR OF ROME. T. in rhyme by J. Crowne. Plot taken fr. Suetonius's "Life of Caligula." Ac. D.L., 1698. Pr. 1698.

CALIPH OF BAGDAD, THE. O. Extrav. 1 a. W. Brough. Strand, December 26, 1867.

CALIPH VALID AMANZOR. See *Almyna*.

CALIRRHOE. Cant. Dr. J. F. Bridge.

CALIRRHOE. D. in verse. Michael Field. Pr. 1884.

CALISTA. O. Pr. 1731.

CALISTHENE. T. Pirou. 1780.

CALISTO; OR, THE CHASTE NYMPH. Masque. J. Crowne. Plot f. on Ovid's "Metamorphoses. Wr. 1675. Several times perf. at Court.

CALISTO AND MELIBEA. Int. Publ. circa 1530.

CALL AGAIN TO-MORROW. M.F. 1 a. Don T. De Trueba v Cosio. Lyceum, July 14, 1834.

CALL TO ARMS. Dom. P. 4 a. Manchester Metro. T., June 30, 1902.

CALL TO ARMS, A. Sk. in 1 sc. H. Edlin. Oxford, May 8, 1909 (mat.).

CALLED BACK. P. in prol. and 3 a. Adap. fr Hugh Conway's novel by the author and Comyns Carr. P.O.W. (late Prince's), May 20, 1884; Hay., November 10, 1890.

CALLED BACK. D. Adap. by John C. Chute fr. Hugh Conway's novel. Eastbourne Dev. Park T., August 25, 1884; Sanger's Amphitheatre, September 20, 1884.

CALLED BACK. D. F. on Hugh Conway's novel. Derby Lecture H., September 1, 1884.

CALLED BACK. See *Called Back Again, Called There and Back, The Scalded Back.*

CALLED BACK AGAIN. Burl. Parody of *Called Back* by Albert Chevalier. Plymouth T.R., July 13, 1885.

CALLED THERE AND BACK. Burl. Parody of *Called Back* by Herman C. Merivale. Gaiety, October 15, 1884.

CALLED TO THE BAR. F. Portman Rooms, May 16, 1892.

CALLED TO THE FRONT. Military D. Sergeant Towner and Frank Beaumont. Britannia, April 29, 1885.

CALTHORPE CASE, THE. D. 4 a. Arthur Goodrich. Vaudeville, December 14, 1887.

CALUMNY. P. 3 a. Adap. by Malcolm Watson fr. the Spanish D. *El Gran Galêoto* by José Echegaray. Shaftesbury, April 4, 1889.

CALVARY. Cant. Spohr. 1784-1859.

CALYPSO. Masque. Pr. 1778. Closely traced fr. Fenelon, but varied fr. Mr. Hughes's.

CALYPSO. O. Richd. Cumberland. M. by Butler. C.G., 1779. Pr.

CALYPSO. C.O. Robt. Houlton. Smock Alley, Dublin, 1785. N.p.

CALYPSO. O. Winter. 1803. See *Gracchus*.

CALYPSO; OR, THE ART OF LOVE. Extrav. Alfd. Thompson. Court, May 6, 1874.

CALYPSO AND TELEMACHUS. O John Hughes. M. by Galliard. Queen's T. in Hay., Pr. 1712.

CALYPSO, QUEEN OF OGYGIA. Burl. 1 a. Sheridan Brookes. Sadler's Wells, April 15, 1865.

CAMARADERIE, LA. C. Scribe. 1837.

CAMARALZAMAN. Fairy C. James. 1848.

CAMARALZAMAN. Burl. D. in prol. and 3 a. F. C. Burnand. Gaiety, January 31, 1884.

CAMARALZAMAN AND BADOURA. 1 a. Brothers Brough.

CAMARALZAMAN AND THE FAIR BADOURA; OR, THE BAD D(J)INN AND THE GOOD SPIRIT. Extrav. 2 a. H. J. Byron. Vaudeville, November 22, 1871.

CAMARONIANS, THE. Standard, November 7, 1863.

CAMBERWELL BROTHERS, THE. Burl. on *The Corsican Brothers*. C. Selby. Olympic, April 20, 1852.

CAMBIALE DI MATRIMONIO, LA. O. Rossini. Venice, 1810.

CAMBIO DELLA VALIZIA, IL. O. Rossini. Venice, 1812.

CAMBRO BRITONS. Hist. P. 3 a. Jas. Boaden. Hay., July 21, 1798. Pr. 1798.

CAMBRO-BRITONS; OR, FISHGARD IN AN UPROAR, THE. Mus. Int. C.G., May 31, 1797. N.p.

CAMBYSES, KING OF PERSIA. P. in old metre. Thos. Preston. Story taken fr. Herodotus and Justin. (N.d.) About 1569. Referred to by Shakespeare, 1 Hen. IV., ii. 4.

CAMBYSES, KING OF PERSIA. T. Elkanah Settle. Duke's T., 1675. Pr. 1671.

CAMERA OBSCURA, A. F. Geo. Walter Browne. Sanger's Amphi., October 24, 1879.

CAMILLA. O. Transl. fr. Italian by Owen MacSwiny. D.L. and Hay., 1706. Pr. 1706.

CAMILLA, THE WILD FLOWER OF THE WILDERNESS. D. Alfred Hillier. Middlesbro' T.R., March 30, 1874; Govan T. of Varieties, June 11, 1877.

CAMILLA OF CAMDEN TOWN. Burl. by Harry Dymond Stuckey. Camden Town Park H., April 3, 1893.

CAMILLA OSSIA IL SOTTERANEO. O. Paër. 1801.

CAMILLA'S HUSBAND. D. 3 a. By Watts Phillips. Olympic, November 10, 1862.

CAMILLE. Italian ver. of Alexandre Dumas' *La Dame aux Camélias*. Lyric, May 24, 1893 (Eleonora Duse's season).

CAMILLE. P. 5 a. Heron. Publ. by J. Dicks.

CAMILLE. D. 5 a. Adap. by B. Hill fr. *La Dame aux Camélias*. Adelphi, September 8, 1902.

CAMILLE; OR, AN AUTUMNAL DREAM. D. 3 a. W. G. Wills. Cambridge T.R., August 20, 1877.

CAMMA. T. Corneille. 1661.

CAMOMILLE, LA. C. 1 a. C. Darantière and M. Soulie. Coronet, October 22, 1900.

CAMP, THE. Mus. Ent. 2 a. Possibly by R. Brinsley Sheridan. D.L., October 15, 1778.

CAMP, THE. Military Div. D.L., October 25, 1825.

CAMP AT CHOBHAM, THE. F. 1 a. Mark Lemon. Adelphi, June 30, 1853.

CAMP AT THE OLYMPIC, THE. Extrav. and Dr. Review. J. R. Planché. Olympic, October 17, 1853.

CAMP DE SILESIE. O. Meyerbeer. Berlin, 1844.

CAMPAIGN, THE. Joseph Addison. 1672-1719.

CAMPAIGN, THE. See *Love and War*.

CAMPAIGN; OR, LOVE IN THE EAST INDIES, THE. O. Mr. Robt. Jephson. N.p. C.G., May 12, 1785. Previously ac. at Dublin.

CAMPAIGNERS; OR, PLEASANT ADVENTURES AT BRUSSELS, THE. C. T. D'Urfey. Plot partly taken fr. novel called "Female Falsehood." D.L., 1698. Pr. 1698.

CAMPAIGNING. F.C. 3 a. Criterion, May 24, 1879.

CAMPANO; OR, THE WANDERING MINSTREL. Mus. C. 3 a. Adap. fr. the Fr. of Henri de Gorsse and Georges Elwall by G. D. Day. M. by Edwd. Jakobowski. Leeds Grand, September 8, 1898.

CAMPASPE. See *Alexander and Campaspê* and *Cupid and Campaspê*.

CAMPDEN WONDER, THE. P. 3 sc. J. Maxfield. Court, January 8, 1907.

CAMPING OUT. P. 4 a. Bronson Howard. Elephant and C., December 13, 1886 (C.P.).

CAMPING OUT. Sk. Hammersmith Pal., January 16, 1909.

CAMPION; OR, A PEARL OF CHRISTENDOM. Hist. and relig. D. 5 a. 8 sc. E. Cox. Oxford Corn Exchange, October 28, 1907.

CAN A WOMAN BE GOOD? Dom. P. 4 a. C. Watson Mill. Chatham R., September 6, 1909.

CAN HE FORGIVE HER? P. Prol. and 4 a. Mrs. Chas. Calvert. Manchester C., September 18, 1891.

CANAL BOAT, THE. D. Swansea T.R., September 20, 1871.

CANARD A TROIS BECS, LA. Fr. O. Bouffe. Jules Moineaux. M. by Emile Jonas. Globe, July 13, 1872.

CANARY, THE. C. 3 a. Geo. Fleming. P.O.W., November 13, 1899; Royalty, January 27, 1900.

CANCER. P. in Latin. Supposed to have been ac. before James I., 1622. Pr. 1648.

CANDIDA. P. 3 a. Geo. Bernard Shaw. South Shields T.R., March 30, 1895 (C.P.); Her M., Aberdeen, July 30, 1897; Strand, July 1, 1900.

CANDIDATE, THE. F. John Dent. Hay., August 5, 1782. See *Rival Candidates.*

CANDIDATE, THE. C. 3 a. Adap. by J. H. M'Carthy fr. *Le Député de Bombignac.* C. in 3 a. by Alexandre Bisson. (Royalty, March 2, 1888, French season.) Criterion, November 22, 1884; rev. May 30, 1894.

CANDLEMAS DAY; OR, THE KILLING OF THE CHILDREN OF ISRAEL. By Ihan Parfre. Wr. 1512.

CANKER IN THE ROSE, A. D. 1 a. Lionel Davis and W. J. Tate. Birkenhead Metro., March 8, 1900.

CANNIE SOOGAH; OR, THE WEARING OF THE GREEN, THE. D. Dublin T.R., May 12, 1873.

CANTAB, THE. F. 1 a. T. W. Robertson. Strand, February 14, 1861.

CANTABS, THE. F. C.G., May 21, 1787. N.p.

CANTEMIR. O. F. E. Fesca. 1789-1826.

CANTERBURIE, HIS CHANGE OF DIOT; WHICH SHEWETH VARIETY OF WIT AND MIRTH. Privately ac. at Westminster. Pr. 1644.

CANTERBURY GUESTS; OR, A BARGAIN BROKEN. C. E. Ravenscroft. T.R., 1695. Pr.

CANTERBURY PILGRIMS, THE. O. 3 a. M. by C. Villiers Stanford. Lib. by Gilbert à Beckett. D.L., April 28, 1884.

CANUTE THE GREAT. P. in verse. Michael Field. Pr. 1887.

CANVASS; OR, THE CHILD IN THE SUDS, THE. C. Ac. at City of Wells. Pr. 1763.

CAP-MAKER'S DAUGHTER, THE. Rom. P. 1 a. Herbt. T. Rainger. Cheltenham Vict. R., February 3, 1905.

CAPE MAIL, THE. D. 1 a. Adap. fr. the Fr. by Clement Scott. Liverpool P.O.W., September 23, 1881; St. James's, October 27, 1881; Court, May, 1894; Vaudeville, October 7, 1897.

CAPE ST. VINCENT; OR, BRITISH VALOUR TRIUMPHANT. Mus. Ent. D.L., March 6, 1797. A rev., with alterations, of *The Glorious First of June.* N.p.

CAPERS. M.F.C. 3 a. Wr. and comp. by Richd. Stahl, with lyrics by Walter Parke. Standard, November 23, 1885.

CAPERS. F.C. Fanny Marriott and Kenward Matthews. Hampstead Vestry H., March 18, 1899.

CAPITAL AND LABOUR. D. 4 a. W. S. Patmore and H. B. Moss. Originally prod. in the provinces. Pav., March 9, 1891.

CAPITAL IDEA, A. F. Frank Arlon and Arthur Rushton. Philharmonic, December 26, 1871.

CAPITAL JOKE, A. Oa. 1 a. Fredk. de Lara and B. Brigata. M. by Landon Ronald. St. Geo. H., May 31, 1889; P.O.W. Club, January 21, 1894.

CAPITAL MATCH, A. F. 1 a. J. Maddison Morton. Hay., November 4, 1852.

CAPITAL MATCH, A. Ca. 1 a. Wm. Parker. Richmond T.R., April 26, 1897.

CAPITALISTE, LE. Monol. M. C. Cros. Royalty, January 31, 1889.

CAPOCHIO AND DORINNA. Mus. Ent. Ascr. to Colley Cibber. Probably an abridgment fr. *The Temple of Dulness.* Pr. (n.d.).

CAPOCHIO AND DORINNA. See *The Happy Captive.*

CAPITOLA; OR, THE MASKED MOTHER AND THE HIDDEN HAND. D. 3 a. C. H. Hazlewood. City of London, 1860.

CAPRICE. P. 4 a. Howard P. Taylor. Rev. by Fred W. Broughton (prod. abroad first), Globe, October 22, 1889.

CAPRICE, A. P. 1 a. Transl. fr. Alfred de Musset by J. H. M'Carthy. V., May 10, 1892; Garrick, November, 1892.

CAPRICE, A. Transl. fr. Alfred de Musset by Miss Irene Fitzgerald. Bayswater Bijou, December 16, 1905.

CAPRICES OF A LOVER, THE. C. Goethe. 1769.

CAPRICIOUS BEAUTY, A. C. 4 a. Adap. fr. the German by Major D'Arcy. Aldershot T.R., March 15, 1886.

CAPRICIOUS LADY, THE. F. Ascr. to Mrs. Pye. D.L., May 10, 1771. N.p.

CAPRICIOUS LADY, THE. C. Alt. fr. Beaumont and Fletcher's *The Scornful Lady* by Wm. Cooke. C.G., January 17, 1783.

CAPRICIOUS LOVERS, THE. C. Mr. Odingsells. L.I.F., December 8, 1725; D.L., 1727. Pr. 1727.

CAPRICIOUS LOVERS, THE. C.O. Robt. Lloyd. M. by Rush. D.L., November 28, 1764. Pd. The groundwork founded on *Caprices d'Amour, ou Ninette à la Cour,* by Favart.

CAPRICIOUS LOVERS, THE. Mus. Ent. Taken fr. the O. of that name by Robt. Lloyd. Pr. 1765.

CAPTAIN, THE. C. Beaumont and Fletcher. Ac. at Court, May, 1613, and previously elsewhere. Pr. 1647.

CAPTAIN, THE. Sensational D. 3 a. Don Carlos. Swindon Mechanics' Inst., February 23, 1883.

CAPTAIN, THE. F.C. 3 a. W. F. Field. Maidenhead Town H., December 27, 1886.

CAPTAIN, THE. See *Tricks.*

CAPTAIN BILLY. Oa. 1 a. Words by Harry Greenbank. M. by François Cellier. Savoy, September 24, 1891.

CAPTAIN BIRCHELL'S LUCK. P. 3 a. L. N. Parker. Alt. by the author from his play *Chris.* Terry's, October 30, 1899; V., March 28, 1892.

CAPTAIN BRASSBOUND'S CONVERSION. Rom. P. 3 a. G. B. Shaw. Manchester Q.T., May 12, 1902; Court, March 20, 1906.

CAPTAIN CHARLOTTE. F. 2 a. Edwd. Stirling. Adelphi, March, 1843.

CAPTAIN COOK. A Serious Panto. C.G., March 24, 1789.

CAPTAIN CUTTLE. D. Sk. 3 a. John Brougham. Gaiety, November 20, 1880.

CAPTAIN DARE. C. 3 a. Robert Wilford. Manchester St. James's T., January 22, 1903.

CAPTAIN DIEPPE. P. 3 a. Anthony Hope and Harrison Rhodes. New T. (C.P.), September 11, 1903; Duke of York's, February 15, 1904.

CAPTAIN DREW ON LEAVE. P. 4 a. Hubert Henry Davies. New, October 24, 1905.

CAPTAIN DREYFUS. Yiddish Melo-d. 4 a. Nahum Rackow. Standard, June 18, 1898.

CAPTAIN DREYFUS. Dr. fr. Military Epis. 5 sc. J. Jackson. Paragon, September 23, 1907.

CAPTAIN FRITZ. M.C.D. 5 a. H. Hamilton. Hammersmith Lyric, April 5, 1897.

CAPTAIN GERALD. D. J. B. Howe. Britannia, November 27, 1867.

CAPTAIN GERALD; OR, THE HIGHWAYMAN'S REVENGE. 3 a. W. Archer. Pav., November 23, 1867.

CAPTAIN IS NOT A-MISS, THE. F. 1 a. Thos. Egerton Wilks. English Op. House, April 18, 1836.

CAPTAIN JOHN HALL, THE FIRST HIGHWAYMAN. D. Liverpool R. Colosseum, February 12, 1872.

CAPTAIN KETTLE. D. 4 a. Malcolm Watson and Murray Carson. F. on Cutcliffe Hyne's story. Adelphi, October 23, 1902.

CAPTAIN KIDD. Sk. W. J. Mackay.

CAPTAIN KIDD; OR, THE BOLD BUCCANEER. C.O. 3 a. M. by E. Solomon. Lib. by G. H. Abbott. Liverpool P.O.W., September 10, 1883.

CAPTAIN KIDD; OR, THE BUCCANEERS. C.O. 3 a. Clare Kummer. Duke of York's (C.P.), July 11, 1898.

CAPTAIN MARIO, THE COMEDIE OF Stephen Gosson. 1577. N.p.

CAPTAIN O'BLUNDER; OR, THE BRAVE IRISHMAN. F. Thos. Sheridan. Goodman's Fields, January 31, 1746. Pr. circa 1748. Partly taken fr. *Sieur Pourceaugnac* of Molière. See *Brave Irishman.*

CAPTAIN OF THE GUARD. C.O. Fredk Wood. M. by Geo. Fox. Margate New T., July 24, 1882. Taken from *Captain of the Watch.*

CAPTAIN OF THE NIGHT HAWK, THE. M. Absurdity. 2 a. Book and lyrics by Albert E. Jecks and Howard de Wing. M. by Arthur Workman. Title changed from *Tit Bits* on production. Balham Assembly R., September 23, 1897.

CAPTAIN OF THE VULTURE, THE. Nautical D. 5 a. Dramatised fr. Miss Braddon's novel of same name by Joseph Lewis and Henry Falconer. Warrington T.R., March 20, 1889.

CAPTAIN OF THE WATCH, THE. F. 1 a. R. Planché. Taken fr. Lockroy's *Le Chevalier Du Guet.* C.G., February 24, 1841; rev. D.L., December 8, 1856, and at Hay., April 1, 1869; Lyceum, 1881. See *Captain of the Guard.*

CAPTAIN PRO TEM. P. Mark Lemon. Olympic, 1841.

CAPTAIN SMITH. F. 1 a. Miss E. Berrie. Charing Cross, April 4, 1870.

CAPTAIN SPENT'S PROPOSALS. F. 1 a. P. J. Barrow. Southsea Portd. H., December 14, 1899.

CAPTAIN STARLIGHT; OR, THE LOST EARL. Sk. 4 scenes. W. J. Mackay. Sadler's Wells, May 22, 1899.

CAPTAIN STEVENS. C. Selby. Strand.

CAPTAIN SWIFT. P. 4 a. C. Haddon Chambers. Hay., June 20, 1888 (mat.); September 1, 1888 (evening bill); Hay., December 2, 1893; H.M.T., May 13, 1899.

CAPTAIN THERESE. C.O. 3 a. Alex. Bissen and F. C. Burnand. M. by Robt. Planquette. P.O.W., August 25, 1890; Criterion, May 30, 1893.

CAPTAIN THOMAS STUKELEY, WITH HIS MARRIAGE TO ALDERMAN CURTEIS' DAUGHTER, AND VALIANT ENDING OF HIS LIFE AT THE BATTAILE OF ALCAZAR, THE LIFE AND DEATH OF. Pr. 1605.

CAPTAIN TOM DRAKE. D. 3 a. W. Stephens. Macclesfield T.R., November 6, 1874.

CAPTAIN UNDERWIT. P. Pr. by A. H. Bullen in his collection of old English plays. Circa 1640.

CAPTAIN'S DAUGHTER. C. 1 a. Mrs. and Archibald Hodgson. Southampton Drill H., December 3, 1890 (C.P.).

CAPTAIN'S GHOST, THE. Reynoldson.

CAPTIFS, LES. C. Rotrou. 1635. Fr. the *Captive of Plautus.*

CAPTIVATING CARMEN. Burl. Martin Byam and Byam Wyke. Folkestone Pier, August 4, 1890.

CAPTIVE, THE. C. Isaac Bickerstaff. M. by Dibdin. Partly taken fr. *Don Sebastian.* Hay., 1769. Pr.

CAPTIVE, THE. Monol. D. M. G. Lewis. C.G., March 22, 1803. N.p.

CAPTIVE; OR, THE LOST RECOVERED. P. Heywood. September 3, 1624.

CAPTIVE MONARCH, THE. T. Richd. Hey. Pr. 1794. N. ac.

CAPTIVE OF SPILSBURG, THE. M. Ent. M. by Dussek. D.L., November 16, 1798. Pr. 1799. An alteration ascr. to Mr. Prince Hoare fr. a Fr. D., *Le Souterrain.* See *Albert and Adelaide.*

CAPTIVE PRINCESS, THE. T. Dr. Smith. N.p. N. ac.

CAPTIVES, THE. P. Pr. by A. H. Bullen in his collection of old English plays. Licensed 1624. Ascr. to T. Heywood.

CAPTIVES, THE. T. J. Gay. D.L., January 15, 1724.

CAPTIVES, THE. C. Transl. fr. Plautus by Richd. Warner. 1767.

CAPTIVES, THE. T. John Delap. D.L., March 9, 1786. Pr. 1786.

CAPTIVI (B.C. 254-184). Plautus C. (Latin). Transl. into blank verse by Thornton, Rich, and Colman, about 1770. See *Captifs* and "Latin Plays."

CAPTIVITY. Orat. Crotch. 1775-1847.

CAPTIVITY, THE. Orat. Goldsmith, 1728-1744.

CAPTURE OF VENUS, THE. M. Phantasy. A. E. Ellis. M. by C. Locknane. Richmond. November 25, 1907.

CAPTURED BY BRIGANDS. Sk. Empress, September 7, 1908.

CAPUCHIN, THE. C. Saml. Foote. Alt. fr. *A Trip to Calais* (1776). Hay., August 17, 1776. Pr. 1778.

CAPULETTI ED I MONTECCHI, I. O. 3 a. Lib. by Romani. M. by Bellini. Prod. in Venice, March 11, 1830. It was wr. for the two Grisis and Rubini. Prod. in London King's T., July 20, 1833.

CARACTACUS. Dr. Poem. W. Mason. Pr. 1759, afterwards alt. and ac. at C.G., December 6, 1776. Pr. 1776. M. by Dr. Arne.

CARACTACUS. Ballet of Action. Invented by D'Egville. M. by Bishop. D.L., 1808. N.p. 1837.

CARACTACUS. Hist. P. 5 a. Alt. fr. Beaumont and Fletcher by the adaptor of *Woman Never Vext.* M. by Balfe. D.L., November 6, 1837.

CARACTACUS. See *Bonduca.*

CARAVAN; OR, CARAVANSERA, THE. M. Piece, advertised as to be prod. at K.T. in the Hay., September 26, 1791, but not brought forward.

CARAVAN; OR, THE DRIVER AND HIS DOG, THE. S.C. Rom. Frederic Reynolds. M. by Reeve. D.L., December 5, 1803. Pr. N.d.

CARAVANNE, LA. O. Grétry. 1783.

CARD BASKET, THE. P. Shirley Brooks. Gallery of Illust., 1861.

CARD CASE, THE. 1 a. H. T. Craven. Liverpool, 1844.

CARD OF FANCY. C. Greene. 1601.

CARDENIO. See *The History of Cardenio.* Ac. at Court, 1613.

CARDINAL, THE. T. Jas. Shirley. Licensed 1641. Ac. at Blackfriars. Pr. 1652.

CARDINAL, THE. D. 4 a. Walter E. Grogan. Torquay T.R., September 8, 1894 (C.P.).

CARDINAL, THE. D. 4 a. Louis N. Parker. C. (C.P.), October 3, 1901; St. James's, August 31, 1903.

CARDINAL BEATON. T. Tennant. 1823.

CARDINAL WOLSEY. P. Ascr. to Henry Chettle. Ac. 1601. A second part ac. 1602. N.p.

CARDINAL'S DAUGHTER. Marylebone, September 27, 1852.

CARDS, THE PLAY OF. D. Ment. in Harington's Apoligie of Poetrie, 1591.

CARDS OF INVITATION. Mus. Sk. Corney Grain. St. Geo. H., June 25, 1888.

CAREFUL SERVANT AND THE CARELESS MASTER, THE. P. 1 a. C.G., October 29, 1816.

CARELESS HUSBAND, THE. C. Colley Cibber. D.L., December 7, 1704. Pr. 1705.

CARELESS LOVERS, THE. C. Edwd. Ravenscroft. Fourth ac. taken fr. Molière's *M. de Pourceaugnac.* Duke's T. and Pr. 1673.

CARELESS SHEPHERD, THE. Pastoral. Without author's name. N.d.; before 1812.

CARELESS SHEPHERDESS, THE. Pastora Tragi-C. Thos. Goffe. Ac. before King and Queen at Salisbury Court. Pr. 1656.

CARES OF LOVE; OR, A NIGHT'S ADVENTURE, THE. C. A. Chaves. L.I.F. Pr. 1705. See *The Lover's Cure.*

CARIB CHIEF, THE. T. 5 a. Twiss (nephew of Mrs. Siddons). D.L., May 13, 1819.

CARINA. C.O. 3 a. E. L. Blanchard and Cunningham Bridgman. F. on *Guerre Auverte; ou Ruse contra Ruse.* M. by Julia Wolff. Op. C., September 27, 1888.

CARL. O. 1 a. Words by Shedden Wilson. M. by Meyer Lutz. Gaiety, May 3, 1886.

CARL THE CLOCKMAKER. Mus. Melo-d. 4 a. Harry Starr. Swansea Star, July 14, 1894; Stratford R., April 15, 1895.

CARL'S FOLLY. Pastoral P. 4 a. Clay M. Greene. Hull T.R., March 26, 1891.

CARLINE. O. Thomas. Paris, 1840.

CARLINE, THE FEMALE BRIGAND. Rom. D. 2 a. Edward Stirling. Pav., January 16, 1837.

CARLO DI BORGOGNA. O. Pacini. Venice, 1834.

CARLO LEONI. Britannia, March 7, 1859.

CARLO MAGNO. O. J. Costanzi. Rome, 1729.

CARLO RE D'ALMAGNA. O. Scarlatti. 1659-1725.

CARLYON SAHIB. P. 4 a. Gilbert Murray. Southport O.H. (C.P.), April 6, 1899; Kennington P.O.W., June 19, 1899.

CARMELITE, THE. T. 5 a. Richd. Cumberland. D.L., December 2, 1784. Pr. 1784.

CARMEN. O. 4 a. By Georges Bizet. Lib. by Meilhac and Halévy. Paris, 1875. H.M.T., June 22, 1878, and adap. into English by Henry Hersee, H.M.T., February 5, 1879. Prod. in Fr. by M. Mayer's Co., H.M.T., November 8, 1886.

CARMEN. P. Dr. ver., by Henry Hamilton, of Prosper Merimée's novel. Gaiety, June 6, 1896.

CARMEN. P. 4 a. Adap. fr. Prosper Merimée's novel Bury St. Edmunds T.R., December 31, 1906.

CARMEN. See *Captivating Carmen.*

CARMEN; OR, SOLD FOR A SONG. Burl. R. Reece. Folly, January 25, 1879.

CARMEN UP TO DATA. Burl. 3 scenes. By Geo. R. Sims and Henry Pettitt. M. by Meyer Lutz. Liverpool Shakespeare, September 22, 1890; Gaiety, October 4, 1890.

CARMENCITA, LA. Playlet by Louis Cohen, founded on Prosper Merimée's novel. (C.P.) Coronet, December 21, 1900. M. by Herman Finck. Oxford M.H., May 13, 1907.

CARMITA. Rom. Mus. C.O. 2 a. Arthur Shirley and Walter Parke. M. Jesse Williams. Broughton Victoria, October 7, 1901; Kennington P.O.W., October 28, 1901.

CARMOSINA. P. 3 a. M. Davies Webster. Adap. and transl. fr. Alfred do Musset's *Carmosine.* Albert H. (West T.), June 13, 1902.

CARNAC SAHIB. P. 4 a. H. A. Jones. H.M.T., April 12, 1899.

CARNAVAL DE VENISE, LE. B.O. J. Campra. 1699.

CARNAVAL DE VENISE, LE. O. Thomas. Paris, 1857.

CARNAVAL DU PARNASSE, LE. O.B. 3 a. M. by Mondonville. September 23, 1749.

CARNEVAL DES REVUES. O. 1 a. M. by Offenbach. 1860.

CARNEVALE DI VENEZIA (PRECAUZIONI). O. Petrella. Genoa, 1862.

CARNIVAL, THE. C. Thos. Porter. T.R., 1664. Pr. 1664.

CARNIVAL; OR, HARLEQUIN BLUNDERER, THE, etc. Charlotte Clarke. L.I.F., 1735. N.p.

CARNIVAL OF NAPLES, THE. V. M. by J. Barnett. C.G., 1830.

CARNIVAL OF VENICE, THE. C.O. Richd. Tickell. D.L., December 13, 1781. Songs only pr. 1781.

CARNIVAL TIME. Mus. Sk. 1 a. Malcolm Watson. M. by Corney Grain. St. Geo. H., April 7, 1890.

CAROLAN. Moral D. 5 a. Howell Victor. Bootle Town H., Liverpool, January 13, 1892 (amat.).

CAROLINE AND HENRIETTA. C. 1 a. Pub. by S. French, Ltd.

CAROLINE'S PUPILS. F. 1 a. Russell Vaughan and Alban Attwood. Bayswater Bijou, December 19, 1896.

CAROONA. Society D. 4 a. Eileen Ray. Torquay T.R. (C.P.), January 20, 1899; St. Geo. H., April 11, 1899.

CARP, THE. Whimsicality. 1 a. Frank Desprez. M. by A. Cellier. Savoy, February 11, 1886.

CARPENTER OF ROUEN; OR, THE MASSACRE OF ST. BARTHOLOMEW. Rom. D. 4 a. J. S. Jones. D.L., March 3, 1853.

CARPET BAG, THE. Protean Ent. E. L. Blanchard. Egyptian H., November 29, 1869.

CARPIO. P. 3 a. John Finnamore. Bradford Prince's T., May 24, 1886.

CARRIER OF LONDON. Strand, January 1, 1855.

CARRON SIDE. O. 2 a. C.G., May 27, 1828.

CARROT AND PA-SNIP; OR, THE KING, THE TAILOR, AND THE MISCHIEVOUS. F. Extrav. Frank W. Green. North Woolwich Gdns., May 11, 1872.

CARROTS. P. 1 a. Alfred Sutro. Taken fr. Fr. of Jules Renard. Dublin T.R., October 18, 1900; Kennington P.O.W., November 21, 1900; Garrick, April 22, 1902.

CARROTTINA. O. Pub. by S. French, Ltd.

CARRY'S BREACH OF PROMISE; OR, THE TWO ADOLPHUSES. F. Maurice de Freece. Liverpool T.R., January 29, 1872.

CARRY'S TRIUMPH. D. Edinburgh O.H., October 14, 1872.

CARTE DE VISITE. F. 1 a. Montague Williams and F. C. Burnand. St. James's, December 26, 1862.

CARTE FORCEE, LA. C. 2 a. Crémieux and Pernetz. Gaiety, June 15, 1883.

CARTER OF LIVERPOOL, THE. D. Liverpool Adelphi, April 28, 1879.

CARTESMUNDA, THE FAIR NUN OF WINCHESTER. T. Brewer. 1655.

CARTHAGINIAN, THE. C. Transl. fr. Plautus. Richd. Warner. Pr. 1772.

CARTHUSIAN FRIAR; OR, THE AGE OF CHIVALRY, THE. T., by a female refugee. Pr. 1793. N. ac.

CARTHUSIANA. "Apropos." 1 a. B. C. Stephenson. Hay., June 26, 1899.

CARTOUCHE. W. Travers.

CARTOUCHE; OR, THE ROBBERS. C. Anonymous. Transl. fr. the Fr. L.I.F. Pr. 1722.

CARTOUCHE, THE FRENCH ROBBER. D. 3 a. Fr. the Fr. of D'Ennery and Dugué. Transl. and adap. by W. R. Waldron. L.I.F., February, 1723.

CARTOUCHE AND CO.; OR, THE TICKET-OF-(FRENCH)-LEAVE MAN. Op. Burl. 2 a. H Chance Newton. M. by Geo. Le Brunn. Birmingham T.R., August 22, 1892.

CARTWRIGHT. P. Wr. by Wm. Haughton. 1602.

CARYNTHIA. D. Prol. and 3 a. Edwd. Towers. Effingham, March 13, 1867.

CARYSWOLD, A STORY OF MODERN LIFE. D. 4 a. H. Herman and J. Mackay. Liverpool P.O.W., September 21, 1877.

CASA DISABITATA, LA. O. L. Rossi. Milan, 1834.

CASCO BAY. Nautical D. 2 a. By W. Bayle Bernard. Olympic, 1827.

CASE FOR EVICTION, A. Ca. 1 a. Theyre Smith. Liverpool Court, September 22, 1882; St. James's, December 20, 1883.

CASE FOR THE LADY, THE. C. 4 a. Florence Warden. Kingsway, March 7, 1909.

CASE IS ALTERED, THE. C. Ben Jonson. 1598. Blackfriars, 1609. Pr. 1609.

CASE OF ARSON, A. P. Howard Peacey. Fr. the Dutch of Herman Heyermans. Royalty, February 11, 1905.

CASE OF COINERS, THE. "Scenic Detective Dramette" in 4 sc. C. D. Carlile. Surrey, October 28, 1907.

CASE OF CONSCIENCE, A. Princess's, November 16, 1857.

CASE OF PICKLES, A. F. G. C. Baddeley. Royalty, May 6, 1871.

CASE OF REBELLIOUS SUSAN. C. 3 a. H. A. Jones. Criterion, October 3, 1894; Wyndham's, May 16, 1901.

CASE OF THE KIDNAPPED KING, THE. Sk. C. Douglas Carlile. Sadler's Wells, December 14, 1908.

CASH BOX, THE. P. 1 a. T. S. Dean Ballin. Dundee Her M., July 3, 1905.

CASH FOR CORONETS. C. 3 a. Ina Leon Cassilis and F. H. Morland. N.E. London Inst. Dalston Lane, June 14, 1894.

CASHEL BYRON'S PROFESSION. See *Admirable Bashville.*

CASINA (B.C. 254-184). C. Plautus. Latin. Fr. Greek C. by Diphilos. Transl. to blank verse by Thornton, Rich, Warner, and Colman. 1769-1774. See "Latin Plays."

CASINO GIRL, THE. M.F. 2 a. Harry B. Smith. M. by Ludwig Englander. Shaftesbury, July 11, 1900.

CASKET, THE. C. Transl. fr. Plautus by Richd. Warner. Pr. 1772. Plautus has called this comedy *Cistellaria.*

CASKET, THE. B.O. M. by Mozart. Adap. by R. Lacy. D.L., March 10, 1829.

CASKET OF JEWELS, THE. D. 3 a. D.L., February 28, 1853.

CASSANDRA, LA. Cant. Marcello. 1686-1739.

CASSANDRA; OR, THE VIRGIN PROPHETESS. O. Lagrange. Ac. at T.R. Pr. 1692.

CASSANDRA PSEUDOMANTIS. By (Fra Gil Arcadi) Aurisco Geresteo. Circa 1803.

CASSANDRE. 17th century T. Calprenède. Transl. by Sir C. Cotterell, 1652.

CASSILDA. Surrey, July 21, 1862.

CASSILIS ENGAGEMENT, THE. C. 4 a. St. John Hankin. Imperial. February 10, 1907.

CASSIOPE. Alexandra, August 20, 1866.

CASSIUS. T. Lagrange. 1677-1758.

CAST ADRIFT. D. 4 a. R. Palgrave and F. Gover. Bristol New T.R., February 27, 1882; Sadler's Wells, April 8, 1882.

CAST ASIDE; OR, LOVING NOT WISELY BUT TOO WELL. D. C. H. Hazlewood. Britannia, October 4, 1871.

CAST KING OF GRANADA, THE. 1 a. Hist. Extrav. by Col. Colomb, F.S.A. Pl. at Gibraltar by officers of the garrison.

CAST ON THE MERCY OF THE WORLD. D. C. H. Hazlewood. Britannia, October 13, 1862.

CAST ON THE WORLD. D. Elliot Galer. Leicester T.R., October 4, 1875, and April 18, 1881.

CASTARA; OR, CRUELTY WITHOUT LUST. P. Ent. on Stationers' Books, November 29, 1653. (?) N.p.

CASTAWAY, THE. D. C. H. Hazlewood. Britannia, March 12, 1866.

CASTAWAYS, THE. Ca. 1 a. Theyre Smith. St. James's, June 10, 1885.

CASTE. C. 3 a. T. W. Robertson. P.O.W. April 6, 1867; Garrick, February 5, 1894; Court, June 10, 1897; Globe, March 18, 1899; Hay., April 26, 1902; Cri., May 23, 1903; rev. Coronet, July 22, 1909.

"CASTE" PLAYS, THE. T. W. Robertson.
Caste. C. 3 a. P.O.W., April 6, 1867.
Birth. C. 3 a. Bristol T.R., May 10, 1870.
Breach of Promise. F.C. 2 a. Globe, April 10, 1869.
Dreams. D. 5 a. Liverpool Alexandra, February 22, 1869. Under the title of *My Lady Clare,* Gaiety, March 27, 1869.
Home. C. 3 a. Hay., January 14, 1869.
M.P. C. 4 a. P.O.W., April 23, 1870.
Nightingale. D. 5 a. Adelphi, January 15, 1870.
Ours. C. 3 a. Liverpool P.O.W., August 23, 1866; P.O.W., September 11, 1866.
Play. C. 4 a. P.O.W., February 15, 1868.
Progress. C. 3 a. Globe, September 18, 1869.
Row in the House. F. 1 a. Toole's, August 30, 1883.
School. C. 4 a. P.O.W., January 16, 1869.
Society. C. 3 a. Liverpool P.O.W., May 8. 1865; P.O.W., November 11, 1865.
War. D. 3 a. St. James's, January 16, 1871.

CASTELL OF PERSEVERANCE, THE. See "Miracle Plays." See *Castle, etc.*

CASTELLAN'S OATH, THE. Melo-d. C.G., June 4, 1824.

CASTELLO DEGLI INVALIDI, IL. O. Donizetti. Palermo, 1826.

CASTILIAN, THE. T. Talfourd. 1853.

CASTILIAN NOBLE AND THE CONTRABANDISTA, THE. Melo. John Oxenford. Adelphi, October, 1835.

CASTING THE BOOMERANG. Eccentric C. 4 a. Adap. by Augustin Daly fr. Franz von Schönthaus' *Schwabenstreich,* originally prod. in America. Toole's, July 19, 1884; Lyceum, June 10, 1890 (Daly's Co. season).

CASTING VOTE, THE. "Electioneering Squib in one Bang," by Walter Helmore. M. by Walter Slaughter. Prince's, October 7, 1885.

CASTLE BANG. O. Publ. by S. French, Ltd.

CASTLE BOTHEREM. A. Law and Hamilton Clarke. St. George's H.

CASTLE GRIM. O. R. Reece. Royalty, September 2, 1865.

CASTLE IN SPAIN. 1 a. Leopold Montague. Publ. by S. French, Ltd.

CASTLE OF ANDALUSIA, THE. C.O. 3 a. John O'Keefe. C.G., 1782; C.G., 1809. Pr. 1798. An alteration from *The Banditti; or, Love's Labyrinth.*

CASTLE OF ANDALUSIA. C.O. M. by Dr. Arnold. Lyceum, July 19, 1815.

CASTLE OF ANDALUSIA. C.O. Compressed into 2 a. Rev. Lyceum, July 28, 1825.

CASTLE OF AVOLA, THE. O. 3 a. Olivia Serres. Pr. 1805.

CASTLE OF AYMON; OR, THE FOUR BROTHERS, THE. O. M. by Balfe. Words by MM. Leuven and Brunswick. Paris Op. C., July 15, 1844; Princess's, November 20, 1844. See *Quatre Fils Aynon.*

CASTLE OF COMO, THE. Rom. O. 3 a. F. on Bulwer Lytton's P. of *The Lady of Lyons.* Lib. by Chas. Searle, with add. and M. by Geo. Cockle, M.B. Op. C., October 2, 1889.

CASTLE OF GLYNDOWER, THE. C. 5 a. D.L., March 2, 1818.

CASTLE OF MONTVAL, THE. T. Rev. T. S. Whalley. D.L., March 23, 1799. Pr. 1799.

CASTLE OF OTRANTO, THE. Burl. G. à Beckett. Hay., April 24, 1848.

CASTLE OF PALUZZI, THE. D. Raymond jun. C.G., May 27, 1818.

CASTLE OF PERSEVERANCE, THE. One of the oldest Morality Plays. Existing only in a MS.

CASTLE OF SORRENTO; OR, THE PRISONER OF ROCHELLE, THE. C.O. 2 a. Hy. Hartwell. Hay., July, 1799. Pr. 1799. F. on *Le Prisonnier, ou La Ressemblance.*

CASTLE OF UDOLPHO, THE. See *Dramatic Appellant.*

CASTLE OF WONDERS, THE. D. Rom Action by Johnson. M. by Tanza. D.L., March 8, 1819.

CASTLE SOMBRAS. Rom. D. 4 a. R. Greenhough Smith and Felix Mansfield. Bayswater Bijou, October 27, 1896 (C.P.).

CASTLE SPECTRE, THE. Rom. D. 5 a. M. G. Lewis. D.L., December 12, 1797; rev., D.L., November 28, 1833.

CASTLE WALSTENFURTH. Dr. Rom. 3 a. Pr. 1801.

CASTLES IN SPAIN. C.O. 2 a. Cosmo Hamilton. Lyrics, Eustace Ponsonby; M., Harry Fragson. Royalty. April 18, 1906.

CASTLES IN THE AIR. Ca. C. M. Rae. V., December 26, 1879.

CASTOR AND POLLUX. O. Bernard. 1770.

CASTOR ET POLLUX. O. Rameau. October 24, 1737.

CASTRUCCIO; OR, THE DEFORMED. D. Edgar Newbound. Britannia, July 24, 1878.

CASUAL ACQUAINTANCE, A. P. Prol. and 3 a. J. F. Cooke. Trafalgar Square, May 25, 1893.

CASUAL WARD. Marylebone, February 12, 1866.

CASUALS, THE. Sk. Fred Karno and Tom Tindall. M. by A. E. Wilson. Stoke Newington Pal., March 30, 1908.

CASWALLON; OR, THE BRITON CHIEF. T. Walker. D.L., January 12, 1829.

CAT AND DOG. F. J. R. Brown. First prod. at Liverpool Alexandra T., May 22, 1871.

CAT AND THE CHERUB, THE. Chinese P. Chester Bailey Fernald. Originally prod. in America. Lyric, October 30, 1897.

CAT LET OUT OF THE BAG; OR, A PLAY WITHOUT A PLOT, THE. F. Notes by Arthur O'Leary, Thomas Paine, etc. Pr. 1792.

CAT'S EYE, THE. Fl. C. 3 a. Partly f. on a German piece by Edward Rose. Oxford New T., May 22, 1893.

CATACLYSM. See *Noah's Flood.*

CATALANA. O. Branca. Florence, 1876.

CATALINA; OR, A LEGEND OF CASTILE. C.O. 3 a. H. Woodville. M. by Clement Lockane. Kilburn T.H., February 23, 1892 (amat.).

CATALINA TRIUMPHANS. C. in Latin of the 17th cent. M. preserved in Library of Trinity College, Cambridge.

CATALINE: HIS CONSPIRACY. T. Ben Jonson. For plot see *Sallust.* Pr. 1611. Ac. by King's servants same year.

CATALINE; OR, ROME PRESERVED. T. Transl. from Voltaire. Pr.

CATALINE. See *Catiline.*

CATALINE'S CONSPIRACY. P. Robert Wilson and Henry Chettle. Ac. 1598. N.p.

CATALINE'S CONSPIRACY. See *Cataline, His Conspiracy.*

CATARACT OF THE GANGES; OR, THE RAJAH'S DAUGHTER, THE. Rom. D. 2 a. W. T. Moncrieff. D.L., March 29, 1824.

CATARINA CORNARO. O. Donizetti. Naples, 1844.

CATASTROPHE, THE. P. 1 a. Hubert C Forraby. Prod. by the Curtain Raisers. Rehearsal, March 11, 1909; Lyceum, September 27, 1909.

CATCH A WEAZEL. F. 1 a. J. M. Morton. Strand, March 17, 1862.

CATCH HIM WHO CAN. F. 2 a. Theodore Hook. M. by his father. Hay., June, 1806.

CATCH OF THE SEASON, THE. M.P. 2 a. S. Hicks and C. Hamilton. Vaudeville, September 9, 1904.

CATCHING A MERMAID. Extrav. 1 a. J. Stirling Coyne. Olympic, October 20, 1855.

CATCHING A WEASEL. Strand, March 17, 1862.

CATCHING AN HEIRESS. F. 1 a. Chas. Selby. Queen's, July 15, 1835.

CATCHING THE IDEA. Ca. Henry W. Hatchman and Herbert C. Cullum. Empire, Blackpool, June 2, 1899.

CATERAN'S SON. D. 2 a. C. Barnett. Pub. by S. French, Ltd.

CATHERINE. D. 1 a. Cecil Fitzroy. Novelty, March 22, 1897.

CATHERINE AND PETRUCHIO. C. 3 a. David Garrick. An alt. of Shakespeare's *Taming of the Shrew*. Pr. 1756. D.L., 1756; Edinburgh, 1781; D.L., June 12, 1821.

CATHERINE DOUGLAS. T. Helps. 1843.

CATHERINE GRAY. O. 3 a. Balfe. D.L., May 27, 1837; Lyceum, 1837.

CATHERINE HOWARD. Rom. D. 3 a. Fr. P. of that title by Dumas. Adap. by W. D. Suter. First perf. at T. Porte St. Martin, Paris, June 2, 1834.

CATHERINE HOWARD; OR, THE TOMB, THE THRONE, AND THE SCAFFOLD. Adap. from the French of Dumas by Mrs. Bandmann-Palmer. Weymouth T.R., January 2, 1892.

CATHERINE HOWARD; OR, UNDER A CRIMSON CROWN. P. 4 a. Kenyon Lyle. Glasgow Queen's, August 15, 1898.

CATHERINE OF CLEVES. D. 3 a. Pub. by S. French, Ltd.

CATHERINE OF HEILBRONN. C. Kleist. 1776-1811.

CATHERINE OF RUSSIA; OR, THE CHILD OF THE STORM. P. Victoria, September, 1850.

CATILINE. T. Geo. Croly. Pr. 1822.

CATILINE. See *Catiline's Conspiracy*.

CATILINE'S CONSPIRACIES. By Stephen Gosson. Circa 1579.

CATO. T. 5 a. Joseph Addison. D.L., March 14, 1712. Pr. C.G., 1824

CATO. T. J. Ozell. L.I.F. Pr. 1716. A transl. from a Fr. P. of same name by Deschamps.

CATO. T. Pr. 1764. This is Addison's *Cato* without the love scenes.

CATO MAJOR. Pr. 1725. This is Cicero 'de Senectute versified.

CATO OF UTICA. T. Transl. fr. Deschamps by John Ozell. Pr. 1716. L.I.F., 1716.

CATON D'UTIQUE. O. Deschamps. M. by Vinci. 1715.

CATONE. O. Bach. Milan, 1758.

CATONE IN UTICA. T. Metastasio. M. by Leo.

CATSPAW, THE. C. Douglas Jerrold. Hay., May 9, 1850.

CATSPAW, THE. D. Fred Jarman. Durham R Albany T., November 3, 1885.

CATSPAW, THE. P. 3 a. John Tresahar. Terry's, July 24, 1889.

CATSPAW, THE. P. 1 a. Sidney Bowkett. Liverpool, April 10, 1893.

CATTARINA. C.O. 2 a. Robt. Reece. M. by Fredk. Clay. Manchester Prince's, August 17, 1874: Charing Cross, May 15, 1875.

CATTLE KING, THE. American D. 5 a. W. H. Young. Bootle Muncaster T., January 2, 1896.

CAUGHT. Ca. 1 a. Thos. Sennett. Sunderland T.R., September 21, 1883.

CAUGHT. C.D. 3 a. Adap. by Stanislaus Calhaem. Comedy, June 29, 1886.

CAUGHT. Ca. Mrs. George Corbett. St. Albans P.H., Acton Green, October 25, 1900.

CAUGHT. Sk. Bristol Pal., April 15, 1909.

CAUGHT AND CAGED. C. E. J. Connell. Southport Cambridge H., February 26, 1877.

CAUGHT AND CAGED. Oa. 1 a. Palgrave Simpson. Pub. by S. French, Ltd.

CAUGHT AT LAST. D. Nelson Lee. City of London, Easter, 1864.

CAUGHT AT LAST. Ca. Adap. by "A. G. C." (Lady Cadogan) fr. *La Souris*, by Armand des Roseaux. The French original prod. Cercle Artistique et Littéraire, Paris, January, 1880, and played in French in London at Comedy, June 24, 1886; Avenue, October 23, 1889.

CAUGHT AT LAST; OR, A CHANGE IN THE WIND. Ca. St. James's, December 20, 1873.

CAUGHT BY THE CUFF. F. 1a. Frederic Hay. Victoria, September 30, 1865.

CAUGHT BY THE EARS. Extrav. 1 a. Chas. Selby. Strand, May 30, 1859.

CAUGHT COURTING. F. Frank Russell. Richmond, July 12, 1880.

CAUGHT IN A LINE; OR, THE UNRIVALLED BLONDIN. 1 sc. Chas. Bolton. Strand, March 3, 1862.

CAUGHT IN A TRAP. C. 2 a. Hay., November 25, 1843.

CAUGHT IN A TRAP. C. 3 a. Blank verse. H. Holl. Princess's, February 8, 1860.

CAUGHT IN HIS OWN TRAP. Ca. 1 a. Mrs. Alfred Phillips. Olympic, October 13, 1851.

CAUGHT IN THE TOILS. J. Brougham. Adap. fr. Miss Braddon's novel, "Only a Clod." St. James's, October 14, 1865.

CAUGHT ON A LINE. Strand, March 3, 1862.

CAUGHT OUT. Ca. Adap. by Florence Bright fr. Pfahl's Ca. *Die Kunstreiterin*. St. Geo. H., July 17, 1888.

CAUGHT OUT. C. 2 a. Edgar H. S. Baines-Austin. Margate Grand, February 14, 1902.

CAULD LAD O' HYLTON, THE. D. Sunderland Lyceum, September 10, 1877.

CAULDRON, THE. Pant. D.L., 1785.

CAUSE, THE. D. Portsmouth T.R., November 29, 1876.

CAUSE AND EFFECT. Surrey, February 20, 1860.

CAVALEARYER COSTERCANA; OR, NEVER INTRODUCE YOUR DONAH TO A PAL. Parody. B. Landeck and E. Turner. Edmonton T.R., June 14, 1893.

CAVALIER, THE. Tragic D. C. Whitehead. Hay., September 15, 1836.

CAVALIER, THE. P. 1 a. J. H. M'Carthy. Belfast R., April 19, 1894.

CAVALIERS AND ROUNDHEADS. D.L., October 13, 1835.

CAVALLERIA RUSTICANA. O. 1 a. Pietro Mascagni. Fd. on one of Verga's Sicilian Tales. Shaftesbury, October 19, 1891; C.G., May 16, 1892. Pl. in Eng. at the Grand, April 9, 1894.

CAVALLERIA RUSTICANA. D. 1 a. Giovanni Verga. Lyric, May 30, 1893; Savoy, October 15, 1904.

CAVALLERIA RUSTICANA. New Vers. by Domenico Monleone. Orig. prod. in Vienna, February, 1907. Coronet, May 10, 1909.

CAVALLERIA RUSTICANA. Perf. by the Sicilian Players. Shaftesbury, February 7, 1908.

CAVALLERIA RUSTICANA. Sk. Richmond Hipp., August 31, 1908.

CAVALLERIA RUSTICANA. See *Rustic Chivalry, Cavalearyer*, etc.

CAVE OF HARMONY, THE. Sketch. Brandon Thomas. Fr. Thackeray. Empire, Leicester Sq., mat., January 30, 1900.

CAVE OF IDRA, THE. T. Henry Jones. Left unfinished. See *The Heroine of the Cave.*

CAVE OF ILLUSION. P. 4 a. Alfred Sutro. Pub. by S. French, Ltd.

CAVE OF NEPTUNE, THE. Dr. Poem. Holford. Pr. 1799.

CAVE OF TROPHONIUS, THE. F.O. Prince Hoare. M. by Storace. D.L., 1791.

CAVERNE, LA. O. 3 a. Méhul. December 4, 1795.

CAYNE. See "Miracle Plays."

CE QUI PLAIT AUX FEMMES. C. Ponsard. 1860.

CEAD MILLE FAILTHE. Irish D. Prol. and 3 a. Mortimer Murdoch. East London, December 22, 1877.

CECCHINA, LA. O. Piccini. Rome, 1760.

CECILIA; OR, THE SACRIFICE OF FRIENDSHIP. C. Transl. from Mdme. de. Genlis's Theatre of Education. Pr. 1781.

CECILIA AND CLORINDA; OR, LOVE IN ARMS. Tragi-C. Thos. Killigrew. Circa 1660.

CELADON AND FLORIMEL; OR, THE HAPPY COUNTERPLOT. C. John Philip Kemble. D.L., 1796. An alt. fr. Cibber's *Comical Lovers.*

CELEBRATED CASE, A. Piece. 1 a. Written for a dr. cosaque by Alfred Arthur. St Geo. H., November 10, 1888.

CELEBRATED CASE, A. See *Proof.*

CELESTIA; OR, THE WORLD IN THE MOON. D. Adap. fr. Fr. by Dalrymple. Adelphi, February, 1835.

CELESTIAL INSTITUTE, THE. Burl. 2 a. E. Howley Sim. M. by Leonard Butler. St. Martin's T.H., May 15, 1896 (amat.).

CELESTIAL INSTITUTE, THE. See *The Institute Abroad.*

CELESTIALS; OR, THE FLOWERY LAND, THE. Anglo-Chinese M.P. Chas. Harrie Abbott, add. lyrics by John W. Houghton. M. by F. Osmond Carr. Blackpool O.H., August 1, 1898.

CELESTINA. See *Spanish Bawd.*

CELESTINA; OR, THE SPANISH BAWD. T.C. Written orig. in Spanish, in 21 a., by Don Mateo Aleman, 1708. Transl. circa 1692. New transl. by J. Savage and reduced to 5 a.

CELESTINA, THE TRAGIC COMEDYE OF. Entd. Stationers' Co., October 5, 1598, by Wm. Aspley.

CELIA, THE GIPSY GIRL. O. 3 a. Elliot Galer. M. by J. E. Mallandine. Leicester R.O.H., October 20, 1879.

CELLINI. O. Berlioz. Paris, 1838.

CENCI, THE. P. 5 a. Percy Bysshe Shelley. 1819. Grand, May 7, 1886. (Private perf. by Shelley Society.)

CENDRILLON. O. Nicolas Isouard. 1810.

CENDRILLON. O. 4 a. Massenet. Paris Opera Comique, May, 1899.

CENERENTOLA, LA. O. Rossini. Lib. by Feretti. Rome, 1817; King's T., January 8, 1820; and in Paris, June 8, 1822.

CENIA; OR, THE SUPPOS'D DAUGHTER. T. Pr. 1752. A literal prose transl., by J. M.D., of *Cenie*, by Mdme. Graffigny, which was afterwards brought on the Eng. stage by Dr. Francis under title of *Eugenia.*

CENOFALLES. THE. P. Ac. at Court. 1567-7.

CENSURE OF THE JUDGES. This is one of the titles of Braithwaite's T.C. of *Mercurius Britannicus; or, The English Intelligence.* 1641.

CENSUS, THE. F. 1 a. A. Halliday and W. Brough. Adelphi, April 15, 1861.

CENT. PER CENT.; OR, THE MASQUERADE. F. By "X. X." C.G., May 29, 1823.

CENT VIERGES, LES. Op. bo. 3 a. John Grantham. M. by Lecocq. Brussels, 1872; Brighton T.R., October 17, 1874.

CENTRAL FIGURE, THE. C. 2 a. H. H. Lloyd. Wolverhampton Drill H., October 27, 1897 (amat.).

CEPHALUS AND PROCRIS. Dr. masque, with panto. int. Harlequin Grand Volgi. D.L. Pr. 1733.

CEPHISA; OR, A STEP OVER THE GIRDLE. C.O. 3 a. Joseph Moser. Wr. circa 1804. N.p. N. ac.

CERAMIQUE, LA. Duol. 1 a. M. E. d'Hervilly. Royalty, March 29, 1888.

CERISE AND CO. F.C. 3 a. Mrs. Musgrave. P.O.W., April 17, 1890.

CERT, THE. Sk. Poplar Queen's, November 2, 1908.

CESARE IN EGITTO. O. Pacini. Rome, 1822.

CESTUS, THE. Seren. Ch. Dibdin. Royal Circus. Pr. 1783.

CETEWAYO IN SOUTH SHIELDS. F. S. Shields T.R., August 28, 1882.

CHABOT (PHILIP), ADMIRAL OF FRANCE. T. Geo. Chapman and Jas. Shirley. Story taken fr. Fr. historian's account reign of Francis I. Lic. 1635. D.L., 1639.

CHACUN SA VIE. C. 3 a. Guiches and Ghensi. Orig. prod. at Française Comédie, September 10, 1907. Royalty, November 4, 1907.

CHAIN GANG; OR, THE CONVICT'S VENGEANCE, THE. D. F. C. Harcourt, S. Shields Siddall's T. and Cirque, July 8, 1881. See *Enlisted.*

CHAIN OF EVENTS, A. D. 8 a. Slingsby Lawrence and Chas. Mathews. Lyceum, April 12, 1852.

CHAIN OF GOLD. P. 3 a. R. B. Peake Publ. by J. Dicks.

CHAIN OF GUILT; OR, THE INN ON THE HEATH, THE. Rom. D. 2 a. Thos. Prochis Taylor. Sadler's Wells, 1836.

CHAINE, UNE. C. Scribe. 1841.

CHAINED TO THE OAR. D. 4 a. H. J Byron, Liverpool P.O.W., June 16, 1873; Gaiety May 31, 1883.

CHAINS. P. 4 a. Eliz. Baker. (Prod. by the Play Actors.) Court, April 18, 1909.

CHAINS OF THE HEART; OR, THE SLAVE BY CHOICE. C.O. 3 a. Prince Hoare. M. by Mazzinghi and Reeve. C.G. Pr. 1802.

CHALET, LE. O. 1 a. Scribe. M. by A. Adam. Paris Op. C., December 25, 1834; Olympic, 1837; D.L., July 16, 1845: Globe, October 7, 1871; before the Queen at Windsor, July 4, 1899; C.G., July 8, 1899.

CHALICE, THE. T. Epis. Harry and Edward Paulton. Daly's, May 25, 1908 (mat.).

CHALK AND CHEESE. Ca. 1 a. Ellie Norwood. Esher New H., January 6, 1888; Vaudeville, November 10, 1899.

CHALK MARK. C. 3 a. Hawley Francks and Algernon Tassin. April 26, 1899.

CHALLENGE, THE. H. M. Milner. Adap. fr. *Le Pré aux Cleres.* M. by T. Cooke. C.G., April 1, 1834.

CHALLENGE AT TILT AT A MARRIAGE, A. Masque. Ben Jonson. 1613. Folio, 1640.

CHALLENGE FOR BEAUTY, A. T.C. Thos. Heywood. Blackfriars and the Globe, 1636. Pr. 1636.

CHAMBER OF HORRORS, THE. F. A. Wood. Holborn, April 18, 1870.

CHAMBERMAID, THE. B.O. 1 a. Edward Phillips. D.L., 1730. Ptd. Taken from *The Village Opera* by C. Johnson.

CHAMELEON; OR, THE ART OF PLEASING, THE. Ca. Wm. Brough. D.L., April 8, 1853.

CHAMILLAC. C. 5 a. Octave Feuillet. Royalty, March 5, 1888; June 10, 1891.

CHAMPAGNE. C. 1 a. Adap. fr. the Fr. by Fredk E. Weatherley and Alfred W. M. Weatherley.

CHAMPAGNE, A QUESTION OF PHIZ. Burl. H. B. Farnie and R. Reece. Strand, September 29, 1877.

CHAMPIGNOL MALGRE LUI. F.C. 3 a. MM. G. Feydean and M. Desyallières. (Prod. at Paris, November 5, 1892.) Adap. entitled *The Other Fellow*, by F. Horner, prod. at Court, September 3, 1893; rev. Royalty, October 14, 1907.

CHANCE. D. 3 a. Chas. Osborne. Belfast T.R., October 4, 1869.

CHANCE, THE. P. 1 a. Frank Vernon. Terry's, December 30, 1907.

CHANCE ACQUAINTANCE, A. Ca. W. H Denny. Richmond T.R., June 28, 1894.

CHANCE DU MARI, LA. 1 a. G. A. de Carllaret and Robert le Gelipaux. Royalty, July 19, 1906.

CHANCE INTERVIEW, A. Duol. 1 a. Mrs. Hughes Bell. St. Geo. H., June 12, 1889.

CHANCE MEDLEY. P. Wilson, Mundy, Drayton, and Dekker. Ac. 1598. N.p.

CHANCE OF WAR; OR, THE VILLAIN RECLAIMED, THE. M.D. 2 a. Archibald Maclaren. Pr. 1801. N. ac.

CHANCE, THE DIPLOMAT. Ep. 1 a. Ada and D. James. West Hartlepool T.H., December 1, 1903.

CHANCE, THE IDIOT. D. Edwin Reynolds. Longton T.R., December 5, 1872.

CHANCE, THE IDOL. P. 4 a. H. A. Jones. Wyndham's, September 9, 1902

CHANCERY SUIT, THE. C. 5 a. R. B. Peake. Publ. by J. Dicks.

CHANCES, THE. C. Fletcher (Beaumont died 1616). Wr. before August, 1625. Pr. Folio 1647. Plot from novel of Cervantes, "The Lady Cornelia." Rev., with alters., by the D. of Buckingham, at Dorset Gardens, 1682. Rev., with alters., by Garrick, at D.L. and pr. 1773. See *The Landlady* and *Don John.*

CHAND D'HABITS. M.P. without words. 1 a and 3 sc. Catulle Mendès. M. by Jules Bouval. H.M.T., May 8, 1897.

CHANDOS; OR, THE JESTER WHO TURNED TRAITOR. D. 5 a. Adap. fr. Ouida's *Chandos* by Hartbury Brooklyn. Adelphi, September 30, 1882.

CHANG-CHING-FOW, CREAM OF TARTAR; OR, THE PRINCE, THE PRINCESS, AND THE MANDARIN. Burl. extrav. Wm. Martin. Luton, April 11, 1864.

CHANGE. C. 2 a. F. H. Pride and F. Grove Palmer. Cavendish Rooms, December 30, 1870.

CHANGE ALLEY. C. 5 a. Louis Parker and Murray Carson. Garrick, April 25, 1899.

CHANGE FOR A SOVEREIGN. F. Horace Wigan. Strand, March 14, 1861.

CHANGE FOR LOVE. Fairy P. 4 a. Pub. by S. French, Ltd.

CHANGE OF AIR. Oa. Edgar Manning and M. Von Leson. Cheltenham Assembly R., October 24, 1878.

CHANGE OF COLOUR, A. Costume ca. 3 a. Mrs. Geo Corbett. Chiswick T.H., May 9, 1901 (amat.).

CHANGE OF CROWNS, THE. P. Edward Howard. Ent. Stationers' Co. N.p. T.R., April, 1667.

CHANGE OF FORTUNE IS THE LOT OF LIFE. C.D. Mdlle. de Latour. Bath T.R., November 10, 1874.

CHANGE OF NAME. F. Arthur Moore. Sadler's Wells, September 14, 1867.

CHANGE OF NAME. 1 a. W. Hancock.

CHANGE OF SYSTEM, A. C. 1 a. Howard Paul. St. James's, April 9, 1860.

CHANGE PARTNERS. F. M. by Horn. D.L., March 10, 1825.

CHANGE PARTNERS. Ca. 1 a. J. W. Morton and T. J. Williams.

CHANGE UPON CHANGE; OR, THE YORKSHIRE LOVER. F. By a gentleman of Leeds. Leeds, 1805.

CHANGED HEART, THE. F. on Fr. D., *Le Comtesse de Noailles.* Surrey, January 23, 1860.

CHANGELING, THE. T. W. Rowley and Thos. Middleton. Plot chiefly fr. story of *Alsemero and Beatrice Yoanna*, in Reynolds's *God's Revenge against Murder.* D.L. and Salisbury Court, 1653. Pt. same year.

CHANGELING, THE. C. Ascribed to Mathew Heywood. N. ac.

CHANGELING, THE. F. 1 a. W. W. Jacobs and H. C. Sargeant. Wyndham's, March 18, 1908.

CHANGEMENT D'UNIFORME. D. Dennery. 1836.

CHANGES. D. 3 a. H. Procter. St. Geo. H., October 12, 1876.

CHANGES. C. 3 a. John Aylmer. Toole's, April 25, 1890.

CHANGES; OR, LOVE IN A MAZE, THE. C. Jas. Shirley. Salisbury Court, 1632. Pr. same year. Partly made use of by Dryden in *Secret Love.*

CHANGES AND CHANCES. D. 2 a. Avenue, March 2, 1891.

CHANSON DE FORTUNIO. Op. bo. Offenbach, 1861.

CHANTEUSE VOITEE, LA. O. Massé. Paris, 1850.

CHAOS IS COME AGAIN. J. M. Morton. F. 1 a. C.G., November, 1838.

CHAPEAU DE L'HORLOGER, LE. See *Betty Martin.*

CHAPEAU DE ST. CATHERINE, LE. See *A Patron Saint.*

CHAPERON, THE. F.C. 3 a. Harry Brummel. Bury T.R., August 3, 1899 (C.P.).

CHAPERON, THE. C. 3 a. A. M. Heathcote. Bayswater Bijou, December 18, 1905 (amat.).

CHAPERON ROUGE, LE. O. Boieldieu. 1818.

CHAPERONE, THE. P. 1 a. Wallett Waller and Chas. Troode. Vaudeville, February 8, 1909 (C.P.).

CHAPERONED. Ca. Miss Eva Harrison. Cheltenham Assembly R., June 3, 1887.

CHAPERONES. L.O. 1 a. J. A. McLaren. Swansea St. Gabriel's H., December 28, 1903.

CHAPERONS, THE. M.C. 3 a. Fredk. Rauken. M. by Isidore Witmark. St. Geo. H., April 23, 1901 (C.P.).

CHAPLET, THE. O. Caldara. 1678-1763.

CHAPLET, THE. M. Ent. 2 Parts. Moses Mendez. M. by Boyce. D.L. Pr. 1749.

CHAPTER OF ACCIDENTS, A. F. 1 a. John Thos. Douglass. Standard, September 26, 1870.

CHAPTER OF ACCIDENTS, THE. C. Miss Lee. Hay., August 5, 1780. Pr. 1780. D.L., April 2, 1816. Built on Diderot's *Père de Famille.*

CHARBONNIERS, LES. C. 1 a. M. Gille. M. by M. Costé. Ac. in French. Gaiety, June 0, 1000.

CHARCOAL BURNER; OR, THE DROPPING WELL OF KNARESBOROUGH, THE. D. 2 a. Geo. Almar. Surrey, December 26, 1832.

CHARIOTEERS; OR, A ROMAN HOLIDAY, THE. D. and M. Spect. Prod. by M. Moore. Lyrics by R. Carse. M. by W. Slaughter. London Coliseum, November 27, 1907.

CHARITABLE ASSOCIATION, THE. C. 2 a. Hy. Brooke. Pr. 1778. N. ac.

CHARITABLE BEQUEST, THE. Ca. 2 a. Newnham Davies.

CHARITABLE MAN, THE. F. Henry Barry. Novelty, February 15, 1887.

CHARITY. P. C. H. Hazlewood. F. on Victor Hugo's *Les Misérables.* Sadler's Wells, November 7, 1862.

CHARITY. P. 4 a. W. S. Gilbert. Hay., January 3, 1874.

CHARITY BEGINS AT HOME. Oa. B. C. Stephenson. M. by Alfred Cellier. Gall. of Illust., February 7, 1872; Gaiety, February 7, 1877; St. George's Hall, June 22, 1892; Shaftesbury, September 12, 1901; St. George's H., March 29, 1902.

CHARITY BOY, THE. M.E. Jas. C. Cross. D.L., 1796. N.p.

CHARITY THAT BEGAN AT HOME, THE. C. 4 a. St. John Hankin. Court, October 23, 1906.

CHARITY TRIUMPHANT; OR, THE VIRGIN-SHOW. E. Gayton. October 29, 1655.

CHARITY'S CLOAK. C. 1 a. Sylvanus Dauncey. Glasgow Royalty, February 25, 1891.

CHARITY'S LOVE. P. John Wilkins. City of London, March, 1854.

CHARLATAN, THE. C. 3 a. Adap. from the German by Mrs. John Aylmer. Torquay, Torre Parish R., Torquay, February 5, 1889.

CHARLATAN, THE. P. 4 a. Robert Buchanan. Hay., January 18, 1894.

CHARLATANISME, LE. Little piece. Scribe. 1822.

CHARLEMAGNE. Chivalric Ent. 2 a. M. of action by Eliason, Vocal M. by Stansbury. D.L., October 22, 1838.

CHARLEMAGNE; OR, THE MOORS OF SPAIN. D. Ducrow. D.L., June 22, 1841.

CHARLES, HIS FRIEND. Sk. Palace, August 5, 1907.

CHARLES I. Hist. T. W. Havard. Pr. 1737. L.I.F.

CHARLES I. T. E. Cobham Brewer. 1828.

CHARLES I. P. Gurney. 1853. See *Cromwell.*

CHARLES I. D. Miss Mitford. Victoria, July 2, 1834. Doncaster T.R., April 21, 1873.

CHARLES I. P. 4 a. W. G. Wills. Lyceum, September 28, 1872. Rev. June 24, 1901. Rev. Shaftesbury, February 15, 1909.

CHARLES I.; OR, THE KING AND THE PROTECTOR. P. C. Flockton. Bath T.R., August 4, 1879.

CHARLES I., KING OF ENGLAND. T. Pr. 1649.

CHARLES I. AND II. T. G. Du Maurier and S. O. N. Frere. Court, October 21, 1901.

CHARLES II. T. Miss Mitford. Pro. by T. J. Serle. Victoria, 1834.

CHARLES II. O. Words adap. by Desmond Ryan. M. by Macfarren. Prod. at Princess's T., October 27, 1849.

CHARLES II.; OR, SOMETHING LIKE HISTORY. Burl. Gilbert à Beckett. Court, November 25, 1872.

CHARLES II.; OR, THE MERRY MONARCH. C. 2 a. Adap. fr. *La Jeunesse de Henri V.* by Howard Payne. C.G., May 27, 1824.

CHARLES VI. O. Halévy. Paris, 1843. Lib. by Delavigne.

CHARLES VII. D. Dumas, 1831.

CHARLES VIII. OF FRANCE; OR, THE INVASION OF NAPLES BY THE FRENCH. Hist. P. J. Crowne. Duke of York's, 1672. Pr. 1672.

CHARLES IX. D. Chénier. 1789.

CHARLES XII.; OR, THE SIEGE OF STRALSUND. His. D. 2 a. J. R. Planché D.L., December 11, 1828.

CHARLES LE TEMERAIRE. D. Guilbert de Pixérécourt. 1814.

CHARLES O'MALLEY. D. 3 a. Macarthy. Olympic, April 12, 1841.

CHARLES O'MALLEY; OR, LOVE, FUN, AND FIGHTING. D. Edmund Falconer. Liverpool Amphitheatre, April 22, 1871.

CHARLES THE BOLD; OR, THE SIEGE OF NANTZ. Hist. Melo.-d. 3 a. Arnold, fr. the French. D.L., June 15, 1815.

CHARLEY STUART. Ca. J. Belverstone. South Shields T.R., August 23, 1875.

CHARLEY'S AUNT. F.C. 3 a. Brandon Thomas. Bury St. Edmunds, February 29, 1892; Royalty, December 21, 1892; trans. to Globe, January 30, 1893; Great Queen Street T., July 10, 1901; Royalty, December 26, 1907.

CHARLEY'S UNCLE. F. 1 a. Louis Honig. Richmond R., April 25, 1894 (C.P.); Royal Standard, April 1, 1907.

CHARLIE. M.Ca. 1 a. Herbert Harraden. Terry's, April 30, 1891.

CHARLIE, THE SPORT. P. 1 a. M. Morton. Fr. the Fr. of Tristan Bernard. Hay., July 25, 1907.

CHARLOT. French V. See *Frolique.*

CHARLOTTE; OR, ONE THOUSAND SEVEN HUNDRED AND SEVENTY-THREE. P. Mrs. Cullum. Pr. 1775.

CHARLOTTE CORDAY. T. Ponsard, 1850.

CHARLOTTE CORDAY. D. 3 a. Bernard. Pub. by J. Dicks.

CHARLOTTE CORDAY. D. J. Mortimer. Dublin T.R., December 14, 1876.

CHARLOTTE CORDAY. D. 4 a. Kyrle Bellew. Calcutta, January, 1894; San Francisco, July, 1894; Islington Grand, December 13, 1897; Adelphi, January 21, 1898.

CHARLOTTE MARIA. F.C. 3 a. Frank Macrae and Mrs. Newton Phillips. Ladbroke H., May 24, 1892.

CHARLOTTE ON BIGAMY. P. 1 a. Edward A. Parry. Kingsway, May 19, 1908.

CHARM, THE. Ca. Walter Besant and W. H. Pollock. St. George's H., July 22, 1884.

CHARM OF IAMBLICHUS, THE. Archaic Melo-mystery. J. Levy. Liverpool Institute, December 18, 1896.

CHARMED LIFE, A. D. Joel Whittaker. Barrow T.R., May 10, 1875.

CHARMER, THE. P. of modern life. 3 a. Arthur Rickett. Scarborough Londesborough T., November 28, 1902; King's Hall, October 13, 1907.

CHARMIAN AND BADOURA. Burl. Chs. Horsman. Edinburgh T.R., May 19, 1873.

CHARMING COTTAGE, THE. Gallery of Illustration. April 6, 1863.

CHARMING MRS. GAYTHORNE. C. 3 a. Chas. Smith Cheltham. Criterion, April 19, 1894.

CHARMING PAIR, A. C. 1 a. Thos. J. Williams. Princess's, May 27, 1863.

CHARMING POLLY, THE. D. 2 a. J. T. Haines. Surrey, June 29, 1838.

CHARMING WIDOW. 1 a. J. Oxenford. Lyceum, March 6, 1854.

CHARMING WOMAN, THE. C. 3 a. Horace Wigan. Olympic, June 20, 1861.

CHARMS. C.D. 4 a. Sir Charles L. Young, Bart. Queen's, July 26, 1871.

CHARMYON. P. 3 a. Sir Charles Young.

CHARTREUSE C.O. R. Ganthony and J. W. Ivimey. Richmond R., July 7, 1899 (C.P.).

CHASSE A ST. GERMAIN, UNE. D. Deslaudes. 1860.

CHASTE MAID OF CHEAPSIDE, THE. C. Thos. Middleton. Ac. at the Swan by Lady Elizabeth's servants, 1620. Pr. 1630.

CHASTE SALUTE, THE. Olympic, October, 1838.

CHASTE SUZANNE, LA. O. 4 a. M. by F. L. H. Monro. December 27, 1840.

CHASTE SUSANNE, LA. See *Madcap.*

CHASTE WOMAN AGAINST HER WILL, THE. C. 1661. Possibly by Stephen Jones. Suppressed.

CHASTELARD. T. Swinburne. 1865.

CHATEAU A TOTO, LE. O. 3 a. Offenbach. 1868.

CHATELET, MDE. DU. V. Ancelot. About 1834.

CHATTE, LA. Op. Bo. 1 a. Offenbach. 1858. First perf. in England, D.L., June 23, 1836.

CHATTERBOX, THE. C. W. B. Jerrold. 1857.

CHATTERBOXES. C. 1 a. Pub. by S. French, Ltd.

CHATTERTON. O. Leoncavallo.

CHATTERTON. P. 1 a. Henry Arthur Jones and Henry Herman. Princess's, May 22, 1884.

CHATTERTON. T. 1 a. Adap. fr. the French of Alfred de Vigny by Joseph Forster. Ladbroke H., January 23, 1888.

CHATTERTON. Hist. Ep. Maurice H. Hoffman. Washington Music H., April 15, 1901.

CHATTERTON. P. 4 a. Professor M. A. Gerothwohl, and Prol. by Professor Edward Dowden. (Prod. by the Dramatic Productions Club and the Revival Co.) Court, April 25, 1909.

CHATTERTON. See *Shattered 'Un.*

CHAUBERT; OR, THE MISANTHROPE. T.D. Ascr. to T. C. Villiers. Pr., 1789.

CHAUCER'S MELIBEE. C. Ralph Radcliff. N.p.

CHAUFFEUR, THE. Episode. Adap. fr. the Fr. of Max Maurey by Gaston Mayer. Playhouse, June 3, 1909.

CHEAP EXCURSION, A. F. 1 a. Edwd. Stirling. Strand, May 19, 1851.

CHEAP JACK; OR, LOVED AND DECEIVED. D. 3 a. Edwd. Towers. Pavilion, April 6, 1874.

CHEAP LIVING. C. Frederic Reynolds. D.L., 1797. Pr. 1797.

CHEAPSIDE; OR, ALL IN THE CITY. C. Hay., 1783. N.p.

CHEAT, THE. C. Transl. fr. Plautus by R. Warner. Pr. 1772. Plautus calls this comedy *Pseudolus.*

CHEAT, THE. D. 4 a. Edward Ferris and B. P. Matthews. Wolverhampton Grand, September 21, 1908; Peckham Crown, September 28, 1908.

CHEAT; OR, THE TAVERN BILKERS, THE. Italian night scene. L.I.F., 1720. C.G., 1733.

CHEATER CHEATED, THE. Int. Pr. N.p Attributed to Robert Cox.

CHEATS, THE. C. John Wilson. Wr. 1662. Pr. 1663. Ac. 1671.

CHEATS OF SCAPIN, THE. F. T. Otway. F. on Molière's *Les Fourberies de Scapin,* the plot from *Phormio* of Terence. Ac. 1677. Pr. same year.

CHEATS OF SCAPIN, THE. C. Ozell. Absolute transl. of Molière's play.

CHECKMATE. C. 2 a. Andrew Halliday. Royalty, July 15, 1869.

CHECKMATED; OR, WAIT AND HOPE. D. 3 a. Portsmouth T.R., March 19, 1869.

CHEER, BOYS, CHEER. D. 4 a. Sir Augustus Harris, Cecil Raleigh, and Henry Hamilton. D.L., September 19, 1895. Transf. to Olympic, December 19, 1895.

CHEERFUL AND MUSICAL. Duo. Ina Leon Cassilis. 1 a. Jersey, St. Peter's H., August 14, 1891.

CHEERFUL KNAVE, THE. P. 3 a. Keble Howard. Margate T.R., May 11, 1908.

CHEFE PROMISES OF GOD UNTO MAN. Miracle P. Bale, 1538.

CHELSEA PENSIONER, THE. C.O. C. Dibdin. Partly taken fr. story of *Belisarius*. C.G., May, 1779. Pr. 1779.

CHELSEA PENSIONER, A. M. sk. Lewis Melville. M. by Fritz Hart. Coliseum, September 8, 1905.

CHEQUE ON MY BANKER. Compressed into 2 a. fr. *Wanted, a Wife*. D.L., August 13, 1821.

CHERIBEL. Burl. 3 a. Frank Green. M. by Hugh Clendon. Manchester P.'s T., May 4, 1885. See *Cherry and Fairstar.*

CHEROKEE, THE. C.O. Jas. Cobb. D.L., December 20, 1794. M. by Storace. Pr. (songs only) 1794. Rev., D.L., 1802. See *Algonah.*

CHERRIES. Ca. Dublin Gaiety, February 22, 1875.

CHERRY. P. 1 a. J. J. Hewson. Liverpool Shakespeare, July 18, 1895; Liverpool P.O.W., September 27, 1897.

CHERRY AND BLUE. D.L., October 22, 1860.

CHERRY AND FAIRSTAR. Extrav. A. Smith and J. Oxenford. Princess's, April, 1844.

CHERRY AND FAIRSTAR. Panto. E. L. Blanchard. Sadler's Wells, December, 1861.

CHERRY AND FAIRSTAR. Burl. C. H. Hazlewood. Britannia, April 25, 1867.

CHERRY AND FAIRSTAR; OR, THE CHILDREN OF CYPRUS. Melo-d. rom. 2 a. C.G., April 8, 1822.

CHERRY AND FAIRSTAR; OR, THE PRETTY GREEN BIRD AND THE FAIRIES OF THE DANCING WATERS. Burl. extrav. F. W. Green. Surrey, April 4, 1874. Prod. as *Cheribel*, Manchester Princes, May 4, 1885; Grand, June 15, 1885.

CHERRY BLOSSOM. Ca. Archer St., W. Victoria H., February 19, 1889.

CHERRY BLOSSOM. Jap. Mus. Epis. Wr. by M. Ring. M. by E. W. Rogers. Richmond, March 25, 1907.

CHERRY BOUNCE. F. 1 a. J. R. Raymond. Sadler's Wells, 1823.

CHERRY GIRL, THE. M.P. 2 a. S. Hicks and I. Caryll. Vaudeville, December 21, 1903.

CHERRY HALL. P. 3 a. Forbes Dawson. Avenue, June 14, 1894.

CHERRY TREE FARM. M. sk. A. Law. M. by Hamilton Clarke. St. Geo. H., May 30, 1881.

CHERUBIN. 3 a. Paris Opera Comique, February 14, 1905.

CHESHIRE COMICS, THE. C. S. Johnson. Ac. 1730.

CHESHIRE HUNTRESS, THE OLD FOX CAUGHT AT LAST, THE. Dr. tale. Pr. 1740.

CHESTER TRAGEDY. P. Middleton. Wr. 1602. Mentioned in Henslowe's Diary.

CHESTER WHITSUN PLAYS. MS. Harleian in British Museum. These Mysteries said to have been written and exhibited in 1328, but the Harleian MS. gives them as they were played in 1600. The different trading companies of Chester were employed three days presenting them. They are the oldest dramatic works in the language. Ascr. to R. Heyden, who died 1363. See "Miracle Plays."

The Ascension. By the Taylors.
Antichrist. By the Clothiers.
The Deluge. By the Dyers.
Day of Judgment. By the Websters.
Descent Into Hell. By the Cooks and Innkeepers.
The Creation. By the Drapers.
The Election of St. Mathias, Sending of the Holy Ghost, etc. By the Fishmongers.
The Fall of Lucifer. By the Tanners.
The Salutation and Nativity. By the Wrightes.
The Shepherds Feeding Their Flocks by Night. By the Painters and Glaziers.
The Three Kings. By the Vinters.
The Obligation of the Three Kings. By the Mercers
The Killing of the Innocents. By the Goldsmiths.
The Purification By the Blacksmiths.
The Temptation. By the Butchers.
The Last Supper. By the Bakers.
The Blind Man and Lazarus. By the Glovers.
Jesus and the Lepers. By the Corvesarys.
Christ's Passion. By the Bowyers, Fletchers, and Ironmongers.
The Resurrection. By the Skinners.
Christ's Entry Into Jerusalem.
Abraham, Melchisedeck, and Lot. By the Barbers.
Moses, Balak, and Balaam. By the Cappers.

CHESTER'S TRIUMPH IN HONOUR OF HER PRINCE. P. Perf. upon St. George's Day, 1610.

CHESTERFIELD THINSKIN. F. 1 a. By author of "A.S.S." Princess's, July 21, 1853.

CHETWYND AFFAIR, THE. P. 3 a. Reginald Kennedy-Cox. Royalty, August 29, 1904.

CHEVAL DE BRONZE, LE. O. Auber. Words by Scribe. Paris, March 23, 1835.

CHEVAL DE BRONZE. See *The Bronze Horse.*

CHEVALEER, THE. C. 3 a. Henry Arthur Jones. Garrick, August 27, 1904.

CHEVALIER A LA MODE. C. Dancourt, 1652.

CHEVALIER DE ST. GEORGE, THE. D. 3 a. Adap. fr. the French of MM. Melesville and Roger de Beauvoir. T. de Varieties, Paris, February 15, 1840. Princess's, May 20, 1845.

CHEVALIER DE ST. GEORGE, THE. C. 3 a. Fredk. Langbridge. Brighton West Pier, October 1, 1906.

CHEVALIER LUBIN, LE. O. Boieldieu, Paris, 1866.

CHEVALIER OF THE MOULIN ROUGE; OR, THE DAYS OF TERROR, THE. Rom. D. 3 a. Adap. fr. the French of Dumas by Colin Hazlewood. Ac. August 1, 1859.

CHEVY CHASE. Hist. Rom. Surrey, July 1, 1816.

CHEVY CHASE. Chivalric Ent. M. by Cooke. D.L., March 3, 1836.

CHI SAFRE SPERI. O. Bo. Mazzocchi and Marazzoli. Probably the first O. Bo. Florence 1639.

CHICAGO, THE CITY OF FLAMES. D. H R. Beverley Liverpool Colosseum, January 29, 1872

CHICHEVACHE AND BYCORNE. Pr. 1780.

CHICKABIDDIES. Burl. Extrav. Darwen O.H., April 1, 1889.

CHICKS, THE. F.C. 3 a. W. F. Field, Brentford, Beach's T. of Varieties, April 15, 1886.

CHICOT THE JESTER. Rom. d. Prol. and 4 a. Founded by H. A. Saintsbury on Alex. Dumas's *La Dame de Monsoreau*. Hastings Gaiety, December 15, 1898 (C.P.).

CHIEF COOK, THE. M. ca. Ernest Leigh. Shepherd's Bush Empire, June 22, 1905.

CHIEF OF STAFF, THE. P. 4 a. Ronald Macdonald. Lyric, February 2, 1909.

CHIEFTAIN, THE C.O. 2 a. F. C. Burnand. M. by Sullivan. An elaboration of *The Contrabandista*, by F. C. B. and A. S. Savoy, December 12, 1894.

CHIEN DE MONTARGIS, LE. D. Guilbert de Pixérécourt. 1814.

CHIENS DU MONT ST. BERNARD. T. Antier. 1838.

CHILD OF CHANCE, A. D. 4 a. Adap. fr. Ouida's novel, *Tricotrin*, by W. Howell-Poole. Liverpool Court, August 6, 1886.

CHILD OF CHARITY. Dom. d. Victoria.

CHILD OF NATURE, A. C. 3 a. Mrs. Inchbald. C.G., 1788. Taken from *Zelie* of Mdme. Genlis. Also bears strong resemblance to *The School for Lovers*. See *The Blue Bells of Scotland*.

CHILD OF THE REGIMENT. O. Donizetti. Gaiety, May 6, 1871. See *Rataplan*.

CHILD OF THE REGIMENT; OR, THE FORTUNE OF WAR, THE. M.C. 2 a. J. B. Buckstone. Founded on Donizetti's O. Hay.

CHILD OF THE STREETS, A. D. 4 a. Frank Price. Walsall Grand, September 20, 1909.

CHILD OF THE SUN, THE. P. John Brougham. M. by Tully. Astley's, October 9, 1865.

CHILD OF THE WRECK, THE. Melo-d. 2 a. Planché. M. by Cooke. D.L., October 7, 1837, and Lyceum, February 16, 1859.

CHILD STEALER, THE. D. 4 parts. Adap. fr. the French by W E. Suter. Birmingham, April 16, 1866; Grecian, June 11, 1866.

CHILDHOOD'S DREAMS. C. 1 a. Adap. fr. Dumas' *L'Invitation à la Valse*, by Sir Chas. L. Young, Bart. Ac.

CHILDREN; OR, GIVE THEM THEIR WAY. C.D. Prince Hoare. M. by Kelly. D.L. Songs only. Pr. 1800.

CHILDREN IN THE WOOD. O. 2 a. Thos. Morton. M. by Dr. Arnold. D.L., 1793. Pr. 1794.

CHILDREN IN THE WOOD. D. D.L., February 8, 1850.

CHILDREN IN THE WOOD; OR, THE VENGEANCE DYER AND THE PAIR OF DIRTY KIDS, THE. Burl. Bayswater Bijou, March 1, 1875.

CHILDREN OF HERCULES, THE. Transl. fr. *Euripides* by Michl. Woodhull. Pr. 1782. See "Greek Plays."

CHILDREN OF ISRAEL. See "Miracle Plays."

CHILDREN OF KINGS, THE. Legend rom. 4 a. F. Langbridge and A. H. Ferro fr. the Ger. of E. Rosmer. Incidental m. by Humperdinck. Dublin T.R., September 4, 1902.

CHILDREN OF THE CASTLE, THE. D. 3 a. Edwd. Fitzball. Marylebone, November 23, 1857.

CHILDREN OF THE GHETTO. D. 4 a. Isrl. Zangwill. Deal Oddfellows H., July 25, 1899 (C.P.); Adelphi, December 11, 1899.

CHILDREN OF THE KING, THE. Fa. tale. 3 a. Transl. by Carl Armbruster fr. the German of Ernest Rosmer (*Königs' Kinder*). Rev. by John Davidson. M. by Englebert Humperdinck. Court, October 13, 1897.

CHILDREN OF THE MIST, THE. D. Adap. fr. Scott's *Legend of Montrose*. Victoria, 1819.

CHILDREN OF THE MIST, THE. D. Paisley R. Exch. Rms., October 26, 1868.

CHILDREN OF THE NIGHT. D. 4 a. A. Skelton. Ventnor Pav., August 3, 1900 (C.P.); Stalybridge Grand, September 10, 1900; Stratford Royal, June 3, 1901.

CHILDREN OF THE WOOD. Pant. E. L. Blanchard.

CHILDREN'S BALL; OR, THE DUEL, THE. C. Fr. Mdme. Genlis's Theatre of Education. Pr. 1781.

CHILI WIDOW, THE. Ver. in 3 a. by Arthur Bourchier and Alfred Sutro of *M. Le Directeur*, by Alex. Bisson and Fabrice Carré. Royalty, September 7, 1895.

CHILPERIC. O. Bouffe. 3 a. Hervé. Adap. by R. Reece. F. A. Marshall and R. Mansell. Lyceum, January 22, 1870.

CHILPERIC. O. 3 a. Hervé. Eng. lib. Adap. by Alex. M. Thompson and R. Mansell, with add. lyrics by H. Beswick and M. Pigott. Notting Hill Coronet, March 9, 1903.

CHILTERN HUNDREDS, THE. C.O. 2 a T. E. Pemberton. M. by Thos. Anderton. Liverpool Alex., April 17, 1882.

CHIMÆRA, THE. F. Thos. Odell. L.I.F., 1720. Pr. 1721.

CHIMES, THE. D. 4 a. An adap. of Dickens's story by Mark Lemon and Gilbert A. Beckett. Adelphi, December 19, 1844. Another ver. by Edward Stirling. Lyceum, January 2, 1845.

CHIMNEY CORNER, THE. M.E. Walsh Porter. M. by Kelly. D.L., October 7, 1797. Principally a transl. fr. the Fr. N.p.

CHIMNEY CORNER, THE. Dom. d. 2 a. H. T. Craven. Olympic, February 21, 1861.

CHIMNEY PIECE, THE. F. 1 a. G. H. Rodwell. D.L., March 23, 1833.

CHIMNEY SWEEPER, THE. B.O. Goodman's Fields, 1736. N.p.

CHINA TALE FROM A DELPH POINT OF VIEW, A. Burl. H. F. McClelland. Belfast T.R., November 11, 1878.

CHINA WEDDING, A. Extrav. West Digges. Duke's, May 21, 1877.

CHINAMAN, THE. F.C. 3 a. J. Tresahar. Sheffield City, July 16, 1894. Prod. as *Naughty Boys*, Trafalgar, September 13, 1894.

CHINESE DIVERTISEMENT. Noble. D.L., April 6, 1824

CHINESE FESTIVAL, THE. Ballet comp. by Mr. Noverre. D.L., November 8, 1755.

CHINESE GIANT, THE. R. Soutar, Marylebone.

CHINESE HONEYMOON, A. M.P. 2 a. G. Dance and Howard Talbot. Orig. prod. Hanley T.R., October 16, 1899; Strand, October 5, 1901

CHINESE IDYLL, A. M.F. 2 a. F. Danvers. Lyrics by J. E. Kiddie. Darlington R., December 17, 1903; Stalybridge Grand, July 18, 1904.

CHINESE LANTERN, THE. Fairy P. 3 a. L. Housman. M. by J. Moorat. Hay., June 16, 1908 (mat.).

CHINESE ORPHAN, THE. Hist. T. Wm. Hatchett. Pr. 1741. D.L., April 21, 1759. See *The Orphan of China*.

CHINESE ROMANCE. 1 a. L. Horne.

CHINESE SORCERER; OR, THE EMPEROR AND HIS THREE SONS, THE. Spec. 2 a. M. by Parry, Cook, and Horn. D.L., April 14, 1823.

CHING CHOW HI. Offenbach. Gall. of Illust. August 14, 1865.

CHINON OF ENGLAND. P. Rose T. January 3, 1595.

CHIP OF THE OLD BLOCK; OR, THE VILLAGE FESTIVAL. F. E. P. Knight. Hay., August 22, 1815.

CHIPS. Playlet. Lechmere Worrall. Piccadilly Hotel, February 23, 1909 (mat.); rev., Hay., June 3, 1909.

CHIROMANCY. Ca. Willis's Rooms, April 18, 1888.

CHIRRUPER'S FORTUNE. M.fl.p. 3 a. Arthur Law. Portsmouth T.R., August 31, 1885.

CHISELLING. F. 1 a. Jas. Albery and Jos. Dilley. Vaudeville, August 27, 1870; Gaiety, May, 1886.

CHISPA. P. Pro and 4 a. Clay M. Greene. Orig. prod. in America. Liverpool Shakespeare, March 18, 1889.

CHIT CHAT. C. Thos. Killigrew, jun. D.L., 1722. Pr. circ. 1719.

CHIT CHAT; OR, THE PENANCE OF POLYGAMY. Int. B. Walwyn. C.G., 1781. N.p.

CHIVALROUS HIGHWAYMAN, THE. R. Hope. M. by Hubt. Bath. Ladywell Par. H., Mary 25, 1905.

CHIVALRY. P. 4 a. Richard Lee. Globe, September 13, 1873.

CHIZZLE'S CHOICE. F. F. Hawley Francks and Mark Wood. Ladbroke H., July 28, 1888.

CHLORIDA (CHLORIDIA); OR, RITES TO CHLORIS AND HER NYMPHS. Masque by Ben Jonson. Presented at Court by Q. and her ladies at Shrovetide, 1630-1. Pr. 1630.

CHLORIS. Mythical P., by E. Newbound. Brit., Dec 18, 1876.

CHOCOLATE MAKERS; OR, MIMICKRY EXPOSED, THE. Int. G. Hayley. Dublin. Pr. 1759.

CHŒPHORÆ, THE. T. Transl. from Æschylus, B.C. 458; by R. Potter, 1777; Buckley, 1849; Plumtre, 1869. See "Greek Plays."

CHOICE. Ca. T. D. M'Cord. Ealing Dean New Public H., February 5, 1887.

CHOICE, THE. C. 2 a. Arthur Murphy. D.L., March 23, 1765. Pr. 1786.

CHOICE, THE. Ca. G. E. H. Bellingham. Dudley O.H., November 29, 1901.

CHOICE OF APOLLO, THE. Serenata. John Potter. Hay. M. by Wm. Yates. Pr. 1765.

CHOICE OF HARLEQUIN; OR, THE INDIAN CHIEF. Pant. Messink. C.G., 1781. Pr. 1782.

CHOLERIC FATHERS, THE. C.O. Thos. Holcraft. C.G. November, 1785. Pr. 1785.

CHOLERIC MAN, THE. C. R. Cumberland. Taken fr. Terence's *Heautonimorumenos*. D.L. Pr. 1775. See *Squire of Alsatia*.

CHOOSING A BRIDE. C. 1 a. E. H. Keating. Publ. by S. French, Ltd.

CHOPPER'S WEDDING MORN. Mono. Eardley F. Turner. St. Geo. H., April 4, 1889.

CHOPS OF THE CHANNEL, THE. F. 1 a. Fredk. Hay. Strand, July 8, 1869.

CHOPSTICKS AND SPIKINS. F. 1 a. Paul Merritt. Grecian, September 25, 1873. Rev. Gaiety, May, 1883.

CHORUS GIRL, THE. Sk. Camberwell Empire, May 24, 1909.

CHORUS LADY, THE. P. 4 a. J. Forbes. Vaudeville, April 15, 1909.

CHOSEN FOR LIFE. D. Henry C. Selby. Merthyr Tydfil Temperance H., January 20, 1882.

CHOSEN ONE, THE. P. 1 a. Neilson Morris. Albert Hall, February 21, 1908 (amat.).

CHOSEN PEOPLE, THE. P. 3 a. in Russian. Eugen Tschirikoff. Avenue, January 21, 1905.

CHOSROES. T. Rotrov. 1649.

CHRIS. See *A Broken Life and Captain Buchell's Luck*.

CHRIST, BIRTH OF, ETC. See "Miracle Plays."

CHRIST TRIUMPHANT. C. in Latin. John Fox, the martyrologist. 1556. Transl. into English by John Day, 1579.

CHRIST WHEN HE WAS TWELVE YEARS OLD, OF. C. Bishop Bale. (Nothing further known.)

CHRISTABEL. D. Coleridge. 1816.

CHRISTABEL; OR, THE BARD BEWITCHED. Extrav. Gilbert A'Beckett. Court, May 15, 1872.

CHRISTALINE. Op. Ex. 1 a. Publ. by S French, Ltd.

CHRISTENING, THE. F. J. B. Buckstone. Adelphi, October 13, 1834.

CHRISTI DESCENSUS AD INFEROS. See "Miracle Plays."

CHRISTIAN, THE. D. Prol. and 4 a. Hall Caine. Douglas Grand, August 7, 1897 (C.P.); Liverpool Shakespeare, October 9, 1899; Duke of York's, October 16, 1899; Lyceum, August 31, 1907.

CHRISTIAN HERO, THE. T. Geo. Lillo. D.L., 1734. Pr. 1734. See *Scanderbeg*.

CHRISTIAN KING, THE; OR, ALFRED OF ENGLELAND. P. 5 a. Wilson Barrett. Bristol Prince's, November 6, 1902; Adelphi, December 18, 1902.

CHRISTIAN SLAVE, THE. T. Mrs. Beecher Stowe. 1855. Fr. *Uncle Tom's Cabin*.

CHRISTIAN TURNED TURK; OR, THE TRAGICAL LIVES AND DEATH OF THE TWO FAMOUS PIRATES, WARD AND DANSIKER, A. T. R. Daborn. Taken fr. Andrew Barker's story. Not divided into acts. Pr. 1612.

CHRISTIANETTA. Play. Richd. Brome. End. on Stationers' books. August 4, 1640. N.p. Ac. 1640.

CHRISTIAN'S CRIME, THE. Dram. sk. 3 sc. L. Mortimer and Peter Wilson. Sadler's Wells, August 14, 1899.

CHRISTIAN'S CROSS, THE. P. 4 a. Adap. fr. Cardinal Wiseman's novel "Fabiola" by the Rev. F. Oakley and rev. by Clarke Claypole. Chester Royalty, April 7, 1897. Prod. as *From Cross to Crown*. Surrey, August 1, 1898.

CHRISTIE JOHNSTONE. See *All Fletcher's Fault*.

CHRISTINA. Rom. d. 4 a. Percy Lynwood and Mark Ambient. P.O.W., April 22, 1887 (mat.); Olympic, March 8, 1888.

CHRISTINE. Melo-d. p'let. A. Tullock Manchester Palace, October 2, 1907.

CHRISTINE. P. Dumas. 1830.

CHRISTINE; OR, A DUTCH GIRL'S TROUBLES D. 3 a. F. W. Broughton and J. Wilton Jones. Newcastle-on-Tyne, Tyne T., May 21, 1879.

CHRISTINE A FONTAINEBLEAU. Dr. rom. Soulié. 1829.

CHRISTINE EN SUEDE. P. Brault, 1829.

CHRISTMAS. Orat. Bach. 1734.

CHRISTMAS. Jephson. 1616.

CHRISTMAS AT BRIGHTON. Ent. by Mr Mathews. Lyceum, February, 1820.

CHRISTMAS BOXES. F. 1 a. Augustus Mayhew and Sutherland Edwards. Strand, January 16, 1860.

CHRISTMAS CAROL. D. 3 a. E. Stirling Adelphi, February 5, 1844.

CHRISTMAS CAROL. Extrav. Adelphi, December, 1859.

CHRISTMAS CAROL; OR, THE MISER'S WARNING, A. Adap. fr. Dickens by C. Z. Barnett. Surrey, February 5, 1844.

CHRISTMAS CHIMES; OR, TROTTY VECK'S DREAM, THE. D. 1 a. A. Williams Pavilion, February 3, 1873.

CHRISTMAS COMES BUT ONCE A YEAR. John Webster. Decker, Heywood, and Chettle. 1602.

CHRISTMAS DINNER, A. P. 1 a. Tom Taylor. Olympic, March 23, 1860.

CHRISTMAS EVE. C. 1 a. W. H. Post Wigan Court, February 2, 1900.

CHRISTMAS EVE; OR, THE DUEL IN THE SNOW. Dom. D. 3 a Edward Fitzball, sug. by Gerome's picture, "Tragedy and Comedy." D.L, March 12, 1860.

CHRISTMAS FAIRY. O. Publ. by S. French, Ltd.

CHRISTMAS GAMBLE, A. C. 1 a. E. H. Keating. Publ. by S. French, Ltd.

CHRISTMAS HAMPER, A. D. 3 a. Mr. and Mrs. McHardy-Flint. Dublin Abbey T., November 28, 1905.

CHRISTMAS IN A WATCH HOUSE. Sk. 1 a. Chas. Smith Cheltnam. St. James's, November 21, 1870.

CHRISTMAS, HIS MASQUE. By Ben Jonson. Pres. at Court, 1616.

CHRISTMAS NIGHT'S DREAM, A. A. Chevalier. M. by A. H. West. Small Queen's H., December 20, 1900.

CHRISTMAS ORDINARY, THE. C. By Trinity Coll., Oxford. Ent. Stationers' Co., June 29, 1660. Pr. 1682. Wr. by "W. R."

CHRISTMAS PANTOMIME, A. F. Extrav. 1 a. W. A. Vicars (Taylor Bilkins). Court. December 26, 1871.

CHRISTMAS STOCKING, A. G. A'Beckett and King Hall.

CHRISTMAS STORM, A. Dr. Epis. H. Scratchard. Smethwick R., May 4, 1907 (C.P.).

CHRISTMAS STORY, A. Victoria, February 10, 1866.

CHRISTMAS TALE, A, in Five Parts, by David Garrick. F. on Favart's *Fée Urgelle*. D.L., December 27, 1773. Pr. 1774.

CHRISTO TRIUMPHANTE DE. T. Latin. J. Foxe, 1551. Transl. 1579.

CHRISTOPHE COLOMB. D. Guilbert de Pixérécourt. 1815.

CHRISTOPHE COLOMBE. O. G. Bottesini (his first O.). Havana, 1847.

CHRISTOPHER JUNIOR. See *Jedbury Junior*.

CHRISTOPHER LOVE, THE TRAGEDY OF Pr. 1651.

CHRISTOPHER TADPOLE. D. Wm. Brown Blackpool P.O.W., September 28, 1877.

CHRISTOPHER'S HONEYMOON. F. 3 a. Malcolm Watson. Strand, July 3, 1889.

CHRIST'S DESCENT INTO HELL. A Miracle P. Represented by the choir boys of Hyde Abbey and St. Swithin's Priory before Henry VII. 1487.

CHRIST'S PASSION T. Geo. Sandys. Not intended for stage. Is only transl. of *Christus Patiens*, by Hugo Grotius. Pr. 1640.

CHRISTUS. Orat. F. Liszt. 1811-86.

CHRISTUS. Orat., unfinished. Mendelssohn. 1847.

CHRISTUS. Sacred O. Rubenstein. 1829-1895.

CHRONICLE HISTORY OF LEIR, KING OF ENGLAND, THE. Tragic D. based upon historical records of the nation's past. Circa 1580.

CHRONONHOTONTHOLOGOS. Mock T. 1 a Harry Carey. Ac. at "little theatre in Haymarket," Feb 22, 1734. Pr. 1734. C.G., 1772; Hay., 1906; D.L., 1815; Gaiety, November 10, 1880.

CHRYSANALEIA, THE, GOLDEN FISHING; OR, HONOUR OF FISHMONGERS. Devised and wr. by Anthony Munday. 1616.

CHRYSANTHEMUMS. C. 1 a. A. C. Wallace. Publ by S. French, Ltd.

CHRYSTABELLE; OR, THE ROSE WITHOUT A THORN. Extrav. Edmund Falconer Lyceum, December 26, 1860.

CHRYSTALINE. Burl. G. M. Layton. King's Cross, March 6, 1871.

CHUCK; OR, THE SCHOOL BOY'S OPERA 1736.

CHUMS. C. 1 a. T. G. Warren. Southport Pavilion T., May 8, 1889.

CHUMS. See *Ned's Chum*.

CHUMS TILL DEATH. Sk. 3 scs. Alfred Marsh. Canterbury, November 23, 1908.

CHURCH AND STAGE. D. 5 a. G. Walter Reynolds. Wolverhampton T.R., January 16 1888; Avenue, April 30, 1888.

CHURCH AND STAGE. P. 1 a. Malcolm Watson. Criterion, December 13, 1900.

CHURCHWARDEN, THE. F. 3 a. Transl from the German of Rudolf Kneisel by Messrs Ogden and Cassell. Adap. for the Engl. stage by Edward Terry. Newcastle T.R., September 17, 1886; Olympic, December 16, 1886. Terry's T. opened with this on October 17, 1887. Rev January 9, 1893.

CHURL, THE. C. Transl. from Plautus by R. Warner. Plautus calls this comedy *Truculentus*. Pr. 1772.

CHYMICAL COUNTERFEITS; OR, HARLEQUIN WORM DOCTOR, THE. Panto. Goodman's Fields, 1734.

CICELEY'S SECRET. Fairy P. 3 a. Mrs. P. L. Hawkins. Bayswater Bijou, January 15, 1895.

CICILIA AND CLORINDA; OR, LOVE IN ARMS. T.C. 2 parts. Thos. Killigrew. Written 1650-1. Pr. 1664.

CID, DER. O. Cornelius. 1824-1874.

CID, LE. O. 4 a. Ad D'Ennery, Louis Gallet, and Edouard Blau. M. by J. Massenet. Paris Grand Opéra, November 30, 1885.

CID, LE. O. Sacchini. 1734-86.

CID, THE. T. Guilhelm de Castro. 1621.

CID, THE. T. Corneille. 1636. See "French Classical Plays."

CID, THE. Tragi C. in 2 parts. A transl. of Corneille. Part I. dedicated to Edward Earl of Dorset; Part II. dedicated to Lady Theophila Cook. By Joseph Rutter. Ac. at Court and at Cockpit. D.L., 1637. Pr. 1637. Part II. dated 1640.

CID, THE. T. A transl. fr. Corneille by a "Captain in the Army." Pr. 1802. N. ac.

CID, THE. By Ross Neil. Pr. 1874.

CID, THE; OR, LOVE AND DUTY. Hist. P. 3 a. J. A. Addison and J. H. Howell. King's Cross, March 25, 1878.

CID, THE: OR, THE HEROIC DAUGHTER. T. John Ozell. Transl. fr. Corneille. Pr. 1714.

CIGALE, LA. C. 3 a. Meilhac and L. Halévy. Gaiety, December 9, 1878; Gaiety, July 3, 1883.

CIGALE, LA. C.O. 3 a. Chivot and Duru. M. Audran. Eng. ver. by F. C. Burnand and Ivan Caryll. Lyric, October 9, 1890.

CIGALE, LA. See *Good Luck*.

CIGARETTE. Oa. G. D'Arcy. M. by Offenbach. Globe, September 9, 1876.

CIGARETTE. O. 3 a. E. Warham St. Ledger and Barry Montour. M. by J. Haydn Parry. Cardiff T.R., August 15, 1892; Lyric, September 7, 1892; Trans. to Shaftesbury, September 26, 1892.

CIGARETTE-MAKER'S ROMANCE. A. P. 3 a. Chas. Hannan (f. on novel by F. Marion Crawford). Court, Feb. 11, 1901; Apollo, May 11, 1901.

CIMENE. Serious O. Hay., 1783.

CINDERELLA. Ballet. D.L., November 10, 1824.

CINDERELLA. Burl. P Taylor and Albert Smith. Publ. by Douglas Cox.

CINDERELLA. Extrav. Harry Lemon. Crystal Palace, April 18, 1870.

CINDERELLA. D. 3 a. E. Towers. Pav., June 4, 1881.

CINDERELLA. C.O. 3 a. Tom Robertson. M. by Rossini. Newcastle R., August 15, 1892; Grand, October 3, 1892.

CINDERELLA. C.O. 3 a. C. Allan Fisher. Macclesfield T.R., May 6, 1895.

CINDERELLA. Burl. 4 scenes. E. S. R. Bayswater Bijou, January 9. 1897.

CINDERELLA. See *Our Cinderella, Pickles, Miss Cinderella*.

CINDERELLA: A LITTLE OPERA FOR BIG CHILDREN, OR A BIG OPERA FOR LITTLE CHILDREN. M. by John Farmer. Lib. by H. S. Leigh. Perf. as an Op. Recit. at Harrow, December, 1883; St. James's H., May 2, 1884.

CINDERELLA: A STORY OF THE SLIP AND THE SLIPPER. Burl. extrav. J. W. Jones. Leicester T.R., October 3, 1878.

CINDERELLA; OR, THE FAIRY QUEEN AND THE GLASS SLIPPER. C.O. 3 a. Rophino Lacy. C.G., April 13, 1830; Newcastle Tyne T., August 15, 1892; Grand, October 3, 1892.

CINDERELLA; OR, THE FAIRY SLIPPER. C.O. M. by Rossini. D.L., January 9, 1837.

CINDERELLA; OR, THE LITTLE GLASS SLIPPER. Spec. D.L., January, 1804. N.p. The groundwork will be found among the *Tales of Mother Goose*. Said to be written by a young Oxonian who had recourse also to heathen mythology.

CINDERELLA; OR, THE LOVER, THE LACKEY, AND THE LITTLE GLASS SLIPPER. Fairy burl. extrav. H. J. Byron. Strand, December 26, 1860.

CINDERELLA IN QUITE ANOTHER PAIR OF SHOES. Burl. Frank W. Green. North Woolwich Royal Gardens, May 20, 1871.

CINDERELLA THE FIRST. C.O. 3 a. M. H. Vernon. Neath Bijou, August 29, 1892.

CINDERELLA THE SECOND. Burla. 2 tableaux. Boyle Lawrence. M. by Ernest Bucalossi. Bayswater Bijou, February 18, 1893.

CINDERELLA THE YOUNGER. Extrav. 3 a. Alfred Thompson. Gaiety, September 23, 1871.

CINDER-ELLALINE. Fairy piece in 3 scs. Wds. and lyrics by L. Shaw. M. by Signor Allegretto. Friern Barnet St. Peter's, April 22, 1909 (amat.).

CINDER-ELLEN UP TOO LATE. Burl. 3 a. A. C. Torr and W. T. Vincent. M. by Meyer Lutz. Originally prod. in Australia. Gaiety, December 24, 1891.

CINDERS. 1 a. Lily Tinsley. Pub. by S. French, Ltd.

CINGALEE; OR, SUNNY CEYLON. M.P. 2 a. J. T. Tanner. M. by Adrian Ross and P. Greenbank. Add. lyrics by Paul Rubens. Daly's, March 5, 1904.

CINNA. T. By Corneille. Prod. 1639. See "French Classical Plays."

CINNA'S CONSPIRACY. T. Anon. (C. Cibber). Plot from Roman history. D.L., February 19, 1713. Pr. 1713. Also ac. at L.I.F.

CINQ-MARS. O. 5 a. Gounod. Paris, 1877. Eng. transl. by S. Adair FitzGerald and W. Van Noorden. Leeds Grand, October 26, 1900; Coronet, November 17, 1900.

CINQ MARS. Hist. D. Alwyne Maude and Maurice Minton. Olympic, January 12, 1883.

CINTHIA'S REVELS. See *Cynthia's Revels*.

CINTHIA'S REVENGE. C. Stephens, 1613.

CIRCASSIAN, THE. C. 3 a. Adap. by F. W. Broughton fr. MM. Emile Blavet and Fabrice Carré's *Le Voyage au Caucase*. Criterion, November 19, 1887.

CIRCASSIAN BRIDE, THE. O. 3 a. D.L., February 23, 1809. M. by Bishop. The night after the performance the theatre was burned down. Score destroyed; songs only pr. 1809.

CIRCASSIENNE, LA. O. 3 a. Auber. Wds. by Scribe. Paris, 1861.

CIRCE. Dr. O. f. on the *Iphigenia in Tauris* of Euripides. By Chas. D'Avenant. Pro. by Dryden. Epil. by Earl of Rochester. M. by Bannister. D. of York's T., 1677. Pr. same year.

CIRCUMSTANCES ALTER CASES. Ca. 1 a. Isidore G. Asher. C. Palace, April 23, 1888. Gaiety, June 27, 1889.

CIRCUMSTANTIAL EVIDENCE. Ca. 1 a. Raymond Carew. Bayswater Bijou, April 6, 1893.

CIRCUS GIRL, THE. M.P. 2 a. J. T. Tanner and W. Palings. M. by Ivan Caryll and Lionel Monckton. Gaiety, December 5, 1896.

CIRO. O. Ariosti. 1721.

CIRO, IL. O. Scarlatti. 1659-1725.

CIRO RICONOSCIUTO. O. Leo, 1739.

CISSY. M.C. 3 a. W. H. Dearlove and Miss Jessie Franklin. Harrogate Town Hall T., January 11, 1890 (produced as *Love's Devotion*), and March 20, 1890.

CISSY'S ENGAGEMENT. Duo. 1 a. Ellen Lancaster-Wallis. Steinway H., November 19, 1895.

CISTELLARIA; OR, THE CASKET COMEDY. C (B.C. 254-184.) Plautus. Latin adap. fr. a Greek P. by Menander. Transl. into blank verse by Thornton, Rich, Warner, and Colman, 1769-74. See "Latin Plays."

CITIZEN, THE. C. 3 a. Also played in 2 a. Arthur Murphy. D.L., July, 1761; Edinburgh, 1782; C.G., 1806. Pr. 1763.

CITIZEN GENERAL, THE. C. Goethe. 1793.

CITIZEN MORAT. P. 1 a. Alice Clayton Greene. Fulham Grand, April 20, 1907. Camden, May 20, 1907.

CITIZEN ROBESPIERRE. P. 4 a. Perth and Condie. Chester Royalty, June 2, 1899.

CITIZEN TURNED GENTLEMAN, THE. Adap. of Molière's *Le Bourgeois Gentilhomme*, reprod. by E. Ravenscroft, 1672. See *Mamamouchi.*

CITIZEN'S DAUGHTER, THE. F. Pr. (n.d.) Circ. 1775.

CITY ASSOCIATION; OR, THE NATIONAL SPIRIT ROUSED, THE. Mus. Ent. Hay., 1780. N.p.

CITY BARGE, THE. Monopolylogue by Mr. Mathews. Lyceum, March 11, 1826.

CITY BRIDE; OR, THE MERRY CUCKOLD, THE. C. Jos. Harris. Borrowed fr. Webster's *Cure for a Cuckold.* L.I.F. Pr. 1696.

CITY DAME. C. Philip Massinger. Blackfriars, 1659.

CITY FARCE, THE. Ascribed to Mr. Weddell. Pr. 1737.

CITY FRIENDS. Strand, February 26, 1855.

CITY GALLANT, THE. P. Ac. by the Queen's Players, 1611. This was the P. of Greene's *Tu Quoque*. Publ. 1614.

CITY GUARD, THE. M. extrav. Birmingham Grand, November 26, 1883.

CITY HEIRESS; OR, SIR TIMOTHY TREATALL, THE. C. Mrs. Aphra Behn. Adap. fr. Middleton's *A Mad World, my Masters*, and Massinger's *Guardian*. Duke's, 1682.

CITY LADY; OR, FOLLY PROCLAIMED, THE. C. Thos. Dilke. D.L. and L.I.F. Pr. 1697.

CITY MADAM, THE. C. 5 a. Philip Massinger. Ac. by King's Co. at Blackfriars, May 25, 1632. Pr. 1659. See *Riches; The Cure of Pride.*

CITY MATCH, THE. C. Jasper Mayne. D.D. Whitehall (before the K. and Q.), 1639; Blackfriars, same year; rev. by Planché at C.G., February 5, 1828. See *The Schemers.*

CITY NIGHT CAP; OR, CREDE QUOD HABES ET HABES, THE. C. Robr. Davenport. Cockpit, 1651; the Phœnix, 1661. Pr. 1661. (A dramatised ver. of *The Curious Impertinent* in "Don Quixote," f. on a tale of the "Decameron," day vii., November 7.)

CITY NIGHT CAP. See *Amorous Prince.*

CITY OF MILLIONS, THE. D. 5 a. Ch. Berte and Wm. Bailey, jun. West London, June 1, 1903.

CITY OF MYSTERY, THE. Romantic Costume Play in Prol. and 4 a. Adap. by Lionel Atwill fr. the novel of that name by A. Clavering Gunter. Luton Grand, January 9, 1908 (C.P.).

CITY OF PLEASURE, THE. D. Pro. and 4 a. F. by G. R. Sims on *Gigolette*, by MM. Tarbé and Decourcelle (Ambigu. Paris, November 25, 1893). Birmingham P.O.W., April 22, 1895; Islington Grand, August 31, 1903.

CITY OF SIN, A. D., 4 a. A. Shirley and W. Muskerry. Barnsley T.R., December 22, 1902; Surrey, February 9, 1903.

CITY OF THE PLAGUE. D. Pm. Wilson, 1816.

CITY OUTCAST, THE. D. Pro. and 3 a. Brandon Ellis. Gateshead T.R., April 18, 1892; Stratford T.R., January 4, 1897.

CITY PAGEANT FOR THE VISIT OF KING CHRISTIAN IV. OF DENMARK, A. John Marston. 1606.

CITY POLITICS. C. John Crowne. Prod. 1673. D.L., 1683. Pr. 1683, rev. 1712.

CITY RAMBLE; OR, A PLAYHOUSE WEDDING, THE. C. E. Settle. Ac. at D.L., August, 1711. Pr. 1712.

CITY RAMBLE; OR, THE HUMOURS OF THE COMPTER, A. F. 2 a. Chas. Knipe. L.I.F., 1715. Pr. 1715. See *The Humours*, etc.

CITY SHUFFLER, THE. P. (?) N.p. Perf. at Salisbury Court, 1633.

CITY WIT; OR, THE WOMAN WEARS THE BREECHES, THE C. Richd. Brome. 1634. Pr. 1653.

CITY WIVES CONFEDERACY, THE. C. Sir John Vanbrugh. D.L.

CIVIL WAR. D. 4 a. Adap. by Herman Merivale from Albert Delpit's *Mdlle. de Bressier* (prod. Aubigu, Paris, April 19, 1887). Gaiety, June 27, 1887.

CIVIL WARS OF FRANCE. P. Decker. Mentioned by Hunslowe. 1598-9.

CIVIL WARS OF HENRY VI., THE. T. Cibber. 1724.

CIVILIAN; OR, THE FARMER TURNED FOOTMAN, THE. Mus. F. Saml. Wm. Ryley. Manchester, 1792. Pr. (n.d.).

CIVILIZATION. D. 5 a. John H. Wilkins. Founded on *Le Huron* and Voltaire's *L'Ingénu*. City of London, November 10, 1852; Strand, January 17, 1853; D.L., April 11, 1853; Marylebone, October 5, 1857.

CIVITATIS AMOR. An ent. by water at Chelsey and White-hall. November 4, 1616.

CLAIMANT; OR, THE LOST ONE FOUND, THE. D. H. P. Grattan. Surrey, April 1, 1872.

CLAIMANTS. C. 1 a. Adap. by Hermann Vezin fr. the German of Kotzebue and Schneider. Worthing Assembly R., September 28, 1891. Matinée T., November 15, 1898.

CLAIRE. Version, 4 a., of M. Georges Ohnet's novel, *Le Maitre de Forges*, by Mrs. Bernhardt Fischer, New Cross Public H., May 7, 1887.

CLAIRVAL. C.D. Cambridge T.R., October 1, 1877.

CLAM. D. 3 a. C. H. Ross. Surrey, April 16, 1870.

CLAMEUR DE HARO. F. A. J. Goudon. Jersey T.R., April 9, 1877.

CLANCARTY. Slightly rev. ver. of *Lady Clancarty; or, Wedded and Wooed.* Lyric, April 16, 1907.

CLANCARTY. See *Lady Clancarty.*

CLANDESTINE MARRIAGE, THE. C. 5 a. G. Colman and D. Garrick. Taken from Hogarth's *Marriage à-la-Mode* and Townley's farce, *False Concord* (1760). D.L., February 20, 1766. Pr. 1766. C.G., 1840; Hay., March 17, 1903.

CLARA SOLEIL.—See *Bad Boys.*

CLARA VERE DE VERE. P. 4 a. F. on Tennyson's poem by Campbell Rae-Brown. P.O.W., June 8, 1888.

CLARAXILLA. See *Claricilla.*

CLARE COTTAGE. P. 1 a. Adap. by Sam James from *La Joie Fait Peur.* Margate T.R., April 16, 1888.

CLARENCE CLEVEDON, HIS STRUGGLES FOR LIFE OR DEATH. D. 3 a. Edwd. Stirling. First perf. at Victoria T., April 9, 1849

CLARI. O. Halèvy. Paris. 1828.

CLARI, THE MAID OF MILAN. M.D. 2 a. J. Howard Payne. M. by Bishop. C.G., May 8, 1823; Saddler's Wells, 1826; City of London, 1838; and Marylebone, 1854.

CLARICE. C. 4 a. Wm. Gillette. Liverpool Shakespeare, September 4, 1905; .D of York's, September 13, 1905.

CLARICE; OR, ONLY A WOMAN. D. Prol. and 4 a. Walter Browne and Frank Roberts. Strand, November 17, 1886.

CLARICE DE CLERMONT; OR, THE COUNT'S TREASURE. Military D. 4 a. Thos. Naden. Wrexham St. James's H., March 16, 1892.

CLARICE ET BELTON. See *Le Prisonnier Anglais.*

CLARICILLA. T.C. Thomas Killigrew. Phœnix. Pr. 1641.

CLARISSA. P. 4 a. Adap by Robt. Buchanan fr. Richardson's *Clarissa Harlowe.* Act three f. partly on French adap. of same novel by MM. Dumanoir, Guillard, and Clairville (Gymnase, Paris, 1842). Vaudeville, June 2, 1890.

CLARISSA; OR, THE FATAL SEDUCTION. T. in prose. Robert Porret. Taken from Richardson's *Clarissa Harlowe.* Pr. 1788 (N.ac.).

CLARISSA HARLOWE. Burla. Olympic, January 3, 1831.

CLARISSA HARLOWE. T.D. 3 a. Adap. fr. the French by T. H. Lacy and G. Courtney. Princess's, September 28, 1846.

CLARISSA HARLOWE. D. 5 a. Adap. fr. Richardson's novel by W. G. Wills. Birmingham T.R., December 16, 1889.

CLARISSE; OR, THE MERCHANT'S DAUGHTER. D. 3 a. E. Stirling. Adelphi, September 1, 1845.

CLARISSIMA'S LOVERS. C.S. W. H. Abbott. N. Cross Goldsmith's Inst., February 1, 1902.

CLASSICAL PLAYS. See—
French Classical Plays.
German Classical Plays.
Italian Classical Plays.
Greek Plays.
Latin Plays.

CLAUD DU VAL. 1 a. A. Morris.

CLAUDE DUVAL. F. 1 a. T. P. Taylor. City of London, May 8, 1842.

CLAUDE DUVAL. Burl. 2 a. Fredk. Bowyer and "Payne Nunn." M. by John Crook and Lionel Monckton. Bristol Prince's, July 23, 1894; P.O.W., September 25, 1894.

CLAUDE DUVAL. Sk. in 3 sc. Wal Pink and Fred Ginnett. Tunbridge Wells O.H., January 4, 1909. Surrey, February 8, 1909.

CLAUDE DUVAL; OR, LOVE AND LARCENY. Rom. and C.O. 3 a. H. P. Stevens. M. by Edwd. Solomon. Olympic, August 24, 1881.

CLAUDE DUVAL; OR, THE HIGHWAYMAN FOR LADIES. Burl. F. C. Burnand. Royalty, January 23, 1869.

CLAUDE MELNOTTE. C.O. 2 a. F. on Lord Lytton's *Lady of Lyons.* Herbert Shelley. Lyrice, Arthur A. Anderson. M., Frank E. Tours. Bayswater Bijou, August 22, 1900 (C.P.).

CLAUDIAN. P. Prol. and 3 a. Story and construction by Henry Herman. Dialogue by W. G. Wills. Princess's, December 6, 1883.

CLAUDIAN. See *Paw Clawdian.*

CLAUDINE; OR, THE BASKET-MAKER. Burl. Chas. Dibdin, jun. Sadler's Wells. Pr. 1801.

CLAUDIO. C.O. 2 a. A. V. Thurgood. M. by Thos. Hunter. Portsmouth T.R., December 1, 1888 (C.P.); Nottingham Grand T., August 5, 1889 (in 3 a.).

CLAUDIUS TIBERIUS NERO, ROME'S GREATEST TYRANT, THE TRAGEDY OF. "Truly represented out of the purest records of those times." Pr. 1607. See *Nero.*

CLAUSE NO. 6. P. 1 a. Charles Windermere. Balham Duchess, December 29, 1902.

CLAVIDGO. T. Transl. from the German of Goethe. Pr. 1798. N.ac.

CLAVIGO. D. Goethe. 1774.

CLAVIGO. The last scene of *Clavidgo* under this title. Transl. and pr. 1790.

CLAVIGO. Transl. of Goethe's play. Manchester Gentleman's Concert H., February 23, 1895.

CLAYCHESTER SCANDAL, THE. C. 4 a. Colchester T.R., December 9, 1898.

CLEAN SLATE, A. C. 3 a. R. C. Carton. Criterion, February 10, 1903.

CLEAN YOUR BOOTS. Surrey, May 10, 1858.

CLEANDER. T. Philip Massinger. Lic. May 7, 1637. Ac. by the King's Co. N.p.

CLEAR AHEAD. D. 4 a. C. A. Clarke. Oldham T.R., August 3, 1885.

CLEAR CASE. F. 1 a. G. A. à'Beckett. St. Jas. T.

CLEAR CONSCIENCE, A. Ca. T. N. Walter. Lincoln T.R., October 14, 1889.

CLEFT STICK, A. C. 3 a. John Oxenford. Olympic, November 8, 1865.

CLEMENTINA. T. Hugh Kelly. C.G., 1771.

CLEMENTINA. F. Edwd. Moncrieffe. Surrey, September 5, 1892.

CLEMENZA; OR, THE TUSCAN ORPHAN. T. Dr. Ainslie. Bath T.R., June 1, 1822.

CLEMENZA DI TITO, LA. O. Metastasio. M. by Leo. 1734.

CLEMENZA DI TITO, LA. O. Glück. 1754.,

CLEMENZA DI TITO, LA. O. Mozart. Prague, 1791; King's T., March 29, 1806.

CLENCH AND WRENCH. F. Bayswater Bijou, June 7, 1879.

CLEODORA. P. Habington's P. of *The Queen of Arrogan.* Pr. 1640.

CLEOMENES, THE SPARTAN HERO. T. J. Dryden and Sothern. Ac. at T.R., 1692 Pr. 1692.

CLEON; OR, CLEAN OUT OF SIGHT OUT OF MIND. M. drollery. A. Maltby. Liverpool Alexandra, March 23, 1874.

CLEONE. T. R. Dodsley. Suggested by the legend of St. Genevieve. C.G., December 2, 1758. Pr. 1758.

CLEONICE, PRINCESS OF BITHYNIA. T. John Hoole. C.G., February, 1775. Pr. 1775.

CLEOPATRA. T. Samuel Daniel. F. on incident in Plutarch's Lives of Anthony and Cleopatra. Pr. 1594.

CLEOPATRA. T. Alfieri. 1773. Ac. 1775. Transl. by C. Lloyd 1815.

CLEOPATRA. O. Enna.

CLEOPATRA. F.C. 3 a. Adap. by Arthur Shirley fr. *Les Amours de Cléopâtre.* Shaftesbury, June 25, 1891.

CLEOPATRA. Sk. 1 a. V. Bridges. Bedford St. Bijou, December 12, 1907.

CLEOPATRA, LA. O. D. Cimarosa. St. Petersburg, 1787.

CLEOPATRA. See *Anthony and Cleopatra.*

CLEOPATRA IN JUDÆA. P. 1 a. A. Symons. Bayswater Bijou, May 5, 1907.

CLEOPATRA, QUEEN OF EGYPT. T. Thos. May. Taken fr. Plutarch's Lives of Anthony and Cleopatra. Pr 1639.

CLEOPATRE. T. Mairet. 1630.

CLEOPATRE. T. 17th Cent. Calprenède. Transl. by R. Loveday, 1668.

CLEOPATRE. T. Marmontel. 1750.

CLEOPATRE CAPTIVE. T. Jodelle. 1550

CLEOPHILUS. C. in Latin. David Waterhouse. 1650. Another edition, 1700.

CLERGYMAN'S DAUGHTER, THE. See *My Girl.*

CLERICAL ERROR, A. Ca. 1 a. H. A. Jones. Court, October 13, 1879.

CLERK OF CLERKENWELL; OR, THE THREE BLACK BOTTLES, THE. Rom. D. 2 a. George Almar, Sadler's Wells, February 3, 1834.

CLERK OF THE WEATHER, THE. F.C. 3 a. Kate Osmond and Agatha Hodgson. Brighton Aquarium, February 26, 1894.

CLEVER ALICE. F.C. 3 a. Adap. fr. the German of Adolf Willbrandt by Brandon Thomas. Royalty, April 6, 1893.

CLEVER CAPTURE, A. Ca. Mark Melford. York T.R., March 7, 1890.

CLEVER DECEPTION, A. Sk. J. B. Andrews. Shrewsbury T.R., December 15, 1903.

CLEVER IMPOSTOR, A. P. 4 a. Emma Litchfield. Macclesfield T.R., December 24, 1906: Stratford R.T., March 2, 1908.

CLEVER LADY JANE. C. 1 a. MS. with Dramatic Authors' Agency.

CLEVER PEOPLE. Ca. Edwd. Rose. Reading County T., September 23, 1889.

CLEVER SIR JACOB. Ca. Paul Grave. Gaiety, December 15, 1873.

CLEVERLY MANAGED. Ca. Andrew Longmuir. Steinway H., June 28, 1887.

CLICQUOT. F.C. 3 a. Brentwood Recreation H., September 29, 1892.

CLIFFORD. T. Clifford. 1817.

CLIFFORD CASTLE. Afterpiece. Glasgow, May 5, 1809. N.p.

CLIMBERS, THE. P. 4 a. Clyde Fitch. Comedy, September 5, 1903.

CLIMBING BOY, THE. D. 3 a. Peake. M. by Mr. Hawes. Olympic, July 13, 1832; D.L., September 18, 1834.

CLIO. P. 5 a. Bartley Campbell. Eleph. and C., August 14, 1885.

CLITANDRE. Corneille. 1632. See "French Classical Plays."

CLITO. T. 5 a. Sydney Grundy and Wilson Barrett. Princess's, May 1, 1886.

CLOACINA. C.T. Anonymous. Possibly by Henry Man. Pr. 1775

CLOCHES DE CORNEVILLE, LES. Op.-bo. Eng. adap. by H. B. Farnie and R. Reece. M. by Planquette. Folly, February 28, 1878; transferred to Globe August 31, 1878; Op. C., February 17, 1890.

CLOCHES DE CORNEVILLE, LES. Spec. Bal 5 sc. Adap. fr. Planquette's C.O. The action inven. by A. Curti. Orig. M. selected and supplemented by Geo. W. Bing. Alhambra, October 7, 1907; rev. Alhambra, August 9, 1909.

CLOCK, THE. D. 1 a. Ch. Harman. Publ. by S. French, Ltd.

CLOCK ON THE STAIRS, THE. Dom. D. 1 a. Colin H. Hazlewood. Britannia, February, 1862.

CLOCKCASE; OR, FEMALE CURIOSITY, THE Int. C.G., May 2, 1777. N.p.

CLOCKMAKER'S HAT, THE. F. 1 a. Adap. fr. *Le Chapeau d'un Horologer* by Mdme. Emile de Girardin. First pl. at T. du Gymnase, December 16, 1854; Adelphi, March 7, 1855, under title of *Betty Martin.*

CLOCKWORK. Burla. R. Reece. Olympic, February 7, 1877.

CLOCKWORK MAN, THE. P. 3 a. Ch. Hannan. Richmond T.R., December 12, 1901.

CLORIDIA; OR, THE RITES TO CLORIS. Masque. Ben Jonson. Pres. by the Q. and her ladies at Court, 1630.

CLORIDON AND RADIAMANTA. P. Ac. at Court by Sir Robert Lane's men, 1571.

CLORILDA, LA. O. Rossi. 1688.

CLORINDE. O. Monteverde. 1568-1643.

CLORIS; OR, PLOTS AND PLANS. Oa. M. by C. Flavell Hayward. Lib. by Magdeline Wycombe and Vernon Shael. Wolverhampton T.R., April 17, 1885.

CLORYS AND ORGASTO. Rose T., February 28, 1591.

CLOSE OF THE POLL, THE. See *The Humours of an Election.*

CLOSE SHAVE, A. F. T. W. Speight. Hay., August 9, 1884.

CLOSE SHAVE, A. F.C. 3 a. F. B. Thalberg Stockton-on-Tees T.R., February 16, 1895.

CLOSE SIEGE. Burla. 1 a. Geo. Dance. St. James's, 1839.

CLOSERIE DES GENETS, LA. D. Soulié, 1846.

CLOSING PRICE, THE. Sk. Maurice Hoffman. Bedford, April 19, 1909.

CLOTHES AND THE WOMAN. C. 3 a. G. Paston. Imperial, May 26, 1907.

CLOTILDE. O. C. Coccia. Venice, 1815.

CLOTILDE. T Soulié, 1832.

CLOUD AND SUNSHINE; OR, LOVE'S REVENGE. D. 4 a. J B. Anderson. D.L., February 22, 1858.

CLOUD KING; OR, MAGIC ROSE, THE. Mus. D. J. C. Cross. Ac. at the Royal Circus. Pr. 1809.

CLOUD OF LIFE. Grecian, May 9, 1859.

CLOUD OF SMOKE, A. F. Chas. Squier. Richmond H.M.T., September 15, 1881.

CLOUDLAND. Dance scena. E. C. Matthews. Hackney Regent, August 27, 1909.

CLOUDS. C.D. Arthur Percival. Exeter T.R., April 1, 1872

CLOUDS, THE. C. Transl. fr. Aristophanes, B.C. 423, by T. Stanley, 1656; J. White, 1759; L. Theobald, 1715; Mitchell, 1820-2; Hickie, 1853; Rudd, 1867. See "Greek Plays."

CLOUDS, THE. C. Aristophanes (in Greek). Oxford New, March 1, 1905.

CLOUDS (OF ARISTOPHANES), THE. C. Richard Cumberland. Pr. N.d. Circa 1797.

CLOUDS; OR, A BROKEN FAITH. C.D. Sidney Bowkett. Brighton Hotel Metropole, January 20, 1894.

CLOUDS AND SUNSHINE IN A LIFE. P. Adolphe Faucquer. Sadler's Wells, October 27, 1862.

CLOVEN FOOT, THE. D. 4 a. Adap. by Fredk. Mouillot and Janet Steer fr. Miss Braddon's novel. Blackburn T.R., January 27, 1890; Pavilion, June 30, 1890; Grand, June 1, 1891.

CLOWN, THE. P. 1 a. Ramsgate Amphitheatre, August 26, 1900.

CLUB BABY, THE. F.C. 3 a. Lawrence Sterner and Edward Knoblauch. Ealing Lyric, September 19, 1895; Parkhurst, October 14, 1895; Avenue, April 27, 1898.

CLUB LAW. C. Clare Hall, 1597-8. A MS. of this title in the library of Dr. Farmer, wr by Geo. Ruggles.

CLUB MEN, THE. A title given to a portion of *Philaster* pl. about 1630.

CLUB RAID, A. Dr. Episode. 3 sc. H. Pleon. Aston T.R., April 20, 1903.

CLUMP AND CUDDEN; OR, THE REVIEW. C.M.P. 1 a. Chas. Dibdin. Royal Circus. Pr. 1785.

CLURICANNE'S TOWER; OR, THE WHITE MAIDEN OF TIERNABOUL. D. John Holmes Grover. Liverpool Royal Colosseum, February 24, 1871.

CLUTTERBUCKS; OR, THE RAILROAD OF LOVE, THE. C.G., 1832. See *Railroad of Love.*

CLYTEMNESTRA. T. Beer. 1823.

CLYTEMNESTRA. Ser. O. Piccini. 1789.

CLYTIE. D. 5 a. Jos. Hatton. Liverpool Amphitheatre, November 29, 1875; Olympic, January 10, 1876.

CLYTOPHON. Latin C. MS. preserved in library of Emanuel College, Cambridge.

COACH-DRIVERS, THE. Poetical C.O. Pr. 1766.

COACHMAN WITH THE YELLOW LACE. P. 4 a. Dram. by C. Hannan from the author's novel. Glasgow Grand T., September 11, 1902. C.P. Hammersmith Lyric, March 25, 1907.

COAL AND COKE. F. Chas. Harding and W. H. Swanborough. Strand, January 27, 1868.

COAL KING, THE. D. 5 a. Ernest Martin and Fewlass Llewellyn. Elephant and Castle, October 24, 1904.

COAL MINE, THE. D. J. B. Johnstone. Pavilion, March 11, 1867.

COALITION. F. Ac. Pr. 1779.

COALITION. M.F. 2 a. Leonard Macnally. C.G., May 19, 1783. N.p.

COALITION. Ca. T. H. Hardman and H. North. Liverpool Alexandra, February 21, 1881.

COALITION; OR, THE OPERA REHEARSED, THE. C. 3 a. Richard Graves. Pr. 1794. Ac. at Bath.

COALITION. See *Echo and Narcissus.*

COALS OF FIRE. C.D. 3 a. H. T. Craven. Court, November 20, 1871.

COASTGUARD; OR, THE LAST CRUISE OF THE VAMPIRE, THE. C.O. J. C. Manning. M. by W. F. Hulley. Neath Robinson's Assembly H., November 27, 1884.

COAT OF MANY COLOURS, A. C. 4 a. Madeline Lucette Ryley. West London, July 22, 1897 (C.P.). First perf. in New York.

COBBLER'S DAUGHTER, THE. D. 4 a. Mrs. S. Lane. Britannia, March 23, 1878.

COBLER, THE. Ac. in 1597 by the Lord Admiral's servants. 1597. Possibly the same as *The Cobler's Prophesie.*

COBLER; OR, A WIFE OF TEN THOUSAND, THE. Ballad O. C. Dibdin. D.L., December 9, 1774. Pr. 1774. Partly fr. *Blaise la Savetier* of Sedaine.

COBLER OF CASTLEBURY, THE. M.Ent. Chas. Stuart. C.G., April 27, 1779. Pr. 1779.

COBLER OF PRESTON, THE. F. 2 a. Chas. Johnson. D.L., February 3, 1716. Pr. 1716.

COBLER OF PRESTON, THE. F. Christopher Bullock. Chiefly fr. Shakespeare's *Taming of the Shrew.* L.I.F., January 24, 1716. Pr. 1716.

COBLER'S OPERA, THE. Lacy Ryan. L.I.F. Pr. 1729. Ac. D.L., 1731, as *The Amours of Billingsgate.*

COBLER'S PROPHECY, THE. C. Robt Wilson. Pr. 1594.

COBWEBS. C. 3 a. Chas. Wills. Vaudeville, March 27, 1880.

COCALUS. C. Aristophanes (B.C. 387). Transl. by Mitchell, 1820-2; Hickie, 1853; Rudd, 1867. See "Greek Plays."

COCARD ET BICOQUET. An adap. of this 3 a. C. by MM. Boucheron and Raymond (prod. at the Paris Renaissance, February 22, 1888). Leeds, March 10, 1888 (C.P.).

COCK ROBIN AND JENNY WREN. Ent. 1 a. M. C. Gillington. M. by Florian Pascall. Royalty, December 12, 1891.

COCKLE. See *Sir John Cockle at Court.*

COCKLE-DE-MOY. P. Presented at Court, 1613.

COCKNEYS IN CALIFORNIA. F. 1 a. Publ. by S. French, Ltd.

COCU IMAGINAIRE. C. Molière. 1660.

CODE OF HONOUR, A. D. 3 a. Gustav Blumberg and Cecil Stephenson. Comedy, February 9, 1903.

CODRUS. T. Pr. 1774. Possible ac. at Manchester.

CŒLIA; OR, THE PERJUR'D LOVER. P. Chas. Johnson. D.L., 1733.

CŒLINA. Masque. Henry Lucas. Pr. 1795. N. ac.

CŒLUM BRITANNICUM. Masque by Thos. Carew. M. by Henry Lawes. Perf. by the K and nobles at Banqueting H., Whitehall, February 18, 1633.

COERCION. F.C. 3 a. W. H. Denny and Thos. Burnside. Gaiety, November 17, 1886.

CŒUR A SES RAISONS, LE. Terry's, November 2, 1908.

CŒUR DE LION. O. Gretry. 1741-1813.

CŒUR DE LION; OR, THE MAID OF JUDAH. D. Chas. Cooke. Victoria, September 4, 1876.

CŒUR DE LION REVISED AND HIS ENEMIES CORRECTED. Burl. 6 sc. John Strachan. Strand, December 22, 1870.

COFFEE HOUSE, THE. C. Rev. Jas Miller. D.L., January 26, 1738. Pr. 1738.

COFFEE HOUSE, THE. C. Transl. fr. Voltaire. Pr. in Dr. Franklin's edition.

COFFEE HOUSE; OR, THE FAIR FUGITIVE, THE. C. Transl. fr. Voltaire. Pr. 1760.

COFFEE-HOUSE POLITICIAN; OR, THE JUSTICE CAUGHT IN HIS OWN TRAP, THE. C. Hy. Fielding. Perf. at "Little Theatre in Haymarket" and at L.I.F., December, 1730. Pr. 1730.

COGGESHALL VOLUNTEER CORPS, THE. F. Anon. Pr. 1804. N. ac.

COINER'S DREAM, THE. D. 1 a. Cecil N. T. Fitzroy (Cecil Noel). Derby Lecture H., May 12, 1890; Standard, July 17, 1899.

COLA'S FURY; OR, LYRENDA'S MISERY. T. Hy. Burkhead. Pr. 1645. N. ac.

COLD MUTTON. F. 1 a. H. W. Mince. Brixton, September 28, 1908.

COLINETTE A LA COUR. O. Grétry. 1774-1826.

COLLABORATORS, THE. F. 1 a. C. Haddon Chambers. Vaudeville, January 7, 1892.

COLLABORATORS, THE. F. 1 a. Lord Kilmarnock. Mat., July 6, 1897.

COLLABORATORS, THE. P. 1 a. W. K. Tarpey, fr. a story by Mrs. K. Tarpey. Criterion, November 5, 1906.

COLLARS AND CUFFS. M.C. Henri R. French. Birkenhead T.R., November 30, 1883.

COLLEEN BAWN; OR, THE BRIDES OF GARRYOWEN, THE. Dom. D. 3 a. Dion Boucicault. F. on Gerald Griffin's novel "The Collegians." Originally prod. in America, December, 1859; Adelphi, September 10, 1860, and November, 1864; Princess's, November, 1867, and January 25, 1896. See *Lily of Killarney*.

COLLEEN BAWN, THE. Extrav. H. J. Byron. Hoxton Variety T., March 14, 1870.

COLLEEN BAWN SETTLED AT LAST, THE. Extrav. 1 a. W. Brough and A. Halliday. Lyceum, July 5, 1862.

COLLEEN GLAS, THE. D. J. D. Logue. Norwich T.R., December 1, 1875.

COLLEDGE OF CANONICALL CLERKES, THE. Int. Entered by John Charlewood on the books of the Stationers' Co. 1566-7. N.p.

COLLEGE CHUMS. Sk. by C. H. Kenney. Bayswater Bijou, March 27, 1895.

COLLEGE CRAMPTON. C. 5 a. Gerhart Hauptmann. Royalty, November 14, 1903.

COLLEGE WIDOW, THE. George Ade's American comedy satire on life in the State of Indiana. Adelphi, April 20, 1908.

COLLEGETTES, THE. Travesty. Wds. and lyrics by Edgar Smith; M. by Maurice Levi. Aldwych, February 27, 1909.

COLLEGIANS, THE. See *The Colleen Bawn*.

COLLIER, THE. P. Ac. at Court, December, 1576. Possibly Fulwell's *Like Will to Like* under another title.

COLLIER OF CROYDON, THE. See *Grim*, etc.

COLLIER'S DAUGHTER, A. D. Pro. and 3 a. Jeffry Fulton. Birmingham Alexandra, June 18, 1909.

COLLIER'S DAUGHTER, THE. D. H. Bosworth. Wolverhampton P.O.W., September 29, 1873.

COLLIER'S WIFE; OR, THE DARK DEEDS OF A COAL PIT, THE. D. H. Beverley. Liverpool R. Colosseum, May 17, 1869.

COLOMBA. Lyrical D. 4 a M. by Sir A. C. Mackenzie. Lib. f. on a story of Prosper Merimée's by Francis Hueffer. D.L., April 9, 1883.

COLOMBE, LA. O. Gounod. Paris, 1866.

COLOMBE'S BIRTHDAY. P. R. Browning. Hay., April 25, 1853.

COLOMBO, IL. O. M. by Morlacchi. 1828.

COLOMBO, THE CORSICAN SISTERS. D. Adelphi, December, 1846.

COLONEL, THE. F. 2 a. C.G., May 4, 1830.

COLONEL, THE. C. 3 a. F. on "Le Mari à la Campagne" by F. C. Burnand. P.O.W., February 2, 1881.

COLONEL CLAY. C. 3 a. F. W. Sydney. Manchester Prince's T., May 25, 1903.

COLONEL CROMWELL. D. 4 a. Arthur Patterson and Charles Cartwright. Globe, October 11, 1900.

COLONEL NEWCOME. P. 4 a. Michael Morton. Adap. fr. Thackeray's novel, "The Newcomes." Terry's, April 25, 1901 (C.P.); H.M., May 29, 1906.

COLONEL SELLERS. Dr. sketch. 5 a. Mark Twain. Gaiety, July 19, 1880.

COLONEL SMITH. C. 4 a. A. E. W. Mason. St. James's, April 23, 1909.

COLONEL SPLIT-TAIL. O. Ac. at Versailles. Pr. 1730.

COLONELL, THE. P. Wm. Davenant. Entered Stationers' Co. by Eph. Dawson, January 1, 1629-30.

COLONEL'S CONSENT, THE. Sk. Camberwell Empire, April 19, 1909.

COLONEL'S HEROIC SIN, THE. M.D. 5 a. T. W. Taylor. Blackpool O.H., March 8, 1905.

COLONEL'S WIFE, THE. D. Prol. and 4 a. Bessie Reid and Lita Smith. Coventry T.R., February 6, 1888.

COLONISTS, THE. P. 1 a. E. C. Ravani. Ideal Club, Tottenham Court Road, March 28, 1895.

COLORADO BEETLE, THE. F. W. Minto. Princess's, October 13, 1877.

COLOUR SERGEANT, THE. P. 1 a. Brandon Thomas. Princess's, February 26, 1885.

COLPORTEUR, LE. O. Onslow. 1784-1853.

COLUMBIA'S DAUGHTER. Dr. Piece. Mrs. S. Rowson

COLUMBUS. John Marston. 1599.

COLUMBUS; OR, A WORLD DISCOVERED. Hist. P. Thos. Morton. C.G., December 1, 1792. See *The Incas; or, The Peruvian Virgin*.

COLUMBUS; OR, THE ORIGINAL PITCH IN A MERRY KEY. Extrav. Elfred Thompson. Gaiety, May 17, 1869.

COMALA. D. poem. 3 a. Taken fr. Ossian by Lady Burrell. Pr. 1793. Wr. in 1784.

COMALA. D. poem fr. Ossian. Pr. 1792. Ac at Hanover Square Rooms.

COMBAT OF CAPPS, THE. Masque. 1582. See "Princeps Rhet." and *The School Moderator*.

COMBAT OF LOVE AND FRIENDSHIP, THE. C. Robt. Mead. Ac. by Students of Christ Church Coll., Oxford, 1651. Pr. 1654.

COMBAT OF THE TONGUE. C. Brewer. 1607. (Cromwell ac. the part of Tactus in this play.)

COME AND SEE. F. 2 a. Langsdorff. Hay., July 18, 1814.

COME HERE; OR, THE DEBUTANTE'S TEST. Dr. sketch. 1 a. Augustin Daly. Hay., May 4, 1876.

COME IF YOU CAN. F. Hay., June 14, 1824.

COME INSIDE. Revue, in 3 scs. Geo. Grossmith, jun. Lyrics by C. H. Bovill; M. comp. and arr. by Cuthbert Clarke. Empire, April 10, 1909.

COME MICHAELMAS. C. 1 a. Keble Howard. Adelphi, April 26, 1909.

COME, SEE A WONDER. P. John Day. T. Dekker. Red Bull, September 18, 1623. N.p.

COMEDIENNE, L'A. C. Audrieux.

COMEDIENS, LES. C. Delavigne. 1819.

COMEDY AND TRAGEDY. C. 1 a. Fr. the French of M. R. Fournier. Transl. by Wm. Robson. Paris Theatre Gymnase, April 15, 1841; and at Lyceum as *The Tragedy Queen*, December 13, 1847.

COMEDY AND TRAGEDY. D. 1 a. W. S. Gilbert. Lyceum, January 26, 1884; Hay., May 7, 1890; Comedy, June 7, 1900; rev., Adel., July 4, 1905; Cri., May 31, 1905.

COMEDY OF ERRORS, THE. C. Shakespeare. 5 a. 1592. Fol., 1623. Partly fr. the Menæchini of Plautus (transl. by W(illiam) W(arner), entered at Stationers' H., June 10, 1594, and called *Historie of Error*, and ac. at Hampton Court on New Year's Day at right 1577). Mentioned by Meres, 1598. Rev. at D.L., September 22, 1866; Gray's Inn H., December 6, 1895. Alt. ver. by Thos. Hull, C.G., 1779. Pr. 1793.

COMEDY OF ERRORS. Bros. Webb. Princess's, 1864.

COMEDY OF ERRORS.—See *O! It's Impossible, Our Strategists, The Twins.*

COMEDY OF GOOD ORDER, THE. John Skelton. N.p.

COMEDY OF SIGHS, A. C. 4 a. John Todhunter. Avenue, March 29, 1894.

COMEDY OF TRIFLES, A. C. 3 a. William Beach. West Norwood Public H., December 2, 1899.

COMEDY OF VIRTUE, THE. John Skelton. N.p.

COMET; OR, DRAMATIC DULNESS, THE. F. 2 a. Joseph Moser. Pr. 1807. N. ac.

COMET; OR, HOW TO COME AT HER, THE. C. 3 a. Hay., 1789. N.p.

COMETE, OR, TWO HEARTS, LA. D. 4 a. A. W. Pinero. Croydon T.R., April 22, 1878.

COMFORTABLE LODGINGS; OR, PARIS IN 1750. F. 2 a. Richd. Brinsley Peake. D.L., March 10, 1827.

COMFORTABLE SERVICE. F. 1 a. T. H. Bayly. Wr. January 1, 1836.

COMICAL COUNTESS, A. F. 1 a. Wm. Brough. Lyceum, November 27, 1854; D.L., December 19, 1855.

COMICAL DISAPPOINTMENT; OR, THE MISER OUTWITTED, THE. B.O. Hay., 1736. N.p.

COMICAL DISTRESSES OF PIERROTT, THE. Pant. D.L., 1729.

COMICAL GALLANT WITH THE AMOURS OF SIR JOHN FALSTAFF, THE. C. John Dennis. A ver. of *The Merry Wives of Windsor*. D.L. Pr. 1702.

COMICAL HASH, THE. C. Duchess of Newcastle. Pr. 1662.

COMICAL HISTORY OF ALPHONSUS, KING OF ARRAGON, THE. 1592. Pr. 1599.

COMICAL HISTORY OF DON QUIXOTE. In 2 parts. C. J. D'Urfey. Dorset Gdns., 1694.

COMICAL LOVERS, THE. C. Colley Cibber, being an adap. of the comic scenes in Dryden's *Marriage à la Mode* and his *Maiden Queen*. Circ. 1707. Queen's T. in Hay., February 4, 1707. Pr. 1712, and rev. at D.L., 1720, 1746, and 1752.

COMICAL RESENTMENT; OR, TRICK FOR TRICK, THE. O.F. C.G., 1759. N.p.

COMICAL REVENGE; OR, LOVE IN A TUB, THE. F. Sir Geo. Etherege. Ac. L.I.F., 1664; Duke of York's and pr., 1669; rev. Hay., December, 1706; D.L., 1713.

COMICAL TRANSFORMATION; OR, THE DEVIL OF A WIFE, THE. F. Thos. Jevon. Queen's T. in Dorset Gardens, 1686.

COMING CLOWN, THE. A "Christmas number." 1 a. By Mark Melford. Royalty, December 21, 1886; rev. Opera Comique, January 2, 1893

COMING EVENTS. "M. prophecy." By R. Reece. M. by Bucalossi. Royalty, April 22, 1876.

COMING HOME. D. 3 a. Geo. Ralph Walker. Globe, July 5, 1873.

COMING MEMBER, THE. Ca. F. Sylvester. St. Albans County Club H., February 13, 1893 (amat.).

COMING OF AGE. Oa. Dr. J. E. Carpenter. M. by E. L. Hime. Charing Cross, June 19, 1869.

COMING OF THE KING, THE. Military Epis. 1 sc. Ivan Patrick Gore. Surrey, September 20, 1909.

COMING RACE, THE. Mag. D. Prol. 3 a. David Christie Murray and Nevil Maskelyne. F. on Lord Lytton's novel of same name. St. Geo. H., January 2, 1905.

COMING THRO' THE RYE. Ca. By J. A. Rosier and W. T. Mainprice. Halifax T.R., October 11, 1886.

COMING WOMAN, THE. C.D. 3 a. Ladbroke H., April 30, 1887.

COMING WOMAN; OR, THE SPIRIT OF SEVENTY-SIX, THE. Prophetic D.

COMMANDANT, THE. C.O. 2 a. Leo and Harry Trevor. M. by Burnham Horner. Richmond T.R., April 26, 1894.

COMME ELLES SONT TONTES. C. 1 a. Royalty, May 17, 1897.

COMMISSARY, THE. C. 3 a. Saml. Foote. Hay., June, 1765. Pr. 1675.

COMMISSION, A. C. 1 a. Weedon Grossmith. Terry's, June 6, 1891; Shaftesbury, Toole's, and tr. to Court, December 2, 1891.

COMMITTED FOR TRIAL. F. 2 a. F. Latour Tomline. Globe, January 24, 1874.

COMMITTED FOR TRIAL. D. 4 a. Edward Towers. E. London, November 30, 1878.

COMMITTEE, THE. C. Sir Robt. Howard. Ac. T.R., and pr. 1665; D.L., February, 1788. Title *The Faithful Irishman* added.

COMMITTEE; OR, HONEST THIEVES, THE. See *Honest Thieves.*

COMMITTEE MAN CURRIED, THE. C. 2 parts. S. Sheppard. Wr. and pr. 1647. 1 a. each part. Chiefly taken fr. Sir John Suckling and Sir Robt. Stapleton's transl. of *Juvenal.*

COMMODITY EXCIS'D; OR, THE WOMEN IN AN UPROAR, THE. B.O. Timothy Smoke. Pr. 1733. Ac. privately.

COMMODORE, THE. Op. bo. 3 a. H. B. Farnie and R. Reece. Taken fr. *La Creole.* M. by Jacques Offenbach. Lib. by Albert Millaud. Avenue, May 10, 1886.

COMMODORE BOUILLI. C.O. 3 a. T. Murray Ford. M. by Dr. John Storer. Bow and Bromley Inst., November 31, 1888.

COMMON CONDITIONS. C. Before 1576. See *Fortune, to Know, etc.*

COMMON SENSE, THE LIFE AND DEATH OF. Prel. Alt. from Fielding's *Pasquin.* Hay., August 13, 1782.

COMMON SENSE; OR, THE SLAVES OF MAMMON. D. 4 a. Edwd. Towers. Pav., May 11, 1878.

COMMONWEALTH OF WOMEN, A. T.C. Thos. D'Urfey. Taken fr. Fletcher's *Sea Voyage.* Ac. at T.R., 1686, and several times to 1746.

COMŒDIA. In rhyme. See *Enterlude of Myndes.*

COMŒDYES AND PASTORALLS. "W. P." Pr. 1610. A book containing:—

The Cuckqueans and Cuckolds Errants; or, The Bearing Down the Inne. C. 1601.
Arabia Sitiens; or, A Dreame of a Drye Yeare. T.C. 1601.
The Faery Pastorall; or, Forrest of Elves.

A Country Tragœdye in Vacuniam; or, Cupid's Sacrifice. 1602.
The Aphrodysial, or Sea Feast. 1602.
Necromantes; or, The Two Supposed Heds. A comical invention.

COMPACT, THE. P. 3 a. D.L., April 5, 1832.

COMPANIONS OF THE ROAD. Sk. Coliseum, July 12, 1909.

COMPETITION; OR, MUCH ADO ABOUT NOTHING (AS USUAL). Burl. skit. 3 sc. F. T. W. Miller. Westminster T.H., April 30, 1889. (Amateurs.)

COMPETITORS; OR, THE NYMPH OF NOZENARO, THE. C.O. 2 a. Sydney Cubitt. M. by Thos. Hackwood. Stroud Subscription R., January 19, 1893.

COMPLAINT OF ROSAMUND. T. Daniel. 1562-1619.

COMPLEAT ANGLER, THE. Duol. S. Craven and J. D. Beresford. Lyceum, June 11, 1907.

COMPLETE CHANGE, A. F. Burnand McDonald. St. Geo. H., January 9, 1896.

COMPOSER, THE. Ca. Arthur Chapman. M. by J. M. Capel. Richmond T.R., October 29, 1891.

COMPOSITEUR TOQUE, LE. Fr. Oa. Lyceum, April 4, 1870.

COMPROMISE; OR, FAULTS ON BOTH SIDES, THE. C. Mr. Sturmy. L.I.F., 1722. Pr. 1723.

COMPROMISED. C. Montague Marks. Fulham Grand, September 27, 1900. C.p.

COMPROMISING CASE, A. C. 1 a. Adap. by Mrs. T. E. Smale fr. *Le Porte Cigare.* Hay., May 26, 1888.

COMPROMISING COAT, A. Ca. J. T. Grein and C. W. Jarvis. Globe, June 27, 1892.

COMPROMISING LETTERS. F. 1 a. C. W. McCabe. Wandsworth Common, St. Luke's Hall.

COMPROMISING MARTHA. C. 1 a. Keble Howard. Royalty, May 20, 1906.

COMRADES. C. 3 a. Brandon Thomas and B. C. Stephenson. Court, February 16, 1882.

COMRADES AND FRIENDS. Military D. 2 a. Isaac Pocock. C.G., February 14, 1831.

COMRADES IN KHAKI. Inc. of the Transvaal War. Chas. Brookfield. Garrick, December 15, 1899.

COMTE CARMAGNOLA, LE. O. Thomas Paris, 1841.

COMTE D'ALBERT. O. Grétry. Fontainebleau, 1786.

COMTE D'ESSEX. See *Robert Devereux.*

COMTE D'ORY, LE. C. Scribe. 1828.

COMTE ORY, LE. O. Rossini. Paris, August 20, 1828; King's T., February 28, 1829.

COMTESSE D'ESCARBAGNAS. C. Molière. 1672. See "French Classical Plays."

COMUS. Masque. 2 a. John Milton. M. by Lawes. Ludlow Castle, September 29, 1634.

COMUS. Milton's Masque. Alt. by Dr. Dalton D.L. and pr., 1738-40. Alt. by Geo. Coleman. C.G. Pr. 1772. Edinburgh, 1782.

COMUS. Masque by Milton. Original M. by Handel and Dr. Arne, with add. by Bishop, 1738. D.L., October 5, 1833; rev. Botanic Gardens, July 1, 1903.

CONCEALED BED IN THE PARLOUR, THE. Ca. Graham Moffat. Glasgow Athenæum, April 23, 1909.

CONCEALED FANCIES, THE. P. Lady Jane Cavendish and Lady Elizabeth Brackley. MS. preserved in the Bodleian Library.

CONCEALED ROYALTY Past. P. R. Carlton. 1674.

CONCEITED DUKE, THE. P. belonging to the Cockpit. Probably no other than *The Noble Gentleman* of Beaumont and Fletcher.

CONCEITED LADIES, THE. C. Transl. fr. Molière. Pr. 1762.

CONCEITED PEDLAR, THE. F. Thos. Randolph. Pr. 1631.

CONCEITED PEDLAR, THE. See *Aristippus.* Dodsley acknowledges taking the hint of his *Toy Shop* fr. this piece.

CONCEITS, THE. P. R. Marriot. Ent. Stationers' Co., November 29, 1653. N.p.

CONCEPTION, THE. See "Miracle Plays."

CONCERNING A COUNTESS. P. 1 a. Criterion, October 15, 1907.

CONDEMNED. C.D. W. Manning. Warrington P.O.W., September 3, 1878.

CONDEMNED; OR, £1,000 REWARD. American D. By Euston Knowles. Castleford T.R., August 25, 1887.

CONFEDERACY, THE. C. Adap. by Sir John Vanbrugh fr. *The Bourgeois à la Mode.* Hay. and Her M., October 3, 1705. Pr. same year. D.L., May 12, 1817; rev. Royalty, November 29, 1904.

CONFEDERATES. D. 1 a. Henry Woodville. Globe, February 25, 1897.

CONFEDERATES. D. 1 a. H. Capper. Publ. by S. French, Ltd.

CONFEDERATES, THE. F. J. Durant Breval. Pr. in name of Joseph Gay, 1717. N. ac.

CONFESSION, THE. C. 5 a. Whyte. Edinburgh, 1799.

CONFESSION, THE. P. R. Cumberland. Pr. 1813.

CONFESSOR. Latin D. T. Sparowe. Wr. about 1666.

CONFIDENCE. Ca. Adap. fr. the Fr. by Dion Boucicault. Hay., May 2, 1848.

CONFIDENCE. D. 3 a. R. Cantwell. Britannia, October 21, 1872.

CONFIDENTIAL CLERK, THE. F.C. 3 a. Sydney Wittman and Shedden Wilson. Adap. fr. Von Moser's *Der Leibrenter.* Gaiety, June 18, 1886.

CONFIDENTIAL CLERK, THE. P. 4 a. W. Elsworthy Stedman. At Gobleville, February 12, 1892.

CONFINED IN VAIN; OR, A DOUBLE TO-DO. F. T. Jones. Pr. 1805.

CONFLICT; OR, LOVE, HONOUR, AND PRIDE, THE. Heroic C. Hannah Brand. Alt. fr. Corneille's Don Sauche d'Aragon. Pr. 1798.

CONFLICT OF CONSCIENCE, THE. Past. 6 a. Rev. Nathaniel Wood. Pr. 1581.

CONFUSION. D. Sk. Francis W. Moore. Royalty, February 23, 1876.

CONFUSION. F.C. 3 a. Joseph Derrick. Vaudeville, May 17, 1883, and May 8, 1891.

CONGENIAL SOULS. F. J. H. Ryley. Edinburgh Princess's, October 3, 1878.

CONGRES DE ROIS, LE. O. 3 a. Méhul February 26, 1793.

CONGRESS; OR, THE CZAR AND THE MINISTER, THE. B. Dover T.R., July 8, 1878.

CONGRESS AT PARIS, A. F. Edwd. Rose. Olympic, July 15, 1878.

CONGRESS OF CRITICS, THE. Int. Pr. 1783.

CONGRESS OF THE BEASTS, THE. F. 2 a. Pr. 1748. In rehearsal at a T. in Germany.

CONJECTURES. P. 1 a. Hay., June 15, 1830.

CONJUGAL FIDELITY. C. Transl. fr. Plautus by Richd. Warner. Pr. 1772. Plautus calls this C. *Stichus*.

CONJUGAL LESSON, A. C.Sc. in 1 a. H. Danvers. Olympic, July 3, 1856.

CONJUROR, THE. F. Miles Peter Andrews. D.L., April 29, 1774. N.p.

CONJUROR; OR, THE ENCHANTED GARDEN, THE. MS. belonging to the library of Arthur Murphy.

CONJUROR; OR, THE SCOTSMAN IN LONDON, THE. F. 3 a. Archibald M'Laren. Pr. 1781.

CONN; OR, OUT OF SIGHT, OUT OF ERIN. B. F. W. Green. Liverpool Alexandra, April 28, 1879.

CONNAN, PRINCE OF CORNWALL. P. Michael Drayton and Thos. Dekker. Ac. 1598. N.p.

CONNAUGHT WIFE, THE. T. 2 a. Smock Alley, Dublin. Pr. 1767. This is Hippisley's *Journey to Bristol* alt.

CONNEMARA. Irish D. J. C. Chute. Warrington P.O.W., May 24, 1880.

CONNOISSEUR; OR, EVERY MAN IN HIS FOLLY, THE. C. Conolly. D.L., 1734. Pr. 1736.

CONQUERED PRIDE. Ca. Ross M'Kenzie and Fred Gover. Bristol Prince's, March 19, 1886

CONQUERING GAME. C. 1 a. W. B. Bernard. Olympic, November 3, 1832.

CONQUERING HERO, THE. Sk. Fredk. Fenn. Metroplitan, December 14, 1908.

CONQUEROR, THE. Rom. D. 4 a. R. E. Fyffe (Duchess of Sutherland). The Scala, September 23, 1905.

CONQUERORS, THE. D. 4 a. Paul M. Potter. Orig. prod. in America. St. James's, April 14, 1898

CONQUEST, THE. P. 3 a. Geo. Fleming. Lyric, April 24, 1909.

CONQUEST OF BRUTE, WITH THE FIRST FINDING OF THE BATH, THE. P. John Singer. Assisted by Day and Chettle. Ac. 1598. N.p.

CONQUEST OF CANADA; OR, THE SIEGE OF QUEBEC. Hist. T. 5 a. Geo. Cockings. Pr. 1766.

CONQUEST OF CHINA, THE. T. Sir Robt. Howard. N.p. N ac.

CONQUEST OF CHINA BY THE TARTARS, THE. T. Elkanah Settle. Duke's T., 1676. Pr. 1676.

CONQUEST OF CORSICA BY THE FRENCH, THE. T. By a lady. Pr. 1771. N. ac.

CONQUEST OF GRANADA BY THE SPANIARDS, THE. T.C. 2 parts. J. Dryden. F. on *Almahide* by Mdlle. de Scudéry. Pr. 1672. T.R., 1678. Ent. on Stationers' Bks., February 1670-71.

CONQUEST OF MAGDALA AND THE FALL OF THEODORE, THE. Spec. D. Mr. Stocqueler. Astley's, September 12, 1868.

CONQUEST OF ST. EUSTATIA, THE. Int. D.L., 1781. N.p.

CONQUEST OF SPAIN, THE. T. Mrs. Pix. Pr. 1705. Chiefly borrowed from *All's Lost by Lust*. Hay., 1705.

CONQUEST OF SPAIN BY JOHN OF GAUNT, THE. Wm. Haughton, in conjunction with Hathwaye Hawkins and Day. Ac. 1601. N.p.

CONQUEST OF TARANTO, THE; OR, ST. CLARA'S EVE. Hist. P. 3 a. W. Dimond. M. by Bishop. C.G., April 15, 1817.

CONQUEST OF THE WEST INDIES, THE. P. Wm. Haughton in conjunction with Wentworth Smith and John Day. Ac. 1601. N.p.

CONRAD. T. Magnocavallo. 1772.

CONRAD AND LIZETTE; OR, LIFE ON THE MISSISSIPPI. P. 4 a. Duke's, March 29, 1880.

CONRAD AND MEDORA. Burl. Pant. W. Brough. Lyceum, December 26, 1856; D.L., April 14, 1857.

CONRAD CONVERTED; OR, THE CORSAIR REFORMED. B. A. W. Allan. St. James's, December 19, 1873.

CONSCIENCE. T. Transl. from Iffland by Benj. Thompson. Pr. 1800. N. ac.

CONSCIENCE. D. Henry Vandenhoff. Sheffield Alexandra, November 13, 1877.

CONSCIENCE. Society D. 4 a. Edwd. Litton. Vaudeville, July 17, 1888.

CONSCIENCE. Wordless piece. 4 sc. Wr. by E. Durel; M. by Colo-Bonet. Palace, December 2, 1907.

CONSCIENCE. P. 3 a. Adapt. fr. the German of Felix Philippi by Jane Wilson. Leicester R.O.H., May 9, 1902.

CONSCIENCE; OR, THE BRIDAL NIGHT. T. Haynes. D.L., February 21, 1821.

CONSCIENCE AND CRIME. D. 4 a. A. Stafford. Fleetwood Queen's, March 12, 1906.

CONSCIENCE MONEY. C.D. 3 a. H. J. Byron. Hay., September 16, 1878.

CONSCIENCE OF A JUDGE, THE. D. 4 a. Madge Duckworth and R. Barrie. Liverpool Queen's, December 10, 1907 (C.P.); Tonypandy R., December 23, 1907; Elephant and Castle, August 17, 1908.

CONSCIENTIOUS CONSTABLE, THE. F. Bernard Macdonald. Kilburn T.R., June 7, 1897.

CONSCIENTIOUS LOVERS. C. C. Gladwell. Included in Mears's Catalogue. Probably n.p.

CONSCIENTIOUS LOVERS. See *Conscious Lovers*.

CONSCILLER RAPPORTEUR, LE. C. Delavigne. 1841.

CONSCIOUS LOVERS. C. 5 a. Sir Richard Steele. Taken from Terence's *Andria*. Pr. and ac. D.L., November 7, 1722. Written some years previously, and intended to be called *The Unfashionable Lovers; or, The Fine Gentleman.*

CONSCRIPT, THE. F. 1 a. W. Oxberry. Queen's, January 18, 1836.

CONSCRIPT, THE. D. 4 a. Wybert Clive. Workington T.R., February 25, 1889; Liverpool Star, July 20, 1903.

CONSCRIPT; OR, THE VETERAN AND HIS DOG, THE. M. by Hughes. D.L., November 17, 1830.

CONSCRIT, LE. Offenbach. See *Breaking the Spell.*

CONSEQUENCES; OR, THE SCHOOL FOR PREJUDICE. C. 3 a. Edmund John Eyre. Worcester and other provincial theatres. Pr. 1794.

CONSPIRACY. P. 4 a. Geo. Lash Gordon. Liverpool P.O.W., June 16, 1882.

CONSPIRACY. D. 5 a. J. Beamul (J. B. Mulholland). Glasgow Princess's, March 5, 1888.

CONSPIRACY: OR, THE CHANGE OF GOVERNMENT, THE. T. W. Whitaker. Ep. by Ravenscroft. Duke's T., 1680. Pr. 1680.

CONSPIRACY, THE. T. Henry Killigrew. Afterwards called *Pallantus and Eudora*, and pr. as such 1653. Blackfryars, 1638.

CONSPIRACY, THE. T. Robert Jephson. D.L. and Pr. 1796 fr. the *Clemenza de Tito* of Metastasio.

CONSPIRACY, THE. P. 1 a. R. Barr and S. Lewis-Ransom. Dublin Royal, November 8, 1907; Adelphi, September 9, 1908; Adelphi, November 23, 1908.

CONSPIRACY AND TRAGEDY OF CHARLES DUKE OF BYRON, MARSHAL OF FRANCE. Two P. in one. Geo. Chapman. Blackfryars, 1608. Pr. 1608.

CONSPIRACY DISCOVERED; OR, FRENCH POLICY DEFEATED, THE. Hist. D. fr. Shakespeare. D.L., 1746. N.p.

CONSPIRACY OF BRUTUS. T. Antoni. 1691 See *Julius Cæsar.*

CONSPIRACY OF GOWRIE, THE. T. Pr. 1800. N. ac.

CONSPIRACY OF THE PAZZI. Alfieri, 1783. Transl. by C. Lloyd, 1815.

CONSPIRATORS, THE. T.C.O. Anon. Ac. in England and Ireland. Pr. 1749.

CONSPIRATORS, THE. P. Louis Dudley. Foresters' M.H., January 5, 1905.

CONSTABLE JACK; OR, THE BOBBY'S BRIDE. Oa. 1 a. M. by C. Forbes Drummond. Words by Stratton Rodney. Bath T.R., May 16, 1889.

CONSTADINA IN CORTE, LA. C.O. M. by Sacchini. King's T. in Hay., 1782.

CONSTANCE. O. Lib. by T. W. Robertson. C.G., January 23, 1865.

CONSTANCE FRERE. P. Pro. and 3 a. Herbert Gough and Morris Edwards. Vaudeville, June 27, 1887.

CONSTANCY. Duol. Cyril Hallward. Comedy, April 21, 1898.

CONSTANT COUPLE; OR, A TRIP TO THE JUBILEE, THE. C. 5 a. Geo. Farquhar, D.L., and pr. 1700, rev. L.I.F. 1731.

CONSTANT LOVERS; OR, THE SAILOR'S RETURN, THE. P. Geo. Duncan. Pr. 1798.

CONSTANT MAID; OR, LOVE WILL FIND OUT THE WAY, THE. C. Jas. Shirley. Ac. at The Nursery in Hatton Garden, probably 1636-9. Pr. 1640. Afterwards repr. as *Love Will Find Out the Way*, 1667. Borr. fr. other plays as a ballet perf. at Royalty T., January, 1788.

CONSTANT MAID; OR, POLL OF PLYMOUTH, THE. Mus. Ent. Royalty. Pr. 1787.

CONSTANT NYMPH; OR, THE RAMBLING SHEPHERD, THE. D. Past. Anon. Duke's, and pr. 1678.

CONSTANT PRINCE, THE. Calderon.

CONSTANTIA. T. 3 a. Mrs. Hughes. Pr. 1790.

CONSTANTINE. P. Rose T., March 21, 1591. N.p.

CONSTANTINE. T. Phil Francis. C.G. Pr. 1754.

CONSTANTINE PALEOLOGUS; OR, THE LAST OF THE CÆSARS. T. Joanna Baillie. Pr. 1804. N. ac.

CONSTANTINE THE GREAT; OR, THE TRAGEDY OF LOVE. T. Nathaniel Lee. T.R., and pr. 1684. F. on hist.

CONSULTATION, THE. F. Hay., April, 1705.

CONSULTATION. Oa. 1 a. Byron and Schubert. Publ. by S. French, Ltd.

CONTE D'ESSEX, IL. O. Mercadante. Milan, 1833.

CONTE ORY, IL. O. Rossini. Paris, 1828.

CONTEMPT OF COURT. Oa. Arthr Matthison and Edward Solomon. Folly, May 5, 1877.

CONTEMPT OF COURT. C. 3 a. Dion Boucicault. Marylebone, October 1, 1879.

CONTENDING BROTHERS, THE. C. Hy. Brooke. Pr. 1778. N. ac.

CONTENTED CUCKOLD; OR, THE WOMAN'S ADVOCATE, THE. C. Reuben Bourne. Pr. 1692. N. ac.

CONTENTION BETWEEN LIBERALITIE AND PRODIGALITIE, THE. C. Pr. 1602. Probably by Greene. Pl. before Her Majestie.

CONTENTION BETWEEN THE TWO FAMOUS HOUSES, LANCASTER AND YORKE, THE WHOLE. 2 parts. Pr. 1600. Shakespeare's Part 2 of *Henry VI.*, publ. 1623, is very like this.

CONTENTION FOR HONOUR AND RICHES, A. Masque. Jas. Shirley. Pr. 1633. Afterwards enlarged and called *Honoria and Mammon.*

CONTENTION OF AJAX AND ULYSSES FOR ACHILLES' ARMOUR, THE. Masque. Jas. Shirley. Taken fr. 13th Book of Ovid's Metamorphoses. Pr. 1659.

CONTES D'HOFFMANN, LES. C.O. Offenbach. Paris, October 30, 1880.

CONTES DE LA REINE DE NAVARRE, LES. Scribe and Legouvé. 1850.

CONTESSA D'AMALFI, LA. Petrella. Turin, 1864.

CONTESSE VILLANE, LE. O. L. Rossi. 1828.

CONTEST OF BEAUTY AND VIRTUE, THE. Masque. Transl. fr. Metastasio by Dr. Arne. C.G. Pr. 1773.

CONTESTED ELECTION. C. 3 a. (Not T. Taylor's.) Harris Arundel. Ptd. 1856.

CONTESTED ELECTION, THE. C. Tom Taylor. Hay., June 29, 1859.

CONTRABANDISTA, THE. O. 2 a. Lib. F. C. Burnand. M. by Arthur Sullivan. St. Geo. H., December 18, 1867.

CONTRABANDISTA, THE. See *The Chieftain.*

CONTRACT, THE. C. 2 a. Dr. Thos. Franklin. Hay., and Pr. 1776. f. on Destouche's *L'Amour Usé.*

CONTRACT, THE. C.O. Robt. Houlton. Dublin, 1783.

CONTRACT, THE. D. 5 a. Harry Croft Hillier. Margate T.R., June 6, 1887.

CONTRACT; OR, FEMALE CAPTAIN, THE. F. D.L., 1779, and afterwards under the latter title at the Hay., 1780. N.p.

CONTRACTOR, THE. C.D. 3 a. G. H. R. Dabbs. Shanklin Lit. Inst., December 15, 1887.

CONTRADICTIONS. Ca. 1 a. Agnes Leigh. Publ. by S. French, Ltd.

CONTRARIETIES; OR, ALL AT CROSS PURPOSES. Int. 1 a. D.L., May 29, 1817.

CONTRARY WINDS. Oa. Lib. by Fredk. Wood. M. by Geo. Fox. Margate New T., July 24, 1882.

CONTRAST, THE. P. Drs. Benjamin and J. Hoadly. L.I.F., April 30, 1731. N.p. The same design is used in *Pasquin.*

CONTRAST, THE. D. Past. Pr. 1782.

CONTRAST, THE. C. 2 a. Ac. at Calcutta, December, 1789.

CONTRAST, THE. C. 5 a. Ac. at New York. Pr. 1790.

CONTRAST; OR, THE JEW AND MARRIED COURTEZAN, THE. F. Waldron. D.L., May 12, 1775. N.p.

CONTRAST; OR, THE MAYORALTY OF TRUEBOROUGH, THE. C. E. Smith.

CONTRETEMPS; OR, RIVAL QUEENS, THE. F. Anon. Ac. at Heidegger's Private T., near Hay. Pr. 1727.

CONTRIVANCES; OR, MORE WAYS THAN ONE, THE. Ballad F. Henry Carey. D.L. August 9, 1715; and C.G. Pr. 1715.

CONTROLEUR DES WAGONS-LITS, LE. C. 3 a. Alex. Bisson. Orig. pr. at the Paris Nouveautés, March 11, 1898. An adap. entitled *On and Off*. Pr. at the Royalty, October 7, 1907; Vaudeville, December 1, 1898.

CONVENIENT LOVER, THE. F. 1 a. Catherine Roxburgh. Glasgow Royalty, April 28, 1909.

CONVENIENT SON-IN-LAW, A. F. Portsmouth T.R., June 4, 1877.

CONVENT, THE. M.D. John Rannie. Pr. No date. N. ac.

CONVENT BELL, THE. D. 4 a. A. Tullock. Surrey, May 30, 1904.

CONVENT BELLES. P. Edwd. Fitzball. Olympic, 1841-4.

CONVENT OF PLEASURE, THE. C. By Margaret Duchess of Newcastle. 1668. N. ac.

CONVERSATION OF A FATHER WITH HIS CHILDREN; OR, THE DANGER OF DISREGARDING THE LAWS, THE. Transl. fr. Gesner. Pr. 1792. N. ac.

CONVERSION OF ENGLAND, THE. Hist. D. Rev. H. Cresswell. Vauxhall St. Peter's H., 1885.

CONVERSION OF NAT STURGE, THE. C.P. 1 a. Malcolm Watson. H.M., June 23, 1904; Garrick, July 9, 1904.

CONVERSION OF ST. PAUL. See "Miracle Plays."

CONVERT, THE. D. 4 a. Sergius Stepoack. Transl. fr. the Russian by Constance Garnett. Avenue, June 14, 1898.

CONVERTED COURTEZAN, THE. The first part of *The Honest Whore*. Originally pr. under this title. Circa 1604.

CONVERTED ROBBER, THE. Past. P. George Wild. Ac. at St. John's College, Oxford, 1637.

CONVERTS; OR, THE FOLLY OF PRIESTCRAFT, THE. O. Anon. Pr. 1690.

CONVICT, THE. D. Perf. J. Wilson, 1816.

CONVICT, THE. P. City of London, November, 1838.

CONVICT, THE. D. H. Neville. Liverpool R. Amphitheatre, August 3, 1868.

CONVICT, THE. D. 4 a. Fred Jarman. Woolwich R.A.T., July 21, 1901; Strat. R., November 18, 1901.

CONVICT; OR, HUNTED TO DEATH, THE. D. Prol. and 4 a. C. H. Stephenson. Pav., February 1, 1868.

CONVICT 99. D. 4 a. J. Denton. Adap. fr. a story. Peckham Crown, June 22, 1908.

CONVICT ON THE HEARTH, THE. P.A. Fredk. Fenn. Court, February 6, 1906; rev Queen's, October 22, 1907; rev. Savoy, December 30, 1907.

CONVICT'S DAUGHTER, THE. D. 4 a. Gordon Holmes. Newcastle-on-Tyne T.R., October 15, 1903 (C.P.); Islington Grand, March 7, 1904.

CONVICT'S ESCAPE, THE. See *A Convict's Wife*.

CONVICT'S WIFE, A. C.D. 3 a. W. Sapte, jun. P.O.W. (under title of *Marah* in prol. and 3 a.), May 31, 1889. Grand, May 19, 1890.

CONVICTS. P. 1 a. Edwin Holland and Robert Hillard. New T. (C.P.), October 24, 1903.

CONVIVADO DE PIEDRA. C. Terso de Molino, whose name was Tellez. 1626. This is the original of all the Don Juans.

COOKETTISH COOK; OR, THE AREA BELL RUNG TOO MANY TIMES, THE. M. Mélange. By F. Wynne Scarlett. Brighton Aq., November 11, 1895.

COOL AS A CUCUMBER. F. 1 a. W. Blanchard Jerrold. Lyceum, March 24, 1851; Gaiety, November, 1872.

COOLEEN DAWN. Martin Dutnall and J. B. Johnstone. Surrey, October 14, 1861.

COOPER, THE. M. Ent. M. by Dr. Arne. Hay., June, 1772. Pr. 1772. Taken fr. a Fr. piece called *Le Tonnelier*.

CO-OPERATIVE MOVEMENT, A. F. Harry Lemon. Hay., April 6, 1868.

COOPER'S HILL. Sir John Denham. Pr. 1643.

COPING STONE, THE. P. 4 a. G. Lawrence. Eastbourne D.P., April 19, 1907.

COPPER CAPTAIN, THE. Kemble and Lewis played in a piece of this name at Dublin.

COQUET, THE. M. Ent. Steph. Storace. Sung at Marylebone Gdns. Pr. 1771. Transl. fr. Ital. of Goldini, and adap. to the original music of Galluppi.

COQUET; OR, THE ENGLISH CHEVALIER, THE. C. Chas. Molloy. L.I.F., and pr. 1718.

COQUET'S SURRENDER; OR, THE HUMOROUS PUNSTER, THE. C. Anon. 1732. Publ. in 1733 under the title of *The Court Lady; or, The Coquet's Surrender*.

COQUETTE, Op. C. 2 a. Wr. by R. E. Pattinson. M. by Daisy Sopwith and Angela Rawlinson. 5, Queen's Gate Place, W., December 17, 1892; Albert H. West T., June 5, 1893; Bayswater Bijou, November 2, 1895.

COQUETTE, THE. Burl. Hay., 1761. N.p.

COQUETTE, THE. P. 3 a. Adap. fr. the Fr. by T. Mead. Hay., July 8, 1867.

COQUETTE, THE. C. 4 a. Capt. Hawley Smart. Cheltenham Assembly Rooms, April 10, 1885.

COQUETTE, THE. Ca. Wm. Poel. Portman Rooms, May 16, 1892.

COQUETTE, THE. C.O. 3 a. Book f. on Garrido-Lefrique's O., *Moliere d'Alcala*, by H. J. W. Dam. Lyrics by Clifton Bingham. M. by Justin Clerice. P.O.W., February 11, 1899.

COQUETTE; OR, THE MISTAKES OF THE HEART, THE. C. Robt. Hitchcock. Ac. at York and Hull. Pr. 1777. Taken fr. Mrs. Heywood's novel, *Betsy Thoughtless*.

COQUETTE DU VILLAGE. C. Dufresny. 1715.

COQUETTES; OR, THE GALLANT IN THE CLOSET, THE. C. Lady Houston. Chiefly a transl. of a P. of Thos. Corneille.

CORA. O. Naumann. 1780.

CORA. O. 4 a. Méhul. 1791.

CORA. D. Prol. and 3 a. Adap. fr. the French *L'Article* 47 by W. S. Wills and Frank Marshall. Globe, February 28, 1877.

CORA; OR, LOVE AND PASSION. D. 4 a. W. G. Wills. Leeds T.R., March 2, 1874.

CORA; OR, THE SLAVES OF THE SOUTH. Grecian, June 26, 1865.

CORA; OR, THE VIRGIN OF THE SUN. Burl. P. J. C. Cross. Royal Circus. Pr. 1809.

CORALIE. P. 4 a. Adap. fr. the French of M. Delpit by G. W. Godfrey. St. James's, May 28, 1881.

CORALINE; OR, SNARES AND PITFALLS. D. 4 a. G. A. Warriner. King's Cross, February 27, 1873.

CORDE SENSIBLE, LA. Royalty, November 5, 1888.

CORDELIA. T. 5 a. Mrs. Hughes. Pr. 1790.

CO-RESPONDENT, THE. F.C. 4 a. G. W. Appleton. Adap. fr. his novel of the same name by the author Afterwards called *Our Kate*. Liverpool P.O.W., June 20, 1896 (C.P.); Birmingham Grand T., August 3, 1896; Camberwell Metropole, September 21, 1896.

CORESUS ET CALLIRHOE. T. Lafosse. 1696.

CORIN; OR. THE KING OF THE PEACEFUL ISLES. Burl. Dublin Queen's, February 6, 1871.

CORINNE. D. 4 a. Robt. Buchanan. Lyceum, June 26, 1876.

CORINNE. D. F. upon Mrs. Otto Von Booth's novel. Standard, May 23, 1885 (C.P.).

CORINNE. Burl. O. 1 a. Philip Scott, A.S.C., and Capt. G. G. Hewlett, A.S.C. M. by Wm. Parker. Dublin Queen's R.T., August 26, 1895.

CORIOLAN. T. Laharpe. 1781.

CORIOLANUS. T. 5 a. W. Shakespeare. 1609. Fol., 1623. Plot taken fr. history—viz., Plutarch's "Life of Coriolanus." Rev. at Lyceum, April 15, 1901.

CORIOLANUS. F. on Haym's D. of Cajo Marzio Coriolano. M. by Attilo Ariosti (a rival of Handel). 1723.

CORIOLANUS. T. James Thomson. C.G. Pr. 1748.

CORIOLANUS; THE INVADER OF HIS COUNTRY. T. John Dennis. D.L., 1720.

CORIOLANUS; OR, THE ROMAN MATRON. T. J. Sheridan. Pr. 1755. Adap. fr. *Coriolanus* of Shakespeare and Thomson. An arrangement prod. by J. P. Kemble at D.L., February, 1789, and pr. 1789, and at C.G., 1806.

CORKONIAN BROTHERS, THE. Burl. Strand, February 27, 1854.

CORKSCREW. Sk. Paragon, July 20, 1908.

CORNARINO'S MISTAKE. Oa. Julian Edwards. Hereford Corn Exchange, September 30, 1872.

CORNELIA. T. Robt. Garnier in Fr. Transl. by Thos. Kyd fr. Garnier's T., *Cornélie*, circa 1594.

CORNELIA. P. Sir W. Bartley. Ac. in Gibbon's Tennis Court, Clare Market, June 1, 1662. N.p.

CORNELIA; OR, A ROMAN MATRON'S JEWELS. D Anecdote. J. P. Roberdean. Chichester, 1805. Pr 1810.

CORNELIE. T. Garnier. 1591.

CORNELIE. T. Henault and Fuscher. 1768.

CORNERED. Sk. New Cross Empire, January 18. 1909.

CORNETTE JAUNE. C. Carmouche. 1864.

CORNEY COURTED. Oa. 1 a. Arthur Waugh, fr. Dickens's "Oliver Twist." M. by Claude Nugent. Ladbroke H.; Comedy, March 6, 1893.

CORNEY RHUE. D. Barry Connor. Brit., August 4, 1879.

CORNISH COMEDY, THE. P. Ac. at Th. in Dorset Gardens and pr. 1696.

CORNISH GIRL, THE. O. 2 a. E. C. Arden. M. by J. H. Wilson and C. Locknane. Folkestone P.G., November 12, 1906.

CORNISH INTERLUDES. 3 on parchment in Bodleian Library and one on paper, 1611. This latter is transl. and called *Creation of the World*.

CORNISH MINERS, THE. Melo-d. 2 a. M. by G. Herbert Rodwell. Lyceum, July 2, 1827.

CORNISH SQUIRE. C. Sir John Vanbrugh, Congreve, and Walsh. F. on Molière's *Sieur Pourceaugnac*. Hay., 1706; D.L., 1734, and pr. See *Monsieur de Pourceaugnac*.

CORONA MINERVÆ. Masque. Pr. 1635. Ac. February 27, 1635. Possibly by Thos. Middleton.

CORONATION, THE. T.C. Either by Beaumont and Fletcher or Jas. Shirley. (Disputed.) Private house, D.L. Pr. 1640.

CORONATION, THE. Ent Archibald Maclaren. Pr. 1804.

CORONATION, THE. Reproduction of Geo. IV. Coronation. D.L., August 1, 1821.

CORONATION MARCH, THE. F. A. Eldred. Birmingham G.T., May 19, 1902.

CORONATION OF DAVID, THE. D. Joseph Wise. 1763. Pr. 1766.

CORONATION OF QUEEN ELIZABETH: OR, THE RESTORATION OF THE PROTESTANT RELIGION AND DOWNFALL OF THE POPE. Hist. P. 3 a. "W. R." Pr. 1680. Played at Bartholomew and Southwark Fairs.

CORONER, THE. D. Prol. and 4 a. J. W. Hemming and Cyril Harrison. Bath T.R., August 4, 1888; Eleph. and C., August 26, 1889

CORPORAL, THE. P. Arthur Wilson, of Trinity College, Oxford. Entered Stationers' Co. September 4, 1646; perf. Blackfriars,.

CORPORAL SHAKO. F. Fredk. Hay. Surrey, June 13, 1879.

CORPORAL'S WEDDING; OR, A KISS FROM THE BRIDE, THE. F. 1 a. J. M. Morton. Adelphi, January 20, 1845.

CORPUS CHRISTI PLAYS. See "Miracle Plays."

CORRECT THING, THE. P. 1 a. Alfred Sutro. D.L., May 29, 1905; Shaftesbury, November 4, 1905.

CORRUPT PRACTICES. C.D. 2 a. Frank Marshall. Lyceum, January 22, 1870.

CORRUPTIONS OF THE DIVINE LAWS. Dr. piece by Bishop Bale.

CORSAIR, THE. O. M. of Herold's O. *Zampa*. First time adap. to English stage. D.L., March 21, 1836.

CORSAIR, THE. Ballet. M. Albert. D.L, September 30, 1844.

CORSAIR, THE. Burl. Adam. 1856.

CORSAIR, THE. English O. 3 a. Chas. Deffell Crystal Palace, March 25, 1873; March 3, 1877.

CORSAIR'S REVENGE. Rom. D. 2 a. Grattan. Victoria T., March 16, 1843.

CORSAIRE NOIR, LE. O. 3 a. Offenbach. Vienna, 1872.

CORSARO, IL. O. Pacini. Rome, 1831.

CORSARO, IL. O. Pappalardo. Naples, 1846.

CORSARO, IL. O. Verdi. Trieste, October 25, 1848.

CORSICAN, THE. F.C. 3 a. J. H. Darnley and H. A. Bruce, Brighton T.R., June 18, 1900.

CORSICAN BROTHER - BABES - IN - THE - WOOD. M. Extrav. G. R. Sims. Hull T.R., March 19, 1881.

CORSICAN BROTHERS, THE. D. 3 a. and 5 tab. Adap. fr. the romance of Dumas' *Les Frères Corses* by E. Grangé and X. de Monté. First performed at Paris T. Historique, August 10, 1850. Adap. to Eng. stage by Dion Boucicault. Princess's, February 24, 1852. Other vers. at Marylebone, March 8, 1852; Surrey, 1852; by G. Almar at Victoria, 1852; Queen's, 1852; Grecian, 1852; City of London, 1852; Standard, 1852; Princess's, by Fletcher, December 15, 1860; Lyceum, Boucicault, September, 1880; Novelty, August 4, 1890; Lyceum, May 12, 1891.

CORSICAN BROTHERS, THE. O. Lib. by Chas. Bradberry. M. by Geo. Fox. Crystal Palace, September 25, 1888.

CORSICAN BROTHERS, THE. New ver. of Alex. Dumas's novel. Birmingham T.R., October 10, 1906; Adelphi, June 17, 1908; Adelphi, September 9, 1908; Adelphi, November 23, 1908.

CORSICAN BROTHERS, THE. See *O Gemini.*

CORSICAN BROTHERS; OR, THE TROUBLESOME TWINS, THE. Burl. extrav. H. J. Byron. Globe, May 17, 1869.

CORSICAN BROTHERS AND CO., LIMITED, THE. F. C. Burnand and H. P. Stephens. Gaiety, November 25, 1880.

CORSICAN PIRATE; OR, THE GRAND MASTER OF MALTA, THE. Burl. J. C. Cross. Ac. at the Circus. Pr. 1803.

CORSICANS, THE. D. 4 a. Transl. fr. the German of Kotzebue. Pr. 1799. N. ac.

CORSICANS, THE. Unfinished Play by Chas. Leftly. Circa 1802.

CORTES. T. Referred to in *The Whim.*

CORTEZ; OR, THE CONQUEST OF MEXICO. O. J. R. Planché. M. by Bishop. C.G., November 5, 1823.

CORYDON AND COCHRANIA. Pas. Alexandre Pennecuik. 1723.

COSA RARA, LA. O. Martini. 1786. Eng. ver. called *The Siege of Belgrade.*

COSAQUE, LA. C. H. Meilhac and A. Millana. M. by Hervé. Perf. in Fr., Gaiety, June 18, 1884; Eng. ver. by Sydney Grundy. Hastings, Gaiety, April 7, 1884; Royalty, April 12, 1884.

COSAQUES, LES. Dr. Spec. 5 a. and 9 sc. M. M. Arnault and Judicis (second time this country). D.L. April 24, 1855.

COSCOLETE. Op. bo. 1 a. Offenbach, 1865.

COSE FAN TUTTE. C.O. Mozart. Vienna, 1790; King's T., May 9, 1811; St. James's H., by students, Lon. Acad. of M., December 19, 1899; Savoy, by students of R. Coll. of M., July 16, 1890.

COSI FAN TUTTE. C.O. Adapt. and arr. by Hawes. Prod. O.H., July 29, 1828.

COSMO. C. Rose T., January 12, 1592. N.p.

COSMO DE MEDICI. T. Horne. 1837.

COSMOGRAPHY. See *Battle of Alcazar, The Blind Lady.*

COSTANZA ET ORINGALDO. O. L. Rossi. Wr. at the request of Barbaja.

COSTER BARON, THE. M.C. 2 a. Harry Pleon. Leeds Colosseum, March 12, 1897 (C.P.).

COSTER GIRL'S ROMANCE, A. P. 1 a. Edward Jewry Spennymoor. Cambridge, March 27 1908.

COSTER-TWIN BROTHERS, THE Burl. Frank Hall. Philharmonic, November 20, 1880.

COSTER'S CHRISTMAS EVE, THE. Sk. Poplar Queen's, May 20, 1908.

COSTLY WHORE, THE. C. Hist. P. Ac. by the Co. of the Revels, and pr. 1633. Said to be by Robt. Mead.

COSY COUPLE, THE. C. 1 a. G. H. Lewes. Lyceum, April, 1854.

COTEAU DE MEDEC, LES. C. Tristan Bernard. Avenue, June 18, 1904.

COTTAGE, THE. Op. F. Jas. Smith. Pr. 1796.

COTTAGE FESTIVAL, THE. O. Leonard MacNally. Dublin, 1796.

COTTAGE IN THE HOLLY, THE. D. Stalybridge, January 22, 1872.

COTTAGE MAID, THE. M.E. C.G., June, 1791.

COTTAGE MAID; OR, THE CUSTOMS OF THE CASTLE, THE. O. R. Sicklemore. Ac. at Brighton, 1798.

COTTAGE OF THE CLIFFS, THE. M.D. John Rannie. Pr. n.d. N. ac.

COTTAGERS, THE. O. Geo. Savile Carey. Pr. 1766.

COTTAGERS, THE. M.E. C.G. Pr. 1768. Not pl. under this title. The same perf. as *William and Nanny.*

COTTAGERS, THE. C.O. 2 a. Miss Anna Ross (aged 15 years). Pr. 1788. N. ac.

COTTON FAMINE; OR, PRESTON IN THE OLDEN TIMES, THE. D. Blackburn T.R., March 10, 1869.

COTTON KING, THE. D. 4 a Sutton Vane. Adelphi, March 10, 1894.

COTTON SPINNER, THE. Dom. C. 4 a. Frank Harvey. Fulham Grand, July 22, 1901.

COUNCELLS OF BISHOPS, OF THE. C. (of the 16th century). Bishop Bale.

COUNSEL FOR THE DEFENCE. P. 5 a Op. C., September 9, 1895 (C.P.).

COUNSEL FOR THE DEFENCE. D. 4 a. Henry Herne. Devonport Metropole T., July 15, 1901.

COUNSEL'S OPINION. P. 1 a. Fredk. Bingham. Richmond T.R., March 24, 1898; H.M.T., May 24, 1898.

COUNT AND THE SECRETARY. C. 1 a. Pub. by S. French, Ltd.

COUNT BASIL. T. Joanna Baillie. Pr. 1798 (N. ac.).

COUNT BENYOWSKY; OR, THE CONSPIRACY OF KOMTSCHATKA. T.C. 5 a. Transl. fr. the German of Kotzebue by Rev. W. Render. Pr. 1798. Another ver. transl. by Benj. Thompson. Pr. 1800. N. ac.

COUNT DE MAROLLES, THE. Ca. Chiswick T. of Varieties, September 8, 1869.

COUNT DE VILLEROI; OR, THE FATE OF PATRIOTISM. T. Pr. 1794. N. ac.

COUNT EGMONT. T. Goethe. 1788. Transl. 1848.

COUNT HANNIBAL. P 4 a. Adap. by F. Langbridge and F. Wills from S. Weyman's novel. Stoke Newington Alex., April 11, 1906.

COUNT HANNIBAL. Ro. P. 4 a. Adap. Norreys Connell and Oscar Ashe. Bristol Prince's, March 18, 1909.

COUNT KOENIGSMARK. D. Transl. fr. Reitzenstein by Benj. Thompson. Pr. 1800. N. ac.

COUNT MORATA. P. 4 a. Robert Wilford. Barrow Royalty, September 10, 1904 (C.P.).

COUNT OF ANJOU; OR, MORE MARRIAGES THAN ONE, THE. M. Rom. 1 a. M. by Cooke. D.L., May 2, 1816.

COUNT OF BURGUNDY, THE. T. 4 a. Transl. fr. the German of Kotzebue by C. Smith. Pr. at New York 1798. By Ann Plumptre. Pr. 1798. N. ac. Alt. fr. latter transl. by Alexander Pope. C.G., 1799. N.p.

COUNT OF NARBONNE, THE. T. 5 a. Capt. Jephson. C.G. Pr. 1781. Evidently f. on Horace Walpole's *The Castle of Otranto*.

COUNT TEZMA. Rom. P. 3 a. A. N. Homer. Comedy, April 20, 1901.

COUNT TREMOLIO. Venetian O. Lib. by Edgar Wyatt. M. by Alfd. R. Watson. Nottingham T.R., September 5, 1887.

COUNT'S DILEMMA, THE. Sk. Empress, July 12, 1909.

COUNTER ATTRACTIONS; OR, STROLLING AND STRATAGEM. "A Trifle light as air." Wm. Harries Tilbury. Punch's Playhouse, November 24, 1851.

COUNTERFEIT, THE. F. Andrew Franklin. D.L., 1804.

COUNTERFEIT BRIDEGROOM; OR, THE DEFEATED WIDOWS, THE. C. Ac. Duke of York's T. and pr. 1677. This is Middleton's *No Wit, No Help Like a Woman's*.

COUNTERFEIT COIN. P. 1 a. Rob Gore. Wigan R. Court T., October 4, 1901.

COUNTERFEIT HEIRESS, THE. F. Taken fr. D'Urfey's *Love for Money*. C.G., April 16, 1762. N.p.

COUNTERFEIT PRESENTMENT. C. Howells. 1876.

COUNTERFEITS, THE. C. Prob. wr. by J. Leonard. Duke of York's T. and pr. 1679. Plot fr. a Spanish novel, "The Trepanner Trepanned," which Cibber also used in *She Would and She Would Not*.

COUNTERFEITS, THE. F. Taken fr. Moore's *Gil Blas* D.L., May 1764. N.p.

COUNTERPLOT. Charade D. Miss Keating. Pub. by S. French, Ltd.

COUNTERPLOT, THE. C. 2 a. Thos. Goodall. Ac. at Bath 1787. N.p.

COUNTESS, THE. D. 3 a. Adap. fr. the Fr. of Adolphe Belot by Lady Monckton Chelsea. Sir Percy Shelley's T., June 2, 1882.

COUNTESS; OR, A SISTER'S LOVE, THE. D. 3 a. By Miss E. Schiff. Alfred T., February 21, 1870.

COUNTESS AND THE DANCER, THE. Alt. ver. of *Jealousy*, adap. by Ch. Reade from Victorien Sardou's *Andrea* or *Agnes*. Olympic, February 27, 1886.

COUNTESS AND THE DRAMA, THE. See *Agnes*.

COUNTESS CATHLEEN, THE. T. W. B. Yeats. Dublin Ancient Concert Rooms, May 8, 1899.

COUNTESS GUCKI, THE. C. 3 a. Adap. by Augustin Daly from the original of Franz von Schonthan. (Originally produced in America.) Comedy, July 11, 1896.

COUNTESS OF ESSARTAGNAS, THE. Transl. fr. Molière by John Ozell.

COUNTESS OF PEMBROKE'S IVY CHURCH, THE. Abraham Fraunce. Pr. 1594. Contains *Aminta's Pastoral*, being a transl. of Tasso's *Aminta*.

COUNTESS OF SALISBURY, THE. T. Hall Hartson. Taken fr. Dr. Leland's rom. *Longsword, Earl of Salisbury*. Pr. 1767. First ac. at Dublin, 1764-5; Hay., Aug. 7, 1767.

COUNTRY, THE. Benham. Terry's, June 2, 1892.

COUNTRY ATTORNEY, THE. C. Richd. Cumberland. Hay., 1787. N.p. See *School for Widows*.

COUNTRY CAPTAIN, THE. C. Wr. by Duke of Newcastle. Blackfryars T. Pr. 1649.

COUNTRY COQUET; OR, MISS IN HER BREECHES, THE. B.O. As it may be ac. at D.L. Pr. 1755.

COUNTRY COUSINS. Ent. by Mr. Mathews. Lyceum, February 28, 1820.

COUNTRY CRICKET MATCH, A. C. 3 a. G. B. Nichols. Taunton Lon. Assembly R., August 5, 1898.

COUNTRY DANCE, A. F.C. 3 a. Ernest Elton. Northampton O.H., March 18, 1896 (C.P.).

COUNTRY DRESSMAKER, THE. C. 3 a. G. Fitzmaurice. Dublin Abbey, October 3, 1907.

COUNTRY ELECTION, THE. F. 2 a. Prob. by Dr. Trusler. Pr. 1768.

COUNTRY FAIR. Oa. 1 a. Gillington and Elliott. Pub. by S. French, Ltd.

COUNTRY FAIR, THE. Prel. C.G., September 20, 1775. N.p.

COUNTRY GAMBOL, THE. C.O. 3 a. MS. In library of Isaac Reed.

COUNTRY GENTLEMAN; OR, CHOICE SPIRITS, THE. D. Wm. Woty. Pr. 1786.

COUNTRY GIRL, THE. C. Anthony Brewer. Pr. 1649. Afterwards (in 1677) called *The Country Innocence; or, the Chambermaid Turned Quaker*.

COUNTRY GIRL, THE. C. 5 a. Alt. fr. Wycherley's *Country Wife* by David Garrick. Pr. 1766. D.L., 1766, and October 18, 1785; C.G., November 23, 1805.

COUNTRY GIRL, THE. Terry's, June 20, 1898, rev.

COUNTRY GIRL; OR, TOWN AND COUNTRY. M.P. T. Tanner. Daly's, January 1, 1894; Daly's, January 18, 1902.

COUNTRY GIRL IN LONDON, A. D. 4 a. Frank Price. Macclesfield R.T., August 1, 1908; rev. Edmonton R., March 15, 1909.

COUNTRY HOUSE, THE. F. By Sir John Vanbrugh. Transl. fr. the French of d'Ancourt, *Maison de Campagne*. Pr. 1715. D.L., June, 1705, and rev. C.G., 1735 and 1758.

COUNTRY INN, THE. C. Joanna Baillie. Pr. 1804. N. ac.

COUNTRY INNOCENCE; OR, THE CHAMBERMAID TURN'D QUAKER. C. John Leonard. T.R., and pr. 1677. See *The Country Girl*, from which it was taken.

COUNTRY LASSES; OR, THE CUSTOM OF THE MANOR, THE. Chas. Johnson. Has two plots, one borr. fr. Fletcher's *Custom of the Country*, the other from Mrs. Behn's *City Heiress* and what she took fr. Middleton's *Mad World My Masters*. D.L. and C.G., 1715. Pr. 1715 and Bath, 1813. See *The Lady of the Manor, The Farm House*, and *Custom of the Manor*.

COUNTRY MADCAP, THE. F. This is Fielding's *Miss Lucy in Town* under another title. C.G., 1772.

COUNTRY MOUSE, THE. P. 3 a. A. Law. Worthing T.R., February 24, 1902; P.O.W., February 27, 1902.

COUNTRY ROSE, A. C.D. 3 a. Mrs. F. G. Kimberley. M. by S. Jones. Leeds T.R., November 1, 1905 (C.P.).

COUNTRY SQUIRE, THE. C. 2 a. Chas. Dance. First perf. C.G., January 19, 1837.

COUNTRY SQUIRE; OR, A CHRISTMAS GAMBOL, THE. C. 3 a. Richd. Gwinnet. Pr. 1732. See *The Glo'stershire Squire.*

COUNTRY WAKE, THE. C. Thos. Dogget, L.I.F. Pr. 1696. Since reduced to B.F., *Flora; or, Hob in the Well*, at D.L., 1767.

COUNTRY WAKE, THE. F. T. Underwood. Pr. 1782. C.G., 1760.

COUNTRY WAKE, THE. C. Robt. Dodesley.

COUNTRY WEDDING; OR, LOVE IN A DALE, THE. F. 1 a. "J. W." Pr. 1750. See *The Deceit.*

COUNTRY WEDDING; OR, THE COCKNEY BIT, THE. F. Hay. Pr. same as E. Hawker's.

COUNTRY WEDDING AND SKIMMINGTON, THE. Ballad F. Essex Hawker. D.L. and pr. 1729. See *The Wedding.*

COUNTRY WIFE, THE. C. 5 a. W. Wycherley. F. partly on Molière's *L'Ecole des Maris* and *L'Ecole des Femmes.* Pr. 1675. D.L., 1683; rev. D.L., 1709, 1735.

COUNTRY WIFE, THE. 2 a. Alt. fr. Wycherley by John Lee. D.L., April 26, 1765. Pr. 1765.

COUNTRY WIT, THE. C. John Crowne. Suggested by Molière's *Le Sicilien, ou L'Amour Peintre.* D. of York's T. and pr. 1675.

COUNTRYMAN, THE. P. Entered Stationers' Co. September 9, 1653.

COUNTY, THE. P. 4 a. Estelle Burney and Arthur Benham. Terry's, June 2, 1892.

COUNTY COUNCILLOR, THE. F.C. 3 a. H. Graham. Ladbroke H., October 7, 1891 (C.P.); Crystal Palace, November 17, 1892; Strand, November 18, 1892; Trafalgar Square, February 4, 1893.

COUNTY FAIR, THE. D. 4 a. Chas. Bernard. Original prod. in America. Brixton April 12, 1897; Princess's, June 5, 1897.

COUP DE MAIN; OR, THE AMERICAN ADVENTURERS, THE. M.Ent. By Archibald Maclaren. Dundee. Pr. 1784.

COUR DE CELIMENE, LA. O. Thomas. Paris, 1855.

COURAGE; THE STORY OF A BIG DIAMOND. D. 4 a. Henry Gascoigne. Marylebone, October 25, 1886.

COURAGE OF LOVE, THE. P. This was the orig. title of Sir Wm. Davenant's P. of *Love and Honour.* 1649.

COURAGE OF SILENCE, THE. P 4 a. Hon. Mrs. Arthur Henniker. Hammersmith King's, May 22, 1905.

COURAGE REWARDED; OR, THE ENGLISH VOLUNTEER. Political D. "A. L. G." Pr. 1798. N. ac.

COURAGEOUS TURK; OR, AMURATH I., THE. Thos. Goff. 1592-1627. Plot fr. "Histories of Turkish Empire." Ac. by students of Christchurch, Oxon. Pr. 1632.

COURIER OF FORTUNE, A. Rom. D. 4 a Arthur W. Marchmont. Bath R., March 30, 1905 (C.P.).

COURIER OF LYONS; OR, THE ATTACK UPON THE MAIL, THE. D. 4 a. C. Reade. Adap. fr. French of Moreau Siraudin and Delacour. First pl. at Paris Theatre de la Gaitê, 1850; Standard, 1851; Princess's, June, 1854; St. James's, 1859; Gaiety, July 4, 1870.

COURIER OF THE CZAR, THE. D. 3 a. Chas. Osborne. Liverpool T.R., May 14, 1877.

COURIER OF THE CZAR, THE. D. 4 a. Hugh Marston. Standard, May 21, 1877.

COURONNE DE BLUETS. Houssaye. 1836.

COURRIER DE LYON, LE. See *The Lyons Mail.*

COURSE DU FLAMBEAU, LA. French D. 4 a. P. Hervieu. Notting Hill Coronet T., June 24, 1904.

COURSING OF THE HARE; OR, THE MADCAP, THE. C. Wm. Heminges. 1632-1633. Probably ac. at the Fortune. N.p.

COURT AND CAMP. D. Adap. fr. the French. Princess's, May 27, 1863.

COURT AND CITY. C. 5 a. R. Brinsley Peake. Adap. fr. scenes in Sir Richard Steele's *Tender Husband* and Mrs. Francis Sheridan's *Discovery.* C.G., November 17, 1841.

COURT AND COTTAGE. C.O. 1 a. Tom Taylor. M. by Fred Clay. November 12, 1861.

Cxxxx AND COUNTRY. P. 7 a. In which will be rev. *The Blundering Brothers*, to which is added *The Comical Humours of Punch*, the whole concluding with the Masque, *The Downfall of Sejanus.* Wr. by a masquerader. Pr. 1735.

COURT AND COUNTRY; OR, THE CHANGELINGS. B.O. Pr. 1743.

COURT AND NO COUNTRY. F. Ent. "Ac. but once these 20 years." Pr. 1753.

COURT BEAUTIES, THE. Dr. Sk. 1 a. J. R. Planché. Olympic. March 12, 1835.

COURT BEGGAR, THE. C. Richd. Brome. Cockpit, 1632. Pr. 1653. See *Tom Hoyden.*

COURT CARDS. C.D. 2 a. J. Palgrave Simpson. Based on Scribe's *La Frileuse.* Olympic, November 25, 1861. See *Delia.*

COURT DRESSMAKER, CORALIE AND CO., THE. F.C. Adeline Votieri. Bayswater Bijou, February 24, 1900 (C.P.).

COURT FAVOUR; OR, PRIVATE AND CONFIDENTIAL. C. 2 a. J. R. Planché. Olympic, September 29, 1836; Strand, August 9, 1858.

COURT FOOL; OR, A KING'S AMUSEMENT. T.D. 3 a. W. E. Burton. Sadler's Wells, May 11, 1840.

COURT GALLANTS. C. C. Selby. Fr. the French. Royalty, August 31, 1863.

COURT JESTER, THE. Ca. Adap. fr. the French by C. J. Mathews. Hay., July, 1832.

COURT LADY; OR, COQUET'S SURRENDER, THE. C. Anon. Pr. 1730. See *The Coquet's Surrender.*

COURT LEGACY, THE. B.O. Pr. 1733. Probably by Mrs. Manley. N. ac.

COURT LOVERS; OR, THE SENTINEL OF THE KING'S GUARD. M.C. 4 a. Julia Agnes Fraser. Pub. by Frend and Co., Plymouth.

COURT MEDLEY; OR, MARRIAGE BY PROXY. B.O. 3 a. Pr. 1733.

COURT OF ALEXANDER, THE. Burl. O. 2 a. Alexander Stevens. C.G. Pr. 1770.

COURT OF AUGUSTUS CAEZAR. P. Durfey, 1679. This is Lee's transl. of *Gloriana.* Pub. 1676.

COURT OF HONOUR, A. P. 3 a. John Lart and Ch. Dickinson. Royalty, May 18, 1897.

COURT OF LYONS; OR, GRANADA TAKEN AND DONE FOR, THE. Burl. 1 a.

COURT OF NASSAU; OR, THE TRIAL OF HUMBUG, THE. C. Geo. Stayley. Pr. 1753.

COURT OF OBERON; OR, THE THREE WISHES, THE. D. Ent. by the Countess of Hardwicke.

COURT OF OLD FRITZ, THE. Burla. Olympic, November, 1838.

COURT OF QUEEN ANNE. D. 2 a. W. T. Moncrieff. Publ. by S. French, Ltd.

COURT OF QUEEN'S BENCH, THE. V. M. by Barnett. Lyceum (by Mme. Vestris).

COURT ROMANCE, A. Ca. 1 a. Herbert H. Cullum. Douglas Grand T., June 14, 1901.

COURT SCANDAL, A. C. 3 a. Aubrey Boucicault and Osmond Shillingford. Fr. the C. of MM. Bayard and Dumanoir, entitled *Les Premières Armes de Richelieu*. Court, January 24, 1899. Transferred to Garrick, May 10, 1899.

COURT SECRET ,THE. T.C. Jas. Shirley. Pr. 1653. Prepared for the Blackfriars, but not ac. until after the Restoration.

COURT, THE PRISON, AND THE SCAFFOLD, THE. D. R. Bell. Britannia, November 30, 1874.

COURTEZANS, THE. C. Transl. fr. Plautus by Richd. Warner. Pr. 1774. Plautus called this C., *Bacchides*.

COURTEZANS, THE. C. 2 a. MS. in possession of Stephen Jones, supposed to be by Cornelius Arnold.

COURTLY MASQUE, A. Masque. Middleton. 1620.

COURTNAY, EARL OF DEVONSHIRE; OR, THE TROUBLES OF QUEEN ELIZABETH. T. Anon. Pr. N.d. N.ac.

COURTSHIP; OR, THE THREE CASKETS. C. 3 a. H. J. Byron. Court, October 16, 1879.

COURTSHIP A LA MODE. C. David Crauford. D.L. Pr. 1700. Prol. by Farquhar.

COURTSHIP OF MORRICE BUCKLER, THE. P. 4 a. Adap. by the author and Miss Isabel Bateman fr. A. E. W. Mason's novel. Grand, December 6, 1897.

COUSIN ADONIS. New Royalty. February 13, 1865.

COUSIN CHARLIE. Ca. 1 a. Miss K. M. Latimer. Eastbourne Dev. Pk. T., February 9, 1889.

COUSIN CHERRY. F. Henry Spicer. Olympic, 1848.

COUSIN DICK. Sk. by Val Prinsep, A.R.A. Court, March 1, 1879. Rev. Criterion, July 3, 1886.

COUSIN FROM AUSTRALIA, THE. F.C. 3 a Sydney Blackburn. Op. C. April 11, 1898.

COUSIN JACK. C. 3 a. Adap. fr. the German of Roderick Benedix by Herman Vezin. Worthing Assembly R., September 30, 1891; Op. C.. November 12, 1891.

COUSIN JOHNNY. C. 3 a. Nisbet and Rae. Strand, July 11, 1885.

COUSIN JOSEPH. F. M. by S. Nelson. Lyceum, May 23, 1835.

COUSIN KATE. C. 4 a. Bronson Howard. Orig. prod. in America. Newcastle-on-Tyne T.R., August 26, 1889.

COUSIN KATE. C. 3 a. H. H. Davies. Hay., June 18, 1903.

COUSIN LAMBKIN. J. M. Morton. C.G.

COUSIN LETTY. C. 1 a. E. H. Keating. Publ. by S. French, Ltd.

COUSIN PETER. C.D. 1 a. T. Egerton Wilks. Olympic, October 11, 1841.

COUSIN TOM. Ca. 1 a. Geo. Roberts. Princess's, June 8, 1863.

COUSIN ZACH (OR ZACHARY). Ca. 1 a. Herbt. Gardner. Canterbury T.R., August, 1883; Windsor T.R., November 28, 1883.

COUSIN'S COURTSHIP. Dr. sk. Mary Collette. Lyric, September 24, 1892; Shaftesbury, September 26, 1892.

COUSINS. C. 3 a. Hamilton Aïdé. Chelsea Shelley T., December 13, 1882.

COUSINS ONCE REMOVED. Ca. 1 a. Arthur M. Heathcote. Terry's, April 10, 1901.

COVENANTERS, THE. Scotch O. 2 a. M. by E. J. Loder. Lyceum, August 10, 1835.

COVENT GARDEN. C. Thos. Nabbs, dedicated to Sir John Suckling. Ac. by the Queen's servants, 1632. Pr. 1638.

COVENT GARDEN THEATRE; OR, PASQUIN TURNED DRAWCANSIR. D. Satire. Charles Macklin. C.G., 1752. N.p.

COVENT GARDEN TRAGEDY, THE. F. Hy. Fielding. D.L. and pr. 1733. A burl. on *The Distrest Mother*.

COVENT GARDEN WEEDED; OR, THE MIDDLESEX JUSTICE OF PEACE. C. Richd. Broome. Pr. 1659. See *The Weeding of C.G.*

COVENTRY ACT, THE. C. Ascr. to J. Plumptre. Ac. at Norwich. Pr. 1793.

COVENTRY PLAYS. *Ludus Coventriæ sive Ludus Corporis Christi*. 40 in number. British Museum (Cottonian MSS., Vesp., D., VIII., p. 113, Plut. IV., A.). In MSS. 1,468. Pr. 1841. Like the Chester Whitsun Plays, they are based on the Old and New Testaments. See "Miracle Plays."

COW DOCTOR, THE. C. 3 a. Pr. 1810.

COWARD CONSCIENCE. P. 4 a. C. A. Byrne and Arthur Wallack. Glasgow Royalty, September 10, 1888.

COWARD OR HERO? Sk. R. Cameron Matthews. Camberwell Empire, September 21, 1908.

COWARDLY FOE, A. Piece. 1 a. Wynne Miller. Criterion, July 12, 1892.

COWBOY AND THE LADY, THE. C. 3 a. Clyde Fitch. D. of York's, June 5, 1899.

COX AND BOX. Rom. 3 a. J. M. Morton and F. C. Burnand. Alt. of *Box and Cox*.

COX AND BOX. C.Oa. 1 a. F. C. Burnand. M. by Sullivan. Adelphi, May, 1867; Gal. Illust., March 29, 1869; Gaiety, January, 1872; Gaiety, July 21, 1880.

COX OF COLLUMPTION. P. Day and Haughton. Wr. November, 1599.

COXCOMB, THE. C. Beaumont and Fletcher Ac. by 1612. Pr. 1647. Rev. at T.R.; perf. at Court about 1613.

COXCOMBS, THE. F. Francis Gentleman. Ac. 1 night at Hay., 1771. N.p. Adap. fr. part of Ben Jonson's *Epicœne*.

COZENERS, THE. C. 3 a. Saml. Foote. Hay., July, 1774. Pr. 1778. Add. sc. commencing A. 3 intro. by author 1776.

COZENING; OR, HALF AN HOUR IN FRANCE. Comic piece. S. Beazley. C.G., May 22, 1819.

COZY COUPLE, A. F. 1 a. Slingsby Lawrence. Lyceum, April, 1854.

CRACK ME THIS NUT. P. Rose T., September 5, 1595. N.p. See *The Nut*.

CRACKED HEADS. Burl. of *Broken Hearts*. A. Clements and F. Hay. Strand, February 2, 1876.

CRADLE, THE. Dom. inc. 1 a. Adap. fr. the Flemish of Emil von Goetham by A. Teixeira de Mattos. St. Geo. H., July 10, 1893. (Independent Theatre.)

CRADLE OF SECURITIE, THE. Int. 1560 1570.

CRAFT. D. Prol. and 4 a. Arthur Sketchley. Leicester T.R., August 19, 1882.

CRAFT AND CREDULITY. C. 3 a. In library of Isaac Reed.

CRAFT OF RHETORIC, THE. C. Anon. Pr. N.d. See *Beauty and Good*, etc.

CRAFTE UPON SUBTILTYE'S BACKE. Int. Entered by Jeffrey Charlton at Stationers' Co., January 27, 1608. N.p.

CRAFTIE CROMWELL; OR, OLIVER ORDERING OUR NEW STATE. T.C. Mercurius Melancholicus. 5 a. Pr. 1648.

CRAFTSMAN; OR, WEEKLY JOURNALISTS, THE. F. John Mottley. Pr. 1728 (not intended for the stage). Ac. at Little French T. in Hay., 1729.

CRAFTY CROMWELL. Political D. Not intended for representation. See *Craftie*, etc.

CRAFTY MERCHANT; OR, COME TO MY COUNTRY HOUSE, THE. C. Wr. by Wm. Bonen. September 12, 1623.

CRAFTY MERCHANT; OR, THE SOULDIER'D CITIZEN, THE. C. Skakerly Marmion. N.p.

CRAINQUEBILLE. P. 3 tableaux. Anatole France. Adelphi, June 28, 1909. See *Down Our Alley*.

CRAMMERS; OR, THE SHORT VACATION, THE. C. 3 a. W. Sapte, jun. Strand, July 2, 1903.

CRAMOND BRIG; OR, THE GUDEMAN O' BALLANGRICH. C.D. 2 a. W. H. Murray. Adap. fr. *Miller of Mansfield* by Sir W. Scott. Edinburgh T.H., February 27, 1826; Lyceum, August 20, 1834; D.L., June 15, 1837; Surrey, April, 1850; Duke's T., April 6, 1878.

CRAZED. Hum. sk. 1 a. A. R. Phillips. Wood Green Assembly R., October 1, 1892.

CRAZED. O. Publ. by S. French, Ltd.

CREATION, THE. An Interlocutory Discourse Concerning the Creation, Fall, and Recovery of Man. Sacred D. Samuel Slater. 1679.

CREATION, THE. Orat. Haydn. Prod. by J. Ashley at C.G. March 28, 1800. Prod. by Salomon at King's, April 21, 1800. D.L., March 2,1814.

CREATION AND FALL OF LUCIFER, THE. See "Miracle Plays."

CREATION OF EVE, THE. A "mystery." Norwich, by Guild of Grocers in reign of Henry VIII.

CREATION OF THE WORLD, THE. See *Cornish Interludes*.

CREATURES OF IMPULSE. M. Fairy tale. 1 a. W. S. Gilbert. Court, April 15, 1871.

CREDIT. Skit on *Money*. By G. à Beckett.

CREED PLAY. See "Miracle Plays."

CREEPING SHADOWS. D. 5 a. Butler Stanhope. Birkenhead T R., April 18, 1887

CREMATION F. R. Height. Liverpool St. James's H., July 14, 1879.

CREMORNE. F.C. 3 a. T. A. Palmer. Strand, November 27, 1876.

CREOLE, THE. C.O. Lib. by R. Reece and H. B. Farnie. M. by Offenbach. Brighton T.R., September 3, 1877; Folly, September 15, 1877.

CREOLE, THE. P. 1 a. Louis N. Parker. Hay., May 6, 1905.

CREOLE; OR, LOVE'S FETTERS, THE. D. 3 a. Shirley Brooks. Lyceum, April 8, 1847.

CRESS. O. G. Abos. London, 1758.

CREUSA IN DELFO. O. Ranzzini. London, 1783.

CREUSA, QUEEN OF ATHENS. T. Wm. Whitehead. F. on "Iön" of Euripides. D.L., April 20, 1754. Pr. 1754.

CRICHTON. Burl. R. Hartley Edgar. Charing Cross, August 30, 1871.

CRICKET MATCH, THE. M.F. 1 a. D.L., April 15, 1850.

CRICKET MATCH, THE. F. Alf. Leslie. Norwich T.R., May 12, 1870.

CRICKET ON THE HEARTH, THE. Dramatised, at request of C. Dickens, by Albert Smith. Lyceum, December 20, 1845.

CRICKET ON THE HEARTH, THE. Adap. by Ed. Stirling, Adelphi, December 31, 1845; another ver., Princess's, January 1, 1846; adap. by W. T. Townsend, City of London, January 5, 1846; adap. by B. Webster, Hay., January 6, 1846; another ver., Grecian, January 13, 1846; and others.

CRICKET ON THE HEARTH, THE. O. Sir A. Mackenzie.

CRICKET ON THE HEARTH, THE. O. 3 a. Carl Goldmark. Eng. lib. by Percy Pinkerton. Brixton T., November 23, 1900.

CRICKET ON THE HEARTH. T. Adap. of Dickens's story, by Napoleon Lambelet. Terry's, December 1, 1906.

CRICKET ON THE HEARTH. THE. See *Dot*.

CRIME; OR, THE BLACK HEART. D. L G. Kean. Victoria, August 6, 1877.

CRIME AND CHRISTENING. F. "Richd. Henry." Op. C., March 10, 1891.

CRIME AND ITS ATONEMENT. D. Don Edgardo Colona. Leeds Amphi., November 15, 1875.

CRIME AND JUSTICE; OR, THE SHADOW OF THE SCAFFOLD. D. 5 a. Burford Delannoy and Norman Harvey. Sadler's Wells, December 15, 1892.

CRIME AND VIRTUE. D. 5 a. Butler Stanhope. Liverpool Adelphi, June 30, 1879.

CRIME FROM AMBITION. P. Transl. fr. the German of Iffland by Maria Geisweiler. Pr. 1799.

CRIMELESS CRIMINAL, A. F. 1 a. Martin Becher. Strand, April 20, 1874; Kilburn T.H., May 26, 1887.

CRIMES OF PARIS, THE. Melo-d. 6 a. P. Meritt and G. Conquest. Surrey, October 22, 1883.

CRIMINAL, THE. D. 5 a. Dover R. Clarence T., December 15, 1884.

CRIMINAL COUPLE, A. F. F. Herbert. Princess's, June 29, 1871

CRIMINAL JUDGE; OR, THE LIGHT OF TRUTH, A. D. Prol. and 4 a. A. Shirley and B. Landeck. Pav., November 5, 1900.

CRIMINALS; OR, FASHION AND FAMINE. D. 5 a. J. H. Clinch. Great Grimsby P.O.W., June 29, 1885.

CRIMSON BLIND, THE. Dr. epis. Sydney Mason. Middlesex, August 26, 1907.

CRIMSON CLUB, THE. D. 5 a. W. Hall and M. James. Oldham T.R., May 11, 1903; Camden, June 15, 1903.

CRIMSON CROSS, THE. D. 4 a. Clement Scott and E. Mauriel. Adelphi, February 27, 1879.

CRIMSON HORSESHOE, THE. D. 4 a. J. Willard. Peckham Crown, June 1, 1903.

CRIMSON MASK, THE. Rom. D. 3 a. Foster Courtenay. Suggested by Capt. Marryat's novel, "The Poacher." Northampton O.H., July 25, 1892.

CRIMSON RAMBLER, THE. P. 3 a. C. C. Young. Cripplegate I. (prod. by amateurs), April 28, 1906.

CRIMSON ROCK, THE. D. 3 a. J. Cross. Pav., May 31, 1879.

CRIMSON SCARF, THE. C.O. Lib. by H. B. Farnie. M. by J. E. Legouix. Alhambra, April 24, 1871; Hay., November 24, 1873.

CRINOLINE. F. 1 a. Rob. B. Brough. Olympic, December 18, 1856.

CRISIS. Ca. 1 a. J. E. Mallock and H. N. Brailsford. Teddington Bijou, July 13, 1903.

CRISIS, THE. C. 4 a. J. Albery. Ver. of Emile Augier's *Les Fourchambault*. Hay., December 2, 1878.

CRISIS; OR, LOVE AND FEAR, THE. C.O. Thos. Holcroft. D.L., May 1, 1778. N.p.

CRISPIN AND CRISPIANUS. Ment. in a dialogue between Dekker and Flecknoe.

CRISPIN GENTILHOMME. C. Montfleury, 1640-85.

CRISPINO E LA COMARE. O. Luigi Ricci (1805-1859), Frederico Ricci (1809-1877). Naples, 1836.

CRISTOFORO COLOMBO. O. Franchetti.

CRITIC; OR, A TRAGEDY REHEARSED, THE. F. 3 a. R. B. Sheridan. D.L., October 29, 1779; D.L., June 23, 1815; December 31, 1827; C.G., 1840; Gaiety, October, 1872, and August, 1883; Great Queen Street, April 24, 1905. Sug. by *The Rehearsal* of the Duke of Buckingham (Sir Fretful Plagiary is meant for Cumberland).

CRITIC; OR, A TRAGEDY REHEARSED, THE. A literary catchpenny by way of prelude to Sheridan's Critic. Pr. 1780. Another in 3 a. perf. same year.

CRITIC ANTICIPATED; OR, THE HUMOURS OF THE GREEN ROOM. F. "R. B. S." Pr. 1779.

CRITIC UPON CRITIC. Dr. medley. 3 a. Leonard MacNully. C.G. Pr. 1792.

CRITICAL DOG, A. O. Signor Tartaglione. Dilettante Club, October 26, 1880.

CRITICAL MINUTE, THE. F. Sir John Hill. See *The Maiden Whim.*

CRITIQUE, LA. C. Molière. 1662.

CROAKING. Int. fr. *The Good-Natured Man.* D.L. Co. at Lyceum, May 2, 1810.

CROCHETS DU PERE MARTIN, LES. Cormon and Grange. 1858. The origin of *Porter's Knot* and *Daddy O'Dowd.*

CROCIATO IN EGITTO. It. O. 2 a. Meyerbeer; was by Rossi. (Venice, 1824.) King's T., 1825.

CROCK OF GOLD, THE. Melo-d. 2 a. Edward Fitzball, on story of M. F. Tupper. City of London, May, 1848.

CROCKERY. F. Victoria, June 11, 1821.

CROCODILE; OR, ACCUSED OF MURDER, THE. Dom. D. Wm. Lowe. Cardiff T.R., March 4, 1882.

CROCODILE'S TEARS. Yuletide Masque. Hampstead Gordon Inst., January 17, 1889 (amat.).

CRŒSUS. T. Wm. Alexander Earl of Sterling. Plot borr. fr. Herodotus, Justin, and Plutarch. Ep. 5 a. Fr. Xenophon's *Cyropaidcia.* Pr. 1604.

CRŒSUS. See *The Monarchic Tragedies.* Pr. 1604.

CRŒSUS, KING OF LYDIA. T. A. B. Richards. Orig. publ. by Pickering, 1845; republ. by Longman and Co., 1861.

CROMWELL. P. Victor Hugo. 1827. See *Charles I.*

CROMWELL. D. 5 a. Alfred Bate Richards. Pr. 1847. Queen's, December 21, 1872.

CROMWELL. T. F. Phillips. Based on Victor Hugo's P. Surrey, February, 1859.

CROMWELL; OR, THE KING. Hist. epis. Worland S. Wheeler. Paragon, March 23, 1908.

CROMWELL, LORD THOMAS. Hist. P. Attrib. to Shakespeare. Pr. 1602. On title page said to be by "W. S." Theobald and other editors of Shakespeare's works have omitted this, together with six pieces more, viz.:—*The Puritan, Pericles Prince of Tyre, The Tragedy of Locrine, The Yorkshire Tragedy, Sir John Oldcastle,* and *The London Prodigal.*

CROMWELL. See *Combat of the Tongue, Life and Death of Thos. Lord Cromwell.*

CROMWELL'S CONSPIRACY. T.C. "Wr. by a person of quality." Pr. 1660.

CROOKED MILE, A. P. 3 a. Miss Clara Lemore. Manchester Comedy T., January 23, 1885; Vaudeville, April 28, 1888.

CROOKED PATHS. D. 4 a. Leonard Dawson. Southampton P.O.W., January 19, 1888.

CROOKED WAYS. D. Worcester T.R., December 18, 1875.

CROOKED WAYS; OR, BASE METAL AND STERLING COIN. D. 4 a. Croydon T.R., September 11, 1882.

CROQUEFER. Op. bo. 1 a. Offenbach. 1857.

CROQUET. Ca. 3 a. Pierre Le Clercq. Mortimer Street Assembly R., November 19, 1868 (amat.).

CROQUET. C. S. Shenton. Cheltenham T.R., June 20, 1877.

CROSS AND THE CRESCENT, THE. D. Herr Bandmann. Huddersfield T.R., September 16, 1876.

CROSS AND THE CRESCENT, THE. O. 4 a. Colin MacAlpin. F. on J. Davidson's *For the Crown.* C.G., September 22, 1903.

CROSS FOR VALOUR, THE. Military D. 4 a. J. Douglass and F. Bateman. Croydon Grand T., July 5, 1897; Brixton, July 12, 1897.

CROSS OF HONOUR, THE. Military D. 5 a. Adap. by Arthur Shirley and Maurice Gally fr. Léopold Stapleaux's D., *Le Couçon* (Beaumarcheus, Paris, November 23, 1889). New Cross P.H., October 28, 1890, under title of *False Witness;* Wakefield T.R. and O.H., March 14, 1892; Royalty, July 29, 1892.

CROSS OF OLGA, THE. Rom. D. 4 a. R. Castleton and G. Gurney. Woodside Park H., January 29, 1896; Longton Queen's, July 18, 1898.

CROSS OF ST. JOHN, THE. D. 3 a. W. T. Lucas.

CROSS PARTNERS. C. By a lady. Partly fr. a novel, "The Kentish Maid," and partly fr. a French piece of Destouches, which also furnished the subject of Dr. Francklin's *Contract.* Hay. Pr. 1792.

CROSS PURPOSES. F. 2 a. Wm. O'Brien. C.G., December 8, 1772. Pr. 1772. (?) F. on the *Trois Frères Rivaux* of La Font.

CROSS PURPOSES. Ca. Adap. by M. Parselle fr. the French. Strand, March 3, 1865.

CROSS QUESTIONS AND CROOKED ANSWERS. Ca. 1 a. F. and F. Bell.

CROSS ROADS. D. 1 a. J. J. Dilley.

CROSS ROADS; OR, DOVE NEST FARM, THE. D. 3 a. John Sargent. Dover R. Clarence T., July 13, 1885.

CROSS ROADS OF LIFE, THE. P. based on Sue's Mystères de Paris. Sadler's Wells, November 13, 1843.

CROSS STROKES. C. Cola Neil. Richmond T.R., April 7, 1894.

CROSSED LOVE. Ca. 1 a. Harry Wolverton. Publ. by S. French, Ltd.

CROSSING SWEEPER, THE. M. and dr. sk. Basil Hood. M. by Walter Slaughter. Gaiety, April 8, 1893.

CROSSING THE LINE; OR, CROWDED HOUSES. F. 2 a. Geo. Almar. Surrey T., December, 1833.

CROSSWAYS, THE. P. 4 a. Mrs. Langtry and J. Hartley Manners (under title of *Virginia*), Manchester T.R.; Imperial, December 8, 1902.

CROTCHET LODGE. F. Thos. Hurlstone. C.G., February 17, 1795. Pr. 1795.

CROTCHETS. F. Fredk. Hay. Strand, June 10, 1876.

CROWN, THE. P. 3 a. Robert Wilford. Leicester O.H., September 5, 1904. (C.P.)

CROWN DIAMONDS, THE. C.O. 3 a. Auber. Princess's, May 2, 1844. English ver. of *Diamants de la Couronne*. Q.v.

CROWN FOR A CONQUEROR, A. D. R. Davenport. 1639.

CROWN FOR LOVE, A. Hist. p. 5 a. Miss J. Evelyn. Edinburgh Princess's, June 17, 1874; Gaiety, October 16, 1875.

CROWN IN-N DANGER! THE. Monol. by Mr. Mathews. Lyceum, March 10, 1825.

CROWN JEWELS, THE. O. 3 a. Adap. fr. Auber's O. *Les Diamants de la Couronne*. D.L., April 16, 1846.

CROWN OF LAUREL, A. P. 1 a. R. Stevens Hammersley. Leek T.H., February 19, 1903.

CROWN OF THORNS, A. D. 4 a. Gilbert Elliott. Originally prod. at Brighton Eden T., September 7, 1896; Olympic, October 10, 1896.

CROWN PRINCE; OR, THE BUCKLE OF BRILLIANTS, THE. D. 2 a. Thos. Egerton Wilkes. Sadler's Wells, July 16, 1838.

CRUCIFIXION, THE. Cant. Dr. Stainer.

CRUEL BROTHER, THE. T. Sir Wm. D'Avenant. Blackfryars. Pr. 1630.

CRUEL CARMEN; OR, THE DEMENTED DRAGOON AND THE TERRIBLE TOREADOR. Burl. Extrav. J. Wilton Jones. Manchester Princess's, March 29, 1880.

CRUEL CITY; OR, LONDON BY NIGHT, THE. D. 4 a. Gertrude Warden and Wilton Jones. Surrey, October 5, 1896.

CRUEL COPPINGER. Sk. R. A. Roberts. Bury R., August 25, 1909.

CRUEL DEBTOR. Int. W. Wager. Entered on books of Stationers' Co., 1565-6.

CRUEL DESTINY; OR, THROWN ON THE WORLD, A. Dom. D. 3 a. Wilfred Carr. Woolwich R. Artillery T., October 23, 1899.

CRUEL FATHER; OR, A TERRIBLE REVENGE, THE D. Pro. and 3 a. Edwin Reading. Coventry Ass. Rooms, October 29, 1885.

CRUEL GIFT; OR, THE ROYAL RESENTMENT, THE. T. Mrs. Centlivre. F. on *Sigismunda and Guiscardo* in Boccace's novel. D.L., 1716. Pr. 1717.

CRUEL HERITAGE; OR, A FLASH IN THE PAN, A. P. 4 a. Allan Upward. Dublin Gaiety (prod. as *A Flash in the Pan*), October 23, 1896; Clapham Shakespeare, May 9, 1898.

CRUEL KINDNESS, THE. P. 5 a. Mrs. Crowe. Hay., June 6, 1853.

CRUEL LAW, THE. C.D. 4 a. Walter S. Craven. Stratford T.R., December 16, 1895.

CRUEL LONDON. D. 5 a. Frank Harvey. Oldham T.R., March 23, 1888. Afterwards renamed *Wicked London*.

CRUEL TEST, A. P. Robt. Hall. Margate T.R., April 19, 1881.

CRUEL TO BE KIND. F. 1 a. T. J. Williams and A. Harris. Princess's, March 6, 1860.

CRUEL WAR, THE. T. Anon. Pr. 1643.

CRUEL WRONG, A. D. J. M. Killick. Cabinet, October 28, 1869 (amat.).

CRUELTY OF A STEPMOTHER, THE. P. Ac. at Court, December, 1578.

CRUELTY OF THE SPANIARDS IN PERU, THE. Sir Wm. D'Avenant. Cockpit, 1658, and pr. 1658.

CRUISE IN THE BAY OF BISCAY, A. Oa. E. A. Williams. M. by A. G. Pritchard. New Cross H., August 30, 1884.

CRUISE OF H.M.S. IRRESPONSIBLE, THE. See *H.M.S. Irresponsible*.

CRUISE OF H.M.S. VICTORY. M.C. Flo Stanley. M. by H. Peterson. Edmonton T.R. (C.P.), September 15, 1906.

CRUISE OF THE CALABAR, THE. M.C. 3 a. Messrs. Percy and Arthur Milton. Warrington Court T., August 3, 1903.

CRUISE OF THE CONSTANCE, THE. C. 2 a. M. by Violet Hatherley and Chs. Winchcomb. Worthing R., June 10, 1909.

CRUISE OF THE CRUSOES, THE. C.O. E. Bryam Wyke. M. by Edwd. Williams. Manchester Queen's, August 8, 1881.

CRUISE TO CARNOUSTIE, A. F.C. 5 sc. Gilbert Payne and Frank Percival. M. by Signor J. de Gabriel. Dundee Empire, July 24, 1905.

CRUISE TO CHINA, A. Op. Bo. Adap. fr. M. Bazin's *Le Voyage en Chine*. Garrick, June 5, 1879.

CRUSADE, THE. English O. Frederic Reynolds. C.G., May 6, 1790.

CRUSADER, THE. O. 4 a. George Tootell (perf. by amateurs). Lytham Pier, November 6, 1906.

CRUSADER AND THE CRAVEN, THE. Mediæval O. 1 a. W. Allison. M. by Percy Reeve. Globe, October 7, 1890.

CRUSADERS, THE. Cant. N. W. Gade.

CRUSADERS, THE. O. 3 a. Alfred Brown and St. Georges. M. by Benedict. D.L., February 26, 1846.

CRUSADERS, THE. D. J. Ebsworth. Marylebone, November, 1849.

CRUSADERS, THE. C. of modern London life. 3 a. H. A. Jones. Avenue, November 2, 1891.

CRUSHED. F. Ladbroke H. April 24, 1890 (C.P.).

CRUSHED TRAGEDIAN, THE. C. 5 a. H. J. Byron. Hay., May 11, 1878.

CRUSOE THE CRUISER. Burl. O. 2 a. Wilton Jones, A. Christensen, and M. Connelly. Parkhurst, July 23, 1894.

CRUTCH AND TOOTHPICK. C. 3 a. Adap. by Geo. R. Sims. Royalty, April 14, 1879; Gaiety, November, 1879.

CRY, THE. Dr. Fable. 3 vols. Pr. 1754. By Mrs. Sarah Fielding or Miss Patty Fielding and Miss Jane Collier.

CRY IN THE DARKNESS; OR, THE COLLISION IN THE MERSEY, THE. D. Liverpool R. Colosseum, December 11, 1871.

CRY OF THE CHILDREN, THE. Dom. and Military D. 4 a. W. Bourne. Stratford T.R., March 9, 1903.

CRY QUITS. D. 1 a. Arr. by H. Austin. Brixton Hall, June 16, 1903.

CRY TO-DAY AND LAUGH TO-MORROW. S.C. after-piece. 2 a. E. P. Knight. M. by Cooke. D.L., November 29, 1816.

CRYPTOCONCHOIDSYPHONOSTOMATA. F. Ch. Collette. O.C. November, 1876.

CRYSTAL GAZER, THE. Ca. 1 a. Leopold Montague. Queen's H., June 5, 1896; Coronet, June 26, 1899.

CRYSTAL GAZER, THE. D. Sk. Leopold Martyn. Albert Hall, November 14, 1906.

CRYSTAL GAZING. Sk. F. Bowyer. Hackney Empire, December 3, 1906.

CRYSTAL GLOBE, THE. D. 5 a. Adap. by Sutton Vane fr. *La Joueuse D'Orgue* of Xavien de Montepin and Jules D'Ornay. Princess's, December 24, 1898.

CRYSTAL QUEEN, THE. D. 4 a. A. W. Parry. Liverpool Adelphi, August 7, 1893.

CRYSTAL RING, THE. F.P. 3 a. Stanger Pritchard. M. by Walter Seward. Norwich Assembly R., October 24, 1903.

CUCK QUEANES, Etc. C. W. Percy. 1601. Pr. 1824.

CUCKOLD IN CONCEIT, THE. C. Sir John Vanbrugh. Queen's T., Hay., March 22, 1706. N.p. Little more than transl. of Molière's *Cocu Imaginaire*.

CUCKOLD'S HAVEN; OR, AN ALDERMAN NO CONJUROR. F. N. Tate. Plot partly fr. *Eastward Hoe* and partly fr. *The Devil's an Ass*, by Ben Jonson. Dorset Gdns., 1685. Pr. 1685.

CUCKOO, THE. Ca. 1 a. Walter Helmore. Criterion, October 5, 1887.

CUCKOO, THE. An adap. in 3 a. by C. H. Brookfield of Meilhac's C., *Décoré*. Avenue, March 2, 1899; Vaudeville, November 26, 1907.

CUCULIO; OR, THE HOOD. B.C. 254-184. Plautus. C. Transl. into blank verse by Thornton, Rich, Warner, and Colman. 1769-1774.

CULPRIT. F. 1 a. T. H. Bayly. St. James's, January 18, 1838.

CULPRITS. F. 3 a. Arthur Law. Liverpool P.O.W., August 29, 1890. Terry's, March 6, 1891.

CULTURE. C. 3 a. Sebastian Evans and Frank Evans. Adap. fr. *Le Monde où l'on s'Ennuie* by Edouard Pailleron. Bournemouth T.R., December 5, 1884; Gaiety, May 5, 1885.

CUNNING LOVERS, THE. C. Alexander Brome. D.L. Pr. 1654. For the plot see *The Seven Wise Masters of Rome* and a novel called "The Fortunate Deceiv'd" and *Unfortunate Lovers*.

CUNNING MAN, THE. M.E. 2 a. Dr. C. Burney. Transl. of Rousseau's *Devin du Village*. D.L., November 21, 1766. Pr. 1766.

CUP, THE. T. 2 a. Alfred Tennyson. Lyceum, January 3, 1881.

CUP OF TEA, A. Ca. 1 a. Princess's, February 15, 1869; rev. at Gaiety, March, 1883.

CUPBOARD LOVE. F. 1 a. Fredk. Hay. Vaudeville, April 18, 1870.

CUPBOARD LOVE. F. 3 a. H. V. Esmond. Court, December 3, 1898.

CUPBOARD SKELETON, THE. F. "Ajax." Ladbroke H., May 14, 1887.

CUPID. Masque. T. Middleton. Pr. 1613.

CUPID. Burl. Adelphi, 1832.

CUPID. Burl. Joseph Graves. Queen's and Strand, 1837.

CUPID. M.C. Henry A. Duffy. Southampton T.R. and O.H., April 14, 1882.

CUPID; OR, TWO STRINGS TO A BEAU. Extrav. H. P. Stephens and C. Harris. Royalty, April 26, 1880.

CUPID AND A CARAVAN. P. 2 a. Arthur Leslie. Crouch End Assem. Rooms, April 22, 1909.

CUPID AND BACCHUS. Pant. John Weaver. D.L., 1719.

CUPID AND CAMPASPE. D. Lyly. 1583.

CUPID AND CO. M.F. 3 a. Horace Leonard. Sheffield City T., August 6, 1894.

CUPID AND COMMONSENSE. P. 4 a. Arnold Bennett. Shaftesbury, January 24, 1908 (C.P.). Prod. by the Incorporated Stage Society. Shaftesbury, January 26, 1908.

CUPID AND DEATH. Masque. Jas. Shirley. Perf. before Ambassador of Portugal, March 26, 1653. Pr. 1659.

CUPID AND FOLLY; OR, THE COURT OF LOVE. Ballet by Noble. D.L., October 2, 1823.

CUPID AND HYMEN. Masque. John Hughes. Pr. 1717.

CUPID AND PSYCHE. P. Thos. Heywood. N.p. Probably same as *Cupid's Mistress*.

CUPID AND PSYCHE. M. Wm. Mason. M. by Giardini. N.p. N. ac.

CUPID AND PSYCHE. L.D. Müller. 19th cent.

CUPID AND PSYCHE. M. Sk. Mary Righton. Bayswater Bijou T., April 20, 1895 (by children).

CUPID AND PSYCHE; OR, BEAUTIFUL AS A BUTTERFLY. Extrav. F. C. Burnand. Olympic, December 26, 1864.

CUPID AND PSYCHE; OR, COLUMBINE COURTEZAN. D. Panto. Ent. D.L., February 4, 1734. Pr. 1734.

CUPID AND THE SCANDALMONGERS. C. 4 a. E. Denny. Wyndham's, February 1, 1904.

CUPID AND THE STYX. C. 3 a. J. Sackville Martin. Manchester Gaiety, February 8, 1909.

CUPID FROM JEWRY. C. 3 a. J. A. Mason. Kilburn T.R., May 3, 1897.

CUPID: HIS CORONATION. Masque. Ac. "at The Spittle" in 1654.

CUPID IN A CONVENT. C.O. 3 a. E. M. Seymour. M. by Mario Di Capri. Fulham Grand, July 18, 1903 (C.P.); Croydon T.R., August 17, 1903.

CUPID IN ARCADY. Fantasy. Mrs. Adrian C. Hope. Royal Botanic Gardens, Regent's Park, July 21, 1909.

CUPID IN CAMP. C.D. 2 a. G. C. Vernon. Criterion, May 22, 1882.

CUPID IN ERMINE. Ca. 1 a. Ellen Lancaster Wallis. Kennington P.O.W., March 27, 1899.

CUPID IN KERRY. C. 3 a. Edmund Leamy. Dublin Queen's, April 19, 1906.

CUPID IN LONDON. Q., 1835.

CUPID IN MISCHIEF. Dr. Ca. 1 a. W. Brett Plummer. Balham Assembly R., April 29, 1901.

CUPID IN WAITING. C. 3 a. Blanchard Jerrold. Royalty, June 17, 1871.

CUPID INCOG. Oa. Cornelius Van-der-Bilt. M. by Martyne Van Lennep. St. George's H., June 12, 1888.

CUPID WINS. Divertisse. Arr. by Alfredo Curti. M. by G. W. Byng. Alhambra, January 27, 1908.

CUPID'S ALLEY. C. 1 a. Drummond Roche. Dublin Gaiety, June 5, 1905.

CUPID'S BANISHMENT. Masque. R. White. Ac. at Greenwich, May 4, 1617.

CUPID'S DIPLOMACY. Int. D.L., January 7, 1840.

CUPID'S DREAM. Int. Henry Austin. Brighton Palace Pier. May 28, 1906.

CUPID'S FROLIC. Dr. Inc. Wilford F. Field. Ealing Vestry H., March 30, 1889.

CUPID'S ISLE. M.C. 2 a. G. Ransley. Liverpool, David Lewis Club, April 3, 1909.

CUPID'S LADDER. D. 2 a. Leicester Buckingham. St. James's, October 29, 1859.

CUPID'S MESSENGER. P. 1 a. Alfred C. Calmour. Novelty, July 22, 1884. Rev. at Vaudeville 1885, and December 2, 1887.

CUPID'S MISTRESS. Masque. Thos. Heywood. 1637. N.p.

CUPID'S ODDS AND ENDS. C. 3 a. Catherine Lewis. Parkhurst, June 1, 1895 (C.P.).

CUPID'S REVENGE. T. Beaumont and Fletcher. Ac. by Children of Revels, January 1, 1612-13. Pr. 1615. Entered Stationers' Co., April 24, 1615. F. on Sidney's *Arcadia*.

CUPID'S REVENGE. Arcadian past. Francis Gentleman. Hay., June 12, 1772. Pr. 1772.

CUPID'S REVENGE. See *Love Despised*.

CUPID'S SACRIFICE. T. W. Percy. 1602. (MS.) N.p.

CUPID'S THRONE. Arcadian C. 1 a. Regent's Park Royal Botanical Gardens, June 17, 1907.

CUPID'S VAGARIES. P. Belonging to the Cock-pit Co. 1639.

CUPID'S WHIRLIGIG. C. By "E.S.," probably Edward Sharpham. Ac. by the children of the King's Revels. Pr. 1607.

CUPS AND SAUCERS. F. Geo. Grossmith. Taken fr. *La Ceramique*. Op. C., August 5, 1878. See *Bric-à-Brac, Under Cover*.

CURATE, THE. C.D. 5 a. and 1 tab. Rase Challis. Gt. Grimsby P.O.W., May 3, 1886.

CURCULIO. Plautus. See "Latin Plays."

CURE, THE. F. 3 a. Weedon Grossmith. Dublin Gaiety, April 18, 1903; Hammersmith King's, June 8, 1903.

CURE FOR A COXCOMB; OR, THE BEAU BEDEVILL'D, A. D. Piece. C.G., May, 1792.

CURE FOR A CUCKOLD, A. C. John Webster and W. Rowley. Pr. 1661. See *The City Bride*.

CURE FOR A SCOLD, A. B.O. Jas. Worsdale. Taken fr. Shakespeare's *Taming of the Shrew*. London and Dublin. Pr. 1738. Ac. D.L., 1735.

CURE FOR COXCOMBS, A. Oa. M. by Mr. Watson. Lyceum, August 30, 1821.

CURE FOR DOTAGE, A. M. Ent. Sung at Marylebone Gdns. Pr. 1771.

CURE FOR FOOLERY, A. F. E. J. Jones and Harry Brashier. Walthamstow Victoria H., January 21, 1888.

CURE FOR JEALOUSY, A. C. John Carey. L.I.F. and D.L., 1705. Pr. 1701.

CURE FOR LOVE, A. C. 2 a. Thos. Parry. Hay., November 29, 1842; rev. 1853.

CURE FOR ROMANCE, A. Oa. M. arr. fr. Vaccari by Mr. Kearns, and other m. by Mr. Solly. Lyceum, August 30, 1819.

CURE FOR ROMANCE, A. C. Thomson. 1819.

CURE FOR THE FIDGETS, A. F. 1 a. Thos. J. Williams. Surrey, September 14, 1867; rev. Gaiety, September, 1876.

CURE FOR THE HEARTACHE, A. C. 5 a. Thos. Morton. C.G., January 10, 1797; D.L., 1824; Royalty, September, 1872.

CURE OF PRIDE, THE. C. This is Massinger's *City Madam*. Alt. N.p.

CURE OF SAUL. O. Arnold. 1770.

CURFEW, THE. P. 5 a. John Tobin. M. by Attwood. D.L., January 19, 1807 (rev.). Pr. 1807.

CURIA, THE. Sc. taken fr. Massinger's T., *The Roman Actor*. D.L., June 3, 1822.

CURING THE DOCTOR. F. Ep. J. H. Darnley. Walsingham Club, February 26, 1905.

CURIO, THE. D. 1 a. Adap. fr. the French. Folkestone Pleasure Gardens T., December 8, 1892.

CURIOSITY. C. W. C. Critton. Dublin Smock Alley, 1785.

CURIOSITY. P. C.G., April, 1798. N.p. Transl. fr. a German p., *Siri Brake; or, The Dangers of Curiosity*.

CURIOSITY. C. 3 a. Transl. fr. the Fr. of Mme. Genlis by Francis Lathom. Norwich, 1801. Pr. 1801.

CURIOSITY. C. 3 a. Joseph Derrick. Vaudeville, September 14, 1886.

CURIOSITY; OR, A PEEP THROUGH THE KEYHOLE. C. W. C. Oulton. Dublin, 1785. N.p.

CURIOSITY CURED; OR, POWDER FOR PEEPING. D. By J. B. Buckstone. D.L., July 21, 1825.

CURIOUS CASE, A. C.D. 2 a. Princess's, 1846; Lyceum, 1853; and Gaiety, October, 1872.

CURIOUS IMPERTINENT, THE. Crowne. Taken fr. *Don Quixote*. See *Amorous Prince*.

CURRENT CASH. D. Prol. and 4 a. C. A. Clarke. N. Shields, May 3, 1886; Greenwich P.O.W., May 24, 1886; Surrey, July 25, 1887.

CURRENT COIN. C. 3 a. Julian Cross. Bristol T.R., February 28, 1879.

CURSE OF CRIME, THE. D. 4 a. J. Rochefort. Surrey, March 21, 1904.

CURSE OF HER LOVE, THE. D. 4 a. Wm. Hibbert. Croydon R., May 22, 1905.

CURSE OF KIVAH, THE. D. 4 a. M. Wallerton and F. Gilbert. Edmonton T.R., June 9, 1902.

CURSE OF SAUL, THE. Orat. Arnold. 1739-1802.

CURSE OF THE CARDS, THE. P. 1 a. E. Harmadale and A. Shelton. Stockport T.R., July 25, 1906.

CURSE OF THE COUNTRY, THE. D. 4 a. Arthur Shirley. Elph. and C., May 22, 1905.

CURSE OF WOMEN, THE. D. G. Ivan Payne. Bayswater Bijou, November 30, 1903.

CUSHLA-MA-CREE. D. a 3. John Levey. Liverpool Adelphi, September 1, 1873; Marylebone, October 18, 1873.

CUSTOM HOUSE, THE. F.C. 3 a. L. A. D. Montague, Vaudeville, March 24, 1892.

CUSTOM OF THE COUNTRY, THE. T.C. Beaumont and Fletcher. Prior to 1628. Pr. 1647. Rev. T.R., 1667. See *Bickerstaff's Burial.*

CUSTOM OF THE COUNTRY, THE. P. 3 a. W. F. Hewer. Cirencester Corn H., April 19, 1901.

CUSTOM OF THE MANOR See *Country Lasses.*

CUSTOM OF ZURICH, THE. C.B. Sadler's Wells, April 17, 1797.

CUSTOM'S FALLACY. Dr. sk. 3 a. James M. Grant. 1805. Pr. 1805. N. ac.

CUT AND COME AGAIN. F. Robert Soutar. Olympic, August 9, 1879.

CUT BY THE COUNTY. See *'Twixt Kith and Kin.*

CUT FOR PARTNERS. F. 1 a. Jas. Bruton. Princess's, April, 1845. See *Paul the Presented.*

CUT MISER, THE. *The Miser* reduced to a F. by Edward Tighe. Pr. 1788.

CUT OFF WITH A SHILLING. Ca. 1 a. S. Theyre Smith. P.O.W., April 10, 1871.

CUTLACKE (GOOD LUCK). Ac. by Lord Admiral's servants, 1594. N.p.

CUTTER OF COLEMAN STREET, THE. C. Abraham Crowley. Ac. 1661. Duke of York's, 1663. Pr. 1663. Previously called *The Guardian.* Now rewritten. N.B.—Cutter signifies "Swaggerer."

CUTTING OUT A PRIZE. P. 1 a. Fenton Mackay. Margate Grand, July 18, 1904.

CUTWELL. P. Ac. 1576.

CYBELE; OR, HARLEQUIN'S HOUR. Panto. Royal Circus. J. C. Cross. Pr. 1804.

CYCLING. Ca. 1 a. Albert Chevalier. Strand, July 11, 1888.

CYCLONE, THE. F. 3 a. W. F. Heatley. Ladbroke H., April 24, 1900 (amat.).

CYCLOPÆDIA, THE. F. Mrs. Hoper. Hay., 1748. N.pr.

CYCLOPS, THE. B.C. 480 407. Transl. fr. Euripides by Potter 1781, Wodhull 1782, Shelley, and with Buckley's prose transl. in Bohn's series. See "Greek Plays."

CYMBELINE, KING OF GREAT BRITAIN. T. Shakespeare. Begun 1608, finished 1610. Pr. first folio 1623. Fd. on Holinshed's *Chronicles* and a novel of Boccaccio (Day 11, novel 9). Story also taken fr. an old story-book, "Westward for Smelts," 1603. Alt. by Ch. March. Pr. 1755. Alt. by W. Hawkins. C.G., 1759. Pr. 1759. Alt. by David Garrick. D.L., 1761 and pr. Alt. by H. Brooke. Pr. 1778. Alt. by Kemble for D.L. Pr. 1801. Rev. and ac. at C.G., 1810. Pr. 1810. Arr. by Henry Irving, Lyceum, September 22, 1896. Manchester Queen's, January 13, 1906, and Glasgow Grand, October 11, 1906. Rev. at Stratford-on-Avon, April 23, 1909.

CYMBRA; OR, THE MAGIC THIMBLE. C.O. 3 a. Harry Paulton. M. by Florian Pascal. Strand, March 24, 1883.

CYMON. D. Rom. David Garrick. D.L., January 2, 1767. Pr. 1767. First perf. as O., 5 a., and pr. 1793.

CYMON. F. 2 a. Alt. fr. David Garrick. D.L., Edinburgh, 1783.

CYMON AND IPHIGENIA. Dryden. 1631-1701.

CYMON AND IPHIGENIA. Lyr. C. Pastoral. 1 a. Adap. fr. David Garrick. J. R. Planché. Lyceum, April 1, 1850.

CYNIC, THE. C. 4 a. Herman Merivale. Suggested by Faust legend. Manchester T.R. (under the title of *The Modern Faust*), November 19, 1881; Globe, January 14, 1882.

CYNIC'S DEFEAT; OR, ALL IS VANITY, THE. Ca. Alfred Thompson. Liverpool P.O.W., August 19, 1878.

CYNICS, THE. C. 3 a. Robert Wilford. Barrow Royalty, September 10, 1904 (C.P.).

CYNTHIA. C. 3 a. H. H. Davies. Wyndham's, May 16, 1904.

CYNTHIA AND CYRUS. T. Hoole. C.G., 1768.

CYNTHIA AND ENDYMION; OR, THE LOVES OF THE DEITIES. Dr. O. 5 a. T. D'Urfey. Story taken fr. Ovid's *Metamorphoses* and Psyche in Apulcius's *Golden Ass.* D.L., 1697. Pr. 1697.

CYNTHIA'S REVELS; OR, THE FOUNTAIN OF SELF-LOVE. C. Ben Jonson. Ac. by the children of Q. Elizabeth's Chapel, 1600. Pr. 1600.

CYNTHIA'S REVENGE; OR, MAENANDER'S EXTACY. T. John Stephens. Plot fr. Lucan's *Pharsalia* and Ovid's *Metamorphoses.* Pr. 1613.

CYNTHIA'S SACRIFICE. Dr. episode. 1 a. Edwin Drew. St. Geo. H., April 11, 1893.

CYPRIAN CONQUEROR; OR, FAITHLESS RELICT, THE. P. In MS. at Brit. Museum.

CYPRUS Q. BLAKE. Piece. 1 a. G. Dayle. Terry's, April 28, 1904.

CYRANO DE BERGERAC. P. 5 a. in verse. Edmond Rostrand. Porte St. Martin, Paris, December 28, 1897; Lyceum, July 4, 1898; Adelphi, June 26, 1899. Adap. by Stuart Ogilvie and L. N. Parker. Blackpool Grand, March 5, 1900; Wyndham's, April 19, 1900; H.M. June 26, 1908.

CYRENE. Dr. fancy. 3 a. Alfd. C. Calmour. Avenue, June 27, 1890.

CYRIL'S SUCCESS. C. 5 a. H. J. Byron. Globe, November 28, 1868, and October 8, 1872; Criterion, January 25, 1890.

CYRUS. Orat. Rossini. D.L., January 30, 1828.

CYRUS. See *Cynthia and Cyrus.*

CYRUS THE GREAT. T. Mentioned in 1784 as offered by Rev. Dr. Stratford to Manager of D.L. Probably a mistake for *Darius.*

CYRUS THE GREAT; OR, THE TRAGEDY OF LOVE. T. John Banks. L.I.F., 1696. Pr. 1696. Plot fr. Scudery's rom. of *The Grand Cyrus.*

CYTHERE ASSIEGEE. O. Glück. Paris, 1775.

CYTHEREA; OR, THE ENAMOUR'D GIRDLE. C. John Smith. Pr. 1677. N. ac.

CZAR, THE. C.O. 3 a. John O'Keefe. C.G., March 8, 1790. Pr. 1798. First called *The Czar Peter.* Finally reduced to a f. and called *The Fugitive.*

CZAR, THE. P. J. Cradock. Pr. 1824.

CZAR OF MUSCOVY, THE. T. Mrs. Mary Pix. D.L., L.I.F. Pr. 1701.

CZAAR UND ZIMMERMANN. O. 3 a. Lortzing (Leipzig, December 22, 1837). Gaiety T., under the title of *Peter the Shipwright,* April 15, 1871.

D

D.T.; OR, LOST BY DRINK. A version of *L'Assommoir*, by E. Romaine Callender. Bradford T.R., August 4, 1879. See *Drink*.

D'ARTAGNAN. See *The Three Musketeers*.

DAD. C. 3a. F. A. Scudamore. Belfast T.R., November 22, 1882.

DAD'S MERMAID. C.D. 1 a. W. Felton. Brompton Hospital, October 20, 1904.

DADDY GRAY. D. 3a. Andrew Halliday. Royalty, February 1, 1868.

DADDY HARDACRE. D. 2a. Adap. by J. Palgrave Simpson. Olympic, March 26, 1857.

DADDY LONGLEGS. Panto. F. Bowyer. Britannia, December 26, 1885.

DAEMON; OR, THE MYSTIC BRANCH, THE. Rom. O. M. fr. Meyerbeer's O., *Robert le Diable*. D.L., February 20, 1832.

DÆMON OF DANESWALL. T. Pr. 1802. Anon.

DAFNE. O. Peri. See *Daphne*.

DAFNE. Schütz. Was a trans. of libretto used by Peri, 1627. All trace lost. See *Daphne*.

DAFNE. O. A. Ariosti. His first O. Was by Apostolo Zeno. Venice, 1686. Pr. 1696.

DAFNE IN ALLORO. B.O. B. Ferrari. Vienna, 1651. (MS. in library at Modena.)

DAGGER AND THE CROSS, THE. D. 4 a. Brownlow Hill. Grecian, October 10, 1867.

DAGGERS DRAWN. Ca. Pryce Seaton. Strand, January 9, 1891.

DAGOBERT. O. Bouffe. 3 a. Richard Sellman. Songs by Frank Green. M. by Hervé. Charing Cross, August 28, 1875.

DAGOBERT, KING OF THE FRANKS. T. Transl. from the German of James Marcus Babo by Benjamin Thompson. Pr. 1800.

DAINTY DRESDEN. C.O. Norah Begbie and P. Knight. (C.P.) Bijou, Bayswater, December 20, 1906.

DAIRYMAIDS, THE. M.P. 3 a. A. M. Thompson and Robert Courtneidge. M. by P. Reubens and A. Tours. Apollo, April 14, 1906; Queen's, May 5, 1908.

DAISY. C. 2 a. E. Manuel. Britannia, October 28, 1878.

DAISY. F.C. 3 a. B. T. Hughes. Glasgow Royalty, July 23, 1883.

DAISY. C.O. F Grove Palmer. M. by Hy. J. Wood. Kilburn T.H., May 1, 1890.

DAISY FARM. D. 4 a. Henry J. Byron. Olympic, May 1, 1871.

DAISY LAND. P. 3 a. H. Graham. Greenwich Lecture H., March 11, 1890.

DAISY'S ESCAPE. Ca. A. W. Pinero. Lyceum, September 20, 1879.

DALHAM FORGE. D. W. Stephens. Warrington Prince of Wales's, October 19, 1874.

DALIBOR. O. Smetana. 1824-1884.

DAME AUX CAMELIAS, LA. D. 5 a. A. Dumas fils. Paris Vaud., February 2, 1852; Gaiety, June 11, 1881; Eng. ver. at Lyceum, July, 1858. See *Camille, Heartsease, Lady of the Camelias*, and *La Traviata*.

DAME BLANCHE, LA. O. 3 a. Boieldieu. Lib. by Scribe. Paris, December 10, 1825. Prod. in English as *The White Maid*. C.G., January 2, 1827. Fd. on a combination of incidents taken fr. Scott's "Monastery" and "Guy Mannering."

DAME DE LA HALLE, LA. See *The Foundlings*.

DAME DE PIQUE, LA. O. Halévy. Paris, 1850.

DAME DE ST. TROPEZ. D. 3 a. Jas. Barber. Olympic, March 4, 1845.

DAME DOBSON; OR, THE CUNNING WOMAN. C. Edwd. Ravenscroft. Transl. fr. Fr. C., *La Divinresse ou, Les faux Enchantmens*. Duke's T., 1684. Pr. 1684.

DAME DU LAC, LA. O. Rossini. Paris, October 21, 1825.

DAME DURDEN'S VISIT. Sk. Re Henry. Steinway H., November 8, 1902.

DAME KOBOLD. C.O. J. C. Raff. Weimar. 1870.

DAMES CAPITAINES, LES. O. 3 a. Reber. June 3, 1857.

DAMNATION; OR, HISSING HOT. Int. Charles Stuart. Hay., August 29, 1781. N.p.

DAMNATION OF FAUST, THE. Dr. Legend. 4 a. and Epilogue (Paris, 1846). Adap. to the English Stage by T. H. Friend. M. by Hector Berlioz. Liverpool Court, February 3, 1894.

DAMOISELLE; OR, THE NEW ORDINARY, THE. C. Richard Brome. Pr. 1653.

DAMOISELLE A-LA-MODE. C. Richard Flecknο. Chiefly transl. fr. *Les Precieuses Ridicules* of Molière, and other pieces of same author. Pr. 1667. N.ac.

DAMON AND DAPHNE. Pastoral. 2 a. Ascr. to Theophilus Cibber. D.L., May, 1733.

DAMON AND PHILLIDA. B.O. 1 a. Colley Cibber. Entirely taken fr. his *Love in a Riddle*. D.L. Pr. 1729.

DAMON AND PHILLIDA. Alt. fr. Cibber into C.O. by C. Dibdin. D.L., Feb. 28, 1769. Pr. 1768.

DAMON AND PHŒBE. M.E. Thos. Horde, jun. Pr. 1774.

DAMON AND PYTHIAS. T.C. Richard Edwards. Ac. 1571. Pr. 1571.

DAMON AND PYTHIAS. P. Henry Chettle. Ac. 1599. Probably an alt. of Edwards' play.

DAMON AND PYTHIAS. T. 5 a. John Banim. C.G., May 28, 1821; Sadler's Wells, November 10, 1836; Marylebone, 1848; Surrey, February 7, 1860.

DAMON AND PYTHIAS. F. J. B. Buckstone. Adelphi, December 19, 1831.

DAMON AND PYTHIAS. Burl. 1 a. Valter Burnet. Soho T., 1860.

DAMON THE DAUNTLESS AND PHILLIS THE FAIR. Burl. Sk. Ch. Dryden. St. George's, December 28, 1869.

DAMP BEDS. Ca. T. Parry. Strand, May, 1832

DAN AND DICK. Eccentric C. 3 a. Herbert Gough and Morris Edwards. Ladbroke H., May 14, 1887 (C.P.) (amat.).

DAN, THE OUTLAW. D. Pro. and 4 a. Kilburn Town H., December 29, 1888.

DAN, THE OUTLAW. D. 3 a. Jessie Robertson. Novelty, May 14, 1892.

DAN, THE RAKE. M.D. 4 a. Myles Warburton, F. Gilbert, and L. Usher. Exeter T.R., June 5, 1903.

DANAIDES, LES. O. Saberi. 1750-1825.

DANAIDES, LES. Ballet. 2 a. M. by Herr Schmidt. D.L., Feb. 4, 1845.

DANCE AT DAWN, A. P. 1 a. Gladys B. Stern. Marlborough, July 31, 1909.

DANCE FOR LIFE, A. Sk. Hammersmith Palace, February 27, 1909.

DANCE OF LOVE, THE. P. 1 a. Steuart Beal. M. by Robert Hilton. Canterbury R., June 23, 1909.

DANCER, THE. Spanish Epis. 1 a. H. C. M. Hardinge. Court, March 20, 1905.

DANCING BARBER. Charles Selby. Adelphi, January 8, 1838.

DANCING DERVISH. Ca. 1 a. F. Kinsey Peile. Gaiety, June, 1894.

DANCING DEVILS; OR, THE ROARING DRAGON, THE. 3 a. Dumb F. Edw. Ward, 1724.

DANCING GIRL, THE. P. 4 a. H. A. Jones, Hay., January 15, 1891; rev. H.M.T., February 16, 1909.

DANCING GIRLS OF SPAIN, THE. M.P. 2 a. Lib. by G. R. Sims. M. comp. by C. C. Corri. Version somewhat rev. and given under a new name of *Miss Chiquita* by the same author and comp. Prod. at Birmingham P.O.W., August 7, 1899, and the following week at the Coronet. Rev. Hull Royal, June 24, 1907.

DANCING MASTER, THE. Ca. Max Pemberton and Milton Wellings. Incidental M. by Milton Wellings. Op. Comique, October 2, 1889.

DANDELION'S DODGES. F. Thos. J. Williams. New Holborn, October 5, 1867.

DANDOLO; OR, THE LAST OF THE DOGES. F. 1 a. Edw. Stirling. City of London, January 8, 1838.

DANDY DAN, THE LIFEGUARDSMAN. M.C. 2 a. Basil Hood. M. by Walter Slaughter. Belfast G.O.H., August 23, 1897; Lyric, December 4, 1897.

DANDY DANVERS, THE. Sk. Middlesex, May 3, 1909.

DANDY DICK. F. 3 a. A. W. Pinero. Court, January 27, 1887; transf. to Toole's, September 12, 1887.

DANDY DICK TURPIN, THE MASHING HIGHWAYMAN. Burl. Geoffrey Thorne. Grand, April 27, 1889; October 7, 1889.

DANDY DICK WHITTINGTON. Op. bo. 2 a. G. R. Sims and Ivan Caryll. Avenue, March 2, 1895.

DANDY DOCTOR, THE. M.F.C. 3 a. E. Marris. M. by Dudley Powell. Sunderland Avenue, March 26, 1900; Balham Duchess, July 16, 1900.

DANDY DUKE, THE; OR, THE MAN WHO WOULDN'T. M.P. 2 a. Vere Smith. Lyrics by D. E. Wilmot, S. Eaton, and Vere Smith. T.R., Brighton, December 17, 1906.

DANDY FIFTH, THE. Mily. C.O. 3 a. G. R. Sims. M. by Clarence Corri. Birmingham P.O.W., April 11, 1898; Duke of York's, Aug. 16, 1898.

DANE'S DYKE. D. 3 a. Mrs. Augustus Bright. Adap. from her novel "Unto the Third and Fourth Generations." Sheffield T.R., August 22, 1881.

DANGER. D. 4 a. Alfred Rayner. Standard, November 7, 1868.

DANGER. C.D. Alfred Davis. Leeds T.R., September 19, 1873.

DANGER. D. 3 a. Horncastle and Ogilvie. Surrey, October 23, 1879.

DANGER AHEAD. C.D. 4 a. Orig. prod. in U.S.A. Nottingham Grand, September 9, 1889.

DANGER SIGNAL, THE. D. 4 a. E. Bryant. Pavilion, October 5, 1867.

DANGERFIELD, '95. Piece. 1 a. Mildred T. Dowling. Garrick, May 26, 1898.

DANGEROUS. C.D. 3 a. C. W. Osborne. Lyceum, Sunderland, September 22, 1873.

DANGEROUS FRIEND, A. C. John Oxenford. Adap. fr. Feuillet's *La Tentation*. Hay., October 31, 1866. See *Led Astray*.

DANGEROUS GAME, A. D. Pro. and 3 a. Sir Randal Roberts. Grand, April 6, 1885.

DANGEROUS RUFFIAN, A. C. 1 a. W. D. Howells. Avenue, November 30, 1895.

DANGEROUS WOMEN. D. 4 a. F. A. Scudamore. Brixton, August 1, 1898.

DANGERS OF A GREAT CITY. Melo-d. 4 a. Oliver North. Oldham Coliseum, September 18, 1905.

DANGERS OF LONDON, THE. D. 4 a. F. A. Scudamore. Cardiff T.R., June 9, 1890; Surrey, June 23, 1890.

DANGERS OF SCIENCE, THE. F. G. J. Courtney. Shoreham Swiss Gardens, April 22, 1896.

DANGERS OF THE WORLD, THE. C. Transl. fr. "Theatre of Education" of Mde. Genlis. Pr. 1781.

DANICHEFF, LE. D. 4 a. Pierre Newsky. St. James's, June 17, 1876 (first perf. Odéon T., Paris, January 8, 1876).

DANIEL. Sacred D. Miss H. More. Pr. 1782.

DANIEL. D. James Scott. Ryde T.R., January 30, 1873.

DANIEL DIBSEY. C. 3 a. Geo. Blagrove. Albert H., May 1, 1905.

DANIEL IN THE LION'S DEN. An alt. of Hannah More's P. to adapt it for the stage. Doncaster, 1793.

DANIEL O'CONNELL. D. J. Robertson. Dublin Queen's, August 14, 1882.

DANIEL O'CONNELL; OR, KERRY'S PRIDE AND MUNSTER'S GLORY. Irish D. 3 a. John Levey. Worcester T.R., June 21, 1880.

DANIEL ROCHAT. See *Roma*.

DANISCHEFFS; OR, MARRIED BY FORCE, THE. C.D. 3 a. Adapt. by Lord Newry fr. A. Dumas and Pierre Newsky's play. St. James's. January 6, 1877.

DANISCHEFFS; OR, MARRIED BY FORCE, THE. D. 3 a. Arthur Shirley. New Cross Hall, 1883.

DANISH TRAGEDY, A. Henry Chettle. Ac. 1602.

DANITES, THE. D. 5 a. Joaquin Miller. Sadler's Wells, April 26, 1880.

DAN'L BARTLETT. See *The Deputy Sheriff*.

DAN'L DRUCE, BLACKSMITH. D. 3 a. W. S. Gilbert. Hay., September 11, 1876; rev. P.O.W. (mat.), February 20, 1894.

DAN'L PEGGOTTY. Adap., H. Kellett Chambers, from Dickens's "David Copperfield." King's, W., March 11, 1907.

DAN'L TRA-DUCED, TINKER. Burl. Arthur Clements. Strand, November 27, 1876.

DAN'L'S DELIGHT. M.Ca. Archie Armstrong. M. by J. W. Elliott. St. George's H., April 1, 1893.

DANSOMANIE, LA. Ballet. D.L., May 12, 1817.

DANTE. Idyll. G. H. R. Dabbs and Edw. Righton. St. George's H., July 10, 1893. (Independent Theatre.)

DANTE. P. in a prol. and 4 a. V. Sardou and E. Moreau. English ver. by Laurence Irving. D.L., April 30, 1903.

DANTE. Rom. P. 4 a. A. C. Calmour. Manchester Queen's T., June 15, 1903; Notting Hill Coronet, September 28, 1903.

DAPHNE. First German O. H. Schutz. 1627. See *Dafne*.

DAPHNE. Italian O. Ottavio Rinuccini, with whom co-operated three musicians, Peri, Giucopo Corsi, and Caccini. This is regarded by Sismondi as the first Italian O. 1594. Privately perf. in 1597. No trace of this work survives.

DAPHNE. Oa. Fk. Huntley. M. by J. Granville. Birmingham Kyrle Society's H., November 16, 1895 (amat.).

DAPHNE AND AMINTOR. C.O. Isaac Bickerstaff. Alt. fr. *The Oracle* of M. St. Foix and Mrs. Cibber. D.L. Pr. 1765.

DAPHNIS AND AMARYLLIS. Past. Pr. 1766. This is Harris's *The Spring* under another title.

DAPHNIS ET ALCIMADURA. O. M. by J. C. Mondonville. December 29, 1754.

DAPHNIS ET CHLOE. Op. bo. 1 a. Offenbach. 1860.

DAPHNIS ET CHLOE. O. 3 a. C. Maréchal. Paris Théâtre Lyrique, 1899.

DARAXES. Past. O. Aaron Hill. 2 a. Not finished. Pr. 1760.

DARBY AND JOAN. Sk. 1 a. Bellingham and Best. Newcastle T.R., September 11, 1885; Terry's, February 11, 1888.

DARBY'S RETURN. Dunlop. 1789.

DARDANUS. O. 5 a and prol. Rameau. October 19, 1739.

DAREDEVIL, THE. D. A. Shirley and H. Leonard. Portsmouth Prince's, October 19, 1894 (C.P.).

DARE-DEVIL DOROTHY. M.D. 4 a. Wilfrid Carr. M. by Sparrow Harris. (Orig. prod. O.H., Coventry, March 5, 1900, as *The Squatter's Daughter*.) Stratford T.R., July 1, 1901.

DARE-DEVIL MAX. Melo-d. 4 a. W. A. Brabner. Camberwell Metropole, December 11, 1800.

DARING DEVICE, A. Ca. A. T. Dancey. Bayswater Bijou, June 7, 1879.

DARIO. O. A. Ariosti. 1725.

DARIUS. T. Rev. Dr. Stratford. N.p., n.ac.

DARIUS. T. Earl of Stirling. Pr. 1603. Publ. with his *Crœsus* and *Aurora* as *The Monarchick Tragedies*.

DARIUS, Int. Taken fr. 3rd and 4th chap. of "Esdras." Pr. 1615.

DARIUS, KING OF PERSIA. T. John Crowne. D.L. and pr. 1688.

DARK CLOUD, THE. D. 2 a. Arthur Sketchley. St. James's, January 3, 1863.

DARK CONTINENT, THE. D. 5 a. Frdk. Mouillot and H. H. Morell. Barnsley T.R., June 11, 1891; Stonehouse Grand T., alt. and rev., February 29, 1892; Grand, October 10, 1892; ac. at Kansas, U.S.A., November, 1893, as *The Heart of Africa*.

DARK DAYS. P. 5 a. J. Comyns Carr and Hugh Conway. f. on Conway's novel. Hay., September 26, 1885.

DARK DAYS IN A CUPBOARD. Ca. 1 a. J. Stirling Coyne. Adelphi, December 29, 1864.

DARK DEEDS. F. Lyceum, 1839.

DARK DEEDS. D. 4 a. Mrs. Fairburn. Adap. fr. Miss Braddon's novel, "The Trail of the Serpent." Belfast T.R., under title of *Jabez North*; Philharmonic, March 11, 1882.

DARK DEEDS OF THE NIGHT. D. 4 a. Edward Thane. Stratford Royal, August 17, 1908.

DARK DOINGS IN THE CUPBOARD. See *Dark Days*, etc.

DARK GLEN OF BALLY FOIHL, THE. D. Edwd. Stirling. Ipswich T.R., October 28, 1871.

DARK HORSE, A. Ca. Croswick Garton. St. Geo. H., March 13, 1868 (amat.).

DARK HOUR, THE. D. Prol. and 4 a. Mrs. Daisy St. Aubyn. St. Geo. H., April 1[illegible] 1885.

DARK HOUR BEFORE DAWN, THE. P. 5 a. John Brougham and Frank B. Goodrich. First played by amateurs. Printed March 16, 1859. New York.

DARK KING OF THE BLACK MOUNTAINS. Britannia, April 2, 1866.

DARK NIGHT'S BRIDAL, A. Poetic C. 1 a. Robert Buchanan, founded on a prose sketch by R. L. Stevenson. Vaudeville, April 9, 1887.

DARK NIGHT'S WORK, A. D. 3 a. Adap. fr. the Fr. by Dion Boucicault. Princess's, March 7, 1870.

DARK PAGE, A. Oa. Written and composed by W. H Breare. Harrogate T.H., January 19, 1885 (amateur minstrels).

DARK PAST, THE. Melo-d. 4 a. Frank Price. Barnsley T.R., October 23, 1890.

DARK SECRET, A. D. Prol. and 4 a. J. Douglass and J. Willing, jun. F. on Sheridan Le Fanu's story "Uncle Silas." Standard, October 28, 1886; Princess's, November 14, 1895.

DARK SECRET, A. Dr. sk. 5 sc. John Douglass. Poplar, Queen's, April 29, 1907.

DARK SECRET, THE. See *The Lucky Shilling*.

DARK SHADOWS AND SUNSHINE OF LIFE. Victoria, April 13, 1857.

DARK SIDE OF THE GREAT METROPOLIS, THE. D. 3 a. W. Travers. Britannia, May 11, 1868.

DARKEST HOUR, THE. P. 3 a. Mrs. Adams-Acton. 8, Langord Place, St. John's Wood, April 6, 1895.

DARKEST LONDON. D. 5 a. Butler Stanhope Birkenhead T.R., April 4, 1891.

DARKNESS. D. 4 a. Adap. by S. B. Rogerson from Guy Thorne's novel "When it was Dark." Grand, Rawtenstall, March 5, 1906; again produced, with fresh dialogue and new scene, T.R., Manchester, March 12, 1906.

DARKNESS AND LIGHT. Pageant in 4 Episodes. J. Oxenham. M. by H. McCunn. Prod. by Hugh Moss. R. Agricultural H., June 4, 1908.

DARKNESS VISIBLE. F. 2 a. Theodore Hook. Hay., September 23, 1811.

DARLING OF THE GODS. David Belasco and J. Luther Long. Eleph. and C., November 7, 1902; His Majesty's, December 28, 1903.

DARLING OF THE GUARDS, THE. "A skittle, in 1 throe and 7 Japanese screens." Burl. introduced into *The School Girl*. P.O.W., February 19, 1904.

DARNLEY; OR, THE KEEP ON THE CASTLE HILL. D. 2 a. T. Egerton Wilks.

DARRACOTT'S WIFE. P. 1 a. Affleck Scott and Alan Carmichael (produced by the Play Actors). Court, March 14, 1909.

DARRY THE DAUNTLESS. Burl. 2 a. Hal Gatward and W. T. Thompson. Reading County T., July 31, 1890.

DARTHULA. T. James Mylne. Pr. 1790.

DARTMOOR. D. Episode. E. Ferris and P. Heriot. Great Queen Street T., June 26, 1900.

DASH; OR, WHO BUT HE? THE. M.F. 2 a. Ascribed to Francis Lathom. M. by Reeve. D.L., October 20, 1804. Probably *Holiday Time; or, The Schoolboy's Frolic*, altered.

DASH FOR FREEDOM, A. D. 5 a. Geo. Roy. Olympic, November 29, 1884.

DASH OF THE DAY, THE. C. Francis Lathom. Ac. at Norwich. Pr 1800.

DASHING LITTLE DUKE, THE. P. Seymour Hicks. M. by Frank E. Tours. Lyrics by Adrian Ross. Nottingham R., February 8, 1909; Hicks's, February 17, 1909.

DASHING PRINCE HAL. M. Trav. 2 a. Huntley Wright. Ealing Lyric, June 16, 1902.

DATAMIS. T. Anthony Davidson. N. ac.

DAUGHTER, THE. D. 1 a. T. H. Bayly. F. on Scribe's *La Lectrice*. Wr. 1836.

DAUGHTER, THE. P. 5 a. J. Sheridan Knowles. D.L., 1836.

DAUGHTER-IN-LAW, THE. C. 1 a. M. Seymour.

DAUGHTER OF ENGLAND, A. Sk. H. Dundas and H. Shelley. Halifax Grand, August 27, 1896 (C.P.).

DAUGHTER OF ERIN, A. Irish C. 4 a. Miss Le F. Robertson. Dublin T.R., August 19, 1901.

DAUGHTER OF EVE. D. 3 a. Paul Meritt. Birmingham P.O.W., July 30, 1877.

DAUGHTER OF EVE, A. Sk. W. M'Cullough. Adapt. of "Lady Audley's Secret." South London, May 1, 1893.

DAUGHTER OF FRANCE, A. P. 3 a. Langford Reed. Kennington, April 18, 1908 (C.P.).

DAUGHTER OF HERODIAS, THE. P. Brinsley Trehane. M. by Granville Bantock. Comedy, February 25, 1907 (C.P.); Royalty, June 10, 1907.

DAUGHTER OF HERODIAS, THE. P. The Hon. Eleanour Norton. Manchester, Midland, April 6, 1908 (rev.).

DAUGHTER OF ISHMAEL, A. D. 4 a. W. J. Patmore. Orig. prod. at St. James's, Manchester, as *Miriam Gray; or, The Living Dead*. Hammersmith Lyric, August 31, 1896; Surrey, March 8, 1897.

DAUGHTER OF ISRAEL, A. Sk. Chas Garry. Canterbury, February 8, 1909.

DAUGHTER OF JAIRUS, THE. Cant. Dr. Stainer.

DAUGHTER OF ST. MARK, THE. O. 3 a. M. by Balfe. D.L., November 27, 1844.

DAUGHTER OF SORROWS, A. P. 2 a. E. Miller. Hay., October 8, 1902.

DAUGHTER OF THE DANUBE, THE. Ballet. 2 a. M. by Adolphe Adam and A. Pilati. D.L., November 21, 1837.

DAUGHTER OF THE DANUBE, THE. Extrav. W. R. Osman. With several original songs imitated fr. the Fr. by W. H. C. Nation. Holborn T., March 3, 1873.

DAUGHTER OF THE PEOPLE, THE. D. 5 a. Frank Harvey. Adap. fr. the French. South Shields T.R., February 16, 1891. Grand, June 29, 1891.

DAUGHTER OF THE REGIMENT, THE. D. 2 a. Edwd. Fitzball. Adap. fr. *La Fille du Regiment*. D.L., November 30, 1843.

DAUGHTER OF THE REGIMENT, THE. C.O. 3 a. Donizetti. Eng. lib. by Fitzball. Surrey, December 21, 1847.

DAUGHTER OF THE REGIMENT, THE. C.O. 3 a. Donizetti. Eng. lib. by Oscar Weil. Bristol Prince's, October 18, 1890.

DAUGHTER OF THE SEA, A. D. 4 a. Lewis Gilbert. Hammersmith Lyric, July 5, 1909.

DAUGHTER OF THE STARS, THE. D. 2 a. Shirley Brooks. Strand, August 5, 1850; Olympic, September 2, 1850.

DAUGHTER OF THE SYNAGOGUE, A. Jewish-Gentile D. S. Downfield and F. E. Stevens. Birkenhead T.R., January 20, 1900 (C.P.).

DAUGHTER OF THE TUMBRILS, THE. P. 1 a. Walter E. Grogan. Albert Hall West T., May 17, 1897.

DAUGHTER TO MARRY, A. Ca. 1 a. J. R. Planché. Hay., 1828; rev. at Olympic, 1832-3.

DAUGHTER'S CRIME, A. D. R. Vaun. Peckham Crown, August 1, 1904.

DAUGHTER'S HONOUR, A. D. 4 a. Benj. Landeck and Arthur Shirley. Surrey, December 17, 1894.

DAUGHTER'S LOVE, A. D. 4 a. W. Armstrong and Richard Lord. Stourbridge Alhambra, December 17, 1902 (C.P.).

DAUGHTERS. F.C. T. G. Warren and W. Edouin. Portsmouth, June 30, 1890. See *Our Daughters*.

DAUGHTER'S SACRIFICE, A. P. 1 a. Neville Doone. Globe, May 17, 1888.

DAUGHTER'S SECRET, A. D. 2 a. Geo. Peel. Britannia, February 26, 1874.

DAUGHTERS OF BABYLON, THE. P. 4 a. Wilson Barrett. Lyric, February 6, 1897, and (rev. ver.) July 12, 1898.

DAUGHTERS OF MEN, THE. P. 3 a. C. Klein. Margate R., June 10, 1907.

DAUGHTERS OF SHEM. P. 1 a. Adapt. by Samuel Gordon and Carmel Goldsmid from story of the same name. Royalty, May 20, 1906.

DAVENANT. French C. Jean Achard. Gaiety, July 12, 1879.

DAVENPORT BROS. AND CO. F. 1 a. Edgar Pemberton. Birmingham T.R., April 24, 1879

DAVENPORT DONE; OR, AN APRIL FOOL. Ca. 1 a. Captain Colomb. Dublin T.R., February 4, 1867.

DAVID. Orat. Anon. 1734.

DAVID. P. 4 a. L. N. Parker and Murray Carson. Garrick, November 7, 1892.

DAVID AND ABSALOM. T. 5 a. Bishop Bale. Among the Stowe MSS.

DAVID AND BASHSHEBA. Stillingfleet. N.P.

DAVID AND BETHSABE: THEIR LOVES, WITH THE TRAGEDY OF ABSALOM. Geo. Peele. Pr. 1599.

DAVID AND GOLIATH. Sacr. D. Hannah More. Pr. 1782. See *Daniel*.

DAVID AND JONATHAN. Orat. Anon. Pr. 1761.

DAVID BALLARD. P. 3 a. Chas. McEvoy (prod. by Author). Imperial, June 9, 1907.

DAVID COPPERFIELD. P. 3 a. Entitled *Born With a Caul*. Strand, October, 1850; another ver., Surrey, November 7, 1850; another ver., Standard, November, 1850.

DAVID COPPERFIELD. American dramatisation of Dickens's novel. 2 a. Grecian, October 3, 1870. Another version, by John Brougham. D. 3 a. Brougham's Lyceum, New York, January 6, 1851. See *Em'ly; or, The Ark on the Sands*, *Little Em'ly*, *Dan'l Peggotty*.

DAVID GARRICK. C. 3 a. Adap. fr. French of Sullivan by T. W. Robertson. Hay., April 30, 1864; Hay., March, 1879; Criterion, November 13, 1886, 1890, 1891, and June 16, 1897; Wyndham's, February, 1900.

DAVID GARRICK. Burl. Chas. Colnaghi and E. Ponsonby. Criterion, May 11, 1888.

DAVID GARRICK. Adap. 1 a. H. M. Holles. Kingston County, June 10, 1901.

DAVID GARRICK. An Inc. 1 sc. Louis Cohen. Alhambra, October 26, 1907.

DAVID GARRICK. See *Garrick, Doctor Davy*.

DAVID MORGAN, THE JACOBITE. D. Aberdare Star T., February 15, 1872.

DAVID RIZZIO. Serious O. 3 a. Col. Hamilton. M. by Braham, Attwood, Cooke, and Reeve. D.L., June 17, 1820.

DAVID RIZZIO. T. Haynes. C.G., November, 1838.

DAVID'S LAMENTATION. Orat. Lockman. 1740.

DAVY. Ro. Sk. Stafford Smith. The Middlesex, February 10, 1902.

DAVY CROCKETT. D. 5 a. Frank Dizance. Edinburgh, Southminster T., September 29, 1873.

DAVY CROCKETT. American D. 4 a. Frank Murdoch. Liverpool, Alexander T., June 9, 1879; Olympic, August 9, 1879.

DAWN. Dram. Duol. Daphne de Rohan. Wimbledon St. Mark's Hall, September 8, 1900 (C.P.).

DAWN. D. 4 a. Geo. Thomas and Frank Oswald. Vaudeville, June 30, 1887. See *Devil Caresfoot, A Mad Match*.

DAWN OF FREEDOM, THE. C. 4 a. J. H. Condell. Goole T.R., April 20, 1900; Aberdare New, February 24, 1902; Surrey, July 28, 1902.

DAWN OF HOPE, THE. D. Prol. and 4 a. Clarence Burnette and Herbert B. Cooper. Orig. prod. in Provinces. Novelty, January 20, 1896.

DAWN OF LOVE, THE. Ca. 1 a. Adap. fr. Besant and Rice's novel, *The Golden Butterfly*. by Russell Rosse. Exeter T.R., January 26, 1885.

DAY AFTER THE FAIR, A. F. 2 a. C. A. Somerset. Sadler's Wells, 1829; Surrey, 1830.

DAY AFTER THE WEDDING; OR, A WIFE'S FIRST LESSON, THE. Int. 1 a. Marie Therese Kemble. C.G., May 18, 1808.

DAY AT AN INN, A. Farcetta, taken from *Killing No Murder*. Int. 1 a. Theodore Hook. Lyceum, August 25, 1823; rev. Lyceum, May 1838; D.L., March 8, 1855.

DAY AT ROME, A. M. Ent. 2 a. Chas. Smith. M. by T. Attwood. C.G., October 11, 1798. Pr. 1798.

DAY AT THE CARNIVAL, A. Ballet. D.L., May 22, 1837.

DAY DREAMS. C. Sir Baldwyn Leighton. Loton Park, Salop, November 5, 1875.

DAY DREAMS. Dr. Episode. 1 a. May Hawthorn. Camden Town, Park H., May 23, 1888.

DAY DREAMS. P. 1 a. Herbert Swears. Brighton, Eden T., December 5, 1894; Opera-Comique, July 6, 1895.

DAY IN KINGSBURY CASTLE, A. A.D. 851. Hist. Pageant, arranged by C. H. Ashdown. St. Albans, County H., April 6, 1899.

DAY IN LONDON, A. C. Andrew Cherry. D.L., April 9, 1807. N.p.

DAY IN PADDY'S MARKET, A. F.P. 3 a. with music. Max Fax. Fleetwood, Queen's, Nov. 14, 1904.

DAY IN PARIS, A. F. 1 a. Chas. Selby. Strand, July 18, 1832. See *Lost, Stolen, or Strayed*.

DAY IN PARIS, A. Bal. in 5 sc. Lieut.-Col. N. Newnham-Davis. M. comp. and arr. by Cuthbert Clarke. Empire, October 19, 1908.

DAY IN TURKEY; OR, THE RUSSIAN SLAVES, A. C. Mrs. H. Cowley. C.G., December 3, 1791. Pr. 1792.

DAY OF RECKONING, THE. D. 3 a. J. R. Planché. Lyceum, December 4, 1851; rev. at Adelphi, 1868.

DAY OF RECKONING, THE. D. Battersea Queen's T., February 17, 1894 (C.P.).

DAY OF RECKONING, THE. D. 4 a. Beatrice Isaacson. Surrey, December 10, 1900.

DAY OF SUNSHINE. See *The Spirit of Poetry*.

DAY TO DAY. D. Pro. and 3 a. C. A. Clarke. Public Hall, Warrington, July 1, 1889. See *Men and Money*.

DAY WELL SPENT, A. F. 1 a. John Oxenford. Lyceum, April 4, 1835.

DAY WILL COME, A. Melo-d. 4 a. W. J. Mackay. Chatham O.H., March 7, 1892; Sadler's Wells, January 12, 1893.

DAY'S FISHING, A. F. 1 a. J. M. Morton. Adelphi, March 8, 1869.

DAY'S SPORT, A. M. Sk. Corney Grain St. Geo. H., January 28, 1889.

DAYBREAK. D. Pro. and 4 a. Jas. Willing. Standard, September 1, 1884.

DAYE AND KNIGHT. M. farcicality. Lib. by Walter Parke. M. by Louise Barone. St. Geo. H., November 4, 1895.

DAYES OF OLDE. C. Pr. and 2 a. Fred Farman. Leamington T.R., November 8, 1892.

DAYLIGHT GHOSTS. 1 sc. J. N. Maskelyne and David Devant. St. Geo. H., September 3, 1906.

DAYS OF ATHENS, THE. A Mirror of History and Science of Past, Present, and Future, invented, arr., and perf. by Ducrow (with others). D.L., November 14, 1831.

DAYS OF CROMWELL, THE. D. Prol. and 3 a. Charles Rogers and E. Carter Livesey. Sunderland Avenue, July 9, 1896 (C.P.); Stratford Borough T., October 19, 1896; alt. to 5 a, West London, November 2, 1896.

DAYS OF DANGER. P. Wm. Bourne. Glasgow G., April 16, 1900; New Cross, Broadway, as *The Invasion of Britain*, July 9, 1900; Dalston T., September 24, 1900.

DAYS OF REPENTANCE. Harry Bruce.

DAYS OF YORE. D. 3 a. Richard Cumberland. C.G., January 13, 1796. Pr. 1796.

DAYS OF TERROR. Rom. D. 4 a. C. A Clarke. Bishop Auckland T.R., March 24, 1891.

DAYS TO COME, THE. D. 4 a. Forbes Dawson. Elephant and Castle, May 29, 1893.

DAYS WE LIVE IN; OR, A TALE OF 1805, The. Dr. piece, with songs. Archibald Maclaren. Pr. 1805.

DE LA PEROUSE; OR, THE DESOLATE ISLAND. Pant. D. 2 parts. M. by Davy and Moorhead. D.L., November 7, 1825.

DE LANCY. P. Augustus Thomas. Vaudeville, September 4, 1905 (C.P.).

DE MONTFORT. T. 5 a. J. Baillie. D.L., March 29, 1800; rev. November 27, 1821.

DE REMEDIO AMORIS. Ovid. See "Latin Plays."

DEACON, THE. C. Sk. 2 a. Henry Arthur Jones. Shaftesbury, August 27, 1890.

DEACON BRODIE; OR, THE DOUBLE LIFE. Melo-d. 4 a and 10 tab. By R. L. Stevenson and W. E. Henley. Bradford, Pullan's T. of V., December 28, 1882; Prince's, July 2, 1884.

DEAD; OR, THE LIVING WILL. D. 5 a. James Scott. Brierley Hill T.H., November 25, 1891.

DEAD ALIVE, THE. F. John Keefe. M. by S. Arnold. Hay., June 16, 1781. Only pr. by piracy, 1783.

DEAD ALIVE, THE. James Bruton, author of *Cut for Partners*, etc.

DEAD ALIVE AGAIN. THE. T.-Comical F. Dr. Collingwood. Pr. (n.d.). N.ac.

DEAD BEAT. D. 5 a. G. Conquest and G. Corner. Surrey, October 22, 1885.

DEAD BOXER, THE. D. Albion, September 20, 1875.

DEAD CALM; OR, THE FISHER'S STORY, A. D. 2 a. J. Douglass, jun. Standard, August 4, 1868.

DEAD DUCHESS. Britannia, March 24, 1856.

DEAD FETCH. See *Death Fetch*.

DEAD GUEST; OR, THE SEXTON'S PROPHECY, THE. C.D. 2 a. M. by Alexander Lee. Lyceum, August 11, 1834.

DEAD HEART, THE. Hist. D. Pro. and 3 a. Watts Phillips. Adelphi, November 10, 1859; rev. at Marylebone, April, 1862, and Lyceum, September 28, 1889.

DEAD HEAT, A. Ca. St. Clair Cooke. Athenæum, Shepherd's Bush, November 11, 1891.

DEAD LETTER, A. D. 1 a. W. A. Brabner. Dublin Gaiety T., April 17, 1891; Op. C., September 9, 1891.

DEAD LETTER; OR, SECOND SIGHT, THE. D. Pro. and 3 a. Walter Roberts. Marylebone, December 11, 1873, and December 3, 1877.

DEAD MAN'S CLIFF; OR, THE BLIND GIRL'S INHERITANCE. Evesham Victoria T., September 23, 1896.

DEAD MAN'S FORTUNE, THE. N.p. Anon. Plot appears in Reed's edition of Shakespeare, 1803, Vol. 3.

DEAD MAN'S GOLD; OR, THE HISTORY OF A CRIME, A. D. 5 a. G. Conquest and Henry Spry. Surrey, November 7, 1887.

DEAD MAN'S HOLLOW, THE. D. M. Wardhaugh. Longton T., October 4, 1869.

DEAD OF NIGHT. Novelty, April 26, 1897.

DEAD O' NIGHT BOYS. Irish D. W. S. Branson. Greenwich, September 19, 1874.

DEAD OR ALIVE. D. 3 a. Tom Taylor. Queen's, July 22, 1872.

DEAD PAST, THE. D. Austin Fryers. Parkhurst, June 24, 1895.

DEAD RECKONING; OR, PRESSED FOR THE NAVY, THE. D. C. H. Hazlewood. Britannia, August 10, 1868.

DEAD ROSES. D. 1 a. W. Reeve.

DEAD SECRET, THE. D. Pro. and 3 a. f. by E. W. Bramwell on Wilkie Collins's novel. Lyceum, August 29, 1877.

DEAD SHOT, A. F. 1 a. J. B. Buckstone. Adelphi, 1830.

DEAD TAKE IN, A. F. Alfred Wigan. Olympic, 1850.

DEAD TO THE WORLD. D. 4 a. G. Conquest and H. Pettitt. Grecian, July 12, 1875.

DEAD WIFE; OR, MARMADUKE, THE SMUGGLER, THE. P. Pav., December, 1838.

DEAD WITHOUT A NAME. Olympic, February 14, 1853.

DEAD WITNESS; OR, SIN AND ITS SHADOW, THE. D. 3 a. Wybert Reeve. f. on "The Widow's Story of the Seven Poor Travellers," by C. Dickens. Sheffield T.R.

DEADLOCK, THE. D. 5 a. Adap. by David Cowis and John Hastings Batson fr. the Russian of Potyeken. Bayswater Bijou, February 7, 1898.

DEADLY FOES. D. Miss Josephine Fiddes. Belfast T.R., November 20, 1868.

DEADLY REPORTS. F. J. Palgrave Simpson. Olympic, October 26, 1857.

DEADLY SAMPSON. D. W. M. Akhurst and Lieut. James Twigg. Pav., September 16, 1876.

DEADLY WEAPONS. D. Woods Lawrence. Pro. and 3 a. Gt. Yarmouth T.R., July 9, 1884; Grimsby T.R., September 14, 1885.

DEADMAN'S POINT; OR, THE LIGHTHOUSE ON THE CARN RUTH. D. 4 a. and 2 tab. F. C. Burnand. Adelphi, February 4, 1871

DEADWOOD DICK. D 5 a. Paul Korrell. Pav., March 12, 1894.

DEAF AND DUMB; OR, ABBE DE L'EPEE. Hist. P. Transl. fr. the French of J. N. Bouilly. Pr. 1801.

DEAF AND DUMB; OR, THE ORPHAN. Hist. D. Fr. the sermon of Kotzebue, by Benj. Thomson. Pr. 1801. Kotzebue's was a transl. of Bouilly's play.

DEAF AND DUMB; OR, THE ORPHAN PROTECTED. Hist. D. 5 a. Taken fr. French of Bouilly by Thomas Holcroft. D.L., February 24, 1801; D.L. (in 3 a), May 27, 1816.

DEAF AS A POST. F. 1 a. John Poole. D.L., February 15, 1823.

DEAF INDEED. F. Edw. Topham. D.L., December 4, 1780. N.p.

DEAF LOVER, THE. F. F. Pilon. C.G., February 2, 1780. Pr. 1779. Alt. of *The Device*.

DEAL BOATMAN, THE. D. 2 a. F. C. Burnand. D.L., September 21, 1863; rev. Sadler's Wells, 1866.

DEAN OF HAZELDENE, THE. D. 4 a. J. Pope Dryden. Nelson Grand T., April 20, 1889.

DEAN'S DAUGHTER, THE. P. 4 a. S. Grundy and F. C. Phillips fr. the latter's novel. St. James's, October 13, 1888.

DEAN'S DILEMMA, THE. Ca. A. J. Dearden. Garrick, January 25, 1906.

DEAR BARGAIN, A. P. 1 a. L. C. Fenn. (Prod. by the Play Actors.) Court, November 8, 1908.

DEAR DEPARTED, THE. Oa., founded by Walter Parke on *Le Clou aux Maris*. Prod. in Paris, 1859. M. by H. Martyn van Lennep. Comedy, May 29, 1890.

DEAR DEPARTED, THE. Ca. Stanley Houghton. Manchester Gaiety, November 2, 1908; Coronet, June 7, 1909.

DEAR FRIENDS. Ca. Mary Righton. Vaudeville, July 24, 1890.

DEAR GIRLS, THE. M.C. 3 a. Harry and Edward Paulton. M. by Knight Pearce, Clement Lockname, T. Fitzgerald, and E. Paulton. Salford, Regent T., September 11, 1899

DEAR HEARTS OF IRELAND. D. 3 a. Peckham Crown, December 3, 1900.

DEAR JACK. Sk. Mrs. Giraud. Colchester T.R., May 30, 1892.

DEAR LADY MARY. P. Lady Violet Greville. Bayswater Bijou, February 21, 1905.

DEAR LITTLE DENMARK. Danish M. Incident. 2 a. Paul A. Rubens. Prince of Wales's, September 1, 1909.

DEAR OLD CHARLEY. C. 3 a. C. H. E. Broogfield, from Célimare le Biendimé, by Labiche and Delacour. Newcastle T.R., May 17, 1906; rev. Vaudeville, January 2, 1908.

DEAR OLD HOMELAND, THE. Melo-d. 5 a. David Muskerry. T.R., Sunderland, August 27, 1906.

DEARER THAN LIFE. C. 3 a. H. J. Byron. Liverpool Alexandra, November 25, 1867; Long Acre, Queen's T., January 8, 1868.

DEAREST FRIENDS. Duo. Mrs. Bradshaw. Steinway H., June 20, 1902.

DEAREST MAMMA! Ca. 1 a. Adap. fr. the French by Walter Gordon. Olympic, May 14, 1860; Criterion, October 13, 1890.

DEATH. Dialogue. Bulleyn. (12 characters.) Pr. 1564.

DEATH AND VICTORY OF LORD NELSON. Melo-d. Cumberland, 1805.

DEATH BY THE LAW. D. Edwd. Towers. Pavilion, August 5, 1876.

DEATH DANCE, THE. Sk. Canterbury, May 3, 1909.

DEATH FETCH; OR, THE STUDENT OF GOTTINGEN, THE. Op. Rom. 3 a. M. by C. E. Horn. Lyceum, July 25, 1826.

DEATH GUEST. Spectral D. Lyceum, 1834.

DEATH OF A SOUL, THE. P. Robert Kelso. Prod. by amateurs. Royalty, February 25, 1906.

DEATH OF ABEL. Orat. Anon. 1768.

DEATH OF ABEL, THE. Orat. Leo. 1694-1745.

DEATH OF ADAM, THE. T. Robt. Lloyd. Transl. fr. German of Klopstock. Pr. 1763.

DEATH OF ADAM, THE. Sacred D., transl. fr. the French of Mme. Genlis by Thos. Holcroft. Pr. 1786

DEATH OF BUCEPHALUS, THE. Burl. T. 2 a. Dr. Ralph Schomberg. Edinburg. Pr. 1765.

DEATH OF CÆSAR, THE. T. Transl. fr. Voltaire. Pr. in D. Francklin's edition.

DEATH OF CAPTAIN COOKE, THE. Hist. pant. ballet. 2 a. C.G. 1789; rev. Lyceum, August 10, 1818.

DEATH OF CAPTAIN FAULKNER; OR, BRITISH HEROISM, THE. M.I. C.G., May 6, 1795. N.p.

DEATH OF DIDO, THE. Masque. by R. C. 1621.

DEATH OF DIDO, THE. Masque. Barton Booth. M. by Dr. Pepusch. D.L. Pr. 1716.

DEATH OF DION, THE. T. Thos. Harwood. Pr. 1787. N. ac.

DEATH OF HANNIBAL, THE. T. Lewis Theobald. N.p. N.ac.

DEATH OF HARLEQUIN, THE. Pant. D.L., 1716.

DEATH OF HEROD, THE. T. By a Gentleman of Hull. Wr. 1785.

DEATH OF MAJOR ANDRE, THE. T., imported fr. America. See *Andre*. Dunlap, 1798.

DEATH OF MARLOW, THE. T. 1 a. R. H. Horne. Orig. publ. in London, and inscribed "To Author's friend, Leigh Hunt. Now dedicated to his memory by R. H. Horne." 1869.

DEATH OF ORSINA AND THE APPEARANCE OF THE ACCUSING SPIRIT. An early play.

DEATH OF ROBERT, EARL OF HUNTTINGTON, THE. Chettle and Anthony Munday. Prod. 1598. Pr. 1601.

DEATH OF SOCRATES. T. E. Harrison. 1756.

DEATH OF THE BLACK PRINCE, THE. T. In library of Dr. Sharpe.

DEATH OF TINTAGILES. T. 4 s. Maurice Maeterlinck. St. George's H., July 22, 1902.

DEATH OF WALLENSTEIN, THE. See *Piccolomini*. Coleridge, 1800.

DEATH OR GLORY. Military D. 5 a. John Mill. Britannia, October 7, 1896.

DEATH OR VICTORY. Military P. John Mill and Harry Mountford. Attercliffe T.R., September 22, 1898.

DEATH PLANK; OR, THE DUMB SAILOR BOY, THE. Melo-d. 2 a. W. J. Lucas. Pavilion, July, 1832.

DEATH TRAP; OR, A CATSPAW, THE. D. 4 a. J. Redding Ware. Grecian, June 6, 1870.

DEATH WALTZ, THE. Sk. Leeds, Queen's, June 3, 1908.

DEATH WARRANT; OR, A RACE FOR LIFE, THE. D. H. P. Grattan. Grecian, October 25, 1879.

DEATH'S BRIDAL. D. 5 a. Charles Osborne. Bolton Temple O.H., June 10, 1878.

DEATH'S HEAD DICK, THE SKELETON PIRATE; OR, THE TIGERS OF THE SEA. D. R. C. Totten. Merthyr Tydfil Cambria T., March 31, 1870.

DEBAUCHEE; OR, THE CREDULOUS CUCKOLD, THE. C. Mrs. Behn. Duke's T., and Pr. 1677. See *The Mad Couple*. Pro. and epil. by Lord Rochester.

DEBAUCHEES; OR, THE JESUIT CAUGHT, THE. C. H. Fielding. D.L. Pr. 1733. An edit. of this P. Pr. 1732, under title of *The Old Debauchées*.

DEBORAH; OR, THE JEWISH MAIDEN'S WRONG. D. 3 a. Chas. Smith Cheltnam. Victoria T., July 12, 1864. Another version of *Leah the Forsaken*.

DEBORAH. Concerto. Handel. 1685-1759.

DEBORAH. Orat. Handel. Words by Humphreys. Completed February 21, 1733; first perf. King's T., Haymarket, March 17, 1733; rev. by the Sacred Harmonic Society, November 15, 1843.

DEBORAH. P. 5 a. Langdon Elwyn Mitchell. Avenue, February 22, 1892.

DEBORAH. See *Ruth*. *The Slave Girl*.

DEBORAH; OR, A WIFE FOR YOU ALL. Ac. D.L., April 6, 1733.

DEBORAH; OR, THE JEWISH OUTCAST. Grecian, February 15, 1864.

DEBT. F.C. 2 a. E. A. De Pass. Gaiety, November 23, 1872.

DEBT. C. Northampton T.R., August 25, 1873.

DEBT, THE. Sk. Hélène Forest. Empress, April 10, 1907.

DEBT OF HONOUR. C. 1 a. Mrs. Bradshaw. Publ. by S. French, Ltd.

DEBT OF HONOUR, A. C. F. W. Broughton. West Hartlepool T.R., January 23, 1879.

DEBT OF HONOUR, A. Piece. 1 a. C. P. Colnaghi. Op. C., December 17, 1891.

DEBT OF HONOUR, A. P. 5 a. Sydney Grundy. St. James's T., September 1, 1900.

DEBT OF HONOUR, A. Sk. 3 sc. Percival H. T. Sykes. Canterbury M.H., May 25, 1903.

DEBT OF HONOUR, THE. C. Elizabeth Ryves. N.p., n.ac.

DEBTOR AND CREDITOR. C. 5 a. Jas. Kenney. C.G., April 20, 1814.

DEBUTANTE, THE (*Père de la Débutante*). Criterion, December 28, 1875. See *The First Night.*

DECADENT DIALOGUE, A. Duol. Mrs. Haig Thomas. Lyceum, March 30, 1909.

DECEIT, THE. F. Henry Norris. Pr. 1723.

DECEIT; OR, THE OLD FOX OUTWITTED, THE, Past. F. 1 a. By J. W. Designed to have been ac. Pr. 1743. Alt. and publ. under the title of *The Country Wedding; or, Love in a Dale.*

DECEIVED; OR, THROUGH LIFE. D. Accrington Prince's, September 9, 1882.

DECEIVER DECEIVED, THE. C. Mrs. Mary Pix. L.I.F. Pr. 1698.

DECEIVERS EVER. F.C. 2 a. Malcolm Chas. Salamon. Strand. November 26, 1883.

DECEMBER AND MAY. Op. F. W. Dimond, from Molière's F., *Barnaby Brittle.* C.G., May, 16, 1818.

DECEPTION. C. Ascr. to Mr. Vaughan. D.L., October 28, 1784. N.p.

DECEPTION. Ca. Maurice de Frece. Liverpool T.R., December 18, 1871.

DECEPTION. F.C. 3 a. Andrew Longmuir. Edinburgh T.R., May 27, 1889.

DECEPTIONS, THE. C. Mrs. Cornelys. Dublin, 1781..

DECIDED CASE. F. 1 a. J. Brougham. Publ. by S. French, Ltd. Wallack's, New York.

DECIDEDLY COOL. P. Bertram Forsyth. Bennington Paroch. H., January 11, 1904.

DECIUS AND PAULINA. Masque. L. Theobald. Pr. 1718.

DECLINED—WITH THANKS. F. J. M. Morton.

DECORUM; OR, VERY SUSPICIOUS. F. 2 a. D.L., March 5, 1831.

DECOY, THE. O. H. Potter. Goodman's Fields, February 5, 1733. Pr. 1733.

DECOY, THE. C.D. 3 a. Fredk. Eastwood. Gaiety, April 18, 1883.

DECOY, THE. Sk. Eugene Magnus. Standard, August 9, 1909.

DECOY BIRD, THE. D. Luton Town H., September 5, 1892.

DECREE NISI, THE. P. 1 a. Joshua Bates. St. James's, October 18, 1904.

DEDALE, LE. P. 4 a. W. L. Courtney. Fr. the French of Paul Hervieu. Comedy, September 21, 1905 (C.P.); Hay., May 25, 1908.

DEED WITHOUT A NAME, A. F. R. Soutar. Olympic.

DEEDS. C. 3 a. Mrs. Freake. Cromwell H., South Kensington, February 25, 1879.

DEEDS, NOT WORDS. D. 2 a. J. Courtney. Surrey, January 15, 1855.

DEEDS OF DREADFUL NOTE. Dr. tale. 1 a. Dubois, fr. the French of De Rosier. Adelphi, 1842.

DEEMING; OR, DOOMED AT LAST. Dom. T. Liverpool Adelphi, June 6, 1892.

DEEMSTER, THE. See *Ben-my-Chree.*

DEENE FARM. Oa. 2 a. Alfred Bateman. M. by Geo. C. Richardson. St. Andrews, Stoke Newington, January 23, 1894; Myddleton H., Islington, April 5, 1894.

DEEP DEEP SEA; OR, PERSEUS AND ANDROMEDA, THE. Burletta. 1 a. J. R. Planché and C. Dance. Olympic, December 26, 1833.

DEEP RED ROVER, THE. Burl. 3 scenes. Fredk. Hay and Westmacott Chapman. Pub. by S. French, Ltd.

DEEP WATERS. P. 1 a. Sydney Grundy. Manchester T.R., September 19, 1889.

DEER SLAYERS; OR, THE FREE ARCHERS OF THE NEW FOREST, THE. D. W. and C. Pitt. Britannia, December 19, 1870.

DEERFOOT. F. 3 a. F. C. Burnand. Olympic, December 16, 1861.

DEFAULTER. A Rom. of Real Life. 1 a. Fr. Hood's Whimsicalities. By a member of the Amateur Theatrical Society of Calcutta. Calcutta, 1858

DEFEAT OF APOLLO. See *The Mirrour.* Anon. 1737.

DEFEATED. C. 3 a. Fredk. Clay. Cardiff T.R., April 11, 1881.

DEFECTIVE DETECTIVE, THE. C.Sk. Frank Melroyd. Southport, Pier Pav., February 29, 1904.

DEFENCE OF LADY ROSA, THE. C. 3 a. Archibald H. Pocock. Bayswater Bijou, May 18, 1905.

DEFENDER OF THE FAITH. Melo.-d. 4 a. and 9 tab. Chas. Darrell. Birmingham Grand, September 20, 1897; Standard, May 9, 1898.

DEFENDING HIS HONOUR. D. 4 a. Lingford Carson. Keighley Queen's, November 10, 1902; Camberwell Metropole, August 17, 1903.

DEFORMED TRANSFORMED, THE. D. Byron, partly f. on *Wood Demon.* Pr. 1824.

DEGEL, LE. See *Adonis Vanquished.*

DEGENERATES, THE. C. 4 a. Sydney Grundy; Hay., August 31, 1899; Garrick, October 16, 1899; rev. Imperial, April 17, 1902

DEIDAMIA. O. Handel. (London, 1741.)

DEIRDRE. Legendary verse in 1 a. W. B. Yeats. New, November 27, 1908 (mat.).

DEL OMBRA; OR, THE SON OF NIGHT. D. J. A. Mercer. Liverpool T.R., April 12, 1879

DEL. TREM.; OR, THE POWER OF DRINK. Ver. of *L'Assommoir.* Walter Banks. West Hartlepool Gaiety, September 22, 1879. See *Drink.*

DELAYS AND BLUNDERS. C. 5 a. Frederic Reynolds. C.G., October 30, 1802. Pr. 1803.

DELIA. Rom. Military C.O. Lib. adap. by F. Soulbieu from Scribe's *La Frileuse.* M. by P. Bucalossi. Bristol Prince's, March 11, 1889. See *Court Cards.*

DELIA DARE'S DEVICE. P. 4 a. Lewis Gilbert. Eastbourne T.R., May 2, 1903.

DELIA HARDING. P. 3 a. Adap. by Comyns Carr fr. the French of V. Sardou. Comedy, April 17, 1895.

DELICATE ATTENTIONS. P. J. Poole. St. James's, December, 1836.

DELICATE BOY. 1 a. S. J. Adair Fitzgerald. Publ. by S. French. Ltd.

DELICATE GROUND; OR, PARIS IN 1793. C.D. 1 a. Chas. Dance. Lyceum, November 27, 1849; rev., Astley's, 1867; Globe, 1870; Criterion, April 23, 1890; Terry's, January 11, 1897; Garrick, July 13, 1903.

DELICATE LOVE. J. G. Shaddick. 1800.

DELIGHT. C. Ac. at Court, 1580.

DELIGHTS O' LONDON. Burl. of *The Lights o' London*. Wallis Mackay, Horace Leonard, and Geo. L. Gordon. Philharmonic, April 8, 1882.

DELILAH; OR, MARRIED FOR HATE. D. Pro. and 3 a. Adap. by James Willing from Ouida's *Held in Bondage*. Park T., October 7, 1880; Sadler's Wells, September 26, 1892.

DELINQUENT; OR, SEEING COMPANY. C. 5 a. Fredk. Reynolds. C.G., November 14, 1805. Pr. 1805.

DELIVERED FROM EVIL. D. 4 a. Frank Dix. Bristol T.R., March 27, 1899.

DELIVERY OF SUSANNAH, THE. T. Ralph Radcliff. N.p.

DELUGE, THE. See *Noah's Flood*. Ecclestone, 1714.

DELUSION. C. Jameson, 1813.

DELUSION. Oxberry. See *Students of Salamanca*.

DEMETER AND PERSEPHONE. P. T. M. Davidson. Dundee, Foresters' H., March 29, 1904.

DEMETRIO. O. Tarchi. M. by Gluck. Milan, 1788.

DEMETRIO E POLIBIO. O. Rossini. Rome, 1812.

DEMETRIUS. O. Transl. from *Metastasio*. John Hoole. Pr. 1768.

DEMETRIUS AND MARSINA; OR, THE IMPERIAL IMPOSTER AND UNHAPPY HEROINE. T. N.p. MS. formerly belonging to Mr. Warburton, and sold about 1759.

DEMETRIUS AND THE THRACIAN PRINCESS. T. Dr. Young.

DEMETRIUS, THE IMPOSTOR. T. Transl. fr. the Russian of Alexander Soumarokove by Eustaphiere. Pr. 1806. N. ac. (The author was born 1727, and died 1777.)

DEMI MONDE, LE. P. A. Dumas. Royalty, November, 1887; D.L., June, 1893.

DEMOCRAT, THE. P. 4 a. Nottingham Grand, March 22, 1893.

DEMOCRATIC RAGE; OR, LOUIS THE UNFORTUNATE, THE. T. Wm. Preston. Dublin, Pr. 1793.

DEMOFOONTE. Or. Leo. Naples, 1735.

DEMOFOONTE. O. Gluck. Milan, 1742.

DEMOISELLE EN LOTERIE, UNE. Op.-bo. 1 a. Offenbach. 1857.

DEMOISELLES DE ST. CYR. See *Two Little Maids from School*.

DEMON, THE. Russian Grand O. Anton Rubinstein. Pl. for first time in England in its orig. language (Russian Opera Co.), Manchester Comedy T., July 2, 1888; Novelty, October 22, 1888.

DEMON; OR, THE MYSTIC BRANCH, THE. O. 5 a. Words by Scribe. M. by Meyerbeer. D.L., February 20, 1832; prod. as *The Fiend Father; or, Robert of Normandy* at C.G., February 21, 1832; as *Robert the Devil* at D.L., March 1, 1845; in Fr. at Her M., June 11, 1832; and in Ital., May 4, 1847.

DEMON BRACELETS; OR, THE MYSTIC CYPRESS TREE, THE. D. C. H. Hazlewood. Britannia, August 16, 1869.

DEMON DARRELL. D. 5 a. Ina Cassilis and Frank H. Morland. Britannia, June 20, 1898.

DEMON DOCTOR, THE. D. 3 a. Edward Towers. Effingham, January 21, 1867.

DEMON DWARF, THE. P. Victoria, January, 1839.

DEMON GIFT, THE. P. J. Brougham and Mark Lemon. Olympic, April, 1841.

DEMON JOCKEY; OR, ARCHER RIDES TO WIN, THE. D. Rotherham T.R., October 16, 1882.

DEMON LOVER, Rom. Ca. 2 a. Brougham. First perf. in Bowery, New York, 1856. Royalty, October 10, 1864.

DEMON OF DARKNESS. Victoria, April 17, 1865.

DEMON OF THE DESERT; OR, THE MURDERER'S SACRIFICE. Melo-d. spec. 2 a. A. L. Campbell. Sadler's Wells.

DEMON OOFBIRD. Panto. Brit., December 26, 1895.

DEMON SPIDER, THE. O. for children. 1 a. Ella Graham Simpson. M. by W. E. Lawson. Newcastle-on-Tyne Art Gal. T., October 29, 1895.

DEMON'S BRIDE, THE. Op. bo. H. J. Byron. M. b G. Jacobi. Alhambra, September 7, 1874.

DEMON'S BRIDE, THE. Min. O. 1 a. Wr. by E. L. Lomax. Comp. by B. Walton O'Donnell. R.A.M., May 22, 1909.

DEMONIO, IL. O. Rubinstein. St. Petersburg, 1875; C.G., June 21, 1881.

DEMOPHOON. O. Transl. fr. *Metastasio*. John Hoole. Pr. 1768.

DENBIGH'S DIVORCE, THE. Sk. Surrey, May 24, 1909.

DENE'S REST. Melo-d. 4 a. Burford Delaunoy. Southend Empire, December 6, 1897.

DENHAM'S FOLLY. D. Henry Beslay. Paisley T.R., February 2, 1894.

DENISE. P. 4 a. Alexandre Dumas fils. (Orig. prod. at the Comédie Française, January 19, 1885.) H.M.T., June 11, 1886.

DENISE. D. 3 a. Adap. by Clement Scott and Sir Aug. Harris fr. the D. of same name by Dumas. Birmingham P.O.W., August 28, 1895.

DENOUNCED; OR, FAITHFUL TO THE END. D. Henry Gascoigne and Frank Jefferson. Eleph. and C., August 11, 1883.

DENTIST, THE. F. 1 a. Frank Lindo. Publ. by S. French, Ltd.

DENTIST'S CLERK; OR, PULLING TEETH BY STEAM, THE. F. 1 a. Everett von Culin. Milton O.H., September 1, 1877.

DEOCH AN DUR'ASS. Irish D. 3 a. R. Dodson. Britannia, October 3, 1877.

DEOCLESYAN. P. Ac. 1594 by the Lord Admiral's men. N.p.

DEORUM DONA. Masque. Part of a Rom. called "The Cyprian Academy," by Robt. Baron. Perf. before K. and Q. of Cyprus at Nicosia. Pr. in London, 1647.

DEPENDANT, THE. C. Richd. Cumberland. D.L., October 20, 1795. N.p.

DEPIT AMOUREUX, LE. Molière. See "French Classical Plays."

DEPOSING AND DEATH OF QUEEN GIN, THE. F. Anon. New T. in Haymarket. Pr. 1736.

DEPUTE DE BOMBIGNAC, LE. C. 3 a. Alexandre Bison. Ac. in Fr., Royalty, March 2, 1888; rev. July 1, 1891. See *The Candidate*.

DEPUTY, THE. F.C. 3 a. J. M. Campbell. Criterion, May 15, 1888.

DEPUTY, THE. F.C. 3 a. Geo. Arliss. South Shields T.R., September 2, 1897.

DEPUTY, THE. Sk. Ivan P. Gore. Shoreditch Olympia, November 9, 1908.

DEPUTY REGISTRAR, THE. F.C. 3 a. Ralph Lumley and Horace Ledger. Criterion, December 7, 1888.

DEPUTY SHERIFF, THE. Piece. 1 a. H. M. Vernon. Garrick, July 21, 1909.

DEPUTY SHERIFF; OR, DAN'L BARTLETT, THE. D. 4 a. Orig. *Dan'l Bartlett.* First prod. under present title at Muncaster T., Bootle, August 8, 1892; Eleph. and C., October 17, 1892.

DERBY CAPTAIN, THE. F. Cooke, 1737. See *The Eunuch.*

DERBY DAY, THE. D. Nelson Lee. Pavilion, February 9, 1867.

DERBY WINNER, THE. D. 4 a. Sir Augustus Harris, Cecil Raleigh, and Henry Hamilton. D.L., September 15, 1894.

DERELICT, THE. P. 4 a. A. W. Nixey. Llanelly, May 5, 1909, under the title of *The Bond of Marriage;* rev., Liverpool Star, June 14, 1909.

DERMOT AND KATHLANE; OR, THE IRISH WEDDING. Ballet. Mr. Byrne. C.G., 1793. Characters the same as those of *The Poor Soldier.*

DERMOT O'DONOGHUE; OR, THE STRANGER FROM BELFAST. D. Pro. and 5a. Miss Julia Agnes Fraser. Strathaven Victoria, July 24, 1872; Whitehaven T.R., March 21, 1877; Belfast T.R., November 25, 1878.

DERNIER JOUR DE POMPEI. O. Joncières. Paris, 1869.

DERNIERE SOIREE DE BRUMMEL, LA. De Georges Maurevert. Royalty, June 29, 1908 (French Season).

DERRY DRISCOLL; OR, THE SPORTSMAN PEARL. Irish D. 3 a. S. J. Mackerne and Barry Aylmer. Liverpool Alexandra, April 16, 1877.

DERVORGILLA. T. 1 a. Lady Gregory. Glasgow King's, December 4, 1907; Court, June 7, 1909.

DESCARTE, THE FRENCH BUCCANEER. M.D. 2 a. Jerrold. Coburg T.

DESCENSUS ASTRAEAE. Pageant by Peele. 1591.

DESCENT OF REGINALD HAMPTON, THE. Story by Hallewell Sutcliff. See *The Blue Dahlia.*

DESCENT OF TREA. M.Piece. Sayers, 1789.

DESERT, THE. Symphonic Past. Ode. Felicien David. H.M.T., 1845.

DESERT; OR, THE IMANN'S DAUGHTER, THE. Orientl. op. spec. M. chiefly by Felicien David. Adap. to Eng. words by J. H. Tully. D.L., April 5, 1847.

DESERT FLOWER, THE. O. 3 a. A. Harris and T. J. Williams. Fr. the French. M. by W. V. Wallace. C.G., October 12, 1863.

DESERT ISLAND, THE. D. Poem. 3 a. Arthur Murphy. D.L. Taken fr. D. *L'Isola Disabitata; or, The Uninhabited Island.* By Abbe Metastasio. Pr. 1760.

DESERTED. D. sk. Cellas Coles. Shepherd's Bush Athenæum, December 13, 1894.

DESERTED DAUGHTERS, THE. C. 5 a. T. Holcroft. C.G., May 2, 1795. Pr. 1795. See *The Steward.*

DESERTED TOWER, THE. M.D. John Rannie. Pr. (n.d.). N.ac.

DESERTED VILLAGE, THE. D. 3 a. F. Fox Cooper. Pub. by J. Dicks.

DESERTER, THE. M.D. 2 a. C. Dibdin. Fr. French piece, *Le Deserteur.* Edinburgh, 1782. D.L. Pr. 1773. Prod. as a ballet at T.R., January, 1788.

DESERTER, THE. D. Berquin, 1793.

DESERTER IN A FIX, THE. F. Bernard Soane Roby. Leicester O.H., February 10, 1879; Grand, March 23, 1885.

DESERTER OF NAPLES, THE. Ballet. Royalty T., 1788. Story same as *The Deserter.* By Dibden.

DESERTER OF NAPLES, THE. Melo-d. F. on O. and ballet of action by that name and on *The Deserter.* Lyceum, July 10, 1817.

DESERTEUR, LE. O. 3 a. M. by Monsigny. March 6, 1769.

DESERTS OF ARABIA, THE. O. spec. Fred Reynolds. C.G., December 26, 1806. M. by G. Lanza, jun. Songs only pr. 1806. Partly fr. Campbell's *Journey Overland to India.*

DESERVING FAVOURITE, THE. T.C. Lodowick Carlell. Ac. before K. and Q. at Whitehall and at Blackfryars. Pr. 1629.

DESIGNERS, THE. F. C. 2 a. F. Zorn. New Cross, Amersham H., April 21, 1904; Torquay O.H., February 6, 1905; Brixton, February 13, 1905.

DESIGNING PEOPLE. P. Sydney Fane. C.G. King's, May 11, 1907.

DESMORE. Pav., September 24, 1866.

DESPATCH BEARER, THE. D. 5 a. Frank Stayton. Richmond T.R., February 25, 1901.

DESPERATE ADVENTURES OF THE BABY; OR, THE WANDERING HEIR, THE. Burl. C. H. Ross and A. C. Freer. Strand, December 14, 1878.

DESPERATE DEED, A. Melo-d. 3 a. Burford Delaunoy. Sadler's Wells, February 7, 1893.

DESPERATE DIFFICULTIES. Sk. Mabel Archdall and Jem Aitken. Empress, June 4, 1908.

DESPERATE DUKE; OR, THE CULPABLE COUNTESS, THE. Burl. D. 1 a. R. Marshall and A. Sutro. Chelsea Hospital Grounds, A.O.F. Garden Party, July 5, 1907.

DESPERATE GAME, A. C.D. 1 a. J. M. Morton. Adelphi, April 9, 1853.

DESPERATE LOVER, THE. C. 1 a. Henry Alexander. Dublin Gaiety, May 12, 1905.

DESPERATE MAN; OR, AT ANY COST, A. American C.D. 4 a. Anson Phelps Pond. Strand, May 15, 1891 (C.P.).

DESPERATE MARRIAGE, A. D. Rosemary Rees. Brighton Grand, March 2, 1908; rev., Hammersmith Lyric, March 16, 1908.

DESPERATE REMEDIES. C. 1 a. F. W. Winckworth. Publ. by S. French, Ltd.

DESPERATION. D. 4 a. Geo. Roy and Bessie Reid. West Bromwich T.R., June 10, 1887.

DESTINY. D. 4 a. Edward Towers. East London, February 24, 1869.

DESTINY. C.D. 3 a. W. F. Lyon. Richmond H.M.T., November 14, 1881.

DESTROYED BY DRINK. Ver. of *L'Assommoir,* by J. W. Lacy. Dublin Queen's, August 25, 1879. See *Drink.*

DESTROYER; OR, FATE'S VICTIM, THE. D. Colosseum, Liverpool, June 15, 1868.

DESTROYER OF MEN, A. Russian D. 4 a. Sydney Spenser and Clarence Burnette. Edmonton R., October 2, 1905.

DESTROYING ANGEL, THE. D. 4 a. F. A. Scudamore. Barnsley T.R. (C.P.), December 8, 1896; Brixton, March 1, 1897.

DESTRUCTION OF JERUSALEM, THE. Thos. Legge. Wr. in time of Q. Eliz. Probably n.p. Mentioned in Kirkman's Catalogue, 1661.

DESTRUCTION OF JERUSALEM BY TITUS VESPASIAN, THE. T. 2 parts. J. Crowne. T.R. and pr. 1677

DESTRUCTION OF THE BASTILE. D. 2 a. Benjamin and F. Webster. Adelphi, 1844.

DESTRUCTION OF TROY, THE. T. John Banks. Duke of York's T. in C.G. and Pr., 1679. f. on hist. and taken fr. Homer, Virgil, etc.

DETECTION: A SKETCH OF THE TIMES, THE. C. Hay., 1780. N.p.

DETECTIVE, THE. P. C. H. Hazlewood. Victoria, July 20, 1863.

DETECTIVE, THE. D. 4 a. Clement Scott and E. Manuel. Mirror, May 29, 1875.

DETECTIVE DEATH; OR, THE SIGN OF THE SCARLET CROSS. D. 1 a. A. E. Halliwell. New Brighton Palace, November 12, 1902.

DETECTIVES. P. Mark Melford.

DETOUR, LE. P. Henri Berustein. Royalty, February 19, 1906.

DEUCE IS IN HER, THE. P. R. J. Raymond. Publ. by J. Dicks.

DEUCE IS IN HIM, THE. F. 2 a. Geo. Colman. Suggested by Marmontel's Tales. Edinburgh, 1762; D.L., November, 1763. Pr. 1763.

DEUX AVARES, LES. O.. Gretry (1741-1813).

DEUX AVEUGLES, LES. Op. bo. 1 a. Offenbach. 1855.

DEUX ECOLES, LES. C. 4 a. Alfred Capus. Garrick, July 21, 1902.

DEUX JOURNEES, LES. O. Cherubini. Paris, 1800.

DEUX NUITS, LES. O. Boieldieu. Paris, 1829.

DEUX PECHEURS, LES. Op. bo. 1 a. Offenbach. 1857.

DEUX SAVOYARDS, LES. O. D'Alayrac. 1753-1809.

DEVICE; OR, THE DEAF DOCTOR, THE. F. F. Pilon. C.G., September 27, 1779. N.p. Taken fr. the French. Afterwards called *The Deaf Lover*.

DEVICE; OR, THE MARRIAGE OFFICE, THE. C.O. Richards. C.G., May 6, 1777. N.p.

DEVICE OF KING JAMES'S PAGEANT, THE. Dekker, Ben Jonson, and Middleton.

DEVICE OF THE PAGEANT BORNE BEFORE WOOLSTONE DIXI. Pageant, by Peele, 1585.

DEVIL, THE. P. by H. Hamilton, fr. the Hungarian of Franz Molnar. Birmingham P.O.W., April 8, 1908 (C.P.); Adelphi, April 17, 1909.

DEVIL AND DOCTOR FAUSTUS, THE. D. 3 a. Leman Rede. See *Faustus*.

DEVIL AND HIS DAME, THE. P. W. Houghton. Mentioned by Henslowe, March, 1600. See *Grim*.

DEVIL AT THE ELBOW; OR, TWO MOTHERS TO ONE CHILD, THE. D. C. H. Hazlewood. Britannia, August 3, 1874.

DEVIL CARESFOOT. P. 4 a. Adap. by C. Haddon Chambers and J. Stanley Little fr. Rider Haggard's novel "Dawn." Vaudeville, July 12, 1887; Strand, August 6, 1887; tr. to Comedy, August 23, 1887.

DEVIL IN LONDON, THE. Extrav. 3 a. R. B. Peake. Adelphi, 1840.

DEVIL IN LOVE, THE. Ballet. 3 a. First time in Engl. D.L., November 21, 1843.

DEVIL IN THE WINE-CELLAR, THE. F. Hay., 1786. N.p. Alt. fr. Aaron Hill's *Walking Statue*.

DEVIL IS AN ASS, THE. C. Ben Jonson. Ac. by His Majesty's servants 1616. Pr. 1631. T.R., 1682.

DEVIL-MAY-CARE. M. Melo-d. Henry Besley. Ealing Lyric H., August 10, 1893.

DEVIL OF A DUKE; OR, TRAPPOLIN'S VAGARIES. Ballad F. Thos. Drury. D.L., September 23, 1732. Pr. 1732. An alteration of a comedy called *Duke and No Duke*.

DEVIL OF A LOVER, THE. M.F. Mowbray. M. by T. Attwood. C.G., 1798. Plot fr. German novel, "The Sorcerer." N.p.

DEVIL OF A WIFE; OR, A COMICAL TRANSFORMATION, THE. F. Thos. Jevon. Dorset Gardens T. Pr. 1686. Partly fr. the story of "Mopsa" in Sir Philip Sidney's *Arcadia*. The plan also used in *The Devil to Pay; or, Wives Metamorphos'd*. Ac. T.R., 1686

DEVIL OF DOWGATE; OR, USURY PUT TO USE, THE. D. J. Fletcher. Licensed 1623. Ac. by the King's Servants, October 17, 1623.

DEVIL ON TOWN. Surrey, April 18, 1863.

DEVIL ON TWO STICKS, THE. Ballet. 3 a. Founded on Le Sage's Romance. M. by Casimir Gide. D.L., December 1, 1836.

DEVIL ON TWO STICKS, THE. Extrav. Adelphi, 1859.

DEVIL ON TWO STICKS, THE. Fantasy. 1 a. Surrey, June 4, 1900.

DEVIL ON TWO STICKS, THE. See *The Devil Upon Two Sticks*.

DEVIL TO PAY, THE. Ballet, founded on the Old English farce. D.L., November 24, 1845.

DEVIL TO PAY; OR, THE WIVES METAMORPHOSED, THE. O. 3 a. Charles Coffey. Pr. 1731. Edinburgh, 1782. From *Devil of a Wife*, by T. Jevon. Altered by Coffey and Mottley, 1730, into ballad o. called *The Devil to Pay*. Altered by Theo. Cibber into 1 a., adding the second title, *The Wives Metamorphosed*, Colley Cibber adding a song. D.L., 1827.

DEVIL UPON TWO STICKS; OR, THE COUNTRY BEAU, THE. B.F. Chas. Coffey. D.L., 1729. An alt. fr. Sir John Vanbrugh's and others' comedy, *The Country Beau*. Ac. one night at Shepheard's Wells, in Mayfair, 1744. Pr. 1745.

DEVIL UPON TWO STICKS. C. 3 a. Saml. Foote. Hay., May 30, 1768. Pr. 1778.

DEVIL UPON TWO STICKS. See *That Doctor Cupid, Last Squil, The Devil On Two Sticks, Asmodeus, Country Squire, Helter-Skelter*.

DEVIL WORSHIPPERS, THE. D. 4 a. Arthur Shirley and Eric Hudson. Leigh T.R., January 29, 1903 (C.P.).

DEVIL'S BARGAIN, A. D. of modern times in 4 a. (F. on Florence Warden's novel of that name.) By Arthur Onslow, the P. prod. by Mr. George Unwin. West London, March 23, 1908.

DEVIL'S BRIDGE, THE. Op. Rom. 3 a. S J. Arnold. M. by C. E. Horn and Braham. Lyceum, May 6, 1812; English O.H., September 2, 1825.

DEVIL'S BROTHER, THE. Melo-dr. O. 2 a. M. fr. Auber's *Fra Diavolo*, adap. by Alex. Lee. D.L., February 1, 1831.

DEVIL'S CHARTER, THE. T. Barnaby Barnes. Ac. before the K. and Pr. 1607.

DEVIL'S DAUGHTER; OR, BEELZEBUB'S BELLES, THE. Lancaster Queen's, November 17, 1839. See *La Tentation.*

DEVIL'S DAUGHTERS; OR, HELL UPON EARTH, THE. Magical Op. Burla. 3 a. Edward Stirling. Victoria, November 11, 1839.

DEVIL'S DEATH, THE. Sk. Tom Gallon. Peckham Hipp., April 19, 1909.

DEVIL'S DECOY, THE. M.C.D. Prol. and 3 a. Fred Monckton. Aberavon Grand, August 2, 1909 (C.P.).

DEVIL'S DEVICE, A. D. 5 a. Percy Warlow. Stalybridge Grand T., August 19, 1895.

DEVIL'S DISCIPLE, THE. D. 3 a. Geo. Bernard Shaw. Bayswater Bijou, November 17, 1897 (C.P.); Kennington P.O.W., September 26, 1899; rev. Savoy, October 14, 1907; trs. to Queen's, November 25, 1907.

DEVIL'S DUCAT; OR, THE GIFT OF MAMMON, THE. Rom. D. 2 a. Douglas Jerrold. Adelphi, December 16, 1830.

DEVIL'S DUPE, A. Sk. 1 sc. Newcastle Grand, July 19, 1909.

DEVIL'S ELIXIR; OR, THE SHADOWLESS MAN, THE. M. Rom. 2 a. Edward Fitz-Ball. M. by G. H. B. Rodwell. C.G., April 20, 1829.

DEVIL'S HOUSE, THE. P. 4 a. H. A. Kennedy. Birmingham Royal, June 15, 1900.

DEVIL'S IN IT, THE. Rom. D. 3 a. T. E. Wilks. Princess's, May, 1843.

DEVIL'S IN IT, THE. C.O. 2 a. M. W. Balfe. Publ. by S. French, Ltd.

DEVIL'S LAW CASE; OR, WHEN WOMEN GO TO LAW THE DEVIL IS FULL OF BUSINESS, THE. T.C. John Webster. Ac. by their Majesties' servants and pr. 1623. Partly fr. *Histoires Admirables* of Goulart.

DEVIL'S LUCK; OR, THE MAN SHE LOVED. D. 5 a. Miss Lily Tinsley and G. Conquest. Liverpool Adelphi, August, 1885; Surrey, September 21, 1885.

DEVIL'S MINE, THE. Amer. Melo-d. 4 a. Fred Darcy. Maidenhead Grand H., April 25, 1894; Pavilion, July 23, 1894. See *The New World.*

DEVIL'S MOUNT; OR, THE FEMALE BLUEBEARD, THE. Rom. D. 2 a. Adap. fr. the French by Thos. Higgie. Queen's, May 24, 1847.

DEVIL'S OPERA, THE. O. 2 a. G. A. Macfarren. Words by G. Macfarren. Lyceum, August 13, 1838.

DEVIL'S OWN LUCK, THE; OR, THE PRINCE OF ROGUES. D. Wilfred Benson and John Douglass. Edmonton T.R., November 11, 1901.

DEVIL'S RING; OR, FIRE, WATER, EARTH, AND AIR, THE. M. Fairy Rom. 3 a. G. H. Rodwell. D.L., April 1, 1850.

DEVIL'S VIOLIN, THE. Extrav. B. Webster. Adelphi, May, 1849.

DEVIL'S WORK, THE; OR, TOLD BY THE CLOCK. D. Sk. 1 sc., by Arthur Wigley. Royal M.H., January 25, 1902.

DEVILISH GOOD JOKE; OR, A NIGHT'S FROLIC, A. Int. 1 a. Thos. Higgie. Victoria T., 1848.

DEVILSHOOF. Victoria, June 9, 1862.

DEVIN DU VILLAGE, LE. O. 3 a. Rousseau. Fontinebleau, 1752. Transl. and adap. as *The Cunning Man* by Dr. Burney. 1766. See *La Serva Padrona*

DEVOTION. D. 3 a. F. G. Cheatham. Sadler's Wells, March 21, 1870.

DEVOTION. P. 4 a. Dion Boucicault, jun. Adap. fr. the French, *Un Duet Sous Richelieu*, by Lockroy and Badon. Court, May 1, 1884.

DEVOTION; OR, A PRICELESS WIFE. D. Pro. and 3 a. Fr. the French by Mrs. S. Lane. Britannia, March 14, 1881.

DEVOTION AND PREJUDICE. C.D. R. Brough and J. V. Bridgeman. Brighton T.R., September 7, 1874.

DEVOUT LOVER, A. See *Quicksands.*

DEY AND THE KNIGHT, THE. Adelphi, October, 1838.

DHRAME; OR, BARNEY'S MISTAKE, THE. F. James Fitzgerald Nugent. Birkenhead T.R., July 10, 1876.

DIABLE AMOUREUX, LE. B.O. Reber. September 23, 1840.

DIADESTE; OR, THE VEILED LADY. Op. bo. Lib. by E Fitzball M. by Balfe. D.L., May 17, 1838.

DIALOGUE BETWEEN A MOTHER AND DAUGHTER. Int. Dublin, 1783. N.p.

DIALOGUE OF DIVES. D. Alluded to Green's *Groatsworth of Wit.* 1592.

DIAMANTS DE LA COURONNE, LES. O 3 a. Words by Scribe and St. George. M. by Auber. Paris, 1841; D.L., July 12, 1845; prod. at London Princess T. as *The Crown Diamonds*, May 2, 1844.

DIAMOND ARROW, THE. Ca. 1 a. W. T. Moncrieff. M. by G. W. Reeve. Olympic T.

DIAMOND CUT DIAMOND. C. 2 a. Lady W(allace). Pr. (n.a.) 1787. Transl. fr. French D., *Guerre Ouverte; ou, Ruse Contre Ruse.* Also used by Mrs. Inchbold in *The Midnight Hour.*

DIAMOND CUT DIAMOND. Int. 1 a. Alt. from *How to Die for Love*, by W. H. Murray. Edinburgh Adelphi, 1838.

DIAMOND CUT DIAMOND; OR, VENETIAN REVELS. Mus. Int. Theodore Hook. C.G. 1797. N.p.

DIAMOND DENE. P. 4 a. Henry J. W. Dam. Vaudeville, March 18, 1891.

DIAMOND EXPRESS, THE. Sk. 1 sc. Cecil Raleigh. Lon. Coliseum, June 3, 1905.

DIAMOND GANG, THE. D. 4 a. Edward Darbey. Bilston T.R., July 30, 1892; Surrey, July 3, 1893.

DIAMOND KING; OR, LIFE IN LONDON, THE. D. Forbes Dawson. Shepherd's Bush Athenæum, May 14, 1893 (C.P.).

DIAMOND QUEEN, THE. F.C. 3 a. Albert Edwards. St. Geo. H., August 6, 1889.

DIAMOND RING, A. C.D. W. J. Wild. Manchester Queen's, March 6, 1885.

DIAMOND RUSH, THE. P. 5 a. G. D. Day and Sidney Bowkett. Cambridge T.R., February 6, 1895 (C.P.).

DIAMOND STATUE; OR, THE KING OF THE GENII, THE. Pant. H. Spry. Britannia, December 26, 1882.

DIAMONDS AND HEARTS. C. Adap. by Gilbert à Beckett. Hay., March 4, 1867.

DIANA. P. 4 a. H. C. M. Hardinge. S. Shields T.R., April 11, 1904.

DIANA; OR, AN ADVENTURESS. D. Charles Vere. Scarborough T.R., March 29, 1880.

DIANA; OR, THE GODDESS OF THE MOON. Burl. Lincoln Masonic T., October, 1882.

DIANA AND ACTÆON. Entert. of Dancing. Roger. D.L., 1730.

DIANA AND ENDYMION. Serenata. Hay., 1739. N.p.

DIANA OF DOBSON'S. C.D. 4 a. Cicely Hamilton. Kingsway, February 12, 1908; rev. Kingsway, January 11, 1909.

DIANA'S GROVE; OR, THE FAITHFUL GENIUS. T.C., Anon. N.a. MS. in Mr. Kemble's collection.

DIANE. P. 5 a. Adap. by James Mortimer fr. Dumas fils' dr., *Diane de Lys*. Toole's, September 9, 1882.

DIARMID. O. 4 a. f. on Celtic legends. Marq. of Lorne. M. by Hamish M'Cunn. C.G., October 23, 1897.

DIARMID AND GRAZIA. Irish P. 3 a. Geo. Moore. W. B. Yeats. Dublin Gaiety, October 21, 1901.

DIARY OF A TRAMP, THE. M. Monol. Corney Grain. St. Geo. H., October 19, 1891.

DIAVOLO COLOR DI ROSA, IL. Retrella. Majella, 1829.

DICE OF DEATH, THE. Rom. D. 3 a. J. Oxenford. M. by E. J. Loder. Lyceum, September 14, 1835; Eng. O.H., June, 1836.

DICK. Comic O. 2 a. A. Murray. M. by Edwd. Jakobowski. Globe, April 17, 1884.

DICK ——? C.O. 2 a. Wr. and comp. by E. W. Pritchard and H. J. Boden. Surrey Masonic H., April 30, 1907.

DICK; OR, THE BEAU OF THE BELLES. Fairy F. Burl. G. D. Lynch. M. by Walter M. George and H. Verrinder. Wimbledon Baths, January 29, 1895.

DICK DRAYTON'S WIFE. C.D. 1 a. Paul Maurice. Ladbroke H., July 24, 1888.

DICK GOODMAN'S REDEMPTION. Dram. P. 1 a. J. E. Tomlinson. Goole Royal, December 26, 1905.

DICK HOPE. P. 3 a. E. Hendrie. Manchester T.R., November 20, 1903; Coronet, December 7, 1903; St. James's, September 16, 1905.

DICK OF DEVONSHIRE. A curious old P. of the 17th century.

DICK SCORNER. Mentioned in Kirkman's Catalogue. ? Hicke Scorner.

DICK SHERIDAN. C. 4 a. Robert Buchanan. Comedy, February 3, 1894.

DICK SWIVELLER. D. 4 a. Chas. Rennell. Brighton T.R., December 5, 1870.

DICK TURPIN AND TOM KING, THE ADVENTURES OF. C.D. W. E. Suter. See *Richard Turpin, Bold Dick Turpin*.

DICK TURPIN THE SECOND. Burl. 2 a. W. F. Goldberg. Gaiety, May 6, 1889.

DICK VENABLES. D. 4 a. Arthur Law. Shaftesbury, April 5, 1890.

DICK WHITTINGTON AND HIS CAT. 3 a. Burl. C. W. McCabe and J. T. Virgo. Battersea Queen's, December 26, 1894.

DICK WHITTINGTON AND HIS CATASTROPHE. Burl. James Horner. Walsall Alexandra, June 16, 1884. See *Dandy Dick Whittington, Whittington*.

DICK WILDER. P. 4 a. Mrs. H. Musgrave. Vaudeville, June 20, 1891.

DICK'S DILEMMA. P. 3 a. James Freeman. Ilford T.H., April 16, 1903 (amat.).

DICK'S HONEYMOON. F.C. 3 a. C. Dawe, Hereford T.R., May 19, 1902.

DICK'S SISTER. Ca. 1 a. Norman McKinnell. Dalston, October 5, 1905; Tivoli, August 31, 1908.

DICKSCHADEL, DER. O. Dvôrák. Bohemia.

DICTATOR, THE. 3 a. Richard Harding Davis. Comedy, May 3, 1905.

DICTIONARY, THE. P. 4 a. Beatrice Harraden. Bournemouth R., June 30, 1905 (C.P.).

DID I DREAM IT? F. 1 a. J. P. Wooler. Strand, November 19, 1860.

DID SHE MEAN IT? C.D. Chas. Rennell. Portsmouth T.R., April 17, 1871.

DID YOU EVER SEND YOUR WIFE TO CAMBERWELL? F. J. Stirling Coyne. Adelphi, March 16, 1846.

DID YOU RING? F. Oa. 1 a. J. W. Houghton and J. W. Mabson. M. by Landon Ronald. P.O.W., June 27, 1892.

DIDDLECOMBE FARM. Extrav. Chas. F. Fuller. Prod. by the Roy. Nav. Artillery Volunteer M. and D. Club on board H.M.S. Rainbow, April 1, 1886.

DIDO. Latin T. Wm. Gager. Pres. by the scholars of St. John's College in Christchurch Hall, Oxford, before a Polish Prince. Palatine. 1583.

DIDO. T. Imitation of Shakespeare's style. Jos Reed. D.L., March 28, 1767. Pr. 1808; rev. 1767 under title of *The Queen of Carthage*.

DIDO. C.O. Thso. Bridges. Hay. Pr. 1771.

DIDO. O. Transl. fr. Metastasio by J. Hoole. Pr. 1800.

DIDO. Burl. 1 a. F. C. Burnand. St. James's, February 11, 1860; N. Royalty, November 8, 1865.

DIDO AND ÆNEAS. P. Ac. by the Lord Admiral's servants, 1597. Probably Marlowe's *Dido*.

DIDO AND ÆNEAS. O. 3 a. N. Tate. M. by Purcell. Priest's Boarding School, Chelsea, 1680. Additional M. by C. Wood. Lyceum, November 20, 1895; Hampstead Conservatoire, May 17, 1900; Purcell's Operatic Soc., Coronet, March 25, 1901.

DIDO AND ÆNEAS. Masq. Barton Booth. D.L., 1716.

DIDO AND ÆNEAS. Masq. J. A. Arne. Hay. T., December 19, 1733.

DIDO AND ÆNEAS. Travestie. 3 a. Strand, October 26, 1893.

DIDO, QUEEN OF CARTHAGE. T. Christopher Marlow. Comp. by Thos. Nash. Ac. by children of Her Majesty's Chapel. Pr. 1594.

DIDO, QUEEN OF CARTHAGE, WITH THE MASQUE OF NEPTUNE'S PROPHESY. O. Writ. by Prince Hoare. M. ascrib. to Storace. Ac. by D.L. Co. at O.H. Pr. 1792.

DIDON. O. Puccini. Fontainebleau, October 16, 1783.

DIDONE. O. G. Colla. 1773.

DIEU ET LA BAYADERE, LE. Auber. Paris, 1830.

DIFFERENT WIDOWS; OR, INTRIGUE A-LA-MODE, THE. Anon. Ac. at New T. in L.I.F., 1703. Pr.

DIGGINGS, THE. F. Jersey T.R., May 14, 1877.

DILIGENCE, LA. Given by Mr. Mathews. Lyceum playbill, March 8, 1819.

DIMITRIUS. O. Joncières. Paris, 1876.

DIMITY'S DILEMMA. F. 1 a. Malcolm C. Salaman. Gaiety, February 19, 1887.

DING DONG BELL. Marylebone, December 26, 1866.

DINGLE'S DOUBLE. F. Sk. Edward Morris. Jersey O.H., May 18, 1908.

DINNA FORGET. P. 1 a. Sidney Barrington. Burslem, February 19, 1901.

DINNER FOR NOTHING. F. 1 a. Chas. Smith Cheltman. P.O.W., October 16, 1865.

DINNER FOR TWO. Ca. R. C. Carton. Brighton T.R., March 9, 1893; Trafalgar Sq., March 22, 1893; Wyndham's, April 2, 1906.

DINNER FOR TWO. Sk. Tivoli, July 12, 1909.

DINORAH. Pastl. O. Meyerbeer. Paris, 1859. With English lib. by H. Chorley. C.G., October, 1859. See *Le Pardon de Ploermel.*

DINORAH UNDER DIFFICULTIES. F. 1 a. Wm. Brough. Adelphi, November 7, 1859.

DIOCLESIAN. P. Prod. Rose T., November, 1594.

DIOCLESIAN; OR, THE PROPHETESS. Dram. O. Thos. Betterton. Pr. 1690. An alt. of Beaumont and Fletcher's *Prophetess.*

DIOCLETIAN. O. Purcell. 1658-95.

DIOGENES. C.O. in German. J. H. Bonawitz. King's Cross Town H., November 3, 1888.

DIOGENES AND HIS LANTERN; OR, A HUE AND CRY AFTER HONESTY. Extrav. by the author of *To Parents and Guardians.* Strand, December 26, 1849.

DIOGENES AND THE DAMSEL. Playlet. May Creagh-Henry. Queen's Gate H., November 17, 1908 (mat.).

DION. T. Fenton. Mentioned as begun by Mr. Pope.

DION. T. Geo. Ambrose Rhodes. Pr. 1806.

DIONE. Pastl. John Gay. Pr. 1720. A counterpart to *Amynta* and *Pastor Fido.*

DIONE. O. Anon. Pr. 1733. New T. in Hay. M. G. Lampe. Taken fr. Mr. Gay's pastoral.

DIONE, THE CANON'S DAUGHTER. F.C. 3 a. Gravesend Public H., October 2, 1895.

DIPHILO and GRANIDA. Attributed to Robt. Cox, 1656.

DIPLOMACY. P. 5 a. B. C. Stephenson and Clement Scott. P.O.W., January 12, 1878. A version of Sardou's *Dora.* Garrick, February 18, 1893.

DIPLOMACY OF SUE, THE. C. 2 a. A. Silas. Victoria St. Studio of Dramatic Art, March 18, 1907.

DIPLOMATIC THEFT, A. D. 1 a. Havelock Ettrick. Garrick, July 17, 1901.

DIPLOMATISTS, THE. 2 a. Sidney Grundy f. on *La Poudre aux Yeux*, by Labiche and Martin. Royalty, February 11, 1905.

DIPLUNACY. See *Dora and Diplunacy.*

DIRCE; OR, THE FATAL URN. O. fr. Metastasio's O., *Demaphoonte.* M. by Horn. D.L., June 2, 1821.

DIRECTOR, THE. F. 3 a. Harry Greenbank. Terry's May 7, 1891.

DISAGREEABLE SURPRISE, THE. F. 2 a. Ac. by pupils of Reading School, 1798.

DISAGREEABLE SURPRISE; OR, TAKEN UP AND TAKEN IN, THE. M.F. 2 a. Geo. Daniel. M. by Reeve. D.L., December 1, 1819.

DISAPPOINTED COXCOMB, THE. C. Bartholomew Bourgeois. Pr. 1765.

DISAPPOINTED GALLANT; OR, BUCKRAM IN ARMOUR, THE. B.O. Edinburgh. Pr. 1738. Ascr. to Adam Thomson.

DISAPPOINTED LADIES. A Court masque. Prod. in the reign of James I.

DISAPPOINTED VILLAINY. Entd. by Thos. Horde. Pr. 1775.

DISAPPOINTMENT; OR, THE MOTHER IN FASHION, THE. C. Thos. Southerne. Part of plot taken from *The Curious Impertinent* in *Don Quixote.* Ac. at the T.R., and pr. 1684. Pro. by Dryden.

DISAPPOINTMENT, THE. C. W. Tavener. Pr. 1708. See *The Maid the Mistress.*

DISAPPOINTMENT, THE. B.O. J. Randal Hay. Pr. 1732. An alt. of Mrs. Cantlivre's *A Wife Well Managed,* with songs.

DISARRANGER, THE. Farc. C. 3 a. J. A. C. Sykes. Carlisle H.M., May 28, 1909.

DISBANDED OFFICER; OR, BARONESS OF BRUCHSAL, THE. C. James Johnstone Hay. 1786. Taken fr. the German of Lessing. Pr. 1786.

DISCARDED SECRETARY; OR, MYSTERIOUS CHORUS, THE. Hist. P. 3 a. Ed. J. Eyre. Pr. 1799.

DISCARDED SON, THE. D. B. Webster. Transl. fr. *Le Fils de Famille.* Adelphi, October 10, 1853.

DISCIPLINE. P. 2 a. F. von Conring. Transl. fr. German by Jean Thore. Royalty, July 25, 1906.

DISCONTENTED COLONEL, THE. Sir J. Suckling. Pr. (circa 1642). The first sk. of *Brennoralt;* which see.

DISCONTENTED MAN, THE. C. Anon. 1804.

DISCOVERY, THE. C. Mrs. Francis Sheridan. D.L., 1763. Pr. 1763.

DISCOVERY, THE. C. Transl. fr. Plantus by R. Warner. Pr. 1773. The author calls it *Epidicus.* First act transl. by Bonnell Thornton.

DISCOVERY OF JOSEPH, THE. Sac. D. Transl. fr. Metastasio. John Hoole. Pr. 1800.

DISCREET PRINCESS; OR, THE THREE GLASS DISTAFFS, THE. F. Extrav. 1 a. J. R. Planché. F. on *L'Adroite Princesse,* by Chas. Perrault. Olympic, December 26, 1855.

DISCREET STATUES. Burl. 3. C. Penruddock. Pub. by S. French, Ltd.

DISGRACE TO HER SEX, A. Melo-d. 4 a. W. Melville. Rotherhithe, Terriss, May 23, 1904.

DISGRACE TO THE FORCE, A. Sk. Holborn Empire, March 30, 1908.

DISGUISE, THE. C. ascr. to Dr. Joddrell. N.ac. 1787.

DISGUISES, THE. Plot. Rose T., October 2, 1595. Stroude's play, *All Plot; or, The Disguises,* prob. taken fr. this. N.p.

DISGUISES, THE. C. Oa. M. by Mr. Jolly. Lyceum, September 8, 1817.

DISHONOUR OF FRANK SCOTT, THE. P. 3 a. M. Hamilton. Belfast T.R., September 7, 1900 (C.P.).

DISHONOURED. Military D. Pro. and 5 a. Arthur St. John. Macclesfield T.R., August 3, 1896; West London, June 20, 1904.

DISINHERITED; OR, LEFT TO HER FATE. D. Rose Evans. Yarmouth T.R., June 1, 1874.

DISINTERESTED LOVE. C. An alt. fr. Massinger's *Bashful Lover,* by Hull. C.G., May 30, 1798.

DISOBEDIENT CHILD, THE. Int. Thos. Ingeland. Pr., Black Letter, 1560.

DISPENSARY, THE. F. Thos. Brown. Pr. in that author's works, 1704.

DISPEROTO PER ECCESSO DI BUON CUORE, IL. O. M. by Morlacchi. 1829.

DISPUTATION AMONG THE DOCTORS. Mention in Hawkin's "Origin of the English Drama," 1773.

DISSEMBLED WANTON; OR, MY SON GETS MONEY, THE. C. Leonard Welsted. L.I.F., December 14, 1726. Pr. 1726.

DISSEMBLERS, THE. P. 3 a. R. Wilford, Sunderland. T.R., May 21, 1902.

DISSIPATION. C. M. P. Andrews. Borr. fr. Garrick's *Bon-Ton* and other pieces. D.L., March 9, 1781. Pr. 1781.

DISSOLVING VIEWS. F. 1 a. C. Selby.

DISTRACTED STATE, THE. T. John Tatham. Written 1641. Pr. 1651.

DISTRACTION. F.C. Chas. Bradley. Cheltenham T.R., June 29, 1885.

DISTRESS UPON DISTRESS; OR, TRAGEDY IN TRUE TASTE. Burl. 2 a. George Alexander Stephen. Pr. 1752. N.ac.

DISTRESS'D INNOCENCE. See *The Unnatural Mother*.

DISTRESS'D INNOCENCE; OR, THE PRINCESS OF PERSIA. T. Elkanah Settle. Last Scene and Epil. written by Montford. Ac. at T.R., 1682. Pr. 1691.

DISTRESSED BARONET, THE. F. Charles Stuart. D.L., May 11, 1787. Pr. 1787.

DISTRESSED FAMILY, THE. D. 4 a. Pr. 1787. Transl. fr. the French of Le Mercier by a lady, and read in Lisle Str. by Le Texier.

DISTRESSED KNIGHT; OR, THE ENCHANTED LADY, THE. Comic O. Dublin, 1791. F. on "The Wife of Bath's Tale," in Vol. III. of Dryden's Miscellaneous Works.

DISTRESSED MOTHER, THE. See *The Distrest Mother*.

DISTRESSED VIRGIN, THE. T. John Maxwell, a blind person. Pr. 1761.

DISTRESSED WIFE. John Maxwell. See *The Distrest Wife*.

DISTRESSES, THE. T.C. Sir Wm. Davenant. Thought to have been the same as *The Spanish Lovers*. Licensed 1639. Pr. 1673.

DISTREST MOTHER, THE. T. Transl. by Ambrose Phillips fr. Racine's *Andromache*. D.L., 1711. Pr. 1712. Rev. at D.L., October 22, 1818.

DISTREST WIFE, THE. C. John Gay. Pr. 1743. Alt. and ac. C.G., 1772.

DISTURBED RENDEZVOUS, A. Burl. pant. 1 sc. Islington Hipp., March 16, 1908.

DIVA, LA. O. 3 a. Offenbach. 1869.

DIVER'S LUCK; OR, THE CRIME BENEATH THE WAVES, THE. D. 4 a. Transl. and adap. to the English stage by Fred Cooke and W. R. Waldron. Jarrow T.R., May 30, 1887. Re-written by Andrew Melville. Birmingham Metropole, August 31, 1908.

DIVERS VANITIES. See *A Stroke of Business*.

DIVERSIONS OF A MORNING, THE. F. Saml. Foote. Hay., 1747; D.L., 1758. N.p. Act one compiled fr. his C. of *Taste*. There were two second acts—one perf. in 1758 at D.L.; the other (in which Whitehead's *Fatal Constancy*, slightly alt., was introduced under the title of *Tragedy à la Mode*) in 1762 at the Hay.

DIVERTISEMENT, THE. M.E. Jas. C. Cross. C.G., 1790. N.p.

DIVERTISEMENT SUISSE. By Mons. Simon. M. fr. Swiss melodies. D.L., April 26, 1831.

DIVES AND LAZARUS. C. Ralph Radcliff. N.p.

DIVES AND LAZARUS. A Droll. Act. at Bartholomew Fair, 17th century. Mentioned in the Wit and Drollery, 1682.

DIVES' DOOM; OR, THE RICH MAN'S MISERY. Geo Lesly. Pr. 1675.

DIVIDED DUTY, A. C.D. 1 a. Silvanus Daunsey. Jewish Inst., Highbury, October 18, 1885; Globe, March 25, 1891.

DIVIDED DUTY. P. 1 a. Gertrude Mouillot. Lyceum Club, March 30, 1909.

DIVIDED WAY, THE. P. 3 a. H. V. Esmond. Manchester T.R., October 31, 1895; St. James's, November 23, 1895.

DIVINA COMMEDIA. See *Epic Poems*.

DIVINE COMEDIAN; OR, THE RIGHT USE OF PLAYS, THE. Sacr. T.C. Richard Tuke. First called *The Soul's Warfare*. Pr. 1672. N.ac.

DIVORCE. C.D. 5 a. Augustin Daly. Ac. in New York, 1871; Edinburgh T.R., December 12, 1881.

DIVORCE. F.C. Adap. fr. an unac. French P. by Robert Reece. Vaudeville, January 29, 1881; Liverpool P.O.W., August 18, 1884.

DIVORCE, THE. P. Entrd. Stationers' Co., November 29, 1653. N.p.

DIVORCE, THE. M.E. Lady Dorothea Dubois. Sung at Marylebone Gardens. Pr. 1771.

DIVORCE, THE. F. Isaac Jackman. D.L., November 10, 1781. Pr. 1781.

DIVORCE, THE. C. 1 a. S. J. Beazley. Adelphi, October 29, 1832.

DIVORCE, THE. D. E. Towers. Southminster T., Edinburgh, November 24, 1873.

DIVORCE; OR, THROUGH THE DIVORCE COURT. D. 4 a. Max Goldberg. Lyric, Hammersmith, March 5, 1902.

DIVORCED. D. 4 a. Reginald Rutter. Imperial, May 19, 1898.

DIVORCED WOMAN, A. Sk. 4 scenes. Fred Maxwell. Bedford, May 17, 1909.

DIVORCONS. Gaiety, July 3, 1882.

DIVORCONS. C. 3 a. Victorien Sardou. Adap fr. the Fr. by Margaret Mayo. Duke of York's, June 12, 1907.

DJAMILCH. O. 1 a. Geo. Bizet. Paris, 1872. Transl. by Jos. Bennett. First time in England. Manchester Prince's T., September 22, 1892.

DOATING LOVERS; OR, THE LIBERTINE TAMED, THE. C. Newburgh Hamilton. L.I.F., and pr. 1715. Pro. by Bullock, jun.

DOBSON AND CO.; OR, MY TURN NEXT. F. 1 a. Stirling Coyne. Adelphi, October 13, 1842.

DOBSON'S DAY OFF. Farc. Sk. Prod. by Maud Elliston. Greenwich Palace, January 12, 1907.

DOCKAN. See *The Miraculous Doll*.

DOCTEUR OX, LE. O. 3 a. Offenbach. 1877.

DOCTOR, THE. F.C. Adap. by F. C. Burnand fr. *La Doctoresse* by MM. Ferrier and Bocage. Globe, July 9, 1887.

DR. AMBROSIAS—HIS SECRET. O. di camera. Words by "H. B.," M. by D'Oyley Carte. St. Geo. H., August 8, 1868.

DOCTOR AND THE APOTHECARY, THE. M. afterpiece by Jas. Cobb. D.L. Pr. 1788. D.L., June 3, 1817.

DR. AND MRS. NEILL. P. 3 a. Clo Graves. T.R., Manchester, September 28, 1894; Grand, September 9, 1895.

DOCTOR AND THE GREAT PROBLEM, THE. D. 4 a. D. M. C. Grandville. Bolton R., June 24, 1909. C.P.

DR. BARLOW. Extra 1 a. W. Heighway.

DR. BELGRAFF. P. Ch Klein. Vaudeville, October 31, 1896 (C.P.).

DR. BILL. F.C. 3 a. Hamilton Aidé. Adap. fr. *Le Docteur Jo-Jo* of Albert Carré. Paris, Cluny, March 16, 1888; Avenue, February 1, 1890; Court, December 8, 1894. See *The Kangaroo Girl.*

DR. BOLUS. Serio C. Int. 1 a. Geo. Daniel. Lyceum, July 21, 1818.

DR. CHETWYND. P. 4 a. F. C. Philips. Cheltenham O.H., January 20, 1896.

DR. CLAUDIUS. C. Prel. and 4 a. F. Marion Crawford and Harry St. Maur. Vaudeville, January 27, 1897.

DR. CLYDE. American C. 5 a. Sheffield Alexandra O.H., July 19, 1880.

DR. D. Comic O. 2 a. M. by Cotsford Dick. Lib. by C. P. Colnaghi. Royalty, May 30, 1885.

DOCTOR DAVY. Ca. Adap. fr. the French by J. Albery. Greenwich, 1865; Lyceum, June, 1866; Op. Comique, 1886. See *David Garrick.*

DOCTOR DILWORTH. F. 1 a. J. Oxenford. Olympic, April 15, 1839.

DR. DODIPOLE. C. Ac. at T.R.

DOCTOR DORA. Ca. F. W. Broughton. Garrick, April 18, 1881.

DR. FAUST AND MISS MARGUERITE; OR, THE YOUNG DUCK WITH THE OLD QUACK. Burl. R. J. Martin and E. A. P. Hobday. Dublin Queen's (amat.), August 24, 1885.

DR. FAUSTUS, LIFE AND DEATH OF, WITH THE HUMOURS OF HARLEQUIN AND SCARAMOUCH. F. W. Mountford Ac. at Queen's, Dorset Gdns., and rev. at L.I.F. Pr. 1697.

DR. FAUSTUS. See *The Necromancer.*

DR. FAUSTUS'S TRAGICAL HISTORY. Christopher Marlow. Wr. in 1588. Pr. 1604. Ent. at Stationers' Co., January 7, 1607; rev. at St. Geo. H., July 2, 1896; rev. Terry's, December 10, 1904.

DOCTOR IN SPITE OF HIMSELF, THE. C. 3 a. Gerald Dixon. Globe, June 23, 1877.

DR. JANET OF HARLEY STREET. P. 4 a. Dramatised by S. Creagh Henry fr. Arabella Kenealy's novel of same. Bayswater Bijou, May 31, 1904; Crystal Pal., March 6, 1905.

DR. JEKYLL AND MR. HYDE. Adaptn. of Robert Louis Stevenson's story of same name. Merthyr Park T., July 26, 1888.

DR. JEKYLL AND MR. HYDE. P. 4 a. Dr. T. Russell Sullivan fr. R. L. Stevenson's story, "The Strange Case of Dr. Jekyll and Mr. Hyde." Lyceum, August 4, 1888.

DR. JEKYLL AND MR. HYDE. P. 4 a. Daniel Baudmann. f. on R. L. Stevenson's story. Op. C., August 6, 1888. See *The Doctor's Shadow, The Phantom.*

DR. JOHNSON. Episode. 1 a. Leo. Trevor. Richmond T.R., May 11, 1896; Strand, April 23, 1897.

DR. KLAUS. German C. 5 a. Adolphe L'Arronge. Ac. in German by members of Ger. Gymnastic Soc. at their H., December 15, 1882; Great Q. St. T., March 12, 1903.

DR. LAST IN HIS CHARIOT. C. 3 a. Isaac Bickerstaff. Transl. fr. Molière's *Malade Imaginaire.* Some new scenes by Saml. Foote. Hay. Pr. 1769.

DR. MAUD'S FIRST. Duol. H. Darnley. Putney Hipp., April 5, 1909.

DR. MEREDITH'S EXPERIMENT. P. 3 a. H. Harding. Liverpool, Balfour Inst., February 23, 1907.

DR. NIKOLO. D. 4 a. Ben Landeck and Oswald Brand. Princess's, March 29, 1902.

DOCTOR OF ALCANTARA, THE. C.O. 2 a. Eichberg. Op. C. (amateurs), February 6, 1897.

DR. PADDY. C.D. Lincoln T.R., April 14, 1884.

DR. PARKER. Sk. Brixton Empress, June 10, 1907.

DOCTOR PRIMROSE. 3 a. Ch. Hannan.

DR. SYNTAX. Mus. C.D. 3 a. Chas. Freeman. St. Leonards R. Concert H., June 3, 1895.

DR. SYNTAX, THE HYPNOTIST. C.D. Wm. Burch. Liverpool Adelphi, September 24, 1894.

DR. WAKE'S PATIENT. C. 4 a. W. G. Mackay and "R. Ord." Liverpool Shakespeare A., September 5, 1904, and Adelphi, September 5, 1905.

DOCTOR'S BOY, THE. F. Roland Grant. Surrey, January 8, 1877.

DOCTOR'S BROUGHAM, THE. F. E. Manuel. Strand, October 9, 1875.

DOCTOR'S DILEMMA, THE. C.F. 3 a. Douglas M. Ford. Scarborough Aquarium, April 13, 1899; St. Geo. H., May 4, 1901.

DOCTOR'S DILEMMA, THE. T. 4 a. and epilogue. G. B. Shaw. Court, November 20, 1906.

DOCTOR'S ENGAGEMENTS. P. 1 a. Hon. M. Pakington. Publ. by S. French, Limited.

DOCTOR'S EXPERIMENT, THE. Sk. Scala. March 10, 1908.

DOCTOR'S SHADOW, THE. D. 4 a. H. A. Saintsbury, suggested by R. L. Stevenson's novel, "Dr. Jekyll and Mr. Hyde." Accrington Prince's, January 2, 1896 (C.P.).

DOCTOR'S STORY, THE. Domestic D. 5 a. Alton Mills. Ladbroke H., December 26, 1894.

DOCTOR'S WARD, THE. F. Oa. Horace Wilton. M. by Alexander Schmidt. Teignmouth Assembly R., February 7, 1899.

DOCTORESSE, LA. C. 3 a. Ferrier and Bocage. Paris Gymnase Dram., October, 1885; Royalty, January 11, 1886. See *The Doctor.*

DOCTORS OF DULHEAD COLLEGE, THE. A droll, by Kirkman, fr. an unpubl. p., *The Father's Own Son.* 1672.

DODGE FOR A DINNER, A. F. 1 a. T. A. Palmer. Strand, December 28, 1872.

DODO; A DETAIL OF YESTERDAY. C. 3 a. E. F. Benson. Scala, November 26, 1905.

DOES HE LOVE ME? C. 3 a. Edmund Falconer. Hay., June 23, 1860.

DOG BETWEEN, THE. P. 1 a. Criterion, July 12, 1909.

DOG DAYS IN BOND STREET. C. 3 a. Attributed to W. Dimond. Hay., August 31, 1820. N.p.

DOG FANCIER, THE. D. A. Lloyd and M. Brahm. Stafford Lyceum, May 19, 1902.

DOG OF MONTARGIS; OR, THE FOREST OF BONDY, THE. Melo-d. 2 a. Adap. fr. the French. C.G., September 30, 1814.

DOGE OF DURALTO; OR, THE ENCHANTED EYES. Exerav. Robert Brough. Olympic, December 26, 1857.

DOGE OF VENICE, THE. Rom. P. 4 a. Bayle Bernard. D.L., November 2, 1867.

DOGS OF ST. BERNARD, THE. D. Clement Scott. Mirror, August 21, 1875.

DOING BANTING. F. 1 a. W. Brough and A. Halliday. Adelphi, October 24, 1864.

DOING FOR THE BEST. Dom. D. 2 a. Rophino Lacy. Sadler's Wells, November 13, 1861.

DOING MY UNCLE. F. 1 a. Rophino Lacy. Surrey, September 8, 1866.

DOING THE HANSOM. F. 1 a. A. Harris. Lyceum, November 3, 1856.

DOING THE SHAH. F. Nugent Robinson. Globe, July 5, 1873.

DOLDRUM; OR, 1803, THE. F. John O'Keeffe. C.G., April 23, 1796. Founded on the idea of a man sleeping from 1796 to 1803. Part of the plot drawn from *Seeing is Believing*. Pr. 1798.

DOLL'S HOUSE, A. P. 3 a. Transl. fr. Henrik Ibsen's *Et Dukkehjem* by Wm. Archer. Novelty, June 7, 1889; Terry's, January 27, 1891; Criterion, June 2, 1891; Avenue, April 19, 1902; rev., Globe, May 10, 1897; pl. in Ital. (Eleonora Duse's season), Lyric, June 9, 1893.

DOLLAR PRINCESS, THE. Mus. p. 3 a. A. M. Willner and F. Grünbaum. Adap. for Eng. stage fr. the Ger. by Basil Hood. Lyrics by Adrian Ross. M. by Leo Fall. Orig. Eng. prod. at Manchester, Prince's, December 24, 1908. Daly's, September 25, 1909.

DOLLARS AND SENSE. C. 3 a. Augustin Daly. Adap. from the German of *L'Arronge*. Originally prod. in America. Toole's, August 1, 1884; Daly's, September 19, 1893.

DOLLDOM. Ca. 1 a. Bingham and Pascal. Publ. by S. French, Ltd.

DOLLS. Piece. 1 a. G. T. Norman. Ladbroke H., July 11, 1892.

DOLLUSIONS. Sk. Wm. Muskerry. "Wonderland," Whitechapel, May 11, 1896.

DOLLY. C.O. 1 a. Adap. for English stage. Cork T.R., December 26, 1860.

DOLLY. C.O. Adolphe Adam. Gaiety, August 22, 1870.

DOLLY. C.O. 2 a. John Bannister. Compiled by Herr Pelzer. Carlisle H.M.T., October 27, 1890.

DOLLY DOLLARS. M.C. 3 a. Harry B. Smith. Bayswater Victoria H., August 26, 1905 (C.P.).

DOLLY REFORMING HERSELF. C. 4 a. Henry A. Jones. Hay., November 3, 1908.

DOLLY VARDEN. D. 4 a. Murray Wood. Bradford T.R., April 29, 1872; Surrey, October 5, 1872.

DOLLY VARDEN. C.O. 2 a. Stanislaus Strange. Orig. prod. in America. Avenue, October 1, 1903.

DOLLY VARDEN. C. 3 a. W. Dexter. Adap. fr. Chas. Dickens's "Barnaby Rudge." Hammersmith King's, December 16, 1907.

DOLLY VARDEN; OR, THE RIOTS OF '80. Comedy O. 2 a. Wr. and composed by E. Cympson. Brighton Aq., November 4, 1889.

DOLLY'S BIRTHDAY. D. and M. episode. Wr. and comp. by Willie Benn. Camberwell Empire, July 15, 1907.

DOLLY'S DELUSION. P. 3 a. R. Reece. Strand.

DOLLY'S DILEMMA. M. Absurdity. Harry Millward and C. Flavell Hayward. Wolverhampton T.R., April 22, 1887.

DOLLY'S ORDEAL. Epis. 1 a. William Toynbee. Court, June 30, 1904.

DOLORES. D. Mrs. S. Lane. Britannia, April 6, 1874.

DOMBEY AND SON. P. 3 a. Brougham. Prod. in America, 1850. Publ. by J. Dicks.

DOMBEY AND SON. Dram. vers. of Dickens's novel. Bradford Royal, October 24, 1907.

DOMBEY AND SON. See ***Heart's Delight***, ***Captain Cuttle***.

DOMENICA. O. 2 a. D.L., June 7, 1838.

DOMENICO THE VILE-UN. Burl. Leigh Thomas. Camberwell Assembly R., April 26, 1872 (amat.).

DOMESTIC ARRANGEMENTS; OR, THE BACHELOR, THE MAID, THE WIFE, AND THE WIDOW. C.Oa. M. by S. Nelson Lyceum, August 10, 1835.

DOMESTIC DIPLOMACY. Ca. James Redmond. Gaiety, Dublin, April 1, 1872.

DOMESTIC ECONOMY. F. 1 a. Mark Lemon. Adelphi, November 8, 1849.

DOMESTIC ECONOMY. C.O. F. C. Burnand and E. Solomon. Based on F. of same name. Comedy, April 7, 1890.

DOMESTIC FOWL, THE. C. 1 a. Nugent Monck. Yeovil O.H., January 26, 1903.

DOMESTIC FOWL, THE. P. Arthur Goodsall. Camberley, February 1, 1905.

DOMESTIC HEARTHSTONE. Burl. 1 a. J. Smith. Publ. by S. French, Ltd.

DOMESTIC HERCULES, A. F. 1 a. Martin Becher. D.L., September 24, 1870.

DOMESTIC MASH, A. F. Tom Park. Cheltenham T.R., November 22, 1888.

DOMESTIC MEDICINE. Ca. Lita Smith. Adap. fr. the Spanish. Grantham T.R., June 2, 1887.

DOMESTIC PROBLEM, A. C. 1 a. Lechmere Worrall. Newquay Victoria H., May 30, 1905; Court, November 12, 1907.

DOMESTIC STRATEGY. Sk. Maurice Casi. Ladbroke H., January 7, 1903.

DOMINICANS, THE. Oa. 2 a. B. Knyvet Wilson. M. by C. Sandford Terry. Art Gallery, Newcastle-on-Tyne, December 13, 1894.

DOMINIQUE. Transl. and adap. by T. J. Serle.

DOMINIQUE; OR, IT IS THE DEVIL. D. 2 a. D.L., October 8, 1831.

DOMINIQUE THE DESERTER; OR, THE GENTLEMAN IN BLACK. C.D. 2 a. W. H. Murray. Adap. fr. the French. T.R., Edinburgh; rev. at Toole's under title of *Old Harry*, 1885.

DOMINIQUE, THE POSSESSED. C. 3. Barnett. Coburg, 1831.

DOMINO; OR, THE FALL OF THE CURTAIN. D. 4 a. Lloyd Clarance. Stockton-on-Tees T.R., March 7, 1879; Darwen T.R., February 26, 1883.

DOMINO NOIR, LE. C.O. 3 a. Scribe. M. by Auber. Paris, 1837; D.L., August 10, 1846.

DOMUS ET PLACENS UXOR ("The House and Pleasing Wife"). P. 1 a. G. Holmes. Margate Grand, November 7, 1904.

DON, THE. C. 3 a. Adap. fr. the German. Written by Mr. and Mrs. Herman Merivale. Toole's, March 7, 1888.

DON ANTONIO; OR, THE SOLDIER'S RETURN. T. Godwin, 1800. See *Antonio*.

DON BUCEFALO. Comic O. 2 a. Antonio Cagnoni. Milan, 1847. C.G., May 29, 1869.

DON CÆSAR DE BAZAN. D. 3 a. G. A. à Beckett and Mark Lemon. Fr. the French of Dumanois and Dennery. Princess's, October 8, 1844.

DON CÆSAR DE BAZAN. Version by D. Boucicault and B. Webster. Adelphi, October 14, 1844.

DON CÆSAR DE BAZAN. 4 a. H. A. Saintsbury. Revised ver. of Dumanois and Dennery. Kennington P.O.W., August 21, 1899.

DON CÆSAR, etc. See *Don César*.

DON CARLOS. T. Transl. fr. Schiller. Pr. 1795.

DON CARLOS. O. 3 a. Words, Tarantini; music, Costa. H.M.T., June 20, 1844.

DON CARLOS. O. 5 a. Words, Méry and Du Locle; music, Verdi. Paris, March 11, 1867. First time in England, C.G., June 4, 1867.

DON CARLOS; OR, THE INFANTE IN ARMS. Burl. Conway Edwardes. S. Shields New T.R., August 6, 1869; Vaudeville, April 16, 1870.

DON CARLOS, INFANT OF SPAIN. T. Fr. the German of Schiller. B. Thompson. Pr. 1801.

DON CARLOS, PRINCE OF SPAIN. T. Thos. Otway. F. on a work by the Abbé de St. Réal. Pr. 1676. Ac. at Duke's T., 1679.

DON CARLOS, PRINCE ROYAL OF SPAIN. Hist. D. Fr. the German of F. Schiller by G. H. Noehden and J. Stoddart. Pr. 1798.

DON CESAR DE BAZAN. O. Massenet. Paris, 1872.

DON DESIDERIO. O. Poniatowski. Pisa, 1839; Paris, 1858.

DON GARCIA OF NAVARRE; OR, THE JEALOUS PRINCE. See "French Classical Plays." Transl. fr. Molière. John Ozell.

DON GIOVANNI. Op. buffa. 2 a. Words, Da Ponte; music, Mozart. Prague, October 29, 1787; Vienna, May 7, 1788, with three extra pieces; King's (London), April 12, 1817; Drury Lane, May 2, 1833.

DON GIOVANNI. Burl. J. C. Brennan. Greenwich T.R., March 11, 1872.

DON GIOVANNI; OR, A SPECTRE ON HORSEBACK. Extrav. T. Dibdin. Rev., Lyceum, July 17, 1820.

DON GIOVANNI D'AUSTRIA. O. Marchetti. Turin, 1880.

DON GIOVANNI IN VENICE. Operatic Extrav. R. Reece. Gaiety, February 17, 1873.

DON GIOVANNI, JUN.; OR, THE SHAKEY PAGE, MORE FUNKEY THAN FLUNKEY. Burl. Greenwich, May 17, 1875.

DON GIOVANNI, M.P. Edinburgh Princess's, April 17, 1874.

DON HORATIO. P. Ac. at the Rose T., February 23, 1591.

DON IGNEZ DE CASTRO. T. John Adamson. Transl. fr. the Portuguese of Nicola Luiz. Pr. 1808.

DON JAPHET OF ARMENIA. C. Transl. fr. Scarron in 1657 by Sir Wm. Lower.

DON JEROME'S TRIP TO ENGLAND. Int. C.G., 1778. N.p.

DON JOHN. See *The Chances*.

DON JOHN; OR, THE TWO VIOLETTAS. C.O. 3 a. F. on *The Chances* by Reynolds. M. by Bishop and Ware. C.G., February 20, 1821 Pr. 1821.

DON JOHN OF AUSTRIA. P. F. on Casimir Delavigne's *Don Juan d'Autriche*. C.G., April 23, 1836.

DON JOHN OF SEVILLE. D. 4 a. Edgardo Colonna. Eleph. and Castle, September 30, 1876.

DON JUAN. Rom. D. 3 a. J. B. Buckstone. Adelphi, December 1, 1828.

DON JUAN. M.D. 3 a. C. Milner. Lyrics by E. Stirling. City of London, 1837.

DON JUAN. Burl. Bradford T.R., November 22, 1870.

DON JUAN. Extrav. H. J. Byron. Alhambra, December 22, 1873.

DON JUAN. Burl. 3 a. J. T. Tanner. Lyrics by Adrian Ross. M. by Meyer Lutz. Gaiety, October 28, 1893.

DON JUAN. See *Convivado*.

DON JUAN; OR, THE FEAST OF THE STATUE. Perf. in England of Moliere's C. Lincoln's Inn H., December 15, 1899.

DON JUAN; OR, THE LIBERTINE DESTROYED. Tragic Pant. Ent. 2 a. Delpini and Oulton. Songs by Reeve. M. by Gluck. Royalty. Pr. circa 1787.

DON JUAN; OR, THE LIBERTINE DESTROYED. Seriò C. Pantomimic Ballet. D.L., Lyceum. (First time for five years.) June 28, 1817. Pr. 1790. Based on Shadwell's *Libertine*.

DON JUAN D'AUTRICHE. Royalty, October 10, 1885.

DON JUAN IN HELL. Dream fr. *Man and Superman*. G. B. Shaw. Court, June 4, 1907.

DON JUAN, JUNIOR. Extrav. Brothers Pendergast. Royalty, November 3, 1880.

DON JUAN, THE LITTLE GAY DECEIVER. Burl. H. Spry. Grecian, June 20, 1870.

DON JUAN'S LAST WAGER. Rom. P. 4 a. Mrs. Cunningham Grahame. Adap. fr. the Spanish of José Zorrilla. P.O.W., February 27, 1900.

DON PADDY DE BAZAN. F. Int. J. Holmes Groves. Pub. by S. French, Limited.

DON PASQUALE. Op. buffa. 3 a. Donizetti. Italiens, Paris, January 4, 1843; Her Majesty's, June 30, 1843; D.L., May 29, 1855.

DON PAULO. M.P. 2 a. Lyrics by W. Forder; M. by J. T. Gouring. Ass. R., Norwich, February 19, 1906.

DON PEDRO. D. 5 a. Richard Cumberland. Hay. Pr. 1796. Probably f. on *The Robbers*.

DON PEDRO. T. Lord Porchester. M. by Bishop. D.L., March 10, 1828.

DON PEDRO. Langdon E. Mitchell. Strand, May 26, 1892.

DON PEDRO. Oa. 2 a. Mrs. Edward Adams. Composed by Frank Idle. New Cross Pub. H., October 18, 1892.

DON QUIXOTE. O. Purcell. 1658-95.

DON QUIXOTE. M. Ent. D. J. Piguenit. C.G. Pr. 1774.

DON QUIXOTE. Orig. O. 2 a. M. by G. A. Macfarren. D.L., February 3, 1846.

DON QUIXOTE. Burl. J. M. Killick. Cabinet. October 28, 1869 (amat.).

DON QUIXOTE. C.O. H. Paulton and Maltby. M. by F. Clay. Alhambra, September 25, 1876.

DON QUIXOTE. C O. H. B. Smith. Composed by Reginald de Koven. Camden Town, Park H., November 8, 1889 (C.P.).

DON QUIXOTE. Burl., 3 a., on the story of Cervantes. A. and P. Milton. Darlington T.R., July 24, 1893; Stoke Newington Alexandra, August 28, 1899.

DON QUIXOTE. Piece. W. G. Wills. F. on an incident in Rom. of Cervantes. Lyceum, May 4, 1895.

DON QUIXOTE. P. 4 a. Constructed by G. E. Morrison and R. P. Stewart. Wr. by G. E. Morrison. Stratford-on-Avon, May 3, 1907; rev. Coronet, March 2, 1908.

DON QUIXOTE. P. 4 a. Justin Huntly McCarthy. Margate R., February 17, 1908 (C.P.).

DON QUIXOTE; OR, THE KNIGHT OF THE ILL-FAVOURED FACE. C. Before 1661

DON QUIXOTE; OR, THE KNIGHT OF the WOEFUL COUNTENANCE. M.D. 2 a. George Almar. Surrey, 1833.

DON QUIXOTE IN BARCELONA; OR, THE BEAUTIFUL MOOR. Ballad F. 2 a. Joseph Moser. Pr. 1808. N.ac.

DON QUIXOTE IN ENGLAND. C. Hy. Fielding. Pr. 1733. Ac. at Little T. in Hay.

DON QUIXOTE, JUNIOR. Ca. 1 a. J. C. Goodman and John Howson. Globe, April 21, 1879.

DON QUIXOTE, THE COMICAL HISTORY OF. The third part with *The Marriage of Mary the Buxom*. C. in three parts. Thos. Durfey. Pr. 1694-6. Dorset Gardens, 1696.

DON QUIXOTE THE SECOND. See *The Fox Hunt*.

DON SANCHE D'ARAGON. Corneille. See "French Classical Plays."

DON SANCHO; OR, THE STUDENT'S WHIM. B.O. 3 a. With *Minerva's Triumph*. Masque. Elizabeth Boyd. Pr. 1739.

DON SAVERIO. M.D. M. (and probably words) by Dr. Arne. D.L. Pr. 1750.

DON SEBASTIAN. See *The Captive*.

DON SEBASTIAN; KING OF PORTUGAL. T. J. Dryden. D.L. Pr. 1690. Rev., D.L., 1753, 1774, and 1794.

DON SEBASTIANO. O. Donizetti. Paris, 1843.

DONA CONSTANZA. O. 3 a. Adolph Golluick. Criterion, November 20, 1875.

DONA IGNEZ. See *Ignez de Castro*.

DONAGH, THE. Irish D. 3 a. Geo. Fawcett Rowe. Grand, April 12, 1884.

DONAGH'S ROMANCE. D. 3 a. Lincoln T.R., October 8, 1883.

DONAH AND THE GOD, THE. Sk. Tivoli, May 15, 1909 (mat.).

DONE BROWN. F. 1 a. H. T. Craven. Edinburgh Adelphi, 1845.

DONE ON BOTH SIDES. F. 1 a. J. M. Morton. Lyceum, February 24, 1847.

DONE TO A CINDERELLA; OR, THE DRUDGE, THE PRINCES, AND THE PLATED GLASS SLIPPER. Burl. Fawcett Lomax. Exeter T.R., September 12, 1881.

DONELLAN. Dom. D. 4 a. Lieut.-Col. P. R. Innes. Strand, June 13, 1889.

DONNA AURORA. O. Morlacchi. Milan, 1821.

DONNA DEL LAGO, LA. O. 2 a. Rossini. F. on Scott's *Lady of the Lake*. San Carlo, Naples, October 4, 1819; London King's, February 18, 1823; Lyceum, June 9, 1823; D.L., June 29, 1855.

DONNA DIANA. Poetical C. 4 a. Westland Marston. Adap. fr. the Ger. ver. of Moreto's *El Desden con el Desden*. Princess's, January 2, 1864. P.O.W., November 4, 1896.

DONNA DIANA. C.O. Fd. on Spanish subject. Reznicek. Recently had successful career in Germany.

DONNA JUANITA. C.O. 3 a. Zell and Génee. M. by Von Suppé. Ladbroke H., February 24, 1880.

DONNA LUIZA. Oa. 1 a. Basil Hood. M. by Walter Slaughter. P.O.W., March 23, 1892.

DONNA MARINA. P. 4 a. Chas. Whitworth Wynne. Great Queen Street, October 5, 1905 (C.P.).

DONNA SERPENTE. See *Die Feen*.

DONNA THERESA. O. Wr. and comp. by Joseph W. Wilson. Wandsworth Church Inst. H., May 21, 1885.

DONNE DISPELTOSE, LE. O. Piccini. Naples, 1755.

DONNYBROOK. Irish M.C. 3 a. Josef Pelzer. Coatbridge T.R., August 5, 1899.

DON'T. P. 1 a. Reginald Arkell. Hove, Aldrington T.H., October 23, 1905.

DON'T DECEIVE YOUR WIFE. C. 3 a. Paul Wilstach. Great Yarmouth Aquarium, January 15, 1897.

DON'T JUDGE BY APPEARANCES. F. 1 a. J. M. Morton. Princess's, October 22, 1855.

DON'T LEND YOUR UMBRELLA. C.D. 2 a. Leicester Buckingham. Strand, January 26, 1857.

DON'T LET THE LADY GO. Ca. 1 a. Publ. S. French, Limited.

DON'T MIND ME. F. Plymouth T.R., December 16, 1872.

DOO BROWN AND COMPANY. F. 3 a. C. M. Rae. Vaudeville. March 11, 1886.

DOOM KISS, THE. Op. Ent. M. by Bishop. D.L., October 29, 1832.

DOOM OF DELILAH, THE. Sk. 1 a. Cecil Raleigh. Hammersmith Palace, March 3, 11, 1907.

DOOM OF DEVORGOIL, THE. P. Sir W. Scott. Pr. 1829.

DOOM OF MARANA; OR, THE SPIRIT OF GOOD AND EVIL, THE. Rom. D. 2 a. J. B. Buckstone. Adelphi, October 10, 1836.

DOOMED. C.D. 3 a. A. H. and A. C. Hodgson. Southampton Philharmonic H., February 8, 1890.

DOOMED BRIDGE. Victoria, March 24, 1856.

DOOR UPON THE LATCH, THE. P. 1 a. F. Kinsey Peile. H.M., June 14, 1907.

DOORWAY, THE. Episode. 1 a. H. Brighouse. Manchester Gaiety, April 10, 1909; Coronet, June 11, 1909.

DORA. D. 3 a. Chas. Reade. F. on Tennyson's poem. Adelphi, June 1, 1867, January, 1883; rev. Hammersmith Lyric, July, 1895.

DORA. C.Oa. Wr. and comp. by W. S. Parker. Doblane School, Newton Heath, Manchester, April 22, 1893.

DORA. See *Diplomacy*.

DORA AND DIPLUNACY; OR, A WOMAN OF UNCOMMON SCENTS. Burl. F. C. Burnand. Strand, February 14, 1878; rev. at Trafalgar Square T., May 6, 1893, as *Diplunacy*.

DORA INGRAM. Dom. D. 4 a. Mortimer Murdock. Pavilion, February 23, 1885.

DORA MAYFIELD. Britannia, February 25, 1878.

DORA'S DEVICE. C. 2 a Robert Reece. Royalty, January 11, 1871.

DORA'S DREAM. O. A. Cellier and Arthur Cecil. Gal. of Illus., June 17, 1873; Op. C., November 17, 1877.

DORA'S LOVE; OR, THE STRUGGLES OF A POOR ENGINEER. D. C. W. Chamberlaine. Wolverhampton P.O.W., August 12, 1872, and July 31, 1876.

DORALICE. O. Mercadante. Vienna, 1824.

DORASTUS AND FAWNIA. Novel by Robt. Green (circ. 1550-1592), on which Shakespeare founded his *Winter's Tale*.

DORCAS. C.D. 3 a. H. and E. A. Paulton. M. by Arditi, Clement, Lochname, and Audran. Kilburn T.R., February 21, 1898.

DORCHLAUCHTING ("Life Picture"). 3 a. F. Reuter. St. George's Hall, February 16, 1900.

DORI, LA. O. Cesti. Perf. in Italy. 1663.

DORIS. C.O. 3 a. B. C. Stephenson. M. by Alf. Cellier. Lyric, April 20, 1889. Ran until November 2, 1889.

DORMEA, THE LAWYER'S DAUGHTER. D. M. Wardlaugh. Longton Victoria, September 2, 1878.

DORO MAYFIELD; OR, LOVE THE LEVELLER. D. 1 a. Edgar Newbound. Britannia, February 25, 1878.

DOROTHY. C.O. Julian Edwards. Leeds, Mechanics' H., April 2, 1877; Ladbroke H., September 24, 1877.

DOROTHY. C.O. 3 a. B. C. Stephenson. M. by A. Cellier. Gaiety, September 25, 1886; transf. to P.O.W. December 20, 1886, then to Lyric December 17, 1888. Ran 930 consecutive performances. Withdrawn April 6, 1889. Revived Trafalgar Square, November 26, 1892. Standard, New York. in 1886; rev. Broadway, September 28, 1908; rev. New, December 21, 1908.

DOROTHY GRAY. D. 5 a. J. F. Nesbit. Princess's, April 10, 1888.

DOROTHY O' THE HALL. P. 4 a. Paul Kester and C. Major. Newcastle T.R., November 3, 1904. New, April 14, 1906; December 24, 1906.

DOROTHY VERNON. Rom. D. 5 a. J. W. Boulding. Ashton-under-Lyne T.R., October 4, 1889; Savoy, October 6, 1892.

DOROTHY'S STRATAGEM. C.D. 2 a. Jas. Mortimer. Criterion, December 23, 1876.

DORVAL; OR, THE TEST OF VIRTUE. C. Transl. fr. Diderot. Pr. 1767.

DOT. D. Dion Boucicault. Vers. of Dickens's *Cricket on the Hearth*. Adelphi, April 14, 1862. Sadler's Wells, 1866; rev. at Queen's T., January 4, 1869, and Garrick, December 1, 1903.

DOT. William Shore. New vers. of Dickens's *Cricket on the Hearth*. Cripplegate Inst., December 22, 1908 (amat.).

DOTHEBOYS' HALL. D. 3 a. J. Daly Besemeres. Court, December 26, 1871.

DOTTY. M.C. A. W. Parry and E. Hugh. Lyrics by C. Blanchard and T. Dodd. M. by C. Blanchard and E. Hugh. Leith Princess's, May 9, 1896 (C.P.).

DOUBLE AMOUR, THE. F. 2 a. Hay., 1791.

DOUBLE AND QUITS. F.C. 3 a. T. Edgar Pemberton. Sunderland, Avenue T., March 4, 1885.

DOUBLE-BARRELLED COURTSHIP, A. P. 1 a. Ch. Blagrove. Bayswater Bijou, May 17, 1902.

DOUBLE-BEDDED ROOM, THE. F. 1 a. J. M. Morton. Hay., June 3, 1843.

DOUBLE CONQUEST, THE. D. Cardiff R., October 27, 1873.

DOUBLE DEALER, THE. C. Wm. Congreve (his second comedy). D.L. and Pr., 1694. Rev. by J. P Kemble and ac. at D.L. Pr. N.d.

DOUBLE DEALING. O. 1 a. F. J. Vigay. Publ. by S. French, Limited.

DOUBLE DEALING; OR, THE RIFLE VOLUNTEER. Duo. 1 a. W. E. Suter.

DOUBLE DECEIT; OR, A CURE FOR JEALOUSY, THE. C. W. Popple. D.L. and C.G., 1736. Pr 1736.

DOUBLE DECEIT; OR, THE HAPPY PAIR, THE. Comic F. Pr. 1745. N.ac.

DOUBLE DECEPTION, A. C. Max Pireau and Lois Royd. Bayswater Bijou, October 25, 1897 (C.P.).

DOUBLE DECEPTION, THE. C. Miss Richardson. Ac. at D.L. for four nights. 1779. N.p.

DOUBLE DISAPPOINTMENT, THE. F. Moses Mendez. C.G., 1747. Pr. 1760.

DOUBLE DISGUISE, THE. D. 2 a. John Murdoch. Pr. 1783. N.ac.

DOUBLE DISGUISE, THE. C.O. 2 a. Probably by Mrs. Hook. M. by Hook. D.L., 1784.

DOUBLE DISTRESS, THE. T. Mrs. Mary Pix. L.I.F. Pr. 1701.

DOUBLE DOSE, A. F. Arthur Shirley. Surrey, March 10, 1890.

DOUBLE DUMMY. F 1 a. N. H. Harrington and Edmund Yates. Lyceum, March 3, 1858.

DOUBLE EPOUVANTE, LA. Sk. Paul Franck. Tivoli, July 6, 1908.

DOUBLE EVENT, A. V. A. Law and A. Reed. M. by Corney Grain. St. Geo. H., February 18, 1884.

DOUBLE EVENT, A. Ca. Alfd. Wilkinson. York T.R., August 7, 1891.

DOUBLE EVENT, THE. D. 4 a. Edward Towers. East London, April 10, 1871.

DOUBLE EVENT, THE. F.C. 3 a. James East. Kilburn Town H., May 6, 1891 (C.P.).

DOUBLE-FACED PEOPLE. C. 3 a. John Courtney. Hay., February, 1857.

DOUBLE FALSEHOOD; OR, THE DISTREST LOVERS, THE. T. Lewis Theobald. Pr. 1727. D.L., 1729. Publ. as Shakespeare's by Theobald in 1728. Some say the same play as *The History of Cardenio.*

DOUBLE GALLANT; OR, THE SICK LADY'S CURE, THE. C. Colley Cibber. Partly fr. *Le Gallant Double*, Burnaby's *Visiting Day*, and Centlivre's *Love at a Venture*. Hay., 1710. D.L. Pr. 1709. Rev., D.L., March 29, 1817; C.G., March 19, 1839.

DOUBLE GIFT, THE. Ladywell P.H., May 31, 1906.

DOUBLE LIFE, A. D. J. C. Elliot. Dundee T.R., October 21, 1872.

DOUBLE LIFE, A. D. 4 a. Marylebone, December 2, 1876.

DOUBLE LIFE, A. D. Pro. and 4 a. Edwd. Cockburn Johnstone. Birkenhead Metropole, April 11, 1892.

DOUBLE LIFE; OR, THE SHADOW OF CRIME, A. D. Lewis Sinclair. Swansea T.R., December 4, 1871.

DOUBLE MARRIAGE, THE. T. Beaumont and Fletcher. Prob. after 1619. Pr. 1647.

DOUBLE MARRIAGE, THE. An adap. of Beaumont and Fletcher by T. J. Serle.

DOUBLE MARRIAGE, THE. 2 a. American D. Adelphi, March 8, 1873.

DOUBLE MARRIAGE, THE. P. 4 a. Charles Reade. Adap. fr. his novel, "White Lies." F. on Masquet's drama, *Le Château Grautier*. Long Acre Queen's T., October 24, 1867. Alt. ver., Worcester T.R., January 2, 1888; P.O.W., June 26, 1888.

DOUBLE MISTAKE, A. F. Frank Thompson. Hastings Pier, June 23, 1884.

DOUBLE MISTAKE, THE. C. Mrs. Eliz. Griffiths. C.G. Pr. 1766.

DOUBLE PERPLEXITY, THE; OR, THE MYSTERIOUS MARRIAGES. C. 3 a. Pr. 1796. N. ac.

DOUBLE ROSE, THE. Hist. P. 5 a. J. W. Boulding. Imperial. Adelphi, June 17, 1882.

DOUBLE SHUFFLE, THE. Ca. A. Kenward Matthews. York T.R., October 25, 1900.

DOUBLE SIXES. P. 1 a. Southampton Grand, July 16, 1900.

DOUBLE STRATAGEM, THE. C.O. Robt. Houlton. Dublin, 1784. N.p. This was *The Contract* of the same author altered.

DOUBLE TRAITOR ROASTED, THE. Scots O. Ac. near Westminster H. Pr. 1748.

DOUBLE ZERO. C. 3 a. J. P. Hurst. Strand, October 10, 1883.

DOUBLEDAY'S WILL. Burnand and King Hall. St. George's H.

DOUBLEDICK. D. 3 a. West Digges. Halifax T.R., October 18, 1875.

DOUBT. Dom. D. 4 a. J. Stanley Little. Strand, June 4, 1889.

DOUBT AND CONVICTION. F. Transl. from the French by James Wild from *La Defiance et Malice* of Dieulafoy. Pr. 1804. N.ac. See *Personation.*

DOUBTFUL HEIR, THE. T.C. Jas. Shirley. Ac. at Dublin as *Rosania; or Love's Victory*, and licensed under that name 1640. Ac. at private house in Blackfryars. Pr. 1652. Part of the story on which this play is founded is in "English Adventures," Part III.

DOUBTFUL PROPOSAL, A. M. "trifle." J. Hickory Wood. M. by Herman Finck. Great Queen Street, June 26, 1900.

DOUBTFUL SON; OR, SECRETS OF A PALACE. P. 5a. Dimond. Hay., July 3, 1810.

DOUBTFUL VICTORY, A. Ca. 1 a. John Oxenford. Olympic, April 20, 1858.

DOUGLAS; OR, THE NOBLE SHEPHERD. T. 5 a. Rev. John Home. Suggested by old Scotch ballad *Gil Morrice*. Also bears strong resemblance to *Merope* of Maffei and Voltaire. Pr. 1757. Edinburgh, 1756. D.L., February 28, 1815; C.G., June 9, 1819.

DOUGLAS TRAVESTIE. Burl. 1 a. Wm. Leman Rede. Adelphi, February 13, 1837.

DOULOUREUX, LA. C. 4 a. Maurice Donnay. Paris Vaud., February 12, 1893. Lyric, June 28, 1897.

DOVE, THE. C. Trans. from the French of Mme. Genlis. Pr. 1781.

DOVE AND THE SERPENT, THE. City of London, March 21, 1859.

DOVE-COT, THE. C. 3 a. Adap. from Bisson and Leclercq's *Jalouse*. Duke of York's, February 12, 1898.

DOVES IN A CAGE. C. 2 a. Douglas Jerrold. Adelphi, February 21, 1835; D.L., February 24, 1855; rev. Charing Cross ,1873.

DOWAGER, THE. Thos. Chatterton.

DOWAGER THE. C. 1 a. Chas. Mathews. Adap. from *Le Chateau de Ma Mère*. Hay., December 3, 1843. Rev. Strand, 1876.

DOWN AMONG THE COALS. F. Taylor Bilkins (W. A. Vicars). Court, November 15, 1873.

DOWN BY THE SEA. M.C. 3 a. Sydney F. Bailey. Bootle T.H., February 5, 1902.

DOWN IN A BALLOON. F. 1 a. John Oxenford. Adelphi, April 10, 1871.

DOWN IN THE MUD. P. 1 a. Una Erie. Rehearsal, W.C., March 26, 1909.

DOWN ON HIS LUCK. F.C. 3 a. John Douglass. Oxford New T., October 4, 1894.

DOWN OUR ALLEY. P. 3 scenes. Adap. by A. Bourchier fr. Anatole France's "Crainquebille." Garrick, July 25, 1906.

DOWN THE SLOPE. American C.D. 4 a. A. E. Berg. Stalybridge Grand T., June 28, 1897.

DOWNFALL OF BRIBERY; OR, THE HONEST MAN OF TAUNTON, THE. Ballad O. 3 a. Mark Freeman. Pr. 1733.

DOWNFALL OF PRIDE, THE. D. C. H. Hazlewood. New Britannia.

DOWNFALL OF ROBERT EARL OF HUNTINGTON, THE. Anthony Munday. Prod. 1598. Pr. 1601.

DOWNFALL OF ST. STEPHEN'S, THE. Political Burla. Pr. 1784.

DOWNFALL OF THE ASSOCIATION, THE. C.T. 5 a. Pr. 1771.

DOWNWARD PATH, THE. D. 4 a. C. A. Clarke and H. R. Silva. Huddersfield T.R., July 17, 1893.

DRAGON, THE. C.O. M. by A. Lee. Lyceum, August 4, 1834.

DRAGON, THE. Oa. 1 a. J. M. Gallatly. Margate R., November 9, 1908.

DRAGON FLY, THE. P. 4 a. J. Luther Long and Edward Childs Carpenter. Broadway, September 15, 1905.

DRAGON KNIGHT; OR, THE QUEEN OF BEAUTY, THE. D. 2 a. E. Stirling. F. on H. Ainsworth's *Crichton*. Adelphi, November 18, 1839.

DRAGON OF HOUGUE BIE; OR, THE LITTLE PRINCE'S TOUR, THE. Burl. J. F. Draper. Jersey Royal H., December 8, 1871 (amat.).

DRAGON OF WANTLEY, THE. Burl. O. 3 a. H. Carey. Set to m. by John Fredk. Lampe. Plot from the old ballad of *Moore of Moorehall*. C.G., October 26, 1737. Pr. 1738. Edinburgh, 1776.

DRAGON'S GIFT; OR, THE SCARF OF FLIGHT AND THE MIRROR OF LIGHT, THE. Melo-d. tale of Enchant. J. R. Planché. M. by Cooke. D.L., April 12, 1830.

DRAGON'S TONGUE, THE. M. Extrav. 2 a Peter Eland. M. by Ralph Illingworth. Morecambe Royal, April 20, 1905.

DRAGONERS, THE. See *Margery.*

DRAGONESS, THE. Burl. O. H. Carey 1743. See *Margery.*

DRAGONETTE. Op. bo. 1 a. Offenbach. 1857.

DRAGONS DE VILLARS, LES. F.O. M. Maillart. Gaiety, June 24, 1875. English ver. by H. Hersee. Folly, May 14, 1879. See *The Dragoons.*

DRAGOONS, THE. C.O. Henry Hersee. Adap. fr. *Les Dragons de Villars*. Folly, April 14, 1879.

DRAMA AT HOME, THE. Revue. 2 a. J. R. Planché. Hay., April 8, 1844.

DRAMA OF LIFE, THE. Dom. D. 4 a. Lingford Carson. Oldham Col., March 21, 1901 (C.P.); Mexborough P.O.W., July 27, 1901; Pav., August 4, 1902.

DRAMA'S LEVEE; OR, A PEEP AT THE PAST, THE. Revue. J. R. Planché. Olympic, April 16, 1838.

DRAMA'S VINDICATION; OR, THE ROMAN ACTOR, THE. Compressed fr. Massinger's play of same name. C.G., November 14, 1799.

DRAMAS OF THE WINE SHOP. Melo-d. B. Webster, jun. Adap. fr. *Les Drames du Cabaret*. Adelphi.

DRAMATIC APPELLANT. A quarterly publication which ran to three numbers only. Publ. in 1808, and contained pieces rejected by theatrical managers. Contents as follows:—

The Barons of Ellenbergh. T. F. F. Weston.
Albert and Rosalie. M.D.
The Wager. M.Ent.
William Tell. T. E. Roche.
The Invasion. P. E. Roche.
Look Before You Leap. F. T. D. Worgan.
The Villagers. C.O. T. D. Worgan.
St. Aubert. T. F. F. Weston.
Two Old Maids of Florence. F. Anon.
Castle of Udolpho. Op. D. Anon.

DRAMATIC DIALOGUE, A, between an English Sailor and a Frenchman. J. S. Munnings. Pr. 1803. N. ac.

DRAMATIC DIALOGUES FOR YOUNG PERSONS. Pr. 1792.

DRAMATIC LOVE. C. Thos. Horde. Pr. 1773. N. ac.

DRAMATIC PASTORAL, A. By a Lady, probably Mrs. Thomas. Pr. 1762.

DRAMATIC PIECE, A. By Charterhouse Scholars in memory of Gunpowder Plot. Charterhouse, November 6, 1732. Pr. 1732.

DRAMATIC PUFFERS, THE. Prel. Henry Bate. C.G., February 9, 1782. Pr. 1782.

DRAMATIC SKETCH in 5 sc. without a title. Prod. by G. Gray. Camberwell Palace, January 21, 1907.

DRAMATIC SKETCH without a name. T. M. Paule. Holloway Empire, August 10, 1908.

DRAMATIC SKETCHES OF ANCIENT NORTHERN MYTHOLOGY. F. Sayers. Pr. 1789. See *Frea, Moina, Starno.*

DRAMATIST; OR, STOP HIM WHO CAN, THE. C. 5 a. Fredk. Reynolds. C.G., May 15, 1789. Pr. 1789. Haymarket, 1806; D.L., May 12, 1818; Lyceum, October 7, 1822; Bijou, October 29, 1903.

DRAPERY QUESTION; OR, WHO'S FOR INDIA? Sketch. 1 a. Chas. Selby. Adelphi, October 28, 1857.

DRAWERS OF DEE PLAYE, THE. See "Miracle Plays."

DRAWING-ROOMS, SECOND FLOOR AND ATTIC. F. 1 a. J. M. Morton. Princess's, March 28, 1864.

DRAWN BATTLE, A. Duol. Malcolm Watson. Op. C. April 17, 1893; Lyric, July 12, 1894.

DREADFULLY ALARMING. F. 1 a. Conway Edwardes and E. A. Cullerne. Philharmonic, September 30, 1871.

DREAM, A. D. 1 a. Lady Bancroft. Liverpool Shakespeare, September 23, 1903.

DREAM, THE. Serio dramatic piece. 2 a. R. Sickelmore. Brighton, August 8, 1796. Pr. 1797.

DREAM; OR, BINK'S PHOTOGRAPHIC GALLERY, A. M. Satire. Nat Childs and Willie Edouin. First prod. in U.S.A. Avenue, July 16, 1883.

DREAM AT SEA, THE. D. 3 a. J. B. Buckstone. Adelphi, November 23, 1835.

DREAM FACES. P. 1 a. Wynn Miller. Ramsgate, Sanger's, October 18, 1888 (C.P.); Terry's, November 1, 1888; Garrick, February 22, 1890.

DREAM FLOWER, THE. Fantasy. 1 a. Aimée Lowther. Comedy (ac. in pant.), June 30, 1898.

DREAM GODDESS, THE. P. 1 a. Arthur H. Westcott. Suggested by a story of Honoré de Balzac. (Prod. by the Rehearsal Co.) Rehearsal, May 23, 1909.

DREAM IN VENICE, A. Ent. T. W. Robertson. Gal. Illustn., March 18, 1867.

DREAM OF DELUSION. D. 1 a. J. P. Simpson. Publ. by S. French, Ltd.

DREAM OF FATE; OR, SARAH THE JEWESS. D. 2 a. C. Z. Barnett. Sadler's Wells, August 20, 1838.

DREAM OF GERONTIUS. Orat. 2 parts. Edward Elgar, Birmingham Festival, October 3, 1900.

DREAM OF HIS LIFE, THE. Fan. M.P., in 1 a., wr. by A. Chevalier; M. by A. H. West. A condensed vers. of *The Land of Nod.* Eastbourne D.P., April 8, 1907.

DREAM OF JUBAL. Cantata. Mackenzie.

DREAM OF LOVE. C. 2 a. John Oxenford. Op. Com., October 21, 1872.

DREAM OF OLD VERSAILLES, A. Fantasy. 1 a. P. Kirwan. Bayswater Bijou, December 31, 1903.

DREAM OF ST. CLOUD, THE. Dram. Poem. Pr. 1797. N.ac.

DREAM OF SCIPIO, THE. O. Transl. by Olivari. Pr. 1797.

DREAM OF SCIPIO, THE. O. Transl. fr. Metastasio by John Hoole. Pr. 1800.

DREAM OF THE FUTURE, A. C. 3 a. Chas. Dance. Olympic, November 6, 1837.

DREAM OF THE WHITEBOY, THE. D. Cheltenham T.R., September 28, 1868.

DREAM OF WHITAKER'S ALMANACK, A. "Up-to-date review of fun, fact, and fancy." Crystal Pal., June 5, 1899.

DREAM SPECTRE, THE. Rom. D. 3 a. T. Egerton Wilks. Victoria T., July 24, 1843.

DREAMER AWAKE; OR, THE PUGILIST MATCHED, THE. F. Edmund John Eyre. C.G., May 6 and 28, 1791. Pr. 1791. Pro. by Peter Pindar.

DREAMLAND. Musical Fantasia. Camberwell Empire, March 23, 1908.

DREAMLAND'S GATEWAY; OR, THE LAND OF NOD. M.F. 3 a. Princess's, October 7, 1902.

DREAMS. D. 5 a. T. W. Robertson. Liverpool Alex., February 22, 1869; under title *My Lady Clare*, Gaiety, March 27, 1869.

DREAMS OF DELUSION. D. 1 a. Pub. by S. French, Limited.

DRED. F. Phillips and John Coleman. Surrey, October, 1856.

DRED. D. Walter Banks. Wolverhampton P.O.W., November 19, 1872.

DRED; A TALE OF THE DISMAL SWAMP. D. 2 a. Fr. Mrs. Beecher Stowe's novel, by W. E. Suter. Queen's T., October, 1856.

DREGS. D. Sk. Alec Nelson. Vaudeville, May 16, 1889.

DREI PINTOS, DIE. O. Weber. Left unfinished. Completed by G. Maher, and prod. Leipzig, January 20, 1888.

DRESDEN CHINA. Fant. 1 a. Miss Alice Chapin and E. H. C. Oliphant. Vaudeville, July 21, 1892.

DRESS. M.D., without words. N. Carlton Hill. M. by Paul Corder. R. Acad. of M., May 5, 1905.

DRESS COAT, THE. F. Frank Green. Strand, June 29, 1876.

DRESS-MAKER, THE. M.O. Adeline Votieri. Grand, April 7, 1902.

DRESS-MAKING. Charade. Stanley Rogers. Pub. by S. French, Limited.

DRESS REHEARSAL. O. 1 a. L. Diehl. Pub. by S. French, Limited.

DRESS REHEARSAL, A. M. Sk. 1 a. Seymour Hicks and A. C. Robatt. M. by A. Lotte and F. Tours. Tivoli, December 2, 1907.

DRIFTED. P. 1 a. H. T. Johnson. Fulham Grand, September 14, 1903.

DRIFTED APART. Dom. Sk. 1 a. Sir Chas. Young. Torquay Bath Saloon, January 16, 1882.

DRIFTING CLOUDS. P. 2 a. Bow and Bromley Inst., October 31, 1894.

DRIFTING DOWN. P. 1 a. J. E. Burfoot. Windsor Conservative Club, April 19, 1900 (amat.).

DRIFTING SPAR, A. D. Sydney Gordon. Edmonton T.R., Aug. 5, 1893.

DRINK. D. 5 a. Adap. by Chas. Reade from Busnach and Gastineau's version of Emile Zola's *L'Assommoir*. Princess's, June 2, 1879; D.L., June 23, 1891; Princess's, July 13, 1896; Adelphi, December 26, 1899, and January, 1900. See *D.T.*, *Del Trem.*, *Destroyed by Drink*.

DRINK; OR, SAVED BY CHILD'S PRAYER. D. 4 a. C. Philips. Cley-next-the-Sea Town Hall, June 14, 1907.

DRIVE LOVE OUT AT THE DOOR, HE'LL GET IN AT THE WINDOW. C. Bal. Rochfort. D.L., May 16, 1815.

DRIVEN FROM HOME. D. 3 a. G. H. Macdermott. Grecian, July 31, 1871.

DRIVEN FROM HOME. Dom. D. 4 a. Birmingham New Grand, October 10, 1884; Pav., June 14, 1886.

DROP BY DROP; OR, OLD ENGLAND'S CURSE. D 4 Tab. By Kate A. Walton. Liverpool, Adelphi, March 24, 18?4.

DROPPED IN. P. 1 a. Walter Boyd. Ladbroke Hall, November 24, 1893.

DROSS. M.D. without words. 1 a. N. Carlton Hill. M. by Paul Corder. R. ac. of M. May 5, 1905.

DROWNED MAN'S LEGACY, THE. D. 3 a. W. Seaman. Britannia, September 23, 1872.

DRUID, THE. Eng. Tragic O. 3 a. Rev. J. M. Capes, St. George's, February 22, 1879.

DRUID'S OAK, THE. Victoria, June 23, 1851.

DRUID'S ELECT, THE. Architectural burl. St. George's H., April 19, 1899.

DRUIDS, THE. Pant. Ent. Woodward. C.G. Pr. (songs only) 1774.

DRUM MAJOR. Ver. of the French lib. of Offenbach's O., *La Fille du Tambour-Majeur*. F. Bowyer and W. E. Sprange. Notting Hill, Coronet T., October 1, 1900.

DRUMCLOG; OR, THE COVENANTERS. D. Edinburgh T.R., September 5, 1871.

DRUMMER; OR, THE HAUNTED HOUSE, THE. C. Joseph Addison. D.L., March 10, 1716. Pr. 1715.

DRUMMER BOY, THE. Song scena. H. Castling and C. W. Murphy. London Pav. (Water Rats' mat.), November 13, 1905.

DRUMMER OF THE 76TH, THE. Hist. playlet. Lewis Coen. Coronet (C.P.), July 3, 1906.

DRUMS OF OUDE, THE. Dram. episode. Austin Strong. Comedy, April 5, 1906; Playhouse, January 28, 1907.

DRUMS OF DOOM, THE. D. 1 a. G. Villiers-Stuart. (Pres. by the English Drama Soc.) Scala, June 23, 1908 (mat.).

DRUNK AND DISORDERLY. F. Audrey Anderson. Brighton W. Pier, November 20, 1908.

DRUNKARD, THE. Dom. D. of American life. 4 a. W. H. Smith and a Gentleman. Boston Museum, 1844.

DRUNKARD, THE. Another ver. of *L'Assommoir* by Benjamin Webster. Birmingham Holte T., Setember 29, 1879.

DRUNKARD'S CHILDREN, THE. D. 2 a. J. B. Johnstone. Pavilion, July, 1848.

DRUNKARD'S DAUGHTER, A. D. 4 a. Clarence Burnette. Blythe R., July 26, 1905.

DRUNKARD'S DOOM. D. 2 a. G. D. Pitt. Victoria, September 24, 1832.

DRUNKARD'S DOOM; OR, THE DEVIL'S CHAIN, THE. Another ver. of *L'Assommoir*. Plymouth T.R., September 8, 1879.

DRUNKARD'S GLASS, THE. D. 1 a. T. Morton. Lyceum, April 21, 1845. Afterwards called *Another Glass*.

DRUNKARD'S LIST, THE. D. Liverpool Colosseum, April 1, 1872.

DRUNKARD'S WARNING, THE. D. 3 a. C. W. Taylor. Ac. at New York 1856. Publ. by J. Dicks.

DRUNKEN NEWS WRITER, THE. Int. Hay. Pr. 1771.

DRUNKEN SWISS, THE. Ballet Dance. Rev. Lyceum, April 9, 1822.

DRYAD, THE. P. J. Huntly McCarthy. Margate March 15, 1905.

DRYAD, THE. Dance Play. 2 tabl. Dora Bright. Playhouse, March 26, 1907 (C.P.); rev. H.M., June 4, 1909.

DU BARRY. David Belasco. Elephant and Castle, December 4, 1901.

DU BARRY. Ch. Brookfield. Adap. from the French. Savoy, January 13, 1905 (C.P.).

DU BARRI. P. Pro. and 3 a. and epilogue of 3 scenes. Ch. St. John. From the French of Jean Richepin. Savoy, March 18, 1905.

DUBLIN BAY. C. T. W. Robertson. Manchester T.R., May 18, 1869. Folly, December 18, 1875.

DUC D'ALBE, LE. O. Donizetti (1798-1848).

DUCHESS ELEANOUR. Haymarket, March 13, 1854.

DUCHESS OF BAYSWATER AND CO. Haymarket, December 8, 1888.

DUCHESS OF BERMONDSEY, THE. See *The Fortunes of Fan*.

DUCHESS OF COOLGARDIE. D. 5 a. Euston Leigh and Cyril Dare. D.L., September 19, 1896.

DUCHESS OF DANTZIC, THE. Rom. O. 3 a. Henry Hamilton. M. by Ivan Caryll. Lyric, October 17, 1903.

DUCHESS OF DEPTFORD, THE. Sk. John Ridding. Standard, November 30, 1908.

DUCHESS OF DEVONSHIRE, THE. C. 4 a. Mrs. Charles A. Doremus. Eleph. and C., April 1, 1903.

DUCHESS OF DIJON. C.O. 2 a. Basil Hood. M. by Walter Slaughter. Portsmouth T.R., September 20, 1897.

DUCHESS OF EUROPE, THE. F.C. 2 a. B. Masters. Brixton T., April 6, 1904.

DUCHESS OF FERNANDIA, THE. T. Henry Glapthorne. Entd. Stationers' Co., June 29, 1660. N.p.

DUCHESS OF MALFEY (OR MALFI), THE. T. John Webster. Blackfriars, 1623. Globe. Pr. 1623. Taken fr. a novel by Bandello, also f. on fact already used by Lope de Vega, and may be found in *Les Histoires Admirables* of Gerelast.

DUCHESS OF MALFI, THE. T. 5 a. Adap. fr. John Webster. Blackfriars, 1640.

DUCHESS OF MALFI, THE. T. Ac. at Duke's T. Pr. 1678. Adapt. of Webster's play.

DUCHESS OF MALFI, THE. Adap. fr. John Webster by R. H. Horne. Sadler's Wells, November 20, 1850; Standard, August, 1859; Sadler's Wells, 1864; Standard, April, 1868.

DUCHESS OF MALFI. Ver. by W. Poel. Op. Com., October 21, 1892.

DUCHESS OF MALFI. See *The Fatal Secret.*

DUCHESS OF MANSFELDT, THE. C.D. 1 a. E. H. Keating. Publ. by S. French, Ltd.

DUCHESS OF MARLBOROUGH, THE. P. 3 a. C. H. Metzler. T.R., Canterbury, February 22, 1906.

DUCHESS OF ORMONDE, THE. D. 3 a. D.L., October 20, 1836.

DUCHESS OF KILLICRANKIE, THE. Skit. H. Fordwych. Terry's, April 13, 1904.

DUCHESS OF SUFFOLK: HER LIFE, THE. Hist. P. Thos. Druce. Pr. 1631. F. on history, and the story may be seen in both Fox's and Clark's Martyrology.

DUCHESS OR NOTHING. Ca. 1 a. Walter Gordon. Olympic, July 9, 1860.

DUCK HUNTING. F. 1 a. J. Stirling Coyne. Hay., September 29, 1862.

DUCKS AND PEAS; OR, THE NEWCASTLE RIDER. F. 1 a. John Lund. Ac. at Pontefract. Pr. 1777.

DUDE AND THE DANCING GIRL, THE. M. Sk. Chas. D. Steele and C. W. Forward. M. by E. W. Eyre. Brixton H., November 4, 1893.

DUE FOSCARI, I. O. Verdi. D.L.

DUE GIORNATE, LE. O. Cherubini, Paris, 1800.

DUE ILLUSTRE RIVALI (GLI). O. Mercadante. Barcelona, 1846.

DUEL, THE. P. Wm. O'Brien, D.L., 1772. Pr. 1773. Taken fr. *Le Philosophe Sans le Scavoir* of Sedaine.

DUEL, THE. P. 3 a. H. Lavedan. Originally prod. Comédie Française, April 17, 1905. Garrick, April 23, 1907; Royalty, October 2, 1907.

DUEL; OR, MY TWO NEPHEWS, THE. F. 2 a. R. B. Peake. C.G., February 18, 1823.

DUEL IN THE DARK, A. F. 1 a. J. Stirling Coyne. Hay., January 31, 1852.

DUEL IN THE SNOW. D. 3 a. E. Fitzball. Publ. by S. French, Ltd.

DUELLIST, THE. C. Wm. Kenrick. C.G. Pr. November 20, 1773. Taken fr. Fielding's *Amelia.*

DUELLISTS, THE. See *Elopement* of Maclaren.

DUENNA, THE. C.O. 3 a. Richd. Brinsley Sheridan. C.G., Feb. 21, 1775. Pr. 1744. Plot seems borrowed fr. *Il Filosofo di Campagna*, fr. Moliere's *Silicien*, and fr. *The Wonder* of Mrs. Centlivre

DUENNA, THE. C.O. 3 a. Parody on Mr. Sheridan's P. Pr. 1776. Supposed author, Israel Pottinger. See *The Governess.*

DUENNA, THE. C.O. D.L., September 14, 1815; Lyceum, September 2, 1815; D.L., 1823.

DUET, A. C. 1 a. A. Conan Doyle. Publ. by S. French, Ltd.

DUFFER, THE. P. 4 a. Weedon Grossmith. Comedy, August 21, 1905.

DUKE, THE. P. James Shirley. Licensed, May 19, 1631.

DUKE AND NO DUKE, A. F. N. Tate. Ac. by their Majesties' servants. Pr. 1685. Plot fr. *Trappolin Suppos'd a Prince.*

DUKE AND NO DUKE, A. Ent. in grotesque characters by Mr. Thurmond.

DUKE AND NO DUKE, A. F. Wr. orig. by Sir Aston Cokaine, since rev. Pr. 1758.

DUKE FOR A DAY; OR, THE TAILOR OF BRUSSELS, A. Ross Neil. Publ. 1874.

DUKE HUMPHREY. T. Stationers' Co., June 29, 1660. Said to be by W. Shakespeare. Destroyed by Mr. Warburton's servant.

DUKE IN DIFFICULTIES, A. C. Tom Taylor. Hay., March 6, 1861.

DUKE OF CODHAM, THE. M. mélange. Wr. by F. Price. Hackney Empire, December 2, 1907.

DUKE OF FLORENCE, THE. T. MS. in library of Mr. Arthur Murphy.

DUKE OF GUISE, THE. Henry Shirley. Stationers' Co., September 9, 1653. N.p.

DUKE OF GUISE, THE. T. Dryden and Lee. T.R., December, 1682. Pr. 1683.

DUKE OF KILLICRANKIE. Rom. F. 3 a. Robert Marshall. Criterion, January 20, 1904.

DUKE OF LERMA, THE. T. Sir Robt. Howard. Pr. 1668.

DUKE OF MILAN, THE. T. 5 a. Philip Massinger. Blackfriars, 1638. Pr. 1623. Plot partly fr. *Guicciardini*, Book 8, and partly fr. Josephus's *History of the Jews.* D.L., March 9, 1816.

DUKE OF MILAN, THE. T.C. Richd. Cumberland. C.G., 1779. N.p. This piece consisted of Massinger's play and Fenton's *Marianne.*

DUKE OF ROCHFORT, THE. T. By A Lady of Quality. Ac. at Edinburgh, 1799.

DUKE OF ROTHSAY, THE. Saml. MacArthur. Wr. 1764. Pr. 1780. N.ac.

DUKE OF SAVOY; OR, WIFE AND MISTRESS, THE. P. Fredk. Reynolds. C.G., 1817.

DUKE OF SWINDLETON, THE. F.C. 3 a. Wm. Burnside. Op. Comique, June 11, 1885.

DUKE OR NO DUKE; OR, TRAPOLIN'S VAGARIES. 2 a. Edin., 1761.

DUKE'S BOAST, THE. P. 3 a. Adap. by H. Osborne Buckle fr. *Mdlle. de Belle Isle*, by A. Dumas *père.* Avenue, March 21, 1889.

DUKE'S COAT; OR, THE NIGHT AFTER WATERLOO, THE. Dr. anecdote. Lyceum Playbill, September 6, 1815. License refused; performance postponed.

DUKE'S DAUGHTER, THE. Op. bo. 3 a. G. M. Layton and L. Vasseur. Royalty, January 10, 1876.

DUKE'S DAUGHTER, THE; OR, THE HUNCHBACK OF PARIS, THE. D. 3 a. and Pro. Dr. by Anicet Bourgeois and Feval fr. Feval's *La Petite Parisien* (Porte St. Martin, Paris, September 8, 1862). Lyceum, January 10, 1863, as the *Duke's Motto.*

DUKE'S DEVICE, THE Same as *Duke's Motto.* Olympic, September 30, 1876.

DUKE'S DIVERSION, THE. 2 a. Planché's *Follies of a Night*, treated musically by Michael Dwyer. Lyrics by Geo. Mudie. W. Norwood Pub. H., May 21, 1892; Parkhurst, June 13, 1892.

DUKE'S MISTRESS, THE. T.C. James Shirley. Ac. at private house in D.L., 1636. Pr. 1638.

DUKE'S MOTTO, THE. Rom. P. John Brougham. Adap. fr. *Le Bossu* by Paul Feval. Lyceum, January 10, 1863; March, 1867.

DUKE'S MOTTO, THE. D. New vers. by Justin Huntly McCarthy. Birmingham R.T., August 31, 1908; Lyric, September 8, 1908.

DUKE'S MOTTO, THE. Adap. by Woods Lawrence.

DUKE'S MOTTO, THE. See *The Duke's Daughter, Duke's Device, The Motto, Motto on the Duke's Crest.*

DUKE'S WAGER, THE. A. R. Slous. A version of Dumas's *Mdlle. de Belle Isle.* Princess's, June 4, 1851.

DULCAMERA; OR, THE LITTLE DUCK AND THE GREAT QUACK. W. S. Gilbert. St. James's, December 29, 1866.

DULCIE DARENDA AFFAIR, THE. Sk. Harry Lowther. Bow Pal., April 13, 1908.

DULVERYDOTTY. F. Mrs. Adams Acton. Ac. at her house at St. John's Wood, March 2, 1894; Terry's, June 15, 1894.

DUMAUR'ALISED TRILBY, A. Duol. Harold Cheverelles. M. by Jennie Franklin. St. Geo. H., December 6, 1895.

DUMB BAWD, THE. Henry Shirley. Stationers' Books, September 9, 1653. N.p.

DUMB BELLE, THE. Ca. 1 a. Wm. Bayle Bernard. Olympic, 1832.

DUMB CAKE, THE. P. 1 a. Wr. or comp. by A. S. Scott-Gatty. Hicks's, June 19, 1907.

DUMB CAKE; OR, THE REGIONS OF FANCY, THE. Pant. C.G., 1787.

DUMB CONSCRIPT; OR, A BROTHER'S LOVE AND A SISTER'S HONOUR, THE. D. 2 a. H. P. Grattan. Astley's, 1835.

DUMB FARCE, THE. Ent. in grotesque characters by Mr. Thurmond. D.L., 1719.

DUMB GUIDE OF THE TYROL, THE. Rom. D. 2 a. T. G. Blake. Adelphi, October 9, 1837.

DUMB KNIGHT, THE. Hist. C. Lewis Machin. Ac. by the Children of the Revels. Pr. 1608. Plot fr. Bandello's Novels, and similar to that in *The Queen; or, The Excellency of Her Sex.*

DUMB LADY; OR, THE FARRIER MADE PHYSICIAN, THE. C. John Lacy. Ac. at T.R. Pr. 1672. Plot fr. Molière's *Le Médecin Malgré Lui* and his *L'Amour Médecin.*

DUMB MAID OF GENOA; OR, THE BANDIT MERCHANT, THE. Melo-d. 1 a. John Farrell. Bath, April 18, 1823.

DUMB MAN, THE. D. 4 a. Pavilion (Jewish season), August 18, 1908.

DUMB MAN OF MANCHESTER, THE. Melo-d. 2 a. B. F. Rayner. Astley's Amphi., under the title of *The Factory Assassin,* September 28, 1837. Adelphi, October, 1837.

DUMB MAN'S CURSE, A. Protean p. 1 sc. J. B. Dickson. Peckham Hippodrome, September 27, 1909.

DUMB PRINCESS, THE. Fairy piece. 2 a. W. C. K. Wilde, Baskcome House, West Kensington, January 17, 1894.

DUMB SAVOYARD AND HIS MONKEY, THE. Melo-d. 1 a. C. Pelham Thompson. M. by Hughes. D.L., April 7, 1828.

DUMB WOOD-MAIDEN, THE. See *Silvana.*

DUMBBELL DAISY. F.C. 3 a. A. P. K. Sidney Carlton, Great Queen Street T., September 25, 1903.

DUN A DAY, A. Oa. M. by Mr. Reeve. Lyceum, September 10, 1823.

DUNBAR; OR, THE KING'S ADVOCATE. T. Blank verse. Chas. Waddie. Glasgow Athenæum, October 2, 1809.

DUNDREARY MARRIED AND DONE FOR. See *Lord Dundreary.*

DUPE, THE. C. Ascribed to Mrs. Frances Sheridan. D.L. Pr. 1763.

DUPES OF FANCY; OR, EVERY MAN HIS HOBBY, THE. F. Geo. Saville Carey. O.H., 1792

DUPLICITY. C. 5 a. Thos. Holcroft. C.G., October 13, 1781. Pr. 1781.

DUPLICITY. D. 3 a. R. Clift. Eclectic T., Soho, December 14, 1871 (amat.).

DUPLICITY. C. 2 a. Mrs. Saker. Birkenhead T.R., May 28, 1883.

DURAZZO. T. 5 a. James Hayn.

DURING HER MAJESTY'S PLEASURE. D. 3 a. G. Conquest and H. Pettitt. Grecian, May 21, 1877.

DURING THE SIEGE. D. 1 a. Ch. Hermann. Bolton Grand, May 5, 1902.

DUSKIE. P. 1 a. Mrs. G. Thompson and Miss Kate Sinclair. Ladbroke H., June 17, 1890. Rev. St. George's H., May 13, 1893.

DUST. F.C. 3 a. Sydney Grundy. Adap. fr. the French of Labiche and Delacour. Royalty, November 12, 1881.

DUST CLOAK, THE. P. 1 a. Octavia Kenmore. Leeds Grand, November 13, 1905.

DUSTMAN'S FIND, THE. C. J. L. Featherstone. Belfast O.H., March 13, 1903.

DUSTMAN'S TREASURE. Britannia, July 16, 1866.

DUTCH ALLIANCE, THE. F. Pr. 1759.

DUTCH COURTEZAN, THE. C. J. Marston. Ac. at Blackfriars by Children of the Revels. Pr. 1605. Alt. 100 years after to *A Woman's Revenge; or, A Match in Newgate,* and four years later to a B.O. called *Love and Revenge; or, The Vintner Outwitted.*

DUTCH FAIR, A. Ballet. M. by Cooke. D.L., September 23, 1826.

DUTCH FLIRTATION, A. Sk. Tivoli, April 1909.

DUTCH GOVERNOR; OR, 'TWOULD PUZZLE A CONJURER, THE. D. Pub. by S. French, Limited. Ac. in U.S.A.

DUTCH JUSTICE. F. 1 a. Harry Pleon. Pub. by J. Dicks.

DUTCH LOVER, THE. C. Mrs. Behn. Duke's, 1673. Pr. 1673. F. on a Spanish novel called "Don Fenise."

DUTCH PAINTER, THE. P. ac. by the Prince's servants. Mentioned by Sir Henry Herbert, June 10, 1622.

DUTCH THE DIVER; OR, BENEATH THE SURFACE. D. Adap. fr. novel by Basil Henry. Liverpool T.R., September 30, 1878; Birkenhead T.R., September 11, 1882.

DUTCHESS OF, etc. See *Duchess of,* etc.

DUTCHMAN, THE. M. Ent. by Thos. Bridges. Hay., September 8, 1775. Pr. 1775.

DUTIFUL DECEPTION, THE. C. 1 a. C.G., April 22, 1778. N.p.

DUTTON'S DILEMMA. F. Sk. Leonard Mortimer. Rawtenstall Grand, September 28, 1906.

DUTY. C. 4 a. Jas. Albery. Adap. fr. Sardou's *Les Bourgeois de Pont Arcy.* P.O.W., September 27, 1879.

DUTY. D. 3 a. Rev. G. D. Rosenthal and J. J. Blood. Birmingham, Balsall Heath Institute, September 27, 1909.

DUTY; OR, BALACLAVA HEROES. Milit. Scena. Harry Bruce. Lyrics by J. Tabrar. Sunderland T.R., December 30, 1889.

DUX REDUX; OR, A FOREST TANGLE. Poetical P. 3 a. Jas. Rhoades. Novelty, January 18, 1887.

DWARF OF NAPLES, THE. T.C. 5 a. D.L., March 13, 1819.

DYCCON OF BEDLAM. Ent. Stationers' Co. by Thos. Colwell. 1562-3. Possibly the first sketch of Gammer Gurton's Needle, which appeared in 1575.

D'YE KNOW ME NOW? F. 1 a. Wm. Martin.

D'YE KNOW ME NOW? F. Capt. Ward Braham and Nitram Wellsey. Reading T.R., June 14, 1872.

DYING FOR LOVE. C. 1 a. J. M. Morton. Princess's, June 25, 1858.

DYKE HOUSE, THE. D. 1 a. Dr. Folkard. Sandgate Assembly R., February 12, 1877.

DYNECOURT'S VENTURE. C. 3 a. Geraldine Kemp. Gt. Yarmouth Royal, October 9, 1907.

E

EACH FOR HIMSELF. F. D.L., October 24, 1816.

EAGLE JOE. Melo-d. 4 a. Henry Herman. Princess's, December 26, 1892.

EAGLE'S WING, THE. C.O. 2 a. Ch Rimington. M. by Robert Forsyth. Folkestone Pier Pav., December 26, 1892.

EAGLES OF EUROPE. C. 1 a.

EARL AND THE GIRL, THE. M.C. 2 a. Seymour Hicks and Ivan Caryll. Lyrics by P. Greenbank. Adelphi, December 10, 1903; Lyric, September 12, 1904.

EARL DOUGLAS, THE. Dr. Essay. Pr. 1760.

EARL GOODWIN. Hist. T. Ann Yearsley. Ac. at Bath, 1789. Pr. 1791.

EARL GOODWIN AND HIS THREE SONS. P. Robert Wilson, in conjunction with Drayton, Chettle, and Dekker. Ac. 1598. A second part of this play ascribed wholly to Drayton ac. same year. Neither pr.

EARL OF ENNIWARE, THE. Soc. Rom. Leonard Mortimer. Surrey, August 21, 1905.

EARL OF ESSEX, THE. T. Henry Brooke. Ac. Dublin, 1748-9; D.L., January 3, 1761. Pr. 1761.

EARL OF ESSEX, THE. T. Henry Jones. C.G., February 21, 1753. Pr. 1753. Author said to have been assisted by Earl of Chesterfield and Colley Cibber.

EARL OF GLOSTER WITH HIS CONQUEST OF PORTUGAL, THE HONOURABLE LIFE OF THE HUMOROUS. P. Anthony Wadeson. Ac. by the Lord Admiral's servants, 1601. N.p.

EARL OF IONA, THE. M.C. 2 a. H. Gerald Ransley. L'pool Balfour Inst., November 24, 1908 (C.P.); L'pool Florence Inst., November 28, 1908.

EARL OF MAR MARR'D, WITH THE HUMOURS OF JOCKEY THE HIGHLANDER, THE. F. J. Phillips. Pr. 1715. N. ac. See *The Pretender's Flight*.

EARL OF MULLIGATAWNY, THE. F.C. 3 a. Mel. B. Spurr and W. Mayne. Greenwich Lecture H., October 22, 1898.

EARL OF PAWTUCKET, THE. C. 3 a. A. Thomas. Playhouse, June 25, 1907.

EARL OF POVERTY; OR, THE OLD WOODEN HOUSE OF LONDON WALL, THE. D. 2 a. Geo. Almer. Surrey, February, 1838.

EARL OF SOMERSET, THE. T. Henry Lucas. Pr. 1779.

EARL OF STRAFFORD, THE. T. W. Russell. 1746-1794. Unf. MS.

EARL OF WARWICK, THE. T. Fr. another of same title by Mons. de la Harpe. Dr. Thomas Franklin. D.L., December, 1766; in 3 a. at C.G., 1796. Pr. 1766.

EARL OF WARWICK; OR, BRITISH EXILE, THE. T. Francis Tolson. D.L. Pr. circa. 1719.

EARL OF WARWICK; OR, THE KING AND SUBJECT, THE. T. Paul Hifferman. Pr. 1764. Transl. of Mons. de la Harpe's play. See *Guy, Earl of W.*

EARL OF WESTMORLAND, THE. T. Henry Brooke. Pr. 1778. Ac. Dublin, 1741, under the title of *The Betrayer of His Country;* and again 1754, under that of *Injured Honour.*

EARL'S DAUGHTER, THE. C.D. 2 a. E. Haslingden Russell. Croydon T.R., July 21, 1899.

EARL'S HOUSEKEEPER, THE. D. W. Seaman. Britannia, April 22, 1872.

EARL'S REVENGE, THE. T. John Wilson Ross (before 1887). F. on the story of Lady Jane Grey.

EARLS OF HAMMERSMITH, THE. P. Olympic, 1813.

EARLY BIRD, THE. F. 2 a. Clara Harriet Sherwood.

EARLY WORM, THE. F. 3 a. Fredk. Lonsdale. Wyndham's, September 7, 1908.

EARNEST APPEAL, AN. F. Frederick Hay. Strand, May 6, 1875.

EARTH, THE. P. 4 a. J. B. Fagan. Torquay O.H., April 8, 1909; Kingsway, April 14, 1909.

EARTHLY TWINS, THE. T. Hanson Lewis. M. by Augustus Bingham. Lyrics by J. M. Bullock. St. James's, July 6, 1896 (C.P.).

EARTHQUAKE; OR, THE PHANTOM OF THE NILE, THE. D. Spectacle. G. H. B. Rodwell. Adelphi, December, 1828.

EAST INDIAN, THE. C. Hay., 1782. N.p. Said to have been a lady's production.

EAST INDIAN, THE. C. Transl. fr. the German by A. Thompson. Pr. 1799.

EAST INDIAN, THE. C. Transl. fr. same original. Anon. Pr. 1799.

EAST INDIAN, THE. C. M. G. Lewis. D.L., April, 1799. Pr. 1800.

EAST LYNNE. Burl. Birmingham T.R., September 16, 1869.

EAST LYNNE. Dom. D. Adap. fr. Mrs. John Wood's novel by T. A. Palmer. Nottingham, November 19, 1874.

EAST LYNNE. D. American ver. of novel of same name. Standard, May 28, 1883. Also vers. as follow:—Standard, 1878; Olympic, 1879; Standard, 1879; Astley's, October, 1879; Olympic, 1888, and April, 1889; Royalty, October, 1891; Eleph. and C., 1901; Op. C., April 10, 1897.

EAST LYNNE. Adaptation of Mrs. Henry Wood's novel (rev.). Princess's, March 7, 1896.

EAST LYNNE. Ver. by Lilla Wilde of Mrs. Henry Wood's novel. Cradley Heath T.R., December 19, 1898.

EAST LYNNE. Adapt. by J. Pitt Hardacre of Mrs. Henry Wood's novel. Olympic, December 26, 1898.

EAST LYNNE. Pro. and 4 a. Herbert Shelley. A ver. of Mrs. Henry Wood's novel. Fulham Grand T., February 20, 1899.

EAST LYNNE. Ver. by Miss Grace Warner. Edmonton R., October 19, 1908.

EAST LYNNE. See *Little Billie Carlyle, Lost Lady of Lynne, New East Lynne.*

EAST LYNNE; OR, ISABEL THAT WAS A BELLE. Burl. Coventry T.R., November 10, 1884.

EASTER EGG, AN. Words and m. by Walter Maynard (Wilbert Beale). Orchestral score by Sydney Ward. Terry's, December 7, 1893.

EASTER MONDAY; OR, THE HOMOURS OF THE FORTH. F. 3 a. Said to have been wr. by a young Newcastle gentleman. Pr. circa 1781.

EASTWARD HO. New ver. of op. burl. *The Black Cat.* Words and lyrics by C. M. Rodney. M. by C. S. Howells. Additions by Willie Younge. Op C., December 24, 1894.

EASTWARD HOE. C. Geo. Chapman, Ben Jonson, and John Marston. Ac. at Blackfriars. Pr. 1605. Fr. this piece Hogarth took the plan of his set of prints *The Industrious and Idle Apprentices.* Alt. and ac. at D.L., 1751, with the add. title *The 'Prentices.* Alt. by Mrs. Lenox later. Also alt. by Tate and called *Cuckold's Haven.* See *Old City Manners.*

EASY SHAVING. F. 1 a. F. C. Burnand and Montagu Williams. Hay., June 11, 1863.

EAU MERVEILLEUSE, L'. O. M. by F. von Flôtow. Perfd. as the work of A. Grisar. 1839.

EBB AND FLOW, THE. D. 4 a. W. F. Field. Brentford T.R., November 19, 1888.

EBONY CASKET; OR, MABEL'S TWO BIRTHDAYS, THE. D. 4 a. T. W. Speight. Gaiety, November 9, 1872.

EBREO L'. O. Apolloni. Prod. in Italy, 1855.

ECARTE. C. 4 a. Lord Newry. Globe, December 3, 1870.

ECCENTRIC GUARDIAN, THE. Oa. M. by Walter R. Quin. Lib. by Henry Zimmermann. New Cross Public H., April 25, 1885.

ECCENTRIC LOVER, THE. C. Richard Cumberland. C.G., April 30, 1798. N.p.

ECCLESIAZUSÆ. Aristophanes. See "Greek Plays."

ECHO. C. 3 a. Arthur M. Heathcote. Trafalgar Square, April 25, 1893.

ECHO AND NARCISSUS. Dr. Past. 3 a. Richd. Graves. Pr. 1760. N.ac. See *The Coalition.*

ECHO ET NARCISSE. O. Gluck. Paris, September 21, 1779, and rev. in August, 1880.

ECHO OF A CRIME, THE. D. 4 a. Herbert Shelley. Liverpool P.O.W.'s, October 12, 1903.

ECHO OF WESTMINSTER BRIDGE, THE. D. Victoria, July, 1835.

ECHOES OF THE NIGHT. D. 4 a. H. P. Grattan and Joseph Eldred. Bradford, Pullan's T., January 7, 1884; Pavilion, July 7, 1884.

ECHOES OF THE OPERA. M. sk. Corney Grain. St. Geo. H., June 15, 1893.

ECLAIR, L'. O. Halévy. Paris, 1835.

ECLIPSE; OR, HARLEQUIN IN CHINA, THE. Pant. J. C. Cross. Pr. 1801.

ECLIPSE TOTALL, L'. O. Nicolas Dalarac. Paris Opéra Comique, 1782.

ECLIPSING THE SON. C.D. 1 a. Fr. the French. W. W. Hartopp. Publ. by S. French, Ltd., St. James's.

ECOLE DES FEMMES, L'. Molière. See "French Classical Plays."

ECOLE DES MARIS, L'. Molière. See "French Classical Plays."

ECUS ET PARCHEMINS. P. 1 a. Comte De St. André. Cambridge Hall, Camberwell Road, S.E., June 30, 1903.

ECUYERE, L'. C. 1 a. Emile Pohl. Adap. by M. Dormic. Terry's, June 7, 1905.

EDDA. Melo-d. E. Fitzball. Ac. Surrey T.

EDDYSTONE ELF, THE. Melo-d. 2 a. Geo. Dibdin Pitt. Sadler's Wells, 1833.

EDELWEISS. B.O. Lib. by F. W. Broughton. M. by Theo Gmur. Cork O.H., April 3, 1893.

EDENDALE. D. 3 a. Chas. Smith Cheltnam. Charing Cross T., June 19, 1869.

EDGAR. O. Puccini. Modern Italy.

EDGAR; OR, CALEDONIAN FEUDS. T. Geo. Manners. C.G., May 9, 1806. Pr. 1806. Plot fr. Mrs. Radcliffe's novel, "The Castles of Athlin and Dunbayne."

EDGAR; OR, THE ENGLISH MONARCH. T. Thos. Rymer. Pr. 1678; also in 1691 under title of *The English Monarch.*

EDGAR AND ALFREDA, KING. T.C. E. Ravenscroft. T.R. Pr. 1677. Plot fr. a nevel called "The Annals of Love."

EDGAR AND EMMELINE. F. 2 a. Dr. Hawkesworth. D.L., January 31, 1761; Edinburgh, 1780. Pr. 1761.

EDGAR HARISSUE. D. 3 a. G. H. Malcolm and Arthur Grahame. Ladbroke H., July 19, 1898.

EDGE OF THE STORM, THE. Pro. and 3 a. Margaret Young. Duke of York's, June 1, 1904.

EDINBURGH BALL, THE. Bal. F. Wm. Whitehead. Wr. circa 1745. N.p.

EDITH; OR, THE FALL OF PRIDE. D. W. Sidney. Richmond H.M.T., August 22, 1870.

EDITH WEST. C.D. Sheffield T.R., April 26, 1875.

EDITH'S FLIGHT. D. Dundee T.R., March 15, 1875.

EDITHA; OR, THE SIEGE OF EXETER. T. Hugh Downman. Ac. at Exeter, 1786. Pr. 1784.

EDITHA'S BURGLAR. P. 1 a. Edwin Cleary. Adap. of Mrs. Frances Hodgson Burnett's story. Princess's, October 28, 1887.

EDITHA'S BURGLAR. D. 3 a. Mrs. Hodgson Burnett and Stephen Townsend. Neath Bijou T. and Assembly R., January 3, 1890.

EDMOND, ORPHAN OF THE CASTLE. T. Anon. Pr. 1799. F. on Miss Reeve's story *The Old English Baron.*

EDMUND IRONSIDE. A. MS. Play wr. about A.D. 1647.

EDMUND KEAN. D. 4 a. Holborn, September 25, 1871.

EDMUND KEAN. T. 5 a. Haddington Templin. Chichester Assembly R., November 20, 1893.

EDMUND KEAN. P. 1 a. Gladys Unger. V., January 10, 1903.

EDMUND KEAN. Sk. Alice Ramsay and Rudolph de Cordova. Hackney Empire, July 29, 1907.

EDMUND KEAN, TRAGEDIAN. P. 5 a. T. Edgar Pemberton. Adap. fr. the French of A. Dumas. West Hartlepool T.R., January 4, 1895; Camberwell Metropole, October 23, 1896.

EDMUND, SURNAMED IRONSIDE. T. Mrs. Jane West. Pr. 1791.

EDOARDO E. CHRISTINA. O. Rossini. Venice, 1819.

EDUCATION. C. 5 a. Thos. Morton. C.G., April 27, 1813.

EDUCATION DE PRINCE. C. 3 a. M. Donnay. Royalty, February 11, 1907.

EDUCATION OF ELIZABETH, THE. P. 4 a. Roy Horniman. Apollo, October 19, 1907. Transferred to the Hay., November 25, 1907; Apollo, January 27, 1908.

EDUCATION OF MR. PIPPS, THE. P. Augustus Thomas. February 16, 1905 (C.P.).

EDWARD I. Hist. P. Geo. Peele. Pr. 1593.

EDWARD II. T. Christopher Marlow. Ac. by the Earl of Pembroke's servants. Pr. 1598. Ent. Stationers' Co., July 6, 1593. Rev. by Elizabethan Stage Society, Oxford New T., August 10, 1903.

EDWARD II. Dr. Poetic Sk. Blake. 1783.

EDWARD II. T. Theophilus Mac. Pr. 1809. N. ac.

EDWARD III; HIS REIGN. Hist. P. Anon. Entd. at Stationers' H., December 1, 1595, and several other times up to February 23, 1625. Pr. 1596, 1599, 1609, 1617, and 1625. Ac. about City of London. Repr. 1760 in a collection of old poetry entitled "Prolusions" as Shakespeare's. See *The Raigne of King Edward the Third.*

EDWARD III. (KING), WITH THE FALL OF MORTIMER, EARL OF MARCH. Hist. P. Anon. Possibly by John Bancroft. Plot fr. Eng. history and a novel called "The Countess of Salisbury." T.R., 1690. Pr. 1691.

EDWARD IV. Hist. P. 2 parts. Thos. Heywood. Pr. circa 1599.

EDWARD VI. P. Edwd. Barnard. Pr. 1757.

EDWARD AND EGWINA. D. poem. Anon. Pr. 1776.

EDWARD AND ELEONORA. T. Jas Thompson. Prohibited to be ac. Pr. 1739.

EDWARD AND ELEONORA. T. Alt. fr. Thompson by Thos. Hull. C.G. Pr. 1775.

EDWARD THE BLACK PRINCE. Hist. P. 3 a. F. on Shirley and Beaumont and Fletcher. M. by Bishop. D.L., January 28, 1828.

EDWARD THE BLACK PRINCE; OR, THE BATTLE OF POICTIERS. T. Mrs. Hooper. Goodman's Fields, 1748.

EDWARD THE BLACK PRINCE; OR, THE BATTLE OF POICTIERS. Hist. T. Wm. Shirley. D.L. Pr. 1750.

EDWARD THE BLACK PRINCE; OR, THE GLORIES OF ENGLAND IN 1356. Hist. D. Victoria, August, 1822.

EDWIN. T. Geo. Jeffreys. L.I.F., 1721. Pr. 1724.

EDWIN AND ANGELINA. Melo-d. Burl. Miss Walford. Gall. of Illus. May 6, 1871 (amat.).

EDWIN AND ANGELINA; OR, THE BANDITTI. O. E. H. Smith. N. York. Pr. 1797.

EDWIN AND CATHERINE; OR, THE DISTRESSED LOVERS. T. Thos. Scott. Pr. 1793.

EDWIN, THE BANISHED PRINCE. T. Rev. Douglas. Pr. circa 1784. N. ac. F. on hist. and on Goldsmith's ballad "Edwin and Angelina."

EDWIN DROOD. See *Mystery of Edwin Drood.*

EDWY. D. Poem. Pr. 1784. Said to be by Thos. Warwick.

EDWY AND ELGIVA. T. Mrs. D'Arblay. D.L., March 21, 1795. N.p.

EFFECTS OF CURIOSITY, THE. C. fr. the French of Mdme. Genlis. Pr. 1781.

EFFIE AND JEANIE DEANS. D. Geo. Hamilton. Albion, October 29, 1877; Marylebone, August 4, 1879.

EFFIE DEANS, THE LILY OF ST. LEONARDS. D. Shepherd. F. on Scott's "Heart of Midlothian." Surrey, February 7, 1863.

EFFIE'S ANGEL. C.D. Sheffield T.R., September 4, 1871.

EFFRONTES, LES. D.L., June 16, 1893.

EGIO. An Interlude wr. about 1560.

EGOTIST, THE. C. 3 a. Herbert J. Leigh Bennett. Brighton Hotel Metropole, February 20, 1895.

EGRIROPHADRON; OR, POLYSCENIC PASTICCIO. D.L., June 8, 1815.

EGYPTIAN, THE. P. 5 a. J. H. Wilkins. City of London T., April 18, 1853.

EGYPTIAN FESTIVAL, THE. C.O. Andrew Franklin. M. by Florio. D.L., March 11, 1800. Pr. 1800.

EGYPTIAN IDOL, THE. P. 4 a. R. Saunders and Maurice E. Bandman. Sunderland T.R., December 16, 1895.

EGYPTIAN WAR; OR, THE FALL OF ARABI, THE. D. B. Stanhope. Birkenhead T.R., October, 1882.

EGYPTOLOGIST'S DAUGHTER, THE. P. 3 a. Carlton. Gloucester T.R., December 7, 1900.

EHRE, DIE. D. 4 a. Hermann Sudermann. D.L., June 18, 1895; Comedy, March 26, 1901.

EHUD. Sacr. D. John Collett. Pr. 1806. N. ac.

EIDER-DOWN QUILT, THE. F.C. 3 a. Tom S. Wotton. Terry's, December 21, 1896.

EIGHT HOURS AT THE SEASIDE. F. 1 a. J. M. Morton.

EIGHT HOURS AT THE SEASIDE. F. W. Sawyer. Brighton, in 1853.

EIGHT POUNDS REWARD. F. John Oxenford. Adap. fr. the French. Olympic, 1855.

£8 10s. 1d., IF QUITE CONVENIENT. F. D.L., May 14, 1823.

1863; OR, THE SENSATIONS OF THE PAST SEASON. F. 1 a. H. J. Byron. St. James's, December 26, 1863.

1870. P. 1 a. Birch Vye. West Hartlepool T.R., August 22, 1896 (C.P.); Birmingham Grand, September 11, 1896.

1870; OR, THE BATTLE OF LIFE. D. Dublin Queen's, October 31, 1870.

1874; OR, HIGH AND LOW, RICH AND POOR. D. John Elphinstone. Hanley T.R., August 17, 1874.

EIGHTEEN YEARS IN ONE HOUR. Oa. G. M. Layton. M. by Lecocq. Park, February 15, 1875.

EIGHTEENTH CENTURY, THE. Fant. P. 3 a. fd. on a C. by E. J. Malyon and C. James. St. James's, July 29, 1907.

EILEEN ALANNAK; OR, THE OUTLAWS OF THE GLEN. Irish D. 4 a. R. Mahoney. Islington Myddleton H., September 5, 1903.

EILEEN DHU. Irish D. Arr. by W. Gordon. Liverpool Sefton T., June 26, 1882.

EILEEN OGE; OR, DARK'S THE HOUR BEFORE THE DAWN. Irish D. 4 a. Edmund Falconer. Princess's, June 29, 1871.

EILY O'CONNOR. P. 2 a. J. T. Haines. City T., October 29, 1832.

EILY O'CONNOR; OR, THE FOSTER BROTHER. Dom. D. 2 a. T. Egerton Wilks. Adap. fr. Griffin's *Collegians*. City T., July 23, 1831.

EILY O'CONNOR. See *Miss Eily O'Connor*.

EIN SCHRITT VON WEGE. St. Geo. H., January 27, 1896.

EINE PARTIE PIQUET. Op. Comique, October 22, 1894.

EINGEBILDETE KRANKE, DER. D.L., July, 1881.

EINSAME MENSCHEN. D. 5 a. G. Hauptmann. Gt. Queen Street T., November 14, 1904.

EITHA AND AIDALLO. Dr. Poem. Pr. 1801. N.ac.

EL CAPITAN. C.O. Chas. Klein. M. by J. P. Sousa Orig. prod. at Boston, U.S.A., April 13, 1896; Lyric, July 10, 1899; Comedy, October 30, 1899.

EL DESDEN CON EL DESDEN. Moreto. Known to the German stage as *Donna Diana*. Introduced to the English stage in 1864 by a ver. of Westland Marston's.

EL FLAMBO. Britannia, December 27, 1875.

EL HYDER, THE CHIEF OF THE GHANT MOUNTAINS. 2 a. Wm. Barrymore. Coburg, November 9. 1818.

EL MAHDI; OR, THE FALSE PROPHET OF THE SOUDAN. D. Gt. Grimsby T.R., March 7, 1885.

ELAINE. P. 1 a. Royston Keith. Kilburn T.H., June 26, 1890; Strand, May 5, 1898; Ealing T., June 22, 1903.

ELAINE O. 4 a. Lib. by P. Ferrier (in Fr.). M. by Bernberg. C.G., July 5, 1892.

ELBOW ROOM STORIES. See *Baby*.

ELDER BROTHER, THE. C. John Fletcher. Blackfriars. Pr. 1637. The first and third editions have Fletcher's name only; in the second Beaumont's is also given. Cibber's *Love Makes a Man*, borrowed fr. this play, perf. at Miss Kelly's T., Dean Street, Soho, 1845 (amat.).

ELDER BROTHER; OR, LOVE AT FIRST SIGHT, THE. C. Fletcher. With alterations. D.L., March 11, 1850.

ELDER MISS BLOSSOM, THE C. 3 a. Ernest Hendrie and Metcalfe Wood. Blackpool Grand, September 10, 1897; St. James's, September 22, 1898; September 16, 1901.

ELDERS, THE. Ascr. to Henry Man. C.G., April 21, 1780. N.p.

ELDORADO. Folie Musicale. H. B. Farnie. Strand, February 19, 1874.

ELDRED; OR, THE BRITISH FREEHOLDER. T. John Jackson. Edinburgh T.R., February 19, 1774; Hay., July 7, 1775. Pr. 1782.

ELEANOR. P. 4 a. Mrs. Humphry Ward. Court, October 30, 1902; June 29, 1905.

ELEANOR'S VICTORY. Dramatisation of Miss Braddon's novel by John Oxenford. St. James's, May 29, 1865.

ELECTION, THE. C. 3 a. Anon. Pr. 1749.

ELECTION, THE. M. Int. Miles Peter Andrews. D.L., October 21, 1774. Pr. 1774.

ELECTION, THE. Ent. 2 a. Richd. Cumberland. Ac. privately at Mr. Hanbury's, Kelmarsh, Northamptonshire, 1778. N.p.

ELECTION, THE. Int. ? by a clergyman in neighbourhood of Yarmouth. Pr. 1784.

ELECTION, THE. C. Joanna Baillie. Pr. 1802. N.ac.

ELECTION, THE. O. Altered fr. Miss Baillie's comedy. Lyceum, June 7, 1817.

ELECTION; OR, THE RIVAL CANDIDATES, THE. O. Ent. D.L. (first time for twenty-five years), December 12, 1832.

ELECTION NOTES. M. Sk. Corney Grain. St. Geo. H., November 9, 1885.

ELECTION OF MANAGERS, THE. Prel. Geo. Colman Hay., June 2, 1784. N.p.

ELECTRA. T. By C. W. (Christopher Wase). Pr. 1649. Transl. fr. Sophocles; also transl. fr. Sophocles as follow:—Lewis Theobald. Pr. 1714. Ac. at D.L. Anon. Pr. 1714. Geo. Adams. Pr. 1729. Dr. T. Franklin. Pr. 1759. W. Shirley. Wr. 1745. Rehearsed at C.G., 1763, but n. lic. Pr. 1765. R. Potter. Pr. 1788. Also transl. fr. Voltaire by Dr. T. Francklin. Pr. 1761. C.G., 1774, and at D.L. Trans. by Gilbert Murray. Court, January 16, 1906. See "Greek Plays."

ELECTRA. T. 1 a. F. on the old Greek story by Hugo von Hufmannsthal. Trans. into English by Arthur Symons. New, November 27, 1908 (mat.).

ELECTRA IN A NEW ELECTRIC LIGHT. Extrav. Ca. Francis Talfourd. Hay., April 25, 1859.

ELECTRIC MAN, THE. F 3 a. C. Hannan. Hammersmith King's, April 4, 1904; Royalty, November 10, 1906.

ELECTRIC SPARK, THE. Op. F. C. F. Pidgin and Chas. D. Blake. Orig. prod. in America. Manchester Prince's, May 28, 1883.

ELECTRIC SPARK, THE. Ca. Elizabeth Bessle. Adap. fr. Pailleron's *L'Etincelle*. Olympic, May 8, 1889.

ELECTROPHOBIA. Ca. H. J. Dixon. Manchester Prince's H., March 26, 1898 (amat.).

ELEONORA. O. Paer. (1771-1839.)

ELEPHANT OF SIAM, THE. Indian Spec. Adelphi, December, 1829.

ELEVENTH COMMANDMENT: AN UNWRITTEN LAW, THE. P. 4 a. R. Castleton. Margate T.R., December 4, 1899; Kingston-on-Thames County, March 28, 1904.

ELEVENTH DAY, THE. C. D.L., July 20, 1835.

ELEVENTH HOUR, THE. D. 4 a. Ronald Macdonald and H. A. Saintsbury. Olympic, July 18, 1896. (C.P.) Birmingham Prince of Wales', September 14, 1896.

ELEVENTH OF JUNE; OR, THE DAGGERWOODS AT DUNSTABLE, THE. F. John O'Keeffe. D.L., June 5, 1798. N.p. A Sequel to *Sylvester Daggerwood*.

ELFIANA; OR, THE WITCH OF THE WOODLAND. Kate Simpson. M. by W. McConnell Wood. Newcastle-on-Tyne Olympia, September 30, 1895.

ELFIE; OR, THE CHERRY TREE INN. D. 3 a. Dion Boucicault. Glasgow T.R., March 10, 1871; Gaiety, December 4, 1871.

ELFIN TREE, THE. Oa. Peyton Wray. M. by Louis Diehl. Alex. P., May 12, 1875.

ELFIN WELL, THE. Oa. 1 a. Bingham and Rogers. Publ. by S. French, Ltd

ELFINELLA; OR, HOME FROM FAIRYLAND. C. 4 a. Ross Neil. Edinburgh Princess's, October 15, 1875; Princess's, June 6, 1878.

ELFRID. T. Jackson. Hay., 1775.

ELFRID; OR, THE FAIR INCONSTANT. T. Aaron Hill. D.L., January 3, 1710. Pr. circ. 1710. Rewritten by the author and ac. at D.L., 1731, as *Athelwold.*

ELFRIDA. Dr. poem. W. Mason. Pr. 1752. Alt. for the stage by Colman in 1772 and by the author himself in 1776. Ac. at C.G., 1773 and 1776.

ELI. Orat. Michael Costa. Birmingham Festival, August 29, 1855.

ELIGIBLE BACHELOR, AN. Ca. 1 a. Strand, December 9, 1871.

ELIGIBLE VILLA, AN. Oa. M. by Gastenel. Gaiety, April 19, 1869.

ELIJAH. Orat. Dupuis. 1789.

ELIJAH. Orat. Mendelssohn. Wr. for Birmingham Festival, August 26. 1846.

ELIJAH RAISING THE WIDOW'S SON. Sacred D. 1 a. Words by Moncrieffe. Adap. to compositions of Winter by J. Addison. D.L., March 8, 1815.

ELISA; OR, LE VOYAGE AU MONTE BERNARD. O. 2 a. Words, Saint Cyr; M., Cherubini. Paris Feydeau, December 13, 1794.

ELISA E CLAUDIO. O. Mercadante. Milan, 1821.

ELISABETH. O. Donizetti. Paris, 1853.

ELISABETTA REGINA D'INGHILTERRA O. Rossini. Naples, 1815. King's T., April 20, 1818.

ELISHA. O. Dr. Arnold (his last O.). Prod. in 1795.

ELISINA. Melo-d. C. M. Klanert. Adap. fr. the Fr. Richmond, Surrey. Pr. 1824.

ELISIR D'AMORE, L'. O. 2 a. Lib., Romand; M., Donizetti. Milan, 1832; London Lyceum, December 10, 1836; also as *The Love Spell* at Drury Lane, June 24, 1839. See *Adina.*

ELIXIR OF LIFE, THE. D. 3 a. G. Conquest. Grecian, September 29, 1873.

ELIXIR OF LOVE, THE. O. 2 a. Adap. fr. Donizetti's *L'Elisir d'Amour*, by T. H. Reynoldson. Surrey, 1839.

ELIXIR OF YOUTH, THE. F.C. 3 a. G. R. Sims and Leonard Merrick. F. on the Bockspruenge of Hirschberger and Kraatz. Vaudeville, September 9, 1899.

ELIZA. M. Ent. Richd. Rolt. Pr. 1754. M. by Dr. Arne. Ac. at Hay., and prohibited; afterwards at D.L., 1757.

ELIZA. Serenata. 3 a. Alt. fr. the O. of same name by Dr. Arne and ed. by his son, Michael Arne. Pr. 1784.

ELIZABETH; OR, THE DON, THE DUCK, THE DRAKE, AND THE INVINCIBLE ARMADA. Burl. F. C. Burnand. Vaudeville, November 17, 1870.

ELIZABETH, QUEEN OF ENGLAND. D. 5 a. Transl. fr. the Italian of Giacometti. Liverpool Amphi., June 14, 1869; Lyceum, December 18, 1869. Transl. by Thos. Williams. D.L., July 14, 1882; rev. Adelphi, September 15, 1902.

ELIZABETH STOREY, THE BRAVE LASS OF HALTWHISTLE. D. Sydney Davis. Newcastle-on-Tyne T.R., May 4, 1868.

ELIZABETH. See *Elisabeth.*

ELLA. See *Ælla.*

ELLA ROSENBERG. Melo-d. 2 a. James Kenney. D.L., November 19, 1807, and June 17, 1814. and 1828. Pr 1807.

ELLA'S APOLOGY. D. 1 a. Alfred Sutro. Publ. by S. French, Ltd. Bloomsbury H., November 8, 1906.

ELLALINE. Duol. Prod. anonymously. Clerkenwell Foresters' H., June 3, 1890.

ELLEN; OR, LOVE'S CUNNING. C. 5 a. W. G. Wills. Hay., April 14, 1879. Afterwards rev. by author and ac. at Hay., June 12, 1879, as *Brag.*

ELLEN WAREHAM. D. 2 a. J. B. Buckstone. F. on tale in Lady Dacre's "Recollections of a Chaperon." Hay., April 24, 1833.

ELLEN WAREHAM, THE WIFE OF TWO HUSBANDS. Dom. D. 2 a. W. E. Burton. Surrey, May, 1833.

ELLIE BRANDON; OR, REVENGE AND LOVE. D. Morton Price. C. of London, April 13, 1868.

ELLINDA; OR, THE ABBEY OF ST. AUBERT. D. Rom. Mrs. Robertson. Newark, 1800. N.p.

ELMERICK; OR, JUSTICE TRIUMPHANT. T. Geo. Lillo. D.L., February 23, 1740 Pr. 1740.

ELMINE; OR, MOTHER AND SON. D. A. C. Jones. West Hartlepool T.R., April 9, 1883.

ELMIRA. Dr. poem. Edward Stanley. Pr. 1790. Taken fr. *The Tales of the Genii.*

ELOISA. T. Fredk. Reynolds. C.G., December 23, 1786. N.p. Taken fr *La Nouvelle Eloise* of Rousseau.

ELOPED; OR, BABES AND BEETLES. See *Babes in the Wood* C. By T. Taylor.

ELOPEMENT, THE. F. Wm. Havard. D.L., April 6, 1763. N.p.

ELOPEMENT, THE. Pant. Ent. Anon. D.L., 1767.

ELOPEMENT. C 2 a. H. A. Jones. Oxford T.R., August 19, 1879; Belfast T.R., August 16, 1880.

ELOPEMENT; OR, CAUTION TO YOUNG LADIES. D. Maclaren. Pr. 1811. See *The Duellists.*

ELOPEMENT OF ELSIE, THE. F.C. a. Austin Fryers. Harrogate O.H., May 22, 1905.

ELOPEMENTS IN HIGH LIFE. C. 5 a. Robert Sullivan. Hay., April 7, 1853.

ELOQUENT DEMPSEY, THE. C. 3 a. Wm. Boyle. (Prod. by amateurs.) Abbey, Dublin, January 20, 1906.

ELPHI BEY; OR, THE ARAB'S FAITH. M.D 3 a. M. by Attwood, Horn and Smart. D.L., April 17, 1817.

ELSA DENE. D. 4 a. A. C. Calmour. Brighton T.R., October 14, 1886; Strand, October 25. 1886.

ELSA'S HAND; OR, THE SQUIRE AND SOMEONE-ELSA. Burl. Victor May. M. by Geo. Bryer. Swansea T.R., March 6, 1893.

ELSIE. D. 1 a. F. Broughton. Globe, September 8, 1883.

ELSIE'S RIVAL. Sk. 1 a. Dora V. Greet (Mrs. Wm. Greet). Strand, May 14, 1888.

ELVES; OR, THE STATUE BRIDE, THE. Fairy Spec. Adelphi, December, 1855.

ELVIRA. T. D. Mallet. D.L., January 19, 1763. Pr. 1763.

ELVIRA; OR, THE WORST NOT ALWAYS TRUE. C. Adap. ascr. to Geo. Digby, Earl of Bristol, of Calderon's *No Sempre lo Peor es Cierto.* Mrs. Centlivre seems to have borrowed fr. this piece for *The Wonder.* Pr. 1667.

ELWINA T. M. Fitzgerald. Dublin T.R., 1792.

ELYSIUM. Prel. Ac. on Her Majesty's birthday at Hanover. Transl. fr. the German. Pr. 1789.

EMBARKATION. M. Ent. Andrew Franklin. D.L., October 3, 1799. M. by Reeve. Songs only Pr. 1799.

EMBARRASSED HUSBAND; OR, LOVE AND HONOUR REWARDED. C. Pr. 1785-7.

EMBASSY, THE. P. 3 a. J. R. Planché. Adap. fr. the French. C.G., March 22, 1841.

EMBLEMATICAL TRIBUTE IN HONOUR OF HER MAJESTY'S NUPTIALS, AN. M. by G. Alex. Macfarren. D.L., February 10, 1840.

EMERALD ISLE; OR, THE CAVES OF CARRIE CLEENA, THE. C.O. 2 a. Basil Hood. M. by Arthur Sullivan and E. German. Savoy, April 27, 1901.

EMERALD QUEEN, THE. D. W. Travers. Britannia, July 18, 1870.

EMIGRANT IN LONDON, THE. D. 5 a. "By an Emigrant." Pr. 1795. N.ac.

EMIGRANT'S DAUGHTER, THE. D. 1 a. R. J. Raymond. Eng. O.H., August 8, 1838.

EMIGRANT'S PROGRESS, THE. City of London, October 4, 1852.

EMIGRATION. Irish D. Barry Connor. Dublin Queen's, July 13, 1880.

EMIGRATION. Irish D. 4 a. Hubert O'Grady. Glasgow Princess's, May 14, 1883.

EMIGRE, L'. P. 4 a. Paul Bourget. (Orig. prod. October 9, 1908, in Paris). Adelphi, June 25, 1909.

EMIGREE'S DAUGHTER. Hay., July 18, 1850.

EMILIA. T.C Anon. Pr. 1672. Suggested by Constanza di Rosamando of Aurelio Aureli.

EMILIA. T. Mark Anthony Meillan. Pr. circa 1771.

EMILIA GALOTTI. T. Transl. fr. the German of Lessing. D.L., October 28, 1794. N.p. Founded on a story similar to that of *Appius and Virginia.*

EMILIA GALOTTI. T. Transl. fr. the German of Gotthold Ephraim Lessing by B. Thompson. Pr. 1860. N.ac.

EMILY. D. 4 a. G. Hamilton. Albion, April 30, 1877.

EMILY. P. 1 a. Margaret M. Mack. H.M.T., December 8, 1908 (mat.).

EMILY. See *Em'ly.*

EMILY; OR, JUVENILE INDISCRETION. Ballet. D.L., February, 1807. The idea probably taken from *The Spoil'd Child.*

EMISSARY; OR, THE REVOLT OF MOSCOW, THE. O. M. chiefly from Onslow's *Le Colporteur.* Adap. by B. Livius, with additions. D.L. May 13, 1831.

EM'LY. 4 a. Adap. T. G. Warren and B. Landeck of *David Copperfield.* Adelphi, August 1, 1903.

EM'LY; OR, THE ARK ON THE SANDS. D. Adap. fr. Dickens's *David Copperfield.* Manchester, Q.T. March 10, 1884.

EMMA. D. On the model of the Greek T. By Geo. Richards. Pr. 1804. N. ac.

EMMA. O. Cavazza. (Bologna, 1877.)

EMMA. C. 3 a. By "A. M." Brighton Aquarium, July 17, 1893.

EMMA VON LEICESTER. O. M. by Meyerbeer. Germany, about 1821.

EMPENOS DE SEIS HORAS, LOS. See *Adventures of a Night, Adventures of Five Hours.*

EMPEROR COMMANDS, THE. M. Ca. Wr. and com by George Cornille-Pescud. Portobello Tower Pav., September 16, 1908.

EMPEROR OF THE EAST, THE. T.C. Philip Massinger. Blackfriars, March 11, 1631, and at the Globe. Pr. 1632. The plot probably used by Lee in *Theodosius.*

EMPEROR OF THE MOON, THE. F. Mrs. Behn. Queen's T. Pr. 1687. Taken fr. *Arlequin Empereur dans le Monde de la Lune.* Orig. transl. fr. the Italian. A dialogue panto. in 3 a adap. fr. this ac. at the Patagonian T. Pr. 1777.

EMPEROR'S DIVORCE, AN. Scena. Arthur Skelton. Cambridge M.H., June 19, 1905.

EMPEROR'S LEGACY, AN. Hist. D. Pro. and 4 a. Sara R. Von Leer and Geo. G. Collingham. Liverpool Shakespeare. April 19, 1905 (C.P.).

EMPEROR'S ROMANCE, AN. P. 4 a. Robt. Barr and Cosmo Hamilton. Adap. fr. R. Barr's novel "The Countess Thekla." West Hartlepool Grand, January 1, 1901.

EMPIRE OF AMBITION, THE. Rom.D. 4 a. Gordon Holmes. West Bromwich Royal, December 5, 1907.

EMPIRIC, THE. A Droll out of Ben Jonson's play of *The Alchemist,* 1672.

EMPIRICK, THE. P. Thos. Horde, jun. Circa 1788.

EMPRESS AND NO EMPRESS; OR, MR. BONY'S WEDDING. F. Maclaren. 1810.

EMPRESS OF MOROCCO, THE. T. Elkanah Settle. Ac Court, 1671; Duke's T. Pr. 1673.

EMPRESS OF MOROCCO, THE. F. A burl. of Settle's P. of same name. Ascr. to Thos. Duffet. T.R. and Pr. 1674.

EMPTY CRADLE, THE. Do.D. 4 a. St. Clair Forbes. Bilston R., November 16, 1908.

EMPTY STOCKING, AN. P. 1 a. F. Wright, jun. Strand, December 5, 1898.

EN BALLON; OR, THE ASCENT OF PRIMROSE HILL. Whimsicality in 3 sc. W. A. Vicars. Ptd. T. Scott.

EN ROUTE. M. Sk. Corney Grain. St. Geo. H., October 23, 1882.

EN ROUTE. M.C. 2 a. Cecil Maxwell. M. by Ernest Bucalossi, lyrics by Walter Parke, add. numbers by Roland Carse and P. Bucalossi. Parkhurst, September 21, 1896.

EN VOYAGE. Petite C. Lewis Coen. Vaudeville, December 20, 1883; National Sporting Club, Covent Garden, April 27, 1903.

ENCHANTED BARBER, THE. Panto. Bros. Grinn. Adelphi, December 22, 1877.

ENCHANTED BEANS, THE. Extrav. Freeman. West Hartlepool New Gaiety, March 22, 1875.

ENCHANTED CASTLE, THE. Panto. Andrews. C.G., 1786.

ENCHANTED CASTLE, THE. T. F. Holcroft. Mentioned in Barker's "Drama Recorded," 1814.

ENCHANTED COURSER; OR, THE SULTAN OF CURDISTAN, THE. Tale of magic. D.L., October 28, 1824.

ENCHANTED DOVE. Panto. Britannia, December 26, 1881.

ENCHANTED FOREST, THE. Burl. C. Dance. Lyceum, 1847.

ENCHANTED FOUNTAIN, THE. Fairy P. 2 a. Mrs. De L. Lacy. M. by Mrs. Lynedock Moncrieff. St. James's, June 22, 1900.

ENCHANTED GARDEN, THE. Ballet Div. Arr. by Mme. Louise. D.L., April 10, 1856.

ENCHANTED HARP; OR, HARLEQUIN FOR IRELAND, THE. D. Spec. J. C. Cross. R. Circus. Pr. 1802.

ENCHANTED HIVE, THE. Playlet. David Devant. St. Geo. H., September 16, 1905.

ENCHANTED HORSE, THE. Burl. A. Smith and T. Taylor. Lyceum, December 26, 1845.

ENCHANTED ISLAND, THE. M.E. Wr. "by a lady," Ac. at Dublin, 1785. N.p.

ENCHANTED ISLAND, THE. Dr. Ballet. John Fawcett. Hay., June 20, 1804. F. on Shakespeare's *Tempest*.

ENCHANTED ISLAND, THE. C.O. 1 a. R. H. O. Bloor. M. by Richd. N. Walthew. St. Geo. H., May 8, 1900.

ENCHANTED ISLAND (OR ISLE), THE. Travesty of *The Tempest*. Wm. and Robert Brough. Liverpool Amphi., 1848. Adelphi, November 20, 1848; rev. in 1860.

ENCHANTED ISLAND; OR, FREE-BORN ENGLISHWOMAN. M.E. Mrs. Robertson. 1796.

ENCHANTED LOVERS, THE. Past. Sir W. Lower. Pr. 1658.

ENCHANTED LUTE, THE. Announced April 13, 1833.

ENCHANTED MAID, THE. Oa. H. Byam Wyke. M. by H. Liston. Sunderland T.R., March 31, 1882.

ENCHANTED ORANGE TREE, THE. Extrav. T. S. Rogers. Liverpool Queen's H., May 10, 1880.

ENCHANTED PRINCE, THE. Pant. J. Douglass. Standard, December 24, 1877.

ENCHANTED ROSE, THE. P. 1 a. E. Harcourt Williams. Fd. on a story by Hans Andersen. Manchester R., April 30, 1907 (C.P.).

ENCHANTED TOWER, THE. Fairy Extrav. Chas. Selby. Marylebone, 1848.

ENCHANTED WOOD, THE. Legendary D. 3 a. Mr. Frances. Hay., July 25, 1792. Pr. 1792. Ideas taken fr. Parnell's *Fairy Tale in the Ancient Style, The Tempest*, and *The Midsummer Night's Dream*.

ENCHANTED WOOD; OR, THE THREE TRANSFORMED PRINCES, THE. Extrav. H. J. Byron. Adelphi, May 4, 1870. F. on the German legend, "The Three Sisters," by Musacus.

ENCHANTER; OR, LOVE AND MAGIC, THE. M.D. 2 a. David Garrick. M. by Mr. Smith. D.L., December 13, 1760. Pr. 1760.

ENCHANTERS; OR, HARLEQUIN SULTAUN, THE. Pant. D.L., 1806-7. N.p. F. on the story of Misnar in "The Tales of the Genii."

ENCHANTRESS, THE. O. M. by Balfe. D.L., May 14, 1845.

ENCHIRIDION CHRISTIADOS. John Cayworth. 1636.

ENCOUNTER, THE. A Droll. Fr. Beaumont and Fletcher's play, *The Knight of the Burning Pestle*. 1672.

Εγχυχλοχορεία; OR, UNIVERSAL MOTION. Part of ent. by Prince de la Grange, Lord Lieutenant of Lincolns's Inn. Ac. before Charles II., Monarch of Great Britain, France, and Ireland. January 3, 1662. Pr. 1662.

END CROWNS ALL, THE. C.D. 4 a. A. Tullock. Ilkeston Foyal, April 22, 1907.

END OF A DAY, THE. P. 1 a. Herbert Barnett. Royalty, December 5, 1891.

END OF A STORY, THE. P. 4 a. J. D. Morgan. Wyndham's, April 12, 1902.

END OF THE LANE, THE. P. 3 a. T. W. Kay. Blackpool Grand, December 14, 1903.

END OF THE STORY, THE. D. 4 a. Ada G Abbott. (Orig. pr. at Cardiff R., June 24, 1907, under title of *The House of Shame*.) W. London, November 1, 1907.

END OF THE STORY, THE. P. 1 a. Neilson Morris. (Pr. by the Amat. Players' Association.) Court, March 3, 1909.

END OF THE TETHER; OR, A LEGEND OF THE PATENT OFFICE. D. 2 a. G. C. Baddeley.

END OF THE WORLD; OR, TABLITSKY SAYS, THE. Playlet. A. Hoffman. May 21. 1908 (C.P.).

ENDIMION AND THE MAN IN THE MOONE. C. J. Lylly. Pr. 1591. Ac. before Q. Eliz. by Children of the Chapel and St. Paul's. Story from Lucian's dialogue between *Venus and the Moon* and other mythologists. See *Lilly's Court Comedies*.

'ENDON WAY. Mus. piece. 1 a. Oswald Brand and Cayley Calvert. M. by Francis W. Woodward. Imperial, October 24, 1898.

ENDYMION; OR, THE NAUGHTY BOY WHO CRIED FOR THE MOON. Extrav. 1 a. Wm. Brough. St. James's, Dec. 26, 1860.

ENDYMION, THE MAN IN THE MOON. Masque. Pr. 1698. Pr. at the end of a C. called *Imposture Defeated*.

ENEA IN CARTAGINE. O. G. Colla. Turin, 1770.

ENEDA; OR, THE MAD PRINCESS. C.O. 3 a. Adeleine Vobieri. Lyrics by H. Morley Park. M. by Denham Harrison. Princess's, May 15, 1902.

ENEMIES. C.D. 3 a. C. F. Coghlan. Adap. from Georges Ohnet's *La Grande Marnière*, P.O.W., January 28, 1886.

ENEMIES. Georgian P. 3 a. John Johnson and Wagner Major. Hildenborough Institute, February 18, 1908 (amat.).

ENEMY OF THE PEOPLE, AN. P. 5 a. Henrik Ibsen. Hay., June 14, 1893; H.M., November 2, 1905; rev. H.M., January 18, 1906; April 30, 1909.

ENEMY'S CAMP, THE. Military D. 4 a. Herbert Leonard. Pavilion, March 26, 1894.

ENEMY'S COUNTRY, THE. P. 1 a. Leopold Montague. Crediton T.H., November 7, 1900 (C.P.).

'ENERY BROWN. Duol. E. Granville. New T (St. Martin's Lane), June 23, 1903.

'ENERY BROWN. C. 1 a. E. Eliot. Pub. by S. French, Limited.

ENFANT PRODIGUE, L'. O. 5 a. Words, Scribe; music, Auber. Academie, Paris, December 6, 1850. In Italian as *Il Prodigo*, at Her M., June 12, 1851. In English, as *Azael the Prodigal*. D.L., February 19, 1851.

ENFANT PRODIGUE, L'. M.P. 3 a, without words. Michel Carré, fils. M. by A. Wormser (Cercle Funambulesque, Paris, June 21, 1890); Bouffes Parisiens, June 21, 1890; P.O.W., March 31, 1891; Criterion, April 11, 1892.

ENGAGED. F.C. 3 a. W. S. Gilbert. Hay., October 3, 1877.

ENGAGED TO APPEAR. Mus. Ca. Trowbridge, Criterion H., March 21, 1879.

ENGAGEMENT, AN. Duol. B. C. Stephenson. Newcastle-on-Tyne T.R., August 29, 1890.

ENGINEER, THE. Victoria, March 23, 1863.

ENGINEERING. Ca. 2 a. Arthur Mathison. Park, June 22, 1878.

ENGLAND. A. P. without a plot. Norman Roe. Ramsgate Victoria, July 4, 1907.

ENGLAND AND GLORY. Mil. D. 4 a. Stafford Grafton. Walsall, Gaiety, October 11, 1888.

ENGLAND, HO! OR, THE BUCCANEERS OF THE ARCTIC REGIONS. D. Marylebone, July 6, 1878.

ENGLAND, HOME, AND BEAUTY. D. 3 a. Joseph Bracewell. Manchester Queen's, August 22, 1882.

ENGLAND IN THE DAYS OF CHARLES THE SECOND. D. 4 a. W. G. Wills. D.L., Sept. 22, 1877.

ENGLAND, MISTRESS OF THE SEAS. M. scena. Invented and wr. by Sydney Blow. M. by Edward Jones. Camberwell Empire, March 30, 1908.

ENGLAND PRESERVED. Hist. P. Geo. Watson. C.G., February 21, 1795. Pr. 1795.

ENGLAND'S COMFORT AND LONDON'S JOY. This pageant comp. by Taylor, the Water Poet, 1641.

ENGLAND'S ELIZABETH. Hist. D. 4 a. Judge Parry and Louis Calvert. Manchester, Royal, April 29, 1901.

ENGLAND'S FLAG. D. 4 a. Harold Whyte. Salford P.O.W., April 15, 1895.

ENGLAND'S GLORY. M.E. M. by James Kremberg. Ac. before Queen Anne. Pr. 1706.

ENGLAND'S GLORY. Naval D. 4 a. Parkhurst, August 20, 1894.

ENGLAND'S GLORY; OR, THE BRITISH TARS AT SPITHEAD. Prel. C.G., May 16, 1795. N.p.

ENGLAND'S JOY. P. Ac. at the Swan, 1602.

ENGLAND'S THRONE. A history. Chandos H., W.C., June 14, 1908.

ENGLEBERT. Joshua Barnes. A piece in rhyme in Library of Emanuel Coll., Cambridge.

ENGLISH BRITONS, THE. F. 1 a. Inscribed to John Wilkes. Pr. 1763.

ENGLISH DAISY, AN. M.C. 2 a. Seymour Hicks and Walter Slaughter. Reading County T., August 11, 1902; Stoke Newington, September 15, 1902.

ENGLISH ETIQUETTE. F.C. 2 a. J. Oxenford. Olympic, Nov. 2, 1840.

ENGLISH FRIAR; OR, THE TOWN SPARKS. C. J. Crowne. Ac. by their Majesties' Servants, 1690.

ENGLISH FUGITIVES, THE. P. Wm. Haughton. Ac. in 1600.

ENGLISH GENTLEMAN; OR, THE EMPTY POCKET, AN. The second title also used, *The Squire's Last Shilling*. C.D. 4 a. (afterwards 3 a.). H. J. Byron. Bristol New T.R., November 8, 1870; Hay., May 13, 1871; rev., Gaiety, October, 1879.

ENGLISH GIRL, AN; OR, A TALE OF INDIA. Mr. E. Crapton Bryant. M. by Miss M. Goyder (Mrs. Herdman Porter). Sutton-in-Ashfield King's, May 8, 1907.

ENGLISH HEARTS. D. 4 a. Matthew Hall and Herbert Green. M. by Charles Harrison. Lincoln T.R., June 10, 1892.

ENGLISH LAWYER, THE. C. E. Ravenscourt. A tragedy of Ruggle's Latin C., *Ignoramus*. This piece had previously been trans. by R. Codrington in 1662. Pr. 1678. T.R. in London, 1678; Westminster Scholars, 1730 and 1747; Merchant Taylor's School, 1763; Bury St. Edmunds School, 1731.

ENGLISH MERCHANT, THE. C. Geo. Colman. D.L., February 21, 1767. Pr. 1767. Plot fr. Voltaire's *Ecossaise*.

ENGLISH MONARCH, THE. See *Edgar*.

ENGLISH MONSIEUR, THE. C. James Howard. Ac. at the T.R., 1666. Pr. 1674.

ENGLISH MOOR; OR, THE MOCK MARRIAGE, THE. C. Richard Brome. Pr. 1659.

ENGLISH NELL. C. 4 a. Anthony Hope and Edward Rose, f. on novel "Simon Dale." P.O.W., August 21, 1900.

ENGLISH PRINCESS; OR, THE DEATH OF RICHARD THE THIRD, THE. T. J. Caryl. Pr. 1667. L.I.F., March 7, 1667.

ENGLISH READINGS. C. Piece. 1 a. Hay., Aug. 7, 1787. Ascribed to James Cobb. Pr. 1787.

ENGLISH ROGUE, THE. C. Thomas Thompson. Ac. Pr. 1668.

ENGLISH ROSE, THE. D. 4 a. G. R. Sims and R. Buchanan. Adelphi, August 2, 1890.

ENGLISH STAGE ITALIANISED, THE. In a new dr. ent. called *Dido and Æneas; or, Harlequin a Butler, a Pimp*, etc. T. Durfey. Pr. 1727.

ENGLISH TAVERN AT BERLIN, THE. C. Pr. 1789. N.ac.

ENGLISH TRAVELLER, THE. T.C. Thos. Heywood. Cockpit, D.L. Pr. 1633. Partly fr. the *Mostellaria of Plautus*.

ENGLISHMAN FROM PARIS, THE. F. Arthur Murphy. D.L., April 3, 1756. N.p.

ENGLISHMAN IN BOURDEAUX, THE. C. Transl. by an English Lady fr. Favart. Pr. 1764.

ENGLISHMAN IN PARIS, THE. C. 2 a. Saml. Foote. C.G., March 24, 1753. Pr. 1753. Edinburgh, 1782.

ENGLISHMAN RETURNED FROM PARIS, THE. C. 2 a. Saml. Foote. C.G., Pr. 1756. A sequel to *The Englishman in Paris*.

ENGLISHMAN'S HOME, AN. P. 3 a. By "A Patriot" (Major Guy du Maurier). Wyndham's, January 27, 1909.

ENGLISHMAN'S HONOUR, AN. Military D. 4 a. Harold Whyte. (Orig. pr. under the title of *True to the Queen* at the Crown, Peckham, November 26, 1900.) Rev. Fulham, May 3, 1909.

ENGLISHMAN'S HOUSE IS HIS CASTLE, AN. 1 a. J. M. Morton. Princess's, May 11, 1857.

ENGLISHMEN FOR MY MONEY; OR, A WOMAN WILL HAVE HER WILL. C. Pr. 1616. An edition in 1631 under 2nd title only.

ENGLISHMEN IN INDIA. O. 3 a. M. by Bishop. D.L., January 27, 1827.

ENGLISHWOMAN, AN. Melo-d. 5 a. St. Aubyn Miller. Chatham O.H., January 1, 1894; Standard, October 1, 1894.

ENID. O. 2 a. M. by Vincent Thomas. Book by Ernest Rhys. Court, November 24, 1908.

ENLISTED. Ca. Windsor T.R., April 7, 1885.

ENLISTED. D. 4 a. Fred C. Harcourt. First acted under title of *The Chain Gang*; rev. by Woods Lawrence and ac. under present title Wolverhampton Star T., June 2, 1890; Sadler's Wells, February 9, 1891.

ENLISTED SHEPHERDS, THE. Past.-d. W. Hawkins. Pr. 1786.

ENOCH ARDEN. D. 4 a. Arthur Mathison. Crystal Palace, December 14, 1876.

ENOUGH'S AS GOOD AS A FEAST. C. Anon. N.d.

ENQUIRE WITHIN. Ent. F. C. Burnand. Gal. of Illus., July 20, 1868.

ENRAGED MUSICIAN, THE. M. by S. Arnold. 1788; rev. at St. Geo. H., March 12, 1855; St. Martin's H., April 2, 1855.

ENRICO DI BORGOGNA. O. Donizetti. 1818

ENROLEMENT D'ARLEQUIN. O. 1 a. Piron. M. by Ramedu. February 29, 1726.

ENSIGN, THE. C. Transl. fr. Schroeder by Benj. Thompson. Pr. 1800. N.ac.

ENSNARED. D. 3 a. Walter Frith. Adap. fr. *Le Drame de la rue de la Paix.* Gaiety, March 8, 1883.

ENTER THE BISHOP. F. 1a. Mrs. J. A. Hobson. South Place Inst., April 2, 1909.

ENTERLUDE OF MYNDES, WITNESSING THE MAN'S FALL FROM GOD AND CHRIST. Set forth by "H. N." (Harry Nicholas). Circa 1574. See *Comœdia.*

ENTERTAINING THE DOWAGER. C. 1 a. G. Colmore (C.P.). D.P. Eastbourne, June 13, 1906.

ENTERTAINMENT, THE HONOURABLE. Given to the Queen in progress at Elenetham, in Hampshire, by the Earl of Hertford. Pr. 1591.

ENTERTAINMENT OF THE QUEEN AND PRINCE, THE, at Lord Spencer's, at Althorpe, June 25, 1603. Ben Jonson. Pr. 1603. See *The Satyr.*

ENTERTAINMENT AT KING JAMES THE FIRST'S CORONATION, THE. Ben Jonson. Pr. 1603.

ENTERTAINMENT TO KING JAMES, QUEEN ANNE, HIS WIFE, AND HENRY FREDERICK, THE PRINCE, upon his passage through London. March 15, 1603. T. Dekker. Pr. 1604.

ENTERTAINMENT OF THE KING AND QUEEN, THE, at Sir W. Cornwallis's house at Highgate on May Day morning, 1604. Ben Jonson. Pr. 1756. See *The Penates.*

ENTERTAINMENT OF THE TWO KINGS OF GREAT BRITAIN AND DENMARK, THE, at Theobalds, July 24, 1606. Ben Jonson. Pr. 1756.

ENTERTAINMENT OF KING JAMES AND QUEEN ANNE, THE, at Theobald's, when the house was delivered up with possession to the Q. by the Earl of Salisbury, May 22, 1607. Ben Jonson. Pr. 1756.

ENTERTAINMENT, THE, given by Lord Knowles at Cawsome (Caversham) House near Reading, to the Q. in her progress toward the Bath, April 27 and 28, 1613. Thos. Campion. Pr. 1613.

ENTERTAINMENT OF KING CHARLES I., THE, at Welbeck on his coming into Edinburgh, June 15, 1633. Pr. 1633. See *Love's Welcome at Welbeck.*

ENTERTAINMENT AT RICHMOND, THE. Masque presented by Prince Charles to their Majesties, 1634.

ENTERTAINMENT ON THE PRINCE'S BIRTHDAY, AN. Thos. Nabbs. Pr. 1639.

ENTERTAINMENT AT RUTLAND HOUSE, AN. Sir W. Davenant. M. by Dr. Chas. Coleman, Capt. Henry Cook, Henry Lawes, and Geo. Hudson. Pr. 1656.

ENTERTAINMENT, AN, designed for Her Majesty's Birthday by R. Dodsley. Pr. 1732.

ENTERTAINMENT, AN, designed for the wedding of Governor Lowther and Miss Pennington, by Robt. Dodsley. Pr. 1732.

ENTERTAINMENTS, THE, set to music for the comic Dr. O. *The Lady's Triumph.* M. by Galliard. Pr. 1718.

ENTFUHRUNG AUS DEM SERAIL, DIE. O. Mozart. Lib. by C. F. Bretzner. Vienna, July 13, 1782.

ENTHUSIAST, THE. C. 1 a. Wm. Lowe. Blackburn, T. R. May 7, 1884.

ENTHUSIAST, THE. Dr. sketch. Vaudeville, March 11, 1892.

ENTHUSIAST, THE. P. Lewis Purcell. Belfast, Clarence Place, H., May 4, 1905.

ENTRANCES AND EXITS. D. Prol. and 3 a. Geo. Spencer. East London, April 27, 1868.

ENTRAPPED. Melod. 2 a. Edgar Newbound. Britannia, July 24, 1880.

ENTREZ, MESSIEURS, MESDAMES. Op. bo. 1 a. Offenbach. 1855.

EOS AND GWEVRIL. Celtic O. 3 a. Vincent Thomas. St. Geo. H., April 18, 1902.

EPHESIAN MATRON, THE. F. 1 a. Chas. Johnson. Pr. 1730. Ac. D.L., April 17, 1732.

EPHESIAN MATRON, THE. C.ser. Isaac Bickerstaff. M. by Dibdin. Ac. at Ranleigh House. Pr. 1769.

EPIC POEMS (Greek, Epos, a song). Narratives in verse.

Homer's "Iliad," "Odyssey," Greek, 8th century B.C.
Virgil's "Æneid," Latin, B.C. 19.
Ovid's "Metamorphoses," Latin, A.D. 1.
Dante (died 1321), "Divina Commedia," Italian, 1472.
Ariosto, "Orlando Furioso," Italian, 1516.
Camoen's "Lusiad," Portuguese, 1569.
Tasso, "Jerusalem Delivered," Italian, 1581.
Spenser's "Faëry Queen," British, 1590-6.
Milton's "Paradise Lost," British, 1667.
Voltaire, "Henriade," French, 1728.
Walter Scott, "Lay of the Last Minstrel," British, 1805.

EPICHARIS. Hist. T. D.L., October 14, 1829.

EPICŒNE; OR, THE SILENT WOMAN. C. Ben Jonson. D.L. Ac. by the children of Her Majesty's Revels, 1609. Pr. 1605; altered by Mr. Colman and ac. 1776.

EPICURE. O. 3 a. Mehul (with Cherubini). O. Comique, March 14, 1800.

EPIDICUS. C. Transl. from Plautus by Rev. Lawrence Echard. N. ac. See "Latin Plays."

EPISODE, AN. P. 1 a. Katherine Stewart. Folkestone Pleasure Gdns. T., May 17, 1895 (C.P.).

EPISODE, AN. P. 1 a. Marion Robertson. Guildhall School, February 25, 1908.

EPONINA (or Epponina). Dr. essay. John Carr. Pr. 1765. Story taken fr. Dion Cassius and Tacitus.

EPSOM WELLS. C. Thos. Shadwell. Duke of York's T. Pr. 1673. Rev. D.L., 1708 and 1715, and at L.I.F., 1726.

EQMITE, L'. D. 2 a. Georges Henriot. Royalty, July 23, 1906.

EQUAL MATCH, AN. A Droll fr. Beaumont and Fletcher's P., *Rule a Wife and Have a Wife.* 1672.

EQUALITY JACK. Nautical Oa. 2 a. Lib. f. on the characters and dialogues of Capt. Marryat's novels by Wm. Poel. M. by Wm. S. Vinning. Ladbroke H., February 28, 1891.

EQUALITY OF CARBERRY, THE. F. C. Beryl Ducker. Jersey O.H., February 19, 1909.

EQUALS. C. 3 a. Edward Rose. Adap. fr. Emile Augier and Jules Sandeau's *Le Gendre de M. Poirier.* Manchester, Prince's, June 28, 1883; Liverpool, R. Alexandra, July 2, 1883; Hammersmith, Iffley H., June 6, 1889.

EQUIVOCO STRAVAGANTE. O. Rossini. Bologna, 1811.

ERASTE ET LUCINDE. Oa. Grétry. 1770.

ERASTUS. Dr. piece. 1 a. Anon. Transl. fr. the German. Pr. in *The Works of Solomon Gessner*, 1802.

ERBE DAS. D. 4 a. Felix Phillippi, Great Queen Street, February 23, 1906.

ERIC'S GOOD ANGEL. P. 1 a. Frank Hird and Cecil Crofton. Newcastle-on-Tyne T.R., May 23, 1894; Eleph. and C., July 4, 1894.

ERIFILE. O. Myshweczek. Munich, 1773.

ERIKSSON'S WIFE. P. 1 a. Christopher St. John. Royalty, September 3, 1904.

ERIN-GO-BRAGH; OR, THE WREN BOYS OF KERRY. D. C. H. Hazlewood. Britannia, April 18, 1870.

ERIN-GO-BRAGH; OR, THE MILESIAN TRUST IN LUCK. D. W. J. Travis. Victoria, May 3, 1873.

ERIPHYLE. O. A. Ariosti. 1697.

ERMINA; OR, THE CHASTE LADY, sometimes called *Ermina; or, The Fair and Vertuous Lady*. T.C. Richard Flecknoe. Pr. 1667. N.ac.

ERMINIE. C.O. 2 a. Claxson Bellamy and Harry Paulton M. by Edward Jakobowski. Birmingham, Grand, October 26, 1885; Comedy, November 9, 1885; Gaiety, February 18, 1886.

ERMIONE. O. Rossini. Naples, Lent, 1819.

ERMYNGARDE IN FAIRYLAND. Fairy C. J. W. Brodie Innes. P.O.W. Club, February 23, 1894.

ERNANI. O. 4 a. Verdi. Venice, 1844; Her M., March 8, 1845.

ERNANI; OR, THE HORNS OF A DILEMMA. Burl. W. Brough. Highbury Alexandra, May 20, 1865.

ERNEST MALTRAVERS. D. 3 a. Miss Rose Medina. Britannia, September 28, 1874.

ERNESTINE. D. 2 a. W. Robertson. Fr. the French of Dennery and Clement. Princess's, 1846.

ERNESTINE; THE ROMANCE OF A TYPIST. P. 4 a. H. F. Maltby. Exeter R.T., May 4, 1908.

ERO E LEANDRO. O. 3 a. Arrigo Boito. M. by Mancinelli. C.G., July 11, 1898.

EROR CINESE, L'. Serious O. Metastasio. M. by Rauzzina. Hay., 1782.

EROS AND PSYCHE. See *The Bride of Love*.

EROSTRATE. O. Reyer. Modern France.

EROSTRATUS. Spec. D. 3 a.

ERRATIC EVANGELINE. Burl. Birmingham P.O.W., March 10, 1884.

ERRING SISTER, AN. Sk. Jas. A. Kilpatrick. Hastings Gaiety, November 5, 1892.

ERRORS EXCEPTED. C. 3 a. T. Dibdin. Hay., August 13, 1807. N.p.

ES LEBE DAS LEBEN. D. 5 a. Hermann Sudermann. Gt. Queen St. T., February 23, 1903.

ESCAPE, THE. Int. D.L., 1798. N.p.

ESCAPE INTO PRISON, AN. M.E. Jas. C. Cross. C.G., November 14, 1797. An adapt. of Mrs. Inchbald's *Hue and Cry*.

ESCAPE OF JOHN MERCHANT, THE. P. 1 a. Philip Gibbs and Cosmo Hamilton. Duke of York's, July 10, 1906.

ESCAPED; OR, THRICE MARRIED. D. 4 a. W. Travers. East London, June 6, 1870.

ESCAPED FROM PORTLAND. D. Pro. and 3 a. Adapt. fr. the French. Princess's, October 9, 1869.

ESCAPES; OR, THE WATER CARRIER, THE. M.F. C.G., October 14, 1801. N.p.

ESCAPES OF HARLEQUIN, THE. Ent. Thurmond. D.L.

ESCARTE. Globe, December 3, 1870.

ESCLARMONDE. O. Massenet. Lib. from old French Ro. 1889.

ESCLAVE DE CAMOENS, L'. O. Flotow. Paris, 1843.

ESMERELDA. O. Poniatowski. Leghorn, 1847.

ESMERALDA. Burl. 2 a. Albert Smith. Adelphi, June 3, 1850.

ESMERALDA. O. Signor Campana. C.G., June 14, 1870.

ESMERALDA. O. 4 a. Goring Thomas. Lib. by A. Randegger and Theo Marzials. F. on Victor Hugo's *Notre Dame*. D.L., March 26, 1883; D.L. (Students of Guildhall Sch. of M.), March 18, 1896; C.G. (first time in Fr.), July 12, 1890.

ESMERELDA. D. 4 a. A. Y. Simon. Moscow, 1902.

ESMERALDA; OR, THE DEFORMED OF NOTRE DAME. D. 3 a. Edward Fitzball. F. on Victor Hugo's novel. Surrey, April 14, 1834.

ESMERALDA; OR, THE SENSATION GOAT. Burl. 1 a. H. J. Byron. Strand, September 28, 1861.

ESMERALDA AND THE HUNCHBACK OF NOTRE DAME. Melo.-d. 4 a. By Battisté. Adapt. to Eng. stage by C. Jefferys. D.L., June 30, 1856.

ESMERALDA. See *Young Folk's Ways*.

ESMOND. Dr. Ver. of W. M. Thackeray's novel in pro. and 3 a. by the late W. G. Wills (completed by Freeman Wills). St. Geo. H. (prod. by Irving Club), June 21, 1893. See *Beatrix*.

ESMONDS OF VIRGINIA, THE. P. 4 a. Cazauran. Originally prod. in America. Royalty, May 20, 1886.

ESOP. C. 2 parts. Sir J. Vanbrugh. D.L. Pr. 1697. Partly fr. a C. of Boursault's. See *Æsop*.

ESOP. F. Probably by R. B. Sheridan, occasioned by Sir J. Vanbrugh's C. of same name. D.L., 1778.

ESOP. Sir John Vanbrugh. Addit. scenes wr. by Moser. Pr. 1808.

ESSEX. Hist rom. 5 a. A. C. Calmour. Manchester Queen's, October 7, 1907.

ESSEX ANTIC MASQUE. Prod. about A.D. 1620.

ESTELLE. It. O. 3 a. Jules Cohen. C.G., July 3, 1880.

ESTHER. The first English Orat. Handel. King's T., May 2, 1732.

ESTHER. Sacr. D. John Collett. Pr. 1806. N.ac.

ESTHER; OR, FAITH TRIUMPHANT. Sacr. T. Thos, Brereton. A transl. of Racine's *Esther*. Pr. 1715. See "French Classical Plays."

ESTHER, THE ROYAL JEWESS; OR, THE DEATH OF HAMAN. Hist. D. 3 a. Eliz. Polack. Pav., March 7, 1835.

ESTHER SANDREZ. P. 3 a. Sydney Grundy. F. on *Femme de Glace*, by Adolphe Belot. P.O.W., June 11, 1889; St. James's, May 3, 1890.

ESTRANGED. C.D. 3 a. H. Williamson. Globe, August 3, 1881.

ESTRELLA. C.O. 3 a. W. Parke. M. by Luscombe Searelle. Manchester Prince's, May 14, 1883; Gaiety, May 24, 1883.

ESTRELLA. Musical wordless P. Wr. and comp. by Marguerite Barreller (Mrs. Barnet) (student, G.S.M.). Guildhall School, December 18, 1908, and July 9, 1909.

ETERNAL CITY, THE. D. Hall Caine. Adap. fr. his novel. Douglas, Gaiety, August 17, 1901 (C.P.); His M., October 2, 1902; Trial sc., therefrom, Crouch End Hipp., March 23, 1908.

ETERNAL MASCULINE, THE. Duo. Horace Newte. Terry's, March 8, 1898.

ETERNAL PURPOSE. THE. P. 3 a. F. E. Archer-Smith. Winslow Oddfellows' H., November 26, 1907.

ETHA. See *Eitha.*

ETHEL; OR, ONLY A LIFE. Adelphi, October 13, 1866.

ETHEL'S REVENGE P. 4 a. Walter Stephens. Taken from Ouida's novel "Strathmore." Court, September 9, 1876.

ETHEL'S TEST. Ca. 2 a. H. W. Williamson. Strand, March 26, 1883.

ETHELINDA; OR, LOVE AND DUTY. T. Matthew West. Pr. 1769. N. ac.

ETHELRED. T. Mrs. Richardson. 1810.

ETHWALD. T. Joanna Baillie. Pr. 1802. N. ac.

ETIENNE MARCEL. O. Saint Saëns. (Lyons, 1879.)

ETIQUETTE. C. C. E. Howells. Alexandra, Walsall, March 1, 1880.

ETOILE, L'. O. 1 a. C. Maréchal. 1881.

ETOILE DU NORD, L'. O. Meyerbeer. (Paris, 1854.)

ETOILE DU NORD, L'. O. Reynolds. Adap. fr. Meyerbeer's O. D.L., February 26, 1855.

ETON BOY, THE. F. 1 a. Edward Morton. D.L., October 29, 1842.

ETON v. HARROW. M. sketch. Corney Grain. St. Geo. H., June 29, 1885.

ETOURDI, L'. Molière. See "French Classical Plays"

ETRANGERE, L'. Alex Dumas. Comédie Française, February, 1876; Adelphi, July 13, 1897.

ETRANGERE, L'. D. 4 a. Eng. Ver. Hay., June 3, 1876.

ETYMOLOGIST, THE. C. 3 a. Anon. Pr. 1785. N.ac.

EUDORA. T. Wm. Hayley. C.G., January 29, 1790. Pr. 1811.

EUGENE ARAM. D. 3 a. W. G. Wills. Lyceum, April 19, 1873.

EUGENE ARAM. D. A. Fancquez. Standard, July 21, 1879.

EUGENE ARAM. M.Ro.P. Pro. and 3 a. T. C. M'Quire. Margate T.R., July 4, 1901.

EUGENE ARAM; OR, SAINT ROBERT'S CAVE. D. 3 a. W. T. Moncrieff. Surrey T.

EUGENE ONEGIN. O. 3 a. Peter Tschaikowsky. Engl. ver. by Mr. and Mrs. Sutherland Edwards. Olympic (1st perf. in England), October 17, 1892; C.G., June 29, 1906.

EUGENIA. T. Philip Francis. D.L., February 17, 1752. Pr. 1752. Adap. fr. the French. C., *Cenia; or, The Supposed Daughter.*

EUGENIA. T. Samuel Hayes and Robert Carr. Pr. 1766.

EUGENIA CLAIRCILLE; OR, THE NEW FOUND HOME. Do.D. 3 a. Tom Parry. Adelphi, September 17, 1846.

EUGENIE. P. 1 a. Dion Boucicault. D.L., January 1, 1855.

EULALIE. Oa. Libretto and Lyrics by Austin Fryers. M. by C. Lecocq. Clerkenwell, Foresters' H., June 3, 1890; Grand, March 26, 1895.

EULALIE, THE LODESTAR. M.P. 3 a. J. Cowper Worden. M. by J. C. Higgin. Blackpool, O.H., December 1, 1902.

EUMENIDES. Æschylus. See "Greek Plays."

EUNICE. P. 4 a. See Arthur and Forrest Halsey. Hicks, June 1, 1909.

EUNICE; OR, LOVE AND DUTY. D. 4 a. Edward Towers. Pavilion, November 6, 1882.

EUNUCH, THE. C. Transl. fr. Terence, by Chas. Hoole. Pr. 1663.

EUNUCH, THE. T. Wm. Hemmings. Pr. 1687. This is *The Fatal Contract* by the same author with a new title.

EUNUCH, THE. C. Transl. by Thomas Newman. Pr. 1627. Transl. by L. Echard. Pr. 1694. Transl. by T. Cooke. Pr. 1734. Transl. by. S. Patrick. Pr. 1745. Transl. by Gordon. Pr. 1752. Transl. by Geo. Colman. Pr. 1765.

EUNUCH; OR, THE DERBY CAPTAIN, THE. F. Thos. Cooke. Pr. circa 1737; D.L., 1737. Taken chiefly fr. the *Eunuchus* of Terence and the *Miles Gloriosus* of Plautus.

EUNUCHUS. C. Transl. by Richard Bernard. Pr. 1598. See "Latin Plays," "Westminster Plays."

EUNUCHUS. See *Bellamira; Beautiful Armenia.*

EUPHORMUS. Latin C. by Geo. Wilde. Ac. at St. John's College, Oxford, February 5, 1634-5.

EUPHROSINE ET CORADIN OU LE TYRAN CORRIGE. O. 3 a. Méhul. September 4, 1790.

EURIBATES. Latin D. of the 17th cent. Wr. by Crouse, of Caius College, Cambridge.

EURIDICE. O. Coccini. (Florence, 1595.)

EURIDICE. O. Peri and Caccini. 1600.

EURIDICE. T. David Mallet. D.L., Pr. 1731. Rev., D.L., 1760.

EURIDICE; OR, THE DEVIL HENPECKT. F. Henry Fielding. D.L., February 19, 1737. Pr. 1735.

EURIDICE HISSED; OR, A WORD TO THE WISE. F. Henry Fielding. Pr. 1736.

EUROPE'S REVELS FOR THE PEACE AND HIS MAJESTY'S HAPPY RETURN. M. int. P. Motteux. M. by J. Eccles. Pr. 1697. L.I.F., 1697.

EURYANTHE. O. Weber. Lib. by Helmine von Chezy. (Vienna, 1823.) D.L., June 7, 1841

EURYDICE; OR, LITTLE ORPHEUS AND HIS LUTE. Burl. Extrav. Second edition of *Orpheus and Eurydice; or, the Young Gentleman who Charmed the Rocks.* H. J. Byron. Strand, April 24, 1871.

EUSTACHE BAUDIN. Orig. D. 3 a. John Courtney. Surrey, January 30, 1854.

EVA. German D. 5 a. Richard Voss. St. Geo. H., January 30, 1896.

EVA'S INHERITANCE. D. Archie Cowper. Liverpool Alexandra, April 6, 1870.

EVADNE; OR, THE STATUE. T. 3 a. Richard Lalor Shiel. Adap. fr. Rivers and Shirley. C.G., February 10, 1819.

EVANDER AND ALCIMNA. Pas. 3 a. Transl. fr. the German. Pr. 1802.

EVANGELIMANN, DER. O. 2 a. Wilhelm Kienzl. C.G., July 2, 1897.

EVANGELINE. Amer. Burl. Liverpool R. Court, June 11, 1883.

EVANTHE. T. Alt. fr. Beaumont and Fletcher's *Wife for a Month*. Not ac. or pr. Mentioned in Barker's Drama Recorded, 1814.

EVE. D. 3 a. B. Webster, jun. Adelphi, May 31, 1869.

EVE. D. 5 a. Adapt. fr. German of Herr Richard Voss. Clapham Shakespeare, November 25, 1901.

EVE OF HER WEDDING, THE. Dom. D. 4 a. C. Watson Mill. Sunderland T.R., May 27, 1907; Ashington Miners', July 13, 1907.

EVE OF MARRIAGE, THE. D. 4 a. A. Shirley and B. Landeck. Hammersmith Lyric O.H., (prod. as *A Great Temptation*), January 20, 1899; Eleph. and C., July 31, 1899.

EVE, THE TEMPTRESS. T. 1 sc. G. B. Nichols and A. Conquest. Surrey, February 24, 1903.

EVE'S TEMPTATION. C.D. 3 a. E. C. Bertrand. Cheltenham T.R., November 22, 1888.

EVELEEN, THE ROSE OF THE VALE. Oa. Birch. Reading T.H., October 21, 1869.

EVELINA. O. In Mr. Oulton's list of plays and Barker's list, 1814.

EVENING AT THE DETECTIVE'S, AN. P. 1 a. J. F. Cooke. B'ham P.O.W., May 19, 1908.

EVENING REVELS. Divert. Mrs. Barrymore. M. by Cooke. D.L., November 10, 1823.

EVENING SHADOWS. C.D. 3 a. Cyril Bowen. Aquarium, August 17, 1878.

EVENING'S ADVENTURES; OR, A NIGHT'S INTRIGUE, AN. C. Fr. the Spanish. Anon. 1680.

EVENING'S INTRIGUE, AN. C. Transl. fr. the Spanish by Capt. John Stevens. Pr. 1709.

EVENING'S LOVE; OR, THE MOCK ASTROLOGER, AN. C. J. Dryden. Taken in part fr. the younger Corneille's *Le Feint Astrologue*, a version of *El Astrologo Fingido* (by Calderon). One scene f. on *Le Dépit Amoureux* of Molière. Also partly from Molière's *Les Precieuses Ridicules* and Quinault's *L'Amant Indiscret*. Pr. and ac. 1668. D.L., October 18, 1717.

EVENTFUL EVE, AN. Ca. 1 a. A. Wilmot.

EVENTIDE. P. 1 a. W. Crichton. Middlesbro' T.R., August 5, 1895; Parkhurst, February 17, 1896.

EVENTS OF A DAY, THE. D. Miss Edmead. Norwich, 1795. N.p.

EVER FAITHFUL. Do.D. 5 a. Edward Darbey. Hastings, July, 1885; Holborn, January 4, 1886.

EVERGREEN. C. 2 a. Adapt. fr. *Le Reveil du Lion* by Jaime and Bayard (the original of *The Roused Lion* by W. H. Pollock). Hay., August 9, 1884.

EVERSLEIGH HOUSE. D. 2 a. E. Newbound. Britannia, March 17, 1879.

EVERY-DAY CHARACTERS. Satirical C. 5 a. Pr. 1805. N.ac.

EVERY INCH A MAN. D. 4 a. Edward Thane. New King's, N.E., February 12, 1906.

EVERY MAN FOR HIMSELF. D. 5 a. Miss May Holt. Gt. Yarmouth Aquarium, June 22, 1885; Pavilion, October 24, 1885.

EVERY MAN IN HIS HUMOUR. C. Ben Jonson. Ac. by the Lord Chamberlain's servants, 1598. Pr. 1601. L.I.F., 1725. Alt. and rev. by David Garrick, C.G., 1751; D.L., June 5, 1816.

EVERY MAN OUT OF HIS HUMOUR. Com. Satire. Ben Jonson. Ac. 1599. Pr. 1600. Rev. by David Garrick, 1751. C.G., 1825.

EVERY WOMAN IN HER HUMOUR. C. Anon. Pr. 1609.

EVERY WOMAN IN HER HUMOUR. F. 2 a. By Mrs. Clive. D.L., March 20, 1760. N.p.

EVERYBODY MISTAKEN. F. 3 a. Wm. Taverner and Dr. Brown. L.I.F., March 10, 1716. See *Presumptuous Love*.

EVERYBODY'S FRIEND. C. 3 a. J. Stirling Coyne. Hay., April 2, 1859. Remodelled and called *A Widow Hunt*. Hay., October, 1867.

EVERYBODY'S HUSBAND. F. 1 a. Richard Ryan. Queen's, February 2, 1831.

EVERYBODY'S SECRET. C. 3 a. Robert Marshall and Louis N. Parker. Adap. fr. *Le Secret de Polichinelle* of Pierre Wolff. Hay., March 14, 1905.

EVERYBODY'S WIDOW. F. 1 a. D.L., October 8, 1836.

EVERYMAN. Morality. Black letter. N.d. Early in the reign of Henry VIII. Rev. and ac., Court T., May 23, 1903; Shaftesbury, April 17, 1905; Garrick, April 9, 1906. See "Miracle Plays."

EVERYONE HAS HIS FAULT. C. 5 a. Mrs. Inchbald. C.G. Pr. 1793. D.L., April 2, 1814; D.L., 1824.

EVICTION, THE. D. 3 a. Hubert O'Grady. Glasgow Princess's, January 24, 1880; Standard, Aug. 9, 1880.

EVIL EYE, THE. M. Rom. M. by G. H. Rodwell. Lyceum (first this season), September 15, 1834.

EVIL EYE, THE. C.O. Leicester T.R., April 21, 1876.

EVIL EYE; A LEGEND OF THE LEVANT, THE. Rom. M.D. 2 a. R. Brinsley Peake. Adelphi, August 18, 1831.

EVIL GENIUS, THE. C. 3 a. Bayle Bernard. Hay., March 8, 1856.

EVIL GENIUS, THE. D. 5 a. Wilkie Collins. Prod. in anticipation of Collins's novel on the same subject. Vaudeville, October 30, 1885.

EVIL HANDS AND HONEST HEARTS Britannia, March 7, 1864.

EVIL LIFE, AN. D. 4 a. F. Brooke Warren. T.R. Smethwick, September 19, 1898; Middlesbrough T.R., July 20, 1903.

EVIL MAY DAY; OR, THE LONDON 'PRENTICES OF 1517, THE. Melo-d. 2 a. W. S. Emden. City of Lon., May 1, 1837.

EXAMPLE, THE. T.C. Jas. Shirley. Ac. at private house in D.L. Pr. 1637. Licensed 1634.

EXCELSIOR. Ballet. 11 tableaux. Manzotti. M. by Marenco. Paris Eden T., January 7, 1884 (after perf. in Italy); H.M.T., May 22, 1885; repro. Lyceum, September 18, 1905.

EXCELSIOR. D. Pro. and 2 a. J. Elliss. Brentford T.R., December 8, 1887.

EXCHANGE ALLEY; OR, THE STOCK JOBBER TURN'D GENTLEMAN; WITH THE HUMOURS OF OUR MODERN PROJECTORS. T.C.F. Pr. 1720.

EXCHANGE NO ROBBERY. C. 3 a. Theodore E. Hook. Hay., August 12, 1820; D.L., January 2, 1826.

EXCHANGE WARE AT THE SECOND-HAND. Anon. Pr. 1615.

EXCISE. T.C.B.O. 3 a. Pr. 1733. (Not for the stage.)

EXCISEMAN, THE. F. Henry Knapp. C.G., November 4, 1780. N.p.

EXCOMMUNICATED PRINCE; OR, THE FALSE RELICK, THE. T. Capt. Wm. Bedloe. Pr. 1679.

EXCURSION TRAIN, THE. F.C. 3 a. Justin Huntley McCarthy and W. Yardley. Adap. fr. Alfred Hennequin, Arnold Mortier, and Albert de Saint Albin's Fr. vaudeville, *Le Train de Plaisir*. Op. C., April 6, 1885.

EXECUTION; OR, MORE FRIGHTENED THAN HURT. M.F. Announced to be ac. C.G., May, 1785. Probably the same as at the Hay., under second title only, during the same year.

EXECUTIONER'S DAUGHTER, THE. See *Monsieur de Paris*.

EXERXES. See *Xerxes*.

EXILE, THE. C. Wm. Duke of Newcastle. ac. at Blackfryars. In Barker's list, 1814.

EXILE, THE. D. 3 a. J. Holmes Grover. Eleph. and C., August 9, 1879.

EXILE, THE. P. 3 a. Lloyd Osbourne and Austin Strong. Royalty, May 9, 1903.

EXILE; OR, THE DESERTS OF SIBERIA, THE. Operatic P. 3 a. Frederick Reynolds. C.G., November 10, 1808. M. by Massinghi, with additions by Bishop. D.L., June 6, 1831, and November 9, 1831.

EXILE FROM HOME, AN. M.F. 1 a. Malcolm Watson. Music by P. E. Fletcher and E. Hess. Savoy, June 12, 1906.

EXILED. D. 4 a. Edward Darbey and Wm. Manning. Keighley Queen's T., February 12, 1891.

EXILED; OR, THE FORCED MARRIAGE. Howard Clarkson. Birkenhead P.O.W., February 12, 1877.

EXILES. Sk. 3 sc. G. M. Marriott. Poplar Queen's, March 21, 1904.

EXILES, THE. M.D. John Rannie. Pr. circa 1806. N.ac.

EXILES OF ERIN; OR, ST. ABE AND HIS SEVEN WIVES, THE. Mormion D. 4 a. and 7 tab. Robert Buchanan. Olympic, May 7, 1881.

EXIT BY MISTAKE. C. 3 a. R. F. Jameson. Hay., July 22, 1816. N.p.

EXPERIENCE TEACHES. Piece. 1 a. Mrs. Merivale Glenridding. October 18, 1892.

EXPERIMENT, THE. C. 2 a. Ascribed to Chas. Stuart. C.G., April 16, 1777. N.p.

EXPERIMENT, THE. F. Chas. Murray. Pr. 1779. Ac. at Norwich.

EXPERIMENT, THE. Sk. Mrs. Albert Bradshaw. Battersea Pal., November 30, 1908.

EXPIATION. D. Pro. and 3 a. E. Manuel. Britannia, June 5, 1876.

EXPIATION. See *Found in Exile*.

EXPLORER, THE. P. 4 a. Wm. Somerset Maugham. Lyric, June 13, 1908; rev. Lyric, May 19, 1909.

EXPOSITION, THE. Scandinavian sketch. 1 a. Shirley Brooks (Punch's Playhouse). Strand T., April 28, 1851.

EXPOSURE. See *A Modern Andromena*.

EXPOSURE, THE. Past. Anon. Licensed in 1598.

EXPRESS. Railway rom. "in the compartment." Adap. fr. the French by J. M. Morton.

EXPRESS; OR, A BROTHER'S SACRIFICE, THE. Ser. C.D. Arthur Masson. St. Geo. H., February 14, 1868 (amat.).

EXPULSION OF THE DANES FROM BRITAIN, THE. T. Elk. Settle. Brought to the managers of D.L., 1723-4, but death of author prevented its being ac. or pr.

EXTRA SHILLING, THE. Bohemian C. 2 sc. Francis Toye. Royalty, June 10, 1907.

EXTRA TURN, AN. Sk. Paul Mill and G. J. Baynes. Brixton Empress, November 11, 1907.

EXTRAORDINARY BEHAVIOUR OF MRS. JALLOWBY, THE. F.C. 3 a. Clive Brooke. Novelty, Dec. 18, 1896.

EXTRAVAGANT JUSTICE. F. James Worsdale (died 1767). N.p.

EXTRAVAGANT SHEPHERD, THE. Past. C. by "T.R." Transl. fr. the French of T. Corneille f. on a Rom. called *Lysis; or, The Extravagant Shepheard*. Pr. 1654.

EXTRAVAGANT SHEPHERD, THE. A complete outline draft of Past. C., conjectured to be in writing of Dodsley in MS. in possession of Stephen Jones.

EXTREME PENALTY, THE. D. 4 a. Gerald Holcroft. Doncaster T.R., December 6, 1886.

EXTREMES. Oa. 1 a. Debenham and Barri. Pub. by S. French, Ltd.

EXTREMES; OR, MEN OF THE DAY. C. 3 a. Edmund Falconer. Lyceum, August 26, 1858; City of Lon., 1859; Glasgow R. Alexandra, March 17, 1869.

EXTREMES MEET. Ca. 1 a. Miss Kate Field. St. James's, March 12, 1877.

EYE FOR AN EYE; OR, PAYING OFF OLD SCORES, AN. D. 4 a. A. F. Robbins and Paul Morris. Crouch End Opera House, February 17, 1902.

EYE-OPENER, AN. American F.C. 3 a. Edward Paulton and Chas. Bradley. Brighton New P. Pav., November 11, 1901.

EYE TO BUSINESS, AN. Ca. Geo. R. Halladay and P. Tardrew. Southampton P.O.W., August 31, 1883.

EYES AND NO EYES; OR, THE ART OF SEEING. Vaud. W. S. Gilbert. M. by T. German Reed. St. Geo. H., July 5, 1875.

EYES IN THE DARK. Effingham. December 3, 1866.

EYES, NOSE, AND MOUTH. Panto. E. L. Blanchard. Marylebone, December, 1847.

EYES OF THE WORLD, THE. Chas. Darrell. Grimsby P.O.W., December 21, 1908; Woolwich R., January 11, 1909; Fulham, March 15, 1909.

EZECHIAS (or EZEKIAS). Sacred D. Nicholas Udall. Ac. before Q. Elizabeth at King's Coll., Cambridge, August 8, 1564.

EZIO. O. Mysliweczek. Munich, 1775.

F

F.F.F.; OR, FIDGET'S FIRST FLOOR. F. Jos. Bracewell. Manchester Queen's, August 22, 1882.

F. M. JULIUS CÆSAR; OR, THE IRREGULAR RUM-UN. Op. Burl. D. 3 a. F. C. Burnand. Royalty, September 7, 1870.

FABII, THE. Hist. D. Circa 1573.

FABIOLA. See *The Christian's Cross*.

FABULIST, THE. F. Wilkinson. Taken fr. Vanbrugh's *Esop*. Ac. at York. N.p.

FACE AT THE WINDOW, THE. D. 4 a. F. Brooke Warren. Blackburn Prince's, June 17, 1897 (C.P.); Salford Regent T., July 26, 1897; West London, May 1, 1899.

FACE IN THE MOONLIGHT, THE. D. Pro. and 3 a. Charles Osborne. Leeds Amphi., October 30, 1871.

FACE TO FACE. D. 2 a. Gilbert à Beckett. Liverpool P.O.W., March 29, 1869.

FACE TO FACE. D. 3 a. Herbert J. Stanley. Dewsbury T.R., April 5, 1875.

FACE TO FACE. D. 4 a. T. Archer. Marylebone, May 19, 1877.

FACE TO FACE. D. H. T. Munns. Birmingham P.O.W., November 27, 1877.

FACE TO FACE; OR, AT HOME AND ABROAD. D. Chas. Irving Hall. Macclesfield T.R., October 24, 1872.

FACE TO FACE; OR, MY AUNT'S LUGGAGE. C. 2 a. A. E. Harbourn. Chiswick T. of Varieties, September 6, 1869.

FACES IN THE FIRE. C. 3 a. Leicester Buckingham. St. James's, February 25, 1865.

FACHEUX, LES. C. Molière. 1661.

FACILE; OR, LOVE THE CONQUEROR. C.D. 3 a. Geo. Rose Norton and Francis Chamier. St. John's Wood Wellington H., December 18, 1905.

FACING THE MUSIC. F.C. 3 a. J. H. Darnley. Liverpool P.O.W., May 22, 1899; Brixton T., June 5, 1899; Strand, February 1, 1900.

FACTIOUS CITIZEN; OR, THE MELANCHOLY VISIONER, THE. C. Duke's T. Pr. 1685.

FACTORY ASSASSIN, THE. See *Dumb Man*.

FACTORY BELLE, THE. M.P.. 1 a. Wr. and comp. by J. Tabrar. Camberwell Empire, October 14, 1907.

FACTORY BOY; OR, THE LOVE SACRIFICE, THE. Dom. D. 3 a. J. T. Haines. Surrey, June 7, 1840.

FACTORY FIRE, THE. P. Adap. fr. the Dutch by Havard Pearcey. (Orig. prod. at Royalty under title *A Case of Arson*, February 11, 1905.) Shaftesbury, November 13, 1905.

FACTORY GIRL, THE. Dom. D. D.L., October 6, 1832. See *All that Glitters*, etc.

FACTORY LAD, THE. Dom. D. 2 a. John Walker. Surrey, July 21, 1834.

FACTORY STRIKE, THE. Dom. D. 3 a. G. F. Taylor. Victoria, October 17, 1836.

FADDIMIR; OR, THE TRIUMPH OF ORTHODOXY. C.O. 2 a. Arthur Reed. M. by Oscar Neville. Vaudeville, April 29, 1889.

FADDISTS, THE. Piece. 3 sc. Edith Balfour, Eliz. Strode, and J. Condurier. St. James's, June 27, 1905.

FADED FLOWERS. P. 1 a. Arthur à Beckett. Hay., April 6, 1872; Garrick, January 19, 1895.

FADETTE. O. 3 a. M. by Maillart. Eng. ver. by W. Grist. Liverpool R. Court (first perf. in Eng.), January 18, 1886.

FADETTE; OR, THE GOLDEN GADFLY. D. T. L. Greenwood. Rochdale P.O.W., October 9, 1871.

FADOROUGH AND THE BLACK PROPHET. D. 4 a. H. J. Stanley. Liverpool Adelphi, July 4, 1898.

FAERY PASTORALL; OR, FORREST OF ELVES, THE. Wm. Percy. 1601.

FAGGOT-BINDER; OR, THE MOCK DOCTOR, THE. C. Transl. fr. Molière by Foote. Pr. 1762.

FAGIN. An Epis. reprod. in a new ver. fr. *Oliver Twist*. Brixton Empress, October 28, 1907.

FAIGALE. P. (in Yiddish). N. Rackow. Standard, August 13, 1898.

FAINT HEART NEVER WON FAIR LADY. Ca. 1 a. J. R. Planché. Olympic, February 28, 1839; D.L., April 11, 1853.

FAINT HEART NEVER WON FAIR LADY Bijou, Bedford Street, W.C., March 9, 1893.

FAINT HEART WHICH DID WIN A FAIR LADY, A. C. 1 a. J. P. Wooler. Strand, February 9, 1863.

FAIR, THE. Panto. Ent. Ascr. to Rich. C.G., 1750; rev. 1752.

FAIR AMERICAN, THE. C.O. F. Pilon. M. by Carter. D.L., May 18, 1782. Pr. 1785.

FAIR ANCHORESS OF PAUSILIPPO, THE. C. Massinger. Ac. by King's Co., January 26, 1640.

FAIR AND FOUL WEATHER. J. Taylor. Hyde's Cata. of the Bodleian Library. 1715.

FAIR AND SQUARE. D. 5 a. Alexander B. Bele. Barnsley T.R., September 7, 1888.

FAIR APOSTATE, THE. T. A. M'Donald. Pr. 1791. N.ac.

FAIR BARGAIN, A. F.C. 1 a. G. Harley. Adap. fr. the French. Whaley Bridge Mechanics' Inst., September 7, 1894.

FAIR BIGAMIST, A. P. 4 a. U. Burford. Royalty, September 20, 1888.

FAIR CAPTIVE, THE. T. L.I.F., 1720. Ascr. to John Gay by Thos. Whincop. (?) Same as Mrs. Heywood's T.

FAIR CAPTIVE, THE. T. L.I.F., March 4, 1721. Pr. 1721. Orig. wr. by Capt. Hurst and rewritten by Mrs. Heywood.

FAIR CHEATING; OR, THE WISE ONES OUTWITTED. M.F. M. by Parry. D.L., June 15, 1814.

FAIR CIRCASSIAN, THE. Dr. perf. Dr. Samuel Croxall. Pr. 1720. A versification of the "Song of Solomon."

FAIR CIRCASSIAN, THE. T. S. J. Pratt. f. on Hawkesworth's "Almoran and Hamet." D.L., November 27, 1781. Pr. 1781.

FAIR CIRCASSIAN; OR, THE CHEVALIER, THE COUNT, AND THE ITALIAN, THE. D. 2 a. C. H. Hazlewood. Britannia, November 25, 1872.

FAIR CONQUEST, A. Dr. Episode. 1 a. A. E. Drinkwater. Gt. Grimsby P.O.W., July 18, 1887.

FAIR CONSTANCE OF ROME. P. 2 parts. Anthony Munday, in conj. with Hathwaye, Drayton, and Dekker. Ac. 1600. N.p.

FAIR CRUSADER, THE. O. 3 a. Pr. 1815. ? N.ac.

FAIR DECEIVERS. Ca. Carr Church. Eastbourne Town H., August 23, 1893.

FAIR EMM, THE MILLER'S DAUGHTER OF MANCHESTER, WITH THE LOVE OF WILLIAM THE CONQUEROR. C. Ac. by Lord Strange's servants. Pr. 1631.

FAIR ENCOUNTER, A. Adapt. fr. *Les Souliers de Bal* by Octave Gastineau. Paris (Th. du Gymnase Dramatique), July, 1868.

FAIR ENCOUNTER, A. Ca. 1 a. Fr. the French. Chas. Marsham Rae. Hay., January 30, 1875.

FAIR EQUESTRIENNE; OR, THE CIRCUS RIDER, A. Mus. trifle. 1 a. Adap. by Haslingden Russell fr. Pfahl's *Die Kunstreiterin* Bristol Prince's, March 14, 1890; Trafalgar Square, March 8, 1893.

FAIR EXAMPLE; OR, THE MODISH CITIZEN, THE. C. R. Estcourt. D.L. Pr. 1706. L.I.F., October 17, 1717.

FAIR EXCHANGE, A. Ca. 1 a. Montagu Williams. Olympic, August 27, 1860.

FAIR FAME. D. 4 a. J. T. Day. Longton T.R., August 8, 1884; Kilburn Town H., February 5, 1885.

FAIR FAVOURITE, THE. T.C. Sir W Davenant. 1673. Lic. 1638. Pr. 1673.

FAIR FRANCE. D. 4 a. West Digges. Queen's, April 18, 1874.

FAIR FUGITIVES. Mus. Ent. Miss Anna Maria Porter. C.G., May 16, 1803. M. by Dr. Busby. N.p.

FAIR GABRIELLE, THE. Oa. M. by Barham Livins. Lyceum, September 5, 1822.

FAIR GAME; OR, FIRST OF OCTOBER. F. 2 a. Bate Dudley. C.G., December 21, 1813.

FAIR HIBERNIAN, THE. T. Anthony Davidson. N.ac.

FAIR LADY. C. Transl. fr. *La Dama Duende* of Calderon. Pr. 1807.

FAIR MAID OF BRISTOL, THE. C. Ac before K. and Q. at Hampton Court. Pr. 1605.

FAIR MAID OF CLIFTON, THE. Extrav. F. R. Goodyer. Nottingham T.R., March 30, 1872.

FAIR MAID OF ITALY, THE. P. Ac. by Earl of Sussex's men, January 12, 1593.

FAIR MAID OF LONDON, THE. Anon. Lic 1598.

FAIR MAID OF PERTH; OR, THE BATTLE OF THE INCH, THE. Hist. D. 3 a. H. M. Milner and T. Lacy. F. on Sir W. Scott's novel. Coburg, June 23, 1828.

FAIR MAID OF THE EXCHANGE, THE C. Thos. Heywood. Pr. 1607.

FAIR MAID OF THE INN, THE. T.C. Beaumont and Fletcher. Possibly by Fletcher only. Ac. 1626. Pr. 1647.

FAIR MAID OF THE WEST; OR, A GIRL WORTH GOLD, THE. C. 2 parts. Thos. Heywood. Ac. and circa 1617, and before the K. and Q. 1631. Pr. 1631. See *A Girl Worth Gold*.

FAIR OF ST. GERMAIN, THE. F. John Ozell. Transl. of Boursault's *Foire de St. Germains*. L.I.F. Pr. 1718.

FAIR ONE WITH THE GOLDEN LOCKS, THE. Fairy Spec. 1 a. J. R. Planché. Hay., December 26, 1843; Marylebone, October, 1853; Sadler's Wells, April, 1857; Adelphi, 1859.

FAIR ORPHAN, THE. C.O. 3 a. Ac. at Lynn. Pr. 1771.

FAIR PARRICIDE, THE. T. 3 a. Anon. Pr. circa 1752. N.ac.

FAIR PARRICIDE, THE. P. Crane. 1761.

FAIR PENITENT, THE. T. 5 a. Nicholas Rowe. Suggested by Massinger's *Fatal Dowry*. L.I.F. Pr. 1703. D.L., November 15, 1814.

FAIR PLAY. Melo-d. 5 a. C. Crozier and Percy Milton. Bradford Prince's, May 6, 1889.

FAIR PRETENDER, A. C.D. 2 a. J. Palgrave Simpson. P.O.W., May 10, 1865.

FAIR PRINCESS, THE. Burl. Wr. and comp. by Fred Bernard. Walsall Gaiety, December 20, 1886.

FAIR QUAKER; OR, THE HUMOURS OF THE NAVY, THE. C. Capt. Edward Thompson. D.L., November 10, 1773. Pr. 1773.

FAIR QUAKER OF DEAL; OR, THE HUMOURS OF THE NAVY, THE. C. C. Shadwell. Pr. 1710. D.L., 1714; C.G., April 13, 1748.

FAIR QUARREL, A. C. T. Middleton and W. Rowley. Pr. 1617. Ac. before the K. by the Prince's servants.

FAIR REFUGEE; OR, THE RIVAL JEWS, THE. C. Hay., 1785. N.p.

FAIR RIVALS, THE. T. 3 a. John Hewitt. Ac. at Bath. Pr. 1729.

FAIR ROSAMOND. D. 3 a. Saville. West London, October 18, 1821.

FAIR ROSAMOND. Hist. O. 4 a. M. by J. Barnett. D.L., February 28, 1837.

FAIR ROSAMOND. P. Michael Field. Pr. 1884.

FAIR ROSAMOND. Pastl. Prol. and 3 a. E. W. Godwin. Adapt. fr. Lord Tennyson's *Becket*. Cannizaro Woods, Wimbledon, July 20, 1886.

FAIR ROSAMOND. Hist. D. 4 a. Brandon Ellis. Widnes Alexandra, August 7, 1893.

FAIR ROSAMOND. See *Fayre Rosamond*.

FAIR ROSAMOND; OR, THE DAYS OF THE PLANTAGENETS. Hist. D. 4 a. W. M. Akhurst. Sanger's Amphi., March 3, 1873.

FAIR ROSAMOND; OR, THE MAZE, THE MAID, AND THE MONARCH. Burl. 1 a. F. C. Burnand. Olympic, April 21, 1862.

FAIR ROSAMOND, ACCORDING TO THE HISTORY OF ENGLAND. Burl. T. P. Taylor. Sadler's Wells, 1838.

FAIR ROSAMOND'S BOWER; OR, THE MONARCH, THE MAIDEN, THE MAZE, AND THE MIXTURE. Burla. 1 a. Fredk. Langbridge. Publ. by S. French, Ltd.

FAIR SINNER, A. P. 5 a. G. W. Appleton. Ipswich T.R., January 23, 1885; Gaiety, March 4, 1885.

FAIR SINNERS; OR, DESPERATE WOMEN. D. 4 a. Paget. Adapt. fr. the French. Wolverhampton T.R., May 2, 1881.

FAIR SPANISH CAPTIVE, THE. T.C. Circa. 1661.

FAIR STAR OF ANTWERP. P. Mentioned in Sir Henry Herbert's MS. Diary, September 15, 1624.

FAIR WOMEN AND BRAVE MEN. P. 4 a. Theodore Tharp. Barnstaple New T., September 23, 1897; Holloway Parkhurst, November 7, 1898.

FAIR WORDS AND FOUL DEEDS. D. 3 a. W. Travers. East London, July 6, 1868.

FAIR, ETC. See *Fayre*.

FAIRIES, THE. O. David Garrick, fr. *Midsummer Night's Dream*. M. by Mr. Smith. D.L. February 3, 1775. Pr. 1755.

FAIRIES' HAUNT, THE. Ballet Div. D.L., July 2, 1856.

FAIRIES' REVELS; OR, LOVE IN THE HIGHLANDS. Burl. Pr. 1802.

FAIRLEIGH'S BIRTHRIGHT. D. 3 a. G. Peel. Britannia, August 26, 1878.

FAIRLY CAUGHT. Ca. 1 a. Geo. D. Day. Parkhurst, May 23, 1892.

FAIRLY FOILED. D. 4 a. Oswald Allan. Grecian, May 29, 1871.

FAIRLY HIT AND FAIRLY MISSED. F. 1 a. J. Martin. Publ. in Duncombe's list.

FAIRLY PUZZLED. V. Oliver Brand. M. by Hamilton Clarke. St. Geo. H., May 19, 1884.

FAIRY AND THE FAWN, THE. Panto. Grecian, 1853.

FAIRY BENISON, THE. Int. Rev. Samuel Bishop. Designed for C.G., but rejected. Wr. 1766. Pr. 1796. See *Fairy Festival.*

FAIRY BLOSSOM. Fairy P. 1 a. F. D. Adams. Publ. by S. French, Ltd.

FAIRY CIRCLE. Adelphi, July 5, 1857.

FAIRY COURT, THE. Int. Francis Gentleman. Ac. at Chester. Circa 1760. N.p.

FAIRY FAVOUR, THE. Masque. Thos. Hull. C.G. Pr. 1767.

FAIRY FAVOUR; OR, HARLEQUIN ANIMATED, THE. Panto. Wrighten. D.L., 1790-1. Songs pr. 1790.

FAIRY FESTIVAL, THE. Masque. D.L., May 13, 1797. F. on Bishop's *Fairy Benison.*

FAIRY GLEN. O. Oliver Brand. M. by P. von Tugginer. St. Geo. H., April 22, 1884.

FAIRY GODFATHER, THE. P. 1 a. L. C. White. Perf. by amateurs. Bijou, Bayswater, January 31, 1906.

FAIRY HILL; OR, MAY DAY. Pastl. O. 3 a. Wm. Mansell. Pr. 1784.

FAIRY KNIGHT, THE. A P. stated to have been wr. by Ford and Decker.

FAIRY LAKE, THE. M. Rom. Adapt. by Alex. Lee, fr. O. of *Le Lac des Fées.* M. by Auber, Hérold, Marschner, and Mercadante. Strand, May 13, 1839, and D.L., October 26, 1839.

FAIRY MADGE. Dr. Sk. 1 a. Claude Trevelyan. Battersea Park Town T., November 28, 1891.

FAIRY MASQUE, THE. A masque prod. at Court about A.D. 1620.

FAIRY OAK, THE. Rom. O. M. by Henry Forbes. D.L., October 18, 1845.

FAIRY OF THE LAKE, THE. John Thelwall. Pr. 1801.

FAIRY PRINCE, A. P. Cyril Clayton. Coronet, April 24, 1902.

FAIRY PRINCE, THE. Masque. Geo. Colman. M. by Dr. Arne. C.G., November 12, 1771. Pr. 1771. Borr. fr. Ben Jonson.

FAIRY QUEEN. See *Epic Poems.*

FAIRY QUEEN, THE. P. Destroyed by Mr. Warburton's servant.

FAIRY QUEEN, THE. O. Anon. Hay. Pr. 1692. M. by Purcell. Fr. *Midsummer Night's Dream.* Orig. prod. Dorset Gardens, 1692; rev. St. Geo. H., June 15, 1901.

FAIRY RING, THE. Burl. Bristol T.R., March 29, 1869.

FAIRY TALE, THE. Dr. Perf. Geo. Colman. Fr. his adpt. of *A Midsummer Night's Dream.* D.L., October 26, 1764. Pr. 1764.

FAIRY TALES OF MOTHER GOOSE, THE. Extrav. Adelphi, April, 1855.

FAIRY UNCLE, THE. Piece. 1 a. Tom Gallon. Adapt. fr. a Christmas story. New T., November 28, 1907. See *Filby the Faker.*

FAIRY. See *Faery.*

FAIRY'S DILEMMA, THE. Dom. Panto. 2 a. W. S. Gilbert. Garrick, May 3, 1904.

FAIRY'S FATHER, A. Dr. Sk. 1 a. C. S. Cheltnam. Olympic, February 24, 1862.

FAIRY'S POST BOX, THE. C.O. 1 a. Palgrave Simpson. M. by Arthur Hervey. Court, May 21, 1885.

FAIRYLAND. Fairy Extrav. 1 a. Alfred Paxton. Publ. by S. French, Ltd.

FAITH. P. F. Wills. Gaiety.

FAITH. C. 1 a. J. H. Lofting. (Perf. by amateurs.) Cripplegate Inst., February 27, 1906.

FAITH; OR, A WIFE AND A MOTHER. D. 3 a. New ver. of *Grace Huntley.* Manchester T.R., August 21, 1879.

FAITH; OR, EDDICATION AND RIGHTS. C.D. 3 a. John Lart. Gaiety, August 27, 1884.

FAITH AND FALSEHOOD; OR, THE FATE OF THE BUSHRANGER. D. 3 a. W. Leman Rede. Queen's, September 22, 1834.

FAITH AND HOPE. D. 4 a. Jas. Rodway. New Cross Pub. H., April 12, 1886.

FAITH, HOPE, AND CHARITY; OR, CHANCE AND CHANGE. Dom. D. 3 a. E. L. Blanchard. Surrey, July 7, 1845.

FAITH UNDER PERIL. D. H. Abel. Pavilion, August 9, 1873.

FAITH'S FRAUD. T. 5 a. R. Landor. Pr. 1841.

FAITHFUL BRIDE OF GRANADA, THE. C. Wm. Tavener. D.L. Pr. 1704.

FAITHFUL FRIEND, A. D. 4 a. L. Gilbert and T. W. Rawson. Liverpool Rotunda, December 15, 1902; Balham Empire, November 9, 1903; West London, July 18, 1904.

FAITHFUL FRIENDS, THE. C. Beaumont and Fletcher. Ent. Stationers' Co., June 29, 1660. N.p.

FAITHFUL GENERAL, THE. T. By a lady ("M. N."). F. on *The Loyal Subject.* Hay, January 3, 1706. Pr. 1706.

FAITHFUL HEART, THE. D. 4 a. R. Palgrave. Bristol New T.R., October 18, 1875.

FAITHFUL IRISHMAN, THE. See *The Committee.*

FAITHFUL IRISHWOMAN, THE. F. Mrs. Clive. D.L., March 18, 1765. N.p.

FAITHFUL JAMES. F.C. 1 a. B. C. Stephenson. Turnham Green H., October 24, 1889; Ealing Lyric H., November 10, 1889; Court, July 16, 1892; December 9, 1893.

FAITHFUL PAIR; OR, VIRTUE IN DISTRESS, THE. T. 3 a. John Maxwell. Ac. at York. Pl. 1740.

FAITHFUL SERVANT, THE. See *The Grateful Servant.*

FAITHFUL SHEPHERD, THE. Past. C. from the Italian, by D. D. Gent. Pr. 1633. Taken from *Pastor Fido* of Guarini.

FAITHFUL SHEPHERD, THE. Past. T.C. Anon., but partly by Sir Richard Fanshaw, trans. from Guarini. Pr. 1736.

FAITHFUL SHEPHERD, THE. D. Past. Trans. by Grove, 1782.

FAITHFUL SHEPHERDESS, THE. Dram. Past. J. Fletcher. Pr. circa 1610. Reproduced before K. and Q. on Twelfth Night, 1633. Rev. Wimbledon, Cannizaro Woods, 1885, and Botanic Gardens, Reg. Pk., July 6, 1903.

FAITHFUL UNTO DEATH. D. E. Newbound. Britannia, March 13, 1876.

FAITHFUL UNTO DEATH. D. E. M. Robson and Edwd. Compton. Bristol New T.R., September 2, 1881.

FAITHLESS FRIENDS. D. Victoria, June 11, 1821.

FAITHLESS WIFE, THE. D. 4 a. Mrs. S. Lane. Britannia, April 15, 1876.

FALCON, THE. P. 1 a. Alfred Tennyson. St. James's, December 18, 1879.

FALCONIERE, IL. O. Benventuo. Venice, 1878.

FALKA. Op. C. 3 a. H. B. Farnie. Adap. fr. the French of Leterrier and Vanloo. M. by F. Chassaigne. Comedy, October 29, 1883.

FALL BABYLONS, DER. O. Sophr. April 9, 1841.

FALL OF ÆGYPT, THE. Or. Hawkesworth. 1774.

FALL OF ALGIERS, THE. O. M. by Bishop. D.L., January 19, 1825.

FALL OF BOB; OR, THE ORACLE OF GIN, THE. T. Timothy Scrub (John Kelly). Hay., Pr. 1736.

FALL OF CARTHAGE, THE. Hist. T. Wm. Shirley. Advertised as int. to be pr. N.ac.

FALL OF CARTHAGE, THE. T. Wm. Watkins. Ac. at Whitby and pr. 1802.

FALL OF CARTHAGE, THE. T. John Joshua, Earl of Carysfort. Pr. 1810.

FALL OF EGYPT, THE. Or. Wainwright. 1780. N.p. See *The Fall of Ægypt*.

FALL OF HAROLD, THE. "A Chaunt fr. Dr. Rom. by Pearce preparing for C.G., by the author of "Hartford Bridge." Pr. November 13, 1792.

FALL OF JERUSALEM, THE. Dr. Poem. H. H. Milman. 1820.

FALL OF JERUSALEM, THE. Hebrew O. 5 a. Latiner. Standard, November 16, 1895.

FALL OF KHARTOUM; OR, THE DEATH OF GENERAL GORDON, THE. D. H. J. Stanley and C. Hermann. Salford P.O.W., April 6, 1885.

FALL OF KHARTOUM, THE. D. Durham R. Albany T. April 11, 1885.

FALL OF MARTINICO; OR, BRITANNIA TRIUMPHANT, THE. Prel. C.G., 1794. N.p.

FALL OF MILAN, THE. T. Hay., 1724. N.p.

FALL OF MORTIMER, THE. Hist. p. A completion of Ben Jonson's imperfect p. of *Mortimer's Fall* (1635). Pr. 1731.

FALL OF MORTIMER, THE. Hist. p. A republication of the foregoing, by Mr. Wilkes. Pr. 1763.

FALL OF MORTIMER, THE. T. Rt. Hon. Morris, Lord Rokeby. Pr. 1806. N. ac.

FALL OF PHAETON, THE. Intermixed with a panto. called *Harlequin Restored; or, Taste à la Mode*, by Mr. Pritchard. M. by Arne. D.L. Pr. 1736.

FALL OF PORTUGAL; OR, THE ROYAL EXILES, THE. T. Ascr. to Dr. Wolcot (*i.e.*, Peter Pindar). Pr. 1808. N.ac.

FALL OF PUBLIC SPIRIT, THE. Dram. Satire. 2 a. Pr. 1757.

FALL OF ROBESPIERRE, THE. Hist. D. S. T. Coleridge. Pr. 1794.

FALL OF SAGUNTUM, THE. T. Phillip Frowde. L.I.F., January 16, 1727. Pr. 1727.

FALL OF TARQUIN; OR, THE DISTRESSED LOVERS, THE. T. Ac. by the D. of Norfolk's servants at Merchant Taylors' H. in York. Wr. by a gentleman of York. Pr. 1713.

FALL OF TARQUIN, THE. T. Wm. Hunt. Pr. 1713. Another edition of foregoing. N. ac. or pr. anywhere but at York.

FALL OF TARQUIN, THE. See *Brutus*.

FALL OF THE EARL OF ESSEX, THE. T. John Ralph. An alt. fr. Bankes's *The Unhappy Favourite*. Goodman's Felds T., February 1, 1731. Pr. 1731.

FALL OF THE FRENCH MONARCHY; OR, LOUIS THE SIXTEENTH. Hist. T. John Bartholomew. Pr. 1794.

FALL OF THE LEAF, THE. P. 2 a. R. C. Carton. Manchester T.R., September 7, 1893.

FALL OF THE MOGUL, THE. T. Rev. T. Maurice. Pr. 1806. N.ac.

FALLACY; OR, THE TROUBLES OF GREAT HERMENIA. In Harleian MSS., No. 6,869.

FALLEN AMONG THIEVES. D. Pro. and 4 a. W. E. Morton. Eleph. and C., March 10, 1888.

FALLEN AMONG THIEVES. D. 5 a. Frank Harvey. Grand, September 29, 1890.

FALLEN AMONG THIEVES. See *From Father to Son*.

FALLEN ANGEL, THE. Sk. 1 sc. Mark Melford. Brixton Empress, November 18, 1901.

FALLING STAR, A. Cant. R. Henry. M. by Algernon Lindo. Steinway H., July 4, 1893.

FALLS OF CLYDE; OR, THE FAIRIES, THE. Dram. Past. 5 a. Ac. at Edinburgh. Pr. 1806.

FALLS OF THE CLYDE, THE. Melo-d. 2 a. Geo. Soane. M. by Cooke. D.L., October 19, 1817.

FALSACAPPA. Op. bo. M. by Offenbach. Eng. ver., fr. the French of Meilhac and Halévy, by Henry S. Leigh. See *The Brigands*. Globe, April 22, 1871.

FALSE ACCUSATION; OR, WHILE THERE'S LIFE THERE'S HOPE, THE. D. F. Fuller. Marylebone, May 3, 1875.

FALSE ALARM. A. F. 1 a. Alf. Young. Holborn, October 5, 1872.

FALSE ALARMS; OR, MY COUSIN. C.O. 3 a. James Kenney. D.L., January 12, 1807; Lyceum, August 27, 1810.

FALSE AND CONSTANT. C. 2 a. Joseph Lunn. Tottenham St. Th., November 23, 1829.

FALSE AND TRUE; OR, THE IRISHMAN IN ITALY. M.C. 2 a. Rev. Moultrie. M. by Dr. Arnold. Hay., August 11, 1798; D.L., June 10, 1816; Rev., C.G., 1842.

FALSE APPEARANCES. C. Fr. Boissey's *Dehors Trompeurs* by General Conway. Epilogue wr. by General Burgoyne. D.L., April 20, 1789. Pr. 1789.

FALSE CARDS. D. Auguste Creamer. Bury Athenæum H., January 11, 1873.

FALSE COLOURS. C. Edward Morris. Ac. by D.L. Co. at the O.H. in the Hay., April 3, 1793. Pr. 1793.

FALSE COLOURS. Ca. G. F. Pass. Royalty, October 8, 1881.

FALSE COLOURS; OR, THE FREE TRADER. Nautical D. 2 a. Edwd. Fitzball. C.G., March 4, 1837.

FALSE CONCORD. F. Rev. James Townley. C.G., March 20, 1764. Part of this was transplanted into *The Clandestine Marriage*. N.p.

FALSE COUNT; OR, A NEW WAY TO PLAY AN OLD GAME, THE. C. Mrs. Behn. A hint taken from *Précieuses Ridicules* f Molière. Duke's T. Pr. 1682. L.I.F., August 11, 1715.

FALSE DELICACIES. C. 3 a. Transl. fr. the French by "J. T." Pr. 1803.

FALSE DELICACY. C. Hugh Kelly. D.L., January 23, 1768 and 1782. Pr. 1768.

FALSE DELICACY. D. Transl. fr. Kotzebue by Benj. Thompson. P. 1800. N.ac.

FALSE DEMETRIUS. P. 5 a. Mr. Cumberland. Announced as in preparation at D.L. in 1802.

FALSE DERVISE, THE. Int. C. Dibdin. N.p. N.ac.

FALSE EVIDENCE. D. 5 a. Manchester St. James', August 19, 1889.

FALSE EVIDENCE. Melo-d. 4 a. Wynn Miller. Pav., September 14, 1891; Bradford Prince's, August 1, 1892.

FALSE FAVOURITE DISGRACED, AND THE REWARD OF LOYALTY, THE. T.C. Geo. Gerbier d'Ouvilly. Pr. 1657. N.ac.

FALSE FRIEND, A. D. 3 a. Shirley Howlett. Gordon Working Lads' Inst., Stanley Road, Liverpool, April 8, 1893.

FALSE FRIEND, THE. C. Sir J. Vanbrugh. D.L. Pr. 1702.

FALSE FRIEND, THE C. Alt. fr. Vanbrugh by J. P. Kemble. D.L., 1789. N.p.

FALSE FRIEND; OR, ASSASSIN OF THE ROCKS, THE. M.D. J. C. Cross. Ac. at the Circu. Pr. 1809. Bath, March 7, 1812.

FALSE FRIEND; OR, THE FATE OF DISOBEDIENCE, THE. T. Mary Pix. L.I.F. Pr. 1699.

FALSE FRIENDS. C. Transl. fr. the French of Mme. Genlis. Pr. 1781.

FALSE GLITTER; OR, THE MANCHESTER GIRL. C.D. Frank Harvey. Huddersfield T.R., April 22, 1875; Manchester Queen's, July 17, 1882.

FALSE GODS. Egypt. P. 4 a. Transl. by J. B. Fagan fr. *La Foi* (by Eugène Brieux). M. by Camille Saint-Saëns. H.M., September 14, 1909.

FALSE GUARDIANS OUTWITTED, THE. B.O. Wm. Goodall. Pr. 1740. ? N.ac.

FALSE HANDS AND FAITHFUL HEARTS. D. Pro. and 3 a. E. Towers. City of London, April 22, 1867.

FALSE HEARTS. D. 4 a. West Bromwich T.R., December 3, 1886.

FALSE HEIR, THE. A Droll out of Fletcher's *Scornful Lady*. 1672.

FALSE IMPRESSIONS. C. 5 a. Richd. Cumberland. Fr. the author's own novel, "Henry." C.G., November 23, 1797. Pr. 1797.

FALSE INDIFFERENCE. Dr. P. Mentioned in "Theatrical Recorder."

FALSE LIGHTS. D. 4 a. T. B. Bannister. Birkenhead T.R., April 9, 1886; Marylebone, November 22, 1886; Pav., August 1, 1887.

FALSE ONE, THE. T. Beaumont and Fletcher. Pr. 1647. F. on the adventures of Julius Cæsar while in Egypt.

FALSE PRIDE. C.D. 4 a. Miss May Holt. Norwich T.R., September 24, 1883; Vaudeville, May 22, 1884.

FALSE SHAME. C. 4 a. Transl. fr. the German of Kotzebue. Pr. 1799. N.ac.

FALSE SHAME. C. 3 a. Frank Marshall. Globe, November 4, 1872.

FALSE SHAME; OR, THE WHITE HYPOCRITE. C. Mackenzie, 1808.

FALSE STEP. P. 3 a. Prohibited p. Pub. by S. French, Limited.

FALSE STEPS. D. Fredk. Vanneck. Bristol T.R., September 19, 1887.

FALSE WIFE, A. D. 4 a. F. Marriott Watson. Pontefract Assmy. R., March 2, 1905; West London, July 10, 1905.

FALSE WITNESS. See *The Cross of Honour*.

FALSELY ACCUSED. D. 4 a. J. Cherry Griffiths. Britannia, August 7, 1876.

FALSELY ACCUSED. D. 4 a. Rita Carlyle. Pav., July 5, 1897.

FALSELY JUDGED. D. 3 a. Such Granville. Connaught, August 7, 1880.

FALSTAFF. C.O. 2 a. Ital. Lib. by Manfredo Maggione, f. on *The Merry Wives of Windsor*. M. by Balfe. H.M., July 19, 1838.

FALSTAFF. O. 3 a. Words fr. Shakespeare by Mosenthal. M. by Otto Nicolai. Prod. Berlin, March 9, 1849; H.M. (in English), May 3, 1864; Adelphi, February 11, 1878.

FALSTAFF. O. Ital. lib. by Arrigo Boito. f. on *The Merry Wives of Windsor*. M. by Verdi. Milan, February 1893; C.G., May 19, 1894; Students R. Coll. of M., December 11, 1896.

FALSTAFF'S WEDDING. C. A sequel to the second part of *King Henry IV*. Imitation of Shakespeare. Dr. Kenrick. Pr. 1766. Rev. and ac. at D.L., 1766.

FALSTAFF'S WEDDING. F. 2 a. The foregoing piece reduced. D.L., May 11, 1803. N.p.

FAME. C. 3 a. Chas. Marsham Rae. Hay., April 7, 1877.

FAMILIAR FRIEND, A. F. 1 a. Mark Lemon. Olympic, February 8, 1840.

FAMILIENTAG DER. C. 3 a. Gustav Kadelburg. Gt. Queen St., October 28, 1905.

FAMILIES SUPPLIED. F. Ernest Cuthbert. Adelphi, August 7, 1882.

FAMILLE PONT-BIQUET, LA. C. 3 a. Alexandre Bisson. Royalty, October 17, 1907.

FAMILY COMPACT, THE. F. Rev. John Rose. Hay., September 6, 1792. N.p.

FAMILY DISTRESS. D. Alt. fr. Kotzebue's *Self Immolation*. Hay., June 15, 1799.

FAMILY DISTRESS. P. Transl. fr. the *Self Immolation* of Kotzebue by H. Neuman. Pr. 1799. N. ac.

FAMILY FAILING, A. F. 1 a. John Oxenford. Hay., November 17, 1856.

FAMILY FIX, A. F. 3 a. Herbert Shelley. Northampton O.H., March 8, 1897.

FAMILY FOOL, THE. C. 3 a. Mark Melford. Edinburgh Prince's, March 6, 1882; Vaudeville, June 23, 1885.

FAMILY GHOST, THE. P. Annie Brunton. Hanley T.R., March 17, 1881.

FAMILY HONOUR. C. 3 a. Frank Marshall. Aquarium, May 18, 1878.

FAMILY JARS. F. 1 a. Joseph Lunn. Hay., August 26, 1822; D.L., April 10, 1824.

FAMILY LEGEND, THE. T. Joanna Baillie. Pr. 1810. F. on same Highland story as *Glenara*. Edinburgh New T.R. Pro. by Walter Scott. Epil. by Mackenzie. D.L., May 29, 1815.

FAMILY LEGEND, THE. Ent. Tom Taylor. Wr. for German Reed. March 31, 1862.

FAMILY MATTER, A. C. 3 a. C. G. Compton and A. G. Hockley. Garrick, June 27, 1894.

FAMILY NOVELETTE, A. F. E. Nesbitt and Oswald Barrow. New Cross P.H., February 21, 1894.

FAMILY OF LOVE, THE. C. Thos. Middleton. Ac. by children of H.M.'s Revels. Pr. 1608.

FAMILY PARTY, A. Mus. Sk. Corney Grain. St. Geo. H., December 26, 1889.

FAMILY PARTY, THE. F. Ac. at Hay., July 11, 1789. Pr. 1789.

FAMILY PICTURES. F. 1 a. E. Stirling. Marylebone, March 11, 1849.

FAMILY POLITICS. C. 3 a. Pr. 1814. ? N.ac.

FAMILY PRIDE. C. 5 a. R. Sullivan. Old p., publ. by S. French, Ltd.

FAMILY PRIDE. D. 2 a. G. Murray. Adap. fr. "Le Pauvre Gentilhomme." Sadler's Wells, May, 1862.

FAMILY QUARRELS. C.O. Thos. Dibdin. M. by J. Moorehead, Braham, and Reeve. C.G., December 18, 1802. Pr. 1802.

FAMILY SECRET, THE. C. 3 a. Edmund Falconer. Hay., May 9, 1860.

FAMILY SECRET, THE. Dom. D. 2 a. H. Leslie. Manchester T.R., March, 1861.

FAMILY TIES. C. 3 a. F. C. Burnand. Strand, September 29, 1877.

FAMINE, THE. P. Pro. and 4 a. Herbert O'Grady. Dublin Queen's, April 26, 1886; Grand, June 28, 1886.

FAMOUS BEAUTY, THE. C.O. 3 a. H. J Stanley. M. by C. R. Engel. Hoyland Paragon, March 15, 1892 (C.P.).

FAMOUS CHRONICLE HISTORY OF EDWARD I. See *Edward I.*

FAMOUS HISTORIE OF SIR THOMAS WYAT, THE. Dekker and Webster. Prob. abridgment of *Ladye Jane*. Pr. 1607.

FAMOUS HISTORIES, THE. D. Pr. 1594.

FAMOUS WARS OF HENRY I. AND PRINCE OF WALES. P. by Drayton, Decker, and Chettle. Wr. in 1598. In Barker's list, 1814.

FAMOUS VICTORIES OF HENRY THE FIFTH, THE. Hist. D. Ac. before 1588.

FAMULUS. See "The Westminster Plays," "Latin Plays."

FANAL, LE. O. Adam. Paris, 1849.

FAN-FAN, THE TULIP; OR, A SOLDIER'S FORTUNE. D. 2 a. W. E. Suter. Adap. fr. the French of Paul Meurice. Th. de l'Ambigu Comique, November 6, 1858. Perf. as *Court and Camp*. Princess's, May 27, 1863; afterwards pl. as *The Days of Louis XV.* and *The King's Butterfly.*

FANATIC, THE. Dram. C. 4 a. John T. Day. Margate T.R., July 23, 1897; Strand, October 21, 1897.

FANATICO PER LA MUSICA. O. Mayer. 1799.

FANCHETTE. C.O. 3 a. Dubreuil, Humbert, and Buraïn. M. by F. Bernicat and A. Messager. Adap. by Oscar Weil. Liverpool R. Court, January 13, 1894.

FANCHETTE; OR, THE WILL-O'-THE-WISP. D. 4 a. Mrs. Bateman. Adap. fr. the German *Die Grille*. Edinburgh T.R., March 6, 1871; Lyceum, September 11, 1871.

FANCHON. O. Himmel. 1765-1814.

FANCHON, THE CRICKET. P. A. Waldauer. Ac. New Orleans, 1860.

FANCHONETTE; OR, THE CRICKET. D. 5 a. F. on *Die Grille*. Originally prod. U.S.A. Standard, September 30, 1871.

FANCIED QUEEN, THE (THE FANCY'D QUEEN). O. Robt. Drury. C.G. Pr. 1733.

FANCIES CHASTE AND NOBLE. T.C. J. Ford. Phœnix, 1638. Lic. 1637. Pr. 1638.

FANCIES (OR FANCY'S) FESTIVAL. Masque. 5 a. Thos. Jordan. Pr. 1657. Ac. privately.

FANCOURT'S FOLLY. C.D. 1 a. B. W. Findon. Folkestone Pleasure Gardens, May 14, 1894.

FANCY BALL, THE. C.Sk. in Hindustani. Gaiety (by Parsee Co.), December 12, 1885.

FANCY BALL, THE; OR, NUBBS, Q.C., THE. O.C. 2 a. R. Wardroper. M. by Wm. W. Meadows. Ipswich O.H., February 11, 1889.

FANCY DRESS BALL, A. Ml. and Mimettic Sk. Corney Grain. St. Geo. H., February 6, 1892.

FANCY FAIR, A. Ca. Ralph Lumley. Ealing Lyric H., September 22, 1892.

FANCY LAND; OR, THE IDEAL KING. Burl. Gunner C. F. Fuller. H.M.S. "Rainbow," April 9, 1884.

FANCY'S FESTIVALS. Masque. 5 a. Thos. Jordan. 1657.

FANCY'S SKETCH. Burla. J. R. Planchè. Adelphi.

FAND. P. in ver. in 2 a. W. S. Blunt. Dublin Abbey, April 20, 1907.

FANISCA. O. 3 a. Cherubini. Words by Sonnleithner fr. the Fr. Prod. at Vienna Kärthnerthor T., February 25, 1806.

FANNETTE; OR, UP IN THE DARK. D. 1 a. J. B. Johnstone. Pav., October 24, 1868.

FANNIKIN. M.C. 1 a. H. F. Maltby. M. by Katherine Barry and H. F. Maltby. Pier Pav., Hastings, May 24, 1906.

FANNY. F. G. R. Sims and Cecil Raleigh. Liverpool P.O.W., April 8, 1895; Strand, April 15, 1895.

FANNY AND THE SERVANT PROBLEM. P. 4 a. Jerome K. Jerome. Aldwych, October 14, 1908.

FANNY LEAR. Royalty, October 26, 1885.

FANNY'S AMERICAN. Sk. Mrs. Frances M. Gostling. Worthing Pier Pavilion, July 13, 1909.

FANNY'S FLIRTATIONS. F. Wynn Miller and Philip Howard. Pav., July 11, 1887.

FANTASIO. O. 3 a. Offenbach. 1872.

FANTASIO. O. M. and lib. by Ethel M. Smyth. Weimar, 1898.

FANTASMA. O. Persiani (Paris, 1843).

FANTASTICKS, THE. Ro.C. 3 a. Adap. by "Geo. Fleming" fr. Rostand's *Les Romanesques*. Royalty, May 29, 1900.

FANTINITZA. C.O. 3 a. Adap. by H. S. Leigh. M. by Von Suppée. Alhambra, June 20, 1878.

FAR AWAY WHERE ANGELS DWELL. D. 3 a. C. H. Hazlewood. Britannia, October 6, 1869.

FAR FETCHED, ETC. See *Farre Fetched, etc.*

FAR FROM THE MADDING CROWD. Past D. 3 a. Adap. by Thos. Hardy and Comyns Carr from Hardy's novel. Liverpool P.O.W., February 27, 1882; Globe, April 29, 1882.

FARCE WRITER, THE. F. C.G., October, 1815.

FARDAROUGHA AND THE BLACK PROPHET. D. 4 a. H. J. Stanley. Liverpool Adelphi, July 4, 1898.

FAREWELL AND RETURN; OR, THE FORTUNE OF WAR, THE. Ballad F. Anon. Circa. 1739.

FAREWELL, FOLLY; OR, THE YOUNGER THE WISER. C. P. A. Motteux. Pr. 1767. (Contains a m. interlude, *The Mountebank: or, The Humours of the Fair*. Ac. at T.R. F. on *The Amorous Miser*.

FAREWELL SUPPER, THE. C. 1 a. A. Schnitzler. Transl. by Edith A. Browne and Mrs. Alix Grein. (Prod. by the New Stage Club.) Bayswater Bijou, March 11, 1908.

FARINAGHOLKAJINGO. Sicilian Amusement. Lyceum (fourth time), November 11, 1835.

FARINELLI! S.C.O. 2 a. Wds. by C. Z. Barnett. M. by J. Barnett. D.L., February 8, 1839.

FARM BY THE SEA, THE. D. 1 a. F. Wedmore. Adap. fr. *Jean-Marie* by André Theuriet. Vaudeville, May 29, 1889.

FARMHOUSE, THE. C. 3 a. J. P. Kemble. D.L. Pr. 1789. Fr. Johnson's *Country Lasses*.

FARMHOUSE STORY, THE. C. 3 a. Anon. Pr. 1803.

FARMER, THE. Mus. F. John O'Keefe. Pr. 1798. C.G., 1787. D.L., May 17, 1814, and May 8, 1822.

FARMER HAYSEED. F. 1 a. Harry Pleon. Pub. by J. Dicks.

FARMER'S DAUGHTER OF THE SEVERNSIDE; OR, MR. AND MRS. TOODLES, THE. Dom. D. 2 a. R. J. Raymond. Coburg, 1832.

FARMER'S JOURNEY TO LONDON, THE. F. 3 a. Pr. 1769.

FARMER'S RETURN FROM LONDON, THE. Int. David Garrick. D.L., March 20, 1762; Pr. 1762.

FARMER'S STORY, THE. Dom. D. 3 a. Bayle Bernard. Lyceum, June 13, 1836.

FARMER'S STORY, THE. See *Ambition*.

FARMER'S WIFE. C.O. 3 a. Chas. Dibdin, jun. C.G., February 1, 1814.

FARMERS, THE. Aristophanes. See "Greek Plays."

FARNLEY. P. 1 a. David Davies. St. Geo. H., October 27, 1894 (amat.).

FARO TABLE, THE. C.G., April 4, 1789. Alt. of *The Gamester*. N.p.

FARO TABLE, THE. C. Tobin. 1795. N.p.

FARRAGO. Burl. Ashton People's O.H., May 14, 1883.

FARRE FETCHED AND DEAR BOUGHT YS GOOD FOR LADIES. P. Ent. Stationers' Co. by Thos. Hackett, 1566. N.p.

FARTHING RUSHLIGHT, THE. D. medley. Oulton. 1810.

FASCHEUX, LES. Molière. See "French Classical Plays."

FASCINATING FELLOWS. F. T. A. Palmer. Olympic, March 18, 1876.

FASCINATING INDIVIDUAL, A; OR, TOO AGREEABLE BY HALF. F. 1 a. H. Danvers. Olympic, June 9, 1856.

FASCINATING MISS KEMP, THE. Light C. 3 a. Gordon Holmes. Margate Grand T., November 7, 1904; Crouch End O.H., December 5, 1904.

FASCINATING MR. VANDERBILT, THE. P. by Alfred Sutro. (C.P.) Comedy, January 4. Prod. Garrick, April 26, 1906.

FASCINATION. C. 3 a. Robt. Buchanan and Harriet Jay. Novelty, October 6, 1887; Vaudeville, January 19, 1888.

FASHION. D. 3 a. Walter Stephens. Olympic, June 21, 1869 (amat.).

FASHION; OR, LIFE IN NEW YORK. C. Mrs. Mowatt. New York, June 24, 1845; Olympic, January, 1850.

FASHION; OR, THE WORLD AS IT GOES. M.E. 2 a. Archibald Maclaren. Pr. 1802. N.ac.

FASHION DISPLAYED. C. Mrs. Philippina Burton. Hay., April 27, 1770. N.p.

FASHIONABLE ARRIVALS. F.C. 2 a. Mark Lemon. C.G., October 29, 1840; Olympic, March, 1859.

FASHIONABLE BEAUTY, THE. M. burla. 3 scenes. George Moore and James M. Glover. Avenue, April 7, 1885.

FASHIONABLE CROP QUIZZ'D, THE. F. Dublin, 1792. Nop.

FASHIONABLE EDUCATION. D. Berguin. 1793.

FASHIONABLE FRIENDS, THE. C. Said to have been found among the papers of Horace Walpole, Earl of Orford. D.L., April 22, 1802. Pr. 1802.

FASHIONABLE FRIENDSHIP. Ballad O. William Shirley. N.ac.

FASHIONABLE INTELLIGENCE. Duol. Percy Fendall. Court, March 5, 1894.

FASHIONABLE LADY; OR, THE HARLEQUIN'S OPERA. J. Ralph. Goodman's Fields, April 2, 1730. Pr. 1730.

FASHIONABLE LEVITIES; OR, NATURE WILL PREVAIL. C. 3 a. Leonard M'Nally. C.G. Pr. 1785. D.L., May 31, 1820

FASHIONABLE LOVER, THE. C. 5 a. Richd. Cumberland. D.L. Pr. 1772. D.L., October 14, 1818.

FASHIONABLE LOVER; OR, WIT IN NECESSITY, THE. C. Anon. Pr. 1706. ? Ac. at D.L.

FAST AND SLOW. C. 3 a. D.L., April 18, 1827.

FAST AND WELCOME. C. Philip Massinger. Ent. at Stationers' Co. June 29, 1660. Destroyed by Mr. Warburton's servant. N.p.

FAST ASLEEP. Mus. Ent. Samuel Birch. D.L., November 28, 1797. N.p. ? fr. *The Narcotic*.

FAST ASLEEP. Eccentric C. 3 a. C. H. Abbott. Adap. fr. *Wide Awake*, a story by W. S. Gilbert. Criterion, March 1, 1892.

FAST BIND FAST BIND. P. Heywood. N.p. 1598.

FAST COACH, THE. F. 1 a. C. J. Claridge and Robert Soutar, jun. Olympic, June 9, 1851; Gaiety, September 29, 1873, and March 20, 1875.

FAST FAMILY, THE. P. 4 a. Adap. fr. *La Famille Benoiton* of Sardou (1865) by B. Webster, jun. Adelphi, May 5, 1866.

FAST FRIEND, A. F. F. Herbert. Olympic, July 2, 1877.

FAST FRIENDS. Ca. 1 a. R. Henry. Steinway Hall, June 14, 1878.

FAST FRIENDS. F.C. Frank Barrett. Nottingham T.R., September 17, 1884.

FAST LIFE, A. D. 4 a. Hubert O'Grady. Rhyl O.H., October 26, 1896; Imperial, October 24, 1898.

FAST MAIL, THE. P. 4 a. Lincoln J. Carter. Orig. prod. in America. Rochdale T.R., December 26, 1891; Grand, June 27, 1892.

FAST TRAIN! HIGH PRESSURE!! EXPRESS!!! A. *A Short Trip.* Lyceum, April 25, 1853.

FASTI. Ovid. See "Latin Plays."

FAT AND FAIR. Sk. Wal Pink. Rotherhithe Hipp., April 13, 1908.

FATA MORGANA. Fairy C. Heiberg. 1838.

FATAL BEAUTY. D. Pro. and 4 a. Gylbert Fisher. Sadler's Wells. April 2, 1892.

FATAL BROTHERS, THE. T. Robt. Davenport. Ent. Stationers' Co., June 29, 1660. N.p.

FATAL CARD, THE. D. 5 a. C. Haddon Chambers and B. C. Stephenson. Adelphi, September 6, 1894.

FATAL CONSTANCY, THE. T. Hildebrand Jacob. Pr. 1723. D.L., April 22, 1723.

FATAL CONSTANCY; OR, LOVE IN TEARS. T. Wm. Whitehead. Pr. 1754. Afterwards part of Foote's f. *The Diversions of the Morning.*

FATAL CONTRACT, THE. French T. Wm. Heminge. Pr. 1653. Taken fr. French hist. Rev. as *Love and Revenge*, and in 1687 as *The Eunuch.*

FATAL CROWN, A. Hist. P. 4 a. Brandon Ellis and J. Bell. Pav., July 22, 1901.

FATAL CURIOSITY, THE. T. 3 a. Geo. Lillo. Hay., 1736. Pr. 1736. Alt. by G. Colman and rev. at Hay., 1782. Pr. 1783. See *The Shipwreck.*

FATAL DANCE, THE. Dr. Epis. Harding Cox. Margate R., June 7, 1909; Comedy, August 23, 1909.

FATAL DISCOVERY, THE. T. John Home. D.L., February 23, 1769. Pr. 1769. Orig. intended to be produced as *Rivine.*

FATAL DISCOVERY; OR, LOVE IN RUINS. T. Anon. Plot fr. Œdipus and Jocasta. D.L., 1698. Pr. 1698. See *Innocence Distress'd.*

FATAL DOWRY, THE. T. 5 a. Massinger and Nathaniel Field. Ac. at Blackfriars and Pr. 1632. The plan of this P. was borrowed by Rowe for his *The Fair Penitent.* Rev. D.L., January 5, 1825. M. by Horn.

FATAL ERROR, THE. T. Benj. Victor Taken fr. *Woman Killed with Kindness.* Pr 1776. N.ac.

FATAL ERROR, THE. Sk. Hall Caine. Poplar Queen's, September 21, 1908.

FATAL EXTRAVAGANCE, THE. T. 1 a. Joseph Mitchell and Aaron Hill. Chiefly fr. *The Yorkshire Tragedy.* L.I.F. and Pr. 1720. D.L. in 5 a., 1726.

FATAL FALSEHOOD. T. Miss Hannah More. C.G., May 6, 1779. Pr. 1779.

FATAL FALSEHOOD; OR, DISTRESSED INNOCENCE. T. 3 a. J. Hewitt. D.L., February 11, 1734. Pr. circa 1734.

FATAL FORTUNE. M.C.D. 5 a. St. Aubyn Miller. Camberwell Met., May 2, 1904.

FATAL FRIENDSHIP. T. Catherine Trotter (afterwards Mrs. Cockburne). L.I.F Pr. 1698.

FATAL FRIENDSHIP, THE. P. Burroughes. Ent. Stationers' Co. September 4, 1646. N.p.

FATAL GLASS; OR, THE CURSE OF DRINK, THE. D. 3 a. J. M'Closkey. Brooklyn Park T., April 1, 1872.

FATAL INCONSTANCY; OR, THE UNHAPPY RESCUE, THE. T. R. Phillips. Pro. by Mr. Johnson. Pr. 1701.

FATAL INTERVIEW, THE. T. Thos. Hull. Partly taken fr. *Pamelia in High Life.* D.L., November 16, 1782. N.p.

FATAL JEALOUSY, THE. T. Duke's T. Anon. Ascribed to Nevil Payne. Plot fr. *The Unfortunate Lovers.* Pr. 1673.

FATAL LEGACY, THE. T. Anon. Transl. of Racine's *Thebais.* L.I.F., 1721. Pr. 1723.

FATAL LETTER; OR, THE MIDNIGHT REVELATION, THE. D. 3 a. W. E. Suter. East London, May 9, 1868.

FATAL LOVE. Fr. T. Geo. Chapman. Ent. at Stationers' Co., June 29, 1660. N.p.

FATAL LOVE; OR, THE DEGENERATE BROTHER. T. Osborne Sidney Wandesford. Pr. 1730. Hay., 1730.

FATAL LOVE; OR, THE FORC'D INCONSTANCY. T. Elk. Settle. Plot partly fr. Tatius's rom. of *Clitophon and Leucippe.* Ac. at T.R. Pr. 1680.

FATAL MARRIAGE, THE. D. Pro. and 3 a. E. Towers. East London, September 10, 1870.

FATAL MARRIAGE; OR, THE INNOCENT ADULTERY, THE. T. Thos. Southerne. Plot fr. Mrs. Behn's novel, "The Nun; or, The Fair Vow Breaker." Ac. at T.R., and pr. 1694; rev. at D.L., 1758, under title, *Isabella; or, The Fatal Marriage.*

FATAL MISTAKE, THE. Dr. Epis. A. H. Rave. Brixton Empress, January 13, 1909 (mat.).

FATAL MISTAKE; OR, THE PLOT SPOILED, THE. T. Joseph Haynes. Pr. 1692. N.ac.

FATAL NECESSITY; OR, LIBERTY REGAINED. T. Robt. Morris. Plot fr. the story of *Appius and Virginia.* Pr. 1742. N.ac.

FATAL PREDICTION; OR, MIDNIGHT ASSASSIN, THE. B. By J. C. Cross. Pr. 1802.

FATAL PROPHECY, THE. Dr. poem. Dr. John Langhorne. Pr. 1766.

FATAL RETIREMENT, THE. T. Anthony Brown. D.L., November 12, 1739. Pr. 1739.

FATAL RING, THE. Blank verse T. 5 a. Francis Henry Cliffe. Ladbroke, September 12, 1893 (C.P.).

FATAL SECRET, THE. Lewis Theobald. F. on Webster's *Duchess of Malfi.* Pr. 1735. C.G.

FATAL SECRET, THE. See *The Rival Brothers.*

FATAL SISTERS; OR, THE CASTLE OF THE FOREST, THE. Dr. Rom. Edmund John Eyre. Pr. 1797.

FATAL SNOWSTORM, THE. Rom. D. 2 a. W. Barrymore. Astley's.

FATAL STOCKINGS, THE. P. 1 a. A. Holmes-Gore. Grand, Blackpool, June 18, 1906.

FATAL TRIUMPH. D. 4 a. J. L. Featherstone and J. C. Hurd. New Cross Pub. H., December 11, 1886.

FATAL VISION; OR, THE FALL OF SIAM, THE. T. Aaron Hill. L.I.F. Pr. 1716.

FATAL WAGER, THE. See *Injured Princess.*

FATAL WEDDING, THE. P. 4 a. Theo Kremer. Princess's, August 25, 1902.

FATALITY. D. 1 a. Caroline Boaden. Hay., September 2, 1829.

FATALITY. D. 5 a. Kate Cameron. Bp Auckland Eden T., January 26, 1898 (C.P.).

FATE. D. Miss H. G. Gregory. Middlesbrough T.R., March 9, 1874.

FATE; OR, DRIVEN FROM HOME. American D. Bartley Campbell. Glasgow Gaiety, February 21, 1876; Ladbroke H., May 6, 1882; Gaiety, August 6, 1884 (mat.).

FATE AND FORTUNE; OR, THE JUNIOR PARTNER. D. 4 a. Jas. J. Blood. Princess's, July 27, 1891.

FATE AND THE FOOTMAN. "Song-salad in three helpings." Olive Tulloch. Littlehampton Terminus H., September 17, 1908 (amat.).

FATE OF AMBITION; OR, THE TREACHEROUS FAVOURITE, THE. T. Dublin, 1733.

FATE OF CALAS, THE. D. 3 a. T. Dibdin. Adap. fr. the French of Victor. Surrey, also rev. there 1835.

FATE OF CAPUA, THE. T. Thos Southerne. L.I.F. Pr. 1700. Pro. by Chas. Boyle. Epil. by Col. Codrington.

FATE OF CORSICA; OR, THE FEMALE POLITICIAN, THE. C. Wr. by "A Lady of Quality." Pr. 1732.

FATE OF FRANKENSTEIN. See *Frankenstein.*

FATE OF SPARTA; OR, THE RIVAL KINGS, THE. T. Mrs. Cowley. Principal events fr. Plutarch. D.L., January 31, 1788. Pr. 1788.

FATE OF THE FALLEN, THE. D. 4 a. T. Hill. Eleph. and C., August 19, 1901.

FATE OF VILLAINY, THE. T. Thos. Walker. Pr. 1730. Goodman's Fields, 1730. See *Love and Loyalty.*

FATE'S DECREE. D. Pro. and 5 tab. H. W. Williamson. Adap. fr. Lytton's novel "Paul Clifford." Sanger's Amphi., September 17, 1883.

FATES AND FURIES. D. 6 tab. G. B. Densmore. Surrey, October 20, 1877.

FATHER, THE. C. Transl. fr. Diderot's *Le Pere de Famille* by the translator of *Dorval.* Pr. 1770.

FATHER; OR, AMERICAN SHANDYISM, THE. C. Ac. at the New York T., pr. 1789. The idea fr. *Tristam Shandy.*

FATHER AND HIS CHILDREN, THE. Melo-d. C.G. Prod. by Bishop, October, 1817.

FATHER AND SON; OR, FAMILY FRAILTIES. C. Pr. 1814. ? N.ac.

FATHER AND SON. Melo-d. E. Fitzball. C.G., February, 1825.

FATHER BAPTISTE. D. 3 a. E. Stirling. Pub. by J. Dicks.

FATHER BUONAPARTE. P. 3 a. C. W. Hudson. Olympic, March 19, 1891.

FATHER GIRARD THE SORCERER; OR, THE AMOURS OF HARLEQUIN AND MISS CADIERE. Tragi-Com. F.O. Goodman's Fields, 1732.

FATHER OF A FAMILY, THE. C. 3 a. Carlo Goldoni. Pr. 1757. Transl. of *Il Padre di Famiglia.* Prod. at Venice, 1750. See *Pamela.*

FATHER OF HER CHILD, THE. Dom. D. 4 a. Arthur Shirley and Forbes Dawson West London, February 9, 1903.

FATHER OF NINETY. M.F. 3 a. Wal Pink and H. Darnley. Brighton Eden T., September 29, 1902; Eleph. and C., December 1, 1902.

FATHER OUTWITTED, THE. Int. Goldoni. See "Theatrical Recorder."

FATHER OUTWITTED, THE. Int. Transl. fr. the Spanish of Lopez de Vega. Pr. October, 1784.

FATHER SATAN. D. 5 a. Harry F. Spiers. Ilkeston New T.R., February 27, 1896 (C.P.); Britannia, June 22, 1896.

FATHER VARIEN. P. 1 a. Monckton Hoffe. Eastbourne D.P., May 9, 1907

FATHER'S CRIME, A. Melo-d. Adap. fr. the French of Edmond Crosnier and St Hilaire. Lyceum, July 6, 1835.

FATHER'S OATH, THE. D. 4 a. F. Gould Glasgow Princess's, October 24, 1892; Surrey May 29, 1893.

FATHER'S OWN SON, THE. P. Belonged to the Cockpit T. See *Doctors of Dulhead College.*

FATHER'S REVENGE, THE. T. Earl of Carlisle. Plot fr. Boccaccio, and may also be found in Dryden, under the title of *Guiscardo and Sigismunda.* The story is the same as *Tancred and Gismund* and *The Cruel Gift.* Pr. 1783. N.ac.

FATHER'S SACRIFICE, A. D. 2 a. W. R. Varty, fr. a novelette by T. W. Speight. School of Dr. Art., Argyll St. February 16, 1887.

FATHER'S SIN, A. D. 4 a. H. Burrows Smith. Woolwich T.R., April 5, 1886.

FATHER'S TRAGEDY, THE. Hist. P. Michael Field. Pr. 1885.

FATHERLAND. D. 5 a. Henry Labouchere. Queen's, January 3, 1878.

FATHERS; OR, THE GOOD-NATURED MAN, THE. C. Henry Fielding. D.L., November 30, 1778. Pr. 1778. See *The Good-natured Man.*

FATHOMS DEEP. D. John B. Cleve. Sadler's Wells. March 24, 1883.

FATINITZA. C.O. 3 a. H. S. Leigh. M. by Suppé. Alhambra, June 20, 1878.

FAUCON, LE. O.C. Sedaine. M. by Monsigny. March 19, 1772.

FAULKNER. T. Wm. Godwin. F. on novel of "Roxana; or, The Fortunate Mistress." D.L., December 16, 1807.

FAULT IN FRIENDSHIP, A. Ac. at the Curtain, 1623. Dr. Anderson states that a play of this name was written by Benjamin, son of Ben Jonson, in conjunction with Richd. Brome. N.p.

FAUSSE MAGIE, LA. O. Marmontel. M. by Grétry. 1775.

FAUST. T. Goethe. 1798. Transl. by A. Hayward 1833, J. Ansted 1835, Sir T. Martin 1870, Bayard Taylor 1871, Miss A. Swanwick 1879.

FAUST. O. Schumann. 1810-1856.

FAUST. O. Spohr. Wds. by Bernhard. Frankfort, 1818. Sc. fr. Prince's, May 21, 1840; at D.L., May 18, 1846; perf. in Italian at C.G., July 15, 1852.

FAUST. O. Lib. by Carré and Barbier. M. by Ch. Gounod. Paris Th. Lyrique, 1859. Eng. lib. by H. F. Chorley. Her M., January 23, 1864.

FAUST. An adap. of first part of Goethe's T. Arr. by W. G. Wills. Lyceum, December 19, 1885; April, 1888; April, 1894; April 26, 1902.

FAUST. An adap. of first part of Goethe's T. 3 a. Sadler's Wells, February 20, 1886.

FAUST. Burl. Standard, July 20, 1891.

FAUST. A new adap. of portions of the first part of Goethe's T., in prol. and 4 a. Stephen Phillips and J. Comyns Carr. H.M., September 5, 1908.

FAUST; OR, MARGUERITE'S MANGLE. Burl. C. H. Hazlewood. Britannia, March 25, 1867.

FAUST; OR, THE DEMON OF THE DRACHENFELS. Rom. D. 2 a. H. P. Grattan. Sadler's Wells, September, 1842.

FAUST; OR, THE FATE OF MARGARET. Rom. P. 4 a. Adap. fr. Goethe by Bayle Bernard. D.L., October 20, 1866; D.L., September, 1867.

FAUST AND CO Burl. Geo. Lash Gordon Greenock T.R., February 27, 1886.

FAUST AND GRETCHEN. O. 1 a. Ross and Thiele. Publ. by S. French, Limited.

FAUST AND LOOSE; OR, BROKEN VOWS. Travestie on Lyceum *Faust* by F. C. Burnand Toole's, February 4, 1886.

FA(U)ST AND LOOSE. Sk. J. J. Hewson. Glagow Hipp., June 8, 1908.

FAUST AND MARGARET. New ver. of Goethe's legend. Brian Daly and C. W. Somerset. Leicester R.O.H., January 30, 1899; West London, February 13, 1899.

FAUST AND MARGUERITE. Rom. D. 3 a. William Robertson. Transl. fr. French of Michel Carré. Gymnase-Dramatique, Paris, August 19, 1850; Princess's, April, 1854, 1858, and April, 1871.

FAUST AND MARGUERITE. Travestie. 1 a F. C. Burnand. St. James's T. July 9, 1864.

FAUST AND MARGUERITE; OR, THE DEVIL'S DRAUGHT. Operatic extrav. J. Halford. Strand, June 8, 1854. Olympia, December, 1866.

FAUST AND THE FAIR IMOGEN. See *Faust Up Too Late.*

FAUST IN FORTY MINUTES. Burl. Fred Locke. Glasgow Gaiety T., August 17, 1885.

FAUST IN THREE FLASHES. M. oddity. J. J. Blood. M. by W. Astley Langston. Birmingham, P.O.W., March 5, 1884.

FAUST REVERSED; OR, THE BELLS ALL GONE WRONG. Travesty. Harry Bruce. Hoxton T., April 2, 1888.

FAUST UP TO DATE. Burl. 3 a. G. R. Sims and H. Pettitt. M. by Meyer Lutz and Robert Martin. Gaiety, October 30, 1888; Globe, June 10, 1889; rev. Gaiety, July 11, 1892.

FAUST UP TOO LATE. Adap. by Flexmore and Furtado fr. Burnand's *Faust and the Fair Imogen.* Ladbroke H., October 22, 1889.

FAUSTINE. D. 3 a. Sir C. Young. Bristol T.R., April 9, 1880; Olympic, June 24, 1880.

FAUSTINE'S LOVE. D. Pro. and 3 a Walter Stanhope. F. on Rita's novel, "Faustine." Strand, June 25. 1889.

FAUSTUS. Rom. D. 3 a. Geo. Soane. M. by Bishop, Horn, and Cooke. D.L., May 16, 1825.

FAUSTUS. See *Doctor Faustus.*

FAUTE, UNE. Petite piece. Scribe. 1822.

FAUTE DE S'ENTENDRE. Royalty, January 30, 1889.

FAUVETTE. C.O. 3 a. Alfred Rae. Adap. fr. *La Fauvette du Temple.* M. by André Massager. Edinburgh Lyceum (first time in England), May 18, 1891; Royalty, November 16, 1891.

FAUX PRODIGUE, LE. O. 2 a. Piron. M. by Rameau.

FAUZ MENAGES, LES. Gaiety, June 1, 1882.

FAVETTE. Ca. 1 a. John Tresahar. Adap. fr. a story of Ouida's. Vaudeville, January 29, 1885.

FAVORITA, LA. O. 4 a. G. Vaez and A. Royer. M. by Donizetti. F. on a T. by Baculard-Darnaud, entitled *Le Comte de Comminges.* Paris, 1840; D.L., August 4, 1846; and at Her M., February 16, 1847.

FAVORITO, IL. O. Pedrotti. Turin, 1870.

FAVOURITE, THE. Hist. T. Fr. Ben Jonson's *Sejanus.* Pr. 1770.

FAVOURITE, THE. O. Donizetti. Adap. by Tully. Paris, 1840; D.L., October 18, 1843.

FAVOURITE, THE. M.F. 1 a. Capt. Coe. M. by Geo. L. Chesterton. Crystal Palace, April 24, 1893.

FAVOURITE, THE. Sporting D. 4 a. By "Riada." Elephant and C. March 13, 1899.

FAVOURITE OF FORTUNE, THE. C. Westland Marston. Hay. April 2, 1866.

FAVOURITE OF THE KING, THE. Hist. P. 4 a. F. S. Boas and Joselyn Brandon Comedy, March 11, 1890.

FAVOURS OF FORTUNE, THE. P. 3 a. Eille Norwood. York G.O.H., February 28, 1902.

FAY O' FIRE, THE. Rom. O. 2 a. Henry Herman. M. by Edward Jones. Op. Comique, November 14, 1885.

FAY O' THE FERN, THE. F. Robert Geo. Legge. Oxford New T., February 4, 1893; Comedy, March 6, 1893.

FAY'S TALE, THE. Dr. Arne. D.L., 1746

FAYRE FOWLE ONE; OR, THE BAYTING OF THE JEALOUS KNIGHT. P. Wr. by Smith. November 28, 1623.

FAYRE MAYDE, etc. See *Fair Maid,* etc.

FAYRE ROSAMOND; OR, THE DAGGER AND THE POISONED BOWL. Burl. T. Cother. Gloucester, T.R., April 19, 1869.

FAZIO; OR, THE ITALIAN WIFE. T. 5 a. Dr. H. H. Milman. Surrey, December 22, 1816 (as *The Italian Wife*); C.G., 1816; D.L., March 3, 1850; Adelphi, March 8, 1865; Strand, July 1, 1890.

FEAR OF ROBERT CLIVE, THE. P. 1 a. Sarah Grand and Haldane M'Fall. Lyceum, July 14, 1896. C.P.

FEARFUL FOG, A. F. Fredk. Hay. Glasgow, P.O.W., February 11, 1871; Vaudeville, April 22, 1871.

FEARFUL JOY, A. F. 3 a. S. Grundy. F. on *Les Plus Heureux de Trois,* by Labiche and Gondinet. Hay., April 18, 1908.

FEARFUL MYSTERY. O. 1 a. W. M. Hutchinson. Pub. by S. French, Limited.

FEARFUL TRAGEDY IN THE SEVEN DIALS. F. Int. 1 a. Chas. Selby. Adelphi, May 4, 1857.

FEARLESS FRED, THE FIREMAN. D. G. Patterson. Sheffield, Alexandra, July 13, 1874.

FEAST OF APOLLO, THE. Int. C.G., May 15, 1810. N.p.

FEAST OF BACCHUS, THE. Ballet. C.G., 1758.

FEAST OF NEPTUNE, THE. D.L., June 8, 1829.

FEAST OF THALIA, THE. Int. C.G., August, 1781. N.p.

FEAST OF THE DRAGON, THE. Chinese festival perf. by Chinese troupe. D.L., March 27, 1854.

FEATHERBRAIN. C. 3 a. J. Albery. Adap. fr. *Tête de Linotte* of Barrière and Goudinet. Criterion, June 23, 1884.

FEDORA. P. 4 a. Victorien Sardou. Ac. in French. Gaiety, July 9, 1883. Engl. ver. by Herman Merivale. Prod. at Hay., May 5, 1883; rev. May 26, 1895; Italian ver. at Lyric, May 26, 1893.

FEDORA. O. 3 a. Umberto Giordano. C.G., November 5, 1906.

FEE AUX ROSES, LA. O. Halévy. Paris, 1849

FEE FAW FUM. D.L., Christmas, 1867.

FEE URGELE, LA. O.C. Favart. 1749-1806.

FEED THE BRUTE. "An uninstructive conversation," in 1 a. "George Paston." (Pr. by the Pioneers.) Royalty, May 24, 1908; rev., Royalty, March 20, 1909.

FEEN DIE. O. 3 a. Wds. and M. by Wagner. Wr. at Würzburg in 1833. Adap. fr. Gozzi's *Donna Serpente*. Pr. at Munich, 1888, 1894 and 1895. Wagner's first O.

FEET OF CLAY. D. 1 a. Hubert S. Ryan. Cripplegate Inst., March 28, 1903 (amat.).

FEIGN'D ASTROLOGER, THE. C. Anon. Pr. 1668. Transl. fr. Corneille, who borrowed fr. Calderon's "El Astrologo Fingido."

FEIGN'D COURTEZANS; OR, A NIGHT'S INTRIGUE, THE. C. Mrs. Behn. Duke's T. Pr. 1679.

FEIGN'D FRIENDSHIP; OR, THE MAD REFORMER. C. Anon. L.I.F., beginning of 18th century. P. Nn.d.

FEIGNED INNOCENCE; OR, SIR MARTIN MAR-ALL. C. J. Dryden. Duke of York's T., 1678. See *Sir Martin Mar-all*.

FEIGN'D SHIPWRECK, THE. See *Strollers' Packet*.

FEINTE PAR AMOUR, LA. C. Dorat. 1734-1780.

FELDLAGER IN SCHESLEN, EIN. O. 3 a. Wds. by Rellstob. M. by Meyerbeer. Wr. and comp. in memory of Frederick the Great for the re-opening of Berlin O.H. on December 7, 1844. (Burnt August 18, 1843.)

FELISE AND PHILOMENE, THE HISTORY OF. Ac. before Her Highness by Her Majesty's servants at Greenwich, 1584-5.

FELIX. O.C. Sedaine. M. by Monsigny. 1777.

FELIX; OR, FESTIVAL OF ROSES. New Royalty, October 24, 1865.

FELLOW SERVANTS. C. 1 a. H. T. Craven. In Douglas Cox's list.

FELMELANEO. P. Henry Chettle and Robinson. Ac. 1602.

FELON'S BOND, THE. D. 3 a. W. E. Suter. Queen's, September 10, 1859.

FEMALE ACADEMY, THE. C. Duchess of Newcastle. Pr. 1662.

FEMALE ADVENTURER; OR, STOP HER WHO CAN, THE. C. Alt. fr. Moore's *Gil Blas*. C.G., April 29, 1790. N.p.

FEMALE ADVOCATES; OR, THE STOCK JOBBERS, THE. C. Wm. Tavener. D.L., January 6, 1713. Pr. 1713. See *Stock Jobbers*.

FEMALE BARBARISM. Oa. E. La Touche Hancock. M. by Clement Locknane. Kilburn T.H., December 17, 1890.

FEMALE CAPTAIN, THE. F. Ascr. to James Cobb. Hay, 1780. D.L., 1779, under title of *The Contract*. Fr. the French of Marivaux.

FEMALE CHEVALIER, THE. C. 3 a. Alt. fr. Taverner by George Colman. Taken from *The Artful Husband*. Hay., 1778. N.p.

FEMALE CLUB, THE. F. John O'Keeffe. Mentioned in *The Monthly Mirror* for February, 1810.

FEMALE DRAMATIST, THE. M.F. Ascr. to Mrs. Gardner and sometimes to younger Colman. Partly fr. "Roderic Random." Hay., August 16, 1782. N.p.

FEMALE DUELLIST, THE. Afterpiece. King's T., Hay. Partly fr. *Love's Cure; or, The Martial Maid*. Songs set to M. by Mr. Suett. Pr. 1793.

FEMALE FALSEHOOD. See *Campaigners*.

FEMALE FOP; OR, THE FALSE ONE JILTED. C. Sandford. New T. in Hay. Pr. 1724.

FEMALE FORTUNE-TELLER, THE. C. Johnson. L.I.F., July, 7, 1726. Pr. 1726.

FEMALE GAMESTER, THE. T. George Edmund Howard. Pr. 1778.

FEMALE HEROISM. T. 5 a. Rev. Matthew West. Pr. 1803. Dublin, May 19, 1804.

FEMALE IAGO, A. F. W. H. Goldsmith. Jersey, T.R., August 6, 1872; Royalty, July 24, 1873.

FEMALE INNOCENCE; OR, A SCHOOL FOR A WIFE. P. 3 a. Ac. at Mrs. Lee's Great Booth on the Bowling Green, Southwark. Plot similar to *Country Wife*. Pr. circa 1730. N.d.

FEMALE JACOBIN CLUB, THE. Pol. C. C. Siber. Liverpool, 1801.

FEMALE JUDAS, A. D. 4 a. Wm. P. Sheen. Leith, Princess's, November 20, 1896; Openshaw, July 5, 1897.

FEMALE MASSARONI; OR, THE FAIR BRIGANDS, THE. Op. D. 2 a. C. A. Somerset. Surrey.

FEMALE OFFICER, THE. C. 2 a. Henry Brooke. Pr. 1778. N.ac.

FEMALE OFFICER, THE. F. J. P. Kemble. Ac. at York, 1779; ac. at D.L., 1786, under the title of *The Projects*. N.p.

FEMALE OFFICER; OR, HUMOURS OF THE ARMY, THE. C. Anon. An alt. of Shadwell's *Humours of the Army*. Ac. at Dublin. Pr. 1763.

FEMALE ORATORS, THE. Prel. C.G., May 12, 1780.

FEMALE PARLIAMENT, THE. Ent. Ac. Pr. 1754.

FEMALE PARRICIDE, THE. T. Edward Crane. F. on the story of Miss Blandy. Pr. 1761.

FEMALE PARSON; OR, THE BEAU IN THE SUDS, THE. B.O. C. Coffey. Pr. 1730. Ac. at Little T. in Hay.

FEMALE PEDANT, THE. Thos. Horde, jun. Ac. at the Grammar School in Stow. Pr. 1782.

FEMALE PIRATE; OR, THE LIONESS OF THE SEA, THE. D. Douglas Stewart, Victoria, October 31, 1870.

FEMALE PRELATE, BEING THE HISTORY OF THE LIFE AND DEATH OF POPE JOAN, THE. T. Elkanah Settle. Taken fr. Platina's *Lives of the Popes* and Cooke's dialogue, *Pope Joan*. T.R. Pr. 1680.

FEMALE RAKE; OR, MODERN FINE LADY, THE. Ballad C. Hay., 1736. Pr. 1736. See *The Woman of Taste*.

FEMALE REBELLION, THE. T.C. 5 a. Wr. seventeenth century. Pr. 1872.

FEMALE SLEEPWALKER, THE. A new ver. of Bellini's O. *La Sonnambula*. Lyceum (first time at this T.), May 18, 1835.

FEMALE SWINDLER, THE. D. 4 a. Walter Melville. Rotherhithe, Terriss, October 12, 1903.

FEMALE VIRTUOSOES, THE. C. Thos. Wright. Ac. at Queen's. Pr. 1693. A transl. of Molière's *Femmes Sçavantes*. See *No Fools Like Wits*. T.R., 1693. Rev. L.I.F., 1721, as *No Fools Like Wits*.

FEMALE VOLUNTEERS; OR, THE DAWNING OF PEACE, THE. D. 3 a. Philo Nauticus (L. H. Halloran). Pr. 1801. N.ac.

FEMALE WITS; OR, THE TRIUMVIRATE OF POETS AT REHEARSAL, THE. C. 3 a By "W. M." D.L. Pr. 1697.

FEMELANCO. T. Chettle and Robinson. Ac. 1602.

FEMININE STRATEGY. Oa. 1 a. Catherine Adams. M. by F. G. Hollis. Basingstoke Drill H., November 16, 1893.

FEMME DE CLAUDE, LA. P. 3 a. Alex Dumas fils. Daly's (in French), July 17, 1894; D.L. (in Italian), June 6, 1895.

FEMME SENTINELLE, LA. Ballet. Miss Barnett. D.L., February 7, 1832. (First time.)

FEMMES NERVEUSES, LES. Royalty, March 1, 1889.

FEMMES SAVANTES, LES. Molière. See "French Classical Plays."

FEMMES VENGEES, LES. C.O. 1 a. F. A. D. Philidor. 1775.

FENCING MASTER, THE. C.O. 3 a. Harry B. Smith. M. by Reginald de Koven. Sadler's Wells, September 26, 1892. C.P.

FENELLA. Rom. Oa. A. R. Cleveland Coliseum, December 18, 1905.

FENELON; OR, THE NUNS OF CAMBRAY D. 3 a. Alt. fr. the French of Robert Merry Pr. 1795. N.ac.

FENIAN, THE. Irish D. 4 a. Hubert O'Grady. Glasgow Princess's T., April 1 1889; Standard, September 2, 1889.

FENNEL. Rom. P. 1 a. Jerome K. Jerome Adap. fr. *Le Luthier de Crémône* of François Coppée. Novelty, March 31, 1888. See *The Violin-Maker of Cremona.*

FERDINANDO. F. Walter Parke. Grand, November 1, 1886.

FERNANDE. D. 4 a. Sutherland Edwards. Adap. fr. V. Sardou's play. St James's, October 15, 1870.

FERNANDE. D. 4 a. J. Schönberg. Adap fr. Sardou. Pub. by J. Dicks.

FERNAND CORTEZ, OU LA CONQUETE DU MEXIQUE. O. 3 a. Wds. by Esménard and De Jouy. M. by Spontini. Pr. Paris, December 18, 1809; Dresden, March, 1812; rev. by composer, Paris, May 28, 1817; Berlin, April 20, 1818.

FERREOL DE MEYRAC. P. 4 a. Herbert Dansey. Adap. fr. *Ferreol* of V. Sardou. Royalty, February 26, 1904.

FERREX AND PORREX. T. 5 a. A. one, two, and three by Thos. Norton, A. four and five by Thos. Sackville (Lord Buckhurst). Ac at Whitehall, January 18, 1561. Pr. 1565. Afterwards alt. and pub. as *Gorboduc.*

FERREX AND PORREX. P. Wm. Haughton. Prob. an alt. of foregoing. N.p. (ac circa 1600).

FERRY GIRL, THE. Oa. 3 a. Dowager Marchioness of Downshire. M. by Lady Arthur Hill. Savoy, May 13, 1890.

FERRYMAN, THE. D. 5 a. R. Landor Pr. 1841.

FERRYMAN'S DAUGHTER, THE. D. 5 a H. J. Johnson and C. Cordingley. Hammersmith Lyric O.H., July 31, 1891.

FERVAAL. O. 3 a. Wds. and M. by Vincent d'Indy. Brussels, March 12, 1897; Paris, May 10, 1898.

FESTA DI BACCO, LA. O. Leo and Vinci. Naples, 1732.

FESTIN DE PIERRE; OR, DON JUAN. Molière. See "French Classical Plays."

FESTIVAL OF APOLLO. Ent. Lyceum September 15, 1817.

FESTIVAL OF BACCHUS. Ballet. Byrne C.G., 1802.

FESTIVE COTTAGERS, THE. Div. Noble. D.L., June 25, 1823.

FESTUS. Dr. Poem. Bailey. In Brewer's list

FETCHES, THE. F. Edmund Falconer Lyceum, August 24, 1861.

FETE AT SEVILLE. A. Div. D.L., November 29, 1844.

FETE DE PAMELIE, LA. Ballet. Rameau. 1754.

FETE DU VILLAGE, LA. Ballet. D.L., June 19, 1820.

FETE NAPOLITAINE, LA. Div. Guerra. D.L., June 20, 1838.

FETE NEAPOLITAINE, UNE. Ballet Div. 1 a. 2 tableaux. M. by Isaacson. D.L., April 12, 1852.

FETES D'HEBE, LES. O. Rameau. May 21, 1739.

FETES DE L'HYMEN ET DE L'AMOUR. O. 3 a and prol. Rameau. March 15, 1747.

FETES DE POLYMIE, LES. O. 3 a. and prol. Rameau. October 12, 1745.

FETES DE RAMIRE, LES. B.O. 1 a. Rameau. Versailles, December 22, 1745.

FETTERED; OR, A GOLDEN FETTER. D. 3 a. Watts Phillips. Holborn, February 17, 1869.

FETTERED FREEDOM. D. 3 a. Milner Kenne and C. H. Stephenson. Vaudeville, September 28, 1887.

FETTERED LIVES. D. 5 a. Harold Whyte. Britannia, July 31, 1893.

FETTERS. D. Burnley. Bradford T.R., December 13, 1875.

FETTERS OF PASSION, THE. D. H. Sydney Warwick and Chas. T. Holderness. Bp Auckland, Eden T., January 12, 1894.

FEUD, THE. P. of Icelandic life of the twelfth century, in 3 a. Ed. Garnet. Manchester Gaiety, April 10, 1909; Coronet, June 11, 1909.

FEUDAL TIMES. T. Rev. Jas. White. Sadler's Wells, February 18, 1847.

FEUDAL TIMES; OR, THE BANQUET GALLERY. D. Geo. Colman, jun. D.L., January 19, 1799. Pr. 1799.

FEUDALISMO. Catalonian D. 3 a. Adapt. into Italian fr. the Spanish P., *Tierra Baja,* by Don Angelo Guimera. Shaftesbury, February 28, 1908.

FEUERSNOTH. O. R. Strauss. 1901.

FEW AND THE MANY, THE. P. 1 a. H. M. Richardson. Manchester Gaiety, May 4, 1908; Coronet, June 9, 1909.

FIAMMA. P. 4 a. J. T. Grein and Henry Hooton. Transl. fr. the French of Mario Uchard. P.O.W., January 9, 1903.

FIANCEE, LA. O. Auber. Paris, 1829.

FIANCEE DU DIABLE, LA. O. Paris, 1854.

FIANDER'S WIDOW. New and original C. 3 a. S. Valentine and M. E. Francis (Mrs. Blundell). Garrick, August 28, 1907.

FIAT OF THE GODS, THE. Idyll. 1 a. Leonard Outram. Adap. of Sonnet's *Le Gladiateur* (Italian version, D.L., May 7, 1875.). Avenue, August 25, 1891; Globe, April 25, 1892.

FIBS. C. 3 a. Welborn Tylar. Toole's, June 14, 1882.

FICKLE FATIMA. Burl. 3 a. W. Graham Robertson. Streatham Town H., February 6, 1892 (amat.).

FICKLE FORTUNE. D. 1 a. Chas. D. Steele. Battersea Park Town H., April 14, 1890 (amat.).

FICKLE SHEPHERDESS, THE. Past. Ac. by women at L.I.F. Pr. 1703. An alt. of Randolph's *Amintas*.

FIDANZATA DI CASTELLAMORE, LA. O. A. Randeger. Trieste, circa 1852.

FIDELE BERGER, LE. O.C. Adam. 1837.

FIDELE AND FORTUNATUS, LE. Thos. Barker. Said to be circa 1690, but Stationers' Co. records a comedy of this name by two Italian gentlemen, transl. into Eng., November 12, 1584.

FIDELIO. O. 3 a. Beethoven. Vienna, November 20, 1805; Paris, May 5, 1860; King's, London (in German), May 18, 1832; Covent Garden (in English), June 12, 1835; Her Majesty's (in Italian), May 20, 1851.

FIDO. C. 3 a. Eva Anstruther. Adap. fr. the French. Playhouse (mat.), November 26, 1907; rev. Playhouse, February 22, 1908.

FIELD OF FORTY FOOTSTEPS, THE. D 3 a. Percy Farren. Tottenham Street T.

FIELD OF THE CLOTH OF GOLD, THE Hist. Extrav. Wm Brough. Strand, April 11, 1868; rev. ver. by F. Flexmore, Kingston County T., September 30, 1901.

FIELD OF THE CLOTH OF GOLD; OR, HENRY THE EIGHTH AND FRANCIS THE FIRST, THE. D. 3 a. Shafto Scott. Astley's, April 24, 1869.

FIEND AT FAULT, THE. Mediæval M Mystery. Sutherland Edwards and Wm. H Taylor. M. by F. Foster Buggen and Wm H. Taylor. Vaudeville, April 4, 1894.

FIEND FATHER, THE. See *Demon*.

FIENDS OF LONDON. D. Herbert Fuller Stratford T.R. (C.P.), January 22, 1902; Batley T.R., August 3, 1903; Surrey, September 21, 1903.

FIERRABRAS. O. 3 a. Schubert. Wds. by Kupelwieser. 1861.

FIERY ORDEAL. Britannia, January 27, 1862.

FIESCO; OR, THE GENOESE CONSPIRACY T. Transl. fr. the German of Schiller. Pr. 1796.

FIESCO; OR, THE GENOESE CONSPIRACY. T. G. H. Noehden and J. Stoddart. Transl. fr. Schiller. Pr. 1798.

FIESCO; OR, THE GENOESE CONSPIRACY Another vers. by Milner. Coburg T.

FIESCO; OR, THE REVOLT OF GENOA Hist. P. Taken fr. Schiller. J. R. Planché. D.L., February 4, 1850; D.L. (in German), June 20, 1881.

FIESTAS DE ARANJUEZ. Masque. Sir Richd. Fanshawe. Transl. fr. the Spanish of Don Antonio de Mendoza. Pr. 1670. Orig. ac. in Spanish at Aranwhez before the King and Queen of Spain, 1623.

FIF; OR, LOST FOR LOVE. D. 4 a. M'Ardle and Gordon. Bradford Pullan's T. of Varieties, December, 1882.

FIFI. P. 1 a. Ella Erskine. Adap. fr. German. Pr. by the Revival Co. Rehearsal, W.C., February 28, 1909; Court, July 31, 1909. See *Zaza*.

FIFTEEN EIGHTY-EIGHT. "Foolish" C. 1 a. Drayton Ogilvy. New, November 5, 1907.

FIFTEEN MINUTES' GRACE. Sk. Walter Goodman. P.O.W.'s Club, February 18, 1894.

FIFTEEN YEARS OF A DRUNKARD'S LIFE. Melo-d. 3 a. D. Jerrold. Victoria, 1828.

FIFTEEN YEARS OF LABOUR LOST; OR, THE YOUTH WHO NEVER SAW A WOMAN. F. 1 a. J. Amherst. Fr. the French. R. Coburg T.; also at D.L. Pub. by J. Dicks.

FIFTEENTH CENTURY, THE. V. 2 a. Ch. F. Fuller. M. by Campbell Williams. H.M.S. Rainbow, April 10, 1883.

FIFTEENTH OF OCTOBER, THE. Op. bo. 1 a. E. Letierrier and A. Vanloo. M. by G. Jacobi. Alhambra, March 22, 1874. Rev. with lyrics by G. Capel. P.O.W., August 8, 1891.

FIFTH OF NOVEMBER, THE. F. 1 a. Publ. by R. Douglas Cox.

FIFTH QUEEN CROWNED. P. 4 a. Adapt. by F. Norreys Connell and Ford Madox Hueffer fr. the latter's novel. Kingsway, March 19, 1909 (mat.).

FIFTY FAFTY, THE TYNESIDE MYSTERY. D. 4 a. C. Freeman. North Shields T R, February 13, 1882; Berwick Queen's Rooms T., December 13, 1895.

FIFTY YEARS AFTER. D. Pro. and 3 a. Albert Alberg. Adap. fr. the Swedish Rom. D. *Efter Femtis Ar* by Z. Topelius. St. Geo. H., February 25, 1888.

FIG FOR MOMUS. Thos. Lodge. Pr. 1595.

FIGARO IN LONDON. F. 2 a. G. A. à Beckett. Strand, November 24, 1834.

FIGHT AGAINST FATE. D. 4 a. Grattan and Dawson. Newport, Mon, Victoria T., March 2, 1885.

FIGHT AT DAME EUROPA'S SCHOOL. F. G. F. Ferneyhough. Derby Lecture H., March 17, 1871. Amateurs.

FIGHT FOR FORTUNE; OR, THE VILLAGE GREEN, A. D. 4 a. Edwin Firth. Inverness T.R., October 27, 1903.

FIGHT FOR FREEDOM, A. M.D. 3 a. B. Landeck and A. Shirley. M. by W. C. Vernon and Edgar Ward. Brighton Aquarium, May 28, 1894.

FIGHT FOR HONOUR, A. Melo-d. 5 a. Frank Harvey. South Shields T.R., March 23, 1892; Surrey, June 13, 1892.

FIGHT FOR LIFE, A. D. 3 a. Saville Clarke and H. du Terreaux. Bradford T.R., August 26, 1876; Park, March 10, 1877.

FIGHT FOR LIFE, A. D. 4 a. F. A. Scudamore. Surrey, July 8, 1895. See *Our Eldorado*.

FIGHT FOR MILLIONS, A. Melo-d. 4 a. Malcolm Douglas. Oldham Colosseum, January 11, 1904; Greenwich Carlton, February 15, 1904.

FIGHT IN THE LIGHTHOUSE, THE. R. Stodart. Standard, July 12, 1909.

FIGHT WITH FATE, A. D. 4 a. Surrey, September, 1864.

FIGHTING BY PROXY. F. 1 a. Jas. Kenney. Olympic, December 9, 1833.

FIGHTING CHANCE, A. Sk. Barry Williams. Euston, September 7, 1908.

FIGHTING FIFTH, THE. D. 5 a. G. Conquest, sen., and Herbert Leonard. Surrey, October 29, 1900.

FIGHTING FOR HONOUR. Dom. D. 4 a. S. Erasmus. Blackburn T.R., March 3, 1903.

FIGHTING FORTUNE. D. 4 a. F. C. Scudamore. Bolton T.R., May 9, 1881; Marylebone, July 24, 1882.

FIGHTING FORTY-FIRST, THE. C. 3 a. C. H. Hazlewood. Britannia, September 11, 1876.

FIGHTING HER FATE; OR, A MAZE OF MYSTERY. D. 4 a. E. E Norris and Fewlass Llewellyn. Elephant and Castle, October 16, 1905.

FIGHTING HOPE, THE. P. 3 a. Wm. J. Hurlbut. Elephant and Castle, August 26, 1908 (C.P.).

FIGLIA DI BOBY, LA. Panto Sk. 4 a. G. Pratesi. M. by Marenco. Crystal Palace, August 4, 1898.

FIGLIA DI JORIO, LA. Pastoral T. 3 a. Gabrielle d'Annunzio. Shaftesbury, February 10, 1908.

FIGLIO PER AZZARDO, IL. O. Rossini. Venice, 1813.

FIGURE OF FUN; OR, THE BLOOMER COSTUME, A. F. 1 a. E. Stirling. Strand, Sept. 22, 1851.

FIGURE OF SPEECH. C. 1 a. H. C. Pemberton. Pub. by S. French, Ltd.

FIGUREHEAD, THE. P. 2 sc. Major W. P. Drury. Plymouth T.R., October 19, 1905.

FILBY THE FAKER. P. 1 a. Adap. fr. a story by Tom Gallon by Leon M. Lion. (Originally known as *The Fairy Uncle.*) Pr. at the New T., November 28, 1907; Wyndham's, September 7, 1908 (rev.).

FILIBUSTIER, LE. D.L., June 17, 1893. ,

FILLE COUPABLE, LA. O. Boieldieu. Words by his father. Rouen, 1793.

FILLE DE MADAME ANGOT, LA. C.O. 3 a. M. by C. Lecocq. Brussels, December, 1872; Paris, February, 1873; St. James's, May, 1873. Lib. by H. J. Byron at Philharmonic, October 4, 1873; D.L., April, 1880. Lib. by H. B. Farnie, Gaiety, November 10, 1873. Lib. by Miss Carry Nelson, Manchester T.R., November 24, 1873. Version by H. F. L. du Terreux, Liverpool P.O.W., February 16, 1874; Globe, May, 1874. Version by Nelson Lee, Liverpool T.R., February 23, 1874. Version by F. Desprez, Royalty, June 4, 1875. Revivals also at Op. Comique, December, 1873; Gaiety, August, 1874; November, 1874; Alhambra, November 12, 1877; Criterion, July 22, 1893; Coronet, February 11, 1901; rev., April 15, 1907.

FILLE DES BOIS. O. Weber, 1800.

FILLE DU REGIMENT, LA. O. Donizetti. Paris, February 11, 1840; London Her Majesty's, May 27, 1847, as *The Daughter of the Regiment;* Surrey, December 21, 1847.

FILLE DU TAMBOUR MAJOR, LA. C.O. 3 a. Offenbach. Eng. ver. by H. B. Farnie. Lib. by MM. Chivot and Dura. Alhambra, April 19, 1880; rev., Shaftesbury, June 1, 1908.

FILLEULE DU ROI, LA. C.O. A. Vozel. Cri., June 7, 1875.

FILLI DI SCIRO; OR, PHILLIS OF SCYROS. Pastl. "J. S., Gent." Transl. fr. Italian of C. G. de Bonarelli. Pr. 1655.

FILLIS OF SCIRUS. A Pastoral written in Italian by Count Guidabaldo de Bonarelli and trans. into Eng. by Sir George Talbot. Dedicated to King Charles II. Preserved in the British Museum. MS. 12128.

FILS DE CORALIE, LE. C. 4 a. Delpit. Gaiety, June, 1881.

FILTHY LUCRE. D. 3 a. Walter Browne.

FIN MACCOUL. C.D. 3 a. Dion Boucicault. Elephant and C., February 2, 1887 (C.P.).

FINAL. Charade. Miss Pickering. Publ. by S. French, Ltd.

FINAL SUPPER, THE. Sk. Chas. F. Kitts. Poplar Queen's, April 19, 1909.

FINANCIER, THE. C. 1 a. Transl. fr. St. Foix. . Pr. 1771.

FINANCIER ET LE SAVETIER, LE. Op. bo. Offenbach. 1819-80.

FIND THE LADY FIRST. Sk. Standard, July 4, 1908.

FINDING OF NANCY, THE. P. 4 a. Miss Netta Syrett. St. James's, May 8, 1902.

FINDING OF THE SWORD, THE. P. 2 sc Countess of Cromartie. Incidental M. comp and arr. by John Ansell. Playhouse, April 30, 1907.

FINE COMPANION, A. C. Shakerley Marmion. Pr. 1663. Ac. at Whitehall and at the Salisbury Court T.

FINE FEATHERS. C.D. Pro. and 3 a. H. J. Byron. Globe, April 26, 1873.

FINE LADIES' AIRS; OR, AN EQUIPAGE OF LOVERS, THE. C. Thos. Baker. D.L., December 14, 1708, and rev. D.L., 1747. Pr. (no date) 1709. Pro. wr. by Motteux.

FINESSE; OR, SPY AND COUNTER-SPY. P. Countess of Giffard. Hay., May 6, 1863.

FINESTRINA, LA. C. Alfieri. Transl. by C. Lloyd. 1815.

FINGER OF FATE, THE. Burl. D. C. Browr and Capt. A. Hill. Walsingham Club, January 15, 1905.

FINISHING SCHOOL, THE. Rom. 4 a. M. Pemberton. Wyndham's, June 16, 1904.

FINNIGAN'S FORTUNE. M.C. 3 a. H. Art. Openshaw, Harte's T., June 12, 1897.

FINTA GIARDINIERA, LA. Op. buffa. 3 a. Mozart. Munich, January 13, 1775.

FINTA PRINCIPESSA, LA. Op. buffa. Cherubini. Hay., 1785.

FINTA SCHIAVA, LA. O. M. by Gluck (in collaboration). Venice.

FINTA SEMPLICE, LA. Op. buffa. 3 a. Lib. by Cottellini. M. by Mozart (comp. when he was twelve, at Vienna, 1768). Apparently never put on the stage.

FINTO PITTORE, IL. O. Spontini. 1798.

FIORELLA. O. Auber. Paris, 1826.

FIORELLA. O. 1 a. Victorien Sardou and G. B. Ghensi. M. by A. Webber. Waldorf, June 7, 1905.

FIRE ALARM, THE. F. 1 a. R. G. Graham. Teddington T.H., February 1, 1893.

FIRE AND BRIMSTONE; OR, THE DESTRUCTION OF SODOM. D. Geo. Lesley. Pr. 1675.

FIRE AND FROST. C.O. 5 a. S. J. Pratt. Pr. 1805. N. ac.

FIRE AND WATER. B.O. Miles Peter Andrews. Hay., July 8, 1780. Pr. 1780.

FIRE AND WATER. C.O. Words by Beazley. M. by Price. Lyceum, August 19, 1817.

FIRE EATER, THE. F. 1 a. Chas. Selby. Olympic, June 30, 1851.

FIRE EATER, THE. V. J. T. Ashton. Royalty, April 15, 1874.

FIRE KING, THE. D. Berguin. 1793.

FIRE KING; OR, ALBERT AND ROSALIE, THE. Ballet. J. C. Cross. Pr. 1801.

FIRE KING; OR, THE YELLOW BOY, THE. Extrav. Liverpool P.O.W.'s, August 3, 1885.

FIRE OF LONDON; OR, WHICH IS WHICH, THE. P. 3 a. Lady Georgiana Fullerton. Pr. 1882.

FIRE-RAISER, THE. Melo-d. 2 a. Geo. ALMAR. Surrey, February 21, 1831.

FIRE WITCH, THE. Mystic D. 4 a. Daisy Halling. Edmonton T.R., June 20, 1904.

FIRE WITCH, THE. Mystic D. 4 a. Norman Towers. Stratford R.T., April 20, 1908.

FIREFLY. D. Pro. and 3 a. Edith Sandford. Fr. Ouida's story, "Under Two Flags." Surrey, May 17, 1869; Britannia, May 16, 1870.

FIREFLY, THE. P. Pro. and 3 a. W. Toynbee. Scala, December 17, 1905.

FIREMAN OF GLASGOW, THE. D. James Dwyer. Glasgow New Adelphi. April 5, 1875.

FIREMAN'S CHILD, THE. Margate Grand, July 7, 1902.

FIRES OF FATE, THE. Mod. Morality P. 4 a. Arthur Conan Doyle. Lyric, June 15, 1909.

FIRESIDE HAMLET, A. Tragic F. Comyns Carr. Prince's, November 27, 1884.

FIRESIDE STORY, A. Ca. 1 a. W. Gordon. In De Witt's List.

FIREWORKS. F.C. 3 a. F. C. Philips and Percy Fendall. Vaudeville, June 29, 1893.

FIRM AS OAK; OR, ENGLAND'S PRIDE. D George Peel. Britannia, June 2, 1873.

FIRMILIAN. "Spasmodic" T. W. E. Aytoun. Pr. 1854.

FIRST AFFECTIONS. Ca. 1 a. J. Palgrave Simpson. St. James's, February 13, 1860.

FIRST AID TO THE WOUNDED. F. 1 a. Harold Montague. Publ. by S. French, Limited.

FIRST ATTEMPT; OR, THE WHIM OF THE MOMENT, THE. C.O. Miss Owenson. Dublin, March 4, 1807. M. by T. Cooke.

FIRST-BORN, THE. Chinese P. 2 a. Francis Powers. Globe, November 1, 1897. Orig. prod. in New York.

FIRST BREEZE, THE. F.C. 1 a. W. R. Denny, West Hartlepool T.R., March 6, 1891.

FIRST CIVIL WARS IN FRANCE, THE. P. in three parts. Michael Drayton and Thos. Dekker. Ac. 1598. N.p.

FIRST-CLASS. D. 4 a. F. A. Scudamore. Greenwich P.O.W., September 14, 1885.

FIRST COME, FIRST SERVED. M.E. Dibdin. Sadler's Wells, April 17, 1797. Pr. 1797.

FIRST COME, FIRST SERVED. Ca. 1 a J. M. Morton. Publ. by S. French, Limited.

FIRST COME, FIRST SERVED; OR, THE BITER BIT. F. 2 a. Sir J. Carr. Haymarket, August 22, 1808. N.p.

FIRST CRIME. City of London, October 20, 1856.

FIRST DAY'S ENTERTAINMENT AT RUTLAND HOUSE, THE. Sir Wm. Davenant. Pr. 1656.

FIRST EXPERIMENT, A. Ca. 1 a J. Wilton Jones. Dewsbury T.R., October 10, 1882. Leeds Grand, March 14, 1883.

FIRST FAULTS. C. Miss Decanys (Mrs. C. Kemble). D.L., May 3, 1799. N.p. See *Natural Faults*.

FIRST FAVOURITE, THE. D. 1 a. C. H. Hazlewood. Britannia. October 25, 1873.

FIRST FLOOR, THE. F. 2 a. Jas. Cobb. D.L., January 13, 1787. Pr. 1787.

FIRST FRANCISCANS, THE. 2 Episodes in the life of St. Francis of Assisi. St. Geo. H., April 6, 1905.

FIRST IMPRESSIONS. C. Pr. in London for the Barbadoes Co. Anon. 1812.

FIRST IMPRESSIONS; OR, TRADE IN THE WEST. H. Smith. D.L., October 30, 1813.

FIRST IN THE FIELD. C. 1 a. C. M. Rae. Adap. fr. Meilhac's *Suzanne et les Deux Vieillards*. Brighton T.R., May 21, 1881. Globe, May 20, 1882.

FIRST LOVE. C. 5 a. Richd. Cumberland. D.L., May 12, 1795. Pr. 1795.

FIRST LOVE; OR, THE WIDOWED BRIDE. D. 3 a. W. E. Sutter. Grecian, June 15, 1863.

FIRST MATE. C.D. 2 a. Richard Henry. Gaiety, December 31, 1888.

FIRST MRS. BANBURY, THE. Sk. Ch. Willmott. Metropolitan M.H., September 7, 1896.

FIRST NIGHT, THE. F. 1 a. T. Parry, Adelphi, November 27, 1834.

FIRST NIGHT, THE. C.D. 1 a. Alfd. Wigan. Adap. fr. *Le Père de la Débutante*. Princess's, October 1, 1849; Olympic, November, 1854; Princess's, October, 1860; Gaiety, February 12, 1870; D.L., July 1, 1872; Folly, July, 1879; Comedy, October, 1887; Hay., 1887, and May, 1888; Her M., May 13, 1899.

FIRST NIGHT, THE. H. A. Saintsbury. Fr. two scenes of *Le Père de la Débutante*. Kennington P.O.W., August 21, 1899.

FIRST NIGHT, THE. Sk. Chs. Baldwin. Richmond, October 2, 1907.

FIRST NIGHT, THE. See *Behind the Scenes, The Débutante*.

FIRST NIGHT'S LODGING, THE. F. Archibald Maclaren. Pr. at Edinburgh and ? ac. before 1812.

FIRST OF APRIL, THE. F. 2 a. Caroline Boaden. Hay., August 31, 1830.

FIRST OF APRIL; OR, THE FOOL'S ERRAND, THE. M. Ent. Archibald Maclaren. Pr. 1802. Ac. in Guernsey.

FIRST OF MAY, THE. F. 1 a. A. Younge. Sadler's Wells, October 26, 1849.

FIRST OF SEPTEMBER; OR, EVERY MAN HIS OWN PARTRIDGE. P. Oliphant. Before 1814.

FIRST PRINTER, THE. D. C. Reade and T. Taylor. Princess's, March 3, 1856.

FIRST REHEARSAL, A. C.O. 1 a. Wr. and comp. by Louis Cottell. Tottenham Ct. Rd. Athenæum, June 1, 1892; Bayswater Bijou, November 2, 1895.

FIRST STOP, LONDON. Sk. Edward Morris. Sadler's Wells, November 30, 1908.

FIRST VIOLIN, THE. D. 4 a. Sidney Bowket. Adap. fr. Jessie Fothergill's novel of same name. First perf. New York, 1898. Peckham Crown, March 27, 1899.

FISCAL POLICY, THE. Sk. 3 sc. Leon Mortimer. Canning Town R. Albert, November 30, 1903.

FISH OUT OF WATER. F. 1 a. Joseph Lunn. Hay., August 26, 1823. Rev. Lyceum, October, 1874.

FISHER GIRL, THE. M.P. 2 a. Oswald Brand. M. by W. T. Gliddon. Hanley T.R., May 27, 1901; Peckham Crown, July 8, 1901.

FISHER GIRL, THE. See *Monsieur Moulon*.

FISHER GIRL; OR, FLYING DUTCHMAN, THE. M. C-D. Wr. by Chs. Fisher. Lyrics by Oswald Brand. M. by W. T. Gliddon. Paragon, June 17, 1907.

FISHER MAIDEN, THE. M.P. Arthur J. Lamb. M. by Harry von Tilzer. Shaftesbury, September 11, 1903 (C.P.).

FISHER MAIDEN, THE. O. 2 a. Geoffrey Blackmore. Additional lyrics by A. Phillips and J. W. Cox. Croydon P.H., November 14, 1904.

FISHERMAN'S DAUGHTER, THE. Dom. D. 2 a. Charles Garvice. Royalty, December 26, 1881.

FISHERMAN'S DAUGHTER, THE. Irish C.D. 3 a. Dr. Montgomery A. Ward. M. by Mrs. Georgina Ayde Curran. Dublin Queen's, February 15, 1892.

FISHERMAN'S DAUGHTER, THE. C.D. 3 a. J. R. Bogue. Goole T.R., August 21, 1902; Grimsby T.R., December 22, 1902.

FISHERMAN'S HUT, THE. M.D. 3 a. Tobin. D.L., October 20, 1819.

FISHERMEN, THE. C.O. 2 a. Jas. Field Stanfield. Ac. circa 1786. N.p.

FISHERS, THE. O. A. Y. Simon. Lib. fr. Vict. Hugo by N. Wilde. Moscow, 1900.

FIT OF THE BLUES, A. Oa. V. Robillard.

FITS AND STARTS. F. 2 a. Wilton Jones and Walter Browne. Gaiety, May 2, 1885.

FITZSMYTHE, OF FITZSMYTHE HALL. F. 1 a. J. M. Morton. Hay., May 26, 1860.

FIVE DEGREES OF CRIME, THE. D. Leman Rede. New City, 1833.

FIVE GALLANTS, THE. C. Thos. Middleton. Blackfriars.

FIVE HUNDRED FRANCS. Oa. Marmaduke Brown. M. by Isidore de Solla. Vaudeville, July 6, 1885.

FIVE HUNDRED POUNDS. C. 2 a. D.L., August 25, 1821.

FIVE HUNDRED POUNDS REWARD. A. Wigan. Adapt. fr. *Le Capitaine de Voleurs.* Lyceum, 1845-47.

FIVE IN ONE. C.D. 1 a. H. Walpole. Publ. by S. French, Ltd.

FIVE LOVERS, THE. C.O. Ascr. to Swift. Dublin, February 22, 1806. M. by T. Cooke.

FIVE MILES OFF; OR, THE FINGER POST. C. 3 a. Thos. Dibdin. Hay. July 9, 1806. Pr. 1806. C.G., May 19, 1807.

FIVE MINUTES TOO LATE; OR, AN ELOPEMENT TO RHEIMS. C. in 3 parts, introd. coronation of Charles X. King of France. M. by Horn, Bishop, and Cooke. D.L., July 5, 1825.

FIVE PLAYS IN ONE. Rose T., April 7, 1597. See *Fyve*, etc.

FIVE POUNDS REWARD. F. 1 a. John Oxenford. Olympic, December 3, 1855.

FIVE THOUSAND A YEAR. C. T. Dibdin. C.G., March 16, 1799. Pr. 1799.

FIVE WITTY GALLANTS, THE. Ac. by the Children of the Chapell. Ent. on the Books of Stationers' Co., March 22, 1608. Probably Middleton's *Your First Gallants.*

FIVE YEARS LATER. Sk. Holborn Empire. June 15, 1908.

FIXED. F.C. J. Wilton Jones. Wigan T.R., March 12, 1883.

FIZZICAL CULTURE, F.Sk. Ewart Beech. Surrey Masonic H., January 3, 1908 (amat.).

FLACHSMANN ALS ERZIEHER. C. 3 a. Otto Ernst. St. Geo. H., November 5, 1901.

FLAG; OR, THE BATTLE FIELD, THE. D. 3 a. Surrey, November 12, 1870.

FLAG LIEUTENANT, THE. Naval C. 4 a. Major W. P. Drury and Leo Trevor. Playhouse, June 16, 1908.

FLAG STATION, THE. D. 1 a. Eugene Walter. Aldwych, October 29, 1908; Hippodrome, August 2, 1909.

FLAGGER'S TELEGRAM. F. W. H. Lonsdale. Gt. Grimsby T.R., February 24, 1871.

FLAME, THE. "Pantomime." Mark Peregrini, Broadway, December 12, 1907 (C.P.).

FLAMINGO; OR, THE ROOK AND THE CAUSE. Folie musicale. F. Hay and F. W. Green. Strand, September 18, 1875.

FLANAGAN AND THE FAIRIES. Extrav. Before 1836.

FLASH IN THE PAN, A. F. Milns. 1798. N.p.

FLASH IN THE PAN, A. P. 4 a. Allen Upward. Dublin Gaiety, October 23, 1896.

FLASH OF LIGHTNING, A. D. 4 a. Murdoch and Daly. Leeds Amphi., August 1, 1870; Grecian, November 21, 1870.

FLASHES. M. Absurdity. 3 a. J. J. Hewson and E. Lewis West. Liverpool New T.R., April 7, 1890; Marylebone, July 20, 1891.

FLATLAND. P. 3 a. W. Reynolds. Bristol T.R., June 11, 1904 (C.P.).

FLATS. F.C. 4 "stories." G. R. Sims. Adap. fr. *Les Locataires de Monsieur Blondeau.* Criterion, July 23, 1881.

FLATTERY, DECEIT, AND FALSEHOOD MISLEAD KING HUMANITY. One of 8 int. by Sir David Lindsay. Pr. 1792.

FLAUTO MAGICO, IL. O. Mozart. Vienna, 1791. See *Die Zauberflote.*

FLEDERMAUS, DIE. C.O. Adap. Hamilton Aidé. M. J. Strauss. Alhambra, December 18, 1876; D.L., June 22, 1895.

FLEETING CLOUDS. Dom. Inc. 1 a. Percy F. Marshall and Charles Dodsworth. Ladbroke H., January 25, 1889.

FLEIRE, THE. C. Edward Sharpham. Blackfriars (by the Children of the Revels). Pr. 1610. Entered Stationers' Co., May 9, 1606. Plot fr. Marston's *Parasitaster.*

FLEUR D'AMOUR, LA. Ballet Div. (new). 2 tab. M. Petit. M. by Alfd. Mellon. D.L., October 6, 1858.

FLEUR DE LYS. Op. bo. Adap. by H. B. Farnie. Philharmonic, April 5, 1873.

FLEUR DE LYS, THE. O. 3 a. C. Lecocq. Adap. by J. H. Jarvis. Newcastle Tyne T., March 15, 1875; Criterion, October 9, 1875.

FLEUR D'ORANGER. Jean Sery. M. by Merril. Royalty, June 29, 1908. (Fr. season.)

FLEURETTE. Oa. Augustus L. Tamplin. Gaiety, March 1, 1873.

FLEURETTE AND FADETTE. M.F. Cardiff Philharmonic, February 24, 1879.

FLIBUSTIER, LE. O. Cui. Paris.

FLIBUSTIER, LE. C. Jean Richepin. D.L. (in Fr.), June, 1893.

FLIEGENDE HOLLANDER, DER. O. 3 a. Words and M. by R. Wagner. Dresden, January 2, 1843. As *L'Orlandese Dannato*, in London, D.L., July 23, 1870. See *The Flying Dutchman.*

FLIES IN THE WEB. C. 3 a. J. Brougham. Circ. 1870. Manchester T.R.

FLIGHT. P. 4 a. Walter Frith. Terry's, February 16, 1893.

FLIGHT FOR LIFE. Surrey, July 8, 1895.

FLIGHT TO AMERICA; OR, TWELVE HOURS in NEW YORK, A. F. Burletta. L. Rede. Adelphi, November, 1830.

FLIGHTY'S FLIRTATION. F. Frank Harvey. Liverpool Amphi., January 25, 1874.

FLINT AND STEEL. F. J. F. M'Ardle. Sheffield Alexandra, May, 1881.

FLIP, FLAP, FLOP. F. Paul Meritt. Adap. fr. the French. Norwich T.R., November 10, 1879; Surrey, September 9, 1882.

FLIP, FLAP FOOTMAN. Adelphi, October, 1840.

FLIRTATION, F. Frank Harvey. Edinburgh T.R., August 11, 1873.

FLIRTATION. C. 3 a. Romer and Bellamy. Globe, July 14, 1877.

FLIRTING. M.C. Ramsgate Sanger's Amphi., July 14, 1884.

FLITCH OF BACON, THE. C.O. Rev. H. Bate Dudley. M. by Shield. Hay., August 17, 1788; D.L., June 22, 1814. Pr. 1779.

FLITCH OF BACON, THE. Sk. Strand, July, 1855.

FLITTING DAY. Mentioned by Brewer.

FLO RIGG. P. 1 a. E. Burney. Royal Albert H., June 3, 1908.

FLO'S FIRST FROLIC. F. Princess's, May 23, 1868.

FLOATING A COMPANY. Ca. 1 a. Julian Cross. Royalty, June 28, 1894

FLOATING BEACON; OR, THE WILD WOMAN OF THE WRECK, THE. Melo-d. 2 a. Edwd. Fitzball. Surrey, April 19, 1824.

FLOATING ISLAND, THE. T.C. Rev. Wm. Strode. M. by Lawes. Ac. before the King and Queen by students of Christchurch, August 29, 1639. Pr. 1655.

FLODDEN FIELD. Dr. Rom. 3 a. Founded on *Marmion*. Johnson. M. by Cooke. D.L., December 31, 1818.

FLODDEN FIELD. D. Prel. and 2 a. Alfred Austin. H.M. (Guy's Hospital ent.), June 8, 1903.

FLOOD TIDE, THE. Melo-f. 4 a. Cecil Raleigh. D.L., September 17, 1903.

FLORA. O. Alteration, probably by John Hippisley, of *The Country Wake*. L.I.F. Pr. 1730.

FLORA. See *Hob; or, The Country Wake*.

FLORA MIRABILIS. O. Samara.

FLORA; OR, HOB IN THE WELL. F. 2 a. Colley Cibber.

FLORA'S VAGARIES. C. R. Rhodes. Ac. by students at Ch. Ch., Oxford, January 8, 1663; and at T.R. Pr. 1670; and D.L., July 26, 1715.

FLORAZENE; OR, THE FATAL CONQUEST. T. James Goodall. Pr. 1754. N.ac.

FLORENCE. D. Plymouth T.R., November 20, 1872.

FLORENTINE FRIEND, THE. P. Entd. Stationers' Co. November 29, 1653. N.p.

FLORENTINE LADIES, THE. In Jordan's Nursery of Novelties. 1660.

FLORENTINE TRAGEDY, THE. P. Oscar Wilde. King's, Covent Garden, June 10, 1906; rev. Cripplegate Inst., October 28, 1907; Manchester Tivoli, June 7, 1909.

FLORENTINE WOOING, A (The Wooing). C. 4 a. Clo Graves. Avenue, July 6, 1898 (C.P.).

FLORENTINES, THE. P. Sadler's Wells, June 2, 1845.

FLORETTA. O. 2 a. Miss Eleanor Farjeon. M. by Harry Farjeon. Founded on a story by Zschökke. St. Geo. H. July 17, 1899.

FLORETTE. O. 3 a. Allen and Bartlett. Publ. by S. French, Limited.

FLORIAN. O. 4 a. Libretto by D. Latham. Dramatised by Grace Latham. M. by Ida Walter. Novelty, July 14, 1886.

FLORIEN. T. 5 a. H. C. Merivale. Pr. 1884.

FLORIMENE. Past. Ac. before the K. at Whitehall. Pr. 1635.

FLORIZEL AND PERDITA. Dr. Past. 3 a. Fr. *A Winter's Tale*, by David Garrick. D.L., 1756. Pr. 1758.

FLORIZEL AND PERDITA; OR, THE SHEEPSHEARING. F. 2 a. Macnamara Morgan. Fr. *A Winter's Tale*. Pr. 1754. Ac. at Dublin and C.G., Edinburgh, 1781.

FLORODORA, M.C. Owen Hall. Lyrics by Ernest Boyd-Jones and Paul Rubens. M. by Leslie Stuart. Lyric, November 11, 1899.

FLOWER GIRL, THE. Oa. MacIvay. Jersey P.O.W.'s R. May 10, 1870.

FLOWER GIRL, THE. C.O. 1 a. J. Parry Cole. Bayswater Bijou, June 20, 1901.

FLOWER GIRL, THE. M.P. 2 a. Books, lyrics, and M. by Wm. T. Gliddon. Lincoln R.T., May 14, 1908; Croydon Grand, November 30, 1908.

FLOWER GIRL; OR, THE CONVICT MARQUIS, THE. P. T. Townsend. Surrey, 1858; rev. Surrey, November 23, 1867. City of Lon., July, 1865.

FLOWER GIRL OF GHENT, THE. Ballet Div. Mme. Louise. M. by Albert. D.L., July 15, 1856.

FLOWER MAKERS AND HEART BREAKERS: A TALE OF TRIAL AND TEMPTATIONS. D. 3 a. C. H. Hazlewood. Grecian, October 7, 1869.

FLOWER O' THE ROSE. Rom. D. 1 a. William J. Locke. Clement Scott *matinée*, H.M., June 23, 1904.

FLOWER OF THE FARM, THE. C. 3 a. Ayr T., November 6, 1896 (C.P.).

FLOWER OF THE FLOCK, THE. D. 3 a. Exeter T.R., November 8, 1880.

FLOWER OF THE FLOCK, THE. C. 3 a. Mark Melford. Grimsby T.R., April 6, 1883.

FLOWERS. A Masque of Flowers was presented by the Gentlemen of Gray's Inn at the Court of Whitehall in the Banqueting House, 1613. Pr. 1614.

FLOWERS OF THE FOREST, THE. D. J. B. Buckstone. Adelphi, March 11, 1847, and August, 1859; rev. Astley's, 1867.

FLUFF; OR, A CLEAN SWEEP. F. 3 a. J. F. M'Ardle. Leicester O.H., August 1, 1881.

FLUTE OF PAN, THE. P. 4 a. J. O. Hobbes. Manchester Gaiety T., April 21, 1904; Shaftesbury, November 12, 1904.

FLY AND THE WEB, THE. C. 2 a. Adolphus C. Troughton. Strand, February 5, 1866.

FLY BY NIGHT, THE. Sk. Paul A. Rubens. Palace, December 14, 1908.

FLY ON THE WHEEL, THE. C. 3 a. Max Beerbohm and Murray Carson. Notting Hill Coronet, December 4, 1902.

FLYAWAY'S RACE. Sk. S. Whitehouse. M. by H. E. Pether. Kilburn T.H., March 9, 1892.

FLYING DUTCHMAN, THE. O. 3 a. Wagner. Dresden, January 2, 1843; as *L'Olandese dannato*, Drury Lane, July 23, 1870. Transl. by John P. Jackson. Lyceum, October 3, 1876; Her M., February, 1882; as *Il Vascello Fantasma*, at Covent Garden, June 16, 1877.

FLYING DUTCHMAN, THE. Burl. R. Reece. Liverpool P.O.W., 1869.

FLYING DUTCHMAN; OR, THE DEMON SEAMAN AND THE LASS THAT LOVED A SAILOR, THE. Burl. W. Brough. Royalty, December 2, 1869.

FLYING DUTCHMAN; OR, THE PHANTOM SHIP, THE. Nautical D. 3 a. Edwd. Fitzball. M. by G. H. B. Rodwell. Adelphi, June, 1825; December 4, 1826; June, 1856.

FLYING DUTCHMAN, THE. See *Vanderdecken*.

FLYING FROM JUSTICE. D. 4 a. Mark Melford. Southampton P.O.W., May 26, 1890; Sadler's Wells, June 15, 1891.

FLYING SCUD; OR, A FOUR-LEGGED FORTUNE, THE. D. 4 a. Dion Boucicault. Holborn T., October 6, 1866; Adelphi, August, 1868.

FLYING VISIT, A. A. Law and Corney Grain. Circa 1865.

FLYING VISIT, A. Ca. 1 a. Mrs. W. Greet. Criterion, November 6, 1889.

FLYING VOICE, THE. P. Ralph Wood. Destroyed by Warburton's servant.

FOGGERTY'S FAIRY. Fairy C. 3 a. W. S. Gilbert. Criterion, December 15, 1881.

FOGGY DAY, A. C. 1 a. M. R. Morand. Belfast T.R., July 23, 1900.

FOIL AND COUNTERFOIL. P. 4 a. Mary Woodifield. St. Geo. H., June 28, 1906 (amat.).

FOILED. C.D. 3 a. H. W. Williamson. Portsmouth T.R., May 4, 1882.

FOILED. D. 3 a. Warwick Buckland. St. Geo. H., October 25, 1890.

FOILED. Dr. Episode. J. R. Alberton. Globe, October 10, 1891.

FOILED. P. 3 a. N. Covertside (Dr. N. Davies). Llandilo Vict. Drill H., September 27, 1900 (amat.).

FOILED. Rom. D. Francis M. Kay. Bingham Harborne Inst., January 28, 1908 (amat.).

FOILED BY FATE. D. 4 a. J. Darlison. West London, October 22, 1900.

FOIRE DE NAPLES, LA. Div. D.L., November 13, 1839.

FOIRE ST. LAURENT, LA. O. 3 a. Offenbach. 1877.

FOLDED PAGE, A. Monol. Mrs. Wm. Greet. Steinway H., May 12, 1891.

FOLIE, UNE. C.O. J. Wild. From *Love Laughs at Locksmiths*. 1803. N.a'c.

FOLIE, UNE. C.O. Méhu. 1763-1817.

FOLLE FARINE. D. W. Avondale. Adap. fr. Ouida's novel of same name. Bishop Auckland T.R., March 10, 1884; Sadler's Wells, October 18, 1884. See *Satan's Daughter*.

FOLLIES OF A DAY; OR, THE MARRIAGE OF FIGARO, THE. C. Thos. Holcroft. Tiansl. of Beaumarchais' *La Folle Journée*. C.G., December 14, 1784. Pr. 1784. Alt. by J. P. Kemble, 1811. Pl. as an afterpiece, D.L., February 12, 1817.

FOLLIES OF A NIGHT, THE. V.C. 2 a. J. R. Planché. D.L., October 5, 1842. See *A Night in Paris, Absurdities of a Day, The Duke's Diversion*.

FOLLIES OF FASHION. C. 5 a. Earl of Glengall. D.L., November 28, 1829.

FOLLIES OF THE DAY; OR, FAST LIFE, THE. D. 4 a. H. P. Grattan and Joseph Eldred. Bristol T.R., October 16, 1882; Pav., July 9, 1883.

FOLLIES OF YOUTH, THE. D. 4 a. Fred L Connynghame and Frank Price. Warrington R.C.T., July 28, 1902; Rotherhithe Terriss, July 13, 1903; rewritten, Windsor T.R., November 28, 1904.

FOLLOW MY LEADER. Duol. H. B. Maxwell. St. Leonard's Pier Pav., November 22, 1899.

FOLLOW THE DRUM. Melo-d. 5 a. Rass Challis. Wakefield O.H., April 2, 1888.

FOLLOW THE LEADER. C. 1 a. C. M. Rae. Charing Cross T., April 12, 1873.

FOLLY AS IT FLIES. C. 5 a. Frederic Reynolds. C.G., Pr. 1802. D.L., November 3, 1821.

FOLLY AS IT FLIES. Ent. H. Thomas. Luxembourg H., July 5, 1870.

FOLLY FETE. Grecian, October 12, 1865.

FOLLY OF AGE, A. C. 1 a. Arthur Ingram. Op. C., November 26, 1894.

FOLLY OF AGE; OR, THE ACCOMPLISHED LADY, A Pant. C.G., 1797.

FOLLY OF PRIESTCRAFT, THE. C. Anon. 1690.

FOLLY'S FORTUNES. M.P. 3 a. Bacup R. Court, August 21, 1899.

FOND HEARTS; OR, A BROTHER'S LOVE. M.D. 3 a. Fred Evanson. Southampton P.O.W., October 7, 1889.

FOND HUSBAND; OR, THE PLOTTING SISTERS, THE. C. T. Durfey. D.L. Duke of York's, 1676. Pr. 1676.

FOND LADY, THE. C. By a "Person of Honour." Pr. 1684. See *Amorous Old Woman*.

FONDLEWIFE AND LETITIA. C. 2 a. Ac. at Dublin. Pr. 1767. Taken from *The Old Bachelor*.

FONTAINEBLEAU; OR, OUR WAY IN FRANCE. C.O. 3 a. John O'Keeffe. C.G., 1784; D.L., February 11, 1814, and October 18, 1819; Lyceum, September 30, 1822. Pr. 1798.

FONTAINVILLE FOREST. P. James Boaden. C.G., March 25, 1794. Pr. 1794. F. on Mrs. Radcliffe's "Romance of the Forest."

FOOL, THE. F. 2 a. Edwd. Topham. C.G., December 14, 1785. Pr. 1786.

FOOL AND HER MAIDENHEAD SOON PARTED, A. P. Probably by Robert Davenport. Belonging to Cockpit. Ent. Stationers' Co., November 29, 1653. N.p.

FOOL AND HIS MONEY, A. C. 3 a. Henry J. Byron. Globe, June 17, 1878.

FOOL MADE WISE, A. O.C. Sam Johnson. Hay., 1741. N.p.

FOOL OF QUALITY. C. Poisson. 1633-1690.

FOOL OF THE FAMILY, THE. C. 3 a. Fergus Hume. D. of York's, January 30, 1896.

FOOL OF THE WORLD, THE. Morality. Arthur Symons. Bayswater Bijou, April 5, 1906.

FOOL TRANSFORMED, THE. C. Advertised "in the press," 1661. ? N.p.

FOOL TURNED CRITIC, THE. C. T. Durfey. Partly fr. *Jealous Lovers*. T.R. Pr. 1678.

FOOL WOULD BE A FAVOURITE; OR, THE DISCREET LOVER, THE. T.C. Lodowick Carlell. Ac. Pr. 1657.

FOOLE WITHOUT BOOKE, THE. P. Wm. Rowley. Entered Stationers' Co.; September 9, 1653. N.p.

FOOL'S FIDELITY, A. D. 3 a. Geo. Capel. Birmingham, March 14, 1887; Dalston N. London Colosseum, June 6, 1887.

FOOL'S MASQUE, THE. Masque. Prod. at Court about A.D. 1620.

FOOL'S MATE. Piece. 1 a. F. W. Broughton. Toole's, December 12, 1889; Avenue, February 1, 1890.

FOOL'S OPERA; OR, THE TASTE OF THE AGE, THE. "Matthew Medley." Aston. Ac. at Oxford. Pr. 1731.

FOOL'S PARADISE. C. Paul Meritt and Alfred Maltby. West Hartlepool T.R., January 20, 1879.

FOOL'S PARADISE, A. P. 3 a. Sydney Grundy. Greenwich P.O.W., October 7, 1887 (C.P. under title of *The Mousetrap*.) New York Wallack's T., October 10, 1887; Gaiety, February 12, 1889; Garrick, January 2, 1892; Coronet, March 18, 1901.

FOOL'S PREFERMENT; OR, THE THREE DUKES OF DUNSTABLE, A. C. T. D'Urfey. Dorset Gardens Queen's T. Pr. 1688. Little more than a transcript of Fletcher's *Noble Gentleman* and one scene fr. novel, *Humours of Basset*.

FOOL'S REVENGE, THE. D. 3 a. Tom Taylor. Sadler's Wells, October 18, 1859; Queen's, December 20, 1869.

FOOL'S TRICK, A. F. Adelene Votieri. St. Geo. H., June 20, 1891.

FOOLED BY FORTUNE. D. 3 a. Henry Walton. Liverpool T.R., September 28, 1874.

FOOLS. F. Eccentricity. 3 a. T. D. M'Cord. Reg. Pk. Lecture H., Camden Town, February 14, 1885.

FOOLS OF NATURE. P. 4 a. H. O. Esmond. Duke of York's, March 11, 1903.

FOOTBALL KING, THE. D. 4 a. Geo. Gray. Eleph. and C., July 13, 1896.

FOOTE, WESTON, AND SHUTER IN THE SHADES. Int. Hay., 1784. N.p.

FOOTLIGHTS. C.D. J. Shenton. Doncaster T.R., September 25, 1872.

FOOTMAN, THE (*The Footman's Opera*). O. Pr. 1732. Ac. Goodman's Fields T., March 7, 1732.

FOOTMAN TURNED GENTLEMAN, THE. F. 2 a. L.I.F., March 13, 1717.

FOOTMARKS IN THE SNOW. D. 3 a. E. Towers. City of London, October 14, 1867.

FOOTSTEP, THE. Sk. C. L. Delph. Brixton Empress, February 1, 1909.

FOR A CHILD'S SAKE. Dom. D. 4 a. H. Herman and M. Turner. Cambridge New T., January 2, 1899; Greenwich Morton's, September 4, 1899; Surrey, December 4, 1899.

FOR A DREAM'S SAKE. P. 1 a. Demain Grange. Brighton W. Pier, November 27, 1902.

FOR A LIFE. D. 4 a. J. J. M'Closkey. Adap. fr. Marcus Clarke's novel, "His Natural Life." Manchester Queen's, July 19, 1886; Surrey, May 6, 1889.

FOR A WOMAN'S HONOUR. Sk. Frank Herbert and E. Sealy. Holborn Restaurant, November 15, 1890.

FOR AN OLD DEBT. Dom. D. 1 a. F. Rawson Buckley and I. Harwood Panting. Bayswater Bijou, February 26, 1895.

FOR AULD LANG SYNE. D. 4 a. Seymour Hicks and Fred G. Latham. Lyceum, Oct. 6, 1900.

FOR BETTER, FOR WORSE. D. 4 a. M. E. Braddon. Suggested by her novel, "Like and Unlike." Whitby W. Cliff Saloon, September 6, 1890 (C.P.). Brighton Gaiety (3 a), April 6, 1891.

FOR BETTER, FOR WORSE. Duol. Frank Farren. Working Men's Club, Aldgate, February 8, 1891.

FOR BETTER OR WORSE. F. 1 a. C. A. Maltby. Croydon T.R., September 18, 1870.

FOR BETTER OR WORSE. D. 4 a. Wm. P. Sheen. Clapham Junction Shakespeare, August 11, 1905 (C.P.); Hyde R., October 23, 1905.

FOR BONNIE PRINCE CHARLIE. D. 4 a. Joseph Clarke. Shaftesbury, January 29, 1897 (C.P.).

FOR BONNIE SCOTLAND. Scottish D. Adap. and arr. by Ernest Stevens. Glasgow G.T., October 12, 1897.

FOR CHARITY'S SAKE. Dom. C.D. 1 a. C. S. Fawcett. (Orig. *Our Lottie.*) Comedy, January 29, 1891; Strand, February 28, 1894.

FOR CHARITY'S SAKE. M.Duol. Fred Bowyer and Walter H. Hedgecock. Terry's, January 9, 1893.

FOR CHURCH OR STAGE. D. 4 a. Rev. Forbes Phillips. Yarmouth Aquarium, June 8, 1903; Savoy, November 12, 1904.

FOR CLAUDIA'S SAKE. C. 3 a. Miss Mabel Freund-Lloyd. Vaudeville, July 2, 1891.

FOR DEAR LIFE. D. 4 a. W. Muskerry. Victoria, June 2, 1873.

FOR ENGLAND. Melo-d. 5 a. Sutton Vane. Manchester Queen's, February 27, 1893; Pavilion, May 15, 1893.

FOR ENGLAND HO! Melo-d. O. 2 a. T. Pocock. C.G., December 15, 1813.

FOR ENGLAND'S GLORY. Military Spectacle. W. J. Mackay. Canterbury, March 2, 1908.

FOR ENGLAND'S SAKE. Military D. 4 a. Henrietta Lindley fr. Robert Cromie's novel. Hay., August 10, 1889 (C.P.).

FOR EVER. D. 7 a. Paul Meritt and Geo. Conquest. Surrey, October 2, 1882.

FOR EVER MINE. C.D. Stevens and Logan. Darlington T.R., June 21, 1889.

FOR FAMILY FAME; OR, THE SEA AND ITS DEAD. Dom. D. Prol. and 3 a. Bernard M'Donald. Royalty, March 25, 1895.

FOR GOLD. D. 5 a. Elliot Galer. Leicester O.H. April 10, 1882.

FOR GOOD OR EVIL. P. 3 a. Mrs. A. J. Macdonnell. Royalty, June 18, 1894.

FOR HALF A MILLION. P. 1 a. Clara Harriet Sherwood. Copyrd. 1891.

FOR HER CHILD'S SAKE. Dr. Episode. 1 a. Sir C. Young. Windsor T.R. (amat.), November 24, 1880; Terry's, March 29, 1890.

FOR HER HUSBAND'S SAKE. Dom. D. 4 a. Millar Anderson. Manchester St. James's, May 20, 1907; Edmonton R., October 12, 1908.

FOR HER SAKE. D. 1 a. Alec Nelson. (E. B. Aveling.) Olympic, June 22, 1888.

FOR HER SAKE. D. 4 a. W. Roberts and Ben Landeck. Cheltenham O.H., April 18, 1907; Fulham G., August 5, 1907.

FOR HIMSELF ALONE. C. 3 a. Holmes Kingston. Adap. fr. T. W. Speight's story. Ladbroke H., May 7, 1888.

FOR HIS SAKE. Society Sk. A. Jefferson. Glasgow R., November 8, 1907 (C.P.).

FOR HONOUR'S SAKE. Rom. Irish D. 3 a. C. H. Hazlewood. Britannia, October 13, 1873.

FOR KING AND COUNTRY. D. Edmund Leathes. Gaiety, May 1, 1883.

FOR KING MONMOUTH. Rom. P. 1 a. Max Pireau. Brighton West P., November 27, 1902; Balham Assembly R., October 28, 1903.

FOR LACK OF GOLD. Oa. Maia. M. by F. von Lesen. Cheltenham Assembly R., December 2, 1880.

FOR LIFE. D. Bath T.R., May 6, 1871.

FOR LIFE. D. 3 a. Charles Coghlan. Adap. fr. *La Morte Civile.* Leeds Grand, August 9, 1880.

FOR LIFE AND AFTER. Melo-d. 4 a. G. R. Sims. Reading County, April 16, 1906; rev. ver. of *The Woman from Gaol*, prod. Pavilion, September 17, 1903.

FOR LIFE THROUGH THICK AND THIN. D. 2 a. J. G. Taylor. Alexandra, March 7, 1868.

FOR LOVE. D. 3 a. T. W. Robertson. New Holborn, October 5, 1867.

FOR LOVE AND THE KING. D. 4 a. C. Watson Mill. Mexborough P.O.W., April 13, 1908; Elephant and Castle, July 20, 1908.

FOR LOVE OF A LADY. Dr. Sk. W. B. Robinson. R. Victoria H., February 11, 1901.

FOR LOVE OF A WOMAN. D. 4 a. Nita Rae. Stafford Lyceum, July 27, 1908; Tyldesley T.R., August 10, 1908.

FOR LOVE OF PRIM. P. 1 a. Eden Phillpotts. Court, January 24, 1899; D. of York's, August 19, 1902.

FOR LOVE OR MONEY. C. 3 a. Andrew Halliday. Vaudeville, April 16, 1870.

FOR LOVE OR MONEY. D. 4 a. John Stanfield. Manchester Victoria, March 5, 1902, and Comedy, August 4, 1902; Pavilion, June 15, 1903.

FOR LOVE'S SAKE. Dom. D. L. E. Stephens. Richmond H.M.T., December 11, 1882.

FOR MILDRED S SAKE. Ca. Chas. D. Steele. West Norwood P.H., May 8, 1895.

FOR OLD LOVE'S SAKE. C.D. 3 a. Stanley Rogers and H. Kimm. Hastings Gaiety, March 17, 1884; Royalty, May 25, 1886; Sch. of Dr. Art, 524, Oxford St., April 30, 1894.

FOR OLD LOVE'S SAKE. See *For the Old Love's Sake*.

FOR OLD SAKE'S SAKE. P. 1 a. A. Demain Grange. Edinburgh Pav., May 7, 1898.

FOR OLD TIMES' SAKE. C.D. 3 a. Manville Morton. Orpington P.H., December 2, 1905.

FOR OLD VIRGINIA. P. 1 a. Henry Herman. Grand, June 4, 1891.

FOR PAPA'S SAKE. C. 1 a. M. B. Spurr. Publ. by S. French, Limited.

FOR QUEEN AND COUNTRY. Military D. 4 a. Evelyn Unsworth. Neath Bijou, December 26, 1890.

FOR SALE. D. 3 a. John T. Douglass, jun. Standard, February 3, 1869.

FOR SWORD OR SONG. Poetical M.P. R. G. Legge and Louis Calvert. M. by Raymond Rose. Newcastle-on-Tyne T.R., September 18, 1902; Shaftesbury, January 21, 1903.

FOR THE COLOURS. Military D. 4 a. W. A. Brabner. Manchester Metropole, August 14, 1899; Greenwich Carlton, April 14, 1902.

FOR THE CROSS; OR, THE DAWN OF CHRISTIANITY. D. 3 a. John Soden. M. by T. C. L. White. Navan Catholic H., July 16, 1898.

FOR THE CROWN. P. 4 a. John Davidson. Adapt. fr. François Coppée's *Pour la Couronne*. Odéon, Paris, January 19, 1895; Lyceum, February 27, 1890; Scala, October 10, 1905.

FOR THE CZAR. T. 1 a. Percival H. T. Sykes. Strand, November 3, 1896.

FOR THE DEFENCE; OR, THE VICTIMS OF THE LAW. D. 4 a. Walter Reynolds, jun., and H. Herne. Leeds T.R., August 4, 1902. Rotherhithe Terriss, September 15, 1902.

FOR THE HONOUR OF THE CLUB. D. 4 a. Fred J. Kirke and Mary Dawson. Liverpool Lyric, June 29, 1901 (C.P.).

FOR THE HONOUR OF THE FAMILY. C.D. 3 a. Adapt. fr. Emile Augier's *Mariage d'Olympe* (Paris Vaudeville, July 17, 1855). Comedy, June 10, 1897.

FOR THE HONOUR OF THE REGIMENT. Sk. 1 sc. W. Felton. Eastern Empire, September 4, 1899.

FOR THE HONOUR OF WALES. Antimasque. Ben Jonson. Circa 1619. Pr. 1692.

FOR THE KING. D. 4 a. Walter Howard and Sydney T. Pease. Windsor T.R., January 21, 1899 (C.P.); Croydon Grand, March 27, 1899; Elephant and Castle, February 26, 1900. See *In Life or Death, Blanche Farreau, Life and Honour*.

FOR THE KING'S SAKE. P. 1 a. Mrs. Challow Hale. Kingston Albany Club (in 3 a.). January 9, 1897 (amat.); Kingston County, October 6, 1898.

FOR THE LOVE OF A CHILD. Dom. D. A. Rose. Middlesbrough T.R., July 21, 1904 (C.P.).

FOR THE LOVE OF A LADY. D. Sk. W. Bevan Robinson. R. Victoria H., February 11, 1901.

FOR THE OLD LOVE'S SAKE. Hastings Gaiety, March 17, 1884.

FOR THE SAKE OF A NAME. D. 4 a. Forester Pilmore and John Holland. F. on the novel "From Gloom to Sunlight." Shoreham Swiss Gardens T., June 1, 1888.

FOR THE SAKE OF A WOMAN. Melo-d. 4 a. W. J. Patmore. Pavilion, September 10, 1900.

FOR THE SAKE OF THE DUCHESS. P. 4 a. Forbes Dawson. Fulham Grand, August 31, 1899.

FOR THE THIRD TIME. C. H. Dickenson. Publ. by S. French, Ltd.

FOR THE WOMAN HE LOVES. D. 4 a. M. Wallerton and F. Gilbert. Bristol T.R., February 23, 1903; Dalston, July 17, 1903.

FOR VALOUR. "Love Story." 1 a. C. S. Fawcett. York T.R., October 16, 1891.

FOR VALUE RECEIVED. P. 1 a. Hammersmith King's, October 3, 1904.

FOR WIFE AND HOME. Melo-d. 4 a. John Power, Manchester Queen's, August 3, 1906.

FOR WIFE AND KINGDOM. Rom. D. 4 a. Ward Bailey. Brighton Grand T., November 19, 1908 (C.P.); Smethwick R., March 8, 1909; Hammersmith Lyric, March 29, 1909.

FOR WIFE AND STATE. See *A Bitter Love*.

FORBIDDEN FRUIT. D. 4 a. F. M. Abbotts. Liverpool P.O.W., June 7, 1869; Lyceum, November 6, 1869.

FORBIDDEN FRUIT. C.D. 3 a. Dion Boucicault. Prod. at Wallack's T., New York. Liverpool St. James's H., October 22, 1877; Adelphi, July 3, 1880; Vaudeville, May 6, 1893.

FORBIDDEN LOVE. D. West Digges. Duke's, May 21, 1877.

FORCE DU NATUREL, LA. See *Adelina*.

FORCE OF CALUMNY, THE. P. Transl. fr. the German of Kotzebue by Ann Plumptre. Pr. 1799. N. ac.

FORCE OF FASHION, THE. H. Mackenzie. C.G., December 5, 1789. N.p.

FORCE OF FRIENDSHIP, THE. T. Chas. Johnson. Hay., April 20, 1710. Pr. 1710. Ac. with a farce *Love in a Chest*.

FORCE OF LOVE. T. Edward Tighe. An alt. of Lee's *Theodosius*. Pr. 1786.

FORCE OF NATURE, THE. P. 2 a. T. J. Thackeray. Hay., July 16, 1830. N.p.

FORCE OF RIDICULE, THE. C. Fr. the French. Thos. Holcroft. D.L., December 6, 1796. N.p.

FORCE OF TRUTH. Orat. Dr. Hoadley. 1744.

FORCED FROM HOME. D. 4 a. W. G. Wills. Duke's, February 2, 1880.

FORCED LADY, THE. T. Massinger. Destroyed by Warburton's servant. See *Minerva's Sacrifice*.

FORCED LADY. See *Forc'd Marriage*.

FORCED MARRIAGE, THE. T. Dr. John Armstrong. Wr. 1754. Pr. 1770.

FORCED MARRIAGE, THE. C. Transl. fr. Molière. Pr. 1762.

FORC'D MARRIAGE, THE. C. John Ozell. Transl. of Molière's "Mariage Forcé." Not intended for the stage.

FORC'D MARRIAGE; OR, THE JEALOUS BRIDEGROOM, THE. T.C. Mrs. Behn. Ac. at Queen's T., 1672. Pr. 1671.

FORCED MARRIAGE; OR, THE RETURN FROM SIBERIA, THE. D. 2 a. Mrs. T. P. Cooke. Surrey, December 5, 1842.

FORC'D PHYSICIAN, THE. C. John Ozell. Transl. fr. Molière's *Le Médecin Malgré Lui*.

FOREBODINGS. P. 1 a. T. A. Palmer.
FORECASTLE FUN; OR, SATURDAY NIGHT AT SEA. M. Ent. C.G., 1798. N.p.
FOREGONE CONCLUSION, A. See *Priest or Painter.*
FOREIGN BUTLER, THE. Ca. 1 a. H. K. Campbell and G. G. Scurfield. Carlisle Her M., February 17, 1906.
FOREIGN POLICY. P. 1 a. Conan Doyle. Terry's, June 3, 1893.
FOREIGN WOMAN, THE. Hist. P. 2 a. G. Vesian Pic. Wolverhampton P.O.W., October 25, 1902; Manchester Queen's, August 31, 1903.
FOREMAN OF THE WORKS, THE. Dom. D. 4 a. Geo. Manville Fenn. Fr. his novel "The Parson o' Dumford." Standard, March 8, 1886.
FOREST, THE. B. Jonson. 1616.
FOREST KEEPER, THE. D. 2 a. H. Holl. D.L., February 15, 1860.
FOREST MAIDEN, THE. O. J. H. Tully. Surrey.
FOREST OF ARDENNES, THE. Mus. D. Wade. Dublin, 1821; Victoria, 1833.
FOREST OF BONDY, THE. Melo-D. C.G., September 30, 1814; Lyceum, November 1, 1824; D.L., July 6, 1835.
FOREST OF HERMANSTADT; OR, PRINCESS AND NO PRINCESS, THE. Melo-d. 2 a. Ac. by C.G. Co., October 7, 1808. Alt. of *La Foret d'Hermanstadt ou La Fausse Epouse.* Arranged as Melo-d. by Dibdin.
FORESTER; OR, THE ROYAL SEAL, THE. D. John Bayley. An imitation of *The Midsummer Night's Dream.* Pr. 1798. N. ac.
FORESTER KING, THE. Hist. Melo-d. 5 a. Dr. Howard. Macclesfield T.R., September 19, 1892.
FORESTER'S DAUGHTER, THE. Oa. W. C. Masters. St. Geo. H., November 13, 1867.
FORESTERS, THE. P. 3 a. T. J. Serle. M. by Loder. C.G., October, 1838.
FORESTERS; A PICTURE OF RURAL MANNERS, THE. P. Bell Plumptre. Transl. fr. the German of Iffland. Pr. 1700.
FORESTERS, ROBIN HOOD, AND MAID MARIAN, THE. Poetic D. 4 a. Tennyson. M. by Sir Arthur Sullivan. Lyceum, March 17, 1892 (C.P.); Daly's, October 3, 1893.
FORESTERS' MASQUE, THE. A Court Masque. Ac. 1574.
FORGE MASTER, THE. D. G. M. Wood. Fr. Georges Ohnet's novel, "Le Maitre de Forges." Lynn T.R., October 23, 1884.
FORGE OF VULCAN, THE. Marylebone Gardens, 1776.
FORGED CHEQUES. D. Edwd. Darbey. Richmond H.M.T., December 7, 1882.
FORGER; OR, GOOD AND EVIL, THE. D. 4 a. Eleph. and C. (first time in London), November 13, 1886.
FORGERY. D. 3 a. J. Carne Ross. Ladbroke H., April 10, 1888.
FORGERY, THE. D. 5 a. Pr. 1814.
FORGERY; OR, ANOTHER MAN'S CRIME. Sk. 3 scenes. C. Stanley Self. Sadler's Wells, September 18, 1899.
FORGERY; OR, THE READING OF THE WILL. J. B. Buckstone. Adelphi, March 5, 1832.
FORGET AND FORGIVE. C.D. 3 a. John Daly Besemeres. Charing Cross, January 5, 1874.
FORGET AND FORGIVE; OR, RENCONTRES IN PARIS. C. 5 a. D.L., November 21, 1827.
FORGET AND FORGIVE; OR, THE ROAD TO HAPPINESS. C. Lindoe. Newcastle, 1804.
FORGET ME NOT. D. 3 a. Herman Merivale and F. C. Grove. Lyceum, August 21, 1879; Avenue, May 21, 1892; Savoy, October 15, 1904.
FORGIVE AND FORGET. Ca. 1 a. D.L., October 31, 1835; Olympic, October 22, 1838.
FORGIVE US OUR TRESPASSES. D. Prol. and 3 a. Naomi Hope. Brighton Gaiety, June 1, 1896.
FORGIVEN. C. 4 a. James Albery. Globe, March 9, 1872.
FORGIVENESS. Ca. J. Comyns Carr. St. James's, December 30, 1891.
FORGOTTEN. P. 4 a. F. Frankfort Moore. Islington Grand, July 5, 1889; Peterborough T.R., October 10, 1889.
FORLORN HOPE, A. Amer. Melo-d. 4 a. Katherine F. Rand. Salford Regent T., April 8, 1901. See *The Golden Prospect.*
FORLORN HOPE, THE. D. 3 a. C. H. Hazlewood, Britannia, May 8, 1871.
FORLORN HOPE, THE. Sk. Clement Scott and J. M. Coward. Oxford M.H., May 22, 1896.
FORMOSA; OR, THE RAILROAD TO RUIN. D. 4 a. Dion Boucicault. D.L., August 5, 1869; Newcastle Tyne T., October 11, 1869; D.L., May 26, 1891.
FORSAKEN; AN EVERY DAY STORY. D. Fredk. Marchant. Victoria, March 27, 1869.
FORT FRIVOLOUS. C.O. E. Byam Wyke. M. by A. Morris Edwards. Weymouth T.R., October 11, 1880.
FORTE THIEVES PLAYED PIANO. Burl. Bruce Smith. Folkestone Town H., October 29, 1889.
FORTITUDE OF JUDITH, THE. T. Ralph Radcliffe. N.p.
FORTRESS, THE. Melo-d. 3 a. T. E. Hook. Hay., July 16, 1807. Pr. 1807.
FORTUNATE DEPARTURE, THE. "Wr. by an Englishman during confinement in Lisbon under the marauders of France." Pr. 1810.
FORTUNATE GENERAL, THE. Richd. Hathwaye. Ac. 1602. N.p.
FORTUNATE ISLES; OR, THE TRIUMPH OF BRITANNIA. Masque, by J. R. Planchè. M. by Sir H. R. Bishop. Prod. in honour of the marriage of Queen Victoria. C.G., January 12, 1840.
FORTUNATE ISLES AND THEIR UNION, THE. Masque. Ben Jonson. Ac. before the Court, Twelfth Night, 1626. Pr. 1756.
FORTUNATE PEASANT; OR, NATURE WILL PREVAIL, THE. C. Benj. Victor. Fr. *Paysan Parvenu* of Mons. de Marivaux. Pr. 1776. N.ac.
FORTUNATE PRINCE; OR, MARRIAGE AT LAST, THE. B.O. 3 a. Pr. 1734. See *Marriage at Last.*
FORTUNATE SAILOR, THE. O. David Morison. Pr. 1790.
FORTUNATE TARS. Burl. Oulton. 1810.
FORTUNATE YOUTH, THE. Sans Pareil. 1818.
FORTUNATUS. Panto. Woodward. D.L., 1753.
FORTUNATUS. Melo-d. Ro. Prod. by Bishop. C.G., April, 1819.
FORTUNATUS. See *Old Fortunatus.*
FORTUNATUS; OR, THE WISHING CAP. C. Not divided into acts. Thos. Dekker. 1600.
FORTUNE BY LAND AND SEA. T.C. Thos. Heywood and Wm. Rowley. Ac. by the Queen's Servants. Pr. 1655.
FORTUNE HUNTER, THE. P. 3 a. W. S. Gilbert. Birmingham T.R., September 27, 1897; Crouch End O.H., October 18, 1897.

FORTUNE HUNTERS, THE. F. Ac. Pr. 1750.

FORTUNE HUNTERS; OR, THE WIDOW BEWITCH'D, THE. F. Chas. Macklin. Ac. circa 1748. N.p.

FORTUNE HUNTERS; OR, TWO FOOLS WELL MET, THE. C. Jas. Carlisle. Ac. by H.M. Servants. Pr. 1689. Hay., June 10, 1707.

FORTUNE IN HER WITS. C. Chas. Johnson. Pr. 1705. N. ac. Transl. of Cowley's *Naufragium Joculare*.

FORTUNE MENDS. C. F. Holcroft.

FORTUNE OF WAR, THE. F. 2 a. J. Kenney. C.G., May, 1815.

FORTUNE OF WAR, THE. Sk. F. C. Philips. Criterion, May 19, 1896.

FORTUNE OF WAR, THE. P. 1 a. Afterwards *Old Crimea*. Cosmo Hamilton. St. James's, July 2, 1901.

FORTUNE OF WAR, THE. Sk. By C. C. Andrews. M. by A. Howells. Canterbury, July 1, 1907.

FORTUNE TELLER, THE. Op. F. D.L., September 29, 1808. N.p.

FORTUNE TELLER, THE. C.O. 3 a. H. B Smith. M. by Victor Herbert. Shaftesbury, April 9, 1901.

FORTUNE TELLERS, THE. Panto. D.L., 1740.

FORTUNE TELLERS; OR, THE WORLD UNMASK'D, THE. Medley. Abel Drugger. (John Hardham.) Pr. No date. (He died September, 1772.)

FORTUNE TO KNOW EACH ONE, THE CONDICIONS AND GENTLE MANORS, AS WELL OF WOMEN AS OF MEN. P. Entered at Stationers' H., 1566. ? N.p. See *Common Conditions*.

FORTUNE'S FOOL. C. Fred Reynolds. C.G., October 29, 1796. Pr. 1796.

FORTUNE'S FOOL. D. 5 a. Chas. Harbury. Adap. fr. the French. Stratford T.R., July 28, 1890.

FORTUNE'S FOOL. Dr. Episode. Monol. Henry Hamilton. Hay., March 28, 1895.

FORTUNE'S FOOL. P. Rathmell Wilson. (Prod. by the Revival Co.) Rehearsal W.C., February 28, 1909.

FORTUNE'S FROLIC. F. 2 a. J. T. Allingham. C.G., May 25, 1799; D.L., November 1?, 1814. Alt. to 1 a.

FORTUNE'S FROLICS. Hay., 1806.

FORTUNE'S TASKE; OR, THE FICKLE FAIR ONE. P. in MS. 1684. John Horne.

FORTUNE'S TRICKS IN FORTY-SIX. Satire. Pr. 1747.

FORTUNE'S WHEEL. M. Ent. Ac. at O.H. in Hay., 1793. N.p.

FORTUNES OF FAN, THE. F.C. 3 a. H. M. Paull. Edinburgh Lyceum, prod. as *The Duchess of Bermondsey*, April 20, 1908; rev. Peckham Crown, May 25, 1908.

FORTUNES OF NIGEL. P. Dramatised by Ball. Surrey, June 25, 1822; Bath, December 7, 1822.

FORTUNES OF SMIKE; OR, A SEQUEL TO NICHOLAS NICKLEBY, THE. D. 2 a. Edwd. Stirling. Adelphi, March 2, 1840.

FORTUNIO AND HARLEQUIN. Pant. C.G., 1815.

FORTUNIO AND HIS SEVEN GIFTED SERVANTS. Fairy Extrav. 2 a. J. R. Planché. F. on Countess d'Alnois's Fairy Tale. D.L., April 17, 1843; Marylebone, 1849; Sadler's Wells, 1851.

FORTY AND FIFTY. Ca. 1 a. T. H. Bayly. March 3, 1836. D.L., April 18, 1836; St. James's, 1876.

FORTY ROBBERS. Wood Green Assembly R., October 1, 1892.

FORTY SHILLINGS. Ca. F. A. Besant Rice. Brixton, April 9, 1906.

FORTY THIEVES, THE. Op. Rom. 2 a. Fr. Arabian Night's Entertainment. The programme sketched by Sheridan. Dialogue wr. by Ward and Colman. M. by Kelly. D.L., April 8, 1806; June 12, 1816; November 19, 1832. N.p.

FORTY THIEVES, THE. Melo-d. Lyceum (first time at this theatre), November 16, 1835

FORTY THIEVES, THE. Burl. Lyceum (Savage Club perf.), March 7, 1860; Lyceum, April, 1860.

FORTY THIEVES, THE. Burl. D. 3 a. Robt. Reece. Gaiety, December 23, 1880.

FORTY THIEVES, THE. Burl. Panto. Extrav. Standard, June 3, 1895.

FORTY THIEVES DOWN TO DATE, THE. Burl. 2 a. and 6 scenes. G. V. Keast. Stonehouse Grand T., Plymouth, June 16, 1890.

FORTY WINKS. Duol. Ca. 1 a. Geo. Roberts. St. James's, June 2, 1862.

FORTY WINKS. Oa. H. B. Farnie. Hay., November 2, 1872.

FORWARD TO THE FRONT. Military and Naval Spec. D. Geo. Fawcett Rowe. Norwich T.R., October 1, 1888.

FORZA DEL DESTINO, LA. O. 4 a. Verdi. Lib. by Piane. St Petersburg, 1862. H.M.T., June 22, 1867.

FOSCARI. T. 5 a. Mary Russell Mitford. C.G., November 4, 1826.

FOSTER BROTHERS. F. C. Burnand and King Hall. St. George's H. Circa 1865.

FOSTER SISTERS OF WICKLOW; OR, TEDDY THE ROLLICKER, THE. D. Birkenhead T.R., July 31, 1882.

FOTHERINGAY, THE. P. 1 a. Adap. fr. Thackeray's "Pendennis" by Patrick Kirwan. Bayswater Bijou, October 29, 1903.

FOUL DEEDS WILL RISE. M.D. S. J. Arnold. Hay., July 18, 1804. Plot fr. "The Traveller's Story" in Miss Lee's Canterbury Tales. Pr. 1804.

FOUL PLAY. D. 4 a. Dion Boucicault and Ch. Reade. Holborn, May 28, 1868; altered to prol. and 5a; Leeds New T.R., June 1, 1868.

FOUL PLAY. Burl. Burnand. See *Fowl Play*.

FOUL WEATHER. Melo-d. 5 a. C. W. Somerset. Glasgow Royalty, May 30, 1881.

FOUND. D. 4 a. F. Haywell. Nottingham T.R., April 9, 1869; Manchester T.R., March 2, 1874; Gaiety, November 14, 1883.

FOUND. D. Prol. and 4 a. Fred Jul. Stein Gateshead T.R., January 16, 1888.

FOUND AT LAST. D. 4 a. Arthur B. Wise. Leamington T.R., February 27, 1899; Greenwich Morton's T., March 6, 1899.

FOUND AT SEA. Victoria, April 19, 1863.

FOUND BRUMMY. F. Alfd. Maltby. Princess's, September 21, 1874.

FOUND DEAD IN THE STREET. D. Prol. and 2 a. W. R. Waldron. Cheltenham T.R., August 30, 1869; Grecian, April 14, 1873; Marylebone, April 10, 1882.

FOUND DROWNED; OR, OUR MUTUAL FRIEND. D. 4 a. G. F. Rowe. Based on Dickens's "Our Mutual Friend." Op. Comique, December 26, 1870. See *Golden Dustman*.

FOUND DYING; OR, THE OLD WATCHMAN'S SECRET. D. 3 a. M. Wardhaugh. Eleph. and C., May 21, 1877.

FOUND DYING IN THE STREETS; OR, A WILL MADE IN A SNOWDRIFT ON THE FLY-LEAF OF A RAKE'S DIARY. D. M. Wardhaugh. Barnsley Queen's, March 21, 1870; Eleph. and C., May 21, 1877.

FOUND FAITHFUL. D. Sk. Pimlico Standard M.H., July 15, 1905.

FOUND IN A FOUR-WHEELER! F. T. J. Williams. New Royalty, April 24, 1866.

FOUND IN A TAXI. Playlet. 1 a. Rehearsal May 30, 1909.

FOUND IN EXILE; OR, NEWS FROM HOME. P. 5 tableaux. Eliot Galer. F. on Phillips Oppenheim's story, "Expiation." Leicester R.O.H., June 11, 1888 (C.P.).

FOUND IN LONDON; OR, PLAYING THEIR GAME. D. Dacre Baldie. Barrow-in-Furness T.R., March 3, 1879.

FOUND ON THE VELT. C. 3 a. Watford Clarendon H., April 8, 1902.

FOUND OUT. F.C. 3 a. James J. Hewson. Liverpool St. Geo. H., January 20, 1888.

FOUNDED ON FACTS. F. 1 a. J. P. Wooler. Olympic, August 7, 1848.

FOUNDED ON FACTS. D. 5 a. H. C. Turner. Keighley Queen's T., February 14, 1890.

FOUNDERED FORTUNE, A. D. Prol. and 4 a. W. E. Morton. Eleph. and C., December 15, 1890.

FOUNDLING, THE. C. 5 a. Edwd. Moore. D.L., February 13, 1748. Pr. 1748.

FOUNDLING, THE. F. 3 a. W. Lestocq and E. M. Robson. Terry's, August 30, 1894.

FOUNDLING OF FORTUNE; OR, NEXT OF KIN, THE. D. Prol. and 3 a. F. G. Cheatham. Victoria, April 22, 1867.

FOUNDLING OF NOTRE DAME, THE. 3 a. W. Banks. Liverpool T.R., August 7, 1876.

FOUNDLING OF THE FOREST, THE. P. 3 a. Wm. Dimond. Hay., July 10, 1809; D.L., June 10, 1815, and June, 16, 1826. M. by Kelly.

FOUNDLINGS, THE. C.D. J. B. Buckstone. Taken fr. the French. Hay., June 16, 1852.

FOUNDLINGS; OR, THE OCEAN OF LIFE, THE. Spec. D. 7 tableaux. Leopold Lewis. Adap. fr. *La Dame de la Halle*. Sadler's Wells, October 8, 1881. See *Chain of Events*.

FOUNTAIN, THE. C. 3 a. Geo. Calderon. (Prod. by the Stage Society.) Aldwych, March 28, 1909.

FOUNTAIN OF BEAUTY; OR, THE KING, THE PRINCESS, AND THE GENI, THE. Burl. Extrav. 2 a. John M. Kingdom. D.L., September 5, 1853.

FOUNTAIN OF NEW FASHIONS, THE. P. G. Chapman. Ac. 1598. N.p.

FOUNTAIN OF SELF LOVE, THE. See *Cynthia's Revels*. B. Jonson. 1600.

FOUNTAIN SEALED, A. See *Only a Quaker Maid*.

FOUR AFTER ONE. C. Sk. Ralph Farr. Publ. by Abel Heywood.

FOUR BROTHERS. See *Quatre Fils Aynon*.

FOUR BY HONOURS. M. Absurdity Huddersfield T.R., October 27, 1879.

FOUR COUSINS, THE. C.D. 2 a. Augustus Mayhew and Sutherland Edwards. Globe, May, 1871.

FOUR FINE GALLANTS. C. Middleton. 1607.

FOUR HONOURED LOVES, THE BOOKE OF THE. C. Wm. Rowley. Entered Stationers' Co., June 29, 1660. N.p. Destroyed by Warburton's servant.

FOUR INNS OF COURT, THE. Ac. before the Court. 1633.

FOUR JUST MEN, THE. D. 4 a. Geo. Wallace. Adap. fr. Edgar Wallace's novel (C.P.) Colchester Royal, August 31, 1906. Prod. at Luton Grand, October 1, 1906; London prod., King's, W., October 8, 1906.

FOUR KINGS, THE. Ac. by the Lord Admiral's servants. 1598.

FOUR KINGS; OR, PADDY IN THE MOON, THE. Burl. C. H. Hazlewood. Britannia, April 14, 1873.

FOUR LEAF CLOVER, A. C. 4 a. Martha Morton. Savoy, September 30, 1905.

FOUR LEAVED SHAMROCK, THE. P. Wm. Travers.

FOUR LITTLE GIRLS. F. 3 a. Walter Stokes Craven. Criterion, July 17, 1897.

FOUR LONDON APPRENTICES. See *Four Prentices*, etc.

FOUR MOWBRAYS, THE. Ca. D.L., February 15, 1854.

FOUR P.'S, THE. Int. John Heywood. Wr. in metre, not divided into acts. One of the first plays that appeared in the English language. Four P.'s—The Palmer, The Pardoner, The Poticary, The Pedlar. Pr. between 1543 and 1547. Prob. wr. circa 1540.

FOUR PLAYS IN ONE; OR, MORAL REPRESENTATIONS. As follows: — *The Triumph of Honour*. T.C. F. on *Boccace*. *The Triumph of Love*. T.C. F. on *Boccace*. *The Triumph of Death*, T., and *The Triumph of Time*, O., F. on *The Fortunate, Deceiv'd, and Unfortunate Lovers*. Beaumont and Fletcher. Pr. 1647.

FOUR PRENTICES OF LONDON, WITH THE CONQUEST OF JERUSALEM, THE. Hist. P. Thos. Heywood. Ac. at Red Bull by the Queen's servants. Pr. 1615. This P. is burlesqued in Beaumont and Fletcher's *Knight of the Burning Pestle*. Ac. 1632.

FOUR SEASONS; OR, LOVE IN EVERY AGE, THE. M. Int. P. M. Motteux. Pr. 1699. Set to music by Jeremy Clarke and pr with the O. of *The Island Princess; or, Generous Portuguese*.

FOUR SISTERS; OR, WOMAN'S WORTH AND WOMAN'S WRONGS, THE. F. 1 a. Bayle Bernard. Strand, May 3, 1832; Lyceum, July 18, 1834.

FOUR SONS OF AMON, THE. P. Robert Shawe. Ac. 1602. N.p.

FOUR SONS OF AYMON, THE. O. Balfe. Princess's. November, 1844.

FOUR SONS OF FABIUS. Ac. by the Earl of Warwick's servants at Whitehall, 1579-80.

FOUR STAGES OF LIFE, THE. D. 4 a. J. Vollaire. Surrey, April, 1862.

FOURBERIES DE SCAPIN. C. Molière. 1671. Royalty, June 30, 1891. See *Cheats of Scapin*. See "French Classical Plays."

FOURCHETTE AND COMPANY. P. 1 a. Brandon Thomas. Northampton Opera H., November 21, 1904; Comedy, December 5, 1904; Terry's, December 26, 1905.

FOURTEEN DAYS. C. 3 a. H. J. Byron. Adap. fr. the French of Gondinet and Bisson. Criterion, March 4, 1882; (Rev.), February 10, 1892.

FOWL PLAY; OR, A STORY OF CHICKEN HAZARD. Burl. F. C. Burnand. Queen's, June 20, 1868.

FOX, THE. See *Volpone; or, The Fox*.

FOX AND THE GOOSE; OR, THE WIDOW'S HUSBAND, THE. C. Oa. 1 a. B. Webster and Dion Boucicault. Adelphi, October 2, 1844.

FOX AND THE GRAPES, THE. Sk. 1 a. E. H. Keating. Publ. by S. French, Ltd.

FOX AND WOLF. F. Gaiety, October 5, 1898.

FOX CHASE, THE. C. 5 a. Dion Boucicault. St. James's, May 11, 1864. First performed in U.S.A. See *The Fox Hunt.*

FOX HUNT; OR, DON QUIXOTE THE SECOND, THE. Dion Boucicault. New York Burton's T., November 23, 1853.

FOX UNCAS'D; OR, ROBIN'S ART OF MONEY-CATCHING, THE. B.O. Ac. privately near St. James's. Pr. 1733.

FOX VERSUS GOOSE. F.C. Wm. Brough and J. D. Stockton. Strand, May 8, 1869.

FOXGLOVE; OR, THE QUAKER'S WILL. O. 3 a. Charles Dyall. M. by G. W. Röhner. Liverpool P.O.W., May 2, 1883.

FRA ANGELO. P. 5 a. W. C. Russell. Hay., August, 1865

FRA DIAVOLO. O. 3a. Auber. Lib. by Scribe. Opera Comique. Paris, January 28, 1830. In English adapted by R. Lacy, Drury Lane, November 3, 1831; in Italian, at the Lyceum, July 4-11, 1857; Gaiety, November 24, 1870.

FRA DIAVOLO; OR, THE BEAUTY AND THE BRIGANDS. Burl. H. J. Byron. Strand, April 5, 1858.

FRA DIAVOLO THE SECOND. Extrav. J. T. Denny. Philharmonic, August 28, 1882.

FRAGMENT, A. Chas. Hannan. Glasgow Royalty, December 11, 1894.

FRAILTY. D. 4 a. Sir Augustus Harris and Paul Meritt. Newcastle Tyne T., July 3, 1893.

FRAILTY AND HYPOCRISY. D. James Wild. Fr. Beaumarchais' *L'Aûtre Tartuffe; ou La Mère Coupable*, and forms a sequel to *The Spanish Barber* and *The Follies of a Day.* Pr. 1804. N.ac.

FRANCESCA. P. E. Falconer. Lyceum, March 31, 1859.

FRANCESCA. P Alaric Burton. Glasgow Athen., February 16, 1903.

FRANCESCA DA RIMINI. T.O. 3 a. Hermann Goetz. The first 2 a. finished and third sketched by composer. Completed and prod. at Mannheim by Ernst Frank, September 30, 1877.

FRANCESCA DA RIMINI. Grand O. 4 a. MM. Barbier and Carré. M. by Ambroise Thomas. Prod. Paris Grand Opera, April 14, 1882.

FRANCESCA DA RIMINI. D. Prol. 4 a. F. Marion Crawford. Shaftesbury, October 1, 1901. Transl. by Marcel Schwob. Garrick (Sarah Bernhardt's season), June 9, 1902.

FRANCESCA DA RIMINI. Ital. T. 5 a. Gabriele D'Annunzio. Adelphi (Eleonora Duse Co.), October 10, 1903.

FRANCILLON. C. 3 a. Arr. fr. the French of Alexandre Dumas fils. Duke of York's, September 18, 1897; Royalty, July 5, 1906.

FRANCIS I. Hist. P. 5 a. Miss Fanny Kemble. C.G., March 15, 1832.

FRANCIS I. O. M. by Loder. D.L., November 6, 1838.

FRANCO-PRUSSIAN WAR, THE. Military Spec. 4 a. J. Elphinstone. Hanley T.R., August 12, 1872.

FRANCOIS THE RADICAL. C.O. J. H. M'Carthy. Fr. the French of Dubreuil Humbert and Burani. M. by Firmin Bernicat and A. Messager. Royalty, April 4, 1885.

FRANK CHARRINGTON'S RETURN. C. 1 a. G. Templeman Norman. Ladbroke H., February 26, 1897.

FRANK FOX PHIPPS, ESQ. F. 1 a. Chas. Selby. Victoria, February 18, 1834.

FRANKENSTEIN. Burl. Bros. Brough. Adelphi, December 26, 1849.

FRANKENSTEIN. Melo-d. Burl. 3 a. "Richard Henry." Gaiety, December 24, 1887.

FRANKENSTEIN. See *Presumption.*

FRANKENSTEIN; OR, THE MAN AND THE MONSTER. Rom. Melo-d. 2 a. H. M. Milner. F. chiefly on Mrs. Shelley's "Frankenstein" and partly on *Le Magician et la Monstre.* Coburg, July 3, 1826; Lyceum, 1839; Sadler's Wells, 1843.

FRANKLIN. D. 5 a. John Brougham. 1868.

FRASQUITA. C.O. 2 a. Meyer Lutz. Gaiety, May 29, 1893.

FRATERNISATION. Adelphi, July 16, 1855.

FRATRUM CONCORDIA SŒVA. Latin T. Apparently by an English author.

FRAUD AND ITS VICTIMS. D. 4 a. J. Stirling Coyne. Surrey, March 2, 1857. See *The Streets of London.*

FRAUS HONESTA. Cambridge Latin P. Philip Stubbe. 1616.

FRAUS PIA. Latin P. Apparently by an English author of the 17th century.

FREA. One of three plays publ. as "Dramatic Sketches of the Ancient Northern Mythology," by F. Sayers. Pr. 1790.

FREAKS AND FOLLIES. F. 2 a. G. H. Rodwell. Publ. by J. Dicks. Ac. in New York, 1832.

FRED FROLIC: HIS LIFE AND ADVENTURES. D. C. Pitt. Britannia, June 17, 1868.

FRED WALTERS, A GRIMSBY FISHING APPRENTICE. D. Barry Stuart. Grimsby T.R., April 13, 1877.

FREDA. P. 3 a. Bernard Bussy and W. T. Blackmore. Strand, July 19, 1887.

FREDEGONDE. O. Guiraud. 1837-1892.

FREDERIC AND BASELLERS (or Basilea). P. Rose T., June 3, 1597. N.p.

FREDERIC DUKE OF BRUNSWICK LUNENBURG. T. Eliz. Haywood. L.I.F., March 4, 1729. Pr. 1729.

FREDERICK OF PRUSSIA; OR, THE MONARCH AND THE MIMIC. Burl. 1 a. Chas. Selby. Queen's, July 24, 1837; rev. Strand, December, 1838.

FREDERICK THE GREAT; OR, THE HEART OF A SOLDIER. Operatic Anecdote. 3 a. M. by T. Cooke. Lyceum, July 22, 1815.

FREDERICK THE GREAT; OR, THE KING AND THE DESERTER. Melo-d. 2 a. J. M. Maddox. Coburg, September 15, 1824.

FREDOLFO. T. C. R. Maturin. C.G., May 12, 1819.

FREE AND EASY. C.O. 2 a. Samuel Jas. Arnold. M. by Addison. Lyceum, September 16, 1816.

FREE KNIGHTS; OR, THE EDICT OF CHARLEMAGNE, THE. Op. D. 3 a. F. Reynolds. C.G., February 8, 1810. Pr. 1810.

FREE LABOUR; OR, PUT YOURSELF IN HIS PLACE. D. 4 a. Charles Reade. Leeds T.R., March 11, 1870; Adelphi, May 28, 1870.

FREE LANCE. P. 5 a. W. A. Tremayne. Britannia, October 20, 1902; Leamington R., April 1, 1907.

FREE LANCE; OR, WHO WINS, THE. D. 3 a. Charles Horsman Alfred. August 2, 1869.

FREE PARDON, THE. Dom. D. 4 a. F. C. Philips and Leonard Merrick. Olympic, January 28, 1897.

FREE WILL. T. Transl. fr. the Italian of Franciscus Niger Bassentinus by "H. C." (Henry Cheeke). One of the old moral plays. Pr. (no date). Circa 1589

FREEBOOTER, THE. Dr. and M.Sk. H. Brockbank. Lyrics by G. Hadath. M. by H. Finck. Paragon M.H., October 20, 1902.

FREEBOOTERS, THE. S.C.O. Freely transl. fr. the original D. M. by F. Paer. Lyceum, August 20, 1827.

FREEDOM. D. Geo. F. Rowe and Augustus Harris. D.L., August 4, 1883.

FREEDOM OF SUZANNE, THE. C. 3 a. Cosmo Gordon Lennox. Criterion, November 15, 1904.

FREEHOLDER, THE. Dr. Int. Joseph Moser. Pr. 1810. N.ac.

FREEMAN'S HONOUR, THE. P. Wm. Smith. Mentioned in the epistle dedicatory of his *The Hector of Germany*. Before 1615.

FREEMASON; OR, THE SECRET OF THE LODGE ROOM, THE. Dom. D. 2 a. J. P. Hart. Queen's, June 3, 1839.

FREEZING A MOTHER-IN-LAW; OR, A FRIGHTFUL FROST. F. 1 a. T. Edgar Pemberton. Birmingham T.R., December 17, 1879; Leeds T.R., September 6, 1880.

FREISCHUTZ, DER. O. Weber. Prod. Berlin, 1822; Paris, 1824.

FRENCH AS HE IS SPOKE. C. 1 a. Adap. by Gaston Mayer fr. the Fr. P. *L'Anglais tel qu'on le Parle*, by Tristan Bernard. Playhouse, August 15, 1907.

FRENCH CLASSICAL PLAYS.

The principal are by Racine, Corneille, Molière, and Hugo.

RACINE, JEAN. A tragic Dramatist of France. 1639-1699.

- LE THEBAIDE, 1663. Palais Royal, June 20, 1664.
- ALEXANDRE LE GRAND, 1665. Palais Royal, December 4, 1665
- ANDROMAQUE. November 10, 1667.
- LES PLAIDEURS. Ca. December 5, 1668.
- BRITANNICUS. December 13, 1669.
- BERENICE 1670.
- BAJAZET. January 4, 1672.
- MITHRIDATE. January 13, 1673
- IPHIGENIE. 1675.
- PHEDRE. Hotel de Bourgogne, January 1, 1677.
- ESTHER. Sac. D. M. by Moreau. 1689.
- ATHALIE. Sac. D. 1690. Pr. 1691.

CORNEILLE, PIERRE. Born at Rouen, June 6, 1606; died October 1, 1684, at Paris.

- MELITE. C. Ac. 1629.
- CLITANDRE. T. Ac. 1632.
- LA VEUVE C. Ac. 1633.
- GALERIE DU PALAIS. C. Ac. 1634.
- LA SUIVANTE. C. 1634.
- LA PLACE ROYAL. D. 1635.
- MEDEE. T. 1635.
- L'ILLUSION COMIQUE. Extra. 1636.
- LE CID. Pr. 1636.
- HORACE. 1639-1640.
- CINNA. Pr. 1639.
- POLYEUCTE. 1640.
- LA MORT DE POMPEE. 1642.
- LE MENTEUR. C. 1642.
- RODOGUNE. 1644.
- THEODORE. T. 1645.
- HERACLIUS. 1647.
- ANDROMEDE. 1650.
- DON SANCHE D'ARAGON. 1650.
- NICOMEDE. 1651.
- PERTHARITE. 1653.
- ŒDIPE. 1659.
- LA TOISON D'OR. 1660.
- SERTORIUS. 1662.
- SOPHONISBE. 1663.
- OTHON. 1664.
- AGESILAS. 1666.
- ATTILA. 1667.
- TITE ET BERENICE. 1670.
- PSYCHE (with Molière and Quinault). 1671.
- PULCHERIE. 1672.
- SURENA. 1674.

MOLIERE (JEAN BAPTISTE POQUELIN). Born at Paris January 15, 1622; died February 17, 1673.

- L'ETOURDI. C. Lyons, 1655; Paris, 1658.
- LE DEPIT AMOUREUX. C. Béziers, 1656; Paris, 1658.
- LES PRECIEUSES RIDICULES. C. November 18, 1659.
- SGANARELLE; OU, LE COCU IMAGINAIRE. May 28, 1660.
- DON GARCIE DE NAVARRE. T.C. February 4, 1661.
- L'ECOLE DES MARIS. June 24, 1662.
- LES FASCHEUX VAUX LE VICOMTE. August 15, 1661.
- L'ECOLE DES FEMMES. December 26, 1662.
- LE MARIAGE FORCE. F. February 15, 1664.
- PRINCESSE D'ELIDE. 1664.
- TARTUFFE. Partially 1664. Complete 1667.
- FESTIN DE PIERRE; OU, DON JUAN. February 15, 1665.
- L'AMOUR MEDECIN. C. September 22, 1665.
- LE MISANTHROPE; OU, L'ATRABILIAIRE AMOUREUX. June 4, 1666.
- LE MEDECIN MALGRE LUI. F. August 6, 1666.
- MELICERTE. December, 1666.
- LA PASTORALE COMIQUE.
- LE SICILIEN.
- AMPHITRYON. January 13, 1668.
- GEORGE DANDIN. July 10, 1668.
- L'AVARE. September 9, 1668.
- M. DE POURCEAUGNAC. September 17, 1669.
- LES AMANTS MAGNIFIQUES. C. Bal. St. Germain, February 10, 1670.
- BOURGEOIS GENTILHOMME. October 23, 1670
- LES FOURBERIES DE SCAPIN. May 24, 1671.
- COMTESSE D'ESCARBAGNAS. February 2, 1672.
- LES FEMMES SAVANTES. February 11, 1672.
- LE MALADE IMAGINAIRE.
- PSYCHE (in collab. with Quinault and Corneile). 1671.

HUGO, VICTOR MARIE VISCOUNT, dramatist and novelist. Born at Besançon, 1802; died at Paris, May, 1885.

- HERNANI. D. 1830.
- MARION DELORME. D. 1831.
- NOTRE DAME DE PARIS. 1831.
- LE ROI S'AMUSE. D. 1832.
- ISTAMINE. T.
- LUCRETIA BORGIA. 1833.
- MARY TUDOR. 1833.
- ANGELO. 1835.
- ESMERALDA. 1836.
- CROMWELL. P. 1837.
- RUY BLAS. 1838.

HUGO, VICTOR, son of preceding. Born at Paris, 1826; died at Bordeaux, 1871.

- JE VOUS AIME. 1862.
- LES MISERABLES. 1863.

FRENCH COMEDY, THE. Rose T., February 11, 1595.

FRENCH CONJUROR, THE. C. by "T. P." Duke of York's. Pr. 1678. Plot fr. two stories in the Rom. of *Gusman de Alfarache, The Spanish Rogue*, the one called *Dorido and Clorinia*, and the other *The Merchant of Sevil.*

FRENCH DANCING MASTER, THE. A Droll out of the Duke of Newcastle's play of variety, 1661.

FRENCH DANCING MISTRESS, THE. May 21, 1662.

FRENCH DOCTOR, THE. Rose T. October 18, 1595.

FRENCH EXHIBITION; OR, THE NOODLES IN PARIS, THE. F. Frederick Hay. Strand, April 1, 1867.

FRENCH FAITH; OR, THE VIRTUOUS INDIVIDUAL. P. 3 a. Transl. fr. the French; prob. fr. the same play as *Jean Hennuyer.* Pr. 1786.

FRENCH FLOGGED; OR, THE BRITISH SAILORS IN AMERICA, THE. F. 2 a. Ascribed to Geo. Alex. Stevens. C.G., March 30, 1761. Pr. 1767. Wr. for Bartholomew Fair.

FRENCH GIRL'S LOVE, A. D. C. H Hazlewood. Britannia, February 12, 1872.

FRENCH HUSSAR, THE. D. J. W. Whitbread. Dublin Queen's, December 24, 1906.

FRENCH IN ALGIERS. Astley's, April 13, 1857.

FRENCH LAW. Ca. Paul Barry. Tot. Court Rd. Athenæum, March 15, 1893.

FRENCH LIBERTINE, THE. C. 5 a. C.G., February, 1826.

FRENCH MAID, THE. M.C. 2 a. Basil Hood. M. by Walter Slaughter. Bath T.R., April 4, 1896; Camberwell Metropole, May 6, 1896; Terry's, April 24, 1897; transferred to Vaudeville, February 12, 1898.

FRENCH REFUGEE, THE. P. Mrs. S. C. Hall. 1836.

FRENCH SCHOOLMASTER, THE. C. 1662. N.p.

FRENCH SPY, THE. Military Spec. M. by Auber. Scarborough Old T., September 13, 1831.

FRENCH SPY, THE. D. 5 a. E. Hill Mitchelson. Greenwich Morton's, March 5, 1900.

FRENCH SPY; OR, THE SIEGE OF CONSTANTINA, THE. D. 3 a. J. T. Haines. Adelphi, December 4, 1837.

FRENCHIFIED LADY NEVER IN PARIS, THE. C. 2 a. Henry Dell. Taken fr. Cibber's *Comical Lovers*, which was borrowed fr. Dryden's *Maiden Queen* and *Marriage à la Mode.* C.G., March 23, 1756. Pr. 1757.

FRENCHMAN IN LONDON. C. Literal transl. of the *François à Londres* of M. de Boissy. Pr. 1755.

FRENCHMAN IN LONDON, A. F. 2 a. J. J. Stafford. Publ. by J. Dicks.

FRERES CORSES, LES. See *The Corsican Brothers.*

FRETFUL PORCUPINE, A. F. Adap. by Leicester Buckingham. Adelphi, April 20, 1867.

FREYA'S GIFT. Masque. J. Oxenford. Comp. by Sir G. A. Macfarren. C.G., 1863.

FREYSCHUTZ, DER. Ital. O. Weber. Dresden, 1819; D.L. (in German), July 6, 1895.

FREYSCHUTZ, DER. O. Weber. M. adap. by Bishop. D.L., November 10, 1824.

FREYSCHUTZ, DER. Rom. O. 4 a. J. Oxenford. M. by Carl Von Weber. Astley's, April 2, 1866.

FREYSCHUTZ, DER; OR, THE BILL, THE BELLE, AND THE BULLETT (OR, THE BELLE, THE BILL, AND THE BALL). Burl. H. J. Byron. P.O.W., October 10, 1866.

FREYSCHUTZ, DER; OR, THE FIEND HUNTSMAN. O. Weber. First time in England in its entire state. M. adap. by R. Lacy. D.L., December 14, 1839.

FREYSCHUTZ, DER; OR, THE SEVENTH BULLET. Fr. the German O. Lyceum, July 22, 1824.

FRIAR, THE. Oa. J. Comyns Carr. M. by Alfred J. Caldicott. St. Geo. H., December 15, 1886.

FRIAR BACON; OR, HARLEQUIN'S ADVENTURES IN LILLIPUT, BROBDIGNAG, ETC. Pant. By Bonnor. Words by O'Keeffe. C.G., 1783. N.p. See *Harlequin Rambler.*

FRIAR BACON AND FRIAR BONGAY, THE HONOURABLE HISTORY OF. C. Robert Greene. Pr. 1594. Ac. 1591.

FRIAR FOX AND GILLIM OF BRENTFORD. P. Thos. Downton and Saml. Ridley. Ac. 1598. N.p. Prob. 1592-3.

FRIAR FRANCIS. P. Rose T., January 7, 1593.

FRIAR SPENDLETON. Rose T., October 31, 1597. N.p.

FRIDOLIN. Cant. A. Randegger.

FRIEND AT COURT, A. C. 2 a. J. R. Planché. Hay., 1831.

FRIEND FELIX. Ca. Norwich T.R., December 1, 1875.

FRIEND FROM LEATHERHEAD. F. Publ. by S. French, Limited.

FRIEND IN NEED, A. M. Ent. Prince Hoare. M. by Kelly. Taken fr. *Le Comte D'Albert et sa Suite*, a M. Ent., chiefly by Gluck. D.L., February 11, 1797. Songs only pr. 1797.

FRIEND IN NEED, A. C. 2 a. Sydney French and Wm. J. Sorrell. St. James's T., April 23, 1860.

FRIEND IN NEED, A. Ca. Frank Runciman. Novelty, April 19, 1897.

FRIEND IN NEED, A. F., by Edgar Selwyn. Adelphi, February 17, 1902.

FRIEND IN NEED, A. Sk. Richard Purdon. Sadler's Wells, July 6, 1908.

FRIEND IN NEED IS A FRIEND INDEED, A. C. D. O'Brien. Hay., May 5, 1783. N.p. Originally in 2 a., then 4 a., and then 3 a.

FRIEND IN THE GARDEN, THE. P. 1 a. E. F. Benson. Savoy, March 7, 1906.

FRIEND INDEED. Mus. Ent. C.G., November, 1817.

FRIEND OF THE FAMILY, A. C. B. H. Dixon. Bijou, Bayswater, September 27, 1894.

FRIEND OF THE FAMILY, A. New 1 a. absurdity. W. H. Cressy and F. Niblo. Palace, April 1, 1907.

FRIEND OF THE FAMILY, THE. C. Henry Siddons. Edinburgh T.R., 1810. N.p.

FRIEND OF THE FLAG, THE. Founded on Ouida's novel. Harry Bruce.

FRIEND OF THE PEOPLE, THE. Rom. D. 5 a. Mary C. Rowsell and H. A. Saintsbury. Hay, February 17, 1898 (C.P.).

FRIEND OR FOE? D. 4 a. Mark Melford. Southampton P.O.W. March 16, 1891.

FRIEND WAGGLES. F. 1 a. J. M. Morton. Strand, April 15, 1850; D.L., July 12, 1850.

FRIENDLY FOE, A. P. Prol. 4 a. Alton Mills. Ladbroke H., April 15, 1895.

FRIENDLY HINTS. F.C. 2 a. Fredk. Bingham. South Acton Parish H., December 9, 1889.

FRIENDLY RIVALS; OR, LOVE THE BEST CONTRIVER. C. Pr. 1752. (Refused by the managers.)

FRIENDS. C.D. 3 a. Alfred D. Parker. Lichfield St. James's H., February 17, 1887.

FRIENDS. C. 2 a. Mary Seymour. Publ. by S. French, Limited.

FRIENDS, THE. T. Mark Anthony Meilan. Pr. circa 1771.

FRIENDS, THE. P. 1 a. Ella Erskine. Adap. fr. the German. (Pr. by the Revival Co.) February 28, 1909.

FRIENDS; OR, THE BENEVOLENT PLANTERS, THE. M. Int. Thos. Bellamy. Hay., August, 1789. Pr. 1789, under latter title only.

FRIENDS AND FOES. C. 2 a. Tom Roberts. Rochester T.R., June 24, 1858; Bayswater Victoria, April 22, 1889.

FRIENDS OF FOOLS, THE. Sk. Leonard Mortimer. Barnard's Pal., Chatham, December 26, 1901.

FRIENDS OR FOES. C. 4 a. Horace Wigan. Adap. alt. fr. the French. St. James' T., March 8, 1862.

FRIENDSHIP; OR, GOLDING'S DEBT. D. 3 a. R. Reece. Alexandra, May 31, 1873.

FRIENDSHIP A LA MODE. C. 2 a. Dublin. An alt. of Vanbrugh's *False Friend*. Pr. 1766.

FRIENDSHIP IMPROVED; OR, THE FEMALE WARRIOR. T. Chas. Hopkins. L.I.F. Pr. 1700.

FRIENDSHIP IN FASHION. C. T. Otway. Duke's T. Pr. 1678. Rev. at D.L., January 22, 1750.

FRIENDSHIP, LOVE, and TRUTH. D. 3 a. Henry Leslie. Surrey, March 14, 1868.

FRIENDSHIP OF PLATO. C. 1 a. Sir W. L. Young.

FRIENDSHIP OF TITUS AND GESIPPUS. C. Ralph Radcliff. N.p.

FRIGHTEN'D TO DEATH. M. Ent. W. C. Oulton. M. by Cooke. D.L., February 27, 1817; Lyceum, December 4, 1835; Olympic, October 6, 1845.

FRIGHTFUL ACCIDENT. Strand, March 5, 1860.

FRIGHTFUL HAIR, THE. Burl. F. C. Burnand. Hay., December 26, 1868.

FRILLED PETTICOATS. C.D. 2 a. Lewis C. Lyne. Gaiety, October 28, 1871.

FRINGE OF SOCIETY, THE. P. 4 a. Adap. fr. Alexandre Dumas fils' *Le Demi-Monde*. Criterion, April 30, 1892.

FRISETTE. See *John and Jeanette*.

FRITZ, OUR COUSIN GERMAN. Andrew Halliday. American D. 3 a. Adelphi, November 30, 1872.

FRITZ, THE OUTLAW; OR, THE WIFE OF TWO HUSBANDS. Melo-d. Pavilion, December 17, 1838.

FRITZ'S FOLLY. Mus. C. 3 a. By Harry Starr. Barnsley T.R., May 4, 1896.

FRITZCHEN. P. 1 a. Hermann Sudermann. Great Queen St. T., December 23, 1902.

FRIVOLI. C.O. 3 a Engl. words by Wm. Beatty-Kingston. M. by Louis Hervé. D.L., June 29, 1886.

FRIVOLITY. F.C. Mark Melford. Liverpool R. Alexandra, August 6, 1883.

FROCKS AND FRILLS. C. 4 a. Adap. by S. Grundy fr. Scribe and Legarive *Les Doigt's de Fée*. Hay., January 2, 1902.

FROG. C.D. 3 a. Alec Nelson (E. B. Aveling). Royalty, October 30, 1893.

FROG HE WOULD A-WOOING GO. Marylebone, December 24, 1875.

FROGGIE GOES TO ETON. Playlet. Mark Ambient. Ealing Lyric H., April 23, 1892.

FROGS, THE. C. Transl. fr. Aristophanes by C. Dunster. Pr. 1785. See "Greek Plays."

FROGS OF ARISTOPHANES, THE. Pr. by Oxford Union Dramatic Society in the original Greek. Oxford New, February 17, 1909 (amat.).

FROLIC, THE. Dr. Piece. 3 a. James Brown. Pr. at Edinburgh, 1783.

FROLIC, OR THE LAWYER CHEATED, THE. C. by "E. P." Dedicated to Prince Rupert. M.S. unpubl.

FROLIC; OR, THE ROMP IN DISGUISE, THE. F. Being a sequel to *The Romp*. Ac. at Dorchester, June, 1792.

FROLICKS IN FRANCE. C. 3 a. Alt. fr. Kenny's *Forget and Forgive*. D.L., March 15, 1828.

FROLICS IN "FORTY-FIVE." C. Extrav. 3 a. D.L., February 10, 1836.

FROLICS OF AN HOUR, THE. M. Int. 1 a. C.G., June 16, 1795. Pr. 1795.

FROLICS OF FORTUNE; OR, THE LORDLY PLOUGHMAN, THE. F. Rev. Lyceum, December 30, 1835.

FROLICS OF THE FAIRIES, THE. Spec. Victoria, 1834.

FROLICSOME FANNY. F. 3 a. Alfred C. Calmour. Gaiety, November 25, 1897.

FROLIQUE. M.C. 1 a. H. J. Byron and H. B. Farnie. Adap. fr. the French V. *Charlot*. Strand, November 18, 1882.

FROM BENEATH THE DEEP. D. Prol. and 3 a. W. H. Abel. Pavilion, February 28, 1876.

FROM CONVENT TO THRONE. P. 4 a. J. A. Campbell. Manchester Osborne, March 31, 1909 (C.P.); Liverpool Rotunda, July 26, 1909; Hammersmith Lyric, September 6, 1909.

FROM CROSS TO CROWN. D. 5 a. Adap. by the Rev. Arthur Whitley from Cardinal Wiseman's *The Church of the Catacombs*. Chester Royalty, April 7, 1897; Longton Queen's T., November 19, 1897. See *The Christian's Cross*.

FROM FATHER TO SON. Arthur à Beckett and Palgrave Simpson. Adap. fr. à Beckett's novel, "Fallen Among Thieves." Liverpool Bijou O.H., October 2, 1882.

FROM GLOOM TO SUNLIGHT. See *For the Sake of a Name*.

FROM GRAVE TO GAY. C. 3 a. Adap. by Benj. Webster, jun. Olympic, December 4, 1867.

FROM GULF TO GULF. Prol. and 4 a. Henry John Smith. Orig. prod. in German at Bremen as *Am Algrund*. Avenue, November 29, 1892

FROM INN TO INN. Op. C. 3 a. James Wild. Transl. of Dupaty's *D'Auberge en Auberge*. Pr. 1804. N. ac.

FROM LIFE TO DEATH. D. 4 a. St. George's, May 22, 1875.

FROM SCOTLAND YARD. D. Prol. and 4 a. John Douglass and Frank Bateman. Accrington Prince's T., August 16, 1897; Parkhurst, September 27, 1897.

FROM SHADOW TO SUNSHINE. D. 4 a. Lilian Revell and Hawley Francks. Eleph. and C., July 22, 1901.

FROM SHOP GIRL TO DUCHESS. D. 4 a. Charles Darrell. Bilston Royal, November 25, 1907; rev. Hammersmith Lyric, January 25, 1909.

FROM SHORE TO SHORE. D. Percy Edwin. Wolverhampton Star T., April 30, 1891.

FROM SHORE TO SHORE. D. Prol. and 4 a. Alfred England and Ch. Rider Noble. Northampton O.H., June 6, 1892.

FROM STEM TO STERN. Nautical D. F. Hay. Surrey, April 15, 1876.

FROM THE JAWS OF DEATH. Dr. Sk. W. J. Patmore. Pavilion, December 7, 1893.

FROM THE LAND OF SILENCE. D. 4 a. D. Moore and L. Clarance. Consett New T., December 19, 1904.

FROM THE UNSEEN WORLD. Melo-d. 4 a. Creagh Henry. Stratford Borough, July 3, 1905.

FROM THE VANISHED PAST. D. 4 a Florence Holton. Upton Park P.H., April 30, 1888.

FROM VILLAGE TO COURT. C.D. 2 a. J. M. Morton. Princess's, June 5, 1854.

FROM WASHERWOMAN TO DUCHESS. C.D. Pro. and 4 a. Milliane Bandmann-Palmer. Muncaster, Bootle, September 7, 1906.

FROMONT JEUNE AND RISLER AINE. See *Partners*.

FROST AND THAW. M.F. Attrib. to Holman. M. by Cooke. C.G., February 25, 1812. N.p.

FROST OF YOUTH, THE. D. J. Wilkins. City of London, 1856.

FROU FROU. D 5 a. Sutherland Edwards. Olympic, April 16, 1870.

FROU FROU. P. 5 a. Adap. Princess's, May 2, 1870.

FROU FROU. D. 5 a. A. Daly. American ver., St. James's, May 25, 1870.

FROU FROU. P. 5 a. Comyns Carr. Princess's, June 4, 1881.

FROU FROU. D. Janet Achurch and C. Charrington. Manchester Comedy T., December 9, 1886.

FROU FROU. New ver. of Meilhac's play. Comedy, March 17, 1894; evening bill, March 31, 1894.

FROU FROU; OR, FASHION AND PASSION. D. 5 a. Benj. Webster, jun. Adap. fr. the French of Meilhac and Halévy (first prod. Theatre du Gymnase, October 30, 1869). Brighton T.R., March 14, 1870; St. James's, April 14, 1870.

FROZEN DEEP, THE. D. 3 a. Wilkie Collins. Tavistock House, January 6, 1857 (amat.); Gal. of Illus. 1857 (amat.); Olympic, October 27, 1866.

FROZEN HEART. Oa. 1 a. Gillington and Carmichael. Publ. by S. French, Ltd.

FROZEN LAKE, THE. M.D. M. by Mr. Reeve. Lyceum, September 3, 1824; C.G., November 26, 1824. See *La Neige*.

FROZEN STREAM; OR, THE DEAD WITNESS, THE. D. 3 a. A. Coates. Britannia, March 4, 1872.

FRUIT AND BLOSSOM. C. 1 a. Adap. fr. the Fr. by Clinton Dent. Playhouse, April 9, 1908 (mat.).

FRUITLESS REDRESS, THE. T. Wr. 1728. MS.

FRUITS OF THE WINE CUP, THE. D. 3 a. J. H. Allen. Publ. by J. Dicks.

FUGITIVE, THE. Mus. F. John O'Keeffe. Alt. of the author's C.O., *The Czar*. C.G., November 4, 1790. N.p.

FUGITIVE, THE. C. Joseph Richardson. Ac. at the O.H. Pr. 1792. Bath, November 30, 1822.

FUGITIVE, THE. D. 4 a. Tom Craven. Barrow-in-Furness Alhambra T., August 1, 1887; Surrey, June 4, 1888.

FUGITIVE; OR, THE HAPPY RECESS, THE. Dr. Past. Thos. Shrapter. Pr. 1790. N.ac.

FUGITIVES, THE. C. Wm. Roberts. Pr. 1791. N.ac.

FUGITIVES, THE. Grecian. November 8, 1858.

FUHRMANN HENSCHEL. D. 4 a. Gerhart Hauptmann. Comedy, October 19, 1900.

FUIMUS TROES. Dr. Jasper Fisher. Pr. 1633. See *The True Trojanes*.

FULGIUS AND LUCRELLA (or Lucrette). Past fr. the Italian. Mentioned by Kirkman in his catalogue, 1661, and prob. very ancient.

FULL PARTICULARS OF THAT AFFAIR AT FINCHLEY. Strand, October 14, 1861.

FULVIUS VALEUS. P. 5 a. T. J. Serle. Pr. 1823.

FUN. Satire. Dr. Kenrick. Pr. 1752. N.ac.

FUN AND FROLIC; OR, THE SAILOR'S REVELS. M. Int. C.G., 1799. N.p.

FUN IN A FOG. F. D.L., October 5, 1872. Rev. Imperial, 1878.

FUN OF ELECTION; OR, THE PATRIOTIC BAKER, THE. C.G., May 15, 1807. A new title for Mr. Andrew's Interlude, *The Election*.

FUN ON A RACECOURSE. Camberwell Empire, December 14, 1908.

FUN ON THE BRISTOL; OR, A NIGHT AT SEA. M.C. Manchester T.R., May 15, 1882; Olympic, August 7, 1882.

FUNERAL; OR, GRIEF A LA MODE, THE. C. Sir Richard Steele. D.L. and C.G. Pr. 1702. C.G., February 16, 1739.

FUNERAL OF RICHARD CŒUR DE LION, THE. Robt. Wilson, in conj. with Chettle Mundy and Drayton. Ac. 1598. N.p.

FUNERAL PILE, THE. C.O. J. S. Dodd. Ac. and pr. in Dublin, 1799. Another title for *Gallic Gratitude*.

FUNNIBONE'S FIX. F. 1 a. Arthur Williams. Surrey, March 27, 1880.

FUNNY FACTS AND FOOLISH FANCIES. Extrav. 1 a. Alfred Paxton. Pub. by S. French, Limited.

FUNNY WORLD, A. M. Sk. Corney Grain. St. Geo. H., March 26, 1894.

FUR CLOAK, THE. P. 1 a. J. H. Irvine, Woolwich Artillery, February 15, 1909.

FURIBOND; OR, HARLEQUIN NEGRO. Panto. D.L., December, 1807.

FURIES, THE. T. Transl. fr. Æschylus by R. Potter. Pr. 1777. Perf. at Court as a Masque; Coronet, March 4, 1905.

FURIES' MASQUE. THE. A Masque perf. at Court about A.D. 1624.

FURIOSO NELL' ISOLA DI SANTO-DOMINGO. O. Donizetti. Rome, 1833.

FURNISHED APARTMENTS. C. Int. 1 a. By "H. A. Y."

FUTURE MRS. SKILLIMORE, THE. F.C. 3 a. Scott Craven. Ramsgate Marina, June 5, 1897.

FUTURITY WINNER, THE. Sk. Shepherd's Bush, May 25, 1908.

FYVE PLAYES IN ONE. Ac. at Greenwich on Twelfth Night, 1585. See *Five Plays*, etc.

G

GAT.P.O., THE. Burl. Fred Karno. Sheffield Empire, October 19, 1908; Paragon, November 16, 1908.

GABERLUNZIE MAN, THE. D. 2 a. W. Leman Rede. Lyceum, September 26, 1836.

GABRIEL GRUB. D. 3 a. Charles Furtado. Lincoln Masonic T., March 15, 1880.

GABRIEL'S PLOT. D. Richmond H.M.T., April 17, 1871.

GABRIEL'S TRUST. D. 1 a. Alfd. C. Calmour. Vaudeville, July 4, 1891.

GABRIELLA. O. 1 a. Mowbray Marras. Italian ver. by C. A. Byrne and Fulvio Fulgonio. St. Geo. H., November 25, 1893 (C.P.).

GABRIELLE. Rom. D. 4 a. Sydney Hodges. Gaiety, March 5, 1884.

GAFFER GREY'S LEGACY. C. 2 a. E. H. Keating. Pub. by S. French, Limited.

GAFFER JARGE. Rustic Study. 1 a. Alicia Ramsay. Com., January 11, 1896.

GAIETE. Op. bo. J. Eldred and H. Aylen. Sheffield T.R., October 26, 1874.

GAIETY GIRL, A. M.C. 3 a. Owen Hall. Lyrics by Harry Greenbank. M. by Sidney Jones. P.O.W., October 14, 1893. Transf. to Daly's, September 10, 1894; rev. Daly's, June 5, 1899.

GAIN. D. 3 a. Henry Sargent. Eleph. and C., June 14, 1880.

GAIN. D. Leeds T.R., June 29, 1885.

GALANT JARDINIER. C. Dancourt. 1667.

GALANTEE SHOW; OR, MR. PEPPERCORN AT HOME, THE. D. Jerrold. Strand, 1837.

GALATEA (or GALATHEA). C. John Lyly. The characters of Galathea and Phillida taken fr. *Metamorphoses*. Ac. before Q. Eliz. at Greenwich on N. Year's Day. Pr. 1592; rev. Regent's Pk. Botanic Gdns., July 6, 1905.

GALATEA. O. Victor Massé. Paris, 1852; Bristol Prince's (1st. t. in England), October 8, 1887.

GALATEA; OR, PYGMALION RE-VERSED. Burl. 1 scene. H. P. Stephens. Gaiety, December 26, 1883.

GALATEA OF OREGON. Stafford T.R., December 4, 1895.

GALE BREEZELY; OR, THE TALE OF A TAR. D. 2 a. J. B. Johnstone. Surrey.

GALEOTTO. Spanish D. 3 a. José Echegaray. Transl. into Ger. by Paul Lindau. St. Geo. H., January 28, 1902.

GALERIE DU PALAIS. C. Corneille. See "French Classical Plays."

GALFRIDO and BERNADO. A play recorded in Henslowe's diary and ac. in May, 1594.

GALIASE. Rose T., June 29, 1594.

GALILEAN'S VICTORY, THE. P. H. A. Jones. Stockport Royal, September 25, 1907 (C.P.).

GALLANT, THE. C. O'Keefe. 1765.

GALLANT, THE. Op. scena. M. Gunn Gwennett. M. by Aiulf Hjorvard. Collins' M.H., July 17, 1905.

GALLANT CAVALIERO, DICKE BOWYER, THIS. Pr. 1605 for Nathaniel Butter.

GALLANT MORISCOES; OR, ROBBERS OF THE PYRENEES, THE. Dr. perf. Pr. 1795.

GALLANT SCHEMERS, THE. C. Mentioned in the *Grub Street Journal*, May 17, 1733.

GALLANTRY; OR, ADVENTURES IN MADRID. C. 5 a. D.L., January 15, 1820.

GALLANTS, THE. C. G. Granville, 1696.

GALLEY SLAVE, THE C.D. 5 a. Bartley Campbell. Hull T.R., November 22, 1880; Grand, February 8, 1886.

GALLIA. Cant. Gounod.

GALLIC GRATITUDE; OR, THE FRENCHMAN IN INDIA. C. 2 a. James Solas Dodd. Taken fr. a 1 a. Fr. F. called *La Naufrage*, by Lafont. C.G., April 30, 1779. Pr. 1779 See *Funeral Pile*.

GALLIGANTUS. Mus. Ent. Taken fr. Brooke's *Jack the Giant Queller*. Pr. 1758. Hay., 1759, and D.L., 1760.

GALLIMAUFRY. D.L., June 21, 1815.

GALWAY GO BRAGH; OR, LOVE, FUN, AND FIGHTING. P. E. Falconer. Adap. fr. C. Lever's "Charles O'Malley." D.L., November 25, 1865.

GAMBLER, THE. P. 3 a. J. W. Boulding. Royalty, December 5, 1891.

GAMBLER'S DAUGHTER, A. D. 4 a. Clarence Burnette. West London, June 25, 1906.

GAMBLER'S FATE, THE. D. 3 a. H. M. Milner. Pub. by J. Dicks.

GAMBLER'S FATE; OR, A LAPSE OF TWENTY YEARS, THE. D. 2 a. C. Thompson. F. on the French P. *La Vie d'un Joueur*. D.L., October 15, 1827.

GAMBLER'S LIFE IN LONDON. P. 3 a. A. L. Campbell. Sadler's Wells.

GAMBLER'S WIFE, THE. Sk. Middlesex, June 16, 1908

GAMBLERS, THE. Surrey, January, 1824.

GAMBLING, FIEND, THE. Sk. Arthur B. Moss. R. Victoria H., February 16, 1901.

GAMBLING HELL, THE. Dr. Sk. H. Francks. Paragon, July 25, 1903.

GAME. D. 4 a. "Richard Henry." Glasgow Royalty, March 9, 1888.

GAME AND COMMERCE; OR, THE ROOKS PIGEONED. A. C. Dibdin. "Sent to the proprietors of D.L., but n.ac." N.p. Previously tried at C.G. under the title of *The Two Houses*, but rejected.

GAME AND GAME. Dr. P. E. L. Blanchard. Olympic, 1841-4.

GAME AT CHESS, A. C. Thos. Middleton. Globe. Pr. 1624.

GAME OF ADVERBS, A. P. 1 a. F. Anstey. Liverpool Royal Court, March 9, 1908; rev. Grand, Fulham, March 30, 1908.

GAME OF BLUFF, A. Sk. Empress, April 3, 1907.

GAME OF BLUFF, A. P. 1 a. H. M. Paull. Liverpool Royal Court, May 11, 1908.

GAME OF BRIDGE, A. C. 1 a. Geo. Trevor. Albert H. West T., July 6, 1903.

GAME OF CARDS. Comedietta. 1 a. L. J. Hollenius. New York, 1875 (a version of same original as *A Quiet Rubber*).

GAME OF CARDS, A. M.C.D. F. Carlyon. M. by G. Dixon. Shrewsbury T.R., January 10, 1898.

GAME OF CHESS. C. 1 a. Alfred Sutro. Pub. by S. French, Limited.

GAME OF DOMINOES, A. R. Reece. Ryde, August, 1867

GAME OF LIFE. Surrey, November 14, 1863

GAME OF LIFE, THE. C. 5 a. J. Brougham. Pub. by J. Dicks. Ac. N.Y., December, 1856.

GAME OF LIFE, THE. D. Pro. and 3 a. W. Howell Poole. Liverpool Court (as a Spec. Melo-d. in 5 a.), August 15, 1887; Grand, December 12, 1887.

GAME OF LIFE AND DEATH, THE. City of London, December 1, 1856.

GAME OF LOVE, THE. C. 5 a. J. Brougham. Pub. by J. Dicks. Ac. N.Y., September 13, 1855.

GAME OF LOVE, THE. Ca. 1 a. Gilbert Dayle. Strand, May 8, 1900.

GAME OF ROMPS, A. F. 1 a. J. M. Morton. Princess's, March 12, 1855.

GAME OF SPECULATION, THE. C. 3 a. "Slingsby Lawrence" (G. H. Lewes). Adap. fr. a posthumous work of H. de Balzac. Lyceum, October 2, 1851; D.L., November 26, 1855; rev. Gaiety, 1872; Op. Comique, May, 1877.

GAME OF SPOOF, A. Sk. Pr. by Leonard Yorke. Manchester Palace, December 15, 1906.

GAMEKEEPER, THE. D. 4 a. Florence Marryat and Herbert M'Pherson. Brighton Aquarium (in 3 a), May 16, 1898; Kilburn T., March 13, 1899.

GAMEKEEPER'S WIFE, THE. C. 1 a. Mrs. Hodgson and Archibald Hodgson. Southampton P.O.W., September 22, 1890.

GAMESTER, THE. C. Jas. Shirley. D.L., 1634. Pr. 1637. Lic. 1633. Several versions appeared afterwards, including *The Wife's Relief; or, The Husband's Cure*, by C. W. Johnson, 1711; *The Gamesters*, by Garrick, 1758; *The Wife's Strategem*, by Poole, 1827.

GAMESTER, THE. C. Mrs. Centlivre. L.I.F. February 22, 1705. Pr. 1705. Plot fr. the French of C. *Le Dissipateur* and fr. Regnard's *Le Joueur*.

GAMESTER, THE. T. 5 a. Edward Moore. Feb. 7, 1753, D.L. Pr. 1753. D.L., January 12, 1819; C.G., 1823; D.L., January 12, 1842; Holborn T., October 16, 1869.

GAMESTER, THE. O. 1 a. Walter Crogan. Composed Aiulf Hjovard. Belfast Royal, June 4, 1906; Canterbury, October 28, 1907.

GAMESTER OF METZ, THE. Rom. D. 5 a. Ch. March. W. Hartlepool Gaiety, July 31, 1897.

GAMESTER OF MILAN, THE. P. 3 a. T. J. Serle. Victoria, April 21, 1834.

GAMESTERS, THE. C. David Garrick. D.L., December 22, 1757. Pr. 1758. See *The Gamester*, by Shirley.

GAMING TABLE, THE. G. à Beckett.

GAMMER GURTON'S NEEDLE. C. 5 a. John Still, afterwards Bishop of Bath and Wells. Pr. 1575. Ac. at Christ's Coll., Cambridge (the second English comedy).

GAMMON. C. James Mortimer. Adap fr. *La Poudre aux Yeux* of Labiche and Martin. Vaudeville, July 13, 1882.

GANDER HALL. F. Andrew Franklin. Hay., August 5, 1799. N.p.

GANDOLFO. O. 1 a. C. Lecocq. 1869.

GANELON. T. Blank verse. Wm. Young. Ac.

GANEM, THE SLAVE OF LOVE. Extrav. Francis Talfourd. Fr. the Arabian Night's Entertainment. Olympic, May 31, 1853.

GANYMEDE AND GALATEA. C.O. W. S. Gilbert. M. by Franz Von Suppé. Gaiety, January 20, 1872.

GAOL GATE, THE. T. 1 a. Lady Gregory. Dublin Abbey, October 22, 1906; Great Queen Street, June 12, 1907.

GARCIA; OR, THE NOBLE ERROR. C. 5 a. F. G. Tomlins. Sadler's Wells, December 12, 1849.

GARDEN OF GLITTER, THE. An Egyptian M.C. extrav. Kenney Allan. Poplar Queen's, May 6, 1907.

GARDEN OF LIES, THE. Rom. 4 a. Adap. fr. the story of J. M. Forman, by S. Grundy. St. James's, September 3, 1904.

GARDEN OF THE GODS, THE. Mus. P. 1 a. Ivan Pat Gore and Chas. H. Williams. M. by Hamilton Weller. Brighton West Pier, March 6, 1909.

GARDEN PARTY, A. Dr. Sk. Chs. S. Cheltnam. Publ. by S. French, Limited.

GARDEN PARTY, THE. Ca. J. M. Morton. Hay., August 13, 1877.

GARDENER OF SIDON, THE. M.D. 3 a. MS. was in Mr. Arthur Murphy's library.

GARDENERS, THE. Song P. 2 a. Fredk. Fenn and Jetta Vogel. M. by R. H. Walthen. Perf. by amateurs. Guildhall School, February 12, 1906; Great Queen Street, June 12, 1907.

GARDIENS DE PHARE. D. 1 a. Paul Autier and Paul Cloquemin. Shaftesbury, March 27, 1908.

GARIBALDI. D. Tom Taylor. Astley's, October, 1859.

GARIBALDI EXCURSIONISTS, THE. F. H. J. Byron, Princess's, November 8, 1860.

GARIBALDI IN SICILY. Mus. D. 1 a. W Sawyer. Adelphi, April 22, 1867.

GAROTTERS, THE. P. 1 a. W. D. Howells. Ac. recently under direction of W. Poel.

GARRET ANGEL, THE. Burla. Ch. Webb. Marylebone, August 11, 1867.

GARRICK; OR, ACTING IN EARNEST. C.D. 3 a. A. G. Daly. Edinburgh Princess's, August 22, 1874.

GARRICK; OR, ONLY AN ACTOR. C. 3 a. Wm. Muskerry. Entirely orig. ver. of Fr. and German pieces on same subject. Prince's, Edinburgh, August 22, 1874. Strand, August 9, 1886.

GARRICK FEVER, THE. F. 1 a. J. R. Planché. Olympic, April 1, 1839.

GARRICK IN THE SHADES; OR, A PEEP INTO ELYSIUM. F. Anon. Pr. 1779.

GARRICK, THE KING'S JESTER; OR, THE EARLY DAYS OF HAMLET. D. C. H. Somerset.

GARRICK'S SACRIFICE. P. 3 a. Frank Lindo and A. Skelton. Harrogate Spa T., September 9, 1897; Stratford T.R., October 14, 1898.

GARRICK'S VAGARY; OR, ENGLAND RUN MAD. Pr. 1769.

GARRYOWEN; OR, THE BELLES OF THE SHANNON. Irish D. 4 a. J. Levey. Victoria, May 21, 1877.

GARTER, THE. C. 1 a. S. L. Ransom. C.P. Shakespeare, May 18, 1906.

GASCON; OR, LOVE AND LOYALTY, THE. D. 5 a. W. Muskerry. Adap. fr. the French of Barrière and L. Davye. Olympic, February 21, 1876.

GASCONADO THE GREAT. O. Jas. Worsdale. Pr. 1759.

GASMAN; OR, FIGHT AGAINST FATE, THE. D. 3 a. Henry Bradford. Oriental, April 14, 1873.

GASPARDO THE GONDOLIER. D. 3 a. Geo. Almar. Surrey, July 2, 1838.

GASTON BOISSIER. P. 2 a. W. L. Courtney. Bushey Herkomer T., January 9, 1893.

GATE OF EDEN, THE. Rom. P. 1 a. Mrs. Vere Campbell. Eastbourne Pier Pav., November 6, 1901.

GATES OF DAWN, THE. Sk. 1 sc. Arthur O'Keene, Canterbury, October 19, 1908.

GATES OF THE MORNING, THE. P. 3 a. Margaret M. Mack. Prod. by Mr. Norman Page. (Prod. by the Stage Society.) Shafesbury, March 1, 1908.

GATHERING OF THE CLANS, THE. Ballet from *Lochinvar*. C. Coppi and G. Jacobs. Alhambra, October 7, 1895.

GAUNTLET, A. P. 3 a. Osman Edwards, adap. by. Geo. P. Hawtrey. Transl. fr. the Norwegian of Björnstjerne Björnson. Royalty, January 20, 1894.

GAVOTTE, THE. Ca. 1 a. Miss Minnie Bell. Adap. fr. the French. Steinway H., April 1, 1890.

GAY CADETS, THE. P. 2 a. and 4 tab. Norman Prescott and J. Thomson. Lyrics by Percy Greenbank and Harold Simpson. M. by Basil Davies. Add. numbers by Chas. Braun and Bernand Johnson. Birmingham P.O.W., June 24, 1901; Camberwell Metropole, June 16, 1902.

GAY CAVALIER, A. Oa. 1 a. Ernest Cuthbert. M. by Arthur Nicholson. Manchester T.R., September 15, 1879.

GAY CAVALIER, THE. M.P. Wr. and comp. by Victor Stevens. Plymouth T.R., November 4, 1902.

GAY CHAPERON, THE. C. 3 a. Shirley Howlett. Bootle Muncaster T., November 22, 1894.

GAY CITY, THE. F.C. G. R. Sims. Nottingham T.R., September 8, 1881.

GAY CITY, THE. Ballet. C. Wilson. M. by G. W. Bing. Alhambra, December 19, 1900.

GAY CITY; OR, A SCENE AT THE SIEGE, THE. F. Royalty, June 12, 1871.

GAY DECEIVER, A. F.C. 3 a. James Mortimer. Royalty, February 3, 1879.

GAY DECEIVERS; OR, MORE LAUGH THAN LOVE, THE. F. Geo. Colman, jun. Plot fr. O. *Les Evènemens Imprévus*. Hay., August 22, 1804. Pr. 1808. D.L., May 10, 1828.

GAY DECEIVERS, THE. Mus. Absurd. 2 a. Margate R.T., June 22, 1908.

GAY DOGS. C. 2 a. F. C. Burnand. Publ. by D. Cox.

GAY DOGS. Sk. Messrs. Stanmore, Leslie Hawkins, and Mark Lester. Stoke Newington Pal., December 7, 1908.

GAY FINANCIER, THE. M.C. 2 a. Geo. Arthurs. Adelphi, July 16, 1904 (C.P.).

GAY GIRL, A. M.P. Edgar Dereve. M. by Guillaume Leone. Maidenhead Grand, May 1, 1905.

GAY GIRL, THE. M.F.C. 3 a. Jack R. Hannan. Matlock T.H., November 23, 1903.

GAY GORDONS, THE. Mus. P. 2 a. Bk. by S. Hicks. M. by G. Jones. Lyrics by A. Wimperis. C. H. Bovill, P. G. Woodhouse, and H. Hamilton. Aldwych, September 11, 1907.

GAY GRISETTE, THE. M.C. 2 a. Geo. Dance. M. by Carl Kiefert. Bradford T.R., August 1, 1898; Camberwell Metropole, December 5, 1898.

GAY HUSBAND, A. D. 3 a. Allerton. Adap. fr. the Fr. of Octave Feuillet. Eastbourne Devonshire Pk. T., May 31, 1886; Criterion, June 15, 1886.

GAY LORD MAYOR, THE. M.P. Herbert Leonard. Lyrics by J. P. Harrington. M. by G. Le Brunn. Camberwell Metropole, September 23, 1902.

GAY LORD QUEX, THE. C. 4 a. A. W. Pinero. Globe, April 8, 1899. D. of York's, May 6, 1902; rev. Garrick, April 30, 1908.

GAY LORD VERGY, THE. Op.-bo. 3 a. C. A. de Caillayet and Robert de Flers. M. by Claude Terrasse. Addl. numbers by Theo Wendt. Eng. ver. by Arthur Sturgess. Apollo, September 30, 1905.

GAY LOTHARIO, THE. Ca. 1 a. Alfred C. Calmour. St. James's, January 31, 1891.

GAY MUSICIAN, THE. C.O. 2 a. Bk. by Ed. Seidle. Lyrics by Chas. J. Campbell. M. by Julian Edwards. Bayswater Bijou, April 3, 1908 (C.P.).

GAY MUSKETEERS; OR, ALL FOR NUMBER ONE, THE. Burl. Eldred and Paulton. Liverpool P.O.W., April 18, 1870.

GAY PARISIENNE, THE. Mus. C. 2 a. Geo. Dance. M. by Ernest Vousden. Northampton O.H., October 1, 1894. New music by Ivan Caryll. Eleph. and C., March 23, 1896; D. of York's, April 4, 1896.

GAY PRETENDER, THE. C.O. 2 a. Geo. Grossmith, jun. M, by Claude Nugent. Globe, November 10, 1900.

GAY TOURISTS, THE. Sk. Southport Empire, August 9, 1909.

GAY WIDOW, A. 3 a. F. C. Burnand. Adap. of Sardou and Deslandes' F.C. *Belle-Maman*. Court, October 20, 1894.

GAY WIDOWER, A. C. 3 a. Sylvain Mayer. Adap. fr. a Ger. P. in 4 a. by Laufs and Kneisel. Vaudeville, March 11, 1892.

GAYEST OF THE GAY; OR, THE LIFE OF A WOMAN, THE. D. 4 a. Arthur Shirley and Eric Hudson. Workington O.H., March 2, 1905 (C.P.); Birkenhead T.R., April 18, 1905; Stratford Borough, November 11, 1907.

GAZETTA, LA. O. Rossini. Naples, 1816.

GAZETTE EXTRAORDINARY, THE. C. 5 a. J. G. Holman. C.G., April 23, 1811.

GAZZA LADRA, LA. O. Rossini. Lib. by Gherardini. Milan, May 31, 1817; King's T., March 10, 1821. Adapt. in English by the Bishops as *Ninetta; or, the Maid of Palaiseau*. C.G., February 4, 1830; D.L., May 4, 1868.

GEESE. Sk. 1 a. Pub. by S. French, Limited.

GEHEIMNISS, DAS. O. Sinetana. 1824-1834.

GEISHA; A STORY OF A TEA HOUSE, THE. Jap. M.P. 2 a. Owen Hall. Lyrics by Harry Greenbank. M. by Sidney Jones. Daly's, April 25, 1896; Daly's June 18, 1906.

GEISHA AND THE KNIGHT, THE. Jap. P. 2 a. Orig. prod. in England at Notting Hill Coronet, May 22, 1900; Criterion (Mr. Otojiro Kawakami's Season), June 18, 1901.

GEISHA'S REVENGE (OSSODE), THE. D. 3 a. in Japanese. Cardiff King's, June 26, 1905.

GELERT. Sk. H. Chance Newton. Canterbury M.H., April 16, 1900.

GELERT; OR, EVERY DOG HAS HIS DAY Sk. D. Basilio. Kilburn T.R., February 3 1896.

GELMINA. O. Poniatowski. C.G., June 4, 1872.

GELOSO RAVVEDUTO, IL. O. Rome Mercadante, 1820.

GELUCINA. Ital. O. 3 a. Prince Poniatowski. C.G., June 4, 1872.

GEM OF A GIRL. Ca. W. T. Le Queux. Brentford Beach's H., June 24, 1886.

GEMEA. D. Pro. and 3 a. Edgar Newbound. Britannia, March 29, 1880.

GEMINI. F. 1 a. R. B. Peake. Lyceum. Pub. by J. Dicks.

GEMMA DI VERGI. O. Donizetti. 1835.

GENDRE M. POIRIER, LE. C. E. Augier and J. Sandeau. Royalty, October 4, 1907.

GENERAL, THE P. Mentioned by Jas. Shirley. N.p.

GENERAL, THE. T.C. MS. in catalogue of library of Dr. Farmer. ? same as mentioned by Shirley. 1664.

GENERAL CASHIER'D, THE. P. Pr. 1712. N.ac.

GENERAL ENGAGEMENT, THE. M.C. Fredk. Faby. M. by Cyril Barry. Chelsea Palace, September 18, 1905.

GENERAL LOVER, THE. C. Theophilus Moss. Pr. 1749. N. ac.

GENERAL JOKE, A. M. Skit. A. Sturgess. Bexhill Kursaal, March 29, 1902.

GENERAL'S PAST, THE. C. 1 a. Clotilde Graves. (Dramatic prod. club. perf.) Court, January 3, 1909.

GENEROUS ARTIFICE;. OR, THE REFORMED RAKE, THE. C. Transl. fr. the French. Pr. 1762.

GENEROUS ATTACHMENT, THE. C. Geo. Smythe. Pr. 1796. N. ac.

GENEROUS CHIEF, THE. T. James Norval. Ac. at Montrose. Pr. 1792.

GENEROUS CHOICE, THE. C. Francis Manning. L.I.F. Pr. 1700.

GENEROUS CONQUEROR; OR, THE TIMELY DISCOVERY, THE. T. Bevil Higgons. Pro. wr. by Lord Lansdown. Ac. at T.R. Pr. 1702.

GENEROUS COUNTERFEIT, THE. C. Wm Davies. Wr. for a private theatre. Pr. 1786.

GENEROUS COURTEZAN, THE. MS. mentioned in catalogue of Mr. Macklin's library.

GENEROUS CULLY, THE. C. ? the same as *The Gentleman Cully*.

GENEROUS ENEMIES, THE. C. Transl. fr. Mme. Genlis's *Theatre of Education*. Pr. 1781.

GENEROUS ENEMIES; OR, THE RIDICULOUS LOVERS, THE. C. J. Corey. Borrowed fr. a variety of sources, chiefly Quinault's *La Généreuse Ingratitude*, Corneille's *Don Bertram de Ciganal*, Randolph's *Muse's Looking Glass*, and Beaumont and Fletcher's *Love's Pilgrimage*. D.L. Pr. 1672.

GENEROUS FREEMASON; OR, THE CONSTANT LADY, THE. B.O. 3 a. Wm. Rufus Chetwood. Pr. 1731. Ac. at Bartholomew Fair.

GENEROUS HUSBAND; OR, THE COFFEE-HOUSE POLITICIAN, THE. C. Chas. Johnson. D.L., January 20, 1711. Pr. circa 1713.

GENEROUS IMPOSTOR, THE. C. Rev. T. L. Obeirne (or O'Burne). (Borrowed from Destouches' *Le Dissipateur*. D.L., November 22, 1780. Pr. 1781.

GENEROUS MOOR, THE. T. Richd. Linnecar. Pr. 1789. Ac. at Wakefield, September 19, 1792.

GENEROUS PORTUGALS, THE. P. Perf. at the King's Playhouse. April 22, 1669.

GENESIUS. O. Weingartner.

GENEVA CROSS, THE. D. 4 a. G. F. Rowe. Adelphi, October 17, 1874.

GENEVIEVE. Oa. F. on the French D. *Kettly*. M. by G. A. Macfarren. Lyceum, November 3, 1834.

GENEVIEVE. D. Miss M. E. Braddon. Liverpool R. Alexandra, April 6, 1874.

GENEVIEVE. R.O. 3 a. Howard C. Cleaver. Fulham Grand, August 3, 1903.

GENEVIEVE; OR, THE LOST WIFE. D Pro. and 2 a. G. Conquest. Grecian, April 22, 1872.

GENEVIEVE; OR, THE REIGN OF TERROR. Adapted fr. Dumas and Maquet's *Le Chevalier de la Maison Rouge*. Adelphi, June, 1853.

GENEVIEVE DE BRABANT. C.O. Offenbach. Adap. by H. B. Farnie. Philharmonic, November 11, 1871.

GENIE DU GLOBE, LE. New Divertt Benj. Barnett. M. by M. Marctzek. D.L, December 15, 1847.

GENIES TUTELAIRES, LES. O. F. Rebel and F. Francœur. 1751.

GENII, THE. Panto. Henry Woodward D.L., 1752.

GENII, THE. Masque. Andrew Becket. Pr. 1814. ? N.ac.

GENII OF THE RING, THE. Ca. 1 a. Ernest Hendrie. Limerick T.R., January, 1882.

GENIUS, THE. C.D. 1 a. H. W. Williamson. Globe, January 26, 1881.

GENIUS, LIMITED. C. 3 a. Mrs. W Christie Gilmer. Barnes Byfield H., May 29 1907.

GENIUS OF GLASGOW, THE. Ac. at Glasgow, 1792.

GENIUS OF IRELAND, THE. Masque. John Macauley. An imitation of *Comus*. Pr. 1785. Ac. at Dublin.

GENIUS OF LIVERPOOL, THE. D. 1 a. T. Harpley. Liverpool. Pr. 1790.

GENIUS OF NONSENSE, THE. Panto Hay., September 2, 1780. Ascribed by some to Colman. N.p.

GENOESE PIRATE; OR, BLACK BEARD THE. Panto. T. C. Cross. C.G., October 15, 1798.

GENOVEVA. O. 4 a. Robert Schumann D.L. (ac. by students of the R. Coll. of M.), December 6, 1893.

GENT FROM LENTON'S, THE. M.F. 3 a E. F. Welch. Dudley Port Colosseum, January 7, 1903 (C.P.).

GENTEEL. Charade. Stanley Rogers. Publ. by S. French, Ltd.

GENTILHOMME PAUVRE, LE. Royalty, November 5, 1888.

GENTLE CRAFT, THE. P. Thos. Dekker. By some ascr. to Barten Holyday. Ac. 1599.

GENTLE CRAFT; OR, THE SHOEMAKER'S HOLIDAY, WITH THE HUMOUROUS LIFE OF SIMON EYRE, SHOEMAKER AND LORD MAYOR OF LONDON, THE. C. 1657. Ac. before the Q. by the Lord Admiral's servants.

GENTLE GERTRUDE; OR, DOOMED, DRUGGED, AND DROWNED AT DATCHET. Another 2nd title used was *The Infamous Redd Lyon Inn; or, Drugged and Drowned in Digbeth*. Melo-d. M. satire. 1 a. T. Edgar Pemberton. M. by T. Anderton. Liverpool Alexandra, January 21, 1881; Gaiety, May 14, 1884.

GENTLE IVY. P. 4 a. Austin Fryers. Strand, May 10, 1894.

GENTLE NELLY. D. Bradford T.R., April 8, 1871.

GENTLE RAIN. P. 1 a. W. Trant, fr. "Petite Pluie." Royalty, February 9, 1904.

GENTLE SHEPHERD, THE. Past. C. Wr. in Scotch dialect by Allan Ramsay. Ac. at Little T. in Hay. Pr. 1729.

GENTLE SHEPHERD, THE. C. Alt. fr. Ramsay by Cornelius Vanderstop. Hay. Pr. 1777.

GENTLE SHEPHERD, THE. Alt. fr. Ramsay by Richard Tickell. M. by Linley. Songs only. Pr. 1781. D.L., May 27, 1789.

GENTLE SHEPHERD, THE. Transl. by W. Ward. Pr. 1785.

GENTLE SHEPHERD, THE. Transl. by Margaret Turner. Pr. 1790. N. ac.

GENTLE SHEPHERD, THE. Ver. ac. at Glasgow Gaiety, November 13, 1876.

GENTLEMAN, THE. C. Sir Richd. Steele. Left. unf. in MS. Pr. 1809.

GENTLEMAN CITIZEN, THE. C. Transl. fr. Molière by John Ozell.

GENTLEMAN CRACKSMAN, THE. Sk. 3 sc. Hammersmith Palace, February 18, 1907; Richmond, June 10, 1907.

GENTLEMAN CULLY, THE. Ascr. by some to Charles Johnson. Ac. at T.R. Pr. 1702. See *Miss in Her Teens*.

GENTLEMAN DANCING MASTER, THE. C. 5 a. Wm. Wycherley. Duke's. Pr. 1673. Partly f. on Calderon's *El Maestro de Danzar*.

GENTLEMAN FROM IRELAND, A. C. 2 a. FitzJames O'Brien. Pub. by S. French, Limited. Ac. in America.

GENTLEMAN GARDENER, THE. B.O. James Wilder. Smock Alley, Dublin; C.G., April 29, 1749. Taken fr. Dancourt, Pr. 1751.

GENTLEMAN IN BLACK, THE. F. 1 a. Mark Lemon. Pub. by J. Dicks.

GENTLEMAN IN BLACK, THE. O.B. 2 a. W. S. Gilbert. M. by F. Clay. Charing Cross, May 26, 1870.

GENTLEMAN IN DIFFICULTIES. F. 1 a. Olympic, 1835 (or) 6. T. H. Bayly. Pub. by J. Dicks.

GENTLEMAN IN GREY, THE. C. 3 a. M. Compton. Edinburgh Lyceum, February 22, 1907.

GENTLEMAN IN KHAKI, A. M.F. Preston Hope and Napoleon Lambelet. D.L., May 15, 1900.

GENTLEMAN JACK. D. 5 a. Fredk. Mouillot. Stratford T.R., October 19, 1888.

GENTLEMAN JACK. D. 5 a. Chas. T. Vincent and Wm. A. Brady. Orig. prod. in America, 1892. D.L., April 21, 1894.

GENTLEMAN JACK. P. 1 a. H. W. C. Newte. Avenue, May 26, 1902.

GENTLEMAN JIM. Ca. W. R. Walkes. Bristol Prince's, October 29, 1894.

GENTLEMAN JOCKEY, THE. P. 3 a. Edward Marris. Inc. M. by Geo. Ess. Jersey St. Julian's, October 18, 1907; Crystal Pal., April 10, 1909.

GENTLEMAN JOE, THE HANSOM CABBY. M.F. Basil Hood. M. by Walter Slaughter. P.O.W., March 2, 1895.

GENTLEMAN OF ALSATIA, THE. C. Shadwell, 1688. Sometimes called *Squire of Alsatia*.

GENTLEMAN OF ENGLAND, A. Rom. P. 4 a. Ernest E. Norris and Fewlass Llewellyn. Eleph. and C., December 2, 1904.

GENTLEMAN OF FRANCE, A. D. 3 a. Harriet Ford. Avenue, June 4, 1904.

GENTLEMAN OF THE ROAD, A. Oa. 1 a. Eleanor Farjeon. M. by Harry Farjeon. St. Geo. H., July 22, 1902.

GENTLEMAN OF VENICE, THE. T.C. Jas. Shirley. Plot taken fr. Gayton's festivous notes on "Don Quixote." Salisbury Court. Lic. 1639. Pr. 1655.

GENTLEMAN OPPOSITE, THE. Ca. Lyceum, July, 1854.

GENTLEMAN USHER, THE. C. Geo. Chapman. Pr. 1606. ? N.a.

GENTLEMAN WHIP, THE. C. 1 a. H. M. Paull. Eastbourne Dev. Pk. T., February 1, 1894; 1st ac. at Terry's, February 21, 1894, to April 14, 1894; Vaudeville, April 16, 1894, to August 8, 1894.

GENTLEMEN, THE KING! Sk. Putney Hippodrome, August 30, 1909.

GENTLEMEN'S MASQUE, THE. Ac. at Court in December, 1613.

GENTYLNES AND NOBILITIE. Op. Int. Pr. (n.d.) by John Rastell. Probably very ancient.

GENUINE FELLOW SAVAGES. Scena. 1 a. J. Ojijatekha Brant-Sero. M. by Harry Child. Bridlington Spa, March 7, 1905.

GENVIERE. Petite piece. Scribe. Ac. before 1822.

GEOFFREY LANGDON'S WIFE. D. 4 a. Nita Rae. Liverpool Queen's, December 18, 1905.

GEOFFREY LANGDON'S WIFE. P. 4 a. Fred C. Somerfield. L'pool Rotunda, June 22, 1908.

GEOFFREY STERLING. P. 4 a. Neville Lynn. Adap. fr. Mrs. de Courcy Laffan's novel. Fulham Grand, July 3, 1905.

GEORGE. F.C. 3 a. Wilfred James. St. Alban's County H., March 11, 1895.

GEORGE-A-GREENE, THE PINDAR OF WAKEFIELD. C. F. on history. Ascr. to Greene. Not in acts. Circa 1592. Pr. 1599. An abridged ver. ac. at York, 1775. N.p.

GEORGE BARNWELL; OR, THE LONDON MERCHANT. T. 5 a. Geo. Lillo. D.L., June 22, 1731. C.G. December 29, 1806; D.L., April 11, 1814. See *The London Merchant*.

GEORGE CAMERON. Sk. Langdon Mitchell. Steinway H., March 13, 1891.

GEORGE DANDIN. F. Taken fr. Molière. D.L., 1747. N.p. See "French Classical Plays."

GEORGE DANDIN; OR, THE WANTON WIFE. C. Ozell. Transl. of Molière's *George Dandin*. Ac. D.L., 1747.

GEORGE DANDIN. See *Barnaby Brittle*.

GEORGE DARVILLE. D. Dion Boucicault. Adelphi, June 3, 1857.

GEORGE DE BARNWELL. Burl. panto. H. J. Byron. Adelphi, December 26, 1862.

GEORGE GARTH. P. 3 a. D. C. Murray, H. Murray, and J. L. Shine. Fulham Grand, July 28, 1902.

GEORGE GEITH; OR, A ROMANCE OF A CITY LIFE. D. 4 a. Wybert Reeve. F. on Mrs. J. H. Riddell's novel. Scarborough T.R. (in 5 a.). August 6, 1877; Crystal Pal., October 30, 1883.

GEORGE GRANDERBURYE, THE TRUE HISTORIE OF. As pl. by the Earl of Oxenforde's servants. N.p.

GEORGE SCANDERBAGE, THE TRUE HISTORIE OF. Prob. by Marlowe. As played by the Earl of Oxenforde's servants. Ent. at Stationers' Co. July 3, 1601. N.p.

GEORGE THE THIRD, THE FATHER OF HIS PEOPLE. D. Victoria, August 30, 1824.

GEORGE'S NATAL DAY. Masque. Pr. at Edinburgh, 1780.

GEORGIENNES, LES. Op. bo. C. J. S. Wilson. M. by Offenbach. Philharmonic, October 2. 1875.

GERALDI DUVAL. THE BANDIT OF BOHEMIA. Dr. piece. 1 a. F. on tale by Mrs. Opie. M. by Cooke. D.L., September 8, 1821.

GERALDINE; OR, THE LOVERS' WELL. C.O. Balfe. Princess's, August, 1843.

GERALDINE; OR, THE MASTER PASSION. D. Mrs. H. L. Bateman. Adelphi, June 12, 1865.

GERALDINE'S ORDEAL. D. T. B. Bannister. Greenock T.R., April 18, 1871.

GERMAN CLASSICAL PLAYS:—

The principal are by Goethe and Schiller.

GOETHE, JOHANN WOLFGANG VON. Born at Frankfort-on-the-Maine, August 28, 1749; died at Weimer, March 22, 1832.

GOETZ VON BERLICHINGEN. Wr. 1771. Pr. 1773.
CLAVIGO. 1774.
IPHIGENIA IN TAURIS. 1780.
DIE FISCHERIN. Oa. 1782.
COUNT EGMONT. Pr. 1788.
TASSO. 1790.
HERMANN AND DOROTHEA. Idyllic Poem. 1796-7.
FAUST. 1806; second part 1830.
STELLA.

SCHILLER, JOHANN CHRISTOPH FRIEDRICH VON. Born at Marbach, in Würtemberg, November 10, 1759; died May 9, 1805.

GEIST-SIEHER. Ro. (unfinished). 1766.
THE ROBBERS. T. Wr. 1777; Mannheim, 1782.
FIESCO. T. 1783.
CABAL AND LOVE. T. 1783.
DON CARLOS. T. 1784.
WALLENSTEIN. T. 1799.
Part 1.—The Camp of Wallenstein.
Part 2.—The Piccolomini.
Part 3.—The Death of Wallenstein.
MARY STUART. 1800.
JOAN OF ARC. 1800.
BRIDE OF MESSINA. 1800.
WILLIAM TELL. D. 1804

GERMAN HOTEL, THE. C. Marshall. C.G. Pr. 1790. Alt. of a German P. by Brandes.

GERMAN PRINCESS, THE. Ac. at Duke's T. in Dorset Gardens, 1663. L.I.F., April 15, 1664.

GERMAN SILVERY KING, THE. Burl. Walter Burnot. Eleph. and C., March 24, 1883.

GERMAN THEATRE AT VENICE, THE. Transl. fr. Meissner by A. Thompson. Pr. 1796.

GERMANIA. Ital. O. in prol. and 2 sc. M. by A. Franchetti. Book by L. Illica. C.G., November 13, 1907 (first prod. in England).

GERMANICUS. T. Thos. Cooke. N.p. N. ac. The MS. was in possession of Sir Joseph Mawbey.

GERMANICUS. T. By a Gentleman of Oxford. Pr. 1775.

GERMANS AND FRENCH; OR, INCIDENTS IN THE WAR OF 1870-1. D. John Douglass, jun. Standard, March 8, 1871.

GERTIE'S BOY. M.C. Tom Elwen. M. by Harry Henderson. Carlisle P. Halls, October 4, 1900 (C.P.).

GERTIE'S GARTER. F. E. H. Sothern. Newcastle T.R., April 12, 1883.

GERTRUDE'S CHERRIES; OR, WATERLOO IN 1835. C. 2 a. Douglas Jerrold. C.G., September 10, 1842.

GERTRUDE'S MONEY BOX. Ca. Harry Lemon. Sadler's Wells, January 9, 1869.

GERTY. D. 4 a. By "Owl." Park, March 26, 1881.

GETTING MARRIED. "Conversation" by G. Bernard Shaw. Hay., May 12, 1908 (mat.).

GHETTO, THE. D. 3 a. Adap. fr. Henry Heijermans, jun.'s, Dutch P. Comedy, September 9, 1899.

GHILLIE CALLUM. Scotch F. Glasgow Royalty, June 26, 1895.

GHOST, A. Sk., "not by Ibsen." Criterion, June 28, 1892.

GHOST, THE. C. 2 a. Dublin. Taken fr. Mrs. Centlivre's P. *The Man's Bewitched.* Pr. 1767. See *The Witchcraft of Love.*

GHOST; OR, THE WOMAN WEARS THE BREECHES, THE. C. Anon. Wr. in 1640. Pr. 1653.

GHOST OF AN IDEA, THE. F. Arthur M. Heathcote. Brompton Hospital, December 20, 1892.

GHOST OF JERRY BUNDLER, THE. F. 1 a. Pub. by D. Cox.

GHOST OF MOLIERE, THE. A transl. of L'Ombre de Molière by Brecourt.

GHOST OF THE HAUNTED INN, THE. F. 1 a. Arthur Hemingway. Knutsford Empire T., June 15, 1900.

GHOST OF THE PAST, A. P. 1 a. Charles Darrell. St. Albans County H., March 1, 1899; Glasgow T.R., May 21, 1900.

GHOST STORY, THE. P. 2 a. T. J. Searle. Adelphi, 1833; rev. Marylebone, October 2, 1863.

GHOSTS. D. 3 a. Henrik Ibsen. Transl. by William Archer. Royalty, March 13, 1891; Athenæum, Tottenham Court Road, January 26, 1893; C.G., King's H., March 11, 1906.

GHOSTS. Burl. By Will Evans. Holloway Empire, September 15, 1902.

GHOSTS, THE. C. Holden. Duke's T., between 1662 and 1665. N.p.

GIACINTA ED ERNESTO. O. Benedict. 1829.

GIANNI DI CALAIS. O. Donizetti. Naples, 1828.

GIANT AND THE DWARF, THE. Britannia, December 26, 1896.

GIANT DEFEATED; OR, THE REWARD OF VALOUR, THE. Panto. Rom. ? by Byrne C.G., June 12, 1795.

GIANT OF PALESTINE, THE. M. Burl. Adelphi, December, 1838.

GIANT OF THE MOUNTAINS, THE. Fredk. Marchant. Britannia, December 27, 1869.

GIANT OF THE MOUNTAINS, THE. Panto. Wr. and invented by J. Addison. Britannia, December 26, 1894.

GIANT'S BRIDE, THE. New ver. of a M. Extrav. in 2 a, 3 sc., by R. N. De Beauvais. (Orig. prod. at Ancaster, February, 1906.) High Wycombe Town H., April 10, 1907.

GIBRALTAR. Com. O. Robert Houlton. Ac. at Dublin, 1784. N.p.

GIBRALTAR. Op. bo. 3 a. Alfred Murray. M. by Louis Varney. F. on *La Reine des Halles.* Hay., August 6, 1881.

GIBRALTAR; OR, THE SPANISH ADVENTURE. C. J. Dennis. D.L., February 16, 1705. Pr. 1705

GIDDY GALATEA. Op. trifle. 1 a. Henry Edlin. M. by Edward Jones. Trafalgar, November 15, 1895.

GIDDY GIRL. F.C. 3 a. F. Jarman. Boscombe Grand T., December 11, 1899.

GIDDY GOAT, THE. F.P. 3 a. Adap. by Augustus Moore for Ferdinand Le Noceur of Léon Gaudillot (Theatre Déjazet, December 19, 1890); Weymouth O.H., August 12, 1901; Terry's, August 22, 1901.

GIDDY GODIVA; OR, THE GIRL THAT WAS SENT TO COVENTRY. Burl. H. C. Newton. Sanger's Amphi., October 13, 1883. See *Lady Godiva.*

GIDDY MISS CARMEN. M. Burl. L. E. Steer (Sidney Lester). M. by J. Crook, Meyer Lutz, Sidney Jones, May Ostlere, J. Glover, and Scott Gatty. Brighton Aquarium, August 27, 1894.

GIFTED LADY, THE. D. 3 a. Skit on Ibsenism by Robert Buchanan. Avenue, June 2, 1891.

GIFTIE, THE. C. 3 a. Margery S. Clarke. Ladbroke H., April 18, 1907 (C.P.).

GIGOLETTE. See *The City of Pleasure.*

GIL BLAS. C. Edwd. Moore. D.L., February 2, 1751. Pr. 1751. Design taken fr. story of "Aurora" in the novel of "Gil Blas."

GIL BLAS! AT 17, 25, 52. O. D. 5 a. F. on the Hist. of the Spanish Adventurer at three different stages of his life. M. by Moss. Lyceum, August 1, 1822. See *Youthful Days of Gil Blas.*

GIL BLAS; OR, THE BOY OF SANTILLANE. Rom. D. 3 a. Geo. Macfarren. D.L.

GILDED FOOL, A. C. 4 a. H. G. Carleton. Shaftsbury, February 10, 1900.

GILDED LOVE. Extrav. Major Yeldham. Ryde T.R., October 8, 1888.

GILDED YOUTH. D. 4 a. Sir C. Young. Brighton T.R., September 30, 1872.

GILDEN AGE, THE. C. Clemens (Mark Twain). 1874.

GILDEROY. D. 2 a. W. H. Murray. Edinburgh T.R., May 18, 1829.

GILDEROY, THE BONNIE BOY. Scotch D. W. Barrymore. Victoria, 1822.

GILESO SCROGGINI. P. Mark Lemon. Olympic, 1841-4.

GILLE ET GILLOTIN. O. Thomas. Paris, 1874.

GILLETTE. Comic O. 3 a. H. Savile Clarke. M. by Audran. Adap. fr. the Fr. Royalty, November 19, 1883.

GIN. Geo. Roberts. A ver. of *L'Assommoir.* Victoria, March 27, 1880.

GIN AND WATER. Victoria, January 23, 1854.

GINECOCRATIA. C. Geo. Puttenham. Mentioned in his "Art of Poetry." N.p.

GINGERBREAD NUT; OR, THE TERMAGANT TAMED, THE. O. Pr. at Dublin 1790.

GIOCHI D'AGRIGENTO, I. O. Paisiello. Venice, 1796.

GIOCONDA, LA. O. Ponchielli. Milan, April 8, 1876; C.G., May 31, 1883; Kennington T., May 6, 1903.

GIOCONDA, LA. T. 4 a. Gabriel D'Annunzio. Done into English by Winifred Mayo. Lyceum (Eleonora Duse's season), May 14, 1900; Bedford Street Bijou, December 8, 1907.

GIORNO ED UN ANNO, UN. O. Benedict. London.

GIOVANNA D'ARCO. O. Verdi. Milan, 1845.

GIOVANNI GISCALA. O. Rossi. Parma, 1855.

GIOVANNI IN IRELAND. Extrav. O. 3 a. M. by Cooke. D.L., December 26, 1821.

GIOVANNI IN LONDON; OR, THE LIBERTINE RECLAIMED. O. Extrav. 2 a. W. T. Moncrieff. Olympic, December 26, 1817; D.L., May 30, 1819.

GIOVENTU DI ENRICO V., LA. O. M. by Morlacchi. 1823.

GIOVENTU DI ENRICO V., LA. O. Mercadante. Venice, 1837.

GIPSIES. Oa. 1 a. Basil Hood. M. by Wilfred Bendall. P.O.W., October 25, 1890.

GIPSIES, THE. C.O. Chas. Dibdin. Hay., August 3, 1778. Pr. 1778. A transl. of *La Bohemienne*, by Favart.

GIPSIES; OR, A CHRISTMAS GAMBOL, THE. 2 a. Joseph Moser. Pr. 1807. N.ac.

GIPSIES METAMORPHOS'D. See *Metamorphos'd Gipsies.*

GIPSY, THE. D. J. Sheridan Knowles. N.p.

GIPSY, THE. P. 1 a. Ch. Hannan. Kidderminster T.R., May 6, 1901; Court, January 21, 1904.

GIPSY EARL, THE. D. 4 a. G. R. Sims. Adelphi, August 31, 1898.

GIPSY FARMER; OR, JACK AND JACK'S BROTHER, THE. D. 2 a. John Beer Johnstone. Surrey, March, 1849.

GIPSY GABRIEL. C.O. 3 a. Walter Parke and Wm. Hogarth. M. by Florian Pascal. F. on story of *Guy Mannering.* Bradford T.R., November 3, 1887.

GIPSY GIRL, THE. O.P. E. Mansel. M. by A. Peterson. Brixton Empress, December 1, 1902.

GIPSY GIRL, THE. C.O. 2 a. Claude Arundale. Lyrics by Follett Thorpe. Add. numbers by Claude Arundale and Tom Hefferman. Liverpool Shakespeare, May 15, 1905; Waldorf, January 28 and March 22, 1907.

GIPSY JACK. Melo-d. 4 a. Henry Bedford. Burnley Victoria T., August 5, 1899; Manchester Queen's, August 14, 1899; Greenwich, Morton's, January 22, 1900.

GIPSY JACK; OR, THE NAPOLEON OF HUMBLE LIFE. Extrav. Moncrieff. Victoria.

GIPSY KING, THE. D. 3 a. J. Bosworth. Queen's, May 25, 1837.

GIPSY PRINCE, THE. C.O. 2 a. Thos. Moore. M. by Kelly. Hay., July, 1801.

GIPSY PRINCESS. Sk. Fredk. Bingham. Middlesex M.H., March 13, 1895.

GIPSY QUEEN, THE. P. 1 a. F. on *The Hunchback of Notre Dame.* West London, June 23, 1903.

GIPSY'S ROMANCE. Victoria, November 29, 1852.

GIPSY'S VENGEANCE, THE. 4 a. Ch. Jeffreys. Eng. ver. of Verdi's O. *Il Trovatore.* D.L., March 24, 1856.

GIPSY'S VENGEANCE, THE. Burl. Melo-d. 1 a Sapte, jun. Publ. by Douglas Cox.

GIPSY'S WARNING, THE. Rom.O. 2 a. M. by Jules Benedict. D.L., April 19, 1838.

GIRALDA. O. 3 a. Adophe Adam (Paris, 1850). Transl. by Arthur Baildon. Lyceum, September 21, 1876.

GIRALDA; OR, THE INVISIBLE HUSBAND. C.D. 3 a. Hy Welstead. Adap. fr. Scribe's O. Olympic, September 12, 1850; City of London, October 19, 1850.

GIRALDA; OR, THE MILLER'S WIFE. P. B. Webster. Hay., September 16, 1850.

GIRALDA; OR, THE SIEGE OF HARLECH. Jackson, 1778. See *British Heroine.*

GIRALDA; OR, WHICH IS MY HUSBAND? C.D. 3 a. Mrs. Davidson. Adap. fr. the French of Scribe. Grecian Saloon, October 25, 1850.

GIRALDO, THE CONSTANT LOVER. Henry Shirley. Ent. Stationers' Co., September 9, 1653. N.p.

GIRL AND THE GOVERNOR, THE. C.O. 2 a. S. M. Brenner. M. by Julian Edwards. C.P. Bayswater Victoria H., October 2, 1906.

GIRL AT THE WHEEL. Extrav. Publ. by Samuel French, Limited.

GIRL BEHIND THE COUNTER, THE. M.C. 2 a. Leedham Bantock and Arthur Anderson. M. by Howard Talbot, add. m. by J. St. A. Johnson and Augustus Barratt, add. lyrics by Percy Greenbank. Wyndham's, April 21, 1906.

GIRL FROM BIARRITZ, THE. P. 1 a. Leonard Robson. Aberdeen H.M., October 29, 1906.

GIRL FROM BOND STREET, THE. M.C. 3 a. R. Oliver. Central T., Northwich. September 5, 1902.

GIRL FROM CHICAGO. American M. F. 3 a. Maidenhead Grand Empire, December 26, 1903.

GIRL FROM CORSICA, THE. M.P. 2 a. Mark Ambrton. Glasgow Athenæum, February 25, 1903; Norwich G.O.H., May 16, 1904.

GIRL FROM JAPAN. M.C. 2 a. Book and lyrics, Wilfred Carr. Dover T.R., April 29, 1903; Crouch End O.H., October 24, 1904.

GIRL FROM KAY'S, THE. M.P. 3 a. Owen Hall. Lyrics by Adrian Ross and Claude Aveling. M. by Cecil Cook. Apollo, November 15, 1902.

GIRL FROM MAXIM'S, THE. F. 3 a. Adap. fr. *La Dame de chez Maxim* of Georges Feydeau. Criterion, March 20, 1902.

GIRL FROM OVER THE BORDER (A Prince's Dream). M. Extrav. Hammersmith King's, May 18, 1908.

GIRL FROM PARIS, THE. F.C. 3 a. H. Durez. Balham Assembly Rooms, February 4, 1902.

GIRL FROM UP THERE, THE. M.E. 3 a. Hugh Morton. M. by Gustave Kerker. (Orig. prod. New York.) Duke of York's, April 23, 1901.

GIRL FROM WHERE? THE. M.F. 1 a. E. Moncrieffe. M. by E. Moncrieffe and W. Dommes. Ilford T.H., September 25, 1903 (amat.).

GIRL GRADUATE: AN IDYLL OF COMMEM, A. Ca. 1 a. Edward Rose. Oxford New T., June 28, 1886.

GIRL HE LEFT BEHIND HIM, THE. A variety. 1 a. Delacour Daubigny. Adap. fr. the French. Vaudeville, November 28, 1881.

GIRL I LEFT BEHIND ME, THE. D. 4 a. David Belasco and Franklyn Fyles. Sadler's Wells, January 6, 1893; Adelphi, April 13, 1895. Orig. prod. U.S.A.

GIRL I LOVE, THE. Dr. Sk. 5 sc. Pimlico Standard, January 21, 1903.

GIRL IN GREY, THE. Sk. Hugo Ames. Metropolitan, September 16, 1907.

GIRL IN STYLE, THE. F. Scawen. C.G., December 6, 1786. N.p.

GIRL IS MINE, HA! HA!, THE. F. 1 a. A. Jefferson. Glasgow Metropole, June 28, 1907.

GIRL NEXT DOOR, THE. M.C. 2 a. Walter Flint. M. by A. S. Taggart. Brighton Aquarium, July 2, 1906.

GIRL OF MY HEART; OR, JACK ASHORE, THE. D. 4 a. Herbert Leonard. Surrey, December 21, 1896.

GIRL OF THE GOLDEN WEST, THE. P. 4 a. David Belasco. Elephant and Castle, September 29, 1905.

GIRL OF THE WOOD, THE. O. Weber. Afterwards publ. under title of *Silvana.* Circa 1800.

GIRL ON THE STAGE, A. A rev. ver. of *The Little Cherub.* Prince of Wales's, May 5, 1906.

GIRL REDEEMED FROM SIN, A. D. In a plot and 4 a. D. Muskerry. (Orig. prod. at South Shields R.T.) Aston R., August 19, 1907; Stratford R.T., February 22, 1908.

GIRL WHO LOST HER CHARACTER, THE. D. 4 a. W. Melville. Standard, October 10, 1904.

GIRL WHO MARRIED FOR MONEY, THE. D. 4 a. Castle, Neath, July 1, 1907.

GIRL WHO TOOK THE WRONG TURNING, THE. P. 4 a. Walter Melville. Standard, October 1, 1906.

GIRL WHO WENT ASTRAY, THE. D. 4 a. W. Hibbert and F. Bulmer. (Orig. prod. at Hyde R.T., April 5, 1907.) Stratford R.T., December 26, 1907.

GIRL WHO WRECKED HIS HOME. P. 4 a. W. Melville. Standard, September 30, 1907.

GIRL WITH THE ANGEL FACE, THE. "Mystery D." in 5 a. James Willard. Shakespeare T., August 3, 1908.

GIRL WITH THE AUBURN HAIR, THE. M.P. 3 a. Wr. and composed by Paul Knox. Walham Green Granville, June 19, 1905.

GIRL WORTH GOLD, A. P. Perf. at King's Arms, Norwich, 1662. The second title of Heywood's play, *The Fair Maid of the West.*

GIRL'S CROSS ROADS, A. P. 4 a. W. Melville. Standard, October 5, 1903. Terriss, December 28, 1903.

GIRL'S FALSE STEP, A. D. 4 a. Harold Wyte. Hoxton King's, January 30, 1905.

GIRL'S FREAK, A. F.C. 2 a. Lilian Feltheimer and Kate Dixey. St. George's H., February 6, 1899.

GIRL'S ROMANCE, A. D. Boucicault, 1879.

GIRL'S TEMPTATION, A. P. 4 a. Mrs. Morton Powell. Liverpool Star, July 12, 1909.

GIRLS, THE. C. 3 a. H. J. Byron. Vaudeville, April 19, 1879.

GIRLS AND BOYS: A NURSERY TALE. C. 3 a. A. W. Pinero. Toole's, November 1, 1882.

GIRLS IN SCARLET, THE. Sk. Royal Standard, May 25, 1908.

GIRLS OF GOTTENBERG, THE. M.P. 2 a. Wr. by G. Grossmith, jun., and L. E. Berman. M. by I. Caryll and Lionel Monckton. Lyrics by A. Ross and Basil Hood. Gaiety, May 15, 1907; rev. Adelphi, August 10, 1908.

GIRLS OF THE PERIOD, THE. M. folly. F. C. Burnand. D.L., February 25, 1869.

GIRLS OF THE PERIOD. By A. B. Publ. by Stanley Rivers.

GIRLS WILL BE GIRLS. M.C. 3 a. Florence Lyndall. M. by Arthur Gatburn and Herbert Sydney. Llanelly Royalty T., March 19, 1900.

GIROFLE-GIROFLA. French Op. bo. by Lecocq. Op. Comique, June 6, 1874. Engl. ver. by Clement O'Neil and Campbell Clarke. Philharmonic, October 3, 1874.

GIRONDIST. City of London, August 14, 1854.

GIROUETTE. Comic O. 3 a. Robert Reece. M. by A. Cœdès. Lib. adap. fr. the orig. of Hemery and Bocage. Crystal Palace and Alexandra Palace; Portsmouth T.R., March 25, 1889; Avenue, June 24, 1889.

GIRTON GIRL. Oa. 1 a. Adams and Caldicott. Publ. by Saml. French, Ltd.

GISELLE. D. 2 a. W. Moncrieff. Publ. by Saml. French, Ltd.

GISELLE; OR, THE SIRENS OF THE LOTUS LAKE. Burl. H. J. Byron. Olympic, July 22, 1871.

GISELLE OU LES WILIS. Ballet. T. Gautier Adap. fr. Heinrich Heine. M. by A. Adam. Paris, 1841; Her M., March, 1842.

GISIPPUS. D. 5 a. Gerald Griffin. M. by Cooke. D.L., February 23, 1842.

GISMONDA. P. 4 a. Victorien Sardou. Daly's, May 27, 1895.

GITANA, LA. D. Pro., 3 a. Edw. Towers. Pavilion, April 15, 1876.

GITANA, LA. 2 a. Leslie Moreton. M. by Stephen Philpots. So. Shields T.R., November 22, 1895; Parkhurst, March 10, 1896.

GITANILLA; OR, THE CHILDREN OF THE ZINCALI, THE. D. 3a. J. Crawford Wilson. Surrey, October 22, 1860.

GIVLIETTA E ROMEO. S.O. 3 a. Wds. by Giuseppe Foppa. M. by Zingarelli. Milan Scala, January 30, 1796.

GIULIETTA E ROMEO. O. 3 a. Wds. by Romani. M. by Vaccaj. Milan, October 31, 1825. Prod. in London at King's T., Haymarket, April 10, 1832.

GIULIO SABINO. O. Sarti. 1781.

GIULIO SABINO. O. Cherubini (a pupil of Sarti). 1784

GIURAMENTO, IL. O. Mercadante. Milan, 1837.

GIUSTINO. T. Metastasio. 1712.

GIVE A DOG A BAD NAME. F. 1 a. "Slingsby Lawrence" (G. H. Lewis). Lyceum, April 18, 1854.

GIVE A DOG A BAD NAME. D. 2 a. Leopold Lewis. Adelphi, November 18, 1876.

GIVE A DOG AN ILL NAME. G. H. Lewes. See *Give a Dog a Bad Name.*

GIVE A MAN LUCK, AND THROW HIM INTO THE SEA. J. Lyly. Ent. Stationers' Co., July 24, 1660. N.p.

GIVE AND TAKE. C. 1 a. Dr. T. J. Price Jenkins. Neath Assembly R.T., November 1, 1894.

GIVE HEED. Modern Morality. Blanche G. Vulliamy. Court, June 29, 1909 (mat.).

GIVE ME MY WIFE. F. 1a. W. E. Suter. Grecian, June 13, 1859.

GLAD TIDINGS. D. Pro. and 5 a. J. Willing and Frank Stamforth. Standard, August 29, 1883.

GLADIATOR, THE. T. Bird. (1803-1854.)

GLADIATOR, THE. T. 5 a. First time on Engl. Stage, D.L., October 17, 1836; D.L., May 7, 1875.

GLADIATORS, THE P. Adap. by T. B. Bannister. Cardiff T.R., June 5, 1839. See *The Fiat of the Gods.*

GLADYS; OR, THE GOLDEN KEY. C. 3 a. Arthur Law. Strand, December 1, 1886; Avenue, August 25, 1888.

GLAMOUR. C.O. 3 a. H. B. Farnie and Alfred Murray. M. by Wm. Hutchison. Edinburgh T.R., August 30, 1886.

GLASHEN GLORA; OR, THE LOVER'S WELL. D. 3 a. R. Dodson. Pavilion, September 25, 1875.

GLASS HOUSES. C. 3 a. F. W. Broughton. Liverpool P.O.W., April 11, 1881; Swansea T.R., March 6, 1893, as a Dr. sketch. 1 a.

GLASS OF FASHION, THE. C. 4 a. Sydney Grundy. Glasgow, Grand T. (in 3 a, by G. R. Sims and Sydney Grundy). March 26, 1883; Globe, September 8, 1883.

GLASS OF GOVERNMENT, THE. T.C. George Gascoigne. Ir. 1575.

GLASS OF WATER; OR, GREAT EVENTS FROM TRIFLING CAUSES SPRING, A. C. 2 a. W. E. Suter. Adap. fr. Scribe's *Verre d'Eau.* Queen's, May 2, 1863. See *The Queen's Favourite.*

GLAUCIS. Burl. F. T. Traill. Olympic, July 5, 1865.

GLAZIER, THE. Fr. Vaude in 1 a. Fulham Grand, August 12, 1907.

GLEAM IN THE DARKNESS. D. 1 a. Hamilton Aidé.

GLEANER; OR, HARVEST HOME, THE. Dr. Ent. 3 a, with songs. Joseph Moser. Wr. 1809. N.p. N.ac.

GLENCOE. T. Sergeant Talfourd. Hay., May 23, 1840.

GLENDALOUGH. Irish D. 4 a. Edmund Gurney. Manchester, Queen's T. December 14, 1891.

GLI ARIBI NELLE GALLIE. O. D.L. (two scenes from). December 16, 1832.

GLI EQUIVOCI. O. Scarlatti. (Rome, Collegio Clementino.) February 8, 1679.

GLI UGONOTTI. See *Les Huguenots.*

GLIMPSE OF PARADISE, A. F.C. 3 a. Joseph J. Dilley. Ealing, Lyric H., January 1, 1887.

GLIMPSE OF THE WORLD, A. D. 1 a. Shirley Howlett. Liverpool, Gordon Lads' Inst., November 23, 1895.

GLIN GATH; OR, THE MAN IN THE CLEFT. D. 4 a. Paul Meritt. Grecian, April 1, 1872.

GLITTER. C. 2 a. Gilbert à Beckett. St. James's, December 26, 1868.

GLITTERING GEM, THE. D. Charles R. Rennel. Oldham T.R., September 21, 1874.

GLITTERING GLORIA. F. 3 a. Hugh Morton. Wyndham's, July 21, 1903.

GLITTERING GOLD. Bal. Crystal Palace, June 7, 1898.

GLOAMING AND THE MIRK, THE. D. Edinburgh Princess's, February 1, 1869.

GLORIANA. C. 3 a. Jas. Mortimer. Adap. fr. *Le Truc d'Arthur* of Chivot and Duru (a modern ver. of *Le Jeu de l'Amour et du Hasard,* by Marivaux). Globe, November 10, 1891.

GLORIANA. See *My Artful Valet.*

GLORIANA; OR, THE COURT OF AUGUSTUS CÆSAR. T. Nathaniel Lee. Ac. at the T.R., 1676. F. on Gomberville's *Cléopatre.* See *Court of Augustus Cæsar.*

GLORIE ASTON. P. 4 a. Forbes Dawson. Wolverhampton Royal Star, March 7, 1898.

GLORIOUS FIRST OF JUNE, THE. M. Ent. D.L., July 2, 1794. Ascr. to Sheridan and Cobb. Songs by the Duke of Leeds, Lord Mulgrave, Mrs. Robinson, Richardson, etc. N.p

GLORY. F. 1 a. H. P. Grattan. Halifax T.R., January 2, 1871; Charing Cr., June 16, 1873.

GLOUCESTERSHIRE SQUIRE, THE. Another title for *The Country Squire*. Pr. 1734.

GLOWWORM, THE. D. Count de la Isla. Adap. fr. his French story. Aberdeen H.M.T., March 10, 1884.

GLUCK IM WINKEL, DAS. D. 3 a. Hermann Sudermann. St. George's Hall, February 2, 1900; Gt. Queen St. T., February 10, 1903.

GNOME; OR, HARLEQUIN UNDERGROUND, THE. Pant. Ascr. to R. Wewitzer. Hay., 1788.

GNOME FLY, THE. Adelphi, 1838.

GNOME FLY, THE. Pant. Geo. Conquest and H. Spry. Grecian, December 24, 1869.

GNOME KING; OR, THE GIANT MOUNTAINS, THE. D. 2 a. C.G., October, 1819.

GNOME KING AND THE GOOD FAIRY OF THE SILVER MINE, THE. Orig. Extrav. Wm. Brough. Queen's, December 26, 1868.

GO-AHEAD LADIES' CLUB, THE. F. Miss Hammond Hills. Bayswater Bijou, October 2, 1901.

GO BANG. Mus. F.C., 2 a. Adrian Ross and Osmond Carr. Trafalgar, March 10, 1894.

GO STRAIGHT; OR, HONEST HEARTS. D. Leonard Outram. Globe, August 2, 1894 (C.P.).

GO TO PUTNEY; OR, A STORY OF THE BOAT RACE. F. Harry Lemon. Adelphi, April 6, 1868.

GOAT'S MASQUE, THE. Ac. at Court about 1611.

GOBLIN AND THE SEXTON, THE. Sk. 3 sc. Cayley Calvert. Collins's M.H., December 24, 1900.

GOBLIN BAT, THE. Pant. F. Bowyer. Britannia, December 27, 1886.

GOBLINS, THE. T.C. Sir John Suckling. Ac. at the Private house in Blackfriars. Pr. 1646. T.R., January 24, 1667.

GOD AND NATURE. Orat. M. by Meyerbeer. 1811.

GOD AND THE MAN. See *Storm Beaten*.

GOD, HYS PROMISES. T. or Int. Bishop Bale. One of the first dramatic pieces pr. in England (1538). Ac. by young men at the Market Cross in Kilkenny on a Sunday in 1552.

GOD OF WAR, THE. D. 4 a. Chas. Whitlock. Wigan T.R., April 18, 1898; Stratford T.R., February 27, 1899.

GOD SAVE THE KING. 1 a. Costume P. Stourbridge Alhambra, November 18, 1908; Crouch End Hipp., February 15, 1909.

GOD SAVE THE QUEEN. D. 5 a. R. Palgrave and F. Glover. Sanger's, September 13, 1886; Bristol Prince's, April 24, 1886.

GOD SPEED THE PLOUGH. Ac. at the Rose T., December 27, 1593. N.p.

GOD'S PROMISES. A tragedy manifesting the chief promises of God unto man. This curious interlude, wr. by John Bale, is reprinted in Dodsley's Collection. See *God, Hys*, etc.

GODDESS OF DESTRUCTION, THE. Rom. Military D. 4 a. Terence Nerrey. Liverpool Queen's, March 6, 1908 (C.P.).

GODDWYN. T. Thos. Rowleie. Pr. 1778. Supposed to be wr. by Thos. Chatterton.

GODFREY OF BULLOIGNE, WITH THE CONQUEST OF JERUSALEM. Int. Danter. En. at Stationers' Co., June 19, 1594. A "Second Part" was ac. at the Rose, July 19, 1594. N.p.

GODIVA; OR, YE LADYE OF COVENTRIE AND YE EXYLE FAYRIE. Burl. Hist. Fancy. 1 a. By the Authors of *The Princesses in the Tower*. Strand, July 7, 1851. See *Lady Godiva*.

GODLY QUEEN HESTER. Mir. P. Anon 1561.

GODOLPHIN, THE LION OF THE NORTH. P. 5 a. B. Thompson. M. by Horne. D.L., 1813.

GODOLPHINS, THE. Surrey, April 9, 1860.

GODPAPA. F.C. 3 a. F. C. Philips and Chas. Brookfield. Comedy, October 22, 1891.

GOETZ OF BERLICHINGEN WITH THE IRON HAND. T. Transl. fr. Goethe by Wm. Scott. Pr. 1799. N.ac.

GOG AND MAGOG. Pant. December 27, 1822

GOGGINS' GINGHAM. Strand, May 4, 1863.

GOING IT! ANOTHER LESSON TO FATHERS. F.C. 3 a. J. M. Morton and W. A. Vicars. Glasgow Royalty, November 13, 1885; Toole's, December 7, 1885.

GOING ON PARADE. Epis. 1 a. H. M. Richardson. Manchester Gaiety, March 15, 1909.

GOING ON THE STAGE. M.C. 1 a. Mrs. Re Henry. M. by Ernest Crook. Corn Exge., Blandford, February 18, 1895.

GOING THE PACE. D. 4 a. Arthur Shirley and Ben Landeck. Star, Wolverhampton (C.P.), August 24, 1898; Pavilion, October 24, 1898.

GOING TO CHOBHAM; OR, THE PETTICOAT CAPTAINS. F. 1 a. C. H. Hazlewood. City of London T., Grecian Saloon.

GOING TO THE BAD. C. 2 a. Tom Taylor. Olympic, June 5, 1858.

GOING TO THE DERBY. F. 1 a. J. M. Morton. Adelphi, May 22, 1848.

GOING TO THE DOGS. F. 1 a. W. Brough and Andrew Halliday. D.L., March 6, 1865.

GOLD. D. 5 a. Chas. Reade. D.L., January 10, 1853. See *It's Never Too Late to Mend*.

GOLD AND GILT. Burl. Sensational D. H. J. Byron. Publ. by French.

GOLD CRAZE. P. 4 a. Brandon Thomas. Princess's, November 30, 1889.

GOLD-DIGGERS, THE. C.O. 3 a. W. W. Petrie. Balham Duchess, June 9, 1902.

GOLD DIGGERS; OR, THE GIRLS FROM UTAH, THE. C.O. 3 a. By W. W. Petre and Claude Aveling. Bath Royal, April 16, 1906.

GOLD DUST. D. James Rymer. Worthing Montague H., July 23, 1878

GOLD DUST. D. 5 a. Geo. De Lara. Blackpool Winter Gardens, April 29, 1887.

GOLD FIEND; OR, THE DEMON GAMESTER, THE. D. 3 a. W. Thompson Townsend. Queen's, May, 1850.

GOLD GUITAR, THE. City of London, September 1, 1851.

GOLD IS NOTHING—HAPPINESS IS ALL. D. John Levey. Leeds Amphi., October 5, 1868; East London, November 29, 1869.

GOLD MINE, A. 3 a. G. H. Jessop and Brander Matthews. First prod. in America. Gaiety, July 21, 1890.

GOLD MINE; OR, THE MILLER OF GRENOBLE. D. 2 a. E. Stirling; D.L., 1854.

GOLD SEEKERS; OR, THE DYING GIFT, THE. P. Victoria T., December, 1838.

GOLD SLAVE, THE. D. 5 a. T. G. Barclay. Longton T.R., July 8, 1886.

GOLDEN ACE; OR, BUBBLES. Sk. L. Mortimer. Bedford, January 4, 1909.

GOLDEN AGE, THE. P. 4 a. Vincent Brown. Worthing T.R., July 7, 1902.

GOLDEN AGE; OR, PIERROT'S SACRIFICE, THE. Mus. Rom. Henry Byatt. M. by Florian Pascal. Savoy, July 5, 1897.

GOLDEN AGE; OR, THE LIVES OF JUPITER AND SATURN, THE. Hist. P. Thomas Heywood. Story fr. Galtruchius and other heathen mythologists. Red Bull T. Pr. 1611.

GOLDEN AGE RESTOR'D, THE. Masque. Ben Jonson. Ac at Court, 1615. Pr. 1641.

GOLDEN APPLE, THE. Mythological O. F. Sylvester. Godalming Pub. H., April 11, 1891.

GOLDEN ASS, AND CUPID AND PSYCHE, THE. P. Henry Chettle and John Day. Ac. 1600.

GOLDEN AXE, THE. Panto. January 25, 1823.

GOLDEN BAIT, THE. C. 3 a. H. C. Lunn. Kilburn T.H., April 6, 1891 (amat.).

GOLDEN BAND, THE. D. 4 a. Henry Herman and the Rev. Freeman Wills. Olympic, June 14, 1887.

GOLDEN BOUGH, THE. C.O. David Scott. M. by Josef Pelzer. Adap. fr. the Countess d'Aulnois' *Le Rameau d'Or*. Broughty Ferry, January 27, 1887 (amat.).

GOLDEN BRANCH, THE. Extrav. 2 a. J. R. Planché. F. on the Countess D'Aulnois' *Le Rameau d'Or*. Lyceum, December 27, 1848.

GOLDEN BUTTERFLY, THE. See *The Dawn of Love*.

GOLDEN CALF, THE. C. 3 a. D. Jerrold. Strand, June 30, 1832.

GOLDEN CALF, OR, DOLLARS AND DIMES, THE. D. Pro. and 3 a. George Howard Coveney. Standard, June 18, 1883.

GOLDEN CASK, THE. Sadler's Wells, December 26, 1866.

GOLDEN CHANCE, THE. D. 6 a. St. Aubin Miller. Gateshead T.R. (in 5 a), November 23, 1891; Standard, August 1, 1892.

GOLDEN CROSS, THE. O. 2 a. Ignaz Brüll. Lib. by Mosenthal. Engl. ver. by J. P. Jackson. Adelphi, March 2, 1878.

GOLDEN DAGGERS. D. 5 a. French. Fletcher and E. Yates. Princess's, April 19, 1862.

GOLDEN DAYS, THE. Oa. 1 a. Wm. Beach, P. Shaw Jeffrey, and W. Teignmouth Shore. M. by Harold S. Moore. Chislehurst, October 17, 1893; Sidcup, February 10, 1897.

GOLDEN DREAM, THE. Manchester T.R., July 11, 1865.

GOLDEN DUSTMAN, THE. P. H. B. Farnie. Adap. fr. Dickens's *Our Mutual Friend*. Sadler's Wells, June 16, 1866; rev. Astley's, October 27, 1866.

GOLDEN FARMER; OR, HARLEQUIN PLOUGHBOY, THE. Panto. J. C. Cross. Pr. 1802. Ac. at the Circus.

GOLDEN FARMER; OR, THE LAST CRIME, THE. Melo-d. 2 a. Benjamin Webster. Coburg, December 26, 1832; rev. Astley's, 1867.

GOLDEN FETTER, A. D. 3 a. Watts Phillips. Holborn, February 17, 1869.

GOLDEN FLEECE; OR, JASON IN COLCHIS AND MEDEA IN CORINTH, THE. Classical Extrav. 2 pts. J. R. Planché. Hay., March 24, 1845.

GOLDEN FRUIT. D. 4 a. Henry Pettitt. East London, July 14, 1873.

GOLDEN GIRL, THE. M.C. 2 a. Basil Hood. M. by Hamish MacCunn. Birmingham P.O.W., August 5, 1905.

GOLDEN GOBLIN, THE. D. 4 a. Frank Marryat. Croydon T.R., March 5, 1888; Marylebone, July 23, 1888.

GOLDEN GULCH, THE. American D. Dover T.R., April 14, 1879.

GOLDEN HARVEST, A. D. 4 a. F. Jarman. Liverpool New T.R., May 26, 1890.

GOLDEN HARVEST, THE. D. G. Bellamy. Queen's Hall, August 17, 1868.

GOLDEN HEARTS. C.D. 4 a. Geo. Roy. Shepherd's Bush Athenæum, September 22, 1892.

GOLDEN KEY, THE. C.D. 3 a. Arthur Law. Leicester R.O.H., April 2, 1888.

GOLDEN KITE, THE. Jap. love playlet. 1 a. Herbert Shelley. M. by Stephen R. Philpot. Bayswater Bijou, March 8, 1905.

GOLDEN LADDER, THE. D. 5 a. Geo. R. Sims and Wilson Barrett. Globe, December 22, 1887.

GOLDEN LEEK, THE. Rom. Op. D. 4 a. Frank E. Wade. Tenby Assembly R., March 5, 1891.

GOLDEN LEGEND, THE. Dr. Pm. Longfellow. 1851.

GOLDEN LEGEND, THE. Dram. Cantata. Sir Arthur Sullivan. Words by Joseph Bennett, from Longfellow's poem. Leeds Festival, 1898.

GOLDEN LIGHT, THE. P 4 a. G. Daring (Mme. Raoul Duval). Savoy, September 29, 1904.

GOLDEN LUCK, THE. D. 4 a. W. G. H. Lees. Hammersmith Lyric, April 7, 1903.

GOLDEN MEAN, THE. M.E. Brewer. N.p. Circa. 1790.

GOLDEN PIPPIN, THE. Burla. Kane O'Hara. 2 a. (orig. in 3 a). C.G., February 6, 1773; Edinburgh, 1776. Pr. 1773.

GOLDEN PLOUGH, THE. D. 4 a. Paul Meritt. Adelphi, August 11, 1877.

GOLDEN PLUME; OR, THE MAGIC CRYSTAL, THE. Extrav. C. E. Howells. Walsall, Alexandra T., May 14, 1883.

GOLDEN PRINCESS AND THE ELEPHANT HUNTERS, THE. Zoolog. and Eques. Spec. A. Ramsey and R. de Cordova. M. by C. Corri. Hippodrome, December 23, 1903.

GOLDEN PROSPECT; OR, A FORLORN HOPE, THE. Amer. D. 4 a. Katherine F. Rund. Rev. and alt. by J. J. Dowling, J. C. Stewart. Orig prod. under title of *A Forlorn Hope*, at Salford Regent, April 8, 1901; Pavilion, July 29, 1901.

GOLDEN RING, THE. Fairy O. M. by F. Clay. Lib. by George R. Sims. Alhambra, December 3, 1883.

GOLDEN ROOK, THE. C.O. 2 a. Wr. by E. Woodhead and Comp. by F. V Lawton. Huddersfield Royal, November 18, 1907.

GOLDEN ROSE; OR, THE SCARLET WOMAN, THE. A "bas-relief." Ian Robertson. Imperial (Stage Society), June 8, 1903.

GOLDEN RUMP, THE. Anon. N.p. N.ac. Suppressed. 1773.

GOLDEN SERPENT, THE. D. 4 a. T. N. Walter. Stratford T.R., November 15, 1897.

GOLDEN SILENCE, THE. D. 4 a. C. H. Chambers. Garrick, September 22, 1903.

GOLDEN SORROW, A. D. 3 a. Albert E. Drinkwater. Ealing, Victoria H., February 2, 1891; Globe, June 16, 1891.

GOLDEN WEBB, THE. C.O. 3 a. F. Corder and B. C. Stephenson. M. by A. Goring Thomas. Liverpool R. Court, February 15, 1893; Lyric, March 11, 1893; Lyric (revised ver.), April 5, 1893.

GOLDEN WEDDING, A. Ca. Sydney Valentine and Cyril Maude. Hay., June 23, 1898.

GOLDEN WEDDING, A. Musical Sc. J. Parry Cole. Wellington H., St. John's Wood, June 5, 1899.

GOLDEN WEDDING, THE. P. 1 a. Eden Phillpotts and Chas. Groves. Playhouse, February 22, 1908.

GOLDENE EVA, DIE. Daly's, June 30, 1897.

GOLD'NE EVA, DIE. C. 3 a. F. von Schoenthan and F. Koppel-Ellfeld. (Ger. season.) Gt. Queen St., April 11, 1907.

GOLDFISCHE. C. 4 a. Franz von Schonthan and Gustave von Kadelburg; Comedy, November 2, 1900; Royalty, January 1, 1904.

GOLDFISH, THE. P. 3 a. A. Teixeira de Mattos. Transl. fr. the Dutch of W. G. van Nouhuys. Op. Comique, July 8, 1892.

GOLDSMITH'S JUBILEE, THE; OR, LONDON'S TRIUMPHS. Thos. Jordan. Perf. October 29, 1674.

GOLIATH. Orat. Anon. Pr. 1773.

GOMBEEN'S GOLD, THE. D. 5 a. Sadler's Wells, March 16, 1891.

GOMMOCH, THE. Irish D. 3 a. Herbert O'Grady. Stockton-on-Tees T.R., March 16, 1877.

GONDIBERT. Poem by Sir Wm. D'Avenant.

GONDIBERT AND BERTHA. T. W. Thompson. Subject fr. D'Avenant. Pr. 1751. N.ac.

GONDOLIER; OR, A NIGHT IN VENICE, THE. O. 2 a. Pr. 1814. ? N.ac.

GONDOLIERS; OR, THE KING OF BARATARIA, THE. Comic O. 2 a. W. S. Gilbert and Sir Arthur Sullivan. Savoy, December 7, 1889; Rev. March 22, 1898, and July 18, 1898; Rev. Savoy, January 22, 1907; Rev. Savoy, January 18, 1909.

GONE AWAY. C. 3 a. Edward Righton and Dalton Stone. Manchester Comedy, August 9, 1886.

GONSALVO DE CORDOVA; OR, THE CONQUEST OF GRANADA. Bal. J. C. Cross. Pr. 1802.

GONZAGA: A TALE OF FLORENCE. T. 5 a. Rev. Henry Solly. St. George's H., April 28, 1877.

GONZANGA. D. 5 a. Pr. 1814 (?N.ac.)

GOOD AS GOLD. Ca. 1 a. Matthews Monk. Imperial, August 13, 1883.

GOOD AS GOLD. Ca. C. F. Coghlan, taken from the Fr. Lyceum, December 18, 1869.

GOOD AS GOLD; OR, A FRIEND IN NEED WHEN OTHERS FAIL. D. 3 a. C. H. Hazlewood. Britannia, September 13, 1869.

GOOD BEGINNING MAY HAVE A GOOD END. P. by Jn. Ford. Mentioned in a list of Warburton's MSS.

GOOD BOY AND THE BAD. P. S. J. Adair Fitz-Gerald. Pub. by S. French, Ltd.

GOOD BUSINESS. F. R. K. Hervey. Novelty, December 14, 1887.

GOOD-BYE. P. 1 a. Arthur Bourchier. Adap. fr. André-Theuriet's *Jean Marie*. Canterbury T., August 6, 1889 (amat.).

GOOD-BYE. P. 1 a. Seymour Hicks. Court, November 25, 1893.

GOOD-BYE. P. 1 a. Henry T. Johnson. Strand, May 21, 1896.

GOOD ENGLISHMAN, THE. B. O. 2 a. Wm. Shirley. N.p. N.ac.

GOOD FAIRY OF ST. HELENS; OR KING COAL AND HIS MERRY MEN, THE. Burl. James Brockbank, jun. St. Helens T.R., April 22, 1872.

GOOD FOR BOTH. Ca. John Kennedy. Londonderry O.H., February 11, 1887. Southampton (P.O.W.), May 5, 1888.

GOOD FOR EVIL; OR, A WIFE'S TRIAL. Do. "Lesson." 2 a. Adapt. fr. the French of Emile Angier. First prod. at Th. Française, 1849. Surrey (as *The Barrister*), March 1, 1852.

GOOD FOR NOTHING. C.D. 1 a. John B. Buckstone. Hay., February 4, 1851. Hay., December 16, 1889; rev. Aldwych, January 18, 1909. See *Nan*.

GOOD FOR NOTHING. F. Yates and Harrington. Adelphi, December 27, 1858.

GOOD FORTUNE. C. C. F. Coghlan. St. James's, December 4, 1880.

GOOD GRACIOUS! Ca. Geo. Hawtrey. Court, January 21, 1885.

GOOD HEART COMPENSATES FOR MANY INDISCRETIONS. D. Berquin, 1793.

GOOD HEARTS. Surrey, November 8, 1858.

GOOD HOPE, THE. P. 4 a. Hermann Heijermans. Trans. by Chris. St. John by arrangt. with J. T. Grein. Imperial, April 27, 1903. Nottingham T.R., April 14, 1904. Hammersmith King's, April 27, 1904.

GOOD HUSBANDS MAKE GOOD WIVES. C. J. B. Buckstone. Hay., June, 1835.

GOOD LITTLE WIFE, A. C. 1 a. Alfred De Musset. Adapt. fr. *Un Caprice*. (Th. Française, November 27, 1847.) Ver. pl. at Lyceum as *A Charming Widow*.

GOOD-LOOKING FELLOW. F. 1 a. J. Kenney and Alfred Bunn. Pub. by S. French, Ltd. Covent Garden, April 17, 1834.

GOOD-LOOKING FELLOW; OR, THE ROMAN NOSE. F 1 a. George Almar. Sadler's Wells, April, 1834; D.L., May 12, 1834.

GOOD LUCK Mus. C. 3 a. J. P. Burnett. Adap. fr. *La Cigale* of Meilhac and Halevy. Strand, April 13, 1885.

GOOD LUCK. D. 3 a. O. Silverstone. Norwich Prince's, February 10, 1902.

GOOD MOTHER, THE. C. Transl. fr. Mme. Genlis' Theatre of Education. Pr. 1781.

GOOD-NATURED MAN, THE. C. 5 a. Oliver Goldsmith. C.G., January 29, 1768. Pr. 1768. C.G. (in 3 a), July, 1804 (N.p.); C.G., 1826; Gaiety, February 2, 1881; Vaudeville, November 16, 1886; Coronet, October 11, 1906.

GOOD-NATURED MAN, THE. See *Fathers*.

GOOD NEWS. D. 3 a. Henry J. Byron, Gaiety, Aug. 31, 1872.

GOOD-NIGHT, SIGNOR PANTALOON. Comic O. 1 a. Taken fr. Oxenford's F., *Twice Killed*. Adap. fr. the French. Op. C., February 19, 1851; Adelphi, May 29, 1851.

GOOD NIGHT'S REST; OR, TWO IN THE MORNING, A. F 1 a. Mrs. C. Gore. Strand, July, 1839.

GOOD OLD BARNES OF NEW YORK. Burl. Walter Burnot. On the story by Archibald Clavering Gunter. Ladbroke H., September 25, 1888 (C.P.). See *Barnes of New York*.

GOOD OLD GADESBY. F.P. 3 a. Adap. for the English stage by Emily Fradersdorff. Hastings Public H., April 24, 1907.

GOOD OLD QUEEN BESS; OR, THE PEARL, THE PEER, AND THE PAGE. Burl. 1 a. Walpole Lewin. M. by William Robins. Vaudeville, June 3, 1891.

GOOD OLD TIMES, THE. D. 4 a. Hall Caine and Wilson Barrett. Princess's, February 12, 1889.

GOOD OR EVIL. D. Ashton O.H., August 24, 1885.

GOOD QUEEN BESS. O. Burl. 2 a. Leo and Harry Trevor. M. by Burnham Horner and Harry Trevor. Richmond T.R., May 1, 1895.

GOOD RUN FOR IT, A. F. 1 a. T. V. Bridgeman. Sadler's Wells. February, 1854.

GOOD TIME; OR, SKIPPED BY THE LIGHT OF THE MOON, A. M.F. 2 a. G. R. Sims. M. by Albert W. Ketelby, H. W. May, and Claude Nugent. Reading County (under second title only), August 24, 1896; Op. C., April 27, 1899.

GOOD TURN, A. C. F. W. Broughton. Chester T.R., September 6, 1880.

GOOD WOMAN IN THE WOOD, THE. Extrav. 2 a. J. R. Planché. F. on Mdlle. De La Force's tale, *La Bonne Femme*. Lyceum, December 27, 1852.

GOOD WOMEN AND BAD. D. 4 a. W. H. Benson. Dover T.R., June 6, 1904.

GOODY TWO SHOES. Sk. Chelsea Palace, June 15, 1908.

GOODY TWO SHOES; OR, HARLEQUIN ALABASTER. Pant. C. Dibdin, jun. Sadler's Wells. Pr. (no date).

GOOSE, THE. F.C. 4 a. Chas. Thornton and Uffington Valentine. Margate R., May 17, 1909.

GOOSE AND GOLDEN EGGS, THE. Burl. J. F. Draper. Jersey R.H., November 19, 1869 (amat.)

GOOSE FAIR. F. F. R. Goodyear. Nottingham T.R., October 2, 1874.

GOOSE FROM HAARLEM. P. 1 a. Louis Cohen. Coronet, August 17, 1907 (c.p.).

GOOSE WITH THE GOLDEN EGGS, THE. F. 1 a. Augustus Mayhew and Sutherland Edwards. Strand, September 1, 1859.

GORBODUC. T. 4 a. Thos. Sackville (Lord Buckhurst) and Thos. Norton. Pr. 1565. Ac. before Q. Elizabeth, January 18, 1562. The first tragedy proper known on the Engl. stage. The first dr. work wr. in English blank verse. See *Ferrex and Porrex.*

GORDIAN KNOT, THE. P. 3 a. Claude Lowther. H.M., May 20, 1903.

GORDIAN KNOT UNTY'D, THE. C. ? ac. in 1691. N.p.

GORDON, THE GYPSEY. Scottish Melo-d. 2 a. M. by Watson. Lyceum, August 6, 1822.

GORE; OR, THE YALLER SEAL. Burl. Melo-d. 1 a. Avenue, July 1, 1889

GORILLA'S REVENGE, THE. Dr. Sk. C. M. Daly, Sunderland Avenue, June 25, 1906.

GOSPEL SHOP, THE. C. 5 a. R. Hill. (? ps.). Pr. 1778.

GOSSIP. C. 2 a. Augustus Harris and T. J. Williams Princess's, November 23, 1859.

GOSSIP. C. 4 a. Clyde Fitch and Leo Dietrichstein. Grand, June 3, 1895; Comedy, February 22, 1896.

GOSSIP'S BRAWL; OR, THE WOMEN WEARE THE BREECHES, THE. A Mock C. 1655. (Not intended for representation.)

GOTHAM ELECTION, THE. F. One long a. Mrs. Centlivre. Pr. 1715. N.a. Another edition, 1737, under the title of *The Humours of Elections.*

GOTOBED TOM! F. 1 a. Thos. Morton. Olympic, November 25, 1852.

GOTTERDAMMERUNG, DIE (*The Dusk of the Gods*). O. Wagner. H.M., May 9, 1882; C.G., July 13, 1892. See *The Nibelung's Ring.*

GOTZEN. D. 4 a. Henri Blau. St. George's Hall, March 2, 1901.

GOVERNESS, THE. C.O. Ac. at Dublin. Pr. 1777. A pirated version of *The Duenna.*

GOVERNESS, THE. Dom. D. Pro. and 4 a. Adolphe Belot. Adap. fr. Miss Multon. Olympic, October 21, 1886.

GOVERNESS, THE. C. 1 a. E. H. Keating. Publ. by S. French, Ltd.

GOVERNESS; OR, BOARDING SCHOOL DISSECTED, THE. D. Pr. 1785 N.a.

GOVERNOR, THE. T. Sir Cornelius Formido. En. Stationers' Co., September 9, 1653. Destroyed by Warburton's servant.

GOVERNOR; OR, CREOLIAN INSURRECTION, THE. Pant. Bal. C.G., March, 1793.

GOVERNOR OF CYPRUS, THE. T. J. Oldmixon. L.I.F. and D.L. Pr. 1703.

GOVERNOR'S BRIDE, THE. Light O. in 3 a. A. S. Manning. Comp. by Robert A. Smith. Newcastle Tyne, March 16, 1908 (amat.).

GOVERNOR'S NEPHEW, THE. Sk. Holborn Empire, August 3, 1908.

GOVERNOR'S WIFE, THE. C. 2 a. Thos. Milldenhall. Lyceum.

GOWRY. T. Ac. 1604. N.p.

GRA GAL MACHREE. Irish D. Barry Connor. Britannia, July 31, 1876.

GRACE. C.D. W. Dutch. Sale T.R., March 5, 1880.

GRACE. C. 3 a. J. S. Dutch, Manchester Prince's, April 24, 1884.

GRACE CLAIRVILLE. P. 3 a. A. Lewis. Publ. by J. Dick.

GRACE DARLING. D. 2 a. Edwd. Stirling. December 3, 1838.

GRACE DARRELL. O. 1 a. Raymond James. M. by F. C. Collinge. Dublin Leinster H., September 12, 1896.

GRACE HOLDEN. D. C. S. Cheltnam. Belfast T.R., August 23, 1869.

GRACE HUNTLEY. Dom. D. 3 a. Hy. Holl. Adelphi, 1833. See *Faith; or, Wife and Mother.*

GRACE ROYAL. D. 4 a. Paul Meritt. Edin. Prince's, May 31, 1876. See *The Golden Plough.*

GRACES, THE. Intermezzo. 1 a. Ascr. to C. Dibdin. Ac. at the Royal Circus. Pr. 1782.

GRACES, THE. F. 1 a. MS. in the library of Mr. A. Murphy.

GRACIOSA AND PERCINET. Fairy Extrav. 1 a. J. R. Planché. Hay., December 26, 1844.

GRAF WALDEMAR. D. 5 a. In German. Gustav Freitag. Op. Comique, September 15, 1894.

GRAN-U-AILLE. Patriotic Sk. Novelty, March 25, 1891.

GRAND ALLIANCE. C.G., June 13, 1814.

GRAND ARMY; OR, THE ATTACK ON MONTERREAU, THE. P. City of London, October, 1838.

GRAND ARMY MAN, A. P. D. Belasco. Elephant and Castle, September 18, 1907 (C.P.).

GRAND DUCHESS, THE. C.O. Offenbach. Prod. in Paris, 1867; Birmingham T.R., April 13, 1868.

GRAND DUCHESS, THE. New ver. of Offenbach's O. By C. H. E. Brookfield. Lyrics by Adrian Ross. Savoy, December 4, 1897.

GRAND DUCHESS ABROAD. Nautical O. Bert Haldane. Barrow Star Palace, September 29, 1902.

GRAND DUCHESS OF GEROLSTEIN. O. by Offenbach. Lib. by Meilhac and Halévy. Adap. for Eng. stage by C. Lamb Kenney. C.G., November 18, 1867. Also ver. at Astley's, March 28, 1870.

GRAND DUKE; OR, CHANGE FOR A SOVEREIGN, THE. M. Extrav. G. L. Gordon. M. by John Gregory. Dundee H.M.T., August 7, 1886.

GRAND DUKE; OR, THE STATUTORY DUEL, THE. C.O. 2 a. W. S. Gilbert and Sir A. Sullivan. Savoy, March 7, 1896.

GRAND DUKE OF CAMBERWELL, THE. Burl. W. M. Akhurst. Eleph. and C., April 17, 1876.

GRAND MOGUL, THE. "Oriental féerie." 3 a. and 3 tableaux. H. B. Farnie. Adap. fr. the French of Chivot and Duon. M. by Audran. Comedy, November 17, 1884.

GRAND MOGUL, THE. C.O. 3 a. Frank Pixey. M. by Gustav Luders. (C.P.) Bayswater Victoria H., November 1, 1906.

GRAND NATIONAL: OR, THE SPORTING YOUTH FROM THE COUNTING HOUSE TO THE HULKS, THE. D. James Elphinstone. Liverpool Colosseum, March 29, 1869.

GRAND REQUIEM. Bochsa. D.L., March 21, 1821.

GRAND SOIR, LE. Fr. vers. By Robert a'Humières of the 3 a. play by Leopold Kampf. (Orig. prod. at the Des Arts, Paris, December 22, 1907.) Tfd. to the Court, November 9; Terry's, November 2 1908.

GRAND TOUR; OR, STOPPED AT ROCHESTER. F. C.G., May 22, 1821. N.p.

GRANDAD'S DARLING. D. 1 a. Edmund Gurney. Publ. by S. French, Ltd.

GRANDBY ENTICED FROM ELYSIUM. C.O. Wm. Watson. Pr. circa 1782.

GRAN'FATHER COQUESNE. P. 1 a. Cosmo Hamilton, Garrick, June 25, 1906.

GRANDFATHER WHITEHEAD. D. 2 a. Mark Lemon. Adap. fr. the French. Hay., September 27, 1842, and rev. at Imperial, 1878.

GRANDFATHER'S CLOCK. D. 3 a. C. E. Bertrand. Pavilion, August 30, 1879.

GRANDFATHER'S CLOCK. F. Joseph Barron. Sadler's Wells, December 17, 1883.

GRANDFATHER'S CLOCK. Sk. Lionel Scudamore. Empress, April 21, 1908.

GRANDFATHER'S LITTLE NELL. D. Bristol T.R., December 13, 1870.

GRANDFATHER'S SECRET. D. 1 a. Surrey, June 6, 1885.

GRANDFATHER'S STORY. S.C.D. 1 a. Publ. by S. French, Ltd.

GRANDMAMMA. C. 3 a. E. Rose. Bayswater Bijou, March 22, 1904.

GRANDMOTHER BROWNING. Skit on *Grandfather Whitehead.* G. à Beckett.

GRANDMOTHER'S GOWN. Duol. Charles Anderson. Matinée T., November 12, 1898.

GRANDPAPA. F. D.L., May 25, 1825.

GRANDPAPA'S PROMISE. C. 1 a. L. Corcoran. Cheltenham T.R., November 4, 1887.

GRANDSIRE, THE. P. 3 a. Archer Woodhouse. Adap. fr. *Le Flibustier* of Jean Richepin. Théâtre Français, May 14, 1888; Terry's, May 15, 1880; Avenue, May 21, 1890; rev. Playhouse, February 9, 1909 (mat.).

GRANNA WAILE AND THE BRIDAL EVE. Irish D. J. Archer. East London, December 26, 1874.

GRANNIE S PICTURE. C. 1 a L. Debenham. Publ. by S. French, Ltd.

GRAPESHOT. "Whimsicality." 1 a. Wilford F. Field. Southall Public H., November 27, 1889.

GRASPING A SHADOW. Ca. 1 a. Tom Craven. West Hartlepool T.R., July 20, 1885.

GRASS WIDOW, THE. C. 2 a. Fawney Fane. Worthing T.R., May 9, 1898.

GRASS WIDOW, THE. F. 3 a. M. L. Ryley. Eastbourne Devonshire Park T., May 26, 1902; Shaftesbury, June 3, 1902.

GRASS WIDOWS. C. J. L. Whittaker. Dublin Queen's, September 19, 1879.

GRASSHOPPER, THE. D. 3 a. Benj. Webster, jun. Adap. fr. "La Petite Fadette," a story by Mdme. Dudevant. Prod. in America. Olympic, August 14, 1867.

GRASSHOPPER, THE. C.D. 3 a. Adap. by John Hollingshead fr. the French. Gaiety, December 9, 1877.

GRASSHOPPER, THE. Duol. by Wilton Heriot. Princess's, January 14, 1902.

GRASSHOPPER'S REVENGE, THE. See *La Revanche des Cigales.*

GRATEFUL. C.D. F. Towers. Exeter T.R., April 23, 1877.

GRATEFUL FAIR; OR, A TRIP TO CAMBRIDGE, THE. C. Christopher Smart. Ac. Pembroke College, Camb., 1747. N.p.

GRATEFUL FATHER, A. F. 1 a. T. Edgar Pemberton. Birmingham P.O.W., April 15, 1878.

GRATEFUL SERVANT, THE. C. James Shirley. Ac. at private house in D.L. Pr. 1630. Licensed 1629 as *The Faithful Servant.*

GRATITUDE; OR, A BATTLE FOR GOLD. D. 3 a. W. H. Pitt. Britannia, June 12, 1869.

GRAUSTARK. D. 4 a. Jeanette L. Gilder, taken fr. G. Barr M'Cutcheon's novel of same name. Globe, February 18, 1902.

GRAVE, THE. C. Ac. at Royal Kentish Bowmen's Lodge. Pro. only pr. See *The Metrical Miscellany,* 1802.

GRAVE-MAKERS, THE. A Droll by Kirkman out of the tragedy of *Hamlet.* Pr. 1672.

GRAY LADY OF FERNLEA, THE. D. C. H. Hazlewood. Britannia, September 9, 1867.

GRAY LADYE OF FERNLEA, THE. D. E. Towers. City of London, August 31, 1867.

GRAZIELLA. Cant. Sir J. Benedict. Birmingham, August 29, 1882.

GRAZIELLA. O. Founded on Sir Julius Benedict's cant. of same name. Crystal Palace, September 29, 1883.

GREAT AWAKENING, THE. D. Pro. and 4 a. Maud Hildyard and Russell Vaun. Sheffield Lyceum, April 5, 1905 (C.P.); Scarborough T.R., July 17, 1905; Pavilion, December 4, 1905.

GREAT BANK ROBBERY, THE. D. 5 a. Edward Darby. Keighley Queen's, March 9, 1896.

GREAT CÆSAR. C. piece. 2 a. G. Grossmith, jun., and Paul Rubens. M. by P. and W. Rubens. Addl. lyrics by H. Ellis. Comedy, April 29, 1899.

GREAT CASIMIR, THE. Vaudeville. 3 a. H. S. Leigh. M. by C. Lecocq. Gaiety, September 27, 1879.

GREAT CATCH, A. C. 3 a. Hamilton Aidé. Olympic mat.), March 17, 1883.

GREAT CITY, THE. C.D. 4 a. A. Halliday. D.L., April 22, 1867, and April 13, 1868; Grecian, August 19, 1867; Surrey, November 8, 1869.

GREAT COMET, THE. P. 3 a. Cotsford Dick. Adap. fr. *Der Grosse Comet*. Bournemouth T.R., December 14, 1896.

GREAT CONSPIRACY, THE. D. 3 a. and 4 sc. P. Berton. Adap. fr. the French by Madeleine Lucette Lyley. D. of York's, March 4, 1907.

GREAT DEMONSTRATION, THE. F. 1 a. I. Zangwill. Royalty, September 17, 1892.

GREAT DETECTIVE, THE. Dr. Sk. 3 sc. Roy Redgrave. Sadler's Wells, January 13, 1902.

GREAT DEVIL; OR, ROBBER OF GENOA, THE. S.C. Spec. C. Dibdin, jun. Sadler's Wells. Pr. 1801.

GREAT DIAMOND ROBBERY, THE. D. Pro. and 4 a. W. R. Waldron and Burford Delannoy. Sadler's Wells, October 10, 1892.

GREAT DIAMOND ROBBERY, THE. D. 4 a. E. M. Elfriend and A. C. Wheeler. Pavilion, May 16, 1898.

GREAT DIVIDE, THE. P. 3 a. Wm. Vaughan Moody (C.P.). Criterion, September 4, 1906; Adelphi, September 15, 1909.

GREAT DIVORCE CASE, THE. C. 3 a. "John Doe and Richard Roe." Criterion, April 15, 1876.

GREAT DUKE OF FLORENCE, THE. A Comical Hist. Philip Massinger. Phœnix, July 5, 1627. Pr. 1636. See *A Mayden-head Well Lost*.

GREAT EXPECTATIONS. D. Pro. and 3 a. W. S. Gilbert. Court, May 29, 1871. See *Pip's Patron*.

GREAT FAVOURITE; OR, THE DUKE OF LERMA, THE. T.C. Sir Robt. Howard. Ac. at T.R., February 20, 1668. Pr. 1668.

GREAT FELICIDAD, THE. C. 3 a. H. M. Paull. Gaiety, March 24, 1887.

GREAT FRIENDS. C. 3 a. G. S. Street. Court, January 30, 1905.

GREAT GLOBE, THE. D. 4 a. J. O. Stewart. Stalybridge Victoria, August 23, 1889; Liverpool New T.R. (in 5 a.), December 11, 1889.

GREAT GUN TRICK; OR, A NIGHT WITH THE LYCEUM WIZARD, THE. A "Magical Squib." 1 a. Christian Le Ros. D.L., December 31, 1855.

GREAT ILLUSION, THE. P. 1 a. Mrs. Hugh Bell. Albert Hall West T., June 28, 1895.

GREAT JUPITER. C.O. 3 a. Rhoda Cameron. Lyrics, Henry M. Mayo; M., H. F. Whermann. Radcliffe Grand T., October 20, 1901.

GREAT MAD CITY, THE. D. Pro. and 3 a. Wm. G. Fortescue. Birkenhead T.R., July 15, 1901.

GREAT MAN, THE. T. Anon. Destroyed by Warburton's servant.

GREAT METROPOLIS, THE. Extrav. F. C. Burnand. Gaiety, April 6, 1874.

GREAT METROPOLIS, THE. Melo-d. 5 a. Teale and Jessop. Rewritten by Wm. Terriss and Henry Neville. Prod. in America, 1889. Princess's, February 11, 1892.

GREAT MILLIONAIRE, THE. D. Mod. Life. 5 a. By Cecil Raleigh. D.L., September 19, 1901.

GREAT MOGUL, THE. C.O. 2 a. Edwd. Oxenford. M. by Wm. W. Meadows. Royalty, June 22, 1881.

GREAT PEARL CASE, THE. C.D. 3 a. S. X. Comte. Birmingham T.R., October 27, 1894. Afterwards called *The Wife of Dives*.

GREAT PICKWICK CASE, THE. Oa. Words of songs by Robt. Pollitt. M. by Thos. Rawson. Publ. 1884.

GREAT PINK PEARL, THE. P. 3 a. R. C. Carton and Cecil Raleigh. Olympic, May 7, 1885.

GREAT POISON CASE, THE. Dr. P. 2 sc. (Previously pl as a M.H. Sk.) Fulham Grand, August 12, 1907.

GREAT POSSESSIONS. P. 4a. Karl Rössler (transl. fr the German) Adelphi, June 10, 1907.

GREAT RUBY, THE. D. 4 a. Cecil Raleigh and Henry Hamilton. D.L., September 15, 1898.

(GREAT) SECRET, THE. D. 4 a. Workington T.R., October 19, 1885.

GREAT SENSATION, A. D. 4 a. Arthur Shirley and Ben Landeck. Pav., August 31, 1903.

GREAT SENSATION TRIAL; OR, CIRCUMSTANTIAL EFFIE-DEANS, THE. Burl. W. Brough on *The Heart of Midlothian*. St. James's, 1864.

GREAT SILENCE, THE. Ep. of Red Indian Life. Basil Hood. Notting Hill Coronet, July 23, 1900.

GREAT STRIKE, THE. Pavilion, October 8, 1866.

GREAT SUCCESS, A. F.C. 1 a. J. James Hewson. Birkenhead T.R., September 19, 1884.

GREAT TAKIN (OR TAYKIN), THE. "Japananza." Arthur Law. M. by Geo. Grossmith. Toole's, April 30, 1885.

GREAT TEMPTATION, A. D. 4 a. Arthur Shirley and Benj. Landeck. Hammersmith Lyric, February 20, 1899. See *The Eve of Marriage*.

GREAT TEMPTATION, THE. F. East London, May 25, 1874.

GREAT TICHBORNE CASE, THE. F. Wm. Mackay. Leicester T.R., May 20, 1872.

GREAT TOM-TOM, THE. C.O. Butler Stanhope. M. by J. R. Reid. Birkenhead T.R., June 14, 1886.

GREAT UNKNOWN, THE. F. Hay., September 9, 1823.

GREAT UNKNOWN, THE. Eccentric C. 3 a. Augustin Daly. An adap. of *Die Berühmte Frau* by Franz von Schönthan and Gustav Kadelberg. Daly's T., New York, October 22, 1889; Lyceum, August 5, 1890.

GREAT UNPAID, THE. 3 a. Fred Horner. An adap. of Alexandre Bisson's *La Famille Pont-Biquet*. Comedy, May 9, 1893.

GREAT WILDERNESS, THE. Melo-d. 4 a. W. Alexander Dallas. Fulham Grand, August 6, 1906.

GREAT WORLD OF LONDON, THE. D. 4 a. G. Lander and W. Melville. Standard, October 31, 1898

GREAT YAH BOO, THE. C.O. 2 a. Lib. and songs by the Rev. H. D. Hinde. M. comp. by Miss L. Stooks, T. R. G. Lyell, and L. Phillipson. Southgate Village H., May 13, 1908 (amat.).

GREATER GLORY, THE. P. 4 a. Estelle Burney. Prod. by the Pioneers. Shaftesbury, January 19, 1908.

GREATER LONDON. Spec. Herr Rousby. Hackney Empire, August 17, 1908.

GREATER LOVE, THE. P. of modern life. 4 a. Vincent Brown. T.R., Brighton, June 10, 1901; Accrington Prince's, June 21, 1909.

GREATEST OF THESE ——, THE. Piece. 4 a. Sydney Grundy. Grand T., Hull. September 13, 1895. Garrick, June 10, 1896.

GREATEST SCOUNDREL LIVING, THE. D. 4 a. McLeod Loader. St. Helens New T., January 29, 1903; St. Helens Opera Ho., March 2, 1903; 5 a. Hammersmith Lyric, November z, 1903.

GRECIAN COMEDY, THE. A P. ac. by Henslowe's Co. December 1, 1594.

GRECIAN DAUGHTER, THE. T. 5 a. Arthur Murphy. D.L., February 26, 1772. Pr. 1772. Founded on a passage in "Valerius Maximus." Rev. by J. P. Kemble and act. C.G., April 29, 1815.

GRECIAN HEROINE; OR, THE FATE OF TYRANNY, THE. T. T. Durfey. 1718 or earlier. Pr. 1721. N.ac. Blank verse.

GREED OF GOLD. D. 4 a. H. R. Silva. Surrey, July 6, 1896. Prod. in the provinces.

GREEK BOY, THE. M.D. Samuel Lover. C.G., September 26, 1840.

GREEK BRIGANDS, THE; OR, THE MASSACRE OF ENGLISH TOURISTS BY THE ARAVANITAKAI. D. Lawrence Meadows. Liverpool Colosseum, July 18, 1870.

GREEK FAMILY, THE. Melo-d. spectacle. 2 a. M. by Cooke. D.L., October 22, 1829.

GREEK MAID, THE. Pastl. P. Ac. by the Earl of Leicester's servants at Richmond, 1579.

GREEK PLAYS.—The greatest dramatic writers and their works are as follows:—

COMEDY.

ARISTOPHANES. Born at Athens circa B.C. 448. He wrote about fifty-four plays, and of these eleven are extant, viz.:—

THE ACHARNIANS, B.C. 425.
THE KNIGHTS, B.C. 424.
THE CLOUDS (Against Socrates), B.C. 423.
THE WASPS, B.C. 422.
THE PEACE, B.C. 421.
THE BIRDS, B.C. 414.
THE LYSISTRATA, B.C., 411.
THE THESMOPHORIAZUCÆ, B.C. 411.
THE FROGS, B.C. 405.
THE ECCLESIAZUSŒ, B.C. 393.
THE PLUTUS, B.C. 388.

The following are among those lost:—

THE BANQUETERS, B.C. 427.
THE BABYLONIANS, B.C. 426.
THE MERCHANTMEN.
THE FARMERS.
THE PRELIMINARY CONTEST (Proagôn)
OLD AGE (Gêras), B.C. 422.
THE ISLANDS.
THE TRIPHALES.
THE STORKS.
ÆOLOSICON, B.C. 387.
COCALUS.

TRAGEDY.

ÆSCHYLUS. This Athenian poet was born at Eleusis B.C. 525. He wrote about seventy tragedies, besides satyric dramas, seven of which are in existence. He was the inventor of the trilogy, *i.e.*, the first who made the three plays represented to constitute parts of a whole. He died B.C. 456.

THE PERSIANS, acted in B.C. 472.
SEVEN AGAINST THEBES.
SUPPLIANTS (one part of a trilogy of which the other parts are lost).
PROMETHEUS BOUND (one part of a trilogy of which the other parts are lost).
ORESTEIA, a trilogy, comprising—
AGAMEMNON,
CHOEPHORI,
EUMENIDES.

See *Orestan Trilogy*.

SOPHOCLES. This poet was born at the village of Colonus B.C. 496. He wrote 113 plays, of which eighty-one were probably produced after the Antigone. Seven only are extant. He died B.C. 405.

ANTIGONE, B.C. 440.
ELECTRA.
TRACHINIAN WOMEN.
ŒDIPUS COLONEUS, acted B.C. 401.
ŒDIPUS TYRANNUS.
AJAX.
PHILOCTETES.

EURIPIDES. This great tragic poet was born at Salamis, October 20, B.C. 480. He wrote in all from seventy-five to ninety-two plays, of which eighteen still exist. He died B.C. 406.

ANDROMACHE.
ALCESTIS.
MEDEA.
HECUBA.
ION MEDIA.
IPHIGENIA IN TAURIS.
IPHIGENIA IN AULIS.
HELEN.
ELECTRA.
ORESTES.
THE TROJAN DAMES.
THE TROJAN CAPTIVES.
THE BACCHANALS.
THE PHŒNICIAN DAMSELS.
THE SUPPLIANTS.
HIPPOLYTUS.
HERCULES DISTRACTED.
THE CHILDREN OF HERCULES.
RHESUS (doubtful).
CYCLOPS, which is the only specimen left of what was called the Satyric Drama.

ANAXANDRIDES was a Greek comic poet, who wrote about 100 plays, of which ten obtained the prize. He was the dramatic poet who introduced intrigues or love adventures upon the stage. He died B.C. 340.

XENOPHON. Greek historian. Wrote:—

ANABASIS OF CYRUS.
THE CYROPÆDIA.
MEMORABILIA OF SOCRATES.
HELLENICA.

POEMS.

HOMER, who lived in the eighth century B.C., wrote:—

ILIAD.
ODYSSEY.

See Bradfield College, Berks, Plays at.

GREEK SLAVE, A. M.C. 2 a. Owen Hall. Lyrics by Harry Greenbank and Adrian Ross. M. by Sidney Jones. Daly's, June 8, 1898.

GREEK SLAVE; OR, THE SCHOOL FOR COWARDS, THE. C. D.L., March 22, 1791. N.p. Alt. fr. *The Humorous Lieutenant*, ascr. to Mrs. Jordan.

GREEK SOPRANO, THE. C. 1 a. Portsmouth T.R., July 12, 1897; Strand, September 13, 1897.

GREEN BUSHES, THE. D. J. B. Buckstone. Adelphi, January 27, 1845; Rev. April 19, 1890; Rev. Grand, September 14, 1903. See *Miami*.

GREEN CLOTH, THE. D. 3 a. A. W. Dubourg. Publ. by Douglas Cox.

GREEN DOMINO. C. Korner. 1810.

GREEN DRAGON; OR, I'VE QUITE FORGOT, THE. Burla. Moncrieff. Adelphi, October 18, 1819.

GREEN ENCHANTRESS, THE. Fairy P. 1 a. Miss Evelyn Sharp. 16, Avenue Road, Regent's Park, July 21, 1898.

GREEN-EYED MONSTER; OR, HOW TO GET YOUR MONEY, THE. F. 2 a. J. Pocock. Lyceum, October 14, 1811.

GREEN-EYED MONSTER, THE. C. 2 a. J. R. Planché. Partly fr. *Les Deux Jaloux*. Hay, August 18, 1828; D.L., October 28, 1828.

GREEN GODDESS. D. 4 a. Russell Vaun. Camberwell Metropole, December 16, 1901.

GREEN GROW THE RUSHES, OH. Sensational D. (Burl.). Henry J. Byron. No date. Publ. by French.

GREEN HILLS OF THE FAR WEST, THE. D. John Wilkins. City of London, 1861.

GREEN IN FRANCE. Extrav. Adelphi.

GREEN ISLE OF THE SEA, THE. Op. bo. 3 a. Princess's, Edinburgh. September 21, 1874.

GREEN LANES OF ENGLAND, THE. D. 4 a. G. Conquest and Henry Pettitt. Grecian, August 5, 1878.

GREEN MAN, THE. C. 3 a. Richd. Jones. Taken fr. the French of D'Augbigny and Ponjol. Hay., August 15, 1818; Hay., July 8, 1826.

GREEN OLD AGE. M.F. 1 a. Robert Reece. Vaudeville, October 31, 1874.

GREEN ROOM, THE. Prel. Finney. Hay., August 27, 1783. N.p.

GREEN ROOM, THE. A "vehicle for imitations." Lyceum, January 29, 1821.

GREEN ROOM CHIT CHAT. Prel. MS. in the library of Isaac Reed.

GREENE'S TU QUOQUE; OR, THE CITY GALLANT. C. J. Cooke. Pr. (n.d.), and also in 1599. L.I.F., 1665. See *Tu Quoque, The City Gallant*.

GREENLEAF THE GRACEFUL; OR, THE PALACE OF VENGEANCE. Burl. W. R. Osman. Royalty, February 26, 1872.

GREENOCK FAIR. M.I. Archibald Maclaren. See *The Humours of Greenock Fair*.

GREENWICH PARK. C. Wm. Mountfort. Ac. at D.L., April 17, 1708. Pr. 1691.

GREENWICH PENSIONER, THE. C.D. 2 a. C. S. Cheltnam. Adelphi, July 21, 1869.

GREGORY VII. T. Horne. 1840.

GRELLEY'S MONEY. D. 4 a. Eric Ross. Salford P.O.W., October 30, 1882. Marylebone, August 8, 1887.

GRENADIER, THE. Int. Ac. at Sadler's Wells. Pr. 1773.

GRENADIER, LA. Bal. O'Keefe. 1798.

GRETCHEN. D. 4 a. W. S. Gilbert. f. on Goethe's *Faust*. Olympic, March 24, 1879.

GRETNA GREEN. M.F. Charles Stuart. Hay., August 28, 1783. Songs only pr. 1783. Lyceum, 1821. M. by Reeve. Lyceum, August 31, 1822.

GRETNA GREEN. C.O. 3 a. J. Murray Ford. M. by John Storer. Comedy, December 4, 1889. Op. C. May 22, 1890.

GRETNA GREEN. Ballet. Alhambra, October 10, 1901.

GREY DOMINO, THE. An 18th century P. in 2 sc. Agnes Egerton Castle. Playhouse, April 30, 1907.

GREY DOUBLET, THE. Burla. 1 a. Mark Lemon. Eng. O.H., August, 1838.

GREY MARE, THE. F.C. 3 a. G. R. Sims and C. Raleigh. f. partly on Roderick Benedix's C. *Das Lügen*. Comedy, January 23, 1892.

GREY MARE THE BETTER HORSE, THE. See *The Welsh Opera*.

GREY PARROT, THE. Ca. W. W. Jacobs and Chas. Rock. Strand, November 6, 1899.

GREY STOCKING, THE. C. 4 a. Maurice Baring. Royalty, May 28, 1908 (mat.).

GREYHOUND AND KING. D. Berquin, 1793.

GREYSTEEL. O. 1 a. Nicholas Gatty. Sheffield T.R., March 1, 1906; London production, Crystal Palace, May 24, 1906; Lyric, September 6, 1907.

GRIEF A LA MODE. C. Steele. 1702.

GRIERSON'S WAY. P. 4 a. H. V. Esmond. Hay., February 7, 1899.

GRIEVING'S A FOLLY. C. 5 a. Richard Leigh. Lyceum, April 21, 1809. Pr. 1809.

GRIF. D. Frank Towers. South Shields T.R., April 9, 1877.

GRIF. D. 4 a. W. Lestocq. Adap. fr. B. L. Farjeon's novel. Surrey, October 5, 1891.

GRIFFITH GAUNT. D. Pro. and 4 a. C. Reade. Leicester T.R., October 9, 1871.

GRIFFITH GAUNT; OR, JEALOUSY. Rom. P. 5 a. Adap. fr. Chas. Reade's novel by Freeman Wills and the Rev. Canon Langbridge. Margate R., October 19, 1908.

GRIFFITH MURDOCH. P. 4 a. Montague H. Spier. St. George's H., March 4, 1893 (C.P.).

GRIM GOBLIN. Grecian, December 23, 1876.

GRIM GRIFFIN HOTEL, THE. F. J. Oxenford and Professor Pepper. Holborn Amphi., May 25, 1867.

GRIM, THE COLLIER OF CROYDON; OR, THE DEVIL AND HIS DAME WITH THE DEVIL AND ST. DUNSTAN. C. By J. T. Ascr. to Ulpian Fulwell. Pr. 1599, re-pr. 1662. See *The Collier of Croydon* and *Thorney Abbey*.

GRIMALDI. T. 5 a. Wm. Bailey. Pr. 1822.

GRIMALDI; OR, THE LIFE OF AN ACTRESS. D. 5 a. Dion Boucicault. Ac. in U.S.A. 1855. Adelphi, March 1, 1862, as "Life of an Actress."

GRIMALKIN; OR, A WOMAN CHANGED INTO A CAT. F. 1 a. G. H. Rodwell. Adelphi, November, 1827.

GRIMALKIN THE GREAT. D.L., December 26, 1868.

GRIMSHAW, BAGSHAW AND BRADSHAW. F. 1 a. J. M. Morton. Hay., July 1, 1851.

GRIMSTONE GRANGE. V. Gilbert and Arthur à Beckett. M. by King Hall. St. George's H., 1879.

"GRIN" BUSHES! OR, THE MRS. BROWN OF THE "MISSIS" SIPPI, THE. Burl. Extrav. 1 a. H. J. Byron. f. on *The Green Bushes*. Strand, December 26, 1864.

GRINGOIRE. P. W. G. Wills. Adap. f. the French P. of same name by Thèodore de Bauville. Prince's, June 6, 1885. Globe, January 24, 1891.

GRINGOIRE. P. 1 a. B. C. Stephenson. Adap. fr. *Théodore de Bauville*. Hay., June 26, 1899.

GRINGOIRE. P. Eliz Bessle and Sydney Herberte-Basing. Adap. fr. *Théodore de Bauville*. Battersea Park T.H., February 4, 1890.

GRINGOIRE. Ver. at Oxford M.H. June 30, 1902.

GRINGOIRE. See *Pity* and *The Ballad-monger.*

GRIP. D. Newcastle Tyne T., April 3, 1871

GRIP OF IRON, THE. Arthur Shirley. Adap. fr. *Les Etrangleurs de Paris.* Surrey, October 17, 1887; rev. Princess's, June 29, 1896.

GRIP OF STEEL, THE. Melo.-d. 4 a. Arthur Shirley and Benj. Landeck. Surrey, December 19, 1892. (Prod. as *A King of Crime.*)

GRIPUS AND HEGIO; OR, THE PASSIONATE LOVERS. Pastoral. 3 a. Robt. Baron. Pr. 1647. Partly fr. Waller's Poems and Webster's *Duchess of Malfy.*

GRISELDA. O. Scarlatti. (His last O.) 1721.

GRISELDA. O. Paer. 1774-1839.

GRISELDA. D. E. Arnold. 1856. See *Patient Grissel.*

GRISELDA; OR, THE PATIENT WIFE. D. 4 a. Miss M. E. Braddon. Princess's, November 13, 1873.

GRISELIDIS. M.C. Massenet. f. on legend of *Patient Grizel.* Paris, 1901.

GRIST TO THE MILL. C.D. 2 a. J. R. Planche. Hay., February 22, 1844.

GRIT. P. 4 a. H. Herman Chilton. Kingsway, November 24, 1908.

GRIZELLE; OR, DANCING MAD. Burl. Ballet. W. H. Oxberry. E. Opera House. Publ. by Barth.

GROATSWORTH OF WIT. Peele. 1592.

GROBIANA'S NUPTIALS. A curious old English P. preserved in the Bodleian Library.

GROSSTE SUNDE, DIE. P. 5 a. Otto Ernst. St. Geo. H., January 7, 1902.

GROTTO ON THE STREAM. D. 2 a. E. Stirling. Publ. by J. Dicks.

GROVE; OR, LOVE'S PARADISE, THE. O. J. Oldmixon. Ac. D.L. Pr. 1700.

GROVES OF BLARNEY, THE. D. 3 a. Mrs. S. G. Hall. Adelphi, April 16, 1838.

GRUB STREET OPERA, THE. H. Fielding. Ac. at the little T. in the Hay., July, 1731. Pr. 1731. See *The Welsh Opera.*

GRUESOME GRANGE; OR, THE BANISHED EARL. T. Act 1 by Capt. R. Marshall; Act 2 by Anthony Hope; Act 3 by Comyns Carr. Regent's Pk. Botanic Gdns., July 6, 1906.

GRUMBLER, THE. C. 3 a. Sir Chas. Sedley. Pr. 1702. Transl. fr. the French. Alt. and ac. D.L., April, 1754.

GRUMBLER, THE. F. Alt. fr. Sedley by Dr. Goldsmith. C.G., May 8, 1773. N.p.

GUARANY, IL. O. 4 a. Gomez. Milan, 1870; C.G., July 13, 1872.

GUARD OF HONOUR, A. P. 1 a. Fredk. A. Hoare. Dundee Her M.T., July 14, 1902.

GUARDED BY HONOUR. Military D. H. J. Stanley. Liverpool R. Sefton T., April 20, 1885.

GUARDIAN, THE. C. Abraham Cowley. Ac. before Prince Charles at Trin. Coll., Cambridge, March 12, 1641. Pr. 1650. See *The Cutter of Coleman Street.*

GUARDIAN, THE. C. Philip Massinger. Partly borr. fr. Boccace's novels and fr. a rom. called *The Roman Matron.* Ac. by K. Co., October, 31, 1633, Blackfryars. Pr. 1655.

GUARDIAN, THE. C. 2 a. David Garrick. Taken fr. Fagan's *Pupille.* D.L., February 3, 1759; also ac. at Edinb. Pr. 1759.

GUARDIAN, THE. See *The City Heiress.*

GUARDIAN ANGEL, THE. F. 1 a. Shirley Brooks. Hay.

GUARDIAN OUTWITTED, THE. C.O. Dr. Thos. A. Arne. C.G., Dec. 12, 1764. Pr. 1764.

GUARDIAN SYLPH; OR, THE MAGIC ROSE, THE. Fairy Int. 1 a. C. Selby. Queen's, 1835: Strand, 1844.

GUARDIANS, THE. C. Tobin. D.L., November 5, 1816.

GUARDIANS; OR, THE MAN OF MY CHOICE, THE. C. Anon. Pr. 1808. N.ac.

GUARDIANS OUTWITTED; OR, A BOLD STROKE FOR A WIFE, THE. O. arr. of Mrs. Centlivre's C. M. by Reeve. Lyceum, September 1, 1823.

GUARDIANS OVERREACHED, THE. Anon. 1741. See *Stroller's Packet.*

GUARDS, THE. D. 5 a. C. E. Dering and John Holloway. Plymouth T.R., October 8, 1883.

GUARDSMAN, THE. F.P. 3 a. G. R. Sims and C. Raleigh. Court, October 20, 1892.

GUBBINS STANDS FOR THE COUNCIL. F. Peckham Public H., January 14, 1889 (amat.).

GUDGEONS. C. 3 a. Thornton Clark and L. N. Parker. Terry's, November 10, 1893.

GUDGEONS AND SHARKS. J. Poole. Hay., July 28, 1827.

GUEBRES. T. Voltaire. 1762.

GUELFES, LES. O. Godard (1849-1895). Posthumous Production in Paris.

GUELPHS AND GHIBBELINES. An old English P. Mentioned in Gayton's notes on "Don Quixote." 1654.

GUERILLA CHIEF AND HIS DAUGHTERS. Military Serio Panto. M. by R. Hughes. D.L., November 19, 1827.

GUERILLERO, LE. O. Thomas. Paris, 1842.

GUGLIELMO RATCLIFF. O. Mascagni. Italy, 1895.

GUIDING STAR, THE. Melo-d. 5 a. Carr Elkington. Great Grimsby P.O.W. T., July 17, 1899; Stratford T.R., June 17, 1901.

GUIDING STAR; OR, THE ADVENTURER'S BRIDE, THE. D. 3 a. W. E. Suter. East London, February 1, 1868.

GUIDO. P. Ac. at the Rose T., March 19, 1597.

GUIDO E GINEVRA. O. 5 a. Halévy. Paris, March 5, 1838.

GUIDO AND IMILDA. D. 3 a. Reginald Moore. Nottingham T.R., February 24, 1869.

GUIDO FAWKES; OR, THE PROPHETESS OF ORDSALL CAVE! Melo-d. 2 a. E. Sterling. Manchester Queen's, June, 1840; afterwards, English O.H. and Queen's.

GUILLAUME TELL. O. 4 a. Rossini. Paris, August 3, 1829. The whole of the music for the first time in England adap. to the English stage by Bishop. The lib. follows Schiller. Rossini's last work. D.L., December 3, 1838; King's T., July 11, 1839. See *William Tell.*

GUILTLESS. D. 4 a. Arthur Shirley. Adap. fr. D'Ennery's novel "Martyne." New Cross Pub. H., January 8, 1887.

GUILTY AT LAST. D. 4 a. W. Harvey. Pelton Fell, September 12, 1898.

GUILTY GOLD. D. 5 a. D. T. Callahan. Dalston, November 26, 1906.

GUILTY GOLD. D. 5 a. and 12 sc. Horace Stanley. Birmingham Alexandra, June 3, 1907.

GUILTY GOVERNESS AND THE DOWNEY DOCTOR. Folly, May 8, 1876.

GUILTY INHERITANCE, A. M.C.D. 4 a. F. J. Kirke and A. Roudry. Widnes Alex. T., August 21, 1902; Stratford T.R., March 14, 1904.

GUILTY MAN, THE. D. 4 a. St. Aubyn Miller. Britannia, July 23, 1900.

GUILTY MOTHER, A. D. 5 a. B. Landeck. Hull T.R., January 8, 1894; Pav., April 9, 1894.

GUILTY OR NOT GUILTY. C. 5 a. Thos. Dibdin. F. on "The Reprobate," a German novel by La Fontaine. Hay., May 26, 1804. Pr. 1804.

GUILTY OR NOT GUILTY. D. Chas. F. Hilder. Grecian, July 24, 1882.

GUILTY PAIR, THE. Sk. Percival H. Sykes and G. W. Byng. Cambridge M.H., November 28, 1899; Oxford M.H., April 7, 1900.

GUILTY SHADOWS. C.D. Prol. and 4 Tab. Emilie de Witt. Imperial, February 6, 1885.

GUINEA GOLD; OR, LIGHTS AND SHADOWS OF LONDON LIFE. D. H. J. Byron. Princess's, September 10, 1877.

GUINEA OUTFIT; OR, THE SAILOR'S FAREWELL, THE. C. 3 a. Pr. 1800. See *The Sailor's Farewell.*

GUINEA PIGS, THE. P. 4 a. Florence Warden. Kennington P.O.W., July 24, 1899.

GUINEA STAMP, THE. D. Globe, March 27, 1875.

GUINEA STAMP, THE. Piece. 1 a. Cyril Hallward. Comedy, April 8, 1896.

GUINEVERE. C.O. 2 a. Stanley Stevens. M. by H. T. Pringuer. Kilburn T.H., March 19, 1890.

GUINEVERE. T. 3 a. Graham Hill. C.P. Court, October 13, 1906.

GUINEVERE. Vera Leslie. Adap. fr. Tennyson's poem. Court, June 2, 1908.

GUIRLANDE, LA. O. 1 a. Rameau, September 21, 1751.

GUISE. Mentioned by Webster as a play of his.

GUISE. Mentioned in Kirkman's Catalogue, 1661. Possibly Henry Shirley's *The Duke of Guise.* See *Guyes, Gwisse.*

GUITARERO, LE. O. Halévy. Paris, 1841.

GUL'S HORNBOOK. C. Dekker. 1609.

GULLIVER IN LILLIPUT. R. Reece.

GULLIVER'S TRAVELS. Spec. Piece. 5 a. Henry J. Byron. Gaiety, December 26, 1879.

GULLIVER'S TRAVELS. Children's Mus. Christmas P. Geo. Grossmith. Avenue, December 23, 1901.

GUNILDA. T. Rev. J. Delap, D.D. Pr. 1803. N.ac.

GUNLOD. O. Cornelius. 1824-1874. Posthumous. Prod. in Germany.

GUNMAKER OF MOSCOW, THE. Melo-d. 3 a. Publ. by S. French, Ltd.

GUNPOWDER PLOT, A. P. 3 a. J. Oxenford. Lyceum, May, 1836.

GUNPOWDER PLOT, A. F. Sydney Hodges. Olympic, May 12, 1873.

GUNTRAM. O. R. Strauss. Germany. 1894.

GURLI. C. 3 a. H. Christiernson. Transl. and adap. by L. P. Nelson and A. Cantam. Croydon Grand T., May 21, 1900.

GUSTAV VASA. O. Neumann. 1783.

GUSTAVE. D. E. H. Brooke. Liverpool Alexandra, May 26, 1873.

GUSTAVE III. O. Scribe. 1833.

GUSTAVUS, KING OF SWETHLAND. Thos. Dekker. Ent. Stationers' Co., June 29, 1660. N.p.

GUSTAVUS THE THIRD. Hist. D. 3 a. H. M. Milner. Victoria, November, 1833.

GUSTAVUS THE THIRD. O. D.L. (last act), April 9, 1835.

GUSTAVUS VASA. T. Piron. 1733.

GUSTAVUS VASA; OR, THE DELIVERER OF HIS COUNTRY. T. 5 a. H. Brooke. Pr. 1739. Intended for D.L., but prohibited; afterwards alt. and ac. as *The Patriot.* C.G., December 28, 1805, under the original title.

GUSTAVUS VASA. T. Kotzelrie. 1797.

GUSTAVUS VASA. P. F. on *Hero of the North.* Dimond. C.G., November 29, 1810.

GUTEM MORGEN, HERR FISCHER. M.P. 1 a. W. Friedrich and E. Stiegmann. Royalty, October 21, 1903.

GUTTER OF TIME. D. 1 a. Alfred Sutro. Eastbourne Pier, August 3, 1908. Publ. by S. French, Ltd.

GUV'NOR, THE. F. C. 3 a. Adap. from the German by "S. G. Lankester" (Robert Reece). Vaudeville, June 23, 1880; January 28, 1893.

GUY CAVALIER, THE. M.P. Victor Stevens. Plymouth T.R., November 5, 1902.

GUY DOMVILLE. P. 3 a. Henry James. St. James's, January 5, 1895.

GUY, EARL OF WARWICK. T. Hist. B. J. Pr. 1661. At Stationer's Co. a play of this name entered January 15, 1619, wr. by John Day and Thomas Dekker. Possibly the same piece. See *The Life and Death of Guy, Earl of Warwick.*

GUY, EARL OF WARWICK. Tolson. Ac. at T.R. 1721.

GUY FAUX: OR, THE GUNPOWDER CONSPIRACY. Melo-d. 2 a. Geo. Marfarren. Coburg, Sept., 1822.

GUY FAWKES. Burl. H. J. Byron. Gaiety, January 14, 1874.

GUY FAWKES. Burl. Albert Smith. Marylebone. Easter, 1840.

GUY FAWKES. See *Ordsall Hall, Guido Fawkes,* and *Gunpowder Plot.*

GUY FAWKES; OR, A MATCH FOR A KING. By T. Taylor, Albert Smith, W. P. Hale, E. Draper, and Arthur Smith. Olympic, March 31, 1855; D.L., May 11, 1855.

GUY FAWKES; OR, A NEW WAY TO BLOW UP A KING. Op. bo. 3 a. J. T. Douglass. Standard, April 16, 1870.

GUY FAWKES: OR, THE FIFTH OF NOVEMBER Dr. Sk. Hay., November 5, 1793. N.p.

GUY FAWKES, ESQ. Burl. 3 a. A. C. Torr (Fr. Leslie) and Herbert F. Clark. Lyrics by Marshall. M. by G. W. Byng. Nottingham T.R., April 7, 1890; Gaiety, July 26, 1890.

GUY FAWKES, THE TRAITOR. D. 4 a. Chas. Whitlock. N. Shields T.R., July 15, 1901.

GUY FAWKES' DAY. Burl. F. C. Burnand. 1854.

GUY MANNERING. O. Sir H. Bishop. C.G., March, 1816; rev. Lyceum, October 2, 1820.

GUY MANNERING. Burl. R. Reece. Edinburgh, December, 1866.

GUY MANNERING. See *Spae Wife; La Dame Blanche.*

GUY MANNERING: OR, THE GIPSY'S PROPHECY. M.P. 3 a. Daniel Terry. Adap. fr. Sir Walter Scott. C.G., March 12, 1816; D.L., October 7, 1819. Pr. 1817.

GUYES, THE TRAGEDY OF THE. Act. at the Rose T., January 30, 1592. This might possibly be Marlow's *Massacre of Paris, with the Death of the Duke of Guise.*

GUZMAN. C. Roger, Earl of Orrery. Pr. 1693. Ac. at the Duke of York's T., 1667-72.

GWENDOLINE. O. Chabrier. Brussels, 1886.

GWENEVERE. "Celtic M.D." 3 a. Ernest Rhyds. M. by V. Thomas. Coronet, November 13, 1905.

GWILTY GOVERNESS AND THE DOWNEY DOCTOR, THE. Burl. G. M. Layton. Folly, May 8, 1876.

GWISSE, THE. Possibly a new version of *The Massacre of Paris*, by John Webster. 1601.

GWYNNE'S OATH. D. 4 a. Nelson Wheatcroft. Stratford T.R., April 2, 1888.

GWYNNETH VAUGHAN. D. 2 a. Mark Lemon. Olympic, 1840-1844.

H

H. B. F. 1 a. R. B. Peake. Publ. by J. Dicks.

H.M.S. IRRESPONSIBLE. M.P. J. F. Cornish and Geo. W. Byng. Chester Royalty (prod. as *The Cruise of*, etc.), August 2, 1900; Broadway, November 26, 1900; Strand, May 27, 1901; Globe (transferred from Strand), July 29, 1901.

H.M.S. MISSFIRE; OR, THE HONEST TAR AND THE WICKED FIRST LUFF. C.O. 3 a. Capt. W. P. Drury. M. by Giovanni Nifosi and Stephen Blythe. Portsmouth T.R., March 11, 1895.

H.M.S. PINAFORE; OR, THE LASS THAT LOVED A SAILOR. C.O. 2 a. W. S. Gilbert. M. by Arthur Sullivan. Op. C., May 25, 1878; Savoy, June 6, 1899; Savoy, July 14, 1908.

H.M. SLOOP SPITFIRE. See *The Alabama.*

H. SAMPSON AGONISTES. T. John Milton. 1671.

HABIT OU REDINGOTE? Royalty, March 29, 1888.

HADDON HALL. Light O. 3 a. Sydney Grundy. M. by Sir Arthur Sullivan. Savoy, September 24, 1892.

HAEUSLICHE KRIEG, DER. Oa. Schubert (1797-1828). Prod. in Germany.

HAFED THE GHEBER. D. 2 a. F. on the story of *Fireworshippers in Lalla Rookh.* D.L., November 29, 1824.

HAGAR. P. 4 a. Adap. fr. *La Fille du Garde Chasse.* G. R. Sims and A. Shirley. Notting Hill Coronet, February 24, 1902.

HAGAR IN THE DESERT. (?) By Mme. Genlis. 1781. See *Theatre of Education, Leah.*

HAGAR IN THE WILDERNESS. Transl. of the foregoing by Thos. Holcroft. Pr. 1786.

HAGAR, THE OUTCAST JEWESS. Another ver. of *Leah.* Britannia, July 5, 1869.

HAGS OF MISCHIEF; OR, HARLEQUIN PLOUGHBOY. Comic Pant. Ac. at Olympic Pav., November 17, 1806.

HAIL FELLOW, WELL MET! Int. Hay., August 9, 1792. N.p.

HAIL FELLOW, WELL MET! D. 5 a. S. J. Pratt. Pr. 1805.

HAIRBREADTH ESCAPE, A. P. 1 a. Claude Askew. Bayswater Bijou, March 21, 1901.

HAJJI BABA; OR, THE STAR OF THE EAST. Persian M.P. Wr. by Geo. Gamble. Comp. by Wm. Robins. St. James's, January 22, 1909 (C.P.).

HAL O' THE WYND. D. 4 a. Leonard Rae. Standard, September 14, 1874.

HAL THE HIGHWAYMAN. P. 1 a. H. M. Paull. Vaudeville, December 15, 1894; Royalty, November 2, 1898.

HALF-A-DOLLAR. Sk. 2 sc. W. A. Haines and A. Borthwick. Granville, March 28, 1907.

HALF AN HOUR AFTER SUPPER. Int Hay., May 25, 1789. Pr. 1789.

HALF CASTE; OR, THE POISONED PEARL, THE. D. 3 a. T. W. Robertson. Adap. fr. the French. Ver. prod. at the Surrey, September 8, 1856.

HALF CROWN DIAMONDS, THE. Burl. Robert Reece. Mirror, September 27, 1875; Imperial (new ver.), October 2, 1880.

HALF MAST HIGH. D. 4 a. Tom Craven. Pavilion, April 1, 1893.

HALF-PAST TEN DOWN EXPRESS, THE. See *Ten Thirty.*

HALF-PAY OFFICERS. F. 3 a. Chas. Molloy. L.I.F., January 11, 1720. Pr. 1720. F. on *Love and Honour* and other old plays.

HALF SEAS OVER. D. Mrs. Mark. Kendal St. Geo. H., June 24, 1882.

HALF-WAY HOUSE, THE. C. 3 a. G. R. Sims. Vaudeville, October 1, 1881.

HALIBLUDE; OR, HOLY BLOOD, THE MYSTERY OF. P. Perf. at Aberdeen, 1445.

HALIDON HILL. Dr. Sk. in 3 a. W. Scott. 1822.

HALL OF HARMONY; OR, THE ROSE, SHAMROCK, AND THISTLE, THE. M. Melange. Lyceum playbill, October 7, 1822.

HALL PORTER, THE. P. 2 a. S. Lover. R.E.O.H., July 25, 1839. Publ. by J. Dicks.

HALLOWE'EN. Dr. Hist. Playlet. By R. Wilford. Lancaster Athenæum, August 7, 1907 (C.P.).

HALLOWEEN; OR, THE CASTLES OF ATHLIN AND DUNBAYNE. Spec. J. C. Cross. Ac. at the Royal Circus. Pr. 1809.

HALT OF THE CARAVAN, THE. Div. Noble. D.L., November 30, 1822.

HALVEI, THE UNKNOWN. D. 3 a. T. Egerton Wilks. City of London, September 30, 1848.

HALVES. P. Pro. and 3 a. A. Conan Doyle. Aberdeen H.M.T., April 10, 1899; Garrick, June 10, 1899.

HAMILTON OF BOTHWELLHAUGH. A. R. Slous. Sadler's Wells, October 24, 1855.

HAMILTON'S SECOND MARRIAGE. P. 4 a. Mrs. W. K. Clifford. Court, October 29, 1907.

HAMLET. A P. with this title ac. at Newington T. by the Lord Admiral's and Lord Chamberlain's Servants, June 9, 1594.

HAMLET, PRINCE OF DENMARK. T. Wm. Shakespeare. F. on an older play now lost; and on the *Hystorie of Hamblett* (Black letter; date of earliest edition unknown), which was trans. fr. one of Belleforest's novels. He took it fr. "Saxo Grammaticus." Wr. 1596. Ent. at Stationers' Hall, July 26, 1602, and November 19, 1607. Pr., quartos, 1603, 1604, 1605, 1611, 1637; first folio, 1628. Alt. by D. Garrick, D.L., 1771; J. P. Kemble, D.L., 1800; Lyceum (H. Irving), October 30, 1874, to June 29, 1875, and December 30, 1878; Princess's (Wilson Barrett), 1884; Globe

(F. R. Benson), March 6, 1890; Olympic (Wilson Barrett), April 13, 1891; Hay. (Beerbohm Tree), January 21, 1892; Her Maj., August 12, 1897; Lyceum (Forbes Robertson), September 11, 1897; Lyceum (Wilson Barrett), December 9, 1899; from the first quarto (played by Eliz. Stage Society), Carpenters' Hall, February 21, 1900; Comedy (F. R. Benson), March 27, 1901; H.M. (Mr. Tree's) March 24, 1905; Adelphi (H. B. Irving), April 4, 1905; Lyric (Martin Harvey), May 22, 1905; H.M., April 26, 1906; Waldorf, May 1, 1907; H.M., April 24, 1908; Shaftesbury (H. B. Irving), February 8, 1909; Lyceum, March 13, 1909; rev. Elephant and C., May 3, 1909.

HAMLET. French ver. by Eugène Morand and Marcel Schwob. Mme. Sarah Bernhardt's season, Adelphi, June 12, 1899.

HAMLET. O. 5 a. Ambroise Thomas. Paris, 1868. R. Ital. O., C.G., June 19, 1869.

HAMLET. See *Rosencrantz and Guildenstern; The Grave-makers.*

HAMLET A LA MODE. Burl. Sk. G. L. Gordon and G. W. Anson. Liverpool P.O.W., October 6, 1876; Op. C., April 21, 1877.

HAMLET IMPROVED; OR, MR. MENDALL'S ATTEMPT TO AMELIORATE THAT TRAGEDY. Burl. Col. Colomb.

HAMLET THE HYSTERICAL. "A Delusion in 5 Spasms." Princess's, November 30, 1874.

HAMLET TRAVESTIE. 3 a. John Poole. C.G., June 17, 1813. Pr. 1810.

HAMLET WHETHER HE WILL OR NO. Burl. George Booth. Sheffield Alexandra, June 2, 1879.

HAMPDEN. T. Lord Dreghorne. Pr. 1799. Mentioned by Oulton.

HAMPSHIRE HOG; OR, NEVER SAY DIE, THE. Sk. 1 a. Mark Melford. Bedford M.H., March 13, 1899.

HAMPSTEAD HEATH. C. Thos. Baker. (Alt. of his *Act at Oxford.*) Pr. 1706. D.L., October 30, 1805.

HAMPTON COURT MASQUE. A True Description of a Royal Masque. Pres. at Hampton Court. January 8, 1603-4.

HAND AND GLOVE; OR, PAGE THIRTEEN OF THE BLACK BOOK. D. 3 a. G. Conquest and P. Meritt. Grecian, May 25, 1874.

HAND AND HEART. P. 1 a. W. Yardley and H. P. Stephens. Gaiety, May 21, 1886.

HAND IN HAND. C.D. 4 a. Edward Darbey. Rotherham T.R., August 5, 1889; Surrey, March 24, 1890.

HAND OF DESTINY, THE. P. 4 a. D. Vincent Buckingham. Guernsey St. Julian's Hall, August 23, 1905.

HAND OF ELMSLEY, THE. D. Barry Lemain. Newcastle Tyne T., August 27, 1877.

HAND OF FATE, THE. D. 4 a. Arthur Shirley. Barrow Alhambra T., March 3, 1884. See *Queen of Diamonds* and *Shadows of Life.*

HAND OF JUSTICE, THE. D. 4 a. Max Goldberg. Sadler's Wells, September 7, 1891; Cardiff Grand T., July 30, 1894. Rev. edit. Brighton Eden, December 2, 1901; West London, December 9, 1901.

HAND OF PROVIDENCE, THE. D. 4 a. T. Gideon Warren. Surrey, August 2, 1897.

HAND OF TIME, THE. D. 5 a. John Glendenning. Darlington T.R., December 20, 1897.

HANDCUFFS, THE. D. 4 a. Reginald Stockton and Eric Hudson. Nottingham T.R., May 11, 1893 (C.P.).

HANDFAST. P. Pro. and 3 a. Henry Hamilton and Mark Quinton. P.O.W., December 13, 1887; Shaftesbury, May 16, 1891.

HANDS AND HEARTS. D. 4 a. J. W. Evelyn. Garston T.R., November 21, 1902.

HANDS ACROSS THE SEA. D. 5 a. Henry Pettitt. Manchester T.R., July 30, 1888; Princess's, November 10, 1888; rev. Dalston, September 21, 1908.

HANDS OF SIN, THE. D. S. Lewis Ransom and H. A. Saintsbury. Wellingborough, Exchange H., December 26, 1905; Widnes Alex., January 1, 1906. See *The Hindoo's Revenge.*

HANDS UP. Revue. Lyrics by M. Pigott, F. Bower, and A. Ross. Dial. by F. Bower. M. by various composers. (Savage Club mat.) H.M., June 4, 1907.

HANDSOME APOLOGY, A. Ca. Andrew Longmuir. Edinburgh T.R., March 2, 1888. P. of W.'s, July 3, 1888.

HANDSOME HERNANI; OR, THE FATAL PENNY WHISTLE. Burl. H. J. Byron. Gaiety, August 30, 1879.

HANDSOME HUSBAND, A. C.D. 1 a. Mrs. Planché. Olympic, February 15, 1836.

HANDSOME HUSBAND, A. Ca., Strand, November 1, 1895.

HANDSOME IS THAT HANDSOME DOES. C. 4 a. C. J. Ribton-Turner. Vaudeville, June 6, 1888.

HANDSOME IS THAT HANDSOME DOES; A STORY OF THE LAKE COUNTRY. C.D. 4 a. Tom Taylor. Manchester Prince's, August 15, 1870; Olympic, September 3, 1870.

HANDSOME JACK. Melo-d. 4 a. J. B. Howe.

HANDSOME JACK, THE HIGHWAYMAN. Marylebone, August 18, 1862.

HANDSOME JIM. P. 4 a. Malcolm Watson. Margate T.R., July 16, 1906.

HANDY ANDY. C.D. 2 a. W. R. Floyd. Publ. by S. French, Ltd.

HANDY ANDY. Hibernian D. 1 a. H. W. Montgomery. Adap. fr. Saml. Lover's novel. New York Wallack's, 1862.

HANDY MAN, THE. M.C. Herbert Shelley. M. by Shelley and Neat. Kingston County T., June 4, 1900.

HANGED MAN, THE. Victoria, April 28, 1866.

HANGING AND MARRIAGE; OR, THE DEAD MAN'S WEDDING. F. Henry Carey. L.I.F., March 15, 1722. Pr. 1722.

HANKEY-HOMEY SHOWMAN, THE. "Operatic agony." Lyrics by Geo. Burnley. Oxford, November 2, 1908.

HANNAH. Orat. Smart. 1764.

HANNAH; OR, THE MISER OF WALREN. O. 2 a. E. Fitzball.

HANNAH HEWITT; OR, THE FEMALE CRUSOE. M. Ent. 2 a. C. Dibdin. Fr. his novel of same name. D.L., May 7, 1798. N.p.

HANNELE. A D. Poem. 2 a. Gerhart Hauptmann. Royalty, February 29, 1904. Presented by the Play Actors. Scala, April 12, 1908. Transl. by William Archer. H.M., December 8, 1908 (mat.).

HANNETONS, LES. C. 3 a. Brieux. Transl. by H. M. Clark. Imperial, March 24, 1907. See *The Incubus.*

HANNIBAL. Hist. D. Professor Nichol. 1873.

HANNIBAL AND HERMES. P. Robt. Wilson in conj. with Dekker and Drayton. Ac 1598.

HANNIBAL AND SCIPIO. P. Wm. Ramkins in conj. with Richard Hathwaye. Ac. 1600. N.p.

HANNIBAL AND SCIPIO. Hist. T. Thos. Nabbs. D.L., 1635. Pr. 1637.

HANS, AN ALSATIAN. M.C. Liverpool Queen's O.H., August 9, 1880.

HANS BEER POT. His Invisible C. of *See Me, and See Me Not.* 3 a. Drawbridge Court Belchier. Pr. 1618.

HANS HEILING. O. H. Marschner. 1796-1861. F. on old legend of the Erzgebirge. Prod. in Germany.

HANS HUCKEBEIN. F. O. Blumenthal and G. Kadelburgh. Great Queen Street, April 22, 1907 (Ger. Season).

HANS ROSENHAGEN. D. 3 a. Max Halbe. St. Geo. H., December 3, 1901.

HANS THE BOATMAN. M.C. 3 a. Clay M. Greene. Sheffield T.R. (first time in England), March 7, 1887; Grand, July 4, 1887; Strand, December 21, 1891.

HANS VON STEIN: OR, THE ROBBER KNIGHT. Melo-d. 2 a. Edwd. Fitzball. Marylebone, August, 1851.

HANSEL AND GRETEL. Fairy O. Adelheid Wette. Fr. Grimm's Fairy Tales. M. by Humperdinck. Daly's, December 26, 1894; Gaiety, January 28, 1895; Princess's, March 4, 1895; Savoy, April 16, 1895; D.L. (in German), June 24, 1895; H.M.T., September 21, 1897.

HANSEMANN'S TOCHTER. C. 4 a. Adolph. L'Arronge. Great Queen Street, March 30, 1906.

HAP; OR, THE MONKEY OF THE NILE. Burl. Crystal Pal., 1881.

HAPPIER DAYS. C.D. 3 a. Miss Sophie Scotti. Ladbroke H., June 17, 1886.

HAPPIEST DAY OF HIS LIFE, THE. P. 1 a. W. F. Downing. Brixton, February 13, 1905.

HAPPIEST DAY OF MY LIFE, THE. F. 2 a. J. B. Buckstone. Hay., July 29, 1829; D.L., October 27, 1829.

HAPPIEST MAN ALIVE, THE. C. 1 a. Wm. Bayle Bernard. Olympic, March, 1840.

HAPPINESS AT HOME. D. C. H. Hazlewood. Britannia, May 29, 1871.

HAPPY ARCADIA. O. W. S. Gilbert and F. Clay. Gal. Illustn., October 28, 1872; St. Geo. H., July 15, 1895.

HAPPY AT LAST; OR, SIGH NO MORE, LADIES. C. Margate T., September 13, 1805. N.p.

HAPPY BUNGALOW. A. Law. St. Geo. H. (circa 1865).

HAPPY CAPTIVE, THE. Eng. O. Lewis Theobald. Plot from *The History of a Slave* in *Don Quixote.* Pr. 1741.

HAPPY CHOICE, THE. Past. MS. in library of Murphy.

HAPPY CONSTANCY, THE. C. H. Jacob. 1738. See *Nest of Plays.*

HAPPY CRUISE, A. Ca. Ernest Cuthbert. Vaudeville, November 17, 1873.

HAPPY DAY, A. F. "Richard Henry." Gaiety, October 6, 1886.

HAPPY DELUSION, THE. C. Ac. at King's T .in Hay. Pr. 1727. Really a pant. in 5 a.

HAPPY DISGUISE; OR, LOVE IN A MEADOW, THE. C.O. W. C. Oulton. Ac. Dublin. Pr. 1784.

HAPPY ENDING, A. C.O. Bertha Moore. Queen's Gate H., July 14, 1901; Court, June 24, 1909 (mat.).

HAPPY FAMILY, A. D. 5 a. Benj. Thompson. Pr. 1799. Fr. the German of Kotzebut.

HAPPY FAMILY, A. S. 1 a. John Jackson. Garston T.R., February 3, 1902.

HAPPY-GO-LUCKY. D. F. Hazleton. Marylebone, July 10, 1875.

HAPPY-GO-LUCKY. P. 3 a. T. Edgar Pemberton. Globe, June 11, 1884.

HAPPY HAMPSTEAD. M.F. 1 a. Frank Duprez. M. by Mark Lynne. Liverpool, Alexandra, July 3, 1876; Royalty, January 13, 1877.

HAPPY HOOLIGAN. M.P. 3 a. Oldham Empire, July 20, 1908. Hammersmith Lyric, September 27, 1909.

HAPPY HYPOCRITE, THE. P. 1 a. Max Beerbohm. Royalty, December 11, 1900.

HAPPY ISLAND, THE. C. Fr. the French of Mme. Genlis. Pr. 1781.

HAPPY LAND, THE. Burl. F. Tomline and Gilbert à Beckett. Court, March 3, 1873.

HAPPY LIFE, THE. C. 3 a. L. N. Parker. Duke of York's, December 6, 1897; Terry's, November 13, 1899.

HAPPY LITTLE ADVENTURE, A. P. 1 a. J. Y. F. Cooke. Eastbourne New Pier Pav., March 28, 1902.

HAPPY LOVERS: OR, THE BEAU METAMORPHOSED, THE. O. Henry Ward. L.I.F. Pr. 1736.

HAPPY MAN, THE. Extrav. 1 a. S. Lover. Publ. by S. French, Ltd.

HAPPY MARRIAGE; OR, THE TURN OF FORTUNE, THE. By "a young gentleman." L.I.F. Pr. 1727.

HAPPY MEDIUM, A. F. 1 a. T. Edgar Pemberton. Hay., November 8, 1875.

HAPPY MEDIUM, A. Ca. Arthur Shirley. New T., November 2, 1905.

HAPPY MEDIUM, THE. C. 3 a. A. Chaplin and Paul Gaye. Ladbroke H., July 29, 1909.

HAPPY NOOK, A. D. 3 a. Fr. Sudermann's "Das Glück in Winkel." Alice Greeven and J. T. Grein. Court, June 25, 1901.

HAPPY PAIR, A. Ca. 1 a. S. Theyre Smith. St. James's, March 2, 1868.

HAPPY PRESCRIPTION; OR, THE LADY RELIEVED FROM HER LOVERS, THE. C. Wm. Hayley. Pr. 1784. N. ac.

HAPPY RETURN, THE. Ca. 1 a. Arthur Law. Court, January 9, 1883.

HAPPY RETURNS. F.C. 3 a. Fred Horner. Fr. *L'Article 231* of Paul Ferrier (Comédie Française, July 11, 1891). Vaudeville, March 1, 1892.

HAPPY THOUGHT, A. P. 1 a. H. Tripp Edgar. Bayswater Bijou, March 2, 1894; Strand, January 12, 1895.

HAPPY VALLEY, THE. C.O. Harold Lee. M. by T. M. Pattison. Warrington P.H., February 10, 1880.

HAPPY VILLAGE, THE. Extrav. Edgar Raynor. Camberwell Drill H., February 17, 1894 (amat.).

HARA KARI, THE. Jap. Play. 3 sc. Savoy, October 2, 1905.

HARBOUR LIGHTS. D. 5 a. G. R. Sims and H. Pettitt. Adelphi, December 23, 1885.

HARBOUR MASTER'S SECRET; OR, THE WRECK OF THE GOLDEN EAGLE, THE. Britannia, December 21, 1868.

HARD AS IRON. D. Burton T. of Varieties, January 16, 1885.

HARD CASE, A. F.C. 3 a. W. Carlton Dawe. Terry's, October 26, 1893.

HARD HANDS AND HAPPY HEARTS. C.D. T. A. Palmer. Plymouth T.R., November 22, 1869.

HARD HEARTS. D. 5 a. A. J. Charleson and Chas. Wilmot. Grand, April 26, 1886; Wolverhampton Star T., September 26, 1892.

HARD HIT. P. 4 a. H. A. Jones. Hay., January 17, 1887.

HARD LINES. D. 4 a. Geo. Comer. Manchester Queen's T., April 16, 1883.

HARD LINES. Petite D. Chas. Dickenson. St. Geo. H., March 19, 1887.

HARD SHIFTE FOR HUSBANDS; OR, BILBOES THE BEST BLADE. C. Saml. Rowley. Circa 1630.

HARD STRUGGLE, A. Dom. D. 1 a. Westland Marston. Lyceum, February 1, 1858.

HARD TIMES. P. 3 a. Cooper. Taken fr. Dickens. Publ. by J. Dicks.

HARD TIMES. See *Under the Earth.*

HARD TIMES IN MANCHESTER. D. Prol. and 4 a. Max Goldberg and E. C. Matthews. Broughton Victoria T., July 6, 1903.

HARD UP. C.D. 2 a. Edwd. Righton. Reading T.R., March 26, 883; Strand, October 20, 1883.

HARDACNUTE. P. Recorded by Philip Henslowe as having been ac. Rose T., October 19, 1597.

HARE AND HOUNDS. F.C. 3 a. Sydney Grundy. Edinburgh Princess's, August 13, 1883.

HAREBELL; OR, THE WAND OF WHITE LILIES. M. Dream P. 2 a. G. Blackmore. West Croydon St. Michael's Parish Hall, April 7, 1904.

HAREY THE FYRSTE, LIFE AND DETH OF. (According to Henslowe.) May 30, 1597.

HARLEKIN PATRIOT, THE. D. Ewald. 1772.

HARLEQUIN ALFRED THE GREAT; OR, THE MAGIC BANJO AND THE MYSTIC RAVEN. Pant. By the author of *Bluff King Hal.* Marylebone, December 26, 1850.

HARLEQUIN AMULET; OR, THE MAGIC OF MONA. Pant. D.L. Pr. 1800.

HARLEQUIN AND ASMODEUS; OR, CUPID ON CRUTCHES. Pant. Farley, 1810.

HARLEQUIN AND FANCY; OR, THE POET'S LAST SHILLING. Pant. M. by Smart. D.L., December 26, 1815.

HARLEQUIN AND FAUSTUS; OR, THE DEVIL WILL HAVE HIS OWN. Pant. C.G., 1793.

HARLEQUIN AND HUMPO. Pant. T. Dibdin. 1812.

HARLEQUIN AND O'DONOGHUE; OR, THE WHITE HORSE OF KILLARNEY. By the author of *Bluff King Hal.* Astley's, December 26, 1850.

HARLEQUIN AND OBERON; OR, THE CHACE TO GRETNA. Pant. C.G., 1796.

HARLEQUIN AND QUIXOTE; OR, THE MAGIC ARM. Pant. J. C. Cross. C.G., December 26, 1797.

HARLEQUIN AND THE DANDY CLUB. Pant. D.L., December 26, 1818.

HARLEQUIN AND THE SWANS; OR, BATH OF BEAUTY. Pant. Farley, 1813.

HARLEQUIN ANNA BULLEN. Ent. Cibber. L.I.F., December 11, 1727.

HARLEQUIN BACCHUS. Pant. Ac. at the Royal Circus, April 15, 1805. Pr. 1805.

HARLEQUIN BARBER. Panto. C.G., April 20, 1741.

HARLEQUIN BENEDICK; OR, THE GHOST OF MOTHER SHIPTON. Pant. Sadler's Wells. Pr. 1801.

HARLEQUIN CAPTIVE; OR, THE MAGIC FIRE. Pant. D.L. Pr. 1796.

HARLEQUIN CARTOUCHE; OR, THE FRENCH ROBBER. Pant. Hay., 1733.

HARLEQUIN COCK ROBIN. Victoria, December 26, 1866.

HARLEQUIN DOCTOR FAUSTUS; WITH THE MASQUE OF THE DEITIES. John Thurmond. D.L. Pr. 1724.

HARLEQUIN DOCTOR FAUSTUS. Panto. Alt. fr. *The Necromancer*, by Woodward. C.G., 1766.

HARLEQUIN ENCHANTED. Pant. D.L., April 25, 1753.

HARLEQUIN ENGLISHMAN; OR, THE FRENCHMAN BIT. Pant. Goodman's Fields, 1742.

HARLEQUIN EXECUTED. Pant. One of John Rich's earliest productions. L.I.F., 1720.

HARLEQUIN FREEMASON. Pant. C.G., 1780. Ascr. to Messink. M. by Dibdin.

HARLEQUIN FUN. Effingham, December 26, 1866.

HARLEQUIN GUY FAWKES. Olympic, March 31, 1855.

HARLEQUIN HAPPY; OR, POOR PIERROTT MARRIED. Pant. D.L., 1728.

HARLEQUIN HARPER; OR, JUMP FROM JAPAN. Pant. C. Extrav. M. by Dibdin. D.L., May 15, 1815; Lyceum, July 18, 1815.

HARLEQUIN HOAX; OR, A PANTOMIME PROPOSED. Extrav. M. by Dibdin. D.L., June 15, 1815. Lyceum, July 18, 1815.

HARLEQUIN HYDASPES; OR, THE GRESHAMITE. Mock O. Asc. to Mrs. Aubert. L.I.F. Pr. 1719.

HARLEQUIN IN CHINA. Pant. Woodward. 1755.

HARLEQUIN IN HIS ELEMENT; OR, FIRE, WATER, EARTH, AND AIR. Pant. T. Dibdin. C.G. Pr. 1808.

HARLEQUIN IN THE CITY; OR, COLUMBINE TURNED ELEPHANT. Pant. Goodman's Fields, 1734.

HARLEQUIN INCENDIARY; OR, COLUMBINE CAMERON. Pant. Anon. M. by Dr. Arne. Pr. 1746. D.L.

HARLEQUIN INVISIBLE; OR, THE EMPEROR OF CHINA'S COURT. L.I.F., April 8, 1724.

HARLEQUIN JUNIOR; OR, THE MAGIC CESTUS. Pant. D.L., 1784.

HARLEQUIN KING, THE. Masquerade. 4 a. Rudolph Lothar. Adap. by Louis N. Parker and Selwyn Brinton. Imperial, January 3, 1906.

HARLEQUIN LITTLE BOY BLUE. Crystal Pal., December 21, 1868.

HARLEQUIN MOUNTEBANK. Pant. D.L., May 11, 1756.

HARLEQUIN MULTIPLIED. Pant. Anon. 1726. In Bathoe's Catalogue. See *Argentina Strega.*

HARLEQUIN MUNGO; OR, A PEEP INTO THE TOWER. Pant. Bate and Oulton. Royalty T., 1789.

HARLEQUIN NOVELTY, AND THE PRINCESS WHO LOST HER HEART. Burl. Pant. 1 a. Leicester Buckingham. Strand, December 24, 1857.

HARLEQUIN ON THE STOCKS; OR, A PANTOMIME LAUNCHED. Pant. Andrew Cherry. Hull T., 1793.

HARLEQUIN ORPHEUS; OR, THE MAGIC PIPE. Panto. D.L., 1735.

HARLEQUIN PADMANABA. Pant. Farley. 1812.

HARLEQUIN PEASANT; OR, A PANTOMIME REHEARSED. Pant. Hay., 1793.

HARLEQUIN PEDLAR; OR, THE HAUNTED WELL. Pant. T. Dibdin. C.G., 1809-10.

HARLEQUIN PREMIER. F. Pr. 1769.

HARLEQUIN QUICKSILVER; OR, THE GNOME AND THE DEVIL. Pant. T. Dibdin. C.G. Pr. 1805.

HARLEQUIN RAMBLER; OR, THE CONVENT IN AN UPROAR. Pant. C.G., 1784. An alt. of *Friar Bacon.*

HARLEQUIN RANGER. Pant. Henry Woodward. D.L., 1751-2.

HARLEQUIN RESTORED; OR, TASTE-A-LA-MODE. Pant. D.L. Songs only. Pr. n.d.

HARLEQUIN ROKOKO. Grecian, December 24, 1879.

HARLEQUIN SHEPPARD. A "night scene." John Thurmond. D.L. Pr. 1724.

HARLEQUIN SHIPWRECKED; concluding with *The Loves of Paris and Œnone.* Pant. Goodman's Fields, 1736.

HARLEQUIN SORCERER, WITH THE LOVES OF PLUTO AND PROSERPINE. Pant. Lewis Theobald. L.I.F., January 21, 1725. Pr. 1725. C.G., 1752.

HARLEQUIN STUDENT; OR, THE FALL OF PANTOMIME WITH THE RESTORATION OF THE DRAMA. Ent. Goodman's Fields, March 2, 1741. M. by Prelleur. Pr. 1741.

HARLEQUIN TEAGUE; OR, THE GIANT'S CAUSEWAY. Pant. Songs by Colman, sen. Hay., 1782. Songs only pr. 1782.

HARLEQUIN, THE PHANTOM OF A DAY. Pant. C. Dibdin. Ac. at the Royal Circus. Pr. 1783.

HARLEQUIN TURN'D JUDGE. Pant. John Weaver. D.L., 1717.

HARLEQUIN'S ALMANACK; OR, THE FOUR SEASONS. Pant. T. Dibdin. C.G. Pr. 1801.

HARLEQUIN'S CHAPLET. Pant. C.G., 1789.

HARLEQUIN'S CONTRIVANCE; OR, THE JEALOUS YEOMAN DEFEATED. Pant. Goodman's Fields, April 21, 1732.

HARLEQUIN'S DEATH AND REVIVAL; OR, THE CLOWN IN PURGATORY. Pant. Sk. West. Lyceum (prob. rev.), April 9, 1822.

HARLEQUIN'S FROLICK; OR, A VOYAGE TO PRUSSIA. Pant. Hay., 1757.

HARLEQUIN'S FROLICKS. Pant. C.G., 1776. An alt. of *Prometheus.*

HARLEQUIN'S HABEAS; OR, THE HALL OF SPECTRES. Pant. T. Dibdin. M. by Moorhead, Braham, and Davy, etc. C.G. Pr. 1802.

HARLEQUIN'S INVASION. "A Christmas Gambol." Dialogue by Garrick. D.L., 1759. Afterwards at Bart. Fair with the title concluding, *The Taylor Without a Head; or, the Battle of the Golden Bridge.*

HARLEQUIN'S JACKET; OR, THE NEW YEAR'S GIFT. Pant. D.L., 1775.

HARLEQUIN'S JUBILEE. Pant. Arr. by Woodward as a burl. on *The Jubilee.* C.G. Pr. 1770.

HARLEQUIN'S MAGNET; OR, THE SCANDINAVIAN SORCERER. Pant. T. Dibdin. M. by J. Davy. C.G., 1806.

HARLEQUIN'S MOUTH OPEN'D. Bentley. 1761. See *Wishes.*

HARLEQUIN'S MUSEUM; OR, MOTHER SHIPTON TRIUMPHANT. C.G., 1792.

HARLEQUIN'S OPERA. Ralph. 1730. See *Fashionable Lady.*

HARLEQUIN'S RACES; OR, TIME BEATS ALL. Pant. C.G., 1803.

HARLEQUIN'S RETURN. Pant. J. C. Cross. C.G., 1798.

HARLEQUIN'S TOUR; OR, THE DOMINION OF FANCY. Pant. C.G. Pr. 1800.

HARLEQUIN'S TREASURE; OR, JEWELS NEW SET. Pant. C.G., 1796.

HARLEQUIN'S TRIUMPH. Pant. John Thurmond. D.L. Pr. 1727.

HARLEQUIN'S VISION. Pant. Rom. Lethbridge. M. by Lanza. F. on *Don Juan.* D.L., December 26, 1817.

HARLEQUINADE; OR, ONLY A CLOWN. M.P. 1 a. Granville Bantock. Eastbourne T.R., October 26, 1899.

HARLEQUINS, THE. C. Pr. at Dublin, 1753.

HARLOT'S PROGRESS; OR, THE RIDOTTO AL FRESCO, THE. Pant. Ent. Theophilus Cibber. D.L., March 31, 1733. Pr. 1733. Adap. fr. Hogarth's Engravings.

HARMLESS HYPOCRITES. C. 4 a. Walter Ellis. Brunswick H.; Dr. Cl., Wandsworth Road, March 26, 1901.

HARMONIOUS DISCORDS. Ca. Op. Comique, March 31, 1873.

HARMONY. Dom. D. 1 a. H. A. Jones. Leeds Grand, August 13, 1879; Strand, June 14, 1884; Royalty, September 25, 1895. Prod. at Leeds as *Harmony Restored.*

HARMONY HALL. Sk. Granville, November 11, 1907.

HARMONY OF THE SPHERES, THE. Cant. Romberg. 1767-1821.

HARMONY RESTORED. See *Harmony.*

HAROLD T. A MS. P. Henry Jones (the bricklayer). See "European Mag.," vol. xxv., p. 260.

HAROLD T. Thomas Boyce. Pr. 1786.

HAROLD. D. 5 a. A. Nance. Portsmouth Prince's, March 29, 1875.

HAROLD. Hist. P. Tennyson. 1876.

HAROLD. O. 5 a. St. Petersburg, 1886.

HAROLD. O. 3 a. Sir Edward Mallett. M. by F. H. Cowen. C.G., June 8, 1895. Originally prod. in Berlin.

HAROLD HAWK; OR, THE CONVICT'S VENGEANCE. Dom. D. 2 a. Chas. Selby. Surrey, September 27, 1858.

HAROLD, THE SAXON. Hist. P. 5 a. J. W. Boulding. Leicester R.O.H., October 21, 1897.

HAROUN ALRASCHID. P. 3 a. C. Dibdin. Publ. by J. Dicks.

HAROUN ALRASCHID. O. Alt. fr. *The Æthiop.* C.G., January, 1813.

HARPER'S DAUGHTER, THE. T. M. G. Lewis. C.G., May 4, 1803. An alt. fr. Schiller's *Minister.* N.p. See *Cabal and Love.*

HARROWING OF HELL. See "Miracle Plays."

HARRY GAYLOVE. See *Sir Harry Gaylove.*

HARRY, LE ROY. Burl. 1 a. Pocock. F. on *The Miller of Mansfield.* C.G., July 2, 1813.

HARRY OF CORNWALL. Rose T., February 25, 1591.

HARRY THE FIFTH. Recorded by Henslowe as ac. November 28, 1595. ? The play entitled *The Famous Victories of Henry the Fifth, containing the Honourable Battle of Agincourt.*

HARRY THE FIFTH: LIFE AND DEATH. Ac. (according to Henslowe) May 26, 1597.

HARTFORD BRIDGE; OR, THE SKIRTS OF THE CAMP. Operatic F. 2 a. M. by Shield. Wm. Pearce. C.G., 1792 and 1811. Pr. (songs only) 1792, (whole piece) 1796.

HARVEST. P. Prol. and 3 a. Henry Hamilton. Princess's, September 18, 1886.

HARVEST HOME. C.O. C. Dibdin. Hay. Pr. 1787.

HARVEST HOME, THE. D. 3 a. Tom Parry. Adelphi, April, 1848.

HARVEST HOME. D. Benjamin Webster. Astley's, 1867.

HARVEST OF CRIME, THE. D. 4 a. Miss Maud Randford. Brierley Hill T.R., May 27, 1897.

HARVEST OF HATE, A. D. Prol. and 3 a. Frank Withers and Henry Eglington. Castleford T.R., February 1. 1899 (C.P.).

HARVEST OF SIN, THE. D. 5 a. G. Daventry. Dalston T., July 25, 1904.

HARVEST OF WILD OATS, A. D. Prol. and 4 a. Hubert Bartlett. Henley-on-Thames St. Mary's H., March 8, 1897.

HARVEST QUEEN. THE. O. 2 a. M. by Phillips. D.L., May 22, 1838.

HARVEST STORM, THE. Dom. D. 1 a. C. H. Hazlewood. Britannia, June, 1862.

HARVEY'S PORTRAIT: TWELVE FOR ONE SHILLING. F. W. J. Sorrell. West Hartlepool New T.R., June 22, 1869.

HASEMANN'S TOCHTER. Adolf L'Arronge. Opera Comique, October 27, 1894; Gt. Queen St., March 30, 1906.

HASKA. D. 3 a. Henry Spicer. D.L., March 10, 1877.

HASTE. C. 3 a. Chas. Wood. St. George's, January 23, 1879.

HASTE TO THE WEDDING. F. W. J. Sorrell. Edinburgh Princess's, December 1, 1873.

HASTE TO THE WEDDING. 3 a. and 5 tab. W. S. Gilbert. M. by Geo. Grossmith. M. ver. of *Un Chapeau de Paille d'Italie*. Criterion, July 27, 1892. Originally prod. under the title of *The Wedding March*, which see.

HASTY CONCLUSION, A. F. 1 a. Mrs. J. R. Planché. Publ. by J. Dicks.

HASTY CONCLUSIONS. C. 2 a. C. Dance. Publ. by J. Dicks.

HASTY WEDDING; OR, THE INTRIGUING SQUIRE THE. C. Charles Shadwell, Pr. 1720.

HAT BOX. Charade. 1 a. H. Hersee. Publ. by J. Dicks.

HATRED. D. 3 a. Oldham T.R., March 1, 1880.

HAUNTED CASTLE, THE. M.E. W. C. Oulton. Ac. in Dublin. Pr. 1784.

HAUNTED FOR EVER. D. 2 a. J. B. Howe. Britannia, February 23, 1880.

HAUNTED GLEN, THE. Burl. 2 a. Harry Webber and Maidlow Davis. M. by Arthur Mills. Woolwich R. Artillery T., April 27, 1888.

HAUNTED GROVE, THE. M.E. Lady Dorothea Dubois. Ac. at Dublin, 1772. N.p.

HAUNTED HOUSE OF LODORE, THE. I. 1 a. and 3 sc. Jefferys C Allen Jefferys. Guildford Town H., February 11, 1895.

HAUNTED HOUSES; OR, LABYRINTHS OF LIFE, A STORY OF LONDON AND THE BUSH. D. Pro. and 4 a. H. J. Byron. Princess's, April 1, 1872.

HAUNTED INN, THE. F. 2 a. R. Brinsley Peake. C.G., D.L., January 31, 1827.

HAUNTED LIVES. D. 5 a. J. Wilton Jones. Hull T.R., April 7, 1884; Olympic, May 10, 1884.

HAUNTED LIVES. See *The Woman in Black*.

HAUNTED MAN, THE. Adelphi, 1849.

HAUNTED MAN, THE. E. Clarence Boielle. Dr. vers. of Dickens's story. Jersey Oddfellows' H., St. Heliers, December 14, 1908 (amat.).

HAUNTED MILL, THE. Oa. 1 a. J. P. Wooler.

HAUNTED TOWER, THE. C.O. 3 a. James Cobb. M. by Storace. D.L., Nevember 24, 1789, and February 24, 1816; Lyceum, April 26, 1809; C.G., 1832.

HAUNTED VILLAGE; OR, THE WAY TO BE HAPPY, THE. Dr. Ent. Young. Ac. at Gainsborough, 1800.

HAVANA. M.P. 3 a. G. Grossmith, jun., and Graham Hill. Lyrics by A. Ross. Additional lyrics by George Arthur. M. by Leslie Stuart. Gaiety, April 25. 1908.

HAVE AT ALL; OR, THE MIDNIGHT ADVENTURES. C. Joseph Williams. D.L., May, 1694. N.p.

HAVE YOU GOT THAT £10 NOTE? F. 1 a. Publ. by S. French, Limited.

HAVEN OF CONTENT, THE. P. 4 a. Malcolm Watson. Bristol Prince's T. October 22, 1896; Garrick, November 17, 1896.

HAVEN OF REST; OR, A MOTHER'S LOVE, THE. D. Miller Walker. Worksop T.R., March 14, 1868.

HAVING A DIP. Musical Extrav. in 1 sc. W. E. Phillips. M. by Joseph Tabrar. Canterbury, August 31, 1908.

HAWAIA; OR, THE BURNING GULF. Alhambra, December 27, 1880.

HAWK'S GRIP, THE. D. 5 a. Loftus Don. Southampton P.O.W.'s, February 14, 1887.

HAWKE'S NEST. D. 3 a. J. Mackay. Park, June 3, 1878.

HAWKSLEY'S LUCK. Dr. Epis. 4 sc. F. Maxwell. Bedford, March 9, 1908.

HAWKWOOD HALL. C.O. 3 a. Lynn Royd. M. by Geo. C. Richardson. Islington, Myddelton H., January 31, 1895.

HAWTHORNE U.S.A. P. 4 a. J. D. Fagan. Imperial, May 27, 1905.

HAY FEVER. F.C. 3 a. W. H. Pollock and Guy Pollock. Princess's, February 27, 1902.

HAYDEE. O. Wds. by Scribe. M. by Auber. Paris, 1847. Prod. in English, Strand T., April 3, 1848, and C.G., November 4, 1848.

HAYMAKERS' MASQUE, THE. A Masque perf. at Court about 1623.

HAYMAKING; OR, THE PLEASURES OF A COUNTRY LIFE. Op. bo. Allwood. Kilmarnock O.H., March 19, 1877.

HAYMARKET SPRING MEETING. Publ. by S. French, Ltd.

HAZARD. F. 1 a. Herbert Burnett. Margate T.R., July 1, 1891.

HAZARD OF THE DIE, THE. T.D. Douglas Jerrold. D.L., February 17, 1835.

HAZEL KIRKE. D. 4 a. Steele Mackaye. Vaudeville (first time in London), June 30, 1886.

HE LIES LIKE TRUTH. C.O. 1 a. F. Kimpton. M. by Kearns. Adap. fr. *Le Menteur Véridique*. Lyceum, July 24, 1828. St. James's, April 1, 1867.

HE LOVES ME; HE LOVES ME NOT. D. 4 a. Eden E. Greville. Maidenhead Grand H., December 16, 1891.

HE MUST BE MARRIED; OR, THE MISER OUTWITTED. Op. piece. 3 a. Pr. 1815. ? N.ac.

HE NEVER TOLD HIS LOVE. Ca. 1 a. Laurence Olde. MS. with Douglas Cox.

HE PROPOSED. Ca. Stephanie Baring and Ernest M. Leigh. M. by C. P. Haselden. Ladbroke H., January 31, 1900.

HE, SHE, AND IT. "Matrimonial scene." 1 a. Wm. Muskerry.

HE, SHE, AND THE MAJOR. F.C. 1 a. Surrey, July 23, 1904.

HE, SHE, AND THE POKER. C. 1 a. Publ. by S. French, Ltd.

HE STOOPS TO WIN. Oa. 1 a. Cunningham Bridgman. M. by Wilfred Bendall. Lyric Club, December 15, 1891.

HE THAT WILL NOT WHEN HE MAY. "Original proverb." 1 a. Herbert Gardner.

HE WOU'D IF HE COU'D; OR, AN OLD FOOL WORSE THAN ANY. Burla. 2 a. Isaac Bickerstaff. D.L. Pr. 1771. Taken fr. *La Serva Padrona.*

HE WOULD BE A BOHEMIAN. Ca. W. R. Garton. Gallery of Illus., March 12, 1870 (amateurs).

HE WOULD BE A FATHER. Sk. M. Melford. Shoreditch. London M.H., January 12, 1903.

HE WOULD BE A SAILOR; OR, BREAKERS AHEAD. D. 2 a. G. H. Hazlewood. Britannia, March 23, 1868.

HE WOULD BE A SOLDIER. C. F. Pilon. C.G., November 18, 1786, and pr. same year.

HE'S A JOLLY GOOD FELLOW. P. 4 a. A. Shirley and E. V. Edmonds. West London, May 28, 1908 (C.P.); Dalston, June 15, 1908.

HE'S A LUNATIC. F. 1 a. Felix Dale. Plot f. on *Le Fou d'en Face.* Queen's, Long Acre, October 24, 1867.

HE'S COMING. F. C. Burnand and German Reed. St. George's H. Circa 1865.

HE'S MUCH TO BLAME. C. 5 a. T. Holcroft; C.G., February 13, 1798; Pr. 1798; rev. Terry's, in 2 a., September 29, 1906.

HE'S SO NERVOUS. F. Maurice De Frece. Liverpool T.R., March 4, 1872.

HEAD OF ROMULUS, THE. Ca. Adap. fr. Scribe by Sydney Grundy. St. James's, May 10, 1900.

HEAD OF THE FAMILY, THE. Ca. 1 a. W. S. Emden. Olympic, November 14, 1859. Fr. *Le Moulin à Paroles.*

HEAD OF THE FAMILY, THE. P. 1 a. B. Knollys. R.A. of Music, May 29, 1908 (amat.).

HEAD OF THE FIRM, THE. C. 4 a. Leslie Faber. Adap. fr. the Danish of Hjalmar Bergstrom. Buxton O.H., June 13, 1908; Vaudeville, March 4, 1909.

HEAD OF THE POLL, THE. V. Arthur Law. M. by Eaton Fanning. St. Geo. H., February 28, 1882.

HEAD OR HEART. Oa. Arthur Chapman. M. by H. Martyn Van Lennep. Comedy, May 29, 1890.

HEADLESS HORSEMAN; OR, THE RIDE OF DEATH, THE. 2 a. C. H. Hazlewood. Adap. fr. Capt. Mayne Reid's novel. Britannia. 1865.

HEADLESS, MAN, THE. Fantastic D. Adelphi, 1857.

HEADLESS MAN, THE. C. 3 a. F. C. Burnand. Adap. fr. the French. Criterion, July 27, 1889, and December 21, 1893.

HEADS AND HEARTS. D. C. Burslem. Dewsbury T.R., August 20, 1877.

HEADS AND TAILS. C. Joseph Barry and W. Griffith. St. Andrew's Hosp., Northampton, April 20, 1900.

HEADS OR TAILS. Ca. 1 a. J. Palgrave Simpson. Olympic, June 29, 1854.

HEADSMAN'S AXE; OR, QUEEN, CROWN, AND COUNTRY, THE. D. 3 a. G. H. Macdermott. Grecian, October 24, 1870.

HEAR BOTH SIDES. C. Thos. Holcroft. D.L., January 29, 1803. Pr. 1803.

HEARD AT THE TELEPHONE. Transl. 2 a. of *Au Téléphone*, by MM. De Lorde and Foley. Wyndham's, March 1, 1902.

HEART OF A BROTHER, THE. D. 2 a. Britannia, May 1, 1871.

HEART OF A HERO, THE. Melo-d. 4 a. Lingford Carson. Originally prod. at T.R., Darwen, August 5, 1899; Pavilion, July 2, 1900.

HEART OF A SONGBIRD, THE. P. 1 a. M. Talfourd. Eastbourne T.R., January 26, 1901.

HEART OF A WOMAN, THE. D. 4 a. W. J. Brabner and J. S. Hardie. Stratford T.R., December 22, 1902.

HEART OF AFRICA. See *The Dark Continent.*

HEART OF GOLD, A. D. 3 a. D. Jerrold. Princess's, October 9, 1854.

HEART OF GOLD. Russo-Japanese P. Beatrice de Burgh and Lawrence Grant. Coronet, February 10, 1905.

HEART OF HEARTS. P. 3 a. H. A. Jones. Vaudeville, November 3, 1887, (evening bill), November 7, 1887.

HEART OF LONDON; OR, THE SHARPER'S PROGRESS, THE. D. Moncrieff. Adelphi, February, 1830.

HEART OF MARYLAND, THE. D. 4 a. David Belasco. Eleph. and C., September 25, 1895 (C.P.); Adelphi, April 8, 1898.

HEART OF MIDLOTHIAN, THE. O. Prod. by H. Bishop. C.G., April, 1819.

HEART OF MIDLOTHIAN; OR, THE LILY OF ST. LEONARDS, THE. D. T. Dibdin. D.L., July 13, 1821.

HEART OF MIDLOTHIAN; OR, THE SISTERS OF ST. LEONARDS, THE. D. 3 a. T. H. Lacy. Adap. fr. Sir Walter Scott.

HEART OF MIDLOTHIAN, THE. See *Jeannie Deans* and *The Trial of Effie Deans.*

HEART OF O HANA SAN, THE. Jap. P. 2 a. Clive Holland. Bournemouth, August 20, 1902.

HEART OF STONE, A. D. 4 a. Fred Moule and Charles H. Longdon. Bootle T., August 11, 1902.

HEART OF THE CITY, THE. P. 1 a. Michael Morton and Julian Wellesley. Birmingham R., March 8, 1909.

HEART OF THE MACHINE, THE. P. 3 a. A. R. Williams. Royalty, June 27, 1907.

HEART OF THE ROSE, THE. C. 3 a. Hope Roman. Kilburn Empire, December 4, 1902.

HEART OF THE WORLD, THE. P. Westland Marston. Hay., October 4, 1847.

HEART STRINGS AND FIDDLE STRINGS. F. David Fisher.

HEART'S ADRIFT. C.D. 4 a. Langdon McCormick. Birmingham Grand, February 20, 1905; Fulham, February 27, 1905.

HEART'S DELIGHT. D. 4 a. Andrew Halliday. F. on Dickens's "Dombey and Son." Globe, December 17, 1873.

HEART'S DESIRE, A. Ro. P. Pro. and 4 a. Sutton-in-Ashford King's, March 26, 1906.

HEART'S ORDEAL. City of London, August 3, 1863.

HEARTHSTONE ANGELS, THE. C. 3 a. A. Garland. Imperial, May 14, 1907.

HEARTLESS. P. Prol. and 3 a. Marion Grace Webb. F. on Ouida's novel, "Puck." Bournemouth T.R. (prod. as *Puck*), August 13, 1883; Olympic, April 18, 1885.

HEARTS. C. 1 a. W. Echard Golden. Copyright, 1592.

HEARTS. C.D. 3 a. J. C. Bertie. Bishop Auckland T.R., July 17, 1874.

HEARTS. D. 1 a. Harry Bruce. Gloucester T.R., April 20, 1891.

HEARTS, THE. C. 4 a. J. Bohun. Manchester T.R., April 29, 1904.

HEARTS AND CORONETS. C. 3 a. W. F. Downing. Worthing T.R., May 11, 1903; Fulham Grand, May 18, 1903.

HEARTS AND HAMPERS. F. Marlande Clarke. Gloucester T.R., November 21, 1881.

HEARTS AND HANDS. Manchester T.R., May 2, 1865.

HEARTS AND HOME. C. York T.R., February 11, 1876.

HEARTS ARE TRUMPS. P. 3 a. Mark Lemon. Publ. by J. Dicks.

HEARTS ARE TRUMPS. C.D. Woods Lawrence. Huddersfield T.R., March 27, 1879.

HEARTS ARE TRUMPS. D. 4 a. Cecil Raleigh. D.L., September 16, 1899.

HEARTS, HEARTS, HEARTS; OR, GOOD AND BAD. D. C. H. Hazlewood. Liverpool R. Colosseum, May 25, 1868.

HEARTS OF ERIN. Rom. Op. P. 4 a. J. Mills. Newcastle-on-Tyne Palace T., February 10, 1902.

HEARTS OF GOLD. D. 5 a. Edwd. Darbey. Keighley Queen's, February 13, 1888.

HEARTS OF GOLD. D. 1 a. Presented by W. T. Ellwanger. Camberwell Palace, January 20, 1908.

HEARTS OF OAK. Int. Merely a song and dance of sailors. Song by G. A. Stevens. 1762.

HEARTS OF OAK. C. J. T. Allingham. D.L., November 19, 1803. Pr. 1804.

HEARTS OF OAK; OR, THE CHIP OF THE OLD BLOCK. D. 2 a. H. A. Jones. Exeter T.R., May 29, 1879.

HEARTS OF THE WEST. D. 4 a. J. R. Cassidy. Darwen T.R., December 3, 1896.

HEARTS OR DIAMONDS. Duol. Ina Leon Cassilis. Steinway H., May 12, 1891.

HEARTSEASE. D. 4 a. James Mortimer. Adap. of *La Dame aux Camélias*. Princess's, June 5, 1875; Court, May 1, 1880; Olympic, January 9, 1892.

HEARTY PARTY. Fairy P. 1 a. E. P. Medley. Publ. by S. French, Ltd.

HEATHEN AND THE CHRISTIAN, THE. O.D. 4 a. F. Maxwell. Edmonton T.R., May 31, 1902; Manchester St. James's, July 8, 1907; Greenwich, January 25, 1909.

HEATHEN GODDESS, A. F.C. 1 a. J. E. McManus. Southend Empire, June 3, 1901; Greenwich Carlton, June 10, 1901.

HEATHEN MARTYR; OR, THE DEATH OF SOCRATES, THE. Hist. T. Geo. Adams. Pr. 1746.

HEATHER FIELD, THE. P. 3 a. Eduard Martyn. Dublin Antient Concert R., May 9, 1899; Terry's, June 6, 1899.

HEAUTONTIMORUMENOS. C. Terence. Transl. by Richard Bernard, 1598; Laurence Echard, pr. 1694; Bentley, 1726; T. Cooke, pr. 1734; S. Patrick, pr. 1745; Gordon, pr. 1752; pro., int. and epil., as ac. at Beverly School, 1756, pr. 1757, wr. by Wm. Warde, the master; G. Colman, pr. 1765; Anon., pr. 1777; Barry, 1857. See *All Fools*. See "Latin Plays."

HEAUTONTIMORUMENOS; OR, THE SELF-TORMENTOR. C. Terence. Transl. by Richard Bernard, pr. 1598; Charles Hoole, pr. 1663.

HEAVEN AND EARTH. Mystery. Byron. 1822.

HEAVY FATHERS. F. Hilton. Folly, April 14, 1879.

HEBER SAYELL. P. 1 a. Dorothea Wilson Barrett. Bristol Prince's, May 24, 1907.

HEBREW, THE. D. 5 a. F. on *Ivanhoe*. D.L., March 2, 1820.

HEBREW, THE. City of London, February 9, 1852.

HECATE'S PROPHECY. D. ? By Wm. Shirley. Pr. 1758.

HECTOR. Dr. Poem. Richard Shepherd. Pr. 1770.

HECTOR. T. Transl. fr. the French of J. C. J. Luce de Lancival by Edward Mangin. Pr. 1810. N.ac.

HECTOR. T. John Galt. Pr. 1815. ? N.ac.

HECTOR: HIS LIFE AND DEATH. Hist. P. Thos. Heywood. 1614.

HECTOR OF GERMAINE; OR, THE PALSGRAVE PRIME ELECTOR, THE. Hist. P. Wm. Smith. Ac. at Red Bull and The Curtain. Not divided into acts. Pr. 1615.

HECTOR'S RETRIBUTION. D. J. Harwood Panting. Walworth Inst., February 9, 1881.

HECTORS, THE. T. Edmund Prestwich. 1650.

HECTORS; OR, THE FALSE CHALLENGE, THE. C. Anon. Pr. 1656.

HECUBA. T. Richard West, Lord Chancellor of Ireland. D.L., February 2, 1726, pr. 1726, transl. fr. Euripides; transl. by Dr. Thos. Morell, pr. 1749; Dr. Delap, pr. 1762, D.L., December 11, 1761; Michael Wodhull, pr. 1782; R. Potter, pr. 1783. See "Greek Plays."

HECUBA A LA MODE. Classical Burl. 2 a. Cranstown Metcalfe. Anerley Vestry H., May 1, 1893.

HECYRA; OR, THE STEPMOTHER. English transl. of Terence's comedy by Richard Bernard. Pr. 1598. For the several translations of Terence's comedies see *Heautontimoroumenos*. See "Latin Plays."

HEDDA GABLER. P. 4 a. Henrik Ibsen. Vaudeville, April 20, 1891; St. Geo. H., November 26, 1901. Italian ver. (Eleanora Duse season), Adelphi, October 7, 1903; Court, March 5, 1907.

HEDGE CARPENTER, THE. D. C. H. Hazlewood. Britannia, February 7, 1870.

HEDONISTS, THE. C. 4 a. Mrs. G. C. Ashton Jonson. Wyndham's, July 4, 1902.

HEEL OF ACHILLES, THE. P. Prol. and 4 a. L. N. Parker and Boyle Lawrence. Globe, February 6, 1902.

HEIGHO FOR A HUSBAND! C. F. G. Waldron. Alt. fr. *Imitation*, by the same author. Hay., July 14, 1794. Pr. 1794.

HEIMATH. See *Magda*.

HEIMCHEN AM HERD, DAS. O. 3 a. Goldmark. Lib. by A. M. Willner. Lib. f. on Dickens's *Cricket on the Hearth*. Prod. in Germany, 1896, and in English at Brixton T. November 22, 1900.

HEIMKEHR AUS DER FREMDE. Oa. Mendelssohn. Wr. to wds. by Klingemann and comp. in London for the silver wedding of Mendelssohn's parents. December 26, 1829.

HEINRICH; OR, FROM FATHERLAND TO THE FAR WEST. D. Pro. and 2 a. Julian Cross. Bristol New T.R., April 3, 1876.

HEIR, THE. C. Thos. May. Ac. 1620. Pr. 1622. ? Some ideas taken from Shakespeare.

HEIR-AT-LAW, THE. C. 5 a. Geo. Colman the younger. Hay., June 15, 1797. Pr. 1808. D.L., September 23, 1815; Hay., October, 1866; Strand, February 5, 1870; Waldorf, 1906. See *The Lord's Warming Pan*.

HEIR FROM THE OCEAN; OR, GOLDEN EVIDENCE, AN. Dublin Queen's, September 25, 1871.

HEIR OF LINN, THE. Rom. Poetical P. 5 a. Chas. Waddie. Glasgow Athenæum, October 9, 1899.

HEIR OF MOROCCO, WITH THE DEATH OF GAYLAND, THE. T. Elkanah Settle. Ac. at T.R. Pr. 1682.

HEIR OF VIRONI. M.D. Pocock. M. by Whitaker, 1817.

HEIRESS, THE. C. Ascr. to Lieut.-Gen. John Burgoyne. F. on Diderot's *Père de Famille*. Pr. 1786. D.L., January 14, 1786; rev., D.L., June 18, 1816.

HEIRESS, THE. Dion Boucicault. C.G., February, 1842.

HEIRESS, THE. C. 2 a. Mary Seymour. Pub. by S. French, Limited.

HEIRESS; OR, THE ANTI-GALLICAN, THE. F. Thos. Mozeen. D.L., May 21, 1759. Pr. 1762.

HEIRESS HUNTING. C. Edwd. Bucknall. Richmond H.M.T., February 27, 1882.

HEIRESS OF BRUGES, THE. P. 2 a. C. Selby. Pub. by J. Dicks.

HEIRESS OF DAVENTRY, THE. Dom. D. W. A. Brabner. Glasgow Metropole, June 28, 1899 (C.P.).

HEIRESS OF HAZLEDENE, THE. D. Edwd. Darbey. Bilston T.R., August 4, 1893.

HEIRESS OF MAES-Y-FELIN; OR, THE FLOWER OF LLANDOVERY, THE. P. 5 a. A. W. Ward. Merthyr Tydfil Victoria T., February 2, 1893 (C.P.).

HEIRS OF RABOURDIN, THE. A. Teixeira de Mattos. Transl. of "Les Héritiers de Rabourdin," by Emile Zola. Op. C., February 24, 1894 (Indept. T. Society).

HELD APART; OR, THE PAINTED WOMAN. D. 5 a. Frank Adair. Revised vers. of *The Painted Woman* (Clapham Shakespeare, July 21, 1902). Clapham Shakespeare, August 27, 1906.

HELD ASUNDER. D. 4 a. Malcolm Watson. P.O.W., April 3, 1888.

HELD AT BAY; OR, THE EXILED MOTHER. D. Marylebone, September 1, 1879.

HELD BY THE ENEMY. D. 5 a. Wm. Gillette. Ladbroke H., February 20, 1886 (C.P.); Princess's, April 2, 1887, (evening bill) April 9, 1887; transferred to Vaudeville, July 2, 1887.

HELD IN HARNESS. C.D. 4 a. C. A. Clarke. Keighley Queen's T., May 29, 1890.

HELD IN JUDGMENT. D. N. S. Campbell. Garston Britannia, November 11, 1891.

HELD IN SLAVERY. D. Martin Haydon. Spennymore Cambridge T., September 3, 1894.

HELD IN TERROR. Dom. D. 4 a. Frank Dix. Bristol T.R., June 21, 1897; Imperial, August 29, 1898.

HELD UP. P. 4 a. Bret Harte and T. Edgar Pemberton. Bedford County, August 3, 1903; Worcester T.R., August 24, 1903.

HELD WITH HONOUR. D. 4 a. Roy Cochrane. Bordesley Imperial T., October 14, 1902.

HELEN. T. Transl. fr. Euripides by Michael Wodhull. Pr. 1782. See "Greek Plays."

HELEN; OR, TAKEN FROM THE GREEK. Burl. 3 scenes. Adap. by F. C. Burnand and M. Williams of *La Belle Hélène*. M. by Offenbach. Liverpool P.O.W., September 30, 1867; Adelphi ?

HELEN AND PARIS. O. Glück. Lib. by Calzabigi. 1768.

HELEN DOUGLAS. D. 5 a. Hay., July 18, 1870.

HELEN OAKLEIGH. P. 2 a. J. S. Coyne. Pub. by J. Dicks.

HELEN OF TROY UP TO DATE; OR, THE STATUE SHOP. F. M. "Absurdetta." Wilton Jones. M. by John Crook. Folkestone Pier T., May 22, 1893.

HELEN'S BABIES. F. Garnet Walch. Gaiety, September 15, 1878.

HELEN'S LITTLE SUBTERFUGE. C. 3 a. Wr. by R. Bottomley. Queen's Gate Hall, June 12, 1907.

HELENA. T. Transl. fr. Euripides by R. Potter. Pr. 1783. Wodhull. 1782.

HELENA IN TROAS. D. 2 a. John Todhunter. Hengler's Circus, May 17, 1886.

HELENE. O. 1 a. Saint Saëns. C.G., June 20, 1904; and Paris Opera Comique, January 18, 1905.

HELIOGABALUS, THE LIFE AND DEATH OF. Int. Ent. by John Danter at Stationers' Co., June 19, 1594. N.p.

HELL'S HIGH COURT OF JUSTICE; OR, THE TRYAL OF THE THREE POLITIC GHOSTS. By J. D. Pr. 1661. N.ac.

HELLAS. Orat. Percy Bysshe Shelley. M. by Dr. Christian Wm. Sellé. Prod. by Shelley Society, St. James's H., November 16, 1886.

HELLO, BILL. Farc. C. 3 a. Llandudno Grand, June 2, 1909 (C.P.).

HELOTS, THE. T. Rev. H. Boyd. Pr. 1793. N.ac.

HELP IN TIME. Mus. sk. C. Rennel. Criterion, June 14, 1879.

HELPING A FRIEND. F.C. 3 a. W. H. Denny. Strand, May 19, 1899.

HELPING HANDS, Do. D. 2 a. Tom Taylor. Adelphi, June 20, 1855.

HELPLESS ANIMALS. F. 1 a. Parry. C.G., November 17, 1819.

HELPLESS COUPLE. Ca. 1 a. M. Hayman. Publ. by S. French, Ltd.

HELPS. Ca. Alfred F. Robbins. Lincoln T.R., December 13, 1877.

HELTER-SKELTER. F.C. 3 a. Walter Browne. Sheffield Alexandra, May 28, 1886.

HELTER-SKELTER; OR, THE DEVIL UPON TWO STICKS. C. E. Ward. 1704.

HELVELLYN. O. Macfarren. 1864.

HELVETIC LIBERTY; OR, THE LASS OF THE LAKES. Op. By a Kentish Bowman. Founded on William Tell. Pr. 1792.

HEN AND CHICKENS, THE. C.D. B. Webster. Adelphi.

HENGES (OR HENGIST). Ac. June 22, 1597.

HENLEY REGATTA. M.Sk. Corney Grain. St. George's H., June 14, 1886.

HENPECK'D CAPTAIN; OR, THE HUMOURS OF THE MILITIA, THE. F. Richd. Cross. D.L., April 29, 1749. Taken fr. Durfey's *Campaigners*.

HENRI QUATRE; OR, THE OLDEN TIME. Hist. P. 2 a. D.L., June 21, 1825.

HENRIADE. See "Epic Poems."

HENRIETTA, THE. C. 4 a. Bronson Howard. Orig. prod. in New York. Eleph. and C., September 23, 1887; Avenue, March 28, 1891.

HENRIETTA, THE FORSAKEN. D. 3 a. Adap. fr. the French by J. B. Buckstone. Adelphi, November, 1832.

HENRIETTE; OR, THE FARM OF SENANGE. Fr. the French *D. Therese, the Orphan of Geneva*. C.G., February 23, 1821. N.p.

HENRIETTE DESCHAMPS. D. Carre. 1863.

HENRIQUE; OR, THE LOVE PILGRIM. O. 3 a. Wds. by T. J. Haines. M. by Rooke. C.G., May 2, 1839.

HENRIQUE, PRINCE OF SICILY. T. Unfinished. Greenfield. Pr. 1790.

HENRIQUEZ. T. Joanna Baillie. D.L., March 19, 1836.

HENRY I. Old Hist. P. Circa 1580.

HENRY I. AND HENRY II. Wm. Shakespeare and Robt. Davenport. Ent. Stationers Co., September 9, 1653. Destroyed by Warburton's servant.

HENRY II. Hist. D. Ascr. to W. H. Ireland. Pr. 1799.

HENRY II.; OR, THE FALL OF ROSAMOND. T. Thos. Hull. C.G., May 1, 1773. Pr. 1774.

HENRY II., KING OF ENGLAND, WITH THE DEATH OF ROSAMOND. T. John Bancroft. Pr. 1693. Epil. by Dryden. Ac. at D.L.

HENRY III. D.L., June 22, 1893.

HENRY III. OF FRANCE, STABBED BY A FRIAR, with the Fall of the Guises. T. Thos. Shipman. D.L. Pr. 1678.

HENRY III. Hist. D. Dumas. 1829.

HENRY IV. Ac. at Lord Essex's house the night before his insurrection and was even then considered an ancient drama.

HENRY IV. (in two parts). W. Shakespeare. F. on Holinshed's "Chronicle" and "The Famous Victories of King Henry the Fifth, containing the Honourable Battle of Agincourt, 1594." Part I. Wr. 1597. Entered at Stationers' H., February 25, 1598. Quartos 1598, 1599, 1604, 1608, 1613, 1622, 1632, and 1639. First folio 1623. Part II. Wr. 1598. Entered at Stationers' H., August 23, 1600. First quarto 1600. First folio 1623. Rev. by J. P. Kemble, C.G. Pr. 1803-4. Part II. alt. by Dr. Valpy, Reading School. Pr. 1801. Part I. rev. at Hay., May 8, 1896; Lyceum (by Irving A.D.C.), March 29, 1890. Part II. rev. by Louis Calvert, Manchester Prince's, March 22, 1898; H.M., April 24, 1906; Coronet, February 25, 1908; rev. 1st part, Lyric, May 11, 1909 (mat.).

HENRY IV., with the Humours of Sir John Falstaff. T.C. Adap. by Thos. Betterton. L.I.F. Pr. 1700.

HENRY IV. O. Balfe. 1834.

HENRY IV. OF FRANCE. T. Chas. Beckingham. Pr. 1719. L.I.F.

HENRY V., THE FAMOUS VICTORIES OF. Ac. by King's servants. Pr. (n.d.).

HENRY V., THE CHRONICLE HISTORY OF. Hist. P. 4 a. Wm. Shakespeare. Wr. 1599. Entered Stationers' H., August 4, 1600 ("to be stayed"); August 14, 1600. F. on same source as *Henry IV*. Quartos 1600 (imperfect), 1602, 1608. First folio 1623. Alt. by J. P. Kemble. D.L. and C.G. ? Pr. 1806. Princess's, March. 1859; staged by Martin Harvey and William Mollison, Lyceum, December 22, 1900; rev. by Martin Harvey, Imperial, January 21, 1905; Coronet, February 26, 1908; rev. Lyric, November 25, 1908.

HENRY V. T. Roger Boyle, Earl of Orrery. Pr. 1672. Ac. at D. of York's T. (n.d.).

HENRY V. Sk. Surrey, April 19, 1909.

HENRY V.; OR, THE CONQUEST OF FRANCE, KING. Hist. T. Pr. 1789. Curtailed fr. Shakespeare by J. P. Kemble. D.L. Ed. by James Wrighten, prompter.

HENRY V.; OR, THE CONQUEST OF FRANCE BY THE ENGLISH. T. Aaron Hill. D.L. Pr. 1723. Borr. fr. Shakespeare.

HENRY VI. Henslowe mentions a P. with this title as having been ac. March 3, 1591.

HENRY VI. Hist. P., in three parts. W. Shakespeare, although generally contended to have been only partly wr. by him. F. on Holinshed's "Chronicles." Part I. Wr. before 1592, when it was ac. by Lord Strange's men at the Rose T. Entered at Stationers' Hall, "*Henry VI.*, First and Second Parts; (2 and 3 *Henry VI.*), April 19, 1602." Part II. "The First Part of the Contention betwixt the Two Famous Houses of York and Lancaster." Entered at Stationers' Hall, March 12, 1594. Quartos 1594, 1600, and 1619 with Part III. Part III. "The True Tragedy of Richard Duke of York." Quartos 1595, 1600, and 1619 with Part II. The three parts are included in the 1st Folio, 1623. See *True Tragedy of Richard, Duke of York.*

HENRY VI. (THE FIRST PART), WITH THE DEATH OF THE DUKE OF GLOUCESTER. T. John Crowne. Duke's T. Pr. 1681. (Partly fr. Shakespeare.)

HENRY VI. (THE SECOND PART); OR, THE MISERIES OF CIVIL WAR. T. John Crowne. Duke's T. Pr. 1681. First pr. by the second title only, 1680. (Fr. Shakespeare.)

HENRY VI. Theophilus Cibber. Pr. (n.d.) circa 1723. An alt. from Shakespeare. D.L.

HENRY VI. Shakespeare's P., rev. by Edmund Kean. D.L., 1817.

HENRY VII.; OR, THE POPISH IMPOSTOR KING. T. C. Macklin. D.L., 1746. Pr. 1746.

HENRY VII. Hist. D. 2 a. J. R. Furness. Conway, November 28, 1900.

HENRY VIII.: THE FAMOUS HISTORY OF HIS LIFE. Hist. P. W. Shakespeare. Ac. as a new P. when the Globe was burned, 1613. Probably wr. 1611. F. on Holinshed's "Chronicle" and Cavendish's "Life of Wolsey." Pr. First Folio 1623. Rev. by J. P. Kemble, C.G. Pr. 1804. Arr. by Henry Irving. M. by Edward German. Lyceum, January 5, 1892.

HENRY VIII. O. 4 a. Camille Saint Saëns. Prod. in Paris, 1883; C.G., July 14, 1898.

HENRY VIII., WITH THE CORONATION OF ANNE BOLEYN. D.L., December 13, 1732.

HENRY VIII. Shakespeare's P. Hist. Notes by Joseph Grove. Pr. 1758.

HENRY AND ALMERIA. T. Andrew Birrel. Pr. 1802.

HENRY AND EMMA. Pastoral Int. Henry Bate. Alt. fr. Prior. C.G., April 13, 1774. N.p.

HENRY AND EMMA; OR, THE NUT-BROWN MAID. M.D. Taken fr. Prior. C.G., 1749. Songs by Dr. Arne were pr. 1749.

HENRY AND ROSAMOND. T. Wm Hawkins. Pr. 1749. N. ac.

HENRY DUNBAR. D. 4 a. Tom Taylor. F. on Miss Braddon's novel. Olympic, December 9, 1865; Adelphi, 1867. See *Jesmond Dene.*

HENRY ESMOND. P. Prol. and 3 a. T. Edgar Pemberton. Adap. fr. Thackeray. Lyceum, Edinburgh, March 5, 1897; Crouch End Queen's O.H., November 26, 1897.

HENRY OF ENGLAND. Rom. p., in prol. and 3 a. Clive Lethbridge and John de Stourton. Bayswater, March 4, 1909 (C.P.).

HENRY OF LANCASTER. Rom. d. Gladys Unger. Nottingham R.T., February 28, 1908; Stratford Borough, April 27, 1908.

HENRY OF NAVARRE. Rom. p. 4 a. Wm. Devereux. Newcastle R., November 5, 1908; New, January 7, 1909.

HENRY OF TRANSTAMARE. T. Anon. Ac. at Edinburgh, November 1, 1805.

HENRY RICHMOND. P. 2 parts. Robert Wilson. Ac. by Lord Admiral's Servants. 1599.

HENWITCHERS. Ca. 1 a. Percy Fitzgerald. Hay., December 2, 1878.

HER ADVOCATE. P. 3 a. Walter Frith. Duke of York's. September 26, 1895.

HER ANSWER. Mus. duol. Wr. by S. Adair Fitzgerald. M. by Napoleon Lambelet. Coronet, July 22, 1907.

HER ATONEMENT: OR, MISS MULTON. American D. Windsor T.R., August 31, 1885.

HER BIRTHDAY. Dr. Sk. Sir C. Young. Lewes Concert H., August 13, 1884.

HER BIRTHDAY. P. 1 a. Gerald Young. Hastings Public H., January 18, 1899.

HER BROTHER. F. Thos. Courtice. Carlisle Her M., July 8, 1901.

HER CONVICT LOVER. Sk. 1 a. A. Jefferson. Glasgow Metropole, January 29, 1907. (C.P.); Camberwell Palace, July 22, 1907.

HER COUNTRY'S ENEMY. Sk. Bedford, June 22, 1908.

HER COUSIN FRANK. F. George Capel. Surrey, June 2, 1879.

HER DEAREST FOE. C.D. 4 a. Miss Henrietta Lindley. Adap. fr. Mrs. Alexander's novel. Criterion, May 2, 1894.

HER DEAREST FRIEND. P. 1 a. Rose mary Rees. Coronet, February 4, 1907.

HER DEVONSHIRE DAD. Sk. 1 sc. Victor Widdicombe. Canterbury, July 29, 1907.

HER FATAL MARRIAGE. P. a. Clarence Brunette and A. Hinton. Aston R., December 28, 1908; Woolwich R., January 25, 1909.

HER FATAL PAST. D. 4 a. Nita Rae. West London. February 15, 1904.

HER FATHER. D. 3 a. E. Rose and J. Douglass. F. on José Echegwray's Spanish D., *Conflicto Entre dos Deberes*. Vaudeville, May 16, 1889.

HER FATHER. P. 4 a. Adap. fr. Albert Guinon and Alfred Bouchinet's *Son Père* by Michael Morton. Orig. prod. Paris Odeon, October 31, 1907. Hay., January 28, 1908.

HER FATHER'S FRIEND. Rom. P. 3 a. H. A. Rudall. Savoy, June 29, 1896.

HER FATHER'S SIN. D. 4 a. Strand, July 23, 1889.

HER FIRST. Sk. Holborn Empire, May 24, 1909.

HER FIRST APPEARANCE. Monol. Haslingden Russell. Liverpool R. Court T., November 7, 1890.

HER FIRST BALL. Monol. John Cutler, Q.C. Terry's, June 29, 1899.

HER FIRST ENGAGEMENT. Ca. Myra Swan. Middlesbrough T.R., March 5, 1894.

HER FIRST FALSE STEP. D. Prol. and 4 a. Myles Wallerton and Francis Gilbert. Shakespeare, January 30, 1905 (C.P.).

HER FORBIDDEN MARRIAGE. D. 5 a. F. Melville. Rotherhithe Terriss, April 4, 1904.

HER GOOD NAME. A "climax" in 1 a. Bernard Espinasse. Imperial, April 17, 1902.

HER GRACE. C. 1 a. Forbes Dawson. Croydon Grand, March 11, 1901; Coronet, May 24, 1906.

HER GRACE THE REFORMER. Ca. 1 a. Mrs. H. de la Pasture. Hay., January 12, 1907.

HER GREAT MISTAKE. Do. D. 4 a. Frank Stuart. East Oxford, September 9, 1907.

HER GUARDIAN. Ca. J. R. Brown. Royalty, March 9, 1895.

HER KING. Rom. P. 4 a. Harold Whyte. Peckham Crown, September 9, 1908 (C.P.).

HER LADYSHIP. P. 3 a. Geo. Manville Fenn. Adap. fr. his own novel, "The Master of the Ceremonies." Strand, March 27, 1889.

HER LADYSHIP'S DAUGHTER. P. 1 a. Miss Everetta Lawrence. Bayswater Bijou, December 6, 1902.

HER LADYSHIP'S GUARDIAN. Liverpool Amphitheatre, July 24, 1865.

HER LAST CARD. P. 3 a. Mrs. K. Donald Rayne. Lincoln T.R., March 18, 1904.

HER LAST CHANCE. Sk. R. Oliver. M. by L. La Rondelle. Chelsea, January 7, 1907.

HER LEVEL BEST. C.D. Prol. and 3 a. Mark Melford. Brighton Eden T., November 9, 1894

HER LOST SELF. D. 4 a. Nita Rae. Portsmouth Prince's, December 18, 1905; Stratford R., April 30, 1906.

HER LOVE AGAINST THE WORLD. Rom. P. 4 a. Walter Howard. Manchester Junction, September 17, 1906; March 30, 1907.

HER LOVE FOR HIM. D. 4 a. Mary Stafford Smith. Hammersmith Lyric, August 27, 1906.

HER LUCK IN LONDON. D. 4 a. Chas. Darrell. Blackpool Grand, November 16, 1905; Castleford T.R., January 1, 1906; London prod., Grand, N., August 27, 1906.

HER MAJESTY'S GUESTS. Kennington, March 26, 1900.

HER MARRIAGE VOW. D. 4 a. Owen Davis. (C.P.) Dudley O.H., October 11; Blyth Royal, August 5, 1907; Pav., December 7, 1908.

HER MOTHER'S RANSOM. D. 4 a. Preston Marchant. Rugby T.R., May 7, 1891.

HER NAMELESS CHILD. D. 4 a. Madge Duckworth and R. Barrie. (C.P.) Tonypandy T.R., June 18, 1906; prod., Devonport Met., July 9, 1906; Shakespeare, July 8, 1907.

HER NEW DRESSMAKER. Ca. W. R. Walkes. Newcastle-on-Tyne T.R., December 18, 1891; St. Geo. H., May 14, 1895, and May 13, 1899.

HER NEXT NOVEL. Ca. Kitty Smart. Prod. by amat. Ladbroke Hall, November 22, 1906.

HER OATH. D. 5 a. Mrs. Harry Wilde. Princess's, November 26, 1891.

HER ONE GREAT SIN. D. 4 a. Frank M. Thorne. Broughton V.T., October 21, 1901; Rotherhithe Terriss, June 29, 1903.

HER OWN ENEMY. D. Adap. fr. Miss Florence Marryat's novel. First prod. in New York under the title of *Pique*. First time in England as *Only a Woman*. Brighton T.R., October 16, 1882; Gaiety (present title), March 26, 1884.

HER OWN RIVAL. Ca. Fred Broughton and Boyle Lawrence. Op. Comique, April 13, 1889.

HER OWN WAY. P. 4 a. Clyde Fitch. Lyric, April 25, 1905.

HER OWN WITNESS. P. 3 a. G. H. R. Dabbs, M.D. Criterion, November 6, 1889.

HER PARTNER IN SIN. D. 4 a. G. B. Nichols and Geo. Conquest. Surrey, November 2, 1903.

HER PRINCELY BETRAYER. Rom. Epis. 1 a. R. Wilton. Stoke Newington Pal., March 9, 1908.

HER PROPER MATE. P. 1 a. Ashton Pearse. Playhouse, February 9, 1909 (mat.).

HER RELEASE. P. 1 a. Henry Edlin. Folkestone Pier T., June 1, 1892.

HER RETALIATION. D. 3 a. Chas. Vorzanzer. Homerton South Hackney Club, November 18, 1889.

HER RETURN. Sk. Middlesex, August 2, 1909.

HER ROAD TO RUIN. D. Fredk. Melville. Terriss's, May 20, 1907.

HER ROYAL HIGHNESS. Extrav. 2 a. Basil Hood. M. by Walter Slaughter. Bournemouth T.R., August 22, 1898; Vaudeville, September 3, 1898.

HER SECOND LOVE. Arthur Shirley. A rev. ver. of *Passion's Power*. Adap. fr. Jules Claretie's *Le Prince Zilah*. Orig. prod. at N. Cross Pub. H., March 25, 1886; Birmingham P.O.W., June 13, 1887.

HER SECOND TIME ON EARTH. D. 4 a. Walter Melville. Standard, October 9, 1902; rev. Adelphi, May 16, 1903.

HER SECRET. P. G. F. Courtney. Shoreham Swiss Gardens, November 24, 1897.

HER SECRET LOVER. P. 4 a. Mrs. F. S. Kimberley. Dudley O.H., December 1, 1908 (C.P.); Wolverhampton R., February 8, 1909

HER SECRET SIN. D. 4 a. A. Shirley and B. Landeck. Dalston, October 27, 1902.

HER SON. C. 4 a. H. A. Vachell, a dr. vers. of his novel of same name. Glasgow T.R., November 15, 1906; Playhouse, March 12, 1907; rev. New, September 4, 1907.

HER TALISMAN. C.D. Fredk. Scott. Surrey Masonic H., Camberwell, January 16, 1896.

HER TRUE COLOURS. Ca. W. A. Brabner. Ruthin Assembly R., November 6, 1891; Avenue, June 10, 1892.

HER TRUSTEE. D. 4 a. James J. Blood. Vaudeville, March 2, 1887.

HER TWO LOVERS. Ca. Keith Lonsdale. Ealing T., May 25, 1903.

HER VOTE. C. 1 a. H. V. Esmond. Playhouse, May 18, 1909 (mat.); Court, June 24, 1909 (mat.).

HER WEDDING DAY. D. 4 a. E. T. de Banzie. Glasgow Royalty, March 28, 1895 (C.P.); Reading R. County, September 30, 1895; Surrey, May 8, 1899.

HER WEDDING DRESS. Oa. F. Llewellyn. M. by A. Wigley. Lyrics by A. Saxby. Putney Assem. Rooms, March 1, 1907.

HER WILD OATS. C. 4 a. J. Bickerdyke and W. G. King. Wallingford Corn Exchange, February 21, 1906.

HER WORLD AGAINST A LIE. D. Pro. and 3 a. Florence Marryat and Geo. F. Neville. Barrow Alhambra, May 24, 1880; Adelphi, February 12, 1881.

HERACLIDÆ, THE. T. R. Potter. Transl. fr. Euripides. Pr. 1781.

HERACLIDES, LES. T. Marmontel. 1752.

HERACLIUS. See "French Classical Plays" transl. fr Corneille. Ac. circa 1664.

HERACLIUS, EMPEROR OF THE EAST. T. Lodowick Carlell. Little more than a transl. fr. Corneille. Pr. 1664. N.ac.

HERBERGPRINSES. O. Block. Antwerp, 1896. Given in French as *Princesse d'Aubérgé* in Brussels and elsewhere.

HERCULES. P. in 2 parts. Martin Slaughter. Ac. by the Lord Admiral's servants, 1598.

HERCULES. M.D. Thos. Broughton. M. by Handel. Hay. Pr. 1745.

HERCULES. T. R. Potter. Transl. fr. Euripides. Pr. 1781.

HERCULES. T. Sir Edw. Sherburne, Bart. Transl. fr. Seneca.

HERCULES AND OMPHALE. Pant. C.G., November 21, 1794.

HERCULES AND OMPHALE; OR, THE POWER OF LOVE. Extrav. Wm. Brough. St. James's T., December 26, 1864.

HERCULES DISTRACTED. Michael Wodhull. Transl. fr. Euripides. Pr. 1782. See "Greek Plays."

HERCULES FURENS. T. Jasper Heywood. Pr. 1561. Transl. fr. Seneca.

HERCULES, KING OF CLUBS. F. 1 a Frederick Cooper. Strand, July 28, 1836.

HERCULES, ŒTÆUS. T. J. Studly. Transl. fr. Seneca. Pr. 1581. Thought by some to be an imitation of the Traxiniai of Sophocles.

HERCULOUS. Two parts. Anon 1595.

HERE AND THERE AND EVERYWHERE. Pant. Hay., 1785.

HERE SHE GOES. Sk. W. Sapte, jun. Princess's, January 25, 1896.

HERE'S ANOTHER GUY MANNERING. Burl. F. C. Burnand. Vaudeville, May 23, 1874.

HEREWARD. Cant. E. Prout.

HERIOD AND MARIAMNE. T. Samuel Pordage. Plot fr. Josephus, the Story of Tyridates in Cleopatra, and the Unfortunate Politic; or, The Life of Herod. Trans. fr. the French. Duke's T. Pr. 1673.

HERITAGE DE MONSIEUR PLUMET, L'. See *Mr. Gull's Fortune*.

HERLEVE OF NORMANDY, MOTHER OF THE CONQUEROR. H.P. Fr. ancient chronicles, by M. Jehan Sawan de Pierrefitte, songs by M. Gaston de Raismes (played in French). St. Leonards-on-Sea, R. Concert H., August 24, 1903.

HERMANI; OR, THE PLEDGE OF HONOUR. P. 5 a. Jas. Kenney. Fr. Victor Hugo. D.L., April 8, 1831.

HERMANN; OR, THE BROKEN SPEAR. M. by John Thomson. Lyceum, October 27, 1834.

HERMESIANAX. Burl. Derby Lecture H., July 9, 1869.

HERMINE. P. 1 a. Chas. Thomas. Court, September 24, 1888.

HERMINIUS AND ESPASIA. T. Ascr. to Chas. Hart. Pr. 1754.

HERMIONE; OR, VALOUR TRIUMPHANT, THE. Inc. Chas. Dibdin. C.G., April 22, 1800. N.p.

HERMIT, THE. C.O. 3 a. Chas. Whitlock. M. by T. G. W. Goddard. Wolverhampton T.R., June 20, 1892.

HERMIT, THE. Ca. Bertha Moore. Royalty, June 6, 1905.

HERMIT; OR, HARLEQUIN AT RHODES, THE. Mr. Love. Pant. D.L., 1766. N.p.

HERMIT; OR, QUARTER DAY. B.O. Anon, 1792.

HERMIT CONVERTED; OR, THE MAID OF BATH MARRIED, THE. Adam Moses Emanuel Cooke. Pr. (n.d.) c. 1771.

HERMIT OF WARKWORTH. T. Anon, 1789.

HERMON, PRINCE OF CHORÆA; OR, THE EXTRAVAGANT ZEALOT. T. Dr. Clancy. Pr. 1746. Ac. in Ireland.

HERMOPHUS. A Latin C. George Wilde. Ac. several times, but n.p.

HERNANI; OR, THE DOUBLE WRONG. D. Chas. Osborne. Belfast T.R., October 5, 1868.

HERNE THE HUNTER. P. 3 a. T. P. Taylor. Publ. by J. Dicks.

HERNE THE HUNTER. Panto. Burl. Robert Reece and W. Yardley. Gaiety, May 24, 1881.

HERNE THE HUNTER. D. 5 a. Kenneth M. Bryant. Burnley Victoria O.H. (C.P.), August 26, 1900.

HERNE THE HUNTER. H.B. 3 a. Harry Rogerson. F. on H. Ainsworth's novel, "Windsor Castle." M. by Alfred Sugden and Arthur Lester. South Shields T.R., July 28, 1902.

HERNE'S OAK; OR, THE ROSE OF WINDSOR. C.O. Walter Parke. M. by J. C. Bond Andrews. Liverpool P.O.W., October 24, 1887.

HERO AND HEROINE. Melo-d. F. 1 a. Scala, December 17, 1905.

HERO AND LEANDER. T. Sir Robert Stapylton. Pr. 1669. ? ac. Plot fr. Ovid's "Epistles" and Musæus's "Erotopaignion."

HERO AND LEANDER. Burl. Isaac Jackman. Royalty T. Pr. 1787.

HERO AND LEANDER. Christopher Marlowe. Completed by Chapman and Petowe.

HERO AND LEANDER. P. 3 a. Kyrle Bellew. Suggested by Grillparzer's ver. of the mythological legend. Manchester Prince's, May 9, 1892; Shaftesbury, June 2, 1892.

HERO OF AN HOUR, A. F. Knight Summers. Charing Cross, September 29, 1869.

HERO OF HEROES, A. D. 5 a. J. W. Whitbread. Dublin Queen's T., August 12, 1889. See *Lured to Ruin*.

HERO OF JAPAN, A. M. Sk. John Morland. Collins's M.H., July 10, 1905.

HERO OF JERUSALEM, THE. D. 4 a., with music. Sigmund H. Fineman. Standard, June 13, 1896.

HERO OF ROMANCE, A. D. Prol. and 5 tab. Westland Marston. Hay., March 14, 1868.

HERO OF THE FLAG, THE. Nav. and Dom. D. Sydney Spenser. Woolwich R. Artillery, March 2, 1903.

HERO OF THE NORTH. P. 3 a. W. Dimond. Pr. 1805.

HERO OF TRAFALGAR, THE. D. 5 tab. W. P. Sheen. Alexandra Palace, October 21, 1905.

HEROD. P. 3 a. Stephen Philips. Her Maj. Th., October 31, 1900.

HEROD AND ANTIPATER, WITH THE DEATH OF FAIR MARIAM. T. Gervase Markham and Wm. Sampson. Red Bull. Plot fr. Josephus's "Antiquities of the Jews." Pr. 1622.

HEROD AND MARIAMNE. See *Heriod and Mariamne*.

HEROD THE GREAT. T. Roger Boyle, Earl of Orrery. Pr. 1694. N.ac.

HEROD THE GREAT. Dr. Poem. Francis Peek. Pr. 1740.

HEROD THE TETRACH. D. Matthew Wardhaugh. Barnsley Queen's, February 16, 1874.

HERODES. A Latin T. Wm. Goldingham. MS. in library at Cambridge. Dedicated to Lord Buckhurst. Another T. on same subject was wr. by Patrick Adamson (afterwards Archbishop of St. Andrews), 1572.

HERODIADE. O. 4 a. Lib. by Paul Milliet and Henry Grémon. M. by Massanet. Brussels, December 19, 1881. Ital. vers. by A. Zanardini, Milan, February 23, 1882; and as *Salome*, C.G., July 6, 1904.

HEROES. C. 3 a. Conway Edwardes. Liverpool P.O.W., November 20, 1876; Aquarium, January 10, 1877.

HEROIC FOOTMAN, THE. F. Hay., 1736. N.p.

HEROIC FRIENDSHIP. T. Ascr. by some to Otway. Pr. 1719. N.ac.

HEROIC LIE, AN. Dr. Episode. 1 a. Mary Costello. Dublin Gaiety, December 14, 1900.

HEROIC LOVE; OR, THE CRUEL SEPARATION. T. Geo. Granville (Lord Lansdowne). L.I.F. and D.L. Pr. 1698. D.L., March 18, 1766, at Mrs. Yates's benefit.

HEROIC LOVER; OR, THE INFANTA OF SPAIN, THE. T. Geo Cartwright. Pr. 1661. ?N.ac.

HEROIC SISTERS, THE. T. MS. in library of Mr. Murphy.

HEROIC STUBBS, THE. P. 4 a. H. A. Jones. Terry's, January 24, 1906.

HEROINE; OR, A DAUGHTER'S COURAGE, THE. Melo-d. 2 a. R. Phillips. M. by Cooke. D.L., February 22, 1819. Pr. 1819.

HEROINE OF CAMBRIA. T. Hayley. Pr. 1811.

HEROINE OF GLENCOE. War P. 4 a. C. March. Liverpool Grand T. and O.H., December 11, 1899.

HEROINE OF LOVE, THE. M. Piece. 3 a. Robertson. Pr. 1778.

HEROINE OF THE CAVE, THE. T. Commenced by Henry Jones under the title of *The Cave of Idra*, and finished by Dr. Hiffernan. D.L., March 19, 1774.

HERPETULUS, THE BLEU KNIGHTE, AND PEROBIA. Ac. by Lorde Klinton's servants, January 3, 1573-4.

HERTFORD. Hist. D. 3 tab. Fredk. Eastwood. Bradford T.R., August 29, 1879; Royalty, March 22, 1880.

HERZOG WILDFANG. O. S. Wagner. Prod. in Germany, 1901.

HESIONE. O. A. Campra (his first O. prod. under his own name). 1700.

HESTER AND AHASUERUS. Ac. by the Lord Admiral's men, June 3, 1594.

HESTER GRAY; OR, BLIND LOVE. D. Pro. and 4 a. H. B. Farnie and R. Reece. Manchester Prince's, October 27, 1877.

HESTER PRYNNE; OR, THE SCARLET LETTER. D. 3 a. Joseph Hatton. Newcastle Tyne, March 27, 1876.

HESTER'S MYSTERY. C.D. 1 a. A. W. Pinero. Folly, June 5, 1880; Toole's, April 23, 1891.

HETTY'S VIOLIN. P. 3 a. Chs. Riminton. Southend Pier Pav., October 7, 1907.

HEWSON REDUC'D; OR, THE SHOEMAKER RETURN'D TO HIS TRADE. Pr. 1661.

HEXE, DIE. O. August Enna. Recently prod. in Germany.

HEXEN AM RHEIN, DIE. Fantastic D. Adelphi (first time), October 4, 1841.

HEY FOR HONESTY, DOWN WITH KNAVERY. C. Thos. Randolph. Ver. of the *Plutus* of Aristophanes. Pr. 1651 (n. ac.). Sir C. Wren perf. in this p.

HEZEKIAH. Sacred D. J. L. Hatton. 1809-86.

HEZEKIAH, KING OF JUDAH; OR, INVASION REPULSED AND PEACE RESTORED. Sacred D. Pr. 1798 (n. ac.).

HIBERNIA FREE'D. T. Captain Wm. Phillips. Pr. 1722. L.I.F.

HIBERNIA'S TRIUMPH. Masque of 2 int. Ac. at Dublin. Pr. 1748.

HIC ET UBIQUE; OR, THE HUMOURS OF DUBLIN. C. Richard Head. Pr. 1663. Ac. privately.

HICK SCORNER. Int. Re-pr. in Hawkins's English Drama, 1773.

HIDDEN. C.D. Pro. and 3 a. Byam Wyke. Stockport Mechanics' Inst., January 21, 1888.

HIDDEN CRIME, THE. American D. 4 a. John M. Lockney. Surrey, May 4, 1903.

HIDDEN ENEMY, A. D. 3 a. Alfred Gray. Woolwich T.R., June 13, 1887.

HIDDEN FOE, A. Melo-d. Pro. and 4 a. Ina Leon Cassilis. Greenwich Lecture H., May 28, 1892.

HIDDEN GOLD. D. 4 a. E. C. Bertrand and Fred Gould. Portsmouth T.R., December 4, 1882.

HIDDEN HAND, THE. D. 4 a. Tom Taylor. Adap. fr. *L'Aieule* of D'Ennery and Edmond. Olympic, November 2, 1864.

HIDDEN PAST, A. Melo-d. Pro. and 3 a. E. Vivian Edmonds. Walsall T.R., May 18, 1896.

HIDDEN TERROR, A. See *The Maelstrom.*

HIDDEN TERROR, THE. Melo-d. Sk. M. Melford. Oxford M.H., November 24, 1902.

HIDDEN TREASURE. P. 3 a. J. Poole. Publ. by J. Dicks.

HIDDEN TREASURE, THE. D. 3 a. Tom Parry and John Oxenford. Adelphi, November 25, 1871.

HIDDEN WORTH. P. Pro. and 3 a. Horace Sedger. F. on Florence Marryat's *Phyllida.* P.O.W., November 3, 1886.

HIDE AND SEEK. M.E. C.G., February 24, 1789.

HIDE AND SEEK. O. 2 a. Joseph Lunn. Hay.

HIDE AND SEEK. F. 1 a. D.L., June 7, 1838.

HIDENSEEK; OR, THE ROMANCE OF A RING. M.P. 3 a. Globe, December 10, 1901.

HIERONIMO IS MAD AGAIN. Continuation of another p. called *First Part of Jeronimo.*

HIGH BID, THE. C. 3 a. H. James. Edinburgh Lyceum, March 26, 1908; H.M.T., February 18, 1909

HIGH JINKS. F. 3 a. Wm. B. Plummer. Dalham Assembly R., October 16, 1902.

HIGH JINKS. 1 scene 2 tab. Wilhelm. Dances by Mdme. Katti Lanner. M. by L. Wenzel. Empire, March 19, 1904.

HIGH JINKS. Sk. Holborn Empire, October 12, 1908.

HIGH LIFE; OR, TASTE IN THE UPPER STORY. Piece. 1 a. By a Gentleman of York. Ac. at Hull, 1801.

HIGH LIFE ABOVE STAIRS. See *Bon Ton.*

HIGH LIFE BELOW STAIRS. F. 2 a. Rev. Jas. Townley. D.L., October 31, 1759, and C.G., April 27, 1787. Pr. 1759. Rev. Terry's, January 14, 1895.

HIGH LIFE IN THE CITY. C. E. J. Eyre. Hay., July 25, 1810.

HIGH, LOW, JACK AND THE GAME. Planchè and C. Dance. Olympic, September 20, 1830.

HIGH METTLED RACER. M. Trifle. Dibdin.

HIGH NOTIONS; OR, A TRIP TO EXMOUTH. M.F. 2 a. M. by Parry. D.L., February 11, 1819.

HIGH ROAD; OR, LIFE. City of London, March 23, 1857.

HIGH ROAD TO MARRIAGE, THE. C. Lumley St. George Skeffington. D.L., May 27, 1803. N.p.

HIGH STREET MYSTERY, THE. Oa. M. by Batchelder. Lib. by L. Machale. Cheetham T.H., September 23, 1885.

HIGH WAYS AND BY WAYS. F. 2 a. Benjamin Webster. Taken from *Mons. Rigaud ou les deux Maris* and *Partie and Revenche.* D.L., March 15, 1831.

HIGHER COURT, THE. P. 3 a. A. C. Fraser Wood. Sutton Coalfield Masonic H., December 11, 1905.

HIGHGATE TUNNEL; OR, THE SECRET ARCH. Burl. op. T. Smith. Pr. 1812. Lyceum playbill, September 7, 1815.

HIGHLAND DROVER, THE. Archibald M'Laren. Pr. in Scotland. N.d. Ac. before 1814.

HIGHLAND FAIR; OR, THE UNION OF THE CLANS, THE. O. Joseph Mitchell. Pr. 1731. D.L., March 20, 1731.

HIGHLAND FLING, A. F. 1 a. Joseph J. Dilley. Vaudeville, January 4, 1879.

HIGHLAND HEARTS. D. Hector C. Gordon. Grand, Glasgow, October 28, 1889.

HIGHLAND LASSIE; OR, TRIP FROM KINGHORNE. M.D. Rannie. 1803.

HIGHLAND LASSIE, THE. See *The Lowland Lassie.*

HIGHLAND LEGACY, A. P. 1 a. Brandon Thomas. Strand (first time at a London theatre), November 17, 1888.

HIGHLAND REEL, The. C.O. John O'Keefe. C.G., November 6, 1788. Pr. same year. D.L., June 14, 1814; Lyceum, July 30, 1822.

HIGHLANDERS, THE. Spec. D. Edgar Bruce. Portsmouth T.R., November 11, 1872.

HIGHLY IMPROBABLE. F. W. S. Gilbert. New Royalty, December 5, 1867.

HIGHWAY KNIGHT, THE. M.C. E. C. Hedmondt and Francis Neilson. Fr. the German of Hanseler and Moller. M. by Gustave Meyer. Liverpool R. Court, March 14, 1898.

HIGHWAY TO HEAVEN, THE. A play mentioned in Greene's "Groatsworth of Wit," 1592.

HIGHWAYMAN, THE. F. 1 a. J. M. Morton. C.G., ? 1843.

HIGHWAYMAN, THE. Ca. J. H. M'Carthy. Op. C. June 5, 1891.

HIGHWAYMAN BOLD, A. C.O. 2 a. Wds., lyrics, and songs by Harry Corrin and Bert Harding. M. by Bert Harding. St. Helens, January 19, 1909 (C.P.).

HIGHWAYMAN'S HOLIDAY, THE. F. 1 a. W. E. Suter. Queen's, September 14, 1863.

HILDA. P. 3 a. Princess's, May 28, 1892.

HILDA; OR, THE MISER'S DAUGHTER. D. 3 a. A. Halliday. F. on Ainsworth's novel. Adelphi, April 1, 1872.

HILDA'S INHERITANCE; OR, LIVINGSTONE'S SIN. D. 4 a. Wm. Muskerry. New Pav., October 21, 1871.

HILL'S HIGH COURT OF JUSTICE; OR, THE TRYAL OF THE POLITE GHOSTS—VIZ., OLIVER CROMWELL, KING OF SWEDEN, AND CARDINAL MAZARINE. T. By J. D. 1661.

HINDOO'S REVENGE, THE. Originally *The Hands of Sin.* Broughton Victoria, March 12, 1906.

HINDUSTANEE; OR, JONES AT JONESEPOORE, THE. M.C. Burl. 2 a., 3 sc. A. F. Allen Tower and Leon Wood. Books and lyrics by A. F. Allen Tower. M. by Leon Wood. Oxford Empire, March 5, 1906.

HINKO; OR, THE HEADSMAN'S BOND. Rom. P. Pro. and 5 a. W. G. Wills. Queen's, Long Acre, September 9, 1871.

HINT TO HUSBANDS, A. C. Richard Cumberland. C.G., March 8, 1806. Pr. 1806. (Blank verse.)

HINTS FOR HUSBANDS. C. 5 a. S Beazley. Hay., 1835.

HINTS FOR PAINTERS. F. C.G., May 10, 1803. N.p.

HIPPOLITUS. T. John Studley. Transl. fr. Seneca. Pr. 1581. Transl. by E. Prestwick. Pr. 1651.

HIPPOLITUS. T. Greek p. of Euripides, transl. by R. Potter, pr. 1781; Michael Wodhull, pr. 1782; Fitzgerald, 1867; Williams, 1871; G. Murray, Lyric, May 28, 1904; and rev. Court, October 18, 1904; March 26, 1906. See "Greek Plays."

HIPPOLYTE ET ARICIE. O. 5 a. Rameau. F. on Racine's *Phèdre*. Academie, October 1, 1733.

HIPSIPILE. O. John Toole. Transl. fr. Metastasio. Pr. 1767.

HIREN; OR, THE FAIR GREEK. T. W. Barksted. Pr. 1611. (Bodleian Library.) See *The Turkish Mahomet.*

HIRONDELLE, L'. C. 3 a. and 4 tab. Durio Nicodemi. Terry's, June 8, 1905.

HIS BEST CHUM. Inc. Geo. Gliddon. Canterbury Royal, August 9, 1907.

HIS BIRTHRIGHT. P. 3 a. C. Clilverd-Young. Cripplegate Inst., November 26, 1907.

HIS BORROWED PLUMES. C. 3 a. Mrs. Geo. Cornwallis-West. Hicks', July 6, 1909.

HIS BOUNDEN DUTY. P. 3 a. P. E. Bodington. Prod. by the Play Actors, Court, May 30, 1909.

HIS BROTHER'S KEEPER. D. 4 a. Lionel Scudamore, Paul Barry. Cambridge T., Spennymoor, December 24, 1900; Rotherhithe, Terriss, July 15, 1901.

HIS CHIEF STUDY. Sk. Empress, August 23, 1909.

HIS CHILD. P. 1 a. Fredk. Fenn and Richd. Pryce. Waldorf, September 10, 1906.

HIS DISHONOURED WIFE. D. 4 a. Harry Tilbury. Stratford Royal, March 30, 1908.

HIS EIGHTIETH BIRTHDAY. Ca. Scott Craven. Grand, March 25, 1901.

HIS EVENING OUT. Ca. W. Kingsley Tarply. Ladbroke H., February 28, 1899. (Amateurs.)

HIS EXCELLENCY. C. 1 a. C. W. Mathews. Hay., July 11, 1860.

HIS EXCELLENCY. C.O. 2 a. W. S. Gilbert. M. by Osmond Carr. Lyric, October 27, 1894.

HIS EXCELLENCY THE GOVERNOR. F. Rom. 3 a. R. Marshall. Court, June 11, 1898. Rev. D. of York's, March 12, 1904.

HIS FATAL BEAUTY. M.C. 3 a. Arthur Shirley. Camberwell Metropole, April 27, 1903.

HIS FATHER'S FRIEND. C. 3 a. H. T. Johnson. Brighton Eden T., April 28, 1902.

HIS FATHER'S WILL. D. 5 a. Geof Thorn. Grand, March 22, 1904 (C.P.).

HIS FIRST CHAMPAGNE. F. 2 a. Wm. Leman Rede. Strand, October 7, 1833; D.L., January 18, 1858.

HIS FIRST LOVE. P. 1 a. Annie Hughes. Hay., May 18, 1905.

HIS FIRST PECCADILLO. F. 1 a. Princess's, October 26, 1848.

HIS FUTURE WIFE. F. F. Hawley Francks. Brighton Aquarium, February 3, 1890.

HIS HELPMATE. P. 1 a. Chs. McEvoy. Manchester Midland, September 23, 1907.

HIS HIDDEN REVENGE. D. 5 a. Florence Holdon. Upton Park P.H., October 10, 1887.

HIS HIGHNESS. C.O. 3 a. J. W. Houghton and Auscal Tate. Op. C., June 13, 1893.

HIS HIGHNESS. F.C. 3 a. Brandon Hurst. Op. C., February 5, 1894. (C.P.)

HIS HIGHNESS MY HUSBAND. F.C. 3 a. Wm. Boosey. Adap. fr. *Le Prince Consort* of Xanrof and Chancel. Comedy, October 1, 1904.

HIS HOUSE IN ORDER. C. 4 a. A. W. Pinero. St. James's, February 1, 1906.

HIS JAPANESE WIFE. P. 1 a. Grace Griswold. Bedford Street Bijou, December 15, 1907.

HIS LANDLADY. F. Geo. Mudie. Parkhurst, June 13, 1892.

HIS LAST CHANCE. O. 1 a. E. Harraden. Publ. by S. French, Ltd.

HIS LAST CRUISE. Oa. 1 a. R. T. Gunton. M. by W. Williams. Hatfield P.H., February 8, 1893 (amat.); St. Albans County H., December 11, 1893.

HIS LAST JEST. Gerald Blake. Standard, July 19, 1909.

HIS LAST LEGS. F. 2 a. W. B. Bernard. Wr. 1839. Hay.

HIS LAST STAKE. D. 1 a. J. Provand Webster. Princess's, April 24, 1888.

HIS LAST VICTORY. D. 2 a. Watts Phillips. St. James's, June 21, 1862.

HIS LIFE FOR HER LOVE. P. 4 a. Geo. S. King. Devonport Metropole, August 24, 1908.

HIS LIFE FOR HERS. P. C. W. Hogg. Scarborough Spa T., July 18, 1908 (C.P.).

HIS LITTLE DODGE. C. 3 a. J. H. McCarthy. Fr. the Fr. of Georges Feydeau and Maurice Hennequin. Royalty, October 24, 1896.

HIS LITTLE MANIA. F. Athenæum H., Tottenham Court Road, July 12, 1890.

HIS LIVING IMAGE. Sk. Stanley Cooke. M. by Arthur Wood. Canterbury, May 22, 1908; Coronet, November 23, 1908.

HIS LORDSHIP. C. 3 a. Armizer Barczinski. Adap. T. W. Speight's novel "A Barren Title." Warlingham School (by students), August 6, 1890.

HIS LORDSHIP. C. Arthur Leverett. M. by J. Greenhill. Bayswater Bijou, July 4, 1901.

HIS LORDSHIP'S BIRTHDAY. M.C. Francis Raphael and Edward Lauri. Parkhurst, March 19, 1894.

HIS LUCKY STAR. P. 1 a. E. Haslingden Russell. 92, Victoria Street, S.W., January 29, 1908.

HIS MAJESTY; OR, THE COURT OF VIGNOLIA. F. C. Burnand and R. C. Lehmann. M. by Sir A. C. Mackenzie. Savoy, February 20, 1897.

HIS MAJESTY'S COASTGUARDS. D. Sk. Edward Ranier. Bow Palace, January 23, 1905.

HIS MAJESTY'S MUSKETEERS. P. 5 a. Frederick Carl. Adap. fr. Alexandre Dumas. St. Geo. H., May 9, 1899.

HIS MAJESTY'S SERVANT. Rom. P. 4 a. Sarah Barnwell Elliott and Maud Horsford. Imperial, October 6, 1904.

HIS MASTERPIECE. M. Sk. Sutton Vane. M. by Edward Jones. St. Geo. H., March 18, 1898.

HIS MOTHER. D. Sk. G. D. Day. Grand, March 23, 1891.

HIS NATURAL LIFE. See *For a Life.*

HIS NEW FRENCH COOK. Ca. By "Wee Tree." St. Geo. H., February 6, 1899.

HIS NOVICE. F. 1 a. Henry Spicer. D.L., December 26, 1878.

HIS ONLY COAT. Oa. 1a. Dallas and Slaughter. Publ. by S. French, Ltd.

HIS OTHER EYES. Ca. M. B. Spurr and W. M. Mayne. Brighton W. Pier Pav., March 4, 1901.

HIS OTHER I. F.C. 3 a. Leonard Outram and W. Heron Brown. Worcester T.R. May 20, 1898 (C.P.).

HIS OWN ENEMY. Ca. 1 a. A. Meadow. Hay., March 8, 1873.

HIS OWN ENEMY. M.D. 4 a. Clara Dillon. Aldershot T.R. December 13, 1898 (C.P.).

HIS OWN GUEST. C. 3 a. A. Ayres and P. Blake. Op. C. May 19, 1883.

HIS OWN WIFE. Folkestone Pleasure Gardens, November 3, 1894.

HIS REAL WIFE. Dom. P. 4 a. Charles A. Clarke. Hammersmith Lyric, September 16, 1909.

HIS RELATIONS. F.C. 3 a. H. A. Saintsbury. Avenue, May 28, 1896.

HIS ROMANCE. C. 4 a. Meyrick Milton. Adap. Michael Klapp's *Rosenkrantz and Guildenstern*. Olympic, February 16, 1888.

HIS SACRIFICE. P. 3 a. Donald F. Buckley Ladbroke H., W., June 26, 1908 (C.P.).

HIS SATANIC MAJESTY. C.O. 2 a. F. Marlow, jun., and H. Barron. Southend Empire, November 13, 1899.

HIS SECOND WIFE. P. 3 a. Vivian Hope. Avenue, June 29, 1892.

HIS SHOP GIRL BRIDE. M.Ca. Roland Oliver. M. and lyrics by Louis la Rondelle. Camberwell Palace, January 13, 1908.

HIS SISTER'S HONOUR. M.D. 4 a Eva Elwes. Fleetwood Queen's, January 14. 1907.

HIS SON-IN-LAW. F. Sk. W. G. Watson and A. Rodman. Herne Bay, September 12, 1890.

HIS SON-IN-LAW. F. 3 a. Robert Fielding Giveen. Reading R. County, November 4, 1896.

HIS SUCCESS. Piece. Walter E. Grogan. Bayswater Bijou, December 3, 1896.

HIS TOAST. Ca. A. M. Heathcote. Court, July 13, 1889.

HIS TREASURES. Dr. Ep. 1 a. Ellis Kingsley. Brompton Hospital, March 9, 1897.

HIS TWIN MATILDA. F. 3 a. John Cleveland. Southend-on-Sea Pier Pav., January 25, 1904.

HIS WIFE. P. 5 a. H. A. Jones. F. on novel "A Prodigal Daughter." Sadler's Wells, April 16, 1881.

HIS WIFE NO LONGER. D. 4 a. Stephen Pritt. Preston R., September 21, 1908.

HIS WIFE'S FATHER. See *The Sleeping Partner*.

HIS WIFE'S LITTLE BILL. Albert Henning. Lyrics by Julian Standish. Bijou, Bedford Street, Strand, May 17, 1894.

HIS WIFE'S PICTURE. P. 1 a. Ernest Cosham. Avenue, May 23, 1900.

HIS WIVES. F.C. 3 a. T. G. Warren. Strand, May 23, 1888.

HIS WIVES. Ellis Cleveland. Avenue, November 16, 1894 (C.P.).

HIS WORSHIP THE MAYOR. M. Sk. 1 sc. A. J. Mills. M. by B. Scott. Collins's, March 18, 1907.

HISPANUS. Latin C. Morrell. Ac. at Cambridge, 1596 MS. wr. in 1600.

HISTORICAL INCIDENT, AN. P. 1 a. 92, Victoria Street, S.W., February 5, 1908.

HISTORICAL REGISTER FOR THE YEAR 1736, THE. C. Henry Fielding. Hay. Pr. 1737.

HISTORY OF A GREEK MAID, THE. See *Turkish Mahomet*.

HISTORY OF ABRAHAM, THE. An old mystery pres. in MS. in Trinity College Library, Dublin, and edited by J. P. Collier.

HISTORY OF ERROR. Ac. at Court, 1577.

HISTORY OF THE TWO MAIDS OF MOORCLACK, THE. C. Robert Armin. Pr. 1609.

HISTORY OF THE TWO VALIANT KNIGHTS, SIR CLYOMON AND SIR CLAMYDES. T. Peele. 1599.

HISTRIOMASTRIX; OR, THE PLAYER WHIPP'D. C. Anon. Pr. 1610.

HIT HIM: HE HAS NO FRIENDS. F. 1 a. E. Yates and N. H. Harrington. Strand, September 17, 1860.

HIT OR MISS. M.F. 2 a. J. Pocock. M. by Chas. Smith. Lyceum, 1810, and rev. there September 8, 1823; D.L., June 26, 1816.

HIT OR MISS; OR, ALL MY EYE AND BETTY MARTIN. Op. Extrav. F. C. Burnand. Olympic, April 13, 1868.

HIT OR MISS; OR, THE LAST OF THE BARONS. Burl. Arthur Milton. Middlesbrough T.R., February 19, 1883.

HIT THE NAILE O' THE HEAD. Int. Mentioned in the tragedy of Sir Thomas More (MSS. Harl., No. 7,368).

HOB; OR, THE COUNTRY WAKE. F. Cibber. D.L. Pr. 1715. This is Dogget's *Country Wake* reduced to a farce. Several songs afterwards added, and produced as *Flora; or, Hob in the Well*.

HOB IN THE WELL. Alt. fr. *Country Wake*. Hippisley. 1755.

HOBB'S VENDETTA. F.C. 3 a. Bert Danson and Geo. Arthur. Worthing R., May 2, 1904.

HOBB'S WEDDING. A sequel to *The Country Wake*. F. John Leigh. Pr. 1720. L.I.F.

HOBBIES. V. H. P. Stephens and W. Yardley. M. by Geo. Gear. St. Geo. H., April 6, 1885.

HOBBINAL, THE HUMOURS OF. A Droll pr. in "The Wits; or, Sport upon Sport." 1672.

HOBBY HORSE, THE. F. Capt. Edwd. Thompson. D.L., April 16, 1766. N.p.

HOBBY HORSE, THE. C. 3 a. A. W. Pinero. St. James's, October 25, 1886; Court, May 15, 1897.

HOBBY HORSES. F. Anon. Hay., July 31, 1789. N.p.

HOBSON'S CHOICE. Ca. Knight Summers. Nottingham Central H., April 24, 1895.

HOBSON'S CHOICE; OR, THESPIS IN DISTRESS. Burla. W. C. Oulton. Royalty, 1787. N.p.

HOCHZEIT DES CAMACHO, DIE. O. 2 a. Mendelssohn. Words by Klingemann, after "Don Quixote." Berlin, April 29, 1827. An early work of this composer, produced in Germany.

HOCK TUESDAY. Old Coventry Play exhib. before Q. Elizabeth, Kenilworth Castle, 1575.

HODGE PODGE; OR, A RECEIPT TO MAKE A BENEFIT. Int. Hay., 1781. N.p.

HOFER; THE TELL OF THE TYROL. Hist. O. M. fr. *Guillaume Tell*, by Rossini. Adap. by Bishop. D.L., May 1, 1830.

HOFFMAN; OR, A REVENGE FOR A FATHER, THE TRAGEDY OF. T. 5 a. Henry Chettle. Ac. at the Phœnix, circa 1602. Ent. Stationers' Co., February 26, 1629. Pr. 1631.

HOGGE HATH LOST HIS PEARLE, THE. C. Robert Tailor. Ac. at Whitefriars, 1613. Pr. 1614. Ac. by 16 London apprentices and stopped by the Sheriffs before the end of the piece.

HOGMANAY; OR, NEW YEAR'S EVE. C. 1 a. Fred W. Sidney. St. Geo. H., June 21, 1898; Globe, August 30, 1898.

HOKEE POKEE. Grecian, December 24, 1878.

HOLD FAST. D. 5 a. Leeds T.R., September 21, 1885.

HOLD YOUR TONGUE. C.D. 1 a. J. R. Planché. Lyceum, March 22, 1849.

HOLDING THE MIRROR. F.C. 1 a. W. Howell Poole. Newcastle Tyne T., October 26, 1885.

HOLE IN THE WALL. F. Poole. 1813.

HOLIDAY GOVERNESS, THE. Sk. Wr. by C. A. Dawson. 92, Victoria Street, S.W., July 2, 1907.

HOLIDAY HUMOUR, A. Rom. 1 a. Stanley Killby. Guildford, February 3, 1904.

HOLIDAY TIME; OR, THE SCHOOL-BOY'S FROLIC. F. Francis Lathom. Pr. 1800. Ac. and pr. at Norwich.

HOLLAND'S LEAGUER. C. Shakerley Marmion. Ac. at the Private House in Salisbury Court, and pr. 1632.

HOLLANDER, THE. C. Hy. Glapthorne. Wr. and ac. at the Cockpit, 1635. Pr. 1640.

HOLLY BRANCH, THE. Oa. 1 a. Ch. Thomas. M. by Harriet Young. This is a M. ver. of Ch. Thomas's Ca. *Breaking the Ice*, which was prod. at the Court T., November 9, 1885. Ealing Lyric H., December 11, 1891.

HOLLY BUSH HALL; OR, THE TRACK IN THE SNOW. D. 2 a. W. E. Suter. Fr. a story of same name in Reynolds' Miscellany. Queen's, February 25, 1860.

HOLLY LODGE. St. Martin's H., April 2, 1855.

HOLLY TREE INN. P. 1 a. Mrs. Oscar Beringer. Fr. Dickens. Terry's, January 15, 1891, and December 28, 1896.

HOLMLEY HOUSE. See *A Maid of Honour*.

HOLOFERNES. An interlude. Ac. at Hatfield 1556. A play so called perf. at Derby 1572.

HOLY GHOST, THE REPRESENTATION (OR DESCENT) OF THE. Anon. Mentioned in the "Theatrical Recorder."

HOLY TRINITY. See "Miracle Plays."

HOLY WAR, THE. Episode. 1 a. G. Carlton Wallace. Woolwich R., June 22, 1908.

HOLYROOD. Scottish O. 3 a. F. on the D. *Cramond Brig*. Arr. by Stewart Bell. M. by John Greig. Glasgow Princess's, October 5, 1896.

HOMBURG. Sk. 1 a. Joseph Hatton. Toole's, May 3, 1893.

HOME. C. 3 a. T. W. Robertson. Story f. on Emile Angier's *L'Aventurière*. Hay., January 14, 1869. See *The Adventurers*.

HOME; OR, A FATHER'S LOVE. D. Victoria, February 7, 1880.

HOME ACCESSORY, THE. P. 1 a. E. F. Yorke. Crystal Palace, July 1, 1909.

HOME AGAIN. D. Hugh Marston. Standard, March 24, 1877.

HOME AGAIN. Dom. D. H. A. Jones. Oxford T.R., August 7, 1881.

HOME AGAIN; OR, THE LIEUTENANT'S DAUGHTERS. Dom. D. 3 a. Edward Fitzball. Lyceum, November, 1844.

HOME CHIMES; OR, THE HOME AND LOVE OF YORE. 1 a. Alfred Arthur. M. by T. Normandale. St. Geo. H., November 10, 1888.

HOME CIRCUIT; OR, COCKNEY GLEANINGS, THE. Ent. by Mr. Mathews. Lyceum, March 12, 1827.

HOME COMING, THE. Piece. 1 a. Ernest Cosham. Comedy, July 4, 1892.

HOME COMING, THE. T. 1 a. Geo. Unwin. West London, March 28, 1908 (C.P.); Liverpool Queen's, April 22, 1908.

HOME FAIRY. Children's P. F. D. Adams. Publ. by S. French, Ltd.

HOME FEUD, THE. P. 3 a. Walter Frith. Comedy, February 14, 1890.

HOME FOR A HOLIDAY. Ca. 1 a. Walter Gordon, Olympic, November 12, 1860.

HOME FOR HOME. Ca. Richard Lee. Vaudeville, August 16, 1879.

HOME FROM THE HONEYMOON. F. Ca. 1 a., 2 sc. Arthur Jefferson. Glasgow Metropole, October 7, 1905 (C.P.); February 16, 1906.

HOME OF LIES, A. Charles Hannan.

HOME OF ONE'S OWN, A. F. 1 a. W. J. Lucas.

HOME ONCE MORE; OR, A FALSE ACCUSATION. Rom. D. 4 a. A. L. Crauford. Britannia, April 6, 1885.

HOME RULE. Irish D. 3 a. E. F. Brady. Liverpool Adelphi, January 12, 1880; Eleph. and C., March 15, 1880.

HOME RULE, A FIRESIDE STORY. C.D. 1 a. J. G. Taylor. Liverpool P.O.W., March 19, 1877; Olympic, December 16, 1886.

HOME SECRETARY, THE. P. 3 a. R. C. Carton. Criterion, May 7, 1895; transf. to Shaftesbury, October 21, 1895.

HOME SPUN. Dom. D. A. C. Calmour. Novelty, November 11, 1884.

HOME STORY, A. See *One Fault*.

HOME, SWEET HOME. P. 2 a. C. A. Somerset. Publ. by J. Dicks.

HOME, SWEET HOME. D. 4 a. B. T. Farjeon, Olympic, June 19, 1876.

HOME, SWEET HOME. F.C. 3 a. Herbert Swears. St. Geo. H. (Irving D. Club), March 2, 1895.

HOME, SWEET HOME. D. 4 a. F. Lindo. Greenwich Carlton, May 18, 1903; Grand, July 4, 1904.

HOME TRUTHS. The original of this piece is *Gabrielle*, C., in 5 a., in verse, by Emile Angier, originally prod. at the Comédie Française in 1849, and played during a French season at the Royalty, March 15, 1888; Princess's, 1859.

HOME WRECK, THE. D. 3 a. Stirling Coyne. Finished by his son, J. Dennis Coyne Suggested by Tennyson's poem "Enoch Arden." Surrey, February 8, 1869; rev. Holborn, 1873.

HOMELESS. D. 4 a. and pro. J. K. Murray and Geo. Comer. Leicester T.R., July 19, 1893.

HOMELY. Charade. Miss Pickering. Publ. by S. French, Ltd.

HOMESTEAD STORY. Princess's, June 22, 1861.

HOMEWARD BOUND. Ca. 1 a. E. Murray. Brighton T.R., November, 1858.

HOMEWARD BOUND. Nautical D. Prol. and 3 a. J. C. Bertie. Sunderland Lyceum, August 28, 1874.

HOMEWARD BOUND. D. Warrington Pub. H., May 6, 1885

HOMEWARD BOUND. F. 1 a. Sydney Grundy. Pr. by Thos. Scott, Warwick Court.

HOMME AUX POUPEES, L'. Coronet, October 22, 1908.

HON'BLE PHIL, THE. M.P. 2 a. G. P. Huntley and Herbert Clayton. M. by H. Samuel. Additional notes by Ralph Nairn. Lyrics by Harold Lawson. Additional lyrics by Bertrand Davis and Claude Aveling. Hicks's, October 3, 1908.

HONEST CHEATS. C. Coyne. 1836.

HONEST CRIMINAL; OR, FILIAL PIETY, THE. D. by G. L. Pr. 1778. Transl. fr. the French.

HONEST ELECTORS; OR, THE COURTIERS SENT BACK WITH THEIR BRIBES, THE. B.O. 3 a. N.d. Pr. circa 1733.

HONEST ELECTORS; OR, THE FREEHOLDER'S OPERA. Pr. 1734. ? above piece with new second title.

HONEST FARMER, THE. 5 a. Berquin (author of *The Children's Friend*). Pr. 1791.

HONEST IN DISTRESS.—See *Honesty in Distress.*

HONEST JOHN. D. C. H. Hazlewood. Britannia, July 19, 1875.

HONEST LABOUR; OR, THE SHIFTING SCENES OF A WORKMAN'S LIFE. D. 3 a. Frederick Marchant. Britannia, August 3, 1870.

HONEST LAWYER, THE. C. By "S. S." Ac. by the Queen's servants. Pr. 1616.

HONEST LIVING, AN. C.D. 3 a. Woods Lawrence. Wakefield O.H., March 13, 1891.

HONEST MAN, AN. D. 1 a. Henry Pettitt. Surrey, November 16, 1878.

HONEST MAN'S FORTUNE, THE. T.C. Beaumont and Fletcher. Ac. in 1613. Pr. 1647.

HONEST SOLDIER, THE. C. J. H. Colls. Pr. 1805. ? N.ac.

HONEST THIEVES, THE. F. 2 a. T. Knight. C.G., May 9, 1797. Pr. same year. Rev. at Lyceum, May 15, 1821. The piece was alt. fr. his *The Committee*.

HONEST WHORE, THE. C. Thos. Dekker. Pr. 1604. The first part contains *The Humours of the Patient Man and the Longing Wife.* The second part, pr. 1630, contains *The Humours of the Patient Man and the Impatient Wife.* (? second part n. ac.) Not divided into acts.

HONEST YORKSHIREMAN, THE. B.O. Hy. Carey. C.G., July 11, 1735. Pr. 1736. See *The Wonder.*

HONESTY. P. Spicer. Olympic, 1848.

HONESTY. P. 1 a. C. Preston Wynne. Oxford New T., December 7, 1900.

HONESTY—A COTTAGE FLOWER. P. 1 a. Margaret Young. Avenue (New Century T. perf.), November 29, 1897.

HONESTY IN DISTRESS, BUT RELIEV'D BY NO PARTY. T. 3 a. By Edward Ward; not intended for the stage. Pr. 1705.

HONESTY THE BEST POLICY. F. Announced for perf. at C.G. in 1791, but withdrawn.

HONESTY THE BEST POLICY. Mus. Ent. M. by Reeve. D.L., May 31, 1815.

HONESTY THE BEST POLICY. D. 2 a. Mark Lemon. Adap. fr. the French. Strand.

HONEYDOVE'S TROUBLES. F. R. Reece. Manchester T.R., September 19, 1867; D.L., December 26, 1867.

HONEYLAND. Fairy Spec. fr. *The Life of the Bee*, by Maeterlinck. Wr. by F. Neville Pigott. M. by Carl Kiefert. London Hippo., December 24, 1907.

HONEYMOON, THE. C.O. W. Linley. D.L., January 7, 1797. M. by the author. Songs only pr. 1797.

HONEYMOON, THE. C. 5 a. John Tobin. D.L., January 31, 1805; also at C.G., the New Queen's, etc.

HONEYMOON, THE. M.P. 3 a. Gilbert Payne. Dundee Empire, September 17, 1906.

HONEYMOON BABY, THE. Sk. Prod. by R. C. Matthews. Camberwell Empire, March 26, 1907.

HONEYMOON IN ECLIPSE, THE. F. on a story publ. in the *World*, "Ugly Barrington," by Mrs. Godfrey. Arr. for the stage by Geo. Moore. St. Geo. H., April 12, 1888.

HONEYMOON TRAGEDY, A. Ca. Mrs. W. K. Clifford. Comedy, March 12, 1896.

HONI SOIT QUI MAL Y PENSE. Ca. Roland Bottomley. Chiswick T.H., May 9, 1901.

HONNETE HOMME, UN. Mme. Camille Clermont. Royalty (Fr. season), June 29, 1908.

HONOR. P. of modern life. 4 a. Alicia Ramsay and Rudolph de Cordova. Kennington T., November 23, 1903.

HONOR AMONG THIEVES. See *Honour* etc.

HONORARY DEGREE, THE. M.F. 2 a. Bks. by H. Rottenberg. M. by J. W. Ivenrey. Extra numbers by Paul Rubens, H. E. Haines, and K. L. Duffield. Cambridge New, June 7, 1907 (amateurs' prod.).

HONORIA and MAMMON. C. Jas. Shirley. Pr. 1659. See *Contention*, etc.

HONOUR. C. R. L. Reed. Newcastle Tyne T., December 1, 1876.

HONOUR. P. 4 a. Maurice H. Barrymore. Adap. fr. Leon Battu and Maurice Desirgue's drama *L'Honour de la Maison*. Court, September 24, 1881.

HONOUR; OR, ARRIVALS FROM COLLEGE. C. 5 a. M. by Cooke. D.L., April 17, 1819.

HONOUR; OR, ONE REDEEMING SPARK. D. 3 a. J. Levey. Grecian, September 4, 1871.

HONOUR AMONG THIEVES. D. 3 a. Edward Towers. Pav., Aug. 4, 1877.

HONOUR AMONG THIEVES. D. 4 a. Charles Hannan, Hastings Pier T., May 6, 1895; Matinée, T., November 15, 1898.

HONOUR AND LOVE. Dialogue. Hey Publ. at York, 1791.

HONOUR BEFORE WEALTH. D. Carlisle H.M.T., September 7, 1885.

HONOUR BEFORE WEALTH; OR, THE ROMANCE OF A POOR YOUNG MAN. D. 4 a. P. Edwards and Lister Wallack. Fr. the French of Octave Feuillet. First ac. at N. York. London Queen's, March 23, 1861.

HONOUR BRIGHT; OR, A STORY OF THE STAGE. D. Pro. and 3 a. E. Towers and W. Paulo. East London, April 18, 1870.

HONOUR BRIGHT. Melo-d. 4 a. Ronald Grahame and E. T. Bauzie and Cecil Harringay. Bilston T.R., September 22, 1897 (C.P.); Nuneaton T.R., March 14, 1898; West London, March 28, 1898.

HONOUR IN THE END. C. Advertised in *Wit and Drollery*, 1661, as in the Press but n.p.

HONOUR OF A ROGUE, THE. Rom. P. 1 a. A. Constance Smedley and Cosmo Hamilton. Royalty, January 31, 1903.

HONOUR OF THE HOUSE, THE. D. 5 a. C. T. Holderness and H. Sidney Warwick. Driffield Corn Exchange, July 25, 1893 (C.P.).

HONOUR OF THE HOUSE, THE. D. 5 a. H. H. Lewis. Nottingham T.R., July 15, 1895; Pavilion, July 29, 1895.

HONOUR OF THE HOUSE, THE. P. 4 a. W. A. Brabner. West Didsbury, The Hall, October 28, 1905 (C.P.).

HONOUR OF THE JOSCELYNS, THE. P. 1 a. Adap. by Herbert Collins. St. John's Wood, All Saints' H., January 28, 1909.

HONOUR OF WALES, THE. Masque. ? Wr. by Ben Jonson.

HONOUR OF WOMEN, THE. Ascr. to Massinger. Now lost. Licensed May 6, 1628. Some think identical with *The Maid of Honour.*

HONOUR OR LOVE? Rom. P. 1 a. Henry Chance Newton. Oldham Empire, February 3, 1898; Camberwell Metropole, February 21, 1898.

HONOUR REWARDED; OR, THE GENEROUS FORTUNE HUNTER. F. 3 a. John Dalton of Clifton. Pr. 1775.

HONOUR THY FATHER. P. 4 a. C. A. Clarke and H. R. Silva. Imperial, September 12, 1898.

HONOURABLE DECEIVERS. C. Mrs. Trotter. 1701. See *Love at a Loss.*

HONOURABLE GHOST, THE. C. 1 a. Frederick Fenn. Ealing, December 29, 1902.

HONOURABLE HERBERT, THE. P. 4 a. C. Haddon Chambers. Vaudeville, December 22, 1891.

HONOURABLE HISTORY OF FRIAR BACON AND FRIAR BUNGAY, THE. Greene. 1591.

HONOURABLE JOHN, THE. C. 3 a. F. Mouillot, C. James, and E. J. Malyon. Crouch End Queen's O.H., December 12, 1898.

HONOURABLE LOVER. Rowley. 1600. See *Four Honoured Loves* (lost).

HONOURABLE MEMBER, AN. C.D. 3 a. A. W. Gattie. Court, July 14, 1896.

HONOURABLE PHIL. See *Hon'ble Phil.*

HONOURS. D. Fawney Vane. Grecian, October 4, 1879.

HONOURS AND TRICKS. C. 3 a. Shirley Brooks. Lyceum.

HONOURS DIVIDED. P. 3 a. C. K. Burrow and Wilson Benington. Lupton St. Benet's Ch. R., May 14, 1895.

HONOURS DIVIDED. P. 4 a. Fergus Hume. Margate G.T., September 1, 1902.

HONOUR'S PRICE. D. 5 a. Mortimer Murdoch. Whitehaven T.R., August 25, 1884; Marylebone, June 27, 1885.

HOODMAN BLIND. Melo-d. 4 a. H. A. Jones and Wilson Barrett. Princess, August 18, 1885, and November 26, 1892.

HOOK AND EYE. Ca. Eille Norwood. Leeds Grand, March 22, 1887; Op. C., November 14, 1891.

HOOLY AND FAIRLY; OR, THE HIGHLAND LAD AND THE LOWLAND LASS. M.I. C.G., April 28, 1798. N.p.

HOOP OF GOLD, THE. D. 3 a. Mortimer Murdoch. Pavilion, March 2, 1878.

HOOPS INTO SPINNING-WHEELS. T.C. J. Blanch. Pr. 1725.

HOP; OR, WHO'S AFRAID? THE. Sk. 1 a. Advertised for perf., D.L., 1791, but withdrawn.

HOP O' MY THUMP O. 1864. Mentioned by Brewer

HOP-PICKERS AND GIPSIES; OR, THE LOST DAUGHTER. D. 3 a. C. H. Hazlewood. Britannia, May 17, 1869.

HOPE. D. 4 a. Arthur Law. Standard, October 2, 1882.

HOPE. Duol. Richard Saunders. Brompton Hosp., January 8, 1895.

HOPE. P. 1 a. Philip B. Kirk Stedman. Primrose Hill, St. Mary's Church Room, April 17, 1909 (amat.).

HOPE. See *Major Hope.*

HOPE OF BRITAIN; OR, THE TWELFTH OF AUGUST, THE. Int. Ac. at Brighton, 1802.

HOPE OF THE FAMILY, THE. C. 3 a. J. Stirling Coyne. Hay., December 3, 1853.

HOPE'S ANSWER. P. 1 a. Herbert Gough and Morris Edwards. South Shields T.R., November 19, 1886.

HOPELESS PASSION, A. C. 1 a. J. Maddison Morton. Strand, September 15, 1851.

HORACE. T. Charles Cotton. Transl. of the *Horace* of Pierre Corneille. Prod. 1639. Pr. 1671. See "French Classical Plays."

HORACE. T. Mrs. Catherine Phillips. Transl. of the *Horace* of Pierre Corneille. The 5th a. add. by Sir John Denham. Ac. at Court. Pr. 1667. Sometimes referred to as *Horace and Pompée.*

HORACE AND LYDIA. C. 1 a. F. Ponsard. Publ. by S. French, Ltd. (Old plays.)

HORATIUS. Roman T. By Sir Wm. Lower. Transl. fr. Corneille. Pr. 1656.

HORATIUS COCLES. O. 1 a. Méhul, February 18, 1794.

HORN OF PLENTY, THE. Ca. Mrs. Gordon Ascher. Acton Central H., December 15, 1897.

HORNETS' NEST, A. Ca. G. L. Gordon. Op. C., January 13, 1876.

HORNETS' NEST, THE. C. 4 a. H. J. Byron. Hay., June 17, 1878.

HORSE AND THE WIDOW, THE. F. Thos. Dibdin. Fr. the German of A. von Kotzebue. C.G., May 30, 1799. Pr. 1799.

HORSE OF THE CAVERN, THE. Astley's, May 12, 1856.

HORTENSIA. T. 5 a. Pr. 1815. N.ac.

HOSPITAL FOR FOOLS, AN. D. Fable. Rev. Miller. Ac. D.L., November 15, 1739. Pr. 1739. Possibly this piece furnished Garrick with the hint for *Lethe.*

HOSPITAL OF LOVERS; OR, LOVE'S HOSPITAL, THE. C. Geo. Wilde. 1636. N.p.

HOT ANGER SOON COLD. P. Henry Chettle, Henry Porter, and Ben Jonson. Ac. 1598.

HOT NIGHT, A. C. 3 a. W. Manning. M. by H. Soutter and J. Bayliss. Preston N.T.R., August 3, 1901.

HOT OLD TIME, A. Sk. Tom Terriss and Robt. Perris. Hammersmith Palace, December 17, 1906.

HOT WATER. F.C. 3 a. H. B. Farnie. Fr. Meilhac and Halévy's *La Boule.* Criterion, November 13, 1876, and rev. August 15, 1894.

HOTEL; OR, SERVANT WITH TWO MASTERS, THE. F. Robert Jephson. Ac. at Dublin. Pr. at Cork, 1783. This piece has the same foundation as Vaughan's. See *Two Strings to Your Bow.*

HOTEL; OR, THE DOUBLE VALET, THE. F. Thos. Vaughan. D.L., November 21, 1776. Partly a transl. of Goldoni's *Il Servitor di due Padroni* and partly fr. *Arlequin Valet de deux Maitres.* Pr. 1776.

HOTEL CHARGES; OR, HOW TO COOK A BIFFIN. F. Sk. 1 a. Chas. Selby. Adelphi, October 13, 1853.

HOUNSLOW HEATH. T. episode. 1 a. Portsmouth T.R., May 7, 1906.

HOUP LA! Ca. T. G. Warren. Comedy, August 18, 1891. Afterwards renamed *Rosabel.*

HOUP LA! TRA-LA-LA! Ca. H. Mainwaring Dunstan. Fr. the German. Royalty, May 20, 1886.

HOUR, THE. C. 3 a. Nugent Monck. Bayswater Bijou, May 6, 1907.

HOUR AT IPSWICH STATION, AN. F. Frank Harvey. Ipswich T.R., Jan. 19, 1874.

HOUR AT SEVILLE, AN. Int. C. Selby. Adelphi, March 10, 1858.

HOUR BEFORE MARRIAGE, AN. F. 2 a. C.G., Jan. 25, 1772. Pr. 1772. Prol. by Woodward.

HOUR GLASS, THE. A morality. 1 a. W. B. Yeats. Queen's Gate H. (amat.), May 2, 1903; Gt. Queen St., June 14, 1907.

HOUR OF HER TRIUMPH, THE. D. pro. and 4 a. Wm. Hibbert. Hammersmith Lyric, February 26, 1906.

HOUSE, THE. P. Geo. Gloriel. Court, December 31, 1907.

HOUSE AGENT'S DILEMMA, THE. F. G. Hyde Lees. Queen's Gate H., May 2, 1902.

HOUSE DIVIDED. F. 2 a. J. T. Haines. Publ. by J. Dicks.

HOUSE DOG, THE. F. 1 a. Thos. Higgie. 1850.

HOUSE IN GREEN STREET, THE. P. 4 a. Mrs. C. Chilvers. King's H., W.C., May 13, 1908.

HOUSE IN THAMES STREET, THE. D. Alexander Dorrell. Ipswich, T.R., May 7, 1885.

HOUSE IN THE VALLEY, THE. Grecian, May 28, 1860.

HOUSE NEXT DOOR, THE. F. 1 a. Austin B. Austin. Tolmers Institute, Hampstead Road, March 16, 1905.

HOUSE OF BONDAGE, THE. P. 3 a. Seymour Obermer. H M.T., March 16, 1909 (mat.).

HOUSE OF BURNSIDE, THE. P. 3 a. Louis N. Parker. Fr. Geo. Mitchell's *La Maison* (originally prod. as *Burnside and Co.; a House of Cards,* Dublin R., October 1, 1903). Terry's, April 28, 1904.

HOUSE OF CARDS, A. 4 a. Sydney Grundy. Condensed fr. V. Sardou's *Maison Neuve.* Brighton T.R., November 13, 1891.

HOUSE OF CLAY, THE. P. 3 a. (Adap. fr. *La Maison d'Argile* of Emile Fabre.) Herbert Swears. Blackpool O.H., April 24, 1908; Coronet, October 2, 1908.

HOUSE OF COLBERG, THE. P. 5 a. T. J. Serle. D.L., October 1, 1832.

HOUSE OF DARNLEY, THE. C. 5 a. Lord Lytton. Rev. by C. F. Coghlan. Court, October 5, 1877.

HOUSE OF DOMBEY, THE. Adap., 5 a., fr. Dickens's novel, by F. T. Shore and W. Dexter. Prod. by amateurs. Cripplegate Inst., November 3, 1906.

HOUSE OF LADIES. Ba. 1 a. Mark Lemon. Olympic.

HOUSE OF LIES, A. D. 4 a. Ch. Hannan. Rugby T.R., November 24, 1892 (C.P.); Hammersmith Lyric, July 20, 1895.

HOUSE OF LORDS, THE. Oa. 1 a. Harry Greenbank. M. by G. W. Byng and Ernest Ford. Lyric, July 5, 1894.

HOUSE OF MORVILLE, THE. C. Luke. 1812.

HOUSE OF MYSTERY, A. D. 4 a. Frank Harvey. Portsmouth, Prince's, May 2, 1898; Imperial, May 12, 1898.

HOUSE OF PIERRE, THE. P. 1 a. Julie Opp. Faversham and Kate Jordon. Dublin Royal, November 8, 1907; Adelphi, September 14, 1908.

HOUSE OF RIMMON, THE. D. 4 a. H. Van Dyke. Bayswater Bijou, March 16, 1908 (C.P.).

HOUSE OF SHADOWS, THE. Dr. phantasy. 2 parts. E. L. Lomax. R. Acad. of M., May 5, 1905.

HOUSE OF SHAME, THE. Modern P. Ada G. Abbott. Cardiff Royal, June 24, 1907. See *The End of the Story.*

HOUSE OF SLEEP, THE. C.D. 4 a. Hubert Warwick. Balham Assembly R., December 6, 1897.

HOUSE OF TERROR, THE. Sk. 1 a. J. G. Brandon. Islington Pal., March 9, 1908.

HOUSE OF THE TRAITOR, THE. P. 1 a. Rathwell Wilson. Adap. fr. the Fr. story *Mateo Falcone* of Prosper Merimée. (Prod. by the Dramatic Debaters.) Court, March 21, 1909.

HOUSE ON THE BRIDGE OF NOTRE DAME, THE. D. 3 a. Colin Hazlewood. Adap. fr. French of Theodore Barrière and Hyde Kock. Ac. at Ambigu Comique, September 22, 1860; Lyceum, February 11, 1861; Marylebone, April 1, 1861.

HOUSE ON THE MARSH, THE. D. 4 a. Adap. fr. her novel of the same name by Miss Florence Warden. Nottingham T.R., March 2, 1885; Standard, June 1, 1885.

HOUSE ON THE MARSH, THE. D. G. M. Wood. Adap. fr. Miss Florence Warden's novel. Derby Lecture H., March 28, 1885.

HOUSE ON THE MARSH, THE. D. Hugh Willoughby. Adap. fr. Miss Florence Warden's novel. Margate T.R., September 28, 1885.

HOUSE OR THE HOME? THE. C. 2 a. Tom Taylor. Adap. fr. Octave Feuillet's *Peril dans la Demeure.* Adelphi, May 16, 1859. See *The Opal Ring.*

HOUSE OUT AT WINDOWS, THE. M. Piece. 1 a. M. by Corri. D.L., May 10, 1817.

HOUSE OUT OF WINDOWS, A. F. 1 a. Wm. Brough. Lyceum, October 18, 1852.

HOUSE ROOM. F. 1 a. R. B. Peake. Publ. by S. French, Ltd. (Old Plays).

HOUSE THAT JACK BUILT. O. 1 a. G. Fox.

HOUSE THAT JACK BUILT. Fairy P. 1 a. E. P. Medley In verse. Publ. by S. French, Ltd

HOUSE THAT JACK BUILT, THE. D.L. December, 1862.

HOUSE THAT JACK BUILT. Fairy P. H. C. Newton. M. by C. E. Howells. Op. C., December 24, 1894.

HOUSE TO BE SOLD, A. M. Piece. 2 a. James Cobb. M. by Kelly. Fr. the French, *Maison à Vendre.* D.L., November 17, 1802. Pr. 1802.

HOUSE TO BE SOLD, A. F. J. Baylis. Transl. fr. the French. Pr. 1804. N.ac.

HOUSE-BOAT, THE. Ca. H. W. Williamson. P.O.W., November 24, 1886.

HOUSEBREAKER, THE. F.C. 3 a. Stanley Rogers. Stockton-on-Tees T.R., March 25, 1892; Eleph. and C., July 31, 1893.

HOUSEHOLD FAIRY, A. Dom. Sk. 1 a. Francis Talfourd. St. James's, December 24, 1859.

HOUSEHOLD WORDS. Ca. W. Bourne. Plymouth T.R., February 13, 1884.

HOUSEKEEPER, THE. F. Hoadly. N.p. (Before 1814.)

HOUSEKEEPER, THE. F. 3 a. Metcalfe Wood and Beatrice Heron-Maxwell. Birmingham P.O.W., November 29, 1904; Camden, December 5, 1904; St. James's, October 12, 1905.

HOUSEKEEPER; OR, THE WHITE ROSE, THE. C. 2 a. Douglas Jerrold. Hay., July 17, 1833; rev., Royalty, 1872.

HOVEL, THE. B.O. D.L., May 23, 1797. N.p

HOW A MAN MAY CHUSE A GOOD WIFE FROM A BAD. C. Anon., but ascr. by Garrick to Joshua Cooke. ? taken fr. Cynthio's novels. Pr. 1602. Ac. by the Earl of Worcester's servants.

HOW DE FIGEAC CAME TO COURT. P. Prol. and 3 a. Arthur Holmes Gore and W. Scarth Dixon. Glasgow King's, August 25, 1905.

HOW DO YOU MANAGE? F. T. H. Bayly. ? Adelphi

HOW DREAMS COME TRUE. Dr. Sk. John Todhunter, M.D. Grosvenor Gallery, July 17, 1890.

HOW GIRLS ARE BROUGHT TO RUIN. D. 4 a. Mrs. Morton Powell. Liverpool Queen's, January 25, 1909.

HOW HE LIED TO HER HUSBAND. Geo. Bernard Shaw, Court, February 28, 1905.

HOW I FOUND CRUSOE; OR, THE FLIGHT OF IMAGINATION. Burl. Alfred Thompson. Olympic, December 28, 1872.

HOW LONDON LIVES. Melo-d. 5 a. Martyn Field and Arthur Shirley. Adap. fr. *Le Camelot* of Paul Andry, Max Maurey, and Georges Jubin. Princess's, December 27, 1897.

HOW MONEY'S MADE. P. 4 a. F. Brook Warren. Salford Regent, July 31, 1899.

HOW NIHILISTS ARE MADE. P. 4 a. A. B. Mackay. Llanelly Royalty, September 21, 1906.

HOW SHE LOVES HIM. C. 5 a. Dion Boucicault. Liverpool P.O.W.'s, 1863; P.O W.'s, December 21, 1867.

HOW STOUT YOU'RE GETTING! P. 1 a. J. M. Morton. Princess's, July 16, 1855.

HOW THE VOTE WAS WON. P. 1 a. Cicely Hamilton and Christopher St. John. Caxton H., April 15, 1909; Shakespeare, July 12, 1909.

HOW TIME FLIES; OR, THINGS THAT HAPPEN EVERY HOUR. D. Elphinstone. Victoria, April 24, 1869.

HOW TO BE HAPPY. C. Geo. Brewer. Hay., August 9, 1794. N.p.

HOW TO BE WISE; OR, FOLLY EXPOSED. Dr. P. Maclaren. Pr. at Dumfries, 1808.

HOW TO CHUSE A GOOD WIFE, ETC. See *How a Man*, etc.

HOW TO DIE FOR LOVE. F. 2 a. Adap. fr. Kotzebue's "Blind Geladin." D.L., May 18, 1814; Lyceum, September 2, 1816, and August 28, 1826.

HOW TO GROW RICH. C. 5 a. Frederic Reynolds. C.G. Pr. 1793.

HOW TO KILL HIM. F. Frederick Robson. Stockton-on-Tees T.R., July 14, 1873.

HOW TO LEARN OF A WOMAN TO WOO. P. Thos. Heywood. Ac. at Court, December, 1605. N.p.

HOW TO MAKE HOME HAPPY. C.D. 1 a. Wm. Brough. Lyceum, November 7, 1853.

HOW TO PAY THE RENT. F. 1 a. T. Power. Publ. by J. Dicks. Hay., April 2, 1840.

HOW TO SETTLE ACCOUNTS WITH YOUR LAUNDRESS. F. J. Stirling Coyne. Adelphi, July 26, 1847.

HOW TO TAKE UP A BILL. V. 1 a. Moncrieff. Publ. by S. French, Ltd.

HOW TO TEASE AND HOW TO PLEASE. G. Ascr. variously to Mrs. Inchbald, Morton, and T. Dibdin. C.G., March 29, 1810. N.p.

HOW TO WIN A WAGER. F. Otley. Bristol T.R., November 30, 1874.

HOW TO WIN HIM. C. 4 a. Adap. fr. Xaraf and Carre's French C., *Pour Etre Aimé*. By Cosmo G. Lennox. Avenue, March 17, 1903 (C.P.).

HOW WE LIVE IN LONDON. J. B. Johnstone.

HOW WE LIVE IN THE WORLD OF LONDON. Surrey, March 24, 1856.

HOW WE SPENT CHRISTMAS DAY IN '69. D. Harry M. Pitt. Surrey, January 30, 1870.

HOW WILL IT END? C. Mrs. West. Pr. 1799. N.ac.

HOW WILL THEY GET OUT OF IT? C. 3 a. Arthur Sketchley. St. James's, August 12, 1864.

HOW WOMEN ARE SLANDERED. D. 4 a. T. G. Bailey. Broughton Victoria, January 14, 1909.

HOW WOMEN RUIN MEN. Dom. D. 4 a. T. G. Bailey. (Orig. prod. at Broughton Victoria, November 9, 1908.) Stratford R., December 28, 1908.

HOW'S THAT, UMPIRE? F. Hayward Bidwell. Richmond, H.M.T., October 19, 1880.

HOW'S YOUR UNCLE? OR, THE LADIES OF THE COURT. F. 1 a. John Egerton Wilkes. Adelphi, August 27, 1855.

HOWARD HOWARD. Ca. Alfred Arthur. St. Geo. H., November 10, 1888.

HUBBY. F.C. 1 a. and 2 scenes. H. A. Sherburn. Ealing Lyric H., April 22, 1884; Shaftesbury, May 25, 1891.

HUBERT, THE BOWYER'S SON. D. Douglas Stewart. Victoria, February 28, 1874.

HUBERT'S PRIDE. C. Miss Julia Agnes Fraser. Strathaven Victoria, July 8, 1872.

HUDIBRASSO. Burl. O. 2 a. Ac. at T.R. at Voluptuaria. Pr. 1741.

HUE AND CRY, THE. F. Mrs. Inchbald. D.L., May 10, 1791. Transl. fr. the French. N.p.

HUE AND CRY, THE. Melo. D. 4 a. A. Shirley and B. Landeck. Pavilion, April 26, 1897.

HUE AND CRY; OR, THE KITHOGUE, THE. D. E. F. Brady. Shields T.R., April 16, 1883.

HUE AND CRY AFTER CUPID, THE. Masque. Ben Jonson. Rev. Botanic Gard., Reg. Pk., July 1, 1903. See *Masque at Lord Haddington's*.

HUE AND DYE. F. Frederick Hay. Strand, January 11, 1869.

HUGGER-MUGGER. F. 1 a. H. Saville Clarke. October 1, 1874.

HUGH WESTON'S WILL. Ca. Hull T.R., December 17, 1880.

HUGUENOT CAPTAIN, THE. D. 3 a. Watts Phillips. Princess's, July 2, 1866, and August 13, 1866.

HUGUENOT LOVER, THE. Ro. C. 4 a. Max Pemberton and J. McArthur. Globe, May 24, 1901.

HUGUENOTS, LES. O. 5 a. Wds. by Scribe and Deschamps. M. by Meyerbeer. Paris, 1836; D.L., July 4, 1845, and D.L., August 15, 1846; King's T., London; as *Gli Ugonotti*, at C.G., July 20, 1848.

HUGUENOTS; OR, THE MASK, THE SURGEON, ETC., THE. D. J. B. Howe. Surrey, June 16, 1873.

HULDA. O. C. Franck (1822-1890). Monte Carlo, 1894.

HULLA. C. Glover. MMS. before 1814.

HUMAN HEARTS. C.D. 4 a. Hal Reid. Kennington, June 5, 1905.

HUMAN NATURE. Ca. Adap. by A. Harris and J. T. Williams. Olympic, July 22, 1867.

HUMAN NATURE. D. Henry Pettitt and Augustus Harris. D.L., September 12, 1885.

HUMAN SPIDER, THE. D. 5 a. Kenyon Lyle. Burnley Gaiety, November 14, 1898.

HUMAN SPORT, A. D. 1 a. Austin Fryers. Globe, May 1, 1895.

HUMAN TERROR, A. D. Pro. and 3 a. Henry Merriman, fr. Sue's *Mysteries of Paris*. Pav., March 9, 1903.

HUMANITIE AND SENSUALITIE. One of the eight int. by Sir David Lindsay. Publ. 1792.

HUMANITY; OR, A PASSAGE IN THE LIFE OF GRACE DARLING. D. 4 a. Hugh Marston and Leonard Rae. Leicester T.R., March 27, 1882; Standard, April 10, 1882.

HUMANITY; OR, LIFE FOR LIFE. D. Chas. Locksley. Sanger's Amphi., October 15, 1881.

HUMBUG. C. 2 a. F. C. Burnand. Idea partly fr. *Les Faux Bonshommes*. Royalty, December 19, 1867.

HUMBUG, THE. F.C. 3 a. Mark Melford. Ladbroke H., October 31, 1901.

HUMBUGS, THE. F. 4 a. Henry de Halsalle. Cripplegate Inst., April 5, 1904.

HUMBUGS OF THE HOUR. Burl. on *Bubbles of the Day*. G. A. Beckett.

HUMOUR OF THE AGE, THE. C. Thos. Baker. D.L. Pr. 1701.

HUMOUR OUT OF BREATH. C. John Day. Ac. by the Children of the Revels. Pr. 1608. Rev. at Hampstead Conservatoire, November 27, 1902.

HUMOURIST, THE. F. James Cobb. D.L., 1785. N.p.

HUMOURIST, THE. P. 1 a. Wilfred Thornely. Winchmore Hill, The Hall, November 15, 1905.

HUMOURISTS, THE. C. Thos. Shadwell. L.I.F., 1670. Ac. by the Duke's servants. Pr. 1671.

HUMOURISTS, THE. Dr. Ent. D.L., 1754. N.p.

HUMOUROUS COURTIER, THE. C. Jas. Shirley. Ac. at a private house in D.L. Pr. 1640.

HUMOUROUS DAY'S MIRTH. C. Geo. Chapman. Pr. 1599.

HUMOUROUS ETHICS. Dr. Bacon. 1757.

HUMOUROUS LIEUTENANT, THE. T.C. Beaumont and Fletcher. Pr. 1647. D.L. (at opening of the T.), April 8, 1663. Plot from Plutarch's "Life of Demetrius." Revived at D.L. as alt. by Reynolds, 1817. See *The Greek Slave*.

HUMOUROUS LOVERS, THE. C. William, Duke of Newcastle. Duke's T. Pr. 1667.

HUMOUROUS PROPOSAL, A. M. Ca. E. A. Rose and W. Melville. Sandgate Alhambra, October 23, 1905.

HUMOUROUS QUARREL; OR, THE BATTLE OF THE GREYBEARDS, THE. F. Ascr. to Israel Pottinger. Ac. at Southwark Fair. Pr., circa. 1761.

HUMOURS, THE COMEDY OF. Ac. at the Rose T., May 11, 1597. ? Ben Jonson's *Every Man in His Humour*.

HUMOURS OF A COFFEE HOUSE THE. C. "As it is daily acted at most of the coffee houses in London." Edward Ward. Pr. 1709.

HUMOURS OF AN ELECTION, THE. F. F. Pilou. C.G. Pr. 1780. First ac. under the title of *The Close of the Poll* or *The Humours*, etc.

HUMOURS OF AN ELECTION, THE. Sk. Adelphi, January, 1837.

HUMOURS OF AN IRISH COURT OF JUSTICE, THE. Dr. Satire. The dedication is signed A. Freeman Barber, and dated December 12, 1750. N.ac.

HUMOURS OF BRIGHTON; OR, THE CLIFF, STEINE, AND LEVEL, THE. Sk., interspersed with songs, etc. J. C. Cross. Ac. at Brighton, 1792.

HUMOURS OF COURT; OR, MODERN GALLANTRY, THE. See *The Humours of the Court*.

HUMOURS OF ELECTIONS, THE. F. Mrs. Centlivre. Pr. 1737. See *Gotham Election, Close of the Poll*.

HUMOURS OF EXCHANGE ALLEY, THE. F. W. R. Chetwode. Pr. 1720. See *The Stock Jobbers*.

HUMOURS OF GREENOCK FAIR; OR, THE TAYLOR MADE A MAN, THE. M.Int. A. M'Laren. Ac. at Greenock. Pr. at Paisley, 1789.

HUMOURS OF HARROGATE. F. Meek. N.p. Wr. before 1814.

HUMOURS OF JOHN BULL, THE. Op. F. Sylvester Otway (John Oswald). Pr. 1789.

HUMOURS OF OXFORD, THE. C. Rev. Jas. Miller. D.L. Pr. 1730.

HUMOURS OF PORTSMOUTH; OR, ALL IS WELL THAT ENDS WELL, THE. F. 3 a. Pr. 1700.

HUMOURS OF PURGATORY, THE. F. Benj. Griffin. L.I.F. and pr. 1716. Borrowed fr. *Fatal Marriage*.

HUMOURS OF THE AGE, THE. G. Finger. 1701.

HUMOURS OF THE ARMY, THE. C. Chs. Shadwell. D.L., January 29, 1713. Pr. 1713. Taken fr. D'Ancourt's *Les Curieux de Campagne*.

HUMOURS OF THE COMPTER, THE. C. Mentioned in a catalogue of books sold by Jonas Brown at the Black Swan Without Temple Bar, 1717. ? *The City Ramble*, of which the above is a second title.

HUMOURS OF THE COURT; OR, MODERN GALLANTRY, THE. B.O. Pr. 1732.

HUMOURS OF THE ROAD; OR, A RAMBLE TO OXFORD, THE. C. Anon. Pr. 1738.

HUMOURS OF THE TIMES; OR, WHAT NEWS NOW? THE. C.O. Pr. 1799. N.ac.

HUMOURS OF WAPPING, THE. F. Pr. 1703.

HUMOURS OF WHIST, THE. Dr. Satire. Not intended for the stage. Pr. 1743. Also pr. 1753, with the second title of *The Polite Gamester; or, Humours of Whist*.

HUMOURS OF YORK, THE. C. Mrs. Davis. L.I.F., 1715. See *Northern Heiress*.

HUMPBACKED LOVER, THE. F. 1 a. C. Mathews. Publ. by J. Dicks.

HUMPHREY, DUKE OF GLOUCESTER. Hist. T. Ambrose Philips. D.L. Pr. 1723.

HUMPTY DUMPTY. Lyceum, December 26, 1868.

HUNCHBACK, THE. P. 5 a. Sheridan Knowles. C.G., April 5, 1832; Princess's, May, 1847.

HUNCHBACK; OR, FROLICKS IN BAGDAD, THE. Revised and altered m. piece f. on a tale fr. "The Arabian Nights." Lyceum playbill, July 8, 1820.

HUNCHBACK BACK AGAIN; OR, PECULIAR JULIA, THE. Burl. F. C. Burnand. Olympic, December 23, 1879.

117, ARUNDEL STREET, STRAND. F. 1 a. Lieut.-Col. H. R. Addison. Lyceum, March 24, 1860.

£100 A-SIDE. F. J. R. Brown. Sadler's Wells (as *Blower Jones*), February 12, 1881; Pavilion, December 8, 1890.

HUNDRED-POUND NOTE, THE. F. 2 a. R. Brinsley Peake. C.G. Lyceum (41st time), November 26, 1828.

HUNDRED THOUSAND POUNDS, A. D. 3 a. H. J. Byron. P. of W.'s, May 5, 1866.

HUNDRED YEARS AGO, A. Pastoral Oa. 1 a. Alec Nelson. M. by J. Wood. Royalty, July 16, 1892.

HUNDRED YEARS HENCE, A. P. 1 a. Margaret S. Clark. Glasgow Royalty, February 18, 1907.

HUNDREDTH WOMAN, THE. Dom. D. 4 a. Marie Hassell. Birmingham, P. of W., May 10, 1904. C.P.

HUNGARIAN LION, THE. Wr. by Gunnel. This play is ment. by Sir Henry Herbert December 4, 1623.

HUNGER. D. W. Raymond. Gt. Grimsby T.R., March 10, 1869.

HUNIADES; OR, THE SIEGE OF BELGRADE. T. H. Brand. Hay., January 18, 1792. See *Agmunda*. Pr. 1798.

HUNT FOR A HUSBAND, A. F. 1 a. J. P. Wooler. Adapt. fr. the French. Strand, Mar. 28, 1864.

HUNT THE SLIPPER. Mus. F. Rev. Henry Knapp. Hay., August 21, 1784. Pr. in a piratical way 1792.

'HUNT THE SLIPPER. F.C. 3 a. F. Locke. Cork T.R. and O.H., April 18, 1887.

HUNTED DOWN; OR, THE ITALIAN'S VENGEANCE. D. Geo. Wynne Bennett. Norwich T.R., January 31, 1881.

HUNTED DOWN; OR, THE TWO LIVES OF MARY LEIGH. D. 3 a. Dion Boucicault. St. James's November 5, 1866.

HUNTED DOWN BY FATE. D. Birkenhead T.R., December 11, 1882.

HUNTED TO DEATH. D. Harwood Cooper. Victoria, October 26, 1867.

HUNTER OF THE ALPS, THE. D. 2 a. Wm. Dimond. Hay., 1804; D.L., July 8, 1835. Pr. N.d.

HUNTERS' MASQUE, THE. P. 1573-4.

HUNTING A FOX. Mus. Ca. 1 a. Wr. and comp. by J. W. Trievnor. Portsmouth T.R., April 5, 1878.

HUNTING A TURTLE. F. 1 a. Chas. Selby. Queen's, September 14, 1835.

HUNTING OF CUPID, THE. C. Peele, 1591, according to Brewer.

HUNTINGDON'S DIVERTISEMENT. See *Huntingdon*, etc.

HUNTINGTON DIVERTISEMENT; OR, AN ENTERLUDE FOR THE GENERAL ENTERTAINMENT AT THE COUNTY FEAST HELD AT MERCHANT TAYLOR'S HALL, THE, June 20, 1678. Pr. The piece has initials, "W. M."

HUNTINGTON, EARL OF. See *John a Kent, The Downfall*, etc., *The Death*, etc.

HUON OF BOURDEAUX. Ac. by the Earl of Sussex's men, December 28, 1593.

HURLOTHRUMBO; OR, THE SUPERNATURAL. P. Sam. Johnson. Pr. 1729. Ac. at the Little T. in the Hay., 1729.

HURLY BURLY. Military pant. and ballet. Empire, December 21, 1885.

HURLY BURLY; OR, NUMBER SEVEN TWENTY EIGHT, THE. F.C. 3 a. Herman Hendriks. Adap. fr. the German *Schwabenstreich* of Franz von Schöthan. New Cross H. (in 4 a.), May 24, 1884; Globe, June 21, 1884.

HURLY BURLY; OR, THE FAIRY OF THE WELL. Pant. D.L., 1785-6. Ascr. to James Cobb and Thos. King.

HURON, LE. O. Marmontel. M. by Grétry. 1769.

HUSBAND AND WIFE. F.C. 3 a. F. C. Philips and Percy Fendall. Criterion (mat.), April 30, 1891; Comedy, July 7, 1891.

HUSBAND AT SIGHT, A. F. 2 a. J. B. Buckstone. Adap. fr. the French, Hay., August 13, 1830.

HUSBAND FOR AN HOUR, A. E. Falconer. Hay., June 1, 1857.

HUSBAND HIS OWN CUCKOLD, THE. C. John Dryden, jun. L.I.F. Pr. 1696. Prol. by Congreve. Pref. and Epil. by Dryden, sen.

HUSBAND IN CLOVER, A. F. 1 a. H. C. Merivale. Lyceum, December 26, 1873.

HUSBAND IN SIGHT, A J. B. Buckstone.

HUSBAND OF AN HOUR, THE. D. in 2 periods. E. Falconer. Hay., May, 1857.

HUSBAND OF MY HEART, THE. C.D. 2 a. Chas. Selby. Hay., October 23, 1850.

HUSBAND TO ORDER, A. S.C.D. 2 a. J. M. Morton. Olympic, October 17, 1859.

HUSBAND'S HUMILIATION, A. Ca. 1 a. Annie Hughes. Criterion, June 26, 1896.

HUSBAND'S VENGEANCE. Marylebone, November 23, 1857.

HUSBAND'S WIVES AND LOVERS. F. 1 a. Publ. by S. French, Limited.

HUSBANDS BEWARE! D.L., October 28, 1865.

HUSBANDS OF ELIZABETH, THE. P. 3 a. Leechmere Worrall. Newquay Victoria H., May 30, 1905.

HUSH! OR, SECRETS AT COURT. C. 2 a. D.L., December 27, 1836.

HUSH-A-BYE, BABY. Pant. Chas. Milward and W. S. Gilbert. First prod. Astley's, December 26, 1866.

HUSH MONEY. F. 2 a. C. Dance. Publ. by J. Dicks.

HUSH MONEY. P. 4 a. Herbert Keith. Terry's. June 23, 1892.

HUSH MONEY; OR, THE DISAPPEARANCE OF SEXTON BLAKE. D. 4 a. Shakespeare, May 3, 1909.

HUSHED UP. C. 1 a. W. Hall. Leeds Grand T., June 4, 1903.

HUSTINGS, THE. Operatic Impromptu. Lyceum playbill announced for June 30, 1818.

HUT OF THE RED MOUNTAINS; OR, THIRTY YEARS OF A GAMBLER'S LIFE, THE. D. 3 a. H. M. Milner. Adap. fr. Victor Ducagne's *Trente ans, ou la Vie d'un Joueur.* Coburg. 1827.

HYACINTH HALVEY. P. Lady Gregory, Gt. Queen St., June 12, 1907.

HYCKE SCORNER. Date and author's name unknown. "Emprynted by me, Wynkyn de Worde" (Blackletter); repr. by Hawkins 1773, in *The Origin of the English Drama.*

HYDASPES; OR, L'IDASPE FEDELE. Italian O. Comp. for a London audience by Francesco Mancini. Hay. T., May 23, 1710.

HYDE PARK. C. James Shirley. Ac. at the private house in D.L. Licensed 1632. Pr. 1637. First occasion of horses brought on the stage on its revival in 1668.

HYDE PARK IN AN UPROAR. Int. E. J. Eyre. 1813. N.p.

HYDER ALI; OR, THE LIONS OF MYSORE. Oriental Spec. M. by Cooke. D.L., October 17, 1831.

HYDROPATHICS. F. 1 a. Tom Wotton. MS. with Douglas Cox.

HYDROPATHY. C.O. 2 a. Wm. Boyce. M. by Alfred C. Davies. Islington Myddleton H., January 26, 1892.

HYMEN. Int. Ascr. to Allen, who was probably the author of *Hezekiah.* D.L., 1764. N.p.

HYMEN IN HALF-AN-HOUR. Sk. Fitzroy Gardner. St. Leonards Pier Pav., July 31, 1902.

HYMEN WINS. F. 1 sc. Wilfred F. Field. Southall Public H., November 17, 1890.

HYMEN'S HOLIDAY; OR, CUPID'S FAGARIES. Masque. Samuel Rowley. Ac. at Court, 1612. Rev. before the King and Queen at Whitehall, 1633. N.p.

HYMEN'S TRIUMPH. Postoral T.C. Samuel Daniel. Ac. at Court, 1614. Pr. 1623. Ent. Stationers' Co., January 13, 1614.

HYMEN'S TRIUMPH; OR, TRICK UPON TRICK. Pant. L.I.F., 1737.

HYMENÆI; OR, THE SOLEMNITIES OF A MASQUE AND BARRIERS AT A MARRIAGE. Ben Jonson. Pr. 1606.

HYMENEAL PARTY; OR, THE GENEROUS FRIENDS, THE. C. Pr. 1789. N.ac.

HYMN OF PRAISE (LOBGESANG). Cant. Mendelssohn. Leipsic, 1840. See *Lobgesang.*

HYPATIA. Poetic D. 4 a. Stuart Ogilvie. F. on Kingsley's novel. Hay., January 2, 1893.

HYPERMNESTRA; OR, LOVE IN TEARS. T. Robert Owen. Pr. 1703. N.ac.

HYPERMNESTRA, THE GIRL OF THE PERIOD. Burl. Frank Sikes. Lyceum, March 27, 1869.

HYPNOTISEE. Royalty, January 31, 1889.

HYPNOTIST, THE. Sk. Brian McCullough. Poplar Queen's, December 30, 1895.

HYPNOTIST, THE. See *Suggestion.*

HYPNOTIST; OR, A BLACK HEART, THE. D. 3 a. B. Copping. Edmonton T.R., April 7, 1903.

HYPOCHONDRIAC, THE. C. John Ozell. A transl. of Mobiere's *Malade Imaginaire.*

HYPOCHONDRIAC, THE. F. Borr. fr. foregoing. N.ac.

HYPOCHONDRIAC, THE. M.E. Andrew Franklin. Ac. at Smock Alley, Dublin, 1785. N.p.

HYPOCHONDRIAC, THE. Ent. by Mathews. Lyceum playbill, March 1, 1821.

HYPOCRITE, THE. C. 3 a. Isaac Bickerstaff. Alt. of Cibber's *Nonjuror,* which was adap. fr. Molière's *Tartuffe.* D.L., November 17, 1768. First time in a new form in 5 a., with M. by Jolly. Lyceum, July 27, 1819. D.L., rev. February 1, 1868.

HYPOCRITE, THE. Sk. 1 scene. Middlesex M.H., May 22, 1905.

HYPOCRITES, THE. P. 4 a. H. A. Jones (C.P.). Hull Grand, August 30, 1906; Hicks', August 27, 1907.

I

I AND MY DOUBLE. F. J. Oxenford. M. by G. A. Macfarren. Lyceum, June 16, 1835.

I AND MY FATHER IN LAW. C. 1 a. H. C. Pemberton. Publ. by S. French, Ltd.

I COULDN'T HELP IT. F. 1 a. John Oxenford. Lyceum, April 19, 1862.

I DEFY THE WORLD. D. 4 a. Wigan T.R., July 20, 1903. Greenwich Carlton, February 22, 1904.

I DINE WITH MY MOTHER. F. R. M. Levey. Dublin T.R., January 23, 1871.

I LOVE YOU. Ca. 1 a. Wybert Reeve. Originally played during Mr. Reeve's tour with the drama *Woman in White.* Newcastle-upon-Tyne T.R., September 18, 1872.

I.O.; OR, LOVE IN A FOG. Sadler's Wells, April 12, 1864.

I.O.U. F. Dublin Gaiety, July 5, 1873.

I.O.U. C. 3 a. Geo. P. Hawtrey. Hove Town H., December 20, 1887.

I.O.U. F.C. Fr. *L'Article* 7. G. Canniage and A. Chevalier. Richmond New T., January 17, 1891.

I.O.U. See *Shylock and Co.*

I.O.U.; OR, THE WAY OF THE WICKED. D. J. Holmes Grover. Sunderland T.R., February 20, 1879. Eleph. and C., June 28, 1879.

I PAGLIACCI (The Strollers). O. 2 a. R. Leoncavallo. C.G., May 19, 1893; Waldorf, May 22, 1905.

I PROMESSI SPOSI. O. 4 a. F. on Manzoni's novel. Transl. of lib. by Henry Hersee. M. by A. Ponchielli. Edinburgh T.R., March 23, 1881.

I RANTZAU. C.G., July 7, 1893.

I SHALL INVITE THE MAJOR. Petite C. 1 a. G. von Moser. Liberally transl. by Sydney Rosenfeld. Publ. by De Witt. New York, 1875.

I WANT TO GO ON THE STAGE. Sk. F. R. Yeulett. Stoke Newington Palace, January 13, 1908.

I WILL HAVE A WIFE. C. Ent. 2 a. M. by Reeve. Lyceum, August 7, 1828.

I WILL IF YOU WILL. St. James's, February 14, 1860.

I'LL BE YOUR SECOND. F. 1 a. G. Herbert Rodwell. Olympic, October 11, 1831.

I'LL SEE YOU RIGHT. Ca. J. R. Crauford. Leicester R.O.H., June 3, 1878; Gaiety, November 30, 1882.

I'LL TELL YOU WHAT! C. Mrs. Eliz. Inchbald. Pr. 1786. Hay., August 4, 1785. Principal incident derived fr. *The English Merchant.*

I'LL TELL YOUR WIFE. F. 1 a. N. S. Webster. Adelphi, March 10, 1855.

I'LL WRITE TO THE TIMES. F. 1 a. J. P. Wooler. Sadler's Wells, October 16, 1856.

I'M NOT MYSELF AT ALL. F. C. A. Maltby. D.L., December 27, 1869.

I'VE EATEN MY FRIEND. F. 1 a. John Bridgeman. Olympic, September 8, 1851.

I'VE TAKEN A HOUSE. M. Monol. Corney Grain. St. Geo. H., November 4, 1889.

I'VE WRITTEN TO BROWNE; OR, A NEEDLESS STRATAGEM. Ca. 1 a. T. J. Williams. Olympic, February 7, 1859.

IB AND LITTLE CHRISTINA. "Picture in three panels." Basil Hood. P.O.W., May 15, 1900; Savoy, November 14, 1901 (M. by F. Leoni). Daly's, January 11, 1904; Lyric, January 19, 1904; rev. Adelphi, September 21, 1908.

IBIS. Ovid. See "Latin Plays."

IBRACIAN WONDER. Webster and Rowley.

IBRAHIM, THE ILLUSTRIOUS BASSA. T. in verse. Elkanah Settle. F. on Georges de Scudery's *L'Illustre Bassa.* Duke's T., 1676. Pr. 1677.

IBRAHIM XII., EMPEROR OF THE TURKS. T. Mrs. Mary Pix. Pr. 1696. D.L., October 20, 1702.

IBSEN CHRISTMAS, AN. Duo. Henry Gibson. Birkbeck Inst. October 20, 1897.

IBSEN'S GHOST; OR, TOOLE UP TO DATE. A new "Hedda" in 1 a. J. M. Barrie. Toole's, May 30, 1891.

ICE WITCH; OR, THE FROZEN HAND, THE. A Tale of Enchantment. 2 a. J. B. Buckstone. M. by Cooke. Taken from *The Ohio.* D.L., April 4, 1831.

ICEBOUND; OR, THE EXILES OF FORTUNE. D. 4 a. Fredk. Cooke. Wolverhampton Star T. (pl. in 5 a.), July 25, 1892. Pavilion, July 3, 1893.

ICI ON (NE) PARLE (PAS) FRANCAIS. F. without words, with m. accomp. by W. S. Robins. Toole's, June 13, 1891.

ICI ON PARLE FRANCAIS. F. 1 a. T. J. Williams. Adelphi, May 9, 1859.

IDALIA; OR, THE ADVENTURESS. D. 3 a. Geo. Roberts. F. partly on Ouida's novel. St. James's, April 22, 1867. See *The Power of England.*

IDEAL, AN. P. 1 a. H. W. C. Newte. Bayswater Bijou, February 9, 1904.

IDEAL HUSBAND, AN. P. of modern life by Oscar Wilde. Hay., January 3, 1895.

IDEALS. Ca. 1 a. M. S. Clark. Publ. by Douglas Cox.

IDELIA; OR, THE FEUDS OF SWITZERLAND. T. Simeons, jun. Ac. at Liverpool, 1802. N.p.

IDIOT OF HEIDELBERG, THE. P. 3 a. Rayner. Pub. by J. Dicks.

IDIOT OF THE MILL, THE. D. 2 a. Pub. by S. French, Ltd.

IDIOT OF THE MOUNTAIN, THE. D. 3 a. Wm. E. Suter. Adap. fr. the French of Eugène Grangé and L. Thiboust. (Theatre de la Gaité, June 3, 1861.) A ver. at the Surrey, September 7, 1861.

IDIOT WITNESS; OR, A TALE OF BLOOD, THE. Melo-d. 2 a. J. T. Haines. Coburg, 1823. Bath, March 22, 1827.

IDLE APPRENTICE. City of London, June 5, 1865.

IDLE BUSINESS; OR, MAN WHO HAS NO TIME. C. Holberg, 1750.

IDLE JACK. D. West Bromwich T.R., November 5, 1883.

IDLE 'PRENTICE, A TYBURNIAN IDYLL OF HIGH LOW JACK AND HIS LITTLE GAME. Burl. H. B. Farnie. Strand, September 10, 1870.

IDLE WORDS; OR, DEATH OR GLORY. D. Julia A. Fraser. Edinburgh Op. H. (amateurs), December 21, 1896.

IDLER, THE. P. 4 a. C. Haddon Chambers. Prod. in New York November 11, 1890. St. James's, February 26, 1891.

IDOL, THE. C. 3 a. Charles Wyndham. Folly, September 21, 1878.

IDOL AND THE HUSBAND, THE. Ca. Mrs. Albert S. Bradshaw. Adelphi, June 25, 1907.

IDOL OF AN HOUR, THE. D. 5 a. Geo. Gervaise Collingham. Adapt. fr. "Sapho," novel by Alphonse Daudet. Windsor T.R., January 16, 1899.

IDOL OF KANO; OR, THE CROCODILE AND THE BRIDE. C.O. 2 a. W. F. Hewer. Comp. T. Pope Arkell. Swindon Queen's T., April 20, 1904.

IDOL OF PARIS. D. 4 a. Chs. Darrell. Middlesbrough O.H., August 12, 1907; Dalston, February 17, 1908.

IDOLATORS, THE. Britannia, June 9, 1862.

IDOLE BRISSEE, L'. Wordless Sk. 3 sc. Percival H. T. Sykes. Collins' M.H., January 2, 1905.

IDOLS. P. 4 a. Roy Horniman. Adap. fr. W. J. Locke's novel. Birmingham R.T., August 24, 1908; Garrick, September 2, 1908.

IDOLS OF THE HEART. P. 1 a. Janette Steer. Liverpool Shakespeare, February 21, 1890; Grand, June 8, 1891; Criterion, July 12, 1892.

IDOMENEO. O. Mozart. Lib. by the Abbé Giambattista Varesco. Munich, January 29, 1781.

IDUNA. C.O. 3 a. Hugh Conway. M. by A. H. Behrend. Manchester Comedy. October 28, 1889.

IDYLL OF NEW YEAR'S EVE, AN. Miss Rosina Filippi. Chelsea Town H., January 31, 1890.

IDYLL OF SEVEN DIALS, AN. Rosina Filippi, P.O.W., May 30, 1899.

IDYLL OF THE CLOSING CENTURY. AN. 1 a. Estelle Burney. Lyceum, November 2, 1896.

IF I HAD A THOUSAND A YEAR! F. 1 a. J. M. Morton, Olympic, October 21, 1867.

IF I WERE KING. P. 4 a. J. H. McCarthy. St. James's, August 30, 1902.

IF I WERE KING. Mythical Fisherman's Rom. A ver. of *Si J'Etais Roi.* Harry Bruce.

IF I WERE RICH. Ca. 1 a. Frank Stainforth. Park, April 16, 1881.

IF IT BE NOT GOOD THE DIVEL IS IN IT. P. Thos. Dekker. Pr. 1612. Ac. at the Red Bull.

IF MEN WERE HONEST. D. 4 a. Albert Ward. Pav., November 11, 1903 (C.P.).

IF THE CAP FITS. Ca. 1 a. N. H. Harrington and Edmund Yates. Princess's, June 13, 1859.

IF WE ONLY KNEW. Rom. P. 4 a. Harry Nicholls and Charles Ross. Fulham Grand, September 28, 1908.

IF YOU KNOW NOT ME YOU KNOW NOBOBY; OR, THE TROUBLES OF QUEEN ELIZABETH. In 2 parts. Thos. Heywood. Part I., 1605; Part II., 1606. Rev. at the Cockpit 21 years later.

IFIGENIA IN AULIDE. O. Cherubini. 1788.

IFIGENIA IN AULIDE. See *Iphigenia*, etc.

IFIGENIA IN AULIDE. O. G. Abos. Naples (1708-1786).

IGNEZ DE CASTRO. T. Benj. Thompson. Transl. fr. the Portuguese of Don Domingo Quita. Pr. 1800. N. ac. See *Dona Ignez*, etc.

IGNORAMUS. Academical C. in Latin. Geo. Ruggle. An imitation of the Italian C. *La Trappolaria*, by G. Porta, which was based on the Pseudolus of Plautus. Ac. at Trin. Coll. H., 1615. Pr. 1630. See "Westminster Plays," "Latin Plays."

IGNORAMUS. C. by R. C. (? Rob. Codrington). Pr. 1662. A transl. of the Latin P. of same name.

IGNORAMUS; OR, THE ENGLISH LAWYER. C. D.L. Pr. 1736.

IHRE FAMILIE. D. with M. 3 a. J. Stinde and G. Engels. St. Geo. H., June 31, 1902.

ILDA D'AVENELLS. O. M. by Morlacchi. 1824.

ILDEGERTE, QUEEN OF NORWAY. P. B. Thompson fr. Kotzebue. 1799.

ILE DE TULIPATAN, L'. Op. bo. [illegible] a. Offenbach. 1868.

ILIAD. See "Greek Plays," "Epic Poems."

ILIAD AND ODYSSEY. See *A Tale of Troy*.

ILKA. C.O. Doppler.

ILL BEGINNING HAS A GOOD END, AND A BAD BEGINNING MAY HAVE A GOOD END, AN. C. John Forde. Pl. at Cockpit, 1613. Ent. Stationers' Co., June 29, 1660. Destroyed by Warburton's servant.

ILL-NATURED MAN, THE. C. Pr. 1773. Ac.

ILL-TREATED IL TROVATORE; OR, THE MOTHER, THE MAIDEN, AND THE MUSICIAN. Burl. Extrav. H. J. Byron. Adelphi, May 21, 1865.

ILLUMINATION; OR, THE GLAZIER'S CONSPIRACY, THE. Prel. F. Pilon. C.G., April 12, 1779. Pr. 1779.

ILLUSION. P. 3 a. Pierre Leclercq. Strand, July 3, 1890.

ILLUSION; OR, THE FRANCES OF NOURJAHAD. Oriental Spec. Lord Byron. M. by Byrne. D.L., November 25, 1813; January 27, 1814.

ILLUSION COMIQUE, L'. Extra. Corneille. See "French Classical Plays."

ILLUSIONS. C. 2 a. Joseph J. Dilley. Charing Cr., May 21, 1870.

ILLUSTRATION ON DISCORD, AN. Brough. Gallery of Illustration, April 3, 1861.

ILLUSTRIOUS STRANGER, THE. C.O. 2 a. Maurice Hardinge; music, H. W. Norman. Dover T.R., July 16, 1906.

ILLUSTRIOUS STRANGER; OR, MARRIED AND BURIED, THE. M.F. 2 a. James Kenney and Millingen. M. by Nathan. From a French D. D.L., August 4, 1827.

ILLUSTRIOUS STRANGER, THE. See *Brown Among*, etc. See *Mummies and Marriage*.

IM BUNTEN ROCK. C. 3 a. Van Schonthan and Von Schlicht. Great Queen Street, November 29, 1902.

IM-PATIENCE. M. travestie. Walter Browne. M. by P. Stanislaus. Liverpool P.O.W., August 25, 1884.

IM VARTESALON ERSTE KLASSE. King's Cross, December 12, 1885.

IM WEISSEN ROSSL. C. 3 a. O. Blumenthal and G. Kadelburg. Royalty, October, 1904.

IMAGE OF LOVE, THE. D. Bishop Bale.

IMAGINARY CONVERSATION, AN. Norreys Connell. Court, June 9, 1909.

IMAGINARY CUCKOLD, THE. C. John Ozell. A transl. of Molière's *Le Cocu Imaginaire*. D.L., April 11, 1733.

IMAGINARY OBSTACLE, THE. C. Transl. fr. the French. Pr. in Foote's Comic Theatre, 1762.

IMELDA. Ballet. 2 a. and 4 tableaux. Barrey. M. by R. Hughes. D.L., April 20, 1846.

IMENEO. O. Handel. 1740.

IMITATION; OR, THE FEMALE FORTUNE HUNTER. C. F. G. Waldron. D.L., May 12, 1783. N.p. An imitation of *The Beaux Stratagem*. See *Heigho for a Husband*.

IMITATION A LA MODE. Int. Ac. at the Earl of Aldborough's private theatre, Stratford Place, 1791. N.p.

IMMANUEL. Orat. Leslie. 1853.

IMOGEN'S NEW COOK. Duo. Mabel S. Mead. Ladbroke H. (amateurs), April 26, 1898.

IMPATIENT POVERTY. C. Pr. B.L. 1560. See *Interlude of Impacyente Poverte*.

IMPEACHED. D. Miss H. L. Walford. Gallery of Illus., May 24, 1873.

IMPERIAL CAPTIVES, THE. T. John Mottley. L.I.F., February 29, 1720. Pr. 1720.

IMPERIAL CONSPIRATOR OVERTHROWN; OR, SPANISH POISON FOR SUBJUGATION, THE. A Serio-burl. perf. P. H. Edwards. Pr. 1808.

IMPERIAL GUARD, THE. D. C. H. Hazlewood. Britannia, September 2, 1872.

IMPERIAL TRAGEDY, THE. Anon. Fr. a Latin play. Ascr. by Jacob to Sir Wm. Killigrew. Ac. at the Nursery in Barbican. Pr. 1669.

IMPERIALE. T. Sir Ralph Freeman. Pr. 1655.

IMPERTINENCE OF NANCY, THE. P. 3 a. Roland Bottomley. Queen's Gate H., January 26, 1905.

IMPERTINENT LOVERS; OR, THE COQUET AT HER WITS' END, THE. C. by "A Citizen of London." D.L., August 16, 1723. Pr. 1723. (? Wr. by Francis Hawling.)

IMPERTINENTS, THE. C. Ozell. Transl. fr. *Facheux*, of Molière.

IMPORTANCE OF BEING EARNEST, THE. "A trivial comedy." 3 a. Oscar Wilde. St. James's, February 14, 1895; Coronet, December 2, 1901; rev. St James's, January 7, 1902.

IMPOSSIBLE TRIO, THE. F. 1 a. Austin Hurgon. Croydon Grand, February 5, 1906.

IMPOSTOR, THE. T. Henry Brooke. Pr. 1778. N.ac. On the same subject as Miller's *Mahomet*.

IMPOSTOR, THE. C. Cumberland, 1789.

IMPOSTOR, THE. Dr. Sk. Alec D. Saville. Walthamstow King's, April 2, 1904.

IMPOSTOR DETECTED; OR, THE VINTNER'S TRIUMPH OVER B[ROOK]E AND H[ELLIE]R. F. Pr. 1712. Political, and not intended for the stage.

IMPOSTORS, THE. C. Richd. Cumberland. D.L., January 26, 1789. Pr. 1789. Partly on same plot as *The Beaux Stratagem*.

IMPOSTORS; OR, CURE FOR CREDULITY, THE. Reed. C.G., March 19, 1776.

IMPOSTURE, THE. T.C. Jas. Shirley. Blackfryars. Licensed 1640. Pr. 1652.

IMPOSTURE DEFEATED; OR, A TRICK TO CHEAT THE DEVIL. C. Geo. Powell Pr. 1698. D.L., 1698.

IMPOSTURES OF THOMAS BECKET, OF THE. Bishop Bale.

IMPRESSARIO, L'. O. Mozart. See *Die Schauspieldirektor*.

IMPRESSARIO, THE. O. 2 a. Fr. Mozart's *Schauspieldirektor*. Adap. into Eng. by W. Grist. Crystal Pal., September 13, 1877, and October 18, 1892.

IMPRESSIONS OF STELLA, THE. F. Nolan and Rolison. Cripplegate Inst., December 6, 1905.

IMPROMPTU OF VERSAILLES, THE. John Ozell. Transl. fr. Molière's comedy of same name.

IMPRUDENCE. C. 3 a. A. W. Pinero. Folly, July 27, 1881.

IMPUDENT PUPPY, AN. C.D. 2 a. D.L., November 7, 1855.

IMPULSE. P. 5 a. B. C. Stephenson. Adap. fr. *La Maison du Mari*. St. James's, December 9, 1882.

IN A BALCONY. P. B. Browning. Prince's H., November 28, 1884. See *A Mighty Error*.

IN A DAY. D. 3 a. Augusta Webster. Terry's, May 30, 1890.

IN A DISTANT LAND. D. 1 a. W. C. Newte. Southend Empire, June 25, 1900.

IN A FOG. Ca. F. Kinsey Peile. P.O.W., January 15, 1901.

IN A LOCKET. Piece. 3 a. Harry and Edward Paulton. Strand. September 16, 1895. See *A World of Trouble in a Locket*.

IN A MIRROR. Mus. Epis. Comp. by Paul Lincke. Adapt. fr. the Ger. by L. E. Berman. Pal., May 3, 1909.

IN A TELEGRAPH OFFICE. Ca. Mrs. Hugh Bell. Parish H., Sloane Square, May 11, 1893.

IN A WOMAN'S GRIP. D. 4 a. Fred Melville. Standard, October 7, 1901.

IN ADVANCE OF THE TIMES. F. J. W. Jones. Leeds Amphi., September 23, 1875.

IN AN AFTERNOON. P. 1 a. Templeman Norman. Ladbroke H., May 13, 1898.

IN AN ARAB GARDEN. C. 1 a. Gladys Unger, adap. fr. the Fr. of P. Elzear. Vaudeville, November 12, 1908.

IN AN ATTIC. Ca. 1 a. Wilton Jones. St. James's, March 25, 1895; Trafalgar, July 29, 1895.

IN AND OUT OF A FIX. No date.

IN AND OUT OF A PUNT. Duo. Henry V. Esmond. St. James's, March 9, 1896.

IN AND OUT OF PLACE. Adelphi, February 23, 1857.

IN AND OUT OF SERVICE. Ca. J. T. Douglass. Standard, October 25, 1869.

IN AND OUT OF TUNE. Mus. afterpiece. D. Lawler, and alt. by Mr. Cherry. D.L., March, 1808. See *Musical Family*.

IN ANOTHER MAN'S CASTLE. P. 1 a. Colin Lundin. Neston T.H. (Amateurs), July 13, 1898.

IN AT THE FINISH. F. Nagi Laczi. Hammersmith Palace, May 13, 1907.

IN BEHANDLUNG. C. 3 a. M. Dreyer. Comedy, March 1, 1901.

IN BELLS AND MOTLEY. Mus. scena. Rita Strauss and T. G. Coates. Lyrics by Roland Carse. M. by Walter Slaughter. Coliseum, December 18, 1905.

IN BLACK AND WHITE. D. 4 a. E. C. Bertrand. Pav., September 18, 1880.

IN CAMP. Extrav. 2 a. Miss Victoria Vokes. Liverpool P.O.W., September 24, 1883.

IN CHANCERY. Eccentric C. 3 a. A. W. Pinero. Edinburgh Lyceum, September 19, 1884; Gaiety, December 24, 1884; Terry's, November 22, 1890.

IN CHARGE. F.C. 3 a. H. Cassel and H. C. Duckworth. Adap. fr. the German. Bradford Prince's, June 29, 1888.

IN CHRYSANTHEMUM LAND. Oa. 2 a. H. T. Moore. M. by Lewis West and Moore. Redruth Druids' H., January 17, 1899.

IN CIVIL. Piece. 1 a. G. Kadelburg (German Season). Comedy, February 22, 1901.

IN CUPID'S COURT. Mus. Ca. T. Malcolm Watson. M. by Alfred J. Caldicott. St. George's H., November 30, 1885.

IN CYDERLAND. M.P. Lyrics by R. Carey Tucker. M. by Edward Sherwood. Cripplegate Inst., May 12, 1909.

IN DAHOMEY. M.C. 3 a. Jesse A. Shipp. Lyrics by Paul Lawrence Dunbar. M. by Will Marion Cook. Shaftesbury, May 16, 1903.

IN DANGER. D. 3 a. W. Lestocq and Henry Creswell. Brighton T.R., October 24, 1887; Vaudeville, November 1, 1887 (evening bill); July 29, 1889.

IN DARK SIBERIA. Anglo-Russian D. 4 a. F. Jarman. West London, February 22, 1904.

IN DAYS OF OLD. Rom. D. 4 a. Edward Rose. St. James's, April 26, 1899.

IN DEADLY PERIL. D. 4 a. Hal Collier. Scarborough People's Pal., February 3, 1890.

IN DR. JOHNSON'S DAYS. Epi. by A. Mackinnon and Lieut.-Colonel N. Davis. Tunbridge Wells O.H., October 16, 1902.

IN DUTY BOUND. D. 4 a. J. Mortimer Murdoch. Pav., August 3, 1878; Sadler's Wells, August 7, 1882.

IN FACE OF THE ENEMY. Dom. D. 1 a. Miss E. White. Wyndham's, October 16, 1902.

IN FACE OF THE FOE. D. 4 a. Originally prod. in the provinces. Marylebone, July 25, 1892.

IN FETTERS. P. 1 a. J. P. Hurst. Strand, November 30, 1885.

IN FOR A HOLIDAY. F. 1 a. F. C. Burnand. Royalty.

IN FOR A PENNY. F.C. 2 a. John Kennedy. Southampton P.O.W., May 5, 1888.

IN FURNISHED ROOMS. Monol. Bertha N. Graham. Amateur Players' Association, Victoria Street, February 6, 1907.

IN GAY ALGIERS. M.C. Herbert Shelley and Reginald Bacchus. Bayswater Bijou (C.P.), May 16, 1903.

IN GAY PAREE. Tom Terriss. Gaiety, February 6, 1901 (C.P.).

IN GAY PICCADILLY. Mus. F. 2 a. Geo. R. Sims and Clarence Corri. Glasgow T.R., October 9, 1899; Stoke Newington Alexandra, November 27, 1899.

IN HARBOUR. See *A Mean Advantage*.

IN HIS POWER. D. 3 a. Mark Quinton. Liverpool Alexandra, September 20, 1884; Olympic, January 21, 1885.

IN HOLY ORDERS. D. 4 a., 12 scenes. Wyn Weaver. Dover T.R., June 18, 1906.

IN HOLY (?) RUSSIA. Russ. D. 4 a. Lillian Clare Cassidy. Salford P.O.W., March 15, 1905 (C.P.); Preston Prince's, May 29, 1905.

IN HONOUR BOUND. C. 1 a. Sydney Grundy. P.O.W., September 25, 1880. Suggested by Scribe's *Une Chaine*.

IN JAPAN. Ballet. S. L. Bensusan. Adap. fr. his tale "Dédé." M. by Louis Ganne. Alhambra, April 21, 1902.

IN LETTERS OF FIRE. D. 5 a. E. M. Seymour. Walthamstow K.T., August 11, 1902.

IN LIFE OR DEATH. D. 4 a. E. A. Elton. Adap. fr. C. Gibbon's novel "For the King." Olympic, March 24, 1885.

IN LILAC TIME. Dom. C. 1 a. Maude Thompson. Crewe Lyceum, September 27, 1909.

IN LONDON TOWN. D. 4 a. Geo. R. Sims and Arthur Shirley. Peckham Crown, August 7, 1899.

IN LONDON'S HEART. D. Llandudno Prince's, November 9, 1899 (C.P.).

IN LOVE. Ca. 1 a. Terry's, May 13, 1890.

IN LOVE, IN DEBT, AND IN LIQUOR; OR, OUR WAY IN WALES. M.D. J. C. Cross. Pr. 1797.

IN LUCK. M.V. A. G. Markham. Hackney Wick Eton Mission H., March 26, 1900.

IN LUCK'S WAY. D. Russell Bogue. Huddersfield Victoria H., December 26, 1895.

IN MARY'S COTTAGE. P. 1 a. Ch. Beckwith. Terry's, December 21, 1896.

IN NELSON'S DAYS. P. 1 a. H. M. Paull. Publ. by S. French, Ltd.

IN OLD KENTUCKY. American D. 4 a. C. T. Dazey. Adap. for Engl. stage by A. Shirley. Hull T.R., February 10. 1894 (C.P.); Bury New T.R., May 7, 1894; Pavilion, June 6, 1898; Princess's, November 6, 1899.

IN OLD MADRID. Mus. D. 4 a. Fred J. Kirk and Walter T. Clifford. Lyrics by Montague Turner. M. by Thos. Hunter. Garston T.R., January 23, 1897 (C.P.); Gainsborough Albert, February 17, 1898; Stratford T.R., November 13, 1899.

IN OLD NEW YORK. P. Miss H. Marsland. Forest Gate P.H., September 19, 1903 (C.P.).

IN OLD VIRGINIA. Spec. and vocal scena. H. Instone. Oldham Royal, September 23, 1907.

IN OLDEN DAYS. C. 1 a. Agatha and Archibald Hodgson. Southampton Philharmonic H., February 8, 1890; Vaudeville, June 5, 1890.

IN ONE DAY. F. Talbot Fell and Gordon Tomkins. Durham Assembly R. T., February 17, 1896.

IN POSSESSION. Oa. R. Reece. M. by Frederic Clay. Gallery of Illus., June 22, 1871.

IN POSSESSION. F. 1 a. Martin F. Becher. D.L., December 26, 1871.

IN QUARANTINE. C. Ware.

IN SEARCH OF A FATHER. M.C. 3 a. Wallace Erskine and A. Stuart. Adap. fr. V. de Cothens and F. Gavault's P. *Le Papa de Françine*. Derby Grand, August 1, 1898; Kingston R. County, August 8, 1898.

IN SEARCH OF AN ENGAGEMENT. M. Sk. Nelly Ganthony. Terry's (rev.), April 13, 1892.

IN SIGHT OF ST. PAUL'S. Melo.-d. 4 a. Sutton Vane. Princess's August 1, 1896; increased to 5 a., rev. there June 26, 1897.

IN SPITE OF ALL. T. 1 a. Gerald Anderson. Margate T.R., July 18, 1898.

IN SPITE OF ALL. P. 3 a. Edna Lyall. Eastbourne Dev. Pk. T., January 4, 1900; Comedy, February 5, 1900.

IN SPITE OF SOCIETY. P. Chas. H. Dickinson. Duke of York's, November 10, 1898.

IN STRICT CONFIDENCE. Ca. Paul Heriot. Comedy, October 9, 1893.

IN SUMMER DAYS. C.D. 3 a. Robert Blackford. M. by Clarence C. Corri. Bradford T.R., March 2, 1891.

IN SUNNY CEYLON. F. 3 a. G. Boothby. Manchester Gaiety T., April 25, 1904.

IN SUNNY SPAIN. M.D. 4 a. W. H. Dearlove and Percy Woodruffe. Walsall St. Geo. T., November 9, 1896.

IN SUNNY SWITZERLAND. M.C. 2 a. Southend Empire, June 3, 1901; M. by J. A. Robertson, Greenwich Carlton, June 10, 1901.

IN THE ARENA. Duol. A. Holmes Gore. Bristol Prince's, July 19, 1906.

IN THE BISHOP'S CARRIAGE. P. 3 a. D. by Channing Pollock, fr. a novel by Miriam Michelson. Waldorf, June 24, 1907.

IN THE CAUSE OF CHARITY. C. 1 a. Leo. Trevor. St. Geo. H., February 3, 1900.

IN THE CLOUDS. F. G. P. Hawtrey. Ealing Lyric H., October 20, 1887.

IN THE CLOUDS: A GLIMPSE OF UTOPIA. Fairy Extrav. Gilbert à Beckett. Alexandra, December 8, 1873.

IN THE CLUTCH OF THE ENEMY. D. Pro. and 2 a. Greenwich, October 4, 1873.

IN THE CORRIDOR. Ca. 1 a. Rudolph Dircks. Court, May 25, 1889.

IN THE DAYS OF KING CHARLES. M. sc. Camberwell Empire, January 7, 1907.

IN THE DAYS OF THE DUKE. D. Pro. and 4 a. Haddon Chambers and Comyns Carr. Adelphi, September 9, 1897.

IN THE DAYS OF THE SIEGE. Rom. O. 3 a. C. B. Nichols. M. by H. A. Jeboult. Afterwards renamed *The Puritan Girl*. Plymouth T.R., July 4, 1898.

IN THE DAYS OF TRAFALGAR. P. 4 a. C. J. Scrymour Nichol. Ampthill Church R., September 12, 1899.

IN THE DEAD OF NIGHT. D. C. C. Vere. Hanley T.R., August 13, 1877.

IN THE DEPTHS OF THE SEA. M. fantasy. 1 a. and 2 scenes. Wm. Gayer Mackay. M. by Angelo Goetz. Avenue, July 5, 1894. See *The Mermaids*.

IN THE EYE OF THE LAW. D. 4 a. T. Crawshaw. Portsmouth Prince's T., April 24, 1893.

IN THE EYES OF THE WORLD. P. 1 a. A. C. Fraser Wood. Globe, March 29, 1894; Brockley St. Peter's H., April 11, 1901.

IN THE FASHION. P. 5 a. Selina Dolars. Ladbroke H., December 28, 1887 (C.P.).

IN THE GLOAMING. Ca. Geo. Capel. Bath T.R., March 17, 1884.

IN THE GLOAMING. P. 4 a. Loie Esmond. Goole R., September 18, 1908 (C.P.); Wellingborough Exchange, September 29, 1908.

IN THE GOLDEN DAYS. P. 4 a. Edwin Gilbert. Adap. fr. Edna Lyall's novel. St. Geo. H., June 17, 1897.

IN THE HEART OF THE STORM. American Melo.-d. 4 a. Herbert Hall Winslow and Will R. Wilson. Twickenham Pub. H., February 29, 1898 (C.P.).

IN THE HOSPITAL. Arthur Schnitzler. Transl. by Christopher Horne. Court, February 28, 1905.

IN THE ITALIAN QUARTER. A Dr. scene. Rosina Fillippi. Vaudeville, November 30, 1899.

IN THE JAWS OF DEATH. D. 4 a. Wm. P. Sheen. Fulham Grand T., May 25, 1903.

IN THE KING'S NAME. Rom. D. 3 a. Foster Courtenay. Fr. Marryat's novel "The Poacher." Eastbourne T.R., June 18, 1888.

IN THE KING'S NAME. Rom. P. Charles Rogers. Hammersmith King's, March 27, 1905.

IN THE KING'S NAVY. D. 4 a. Gilbert Heron. Greenock Alexandra, September 23, 1905 (C.P.).

IN THE LAND OF THE CZAR. D. E. L. Noel. (C.P.) Brixton, April 19, 1906.

IN THE LION'S MOUTH. D. 5 a. Miss Florence Warden. Bath T.R., September 25, 1885.

IN THE MIDDLE OF JUNE. D. 4 a. Wilson Barrett. Middlesbrough T.R., June 11, 1903.

IN THE MIDST OF LIFE. D. 5 a. Fred Victor. Belfast T.R., July 15, 1901; West London, April 21, 1902.

IN THE MIDST OF LIFE. Sk. H. E. Terry. Shoreditch Empire, December 14, 1908.

IN THE MOONLIGHT. D. 4 a. Mark Melford. Rev. ver. of his *The Nightingale*. Surrey, October 16, 1893.

IN THE NAME OF THE CZAR. P. 1 a. Marah Aymet. Kingsway, March 19, 1909 (mat.).

IN THE NICK OF TIME. D. 5 a. Della Clarke. Hay., August 26, 1908 (C.P.).

IN THE OLD TIME. P. 4 a. Walter Frith. St. James's, May 31, 1888.

IN THE ORCHARD. Ca. 1 a. G. R. Walker. Folly, February 14, 1880.

IN THE QUEEN'S NAME. D. Pro. and 3 a. Wm. Trevor and John Douglas Delille. Colchester T.R., February 5, 1890; Sadler's Wells, December 15, 1890.

IN THE RANKS. D. 5 a. G. R. Sims and H. Pettitt. Adelphi, October 6, 1883.

IN THE RING. M.F. J. T. Tanner. Gaiety, May 27, 1896 (C.P.).

IN THE ROCKIES. Panto. Sk. L. Morgan. Crystal Palace, May 19, 1902.

IN THE SEASON. Society P. 1 a. Langdon Elwyn Mitchell. Strand, May 26, 1892.

IN THE SHADOW OF NIGHT. D. 4 a. J. Willard. Britannia, December 5, 1898.

IN THE SHADOW OF THE GLEN. P. 1 a. J. M. Synge. Royalty, March 26, 1904; St. George's H., November 28, 1905.

IN THE SILENCE OF THE VELDT. P. 1 a. Horace Collins. (Prod. by the Dramatic Debaters.) Court, March 21, 1909.

IN THE SOUP. F.C. 3 a. Ralph Lumley. Northampton O.H., August 16, 1900; Strand, August 28, 1900.

IN THE SPIDER'S WEB; OR, THE COCKNEY FARMER. D. 4 a. Henry Pettitt. Glasgow Grand, May 28, 1883.

IN THE STATIONERY LINE. F. J. M. Killick. Cabinet, February 19, 1870 (amateurs).

IN THE STUDIO Sk. Middlesex, December 5, 1908.

IN THE SULKS. Oa. Frank Desprez. M. by Alfred Cellier. Opera Comique, February 21, 1880.

IN THE TOILS. D. Oxford Victoria, January 13, 1869.

IN THE TRAIN. Ca. Ernest Radford. Adap. fr. *En Wagon*. Athenæum H., Tottenham Court Road, April 18, 1888.

IN THE TWILIGHT. Episode. 1 a. Cyril Harrison. Scarborough People's Palace, December 5, 1900.

IN THE WOLF'S DEN: A STORY OF THE WELSH COAST. D. 3 a. Swansea T.R., April 30, 1869.

IN THE WRONG BOX. F. 2 a. R. B. Peake. Publ. by J. Dicks.

IN THE WRONG BOX. Ca. Richard Leach. Lowestoft T.R., January 4, 1889.

IN THREE VOLUMES. F. 1 a. Taylor Bilkins. Strand, February 27, 1871.

IN THREE VOLUMES. Ca. Arthur Law. P.O.W., January 6, 1893.

IN TOWN. M.F. 2 a. Adrian Ross and James T. Tanner. M. by F. Osmond Carr. P.O.W., October 15, 1892; Garrick, August 9, 1897.

IN TWO MINDS. Duol. 1 a. Arthur M. Heathcote. Garrick, June 27, 1894; Belfast Wellington Minor H., December 4, 1903.

IN WANT OF A WIFE. F. G. A. Toplis. Regent's Park Lecture H., Camden Town, February 14, 1885.

IN WASHINGTON'S DAYS. Rom. C. 3 a. H. Gerald Ransley. Liverpool, St. Francis Xavier's College H., September 25, 1907.

INA. T. 5 a. D.L., April 22, 1815.

INA. P. 4 a. R. O. Prowse. Court, May 15, 1904.

INCA, THE. An alt. fr. *The Virgin of the Sun*. Victoria, June, 1819.

INCAS. See *Columbus*.

INCAS; OR, THE PERUVIAN VIRGIN, THE. Hist. O. John Thelwall. N.ac., n.p. in full. 1792.

INCENDIARIES. Britannia, August 29, 1859.

INCH VERRA; OR, THE VERDICT OF THE WORLD. Irish D. G. M. Lander. Albion, February 22, 1875.

INCHANTED LOVERS, THE. See *Enchanted Lovers*.

INCHAVOGUE. D. 4 a. W. B. Cahill. East London, April 21, 1873.

INCHCAPE BELL, THE. Nautical D. 2 a. Edward Fitzball. Surrey, 1828.

INCLE AND YARICO. See *Inkle and Yarico*.

INCOG. See *Tom, Dick, and Harry*.

INCOG; OR, THREE DAYS AT A WELL-KNOWN HOTEL. Afterpiece D.L., June 11, 1817.

INCOG! "WHAT'S IN A NAME?" F. 2 a. Lyceum, July 20, 1829.

INCOGNITA. D. Edward Rose. Ipswich T.R., February 17, 1879.

INCOGNITA. C.O. 3 a. F. C. Burnand. M. by Lecocq Yvolde and Bunning. Lyrics by Harry Greenbank. F. on *Le Cœur et la Main*. Lyric, October 6, 1892.

INCOGNITO. D. Mdlle. Antonini. Richmond H.M.T., June 11, 1881.

INCOGNITO. P. 3 a. Hamilton Aïdé. Hay., January 11, 1888.

INCOMPATIBILITY OF TEMPER. F. 1 a. W. E. Suter.

INCONSOLABLES; OR, THE CONTENTED CUCKOLD, THE. Dr. F. 3 a. Anon. Pr 1738 N.ac.

INCONSTANT; OR THE WAY TO WIN HIM, THE. C. 5 a. Geo. Farquhar. Fr. *The Wild Goose Chase.* Ac. at T.R., 1703; rev. 1747; D.L., 1812, and February 15, 1817; and Hay., September 20, 1856. Pr. 1702.

INCONSTANT LADY, THE. C. Arthur Wilson. Entered Stationers' Co., September 9, 1653. N.p. Destroyed by Warburton's servant.

INCORRIGIBLES; OR, LIFE IN 1796, THE. P. Scarborough Londesborough T., May 29, 1882.

INCREDULITY OF ST. THOMAS. Ac. by the Scriveners of York. First pr. in the 15th century, and again by J. P. Collier, 1859.

INCUBUS, THE. (Eng. ver. of *Les Hannetons.* Brieux. Prod. under the orig. Fr. title, transl. by H. M. Clark, by Stage Society at Imperial, March 24, 1907). Rev. Coronet, June 25, 1907; Court, October 1, 1907.

INDECIS, L'. Ca. Mrs. Hughes Bell. Adap. fr. her *Between the Posts.* Royalty, November 10, 1887.

INDECISION OF MR. KINGSBURY, THE. P. 4 a. Cosmo Gordon Lennox. Fr. the French *L'Irrésolu* of Georges Berr. Hay., December 6, 1905.

INDEPENDENCE; OR, THE TRUSTEE. C. J. T. Allingham. Hay., March 9, 1809. N.p.

INDEPENDENT MEANS. D. 4 a. Stanley Houghton. Manchester Gaiety, August 30, 1909.

INDEPENDENT PATRIOT; OR, MUSICAL FOLLY, THE. C. Francis Lynch. L.I.F., February 12, 1733. N.p. 1737.

INDES GALANTES, LES. O. Rameau. August 23, 1735.

INDIA IN 1857. Surrey, November 9, 1857.

INDIAN, THE. F. John Fenwick. D.L., October 6, 1800. Pr. 1800. F. on *Art and Nature,* which came fr. a French O. called *Arlequin Sauvage.*

INDIAN CAPTIVE; OR, THE DEATH OF DUCOMAR, THE. Hist. P. fr. *The Tarish Mogulisatan; or, The History of the Mogul Tartars.* Dublin, 1796.

INDIAN CHIEF, THE. M. Ent. John Williams. Intended for perf. at Dublin. N.p. N.ac.

INDIAN EMPEROR; OR, THE CONQUEST OF MEXICO BY THE SPANIARDS, THE. T.C. J. Dryden. A sequel to *The Indian Queen.* Ac. at the T.R., 1670. Pr. 1667.

INDIAN EMPEROR; OR, THE CONQUEST OF PERU BY THE SPANIARDS, THE. T. Francis Hawling. Ac. 1728.

INDIAN EXILES, THE. C. Benj. Thompson. Transl. fr. Kotzebue. Pr. 1800. N.ac.

INDIAN GIRL, THE. Rom. D. 2 a. M. by Eliason. D.L., October 28, 1837.

INDIAN MUTINY. Burnley, December 26, 1892.

INDIAN NUPTIALS. Ballet. M. Rochfort. D.L., February 20, 1815.

INDIAN PRINCE. M. Sporting C. 3 a. T. Gilbert Perry. M., Harry Richardson. Walsall Grand T., July 26, 1897.

INDIAN QUEEN, THE. T. Sir Robert Howard and Dryden. Pr. 1665. See *The Indian Emperor.*

INDIAN QUEEN; OR, A HOME IN THE MOUNTAINS, THE. D. 5 a. Matthew Wardhaugh. Victoria, December 24, 1877.

INDIANA. C.O. 3 a. Fr. the French by H. B. Farnie. M. by Audran. Manchester Comedy, October 4, 1886; Avenue, October 11, 1886.

INDIANS, THE. T. Richardson. Pr. 1790 Ac. at Richmond.

INDIANS IN ENGLAND, THE. C. 3 a. A. Thompson. Transl. fr. Kotzebue. Pr. at Perth 1796. N.ac.

INDISCREET LOVER, THE. C. Abraham Portal. Ac. at King's T., in Hay. Pr. 1768.

INDISCRETION. C. Prince Hoare. D.L., May 10, 1800. Pr. 1800.

INDISCRETION. F.C. 3 a. Fergus Hume. Folkestone Exhibition Pal., November 13, 1888.

INDISCRETION OF ELIZABETH, THE. P. 3 a. Mrs. C. Campbell Wardrop. Liverpool Balfour Inst., April 17, 1909 (amat.).

INEZ. T. Ascribed to the Rev. Charles Symmonds. Pr. 1796. N.ac.

INEZ. See *Loyal Love.*

INEZ; OR, THE BRIDE OF PORTUGAL. Ross Neil. Pr. 1871.

INEZ DE CASTRO. T. 5 a. M. R. Mitford Publ. by J. Dicks.

INEZ DE CORDONE. T. Bernard. 1696.

INEZ MENDO. O. 3 a and 4 tableaux, fr. the French of Merimée, Decourcelle, and Liorat. M. by D'Erlanger. Engl. ver. by Beatty-Kingston. C.G., July 10, 1897.

INEZ, THE DANCING GIRL. O. 3 a. Wallace Pringle. Stafford Lyceum, August 3, 1896.

INFANCY OF CHRIST. Sacred Triology. Berlioz. 1803-69.

INFANT PHENOMENON. F. 1 a. H. Horncastle. Publ. by J. Dicks.

INFANTICIDE; OR, A TRIAL FOR LIFE, THE. D. W. Travers and Nelson Lee, jun. Liverpool Colosseum, March 16, 1868.

INFATUATION. D. 4 a. Sir Charles Young. Fr. the French of Dinaux and Legouvé. Bristol Old T.R., April 25, 1879; Hay., May 1, 1879.

INFLEXIBLE CAPTIVE, THE. T. Miss Hannah More. Pr. 1774; ac. at Bath. F. on Metastasio's *Regulus.*

INFORMERS. P. Auguste Creamer. Leeds T.R., August 31, 1883

INFORMERS OUTWITTED, THE. T.C.F. Anon. Pr. 1738. N.ac.

INGANNO FELICE, L'. O. Rossini. Venice, 1812. King's T., July 1, 1819.

INGANNO FORTUNATO, A HAPPY DELUSION. C. Anon. Pr. 1727.

INGOMAR. Burl. G. E. Jeffrey. Douglas T.R., September 2, 1868.

INGOMAR, SON OF WILDERNESS. P. 5 a. Publ. by S. French, Ltd.

INGOMAR, THE BARBARIAN. P. 5 a. Maria Lovell (Miss Lacy). Transl. fr. the German. D.L., June 9, 1851.

INGOMAR, THE IDIOTIC; OR, THE MISER, THE MAID, AND THE MANGLE. Burl. Allan and Howard. Alfred, August 19, 1871.

INGRANNO INFELICE. O. Rossini. 1812.

INGRATITUDE; OR, THE ADULTERESS. T.D. 3 a. Joseph Moser. F. on Heywood's *Woman Killed with Kindness.* Pr. 1810.

INGRATITUDE OF A COMMONWEALTH; OR, THE FALL OF CAIUS MARTIUS CORIOLANUS. T. Nahum Tate. F. on Shakespeare's *Coriolanus.* Ac. at T.R. Pr. 1682.

INGULPH. D. 1 a. Edgar Newbound. Britannia, December 15, 1879.

INGWELDE. O. Schillings. Prod. in Germany.

INHERITANCE, THE. A moral and Dr. P. Transl. fr. the French of Bret. Pr. 1786.

INHERITANCE, THE. P. 3 a. Cecil Raleigh. Comedy, May 16, 1889.

INJURED FEMALE, AN. F. H. T. Arden. Park, November 6, 1876.

INJURED HONOUR. T. Henry Brooke. Pr. Dublin, 1751. See *The Earl of Westmorland.*

INJUR'D INNOCENCE. T. Fettiplace Bellers. D.L., February 3, 1732. Pr. 1732.

INJURED LOVE; OR, THE CRUEL HUSBAND. T. Nahum Tate. Intended for D.L., but n.ac. F. on Webster's *White Devil.* Pr. 1707.

INJURED LOVE; OR, THE LADY'S SATISFACTION. C. Ac. at D.L. and L.I.F., December 18, 1721. Pr. (n.d.) circa 1711.

INJURED LOVERS; OR, THE AMBITIOUS FATHER. T. W. Mountford. D.L. Pr. 1688.

INJURED PRINCESS; OR, THE FATAL WAGER, THE. T.C. T. D'Urfey. Ac. at the T.R. Pr. 1682. F. on Shakespeare's *Cymbeline.* The author has used the epil. to *Fool Turn'd Critic* by way of prol. Its running title is *The Unequal Match; or, The Fatal Wager.*

INJURED VIRTUE; OR, THE VIRGIN MARTYR. T. Benjamin Griffin. Ac. at Richmond. Pr. 1715. An alt. of a p. by Massinger and Dekker called *The Virgin Martyr.*

INKLE AND YARICO. T. 3 a. Ascr. to Mr. Weddel, supposed author of *The City farce.* Story fr. *The Spectator.* Pr. 1742. N.ac.

INKLE AND YARICO. O. 3 a. Geo. Colman, jun. Hay., August 4, 1787. Story fr. the *Spectator.* Also ac. at C.G., 1790; D.L., June 14, 1814; and Lyceum, September 23, 1819.

INKSLINGER, THE. Ca. Chas. Whitlock and E. T. De Banzie. Adapt. fr. a story by Max Adeler. Glasgow Royalty, February 22, 1893

INNER TEMPLE MASQUE, THE. Wm. Browne. Ac. circa 1620. Pr. fr. a MS. in Emanuel Coll. Libr., 1772. Warton supposes this masque to have suggested a hint to Milton in his *Masque of Comus.*

INNER TEMPLE MASQUE; OR, MASQUE OF HEROES, THE. Thos. Middleton. Pr. 1619. Mrs. Behn borr. fr. this in her *City Heiress.*

INNISFALLEN; OR, THE MAN IN THE GAP. D. 3 a. Edmund Falconer. Lyceum, September 17, 1870.

INNKEEPER OF ABBEVILLE; OR, THE OSTLER AND THE ROBBER, THE. D. 2 a. Edward Fitzball. Surrey, 1826.

INNKEEPER'S DAUGHTER; OR. MARY, THE MAID OF THE INN, THE. Melo-d. 2 a. Geo. A. Soane. M. by Cooke. D.L., April 7, 1817; Lyceum, September 16, 1820; D.L., February 11, 1851.

INNOCENCE. C. Gloucester T.R., October 22, 1874.

INNOCENCE; OR, A LIGHTNING'S FLASH. D. Mortimer Murdoch. Scarborough T.R., August 4, 1884.

INNOCENCE BETRAY'D; OR, THE ROYAL IMPOSTOR. Dr. Ent. Daniel Bellamy, sen. and jun. Pr. 1746. N.ac.

INNOCENCE DISTRESS'D; OR, THE ROYAL PENITENTS. T. Robt. Gould. Pr. 1737 (n.ac.). On the same subject as *The Fatal Discovery; or, Love in Ruins,* and *The Mysterious Mother.*

INNOCENT; OR, LIFE IN DEATH. D. Pro. and 4 a. Murray Wood. Surrey, April 14, 1873.

INNOCENT ABROAD, AN. F. 3 a. W. Stokes Craven. Belfast T.R., September 9, 1894; Terry's, January 14, 1895.

INNOCENT MISTRESS, THE. C. Mrs. Mary Pix. L.I.F., November 24, 1718. Pr. 1697. Party fr. *Man of Mode.* Pro. and epil. by Motteux.

INNOCENT USURPER; OR, THE DEATH OF LADY JANE GRAY, THE. T. J. Banks. Pr. 1694. (Prohibited.)

INNOCENTINEZ; OR, THE MAGIC PIPE AND THE FATAL I.O.U. Burl. H. Adams. King's Cross, March 29, 1876.

INNOCENTS ABROAD; OR, GOING OVER TO ROME. Oa. J. F. M'Ardle. M. by W. H. Jude. Liverpool Bijou O.H., May 15, 1882.

INNOCENTS ALL ABROAD. O. absurdity. A. C. Clark. M. by John Geffory. Blackpool Winter Gardens, June 9, 1886.

INNOCENZA GRATIFICATA, L'. O. Gluck. Vienna, December 8, 1755.

INNODELLE NAZIONI. O. Verdi. Her M., 1862.

INO; OR, THE THEBAN TWINS. Burl. B. J. Spedding. Liverpool P.O.W., August 30, 1869; Strand, October 30, 1869.

INOCULATION. F. A. W. Gattie. Ladbroke H. (amat.), February 18, 1892.

INOCULATOR, THE. C. Geo. Saville Carey. Pr. 1766.

INQUIRE WITHIN. See *Enquire,* etc.

INQUISITION, THE. F. J. Philips. Pr. 1717. N.ac. See *Pretender's Flight.*

INQUISITOR, THE. T. 5 a. James Petit Andrews and Henry James Pye. Alt. fr. the German. Pr. 1798. N.ac.

INQUISITOR, THE. P. Ascribed to Holcroft. Hay., June 23, 1798. Pr. same year. Transl. from the German.

INSATIATE COUNTESS, THE. T. John Marston. Pr. 1613. Some say the author was Wm. Barksted. Ac. at Whitefryars 1603.

INSECT-SELLER OF FUCHIYAMA, THE. Japanese idyll. 1 a. G. A. Peacock and W. W. Macfarlane. Edinburgh Lyceum, May 11. 1900.

INSIGNIFICANTS, THE. C. 5 a. Dr. Bacon. Pr. 1757.

INSOLVENT; OR, FILIAL PIETY, THE. T. Aaron Hill. Hay., March 6, 1758. Pr. 1758. Alt. from *The Guiltless Adulteress; or, Judge in His Own Cause.* Supposed to have been written by Sir Wm. Davenant. The opening of the piece f. on Massinger's *Fatal Dowry.*

INSOLVENTS, THE. Prel. Announced for perf. at C.G. May, 1785, but (?) laid aside.

INSPECTOR. Oa. 1 a. Ross and Carr. Publ. by S. French, Ltd

INSPECTOR. Charade P. Miss Keating. Publ. by S. French, Ltd.

INSPECTOR-GENERAL, THE. F.C. 3 a. N. F. Gogol. Scala, June 17, 1906.

INSPIRATION. Ballet. Alhambra, June 8, 1901.

INSPIRATION. P. of modern life. Edwd. Locke. Inci. M. by Joseph Carl Breil. Bayswater Bijou, February 15, 1909 (C.P.).

INSPIRATION OF NANCE. P. 1 a. Blanche Wills Chandler. (Prod. by the Play Actors.) Court, May 9, 1909.

INSTITUTE ABROAD, THE. An adap. of *The Celestial Institute*. Alfred Stalman and G. B. Carvill. M. by Leonard Butler. St. Geo. H., May 6, 1897.

INSTITUTION OF THE GARTER; OR, ARTHUR'S ROUND TABLE RESTORED, THE. Masque. D.L., October 28, 1771. Pr. 1771. An alt. by Garrick of West's poem, "Institution of the Order of the Garter."

INSTITUTION OF THE ORDER OF THE GARTER, THE. Dr. poem. Gilb. West. Pr. 1742.

INSURANCE MONEY. D. Corrie Burns (Edwd. Righton). Hammersmith Lyric, June 4, 1894.

INSURED AT LLOYDS. D. 4 a. T. A. Palmer. Manchester New Queen's, November 5, 1870; Plymouth T.R., October 4, 1875.

INSURGENT CHIEF, MICHAEL DWYER, THE. R.S. 5 a. J. W. Whitbread. Dublin Q.R.T., March 31, 1902.

INSURING HIS LIFE. F. Ben Brierly. Manchester T.R., March 24, 1875.

INTEGRITY. D. Anon. C.G., October 8, 1801. N.p.

INTEMPERANCE; OR, A DRUNKARD'S SIN. D. 4 a. Fred Hazleton. Elephant and Castle, July 19, 1879.

INTERLUDE, AN. Ralph Wood. Name and date unknown. Destroyed by Warburton's servant.

INTERLUDE, AN. P. 1 a. Mrs. W. K. Clifford and Walter H. Pollock. Terry's, June 3, 1893.

INTERLUDE BETWEEN JUPITER, JUNO, AND MERCURY, AN. H. Fielding. This piece was introduction to a projected C. entitled *Jupiter Upon Earth*. Pr. 1743. N.ac.

INTERLUDE CONCERNING THE LAWS OF NATURE. See *The Three Laws of Nature*.

INTERLUDE OF IMPACYENTE POVERTE, NEWLYE IMPRINTED, A NEWE. MVLX. (? 1560).

INTERLUDE OF THE FOUR ELEMENTS. See *Nature of the Four*, etc.

INTERLUDE OF WELTH AND HELTH, FULL OF SPORT AND MERY PASTYME, AN. Black letter (n.d.).

INTERLUDE OF YOUTH, THE. Wr. in verse. Black letter. Circa 1565; Gt. Queen St., January 8, 1906.

INTERMEDES DE LA PRINCESSE DE NAVARRE, LES. C. Rameau. 1745.

INTERRUPTED ELOPEMENT, AN. Sk. Islington Hipp., May 11, 1908.

INTERRUPTED HONEYMOON, AN. C. 3 a. F. Kinsey Peile. Avenue, September 23, 1899.

INTERRUPTED REHEARSAL, AN. P. 1 a. W. H. Squire and J. Randall. Croydon Grand, July 20, 1900; St. George's H., April 12, 1902.

INTERVENTION OF DR. METZLER, THE. P. 1 a. J. Pollock. Scala, June 17, 1906.

INTERVIEW, AN. Herbert Swears. Small Queen's H., November 29, 1895.

INTERVIEW, THE. Ca. T. Gideon Warren. Garrick, November 11, 1895.

INTERVIEWED P. 1 a. Josephine Rae and Thos. Sidney. Brighton West P., September 1, 1896.

INTERVIEWED. C. 1 a. Ina Cassilis. Publ. by S. French, Ltd.

INTIMIDAD; OR, THE LOST REGALIA. M. Bouff. H. B. Farnie. Strand, March 8, 1875.

INTO THE LIGHT. Rom. C. 4 a. Gerald Lawrence. Bradford R.T., February 23, 1908; Court, November 30, 1908.

INTRIGUE; OR, THE BATH ROAD. Int. 1 a. John Poole. D.L., April 26, 1814, and May 24, 1826.

INTRIGUE; OR, THE LOST JEWELS. C. 5 a. By "An Old Author." Printed by Hall and Lovitt, 88, Camden Road, N.W. 1876.

INTRIGUE AND LOVE. T. Schiller. 1783.

INTRIGUE IN A CLOISTER. F. T. Horde, jun. Pr. 1783.

INTRIGUERS, THE. D. 4 a. F. Nasmith and S. Houghton. Prod. by amateurs. Manchester Athenæum, October 20, 1906.

INTRIGUES AT VERSAILLES; OR, A JILT IN ALL HUMOURS, THE. C. T. Durfey. L.I.F. Borrowed fr. *The Double Cuckold*. Pr. 1697.

INTRIGUES OF A DAY; OR, THE POET IN LIVERY, THE. C. 5 a. Pr. 1814. ? N.ac.

INTRIGUES OF A MORNING; OR, AN HOUR IN PARIS. F. Mrs. Parsons. Pr. 1792. C.G., April 18, 1792. Chiefly alt. fr. Molière.

INTRIGUING CHAMBERMAID, THE. C. 2 a. H. Fielding. D.L.; Edinburgh, 1781. Pr. 1734. Borrowed fr. the *Dissipateur*, and *Le Retour Imprevu* of M. Regnard. First ac. February, 1700. Alt. of Fielding's farce, ac. at D.L., November 3, 1790. Pr. 1790.

INTRIGUING COURTIERS; OR, THE MODISH GALLANTS, THE. C. Anon. An int. is introduced herein called *The Marriage Promise; or, The Disappointed Virgin*. Pr. 1732. N.ac.

INTRIGUING FOOTMAN; OR, THE HUMOURS OF HARRY HUMBUG, THE. Ent. Ac. at Sheffield, 1791, but not then new. Probably the P. wr. by James Whiteley, and fr. which Macready took his farce *The Irishman in London*.

INTRIGUING MILLINERS AND ATTORNIES' CLERKS, THE. Mock T. 2 a. Robinson, of Kendal. 1738. Designed to be ac. at D.L. Pr. 1738.

INTRIGUING WIDOW; OR, HONEST WIFE, THE. C. Pr. 1705, and dedicated to Lady Rivers by J. B.

INTRUDER, THE. D. 1 a. Engl. ver. of *L'Intruse*, by Maurice Maeterlinck. Hay., January 27, 1892.

INTRUDERS. C. 4 a. John T. Day. Prod. at Colchester December 9, 1898, as *The Claychester Scandal*. Worcester T.R., January 16, 1899; Brixton T., February 6, 1899.

INTRUSE, L'. D. 1 a. Maurice Maeterlinck. Opera Comique, March 25, 1895.

INUNDATION; OR, THE MISER OF THE HILL FORT, THE. D. 3 a. T. Archer. City of London T., April 5, 1847.

INVADER OF HIS COUNTRY; OR, THE FATAL RESENTMENT, THE. T. John Dennis. D.L., November 11, 1719. Alt. of Shakespeare's *Coriolanus*. Epil. by Cibber. Pr. 1720.

INVALIDES DU MARIAGE, LES. Royalty, December 11, 1884.

INVASION, THE. F. Anon. Pr. 1759. N.ac.

INVASION, THE. P. E. Roche. Pr. 1808.

INVASION, THE. See *Dramatic Appellant*.

INVASION; OR, A TRIP TO BRIGHTHELMSTONE, THE. F. F. Pilon. C.G., November 4, 1778. Pr. 1778. D.L., May 26, 1804.

INVASION; OR, ENGLAND'S GLORY. D. Boeling. Pr. 1798.

INVASION OF BRITAIN; OR, THE SIEGE OF GLASGOW, THE. Spec. D. Glasgow Grand, April 16, 1900.

INVASION OF ENGLAND, THE. F. 3 a. Anon. Pr. 1803. N.ac.

INVASION OF RUSSIA. P. Publ. by S. French, Ltd.

INVENTION OF DR. METZLER, THE. P. 1 a. John Pollock. Scala, June 17, 1906.

INVENTORIES, THE. Sk. H. Savile Clarke. Strand, July 8, 1885.

INVINCIBLES, THE. M.F. 2 a. Thos. Morton. M. by A. Lee. C.G., February 28, 1828, and Lyceum.

INVISIBLE AVENGERS, THE. Melod. Spec. Surrey, 1809.

INVISIBLE BRIDEGROOM, THE. F. 2 a. Attributed to Jameson. C.G., November 10, 1813. N.p.

INVISIBLE CLIENT, THE. F. E. L. Blanchard. Edinburgh Princess's, March 1, 1875.

INVISIBLE GIRL, THE. C.P. 1 a. Theodore Edward Hook. Adap. fr. *Le Babillard*. D.L., April 28, 1806. Pr. 1806.

INVISIBLE KNIGHT. P. Anon. Before 1814.

INVISIBLE PRINCE; OR, THE ISLAND OF TRANQUIL DELIGHTS, THE. Fairy Extrav. 1 a. J. R. Planché. Hay., December 26, 1846. F. on Countess D'Aulnoy's tale, "Prince Tutin."

INVISIBLE RING; OR, THE WATER MONSTER AND FIRE SPECTRE. Melo. Dr. Rom. Ac. at Aquatic T., Sadler's Wells, September 3, 1806.

INVISIBLE SMIRK, THE. A Droll formed out of *The Two Merry Milkmaids*. Pr. 1672.

INVITATION A LA FETE, L'. Ballet. Barnett and Maretzek. D.L., January 29, 1848.

INVOLUNTARY UNDERSTUDY, AN. P. 1 a. Percival Pollard. Dram. fr. a story. Terry's, May 23, 1909.

IOCASTA. Gascoigne, assisted by Kinwelmarsh and Yelverton. A tolerably free adap. of the *Phœnissœ* of Euripides. This was the second English P. in blank verse. Ac. at Gray's Inn, 1566.

IOLANTHE. An Idyll in 1 a. W. G. Wills. Lyceum, May 20, 1880.

IOLANTHE; OR, THE PEER AND THE PERI. Fairy O. 2 a. W. S. Gilbert. M. by Arthur Sullivan. Savoy, November 25, 1882; rev., Savoy, December 7, 1901; rev., Savoy, June 11, 1907; rev., Savoy, October 19, 1908.

ION. T. Transl. fr. Euripides by R. Potter. Pr. 1781 by Michael Wodhull. Pr. 1782. See "Greek Plays."

ION. Classical P. by Talfourd. D.L., February 27, 1850.

IPERMNESTRA. O. Glück. 1742.

IPERMNESTRA. Metastasio. 1744.

IPERMESTRO. O. Naumann. Venice. 1774.

IPHIGENIA. T. John Dennis. L.I.F. Pr. 1700.

IPHIGENIA; OR, THE VICTIM. T. Thos. Hull. C.G., March 23, 1778. N.p. See *Achilles*.

IPHIGENIA IN AULIDE. See *Ifigenia*, etc.

IPHIGENIA IN AULIS. O. Transl. fr. Algarotti. Pr. 1767.

IPHIGENIA IN AULIS. Transl. fr. Euripides. Ascr. to Bannister. Pr. 1780; by M. Wodhull. Pr. 1782; by R. Potter. Pr. 1783. See "Greek Plays."

IPHIGENIA IN TAURIS. T. Transl. fr. Euripides by Gilbert West. Pr. 1749; by M. Wodhull. Pr. 1782; by R. Potter. Pr. 1783. See "Greek Plays."

IPHIGENIA IN TAURIS. T. Transl. fr. the German of Goethe by Taylor, of Norwich. Pr. at Norwich, 1793.

IPHIGENIE. See *Achilles*.

IPHEGENIE. German T., by Goethe. Rev. at D.L. June 18, 1881.

IPHIGENIE. O. B. Aliprandi. Munich. 1739.

IPHIGENIE. Racine. See "French Classical Plays."

IPHIGENIE EN AULIDE. O. Glück. F. on Racine's P. taken fr. Euripides. Paris, 1774.

IPHIGENIE EN TAURIDE. O. Glück. Paris. 1779.

IPHIS AND IANTHE; OR, A MARRIAGE WITHOUT A MAN. C. Ent. Stationers' Co. June 29, 1660, in the name of William Shakespeare. N.p.

IPPOLITO. O. Glück. Milan. January, 1745.

IPSITHILLA. 1 a. Suggested by "L'Ilote" of Paul Arène. Justin McCarthy.

IRATO, L'. Op. bo. Méhul. An imitation of Italian op. buffa. 1807. Recently rev. at Brussels.

IRELAND—AS IT WAS. D. 2 a. J. A. Amherst. Publ. by S. French, Ltd. New York, 185—.

IRELAND PRESERVED; OR, THE SIEGE OF LONDONDERRY. T.C. John Michelborne. Pr. 1707.

IRENA. T. Anon. Pr. 1664. ? N.ac.

IRENE. See *The Queen of Sheba*.

IRENE. T. Swinhoe. 1658. Mentioned by Brewer.

IRENE. T. Samuel Johnson. Ac. at D.L. February 6, 1749. Pr. 1749.

IRENE. Engl. O. 5 a. H. B. Farnie. M. by Gounod. Manchester T.R., March 10, 1880.

IRENE. See *Mahomet and Irene*.

IRENE; OR, THE FAIR GREEK. T. Chas. Goring. Ac. at D.L. February 9, 1708. Pr. 1708.

IRENE WYCHERLEY. D. 3 a. A. P. Wharton. Kingsway, October 9, 1907.

IRIS. O. Lulli. Paris, 1677.

IRIS. O. Mascagni. 1898.

IRIS. D. 5 a. A. W. Pinero. Garrick, September 21, 1901.

IRISH AMBASSADOR. C. 2 a. J. Kenney. Philadelphia. Publ. by J. Dicks.

IRISH ARISTOCRACY. American C. 3 a. St. Helen's T.R., June 2, 1884; Stratford T.R., February 22, 1886.

IRISH ASSURANCE. F. Orig. as *His Last Legs*, Hay., October 15, 1839; Wyndham's, March 1, 1902.

IRISH ATTORNEY, THE. F. 2 a. W. B. Bernard. 1839. Hay., May 6, 1840.

IRISH ATTORNEY, THE. P. Father Irwin. St. Mary's H., E., June 1, 1909 (amat.).

IRISH BELLE. F. Rev. vers. of *Irish Widow*. David Garrick. Charing Cross, 1873.

IRISH CHAIRMAN. C. Dibdin.

IRISH DIAMOND. Hay., October 29, 1850.

IRISH DOCTOR; OR, THE DUMB LADY CURED, THE. F. 1 a. G. Wood. Queen's, November 19, 1844. Fr. Molière's *Le Medecin Malgre Lui*.

IRISH DRAGOON. F. 1 a. Selby. Publ. by J. Dicks

IRISH DRAGOON, THE. Rom. Irish D. 4 a. J. W. Whitbread. Dublin Queen's, December 26, 1905.

IRISH ELOPEMENT, AN. F.C. 3 a. Manchester Queen's, April 11, 1887.

IRISH EMIGRANT, THE. Comic D. 2 a. John Brougham. New York Burton's T.

IRISH EYES. Ca. Kelso Corn Exch. H., January 4, 1889.

IRISH FINE LADY, THE. F. Chas. Macklin. C.G., November 28, 1767. Ac. in Ireland as *The Trueborn Irishman.*

IRISH FOOTMAN; OR, TWO TO ONE, THE. F. A. Clements. Sadler's Wells, December 17, 1872.

IRISH GENTLEMAN, AN. P. 3 a. D. C. Murray and J. L. Shine. Globe, June 9, 1897.

IRISH HEIRESS, THE. Also called WEST END. C. 5 a. D. Boucicault. C.G., February, 1842.

IRISH HOSPITALITY; OR, VIRTUE REWARDED. C. Chas. Shadwell. Pr. 1720. Ac. at Dublin. Rev. at D.L. March 15, 1766.

IRISH INTRIGUE, AN. F. Thos. F. Doyle Sunderland T. of Varieties. September 29, 1873

IRISH KNIGHT, THE. P. Ac. by the Earl of Warwick's servants, 1576.

IRISH LAND AGENT, THE. D. 3 a. Ashton-under-Lyne St. Ann's H., May 5, 1903.

IRISH LEGACY, THE. M.F. S. J. Arnold. M. by Dr. Arnold. Hay., June 26, 1797. N.p.

IRISH LIFE. D. 4 a. Auguste Creamer and L. Downey. Lowestoft T.R., October 22, 1888; Sadler's Wells, November 17, 1890.

IRISH LION, THE. F. 1 a. J. B. Buckstone. Hay., June 13, 1838.

IRISH MASQUE AT COURT, THE. Ben Jonson. Pr. 1640. Presented by gentlemen, the King's servants, 1613.

IRISH MIMIC; OR, BLUNDERS AT BRIGHTON, THE. M. ent. by John O'Keefe. C.G., April 23, 1795. Pr. 1795.

IRISH MINSTREL, THE. D. Count. Cheltenham T.R., January 31, 1867.

IRISH POST, THE. Comic D. 2 a. J. R. Planché. Hay., February 28, 1846.

IRISH REBELLION, THE. Anon. Ac. circa 1623. Sir H. Herbert lic. a "New Play" by Kirke under this title, 1642.

IRISH TAR; OR, WHICH IS THE GIRL? THE. M. Int. W. C. Oulton. Hay., August 24, 1797. N.p.

IRISH TIGER, THE. F. 1 a. J. M. Morton. Hay., April, 1846.

IRISH TUTOR; OR, NEW LIGHTS, THE. C.P. 1 a. Earl of Glengall. Adap. fr. the French. Cheltenham T., July 12, 1822; C.G., October 28, 1822; Lyceum, May 11, 1825; D.L., June 12, 1830.

IRISH WIDOW, THE. C. 2 a. D. Garrick. D.L. Ac. also at Edinburgh, 1787, and D.L., May 11, 1814. Pr. 1772. See *The Irish Belle.*

IRISHMAN, THE. D. 5 a. J. W. Whitbread. Eleph. and C., November 4, 1889.

IRISHMAN IN ITALY (FALSE AND TRUE), THE. C. Moulter. 1806.

IRISHMAN IN LONDON; OR, THE HAPPY AFRICAN, THE. F. 2 a. Wm. Macready. Adap. fr. *The Intriguing Footman.* C.G., April 21, 1792. Pr. 1793. D.L., February 3, 1814; Lyceum, May 15, 1822; C.G., 1823.

IRISHMAN IN SPAIN, THE. F. Taken fr. the Spanish by C. Stuart. Hay., August 3, 1791. Pr. 1791. (First called *She Would be a Duchess.*)

IRISHMAN'S HEART; OR, A KISS O' THE BLARNEY, AN. Ca. John Levey. Britannia, September 29, 1879.

IRISHMAN'S HOME, THE. D. Westminster T., May, 1833.

IRISHMAN'S HOME, THE. D. Scarborough T.R., April 12, 1875.

IRISHMAN'S MANŒUVRE. C. 2 a. Publ. by S. French, Ltd.

IRISHMAN'S POLICY, AN. F. H. Richardson. Barnsley Mechanics' H., September 9, 1875.

IRMA. O. M. and lib. by J. H. Bonawitz. St. Geo. H., March 17, 1885.

IRMENGARDA. Grand O. Leonhard Emil Bach. Italian ver. of original German lib. by Zanardini. Engl. ver. by W. Beatty Kingston. C.G., December 8, 1892.

IRON AGE, THE. History, in 2 parts. Thos. Heywood. Pr. 1632.

IRON ARM, THE. Surrey, April 13, 1857.

IRON BEFORE GOLD. D. 3 a. Charles Osborne. Belfast T.R., February 12, 1872.

IRON CASKET; OR, THE BURNING MOUNTAIN, THE. D. Liverpool Colosseum, February 10, 1868.

IRON CHEST, THE. P. 3 a. Geo. Colman the Younger. Taken fr. Godwin's *Caleb Williams.* D.L., March 12, 1796; Hay., 1806; Lyceum, April 10, 1822; D.L., June 7, 1831. M. by Storace.

IRON DUKE. D. 1 a. W. Frith. Comedy, October 9, 1902.

IRON GATES. D. 2 a. John Henderson. Todmorden T.R., October 20, 1883.

IRON HAND AND VELVET GLOVE. P. 4 a. Chas Hannan. Douglas, Gaiety, June 24, 1909.

IRON HANDS. D. 4 a. Harry M. Pitt. Edinburgh Princess's, September 29, 1873; Grecian, October 12, 1874.

IRON MAIDEN, THE. D. 4 a. Matt. Wilkinson and W. H. Hallatt. Hanley T.R., June 3, 1896; Southampton P.O.W., December 31, 1896; Stratford T.R., January 17, 1898.

IRON MASK, THE. See *The Island of Marguerite.*

IRON STATUE, THE. Victoria, 1868.

IRON TRUE; OR, CONVICTED. D. Prol. and 3 a. Thos. Sennett. Stratford T.R., May 3, 1886.

IRONFOUNDER, THE. P. 4 a. Wm. Muskerry. Fr. Geo. Ohnet's novel, "Le Maitre de Forges." Eastbourne, Devonshire Park, December 6, 1907.

IRONMASTER, THE. P. 4 a. A. W. Pinero. Adap fr. the French D. *Le Maître de Forges*, by Georges Ohnet (Gymnase T., Paris, December, 1883). St. James's, March 17, 1884; Avenue, March 2, 1893.

IRONY OF FATE, THE. Dr. epis. J. G. Levy. Bedford, April 13, 1908.

IROQUOIS; OR, CANADIAN BASKET-MAKER. M.P. Taken fr. O'Keefe's *Basket-maker.* C.G., November 20, 1820. N.p.

IRVINGMANIA; OR, TRAGEDY IN TROUSERS. F. Glasgow T.R., July 12, 1877.

IS BROWN AT HOME? F. Maurice de Freece. Liverpool T.R., February 24, 1873.

IS HE A CHRISTIAN? Emotional P. 4 a. Fred. L. Connynghame and Frank Price. Liverpool Rotunda, December 10, 1900.

IS HE A PRINCE? F. Ascr. to Greffulhe. Hay., February, 1809; C.G., September 19, 1809.

IS HE ALIVE? OR, ALL PUZZLED. F. D.L., December 10, 1818.

IS HE JEALOUS? Oa. 1 a. Samuel Beazley. English O.H. (Lyceum), July 2, 1816; D.L., November 14, 1822.

IS IT THE KING? Strand. November 14, 1861.

IS LAW JUSTICE? D. 4 a. M. Wilkinson. Walsall Grand, December 21, 1903.

IS LIFE WORTH LIVING? D. 4 a. F. A. Scudamore. Bristol Prince's, September 1, 1887; Surrey, July 9, 1888.

IS LIFE WORTH LIVING? Monol. Paul Pelham. Empress, October 12, 1908.

IS MADAME AT HOME? Ca. Minnie Bell. Adap. fr. the French. Prince's H., May 23, 1887.

IS MARRIAGE A FAILURE? C. 1 a. Sir W. L. Young. Pub. by S. French, Ltd.

IS MARRIAGE A FAILURE? F.C. 3 a. Russell Vaun and Alban Atwood. Worthing Royal, October 10, 1907; Terry's December 23, 1907.

IS MARRIAGE A FAILURE? F.C. 3 a. Hal Collier-Edwards and F. H. Dudley. Adap. fr. the German P. *Harun Alraschid*, the original of "The Arabian Nights." Woolwich T.R., November 19, 1888.

IS OUR NAVY READY? Spectacular Naval Scena. F. Cornelius Wheeler and J. Herbert Jay. Olympia, May 10, 1909.

IS SHE GUILTY? D. A. Fanequez. Britannia, June 23, 1877.

IS SHE HIS DAUGHTER? OR, BEAUJOLAIS THE NECROMANCER. D. 3 a. Gaston Murray and T. H. Hipkins. Adap. fr. the French.

IS SHE HIS WIFE? OR, SOMETHING SINGULAR. F. C. Dickens. St. James's, March 6, 1837.

ISAAC. Orat. Himmel (1765-1814).

ISAAC ABROAD; OR, IVANHOE SETTLED AND REBECCA RIGHTED. Burl. Thos. F. Plowman. Oxford T.R., January 15, 1878.

ISAAC OF YORK; OR, SAXONS AND NORMANS AT HOME. Burl. T. F. Plowman. Court, November 29, 1871.

ISAAC'S WIFE. D. 3 a. F. D. Bone and Teignmouth Shore (The Dramatic Productions Club). Court, December 6, 1908.

ISABELLA. See *Night Walker*.

ISABELLA; OR, THE FATAL MARRIAGE. P. 5 a. Alt. fr. Southern by David Garrick. Pr. 1758. Southern was indebted for the plot to Mrs. Behn. The tragical portion of *Isabella* taken fr. *The Nun; or, The Fair Vowbreaker*. Other incidents fr. Fletcher's *Little Thief*. D.L., December 28, 1818, and May 3, 1828; C.G., 1824, and April 28, 1830.

ISABELLA; OR, THIRTY YEARS OF A WOMAN'S LIFE. J. B. Buckstone. Adelphi, 1834.

ISABELLE, O. Rossini.

ISABELLE; OR, WOMAN'S LIFE. D. Buckstone. Circa 1836.

ISABELLE ET GERTRUDE. O. Grétry.

ISALDA. P. 1 a. Fred Horner. Toole's, February 14, 1890.

ISAURE. Melo-d. 3 a. B. Webster.

ISIDORE DE MERIDA; OR, THE DEVIL'S CREEK. O. f. on the O. of *Pirates*. Original M. by S. Storace. New M. by Cooke and Braham. D.L., November 29, 1827.

ISLAND, THE. S.C.D. Sadler's Wells, 1833.

ISLAND NYMPH, THE. Ballet. 2 a. and 4 tab. Barrez. M. by Schira. D.L., February 12, 1846.

ISLAND OF BACHELORS, THE. Op.-bo. Robert Reece and Lecocq. Gaiety, September 14, 1874.

ISLAND OF FOOLS, THE. F. 2 a. MS. fr. the library of Isaac Reed.

ISLAND OF JEWELS, THE. Fairy Extrav. J. R. Planché. Lyceum, December 26, 1849. F. on Countess D'Aulnoy's tale "Serjcentin Vert."

ISLAND OF PHAROS, THE. C.O. 2 a. W. Caine. M. by O. Roberts. Chelsea Town H., May 18, 1904; rev. Plymouth T.R., July 11, 1904.

ISLAND OF ST. MARGUERITE, THE. O. Hon. John St. John. F. on the story of "The Iron Mask" related by Voltaire. D.L. Pr. 1789.

ISLAND OF SLAVES, THE. C. 2 a. 1761. A transl. of Marivaux's *Isle des Esclaves*. (?) Ac.

ISLAND OF TOBE-HANG. M. Extrav. 3 a. Lib. by Sir F. Barrow. M. by Cuthbert Hanley. Boscombe G.T., October 20, 1902.

ISLAND PRINCESS, THE. T.C. Beaumont and Fletcher. (Ascr. to Fletcher only.) Prod. 1621; (?) rev. D.L., 1687. Pr. 1647.

ISLAND PRINCESS, THE. T.C. N. Tate. Alt. fr. Beaumont and Fletcher. Pr. 1687.

ISLAND PRINCESS; OR, THE GENEROUS PORTUGUESE, THE. O. Peter Motteux. F. Beaumont and Fletcher's *The Island Princess*. M. by Daniel Purcell, Clarke, and Leveridge Ac. at the T.R. Pr. 1699.

ISLAND QUEENS; OR, THE DEATH OF MARY QUEEN OF SCOTLAND, THE. T. S. Banks. Prohibited. Pr. 1684. Repr. 1704 with title *The Albion Queens; or, The Death*, etc.

ISLANDERS, THE. C.O. Chas. Dibdin. F. on two French C.'s of St. Foix, *L'Isle Sauvage* and *La Colonie*. C.G., November 25, 1780. Songs only pr. 1780.

ISLANDERS, THE. Ballet. M. by Byrne. D.L. June 4, 1816.

ISLANDS, THE. Aristophanes. See "Greek Plays."

ISLE OF BOY, THE. C. Bolton T.R., April 15, 1903 (C.P.).

ISLE OF CHAMPAGNE, THE. D.D. 4 a. J. F. Stanfield. Stourbridge Alhambra, August 4, 1902.

ISLE OF CHAMPAGNE. M.C. 3 a. Lib. by T. G. Perry. Balham Duchess, January 19, 1903.

ISLE OF DOGS, THE. C. Thos. Nash. Circa 1599. N.p.

ISLE OF GULLS, THE. C. J. Daye. Ac. at Blackfryars by the children of the Revels. Plot fr. Sir Ph. Sidney's *Arcadia*. Pr. 1606.

ISLE OF PALMS. Wilson. 1812.

ISLE OF ST. TROPEZ, THE. D. 4 a. Montagu Williams and F. C. Burnand. St. James's, December 20, 1860.

ISLE OF TEARS. P. 1 a. E. Bliss. Littlehampton Terminus H., May 8, 1902.

ISLE OF UTOPIA. Extrav. Geo. St. Cloud. M. by Claude Nugent. Eastbourne Devonshire Park T., December 26, 1892; Comedy, March 6, 1893.

ISLINGTON; OR, LIFE IN THE STREETS. Another ver. of *The Streets of London*. D. Prol. and 4 a. W. R. Osman. Sadler's Wells, May 11, 1867.

ISMENE. O. F. Rebel and F. Francœur, 1750.

ISOFEL. P. 4 a. Eweretta Lawrence. Ipswich T.R., February 2, 1887.

ISOLDA. D. 5 a. Publ. by S. French, Ltd.

ISOLINE OF BAVARIA. D. 4 a. W. E. Suter. Sadler's Wells, November 13, 1869.

ISRAEL IN BABYLON. Orat. Anon. Pr. 1764.

ISRAEL IN EGYPT. Orat. Handel. 1738. D.L., March 6, 1816.

ISRAELITES; OR, THE PAMPERED NABOB, THE. F. C.G., April 1, 1785. Ascr. to Smollett.

ISRAELITES ON MOUNT HOREB. Orat. Anon. 1773.

ISSE. Past. O. Lamotte. 1699.

ISSIPILE. O. Metastasio. 1732.

ISSIPILE. O. Gluck. Prague, 1752.

IT ALL DEPENDS ON MARY. C. Ellis Kingsley. Manchester Prince's, September 25, 1903.

IT IS JUSTICE. D. Mrs. Claude Robinson (Miss Marie Zech). Bury St. Edmunds T.R., December 26, 1890.

IT IS NOT ALWAYS MAY. See *The Spirit of Poetry*.

IT MUST BE TRUE. Lyceum, October 20, 1862.

IT NEVER RAINS BUT IT POURS. Ca. P. Meritt. Liverpool Alexandra, April 16, 1877.

IT SHOULD HAVE COME SOONER, BEING THE HISTORIC SATIRIE TRAGIC COMIC HUMOURS OF EXCHANGE ALLEY. F. Fras. Hawling. D.L., July 30, 1723.

IT WAS A DREAM. C.D. 1 a. "XL." Birmingham P.O.W., September 18, 1890.

IT WAS RIGHT AT THE LAST. F. T. Hoade, jun. Taken fr. *The Twin Rivals* of Farquhar. N.d.

IT'S AN ILL WIND THAT BLOWS NOBODY GOOD. Adelphi, May 14, 1860.

IT'S NEVER TOO LATE TO MEND. D. 4 a. Chas. Reade. Leeds T.R., 1864; Princess's, October 4, 1865; D.L., April 11, 1891; first version at D.L., under title of *Gold*. This did not contain prison scene.

IT'S NEVER TOO LATE TO REPENT. D. G. Lewis. Britannia, August 18, 1875.

IT'S NEVER TOO LATE TO WED. P. 1 a. Montague Samuel. Brondesbury Synagogue, February 22, 1909 (amat.).

ITALIAN, THE. T. W. Gifford. An old P.

ITALIAN CLASSICAL PLAYS AND POEMS. The principal are by Tasso, Ariosto, Dánte, and Metastasio:—

TASSO. Born at Sorrento, 1544, and died 1595. He wrote:—

Rinaldo. Poem. Circa, 1560.
Aminta. Past D.
Il Torrismondo. T.

ARIOSTO (*Lodovico*). Born at Reggio, 1474; died, 1533. He wrote:—

Orlando Furioso. Pr. 1532. He also wrote several comedies.

DANTE, Alighieri. Born at Florence, May, 1265; died at Ravenna, September 14, 1321.

His chief work was *Divina Commedia*, a triple poem on Paradise, Purgatory, and Hell.

METASTASIO, Pietro Antonio Domenico Buonaventura. Born at Assisi, 1698; died, 1782. Wrote twenty-six operas and eight sacred dramas. He wrote:—

Didone. Naples, 1724.
Achille in Sciro. 1736.
See *Adrian in Siria*.

ITALIAN HUSBAND, THE. T. 3 a. Edwd. Ravenscroft. L.I.F., 1697. Pr. 1698.

ITALIAN HUSBAND; OR, THE VIOLATED BED AVENGED, THE. D. Edward Lewis, M.A. Pr. 1754. N.ac.

ITALIAN MONK, THE. P. James Boaden. Hay., August 15, 1797. Pr. 1797.

ITALIAN NIGHT PIECE; OR, THE UNFORTUNATE PIETY, THE. Philip Massinger. Entered Stationers' Co. September 9, 1653. Destroyed by Warburton's servant.

ITALIAN PATRIOT; OR, THE FLORENTINE CONSPIRACY, THE. T. Chas. Gildon. This is the same p. as *The Patriot*. D.L. Pr. 1703.

ITALIAN QUARTER. Criterion.

ITALIAN ROMANCE, AN. Ca. Philip Darwin Middlesex County Asylum T., November 14, 1889.

ITALIAN VILLAGERS, THE. C.O. Prince Hoare. M. by Shield. C.G., April 25, 1797. Songs pr. 1797.

ITALIANA IN ALGIERI. Op. bo. Wds. by Anelli. M. by Rossini. Venice, 1813; King's T. Prod. in English December 30, 1844.

ITALIANA IN LONDON, L'. O. Cimarosa. Rome, 1779.

ITALIANS; OR, THE FATAL ACCUSATION, THE. T. 5 a. Bucke. M. by Cooke. D.L., April 3, 1819.

ITE IN VINEAM. C. John Bourchier, Lord Berners. Ac. at Calais. N.p.

ITINERANT, THE. P. Riley.

IVAN SAFFERI. Surrey, April 17, 1854.

IVANHOE. Extrav. H. J. Byron. Strand, December 26, 1862.

IVANHOE. P. 3 a. Fox Cooper. Taken fr. Sir W. Scott. Pub. by J. Dicks.

IVANHOE. D. R. Cowie, sen. Dundee T.R., February 15, 1875.

IVANHOE. O. 4 a. Julian Sturgess. M. by Sir Arthur Sullivan. F. on Sir W. Scott's novel. R. Eng. O.H., January 31, 1891.

IVANHOE. D. Adap. fr. Sir Walter Scott's novel by Ernest Stevens. Glasgow Grand, March 14, 1896.

IVANHOE. Dram. ver. of Sir Walter Scott's novel by Wm. Palmer. Manchester Queen's, September 10, 1906.

IVANHOE; OR, THE JEW'S DAUGHTER. Rom. Melo-d. 3 a. Thos. Dibdin. Surrey, January 20, 1820; fr. Sir Walter Scott's "Ivanhoe."

IVANHOE; OR, THE MAID OF YORK. D. R. Edgar. Liverpool Amphitheatre, November 27, 1871.

IVAR. T. Anon. Pr. Exeter, 1785.

IVER AND HENGO; OR, THE RIVAL BROTHERS. Dr. Rom. T. D. Rees. Pr. 1795. N.ac.

IVERS DEAN. C.D. Sir Charles Young and Bronson Howard. Hanley T.R., November 12, 1877.

IVOR; OR, THE SIGHS OF ULLA. T. W. H. Hitchener. Ac. at Henley-on-Thames. Pr. 1808.

IVORY TABLETS, THE. D. 3 a. Margate T.R., July 7, 1898.

IVY. C.D. 3 a. Mark Melford. Manchester T.R., April 4, 1887; Royalty, April 16, 1887.

IVY HALL. D. Adap. by J. Oxenford. Princess's, September 24, 1859.

IXION. Masque. W. Taverner. Mentioned in Mears's catalogue. (?) The masque inserted in Ravenscroft's *Italian Husband.*

IXION; OR, THE MAN AT THE WHEEL. Extrav. F. C. Burnand. New Royalty, September 28, 1863; rev. Sadler's Wells, April 1, 1866; (partly re-wr.), Charing Cross, February 28, 1870.

IXION RE-WHEEL'D. Op.-bo. F. C. Burnand. Opera Comique, November 21, 1874.

IZAAK WALTON. D. 4 a. C. Dance. Publ. by J. Dicks.

IZEYE. Daly's, June 18, 1894.

J

J.P., THE. F.C. 3 a. Fenton Mackay. Opera Comique, March 16, 1897 (C.P.); Bury St. Edmunds T.R., March 22, 1897; Clapham Shakespeare, March 14, 1898; Strand, April 9, 1898.

JABEZ NORTH. See *Dark Deeds.*

JACK. C. 4 a. Mrs. Harry Beckett. Royalty, June 14, 1886.

JACK. Sk. Brien McCullough. Surrey, June 10, 1907.

JACK; OR, THE MAGIC KEY. Burl. Dublin Queen's, April 14, 1879.

JACK AND GILL. Panto. Arthur Clements and R. Soutar. Victoria.

JACK AND JILL. Christmas Masque. E. L. Blanchard. Crystal Palace, December 21, 1872.

JACK AND JILL. Sk. 1 a. Sutton Vane. Brighton Pier Palace, August 9, 1902.

JACK AND JILL. C.D. 1 a. Marcus. Transl. fr. the French. Britannia, May 8, 1882.

JACK AND JILL. M.F. 3 a. Barton White. Manchester Gaiety, October 29, 1906.

JACK AND JILL AND THE SLEEPING BEAUTY. Surrey, December 26, 1868.

JACK AND THE BEANSTALK. F. 1 a. W. Hodson. Publ. by S. French, Ltd.

JACK AND THE BEANSTALK. D.L., December 26, 1859.

JACK AND THE BEANSTALK. Burl. Chas. Millward. Adelphi, December 26, 1872.

JACK AND THE HANDYMAN. P. W. Boznet and G. W. Appleton. Brixton, June 6, 1900 (C.P.).

JACK ASHORE. Div. 1 tab. C. Wilson, Sig. Practesi, G. W. Byng. Alhambra, August 8, 1898.

JACK BRAG. F. 2 a. Gilbert A. à Beckett. St. James's, May, 1837.

JACK CADE, THE CAPTAIN OF THE COMMONS. T. 4 a. Robert T. Conrad. New York Niblo's Garden, February 18, 1861; Dublin Queen's, March 13, 1868.

JACK CRAUFORD. D. Sunderland Lyceum, October 1, 1877.

JACK DRUM'S ENTERTAINMENT; OR, THE PLEASANT COMEDY OF PASQUIL AND KATHARINE. Anon. Ac. by the children of St. Paul's. Partly borrowed from Demagora's treatment of Parthenia in *Argalus and Parthenia.* Pr. 1601.

JACK IN A BOX. Ca. 1 a. J. Palgrave Simpson. St. James's, June 11, 1866.

JACK IN THE BOX. D. 4 a. E. Towers. Pavilion, November 5, 1881.

JACK IN THE BOX. M. Variety D. 4 a. Geo. R. Sims and Clement Scott. Brighton T.R., August 24, 1885; Strand, February 7, 1887.

JACK IN THE GREEN; OR, HINTS ON ETIQUETTE. F. Mark Lemon. Adelphi, May 23, 1850.

JACK IN THE WATER. D. 3 a. W. L. Rede. Publ. by J. Dicks.

JACK IN WONDERLAND. Crystal Palace, December 22, 1874.

JACK JUGGLER AND MRS. BOUNDGRACE. Int. Copland. Ent. Stationers' Co., 1562-3. See *Amphitryon.*

JACK KETCH. D. 3 a. G. Almar. Publ. by J. Dicks.

JACK LONG; OR, SHOT IN THE EYE. D. 2 a. J. B. Johnstone.

JACK MINGO, Britannia, August 11, 1866.

JACK O' HEARTS. A "Blend of Drama and Burlesque." Sidney Vereker and W. H. Dearlove. Swindon Mech. Inst., March 26, 1894.

JACK O' LANTERN. D. C. H. Hazlewood. Britannia, June 8, 1867.

JACK O' THE HEDGE. D. 2 a. W. E. Suter. Queen's, November 19, 1862.

JACK OF ALL TRADES, A. P. 1 a. Sumerville Gibney. Bradford T.R., March 30, 1896.

JACK OF NEWBURY. Op. T. E. Hook. D.L., May 6, 1795. Concluding with a Masque called *The Triumph of Hymen.* M. by the author's father. Songs only pr. 1795.

JACK ROBINSON AND HIS MONKEY. Melo-d. 2 a. C. Pelham Thompson. Surrey, August 20, 1829.

JACK ROBINSON CRUSOE; OR, THE GOOD FRIDAY THAT CAME ON A SATURDAY. Burl. J. W. Jones. Windsor T.R., October 14, 1876.

JACK SHEPPARD. D. 4 parts. J. B. Buckstone. Adap. fr. Ainsworth's novel. Adelphi, October 28, 1839.

JACK SHEPPARD. Ver. by Moncrieff. Victoria, October, 1839.

JACK SHEPPARD. D. 3 a. Ver. by J. T. Haines. Publ. by S. French, Ltd.

JACK SHEPPARD. D. 4 a. Joseph Hatton. Pav., April 9, 1898.

JACK SHEPPARD. See *Jonathan Wild.*

JACK SHEPPARD; OR, THE BURGLARY AT THE GRANGE. Vocal scs. by A. Voyce. Bow Palace of Varieties.

JACK SPRAT. Astley's, December 26, 1864.

JACK STEDFAST; OR, WRECK AND RESCUE. D. 3 a. Cecil Pitt. Britannia, August 30, 1869.

JACK STRAW. C. 3 a. W. Somerset Maugham. Vaudeville, March 26, 1908.

JACK STRAW'S LIFE AND DEATH. 4 a. Danter. Ent. Stationers' Co., October 23, 1593. Pr. 1593. Another edition was pr. for Thos. Pavier, 1604.

JACK TAR. D. 5 a. A. Shirley and B. Landeck. Pav., October 12, 1896.

JACK TAR AND JOHN CHINAMAN; OR, MOLLY AND THE ALIEN. M. Sk. by Lady Colin Campbell, lyrics by Hugo Ames, M. by H. Bunning. Alhambra, February 13, 1903.

JACK THE GIANT KILLER. F. 1 a. Anon. Hay. Pr. 1730.

JACK THE GIANT KILLER. Ballet. Lyceum (eighth perf.), August 25, 1810.

JACK THE GIANT KILLER; OR, HARLEQUIN KING ARTHUR AND YE KNIGHTS OF YE ROUND TABLE. Burl. Extrav. H. J. Byron. Princess's, December 26, 1859.

JACK THE GIANT QUELLER. Operatic P. Henry Brooke. Ac. Dublin, 1748. Prohibited after first night. Alt. in 1754 and ac. again at Dublin. Pr. 1778 under the title of *Little John and the Giants.*

JACK, THE TALE OF A TRAMP. D. Blackpool T.R., November 12, 1877.

JACK TREMAINE, V.C. P. 1 a. W. Heriot. Lancaster Athenæum, August 3, 1901.

JACK WHITE'S TRIAL. D. 1 a. F. C. W. Parr. Sheffield Alexandra, March 16, 1883.

JACK'S DELIGHT. F. 1 a. T. J. Williams. Strand, November 3, 1862.

JACK'S SWEETHEART. M.C. 3 a. Fletcher Sansome. Workington T.R., February 2, 1903; Woolwich R. Artil., June 15, 1903.

JACK'S THE LAD. D. 2 a. W. Rogers. Publ. by J. Dicks.

JACKAL, THE. C. 3 a. Alec Nelson. Adap. fr. the French. Strand, November 28, 1880.

JACKDAW, THE. C. 1 a. Lady Gregory. Dublin Abbey, February 22, 1907; Great Queen Street, June 11, 1907 (mat.).

JACKET OF BLUE, THE. Comic Orig. Burla. 1 a. T. Egerton Wilks. Pav., February 14, 1838.

JACKEYDORA; OR, THE LAST WITCH. C.O. 3 a. Mark Melford. M. by Popsie Rowe. Leamington T.R., December 26, 1890.

JACKO. M. Absurdity. 2 a. H. Rogerson. Staleybridge Grand, April 11, 1898; in 3 a. under title *Jacko; or, Comical Complications.* Stratford T.R., July 29, 1901.

JACKS AND JILLS. C. 3 a. James Albery. Vaudeville, May 29, 1880.

JACKSON'S BOY. Melo-d. 5 a. Mrs. Wm. Greet. Carlisle H.M.T., May 28, 1891.

JACOB. Orat. H. Smart (1813-79).

JACOB AND ESAU. Int. Pr. Wr. in metre. Black letter. Pr. 1568.

JACOB FAITHFUL. D. 3 a. Haines. Taken fr. Marryat. Publ. by J. Dicks.

JACOB GUNSON, AGITATOR. D. Pro. and 3 a. L. Clarance and V. Wray. Consett New T.R., May 1, 1902.

JACOB'S LADDER. D. C. S. Watson. Derby Grand, August 27, 1902 (C.P.).

JACOBI; OR, THE FATAL PEA-NUT, IL. Burl. O. Lyrics and M. by L. Hansay. Bayswater Bijou, February 26, 1895.

JACOBIN CLUB. Pol. C. J. C. Siber. Pr. Liverpool, 1801.

JACOBITE, THE. C.D. 2 a. J. R. Planché. Hay., June 12, 1847.

JACOPO THE BRAVE. D. 3 a. Buckstone. Adelphi, February, 1833.

JACQUELINE. Op. bo. 1 a Offenbach. 1862.

JACQUELINE. D. Pro. and 4 a. Frank Harvey. Leeds Amphi., May 8, 1874.

JACQUES DAMOUR. Royalty, February 4, 1889.

JACQUES STROP; OR, A FEW MORE PASSAGES IN THE LIFE OF THE RENOWNED AND ILLUSTRIOUS ROBERT MACAIRE. Dom. D. 3 a. Chs. Selby. Strand, September 28, 1838.

JAILBIRD, THE. C. of Crime. M. Maartins. Wyndham's, February 9, 1904.

JALOUSE. See *The Dove-Cot.*

JAQUIRITA L'INDIENNE. O. Halévy. Paris, 1855.

JAM OF POTANA, THE. Ca. 2 sc. Mrs. Fortune. Camberwell Empire, June 3, 1907.

JAMES IV., THE SCOTTISH HISTORY OF. Robt. Greene. Ent. Stationers' Co., May 13, 1594. Pr. 1599.

JAMES (KING), HIS ENTERTAINMENT AT THEOBALD'S. J. Saville. P. 1603.

JAMIE AND BESS; OR, THE LAIRD IN DISGUISE. Past. C. 5 a. Andrew Shirrefs. Ac. Edinburgh, 1796. Pr. 1787.

JAN, THE ICELANDER; OR, HOME, SWEET HOME. D. 3 a. H. Caine. W. Hartlepool Grand, November 24, 1900.

JAN THE JESTER. Rev. ver. of M.P. prod. in 1902. Now in 2 a. Wr. and comp. by Geo. H. Chester. West Hampstead T.H., October 24, 1902; C.G. King's Hall, May 19, 1905.

JANUS. Masque pres. at Court, 1573.

JANE. F.C. 3 a. Harry Nicholls and W. Lestocq. Comedy, December 18, 1890; Terry's, December 26, 1899.

JANE. D. 2 a. J. P. Hart. Publ. by S. French, Ltd.

JANE ANNIE; OR, THE GOOD CONDUCT PRIZE. J. M. Barrie and Conan Doyle. M. by Ernest Ford. Savoy, May 13, 1893.

JANE EYRE. D. 2 a. Surrey, November 16, 1867.

JANE EYRE. D. 5 a. J. Brougham. Adap. fr. Charlotte Brontë's novel. Publ. by J. Dicks.

JANE EYRE. D. 3 a. T. H. Paul. Oldham Amphi., October 13, 1879.

JANE EYRE. D. 4 a. W. G. Wills. Adap. of Miss Charlotte Brontë's novel. Globe, December 23, 1882.

JANE JENKINS; OR, THE GHOST OF THE BACK DRAWING-ROOM. G. à Beckett.

JANE LOMAX. D. Adelphi, February, 1839.

JANE OF FLANDERS; OR, THE SIEGE OF HENNEBONNE. D. 2 a. By "S. W." Pr. 1800-1.

JANE SETON. D. Liverpool Amphi., May 25, 1878.

JANE SETON; OR, THE WITCH OF EDINBRO'. D. S. Nicholson. Leith T.R., March 28, 1870.

JANE SHORE. P. Henry Chettle, in conjunction with John Day. Ac. 1602 (? previously.

JANE SHORE. T. 5 a. Nicholas Rowe. Pr. 1713. D.L., February 2, 1714; C.G., 1824.

JANE SHORE. D. 5 a. W. G. Wills. Leeds Amphi., March 8, 1875. Princess's, September 30, 1876.

JANE SHORE. P. 4 a. J. W. Boulding and R. Palgrave. Liverpool R. Court (under the title of *The King's Favourite*), August 31, 1885; Grand, March 15, 1886.

JANE SHORE. Burl. Strand, March 26, 1894.

JANE SHORE; OR, THE FEARFUL PENANCE AND THE FATAL PENNY ROLL. Burl. J. Wilton Jones. Liverpool Princess of Wales, August 16, 1880.

JANE, THE LICENSED VICTUALLER'S DAUGHTER. D. 2 a. J. P. Hart. Pub. by J. Dicks.

JANET O'BRIEN. D. 3 a. Nugent Robinson. Dublin T.R., February 27, 1869.

JANET PRIDE. D. 4 a. Dion Boucicault. First acted in U.S.A. Adelphi, February 5, 1855; Princess's, July, 1874.

JANET'S RUSE. C. Royalty, 1872.

JANETTA. O. Auber. 1840.

JAPANESE DANCE. A. D.Sk. W. G. H. Lees. Chiswick T.H., May 15, 1906.

JAPANESE GIRL, THE. Mus. C. 2 a. Austin Fryers. M. by Charles J. Lacock. Plymouth T.R., June 26, 1897.

JAPANESE LAMP, A. Ca. By Lisa Dorisi. Tiverton Drill H., February 25, 1897.

JAPANESE REVENGE, A. Sk. Metropolitan, August 12, 1907.

JAPS; OR, THE DOOMED DAIMIO, THE. Burl. d. 2 a. H. Paulton and Mostyn Tedde. Bristol, Princes's, August 31, 1885; Novelty, September 19, 1885.

JARDINIER, LE. Op. C. Sedaine, 1771.

JARGONELLE. C. 1 a. Mrs. H. Parker. Pub. by J. Dicks.

JASON. T. R. Glover. Pr. 1799. N. ac.

JASON. Cantata. Sir A. C. Mackenzie.

JASPER BRIGHT: BY SPECIAL APPOINTMENT. P. 3a. Arthur Sturgess. Adap. fr. Ger., *Herren Söhne*, of Oscar Walter and Leo Stein. Folkestone Pleasure Gardens, May 1, 1905; Avenue, May 6, 1905.

JASPER'S REVENGE. P. 1 a. Wynn Miller. Shaftesbury, June 25, 1891.

JAUNTY JANE SHORE. Burl. 2 a. "Richard Henry." M. by John Crook. Strand, April 2, 1894.

JEALOUS CLOWN; OR, THE LUCKY MISTAKE, THE. O. 1 a. Thos. Gataker. Goodman's Fields. Pr. 1730.

JEALOUS FARMER OUTWITTED; OR, HARLEQUIN STATUE, THE. Panto. C.G. Before 1814.

JEALOUS HUSBAND, THE. C. C.G., April 7, 1777. Founded on *The Spanish Fryer*. N.p.

JEALOUS HUSBANDS, THE. Leonard. Pr. 1678. See *Rambling Justice*.

JEALOUS IN HONOUR. P. 4 a. Basil Broke. Garrick, April 27, 1893.

JEALOUS LOVER CURED, THE. Ent. 2 a. Anon. Pr. 1788.

JEALOUS LOVERS, THE. C. Thos. Randolph. Pr. 1632. Acted by the Students of Trin. Coll., Cambridge. Rev. 1682.

JEALOUS MISTAKE, A. Dom. sketch. S. J. Adair Fitz-Gerald. Globe, April 27, 1899.

JEALOUS OF THE PAST. Ca. 1 a. Miss Alice Chandos. New Cross H., September 17, 1885.

JEALOUS ON ALL SIDES; OR, THE LANDLORD IN JEOPARDY. C.O. 2 a. M. by Jolly. Lyceum, August 19, 1818.

JEALOUS WIFE, THE. C. 5 a. George Colman. Pr. 1761. D.L., February 12, 1761. F. on Fielding's "Tom Jones." D.L., June 28, 1816, and June 30, 1820; C.G., 1824; Strand, July 26, 1892.

JEALOUS WIFE'S REVENGE, A D. Epis. Louis H. Carlton. Collins's M.H., May 12, 1905.

JEALOUSY. D. 4 a. Charles Reade. Olympic, April 22, 1878.

JEALOUSY. C. 2 a. C. and Mrs. F. S. Shannon. Publ. by J. Dicks. C.G., November, 1838.

JEALOUSY. Humorous Rom 1 a. W. H. Dearlove. Harrogate Spa, January 17, 1891.

JEALOUSY. M.P. Performed by German Reed Co. at St. George's Hall.

JEALOUSY. O. 1 a. Watson and Solomon. Publ. by S. French, Ltd.

JEALOUSY. Wordless P. Marc Aubry. M. by Lucien de Flagny. (Prod. by the Argonauts.) Rehearsal, W.C., November 13, 1908 (mat.).

JEALOUSY. See *The Countess and the Dancer, Andrea, Agnes*.

JEAMES. C. 3 a. F. C. Burnand. Gaiety, August 26, 1878.

JEAN DE COUVIN. O. Auber, 1812.

JEAN DE NIVELLE. O. Delibes. Paris, March 8, 1880.

JEAN DE PARIS. O. Boieldieu. Paris, 1812.

JEAN DE PARIS. Comic D. 2 a. Fr. the French. D.L., November 1, 1814.

JEAN ET GENEVIEVE. O. J. P. Soulier. 1792 (his last O.).

JEAN HENNUYER, BISHOP OF LIZIEUX; OR, THE MASSACRE OF ST. BARTHOLOMEW. Dr. Ent. 3 a. Taken from the French. Pr. 1773.

JEAN MARIE. See *Auld Robin Gray*.

JEAN MAYEUX. Mimo D. 3 a. Blanchard de la Bretesche. M. by Chas. Thony. Princess's, May 12, 1894.

JEAN ON LA REPUBLIQUE. D. 4 a. Adap. fr. the French. Sadler's Wells, October 28, 1882.

JEANIE DEANS. O. 4 a. and 7 tab. Joseph Bennett. M. by Hamish M'Cunn. F. on Sir Walter Scott's "Heart of Midlothian." Edinburgh Lyceum, November 15, 1894; Daly's, January 22, 1896.

JEANNE D'ARC. O. Gounod. Paris, 1873.

JEANNE D'ARC. O. Mermet. Paris, 1876.

JEANNE D'ARC. Her M.T., June 23, 1890.

JEANNE D'ARC. P. 5 a. Percy MacKaye. Waldorf, April 24, 1907.

JEANNE DUBARRY. D. 3 a. H. Hermann. Charing Cr., May 15, 1875.

JEANNE JEANNETTE JEANNETON. O.C. in Prol. and 3 a. R. Reece. Fr. the French of Clairville and Delacour. M. by P. Lacome. Alhambra, March 28, 1881.

JEANNE QUI PLEURE ET JEAN QUI RIT. Op. bo. 1 a. Offenbach. 1865.

JEANNETTE AND JEANNOT; OR, THE VILLAGE PRIDE. M.D. 2 a. Edward Stirling. Olympic, October 26, 1848.

JEANNETTE'S WEDDING. Oa. 1 a. Leicester Buckingham and A. Harris.

JEANNETTE'S WEDDING DAY. Mus. F. 1 a. T. H. Lacy. Adap. fr. *Les Noces de Jeannette* by Carri and Jules Barbier. T. Imperial de l'Opera Comique, February 4, 1853; Princess's (as *Jeannette's Wedding*).

JEANNIE DEANS. See *Jeannie Deans* and *The Trial of Effie Deans*.

JEANNIE DEANS; OR, THE HEART OF MIDLOTHIAN. P. Princess's, March, 1868.

JEDBURY JUNIOR. C. 3 a. Madeleine Lucette Ryley. New York Empire T. (as *Christopher Junior*), September 23, 1895; Terry's, February 14, 1896; Globe, December 21, 1896; rev. Shaftesbury, June 16, 1902.

JEDEDIAH THE SCARECROW. Oa. 2 a. Bernard Page. M. by Geo. G. Vincent. Cripplegate Inst., May 23, 1905.

JEDORKA (The Jewess). Dr. Sk. J. Clempert. Manchester Palace, April 15, 1907.

JEHOSAPHAT. Orat. Anon. Before 1814.

JEHU. F. Anon. D.L., February 20, 1779. N.p.

JEMMY. P. 1 a. Louis N. Parker. Adelphi, April 25, 1907.

JENKINS' LOVE COURSE. A Droll formed out of Shirley's *School of Compliments*, and pr. 1672.

JENKIN'S WIDOW. .P 1 a. Priscilla Craven (Mrs. Teignmouth Shore). (Prod. by the Dramatic Debaters.) Court, March 21, 1909.

JENKINSES; OR, BOARDED AND DONE FOR, THE. F. 2 a. J. R. Planché. D.L., December 9, 1830; Lyceum, December 6, 1852.

JENNY BELL. O. Auber. Paris, 1855.

JENNY FOSTER, THE SAILOR'S CHILD; OR, THE WINTER ROBIN. 2 a. C. H. Hazlewood. Britannia, October, 1855.

JENNY JONES. Oa. 1 a. F. Cooper. Publ. by S. French, Ltd.

JENNY LIND AT LAST; OR, THE SWEDISH NIGHTINGALE. An apropos operatic bagatelle in 1 a. by Angus B. Reach. Lyceum, about 1851.

JENNY THE BARBER. C. 1 a. Wilson Barrett. Bristol Prince's, December 10, 1891.

JENNY'S WHIM; OR, THE ROASTED EMPEROR. F. John O'Keeffe. Advertised for perf. at the Hay., 1794, but withdrawn. N.p.

JENSEN FAMILY, THE. C. 4 a. Edward Höyer. May Morrison. A translation. Criterion, April 23, 1901.

JEPHTHA. T. Christopherson. 1546.

JEPHTHA. T. Buchanan. 1554.

JEPHTHA. P. Henry Chettle. Ac. 1602.

JEPHTHA. Orat. G. Carissimi (1582-1673).

JEPHTHA. Orat. Handel. 1751.

JEPHTHA'S DAUGHTER. Dr. Poem. Mrs. Ann Wilson. Pr. 1783.

JEPHTHA'S RASH VOW. Perf. at Bartholomew Fair, 1698.

JEPHTHA'S VOW. O. M. by Meyerbeer (his first O.), Munich, 1813.

JERONYMO; OR, THE SPANISH TRAGEDY, WITH THE WARS OF PORTUGAL. Anon. Probably by Thos. Kyd. This is in two parts. Part 2 called *Jeronymo's Mad Again; or, The Spanish Tragedy*. Probably written before 1588. Pr. 1605. See *Spanish Tragedy*.

JERRY AND A SUNBEAM. P. 1 a. Cosmo Hamilton. Adap. fr. a story in his "Furrows." Strand, September 26, 1898.

JERRY BUILDER, THE. F.c. 3 a. Mark Melford. Suggested by Wm. Miller. Southampton, P.O.W., June 13, 1892; Grand, June 11, 1894.

JERRY BUILDER, SOLNESS. Parody, by Mrs. Hugh Bell, of Ibsen's *Master Builder*. St. Geo. H., July 10, 1893.

JERRY IN THE SUDS. F. Milns, 1799. N.p.

JERRY, THE BURGLAR. Sk. H. Percival. Middlesex, January 7, 1901.

JERRY'S WAGERS. C. 2 a. F. Haywell. Manchester T.R., August 3, 1874.

JERSEY GIRL; OR, LES ROUGE VOLEURS, THE. Melo. d. 2 a. G. Dibdin Pitt. Surrey.

JERUSALEM. Ac. March 22, 1591. Possibly Legg's "Destruction of Jerusalem."

JERUSALEM. O. Verdi. Wds. by Royer and Waez.

JERUSALEM DELIVERED. See Epic Poems.

JERUSALEM INFIRMARY; OR, A JOURNEY TO THE VALLEY OF JEHOSAPHAT, THE. F. Anon. Pr. 1749. N. ac.

JESMOND DENE. D. 4 a. Adap. fr. Miss Braddon's novel, "Henry Dunbar." Ipswich, T.R., October 9, 1890; Shepherd's Bush Athenæum, March 5, 1892.

JESS. D. 4 a. Eweretta Lawrence and J. J. Bisgood. Adap. fr. H. Rider Haggard's novel. Adelphi, March 25, 1890.

JESSAMY'S COURTSHIP. F. 1 a. C. H. Hazlewood. Philharmonic, April 12, 1875.

JESSIE ASHTON. D. W. Sawyer. Surrey, December, 1862.

JESSIE BROWN; OR, THE RELIEF OF LUCKNOW. D. 3 a. Dion Boucicault. Plymouth T.R., November, 1858.

JESSIE FARLEIGH. City of London, February 9, 1863.

JESSIE GRAY. R. Brough and Bridgman. Adelphi, 1850.

JESSIE LEE. See *Jessy Lea*.

JESSIE, THE FLOWER OF DUMBLANE; OR, WEEL MAY THE KEEL ROW. Oa. By the author of *Lo Zingaro*. Lyceum playbill (first time this season), August 7, 1834.

JESSIE, THE MACHINE GIRL. D. 4 a. Northampton T.R., February 17, 1868.

JESSIE TYRRELL. Victoria, March 3, 1866.

JESSONDA. O. Wds. by Edouard Gehe. M. by Spohr. Vienna, 1825, D.L., March 18, 1841; prod. in Italian C.G., August 6, 1853.

JESSY LEA. O. Macfarren. 1863.

JESSY VERE; OR, THE RETURN OF THE WANDERER. Dom. D. 2 a. C. H. Hazlewood. Britannia, February, 1856.

JEST, THE. P. 3 a. Murray Carson and Louis N. Parker. Criterion, November 10, 1898.

JESTER, THE. H.P. 3 a. R. Wilford. Sunderland T.R., May 22, 1902.

JEU DE BARRIS, LE. D.L., March 30, 1848.

JEUNE HENRI, LE. O.C. 2 a. Lib. by Bouilly. M. by Méhul. Paris, Théâtre Favart, May 1, 1797.

JEVAN THE PRODIGAL SON. Rom. P. 4 a. Alfred C. Calmour. Manchester Queen's, October 30, 1905. Produced at the Scala as *The Judgment of Pharaoh*, April 20, 1907.

JEW, THE. P. Anon. 1579. N.p.

JEW, THE. C. 5 a. Richard Cumberland. D.L. Pr. 1793. Rev. D.L., May 22, 1815; June 9, 1818; August 8, 1821.

JEW AND GENTILE, THE. Burl. J. C. Cross. Ac. at the Circus.

JEW AND THE DOCTOR, THE. F. 2 a. Thos. Dibdin. C.G., 1800; D.L., December 18, 1819; and May 25, 1832.

JEW DECOY'D; OR, THE PROGRESS OF AN HARLOT, THE. Bal. O. Pr. 1733. N.ac. Founded on Hogarth's Prints, the "Harlot's Progress."

JEW OF CONSTANTINE, THE. Victoria, June 9, 1855.

JEW OF LUBECK; OR, THE HEART OF A FATHER, THE. Melo-d. 2 a. H. M. Milner. M. by Cooke, action by Johnson, D.L., May 11, 1819.

JEW OF MALTA, THE (or, *The Rich Jew of Malta*). T.C. Christopher Marlowe. Publ. after the author's death. Ent. Stationers' Co., May 17, 1594. (?) Wr. in 1589. Rose T., February 26, 1591; Newington T., June 12, 1594; Cockpit, 1633. Pr. 1633. Probably a P. on which Shakespeare partly f. his ***Merchant of Venice***.

JEW OF MALTA, THE. Hist. T. W. Shone. Repr. with Notes, 1810.

JEW OF MALTA, THE. F. on Marlowe's T. D.L., April 24, 1818.

JEW OF MOGADORE, THE. O. Richard Cumberland. D.L. Pr. 1808.

JEW OF VENICE, THE. Thos. Dekker. Ent. Stationers' Co., September 9, 1653. N.p.

JEW OF VENICE, THE. C. Rt. Hon. Geo. Granville, Lord Lansdowne. L.I.F. Pr. 1701. An alt of Shakespeare's ***Merchant of Venice***. Prol. by Bevil Higgons. A masque called ***Peleus and Thetis*** was introd. in act two.

JEW OR GENTILE. P. 1 sc. Moses Hoffman and G. Le Brunn. Paragon M.H., August 7, 1899.

JEW REVOLUTIONIST, THE. Dr. Episode by J. Jackson. Paragon, August 19, 1907.

JEW'S DAUGHTER, THE. D. 2 a. Edwd. Stirling. Strand, January 5, 1857.

JEW'S EYE, THE. P. 3 a. Florence Lane-Fox. Bayswater Victoria H., June 4, 1889.

JEW'S REVENGE, THE. Sk. 1 a. D. Mahomed. Surrey, July 21, 1904.

JEW'S TRAGEDY; OR, THEIR FATAL AND FINAL OVERTHROW BY VESPASIAN AND TITUS HIS SON, THE. Wm. Heminge. Founded on the siege and destruction of Jerusalem as related by Josephus. Pr. 1662.

JEWEL MAIDEN, THE. Japanese O. 3 a. M. C. Gillington. M. by Florian Pascal. Forest Hill St. Geo. Parish H., December 13, 1899.

JEWELLER OF AMSTERDAM; OR, THE HAGUE, THE. P. John Fletcher, Nathaniel Field, and Philip Massinger. Ent. Stationers' Co., April 8, 1654. N.p.

JEWELLER OF ST. JAMES'S, THE. C. 3 a. W. E. Suter. Adap. fr. the French of H. de Saint Georges and A. de Leuven. Op. C., February 17, 1862.

JEWELS, THE. P. 4 a. Dr. G. H. R. Dabbs. Shanklin Inst., August 31, 1893.

JEWELS AND DUST; OR, THE ROMANCE OF A COUNT. C. 4 a. Geo. Manville Fenn. Crystal Pal., May 18, 1886.

JEWESS, THE. Op. D. F. on Scribe's O., *La Juive*. M. by Halevy. Arr. for the Engl. stage by Cooke. D.L., November 16, 1835.

JEWESS, THE. O. Balfe. 1835.

JEWESS, THE. Spectacle. Victoria, December, 1835.

JEWESS, THE. D. 3 a. W. T. Moncrieff. Publ. by J. Dicks.

JEWESS, THE. D. 4 a. Louis Ludovici. Adap. from Mosenthal's P. ***Deborah***. Shaftesbury, June 27, 1899.

JEWESS, THE. T. 5 a. M. Lerner. Pav., September 20, 1907.

JEWESS, THE. See *Jedorko*.

JEWESS; OR, THE COUNCIL OF CONSTANCE, THE. Rom. D. 3 a. T. H. Lacy. Adap. fr. Scribe's ***La Juive***. Academie Royal de Musique, 1828. D.L., November 16, 1835; Lyric, August 29, 1908. See *La Juive*.

JEWESS AND CHRISTIAN; OR, THE LOVE THAT KILLS. D. 4 a. E. Manuel. Britannia, April 2, 1877.

JEWISH COUNTESS, THE. Sk. J. W. Jackson. M. by F. Bradsell. Cambridge, November 18, 1907.

JEWISH GENTLEMAN, THE. P. Richd. Brome. En. Stationers Co., August 4, 1640. N.p.

JEW-MANITY. Travesty. J. Hickory Wood. Canterbury M.H., January 13, 1902.

JEZEBEL; OR, THE DEAD RECKONING. D. 3 a. Dion Boucicault. F. on ***Le Pendu***. P. by Michel Masson and Anicet Bourgeois. Holborn T., December 5, 1870.

JEZEBEL'S HUSBAND. D. 1 a. Bernard Dale. Middleton T.R., December 1, 1893.

JILT, THE. C. 5 a. Dion Boucicault. Eleph. and C., July 13, 1885; P.O.W., July 29, 1886.

JILTED. C. 2 a. Alfred Maltby. Liverpool. P.O.W., June 18, 1877; Criterion, July 28, 1879.

JIM. P. 1 a. Stanley Hall, N., April 17, 1902.

JIM, A ROMANCE OF COCKAYNE. D. 4 a. H. A. Saintsbury. Kingston County T., July 6, 1903.

JIM BELMONT. P. 3 a. Mrs. Oscar Beringer. Camberwell Metropole, October 1, 1900.

JIM CROW. Burl. 1 a. T. P. Taylor. Pub. by S. French, Ltd.

JIM DRAGS, THE DRAYMAN. D. F. Hay. Liverpool P.O.W., May 26, 1870.

JIM THE PENMAN. Ro. 4 a. Sir Chas. Young. Hay., March 25, 1886; evening bill, April 3, 1886.

JIM'S LITTLE JOKE. Sk. Metropolitan, October 7, 1907.

JIM'S WIFE. D. Epis. Vic. C. Rolfe. Surrey, December 19, 1904.

JIMES. Monol. Bertha Graham. Amateur Players' Association, February 7, 1906.

JIMMY WATT. D. 3 a. Dion Boucicault Eleph. and C., August 1, 1890. (C.P.)

JIMMY'S MOTHER. P. 1 a. Hope Merrick (Mrs. Leonard Merrick). Eastbourne Pier, January 19, 1904 (C.P.); the Scala, November 26, 1905.

JINGLE. F.C. James Albery. Lyceum, July 8, 1878.

JO. D. 3 a. J. P. Burnett. F. on Charles Dickens's "Bleak House." Globe, February 21, 1876; D.L., May 13, 1896. See ***Bleak House***.

JO THE WAIF. See *Joe the Waif*.

JO THE WAIF; OR, THE MYSTERY OF CHESNEY WOLD. D. Liverpool Rotunda, July, 1881.

JO v. JO. Surrey, September 25, 1876.

JOAN. D. 6 a. Charles Reade. Liverpool Amphi., August 31, 1878.

JOAN; OR, THAT LASS O' LOWRIE'S. D. G. H. Coveney. A version of Mrs. Burnett's novel. Coventry T.R., July 8, 1878.

JOAN; OR, THE BRIGANDS OF BLUEGORIA. C.O. Robert Martin. M. by Ernest Ford. Op. Comique, June 9, 1890 (amat.).

JOAN AND ANGELINA. O. 1a. Lathair and Elliott. Published by S. French, Limited.

JOAN AS GOOD AS MY LADY. P. Thos. Heywood. Ac. in 1598. N.p.

JOAN LOWRIE. D. Blackburn T.R., February, 11, 1878.

JOAN OF ARC. Hist. O. 3 a. M. by Balfe. Wds. by A. Bunn. D.L., November 30, 1837.

JOAN OF ARC. 2 a. T. J. Serle. C.G.

JOAN OF ARC. Extrav. William Brough. Strand, March 29, 1869.

JOAN OF ARC. D. 4 a. Tom Taylor. Queen's, April 10, 1871.

JOAN OF ARC. D. 5 a. E. Villiers. East London, August 26, 1871.

JOAN OF ARC. D. G W. Innes. Sadler's Wells, September 15, 1890.

JOAN OF ARC. Burl. 2 a. J. L. Shine and Adrian Ross M. by F. Osmond Carr. Op. Comique, January 17, 1891; Gaiety, September 30, 1891; transf. to Shaftesbury, December 21, 1891.

JOAN OF ARC. Piece in four Chronicles. John Henderson. Bayswater Bijou, July 24, 1896 (C.P.).

JOAN OF ARC. Burl. J. H. Maxwell. Brighton Aquarium, August 27, 1900.

JOAN OF ARC; OR, THE MAID OF ORLEANS. Hist. Bal. of Action. Ascribed to J.C. Cross. C.G. Songs and Choruses. Pr. 1798.

JOAN OF ARC; OR, THE MAID OF ORLEANS. Melo. D. 3 a. E. Fitzball. Sadler's Wells, August 12, 1822.

JOAN OF ARC; OR, THE MAID OF ORLEANS. Hist. D. 3 a. M. Grace. Manchester Queen's, July 30, 1904.

JOAN OF ARC; OR, THE MAID, THE AMAZON, AND THE MARTYR. D. 3 a. Charles A. Clarke. Victoria, August 7, 1871.

JOAN OF HEDINGTON. T.C. 5 a. Dr. Wm. King. Pr. 1776.

JOAN'S KISS. P. 1 a. Frances Gostling. Worthing R., January 25, 1909 (amat.).

JOANNA OF MONTFAUCON. Dr. Rom. Ascr. to Maria Geisweiler. The original transl. of the MS. by Kotzebue fr. which Cumberland formed his dr. Pr. circa 1799. N.ac.

JOANNA OF MONTFAUCON. Dr. Rom. Formed on the plan of the German D. by Kotzebue by Richard Cumberland. C.G. January 16, 1800. Pr. 1800. M. by Busby.

JOANNA OF SURINAM. Spec. J. C. Cross. Pr. 1804.

JOB. Sacred D. Rannie. Pr. n.d. N.ac.

JOB. Orat. Sir C. Hubert H. Parry. Gloucester Musical Festival, 1892.

JOBE, THE HISTORY OF. Robert Green. Ent. Stationers' Co., 1594. N.p. Destd. by Warburton's servant.

JOB'S AFFLICTIONS. T. Ralph Radcliff. N.p.

JOBSON'S CHOICE. P. 1 a. Sydney Low. Aldwych, May 7, 1909 (mat.).

JOCASTA. T. Geo. Gascoigne and Francis Kinwelmarshe. Transl. fr. Euripides. Ac. at Gray's Inn, 1566. Pr. 1575. See *Phœnissœ*.

JOCELYN, THE JESTER. C. 1 a. Ronald MacDonald. Crys. Pal., March 4, 1907; Croydon Grand, February 17, 1908.

JOCHEN PASEL, WOT BIST FOR'N ESEL. (Herr Junkermann's season.) St. George's Hall, February 16, 1900.

JOCKEY, LE. O. J. P. Soulier, January 6. 1879.

JOCKEY, THE. F.C. 3 a. Fred Bousfield. Walthamstow Victoria H., October 22, 1894.

JOCKEY AND JENNY. Panto F. Ac. at Astley's Olympic, December 29, 1806.

JOCKEY CLUB, THE. Sk. Geo. Sanger. Water panto. and circus perf. Sanger's, December 26, 1892.

JOCONDE. F. 3 a. W. T. Moncrieff. Pub. by J. Dicks.

JOCONDE. O. 3 a. Nicolo Isonard. Transl. by Santley. Lyceum, Oct. 25, 1876.

JOCONDO and ASTOLFO, THE TALE OF. C. Thos. Dekker. Ent. at Stationers' Co., June 29, 1660. N.p. Destroyed by Warburton's servant.

JOCRISSE, THE JUGGLER. D. 3 a. Adap. fr. the French of D'Ennery and Jules Bresil. Paris Gaité, October 12, 1860; Adelphi, April 1, 1861.

JOE MILLER AND HIS MEN. Burl. G. à Beckett. Princess's, December, 1844.

JOE STERLING; OR, A RAGGED FORTUNE. D. 3 a. C. H. Hazlewood. Victoria, November 7, 1870.

JOE THE MINER. D. 3 a. Berte Thomas. Margate T.R., June 12, 1893.

JOE THE WAIF. D. Herbert Rhoyds. Greenwich, April 24, 1876.

JOFFIN'S LATCHKEY. F. 1 a. N. Robinson. Publ. by Douglas Cox.

JOHAN TYB AND SIR JHAN. P. John Heywood, 1533.

JOHANNISFEUER. D. H. Sudermann. Comedy, January 18, 1901; Gt. Queen St. T., November 24, 1904.

JOHN. F. 3 a. Cecil Proctor. Burslem Wedgwood, February 20, 1902.

JOHN-A-DREAMS. P. 4 a. C. Haddon Chambers. Hay., November 8, 1894.

JOHN A KENT AND JOHN A CUMBER. Anthony Munday. M.S. 1595.

JOHN AND ANGELINA. Oa. 1 a. Henry Lathair. M. by Lionel Elliott. Kilburn Town H., April 16, 1890.

JOHN AND JEANNETTE. Oa. L. Machale. M. by J. Batchelder. Adap. fr. Labiche's *Frisette*. Cheetham Town H., September 23, 1885.

JOHN AYLMER'S DREAM. P. 1 a. E. J. Burbey. Sheffield T.R., September 6, 1886.

JOHN BON AND MAST PARSON. A satire on the Real Presence. Repr. of a rare interlude, 1548.

JOHN BROWN. F. D.L., February 21, 1826.

JOHN BULL. Boucicault's ver. of Colman's c. of the same name. Gaiety, July, 1872.

JOHN BULL; OR, AN ENGLISHMAN'S FIRESIDE. C. 3 a. Geo. Colman, jun. C.G., March 5, 1803; D.L., January 21, 1867. Pr. circa 1805.

JOHN BULL ABROAD. Sk. Corney Grain. St. Geor. H., October 15, 1888.

JOHN BULL AND BUONAPARTE; OR, A MEETING AT DOVER. Burl. Serenata, by J. C. Cross. Pr. 1803.

JOHN BULL AT MARKET. P. E. W. A. B. Station. Oxford. East Oxford, August 3, 1907 (C.P.).

JOHN BULL'S OTHER ISLAND. P. 4 a. Bernard Shaw. Court, November 1, 1904; rev. Court, September 11, 1905, and September 17, 1906.

JOHN BUTT. F. E. Smith. Pr. Edin, 1798.

JOHN CHILCOTE, M.P. P. 4 a. E. Temple Thurston. Adap. fr. story of Katherine Cecil Thurston. St. James's, May 1, 1905.

JOHN COX OF COLMISTON. T. Wm. Haughton, assisted by John Day. Ac. 1599. N.p.

JOHN DOBBS. F. 1 a. J. M. Morton. Strand, April 23, 1849. D.L., June 11, 1851.

JOHN DRAYTON, MILLIONAIRE. C. 3 a. H. M. Walbrooke. Dover T.R., June 25, 1906.

JOHN DURNFORD, M.P. P. 4 a. Stuart Ogilvie. Court, September 5, 1901.

JOHN ERMINE. D. L. E. Shipton. Based on story of Fredk. Remington. Comedy, July 30, 1903 (C.P.).

JOHN FELTON. Hist. P. Stirling, 1852.

JOHN GABRIEL BORKMAN. P. 4 a. Wm. Archer. A transl. of Ibsen's play. Strand, May 3, 1897.

JOHN GLADYE'S HONOUR. P. 4 a. Alfred Sutro. St. James's, March 8, 1907.

JOHN JASPER'S WIFE. C.D. 4 a. Frank Harvey. Ipswich T.R., January 12, 1876; Standard, May 8, 1876.

JOHN JAY, JUNIOR. Sk. Hackney Empire, May 10, 1909.

JOHN JONES. F. 1 a. J. B. Buckstone. Hay., September 15, 1831.

JOHN, KING OF ENGLAND. See *King John.*

JOHN, KING OF ENGLAND. Dr. Piece. Bishop Bale.

JOHN, KING OF ENGLAND; WITH THE DISCOVERIE OF KING RICHARD CORDELION'S BASE SON, VULGARLY NAMED THE BASTARD FAWCONBRIDGE; ALSO THE DEATH OF KING JOHN AT SWINSTEAD ABBEY. THE TROUBLESOME RAIGNE OF. Ac. in the City of London, etc., 1591. Black letter. Republ. 1611. In two parts. Possibly the work of Marlowe.

JOHN LESTER, PARSON. P. 3 a. Knight Rider and Layton Foster. Lyric, January 20, 1892.

JOHN MALONE'S LOVE STORY. P. 4a. Rachael Penn. Court, January 10, 1909. (Prod. by the Play Actors.)

JOHN MARTIN'S SECRET. D. 4 a. Sutton Vane. R. Artillery T., Woolwich, September 30, 1895.

JOHN OF PARIS. C.O. 2 a. J. Pocock. Adap. fr. French O., *Jean de Paris,* by Saint Just. C.G., November 14, 1814; D.L., May 17, 1830; Olympic, July 31, 1869.

JOHN OF PROCIDA; OR, THE BRIDALS OF MESSINA. See *John Procida.*

JOHN OVERY; THE MISER OF SOUTHWARK FERRY. D. 3 a. Douglas Jerrold. Surrey.

JOHN PROCIDA. P. 5 a. J. Sheridan Knowles. C.G., September, 1840.

JOHN SMITH. D. 2 a. T. E. Wilkes. Pub. by J. Dicks.

JOHN SMITH. F. 1 a. W. Hancock. Strand, January 13, 1862.

JOHN SMITH. Oa. 1 a. Alfred Law. M. by Alfred J. Caldicott. P.O.W., January 28, 1889.

JOHN STREET, ADELPHI. F. 2 a. J. B. Buckstone. Bath, January 12, 1828.

JOHN THE BAPTIST. Int. Bishop Bale. Pr. 1538. One of the earliest dr. pieces pr. in Engl. In metre, and black letter. 1538. Ac. by young men at the Market Cross in Kilkenny on a Sunday in 1552.

JOHN THE BAPTIST. Cant. Macfarren. 1873.

JOHN THE EVANGELIST. Int. Anon. Pr. 1566.

JOHN THE HUSBAND, ETC. Heywood. 1532. See ***Play Between,* etc.**

JOHN THURGOOD, FARMER. D. 1 a. Henry Byatt. Globe, June 26, 1893.

JOHN WHARTON; OR, THE WIFE OF A LIVERPOOL MECHANIC. D. Miss Mary Fielding. M'ch'r Queen's, October 5, 1868.

JOHN WOODVIL. T. 5 a. C. Lamb. Pr. 1802. N. ac.

JOHN WOPPS. F. 1 a. W. E. Suter. Publ. by S. French, Ltd.

JOHNNE THE EVANGELISTE. See *John the Evangelist.*

JOHNNY GILPIN. F. M. by Smart. D.L., April 28, 1817.

JOI FAIT PEUR, LA. Royalty, June 30, 1891.

JOINING THE COMPANY. F.P. 1 a. N. Lynn. Bayswater Bijou, December 19, 1903 (C.P.).

JOINT HOUSEHOLD, A. Ca. 1 a. Mrs. Hugh Bell. Steinway Hall, March 13, 1891. Grand, May 2, 1892.

JOKE'S A JOKE; OR, TOO MUCH FOR FRIENDSHIP, A. F. 2 a. D.L., May 3, 1830.

JOKER, THE. F.C. 3 a. M. H. Tennyson. Avenue, November 13, 1894.

JOKING GIRL, THE. Mus. F.C. Robert A. Williams. M. by J. Capel Woodruffe. Gainsborough Albert T., March 9, 1899.

JOLIE PARFUMEUSE, LA. O. 3 a. Offenbach, 1873.

JOLLIBOY'S WOES. F. 1 a. Chas. A. Fawcett. Olympic, December 26, 1878.

JOLLY AMERICAN TRAMP, A. M.C.D. 4 a. Ed. E. Kidder. M. by Fred Gagle. Southend Empire, July 21, 1902.

JOLLY CREW; OR, TARS AT ANCHOR, THE. Int. C.G., 1799.

JOLLY GOOD SORT, A. P. 1 a. J. Farries Moss. Ladywell Parish H., May 17, 1905.

JOLLY JOE. D. H. C. Hazlewood, jun. Alexandra, November 21, 1868.

JOLLY MILLER OF STRATFORD; OR, HARLEQUIN OLD DAME GOODNESS, THE. Panto. Alfred Giovannelli. Oriental, July 5, 1869.

JOLLY WIDOW, THE. M.C. 3 a. Edith Ellis Baker, Handel V. Phasep, and Carlile. May 19, 1908 (C.P.).

JONAH. Orat. G. Carissimi. 1582-1673.

JONAS, T. Ralph Radcliffe. N.p.

JONATHAN. F. 1 a. J. Barber. Publ. by J. Dicks.

JONATHAN. Orat. Piccini. 1728-1800.

JONATHAN BRADFORD; OR, THE MURDER AT THE ROADSIDE INN. Melo.-d. 2 a. Edward Fitzball. Surrey, June 12, 1833. Victoria.

JONATHAN IN ENGLAND. F. 2 a. G. Colman. Lyceum, September 3, 1824; D.L., May 24, 1826.

JONATHAN WILD. D. 5 a. Henry Young. A ver. of Harrison Ainsworth's "Jack Sheppard." Eleph. and C., November 27, 1886.

JONATHAN WILD; OR, THE STORM ON THE THAMES. D. 4 a. Mrs. H. Young. East London, July 13, 1868.

JONATHAN WITHOUT A DAVID, A. P. 4 a. Leighton Foster. Clacton-on-Sea Town H., July 19, 1894.

JONE. O. Petrella. Milan, 1848.

JONES, F. C. Arthur Shirley and Benjamin Landeck. Bury T.R., October 16, 1891.

JONES AND CO. Ca. Clifton Bingham. Croydon Pub. H., February 4, 1893.

JONES AND CO. Ca. Adap. fr. the Fr. by Miss Frances Burleigh. Islington, Myddelton H., November 30, 1893.

JONES, THE AVENGER. Olympic, November 24, 1856.

JONES'S JAUNT. F.C. 3 a. Glen-Macdonough. Aberdeen, Her Maj. T., September 12, 1904.

JONES'S NOTES, THE. F.C. 3 a. Joseph Tabrar. Bournemouth T.R. June 14, 1886. Gaiety, July 12, 1886.

JONGLEUR DE NOTRE DAME, LA. O. Massenet, 1902.

JOSEPH. Mentioned in Catalogues. This is Goldsmith's *Sophompaneas*.

JOSEPH. Sacred D. Fesch. Pr. 1745.

JOSEPH. Orat. Handel. 1746.

JOSEPH. Sacred D. W. T. Procter. Pr. 1802.

JOSEPH. O. Méhul, 1807. Lib. follows Biblical Story.

JOSEPH. Orat. Stillingfleet. N.d.

JOSEPH. O. Raimondi. August 7, 1852.

JOSEPH AND HIS BRETHREN. O. J. Miller. M. by Handel. 1747.

JOSEPH AND HIS BRETHREN. Arthur Shirley. M. by Walter Slaughter and Roland Carse. Coliseum, September 25, 1905.

JOSEPH ANDREWS. F. S. J. Pratt. D.L., April 20, 1778. N.p.

JOSEPH CHAVIGNY. D. Watts Phillips. Adelphi, May, 1856.

JOSEPH ENTANGLED. C. 3 a. H. A. Jones. Haymarket, January 19, 1904.

JOSEPH IN EGYPT. Orat. M. by Méhul. 1807. First time in England at D.L., April 7, 1841.

JOSEPH MADE KNOWN TO HIS BRETHREN. Sacred D. T. Holcroft. Transl. fr. Mdme. Genlis. Pr. 1786.

JOSEPH SHARK. F. 1 a. G. Phillips. Publ. by S. French, Limited.

JOSEPH SOLD BY HIS BRETHREN. Sacred D. Anon. Pr. 1789.

JOSEPH'S AFFLICTIONS. (Probably a misprint in old catalogues for *Job's Afflictions*.)

JOSEPH'S SWEETHEART. C. 5 a. Robert Buchanan. F. on Fielding's novel. Vaudeville, March 8, 1888.

JOSEPHINE. D. 2 a. C. E. Wallis. Publ. by S. French, Limited.

JOSEPHINE. Political Extrav. 3 scenes. J. M. Barrie. Comedy, April 5, 1906.

JOSEPHINE, THE CHILD OF THE REGIMENT; OR, THE FORTUNE OF WAR. Mus. C. 2 a. J. B. Buckstone. Hay.

JOSHUA. Sacred D. Saml. Rowley. Ac. 1602.

JOSHUA. Orat. Handel. 1747.

JOSHUA HAGGARD. D. Jesmond L. Young. Cheltenham T.R., May 19, 1879. See *Recommended to Mercy*.

JOSIAH'S DREAM; OR, THE WOMAN OF THE FUTURE. F.C. 3 a. Charles Rogers. Strand, May 21, 1896.

JOURNEY TO BRISTOL; OR, THE HONEST WELCHMAN, A. F. John Hippisley. L.I.F. Pr. 1729. See *Connaught Wife*.

JOURNEY TO LONDON, A. Part of a C. by Sir John Vanbrugh. Pr. 1728. Left unfinished, and completed by Cibber as *The Provok'd Husband*.

JOURNEY'S END, THE. P. 1 a. Horace W. C. Newte. Ladbroke H., June 11, 1891; Globe, January 30, 1895; Birmingham T.R., March 14, 1895; Gt. Queen St., November 4, 1901.

JOURNEYS END IN LOVERS MEETING. P. 1 a. John Oliver Hobbes and Geo. Moore. Daly's, June 5, 1894.

JOV, JO. M.F. 1 a. Frank W. Green and Oswald Allan. Surrey, September 25, 1876.

JOVIAL COBLER; OR, A LIGHT HEART'S BETTER THAN A HEAVY PURSE, THE. Burla. Pr. circa 1749.

JOVIAL CREW. C.O. Roome. 1731.

JOVIAL CREW; OR, THE DEVIL TURN'D RANTER, THE. Int. Anon. Pr. 1598.

JOVIAL CREW; OR, THE MERRY BEGGARS, THE. C. Richd. Brome. Cockpit, 1641. Pr. 1652. Converted into a B.O. and ac. at D.L., 1731; Lyceum, September 7, 1815. ? F. on *The Beggar's Bush*.

JOY. C. 3 a. J. Galsworthy. Savoy, September 24, 1907 (mat.).

JOY COMETH; OR, AN INNOCENT SINNER. D. J. Wrangham and D. Knight. Douglas Grand, September 5, 1903 (C.P.).

JOY IS DANGEROUS. C. 2 a. J. Mortimer. D.L., February 9, 1872.

JOY OF LIVING, THE. 5 a. Edith Wharton. Transl. of Hermann Sudermann's *Es Lebe das Leben*. New T., June 24, 1903.

JOY OF THE HOUSE. Dom. D. John Douglass. Northwich Central T., October 24, 1898.

JUAN JOSE. Spanish D. 4 a. Joaquin Dicenta. Shaftesbury, February 12, 1908.

JUAN'S EARLY DAYS. Op. extrav. F. on Byron's poem. M. by Reeve. D.L., February 18, 1828.

JUANA. P. 4 a. W. G. Wills. Court, May 7, 1881. See *Juanna*.

JUANITA; OR, A LOVE'S STRATEGY, Mus. C. H. C. Newland. M. and lyrics by Austin Wellnone. Southend Empire, November 15, 1894.

JUANITA; OR, A NIGHT IN SEVILLE. C.O. 2 a. J. B. Cooper. Liverpool, April 2, 1872.

JUANNA. T. 3 a. Rev. ver. of W. G. Wills's p. Op. Comique, April 16, 1890. See *Juana*.

JUBE, THE SANE. P. Temp. Edw. VI. Mentioned by Brewer.

JUBILATION. "Musical mixture." 1 a. "Richard Henry." M. by Ivan Caryll and H. J. Leslie. P.O.W., May 14, 1887.

JUBILEE, THE. Dr. Ent. David Garrick. D.L., 1769. M. by Ch. Dibdin. MS. was in possession of Mr. Kemble. N.p.

JUBILEE, THE. Mus. sk. Ascribed to T. Dibdin. C.G., October 25, 1809. M. by Reeve.

JUBILEE, THE. Mus sk. Arnold. 1809.

JUBILEE, THE. Ent. By Joseph Kemp. Hay., October 25, 1809. Music by the author and D. Corri.

JUBILEE; OR, JOHN BULL IN HIS DOTAGE, THE. Panto. By the author of "Operations of the British Army in Spain." As it was to have been ac. on October 25, 1809

JUBILEE NOTES. Mus. sk. Corney Grain. St. Geo. H. April 11, 1887

JUBILEE OF 1802; OR, PRESTON GUILD, THE. J. C. Cross. Pr. 1802.

JUDAEL. Ro. D. 5 a. Mrs. Julius Pollock. Olympic, May 14, 1885.

JUDAH. P. 3 a. H. A. Jones. Shaftesbury, May 21, 1890; Avenue, January 30, 1892.

JUDAS. P. Wm. Haughton, in conj. with Samuel Rowley and Wm. Borne. Scriptural subject. Ac. 1601. N.p.

JUDAS ISCARIOT. Mir. P. Horne. 1848.

JUDAS MACCABÆUS. Orat. Handel. 1746.

JUDAS MACCABÆUS. O. Goldfaden, in Yiddish. Novelty, March 30, 1896.

JUDGE, THE. C. Philip Massinger. Ac. by the King's Co. Licensed June 6, 1627. Destroyed by Warburton's servant.

JUDGE, THE. C. Anon. Pr. 1781.

JUDGE, THE. F.C. 3 a. Arthur Law. Terry's, July 24, 1890. Transf. to Op. Comique, September 15, 1890

JUDGE LYNCH. D. 5 a. J. P. Lallen. Brierley Hill T.R., June 10, 1897.

JUDGE NOT. Dom. D. 5 a. Frank Harvey. Pavilion, August 13, 1888.

JUDGE NOT; OR, THE SCALES OF JUSTICE. D. Sterling. (?) 1900.

JUDGE'S EYE, THE. Ca. H. H. Lloyd. Wolverhampton Grand, December 19, 1898 (amat.).

JUDGE'S MEMORY, A. P. 3 a. Brandon Thomas. Terry's, March 13, 1906.

JUDGE'S WOOING, THE. Amer. sk. Tivoli, May 7, 1898.

JUDGED BY APPEARANCES. P. 1 a. F. Fenn. Comedy, March 22, 1902.

JUDGMENT. D. Prol. and 4 a. J. Douglass. Standard, September 19, 1885.

JUDGMENT OF BOLINAS PLAIN, THE. See *Sue.*

JUDGMENT OF HERCULES, THE. Masque. Dr. Greene. Pr. 1740.

JUDGMENT OF MIDAS, THE. Masque. Christopher Smart. Pr. 1752. See *Jugement of*, etc.

JUDGMENT OF PARIS, THE. Masque. W. Congreve. Pr. 1701. M. by John Eccles, Finger, Purcell, and Weldon. Dorset Gardens T., early in 1701.

JUDGMENT OF PARIS, THE. Entert. of 5 Interludes. Abraham Langford. Pr. 1730.

JUDGMENT OF PARIS, THE. Panto. John Weaver. 1732.

JUDGMENT OF PARIS, THE. Burla. 2 a. Dr. Ralph Schomberg. Hay. Pr. 1768.

JUDGMENT OF PARIS, THE. O. F. on *Les Charbonniers.* Lyrics by W. G. Rothery. Lyric, October 30, 1897.

JUDGMENT OF PARIS; OR, THE TRIUMPH OF BEAUTY, THE. Past. Ballad O. 1 a. L.I.F., May 6, 1731. Pr. 1731.

JUDGMENT OF PHARAOH, THE. Rom. Spec. P. 4 a. A. C. Calmour (prev. prod. under the title of *Jevan; the Prodigal Son*, at Queen's, Manchester, October 30, 1905). Scala, April 20, 1907.

JUDICIAL SEPARATION, A. P. W. A. Chandler. Macclesfield T.R., October 10, 1885.

JUDICIAL SEPARATION, A. Sk. Holborn Empire, June 17, 1907.

JUDITH. Orat. Huggins. 1733.

JUDITH. Orat. Bickerstaff. M. by Arne. February 29, 1764.

JUDITH. Orat. Leslie. 1857.

JUDITH. Cant. Hubert Parry.

JUDITH. Dr. Sk. 1 a. Augusta Tullock. Altrincham Central, June 15, 1908; perf. under the title of *The Woman Who Sinned*, in 4 a., Boston Pal., December 7, 1908; Edmonton R., May 10, 1909.

JUDITH SHAKESPEARE. D. 1 a. Alec Nelson. F. on an incident in William Black's novel. Royalty, February 6, 1894.

JUDY. P. 3 a. Roy Horniman. Adap. fr. Percival Pickering's novel, "A Life Awry." P.O.W., May 15, 1899.

JUDY; OR, A CHILD OF THE STREETS. Melo-d. 4 a. Standard, December 15, 1902.

JUGEMENT DE MIDAS. O. Grétry. Stoke, Gordon T., November 10, 1902

JUGEND. O. M. Halbe. St. Geo. H., March 10, 1900.

JUGEND VON HEUTE. C. O. Ernst. Comedy, November 30, 1900.

JUGENFREUNDE. C. Comedy, October 12, 1900; Great Queen Street T., November 15, 1904.

JUGGLER OF PARIS, THE. Pav., September 10, 1866.

JUGURTHA. P. William Boyle. Ac. in 1529. N.p.

JUGURTHA. T. Dr. Gloster Ridley. In MS. 1761. Mentioned in "The Gentleman's Magazine," vol. 44.

JUIF ERRANT, LE. O. Halévy. Paris, 1852.

JUIF ERRANT, LE. D. Eugène Sue. Ac. in Australia. See *All for Gold.*

JUIF POLONAIS, LE. Royalty, November 7, 1887. See *The Sleigh Bells.*

JUIVE, LA. O. Scribe. M. by Halévy. Paris, 1835; D.L. 1846, and April 11, 1893; C.G., 1850. See *The Jewess.*

JULIA. P. 3 a. A. Sturgess. M'ch'r Comedy, March 28, 1898; Royalty, April ., 1898.

JULIA; OR, SUCH THINGS WERE. T. Prince Hoare. D.L., 1796. N.p. See *Such Things Were.*

JULIA; OR, THE ITALIAN LOVER. T. R. Jephson. D.L., April 14, 1787. Pr. 1787.

JULIA AGRIPPINA, EMPRESSE OF ROME. T. Thos. May. Ac. 1628. Pr. 1639.

JULIA DE ROUBIGNE. T. Catherine Metcalfe. F. on Mackenzie's novel. Ac. at Bath December 23, 1790. N.p.

JULIA OF LOUVAIN; OR, MONKISH CRUELTY. J. C. Cross. Ac. at the R. Circus. Pr. 1809.

JULIAN. T. 5 a. Mary Russell Mitford. C.G., 1823. Pr. 1823.

JULIAN AND AGNES; OR, THE MONKS OF THE GREAT ST. BERNARD. T. Wm. Sotheby. D.L., April 25, 1801. Pr. 1801.

JULIAN OF BRENTFORD. Ac. at Rose T., Jan. 5, 1592.

JULIAN THE APOSTATE. Ac. at Rose T., April 29, 1596.

JULIANA, PRINCESS OF POLAND. T.C. John Crowne. D. of York's T., 1671. Pr. 1671.

JULIE. O. Auber. 1811.

JULIE. P. Octave Feuillet. Lyric, June 30, 1898.

JULIE BON-BON. P. 4 a. Clara Lipman. Waldorf, November 26, 1906.

JULIUS CÆSAR. T. Wm. Shakespeare. Wr. about 1600; again prod. 1607, and, in present abridged form, 1613. Pr. in 1st folio, 1623. F. on North's translation of Plutarch's Lives of Julius Cæsar, Marcus Brutus, and Marcus Antonius. Recent revivals include Olympic (Edmund Tearle), April 16, 1892; H.M., April 29, 1905; April 25, 1907. Version in 3 a. arranged by Beerbohm Tree, H.M.T., January 22, 1898.

JULIUS CÆSAR. T. Alexander, Earl of Stirling. Pr. 1604. See *The Monarchie Tragedies*..

JULIUS CÆSAR. T. J. Sheffield, Duke of Buckingham, with prol. and chorus. Pr. 1722.

JULIUS CÆSAR. Tr. fr. Voltaire. See *Death of Cæsar, Monarchie Tragedies, F. M. Julius*, etc.

JULIUS SEE SAW; OR, DAUNTLESS DECIUS, THE DOUBTFUL DECEMOIR. Burl. Harry M. Pitt. Sheffield T.R., March 29, 1869.

JULIUS STERNE. P. 4 a. Taken fr. Sidney Grundy's *An Old Jew*. Coronet, November 22, 1905.

JULYUS SESAR. A French *César*, by Jacques Grévin, had appeared in 1560, but nothing is known about this piece except the date of its production, viz., February 1, 1562.

JUMP A LITTLE WAGTAIL. Bower, December 26, 1868.

JUMPING AT CONCLUSIONS. F. Alec Van Homrigh. Wandsworth Town H., November 23, 1892 (amat.).

JUNCTO, THE. F. A political and religious satire. Pr. 1715.

JUNGLE, THE. Melo-d. 4 a. C. W. Somerset. Liverpool Queen's, November 26, 1906; Dalston, December 10, 1906.

JUNIOR PARTNER, THE. F.C. 3 a. Sidney Russ. Northampton Berry Wood Asylum, April 21, 1887.

JUNIOR PARTNER, THE. F.C. 3 a. Thos. Naden. Windsor T.R., September 22, 1890.

JUNIUS; OR, THE HOUSEHOLD GODS. P. 5 a. Lord Lytton. Princess's, February 26, 1885.

JUNIUS BRUTUS. See *Lucius Junius Brutus*.

JUNTO; OR, THE INTERIOR CABINET LAID OPEN. F. A political piece. Pr. 1778.

JUPITER. Burla. Sheridan and Halked. 1771.

JUPITER AND ALCMENA. C.O. Chas. Dibdin. C.G., October 27, 1781. Songs only pr. Taken fr. Dryden's "Amphytrion."

JUPITER AND EUROPA; OR, THE INTRIGUES OF HARLEQUIN. Panto. L.I.F., 1723. N.p.

JUPITER AND IO. D. Thos. Heywood. Taken fr. Ovid. Pr. 1637.

JUPITER AND IO, with a comic int. called *Mother Shipton's Wish; or, Harlequin's Origin*. Goodman's Fields, 1735. N.p.

JUPITER IN ARGOS. O. Handel. 1739.

JUPITER UPON EARTH. See *Interlude between Jupiter*, etc.

JURA; OR, THE WILD FLOWER OF MEXICO. D. Leeds T.R., October 30, 1868.

JUROR, THE. F. by "W.B.," of St. John's Coll., Cambridge. Pr. 1718. N.ac.

JURY OF FATE, THE. P. 7 tab. C. M. S. McLellan. Shaftesbury, January 2, 1906.

JUST A LITTLE CHANGE. Epis. Bertha Moore. Royal Albert H., June 28, 1907.

JUST A MAN'S FANCY. P. 1 a. W. Gayer Mackay. Court, May 2, 1901.

JUST AS WELL. M.R.C. 1 a. J. Hartley Manners. Shaftesbury, July 8, 1902.

JUST GENERAL, THE. T.C. Cosmo Manuche. Pr. 1650. N.ac.

JUST IN TIME. Comic O. Thos. Hurlstone. C.G., May 10, 1792. Pr. 1792.

JUST IN TIME. D. Pro. and 3 a. F. C. Burnand. Avenue. November 12, 1884.

JUST IN TIME. Mus. C. 1 a. Chas. Anderson. M. by Harold M. M'Nay. Arranged by Argyll Saxby. Guildford, St. Nicholas H., July 21, 1897.

JUST IN TIME. Far. Sk. 1 sc. Eric Albury. Empress, February 18, 1907.

JUST ITALIAN, THE. T.C. Sir W. Davenant. Ac. at Blackfryars. Pr. 1630.

JUST LIKE A WOMAN. C. 3 a. A. W. Dubourg. Gaiety, November 22, 1879.

JUST LIKE CALLAGHAN. F. 3 a. Cosmo Gordon Lennox. Adap. fr. *Le Coup de Fouet*. Criterion, June 3, 1903.

JUST LIKE ROGER. F. 1 a. W. Webster. Adelphi, April 15, 1872.

JUST MY LUCK. F. Alfred Maltby. Lyceum, October 29, 1877.

JUST ONE WORD. F. Op. Comique, May 31, 1873.

JUST RETRIBUTION. Sk. 4 tab. Ronald Bayne. Bedford Bijou H., October 27, 1893.

JUSTICE. Christina Dening. Westminster T.H., May 12, 1893 (amat.).

JUSTICE; OR, THE CALIPH AND THE COBBLER. Mus. D. 3 a. M. by Cooke and Horn. D.L., November 28, 1820.

JUSTICE AT LAST. D. 1 a. George Roberts. North Camp Theatre, Farnborough, Nov. 24, 1894.

JUSTICE AT LAST. D. 4 a. John Addison. Woolwich, R. Artil., April 11, 1903.

JUSTICE BUSY. C. John Crowne. L.I.F. Circa 1699. N.p.

JUSTICE NELL. Humorous Sk. J. Farren Soutar and Robb Harwood. Wr. for the return of Miss Nellie Farren to the stage on the occasion of Miss Lydia Thompson's farewell benefit. Lyceum, May 2, 1899.

JUSTICE TRIUMPHANT; OR, THE ORGAN IN THE SUDS. F. 3 a. Pr. 1747.

JUVENILE FRIENDSHIP; OR, THE HOLIDAYS. D. 3 a. Pr. 1802. N. ac.

K

KAFFIR WAR, THE. D. Sanger's Amphi., April 26, 1879.

KAIS; OR, LOVE IN THE DESERTS. O. 4 a. I. Brandon. Pr. 1808. D.L., February 11, 1808. F. on *The Loves of Mejnoun and Leila*, a Persian rom. by D'Israeli. M. by Braham and Reeve.

KALTWASSER. C. 3 a. L. Fulda. Royalty, November 7, 1903.

KAMTCHATKA; OR, THE SLAVE'S TRIBUTE. M.D. 3 a. C. Kemble. Adap. fr. Kotzebue. C.G., October 16, 1811.

KANGAROO GIRL, THE. A M. Ver. of *Dr. Bill*. M. by Oscar Barrett. Folkestone Pleasure Gardens, July 12, 1897; Camberwell Metropole, July 19, 1897.

KARIN. P. 2 a. Mrs. Hugh Bell. Transl. fr. the Swedish of Alfhild Agrell. Vaudeville, May 10, 1892.

KARL; OR, THE LOVE THAT WINS. P. 5 a. Herbert Mooney. Standard, June 23, 1884.

KASSA. P. 4 a. John Luther Long. Hay., January 5, 1909 (C.P.).

KASSYA. O. Delibes (1836-1891). Left unfinished. Orchestrated by Massanet. Prod. 1893.

KATAWAMPUS. P. Louis Calvert and Judge Parry. P.O.W., December 23, 1901.

KATAWOMPOS. Oa. Extrav. Knight Summers. M. by Louis Konig. Brighton West Pier Pav., November 24, 1896.

KATCHELL. Bal. Anon. 1813.

KATCHEN VON HEIDBRONN, DAS. Rom. D. 4 a. Heinrich von Kleist. D.L., June 27, 1881; Court, February 26, 1909.

KATE KEARNEY; OR, THE FAIRY OF THE LAKES. M. Rom. 2 a. Wm. Collier. Queen's, October 3, 1836.

KATE PAYTON'S LOVERS. D. 1 a. Chas. Reade. Queen's, December 20, 1873.

KATHERINE AND PETRUCHIO. C. 3 a. Alt. by David Garrick (in 1 a.) fr. Shakespeare's *Taming of the Shrew*. C.G., 1838; H.M.T., November 1, 1897.

KATHLEEN MAVOURNEEN. D. 4 a. W. Travers. Old Bowery Theatre, New York, 1868; New B.T., 1865 (?).

KATHLEEN NI HOULIHAN. P. 1 a. W. B. Yeats. Queen's Gate H. (under direction of Irish National T. Society), May 2, 1903; St. George's H., November 27, 1905; Gt. Queen St., June 13, 1907.

KATIE'S BIRTHDAY. C. Henry Shield. Newcastle-upon-Tyne T.R., February 21, 1873.

KATTI, THE FAMILY HELP. C. 3 a. Chas. S. Fawcett. F. on Meilhac's *Gotte* (Palais Royal, December 2, 1886). Glasgow T.R., September 30, 1887; Strand, February 25, 1888, and rev. there June 27, 1891.

KEELEY WORRIED BY BUCKSTONE. F. 1 a. Mark Lemon and B. Webster. Hay., June 5, 1852.

KEEN BLADES. D. 3 a. A. F. Cross and J. F. Elliston. Sheffield T.R., May 22, 1893.

KEEP TO THE RIGHT. D. 4 a. Walter Reynolds. Leeds T.R., August 7, 1899.

KEEP YOUR DOOR LOCKED. Adelphi, August 29, 1866.

KEEP YOUR EYE ON HER. F. 1 a. T. J. Williams. Olympic, September 30, 1876.

KEEP YOUR OWN COUNSEL. Duo. Henry Bellingham and Wm. Best. Terry's, January 14, 1895.

KEEP YOUR OWN SECRET. C. Transl. fr. *Nadie Fie su Secreto* of Calderon. Pr. 1807. N.ac.

KEEP YOUR PLACES. Oa. Robt. Reece. M. by G. B. Allen. St. George's H., February 15, 1886.

KEEP YOUR TEMPER. F. 1 a. J. P. Wooler. Strand, July 5, 1862.

KEEPER OF THE SEALS. Ca. 1 a. Lionel S. Gordon.

KEEPERS DISTRACTED, THE. F. Mentioned in Mears's catalogue. N.p.

KEEREDA AND NENA SAHIB. Victoria, November 18, 1857.

KENILWORTH. D. 2 a. Thos. Dibdin and A. Bunn. F. on Sir Walter Scott's novel. C.G., March 8, 1821; rev. D.L., October 22, 1832.

KENILWORTH. D. Manchester T.R., April 8, 1871.

KENILWORTH. D. Edinburgh T.R., July 17, 1871.

KENILWORTH. Burl. C. J. Archer and A. E. Aubert. M. by John Reille. Croydon T.R., April 1, 1893.

KENILWORTH. Burl. Extrav. 3 a. R. Reece and H. B. Farnie. Avenue, December 19, 1885.

KENILWORTH. D. Pro. and 4 a. Max Goldberg. Dr. fr. Sir Walter Scott's novel. Hammersmith Lyric, November 25, 1895.

KENILWORTH. D. 5 a. J. S. Blythe. Glasgow T.R., June 5, 1899.

KENILWORTH. 5 a. 17 scenes. F. on Sir Walter Scott's novel. Kennington Princess of Wales, June 4, 1900.

KENILWORTH; OR, THE GENTLE AMY ROBSART. D. 3 a. Royal Alfred, November 12, 1870.

KENILWORTH; OR, YE QUEENE, YE EARLE, AND YE MAYDENNE. C.O. Extrav. 1 a. Andrew Halliday and Fredk. Lawrance. Strand, December 27, 1858.

KENNETH DUNBAR, A CITY MAN. D. 3 a. W. A. Brabner. Manchester Athenæum H. March 29, 1893 (amat.).

KENNETH, KING OF SCOTS; OR, THE FEMALE ARCHERS. M.D. Archibald M'Laren. Edinburgh T.R. Pr. 1807.

KENNYNGTON CROSSE; OR, THE OLD HOUSE ON THE COMMON. Rom. D. 2 a. T. Egerton Wilks. Surrey, June 12, 1848.

KENSINGTON GARDENS; OR, QUITE A LADIES' MAN. 2 a. Robt. B. Brough. Adap. fr. the French. Strand, May 12, 1851.

KENSINGTON GARDENS; OR, THE PRETENDERS. C. John Leigh. L.I.F., November 26, 1719. Pr. 1720.

KENSINGTON GARDENS; OR, THE WALKING JOCKEY. Int. Jas. Cobb. Hay., 1781. N.p.

KENTISH BARONS, THE. O. Hon. Francis North. Hay., June 25, 1791. Pr. 1791.

KENTISH ELECTION, THE. C. "L. N." Pr. 1735.

KENTISH FAYRE; OR, THE PARLIAMENT SOLD TO THEIR BEST WORTH. Pr. Rochester, 1648. Sat. P. Wr. to expose Oliver Cromwell.

KENTUCKIAN, THE. American D. W. B. Bernard. C.G., 1833.

KENYON'S WIDOW. C. 3 a. C. Brookfield. Comedy, May 10, 1900.

KEOLANTHE; OR, THE UNEARTHLY BRIDE. Balfe. Wds. by Rizball. Lyceum, March, 1841.

KEPT IN. Duol. Mark Ambient. Queen's H., February 25, 1895.

KERIM. O. Bruneau. His first work. Modern France.

KERMOPHUS. Latin P. Ac. before the University at Oxford.

KERRY; OR, NIGHT AND MORNING. P. Adap. by Boucicault fr. *La Joie Fait Peur* of Mde. de Girardin. Rev. at Terry's, January 9, 1893.

KESA; THE WIFE'S SACRIFICE. Japanese P. Coronet, July 22, 1900. Criterion, June 18, 1901.

KEVIN'S CHOICE. O. 2 a. Miss Hazlewood. M. by T. A. Wallworth. St. George's H., December 2, 1867. Adelphi, March 25, 1882.

KEY OF LIFE, THE. Phantasy. Viscountess Maitland. M. of pro. and epi. by Reginald Somerville. Scala, May 28, 1908 (amat.).

KEY OF THE GARDEN, THE. T.C. Young. Pr. 1801 at Dundee. N. ac.

KEY OF THE STREET, THE. Surrey, March 30, 1866.

KEY TO KING SOLOMON'S RICHES, LIMITED. D. 4 a. Miss Abbey St. Ruth. Op. C., December 24, 1896.

KEY TO THE LOCK, A. C. 2 a. O'Keeffe. Transl. fr. the *Gageure Imprévue* of Sedaine. Hay., August 18, 1788. Pr. 1788.

KEY TO THE SITUATION, THE. Duol. by Sydney Keith. Vict. Hall, W., April 28, 1906.

KHARTOUM. See *At Duty's Call.*

KHARTOUM; OR, THE STAR OF THE DESERT. Spec. Military D. in 9 tab. Wm. Muskerry and John Jourdain. Sanger's Amphi., March 14, 1885.

KIARTAN, THE ICELANDER. P. 5 a. E. Newman Howard. Boscombe Grand, November 29, 1901 (C.P.).

KICKS AND HALFPENCE. Lyceum, September 1, 1858.

KIDDIE. P. 1 a. Cyril Twyford. Garrick, January 19, 1909.

KIDDIES ON THE SANDS. Sk. Battersea Palace, June 7, 1909.

KIDDLE A WINK. Victoria, January 30, 1864.

KIDNAPPER, THE. F.C. 3 a. H. Graham. Greenwich Lecture H., May 29, 1888.

KILL OR CURE. F. 1 a. C. Dance. Publ. by S. French, Ltd. Olympic, Oct. 29, 1832.

KILLARNEY; OR, THE MAIDEN'S WISH AND THE FAIRY OF THE LAKE. D. 2 a. G. H. George. Oriental, August 29, 1872.

KILLIECRUMPER. Oa. 1 a. Malcolm Watson. M. by Edwd. Solomon. St. Geo. H., March 30, 1891.

KILLIGREW. D. Adelphi, October 10, 1825.

KILLING NO MURDER. F. 2 a. Theodore Edwd. Hook. Hay. Rev., D.L., April 6, 1824. Pr. 1809. See *A Day at an Inn.*

KILLING OF THE CHILDREN. See "Miracle Plays."

KIMBERLEY MAIL; OR, THE ROBBERY OF THE CAPE DIAMONDS, THE. D. 4 a. Ch. H. Longden. Blackburn Prince's, April 8, 1892.

KIMONA GIRL, THE. Oa. Osmond Carr. Glasgow Pav., October 2, 1905.

KIMONA SAN. Jap. operettina. Wr. and comp. by Chas. Thomason and Fredk. Lane. Aberystwyth Col., June 28, 1909.

KIND HEART WITH A ROUGH COVERING, A. D. W. H. Pitt. Pav., July 3, 1875.

KIND IMPOSTOR, THE. Operatic D. F. on Cibber's *She Wou'd and She Wou'd Not.* M. by Cooke and Horn. D.L., May 8, 1821.

KIND KEEPER; OR, MR. LIMBERHAM, THE. C. J. Dryden. Duke's T. Pr. 1680.

KIND TO A FAULT. C. 2 a. Wm. Brough. Strand, November 11, 1867.

KINDER DER EXCELLENZ, DIE. C. 4 a. Ernst von Wolzogen and Wm. Schumann. Gt. Queen St., March 2, 1906.

KINDHEART'S DREAM. C. Chettle. 1592.

KINDRED SOULS. F. C. W. Manning. Sturton. Cambridge Town T.R., February 4, 1884.

KINDRED TIES. Sk. Wilfred H. Benson. Inci. M. by R. E. Lawson. Hammersmith Pal., July 1, 1907.

KING AHASUERUS AND QUEEN ESTHER. Int. Attributed to Robert Cox. Publ. in second part of *Sport upon Sport.* 1672.

KING ALFRED. Dram. Cantata. Ebenezer Prout.

KING ALFRED. O. Carl Reinecke.

KING ALFRED THE GREAT; OR, THE FIRST MAN. Rom. P. 4 a. H. Byatt, Bedford County T., July 10, 1901.

KING AMONG MEN, A. D. 4 a. Ch. Aldin. Garston T.R., December 21, 1903. Salford P.O.W., January 11, 1904.

KING AND CARPENTER. P. 1 a. Lawrence. Publ. by S. French, Ltd.

KING AND I, THE. F. 1 a. J. M. Morton. Hay., June 4, 1845.

KING AND NO KING, A. T.C. Beaumont and Fletcher. Licensed 1611. Ac. at D.L., June 15, 1704. Pr. 1619.

KING AND QUEEN'S ENTERTAINMENT AT RICHMOND AFTER THEIR DEPARTURE FROM OXFORD, THE. Masque. September 12, 1634. Dances by Simon Hopper. M. by Chas. Colman.

KING AND REBEL. Hist. D. Pro. and 4 a. Dr. Vellère.

KING AND THE ANGEL, THE. Ross Neil. Publ. 1874.

KING AND THE COUNTESS, THE. An Episode in the p. of *King Edward the Third.* St. George's H., July 9, 1897.

KING AND THE MILLER. F. Murray.

KING AND THE MILLER OF MANSFIELD, THE. Dr. Tale. Robt. Dodsley. F. on a traditional story in the reign of Henry II. D.L., 1736. Pr. 1737. D.L., April 26, 1820.

KING AND THE SUBJECT, THE. T. Philip Massinger. Ac. by the K.'s Co. June 5, 1638. The title is thought to have afterwards been alt. to *The Tyrant,* which piece was destroyed by Warburton's servant.

KING AND THE VAGABOND, THE. Laurence Irving. Adapt fr. Theodore de Bauville's *Gringoire.* London Coliseum, December 7, 1908.

KING ARTHUR. O. Dr. Arne (1710-78).

KING ARTHUR. P. Pro. and 4 a. J. Comyns Carr. M. by Sir A. Sullivan. Lyceum, January 12, 1895.

KING ARTHUR. An examination of the past burls. by Arthur W. Earle and E. Howley Sim. James Street, Buckingham Gate, May 16, 1895.

KING ARTHUR; OR, THE BRITISH WORTHY. O. John Dryden. Ac. at Dorset Gardens 1691. Pr. 1691. A kind of sequel to the author's *Albion and Albanius.* Largely borr. fr. *Tasso.* M. by Purcell. Alt. by David Garrick and ac. at D.L. Pr. 1770. Rev. D.L., November 16, 1842.

KING ARTHUR; OR, THE DAYS AND KNIGHTS OF THE ROUND TABLE. Christmas Extrav. 1 a. Wm. Brough. Hay., December 26, 1863.

KING ARTHUR AND THE KNIGHTS OF THE ROUND TABLE. Ent. 3 a. M. by T. Cooke. D.L., December 26, 1834.

KING CAMBISES. One of the earliest T. wr. by Thos. Preston. Circa 1563.

KING CANNOT ERR, Etc. C. Ame (*i.e.,* Adam Moses Emanuel) Cooke. Pr. circa 1762.

KING CHARLES I. See *Charles I., King.*

KING CHARMING; OR, THE BLUE BIRD OF PARADISE. Extrav. J. R. Planché. F. on the Countess D'Aulnoy's tale, *L'Oiseau Bleu.* Lyceum, December 26, 1850.

KING CHRISTMAS. "Fancy-full Mortality." J. R. Planché. Gallery of Illus., December 26, 1871.

KING CHRISTMAS. Fairy Masquerade. 1 a. Catherine Tudor. Publ. by S. French, Ltd.

KING COFFEE; OR, THE PRINCESS OF ASHANTEE. Burl. Southport Bijou T., December 8, 1873.

KING DARYUS. Peele. Pr. B.L. 1565.

KING DAVID AND ABSALOM. Sacr. D. Peele. Pr. 1599.

KING DAVID AND KING SAUL. Hebrew O. 5 a. Latimer. Standard, December 7, 1895.

KING DOO-DAH. Britannia, December 26, 1900.

KING EDGAR AND ALFREDA. See *Edgar and Alfreda King.*

KING EDWARD IV. See *Edward IV.*

KING FAREWELL. T. Bristowe. 1799.

KING FOO. Extrav. E. Adams. Philharmonic, December 26, 1873.

KING FOR A DAY. Rom. O. 3 a. Valentine Smith. Adap. fr. *Si J'Etais Roi*, by Adolphe Adams. Newcastle-on-T. Art Gallery T., February 20, 1893; Parkhurst, May 23, 1893.

KING FOR A DAY. M.C. 1 a. Geo. Sheldon. Ardwick Empire, April 15, 1907.

KING FREEWILL. T. Transl. fr. the French by Francis Bristowe. 1635.

KING GEORGE'S SHILLING. D. 3 a. Edward Stirling. Grecian, April 28, 1879.

KING HAL'S EARLY DAYS. D. 2 a. F. on an hist. anecdote. D.L., March 31, 1837.

KING HAROLD; OR, THE BATTLE OF HASTINGS. D. 3 a. Haines. Victoria, September 16, 1839.

KING HENRY IV., V., VI., Etc. See *Henry IV., V., VI.*, etc.

KING IN DISGUISE. Juvenile P. F. D. Adams. Publ. by S. French, Ltd.

KING IN THE COUNTRY, THE. Dr. Piece. 2 a. F. G. Waldron. Ac. at Richmond and Windsor 1788. Pr. 1789. Taken fr. the under plot of Part 1 of *King Edward the Fourth.*

KING INCOG., THE. F. 2 a. G. à Beckett. Queen's.

KING INDIGO. Op. bo. 3 a. F. C. Burnand. M. by Johann Strauss. Alhambra, September 24, 1877.

KING JAMIE; OR, THE FORTUNES OF NIGEL. D. Manchester Queen's, September 15, 1879.

KING JOHN. T. Wm. Shakespeare. 1595. First folio, 1623. F. on "The Troublesome Raigne of John. King of England, with the Discoverie of King Richard, Cordelion's base son, vulgarly named the Bastard Fawconbridge; also the Death of King John at Swinstead Abbey, 1591." C.G., February 26, 1737. D.L., March 16, 1747. Alt. fr. Shakespeare by R. Valpy. Ac. at Reading School by Dr. Valpy's scholars. Pr. 1800. By J. P. Kemble. Ac. at D.L. Pr. 1800; Revised by J. P. Kemble. Ac. at C.G. Pr. 1804; Rev. at Princess's, February 9, 1852. D.L., September 22, 1866. Arr. by Beerbohm Tree and ac. at H.M.T., September 20, 1899.

KING JOHN. See *John, King*, etc., *Kynge Johan.*

KING JOHN AND MATILDA. T. Robert Davenport. Cockpit, 1655. Pr. 1655. Borr. fr. *The Death of Robert, Earl of Huntington.*

KING JOHN WITH THE BENEFIT OF THE ACT. Burl. G. à Beckett. 1837.

KING JONATHAN. M. Phantasy. A. M. Lee. Perf. by amateurs. Bayswater Bijou, January 23, 1906.

KING KLONDIKE. Britannia, December 26, 1898.

KING KODAK. Extrav. Arthur Branscombe. M. by John Crook, Walter Slaughter, Edward Solomon, Alfred Plumpton, Milton Wellings, Von der Fink, and Lionel Monckton. Terry's, April 30, 1894.

KING KOFFEE; OR, THE ASHANTEE WAR. D. J. Elphinstone. Hanley T.R., March 16, 1874.

KING KOKATOO; OR, WHO IS WHO AND WHICH IS WHICH? Burl. F. C. Burnand. Leeds T.R., March 4, 1872. Alt. and Reprod. at the Op. C., under the title of *Kissi-Kissi.*

KING KOOKOO. Britannia, December 26, 1884.

KING LEAR. Ac. at the Rose T., April 6, 1593.

KING LEAR. Wm. Shakespeare. 1605. 1st qto., 1608; 2nd qto., 1608; 1st folio, 1623. F. on Holinshed's *Chronicle* and *The True Chronicle*, History of King Leir and his three daughters, Gonorill, Ragan, and Cordella. Entd. 1594. Played 1605. Entd. at Stationers' Co., November 26, 1607, as having been played in 1606. Probably prod. early 1605, as the old play was then repr. and entd. May 8 as "lately acted." L.I.F., 1662 and 1665. An alt. by N. Tate. Duke's T. Pr. 1681; an alt. of Shakespeare and Tate. Geo. Colman. C.G. Pr. 1768; Edited by J. Ambrose Eccles. Pr. Dublin, 1793; Alt. J. P. Kemble. D.L. Pr. 1800; Revised by J. P. Kemble. C.G. Pr. 1808; Lyceum, November 10, 1892. Rev. by Herbert Trench, Hay., September 8, 1909.

KING LEAR. See *Kynge Lear.*

KING LIBERTY. City of London, September 29, 1851.

KING LUD. Anon. 1594. N.p.

KINGMAKER, THE. Hist. D. 4 a. J. W. Boulding. Adelphi, April 15, 1882.

KING MAKER; OR, THE LAST OF HIS RACE, THE. D. 4 a. R. Dodson. Victoria, October 4, 1873.

KING O'NEIL. C. 2 a. Mrs. C. Gore. Publ. by S. French, Ltd.

KING O' SCOTS (OR, KING OF SCOTS). D. 3 a. Andrew Halliday. D.L., September 26. 1868. Liverpool Alexandra, Easter Monday, 1869; Sadler's Wells, October 16, 1869; Astley's, March 21, 1870; Princess's, February, 1876.

KING O' THE CASTLE, THE. Britannia, December 26, 1893.

KING O' THE CASTLE, THE. Sk. Wal Pink. Camberwell Palace, May 27, 1907.

KING O'TOOLE'S GOOSE; OR, THE LEGENDS OF GLENDALOUGH. Extrav. Edwd. Trivin. Queen's, Dublin, March 24, 1856.

KING OF BORNEO, THE. F. 1 a. Henry Allen Ashton. Rehearsal, W.C., May 23, 1908.

KING OF CADONIA, THE. M.P. 2 a. Fredk. Lonsdale. Lyrics by Adrian Ross. M. by Sidney Jones P.O.W., September 3, 1908.

KING OF CELARIA, THE. C.O. 2 a. Norman D. Slee. Composed by J. Ansell. Walsall Her Majesty's T., May 2, 1901.

KING OF CLUBS, THE. Duol. Annette L. Conrad. St. Geo. H., May 7, 1901.

KING OF CRIME, THE. See *Midnight; or, The Bells of Notre Dame.*

KING OF DIAMONDS; OR, THE HISTORY OF A ROUGH GEM, THE. D. Paul Meritt and Geo. Conquest. Surrey, April 12, 1884.

KING OF FOOLS, A. Rom. D. H. J. W. Dam, C. Cartwright, and Ben Landeck. Based on Dumas's character of Chicot. Grand, September 25, 1899.

KING OF KENT, THE. P. Keningale Cook. Richmond H.M.T., October 28, 1881.

KING OF LOMBARDY. T. Anon. MS. in possession of J. Barker. 1814.

KING OF STEEL; OR, THE BUILDING OF THE SHIP, THE. D. 4 a. Edmund Gurney. Preston T.R., December 12, 1898.

KING OF TERRORS. D. 4 a. Dover T.R., July 24, 1899.

KING OF THE ALPS, THE. Rom. D. 3 a. J. B. Buckstone. Adap. fr. the German. Adelphi, January 24, 1831.

KING OF THE COMMONS, THE. Hist. P. Rev. Jas. White. Princess's, May, 1846.

KING OF THE DANUBE, THE. Spec. Burl. Adelphi, 1837.

KING OF THE HUGUENOTS. D. 4 a. H. A. Saintsbury. Croydon Grand T., January 21, 1901.

KING OF THE MERROWS; OR, THE PRINCE AND THE PIPER, THE. Extrav. F. C. Burnand. Fr. an original plot constructed by J. Palgrave Simpson. Olympic, December 26, 1861.

KING OF THE MINT; OR, OLD LONDON BRIDGE BY NIGHT, THE. D. Victoria, February 17, 1873.

KING OF THE MIST; OR, THE MILLER OF THE HARTZ MOUNTAINS, THE. Melo-d. 2 a. M. by Stansbury. D.L., April 1, 1839.

KING OF THE PEACOCKS, THE. Fairy Extrav. 2 a. J. R. Planché. F. on the Countess D'Aulnoy's story, *La Princess Rosette*. Lyceum, December 26, 1848.

KING OF THIEVES, THE. D. 4 a. M'Leod Loader. Liverpool Star, November 19, 1903. (C.P.) St. Helens T.R., April 18, 1904; Peckham Crown, July 11, 1904.

KING OF TRUMPS, THE. Victoria, December 24, 1873.

KING PEPIN'S CAMPAIGN. Burl. O. W. Shirley. 1755.

KING PHILIP OF SPAIN. T. Anon. 1740. N.p.

KING QUEER. Strand, April 9, 1855.

KING RENE'S DAUGHTER. Cantata. H. Smart. 1813-79.

KING RENE'S DAUGHTER. Lyric D. Hon. Edmund Phipps. Ver. fr. the Danish of Henrik Herz. Dublin T.R., November 28, 1849. Arr. for the stage by Sir Henry Irving. Orig. prod. at Lyceum, May 20, 1880; rev. Shaftesbury, December 7, 1908.

KING RENE'S DAUGHTER. Theodore Martin. Fr. the Danish of Herz. First prod. in the provinces. Hay., July 6, 1855; Botanic Gardens, June 17, 1902.

KING RENE'S DAUGHTER. T. Fred E. Weatherby. Edinburgh T.R., October 2, 1873.

KING RICHARD II. AND III. See *Richard II. and III.*

KING RICHARD YE THIRD; OR, YE BATTEL OF BOSWORTH FIELD. "Merrie Mysterie." 1 a. Chas. Selby. A travestie on Shakespeare. Strand, February 26, 1844.

KING SAUL. T. Armstrong. Mentioned by Brewer. 1703 (?).

KING SAUL. Orat. Sir C. Hubert H. Parry. Birmingham Festival, 1894.

KING SIGMUND. Boje. Probably not transl.

KING SOLOMAN. P. in Yiddish. Novelty, April 2, 1896.

KING SOLOMON'S WISDOM. Cox. 1672.

KING, THE RING, AND THE GIDDY YOUNG THING; OR, HERNE THE HUNTER, ANNE BOLEYN, AND THE FAIR MAID OF THE RIVER DEE, THE. Burl. Geo. Reeves. Elephant and Castle, April 8, 1882.

KING THRUSHBEARD; OR, A LITTLE PET AND THE GREAT PASSION. Extrav. Francis Talfourd. Lyceum, December 26, 1859.

KING ZANY'S DAUGHTER. Burl. 1 a. Bosbacca. Publ. by S. French, Ltd.

KING'S BANNER, THE. D. Mrs. S. Cresswell. Dublin T.R., December 6, 1872.

KING'S BEGGAR, THE. D. Edinburgh Princess's, March 15, 1873.

KING'S BENCH, THE. Holman. 1796. See *Abroad and at Home*.

KING'S BUTTERFLY, THE. Rom. D. Lyceum, October 22, 1864. See *Fan Fan*.

KING'S COMMAND, THE. D. 2 a. C. Pelham Thompson. Adelphi, October 15, 1835.

KING'S COMMAND, THE. Oa. 1 a. Knight Summers. M. by Louis Honig. Lowestoft Pier Concert R., September 7, 1893; Salle Erard, May 19, 1898.

KING'S CURE, THE. C.O. 3 a. Rev. J. H. Turner. Warrington R. Court, December 19, 1892.

KING'S DEATH TRAP, THE. D. 2 a. C. H. Hazlewood. Britannia, November 25, 1867.

KING'S DIAMOND, THE. C.O. 3 a. Chas. Harbury. M. by M. Ball. Kingston-on-Thames County, May 23, 1904.

KING'S DRAGOONS, THE. O. 3 a. J. Wilton Jones. M. by John Crook. Manchester T.R., November 1, 1880.

KING'S ENTERTAINMENT AT WALBECK, THE. Ben Jonson. 1633. Pr. 1640. Given in Nottinghamshire, a seat of the Earl of Newcastle.

KING'S FAVOURITE, THE. See *Jane Shore*.

KING'S FAVOURITE; OR, THE FOOL OF FORTUNE, THE. Manchester T.R., May 29, 1873.

KING'S FIRESIDE, A. An Hist. Anecdote. 1 a. D.L., December 17, 1830.

KING'S FOOL. P. 3 a. Mullingen.

KING'S GARDENER. F. 1 a. C. Selby.

KING'S GLOVE, THE. P. 3 a. Brenda Girvin. M. by Archibald H. Benwell. Sydenham. Ashbourne, Lawrie Park, July 3, 1909 (amat.).

KING'S GUARDSMEN, THE. Ca. Edinburgh Princess's, January 31, 1876.

KING'S HARD BARGAIN, A. P. 1 a. ham. Ashbourne, Lawrie Park, July 3, 1909 (mat.).

KING'S HAT, THE. Dr. Episode. Chas. Cunningham. Hackney Empire, December 12, 1904.

KING'S HIGHWAY, THE. D. 4 a. Geo. Roberts and Frank Gerald. Adap. fr. Harrison Ainsworth's "Rookwood." West London, August 24, 1896.

KING'S HIGHWAY, THE. M.P. Miss B. M. Leyton. Jersey O.H., December 8, 1903.

KING'S HIGHWAY, THE. P. 1 a. E. Nesbit. Woolwich Freemasons' H., May 11, 1905.

KING'S MAIL, THE. Britannia, June 18, 1866.

KING'S MESSENGER, THE. Oa. S. Levey. Westminster Caxton H., May 19, 1903.

KING'S MISTRESS, THE. Entd. Stationers' Co., September 9, 1653. N.p.

KING'S OUTCAST, THE. P. 4 a. W. Gayer Mackay. Camberwell Metropole, April 24, 1899.

KING'S PASSWORD, THE. P. 3 a. Mrs. Vere Campbell. Liverpool Shakespeare, May 21, 1900; Camberwell Metropole, May 28, 1900.

KING'S PLEASURE, THE. D. 1 a. Alfred Thompson. Gaiety, April 12, 1870 (amat.).

KING'S PLEDGE; OR, A MISSION OF MERCY, THE. D. G. F. Charles. Barnsley Queen's, January 3, 1870.

KING'S PORTRAIT, THE. Dram. Sk. Jas. Malam. Camberwell Empire, March 16, 1908.

KING'S PRIZE, THE. O. 3 a. Alick Maclean. Royalty, April 29, 1904.

KING'S PROXY; OR, JUDGE FOR YOURSELF, THE. C.O. 3 a. M. by T. Cooke. Lyceum, August 19, 1815.

KING'S RIVAL, THE. Tom Taylor and Chas. Reade. St. James's, October 2, 1854.

KING'S SEAL, THE. D. 2 a. H. R. Addison. D.L., January 10, 1835, and January 25, 1855.

KING'S SECRET, THE. P. 4 a. Charles Whitlock. Yarmouth Aquarium, April 5, 1906.

KING'S SECRET; OR, DUDLEY CASTLE IN THE OLDEN TIME, THE. D. C. H. Hazlewood. Bilston T.R., June 20, 1878.

KING'S SIGNET, THE. Rom. P. 4 a. Watson Bay. Fulham Grand, September 17, 1906.

KING'S SWEETHEART; OR, REGINA B.A., THE. C.O. 2 a. A. Sturgess. M. by J. Glover. Birmingham Grand, August 2, 1897; Camberwell Metropole, March 7, 1898.

KING'S THRESHOLD, THE. P. 1 a. W. B. Yeats. Royalty (Irish National T. Society), March 26, 1904.

KING'S WAGER; OR, THE COURT, THE CAMP, AND THE COTTAGE, THE. D. in 3 parts. T. Egerton Wilks. Victoria, December 11, 1837.

KING'S WORD, THE. Int. D.L., January 20, 1835.

KINGDOM OF HIS HEART, THE. D. 4 a. Wilson Howard. Hebburn R., March 18, 1909; Methil Gaiety, April 8, 1909.

KINGDOM OF KENNAQUHAIR, THE. M. and Satirical P. in 3 sc. V. Park. Several songs wr. by W. H. C. Nation. Royalty, December 26, 1908.

KIOLANTHE. O. Balfe. 1840.

KIPPER, THE. Duo. Bertha Moore. Royalty, June 6, 1905.

KISMET. D. 4 a. J. Wilton Jones. Hull T.R., February 20, 1888.

KISS, THE. Piece. 1 a. John Gray. A transl. fr. *Le Baiser* of Theodore de Banville. Royalty, March 4, 1892 (Independent T. perf.).

KISS, THE. Sk. Canterbury, November 23, 1908.

KISS ACCEPTED AND RETURNED, THE. Oa. James Ayre. Hay., 1744. N.p.

KISS AND BE FRIENDS. F. 1 a. J. M. Morton.

KISS AND THE ROSE. V. 1 a. W. T. Moncrieff.

KISS IN THE DARK, A. F. 1 a. J. B. Buckstone. Hay., June 13, 1840.

KISS OF DELILAH, THE. P. 3 a. Geo. Grant and James Lisle. D.L., November 27, 1896.

KISS OF JUDAS, THE. D. 4 a. Herbert Leonard. Aston R., October 19, 1908.

KISSI-KISSI. See *King Kokotoo.*

KISSI-KISSI; OR, THE PA, THE MA, AND THE PADISHAH. Extrav. F. C. Burnand. Opera Comique, July 12, 1873.

KISSING CUP'S RACE. D. 4 a. Campbell Rae-Brown. Ealing Lyric H., April 20, 1891; Glasgow Grand, April 14, 1905.

KISSING GOES BY FAVOUR. F. 1 a. Edward Stirling. Surrey, April 5, 1847.

KISSING, KISSING. Ca. Dover Apollonian H., November 13, 1873

KISSING THE ROD. See *The Millionaire.*

KIT MARLOWE. P. 1 a. W. L. Courtney. Shaftesbury, July 4, 1890; St. James's, October 31, 1892.

KIT'S WOMAN. P. 3 a. Mrs. Havelock Ellis and Joshua Bates, dram. from Mrs. Havelock Ellis's novel of same name. (Prod. by the Play Actors.) Court, June 27, 1909.

KITCHEN BELLES, THE. "Saltatorial Burlesque." Standard, February 27, 1869.

KITCHEN GIRL, THE. F. James East. Taunton Assembly R., October 26, 1899; Surrey, September 24, 1900.

KITCHEN LOVE. F. Robert Courtneidge. Olympic, September 29, 1888.

KITCHEN STUFF WOMAN, THE NEW JIG OF THE. Wm. Kempe. Entd. Stationers' Co. in 1595.

KITCHEN TRAGEDY, A. F. Edwin R. Barwick. Sanger's, May 21, 1887.

KITTENS. M.P. Fred Lyster and J. M. Glover. Brighton T.R., April 4, 1887.

KITTY. F.C. 3 a. Richmond New T., February 25, 1891.

KITTY. C.O. 3 a. Walter Parke. M. by Henry Parker. Cheltenham O.H., August 30, 1897; Kilburn T.R., October 11, 1897.

KITTY CLIVE, ACTRESS. C. 1 a. Frankfort W. Moore. Royalty, October 11, 1895; Strand, April 17, 1897.

KITTY GREY. C. 3 a. J. Smyth Pigott. Adap. fr. MM. Mars and Hennequin's *Les Fêtards.* M. by Augustus Barratt, Howard Talbot, and Lionel Monckton. Vaudeville, April 25, 1900; Bristol Prince's, August 27, 1900; Apollo, September 7, 1901.

KLEPTOMANIA. F.C. 3 a. Mark Melford. Southsea Portland H., April 30, 1888; Strand, June 12, 1888 (*matinée*), and September 15, 1888 (evening bill); Novelty, January 27, 1890.

KLEPTOMANIACS. F. Sk. H. Hall Winslow. Brighton Hipp., May 27, 1907.

KLONDYKE NUGGET, THE. Spec. D. 5 a. S. F. Cody. Walsall St. George's H., December 5, 1898; Elephant and Castle, August 7, 1899.

KLONDYKE RUSH, THE. D. 4 a. Henry E. Fielding. Britannia, May 30, 1898.

KLU, KLUX, KLAW. D. 3 a. G. H. Macdermott and H. A. Major. Britannia, May 12, 1873; Liverpool Amphi., October 20, 1876.

KNACKE HOW TO KNOWE A KNAVE, A. C. Anon. Pr. 1594.

KNACKE HOW TO KNOWE AN HONEST MAN, A. C. Anon. Several times ac. Pr. 1596. Entd. Stationers' Co., November 26, 1596.

KNAPSACK, THE. See *Such is Life.*

KNAPSACK; OR, TAKEN FROM THE RANKS, THE. D. Elephant and Castle, April 14, 1884.

KNAPSCHOW, THE FOREST FIEND. Panto. Bal. Lyceum, 1809. M. by C. Smith. N.p.

KNAVE IN GRAINE; OR, JACK COTTINGTON, THE. P. Entd. Stationers' Co., June 18, 1639. ? N.p.

KNAVE IN GRAINE NEW VAMPT, THE. C. by "J. D." Ac. at Fortune T. Pr. 1640.

KNAVE IN PRINT; OR, ONE FOR ANOTHER, A. C. Wm. Rowley. Entd. Stationers' Co., September 9, 1653. N.p.

KNAVE OF DIAMONDS, THE. Melo-d. 5 a. S. Creagh Henry. Kingston-on-Thames County, April 8, 1901.

KNAVE OF HEARTS. O. 1 a. Yardley and Elliott. Publ. by S. French, Limited.

KNAVE OF HEARTS. C. 1 a. F. E. Potter. Perf. by amateurs. Ladbroke H., November 22, 1906.

KNAVE OF HEARTS, THE. Drawing-room Melo-d. 4 a. Gladys-Unger. Glasgow Royalty, September 16, 1907. Croydon Grand, November 4, 1907.

KNAVE OR NOT. C. Thos. Holcroft. D.L., January 25, 1798. Pr. 1798.

KNAVERY IN ALL TRADES; OR, THE COFFEE-HOUSE. C. Anon. Pr. 1664. Ac. by apprentices of London.

KNAVES, THE. P. Anon. Ac. 1613. N.p.

KNAVES AND FOOLS. C. 1 a. Walter Reynolds. Adap. fr. the French. Leeds T.R., June 9, 1899.

KNIGHT AGAINST ROOK. C. 4 a. Owen Dove and J. G. Lefebre. Gaiety, July 23, 1886; Ladbroke H., April 18, 1893.

KNIGHT ERRANT, A. Rom. 1 a. Rutland Barrington. M. by A. J. Caldicott. Lyric, November 14, 1894.

KNIGHT ERRANT, A. C.O. 2 a. Lyrics A. and H. Chaplin. M., Frank Corrie. Falkirk Grand, August 6, 1906.

K(NIGHT) IN ARMOUR, A. M.D. Leigh T.R., August 5, 1895. See *A Night in Armour*.

K-NIGHT IN ARMOUR; OR, LITTLE MR. NOBODY. M. Ca. Harry Bruce. Chatham T.R., February 4, 1889.

KNIGHT IN THE BURNING ROCK, THE HISTORY OF THE. Perf. by the Earl of Warwick's Servants at Whitehall. Revels' Accounts, 1578.

KNIGHT OF ARVA, THE. Dion Boucicault. Hay., November 22, 1848.

KNIGHT OF MALTA, THE. T.C. Beaumont and Fletcher. Pr. 1647.

KNIGHT OF MALTA, THE. T.C. M'Nally. Alt. fr. Beaumont and Fletcher. C.G., April 23, 1783. N.p.

KNIGHT OF SNOWDEN, THE. O. Sir H. Bishop. (1782-1855.)

KNIGHT OF SNOWDOWN, THE. M.D. Morton. 1811. F. on the poem of "The Lady of the Lake." Lyceum (rev.), July 14, 1823.

KNIGHT OF THE BATH, THE. F. 3 a. Arthur Applin. Terry's, May 1, 1906.

KNIGHT OF THE BURNING PESTLE, THE. C. Beaumont and Fletcher. Wr. 1611. Pr. 1613. Rev. after the Restoration with a pro. spoken by Mrs. Ellen Gwynn. Rev. Royalty, November 13, 1904; rev., pro. spoken by Miss Carmen Woods. Manchester Gaiety, December 24, 1908. See *The Encounter*.

KNIGHT OF THE GARTER, THE. C.Oa. J. Sheldon Wilson. M. by Meyer Lutz. Gaiety, December 7, 1882.

KNIGHT OF THE LEOPARD. O. Balfe. D.L., July 11, 1874.

KNIGHT OF THE ROAD, A. C.D. 4 a. Ina L. Cassilis; Bayswater Bijou, May 2, 1904; Kingston R.C., June 3, 1907.

KNIGHT OF THE ROAD, THE. Irish C.O. W. Percy French. M. by W. Houston Collison. Dublin Queen's, April 27, 1891.

KNIGHT OF THE ROAD, THE. M.C. Haslingden Russell. Wolverhampton T.R., December 9, 1892.

KNIGHT'S CONJURING. C. Day. 1607.

KNIGHTS, THE. C. 2 a. Samuel Foote. Pr. 1754. Little T. in the H. Circa 1747. Also at D.L., February 9, 1754.

KNIGHTS, THE. (Aristophanes.) Transl. by Mitchell, 1820-2; Hickie, 1853; Rudd, 1867. See "Greek Plays."

KNIGHTS; OR, FRESH TEA FOR MR. FOOTE, THE. A Satire. Pr. in Dublin. Repr. in London 1758.

KNIGHTS OF ST. JOHN; OR, THE FIRE BANNER, THE. Melo-d. 2 a. Geo. Almar. Sadler's Wells, August 26, 1833.

KNIGHTS OF THE CROSS. Cant. R. Reece.

KNIGHTS OF THE CROSS; OR, THE HERMIT'S PROPHECY, THE. Rom. D. 3 a. fr. Sir Walter Scott. D.L. May 29, 1826.

KNIGHTS OF THE POST; OR, THE BLACKMOOR WASHED WHITE. F. Fr. the novel "Gil Blas." Ac. at Newcastle, 1797.

KNIGHTS OF THE ROAD, THE. Oa. Lib. Henry A. Lytton. M. by A. C. Mackenzie. Palace, February 27, 1905.

KNIGHTS OF THE ROAD; OR, THE GIPSY'S PROPHECY, THE. D. 3 a. W. Travers. Marylebone, April 13, 1868.

KNIGHTS OF THE ROUND TABLE, THE. D. 5 a. J. R. Planché. Hay., May 20, 1854.

KNOCKING AT THE GATE, THE. P. 4 a. A. L. Casserley. Cripplegate Institute, January 28, 1904.

KNOT OF FOOLS, THE. P. Ac. in 1613.

KNOTTING 'EM BROS. P. Publ. by S. French, Ltd.

KNOTTY QUESTION, A. Piece. 1 a. F. C. Thomas. Woking Public H., November 26, 1904.

KNOW YOUR OWN MIND. C. 5 a. Arthur Murphy. C.G., February 22, 1777. Pr. 1778. D.L., January 16, 1817. F. on *The Irrésolu* of Destouches.

KNOWING ONES TAKEN IN, THE. M. Piece. 2 a. Taken fr. Holman's C.O. *Abroad and at Home*. Ac. at Edinburgh, 1797.

KNOWLEDGE. C. 3 a. Gaiety. May 8, 1883.

KNOWN TO THE POLICE. D. Pro. and 3 a. John Douglass. Portsmouth Prince's, December 10, 1897; Surrey, March 6, 1899.

KNUCKLE DUSTER, THE. F. J. C. Wilson. Strand, 1863.

KO AND ZOA; OR, LA BELLE SAUVAGE. Bal. C. Dibdin, jun. 1812.

KOLAF; OR, THE FROZEN GIFT. Extrav. W. M. Akhurst. Sanger's Amphi., April 1, 1876.

KOLLEGEN. C. 1 a. A. Neumann-Hofer. Royalty, February 29, 1904.

KOMTESS GUCKERL. C. 3 a. Franz von Schönthau and Franz Kadelburg. Royalty, February 22, 1904.

KONIG SAUL. O. Gutzikow. 1839. See *Saul*.

KONIGIN NON SABA, DIE. O. 4 a. Lib. by J. Mosenthal, M. by Goldmark. Vienna, March 10, 1875.

KONIGSKINDER. O. Wds. by Ernst Rosmer, with M. by Humperdinck. Munich, January 23, 1897. In English at Court T., October 13, 1897.

KORANZO'S FEAST. T. Hayes. 1811.

KRIEG IM FRIEDEN. C. 5 a. G. von Moser and F. von Schönthau. St. George's H., December 17, 1901. See *Peaceful War*.

KUNIHILD. O. Kistler. 1883.

KUONI, THE JESTER. D. 1 a. Stephanie Baring and Raphael Sabatini. Luton Grand, June 12, 1903.

KUSS DER. O. Smetana (1824-1884).

KYNGE JOHAN. T. Bishop Bale. 1550.

KYNGE LEAR AND HIS THREE DAUGHTERS QUEER. E. Elton. Britannia, March 20, 1871.

KYRITZ PYRITZ. M.P. 3 a. H. Wilken and O. Justinius. Royalty, December 26, 1903.

L

L.S.D. Arthur à Beckett.

L.S.D. C.D. 3 a. Bertie Vyse. Royalty, June 29, 1872.

L.S.D.; OR, FACE TO FACE. 4 a. By "Thespis." Pav., July 15, 1889.

LABOUR MEMBER, THE. F. 2 a. H. Ramsbottom. Bayswater Bijou, May 8, 1906.

LABOUR OF LOVE, A. Ca. F. W. Broughton. Birmingham P.O.W., October 22, 1875.

LABOUR OF LOVE, A. P. 1 a. Horace W. C. Newte. Comedy, July 26, 1897.

LABYRINTH; OR, THE FATAL EMBARRASSMENT, THE. T. fr. Corneille. Pr. 1795.

LABYRINTH; OR, THE MAD CAP, THE. Ball. D.L. Pr. 1796.

LABYRINTH FARM; OR, FASHIONABLE RECLUSE. Anon. Pr. Glasgow 1811.

LABYRINTH, THE. P. Perf. at the King's Playhouse, 1664.

LABYRINTHUS. C. Hawkesworth. Pr. 1636.

LACKEY'S CARNIVAL, THE. C. 4 a. H. A. Jones. Duke of York's, September 26, 1900.

LAD FROM THE COUNTRY, A. F. 1 a. J. M. Morton. Olympic, June 5, 1863.

LAD OF THE HILLS; OR, WICKLOW GOLD MINES, THE. C.O. John O'Keeffe. C.G., April 9, 1796. Reduced to an afterpiece and called *Wicklow Gold Mines*. Pr. 1798 under title *The Wicklow Mountains*.

LADDER OF LIFE, THE. D. Croydon T.R., March 3, 1884.

LADDER OF LIFE; OR, GORDONS TO THE FRONT, THE. Military D. 4 a. Charles Rogers and Wm. Boyne. Stratford Borough T., May 30, 1898.

LADDER OF LOVE, THE. M.D. 1 a. T. H. Bayly. Filed at British Museum, May 31, 1852.

LADDER OF WEALTH, THE. M.D. 4 a. J. R. Orchard. Guildford County H., October 23, 1899.

LADIES A-LA-MODE. P. Dryden. Mentioned by Pepys 1668, and distinguished from *Marriage-à-la-Mode*.

LADIES AT HOME; OR, GENTLEMEN WE CAN DO WITHOUT YOU. Female Int. 1 a. J. V. Millingen. Hay., August 7, 1819.

LADIES, BEWARE. Princess's, 1857.

LADIES OF CASTILE, THE. T. 5 a. M. Warren. Pr. in America, 1790.

LADIES OF ST. CYR; OR, THE RUNAWAY HUSBAND, THE. C. 3 a. Adap. fr. the French of Alexander Dumas. Théâtre Française, July 25, 1843.

LADIES OF THE PALACE; OR, THE NEW COURT LEGACY, THE. B.O. 3 a. Pr. 1735.

LADIES ONLY. Sk. Chas. Darrell. Greenwich Pal., November 30, 1908.

LADIES' BATTLE. C. 3 a. T. W. Robertson. 1851.

LADIES' BATTLE, THE. C. 3 a. G. B. Coale. Pub. by S. French, Ltd.

LADIES' BATTLE; OR, UN DUEL EN AMOUR, THE. C. 3 a. C. Reade. Fr. Scribe and Legouvé's C., *La Bataille des Dames*. Olympic, May 7, 1851; D.L., January 5, 1857; Op. C., circa 1872, and June 5, 1891.

LADIES' CHAMPION, THE. Ca. Harold Gwindon. Hay., May 18, 1868.

LADIES' CHANCE. O. Pub. by S. French, Ltd.

LADIES' CHOICE, THE. See *The Lady's Choice*.

LADIES' CLUB, THE. C.D. 2 a. Mark Lemon. Olympic, March, 1840.

LADIES' FROLICK, THE. O. Jas. Love (Dance). Alt. fr. *The Jovial Crew*. D.L., May 4, 1770. N.p.

LADIES' GALLERY, THE. See *The Binbian Mine*.

LADIES' HOUSE OF COMMONS. Sk. Wal Pink. M. by G. Le Brunn. Royal M.H., May 19, 1902.

LADIES' IDOL, THE. Bournemouth T.R., March 28, 1895.

LADIES' LAST STAKE; OR, THE WIVES' RESENTMENT, THE. See *The Lady's*, etc.

LADIES' MASQUE, THE (The Masque of Ladies.) Conducted by Lady Hay. Perf. at Court early in 1618.

LADIES' PARADISE, THE. Ro. P. 2 a. G. Dance and I. Caryll, Hanley T.R., March 11, 1901.

LADIES' PRIVILEGE, THE. Ro. C. Henry Glapthorne. Ac. at D.L., and twice at Whitehall before their Majesties. Pr. 1640.

LADIES' STRATAGEM, THE. Hitchcock 1775.

LADIES' SUBSCRIPTION, THE. Perf. designed for an introduction to a dance. John Cleland. Pr. 1755.

LADIES' TRIAL, THE. T.C. John Ford. D.L. Pr. 1639. Prol. by Mr. Bird. Cockpit, May, 1638.

LADIES' TRIUMPH, THE. See *Lady's Triumph*.

LADIES' VISITING DAY, THE. See *Lady's Visiting Day*.

LADLE, THE. Ent. of music, alt. fr. Prior (By Chas. Dibdin). Pr. 1773. Int. perf. at Sadler's Wells.

LADY ALIMONY; OR, THE ALIMONY LADY, THE. C. Anon. Possibly by Lodge and Green. Pr. 1659. ? Ac.

LADY AND GENTLEMAN IN A PECULIARLY PERPLEXING PREDICAMENT, A. F. 1 a. Chas. Selby. English O.H., August 9, 1841.

LADY AND THE BATH, THE. Sk. Kenyon Musgrave. Bedford, September 16, 1907.

LADY AND THE BURGLAR, THE. C. Sk. Fred Monckton and Ch. D. Hickman. Hulme Hipp., September 27, 1905.

LADY AND THE DEVIL, THE. Ro. Mus. D. 2 a. Wm. Dimond. M. by Kelly. Suggested by a Spanish C. of the seventeenth century, *La Dama Duende*. D.L., May 3, 1820; Lyceum, June 26, 1820, and June 3, 1825.

LADY AND THE LIONS. P. 3 a. A. Hare and A. Pearse. Manchester Prince's, June 14, 1904.

LADY AND THE MAGISTRATE, THE. Ca. Theodore A. Sharp. Bexhill York T., July 20, 1897.

LADY ANNE'S WELL; OR, THE WARNING SPIRIT. D. W. Travers. Britannia, July 20, 1868.

LADY AUDLEY'S SECRET. D. 2 a. W. E. Suter. Adap. fr. Miss Braddon's novel. ueen's, February 21, 1863.

LADY AUDLEY'S SECRET. D. Geo. Roberts. Adap. fr. Miss Braddon's novel. St. James's, February 28, 1863.

LADY AUDLEY'S SECRET. Sk. Adap. fr. the novel. Poplar Q., January 7, 1907.

LADY AURORA, THE. Oa. 1 a. J. Wilson Woodward. M. by F. Wilson Woodward. Chatham O.H., November 19, 1894.

LADY BANDITS, THE. Topical and F. O. H. C. Sargeant and E. Lauri. Kingston R.C., April 15, 1908.

LADY BANDITS, THE. Sk. Holborn Empire, April 27, 1908.

LADY BANKRUPT, THE. M.C. 1 a. Owen Hall. Brixton Empress, November 24, 1905.

LADY BARBARA. P. Perf. by Sir Robert Lane's men. 1571.

LADY BARBARA'S BIRTHDAY. Ca. Miss Barker. Brighton T.R., February 12, 1872 (amat.).

LADY BARBARITY. Ver. 4 a. R. C. Carton. Adap. fr. J. C. Snaith's novel of same name. Comedy, February 27, 1908.

LADY BARTER. C. 3 a. Chas. Coghlan. Princess's, February 28, 1891.

LADY BELLE BELLE; OR, FORTUNIO AND HIS SEVEN MAGIC MEN. Extrav. 1 a. H. J. Byron. Adelphi, December 26, 1863.

LADY BEN. C. 4 a. Geo. P. Bancroft. Comedy, March 28, 1905.

LADY BOOKIE, THE. Duo. Cyril Hallward. Terry's, November 9, 1898.

LADY BOUNTIFUL. P. 4 a. A. W. Pinero. Garrick, March 7, 1891.

LADY BROWNE'S DIARY. 3 a. Miss Minnie Bell. Adap. of Octave Feuillet's *La Crise*. Strand, June 28, 1892.

LADY BURGLAR, THE. P. 1 a. E. J. Malyon and Chas. James. Kilburn T.R., May 3, 1897; Avenue, October 16, 1897.

LADY BURGLAR, THE. C. 1 a. C. H. Brookfield. Liverpool Court, November 3, 1904; rev. Kingston County, December 7, 1904; Terry's March 31, 1906.

LADY BY BIRTH, A. Ca. 1 a. W. Gordon Smythies. Cardiff T.R., January 9, 1893.

LADY CECIL. Juvenile P. F. D. Adams. Pub. by S. French, Ltd.

LADY CLANCARTY; OR, WEDDED AND WOOED. D. 4 a. Tom Taylor. Olympic, March 9, 1874.

LADY CLARA VERE DE VERE. P.O.W., June 8, 1888.

LADY CLARE. D. 5 a. Robert Buchanan. Adap. fr. Georges Ohnet's *Le Maitre de Forges*. Globe, April 11, 1883.

LADY CLERK, THE. Ca. Cyril Hurst. M. by Ada Cleveland. Forest Gate Earlham H., October 27, 1899.

LADY COMMERCIALS, THE. Sk. 1 sc. Fredk. Faby. M. by Cyril Barry. Chelsea Palace, September 11, 1905.

LADY CONTEMPLATION, THE. C. 2 parts. Duchess of Newcastle. Pr. 1662. Sc. 3 in the first part and sc. 2 in the second part written by the Duke.

LADY COUNCILLOR; OR, URBAN URBANITY, THE. Oa. Wr. and comp. by J. F. Swift (Godfrey Marks). Liscard Concert H., April 2. 1900.

LADY CYCLIST; OR, A BICYCLE BELLE, THE. M.C. 2 a. St. Aubyn Miller. M. by Geo. D. Fox. Luton T. H., April 24, 1897.

LADY D'ARCY. C. B. H. Hilton. Bristol T.R., May 25, 1870.

LADY DAISY. Panto. burl. Bert Dent. Grimsby Temperance H., February 12, 1896.

LADY DANDIES, THE. The Merveilleuses played under this title. Daly's, January 31, 1907.

LADY DEADLOCK'S SECRET. P. 4 a. J. Palgrave Simpson. Adap. of Ch. Dickens's "Bleak House." Aberdeen O.H., April 3, 1874; Windsor T.R., November 28, 1883; Op. C., March 26, 1884.

LADY DEANE, Dom. P. 4 a. Alfred A. Wilmot. St. Geo. H., May 26, 1887.

LADY DENTIST, THE. F. 3 a. Leopold Montague and Alban Atwood. Broadway, April 10, 1905.

LADY DETECTIVE, THE. Renamed fr. *Bilberry of Tilbury*. Hanley T.R., March 13, 1899.

LADY DI'S VISIT. Duol. Ch. Thursby. Chatham O.H., April 26, 1897.

LADY DOCTOR, THE. Duol. E. N. Yorke. Brighton Pier T., October 12, 1903.

LADY DOLLY AND THE DECALOGUE. P. 3 a. Joseph Fletcher and Marcus Ellis. Paignton Pier Pav., September 17, 1908.

LADY DOROTHY'S SCHEME. M.C. 1 a. Tom Walton. M. by Wilfred Bendall. Newcastle-on-Tyne Art Gallery T., June 24, 1895.

LADY ELIZABETH POOLE GUBBINS. 1 a. "A. L. H." Pub. by S. French, Ltd.

LADY ELLA. Juvenile Oa. E. O. Gilbert. Publ. by S. French, Ltd.

LADY EPPING'S LAWSUIT. C. 3 a. Hubert Henry Davies. (Rehearsed and prod. under the direction of Sir Chas. Wyndham.) Criterion, October 12, 1908.

LADY ERRANT, THE. T.C. Wm. Cartwright. Pr. 1651.

LADY EXMORE'S EMBARRASSMENT. C. 3 a. Herbert G. Phillips. Adap. fr. a story by Claude and Alice Askew. St. Leonards Concert H., February 20, 1909 (amat.).

LADY FEATHERBRAIN. C. 3 a. Mrs. Geo. Corbett. Queen's Gate H., February 23, 1905.

LADY FLIRT. C. 3 a. Paul Gavault and G. Berr. Adap. fr. the French C.O., *Mdme. Flirt*. Paris Athenée, December 27, 1901; Haymarket, 1901; Hay., May 25, 1904.

LADY FLORA. C. 4 a. C. F. Coghlan. Court, March 13, 1875.

LADY FOLLY. P. 4 a. Stephen Pritt. Preston New T.R., November 18, 1901; Fulham Grand, August 25, 1902.

LADY FORGER, THE. F. 1 a. Bayswater Bijou, February 17, 1906.

LADY FORTUNE. P. 1 a. Ch. Thomas. Globe, September 17, 1887; Comedy. February 18, 1892.

LADY FREDERICK. C. 3 a. W. Somerset Maugham. Court, October 26, 1907; tfd. Garrick, March 10, 1908; tfd. to Criterion, April 27, 1908; trns. to Haymarket, August 1, 1908.

LADY FROM LONDON, THE. F. 2 a. Cyril Depoir. Warrington Court, December 4, 1905.

LADY FROM TEXAS, A. C. 3 a. Mrs. T. P. O'Connor. Great Queen Street T., June 1, 1901.

LADY FROM THE SEA, THE. D. 5 a. Henrik Ibsen. Trans. by Eleanor Marx-Aveling. Terry's, May 11, 1891; trans. by Mrs. F. E. Archer. Royalty May 5, 1902.

LADY GERALDINE'S SPEECH. Ca. Beatrice Harraden. Guildhall Sch. of M., July 15, 1909 (amat.).

LADY GLADYS. C. Rob. Buchanan. Op. C., May 7, 1894 (C.P.).

LADY GODIVA. Burl. Strand, July, 1851.

LADY GODIVA. Burl. Fred. Robson. Middlesboro' T.R., May 5, 1873; Sadler's Wells, December 6, 1873.

LADY GODIVA. P. Max Goldberg. 1894.

LADY GODIVA. P. J. C. Clarke. Imperial, April 23, 1902.

LADY GODIVA. See *Giddy Godiva.*

LADY GODIVA; OR, FOR THE PEOPLE. D. 4 a. H. P. Grattan. Greenwich T.R., October 2, 1885.

LADY GODIVA; OR, ST. GEORGE AND THE DRAGON AND THE CHAMPIONS OF CHRISTENDOM. Wm. Muskerry. Sanger's, December 26, 1889.

LADY GODIVA AND PEEPING TOM. Sanger's, December 27, 1875.

LADY GUIDE, THE. P. 3 a. Terry's, April 15, 1891.

LADY HAMILTON; OR, THE LAST SIGNAL. P. 3 a. H. F. Wood. Islington Grand, November 22, 1904.

LADY HATTON. D. St. Helen's T.R., September 3, 1883.

LADY HENRIETTA; OR, THE STATUTE FAIR. Ballet. M. by Burgmuller Flotow and Deldevez. D.L., April 15, 1844.

LADY HUNTWORTH'S EXPERIMENT. C. 3 a. R. C. Carton. Criterion, April 26, 1900; Haymarket, January 12, 1907

LADY IN DIFFICULTIES, A. C.D. 2 a. J. R. Planché. Lyceum, October 15, 1849.

LADY IN RED, THE. Sk. Frank Dix. Walham Green Granville, July 17, 1905.

LADY IN SEARCH OF AN HEIRESS. P. 1 a. Agnes Leigh. Pub. by S. French, Ltd.

LADY INGER OF OSTRAT. P. 5 a. H. Ibsen. Transl. by Chs. Archer. Scala, January 28, 1906.

LADY INTERVIEWER, THE. Sk. Herbert Swears. Richmond T.R., December 14, 1896.

LADY ISABEL. D. 5 a. Alfred Kempe. Holborn, January 16, 1873.

LADY JANE. P. 2 parts. Henry Chettle, in conjunction with Dekker, Heywood, and Webster. Ac. 1602. N.p.

LADY JANE GRAY. T. by Calprinède, 1638; T. by Rowe, 1715; T. by Tennyson, 1876.

LADY JANE GRAY. T. Nicholas Rowe. D.L., April 20, 1715. Pr. 1715. Partly based on an unfinished play on same subject by Edmund Smith.

LADY JANE GREY. Ross Neil. Pr. 1871.

LADY JANE GREY. D. C. H. Hazlewood. Britannia, May 25, 1874.

LADY JANE GREY. D. Warrington P.O.W., February 12, 1875.

LADY JANE GREY. Dr. fragment. 1 a. Wm. Poel. St. Geo. H., June 12, 1885.

LADY JANE'S CHRISTMAS PARTY. Epi. 1 a. Tom Gallon. Garrick, December 21, 1904.

LADY JEMIMA. Do. C. 3 a. Noel Grant. Whitstable Assembly R., August 29, 1888.

LADY JOURNALIST, THE. Duo. I. Zangwill. M. by Algernon Lindo. Steinway H., July 4, 1893.

LADY KILLER, THE. F.C. 3 a. A. Chevalier and W. Mackintosh. Plymouth T.R., July 13, 1885.

LADY KILLER, THE. F.C. 3 a. Ch. S. Fawcett. Adap. fr. Bisson's 115, *Rue Pigalle.* Liverpool P.O.W., September 25, 1893; Strand, October 17, 1893.

LADY KILLER, THE. Hist. P. J. Hickory Wood. Kennington T., June 22, 1903.

LADY KINTON'S NECKLACE; OR, THE HYPNOTIST. P. 3 a. G. H. Trotman. Ilkeston T.R., October 15, 1906.

LADY LANIGAN; LAUNDRESS. C.D. 1 a. J. Russell Bogue. Liverpool R.T., April 9, 1908.

LADY LAURA'S ARCADIA. Ro. C.O. 1 a. F. Broughton. M. by Florian Pascal. Bayswater Bijou, July 10, 1897.

LADY LAWYER, THE. Oa. 1 a. G. D. Lynch. M. by J. W. Ivimey. Garrick, March 8, 1897.

LADY LILIAN; OR, FLOWERS OF JOY AND FLOWERS OF SORROW. D. 4 a. Edward Towers. Pavilion, March 29, 1880.

LADY LILLIAN. D. Huddersfield O.H., June 15, 1885.

LADY LOVINGTON; OR, A SOIREE DRAMATIQUE. Ca. 1 a. 3 sc. Geo. Villars. Athenæum H., Tottenham Court Road, June 28, 1888; Ladbroke H., March 24, 1890; St. Geo. H., June 28, 1894.

LADY LUCKY. M.C. 3 a. F. Jarman. Weymouth O.H., July 12, 1906.

LADY MADCAP. M.P. P. Rubens and N. N. Davis. M. by P. Rubens. Lyrics by P. Rubens and P. Greenbank. P.O.W., December 17, 1904.

LADY MARJORIE'S WAGER. P. 1 a. A. Demain Grange. Marlboro', April 26, 1905.

LADY MARY WORTLEY MONTAGU. D. Lyceum, 1839.

LADY MAYORESS, THE. C. 3 a. H. D. Rowan. East Finchley All Saints' Parish H., May 19, 1908 (amat.).

LADY MELVILL. O. F. Flotow. 1838.

LADY MOTH. A curious p. of the 17th century. MS. pres. in private library in Ireland.

LADY OF BAYONNE, THE. T.O. 1 a. Dr. W. S. Macgowan. M. by Dr. Dyer. Cheltenham O.H., February 9, 1897.

LADY OF BELLEISLE; OR, A NIGHT IN THE BASTILLE. D. 3 a. J. M. Gully. Adap. fr. Dumas's *Mademoiselle de Belleisle.* D.L., December 4, 1839.

LADY OF HAIGH; OR, A WIFE'S PENANCE. Hist. legend. Rom.D. 4 a. and 9 sc. Alard Bensell. Wigan Court, May 1, 1907 (C.P.); Wigan R., July 22, 1907.

LADY OF KENSINGTON, THE. P. 5 a. Sutton-Vane. Hammersmith Lyric, April 3, 1908 (C.P.).

LADY OF KILDARE; OR, MARRIED IN MISTAKE, THE. D. Salisbury Queen's, March 4, 1872.

LADY OF LEEDS, THE. Fro. 3 a. Robt. Marshall. Wyndham's, February 9, 1905.

LADY OF LONGFORD, THE. O. 1 a. Sir Augustus Harris and Fredk. Weatherly. M. by Emil Bach. C.G., July 21, 1894; D.L., April 20, 1896.

LADY OF LOYAL HOUSE, THE. P. J. H. McCarthy. Margate Grand T., September 21, 1904.

LADY OF LYONS, THE. Burl. W. Younge. Imperial, April 23, 1879.

LADY OF LYONS, THE. See *The Castle of Como, Bellows Menders, Pauline.*

LADY OF LYONS; OR, LOVE AND PRIDE, THE. P. 5 a. Lord Lytton. C.G., February 15, 1838. The title used prior to perfce. was *The Adventurer.* Chief incidents suggested by a tale named "The Bellows Menders"; D.L., January 17, 1843, and January 4, 1850; Lyceum, April 17, 1879; Adelphi, February 9, 1898.

LADY OF LYONS; OR, TWOPENNY PRIDE AND PENNY-TENCE, THE. Burl. extrav. H. J. Byron. Strand, February 1, 1858.

LADY OF LYONS MARRIED AND CLAUDE UNSETTLED, THE. Absurdity. R. Reece. Glasgow Royalty, September 27, 1884.

LADY OF LYONS MARRIED AND SETTLED, THE. Vaudeville in 3 sc. H. C. Merivale. Gaiety, October 5, 1878.

LADY OF MAY, THE. Masque. Sir Philip Sidney. Presented to Queen Elizabeth in the Gardens at Wanstead, Essex. ? Pr.

LADY OF OSTEND, THE. F. 3 a. F. C. Burnand. Fd. on German P. of Oscar Blumenthal and Gustave Kadelburg. Bournemouth Royal, June 19, 1899; Terry's, July 5, 1899; and November 29, 1800.

LADY OF PLEASURE, THE. C. *Jas. Shirley. Ac. at the private house in D.L. 1638. Licensed 1635. Pr. 1637.

LADY OF QUALITY, A. D. 5 a. Adap. by Frances Hodgson Burnett and Stephen Townesend fr. Mrs. Burnett's novel. Ladbroke H., March 7, 1896 (C.P.); Cambridge New T., February 23, 1899; Comedy, March 8, 1899.

LADY OF THE CAMELLIAS, THE. T.D. 4 a. Adap. fr. Dumas's *Dame aux Camelias.* Vaudeville, February 2, 1852.

LADY OF THE DESERT. D. Stirling. 1859.

LADY OF THE LAKE, THE. E. J. Eyre. Pr. (Edinburgh), 1811.

LADY OF THE LAKE, THE. M.D. M. by Cooke. D.L. January 4, 1827.

LADY OF THE LAKE, THE. C. 3a. Dibdin. Pub. by S. French, Ltd.

LADY OF THE LAKE, THE. Burl. R. Reece. F. on Sir Walter Scott's poem. Royalty, September 8, 1866.

LADY OF THE LAKE, THE. Cantata. Sir Geo. Macfarren. 1813-88.

LADY OF THE LAKE, THE. D. 4 a. Chas. Webb. Glasgow T.R., August 14, 1871.

LADY OF THE LAKE, THE. D. 1 a. Andrew Halliday. D.L., September 21, 1872.

LADY OF THE LAKE, THE. Ro. D. 3 a. Adap. fr. Sir Walter Scott's poem. Surrey.

LADY OF THE LAKE, THE. See *Knight of Snowdown* and *La Donna del Lago.*

LADY OF THE LANE, THE. Burl. H. J. Byron. Strand, October 31, 1872.

LADY OF THE LOCKET, THE. C.O. 3 a. H. Hamilton. M. by Wm. Fullerton. Empire, March 11, 1885.

LADY OF THE MANOR, THE. C.O. 3 a. Dr. Kenrick. C.G., November 23, 1778. Pr. 1778. T. fr. Chas. Johnson's *Country Lasses; or, The Custom of the Manor.* D.L. (rev., with new m. by Hook, the original composer), April 23, 1818.

LADY OF THE MAY, THE. See *Lady of May.*

LADY OF THE PAGEANT, THE. F.C. 3 a. Max Pemberton and Cyril Wentworth. Eastbourne D.P., July 20, 1908.

LADY OF THE ROCK, THE. Melo-d. Thos. Holcroft. D.L., February 12, 1805. Pr. 1805.

LADY OR THE TIGER, THE. 3 a. Sidney Rosenfeld. Adap. fr. F. R. Stockton's story. Elephant and Castle, May 7, 1888 (C.P.).

LADY OF THE TOWER. Burl. Anon. 1811.

LADY PADDINGTON. F.C. 3 a. F. C. Philips and Walter Parke. Adap. fr. *Le Truc d'Arthur.* Hastings Pier Pav., July 26, 1902.

LADY PHILOSOPHER, THE. M.C. 2 a. Henry Hughes. M. by A. A. Bancroft. Heaton Moor Conservative H., March 4, 1898. Dalston, Oct. 1898.

LADY SATAN. D. 4 a. Wm. P. Sheen. Openshaw Harte's T., June 28, 1897.

LADY SELINA OF "K." M.C. 3 a. Bks. and lyrics by E. C. Mabel Leeds, M. by C. Blakesley Yearsley. Kingston R. County, May 5, 1907.

LADY SLAVEY, THE. M.P. 2 a. G. Dance. M. by John Crook. Northampton O.H., September 4, 1893; Avenue, October 20, 1894.

LADY SWINDLER, A. Sk. Rose Vane. Greenwich Palace, September 9, 1907.

LADY TATTERS. Rom. mus. play. 3 a. Book Herbert Leonard, lyrics Roland Carse, music Walter Slaughter. Marlborough, August 31, 1906 (C.P.); Shaftesbury, May 1, 1907.

LADY TEMPLEMORE'S FUTURE. Society P. 4 a. G. B. Nichols. Taunton London Association R., April 8, 1901 (C.P.).

LADY TETLEY'S DIVORCE. P. Pro. and 3 a. Mr. and Mrs. W. F. Downing. Bristol Prince's, August 26, 1901; Royalty, *Lady Tetley's Scheidung*, March 7, 1904.

LADY VOLUNTEERS, THE. C. 1 a. Miss Sydney Phelps. Parkhurst, July 13, 1896; Vaudeville, April 25, 1900.

LADY WHO DWELT IN THE DARK. P. 1 a. Monckton Hoffe. Southampton Grand, June 8, 1903; Holloway Marlborough, August 8, 1904; Collins's M.H., May 15, 1905.

LADY WINDERMERE'S FAN. C. 4 a. Oscar Wilde. St. James's, February 20, 1892, and November 19, 1904. See *The Poet and the Puppets.*

LADY WITH A TEMPER, THE. 1857.

LADY WRANGLER, THE. M.C. Seymour Hicks. M. by Ellaline Terriss. Duke of York's, March 4, 1898.

LADY'S CHOICE, THE. P. 2 a. Paul Hiffernan. C.G., April 20, 1759. Pr. 1759.

LADY'S IDOL, THE. F.C. 3 a. Arthur Law. Bournemouth T.R., March 28, 1895; Vaudeville, April 18, 1895; and Terry's

LADY'S LAST FROLIC. Love. 1774.

LADY'S LAST STAKE; OR, THE WIFE'S RESENTMENT, THE. C. Colley Cibber. Queen's T. in Hay., December 13, 1707. Pr. 1708. A kind of pendant to *The Careless Husband.*

LADY'S LAST STROKE, THE. C. Theo. Cibber.

LADY'S LECTURE, THE. Dialogue between Sir Chas. Easy and his marriageable daughter. C. Cibber. Pr. 1748.

LADY'S MAID, THE. C. 3 a. Henry Hamilton. Liverpool P.O.W., April 17, 1893.

LADY'S MAID, THE. M.P. 2 a. C. A. Lord. M. by E. Hastings. Swindon, December 21, 1901; Cambridge New T., December 26, 1901; Balham Duchess, February 10, 1902.

LADY'S MAID, THE. M.C. 2 a. E. A. Sykes and R. G. Neal. M. by E. A. Sykes. Northampton St. Michael's H., November 16, 1905.

LADY'S OPERA, THE. C.G. 1781. This was *The Beggar's Opera,* with the characters entirely impersonated by females.

LADY'S REVENGE; OR, THE ROVER RECLAIM'D, THE. C. Wm. Popple. C.G., January 9, 1734. Pr. 1734.

LADY'S TRIAL, A. D. Ford. 1639. Pr. 1639.

LADY'S TRIUMPH, THE. C.O. Elkanah Settle. L.I.F. Pr. 1718.

LADY'S VISITING DAY, THE. C. Chas. Burnaby. Pr. 1701. Ac. one night at L.I.F.

LADYLAND. C.O. 2 a. and 3 scenes. E. Ponsonby. M. by F. Lambert. Avenue, December 12, 1904.

LÆLIA. A Latin P. Ac. at Queen's Coll., Cambridge, 1590. MS. Lambeth, 838.

LAGGARD, THE. Orig. P. 1 a. William Senior. Bedford Street Bijou, November 10, 1907.

LAGGARD IN LOVE, A. F. Horace Lennard. Trafalgar Square, April 27, 1893.

LAID UP IN PORT! OR, SHARKS ALONGSHORE. Nautical D. 3 a. Thos. Higgie.

LAKERS, THE. Comic O. 3 a. J. Plumptre. Pr. 1798. N.ac.

LAKME. O. Lib. by MM. Gondinet and Gilli. L. Delibes. Prod. in Paris, April 14, 1883, and in London, Gaiety T., June 6, 1885.

LALLA ROOKH. O. C. E. Horn. Dublin, 1822.

LALLA ROOKH. Extrav. 3 a. Vincent Amcotts. Gallery of Illust. June 19, 1868.

LALLA ROOKH. P. 2 a. B. F. Rayner. Publ. by S. French, Ltd.

LALLA ROOKH. Extrav. Frank Hall. Philharmonic, December 26, 1879.

LALLA ROOKH. Burl. Extrav. Horace Lennard. Novelty, May 1, 1884.

LALLA ROOKH. O. F. David (1810-1876). A setting of Moore's story.

LALLA ROOKH. See *The Veiled Prophet*, *Zelica*.

LALLA ROOKH; OR, THE PRINCESS, THE PERI, AND THE TROUBADOUR. Burl. and Pant. 1 a. Wm. Brough. Lyceum, December 24, 1857.

LALLAPALOOSA. Sk. Holborn Empire, May 31, 1901.

LAMBERT SIMNEL. O. Left unf. by F. L. H. Monro and completed by Adolfe Adam. September 16, 1843.

LAMBERTAZZI, I. O. Poniatowski. Florence, 1845.

LAME COMMONWEALTH, THE. A Droll taken from *The Beggar's Bush*.

LAME EXCUSE, A. F. 1 a. Fredk. Hay. P.O.W., April 19, 1869.

LAME LOVER, THE. C. 3 a. Samuel Foote. Hay., August 27, 1770. Pr. 1770; rev. Royalty, 1872.

LAMED FOR LIFE. C. 2 a. Westland Marston. Royalty, June 12, 1871; rev. Holborn, 1873.

LAMPLIGHTER, THE. F. 1 a. C. Dickens.

LANCASHIRE LAD, THE. Dom. melo-d. 4 a. G. Carlton Wallace. Broughton Vic., September 16, 1907; rev. Hammersmith Lyric, April 27, 1908.

LANCASHIRE LASS; OR, TEMPTED, TRIED, AND TRUE, THE. D. Pro. and 4 a. H. J. Byron. Liverpool Amphi., October 28, 1867; Queen's, July 24, 1868.

LANCASHIRE LIFE; OR, POOR JOE THE FACTORY LAD. D. Edward Towers. Pav., May 15, 1875.

LANCASHIRE SAILOR, THE. D. 1 a. Brandon Thomas. Terry's, June 6, 1891; afterwards transf. to Shaftesbury and Toole's. York Royal, April 20, 1907; rev. Royalty, December 26, 1907.

LANCASHIRE WEAVER LAD, THE. D. 3 a. Ben Brierley. Manchester Free Trade H., October 10, 1877; Manchester Comedy, November 13, 1885.

LANCASHIRE WITCHES, THE. C. Thos. Heywood and Richd. Brome. Globe. Pr. 1634. Called on title page *The Late Lancashire Witches*, and the running title is *The Witches of Lancashire*.

LANCASHIRE WITCHES, THE. P. 3 a. E. Fitzball.

LANCASHIRE WITCHES, THE. O. 3 a. R. T. Gunton. M. by F. Stanislaus. Manchester T.R., October 20, 1879.

LANCASHIRE WITCHES; OR, THE DISTRESSES OF HARLEQUIN, THE. Pant. Chas. Dibdin. Ac. at the Circus. Songs, etc., only pr. 1783. See *Amorous Bigot*.

LANCASHIRE WITCHES AND TEAGUE O'DIVELLY, THE IRISH PRIEST. C. Thos. Shadwell. Duke's T. Pr. 1682. See *The Amorous Bigot*.

LANCELOT AND ELAINE. Cant. A. Barratt and J. St. A. Johnson. F. on Tennyson's poem. Alexandra Pal., July 23, 1898.

LANCELOT DU LAC. O. Joncières. 1900.

LANCELOT THE LOVELY; OR, THE IDOL OF THE KING. Burl. 2 a. Richard Henry. M. by John Crook. Avenue, April 22, 1889.

LANCERS, THE. Int. 1 a. John Howard Payne. D.L., November 29, 1827.

LANCERS, THE. D. 3 a. Capt. Leicester Vernon. Adap. fr. the French (Gymnase, 1852). Princess's, November 1, 1853.

LANCIOTTO AND CECILIA. O. 3 a, F. M. Kay. M. by Seymour Reeves. Birmingham. Wretham Road Assem. Rms. December 8, 1906 (amat.).

LANCY, DE. P. Augustus Thomas. Vaudeville, September 4, 1905. C.p.

LAND, THE. P. 3 a. Padriac Colum. Irish Players, St. Geo.'s H., November 28, 1905.

LAND AHEAD. D. 4 a. Geo. Manville Fenn. Hull T.R., March 4, 1878; Sanger's Amphi., September 30, 1878.

LAND AND LOVE. C. 3 a. A. W. Dubourg. Globe, May 26, 1884

LAND AND THE PEOPLE, THE. D. Pro. and 4 a. Arthur B. Moss and W. J. Patmore. New Cross Public H., October 16, 1893.

LAND OF CHERRY BLOSSOM, THE. Japanese M.P. 2 a. Fredk. G. Turner and Maude Smyth. M. by Sydney H. Smyth. Stoke Newington Library H., February 25, 1909 (amat.).

LAND OF DIAMONDS, A. D. Louis Coen. Sadler's Wells, June 2, 1884.

LAND OF GOLD, THE. D. 6 a. Geo. Lander. Eleph. and C., February 25, 1888.

LAND OF HEART'S DESIRE, THE. Poetic P. 1 a. W. B. Yeats. Avenue, March 29, 1894.

LAND OF NOD, THE. Mus. C. 2 a. Albert Chevalier. M. by Alfred H. West. Lincoln T.R., May 24, 1897; Royalty, September 24, 1898. See *The Dream of His Life*.

LAND OF PIE, THE. Oa. 2 a. H. C. Bunner. M. by C. R. W. Cuckson. Leicester Great Meeting Sch., January 17, 1899.

LAND OF SIMPLICITY, THE. C. Dibdin. Ac. at the Circus. N.p.

LAND OF THE LIVING. D. 5 a. Frank Harvey. Gt. Grimsby P.O.W., March 16, 1889; Grand, July 29, 1889; Surrey, June 8, 1891.

LAND OF THE WEST, THE. Sk. J. Henderson. Bedford M.H., September 2, 1907.

LAND RATS AND WATER RATS. D. 3 a. Watts Phillips. Surrey, September 5, 1868.

LAND WE LIVE IN, THE. C. Holt. 1805.

LANDGARTHA. T.C. Henry Burnell. Ac. at Dublin 1639. Pr. 1641. Plot fr. Swedish history.

LANDGARTHA; OR, THE AMAZON QUEEN OF DENMARK AND NORWAY. Ent. Joshua Barnes. MS. in library of Emanuel Coll., Cambridge. The play was finished May 29, 1683.

LANDGRAVE'S LEAP; OR, THE ANCESTOR OF LEOPOLD. D. Victoria.

LANDLADY, THE. Ca. Alec Nelson. Taken fr. *The Chances*. Shaftesbury, April 4, 1889.

LANDLORD, THE. Dom. D. 4 a. W. J. Colling Hall. Sunderland T.R., February 8, 1886.

LANGUISHING LOVER; OR, AN INVOCATION TO SLEEP, THE. Mus. Int. D. Bellamy. Pr. 1746.

LANNIVE'S FESTIVALS. Mentioned in Barker List, 1814.

LANSDOWN CASTLE; OR, THE SORCERER OF TEWKESBURY. Oa. A. C. Cunningham. M. by Gustav Van Holst. Cheltenham Corn Exchange, February 7, 1893 (amat.).

LANTERN LIGHT. D. Pro. and 4 a. G. D'Arcy and C. H. Ross. Eleph. and C., February 15, 1873.

LANVAL. D. 4 a. T. E. Ellis. (Prod. at Acton Bond's invitation performance.) Playhouse, May 14, 1908; Aldwych, May 21, 1908.

LAODAMIA. T. Miss Bernard. 1689.

LAOEUDAIMONOS; OR, A PEOPLE MADE HAPPY. Masque. D.L., May 19, 1789. N.p.

LARA. Cormon. 1864.

LARA. Her M.T., January, 31, 1865.

LARGESSE OF THE SEA, THE. P. 1 a. Ada and D. James. West Hampstead Town H., December 1, 1903.

LARK IN THE TEMPLE. Alexandra, November 5, 1866.

LARKIN'S LOVE LETTERS. F. J. T. Williams. Holborn, October 6, 1866.

LARKS. M.F. Burl. C. 3 a. J. Wilton Jones. F. on a German C. Southport Winter Gardens, February 22, 1886; Grand, March 29, 1886.

LARKS IN LONDON. New ver. of above. M. by J. Greebe. Hammersmith Lyric, July 17, 1899.

LARUM FOR LONDON; OR, THE SIEGE OF ANTWERP, A. Anon. Pr. 1602.

LASANDER AND CALISTA. Sir Humphrey Mildmay. 1634.

LASHED TO THE MAST; OR, ICEBOUND IN THE NORTHERN SEA. D. C. P. Emery. Entered at Stationers' H., April 20, 1893.

LASS OF RICHMOND HILL, THE. C.O. 2 a. Harry Trevor. M. by Burnham Horner. Richmond T.R., April 12, 1893.

LASS THAT LOVED A SAILOR, THE. Oa. Neville Doone. M. by Bond Andrews. Folkestone Pier T., May 22, 1893.

LASS THAT LOVES A SAILOR; OR, THE PERFIDIOUS PIRATE, THE MODEST MAIDEN, AND THE TRUSTY TAR, THE. P. 3 a. J. T. Haines.

LAST ACT, THE. F. 2 a. Pr. 1814. ? N.ac.

LAST ACT, THE. Dr. Monol. Ernest M. Leigh. St. Andrews T.H., November 2, 1899.

LAST APPEAL, THE. Britannia, July 4, 1859.

LAST CALL, THE. D. Pro. and 4 a. H. Charles and H. J. S. Greiff. Adap. fr. the French. Liverpool Shakespeare, April 1, 1895.

LAST CAUSE; OR, THE ADVOCATE, THE. D. 2 a. Liverpool Amphi., March 25, 1868.

LAST CHANCE, THE. D. 5 a. Geo. R. Sims. Adelphi, April 4, 1885.

LAST CHAPTER, THE. P. 4 a. G. H. Broadhurst. Strand, September 4, 1899.

LAST CHAPTER, THE. P. 1 a. Sidney H. Swan. Passmore Edwards Settlement, Tavistock Place, March 4, 1905.

LAST COMMAND, THE. Dramatic epis. Wr. by Fredk. Maxwell. Bedford, March 30, 1908.

LAST DAYS OF POMPEII, THE. Adap. by Fitzball fr. Lord Lytton's novel. Victoria, December, 1834.

LAST DAYS OF POMPEII, THE. D. 3 a. Dr. by J. B. Buckstone. Adelphi, December, 1834.

LAST DAYS OF POMPEII, THE. D. 5 a. John Oxenford. Queen's, January 8, 1872.

LAST DAYS OF POMPEII, THE. See *Nydia*.

LAST EXPRESS, THE. D. 3 a. W. H. Abel. East London, June 19, 1871.

LAST FEAST OF THE FIANNA, THE. A. Milligan. Dublin Gaiety T., February 19, 1900.

LAST GUERRILLA, THE. Melo-d. 2 a. M. by M. Moss. Lyceum, July 6, 1826.

LAST HALT, THE. Sk. W. H. Benson. Poplar Queen's, November 16, 1908; Bow Pal., January 25, 1909.

LAST HEIR, THE. P., in prose, in 4 a. and a tab. Adap. fr. Sir Walter Scott's novel, *The Bride of Lammermoor*, by Stephen Phillips (orig. prod. at the King's, Glasgow, March 23, 1908). Adelphi, October 5, 1908.

LAST HOPE, THE. D. 3 a. W. H. Abel. East London, December 26, 1873; Lyceum, February 16, 1908.

LAST HOPE, THE. Sk. W. Howard. Holloway Empire, February 15, 1909.

LAST HOUR, THE. Dr. Epis. 1 a. Herbert Darnley. Dover T.R., July 30, 1906.

LAST JUDGMENT, THE. Cantata. Spohr, 1825.

LAST LIFE, THE. D. 3 a. T. A. Palmer. Alt. fr. one of Mrs. Hall's stories of Irish life. Greenwich T., February 9, 1874.

LAST LILY, THE. Ca. Clement Scott. Alt. fr. *L'Œillet Blanc*. Kilburn T.H., February 23, 1886.

LAST LINK OF LOVE, THE. D. 2 a. C. H. Hazlewood. Britannia, February 25, 1867.

LAST LOAD, THE. Mus. Sca. Arthur Sturgess. M. by Napoleon Lambelet. Coliseum, December 24, 1904.

LAST MAN, THE. Mus. C. 3 a. Victor Stevens. M. by Geo. Burton. Bradford Prince's, February 26, 1897 (C.P.).

LAST MOMENT, THE. D. 3 a. W. Travers. New East London, October 26, 1867.

LAST MOMENT, THE. D. Portsmouth Prince's, October 11, 1875.

LAST MUSTER, THE. Sk. J. W. Tate and J. P. Harrington. M. by O. Powell. Oxford, July 13, 1908.

LAST NAIL. D. 2 a. G. D. Pitt.

LAST OF HIS RACE, THE. Indian Rom. 4 a. D. McLaren. M. by A. Farewell. (Orig. prod. in America under the title of *The Redskins*). Glasgow R., April 8, 1907; D.L., May 18, 1907.

LAST OF THE BARONS, THE. Burl. L. H. Du Terreaux. Strand, April 18, 1872.

LAST OF THE DANDIES, THE. P. 4 a. Clyde Fitch. H.M., October 24, 1901.

LAST OF THE DE MULLINS, THE. C. 3 a. St. John Hankin. Pres. by the Incorporated Stage Society. Haymarket, December 6, 1908.

LAST OF THE FAMILY, THE. C. Richd. Cumberland. D.L., May 8, 1797. Pr. 1797.

LAST OF THE LATOUCHES. D. 4 a. Mrs. R. Ellis and Chas. Rennell. Croydon T.R., December 3, 1877.

LAST OF THE LEGENDS; OR, THE BARON, THE BRIDE, AND THE BATTERY, THE. Extrav. Gilbert à Beckett. Charing Cross T., September 1, 1873; rev. Terry's, March 9, 1907.

LAST OF THE MOHICANS, THE. See *Uncas*.

LAST OF THE PALADINS, THE. Mus. Extrav. R. Reece. Gallery of Illus., December 23, 1868.

LAST OF THE PIGTAILS, THE. C. 1 a. Chas. Selby. Strand, Septemberr 6, 1858.

LAST OF THE RACE; OR, THE WARRIOR WOMEN, THE. Equestrian Dr. Spec. Geo. Sanger. Astley's, October 21, 1871.

LAST OF THE WELSH BARDS, THE. D. Bridgend, S. Wales, Pavilion T., April 21, 1873.

LAST ON THE PROGRAMME. M. Sk. Nellie Ganthony. Ealing Lyric H., September 24, 1892.

LAST PITCH, THE. Ep. Croydon R., December 10, 1904.

LAST POST, THE. Episode. 1 a. Geo. Unwin. Stafford Lyceum, September 26, 1902; Marlborough, June 12, 1905.

LAST RECRUIT, THE. Mrs. Geo. Corbett. Acton St. Albans Par. H., December 6, 1908 (amat.).

LAST ROSE OF SUMMER, THE. P. 1 a. P. Robinson. Margate R.T., May 11, 1908.

LAST SACRIFICE, THE. D. Great Yarmouth T.R., October 12, 1874.

LAST SERENADE, THE. Episode of love, song, and sword. Pimlico Standard, November 6, 1905.

LAST SHILLING, THE. D. 3 a. J. F. Saville.

LAST SHOT, THE. Sk. 1 a. Ernest Leicester. Surrey, July 21, 1904.

LAST STRAW, THE. Dom. D. 1 a. C. H. Dickinson. St. George's H., March 3, 1888.

LAST STROKE OF MIDNIGHT, THE. D. 4 a. James Guiver. Grecian, March 18, 1879.

LAST TEMPTATION, THE. Sk. Percival T. H. Sykes. Novelty, April 5, 1897.

LAST TRAIN, THE. F.C. 3 a. Fred F. Forshaw. Richmond T.R., May 7, 1898.

LAST WHISTLE, THE. C. Sk. By author of *Tam o' Shanter*, fr. Robert Burns's poem. D.L., May 6, 1835.

LAST WORD, THE. C. 4 a. Augustin Daly. Adap. fr. Ger. of Franz von Schoenthan. Lyceum, September 19, 1891; Daly's, October 13, 1893.

LAST YEAR. J. B. Buckstone. Mentioned by Brewer.

LASTING LOVE. D. 3 a. Edgar Newbound. Britannia, July 15, 1878.

LATCH, THE. P. 1 a. Mrs. W. K. Clifford. Kingsway, May 19, 1908.

LATE LAMENTED, THE. 3 a. Fred Horner. Adap. of *Feu Toupinel*, by Bison. (Paris Vaudeville, February 27, 1890). Court, May 6, 1891

LATE LANCASHIRE WITCHES, THE. See *The Lancashire Witches* (Heywood).

LATE LOVE. C.D. Pro. and 4 a. Leonard S. Outram. Adap. fr. *L'Aventurière* of Emile Augier. Reading T.R., January 7, 1886.

LATE MR. BLACKTHORNE, THE. F.C. 1 a. H. Hunter. Hastings Pier P., July 15, 1903.

LATE MR. CASTELLO, THE. F. 3 a. Sydney Grundy. Comedy, December 28, 1895; rev. Great Queen Street, September 4, 1905.

LATE MURTHER OF THE SONNE UPON THE MOTHER, THE. T. John Webster and Ford. Licensed 1624.

LATE RALPH JOHNSON, THE. C. 3 a. Sutherland Edwards. Adap. fr. *Le Testament de César Girodot* (a stock piece at the Comédie Francaise). Adolphe Bélot. Royalty, February 26, 1872. Scala, February 15, 1908.

LATE REVOLUTION; OR, THE HAPPY CHANGE, THE. T.C. Political. Wr. by "a person of quality." Ac. 1688. Pr. 1690.

LATE SIR BENJAMIN, THE. C. 1 a. Sir Chas. Young. Adap. fr. the French of Edouard Romberg. Torquay Bath Saloon, January 16, 1882.

LATEST EDITION OF BLACK EYED SUSAN; OR, THE LITTLE BILL THAT WAS TAKEN UP, THE. F. C. Burnand and M. Williams. Royalty, November, 1866.

LATEST YARN OF THE CRUSOE CREW, THE. Burl. Ashton People's O.H., July 16, 1883.

LATIN PLAYS.—The greatest dramatic writers and their works are as follows:—

COMEDY.

PLAUTUS T. MACCIUS.—This Roman poet was born at Sarsina, circa B.C. 255. He began to write plays about B.C. 220. Twenty of his comedies are still extant out of the twenty-five pronounced by Lemprière as genuine. One hundred and thirty were current under his name. He died B.C. 184.

AMPHITRUO
ASINARIA
AULULARIA
BACCHIDES (incomplete)
CAPTIVI
CURCULIO
CASINA
CISTELLARIA
EPIDICUS
MENÆCHMI
MOSTELLARIA
MILES GLORIOSUS
MERCATOR
PSEUDOLUS
PŒNULUS
PERSA
RUDENS
STICHUS (incomplete)
TRINUMMUS
TRUCULENTUS

Fragments only of Vidularia are preserved.

TERENCE (Terentius Afer, Publius).—This Roman poet was probably born at Carthage about B.C. 195. Six of his comedies have come down to us, and all are translations or adaptations from the comedies of Menander, whose entire collection of 108 comedies Terence is said to have translated. He died circa B.C. 158.

ANDRIA, B.C. 166.
HECYRA; OR, THE STEPMOTHER, B.C. 165.
HEAUTON - TIMOROUMENOS; OR, SELF-TORMENTOR, B.C. 163.
EUNUCHUS, B.C. 162.
PHORMIO, B.C. 162.
ADELPHI; OR, THE BROTHERS, B.C. 160.

TRAGEDY.

SENECA (Lucius Annæus).—Born at Corduba, in Spain, B.C. 7. His 8 tragedies, together with 2 sc. from *Thebais*, being rhetorical and undramatic in style, are not suited to the stage. He died A.D. 65.

MEDEE.
HIPPOLYTE.
LES TROYENNES.
ŒDIPE.
THYESTE.
HERCULE FURIEUX.
HERCULE S L'ŒTA.
AGAMEMNON.

POEMS AND PLAYS.

OVID (Publius Ovidius Naso).—Born at Sulmo, B.C. 43. He died A.D. 17. His writings comprise:—

AMORES.
DE ARTE AMANDI.
FASTI.
METAMORPHOSES.
MEDEA (lost).
TRISTIA.
RE REMEDIO AMORIS.
IBIS.

See *The Westminster Plays*.

LAUDA ZION. Orat. Mendelssohn. 1809-47.

LAUGH WHEN YOU CAN. C. 5 a. Frederic Reynolds. C.G., December 8, 1798. Pr. 1799. Hay., 1829.

LAUGHABLE LOVER, THE. C. 5 a. Carol O'Caustic. Pr. 1805.

LAUGHING HYENA, THE. F. 1 a. B. Webster. Glasgow Colosseum T. and O.H., November 28, 1867; Hay., .

LAUGHING PHILOSOPHER, A. Play. 1 a. R. C. Henry. Ladbroke H., April 11, 1889.

LAUGHS. Burl. Mus. C. A. R. Marshall and Arthur Alexander. M. by C. E. Howells. Edinburgh T.R., June 30, 1894; Parkhurst, April 8, 1895.

LAUGHTER IN COURT. Piece. 1 a. John Kendall. D.L., May 11, 1909 (mat.).

LAUGHTER LAND. M.C. 3 a. W. T. and W. McClelland. Woolwich R. Artillery, February 9, 1903.

LAUGHTER OF FOOLS, THE. C. 3 a. H. F. Maltby. Carlisle H.M., May 21, 1909.

LAUNDRY BELLE, THE. Burla. F. on Maddison Morton's farce *Betsy Baker*. Lyrics by Sheldon Wilson. M. by W. M. Lutz. Gaiety, December 5, 1883.

LAURA; OR, LOVE'S ENCHANTMENT. C. 3 a. Novelty, June 20, 1888.

LAURA; OR, WHO'S TO HAVE HER? O. 3 a. John Sharpe. Ac. at Sheffield 1791. ? N.p.

LAURENCE'S LOVE SUIT. Ca. 2 a. J. P. Wooler. Strand, January 9, 1865.

LAURETTE'S BRIDAL. Britannia, November 26, 1866.

LAVINIA. Dram. poem. 5 a. Wr. on the model of the ancient Greek tragedy. Circa 1791. ? N.p.

LAW AGAINST LOVERS, THE. T. C. Sir W. Davenant. An amalgamation of Shakespeare's *Measure for Measure* and *Much Ado About Nothing*. Pr. 1673. L.I.F., February 18, 1662.

LAW AND LIONS. F. 2 a. Douglas Jerrold.

LAW AND ORDER. Farc. Duol. Tom Gallon. Palace, January 13, 1908.

LAW AND PHYSIC. Duol. 1 a. W. Best. Terry's, April 20, 1888.

LAW AND THE MAN. D. Arthur J. Charleson. Woolwich Alexandra, July 30, 1900.

LAW CASE, THE. P. Entd. Stationers' Co. November 29, 1653. N.p.

LAW, NOT JUSTICE. D. A. C. Calmour. Surrey, July 27, 1882.

LAW OF JAVA, THE. M.D. Colman.

LAW OF JAVA, THE. O. Sir H. Bishop. 1782-1855.

LAW OF LOMBARDY, THE. T. Robt. Jephson. D.L., February 8, 1779. Pr. 1779.

LAW SUIT. C. Brenan. N.p.

LAW TRICKS; OR, WHO WOULD HAVE THOUGHT IT? C. John Day. Ac. by Children of the Revels. Pr. 1608.

LAW VERSUS LOVE. Ca. 1 a. Geo. Linley. Princess's, December 6, 1862.

LAWLESS WITNESS; OR, THE CONVICT'S VOW, THE. D. Sunderland Lyceum, March 7, 1871.

LAWS OF CANDY, THE. T.C. Beaumont and Fletcher. Pr. 1647.

LAWS OF NATURE, THE. C. Possibly by Lodge and Green. Circa 1660.

LAWYER, THE. C. 2 a. Williamson. Hay., 1783. N.p.

LAWYER'S FEAST, THE. F. Jas. Ralph. Pr. 1744. D.L., December 12, 1743. Fr. Beaumont and Fletcher's *Spanish Curate*.

LAWYER'S FORTUNE; OR, LOVE IN A HOLLOW TREE, THE. C. Wm. Lord Viscount Grimstone. Ac. by a strolling company of comedians at Windsor. Pr. 1705. Republ. by the Duchess of Marlborough 1736.

LAWYER'S LOVE, THE. P. 3 a. F. G. Young.

LAWYERS, THE. D. C. Ludger. Transl. fr. the German of Iffland. Pr. 1799. N.ac.

LAWYERS, THE. C. 3 a. Slingsby Lawrence. Lyceum, May 19, 1853.

LAWYERS' PANIC; OR, WESTMINSTER HALL IN AN UPROAR, THE. Prel. John Dent. C.G., May 7, 1785. Pr. 1785.

LAY OF A LADY, THE. P. 1 a. Kennington Princess of Wales, May 14, 1900.

LAY OF THE BELL, THE. Cantata. Romberg. 1767-1821.

LAY OF THE LAST MINSTREL. See *Epic Poems*.

LAYETTE, LA. French C. 3 a. A. Sylvane. Avenue, July 1, 1904.

LAZARUS RAIS'D FROM THE DEAD, OF. C. Bishop Bale.

LAZY LIFE, A. C. 3 a. Arthur Shirley. New Cross Public H., October 12, 1882; Ramsgate St. James's T., August 6, 1883.

LAZZARONE, IL. Op. bo. Randegger. Lib. by G. Rossi. Trieste, 1854.

LEADER OF MEN, A. C. 3 a. Charles E. D. Ward. Comedy, February 9, 1895.

LEADING LADY, THE. F.C. 3 a. Michael Morton. Gaiety, May 15, 1896.

LEADING STRINGS. C. 3 a. Adolphus C. Troughton. Olympic, October 19, 1857.

LEAF IN THE LIFE OF OUR AMERICAN COUSIN, A. C. Sk. Reading T.R., November 22, 1871.

LEAH. Burl. Edinburgh Southminster T., June 15, 1868.

LEAH. Fr. ver. of Dr. S. H. Mosenthal's *Deborah*. Hamburg T., January 15, 1849. Albert Darmont. Sarah Bernhardt's season. R. Eng. O.H., June 25, 1892.

LEAH: A HEARTY JOKE IN A CAB-AGE. Burl. W. Routledge. Gallery of Illus., January 23, 1869 (amat.).

LEAH HOWARD. Boston, U.S.A., Athenæum, December 9, 1862.

LEAH KLESCHNA. P. 5 a. C. M. S. McLellan. New T., May 2, 1905.

LEAH THE FORSAKEN. P. 5 a. Augustin Daly. Adap. fr. Mosenthal's *Deborah*. Harvard Athenæum, Boston, U.S.A., December 9, 1862; Adelphi, October 1, 1863; Lyceum, May, 1872; Opera Comique, April 27, 1897. See *Deborah, Hagar, The Outcast Jewess.*

LEANDER. Latin P. First ac. at the University of Cambridge, 1598, and again 1602. ? By William Johnson.

LEANDER AND HERO. T. Anon., but prod. by Thomas Horde. In prose. Pr. 1769.

LEANDER AND LEONORA. Ballet dance fr. Padlock Byrne. D.L., February 16, 1814.

LEAP FOR LIFE, THE. Mus. C.D. 4 a. Sutton Vane and Charles Callahan. Hebburn Grand, April 2, 1898 (C.P.); Imperial, June 13, 1898.

LEAP IN THE DARK, A. Dom. D. Buckstone. 1850.

LEAP YEAR. Dom. D. J. B. Buckstone. Hay., January 15, 1850.

LEAP YEAR. Duol. Fredk. Kerr. Ladbroke H., August, 1892; Terry's, November 10, 1893.

LEAP YEAR IN THE WEST. P. Johanna Redmond. Court, July 2, 1908.

LEAP YEAR'S COMEDY, A. J. Redfern Kenyon. Bootle Muncaster T., October 23, 1899.

LEAR. See *King Lear*.

LEAR OF PRIVATE LIFE, THE. D. 3 a. W. T. Moncrieff. F. on Mrs. Opie's story *Father and Daughter*. Victoria.

LEARNED LADIES, THE. C. Ozell Transl. of Molière's *Femmes Scavantes*.

LEARNED LADY, THE. C. 2 a. R. Oliphant. Ac. at Liverpool 1789. N.p.

LEARNED PROFESSOR, THE. Satirical F. H. Farnsworth Jervis. Sheffield Surrey Street H., May 3, 1909.

LEATHERLUNGOS THE GREAT: HOW HE STORM'D, REIGNED, AND MIZZLED. Extrav. Chas. S. Cheltnam. Adelphi, July 1 1872.

LEAVE IT TO ME. F. 1 a. C. H. Hazlewood and Arthur Williams. Surrey, December 26, 1870.

LEAVE IT TO ME. F. Liverpool Rotunda April 23, 1877.

LEAVENWORTH CASE, THE. D. Adap fr. the story of the same name. Halifax T.R., February 9, 1885.

LEAVES OF MEMORY, THE. Sk. Euston, December 14, 1908.

LEAVES OF SHAMROCK. D. 5 a. J. P. Sullivan. Originally prod. in the provinces. Sadler's Wells, June 22, 1891.

LED ASTRAY. D. 6 a. Dion Boucicault. Adap, fr. *La Tentation* of Octave Feuillet Gaiety, July 1, 1874. See *A Dangerous Friend.*

LEEDS MERCHANT, THE. C. Wallis. 1776.

LEFT IN A CAB. F. 1 a. Edwd. Stirling. Surrey, August 11, 1851.

LEFT THE STAGE; OR, GRASSOT TORMENTED BY RAVEL. A "personal experiment." 1 a. Transl. fr. Siraudin for the English stage.

LEGACY, THE. C.O. W. P. Godfrey. Bedford Grammar School, December 18, 1879.

LEGACY, THE. Ca. 1 a. Frank Lindo. Royalty, February 6, 1894; Parkhurst, June 17, 1895.

LEGACY; OR, THE FORTUNE HUNTER, THE. C. Foote. Transl. fr. the French. Pr. 1762.

LEGACY LOVE. Ca. Ernest Cuthbert. Vaudeville, December 7, 1872.

LEGACY OF HONOUR, THE. D. 2 a. Edwd. Stirling. D.L., April 13, 1853.

LEGAL IMPEDIMENT, A. F. 1 a. John Oxenford. Olympic, October 28, 1861.

LEGAL WRECK, A. P. 4 a. Wm. Gillette. Ladbroke H., August 13, 1888 (C.P.).

LEGEND OF FLORENCE, A. P. 5 a. Leigh Hunt. C.G., 1840; Sadler's Wells, 1850.

LEGEND OF MAB'S CROSS, THE. D. Wigan T.R., April 20, 1883.

LEGEND OF MONTROSE. See *Children of Mist.*

LEGEND OF NOTRE DAME, A. D. J. C. Smith. Birmingham T.R., September 25, 1871; Surrey, November 9, 1872.

LEGEND OF ST. CECILIA, THE. Cant. Jules Benedict. Exeter H., March 29, 1867.

LEGEND OF SPRING, A. E. Redwood. W. Hampstead Town H., January 4, 1906 (amat.)

LEGEND OF SPRING; OR, THE VICTORY OF THE SUNBEAM. Crystal Palace, Easter, 1872.

LEGEND OF THE DEVIL'S DYKE, A. D. 4 a. Dion Boucicault.

LEGEND OF THE HEADLESS MAN, THE. Adelphi, November 16, 1857.

LEGEND OF VANDALE, A. Ca. Albert E. Drinkwater. Grand, September 1, 1890.

LEGEND OF WEHRENDORF, A. D. Edgar Newbound. Britannia, December 16, 1878.

LEGERDEMAIN. D. 2 a. J. Oxenford.

LEGETAIRE UNIVERSEL, LE. P. Regnard. Royalty, February 4, 1907.

LEGION OF HONOUR, THE. Op. D. 2 a Alex. Lee. D.L., April 16, 1831.

LEICESTER. O. Auber. 1822.

LEIDA. P. 3 a. Josine Holland. A. Teixeira de Mattos. Transl. fr. the Dutch. Comedy, June 2, 1893.

LEILA. O. F. E. Fesca. 1789-1826.

LEILA. See *Les Pecheurs de Perles.*

LEILA; OU, LES PECHEURS DE PERLES. O. 3 a. Caire and Cormor. M. by Bizet. C.G., April 22, 1887.

LEKINDA; OR, THE SLEEPLESS WOMAN. D. Adelphi, September, 1833.

LELA'S LOVE LETTERS. Ca. John H. Soden and Alfred Ganthony. St. George's H., May 31, 1888.

LELAMINE. S.C.O. 3 a. Edwd. Krusard. M. by Alfred R Moulton. Hastings Gaiety, February 14, 1889.

LELIA. C. Anon. 1590. N.p.

LELIO. D. 3 a. Geo. D'Arcy. Olympic, August 15, 1885.

LEMONADE BOY, THE. P. 1 a. Gladys Unger. Criterion, October 13, 1906; Glasgow Athenæum, January 23, 1908 (amat.).

LENA. D. 4 a. Adap. in French fr. the novel *As in a Looking Glass* by Mdme. Van de Velde and Berton. (Originally prod. at Porte St. Martin T., Paris.) Lyceum (Mme. Sarah Bernhardt's season), July 9, 1889.

LENA AND GERTRUDE. D. 1 a. E. H. Keating. Pub. by S. French, Ltd.

LEND ME FIVE SHILLINGS. F. 1 a. J. Maddison Morton. Hay., 1846.

LENDING A HAND. F. 1 a. Gilbert Arthur à Beckett. Strand, January 22, 1866.

LENORE. O. 3 a. Otto Bach. December 25, 1874.

LEO; OR, THE GYPSY. D. Sheridan Knowles.

LEO THE TERRIBLE. Burl. 1 a. J. Stirling Coyne. Hay., December 27, 1852.

LEOCADEA. Op. D. 3 a. M. by Auber arr. by Livius. D.L., December 17, 1825.

LEOCADIE. O. Auber. Paris, 1824.

LEOLA COLOMBA, THE CORSICAN MAID. D 3 a. R. B. Pearce.

LEOLINE, O. F. von. Flôtow. Princess's, October 16, 1848.

LEOLINE. Ballet Fantastique. 1 a. and 2 tableaux. D.L., August 22, 1853.

LEONA; OR, LOVE AND STRATAGEM. D. 3 a. Oswald Brand and E. W. Linging. Gaiety (at a *matinée*, prod. as *Love and Stratagem*), March 15, 1886; Sadler's Wells, June 20, 1892.

LEONARD; OR, THE SECRET OF TWENTY YEARS. D. 4 a. R. Dodson. Liverpool T.R., August 21, 1876.

LEONIDAS. See *The Patriot*, by Joseph Simpson. 1785.

LEONIE. O. Henri Drayton. M. by J. F. Duggan. D.L., March 14, 1854.

LEONIE, THE SUTLER GIRL. Sadler's Wells, February 9, 1863.

LEONORA. T. (with Eitha and Aidallo). Pr. 1801. No. ac.

LEONORA. O. Mercadante. 1850.

LEONORE. P. 1 a. Horace W. C. Newte. Ladbroke H., May 11, 1892.

LEONORE. C.O. 3 a. Wr. and comp. by John H. E. Ashworth. Folkestone Pleasure Gardens T., April 10, 1894.

LEONTINE; OR, CLORINDE'S REVENGE. D. Bath T.R., November 7, 1870.

LEPRACHAUN; OR, THE LOVERS OF TARA'S VALE. D. John Levey. Liverpool T.R., February 19, 1877.

LESBIA. Classical C. 1 a. Richd. Davey. Lyceum, September 17, 1888.

LESBIA, THE VESTAL VIRGIN. P. Torquay T.R. and O.H., June 13, 1881.

LESSON, A. C. 1 a. F. C. Burnand. Adap. fr. *Lolotte* by Meilhac and Halévy. Hay., November 26, 1881.

LESSON FOR LADIES, A. J. B. Buckstone. Hay.

LESSON FOR LIFE, A. C. Tom Taylor. Hay., January, 1867.

LESSON IN ACTING, A. F. Austin Fryers. Sadler's Wells, June 9, 1883.

LESSON IN ACTING. C. 1 a. Hamilton Aidé. Publ. by S. French, Ltd.

LESSON IN COURTSHIP. C. 1 a. Ina L. Cassilis. Publ. by S. French, Ltd.

LESSON IN HARMONY, A. Ca. 1 a. A. Austin. Garrick, June 16, 1904.

LESSON IN LOVE, A. C. 3 a. Chas Smith Cheltham. St. James's. December 22, 1864.

LESSON IN LOVE, A. Oa. 1 a. P. Felix. M. by F. W. Courtenay. New Cross H., December 3, 1903.

LESSON IN MAGIC, A. Oa. 1 a. T. M. Watson. M. by L. Zavertal. Woolwich R. Artillery T., April 27, 1883.

LESSON IN MANNERS, A. P. 1 a. E. J. Malyon and Chas. James. Portsmouth T.R., October 25, 1897.

LESSON IN PEARLS, A. Ca. 1 a. Mrs. Barry Pain. Bath T.R., September 24, 1906.

LESSON IN SHAKESPEARE, A. P. 1 a. Eric Lewis. Playhouse, November 26, 1907.

LESSON OF LIFE; OR, THE WOODMAN'S DREAM, THE. D. Marylebone. December 5, 1877.

LESSON TO LANDLORDS, A. "Rustic absurdity." 5 a. Strand, July 10, 1888.

LESSONS IN HARMONY. Ca. Miss Ella Dietz. Adap. fr. the French. St. George's T., June 26, 1875.

LESTOCQ; OR, THE FETE AT THE HERMITAGE. Hist. O. 3 a. Geo. Macfarren. Adap. fr. Scribe. M. by Auber. C.G., February 21, 1835.

LET FURNISHED. P. G. S. Tanner. Guildford County H., November 27, 1908 (amat.).

LET NOT YOUR ANGRY PASSIONS RISE. D. 1 a. James Schonberg. Royalty, June 22, 1881.

LETHE. Dr. Satire. David Garrick. D.L., April 15, 1740; Goodman's Fields, 1741. Pr. 1745 under the title of *Lethe; or, Æsop in the Shades*. Rev. and ac. March 27, 1756; again rev. 1777; Edinburgh, 1782.

LETHE REHEARSED. Burl. Anon. Pr. 1749.

LETTER, THE. Ca. W. H. Vernon, junr. Gateshead T.R., May 6, 1891.

LETTER-BOX, THE. Ca. Wm. B. Harrison and Beta Harrison. Steinway H., May 27, 1895.

LETTER-WRITERS; OR, A NEW WAY TO KEEP A WIFE AT HOME, THE. F. 3 a. Henry Fielding. Little T. in Hay., and Pr. 1732.

LETTERS ADDRESSED HERE. F. H. Chance Newton. Shaftesbury, February 14, 1893.

LETTY. D. 4 a. and epil. A. W. Pincro. Duke of York's, October 8, 1903.

LEUCOTHOE. Dr. poem. Isaac Bickerstaff. Pr. 1756. N.ac. Story fr. Ovid's *Metamorphoses*. Pr. 1756. N.ac.

LEVEE, THE. F. John Kelly. Denied a license. Pr. 1741. N.ac.

LEVEE, THE. F. Anon. Pr. 1744. Mentioned in Oulton's list.

LEVELLERS LEVELL'D; OR, THE INDEPENDENTS' CONSPIRACY TO ROOT OUT MONARCHY, THE. Int. Mercurius Pragmaticus. Pr. 1647. (The author was Marchmont Nedham.)

LEWES MAID; OR, A TRIP TO BRIGHTON, THE. M. Ent. Young. Ac. at Lewes 1792. ? By the Mr. Young who wrote *The Haunted Village*.

LEWIS ARUNDEL. D. 4 a. Pub. by S. French, Ltd.

LEWIS XI., KING OF FRANCE, THE HISTORY OF. T.C. Advertised at the end of *Wit and Drollery*. Pr. 1661. ? Never appeared.

LI 'IGGS. Dr. Sk. Geo. S. Tanner. Bayswater Bijou, January 23, 1908.

LIAR, THE. C. 2 a. Samuel Foote. Borrowed from Sir R. Steele's *Lying Lover*, itself borrowed from *The Mistaken Beauty*, f. on *Le Menteur* of Corneille. C.G., January 12, 1762; Edinburgh, 1780; D.L., June 9, 1818, and December 23, 1819. Pr. 1864. Alt. by Ch. Mathews, and rev. at Olympic, March 9, 1867; Royalty, July 9, 1896. See *The Lyar*.

LIARS, THE. C. 4 a. Henry Arthur Jones. Criterion, October 6, 1897; rev. New, June 16, 1904; rev. Criterion, April 13, 1907.

LIBATION BEARERS, THE. See Orestean Trilogy. Coronet, March 4, 1905.

LIBERAL OPINIONS. C. 3a. Thos. Dibdin. C.G., May 12, 1800. See *The School for Prejudice*. N.p.

LIBERALITY AND PRODIGALITY. C. Lodge and Green. (?) 1660.

LIBERATION OF GERMANY, THE. Cant. M. by Winter. D.L., May 13, 1815.

LIBERTINE, THE. T. Thos. Shadwell. Ac. by their Majesties' servants. Pr. 1676. D.L., July 3, 1708. Derived f. *Il Atheisto Fulminato* and Molière's *Le Festin de Pierre*.

LIBERTINE, THE. Pocock. C.G., May 20, 1817.

LIBERTINE, THE. T. Trans. by Ozell.

LIBERTINE, THE. Op. D. F. on the story of Don Juan. Lyceum rev., July 30, 1825.

LIBERTINE, THE; OR, THE HIDDEN TREASURE, THE. C. Foote. Trans fr. the French. Pr. 1762.

LIBERTINE LOVERS, THE. C. Blacket. 1811. Pr.

LIBERTINE'S BET. St. James's, January 23, 1857.

LIBERTINE'S LESSON. D. 2 a. Fitzball. Pub. by J. Dicks.

LIBERTY. D. Pro. and 4 a. C. A. Clarke. Bromley Grand H., August 25, 1890.

LIBERTY; OR, THE DHU COLLEEN OF BALLYFOYLE. D. Henry Richardson. Victoria, September 16, 1876; Eleph. and C., June 14, 1879.

LIBERTY ASSERTED. T. John Dennis. L.I.F., February 24, 1704. Pr. 1704.

LIBERTY CHASTISED; OR, PATRIOTISM IN CHAINS. Tragi-comi-political F. Modernised by "William Tell Truth." Pr. 1768. (?) by Geo. Saville Carey.

LIBERTY HALL; OR, THE TEST OF GOOD FELLOWSHIP. O. 2 a. C. Dibdin. D.L., February 8, 1785. (?) Plot fr. Fielding's *Intriguing Chambermaid*.

LIBERTY HALL. C. 4 a. R. Claude Carton. St. James's, December 3, 1892, and rev. November 7, 1895.

LIBRARIAN, THE. C. 4 a. Miss Dulcie Douglas. A literal transl. of Von Mozer's *Der Bibliothekar*. Limerick Athenæum, May 22, 1885.

LIBUSA. O. Smetana. 1824-1884.

LICK AT THE TOWN, A. Dr. Prel. Henry Woodward. D.L., March 16, 1751. N.p.

LIE OF THE DAY; OR, A PARTY AT HAMPTON COURT, THE. C. John O'Keeffe. C.G., March 19, 1796. N.p. (A reduction of *The Toy* to 3 a.) Rev. D.L., May 19, 1819.

LIEBELI. D. 3 a. A. Schnitzler. Great Queen Street T., January 6, 1903. See *Light o' Love*.

LIEBENVERBOT DAS. O. Wagner. Lib f. on Shakespeare's *Measure for Measure* Magdeburg, 1836.

LIEN OF LIFE, THE. D. 3 a. Lee Wilson Dodd. Court, July 31, 1909.

LIFE. C. Fredk, Reynolds. C.G., November 1, 1800. Pr. 1801.

LIFE. C. J. Brockbank. Cambridge T.R., October 7, 1873.

LIFE. D. 4 a. Herbert Barrs (originally prod. at Swansea in 1894. Stratford T.R., July 22, 1901.

LIFE; ITS MORN AND SUNSET. D. 3 a. C. H. Hazlewood. Britannia, October 2, 1872, and October 1, 1879.

LIFE AND DEATH. D. 5 a. Frank Harvey. Adap. fr. Hector Crémieux and D'Ennery's *Germaine* (Paris Gaîté, April 3, 1858). Grand, August 16, 1886.

LIFE AND DEATH OF CAPTAIN THOMAS STUKELEY, THE. Anon. Pr. 1605.

LIFE AND DEATH OF CHATTERTON, THE. P. 1 a. Geo. Marsh. Liverpool Rotunda, July 31, 1885.

LIFE AND DEATH OF COMMON-SENSE, THE. Alt. fr. Fielding's *Pasquin*. Hay., August 13, 1782. N.p.

LIFE AND DEATH OF JO, THE. D. Edwd. Price. Coventry T.R., May 15, 1876.

LIFE AND DEATH OF MARTYN SWARTE, THE. Ac. at Rose T., June 30, 1597. N.p.

LIFE AND DEATH OF MRS. RUMP. Political T. Pr. 1660.

LIFE AND DEATH OF SIR MARTIN SKINK, etc. Brome. N.p.

LIFE AND HONOUR. Milit. D. 4 a. W. Calvert. Adap. fr. Chas. Gibbons's novel, "For the King." Orig. prod. as *Blanche Farreau* at Liverpool T.R., October 6, 1890. Elephant and Castle, December 18, 1893.

LIFE AND LOVE. Sk. E. Dalvery. Stoke Newington Pal., October 12, 1908.

LIFE AS IT IS. D. 2 a. Blake. Publ. by J. Dicks.

LIFE BEYOND, THE. P. 4 a. H. Montgomery. Leith Gaiety T., May 30, 1904.

LIFE CHASE, A. D. 5 a. John Oxenford and Horace Wigan. Gaiety, October 11, 1869.

LIFE CHASE, A. D. 2 a. J. Courtney. Publ. by S. French, Ltd.

LIFE, DEATH, AND RENOVATION OF TOM THUMB. Burl. 1785. Anon.

LIFE DOWN SOUTH. D. 4 a. R. F. Cantwell. Britannia, June 15, 1874.

LIFE DRAMA, THE. Dr. Pm. A. Smith. 1852.

LIFE FOR A LIFE, A. D. 5 a. W. Beaumont and S. Baring. Manchester Royal Osborne T., July 10, 1899; Islington Grand, June 8, 1903.

LIFE FOR LIFE. D. 4 a. Dr. Westland Marston. Lyceum, March 6, 1869.

LIFE FOR LIFE. Sk. 3 sc. Herbert Cole and T. C. Glenville. Sadler's Wells, May 27, 1901.

LIFE FOR THE CZAR. Russian O. Michele Glinka. (Orig. prod. at St. Petersburg, November 27, 1836.) Manchester Comedy, July 9, 1888; ver. in Italian, C.G., July 12, 1887.

LIFE IN AUSTRALIA. Olympic, February 21, 1853.

LIFE IN NEW YORK. D. In Hebrew. Standard, September 24, 1896.

LIFE IN PARIS. Victoria, 1821.

LIFE IN THE CLOUDS. Extrav. John Brougham. Lyceum, 1840.

LIFE IN THE COAL-PITS. D. 4 a. J. C. Levey. Victoria, February 26, 1867.

LIFE OF A POTTERY LASS, THE. D. Walters. Hanley R. Pottery T., March 9, 1869.

LIFE OF A SHINGLER; OR, A PUDDLER'S REVENGE, THE. D. Hall. Coatbridge Adelphi, December 2, 1870.

LIFE OF A SHOWMAN, THE. D. 4 a. Chas. Darrell and Geo. Testo Sante. West London, June 12, 1905.

LIFE OF A WEAVER, THE. D. C. H. Hazlewood. Britannia.

LIFE OF A WOMAN, THE. D. Liverpool T.R., May 19, 1879. D. 3 a. Haines. Publ. by J. Dicks.

LIFE OF AN ACTOR, THE. F. 2 a. Peake. Adelphi, 1824.

LIFE OF AN ACTRESS, THE. D. 5 a. Dion Boucicault. First ac. in America. Adelphi, March 1, 1862.

LIFE OF CAMBYSES. T. Thos. Preston.

LIFE OF DORA THORNE. D. 4 a. L. M. Parker. Lincoln T.R., November 17, 1905. C.p.

LIFE OF PLEASURE, A. Melo-d. 5 a. H. Pettitt and Sir Aug. Harris. D.L., September 21, 1893.

LIFE OF THE BEE, THE. See *Honey Land*.

LIFE ON THE OCEAN. Nautical D. Barrow T.R., September 12, 1868.

LIFE POLICY, A. P. 4 a. Helen Davis. Adap. fr. the author's novel "For So Little." Terry's, July 20, 1894.

LIFE PRESERVER, A. F. Manchester Queen's, May 22, 1876.

LIFE RACE, A. D. 3 a. Miss Evelyn Alfred. February 19, 1872.

LIFE SIGNAL, THE. D. 2 a. C. H. Hazlewood. Britannia, April 22, 1867.

LIFE THAT KILLS, THE. P. 5 a. Fred Moule. Smethwick T.R., June 21, 1901. Dewsbury, December 16, 1901; Surrey, June 9, 1902.

LIFE WE LIVE, THE. D. 4 a. Fenton Mackay and Louis Denbigh. Princess's, April 16, 1892.

LIFE'S A LOTTERY; OR, JOLLY DICK THE LAMPLIGHTER. Dom. Burla. 3 a. Wm. Leman Rede.

LIFE'S BATTLE. C. D. 4 a. Geo. Comer. Lytham Pavilion, August 3, 1891.

LIFE'S BATTLE: A STORY OF THE RIVER THAMES. D. 5 a. Henry F. Saville. Victoria, August 3, 1878.

LIFE'S BONDAGE, A. D. 4 a. Harry Byrton and Arthur Shirley. Marylebone, May 12, 1891.

LIFE'S DEBT, A. D. 4 a. J. F. Graham. Chester Royalty, November 17, 1887. (C.P.) Burnley Victoria, August 27, 1888.

LIFE'S DEVOTION, A. D. Prol. and 3 a. W. H. Abel. East London, November 2, 1870.

LIFE'S HANDICAP. D. 4 a. W. J. Patmore. Pavilion, September 10, 1900.

LIFE'S HARVEST, A. Melo-d. 3 a. Edwd. A. Shute. Nuneaton Drill H., February 25, 1891 (amat.).

LIFE'S IRONY. Ca. F. C. T. Mann. Woking Public H., April 21, 1904.

LIFE'S MEASURE. Morality P. Nugent Monck. Bayswater Bijou, June 8, 1905.

LIFE'S MISTAKES; OR, THE HOOSE O' M'AULD. D. 4 a. J. C. Edwards. Glasgow Princess's, July 27, 1885.

LIFE'S PARTING WAYS. D. 4 a. Julia Gilbert Gilmer (Miss Julia Gilbert). Parkhurst, September 9, 1893 (C.P.); Hackney Manor Rooms, May 31, 1894.

LIFE'S PERIL, A. D. 3 a. Herbert Stanley. Barnsley, January 19, 1874.

LIFE'S RANSOM, A. D. 3 a. Dr. Westland Marston. Lyceum, February 16, 1857.

LIFE'S REVENGE, A. D. 4 a. Walter Howard. Shaftesbury, June 11, 1897 (c.p.); Manchester Metropole, January 16, 1899; Greenwich, Morton's, June 5, 1899.

LIFE'S REVENGE; OR, TWO LOVES FOR ONE HEART, A. D. 3 a. W. Suter. Grecian, October 18, 1858.

LIFE'S REVERIE. Oa. 1 a. Lyrics by H. Woodrow and C. D. Hickman. M. by Léon Bassett and H. French. Eleph. and C., August 28, 1900.

LIFE'S SARCASM. Duo. Cicely M'Donnell and Russell Vaun. Matinée T., May 6, 1898.

LIFE'S STEPPING-STONES. Melo-d. 4 a. F. E. Archer-Smith. Wolverhampton P.H., April 19, 1909.

LIFE'S STORY, A. D. 4 a. F. Benton. Nottingham Grand, June 12, 1902; Darwen T.R., December 15, 1902; Stratford T.R., February 9, 1903.

LIFE'S SWEETEST SINS. P. 4 a. W. A. Brabner. Eccles Lyceum, January 25, 1904; rev. Stratford R., April 3, 1905.

LIFE'S TRIAL, A. D. 3 a. Bayle Bernard. Hay., March, 1857.

LIFE'S TROUBLES. Effingham, August 13, 1866.

LIFE'S VAGARIES; OR, THE NEGLECTED SON. C. John O'Keefe. C.G., March 19, 1795. Pr. 1795.

LIFE'S VICTORY, A. C.D. 3 a. Loftus Don. Adap. fr. B. L. Farjeon's novel "A Love's Victory." Oxford T.R., July 15, 1885.

LIFEBUOY, THE. D. Hoskins. Swansea T.R., May 12, 1869.

LIFT'EMS, LIMITED. Sk. Chris Davis. Holborn Empire, September 14, 1908.

LIGHT. D. 4 a. Arthur J. Flaxman. Gaiety, November 3, 1877.

LIGHT. Dom. Idyll. 1 a. Lionel Dalton. Bayswater Bijou, April 27, 1893. See *My Darling*.

LIGHT AHEAD. D. 4 a. Herbert Leonard. Surrey, November 23, 1891.

LIGHT AND DARK; OR, THE WRECK OF THE SHIP SILVER STAR. D. Matthew Wardhaugh. Longton Victoria, October 30, 1871; Barnsley Queen's, January 29, 1872.

LIGHT AND SHADE. C. 3 a. F. W. Broughton. Birmingham P.O.W., November 9, 1877; Imperial, October 29, 1879.

LIGHT AND SHADOW. A. R. Slous.

LIGHT AS AIR. Ca. Crewe R. Albion, September 1, 1870.

LIGHT AT LAST. C. D. Oldham T.R., September 7, 1874.

LIGHT AT LAST. C. D. 5 a. W. J. Patmore. Manchester T.R., July 28, 1890.

LIGHT FANTASTIC, THE. F. H. J. Byron. Folly, November 20, 1880.

LIGHT HEART. Jonson.

LIGHT IN THE DARK. D. 4 a. W. Sidney. Greenwich, March 11, 1867.

LIGHT IN THE DARK. D. Manchester Queen's, July 16, 1883.

LIGHT IN THE DARKNESS. M. D. 4 a. W. Watkin Wynne. Birmingham Queen's, June 25, 1902 (C.P.); Hammersmith Lyric, August 10, 1908.

LIGHT IN THE WINDOW, THE. Dr. Episode. Frank Dix. Camberwell Empire, February 11, 1907.

LIGHT O' DAY. C. D. 4 a. Brien M'Cullough. Burnley Gaiety, June 18, 1888; Novelty, August 30, 1890.

LIGHT O' LOVE. D. 3 a. An Eng. transl. of Arthur Schnitzler's *Liebelei* by G. Valentine Williams. H.M., May 14, 1909.

LIGHT OF ASIA, THE. O. De Lara. See *La Luce dell'Asia.*

LIGHT OF HIS EYES, THE. D. 3 a. Henry Bellingham and Wm. Best. Bury O.H., February 22, 1895; Blackpool O.H., November 26, 1897.

LIGHT OF LOVE, THE. D. 3 a. Mrs. H. Young. Effingham, February 25, 1867.

LIGHT OF OTHER DAYS, THE. Dr. Episode. 1 scene. Rose Meller. Middlesex County Asylum T., November 14, 1889.

LIGHT OF PENGARTH, THE. Piece. 1 a. Ina Leon Cassilis. Op. Comique, December 17, 1891.

LIGHT OF THE ISLES, THE. Burl. Oswald Allan. Dublin Queen's, August 21, 1876.

LIGHT OF THE WORLD, THE. Orat. Sir A. Sullivan. Birmingham Festival, 1873.

LIGHT OF THE WORLD, THE. Rom. P. 4 a. May Irene Wright. Darlington Royal, July 1, 1907.

LIGHT THAT FAILED, THE. P. 1 a. C. Thorpe. Adap. fr. Rudyard Kipling's story. Manchester Comedy. Rev. Royalty, April 7, 1898.

LIGHT THAT FAILED, THE. P. Prol. and 3 a. Adap. by "Geo. Fleming" fr. Rudyard Kipling. Lyric, February 7, 1903; New T., April 20, 1903.

LIGHT THAT LIES IN A WOMAN'S EYES, THE. P. E. H. Sothern. Criterion, September 11, 1903 (C.P.).

LIGHTHOUSE, THE. D. 2 a. Wilkie Collins. Olympic, July 25, 1857.

LIGHTHOUSE, THE. D. 3 a. J. C. Levey. East London, April 29, 1871.

LIGHTHOUSE ON THE CRIMSON ROCK, THE. D. Birkenhead T.R., May 14, 1883.

LIGHTHOUSE ROBBERY, THE. D. 4 a. Hammersmith Lyric, December 31, 1906.

LIGHTNING'S FLASH, THE. D. 4 a. Arthur Shirley. Surrey, December 17. 1891; (new ver.) Saltley, August 3, 1903.

LIGHTNING'S FLASH; OR, THE WILD STEED OF THE PRAIRIES, THE. Hippo. Dr. spec. C. H. Hazlewood. Edinburgh Princess's, June 5, 1871.

LIGHTS O' LONDON, THE. D. 5 a. G. R. Sims. Princess's, September 10, 1881; Olympic, February 9, 1891.

LIGHTS O' LONDON, THE. See *Delights o' London.*

LIGHTS OF HOME, THE. D. 5 a. G. R. Sims and Robert Buchanan. Adelphi, July 30, 1892.

LIGHTS OUT. Military Dom. P. 1 a. Charles Clayton. Crowborough Oddfellows' H., July 26, 1905 (C.P.).

LIGHTS OUT. P. 4 a. Fr. the Ger. *Zapfenstreich* of Franz Adam Beyerlein. Waldorf, October 25, 1905; Savoy, January 15, 1906.

LIKE AND UNLIKE. Adelphi, April 14, 1857. See *For Better for Worse.*

LIKE FATHER LIKE SON. F. 1 a. R. J. and G. Raymond. Publ. by J. Dicks.

LIKE FATHER LIKE SON. D. 5 a. J. Eaton and E. E. Norris. Globe, August 20, 1901; Eleph. and C., December 9, 1901.

LIKE MASTER LIKE MAN. C. 2 a. Ac. at D.L. April 12, 1768, and at Smock Alley. Pr. 1770. Fr. Vanbrugh's *Mistake.* ? by Thomas Ryder.

LIKE NO OTHER LOVE. P. 4 a. Mark Melford. Croydon Grand, December 11, 1905.

LIKE QUITS LIKE. P. Chettle and Heywood. Ment. by Henslowe, 1602-3.

LIKE UNTO LIKE. P. Ac. Rose T., 1600.

LIKE WILL TO LIKE, QUOTH THE DEVIL TO THE COLLIER. Int. Ulpian Fulwell. Pr. 1568 (black letter).

LIKENESS OF THE NIGHT, THE. P. 4 a. Mrs. W. K. Clifford. Liverpool Court, October 18, 1900; Fulham Grand, November 12, 1900; St. James's, October 28, 1901.

LIKES O' ME, THE. Epis. Wilfred T. Coleby. Kingsway, April 13, 1908.

LILI. C. 3 a. Hennequin, Millaud, and Blum. Ac. in Fr. Gaiety, June 4, 1883.

LILI; OR, THE SAVOY GIRL. C.O. Arthur Weld and H. B. Smith. Richmond, October 18, 1901.

LILIAN GERVAIS. D. 3 a. Morris Barnett. Olympic, January 17, 1853.

LILIAN, THE SHOW GIRL. D. 2 a. Soane. Publ. by J. Dicks.

LILIES; OR, HEARTS AND ACTRESSES. F.C. 3 a. Harry Paulton. Liverpool P.O.W., November 10, 1884; Gaiety, November 22, 1884.

LILINE AND VALENTIN. Gaiety, September 13, 1875.

LILLIPUT. Dr. Ent. D. Garrick. D.L., December 3, 1756. Pr. 1757. Rev. Hay., 1777, with an additional scene.

LILLIPUT. Dr. Rom. 2 a. F. on Garrick's Lilliput. D.L., Dec. 10, 1817.

LILLY DAWSON; OR, A POOR GIRL'S STORY. Dom. Dr. 3 a. Edward Stirling. Surrey, March 8, 1847.

LILLY'S COURT COMEDIES:—*Alexander and Diogenes, Edimion and the Man in the Moon, Sappho and Phao, Galathea* (played before Q. at Greenwich, January 1, 1592), *Midas, Mother Bombie.* All circa 1591-1620.

LILY. D. Edwd. Darbey. Greenwich, February 4, 1878.

LILY. C.D. 3 a. H. A. Delille. Leicester R.O.H., February 27, 1888.

LILY DALE. Melo-d. J. H. Delafield. Leeds Amphi., April 12, 1869.

LILY OF FRANCE. New York Booth's T., December 16, 1872.

LILY OF KILLARNEY. O. Benedict. Wds. by J. Oxenford. F. on Boucicault's *Colleen Bawn* London, Royal English Opera, C.G., February 2, 1862.

LILY OF LEOVILLE, THE. C.O. 3 a. Alfred Murray and Felix Remo. Lyrics by Clement Scott. M. by Ivan Caryll. Birmingham Grand, May 3, 1886; Comedy, May 10, 1886.

LILY OF ST. LEONARDS. D. 2 a. Pitt. Publ. by J. Dicks.

LILY OF THE DESERT, THE. Rom. D. Stirling, 1859.

LILY OF THE FIELD, THE. P. 1 a. C. Hannan. Ayr T., November 6, 1896 (C.P.).

LILY'S LOVE; OR, WEARY OF WAITING. D. W. H. Abel. Pavilion, August 17, 1872.

LIMBERHAM; OR, THE KIND KEEPER. C. Dryden. Stopped after third performance. Ac. 1678.

LIMBS OF THE LAW. F. Edinburgh T.R., August 18, 1879.

LIMITED. C. 3 a. Robert Blake. Originally prod. at Richmond T.R. as *Skittles, Limited.* Alt. and rev. Hammersmith Lyric, April 18, 1896.

LIMITED LIABILITY. F.C. 3 a. Angelo Thomas Naden. Stratford T.R., May 4, 1888.

LINA. O. Pedrotti (his first O.). Verona, 1840.

LINA. O. Ponchielli. Milan, 1877.

LINA AND GERTRUDE. D. 1 a. Publ. by S. French, Ltd.

LINCO'S TRAVELS. Int. David Garrick. D.L., April, 1767. Pr. 1785.

LINDA DI CHAMOUNI. O. Donizetti. Vienna, 1842; H.M.T., March 25, 1843; D.L., January 12, 1848.

LINDA DI CHAMOUNI; OR, NOT A FORMOSA. Burl. A. Thompson. Gaiety, September 13, 1869.

LINDA DI CHAMOUNI; OR, THE BLIGHTED FLOWER. Burl. Conway Edwardes. Bath T.R., February 20, 1869.

LINDA GREY. D. 4 a. Sir C. L. Young. Margate T.R., June 9, 1885. Princess's, April 8, 1891.

LINDA, THE PEARL OF SAVOY. D. 3 a. Barnet. Publ. by J. Dicks.

LINDAMIRA; OR, TRAGEDY A LA MODE. Burl. Samuel Foote. Pr. 1805. See *Tragedy à la Mode.*

LINDOR AND CLARA; OR, THE BRITISH OFFICER. C. Fennell. Pr. 1791. Ac. at provincial theatres.

LINDOVE'S ABBEY. D. Dundee T.R., March 27, 1877.

LINDSAY'S PLAY. See *Play.* Edinburgh, 1602.

LINE OF FATE, THE. D. 4 a. J. J. Hewson. Macclesfield T.R., March 26, 1894.

LINE OF LIFE; OR, MIND YOUR POINTS. D. W. Sidney and H. Grattan. Glasgow P.O.W., October 28, 1871; Norwich T.R., October 8, 1877

LINEN DRAPER, THE. C. Transl. fr. the French of Mme. Genlis. Pr. 1781.

LINEN DRAPER, THE. F.C. 3 a. J. R. Brown and J. F. Thornthwaite. Comedy, April 17, 1890; Royalty, July 23, 1894.

LINGO IN LOVE. Ballet. Hay., August, 1804.

LINGUA; OR, THE COMBAT OF THE TONGUE AND THE FIVE SENSES FOR SUPERIORITY. C. Anon. Attributed to Anthony Brewer. Pr. 1607.

LINK BY LINK. D. 4 a. F. Hay and F. Fenton. Surrey, October 8, 1870.

LINK IN THE CHAIN, THE. Sk. Cambridge, March 18, 1907.

LINK O' GOLD. D. 3 a. Geo. Capel, Sheffield Alexandra, April 6, 1882.

LINK OF LOVE, A. C. D. 4 a. W. F. Colville. Spennymoor Cambridge T., July 18, 1882.

LINKED BY LOVE. Dom. C. 3 a. P. Meritt. Grecian, July 29, 1872.

LINKMAN; OR, GAIETY MEMORIES, THE. Dia. G. Grossmith, jun. Old Gaiety, February 21, 1903.

LINKS. P. 4 a. Herman Heijermans. Transl. by H. Peacey and W. R. Brandt. Prod. by the Stage Society, Scala, May 31, 1908.

LINNET'S LARK. Ca. Fredk. Hay. Park, September 14, 1878.

LINUS. Amer. Epis. Empress, October 21, 1907.

LION AND THE BEAR, THE. Dr. Epis. Hammersmith Pal., May 6th, 1907.

LION AND THE MOUSE, THE. P. 4 a. Chas. Klein, Duke of York's, May 22, 1906.

LION AND THE UNICORN, THE. Hist. F. 1 act. Laurence Irving and Tom Hesslewood, Bolton Royal, August 28, 1907.

LION AT BAY, A. D. 1 a. Watts Phillips. 1869.

LION HUNTER, THE. C. 3 3. J. T. Grein and Martha Leonard. Terry's, March 10, 1901.

LION LIMB. D. Cecil Pitt. Britannia, September 25, 1867.

LION QUEEN. Victoria, September 6, 1852.

LION SLAYER; OR, OUT FOR A PROWL, THE. F. 1 a. T. H. Williams. Hay., November 22, 1860.

LION TAMER, THE. D. 2 a. Marcus Grey and H. B. Wilson. Wolverhampton Star, July 10, 1902.

LION'S DEN, THE. D. 3 a. Victoria, July 22, 1871.

LION'S HEART, THE. Melo-d. Prol. and 4 a. A. Shirley and B. Landeck. Parkhurst, July 25, 1892; Princess's, October 14, 1895.

LION'S LADY, THE. Burla. 2 a. Publ. by S. French, Ltd.

LION'S LOVE, THE. Grecian, July 16, 1866.

LION'S MOUTH, THE. Op.bo. 3 a. A. Thompson. M. by V. Gabriel. Lady Collier's House, Eaton Place, May 2, 1867.

LION'S TAIL AND THE NAUGHTY BOY WHO WAGGED IT, THE. Burl. R. Reece. Globe, June 16, 1877.

LIONEL AND CLARISSA. C. O. Isaac Bickerstaff. Pr. 1768. Ac. at C.G., February 25, 1768. Alt. and ac. D.L., as *The School for Fathers,* May 4, 1814. M. by Sir J. Stevenson, Horne, and Reeve. Lyceum, August 8, 1818.

LIONESS OF THE NORTH. D. 2 a. Selby. Publ. by J. Dicks.

LISBETH. O. 3 a. Gretry. 1797.

LISBETH. O. Mendelssohn. Paris, 1865.

LISELOTT. C. 4 a. Heinrich Stobitzer, Great Queen Street, Jan. 19, 1906.

LISETTE. Oa. Herr Lauber. Op. C., April 26, 1873.

LISTENERS, THE. Ca. Constance Smedley. Portsmouth T.R., March 17, 1904.

LITA. C. 3 a. Adapt. by A. G. Conway fr. Lord Lorne's novel. New Cross H., January 7, 1888.

LITERARY NEPHEW, THE. F. Harry Seed. Sussex H., Bouverie Street. February 6, 1868 (amat.).

LITERATURE. C. 1 a. A. Schnitzler. Transl. by Edith A. Brown and Mrs. Alix Grein. Prod. by the New Stage Club, Bayswater Bijou, March 11, 1908.

LITIGANTS, THE. C. John Ozell. Transl. fr. the *Plaideurs* of Racine and fr. *The Wasps* of Aristophanes. Pr. 1715.

LITIGIOUS SUITOR DEFEATED; OR, A NEW TRICK TO GET A WIFE, THE. F. Pr. 1741. Inserted in *The Stroller's Packet Broken Open.*

LITTLE ADMIRAL, THE. Pin pro and 3 a. Horace Hodges and T. W. Percyval, Lyric, March, 9, 1907.

LITTLE AMY ROBSART, FROM A COMIC POINT OF VIEW. Burl. Liverpool P.O.W., February 22, 1872.

LITTLE ANN'S BIRTHDAY. F. 1 a. W. E. Suter. Grecian.

LITTLE ASCOT HERO, THE. Sk. Tom Petrie. Sadler's Wells, June 29, 1908.

LITTLE BACK PARLOUR, THE. F. 1 a. E. Stirling. English O.H., August 17, 1839.

LITTLE BARONET, THE. P. 4 a. Maurice H. Hoffmann. Edinburgh Pav., October 14, 1897; Brighton New Palace Pier, December 1, 1902.

LITTLE BEN BOLT; OR, THE MERITORIOUS MAIDEN AND THE MILL-ICIOUS MILLER. Burl. Edwin Keene. Gravesend Theatre Subscription Ground, June 24, 1879; Colchester T.R., August 2, 1880.

LITTLE BILLIE CARLYLE; OR, THE BELL AND THE HARE. Burl. of *East Lynne*. W. J. Harbon. Wolverhampton P.O.W., April 18, 1881.

LITTLE BLACK SAMBO AND LITTLE WHITE BARBARA. Children's Ent. 2 a. Rutland Barrington. M. by Wilfred Bendall and F. Rosse. Garrick, December 21, 1904.

LITTLE BLUE BOTTLE, THE. F. G. C. Baddeley. Bijou, Archer Street, W., December 15, 1873.

LITTLE BO-PEEP Hay., December 26, 1854.

LITTLE BOY BLUE. Burl. J. F. Watts. Shoreham Swiss Gardens, May 17, 1875.

LITTLE BREADWINNER, THE. D. 4 a. J. A. Campbell. Birmingham Alexandra, December 11, 1905; Standard, March 19, 1906.

LITTLE BROWN BRANCH, A. C. 3 a. B. Thomas. Court, December 14, 1904.

LITTLE CAPTIVE, THE. Div. D.L., December 18, 1828.

LITTLE CARMEN. Burl. Alfred Murray. Globe, February 7, 1884.

LITTLE CHANG. Op. bo. F. C. Burnand. Newcastle Tyne T., May 6, 1872.

LITTLE CHANGE, A. Ca. 1 scene. Sydney Grundy. Hay., July 13, 1872.

LITTLE CHAP—CURLY AND BROWN, A. Dr. Incident. 1 a. W. J. Rix and F. J. Gillett. Adap. fr. a poem by H. L. Childe-Pemberton. Kilburn Town H., January 29, 1895.

LITTLE CHARWOMAN, THE. Sk. J. L. Shine. M. by H. Trotére. Walham Green Granville, November 16, 1903.

LITTLE CHERUB, THE (afterwards known as A GIRL ON THE STAGE). Mp. 3 a. Owen Hall; lyrics, Adrian Ross. M. Ivan Caryll, Prince of Wales, January 13, 1906.

LITTLE CHRISTIANS, THE. D. Pro. and 3 a. W. C. Bellows. Eleph. and C., March 11, 1903 (C.P.).

LITTLE CHRISTOPHER COLUMBUS. Burl. 3 a G. R. Sims and C. Raleigh. M. by Ivan Caryll. Lyric, October 10, 1893.

LITTLE CINDERELLA. Burl. J. W. Jones. Newcastle Tyne T., June 25, 1887.

LITTLE COQUETTE, A. Burl. 3 a. Lib. and lyrics by J. L. Barry. M. comp. and arr. by Arthur Langstaffe. Widnes Alexandra T., July 31, 1899.

LITTLE CORPORAL, THE. Dr. Epis. A. Shirley. Richmond T.R., May 4, 1901.

LITTLE CORPORAL; OR, THE SCHOOL OF BRIENNE, THE. Hist. D. D.L., May 30, 1831.

LITTLE COUNTESS, THE. P. 4 a. G. P. Bancroft. Avenue, May 2, 1903.

LITTLE COWHERD OF SLAINGE, THE. P. Leosamb MacCathmhavil. Belfast Clarence Place H., May 4, 1905.

LITTLE CRICKET. D. 3 a. James Mortimer. Brighton T.R., March 11, 1878; Duke's, June 8, 1878.

LITTLE CRIPPLE, THE. D. 4a. Beverley George. Runcorn R., July 22, 1905 (C.P.).

LITTLE CULPRIT, THE P. 1 a. Russell Vaun and Alban Atwood. Folkestone Pleasure Gardens T., November 19, 1897; St. Geo. H., May 6, 1898; rev. Broadway, May 10, 1905.

LITTLE DAISY. C. D. 1 a. T. J. Williams. Hay., November 9, 1863; H.M.T., December 22, 1865.

LITTLE DEVIL CHOOSES, THE. Kate Goddard and F. A. Stanley. Wembley St. John's H. December 2, 1908.

LITTLE DINNER, A. M. Sk. Corney Grain. St. Geo. H., April 14, 1884.

LITTLE DR. FAUST. Burl. H. J. Byron. Gaiety, October 13, 1877.

LITTLE DON CÆSAR DE BAZAN. Extrav. H. J. Byron. Gaiety, August 26, 1876.

LITTLE DON GIOVANNI; OR, LEPORELLO AND THE STONE STATUE. Op. Extrav. H. J. Byron. P.O.W., December 26, 1865.

LITTLE DON QUIXOTE. Burl. Cheltenham T.R., April 9, 1883.

LITTLE DOROTHY. City of London, June 8, 1868.

LITTLE DUCHESS, THE. C. Coster O. 2 a. F. W. Marshall and F. Mouillot. M. by Congden. Stockton-on-Tees T.R., September 9, 1897; Stratford Borough T., August 8, 1898.

LITTLE DUKE, THE. O. 3 a. Meilhac, Halévy, and Lecocq. Engl. adap. by Saville Rowe and Bolton Rowe. Philharmonic, April 27, 1878.

LITTLE 18-CARAT; OR, A ROUGH NUGGET. M. C. Augustin Dawtrey. M. by R. W. Manning. Sunderland T.R., November 16, 1885.

LITTLE EMILY'S TRIALS. D. E. H. Brooke. Sadler's Wells, March 4, 1871.

LITTLE EM'LY. D. 4 a. Andrew Halliday. Fr. C. Dickens's "David Copperfield." Olympic, October 9, 1869; Adelphi, 1875.

LITTLE EMPTY STOCKING. A.p. 5 scenes. Adapted by Maud Lilly from a story by John Strange Winter, Coronet, September 20, 1906 (C.P.).

LITTLE EYOLF. P. 3 a. Henrik Ibsen. Transl. by Wm. Archer. Avenue, November 23, 1896.

LITTLE FAMILY, THE. See *The Little Gamester*.

LITTLE FATHER OF THE WILDERNESS. C. 1 a. Lloyd Osbourne and Austin Strong. Comedy, November 21, 1905.

LITTLE FIBS. Ca. Miss E. Berrie. Charing Cross. October 11, 1869.

LITTLE FOLKS' WORK. Fa. 1. F. D. Adams. Publ. by S. French, Ltd.

LITTLE FREEHOLDER, THE. Dr. Ent. by Lord Hailes. Pr. 1790. N.ac.

LITTLE FRENCH LAWYER, THE. C. Beaumont and Fletcher. Plot fr. *Gusman de Alfarache; or, The Spanish Rogue*. Pr. 1647. D.L., June 30, 1720.

LITTLE FRENCH LAWYER, THE. Arr. as a F. and ac. at D.L., October 7, 1749. N.p.

LITTLE FRENCH LAWYER, THE. C. 2 a., fr. Beaumont and Fletcher. ? by Mrs. Booth. Ac. at C.G., April 27, 1778. N.p.

LITTLE FRENCH MILLINER. F. 3 a. Adap. fr. Maurice Hennequin and Albin Valabrique. Avenue, April 8, 1902,

LITTLE GAMBLERS, THE. D. Berquin. 1793.

LITTLE GAMESTER, THE. One of two short dramas introduced in *The Little Family*. Charlotte Sanders. Pr. 1797.

LITTLE GENIUS, THE. C. O. 3 a. Sir Aug. Harris and A. Sturgess. M. by Eugen von Taund, J. M. Glover, and Landon Ronald. Shaftesbury, July 9, 1896.

LITTLE GERTY. D. 4 a. Lander. Publ. by J. Dicks.

LITTLE GIL BLAS AND HOW HE PLAYED THE SPANISH D(J)EUCE. Extrav. H. B. Farnie. Princess's, December 24, 1870.

LITTLE GIPSY, THE. Ca. M. Lemon. Olympic, April 12, 1841.

LITTLE GIRL WHO TELLS FIBS. C. 1 a. E. H. Keating. Publ. by S. French, Ltd.

LITTLE GISELLE. Burl. 1 a. H. J. Byron. Publ. by S. French, Ltd.

LITTLE GLEANER. D. Berquin. 1793.

LITTLE GOODY TWO SHOES. Rustic Burl. M. by R. Hughes. D.L., February 27, 1829.

LITTLE GOODY TWO SHOES. Fairy P. 5 scenes. Dr. by Rosina Filippi. Court, December 26, 1888.

LITTLE HANS ANDERSON. Fairy p. 2 a and 7 scenes. Hood. M. by W. Slaughter. Adelphi, December 23, 1903.

LITTLE HERMIT; OR, THE RURAL ADVENTURE, THE. D. 3 a. Mrs. Trimmer. Pr. 1788.

LITTLE HEROES. D. 4 a. C. H. Longden and Eric Hudson. Coluseum, Oldham, March 29, 1900; Hammersmith Lyric, September 24, 1900.

LITTLE HEROINE, A. American M. D. 4 a. J. K. Royden. Sutton-in-Ashfield Town H., October 30, 1902.

LITTLE HOBBY, A. Ca. 1 a. C. Agnew. Elephant and Castle, November 2, 1903.

LITTLE HUNCHBACK, THE. C. Ballet. 1 a. M. by Eliason. D. L., March 7, 1839.

LITTLE HUNCHBACK; OR, A FROLIC IN BAGDAD, THE. F. John O'Keefe. C.G., 14, 14, 1789. Pr. 1788. Fr. The Arabian Nights' Entertainments.

LITTLE INNOCENTS, THE. C.O. 2 a. H. Stanger. Addl. numbers by E. C. Thurston and Paul Powell. M. by Louis Varney. Adap. fr. *Les Petites Brébis*, by MM. Armand Livrat and Louis Varney; Paris Théâtre, Cluny, June 5, 1895; Grand, October 28, 1901.

LITTLE INTERVENTION, A. C. Sk. Gladys Ffolliott. Royal M.H., November 23, 1901.

LITTLE INTRUDER, THE. Farc. C. 3 a. J. H. Darnley and A. H. Bruce. Kingston-on-Thames County T., December 10, 1900.

LITTLE JACK CARPENTER. Burl. Extrav. Liverpool T.R., May 15, 1875.

LITTLE JACK HORNER. D.L. December, 1857.

LITTLE JACK SHEPPARD. Burl. 3 a. H. P. Stephens and W. Yardley. M. by Meyer Lutz and others. Gaiety, December 26, 1886, and August 11, 1894.

LITTLE JAPANESE GIRL, THE. P. 1 a. Adap. from Japanese by Loie Fuller, incidental music by John Crook. Duke of York's, August 26, 1907.

LITTLE JESSIE. Duol. "Frederic Darâle." Steinway H., July 2, 1891.

LITTLE JIM. Melo-d. 4 a. A. Shirley and B. Landeck, fr. the French. Dalston T., April 28, 1902; Bolton R., July 26, 1902.

LITTLE JOCKEY, THE. F. 2 a. Dimond. Olympic, January 3, 1831.

LITTLE JOHN AND THE GIANTS. Henry Brooke. 1778. See *Jack the Giant-Queller*.

LITTLE KING PIPPIN. D.L., December 26, 1865.

LITTLE LADY LOO. M.C. 3 a. W. H. Dearlove. M. by Sidney Shaw. Harrogate Grand Opera H., May 10, 1900; (rev.) Plymouth Grand, March 7, 1904.

LITTLE LALLA ROOKH. Burl. Extrav. J. T. Denny. Hastings Gaiety T., August 31, 1885; Grand, September 14, 1885.

LITTLE LOHENGRIN; OR, THE LOVER AND THE BIRD. Burl. of Wagner's O. Fredk. Bowyer. Holborn T. (The International), August 16, 1884.

LITTLE LORD FAUNTLEROY. C. 3 a. E. V. Seebohm. Adap. fr. Mrs. Frances Hodgson Burnett's story. P.O.W., February 23, 1888; Terry's, May 14, 1888; Wyndham's, December 26, 1901; Brixton, January 4, 1904; (rev.) Court, December 26, 1908.

LITTLE LORD FAUNTLEROY. See *The Real Little Lord Fauntleroy*.

LITTLE LOST CHILD, THE. Burl. H. Hume. Publ. by S. French, Ltd.

LITTLE MADCAP, A. C.D. 1 a. C. S. Cheltnam. Sadler's Wells, March 2, 1846.

LITTLE MARCHIONESS, THE. Sk. adap. by B. Soane Roby fr. Dickens' "Old Curiosity Shop." Liverpool Olympia, October 2, 1905; Shepherd's Bush Empire, November 6, 1905.

LITTLE MARY. "An uncomfortable P." Prol. 2 a. J. M. Barrie. Wyndham's, September 24, 1903.

LITTLE MICHUS, THE. M. P. 3 a. A. Vanloo and G. Duval. M. by André Messager. Adap. for Engl. stage by Henry Hamilton. Lyrics by P. Greenbank. Daly's, April 29, 1905.

LITTLE MINISTER, THE. P. 4 a. J. M. Barrie. F. on his novel. Hay., November 6, 1897.

LITTLE MISS CUTE. C. 4 a. C. T. Vincent. Arr. for Engl. stage by E. B. Norman. Royalty, September 14, 1894.

LITTLE MISS MUFFET. C. 3 a. James Albery. Adap. fr. *La Femme à Papa* of A. Hennequin. Crystal Pal., December 24 1866; Brighton T.R. (called *The Mulberry Bush*), June 19, 1882; Criterion, September 2, 1882.

LITTLE MISS MUFFET. C. 1 a. Mrs. Lancaster Wallis. Publ. by S. French, Ltd.

LITTLE MISS NOBODY. M. C. 2 a. H. Graham. M. by A. E. Godfrey, with additional numbers by Landon Ronald. Cheltenham O.H., March 5, 1898; Lyric, September 14, 1898.

LITTLE MISTER FAUST. Burl. O. 2 a. A Leslie. M. by A. Leslie and F. Foster. Parkhurst, August 18, 1894 (C.P.).

LITTLE MORE, THE. C. 3 a. H. C. M. Hardinge. Court, March 20, 1905.

LITTLE MOTHER. C. 2 a. J. Maddison Morton. Royalty, April 21, 1870.

LITTLE MOTHER. P. 3 a. Haidée Wright and F. Wright, jun. Brixton, April 3, 1902.

LITTLE MOTHER, THE. D. 4 a. Gordon Holmes, Shakespeare, S.W., July 15, 1907.

LITTLE NEEDLEWOMAN. D. Berquin. 1798.

LITTLE NELL. P. 4 a. D. James. Fr. Dickens's "Old Curiosity Shop." St. Leonards Pier Pavilion, January 20, 1902.

LITTLE NELL. P. 4 a. O. Brand. Fr. Dickens. Grand, February 23, 1903.

LITTLE NELLY. D. 4 a. Murray Wood. Surrey, November 23, 1872.

LITTLE NOBODY. C. 1 a. Mary Righton. Vaudeville, July 24, 1890.

LITTLE NUT TREE. Fairy P. Annie Dymond and Blanche Penley. Playhouse, April 9, 1908. Publ. by S. French, Ltd.

LITTLE OLD MAN, THE. F. P. 3 a. C. Windermere. Brighton Eden, August 6, 1901.

LITTLE ONE, THE. D. 1 a. Arthur Ayers. Vaudeville, January 22, 1885.

LITTLE ORPHAN OF THE HOUSE OF CHAO, THE. Chinese T. Transl. fr. French ver. of P. Du Halde's *Description de l'Empire de la Chine*. By Dr. Percy. Pr. 1762.

LITTLE OUTCAST: A CHILD'S STORY, A. D. 4 a. C. A. Clarke and H. R. Silva. Grand, July 15, 1901.

LITTLE PAUL. D. W. Stephens. Rochester Lyceum, March 6, 1871.

LITTLE PEACEMAKER, THE. Sk. Ivan P. Gore and Ronald Bayne. Bedford, November 2, 1908.

LITTLE PEGGY'S LOVE. Scotch Ball. Sig. Rossi. D.L., 1796.

LITTLE PEST, THE. F. H. Richardson. Halifax T.R., October 11, 1875.

LITTLE PIECE OF CAKE, A. Max Rae and Leo Diensis. M. by Louis Hillier. Ealing Hipp., July 19, 1907.

LITTLE PIGS, THE. C. Sketch. D.L., June 4, 1830.

LITTLE PILGRIM, THE. 2 a. W. G. Wills. Ver. of Ouida's novel, "Two Little Wooden Shoes." Criterion, July 3, 1886.

LITTLE POSTMISTRESS, THE. C. 3 a. C. Gregory and Wilson Fisher. Adap. fr. *La Petite Fonctionnaire* of Alfred Capus. Terry's, December 31, 1902.

LITTLE PRINCESS, A. *A Little Un-Fairy Princess* renamed on transference fr. Shaftesbury to Terry's, January 19, 1903.

LITTLE RAGAMUFFIN; OR, THE WORLD'S WAIF, THE. D. 3 a. Pavilion, June 27, 1868.

LITTLE RAY OF SUNSHINE, A. C. 3 a. Mark Ambient and W. Heriot. Yeovil Assembly R., May 3, 1898; Royalty, December 31, 1898; Great Queen Street T., May 24, 1900.

LITTLE REBEL, THE. F. 1 a. J. Stirling Coyne. Olympic, April 1, 1861. Sheffield Alexandra, March 17, 1869.

LITTLE RED CROSS, THE. D. 3 a. Jas. Gower. Wigan Alhambra, July 16, 1885.

LITTLE RED RIDING HOOD. Fa. 1. E. H. Keating. Publ. by S. French, Ltd.

LITTLE RED RIDING HOOD; OR, THE DEY AND THE NIGHT. Burl. Extrav. 2 a. V. Mathews and A. Manley. Bedford Park Club, January 8, 1901.

LITTLE RED RIDING HOOD AND THE FAIRIES OF THE ROSE, SHAMROCK, AND THISTLE. Burl. Extrav. 1 a. L. Buckingham. Lyceum, December 26, 1861.

LITTLE ROBIN HOOD; OR, QUITE A NEW BEAU! Burl. 3 a. R. Reece. Royalty, April 19, 1871; Gaiety, September 15, 1882.

LITTLE ROBINSON CRUSOE. Burl. David James, jun. Oxford T.R., April 13, 1885.

LITTLE SAVAGE, THE. F. 1 a. J. M. Morton. Strand, November, 1858.

LITTLE SENTINEL, THE. Ca. 1 a. T. J. Williams. St. James's, May 4, 1863.

LITTLE SINS AND PRETTY SINNERS. Int. 1 a. C. Selby. Strand, June 4, 1838.

LITTLE SNOW WHITE. Burl. Extrav. C. Millward. Adelphi, December 26, 1871.

LITTLE SQUIRE, THE. C. 3 a. Wm. Greet and H. Sedger. Adap. fr. a novel by Mrs. De La Pasture. Lyric, April 5, 1894.

LITTLE STOWAWAY, THE. D. C. P. Emery. Ent. at Stationers' H., June 1, 1894.

LITTLE STOWAWAY, THE. Sk. 2 sc. Fred Bowyer. Canterbury, March 27, 1905; New Cross Empire, February 25, 1907.

LITTLE STRANGER, THE. C. 3 a. Michael Morton. Middlesbrough Grand, October 9, 1905, Criterion, February 14, 1906.

LITTLE SUNBEAM. C.D. Mrs. Henry Wylde. Lyric, June 30, 1892.

LITTLE SUNSHINE. Play. 5 a. Bartley Campbell. Rhode Island O.H., November 21, 1873.

LITTLE SUPPER, A. F. Harold Ellis. Globe, December 6, 1900.

LITTLE SURPRISE, A. Playlet. Rehearsal May 30, 1909.

LITTLE THIEF, THE. Occurs in Bentley's Catalogue of Plays. Possibly only Fletcher's *Night Walker; or, Little Thief*. Occurs in a list of plays ac. at the King's Arms, Norwich, in 1662.

LITTLE TIFF, A. D. Duo. Victoria St. Women's Institute, December 21, 1904.

LITTLE TODDLEKINS. C.D. 1 a. C. Matthews. Lyceum, December 15, 1852; D.L., December 26, 1855.

LITTLE TOM BOWLING. M. Nautical C. 3 a. Fisher Simpson. M. by Herbert Simpson. Gainsborough R. Albert T., August 5, 1889.

LITTLE TOM TUCKER. Elephant and Castle, December 23, 1876.

LITTLE TOM TUG; OR, THE FRESH WATERMAN. Extrav. F. C. Burnand. Op. Comique, November 12, 1873.

LITTLE TREASURE, THE. C. 2 a. A. Harris. Hay., October 11, 1855.

LITTLE TYRANT. Children's P. S. J. Adair FitzGerald. Publ. by S. French, Ltd.

LITTLE TYRANT. Sk. Middlesex, June 17, 1907.

LITTLE UN-FAIRY PRINCESS, A. P. 3 a. Mrs. Frances Hodgson Burnett. Avenue, September 18, 1902; Shaftesbury, December 20, 1902. See *A Little Princess*.

LITTLE VAGRANT, A. D. 4 a. F. Moule and E. W. Avery. Cleethorpes Alexandra, July 8, 1897; Boscombe Grand, March 19, 1900; Greenwich Morton's, July 16, 1900.

LITTLE VISCOUNT, THE. C. 2 a. Hermann Vezin. Adap. fr. Bayard's *Le Vicomte de Letorrières*. Gaiety, August 2, 1884.

LITTLE VIXEN, THE. Ca. 1 a. G. F. Neville. Olympic, February 2, 1878.

LITTLE VIXEN, THE. F.C. G. Capel. Huddersfield T.R., July 21, 1884.

LITTLE WIDOW, THE. F.C. 3 a. Fred Jarman. Liverpool T.R., February 2, 1891. Hammersmith Lyric O.H., April 20, 1891; rev. Royalty, 1894.

LITTLE WITNESS. D. 4 a. J. Bainbridge. Ton-y-pandy T.R., October 2, 1902.

LITTLE WONDER, THE. Mus. Absurdity. 1 a. J. W. Jones. Gravesend T.R., March 14, 1874.

LITTLEST GIRL, THE. P. 1 a. Dr. by R. Hilliard fr. R. H. Davis's story "Her First Appearance." Court, July 15, 1896.

LIVE LUMBER; OR, UNBURIED DEAD. Prel. Anon. Alt. 1796. N.p. See Bickerstaffe's *Unburied Dead.*

LIVELY HAL. C.O. 3 a. Ada G. Yabsley. M. by Mrs. Brooks and Mr. Treleavan. Plympton District H., April 11, 1893.

LIVELY HONEYMOON, A. Ca. Alton Ignis (E. Stuart-Smith). Merthyr Drill H., July 14, 1897.

LIVERPOOL PRIZE, THE. F. F. Pillon. C.G. Pr. 1779.

LIVERY RAKE AND COUNTRY LASS, THE. Ballad O. Edward Philips. Hay., October 15, 1733; D.L., 1734. Pr. 1733.

LIVING AT EASE. C. 3 a. A. Sketchley. Strand, October 5, 1870.

LIVING CLUE, A. D. Pro. and 4 a. A. Harvey and H. Hoken. Eleph. and C., March 9, 1903.

LIVING FLOWERS. B.O. 1 a. Simon.

LIVING IN A FLAT. Ca. Albert Ward. W. Hartlepool G.T., March 11, 1909 (C.P.).

LIVING LIE; OR, SOWING AND REAPING, A. D. 5 a. Miss Fanny Dickens. Blackburn Royalty T., June 18, 1883.

LIVING MODEL OF ANTIQUES, THE. A series of compositions of ancient sculpture represented by Mr. Ducrow. D.L., October 5, 1829.

LIVING MODELS. M. Eccentric C. 1 a. G. Walton. Maidenhead T.R., May 5, 1898.

LIVING OR DEAD. P. 5 a. W. Stephens. Adap. fr. a story by Hugh Conway. Sadler's Wells, October 9, 1886.

LIVING SKELETON, THE. F. D. Jerrold. Victoria.

LIVING STATUES. F. 1 a. Grattan. Publ. by J. Dicks.

LIVING TOO FAST; OR, A TWELVEMONTH'S HONEYMOON. Ca. 1 a. A. C. Troughton. Princess's, October 9, 1854.

'LIZ. Playlet. May Creagh-Henry. Queen's Gate H., November 17, 1908 (mat.).

LIZ; OR, THAT LASS O' LOWRIE'S. D. in Pro. and 3 a. A. Matthison and J. Hatton. F. on Mrs. Burnet's "That Lass o' Lowrie's." Liverpool R. Amphi., July 9, 1877. Op. Comique, September 1, 1877.

LIZ'S BABY. P. 1 a. R. Pryce and F. Fenn. Camberwell Metropole, April 22, 1901.

LIZA'S BILL. Monol. Laura Leycester. Metropolitan, September 20, 1909.

LIZER'S NEW LODGER. F. Ellis Kingsley. Brompton Hospital, March 9, 1897.

LIZZIE LEIGH; OR, THE MURDER NEAR THE OLD MILL. Dom. D. 3 a. W. R. Waldron. September 14, 1863. See *The Long Strike*. City of London, August 27, 1866.

LIZZIE LYLE; OR, THE FLOWER GIRL'S TEMPTATION. D. C. H. Hazlewood. Marylebone, February 9, 1874.

LIZZIE LYLE; OR, THE FLOWER MAKERS OF FINSBURY. Dom. D. 3 a. C. H. Hazlewood. Grecian, October 7, 1869.

LLEWELLYN. Melo-d. Surrey.

LLEWELLYNE IN LLYW OLAF. Welsh hist. p. B. G. Evans. M. by J. Parry and A. Ddu. Llandudno Prince's, May 28, 1903.

LLEWELYN, THE LAST KING OF WALES. D. Carmarthen Warren's T., November 25, 1872.

LO ZINGARO. D. H. R. Addison. Adelphi.

LO ZINGARO. Melo-d. Opera. M. by A. Lee. Lyceum (rev.), October 7, 1834.

LOADSTONE, THE. D. 4 a. T. E. Pemberton and W. H. Vernon. Lyceum, April 7, 1888.

LOAN OF A LOVER, THE. Vaudeville. J. R. Planché. Olympic, September 29, 1834.

LOAN OF A WIFE, THE. F. 1 a. A. Wigan. Alt. fr. the French. Lyceum, July 7, 1846.

LOBGESANG. Hymn of Praise. Symphonia Cant. Mendelssohn. Leipsic, St. Thomas's Church, 1840.

LOCAL AMATEURS, THE. George Dance's M.C. Sk. Richmond Hippodrome, August 24, 1908.

LOCAL VETO VILLA. Operatic C. 3 a. H. D. Stuckey. Weston-super-Mare Assembly R., October 30, 1895.

LOCANDIERA, LA. C. Goldoni. (Venice, 1741.) Lyric, May 30, 1893 (Eleonora Duse season).

LOCHINVAR. D. 2 a. W. T. Moncrieff. Publ. by S. French, Ltd.

LOCK AND KEY. M. Ent. 2 a. Prince Hoare. Hay., 1791; Pr. 1796; D.L., July 8, 1814; Lyceum, August 15, 1818, and August 23, 1826.

LOCK OUT, THE. D. Glasgow New Adelphi, July 6, 1874.

LOCK-KEEPER'S DAUGHTER, THE. D. 1 a. Geo. Corner. Stratford T.R., September 4, 1886.

LOCKED IN. F. J. P. Wooler. P.O.W., September 17, 1870.

LOCKED IN. M. C. Walter Frith. Savoy, May 28, 1889.

LOCKED OUT. Comic Scene. Howard Paul. D.L., March 22, 1855; Hay., July 12, 1875.

LOCKSMITH. Charade. Stanley Rogers. Publ. by S. French, Ltd.

LOCKSMITH. Charade. 1 a. Romona. Publ. by J. Dicks.

LOCOMOTION. F. 1 a. Bernard. Publ. by J. Dicks.

LOCRINE. Publ. anonymously 1595. ? by Marlowe. "Corrected by W. S." and by some ascribed to Shakespeare; but this is improbable.

LOCRINE. T. 5 a. A. C. Swinburne. (Elizabethan Stage Soc.) St. George's H., March 20, 1899.

LODGERS, THE. F. 3 a. B. Thomas and Maurice de Verney. Adap. fr. *Ma Nièce et mon ours*. Globe, January 18, 1887.

LODGERS AND DODGERS. F. 1 a. Fredk. Hay. Strand, May 13, 1871.

LODGINGS AT CLEETHORPES. F. Grimsby T.R., August 30, 1878.

LODGINGS FOR SINGLE GENTLEMEN. F. 1 a. John Poole. Hay., June 15, 1829.

LODGINGS TO LET. O. 1 a. Ross and Kron. Publ. by S. French, Ltd.

LODOISKA. O. Cherubini. Paris, 1791.

LODOISKA. M. Rom. 3 a. J. P. Kemble. M. by Storace. Principally fr. the French. D.L., June 9, 1794; D.L., 1824. Pr. 1794.

LODOISKA. Hist. Rom. John Baylis. Transl. fr. the French. Pr. 1804. N.ac.

LODOWICK SFORZA, DUKE OF MILAN. T. Rev. Robert Gomersall. Pr. 1632. F. on story in Guicciardini, Philip de Comines, and Mezeray.

LOHENGRIN. O. 3 a. Richard Wagner. Weimar, 1850; C.G., May 8, 1875. Transl. by J. P. Jackson, H.M.T. (first time in English), February 7, 1880.

LOHENGRIN. See *Little Lohengrin.*

LOI DE L'HOMME, LA. C. 3 a. Paul Hervieu. Shaftesbury, May 18, 1908.

LOILOLA. C. Hackett. 1648.

LOIOLA. Latin C. Geo. Ruggle. Pr. 1648 and act. before King James I.

LOLA MONTEZ. P. 1 a. H. Chance Newton and J. Searle Dawley. Richmond, October 18, 1901.

LOLA, THE BELLE OF BACCARATO. C.O. 2 a. Lib. by Frank Marshall. M. by Antonio Orsini. Olympic, January 15, 1881.

LOLANDESE DANNATO, L'. D.L., July 23, 1870.

LOLLYPOP LANE. O. 3 a. Keswick Pav., April 30, 1909.

LOLO. C.O. 2 a. A. Sturgess and J. M. Glover. Mchr. Prince's, September 8, 1900. See *Loloh.*

LOLOH; OR, THE FALSE ORACLE. C.O. 2 a. A. Sturgess and J. Hickory Wood. M. by J. M. Glover. A rev. vers. of *Lolo.* Bradford T.R., May 13, 1901; Peckham Crown, March 3, 1902.

LOLOTTE. St. James's, November 3, 1890.

LOMBARDI ALLA PRIMA CROCIATA I. O. Verdi. Milan, 1843.

LONDON; OR, THE LIFE OF A STREET BOY. D. 4 a. L. E. B. Stephens. Barnstaple T.R., January 1, 1885.

LONDON ACTRESS, A. D. 4 a. Emma Litchfield. Rotherhithe Terriss, January 11, 1904.

LONDON ARAB, A. D. 5 a. Miles Wallerton and Francis Gilbert. Folkestone Pleasure Gdns., March 20, 1899; Surrey, April 10, 1899.

LONDON ARAB, THE. D. Grecian, June 10, 1878.

LONDON ASSURANCE. C. 5 a. Dion Boucicault. C.G., March 4, 1841; D.L., October 21, 1856; Criterion, November 27, 1890.

LONDON BANKER. D. 2 a. Campbell. Publ. by J. Dicks.

LONDON BRIDGE 150 YEARS AGO: OR, THE OLD MINT. Rom. D. 5 a. Adap. fr. *Les Chevaliers du Brouillard* by James Macnab, author of *Our Future King,* etc. Queen's, February 5, 1873.

LONDON BY DAY AND NIGHT. See *Bootblack.*

LONDON BY GASLIGHT. D. 5 a. Miss Hazlewood. Adap. fr. Aug. Daly's American play, *Under the Gaslight,* Sadler's Wells, September 19, 1868.

LONDON BY NIGHT. D. 3 a. Selby. Publ. by J. Dicks.

LONDON CARRIER, THE. Dom. Burla. Adelphi, September 28, 1835.

LONDON CHANTICLEERS. C. Not divided into acts. Anon. Frequently ac. 1659. Pr. same year.

LONDON CUCKOLDS, THE. C. Edwd. Ravenscroft. Duke's T., 1683. Pr. 1682, and rev. L.I.F., November 12, 1731.

LONDON DAY BY DAY. D. 4 a. Geo. R. Sims and Henry Pettitt. Adelphi, September 14, 1889.

LONDON FIREMAN, THE. D. 4 a. A. Shirley and G. Conquest. Surrey, October 13, 1902.

LONDON FLORENTINE, THE. P. 2 a. Henry Chettle (assisted by T. Heywood). Ac. in 1602.

LONDON GALATEA, A. Sk. Middlesex, November 23, 1908.

LONDON GENTLEMAN, THE. C. E. Howard. Entered Stationers' Co., August 7, 1667. N.p.

LONDON HERMIT; OR, RAMBLES IN DORSETSHIRE, THE. C. 3 a. John O'Keeffe. Hay., June 29, 1793. Pr. 1793. D.L., June 12, 1815.

LONDON IMP; OR, LONDON MERCATOR. T. Heywood. 1633.

LONDON LIFE. D. 4 a. By T. G. Clark. Grecian, September 24, 1881.

LONDON MERCHANT, THE. P. John Ford. Entered Stationers' Co., June 29, 1660 N.p. Destroyed by Warburton's servant.

LONDON MERCHANT; OR, THE HISTORY OF GEORGE BARNWELL, THE. T. Geo. Lillo. Pr. 1730. D.L., 1731.

LONDON MYSTERY, A. D. 4 a. Wm Bourne. Pavilion, July 15, 1895.

LONDON NIGHT HAWKS. D. 4 a. T. B Brabazon. Arbroath P. Hall, September 27 1909.

LONDON OUT OF TOWN, etc. F. Maclaren, 1809.

LONDON 'PRENTICE, THE Engl. Oa. D.L., March 17, 1754. N.p.

LONDON PRIDE. D. G. L. Gordon and Jos. Mackay. Philharmonic, February 28, 1882.

LONDON PRODIGAL, THE. C. "W. Shakespeare." Pr. and ac. by His Majesty's servants, 1605. Not by Shakespeare, his name being improperly used by the printer.

LONDON STREETS. Sk. 3 sc. Matthews Monck. Canterbury M.H., May 22, 1899.

LONDON WITH THE LID OFF. D. 4 a. Arthur Shirley. Stratford R.T., August 3, 1908.

LONDON'S ANNUAL TRIUMPH. Pageants, Speeches, and Songs on the Inauguration of Lord Mayor's Day:—1585, 1590, 1591, by G. Peele; 1604, by Dekker; 1605, 1610, 1611, by A. Munday; 1612, by Dekker; 1613, by Middleton; 1614, 1615, by A. Munday; 1616, 1619, by Middleton; 1620, by J. Squire; 1621, by Middleton; 1624, by Webster; 1626, by Middleton; 1631 to 1633, by Heywood; 1634, by J. Taylor; 1637 to 1639, 1641, by Heywood; 1655, by Gayton; 1656, by J. B.; 1657 to 1661, by J. Tatham; 1661, by Ogilby; 1662, 1663, 1664, by Tatham; 1671 to 1684, by T. Jordan; 1685 to 1689, by M. Taubman; 1691 to 1695, 1698 to 1701, 1708, by Elk. Settle. All were pr. either 4to or fol.

LONDON'S CURSE. P. Prol. 3 a. E. Hoggan-Armadale. Darlington T.R. (in 4 a), May 4, 1900; Liverpool Star, July 30, 1900; Surrey, July 15, 1901.

LONDON'S GLORY See "Pageants," etc.

LONDON'S LOVE TO THE ROYAL HENRIE. "Meeting him on the River Thames at his Returne from Richmonde with a Worthie Fleete of her Citizens. With a brief Reporte of the Water Fight and Fireworks." 1610.

LONDONERS, THE. F. 3 a. Adap. by H. Whitestone fr. R. Hichens' novel. Apollo, March 26, 1903.

LONE HOUSE ON THE BRIDGE OF NOTRE DAME, THE. D. 3 a. C. Webb. Transl. fr. the French. Dublin Queen's.

LONE HUT. D. 2 a. Raymond. Publ. by J. Dicks.

LONE MAN. Dom. C. 3 a. C. H. Voss-Bark. Bridlington Pavilion, March 14, 1907. Prod. by amateurs.)

LONELY LIFE, THE. P. 1 a. A. H. Close. Hammersmith King's, May 25, 1903.

LONELY LIFE, THE. P. 1 a. Alfred Sutro. Manchester Queen's, July 22, 1907.

LONELY LIVES. D. 5 a. Mary Morrison. Transl. fr. Gerhart Hauptmann's *Einsame Menschen.* Strand, April 1, 1901.

LONELY MAN OF THE OCEAN; OR, THE NIGHT BEFORE THE BRIDAL, THE. D. 3 a. T. G. Blake. Olympic, 1851.

LONELY MILLIONAIRES, THE. C. 3 a. Mrs. Henry de La Pasture. Court, February 25, 1905; rev. Adelphi, May 15, 1906.

LONG AGO. D. 1 a. Arthur à Beckett. Royalty, April 22, 1882.

LONG AND SHORT. F. 1 a. Oxberry. Publ. by J. Dicks.

LONG ARMS, THE. Sk. Beatrice Heron Maxwell. Tivoli, July 17, 1909.

LONG DUEL, A. C. 4 a. Mrs. W. K. Clifford Garrick, August 16, 1901.

LONG JOURNEY, A. P. 1 a. Marie Muggeridge. Birkenhead R., October 5, 1908.

LONG LIVE THE KING. Sk. Reading Pal., June 21, 1909.

LONG LIVE THE QUEEN. Jubilee Spec. D. 4 a. E. J. Brady. Hednesford T.R., February 17, 1887 (C.P.).

LONG MEG OF WESTMINSTER. Ac. at Rose T., February 14, 1595. N.p.

LONG ODDS. C.D. 3 a. Conway Edwardes. Bath T.R., February 10, 1883; Op. Comique, February 1, 1887.

LONG ODDS, THE. Serenata. C. Dibdin. Pr. 1783. Ac. at the R. Circus.

LONG PACK, THE. D. Sunderland Lyceum, March 17, 1879.

LONG STRIKE, THE. D. 4 a. Dion Boucicault. F. partly on *Mary Barton* and partly on *Lizzie Leigh.* Lyceum, September 15, 1866; Adelphi, November 29, 1869.

LONG STRIKE, THE. See *The Strike.*

LONGER THOU LIVEST, THE MORE FOOL THOU ART, THE. C. Wm. Wager. Black letter. Pr. N.d.

LONGSHANK. Ac. at the Rose T., August 29, 1595. Possibly Peele's *Edward I.*

LOO, AND THE PARTY WHO TOOK MISS "Bouffounerie musicale." H. B. Farnie. Strand, September 28, 1874.

LOOEY NAPOLEONG. F. N. Robinson. Dublin T.R., September 12, 1868.

LOOK ABOUT YOU. C. Anon. Ac. by Lord High Admiral's servants, 1600. Pr. 1600.

LOOK BEFORE YOU LEAP. C. 2 a. Announced for C.G., March 31, 1789. Not ac. on that date. ? Same as the following.

LOOK BEFORE YOU LEAP. C. 1 a. Horatio Robson. Hay. Pr. 1788. F. on *La Bonne Mère* of M. de Florian.

LOOK BEFORE YOU LEAP. F. Worgan. 1808.

LOOK BEFORE YOU LEAP. C. G. W. Lovell. Hay., October 29, 1846.

LOOK ON THE BRIGHT SIDE. City of London, July 28, 1866.

LOOKE TO THE LADIE. C. J. Shirley. Ent. Stationers' Co. March 10, 1639. N.p.

LOOKING-GLASS FOR LONDON AND ENGLAND, A. T.C. Thos. Lodge and Robert Green. F. on the story of Jonah and the Ninevites. 1592. Pr. 1594.

LOOSE TILES. F.C. 3 a. J. P. Hurst. Vaudeville, January 28, 1885.

LOOSE TILES. Sk. H. A. Langlois. Poplar Queen's, June 17, 1907.

LORD ALLANGFORD. D. 4 a. Walter E. Grogan. Torquay T.R., May 16, 1895.

LORD AND LADY ALGY. C. 3 a. R. C. Carton. Comedy, April 21, 1898; tfd. to Avenue, September 5, 1898.

LORD AND LADY GUILDEROY. C.D. 3 a. Hamilton Aidé. Brighton T.R., April 9, 1896.

LORD AND THE LOUT, THE. Victoria, January 31, 1859.

LORD ANERLEY. P. 4 a. H. Hamilton and M. Quinton. St. James's, November 7, 1891.

LORD BATEMAN. Extrav. 4 a. Sydney French. Alhambra, December 24, 1875.

LORD BATEMAN. Burl. Charles Daly. Seaham Harbour T.R., April 17, 1876.

LORD BATEMAN; OR, PICOTEE'S PLEDGE. C.O. 2 a. H. P. Stephens. M. by Edward Solomon. Gaiety, April 29, 1882.

LORD BATEMAN; OR, THE PROUD YOUNG PORTER AND THE FAIR SOPHIA. Burl. Henry J. Byron. Globe, December 27, 1869. F. on the ballad "Lord Bateman."

LORD BATEMAN'S JOURNEY. Extrav. Old play publ. by S. French, Ltd.

LORD BATEMAN'S OVERLAND JOURNEY. Adelphi, April 17, 1854.

LORD BLUNDER'S CONFESSION; OR, GUILT MAKES A COWARD. Ballad O. Anon. Written by the author of *Vanelia.* Pr. 1733. N.ac.

LORD CROMWELL. Hist. P. Anon. 1602. See *Cromwell.*

LORD DANBY'S LOVE AFFAIR. P. 4 a. Rev. Forbes Phillips. Leamington R., April 24, 1905; Coronet, May 22, 1905.

LORD DARCY; OR, TRUE TILL DEATH. Hist. P. 2 a. A. E. Greene. Cheltenham Corn Exch., December 1, 1896.

LORD DARNLEY; OR, THE KEEPER OF CASTLE HILL. Rom. D. 2 a. T. E. Wilks. Surrey, September 11, 1837.

LORD DOLLY. F.C. 3 a. C. Anderson. Wallington Parish H., June 18, 1898, Matinée T., November 12, 1898.

LORD DUNDREARY MARRIED AND DONE FOR. C. H. J. Byron and Sothern. Hay., June 13, 1864.

LORD DUNNOHOO. R. Redgrave. Additional lyrics by M. Turner. M. by G. O. Walker. Aldershot T.R., July 5, 1897.

LORD EDWARD; OR, '98. Irish D. 5 a. J. W. Whitbread. Dublin Queen's T., March 26, 1894. Pav., August 6, 1894.

LORD FITZHARRIS. Ca. Miss H. L. Walford. Gallery of Illus., May 24, 1873.

LORD HALIFAX. D. 4 a. M. Wardlaugh. Barnsley Queen's T., February 8, 1875; Longton T.R., October 14, 1878.

LORD HARKAWAY. Sk. Fredk. Maxwell. Standard M.H., November 24, 1902.

LORD HARRY, THE. Rom. D. 5 a. H. A. Jones and Wilson Barrett. Princess's, February 18, 1886.

LORD IN WAITING, A. C. 1 a. A. O'D. Bartholeyns. Avenue, July 8, 1893.

LORD LOVEL AND LADY NANCY BELL; OR, THE BOUNDING BRIGADE OF THE BAKUMBOILUM. Burl. 1 a. F. C. Burnand. Cambridge A.D.C. Rooms, November, 1856.

LORD MACNINNY. F. Vaudeville, December 21, 1887.

LORD MARPLE'S DAUGHTER. C.D. 3 a. Frank Harvey. Adap. fr. the French. Grand, November 29, 1886.

LORD MAYOR, THE. 3 a. W. E. Bradley, Harry and Edward Paulton. Strand, November 1, 1895.

LORD MAYOR'S DAY. F.C. 3 a. Folly, June 30, 1879.

LORD MAYOR'S DAY; OR, A FLIGHT FROM LAPLAND. Panto. C.G., 1782. Songs and dial. by O'Keeffe.

LORD MAYOR'S PAGEANT. See *London's Annual Triumph.*

LORD OF ELLINGHAM, THE. P. Spicer, Olympic, 1848.

LORD OF HIS HOUSE. C. 3 a. G. Hawtrey. Coventry O.H., June 9, 1902; Comedy, June 12, 1902.

LORD OF LATIMER STREET, THE. P. 4 a. Oliver Madox Hueffer. Terry's, February 26, 1908.

LORD OF THE ISLES, THE. M. by G. H. B. Rodwell. 1834.

LORD OF THE ISLES, THE. Dr. Cantata. Fd. on Scott's poem. M. by Henry Gadsby. Brighton, February 13, 1879.

LORD OF THE LAST, THE. M.C. 3 a. F. A Ellis. M. by P. Knight and Denham Harrison. Worthing T.R., August 23; London prod., Camden, August 27, 1906.

LORD OF THE MANOR, THE. C.O. 3 a. John Burgoyne. D.L., 1781. Pr. 1781. M. by Jackson. The leading incident taken from *Silvain* of Marmontel. (Rev.) D.L., December 20, 1820; Lyceum, November 12, 1834. C. 3 a. By Dibdin. Publ. by J. Dicks.

LORD OF THE MANOR, THE. P. 3 a. Herman Merivale. Imperial, January 3, 1880.

LORD RUSSELL. T. Rev. Dr. Stratford. D.L., August 20, 1784. Advertised in 1792 as about to be publ.

LORD RUSSELL. T. Wm. Hayley. Hay., August 18, 1784. Pr. 1784.

LORD TOM NODDY. Mus. Piece. 2 a. Geo. Dance. M. by F. O. Carr. Bradford T.R., April 6, 1896; Garrick, September 15, 1896.

LORD'S MASQUE, THE. Dr. Thomas Campion. 1612-13.

LORD'S SUPPER AND WASHING THE FEET. C. Bishop Bale. N.p.

LORD'S WARMING PAN, THE. Title adopted by B. Webster for *The Heir at Law* when pl. at the Tottenham Street T.

LORDS AND COLONELS. C. 3 a. Rev. A. J. Steed, M.A. Aylsham T.H., April 28, 1903.

LORDS AND COMMONS. C. D.L., December 20, 1831.

LORDS AND COMMONS. C. 4 a. A. W. Pinero. Hay., November 24, 1883.

LORDS OF CREATION. Ca. A. E. Drinkwater. Oxford New T., February 4, 1895; Kilburn T.R., February 17, 1896.

LORELEI, DIE. O. Mendelssohn. (Unfinished.)

LORELEY. First prod. in England of O., 3 a. (in Italian). Words by Carlo D'Ormeville and A Zanardini English vers. by Alfred Kalisch. M. by Alfredo Catalani. C.G., July 12, 1907.

LORENZACCIO. D. 5 a. Alfred Musset. Adap. by Armand D'Artois. Adelphi (Mdme. Sarah Bernhardt's season), June 17, 1897.

LORENZINO DI MEDICI. D. 5 a. Wm. Rough. Pr. 1797. N.ac.

LORENZO. T. Robert Merry. C.G., April 5, 1791. Pr. 1791.

LORNA DOONE. P. 5 a. Mildred Dowling. Royalty, June 13, 1901 (C.P.).

LORNA DOONE. D. Mary Ford and Leonard Rayne. F. on R. D. Blackmore's novel. Princess's, December 19, 1901.

LORNA DOONE. Rom. D. 5 a. Horace Newte. Crouch End O.H., February 4, 1902.

LORNA DOONE. P. 4 a. Adap. from R. D. Blackmore's novel. Tunbridge Wells O.H., January 1, 1903.

LORNA DOONE. P. 4 a. Annie Hughes. Avenue, June 20, 1903.

LORRAINE. O. 1 a. Walter E. Grogan. M. by Giovanni Clerici. Torquay T.R., January 10, 1898; St. Geo. H., October 31, 1899.

LOSE NO TIME. C. Skeffington. 1811.

LOSING HAZARD, A. Dr. Sk. Brandon Hurst. Parkhurst, April 11, 1892.

LOSS OF THE ROYAL GEORGE. D. 2 a. Barnett. Publ. by J. Dicks.

LOST. D. Lambert Thiboust. Standard, October 16, 1871.

LOST. C.D. C. Wyndham. Bristol T.R., February 2, 1874.

LOST AND FOUND. C. M. K. Masters. 1811.

LOST AND FOUND. Oa. 1 a. G. Marsh. M. by Miss Virginia Gabriel. Gallery of Illus., February 5, 1870; Liverpool Alexandra, June 27, 1870.

LOST AND FOUND. D. 5 a. J. C. Wilson. Norwich T.R., March 17, 1873; Hull T.R., April 8, 1878.

LOST AND WON. D. 2 a. Lemon. Publ. by J. Dicks.

LOST AT SEA; A LONDON STORY. D. 4 a. D. Boucicault and H. J. Byron. Adelphi, October 2, 1869.

LOST BY DRINK. D. See *Drink.*

LOST CAUSE, THE. Hist. D. 5 a. Malcolm E. Boyd. Torquay T. (under title *Bonnie Dundee*), February 24, 1881; Olympic, July 22, 1884.

LOST CHANCE, A. Sk. Bertha N. Graham. Empress, May 6, 1908.

LOST CHILD, THE. F. 1 a. W. E. Suter. Lyceum, December 26, 1863.

LOST CHORD, THE. M. Sk. Maxwell Ryder. W. London, March 24, 1900.

LOST CHORD, THE. P. Sutton Vane and Arthur Carlton. (C.P.). Worcester T.R., November 23, 1906.

LOST DEWDROPS, THE. C.O. 2 a. H. D. Hinde. M. by Misses F. Wykes and E. McLean. Prod. by amateurs, Edmonton Town Hall, February 29, 1908.

LOST DIAMONDS, THE. D. 2 a. E. Stirling. Olympic, February, 1849.

LOST DISCHARGE, THE. Oa. C. P. Mann. St. George's, June 20, 1873.

LOST EDEN, A. D. 1 a. Miss Hammond Hills. Novelty, June 1, 1897.

LOST EMILY. D. G. Murray. Birmingham P.O.W.'s, June 30, 1870.

LOST EM'LY. D. 5 a. Murray Wood. Surrey, March 8, 1873.

LOST FOR EVER; OR, MILLY, THE COLLIER'S WIFE. D. G. Nicholson. Barnsley Queen's T., January 11, 1869.

LOST FOR GOLD; OR, OAKMERE HOLD. D. J. H. Illingworth. At Agra, Bengal, March 21, 1879; Winchester Guildhall, December 26, 1885.

LOST HEIR, THE. D. 3 a. T. B. Henderson. Kendal T., December 7, 1868.

LOST HEIR, THE. D. Edward Price. Aberdeen T.R., March 20, 1872.

LOST HEIR OF MACCLESFIELD, THE. D. T. M. Dakin. Macclesfield T.R., February 15, 1875.

LOST HUSBAND, THE. D. 4 a. Adap. fr. the French by the author of *The Ladies' Battle*. Strand, April 26, 1853.

LOST HUSBAND, THE. C.O. 1 a. M. by Lady Arthur Hill. Devonshire Ho., Belgrave Square, November 21, 1884; Brighton T.R., February 16, 1885; Criterion, February 28, 1885.

LOST IN LONDON. D. 3 a. Watts Phillips. Adelphi, March 16, 1867.

LOST IN NEW YORK. C.D. 5 a. Leonard Grover. Olympic, August 3, 1896.

LOST LADY, THE. T.C. Sir Wm. Berkley. Pr. 1638.

LOST LADY OF LYNNE, THE. Dr. ver. of *East Lynne*, by A. Willoughby. Coventry T.R., January 24, 1883.

LOST LEGION, THE. P. 1 a. W. J. Locke. Liverpool Shakespeare, November 7, 1898; Brixton T., November 14, 1898.

LOST LETTER. Mentioned by Pascoe. Rev. C.G., December, 1871.

LOST LIFE. C. 3 a. D.L., November 13, 1821.

LOST LIFE, A. D. 3 a. H. L. Walford. Gallery of Illus., November 24, 1870 (amat.).

LOST LOVE. D. 4 a. Mortimer Murdoch. Pavilion, March 8, 1879.

LOST LOVER; OR, THE JEALOUS HUSBAND, THE. C. Mrs. De La Riviere Manley. T.R., 1696. Pr. 1696.

LOST MEMORY, A. P. 3 a. J. S. Blythe. Bradford T.R., June 14, 1902; M'chr Prince's, August 4, 1902.

LOST OR FOUND. D. 5 a. Crawford Wilson. Holborn, December 21, 1872.

LOST OVERTURE, THE. M.Ca. Middlesbrough T.R., March 25, 1892.

LOST PARADISE, THE. P. Henry C. De Mille. Adap. fr. Ludwig Fulda's *Das Verloren Paradies*. (Prod. in November, 1890, at Deutsches T., Berlin.) Adelphi, December 22, 1892.

LOST PARADISE, THE. D. 3 a. Transl. fr. Fulda by Janet Achurch. Alexandra Pal., May 1, 1902 (C.P.); M'ch'r Queen's, May 26, 1902.

LOST POCKET BOOK. C. 1 a. Reynoldson. Publ. by J. Dicks.

LOST PRINCE, THE. Oa. H. W. Rendell. Crystal Pal., May 18, 1895 (by boys).

LOST PRINCESS, THE. T. Murrough Boyle, Lord Visc. Blessington. Wr. in 18th century. N.p.

LOST SHEEP, A. F.C. 3 a. W. Parke and A. Shirley. Bradford T.R., July 13, 1891; Op. C., July 30, 1892.

LOST SHIP; OR, THE MAN OF WARSMAN AND THE PRIVATEER, THE. Nautical D. 3 a. Thompson Townsend.

LOST, STOLEN, OR STRAYED, afterwards called *A Day in Paris*. M.F. 3 a. J. Cheever Goodwin. Adap. fr. the French. M. by Woolson Morse. D. of York's, April 27, 1897.

LOST, £30,000. Marylebone, March 24, 1856

LOST THREAD, A. Sk. Mrs. Hugh Bell Prince's H., May 20, 1890.

LOST TO LIFE. D. 4 a. James Horner. Leicester T.R., March 3, 1884.

LOST TO THE WORLD. D. Pro. and 4 a. Mrs. Talbot Hunter. Crewe Lyceum, February 15, 1892; Marylebone, July 4, 1892.

LOST WAGER, THE. C. 1 sc. Wm. Felton. Brompton Cancer Hospital, November 23, 1905.

LOST WIFE; OR, A HUSBAND'S CONFESSION, THE. Dom. D. 3 a. C. H. Hazlewood. Britannia, August 7, 1871.

LOST WITNESS, THE. D. 4 a. H. Pettitt and P. Meritt. Grecian, May 22, 1880.

LOST WOMAN, A. Dr. Sk. Dora Deane and F. G. Brooke. Canning Town Royal Albert, November 2, 1903.

LOT No. 1; OR, THE MAN IN POSSESSION. S.C.D. 1 a. Nelson Lee. Liverpool T.R., October 5, 1874.

LOT No. 49. F. 1 a. W. J. Fisher. Adap. from the German of G. Von Moser. Gaiety, January 17, 1888.

LOTA; OR, A MOTHER'S LOVE. D. Pro. and 4 a. Fred Jarman. Sadler's Wells, August 8, 1892.

LOTHAIR, BATTI BATTI; AND SHAH DEE DOO. R. Soutar and F. Green. Liverpool T.R., October 13, 1873.

LOTS, THE. C. Richd. Warner. Transl. from *Casina* of Plautus. Pr. 1774.

LOTTERY, THE. C. Ac. at New T. in Hay. Pr. 1728.

LOTTERY, THE. B. F. H. Fielding. D.L., January 1, 1732. Pr. 1731.

LOTTERY, THE. D. 1 a. E. H. Brooke. Brighton T.R., June 12, 1903.

LOTTERY CHANCE; OR, THE DRUNKARD RECLAIMED, THE. M.D. Archibald M'Laren. Pr. 1803. Ac. at Aberdeen.

LOTTERY OF LIFE; A STORY OF NEW YORK. D. 5 a. John Brougham. Ac. at Wallack's T. Publ. by J. Dicks.

LOTTERY TICKET; OR, THE LAWYER'S CLERK, THE. F. 1 a. Saml. Beazley. D.L., December 13, 1826; January 12, 1829; March 16, 1850; and at Strand T.

LOTTIE. C. 3 a. Novelty, November 20, 1884.

LOTTIE'S LOVE; OR, HOW TO CHOOSE A HUSBAND. F. Alfd. Davis. Glasgow P.O.W., May 15, 1868.

LOUIS IX. T. Ancelot. 1819.

LOUIS XI. Hist. D. 3 a. W. R. Markwell. Adap. from Casimir Delavigne. D.L., February 14, 1853.

LOUIS XI. (or *Louis Onze*). Dion Boucicault. Ver. of C. Delavigne's play. New York, 1854; Lyceum, March 9, 1878; Rev., Lyceum, July 1, 1901; D.L., June 6, 1905; Manchester T.R., September 26, 1907; rev. Shaftesbury, February 22, 1909.

LOUIS XI.; OR, THE TRICKSEY MONARCH AND THE WICKSEY WARRIOR. Burl. Harry M. Pitt. West Hartlepool T.R., July 9, 1869.

LOUIS XVI. P. Philip J. Dear. Bath T.R., February 7, 1895 (C.P.).

LOUIS AND ANTOINETTE. T. Geo. M. Hunter. Pr. 1794. N. ac.

LOUIS IN THE ELYSIAN FIELDS. D. Transl. fr. the French by Thos. Holcroft. Pr. 1785.

LOUISA MILLER. O. Verdi. Naples, December 8, 1849.

LOUISA OF LOMBARDY; OR, THE SECRET NUPTIALS. Spec. by J. C. Cross. Pr. 1803. Ac. at the R. Circus.

LOUISE. O. 4 a. and 5 Tab. (in Fr.). Lib. and M. by Gustave Charpentier. Paris Opéra Comique, February 2, 1900.

LOUISE DE LIGNEROLLES. T.D. 5 Parts. Adap. fr. the French of Denaux and Ernest Legouvé.

LOUISIANA CREOLE; OR, ARTICLE 47. Adap. fr. the French. Preston T.R., May 30, 1891.

LOUISON. Ver. of *The Angel of the Attic*. D 1 a. Bernard. Publ. by J. Dicks.

LOVE, THE PLAY OF. An interlude. John Heywood. 1533.

LOVE. P. 5 a. J. Sheridan Knowles. C.G., 1839, 1840; D.L., September 25, 1856; Princess's, October 20, 1862.

LOVE. C. George Lester. Gloucester T.R., December 11, 1876.

LOVE-A-LA-MODE. C. By "T. S." Pr. 1663. Ac. at Middlesex House.

LOVE-A-LA-MODE. F. Chs. Macklin. D.L., December 12, 1759. Pr. 1793. D.L., November 3, 1817.

LOVE AMONG THE ROSES; OR, THE MASTER KEY. Oa. M. by Dr. Kitchiner. Lyceum, July 1, 1822.

LOVE AMONGST THE ONIONS. Sk. 1 sc. Balham Duchess, December 26, 1905.

LOVE AMONGST THE ROSES. O. 3 a. Capt. Erskine. Publ. by S. French, Ltd.

LOVE AMONGST THE ROSES. Fantastic O. Leopold Montague. M. by T. H. Bairnstather. Bideford Public R., December 17, 1902 (amat.).

LOVE AND A BOTTLE. C. Geo. Farquhar. D.L., 1699. Pr. 1699. The part of Mockmode probably borrowed fr. Molière's *Bourgeois Gentilhomme.*

LOVE AND A SHADOW. P. 4 a. Archibald H. Pocock. Hampstead Conservatoire, May 30, 1907.

LOVE AND AMBITION. T. James Darcy. Pr. 1732. Ac. at Dublin.

LOVE AND ART; OR, THE ARTIST'S GHOST. Ca. 1 a. Alfred A. Wilmot. Hammersmith Lyric H., March 28, 1889; Novelty, March 9, 1891.

LOVE AND AVARICE. Olympia, June, 27, 1853.

LOVE AND BE SILENT. P. 1 a. Mrs. Chs. Sim. Garrick, May 17, 1901. Rehearsal, February 28, 1909.

LOVE AND CHARITY. F. 1 a. Lemon. Publ. by J. Dicks.

LOVE AND CRIME. Grecian, May 24, 1858.

LOVE AND DENTISTRY. Duol. H. Swears. Greenwich Lecture H., December 5, 1893; Op. C., May 8, 1895.

LOVE AND DUTY. T. John Slade. Pr 1756. Ac. one night at the Hay.

LOVE AND DUTY; OR, THE DISTRESS'D BRIDE. T. J. Sturmy. L.I.F., 1721. Pr. 1722.

LOVE AND FOLLY. Serenata. 3 Int. M. by Galliard. Ac. at King's T. in Hay. Pr. 1739.

LOVE AND FORTUNE, HISTORY OF. Perf. before Her Majesty at Windsor, 1589.

LOVE AND FORTUNE. Extrav. J. R. Planché. Princess's T., September 24, 1859.

LOVE AND FRIENDSHIP. P. Sir William Killigrew. 1666.

LOVE AND FRIENDSHIP. Serenata. M. by W. Defesch. Pr. 1744.

LOVE AND FRIENDSHIP. Op. D.L. Pr. 1746.

LOVE AND FRIENDSHIP; OR, THE LUCKY RECOVERY. C. Pr. 1754. N.ac.

LOVE AND FRIENDSHIP; OR, THE RIVAL PASSIONS. Pr. 1723.

LOVE AND GLORY. Masque. Thos. Philips. M. by T. Arne. D.L., March 28, 1734. Pr. 1734.

LOVE AND GOUT. C. 3 a. Jameson. Hay., August 23, 1814. N.p.

LOVE AND HALFPENCE. Ca. Wm. Poel. Adap. fr. Clairville and Lambert Thiboust's *L'Histoire d'un Sou.* St. Geo. H., January 31, 1888.

LOVE AND HATE. D. 2 a. Horace Wigan. Olympic, June 23, 1869.

LOVE AND HATE. D. Britannia, April 12, 1875.

LOVE AND HATE IN CORSICA. P. 1 a. E. Hamilton Moore. Bayswater Bijou, December 4, 1906 (C.P.).

LOVE AND HONOUR. T.C. Sir W. Davenant. Little L.I.T., Dorset Gardens T., Blackfriars T. Licensed 1634. Pr. 1649. Originally called *The Courage of Love*, and afterwards *The Nonpareilles; or, The Matchless Maids.*

LOVE AND HONOUR. Dr. Poem. Thos. Delamayne. Pr. 1742. Consisting of 7 Cantos or Acts introducing the principal personages of the Æneid as interlocutors.

LOVE AND HONOUR. Op. Piece. C.G., May 9, 1794. N.p.

LOVE AND HONOUR. C.D. Campbell Clarke. Birmingham T.R., June 30, 1875; Globe, August 14, 1875.

LOVE AND HONOUR; OR, SOLDIERS AT HOME—HEROES ABROAD. Dom. D. 3 a. J. E. Carpenter. Surrey, November 5, 1855.

LOVE AND HONOUR; OR, THE PRIVATEER. F. Pr. 1753 at Ipswich.

LOVE AND HUNGER. F. 1 a. J. M. Morton. Adelphi, September 26, 1859. Hay.

LOVE AND INNOCENCE. Past. Serenata. Marylebone. Pr. 1769.

LOVE AND LAW. Oa. 1 a. Frank Latimer. M. by Ivan Caryll. Lyric, March 4, 1891.

LOVE AND LIBERTY. T. Chas. Johnson. Pr. 1709. N. ac. Intended for D.L.

LOVE AND LOYALTY. Walker. See *Fat of Villainy.*

LOVE AND LOYALTY. O. A. Macdonald. Pr. 1791. N. ac.

LOVE AND LOYALTY. W. J. Robson. D.L., March 22, 1855.

LOVE AND MADNESS. An antique dr. tale. F. G. Waldron. Hay., September 21, 1795. N.p. F. on *The Two Noble Kinsmen.*

LOVE AND MAGIC; OR, HARLEQUIN'S HOLIDAY. Pant. D.L., March, 1802. N.p.

LOVE AND MONEY. D. Prol. and 5 a. C. L. Reade and H. Pettitt. Adelphi, November 18, 1882.

LOVE AND MONEY. D. 4 a. J. F. Stanfield. Manchester, March 5, 1902.

LOVE AND MONEY; OR, THE FAIR CALEDONIAN. M.F. 1 a. Benson. Hay., 1795. Pr. 1798.

LOVE AND MURDER. F. 3 a. Buckstone. Publ. by J. Dicks.

LOVE AND NATURE. Mus. Piece. 1 a. Geo. Monck Berkeley. Dublin, March, 1789. Pr. 1797. This is the story of Prior's *Henry and Emma*, curtailed. M. by Shields.

LOVE AND POLITICS. Ca. H. T. Johnson. Op. C., February 9, 1888.

LOVE AND PRIDE. D. Rodwell. Adelphi, February, 1843.

LOVE AND RAIN. F. 1 a. Adap. fr. the French. Another translation, called *Killing Time*, played at Princess's.

LOVE AND REASON. C. 3 a. Taken fr. the Fr. and adap. to Eng. stage by M. R. Lacy. C.G., May 22, 1827.

LOVE AND REVENGE. T. Elkanah Settle. Duke of York's T., 1675. Pr. 1675. Partly fr. *The Fatal Contract*, by Heminge.

LOVE AND REVENGE; OR, THE VINTNER OUTWITTED. Ballad O. Anon. Ac. at the little T. in Hay., 1729. This is *The Match in Newgate* altered, and with songs added.

LOVE AND RICHES RECONCILED. Masque. Harris. 1699. See *Love's a Lottery.*

LOVE AND STRATAGEM. See *Leona.*

LOVE AND THE LAW. Oa. 1 a. H. Millward. M. by C. F. Hayward. Wolverhampton Exch. H., February 26, 1886.

LOVE AND THE LAW. P. 3 a. Charlotte Eliza Wells. Bayswater Bijou, March 16, 1908 (C.P.)

LOVE AND VALOUR; OR, THE TWO NOBLE KINSMEN. T. Altered fr. Beaumont and Fletcher. Ac. at Richmond, 1779. N.p.

LOVE AND WAR. T. Thos. Meriton. Pr. 1658. N. ac.

LOVE AND WAR. M. Ent. Robert Jephson. Abridgment of *The Campaign.* C.G., March 15, 1787. N.p.

LOVE AND WAR. M. Rom. C.O. by Lawrence Olde and Basil Gotto. M. by Evan Kefe. Portsmouth T.R., June 17, 1895; Eleph. and C., July 15, 1895.

LOVE AND WINE. A Sequel to *Love and Friendship.* C. Pr. 1754. By the author of *The Friendly Rivals.*

LOVE APPLE. Oa. Offenbach. Gaiety, September 24, 1874.

LOVE AT A LOSS; OR, MOST VOTES CARRY IT. C. Mrs. Catherine Trotter, afterwards Cockburne. D.L. Pr. 1701. Rewritten and intended for production as *The Honourable Deceivers; or, All Right at the Last.*

LOVE AT A VENTURE. C. Mrs. Centlivre. Ac. at Bath New T. Transl. fr. *Le Gallant Double.* Pr. 1706. See *The Double Gallant.*

LOVE AT A VENTURE; OR, THE RAKE RECLAIMED. C. 5 a. Hay., 1782. N.p.

LOVE AT FIRST SIGHT. C. David Crawford. L.I.F., 1704. Wr. 1700. Pr. N.d.

LOVE AT FIRST SIGHT. Ballad F. Thos. King. D.L., October 17, 1763.

LOVE AT FIRST SIGHT. Ca. Major Jocelyn, R.A. Woolwich Royal Artillery T., May 3, 1889.

LOVE AT FIRST SIGHT; OR, THE WIT OF A WOMAN. B.O. 2 a. Joseph Yarrow. Pr. 1742. Ac. by the York Co. of Comedians. ? a hint taken from Mrs. Centlivre's *Busy Body.*

LOVE AT FIRST SIGHT. P. Pro. and 4 a. E. Martin and F. Llewellyn. Bayswater Bijou, July 26, 1906.

LOVE AT HOME. C. 1 a. Sylvanus Dauncey. F. on *T.K. et P.K.*, by Aug. Hendrix. West Hartlepool T.R., May 14, 1891.

LOVE BETRAYED; OR, THE AGREEABLE DISAPPOINTMENT. C. Chs. Burnaby. Pr. 1703. L.I.F., 1703. Partly fr. *Twelfth Night.*

LOVE BIRD. Oa. Lib. by Conway Edwardes. M. by A. Nicholson. Vaudeville, June 19, 1872.

LOVE BIRDS, THE. M.C. 3 a. George Grossmith, jun. M. by Raymond Roze, addl. lyrics by P. Greenbank. Savoy, February 10, 1904.

LOVE BY LANTERN LIGHT. Oa. 1 a. Adap. fr. *Le Mariage aux Lanterns*, by M. Carré and L. Batter. Soho T., 1862.

LOVE CHARM; OR, THE VILLAGE COQUETTE, THE. C.O. 2 a. M. by Auber, adap. by Bishop. Taken fr. French of Scribe. D.L., November 3, 1831.

LOVE CHASE, THE. C. 5 a. J. Sheridan Knowles. Hay., 1837; D.L., January 25, 1850; Shaftesbury, June 1, 1891.

LOVE CONQUERS; OR, NO SPY. P. 1 a. A. Houghton Townley. Camden Town Park H., February 21, 1889.

LOVE CROWNS THE END. Past. John Tatham. Pr. 1640. Not divided into acts. In 1657 edition called a T.C. ? written for and ac. by Scholars of Bingham, Nottinghamshire, in 1632.

LOVE DESPISED. Another title for *Cupid's Revenge* 1668

LOVE DRAGOONED. F. Motteux. Circa 1700.

LOVE EXTEMPORE. C. 2 a. Kenny. Publ. by J. Dicks.

LOVE FINDS A WAY. Keith. Jersey O.H., November 30, 1903.

LOVE FINDS THE WAY. C.O. Thos. Hull. C.G., November 12, 1777. An abridgment of *The School for Guardians.* Songs only pr.

LOVE FOR LOVE. C. 5 a. Wm. Congreve. New T. in L.I.F., 1693; C.G., 1807; D.L., January 23, 1816; D.L., October 20, 1825. Pr. 1695. See *Buxom Joan.*

LOVE FOR MONEY; OR, THE BOARDING-SCHOOL. C. Thos. Dungey. Ac. at the T.R., 1691. Pr. 1691. *The Boarding-School* by Coffey f. on this piece.

LOVE FREED FROM IGNORANCE AND FOLLY. Masque. Ben Jonson. Circa 1610-11. Pr. 1640.

LOVE GAME, A. Oa. Walter Browne. M. by A. Thompson M'Evoy. Ealing Lyric H., February 16, 1885.

LOVE GERMS. Sk. Prod. by the Smythsons. Royal Standard, December 3, 1906.

LOVE GIVES THE ALARM. C. J. G. Holman. C.G., February 23, 1804. N.p.

LOVE HATH FOUND OUT HIS EYES. P. Thos. Jordan. Ent. Stationers' Co., June 29, 1660. Destroyed by Warburton's servant.

LOVE HIS METAMORPHOSIS. John Lyly Pr. 1601.

LOVE, HONOUR, AND INTEREST. C. 3 a. John Galt. Pr. 1814. ? N. ac.

LOVE IN A BLAZE. C.O. Joseph Atkinson. Ac. at Dublin. Pr. 1800. Idea possibly fr. *The Widow of Malabar.*

LOVE IN A CAMP; OR, PATRICK IN PRUSSIA. M.F. John O'Keeffe. A sequel to *The Poor Soldier.* C.G., February 17, 1786. Pr. 1798. D.L., February 15, 1814.

LOVE IN A CHEST. F. Chs. Johnson. Ac. and pr. with *The Force of Friendship.* 1710.

LOVE IN A COFFEE SHOP. Sk. Bedford, May 10, 1909.

LOVE IN A CONVENT. C. By the Margravine of Anspach. Ac. at Brandenburgh House, July, 1805. N.p.

LOVE IN A COTTAGE. Past. Joseph Waker. Pr. at Dublin, 1785.

LOVE IN A COTTAGE. Burl. D.L., June 28, 1836.

LOVE IN A COTTAGE. C. 4 a. B. Hood. Terry's, January 27, 1904.

LOVE IN A FLAT. Duol. by S. Lounde. Fulham Grand, February 13, 1899.

LOVE IN A FOREST. C. C. Johnson. Pr. 1723. Ac. at D.L., January 9, 1723. Partly fr. *As You Like It.* Dedicated to the Fraternity of Free Masons.

LOVE IN A HURRY. C. A. Aston. Ac. at Dublin. Circa 1709.

LOVE IN A MAZE. C. James Shirley. Licd. 1631.

LOVE IN A MAZE. C. Ac. at King's T. Circa 1672. N.p.

LOVE IN A MAZE. Dion Boucicault. Princess's, 1851.

LOVE IN A MIST. F. Cunningham. 1747.

LOVE IN A MIST. M. Fairy P. 3 a. L. N. Parker. Orig. prod. in the provinces. Crystal Palace, July 9, 1891.

LOVE IN A MYSTERY. F. T. Horde. Pr. 1786.

LOVE IN A NUNNERY. Drydon's Play of the Assignation. 1673.

LOVE IN A PUDDLE. C. Anon. N.d., but since 1700.

LOVE IN A RIDDLE. Past. O. Colley Cibber. D.L., January 7, 1729. An imitation of *The Beggar's Opera.* Pr. 1729 (not 1719 as on title).

LOVE IN A SACK. F. 2 a. Benjamin Griffin. L.I.F., June 14, 1715. Pr. 1715.

LOVE IN A TUB. C. Etherage. 1664.

LOVE IN A TUB. Lyceum, April 24, 1809.

LOVE IN A VEIL. C. Richd. Savage. D.L., July 22, 1718. Pr. 1719.

LOVE IN A VILLAGE. C.O. 3 a. Isaac Bickerstaffe. C.G., 1762. Pr. 1763. Compiled fr. C. Johnson's *Village Opera*, Wycherley's *Gentleman Dancing-Master*, Marivaux's *Jeu de l'Amour et du Hazard*, and other pieces. D.L., July 5, 1814; Lyceum, July 22, 1817; Lyceum, 1827; D.L., 1829; City, 1831; Princess's, November, 1848.

LOVE IN A WOOD; OR, ST. JAMES'S PARK. C. Wm. Wycherley. Ac. at the T.R. Pr. 1672. D.L., August 15, 1718.

LOVE IN A WOOD; OR, THE COUNTRY SQUIRE. F. By "G. J." (Giles Jacob). Pr. 1714. N. ac.

LOVE IN ALL SHAPES. F. Anon. Pr. 1739. ? N. ac.

LOVE IN AUTUMN. C. 4 a. A. H. Pocock. Bayswater Bijou, July 12, 1904.

LOVE IN DISGRACE. O. Henry Lucas Dublin. Circa 1776. N.p.

LOVE IN HUMBLE LIFE. C. 1 a. J. Howard Payne. Adap. fr. Scribe's *Michel and Christine.* D.L., February 14, 1822.

LOVE IN IDLENESS. C. 3 a. L. N. Parker and Edward J. Goodman. Brighton T.R., March 13, 1896; Terry's, October 21, 1896, and December 28, 1896.

LOVE IN ITS EXTASY; OR, THE LARGE PREROGATIVE. Dr. Past. Wm. Peaps. Pr. 1649. N. ac.

LOVE IN MANY MASKS. C. J. P. Kemble. An alt. of the first part of Mrs. Behn's *Rover.* D.L., 1790. Pr. 1790.

LOVE IN SEVERAL MASKS (MASQUES). C. Henry Fielding. D.L., 1727. Pr. 1728.

LOVE IN SHORT FROCKS. F. Sk. Camberwell Empire, April 1, 1907.

LOVE IN TANDEM. Eccentric C. 3 a. Aug. Daly. Adap. fr. *La Vie à Deux* (Paris Odéon, 1890). Daly's, July 18, 1893.

LOVE IN THE CITY. C.O. Isaac Bickerstaffe, part of M. by Dibdin. C.G., February 21, 1767. Pr. 1767. See *The Romp.*

LOVE IN THE DARK; OR, THE MAN OF BUSINESS. C. Sir Francis Fane. Ac. at the T.R. Pr. 1675. Borrowed fr. Scarron's novel *The Invisible Mistress*, Boccace's *The Devil's an Ass, The Busy Body,* and *The Loves of Great Men.*

LOVE IN THE EAST; OR, THE ADVENTURES OF TWELVE HOURS. C.O. James Cobb. D.L., February 25, 1788. Pr. 1788.

LOVE IN WRINKLES; OR, THE RUSSIAN STRATAGEM. C.O. 2 a. M. R. Lacy. D.L., December 4, 1828.

LOVE IS THE CONQUEROR. C. Ashton. N.p.

LOVE IS THE CONQUEROR; OR, THE IRISH HERO. MSS. Play in Charles Macklin's library.

LOVE IS THE DOCTOR. C. 1 a. Taken fr. *L'Amour le Medecin* of Molière. L.I.F., April 4, 1734.

LOVE KING, THE. D. 4 a. Gilbert Elliott. Reading R. County T., March 9, 1893.

LOVE KNOT, THE. C. 3 a. J. Stirling Coyne. D.L., March 8, 1858.

LOVE KNOT, THE. P. 4 a. Louis N. Parker. York T.R., October 7, 1892.

LOVE LAUGHS AT LOCKSMITHS. M.F. 2 a. Geo. Colman the younger. Fr. the French of Bouilly's *Une Folie.* Hay., July 25, 1803. Pr. 1808. D.L., October 6, 1818; Lyceum, August 1, 1820.

LOVE LAUGHS AT LOCKSMITHS. T. Transl. Anon. 1803.

LOVE LAUGHS AT LOCKSMITHS. Duol. by Elsie Fogerty. Albert H. West T., May 13, 1899.

LOVE, LAW, AND PHYSIC. F. 2 a. James Kenney. 1812. C.G. D.L., March 15, 1823.

LOVE LETTER, A. Dom. D. 1 a. Mrs. E. Argent Lonergan. Strand, May 10, 1894.

LOVE LIES BLEEDING. Ca. 1 a. Charles Daly. Bayswater Bijou, April 30, 1900.

LOVE LIMITED; OR, A PROVOKING PREDICAMENT. C. Oa. 1 a. A. F. Knight. M. by Ernest W. Brown. Reading Old Town H.T., November 10, 1894.

LOVE LOCK. Olympic, February 13, 1854.

LOVE LOST IN THE DARK; OR, THE DRUNKEN COUPLE. F. Pr. 1680. See *The Muse of Newmarket.*

LOVE LOYAL. Duol. Oa., with M. J. Greenhill. Bayswater Bijou, July 4, 1901.

LOVE MAKES A MAN; OR, THE FOP'S FORTUNE. C. 5 a. C. Cibber. Pr. 1701. Partly fr. Beaumont and Fletcher's *Custom of the Country* and their *The Elder Brother*. L.I.F., 1700. C.G. D.L., 1828; November 13, 1818; D.L., October 30, 1828.

LOVE MAKES THE MAN. Sadler's Wells, September 22, 1853.

LOVE MARRIAGE, THE. O. Wm. Russel. Left unfinished in MS.

LOVE MATCH, THE. F. Anon. C.G., March 13, 1802. N.p.

LOVE MY DOG. F.C. 3 a. A. Yorke and Russell Vaun. Hay., July 9, 1903.

LOVE OF A GRECIAN LADY, THE. Rose T., October 4, 1594. N.p.

LOVE OF A LIFE. D. 4 a. Eugene Gotère. Rotunda, Liverpool. June 24, 1907.

LOVE OF A PRINCE. D. 3 a. Gayler. Publ. by J. Dicks.

LOVE OF ARCADIA, THE. Ca. Miss Braddon. 1860.

LOVE OF KING DAVID AND FAIR BETHSABE WITH THE TRAGEDIE OF ABSALON, THE. George Peele. Pr. 1599.

LOVE OF SIN, THE. D. Pro. 3 a. Harry Marlow and Fred Morgan. Eleph. and C., May 18, 1905 (C.P.); Southend Empire, July 17, 1905.

LOVE OF THE PRINCESS, THE. D. 4 a. C. Watson Mill Nelson. Grand, April 13, 1908; Elephant and Castle, September 14, 1908.

LOVE OF WOMAN, THE. P. 1 a. Mrs. George Norman. Prod. by the Play Actors. Court, May 9, 1909.

LOVE ON CRUTCHES. C. 3 a. Aug. Daly. F. on a German piece by Heinrich Stobitzer. (Orig. prod. in America.) Comedy, July 28, 1896.

LOVE ON WHEELS. O. M. Hopkins. M. by Harold Jenner. Queen's Gate Hall, May 30, 1901.

LOVE OR HATE. D. Pro. and 4 a. W. J. Wild and F. Williams. Salford P.O.W., April 19, 1886.

LOVE OR LIFE. Dom. D. 3 a. T. Taylor and P. Meritt. Dramatised fr. one of Crabbe's "Tales of the Hall." Olympic, June 10, 1878.

LOVE PARTS FRIENDSHIP. P. H. Chettle, assisted by Wentworth Smith. Ac. 1601.

LOVE PHILTRE, THE. D. 1 a. Alec Nelson. Torquay T.R., January 7, 1888.

LOVE PREVENTED. P. Henry Porter Ac. 1598. N.p.

LOVE RESTOR'D. Masque, by Ben Jonson. Ac. by gentlemen, the King's servants, 1610-11. Pr. 1640.

LOVE RULES THE WORLD. Dom. d. 4 a. By T. G. Bailey. Star, Liverpool, July 1, 1907; Elephant and Castle, December 14, 1908.

LOVE RUNS ALL DANGERS. Panto. Anon. 1733.

LOVE SHOP, THE. Sk. C. P. Coughlan. Canterbury M.H., September 14, 1905.

LOVE SPELL; OR, THE MOUNTEBANK OF RAVENNA, THE. Transl. of O. *L'Elisir d'Amour*, by Donizetti. Arr. by Reynold, sen., D.L., June 24, 1839.

LOVE STORY, THE. P. 4 a. Pierre Leclercq. Strand, May 23, 1888.

LOVE SUIT, A. Duol. W. G. Smythies.

LOVE TANGLE, A. Pastoral Duol. Maud Stepney-Rawson. M. by Geo. H. Clutsam. Wyndham's T., June 17, 1901.

LOVE TEST, THE. Ca. 1 a. Walter Leslie. Gaiety, June 22, 1873.

LOVE TESTS. Oa. 1 a. Vamcott's. Publ. by S. French, Ltd.

LOVE THAT CONQUERS, THE. P. 4 a. Dudley Beresford. Bayswater Bijou, November 23, 1908 (C.P.).

LOVE THAT KILLS, THE. Poetical Fancy. 3 a. Joselyn Brandon. Adap. fr. Alphonse Daudet's "L'Artésienne." M. by Geo. Bizet. P.O.W., January 27, 1888.

LOVE THAT LASTS, THE. D. 5 a. Frank Harvey. Adap. fr. the French. Northampton T.R., January 10, 1881.

LOVE THAT WOMEN DESIRE, THE. P. 4 a. G. Carlton Wallace. Leeds Queen's, April 28, 1905 (C.P.); Leigh R., July 24, 1905; Grand, July 23, 1906.

LOVE, THE BEST PHYSICIAN. C. John Ozell. Transl. fr. Molière's *Amour Medecin*. N.ac.

LOVE, THE CAUSE AND CURE OF GRIEF. T. 3 a. Thos. Cooke. D.L., December 19, 1743. Pr. 1744.

LOVE, THE CONQUEROR. Ro. P. 5 a. Frank Lindo. Newcastle Pal., December 15, 1908.

LOVE, THE CURE OF ALL WOES. T. Cooke. 1739. See *The Mournful Nuptials*.

LOVE, THE LEVELLER; OR, THE PRETTY PURCHASE. G. B. Gent. Pr. 1704. D.L., January 26, 1704.

LOVE, THE MAGICIAN. P. 3 a. Josephine Rae and Thomas Sidney Shaftesbury, July 7, 1892.

LOVE TRAP, THE. Ca. Hugh Moss. Bristol New T.R., September, 1883.

LOVE TRICKS; OR, THE SCHOOL OF COMPLIMENTS. C. Jas. Shirley. Formerly pl. as *The School for Compliments*. D. of York's T., Little Lincoln's Inn Fields. Pr. 1667. Licensed 1625.

LOVE TRIUMPHANT; OR, NATURE WILL PREVAIL. T.C. J. Dryden. Ac. at the T.R., 1694. Pr. 1694. The last piece Dryden wrote for the stage. F. on the story of Fletcher's "King and No King."

LOVE TRIUMPHANT; OR, THE RIVAL GODDESSES. Past. O. D. Bellamy, sen., and D. Bellamy, jun. Ac. by the young ladies of Mrs. Bellamy's Boarding School. Pr. 1740.

LOVE TRUST, A. Ca. 1 a. Lloyd Williams. MS. with Douglas Cox.

LOVE VERSUS LAW. Princess's, December 8, 1862.

LOVE VERSUS SCIENCE. Sk. Mrs. Argent Lonergan. S.W. Lon. Polytechnic, May 9, 1896.

LOVE WATCHES. C. 4 a. Robert de Fiers and Armand de Caillavet. Adap. by Gladys Unger. Hay., May 11, 1909.

LOVE WILL FIND OUT THE WAY. C. by T. B. Pr. 1661. Shirley's *Constant Maid* under a new title.

LOVE WILL FIND OUT THE WAY. C.O. Hull. N.p.

LOVE WINS. C. 3 a. Savile Clarke and H. F. du Terreaux. Cambridge T.R., August 11, 1873; Croydon, October 12, 1874; Surrey, May 26, 1877.

LOVE WINS THE DAY. D. 3 a. Edward Towers. Pav., July 12, 1879.

LOVE WISELY; OR, THE SETTING OF THE SUN. Chas. Hannan. Liverpool Court T (prod. as *The Setting of the Sun*), October 12, 1892; Avenue, April 22, 1898.

LOVE WITHOUT INTEREST; OR, THE MAN TOO HARD FOR THE MASTER. C. Pr. 1699. Ac. at the T.R. Author unknown.

LOVE-CROWNED KING, A. P. 1 a. Philip B. Kirk Stedman. Primrose Hill, St. Mary's Church Room, April 17, 1909 (amat.).

LOVE-SICK COURT; OR, THE AMBITIOUS POLITICK, THE. C. Richd. Brome. Pr. 1658.

LOVE-SICK KING, THE. English Tragical Hist., WITH THE LIFE AND DEATH OF CARTESMUNDA, THE FAIR NUN OF WINCHESTER. Anth. Brewer. Pr. 1655. Afterwards renamed *The Perjur'd Nun*. Ac. at the King's T. in 1680 and repr.

LOVE-SICK MAID; OR, THE HONOUR OF YOUNG LADIES, THE. C. Richd. Brome. Ent. Stationers' Co. September 9, 1653. Ac. at Court in 1629 Licensed February, 1628-9. N.p.*

LOVE'S A JEST. C. Peter Molteux. L.I.F., 1696. Pr. 1696.

LOVE'S A LOTTERY, AND A WOMAN THE PRIZE. C. Jos. Harris. L.I.F. Pr. 1699. A masque annexed called *Love and Riches Reconcil'd*.

LOVE'S ADVENTURES. C. in 2 parts. Margaret Duchess of Newcastle. Pr. 1662.

LOVE'S AFTERGAME. Also called *The Proxy*. Ac. at Salisbury Court, 1634-5.

LOVE'S ALARMS. Ca. 1 a. Chas. Marsham Rae. Royalty, January 1, 1878.

LOVE'S ANGUISH. D. 4 a. Oscar H. Schow. Adap. fr. the French novel "Serge Panine." Adelphi, May 3, 1882.

LOVE'S ARTIFICE; OR, THE PERLEX'D SQUIRE. F. 2 a. John Wignell. Pr. 1762. Abridgment of Taverner's *Maid the Mistress*.

LOVE'S CARNIVAL. 5 a. English ver., by R. Bleichmann, of Hardleben's play *Rosenmontag*. Edinburgh Royal Lyceum, November 12, 1903; St. James's, March 17, 1904.

LOVE'S CHANGELING CHANGED. An old English P. pres. in a MS. of the 17th century in a private library in Ireland.

LOVE'S COMEDY. P. 1 a. L. M. Lion and F. Sargent. Leicester R.O.H., February 8, 1904.

LOVE'S COMEDY. P. 3 a. Henrik Ibsen. Cripplegate Inst., November 28, 1905; Manchester Gaiety, February 22, 1909.

LOVE'S CONTRIVANCE; OR, LE MEDECIN MALGRE LUI. C. Mrs. Centlivre. D.L., June 4, 1703. Pr. 1703. Almost a transl. of Molière's C. *Le Médecin*, etc.

LOVE'S CRONES. Wolverhampton T.R., January 28, 1881.

LOVE'S CROSSES. Ca. J. Day. Wolverhampton T.R., January 28, 1881.

LOVE'S CRUELTY. T. James Shirley. Ac. at the private house in D.L. Licensed 1631. Pr. 1640.

LOVE'S CURE; OR, THE MARTIAL MAID. C. Beaumont and Fletcher (or ? by Fletcher only). Prod. 1622-3. Pr. 1647.

LOVE'S DEVOTION. See *Cissy*.

LOVE'S DISGUISES. C. Knowles. 1838.

LOVE'S DISGUISES; OR, THE MOB CAP. Dom. D. 2 a. Howard Paul. D.L., April 13, 1853.

LOVE'S DOCTOR. D. 2 a. Andrew Halliday. Royalty, January 27, 1870.

LOVE'S DOMINION. Dr. Past. Richard Flecknoe. Pr. 1654. See *Love's Kingdom*.

LOVE'S DREAM. Piece. 2 a. M. by M. Moss. Lyceum, July 5, 1821.

LOVE'S ERROR. C. D. 2 a. Francis H. Manby. Southampton T.R., December 20, 1870 (amat.).

LOVE'S EYES. Ca. E. Lawrence Levey. Birmingham P.O.W. T., March 5, 1891.

LOVE'S FRAILTIES. D. 2 a. J. J. Stafford. M. by Mr. Jolly. Lyceum, November 9, 1835.

LOVE'S FRAILTIES; OR, PRECEPT AGAINST PRACTICE. C. Thos. Holcroft. C.G., February 5, 1794. Pr. 1794. Fr. the German *Hausvater*, which was borr. fr. Diderot's *Père de Famille*.

LOVE'S GOLDEN DREAM. P. 4 a. Frances Delavel. Stratford R.T., February 10, 1908.

LOVE'S HAZARD. P. 1 a. and 3 sc. Mrs. M. French Sheldon. Bayswater Bijou, November 7, 1901.

LOVE'S HOSPITAL. Geo. Wilde. Ac. before the King and Queen by the Students of St. John the Baptist's College, Oxford, August 29, 1636.

LOVE'S INTERLUDE. P. 1 a. Geo. D. Day. Bayswater Bijou, December 16, 1905.

LOVE'S KINGDOM. Past. T.C. R. Flecknoe. Pr. 1664. Little more than an alt. of *Love's Dominion*.

LOVE'S KNOTS. Oa. Libretto by C. V. Bridgman. M. by Wilfred C. Bendahl. St. Geo. H., May 5, 1880.

LOVE'S LABOUR WON. C. Meres mentions a play wr. by Shakespeare under this title. (?) *All's Well that Ends Well*.

LOVE'S LABOUR'S LOST. C. Wm. Shakespeare. Ac. at the Blackfriars and the Globe. Prod. 1591, rev. 1597. Pr. qto. 1598 as "presented before Her Highness (Q. Eliz.) last Christmas (1597) and newly corrected and augmented." Entd. Stationers' Co., January 22, 1607, and November 19, 1607. Pr. 1st folio, 1623. Pr. 2nd qto from 1st folio, 1631. Rev at Stratford-on-Avon Memorial, April 23, 1907.

LOVE'S LABYRINTH. Ca. 1 a. W. S. Emden. Strand, 1834.

LOVE'S LABYRINTH; OR, THE ROYAL SHEPHERDESS. T.C. Thos. Ford. Pr. 1660. ? N.ac. Partly borr. fr. Gomersal's tragedy of *Sforza Duke of Milan*.

LOVE'S LAST SHIFT; OR, THE FOOL IN FASHION. C. Colley Cibber. D.L., 1696. Pr. 1696. See *The Relapse*.

LOVE'S LIMIT. O. R. Reece. New Royalty, January 5, 1866.

LOVE'S LIVERY F. 1 a. J. Brougham. Publ. by S. French, Limited.

LOVE'S LOADSTONE. Anon., 1630. See *Pathomachia*.

LOVE'S LOTTERY. See *Love is a Lottery*.

LOVE'S LOYALTY. D. Pro. and 3 a. Harold Jaye. Greenwich, September 2, 1876.

LOVE'S MAGIC. Oa. 1 a. Major J. R. J. Jocelyn, R.A. M. by Cavaliere L. Zavertal. Woolwich, R. Artillery T., February 18, 1890.

LOVE'S MAGNET. P. 1 a. W. H. Pollock. Manchester Prince's, October 9, 1903; Alexandra, N., November 23, 1903.

LOVE'S MAISTRESSE, ETC. See *Love's Mistress*, etc.

LOVE'S MARTYR. D. 4 a. Leicester Buckingham. Olympic, April 25, 1866.

LOVE'S MARTYR; OR, WIT ABOVE CROWNS. P. Mrs. Anne Wharton. N.p. Ent. Stationers' Co., February 3, 1685.

LOVE'S MARTYRDOM. John Saunders. Hay., June 12, 1855.

LOVE'S MARTYRDOM. T. 1 a. A. C. Calmour. Criterion, July 3, 1886.

LOVE'S MASTERPIECE. C. Heywood. Ent. Stationers' Co., May 22, 1640. ? N.p.

LOVE'S METAMORPHOSIS. Dr. Past. John Lyly. Ac. by the Children of St. Paul's and by the Children of the Chapel, 1601. Ent. Stationers' Co., November 25, 1600. Pr. 1601.

LOVE'S METAMORPHOSIS. F. Vaughan. 1776. N.p. See *Love's Vagaries.*

LOVE'S MISTRESS; OR, THE QUEEN'S MASQUE. Between a D. and a Masque. T. Heywood, assisted in inventions by Inigo Jones. Pr. 1636. Ac. before their Majesties and at the Phœnix. The design taken fr. Apuleius's *Golden Ass.*

LOVE'S OLD SWEET SONG. C. 1 a. Ina Cassilis. Publ. by S. French, Limited.

LOVE'S ORDEAL; OR, THE OLD AND NEW REGIME. E. Falconer. D.L., May 4, 1865.

LOVE'S PILGRIMAGE. C. Beaumont and Fletcher. Pr. 1647. F. on a novel by Cervantes called "The Two Damsels," and from Ben Jonson's "New Inn." See *Lover's Pilgrimage.*

LOVE'S POWER. D. 3 a. Geo. H. Blagrove. Bayswater Bijou, July 25, 1901.

LOVE'S QUARREL. Ac. for the first time, April 6, 1661.

LOVE'S RANSOM. O. J. L. Hatton. 1809-86.

LOVE'S RETRIBUTION. C.D. 4 a. H. A. Langlois. Middlesbrough T.R., December 4, 1882.

LOVE'S REVENGE. Dr. Past. Dr. J. Hoadly. M. by Dr. Green. Pr. 1737.

LOVE'S REVENGE. D. 3 a. Bayle Bernard. Greenwich, November 21, 1868.

LOVE'S REVENGE. D. 3 a. W. F. Morton. Portsmouth T.R., February 13, 1882.

LOVE'S RIDDLE. Past. C. Abraham Cowley. Pr. 1638. (Author 15 years of age.)

LOVE'S SACRIFICE. T. John Forde. Phœnix, 1633. Pr. 1633.

LOVE'S SACRIFICE; A STORY OF THE COMMUNE. D. 1 a. J. Macer Wright. Hastings Pier Pav. November 25, 1896 (C.P.).

LOVE'S SACRIFICE; OR, THE RIVAL MERCHANTS. P. 5 a. G. W. Lovell. C.G., September 12, 1842; Holborn, December 11, 1869.

LOVE'S SECRET. Ca. J. R. Brown. Ladbroke H., January 2, 1888.

LOVE'S STRATAGEM. F. W. M. Alexander. Eccles Assembly R., February 12, 1904.

LOVE'S STROKE OF GENIUS. Vaudeville. Hertz.

LOVE'S SYSTEMS. P. Wm. Vane. Ac. by persons of fashion at Fobsey Magnus, the seat of Sir J. Knowles in Cornwall, December 22, 1807. ? N.p.

LOVE'S TELEGRAPH. C. 3 a. Princess's, September 9, 1846.

LOVE'S TEST. Oa. Julian Edwardes. Norwich, Victoria H., September 4, 1874.

LOVE'S TRIAL. O. H. W. Moore. M. by Sidney Shaw. Part perf. at Liverpool Bijou O.H., May 5, 1882.

LOVE'S TRIAL. P. 5 a. Publ. by S. French, Limited.

LOVE'S TRIALS; OR, THE TRIUMPHS OF CONSTANCY. C.O. S. J. Pratt. Pr. 1805. F. on Prior's "Nut-Brown Maid" and partly taken fr. the ballad of "Argentile and Curan," in "The Reliques of Antient Poetry." N.ac.

LOVE'S TRICKERY. Oa. 1 a. Cunningham Bridgman. M. by Ivan Caryll. Lyric, August 31, 1889.

LOVE'S TRIUMPH. O. P. Motteux. Hay. Pr. 1708.

LOVE'S TRIUMPH. O. 3 a. Wds. by J. R. Planché, M. by W. V. Wallace. R. Eng. O. at C.G., November 3, 1862.

LOVE'S TRIUMPH; OR, THE ROYAL UNION. T.C. Edward Cooke. Pr. 1678. Plot fr. the rom. of Cassandra, Part V., Book 4. N.ac.

LOVE'S TRIUMPH THRO' CALLIPOLIS. Masque. Ben Jonson. Perf. at Court, 1630. Decorations by Inigo Jones. Pr. 1640.

LOVE'S VAGARIES; OR, THE WHIM OF THE MOMENT. Dr. P. 2 a. T. Vaughan. D.L., April, 1776, under the title of *Love's Metamorphoses.* Pr. 1791. Same plot afterwards used in *Tit for Tat.*

LOVE'S VICTIM; OR, THE QUEEN OF WALES. T. Charles Gildon. L.I.F., 1701. Pr. 1701.

LOVE'S VICTORIE. P. Shirley. 1653.

LOVE'S VICTORY. T.C. Wm. Chamberlaine. Pr. 1658. Acted 1678 as *Wits Led by the Nose; or, A Poet's Revenge.* See *A Life's Victory.*

LOVE'S VICTORY, A. See *A Life's Victory.*

LOVE'S WELCOME. Ent. for the K. and Q. by Ben Jonson. Ac. at Bolsover at the Earl of Newcastle's, July 30, 1634. Pr. 1640.

LOVE'S YOUNG DREAM. P. 1 a. Eva Bright. Strand, April 21, 1891.

LOVED AND LOST. D. Pro. and 3 a. J. Hatton and A. Mathison. Manchester Queen's, November 3, 1879.

LOVELORNIA; OR, WITCH VERSUS CUPID, THE. O.A. Kate A. Simpson. Newcastle-on-Tyne Tyne T., June 17, 1901.

LOVELY. C. 1 a. Grattan. Publ. by J. Dicks.

LOVELY LIARS, THE. F.Ca. Camberwell Empire, September 30, 1907.

LOVER, THE. C. Theophilus Cibber. Pr. 1730. D.L., 1733.

LOVER BY PROXY. C. 1 a. Dion Boucicault.

LOVER HIS OWN RIVAL, THE. B.O. Abraham Langford. Goodman's Fields T. Pr. 1736.

LOVER LOST, THE. C. Mrs. De La Rivier Manley. 1696.

LOVER OF TWO, A. Military C. 3 a. Stephen Pritt. Preston T.R., July 27, 1896.

LOVER'S AMAZEMENT. Leigh Hunt. Lyceum, January 20, 1858.

LOVER'S CURE, THE. C. A. Chaves. 1705. See *The Cares of Love.*

LOVERS' KNOTS. O. 1 a. C. Bridgman. Publ. by S. French, Ltd.

LOVER'S LEAP, THE. D. T. Downey. Glasgow P.O.W., February 16, 1874.

LOVER'S LUCK, THE. C. Thos. Dilke. Ac. at T. in Little L.I.F., 1696. Pr. 1696.

LOVER'S MELANCHOLY, THE. T.C. John Forde. Blackfriars and Globe, November 24, 1628. Pr. 1629. D.L., 1747.

LOVER'S OPERA, THE. Wm. Rufus Chetwood. D.L., May 14, 1730. Pr. 1729.

LOVER'S PILGRIMAGE, THE. C. Beaumont and Fletcher, Fletcher and Shirley. After 1625.

LOVER'S PROGRESS, THE. T.C. Beaumont and Fletcher. Circa 1625. Pr. 1647. F. on a French rom. called *Lisander and Calista*, wr. by Daudiguier.

LOVER'S RUSE, A. F. Chas. Burslem. Dewsbury, T.R., October 27, 1873.

LOVER'S WATCH, THE. C. Mrs. Behn 1686.

LOVERS. Rom. M.P. 3 a. W. E. Morton, F. H. Herbert, and H. Crichton. M. by G. D. Fox. Cork T.R. and O.H., May 5, 1886.

LOVERS AT PLAY Strand, May 5, 1856.

LOVERS OF LOODGATE. P. Anon. Destroyed by Warburton's servant.

LOVERS OF PALMA, THE. See *Paul and Virginia.*

LOVERS OF THEIR COUNTRY. Anon. 1770. N.p.

LOVERS' QUARRELS. Int. 1 a. T. King. 1790. D.L., June 19, 1816. Alt. fr. *The Mistake.*

LOVERS' RESOLUTIONS. C. Richard Cumberland. D.L. March 2, 1802. N.p.

LOVERS' VOWS. P. 5 a. Mrs. Inchbald. C.G. Pr. 1798. D.L., September 26, 1815; C.G., 1816. Alt. fr. Kotzebue's *Natural Son.*

LOVERS' VOWS; OR, THE CHILD OF LOVE. P. 5 a. Transl. fr. Kotzebue by Stephen Porter. Pr. 1798. N.ac.

LOVERS' VOWS; OR, THE NATURAL SON. D. Transl. fr. Kotzebue by Benjamin Thompson. Pr. 1800. N.ac. See *Natural Son.*

LOVES AND GLOVES. Ca. E. B. Wyke. Newcastle Tyne T., March 23, 1878.

LOVES OF ARCADIA. See *Love of Arcadia.*

LOVES OF DIDO AND ÆNEAS. See *Dido and Æneas.*

LOVES OF EMILIUS AND LOUISA, THE. T. Maxwell, 1755.

LOVES OF ERGASTO, THE. Dr. Pas. G. Greber. Ac. at opening of Q.T., Hay. Pr. 1705.

LOVES OF MARS AND VENUS, THE. P. 3 a. Set to M. P. Motteux. Little L.I.F., 1696. Pr. 1696. Story fr. Ovid. M. by Finger and J. Eccles. Wr. to be inserted in Ravenscroft's *Anatomist.*

LOVES OF MARS AND VENUS, THE. Dr. ent. of dancing in imitation of the ancient Greeks and Romans. John Weaver. D.L. Pr. 1717.

LOVES OF PRINCE EMILIUS AND LOUISA, THE. T. John Maxwell (who was blind). Pr. 1755 at York by subscription for benefit of author.

LOVES OF THE ANGELS, THE. Burletta. Strand, 1832.

LOVES OF THE DEVILS, THE. Burletta. Strand, 1832.

LOVING AND SCHEMING. C. 3 a. Ralph Walker. Brighton T.R., March 16, 1874.

LOVING CUP, THE. S.C.D. 2 a. Andrew Halliday. Royalty, November 2, 1868.

LOVING ENEMIES, THE. C. L. Maidwell. D. of York's, 1680. Pr. 1680. Epil. by Shadwell, fr. whose *Virtuoso* the idea of this C. originated.

LOVING HEARTS. C. 3 a. G. F. Neville. Strand, May 21, 1870.

LOVING LEGACY, A. F.C. 3 a. F. W. Sidney. Eastbourne Devonshire Park T., January 28, 1895; Strand, March 12, 1895. See *That Terrible Turk and His Loving Legacy.*

LOW LIFE ABOVE STAIRS. F. Anon. Pr. 1759. N.ac.

LOW WATER. C. 3 a. A. W. Pinero. Globe, January 12, 1884.

LOWER DEPTHS, THE. 4 a. L. Irving. Transl. of Maxim Gorky's work. Great Queen Street T. (Stage Soc.), November 30, 1903.

LOWLAND LASSIE; OR, A TRIP FROM KINGHORN. Mus. D. John Rannie. D.L., 1803, under the title of *The Highland Lassie.* Pr. N.d.

LOYAL. P. 1 a. H. T. Johnson. Vaudeville, September 9, 1894; Terry's, 1894.

LOYAL BROTHER; OR, THE PERSIAN PRINCE, THE. T. T. Southern. Pr. 1682. Plot fr. a novel called *Tachmas Prince of Persia.* Pro. and Epil. by Dryden.

LOYAL BROTHER; OR, THE REVENGER'S TRAGEDY, THE. Cyril Turner. Ac. several times by the King's servants.

LOYAL CITIZENS, THE. A Droll out of the play *Philaster*, 1672.

LOYAL EFFUSION, A. Dr. Ent. Charles Dibdin. C.G., 1797. N.p.

LOYAL GENERAL, THE. T. Nahum Tate. Pr. 1680. Duke's T., 1680.

LOYAL LOVE. Rom. Play. 4 a. Originally called *Inez; or, The Bride of Portugal.* Ross Neil. Gaiety, August 13, 1887.

LOYAL LOVERS. C. 4 a. C. Garick and A. F. Guibal. Adapt. fr. "Le Voyage de M. Perrichon." Vaudeville, December 2, 1885.

LOYAL LOVERS, THE. T.C. Cosmo Manuche. Pr. 1652.

LOYAL LOVERS. See *The Alps.*

LOYAL PEASANTS, THE. C. J. Straycock. Pr. 1804. N.ac.

LOYAL SALOPIAN; OR, THE KING IN THE COUNTRY, THE. F. J. H. Colls. Ac. at Shrewsbury, 1795. N.p.

LOYAL SHEPHERD; OR, THE RUSTIC HEROINE, THE. Dr. Past. Poem. 1 a. T. Goodwin. Pr. 1779.

LOYAL SUBJECT, THE. T.C. Beaumont and Fletcher (? entirely by Fletcher). Pr. 1647. Ac. in 1618. Dublin (circa 1795). See *Faithful General.*

LOYAL SUBJECT, THE. Alt. T. Sheridan. N.p.

LOYAL TO THE LAST. D. 3 a. T. E. Pemberton. Birmingham T.R., June 16, 1896.

LOYAL TRAITOR, A. P. 1 a. Beatrice De Burgh. St. James's, May 10, 1900.

LOYALIST, THE. Piece. 1 a. Notting Hill Coronet T., May 22, 1900.

LOYALTY. C.D. 3 a. H. P. Lyste. Criterion, March 13, 1876.

LOYALTY. P. Douglas New Grand, September 25, 1882.

LOYALTY. Light Dom. C. 3 a. Hugh de Sélincourt. Court, June 21, 1909 (mat.).

LOYALTY; OR, INVASION DEFEATED. Hist. T. John Charnock. Pr. 1810. N.ac.

LOYALTY AND BEAUTY. Ac. by the Children of "Queenes Majesties Chappell," 1578.

LOYALTY HOUSE; INCLUDING THE SIEGE OF MANCHESTER. Hist. P. 4 a. Manchester Queen's, June 8, 1908.

LUCE DELL'ASIA, LA. O. 4 a. F. on Arnold's *The Light of Asia.* M. by De Lara. C.G., June 11, 1892.

LUCETTE'S LEGACY. Oa. B. Wyke. M. by F. Kessler. Brighton T.R., February 18, 1884.

LUCIA DI LAMMERMOOR, Italian O. 3 a. Donizetti. Naples, 1835. D.L., July 16, 1845. Eng. ver. Princess's, July 13, 1844. Plot fr. *The Bride of Lammermoor.*

LUCIA DI LAMMERMOOR; OR, THE LAIRD, THE LADY, AND THE LOVER. Op. Burl. Extrav. F. on Donizetti's O. H. J. Byron. P. of W. T., September 25, 1865.

LUCIFER. Orat. Benoit. Perf. in Brussels, 1860; Paris, 1883; Albert Hall, April 3, 1889.

LUCIFER. 1 a. Charles McEvoy. Midland, Manchester, November 9, 1907.

LUCIFER, SON OF THE MORNING. Adapt. of Marie Corelli's novel "The Sorrows of Satan," in 3 a. R. Castleton. Stratford Lyceum, December 15, 1898.

LUCILLE; OR, THE STORY OF THE HEART. D. 3 a. Bayle Bernard. Lyceum, April 4, 1836.

LUCINDA. Dr. Ent. 3 a. (with songs). Charles Jenner. Pr. 1770.

LUCIO PAPIRIO. O. Leo. Naples, 1720.

LUCIO SILLA. O. Mozart. Milan, 1773.

LUCIUS DAVOREN. Miss Braddon. See *The Outlawed Son.*

LUCIUS JUNIUS BRUTUS. T. Duncombe. D.L., November, 1734. Pr. 1735. F. on Voltaire's tragedy of Brutus.

LUCIUS JUNIUS BRUTUS; OR, THE EXPULSION OF THE TARQUINS. Hist. P. Hugh Downman. Pr. 1779. N.ac.

LUCIUS JUNIUS BRUTUS FATHER OF HIS COUNTRY. T. Nathaniel Lee. Duke's T., 1681. Pr. 1681. F. on real histories of Florus, Livy, Dionys, Halic, etc., and the rom. of Clelia by Mlle. de Scudéry.

LUCIUS, THE FIRST CHRISTIAN KING OF BRITAIN. T. Mrs. De La Rivier Manley. D.L., 1717. Pr. 1717. Prol. by Richard Steele. Epil. by Prior.

LUCIUS VERUS. O. A. Ariosti. 1727.

LUCK. Ca. Claude Templar. Imperial, November 15, 1879.

LUCK. P. 4 a. Lady Violet Greville. Ryde Royal T., November 19, 1900.

LUCK, OR A STORY OF PASTORAL LIFE. Britannia, July 19, 1869.

LUCK; OR, THE YORKSHIRE LASS. D. J. Levey. Leeds Amphi., March 8, 1869; Britannia (with second title, *or, A Story of Pastoral Life*), July 19, 1869.

LUCK OF LIFE, THE. Rom. D. 5 a. J. K. Murray. Manchester Royal Osborne T. (6 a.), May 30, 1898; Standard, August 15, 1898.

LUCK OF ROARING CAMP. D. 4 a. Fulham, March 1, 1909.

LUCK OF THE BRIANS, THE. D. John Johnson and Dagney Major. Hildenboro' Drill Hall, January 30, 1905

LUCK'S ALL. A. Wigan.

LUCKY BAG, THE. M.P. 1 a. Rachel Penn. Lyrics and M. by L. Parker. Savoy, June 8, 1893.

LUCKY CHANCE; OR, AN ALDERMAN'S BARGAIN, THE. C. Mrs. Aphra Behn. D.L., 1687. Pr. 1687. L.I.F., July 24, 1718.

LUCKY DISCOVERY; OR, THE TANNER OF YORK, THE. Ballad O., J. Arthur. C.G., April 24, 1738. Pr. 1738. Rev. at C.G., 1754.

LUCKY DOG, A. F.P. 3 a. W. Sapte, jun. Strand (mat.), July 4 1892; Terry's, October 3, 1892.

LUCKY DURHAM. P. 4 a. Wilson Barrett. Liverpool Shakespeare, June 9, 1904; Hammersmith King's, August 28, 1905.

LUCKY ESCAPE, A. C.D. 1 a. C. S. Cheltenham. Strand, September 9, 1861.

LUCKY ESCAPE, THE. M.F. Mrs. Robinson. D.L., April 30, 1778. Songs only pr.

LUCKY ESCAPE, THE. C. R. Linnecar. Pr. Leeds, 1789. N.ac.

LUCKY GIRL, A. M. Melo. D. 3 a. S. J. Adair Fitzgerald. M. numbers by Fitzgerald and L. Barone. Liverpool New T.R., November 18, 1889.

LUCKY GIRL, A. M.C. 3 a. Originally known as *In Search of a Father.*

LUCKY HIT, A. C.D. 1 a. Edward Stirling. D.L., February 1, 1858.

LUCKY HIT, A. C. 1 a. H. Paul. Princess's. Pub. by S. French, Limited.

LUCKY HIT, A. C. 3 a. Charles Appleyard. Royalty, November 21, 1872.

LUCKY HIT; OR, LOVE AT A VENTURE, THE. F. MS. in the possession of Stephen Jones (before 1812). N.p. N.ac.

LUCKY HORSE SHOE; OR, WOMAN'S TRIALS, THE. Dom. D. 3 a. Tom Parry. D.L., November 27, 1839.

LUCKY JIM. Sk. Walthamstow Palace, August 3, 1908.

LUCKY LIZA. M.F. Absurdity. F. Locke. M. by J. W. Hallon. Paisley Paisley, May 7, 1906.

LUCKY MISS DEAN. C. 3 a. Sidney Bowkett. Cri., August 3, 1905; rev. Hay., November 11, 1905.

LUCKY PRODIGAL; OR, WIT AT A PINCH, THE. F. 2 a. L.I.F., October 24, 1715. See second title.

LUCKY SHILLING, THE. D. 5 a. By the authors of *The Dark Secret.* Standard, February 20, 1888.

LUCKY SIXPENCE, A. F. 1 a. E. J. Browne.

LUCKY SPILL, A. C. 1 a. H. A. L. Rudd. Criterion, June 8, 1908.

LUCKY STAR. D. 4 a. Geo. Comer. Darlington T.R., August 1, 1887; Elephant and Castle, May 6, 1889.

LUCKY STAR, A. Mus. and satirical play. 1 a. 3 sc. By W. G. Rothery, music W. H. C. Nation. Scala, December 18, 1907.

LUCKY STAR, THE. C.O. 3 a. Dialogue by C. H. E. Brookfield. Lyrics by A. Ross and A. Hopwood. M. by Ivan Caryll. Savoy, January 7, 1899.

LUCKY STARS; OR, THE COBBLER OF CRIPPLEGATE. Burletta. 1 a. Geo. Dance. Strand, July, 1842.

LUCKY STONE, THE. Irish D. Britannia, July 16, 1877.

LUCRETIA. T. R. C. Dallas. Pr. 1797 N.ac.

LUCRETIUS. Dr. Monol. Tennyson.

LUCREZIA BORGIA. O. Donizetti. Milan, 1834. First time in Italian, D.L., June 5, 1855; first time in Eng., D.L., March 12, 1852.

LUCREZIA BORGIA. Burl. Sydney French. Marylebone, July 20, 1867.

LUCREZIA BORGIA. D. 3 a. Frederick Belton. Sadler's Wells, November 4, 1871.

LUCREZIA BORGIA. D. 3 a. Weston. Pub. by J. Dicks.

LUCREZIA BORGIA! AT HOME AND ALL ABROAD. Burl. 1 a. Leicester Buckingham. St. James's, April 9, 1860.

LUCREZIA BORGIA, M.D.; OR, LA GRANDE DOCTRESSE. Burl. Extrav. F. on the opera. H. J. Byron. Holborn, October 28, 1868.

LUCY. Dr. Poem. Henry Jones. Mentioned in Biographia Dramatica, 1812. Pr. N.d.

LUCY BRANDON. P. 4 a. Robert Buchanan. Adap. fr. Lord Lytton's *Paul Clifford*. Imperial, April 8, 1882.

LUCY HATTON. Marylebone, November 2, 1863.

LUD. Anon. 1594. N.p. See *King Lud.*

LUDI BEATÆ CHRISTINÆ. See "Miracle Plays."

LUDUS FILIORUM ISRAELIS. Anon. 1355. Represented by the Guild of Corpus Christi at Cambridge. N.p. See "Miracle Plays."

LUGARTO THE MULATTO. D. 4 a. C. O'Bryan. Surrey, May 20, 1850.

LUGGAGE PER RAIL. F. J. Russell. Richmond H.M.T., July 12, 1882.

LUISA MILLER. O. 4 a. Lib. by Camarran. M. by Verdi. Naples, December 8, 1849; as *Louise Miller* in Paris, February 2, 1853; Sadler's Wells, June 3, 1858; Her M., June 8, 1858.

LUKE RAEBURN, SINNER. M.D. 4 a. E. Cosair. Crouch End O.H., September 19, 1902 (C.P.); Garston T.R., November 24, 1902; Greenwich Carlton, July 20, 1903.

LUKE SHARP OF LONDON. M.C. Sk. R. P. Sheen. M. by Guillaume Leone. The Surrey, April 29, 1907.

LUKE THE LABOURER; OR, THE LOST SON. Dom. D. 2 a. J. B. Buckstone. Surrey, 1826; Adelphi, October 7, 1826, and 1828.

LUMINALIA; OR, THE FESTIVAL OF LIGHT. Masque. Presented at Court, Shrove Tuesday night, 1637. Ascr. by Winstanley and Wood to T. Lodge and R. Green. Contrivance of machinery by Inigo Jones.

LUN'S GHOST; OR, THE NEW YEAR'S GIFT. Panto. D.L., 1782. Compiled fr. *Harlequin's Jacket* and similar pieces.

LUNACY COMMISSION, A. F. John Anderton. Birmingham P.O.W., March 10, 1876.

LUNATIC, THE. C. 1 a. Agnes Leigh. Pub. by S. French.

LUNATIC, THE. F.C. 2 a. P. J. Barrow. Bournemouth T.R., August 30, 1898 (C.P.).

LUNATICK, THE. C. Dedicated to the Three Ruling B——s at the new house in L.I.F. Pr. 1705.

LUNATICS, THE. M.C. 3 a. Nita Rae. Woolwich Royal Artillery T., June 8, 1903.

LUPA, LA (*The She Wolf*). D. 2 a. G. Verga. Shaftesbury, February 18, 1908.

LUPONE; OR, THE INQUISITOR. Alexander Gordon. C. Pr. 1731.

LURED TO LONDON. D. 4 a. W. J. Patmore and A. B. Moss. Crewe Lyceum, February 14, 1889.

LURED TO LONDON; OR, NATTY, THE HOXTON BOY. P. 4 a. E. Thane. Hoxton King's, October 1, 1906.

LURED TO RUIN; OR, A HERO OF HEROES. D. 5 a. J. W. Whitbread. Dublin Q.T. (under second title); Glasgow Princess's, June 30, 1890; Britannia, July 4, 1892.

LURETTE. C.O. 3 a. F. Desprez and A. Murray. Lyrics by H. S. Leigh. M. by J. Offenbach. Avenue, March 24, 1883.

LURIA. T. R. Browning.

LURLINE. M.D. 1 a. D. Pitt. Adelphi, 1834.

LURLINE. O. 3 a. M. by Wallace. Words by E. Fitzball. Roy. Eng. O., C.G., February 23, 1860.

LURLINE. Burl. 3 a. R. Reece and H. B. Farnie. Avenue, April 24, 1886.

LUSIAD. See "Epic Poems."

LUSIUNCULA. Latin P. Said to be constructed on same story as *Macbeth.*

LUST OF GOLD, THE. D. 4 a. H. C. Sargent. Edmonton Royal T., June 23, 1902.

LUST'S DOMINION; OR, THE LASCIVIOUS QUEEN. T. Christopher Marlow. Pr. 1657. Afterwards alt. by Mrs. Behn and ac. under the title of *Abdelazer; or, The Moor's Revenge.* Ascr. by Ward to Haughton Day and Dekker. See *Spanish Moor's Tragedy.*

LUSTIGEN WEIBER VON WINDSOR, DIE. O. Nicolai. 1810-1849. An adapt. of Shakespeare's *Merry Wives of Windsor.*

LUSTY JUVENTUS, DESCRIBING THE FRAILTIE OF YOUTH, ETC. Int. Robert Wever. Black letter. N.d. Circa 1561.

LUSTY LONDON. Int. G. Puttenham. Mentioned in his *Arte of English Poesie.* N.p. Circa 1589.

LUTE PLAYER, THE. R. M. Percival. Dram. fr. Andrew Lang's "Violet Fairy Book." St. John's Wood, All Saints' H., January 28, 1909.

LUTTIER DE CREMONE, LE. D.L., June 23, 1893.

LYAR, THE. C. Pr. 1661. See *Mistaken Beauty.*

LYAR, THE. C. 2 a. Samuel Foote. See *The Liar.*

LYAR, THE. C. 3 a. Pr. 1763. Not Foote's P. An imposition.

LYCIDAS. Masque. Pr. 1762. N.ac.

LYCIDAS. M. Ent. C.G., November 4, 1767. Pr. 1767. Words alt. fr. Milton by Jackson, of Exeter (the composer).

LYDIA'S LOVER'S LODGINGS. F. 1 a. Wilks. Pub. by J. Dicks.

LYIENSHEE LOVEL; OR, THE GIPSY OF ASHBURNHAM DELL. Melo-d. 3 a. A. L. Campbell.

LYING DUTCHMAN, THE. Burl. F. W. Green and W. Swanborough. Strand, December 21, 1876.

LYING IN ORDINARY. F. 1 a. Peake. Pub. by J. Dicks.

LYING LOVER; OR, THE LADIES' FRIENDSHIP, THE. C. Sir R. Steele. D.L., December 2, 1703. Pr. 1704. Chiefly taken fr. the *Menteur* of P. Corneille and indirectly fr. *Alarcon.* See *The Liar.*

LYING MADE EASY. C.Oa. M. by Hawes. Lyceum, August 1, 1826.

LYING VALET, THE. C. 2 a. D. Garrick. Goodman's Fields T., November 30, 1741; Edinburgh, 1782. Pr. 1741. Also ac. at D.L. ? An alt. of *All Without Money,* a short C. forming the second of the five pieces in Motteux's *Novelty; Every Act a Play.* Pr. 1697.

LYLLY'S COMEDIES. See *Lilly's Court Comedies.*

LYNCE AND POLLIDORE. Past. Ent. Ac. at Vyse's Academy, Mitcham, Surrey. Pr. 1781.

LYNCH LAW. D. H. Pettitt. West Hartlepool T.R., September 19, 1874.

LYNCH LAW. Dr. Sk. 3 sc. By Sara B. Von Leer and E. P. Clift. Royal, Leeds, May 22, 1907 (C.P.).

LYNCH LAW; OR, THAT AWFUL YANKEE. D. Hull T.R., August 22, 1881.

LYONS MAIL, THE. P. 3 a. C. Reade. A re-arrangement fr. *Le Courier de Lyon*, by MM. Moreau, Siraudin, and Delacour (Paris Gâité, March 16. 1850; Princess's, June 26, 1854; St. James's (in Fr.), May, 1859; Shaftesbury, October 15, 1908.

LYRE AND LANCET. C. 2 a. F. Anstey and K. Pelle. Royalty, November 8, 1902.

LYRIC NOVELIST; OR, LIFE EPITOMISED, THE. Ent. by A. Cherry.

LYRIC ODE, A, on the Fairies, Aerial Beings and Witches of Shakespeare. Pr. 1776.

LYRICAL LOVER, A. Ca. 1 a. H. S. Clarke. Imperial T., March 24, 1881.

LYSANDER. MS. under this title, probably a drama, in Charles Macklin's library.

LYSIANE. P. 4 a. M. Romain Coolus. Paris Renaissance, April 10, 1898; Lyric, June 21, 1898.

LYSISTRATA. C. Transl. fr. the Greek by Mitchell, 1820-22, and by Hickie, 1853, and by Rudd. 1867. See "Greek Plays."

M

M.D. M. Absurdity. Odoardo Barri. Garrick, June 9, 1879.

M.D. M.D. 3 a. H. Paulton and M. Tedde. Adap. fr. the German of Von Moser. Doncaster T.R., April 2, 1888.

M.D.; OR, SWEETS AND BITTERS. F. by N. Lee. Liverpool T.R., March 7, 1874.

M.I., THE (*i.e.*, Mounted Infantry). M. Sk. H. Grattan and H. Clayton. M. by A. Barratt. Comedy, March 24, 1903.

M.P. C. 4 a. T. W. Robertson. P. of W.'s, April 23, 1870.

M.P.; OR, THE BLUE STOCKING. C.O. 3 a. T. Moore, Pr. 1811. Lyceum, July 12, 1815.

M.P. FOR PUDDLETON; OR, THE BOROUGH ELECTION. F. K. Summers. Sadler's Wells, November 23, 1868.

M.P. FOR THE ROTTEN BOROUGH, THE. F. 1 a. M. Lemon. Publ. by J. Dicks.

M.P.'S WIFE, AN. P. 4 a. Adap. fr. Tenell's novel, "A Woman of Heart." Op. C., February 16, 1895.

MA COUSINE. C. 3 a. Henri Meilhac. (Mme. Réjane's season) Garrick, July 1, 1895.

MA MIE ROSETTE. Ro. O. 2 a. G. Dance. M. by I. Caryll. Adap. fr. the French O. of same name. Lib. by Préval and Liorat. M. by Paul Lecôme (Folies Dram., Paris, February, 1890). Globe, November 17, 1892.

MA TANTE. C. 1 a. M. Stop. Notting Hill Coronet, June 29, 1903.

MA TANTE AURORE. O. Boieldieu. 1802.

MA'S MISTAKE. F.C. 1 a. Wm. Parker. Dublin Queen's, August 26, 1895.

MA'S OLD BEAU. Ca. Hilton Hill. Leigh T.R., October 16, 1888; Nottingham Grand, May 14, 1891.

MABEL. D. 3 a. F. Hay. Olympic, October 10, 1880.

MAB'S MANGLE. D. Liverpool Royal Sefton Theatre, August 27, 1883.

MABEL LAKE. D. 3 a. C. H. Hazlewood. Britannia, February 10, 1873.

MABEL, THE FORSAKEN. D. H. Lloyd. Longton Theatre, September 27, 1869.

MABEL'S CURSE. D. 2 a. Mrs. S. C. Hall. Publ. by J. Dicks.

MABEL'S LIFE; OR, A BITTER BARGAIN. D. 4 a. H. J. Byron. Adelphi, November 2, 1872.

MABEL'S SECRET. C.D. G. F. Ferneyhough. Derby Drill Hall, March 1, 1870.

MACAIRE. Ro. O. 2 a. Geo. Fox. Crystal Palace (in 3 a.), September 26, 1887; Standard, February 11, 1888.

MACARONI, THE. C. R. Hitchcock. Ac. at York, and once at the Hay. Pr. 1773.

MACARONI, THE. F. Between 1770 and 1780. Possibly abridgment of above. N.p. ? N.ac.

MACBETH. T. William Shakespeare. Founded on Holinshed's "Chronicle" and Reginald Scot's "Discovery of Witchcraft." 1st folio 1623. An adap. by Wm. Davenant. M. by Lock (different M. fr. that popularly called by his name). Duke's Theatre. Pr. 1673. Hay., December 27, 1707. Collated with the old and modern editions. Pr. 1773. D.L., January 7, 1744. Alt. by J. Lee. Pr. 1753. Another edition by H. Rowe. Pr. 1799. Rev. by J. P. Kemble, C.G. Pr. 1803. Rev. (by Kean), Princess's, February 14, 1853. Lyceum, November, 1875, and September 17, 1898. Rev. by A. Bourchier, Stratford-on-Avon Memorial, November 13, 1906; Garrick, December 11, 1906. Adap. for Mdme. Sarah Bernhardt and the French stage by Jean Richepin, Edinburgh T.R., June 24, 1884; Garrick, December 11, 1907; Garrick, May 7, 1909 (mat.).

MACBETH. Travestie. Anon. Pr. 1813.

MACBETH. O. H. A. J. B. Chelard. Lib. by Rouget de L'Isle. Paris Grand O., June 29, 1827.

MACBETH. Travestie. 2 a. Francis Talfourd. Henley-on-Thames, June 17, 1847; Olympic, April, 1853.

MACBETH. O. Verdi. Florence, 1847; Paris, April 21, 1865.

MACBETH. Travestie. Royal Naval School, New Cross, June 3, 1889.

MACBETH. See *Lusiuncula*

MACBETH MYSTIFIED. Burl. W. H. Mason and J. E. Roe. Brighton T.R., May 3, 1869.

MACCABAER. O. Rubinstein. Berlin, 1875.

MACCARTHY MORE; OR, POSSESSION NINE POINTS OF THE LAW. C.D. 2 a. Samuel Lover. Lyceum, April 1, 1861.

MACDUFF'S CROSS. D. 1 a. Sir Walter Scott. St. Geo. H., December 8, 1887 (amat.).

MACFARLANE'S WILL. Panto. V. 3 a. J. Mackay and H. Agoust. Imperial, December 26, 1881.

MACFLECKNOE; OR, A SATIRE ON THE TRUE BLUE PROTESTANT POET T. S. Dryden.

MACHAGGIS, THE. F. 3 a. J. K. Jerome and E. Phillpotts. Peterborough T.R., February 22, 1897; Globe, February 25, 1897.

MACHEATH IN THE SHADES; OR, BAYES AT PARNASSUS. Ser. C.O. Anon. 1735. N.p.

MACHIAVEL. P Ac. at the Rose T., 1591. In 1613 Daborne and Henslowe had a P. called *Machiavel* and *The Devil.*

MACHIAVELLUS. Latin D. D. Wilburne. Ac. at Cambridge, 1597.

MACHINE MADE. "F. impossibility." J. L. Balbi. Bayswater Bijou, October 10, 1903 (C.P.).

MACKE, THE (A game at cards). P. Ac. by Henslowe's Co. February 21, 1594. N.p.

M'KENNA'S FLIRTATION. F. 3 a. E. Selden. Coventry O.H., August 1, 1892

MACLEANS OF BAIRNESS, THE. P. 4 a. Edith Lyttleton. Criterion, June 19, 1906.

MACON, LE. C.O. 3 a. Scribe and Delairgne. M. by Auber. Paris Op. Com., May 3, 1825; St. James's, May 13, 1850.

McTAVISH. THE. F. Glasgow Princess's. October 5, 1896.

MAD. Ca. E. Rose. Olympic, June 12, 1880.

MAD; OR, BACK TO LIFE. Melo-d. 4 a. W. H. Dearlove. Castleford T.R., January 2, 1893.

MAD ACTOR, THE. C. Int. Lyceum playbill, June 8, 1825.

MAD AS A HATTER. F. 1 a. Francis A. Marshall. New Royalty, December 7, 1863.

MAD AS A HATTER. F. A. C. Thorp. Dublin Alexandra Hall, March 12, 1872 (amat.).

MAD AUTHOR, THE. P. Wm. Armstrong. Colen R.T., March 18, 1909 (C.P.).

MAD CAPTAIN, THE. O. Robt. Drury. Goodman's Fields. Pr. 1733.

MAD CAPTAIN; OR, THE LOVER HIS OWN RIVAL, THE. C. Langford. Goodman's Fields, March 5, 1733.

MAD COUPLE, THE. Burl. G. A. Stevens. 1769.

MAD COUPLE WELL MATCHED, A. C. Richard Brome. Pr. 1653. Afterwards renamed *The Debauchee; or The Credulous Cuckold.* Pr. 1677.

MAD GUARDIAN; OR, SUNSHINE AFTER RAIN, THE. F. 2 a. T. Merchant. Pr. 1795. (The name "Merchant" probably assumed by Thos. Dibdin.) Rev. at C.G. under latter title only.

MAD HOUSE, THE. A rehearsal of B.O. burlesque called *The Madhouse.* R. Baker. L.I.F., April 22, 1737. Pr. 1737.

MAD HOUSE, THE. M. Ent. W. C. Oulton Ac. in Dublin. Pr. 1785.

MAD LOVER, THE. T.C. Beaumont and Fletcher. Pr. 1647. Prod. before March, 1619. Plot fr. story of "Mundus and Paulina in Josephus."

MAD LOVER, THE. O. Mentioned in *Acis and Galatea*, masque, by Motteux.

MAD LOVER, THE. Massinger. 1637.

MAD LOVERS, THE. C. S. Johnson. 1732.

MAD MARRIAGE, A. D. 4 a. Adap. fr. the French by Frank Harvey. Northampton T.R. (5 a), January 16, 1884; Grand, August 21, 1885.

MAD MATCH, A. D. 4 a. Hugh Moss. Adap. fr. H. Rider Haggard's novel "Dawn." Gt. Malvern Assembly R., October 28, 1887.

MAD MEG. D. 3 a. By Clarence Burnette. Workington T.R., Nov. 9, 1885.

MAD MOTHER AND HER LOST SON, THE. Burl. of *Il Trovatore.* Scarborough T.R., April 21, 1884.

MAD PAINTER, THE. F. Alhambra, Oct. 6 1879.

MAD PASSION, A. D. 4 a. By E. H. Lampard. Castleford T.R., Jan. 23, 1888.

MAD REVENGE, A. See *Uncle Zac.*

MAD RUTH OF WILTON; OR, THE PROPHET OF STONEHENGE. D. By C. Belmore. Salisbury Pavilion, Jan. 29, 1872.

MAD TOM OF BEDLAM. Droll Dogget. N.p. Mentioned by Barker, 1814.

MAD WOMAN THROUGH LOVE; OR, THE CHILD OF THE ISLAND, THE. Manchester Free Trade H., August 10, 1885.

MAD WORLD. Beaumont and Fletcher 1608.

MAD WORLD, MY MASTERS, A. C. Thos. Middleton. Pr. 1608. See *City Heiress* and *Country Lasses.*

MADAME. Absurdity. 3 a. J. T. Tanner. Op. Comique, Dec. 7, 1895.

MADAME ANGOT. New ver. op. bouffe. 2 a. F. Desprez. Royalty, June 4, 1875.

MADAME ARCHIDUC. O. 3. a. Offenbach. 1874.

MADAME BERLIOT'S BALL; OR, THE CHALET IN THE VALLEY. C.D. 2 a. F. C Burnand. New Royalty, Dec. 26, 1863.

MADAME BONIVARD. F. 3 a. Alexandre Bisson. Comedy, Nov. 16, 1900.

MADAME BUTTERFLY. P. 1 a. David Belasco. From story of Japanese life by John Luther Long. Orig. prod. in America. D. of York's, April 28, 1900.

MADAME BUTTERFLY. O. 2 a. Giacomo Puccini. In Italian. C. G., July 10, 1905. In 3 a. (founded on a magazine story by John Luther Long, dramatised by the author and David Belasco, and adapted to the uses of the O. by Signori Illica and Giacosa). English version by Mrs. Elkin. Lyric (Moody-Manners Co.), Aug. 16, 1907.

MADAME CARTOUCHE. C.O. 3 a. Busnach and Decourcelles. M. by L. Vasseur. Adap. by H. Sutherland Edwards. (Paris, 1886.) Leicester R.O.H., Sept. 21, 1891.

MADAME DE RAIMONT. D. 1 a. R. Henry. Gaiety, May 8, 1883.

MADAME DU BARRY. Vaudeville. Ancelot, 1836.

MADAME DU CHATELET. Vaudeville. Ancelot, circa 1834.

MADAME FAVART. O. 3 a. Offenbach. Adap. by H. B. Farnie. Strand, April 12, 1879; rev. Criterion, Nov. 9, 1893.

MADAME FICKLE; OR, THE WITTY FALSE ONE. C. T. Durfey. Duke of York's T., 1677. Borrowed partly from *The Antiquary, The Walks of Islington and Hogsden,* and *Fawn.*

MADAME FLIRT. C. 3 a. Paul Gavault and Georges Berr. Paris Athenée, Dec. 27, 1901; Eng. ver., Hay., May 25, 1904; original French, Royalty, Nov. 21, 1907.

MADAME LAFARGE. Dom. D. Adelphi, Nov., 1840.

MADAME L'ARCHIDUE. Op. bo. 3 a. H. B. Farnie. M. by Offenbach. Op. Comique, Jan. 13, 1876.

MADAME MIDAS. D. 5 a. P. Beck and F. Hume, from latter's novel. Stratford T.R., July 7, 1888, c.p.; Exeter Victoria H. (in 4 a), Dec. 5, 1888.

MADAME OR MISS. Mus. ca. Lyrics by Ernest Leigh, M. by E. Nicholls. Bayswater Bijou, Nov. 14, 1900.

MADAM PAPILLON. C.O. 1 a. Offenbach, 1855.

MADAME RECOIT-ELLE? Duol. Emile de Najac. P.O.W., May 24, 1886.

MADAME SANS-GENE. P. 4 a. V. Sardou and E. Moreau. (Paris Vaudeville, Oct. 27, 1893.) Gaiety, June 23, 1894; Terry's, June 12, 1905.

MADAME SANS-GENE. C. Prol. and 3 a. Adap. by J. C. Carr fr. Sardou and Moreau. Lyceum, April 10, 1897; rev. June 10, 1901.

MADAME SANS-GENE. See *Duchess of Danzic.*

MADAME SHERRY. M.P. 3 a. M. Ordonneau. Book adap. by C. E. Hands. Apollo, Dec. 23, 1903.

MADAME X. P. Pro. and 3 a. Alexandre Bisson. Globe, September 1, 1909.

MADCAP. Bouffonnerie Musicale. Adap. of *La Chaste Susanne.* R. Reece and H. B. Farnie. Royalty, Feb. 7, 1878.

MADCAP. Ca. 1 a. Alec Nelson (E. B. Aveling). Comedy, Oct. 17, 1890.

MADCAP, THE. D. Mentioned in Herbert's Diary. May 3, 1624.

MADCAP MADGE. C.D. Pro. and 4 a. L. E. B. Stephens. Edmonton T.R., June 22, 1895; Imperial, Oct. 5, 1898.

MADCAP MIDGE. Dom. C. 3 a. Chas. S. Fawcett. Op. Comique, Dec. 5, 1889.

MADCAP PRINCE, A. C. 3 a. Robert Buchanan. Hay., Aug. 3, 1874.

MADCAP PRINCE, THE. P. 3 a. Mrs. A. M. Allen. Folkestone Pleasure Gardens, April 13, 1894 (amat.).

MADCAP VIOLET. C.D. 4 a. Dr. fr. Black's novel by Miss Ella Stockton. Sadler's Wells, March 18, 1882.

MADEIRA; OR, W(H)INES FROM THE WOOD. Extrav. H. Adams. King's Cross. Oct. 25, 1875.

MADELAINE MOREL. D. 5 a. D. E. Bandmann. Queen's, April 20, 1878.

MADELEINE. D. 3 a. J. Mortimer. Vaudeville, Feb. 1, 1873.

MADELEINE, LA. P. 3 a. H. W. Dam. Shaftesbury, Dec. 27, 1901.

MADELINE. D. C. Cooke. Sheffield Alex. O.H., Nov. 30, 1874.

MADELINE MARTEL; OR, WOMAN WRONGED BY WOMAN. D. Prol. and 4 a. Adap. fr. the French by F. Harvey. Northampton T.R., Feb. 9, 1882.

MADEMOISELLE CLEOPATRA. P. 1 a. W. Sapte, jun. Avenue, March 2, 1891.

MDLLE. DE LA SEIGLIERE. C. G. J. Sandeau. (M. Coquelin's Season.) Adelphi (rev.), July 5, 1899.

MADEMOISELLE DE LIRA. P. 1 a. Mrs. G. Thompson and Miss K. Sinclair. Comedy, Jan. 7, 1890.

MADEMOISELLE DELPHINE. C. 1 a. M. Eaton. Camberwell Metropole, June 11, 1900.

MADEMOISELLE FIFI. P. 1 a. Joan Pereira. Adap. fr. the Fr. of Guy de Maupassant. Prod. by Le Cercle Artistique. Rehearsal, W.C., December 13, 1908.

MADEMOISELLE MARS. P. 4 a. P. Kester. Imperial, Jan. 25, 1902.

MADEMOISELLE NAPOLEON. M.C. 3 a. J. Richepin. Adap. by J. Herbert. Bayswater Bijou, Oct. 20, 1903. C.p.

MADEMOISELLE NITOUCHE. See *Mam'zelle Nitouche* and *Nitouche.*

MADEMOISELLE SQUALLINO. F. 1 a. Featherstone.

MADEMOISELLE ZAMPA. F. W. S. Maugham. Avenue, Feb. 18, 1904.

MADEMOISELLE. See *Ma'mzelle.*

MADGE. Dom. D. 4 a. F. Rodgers. Middlesbrough T.R., March 24, 1888.

MADGE. C.S. H. Austin and Florence Wade. St. Geo. H., March 10, 1891. Royalty, Sept. 3, 1892.

MADGE WILDFIRE. D. 4 a. E. Stirling. Standard, Oct. 18, 1868.

MADMAN, THE. Burla. Anon. Marylebone Gardens, 1770. Pr. 1770.

MADMAN, THE. D. G. R. Walker. Gloucester T.R., May 6, 1881.

MADMAN'S MORRIS, THE. P. Robt. Wilson (with Dekker and Drayton). Ac. 1598. N.p.

MADOR, KING OF BRITAIN, THE HISTORY OF. F. Beaumont. Ent. Stationers' Co., June 29, 1660. N.p.

MADRE DEI MACCABEI, LA. O. Ariosti. Wr. for Venice. 1704.

MADRIGAL AND TRULLETTA. Mock T. Reed. C.G., July 6, 1758. Pr. 1758.

MAELSTROM, THE. D. 4 a. M. Melford. Southampton P.O.W. (prod. as *A Hidden Terror,* March 16, 1891); Shaftesbury, April 9, 1892.

MAESTRO DI CAPPELLA, IL. Op. bo. 1 a. In Italian. M. by Ferdinand Paër. P.O.W., Feb. 16, 1897.

MAEVE. Physl. D. 2 a. E. Martyn. Dublin Gaiety, Feb. 19, 1900.

MAFEKING. Rom. of the Siege. D. 4 a. H. Bedford. Leeds Queen's, May 10, 1902; Greenwich Carlton, June 9, 1902.

MAFEKING NIGHT. F. Chas. Brookfield and Harold Ferrar. Balham Duchess, Oct. 15, 1900.

MAGDA. P. 4 a. Adap. by Louis N. Parker fr. Sudermann's P. *Heimath.* 1st prod. in orig. German in London at D.L. by the Ducal Court Co. of Saxe-Coburg, June 25, 1895; Ital. ver. *Magda* (Eleonora Duse's season), D.L., June 12, 1896; Fr. ver. *Magda,* by W. Rémon (Sarah Bernhardt's season), Daly's, June 10, 1895; Lyceum, June 3, 1896; Italian ver., Lyceum, May 10, 1900.

MAGDA. 3 a. Ver. of Sudermann's *Heimath* by G. E. A. Winslow. Adelphi, Sept. 1, 1902; Notting Hill Coronet, Dec. 1, 1903.

MAGDA. New transl. by Claude Sykes of Hermann Sudermann's P. Eastbourne Devonshire Park, Dec. 12, 1907.

MAGDALEN MARRIED, A. Dr. Epis. P Barry Lewers. Middlesex, January 20, 1909.

MAGE, LE. O. 5 a. Massenet. Paris. March 16, 1891.

MAGENTA. O. Auber. 1859.

MAGGIE LORME. D. 3 a. Olympic, Feb. 3, 1873.

MAGGIE'S SITUATION. Ca. 1 a. J. M. Morton. Court, Jan. 27, 1875.

MAGIC BANNER; OR, TWO WIVES IN ONE HOUSE, THE. M.D. O'Keeffe. 1810. N.p.

MAGIC BANNER, THE. See *Alfred.*

MAGIC BEANS, THE. Extrav. H. and E. Paulton. Brighton Palace Pav., April 15, 1901.

MAGIC CAR; OR, THREE DAYS' TRIAL, THE. Oriental Spec. M. by Cooke. D.L., April 23, 1832.

MAGIC CAVERN; OR, VIRTUE'S TRIUMPH, THE. Pant. Wewitzer. C.G., Dec. 27, 1784. Pr. 1785.

MAGIC CLOAK, THE. Sk. Espanasse and Turman. Camberwell Empire, April 6, 1908.

MAGIC CUP, THE. O. 2 a. Words and M. by M. Johnson. Morley Town H., Oct. 21, 1895.

MAGIC EYE, THE. Sk. Eastern Epis. London M.H., December 31, 1906.

MAGIC EYE, THE. Miniature Grand O. Metropolitan M.H., April 20, 1908.

MAGIC FAN, THE. Oa. Bishop. Vauxhall Gardens, 1832.

MAGIC FIFE, THE. Oa. Offenbach. Gaiety, Jan. 25, 1873.

MAGIC FLUTE, THE. Panto. J. C. Cross. 1800.

MAGIC FLUTE, THE. Fairy O. 2 a. Mozart. Adap. to English stage by Cooke. D.L., March 10, 1838; Lyceum, Dec. 12, 1899. See *Die Zauberflötte.*

MAGIC FOUNTAIN, THE. O. Prol. and 3 a. J. R. J. Johnston. M. by H. S. Moore. St. Geo.'s H., Feb. 1, 1894; ? previously pl. at Sidcup.

MAGIC GIRDLE, THE. Burla. G. S. Carey. Marylebone Gardens. Pr. 1770.

MAGIC GLASS, THE. O. 1 a. H. Merivale. M. by Harriet Young. Hove T.H., Nov. 8, 1887.

MAGIC KISS. Children's P. L. Debenham. Pub. by S. French, Ltd.

MAGIC LOVE-PHILTRE, THE. Mus. Com. 1 a. S. E. Lees. M. by R. Brown. Upper Clapton St. Matthew's Parish R., Nov. 20, 1896.

MAGIC MIRROR, THE. Burl. spec. G. à Beckett. Princess's, Dec., 1843.

MAGIC MOONSTONE, THE. Britannia, December 26, 1899.

MAGIC MULE, THE. Britannia, December 26, 1878.

MAGIC OAK; OR, HARLEQUIN WOODCUTTER, THE. Panto. C.G. Songs only. Pr. 1799.

MAGIC OPAL, THE. Light O. 2 a. Arthur Law. Comp. by Señor Albeniz. Lyric, Jan. 19, 1893; P.O.W., April 11, 1893; revised ver. as *The Magic Ring.*

MAGIC PEARL, THE. O. 2 a. E. Fitzball. M. by T. Pede. Alexandra, Sept. 29, 1873.

MAGIC PICTURE, THE. Alt. of Massinger's *Picture* by the Rev. Henry Bate. C.G., Nov. 8, 1783. Pr. 1783.

MAGIC RING, THE. Com. O. 2 a. O. Brand. M. by I. Liebich. Grand, Oct. 11, 1886.

MAGIC RING, THE. See *The Magic Opal.*

MAGIC TOYS, THE. Ballet F. 1 a. J. Oxenford. St. James's, Oct. 24, 1859.

MAGIC WHISPER, THE. D. 2 a. C. H. Hazelwood. Britannia, Nov. 14, 1870

MAGICAL MASTER, THE. F. St. Geo. H., Dec. 6, 1907.

MAGICIAN; OR, THE BOTTLE CONJUROR, THE. C.D. Star and Garter Tavern, 1749. N.p.

MAGICIAN AND THE RING, THE. F. 1 a. F. D. Adams. Pub. by S. French, Ltd.

MAGICIAN NO CONJUROR, THE. C.O. Robert Merry. C.G., Feb. 2, 1792. N.p.

MAGICIAN OF THE MOUNTAIN, THE. Panto. Anon. D.L., 1763.

MAGICIAN'S DAUGHTER, THE. C.O. 3 a. C. V. France. M. by W. Wadham. Bradford T.R., Dec. 16, 1889.

MAGICIAN'S HEART, THE. Fairy P. 3 a. E. Nesbit. St. Geo. H., Jan. 14, 1907.

MAGICIENNE, LA. O. Halévy. Paris, 1858.

MAGISTRATE, THE. F.C. 3 a. A. W. Pinero. Court, March 21, 1885; Terry's, April 13, 1892.

MAGLOIRE, THE PRESTIGITATOR. Adelphi, April 1, 1861.

MAGNA CHARTA; OR, A ROMANCE OF RUNNYMEDE. O. 3 a. Wr. by "M.A.Oxon." M. by F. Dean. Lancaster Athenæum, Jan. 12, 1888.

MAGNET, THE. M. Ent. Marylebone Gardens. Pr. 1771.

MAGNET, THE. F. 3 a. Lionel Dalton. Bayswater Bijou T., April 27, 1893.

MAGNETICK LADY; OR HUMOURS RECONCIL'D, THE. C. Ben Jonson. Blackfryars, 1632. Pr. 1640.

MAGNETISM OF THE KING, THE. Mythical Rom. P. Harry Bruce.

MAGNIFICENCE. Int. Skelton. Pr. 1533 (Bk. Letter). This and *The Nigramansir* are the first of the Moralities that bear the name of the author.

MAGNIFICENT LOVERS, THE. Transl. of *Les Amants Magnifiques* fr. Molière by John Ozell. Circa 1710.

MAGNIFIQUE, LE. O. 3 a. Gretry. 1773.

MAGO AND DAGO; OR, HARLEQUIN THE HERO. Panto. M. Lonsdale. C.G., 1794. N.p.

MAGPIE OR THE MAID? THE. Melo-d. 3 a. J. Pocock. Fr. the French. C.G., 1830.

MAGPIE; OR, THE MAID OF PALAISIAN, THE. Melo-d. Rom. M. by T. Cooke. D.L., Sept. 9, 1815.

MAGPIE AND THIMBLE, THE. Ca. T. Smelt. Globe, March 17, 1877.

MAGUELONE, O. 1 a. M. Missa. Lib. by M. Carré. C.G., July 20, 1903.

MAHATMA, THE. Esoteric C. 3 a. L. A. D. Montague. Lichfield St. James's H., Feb. 15, 1894.

MAHMOUD; OR, THE PRINCE OF PERSIA. O. Prince Hoare. M. by Storace, introd. herein by Braham. D.L., April 30, 1796.

MAHOMET. P. Peele. Ac. by Henslow's company, Aug. 15, 1594. Possibly *The Turkish Mahomet.*

MAHOMET. T. Voltaire. Transl. under the name of Dr. Francklin. Pr.

MAHOMET AND IRENE. T. Dr. Johnson. D.L., Feb. 6, 1749.

MAHOMET, THE IMPOSTOR. T. Rev. J. Miller. F. on Voltaire's *Mahomet.* D.L., 1743 Pr. 1744. D.L., 1765, as alt. by Garrick.

MAID AND THE BLACKBIRD, THE. O. 1 a. Gillington and Solomon. Pub. by S. French, Ltd.

MAID AND THE MAGPIE, THE. C. Payne. Mentioned by Brewer.

MAID AND THE MAGPIE, THE. P. 3 a. I. Pocock. See *Magpie and the Maid.*

MAID AND THE MAGPIE; OR, THE FATAL SPOON, THE. Burl. H. J. Byron. F. on O. of *La Gazza Ladra.* Strand, Oct. 11, 1858.

MAID AND THE MAGPIE; OR, WHICH IS THE THIEF, THE. M. afterpiece fr. a Fr. M.D. Lyceum Playbill, Aug. 28, 1815.

MAID AND THE MINSTREL, THE. M.C. 2 a. S. Cubitt. M. by C. St. Amory. Lyric, Nov. 19, 1904.

MAID AND THE MOTOR MAN, THE. M.C. Lib. by J. Hickory Wood. M. by A. Romilli. Cardiff New, May 27, 1907.

MAID FROM SCHOOL. O. 3 a. F. Stayton. Folkestone Pleasure Gardens T., Nov. 30, 1903; Terry's, March 31, 1904.

MAID IN THE MILL, THE. C. Beaumont and Fletcher. See *The Surprise*. Partly bor. fr. the Spanish Rom. *Gerards* and from Belleforest's Histoires Tragiques. Globe, 1623. Pr. 1647. D.L., March 23, 1710. See *The Maid of the Mill*.

MAID IN THE MOON. M. Scena. A. Voyce. Coliseum, Sept. 25, 1905.

MAID IN THE MOON, THE. "Fantasy." 2 a. and 4 sc. Ralph T. Butler. M. by Herbert Hart. Bayswater Bijou, February 1, 1908.

MAID MARIAN Bishop. Mentioned by Brewer.

MAID MARIAN. C.O. 3 a. H. B. Smith. M. by R. de Koven. Camden Town Park Hall, Sept. 20, 1890; P.O.W., Feb. 5, 1891.

MAID OF ARTEMIS, THE. Past. P. A. Dillon. M. by C. Baughan. Kingston Albany Club, July 13, 1895.

MAID OF ARTOIS, THE. O. 3 a. Balfe. Words by Bunn. D.L., May 27, 1836.

MAID OF ATHENS, THE. P. 4 a. Buckstone. Pub. by J. Dicks.

MAID OF ATHENS, THE. M.P. 2 a. C. Edmond and H. C. Newton. M. by F. O. Carr. Op. Comique, June 3, 1897.

MAID OF BATH, THE. C. S. Foote. Hay., 1771. Pr. 1778.

MAID OF BIGGAR; OR, LOVE AGAINST MONEY, THE. D. James Skea. Barrow T.R., Sept. 9, 1872. See *The Maid of St. Aubins*.

MAID OF BRISTOL, THE. P. 3 a. J. Boaden. Hay., Aug. 24, 1803. Pr. 1803.

MAID OF CASHMERE, THE. B.O. F. on Scribe's *Le Dieu et La Bayadère*. M. by Auber. Adap. by Bishop. D.L., March 16, 1833, and Oct. 31, 1846.

MAID OF CEFN YAFA, THE. Welsh traditional D. 3 a. J. C. O'Dowd. Aberdare Model Th., April 21, 1870.

MAID OF CEFN YAFA, THE. M.P. 3 a. J. Bennett. M. by J. Parry. Cardiff Grand, Dec. 13, 1902.

MAID OF CROISSEY, THE. D. 2 a. Mrs. C. Gore. Pub. by J. Dicks.

MAID OF CROXDALE, THE. D. R. Richley. Spennymoor Cambridge T., Jan. 8, 1877.

MAID OF FRANCE, A. P. Rev. F. Phillips. Yarmouth R., July 10, 1905.

MAID OF GENOA. See *The Dumb Girl of Genoa*.

MAID OF GLENDALOUGH, THE. Orig. O. 2 a. M. by T. A. Wallworth. Based on the composer's "Keven's Choice." Lib. by Miss Hazlewood. Adelphi, March 25, 1882; P.O.W., June 13, 1899.

MAID OF HONOUR, A. P. 1 a. Edward Denby (E. C. Hemmerde, K.C.). F. on an incident in G. J. Whyte Melville's novel, "Holmby House." Queen's, September 22, 1909.

MAID OF HONOUR, THE. T.C. 5 a. Ph. Massinger. Phœnix, 1632. Pr. 1632. Alt. and rev. by Kemble at D.L., 1785. Pr. 1785.

MAID OF HONOUR, THE. O. 3 a. Lib. by Fitzball. M. by Balfe. D.L., Dec. 20, 1847.

MAID OF HONOUR, THE. Ca. 1 a. J. P. Wooler. Strand, May 16, 1864.

MAID OF HONOUR, THE. Cost. P. 1 a. J. Waters. Dublin T.R., Feb. 25, 1899.

MAID OF JUDAH, THE. O. C.G., March 7, 1829; Victoria, 1834.

MAID OF JUDAH; OR, THE KNIGHT TEMPLARS, THE. O. 3 a. Fr. Sir Walter Scott's *Ivanhoe* by M. R. Lacy. C.G., March 7, 1829.

MAID OF KENT, THE. C. F. G. Waldron. Founded on a story in the *Spectator*. D.L., May 17, 1773. Pr. 1778.

MAID OF LOCHLIN, THE. Lyrical D. Wm. Richardson, M.A. Pr. 1801. N.ac.

MAID OF MANY PARTS, A. C. 1 a. Mrs. Langtry and G. Hill. Court, Oct. 13, 1906. (C.P.)

MAID OF MARIENBURG, THE. D. 5 a. Anon. Fr. the German of Kratter. Pr. 1798. N.ac.

MAID OF MARIENDORPT, THE. P. 5 a. J. Sheridan Knowles. Hay., 1838.

MAID OF MILAN. Mentioned by Brewer.

MAID OF NORMANDY; OR, THE DEATH OF THE QUEEN OF FRANCE, THE. T. 4 a. E. J. Eyre. Pr. 1793. Act. at Dublin.

MAID OF ORLEANS. T. Schiller. 1801. See *Joan of Arc*.

MAID OF PALAISIAN, THE. O. With Rossini's *Gazza Ladra*. Adap. to Engl. stage by Bishop. D.L., Oct. 13, 1838.

MAID OF ST. AUBINS; OR, LOVE AGAINST MONEY, THE. D. 2 a. J. Skea. Jersey Royal H., March 15, 1870 (amat.). See *The Maid of Biggar*.

MAID OF SAXONY. O. George Morris. 1842.

MAID OF SEVILLE, THE. Sk. Wr. and comp. by J. M. Down and E. Woodville. Prod. by R. Temple. Metropolitan M.H., Oct. 7, 1907.

MAID OF SWITZERLAND, THE. D. 1 a. C. B. Wilson. Pub. by J. Dicks.

MAID OF THE MILL, THE. P. J. Fletcher, assisted by Rowley. Globe, 1623. See *The Maid in the Mill*.

MAID OF THE MILL, THE. C.O. 3 a. Isaac Bickerstaffe. C.G. Pr. 1765. D.L., Nov. 8, 1815, and Nov. 6, 1824. Taken fr. Richardson's "Pamela." Since reduced to afterpiece.

MAID OF THE MILL, THE. C.O. 2 a. B. Carter. M. by R. Forsyth. Folkestone Pleasure Gardens, Jan. 5, 1897.

MAID OF THE MILL; OR, THE COUNTRY REVELS, THE. F. Anon. Taken fr. Beaumont and Fletcher. C.G., 1750. N.p.

MAID OF THE OAKS, THE. Alt. to an afterpiece. 2 a. By a Gentleman of the T.R., Edinburgh. Edinburgh.

MAID OF THE OAKS, THE. D. Ent. J. Burgoyne. D.L. Pr. 1774. Reduced to a farce in 1782.

MAID OF THE VALE, THE. C.O. Trans. and alt. fr. *La Buona Figliuola*. Dublin, 1775.

MAID OF YESTERDAY, THE. Duol. Mrs. Vere Campbell. Queen's Gate H., S. Kensington, May 11, 1896; Garrick, Nov. 19, 1896.

MAID OR WIFE; OR, THE DECEIVER DECEIVED. M.C. 2 a. B. Livius. D.L., Nov. 5, 1821.

MAID THE MISTRESS, THE. C. W. Taverner. D.L., June 5, 1708. Pr. 1708. The running title is *The Disappointment; or, The Maid the Mistress*.

MAID THE MISTRESS, THE. Burla. C.G., 1783. N.p. A transl. of *La Serva Padrona*, by O'Keefe.

MAID THE MISTRESS, THE. O. M. by Dibdin. 1769.

MAID WITH THE MILKING PAIL, THE. C.D. 1 a. J. B. Buckstone. T.R., Hay., and Adelphi.

MAID'S LAST PRAYER; OR, ANYTHING RATHER THAN FAIL, THE. C. T. Southern. Contains a song by Congreve. Ac. T.R., 1693. Pr. 1693.

MAID'S METAMORPHOSIS, THE. C. in verse. J. Lyly. Ac. Pr. 1600.

MAID'S REVENGE, THE. T. J. Shirley. Plot fr. a story in Reynolds's *God's Revenge against Murder*. Ac. at the Private House in D.L., 1638. Lic. 1626. Pr. 1639.

MAID'S TRAGEDY, THE. Beaumont and Fletcher. Ac. at Blackfriars T. Pr. 1619. Originally called *The Bridal*.

MAID'S TRAGEDY, THE. An adapt. of Beaumont and Fletcher's P. E. Waller. 1682. Pr. 1690.

MAID'S TRAGEDY, THE. Beaumont and Fletcher. Rev. at Royalty, Dec. 5, 1904; prod. by the Play Actors (rev.), Court, October 18, 1908.

MAIDEN QUEEN. See *The Comical Lovers*.

MAIDEN QUEEN, THE. C.O. 2 a. R. Buchanan and "Charles Marlowe." M. by F. Pascal. Ladbroke H., April 6, 1905 (C.P.).

MAIDEN WHIM; OR, THE CRITICAL MINUTE, THE. F. Dr. Hill. D.L., April 24, 1756. N.p.

MAIDEN WIDOW, A. F.C. 1 a. F. M. Reece. Salford P.O.W., January 25, 1906 (C.P.).

MAIDEN WIFE, A. New ver., 2 a., of De Leuven and Brunswick's opera *Le Postillon de Lonjumeau*. M. by A. Adam. Engl. title alt. to original French, Aug. 30, 1886. Empire, Aug. 21, 1886.

MAIDEN'S FAME, A. D. 2 a. W. B. Bernard.

MAIDEN'S HOLIDAY, THE. C. C. Marloe and J. Day. Ent. Stationers' Co., April 8, 1654. Destroyed by Warburton's servant.

MAIDENLY MANŒUVRES. F. Godfrey Drayton. Hackney Manor T., Nov. 14, 1900.

MAIDENS, BEWARE. F. 1 a. J. T. Haines. Publ. by J. Dicks.

MAIDS; OR, THE NUNS OF GLOSSENBURY. F. 1 a. Transl. fr. *Les Dragons et les Benedictines* of M. Le Brun by J. Wild. Ac. 1804.

MAIDS AND BACHELORS; OR, MY HEART FOR YOURS. C. Lumley St. George Skeffington. C.G., June 6, 1806. An alt. of *The High Road to Marriage*.

MAIDS AS THEY ARE. C. Inchbald. 1797.

MAIDS OF HONOUR. Ca. C. L. Kenney. Mirror, April 24, 1875.

MAIL COACH ADVENTURES. Monol. given by Mr. Mathews. Lyceum, April 2, 1818.

MAIL COACH PASSENGERS. F. 2 a. D.L., Feb. 13, 1816.

MAIN, LA. Wordless P. Henri Berény. Coronet, October 22, 1900; Waldorf, October 25, 1905.

MAIN CHANCE. C. B. Tweedale. Blackpool Nortreck H., March 31, 1902.

MAIN CHANCE, THE. C. 2 a. H. B. Farnie. Liverpool P.O.W., Dec. 6, 1873; Royalty, April 15, 1874.

MAIN HOPE, THE. D. Prol. and 3 a. G. Comer. West Bromwich T.R., Aug. 31, 1885; Britannia, Aug. 30, 1886.

MAINACHT, DIE. O. Rimsky-Korsakor.

MAINTOP WATCH, THE. Nautical D. Liverpool Colosseum T., Sept. 14, 1868.

MAISIE. P. 4 a. F. Davenporte and J. W. Boyling. Southampton Grand, Feb. 4, 1905.

MAISON D'ARGELE, LA. See *The House of Clay*.

MAITRE DE CHAPPELLE, LE. C.O. 2 a. Ferdinando Paër. Paris, March 29, 1821; D.L., July 12, 1845. Afterwards reduced to 1 a. and ac. in France and Germany. Eng. vers. prod. P.O.W., February 16, 1897.

MAITRE DE FORGES, LE. D. Georges Ohnet. Paris, December, 1803; Royalty, January 8, 1885; Notting Hill, May 26, 1902.

MAITRE EN DROIT, LE. O. P. A. Monsigny. Paris, February 13, 1760.

MAITRE GRIFFARD. C.O. C. P. L. Delibes. Paris, 1857.

MAITRE PERONILLA. O. 3 a. Offenbach, 1878.

MAITRE SEILER. O. in Eng. 1 a. Alick Maclean. Lyric, August 20, 1909.

MAJESTY MISLED; OR, THE OVERTHROW OF EVIL MINISTERS. T. Pr. 1734. Ascribed to John Wilkes. Alt. and repr. 1770.

MAJOR, THE. F.C. Mark Melford. Wolverhampton P.O.W., Oct. 20, 1882.

MAJOR, THE. C.Oa. 3 a. J. McL. Jones. M. by the Misses Gregory. Holywell Assembly H., April 8, 1890.

MAJOR AND MINOR. C.D. 2 a. W. Ellis. Olympic, Aug. 6, 1881.

MAJOR BAGGS. F.C. 3 a. Arthur Lloyd. Barrow T.R., Sept. 2, 1878; Philharmonic, June 5, 1882.

MAJOR BARBARA. P. 3 a. Geo. Bernard Shaw. Court, Nov. 28, 1905.

MAJOR HOPE. C. 3 a. Liverpool P.O.W., Sept. 25, 1891; as *Hope*, Vaudeville, Feb. 11, 1892.

MAJOR JENNINGS. F. 3 a. F. A. Besant Rice. Camden, Feb. 11, 1907.

MAJOR MARIE ANNIE. Ca. 2 a. Edgar Newbound. Britannia, May 17, 1880.

MAJOR PROPOSES, THE. Ca. H. T. Milner. Rotherham T.R., March 17, 1884.

MAJOR RAYMOND. Play. 4 a. P. Havard. Terry's, June 25, 1896.

MAJOR'S DAUGHTER, THE; OR, A HOPELESS SIN. Mil. D. 3 a. H. Hewitt. Inverness T.R., Sept. 24, 1902.

MAJOR'S DILEMMA; OR, FINE FEATHERS MAKE FINE BIRDS, THE. C. Evagone. Jersey T.R., Sept. 26, 1894.

MAJOR'S DOUBLE, THE. F.C. 3 a. C. W. McCabe. Brunswick Inst., Vauxhall, Nov. 11, 1901; Croydon Grand, Oct. 21, 1905; Belfast T.R., June 4, 1906.

MAJOR'S MANŒUVRE, THE. Sk. Bedford, June 29, 1908.

MAJOR'S MIDDY, THE. M.C. Sk. Camberwell Empire, Aug. 19, 1907.

MAJOR'S NIECE, THE. F. sk. in 1 sc. John Beauchamp. Hammersmith Pal., December 7, 1908.

MAKE A NOISE TOM. F. Pr. 1718. Of local interest in Wakefield.

MAKE BELIEFS. Duol. fr. the Danish of Otto Benzon. Dagmar Holberg and J. T. Grein. Royalty, May 27, 1892.

MAKE YOUR WILLS. F. 1 a. E. Mayhew and G. Smith. Hay., 1836.

MAKE YOURSELF AT HOME. F. A. Maltby. Mirror, April 24, 1875.

MAKER OF COMEDIES, A. C. 1 a. Clo. Graves. Shaftesbury, Feb. 9, 1903.

MAKER OF MEN. P. 1 a. A. Sutro. St. James's, Jan. 27, 1905.

MAKER OF WOMEN, A. P. Edith A. Browne. Prod. by Ama., Royalty, Feb. 25, 1906.

MAKESHIFTS, THE. Ca. G. L. Robins. Manchester Gaiety, October 5, 1908; Coronet, June 8, 1909.

MAKING A GENTLEMAN. P. 4 a. Alfred Sutro. Garrick, September 11, 1909.

MAKING IT PLEASANT. F. Will Clement. Woolwich T.R., Aug. 22, 1887.

MAKINGS OF A MAN, THE. D. 4 a. Tom Craven. F. on a story by the same author. Pav., September 27, 1909.

MALADE IMAGINAIRE, LE. C. Molière. 1673. D.L., June 12, 1893. See *Dr. Last iu His Chariot*. See "French Classical Plays."

MALALA. Extrav. Offenbach. Gaiety, April 8, 1781.

MALCOLM. T. John Roberts. Pr. 1779. N.ac.

MALCOLM KING OF SCOTS. P. Charles Massey. Ac. in 1602. N.p.

MALCONTENT, THE. T.C. John Marston. Ac. by the King's Servants. Pr. 1604. Olympic, Aug., 1850.

MALE COQUETTE; OR, SEVENTEEN HUNDRED FIFTY-SEVEN, THE. F. D. Garrick. D.L., March 24, 1757. Pr. 1757.

MALEK ADEL. O. 3 a. Count Pepoli. M. by M. Costa. Paris, January 14, 1837; Her M., May 18, 1837.

MALEK ADEL. O. Poniatowski. Genoa, 1846.

MALIA. Sicilian D. 3 a. Luigi Capuana. Shaftesbury, February 3, 1908.

MALL; OR, THE MODISH LOVERS, THE. C. by J. D. Ascr. by some to Dryden. Ac. at the T.R., 1674. Pr. 1674.

MALVINA. O. 3 a. G. Macfarren. D.L.

MALVINA. T. Anon. Pr. at Glasgow, 1786.

MALVINA. B.O. Subject fr. Ossian. M. arr. by Cooke. D.L., Jan. 28, 1826.

MAMA. C. 3 a. Mrs. Chippendale. Dublin Gaiety, May 8, 1876.

MAMAMOUCHI; OR, THE CITIZEN TURN'D GENTLEMAN. C. E. Ravenscroft. Pr. 1675, and under latter title only 1672. Duke's T., 1675. Taken fr. *Mons. Pourceaugnac* and the *Bourgeois Gentilhomme* cf Molière.

MAMILLA. Greene. 1593. Recorded by Brewer.

MAMMA. F.C. 3a. Adap. by Sydney Grundy fr. Bisson and Mars's *Les Surprises du Divorce*. Dublin Gaiety, May 8, 1876 (the orig. C. prod. at Vaudeville, Paris, March 2. 1888); first time in England, under direction of M. Coquelin, Royalty, April 16, 1888; (New) Court, September 24, 1888 (opening night); Criterion. March 12, 1901.

MAMMA'S OPINIONS. Ca. 1 a. St. Geo. H., Jan. 31, 1893.

MAMMA'S. See *Ma's*.

MAMMON. C. 3 a. S. Grundy. Strand, April 7, 1877.

MAMON. D. in Hebrew. Mr. and Mrs. Sigmund Fineman's Co. Standard, Sept. 21, 1896.

MAM'ZELLE; OR, THE LITTLE MILLINER. M.C. 3 a. W. Gill. Orig. prod. in America. Liverpool P.O.W.'s, Oct. 22, 1894.

MAM'ZELLE NITOUCHE. M.C. 3 a. H. Meilhac and A. Millaud. (Paris Variétés, Jan. 26, 1883); Trafalgar Square, May 6, 1893.

MAM'ZELLE. See *Mademoiselle*.

MAN. D. H. A. Glyn. Gloucester T.R., Jan. 5, 1874.

MAN; OR, GOLDEN FETTERS. D. H. Pettitt. Leeds Amphi., Nov. 10, 1873.

MAN ABOUT TOWN, A. An Episode. S. Stange. Strand, May 1, 1899.

MAN ABOUT TOWN, A. M.F. 3 a. "Huan Mee." M. by A. Carpenter. Avenue, January 2, 1897.

MAN ABOUT TOWN, THE. F. 1 a. W. B. Bernand. Eng. O.H., May 5, 1835; Lyceum, 1836.

MAN AGAINST MOTOR. Sk. 2 sc. Paragon, August 3, 1903.

MAN AND HIMSELF. P. 4 a. M. Carson and N. Keith. Kennington T., November 16, 1903.

MAN AND HIS MAKERS. P. of Modern Life. 4 a. Wilson Barrett and L. N. Parker. Lyceum, October 7. 1899.

MAN AND HIS MASTER. D. 3 a. People's O.H., Ashton, July 16, 1883.

MAN AND HIS PICTURE, THE. P. 5 a. Adap. fr. Hermann Sudermann's P., *Sodoms Ende*. Folkestone Pleasure Gdns., March 11, 1903; Gt. Queen's St. T., March 18, 1903.

MAN AND HIS WIFE, A. C. 3 a. Liverpool Shakespeare T., August 8, 1904.

MAN AND SUPERMAN. P. 3 a. G. B. Shaw. Court, May 23, 1905; rev. October 23, 1905; May 27, 1907. See *Don Juan in Hell*.

MAN AND THE SPIRIT, THE. D. 1 a. C. H. Hazelwood, Britannia, February 28, 1881.

MAN AND THE WOMAN. D. 3 a. R. Buchanan. Criterion, December 19, 1889.

MAN AND WIFE. C. C. H. Stephenson. Belfast T.R., September 2, 1870.

MAN AND WIFE. D. 4 a. W. Collins. P.O.W., February 22, 1873.

MAN AND WIFE. D. 4 a. W. Howard. Kidderminster T.R.. April 16, 1900; Liverpool Star, April 23, 1900; Stratford T.R., September 10, 1900.

MAN AND WIFE. See *Wife or No Wife*, *Matrimony*.

MAN AND WIFE; OR, A SCOTCH MARRIAGE. D. David James jun. Adap. fr. Wilkie Collins's novel. Margate T.R., June 29, 1885.

MAN AND WIFE; OR, MORE SECRETS THAN ONE. C. S. J. Arnold. P. 1809. D.L., October 4, 1814; Lyceum, May 15, 1822.

MAN AND WIFE; OR, THE SHAKESPEARE JUBILEE. C. G. Colman. (See Garrick Jubilee.) C.G., 1770.

MAN AND WOMAN. C.D. 4 a. H. C. de Mille and D. Belasco. Fourth act rewritten by Malcolm Watson. Orig. prod. in America. Op. Comique, March 25, 1893.

MAN AND WOMAN. P. Mrs. James Ward. Brondesbury H., January 14, 1909 (mat.).

MAN AS WOMAN MAKES HIM. Sk. Harry Bruce. Greenwich Palace, October 21, 1907.

MAN BEWITCHED. See *The Ghost*.

MAN FIEND, THE. D. 4 a. C. S. Kitts. Bilston R.T., April 6, 1903.

MAN FOR THE LADIES, THE. F. 2 a. D. Jerrold. Publ. by J. Dicks.

MAN FRED. See *Manfred*.

MAN FROM ADEN, THE. D. Episode. 3 sc. G. H. Inglis. Victoria H., May 6, 1905.

MAN FROM AUSTRALIA, THE. P. 3 a. G. Dayle. Llandudno, Princess T., June 2, 1902.

MAN FROM BLANKLEY'S, THE. C. 3 a. F. Anstey. P.O.W., April 25, 1901. Revived, Haymarket, March 24, 1906.

MAN FROM CEYLON, THE. F. F. Dawson. Worthing T.R., October 28, 1901.

MAN FROM DOWN THERE, THE. M. Burl. Extrav., in two spasms. S. T. Pease, Oxford Empire, March 3, 1902.

MAN FROM MEXICO, THE. F.C. 3 a. H. A. du Souchet. Orig. prod. in America and Australia. Eastbourne D.P., November 9, 1908; Coronet, November 23, 1908.

MAN FROM PARIS, THE. Sk. H. W. Barker. Muncaster, Bootle, February 22, 1909.

MAN FROM THE MINT, A. F. 3 a. F. D. Head. Worthing T.R., December 22, 1902.

MAN HIS OWN MASTER, THE. F. 1 a. D.L., June 12, 1816.

MAN HUNTER, THE. D. of Australian life, by F. Jarman. Newport (Mon.) Victoria T., May 11, 1891.

MAN IN A THOUSAND, THE. D. 4 a. C. Burnette. North Shields T.R., August 11, 1890; 5 a., Surrey, March 7, 1892.

MAN IN BLACK, A. Rom. D. 4 a. H. E. Williams. F. on Stanley Weyman's novel. Vaudeville, September 3, 1897 (C.P.).

MAN IN LOVE, A. C. 3 a. E. Rassendyll Wimbledon New T., November 1, 1895.

MAN IN MOTLEY, A. Duo. Tom Gallon. Birmingham Grand, January 13, 1908; Coliseum, January 20, 1908.

MAN IN MOURNING FOR HIMSELF, A. M.E. 2 a. M. by H. Smart and M. P. Corri. Lyceum, July 20, 1816.

MAN IN POSSESSION, THE. Comic D. 3 a. J. Albery. Gaiety, December 4, 1876.

MAN IN POSSESSION, THE. D.Ca. Robert Overton. Leytonstone Assembly R., December 10, 1892.

MAN IN RAGS, THE. P. 1 a. N. Monck. St. George's H., July 12, 1901.

MAN IN THE CLOAK; OR, THE ASSASSIN, THE. D. 2 a. F. Marchant. Victoria, February 7, 1870.

MAN IN THE HOUSE, A. Ca. M. Melford. Huddersfield T.R. and O.H., August 4, 1884.

MAN IN THE IRON MASK, THE. Marylebone, February 5, 1855.

MAN IN THE IRON MASK, THE. D. 5 a. Adap. fr. Dumas' rom. by M. Goldberg, and suggested partly by an episode in "The Vicomte de Bragelorme." Huddersfield T.R., March 7, 1899 (C.P.); Hammersmith Lyric, April 24, 1899; Adelphi, March 11, 1899.

MAN IN THE IRON MASK, The. P. 4 a. Perth and Condie. Walsall G.T., March 17, 1899.

MAN IN THE IRON MASK, THE. D. 5 a. Transl. and adap. by T. J. Serle. Publ. by J. Dicks.

MAN IN THE IRON MASK. See *The Prisoner of the Bastille.*

MAN IN THE MOON, THE. D. Sk. 1 a. Advertised for the opening of the Hay., 1799, but withdrawn. Written by Brewer. N.p.

MAN IN THE MOON, THE. F. D.L., December 8, 1817.

MAN IN THE MOON, THE. Freak of fancy by E. L. Blanchard. Princess's, April 10, 1871.

MAN IN THE MOON, THE. Panto. by J. Addison. Britannia, December 26, 1892.

MAN IN THE MOON, THE. See *Endemion.*

MAN IN THE STREET, THE. P. 1 a. L. N. Parker. Avenue, May 14, 1894.

MAN IN THE ULSTER, THE. F. Manuel. Britannia, November 16, 1874.

MAN IS NOT PERFECT. D. Adap. by B. Webster, jun. Adelphi, October 14, 1867.

MAN MILLINER, THE. Mus. F. John O'Keefe. C.G., 1787. Pr. 1798.

MAN O' AIRLIE, THE. D. 4 a. W. G. Wills. Princess's, July 20, 1867; Globe, May 16, 1870; Grand, March 3, 1890.

MAN O' WAR'S MAN, THE. P. 4 a. H. Dellow and C. Livesay. Mexborough P.O.W.'s, August 10, 1894.

MAN OF BUSINESS, A. P. 4 a. Transl. fr. the Swedish *En Fallat* of Björnsterne Björnson by W. Olaf and W. Chapman. St. George's H., March 26, 1887.

MAN OF BUSINESS, THE. C. George Colman. Pr. 1774. C.G., 1774.

MAN OF DESTINY, THE. P. 1 a. G. Bernard Shaw. Croydon G.T., July 1, 1897; Comedy, March 29, 1901; Court, June 4, 1907.

MAN OF ENTERPRISE, THE. F. Chas. Shillito. Ac. at Norwich. Pr. 1789.

MAN OF FAMILY, THE. Sentimental C. C. Jenner. Fr. Diderot's *Père de Famille.* Pr. 1771.

MAN OF FORTY, THE. Ca. in 1 a. Wm. Poel. Adap. fr. Kotzebue. King's Cross T., June 29, 1880.

MAN OF FORTY, THE. P. 4 a. W. Frith. Manchester T.R., October 27, 1898; St. James's, March 28, 1900.

MAN OF HER CHOICE, THE. P. 4 a. Wr. by Ada G. Abbott (Mrs. Ernest R. Abbott), Broadway, July 27, 1908.

MAN OF HIS WORD, A. P. 3 a. B. Lawrence. Imperial, August 21, 1901.

MAN OF HONOUR, A. P. 4 a. W. S. Maugham. Originally prod. by the Stage Society at the Imperial, February 22, 1903; Avenue, February 18, 1904.

MAN OF HONOUR, THE. C. Francis Lynch. Circa 1730.

MAN OF HONOUR, THE. C. Wm. Davies. Pr. 1786. N.ac.

MAN OF IDEAS. C. 1 a. Ada Rose. Publ. by S. French, Ltd.

MAN OF IRON, A. D. 5 a. Adap. fr. Ohnet's novel "Le Maitre de Forges." Grimsby T.R., June 15, 1885.

MAN OF LAW, THE. Hay., December 9, 1851.

MAN OF MANY FRIENDS, THE. C. 3 a. J. Stirling Coyne. Hay., September 1, 1855.

MAN OF MODE; OR, SIR FOPLING FLUTTER, THE. C. Sir Geo. Etherege. Duke's, 1676. Pr. 1676.

MAN OF MYSTERY, A. Melo-d. 4 a. F Redgrave and A. Bell. Broughton Victor July 29, 1901; Grand, August 12, 1901.

MAN OF NEWMARKET. C. The Hon. E Howard. T.R., 1678. Pr. 1678.

MAN OF NO PRINCIPLE, A. Melo-d 4 a. John H. Brownson. Hyde T.R., March 4, 1895.

MAN OF PARTS; OR, A TRIP TO LONDON, THE. F. I. Jackman. Ac. at Dublin Crow Street T. Pr. 1795.

MAN OF QUALITY, THE. F. Lee. An alt. of Vanbrugh's *Relapse.* D.L., March 15, 1774 Pr. 1776.

MAN OF QUALITY, THE. C. Adap. fr Sir John Vanbrugh's *The Relapse; or, Virtue in Danger* by John Hollingshead. Gaiety, May 7, 1870.

MAN OF REASON, THE. C. Hugh Kelly. C.G., February 9, 1776.

MAN OF SPIRIT, A. Sk. Frank Price. Hackney Empire, August 9, 1909.

MAN OF TASTE, THE. C. Rev. J. Miller. Plot partly fr. *Ecole des Maris*, fr. *Precieuses Ridicules* of Molière. D.L., March 6, 1735. Pr. 1735.

MAN OF TASTE, THE. Ac. near Twickenham. Pr. 1733. The running title is *The Poetical Fop; or, The Modes of the Court.* Previously publ. in 1732 as *Mr. Taste, the Poetical Fop.*

MAN OF TASTE, THE. F. Anon. This is Miller's C. of same name abbreviated. D.L., March 10, 1752.

MAN OF TEN THOUSAND, THE. C. T. Holcroft. D.L., January 23, 1796. Pr. 1796.

MAN OF THE MILL, THE. Burl. T.O. Signor Squalline. Pr. 1765. A parody on *The Maid of the Mill.*

MAN OF THE MOMENT. P. 4 a. H. Melville. Adap. fr. *L'Adversaire* of A. Capus and Emmanuel Arene. St. James's, June 13, 1905.

MAN OF THE PEOPLE, A. P. 4 a. Louis B. Goldman. Treharris Public H., March 7, 1894.

MAN OF THE PEOPLE. D. Sk. A. Thomas. Cardiff R., September 18, 1905; Comedy, September 27, 1905.

MAN OF THE PEOPLE. See *The Owner of the Works.*

MAN OF THE PEOPLE; OR, THE TOP OF THE LADDER AND HOW TO GET THERE HONESTLY, A. D. Pro. and 3 a. W. S. Bronson. Liverpool T.R., March 17, 1879.

MAN OF THE WORLD, A. D. Sk. Augustus Thomas. Cardiff R., September 18, 1905; Comedy, September 27, 1905.

MAN OF THE WORLD, THE. C. 5 a. C. Macklin. C.G., May 10, 1781. Originally pl. in Ireland about seventeen years before under the title of *The True-Born Scotchman.* D.L., 1822; C.G., 1824.

MAN OF TWO LIVES, THE. Rom. P. 3 a. Adap. fr. Victor Hugo's "Les Miserables" by B. Bernard. D.L., March 29, 1869.

MAN OF TWO LIVES, THE. D. L. Thompson. Liverpool T.R., June 16, 1879.

MAN ON THE BOX, THE. Light C. 3 a. Grace Livingstone Furniss. F. on Harold McGrath's novel of same name. Eastbourne Pier, August 6, 1908; Marlborough, July 31, 1909.

MAN ON THE KERB, THE. P. 1 a. A. Sutro. Aldwych, March 24, 1908.

MAN OR BEAST? D. 4 a. Chas. H. Phelps. Orig. prod. at Swansea, July 27. Stratford R., November 30, 1908.

MAN OR MONEY? Surrey, May 7, 1860.

MAN PROPOSES. C. 1 a. S. Grundy. Duke's T., March 18, 1878.

MAN PROPOSES. Ca. 1 a. F. Langbridge.

MAN SHE LOVES. D. 4 a. G. B. Nichols and F. Herbert. Surrey, November 24, 1902.

MAN THAT HESITATES, THE. Adap. by G. W. Godfrey fr. Mrs. Hughes Bell's *L'Indécis*, produced Royalty, November 10, 1887. The original Eng. ver. of *Between the Posts*, also by Mrs. Bell. Prod. Newcastle T.R., September 9, 1887; St. George's H., February 28, 1888.

MAN, THE BRUTE. Tivoli, July 15, 1907.

MAN THE LIFEBOAT. Leedham Bantock and Percy Greenbank. Metropolitan, April 19, 1909.

MAN TO MAN. D. 5 a. W. Bourne. Manchester Q.T., March 24, 1884; Surrey, July 4, 1887(4 a.); rev., Stratford T.R., January 4, 1904.

MAN TOO HARD FOR THE MASTER, THE. C. Anon. Publ. since the Restoration, and mentioned in the Appendix to the "British Theatre. See *Love Without Interest.*

MAN WHO FOLLOWS THE LADIES, THE. "Piece of Impudence." F. 1 a. Howard Paul. Strand, July 19, 1856.

MAN WHO MISSED THE TIDE, THE. W. F. Casey. Dublin Abbey, February 13, 1908.

MAN WHO STOLE THE CASTLE, THE. Christmas episode. 1 a. T. Gallon and L. M. Lion. Garrick, December 26, 1900, and rev. December 14, 1901.

MAN WHO WAS, THE. Kinsey Peile. D. ver. of story by Rudyard Kipling. H.M. (Guy's H. net.), June 8, 1903; H.M., January 18, 1906.

MAN WHO WASN'T, THE. F. 1 a. H. A. V. Ransom. Bayswater Victoria H. (Bijou), February 22, 1895.

MAN WHO WON, THE. D. 3 a. A. M. Heathcote. F. on novel of same name by Mrs. Baillie Reynolds. Scala, May 24, 1908.

MAN WITH A GENERAL FACE, THE. F. 1 a. T. Townsend. Publ. by J. Dicks.

MAN WITH A PAST, A. Strand (C.P.), September 9, 1895.

MAN WITH A PAST, A. Mono. Charles Brookfield. Garrick, December 11, 1900.

MAN WITH A PAST, A. F.C. 3 a. H. and E. Paulton. Worthing T.R., May 9, 1901.

MAN WITH MANY FRIENDS, THE. C. Stirling Coyne. Hay., September 3, 1855.

MAN WITH THE CARPET BAG, THE. F. 1 a. Gilbert à Beckett. Strand, 1835.

MAN WITH THE IRON MASK, THE. W. J. Lucas. Adap. fr. the French. In 4 epochs. R. Pavilion T.

MAN WITH THREE WIVES, THE. F. 3 a. C. M. Rae. Adap. fr. *Trois Femmes pour un Mari* of Grenet Dancourt (Cluny T., Paris, January 11, 1884). Criterion, March 21, 1886.

MAN WITH TWO WIVES; OR, WIGS FOR EVER. Dr. fable. F. G. Waldron. (?) Pl. in provinces, 1798. N.p.

MAN, WOMAN, AND FATE. D 4 a. Wm. P. Sheen. Broughton Victoria, February 26, 1904. C.p.

MAN'S A MAN FOR A' THAT, A. Sk. Belfast Hippodrome, December 7, 1908; Oxford, December 21, 1908.

MAN'S BEWITCHED; OR, THE DEVIL TO DO ABOUT HIM, THE. C. Mrs. Centlivre. Queen's T. in Haymarket, December 12, 1709. Pr. N.d. Taken fr. a French C. *Le Deuil.* ? By Corneille, 1672.

MAN'S ENEMY; OR, THE DOWNWARD PATH. D. 4 a. C. H. Longden and Eric Hudson. Blackburn Prince's, January 14, 1897; Wigan T.R., February 25, 1897; West London, April 25, 1898.

MAN'S FOES, A. P. 1 a. Diana Cholmondeley. Imperial, May 26, 1907.

MAN'S IDOL. P. C. A. Lee. Belfast R., April 25, 1902.

MAN'S INHUMANITY. D.D. 4 a. C. H. Phelps and Florence Gerard. Burnley G.T., July 7, 1902.

MAN'S LOVE, A. P. 3 a. J. T. Grein and C. W. Jarvis. Adap. fr. the Dutch of J. C. De Vos. P.O.W., June 25, 1889 (*matinée*); Opera Comique, March 15, 1895; Walsingham Club, March 27, 1905.

MAN'S MERCY. D. W. H. Pitt. Darlington T.R., May 5, 1874.

MAN'S SHADOW, A. D. 4 a. Robert Buchanan. Adap. fr. Jules Mary and Geo. Grisier's d. *Roger la Honte* (Ambigu, September 28, 1888); Elephant and Castle, November 29, 1888 (C.P.), under title of *Roger la Honte; or, Jean the Disgraced.* Haymarket, September 12, 1889; Her Majesty's Theatre, November 27, 1897; H.M., March 25, 1905.

MAN'S SHIRT, A. P. 1 a. E. Hamilton Moore. Bayswater Bijou, December 4, 1906. C.P.

MAN'S TALISMAN—GOLD. D. E. Newbound, Britannia, December 17, 1877.

MAN'S THE MASTER, THE. C. Sir W. Davenant. Ac. L.I.F., March 26, 1668. Pr. 1669. F. on two plays of Scarrow, *Jodelet; ou, le Maitre Valet*, and *L'Heritier Ridicule.*

MAN'S THE MASTER, THE. C. Alt. fr. Davenant by Woodward. C.G., November 3, 1775. Pr. 1775.

MAN'S TREACHERY, A. Sk. H. Young. Greenwich Carlton, December 17, 1901.

MAN'S WIT. Moral P. Mentioned in Greene's "Groatsworth of Wit," 1592.

MAN-HATER, THE. Transl. fr. Molière's "Misanthrope" by John Ozell.

MAN-HATER, THE. Transl. fr. the French. Prod., 1762, in Foote's Comic Theatre.

MAN-TRAP, THE. Dom. D. 3 a. Montague Marks. Adap. fr. Sir Wm. Magnay's novel. Royalty, April 3, 1903 (C.P.).

MANAGEMENT. C. Fredk. Reynolds. C.G., August 31, 1799. Pr. 1799.

MANAGEMENT. C. 4 a. Curtis Brown. (Pres. by the English Play Society.) Kingsway, December 20, 1908.

MANAGEMENT; OR, THE PROMPTER PUZZLED. C.Int. 1 a. J. Lunn. Haymarket, September 29, 1828.

MANAGEMENT, ETC. Trans. from *Le Beneficiare* by Theaulon and Etienne.

MANAGER, THE. F.p. 3 a. F. C. Burnand. F. on Meillac and Halevy's *Le Mari de la Débutante.* Court, February 15, 1882.

MANAGER AN ACTOR IN SPITE OF HIMSELF, THE. Int. C. Bonnor. C.G., May 6, 1785. F. on *La Fête de Campagne; ou, L'Intendant Comédien Malgré Lui, Comédie Episodique* (by Dorvigny).

MANAGER IN DISTRESS, THE. Prel. G. Colman the Elder. Haymarket, May 15, 1780. Pr. 1780.

MANAGER IN LOVE, THE. F. Haymarket, February 3, 1873.

MANAGERESS IN A FIX. F 1. Pub. by S. French, Ltd.

MANAGERS, THE. C. Anon. Pr. 1768. Relates to the differences existing between proprietors of C.G.

MANAGING DIRECTOR, THE. Victoria, March 16, 1863.

MANASSEH. Orat. Anon. Pr. 1766.

MANCHESTER BY DAY AND NIGHT. Melo-d. 4 a. Wm. B. Broadhead. Manchester Metropole T., September 17, 1900.

MANCHESTER HANDICAP. MF. 1 a. MS. with Douglas Cox.

MANDARIN, THE. Melo-d. 5 a. Alicia Ramsey and Rudolph De Cordova. Grand, April 15, 1901.

MANDARIN'S DAUGHTER; BEING THE SIMPLE STORY OF THE WILLOW PATTERN PLATE, THE. A Chinese tale by author of *Godiva*, etc. Punch's Playhouse and Strand, December 26, 1851.

MANDRIN. Burla. D. 3 a. C. Mathews. Adelphi, 1835.

MANFRED. O. Schumann. 1810-56.

MANFRED. Choral T. 3 a. Lord Byron. D.L., October 10, 1863; Princess's, August 16, 1873.

MANFRED. Burl. Ballet O. G. à Beckett, Strand.

MANFREDI. T. Monti, 1825. Fr. ver. by Duplisses, 1854.

MANFREDO. O. Petrella. Rome, 1873.

MANGORA, KING OF THE TIMBUSIANS; OR, THE FAITHFUL COUPLE. T. Sir T. Moore. L.I.F., December 14, 1717. Pr. 1718.

MANHOOD. D. Pitt. St. Helen's T.R., March 27, 1876.

MANHOOD. D. 5 a. J. James Hewson. Burnley Gaiety, September 20, 1888; Marylebone, July 29, 1889; Sadler's Wells, January 18, 1891.

MANHOOD AND WISDOME; A MASQUE OF MUCHE INSTRUCTIONE. Anon. Pr. 1563.

MANIAC, THE. O. Bishop. 1810.

MANIAC; OR, SWISS BANDITTI, THE. S.C.O. S. J. Arnold. M. by Bishop. Lyceum, 1810. N.p.

MANIAC MAID; OR, EUPHEMIA'S FLIGHTS, THE. M.Int. J. P. Roberdeau. Ac. at Portsmouth T., 1804. N.p.

MANKIND. Hynghm. Mentioned by Brewer.

MANKIND; OR, BEGGAR YOUR NEIGHBOUR. Do.D. in 7 tableaux. P. Meritt and G. Conquest, Surrey, October 3, 1881; rev. May 22, 1893.

MANLIUS CAPITOLINUS. T. Lafosse. An imitation fr. Otway's *Venice Preserved.*

MANLIUS CAPITOLINUS. T. John Ozell. Trans. fr. the French of Lafosse (? 1684). 1715.

MANNEQUIN DE BERGAME, LE. O. F. J. Fétis. Paris, 1832.

MANŒUVRES OF JANE, THE. P. 4 a. H. A. Jones. Haymarket, October 29, 1898.

MANŒUVRING. C. 5 a. Taken fr. Miss Egworth's tale. Pr. 1814. ? N.ac.

MANOLA. C.O. 3 a. H. B. Farnie. Adap. fr. the French of Leterrier and Vanloo. M. by Lecocq. Strand, February 11, 1882.

MANOLO; OR, THE GITANA'S LOVE. D. 5 a. Sergeant Lucas (R. Marines). Plymouth T.R., October 21, 1872.

MANON. O. 4 a. J. Bennet. Adap. fr. the French of Meilhac and Gille. Founded on the Ro. of the Abbé Prevost's *Manon Lescant.* M. by M. J. Massenet. Paris Opera Comique, January 19, 1884; Liverpool R. Court, January 17, 1885; D.L., May 7, 1885. Perf. in French at C.G., May 19, 1891.

MANON LESCAUT. O. Bal. 3 a. Halévy. Paris O., May 3, 1830.

MANON LESCAUT. O. Balfe. Paris, 1836.

MANON LESCAUT. O. 3 a. Auber. Lib. by Scribe. Paris Op. Com., February 23, 1856.

MANON LESCAUT. O. 4 a. G. Puccini. Turin, February 1, 1893; C.G., May 14, 1894.

MANRU. O. Paderewski.

MANTEAU, LE. C. Andrieux. 1826.

MANTEAUX NOIR, LES. C.O. 3 a. W. Parke and Harry Paulton. Adap. fr. the French of Scribe. M. by Bucalossi. Avenue, June 3, 1882.

MANTUAN REVELS. C. Chenevix, 1812.

MANUEL. T., by Maturin. M. by Cooke. D.L., March 8, 1817.

MANUSCRIPT, THE. Int. Wm. Cooke. Pr. 1809. N.ac.

MANUSCRIPTS. Int. Lucas. Pr. 1809.

MANXMAN, THE. P. 5 a. Wilson Barrett. Adap. fr. Hall Caine's novel of same name. Leeds Grand, August 22, 1894; Shaftesbury, November 18, 1895; Lyric, November 16, 1896; Lyceum, November 25, 1899; Adelphi, January 11, 1908. See *Pete*.

MANY HAPPY RETURNS. M.Sk. Gilbert à Beckett and Clement Scott. M. by Lionel Benson. St. George's H., March 28, 1881.

MAOMETTO SECUNDO. O. Rossini. Prod. during the carnival at San Carlo, Naples, 1820. Adap. and extended as *Le Siege De Corinthe*.

MAQUELONE. O. 1 a. In French. Lib. by M. Carré. M. by E. Missa. C.G., July 20, 1903.

MARAH. See *A Convict's Wife, Convict's Escape*.

MARAQUITA. Michael Merrick. (Prod. by the Play Actors.) Court, November 8, 1908.

MARAUDERS; OR, THE POWER OF LOVE, THE. S.C.O. 3 a. Lib. and lyrics by A. E. Siedle. Swansea G.T. April 28, 1903.

MARBLE ARCH, THE. Ca. 1 a. Edward Rose and Agnes J. Garraway. Adap. fr. *Versucherin* (Von Moser). P.O.W., February 2, 1882.

MARBLE BRIDE; OR, THE ELVES OF THE FOREST, THE. D. 2 a. Adap. fr. *Les Elves* by C. H. Hazlewood. Britannia Saloon.

MARBLE GUEST, THE. O. Dargomishky 1813-1868.

MARBLE HEART; OR, THE SCULPTOR'S DREAM, THE. Rom. of real life in five chapters. C. Selby. Adap. fr. *Les Filles de Marbre* (Barrière and Thiboust). Adelphi, May 20, 1854.

MARBLE MAIDEN, THE. Ballet Fantastique. 3 a. St. George's and Albert. M. by Adolphe Adam. D.L., September 27, 1845.

MARBLE MAIDEN; OR, ZAMPA IN MINIATURE, THE. Burl. G. M. Layton. Royalty, July 24, 1873.

MARBLE PALLAS; OR, THE MANNIKINS. C.O. R. T. Nicholson and A. Wimperis. Loughton Lopping H., November 30, 1908 (C.P.).

MARCEL. Adap of the French p. *Marcel* (Sandeau and Decourcelle). See *Awaking*.

MARCELIA; OR, THE TREACHEROUS FRIEND. T.C. Mrs. Frances Boothby. Ac. at the T.R. Pr. 1670.

MARCELINE. D. 1 a. C. Selby. Pub. by J. Dicks.

MARCELLA. T. Wm. Hayley. D.L., November 7, 1789. C.G., November 10, 1789. Pr. 1784.

MARCH HARE, THE. F.C. 3 a. Harold Smith. Birkenhead R., April 26, 1909 (amat.).

MARCH HARE HUNT, A. Ca. F. F. Moore. Lyceum, August 29, 1877.

MARCH ON MAGDALA, THE. D. F. Warrington. Dublin Queen's, February 21, 1870.

MARCH WINDS AND APRIL SHOWERS. Marylebone, May 21, 1860.

MARCHE NUPTIALE, LA. P. 4 a. H. Bataille. Royalty, February 15, 1906.

MARCHES DAY. D.E. Anon. Pr. Edinburgh, 1771.

MARCHESE DI TULIPANO, IL. O. Paisiello. Rome, 1792.

MARCHIONESS, THE. O. B. W. Findon and E. Jones. H. M. T., June 23, 1904.

MARCIANO; OR, THE DISCOVERY. Pr. at Edinburgh, 1663. The Mercurius Publicus, January 15, 1663, says by W. Clerke. Ac. at the Abbey of Holyrood House, Edinburgh, on St. John's Night.

MARCO SPADA. D. 3 a. J. Palgrave Simpson. Adap. fr. Scribe's lib. of Auber's O. Princess's, March 28, 1853.

MARCO VISCONTI O. Petrella, Milan, 1855.

MARCUS BRUTUS. T. J. Sheffield, Duke of Buckingham. Pr. 1792. Two Choruses by Mr. Pope.

MARCUS GEMINUS. Latin C. Ac. in Christchurch H., Oxford, before Q. Eliz., 1566.

MARCUS TULLIUS CICERO. T. Patsall. Part publ. in the "Oxford Magazine," January, 1773.

MARCUS TULLIUS CICERO, THAT FAMOUS ROMAN ORATOR, HIS TRAGEDY. Pr. 1651. Ascr. by some to Fulk Greville, Lord Brook.

MARDEN GRANGE. Queen's, December 4, 1869.

MARDO; OR, THE NIHILISTS OF ST. PETERSBURG. Hist. Rom. 4 a. F. J. Frayne. Queen's, Manchester, July 7, 1883.

MARE'S NEST, A. F.C. 3 a. H. Hamilton. Adap. fr. the German of Julius Rosen. Vaudeville, November 17, 1887.

MARE'S NEST, A. Ca. 1 a. F. Mouillot. Norwich T.R., October 2, 1889.

MARFORIO. Satire; being a T.C. farce called *The Critic of Taste; or, A Tale of a Tub*. C.G., April 10, 1736. N.p.

MARGARET BYNG. P. 4 a. F. C. Philips and P. Fendall. Criterion, December 8, 1891.

MARGARET CATCHPOLE, THE HEROINE OF SUFFOLK; OR, THE VICISSITUDES OF REAL LIFE. D 3 a. Adap. fr. work of same title. E. Stirling. Surrey, March, 1845.

MARGARET OF ANJOU. Hist. Int. E. Jerningham. D.L., March 11, 1777.

MARGATE. F.C. 3 a. Barton White. Terry's, February 5, 1895.

MARGATE SANDS. F. 1 a. Wm. Hancock. Strand, January 10, 1864.

MARGERITE D'ANGOU. O. Cherubini. 1790.

MARGERY; OR, A WORSE PLAGUE THAN THE DRAGON. Burl. O. H. Carey. Pr. 1738. A Sequel to *The Dragon of Wantley*. C.G., December 9, 1738. Pr. 1743 as *The Dragoness*.

MARGERY DAW; OR, THE TWO BUMPKINS. F. J. M. Morton. Adelphi, Haymarket.

MARGERY'S LOVERS. C. 3 a. B. Matthews. Court, February 18, 1884.

MARGHERITA D'ANJOU. O. Meyerbeer. Milan, 1820.

MARGOT. D. Pro. and 3 a. E. Manuel, Britannia, March 29, 1875.

MARGOT. P. 3 a. Adap. by May Pardoe fr. the Fr. of Alph. Daudet. Windsor T.R., May 18, 1903; Camberwell Metropole, May 25, 1903; Court, December 12, 1904.

MARGOT. C. 3 a. Henry Meilhac (Comédie Française, January 18, 1890). Royalty, June 22, 1891; November 11, 1907.

MARGUERITE. O. Boieldieu. Paris, 1838.

MARGUERITE. Oa. Thorpe Pede. Alexandra, May 31, 1873.

MARGUERITE. Piece. 4 a. Michael Morton (adap. fr. *La Montansier* of G. A. De Gaillavet, Robert De Flers, and Jeoffrin. Paris, March 24, 1904). Notting Hill Coronet, September 5, 1904.

MARGUERITE; A LEGEND OF LOVE. M.sk. J. Halford. M. by J. H. Tully. Adap. fr. Goethe's *Faust*. D.L., March 24, 1856.

MARGUERITE'S COLOURS; OR, PASSING THE FRONTIER. C.D. 2 a. Adap. by Thos. Archer. Lyceum, July 5, 1847.

MARI A LA CAMPAGNE, LE. Gaiety, June 30, 1882. See *The Colonel*.

MARIA. F. Sk. John Meighan. Rutherglen T.H., December 5, 1890.

MARIA; OR, THE MAID OF THE ROCK. C.O. Anthony Davidson. Ac. at Lymington. N.p.

MARIA DI GRAND. It.O. 4 a. Tito Mattei. St. George's, July 18, 1877; H.M.T., November 25, 1880.

MARIA DI ROHAN. O. 3 a. M. by Donizetti. Vienna, June 5, 1843; Paris, November 20, 1843; C.G., May 8, 1847.

MARIA MARTIN; OR, THE MURDER IN THE RED BARN. D. 2 a. Swansea Star T.

MARIA PADILLA. O. Donizetti. Milan, 1841.

MARIA STUARDA. T. Alfieri, 1785. Trans. by C. Lloyd, 1815.

MARIA STUARDA. O. Mercadante Bologna, 1821.

MARIAGE BLANC. D. 3 a. Jules Lemaitre (Th. Française, March 20, 1891). Royalty, June 15, 1891.

MARIAGE D'ARGENT, LE. C. Scribe. 1827.

MARIAGE DE FIGARO, LE. Royalty, March 12, 1888.

MARIAGE FORCE. C. Molière. 1664. See *Forced Marriage*. See "French Classical Plays."

MARIAGE OF WITTE AND SCIENCE, THE. Int. Anon. Circa 1570.

MARIAGES SAMNITES, LES. O. Gretry.

MARIAM, THE FAIR QUEEN OF JEWRY T. Lady Eliz. Carew. Pr. 1613. ? N.ac.

MARIAMNE. T. Hady. 1623.

MARIAMNE. T. Voltaire. 1724. See *Herod and Mariamne*.

MARIAMNE. T. Trans. fr. Voltaire by Dr. Francklin.

MARIAMNE. T. Elijah Fenton. L.I.F., February 22, 1723, and C.G., April 13, 1733. Pr. 1723. F. on story in Josephus, books 14 and 15. See *Herod and Mariamne*.

MARIAN. M.Ent. Mrs. Frances Brooke. C.G., May 26, 1788. Pr. 1788.

MARIAN. O. Shield.

MARIAN AND THE KNIGHT TEMPLAR; OR, THE EARLY DAYS OF WALLACE. D. 4 a. Charles Cooke. Edinburgh Southminster T., June 6, 1870. Greenwich, November 25, 1871.

MARIANA. P. 4 a. José Echaragay. Adap. by J. M. Graham. Court, February 22, 1897. Royal, May 23, 1901.

MARIANNE, THE CHILD OF CHARITY. Do.D. 3 a. G. D. Pitt. Victoria.

MARIANNE THE VIVANDIERE; OR, THE MYSTERY OF TWENTY YEARS. D. Pro. and 3 a. L. Phillips. Standard T., February 8, 1851.

MARIE. Oa. D'Oyley Carte. Op. C. August 26, 1871.

MARIE. D. 1 a. H. R. Addison. Pub by J. Dicks.

MARIE; OR, THE PEARL OF CHAMONNY. D. 5 parts. D.L., February 5, 1855.

MARIE; OR, THE PEARL OF SAVOY. Adelphi, October 2, 1843.

MARIE ANTOINETTE. D. 4 a. J. Palgrave Simpson. Dublin T.R., October 12, 1868; Princess's, October 12, 1868.

MARIE ANTOINETTE. Hist. d. Pro. and 5 a. Italian transl. Paolo Giacommetti. Prod. in England, D.L., June 20, 1873.

MARIE ANTOINETTE, QUEEN OF FRANCE. Hist. D. Prog. and 5 a H. Forest. Taken from the Italian transl. of same title. 1867. Philadelphia, Walnut Street T., October 6, 1868.

MARIE DE BRABANT. Dram. pm. Ancelot. 1825.

MARIE DE COURCELLES; OR, A REPUBLICAN MARRIAGE. D. 5 a. Mrs. Holford. Olympic, November 9, 1878.

MARIE DUCANGE. Dom. D. 3 a. Bayle Bernard. Wr. 1837. Hay., May 29, 1841.

MARIE JEANNE. D. 3 a. Bandmann. Bristol T.R., March 10, 1879.

MARIE MAGDALENE. Mystery. MS. anon. 1512.

MARIE MAGDALENE, THE LIFE AND REPENTANCE OF. Lewis Wager. Pr. 1567.

MARIE STUART. T. Schiller. 1800. See *Mary Queen of Scots*.

MARIE STUART. W. G. Wills.

MARIE STUART EN ECOSSE. O. F. J. Fétis. Paris, 1823.

MARIE TUDOR. See *Two Women*.

MARIETTE'S WEDDING. Oa. W. E. Morton and Haydn Millars. Adelphi, September 30, 1882.

MARIGOLD. C.O. 3 a. A. Matthison. M. by Leon Vasseur. Olympic, October 29, 1879.

MARIGOLD FARM; OR, THE SIMPLE SQUIRE AND THE EVIL EYE. Lyrical P. 3 a. W. Sapte, jun. M. by H. Parry. Op. Comique, February 7, 1893 (C.P.).

MARINA. P. 3 a. Lillo. C.G., August 1, 1738. Pr. 1738. fr. *Pericles, Prince of Tyre*.

MARINA. P. 4 a. John Coleman. fr. Archibald Clavering Gunter's story *Mr. Barnes of New York*. Gaiety, August 4, 1888.

MARINA. See *Mariana*.

MARINE MANSION. Greenwich Lecture H., April 17, 1902.

MARINER'S COMPASS, THE. D. Pro. and 3 a. H. Leslie. Astley's, March 4, 1865.

MARINERS, THE. M. Ent. Samuel Birch. Act. at the O.H., 1793. N.p.

MARINERS OF ENGLAND, THE. Nautical D. 4 a. and 10 tab. R. Buchanan and Ch. Marlowe. Nottingham Grand, March 1, 1897; Olympic, March 9, 1897.

MARINO FALIERO, THE DOGE OF VENICE. T. Lord Byron. D.L., April 25, 1821, and May 20, 1842.

MARINO FALIERO, THE DOGE OF VENICE. O. Donizetti. 1835.

MARION. Dom. P. W. Ellis and P. Greenwood. Dr. fr. Dickens's Christmas story, *The Battle of Life*. Royalty, December 6, 1898.

MARION DE L'ORME. Rom. D. Victor Hugo. 1829.

MARION DE L'ORME. D. Transl. fr. Emile de la Roche's P. Lyceum, 1859.

MARION DE L'ORME. O. 3 a. Ponchielli. Milan Scala, March 17, 1885.

MARION DE L'ORME. 5 a. Richd. Davey. Adap. of Victor Hugo's P. Princess's, June 28, 1887.

MARIONETTES, THE. M.F. R. Reece and J. F. McArdle. Haymarket, June 16, 1879.

MARISHKA. Russian D. 5 a. Wanda Zaleska. Grimsby T.R., August 4, 1890; Sadler's Wells, May 4, 1891.

MARITANA. O. 3 a. F. on *Don César de Bazan*. Words by Fitzball. M. by W. V. Wallace. D.L., November 15, 1845. First t. in English, D.L., August 4, 1855.

MARIUS. T. Otway. 1680.

MARIUS. T. Arnault. 1791.

MARIUS AND SYLLA. Hist.P. Lodge. 1594.

MARJOLAINE, LA. O. 3 a. S. Edwards. M. by Lecocq. Royalty, October 11, 1877.

MARJORIE. C.O. 3 a. L. Clifton and J. J. Dilley. M. by W. Slaughter. Prince of Wales's (mat.), July 18, 1889; January 18, 1890; and August 1, 1890.

MARJORIE'S COUSIN. P. 3 a. A. F. Major. Temperance H., Regency Street, Westminster, May 10, 1886.

MARJORY GILZEAN; OR, THE LIFE AND ADVENTURES OF GENERAL ANDERSON. D. 3 a. James Gower, Elgin T.H., November 16, 1888.

MARJORY STRODE. C. 4 a. A. E. W. Mason. Playhouse, March 19, 1908.

MARK OF CAIN, THE. D. 5 a. F. Jarman. Greenwich, P.O.W.'s, July 25, 1887.

MARKED FOR LIFE. Amer.D. 4 a. G. France. First time in England, Walthamstow Victoria T., October 29, 1900.

MARKED MAN, A. Melo-d. 4 a. J. J. Hewson. Colchester T.R., January 2, 1893. Pavilion, September 30, 1901.

MARKHEIM. Dram.Ep. 1 sc. Adap. fr. W. L. Courtney fr. a story by R. L. Stevenson, Lyric, April 14, 1906.

MARLBOROUGH; OR, THREE PHASES OF A LIFE. D. 4 a. Watts Philipps. Brighton T.R., October 21, 1872.

MARLEYVALE. Ca. C. Searle. Eastbourne Devonshire Pk. T., May 31, 1886.

MARMADUKE MAXWELL. See *Sir Marmaduke Maxwell*.

MARMADUKE SNOOKS. F. Bernard Leslie. Leicester R.O.H., February 10, 1879.

MARMION. 5 a. R. Buchanan. Dramatisation of Sir Walter Scott's poem. Glasgow T.R., April 8, 1891.

MARMION; OR, THE BATTLE OF FLODDEN FIELD. Dr. P. Grosette. 1811. N.p.

MARPLOT; OR, THE SECOND PART OF THE BUSY-BODY. C. Mrs. Centlivre. D.L., December 30, 1710. Pr. 1711.

MARPLOT IN LISBON. C. Mrs. Centlivre's P. alt. by H. Woodward. Dublin, Crow Street T. Later reduced to 3 a. and pl. as a F. at C.G., April 29, 1762. Pr. 1760.

MARQUESA, THE. D. of Spanish life. 4 a. John Uniacke. Op. C., July 11, 1889.

MARQUIS, THE. F. 3 a. Cecil Raleigh and Sidney Dark. Scala, February 9, 1908. Prod. by the Play Actors.

MARQUIS CAPORAL. D. Sejour. 1864.

MARQUIS D'ARGENCOURT. D. Dupenty. 1857.

MARQUIS DE PRIOLA, LE. P. 3 a. Henri Lavedan. Royalty, January 21, 1907.

MARQUIS ST. VALERY, LE. C.O. J. Edwards. Reading Town H., January 20, 1876.

MARQUISE, LA. Watteau P. Regent's Pk. Botanic Gardens, July 25, 1905.

MARRIAGE. R. Bell. Hay.

MARRIAGE. P. 3 a. B. Thomas and H. Keeling. Court, June 7, 1892; rev. May 17, 1894.

MARRIAGE A LA MODE. C. J. Dryden. T.R., 1673. Pr. 1673. Partly fr. *The Grand Cyrus, The Annals of Love,* and *Les Contes d'Ouville*.

MARRIAGE A LA MODE. F. Being Capt. Boden's *Modish Couple* reduced to a F. D.L., March 24, 1760. N.p.

MARRIAGE A LA MODE. Duol. Cotsford Dick. Small Queen's H., November 29, 1895.

MARRIAGE A LA MODE. See *The Clandestine Marriage* and *The Comical Lovers*.

MARRIAGE A LOTTERY. C. 2 a. C. Dance. Strand, May 20, 1858.

MARRIAGE ACT, THE. F. Ascr. to C. Dibdin. C.G. Pr. 1781. Taken fr. *The Islanders*.

MARRIAGE AT ANY PRICE. F. 1 a. J. P. Wooler. Strand, July 28, 1862.

MARRIAGE AT LAST; OR, THE FORTUNATE PRINCE. O. Pr. 1733. In following year repr. with title transposed. See *The Fortunate Prince*.

MARRIAGE AUX LANTERNS, LE. New Royalty, January 18, 1862.

MARRIAGE BELLS. D. 1 a. Herbert Gough. Vaudeville, November 28, 1881; Op. C., July 30, 1892.

MARRIAGE BROKER; OR, THE PANDER, THE. C. "M. W." Pr. 1662. One among the *Ternary of Plays*.

MARRIAGE BY LANTERNS. Op. C. By Offenbanch. Albert H. West T., May 7, 1902.

MARRIAGE CERTIFICATE, THE. D. 3 a. C. H. Hazlewood. Britannia, June 10, 1867.

MARRIAGE CONTRACT, THE. C. 2 a. H. Brooke. Pr. 1778. N.ac.

MARRIAGE, 1892. P. 3 a. and Epil. Clyde Fitch. Royalty, October 28, 1892.

MARRIAGE HAS BEEN ARRANGED, A. Duol. A. Sutro. Hay., May 6, 1902.

MARRIAGE HATER MATCH'D, THE. C. T. Durfey. Pr. 1692. T.R., 1693. D.L., March 8, 1708.

MARRIAGE KNOT, THE. C. 3 a. F. Jarman. Ramsgate Amphi., June 8, 1894.

MARRIAGE LINES. D. 3 a. J. D. Besemeres. Court, March 17, 1873.

MARRIAGE MARKET, THE. F.C. 3 a. F. Jarman. Torquay R.T., January 16, 1901.

MARRIAGE NIGHT, THE. T. Lord Falkland. Pr. 1664. Ac. L.I.F., March 21, 1667.

MARRIAGE NOOSE. Charade. 1 a. H. B. Farnie. Pub. by J. Dicks.

MARRIAGE, NOT DIVORCE; OR, THE LOVE THAT BLOOMS FOR EVER. D. 3 a. J. Levy. Britannia, May 2, 1870.

MARRIAGE OF BACCHUS. O. Anon. 1673.

MARRIAGE OF CAMACHO, THE. Victoria, 1868.

MARRIAGE OF CONVENIENCE, A. P. 4 a. S. Grundy. Adap. fr. Alexandre Dumas' 4 a. com. *Un Mariage sous Louis Quinze*. Haymarket, June 5, 1897. Rev., Imperial, March 8, 1904. Terry's, November 2, 1905.

MARRIAGE OF FIGARO, THE. C.O. Mozart. Lyceum, May 19, 1822; D.L., March 15, 1823; Adelphi, March 28, 1878; Lyric, July 23, 1907. See *Le Nozze di Figaro, Mariage de Figaro*.

MARRIAGE OF GEORGETTE, THE. C.G., November 16, 1860.

MARRIAGE OF KITTY, THE. P. 3 a. Fr. the French of De Grèsac and De Croisset (*La Passerelle*, Paris Vaud., January 31, 1902), by Cosmo Gordon Lennox. Duke of York's, August 19, 1902. Trans. Wyndham's, October 27, 1902. Trans. Criterion, March 27, 1903; D. of Y., June 9, 1906.

MARRIAGE OF MIGNON, THE. P. 3 a. Herbert Shelley. Adap. fr. novel of same name. M. by S. R. Philpot. Fulham, July 31, 1909.

MARRIAGE OF MIND AND MEASURE. Morale. Ac. at Richmond on first Sunday in the year 1579 by "Children of Pawles."

MARRIAGE OF OCEANUS AND BRITANNIA, THE. Masque. R. Flecknol. Pr. 1659.

MARRIAGE OF SIR GAWAINE, THE. O. Dr. John Seally. Pr. 1782 in "The European Mag." N.ac.

MARRIAGE OF THE THAMES AND THE RHINE. Masque of the Inner Temple and Gray's Inn by Sir F. Bacon. 1613.

MARRIAGE OF VENGEANCE. P. 4 a. A. J. Charleson. Pontypridd, Clarence T., December 21, 1903; Stratford R., February 8, 1904.

MARRIAGE OF WILLIAM ASHE, THE. P. 5 a. Mary Ward and Margaret Mayo. Adap. fr. novel of same name. Terry's, April 22, 1908.

MARRIAGE OF WIT AND WISDOM. Pr. 1579. Repr. for the Shakespeare Society 1846.

MARRIAGE PROJECTS. C. See "Theatrical Recorder."

MARRIAGE PROMISE, THE. Int. Anon. 1732. See *The Intriguing Courtiers.*

MARRIAGE PROMISE, THE. C. J. T. Allingham. D.L., April 16, 1803. Pr. 1803.

MARRIAGE TRAP, THE. P. 4 a. Myles Wallerton. Sunderland Av., June 4, 1906.

MARRIAGE. See *Mariage.*

MARRIAGES ARE MADE IN HEAVEN. Epis. 1 a. Basil Dean. Manchester Gaiety, September 7, 1908; Coronet, June 21, 1909.

MARRIAGES OF MAYFAIR, THE. D. of modern life in 4 a. Cecil Raleigh and Henry Hamilton. Prod. by Arthur Collins. Inci. M. by J. M. Glover. D.L., September 21, 1908.

MARRIED. C. 3 a. James Albery. Royalty, November 29, 1873.

MARRIED A MONTH. Monol. Clare Shirley Amateur perf., Cripplegate Institute, April 28, 1906.

MARRIED ALL OF A SUDDEN. Sk. Hammersmith Palace, December 31, 1906.

MARRIED AND SINGLE. J. Poole. Hay., July 16, 1824.

MARRIED AND UNMARRIED; OR, THE WIDOWED WIFE. Hay., September 1, 1796. J. C. Cross. Afterwards pr. under the title of *The Way to Get Unmarried.*

MARRIED ANOTHER. Ca. 1 a. G. Dixon. Op. C., September 1, 1877.

MARRIED BACHELOR; OR, MASTER AND MAN. F. 1 a. P. P. O'Calligan. Publ. by S. French, Ltd.

MARRIED BEAU; OR, THE CURIOUS IMPERTINENT, THE. C. (blank verse). J. Crowne. Ac. at the T.R. Pr. 1694. Story fr. *Don Quixote.*

MARRIED BENEATH HIM. P. 1 a. E. V. Edmonds. Workington Queen's O.H., October 12, 1900.

MARRIED BY PROXY. F.C. 3 a. A. W. Yeuill. Greenock T.R., January 19, 1894; Toole's, October 18, 1894.

MARRIED COQUET, THE. C. Dr. John Baillie. Pr. 1746. N.ac.

MARRIED DAUGHTERS AND YOUNG HUSBANDS. Orig. C.D. 2 a. John Daly. Lyceum.

MARRIED FOR MONEY. C. Buckstone.

MARRIED FOR MONEY. C. 3 a. Charles Mathews. Alt. fr. *The Wealthy Widow.* D.L., October 10, 1855.

MARRIED FOR MONEY. D. 4 a. E. Towers. Pav., March 12, 1873.

MARRIED FROM SCHOOL. C. W. Brown. Manchester Queen's, March 10, 1876.

MARRIED IN HASTE. C. 4 a. H. J. Byron. Hay., October 2, 1875.

MARRIED LIBERTINE, THE. C. C. Macklin. 1761. Ac. at C.G., January 28, 1761.

MARRIED LIFE. C. 3 a. J. B. Buckstone. Hay., August, 1834; Surrey, November 15, 1869.

MARRIED MAN, THE. C. 3 a. Mrs. Inchbald. Hay., July 15, 1789. Taken fr. *Le Philosophe Marié* of Destouches. Pr. 1789.

MARRIED MICROBE, A. Sk. Prod. by Miss Kate Chard. Chelsea Palace, December 17, 1906.

MARRIED, NOT MATED. D. 4 a. F. Harvey. Brighton T.R., August 31, 1877; Olympic, April 27, 1879.

MARRIED PHILOSOPHER, THE. C. John Kelly. L.I.F. and D.L. Pr. 1732. A transl. fr. the same source as *The Married Man.*

MARRIED RAKE, THE. F. 1 a. C. Selby. Queen's, February 9, 1835.

MARRIED TO THE WRONG MAN. D. 4 a. By Frederick Melville. Elephant and Castle, August 3, 1908.

MARRIED TO-MORROW. F.C. 3 a Adap. fr. the German. Chatham O.H., March 28, 1898.

MARRIED UNMARRIED. D. 2 a. Morris Barnett. Princess's, March 25, 1854.

MARRIED WOMAN, A. D.P. 4 a. F. Fenn. (Orig. prod. at Dundee, Her M. T., October 30, 1902); Camberwell Metropole, November 24, 1902.

MARRY AUDREY. Mentioned in Pepy's Diary, 1668. See *Merry Andrew.*

MARRY, OR DO WORSE. C. Wm. Walker. Pr. 1704, L.I.F., and rev. 1747.

MARRY YOURSELVES. F. Herbert Prior. Edinburgh T.R., March 4, 1873.

MARRYING OF ANNE LEETE, THE. C. 4 a. G. Barker. Royalty, January 26, 1902.

MARSAC OF GASCONY. C. 3 a. Eduard Vroom. Birmingham P.O.W., November 11, 1899; D.L., April 21, 1900.

MARSEILLAISE, LA. Rom. P. 1 a. Frank Ernest Potter. Worcester T.R., September 6, 1906.

MARSEILLAISE; OR, THE STORY OF A SONG, LA. Sk. 1 sc. Geo. Roy. M. by Josef Pelzer. Middlesex, March 12, 1907.

MARSHAL, THE. Hist. P. 4 a. R. Wilford. Liverpool Royal Court T., May 8, 1902.

MARSHAL NEY; OR, THE SOLDIERS OF FRANCE. P. 1 a. L. Coen. National Sporting Club, Cov. Gar., W.C., April 27, 1903; Wyndham's, July 28, 1903.

MARSHAL OF LUXEMBOURG UPON HIS DEATH-BED. T.C. Pr. 1695. Fr. the French.

MARSHAL OSRICK. P. Thos. Heywood, assisted by Wentworth Smith. Ac. 1602. N.p.

MARTHA. O. 4 a. Flotow. Vienna, November 25, 1847. An extention of *Lady Henriette*. D.L., June 4, 1849; first time in English, D.L., October 11, 1855. Prod. as *Marta*, C.G., July 1, 1858; Paris, December 16, 1865.

MARTHA. Burl. Robt. Reece. Gaiety, April 14, 1873.

MARTHA. "Eccentricity." 3 a. Wilford F. Field. Tottenham (produced as *The Bishop*), October 25, 1894; St. Geo. H., November 24, 1894.

MARTHA PLAYS THE FAIRY. C. 1 a. Keble Howard. Hay., May 28, 1907.

MARTHA WILLIS, THE SERVANT MAID. D. 2 a. D. Jerrold. Pavilion, April 4, 1831.

MARTHA'S DOUBLE. P. G. E. Wright-Matron. Bayswater Bijou, July 24, 1896 (C.P.).

MARTIAL MAID, THE. C. Beaumont and Fletcher. Pr. 1647. See *Love's Cure*.

MARTIAL QUEEN, THE. T. R. Carleton, 1675. MS. copy in the Bodleian Library. M. S. Rawl, poet, 126.

MARTIN CHUZZLEWIT. Stirling. Adap. fr. Dickens's novel. Lyceum, 1844-7.

MARTIN CHUZZLEWIT. D. 4 a. H. Simms. Publ. by J. Dicks.

MARTIN CHUZZLEWIT. D. 4 a. H. Wigan. Olympic, March 2, 1868.

MARTIN CHUZZLEWIT. See *Tom Pinch*.

MARTIN GUERRE; OR, THE GUILTY CLAIM. D. E. M. Pearl. Woolwich T.R., September 13, 1873.

MARTIN PRYOR'S MILLIONS; OR, DON'T DO AS SHE DID. Devonport Metropole, July 15, 1907.

MARTIN SWART, THE LIFE AND DEATH OF. P. Mentioned by Henslowe under date of 1597.

MARTINUZZI. Tragic burla. Lyceum, August 26, 1841.

MARTIRI. See *Les Martyrs*.

MARTIRIO DI SANTA CECILIA. O. seria, 3 a. Scarlatti. Rome, 1709.

MARTYN SWARTE. Anon, 1597. N.p. See *Martin Swarte*.

MARTYNE. See *Guiltless*.

MARTIRE LA. O. Samara.

MARTYR, THE. F. Templeton Lucas. Orig. prod. as *Browne the Martyr* at Court T., January, 1872. Revived November 3, 1892.

MARTYR; OR, POLYEUCTE, THE. T. Sir W. Lower. 1655.

MARTYR OF ANTIOCH. Dr. poem. H. H. Milman. 1822.

MARTYR OF ANTIOCH, THE. Dr. ver. of Sir A. Sullivan's cantata (1880). Edinburgh Lyceum, February 25, 1898.

MARTYR OF FREEDOM, THE. D. Coatbridge T.R., August 28. 1882.

MARTYR TO SCIENCE. F. 1 a. F. Weston. Publ. by S. French, Ltd.

MARTYR'D SOLDIER, THE. T. H. Shirley. Ac. at private house in D.L., 1638. Pr. 1638.

MARTYRDOM OF IGNATIUS, THE. T. John Gambold (1740) Pr 1773. Ac. at Hull after slight alt. December 29, 1781.

MARTYRS, LES. O. 4 a. Scribe M. by Donizetti. Prod. as *I Martiri*. Paris, April 10, 1840; London R. Italian O., April 20, 1852; fr. Corneille's *Polyeucte*.

MARVELS OF ELECTRICITY, THE. Spec. extrav. Holborn Amphi., December 28, 1868.

MARY. Ca. H. J. Wynter. Avenue, February 16, 1897.

MARY AND SAIREY, O. 1 a. Ross and Thiele. Publ. by S. French, Ltd.

MARY BARTON See *The Long Strike*.

MARY EDMONSTONE. Rom. D. C. H Hazlewood. Britannia, December 22, 1862.

MARY GRAHAM. Grecian, December 8, 1862.

MARY JONES. Ca. Queen's March 30, 1868.

MARY MAGDALEN. Orat. Jules Massenet.

MARY MAGDALEN. See *Marie Magdalene*.

MARY MAGDALENE. Cantata. Dr. J. Stainer.

MARY MELVYN. D. 3 a. E. Fitzball. Publ. by J. Dicks.

MARY PENNINGTON, SPINSTER. C. 4 a. W. R. Walkes. St. James's, April 24, 1896.

MARY PRICE; OR, THE ADVENTURES OF A SERVANT GIRL. Dom. D. 2 a. F. on G. W. Reynolds's novel. Queen's.

MARY QUEEN OF SCOTLAND. Anon. Advertised as sold by Wellington in St. Paul's Churchyard in 1703.

MARY QUEEN OF SCOTS. T. Philip Duke of Wharton. Left unfinished. Lady Mary Wortley Montague wrote epil.

MARY QUEEN OF SCOTS. T. Dr. Francklin. MS. in Mr. Stephen Jones's collection.

MARY QUEEN OF SCOTS. Banks. 1684.

MARY QUEEN OF SCOTS. T. Hon. John St. John. Pr. 1789. Ac. at D.L., March 20, 1789.

MARY QUEEN OF SCOTS. T. Mrs. M. Deverell. Pr. 1792

MARY QUEEN OF SCOTS. D. 5 a. W. G. Wills. Lyceum, January 8, 1870; Princess's, February 23, 1874.

MARY QUEEN OF SCOTS. T. 3 a. Robt. Blake. T.R., Richmond, December 10, 1894.

MARY QUEEN OF SCOTS. Rom. 4 a. R. Kennedy Cox. King's W., May 21, 1906.

MARY QUEEN OF SCOTS; OR, THE ESCAPE FROM LOCH LEVEN. D. 2 a. Wm. Murray. Edinburgh, October 3, 1825; Olympic, January 3, 1831.

MARY ROPER. Duo. John Douglass. Cavendish Rooms, May 5, 1908 (amat.).

MARY STEWART QUEEN OF SCOTS. D. N.ac. Pr. 1801.

MARY STUART. Frederick Schiller. Trans. by J. C. M. Pr., no date; circ. 1801. N.ac.

MARY STUART. D. Poem. James Grahame. 1807.

MARY STUART. T. J. Haynes. M. by A Lee. D.L., January 22, 1840.

MARY STUART. D. 5 a. Hon. Lewis Wingfield. Court, October 9, 1880.

MARY STUART. See *Mary Queen of Scots*.

MARY STUART; OR, THE CASTLE OF LOCHLEVEN. D. D.L., March 18, 1850.

MARY STUART, THE CHILD OF MISFORTUNE. A skit on ancient melodrama. Strand, October 17, 1893.

MARY TUDOR. T. Victor Hugo. 1833.

MARY TUDOR. T. Vere. 1847.

MARY TUDOR. Hist.P. Miss Dickenson. 1876.

MARY TURNER; OR, THE WICIOUS WILLIN AND WICTORIOUS WIRTUE. Bur.A. F. C. Burnand. New Holborn, October 25, 1867.

MARY WARNER. D. 4 a. Tom Taylor. Haymarket June 21, 1869; Olympic, May 23, 1870.

MARY'S DEVOTION. D. 1 a. C. Frere. Surrey, April 29, 1898.

MARY'S DREAM; OR, FAR, FAR AT SEA. Melo.d. 3 a. Thompson Townsend. Pavilion, July 24, 1837.

MARY'S HOLIDAY. F. W. F. Vandervell. Surrey, June 29, 1879.

MARY'S SECRET. C.D. Arthur Matthison. Criterion, May 15, 1876.

MASANIELLO. Burl. Publ. by S. French, Ltd.

MASANIELLO. D. Milner. D.L., February 17, 1825; Victoria, May, 1829.

MASANIELLO. O. 5 a. Scribe and Delavigne, under the title *La Muette de Portici.* M. by Auber. Paris, February 29, 1828. Prod. in 3 a., D.L., May 4, 1829; as *Masaniello; or, The Dumb Girl of Portici*, C.G., March 15, 1849. Prod. as *La Muta di Portici*, Her M., April 10, 1851.

MASANIELLO; OR, THE FISH'O'MAN OF NAPLES. F. 1 a. R. B. Brough. Olympic, July 2, 1857.

MASCHERE, LE. O. Mascagni. 1901.

MASCOTTE, THE. Op. C. 3 a. H. B. Farnie and R. Reece. M. by Audran. Adap. fr. the French of Chivot and Duru. Brighton T.R., September 19, 1881; Comedy, October 15, 1881; Gaiety, September 9, 1893; transf. to Criterion, October 16, 1893.

MASK OF DEATH, THE. Melo-d. 4 a. H. Ford. Burslem Wedgwood T., July 19, 1897.

MASK OF GUILT, THE. D. 4 a. S. Vane and A. Shirley. Surrey, June 21, 1894 (C.P.). See *Under the Masque of Truth.*

MASK, etc. See *Masque*, etc.

MASKED. D. 4 a. Britannia, April 18, 1870.

MASKED BALL, THE. F.C. 3 a. Clyde Fitch, fr. A. Bisson's and A. Carrè's C. Criterion, January 6, 1900.

MASKED FESTIVAL in commemoration of the Battle of Waterloo. D.L., June 18, 1821.

MASKED GIRL, THE. P. 1 a. A. Applin. (Prod. by the Play Actors.) King's Hall, W.C., March 22, 1908.

MASKED MAN, THE. Effingham, July 23, 1866.

MASKED RIDOTTO, A. Consisting of songs, dances, etc. D.L., April 14, 1821.

MASKERADE. P. 4 a. Ludwig Fulda. Gt. Queen Street, February 15, 1905.

MASKS AND FACES. C. C. Reade and T. Taylor. Hay., November 20, 1852; Adelphi, April, 1853; Olympic, April 14, 1869.

MASKS AND FACES. See *Peg Woffington.*

MASNADIERI, I. O. 4 a. Lib. by Maffei fr. Schiller's *Die Rauber.* M. by Verdi. Her M., July 22, 1847.

MASQUE, A. R. Govell. Destroyed by Warburton's servant.

MASQUE, A. For the Right Hon. Viscount Montacute, on account of the marriage of his son to the daughter of Sir W. Dormer. Geo. Gascoigne. Pr. 1587.

MASQUE, A. For Lord Hayes, in honour of his daughter's marriage to the Hon. the Lord Dennye. Thos. Campion. Pr. 1607.

MASQUE, A, at Lord Viscount Haddington's marriage at Court on Shrove Tuesday, 1608. Ben Jonson. Pr. 1640. See *Hue and Cry After Cupid.*

MASQUE, A. Presented at Whitehall on St. Stephen's night last at the marriage of Right Hon. the Earl of Somerset and the Right Noble the Lady Francis Howard. T. Campion. Pr. 1614.

MASQUE, A. Presented at the house of Lord Hayes for ent. of Le Baron de Tour on February 22, 1617. Ben Jonson. Pr. 1617.

MASQUE, A. Presented at Ludlow Castle 1634, on Michaelmas Night, before the Earl of Bridgewater. John Milton. Pr. 1637. See *The Old Wives' Tale.*

MASQUE, A. Presented at Hunsdon House by T. Heywood. Pr. 1637.

MASQUE, A. Presented at Bretbie, in Derbyshire, Twelfth Night, 1639, by Sir Aston Cokain. Pr. 1659.

MASQUE, A. Wr. at Lord Rochester's request for his T. of Valentinian by Sir Francis Fane. Pr. 1685.

MASQUE, A, in the O. of *The Prophetess*, by Thos. Betterton. Pr. with same, 1690.

MASQUE, A, in honour of the nuptials of the Prince and Princess of Wales. Rev. J. Hook. Pr. 1795. See *Jack of Newbury.*

MASQUE, A. Chas. Leftly. Pr. 1802. in the "Poetical Register."

MASQUE OF AUGURES, THE. Ben Jonson. Presented with several anti-masques on Twelfth Night, 1612. Pr. 1621.

MASQUE OF BEAUTY. Ben Jonson. 1609.

MASQUE OF BLACKNESS, THE. Presented at Whitehall. Ben Jonson, assisted by Inigo Jones. Twelfth night, 1605. See *Twelfth Night's Revels.*

MASQUE OF CALISTO Crowne. 1676.

MASQUE OF FLOWERS, THE. Presented at the Banqueting Ho. in Whitehall by the Gentlemen of Gray's Inn on Twelfth Night, 1613.

MASQUE OF HEROES. Middleton. 1619.

MASQUE OF LETHE, THE. Ben Jonson, 1617. Contains an anti-masque.

MASQUE OF LOVE, THE. D. 3 a. Ch. Osborne. Plymouth T.R., May 23, 1877.

MASQUE OF LOVE, THE. Fr. the opera of Dioclesian. Henry Purcell. Notting Hill (Purcell Operatic Society), March 25, 1901.

MASQUE OF MAY. Cantata. Publ. by S. French, Ltd.

MASQUE OF OWLS AT KENELWORTH, A. Perf. by the Ghost of Capt. Cox, mounted on his Hobby Horse. Ben Jonson. 1626.

MASQUE OF PATRIOTISM AND TRUTH; OR, THE COURT FOOL, THE. Presented before the King. Anon. Pr. 1742.

MASQUE OF QUEENS. Celebrated at Whitehall October 2, 1609. Ben Jonson. Pr. 1640. Assisted in the invention of machinery by Inigo Jones.

MASQUE OF THE FOUR INNS OF COURT. Perf. about Allhollandtide, 1633. Anon. ? N.p.

MASQUE OF THE GYPSIES, THE. Ben Johnson. Pr. 1640. Thrice presented before the King (James I.) at Burleigh-on-the-Hill, at Belvoir Castle, and the last time at Windsor, August, 1621. Afterwards called a masque of the *Metamorphosed Gypsies.*

MASQUE OF THE INNER TEMPLE AND GRAYE'S INN, GRAYE'S INN, AND THE INNER TEMPLE. Presented before the Queen at Whitehall, February 20, 1612. Francis Beaumont. Pr. N.d.

MASQUE OF THE MIDDLE TEMPLE AND LYNCOLN'S INNE. Geo. Chapman. Presented before the King at Whitehall, February 5, 1613. Machinery and decorations by Inigo Jones. This masque cost the Society of Lincoln's Inn £2,400.

MASQUE OF WAR AND PEACE, THE. O. H. MacCunn. Lib. by L. N. Parker. A single performance for the benefit of the Household Troops. Her M., February 13, 1900.

MASQUE OF WAR AND PEACE, THE. Scala. May 28, 1908 (amat.).

MASQUED FRIEND, A. C. This was Holcroft's *Duplicity*. Reduced to 3 a. C.G., May 10, 1803.

MASQUERADE, THE. C. Chs. Johnson. D.L., January 16, 1719 Pr. circa 1719.

MASQUERADE, THE. C. 5 a. John Galt. Pr. 1814. ? N.ac.

MASQUERADE; OR, AN EVENING'S INTRIGUE, THE. F. 2 a. Benjamin Griffin. Pr. 1717. L.I.F., May 16, 1717.

MASQUERADE; OR, THE HUMOROUS CUCKOLD, THE. Mrs. Aubin. 1730. See *The Merry Masqueraders Maskerade.*

MASQUERADE DU CEIL. Masque. "A Celestial map, representing the true site and motions of the heavenly bodies through the years 1639, 1640, etc." By J. S. (*i.e.*, J. Sadler). P. 1640.

MASQUERADERS, THE. P. 4 a. H. A. Jones. St. James's, April 28, 1894.

MASSACRE OF ABERGAVENNY, THE. D. 5 a. J. R. Furness. Llandudno St. Geo. T., September 18, 1897 (C.P.).

MASSACRE OF AMBOYNA, THE. Dryden.

MASSACRE OF PARIS, THE. T. Nathaniel Lee. Ac. at the T.R., 1690. Pr. 1690. C.G., November 1, 1745.

MASSACRE OF PARIS, WITH THE DEATH OF THE DUKE OF GUISE, THE. P. Not divided into acts. Christopher Marlowe. Pr. (no date). Wr. after August 2, 1589, probably about 1590. See *The Gwisse, Guise.*

MASSANIELLO. Kenney. Mentioned by Brewer.

MASSANIELLO; OR, THE REBELLION OF NAPLES. T. 1631.

MASSANIELLO, THE FAMOUS HISTORY OF THE RISE AND FALL OF. In 2 parts. Thos. Durfey. Pr. 1700. L.I.F., July 31, 1724. Partly borr. fr. *The Rebellion of Naples.*

MASSANIELLO, THE FISHERMAN OF NAPLES. P. 5 a. M. by Bishop. D.L., February 17, 1825.

MASSARONI. Rom. O. 3 a. F. L. Moreton. M. by F. Bucalossi. F. on J. R. Planché's D. in 2 a. entitled *The Brigand* (November 23, 1829). Dublin Leinster H., January 23, 1894.

MASSE-EN-YELL-OH. Travestie in 3 sc. H. Paulton and "Mostyn Tedde." M. by Jakobowski. Comedy, March 23, 1886.

MASTER, THE. C. 3 a. G. S. Ogilvie. Globe, April 23, 1898.

MASTER AND MAN. D. 4 a. H. Pettitt and G. R. Sims. Birmingham P.O.W., March, 1889 (in 5 a.); Pav., September 16, 1889; Grand; Princess's, December 18, 1889.

MASTER ANTHONY. C. Roger Boyle, Earl of Orrery. Pr. 1690. Duke's T., L.I.F., probably many years before.

MASTER BUILDER, THE. P. 3 a. Transl. fr. the Norwegian of H. Ibsen by W. Archer and E. Gosse. Trafalgar Square T., February 20, 1893; Vaudeville, March 6, 1893; Bayswater Bijou, September 17, 1907; rev., Court, March 16, 1909.

MASTER BUILDER. See *Jerry Builder Solness.*

MASTER CARVER, THE. P. 4 a. Mrs. John Greathead. Southend All Saints' Parish R., November 21, 1905.

MASTER CHRISTIAN. P. 4 a. Marie Corelli. Leeds Grand T., August 18, 1900.

MASTER CLARKE. P. 5 a. T. J. Serle. Hay., 1840.

MASTER CRIMINAL, THE. P. 4 a. Henry Merriman. Margate Grand T., May 16, 1904; Elephant and C., May 23, 1904.

MASTER HUMPHREY'S CLOCK. D. 2 a. F. F. Cooper. Publ. by J. Dicks.

MASTER JONES'S BIRTHDAY. F. 1 a. J. M. Morton. Princess's, August 24, 1868.

MASTER MUMMER. E. Phillips Oppenheim.

MASTER MUSICIAN, THE. Playlet. 1 a. Prod. by Auguste van Biene. Hackney Empire, January 7, 1907.

MASTER OF HOPE, THE. Dom. D. 4 a. Lanwarne Hawkins. Stalybridge Grand, December 3, 1898.

MASTER OF KINGSGIFT, THE. Rom. D. Mrs. Tom Kelly. Avenue, October 17, 1904.

MASTER OF RAVENSWOOD. Lyceum, December 23, 1865. See *Ravenswood.*

MASTER OF THE CEREMONIES, THE. See *Her Ladyship.*

MASTER OF THE CHAIN. D. 4 a. J. Sargent. Plymouth T.R., February 21, 1900 (C.P.); Greenwich Carlton, December 17, 1900.

MASTER OF THE KING'S COMPANY. Rom. C. 4 a. October 9, 1902.

MASTER OF THE SITUATION. "Comedy of Morals." 4 a. Charles Hannan. St Leonards Pavilion, July 24, 1899.

MASTER PASSION, THE. C. 2 a. Mrs. Alfred Phillips. Olympic, September 1, 1852.

MASTER PASSION, THE. E. Falconer. Princess's, November 2, 1859.

MASTER TOMMY'S SCHOOL. M. Sk. Corney Grain. St. Geo. H., December 22, 1883.

MASTER TOMMY'S THEATRICALS. M. Sk. Corney Grain. St. Geo. H., December 26, 1881.

MASTER TURBULENT; OR, THE MELANCHOLICS. C. Anon. Pr. 1682.

MASTER'S LODGE NIGHT. F. G. Hodgson. Surrey, February 24, 1872.

MASTER'S RIVAL; OR, A DAY AT BOULOGNE. F. 2 a. R. B. Peake. M. by Mr. Hawes. D.L., February 12, 1829; C.G., May 6, 1829; Lyceum, July 7, 1829.

MASTERPIECE, THE. Ca. 1 a. Mrs. Hugh Bell. Royalty, April 15, 1893.

MATAMOROS; OR, A NIGHT IN SPAIN. D. 1 a. Frank Desprez. Ealing Lyric H., December 18, 1889.

MATCH AT MIDNIGHT, A. C. Wm. Rowley. Ac. by the Children of the Revels. Pr. 1633.

MATCH FOR A MOTHER-IN-LAW, A. Ca. 1 a. Wybert Reeve. Manchester T.R., June 20, 1859.

MATCH FOR A WIDOW; OR, THE FROLICS OF FANCY, A. Com. O. Joseph Atkinson. Pr. 1788. Ac. in Dublin.

MATCH IN THE DARK, A. F. 1 a. C. Dance. Publ. by J. Dicks.

MATCH ME IN LONDON. T.C. Thos. Dekker. Bull T. in John Street; Phœnix T.; D.L. Pr. in 1631.

MATCH OR NO MATCH, A. Mentd. in Herbert's Diary, April 6, 1624.

MATCH-MAKER, A. C. 4 a. C. Graves and Gertrude Kingston. Shaftesbury, May 9, 1896.

MATCH-MAKER, THE. F.C. 2 a. C. S. Cheltnam. Gaiety, October 11, 1871.

MATCH-MAKER FITTED; OR, THE FORTUNE HUNTERS RIGHTLY SERVED, THE. Pr. 1718. Intended for the stage, but not accepted by the performers.

MATCH-MAKING. C. 1 a. John Poole. Taken fr. the French. Hay., August 25, 1821.

MATCH-MAKING; OR, 'TIS A WISE CHILD THAT KNOWS ITS OWN FATHER. C.G., May 24, 1808. N.p. Ascr. to Mrs. C. Kemble.

MATCHAVELL (MACHIAVEL). P. So-called by Henslowe. Ac. May 2, 1591.

MATCHED AND MATCH. F. C. Burnand and German Reed. St. Geo. H. Circa 1865.

MATCHES. C. 3 a. Charles Glenney and A. E. Bagot. Comedy, January 17, 1899.

MATCHES. D. Duo. H. A. Moore. Manchester P., January 28, 1905.

MATCHES—MADE IN ENGLAND. Duo. 1 a. Margaret Young. Steinway Hall, March 10, 1902.

MATCHLOCK. Charade. Miss Keating. Publ. by S. French, Ltd.

MATE. P. 1 a. W. E. Grogan and F. A. Major. Ladbroke H., January 31, 1895.

MATE IN THREE MOVES. Duo. Ac. at 92, Victoria St., S.W. January 29, 1908.

MATE OF THE MOUNTJOY, THE. Nautical D. J. Dilley and J. Albery.

MATED. C.D. 3 a. Mrs. Vaughan. Criterion, June 28, 1879.

MATEO FALCONE. See *The House of the Traitor.*

MATERNAL INSTINCT, THE. P. 3 a. Thos. Bedding. D. of York's, June 9, 1898.

MATERNITE. P. 3 a. Eugene Brieux. C.G., King's T., April 8, 1906.

MATES. D. F. Broughton. Burnley T.R., June 20, 1881.

MATES. Oa. 1 a. Walter Browne. M. by Hamilton Clarke. St. Geo. H., March 27, 1890.

MATHEWS' DREAM; OR, THE THEATRICAL GALLERY. Monolopylogue by Mr. Mathews. Lyceum, playbill, March 12, 1827.

MATILDA. T. Wr. in the reign of Henry VII., according to Jacob's Poetical Register. If this be true, it is the earliest dramatic piece we know of. Henry VII. died in 1509.

MATILDA. T. Dr. Thomas Francklin. D.L., January 21, 1775. Pr. 1775. Almost a transl. of Voltaire's *Duc de Foix.*

MATILDA. D. 5 a. Transl. by Eleanor H—— fr. the French of Monvel. Pr. 1803. Orig. f. on a French transl. of Mrs. Inchbald's *Simple Story.*

MATILDA. T. J. Delap. N.ac. Pr. at Lewes, 1803.

MATILDA DI SHABRAN. O. Rossini. Rome, 1821. King's T., July 3, 1823. (Paris, 1857.)

MATILDA OF HUNGARY. O. 3 a. Lib. by Alfd. Bunn. M. by W. V. Wallace. D.L., February 15, 1847.

MATRIMONIAL. C. 3 a. Novelty, June 9, 1891 (C.P.).

MATRIMONIAL—A GENTLEMAN, ETC. F. 1 a. J. V. Bridgeman. Olympic, February 18, 1852.

MATRIMONIAL ADVERTISEMENT, A. F. R. Clarke. Metropole, October 28, 1895; rev. Marlborough, December 3, 1906.

MATRIMONIAL AGENCY, A. Oa. By Louis Collett. Athenæum, Tottenham Court Road, June 1, 1892; Bayswater Bijou, July 10, 1897.

MATRIMONIAL AGENCY, A. M.P. 3 a. S. F. Bailey. Bootle County H., March 21, 1901.

MATRIMONIAL AGENCY, THE. F. Charlotte E Morland. Bayswater Victoria H., November 15, 1888.

MATRIMONIAL AGENCY, THE. Piece. 1 a. Emily Beauchamp. Strand, December 8, 1897.

MATRIMONIAL BREAKFAST, A. Burl. B. Walwyn. M. by Reeve. Royalty T. Pr. N.d.

MATRIMONIAL BUREAU, A. F. 1 a. "Sparrowdrop." Dublin Queen's, February 11, 1907.

MATRIMONIAL FEE, THE. Metropolitan, June 28, 1909.

MATRIMONIAL NOOSE, THE. F.C. 3 a. M. H. Spier. Prince's, May 1, 1885.

MATRIMONIAL PROSPECTUSES. Ca. 1 a. J. P. Simpson. Punch's Playhouse and Strand T., March 4, 1852.

MATRIMONIAL TROUBLE, THE. In 2 parts, first comedy, second comic tragedy. Margaret Duchess of Newcastle. Pr. 1662.

MATRIMONIO PER CAMBIALE, IL. O. C. Coccia. Rome, 1818.

MATRIMONIO SEGRETO, IL. C.O. 2 a. Bertotti, M. by Cimarosa. Adap. fr. Colman's *Clandestine Marriage.* Viennia, 1792; Paris, May 10, 1801; King's, January 25, 1803; in English at C.G., November 1, 1842; D.L., April 30, 1844 (1st act).

MATRIMONY. Petit O. 1 a. James Kenney. M. by King Alt. fr. the French O., *Adolphe et Clare.* D.L., November 20, 1804. Pr. 1804. See *Adolphus and Clara.*

MATRIMONY. M.E. 1 a. D.L., April 23, 1814; Lyceum, August 1, 1817; D.L., June 14, 1824; D.L., May 29, 1851.

MATRIMONY. C.D. Chas. Cameron. Adap. fr. Wilkie Collins's novel, "Man and Wife." Barrow-in-Furness R. Alhambra (5 a.), September 6, 1886; New Pub. H. (4 a.), November 8, 1890.

MATRIMONY. C.O. 1 a. G. Parsons Norman. M. by F. St. John Lacy. Ladbroke H., June 22, 1893.

MATRIMONY; OR, SIX AND SIX WHERE SUITED. Oa. Huddersfield T.R. and O.H., May 14, 1883.

MATRIMONY; OR, THE SLEEP WALKER. Petite piece fr. the French. C.G., April 26, 1798. N.p.

MATRIMONY, LIMITED. Ca. Ernest Martin. Putney Assem. R., March 1, 1907 (amat.)

MATT OF MERRYMOUNT. P. 4 a. B. M. Dix and E. S. Sutherland. Newcastle T.R., October 11, 1906; New., February 20, 1908.

MATTEO FALCONE; OR, THE BRIGAND AND SON. Melo-d. 1 a. W. H. Oxberry. Adap. fr. the French. English O.H., June 6, 1836.

MATTER-OF-FACT HUSBAND, A. C. 1 a. John Cutler, K.C. Lyceum, July 14, 1908.

MATTER OF £20, A. F. Sk. E. L. Furst. Tivoli M.H., February 21, 1903.

MAUD. Dr. Poem. Tennyson. 1855.

MAUD, CHIEF JUSTICE. Cairns James and Vivian Matthews. Steinway H., May 21, 1903.

MAUDE BOWEN. P. 1 a. Ethel Griffiths F. on the local legend of "Maude's Elm." Cheltenham O.H., May 18, 1909 (C.P.).

MAUD'S PERIL. P. 4 a. Watts Phillips. Adelphi, October 23, 1867.

MAUDE MULLER. Dom. D. Walsall Alexandra T., November 1, 1883.

MAUREEN NA LAVEEN. D. 3 a. Fred. Cooke. Greenock T.R., February 7, 1873.

MAURICE THE WOODCUTTER. D. 3 a. Publ. by S. French, Ltd.

MAURICETTE. P. 3 a. Transl. by H. B. Irving fr. André Picard's *Jeunesse*. Lyric, March 31, 1906.

MAUSOLEUM, THE. C. Wm. Hayley. Pr. 1784. N.ac.

MAWE, THE. (A game at cards.) Recorded by Henslowe as having been ac. December 14, 1594.

MAXIMIAN. T. fr. Corneille by Lady Sophia Burrell. Pr. 1800. N.ac.

MAY; OR, DOLLY'S DELUSION. Dom. D. 3 a. R. Reece. Strand, April 4, 1874.

MAY AND DECEMBER. Adap. fr. Meilhac and Halévy C., *La Petite Marquise*. P. of W.'s, 1865.

MAY AND DECEMBER. F.C. 3 a. Adap. fr. Meilhac and Halévy's C. *La Petite Marquise*. Originally adap. by Sydney Grundy and Joseph Mackay as *A Novel Reader*, and privately ac. September, 1882, but the license was refused by the Censor. Criterion, April 25, 1887; Comedy, November 15, 1890.

MAY AND DECEMBER. Oa. Tunbridge Wells Assembly R., March 16, 1875.

MAY LORD, THE PASTORAL. Ben Jonson. Circa 1633.

MAY MEETINGS. Oa. H. Nowell and H. Wynne. Reading T.H., September 6, 1894.

MAY MORNING, A. Duo. G. Templeton Norman. Bayswater Bijou, December 3, 1895.

MAY MYRTLE. D. Dundee T.R., April 26, 1875.

MAY QUEEN, THE. J. B. Buckstone. Adelphi, October, 1828.

MAY QUEEN, THE. O. Adap. fr. Cant. of same name. M. by Sir W. Sterndale Bennett. Crystal Palace, October 18, 1883.

MAY QUEEN, THE. Vocal ballet div. 3 sc. Manchester Palace T., December 19, 1898.

MAY QUEEN; OR, THE FOLLY FETE, THE. D. Leicester T.R., March 2, 1874.

MAY-DAY. C. Geo. Chapman. Blackfriars, 1611. Pr. 1611.

MAY-DAY; OR, THE LITTLE GYPSEY. M.F. 1 a. David Garrick. D.L., August 28, 1775. Pr. 1775.

MAYDES METAMORPHOSES THE. Myth D. J. Lyly. 1600. See *The Maids*, etc.

MAYFAIR. P. 5 a. A. W. Pinero. Adap. fr. Sardou's *Maison Neuve*. St. James's, October 31, 1885.

MAYFAIR AND RAGFAIR. D. 2 a. J. Mackay. Globe, August 31, 1878.

MAYFLOWER, THE. C. 4 a. F. Frankfort Moore. F. on Longfellow's *Courtship of Miles Standish*. Op. C., January 9, 1892.

MAYFLOWER, THE. P. 3 a. L. N. Parker. Camberwell Metropole, March 6, 1899.

MAYOR AND THE MERRY MAIDS OF MELMERBY, THE. M.P. T. Williamson. M. by A. Williamson. Ripon Victoria H., November 12, 1903.

MAYOR OF GARRATT, THE. F. 2 a. S. Foote. The characters of Sneak and Bruins suggested by Bisket and Fribble in Shadwell's comedy, *Epsom Wells*. Hay., June 20, 1763. Pr. 1764. Edinburgh, 1780; Lyceum, April 24, 1809; D.L., March 3, 1814; Lyceum, June 9, 1823; Hay., 1824.

MAYOR OF MONTILLADO, THE. M.P. 2 a. D. Clapham. M. by L. Butler. St. Geo. H., May 9, 1900.

MAYOR OF QUINBOROUGH, THE. C. Thos. Middleton. Blackfriars. Pr. 1661. Hay., April 29, 1710.

MAYOR OF ROCHESTER, THE. F. 1 a. W. T. Moncrieff. Publ. by J. Dicks.

MAYPOLE; OR, MAD FOR LOVE, THE. C.O. 2 a. C. B. Wade and S. Elliott. Limerick T.R., October 6, 1887.

MAYSIE. P. 1 a. J. F. Nolan and F. Robison. Cripplegate Inst., April 13, 1904.

MAZEPPA. Burl. extrav. 1 a. H. J. Byron. Olympic, December 26, 1859.

MAZEPPA. Burl. 3 a. F. C. Burnand. Gaiety, March 12, 1885.

MAZEPPA. Russian O. Lib. f. by Bourenin and others on the poem by Puschkine entitled *Poltava*. M. by Peter Tschaikowsky. Moscow and St. Petersburg, 1883; Liverpool Alexandra, 1888; and Manchester Comedy, August 27, 1888.

MAZEPPA. An Eq. Spec. East Ham Palace, December 7, 1908.

MAZEPPA; OR, THE WILD HORSE OF TARTARY. Rom. D. 3 a. H. M. Milner. Dramatised fr. Lord Byron's poem. Westminster Bridge Amphi. T., 1831.

MAZOURKA; OR, THE STICK, THE POLE, AND THE TARTAR. Burl. extrav. 1 a. H. J. Byron. F. on *Le Diable à Quatre*. Strand, April 27, 1864.

MEADOW SWEET. C. 1 a. By "Terra Cotta" (Miss C. M. Prevost). Vaudeville, March 5, 1890.

MEAN ADVANTAGE, A. Ca. Rudolf Dircks. Adap. fr. the German *Einer muss Heirathen* (already adap. into English under the title of *One of You Must Marry*). Newcastle-on-Tyne T.R., June 29, 1889 (amat.); Blackpool P.O.W., September 6, 1889.

MEAN ADVANTAGE, A. P. 1 a. Fritz B. Hart and Galwey Herbert. Afterwards renamed *In Harbour*. Chester Royalty, June 11, 1897.

MEASURE FOR MEASURE. Fd. on Whetstone's *Promos and Cassandra*. 1578. Pr.

MEASURE FOR MEASURE. C. William Shakespeare. Fol. 1623. The plot is f. on a novel of Cinthio Giraldi. Ac. Whitehall, 1604; L.I.F., December 8, 1720; rev. by J. P. Kemble, C.G. Pr. 1803. Miss Wallis's rev., Kennington P.O.W., March 27, 1899. Oscar Asche's season, Adelphi, March 20, 1906.

MEASURE FOR MEASURE; OR, BEAUTY THE BEST ADVOCATE. C. Chas. Gildon. L.I.F., 1700. Pr. 1700. Alt. fr. Shakespeare.

MEASURE FOR MEASURE. See *Beauty the Best Advocate, Law Against Loves, Promos and Cassandra.*

MECHANIC, THE. Rom. P. 1 a. Frank Lindo. Ladbroke H., September 28, 1889.

MECHANIC'S WIFE, THE. D. Liverpool Rotunda, August 13, 1883.

MECHANICAL PARTNER, A. Burla. James Redmond. Dublin Gaiety, May 10, 1873.

MECHANICAL TOY, THE. V. Miss Marian Taylor. Britannia, March 21, 1870.

MEDAL, THE. Dryden.

MEDAL AND THE MAID, THE. C. 2 a. Owen Hall. Lyrics by C. H. Taylor, G. Rollit, and P. Rubens M. by Sydney Jones. Lyric, April 25, 1903.

MEDAL OF DEATH, THE. Effingham, November 19, 1866.

MEDAL OF JOHN BAYES, THE. Thos. Shadwell. Being a reply to Dryden's *The Medal.*

MEDDLE AND MUDDLE. F. 1 a. Bellingham and W. Best. Glasgow Royalty, June 3, 1887; Terry's, October 17, 1887.

MEDEA. A favourite subject with the ancients. Ennius transl. this P. into Latin, Ovid wrote a T. on the same story, and Mæcenas is said to have added to the number. These are all lost. Seneca has also left us a P. on this subject, which Corneille has followed in preference to Euripides. See "French Classical Plays." T. Sir Edward Sherborne. Pr. 1648. Transl. fr. Seneca. Not intended for the stage. See "Greek Plays."

MEDEA. T. John Studly, fr. Seneca. Pr. 1563.

MEDEA. T. Charles Johnson. D.L., December 11, 1730. Pr. 1731.

MEDEA. T. Richard Glover. D.L. and C.G. Pr. 1761.

MEDEA. O. Benj. Stillingfleet. Pr. with 3 oratorios in an 8vo. vol., but not publ.

MEDEA. T. R. Potter. Transl. fr. Euripides. Pr. 1781.

MEDEA. T. Michael Wodhull. Transl. fr. Euripides. Pr. 1782.

MEDEA. O. Benda. 1721-95.

MEDEA. O. Cherubini. Paris, 1797. See *Medee.*

MEDEA. T. Transl by Wheelwright 1810, Morgan 1865, Giles 1865, Lee 1867, Webster 1868, Williams 1871.

MEDEA. O. Pacini. Palermo, 1843.

MEDEA. J. A. Heraud. Adap. fr. Legouvés *Tragedy of Medea.* Sadler's Wells, 1857.

MEDEA. T. 3 a. Matilde Heron. Transl. fr. the French of Legouvé. D.L., November 5, 1861.

MEDEA. T. 3 a. W. G. Wills. Adap. fr. the "Medea in Corinth." Lyceum, June, 1872. Rev. as *Medea in Corinth.* Court, July 2, 1907.

MEDEA. T. Adap. fr. the French of Legouvé. Olympic, March 3, 1883.

MEDEA. T. Pro. and 3 a. T. W. Broadbent. Ealing New, June 2, 1905 (C.P.).

MEDEA. Transl. by Gilbert Murray fr. Euripides. Savoy October 22, 1907.

MEDEA; OR, THE BEST OF MOTHERS, WITH A BRUTE OF A HUSBAND. Burl. 1 a. R. B. Brough. Olympic, July 14, 1856.

MEDEA AND JASON. Ballet. Hay., 1781. Burlesquing an Italian perf. at the King's T.

MEDEA IN CORINTH. See *Medea.*

MEDECIN MALGRE LUI, LE. Molière. See "French Classical Plays."

MEDECIN MALGRE LUI, LE. O. Gounod. An O. ver. of Molière's C. Arr. by Carré and Barbier. Paris, January 15, 1858. Pl. in England as *The Mock Doctor, Physician Against His Will.* Q.v.

MEDEE. T. 5 a. and pro. Charpentier. Wds. by J. Corneille. Paris, December 4, 1693. See "French Classical Plays."

MEDEE. O. 3 a. Hoffman. M. by Cherubini. Paris, March 13, 1797. Prod. in Italian at Her M., June 6, 1865.

MEDICAL MAN, A. W. S. Gilbert. St. George's T., October 24, 1872.; rev. by Geo. Groves at Birmingham P. of W.'s, September 2, 1895.

MEDICAL STUDENT, THE. C. 3 a. Beard Frances and H. J. Laeland. Strand, July 4, 1893; Crown, June 11, 1906.

MEDICI I. O. Leoncavallo. Modern Italy.

MEDICINE FOR A CURST WIFE, A. P. Thos. Dekker. Ac. 1602. N.p.

MEDICINE MAN, THE. Melo-d. C. 5 a. H. D. Traill and Robert S. Hichens. Lyceum, May 4, 1898.

MEDICO, THE. F. Frederick Lane. Ladbroke Hall, May 7, 1894.

MEDIUM, THE. F.C. 3 a. J. R. Brown. St. Alban's Hall, Acton Green, October 12, 1899.

MEDLEY; OR, HARLEQUIN HAVE AT ALL, THE. Pant. C.G., 1778.

MEDOR. C. 3 a. Henri Malin. Paris Gymnase, November 8, 1897; Royalty, October 10, 1907.

MEDUSA. Ca. 1 a. F. W. Hayes. St. James's, March, 1882.

MEDUSA. F. Guildhall S. of M., March 15, 1902.

MEDUSE. O. Lagrange.

MEETING, THE. Duol. R. Ganthony. P.O.W., June 25, 1903.

MEETING OF THE COMPANY; OR, BAYES'S ART OF ACTING, THE. Prel. D. Garrick. D.L., ac. at the opening of this theatre September 17, 1774. N.p.

MEFISTOFELE. Gr. O. Prol. and 5 a. Words (after Goëthe) and M. by A. Boito. Milan, March 5, 1868. Remodelled (pro. and 4 a.) at Bologna, October 4, 1875; Her M.T., July 6, 1880; adap. to the English stage and ac. at Dublin Gaiety, August 21, 1884.

MEFISTOFELE II. C.O. English lib. By A. Maltby. M. by Hervé. Alhambra, December 20, 1880.

MEG MERRILEES. D. Henry Leslie. A new ver. of *Guy Mannering.* Glasgow T.R., November 10, 1873.

MEG'S DIVERSION. D. 2 a. H. T. Craven. Royalty, October 17, 1866; rev. Royalty, 1872.

MEHALAH. P. 4 a. Rev. A. Whitley, fr. Baring-Gould. Manchester Comedy, November 14, 1900.

MEHALAH. P. P. M. Lang and A. E. Anson, fr. Baring-Gould. Croydon G., June 12, 1905.

MEHALAH; OR, THE POWER OF WILL. Rom D. 5 a. W. Poel and W. H. G. Palmer. Adap. fr. Baring-Gould's novel. Gaiety, June 11, 1886.

MEIN LEOPOLD. Opera Comique, October 13, 1894.

MEIN LEOPOLD. Volsstück. 3 a. A. L'Arronge. Great Queen Street T., February 22, 1905.

MEINEDBAUER. P. 3 a. L. Gruler. Opera Comique (German season), October 13, 1894.

MEISTERSINGER VON NURNBERG, DIE. O. 3 a. R. Wagner. Completed October, 1867. Munich, June 21, 1868; D.L., May 30, 1882; C.G., July 13, 1889 (in Italian).

MEISTERSINGERS, THE. Wagner's O. in English. Manchester T.R., April 16, 1896.

MELANCHOLICKS. Anon. Pr. before 1812.

MELANCHOLY KNIGHT. S. Rowlands. Ent. on books of Stationers' Co., December 2, 1615.

MELANTHE. Latin pastoral. Brookes, Ac. at Trinity Coll., Cambridge. 1615.

MELCOMBE MARRIAGE, THE. P. 3 a. Winifred Dolan. Brighton R., February 15, 1907.

MELEAGER. Lat. T. Wm. Gager. Ac. at Christchurch Coll., Oxford, before Lord Leicester, Sir Philip Sydney, and other distinguished persons, 1581.

MELIA, 'ENERY, AND IT. Epis. in humble life B. W. Findon. His Majesty's, June 15, 1905.

MELICERTA. Pastoral. Ozell. Transl. of Molière's p.

MELICERTE. Molière. See "French Classical Plays."

MELIDE OU LE NAVIGATEUR. C. O. 2 a. F. A. D. Philidor, 1766.

MELITA; OR, THE PARSEE'S DAUGHTER. C.O. Juba Kennerley. M. by H. Pontet. Novelty, December 9, 1882.

MELITE. C. See "French Classical Plays." Transl. fr. Corneille. Pr. 1776.

MELMOTH THE WANDERER. P. 3 a. Publ. by S. French, Ltd.

MELNOTTE. C.O. 2 a. H. Shelley. Partly adap. fr. *The Lady of Lyons*. Lyrics by A. Anderson. M. by F. E. Tours. Coronet, September 30, 1901.

MELOCOSMIOTES. Int. C.G., 1796. N.p.

MELODRAMA, THE. Skit. Lydia Thompson's farewell benefit, Lyceum, May 2, 1899.

MELODRAMANIA, Burla. 3 a. Malcolm Watson. M. by Walter Slaughter. St. Geo. H., December 20, 1894.

MELPOMENE'S OVERTHROW; OR, THE COMIC MUSE TRIUMPHANT. Mock masque. J. Cawdell. Pr. 1778.

MELTING MOMENTS. Ca. 1 a. T. Pemberton. Birmingham P.O.W., February 18, 1884.

MELTING POT, THE. D. 4 a. Israel Zangwill. Terminus H., Littlehampton, August 21, 1908 (C.P.).

MELTONIANS, THE. D. F. on some sporting subjects. M. fr. Mozart, Bellini, etc. D.L., April 16, 1838.

MELUSINE. O. bouffe. 3 a. G. M. Layton. M. by Hervé. Holborn Amphi., October 17, 1874.

MEM 7. Ca. W. Lisle. Royalty, October 20, 1879.

MEMBER FOR SLOCUM. C. 3 a. G. R. Sims. Adap. fr. *Le Supplice d'un Homme*. Royalty, May 4, 1881.

MEMNON AND MANDANE. T. Dr. Young.

MEMOIRS OF AN UMBRELLA. M. by G. H. B. Rodwell. Circa 1831.

MEMOIRS OF THE D—— C——; OR, THE MYSTIC BELL OF RONQUEROLLES, THE. Eccentric D. 3 a. J. Barber. Surrey, August 8, 1842.

MEMORABLE MASKE OF THE TWO HONOURABLE INNS OF COURT, THE. Chapman. 1614.

MEMORIES. C. 3 a. T. A. Palmer. Court, October 12, 1878.

MEMORIES. Sk. R. Standard M.H., December 9, 1907.

MEMORIES. P. 1 a. Geo. Wilding. New, December 16, 1907.

MEMORY'S GARDEN. P. 3 a. A. Chevalier and T. Gallon. Comedy, February 18, 1903.

MEN AND MONEY. D. Pro. and 3 a. C. A. Clarke. Warrington Pub. H., under the title of *Day to Day*; Pav., July 7, 1890.

MEN AND WOMEN. D. 6 tab. Mrs. R. Fairbairn. Surrey, July 17, 1882.

MEN AND WOMEN. P. 1 a. Arthur Lindo. Ladbroke H., June 17, 1890.

MEN AND WOMEN. P. 3 a. James Buckland. Kilburn, June 3, 1899 (C.P.).

MEN O' SENSE. C. Ch. Burslem. Dewsbury T.R., April 5, 1876.

MEN OF GOTHAM. A "merriment." Wm. Kempe. N.p.

MEN OF METAL. D. 4 a. C. A. Clarke and H. R. Silver. Barnsley T.R., October 3, 1890; Pavilion, July 20, 1891.

MEN OF PLEASURE. New C. D.L., December 11, 1832.

MENÆCHMI. C. by 'W. W." Pr. 1595. A transl. fr. Plautus. Ascr. to William Warner. From this play the plot of *The Comedy of Errors* is borrowed. Repr. 1779. In the running title it is called *Menechmus*. Translations into blank verse by Thornton, Rich, Warner and Colman. See "Latin Plays."

MENASSAH BEN ISRAEL. Hebrew D. 5 a. Liverpool Bijou O.H., August 10, 1885.

MENDER OF NETS, A. P. 1 a. Cosmo Hamilton. Orig. prod. as *The Escape of John Merchant*. Duke of York's, July 10, 1906; Court, December 31, 1907.

MENDICANT, THE. D. 2 a. Gilbert à Beckett. St. James's, February 1, 1836.

MENESTRELS, LES. O. 3 a. J. P. Soulier. 1811. (His last O.)

MENETRIER A LA COUR, LE. C.O. Reber. 1875.

MENTALIST, THE. D. satire. F. Gentleman. Ac. at Manchester, circa 1759. N.p.

MENTEUR, LE, by Corneille, furnishes subject of comedies by Steele and Foote. See "French Classical Plays."

MEPHISTO. Travestie. Byron M'Guiness. Royalty, June 14, 1886.

MEPHISTOPHELES; OR, AN AMBASSADOR FROM BELOW. Extrav. 1 a. Robert Brough and Sutherland Edwards. Adelphi, December, 1852.

MEPRISES PAR RESSEMBLANCE, LES. O. 3 a. Gretry. 1786.

MERCANTILE LOVERS, THE. D. satire. G. Wallis. Ac. at York. Pr. 1775.

MERCATOR; OR, THE MERCHANT. C. Plautus. Adap. fr. a Greek P. by Philemon. Transl. into blank verse by Thornton, Rich, Warner, and Colman. See "Latin Plays."

MERCEDES. O. 3 a. Augusto Ardori. F. on Longfellow's *Spanish Student*. M. by Damele Pellegimi. Engl. adap. by F. Wood. Dublin Leinster H., January 11, 1896; Grand, March 24, 1896

MERCEDES. D. 1 a. 2 c. T. B. Aldrich. Royalty, April 17, 1902.

MERCHANT, THE. C. Transl. fr. Plautus by G. Colman. Pr. 1767. See *Mercator*.

MERCHANT AND HIS CLERKS, THE. D. S. Coyne. Adelphi, December, 1842.

MERCHANT OF BRUGES; OR, BEGGAR'S BUSH, THE. Hon. D. Kinnaird and Ed. Kean. Ver. of Beaumont and Fletcher's *The Beggar's Bush*. M. by Cooke. D.L., December 14, 1815.

MERCHANT OF CAMDEN, THE. Mentioned by Henslowe as having been ac. July 30, 1594. N.p.

MERCHANT OF GUADALOUPE, THE. P. 3 a. John Wallace fr. the French of Mercier. Ac. at Margate, October 5, 1802.

MERCHANT OF LONDON, THE. P. 5 a. T. J. Serle. D.L., April 26, 1832.

MERCHANT OF PAISLEY; OR, THE FALSE BRIDE, THE. D. Paisley T.R., November 7, 1870.

MERCHANT OF VENICE, THE. T.C. Wm. Shakespeare. Wr. 1596. Ent. at Stationers' Hall July 22, 1598, and October 28, 1600. Pr.—1st quarto, 1600; 2nd quarto, 1600; 1st folio, 1623; 3rd quarto, 1637; 4th quarto, 1652. Mentioned by Meres 1598. Main plot fr. *Pecorene* of San Giovanni Fiorentino. Fourth day, first novel. *Gianetta* (1378). Casket story fr. an old transl. of the *Gesta Romanorum* (1577). Gosson (1579) mentions *The Jew*, performed at the Bull. Malone identifies this play with "The Venesyan Comedy" acted at the Rose, 1594, but Shakespeare's plays were never acted there. Alt. by J. P. Kemble. Pr. 1795. Rev. 1810. Alt. by Dr. Valpy, and ac. at Reading School October, 1802. Pr. 1802. Pr. at Dublin, with notes and illustrations by Eccles, 1804. Rev. at Olympic May 26, 1897; Comedy, January 16, 1901; D.L., July 14, 1903, May 22, 1905; Garrick October 11, 1905; rev. by Forbes Robertson Manchester T.R., August 31, 1906; Royalty, February 10, 1908; Coronet, February 26, 1908; H.M. (Mr. Tree), April 4, 1908; (arranged in 3 sc.), Birmingham Grand, September 21, 1908; rev. Court, April 26, 1909. See *Jew of Malta*, *Jew of Venice*.

MERCHANT OF VENICE. Burl. F. Talfourd. Olympic, July, 1853.

MERCHANT PIRATE. D. Stirling.

MERCHANT'S DAUGHTER OF TOULON, THE. Mrs. Edward Thomas.

MERCHANT'S SACRIFICE, THE. Mentioned in Warburton's list, but title afterwards cancelled. Prob. the orig. title of Marmion's *Crafty Merchant*.

MERCHANT'S VENTURE, A. D. Reginald Moore. Nottingham T.R., February 3, 1868.

MERCHANT'S WEDDING; OR, LONDON FROLICS IN 1638. C. 5 a. J. R. Planché. C.G., February 5, 1828.

MERCHANTMEN, THE. Aristophanes. See "Greek Plays."

MERCIFUL LIE, THE. P. 1 a. J. Morton Lewis and Frank Bentz. Dram. fr. a story by the former. Palmer's Green, St. John's H., April 29, 1909 (amat.).

MERCILESS WORLD, A. D. 4 a. H. Leonard. Hammersmith Lyric, October 12, 1896.

MERCURIUS BRITANNICUS; OR, THE ENGLISH INTELLIGENCER. T.C. Ac. at Paris. Pr. 1641. Fr. the French. Ascr. to Richard Braithwaite. See *Censure of the Judges*.

MERCURY HARLEQUIN. Panto. H. Woodward. D.L., 1756.

MERCURY VINDICATED FROM THE ALCHEMISTS AT COURT. Masque. Ben Jonson. Ac. by the King's servants. Pr. 1640.

MERCY. D. Goodwin. Norwich T.R., November 17, 1879.

MERE CHILD. Hay., December 26, 1866.

MERE MAN. C. 1 a. H. Swears. Publ. by S. French, Limited.

MERE QUESTION OF TIME, A. C. E. J. Malyon and C. James. Kilburn T.R., July 14, 1897 (C.P.).

MEREDITH MARRIAGES. Skit. Elephant and Castle, December 2, 1904.

MERELY ACTING. Duol. Quinton Ashlyn. French Room, St. James's H., June 28, 1898.

MERELY MARY ANN. C. 4 a. I. Zangwill. Wallingford Town H., October 22, 1903 (C.P.); Duke of York's, September 8, 1904.

MERLIN. O. 3 a. Lib. by Siegfried Lippiner. M. by Carl Goldmark. Vienna, November 19, 1886.

MERLIN; OR, THE BRITISH INCHANTER AND KING ARTHUR, THE BRITISH WORTHY. Dr. O. Goodman's Fields. Pr. 1736. An alt. of Dryden's *King Arthur* by Giffard.

MERLIN; OR, THE DEVIL OF STONEHENGE. L. Theobald. D.L., December 14, 1734. Pr. 1734. This is the musical part of a panto.

MERLIN IN LOVE; OR, YOUTH AGAINST MAGIC. Past. O. Aaron Hill. Pr. 1759.

MERMAID. D. 3 a. Stebbings Heath. Ladbroke H., February 15, 1887 (amat.).

MERMAID, THE. F. Andrew Franklin. C.G., March 26, 1792. Pr. 1792.

MERMAID, THE. Int. 2 a. John Galt. Pr. 1814. ? N.ac.

MERMAID, THE. Mus. C.D. 3 a. T. Norman Walter. M. by R. W. Manning. Sheffield Alexandra, May 31, 1898; Chorley Grand, December 26, 1898.

MERMAID OF MARGATE, THE. Sk. Alice Rix. Lyrics by Ballard Macdonald. M. by Donovan Meher. Poplar Queen's, July 1, 1907.

MERMAIDS, THE. Submarine fantasy. G. Mackay. M. by C. Nugent. Add. lyrics by C. Brookfield. (Originally prod. as *In the Depths of the Sea.*) Avenue, October 2, 1897.

MEROFLEDE; OR, LOVE'S AWAKENING. Rom. P. 4 a. G. G. Collingham. Preston T.R., December 31, 1892.

MEROPE. T. of the Marquis Scipio Maffei. Transl. by Ayre. Pr. 1740. The original author notices the several plays on the same subject which had then appeared—viz., those of Euripides, John Battista Liviera, and Count Pomponio Torelli.

MEROPE. T. Jeffreys. 1731.

MEROPE. T. by Voltaire. Transl. by Dr. John Theobald. Pr. 1744. N.ac.

MEROPE. T. Aaron Hill. D.L., April 15, 1749. Pr. 1749. Borr. fr. p. of same name by Voltaire.

MEROPE. O. N. Sala. 1769.

MEROPE. T. Transl. fr. Voltaire. Pr. in Dr. Francklin's edition of that author. Also translations by Lloyd, 1815, and Matthew Arnold, 1858.

MEROPE. See *Barbarossa*.

MERRIE ENGLAND. C.O. 2 a. Basil Hood. M. by Ed. German. Savoy, April 2, 1902.

MERRIE FAMILIE, A. C.D. 3 a. W. F. Field. Bradford T. of Varieties, March 3, 1886.

MERRIE PRINCE HAL. Burl. 2 a. W. Thomas. M. by C. C. Corri. Sadler's Wells, August 31, 1891.

MERRIFIELD'S GHOST. Ca. 1 a. H. M. Paull. Vaudeville, November 13, 1895.

MERRY ANDREW. It is supposed that this is the title of the play referred to by Pepys, 1668. See *Marry Andrey*.

MERRY BLACKSMITH, THE. Oa. E. C. Dunbar. Adap. fr. Longfellow's "The Village Blacksmith." Vaudeville, September 25, 1893.

MERRY CHRISTMAS, A. M. Sk. A. Law. M. by K. Hall. St. Geo. H., December 27, 1880.

MERRY CHRISTMAS, A. Ca. Clement Scott. An adap. of the French Ca. *Je Dîne chez ma mère*. Strand, February 1, 1897.

MERRY COBBLER, THE. (The second part of *The Devil to Pay*.) F.O. 1 a. Charles Coffey. D.L., May 6, 1735. Pr. 1735.

MERRY COMBAT. Burl. W. C. Oulton. 1787.

MERRY COUNTERFEIT; OR, THE VISCOUNT A LA MODE, THE. F. Taken fr. Mrs. Behn. C.G., March 29, 1762. N.p.

MERRY DEVIL, A. Florentine F. of the 16th cent. 3 a. Jas. Bernard Fagan. Playhouse, June 3, 1909.

MERRY DEVIL OF EDMONTON, THE. C. Anon. Ent. Stationers' Co., 1608, and September 9, 1653. Attributed by Kirkman to Shakespeare and by Coxeter to Michael Drayton. The second entry at Stationers' H. gives the author as "T. B.," possibly standing for Tony or Antony Brewer. Globe. Pr. 1608.

MERRY DUCHESS, THE. C.O. 2 a. G. R. Sims. M. by F. Clay. Royalty, April 23, 1883.

MERRY-GO-ROUND, THE. M.P. 2 a. C. Fitch and F. K. Peile. M. by Peile. Gaiety, January 13, 1898.

MERRY-GO-ROUND, THE. M.C. 2 a. Seymour Hicks. M. by Meyer Lutz. Notting Hill Coronet, April 24, 1899.

MERRY MADCAP, A. M.C. 2 a. By Victor Stevens. Lyrics partly by Albert Birch. Grantham T.R., July 30, 1896 (C.P.); Ealing Lyric, August 3, 1896.

MERRY MAID, A. M.C. Chorley Grand T., August 3, 1908.

MERRY MAID MARIAN. M. Ca. Geo. Burton. South Shields Cosy Corner, June 29, 1908.

MERRY MARCHIONESS, THE. M.F. 2 a. C. W. McCabe. M. by Spencer Dickenson. Walmer Globe; Balham Assembly R.T., June 21, 1897.

MERRY MARGATE. F. 3 a. S. Grundy. Comedy, March 27, 1889.

MERRY MASQUERADERS; OR, THE HUMOROUS CUCKOLD, THE. C. Mrs. Aubin. Hay., Pr. 1730.

MERRY MEETING, A. F. 1 a. W. Lestocq. Op. C. February 26, 1887.

MERRY MIDNIGHT MISTAKE; A COMFORTABLE CONCLUSION, THE. C. David Ogborne. Pr. 1765. Ac. at the Saracen's Head, in Chelmsford.

MERRY MIGNON; OR, THE BEAUTY AND THE BARD. Op. burl. extrav. J. W. Jones. M. by J. Crook. Liverpool Court T., April 26, 1882.

MERRY MILKMAID OF ISLINGTON, THE. Pr. 1680. See *Muse at Newmarket*.

MERRY MILLER; OR, THE COUNTRYMAN'S RAMBLE TO LONDON, THE. F. Thos. Sadler. Pr. 1766.

MERRY MR. MERLIN; OR, GOOD KING ARTHUR. Burl. 2 a. E. H. Paterson and H. Grattan. Eleph. and C., February 11, 1895.

MERRY MONK, THE. C.O. 2 a. M. Dure and M. Bell. M. by A. Llewellyn. St. Geo. H. (mat.), July 15, 1897.

MERRY MOUNTAINEERS, AN ALPINE FROLIC, THE. Sk. Greenwich Barnard's Pal. of Varieties, June 18, 1908.

MERRY PIPER OF NUREMBERG, THE. Legendary fancy. 1 sc. Rachel Penn. Savoy, June 8, 1893.

MERRY PLAY BETWEEN THE PARDONER AND THE FRERE, THE CURATE AND NEYBOUR PRATTE, A. John Heywood. Pr. April 5, 1533. See *Play Between*, etc.

MERRY PRANKS; OR, WINDMILL HILL. F. Anon. 1704.

MERRY SAILORS; OR, LANDLORD BIT, THE. F. 1707. Mentioned in *The British Theatre*

MERRY SELL, A. Oa. W. Sallenger. M. by B. J. Hancock. Woolwich R. Artillery T., May 21, 1888.

MERRY SHERWOOD; OR, HARLEQUIN FORESTER. Panto. C.G., 1795.

MERRY TERRITORIAL; OR, A MILITARY MUDDLE, THE. Farc C. 3 a. Weymouth Pav., May 8, 1909 (C.P.).

MERRY VAGABONDS, THE. Sk. Brighton Alhambra, April 2, 1909.

MERRY WAR, THE. C.O. R. Reece. Fr. the German of F. Bell and R. Genée. M. by Johann Strauss. Alhambra, October 16, 1882.

MERRY WIDOW, THE. C. 2 a. Leicester Buckingham. Adap. fr. the French, *Jeanne qui Pleure et Jeanne qui rit*. St. James's, January 21, 1863.

MERRY WIDOW, THE. M.P. 3 a. English ver. of Victor Léon and Leo Stein's *Die Lüstige Witwe*. Attributed on programme of first perfce. to Ed. Morton. A controversy with Capt. Basil Hood as to authorship resulted in Mr. Morton's name being withdrawn. Lyrics by Adrian Ross. Daly's, June 8, 1907.

MERRY WIDOW TWANKEY, THE. M.C F. 1 a. Roy Redgrave. Wolverhampton R., April 28, 1909 (C.P.).

MERRY WIVES OF WINDSOR, THE. C. Wm. Shakespeare. Said to have been wr. by Command of Q. Elizabeth, who desired to see Falstaff in love. Probably taken fr. the story of the lovers of Pisa, in an old piece, called *Tarlton's Newes Out of Purgatorie* (1589). Wr. (first draft) 1598. Ent. Stationers' Hall, January 16, 1602. Completed 1605. Pr. 1st 4to (imperfect), 1602; 2nd 4to, 1619; 1st folio, 1623; 3rd 4to, 1630. Alt. by J. P. Kemble. Pr. 1797. Rev. and ac. at C.G. Pr. 1804. Rev. Princess's, November 22, 1851; Comedy, December 19, 1900; H.M., June 10, 1902; January 17, 1903; April 25, 1905; April 27, 1906; April 27, 1907; April 20, 1908; and May 30, 1908.

MERRY WIVES OF WINDSOR, THE. See *Comical Gallant; Falstaff*.

MERRY WIVES OF WINDSOR, THE. O. 3 a. Otto Nicolai. Berlin, March 9, 1849. Adap. into English by H. Hersee. D.L., February 20, 1824; Aberdeen H.M.O.H., October 10, 1877; Adelphi, February 11, 1878; rev. Edinburgh Lyceum, October 11, 1906; rev. Lyric, July 15, 1907.

MERRY ZINGARA: OR, THE TIPSY GIPSY AND THE PIPSY WIPSY, THE. Burl. W. S. Gilbert. Royalty, March 21, 1868

MERRYMAKING; OR, BIRTHDAY FESTIVITIES Ent. J. Perry. Gallery of Illus., May 13, 1867.

MERVEILLEUSES, THE. P. Vte Sardou. Adap. fr. the French by Basil Hood. Lyrics by Adrian Ross. M. by Hugo Felix. Daly's, October 27, 1906. See *The Lady Dandies*.

MESMERIC MYSTERY, A. F. W. R. Osman. Victoria, August 17, 1867.

MESMERISM. F. 1 a. Carrol Clyde. Opera Comique, May 22, 1890.

MESMERIST, THE. D. G. Conquest and H. Robinson. Grecian, October 4, 1879.

MESMERIST, THE. F.C. 3 a. F. Jarman. Bath T.R., May 5, 1890.

MESSAGE FROM MARS, A. P. 3 a. Richard Ganthony. Avenue, November 22, 1899; transf. to P.O.W., April 6, 1901; rev. Avenue, June 19, 1905.

MESSAGE FROM THE SEA, A. D. Birmingham P.O.W., August 30, 1869.

MESSAGE FROM THE SEA, A. D. 3 a. Surrey, February 1, 1873.

MESSALINA. D. Pietro Cossa.

MESSALINA, THE ROMAN EMPRESS. T. N. Richards. Ac. by His Majesty's Revels 1640. Pr. 1640.

MESSALINE. O. 3 a. G. M. V. Blackburn. Fr. the French of Armand Silvestre and Eugène Morand. M. by Isidore De Lara. Orig. prod at the Casino, Monte Carlo, March 21, 1899. C.G., July 13, 1899.

MESSENE FREED; OR, THE CRUEL VIRTUE. T. W. Preston. Pr. 1793. Story fr. Barthélemy's *Travels of Anacharsis.*

MESSENGER BOY, THE. M.P. 2 a. J. T. Tanner and A. Murray. M. by I. Caryll and L. Monckton. Gaiety, February 3, 1900.

MESSIAH, THE. Orat. Handel. Words selected by Jennens. 1741. Pr. 1755. D.L., March 2, 1827.

MESSIDOR. O. Bruneau. Prose lib. by Zola. 1897.

METAMORPHOSED GYPSIES, THE. Masque. Ben Jonson. Presented before the K. at Burleigh-on-the-Hill and Windsor Castle, 1621. See *The Masque of the Gypsies.*

METAMORPHOSES. C.O. C. Dibdin. Hay. Pr. 1776. Taken fr. Molière's *Sicilien* and *George Dandin.*

METAMORPHOSES. Ovid. See also *Midas.*

METAMORPHOSES. Ent. Egyptian H., May 6, 1867.

METAMORPHOSES. See *Acis and Galatea, Actaeon and Diana, The Brazen Age, Calisto. Midas,* "Latin Plays," "Epic Poems."

METAMORPHOSIS. C.O. 3 a. D.L., December 5, 1783. Attributed to Jackson. Songs (?) by Tickel. N.p.

METAMORPHOSIS; OR, HARLEQUIN CATS. C. Pr. 1723.

METAMORPHOSIS; OR, THE OLD LOVER OUTWITTED. C. John Corey. L.I.F., August 2, 1704. An alt. of *Albumazar.*

METAMORPHOSIS OF PIGMALION'S IMAGE AND CERTAIN SATYRES, THE. Publ. under the ps. of Wm. Kinsayder (John Marston). Pr. 1598.

METED OUT. D. 4 a. Dr. Vellère.

METEMPYSCHOSIS, THE. D. W. Bayle Bernard. Tottenham Street T., 1830.

METEOR; OR, A SHORT BLAZE FOR A BRIGHT ONE. F. Gent. 1809.

METHINKS I SEE MY FATHER; OR, WHO'S MY FATHER? F. 2 a. T. Morton. C.G.

METHODIST, THE. C. Supplement to *The Minor,* by Israel Pottinger. Pr. circa 1761. N.ac.

METHODIST PREACHER, THE. Int. Ac. at Richmond, 1775. N.p.

METOPEMANIA; OR, A SPARING USE OF ART. Mus. and Dr. "Prophecy." M. by Claude Kelly. Gaiety Restaurant, Georgian Hall, February 26, 1908 (amat.).

METROPOLIS CORONATA; THE TRIUMPHS OF ANCIENT DRAPERY; OR, RICH CLOATHING OF ENGLAND. Devised and wr. by Anthony Munday (citizen and draper of London), 1615.

METUREF, THE. D. 4 a. Jacob Gordin. Pavilion, August 17, 1908. (Jewish season.)

MEXICAN BILL; OR, LIFE IN THE FAR WILD WEST. D. 5 a. Butler Stanhope. Birkenhead T.R., August 29, 1887.

MIAMI. Melo-d. O. 3 a. J. Hollingshead. Lyrics by W. St. Ledger. M. by H. Parry. F. on Buckstone's *Green Bushes.* Princess's, October 16, 1893.

MICE AND MEN. P. 4 a. Madeleine Lucette Ryley. Manchester T.R., November 27, 1901; Lyric, January 27, 1902; rev. D. of York's, June 18, 1904.

MICHAEL AND HIS LOST ANGEL. P. 5 a. H. A. Jones. Lyceum, January 15, 1896.

MICHAEL CENO. Victoria, June 5, 1854.

MICHAEL DANE'S GRANDSON. P. 1 a. Ina Leon Cassilis. Hammersmith Lyric, April 18, 1896.

MICHAEL ERLE, THE MANIAC LOVER; OR, THE FAYRE LASS OF LICHFIELD. Rom. D. 2 a. T. E. Wilks. Surrey, December 26, 1839.

MICHAEL STROGOFF. D. Prol. and 5 a. H. J. Byron. Adap. fr. the French of D'Ennery and Jules Verne. Adelphi, March 14, 1881.

MICHAELMAS TERM. C. Thos. Middleton. Pr. 1607. Ac. by the Children of Paul's.

MICROCOSMUS. Masque. Thomas Nabbes. Salisbury Court, 1637. Pr. 1637.

MICROCOSMUS. Lat. T. J. Arthur, of St. John's College, Cambridge. 16th century.

MID-CHANNEL. P. 4 a. Sir Arthur W. Pinero. St. James's, September 2, 1909.

MID-OCEAN. D. 4 a. M. H. Hoffman. Southend Alexandra, June 26, 1889.

MIDAS. C. Ascr. to J. Lyly. Ac. before the Q. by the Children of Paul's on Twelfth Day. Pr. 1592. The story is also used by Apuleius in his *Golden Ass.* See also Ovid's *Metamorphoses.*

MIDAS. Burla. 2 a. K. O'Hara. Dublin, 1762; C.G., February 22, 1764. Pr. 1764. Edinburgh, 1782; Lyceum, August 4, 1817; Hay., July 23, 1825.

MIDAS. Burl. 2 a. C.G. Pr. 1771.

MIDDLE DISH; OR, THE IRISHMAN IN TURKEY, THE. F. W. C. Oulton. D.L., April 16, 1804. N.p.

MIDDLE TEMPLE, THE. Masque. Geo. Chapman. Presented before the King at Whitehall, February 15, 1613. This masque cost the Society of Lincoln's Inn no less than £2,400.

MIDDLE TEMPLE, THE. F. 1 a. R. B. Peake. Pub. by J. Dicks.

MIDDLE TEMPLE, THE; OR, WHICH IS MY SON? THE. Oa. M. by G. H. Rodwell. Lyceum, June 27, 1829.

MIDDLEMAN, THE. P. 4 a. H. A. Jones. Shaftesbury, Aug. 27, 1889; Comedy, 1894.

MIDDY ASHORE, THE. F. 1 a. W. B. Bernard. Engl. O.H., May 23, 1836; rev. Astley's, 1867.

MIDGE. C. 3 a. R. J. Martin and J. P. Burnett. Dublin Gaiety, May 23, 1879; Royalty, Jan. 12, 1880.

MIDGELET; OR, A DAY UP THE RIVER. Sk. E. Benson. Strand, July 11, 1893.

MIDNIGHT; OR, THE BELLS OF NOTRE DAME. D. 4 a. A. Shirley and B. Landeck. Afterwards called *The King of Crime.* Surrey, Dec. 19, 1892.

MIDNIGHT; OR, THE WOOD CARVER OF BRUGES. J. W. Furrell and E. C. Stafford. Princess's, May 24, 1888.

MIDNIGHT; THE THIRTEENTH CHIME, OR OLD SAINT PAUL'S. Melo-d. 3 a. C. Z. Barnett. Surrey, Feb., 1845.

MIDNIGHT BRIDAL, A. P. 1 a. Mrs. F. R. Benson and H. O. Nicholson. Adap. fr. the story of Halliwell Sutcliffe. Coronet, February 19, 1909.

MIDNIGHT CHARGE, THE. P. 4 a. W. E. Stedman.

MIDNIGHT HOUR, THE. C. 3 a. Mrs. Inchbald. C.G., 1788. Taken fr. the Fr. of Damaniant. Pr. 1788. Fr. the same source as Lady Wallace's *Diamond Cut Diamond.*

MIDNIGHT HOUR; OR, WAR OF WITS, THE. F. Rehearsed at C.G. Pr. 1787. An anon. transl. of *La Ruse contre Ruse, ou Guerre Ouverte.* D.L., April 16, 1814; November 23, 1814; November 12, 1816.

MIDNIGHT MAIL, THE. D. 5 a. A. Shirley. Hammersmith Lyric, October 20, 1902.

MIDNIGHT MAIL; OR, ELLA'S LOVE, THE. D. Mark Melford. Dumfries T.R., April 30, 1877.

MIDNIGHT MARRIAGE, A. Rom. D. 4 a. Chas. Osborne. Margate T.R., August 30, 1883.

MIDNIGHT MUDDLE, A. C. Mrs. A. Wallis. Acton Central Hall, May 2, 1900.

MIDNIGHT PARIS. D. 4 a. A. Shirley. Adap. fr. *La Legion Etrangère* by M. La Rose and A. Levy. Ambigu, May 10, 1899; Pavilion, May 14, 1900.

MIDNIGHT SHRIEK, A. Burl. D. Dorothea Payn. Dublin Gaiety, January 5, 1896.

MIDNIGHT SUN, THE. M.P. 3 a. W. David. Devonport M'pole, April 2, 1903.

MIDNIGHT TRUST, A. D. 5 a. W. R. Waldron and L. Ellis. Britannia, May 1, 1899.

MIDNIGHT WANDERERS, THE. Com. O. 2 a. Wm. Pearce. C.G., Feb. 25, 1793. Pr. 1793.

MIDNIGHT WATCH, THE. D. 1 a. J. M. Morton. Marylebone, October 16, 1848.

MIDNIGHT WEDDING, THE. P. 4 a. W. Howard. Manchester Grand Junction, October 20, 1905; W. London, February 25, 1907; Lyceum, June 15, 1907.

MIDST LONDON'S CRIMINALS. D. 4 a. Horwich New Prince's, April 13, 1903.

MIDSUMMER DAY. C. 1 a. W. Frith. St. James's, March 30, 1892.

MIDSUMMER EVE. O. for children. 2 a. A. Kaye. M. by Wm. Boyd. Albemarle Coll., Beckenham, April 7, 1893.

MIDSUMMER FIRES. P. 4 a. Adap. fr. Herman Sudermann's German by Mr. and Mrs. J. T. Grein. Scala, May 13, 1906.

MIDSUMMER FROLIC, A. Fa. 1 a. F. D. Adams. Publ. by French, Ltd.

MIDSUMMER NIGHT'S DREAM, A. C. William Shakespeare. Ac. by the Lord Chamberlain's Servants. Mentioned by Meres, 1598. Wr. 1592. Revised 1599. Ent. Stationers' Hall Oct. 8, 1600. Hints for Theseus and Hippolyta probably taken fr. Chaucer's "Knight's Tale"; for the interlude of Thisbe fr. Chaucer's "Thisbe of Babylon"; for the Fairies fr. "Popular Tales of Robin Goodfellow"; and Oberon fr. Greene's "James IV." Oberon and Titania were introduced in a Dr. Ent. before Queen Elizabeth, 1591. Pr. 1st qto., 1600; 2nd qto., 1600; 1st folio, 1623. An alt. by D. Garrick, D.L. Pr. 1763. Afterwards, by the advice of Colman, reproduced in 2 a. as *A Fairy Tale.* Rev. Globe (F. R. Benson), Dec. 19, 1889; Daly's, July 9, 1895; Lyceum, Feb. 22, 1900; Adelphi (Oscar Asche), Nov. 25, 1905; Adelphi (Otho Stuart), Dec. 5, 1906; Oxford, New (O.U.D.S.), February 26, 1908. (Mendelssohn wrote music for this play.)

MIDSUMMER NIGHT'S DREAM, A. Adap. of Shakespeare's play as an O. M. by Purcell.

MIDSUMMER NIGHT'S DREAM, A. See *Puck.*

MIDSUMMER'S EVE. Oa. 1 a. E. Genet. Lyrics by Geo. White; M. by Tito Mattei. Camden, June 11, 1902.

MIDSUMMER'S EVE. C. 4 a. Waldorf, October 17, 1906 (C.P.).

MIDSUMMER'S MADNESS. M.C. W. P. French. M. by W. H. Collisson. Dublin Leinster H., Nov. 7, 1892.

MIETJE. O. 2 a. Wr. and comp. by Benoit Hollander. Hampstead Conservatoire, May 11, 1909.

MIGHT AND RIGHT. Rom. D. Pro. and 3 a. F. A. Scudamore. Bolton T.R., Nov. 23, 1881.

MIGHT OF RIGHT. Astley's, January 30, 1864.

MIGHTY DOLLAR, THE. P. 4 a. B. E. Woolf. Gaiety, Aug. 30, 1880

MIGHTY ERROR, A. Mediæval Rom. 2 a. Leonard Outram. Suggested by R. Browning's poem, *In a Balcony.* Avenue, July 14, 1891.

MIGHTY HAND, THE. Dom. D. Pro. and 3 a. H. Shelley. Reading R. County, June 12, 1899.

MIGHTY MOTIVE, THE. D. Barry Williams. Stafford Lyceum, Aug. 11, 1899.

MIGNON. O. 3 a. Lib. by Michel Carré and Jules Barbier. M. by A. Thomas. Subject based on Goethe's story of Wilhelm Meister's wanderings. Paris Op. Comique, 1866; D.L., July 5, 1870.

MIGNONETTE. C.O. 3 a. O. Brand. M. by H. Parker. Royalty, Aug. 4, 1889.

MIKADO; OR, THE TOWN OF TITIPU, THE. Japanese O. 2 a. W. S. Gilbert. M. by Sir A. Sullivan. Savoy, March 14, 1885; Nov. 6, 1895; May 27, 1896; and April 28, 1908.

MIKALAY, THE. C.O. 3 a. A. Leeds and Gertrude Reade. Devonport Met., Dec. 10, 1896 (C.P.).

MIKE; OR, THE MILLER'S TRIALS. D. M. Pletts. Albion, May 12, 1876.

MILADY, D. 3 a. O. Brand. Avenue, May 28, 1885.

MILDRED'S WELL. Burnand and German Reed. Gallery of Illustration, May 5, 1873.

MILES C. Plautus' transl. into blank verse. Thornton, Rich, Warner, and Colman. Circa 1796. See "Latin Plays."

MILES CAREW, HIGHWAYMAN. Rom. P. 3 a. H. and E. Paulton. Cheltenham O.H., September 3, 1906.

MILESIAN, THE. C.O. Isaac Jackman. Pr. 1777. D.L., March 20, 1777.

MILESTONES OF LIFE, THE. Dom. D. 5 a. Frank Harvey. Manchester Comedy, August 3, 1901; Pavilion, August 19, 1901.

MILITANT COUPLE. F. (Battle of Sedgmoor.) D. of Buckingham. 1714.

MILITARY ACADEMY. D. Berguin. 1793.

MILITARY BILLY TAYLOR; OR, THE WAR IN THE CARIBOO ISLANDS, THE. F. Extrav. F. C. Burnand. Royalty, April 22, 1869.

MILITARY MANŒUVRE, A. F. J. J. Dilley and L. Clifton. Vaudeville, December 26, 1879.

MILITARY MANŒUVRE; OR, THE LADY'S MAID, A. M.P. 2 a. G. Elmer. Hackney Manor T., September 15, 1899.

MILITARY MANŒUVRES. Oa. 1 a. A. O'D. Bartholeyns. M. by F. Idle. Avenue, July 8, 1893.

MILITARY PICKLE, A. C. 4 a. Marjorie Hawkins. Cripplegate Inst., April 25, 1908 (amat.).

MILITARY TACTICS. C. Oa. Adap. fr. the Fr. C. in 1 a, *Les Projets de Marriage.* M. by Reeve. Lyceum, July 6, 1824.

MILITARY TOURNAMENT, A. M. Sk. 1 a. A. E. Jecks. West Hartlepool T.R., February 7, 1898.

MILITIÀ MUSTER, THE. Ent. D.L., November 17, 1832.

MILK MAID, THE. Serenata. C. Dibdin. Ac. at the Circus. N.p.

MILKY WHITE. S.C.D. 2 a. H. T. Craven. Liverpool P.O.W., June 20, 1864; Strand, September 28, 1864; rev., Royalty, 1872, and October 4, 1902.

MILL, THE. P. 3 a. Nugent Monck. (Presented by the Eng. Drama Soc.). Scala, June 23, 1908 (mat.).

MILL GIRL, THE. D. Brinsley Sheridan. Coventry T.R., June 23, 1884.

MILLENNIUM, THE. M. Extrav. Wr. and composed by Harvey de Montmorency. Appleby Market H., April 4, 1907 (amat.).

MILLER, THE. P. Robert Lee. Ac. 1598. N.p.

MILLER AND HIS MEN, THE. Melo-d. 2 a. J. Pocock. M. by Bishop. C.G., October 21, 1813.

MILLER AND HIS MEN, THE. Burl. Melo-d. F. Talfourd and H. J. Byron. Strand, April 9, 1860.

MILLER AND HYS MENNE. Geo. Thorne and F. Grove Palmer. Maidstone Corn Exchange, December 26, 1893.

MILLER AND THE MAID, THE. Burl. Cambridge Conservative Club, May 4, 1898 (amat.).

MILLER OF DERWENT WATER, THE. D. 3 a. E. Fitzball. Olympic, May 2, 1853.

MILLER OF FIFE; OR, CROMWELL IN SCOTLAND, THE. D. 3 a. Lowe. Glasgow R. Colosseum, March 24, 1869.

MILLER OF HAZLEBURY, THE. Oa. 2 a. W. Carnegie. M. by L. Marx. Cannon Street Hotel, March 26, 1890 (amat.); St. Geo. H., April 10, 1894.

MILLER OF MANSFIELD, THE. Dr. Ent. Dodsley, 1737. (The second part is *Sir John Cockle at Court.*)

MILLER OF MILLBERG, THE. C.O. Meyer Lutz. Gaiety, April 13, 1872.

MILLER OF MONMOUTH, THE. Duol. 1 a. H. O. Hughes. Newport Lyceum, October 12, 1906.

MILLER OF WHETSTONE; OR, THE CROSS BOW LETTER, THE. C. Burl. 1 a. T. E. Wilks. Strand.

MILLER OUTWITTED, THE. F. C.G., May 30, 1752. N.p.

MILLER'S DAUGHTER. Hay., May 5, 1865.

MILLER'S MAID, THE. C.O. 2 a. Ascr. to Waldron. Hay., Aug. 25, 1804. N.p. F. on one of the *Rural Tales* of Robert Bloomfield. M. by Davy.

MILLER'S MAID, THE. Melo-d. 2 a. J. F. Saville. M. by Jolly. Lyceum, August 16, 1821; D.L., July 12, 1824; Strand, January 26, 1832.

MILLER'S MAN, THE. John Emery (1777-1822) ac. in this piece.

MILLICENT. D. 3 a. Williams (of Birmingham). Birmingham P.O.W., November 2, 1868.

MILLINER, THE. C. Transl. fr. the French of Mme. Genlis. Pr. 1781.

MILLINER, THE. F.C. 3 a. A. C. F. Wood. Walsall Grand, August 11, 1893.

MILLINER'S HOLIDAY, THE. F. 1 a. J. M. Morton. Hay., July 1, 1844.

MILLINERS; OR, FEMALE REVENGE, THE. Burl. 2 a. T. Harpley. Pr. 1790. Ac. and pd. at Liverpool.

MILLION OF MONEY, A. D. 5 a. H. Pettitt and Aug. Harris. D.L., September 6, 1890; Grand, February 23, 1891.

MILLIONAIRE, THE. D. 4 a. Edward Towers. Pav., May 25, 1874.

MILLIONAIRE, THE. C. 4 a. G. W. Godfrey. Adap. fr. Edmund Yates's novel "Kissing the Rod." Court, September 27, 1883.

MILLIONAIRES, THE. M.P. 2 a., J. E. Gravēlins. M. by E. and G. Scott. Cripplegate Inst., February 15, 1904.

MILLIONS IN IT. C.D. 3 a. G. L. Gordon. Liverpool P.O.W., April 16, 1877.

MILLIONS OF MONEY; OR, THE SOLDIER'S TRUST. Adap. of Eugène Sue's *Le Juif Errant*. A. Melville. Sanger's, March 1, 1886.

MILLS OF GOD, THE. D. 4 a. R. Overton. Greenwich Lecture H., February 6, 1892 (C.P.); Bayswater Bijou T., May 25, 1893.

MILORD SIR SMITH. M.C. 3 a. G. D. Day. Fr. the French of Henry de Grosse and Georges Elwall. M. by Edwd. Jakobowski. Leeds Grand, September 8, 1898, as *Campano; or, The Wandering Minstrel;* Comedy, December 15, 1898.

MILORD SIR SMITH. See *The Tree Dumas Skitters*.

MILORD'S DILEMMA. C. 4 a. M. C. Martyn. Bayswater Bijou, May 20, 1905

MILTON. O. Spontini. Paris, 1804.

MIMI. Ro. D. 3 a. D. Boucicault. Partly f. on Henri Murger's *Scènes de la Vie de Bohème*. Court, October 7, 1881.

MINC'D PIE, THE. Dr. Inanity. 1 a. Joseph Moser. Pr. 1806. N.ac.

MIND THE SHOP. C. Burl. R. Reece and E. Righton. Globe, April 22, 1878.

MIND, WILL, AND UNDERSTANDING. MS. Anon. Mentioned by Brewer.

MIND YOUR OWN BUSINESS. C. 3 a. J. L. Toole played in this piece at H., 185—.

MIND YOUR STOPS. Olympic, December 2, 1850.

MINDING THE SHOP. Sk. Tivoli, July 15, 1907

MINDS. C. H. Nicholas. Pr. abroad. Circa 1550.

MINE, THE. Dr. Poem. J. Sargent. Pr. 1785. N.ac.

MINE, THE. Dr. Burl. S. J. Pratt. N.p. N.ac.

MINE; OR, BLACK FOREST OF ISTRIA, THE. Spec. By J. C. Cross. Pr. 1800.

MINE HOSTESS. Miss Davies Webster. Adap. transl. of Goldoni's c. *La Locandiera*. Bayswater Bijou, June 12, 1899.

MINE OF WEALTH, A. D. 3 a. E. Towers. City of London, July 1, 1867.

MINER'S DOG; OR, THE MURDER AT THE PIT'S BANK, THE. D. Barnsley Queen's, June 28, 1872.

MINER'S LUCK; OR, THE SONS OF TOIL, A. D. 5 a. F. Edwards. Pontypridd Clarence, June 4, 1894.

MINERS' QUEEN, THE. D. Pro. and 4 a. F. Jarman. Lincoln T.R., January 25, 1892.

MINERAL WORKERS, THE. P. 3 a. Wm. Boyle. Dublin Abbey, October 22, 1906.

MINERALI; OR, THE DYING GIFT, THE. Ro. D. 2 a. H. G. Plunkett. Victoria Lyceum, December 21, 1835.

MINERVA'S SACRIFICE; OR, THE FORC'D LADY. T. Philip Massinger. Ent. Stationers' Co., September 9, 1653. Ac. by King's Co., November 3, 1629. Destroyed by Warburton's servant.

MINERVA'S TRIUMPH. S. Shaw, 1679.

MINERVA'S TRIUMPH. Masque. Boyd, 1739. See *Don Sancho; or, The Student's Whim*, and *Words Made Visible*.

MINGLED THREADS. P. 1 a. H. Farrington. St. Geo. H., February 14, 1901.

MINIATURE PICTURE, THE. C. Lady Craven. D.L., May 24, 1780. Pr. 1781. Ac. at private T. near Newbury and at D.L. Pro. by Sheridan.

MINISTER, THE. T. M. G. Lewis. Transl. fr. the German of Schiller. Pr. 1797. N.ac. Taken fr. *Cabal and Love*.

MINISTER AND THE MERCER, THE. Hist. C. 5 a. D.L., February 8, 1834.

MINISTER OF SPAIN, THE. Standard, February 28, 1863.

MINISTER'S CALL, THE. P. 1 a. Royalty (Independent T.), March 4, 1892.

MINISTERING ANGEL, A. D. 1 a. Neville Doone and H. W. C. Newte. Bayswater Bijou T., June 6, 1893.

MINNA; OR, THE FALL FROM THE CLIFF. Oa. 1 a. Sutherland Edwards and Isidore de Lara. Crystal Pal., July 20, 1886.

MINKALAY, THE. Devonport, December 10, 1896.

MINNA VON BARNHELM. F. Holcroft. 1781.

MINNA VON BARNHELM. C. 5 a. Gottbold Ephraim Lessing. Royalty (German season), May 2, 1908.

MINNIE; OR, LEONARD'S LOVE. D. 3 a. H. J. Byron. Globe, March 29, 1869.

MINNIGREY. D. 4 a. H. Young and G. Roberts. Eleph. and C., June 14, 1886.

MINOR, THE. C. 3 a. S. Foote. Pr 1760. Ac. at the Little T. in the Hay. and at D.L. An additional scene pr. 1761.

MINORCA. T. H. Dell. Pr. 1756.

MINSTREL, THE. Fant. O. 1 a. Mr. Fleackley and Father Downs. Scala, November 16, 1906 (amat.).

MINSTREL; OR, THE HEIR OF ARUNDEL, THE. T. Mrs. West. Pr. 1805. N.ac.

MINSTREL OR PRINCE? Children's P. L. Debenham. Wr. in Verse. Pub. by S. French, Ltd.

MINT OF MONEY, A. F. C. 3 a. Arthur Law. Toole's, January 10, 1884.

MINX AND MAN, THE. Burl. 4 a. F. Lindo. Lyrics by R. H. Lindo and A. W. Skelton. M. by T. Prentis. Carlisle H.M.T., April 15, 1895; Parkhurst, June 17, 1895.

MIQUETTE. P. 3 a. Adap. fr. the French of G. A. Caillavet and Robert de Flers by Cosmo Gordon Lennox. Paris Variétés, November 2, 1906; Duke of York's, October 26, 1907.

MIRABEL. C.D. 4 a. E. Dering and J. Holloway. Adap. fr. Miss Braddon's novel, "Sir Jasper's Tenant." Macclesfield T.R., January 24, 1883.

MIRACLE, A. P. 1 a. Geo. de Lara. Brighton R., June 15, 1908.

MIRACLE PLAYS:—

The principal miracle plays are known as:

YORK PLAYS, 48 in number. (Corpus Christi plays.) 1360-1579.

CHESTER PLAYS, 25 in number. 1328-1577 and 1600.

WAKEFIELD PLAYS (Towneley Plays), 32 in number. Early 15th century.

COVENTRY PLAYS, 40-42 in number. Circa 1468.

Miracle plays were also performed as follows:—

Dunstable, 12th century.
ST. CATHERINE.

Cambridge, 1350
LUDAS FILIORUM ISRAEL.

London, Skinners' Well, Clerkenwell, 1390.
PASSION OF OUR LORD.
CREATION OF WORLD.
GREY FRIARS. 1557.
PASSION OF CHRIST. 14th and 15th centuries.
HOLY TRINITY.
ST. FABYAN.
ST. SEBASTIAN.
ST. BOTULF.
THE 'TEREMENT (BURIAL OF CHRIST).

Canterbury, temp. Henry VI.
CORPUS CHRISTI PLAYS, 1501-2.
THREE KINGS OF COLEYN.

Winchester, 1487.
CHRISTI DESCENSUS AD INFEROS.

Worcester, 1467.
FIVE PAGEANTS.

Sleaford, 1477.
THREE KINGS OF COLOGNE.

Leicester, 1477.
PASSION PLAY.

Aberdeen, 1442-1531.
OFFERAND OF OUR LADY AND CORPUS CHRISTI.

Edinburgh, 1503.

Bassingbourne (Cambridgeshire), 1511.
PLAY OF ST. GEORGE.

Betherdon (Kent), 1522.
LUDI BEATÆ CHRISTINÆ.

Heybridge (Essex), 1532.

Wymondham (Norfolk), 1549.

Reading, 1498-1557.
THREE KINGS,
RESURRECTION, AND
PASSION PLAYS.
ADAM.
CAYME.
CORPUS CHRISTI PLAYS.

Lincoln, 1564.
OLD TOBIT.

Shrewsbury, 1574.

Tewkesbury, 1578, 1585.

Witney (Oxfordshire), 16th century.
THE RESURRECTION.

Preston, Lancaster, Kendall.
CORPUS CHRISTI PLAYS.

Beverley, 1407-1604.
36 CORPUS CHRISTI PLAYS.

Newcastle-on-Tyne, 1426-1589.
Cycle of plays, 16 known. Only one play exists—viz., *Noah's Ark*.

Dublin, 15th century.
14 plays known. Only one exists—viz., *Abraham and Isaac*.

Norfolk and Suffolk, 15th century.
ABRAHAM AND ISAAC.

Croxton, 1461.
THE PLAY OF THE SACRAMENT.

Cornwall, 14th century.
ORIGO MUNDI.
PASSIO DOMINI NOSTRI.
RESURREXIO DOMINI NOSTRI, 1504.
LIFE OF ST. MERIASEK. 1611 (? older).
CREATION OF THE WORLD.

The following plays are also known:—
HARROWING OF HELL. MS. Harl. 2253 fo. 55b. Temp. Edward II. or III. In southern dialect.
BURIAL OF CHRIST.
RESURRECTION.
KILLING OF THE CHILDREN.
CONVERSION OF ST. PAUL.
MARY MAGDALENE.
THE CREATION AND FALL OF LUCIFER (York plays).

(Chester Plays.)

NOAH'S FLOOD.
THE WATTER LEADERS.
THE DRAWERS OF DEE PLAYE.
THE SACRIFICE OF ISAAC.
ECUNDA PASTORUM (a Towneley play).

(Coventry Plays.)

THE SALUTATION.
THE CONCEPTION.
MARY MAGDALEN.
THE CASTELL OF PERSEVERANCE.
EVERYMAN.
INTERLUDE OF THE FOUR ELEMENTS.
SKELTON'S MAGNYFYCENCE.
HEYWOOD'S THE PARDONER AND THE FRERE.
THERYSTES.
BALE'S KING JOHN.
BROME PLAY OF ABRAHAM AND ISAAC.
CHILDREN OF ISRAEL, ac. at Cambridge, 1350
ST. GEORGE OF CAPPADOCIA, ac. at Windsor, 1416.
PLAY OF OUR LORD'S PRAYER, York, 1384.
CREED PLAY, York, 1446.
THE SHEARMEN.
TAYLOR'S PLAY-BIRTH OF CHRIST AND OFFERING OF THE MAGI WITH THE FLIGHT INTO EGYPT AND MURDER OF THE INNOCENTS, Coventry, 1534.

MIRACLE, THE. D. 4 a. W. Howell-Poole. Surrey, March 24, 1883.

MIRACULOUS CURE; OR, THE CITIZEN OUTWITTED, THE. F. Brownlow Forde. Pr. 1771. Taken fr. Cibber's *Double Gallant.*

MIRACULOUS DOLL, THE. C.O. W. Wardroper. Adap. to the Engl. stage fr. a Swedish ver. of Dockan. M. by Adolphe Adam. Sheffield T.R., July 12, 1886.

MIRAGE. P. 4 a. Edwin Cleary. Adap. fr. F. C. Philips's *As in a Looking Glass.* Princess's, February 9, 1888.

MIRANDA. Ballet. D.L., June 26, 1855.

MIRANDA OF THE BALCONY. P. 4 a. Adap. by Anne Crawford Elexner fr. A. E. Alason's novel. Huddersfield E.T., September 2, 1901.

MIRANDOLA. T. Procter. 1821.

MIREILLE. O. 5 a. Gounod. Words by M. Carré. Paris, 1864. Prod. in 5 a. as *Mirella,* Her M., July 5, 1864. Perf. by students of the Guildhall S. of M., December 6, 1899.

MIRETTE. O. 3 a. Michel Carré. Engl. lyrics by F. E. Weatherly. Engl. dialogue by Greenbank. M. by André Messager. Savoy, July 3, 1894; new ver., October 6, 1894; Scala, July 2, 1906.

MIRIAM, QUEEN OF JERUSALEM. P. 4 a. Dr. Sifert. Standard, July 6, 1896.

MIRIAM GRAY; OR, THE LIVING DEAD. See *A Daughter of Ishmael.*

MIRIAM'S CRIME. D. 3 a. H. T. Craven. Strand, October 9, 1863.

MIRKA, THE ENCHANTRESS. Pant. P. Craig-y-nos Castle T., July 22, 1895.

MIRRA. Alfieri, 1783. Transl. by C. Lloyd, 1815.

MIRROR, THE. Jap. P. 1 a. R. Filippi. Criterion, September 15, 1903.

MIRROR OF THE TIME, THE. P. 1 a. C. W. Hogg. Manchester T.R., April 9, 1906.

MIRROUR, THE. Dr. Satire. With the practice of a dr. ent. called *The Defeat of Apollo; or, Harlequin Triumphant,* and a farce called *The Mob in Despair.* Hay., 1737.

MIRROUR, THE. C. 3 a. H. Dell. Pr. 1757. N.ac. An alt. of Randolph's *Muses' Looking Glass.*

MIRROUR; OR, HARLEQUIN EVERYWHERE, THE. Pant. burla. C. Dibdin. C.G. Pr. 1779.

MIRZA. T. R. Baron. Pr. 1647, in the reign of Charles I. ? N.ac. Same story as that of Denham's *Sophy.*

MIRZA. Society P. 4 a. W. Bryant. Op. C., November 4, 1893.

MISANTHROPE, THE. C. A transl. fr. Voltaire by J. Hughes. Pr. 1709. Afterwards reprinted with Molière's other plays. Transl. by Ozell. See "French Classical Plays."

MISANTHROPE AND REPENTANCE. D. Kotzebue. 1797. Called in English *The Stranger.*

MISCARRIAGE OF JUSTICE. D. 4 a. G. Roy. Sadler's Wells, May 27, 1882.

MISCELLANEOUS ACT. Orat. D.L., February 25, 1814.

MISCHANCE, THE. Int. C. Dibdin. Sadler's Wells, 1772. Story fr. *The Barber of Bagdad.*

MISCHIEVOUS ANNIE; OR, A LESSON FOR HUSBANDS. Protean sk. D.L., May 12, 1856.

MISCHIEF. C 3 a. C. Bridgman. Gaiety, June 23, 1886

MISCHIEF MAKER, THE. F.C. 3 a. Edith Henderson. Globe, June 12, 1891; Vaudeville, July 4, 1891.

MISCHIEF-MAKERS, THE. Sk. Leonard Mortimer. Camberwell Pal., September 28, 1908.

MISCHIEF MAKING. F. 1 a. J. B. Buckstone. Adelphi, 1830; Surrey, May 12, 1835.

MISCHIEF MAKING Princess's, September 10, 1877.

MISCONCEPTION; OR, LOVE ME, LOVE MY DOG. C. E. Rose. Portsmouth T.R., August 27, 1873.

MISDEAL, A. P. 1 a. G. Lindley. Great Malvern Ássembly Rooms, March 19, 1901.

MISER, THE. C. T. Shadwell. Pr. 1672. F. on the *Avare* of Molière, which is itself built on the "Aulularia" of Plautus. Ac. at the T.R., 1672; D.L., June 5, 1704.

MISER, THE. C. J. Ozell. Transl. fr. Molière. Pr. 1732.

MISER, THE. C. Henry Fielding. Pr. 1733. Transl. fr. Molière. D.L., February 17, 1733.

MISER, THE. C. J. Hughes. 1st a. only. Transl. fr. Molière. Pr. 1735.

MISER, THE. Molière. Transl. by Michael de Boissy. Pr. 1752.

MISER, THE. C. Bonnell Thornton. Transl. fr. Plautus. Pr. 1767. Plautus called the play *Aulularia,* of which an imitation in verse was wr. by G. B. Gelli and pr. at Florence 1550.

MISER, THE. For the use of private theatres. Pr. 1788. This is *The Miser* converted into a farce by Edward Tighe. It has been called *The Cut Miser.*

MISER, THE. C. 3 a. J. Wild. An abridged ver. of Fielding's *Miser.* C.G. Pr. 1792.

MISER, THE. C.Oa. 1 a. E. H. Gomm. M. by W. Fullerton. Prince's, July 17, 1884.

MISER, THE. D. 1 a. Julian Cross. Brighton T.R., November 16, 1887. Globe, May 5, 1890.

MISER, THE. Fantasy. 1 a. S. W. Mitchell. Olympic, May 9, 1891.

MISER; OR, WAGNER AND ABERICOCK, THE. Grotesque ent. John Thurmond. Pr. 1727.

MISER OF SHOREDITCH, THE. Rom. D. 2 a. T. P. Prest. Standard, November 2, 1854.

MISER'S CONSCIENCE, THE. Sk. Edmonton Empire, July 26, 1909.

MISER'S DAUGHTER, THE. D. D.L., February 24, 1835.

MISER'S DAUGHTER, THE. D. 3 a. E. Stirling. F. on Ainsworth's novel. Adelphi, October 24, 1842.

MISER'S DAUGHTER, THE. Rom. D. 4 a. F. A. Talbot and Jessie Warner. Tunbridge Wells Great H., October 16, 1900.

MISER'S LEGACY, THE. Do. D. H. F. Maltby. Llanelly R.T., May 20, 1907.

MISER'S RETREAT, THE. F. Anon. 1734. See *The Whim.*

MISER'S TREASURE, THE. C.D. 2 a. J. Mortimer. Olympic, April 29, 1878.

MISER'S WILL, THE. D. 4 a. T. Craven. Hastings Gaiety, December 3, 1888; Surrey, November 4, 1889.

MISERABLE. Charade. Stanley Rogers. Publ. by S. French, Ltd.

MISERABLE MARRIAGE, A. D. 4 a. A. Pringle. Lincoln T.R., September 17, 1906.

MISERABLES, LES. Victor Hugo. See *Saint or Sinner? After Ten Years, The Barricade, Revelations of London.*

MISERIES OF HUMAN LIFE, THE. F. C.G., May 19, 1807. N.p.

MISERIES OF INFORCED MARRIAGE, THE. G. Wilkins. Pr. 1607. Mrs. Behn took fr. this some part of her plot of *Town Fop; or, Sir Timothy Tawdry.*

MISERY OF CIVIL WAR, THE. T. J. Crowne. Pr. 1680. See *Henry VI.*, part II.

MISFIT MANTLE, THE. F.C. Prol. and 3 a. Chas. Gleig. Cork O.H., February 9, 1903.

MISFORTUNES OF ARTHUR, THE. T. By eight members of the Society of Gray's Inn, including Thos. Hughes, Nicholas Trotte, Francis Flower, William Fulbeck, Christopher Yelverton, John Lancaster, and "Maister Francis Bacon." Ac. before Q. Eliz. at Greenwich, 1587. Pr. 1587.

MISJUDGED. D. 3 a. Edmund Gilbert. Manchester Q., April 4, 1884.

MISLED. F. A. A. Wilmot. St. Geo. H., May 26, 1887.

MISOGONUS. C. ? by Thos. Rychardes. Circa 1560.

MISOGYNIST, THE. 1 a. G. W. Godfrey. Orig. prod. at Manchester T.R. as *The Woman Hater.* St. James's T., November 23, 1895.

MISS ANGEL. C. A. D. Furniss and M. D. Gibbs, fr. Miss Thackeray's novel. King's, C.G., May 10, 1906 (C.P.).

MISS BRAMSHOTT'S ENGAGEMENT. F. 1 a. G. S. Street. P.O.W., April 30, 1902.

MISS CHESTER. D. 3 a. Miss Florence Marryat and Sir Charles Young. Holborn T., October 6, 1872.

MISS CHIQUITA. M.P. 2 a. G. R. Sims. M. by Clarance Corri. Birmingham P.O.W., August 7, 1899; Notting Hill Coronet, August 14, 1899. See *The Dancing Girls of Spain.*

MISS CINDERELLA. Ca. W. R. Walkes. Avenue, March 15, 1890.

MISS CINDERELLA, Ca. Gertrude Warden. Strand, May 29, 1900.

MISS CLEOPATRA. F. 3 a. Arthur Shirley. Publ. by S. French, Ltd.

MISS DECIMA. Operatic C. 3 a. F. C. Burnand. Lyrics by Percy Reeve. Adap. fr. *Miss Helyett* of Boucheron. M. by Audran. Bouffes Parisiens, November 12, 1890; Criterion July 23, 1891; P.O.W., November 26, 1891; Tr. to Toole's, January 27, 1892.

MISS EILY O'CONNOR. Burl. H. J. Byron. F. on *The Colleen Bawn.* D.L., November 25, 1861.

MISS ELIZABETH'S PRISONER. Ro. C. 3 a. R. N. Stephens and E. L. Swete. Imperial. April 16, 1904. Pro. added, September 1, 1904.

MISS ESMERALDA. Melo. Burl. A. C. Torr (Fred J. Leslie) and H. Mills. M. by Meyer Lutz and R. Martin. Gaiety, October 8, 1887.

MISS FLIPPER'S HOLIDAY. C. 1 a. Harriet F. Bell. Publ. by S. French, Ltd.

MISS FRANCES OF YALE. F.C. 3 a. Michael Morton. St. Leonards R. Opera H., August 18, 1897; Globe, September 7, 1897.

MISS GALATEA OF OREGON. P. Prol. and 3 a. E. A. Cleveland. Avenue, November 16, 1894 (C.P.), Stafford Lyceum, December 4, 1895.

MISS GWILT. D. 5 a. Wilkie Collins. Adap. fr. his novel, "Armadale." Liverpool Alex., December 9, 1875; Globe, April 15, 1876.

MISS HELYETT. See *Miss Decima.*

MISS HOBBS. C. 4 a. Jerome K. Jerome. D. of York's, December 18, 1899.

MISS HONEY'S TREASURE. C. 1 a. Anon. Publ. by S. French, Limited.

MISS HOOK OF HOLLAND. M.P. 2 a. Paul A. Rubens and Austen Hurgon. M. by Paul A. Rubens. P.O.W., January 31, 1907.

MISS HOYDEN'S HUSBAND. C. 1 a. Arr. by Aug. Daly fr. Sheridan's *Trip to Scarborough.* Shaftesbury, July 4, 1890.

MISS HURSEY FROM JERSEY. M.C. Lancaster Athenæum, January 14, 1905 (C.P.).

MISS IMPUDENCE. Edward A. Morton. Terry's, June 2, 1892.

MISS IN HER TEENS; OR, THE MEDLEY OF LOVERS. F. 2 a. D. Garrick. C.G., January 17, 1747. Pr. 1747. Edinburgh, 1782; rev. Sadler's Wells, April, 1866. The idea of the piece taken fr. D'Ancourt's *La Parisienne.* See *The Gentleman Cully.*

MISS JACK. P. 3 a. Adap. for Engl. stage by Mrs. Lewis Waller fr. a story in the *Smart Set.* Manchester St. James's, December 14, 1904; Ealing New, February 10, 1905.

MISS JEKYLL AND MISS HYDE. Fantastic sequel. 1 a. Scarborough Londesborough, May 6, 1901.

MISS LANCASHIRE, LIMITED. M.F. 2 a. Sydney Sydney. Croydon Grand, September 4, 1905.

MISS LEAR. Surrey, April 11, 1864.

MISS LUCY IN TOWN. F. H. Fielding. D.L., May 5, 1740. Pr. 1742. A sequel to *The Virgin Unmasked.*

MISS MARITANA. Op. Burl. 3 a. Lieut. G. Nugent and J. W. Whitbread. Dublin Queen's R.T., April 21, 1890.

MISS MISCHIEF. M.C. 2 a. R. Bacchus and F. O. Carr. West London, October 31, 1904.

MISS MULTON. D. 5 a. Duke's, November 23, 1878. See *The Governess.*

MISS OR MRS? Ca. Bertha Moore. Queen's Gate H., June 14, 1901.

MISS RUTLAND. P. of modern life. 3 a. R. Pryce. Gaiety, April 3, 1894.

MISS SELINA OF "K." M.C. 3 a. Bk. and lyrics by E. C. Mabel Leeds. M. by Claude Blakesley Yearsley. Kingston County T., May 4, 1907.

MISS SMITH OF PINE RIDGE. P. 1 a. Ivan Pat Gore. Aberdeen H.M., July 31, 1909.

MISS TIBBETT'S BACK HAIR. F. 1 a. N. Robinson. Dublin T.R., December 5, 1870.

MISS TOMBOY. C. 3 a. R. Buchanan. F. on Vanbrugh's comedy, *The Relapse.* Vaudeville, March 20, 1890, and May 26, 1891.

MISS VERE D'ARSAY. P. F. M. Mayor. Prod. by Amateurs. Royalty, February 25, 1906.

MISS WALKER, OF WOOLOOMOOLOO. M.C. 2 a. E. Paulton. M. by E. Jakobowski. Globe, October 5, 1900.

MISS WINGROVE. M.P. 2 a. W. H. Risque and H. Talbot. Strand, May 4, 1905.

MISS WRIGHT; OR, COURTING BY PROXY. F. 2 a. M. by Mr. Hawes. Lyceum, August 28, 1828.

MISSING. Semi-M.D. Prol. and 4 a. Mark Melford. Huddersfield T.R., June 2, 1890.

MISSING. Ent. 1 a. S. Gibney. St. Geo. H., July 9, 1894.

MISSING; OR, SAVED FROM THE SCAFFOLD. D. 4 a. E. Newbound. Britannia, June 6, 1881.

MISSING LINK, THE. D. 4 a. Hal Collier. Workington T.R., February 22, 1886.

MISSING LINK, THE. F. A. Shirley. Surrey, March 24, 1894.

MISSING MISS, THE. Sk. Frank Couch and Wal Pink. M. by J. S. Baker. London M.H., November 4, 1907.

MISSING MORTGAGE. D. Sunderland T.R., September 3, 1883.

MISSION FROM ROME INTO GREAT BRITAIN IN THE CAUSE OF POPERY AND THE PRETENDER. Scenically represented. N.d. Circa 1746.

MISSIONARY, THE. D. C. Whitlock. Ilkeston New T.R., May 19, 1900 (C.P.); Warrington Court, July 23, 1900.

MISSIS IS OUT. F. Princess's, December 2, 1901.

MISSIVE FROM THE CLOUDS, A. F. Princess's, September 18, 1871.

MIST BEFORE THE DAWN, THE. D. 3 a. Leeds R. Amphi., August 31, 1868.

MISTAKE, THE. C. Sir John Vanbrugh. Hay., December 27, 1705. Pr. 1706. Partly fr. Molières *Le Dépit Amoureux.* Epil. by Motteux.

MISTAKE OF A MINUTE, THE. M.D. D.L., April 23, 1787. N.p.

MISTAKE UPON MISTAKE. F. Mrs. Inchbald. 1786. See *Appearance is Against Them.*

MISTAKEN. C.D. 3 a. J. M. Killick. St. George's H., November 15, 1872, and October 25, 1877 (amat.).

MISTAKEN. Duol. 1 a. W. F. Field. Southall Public R., April 9, 1888.

MISTAKEN. Charade. "Quill." Publ. by J. Dicks.

MISTAKEN BEAUTY; OR, THE LYAR. C. Transl. of the *Menteur* of Corneille. Pr. 1685. An earlier edition was pr. under the latter title only, 1661.

MISTAKEN HUSBAND. C. Anon. Adap. by J. Dryden. Ac. at the T.R. Pr. 1675. On the model of Plautus's *Menœcluni.*

MISTAKEN IDENTITY. C. J. B. Bannister. Runcorn T.R., February 12, 1883.

MISTAKEN IDENTITY. F. A. Murray. Gaiety, February 4, 1886.

MISTAKEN IDENTITY. F. Lewis Gilbert. Gloucester R.T., May 23, 1900.

MISTAKEN IDENTITY. C. 1 a. Kate Goddard. Publ. by S. French, Ltd.

MISTAKEN STORY, A. F. 1 a. T. E. Wilks. Princess's, 1844.

MISTAKES. P. 2 a. Mrs. Christina Dering. Pioneer Club, Cork Street, Piccadilly, October 19, 1893.

MISTAKES; OR, THE FALSE REPORT, THE. T.C. Joseph Harris. Pr. 1691. Wr. originally by an anonymous gentleman. Prol. by Dryden. Epil. by Tate.

MISTAKES; OR, THE HAPPY RESENTMENT, THE. C. Lord Cornbury. Pr. 1758. N.ac.

MISTAKES OF A DAY, THE. M.F. Ac. at Norwich. Circa 1786.

MISTAKES OF A NIGHT, THE. C. Dr. Goldsmith.

MR. AND MISS. Ca. 1 a. Publ. by S. French, Ltd.

MR. AND MRS. DAVENTRY. P. 4 a. Frank Harris. Royalty, October 25, 1900, February 4, 1901.

MR. AND MRS. GRUBB. Olympic, February 8, 1840.

MR. AND MRS. JOHN BULL. Duo. E. C. Matthews. Hackney Regent, July 15, 1909 (C.P.).

MR. AND MRS. MUFFITT; OR, A DOMESTIC EXPERIMENT. Ca. Lita Smith. Hastings Gaiety T., June 6, 1892.

MR. AND MRS. PRINGLE. Com. Interlude. 1 a. Don Ide Trueba Cosio. D.L., October 9, 1832.

MR. BACON. Sk. 1 s. A. Desword. Cambridge Music Hall, May 13, 1899.

MR. BARNES OF NEW YORK. See *Barnes of New York, Marina, To the Death, The Vendetta.*

MR. BUCKSTONE'S ASCENT OF MOUNT PARNASSUS. Panoramic Extrav. 1 a. J. R. Planché. Hay., March 28, 1853.

MR. BUCKSTONE'S VOYAGE ROUND THE WORLD. IN LEICESTER SQUARE. Extrav. 1 a. and 4 quarters. J. R. Planché. Hay., April 17, 1854.

MR. CYNIC. Ca. W. J. Locke and G. Roper. Trafalgar Sq., May 2, 1893.

MR. DICK'S HEIR. P. 1 a. C. Crofton and H. Brooke Chatsworth. January 1, 1895.

MR. DONAH. Sk. Islington Empire. August 1, 1907.

MR. DONNITHORPE'S RENT. C. Rose Seaton. Chatham O.H., June 9, 1890.

MR. FITZ W——? Oa. Horace W. C. Newte. Lyrics by Walter Parke M. by Bond Andrews. Bayswater Bijou, February 1, 1894.

MR. FLIMSEY'S FAMILY. C. Glasgow P.O.W., September 22, 1868.

MR. GEORGE. C. 3 a. Louis N. Parker. Vaudeville, April 25, 1907.

MR. GORILLA. Adelphi, July 1, 1861.

MR. GRADGRIND'S SYSTEM. P. 4 a. S. Hanworth. Fr. Dickens's *Hard Times*. Llandudno Prince's, July 3, 1906 (C.P.).

MR. GREENFINCH. C. 2 a. T. H. Bayly.

MR. GUFFIN'S ELOPEMENT. M.F. Arthur Law and George Grossmith. Liverpool Alexandra T., September 29, 1882; Toole's, October 7, 1882.

MR. GUFFIN'S ELOPEMENT. F. 1 a. H. J. Byron. Publ. by S. French, Ltd.

MR. GULL'S FORTUNE. C. 3 a. Adap. fr. Theodore Barriére's *L'Heritage de Monsieur Plumet* by H. Chance Newton. Terry's, February 6, 1907.

MR. H. F. Charles Lambe. D.L., December 10, 1806. N.p.

MR. HOPKINSON. F 3 a. R. C. Carton. Avenue, February 21, 1905.

MR. HUGHES AT HOME. Hay., July 2, 1856.

MR. JERICHO. Oa. Harry Greenbank. M. by Ernest Ford. Savoy, March 24, 1893.

MR. JOFFIN'S LATCH-KEY. F. 1 a. Nugent Robinson. Charing Cr., January 23, 1875.

MR. MALONY. See *Turkish Mahomet*.

MR. MARTIN. P. 3 a. C. Hawtrey. Comedy, October 3, 1896.

MR. POPPLE OF IPPLETON. M.C. 3 a. Wr. and comp. by Paul Rubens. Apollo, November 14, 1905.

MR. POTTER OF TEXAS. P. Wilford Stephens. Adap. fr. Archibald Clavering Gunter's novel. Liverpool Adelphi, August 20, 1888.

MR. PREEDY AND THE COUNTESS. F. in 3 a. R. C. Carton. Criterion, April 13, 1909.

MR. RICHARDS. P 3 a. Arthur Bourchier and James Blair. Shaftesbury, March 10, 1892.

MR. RIGGLES JOINS THE CHOIR. P. 1 a. E. Rynd and Amy Nankivell. Royal Albert H., November 7, 1908. The Pivot Club's Perf.

MR. ROBERT ROY HIELAN HELEN, HIS WIFE, AND DOUGAL the DODGER. Burl. Wm. Lowe. Glasgow P.O.W. Pav., December 11, 1880.

MR. SCROGGINS; OR, CHANGE OF NAME. F. 1 a. Wm. Hancock and Arthur Moore. Sadler's Wells, September 14, 1867; Dublin T.R., February 6, 1871.

MR. SHERIDAN. C. 4 a. Gladys Unger. Brighton T.R., August 29, 1904; Garrick March 6, 1907.

MR. SMITH. F.C. 1 a. Stanley Dark. Alexandra, April 26, 1900.

MR. SMITH. C.D. 3 a. W. Reynolds. Nottingham R., February 27, 1905; Camden, March 6, 1905.

MR. STEINMANN'S CORNER. D. 1 a. A. Sutro. H.M., June 4, 1907. Published by S. French, Ltd.

MR. SYMPKYN. F. 3 a. A. J. Flaxman and Wm. Yonnge. Globe, May 1, 1897.

MISTER TASTE, THE POETICAL FOP; OR, THE MODES OF THE COURT. C. By the author of "Vanella." Pr. 1732. Afterwards called *The Man of Taste*.

MR. TIBBS. F. 1 a. Thomson. D.L., March 8, 1821.

MR. TODD OF LONDON. Epis. 4 tabl. J. Lawson. Bristol Palace, October 24, 1904.

MR. VERSUS MRS. Duo. Arthur Bourchier and "Mountjoy." Royalty, December 4, 1895.

MR. WIX OF WICKHAM M.C. 2 a. H. Darnley. M. by G. Everard, F. Seddon, and F. Tours. Stratford Borough, July 21, 1902.

MISTLETOE BOUGH, THE. Burl. H. B. Farnie. Adelphi, December 26, 1870.

MISTLETOE BOUGH; OR, THE FATAL CHEST, THE. Melo-d. 2 a. C. Somerset. Garrick, 1834.

MISTRESS AND MAN. Children's P. L. Debenham. Wr. in verse. Publ. by S. French, Ltd.

MISTRESS CLARE. C.O. 3 a. W. Cooper Lissenden and R. Gardner Gillman. M. by Mme. F. Schulz. Bayswater Bijou, October 25, 1900; St. Geo. H., June 18, 1901.

MISTRESS DOGGREL IN HER ALTITUDES; OR, THE EFFECTS OF A WEST INDIA RAMBLE. Prel. Hay., 1795.

MISTRESS NONSUCH'S NONSENSE. Int. Advertised for perf. at Hay. 1790, but n.a.

MISTRESS OF CRAIGNAIRN, THE. R.P. 3 a. Alfred C. Calmour. Liverpool Royal C.T., February 26, 1900

MISTRESS OF THE MILL, THE. Ca. 1 a. W. T. Moncrieff. A transl. fr. *La Munière de Marly*. Sadler's Wells, October 17, 1849; Holborn, May 1, 1869.

MISTRESS OF THE ROBES, THE. C. 4 a. C. Graves, Liverpool Court, November 3, 1903.

MISTRESS OF THE SEAS, THE. D. 4 a. John Douglass. West London, February 27, 1899.

MISTRESS PARLIAMENT, HER GOSSIPPING. Pr. 1648. By Mercurius Melancholicus. ? Same piece as *Newmarket Fayre*.

MISTRESS PEG. Dr. inc. Lita Smith. F. on supposed event in the life of Peg Woffington. Vaudeville, February 23, 1892.

MISTRESS WIGGINS. C.P. 2 a. J. T. Allingham. Hay., May 27, 1803. Pr. 1803.

MRS. ANNESLEY. P. 3 a. J. F. Cooke. Criterion, July 1, 1891.

MRS. BAILEY'S DEBTS. C. 3 a. Charles Eddy. Fd. on his novel. Garrick, October 27, 1908.

MRS. BEFLAT'S BLUNDER. F. W. Routledge. Gallery of Illus., January 23, 1869 (amat.).

MRS. BILL. Slight c. of pleasant people. Capt. J. Kendall. Court, March 9, 1908.

MRS. BROWN. Ca. Miss J. H. Wilton. Britannia, May 11, 1874.

MRS. CAUDLE'S CURTAIN LECTURES. F. 1 a. E. Stirling. Publ by S. French, Ltd.

MRS. DAINTREE'S DAUGHTER. P. 4 a. Janet Achurch. Manchester T.R., May 15, 1903.

MRS. DANE'S DEFENCE. P. 4 a. Hy. A. Jones. Wyndham's, October 2, 1900; June 5, 1902.

MRS. DEERING'S DAUGHTERS. D. 1 a. MS. with Douglas Cox.

MRS. DERING'S DIVORCE. C. 3 a. P. Fendall. (First in London.) Camden, November 14, 1904; Terry's, January 18, 1905.

MRS. DEXTER. F.C. 3 a. J. H. Darnley. Liverpool Court, December 26, 1891; Strand, February 28, 1894.

MRS. DOT. C. 3 a. W. Somerset Maugham. Comedy, April 27, 1908.

MRS. DUNCOMBE'S PAST. P. 3 a. G. S. Tanner. Godalming Bor. H., April 22, 1905.

MRS. ELLISTREE'S ANSWER. Serious C. 3 a. Rowan Orme. New, November 5, 1907.

MRS. EVERSLEY—WEDNESDAYS. Duo. Malcolm Bell. Steinway H., April 18, 1893.

MRS. GARTH'S JEALOUSY. P. 4 a. W. Ellis. Brunswick House, Wandsworth Road, December 8, 1902 (amat.).

MRS. GORRINGE'S NECKLACE. P. 4 a. H. H. Davies. Wyndham's, May 12, 1903; rev. New T., September 23, 1903; rev. Criterion, January 6, 1909.

MRS. GREEN'S SNUG LITTLE BUSINESS. F. 1 a. C. S. Cheltnam. Strand, January 16, 1865.

MRS. GRUNDY. Dom. P. 4 a. Madeleine Lucette Ryley. The Scala, November 16, 1905.

MRS. H—— WILL GIVE LESSONS IN LOVEMAKING. Ca. A. Atwood and R. Vaun. Parkhurst, March 12, 1897.

MRS. HAMILTON'S SILENCE. P. 3 a. Adap. by Jane Wilson fr. the German (Felix Phillipi). Fulham Grand T., June 12, 1902.

MRS. HILARY REGRETS. Ca. 1 a. T. Smith. Criterion, June 21, 1892.

MRS. HONEY'S TREASURE. Ca. 1 a. F. Gourlie. Pub. by S. French, Ltd.

MRS. JARRAMIE'S GENIE. Oa. F. Desprez. M. by A. and F. Cellier. Savoy, February 14, 1888.

MRS. JOFFIN'S LATCH KEY. F. N. Robinson. Charing Cr., January 25, 1875.

MRS. JOHNSON. F. D.L., February 26, 1852.

MRS. JOLLYBUTT'S OUT; OR, A DAY AT BLACKPOOL. C. 3 a. W. Brown. Rochdale P.O.W.'s, December 15, 1876.

MRS. JORDAN; OR, ON THE ROAD TO INGLEFIELD. P. 1 a. A. Constance Smedley. Royalty, February 19, 1900.

MRS. LESSINGHAM. P. 4 a. Geo. Fleming. Garrick, April 7, 1894.

MRS. L'ESTRANGE. P. 3 a. F. K. Peile. Shaftesbury, May 22, 1905.

MRS. M.P. F. H. Vezin. Adap. fr. the German of Julius Rosen. Worthing Assembly R., September 28, 1891. Op. C., December 1, 1891.

MRS. MACKENZIE NO. 2. Ca. K. Harrison and Beta Harrison. S. Kensington Queen's Gate H., May 11, 1896.

MRS. OAKLEIGH. P. 3 a. Lady Trowbridge. New, December 3, 1903.

MRS. OR MISS? Ca. 1 a. Mme. Bertha Moore, Queen's Gate H., June 14, 1901.

MRS. OTHELLO. F. 3 a. F. Leslie and A. Shirley. Adap. fr. the French of Boucheron and Morel. Toole's, November 11, 1893.

MRS. PONDERBURY'S PAST. F.C. 3 a. Adap. by F. C. Burnand from Blum and Toche's *Madame Mongodin*. Avenue, November 2, 1895; Court, February 20, 1896 (prod. as *Mrs. Ponderbury*); Vaudeville, June 18, 1907.

MRS. RIGGLES MAKES A MATCH. F. 1 a. E. E. Rynd. Croydon Pembroke H., October 17, 1907.

MRS. SLIMMER'S LODGERS. F. 1 a. Wm. Holles. Bolton T.R., July 17, 1893.

MRS. SMITH; OR, THE WIFE AND THE WIDOW. F. 1 a. J. H. Payne. Hay., June 18, 1823.

MRS. SWALLOW. F. 3 a. E. J. Hart. Manchester Gaiety, March 16, 1908.

MRS. TEMPLE'S TELEGRAM. F. 3 a. F. Wyatt and Wm. Morris. Waldorf, September 10, 1906.

MRS. THOMAS BROWN. F. 1 a. MS. with Douglas Cox.

MRS. VANCE. P. 1 a. Ciceley Hamilton. Bedford St. Bijou, October 27, 1907.

MRS. WARREN'S PROFESSION. P. 4 a. G. B. Shaw. New Lyric Club, January 6, 1902.

MRS. WEAKLY'S DIFFICULTY. Ca. Wm. Poel. Vaudeville, July 5, 1887.

MRS. WESTERFIELD ——? Dom. D. 4 a. C. Hannan. Batley R., July 2, 1900.

MRS. WHITE. F. 1 a. R. J. Raymond. Eng. O.H., July, 1836.

MRS. WIGGINS. F. 1 a. J. T. Allingham. Hay., 1806.

MRS. WIGGS OF THE CABBAGE PATCH. C. 3 a. A. H. Rice and Anne Crawford Flexner. Terry's, April 27, 1907. Tfd. to Adelphi, September 9, 1907.

MRS. WILLIS'S WILL. C.D. 1 a. Adap. fr. the French of Emile Souvestre.

MRS. WILLOUGHBY'S KISS. P. 4 a. F. Stayton. Brighton R., May 2, 1901; Avenue, October 18, 1902.

MISUNDERSTOOD. Duo. Julia B. Nordan. Steinway H., May 6, 1899.

MIT FREMDEN FEDERN. F.C. 4 a. Herr Carl Schonfield. St. Geo.'s H., October 27, 1900.

MITHRIDATE. T. Racine. 1673. From Euripides. See "French Classical Plays."

MITHRIDATE. O. Scarlatti. Venice, 1707.

MITHRIDATE. O. B. Aliprandi. Munich, 1738.

MITHRIDATE, RE DI PONTO. O. Mozart. 1770.

MITHRIDATES, KING OF PONTUS. P. N. Lee, Ac. at the T.R., 1678. F. on history, for which see *Appian, Florus and Plutarch*. Epil. by Dryden.

MITRANE. O. Rossi. 1689.

MIXED; OR, ALL IN THE WRONG. F.C. 3 a. Lloyd Clarance. Blackpool Raike's H. Gardens T., June 2, 1884.

MIXED ADDRESSES. C. 1 a. Sydney Fane. Publ. by S. French, Ltd.

MIXED MARRIAGES. F.C. 3 a. Alfred Robbins. Hastings Pier Pav., June 3, 1895.

MIXED PICKLES. F.C. 3 a. W. S. Blessley. Cardiff T.R., December 19, 1899.

MIXED PICKLES. M.C. Nita Rae. Rawtenstall Grand, January 25, 1901.

MIXED RELATIONS. P. 3 a. Miss K. Santley. Adap. of Sardou and Najac's *Divorçons*. Royalty, February 4, 1902.

MIXED UP. Sk. by Chs. Stephenson. Cambridge, March 11, 1907.

MIZPAH. D. Prol. and 4 a. B. Sykes. International T. (Holborn), December 22, 1883.

MIZPAH. D. 4 a. Wood Lawrence, H. W. Hatchman, and J. B. Mulholland. Stirling Arcade T., December, 1885; Grimsby T.R., January 25, 1886; Britannia, May 18, 1891.

MOB CAP; OR, LOVE'S DISGUISES, THE. Do. D. 2 a. Howard Paul. D.L., April 13, 1853.

MOB IN DESPAIR, THE. Dr. satire. Anon. 1737. See *The Mirrour*.

MOBSWOMAN, THE. D. 1 a. Leon M. Lion and W. Strange Hall. Playhouse, August 31, 1909.

MOCK COUNTESS, THE. F. Anon. 1727. Taken fr. Breval's *Play is the Plot*. See *The Strollers*.

MOCK DOCTOR, THE C.O. 3 a. Gounod. F. on Molière's *Le Medécin Malgre lui.* English ver. by C. Lamb Kenney. C.G., February 27, 1865; rev. Avenue, February 26, 1891; R.A.M., December 10, 1896; Guildhall S. of M., February 24, 1899.

MOCK DOCTOR; OR, THE DUMB LADY CURED, THE. F. 2 a. H. Fielding. Fr. Molière's *Le Medécin Malgre lui.* D.L., September 8, 1732; Edinburgh, 1781; D.L., March 28, 1814. Pr. 1732. Compressed into 1 a. Lyceum, October 11, 1824.

MOCK DOCTRESS, A F. J. S. Battams. Ealing Lyric H., May 7, 1887.

MOCK DUELLIST; OR, THE FRENCH VALET, THE. C. By P. B. Ac. at T.R. and pr. 1675. Attributed to Peter Beton.

MOCK LAWYER, THE. Ballad O. E. Phillips. C.G., April 28, 1733, and D.L. Pr. 1733.

MOCK MARRIAGE, THE. C. T. Scott. Dorset Gardens. Pr. 1696.

MOCK OFFICER; OR, THE CAPTAIN'S A LADY, THE. F. A p. under this title ascribed to Theophilus Cibber in the "Grub Street Journal" of May 24, 1733, and said to have been ac. at D.L.

MOCK ORATORS, THE. F. Ac. at D.L., April 10, 1756. N.p.

MOCK PHILOSOPHER, THE. C. S. Harper. Pr. 1737.

MOCK PILGRIM, THE. F. 1 a. Alt. fr. Beaumont and Fletcher.

MOCK POMPEY. This seems to have been a Droll. 1674.

MOCK PREACHER. Sat. C. Anon. 1739.

MOCK TEMPEST; OR, THE ENCHANTED CASTLE, THE. F. T. Duffet. Ac. at T.R. Pr. 1675.

MOCK TESTATOR, THE. Taken fr. *The Spanish Curate.*

MOCK THYESTES. F. burl. J. Wright. Pr. 1674. F. on his transl. of "Seneca."

MOCK TRIAL; OR, BREACH OF PROMISE. Sc. 1 a. Publ. by S. French, Ltd.

MOCK TURTLES. Vaud. 1 a. F. Desprez. M. by E. Fanning. Savoy, October 17, 1881.

MOCKERY OF MARRIAGE, THE. D. 4 a. E. Thane. Chorley G.T., January 31, 1901; West London, March 10, 1902.

MODE, THE. C. Wm. Davies. Pr. 1786. N.ac.

MODEL HUSBAND, A. F. 1 a. J. P. Wooler. Sadler's Wells, September 9, 1853.

MODEL HUSBAND, THE. Ca. Miss Braddon. Rev. Surrey, October, 1868.

MODEL OF A WIFE, A. F. 1 a. A. Wigan, Lyceum, January 27, 1845.

MODEL OF PROPRIETY. M. Ca. Tom Hefferman and F. Rosse. Avenue, May 6, 1905.

MODEL TRILBY; OR, A DAY OR TWO AFTER DU MAURIER, A. M. Sk. 1 a. C. H. Brookfield and W. Yardley. M. by Meyer Lutz. Op. Comique, November 16, 1895.

MODEL UNCLE, A. F. Dr. S. Z. M. Strauss. D.L., October 26, 1868.

MODERN ADVENTURESS, A. D. 4 a. Lingford Carson. Keighley Queen's, December 26, 1903; Stratford R., August 21, 1905.

MODERN ANDROMENA, A. Dr. Epis. 1 sc. Leo Stormont and J. E. Macmanus. Formerly called *Exposure.* New Cross Empire, September 6, 1909.

MODERN ANTIQUES; OR, THE MERRY MOURNERS, THE. F. 2 a. J. O'Keeffe. C.G., 1789. Pr. 1798. Hay, 1806; D.L., February 16, 1814, and October 22, 1825.

MODERN ARRIA, THE. T. Transl. from the German of F. M. Klinger. Pr. 1795. N.ac.

MODERN ASPASIA, A. C. 3 a. H. Hamilton Fyfe. Prod. by the Stage Society, Aldwych, June 4, 1909 (C.P.); Aldwych, June 6, 1909.

MODERN BREAKFAST; OR, ALL ASLEEP AT NOON. Int. H. Siddons. Hay, August 11, 1790. Pr. 1790.

MODERN CHARACTER. A.—Introduced into Æsop as ac. at the Hay. Pr. 1751.

MODERN COMEDY; OR, IT IS ALL A FARCE. Dr. afterpiece. 3 a. Anon. Pr. 1792. N.ac.

MODERN COURTSHIP. C. 2 a. Pr. 1768.

MODERN CRAZE, THE. Ca. Mrs. Henry De La Pasture. St. George's H., November 2, 1899.

MODERN DAUGHTER, A. C. Mrs. Tom Godfrey. Court, July 14, 1908.

MODERN DON QUIXOTE, A. M.F. 2 a. G. Dance. M. by J. Crook. Nottingham T.R., July 17, 1893; Strand, September 23, 1893; Lyric (revised ver.), May 21, 1898.

MODERN EVE, A. P. 3 a. M. C. Salaman. Hay., July 2, 1894.

MODERN FAUST, THE. See *The Cynic.*

MODERN HELEN; OR, SCHOOL FOR FASHION, THE. Pr., but not publ.

MODERN HERCULES, A. F. O. Brand. Transl. fr. the German F., *Monsieur Herkules.* Grand, October 11, 1886.

MODERN HONEYMOON. F. Anon. N.p. Before 1812.

MODERN HONOUR; OR, THE BARBER DUELLIST. C.O. 2 a. Anon. Ac. at Smock Alley, Dublin. Pr. 1775.

MODERN HUSBAND, THE. Burnaby. Pr. 1702.

MODERN HUSBAND, THE. C. H. Fielding. Pr. 1732. Ac. at T.R. in D.L., February 21, 1732.

MODERN HYPATIA; OR, A DRAMA OF TO-DAY, A. P. Mabel Collins. Bayswater Bijou, February 22, 1894 (C.P.); Terry's, June 17, 1895.

MODERN IRELAND. D. R. F. Sagar. Bacup T.R., September 13, 1890.

MODERN JUDAS, A. D. 4 a. Nellie Cortelyon Guion. Vaudeville, February 25, 1892.

MODERN JULIET; OR, ROMEO REVISED, A. Sk. by "Triplet." Terry's, July 26, 1893.

MODERN LIFE. C. W. Russell. Left unfinished in MS.

MODERN MAGDALEN, A. D. 5 a. W. H. Ware. Southport O.H., January 20, 1902.

MODERN MARRIAGE, A. P. 4 a. Neville Doone. Comedy, May 8, 1890.

MODERN MARTYR, A. P. 4 a. 13 sc. J. Stevenson, jun. Nuneaton P.O.W., August 31, 1905.

MODERN MIRACLE, THE. P. 3 a. J. S. Macnab. Glasgow Athenæum, October 9, 1902.

MODERN POETASTERS; OR, DIRECTORS NO CONJURORS. F. Isaac Bickerstaffe, jun. Circa 1720.

MODERN PROPHETS; OR, NEW WIT FOR A HUSBAND, THE. C. Thos. Dwyer. D.L., May 3, 1709. Pr. circa 1709.

MODERN RECEIPT; OR, A CURE FOR LOVE, THE. C. By J. C. An alt. of Shakespeare's *As You Like Lt.* Pr. 1730.

MODERN TUTOR, THE. C. Wilford F. Field. Southall, February 8, 1892.

MODERN WIFE, THE. C. Alt. fr. Gay. C.G., April 27, 1771. N.p.

MODERN WIFE; OR, THE VIRGIN HER OWN RIVAL, THE. C. Brought out by J. Stevens, but authorship uncertain. Pr. 1744. As it was to have been ac. at the New T., Hay., 1745. Alt. 1771. N.p.

MODERN WIVES. F.C. 3 a. E. Warren. Adap. fr. *Le Bonheur Conjugal* of Albin Valabrègne. Royalty, January 20, 1887.

MODERN WIZARD, A. M.F. 3 a. John Henderson. Torquay T.R. and O.H., December 26, 1895.

MODISH COUPLE, THE. C. Capt. Charles Bodens. D.L., January 10, 1732. Pr. 1732. Fr. this was taken a F., *Marriage à la Mode*. Ac. 1760.

MODISH GALLANTS, THE. C. Pr. 1733. This is *The Intriguing Courtiers*, with a new title-page.

MODISH HUSBAND, THE. C. Charles Burnaby. Pr. 1702. Ac. at D.L., 1702.

MODISH WIFE, THE C. Francis Gentleman. Hay., September 18, 1773. Pr. 1774. First ac. at Chester circa 1760.

MODUS VIVENDI, A. Duol. L. Fomm. Bayswater Bijou, December 6, 1902.

MOGGY AND JENNY. Bal. Roffey. D.L., 1799.

MOGUL TALE, THE. F. 2 a. Mrs. Eliz. Inchbald. Hay., July 6, 1784.

MOHICANS OF PARIS, THE. D. Pro. and 2 a. Britannia, July 14, 1873.

MOHOCKS, THE F. John Gay. Ac. "near the watch house in Covent Garden." Pr. 1712.

MOINA. O. De Lara.

MOINA. One of three plays published as "Dramatic Sketches of the Ancient Northern Mythology." F. Sayers, M.D. Pr. 1790.

MOISE. O. Rossini. March 25, 1827.

MOISE IN EGITTO. O. Rossini. 1818. Paris, March 25, 1827.

MOLIERE. P. 1 a. Walter Frith. St. James's, July 17, 1891

MOLINARA, LA. O. Paisiello (Naples, 1788); King's T., March 22, 1803.

MOLL THE ROGUE. M.P. 3 a. Rev. ver. Cheltenham O.H., September 27, 1905.

MOLLENTRAVE ON WOMEN. P. 3 a. A. Sutro. St. James's, February 13, 1905.

MOLLUSC, THE. C. 3 a. Hubert H. Davies. Criterion, October 15, 1907.

MOLLY AND THE MASTER. C. 3 a. P. V. Hughes. Worthing Pier Pav., May 22, 1909 (C.P.).

MOLLY AND THE MODEL. M.F. 1 a. Cairns James and Claude Aveling. Steinway H., May 26, 1902.

MOLLY OF THE DUKE'S. D. G. R. Sims and A. Shirley. Court, March 11, 1901.

MOMENT OF TERROR. Grecian, June 9, 1862.

MOMENTOUS QUESTION, THE. Do. D. 2 a. E. Fitzball. Lyceum, June 17, 1844.

MOMUS TURN'D FABULIST; OR, VULCAN'S WEDDING. O. L.I.F., December 3. 1729. Pr. 1720.

MONA, THE BRIDE OF GLEN MAY. C.O. 3 a. A. Slater. Songs and M. by J. Broadbent. Hyde T.R., December 11, 1893.

MONARCH OF THE WORLD, THE. D. Royal, Barry Dock, May 29, 1908.

MONARCHICAL IMAGE; OR, NEBUCHADNEZZAR'S DREAM. Dr. P. R. Fleming. Pr. 1691.

MONARCHIE TRAGEDIES, THE. Four Tragedies by Wm. Alexander, afterwards Earl of Stirling. See *Tragedy of Darius, Crœsus, Julius Cæsar*, and *The Alexandræan Tragedy*. Pr. 1607.

MONASTERY. Seith. See *La Dame Blanche*.

MONASTERY OF ST. JUST, THE. P. 3 a. J. Oxenford. Adap. fr. the French of C. Delavigne. Princess's, June 27, 1864.

MONCRIEFF. T. Alfred Millard. Wigan R. Court, April 22, 1896 (C.P.).

MONDE OU L'ON S'ENNUIE, LE. C. 3 a. Maria Leonard and J. T. Grein. Transl. E. Pailleron. Com. Franc., April 25, 1881; Strand, February 12, 1901.

MONEY. C. 5 a. Sir E. L. Bulwer. Hay., December 8, 1840; rev. P.O.W. May, 1872; Vaudeville, April 9, 1891; rev. Garrick, May 19. 1894; Comedy, January 25, 1900.

MONEY. See *Credit*.

MONEY AND MAN. Modern P. in pro. and 3 a. Adap. by H. Comber Wiatt fr. F. Marion Crawford's novel, "Whosoever Shall Offend." Bradford R., April 5, 1909; Eleph. and C., April 19, 1909.

MONEY AT A PINCH; OR, THE IRISHMAN'S FROLICS. M. Ent. H. Robson. C.G., April 25, 1793.

MONEY BAGS. F.C. 3 a. E. Pemberton and Shannon. Adap. fr. the German. Novelty. November 5, 1885.

MONEY GRABBER, THE. Society satire. 3 a. Hester Stanhope. Kingsway, February 27, 1908.

MONEY IS AN ASS. C. Thos. Jordan. Pr. 1668.

MONEY LENDER, THE. Melo-d. 5 a. T. M. Ford. Warrington Public H., August 6, 1888.

MONEY MAD. D. 5 a. Steele Mackay. First prod. in America. Surrey, April 3, 1893.

MONEY MAKERS, THE. F.C. 3 a. Geo. Rollit. Royalty, May 13, 1904.

MONEY SPIDER, THE. C.O. 2 a. A. Eliot. M. by C. Lucas. St. Geo. H., April 19, 1897; Coliseum, June 20, 1908.

MONEY-SPINNER, THE. C. 2 a. A. W. Pinero. Manchester Prince's, November 5, 1880; St. James's, January 8, 1881.

MONEY THE MISTRESS. P. Thos. Southern. Pr. 1726. L.I.F., February 19, 1726. Plot from Mme. Dunois's *Lady's Travels in Spain*.

MONEY'S AN ASS. See *Money is an Ass*.

MONFORT. T. Joanna Baillie. Pr. 1798. Partly fr. *Les Frères Ennemis*, or *La Thebaide* of Racine.

MONFORT. See *De Monfort; Montfort*.

MONICA. Sk. J. W. Swarbreck. Hatfield. Pub. H., February 8, 1893 (amat.).

MONIMIA. T. John Joshua, Earl of Carysfort. Pr. 1810. First two acts wr. in 1784.

MONK. See *La Nonne Sanglante*.

MONK OF SAN MARCO, THE. The third a. of a new Ro. D., in 3 a. By Sybil Ruskin. Bedford Street Bijou, September 29, 1907.

MONK'S ROOM, THE. P. 3 a. John Lart. P.O.W. (with pro and 4 a.), December 20, 1887; Olympic, April 18, 1888; Globe, October 2. 1888.

MONKEY ISLAND; OR HARLEQUIN AND THE LOADSTONE ROCK. Pant. Lyceum, July 3, 1824.

MONKEY'S PAW, THE. Story. 3 sc. W. W. Jacobs. Dram. by L. N. Parker. Haymarket, October 6, 1903, and March 4, 1905.

MONMOUTH UP TO DATE. Burl. D. M'Kay. Shepton Mallet, April 23, 1895.

MONNA VANNA. P. 3 a. M. Maeterlinck. Bayswater Bijou, June 19, 1902.

MONOPOLISER OUTWITTED. M.E. By A. M'Laren. Pr. 1800. N.ac.

MONSIEUR ALPHONSE.

MONSIEUR AND MADAME PIERROT. P. without words. J. Hubert. M. by A. Bert. Royalty (Mlle. Jane May's season), May 20, 1897.

MONSIEUR BEAUCAIRE. Rom. C. 4 a. B. Tarkington and E. G. Sutherland. Liverpool Shakespeare T., October 6, 1902; Comedy October 25, 1902; Imperial, June 10, 1905; Lyric, June 28, 1906; Lyric, July 4, 1907; Lyric, December 2, 1907.

MONSIEUR D'OLIVE C. Geo. Chapman. Pr. 1606. Ac. by Her Majesty's children at Blackfriars.

MONSIEUR DE PARIS. P. 1 a. Alicia Ramsay and Rudolph de Cordova. Hastings Gaiety (prod. as *The Executioner's Daughter*), April 6, 1896, Royalty, April 16, 1896; rev. Garrick, July 25, 1906.

MONSIEUR DE POURCEAUGNAC; OR, SQUIRE TRELOOBY. C. Anon. Ascr. to Dr. Garth. Transl. fr. Molière's C. See "French Classical Plays." L.I.F., March 20, 1704. Pr. 1704. See *The Cornish Squire.*

MONSIEUR DE POURCEAUGNAC; OR, SQUIRE TRELOOBY. C. John Ozell. A transl. of Molière's P. N.ac.

MONS. ET MAD. GALOCHARD! French V. D.L., July 8, 1836.

MONSIEUR JACQUES. M.P. 1 a. Morris Barnett. Fr. *Le Pauvre Jacques,* of Cogniard (Paris Gymnase, September 15, 1835). St. James's, January 12, 1836; rev. O.C., November 5, 1892.

MONSIEUR JEAN. C. 1 a. G. Manteine. Shaftesbury, March 27, 1908.

MONSIEUR LE DUC. P. 1 a. Val Prinsep,

MONSIEUR LE MINISTRE. Gaiety, June 18, 1883.

MONSIEUR LEPINARD. Sk. Foresters', April 18, 1907.

MONSIEUR MALLET; OR, THE POST OFFICE MISTAKE. F. 3 a. W. T. Moncrieff. D.L., December 10, 1839.

MONSIEUR METHUSELAH. C. 1 a. Toynbee.

MONSIEUR MOULON; OR, THE SHADOW OF DEATH. P. 4 a. C. Hannan. Ladbroke H. (in 4 a., under the title of *The Fisher Girl*), January 6, 1890 (C.P.); Shaftesbury, October 28, 1890.

MONSIEUR RAGOUT. C. Lacy. About 1669.

MONSIEUR THOMAS. C. John Fletcher (Beaumont and Fletcher). Ac. at Blackfriars before August 1625. Pr. 1639. Rev. by Durfey as *Trick for Trick.*

MONSIEUR TONSON. F. 2 a. Moncrieff. D.L., September 20, 1821.

MONSIEUR TONSON. Ent. Mr. Mathews. 2 a. Rev. Lyceum, August 18, 1823.

MONSTER OF THE WOOD, THE. Pant. M. by J. A. Fisher. 1772.

MONT BLANC. C. 3 a. H. and A. Mayhew. Hay., May 25, 1874.

MONT ST. MICHEL; OR, THE FAIRY OF THE SANDS. Rom. melo-d. B. Bernard. Princess's, 1852.

MONTACUTE MASQUE, THE Geo. Gasgoine. 1587.

MONTALTO T. 5 a. Anon. D.L., November 8, 1821.

MONTANSIER, LA. French C. Pro. and 3 a. G. A. de Caillavet, R. de Fiers, and Jeoffrin. P.O.W., June 17, 1904.

MONTBAR; OR, THE BUCCANEERS. T. Moore. 1804.

MONTCALM. Rom. D. 5 a. Sir C. Young. Queen's, September 28, 1872.

MONTE CARLO. M.C 2 a. S. Carlton. H. Greenbank. M. by Howard Talbot. Strand, September 20, 1894 (C.P.); Avenue, August 27, 1896.

MONTE CARLO. Dr. Inc. Mr. and Mrs. Geo. Daventry. Poplar Queen's, January 7, 1907.

MONTE CARLO. M. Burla. Britannia, October 7, 1907.

MONTE CHRISTO. D. Pro. and 4 a. Adap. fr. Dumas. Woking Public H., February 6, 1899.

MONTE CHRISTO. D 5 a. T. H. Lacy. Publ. by S. French, Ltd.

MONTE CHRISTO; OR, THE PRISONERS OF THE CHATEAU D'IF. P. O. Brand. F. on story by Alex. Dumas the elder. Islington Grand, November 2, 1903.

MONTE CRISTO. D. 10 a. A. Dumas and A. Magret. M. by V. Stopel and Mangeant. (Occupying two evenings in performance). D.L. (1st part), June 14, 1848.

MONTE CRISTO. Rom. D. 5 a. Adap. fr. Dumas. Produced in Paris, December 3, 1848; Adelphi, October 17, 1868; Avenue, February 7, 1891.

MONTE CRISTO, JUNIOR. Burl. Melo-d. 3 a. Richard Henry. M. by Meyer Lutz, I. Caryll, H. Clarke, G. W. Hunt, and H. J. Leslie. Gaiety, December 23, 1886.

MONTEM, THE. M. ent. 2 a. Rev. Henry Rowe, LL.B. Pr. 1808.

MONTEZUMA. O. Sacchini, 1772.

MONTEZUMA. T. Henry Brooke. Pr. 1778. N.a. The production of a friend, but corrected by him.

MONTEZUMA. O. Verdi. 1878.

MONTFORT. T. Partly f. on Shakespeare's *King John.* Ac. by gentlemen of the Naval Academy, Gosport, 1803.

MONTH AFTER DATE, A. C.D. 1 a. Silvanus Dauncey. Ac. at Highbury by members of the Princess's company, October 15, 1885; Reading R. County, February 27, 1888; Globe, March 25, 1891.

MONTH FROM HOME, A. Gallery of Illustration, April 27, 1857.

MONTILLADIOS, THE. M.C. 2 a. Bedford Town H., January 18, 1897 (amat.).

MONTONI. Sheil. 1820.

MONTROSE. Pocock.

MONUMENT IN ARCADIA, THE. Dr. poem. 2 a. George Keate. Pr. 1773.

MONUMENTS OF HONOUR. Pageant. John Webster. 1624.

MOON SLAVE, THE. Terpsichorean fantasy. 1 tab. F. on a tale by Barry Pain. Wr. and comp. by Paul Corder. St. George's H., July 22, 1902.

MOON SPELL, THE. D. and M. Sk. Beatrice H. Maxwell and Philip Yorke. M. by V Lloyd. Tivoli, December 21, 1903.

MOONBEAMS Ca Haslingden Russell. Liverpool Shakespeare, July 30, 1891.

MOONLIGHT BLOSSOM, THE. Japanese Rom. 3 a. G. Chester-Bailey Fernald. P.O.W., September 21, 1899

MOONSHINE. C. 5 a. E. S. Wortley. Publ. by J. Dicks.

MOONSHINE. M. fantasy. 4 sc. Book by Eustace Baynes. M. by Herman Finck Palace, December 26, 1905

MOONSHINE; OR, THE PIRATE'S PLUNDER. Burl. 2 a. J. H. Booth. Hereford Athenæum, December 8, 1892.

MOONSTONE, THE. D. 4 a. Wilkie Collins. Olympic, September 17, 1877.

MOONSTRUCK. Oa. R. Reece. M. by Thorpe Pede. Alexandra, November 10, 1873.

MOOR'S MASQUE, THE. 1636.

MOORS. Refers to Ben Jonson's Masque of *Blackness*. 1605.

MOORS. P. Cunningham. Twelfth Night. 1605.

MORAL QUACK, THE Dr. satire. Dr. Bacon. Pr. 1757. Contains no female character.

MORAL SUASION. C. T. A. Palmer. Nottingham T.R., January 4, 1875.

MORALS OF MARCUS, THE. P. 4 a. W. J. Locke. Dr. fr. his novel, "The Morals of Marcus Odeyne." Garrick, August 30, 1906.

MORAYS; OR, A LIE FOR A LIFE, THE. C.D. Blackpool P.O.W., June 24, 1884.

MORDECAI LYONS. D. Edward Harrigan. Richmond H.M.T., October 26, 1882.

MORDECAI'S BEARD. Int. D.L., April 20, 1790. N.p.

MORDEN GRANGE. D. 4 a. F. C. Burnand. Queen's, December 4, 1869.

MORE BLUNDERS THAN ONE. F. 1 a. T. G. Rodwells. Adelphi, December 13, 1824; D.L., October 31, 183[illegible].

MORE DISSEMBLERS BESIDES WOMEN. C. Thos. Middleton. Ac. before 1623. Pr. 1657.

MORE FREE THAN WELCOME. F. W. E. Suter. Adap. fr. the French. Prod. at the Strand T. as *Lending a Hand*.

MORE FRIGHTENED THAN HURT. M.F. Hay., 1785 N.p. See *Execution*.

MORE KOTZEBUE; OR, MY OWN PIZARRO. Mono. dr. Pr. 1799.

MORE PRECIOUS THAN GOLD. C. 2 a. C. S. Cheltnam. Strand, July 8, 1861.

MORE THAN EVER. Burl. melo-d. A. Matthison. Gaiety, November 1, 1882; rev., Avenue, October 16, 1897.

MORE WAYS THAN ONE. C. Mrs. Cowley. C.G., December 6, 1783. Pr. 1784.

MORETON PEARLS, THE. Sk. Russell Vann. Hammersmith Palace, July 20, 1908.

MORGIANA. Burl. Guy du Maurier. Woolwich R. Fusilier Barracks, January 8, 1892.

MORMON, THE. F.C. 3 a. W. D. Calthorpe. Vaudeville (mat.), March 10, 1887; Comedy, March 28, 1887. See *Teddy's Wives, Moses and Son*.

MORNING CALL, A. Ca. 1 a. C. Dance. D.L., March 17, 1851

MORNING DRIVE, A. D. 1 a. F. W. Plant. Stockport Mechanics' Inst., December 2, 1896.

MORNING POST, THE. See *The Agony Column*.

MORNING POST AND MORNING CHRONICLE, THE. Int Anon. 1811.

MORNING RAMBLE, THE. C. Anon. Pr. 1673. Ascr. by Downes to Nevil Payne. Some compilers have given a second title, *The Town Humours*. Ac. at the Duke's T., 1673.

MORO. O. Prol. and 3 a. W. A. Barrett. M. by M. W. Balfe. H.M.T., January 28, 1882.

MOROCCO BOUND. M.F.C. 2 a. Arthur Branscombe. Lyrics by Adrian Ross. M. by F. Osmond Carr. Shaftesbury, April 13, 1893; rev. Comedy, December 19, 1901.

MOROSINA. O. Petrella. 1862.

MORS. Lat. C. Wm. Drury. Pr. 1628.

MORS ET VITA. Orat. Gounod. Paris, May 22, 1886.

MORT D'ABEL. T. Legouvé. 1792. Imitated fr. Gesser and Klopstock.

MORT DE CALAS. T. Chénier. 1791.

MORT DE CLEOPATRE, LA. O. Wr. by Mansé.

MORT DE HENRI IV. T. By Legouvé. 1806.

MORT DE POMPEE, LA. Corneille. See "French Classical Plays."

MORTE CIVILE (*La Morte Legale*). D. 5 a. P. Giacometti. Shaftesbury, February 13, 1908. See *A New Trial*.

MORTGAGE DEEDS, THE. D. C. H. Hazlewood. Britannia, February 22, 1875.

MORTIMER. P. Ac. by Henslowe's company. 1602.

MORTIMER. P. Ac. by Henslowe's Co. 1602.

MORTIMER'S FALL. T. Ben Jonson. Pr. 1640. Left unfinished. See *The Fall of Mortimer*.

MOSCOW DOCTOR, THE. P. H. P. Gardiner. Adap. fr. H. S. Merriman's novel, "The Sowers." Brighton West Pier, April 27, 1903.

MOSE IN EGITTO. O. Rossini. Lib. by Tottola. Naples, Lent, 1818; Paris, 1827.

MOSES. O. Süzsmayer. May 4, 1792; rev. in 1796 and 1800.

MOSES. Sacred O. Rubinstein. 1829-1895.

MOSES AND SON. "Up-to-date Mosaic." 3 a. J. Gordon. Royalty, June 11, 1892. See *The Mormon*.

MOSES AND SON. Sk. Fred Karno, Fred Kitchen, and Harold Gatty. M. by Dudley Powell. Bordesley Palace, December 18, 1905.

MOSES AND ZIPPORAH. O. Stillingfleet. 1760. N.p.

MOSES IN EGYPT. See *Mose in Egitto*.

MOSES IN THE BULRUSHES. Sacred D. Miss H. More. Pr. 1782. Not intended for the stage.

MOSES IN THE BULRUSHES. An alt. of the foregoing "by a gentleman in the neighbourhood of Doncaster," and ac. in that town 1793.

MOSS ROSE RENT, A. Vaudeville. 1 a. A. Law. M. by A. J. Caldicott. St. Geo. H., December 17, 1883.

MOSSOO IN LONDON. M. Sk. Corney Grain. St. Geo. H., April 2, 1888.

MOST BEAUTIFUL WOMAN IN THE WORLD, THE. P. 4 a. G. S. King. Hoyland Metropole, September 25, 1905.

MOST UNWARRANTABLE INTRUSION, A. C. int. 1 a. J. M. Morton. Adelphi, June 11, 1849.

MOSTELLARIA; OR, THE HAUNTED HOUSE. C. Plautus. Transl. into blank verse by Thornton, Rich. Warner, and Colman. 1769-74. See "Latin Plays."

MOSTLY FOOLS. P. 3 a. B. White. Fulham Grand, April 1, 1901.

MOTH AND FLAME. C. 3 a. F. Frankfort Moore. Hull T.R., May 20, 1878.

MOTH AND THE CANDLE, THE. P. 3 a. Lady Violet Greville and M. Ambient. Wyndham's, December 18, 1901 (C.P.).

MOTHER. Dom. d. 4 a. Sheila Walsh. Coventry O.H., January 15, 1909; Wakefield O.H., February 8, 1909.

MOTHER, THE. P. 5 a. F. Harvey. Olympic, April 14, 1879. See *The Mothers*.

MOTHER AND CHILD. D. 1 a. J. M. Morton. Edinburgh Princess's, November 17, 1879.

MOTHER AND DAUGHTERS. St. Leger. 1805.

MOTHER AND HOME. P. 4 a. Geo. S. King. Devonport Metropole, June 21, 1909.

MOTHER AND SON. D. 3 a. D.L. April 24, 1821.

MOTHER AND SON. D. Pro. and 3 a. S. Bell. Manchester Princess's, September 14, 1883.

MOTHER BOMBIE. C. J. Lyly. Pr. 1594. Ac. by the children of S. Paul's.

MOTHER BUNCH. Surrey, December 24, 1881.

MOTHER GOOSE; OR, THE GOLDEN EGG. Pant. T. Dibdin, assisted by Mr. Farley. C.G., 1806-7.

MOTHER OF THREE, A. F. 3 a. Clo. Graves. Comedy, May 8, 1896.

MOTHER PANTOM. C. Dibdin.

MOTHER REDCAP. P. Drayton and Mundy. N.p.

MOTHER SHIPTON. Panto. C.G. Pr. 1770.

MOTHER SHIPTON, HER LIFE. C. T. Thompson. Pr. (no date). Partly f. on Massinger's *City Madam* and Middleton's *Chaste Maid in Cheapside*

MOTHER'S DREAM. Adelphi, March 19, 1850.

MOTHER'S DYING CHILD, THE. D. 3 a. C. H. Hazlewood. Britannia, October, 1864.

MOTHER'S LOVE, A. D.P. 4 a. Fred L. Connynghame and F. Price. S. Shields R.T., August 13, 1900; Stratford T.R., August 18, 1902.

MOTHER'S SACRIFICE, A. D. 4 a. H. Darnley. Mansfield Hipp., September 9, 1907.

MOTHER'S SALVATION. A. Melo-d. 4 a. Nita Rae. Wednesbury R., April 27, 1908; Stratford R., May 18, 1908.

MOTHER'S SIN, A. D. 6 tabl. W. Reynolds. Eleph. and C., July 25, 1885 (C.P.); Grand, July 26, 1886.

MOTHER-IN-LAW. C. 3 a. G. R. Sims. Liverpool P.O.W., May 23, 1881; O.C., December 31, 1881.

MOTHER-IN-LAW; OR, THE DOCTOR THE DISEASE, THE. C. Rev. J. Miller, assisted by H. Baker. Pr. 1734. Ac. at the Little T. in the Hay., February 12, 1734. Little more than a transl. of Molière's "Malade Imaginaire."

MOTHERING SUNDAY. P. 3 a. T. E. Pemberton. Belfast O.H., October 10, 1901.

MOTHERS, THE. C. Anon. 1805.

MOTHERS, THE. P. 5 a. F. Harvey. Rochdale R.A., July 5, 1909. See *The Mother*.

MOTHERS AND DAUGHTERS. C. 5 a. R. Bell. Publ. by J. Dicks.

MOTHS. P. 4 a. H. Hamilton. Adap. fr. Ouida's novel. Globe, March 25, 1882; re-wr. ver., King's W., October 14, 1907.

MOTHS. C. John Chute. Croydon T.R., August 28, 1882.

MOTHS. D. 4 a. Adap. fr. Ouida's novel. Sadler's Wells, September 4, 1882.

MOTHS. D. W. F. Lyon. Peterboro' T.R., February 12, 1883.

MOTHS. D. M. A. Seaton. Liverpool Rotunda, March 19, 1883.

MOTHS. Rom. D. 4 a. Mervyn Dallas. Strand, June 26, 1884.

MOTHS. Society episode. 3 scenes. Fd. on Ouida's novel of that name. Euston, October 17, 1904.

MOTHS A LA MODE. Burl. F. H. Herbert. Edinburgh Princess's, March 5, 1883.

MOTHS QUITOS; OR, OUIDA'S MOTHS. Burl. D. W. Edgar. Middlesbrough T.R., April 21, 1882.

MOTIVES, THE. C. Mentioned by Wood (*Athenæ Oxonienses*) as by Ben Jonson and pr. 1622.

MOTOR MAN, THE. F. Sk. Clare Shirley. Brotton Cleveland H., April 9, 1908.

MOTTO: I AM "ALL THERE," THE. Burl. H. J. Byron. Fd. on Lyceum D. *Duke's Motto*. Strand, July 16, 1863.

MOTTO ON THE DUKE'S CREST. Grecian, July 20, 1863.

MOUNT MORIAH. Orat. D. J. F. Bridge.

MOUNT OF OLIVES, THE. Orat. Beethoven. 1803. D.L. (first time in this country), February 25, 1814.

MOUNT ST. BERNARD; OR, THE GOLDSMITH OF GRENOBLE. D. 4 parts. Adelphi, October, 1839.

MOUNT SINAI. Orat. Chevalier Newkomm. D.L., March 18, 1836.

MOUNTAIN BELLE, THE. M. Sk. Laurence Anarto and Harry Rushworth. Richmond Hippodrome, October 19, 1908.

MOUNTAIN CHIEF, THE. D. Rom. 3 a. M. by Lanza. D.L., April 30, 1818.

MOUNTAIN CLIMBER, THE. F. 3 a. Cosmo Hamilton. Adap. fr. the German of *Curt Kraatz*. Comedy, November 21, 1905.

MOUNTAIN DEVIL, THE. Sk. G. Reeves. Surrey, March 26, 1879.

MOUNTAIN DHU. Burl. A. Halliday. Travestie of *The Lady of the Lake*. Adelphi, December, 1866.

MOUNTAIN HEIRESS, A. Gilbert à Beckett. M. by L. Benson. St. Geo. H., March 7, 1883.

MOUNTAIN KING, THE. Oa. A. Nance and J. Winterbottom. Portsmouth T.R., January 25, 1875.

MOUNTAIN OF MISERIES; OR, HARLEQUIN TORMENTOR, THE. Panto. Sadler's Wells, April 17, 1797.

MOUNTAIN ROBBERS; OR, THE TERRIFIC HORN, THE. "Ballad or Melo-d." D.L., June, 1806. N.p.

MOUNTAIN SYLPH, THE. Rom. Grand O. 2 a. J. Barnett. Wds. by J. T. Thackeray. Lyceum, August 25, 1834; D.L., January 28, 1837, and February 17, 1840; Guildhall Sch. of M., July 5, 1906.

MOUNTAINEERS. THE. P. 3 a. G. Colman, jun. F. on Adventure of Don Quixote. Hay. Pr. 1795. D.L., July 4, 1815; C.G., May 29, 1817.

MOUNTAINEERS, THE. Rom. C.O. 3 a. Guy Eden and Reginald Somerville. Lyrics by Guy Eden. M. by Reginald Somerville. Savoy, September 29, 1909.

MOUNTEBANK; OR, THE HUMOURS OF THE FAIR, THE. M. Int. Pr. with *Farewell Folly*, 1707.

MOUNTEBANK'S MASK, THE. Masque. John Marston. Gray's Inn. Not before 1600.

MOUNTEBANKS, THE. Comic O. 2 a. W. S. Gilbert. M. by A. Cellier. Lyric, January 4, 1892.

MOURNFUL NUPTIALS; OR, LOVE THE CURE OF ALL WOES, THE. T. T. Cooke. Pr. 1739. N.ac. Afterwards alt. and ac. in 1744 at D.L. under the title of *Love, the Cause and Cure of Grief; or, The Innocent Murderer.*

MOURNING BRIDE, THE. T. W. Congreve. M. by G. Finger. L.I.F., 1606. Pr. 1697. The only T. by this author. Blank verse. D.L. See *Barbarossa.*

MOUSE, THE. C. 3 a. Transl. fr. Pailleron's *Le Souris* by J. T. Grein and H. Hooton. Comedy, December 11, 1902.

MOUSE AND THE MAN. Ca. 1 a. Publ. by S. French, Limited.

MOUSETRAP, THE. F. Mrs. Burton Harrison. "The Sea Urchins." Bar Harbour, August, 1886.

MOUSETRAP, THE. Manchester Palace, May 19, 1909.

MOUSETRAP, THE. See *A Fool's Paradise.*

MOUSQUETAIRES, LES. O. Com. 2 a. P. Ferrier and J. Prevée. Adap. by H. B. Farnie. M. by Varney. Globe, October 31, 1880.

MOUSQUETAIRES DE LA REINE, LES. C.O 3 a. Wds. by St. Georges. M. by Halevy. Paris, February 3, 1846.

MOUSTACHE MOVEMENT, THE. F. 1 a Robt. Brough. Adelphi, March 30, 1854.

MOUTH OF THE NILE; OR, THE GLORIOUS FIRST OF AUGUST, THE. M. Ent. T. Dibdin. C.G., April 6, 1798. Pr. 1798.

MOUTH OF THE PIT, THE. D. 4 a. W. Miller (afterwards called *Birds of Prey*). Middlesbrough T.R., February 8, 1892.

MOVE ON; OR, THE CROSSING SWEEPER. D. 3 a. James Mortimer. Adap. fr. *Bleak House.* Grand, September 1, 1883.

MOVING TALE, A. F. 1 a. Mark Lemon. Adelphi, June 7, 1854.

MOYNA A-ROON; OR, THE RAPPAREE'S BRIDE. D. J. Levey. Chester T.R., October 25, 1875; Eleph. and C., November 8, 1875.

MUCEDORUS, THE KING'S SONNE OF VALENTIA, AND AMADINE, THE KING'S DAUGHTER OF ARRAGON, WITH THE MERRY CONCEITS OF MOUSE. C. Ac. at Whitehall on Shrove Sunday night. Pr. 1598. Attributed to Shakespeare. A Christmas diversion.

MUCH ADO. A scena in dial. in the second volume of Miss Fielding's *Letters.*

MUCH ADO ABOUT NOTHING. C. W. Shakespeare. Wr. 1599. Entered Stationers' H. August 4, 1600 (to be staged); August 23, 1600. Pr. qto. 1600; first folio, 1623. Taken indirectly fr. a novel of Belleforest's, after Bandello. Similar story in Ariosto's *Orlando Furioso*, Book V., and in the Geneura of Turbervil Alt. by J. P. Kemble. Pr. 1799. Holborn, 1873; Lyceum, January 5, 1891; St. James's (Geo. Alexander's production), February 16, 1898; Imperial, May 23, 1903; H.M., January 24, 1905; Coronet (F. R. Benson's rev.), February 17, 1908.

MUCH ADO ABOUT NOTHING. Eng. O. 4 a. Julian Sturgis. M. by Dr. V. Stanford (f. on Shakespeare's C.). C.G., May 30, 1901.

MUCH ADO ABOUT NOTHING. See *Béatrice et Bénèdict; Benedick and Beatrice.*

MUCH TOO CLEVER; OR, A FRIEND INDEED. C. 1 a. and 3 scenes. J. Oxenford and J. Hatton. Adap. fr. the French Gaiety, February 23, 1874.

MUDBOROUGH ELECTION. F. 1 a. W. Brough and A. Halliday. P.O.W., July 13, 1865.

MUDDLE-UP, THE. Amer. M.C. S. Sidney. M. by H. Vernon. Add. lyrics by J. J. Hewson and L. Stuart. Oldham Colosseum, September 10, 1900.

MUDDLER, THE. F.C. 3 a. Nottingham Grand, July 18, 1890.

MUDDLES. F.C. 3 a. Jessop and Gill. Imperial, March 2, 1885.

MUETTE DE PORTICI, LA. O. Auber. The Italian ver. of *Masaniello*, which see.

MUFF OF THE REGIMENT, THE. P. 1 a. H. T. Johnson. Strand (produced as *Good Bye*); Globe, November 21, 1896.

MUGWUMP, THE. Ca. 1 a. "X.L." Court, October 19, 1898.

MUIRGHEIS. Irish grand O. Lib. Nora Chesson. Dublin T.R., December 7, 1903.

MULBERRY BUSH, THE. See *Little Miss Muffet.*

MULBERRY GARDEN, THE. See *The Wandering Ladies.*

MULBERRY GARDEN, THE. C. Sir C. Sedley. D.L. Pr. 1668. Partly f. on Molière's *L'Ecole des Maris.*

MULDOON'S PICNIC; OR, IRISH LIFE IN AMERICA. F. Pleon Marylebone (first time in London), November 8, 1886.

MULEASSES THE TURK. T. John Mason. Ac. by the children of His Majesty's Revels, 1610.

MULETEER OF TOLEDO; OR, KING, QUEEN, AND KNAVE, THE. C.D. 2 a. J. M. Morton. Princess's, April 9, 1855.

MULETEER'S VOW, THE. Rom. melo-d. Lyceum, October 19, 1835.

MULLIBALOO. Op. bouffe. F. Green. Brighton T.R., September 21, 1874.

MULMUTIUS DUNWALLOW. P. W. Ramkins. Ac. by the Lord Admiral's servants in 1598. N.p.

MULO MURCO; OR, MULAMULLUCO. Ac. February 20, 1591. Possibly the same as *The Battle of Alcazar.*

MUMBY. 1 a. Geo. H. Balgrove. Kingsway, December 20, 1908.

MUMMER'S WIFE, THE. P. 1 a. Kinsey Peile. Tunbridge Wells O.H., August 2, 1906; Shakespeare, August 13, 1906.

MUMMERS, THE. D.C. 3 a. J. Edwardes and F. R. Cullingford. Ladbroke H., May 24, 1900 (amat.).

MUMMIES AND MARRIAGE. M. adap. of *An Illustrious Stranger.* 2 a. A. M. Mackinnon and J. G. Adderley. M. by Leslie Mayne. Folkestone Exhibition Pal., December 6, 1888.

MUMMY, THE. F. 1 a. W. B. Bernard. M. by Hawes. Lyceum, 1833; rev. July 28, 1834.

MUMMY, THE. Oa. O. Brand. M. by L. Gautier. St Geo. H.. April 22, 1884.

MUMMY, THE. F.C. 3 a. G. D. Day, A. Reed, and S. Bowkett. Chester Royalty, September 6, 1895 (C.P.); Comedy, July 2, 1896 (evening bill); August 11, 1896.

MUMMY AND THE HUMMING BIRD, THE. P. 4 a. Isaac Henderson. Wyndham's, October 10, 1901.

MUMMYDOM. Fan. 1 a. Rutland Barrington and W. Bendall. Gt. Queen St. T., September 25, 1903.

MUMPS THE MASHER. F. T. Craven and R. Nelson. Nottingham T.R., June 2, 1884; Pavilion, August 11, 1884.

MUNDUNGAS. Anon.

MUNDUS PLUMBEUS. Latin T. Thomas Arthur, of St. John's College, Cambridge. Sixteenth century.

MURDERED GUEST, THE. D. 2 a. M. by Horn. D.L., December 27, 1826.

MURDEROUS MICHAEL. Probably an early work on *Arden of Feversham.* ? 1578.

MURIEL; OR, THE WARNING VOICES. D. 3 a. H. Leslie. Liverpool Amphi., April 16, 1870.

MURPHY'S AFFINITY. Sk. The Surrey, March 2, 1908.

MUSE IN LIVERY. C. Dodsley. 1732.

MUSE OF BRITAIN Ode. Inscribed to the Rt. Hon. Wm. Pitt. Pr. 1785.

MUSE OF NEWMARKET, THE. Containing 3 Drolls, viz., *The Merry Milkmaid of Islington; or The Rambling Gallants Defeated; Love Lost in the Dark; or, the Drunken Couple; The Politick Whore; or, the Conceited Cuckold.* Probably based on other plays. Pr. 1680.

MUSE OF OSSIAN, THE. D. Poem. 3 a. Extracted fr. the Poems of Ossian by D. E. Baker. Ac. at Edinburgh. Pr. 1763.

MUSES GALANTES, LES. O. Rousseau. Paris, 1745.

MUSES IN MOURNING, THE. O. A. Hill. Pr. 1760. N.ac.

MUSES' CHAPLET; OR, FEAST OF THALIA, THE. Medley Duo West. Lyceum, April 9, 1822.

MUSES' LOOKING-GLASS, THE. C. Thos. Randolph. Pr. 1638. First called *The Entertainment.* In an edition in 1706 it has the second title of *The Stage Reviv'd.*

MUSES' LOOKING-GLASS, THE. Dr. Ent. taken fr. foregoing. C.G., 1748. Not pr.

MUSETTE. Dr. Story. F. Marsden. Orig. prod. in America. Op. Comique, December 22, 1883.

MUSIC: OR, A PARLEY OF INSTRUMENTS. Pr. 1676. A piece composed by some master of music for his scholars.

MUSIC A LA MODE. M. Sk. Corney Grain. St. Geo. H., February 11, 1895.

MUSIC AT HOME. C. Rose Seaton. Chatham O.H., June 9, 1890.

MUSIC AT HOME. Ca. (Variety Ent.). Op. Comique, July 30, 1892.

MUSIC HATH CHARMS. C. 1 a. D. Fisher. Princess's, July 7, 1856.

MUSIC IN ZARA. Dr. Arne. 1736.

MUSIC MAD. Dr. Sk. 1 a. T. E. Hook. Hay. Pr. 1808. Principal character taken fr. *Il Fanatico per la Musica.*

MUSIC MASTER, THE. Ca. Flavell Haward. Wolverhampton Exchange H., November 19, 1887.

MUSIC MASTER, THE. P. C. Klein. Elephant and Castle, August 31, 1904 (C.P.).

MUSIC MASTER, THE. M. Sk. Prod. by Ch. Fisher. Chelsea Palace, January 7, 1907.

MUSIC MASTER, THE. M.F. 1 a. W. Mallett. Bayswater Bijou, March 22, 1908 (amat.).

MUSICAL BOX, THE. F. F. C. Burnand. Gaiety, October 1, 1877.

MUSICAL CLOCK, THE. Christmas Extrav. Hon. C. Leigh. Stoneleigh Abbey, January 22, 1883 (amat.).

MUSICAL DISCORD, A. Sk. 1 a. C. M. Greene. Hull Grand, May 14, 1897; Stratford Borough, July 9, 1897.

MUSICAL FAMILY. F. Lawler. Before 1812. N.p.

MUSICAL FAMILY, A. M. Sk. C. Grain. St. George's H., December 27, 1880.

MUSICAL FAMILY, THE. See *In and Out of Tune.*

MUSICAL ENTERTAINMENT, A. Masque. E. Ward. Pr. 1718. N.ac.

MUSICAL ENTERTAINMENT IN THE VIRGIN PROPHETESS; OR, THE FATE OF TROY, THE. Composed by Finger. Pr. 1701.

MUSICAL INTERVIEW WITH THE PARISH PUMP, A. M. Sk. C. Grain. St. George's H., January 16, 1894.

MUSICAL LADY, THE. F. 2 a. G. Colman. D.L., March 6, 1762; Edinburgh, 1772. Pr. 1762. Prol. by Garrick.

MUSICAL MARIONETTES, THE. C. 2 a. F. McArdle. Liverpool P.O.W., October 6, 1876.

MUSICAL VILLAGE, THE. Oa. M. Johnston. Morley Co-operative H., December 28, 1893.

MUSICIAN'S DAUGHTER, THE. Sk. Canterbury M.H., July 13, 1908.

MUSICIAN'S ROMANCE, A. P. 3 a. F. Harvey. Halifax Grand, March 21, 1898; Camberwell Metropole, June 13, 1898.

MUSICO, THE. F. P. Joddrell. Pr. 1787. N.ac.

MUSKETEERS, THE. P. in 10 tableaux. Sydney Grundy. Adap. fr. Dumas' *Three Musketeers.* H.M.T., November 3, 1898.

MUSTAPHA. T. Fulk Greville, Lord Brooke. Pr. 1609, and 1633, corrected and complete.

MUSTAPHA. T. David Mallett (also known as David Malloch). D.L., and pr. 1739.

MUSTAPHA, THE SON OF SOLYMAN, THE MAGNIFICENT. T. Roger, Earl of Orrery. Ac. at the Duke of York's T., 1665. Pr. 1668. F. on *Mustapha et Zéangir* (by Georges de Scudéry ?).

MUTA DI PORTICI. O. Auber. (Paris, 1828.) See *Masaniéllo.*

MUTE PRINCESS, THE. Oa. Latiner. In Yiddish. Standard, December 19, 1899.

MUTINES, THE TRAITOR. Liverpool, November 14, 1898.

MUTINY AT THE NORE, THE. Nautical D. 2 a. D. Jerrold. Pavilion, 1830; Victoria, 1830.

MUTIUS SCÆVOLA. Ac. by the children of Windsore and the Chappell, 1576.

MUTIUS SCAEVOLA; OR, THE ROMAN PATRIOT. Hist. D. W. H. Ireland. Pr. 1801. N. ac.

MUTUAL DECEPTION, THE. C. J. Atkinson. Ac. and pr. in Dublin, 1785. Partly f. on *Le Jeu de l'Amour et du Hazard,* of the Théatre Italien. See *Tit for Tat.*

MUTUAL MISTAKE, A. F. W. H. Denny. Court, March 21, 1891.

MUTUAL MISUNDERSTANDING, A. Ca. 1 a. H. Lee. Liverpool P.O.W., January 31, 1876.

MUTUAL SEPARATION, A. Ca. 1 a. E. Compton. Edinburgh Princess's, December 7, 1877; Bayswater Bijou, January 10, 1879.

MUTURES, THE TRAITOR. Hist. D. 5 a. J. Downs. M. by E. Watson. Liverpool St. Geo. H., November 14, 1898.

MUZIO SCEVOLA. O. The three rival composers, Handel, Bononcini, and Ariosti, wrote one act each to try and settle their merits. The result was that Handel was declared first and Bononcini second. 1720.

MY ARTFUL VALET. F.C. 3 a. J. Mortimer. Adap. fr. *Le True d'Arthur* of Chivot and Duru (Palais Royal), October 14, 1882); Globe (prod. as *Gloriana*), November 10, 1891; Terry's, August 22, 1896; (rev.) December 4, 1901.

MY ASTRAL BODY. F. 3 a. W. C. Hudson and Nicholas Colthurst. Court, April 22, 1896.

MY AUNT. M.F. M. by Addison. Lyceum, August 1, 1815; Bath, October 21, 1815; D.L., May 18, 1827.

MY AUNT FROM CALIFORNIA. F. 1 a. M. Barnum. Publ. by S. French, Ltd.

MY AUNT GRUMBLE. Ca. Mrs. Ellen Johnson. Brighton T.R., April 21, 1877.

MY AUNT IN TOWN. M. Sk. C. Grain. St. George's H., June 10, 1889.

MY AUNT'S ADVICE. D.L., March 17, 1890.

MY AUNT'S HEIRESS. C. 1 a. E. H. Keating. Pub. by S. French, Limited.

MY AUNT'S HUSBAND. D. 1 a. C. Selby. Strand, September 27, 1858.

MY AUNT'S SECRET. Burnand and Mollay. Gall. of Illustration, March 3, 1872.

MY AWFUL DAD. C. 2 a. C. Matthews. Gaiety, September 13, 1875.

MY AWFUL LUCK. Neville Doone. Lyric Club, January 24, 1892.

MY BACHELOR DAYS. F. 1 a. J. M. Morton.

MY BACHELOR PAST. C. 3 a. J. Mortimer. F. on *Celimare le Bien-Aimé* by Labiche and Delacour. Wyndham's, August 1, 1901.

MY BEAUX; OR, THE FIRST OF APRIL. F. T. A. Stack. Marylebone, April 1, 1868.

MY BENEFACTOR. F. 1 a. E. Rose. Strand, November 21, 1883.

MY BEST FRIEND; OR £277 7s. 7d. P. 1 a. D.L., January 23, 1827.

MY BONNY BOY. F.C. 3 a. T. G. Warren. Criterion, December 2, 1886. See *Bonny Boy*.

MY BOY. Dom. C. 3 a. Gospodin A. Lubinoff. Adap. fr. Adolph L'Arronge's "lebensbild" *Mein Leopold*. Ryde T.R. (C.P.); Bournemouth, November 12, 1886; Vaudeville, January 5, 1888.

MY BRACES. F.C. Sk. By Leonard Robson. Hastings Hippo., April 20, 1907.

MY BRAVE LITTLE WIFE. C.D. 1 a. A. M. Seaton. Toole's, July 24, 1882.

MY BROTHER-IN-LAW. C. 1 a. Beatrice Knollys. Queen's Gate H., February 14, 1903.

MY BROTHER'S SISTER. P. 3 a. Liverpool Alexandra (C.P.); Manchester Prince's, September 3, 1888; Crystal Pal.; Gaiety, February 15, 1890.

MY CALIFORNIAN SWEETHEART. M.C.D. Book, lyrics, and M. by A. Bardwell-Challier. Burnham Town H., August 25, 1908 (C.P.).

MY BUTLER. Sk. Ivan Gore. Crouch End Hippodrome, April 18, 1908.

MY CALIFORNIAN SWEETHEART. M.C.D. by A. Bardwell-Challier. Town Hall, Burnham, August 26, 1908.

MY COLLABORATOR. F. Kennedy Jones. Birmingham P.O.W., March 8, 1892.

MY COMRADE; OR, THE LAST COMMAND. D. Pro. and 3 a. C. Horsman. Adap. fr. *La Vie Caporal*. Stratford T.R., May 18, 1885.

MY COOK AND HOUSEKEEPER. F. D.L., March 9, 1854.

MY COUNTRY COUSIN. C. Sk. 1 a. D.L., May 29, 1827.

MY COURIER. Manchester Comedy, August 23, 1886.

MY COUSIN. Ca. 1 a. J. J. Hewson. Belfast T.R., October 16, 1885; Olympic, March 21, 1887.

MY COUSIN. C. 4 a. Miss Jennie Le Terrier. Adap. fr. the German. Manchester Comedy, August 23, 1886.

MY COUSIN MARCO. F. 3 a. Arthur Law. Canterbury T.R., January 26, 1906.

MY DARLING. C.D. 3 a. E. R. Callender. Sheffield T.R. (originally as *Light*), August 7, 1882; Gaiety, February 13, 1883.

MY DARLING. M.P. 2 a. Seymour Hicks and Herbert E. Haines. Lyrics by C. H. Taylor; add. numbers by Evelyn Baker; add. lyrics by P. S. Wodehouse. Hicks T., March 2, 1907.

MY DAUGHTER. F. A. Chapman. Shepherd's Bush Athenæum, April 9, 1888.

MY DAUGHTER. P. 1 a. Mrs. Bancroft. Adap. fr. the German. Garrick, January 2, 1892.

MY DAUGHTER, SIR! OR, A DAUGHTER TO MARRY. F. 1 a. J. R. Planché. Hay.

MY DAUGHTER THE DUCHESS. C. 4 a. A. Meadow. Vaudeville, October 30, 1884.

MY DAUGHTER'S DAUGHTER. C. 1 a. E. H. Keating.

MY DAUGHTER'S DEBUT. M.C. 1 a. H. T. Craven.

MY DAUGHTER-IN-LAW. An adap. of F. Carré and P. Bilhaud's comedy *Ma Bru*. Criterion, September 27, 1899.

MY DEAR OLD DUTCH. Sk. South London, November 30, 1908.

MY DRESS BOOTS. F. 1 a. T. J. Williams. Royalty, September 5, 1834.

MY ENEMY. F.C. 2 a. R. Reece. Olympic, January 15, 1880.

MY FAIRY FANCIFUL. Pant. C. Ross and E. Martin. Kingston County, April 15, 1904 (C.P.).

MY FATHER'S WILL. C. 1 a. Pub. by S. French, Limited.

MY FELLOW CLERK. F. 1 a. J. Oxenford. M. by Tutton. Lyceum, April 20, 1835.

MY FIRST CASE. Ca. T. Courtice. M. by E. Ramsay. Chatham O.H., March 25, 1897.

MY FIRST CLIENT. C. 1 a. Mary Openshaw. Pub. by S. French, Limited.

MY FIRST FIT OF THE GOUT. F. 1 a. J. M. Morton. Queen's, March, 1835.

MY FIRST PATIENT. F. H. Cassel and C. Ogden. Taken fr. the German. Bradford Theatre of the Technical College, February 12, 1887.

MY FIRST PATIENT. F. 1 a. Vincent Collier. Ealing New T., October 23, 1905.

MY FRIEND. C. J. Tabrar. Vaudeville, November 17, 1885.

MY FRIEND FROM INDIA. See *My Friend the Prince.*

MY FRIEND FROM LEATHERHEAD. F. 1 a. E. Yates and N. H. Harrington. Lyceum, February 23, 1857.

MY FRIEND GOMEZ. Oa. Lita Smith. M. by E. Stanley. Brighton Preston Assembly R., May 28, 1896.

MY FRIEND IN THE STRAPS. Hay., October 24, 1850.

MY FRIEND JARLET. C. 1 a. A. Goldsworthy and E. B Norman. Canterbury T.R. (perf. by the "Old Stagers"), August 2, 1887; Terry's, November 5, 1890.

MY FRIEND THE CAPTAIN. F. 1 a. J. S Coyne. Publ. by J. Dicks.

MY FRIEND THE DEVIL. Fantasy. Geo. Rollit. Palace, April 27, 1907.

MY FRIEND THE GOVERNOR. F. 1 a J. R. Planché. Publ. by J. Dicks.

MY FRIEND THE MAJOR. F. 1 a. C. Selby. St. James's, October 2, 1854.

MY FRIEND THE PRINCE. P. 3 a. J. H. McCarthy. Suggested by the American f., *My Friend from India.* Garrick, February 13, 1897.

MY GIRL. M.P. 2 a. J. T. Tanner. Lyrics by A. Ross. M. by F. O. Carr. Birmingham T.R. (prod. as *The Clergyman's Daughter*), April 13, 1896; Gaiety July 13, 1896; Clapham Shakespeare, November 16, 1896; Garrick, December 1, 1896.

MY GOOD NAME. P. 1 a. E. Turner. Woolwich R. Artillery, February 24, 1896; Hammersmith Lyric, July 27, 1896.

MY GRANDFATHER. C. Oa. M. by A. Lee. Lyceum, September 29, 1834.

MY GRANDFATHER'S WILL. C. 5 a. F. Reynolds. Publ. by J. Dicks.

MY GRANDMOTHER AND OTHER FAIRIES. M.F. 2 a. Prince Hoare. The idea of this piece previously used in *The Portrait.* Hay., December 16, 1795; D.L., March 19, 1814, and April 28, 1824.

MY GREAT AUNT; OR, RELATIONS AND FRIENDS. C. 1 a. J. R. Planché. Olympic, March 1, 1831.

MY GUARDIE. C.D. 1 a. C. Trevelyan. Kew Bridge Prince's, December 19, 1896.

MY HEART'S DARLING. D. B. Ellis. Bath T.R., February 14, 1876.

MY HEART'S IDOL; OR, A DESPERATE REMEDY. C. 2 a. J. R. Planché. Lyceum, October 16, 1850.

MY HEART'S IN THE HIGHLANDS. F. 1 a. W. Brough and A. Halliday. D.L., November 9, 1863.

MY HUSBAND'S GHOST. F. 1 a. J. M. Morton. Hay., 1836.

MY HUSBAND'S SECRET. F. 1 a. W. D. Whitty. Vaudeville, April 22, 1874.

MY HUSBAND'S SECRET. F. 1 a. Meadows. Publ. by S. French, Ltd.

MY HUSBAND'S WIFE; OR, T.T.T., TOM TRIMMER'S TRIALS. F.C. 3 a. R. D. Perry. Greenwich P.O.W., March 19, 1885.

MY INNOCENT BOY. F.C. 3 a. G. R. Sims and L. Merrick. Royalty, May 11, 1898.

MY JACK. Ca. 1 a. Miss Emily Coffin. Princess's, October 6, 1887.

MY JACK. Nautical D. 5 a. B. Landeck. Surrey, September 9, 1889.

MY KNUCKLEDUSTER. Strand, February 2, 1863.

MY LADY. Dr. Sk. A. Shirley. Adap. fr. *The Three Musketeers.* Holborn Empire, February 24, 1908.

MY LADY BARBARA. P. 1 a. G. W. Boyle. MS. with Douglas Cox.

MY LADY BETTY. Rom. C. Epis. by Vincent Gordon Corelli. Standard, October 14, 1907.

MY LADY CLARA. D. 5 a. T. W. Robertson. Liverpool Alexandra, February 22, 1869.

MY LADY DAINTY. O.P. 4 a. Madeleine Lucette Ryley. Brighton R.T., July 2, 1900.

MY LADY FANCIFUL. M. Past. Amabel Jenner. M. by W. Dry. Margate Old Tivoli Gardens. August 15, 1899.

MY LADY HELP. Ca. 1 a. A. Macklin. Shaftesbury, November 24, 1890; Avenue, April 7, 1891.

MY LADY HILDA; OR, THE BURIED SECRET. D. 3 a. H. F. Saville. Nottingham T.R., March 21, 1870.

MY LADY M.D. Oa. G. D. Lynch. M. by W. M. George. Wimbledon Baths, January 29, 1895.

MY LADY MOLLY. C.O. 2 a. G. H. Jessop, add. lyrics by P. Greenback and C. Taylor. M. by S. Jones. Brighton T.R., August 11, 1902; Terry's, March 14, 1903.

MY LADY OF ROSEDALE. P. 4 a. J. C. Carr. Adap. fr. *La Chatelaine* by A. Capus. New, February 13, 1904.

MY LADY VIRTUE. P. 4 a. H. V. Esmond. Garrick, October 27, 1902.

MY LADY VISITOR. C. Nellie Dallas. Brighton New Palace, Pav., July 14, 1902.

MY LADY'S BOWER. Sk. Canterbury, September 7, 1908.

MY LADY'S CHAMBER. C. Sk. R. Royston-Dene. Bedford, July 22, 1907.

MY LADY'S GLOVE. C. 1 a. N. Morris. (Pr. by the Curtain Raisers.) Rehearsal, March 11, 1909.

MY LADY'S ORCHARD. P. 1 a. Mrs. Oscar Beringer and G. P. Hawtry. Glasgow T.R., August 23, 1897; Avenue, October 2, 1897.

MY LANCASHIRE WIFE. Sk. Middlesex, November 16, 1908.

MY LANDLADY'S DAUGHTER. Ca. 1 a. P. M. Berton. Maidenhead Grand H., January 2, 1893.

MY LATEST OPERA. Burla. St. George's H., November 24, 1894.

MY LIFE. D. 4 a. Miss Archer. Gaiety, December 6, 1882.

MY LIFE BY MYSELF. F. Harry St. Maur. Liverpool P.O.W., July 8, 1876.

MY LITTLE ADOPTED. F. 1 a. T. H. Bayly. Pub. by J. Dicks.

MY LITTLE GIRL. Ca. 1 a. D. G. Boucicault. Adap. fr. Besant and Rice's novel. Court, February 15, 1882.

MY LITTLE MAID, SINCE GROWN TALL. Duol. "Basel." Hampstead Road, Tolmers Inst., March 16, 1905.

MY LITTLE RED RIDING HOOD. P. 1 a. J. Rae and T. Sidney. St. Leonards Pier Pav., October 16, 1895.

MY LITTLE WILLIAM. F. B. McCullough. Wolverhampton P.O.W., April 17, 1876.

MY LIVING STATUTE. Inc. 1 a. R. Barrie. Birkenhead Metropole T., August 12, 1901.

MY LORD ADAM. C. 3 a. Mrs. De Lacy Lacy. Royalty, January 15, 1901.

MY LORD AND MY LADY; OR, IT MIGHT HAVE BEEN WORSE. C. 5 a. J. R. Planché. Hay., July 12, 1861.

MY LORD CARDINAL. G. Alexander. Avenue, November 16, 1894 (C.P.).

MY LORD FROM TOWN. Past. P. 2 a. H. M. Paull. Worcester Coll., Oxford Gardens, June 18, 1904.

MY LORD IN LIVERY. F. 1 a. S. T. Smith. Princess's, October 9, 1886.

MY LORD *IS NOT* MY LORD. C.O. 1 a. M. by Boieldieu. D.L. (first time in England), January 29, 1840.

MY LORD OF PURSLOW. M.P. 3 a. L. Bailey. Bootle T.H., January 14, 1903.

MY LOVE AND I. Duol. H. Bellingham and W. T. Best. P.O.W., April 3, 1886.

MY MAGGIE. D. Miss Helen Thompson. Orig. prod. in America. Liverpool R. Sefton, October 22, 1884.

MY MAN TOM. Olympic, February 8, 1840; D.L., April 18, 1853.

MY MILLINER'S BILL. Duol. 1 a. G. W. Godfrey. Court, March 6, 1884; St. George's H., December 26, 1898.

MY MIMOSA MAID. Mus. P. 2 a. Paul A. Rubens and Austen Hurgon. M. by Paul A. Rubens. P.O.W., April 21, 1908.

MY MISSING SPECTACLES. C. 1 a. H. C. Pemberton. Pub. by S. French, Limited.

MY MISSIS. Dom. D. Catherine Lewis and D. Robertson. Op. C., October 8, 1886 (C.P.).

MY MOTHER. F. 3 a. Amy Steinberg. Toole's, April 20, 1890.

MY MOTHER'S MAID. Hay., November 18, 1858.

MY MOTHER-IN-LAW. C. 3 a.

MY NADINE; OR, ANDRE, THE MOUNTAINEER. C.D. H. Collier. M. by Jules de Croix. Folkestone Exhibition Pal., April 20, 1889.

MY NAME IS JONES. F. Joel H. G. Whittaker. Leeds Amphi., October 28, 1872.

MY NAME IS NORVAL. St. James's, January 18, 1860.

MY NATIVE LAND. Anglo-American D. 4 a. Wm. Manning. Coatbridge T.R., October 29, 1891; Hammersmith Lyric, December 5, 1892.

MY NEIGHBOUR'S WIFE. F. 1 a. Alfred Bunn. Adap. fr. the French. C.G., October 5, 1833; D.L., November 12, 1833.

MY NEW COOK. Sk. London Pav., February 10, 1908.

MY NEW MAID. Oa. Lecocq. St. George's. June 22, 1878.

MY NIECE AND MY MONKEY. C.T. 3 a H. Herman. Folly, June 10, 1876.

MY OFFICIAL WIFE. P. 5 a. A. C. Gunter. Lyric, September 10, 1892 (C.P.). See *The Passport*.

MY OLD WOMAN. F. 3 a. G. Macfarren. Publ. by J. Dicks.

MY ONLY DAUGHTER. P. Waldorf, September 10, 1906 (C.P.).

MY OWN BLUE BELL. F. 1 a. G. D. Pitt. Publ. by J. Dicks.

MY OWN FAMILIAR FRIEND. Curtain-raiser. P. Doveton Maxwell. Dumfries Royal, November 24, 1898.

MY OWN LOVER. M.D. M. by G. H. B. Rodwell. D.L., January 11, 1832.

MY OWN RIVAL: OR, SOPHY LUCY, AND LUCY SOPHY. M.C. 2 a. M. by Hart. Lyceum, June 28, 1819.

MY OWN TWIN BROTHER. C.Oa. Lyceum, September 9, 1834.

MY PARTNER. D. 4 a. B. Campbell. Orig. prod. in America. West Hartlepool T.R., March 17, 1884; Olympic, April 10, 1884.

MY PAYING GUEST. Duol. Marion Crofton. Queen's H., February 25, 1895.

MY PLAYMATE. M. and Rom. C.D. F. Evanson. M. by H. W. May. Seaham Harbour T.R., November 8, 1888.

MY POLL AND MY PARTNER JOE. Nautical D. 3 a. J. T. Haines. Surrey, September, 1835. F. on Dibdin's song.

MY PRECIOUS BETSY. F. 1 a. J. M. Morton. Adelphi, February, 1850; Hay.

MY PRESERVER. C. 1 a. H. T. Craven. Strand, March 2, 1863.

MY PRETTY LITTLE COZ. D. Agnes Platt. St. George's H., February 5, 1909.

MY PRETTY MAID. C. 4 a. Basil Hood. Terry's, April 5, 1902.

MY PRINCESS OF JAPAN. Sk. Holborn Empire, December 21, 1908.

MY QUEEN. P. Pro. and 3 a. H. Poole. Gaiety, March 20, 1884.

MY QUEENIE. C.D. 4 a. H. W. Williamson. Vaudeville. April 9, 1889.

MY RETRIBUTION. D.S. 1 a. E. C. Mathews. Tunbridge Wells Gt. H., September 18, 1902; Notting Hill Coronet, September 22, 1902.

MY RUNAWAY DAUGHTER. F. 3 a. E. Moncrieffe. Ilford Town H., September 12, 1902.

MY SIN. C.D. T. R. Bogue. Spennymoor Cambridge T., January 2, 1888.

MY SISTER AND I. Ca. J. J. Hewson. Liverpool P.O.W., November 29, 1897.

MY SISTER FROM INDIA. F. 1 a. C. Selby. Strand, January 5, 1852.

MY SISTER KATE. F. 1 a. M. Lemon. Publ. by J. Dicks.

MY SOLDIER BOY. F.C. 3 a. A. Maltby and F. Lindo. Fulham Grand, July 11, 1898; Criterion, January 3, 1899.

MY SON AND I. P. 1 a. Ellen Lancaster Wallis. Steinway H., May 25, 1894

MY SON DIANA. F. 1 a. A. Harris. Hay., May 25, 1857.

MY SON'S A DAUGHTER. C.D. 2 a. J. Parselle. Strand, September 15, 1862.

MY SPOUSE AND I. M.F. 2 a. C. Dibdin M. by Whittaker. D.L., December 7, 1815 Lyceum, October 27, 1835.

MY SWEETHEART. M.C. 3 a. F. G. Maeder and W. Gill. Orig. prod. in America. Glasgow Princess's, June 4, 1883; Grand, September 17, 1883.

MY TURN NEXT. F. T. J. Williams. New Holborn, December 17, 1866. See *Dobson and Co*.

MY UNCLE. Oa. Lyceum, June 23, 1817.

MY UNCLE. P. D. S. James and W. Y. Stewart. Torquay T.R. and O.H., May 28, 1883.

MY UNCLE. F.C. 3 a. Amy Steinberg (Mrs. John Douglass). Terry's, July 1, 1889.

MY UNCLE FROM TEXAS. Sk. Middlesex, April 26, 1909.

MY UNCLE GABRIEL. Operatic F. 2 a. M. by Parry. D.L., April 29, 1825.

MY UNCLE THE GHOST. O. 1 a. Lathair, Lecocq, etc. Publ. by S. French, Ltd.

MY UNCLE'S CARD; OR, THE FIRST OF APRIL. F. H. P. Grattan. Surrey, January 26, 1873.

MY UNCLE'S PARLOUR. Op. P. Ac. by amateurs at Sir James Knowles' house in Cornwall, December 22, 1807, by way of afterpiece to *Love's Systems*. N.p.

MY UNCLE'S WILL. Ca. 1 a. S. Theyre Smith.

MY UNFINISHED OPERA. Gallery of Illustration, April 27, 1857.

MY UNKNOWN FRIEND. P. 3 a. Shafto Scott. Taken fr. Dickens. Publ. by J. Dicks.

MY VALET AND I. F. 1 a. T. E. Wilks. Publ. by J. Dicks.

MY VERY LAST PROPOSAL. F. 1 a. A. J. Phipps. Belfast T.R., March 30, 1874.

MY VILLA IN ITALY. F. 1 a. C. M. Rae. Charing Cross T., August 14, 1871.

MY WIFE. C. 3 a. Michael Morton. Fr. the French, MM. Gavault and Charnay. Haymarket, May 28, 1907.

MY WIFE. F. A. E. Cowell. Eastbourne Pier Pav., October 17, 1892.

MY WIFE; OR, SUNSHINE THROUGH THE MIST. D. G. Roberts. Burnley Gaiety, April 6, 1885.

MY WIFE! WHAT WIFE? F. 1 a. J. Poole. D.L., April 2, 1829.

MY WIFE'S BABY. F. F. Hughes. Royalty, September 7, 1872.

MY WIFE'S BONNET. F. 1 a. J. M. Morton. Olympic, November 2, 1864.

MY WIFE'S COME. F. 1 a. J. M. Morton. D.L., October 18, 1843.

MY WIFE'S DAUGHTER. C. 2 a. J. S. Coyne. Olympic, October 14, 1850.

MY WIFE'S DENTIST. F. 1 a. T. E. Wilks. Hay., 1840.

MY WIFE'S DIARY. F. 1 a. W. Robertson. Adap. fr. *Les Memoirs de deux Jeunes Mariées* of Dennery and Clairville (Palais Royal, December 10, 1843). Olympic, 1854, as *A Wife's Journal*.

MY WIFE'S FATHER'S SISTER. Ca. 1 a. T. E. Pemberton. Brighton T.R., October 21, 1878.

MY WIFE'S HUSBAND. Sk. by G. D. Lynch. Collins's, March 25, 1907.

MY WIFE'S HUSBAND. Sk. Oxford M.H., May 2, 1908.

MY WIFE'S INTENDED. F. Malyon and A. Seymour. Worthing T.R., January 16, 1902.

MY WIFE'S JOURNAL. A. Wigan.

MY WIFE'S JOURNAL. See *My Wife's Diary*.

MY WIFE'S MAID. F. 1 a. T. J. Williams. Adelphi, August 8, 1864.

MY WIFE'S MOTHER. C.D. 2 a. C. J. Matthews. Hay., July 3, 1833.

MY WIFE'S OUT. F. 1 a. G. H. Rodwell. C.G., October 2, 1843.

MY WIFE'S PARTY. M. Sk. C. Grain. St. George's H., May 23, 1892.

MY WIFE'S RELATIONS. Ca. 1 a. W. Gordon. Olympic, December 1, 1862.

MY WIFE'S SECOND FLOOR. F. 1 a. J. M. Morton. Princess's, June 22, 1853.

MY WIFE'S STEPHUSBAND. F.C. 3 a. H. A. du Souchet. Tenby Assembly R., September 14, 1897 (C.P.).

MY WIFE'S SWEETHEART. F. Sk. H. Leonard. Met. M.H. December 2, 1907.

MY WIFE'S VICTIM. Melo. D. Travesty. Manchester Osborne, May 22, 1905.

MY YOUNG WIFE AND MY OLD UMBRELLA. F. 1 a. B. Webster. Pub. by S. French, Limited.

MYDAS. See *Midas*.

MYFISTO. Burl. Extrav. V. Montague and F. St. Clare. Colchester T.R., January 24, 1887.

MYNHEER JAN. C.O. 3 a. H. Paulton and "Mostyn Tedde." M. by E. Jakobowski. Birmingham Grand, February 7, 1887; Comedy, February 14, 1887.

MYRA. D. 5 a. Mrs. Noel Tompson. Richmond H.M.T., September 27, 1880.

MYRRHA. T. Alfieri. Transl. by C. Lloyd.

MYRROUR. See *Mirror*.

MYRTILLO. Past. Int. Colley Cibber. M. by Dr. Pepusch. D.L. Pr. 1716.

MYRTLE. C.D. 3 a. P. Havard. Birmingham T.R., April 8, 1889.

MYSTERIE OF INYQUYTE (INIQUITY). P. Bishop Bale.

MYSTERIES OF AUDLEY COURT. Astley's, August 11, 1866.

MYSTERIES OF CALLOW ABBEY; OR, OLD FIDELITY, THE. D. Liverpool T.R., May 15, 1876.

MYSTERIES OF LONDON, THE. Melo. D. 4 a. L. Gilbert. Edinburgh Pavilion, April 22, 1901; Surrey, August 5, 1901.

MYSTERIES OF PARIS, THE. D. 3 a. C. Dillon. Marylebone, September, 1844.

MYSTERIES OF PARIS, THE. See *A Human Terror*.

MYSTERIES OF PRINCE'S TOWER, THE. D. A. Mayne. Jersey T.R., June 9, 1879.

MYSTERIES OF THE CASTLE, THE. D.T., M. P. Andrews. C.G., January 31, 1795. Pr. 1795.

MYSTERIES OF THE THAMES. D. 4 a. F. B. Warren. Stalybridge Grand, July 20, 1901; West London, September 26, 1904.

MYSTERIES OF UDOLPHO; OR, PHANTOM OF THE CASTLE, THE. D. J. Baylis. Transl. fr. the French. Pr. 1804. N. ac.

MYSTERIOUS BRIDE, THE. P. 3 a. L. St. G. Skeffington. D.L., June 1, 1808. N.p.

MYSTERIOUS DISAPPEARANCE, A. F. Norwich St. Andrew's H., May 11, 1809.

MYSTERIOUS DRAMA; CAMDEN TOWN MURDER, THE. Ac. at Whitstable by W. G. B. Bell's company on September 5, 1908, without license from Lord Chamberlain.

MYSTERIOUS FAMILY, THE. F. 2 a. G. H. Rodwell. Publ. by J. Dicks.

MYSTERIOUS HOME OF CHELSEA, THE. D. 3 a. J. A. Cave and G. Roberts. Marylebone, September 30, 1876

MYSTERIOUS HUSBAND, THE. P. R. Cumberland. C.G., January 28, 1783. Pr. 1783. Partly f. on *The Mysterious Mother*.

MYSTERIOUS LADY; OR, WORTH MAKES THE MAN, THE. C. 2 a. J. R. Planché. Lyceum, October 18, 1852.

MYSTERIOUS MARRIAGE; OR, THE HEIRSHIP OF ROSALVA, THE. P. 3a. Harriet Lee. Pr. 1798. N.ac.

MYSTERIOUS MR. BUGLE, THE. F. 3 a. Madeleine Lucette Ryley. Strand, May 29, 1900.

MYSTERIOUS MRS., THE. Sk. 4 sc. C. Berte. Richmond, May 22, 1905.

MYSTERIOUS MOTHER, THE. T. Horace Walpole. Pr. 1768.

MYSTERIOUS MUSICIAN, THE. M.P. 1 a. G. G. Eden. M. by G. W Byng. Terry's, June 27, 1899.

MYSTERIOUS MUSICIANS, THE. Rom. Society. Mus. C.D. Louis H. Carlton. Northampton O.H., December 2, 1904.

MYSTERIOUS WIDOW, THE. F.C. 2 a. F. Fripp. Neville Dramatic Studio (Oxford St.), July 26, 1897.

MYSTERIOUS STRANGER. M.R. F. C. Gordon. 1812.

MYSTERIOUS STRANGER, THE. D. 2 a. C. Selby. Publ. by J. Dicks.

MYSTERY, THE. Surrey, September 19, 1863.

MYSTERY; OR, GREED FOR GOLD. D. 4 a. W. Stephens. Olympic, April 5, 1873.

MYSTERY OF A GLADSTONE BAG, THE. F. F. H. Francks. Pavilion, June 24, 1889.

MYSTERY OF A HANSOM CAB, THE. D. 4 a. F. Hume and A. Law. Adap. fr. Hume's story. Princess's, February 23, 1888.

MYSTERY OF DESBOROUGH, THE. D. 3 a. Mrs. Catherine Bater. Bootle Muncaster T., January 22, 1900.

MYSTERY OF EDWIN DROOD, THE. D. 4 a. W. Stephens. Surrey, November 4, 1871.

MYSTERY OF EDWIN DROOD, THE. D. G. H. Macdermott, Britannia, July 22, 1872.

MYSTERY OF EDWIN DROOD, THE. D. 4 a. J. Comyns Carr. F. on Dickens's unfinished novel. Cardiff New, November 21, 1907; H.M., January 4, 1908.

MYSTERY OF EDWIN DROOD, THE. D. 4 a. C. A. Clarke and S. B. Rogerson. (F. on Dickens's novel.) Manchester Osborne, March 2, 1908.

MYSTERY OF EDWIN DROOD, THE. Sk. Adap. fr. Dickens's novel. Bedford M.H., March 2, 1908.

MYSTERY OF MARCUS; OR, ANTHONY AND CLEOPATRA IN A NEW LIGHT. Architectural hash in 3 courses. W. J. H. Leverton. Guildhall Sc., February 12, 1907.

MYSTERY OF MUDDLEWITZ. C. 2 a. E. H. Keating. Publ. by S. French, Ltd.

MYSTERY OF REDWOOD GRANGE, THE. P. 1 a. By "An Englishman." Portsmouth R., March 1, 1909; Stratford R., March 8, 1909.

MYSTERY OF THE RED WEB, THE. Sk. Fergus Hume and Newman Harding. Liverpool Olympia, April 13, 1908; Canterbury M.H., May 18, 1908.

MYSTERY OF THE SEA, THE. D. Pro. and 5 a. Bram Stoker. Lyceum, March 17, 1902.

MYSTERY OF THE SEVEN SISTERS. D. 4 a. F. A. Scudamore. Surrey, October 27, 1890.

MYSTERY PLAYS. See "The Chester Plays," "The Coventry Plays," etc.

MYSTIC MAHATMA, THE. Oa. 1 a. T. M. Taylor. M. by Vivian Phillips. St. Geo. H., January 5, 1892.

MYSTIC RING, THE. Pant. Burl. 1 a. E. Cockburn Johnston. Birkenhead Pavilion, March 17, 1893.

MYSTICAL MISS, THE. C.O. 3 a. Chs. Klein. Comp. by John Philip Sousa. Comedy, December 13, 1899.

MYSTICAL MISS, THE. Comedy. Shaftesbury, January 1, 1900.

MYSTIFICATION. C. 1 a. D.L., April 7, 1821; Strand, January 26, 1832.

MYTHOLOGY RUN MAD; OR, LES CHUMPS DE MARS. Medley. Prol. and 2 a. T. Moore and E. Runtz. Westminster Town H., May 17, 1893 (amat.).

N

NAAMAN. Orat. Costa. Wds. by W. Bartholomew. September 7, 1864.

NABAL. Orat. Morell. 1764.

NABOB, THE. C. S Foote. Hay., June 29. 1772. Pr. 1778.

NABOB; OR, THE INDIAN LOVERS. THE. Bal. Lyceum, 1809.

NABOB FOR AN HOUR, A. F. 2 a. J. Poole. C.G., March 21, 1832.

NABOB'S FORTUNE; OR, THE ADVENTURES OF A SEALED PACKET, THE. C. H. Pettitt. Plymouth T.R., July 16, 1881.

NABOBS OUTWITTED, THE. F. Anon. Ac. at Tewkesbury, 1797. N.p.

NABOTH. Sacred D. J. Collett. Pr. 1806. N. ac.

NABUCADONOSOR. O. A. Ariosti. Vienna, 1706.

NABUCADONOSOR. O. Verdi. Lib. by Solero. Milan, 1842. Prod. as *Nino*, Her M., March 3, 1846

NACHTLAGER VON GRANADA, DAS. O. 3 a. M. by C. Kreutzer, 1782-1849. D.L., May 9, 1849.

NADEJA. O. Rossi. Prague. 1903.

NADEL. Poetic Rom. 1 a. W. F. Lyon. Coventry T.R., March 11, 1886.

NADESHDA. O. 4 a. Julian Sturgis. M. by Goring Thomas. D.L., April 16, 1885.

NADGY. C.O. 3 a. A. Murray. M. by A. Chassaigne. Adap. fr. *Les Noces Improvisées* (Bouffes Parisiens, February 13, 1886) of A. Liorat and A. Fonteny. The original had two other titles, *Les Noces de Nadgy* and *La Mariée d'un Jour*. Greenwich P.O.W., October 19, 1887 (C.P.); Avenue, November 7, 1888.

NADIA. P. 3 a. Lady Violet Greville. An adap. of H. Greville's novel, *Les Epreuves de Raissa*. Lyric, May 3, 1892.

NADINE. P. 4 a. F. Rogers. Vaudeville, March 5, 1885.

NADINE. C. 3 a. L. Grover. Liverpool R. Alexandra, October 22, 1887.

NADIR. Dr. Poem. Rev. Joseph Wise. Pr. 1779.

NADJEZDA. P. Pro. and 3 a. M. Barrymore. Hay., January 2, 1886.

NAIAD QUEEN; OR, THE REVOLT OF THE WATER NYMPHS, THE. Spec. D. Manchester Princess's, August 27, 1883.

NAIADS. Cant. Sir W. Sterndale Bennet. (1816-75.)

NAIDA. O. Flotow. St. Petersburg, 1873.

NAILING NOTION. M.P. 1 a. F. C. Burnand. Publ. by Douglas Cox.

NAIM. Grand O. 5 a. Reber. 1875.

NAIS. O. Pro. and 3 a. Rameau. April 22, 1749.

NAKED TRUTH, A. C. 3 a. F. Wyatt. Sunderland Avenue T., May 13, 1901.

NAKED TRUTH, THE. Op. Fant. 1 a. Edwd. A. Paulton. London Coliseum, May 17, 1909.

NAMESAKES. F. 1 a. H. Lennard. Toole's, February 24, 1883.

NAN. M. Adap. of *Good-for-Nothing*, by R. André. M. by Isidore de Solla. Coronet, September 12, 1905 (C.P.).

NAN. P. 3 a. John Masefield. Royalty (private), May 24, 1908; Haymarket (public), June 2, 1908.

NAN, A CHILD OF SHAME. D. 4 a. J. Cooper. Cinderford Town H., March 14, 1903.

NAN PILGRIM. P 4 a. Mabel Dearmer. Court, March 8, 1909.

NANA. M.S.S.P. M. by H. Simpson, J. Crook, and H. May. Lyrics, B. Daly. Birmingham Grand, May 1, 1902.

NANA. See *Nina*.

NANA SAHIB. Victoria, November 2, 1863.

NANCE. D. Pro. and 3 a. J. Douglass. Pavilion, November 13, 1893.

NANCE ARDEN; OR, THE WOMAN WHO DID. Sk. 1 sc. Wr. by Cecil Raleigh. Empress, March 30, 1908.

NANCE OLDFIELD. C. 1 a. C. Reade. Rev. at Lyceum, May 12, 1891

NANCY. Dr. Sk. A. Buckland. F. on an incident in *Oliver Twist*. Strand, July 11, 1901.

NANCY. See *Sweet Nancy*.

NANCY; OR, THE COUNTRY GIRL AT COURT. In Oulton's list, and dated 1781.

NANCY; OR, THE PARTING LOVERS. M. Int. H. Carey. Pr. 1739. D.L., 1739.

NANCY; OR, THE PARTING LOVERS. M. Int. Joseph Yarrow. Pr. 1742 at York. ? A piracy of foregoing.

NANCY AND CO. F.C. 4 a. Aug. Daly. Adap. fr. the German of J. Rosen. Orig. prod. in America. Strand, July 7, 1886; Daly's, July 29, 1895.

NANCY SIKES. D. 5 a. C. Searle. Olympic, July 9, 1878.

NANETTE. Oa. 1 a. Kate Simpson and Elva Lorence. Newcastle-on-Tyne Assembly R., November 12, 1895.

NANINE. C. Transl. fr. Voltaire by D. Francklin. ? Pr.

NANNETTE; OR, BETTER LATE THAN NEVER. Oa. H. Drayton. Standard, August 24, 1868.

NANNIE. C. 2 a. T. G. Warren. Op. C., November 10, 1895.

NANON. C.O. 3 a. R. Genée. Orig. prod. in America. Birmingham Grand, September 16, 1889.

NAOMI, THE GIPSY GIRL. D. 3 a. C. H. Hazlewood. Britannia, August 19, 1872.

NAOMI'S SIN; OR, WHERE ARE YOU GOING TO, MY PRETTY MAID? D. 3 a. Mrs. Augustus Bright. Sheffield Alexandra, May 7, 1879.

NAP; OR, A MIDSUMMER NIGHT'S SCREAM. Burl. S. Rogers. M. by G. Salmon and M. Adeson. Blyth T.R., April 5, 1890; Eleph. and C., July 21, 1890.

NAPLES BAY; OR, THE BRITISH SAILORS AT ANCHOR. M. Ent. C.G., May, 1794. Attributed to Cross. N.p.

NAPOLEON. D. 1 a. J. Walker. Pub. by J. Dicks.

NAPOLEON. Dr. Epis. and Sca. Sadler's Wells, December 5, 1904.

NAPOLEON; OR, THE STORY OF A FLAG. D. 5 a. C. H. Hazlewood. Britannia, April 14, 1873.

NAPOLEON AT WATERLOO. Sk. Standard, May 24, 1909.

NAPOLEON BONAPARTE. D. 4 a. A. Skelton. Dudley Colosseum, June 19, 1899; Stratford T.R., October 16, 1899.

NAPOLEON BONAPARTE'S INVASION OF RUSSIA; OR, THE CONFLAGRATION OF MOSCOW. Milit. and equestr. spec. 3 a. A. J. Amherst. Astley's Amphi., April 4, 1825.

NAPOLEON THE GREAT. D. 4 a. F. M. Thorne. Blackburn Prince's T., April 15, 1903 (C.P.); Preston P.O.W.'s, August 29, 1904; West London, August 20, 1906.

NAPOLEON, THE MAN. D. 1 a. Harry Starr. Preston Prince's T., April 7, 1905.

NAPOLIO. Ballet. Geovaumi Praetesi. G. W. Boyng. Alhambra, August 21, 1899.

NARCISSE. D. 3 a. A. E. Brachvogel. F. on Diderot's story, *Neveu de Rameau*. Circa. 1760. Publ. by Goethe in 1805. Transl. into English. Lyceum, February 17, 1868.

NARCISSE, THE VAGRANT. T. 5 a. J. Schönberg. Fr. the German of A. E. Brachvogel. Booth's T., New York, February 20, 1869; Vaudeville (in 4 a), July 3, 1883.

NARCISSUS. P. Alluded to in Heywood's Apology for Actors. 1610.

NARCISSUS; OR, THE SERF ADMIRER. C. Trans. fr. J. J. Rousseau. Pr. 1767. (First ac. in Paris, December 18, 1752.)

NARCOTIC, THE. F. J. Powell. Pr. circa. 1787. N.ac.

NARENSKY; OR, THE ROAD TO YAROSLAF. Serio c.o. 3 a. M. by Braham and Reeve. First ac., D.L., January 11, 1814.

NARROW ESCAPE, A. Ca. 1 a. Re Henry.

NARROW ESCAPE, A. C.D. 4 a. J. A. Stevens. March 20, 1888 (C.P.).

NARROW SQUEAK, A. F. 1 a. J. M. Morton.

NATALIA AND MENZIKOFF; OR, THE CONSPIRACY AGAINST PETER THE GREAT. T. Fr. the German of Kratter. Pr. 1798. N.ac.

NATALIE. O. J. L. Mackay. Glasgow Burgh H., April 28, 1892.

NATALIE; OR, LAITIERE SUISSE. C. ballet. 2 a. D.L., June 16, 1845.

NATHAN DER WEISE. D. poem. fr. the German of Lessing by the translator of Goethe's *Iphigenia* and Bürger's *Ellenore*. Pr. 1805.

NATHAN DER WEISE. D. poem. 5 a. and 12 sc. G. E. Lessing. Comedy, November 9, 1900.

NATHAN THE SAGE. D. By Lessing. 1779.

NATHAN THE WISE. D. R. E. Raspe. Transl. fr. the German by G. E. Lessing. Pr. 1781. Not wr. for the stage.

NATION IN ARMS, A. Military P. B. S. Townroe. Warrington R. Court, September 20, 1909.

NATIONAL GRATITUDE. Spec. to commemorate Admiral Lord Nelson. C.G., May 15, 1806.

NATIONAL GUARD; OR, BRIDE AND NO BRIDE, THE. C.O. 2 a. Cooke. Alt. fr. Scribe's O., *The Fiancée*. M. by Auber. D.L., February 4, 1830.

NATIONAL PREJUDICE. C. 2 a. P. Hiffernan. An alteration of *The Englishman in Bourdeaux*. D.L., April 6, 1768. N.p.

NATIONAL PREJUDICE. C. Simon. C.G., May 9, 1791. N.p.

NATIONAL QUESTION, A. F. R. Reece. Globe, March 16, 1878.

NATIONALIST, THE. Irish D. 4 a. J. W. Whitbread. Dublin Queen's T., December 21, 1891.

NATIVE LAND. O. Bishop. 1823.

NATURAL DAUGHTER, THE. C. Goethe. 1792.

NATURAL FAULTS. C. Wm. Earle, jun. Pr. 1799. N. ac.

NATURAL MAGIC. F. Motteux. 1697. See *The Novelty*.

NATURAL SON, THE. C. R. Cumberland. Ac. at D.L., December 22, 1784. Pr. 1785.

NATURAL SON, THE. T. J. Mason. Pr. at Liverpool, 1805.

NATURAL SON; OR, A LOVER'S VOWS, THE. P. 5 a. Anne Plumptre. Transl. fr. the German of Kotzebue. Pr. 1798. N. ac. See *Lover's Vows*.

NATURALIST, THE. Mus. Piece. 1 a. J. C. Carr. M. by K. Hall. St. George's H., April 11, 1887.

NATURE, A GOODLY INTERLUDE OF. H. Medwall. Pr. N.d. 1538.

NATURE AND PHILOSOPHY. Ca. 1 a. Lyceum, April 18, 1876.

NATURE OF THE IIIJ ELEMENTS. A NEW INT. AND A MERY OF THE. Assigned by Wood to Rastall. Pr. circa 1510.

NATURE WILL PREVAIL. Dr. Proverb. H. Walpole, Earl of Orford. Hay., June 10, 1778. Pr. 1798.

NATURE WILL PREVAIL. F. T. Hoarde. Pr. 1784. N. ac.

NATURE'S ABOVE ART. C. E. Falconer. D.L., September 12, 1863.

NATURE'S NOBLEMAN. Rom. D. J. F. Scudamore. Dublin Gaiety, July, 1882.

NATURE'S THREE DAUGHTERS, BEAUTY, LOVE, AND WIT. C. in 2 parts. Margaret Duchess of Newcastle. Pr. 1662.

NAUFRAGIUM JOCULARE; THE MERRY SHIPWRECK. Latin C. Abraham Cowley. Ac. by the members of Trin. Coll., Cambridge, 1638. Transl. by C. Johnson, and called *Fortune in Her Wits*, 1705.

NAUGHTY BOYS. See *The Chinaman*.

NAUGHTY ELIZABETH. "Musical Farcical Absurdity." 2 a. Norman H. Lee. Bromsgrove Ass. Rooms, February 15, 1909.

NAUGHTY FORTY THIEVES. Grand, December 26. 1892.

NAUGHTY LADY CECIL. Playlet. 1 a. New Cambridge, December 11, 1905.

NAUGHTY MEN. F.C. 3 a. F. Harvey. Dublin Gaiety, June 1, 1885.

NAUGHTY NANCY. M.C. 2 a. O. Bath and G. W. Preston. M. by R. E. Lyon and G. W. Preston. Southend Empire, March 31, 1902; Savoy, September 8, 1902.

NAUGHTY ROSINA. F.C. 3 a. L. Montague and A. Atwood. Brixton T., August 15, 1898.

NAUGHTY TITANIA. Burl. S. Rogers and J. Rushworth. M. by J. H. Yorke. Aston New T., August 7, 1893; Leamington T.R., April 6, 1896.

NAULAHKA, THE. P. Fr. Kipling and Balostier's novel. O.C., October 26, 1891 (C.P.).

NAUTCH GIRL; OR, THE RAJAH OF CHUTNEYPORE, THE. C.O. 2 a. G. Dance. M. by E. Solomon. Lyrics by G. Dance and F. Desprez. Savoy, June 30, 1891.

NAVAL CADETS, THE. Op. C. 3 a. M. by R. Génee. Globe, March 27, 1880.

NAVAL DETECTIVE, THE. P. F. J. Kirke. Eccles Lyceum, July 28, 1904.

NAVAL ENGAGEMENTS. Burla. C. Dance. D.L., June 25, 1838.

NAVAL ENGAGEMENTS. C. 2 a. P.O.W., September 25, 1865.

NAVAL PILLAR; OR, BRITANNIA TRIUMPHANT, THE. M. ent. T. Dibdin. C.G., August 7, 1799. Pr. 1799.

NAVAL VOLUNTEERS; OR, BRITAIN'S GLORY. Prel. C.G., May 7, 1795. N.p.

NAVARRAISE, LA. O. 2 a. J. Clarétie and H. Cain. M. by J. Massenet. C.G., June 20, 1894.

NEALE O'NEAL. C. W. Sidney. Liverpool P.O.W., July 20, 1874.

NEAR RELATIONS. A Sketchley. Gall. of Illustration, August 14, 1871.

NEAR SHAVE, A. M.F. G. D. Day and E. Jones. Court, May 6, 1895.

NEARLY LOST. D. W. Travers. City of London, August 5, 1867.

NEARLY SEVEN. Monologue. C. Brookfield. Hay., October 7, 1882.

NEARLY SEVERED. P. 1 a. J. P. Hurst. Manchester Comedy, August 31, 1885; Vaudeville, September 12, 1885.

'NEATH THE SHADOW OF GREAT BIG BEN. Scena. H. Cole. Middlesboro' T.R., February 8, 1904.

NEBUCADONIZER. Mentioned by Henslows as ac. by his company December 19, 1596.

NECESSITY KNOWS NO LAW. P. 4 a. W. Toynbee. Court, June 30, 1904.

NECK OR NOTHING F. 2 a. D. Garrick. D.L., November 18, 1766. Pr. 1766. An imitation of Le Sage's *Crespin Rival de son Maître*.

NECK OR NOTHING. D. 3 a. G. Conquest and H. Pettitt. Grecian, August 3, 1876.

NECROMANCER; OR, HARLEQUIN DR. FAUSTUS, THE. Panto. L.I.F., December 20, 1724. Pr. 1723.

NECROMANTES; OR, THE TWO SUPPOSED HEADS. Comical Invention by Wm. Percy. Ac. by children of St. Paul's. MS. in private hands. Wr. about 1602.

NECROMANTIA. Dial. Pr. (n.d.) by John Rastall. ? by Sir Thos. More.

NECTAR AND AMBROSIA. T. Campion. N.p.

NED KELLY; OR, THE BUSHRANGERS. D. 4 a. B. Espinasse and H. Leader. Vaudeville, September 25, 1902.

NED KNOWLES. Ca. T. G. Warren. O.C., February 5, 1887.

NED'S CHUM. C.D. 3 a. D. C. Murray. Auckland (N.Z.) O.H. (called *Chums*), March 4, 1890; Globe, August 27, 1891, and July 4, 1892.

NEEDFUL, THE. C. 5 a. H. T. Craven. Liverpool P.O.W., June 4, 1866; St. James's, January 1, 1868.

NEEDLES. F.C. 3 a. J. H. Darnley. MS. with Douglas Cox Worthing T.R., December 10, 1903.

NEEDLES AND PINS. F.C. 4 a. Aug. Daly. Adap. fr. the German of Rosen. Orig. prod. in America. Crystal Pal., August 12, 1884.

NEEDLES AND PINS. P. 4 a. J. H. McCarthy. Margate Hippo, April 23, 1907.

N'ER-DO-WEEL. C. 3 a. W. S. Gilbert. Olympic, February 25, 1878. Title changed to *The Vagabond*, and played at Olympic March 25, 1878.

NE'ER-DO-WELL, THE. Piece. 1 a. S. Bowkett. Strand, May 22, 1894.

NEGLECTED VIRTUE; OR, THE UNHAPPY CONQUEROR. T. Publ. by Hildebrand Horden, 1696, who wrote the pro. Epil. by Motteux. Ac. at the T.R.

NEGRO SLAVES, THE. D.P. 3 a. Transl. fr. the German of Kotzebue. Pr. 1796.

NEGRO SLAVES; OR, THE BLACKMAN AND BLACKBIRD, THE. M. ent. A. M'Laren. Ac. at Edinburgh. Pr. 1799.

NEHEMIAH. Sacr. D. Macket. 179—.

NEHEMIAH. Orat. Josiah Booth. Words by A. J. Foxwell. Pr. by J. Curwen and Sons. Perf. by South London Choral Association.

NEIGE, LA. C.O. 4 a. Scribe and Delavigne. M. by Auber. Paris, October 8, 1823. Prod. as *The Frozen Lake*, C.G., November 26, 1824.

NEIGHBOURS. C. 2 a. J. Oxenford. Strand, November 10, 1866.

NEIGHBOURS. M.C. H. S. Edwards. M. by Vera Leslie. St. Albans County H., September 2, 1904.

NEITHER OF THEM. C. 1 a. Miss Cowen. Publ. by S. French. Ltd.

NEITHER'S THE MAN. C. 5 a. Mrs. Holford. Pr. 1799. Ac. by the Chester Co., but never reached London.

NELL. O. 1 a. Publ. by S. French, Ltd.

NELL. P. 1 a. Charles Vane. Edinburgh T.R., November 13, 1905.

NELL; OR, THE OLD CURIOSITY SHOP. D. 4 a. A. Halliday. Olympic, November 19, 1870.

NELL GWYN. P. 4 a. W. E. Grogan. Torquay R., May 9, 1905.

NELL GWYNNE. C.O. 3 a. H. B. Farnie. M. by A. Cellier. Manchester Prince's, October 16, 1876.

NELL GWYNNE. C. 4 a. W. G. Wills. Royalty, May 1, 1878.

NELL GWYNNE. C.O. 3 a. H. B. Farnie. M. by R. Planquette. Avenue, February 7, 1884.

NELL GWYNNE. C. 1 a. E. H. Vanderfelt. Camberwell Metropole, May 7, 1900.

NELL GWYNNE. P. 4 a. M. Goldberg. Croydon R., September 3, 1900.

NELL GWYNNE; OR, THE KING AND THE ACTRESS. Extrav. H. T. Arden. Royalty, June 12, 1871.

NELL GWYNNE: OR, THE PROLOGUE. C. 2 a. D. Jerrold. C.G., January 9, 1833.

NELL GWYNNE, THE ORANGE GIRL OF DRURY LANE; OR, A HEART OF GOLD. Rom. C. 3 a. A. Burton. Glasgow Athenæum, November 2, 1906.

NELL GWYNNE, THE PLAYER. C. 1 a. Catherine Lewis. New, November 17, 1908.

NELL SNOOKS. D. 4 a. C. Russell and J. Lawson. W. London, April 3, 1899.

NELLIE'S FLIGHT. C. 3 a. H. S. Edwards and B. Thomas. Crystal Palace, July 20, 1886.

NELLIE'S TRIALS. Strand, January 8, 1866.

NELLY NEIL. M.P. 3 a. C. M. S. McLellan. M. by Ivan Caryll. Aldwych, January 10, 1907.

NELSON. D. 2 a. E. Fitzball. Publ. by J. Dicks.

NELSON. Playlet by L. Cohen. Coronet, February 2, 1907; Croydon R.T., July 26, 1907.

NELSON TOUCH, THE. P. 1 a. Fredk. Fenn. Haymarket, October 21. 1907.

NELSON'S ENCHANTRESS. P. 4 a. R. Horne. Avenue, February 11, 1897.

NELSON'S GLORY. Int. T. Dibdin. C.G., November 7, 1805. N.p.

NEMESIS; OR, NOT WISELY, BUT TOO WELL. Extrav. H. B. Farnie. Strand, April 17, 1873.

NEPHEWS, THE. P. H. E. Lloyd. Transl. fr. the German of Iffland. Pr. 1799. N.ac.

NEPOS. See *Alcibiades.*

NEPTUNE AND AMPHITRITE. M. Ent. D.L., 1746. N.p.

NEPTUNE'S PROPHECY. Masque. See *Dido, Queen of Carthage,* by P. Hoare. 1792.

NEPTUNE'S TRIUMPH FOR THE RETURN OF ALBION. Masque. Ben Jonson. Ac. at Court on Twelfth Night. 1624. Pr. 1756.

NERO. Gwinne. Pr. 1603.

NERO. O. Handel. February 25, 1705.

NERO. O. 4 a. M. by Rubenstein. Hamburg, 1879.

NERO. Poetic P. 4 a. Stephen Philips H.M., January 25, 1906.

NERO. T. Unfinished. ? by Butler. Mentioned in *The British Critic,* September, 1793

NERO, THE TRAGEDY OF. Anon. Pr 1624. Repr. 1676, under the title, *Piso's Conspiracy.*

NERO, THE TRAGEDY OF. See *Claudius Tiberius Nero,*

NERO AND CO. C.O. 2 a. M. by Bernard Page. Nottingham Mechanics' H., May 11, 1908.

NERO, EMPEROR OF ROME. T. N. Lee. Ac. at the T.R. Pr. 1675.

NERO'S NIECE. Ca. 3 a. L. S. Palmer. Worthing T.R., June 26, 1899.

NERONE. D. 5 tab. Pietro Cossa. 1871.

NERONE. O. 4 a. Rubinstein. Words by Barbier. Stadttheater, 1879.

NERONE DETRONATO. O. Pescetti. 1725.

NERVES. F.C. 3 a. J. C. Carr. Adap. fr. *Les Femmes Nerveuses* of E Blum and R. Toché. Comedy, June 7, 1890.

NERVOUS MAN AND THE MAN OF NERVES, THE. F. 2 a. W. B. Bernard. D.L., January 26, 1833.

NEST OF NINNIES, A. C By Armyn. 1608

NEST OF PLAYS, THE. Consisting of 3 plays. Hildebrand Jacob. C.G., January 25. 1738. The three distinct comedies intended to form the evening's amusement are *The Prodigal Reformed, The Happy Constancy,* and *The Trial of Conjugal Love.* This was the 1st dr. ent. licensed by the Lord Chamberlain after the passing of the Act for restraining the liberty of the stage.

NETLEY ABBEY. Op F. 2 a. W. Pearce C.G., April 10, 1794; D.L., November 28, 1812. Pr. 1794.

NETTLE, THE. Ca. 1 sc. E. Warren. Court, October 13, 1886.

NETTLEWIG HALL; OR, TEN TO ONE. M.F. 2 a. C. M. Westmacott. D.L., April 7, 1831.

NEUCHARS JUNCTION. Ca. 1 a. Bertha Moore. Queen's Gate H., June 14, 1901.

NEUE VORMUND, DER. P. 1 a. Gustave Hadelburg (Ger. Sea.) Comedy, February 22, 1901.

NEUTRAL GROUND. Ca. G. F. Brodie. Princess's, August 7, 1875.

NEVADA. M.C.D. 3 a. S. F. Cody. Saltley Carlton T., January 8, 1904 (C.P.).

NEVER AGAIN. D. R. E. Hall. Coatbridge Prince's, December 1, 1873.

NEVER AGAIN. F.C. 3 a. M. Desvallières and A. Mars. Adap. fr. *Le Truc de Séraphin.* Birmingham T.R., October 4, 1897; Vaudeville, October 11, 1897.

NEVER DESPAIR. D. 4 a. W. James. Grecian, December 7, 1871.

NEVER DESPAIR. D. Norwich T.R., October 22, 1875.

NEVER DESPAIR. D. Pro. and 4 a. G. Comer. Halifax Gaiety, May 5, 1887; Sadler's Wells, March 9, 1889.

NEVER DESPAIR, FOR OUT OF EVIL COMETH GOOD. D. 4a. C. H. Stephenson. Victoria, August 30, 1869.

NEVER, NEVER LAND, THE. D. 4 a. W. Barrett. Broughton V.T., April 9, 1902; Hull Grand, February 1, 1904; Hammersmith King's, March 21, 1904.

NEVER RECKON YOUR CHICKENS BEFORE THEY ARE HATCHED. F. 1 a. W. Reeve. Olympic, December 26, 1871.

NEVER TASTE WINE AT THE DOCKS. R. Soutar. Strand.

NEVER TO KNOW. Pl. 1 a. M. Fairfax. Reading R. County, May 15, 1899.

NEVER TOO LATE. C. By Greene. 1590.

NEVER TOO LATE TO LEARN. D. W. S. Branson. Greenwich, November 14, 1874.

NEVER TOO LATE TO MEND. See *It's Never*, etc.

NEW ACADEMY; OR, THE NEW EXCHANGE, THE. C. R. Brome. Circa 1645. Pr. 1658.

NEW ACTRESS, THE. D. 1 a. Edwin Drew. Athenæum, Tottenham Ct. Rd., July 24, 1888.

NEW ADAM, THE. F.C. 3 a. M. Melford. Southend Empire, May 27, 1897.

NEW AGENT, THE. Mus. ca. R. Lindo. M. by A. Lindo. Novelty, April 6, 1896.

NEW ALADDIN, THE. M. extrav. 2 a. J. T. Tanner and W. H. Risque. Lyrics by Adrian Ross, Percy Greenbank, W. H. Risque, and Geo. Grossmith, jun. M. by Ivan Caryll and Lionel Monckton. Gaiety, September 29, 1906.

NEW APOLLO, A. C. 1 a. C. Gray. Everton Liverpool New T., June 10, 1889.

NEW ATHENIAN COMEDY, THE. By "E. S." (Elkanah Settle). Pr. 1693. 3 a. Not intended for the stage.

NEW ATLANTIS. Bacon. Publ. 1627.

NEW BABY, THE. F. 3 a. A. Bouchier. Adap. fr. the German *Der Rabenvater* (Residenz Theatre, Berlin, September 18, 1895) of H. J. Fischer and J. Jarno. Royalty, January 8, 1896 (C.P.); Hastings, Gaiety, April 6, 1896; Royalty, April 28, 1896.

NEW BABYLON. D. Pro. and 4 a. P. Meritt and G. F. Rowe. Manchester Queen's, June 10, 1878; Duke's, February 13, 1879.

NEW BARMAID, THE. Mus. P. 2 a. F. Bowyer and W. E. Sprange. M. by J. Crook. Southport O.H., July 1, 1895; Camberwell Metropole, August 19, 1895; Avenue; Op. C. (tr. fr. Avenue), June 8, 1896.

NEW BEGGAR'S OPERA, THE. M.E. 3 a. Cervantes Hogg. A parody on *The Beggar's Opera*. Pr. 1809.

NEW BOARDER, THE. F.M. Absurdity. F. Stanmore. M. by F. A. Armstrong. Paragon, March 30, 1908

NEW BOY, THE. C.D. 4 a. R. R. Lumley. Margate T.R., May 29, 1893.

NEW BOY, THE. F.C. 3 a. A. Law. Eastbourne Dev. Park T. (prod. as *The Boy*), February 1, 1894; Terry's, February 21, 1894; Vaudeville (tr. fr. Terry's), April 16, 1894; rev. December 3, 1895; New, November 28, 1907.

NEW BRAWL; OR, TURNMILL STREET AGAINST ROSEMARY LANE, THE. Mock C. (Not intended for representation.) 1654.

NEW BRIGHTON SANDS. F. W. Harrison. Liverpool Rotunda, June 27, 1881.

NEW BROOMS. Occ. Prel. G. Colman. D.L. (at opening of the theatre), September 21, 1776.

NEW BROOMS. F. Piece. H. J. Byron. Dublin Gaiety, July 18, 1881.

NEW BULL BAYTING; OR, MATCH PLAY'D AT THE TOWN BULL OF ELY, etc. A. Anon. Pr. 1649.

NEW CINDERELLA, THE. C. 2 a. J. P. Simpson. Royalty, January 1, 1879.

NEW CLOWN, THE. F. 3 a. H. M. Paull. Margate Grand T., February 3, 1902; rev. Terry's, March 31, 1906.

NEW COACHMAN, THE. Sk. Grace Gardner. London Pav., July 8, 1907.

NEW COMEDY, A. Ac. by the French K. and his Privy Council. Transl. fr. the French. Pr. 1704.

NEW COMMANDER, THE. Naval M.C. 2 a. E. Mervyn. Hastings Gaiety, February 22, 1904; Crystal Pal., March 7, 1904.

NEW COMPANION, THE. P. 1 a. T. Cheek (C.P.). Gravesend P.H., October 10, 1906.

NEW CORSICAN BROTHERS, THE. Extrav. 3 a. C. Raleigh and W. Slaughter. Liverpool P.O.W., November 11, 1889; Royalty, November 20, 1889.

NEW COSMETIC; OR, THE TRIUMPH OF BEAUTY, THE. C. C. Melmoth (S. J. Pratt). Pr. 1790.

NEW CUSTOM. An int. on morality in 3 a. Anon. Black letter. Pr. 1573.

NEW DEAN, THE. P. H. Ellis. M. by J. W. Ivimey. Cambridge New T., June 11, 1897 (amat.).

NEW DIVERTISEMENT, A. M. by Carey. D.L., December 19, 1843.

NEW DIVERTISEMENT, THE. ? Pupils of Hullins. D.L., October 25, 1824.

NEW DON QUIXOTE, THE. P. 4 a. R. Buchanan and C. Marlowe. Royalty, February 19, 1896 (C.P.).

NEW DROLL, A. Masque. Jordan. 1660.

NEW EAST LYNNE, THE. Dr. Pro. and 4 a. Edmund Gurney. An adap. of Mrs. Henry Wood's novel. Birkenhead Metropole, June 6, 1898; Standard, July 18, 1898.

NEW EDITION OF THE CORSICAN BROTHERS; OR, THE KOMPACT, THE KICK, AND THE KOMBAT, A. Burl. W. H. Mason. Brighton T.R., June 18, 1870.

NEW ENDYMION; OR, EASTERN DIPLOMACY, THE. P. Perth New Public H., November 1, 1882.

NEW EXCHANGE, THE. Brome. 1658. See *The New Academy*.

NEW FELICITY, THE. C. 3 a. L. A. Tadema. Royalty, June 25, 1905.

NEW FOOTMAN, THE. Burla. 1 a. C. Selba. Strand, March 28, 1842.

NEW GENEVRA, A. P. 1 a. Frances C. Deverell. Ladbroke Hall, January 31, 1908.

NEW GOVERNESS, THE. F.C. Walter Frith. F. on a short story by G. S. Layard. Malvern Association Rooms, November 19, 1908.

NEW GROOM, THE. C. 1 a. C. Hannan. Chester Royalty, October 13, 1899.

NEW GUN, THE. Dr. sk. R. Rees. Crystal Pal., November 25, 1901; Collins's M.H., December 8, 1902.

NEW HAY AT THE OLD MARKET. Occ. D. 1 a. G. Colman the younger. Hay. (at opening of the theatre), June 9, 1795. Pr. 1795. Reduced and ac. as *Sylvester Daggerwood*.

NEW HAYMARKET SPRING MEETING, THE. Extrav. 1 a. J. R. Planché. Hay., April 9, 1855

NEW HIPPOCRATES, THE. F. Ascr. to Dr. Hifferman. Ac. at D.L., 1761.

NEW HOUSEMAID, THE. F.C. 3 a. C. Dewar. Islington Myddelton H., February 15, 1895.

NEW HOUSEKEEPER, THE. Ca. 1 a. F. L. Hare. M. by D. Barone. Ealing Lyric, June 11, 1896.

NEW HOUSEMAID, THE. F.C. 3 a. C. Windermere. Margate, October 19, 1893; Peckham Crown, May 9, 1904.

NEW HUSBAND, THE. Duo C. Dick. Hay., December 16, 1895.

NEW IDOL, THE. P. 3 a. Transl. by Maurice Durand and Hugh Stokes of *La Nouvelle Idole* by F. De Curel. Royalty, March 17, 1902.

NEW INN; OR, THE LIGHT HEART, THE. C Ben Jonson. Ac. by the King's servants, January 19, 1629. Pr. 1631.

NEW INVENTIONS. F. 1 a. W. E. Emden. Publ. by J. Dicks.

NEW KING RICHARD THE THIRD. THE. Burl. C. H Hazlewood. Britannia, April 1, 1878.

NEW LAMPS FOR OLD. P. 3 a. J. K. Jerome. Terry's, February 8, 1890.

NEW LEAF, A. Do. P. 1 a. H. Darnley. Royalty, November 20, 1897.

NEW LIFE, A. D. L. Clarance. Barnsley T.R., March 3, 1884.

NEW LIFE, THE. P. 1 a. W. G. Mackay. Avenue, July 5, 1894.

NEW LODGER, THE. F. 1 a. H. Louther. Dumbarton T.R., November 22, 1894.

NEW MAGDALEN, THE. D. Prol. and 3 a. Wilkie Collins. Olympic, May 19, 1873.

NEW MAID OF THE OAKS, THE. T. Ahab Salem. 1778. Ac. near Saratoga, under the direction of the author of *The Maid of the Oaks.*

NEW MAN, THE F.C. 3 a. H. Woodgates and P. M. Berton. Ladbroke H., December 20, 1895 (C.P.)

NEW MAZEPPA, THE. Rom. D. Pro. and 3 a. F. Cooke and W. J. Waldron. Croydon T.R., March 10, 1890; Sadler's Wells, September 22, 1890.

NEW MEN AND OLD ACRES; OR, A MANAGING MAMMA. C 3 a. Tom Taylor and A. W. Dubourg. Manchester T.R., August 20, 1869; Hay., October 25, 1869.

NEW MEPHISTO. M.C. 2 a. Orig. prod. as *The New Mephistopheles.* Brixton, October 4, 1897.

NEW MEPHISTOPHELES, THE. G. Dance. M. by E. Vousden and others. Leeds Grand, March 29, 1897. See *The New Mephisto.*

NEW MOON, THE. O. fancy. 3 phases. R. André. M. by Isidore de Solla. Recited at Savoy Hotel, February 6, 1893.

NEW OCCASIONAL ORATORIO. Anon. Pr. 1746.

NEW PEERAGE; OR, OUR EYES MAY DECEIVE US, THE. C. Miss Harriet Lee. D.L., November 10, 1787. Pr. 1787.

NEW POLICE; OR, GIRLS FROM THE AMAZON CLUB, THE. M.C. 3 a. Towyn. M. by O. Trevine and J. Armstrong. Nottingham R., May 22, 1905.

NEW REGIME, THE. P. 1 a. C. Brookfield. P.O.W., June 25, 1903; Royalty, January 22, 1908.

NEW REHEARSAL; OR, BAYES THE YOUNGER, THE. Anon. Pr 1714. Ascr. to Charles Gildon. Wr. in imitation of the Duke of Buckingham's *Rehearsal*, and bears upon *The Ambitious Stepmother, Tamerlane, The Biter, Fair Penitent, Royal Convert, Ulysses, Jane Shore*, and *The Rape of the Lock.*

NEW SERVANT, THE. M.C. F. A. Barnes. Colchester T.R., April 29, 1889.

NEW SPAIN; OR, LOVE IN MEXICO. O. Hay. Pr. 1790. Ascr. to Seawen, author of *The Girl in Style.*

NEW SUB, THE. P. 1 a. S. Hicks. Suggested by L. Trevor's story, *The Mistletoe Bough.* Court, April 27, 1892.

NEW TENANTS, THE. C. 3 a. Geoffrey Wilkinson. Rehearsal Theatre, July 30, 1908.

NEW TRIAL, A. P. 4 a. C. F. Coghlan. Adap. fr. *La Morte Civile* of P. Giacornetti (played at H.M.T., March 7, 1884). P.O.W., December 18, 1880.

NEW TRICK TO CHEAT THE DEVIL, A. C. R. Davenport. Pr. 1639. Partly fr. Ovid, *de Arte Amandi*, lib. ii. See *Trick to Catch*, etc.

NEW TROOP, THE. A Soliloquy quoted from this P. in Dr. King's Works, Vol. iii., p. 243, Edit. 1776

NEW WAY OF WOOING. F. Meek. N.p.

NEW WAY TO KEEP A WIFE AT HOME, A. F. W. C. Oulton. Alt. fr. Fielding's *Letter Writers.* Ac at Smock Alley, Dublin, 1785. Pr. 1787.

NEW WAY TO PAY OLD DEBTS. C. P. Massinger. A few hints borr. fr. *A Trick to Catch the Old One* Ac. at the Phœnix, D.L., 1633; D.L., August 19, 1748; C.G., April 18, 1781; alt. by J. P. Kemble, 1810; D.L., January 12, 1816; Victoria, 1844.

NEW WING, THE. F.C. 3 a. H. A. Kennedy. Strand (mat.), May 27, 1890; (evening bill), January 9, 1892.

NEW WOMAN, THE. C. 4 a. S. Grundy. Comedy, September 1, 1894.

NEW WONDER—A WOMAN HOLDS HER TONGUE. F. W. C. Oulton. 1784. N.p.

NEW WONDER—A WOMAN NEVER VEXT, A. C. W. Rowley. Pr. 1632.

NEW WORLD, THE. D. E. France. Windsor T.R., September 27, 1880.

NEW WORLD, THE. Rom. 4 a. F. Darcy. Maidenhead Grand H., under title of *Devil's Mine*, April 25, 1894; West London, May 23, 1898.

NEW WORLD; OR, UNDER THE SOUTHERN CROSS, THE. P. 4 a. F. Dawson. Bath T.R., March 21, 1893.

NEW WORLD'S TRAGEDY. P. Ac. at Rose T., 1595.

NEW YEAR; OR, PEACE WITH HONOUR, THE. Pantomimic Patriotic Spec. 1 a. 3 sc. Reginald Clarence. M. by T. Le Brunn. Assembly R.T., Balham, December 27, 1899.

NEW YEAR'S CHIMES. D. 4 a. A. Shirley. Bradford T.R., January 30, 1891 (C.P.).

NEW YEAR'S EVE. Duo. F. Lindo. Grosvenor Club, New Bond Street, July 12, 1894.

NEW YEAR'S LESSON. Dream. 1 a. Lauderdale Maitland. Coronet, May 24, 1906.

NEW YEAR'S MORNING. P. 1 a. A. Law. Norwich T.R., January 1, 1900.

NEW YORK DIVORCE. F. 3 a. W. Clarke. Taken fr. the French. Strand, August 19, 1895.

NEW YORK IDEA, THE. Amer. C. 4 a. Langdon Mitchell. Queen's, November 27, 1907.

NEW YORK POLITICS. F.C. J. Aikin. Brentford T.R., August 28, 1890 (C.P.).

NEWEST WOMAN, THE. M. Ca. H. C. Newton. M. by G. Jacobi. Avenue, April 4, 1895.

NEWINGTON BUTTS. F. 2 sc. J. M. Morton. St. James's, November 2, 1866.

NEWMARKET. Racing c. Lyrics by E. B. Jones. M. by Mrs. Frank Taylor. Manchester Prince's, June 22, 1896; Opera Comique, August 22, 1896.

NEWMARKET; A TALE OF THE TURF. W P. Isaacson. Holborn, October 17, 1874.

NEWMARKET; OR, THE HUMOURS OF THE TURF. C. 2 a. G. Downing. Ptd. 1763. D.L.

NEWMARKET FAYRE; OR, A PARLIAMENTARY OUTCRY OF STATE COMMODITIES SET TO SALE. T.C., Part 1. Pr. 1649.

NEWMARKET FAYRE; OR, MRS. PARLIAMENT'S NEW VAGARIES. T.C. Part II. Pr. 1649.

NEWS FROM PARNASSUS. Prel. A. Murphy. C.G., September 23, 1776. Pr. 1786.

NEWS FROM PLYMOUTH. C. Sir W. Davenant. Licensed 1635. Pr. 1673. Globe T.

NEWS FROM THE NEW WORLD DISCOVER'D IN THE MOON. Masque. Ben Jonson. Pr. 1640. Presented at Court before James I., 1620.

NEWS OUT OF THE WEST; OR, THE CHARACTER OF A MOUNTEBANK. Int. Pr. 1647.

NEWS THE MALADY. C. 3 a. W. Davies. Pr. 1786.

NEWSBOY, THE. Sk. John Jackson. Forester's M.H., May 6, 1901.

NEWSPAPER NUPTIALS. Ca. 1 a. Eille Norwood. Strand, August 10, 1901.

NEWTON FORSTER. D. 3 a. J. F. Saville. Publ. by J. Dicks.

NEXT DOOR. T.F. 3 a. Eardley Turner. Newcastle T.R., September 7, 1908.

NEXT OF KIN. C.D. 2 a. E. Falconer. Lyceum, April 9, 1860; D.L., December 26, 1862.

NEXT OF KIN. Melo-d. 4 a. R. Overton. Sanger's (1st time in London), February 28, 1887.

NEXT, PLEASE. Duo. 1 a. W. Edouin. MS. with Douglas Cox.

NEXT-DOOR NEIGHBOURS. C. Mrs. Inchbald. Haymarket, July 9, 1791. Pr. 1791. Taken fr. two Fr. plays, *Le Dissipateur* and *L'Indigent*.

NIBELUNGEN RING, THE. Tetralogy by Richard Wagner. First Part.—*Das Rheingold*. O. 2 a. Munich, 1869; H.M.T., May 5, 1882. Second Part.—*Die Walkure*. O. 3 a. Munich, 1870; H.M.T., May 6, 1882. Third Part.—*Siegfried*. O. 3 a. H.M.T., May 8, 1882. Fourth Part.—*Götterdammerung*. O. 3 a. H.M.T., May 9, 1882. Complete form Beyreuth, 1876. Incidents of the O. taken fr. the old Norse Sagas, principally from the 2 Eddas.

NICANDRA. F. 3 a. R. Vaun. Cambridge New T., June 2, 1898; Parkhurst, October 3, 1898; Avenue, April 6, 1901.

NICCOTO DI LAPI. O. Pacini. Florence, 1873.

NICE BOY, JIM. Oa. 1 a. A. E. Drinkwater. M. by Wm. S. Vinning. Bayswater Bijou, November 16, 1893.

NICE FIRM, A. Comic D 1 a. T. Taylor. Lyceum, November 16, 1853.

NICE GIRL, A. Ca. Gaiety, February 8, 1873.

NICE LADY, THE. C. G. S. Green. Pr. 1762. N. ac.

NICE QUIET CHAT. C. 1 a. M. J. W. Publ. by S. French, Limited.

NICE QUIET DAY, A. F. 1 a. H. J. Hipkins. Royalty, December 26, 1861.

NICE QUIET MORNING, A. Sk. Tivoli, February 17, 1908.

NICE VALOUR; OR, THE PASSIONATE MADMAN, THE. C. Beaumont and Fletcher. Ac. circa 1624. Pr. 1647.

NICE WANTON, THE. Int. Black letter. Pr. 1560.

NICETTE. Oa. E. Rose. M. by R. Labrocetta. Royalty, June 2, 1879.

NICHOLAS FLAM. Comic D. Buckstone.

NICHOLAS NICKLEBY. D. 3 a. A. Halliday. Dramatised version of Dickens's novel. Adelphi, November, 1838; Adelphi, March 20, 1875.

NICHOLAS NICKLEBY. D. 4 a. American version. Liverpool Amphi., August 28, 1875.

NICHOLAS NICKLEBY. Episodic Sk. Taken fr. Dickens. Strand, September 10, 1885.

NICHOLAS NICKLEBY. D. 8 tab. Rehearsal, July 4, 1909.

NICHOLAS NICKLEBY. See *The Fortunes of Smike*.

NICHOLSON'S NIECE. F.C. 3 a. Mrs. Hugh Bell. Terry's, May 30, 1892.

NICK OF THE WOODS. D. 3 a. Miss L. H. Medina. From Dr. Bird. Publ. by J. Dicks.

NICK OF TIME, THE. Guards' Burl. Sir E. Colville. Chelsea Barracks, March 23, 1896.

NICKNAMES. C. 1 a. H. C. Pemberton. Publ. by S. French, Limited.

NICODEMUS IN DESPAIR. F. Margravine of Anspach. Hay., August 31, 1803. Fr. the French. Previously ac. at the Margravine of Anspach's T. as *Poor Nony*. N.p.

NICOLETE. Rom. P. 1 a. E. Ferris and A. Stuart. Criterion, January 3, 1899.

NICOLO DE' LAPI. O. Gammieri. St. Petersburg, 1877.

NICOMEDE. Pierre Corneille. Transl. by Colton. See "French Classical Plays."

NICOMEDE. T.C. J. Dancer. Transl. fr. Corneille. Dublin T.R., and pr. 1671. The story is from Justin, Book xxxiv., last chapter.

NIGEL. R.O. 2 a. Percy Pinkerton. M. by S. P. Philpott. Birmingham Grand, January 25, 1907; Shakespeare, S.W., February 8, 1907.

NIGEL; OR, THE CROWN JEWELS. P. 5 a. C.G., January 28, 1823. Pr. 1823.

NIGHT; OR, PERILS OF THE ALPS. Pav., January 26, 1863.

NIGHT AIR, THE. P. 3 a. R. Steel. Royalty, September 24, 1904 (C.P.).

NIGHT AND DAY; OR, THE HAUNTS OF THE HUNTED DOWN. D. Pavilion, October 3, 1868.

NIGHT AND MORN. E. Falconer. D.L., January 9, 1864.

NIGHT AND MORNING. D. 1 a. D. Boucicault. F. on *La Joie fait Peur*. Manchester Prince's, September 7, 1871; Gaiety, November 19, 1871; May 4, 1872.

NIGHT AND MORNING. D. 5 a. F. Lindo Salford P.O.W., January 21, 1901; Stratford T.R., February 4, 1901.

NIGHT AT NOTTING HILL, A. Sk. E. Yates and H. Harrington. Adelphi, January 5, 1857.

NIGHT AT THE BAL MASQUE. Surrey, March 10, 1866.

NIGHT BEFORE CHRISTMAS, THE. American Domestic D. 4 a. Hal Reid. Coventry O.H., March 1, 1909; Greenwich, March 15, 1909.

NIGHT BIRDS. D. 4 a. G. L. Gordon and J. Mackay. Northampton T.R., February 24, 1881; Philharmonic, April 8, 1882.

NIGHT BIRDS OF LONDON. Melo-d. 4 a. G. England and M. Bode. New Cross Broadway, August 6, 1900.

NIGHT COMETH, THE. P. 1 a. W. E. Grogan. Ladbroke H., January 31, 1895.

NIGHT DANCERS, THE. Ro. O. G. Soane. M. by E. J. Loder. Pr. as *The Wilis; or, The Night Dancers.* Princess's, October 28, 1846; C.G., October 10, 1860.

NIGHT EXPRESS, THE. P. Prol. and 3 a. G. Holcroft. Edmonton T.R., October 10, 1890.

NIGHT GUARD; OR, THE SECRET OF THE FIVE MASKS, THE. D. C. Pitt. Britannia, September 23, 1868.

NIGHT IN ARMOUR, A. M.C.D. 4 a. W. Burnot and H. Bruce. M. by P. Wilson. Orig. prod. as *A K(Night) in Armour.* Surrey, July 5, 1897.

NIGHT IN GRANADA, A. O. Kreutzer. D.L., April 30, 1841.

NIGHT IN PARIS, A. F.C. 3 a. Adap. fr. the French. *Follies of a Night* was adap. fr. the same. Cheltenham T.R., October 3, 1889.

NIGHT IN PARIS, A. F.C. 3 a. Adap. fr. *L'Hotel du Libre-Exchange* by G. Feydeau and M. Desvallières. Newcastle T.R., April 13, 1896. Afterwards prod. at Vaudeville, April 29, 1896, as *A Night Out.*

NIGHT IN THE BASTILLE, A. P. 3 a. Archer. D.L., December 4, 1839.

NIGHT IN TOWN, A. F.C. 3 a. H. A. Sherburn. Strand (mat.), April 21, 1891; Royalty, June 28, 1894.

NIGHT IN WALES, A. V. Adap. fr. the French of Vercousen by H. Gardner. M. by Corney Grain. St. Geo. H., June 1, 1885.

NIGHT MAIL, THE. C. 1 a. H. Pierson. Keighley Queen's T., June 8, 1903.

NIGHT OF SUSPENSE, A. Monol. Strand, August 21, 1843.

NIGHT OF TERROR; A MUSICAL MADNESS IN THREE FYTTES. A. C. Wyndham and A. Matthison. Folly, December 22, 1877.

NIGHT OF THE PARTY, THE. F.C. 3 a. W. Grossmith. Southend Empire, April 1, 1901; Brixton T., April 8, 1901; Avenue, May 1, 1901; Apollo, December 23, 1907.

NIGHT OFF; OR, A PAGE FROM BALZAC, A. Ecc. C. 4 a. Aug. Daly. F. on Franz von Schonthau's *Der Raub der Sabinerinnen.* Prod. in America. Strand, May 27, 1886.

NIGHT ON SNOWDON, A. F. 1 a. Herbert Gardner.

NIGHT OUT, A. F.C. 3 a. C. Klein. Rev. by S. Hicks. Adap. fr. *Hôtel du Libre Echange* of Georges Feydeau and Maurice Desvallières. Newcastle-on-Tyne T.R., (as *A Night in Paris*), April 13, 1896; Vaudeville, April 29, 1896; rev. Cri., July 30, 1907.

NIGHT OUT, A. C.F. Manville Morton. Greenwich, Morton's T., November 27, 1905.

NIGHT OWLS, THE. Sk. Pr. by Wm. Lee. Tivoli, December 3, 1906.

NIGHT PATROL, THE. F. 2 a. D.L., October 1, 1835.

NIGHT SESSION, A. F. Adap. fr. the French of G. Feydeau. Globe, November 1, 1897.

NIGHT WALKER; OR, THE LITTLE THIEF, THE. C. J. Fletcher (Beaumont and Fletcher), possibly assisted by Shirley. D.L., after August, 1625. Pr. 1640. Ac. at Court, 1634. See *Isabella*, etc.

NIGHT WATCH, THE. P.D. R. Buchanan. Southend Empire, April 8, 1902.

NIGHT WITH THE STARS, A. Up-to-date M.C. "Hotch Potch" by Max Goldberg. Scala, February 11, 1907.

NIGHT'S ADVENTURE, A. D. T. W. Robertson. Olympic, 1851.

NIGHT'S FROLIC, A. F. C. 3 a. G. Thomas and Helen Barry. Adap. fr. the German. Prod. in America. Strand, June 1, 1891.

NIGHT'S INTRIGUE, A. F. Anon. Pr. (n.d.) since 1700. Probably *The Evening's Intrigue*, by Captain Stevens.

NIGHT'S SURPRISE, A. West Cromer and German Reed. St. Geo. H., circa 1865.

NIGHTINGALE, THE. D. 5 a. T. W. Robertson. Adelphi, January 15, 1870.

NIGHTINGALE, THE. D. 5 a. M. Melford. Edinburgh Lyceum, July 10, 1884; Standard, August 25, 1884.

NIGHTINGALE, THE. P. 4 a. H. A. Vachell and H. Wyndham. Adap. fr. Mr. Vachell's *The Shadowy Third.* Imperial, April 25, 1902.

NIGHTINGALE, THE. See *In the Moonlight.*

NIGHTINGALE'S WOOING. Extrav. A. Rushton and F. Arlon. Philharmonic, April 10, 1871.

NIGHTMARE. P. 1 a. Miss Keating. Publ. by S. French, Ltd.

NIGHTSHADE. D. 3 a. K. E. Hall. Coatbridge Prince's, July 12, 1873.

NIGRAMANSIR, THE. Int. Skelton. Pl. before the King (Henry VII.) at Woodstoke on Palm Sunday. Pr. 1504.

NIHILIST, THE. D. 4 a. E. J. Towers. Abertillery The Castle, February 25, 1897.

NIHILIST QUEEN; MASTER OF THE CHAIN, THE. D. 4 a. J. Sargent and J. W. Carson. (Orig. prod. under second title at Greenwich Morton's, December 17, 1900; Balham Duchess, August 25, 1902.

NIJE-NOVGORODIANS, THE. O. 4 a. St. Petersburg, 1868; rev. 1888.

NIMBLE SHILLING, THE. D. J. Levey. Elephant and C., June 11, 1877.

NINA. Op. piece. C.G., April 24, 1787. Ascr. by some to Peter Pindar (Dr. Wolcot). A transl. N.p.

NINA. O. D'Alayrac. (1753-1809.)

NINA; OR, THE LOVE-DISTRACTED MAID. C. 1 a. Pr. 1787. N.ac.

NINA; OR, THE MADNESS OF LOVE. C. 2 a. Transl. fr. the French by G. M. Berkeley. Pr. 1787. N.ac.

NINA, O LA PAZZA PER AMORE. O. Paisiello. Naples, 1787.

NINA; OR, THE STORY OF A HEART. P. 5 a. Mrs. Kennion. Taken fr. *La Dame aux Camélias* and E. Zola's *Nana.* Wigan T.R., April 13, 1885; Strand, July 13, 1887.

NINA SFORZA. T. Z. Troughton. Hay.

NINE DAIES' WONDER. Perf. in a daunce fr. London to Norwich. Wm. Kempe. Blackletter pr. 1600.

NINE DAYS' QUEEN, THE. Rom. poetical D. 4 a. R. Buchanan. Gaiety, December 22, 1880.

NINE DAYS' WONDER, A. C.D. 3 ar. H. Aidé. Court, June 12, 1875.

NINE POINTS OF THE LAW. Ca. 1 a. T. Taylor. F. on Savage's story, *Clover Cottage*. Olympic, April 11, 1859.

1920. Sk. Brien McCulloch. Surrey, June 28, 1909.

1934; OR, A HUNDRED YEARS HENCE. F. Queen's, 1834.

1990. Oa. 1 a. B. Arthur. M. by A. Roby. Islington Myddelton H., October 16, 1895.

NINETEENTH CENTURY, THE. D. Morell and F. Mouillot. Chester Royalty, May 12, 1894 (C.P.).

NINETEENTH CENTURY, THE. M. Duol. P. A. Rubens. St. James's, December 3, 1900.

NINETTA. O. Pugno. Paris, 1882.

NINETTA. See *La Gazza Ladra*.

NINETTE A LA COUR. Op. C. Favart. French lib. Duni, Paris, 1755.

'98; OR, FAUGH A BALLAGH. Irish D. F. Cooke. Rochdale P.O.W., July 13, 1874.

NINETY-NINE. P. 5 a. D. Boucicault. Standard, October 5, 1891.

NINEVAH'S REPENTANCE. Mentioned in catalogue annexed to *The Careless Shepherdess*, 1656.

NINICHE. C. 3 a. Hennequin and Milland. (Ac. in French.) Gaiety, June 6, 1883.

NINO. See *Nabucadonosor*.

NINON. D. 4 a. W. G. Wills. Adelphi. February 7, 1880.

NINTH STATUE; OR, THE IRISHMAN IN BAGDAD, THE. M.Rom. 2 a. Fr. *The Arabian Nights*. D.L., November 29, 1814.

NINTH WALTZ, THE. Duol. R. C. Carton. Garrick, December 11, 1900.

NINUS AND SEMIRAMIS, THE TRAGEDIE OF. Ent. Stationers' Co., May 10. 1595, by John Hardye. N.p.

NIOBE. C. 3 a. H. and E. Paulton. Originally played in America. Liverpool P.O.W., September 1, 1890; Strand, April 11, 1892; and rev. November 14, 1895.

NIOBE; OR, HARLEQUIN'S ORDEAL. Panto. J. C. Cross. Ac. 1797.

NIPPED IN THE BUD. Ca. W. C. Sullivan. Birmingham P.O.W., March 15, 1883.

NIPPED IN THE BUD. Mus.F. J. Hewson and V. Champion. Brighton Aquarium, November 28, 1892.

NITA THE DANCER. D. 1 a. Weller and Raphael. Publ. by S. French, Ltd.

NITA'S FIRST. F.C. 3 a. T. G. Warren. Oxford T.R., December 14, 1883; Novelty, March 4, 1884, and March 31, 1888.

NITOCRIS. Egyptian P. E. Fitzball. In 6 tableaux. D.L., October 8, 1855.

NITOCRIS. P. 5 a. Miss Clo Graves. D.L., November 2, 1887.

NITOUCHE. M.C. 3 a. Adap. fr. the French *Mlle. Nitouche* of H. Meilhac, A. Millaud, and Hervé. Op. C., May 12, 1884; Court, June 1, 1896.

NIXIE. P. 3 a. Mrs. Hodgson Burnett and S. Townsend. Suggested by *Editha's Burglar*. Terry's, April 7, 1890.

NO!!! Oa. 1 a. D.L., October 29, 1829.

NO. O. F. G. Pentreath. M. by McLean. Kennington Horns Concert R., January 25, 1881.

NO ACTRESS. F. H. Bartlett. Surrey, June 6, 1898.

NO APPEAL. C.D. 4 a. W. T. Craven. Brighton Eden, December 6, 1897.

NO ASSETS. Ca. St. Albans County H., May 17, 1898.

NO CARDS. F. J. Oxenford. Adelphi, November 30, 1872.

NO CARDS. W. S. Gilbert. Gallery of Illus., March 29, 1869; rev. St. George's H., March 29, 1902.

NO CATS. F. sk. Gilbert Wells. Camberwell Empire, April 13, 1908.

NO CORONET. C. 3 a. H. Hamilton. Sheffield T.R., September 5, 1883.

NO CREDIT. Ca. Miss Emily Coffin. Strand, April 11, 1892.

NO CROSS, NO CROWN. D. 4 a. B. Williams and H. Sorrell. Sheffield, Attercliffe, People's T., July 26, 1897; Peckham Crown T., June 11, 1900.

NO CURE, NO PAY; OR, THE PHARMACOPOLIST. M.F. H. Rowe. Pr. at York, 1794.

NO ESCAPE. D. R. C. Davies. Preston T.R., July 2, 1888.

NO EVIDENCE. D. G. L. Gordon. Belfast T.R., January 15, 1886.

NO FARCE. 1 a. Publ. by S. French, Ltd.

NO FOOLS LIKE WITS; OR, THE FEMALE VERTUOSOES. C. J. Gay. A republication of Wright's *Female Virtuosoes*, taken fr. the *Femmes Sçavantes* of Molière. See *The Refusal*. L.I.F., 1720. Pr. 1721.

NO GREATER LOVE. P. 1a. M. Lang. Inverness T.R., June 9, 1902.

NO IRISH NEED APPLY. Strand, February 19, 1854.

NO' JUSTICE Harry Bruce.

NO MAN'S LAND. D. 5 a. J. Douglass. Leicester T.R., November 21, 1890; Grand, April 3, 1893; Collins's M.H., January 20, 1902.

NO MATTER WHAT. F. D.L., 1758. N.p.

NO MERCY. D. 5 a. M. Melford. Dundee T.R., August 31, 1883; Eleph. and C., May 18, 1885.

NO NAME. D. 4 a. W. Reeve. Newcastle-on-Tyne T.R., October 26, 1877.

NO ONE'S ENEMY BUT HIS OWN. C. Murphy. C.G. Pr. 1764. F. on Voltaire's *L'Indiscret*.

NO OTHER WAY. Dr. Epis. Shrewsbury T.R., March 18, 1907.

NO PAIN, NO GAIN. D. 4 a. R. F. Cantor, *The History of the General Deluge*.

NO PLOT WITHOUT DANGER. C.O. M. by Mercadante. F. on the O. of *Eliza and Claudio*. Lyceum, September 5, 1835.

NO PRELUDE. Dial. Colman, Jun. 1803. N.p.

NO QUARTER. Military C. R. Overton. Brentwood Drill H., March 3, 1900 (C.P.).

NO ROSE WITHOUT A THORN. M.Ca. M. Melford. Nottingham T.R., August 2, 1886.

NO SONG, NO SUPPER. M.F. 2 a. P. Hoare. M. by Storace. D.L., April 16, 1790; Lyceum, October 19, 1809; D.L., June 14, 1817; Manchester T.R., July 11, 1870. Songs only. Pr. 1790.

NO SURRENDER. Dr. sk. John Henderson. Poplar Queen's, January 28, 1907.

NO THOROUGHFARE. D. C. Dickens and W. Collins. Fr. story of same name. Adelphi, December 26, 1867; Standard, June 27, 1868.

NO THOROUGHFARE. Burl. G. Grossmith. Victoria, March 22, 1869.

NO THOROUGHFARE; OR, THE STORY OF A FOUNDLING. P. Prol. and 4 a. O. Brand. Taken fr. Dickens and Collins. Islington Grand, May 11, 1903.

NO THOROUGH-FAIR BEYOND HIGHBURY; OR, THE MAID, THE MOTHER, AND THE MALICIOUS MOUNTAINEER. Burl. Hazlewood, jun. Alexandra, April 13, 1868.

NO WEDDING BELLS FOR HER. P. of London and Japan, by Frank Bateman and John Douglass. Cardiff King's, December 26, 1905.

NO WIT LIKE A WOMAN'S. F. Fr. Molière's *George Dandin*. D.L., 1769. N.p.

NO WIT, NO HELP LIKE A WOMAN'S. C. T. Middleton. Ac. 1638. Pr. 1657. See *Counterfeit Bridegroom*.

NOAH'S ARK. C. 3 a. H. Paulton. Bath T.R., May 30, 1885; Royalty, October 27, 1886.

NOAH'S ARK. F.P. 2 a. P. French and B. Stuart. M. by Houston Collison and J. St. A. Johnson. Waldorf, January 1, 1906.

NOAH'S ARK. M. Extrav. 2 a. Wds. and M. by Clare Kummer. Bayswater Bijou, April 22, 1907.

NOAH'S FLOOD. Geo. Bayley. License for this play granted in 1662.

NOAH'S FLOOD; OR, THE DESTRUCTION OF THE WORLD. O. E. Eccleston. Pr. 1679. Afterwards pub. under different titles, viz.:—1685, *The Cataclysm; or, General Deluge of the World*. 1691, *The Deluge; or, The Destruction of the World*. 1714, *Noah's Flood*. See *Miracle Plays*.

NOBLE ART, THE. F.P. 3 a. E. Norwood. York T.R., April 11, 1892; Terry's, May 25, 1892.

NOBLE ATONEMENT, A. D. 4 a. Ina Leon Cassilis. Op. Comique, January 21, 1892.

NOBLE BONDMAN, THE. T. Philip Massinger. Cockpit D.L., December 3, 1623. Pr. under the title of *The Bondman*.

NOBLE BROTHER, A. M.C.D. 4 a. W. J. Summers. Orig. prod. in America. Liverpool Shakespeare, October 28, 1889; Op. Comique, February 3, 1890.

NOBLE CHOICE; OR, THE ORATOR, THE. T.C. P. Massinger. Ent. Stationers' Co., September 9, 1653. N.p. Destroyed by Warburton's servant.

NOBLE COWARD, A. D. 4 a. T. Naden. Grimsby T.R., February 23, 1891.

NOBLE DEED, A. Sk. 4 scenes. Oxford Music Hall, November 6, 1899.

NOBLE FALSEHOOD, A. P. 1 a. E. Drew. St. Geo. H., June 2, 1894.

NOBLE FORESTERS; OR, HUMAN LIFE REFLECTED, THE. Int. Adam Smith. Taken fr. *As You Like It*. Pr. 1776.

NOBLE GENTLEMAN, THE. C. Beaumont and Fletcher. Pr. 1647. Ac. 1626. Rev., with little alt., by Durfey under the title of *The Fool's Preferment*.

NOBLE HEART, THE. T. 5 a. G. H. Lewes. Olympic, February, 1850.

NOBLE INGRATITUDE, THE. Past. T.C. Sir W. Lower. Circa 1656. Pr. 1659. Transl. fr. the French of Quinault.

NOBLE LIE, A. P. 4 a. F. Jarman. Jersey T.R., July 23, 1890.

NOBLE LIE, THE. C. 1 a. Transl. fr. the German of Kotzebue. Anon. Pr. 1799. N. ac. A sequel to *The Stranger*.

NOBLE LIE, THE. D. 1 a. Transl. fr. Kotze by Maria Geisweiler. Pr. 1799. N.ac.

NOBLE LORD, THE. F.C. 3 a. R. Marshall. Criterion, October 18, 1900.

NOBLE LOVE. D. 4 a. C. A. Clarke and J. J. Hewson. Goole T.R., January 27, 1890; Eleph. and C., July 20, 1891.

NOBLE PEASANT, THE. C.O. T. Holcroft. Hay., August 2, 1784. Pr. 1784. Probably suggested by *As You Like It*. Afterwards abridged.

NOBLE PEDLAR, THE. Burl. 2 a. G. S. Carey. Ac. at Marylebone Gardens and at D.L., May 13, 1771. Pr. 1770.

NOBLE RAVISHERS, THE. P. Ent. Stationers' Co., November 29, 1653. N.p.

NOBLE REVENGE, A. P. 1 a. Albert Ward. Croydon T.R., December 10, 1904.

NOBLE SAVAGE, THE. Oa. 1 a. Mr. and Mrs. F. Corder. Brighton R. Aquarium, October 3, 1885; Standard, April 30, 1887.

NOBLE SLAVES, THE. Mentioned in Oulton's list.

NOBLE SOLDIER; OR, A CONTRACT BROKEN JUSTLY REVENGED, THE. T. S. Rowley. Pr. 1634. Ac. The running title is *The Noble Spanish Soldier*, and Nicholas Vavasour, the publisher, on December 9, 1633, entered it under that title as written by Thos. Dekker. See *The Spanish Soldier*.

NOBLE SPANIARD, THE. Victorian F. 3 ac. W. Somerset Maugham. Adap. fr. the Fr. of Grenet-Dancourt. Royalty, March 20, 1909.

NOBLE SPANISH, THE. See *The Noble Soldier*.

NOBLE STRANGER, THE. C. L. Sharpe. Ac. at private house in Salisbury Court. Pr. 1640.

NOBLE TRYAL, THE. T.C. H. Glapthorne. Ent. Stationers' Co., June 29, 1660. N.p. Destroyed by Warburton's servant.

NOBLE VAGABOND, THE. Rom. D. 4 a. H. A. Jones. Princess's, December 22, 1886.

NOBLEMAN, THE. T.C. C. Tournier. En. Stationers' Co., February 15, 1611. N.p. Destroyed by Warburton's servant.

NOBLEMAN, THE. C. Eliz. Cooper. Hay., May, 1730. N.p.

NOBLEMAN OF NATURE, A. D. 4 a. Whitmore Ledger. Ferndale Tudor, July 4, 1907.

NOBLESSE OBLIGE. C.D. Prol. and 3 a. Mrs. Augustus Bright. Exeter T.R., October 4, 1878.

NOBLY WON. D. C. Bradley. Cheltenham T.R., June 22, 1885.

NOBODY. C. 2 a. Mrs. Robinson. D.L., November 29, 1794. N.p.

NOBODY AND SOMEBODY. C. Trundell. 1606.

NOBODY AND SOMEBODY, WITH THE TRUE CHRONICAL HISTORIE OF ELYDURE, WHO WAS FORTUNATELY THREE SEVERAL TIMES CROWNED KINGE OF ENGLAND. Ac. by the Queen's servants. Pr. N.d. Not divided into acts.

NOBODY IN LONDON. Panto Eccentricity. E. L. Blanchard. D.L., September 20, 1873.

NOBODY'S CHILD. Ro. D. 3 a. Watts Phillips. Surrey, September 14, 1867. Princess's, 1868.

NOBODY'S CHILD. Burl. H. T. Arden. Cremorne, August 10, 1868.

NOBODY'S CLAIM. D. 5 a. E. A. Lock. Prod. in America. Greenock T.R., July 31, 1886.

NOBODY'S FAULT. V. A. Law. M. by H. Clarke. St. Geo. H., June 5, 1882.

NOBODY'S FORTUNE. D. 3 a. H. P. Grattan. Surrey, February 5, 1872.

NOBODY'S SON. Effingham. February 12, 1866.

NOCES DE GAMACHE. O. Mendelssohn. 1827.

NOCES D'OLIVETTE, LES. O. E. Audran. Paris Bouffes, November 13, 1879. Ac. in Eng. as *Olivette*.

NOCES DE VENUS, LES. O. A. Campora. (His last O.) 1740.

NOCTURNE. P. 1 a. By Anthony P. Wharton. Kingsway, May 19, 1908.

NOEL AINSLIE, V.C. P. 1 a. W. E. Grogan and N. V. Norman. Ladbroke H., February 26, 1897.

NOEMI. D. 2 a. W. Robertson. Transl. fr. the French of Dennery and Clement. Theatre du Gymnase, October 31, 1845; Princess's (under the title of *Ernestine*), April 14, 1846.

NOMINATION DAY; OR, THE ELECTION AT ROTTENBURGH, THE. Greenwich T.R., February 28, 1873.

NOMISSES; OR, IT'S TWO TO ONE. F. Liverpool T.R., August 25, 1873.

NONDESCRIPT. M.F. Devis, 1813.

NON-JUROR, THE. C. C. Cibber. Taken fr. Molière's *Tartuffe*, a transl. of which, called *The English Puritan*, was ac. in Charles II.'s reign. D.L., December 6, 1717. Pr. 1718.

NON-SUITED. F. W. C. Rhodes. Tooting Vestry H., April 7, 1891.

NONE BUT THE BRAVE. D. 5 a. S. Vane and A. Shirley. Brighton T.R., August 12, 1898 (C.P.); Peckham Crown T., April 2, 1900.

NONE SO BLIND AS THOSE WHO WON'T SEE. M.F. C. Dibdin. Hay., 1782. N.p. A close imitation *L'Avengle Prétendu*.

NONESUCH, THE. C. Wm. Rowley. En. Stationers' Co., June 29, 1660. Destroyed by Warburton's servant.

NONNE SANGLANTE, LA. O. 5 a. Wds. by Scribe and Delavigne. Fd. on Lewis's legend, "Monk." M. by Gounod. Paris, October 18, 1854.

NONPAREILLES; OR, THE MATCHLESS MAIDS, THE. See *Love and Honour*.

NOODLEHAM. Burl. E. Marshall. Lecture H., Carter Street, Walworth, January 10, 1877.

NOOTKA SOUND; OR, BRITAIN PREPARED. F. C.G., June 7, 1790.

NORA. P. Miss Frances Lord. Adap. fr. Ibsen's *Elt Dukkehjem*. Sch. of Dr. Art. Argyle Street, March 25, 1885.

NORA. P. Adap. fr. H. Ibsen's German version, *Doll's House*. St. Geo. H., October 5, 1900.

NORAH. C. 1 a. R. Henry. Grand, October 30, 1897.

NORAH. See *Breaking a Butterfly*.

NORAH O'NEAL. Irish D. W. Travers. East London, December 22, 1876.

NORAH'S VOWS. Irish D. 4 a. D. Boucicault. Brighton T.R., July 6, 1878.

NORDISA. Rom. O. 3 a. M. by Fredk. Corder. Lib. f. on French D. *La Bergère des Alpes*. Liverpool Royal Court, January 26, 1887; D.L., May 4, 1887.

NORMA. O. 2 a. Wds. by Romani. M. by Bellini. Milan, December 26, 1831. Paris, December 8, 1835. In Ital. at King's T., June 20, 1833. In Eng., D.L., June 24, 1837.

NORMA. Tragic O. 2 a. Fr. the Italian. J. R. Planché. C.G.; Lyceum.

NORMA. Burl. Gilbert. Charing Cr., June 19. 1869.

NORMA. T. Colonel A. B. Richards. Belfast T.R., February 5, 1875.

NORMA. Burl. J. H. Draper. Jersey Royal H., March 5, 1875.

NORMA, TRAVESTIE. Burla. 1 a. W. H. Oxberry. Adelphi, December 6, 1841.

NORMAN INVASION, THE. Burl. J. M. Killick. St. Geo. H., October 26, 1870 (amat.).

NORMANDELLE. C.O. 2 a. P. Cole. Bayswater Bijou, June 21, 1904.

NORMANDY PIPPINS. M. Extrav. H. J. Byron. Criterion, April 18, 1874.

NORTH AND SOUTH. Dr. Sk. H. Forrest. Newcastle Tyne T., September 24, 1877.

NORTH AND SOUTH. F. F. H. Francks. Ladbroke H., July 28, 1888.

NORTH POLE, THE. D. Victoria, 1868.

NORTH POLE, THE. Illusion Sk. David Devant. St. Geo. H., September 15, 1909.

NORTHERN CASTLE, THE. P. Ment. in Pepys's Diary, September, 1667.

NORTHERN ELECTION; OR, NEST OF BEASTS, THE. D. 6 a. Pr. 1749. N.ac.

NORTHERN HEIRESS; OR, THE HUMOURS OF YORK, THE. C. Mrs. Mary Davys. L.I.F. Pr. 1716 and 1725.

NORTHERN HEROES; OR, THE BLOODY CONQUEST BETWEEN CHARLES THE TWELFTH, KING OF SWEDEN, AND PETER THE GREAT, CZAR OF MUSCOVY, THE. With a C. Int. called THE VOLUNTEERS; OR, THE ADVENTURES OF RODERICK RANDOM AND HIS FRIEND STRAP. Ac. at Bartholomew Fair. Pr. 1748.

NORTHERN INN; OR, THE GOOD TIMES OF QUEEN BESS, THE. F. Alt. by S. Kemble fr. Heywood's *Fair Maid of the West*. Hay., August, 1791. N.p.

NORTHERN LASS, THE; OR, A NEST OF FOOLS. C. R. Brome. Globe and Blackfriars. Pr. 1632. Revived and repr. 1684, with M. by Purcell. Repr. in 1706.

NORTHERN ROMANCE, A. P. 4a. Cicely Wroughton, Creaton, April 20, 1906 (amat.); Comedy, February 5, 1907.

NORTHUMBERLAND. T. M. A. Meilan. On the same story as Rowe's *Lady Jane Gray*. Pr. N.d. N.ac.

NORTHWARD HOE. C. T. Dekker and J. Webster. Ac. by the children of St. Paul's. Pr. 1607.

NORWICH MERCHANT; OR, THE HAPPY RECONCILIATION, THE. F. Pr. at Norwich.

NORWOOD GYPSIES, THE. Panto. M. by J. A. Fisher. C.G., 1777. N.p.

NOS INTIMES. Sardou. Engl. ver. Prod. at Olympic, May, 1872. See *Peril*.

NOSEGAY OF WEEDS; OR, OLD SERVANTS IN NEW PLACES, A. F. J. O'Keeffe. D.L., June 6, 1798. N.p.

NOT A BAD JUDGE. C.D. 2 a. J. R. Planché. Lyceum, March 2, 1848; D.L., February 25, 1856; Royalty, July 23, 1894.

NOT A WORD. F.C. 3 a. O. Dove. Adap. fr. Civot and Duru's *Le Carnaval d'un Merle Blanc*. Avenue, April 28, 1884.

NOT A WORD TO THE WIFE. Sk. Camberwell Empire, November 11, 1907.

NOT ALL SMOKE. Ca. 1 a. B. M'Donald. Bayswater Bijou, May 12, 1898.

NOT ALONE. D. 5 a. G. Lander and Mrs. Weldon. Birmingham Grand (prod. as the sole work of Geo. Lander), October 12, 1885; Grand, October 19, 1885.

NOT AT ALL JEALOUS. F. 1 a. T. W. Robertson. Court, May 29, 1871.

NOT AT HOME. Dr. Ent. R. C. Dallas. Lyceum (by the D.L. Co.), November, 1809. Pr. 1809.

NOT AT HOME. Oa. 1 a. H. Aidé. M. by A. S. Gatty. Grosvenor H., June 1, 1886.

NOT DEAD; OR, SAVED FROM THE SEA. D. A. Rousby. Bolton T.R., March 16, 1874.

NOT FALSE, BUT FICKLE. C.D. 1 a. Mrs. Augustus Bright. Sheffield Alexandra, March 22. 1878; Philharmonic, March 10, 1880.

NOT FOR ME; OR, THE NEW APPLE OF DISCORD. Ballad O. 2 a. Fr. the French. M. by L. Maurer. Lyceum, August 23, 1828.

NOT FOUND. D. 3 a. E. Towers. East London, February 7, 1870.

NOT GUILTY. C. Gilbert à Beckett. Adap. fr. the French. Manchester Prince's, December 9, 1867.

NOT GUILTY. D. 4 a. Watts Phillips. Queen's, February 13, 1869.

NOT GUILTY; OR, WRONG MADE RIGHT. D. Warrington P.O.W., May 18, 1875.

NOT IF I KNOW IT. F. Extrav. 1 a. H. J. Byron. Hay., June 17, 1871.

NOT IN SOCIETY. P. 1 a. R. Henry. Bayswater Bijou, December 2, 1899.

NOT IN VAIN. D. P. Meritt. Grecian, October 5, 1871.

NOT PEACE, BUT A SWORD. D. 4 a. Bishop Auckland Eden T., June 4, 1900.

NOT PROVEN C.D. 3 a. H. Pettitt. Leeds T.R., March 15, 1880.

NOT REGISTERED. Dom.D. 2 a. A. Matthison. Royalty, April 10, 1882.

NOT SO BAD AFTER ALL. C. 3 a. W. Reeve. Charing Cross, January 8, 1870.

NOT SO BAD AS WE SEEM; OR, MANY SIDES TO A CHARACTER. P. Lord Lytton. Wr. for some distinguished amat. perf. at Picture Gallery of Devonshire House, May 14, 1851. Hay., February 12, 1853.

NOT SO MAD AS HE LOOKS. F. M. De Frece. Liverpool T.R., May 20, 1872.

NOT SUCH A FOOL AS HE LOOKS. C. 3 a. H. J. Byron. Manchester T.R., December 4, 1868; Globe, October 23, 1869; Adelphi, February, 1870.

NOT TO BE DONE. F. 1 a. H. T. Craven. Publ. by S. French, Ltd.

NOT WHOLLY BAD. P. 1 a. W. E. Grogan. Torquay Public Hall, April 13, 1893; Bayswater Bijou, March 2, 1894.

NOT WISELY, BUT TOO WELL. P. 4 a. Walter Frith. Glasgow Royalty, April 1, 1898; Fulham Grand, April 25, 1898.

NOT YET. D. M. Ouseley. Croydon T.R., March 19, 1886.

NOTA-BENE. F. D.L., December 12, 1816.

NOTAIRE OBLIGEANT. C. By Dancourt. 1650.

NOTE OF HAND, THE. P. 1 a. H. Keith. Vaudeville, January 13, 1891.

NOTE OF HAND; OR, TRIP TO NEWMARKET, THE. F. R. Cumberland. D.L. Pr. 1774.

NOTE-FORGER, THE. Melo-d. 2 a. E. Fitzball. D.L., April 21, 1835; C.G.

NOTES AND GOLD. D. 4 a. A. F. Robbins. Bradford Pullan's T., August 31, 1885.

NOTHING IMPOSSIBLE TO LOVE. T.C. Ent. Stationers' Co. June 29, 1660, and ascr. to Sir Robert Le Greece (Le Grys). Destroyed by Warburton's servant.

NOTHING TO NURSE. F. 1 a. C. M. Walcot. First prod. in America September, 1857.

NOTHING VENTURE, NOTHING WIN. C.D. 2 a. J. S. Coyne. Strand, April 5, 1858.

NOTICE TO QUIT; OR, IN THE CLUTCH OF THE LAW. D. 3 a. G. Conquest and H. Pettitt. Grecian, April 20, 1878.

NOTORIETY. C. 5 a. F. Reynolds. C.G., 1792. Pr. 1793

NOTORIETY CLAUSE, THE. Sk. Cosmo Hamilton. Palace Music Hall, April 9, 1900.

NOTORIOUS MRS. EBBSMITH, THE. P. 4 a. A. W. Pinero. Garrick, March 13, 1895; Royalty, February 27, 1901.

NOTRE DAME; OR, THE GIPSY GIRL OF PARIS. D. 3 a. F. on Victor Hugo's novel. A. Halliday. Adelphi, April 10, 1871.

NOTRE EDOUARD. P. 1 a., in French. By Constance Meredyth. Criterion, December 18, 1908.

NOTRE JEUNESSE. C. 4 a. A. Capus. Shaftesbury, June 9, 1905.

NOTTINGHAM CASTLE. Burl. F. R. Goodyer. Nottingham T.R., September 22, 1873.

NOTTOLA. Lat. C. 5 a. MS. of the 17th century.

NOUGHTOLOGY; OR, NOTHING. S.C.D. 4 a. F. Stanford. St. Geo. H., November 5, 1880.

NOURJAD. Dr. Piece. 3 a. Margravine of Anspach. Ac. at Brandenburgh House, 1803. N.p.

NOURJAHAD. O. M. by E. J. Loder. F. on Sheridan's Persian tale. Lyceum, July 21, 1834.

NOURMAHAL, EMPRESS OF HINDOSTAN. Melo-d. 2 a. J. Moser. Pr. in the "European Magazine," 1808. N. ac.

NOUVEAU SEIGNEUR DU VILLAGE. O. Boieldieu. 1813.

NOUVELLE ECOLE DES FEMMES, LA. C.O. 2 a. F. A. D. Philidor. 1770.

NOVEL EXPEDIENT, A. Ca. 1 a. (By permission of B. Webster). D.L., February 1, 1858.

NOVEL EXPEDIENT, THE. See *Book the Third, Chapter the First.*

NOVEL READER, A. See *May and December.*

NOVEL READER, THE. C. 3 a. J. Mackay and S. Grundy. Adap. fr. Meilhac and Halévy's *La Petite Marquise.* Globe, August 28, 1882.

NOVELLA. C. R. Brome. Ac. at Blackfriars, 1632. Pr. 1653.

NOVELTY; OR EVERY ACT A PLAY, THE. P. Motteux. L.I.F., 1697. Pr. same year. After the fashion of Davenant's *Playhouse to be Let.* It consists of five distinct pieces, as:— 1. A Past. *Thyrsis*, by Oldmixon. 2. C. *All Without Money*, by Motteux. 3. Masque. *Hercules*, by Motteux. 4. T. *The Unfortunate Couple*, being the latter part of Dr. Filmer's *Unnatural Brother.* 5. F. *Natural Magic.* An imitation of a French C.

NOVELTY FAIR; OR, HINTS FOR 1851. A Revue. By the authors of "Valentine and Orson." Lyceum, May 21, 1850.

NOVICE, THE. 1837.

NOVICE, THE. P. Lady Townsend. Maidenhead Town H., February 22, 1909.

NOW ON! Sk. 2 sc. Harry Leighton and Gilbert Wells. Brixton Empress, February 24, 1908.

NOW OR NEVER! F. 1 a. D.L., January 15, 1839.

NOW-A-DAYS. C. 3 a. W. Craven. Croydon T.R., March 2, 1882.

NOW-A-DAYS; A TALE OF THE TURF. D. 4 a. W. Barrett. Princess's, February 28, 1889.

NOW'S YOUR TIME, TAYLORS! C. Sk. Announced for perf. at C.G., 1794, but withdrawn before perf.

NOYADES; OR, LOVE AND GRATITUDE, THE. Hist. Anecdote. 2 a. Peake. M. by Moss. Lyceum, July 14, 1828.

NOZZE DI FIGARO, LE. C.O. 4 a. Lib. by L. da Ponte. M. by Mozart. Vienna, April 29, 1786. Paris (in 5 a.), March 20, 1793. In Ital., at King's T., June 18, 1812. Alt. by Sir H. Bishop, Her M., 1817.

NOZZE DI TELEMACO ED ANTIOPE, LE. O. Mercadante. Vienna, 1824.

NUIT BLANCHE, UNE. Op. bo. 1 a. Offenbach, 1855.

NUIT DE NOEL, LA. O. 3 a. Reber, February 9, 1848.

NUITS DER HAMPTON CLUB, LES. D. 3 tabl. Movezy and Armont. Adap. fr. novel by R. L. Stevenson. Shaftesbury, March 21, 1908.

NUITS TERRIBLES. Op.C. St. George's, 1821.

NUMBER ONE ROUND THE CORNER. F. 1 a. W. Brough. Lyceum, March 12, 1854.

NUMBER TWO. F.C. 3 a. H. C. Hiller. Vaudeville, March 24, 1890.

NUMBER TWO. Sk. 1 a. Geo. Bellamy and Sydney Blow. Palace, January 25, 1909.

NUMBER SIX, DUKE STREET. F. M. Becher. D.L., September 23, 1871.

NO. 9. Sk. Shepherd's Bush Empire, May 22, 1909.

NO. 12. Ca. J. Français. Novelty, July 31, 1886.

NO. 17. C. 1 a. Agnes Leigh.

NUMBER TWENTY; OR, THE BASTILLE OF CALVADOS. D. 4 a. J. Hatton and J. Albery. Princess's, November 30, 1878.

NUMBER FORTY-NINE. St. James's, March 5, 1860.

NO. 50: A TALE OF THE COMMUNE. D. 1 a. F. A. Marshall. Glasgow Gaiety, September 21, 1876.

NUMBER FIFTY-ONE; OR. CIRCUMSTANTIAL EVIDENCE. D. 4 a. E. R. Callender. Liverpool, August 30, 1880.

NO. 72. Ca. W. J. Patmore. Bath T.R., December 11, 1893.

NUMBER 90. Dr. Sk. Fred Kitchen and Frank Lister. Granville M.H., January 14, 1907.

NUMBER NINETY-NINE; OR, THE DIAMOND NECKLACE. F. Glasgow Gaiety, March 16, 1882.

NO. 204. An Ent. F. C. Burnand and German Reed. St. George's H.,

NO. 442—HIS ESCAPE. O. 1 a. Rutland Barrington. M. by H. M. Higgs. Coronet, July 15, 1907.

NUMBER NIP. Extrav. S. Brooks and M. Lemon. Adelphi, December, 1853.

NUMBER NIP; OR, THE ELFIN KING OF THE GIANT MOUNTAINS. T.S. by J. C. Cross. Pr. 1803.

NUMP'S COURTSHIP; OR, LOVE MAKES A PAINTER. D.P. Hay., 1758. N.p.

NUN; OR, THE FAIR VOW-BREAKER, THE. See *Isabella*, etc.

NUN AND THE BARBARIAN, THE. Adap. fr. Spanish play *La Loca de la Coas* of Galdo; transl. by Osmond Shillingford. Margate T.R., November 26, 1906.

NUNKEY. F.C. 3 a. A. A. Wilmot. Shepherd's Bush Athenæum, April 4, 1892.

NUNNERY, THE. C. O. W. Pearce. C.G., April 12, 1785. Songs only pr. 1785.

NUPTIAL NOOSE, THE. C. O. 2 a. W. H. Brown. M. by C. Dubois. Gaiety, February 20, 1884.

NUPTIALS, THE. Masque on the marriage of James, Duke of Hamilton and Lady Anne Cochran. Pr. 1723. Allan Ramsay. Ac. February 11, 1723.

NUPTIALS, THE. M.D. Lieut. T. P. Christian. Pr. 1791. N.ac.

NUPTIALS OF PELEUS AND THETIS, THE. Masque. J. Howell. Ac. at Paris 1654. Borr. fr. an Italian C. Story is in Ovid's "Metamorphoses," Book XI.

NUPTIALS OF PELEUS AND THETIS, THE. C. J. Howell, fr. which preceding was taken.

NURMAHEL. D. 2 a. Lib. by Herklot. Berlin, May 27, 1822.

NURSE. F. 2 a. Clo Graves. Globe, March 17, 1900.

NURSE AGATHA. P 1 a. Camberwell Met., October 14. 1901

NURSE MARJORIE. P. 4 a. Israel Zangwill. Criterion, September 14, 1906 (C.P.).

NURSERY GOVERNESS, THE. P. 1 a. Adap. by P. G. Duchesne fr. *La Gouvernante* of M. Provins. Kennington, October 26, 1908.

NURSERY PASTORAL. F. 1 a. A. Paxton.

NURSERYRHYMIA. F. 1 a. A. W. Paxton.

NURSEY CHICKWEED. F. 1 a. T. J. Williams. Princess's, November 12, 1859.

NUT, THE. P. Ment. in Henslowe's Diary. December, 1601. Mr. Collier thinks it probably a rev. of *Crack Me This Nut*, which was prod. 1595.

NUTBROWN MAID, THE. C.O. Geo. Savile Carey. Pr. 1770.

NYDIA, THE BLIND GIRL OF POMPEII. D. Dublin Queen's, October 18, 1869 See *The Last Days of Pompeii.*

NYDIA, THE BLIND GIRL OF POMPEII. Grand O. 5 a. G. Fox. Lib. f. on Lord Lytton's *The Last Days of Pompeii.* Crystal Pal., May 10, 1892

NYMPH OF THE DANUBE. Op. bo. Extrav. G. Capel, Sunderland T.R., July 31, 1882.

NYMPH OF THE FOUNTAIN, THE. Pant. J. C. Cross. Ac. 1797.

NYMPH OF THE GROTTO. O. 3 a. Dimond. C.G., January 15, 1829.

NYMPH OF THE LURLEYBERG; OR, THE KNIGHT AND THE KNIGHT OF THE NAIADS, THE. Extrav. H. J. Byron. Adelphi, December 26, 1859; rev. Astley's, 1867.

NYMPHIDIA. M. Fairy P. 3 a. Wr. by Harry de Koningh. M. by Fredk. Leeds. Brockley, St. Peter's H., January 9, 1909 (amat.).

O

O'DONNELL ABOO. D. B. Stanhope. St. Helens T.R., February 3, 1875.

O'DONOGHUE'S WARNING, THE. Irish D. E. Falconer. Dublin T.R., October 28, 1878.

O'DORA; OR, A WRONG ACCENT, THE. Travestie of Sardou's *Théodora*. F. C. Burnand. Toole's, July 13, 1885.

O'DOWD, THE. Irish D. 4 a. D. Boucicault. Adelphi, October 21, 1880.

O'FLANNIGAN AND THE FARIES. Extrav. Publ. by S. French, Ltd.

O'GEMINI. Burl. on *The Corsican Brothers*. G. à Beckett.

O'GRINDLES, THE. P. 3 a. H. V. Esmond. January 21, 1908.

O'HOOLIGAN'S HOLIDAY. F.C. 4 a. J. R. Bogue West Stanley Victoria, February 12, 1894.

O'JUPITER; OR, THE FIDDLER'S WIFE. Burl. F. Hall. Philharmonic, October 2, 1880.

O.K. C. Sk. Ina Leon Cassilis. Bethnal Green Excelsior H., February 23, 1901.

O NANA SAN. M.C. 2 a. W. A. Forder. Norwich Agricultural H., December 10, 1903.

O'NEAL THE GREAT. D 3 a. Publ. by S. French, Ltd.

O.P. VICTORIOUS; OR, WHO DARE SNEEZE? F. 2 a. Intended for representation at C.G., but not ac. Pr. 1810.

OAKDELL MYSTERY, THE. Melo.-d. F. A. Scudamore. Eastbourne T.R. and O.H., August 25, 1884.

OAKWOOD HALL; OR, A CURIOUS WILL. D. W. Lane. Worcester T.R., April 1, 1871.

OAKS; OR, THE BEAUTIES OF CANTERBURY, THE. C Mrs. Burgess. Canterbury T.R. Pr. 1780.

OATH, THE. Rom. D. Pro. and 4 a. J. A. Meade. Manchester Queen's, April 4, 1887; Strand, June 14, 1887.

OBED SNOW'S PHILANTHROPY. P. 3 a. G. Newton. P.O.W., July 11, 1887.

OBERINE; OR, THE NYMPH OF THE ADRIATIC. Extrav. W. Summers. Liverpool Court, December 21, 1901.

OBERON. O. 4 a. Lib. by J. R. Planché. M. by Weber. C.G., April 12, 1826; D.L., April 19, 1841; C.G., November 5, 1870. It Ital. by Maggione. Her M., July 3, 1860. In German, Leipsic, December 23, 1826.

OBERON; OR, HUON DE BOURDEAUX. Masque. 5 a. W. Sotheby. Pr. at Bristol, 1802. N.ac. Story fr. Wieland's poem of same name.

OBERON; OR, THE CHARMED HORN. Ro. fairy tale. 2 a. D.L., March 27, 1826. F. on Wieland's poem.

OBERON, THE FAIRY PRINCE. Masque of Prince Henry's, by B. Jonson. Circa 1611. Pr. 1640.

OBERON'S OATH; OR, THE PALADIN AND THE PRINCESS. Fairy tale. 2 a. M. by Parry. D.L., May 21, 1816.

OBERTO DI BONIFAZIO. O. Verdi, 1839.

OBI; OR, THREE-FINGER'D JACK. Pant. D. 2 a. Haymarket. Pr. 1800. D.L., March 14, 1818; Victoria, 1819. Story fr. Dr. Moseley's "Treatise on Sugar." Ascr. to Fawcett.

OBJECT OF INTEREST, AN. F. 1 a. J. H. Stocqueler. Lyceum, July 14, 1845.

OBLIGING A FRIEND. F. Adap. by G. Conquest. Grecian, November 11, 1867.

OBLIGING A FRIEND. F. 1 a. W. Reeve. Newcastle-on-Tyne T.R., September 9, 1872.

OBLIGING HIS LANDLADY. F. Monol. C. D. Hickman. Birmingham Grand.

OBSERVATION AND FLIRTATION. C. 1 a. H. Wigan. Strand, July 26, 1860.

OBSTINATE FAMILY, THE F 1 a. Transl. and adap. fr. the German. Sadler's Wells, February 21, 1853.

OBSTINATE LADY, THE. Rom. C. Sir A. Cokain. Pr. 1657. In imitation of Massinger's *Very Woman*.

OBSTINATE WOMAN. P. 1 a. Jessie Corrie. Publ. by S. French, Limited.

OCA DEL CAIRO. L. Unfinished O. Mozart. Lib. by Varesco, 1783. Paris, June 6, 1867; Vienna, 1868; D.L. (in Ital.), May 12, 1870. See *L'Oie du Caïre*.

OCCASIONAL ORATORIO, THE. Handel. 1747.

OCCASIONAL PRELUDE. Colman, 1776. N.p.

OCCASIONAL PRELUDE. Cumberland, 1792.

OCCASIONE FA IL LADRO, L'. M.F. Rossini. Venice, 1812.

OCCULT SCIENCE, THE. Ca. 1 a. A. Clayton Greene. Camden, May 1, 1905.

OCEAN OF LIFE; OR, EVERY INCH A SAILOR, THE. Nautical D. 3 a. J. T. Haines. Surrey, April 4, 1836.

OCEAN WAIF, THE. D. 5 a. Grace Temple and H. M. Le Blonde. Wrexham, St. James's, May 16, 1893.

OCTAVE. Mirande et Henri Geroule. Royalty, June 29, 1908.

OCTAVIA. T. Thos. Nuce. A transl. of the Octavia of Seneca. Black letter. Pr. 1581.

OCTAVIA. T. Alfieri, 1783. Transl. by C. Lloyd, 1815. See *Virtuous Octavia*.

OCTAVIA. Transl. by C. Lloyd, 1815.

OCTAVIUS. Hist.D. Kotzebue.

OCTOROON; OR, LIFE IN LOUISANA, THE. P. 4 a. D. Boucicault. New York Winter Gardens, December, 1859; Adelphi, November 18, 1861; Princess's, February, 1868.

OCULIST, THE. F. Anon. Pr. 1747. N.ac.

OCULIST, THE. Ent. 2 a. Dr. Bacon. Pr. 1757.

OCULIST, THE. D. 1 a. L'Estrange. North Camberwell Progressive Club, August 25, 1894.

ODD GIRL, THE. P. 1 a. Mrs. Hope Merrick. Hammersmith King's, April 4, 1904.

ODD LOT, AN. F. 1 a. W. Gordon. Royalty, March 28, 1864.

ODD MAN OUT. M.F. 3 a. M. Turner and F. Dix. Lyrics by M. Turner and W. L. Clement. M. by T. Hunter and S. Shaw. Special songs by G. Le Brunn and A. G. Spry. Nottingham Grand, April 19, 1897.

ODD PAIR, AN. M.P. 1 a. M. Watson. M. by A. J. Caldicott. St. George's H., July 10, 1893.

ODD, TO SAY THE LEAST OF IT. F.C. 3 a. E. Rose. Novelty, November 6, 1886 (C.P.); Oxford New T., June 21, 1887.

ODD TRICK, AN. C. 1 a. W. Muskerry. Adap. fr. *La Partie de Piquet*. Bradford T.R., May 27, 1895.

ODD WHIMS; OR, TWO AT A TIME. C. H. Repton. Ac. at Ipswich. Pr. 1804.

ODDS; WHAT THEY WERE, WHO WON, AND WHO LOST THEM. D. 4 a. Sefton Parry. Holborn, October 1, 1870.

ODDS ARE EVEN, THE. C. Mrs. Jameson. Adap. fr. *Le Burgeoir*. Northampton T.R., June 22, 1893.

ODE upon dedicating a building and erecting a statue to Shakespeare at Stratford. D. Garrick. Pr. 1769. Rec. at D.L. about that time; also on April 23, 1816.

ODE, THE REJECTED. C. See *Earl Goodwin*, by Ann Yearsley.

ODE TO ST. CECILIA'S DAY. Concerto. Handel. 1685-1759.

ODETTE. D. Déaddé. 1832.

ODETTE. C. 4 a. V. Sardou. Eng. ver. Haymarket, April 25, 1882.

ODETTE. Clement Scott. Adap. fr. Sardou's play. Princess's (new), September 29, 1894.

ODIN. D. G. Richards. On the model of the Greek Theatre. Pr. 1604. N.ac.

ODYSSEY. See "Greek Plays," "Epic Poems."

ŒDIPE. T. Corneille. 1659. See "French Classical Plays."

ŒDIPE. T. Voltaire. 1718.

ŒDIPE. O. Sacchini. 1781.

ŒDIPE ROI. D.L., 1893.

ŒDIPUS. T. A. Neville. Transl. fr. Seneca, who took part of it from Sophocles. Pr. 1581.

ŒDIPUS. T. Dryden and Lee. D.L., 1679.

ŒDIPUS. T. W. Whitehead and W. Mason. N.p. N.ac.

ŒDIPUS AT COLONUS. T. Sophocles.

ŒDIPUS AT COLONUS. T. Transl. fr. Sophocles. R. Polter. Pr. 1788. Dale, 1824; Doyle, 1849; and Plumtree, 1865.

ŒDIPUS COLONEUS. T. G. Adams. Transl. fr. Sophocles. Pr. 1729.

ŒDIPUS COLONEUS. T. T. Francklin. Pr. 1759. Pr. in Dr. Francklin's editions of Sophocles. See "Greek Plays."

ŒDIPUS, KING OF THEBES. T. J. Dryden and N. Lee. Ac. at Duke of York's T., 1678. Pr. 1679. (First and third acts by Dryden, remainder by Lee.)

ŒDIPUS, KING OF THEBES. T. L. Theobald. Transl. fr. Sophocles. Pr. 1715.

ŒDIPUS, KING OF THEBES. T. R. Potter. Transl. fr. Sophocles. Pr. 1788.

ŒDIPUS, KING OF THEBES. T. G. S. Clarke. Transl. fr. Sophocles. Pr. 1790.

ŒDIPUS TYRANNUS. T. G. Adams. Transl. fr. Sophocles. Pr. 1729. See "Greek Plays."

ŒDIPUS TYRANNUS. T. Dr. Francklin's editions of Sophocles. Pr. 1759.

ŒDIPUS TYRANNUS. T. T. Maurice. Transl. fr. Sophocles. Pr. 1779.

OEIL CREVE, L'. Op. bo. Herve. Globe, June 15, 1872.

OEIL CREVE, L'. English ver. by H. B. Farnie. O.C., October 21, 1872.

OEILLET DE NINETTA, L'. P. 2 Epis. Lady Clarke Jervoise. Adelphi, January 27, 1902.

ŒNONE. Past. R. Cox. 1656. N.d.

ŒNONE. O. By Kalkbrenner. 1804.

O'ER LAND AND SEA. D. 4 a. Leeds T.R., September 30, 1899 (C.P.).

OF A CLOWN. P. 1 a. V. Jones. Dudley O.H., December 14, 1903.

OF AGE TO-MORROW. M. Ent. 2 a. T. Dibdin. D.L. M. by Kelly. Pr. 1805. D.L., October 17, 1814; Lyceum, September 3, 1817. Fr. a drama of Kotzebue (? *The Baron*).

OF BAPTISM AND TEMPTATION. Two C. by Bishop Bale.

OF GLOUCESTER PLACE. Inc. 1 a. Mrs. Dering White. F. on story by James Payn. Brompton Hospital, March 15, 1904.

OF NOBLE BIRTH. Op. bo. 1 a. W. Heighway. Publ. by S. French, Ltd.

OFF DUTY. Dom. C. 1 a. T. E. Pemberton. Toole's, September 9, 1884.

OFF THE CORNISH COAST. P. 1 a. Estelle Burney. Kingsway, March 2, 1908.

OFF THE LINE. F. C. Scott. Gaiety, April 1, 1871

OFF THE RANK. F.C. 3 a. L. Sterner. Douglas Gaiety T., June 16, 1904; Strand, March 11, 1905.

OFF TO GRETNA GREEN. C.O. in 30 mins. Wellesley Smith. M. by Geo. Ess and Julian Rutt. Poplar Queen's M.H., April 8, 1907.

OFFA AND ETHELBERT; OR, THE SAXON PRINCES. T. W. Preston. Pr. 1791. N.ac.

OFFER OF MARRIAGE, AN. L. Fomm. Orig. prod. at Globe April 27, 1899, as *Ambition*. Wyndham's, June 26, 1900.

OFFERAND OF OUR LADY. See "Miracle Plays."

OFFERING OF ISAAC. Sacr. D. (with poems). Anon. 1811.

OFFICER OF FORTUNE, THE. D. A. Stanley. Newcastle Tyne T., April 19, 1875.

OFFICER'S CALL. Military C. 3 a. T. Blair. Richmond R., September 16, 1901.

OFFICERS' MESS AND HOW THEY GOT OUT OF IT. By C. Hurst. M. by M. Strong. Add. nos. by Emily Beatrice Gadsdon. Terry's, April 3, 1905.

OFFSPRING OF FLOWERS, THE. Ballet. 2 a. M. by Scaramelli. D.L., October 3, 1846.

OGNI ECCESSO' E VIZIOSO. O. V. Floravanti. Naples, 1823.

OGRE AND LITTLE THUMB; OR, THE SEVEN LEAGUE BOOTS. Ballet. C.G. Songs only pr. 1807.

OGRE AND THE WITCH, THE. M.C. 2 a. P. M. Faraday. Islington Myddelton H., December 21, 1897.

OH, INDEED! Revue. Geo. Grossmith, jun. Lyrics H. C. Bovill. M. by Cuthbert Clarke. Empire, March 7, 1908.

OH! IT'S IMPOSSIBLE. C. J. P. Kemble. An alt. of Shakespeare's *Comedy of Errors*. Ac. at York 1780. N.p.

OH! 'LIZA. "Comedy miniature." A. Fryers. Crystal Pal., November 22, 1899.

OH! MISS. F.C. 3 a. Woolwich Artillery T., July 2, 1900.

OH! MY HEAD. F. F. Allen. Alhambra Pal. of Varieties, April 24, 1871.

OH, MY WIFE! Duol. Daphne De Rohan. Ealing Lyric, August 30, 1897.

OH! SOCIETY. F.C. 3 a. J. H. Darnley. Liverpool P.O.W., May 28, 1900.

OH, SUSANNAH! F.C. 3 a. M. Ambient, A. Atwood, and R. Vaun. Brighton Eden, September 6, 1897; Royalty, October 5, 1897.

OH, THAT MAJOR! Farcical Sk. J. Hamilton Urquhart. Leven Town H., September 10, 1906.

OH! THESE WIDOWS. F.C. 3 a. J. Mortimer. Adap. fr. the French of Michel and Labiche. Terry's May 1, 1889.

OH! THIS LOVE; OR, THE MASQUERADERS. C.O. J. Kenney. M. by King. Lyceum, 1810 (23rd time on August 28, 1810). N.p.

OH! THOSE BABES; OR, THE UNHAPPY UNCLE, THE VIRTUOUS VILLAINS, AND THE CHEEKY CHILDREN. Burl. W. Clements. Woolwich T.R., June 18, 1888.

OH! THOSE GIRLS. M.P. 1 a. R. Soutar. Adap. fr. the German. M. by Meyer Lutz. Gaiety, March 4, 1882.

OH! WHAT A NIGHT. M.C. 2 a. W. Terriss. Adap. fr. the German. Lyrics by Clement Scott. M. by J. Crook. Wakefield O.H., January 15, 1898 (C.P.).

OH! WOMAN! Sk. F. Hardie. Balham Assembly R., March 20, 1895.

OH! YOU WILLIAM. Sk. London Col., June 7, 1909.

OIE DU CAIRE, L'. See *L'Oca de Cairo*.

OIL AND VINEGAR. C. 2 a. H. J. Byron. Gaiety, November 4, 1874.

OISEAU DE PASSAGE. P. 4 a. M. Donnay and L. Descaves. Royalty, November 25, 1907.

OITHONA. Dr. Poem. Taken fr. Ossian M. by Barthelemon. Hay. Pr. 1768.

OJIBBEWAY INDIANS, THE.

OKUTOKO; OR, THE PRINCIPALITY OF THE SIMPLE LIFE. M.C. Wr. and comp. by Dr. H. de Montmorency. Appleby Market H., April 19, 1906 (amat.).

OLAF AND THE LITTLE MAID. C. 1 a. M. E. Francis. Hay., May 8, 1906.

OLANDESE DANNATO, L'. O. 3 a. R. Wagner. D.L., July 23, 1870.

OLD ADMIRER, AN. P. 1 a. C. H. Brookfield. Avenue, September 23, 1899.

OLD AGE (GERAS). See "Greek Plays."

OLD AND YOUNG; OR, THE 4 MOWBRAYS. F. 1 a. D.L., December 5, 1822, and 1826.

OLD AND YOUNG STAGER, THE. F. 2 a. W. L. Rede. Olympic, December 7, 1835.

OLD BACHELOR, THE. C. W. Congreve. T.R., 1691. Pr. 1693.

OLD BACHELOR'S BIRTHDAY, THE. C. 3 a. F. Harvey. Preston T.R., March 7, 1873.

OLD BAILE'S STRAND. P. 1 a. W. B. Yeates. Gt. Queen St., June 12, 1907.

OLD BISHOPSGATE. City of London, August 25, 1851.

OLD BOGEY OF THE SEA. Britannia, December 26, 1891.

OLD BOYS AND THE NEW, THE. C. 1 a. H. M. Lewis. Twickenham Town H., May 14 1898.

OLD BRIGADE, THE. Dr. Epis. Bedford M.H., December 9, 1907.

OLD BUREAU, THE. Ent. 1 a. H. M. Paull. M. by A. J. Caldicott. St. Geo. H., November 18, 1891.

OLD CABIN HOME; OR, CAROLINA, THE. P. 4 a. Grattan Donnelly. C.P. Darwen T.R., September 29, 1906.

OLD CHATEAU; OR, A NIGHT OF PERIL, THE. D. 3 a. J. Coyne. Hay., July 22, 1854.

OLD CHERRY TREE. Britannia, October 3, 1866.

OLD CHINA. Ballet in 2 tab, designed by Wilhelm, dances by Katti Lanner and L. Wenzel. Empire, November 6, 1901.

OLD CHINA'S IN CHINA. Sk. Morton Davis and Lew Lake. Shoreditch Olympia, July 19, 1909.

OLD CHUMS. C. 3 a. H. J. Byron. Op.C., December 16, 1876.

OLD CHURCH WALLS. Marylebone, November 29, 1852.

OLD CITY MANNERS. C. Mrs. Charlotte Lennox. D.L., November 9, 1775. Pr. 1775. An adap. of *Eastward Hoe*.

OLD CLAY PIPE, THE. Melo-d. Pro. and 2 a. J. L. Avondale. Shoreham Swiss Gardens, September 30, 1878.

OLD CLAY PIPE, THE. M.D. John Henderson. Todmorden T.R., November 19, 1883.

OLD CLO'. P. 1 a. C. Mackay. Birkenhead Metropole, December 7, 1894.

OLD CLO' MAN, THE. M.P. - a, 3 sc. E. Catulle Mendes. Her Majesty's, March 8, 1897.

OLD CLOTHES. P. 1 a. Eva Anstruther. Garrick, February 16, 1904.

OLD CLOTHESMAN, THE. M. Ent. 3 a. Anon. C.G., April 3, 1799. M. by Attwood. (Ascr. to Holcroft, but repudiated by him.)

OLD CLOWN'S CHRISTMAS, AN. Collins's, April 8, 1905.

OLD COUPLE, THE. C. in verse. T. May. Pr. 1658.

OLD CREATION OF THE WORLD, THE. O. (Reign of Q. Anne.)

OLD CRIMEA. New title for *The Fortune of War*.

OLD CRONIES. Duol. Ca. S. T. Smith. St. James's, March 6, 1880.

OLD CURIOSITY SHOP, THE. D. 2 a. E. Stirling. Adelphi, November 9, 1840.

OLD CURIOSITY SHOP, THE. D. F. on Dickens's work. D.L., October 4, 1853.

OLD CURIOSITY SHOP, THE. D. C. Dickens, jun. Adap. fr. his father's story. Op. C., January 12, 1884.

OLD CURIOSITY SHOP. Arr. 4 a. fr. Dickens's novel. Cripplegate Inst., April 12, 1906 (amat.).

OLD CURIOSITY SHOP, The. See *An Angel on Earth*.

OLD CURIOSITY SHOP; OR, THE LIFE AND DEATH OF LITTLE NELL, THE. D. W. Sidney. Norwich T.R., February 6, 1871.

OLD CUSTOMS OR NEW YEAR'S GIFTS. C. Oa. Lyceum playbill, August 5, 1816.

OLD DEBAUCHEES; OR, THE JESUIT CAUGHT, THE. C. H. Fielding. D.L., 1733. Pr. 1732. See *The Debauchees*.

OLD ENGLAND FOR EVER; OR, A FIG FOR INVASION. C.O. 2 a. A. M'Laren. Pr. 1799 at Bristol. N.ac.

OLD FATHER TIME; OR, THE CLOCKMAKER OF MARDYK. P. 3 a. E. A. Shute. Adap. fr. R. E. Francillon's Dutch story. Nuneaton Drill H., November 7, 1889.

OLD FERRIER'S DISCOVERY. P. 1 a. Guildhall Sch. of M., July 16, 1900.

OLD FIRM, THE. F. Comedy. 3 a. H. and E. Paulton. Newcastle R., August 17, 1908; Queen's, September 4, 1908. (Orig. prod. in America).

OLD FLAME, AN. Ca. W. T. Blackmore. Adap. fr. *Le Passé de Nichette*. Gaiety, September 16, 1882.

OLD FLAMES. F.P. 3 a. A. Maltby. Adap. fr. the French *No. 115, Rue Pigalle* of Embisson. Op. C. February 26, 1884.

OLD FLAMES. F.C. 3 a. A. Reed and G. D. Day. Fulham Grand, December 8, 1902.

OLD FOLKS, THE. Ca. Howard Paul. Strand, September 16, 1867.

OLD FOLKS AT HOME, THE. Melo-d. 4 a. J. A. Campbell. Manchester Junc., September 30, 1907; Hammersmith Lyric, October 5, 1908.

OLD FORGE, THE. D. 3 a. C. Osborne. Gaiety, June 22, 1872.

OLD FORTUNATUS. C. T. Dekker. Ac. before the Q. at Christmas by the Earl of Nottingham's servants. Black letter. Pr. 1600. Not divided into acts.

OLD FOX INN, THE. D. 3 a. C. H. Hazlewood. Britannia, August 2, 1875.

OLD FRIENDS. C. 1 a. Lady Violet Greville. St. James's, June 26. 1890.

OLD GARDEN, AN. C. 1 a. H. Davies. Brighton T.R., October 14, 1895; Terry's, November 12, 1895.

OLD GOOSEBERRY. F. 1 a. T. J. Williams. Olympic, October 9, 1869.

OLD GRIMEY; OR, LIFE IN THE BLACK COUNTRY. D. Pro. and 3 a. J. M. Murdock. Grecian, September 23, 1872.

OLD GUARD, THE. D. 1 a. Boucicault. Princess's, October, 1843.

OLD GUARD, THE. C.O. 3 a. H. B. Farnie. Adap. fr. *Les Voltigeurs de la 32 Eme* of E. Goudinet and G. Duval. M. by R. Planquette. Orig. French production. Renaissance, January 7, 1880; Birmingham Grand, October 10, 1887; Avenue, October 26, 1887.

OLD HARLEQUIN'S FIRESIDE. Pant. D.L., December 26, 1804. Short piece, playing about 15 minutes.

OLD HEADS AND YOUNG HEARTS. C. 5 a. D. Boucicault. Hay., November 18, 1844.

OLD HEIDELBERG. 5 a. R. Bleichmann. A ver. of Wilhelm Meyer Forster's C. *Alt Heidelberg.* St. James's, November 19, 1903, and rev. March 22, 1904; rev. St. James's, May 24, 1909.

OLD HOME, THE. C.D. 3 a. Robt. Buchanan. Vaudeville, June 19, 1889.

OLD HOME, THE. Dom. D. 4 a. Roland Yorke. Salford P.O.W., May 11, 1908.

OLD HONESTY. D. 2 a. J. M. Morton. Hay.

OLD HOUSE AT HOME. D. 2 a. Publ. by S. French, Ltd.

OLD HUSBANDS AND YOUNG WIVES. F. H. Seed. Cavendish Rooms, July 7, 1868 (amat.)

OLD INTEREST. F. "of 43 acts." Oxford. Pr. 1753.

OLD JEW, AN. C. 5 a. S. Grundy. Garrick, January 6, 1894.

OLD JOE AND YOUNG JOE. C.D. 2 a. John Courtney. Surrey, October 31, 1853.

OLD KENT ROAD, THE. "Wordless scena." C. Baldwin, Metropole, April 3, 1905.

OLD KING COLE AND GOOD QUEEN COLE. Ent. O. 1 a. W. Younge. M. by F. Pascall. Royalty, December 12, 1891.

OLD KNOCKLES. O. 1 a. V. A. Law. M. by A. J. Caldicott. St. Geo. H., November 24, 1884.

OLD KNOCKLES. Sk. Empress, September 14, 1908.

OLD LADY, THE. C. 3 a. C. H. Chambers. Criterion, November 19, 1892.

OLD LADY, THE P. 3 a. Geo. S. Tamner. Guildford T.H., October 15, 1907.

OLD LAND, THE. Rom. Irish D. 5 a. R. Johnston. Dublin Queen's T., April 13, 1903.

OLD LAW; OR, A NEW WAY TO PLEASE YE, THE. C. P. Massinger, Thos. Middleton, Wm. Rowley. Ac. at Salisbury Court, 1656. Pr. same year.

OLD LEAP YEAR. C. 3 a. H. T. Craven. MS. with Douglas Cox.

OLD LONDON. Rom. D. 5 a. F. Boyle. Adap. fr. *Les Chevaliers du Brouillard*, a French dramatisation of Harrison Ainsworth's *Jack Sheppard.* Queen's, Long Acre, February 5, 1873; Bristol New T.R., 1873.

OLD LONDON. D. Pro. and 3 a. A. Shirley and W. M. Tilson. Adap. fr. Harrison Ainsworth's novel. Manchester Queen's, July 25, 1891; Marylebone, August 29, 1892.

OLD LONDON BRIDGE IN THE DAYS OF JACK SHEPPARD AND JONATHAN WILD. Ver. of Harrison Ainsworth's novel. Standard, March 12, 1894.

OLD LOVE, THE. C. 3 a. J. S. Pigott. Globe, May 31, 1900.

OLD LOVE AND NEW FORTUNE. H. F. Chorley. Surrey, February 18, 1850.

OLD LOVE AND THE NEW, THE. C. Sullivan. D.L., January 16, 1851.

OLD LOVE AND THE NEW, THE. C. 5 a. B. Howard. Adap. to the Eng. stage by J. Albery. Court, December 15, 1879.

OLD LOVE LETTERS. C. 1 a. B. Howard. Publ. by S. French, Ltd.

OLD LOVE RENEWED. C. W. Nation. Pr. at Plymouth, 1789.

OLD MAID, THE. C. 2 a. A. Murphy. Partly fr. *L'Étourderie* of Fagan. D.L., July 2, 1761. Edin., 1782. Pr. 1761.

OLD MAID'S CORNER. 1 a. Maude Thompson. R., Plymouth, November 16, 1908.

OLD MAID'S WOOING, AN. P. 1 a. A. Goldsworthy and E. B. Normon. St. Geo. H., January 28, 1888; Lyric, July 12, 1890.

OLD MAIDS. 5 a. J. Sheridan Knowles. C.G., 1841.

OLD MAN, AN. Dom. D. 2 a. R. Reece. Duke's, March 25, 1876.

OLD MAN OF THE MOUNTAINS; OR, A TALE OF THE ELEVENTH CENTURY. C. Dibdin, jun. Sadler's Wells. Pr. N.d.

OLD MAN TAUGHT WISDOM; OR, THE VIRGIN UNMASKED, THE. F. H. Fielding. D.L. 1734. Pr. 1734. Afterwards known under second title only.

OLD MAN'S BLESSING, AN. D. Gallery of Illus., June 13, 1868.

OLD MAN'S DARLING, AN. C. 1 a. H. Pettitt. Grecian, November 12, 1879.

OLD MAN'S DARLING, AN. P. 1 a. F. Morris. Royal Park H., May 4, 1893.

OLD MAN'S DARLING, AN. Dom. D. 1 a. E. Oliver. Ladbroke H., March 19, 1895.

OLD MAN'S DARLING, AN. M.F. 1 a. H. Francks. M. by T. Warden-Reed. West London, November 24, 1900.

OLD MAN'S DARLING, AN. Sk. J. Chandler. Middlesex, December 9, 1908.

OLD MAN'S DARLING, AN. Dom. D. D. M. C. Granville. Preston Prince's, March 18, 1909 (C.P.); Liverpool Queen's, April 10, 1909.

OLD MAN'S DREAM, AN. D. 1 a. F. Lindo. Ladbroke H., September 27, 1889.

OLD MAN'S LESSON AND A YOUNG MAN'S LOVE, AN. Int. (Pr. by Nicholas Breton). Author unknown. Pr. 1605.

OLD MANCHESTER; OR, WHEN JAMES I. WAS KING. D. 3 a. W. Wade. Manchester Queen's T., May 28, 1904.

OLD MARTIN'S TRIALS. Dom. D. Stirling.

OLD MASTER, AN. C. 1 a. H. A. Jones. Princess's, November 6, 1880.

OLD MASTER, AN. P. Betty Brandon. Cambridge New, May 10, 1907 (C.P.).

OLD MILL STREAM, THE. D. C. H. Hazlewood. Britannia, June 14, 1875.

OLD MINT, THE. J. B. Johnstone,

OLD MODE AND THE NEW; OR, COUNTRY MISS WITH HER FURBELOE. C. T. Durfey. Ac. at D.L., March 11, 1703. Pr. N.d., ? 1709.

OLD MORTALITY; OR, THE HEIR OF MILNWOOD. D. 3 a. W. E. Suter. Sadler's Wells, September 13, 1869.

OLD MOSS. F 1 a. F. H. Head. Bayswater Bijou, May 24, 1894.

OLD MUSICIAN, AN. P. 1 a. L. Wagner. Forest Gate Earlham H., April 12, 1902.

OLD OAK CHEST; OR, THE SMUGGLER'S SONS AND THE ROBBER'S DAUGHTER, THE. D. 2 a. Sans Pareil. February, 1816.

OLD OAK TREE, THE. D. 2 a. F. on the incidents of the remarkable escape of De Latude fr. the Bastille 1750. M. by G. A. Macfarren. Lyceum, August 24, 1835.

OLD OFFENDER, AN. C.D. 2 a. J. R. Planché. Adelphi, July 22, 1859.

OLD, OLD STORY, THE. Sk. 1 a. and 3 sc. G. B. Nichols. Surrey, May 25, 1903.

OLD, OLD STORY. D. 4 a. Edmonton T.R., March 18, 1907.

OLD, OLD STORY; OR, THE FALL OF A SHATTERED FLOWER, THE. D. F. Marchant. Britannia, October 7, 1868.

OLD PALS. O. Burl. L. Clarance. M. by W. Haunt. South Shields T.R., August 7, 1884.

OLD PALS. C. 1 a. W. A. Mackersey. Publ. by S. French, Ltd.

OLD PATIENT GRISSEL. C. Mentioned in Kirkman's Catologue, 1661, probably same P. as *Patient Grissel.*

OLD PHIL'S BIRTHDAY. S.C.D. 2 a. J. P. Wooler. Strand, Jan. 20, 1862.

OLD PROMISE, AN. P. 1 a. C. Crozier. Ladbroke H., May 13, 1898.

OLD QUIZZES; OR, WHAT'S THE NEWS? M.F. R. Hall. Dublin. Pr. 1779.

OLD RAG SHOP, THE. D. Pro. and 3 a. F. Marchant, Victoria, October 23, 1869.

OLD REGIMENTALS, THE. Hist. D. 1 a. W. B. Bernard. Eng. O.H. 1831.

OLD ROSCIUS. M.F. McLaren. 1805.

OLD SAILORS. C. 3 a. H. J. Byron. Strand, October 19, 1874.

OLD SALT. S.C.D. 2 a. J. Daly. Strand, January 11, 1868.

OLD SARAH. Oa. 1 a. H. Greenbank. M. by François Cellier. Savoy, June 17, 1897.

OLD SARUM; OR, HUNTED TO DEATH BY A WOMAN. D. A. J. Hough. Salisbury T., September 21, 1868.

OLD SCAPEGOAT, AN. C.D. 2 a. A. Fryers. Imperial, November 22, 1884.

OLD SCORE, AN. C.D. 3 a. W. S. Gilbert. Gaiety, July 19, 1869.

OLD SCORES. P. 4 a. Messrs. A. F. Robbins and P. Morris. Camberwell Metropole, February 25, 1901.

OLD SCORES. Ca. 1 a. R. A. Roberts. Liverpool Empire, November 21, 1903.

OLD SINNERS. 4 a. J. Mortimer. An adap. of Sardou's *Les Vieux Garcons.* Gaiety, June 16, 1886.

OLD SOLDIERS. C.D. 3 a. H. J. Byron. Strand, January 25, 1873.

OLD SONG, AN. P. 1 a. Rev. F. Wills and A. F. King. Tunbridge Wells Great H., August 2, 1894; Criterion, December 10, 1896.

OLD SPOONS. Ca. Mrs. T. E. Smale. Turnham Green Vestry H., February 2, 1899.

OLD SPORT, THE. C.D. 4 a. C. Riminton and J. P. Clairemont. Folkestone Pier T., November 27, 1893.

OLD STEADY. D. 4 a. M. Murdock. Pav., September 3, 1881.

OLD STORY, THE. C. 2 a. H. J. Byron. Strand, April 29, 1861.

OLD TIME STORY, THE. D. Chs. Elderton. Douglas G.T., December 22, 1902.

OLD TOBIT. See "Miracle Plays."

OLD TOLL HOUSE, THE. Marylebone, September 30, 1861.

OLD TROOP; OR, MONSIEUR RAGOUT, THE. C. J. Lacy. Circa 1665. Act. at T.R., Pr. 1672.

OLD TRUSTY. C.D. 1 a. W. Gordon. Olympic, January 25, 1861.

OLD TYME HALLOWE'EN, AN. Sk. Lond. Col., January 11, 1909.

OLD VIOLIN, THE. Dom. D. 1 a. F. P. Dempster. Stratford Town H., January 19, 1900.

OLD VIRGINIA. P. 1 a. H. Herman, Liverpool Shakespeare, March 25, 1891.

OLD VIRGINIA. M.Ca. Lib. by K. Allen and E. Adeler, lyrics K. Allen, F. Dunlop, and A. W. Parry. Rock Ferry Olympian Gardens, June 8, 1908.

OLD WIDOW, THE. A Droll formed out of Cartwright's P., *Ordinary.* Pr. 1662.

OLD WILLOW PLATE, THE. Op. fantasy. M. Strong. Camberwell Empire, October 19, 1908.

OLD WIVES' TALE, THE. C. G. Peele. Pr. 1595. Ac. by Her Maj. Players.

OLD WOMAN OF EIGHTY. Burl. C. Dibdin.

OLD WOMAN WHO LIVED IN A SHOE, THE. Bayswater All Saints' H., January 9, 1900.

OLD WOMEN WEATHER-WISE, THE. Int. G. S. Carey. D.L. Pr. 1770. Miscalled in some old lists *The Three Old Women Weather-Wise.*

OLEMPEO AND HENGENYO. P. Mentioned by Henslowe. 1595.

OLIMPIADE. O. by Leo. 1719.

OLIMPIADE. Ital. O. Metastasio, 1733-Trans. by Dr. Arne. King's T., 1764.

OLIMPIADE. See *Olympiade.*

OLINDO AND SOPHRONIA. T. A. Portal. Pr. 1758. N.ac. Plot fr. Tasso's *Giervsalemme Liberata.*

OLITORIO. O. Scarlatti. Circa 1700.

OLIVE BRANCH. D. 3 a. P. Meritt. Leicester T.R., March 15, 1875.

OLIVE LATIMER'S HUSBAND. P. 1 a. R. Besier. Vaudeville, January 19, 1909.

OLIVER CROMWELL. Hist. P. G. S. Green. Pr. 1752. N.ac.

OLIVER CROMWELL'S SOFA. F. Queen's, December 3, 1877.

OLIVER GOLDSMITH. P. 1 a. F. F. Moore. Limerick T.R., June 24, 1892.

OLIVER GRUMBLE. Burl. 2 a. G. Dance. Liverpool P.O.W., March 15, 1886; Novelty, March 25, 1886.

OLIVER TWIST. Adapt. of Dickens's novel. Adelphi, March, 1839.

OLIVER TWIST. D. 3 a. J. Oxenford. Queen's, April 11, 1868.

OLIVER TWIST. D. J. B. Johnstone. Surrey, May 18, 1868.

OLIVER TWIST. D. J. Mordaunt. Alexandra, April 10, 1869.

OLIVER TWIST. D. 5 a. G. Collingham. Olympic, December 21, 1891.

OLIVER TWIST. 4 a. O. Brand. Grand. March 30, 1903.

OLIVER TWIST. 4 a. ver. Eleph. and C., April 13, 1903.

OLIVER TWIST. D. 5 a. J. C. Carr. H.M., July 10, 1905; September 4, 1905.

OLIVER TWIST. New and original vers. 4 a. H. Whyte and R. Balmain. Walthamstow King's, October 2, 1905.

OLIVER TWIST. See *Bumble, Bumble's Courtship, Fagin.*

OLIVER TWIST; OR, THE PARISH BOY'S PROGRESS. D. 3 a. Pavilion, May, 1838.

OLIVER TWISTED; OR, DICKENS UP A TREE. Sk. Words by Wal Pink. M. by J. S. Baker. London Pavilion, November 13, 1905.

OLIVETTE. C.O. 3 a. H. B. Farnie. Adap. fr. the French of Chivot and Durn. Strand, September 18, 1880. See *Les Noces d'Olivette.*

OLIVIA. P. 4 a. W. G. Wills. F. on incidents in Oliver Goldsmith's "Vicar of Wakefield. Court, March 28, 1878; Lyceum, April 22, 1891; January 30, 1897; June 16, 1900.

OLIVIA. See *The Vicar of Wide-awake-field.*

OLIVIA'S ELOPEMENT. C. 1 a. Affleck Scott. King's, December 17, 1908.

OLIVIA'S LOVE. D. 4 a. J. F. McArdle and R. Mansell. Liverpool T.R., May 6, 1878.

OLLA PODRIDA. O. 1 a. Banbury and Dichl. Publ. by S. French, Ltd.

OLLANTA. D. Markham. 1871.

OLYMPIA. T. Transl. fr. Voltaire. Pr. in Francklin's edition of that author.

OLYMPIAD. O. J. Hoole. Transl. fr. Metastasio. Pr. 1767.

OLYMPIADE. O. Piccini. 1761.

OLYMPIC. T. 3 a. Imitated fr. Voltaire by Dieulafoy and Briffant. M. by Sponlini. Paris, February 2, 1819; in Ger., Berlin, May 5, 1821.

OLYMPIC DEVILS; OR, ORPHEUS AND EURYDICE. Burl. Burla. 1 a. J. R. Planché and C. Dance. Olympic, December 26, 1831.

OLYMPIC FRAILTIES. Burl. Olympic, April 12, 1841.

OLYMPIC GAMES. Burl. F. C. Burnand. Olympic, April 22, 1867.

OLYMPIC REVELS; OR, PROMETHEUS AND PANDORA. Burl. 1 a. J. R. Planché and C. Dance. Fr. G. W. Colman's tale "The Sun Poker." Olympic, January 3, 1831.

OLYMPIE. O. By Kalkbrenner. 1800.

OLYMPIE. O. Brifaut. M. by Spontini. 1820.

OLYMPUS. Mythological M.P. Mrs. Christina Dening. Somerville Club, 231, Oxford Street, February 21, 1893.

OLYMPUS IN A MUDDLE. Hay., August 23, 1855.

OLYMPUS IN AN UPROAR. Burl. Partly fr. O'Hara's *Golden Pippin.* C.G., November 5, 1796. N.p.

OMADHAUN, THE. D. 3 a. H. P. Grattan. Queen's, November 24, 1877.

OMAI; OR, A TRIP ROUND THE WORLD. Panto. J. O'Keeffe. M. by Shield. C.G., December 20, 1785. Pr. 1785.

OMBA. Dram. Rom. Bigsby. 1853.

OMBRA, L'. Eng. O. 3 a. Flotow. Adap. by Gilbert à Beckett. H.M., January 12, 1878.

OMBRE, L'. O. Flotow, Paris, 1870.

OMELETTE MAKER, THE. M.C. 2 a. C. Gouldsbury and T. Holland. Kingsway, March 17, 1908.

OMNIBUS; OR, A CONVENIENT DISTANCE, THE. F. 1 a. Alt. fr. Raymond's *Cherry Bounce.* C.G.

OMNIPOTENCE. Orat. Anon. 1774.

OMOO; OR, THE SEA OF ICE. D. D. Boucicault. Liverpool R. Amphi., October 30, 1864.

ON ACTIVE SERVICE. Naval Mil. D. H. Leonard. Surrey, October 23, 1899.

ON AN ISLAND. Ca. 1 a. J. W. Jones. Bradford T.R., March 8, 1879; Vaudeville, February 4, 1882.

ON AN OLD HARPSICHORD. Poetic fancy. 1 tab. Brighton T.R., November 18, 1897.

ON AND BETWEEN THE BOARDS. M. duol. F. W. Ward. Royal M.H., December 18, 1902.

ON AND OFF F. 1 a. T. J. Williams. Strand, June 6, 1861.

ON AND OFF. Adap. of A. Bisson's *Le Contrôleur des Wagons-Lits.* Vaudeville, December 1, 1898.

ON BAIL. Farcl. C. 3 a. W. S. Gilbert. Adap. fr. *Le Reveillon.* Criterion, February 12, 1877.

ON BAILIE'S STRAND. P. 1 a. W. B. Yeat's Irish Players. St. Geo. H., November 27, 1905; Gt. Qn. St., June 12, 1907.

ON BUSINESS. F. F. Desprez. Aberdeen H.M.T., August 30, 1880.

ON 'CHANGE. F. 3 a. Miss Eweretta Lawrence. Adap. fr. G. Von Moser's *Ultimo.* Strand, July 1, 1885; Toole's, August 22, 1885; Strand, February 15, 1896.

ON CIRCUMSTANTIAL EVIDENCE. M.P. 4 a. C. Clifford. Perth T., April 3, 1902; Aberdare New T., July 11, 1902.

ON CONDITION. Oa. R. Reece. M. by Meyer Lutz. Op. C., October 9, 1882.

ON DEMANDE DES DOMESTIQUES. St. Geo. H., June 30, 1885.

ON DISTANT SHORES. D. 4 a. W. Burnot and H. Bruce. Woolwich Artillery, April 18, 1897; Aldershot T.R., May 2, 1898; Stratford T.R., April 29, 1901.

ON GUARD. C. 3 a. W. S. Gilbert. Court, October 28, 1871.

ON GUY FAWKES DAY. F.C. 3 a. J. H. Darnley and H. Bruce. Liverpool P.O.W., November 29, 1897.

ON HER MAJESTY'S SERVICE. D. 4 a. H. W. Hatchman and H. G. May. Sunderland Avenue T., November 20, 1891 (C.P.).

ON HER MAJESTY'S SERVICE. P. 4 a. W. Jones. Rev. by W. Melville, January 22, 1900.

ON HIS OATH. D. Pro. and 4 a. C. A. Aldin. Scarborough T.R., January 18, 1887.

ON JHELUM RIVER. Indian mus. love story. Bk. by Nydia, lyrics by F. John Fraser, M. by Amy Woodforde-Finden. Aldwych, June 22, 1909.

ON LEAVE. F. 3 a. F. Horner. Adap. fr. *Le Sursis* of Sylvane and Gascoyne. Avenue, April 17, 1897.

ON PARADE; OR, A SAILOR'S SWEETHEART. M. Spec. D. 3 a. F. W. Scarlett. Wolverhampton Star T., April 8, 1895.

ON PROBATION. C. 4 a. Brander Matthews and G. H. Jessop. Eleph. and C., September 5, 1889 (C.P.).

ON RUIN'S BRINK. Melo-d. E. Newbound. Leicester T.R., February 28, 1881.

ON SERVICE; OR, A SOLDIER'S LIFE. S.C. D. 3 a. W. Digges. Derby Lecture H., December 26, 1878.

ON SHANNON'S SHORE; OR, THE BLACK-THORN. Irish Melo-d. F. Cooke. Reading Prince's T., February 14, 1895; Greenwich Carlton, June 29, 1903.

ON SHORE FROM THE HERCULES. Ca. Greenock T.R., January 19, 1880.

ON STEPPING-STONES. Ca. 1 a. Victor Jones. Publ. by Douglas Cox.

ON STRIKE. A Social Problem. A. à Beckett. Court, October 14, 1873.

ON STRIKE. Oa. 2 a. Anna Goldschmidt. M. by Julia Goldschmidt. Nottingham Mechanics' H., November 15, 1894. Amateurs.

ON THE BENCH; OR, DISTANT COUSINS. C.D. 3 a. T. Pemberton. Liverpool Alexandra, February 22, 1883.

ON THE BORDER. D.E. 1 a. J. E. Willmott. Birmingham Kyrle H., February 28, 1903.

ON THE BRINK. C.D. 1 a. Miss Emma Schiff. Liverpool Amphi., October 23, 1875.

ON THE BRINK. Ca. 1 a. J. T. Grein.

ON THE CARDS. C.D. 3 a A. Thompson. Adap. fr, the French *L'Escamoteur*. Gaiety, December 21, 1868.

ON THE CLYDE. D. 3 a. W. S. Scott Dundee T.R., January 27, 1875.

ON THE CONTINONG. F.C. 3 a Max O'Rell. Adap. fr. *Le Voyage de M. Perrichon*. Liverpool Court, April 5, 1897; Crouch End O.H., May 1, 1899.

ON THE EAST SIDE. P. by Christopher St. John. Court, July 7, 1908.

ON THE FRONTIER. D. Anne L. Johnstone. F. on two Indian stories by J. Fennimore Cooper. Orig. prod. in America. Greenwich Morton's, July 27, 1891.

ON THE FRONTIER. Melo-d. 5 a. American. Liverpool Shakespeare T., March 30, 1891.

ON THE HEATH. Revue divert. Pr. by Miss Elsie Clerc fr. scenario arr. by Fred Bowyer, M. by Geo. W. Byng. Alhambra, September 20, 1909.

ON THE INDIAN OCEAN. Ca. H. Lee. Liverpool Alexandra, March 11, 1878.

ON THE JURY. D. 4 a. W. Phillips. Princess's, December 14, 1871.

ON THE LOVE PATH. P. 3 a. C. M. S. McLellan. Hay., September 6, 1905.

ON THE MARCH. Mus. C. 2 a. W. Yardley, B. C. Stephenson, and C. Clay. M. by J. Crook, E. Solomon, and F. Clay. Sheffield T.R., May 18, 1896; P.O.W., June 22, 1896.

ON THE QUIET. C. 3 a. A. Thomas. Cardiff R., September 18, 1905; Comedy, September 27, 1905.

ON THE RANCH. Lieut.-Col. H. Everitt. Dram. fr. the story by Iza Duffus Hardy. St. Geo. H., February 1, 1896 (amat.).

ON THE RIGHT ROAD. P. 1 a. Mrs. de Courcy Laffan. Court, June 2, 1908.

ON THE RINK; OR, THE GIRL HE LEFT BEHIND HIM. Burl. F. C. Burnand. Duke's, February 26, 1876.

ON THE ROAD. Burla. E. Dowsett. M. by Amy Davis. Edmonton T.H., May 15, 1894.

ON THE SANDS. M. Sk. P. F. Marshall. Harwich Public H., July 14, 1887.

ON THE SIDE OF THE ANGELS. P. 4 a. W. L. Courtney. Royalty, December 16, 1906.

ON THE SLY. F. 1 a. J. M. Morton. Hay., October 24, 1864.

ON THE SQUARE. Ball. divert. Arr. and pr. Elise Clerc. M. comp., selected, and arr. by Geo. Byng. Alhambra, February 22, 1909; Alhambra, June 7, 1909.

ON THE STROKE OF TWELVE. C.M. 4 a. J. Le Brandit. Nottingham Grand, May 12, 1902; Greenwich Carlton, March 23, 1903.

ON THE THAMES. M. Sk. C. Grain. St. Geo. H., October 22, 1883.

ON THE THRESHOLD. Fairy Allegory. Mrs. G. Corbett. Bayswater Bijou, April 30, 1900.

ON THE TILES. F. 1 a. E. Stirling. Surrey, April 13, 1846.

ON THE TRACK. D. 4 a. E. Towers. East London, November 24, 1877.

ON THE VERGE. Wolverhampton T.R. March 10, 1888.

ON THORNS. C.D. 3 a. D. Robinson. Richmond H.M., November 8, 1880.

ON TOAST. Ca. 1 a. F. Horner. Avenue, July 16, 1888; Toole's, October 7, 1889.

ON TOUR. Ca. J. Mortimer. Adap. fr. the French. Strand, March 30, 1886.

ON TOUR. M.F. 1 a. Kilburn T.H., February 23, 1895.

ON TOUR; OR, A TRIP TO HEIDELBERG. M.C. 1 a. W. F. Field. Ealing Drill H., January 5, 1887.

ON TRUST. F. 1 a. Manville Morton. Cambridge Hipp., November 18, 1905.

ON WATCH. D. H. Russell. Plymouth Grand T., June 27, 1904.

ON ZEPHYR'S WINGS. Past. P. 2 a. Agatha and Archibald Hodgson. Teddington T.H., July 30, 1891.

ONCE A LOVER AND ALWAYS A LOVER. C. G. Granville (Lord Lansdowne). An alt. of his *The She-Gallants*. Pr. 1736. ? N.ac.

ONCE A WEEK. F. 1 a. Wilmot and Harrison. Rochester T.R., May 5, 1881.

ONCE AGAIN. Ca. E. Cuthbert. Vaudeville, January 25, 1879.

ONCE AGAIN. Ca. 1 a. F. W. Broughton and W. Browne. Liverpool Alexandra, March 24, 1884; Ealing Lyric H., February 17, 1885; Toole's, August 22, 1885.

ONCE BIT. Duol. G. Aitken. Kensington Philbeach H., July 19, 1904.

ONCE IN A CENTURY. G. à Beckett and Vivian Bligh.

ONCE TOO OFTEN. D.L., January 20, 1862.

ONCE UPON A TIME. Ca. H. Russell and H. Furnival. Brighton T.R., July 12, 1889.

ONCE UPON A TIME. P. L. N. Parker and H. B. Tree. Adap. fr. Ludwig Fulda's *Der Talisman*. Hay., March 28, 1894.

ONCE UPON A TIME. Fa. Ca. F. on *The Sleeping Beauty*, by G. H. Jessop. Langham Place Queen's H., January 22, 1903.

ONCE UPON A TIME; OR, A MIDSUMMER NIGHT'S DREAM IN MERRIE SHERWOOD. Extrav. F. R. Goodyer. Nottingham T.R., April 13, 1868.

ONCE UPON A TIME THERE WERE TWO KINGS. Fairy Extrav. 2 a. J. R. Planché. F. on Countess D'Aubnay's story *La Princess Carpillon.* Lyceum, December 26, 1853.

ONCLE VALET. O. Comique. Dellamaria. 1798.

ONDINE. O. Hoffman. 1816.

ONDINES DE CHAMPAGNE, LES. O. C. Lecocq. Folly, September, 1877.

ONE; OR, A MONARCHY. Alfieri. Transl. by C. Lloyd. 1815.

ONE AGAINST THE WORLD. Harry Bruce.

ONE AND ALL. F. R. P. Joddrel. Pr. 1787. N.ac.

ONE BIRD IN THE HAND WORTH TWO IN THE BUSH. Short M.P. Cheshire Crewe H., January 5, 1803.

ONE BLACK SPOT. D. 2 a. C. H. Hazlewood. Britannia, April 4, 1870.

ONE CHRISTMAS EVE. Sk. M. Ryder. West London, December 17, 1900.

ONE CHRISTMAS EVE. Dr. Sk. 1 a. L. Townrow. Camberwell Met., May 28, 1904.

ONE DAY IN JUNE. P. 1 a. R. M. Heath. Surrey Masonic H., December 8, 1902 (amat).

ONE-DAY MILLIONAIRE, THE. C.O. 1 a. Francis Reeve, M. by Basil Rideaux. Surrey Masonic Hall, January 3, 1908 (amat.).

ONE DAY MORE. D. 1 a. J. Conrad. Royalty, June 25, 1905.

ONE FAIR DAUGHTER. D. 4 a. Mrs. W. C. Gilmer. Barnes Inst., April 9, 1904.

ONE FALSE STEP. Guernsey T.R., May 9, 1873.

ONE FALSE STEP. D. 1 a. W. J. Mackay. Sadler's Wells, February 9, 1893.

ONE FALSE STEP; OR, THE PERILS OF A BEAUTY. D. 4 a. W. Travers. Pavilion, July 13, 1874.

ONE FAULT. Transl. fr. the French. City T., July, 1831.

ONE FAULT: "A HOME STORY." P. 1 a. E. Warren and Charlotte Elliott. Wigan T.R., October 9, 1885.

ONE FOOL MAKES MANY. C. Transl. fr. *Un Bobo hace Ciento* of De Solis, Spanish dramatist. Pr. 1807. N.ac.

ONE FOR ANOTHER. 1604. Not pr. under this title.

ONE FOR HIS NOB; OR, 39, HONEYSUCKLE VILLAS, N.W. Ca. E. Manuel. Britannia, February 16, 1874.

ONE GOOD TURN DESERVES ANOTHER. Princess's, November 10, 1862.

ONE HALF-HOUR. Sk. G. T. Norman. Ladbroke H., July 11, 1892.

ONE HOUR! OR, A CARNIVAL BALL. Burl. T. H. Bayly. June 7, 1839.

ONE HUNDRED AND TWO; OR, THE VETERAN AND HIS PROGENY. D. 1 a. Milner. D.L., June 6, 1838.

117, ARUNDEL STREET. F. 1 a. Publ. by S. French, Ltd.

ONE HUNDRED YEARS AGO. D. Olympic, July 10, 1875.

ONE HUSBAND FOR ONE WIFE. D. 4 a. G. B. Nichols. Britannia, November 10, 1902.

ONE IN HAND IS WORTH TWO IN THE BUSH. Ca. 1 a. G. March.

ONE LAW FOR MAN. P. F. by C. H. E. Brookfield on *La Loi der Homme*. Criterion, December 12, 1899.

ONE O'CLOCK; OR, THE KNIGHT AND THE WOOD DEMON. O. Rom. 3 a. Matthew Gregory Lewis. Lyceum, 1811; August 3, 1815; 1824; and D.L., October 15, 1833.

ONE OF OUR GIRLS. C. 4 a. B. Howard. Eleph. and C., November 4, 1885.

ONE OF THE BEST. D. 4 a. S. Hicks and G. Edwardes. Adelphi, December 21, 1895; Princess's, June 1, 1899; rev. Aldwych, May 1, 1909.

ONE OF THE BOYS. D. 4 a. W. Summers. Stonehouse Grand T., July 20, 1896.

ONE OF THE BOYS. C. 3 a. J. T. Tanner. (Renamed *On the Move*). Burnley Victoria Op. H. October 9, 1899.

ONE OF THE BRAVEST. American Mus. D. 3 a. Britannia, December 2, 1895.

ONE OF THE FAMILY. Mus. F.C. 3 a. G. Capel and F. Benton. Lyrics by F. Dix and F. Ayrton. M. by H. W. May and A. Cooke. Boscombe Grand, April 9, 1898.

ONE OF THE GIRLS. M. F. C. 2 a. H. Darnley and S. A. Lladd (J. J. Dallas). M. by J. Crook, S. Jones, and M. Lutz. Birmingham Grand, March 9, 1896; Camberwell Metropole, June 1, 1896.

ONE OF THE RIGHT SORT. D. 4 a. G. V. Wybrow. Rochdale T.R., March 6, 1902 (C.P.); Salford Regent, September 29, 1902.

ONE OF THEM. F.C. 2 a. C. H. Chambers. Margate T.R., September 10, 1886 (C.P.).

ONE OF THESE LITTLE ONES. P. 1 a. Clifford Mills. Albert H., July 2, 1909.

ONE OF US. D. 4 a. M. Melford. Liverpool St. James's H. and Comedy T., June 20, 1884.

ONE OF YOU MUST MARRY. Adap. fr. the German of Alexander Wilhelme. See *A Mean Advantage*.

ONE PEOPLE. P. 3 a. C. Ward. Liverpool Court T., March 19, 1903; Notting Hill Coronet, May 1, 1903.

ONE SHADE DEEPER. Effingham, February 16, 1863.

ONE SNOWY (?) KNIGHT. C. Ware. Transl. fr. the French.

ONE SUMMER HOLIDAY. C. 2 a. F. Morris. Clifton Alexandra H., November 25, 1886 (amat.).

ONE SUMMER'S DAY. Love story. 3 a. H. V. Esmond. Comedy, September 16, 1897.

ONE SUMMER'S NIGHT. C. 1 a. F. W. Broughton. Worcester T.R., March 20, 1882; Comedy, November 23, 1889.

ONE SWEET SEPTEMBER DAY. F.C. 3 a. H. D. Bradley. St. Geo. H., May 1, 1902.

ONE TOO MANY. O. 1 a. Burnand and Cowen. Publ. by S. French, Ltd.

ONE TOO MANY. F. 1 a. Desmond L. Ryan. Princess's, April 29, 1872.

ONE TOO MANY, THE. Dr. Sk. 1 sc. Percival H. T. Sykes. Chelsea Palace, July 2, 1904.

ONE TOO MANY FOR HIM. F. 1 a. T. J. Williams. Surrey, February 10, 1868.

ONE TOUCH OF NATURE. D. 1 a. Adelphi, August 6, 1859.

ONE TREE HILL. D. 2 a. H. T. Craven. Strand, April 17, 1865; Royalty, April, 1865; Greenwich, April 11, 1868.

ONE TRUE HEART. D. Willington T.R., February 8, 1875.

ONE, TWO, THREE, FOUR, FIVE; BY ADVERTISEMENT. M. Ent. 1 a. Bath, May 21, 1825.

ONE WOMAN'S WICKEDNESS. D. 4 a. C. H. Phelps. Smethwick T.R., December 15, 1902.

ONKEL BRASIG. St. Geo. H., February 1, 1900.

ONLY A CLOD. C.D. 1 a. J. P. Simpson. Lyceum, May 20, 1851.

ONLY A DREAM. P. 4 a. A. C. Forde. Ipswich T.R., April 13, 1885.

ONLY A DREAM. An Idyll. 1 a. J. Brandon. Criterion, December 7, 1888.

ONLY A FARMER'S DAUGHTER. C.D. E. Barnes and F. Levick. Origin. prod. in New York. Birkenhead T.R., February 22, 1897.

ONLY A HALFPENNY. F. 1 a. J. Oxenford. Hay., May 30, 1855.

ONLY A HEAD; OR, THE HEMPEN CRAVAT. D. 4 a. E. Newbound. Britannia, November 20, 1880.

ONLY A JEST. C. 1 a. M. Seymour. Publ. by S. French, Ltd.

ONLY A LITTLE BOY. P. 4 a. F. Marriott Watson and Jas. Ussher. Liverpool Rotunda, September 6, 1909.

ONLY A MODEL. Piece. 1 a. Vaudeville, February 23, 1892.

ONLY A MODEL. Ca. L. Stiles. Chelsea Town H., April 10, 1902.

ONLY A PENNY-A-LINER. Ca. 1 a. Hy. P. Lyste.

ONLY A PENNY-A-LINER. C. 1 a. H. P. Stephens. Publ. by S. French, Ltd.

ONLY A PLAYER. C. Bandmann. Princess's, March 1, 1873.

ONLY A QUAKER MAID. P. 1 a. F. Llewellyn. F. on an incident in Sir Walter Besant's novel "A Fountain Sealed." Orig. prod. Fulham Grand, July 19, 1898. Assembly Rooms, Putney, February 26, 1908.

ONLY A SHILLING. D. 3 a. W. H. Abel. Pavilion, April 22, 1872.

ONLY A WAIF; OR, THE LION AND THE MOUSE. D. 4 a. W. Clement. Woolwich T.R., May 28, 1888.

ONLY A WOMAN. Dom. D. 4 a. Percy Ballard. Central, Altrincham, January 20 1908; West London, April 13, 1908.

ONLY A WOMAN. See *Her Own Enemy*.

ONLY A WOMAN'S HAIR. D. H. Vandenhoff. Warrington T.R., October 21, 1873.

ONLY AMATEURS. F. 1 a. H. Montague. Liverpool Balfour Inst., April 17, 1909 (amat.) Publ. by S. French, Limited.

ONLY AN ACTRESS. C. 1 a. Mlle. Gratienne. Adap. fr. the same French source as *Nance Oldfield*. Bournemouth Mont Dore H., January 12, 1898.

ONLY FOR LIFE; OR, A CONVICT'S CAREER. D. C. H. Hazlewood. Britannia, August 6, 1877.

ONLY HALF WAY. F. 3 a. Stanley Cooke, Dunfermline T.R., November 7, 1905 (C.P.).

ONLY HUMAN. D. W. H. Harrison. Sunderland Avenue, April 25, 1906 (C.P.).

ONLY MY COUSIN. Ca. E. Newbound. Britannia, April 19, 1880.

ONLY THE GOVERNESS. Ca. A. Sketchly Holborn, March 30, 1872.

ONLY THREE YEARS AGO. P. 1 a. C. H Dickinson, Duke of York's, November 10, 1898

ONLY WAY: A TALE OF TWO CITIES, THE. Rom. P. Prol. and 4 a. Adap. by F. Wills fr. Charles Dickens. (Martin Harvey's season.) Lyceum, February 16, 1899; rev. Apollo, May 25, 1901; rev. Adelphi, June 24, 1907; rev. Adelphi, October 26, 1908.

ONORE VINCE AMORE. O. Leo. Naples, 1736.

ONY-NA-POCAS. Irish D. 3 a. B. Connor, Limerick T.R., September 27, 1879.

OONAGH. Irish D. 5 a. E. Falconer H.M.T., November 19, 1866.

OOP AT KIERSTENAN'S. P. 3 a. Bertha N. Graham. Court, December 20, 1908.

OOR GEORDIE; OR, THE HORRID BARBARIAN. F. 1 a. J. Cooper. Glasgow T.R. 1872.

'OP O' ME THUMB. P. 1a. F. Feron and R. Pryce. Court, March 13, 1904; St. James's, April 23, 1904.

OPAL RING, THE. C. 2 a. G. W. Godfrey. Adap. fr. Octave Feuillet's *Péril en la Demeure* (the original of Tom Taylor's *The House or the Home*). Court, January 28, 1885.

OPEN GATE, THE. Dom. D. 1 a. C. H. Chambers. Comedy, March 25, 1887.

OPEN HOUSE. F.C. 3 a. H. J. Byron, Vaudeville, April 16, 1885.

OPEN HOUSE; OR, THE TWIN SISTERS. F. 2 a. J. B. Buckstone. Haymarket, 1833.

OPEN SEA, THE. Spanish P. 3 a. Angel Guimera. Trans. by Frank Ross and Gerald Ames. Manchester R., April 5, 1909; Marlborough, May 10, 1909.

OPEN SESAME. Standard, December 26, 1876.

OPEN TO CORRECTION. F. R. Brough. Adelphi, January 10, 1870.

OPEN WAY, THE. P. 1 a. F. Lynton. St. Geo. H., February 16, 1905.

OPEN WINDOW, THE. P. 1 a. Ford Lynton. St. Geo. H., February 16, 1905.

OPERA, AN. Epil. to the T. of *Richard III*. Dublin, 1756.

OPERA ALLUDING TO THE PEACE, AN. Grimes. Ac. by his scholars at Cordwainers' H. Pr. 1712.

OPERA CLOAK, THE. Ca. 1 a. L. D. Powles and Aug. Harris. Drury Lane, September 8, 1883.

OPERA COMIQUE. O. Comique by Dellamaria. 1799.

OPERA DANCER. D. Pr. Carmontel. ("Theatrical Recorder.") 1805.

OPERA DI CAMERA OF JESSY LEA. O. by McFarren. 1863.

OPERA DU GUEUX. T. Hallam, 1750.

OPERA MAD. F. Evelyn Martell. Dumfries T.R., May 14, 1877.

OPERA OF OPERAS; OR, TOM THUMB THE GREAT, THE. O. Mr. Hatchet and Mrs. Haywood. D.L., November 9, 1733. Pr. 1733. This is Fielding's *Tragedy of Tragedies* converted into an opera.

OPERATOR, THE. Ballad O. Pr. 1740.

OPFERLAMM, DAS. F. 3 a. Oscar Walther and Leo Stein. Gt. Queen St., March 10, 1906.

OPIUM EATER, THE. P. 3 a. C. Hannan. Orig. prod. in America. Ayr T., December 31, 1894 (C.P.); Richmond T.R., July 31, 1895.

OPPORTUNITY, THE. C. J. Shirley. Ac. at the private house in D.L. by Her Maj. servants. Licensed 1634. Pr. 1640. Partly f. on Shakespeare's *Measure for Measure*. See *A Prince in Conceit*.

OPPOSITE NEIGHBOURS. F. 1 a. H. Paul. Strand, July 24, 1854.

OPPOSITES. C. 1 a. L. Fomm. Queen's Gate H., May 2, 1902.

OPPOSITION. C.P. 1 a. Hay., August 6, 1790. Alt. fr. *Sir Courtly Nice*. Ascr. to Mr. Ryder, at whose benefit it was ac. N.p.

OPPOSITION. F. R. Henry. M. by I. Caryll. Lyric, June 28, 1892.

OPTICAL DELUSION, AN. F. 1 a. J. R. O'Neill. St. James's T.

ORACLE, THE. C. Anon. Pr. 1741 "for J. Roberts." ? N.ac.

ORACLE, THE. C. 1 a. Mrs. Cibber. Fr. the French. C.G., March 17, 1752. Pr. 1752.

ORACLE; OR, THE INTERRUPTED SACRIFICE, THE. S.C.O. Transl. fr. Winter's O. *Das Unterbrochene Opferfest.* Lyceum, August 7, 1826; C.G., February 20, 1827.

ORACOLO, L'. M.D. 1 a. C. B. Fernald. F. on *The Cat and the Cherub.* Italian lib. by C. Zanoni. Engl. transl. by P. Pinkerton. M. by F. Leoni. C.G., June 28, 1905.

ORANGE BLOSSOM, THE. C. 3 a. V. Widnell. Strand, January 18, 1904; Terry's, January 23, 1908. C.P.

ORANGE BLOSSOMS. Ca. 1 a. J. P. Wooler. Strand, February 20, 1862.

ORANGE BLOSSOMS. M. Sk. Capt. Royston Fleet. London Pav., June 21, 1909.

ORANGE BOVEN; OR, MORE GOOD NEWS. C. Div. T. Dibdin. 1813. Ac. January 4, 1814.

ORANGE GIRL, THE. D. Prol. and 3 a. H. Leslie and N. Rowe. Surrey October 24, 1864; East London, May 14, 1870.

ORANGE NELL. "Historical incident." Adelaide Farren. Metropolitan, December 4, 1905.

ORANGE TREE AND THE HUMBLE BEE; OR, THE LITTLE PRINCESS WHO WAS LOST AT SEA, THE. Extrav. H. J. Byron. Vaudeville, May 13, 1871.

ORATOR, THE. P. Massinger. Ac. by King's Co. June 10, 1635. (Lost.)

ORATORS, THE. C. 3 a. S. Foote. Pr. 1762. Hay., 1762 and 1767.

ORAZI ED I CURIAZI GLI. O. 3 a. Lib. by Sografi, M. by Cimorosa. Venice, 1794; Paris, June 16, 1813.

ORAZZI E CURIAZI. O. Mercadante. (Vienna, 1830.)

ORBIS; OR, THE WORLD IN THE MOON. Dr. Satire. 3 a. J. Moser. Pr. 1810. N.ac.

ORCHARD OF THE KING, THE. P. 1 a. E. Day and M. H. Footman. Lincoln T.R. (amat.); November 20, 1889.

ORCHID, THE. M.P. 2 a. J. T. Tanner. Lyrics by Adrian Ross and Percy Greenbank. M. by Ivan Caryll and Lionel Monckton. Addl. numbers by Paul Rubens. New Gaiety, October 26, 1903.

ORDEAL, THE. D. 1 a. T. S. Wotton. Comedy (Sch. of Dr. Art Perf.), June 20, 1893.

ORDEAL BY TOUCH. C. 5 a. R. Lee. Queen's, May 4, 1872.

ORDEAL OF THE HONEYMOON, THE. Duol. Miss Estelle Burney. P.O.W., May 9, 1899.

ORDER OF THE GARTER, THE. Dr. Pm. West. 1742.

ORDER OF THE NIGHT; OR, TWENTY YEARS OF A SOLDIER'S LIFE, THE. D T. Mead. Eleph. and C., September 22, 1873.

ORDERED SOUTH: A SKETCH IN KHAKI. A. Ross. M. by A. Barrett. Forest Hill St. Geo. Lawn Tennis Club, July 28, 1900.

ORDERED TO THE FRONT. D. Sk. Wm. Bourne. Stratford Empire, May 6, 1907.

ORDINARY, THE. C. W. Cartwright. Pr. 1651. Part of Act 1 afterwards transcribed and pr. as *The Old Widow.*

ORDSALL HALL. D. C. Hermann. F. on Harrison Ainsworth's novel *Guy Fawkes.* Salford P.O.W., August 27, 1883.

ORESTAN TRILOGY. (*The Agamemnon*; *The Libation Bearers*; *The Furies*) Æschylus. Engl. transl. by E. D. A. Morshead. Coronet, March 4, 1905.

ORESTE. T. Voltaire. 1750.

ORESTE ET PYLADE. T. Lagrange. 1695.

ORESTEIA. See "Greek Plays."

ORESTES. T. J. Hughes. Taken fr. Euripides. Unfinished at decease of Author. Pr. 1717. N.ac.

ORESTES. T. Rev. T. Goffe. Ac. by students of Christchurch, Oxford. Plot fr. the *Orestes* of Euripides and the *Electra* of Sophocles. Pr. 1633.

ORESTES. Dram. O. L. Theobald. L.I.F., April 3, 1731. Pr. 1731. (A 5 a. T. with music.)

ORESTES. T. Dr. Francklin. Transl. fr. Voltaire. C.G., March 13, 1769, and at D.L. Paris, January 12, 1750.

ORESTES. T. M. Wodhull. Transl. fr. Euripides. Pr. 1782.

ORESTES. T. R. Potter. Transl. fr. Euripides. Pr. 1783.

ORESTES. T. Ascr. to James Banister. Transl. fr. Euripides. Pr. 1786.

ORESTES. T. W. Sotheby. Pr. 1802. N.ac.

ORESTES. T. Fr. Alfieri. Transl. by C. Lloyd. Transl. by Warren. 1871.

ORESTES IN ARGOS. T. 5 a. P. Bayley. C.G., April 20, 1825. Partly fr. Sophocles, Voltaire, and Alfieri.

ORESTES' FURIES. P. T. Dekker. Ac. 1598.

ORFEO. Poliziano. 1472. See *Orpheus.*

ORFEO. O. Monteverde. (1568-1643.)

ORFEO. O. Glück. Prod 1762. C.G., November 6, 1890.

ORFEVRE, L' C.O. F. L. H. Monro. N.ac.

ORGAN-GRINDER, THE. Melo-d. 5 a. A. Shirley and C. H. Longden. Adap. fr. the French D. *Fualdes.* Leicester T.R., June 24, 1898 (C.P.).

ORGAN-GRINDER, THE. Sk. 4 sc. Alicia Ramsey and Rudolph de Cordova. New Cross Empire, August 24, 1908.

ORGANIC AFFECTION, AN. F. 1 a. Mrs. Alfred Phillips. Olympic, January 15, 1852.

ORGANIST, THE. Rom. C.D. 4 a. H. Wilton and A. B. Moss. New Cross H., November 14, 1887.

ORGANISTE, L'. Oa. 1 a. G. V. Fanvré. Salle Duprez, 1885.

ORGULA; OR, THE FATAL ERROR. T. by "L. W." Pr. 1658.

ORIANA. C. 3 a. J. Albery. Globe, February 15, 1873.

ORIENT EXPRESS, THE. C. 3 a. F. C. Burnand. Daly's, October 25, 1893.

ORIENTALES, LES. Rom. D. V. Hugo. 1828.

ORIGINAL, THE. J. M. Morton. C.G.

ORIGINAL AFFECTION. Olympic, January 12, 1852.

ORIGINAUX, LES. Lamotte. 1693.

ORIGO MUNDI. See "Miracle Plays."

ORIONE. O. J. C. Bach. (Clarinets first introduced) 1760.

ORLANDESE DANNATO, L'. See *Der Fliegende Holländer, The Flying Dutchman.*

ORLANDO. O. Handel. 1733.

ORLANDO AND SERAPHINA; OR, THE FUNERAL PILE. D. 3 a. F. Lathom. Taken fr. Tasso's *Jerusalem Delivered.* Ac. at Norwich. Pr. 1800 (? previously without date).

ORLANDO DANDO. M.C. 2 a. B. Hood and W. Slaughter. Fulham Grand, August 1, 1898.

ORLANDO FURIOSO. O. Purcell. Hay., 1705.

ORLANDO FURIOSO. See "Italian Classical Plays," "Epic Poems."

ORLANDO FURIOSO, THE HISTORIE OF. R. Greene. Not divided into acts. Taken fr. Ariosto's *Orlando Furioso*. Ac. before the Queen (? 1591). Pr. 1594.

ORMASDES; OR, LOVE AND FRIENDSHIP. T.C. Ac. Sir William Killigrew. Pr. 1665 as *Ormasdes* only. Repr. 1666 under second title only. Running title in latter edition unites the two.

OROONOKO. T. 5 a. T. Southern. F. on Mrs. Aphra Behn's novel. Epil. by Congreve. Ac. T.R., 1696. Pr. 1696.

OROONOKO. T. J. Hawkesworth. An alt. of foregoing. Pr. 1759. Ac. at D.L. December 1, 1759.

OROONOKO. T. Anon. Alt. fr. Southern. Pr. 1760.

OROONOKO. See "Victorious Love."

OROONOKO; OR, THE ROYAL SLAVE. F. Gentleman. Alt. fr. Southern. Ac. at Edinburg. Pr. in Glasgow, 1760.

ORPHAN; OR, THE HAPPY MARRIAGE, THE. T. 3 a. J. Ferrar. In rhyme. Pr. at Limerick, 1765.

ORPHAN; OR, THE UNHAPPY MARRIAGE, THE. T. T. Otway. In blank verse. Ac. at the Duke's T. Pr. 1680. Plot f. on a novel called "English Adventures." Publ. in 1667. Ac. at D.L.

ORPHAN AND THE OUTCAST; OR, THE PERILS OF A STEAM FORGE HAMMER, THE. D. 3 a. J. Mortimer. Blackburn T.R., and O.H., October 20, 1871

ORPHAN HEIRESS, THE. Melo-d. 4 a. A. Jefferson. Bp. Auckland Eden T., December 23, 1895; Surrey, Sept 25, 1899.

ORPHAN OF CHINA, THE. T. Transl. fr. Voltaire. Pr. in Dr. Francklin's edition of that author's works.

ORPHAN OF CHINA, THE. T. A. Murphy. Ac. at D.L. April 21, 1759. Pr. 1759. F. on Chinese D. piece in Du Halde's *History of China*. (Previously treated by Voltaire.) C.G., 1777, after some alterations.

ORPHAN OF THE FROZEN SEAS. Naut. D. Stirling. 1856.

ORPHAN OF VENICE, THE. T. J. Darcy. Dublin T.R., 1749.

ORPHAN'S LEGACY, THE. D. 4 a. A. Fancquez. Grecian, June 10, 1867.

ORPHAN'S TRAGEDY, THE. P. H. Chettle. Ac. in 1601. N.p.

ORPHANS, THE. Surrey, May 15, 1866.

ORPHANS; OR, GENEROUS LOVERS, THE. O. H. Shepherd. Pr. 1800. N.ac.

ORPHANS; OR, THE BRIDGE OF NOTRE DAME, THE. D. 4 a. A. Shirley and C. H. Longden. Adap. fr. the French. Pavilion, July 8, 1898 (C.P.).

ORPHEE. O. Lagrange.

ORPHEE AUX ENFERS. Op. bo. 2 a. and 4 tab. Wds. by Hector Crémieux, M. by Offenbach. Paris, October 21, 1858. In Fr., by Schneider, St. James's, July 12, 1869.

ORPHEUS. Fragment of a D. in the British Museum. Probably very old.

ORPHEUS. P. under this title destroyed by Warburton's servant.

ORPHEUS. English O. J. Hill. Pr. 1740.

ORPHEUS. Burla. Anon. Pr. 1749.

ORPHEUS. O. Glück. Paris, 1774.

ORPHEUS. O. 3 parts. J. Galt. Pr. 1814. ? N.ac.

ORPHEUS AND EURIDICE. Masque. M. Bladen. Pr. 1705. Publ. in Act III. of T.C. called *Solon*.

ORPHEUS AND EURIDICE. Masque. J. Dennis. Pr. 1707.

ORPHEUS AND EURIDICE. D. Ent. of Dancing. J. Weaver. D.L. 1717. Pr. 1718. F. on story in Ovid's "Metamorphoses."

ORPHEUS AND EURIDICE. O. J. F. Lampe. Pr. 1739.

ORPHEUS AND EURIDICE. With the Pant. Ent. Henry Sommer. L.L.F. Pr. 1740.

ORPHEUS AND EURIDICE. Masque. J. E. Weekes. Pr. at Cork. 1743.

ORPHEUS AND EURIDICE. Serious O. F. Gentleman. Reduced to an afterpiece C.G., February 28, 1792. Ac. at Smock Alley, Dublin, 1783. Transl. fr. the Italian.

ORPHEUS AND EURIDICE. Burl. O. R. Houlton. Ac. at Capel Street, Dublin, 1784. N.p.

ORPHEUS AND EURIDICE. M.D. Poetry by Calsabigi. Alt. by Andrei. Preface by Tenducci. Pr. 1785. Ac. at King's T. in Hay.

ORPHEUS AND EURYDICE. O. Reeve (partly adapted fr. Glück). 1792.

ORPHEUS AND EURYDICE; OR, THE YOUNG GENTLEMAN WHO CHARMED THE ROCKS. Classical Love Tale. 1 a. H. J. Byron. Strand, December 26.

ORPHEUS AND (P)EURYDICE. Burl. 3 a. E. Rose and "Coe." Yarmouth R. Aquar., July 20, 1891.

ORPHEUS IN THE HAYMARKET. Op. bo. 3 tableaux and a last scene. J. R. Planché. Fr. the French of H. Cremieux. Hay., December 26, 1865.

ORSON. Ca. H. P. Grattan. Adelphi, August 12, 1876.

ORTI ESPERIDI. Gli.

OSCAR AND MALVINA. Ballet Pant. Fr. Ossian. M. by W. Reeve. C.G., August 20, 1791.

OSCAR AND MALVINA. O. By Shield.

OSCAR THE BANDIT. Adelphi, 1834.

OSERYCK. Recorded by Henslowe as having been ac. by his comp. February 5, 1597. Possibly Heywood's *Marshal Osrick*.

OSMAN. T. C. Arnold. F. on a catastrophe which occurred in Constantinople. 1624. Pr. 1757. N.ac.

OSMAN. T. F. Gentleman. Bath (circa), 1751. Intended for perf. at the Little Theatre in the Hay. N.p.

OSMOND, THE GREAT TURK; otherwise called THE NOBLE SERVANT. T. L. Carlell. F. on the taking of Constantinople by Mahomet II., 1453. Pr. 1657.

OSMYN AND DARAXA. M. Rom. J. Boaden. Ac. by the D.L. Co. at the O.H. Plot probably taken fr. one of Le Sage's romances. Songs only pr. 1793.

OSTROLENKA. O. 4 a. Wetherill and Tryon. Transl. fr. the German of P. Haimbach. M. by Bonawitz. St. Geo. H., April 2, 1885.

OSWALD. Mor. D. Sayers, 1783.

OSWAY. T. J. Plumtre. F. on story of Dionysius, Damon and Pythias, told by Valerius Maximus. Pr. 1795 at Norwich. N.ac.

OTAGE, L'. See "The Shadow of the Surplice."

OTAKE. Sk. W. Shiko and Louie Fuller. London Hippo., July 20, 1908.

OTELLO. O. Rossini. Naples, December 4, 1816; King's, May 16, 1822; D.L., July 19, 1833; in Fr. as *Othello*, September 2, 1844; C.G., November 22, 1892.

OTELLO. Grand O. 4 a. Arrizo Boito. F. on Shakespeare's *Othello.* M. by Verdi. La Scala, Milan, February, 1887; Lyceum, July 5, 1889; C.G., July 15, 1891; first time in English at Manchester Prince's T., October 8, 1892.

OTHELLO. Burl. Strand, 1836.

OTHELLO, THE MOOR OF VENICE. T. Wm. Shakespeare. 1604. Ent. Stationers' H., October 21, 1621. Pr. Qto., 1620, 1630. 1st Folio, 1623. F. on novel by Giraldi Cinthio (Decade iii., Novel 3). The names Othello and Iago occur in Reynold's "God's Revenge Against Adultery." Ac. at Harefield, 1602, and at Globe and Blackfriars. C.G. (J. P. Kemble). Pr. 1804. Lyceum, February, 1876; Olympic (Edmund Tearle's season), May 21, 1892; Lyric (Wilson Barrett), May 22, 1897; rev. Lyric December 15, 1902, and April 8, 1905; rev. by Lewis Waller Lyric, May 17, 1906; Manchester Queen's, January 12, 1907; Kennington (Oscar Asche), February 28, 1907; H.M., November 7, 1907.

OTHELLO. Anon. Pr. 1812.

OTHELLO. O. English ver. of Verdi's *Otello.* Played by the Carl Rosa Opera Co., Marlborough T., April 26, 1907.

OTHELLO. See *Otello.*

OTHELLO TRAVESTIE. O. Burl. Bula. M. G. Dowling. Liverpool T., March, 1834.

OTHER CHARLIE, THE. Sk. M. Anderson. Belfast Alhambra, December 16, 1903.

OTHER DAYS. P. 3 a. T. W. Robertson. Hull T.R., April 12, 1883.

OTHER FELLOW, THE. F. 3 a. F. Horner. Fr. Feijdeau and Desvallière's *Champignol Malgré lui.* Court, September 9, 1893; tr. to Strand, November 18, 1893.

OTHER HALF OF THE WORLD, THE. E. 1 a. Balham Assembly R., February 4, 1902.

OTHER HEIR, THE. Ca. 1 a. E. H. G. Cox. Blackpool O.H., November 5, 1906.

OTHER LADY, THE. C. 3 a. F. Horner. Edinburgh Lyceum, June 20, 1898.

OTHER LITTLE LORD FONDLEBOY, THE. Travestie by F. Bowyer. Avenue, June 18, 1888.

OTHER MAN'S BUSINESS, THE. F. 3 a. G. W. Elton and E. S. Petley. Kingston-on-Thames County T., June 18, 1900; Camberwell Metropole, September 24, 1900.

OTHER MAN'S WIFE, THE. C. F. K. Peile. Worcester T.R., May 16, 1898.

OTHER MRS. HUDSON, THE. F.C. 3 a. J. F. Nolan and F. Rolison. Cripplegate Inst., April 8, 1905 (C.P.).

OTHER PEOPLE'S MONEY. D.D. 4 a. A. E. Pringle. Bradford P.T., March 21, 1901; Garston T.R., October 14, 1901.

OTHER SIDE, THE. P. 3 a. Clo Graves. Manchester Prince's, October 25, 1907; rev. Grand, Croydon, February 26, 1908; Fulham Grand, March 5, 1908.

OTHER TENTH OF THE LAW, THE. P. 1 a. Edith A. Browne. Court, March 21, 1909. (Prod. by the Dramatic Debaters.)

OTHER WOMAN, THE. Duol. 1 a. Miss Ellis Kingsley. H.M., November 11, 1897.

OTHER WOMAN, THE. P. 3 a. Herbert Leonard. Hastings Pier Pav., January 6, 1908.

OTHO. P. Corbet Owen. 17th Century MS. trans. fr. Corneille.

OTHO AND RUTHA. Dr. Tale. Miss Edwards. Pr. 1781.

OTHO THE GREAT. T. by Keats and Brown.

OTHON. T. Corneille, 1664. See "French Classical Plays."

OTHRYADES. Melo-d. Pr. in "The Poetical Register," 1803.

OTTO, A GERMAN. C.D. 3 a. J. F. Marsden. Birmingham P.O.W. July 28, 1879; Sadler's Wells, July 12, 1880.

OTTO OF WITTELSBACH; OR, THE CHOLERIC COUNT. T. B. Thompson. Transl. fr. the German of James Marcus Babo. Pr. 1800. N.ac.

OTTO THE OUTCAST; OR, THE BIRD-SELLER OF PARIS. C.D. H. Starr. Nelson Grand, April 4, 1898.

OUDE DOULLAGH. D. J. A. Avondale. Shoreham Bijou T., Swiss G., June 7, 1879.

OUGHT WE TO VISIT HER? C. 3 a. Mrs. Edwards and W. S. Gilbert. Royalty, January 17, 1874.

OUGHTS AND CROSSES. F.C. G. L. Gordon. Jersey T.R., July 28, 1884.

OULITA, THE SERF. P. Helps. 1858.

OUR ACCOMPLISHED DOMESTIC. F. E. Dale. Strand, August 21, 1878.

OUR AGENCY. M.C. 4 a. B. Brumell and W. G. Matchem. Avenue, July 19, 1886.

OUR AMATEUR THEATRICALS. Extrav. 2 a. H. L. Hilliard. M. by O. Barri. Croydon T.R., July 23, 1894.

OUR AMERICAN COUSIN. D. 4 a. T. Taylor. New York, October 18, 1858; Hay., November 11, 1861; Novelty, February 3, 1890.

OUR ANGELS. D. 3 a. and 4 tableaux. G. H. R. Dabbs and E. Righton. Vaudeville, March 3, 1891.

OUR AUNT FROM CALIFORNIA. Ca. 1 a. Publ. by S. French, Ltd.

OUR AUTUMN MANŒUVRES. F. C. L. Kenney. Adelphi, October 21, 1871.

OUR AWFUL LADS. Ca. E. B. Wyke. West Hartlepool Gaiety, March 15, 1878.

OUR BABES IN THE WOOD; OR, THE ORPHANS RELEASED. Burl. F. C. Burnand. Gaiety, April 2, 1877.

OUR BABIES. M.C. 3 a. W. E. Morton. M. by G. D. Fox. Eastbourne T.R., November 26, 1888.

OUR BAIRN. F. F. H. Francks. Kilburn Town H., December 4, 1889.

OUR BAZAAR. O. 1 a. Diehl. Publ. by S. French, Ltd.

OUR BEST SOCIETY. C. 4 a. Publ. by S. French, Ltd.

OUR BETTER SELVES. D. Ent. 1 a. H. Furnival. Wakefield O.H., November 6, 1903.

OUR BITTEREST FOE. D. 1 a. H. Gardner. Publ. by S. French, Ltd.

OUR BITTEREST FOE. An incident of 1870. D. 1 a. G. C. Herbert. Globe, April 1874; rev., Bayswater Bijou, May 8, 1906.

OUR BOARDING SCHOOL. American C. F. Rogers. International T. (Holborn), February 1, 1884.

OUR BONNIE PRINCE. Hist. D. 4 a. J. Chute and J. Colman. Glasgow T.R., October 24, 1887.

OUR BOYS. C. 3 a. H. J. Byron. Vaudeville, January 16, 1875 (ran for 4 yrs. and 3 mos. until April 18, 1879); Criterion, February 11, 1890; Terry's, July 26, 1898; (rev.) Vaudeville, September 14, 1892.

OUR BRITISH EMPIRE; OR, THE GORDON HIGHLANDERS. D. 5 a. C. A. Aldin. Bootle Muncaster T., August 1, 1898; Stratford T.R., December 12, 1898.

OUR BURLESQUE BABY. F. 1 a. E. T. De Banzie. Glasgow T.R., February 13, 1895.

OUR CARD BASKET. Shirley Brooks. Gall. of Illustration.

OUR CINDERELLA. Burl. 2 a. R. Reece. Gaiety, September 8, 1883.

OUR CLERKS; OR, NO. 3, FIG TREE COURT TEMPLE. F. 1 a. Tom Taylor. Princess's, March 6, 1853.

OUR CLUB. C. 3 a. F. C. Burnand. Strand, May 9, 1878.

OUR COASTGUARDS. Melo-d. 4 a. J. Worden. Manchester St. James's, November 14, 1892.

OUR COLONIAL RELATIVE. Ca. Newcastle Tyne T., July 9, 1886.

OUR COURT. "Operatic drametta." 1 a. E. Humphrey and J. Addison. M. by J. Weaver. Woolwich R. Artillery, November 17, 1888.

OUR COUSINS. C. 3 a. A. Romer. Bayswater Bijou (amat.), June 14, 1869.

OUR COUSINS. F.C. 3 a. A. Argles and F. Stayton. Torquay T.R., April 25, 1898.

OUR CURATE. "Miniature D." 6 sc. C. Stanley Self. Sadler's Wells, July 27, 1903.

OUR DAILY BREAD. D. 3 a. H. C. Hazlewood. Wolverhampton T.R., October 5, 1885.

OUR DANCING DAYS. Bal. Byrne. D.L., February, 1801.

OUR DAUGHTERS. C. 3 a. T. G. Warren and W. Edouin. Portsmouth T.R. (prod. as *Daughters*), June 30, 1890; Strand, April 15, 1891; tr. to evening bill, April 22, 1891.

OUR DEAR OLD HOME. D. W. Archer. City of London, June 20, 1868.

OUR DIVA. C.O. 3 a. C. M. Rae. Fr. Paul Ferrier and Fabrice Carré's *Joséphine Vendue par ses Sœurs*. M. by V. Roger. Op. C., October 29, 1886.

OUR DOCTORS. F.C. 3 a. Sir R. H. Roberts and J. Mackay. Terry's, March 24, 1891.

OUR DOLLS' HOUSE. See *Our Toys*.

OUR DOMESTICS. C.F. 2 a. F. Hay. An adaptation. Strand, June 15, 1867.

OUR ELDORADO. D. 4 a. F. A. Scudamore. Northampton O.H., August 6, 1894; Pav., August 13, 1894. See *Fight for Life*.

OUR EMMIE. P. 1 a. M. Clark. Op. Comique, August 1, 1892.

OUR FAMILY LEGEND. Oa. R. Stockton. M. by J. S. Jones, jun. Brighton Aquar., October 8, 1892.

OUR FAMILY MOTTO; OR, NOBLESSE OBLIGE. P. 1 a. Heloïse Durant. Queen's Gate H., February 27, 1889.

OUR FARM. Ca. E. Rose. Queen's, June 29, 1872.

OUR FLAT. F.C. 3 a. Mrs Musgrave. Southport Winter Gardens, April 10, 1889; P.O.W.'s, June 13, 1889; tr. to Op. Comique, June 25, 1889; rev. Strand, July 2, 1894; Comedy, February 14, 1905.

OUR FLOSSIE. C. 1 a. W. F. Field. Addlestone New T., April 2, 1888.

OUR FOLKS. Duol. E. Drew. St. George's H., July 26, 1900.

OUR FRENCH LADY'S MAID. Adelphi, May 22, 1858.

OUR FRIEND THE JEW. C. 4 a. A. Paumier. Merthyr Tydvil T.R., August 12, 1904 (C.P.).

OUR FRIENDS (*Nos Intimes*). C.D. 4 a. G. March. Olympic, May 6, 1872.

OUR FRIENDS. Ca. 1 a. Mary Righton. Ladbroke H., March 16, 1888.

OUR GAL. F. 1 a. Publ. by S. French, Ltd.

OUR GARDEN. Oa. 3 a. Annie M'Namara. M. by C. Schäfer. Parkhurst, December 15, 1894.

OUR GEORDIE. F. Newcastle-upon-Tyne T.R., March 7, 1872.

OUR GIRLS. C. H. J. Byron. Vaudeville, April 19, 1879.

OUR GOBLINS; OR, FUN ON THE RHINE. M.C. Leamington Circus Pav., September 18, 1882.

OUR GREAT SURPRISE. P. 1 a. H. Blyth. Glasgow T.R., February 20, 1890.

OUR GUARDIAN ANGEL. D. 4 a. C. Burnette. Prod. in provinces, August, 1895; Novelty, January 6, 1896.

OUR HATED RIVAL. Ca. Capt. R. L. and C. M. A. Bayliff. Richmond T.R., December 17, 1891.

OUR HELEN. Burl. D. 3 a. R. Reece. Adap. fr. Meilhac and Halévy's *La Belle Helène*. Gaiety, April 8, 1884.

OUR HOME DEFENDERS. Dr. Sk. Cayley Calvert. East Ham Pal., February 22, 1909.

OUR HOSTESS. A. O'D. Bartholeyns. Eng. ver. of Goldoni's *La Locandiera*. Kilburn T.R., April 5, 1897.

OUR HOUSEMAID. C. Sk. Chas. Windermere. Middlesex, May 10, 1909.

OUR ISLAND HOME. Ent. W. S. Gilbert. Gallery of Illus., June 20, 1870.

OUR JOAN. D. 3 a. Mr. and Mrs. Herman Merivale. Birmingham P.O.W.'s, August 22, 1887; Grand, October 3, 1887.

OUR JOHN. P. 1 a. P. Murray. Garrick, June 10, 1899

OUR KATE. See *The Co-Respondent*.

OUR LADS IN BLUE; OR, UNDER THE UNION JACK. D. C. P. Emery. Ent. at Stationers' Hall, March 13, 1891.

OUR LASS. D. Prol. and 4 a. W. Stevens. Salford P.O.W.'s, April 30, 1886. Sadler's Wells, July 28, 1888.

OUR LAST REHEARSAL. M.C. Miss Perry. M. by A. Oake. Folkestone Pleasure Gdns. T., April 25, 1893.

OUR LODGER. Eccentric C. 3 a. J. J. Blood. Brighton T.R., May 27, 1885.

OUR LODGERS. F. Mme. Brunner. Sunderland Lyceum, June 26, 1868.

OUR LORD'S SUPPER. See "Miracle Plays."

OUR LOT IN LIFE. Military D. 4 a. D. Henger. Lancaster Athenæum, April 2, 1900.

OUR LOT IN LIFE. D. C. H. Hazlewood. New Britannia.

OUR LOTTIE. Dom. C.D. 1 a. C. S. Fawcett. Paignton Bijou. See *For Charity's Sake*.

OUR LUCK. S.C.D. 1 a. C. D. Friel. Doncaster T.R., September 22, 1876.

OUR MARY ANNE. F. 1 a. J. B. Buckstone. D.L., January 18, 1837.

OUR MASTER. F. C. Sk. 1 sc. Poplar Queen's, March 30, 1908.

OUR MESS. M. Sk. C. Grain. St. Geo. H., 1883.

OUR MISS GIBBS. M.P. in 2 a., by "Cryptos." Constructed by Jas. T. Tanner. Lyrics by Adrian Ross and Percy Greenbank. M. by Ivan Caryll and Lionel Monckton. Gaiety, January 23, 1909.

OUR NATIVE HOME. D. 5 a. Chas. Whitlock and J. Sargent. Surrey, September 19, 1892.

OUR NATIVE LAND AND GALLANT PROTECTORS. D. J. C. Cross. Pr. 1803.

OUR NELLY. Dom. D. 2 a. H. T. Craven. Surrey, 1853.

OUR NEW BUTLER. F. 1 a. H. Nicholls. Publ. by S. French, Ltd.

OUR NEW DOLLS' HOUSE. W. Yardley and Cotsford Dick.

OUR NEW GOVERNESS. C. 2 a. S. Brooks. Lyceum.

OUR NEW MAN. F. 1 a. W. E. Suter. Surrey. Other vers. entitled *The Waiter of Cremorne* and *The Waiter of the Eagle Tavern.*

OUR NURSE DOROTHY. F. D.L., January 25, 1855.

OUR OLD HOUSE AT HOME. Dom. D. 2 a. T. Blake. Sadler's Wells.

OUR OWN ANTHONY AND CLEOPATRA. Absurdity. F. C. Burnand. Gaiety, September 8, 1873.

OUR OWN CORRESPONDENT. F. J. Strachan. Charing Cr. T., August 14, 1871.

OUR PAL. D. 1 a. Dr. G. H. R. Dabbs. Shanklin Inst., April 24, 1889 (amat.).

OUR PARTY. F.C. A. Lloyd. Croydon T.R., August 4, 1884.

OUR PET. C. 3 a. C. Edwards. Charing Cr., November 12, 1873.

OUR PICNIC. Duol. Bertha Graham. Amateur Players' Association, February 7, 1906.

OUR PLAY. Ca. R. G. Graham. Teddington T.H., February 1, 1893; Vaudeville, March 13, 1893.

OUR PLEASANT SINS. C.D. 4 a. W. Barrett and C. Hannan. Leeds Grand, February 13, 1893 (C.P.), and July 12, 1893; St. Leonards Pier Pav., August 3, 1896.

OUR POLLY. D. 3 a. E. Towers. Pav., April 16, 1881.

OUR QUIET CHATEAU. R. Reece. Gall. of Illustration, December 26. 1867.

OUR REGIMENT. F.C. 3 a. H. Hamilton. Adap fr. Von Moser's *Kriegim Frieden.* Vaudeville (mat.), February 13, 1883; Globe, January 21, 1884; Toole's, January 27, 1891.

OUR RELATIONS. F.C. 3 a. F. Jarman. Brighton Aquarium, October 5, 1891.

OUR RELATIVES. Dom. C. 1 a. W. Ellis. Olympic, Dec. 11, 1880.

OUR SAILOR LAD. Mus. C. 3 a. F. J. Kirke. M. by G. Dixon. Bootle Muncaster T., May 6, 1895; Novelty, January 13, 1896.

OUR SERVANT GIRL. Mus. C. 2 a. F. Lawrence and C. A. Vane. M. by J. L. S. Moss and J. S. Baker. Edmonton T.R., June 15, 1896.

OUR SERVANT'S BALL. Sk. C. Grain. St. Geo. H. (first time in London), December 26, 1887.

OUR SILVER WEDDING. D. 5 a. J. Willing. Standard, March 27, 1885.

OUR SISTERS. Oa. M. by A. Lee. Lyceum (first time this season), August 11, 1834.

OUR SONS AND DAUGHTERS. C.D. 3 a. J. F. Cooke. Glasgow P.O.W.'s, October 31, 1879.

OUR SQUARE. F.C. 3 a. E. Rose. Southport Winter Gdns., February 11, 1884; Gaiety, April 30, 1884.

OUR STRATEGISTS. Modern "Comedy of Errors." Dr. Sayre. Orig. prod. in America. Op. Comique, May 29, 1886.

OUR SUBURB. C. C. Richins. Hanwell Park H., March 12, 1902.

OUR SUMMER HOLIDAY. Clifton, November 25, 1886.

OUR TOM. F. R. Clothier. Leicester T.R., February 8, 1875.

OUR TOWN; OR, THE FIRST OF NOVEMBER. C. J. Davies (local). Warrington Public H., November 16, 1871, and January, 1884.

OUR TOYS. Fairy piece. 1 a. W. Yardley. Originally *Our Doll's House.* St. James's T., July 16, 1895

OUR TUNER. F.C. T. G. Warren. Shrewsbury T.R., October 15, 1885.

OUR TUTOR. F. Sk. 1 a. Abbey Wood. Leytonstone Assembly R., October 25, 1890.

OUR VILLAGE; OR, THE LOST SHIP. Dom. D. 3 a. W. L. Rede. D.L., April 18, 1853.

OUR VOLUNTEERS. D. 4 a. F. Maxwell. Brighton Eden T., July 19, 1897.

OUR VOLUNTEERS; OR, THE CAPTAIN'S NOT AMISS. Burla. J. E. Wilks. Brighton West Pier Pav., July 6, 1896.

OUR WAR CORRESPONDENT. Burl. Leicester R.O.H., May 27, 1878.

OUR WIFE; OR, THE ROSE OF AMIENS. C.D. 2 a. J M. Morton Princess's, November 18, 1856.

OUR WIVES. C. F. Blanshard. Adap. fr. *Trois Femmes pour un Mari.* Eastbourne T.R., September 16, 1885 (afterwards interdicted as an infringt. of copyright).

OURAGAN, L'. O. 4 a. Lib. by Emile Zola. M. by A. Bruneau. Paris O. Com., April 29, 1901.

OURANG-OUTANG; OR, HIS DOUBLE, THE. Adelphi, December 29, 1842. See *As in a Glass.*

OURS. C. 3 a. T. W. Robertson. Liverpool P.O.W.'s, August 23, 1866; P.O.W.'s, September 15, 1866; Globe, February 18, 1899; Coronet, July 12, 1909.

OURSELVES. C. Miss Chambers. 1811.

OURSELVES. C. 3 a. F. C. Burnand. Vaudeville, January 29, 1880.

OUT ALL NIGHT. Sk. 1 sc. W. Pink. Camberwell Palace, March 13, 1905.

OUT AT ELBOWS. An "improbability." 1 a. Aylmer H. Dove. Toole's, March, 1882.

OUT FOR A HOLIDAY. F. Northampton T.R., November 29, 1870.

OUT FOR A HOLIDAY. F. A. Willoughby. Wolverhampton P.O.W.'s, June 9, 1884.

OUT FOR THE DAY. F. 3 a. W. E. Morton. Oxford New T., August 2, 1886.

OUT OF EVIL. D. 4 a. A. Forrest. Battersea Queen's, December 4, 1893.

OUT OF PLACE; OR, THE LAKE OF LAUSANNE. M.F. F. Reynolds. C.G., February 28, 1805.

OUT OF SIGHT. O. 1 a. C. B. Stephenson. M. by F. Clay. Cromwell Ho., July 8, 1881

OUT OF SIGHT. Ca. Fredk. Fenn and Richd. Pryce. Royalty, May 20, 1906.

OUT OF SIGHT, OUT OF MIND. F.C. Sk. K. Summers. Nottingham Sneinton Inst., May 29, 1894.

OUT OF SORTS F.C. 3 a. Windsor T.R., September 20, 1884.

OUT OF THE BEATEN TRACK. C. 4 a. M. Milton. Adap. fr. the German of E. Wichert. Strand, July 11, 1889.

OUT OF THE DARKNESS. Rom. P. 4 a. M. and lyrics by C. Baxter. Stafford Lyceum, June 5, 1905.

OUT OF THE DARKNESS. D. 4 a. Ivan Patrick Gore. West Stanley R., July 12, 1909.

OUT OF THE FRYING PAN. C. 1 a. Transl. fr. the Danish by P. Toft. Adap. by A. P. Graves. Holborn, May 4, 1872.

OUT OF THE FRYING PAN INTO THE FIRE. F. B. Wright. City of London, July 8, 1867.

OUT OF THE HUNT. F.C. R. Reece and T. Thorpe. Adap fr. the French of Barrière and Bernard. Royalty, October 8, 1881.

OUT OF THE PAST. P. 1 a. P. Grayle. St. Geo. H., June 6, 1893 (amat.).

OUT OF THE PAST. Dram. Dr. Ep. 1 a. H Nolan. Barrow Royalty T. and O.H., February 4, 1898.

OUT OF THE RANKS. Burl. R. Reece. Strand, June 3, 1884.

OUT OF THE SHADOWLAND. Ca. 1 a. Mary Stuart Bayswater Bijou. June 17, 1899

OUT OF THE WORLD. Piece. 1 a. H. Burnett. Vaudeville, February 23, 1892.

OUT ON THE LOOSE. F. 1 a. M. and B. Barnett. Strand, March 11, 1850.

OUTCAST FORTUNE TELLER, THE. D. Birkenhead T.R., December 18, 1882.

OUTCAST JOE; OR, THE STREET ARAB. D. W. R. Waldron. Bolton T.R., March 28, 1870.

OUTCAST LONDON. Dom. D. 4 a. H. Young and G. Roberts. Rev. and alt. by A. West Eleph. and C., Oct. 2, 1886; West London, Feb 14, 1898.

OUTCAST LONDON. D. 4 a. Liverpool Rotunda T.. April 3, 1899.

OUTCAST POOR; OR, THE BYEWAYS OF LONDON. D. 4 a. J. Cross. Surrey, August 25, 1884.

OUTCASTS, THE. Effingham, February 6, 1864.

OUTCASTS; OR, POOR BESS AND LITTLE DICK, THE. O. A. Cherry. Dublin, Manchester, etc., 1796. N.p.

OUTCAST OF THE FAMILY, THE. D. 4 a. H. Foxwell. Salford P.O.W., June 25, 1908.

OUTCAST OF THE STREETS. City of London, February 18, 1886.

OUTCASTS OF THE CITY. D. 4 a. J. Eldred and H. P. Grattan Jarrow T.R., November 3, 1884.

OUTLAW OF THE ADRIATIC; OR, THE FEMALE SPY AND THE CHIEF OF THE TEN, THE. Rom. D. 3 a. Adap. fr. the French of Victor Sejour. Th. Porte St. Martin, May 8, 1855; Princess's (a version under title of *Master Passion*), November 2, 1859.

OUTLAWED SON, THE. D. W. F. Lyon, Adap. fr. Miss Braddon's novel "Lucius Davoren." H.M.T., Richmond, July 30, 1881.

OUTLAWS, THE. M.D. A. Franklin. D.L., October 18, 1798. N.p.

OUTPOST, THE P. 1 a. W. Ackerman. Lyric, January 19, 1904.

OUTSIDE PASSENGER. F. Attributed to Brewer. Hay., July 4, 1811. N.p.

OUTSIDER, AN. C. 3 a. Mayne Lindsay and Robert Marshall. Manchester R., October 15, 1908.

OUTSIDER, THE. Sporting Melo-d. 5 a. F. Dawson. Yarmouth Aquarium T., March 2, 1891.

OUTWARD BOUND. M. Sk. Nellie Ganthony. Terry's, March 21, 1896.

OUTWARD BOUND; OR, NOT GUILTY. D. Liverpool Colosseum, May 17, 1875.

OUTWITTED. C. 3 a. Mrs. Vaughan. St. Geo. H., July 14, 1871.

OUTWITTED. C. B. Aylmer. Holborn, January 21, 1873.

OUTWITTED. Playlet. 1 a. W. G. Smythies. May Street H., West Kensington, December 16, 1891.

OUTWITTED. P. 1 a. G. Anderson. Margate T.R., July 13, 1899.

OUTWITTED AT LAST. C.O. 3 a. M. by Lanza. D.L., December 11, 1817.

OVER HEADS AND EARS. Burla. R. Reece. Park, June 10, 1876.

OVER NIAGARA FALLS. Melo-d. 4 a. Joseph le Brandt. Islington Grand, April 27, 1903.

OVER-PROOF; OR, WHAT WAS FOUND IN A CELEBRATED CASE. Burl. F. C. Burnand. Royalty, November 6, 1878. See *Proof*.

OVER THE BORDER. Ent. Eyre Arms, St. John's Wood, November 16, 1870.

OVER THE CLIFF; OR, BY ACCIDENT OR DESIGN. D. 4 a. A. T. Robbins. Grimsby T.R., February 11, 1884

OVER THE GARDEN WALL. F. S. Grundy. Folly, July 20, 1881.

OVER THE HILLS TO THE POOR-HOUSE. P. 1 sc. A. R. Callender. Birmingham Gaiety, February 24, 1905.

OVER THE WAY. F. P. Meritt. Strand, February 14, 1878.

OVER THE WAY. Ca. T. W. Robertson. F. on Henri Murger's *Bonhomme Jadis*. Court, January 20, 1893.

OVER. See *O'er*.

OVERLAND JOURNEY TO CONSTANTINOPLE AS UNDERTAKEN BY LORD BATEMAN, WITH INTERESTING PARTICULARS OF THE FAIR SOPHIA. Extrav. 2 a. R. B. Brough. Adelphi, April 17, 1854.

OVERLAND ROUTE, THE. C. 3 a. T. Taylor. Hay., February 23, 1860.

OVERTHROW OF REBELS, THE. P. with this title ac. 1602. N.p.

OVID, THE TRAGEDY OF. Sir A. Cokain. F. partly on Molière's *Dom Juan ou Le Festin de Pierre*, itself not original, and partly taken from Ovid's Elegies and an Italian play called *Il Atheisto Fulminato*. Pr. 1669.

OWEN, PRINCE OF POWYS; OR, WELSH FEUDS. T. D.L., January 25, 1822.

OWEN TUDOR. P. R. Wilson, assisted by Drayton, Hathwaye, and Mundy. N.p.

OWL, THE. P. D. Daborne. Wr. 1613.

OWL SISTERS; OR, THE HAUNTED ABBEY RUINS, THE. Melo-d. Rom. E Fitzball. Adelphi, September, 1842.

OWLS. Masque. Ben Jonson. 1624.

OWNER OF THE WORKS, THE. D. 4 a. L. B. Goldman. Orig. prod. as *A Man of the World* at Treharris Publ. H., March 7, 1894; Leamington T.R., March 18, 1895.

OXFORD ACT, THE. Ballad O. Pr. 1733.

OXFORD AGREEMENT, THE. P. 1 a. L. Hawkins. Barnsley T.R., October 29, 1897.

OXFORD LADIES; OR, THE NOBLEMAN, THE. C. Thos. Brereton. (Left unfinished.)

OXONIAN IN TOWN, THE. C. Geo. Colman. C.G., November 7, 1767. Pr. 1770.

OXYGEN; OR, GAS IN BURLESQUE METRE. Burl. R. Reece and H. B. Farnie. Folly, March 31, 1877.

P

P.P.; OR, THE MAN AND THE TIGER. F. 1 a. T. Parry. Adelphi, October 21, 1833.

P.U.P.; OR, THE DOG IN THE MANGER. F. 1 a. H. Moss. Leeds Grand, August 6, 1883; Huddersfield T.R. and O.H., September 3, 1883.

PA'S ODD TRICK; OR, HERO AND ERROR WIN. M. P. J. P. Kennedy. M. by J. Armstrong. Nottingham T.R., February 4, 1897 (C.P.).

PA'S PILLS. F. C. 3 a. C. A. Fisher. Aberystwith Bijou T., June 1, 1894.

PACE THAT KILLS; OR, FAST LIFE AND NOBLE LIFE, THE. D. 3 a. C. H. Hazlewood. Britannia, March 7, 1870.

PACHA OF PIMLICO, THE. F. Extrav. 1 a. J. M. Morton. St. James's, April 15, 1861.

PACKET BOAT; OR, A PEEP BEHIND THE VEIL, THE. M. Ent. S. Birch. C.G., May 13, 1794. N.p.

PACKET FROM ENGLAND, A. P. 1 a. W. O. Tristram. Bayswater Bijou, April 24, 1895.

PACKING UP. F. 1 a. H. Grattan. Publ. by S. French, Ltd.

PACQUITA; OR, LOVE IN A FRAME. C.O. 2 a. R. Reece. Royalty, October 21, 1871.

PAD, THE. F. 1 a. R. Woodbridge. C.G., May 27, 1793. Ptd. 1793.

PADDY CAREY; OR, THE BOY OF CLOGHEEN. F. 1 a. T. Power. C.G., May 29, 1833.

PADDY MILES, THE LIMERICK BOY. F. 1 a. J. Pilgrim. Sadler's Wells, April 22, 1836.

PADDY THE PIPER. C. 1 a. Publ. by S. French, Ltd.

PADLOCK, THE. C.O. 2 a. Isaac Bickerstaffe. M. by C. Dibdin. Plot fr. Cervantes's novel *The Jealous Husband*. Pr. 1768. D.L., October 3, 1768; Edinburgh, 1783; Lyceum, August 16, 1817; C.G., 1825; D.L., June 8, 1829.

PÆTUS AND ARRIA. T. Pr. 1809. N.ac.

PAGE. D. Berquin, 1793.

PAGE, THE. C By Reynolds.

PAGE 97. P. 1 a. "T. K." Newport Lyceum, December 23, 1907; Garrick, January 11, 1908; Tivoli, March 16, 1908.

PAGE OF PLYMOUTH. T. Ben Jonson and Decker. 1599.

PAGEANT OF LLOYDS. A. W. H. Leslie. Savoy Hotel, February 25, 1908 (amat.).

PAGEANTS performed at the Inauguration of the Chief Magistrates of the City of London, etc.:—

1. When Henry III.'s Queen Eleanor rode through the City to her Coronation. 1236.
2. For Edward I.'s Victory over the Scots. 1298.
3. When Black Prince made his entry with his Royal prisoner. 1357.
4. When Richard II. passed along Cheapside. 1392.
5. When Henry V. made his entry after the Battle of Agincourt. 1415.
6. When Princess Catherine came through London to be married to Prince Arthur. 1501.
7. When Henry VIII. received the Emperor Charles V. 1522.
8. When Henry VIII. and Ann Boleyn passed through the City to her coronation. 1532.
9. The passage of our Most Sovereign Lady Queen Elizabeth through the City of London to Westminster the day before her Coronation. Pr. 1558.
10. The Device of the Pageant borne before Sir Wolstone Dixie, Lord Mayor, October 29, 1585. G. Peele. Pr. 1585.
11. POLYHYMNIA. G. Peele. Describing a triumph at tylt before Her Majesty on November 17. Pr. 1590.
12. DESCENSUS ASTRÆÆ. G. Peele. A pageant borne before William Web, Lord Mayor of London, October 29, 1591. Pr. 1591.
13. THE WHOLE MAGNIFICENT ENTERTAINMENT given to King James and Queen Anne and Henry Frederick, the Prince, on their passage through the City, March 15, 1603. By T. Dekker. Pr. 1604.
14. THE TRIUMPHS OF REUNITED BRITANNIA. Performed on the entry of Sir Leonard Hethday as Lord Mayor of London. October 29, 1605. Wr. by A. Munday. Pr. 1605.
15. LONDON'S LOVE TO THE ROYAL PRINCE HENRIE. Meeting him on his return fr. Richmond. Munday. May 31, 1610. Pr. same year.
16. HRRYSO-THRIAMOS; THE TRIUMPHES OF GOLDE. On inauguration of Sir James Pemberton as Lord Mayor of London. October 29, 1611. By A. Munday. Pr. 1611.
17. TROIA NOVA TRIUMPHANS. On receiving Sir John Swinnerton into the City of London. By T. Dekker. Pr. 1612.
18. THE TRIUMPHS OF TRUTH. On installation of Sir Thomas Middleton as Lord Mayor of London. October 29, 1613. By T. Middleton. Pr. 1613.
19. TRIUMPHS OF OLD DRAPERY; OR, THE RICH CLOTHING OF ENGLAND. At the installation of Thomas Hayes as Lord Mayor. By A. Munday. Pr. 1614.
20. METROPOLIS CORONATA. THE TRIUMPHES OF ANCIENT DRAPERY; OR, RICH CLOATHING OF ENGLAND. On installation of Sir John Jolles as Lord Mayor of London, October 30, 1615. By A. Munday. Pr. 1615.
21. CHRYSANALEIA. THE GOLDEN FISHING; OR, HONOUR OF FISHMONGERS. On installation of John Lernan as Lord Mayor of London. October 29, 1616. By A. Munday. Pr. 1616.
22. CIVITATIS AMOR; THE CITY'S LOVE. Middleton. On entry of Charles to be created Prince of Wales. 1616.
23. THE TRIUMPHS OF LOVE AND ANTIQUITY. On installation of Sir William Cockayn as Lord Mayor of London, October 29, 1619. By T. Middleton. Pr. 1619.
24. LES IRENES TROPHÆA; OR, THE TRYUMPHS OF PEACE. On installation of Sir Francis Jones as Lord Mayor of London, October 30, 1620. By J. Squire. Pr. 1620.
25. SUN IN ARIES, THE. On installation of the Right. Hon. Edward Barkham as Lord Mayor of London, October 29, 1621. By T. Middleton. Pr. 1621.
26. MONUMENT OF HONOUR, THE. On confirmation of John Goare. By J. Webster. Pr. 1624.

27. TRIUMPH OF HEALTH AND PROSPERITY, THE. At the installation of the Right Hon. Cuthbert Hasket. By T. Middleton. Pr. 1626.

28. LONDON'S JUS HONORARIUM. On installation of the Right Hon. George Whitmore. By T. Heywood. Pr. 1631.

29. LONDINI ARTIUM ET SCIENTIARUM SCATURIGO; OR, LONDON'S FOUNTAIN OF ARTS AND SCIENCES. On installation of the Right Hon. Nich. Raynton as Lord Mayor. By T. Heywood. Pr. 1632.

30. LONDON IMP.; OR, LONDON MERCATOR. On installation of the Right Hon. Ralph Freeman. By T. Heywood. Pr. 1633.

31. TRIUMPHS OF FAME AND HONOUR. At installation of Robert Parkhurst. By J. Taylor. Pr. 1634.

32. LONDINI SPECULUM; OR, LONDON'S MIRROR. On installation of the Right Hon. Richard Fenn as Lord Mayor. By T. Heywood. Pr. 1637.

33. PORTA PIETATIS; OR, THE PORT OR HARBOUR OF PIETY. On installation of the Right Hon. Sir Maurice Abbot as Lord Mayor. By T. Heywood. Pr. 1638.

34. LONDINI STATUS PACATUS; OR, LONDON'S PEACEABLE ESTATE. On installation of the Right Hon. Henry Garaway as Lord Mayor. By T. Heywood. Pr. 1639.

35. OVATIO CAROLI; THE TRIUMPH OF KING CHARLES. T. Heywood. On entry of His Majesty into the City, November 25, 1641. Pr. 1641.

36. CHARITY TRIUMPHANT; OR, THE VIRGIN SHOW. On installation of Alderman Déthicke as Lord Mayor, October 29, 1655. By E. Gayton. Pr. 1655.

37. LONDON'S TRIUMPH. On installation of Robert Titchburn as Lord Mayor. By "J. B." Pr. 1656.

38. LONDON'S TRIUMPH. On installation of Richard Chiverton as Lord Mayor, October 29, 1657 By J. Tatham. Pr. 1657.

39. LONDON'S TRYUMPH PRESENTED BY INDUSTRY AND HONOUR. On installation of the Right Hon. Sir John Ireton as Lord Mayor, October 29, 1658. By J. Tatham. Pr. 1658.

40. LONDON'S TRIUMPH. On installation of Thomas Allen as Lord Mayor, October 29, 1659. By J. Tatham. Pr. 1659.

41. LONDON'S GLORY. An entertainment in honour of Charles II., the Dukes of York and Gloucester, the two Houses of Parliament, Privy Council, Judges, etc., at Guildhall, July 5, 1660. By J. Tatham. Pr. 1660.

42. LONDON'S TRYUMPHS. On installation of Sir John Frederick as Lord Mayor. By J. Tatham. Pr. 1661.

43. ENTERTAINMENT OF HIS MOST EXCELLENT MAJESTY CHARLES II. IN HIS PASSAGE THROUGH THE CITY OF LONDON TO HIS CORONATION, THE. By John Ogilby. Pr. 1661. Afterwards enlarged and pr. 1685 under title of *The King's Coronation*.

44. AQUA TRIUMPHALIS. On entertaining Their Majesties, August 23, 1662. By J. Tatham. Pr. 1662

45. LONDON'S TRIUMPH. On installation of Sir John Robinson as Lord Mayor. Ascr. to J. Tatham. Pr. 1662.

46. LONDINUM TRIUMPHANS; OR, LONDON'S TRIUMPH. On installation of Sir Anthony Bateman as Lord Mayor on October 29, 1663. By J. Tatham. Pr. 1663.

47. LONDON'S TRIUMPHS. On installation of Sir John Lawrence as Lord Mayor, October 29, 1664 By J. Tatham. Pr. 1664.

48. LONDON'S RESURRECTION TO JOY AND TRIUMPH. On installation of Sir George Waterman as Lord Mayor. By T. Jordan. Pr. 1671.

49. LONDON TRIUMPHANT; OR, THE CITY IN JOLLITY AND SPLENDOUR. On installation of Sir Robert Hanson as Lord Mayor. By T. Jordan. Pr. 1672.

50. LONDON IN ITS SPLENDOUR. On installation of Sir William Hooker as Lord Mayor. By T. Jordan. Pr. 1673.

51. GOLDSMITH'S JUBILEE; OR, LONDON'S TRIUMPHS, THE. On installation of the Right Hon. Sir Robert Vyner as Lord Mayor. T. Jordan. Pr. 1674.

52. TRIUMPHS OF LONDON, THE. On installation of Sir Joseph Sheldon as Lord Mayor, October 29, 1675. T. Jordan. Pr. 1675.

53. LONDON'S TRIUMPHS. On installation of the Right Hon. Sir Thomas Davies as Lord Mayor, October 30, 1676. T. Jordan. Pr. 1676.

54. LONDON'S TRIUMPHS. On installation of the Right Hon. Sir Francis Chaplin as Lord Mayor, October 29, 1677. T. Jordan. Pr. 1677.

55. TRIUMPH OF LONDON, THE. On installation of Sir James Edwards as Lord Mayor. By Thomas Jordan. Pr. 1678.

56. LONDON IN LUSTER. On installation of the Right Hon. Sir Robert Clayton as Lord Mayor, October 29, 1679. T. Jordan. Pr. 1679.

57. LONDON'S GLORY; OR, THE LORD MAYOR'S SHOW. On installation of the Right Hon. Sir Patience Warde as Lord Mayor, October 29, 1680. T. Jordan. Pr. 1680.

58. LONDON'S JOY; OR, THE LORD MAYOR'S SHOW. On installation of the Right Hon. Sir John Moore as Lord Mayor, October 29, 1681. T. Jordan. Pr. 1681.

59. LORD MAYOR'S SHOW, THE. On installation of the Right Hon. Sir William Pritchard as Lord Mayor, September 30, 1682. T. Jordan. Pr. 1682.

60. TRIUMPHS OF LONDON, THE. On installation of the Right Hon. Sir Henry Tulse as Lord Mayor, October 29, 1683. Ascr. to T. Jordan. Pr. 1683.

61. LONDON'S ROYAL TRIUMPH FOR THE CITY'S LOYAL MAGISTRATE. On installation of the Right Hon. Sir James Smith as Lord Mayor, October 29, 1684. T. Jordan. Pr. 1684.

62. LONDON'S ANNUAL TRIUMPH. On installation of the Right Hon. Sir Robert Jeffreys as Lord Mayor, October 29, 1685. By M. Taubman. Pr. 1685.

63. LONDON'S YEARLY JUBILEE. On installation of the Right Hon. Sir John Peake as Lord Mayor, October 29, 1686. M. Taubman. Pr. 1686.

64. LONDON'S TRIUMPH; OR, THE GOLDSMITHS' JUBILEE. On installation of Sir John Shorter as Lord Mayor, October 29, 1687. M. Taubman. Pr. 1687.

65. LONDON'S ANNIVERSARY FESTIVAL. On installation of the Right Hon. Sir John Chapman as Lord Mayor, October 29, 1688. M. Taubman. Pr. 1688.

66. LONDON'S GREAT JUBILEE. On installation of the Right Hon. Sir Thomas Pilkington as Lord Mayor, October 29, 1689. M. Taubman. Pr. 1689.

67. TRIUMPHS OF LONDON, THE On installation of the Right Hon. Sir Thomas Stamp as Lord Mayor, October 29, 1691. E. Settle. Pr. 1691.

68. TRIUMPHS OF LONDON, THE. On installation of the Right Hon. Sir John Fleet as Lord Mayor, October 29, 1692. E. Settle. Pr. 1692.

69. TRIUMPHS OF LONDON, THE. On installation of the Right Hon. Sir William Ashurst as Lord Mayor, October 30, 1693. E. Settle. Pr. 1693.

70. TRIUMPHS OF LONDON, THE. On installation of Sir Thomas Lane as Lord Mayor, October 29, 1694. E. Settle. Pr. 1694.

71. TRIUMPHS OF LONDON, THE. On installation of the Right Hon. Sir John Houblon as Lord Mayor, October 29, 1695. E. Settle. Pr. 1695.

72. TRIUMPHS, Etc., for Sir Humphry Edwin in 1698. E. Settle. Pr. 1698.

73. TRIUMPHS OF LONDON. On installation of Sir Richard Levett as Lord Mayor, October 30, 1699. E. Settle. Pr. 1699.

74. TRIUMPHS OF LONDON, THE. On installation of Sir T. Abney as Lord Mayor, October 29, 1700. E. Settle. Pr. 1700.

75. TRIUMPHS OF LONDON, THE. For Sir William Gore. 1701. E. Settle. Pr. 1701.

76. TRIUMPHS OF LONDON, THE. On installation of the Rt. Hon. Sir Charles Duncombe. October 29, 1708. E. Settle. Pr. 1708. This was never performed, owing to Prince George of Denmark's death on October 28, 1708.

See *Warwick Pageant*.

PAGES OF THE DUKE DE VENDOME, THE. Ballet. D.L., May 21, 1838.

PAGLIACCI, I. O. 2 a. Lib. and M. by R. Leoncavallo. Milan, May 21, 1892. (As *The Strollers*) first time in England, C.G., May 19. 1893; Grand T., April 23, 1894.

PAGLIACCI. Dr. ver. Chas. Brookfield, taken fr. Leoncavallo's O. Savoy, December 6, 1904.

PAGLIACCI. Condensed ver. of Leoncavallo's O., in 2 a. London Col., February 22, 1909.

PAID IN FULL. D. 3 a. St. A. Miller. Ladbroke H., November 14, 1887.

PAID IN FULL. 4 a. Eugene Walter. Aldwych, September 26, 1908.

PAID IN FULL; OR, A LIFE'S REPENTANCE. Oldham T.R., November 3, 1873.

PAID IN HIS OWN COIN. C. 3 a. Thomas King Moylan. Dublin Abbey, April 22, 1909 (amat.).

PAILLASSE, LA. See *The Acrobat, Belphegor*.

PAINFUL PILGRIMAGE, THE. P. Ac. before Queen Elizabeth. 1568.

PAINFUL PREDICAMENT OF SHERLOCK HOLMES. Fantasy. Duke of York's, October 3, 1905.

PAINLESS DENTISTRY. F. M. Becher. Adelphi, June 12, 1875.

PAINTED WOMAN, THE. D. 4 a. By "Riada." Clapham Shakespeare, July 21, 1902. See *Held Apart*.

PAINTER OF GHENT, THE. D. 1 a. D. Jerrold, April 25, 1836. Strand, May 1, 1836.

PAINTER'S BREAKFAST, THE. Dr. Satire. Mr. Brenan. Pr. at Dublin, 1756. ? N.ac.

PAINTER'S DAUGHTER, THE. P. Ac. at Court, 1576.

PAIR O' WINGS. C. D. 3 a. P. Meritt and H. Girnot. Dublin Gaiety, December 13, 1878; Portsmouth T.R. (Meritt and Righton), May 27, 1881.

PAIR OF BOOTS, A. F. Olympic, October 4, 1873.

PAIR OF KIDS, A. M. Absurdity. J. J. Hewson. Manchester Comedy T., July 2, 1888.

PAIR OF KNICKERBOCKERS, A. C. 1 a. E. Phillpotts. St. George's H., December 26, 1899.

PAIR OF LUNATICS, A. Dr. Sk. 1 a. W. R. Walker. D.L., 1889.

PAIR OF PARROTS, A. F. C. 3 a. F. H. Morland. Belfast O.H., October 21, 1901.

PAIR OF PIGEONS, A. Dr. Sk. 1 a. E. Stirling. Lyceum, November, 1857.

PAIR OF SPECTACLES, A. C. 3 a. S. Grundy. Adap. fr. Labiche and Delacour's C. *Les Petites Oiseaux*. Garrick, February 22, 1890; rev. June 20, 1892, and January 17, 1895; Criterion, January 4, 1902; rev. Comedy, March 14, 1906; rev. Garrick, June 15, 1908.

PAIR OF THEM, A. M. piece. 1 a. P. Wrey. M. by M. Lutz. Gaiety, March 1, 1879.

PAIR OF WINGS. See *Pair o' Wings*.

PAIR'D OFF. Ca. Geo. Buckle. Licensed by Lord Chamberlain February 27, 1885. Stratford T.R., April, 1885.

PALACE OF PEARL, THE. M. spec. extrav. W. Younge and A. Murray. M. by Jakobowski and Stanislaus. Empire, June 12, 1886.

PALACE OF PLEASURE. Paynter.

PALACE OF PUCK, THE. Fan. C. 3 a. W. J. Locke. Hay., April 2, 1907. See *Butterflies*.

PALACE OF TRUTH, THE. Fairy c. 3 a. W. S. Gilbert. Hay., November 19, 1870; rev. Prince's; rev. Great Queen Street, May 23, 1905.

PALACE REVIEW, THE. "Fantastic forecast." 5 sc. G. R. Sims. M. by H. Finck. Palace, September 25, 1905.

PALADINS, LES. O. 3 a. Rameau, February 12, 1760.

PALAGIO D'ATLANTE. Il. O. Rossi. Wds. by G. Ruspigliosi. Circa 1642.

PALAMON AND ARCITE. D. Rose T., September, 1594 (probably an alt. of R. Edwards's c.).

PALÆMON AND ARCYTE. C. in 2 parts. Richard Edwards. Ac. before Q. Elizabeth in Christ Church H., Oxford, September 2, 1566. Probably not pr. Story taken fr. Chaucer's poem of *The Knight's Tale*.

PALAST REVOLUTION, EINE. F. C. 4 a. R. Showronnek. Gt. Queen St., March 13, 1905.

PALE JANET. D. 4 a. C. H. Hazlewood. Pavilion, August 31, 1867.

PALESTINE. Orat. Crotch (1775-1847).

PALLADIUS AND IRENE. D. 3 a. Pr. 1773. N. ac.

PALLANTUS AND EUDORA. T. H. Killigrew. Pr. 1653. See *The Conspiracy* and *The Tyrant King*.

PALLETTARIA. "An anachronism." 1 a. Brush. St. George's H., June 4, 1895.

PALMER'S MASQUE, THE. Ac. at Court in the early part of Henry VIII.

PALMISTRY. Ca. 1 a. R. R. Lumley. P.O.W., April 13, 1888.

PALMISTRY. Ca. A. Bonnin. Middlesbrough T.R., June 19, 1901.

PAMELA. C. Dance. Goodman's Fields, November 9, 1741. Pr. 1742. D.L. Taken fr. Samuel Richardson's novel.

PAMELA. C. C. Goldoni. Pr. 1756. F. on Richardson's novel. Orig. in Italian.

PAMELA. C. 3 a. Miss Johnston Douglas. Falkirk Town H., November 7, 1898.

PAMELA; OR, VIRTUE TRIUMPHANT. C. Anon. On same plan as foregoing. Pr. 1742. N.ac.

PAMELA'S PREJUDICE. Ca. 1 a. Mrs. M. Davis. Publ. by S. French, Ltd.

PAMELA'S PRODIGY. C. 3 a. C. Fitch. Court, October 21, 1891.

PAMMACHIUS. Latin C. B. P. Gardiner. 1544.

PAMPERED MENIALS. F. 1 a. H. J. Byron. Publ. by S. French, Ltd.

PAN; OR, THE LOVES OF ECHO AND NARCISSUS. H. J. Byron. Adelphi, April 10, 1865.

PAN AND HIS SYRIAX. Warner. Lic. 1584.

PAN AND SYRINX. O. 1 a. L. Theobald. Pr. 1717. L.I.F., 1717. M. by Galliard. Story taken fr. Ovid's *Metamorphoses*. Book I., fab. 12

PAN AND THE YOUNG SHEPHERD. Past. P. 2 a. Maurice Hewlett. Court, February 27, 1906.

PAN'S ANNIVERSARY; OR, THE SHEPHERD'S HOLIDAY. Mas. Ben Jonson. Presented at Court before King James, 1625. Assisted by Miss Jones. Pr. 1640.

PANACHE, LE. C. Edmond Goudinet. Royalty, October 23, 1876.

PANDORA. C. Transl. fr. Voltaire and pr. in Dr. Franklin's edition of that author.

PANDORA. M. Ent. C. Dibdin. Ac. at the Circus. N.p.

PANDORA; OR, THE CONVERTS. T. C. Sir W. Killegrew. Second title only appears in follo edition. Pr. 1664. ? Ac.

PANDORA'S BOX. Extrav. 1 a. H. J. Byron. P.O.W., December 26, 1866.

PANECIA. P. Ac. at Court, 1574.

PANEL PICTURE, THE. P. 4 a. W. O. Tristram. O. Comique. March 28, 1889.

PANGS OF JEALOUSY, THE. F. 1 a. E. Hine. Croydon Pub. H., May 22, 1905.

PANIER FLEURI, LE. Petite O. D.L., July 23, 1845.

PANNE. F. 3 a. Richard Skowronnek. Royalty, German Season, May 4, 1908.

PANNEL, THE. F. J. P. Kemble. D.L. Pr. 1788. D.L., January 29, 1817. Taken fr. Bickerstaffe's *'Tis Will It's No Worse*.

PANSIES. C. D. Cooke. Hackney Manor T., November 14, 1900.

PANSY. C. 1 a. H. Swears. Playhouse, June 6, 1907.

PANSY. P. 1 a. F. Jarman. Preston T.R., February 28, 1890.

PANTALOON; A PLEA FOR AN ANCIENT FAMILY. P. 1 a. J. M. Barrie. Duke of York's, April 5, 1905; rev. Duke of York's, June 9, 1906.

PANTHEA. T. Ascr. to James Hurdis. F. on the story in Xenophon's *Cyropædia*. N.pr. Afterwards transformed into a poem and pr.

PANTHEA; OR, THE CAPTIVE BRIDE. T. Ascr. to the Rev. T. Maurice. Pr. 1789. N. ac.

PANTHEA; OR, THE SUSIAN CAPTIVE. T. Nicholas Ashe. Pr. 1803 at Dublin. N.ac.

PANTHEA, QUEEN OF SUSIA. T. Anon. Pr. 1809.

PANTHEONITES. Dr. Ent. F. Gentleman. Hay., September 3, 1773. Pr. 1773.

PANTINS DE VIOLETTO, LES. O. Adolphe Adam. Princess's, June 27, 1870.

PANTOMIME PRINCE, A. Ca. John Glendinning. Belfast T.R., March 15, 1897.

PANTOMIME REHEARSAL, A. C. Sk. C. Clay. Terry's, June 6, 1891; Shaftesbury; Toole's; Court, December 2, 1891, and January 20, 1903.

PANTOMIME. This form of entertainment was first introduced on the English stage when *Tavern Bilkers*, by John Weaver, was produced at D.L. in 1702. The same author also produced:—

The Loves of Mars and Venus. 1716.
Perseus and Andromeda. 1716.
Orpheus and Eurydice. D.L., 1717.
Harlequin Turn'd Judge. D.L., 1717.
Cupid and Bacchus, D.L., 1719.

It was, however, John Rich who brought pantomime into popularity. Some of his earliest productions were:—

Harlequin Executed: A New Italian Mimic Scene Between a Scaramouch, a Harlequin, a Country Farmer, His Wife, and others, 1717; and *The Necromancer*, or *History of Dr. Faustus*. L.I.F., 1724.

At the end of the eighteenth century pantomime was usually to be seen after a drama or other play at Christmas-time, both at Covent Garden and Drury Lane Theatres.

The following is a list of the more recent pantomimes produced at the National Theatre, Drury Lane, commencing with the first from the pen of E. L. Blanchard:—

1852.—*Harlequin Hudibras; or, Old Dame Durden and the Droll Days of the Merry Monarch.* E. L. Blanchard.

1853.—*Harlequin King Humming-Top and the Land of Toys.* E. L. Blanchard.

1854.—*Jack and Jill; or, Harlequin King Mustard and Four-and-Twenty Blackbirds Baked in a Pie.* E. L. Blanchard.

1855.—*Hey-Diddle-Diddle; or, Harlequin King Nonsense and the Seven Ages of Man.* E. L. Blanchard.

1856.—*See-Saw, Margery Daw; or, Harlequin Holiday and the Island of Ups and Downs.* E. L. Blanchard.

1857.—*Little Jack Horner; or, Harlequin A.B.C.* E. L. Blanchard.

1858.—*Robin Hood and the Merry Men of Sherwood Forest.* E. L. Blanchard.

1859.—*Jack and the Beanstalk; or, Harlequin Leap-Year and the Merry Pranks of the Good Little People.* E. L. Blanchard.

1860.—*Peter Wilkins; or, Harlequin and the Flying Women of the Loadstone Island.* E. L. Blanchard.

1861.—*The House that Jack Built; or, Old Mother Hubbard and Her Dog.* E. L. Blanchard.

1862.—*Little Goody Two Shoes; or, Harlequin Cock Robin.* E. L. Blanchard.

1863.—*Harlequin Sinbad the Sailor; or, The Great Rock of the Diamond Valley and the Seven Wonders of the World.* E. L. Blanchard.

1864.—*Hop o' My Thumb and His Eleven Brothers.* E. L. Blanchard.

1865.—*Little King Pippin; or Harlequin Fortunatus and the Wishing Cap.* E. L. Blanchard.

1866.—*Number Nip; or, Harlequin and the Gnome King of the Giant Mountains.* E. L. Blanchard.

1867.—*Faw, Fee, Fo, Fum; or, Harlequin Jack the Giant Killer.* E. L. Blanchard.

1868.—*Grimalkin the Great; or Harlequin Puss in Boots and the Miller's Men.* E. L. Blanchard.

1869.—*Beauty and the Beast; or, Harlequin and Old Mother Bunch.* E. L. Blanchard.

1870.—*The Dragon of Wantley; or, Old Mother Shipton.* E. L. Blanchard.

1871.—*Tom Thumb; or, Harlequin King Arthur and the Knights of the Round Table.* E. L. Blanchard.

1872.—*The Children in the Wood.* E. L. Blanchard.

1873.—*Jack in the Box.* E. L. Blanchard.

1874.—*Aladdin; or, the Wonderful Lamp.* E. L. Blanchard.

1875.—*Whittington and His Cat.* E. L. Blanchard.

1876.—*The Forty Thieves.* E. L. Blanchard.

1877.—*The White Cat.* E. L. Blanchard.

1878.—*Cinderella.* E. L. Blanchard.

1879.—*Bluebeard.* Brothers Grinn.

1880.—*Mother Goose and the Enchanted Beauty.* E. L. Blanchard.

1881.—*Robinson Crusoe.* E. L. Blanchard.

1882.—*Sinbad.* E. L. Blanchard.

1883.—*Cinderella.* E. L. Blanchard.

1884.—*Whittington and His Cat.* E. L. Blanchard.

1885.—*Aladdin.* E. L. Blanchard.

1886.—*The Forty Thieves.* E. L. Blanchard.

1887.—*Puss in Boots.* E. L. Blanchard.

1888.—*Babes in the Wood and Robin Hood and His Merry Men and Harlequin Who Killed Cock Robin?* E. L. Blanchard.

1889.—*Jack and the Beanstalk; or, Harlequin and the Midwinter Night's Dream.* Harry Nicholls and Augustus Harris.

1890.—*Beauty and the Beast.* William Yardley and Augustus Harris.

1891.—*Humpty Dumpty.* Harry Nicholls and Sir Augustus Harris.

1892.—*Little Bo-Peep, Little Red Riding Hood, and Hop o' My Thumb.* Sir Augustus Harris and Wilton Jones.

1893.—*Robinson Crusoe.* Harry Nicholls and Sir Augustus Harris.

1894.—*Dick Whittington.* Sir Augustus Harris, Cecil Raleigh, and Henry Hamilton.

1895.—*Cinderella.* Sir Augustus Harris, Cecil Raleigh, and Arthur Sturgess.

1896.—*Aladdin.* Arthur Sturgess and Horace Lennard.

1897.—*Babes in the Wood.* Arthur Sturgess and Arthur Collins.

1898.—*Forty Thieves.* Arthur Sturgess and Arthur Collins.

1899.—*Jack and the Beanstalk.* Arthur Sturgess and Arthur Collins.

1900.—*Sleeping Beauty and the Beast.* Jay Hickory Wood and Arthur Collins.

1901.—*Blue Beard.* Jay Hickory Wood and Arthur Collins.

1902.—*Mother Goose.* Jay Hickory Wood and Arthur Collins.

1903.—*Humpty Dumpty.* Jay Hickory Wood and Arthur Collins.

1904.—*The White Cat.* Jay Hickory Wood and Arthur Collins.

1905.—*Cinderella.* Sir F. C. Burnand, J. Hickory Wood, and Arthur Collins.

1906.—*Sinbad.* J. Hickory Wood and Arthur Collins.

1907.—*Babes in the Wood.* J. Hickory Wood and Arthur Collins.

1908.—*Dick Whittington.* J. Hickory Wood and Arthur Collins.

PANTRY BELL, THE. S. C. Windermere. Barrow T.R., October 3, 1902.

PANURGE. O. Grétry. 1785.

PAOLA. C. O. 2 a. H. Paulton and M. Tedde. M. by E. Jakobowski. Edinburgh R. Lyceum, December 16, 1889.

PAOLO AND FRANCESCA. T. 4 a. S. Phillips. St. James's, March 6, 1902.

PAON, LE. C. 3 a. François de Croisset, in verse. Royalty, January 15, 1906.

PAP WITH A HATCHET, ALIAS A FIG FOR MY GODSON; OR, CRACK ME THIS NUT; OR, A COUNTRY CUFF THAT IS A SOUND BOX ON THE EAR FOR THE IDEOT MARTIN TO HOLD HIS PEACE. John Lyly. Pr. 1593.

PAPA. F. C. 3 a. J. B. Booth. Adap. fr. the French. Dover Tivoli, March 21, 1898.

PAPA'S DAY OFF. Sk. London Hipp., April 19, 1909.

PAPA'S HONEYMOON. C. 3 a. S. Mayer and W. B. Tarpey. Adap. fr. the German. Criterion, June 28, 1890.

PAPA'S WIFE. Duol. S. Hicks and F. C. Philips. M. by Ellaline Terriss. Lyric, January 26, 1895.

PAPAL TYRANNY IN THE REIGN OF KING JOHN. T. C. Cibber. C.G., February 15, 1745. Pr. 1745.

PAPATU, DE. T. N. Udall. 1540.

PAPER CHASE, THE. F. C. 3 a. C. Thomas. S. Geo. H., May 1, 1888 (C.P.); Strand (mat.), June 9, 1888; Toole's, July 9, 1888; transferred to Royalty, August 20, 1888.

PAPER WINGS. C. W. Phillips. Rev. Olympic, February 15, 1869.

PAPERHANGER, THE. Sk. Empire, June 7, 1909.

PAPHIAN BOWER; OR, VENUS AND ADONIS, THE. Burla. 1 a. J. R. Planché and C. Dance. Olympic, December 26, 1832.

PAPILLIONS, LES. Ballet in 2 tab. Designed by Wilhelm. M. by L. Wenzel, M. Katti Lanner. Empire, March 18, 1901.

PAPILLON, LE. Pant. Bal. M. by Offenbach. Paris, November 26, 1860.

PAPILLONETTA; OR, THE PRINCE, THE BUTTERFLY, AND THE BEETLE. Burl. Extrav. W. Brough. P.O.W., December 26, 1865.

PAPILLONNE, LA. See *Butterfly Fever.*

PAPILLONS, LES. Bal. O. Pugno. 1881.

PAPILLOTES DE M. BENOIT, LES. O. 1 a. Reber., December 28, 1853.

PAQUITA. Ballet. M. by Deldevez. First time in England. D.L., June 3, 1846.

PAQUITA. D. 5 a. B. Campbell. Eleph. and C., August 20, 1884.

PAQUITA. Rom. Bal. in 3 sc. Arr. and prod. by Alfredo Curti. M. by Geo. W. Byng. Alhambra, October 12, 1908.

PAQUITA; OR, LOVE IN A FRAME. C. O. 2 a. R. Reece. M. by Mallandaine. Royalty, October 21, 1871.

PAR LE GRAIVE. D.L., June 14, 1893.

PARACELSUS. Dram. Pm. R. Browning. 1836.

PARADISE. Orat. J. Fawcett. Pr. 1853.

PARADISE AND THE PERI. O. Schumann (1810-1856).

PARADISE AND THE PERI. Cantata. J. F. Barnett (b. 1838). Birmingham Festival.

PARADISE AND THE PERI. Cantata. Sir W. Sterndale Bennett (1816-75).

PARADISE LOST. Orat. Stillingfleet. 1760.

PARADISE LOST. See "Epic Poems," *Adam.*

PARADISE OF FOOLS, THE. T. Horde, jun.

PARADISE UP TO DATE. M. F. 2 a. W. R. Clements. M. by Jeffrey Jones. Gravesend Pub. H., March 26, 1894.

PARADOX, THE. Ac. by Henslowe's Co. July 1, 1596. N.p.

PARADOX, THE. C. P. C.G., April 30, 1799. N.p.

PARAGRAPH, THE. M. Ent. P. Hoare. C.G., March 10, 1804. Pr. 1804.

PARALLEL ATTACKS. Ca. F. James. Strand, July 11, 1893.

PARASIDE; OR, REVENGE FOR HONOUR, THE. H. Glapthorne. Ent. Stationers' Co. November 29, 1653. N.p.

PARASITASTER; OR, THE FAWN. C. J. Marston. F. partly on stories in Boccace's *Decameron*, and fr. Ovid. Blackfriars. Pr. 1606.

PARASITE, THE. C. R. Warner. Transl. fr. Plautus. Pr. 1772.

PARASITE, THE. 1 a. E. C. Ravani. Athenæum H., Tottenham Court Road, January 15, 1894.

PARASITES. A 2, sc. 1. Miss Rose Matthews. Bedford St. Bijou, June 23, 1907; rev. Scala. June 25, 1908.

PARCELS POST, THE. F. C. A. Shirley. Belfast T.R., February 4, 1884.

PARDON DE PLOERMEL. C.O. 3 a. Wds. by Barbier and Carre. M. by Meyerbeer. Paris, April 4, 1859. In Ital. as *Dinorah*, C.G., July 26, 1859; in Eng. as *Dinorah*, C.G., October 3, 1859.

PARDONER, THE. See "Miracle Plays."

PARDONER AND THE FRERE, THE CURATE AND NEIGHBOUR PRATT. P. Heywood, 1533.

PARENTS AND GUARDIANS.

PARIA. Ser. Vincent. 1648.

PARIA, LE. T. By Delavigne, 1821, and transl. into English by Beer, 1826.

PARIDE E ELENA. O. Glück. Lib. by Calzabigi. 1770.

PARIS. Monol. A. Sketchley. Egyptian H., February, 1864.

PARIS. H. C. Burnand and M. Williams Strand, 1866.

PARIS; OR, VIVE LEMPRIERE. Burl. F. C. Burnand. Strand, April 2, 1866; Greenwich, April 11, 1868.

PARIS AND ÆNONE. T. 1 a. Laurence Binyon. Savoy, March 8, 1906.

PARIS AND LONDON. Planché. Adelphi, 1828.

PARIS AND PLEASURE; OR, HOME AND HAPPINESS. Fantastic D. 4 a. C. Selby Adap. fr. the French. Lyceum, November 28, 1859.

PARIS AND VIENNA. Perf. by the Children of Westminster. Circa 1571.

PARIS FEDERATION, THE. P. Royalty Pr. 1790.

PARISH CLERK, THE. 3 a. Boucicault. Wr. expressly for Mr. Joseph Jefferson. Manchester, May, 1866.

PARISEN, UN. Royalty, October 24, 1887.

PARISIAN ROMANCE, A. 5 a. Transl. of Octave Feuillet's play, *Un Roman Parisien*. Lyceum (first time in England), October 1, 1888.

PARISINA. O. 3 a. Lib. by Romani. Fd. on Byron's poem. M. by Donizetti. Florence, March 18, 1833; Paris, February 24, 1838; Her M., June 1, 1838.

PARLATORE ETERNO, IL. O. Ponchieli Lecco. October 18, 1872.

PARKER, P.C. Sk. Chas. Austin and Chas. Ridgwell. Islington Hipp., May 18, 1908.

PARLAMENTS WAHL, DIE. German M. Sk. 3 a. A. Loewenthal and H. Schmidt. St. Pancras Germ. Gym., March 8, 1890.

PARLEZ-VOUS FRANCAIS? C. 3 a. Florence Warden. Gt. Queen St., March 3, 1906.

PARLIAMENT OF BEES, THE. Masque John Day. Pr. 1641. ? Ac. 1607.

PARLIAMENT OF CORRECTION, THE One of 8 Int. by Sir D. Lindsay. Pr. 1792.

PARLIAMENT OF LOVE, THE. C. 4 a. (Incomplete.) P. Massinger. Cockpit, D.L., November 3, 1624.

PARLIAMENT OF LOVE, THE. C. W. Rowley. Ent. Stationers' Co., June 29, 1660. Destroyed by Warburton's servant.

PARLIAMENT OF SPRITES, THE. Int. T. Chatterton, although under the names of Rowley and John Isram. Repr. 1789.

PARLOUR MATCH, A. M. F. 3 a. C. H. Hoyt. Terry's, October 4, 1900.

PARLOURS. F. C. 3 a. R. Reece. Royalty, July 24, 1880.

PARMA VIOLETS. See *Baffled.*

PAROLE OF HONOUR. 2 a. T. J. Serle. C.G.

PAROLLE ET ISIDORA. C. By Theo Cibber.

PARRICIDE, THE. T. J. Sterling. Goodman's Fields, January 29, 1736. Pr. 1736.

PARRICIDE, THE. P. 5 a. T. J. Serle. Dover.

PARRICIDE, THE. See *Paraside.*

PARRICIDE, THE; OR, INNOCENCE IN DISTRESS, THE. T. W. Shirley. C.G., January 17, 1739. Pr. 1739.

PARSIFAL. M. D. 3 a. R. Wagner. Bayreuth, July 28, 1882. R. Albert H., November 10, 1884.

PARSON, THE. F. C. 3 a. S. J. Adair Fitzgerald. Globe, October 10, 1891.

PARSON AND A MAN, A. Melo-d. 1 a. Manville Morton. November 18, 1905.

PARSON JIM. D. 1 a. Suggested by American story of same name. Terry's, May 24, 1889.

PARSON O' DUMFORD, THE. See *Foreman of the Works.*

PARSON THORN. D. 3 a. Rass Challis. Wakefield R.O.H., April 3, 1891.

PARSON WYNNE'S TRUST. Dr. Idyll. 1 a. P. Heriot. Comedy, April 22, 1808.

PARSON'S PLAY, THE. C. 1 a. S. Battams. Grand, July 8, 1889.

PARSON'S WEDDING, THE. C. T. Killigrew. Partly fr. Calderon's *Dama Ducnde*. Pr. 1664. Rev. at L.I.T. same year.

PART DU DIABLE, LA. C. O. 3 a. Wds. by Scribe. M. by Auber. Paris, January 16, 1843; D.L., July 9, 1845; Eng. vers., Plymouth T.R., May 7, 1870.

PARTED; AN ENGLISH LOVE STORY. C. D. 4 a. W. Reeve. Scarborough T.R., September 2, 1874.

PARTED AND REUNITED. D. 3 a. C. H. Hazlewood. Britannia, June 24, 1872.

PARTED ON THE BRIDAL HOUR. D. 4 a. L. J. Libbey. Sadler's Wells. February 8, 1888 (C.P.).

PARTHENIA; OR, THE LOST SHEPHERDESS. Arcadian D. 3 a. Pr. 1764.

PARTHIAN EXILE, THE. T. G. Downing. Ac. at Coventry and Worcester. Pr. 1774.

PARTHIAN HERO, THE. T. M. Gardiner. Pr. 1741. N.ac. in London; ? in Dnblin.

PARTIC'LER PET, THE. F. 1 a. Edward Knoblanch, taken fr. Max Maurey's *Asile de Nuit*. Brighton Royal, December 18, 1905; Waldorf, January 17, 1906.

PARTING, THE. Ca. S. J. Adair Fitzgerald. Hotel Cecil, May 15, 1899.

PARTING OF THE WAYS, THE. C. 1 a. F. Bowyer and W. Sprange. Terry's, February 8, 1890.

PARTITION WAR. Ca. 1 a. R. Pryce. MS. with Douglas Cox.

PARTIZANS; OR, THE WAR OF PARIS IN 1649, THE. P. 3 a. D.L., May 21, 1829.

PARTNER OF MY JOYS, THE. Sk. Crouch End Hipp., May 18, 1908.

PARTNERS. C. D. 5 a. R. Buchanan. Partly f. on Alphonse Daudet's *Fromont Jeune and Risler Aîné*. Hay., January 5, 1888.

PARTNERS, THE. C. 3 a. P. Hoare. Hay., June 28, 1805. N.p.

PARTNERS FOR LIFE. C. 3 a. H. J. Byron. Globe, October 7, 1871.

PARTS AND PLAYERS. P. 3 a. F. Harlowe. St. Andrew's Parish R., Stoke Newington, April 11, 1887.

PARTY AT NO. 4, THE. Sk. Chas. Ross. Cambridge M.H., November 16, 1901.

PARVENU, THE. C. 3 a. G. W. Godfrey. Court, April 8, 1882; Globe, February 18, 1891.

PAS DE BERGERS. Dance. D.L., May 12, 1846.

PAS DE FASCINATION, THE. F. 1 a. D.L., October 23, 1856.

PAS HONGROIS. Dance. D.L., May 27, 1846

PASCAL BRUNO. Ro. O. 3 a. M. by J. L. Hatton. Vienna, March 2, 1844.

PASHA, THE. C. 4 a. Alan Grey. Kilburn T.R., February 28, 1898.

PASHA, THE. F. 3 a. W. Ellis and P. Greenwood. Hounslow Town H., December 11, 1899.

PASQUIN. C. H. Fielding. Hay., 1735. Pr. 1736. Olympic, August, 1850.

PASSE LE PLAY. P. 4 a. George de Porto Riche. Royalty, July 2, 1906.

PASSERELLE, LA. (Original of *The Marriage of Kitty*.) F. C. 3 a. Mme. Gresac and Mlle. Croisset. Garrick, June 29, 1903.

PASSING CLOUD, A. C. 1 a. Annie Saker. Carlisle Her M. T., June 5, 1903.

PASSING CLOUD, THE. D. 2 a. B. Bernard. D.L., April 8, 1850.

PASSING HOUR, THE. D. Edinburgh Southminster T., December 13, 1873.

PASSING OF PAUL, THE. Sk. Leonard Mortimer. Sadler's Wells, January 6, 1908.

PASSING OF PAUL DOMBEY, THE. D.E. 1 a. Claude Trevelyan. Borough, Stratford, April 22, 1909.

PASSING OF THE THIRD FLOOR BACK, THE. P. 4 a. Jerome K. Jerome. Harrogate O.H., August 17, 1908, and St. James's, September 1, 1908; Terry's, November 9, 1908.

PASSING THROUGH THE FIRE. D. 4 a. T. Mead. Eleph. and C., September 1, 1873.

PASSIO DOMINI NOSTRI. See "Miracle Plays."

PASSION. Orat. Book fr. Metastasio. M. by Morlacchi, 1812.

PASSION. D. 4 a. W. Stephens. Vaudeville, February 8, 1873.

PASSION. D. 4 a. G. Roberts. Newcastle Tyne T., December 3, 1874.

PASSION, THE. Orat. H. Schutz (1585-1672).

PASSION, THE. Orat. Handel, 1717.

PASSION AND PRINCIPLE. D. 5 a. L. Wagner. Sadler's Wells, June 9, 1883.

PASSION FLOWER, THE. P. 1 a. C. Thursby and A. Applin. Wyndham's Theatre, June 15, 1900. Balham Duchess, May 22, 1900.

PASSION FLOWER; OR, WOMAN AND THE LAW, THE. D. 3 a. Adapt. fr. the Spanish play *La Passionaria* of Leopoldo Cano y Massas. Engl. ver. first prod. at Hull T.R., July 28, 1884; Olympic, March 13, 1885.

PASSION FLOWERS. D. T. W. Robertson. Hull T.R., October 28, 1868.

PASSION MUSIC. Bach. St. Matthew, 1729; St. John, 1733.

PASSION OF CHRIST. See "Miracle Plays."

PASSION OF CHRYST, OF THE. 2 Comedies. Bishop Bale. (1495-1563.)

PASSION OF LIFE. D. 5 a. H. Fuller. Merthyr Tydvil T.R., July 31, 1899; Edmonton Royal, August 6, 1900; West London, March 4, 1901.

PASSION, POISON, AND PETRIFICATION; OR, THE FATAL GASOGENE. Burl. T. G. B. Shaw. Regent's Park Botanic Gardens, July 14, 1905.

PASSION'S PENALTY. D. Swansea New T., April 16, 1884.

PASSION'S PERIL; OR, THE BROKEN MARRIAGE. D. M. Faucquez. Britannia, May 23, 1874.

PASSION'S POWER. D. 4 a. Adapt. fr. *Le Prince Zilah* of Jules Clarétie by A. Shirley. New Cross Pub. H., March 25, 1886; Birmingham P.O.W., 1888; Parkhurst, April 3, 1893.

PASSION'S SLAVE. D. 4 a. J. A. Stevens. Orig. prod. in America. Bradford T.R. (first time in England), November 1, 1886; Standard, August 1, 1887.

PASSIONARIA, LA. See *Passion Flower*.

PASSIONATE LOVERS, THE. T. C. 2 parts. L. Cartell. Somerset H., 1655. Pr. 1655. Also ac. at the Blackfriars.

PASSIONS, THE. M. Ent. C. Dibdin. Ac. at the Circus. N.p.

PASSIONS OF LOVE, THE. Melo. 1 a. Manville Morton. Orpington P.H., December 4, 1905.

PASSIONS OF THE HEART; OR, NATURE AGAINST THE WORLD, THE. D. Albion, June 26, 1876.

PASSIVE HUSBAND, THE. P. R. Cumberland. Advertised as intended for publication by subscription.

PASSPORT, THE. C. 3 a. B. C. Stephenson and W. Yardley. Partly f. on Col. Savage's novel "My Official Wife." Globe, October 15, 1894 (C.P.); Terry's, April 25, 1895; Trafalgar, July 29, 1895; rev. Terry's, April 14, 1900.

PASSWORD, THE. M. P. 3 a. W. Livingstone and W. B. Reynolds. Belfast Ulster H., April 8, 1903.

PASSWORD, THE. P. 1 a. Alicia Ramsey and R. De Cordova. Imperial, July 7, 1904.

PAST AND FUTURE; OR, THREE TIMES ON EARTH. Serio-comic O. Wds. and M. by Dr. H. A. Speed. Douglas H. M., December 10, 1908 (mat.).

PAST AND PRESENT; OR, THE HIDDEN TREASURE. D. 3 a. Adapt. fr. the French by J. Poole. D.L., February 23, 1830.

PAST MASTER, THE. C. O. Prol. and 2 a. Lib. N. Prescott. Lyrics by B. Davies. Strand, December 21, 1899.

PAST REDEEMED, A. D. 4 a. J. Hewson. Pavilion, October 5, 1903.

PAST TEN O'CLOCK AND A RAINY NIGHT. F. 2 a. T. Dibdin. D.L., March 11, 1815.

PASTICCIO, A. Dr. Arne. Consisting of select airs. C.G. Pr. 1773.

PASTO FIDO, IL. See *Faithful Shepherdess*.

PASTOR FIDO; OR, THE FAITHFUL SHEPHERD (Il Pastor Fido). Dymock. Transl. from the Italian of Guarini. Pr. 1602 and 1633.

PASTOR FIDO; OR, THE FAITHFUL SHEPHERD. Past. Sir R. Fanshaw. Pr. 1648. Translation of Guarini.

PASTOR FIDO; OR, THE FAITHFUL SHEPHERD. Past. E. Settle. Pr. 1677 and 1694. Foregoing alt. Ac. at D. of York's.

PASTOR FIDO; OR, THE FAITHFUL SHEPHERD. Past. T. C. in English blank verse. Taken fr. It. of Guarini. Pr. 1809.

PASTOR FIDUS. D. in Latin. Ac. at King's Coll., Cambridge. MS. preserved in University Library.

PASTOR LORM. P. 3 a. A. Schirokauer (German season). Royalty, September 21, 1903.

PASTORA; OR, THE COY SHEPHERDESS. O. A. Aston. Ac. at Tunbridge Wells, 1712. Pr. 1712.

PASTORAL, LA. The first French O. Cambert, 1659.

PASTORAL BALLET. Noble. D.L., July 21, 1824.

PASTORAL COMIQUE. Molière. 1666. See "French Classical Plays."

PASTORAL MASQUE, A. Tr. Fanshaw. 1648 (rev.); Settle, 1677.

PASTORAL MASQUE, A. J. Hughes. Pr. 1735.

PASTORAL POSTPONED, A. Playlet. Mr. Creagh-Henry. Queen's Gate H., November 17, 1908 (mat.).

PAT. M. C. D. 3 a. G. Roberts, H. Erwin, and H. Monkhouse. Lyrics by M. Ambient and F. Wood. Woolwich Artillery T., November 16, 1891; Yarmouth R. Aquarium, August 1, 1892; Parkhurst, September 12, 1892.

PAT AND THE GENIE. Sk. Alhambra, August 3, 1908.

PAT OF MULLINGER; OR, AN IRISH LOTHARIO. Irish C.D. 3 a. Julia Agnes Fraser. Publ. at the *Greenock Advertiser* Office, Greenock.

PAT, THE IRISH LANCER. Irish D. 3 a. Sadler's Wells, March 12, 1888.

PAT'S THANKSGIVING. F. Maurice de Frece. Liverpool T.R., March 18, 1872.

PATCHED-UP AFFAIR, A. P. 1 a. Florence Warden. St. James's, March 10, 1900.

PATENT LOVE LOCK, THE. Duol. Ca. K. Howard. Court, July 5, 1901.

PATENT OF GENTILITY, THE. C. 4 a. Glasgow R. Colosseum T., February 6, 1869.

PATENT SEASONS. Sk. Lyceum, August 21, 1820.

PATER, LE. P. in verse. 1 a. François Coppèe. Op. Comique, October 27, 1893.

PATER NOSTER. P. 1 a. Adap. f. French of F. Coppée. St. James's, February 20, 1908.

PATH OF LIFE, THE. D. 4 a. W. H. Dearlove. Halifax T.R., June 9, 1896; Grantham, June 7, 1897.

PATH OF THORNS. D. 4 a. A. Shirley and S. Vane. Camden, August 31, 1903.

PATHOMACHIA; OR, THE BATTLE OF AFFECTIONS, SHADOWED BY A FEIGNED SIEGE OF THE CITIE OF PATHOPOLIS. C. Anon. Pr. 1630. The running title is *Love's Loadstone*. MS. copy in British Museum.

PATIE AND PEGGY; OR, THE FAIR FOUNDLING. Scotch B. O. T. Cibber. D.L., May 31, 1731. Pr. 1730. This is Ramsay's *Gentle Shepherd* reduced to 1 a.

PATIENCE. Sadler's Wells, October 27, 1866.

PATIENCE; OR, BUNTHORNE'S BRIDE. Æsthetic O. 2 a. W. S. Gilbert. M. by A. Sullivan. Op. Comique, April 23, 1881; Savoy, November 7, 1900; Savoy, April 4, 1907.

PATIENT, THE. O. 1 a. Parke, Gillington, and Delibes. Publ. by S. French, Ltd.

PATIENT GRISELD. C. Ralph Radcliffe. N.p., unless it is the same piece as mentioned in Kirkman's Catalogue as *Old Patient Grissel*.

PATIENT GRISSEL. C. Haughton Chettle and Dekker. Plot f. on Boccace's Novels, December 10, November 10. Story is also told in a poem called "Gualtherus and Grisalda," which is modernised version of one of Chaucer's Canterbury Tales. Entered at Stationers' Hall, March 28, 1600. Ac. Circa., 1600. Pr. 1603.

PATIENT GRISSEL. P. Mentioned by Pepys as perf. at Bartholomew Fair, August, 1667.

PATIENT MAN AND HONEST WHORE, THE. P. T. Dekker. Ac. 1602. Afterwards called *The Honest Whore*.

PATIENT PENELOPE; OR, THE RETURN OF ULYSSES. Burl., 1 a. F. C. Burnand and M. Williams. Strand, November 25, 1863.

PATRICIA IN A QUANDARY. Sk. by C. Hamilton. Strand, December 19, 1899.

PATRICIAN AND THE PARVENU; OR, CONFUSION WORSE CONFOUNDED. C. 5 a. J. Poole. D.L., March 21, 1835.

PATRICIAN'S DAUGHTER, THE. P. 5 a. Westland Marston. Prod. by Charles Dickens. D.L., December 10, 1842; Hay., October 23, 1848.

PATRICK IN PRUSSIA. See *Love in a Camp*.

PATRICK'S RETURN. Past Ballet. Byrne. D.L., February 5, 1817.

PATRICK'S VOW. D. 5 a. Miss J. A. Fraser. Strathaven, Vict. T., May 23, 1873.

PATRIE. O. Paladilhe. F. on Sardou's D.

PATRIOT, THE. Dr. History of William Prince of Orange, by "A Lover of Liberty." Ascr. to Baillie. Pr. 1736.

PATRIOT, THE. T. W. Harrod. Pr. 1769. N.ac.

PATRIOT, THE. C. Ac. at the Hay., 1784. First advertised as *The Artful Patriot; or, The Rage of the People*. N.p.

PATRIOT, THE. T. C. Hamilton. A't. fr. Metastasio's *Themistocles*. Circa., 1784.

PATRIOT, THE. T. J. Simpson. Pr. 1785. Advertised to be published about the year 1764 under the title of *Leonidas*, but postponed through death of author. Story taken from Glover's poem, "Leonidas."

PATRIOT, THE. P. 1 a. H. R. Trowbridge. Passmore Edwards Settlement, Tavistock Place, November 12, 1902; Fulham Grand, April 6, 1903; Newport Lyceum, February 20, 1905.

PATRIOT; OR, THE ITALIAN CONSPIRACY, THE. T. C. Gildon. D.L. Pr. 1703. Taken fr. Lee's *Lucius Junius Brutus*. Prol. by Dennis. Epit. by Farquhar. See *Italian Patriot*.

PATRIOT CHIEF, THE. T. Macroe. Pr. 1784

PATRIOT KING; OR, ALFRED AND ELVIDA, THE. T. A. Bicknell. Pr. 1788. N.ac.

PATRIOT KING; OR, THE IRISH CHIEF, THE. T. F. Dobbs. Ac. at Smock Alley, Dublin. Pr. 1774.

PATRIOT'S DAUGHTER; OR, TRIED AND TRUE, THE. D. 3 a. E. Stirling. Portsmouth R. Albert T., January 15, 1872.

PATRIOTIC SPY, THE. Standard, March 3, 1866.

PATRIOTISM! F. Ac. by His Majesty's Servants. Pr. 1763.

PATRIOTISM. Rom. P. 1 a. Miss E. White. Herne Bay Pier Pav., October 2, 1903.

PATRON, THE. B.O. T. Odell. Little Theatre in Hay., 1729.

PATRON, THE. F. 3 a. Sam. Foote. Hay., 1764, and September 5, 1774.

PATRON; OR, THE DISINTERESTED FRIEND, THE. Anon. Edinburgh, 1793.

PATRON SAINT, A. C. 1 a. By C. Thomas. Suggested by *Le Chapeau de St. Catharine* of Edmund About. St. James's, October 17, 1888.

PATTER VERSUS CLATTER. F. 1 a. C. Matthews. Olympic, May 21, 1838; D.L., December 6, 1855.

PATTIE AND PEGGY. Ballad. T. Cibber. 1730.

PATTY; OR, THE SHIPWRIGHT'S LOVE. Oa. Bayswater Bijou, June 6, 1872.

PAUL, ST. Orat. Mendelssohn. 1836.

PAUL AND VIRGINIA. O. Mazzinghi.

PAUL AND VIRGINIA. M.E. 2 a. J. Cobb. C.G., 1800.

PAUL AND VIRGINIA. M. afterpiece. D.L., May 26, 1817.

PAUL AND VIRGINIA. M.E. Lyceum playbill. Rev. July 11, 1823.

PAUL AND VIRGINIA. B. A. Wood. Olympic, October 15, 1870.

PAUL AND VIRGINIA. P. 3 a. Ross Neill. Afterwards entitled *The Lovers of Valma*. Dublin Gaiety, September 23, 1881.

PAUL AND VIRGINIA. D. 5 a. R. Davey. F. on Bernardin de St. Pierre's novel. Novelty, November 17, 1886.

PAUL ET VIRGINIE. Italian O. 3 a. Lib. J. Barbier and M. Carré. M. by V. Massé. Paris, 1876; C.G., June 1, 1878.

PAUL CLIFFORD. Adaptation. B. Webster. Victoria, 1832.

PAUL CLIFFORD. See *Fate's Decree* and *Lucy Brandon*.

PAUL CLIFFORD; OR, THE HIGHWAYMAN OF LIFE. D. 4 a. H. M. Pitt. Victoria, July 2, 1870.

PAUL JONES. Ca. 3 a. Adap. by H. Farnie fr. Surcouf (Folies Dramatiques, Paris, October 6, 1887), by Chivet and Duru. M. by R. Planquette. Bolton T.R., December 10, 1888; P.O.W., January 12, 1889 (ran for 370 nights).

PAUL KAUVAR. D. Steele Mackaye. Pr. in America under title of *Anarchy*. D.L., May 12, 1890.

PAUL LAFARGE; OR, SELF-MADE. D. 2 a. Adap fr. French by D. Boucicault. Princess's, March 7, 1870.

PAUL LAZARO. D.L., January 9, 1854.

PAUL O' THE ALPS. Rom. D. C. Murray and C. Arnold. Colchester T.R., April 15, 1898.

PAUL PRY. C. 3 a. J. Poole. Hay., September 13, 1825; D.L., June 13, 1829.

PAUL PRY. C. 2 a. D. Jerrold. Coburg.

PAUL PRY. Sk. Kingston County, April 19, 1909.

PAUL PRY MARRIED AND SETTLED. F. 1 a. C. Matthews. Hay. T., October 3, 1861.

PAUL, THE PRESENTED. Jas. Bruton (author of *Cut for Partners*).

PAUL, THE SPANISH SHARPER. F. 2 a. J. Wetherby. 1730. N.a.

PAUL ZEGERS; OR, THE DREAM OF RETRIBUTION. D. 3 a. F. C. Burnand. Alfred, November 13, 1871.

PAUL'S RETURN. C. 3 a. Watts Phillips. Princess's T., February 15, 1864.

PAULA: A DEAD LOVE. D. in a pro. and 3 a. Lewis Willougby and Alice Chapin. Seacombe Irving T., November 28, 1902.

PAULA LAGARRO; OR, THE LADRONE'S DAUGHTER. D. 3 a. Mark Lemon. M. by Alfred Mellon. D.L., January 9, 1852.

PAULINE. D. 5 a. and 7 tab. Adap. fr. the French by J. Oxenford. Theatre Historique, June 1, 1850; Princess's, March 17, 1851.

PAULINE. O. 4 a. Henry Hersee. Fd. on Lytton's *Lady of Lyons*. M. by H. Cowen. Lyceum, November 22, 1876.

PAULINE. Sk. Portman Rooms, Baker Street, May 16, 1892.

PAULINE. C. 4 a. George Hirschfeld. German Season.) St. George's H., November 12, 1901.

PAULINE See *'Twixt Love and Art*.

PAULINE BLANCHARD. D. 6 a. Albert Darmont and Hamblot, fr. novel by M. Jules Case Mme. Sarah Bernhardt's season). R E. Opera House, June 16, 1892.

PAULINE PAULOVNA. Rom. Duol. R. Aldrich. West Town H., February 4, 1896 (amat.).

PAUPER OF LAMBETH. Victoria, April 21, 1851.

PAUSANIAS, THE BETRAYER OF HIS COUNTRY. T. Norton. T.R., 1696. Pr. 1696.

PAVED WITH GOLD. D. 3 a. J. B. Johnstone. City of London, May 16, 1868.

PAVILION. M.E W. Linley. D.L., 1799. N.p.

PAVING THE WAY. Ca. 1 a. Herbert Thomson. Shrewsbury T.R., April 8, 1901.

PAW CLAUDIAN; OR, THE ROMAN AWRY. Travestie of Wills and Herman's *Claudian*. F. C. Burnand. Toole's, February 14, 1884.

PAWNBROKING. Sk. Hilton Francis. Camberwell Empire, August 26, 1907.

PAY TO THE BEARER A KISS. F. Walter Gordon. Hay., July 16, 1868.

PAYABLE AT SIGHT. F. 1 a. Publ. by S. French, Ltd.

PAYABLE ON DEMAND. Dom. D. 2 a. Tom Taylor. Olympic, July 11, 1859.

PAYING GUEST. C. 1 a. W. H. Johnson. Publ. by S. French, Limited.

PAYING GUESTS. F. H. Leslie Bell and Chas. D. Hickman. Lyrics by Hickman and Woodin. M. by R. E. Lawson. Islington Hip., June 15, 1908.

PAYING THE DEBT. Harold B. Lewis. Royal, Ashton-under-Lyne, December 19, 1908 (C.P.).

PAYSANNE DU NORD, LA. Ballet. D.L., September 9, 1854. N.B.—Notice on playbill (in ink) intimating that this and other performances announced for same night did not take place.

PEACE. C. Aristophanes. Transl. fr. Greek by Mitchell, 1820-22; Hickie, 1853; and by Rudd, 1867. See "Greek Plays."

PEACE AND QUIET. F. 1 a. T. J. Williams. Strand, June 29, 1861.

PEACE AT ANY PRICE. F. 1 a. Adap. fr. French by T. W. Robertson. Another version pl. at Hay.

PEACEABLE KING, THE. D. Mentioned in Herbert's Diary, August 19, 1623.

PEACEFUL WAR. Adap. by S. Scotti and L. Wagner from Von Moser and Schönthan's "Krieg im Frieden." P.O.W., May 24, 1887.

PEACEMAKER, THE. P. Ipswich Public H., September 30, 1887.

PEACEMAKER, THE. C. 1 a. E. M. Bryant. Apollo, January 22, 1907.

PEACEMAKER, THE. Sk. London Pavilion, June 10, 1907.

PEACOCK'S HOLIDAY. F. C. 2 a. H. C. Merivale. Court, April 16, 1874.

PEARL AMONG WOMEN. Liverpool Amphi., March 11, 1870.

PEARL AND THE GIRL, THE. Burl. 1 a. Lieut. H. O. Wanton. Prod. on H.M.S. Bulwark at Chatham, November 13, 1907.

PEARL DARRELL. Irish D. Miss Kate Wilton. Liverpool Sefton T., September 17, 1883.

PEARL OF PARIS, THE. D. J. B. Johnstone. Portsmouth Albert T., December 18, 1871.

PEARL OF THE OCEAN, THE. Adelphi, 1848.

PEASANT BOY, THE. O.D. 3 a. W. Dimond. Lyceum, 1811; D.L., June 30, 1815; rev. D.L., September, 29, 1819.

PEASANT QUEEN. C. 1 a. E. H. Keating. Publ. by S. French, Ltd.

PECHEURS DE PERLES, LES. O. 3 a. Lib. by Cormon and Carré. M. by Georges Bizet. Paris, September 29, 1863. Prod. as *Leila*. C.G., April 22, 1887, and May 18, 1889.

PECK'S BAD BOY. M. Singularity. Pleon. Britannia, June 1,1891.

PECKHAM FROLIC; OR, NELL GWYNNE. C. P. Jerningham, 1799.

PECKSNIFF. C. D. 3 a. H. Paulton. Folly, October 23, 1876.

PECULIAR CASE, A. V. A. Law. M. by G. Grossmith. St. Leonards Warrior Square Concert H., December 2, 1884; St. George's H., December 6, 1884.

PECULIAR FAMILY, THE. Ent. Mr. and Mrs. German Reed. Gall. of Illus., March 15, 1865.

PECULIAR PROPOSALS. F. 1 a. J. M. Lowry. Dublin Gaiety T., March 9, 1876.

PEDANT LE BAL. Ca. Pailleron. Royalty, October 10, 1907.

PEDANTIUS. C. Wingfield. 1631.

PEDIGREE. C. 3 a. C. C. Bowring and F. H. Court.Derby, Decembr, 1889 (amat.); Toole's, March 28, 1890.

PEDLAR; OR, FRIENDS IN NEED, THE. C.D. 4 a. R. C. Dacres. Lowestoft T.R., December 30, 1889.

PEDLAR BOY, THE. Standard, January 27, 1862.

PEDLAR BOYS; OR, THE OLD MILL RUINS. D. 1 a. R. Harrington. Sadler's Wells, January 22, 1866.

PEDLAR SAM. Sk. 1 a. Felton. Rev. Camberwell Empire, July 27, 1908.

PEDLAR'S ACRE; OR, HARLEQUIN MENDICANT, THE. Pant. J. C. Cross. Royal Circus. Pr. 1804.

PEDLAR'S PROPHECY. C. Anon. 1595.

PEDLER, THE. C. R. Davenport. Ent. Stationers' Co., April 8, 1630. N.p.

PEDLERS' MASQUE, THE. Ac. at Court, 1574.

PEDRILLS; OR, A SEARCH FOR TWO FATHERS. D. 2 a. Adapt. fr. French by J. B. Johnstone. Marylebone, November 16, 1857.

PEDRO DE ZALAMEA. O. B. L. P. Godard. Wr. on a tale by Silvestre and Détroyat. Paris, January 31, 1884.

PEEBLES. C. Glasgow Gaiety T., August 14, 1882.

PEEP BEHIND THE CURTAIN; OR, THE NEW REHEARSAL, A. F. D. Garrick. D.L., October 23, 1767. Pr. 1767.

PEEP O' DAY. Irish D. E. Falconer. Lyceum, November 9, 1861; rev. D.L., February 28, 1870.

PEEPING TOM OF COVENTRY. M. Ent. J. O'Keefe. Hay., 1784. N.p. (Piratically, 1787.) D.L., October 11, 1823, and 1826; and December 18, 1837.

PEEPSHOW MAN, THE. D. 2 a. T. J. Williams. New Surrey, February 10, 1868.

PEER AND PEASANT. D. W. T. Moncrieff. Yarmouth T.R., 1884.

PEER OF THE REALM, A D. 4 a. F. W. Broughton. Bolton T.R., June 4, 1890 (C.P.).

PEER OR PAUPER. D. Pro. and 4 a. A. M. Green. Olympic, September 21, 1885.

PEERLESS AND PEERLOT. C.O. 2 a. G. B. Nicols. M. by H. A. Jeboult. Taunton Assembly R., February 7, 1901.

PEEVISH MAN, THE. D. 4 a. Transl. fr. Kotzebue by C. Ludger. Pr. 1799.

PEG OF PLYMOUTH. T. T. Downton. 1599.

PEG THE RAKE. "Rita" and A. Grey. F. on novel of same name. Bayswater Bijou T., October 25, 1897.

PEG WOFFINGTON. P. 3 a. Adap. fr Ch. Reade's novel. P.O.W., February 13, 1901.

PEG WOFFINGTON. Laurence Irving. Arranged fr. Tom Taylor's D., *Masks and Faces*. Birmingham G., January 27, 1908; Coliseum, February 17, 1908.

PEG WOFFINGTON. See *Mistress Peg*.

PEGGIE MACHREE. M.P. 3 a. P. Bidwell. Grimsby P.O.W., November 7, 1904; Wyndham's, December 28, 1904.

PEGGY. D. J. Mackay. Royalty, February 14, 1881.

PEGGY. C. 4 a. Atholie Robertson. Brighton Palace Pier, June 25, 1906.

PEGGY. P. 1 a. Stella Perugini. Broadway, December 12, 1907 (C.P.).

PEGGY DOYLE. P. 3 a. Mirabel Hillier. Rehearsal, June 26, 1908.

PEGGY GREEN. C.D. 1 a. C. Selby. Lyceum, December 1, 1847.

PEGGY'S LITTLE GAME. F. G. S. Hodgson. Greenwich New, May 18, 1868.

PEGGY'S PLOT. Ent. 1 a. S Gibney. M. by W. Slaughter. St. Geo. H., December 20, 1893.

PELAGIO, IL. O Mercadante. (Naples, 1857.)

PELERIN BLANC, LE. Guilbert de Pinérécourt. 1811.

PELEUS AND THETIS. Masque. Lord Lansdowne. Perf. at end of *Jew of Venice*. 1701.

PELEUS AND THETIS. (In Windsor Castle.) Pearce. 1795.

PELOPIDARUM SECUNDA. Eng. T. in blank verse. Ac. at Winchester School in the 17th century. MS. in Brit. Museum.

PELOPIDES. T Voltaire. 1763.

PELLEAS ET MELISANDE. T. Rom. 5 a. Maurice Maeterlinck. Transl. by J. W. Mackail. Special m. by Faure. P.O.W., June 21, 1898; Lyceum, October 29, 1898; Royalty, June 21, 1900.

PELLEAS ET MELISANDE. O. 5 a, in French, based on Maurice Maeterlinck's play. Music by Claude Debussy. Covent Garden, May 21, 1909.

PELLEAS ET MELISANDE. Presented in original French by Mme. Sarah Bernhardt and Mrs. Patrick Campbell. Vaudeville, July 1, 1904; July 18, 1904. Matinée and evening perf.

PENAL CODE, THE. D. Aug. Daly. Dublin Gaiety T., February 11, 1878.

PENAL LAW. D. 3 a. R. Hodson. Britannia, March 24, 1879.

PENAL SERVITUDE; STORY OF MANCHESTER LIFE. D. F. Cross. Salford P.O.W., November 29, 1883.

PENALTY, THE. P. 3 a. J. Cross. Terry's, December 2, 1890.

PENALTY OF CRIME. Melo.-d. 4 a. L. Gilbert. Devonport Metropole, November 2, 1896.

PENATES, THE. Masque. Ben Jonson. Sir W. Cornwallis's, Highgate, 1604.

PENDAROON. D. A. E. T. Watson and S. Clarke. Liverpool Alexandra, March 2, 1874.

PENDRUDGE v. PRETTIWON. C. 1 a. J. Wallace, jun. Publ. by S. French, Ltd.

PENELOPE. Dr. O. T. Cooke and J. Mottley. French transl. in Hay., 1728.

PENELOPE. O. Marmontel. M. by Piccini. 1785.

PENELOPE. O. D. Cimarosa. 1795.

PENELOPE. Dr. cantata. B. Horner. Colchester T.R., May 30, 1892 (amat.).

PENELOPE. Mus. ver., 1 a., by G. P. Hawtrey of *The Area Belle*, by Brough and Halliday. M. by E. Solomon. Comedy, May 9, 1889 (mat.); Comedy, September 24, 1889; evening bill, Royalty, January 20, 1894.

PENELOPE. C. 3 a. W. Somerset Maugham. Comedy, January 9, 1909.

PENELOPE'S LOVERS. P. 1 a. Geo. P. Bancroft. Rehearsal, Maiden Lane, July 17, 1908.

PENNY HEDGE; OR, THE MURDER OF THE ESKDALE HERMIT, THE. P. F. de Vere. Scarborough T.R., October 29, 1883.

PENSIONER SCHOLLER. F.C. 3 a. Carl Laufs. Great Queen Street, December 23, 1902

PENTLANDS, THE. D. 4 a. E. S. France. Wakefield T.R., April 23, 1872.

PEOPLE'S HERO, A. D. 4 a. W. H. Poole. F. on Ouida's novel "Triçotrin." Vaudeville, June 12, 1890; Glasgow Grand T., February 21, 1889.

PEOPLE'S IDOL, THE. D. 4 a. W. Barrett and V. Widnell. Olympic (new), December 4, 1890.

PEOPLE'S ROSE, THE. P. 4 a. A. Clarke and C. Caldcleugh. Sutton-in-Ashfield King's, July 1, 1905.

PEOPLE'S WILLIAM; OR, RANDY THE (W)RECKLESS, AND THE GRAND OLD MAN ALL AT SEA, THE. Burl. Birkenhead T.R., May 12, 1884.

PEPA. C. 3 a. Meilhac and L. Ganderax. Comédie Française, October 31, 1888; Royalty, April 1, 1889, and rev. June 16, 1891, November 18, 1907.

PEPITA. C.O. 3 a. Lib. by Chivot and Durm. Adap. by "Mostyn Tedde" from *La Princesse des Canaries*. M. by C. Lecocq. Prod. originally Folies Dramatiques, Paris, February 9, 1883. Liverpool Court T., December 30, 1886; Toole's T., August 30, 1888.

PEPPER'S DIARY. Ca. A. Morris. Royalty, October 6, 1890.

PEPPERPOT'S LITTLE PETS. 1 a. J. M. Morton.

PER PARCELS POST. Oa. G. D. Fox and W. E. Morton. Accrington Prince's T., November 26, 1883.

PERCY. D. 3 a. L. Towne. Globe, April 29, 1877.

PERCY. T. Hannah More. Hay., July 6, 1780.

PERCY, THE LADY-KILLER. M.F. 4 a. J. H. Wood. Tunbridge Wells O.H., May 25, 1903.

PERDITA; OR, THE ROYAL MILKMAID. (Legend upon which Shakespeare is supposed to have founded *A Winter's Tale*.) Burl. W. Brough, Lyceum T., September 15, 1856.

PERE DE FAMILLE. C. Diderot. 1758.

PERE GAILLARD, LE. O. 3 a. Reber. September 7, 1852.

PERE LEBONNARD, LE. P. 4 a. Jean Aicard. Royalty, January 25, 1906.

PERE PRODIGUE, UN. D.L., June 13, 1883.

PEREGRINATIONS OF PICKWICK, THE. Adelphi, April, 1837.

PERFECT CURE, A. F. 1 a. W. Sapte, jun. Cheltenham O.H., August 1, 1898.

PERFECT LOVE; OR, OBERON'S TRIUMPH. Spec. Fairy P. R. Reece. Olympic, February 25, 1871.

PERFECT LOVER, THE. P. 4 a. A. Sutro. Imperial, October 14, 1905.

PERFECT TREASURE, A. C. 1 a. Adap. fr. the French of Labiche by H. Williamson. Darlington T.R., January 26, 1900.

PERFECTION. F. Scarborough Old T., 1839.

PERFECTION. C. 1 a. T. H. Bayly. D.L.

PERFECTION; OR, THE LADY OF MUNSTER. F. 2 a. D.L., March 25, 1830.

PERFIDIOUS BROTHER, THE. T. L. Theobald. L.I.F., February 21, 1716.

PERFIDIOUS BROTHER, THE. T. H. Mestayer, a watchmaker, who complains that Theobald purloined his piece. 1716.

PERFIDIOUS ROBINSON. F. Woods Lawrence.

PERFIDUS HETRUSCUS. Latin T. MS. preserved in Bodleian Library.

PERFIDY. D. 4 a. E. Falconer. Rev. and alt. by W. J. Connel. Bolton T.R., November 10, 1887.

PERI, THE. Ballet. Coralli and Gautier. M. by Burgmuller. D.L., September 30, 1843, and May 16, 1855.

PERIANDER; KING OF CORINTH. T. J. Tracy. L.I.F., January 13, 1731.

PERICHOLE, LA. Op. bo. 3 a. Offenbach. Princess's, June 27, 1870; Royalty, January 30, 1875 (new ver.); Alhambra, November 9, 1878 (new ver. by Alfred Murray); Garrick, September 14, 1897.

PERICHON. F. L. E. B. Stephens. Richmond H.M.T., June 19, 1882.

PERICLES, PRINCE OF TYRE. T. W. Shakespeare. Unfinished and completed by others. Wilkins and Rowley possibly contributed. Fd. on novel by T. Twine, "The Patterns of Painful Adventures, etc., that Befel Unto Prince Appolonius, the Lady Lucina his Wife, and Tharsis his daughter, etc." Rep. in 1607. Ent. at Stationers' Hall, 1576. Gower tells the story in "Confessio Amantis," 1554. Partly wr. 1607. Ent. at Stationers' Hall, May 20, 1608. Pr. 4to 1609, second 4to 1609, third 4to 1611, fourth 4to 1619, fifth 4to (incomplete) 1630, sixth 4to 1635. Ac. 1609.

PERIL. P. Adap. fr. Sardou's *Nos Intimes* by Saville and Bolton (B. C. Stephenson Rowe) P.O.W., Tottenham Ct. Rd., September 30, 1876; Haymarket, April 23, 1892; Garraick, February 14, 1901

PERILOUS PASS. Britannia, August 11, 1862.

PERILOUS PICNIC, A. Ca. E. B. Wyke. Dundee T.R., June 16, 1879.

PERILS OF CRINOLINE. Strand, January 9, 1857.

PERILS OF FLIRTATION, THE. P. 4 a. W. Frith, Glasgow Royalty T., November 16, 1903; Avenue, January 26, 1904.

PERILS OF LIFE, THE. M.C.D. 1 a. T. C. McGuire. Hartlepool Empress T., September 11, 1899.

PERILS OF PARIS, THE. Dom. d. Prol. and 3 a. Adap. by A. Shirley fr. *La Porteuse de Pain* of De Montepin and Dornay. Prod. at Paris Ambigu, January 11, 1889. Hammersmith Lyric, September 20, 1897.

PERILS OF PEPPIUS, THE. D. Jerrold. Strand. Fr.

PERJUR'D DEVOTEE; OR, FORCE OF LOVE, THE. C. D. Bellamy, sen. and jun. Pr. 1739.

PERJURED HUSBAND; OR, THE ADVENTURES OF VENICE, THE. T. Susanna Centlivre. Blank verse. D.L., 1700.

PERJUR'D NUN, THE. See *Love-Sick King.*

PERJUROR, THE. F. 1 a. C. Bullock. L.I.F., December 12, 1717.

PERKIN WARBECK, THE CHRONICLE HISTORIE OF. Hist. D. J. Ford. Phœnix D.L., 1745.

PERKINS, M.P. Sk. 3 sc. Fred Karno, Hickory Wood, and Fred Kitchen. Leicester Pal., July 12, 1909; Holborn Empire, August 2, 1909.

PERLA; OR THE COURT BELL(E). Past. O. Sk. 2 a. H. E. Manuel. Britannia, November 1, 1875.

PERLE DU BRESIL. LA. Lyric D. 3 a. Wds. by Mons. St. Etionne. M. by Felicien David. Paris, November 22, 1851.

PERLE NOIRE. Sardou. 1862.

PEROLA; OR, THE JEWEL AND THE DUEL. Burl. Rotherham T.R., March 19, 1883.

PEROLLA AND IZIDORA. T. (blank verse). C. Cibber. F. on Lord Orrery's novel. Parthenissa T.R., 1706; D.L., December 3, 1705.

PEROUSE, LA. D. 2 a. Transl. fr. Kotzebue by B. Thomson, 1799. Also transl. by Anne Plumptre.

PEROUSE; OR, THE DESOLATE ISLAND. Panto. D. J. Fawcett. C.G., May 5, 1801. Rev. as *ballet d'action* D.L., April 13, 1846.

PEROUSE; OR, THE DESOLATE ISLAND. Hist. Ballet. D. 2 a. M. by Davy and Morehead. Lyceum, July 8, 1818, and July 17, 1820.

PERPLEX'D COUPLE; OR, MISTAKE UPON MISTAKE, THE. Co. C. Molloy. Chiefly transl. fr. French. L.I.F., February 16, 1715.

PERPLEX'D HUSBAND, THE. Pant. C.G., 1748.

PERPLEX'D LOVERS, THE. C. Susanne Centlivre. Partly fr. Spanish p. D.L., January 19, 1712.

PERPLEX'D LOVERS; OR, THE DOUBLE MARRIAGE, THE. M.P. 2 a. M. selected by Mr. Gaudry. Salisbury T., 1776.

PERPLEXITIES, THE. C. T. Hull. Alt. of Sir S. Tuke's *Adventures of Five Hours.* C.G., January 31, 1768.

PERSA; OR, THE PERSIAN. C. Plautus. Transl. into blank verse by Thornton, Rich, Warner, and Colman. 1769-74. See "Latin Plays."

PERSECUTED DUTCHMAN. F. 1 a. Publ. by S. French, Ltd.

PERSECUTION OF JEWS IN PALERMO, THE. Hist. D. Taken fr. Hebrew and perf in German. International T. (Holborn), January 22, 1884.

PERSECUTION OF JEWS IN PORTUGAL, THE. M.P. in Yiddish. Novelty, April 1, 1896.

PERSEE. O. 5 a. Lulli. April 17, 1682.

PERSEE. O. 3 a. F. A. D. Philidor. October 27, 1780.

PERSEUS AND ANDROMEDA. P. Ac. at Court, 1574.

PERSEUS AND ANDROMEDA; OR, THE MAIDS AND THE MONSTER. Classical Extrav. W. Brangl. St. James's T., December 26, 1861.

PERSEUS AND ANDROMEDA WITH RAPE OF COLUMBINE; OR, THE FLYING LOVERS. 5 Int. (3 serious, 2 comic). S. by Mons. Roger and C. by John Weaver. D.L., 1716.

PERSEUS AND ANDROMEDA. Pant. "Same as prod. at C.G." L.I.F.

PERSEUS AND DEMETRIUS. Latin T. J. Banister. 1664. MS. preserved.

PERSEVERANCE. M.F. Hay., 1802.

PERSEVERANCE; OR, THE THIRD TIME THE BEST. M. W. C. Oulton. M. by Giordani. Crow Street, Dublin. C.G., June 2, 1789.

PERSIAN, THE. C. Transl. by R. Warner fr. Plautus's *Persa*, q.v.

PERSIAN CAT, THE. C.O. 3 a. V. H. Sutton Vane. Music by Harold Bailey. Hippodrome, Brighton, January 26, 1909.

PERSIAN HEROINE, THE. Hist. T. R. P. Jodrell. D.L., June 2, 1819; Lyceum, June 3, 1825.

PERSIAN HUNTERS, THE; OR, THE ROSE OF PURGISTAN, THE. S.C.O. M. by Horn. Lyceum, August 13, 1817.

PERSIAN PRINCE, THE. T. Southerne. 1682.

PERSIAN PRINCE AND MOORISH BOY, THE (Equestrian Act). Ducrow. D.L., June 28, 1836.

PERSIAN PRINCESS; OR, THE ROYAL VILLAIN, THE. T. L. Theobald. D.L., May 31, 1708. Pr. 1715.

PERSIAN PRINCESS, A. Oriental Mus. P. Wr. by Leedham Bantock and P. J. Barrow. Lyrics by Percy Greenbank. M. by Sydney Jones. Addit. numbers by Marie Horne. Queen's, April 27, 1909.

PERSIANS, THE. T. Transl. fr. Æschylus by R. Potter, 1777; Buckley, 1849; and Plumtre, 1869. See "Greek Plays."

PERSIANS, THE. P. Æschylus. Perf. by Literary Theatre Society. Terry's, March 23, 1907.

PERSONATION. F. D.L., April 17, 1828.

PERSONATION; OR, FAIRLY TAKEN IN. C. Int. 1 a. Adap. fr. the French (*Defiance and Malice*) by Marie Theresa Decamp. D.L., April 29, 1805; D.L., May 12, 1817. See *Doubt and Conviction.*

PERTHARITE. T. Corneille. 1693. See "French Classical Plays."

PERUGINA. O. F. L. H. Monro. December 20, 1838.

PERUVIAN, THE. C.O. Taken fr. Marmontel's novel "L'Amitié à l'Epreuve." M. by Hook. C.G., March 18, 1786.

PERUVIAN, THE. Adap. 1 a. Mme. Anna de Naucaze. Op. C., November 12, 1891.

PERUVIAN LOVERS, THE. Div. Noble. D.L., March 6, 1827.

PERUVIANS, THE. C. L. N. Parker. Bayswater Bijou T., May 7, 1895 (C.P.).

PET DOVE, THE. O. 2 a. Gounod. Crystal Pal., September 20, 1870.

PET LAMB, THE. Ca. 1 a. C. Selby. Strand, September 10, 1860.

PET OF NEWMARKET, THE. C.O. 2 a. Lib. by H. Mooney. M. by Camille. Sadler's Wells, November 12, 1881.

PET OF THE EMBASSY, THE. M.P. 2 a. S. F. Bailey. M. by A. E. Wilson. Bootle Muncaster, December 3, 1906 (amat.); Eccles Grand, March 30, 1907.

PET OF THE PETTICOATS, THE. C.O. M. by J. Barnett. D.L., June 19, 1834.

PET OF THE PUBLIC, A. F. 1 a. E. Stirling. Strand, 1853.

PET OF THE 21ST, THE. Op. Sk. Bedford, December 18, 1905.

PETALS OF A ROSE, THE. Rom. P. 2 a. E. Hine. M. by F. E. Hine. Croydon P.H., May 22, 1905.

PETE. P. 4 a. Hall Caine and Louis N. Parker. D. from *The Manxman*. Lyceum, August 29, 1908.

PETER AND PAUL. Hook.

PETER AND PAUL; OR, LOVE IN THE VINEYARDS. Oa. 2 a. Planché. Hay., July 4, 1821.

PETER BELL, THE WAGGONER; OR, MURDERERS OF MASSIAC. Melo-d. 3 a. J. B. Buckstone. Coburg T., 1826.

PETER KLAUS. Past. P. Lucie d'Aymant. An orig. dr. ver. of the old German legend fr. which *Rip Van Winkle* was derived. Langley Park, Bucks, June 11, 1902.

PETER PAN; OR, THE BOY WHO WOULDN'T GROW UP. P. 3 a. J. M. Barrie. Duke of York's, December 27, 1904; December 19, 1905; December 16, 1908.

PETER PRY. Sk. Victoria, 1821.

PETER SMINK; OR, THE ARMISTICE. C.D. 1 a. Adap. fr. the French by H. Payne. Surrey T., July, 1822.

PETER THE GREAT. P. 5 a. L. Irving. Lyceum, January 1, 1898.

PETER THE GREAT; OR, THE BATTLE OF PULTOWA. P. 3 a. M. by Dr. Carnaby and Cooke. D.L., February 21, 1829.

PETER THE GREAT; OR, THE WOODEN WALLS. Op.D. 3 a. A. Cherry. M. by Jouve. C.G., May 8, 1807.

PETER THE SHIPWRIGHT. O. 3 a. Lortzing. Gaiety, April 15, 1871. See *Czaar und Zimmermann*.

PETER WILKINS. G. A. à Beckett. Adelphi, 1845.

PETER WILKINS; OR, THE FLYING ISLANDERS. Melo-d. Spec. 2 a. C.G., April 16, 1827.

PETER'S MOTHER. P. 3 a. Mrs. H. de la Pasture. Wyndham's, September 12, 1906; Apollo, December 10, 1906; Comedy, February 8, 1907; Hay., March 2, 1907; Hay., June 8, 1909.

PETER'S PICTURE. Sk. C. C. Horton. Bedford, September 14, 1908.

PETERKIN. C.O. 3 a. Will Ladislaw. M. by L. Camerana. Royalty, September 4, 1893.

PETIT CHAGRIN. C. 3 a. Maurice Vaucaire, Royalty, July 12, 1906.

PETIT CHAPERON ROUGE, LE. P. without words. By A. De Sanson and H. de Brisay. M. by C. de Sivry. Royalty, May 27, 1892.

PETIT DUC, LE. C.O. By Meilhac and Halévy. Music by Charles Lecocq. Coronet, April 8, 1907. See *The Little Duke*.

PETIT FAUST, LE. Op. bo. 3 a. M. by Hervé. Adap. by H. B. Farnie. Lyceum, April 18, 1870.

PETIT HOTEL, LE. P. By H. Meilhac and L. Helévy. Royalty, February 4, 1907.

PETIT SOUPRE, LE. C.O. Nicolas Dalayrac. First prod. at the Fr. Court, 1781.

PETITE BOHEMIENNE, LA. Epis. Alfd. Moul. M. by Francis Thomé. Alhambra, January 4, 1909.

PETITE FADETTE, LE. V. 2 a. Fr. George Sand's Novel. Royalty, March 17, 1897.

PETITE FONCTIONNAIRE, LA. C. 3 a. Alfred Capus. Royalty, February 1, 1906.

PETITE MADEMOISELLE, LA. C.O. Lecocq. Adap. by R. Reece and H. S. Leigh. Alexandra, October 6, 1879.

PETITE MAISON, LA. O. 3 a. Spontini. June 23, 1804.

PETITE MARIEE, LA. Op. C. 3 a. M. Lecocq. Op. Comique, May 6, 1876.

PETITE MARQUISE, LA. See *May and December*.

PETITES OISEAUX, LES. See *A Pair of Spectacles*.

PETRONELLA. See *White Roses*.

PETRONELLA; OR, A ROYAL ROMANCE. C.O. 2 a. M. Turner and S. Smith. M. by W. T. Gliddon. Gt. Queen Street, May 26, 1906.

PETRONIUS MAXIMUS. Blank Verse. By W. S. Pr. by Wm. Brent. 1619.

PETROVNA; OR, THE PRICE OF FREEDOM. D. Prol. and 2 a. S. Hodges. Colchester T.R., April 6, 1885.

PETS. C. B. Ellis. St. Geo. H., May 31, 1889.

PETS. Sk. H. Graham. St. Geo. H., December 18, 1899 (amat.).

PETS OF THE PARTERRE; OR, LOVE IN A GARDEN, THE. Ca. 1 a. J. S. Coyne. Lyceum, November 11, 1860.

PETTICOAT GOVERNMENT. Int. 1 a. G. Dance. D.L., November 12, 1832.

PETTICOAT GOVERNMENT. C. Baroness Orczy and Montague Barstow. Wyndham's, August 12, 1909 (C.P.).

PETTICOAT KNIGHT, THE. C. Anne Yearsley. 1791

PETTICOAT PERFIDY. Ca. 1 a. Sir C. L. Young. Court T., May 21, 1885.

PETTICOAT PLOTTER, THE. C. 2 a. N. Hamilton. D.L. and L.I.F., 1720.

PETTICOAT PLOTTER; OR, MORE WAYS THAN ONE FOR A WIFE, THE. C. H. Ward. York, 1746.

PETTIPHER'S BABY. Ca. W. Wainwright. Richmond R., April 1, 1901.

PEWTERER, THE. Burl. c. Holbery. 1747.

PFARRER VON KIRCHFELD, DER. D. 5 a. L. Gruber. O. Com., September 20, 1894.

PHADREG, THE BOCANN. Irish c. C. J. Werner. Kilkenny Athenæum H., May 9, 1879.

PHAEDRA. T. Transl. fr. Racine. Anon. 1776.

PHÆDRA AND HIPPOLITUS. T. Transl. fr. "Seneca" by Sir E. Sherburne. 1701.

PHAEDRA AND HIPPOLYTUS. T. Pradon. 1677.

PHAEDRA AND HIPPOLYTUS. T. Edmund Smith. Hay., April 21, 1707.

PHAEDRA AND HIPPOLYTUS. O. T. Roseingrave. The foregoing T. abbreviated and songs added. Pr. at Dublin, 1753.

PHAETON. P. T. Dekker. Ac. by Lord Admiral's servants, 1597.

PHAETON. O. Lulli. 1663.

PHAETON; OR, THE FATAL DIVORCE, THE. T. C. Gildon. D.L., 1698.

PHANATIC PLAY, A. First part. Ac. Pr. 1660.

PHANTOM, THE. H. C. Edwards. Suggested by R. L. Stevenson's "Dr. Jekyll and Mr. Hyde." Liverpool Adelphi T., October 22, 1888.

PHANTOM BREAKFAST, THE. F. 1 a. C. Selby. Adelphi T., January 15, 1846.

PHANTOM BRIDE. Melo D. 2 a. Publ. by S. French, Ltd.

PHANTOM CAPTAIN, THE. Grecian, September 28, 1864.

PHANTOM DANCERS, THE. Fairy Spec. 2 a. Adelphi. December, 1846.

PHANTOM EARL, THE. Sk. 2 sc. and tab. A. E. Pringle. Salford Regent, March 19, 1907.

PHANTOMS. D. 5 a. G. Conquest and A. Shirley. Surrey, October 1, 1894.

PHANTOMS; OR, THE IRISHMAN IN ENGLAND. F. 2 a. T. Jones. Pr. 1803.

PHARAMOND. T. Calprenède. Transl. by Phillips. 1677.

PHARAMUS. T. Snelling. 1651.

PHARAOH. P. 4 a. W. Barrett. Leeds Grand T., September 29, 1892.

PHARAOH'S DAUGHTER. O. 1 a. Ethel Ra-Leslie. M. by J. Tabrar. Bijou, Bayswater, September 2, 1907 (C.P.); Camberwell Empire, September 16, 1907.

PHARISEE, THE. P. 3 a. M. Watson and Mrs. Lancaster Wallis. Shaftesbury, November 17, 1890; Kennington P.O.W., March 29, 1899.

PHARISEE'S WIFE, THE. P. 3 a. G. Paston. Duke of York's, July 12, 1904.

PHARISEES. C.D. 4 a. J. Day. Llanelly T.R., December 8, 1884.

PHARNACES. O. Alt. fr. Italian by T. Hull. D.L., 1765.

PHARO TABLE, THE. C. Alt. Anon. 1789. N.p. See *Faro Table.*

PHARSALIA. P. by Lucan. Transl. by Th. May.

PHEDRE. T. Racine transl. into prose. A. W. Momerie. Princess's, April 16, 1000. See "French Classical Plays."

PHEDRE. O. Massenet. Paris, Sarah Bernhardt T., 1901.

PHEDRE. Racine's T.; rev. Royalty, October 30, 1907.

PHEDRE. See *Phaedra* and *Hyppolyte*.

PHENOMENON IN A SMOCK-FROCK, A. C.D. 1 a. W. Brough. Lyceum, December 13, 1852.

PHIALS. C. Anon. 1781.

PHIL'S FOLLY. Ca. F. Haywell. Royalty, April 30, 1877.

PHILANDER. D. Past. Lennox. 1757.

PHILANDER AND ROSE. M. Past. Songs only pr. Manchester, 1785.

PHILANDERER, THE. C. 4 a. G. B. Shaw. Cripplegate Inst., February 20, 1905; Court, February 5, 1907.

PHILANDERING; OR, THE ROSE QUEEN. New C.O. M. by Horn. D.L., December 16, 182[illegible].

PHILANDRIST; OR, LADY FORTUNE-TELLER, THE. P. 1 a. E. Nesbit and Dorothea Deakin. Woolwich Freemasons' H., May 11, 1905.

PHILANTHROPIC EXPERIMENT, A. Ca. Mrs. Bradshaw. Nottingham Exchange H., April 23, 1905.

PHILANTHROPIST, THE. P. 5 a. Capt. J. Jones. Hay., 1801.

PHILANTHROPISTS, THE (*Les Bienfaiteurs*). C. 4 a. M. Brieux. C.G., King's H., King Street, February 2, 1904.

PHILANTHROPY. F. A. D. Livondais (Miss Alice Chandos). Princess's, September 3, 1888.

PHILANTHROPY. Orig. C. 3 a. W. Maurice and J. Rice.

PHILASTER. T. Alt. fr. Beaumont and Fletcher. D.L., December 31, 1715, and C.G., November 23, 1767.

PHILASTER; OR, LOVE LIES A BLEEDING. T.C. Beaumont and Fletcher, 1608 or 1609. Globe. (Not old T. in L.I.F.) Rev. and last 2 a. re-written by E. Settle. T.R., 1695. See *The Club Man.*

PHILEMON AND PHILECIA. Pl. by the Earl of Leicester's men, 1574.

PHILEMON ET BAUCIS. O. 3 a. Afterwards reduced to 2 a. Words by Barbier and Carre. M. by C. Gounod. Paris, February 18, 1860; C.G., October 24, 1891, and May 16, 1892.

PHILENZO and HIPPOLITA. T.C. Massinger. Ent. Stationers' Co., September 9, 1653. Destroyed by Warburton's servant.

PHILETUS AND CONSTANTIA. Supposed Robert Cox. Pr. in second part of *The Wits; or Sport upon Sport*, 1672.

PHILIP. D. 4 a. H. Aidé. Lyceum, February 7, 1874.

PHILIP AND HIS DOG. Sadler's Wells.

PHILIP OF FRANCE AND MARIE DE MERANIE. Hist. t. Westland Marston. Olympic, November 5, 1850.

PHILIP OF MACEDON. T. D. Lewis L.I.F., April 29, 1727.

PHILIP OF SPAIN, KING. T. Tennis Court St. James's, 1740.

PHILIP STRONG; OR, IN HIS STEPS. D 4 a. G. F. Neilson. Garrick, November 16 1899 (C.P.).

PHILIP THE SECOND. T. See "Theatrical Recorder."

PHILIP THE SECOND. T. Alfieri. Transl by C. Lloyd. 1815.

PHILIP VAN ARTEVELDE. P. H. Taylor Princess's November, 1847.

PHILIPPE. O. 1 a Publ. by S. French, Ltd.

PHILIPPO AND HIPPOLITIA. P. Henslow's company. Suggested that it and *Philenzo and Hippolita* are same. (Could not be, as Massinger would only be ten years.) July 9 1594.

PHILISTINES; OR, THE SCOTCH TOCSIN SOUNDED, THE. Scene at Jacobin Club. 1793.

PHILLIDA AND CHORYN. Pastoral P. Ac. at Court, 1584.

PHILLIPI; OR, THE SECRET MARRIAGE. A STORY OF THE REVOLUTION. Dom. d. 1 a. Adap. fr. French by W. Murray. Edinburgh T.R.

PHILLIS. O. Michael Arne. 1776.

PHILLIS AT COURT. C.O. 3 a. Alt. of *Capricious Lovers*, by Lloyd. M. by Giardini. Dublin, Crow Street, 1767.

PHILLIS MAYBURN. D. C. H. Hazlewood. Britannia, July 28, 1873.

PHILLIS OF SEYROS. Dr. past. Shirley. 1655.

PHILOCLEA. T. McNamara Morgan. F. on Sidney's *Arcadia*. C.G., January 20, 1754.

PHILOCTETES. T. Transl. fr. Sophocles by Dr. T. Sheridan. 1725. Same transl. by G. Adams, 1729; Sir Th. Francklin, 1759; and R. Potter, 1788; and Plumptre. See "Greek Plays."

PHILOCTETES IN LEMNOS. D. 3 a. Pr. 1795.

PHILODAMUS. T. T. Bentley. C.G., December 14, 1782.

PHILOMAR; OR, LOVE'S VICTORY. Christmas Fantasy. 3 a. Alicia A. Leith. Albert H., January 10, 1906 (amat.).

PHILOMEL. Rom. D. 3 a. H. T. Craven. Globe, February 10, 1870.

PHILOPOENA. A Farrago of Fun, etc. 2 a. Edgar Smith. Music by Maurice Levi. Aldwych, February 27, 1909.

PHILOSOPHER IN THE APPLE ORCHARD, THE. Past. Adap. fr. a story of Anthony Hope by E. H. Williams. Garrick, April 22, 1902.

PHILOSOPHER'S DIAMOND, THE. C. of Marvels. By Nevil Maskelyne. St. George's Hall, August 5, 1908.

PHILOSOPHER'S OPERA, THE. Lord Dreghorn.

PHILOSOPHER'S STONE, THE. M. J. Moorehead. Sadler's Wells, 1795.

PHILOSOPHER'S STONE, THE. Extrav. By author of *Diogenes*. Strand, May 20, 1850.

PHILOSOPHER'S STONE, THE. Mag. F. Sk. N. Maskelyne. Egyptian H., December 22, 1902.

PHILOSOPHER'S STONE, THE. Fantasy Drama. 4 a. Isaac York. Royalty, March 1, 1908.

PHILOSOPHIC WHIM; OR, ASTRONOMY A FARCE, THE. Dr. Hefferman. Pr. 1774. N.ac.

PHILOTAS. T. S. Daniel. Circa 1605.

PHILOTAS. T. P. Frowde. L.I.F., February 3, 1731.

PHILOTUS. R. Semble. 1603.

PHILOTUS. C. 1616.

PHILTRE, LE. C.O. 2 a. By Scribe. M. by Auber. D.L., August 10, 1846.

PHOBUS'S FIX. F. D.L., February 28, 1870.

PHOCAS. T. M. Slaughter. May 19, 1596, and in 1598.

PHŒBE. Past. O. J. Hoadley. M. by Dr. Greene. 1748.

PHŒBE; OR, THE BEGGAR. D.L. See *The Beggar's Wedding*.

PHŒBE AT COURT. Oa. Alt. by Dr. T. A. Arne fr. Lloyd's *Capricious Lovers*. 1776.

PHŒNICIAN DAMSELS, THE. T. Transl. fr. Euripides by M. Wodhull. 1782. See "Greek Plays."

PHŒNICIAN VIRGINS, THE. T. Transl. fr. Euripides by R. Potter. 1781.

PHŒNISSŒ. T. Transl. fr. Euripides by J. Banister, 1780; Potter, 1781; Wodhull, 1782; Morgan, 1805; and Giles, 1865.

PHŒNISSŒ. See *Iocasta*.

PHŒNIX, THE Tragi C. T. Middleton. F. on a Spanish novel, "The Force of Love." Ac. by children of St. Paul's and also before His Majesty. 1607.

PHŒNIX, THE. P. 1 a. By Laurence Irving. Coronet, June 25, 1907.

PHŒNIX IN HER FLAMES, THE. T. Sir W. Lower. 1639.

PHONOGRAPH, THE. Ca. A. C. F. Wood. Walsall St. Geo. H., November 20, 1889.

PHONOGRAPH GIRL, THE. Sk. Camberwell Empire, November 18, 1907.

PHORMIO. Eng. transl. of Terence's C. by R. Bernard, 1598. Transls. by Hoole, Patrick, Echard, Cooke, Gordon, and Colman. See "Latin Plays," "Westminster Plays."

PHOTOGRAPHIC FIX, A. F. 1 a. F. Hay. R. Victoria T., November 4.

PHRENOLOGIST, THE. F. J. S. Coyne. Dublin T.R., 1835.

PHRONTISTERION; OR, OXFORD IN THE NINETEENTH CENTURY. D. Mansel. 1852. (Left unfinished.)

PHROSINE ET MELIDOR. O. 3 a. Méhul. Op. Comique, May 4, 1794.

PHUNNYGRAPH, THE. Sk. F. Bowyer and H. Sparing. Folkestone Pl. Gardens T., May 28, 1894.

PHYLLIDA. See *Hidden Worth*.

PHYLLIS. Dr. P. 4 a. Frances Hodgson-Burnett. Globe, July 1, 1889.

PHYLLIS. C.O. M. Blatchford. M. by A. T. M'Evoy. Halifax T.R. April 14, e890.

PHYLLIS. C. 3 a. Max Pireau (Mabel Pineo). Bayswater Bijou, June 17, 1899.

PHYSIC LIES A-BLEEDING; OR, THE APOTHECARY TURNED DOCTOR. C. Ac. in apothecaries' shops by T. Brown. 1697.

PHYSICAL CULTURE. Previously presented as a M.H. Sk. Aldwych, June 22, 1909.

PHYSICAL METAMORPHOSIS, THE; OR, A TREBLE DISCOVERY. F. F. Stretler. Rochester, 1778

PHYSICIAN, THE. P. 4 a. H. A. Jones. Criterion, March 25, 1897.

PHYSICIAN AGAINST HIS WILL. Anon. Prob. a transl. of Molière's *Le Medecin Malgré Lui*.

PHYSICIAN'S WIFE, THE. Grecian, October 4, 1858.

PICCADILLETTANTE. F. 2 fits. U. F. Heatly. Ladbroke H., April 24, 1900 (amat.).

PICCALILLI Jap. M.P. Wr. and comp. by Catherine Adams. Basingstoke Drill H., May 10, 1906 (amat.).

PICCOLINO. O. 3 a. M. by M. Guiraud. Lib. MM. Nuiter and Victorien Sardou. Adap. into Engl. by Sydney Samuel. Dublin Gaiety, January 4, 1879; H.M.T., January 29, 1879.

PICCOLO HAYDN, IL. Lyric O. 1 a. A. and G. Cipollini. Lyric, November 16, 1897.

PICCOLOMINI; OR, THE FIRST PART OF WALLENSTEIN (? OR, THE DEATH OF WALLENSTEIN). 5 a. Transl. fr. German of Schiller by S. T. Coleridge. Pr. 1800.

PICCOLOMINIS, THE. D. 5 a. Prel., "Wallenstein's Camp." Transl. fr. Fr. Schiller by a gentleman. Pr. 1806.

PICK ME UP. C. M. Capper. Ipswich T.R., September 18, 1882.

PICK OF THE BUNCH, THE. M.C. 2 a. By Charles Carey, Buckstone Clair, Charles Wilmot. M. by L. Lasel and H. Wellmon. Kingston, April 8, 1907.

PICKING UP THE PIECES. Ca. 1 a. J. Sturgis. Court, November 14, 1882.

PICKLES. C. 3 a. P. Meritt. Preston T.R., March 15, 1879.

PICKLES. M. conceit. 2 a. F. on story of *Cinderella*. H. Mills and T. W. Charles. Liverpool P.O.W., April 9, 1894.

PICKLOCK OF PARIS, THE. Effingham, October 27, 1866.

PICKPOCKET, THE. F.C. 3 a. Adap. fr. Baron Von Moser's *Mit Vernügen* by G. P. Hawtrey. Globe, April 24, 1886.

PICKPOCKETS, THE. P. 4 a. C. M.S. McLellan. Garrick, December 14, 1908 (C.P.).

PICKWICK. P. 4 a Fr. Dickens, by J. Albery. Lyceum, October 23, 1871.

PICKWICK. Dr. cant. 1a. F. C. Burnand. M by E. Solomon. Comedy, February 7, 1889; Trafalgar, December 13, 1893.

PICKWICKIANS. C.O. 3 a. Publ. by S. French, Ltd.

PICOTIN'S REVENGE. Dr. epi. of Viennese life. Pimlico Standard, July 21, 1902.

PICTURE, THE. T.C. P. Massinger. Fr. novel in Painter's *Palace of Pleasure* and *A Lady of Boeme*. Globe, June 8, 1629; Blackfriars, 1636. Pr. 1630.

PICTURE; OR, MY OWN CHOICE. C. Wood. 1796.

PICTURE; OR, THE CUCKOLD IN CONCEIT, THE. C. 1 a. Fr. *Cocu Imaginaire*, by Molière. J. Miller. D.L., February 11, 1744. Pr. 1745.

PICTURE DEALER, THE. F.C. 3 a. H. Reichardt and A. Golsworthy. Ladbroke H., June 30, 1892 (C.P.); Strand, July 4, 1892; Parkhurst, June 24, 1895.

PICTURE OF PARIS, THE. Pant. Mr. Bonnor. Dial. and songs, Mr. Merry. M., Shield C.G., December 20, 1790. N.p.

PICTURE OF THE YEAR, THE. P. 1 a. George Paston and Henriette Cockeran. King's Hall, March 22, 1908.

PIE VOLEUSE, LA. O. Rossini. Paris, 1822

PIED PIPER. O. 1 a. Bartholeyns and Farmer. Publ. by S. French, Ltd.

PIEL CASTLE, IN THE OLDEN TIME. D. E. Lawson. Barrow T.R., September 19, 1873.

PIERCE OF EXTON. P. R. Wilson, assisted by Drayton, Chettle, and Dekker. 1598.

PIERCE OF WINCHESTER. P. R. Wilson, in conjunction with Dekker and Drayton. 1598.

PIERRE DE MEDICIS. O. Poniatowski. Paris, 1860.

PIERRE LE GRAND. O. Grétry. Paris, 1790.

PIERRE LE GRAND. O. Meyerbeer. 1854.

PIERRETTE; OR, THE VILLAGE RIVALS. C. Oa. 1 a. E. Fitzball. Pyne and Harrison, March 6, 1858.

PIERRETTE'S BIRTHDAY. Episode, with music, by Colin Neil Rose. Music by Clement Locknane. New, June 24, 1908.

PIERROT AND PIERRETTE. Dr. Sk. 1 a. T. MacDonald. Publ. by S. French, Limited.

PIERROT AND PIERRETTE. P., without words. F. Wyatt and G. Jacobi. Albert H., West T., May 7, 1902.

PIERROT OF THE MINUTE, THE. Fantasy. Ernest Dowson. Bayswater Bijou, December 16, 1905.

PIERROT'S DREAM. M.P. 1 a. H. Byatt. M. by H. Grey. Birmingham T.R., February 17, 1893.

PIERROT'S LIFE, A. P., without words. 3 a. F. Boissier. M. by M. Costa. P.O.W. (first time in England), January 8, 1897.

PIERROT'S LIFE, A. F. Boissier. M. by Signor V. Monti. Adapt. by C. Lauri. Lyric, April 11, 1900.

PIETRA. D. 3 a. Adap. of Dr. Mosenthal's T. by J. Oxenford. Hay., July 12, 1868.

PIETRA DEL PARAGON, LA. O. Rossini. Milan, September 26, 1812.

PIETRO IL GRANDE. Hist. O. Desmond Ryan and Maggioni M. by Jullien. C.G., August 17, 1852.

PIETRO WILKIN; OR, THE CASTAWAYS, THE WILD MEN, AND THE WINGED BEAUTY. Burl. F. Eyles, jun. Shoreham Swiss Gardens, August 18, 1870.

PIETRO'S VIOLIN. Sk. Sheffield R., August 30, 1907.

PIETY AND VALOUR; OR, DERRY DEFENDED. T.C. Anon. ? Same as *Siege of Derry* which appeared at the time. 1692.

PIETY IN PATTENS. C. S. Foote. Introd. in an ent. *The Primitive Puppet-Show*. Hay., February 15, 1773. Rev. March 6, 1773, as *The Handsome Housemaid; or, Piety in Pattens.*

PIFF PAFF; OR, THE MAGIC ARMOURY. Extrav. H. B. Farnie. Criterion, January 31, 1876.

PIGEON HOUSE, THE. F. 3 a. Miss Molly E. Seawell. Dr. by E. Hope. Bayswater Bijou, July 2, 1902.

PIGMY REVELS. Pant. D.L., 1773.

PIGS IN CLOVER. Sk. J. J. S. Sutcliffe. Putney Hipp., October 5, 1908.

PIKE O'CALLAGHAN; OR, THE IRISH PATRIOT. D. 3 a. W. Reeve. Scarborough T.R., September 29, 1868; Surrey, February 7, 1870.

PILATE AND OVID'S DAUGHTER. Classl. D. 4 a. Mrs. M. French Sheldon and Acton Bond. Victoria Hall, W., October 9, 1900; Bijou, Bayswater, July 30, 1900.

PILGRIM, THE. C. Beaumont and Fletcher. Ptd. 1647.

PILGRIM, THE. T. T. Killigrew. Pr. 1664.

PILGRIM, THE. Foregoing P. rev. with Prol. and Epil by Dryden by Sir J. Vanbrugh. Drury Lane T.R., 1700, and rev. as late as 1812.

PILGRIM OF LOVE, THE. Fairy R. 1 a. H. J. Byron. Hay., April 9, 1860.

PILGRIM'S PROGRESS, THE. Mystery P. 4 a. (F. on Bunyan's Allegory.) M., George Gervase Collingham. Olympic, June 10, 1896 (C.P.); December 24, 1896; (and rev.), March 1, 1897.

PILGRIM'S PROGRESS, THE. Version by Mrs. W. Hadley and Miss E. Ouless. Imperial, March 16, 1907.

PILGRIM'S REST, THE. Prol. and 3 a. by Dagney Major. Peterborough Drill H., February 5, 1906 (amat.).

PILGRIM'S WAY, THE. M. Allegory. 3 a. 4 sc. Daisy Elliott (Margaret Meredith). Court, March 27, 1905.

PILGRIME VON MEKKA, DIE. C.O. Transl. fr. Darcourt's *Rencontre Imprévue*. M. by Gluck. In Fr. at Schonbrunn, 1764; Ger., 1766; rev., 1780.

PILGRIMAGE OF THE ROSE, THE. Cant. Schumann. 1810-56.

PILGRIMAGE TO PARNASSUS, THE. C. Same author as *The Return from Parnassus*. N.p.

PILGRIMS; OR, THE HAPPY CONVERTS, THE. T. W. Harrison. Queen Anne's reign. ? 1701. Pr. N.ac.

PILGRIMS; OR, THE WORLD BETWEEN THEM. D. F. Jefferson. Scarborough T.R., August 18, 1884.

PILKERTON'S PEERAGE. C. 4 a. Anthony Hope. Garrick, March 18, 1901 (C.P.); and January 28, 1902.

PILL AND DROP. P. Ascr. to J. Kerry. N.p. 1735.

PILL FOR THE DOCTOR; OR, THE TRIPLE WEDDING, A. M. ent. Anon. Royalty. Pr. 1790.

PILLARS OF SOCIETY, THE. P. 4 a. Transl. fr. Ibsen's Norwegian piece, *Samfundetz Stölter*. W. Archer. O.C., June 17, 1889.

PILLS OF WISDOM. Extrav. 1 a. W. Heighway. Publ. by S. French, Ltd.

PILOT, THE D. Ver. of Cooper's novel. E. Fitzball. Adelphi, October 31, 1825; Bath, February 11, 1829.

PIM POM. M.F. 1 a. E. T. De Banzie Glasgow Princess's, February 21, 1890.

PIMPLE THE PIRATE. Absurdity. 4 a. H. Mills. M. by J. G. Wingrove. Woolwich Bijou, December 10, 1885.

PIN AND THE PUDDING, THE. P. 3 a. Barton White. R., Margate, June 7, 1909; Comedy, August 23, 1909.

PINAFORE. See *The Wreck of the Pinafore*, *H.M.S. Pinafore.*

PINDAR OF WAKEFIELD, THE. See *George A. Greene, Pindar*, etc.

PINDEE SINGH. D. C. H. Stephenson. Royal Alfred (late Marylebone), October 10, 1868.

PINK DOMINOS, THE. F.C. Adap. fr. Hennequin and Delacour's *Les Dominos Roses*. J. Albery. Criterion, March 31, 1877; rev. October 10, 1902

PINK LETTER, THE. C. 1 a. Mrs. Douglas Cox. Maidenhead T.R., January 27, 1898.

PINK OF POLITENESS, THE. Selby. Olympic, February 8, 1840.

PINKIE AND THE FAIRIES. Fairy P. 3 a. W. Graham Robertson. M. by Frederick Norton. His Majesty's, December 19, 1908.

PIONEERS OF AMERICA. October 22, 1860.

PIP'S PATRON. Dr. ver. of Dickens's *Great Expectations*. W. J. Rix. Beccles Public H., January 26, 1892.

PIPER, THE. P. 1 a. F. Noreys Connell. Dublin Abbey, February 13, 1908.

PIPER OF HAMELIN, THE. O. 5 a. Lib. by H. Hersee. M. by V. E. Nessler. Dresden, 1879; Manchester Queen's, November 16, 1882; C.G., January 7, 1884.

PIPER OF HAMELIN, THE. Fantastic O. 2 a. R. Buchanan. M. by F. W. Allwood. Comedy, December 20, 1893.

PIPES AND THE DRYAD; A SPRING IDYL. O. 3 a. Florence Campbell Perugini. M. by H. A. S. Campbell. Acton St. Albans Par. R., February 27, 1905.

PIPKIN'S RUSTIC RETREAT. F. 1 a. T. J. Williams. Adelphi, January 18, 1866.

PIPPA PASSES. D. R. Browning. 1842. Fortune Playhouse, January 25, 1909.

PIQUE. See *Her Own Evening.*

PIRATE, THE. P. R. Davenport. (See Malone's "Attempt to Ascertain the Dates of Shakespeare's Plays.") Written about 1660 N.p.

PIQUILLO. O. 3 a F. L. H. Monro. October 31, 1837.

PIRATE, THE. D. with M. by Rooke. F on novel, "The Pirate." D.L., January 15 1822.

PIRATE; OR, THE WICKED FATHER WHO SOLD HIS DAUGHTER AND THE DON WHO BOUGHT HER, THE. Extrav. Leigh Thomas. So. London Assembly R., December 8, 1871 (amat.).

PIRATE KING, THE. M. Extrav. N. Lamont. M. and lyrics by J. James. Britannia. August 7, 1905.

PIRATE OF GENOA, THE. Adap. of Weigh's O., *Gli Amon. Marinari*. C.O. Lyceum playbill, September 5, 1828.

PIRATE'S HOME, THE. G. à Beckett and V. Bligh. St. Geo. H., 1884.

PIRATE'S LOVE, THE. Grecian, September, 1860.

PIRATE'S WIFE; OR, THE TWIN BROTHERS, THE. D. Newcastle-on-Tyne T., April 16, 1870.

PIRATES, THE. C.O. J. Cobb. M. by Storace. Ac. by D.L. company at Opera Ho. Pr. (songs only) 1792.

PIRATES OF PENZANCE; OR, LOVE AND DUTY (OR, SLAVES OF DUTY, THE), THE. C.O. 2 a. W. S. Gilbert. M. by A. Sullivan. Penzance Bijou, December 30, 1879; Op. Com., April 3, 1880: Savoy, June 30, 1900; Savoy, December 1, 1908.

PIRATES OF PUTNEY, THE. Naut. Extrav. 1 a. C. Selby. Royalty, August 31, 1863.

PIRATES OF SAVANNAH; OR, THE TIGER HUNTER OF THE PRAIRIES, THE. Rom. D. 3 a. Fr. the French of A. Bourgeois and F. Dugué. Adap. by W. Luter. Effingham R., April 29, 1861.

PIRATICAL PIRATE OF THE PRECIPITOUS PRECIPICE. Crystal Pal., August 1, 1863.

PIRATO, IL. O. 2 a. Lib. by Romani. M. by Bellini. Milan Scala, October 27, 1827; Paris, February 1, 1832; King's, April 17, 1830.

PIRITHOUS, THE SON OF IXION. Burl. F. C. Burnand. New Royalty, April 13, 1865.

PISCATOR; OR, THE FISHER CAUGHT. C. J. Hoker. Wr. about 1535. N.p.

PISCATORY, THE. Eng. C. P. Fletcher. Cambridge King's Coll., 1615. See *Sicelides*, of which probably this was the second title.

PISH O'POGUE. Irish D. T. W. Lord. South Shields Royal Amphitheatre, May 22, 1876.

PISO'S CONSPIRACY. T. Anon. Duke of York's, 1676. Same as *Tragedy of Nero*, except for slight alt.

PISTE, LA. C. 3 a. Victorien Sardou. Royalty, July 23, 1906.

PIT'S MOUTH; OR, LIFE IN THE MINE, THE. D. 1 a J. Lewis. Dunstable Corn Exch., August 24 1895.

PITCAIRN'S ISLAND. Ballet. Action and dances by Byrne M. (partly), Corri. D.L., April, 1816.

PITCH AND TOSS. C.D. By Bertha N. Graham. Amateur Players' Assoc., Victoria St., February 6, 1907.

PITMAN'S DAUGHTER, THE. D. H. S. Springate. Wolverhampton P.O.W., May 12, 1879.

PITTY THE MAID. P. Ent. Stationers' Co November 29, 1653. N.p.

PITY; OR, GRINGOIRE THE BALLAD-MONGER. Pathetic p. Adap. fr. De Banville's *Gringoire*. A. Shirley. New Cross P.H., November 18, 1882; Crystal Pal., February 27, 1883.

PITY IS AKIN TO LOVE. Unfinished sk. J. K. Jerome. Olympic, September 8, 1888.

PITY OF IT, THE. Inc. 1 a. Ian Robertson. Ealing Lyric, April 15, 1896; Savoy, June 29, 1896.

PITY PODDLECHOCK. F. O. Allen. Liverpool Alexandra, June 27, 1881.

PITY THE SORROWS OF A POOR OLD MAN. Strand, 1862.

PIU GLORIOSA TATICA D'ERCOLE, LA. O. A. Ariosti. Bologna, 1706.

PIXIES' REVEL, THE. Sk. Brixton Empress, May 11, 1908.

PIZARRO. T 5 a. Adap. fr. Augustus von Kotzebue's d. *The Spaniard in Peru*. R. B. Sheridan. M. by Kelly. D.L., May 24, 1799; D.L., May 31, 1819; 1827; Victoria, 1834.

PIZARRO. Sheridan's transl into German by C. Geisweiler Pr. 1799.

PIZZARO. T. Blank verse. M. West. Pr. 1799, Dublin.

PIZZARO. T. 5 a. "North Briton." N.d.

PIZZARO. City of London, January 22, 1866.

PIZARRO; OR, THE DEATH OF ROLLA. Transl. fr. Kotzebue by R. Heron. Pr. 1799.

PIZZARO; OR, THE DEATH OF ROLLA. Rom. t. Transl. fr. Kotzebue by B. Thompson. 1800.

PIZARRO IN PERU; OR, THE DEATH OF ROLLA. Transl. fr. Kotzebue by T. Dutton. 1799. N.ac.

PLACE ROYALE, LA. Corneille. See "French Classical Plays."

PLAGUE, THE. Mystic M.P. 1 a. Ian Robertson. M. by L. Drysdale. Edinburgh Lyceum, October 16, 1896.

PLAGUE OF MY LIFE, THE. F. 1 a. I. Davean.

PLAGUE OF RICHES; OR, L'EMBARRAS DES RICHESSES. C. French and English. Transl. by Ozell. Pr. 1735.

PLAIDEURS, LES. C. Racine. Imitated fr. Aristophanes' *Wasps*. See "French Classical Plays."

PLAIN DEALER, THE. C. W. Wycherley. F. on Molière's *La Critique de L'École des Femmes* and *Le Misanthrope* and Jean Racine's *Les Plaideurs*. T.R., 1674.

PLAIN DEALER, THE. C. Alt. fr. Wycherley and adap. to stage by Isaac Bickerstaff. Pr. 1766. D.L.

PLAIN ENGLISH. C. 3 a. T. Morton. Holborn, September 29, 1869.

PLAINTIFF. Comical Cha. Stanley Rogers. Publ. by S. French, Ltd.

PLAINTIFF. 1 a. H. W. Smith. Publ. by S. French, Ltd.

PLANCHETTE. C.O. Rev. ver. in 2 a. George Quain. M. by H. W. Norman. Dover R.T., December 18, 1907.

PLANETOMACHIA; OR, THE FIRST PART OF THE GENERAL OPPOSITION OF THE SEVEN PLANETS. C. R. Green. Pr. 1585.

PLANTATION OF VIRGINIA, THE. P. Ment. in Sir Henry Herbert's Diary under the date August, 1623.

PLANTATION THOMASSIN, LA. By Maurice Ordinneau. See *Too Much Johnson*.

PLANTER, THE. F.C. 3 a. Adap. fr. Ordinneau's *La Plantation Thomassin* (Folies Dramatiques, June 1, 1891). W. Yardley P.O.W., October 31, 1891.

PLANTERS OF THE VINEYARD; OR, THE KIRK SESSIONS CONFOUNDED, THE. C. Pr. 1771.

PLANTEUR, LE. O. 2 a. M. by F. L. H. Munro. March 1, 1839.

PLATEE. O. 3 a. and prol. Rameau. February 4, 1749.

PLATONIC ATTACHMENTS. F. 1 a. B. Bernard. Princess's, September 28, 1850.

PLATONIC ATTACHMENTS. C. 3 a. E. Philpotts. Ealing Lyric H., February 20, 1889.

PLATONIC FRIENDSHIP, A. Duol. J. M. Barrie. D.L., March 17, 1908.

PLATONIC LADY, THE. C. Pro. by Capt. G. Farquhar. Susanna Centlivre. Hay., November 25, 1706; T.R., 1710.

PLATONIC LOVE. C. Centlivre. 1707.

PLATONIC LOVERS, THE. T.C. Sir W. Davenant. Pr. 1636. Blackfriars.

PLATONIC WIFE, THE. C. Mrs. Griffiths. Taken fr. Marmontel's *L'Heureux Divorce*. D.L., January 24, 1765. Pr. 1765.

PLAUTO E IL SUO SECOLO. D. Pietro Cossa.

PLAY. Lindsay. 1602.

PLAY. C. 4 a. T. W. Robertson. P.O.W., February 15, 1868.

PLAY ACTOR, THE. F.C. 3 a. C. Rimington. Preston R.T., September 12, 1907.

PLAY ACTRESS, THE. P. R. D. Scott. Adap. fr. S. R. Crockett's novel. Grand, January 28, 1890 (C.P.).

PLAY ACTRESS, THE. P. 3 a. R. D. Mackintosh. Richmond Castle Assembly R., April 26, 1905.

PLAY BETWEEN JOHAN, TYB, AND SIR JOHAN. J. Heywood. 1533. (B.L.).

PLAY BETWENE THE PARDONER AND THE FRERE, THE CURATE AND NEYBOUR PRATTE. Int. J. Heywood. Pr. 1533. Apparently wr. before 1521.

PLAY BOY OF THE WESTERN WORLD, THE. See *Playboy*.

PLAY IN A LITTLE, A. P. 1 a. Ian Robertson. Shaftesbury, June 2, 1892; Birmingham P.O.W., April 26, 1909.

PLAY IS OVER, THE. D. proverb. Transl. fr. Carmentel by Thos. Holcroft. Pr. 1804.

PLAY IS THE PLOT, THE. C. J. D. Breval. D.L., February 19, 1718. Pr. 1718.

PLAY OF A WOMAN, THE. H. Chettle. 1598.

PLAY OF CARDS, THE. N.p.

PLAY OF GENTLENESS AND NOBILITY. Int. in 2 parts. J. Heywood. 1535. N.d.

PLAY OF LOVE, A. Int. J. Heywood. Pr. 1533.

PLAY OF ST. CATHERINE'S, THE. Geoffrey of Dunstable. Ac. by his scholars. N.p.

PLAY OF THE WEATHER, CALLED A NEW AND MERRY INTERLUDE OF ALL MANNER OF WEATHERS, A. J. Heywood. Pr. 1533.

PLAY WITHOUT A NAME, A. Society D. T. M. Paule. East Oxford, July 20, 1909.

PLAY'S THE THING, THE. Ca. E. Drew. Athenæum, Tott. Ct. Rd. January 28, 1889.

PLAY'S THE PLOT, THE. C. J. D. Breval. D.L., 1717.

PLAYE CALLED THE FOURE P.P., THE. J. Heywood. N.d. See *The Four P's.*

PLAYBOY OF THE WESTERN WORLD, THE. C. 3 a. J. M. Synge. Gt. Queen Street, June 10, 1907.

PLAYED AND LOST. D. W. J. Wild. N. Shields T.R., August 1, 1887

PLAYER QUEEN, THE. C. 1 a. Adap. fr. French by W. Farren, jun. Bath T.R., November 21, 1892.

PLAYERS' REHEARSAL, THE. C. 2 a. Dean Swift, and sent to Gray to finish.

PLAYHOUSE TO BE LET, A. C. Sir Wm. Davenant. 2 a. F. on Molière's *Sganarelle.* Composed of series of more or less heterogeneous materials. Four p. in one, two of which had been previously prod. 1663.

PLAYING AT LOO-LOO. F. G. H. Macdermott. Grecian, May 8, 1871.

PLAYING FIRST FIDDLE. Adelphi, April 1, 1850.

PLAYING THE GAME. F.C. 3 a. W. Younge and A. Flaxman. M. by F. Eplett. Strand, June 18, 1896.

PLAYING WITH FIRE. C. 5 a. J. Brougham. Princess's, September 28, 1861. Prod. in America.

PLAYLETS, LTD.; OR, PERCY'S PROPOSAL. M.Ca. 1 a. Victor Stevens. Rehearsal, W.C., November 4, 1908 (mat.).

PLAYMATES. D.Sk. 1 a. H. Warburton. Stratford T.R., August 18, 1888 (C.P.).

PLAYWRIGHT, THE. 3 a. A. E. Hiscock. Hull T.R., October 26, 1901 (amat.).

PLAYS ACTED AT PARIS. Anon. (4 vols.) 1800.

PLAYS WRITTEN FOR A PRIVATE THEATRE. Davies. 1786.

PLEASANT DREAMS. F. 1 a. C. Dance. C.G., May 24, 1834.

PLEASANT HOUR, A. F. A. T. Robbins. Bradford Pullan's, September 6, 1878.

PLEASANT NEIGHBOUR. F. 1 a. Mrs. Planche. Publ. by S. French, Ltd.

PLEASE TO REMEMBER THE GROTTO; OR, THE MANAGERESS IN A FIX. Extrav. J. Oxenford. St. James's, December 26, 1865.

PLEASURE. Spec. C.D. 6 a. P. Meritt and Aug. Harris. D.L., September 3, 1887.

PLEASURE AT KENILWORTH CASTLE. Masque. G. Gascoign. Perf. before Q. Eliz. Pr. 1587.

PLEASURE RECONCILED TO VIRTUE. Masque. Ben Jonson. Additional masque, *For the Honour of Wales,* at end. Perf. before James I., 1619.

PLEASURES OF ANARCHY. Dr. Sermon, to which is prefixed a map illustrative of work. 5 a. Pr. 1809.

PLEASURES OF LONDON, THE. P. H. Whyte. Sydenham P.H., November 11, 1901.

PLEBEIAN, THE. Co. D. 4 a. Vaudeville, July 28, 1891.

PLEBEIANS. C. 3 a. J. Derrick, Vaudeville, January 12, 1886.

PLEDGE; OR, CARTELIAN HONOUR, THE. T.D. 5 a. D.L., April 8, 1831.

PLIGHTED TROTH. P. D.L., April 20, 1842.

PLOT; OR, PILL AND DROP. F. J. Kelly. D.L., 1733.

PLOT AND COUNTERPLOT; OR, THE PORTRAIT OF CERVANTES. F. 1 a. C. Kemble. Adap. fr. French. D.L., 1832.

PLOT AND NO PLOT; OR, JACOBITE CREDULITY. C. J. Dennis. D.L., 1695; C.G., April 23, 1746.

PLOT AND PASSION. D. T. Taylor and J. Lang. Olympic, October 17, 1853.

PLOT FOR PLOT. Ca. 1 a. Sir C. L. Young, Bart.

PLOT OF HIS STORY, THE. P. 1 a. Mrs. Oscar Beringer. Garrick, December 15, 1899.

PLOT OF POTZENTAUSEND, THE. Co. D. 1 a. Publ. by S. French, Ltd.

PLOTS; OR, THE NORTH TOWER. Melod. O. S. J. Arnold. Lyceum, September 3, 1810

PLOTS FOR PETTICOATS. F. 1 a. J. Wooler. Sadler's Wells, September 17, 1849.

PLOTTING LOVERS; OR, THE DISMAL SQUIRE, THE. F. Ch. Shadwell, 1720. Transl. fr. Molière's *Mons. de Pourceaugnac.*

PLOTTING MANAGERS, THE. Peter Pindar, jun. N.d.

PLOTTING SISTERS, THE. C. D'Urfey. 1676.

PLOTTING WIVES, THE. C. 2 a. R. Linnecar York. Pr. 1789.

PLOWDENS, THE. C. 4 a. O. Benyon and E. Rose. P.O.W., March 8, 1892.

PLUCK: A STORY OF £50,000. D. 7 tab. H. Pettitt and Aug. Harris. D.L., August 5, 1882.

PLUCKY JAPAN. Spec. Sk. M. Goldberg. Manchester Metropole, May 8, 1905.

PLUCKY NANCY. P. 1 a. Mrs. C. Thompson and Kate Sinclair. Kilburn Town H., March 16, 1889.

PLUCKY NIPPER, THE. C.D. Greenwich Carlton, May 7, 1906.

PLUCKY PARTHEINA. Burl. R. Reece. Portsmouth T.R., February 26, 1874.

PLUM CAKE, THE. Fantasy. Miss C. M. Whelpton. Eastbourne, St. Saviour's Ch. R., January 13, 1903.

PLUNGE IN THE DARK, A. (Revised, remodelled, and renamed). D. 4 a. G. Roberts, Sadler's Wells, March 26, 1888.

PLUNGER, THE. Sporting F.C. W. Sapte, Jun., and E. Spencer. Ladbroke H., October 24, 1888 (C.P.).

PLUNGER, THE. Melod. 5 a. D. H. Heggins. Burnley Victoria Old H., August 5, 1893 (as D. 4 a.), Eleph. and C., October 2, 1893.

PLUS BEAU JOUR DE LA VIE, LE. P. Scribe before 1822.

PLUS QUE REINE. P. 6 a. E. Bergerat (Madame Sarah Bernhardt's season), Adelphi, June 29, 1903.

PLUTARCH. See Alcibiades.

PLUTO; OR, LITTLE ORPHEUS AND HIS LUTE. Rewr. fr. his Burl., *Orpheus and Eurydice.* H. J. Byron. Royalty, December 26, 1881.

PLUTO AND PROSERPINE; OR, THE BELLE AND THE POMEGRANATE. Extrav. in one vol. F. Talfourd. Hay., April 5, 1858.

PLUTO FURENS ET VINCTUS; OR, THE RAGING DEVIL BOUND. Modern F. Pr. 1669.

PLUTUS. Transl. fr. Aristophanes C. by Randolph, 1651; Fielding and Young, 1812; Mitchell, 1820-22; Cunningham, 1826; and Rudd, 1857.

PLUTUS; THE GOD OF RICHES. C. fr. Aristophanes. H. Fielding and R. Young. Pr. 1742.

PLUTUS; OR, THE WORLD'S IDOL. C. Transl. fr. Aristophanes. L. Theobald. Pr. 1715. See "Greek Plays."

PLYMOUTH IN AN UPROAR. M.F. Mr. Neville. C.G., October 20, 1779; Pr. 1779.

POACHER, THE. Lortzing. 1803-1852.

POACHER, THE. See *The Crimson Mask*, *In the King's Name*.

POACHER AND HIS DOG, THE. D. F. on *Three Courses and a Dessert*. M. Hawes. Lyceum playbill, November 23, 1835.

POACHER BILL; OR, THE GIPSY OUTCAST. D. A. Coates. Britannia, April 1, 1872.

POACHERS, THE. D. 1 a. A. F. Cross. Nuneaton P.O.W., November 29, 1901.

POCAHONTAS. C.O. 2 a. M. by E. Solomon. Lib. by S. Grundy. Empire, December 26, 1884.

POCAHONTAS. J. Brougham.

POCCAHONTAS; OR, THE INDIAN PRINCESS. Amer. D. 3 a. D.L., December 15, 1820.

POCKET MISS HERCULES, THE. F. 3 a. J. S. Clouston. Royalty, June 28, 1907; July 22, 1907.

PODESTA DI BURGOS, IL. O. Mercadante. Vienna, about 1824

PŒNULUS. C. Plautus. Transl. into blank verse by Thornton, Rich, Warner, and Colman, 1769-74.

POET, THE. C 1 a. F. W. Broughton. Vaudeville, January 4, 1889.

POET; OR, THE PUPPETS, THE. A Travestie on *Lady Windermere's Fan*. C. Brookfield. M. by J. M. Glover. Comedy, May 19, 1892.

POET'S DREAM, A. O. 3 a. Adap. for Eng. stage by W. Beatty Kingston from *Le Songe d'une Nuit d'Eté*, by Ambroise Thomas. Royalty, Glasgow, February 18, 1898.

POET'S SLAVE, THE. Olympic, February 25, 1850.

PŒTA INFAMIS; OR, A POET NO WORTH HANGING. Pr. 1692.

POETASTER; OR, HIS ARRAIGNMENT, THE. Comical Satire. Ben Jonson. Ac. by children of the Q. Chapel, 1601.

POETIC JUSTICE. M. by Mrs. M. French Shelton. Bijou, Bayswater, November 7, 1901.

POETIC PROPOSAL, A. F. 1 a. M. Becher. Globe T. March 20, 1872.

POETICAL FOP; OR, THE MODES OF THE COURT, THE. See *The Man of Taste*.

POETRY AND POISON F. Plymouth T.R., September 11, 1876.

POETS, THE. F Alfieri. Transl. by C. Lloyd, 1815.

ΠΟΙΚΙΛΟΦΡΟΝΗΣΙΣ, OR THE DIFFERENT HUMOURS OF MEN, REPRESENTED IN AN INT. AT A COUNTRY SCHOOL. S. Shaw. December 15, 1691. Adap. fr. *The Muse's Looking Glass*.

POINT AT HERQUI; OR, BRITISH BRAVERY TRIUMPHANT, THE. O. Int. to celebrate daring exploit of Sir W. Sydney Smith. C.G., April, 1796. N.p.

POINT OF HONOUR, A. P. 1 a. A. F. Owen-Lewis and Eille Norwood. Dublin R. Hospital, February 27, 1902; Adelphi, May 22, 1903.

POINT OF HONOUR, THE. C. 3 a. Chas. Kemble. Taken fr. Mercier's *Le Deserteur*. C.G., 1805; D.L., October 16, 1816; and January 25, 1842.

POINT OF HONOUR, THE. F. 2 a. J. P. Roberdeau. C.G., 1792. Title alt. to *The Spirit of the Times*.

POINT OF LAW, A. Ca. 1 a. Paxton and Woodville. Park, March 26, 1881.

POINTSMAN, THE. D. Prol. and 3 a. R. C. Carton and C. Raleigh. Olympic, August 29, 1887.

POISON DOCTOR OF PARIS, THE. D. B. Ellis. Southampton T.R., October 31, 1870.

POISON FLOWER, THE. P. 3 a. Adapt. fr. N. Hawthorne's "Rappacini's Daughter" by Dr. Todhunter. Vaudeville, June 15, 1891.

POISON TREE, THE. D. R. Clarke. Pr. 1810.

POISONED CUP, THE. D. B. Ellis. Weymouth T.R., January 13, 1869.

POISONED CUP, THE. Ca. 1 a. Lord Kilmarnock (MS.). Publ. by Mrs. Douglas Cox.

POISONER OF MILAN, THE. D. 4 a. T. B. Warren. Darwen T.R., November 7, 1898; Stratford T.R., July 10, 1899.

POLICE TRAP, THE. Sk. Cecil Raleigh. Tivoli, June 15, 1908.

POLICEMAN, THE. F.C. 3 a. W. Helmore and E. Philpotts. Ealing Lyric H., January 12, 1887; Terry's, November 1, 1888.

POLICEMAN'S LOT, THE. Oa. Rev. S. N. Sedgwick. Leatherhead, January 18, 1905.

POLICY. C. 2 a. T. W. Robertson. Glasgow T.R., February 13, 1871.

POLICY; OR, THUS RUNS THE WORLD AWRY. New C. 5 a. Attributed to Henry Siddons. N.p. D.L., October 15, 1814.

POLICY OF THE OSTRICH, THE. P. 1 a. C. Hamilton. Terry's, January 22, 1900.

POLIDUS; OR, DISTRESSED LOVE. T. Moses Browne. Annexed to it, *All Bedevelled; or, The House in a Hurry*. F. Pr. 1723.

POLINICE. T. Alfieri. Transl. by C. Lloyd. 1815.

POLISH JEW, THE. D. 3 a. J. R. Ware Grecian, March 4, 1872.

POLISH JEW, THE. D. S. Emery. Bradford T.R., March 18, 1872.

POLISH JEW, THE. See *The Bells*. See *The Bells of the Sledge*.

POLITE CONVERSATION. Dean Swift. 2 D. Dialogues. D.L., April 23, 1740. N.p.

POLITE GAMESTER; OR, THE HUMOURS OF WHIST, THE. Satire. "S—— F——, Esq." 1753. Republication of *Humours of Whist*.

POLITIC BANKRUPT; OR, WHICH IS THE BEST GIRL, THE. C. Ent. Stationers' Co. September 9, 1653. N.p.

POLITIC FATHER, THE. P. Shirley. Licensed in 1641.

POLITIC QUEEN; OR, MURTHER WILL OUT, THE. R. Davenport. Ent. Stationers' Co., June 29, 1660. N.p.

POLITIC WHORE; OR, THE CONCEITED CUCKOLD, THE. Stolen from other plays. See *The Muse of Newmarket*. Newmarket. Pr. 1680.

POLITICAL REHEARSAL; HARLEQUIN LE GRAND; OR, THE TRICKS OF PIERROT LE PREMIER, THE. T.C. Panto. perf. 2 a. Pr. 1742.

POLITICIAN, THE. T. J. Shirley. Salisbury Court, (?) 1639. Pr. 1655.

POLITICIAN CHEATED, THE. C. A. Green. Pr. 1663.

POLITICIAN OUTWITTED, THE. C. Pr. 1789.

POLITICIAN REFORMED, THE. D. 1 a. Pr. 1774 in "An Appeal to the Public from the Judgment of a Certain Manager (Mr. Garrick) with Original Letters."

POLITICS IN MINIATURE; OR, THE HUMOURS OF PUNCH'S RESIGNATION. Puppet show. Pr. with *The Political Rehearsal*, 1742.

POLITICS ON BOTH SIDES. F. C.G., July 30, 1735. Anon. N.p.

POLKA, THE. Ca. R. Vaun. Ladbroke H., March 19, 1895; Grand, June 3, 1895.

POLL AND MY PARTNER JOE. Surrey.

POLL AND MY PARTNER JOE. Burl. F. C. Burnand. St. James's, May 6, 1871.

POLLY. O. John Gay. Second part of *The Beggar's Opera*. Suppressed 1728.

POLLY. O. Alt. fr. Gay by G. Colman. Hay., July 11, 1782. Pr. 1777. D.L., June 16, 1813.

POLLY. C. 3 a. E. H. Keating. Pub. by S. French, Ltd.

POLLY. C.O. 2 a. M. by E. Solomon. Lib. by J. Mortimer. Novelty, October 4, 1884.

POLLY HONEYCOMBE. F. 2 a. G. Colman. D.L., December 5, 1760. Pr. 1760.

POLLY LOWE'S LOVER. P. 1 a. A. Leslie. Crouch End Assembly Rooms, April 22, 1909.

POLLY PACKET, THE. Monopologue. C. Matthews. Lyceum, 1823.

POLLY PICKLE'S PETS IN PETLAND. Sk. London Coliseum, December 21, 1908.

POLLY'S BIRTHDAY. Ca. C. Fawcett. Gaiety, March 3, 1884.

POLLY'S LUCK. Duol. E. Drew. St. George's H., October 9, 1900.

POLLY'S VENTURE. Dom. C. 1 a. M. Watson. Gaiety, August 9, 1888.

POLUSCENICON. Pant.-Selection. C.G., June, 1789.

POLYEUCTE. T. Pierre Corneille. See "French Classical Plays." Prod. 1640.

POLYEUCTE. O. 5 a. Wds. by Barbier and Carré. M. by Gounod. Paris, October 7, 1878.

POLYEUCTE; OR, POLIUTE. O. 3 a. Lib. by A. Nourrit and Cammarano. M. by Donizetti. 1838. Transl. in Fr. as *Les Martyrs*. 4 a., by Scribe. Paris, April 10, 1840. As *I Martiri*, in London, Royal Italian O., April 20, 1852.

POLYEUCTES; OR, THE MARTYR. T. Sir W. Lower. Pr. 1655.

POLYHYMNIA. George Peele. 1590.

POLYPHEMUS. T. Chettle, 1598. N.p.

POLYPHOMUS. Nonsensical satire. J. M. Killick. St. George's H., November 15, 1872 (amat.).

POLYXENA. T. J. Joshua. Earl of Carysfort. Pr. 1810.

POLYXENE. T. Lafosse. 1686.

POM. Com. O. M. and lib. Signor Bucalossi.

POMONA. D. in prol. and 3 a. E. Towers. E. London, January 13, 1877.

POMONE. O. Cambert. Paris about 1655.

POMPADOUR, THE. Rom. pl. 4 a. F. partly on Brachvogel's German piece, *Narcissi* (ad. fr. Diderot's *Neveu de Rameau*).—W. G. Wills and S. Grundy. Hay., March 31, 1888.

POMPEY. T. Mrs. Catherine Philips. Transl. fr. Corneille's *Pompée*. Followed by "Travestie," which forms 5th a. of Davenant's *Playhouse to be Let*. Duke's, 1678.

POMPEY THE GREAT. Transl. fr. Corneille's *Pompée*, by Earl of Dorset and Middlesex. E. Waller. Ac. by Duke's servants, 1664.

POMPEY THE GREAT. Samuel Johnson. N.p.

POMPEY THE GREAT, HIS FAIR CORNELIA'S TRAGEDY EFFECTED BY HER FATHER AND HUSBAND'S DOWNCAST DEATH AND FORTUNE. T. Transl. fr. French of Robert Garnier by Thos. Kyd. Pr. 1594 as *Cornelia*.

POMPILIOUS; OR ROME AS IT WASN'T. C.Oa. F. Forbes Glennie. Guildford St. Nicholas H., December 7, 1907 (amat.).

POMPON, LE. O. 3 a. C. Lecocq. 1875.

PONSONBY HALL. Melo-d. 5 a. G. L. Cartwright. Wolverhampton St. Geo. H., October 10, 1892 (amat.).

PONT DE LODI, LE. O. 1 a. Méhul. O. Comique, December 15, 1797.

PONTEACH; OR, THE SAVAGES OF AMERICA. T. Major R. Rogers. Pr. 1706.

PONTER'S WEDDING. F. 1 a. J. M. Morton. St. James's, June 19, 1865.

PONTIUS PILATE. P. 1602. Anon. Prol. and Epil, said to be wr. by Deker in January, 1601-2.

POOR AUTHOR. F.C. Adap. fr. Sydney Grundy's ver. of *The Arabian Knights*. Richmond Hippo., November 16, 1908.

POOR COUSIN WALTER. D. 1 a. J. P. Simpson. Strand, April 8, 1850.

POOR COVENT GARDEN; OR, A SCENE REHEARSED. Occ. prel. Pr. 1792.

POOR EM'LY. D. B. Ellis. Southampton T.R., October 10, 1870.

POOR FIDLER'S WINDFALL, THE. Sk. Barrow Tivoli, June 22, 1908.

POOR GENTLEMAN, THE. C. 5 a. G. Colman, jun. C.G., February 11, 1801; Hay., 1806; D.L., June 4, 1816.

POOR GENTLEMAN, THE. C. 2 a. Adapt. by A. Wigan of *Le Gentilhomme Pauvre*. Dumanoir and Lafargue. (Played during French season at Royalty, November 5, 1888.) St. James's, 1861. See *Brave Hearts*.

POOR GENTLEWOMAN. C. Miss Isdell. 1811. N.p.

POOR GIRL'S TEMPTATIONS; OR, A VOICE FROM THE STREETS, A. D. W. Travers. City of London, 1857.

POOR HUMANITY. D. Pro. 4 a. Mr. Robinson. Surrey, April 11, 1868.

POOR JACK. D. Buckstone. Adelphi. February, 1840.

POOR JACK; OR, THE BENEVOLENT TARS OF OLD ENGLAND. Bal. C.G., February, 1808.

POOR JACK; OR, THE WRECK OF THE VAMPYRE. Yarmouth T.R., April 26, 1875.

POOR JO. D. H. Davenport. Southampton T.R., February 25, 1878.

POOR JONATHAN. M.C. 2 a. Adap. C. H. E. Brookfield. Lyrics by H. Greenbank. M. by Millocken and Albeniz. Prod. in America. P.O.W., June 15, 1893.

POOR LAW BOARD, THE. F. R. Callender. Bolton O.H., October 25, 1875.

POOR LITTLE JO. D. Park, July 2, 1877.

POOR LOST EMILY; OR, THE WRECK OF THE ROSA. D. 3 a. W. Stephens. Uxbridge T.R., December 5, 1870.

POOR MAN'S COMFORT, THE. T.C. Robert Daborne. Cockpit in D.L. Circa 1612. Pr. 1655.

POOR MAN'S PARADISE, THE. P. W. Haughton. 1599. N.p.

POOR MARIA. Int. W. C. Oulton. Dublin Crow Street, 1785. N.p.

POOR MARY; OR, THE MAID OF THE INN. M.D. Richmond T., June 24, 1806.

POOR MASTER. F.C. Sk. 1 a. Poplar Queen's, March 30, 1908.

POOR MIGNONETTE. Oa. Adapt. fr. Offenbach's *Pomme d'Api* by A. Schade. Lyrics by P. Reeve. Criterion, August 2, 1892.

POOR MISS FINCH. D. S. Dairs. Sunderland Lyceum, March 13, 1873.

POOR MR. POLTON. F. 3 a. C. Hamlyn and H. M. Paull. Vaudeville, October 10, 1895.

POOR MUST LIVE, THE. D. Prol. and 4 a. D. Muskerry. Longton Queen's, January 23, 1905; Greenwich, February 13, 1905.

POOR NEEDLEWOMAN OF LONDON. Marylebone, June 14, 1858.

POOR NELL. D. E. Price. Aberdeen T.R., November 18, 1872; Liverpool T.R., May 1, 1875.

POOR NOBLEMAN, THE. See *Brave Hearts*. Serio Comic D. 2 a. Chas. Selby. St. James's, November 14, 1861; rev. Queen's, May 13, 1868.

POOR NONY. F. 2 a. Transl. fr. French. Brandenburgh House T., 1803. Hay., August 31, 1803, as *Nicodemus in Despair*.

POOR OF LIVERPOOL. Liverpool Amphitheatre, February 11, 1864.

POOR OF NEW YORK, THE. D. 5 a. Publ. by S. French, Ltd.

POOR OLD DRURY. Occ. Prel. J. Cobb. O.H. by D.L. Co., September 22, 1791. N.p.

POOR OLD HAYMARKET; OR, TWO SIDES OF THE GUTTER. Prel. G. Coleman, jun. Hay., June 15, 1792. Pr. 1792.

POOR OLD PERKINS. F.C. 3 a. P. H. 1. Sykes. Strand, November 3, 1896.

POOR PARISHEEN; OR, THE FUGITIVES OF DERRINANE, THE. D. 3 a. J. B. Howe. Britannia, September 27, 1869.

POOR PHIL GARLIC. Sk. Roy Redgraves. Cambridge M.H., December 15, 1900; Richmond M.H., December 3, 1906.

POOR PIANO. M. Sk. C. Grain. St. Geo. H., April 1, 1893.

POOR PILLICODDY. F. 1 a. J. M. Morton. Lyceum, July 12, 1848.

POOR PLAYER, THE. S.C. Dom.D. 3 a. W. Digges. Plymouth T.R., September 22, 1884.

POOR PUNCHINELLO. Dram. Epis. 1 a. W. S. Barnett-Garrett. Hastings Public H., April 24, 1907.

POOR RELATION, THE. Co.D. 2 a. Pub. by S. French, Ltd.

POOR RELATIONS. M.F. 2 a. M. by Horn. D.L., February 25, 1815.

POOR RELATIONS; OR, JANE EYRE. D. in prol. 4 a. J. Willing. Park, August 27, 1879.

POOR SAILOR; OR, LITTLE BOB AND LITTLE BEN. M.E. Bernard. 1795. N.p.

POOR SCHOLAR, THE. C. R. Nevile. Written after 1661.

POOR SOLDIER, THE. C.O. 1 a. J. O'Keeffe. Same as *Shamrock*. C.G., 1783; September 20, 1809; D.L., February 19, 1816; Lyceum Playbill, July 1, 1823.

POOR STROLLERS, THE. D. W. Phillips. Adelphi, January 18, 1858. Rev. Sadler's Wells, 1866.

POOR TOMMY. F.C. 3 a. Chatham Op. H., April 26, 1897. Prod. as *The Triple Alliance*, Strand, December 6, 1897.

POOR TRAGEDIAN. Ca. 1 a. Mrs. Merivale. MS. with Douglas Cox.

POOR VULCAN. Burl. C. Dibdin. Taken fr. *The Loves of Mars and Venus*, by Motteux. C.G., February 4, 1778. Pr 1778.

POORHOUSE, THE. P. 1 a. (Story transl. by Lady Gregory fr. the Irish). Douglas Hyde. Passmore Edwards Settlement, June 4, 1904.

POPE ALEXANDER THE SIXTH, THE TRAGEDIE OF. Entered Stationers' H., October 15, 1607.

POPE ALS METAPHYSIKER. Lessing. M. by Mendelssohn. 1754.

POPE JOAN. P. March 1, 1591. See *Female Prelate*.

POPINJAY, THE P. 4 a. Boyle Lawrence and Fred Mouillot. Newcastle R., October 24, 1907.

POPOCATAPET, L'. Oa. F. Robson. M. by G. Richardson, Holborn, December 18, 1872; Philharmonic, May 4, 1874.

POPPING THE QUESTION. F 1 a. J. B. Buckstone (idea taken fr. one of the annuals). D.L., March 23, 1830; D.L., March 15, 1847; Strand, 1851.

POPPLETON'S PREDICAMENTS. F. 1 a. C. M. Rae. Royalty, July 21, 1870. Publ. by S. French, Limited.

POPSY. Mus. Folly. 1 a. Lib. S. Grundy. M. by E. Solomon. Royalty, October 4, 1880.

POPSY. Ca. Dr. Dabbs. Shanklin Inst., April 13, 1888.

POPULAR WORKHOUSE, THE. Fred Karno and Wal Pink. M. by J. S. Baker. London Pav., November 25, 1907.

POPULARITE. C Delavigne. 1838.

PORK CHOPS; A DREAM OF HOME. F. extrav. 1 a. E. L. Blanchard. Olympic, February 13, 1843.

PORO. O. Glück. Turin, 1744.

PORSENNA'S INVASION; OR, ROME PRESERVED. T. Pr. 1748.

PORT ADMIRAL. Burl. T. G. Bowles. Publ. by S. French, Limited.

PORTER OF HAVRE, THE. O. Lib. J. Oxenford. M. by Sig. Cagonini. Princess's, September 15, 1875.

PORTER'S KNOT, THE. S.C. D. 2 a. J. Oxenford's adaptation of *Les Crochets du Père Martin*. Olympic, December 2, 1858. Extended into 3 a. and revised by C. Carton. Crystal Pal., April 18, 1892.

PORTEUSE DE PAIN, LA. See *The Perils of Paris*, April 20, 1904.

PORTIA PIETATIS; OR, THE PORT OR HARBOUR OF PIETY. T. Heywood. 1638.

PORTIA UP TO DATE. P. 1 a. L. Fomm. Albert Hall West T., April 20, 1904.

PORTIO AND DEMORANTES. P. Ac. at Court, 1580.

PORTMANTEAU PREDICAMENT. F. F. Bingham. Richmond H.M., October 31, 1881.

PORTRAIT, THE. Burl. G. Colman. Fd. on the French, *Le Tableau Parlant*, C.G. (Pr. 1770.)

PORTRAIT, THE. C. Hay., 1784. N.p.

PORTRAIT, THE. Ca. W. Sapte, jun. Olympic, May 15, 1888.

PORTRAIT; OR, THE GENEROUS RIVALS, THE. C. Fr. the French of Mme. Genlis. Pr. 1781.

PORTRAIT DE MANON, LE. Oa. 1 a. Massenet. Paris O. Com., May 8, 1894.

PORTRAIT OF CERVANTES; OR, THE PLOTTING LOVERS, THE. F. Greffulhe. C.G., June 21, 1808. N.p.

PORTSMOUTH HEIRESS; OR, THE GENEROUS REFUSAL, THE. C. Anon. Pr. 1704.

POSITIVE MAN, THE. F. J. O'Keeffe. C.G., 1782. Rev. D.L., May 21, 1822.

POSSESSION. M. Sk. W. Browne. M. by A. J. Caldecott. St. George's H., December 1, 1890.

POST BOY, THE. D. 2 a. H. T. Craven. Strand, October 31, 1860; New Holborn, April 13, 1868.

POST OF HONOUR, THE. C.D. 1 a. T. Mildenhall. Lyceum, May 8, 1844.

POST OFFICE FRAUDS. D. Blackburn T.R. and O.H., October 24, 1870.

POST OFFICE GIRL, THE. Sk. The Granville, February 10, 1908.

POSTAL CARD, THE. F. Edinburgh T.R., February 13, 1871.

POSTBAG, THE. Ca. A. P. Graves. Court, July 3, 1908.

POSTERITY: AN OPERATIC ANDISSIPATION. 1 a. A. M. Moore. M. by Meyer Lutz. Newcastle-on-Tyne T.R., March 10, 1884.

POSTERN GATE, THE. 1 a. B. Iden Payne. P.O.W., Birmingham, August 13, 1909.

POSTHEEN PHEURI, THE. D. 3 a. J. H. Grover. Cardiff T.R., February 19, 1872.

POSTILION, THE. O. 3 a. G. A. à Beckett. St. James's, March 13, 1837.

POSTILLION! THE. C.O. A. Adam. Active prep. (not prod.) February 27, 1837.

POSTILLION OF LONGUMEAU, THE. O. 3 a. M. by A. Adam. 1803-1856. De Luven and Brunswick, Paris, 1836; D.L., July 9, 1845, and July 18, 1846; Edinburgh Lyceum, December 10, 1892.

POSTMAN, THE. Ca. T. E. Pemberton. Strand, July 26, 1892.

POSTMAN'S KNOCK, THE. M. F. 1 a. L. M. Thornton. Hay., April 7, 1856.

POSTMARK. Co. Char. Stanley Rogers. Publ. by S. French, Ltd.

POSTSCRIPT, THE. Ca. 1 a F. H. Knight. P.O.W., February 14, 1888 (mat.); Vaudeville, August 24, 1889.

POT OF BROTH, THE. W. B. Yeats. Court, February 28, 1905.

POT OF CAVIARE, A. Dramatised by Mrs. Arthur Mortimer, by special permission of Sir Arthur Conan Doyle. Jersey O.H., November 13, 1908.

POT OF MONEY. C. D. J. Swift. Richmond H.M., March 15, 1881.

POT-POURRI. "Revue" of 1899. 2 parts and [illegible] sc. [illegible]y J. T. Tanner. Lyrics by W. H. Risque. M. by Napoleon Lambelet. Notting Hill Coronet, April 3, 1899; Avenue, June 9, 1899.

POUDRE AUX YEUX, LA. By Labische and Martin. See *Gammon*.

POUL A-DHOIL; OR, THE FAIRY MAN. Orig. Hibernian D. 3 a. C. H. Hazlewood. Britannia, October, 1865.

POULE AUX ŒUFS D'OR, LA. Fairy Extrav. Prol. and 3 a. Dennery and Clairville. Adap. by Frank Hall. Alhambra, December 23, 1878.

POULET and POULETTE. C.O. 3 a. M. by Hervé. Gaiety, March 29, 1879.

POUNDS, SHILLINGS, AND PENCE. Drawing-room Sk. Mrs. G. Thompson and Miss Kate Sinclair. Kilburn Town H., January 18, 1892.

POUPEE, LA. C.O. 3 a. A. Maurice Ordonneau. M. by E. Audran. (Paris Gaité, October 21, 1896.) Engl. adapt. by A. Sturgess. P.O.W., February 24, 1897, and April 12, 1904.

POUPEE DE NURNBERG, LA. O. Adam.

POUTER'S WEDDING. F. 1 a. J. M. Morton. Publ. by S. French, Ltd.

POVERTY AND NOBLENESS OF MIND. P. 3 a. Transl. fr. Kotzlbue by Maria Geisweiler. Pr. 1799.

POVERTY AND WEALTH. C. 5 a. Transl. fr. Danish of P. A. Heiberg by C. H. Wilson. Pr. 1799.

POVERTY OF RICHES. C. 4 a. E. Hendrie and M. Wood. Blackpool Grand T., April 7, 1899.

POWDER AND BALL. F. Adelphi, 1845.

POWDER AND SHOT. F. Miss B. Chandler. Basingstoke Drill H., January 21, 1896.

POWDER AND SHOT. Mrs. George Corbett and Agatha Roze. Acton St. Alban's Par. H., December 6, 1900. (amat.).

POWER AND PRINCIPLE. D. 3 a. F. on Schiller's *Kabale und Liebe*, by M. Barnett. Strand, June 10, 1850.

POWER AND THE GLORY, THE. Melo. D. 4 a. Chas. Darrell. Leeds T.R., April 29, 1898 (C.P.); New Cross Broadway T., February 20, 1899.

POWER OF CONSCIENCE, THE. P. 4 a. R. P. Rulter. Stalybridge Grand, July 23, 1891.

POWER OF DARKNESS, THE. P. 5 a. Leo Tolstoy. Transl. by Louise and Aylmer Maude. Royalty, December 18, 1904.

POWER OF ENGLAND, THE. D. Adap. fr. Ouida's novel, "Idalia." C. E. Dering. Imperial, June 17, 1885.

POWER OF GOLD, THE. M.D. 3 a. W. Sanford. Orig. prod. in America. Birmingham Grand, March 29, 1897; Stratford T.R., February 20, 1899.

POWER OF HATE, THE. D. 4 a. O. Silverstone. Warrington R.C.T., February 14, 1901.

POWER OF HATE; OR, HONESTY IS THE BEST POLICY, THE. D. 3 a. W. R. Osman. Surrey, February 19, 1870.

POWER OF LIES, THE. D. Prol. and 3 a. Mary Ford. West Bromwich T.R., February 5, 1901.

POWER OF LIES. Dom. D. 4 a. M. by Michael Connelly. Prod. by Marshall Moore. Shakespeare, July 27, 1908.

POWER OF LOVE, THE. D. 4 a. Adap. fr. Mr. Panton's novel, "A Tangled Chain," by Henrietta Lindley. P.O.W., March 6, 1888.

POWER OF THE CROSS; OR, THE LAST OF THE VAMPIRES, THE. Melo-d. 4 a. G. A. de Gray. Chester R., April 22, 1905.; Keighley Queen's, December 23, 1905; Elephant and Castle, October 14, 1907.

POWER OF THE EYE, THE. Melo-d. 4 a. H. Thomson. Hastings Gaiety, December 16, 1901; Alexandra Pal., January 6, 1902.

POWER OF THE HEART. D. A. Davis. Sunderland Lyceum, March 21, 1873.

POWER OF THE IDOL, THE. Laura Leycester. Richmond, April 6, 1908.

POWER OF THE KING, THE. D. 4 a. Mrs. F. G. Kimberley. Longsight King's, October 9, 1907 (C.P.); Manchester Junc., December 2, 1907; Broadway, March 30, 1908.

POWER OF THE PRESS, THE. American D. 5 a. A. Piton and G. H. Jessop. Glasgow Princess's, August 3, 1896.

POWER OF WOMAN, THE. C.D. 4 a. W. H. Benson and L. Forster. Macclesfield T.R., October 7, 1901.

PRACTICAL JOKER, A. Ca. C. L. Hume. Comedy, June 15, 1895.

PRACTICAL MAN, A. F. 1 a. B. Bernard. Lyceum, October 20, 1849.

PRACTICAL MAN, A. D. D.L., March 8, 1856.

PRAGMATICAL JESUIT NEW LEAVENED, THE. C. R. Carpenter. Pr. N.dr.

PRAIRIE FLOWER, THE. R.P. Prol. and 3 a. B. Ellis and A. Carlton. Jersey T.R., March 14, 1895.

PRAISE AT PARTING. Morality. Stephen Gosson. N.p. 1580.

PRANCING GIRL, THE. Travestie. C. R. Brown. M. by B. Brigata. P.O.W., November 26, 1891.

PRANK OF CUPID. C. 1 a. W. Poynbee. Publ. by S. French, Limited.

PRAYER, THE. P. 1 a. Adap. fr. the French of F. Coppée by H. Child. Birmingham T.R., September 1, 1898.

PRAYER OF THE SWORD, THE. P. 5 a. B. Fagan. Adelphi, September 19, 1904.

PRE AUX CLERCS. O. 3 a. A. L. J. Ferdinand. C.G., June 26, 1880.

PRE AUX CLERCS, LE. C.O. 3 a. Words by Planard. M. by Hèrold. Paris, December 15, 1832 (in French); Princess's, May 2, 1849 (in Italian).

PRECAUZIONE, LE. O. Petrella. (Genoa, 1862.) Lyceum, March 22, 1871.

PRECAUZIONE, THE. C. 2 a. T. Warboys. Taken fr. D'Ancourt's *Besoin de l'Amour*. Pr. 1777.

PRECEPTOR; OR, THE LOVES OF ABELARD AND HELOISE, THE. B.O. 1 a. W. Hammond. Dublin Smock Alley. Pr. 1740.

PRECIEUSES RIDICULES. C. Molière. 1659. See "French Classical Plays."

PRECIOSA. O. A. Wolff. M. by Weber. (Dresden, 1822.) D.L., July 4, 1881.

PRECIOSITA. Oa. Mlle. Lisa Dorisi. St. George's Hall, July 4, 1893.

PRECIOUS RELICS; OR, THE TRAGEDY OF VORTIGERN REHEARSAL. D.P. 2 a. W. C. Oulton. Imitation of *The Critic*. Pr. 1796

PREDOR AND LUCIA. 1573.

PREFERENCE BOND, A. Ca. J. B. Maclaren. Nottingham T.R., August 15, 1887.

PREFERMENT. C. 3 a. By E. B. Jones. Wyndham's, October 16, 1902.

PREHISTORIC LORD MAYOR'S SHOW. Arr. by J. Reed and Edmund Payne. D.L., March 7, 1907.

PREJUDICE. See *Sons of Erin*.

PREJUDICE OF FASHION, THE. F. Hay., February 22, 1779. N.p.

PREJUDICES, THE. C. B. F. Cherensi. Hereford, December 19, 1798.

PRELIMINARY CONTEST (PROAGON), THE. See "Greek Plays."

PRELUDE. Foote. 1767.

PRELUDE. Colman. 1776.

PRELUDE. L. MacNally. C.G., September 23, 1782 N.p.

PRELUDE. Cumberland. 1792.

PRELUDIO; OR, THE SCHOOL OF SHAKESPEARE. 3 sc. of dialogue. G. Keate. Hay., August 7, 1781 N.p.

PREMIER JOUR DE BONHEUR, LE. O. Auber. 1868.

'PRENTICE PILLAR, THE. O. 1 a. G. Eden. M. by R. Somerville. Colchester T.R., February 13, 1895 (C.P.); H.M., September 24, 1897.

PRES AUX CLERCS, LES. O. Herold. (1791-1833.) See *Le Pre*, etc.

PRES ST. GERVAIS, LES. C.O. 3 a. Lib. by R. Reece. M. by C. Lecocq. Criterion, November 28, 1874.

PRESBYTERIAN LASH; OR, NOCTROFFE'S MAID WHIPP'D, THE. T.C. 13 scenes. Anon. Great Room, Pye Tavern, Aldgate. Kirkman is said to be the author. Pr. 1661. Perf. by Noctroff, the priest, and parishioners.

PRESCRIBED. C.Oa. 1 a. Lib. G. Stanford. M. by C. Hardie. Bayswater Victoria H., April 22, 1889.

PRESENCE, THE. C. Margaret Duchess of Newcastle. 1668.

PRESENCE OF MIND. D. 1 a. F. A. Scudamore. Edinburgh Princess's, August 19, 1881.

PRESENTATION, A. Int. T. Nabbs. Intended for Prince Charles' birthday. Pr. 1638.

PRESENTATION IN THE TEMPLE, A. MS. copy, 1534; probably modernised and pr. Edinburgh, 1836.

PRESENTATION ON THE PRINCE'S BIRTHDAY, A. T. Nabbes. 1638. Pr. 1639.

PRESENTED AT COURT. C. J. S. Coyne. 1848.

PRESIDENT, THE. M.C. 2 a. J. M. Fisher and E. Turner. M. by H. Vernon. Maidenhead Grand H., October 19, 1896.

PRESIDENT, THE. M.F. 3 a. F. Stayton. P.O.W., April 30, 1902.

PRESIDENT'S DAUGHTER; OR, A SOLDIER'S SWEETHEART, THE. M.C. L. Hawkins and V. Lawton. Morecambe Royalty, June 17, 1901

PRESS CUTTINGS. Topical Sk. G. B. Shaw. Court, July 9, 1909; Manchester Gaiety, September 27, 1909.

PRESS GANG; OR, LOVE IN LOW LIFE, THE. B.F. Alt. fr. H. Carey. Enlargement of "Nancy; or, The Parting Lovers." Perf as int. under title of *True Blue*. Pr. 1755.

PRESUMPTION! OR, THE FATE OF FRANKENSTEIN. Rom. D. R. B. Peake. M. by Mr. Watson. Lyceum playbill, July 28, 1823. C.G., July 9, 1824. Publ. by Dicks.

PRESUMPTIVE EVIDENCE. D. 2 a. D. Boucicault. Princess's, May 10, 1869.

PRESUMPTIVE EVIDENCE; OR, MURDER WILL OUT. Dom. D., 2 a. J. B. Buckstone. Adapt. of "Card Drawing" in "Tales of Munster Festivals." Adelphi, September 29, 1828; Bath, March 16, 1829.

PRESUMPTUOUS LOVE. Dram. Masque. Anon. L.I.F. as C. *Everybody Mistaken*. Pr. 1716.

PRETENCE. P. 1 a. S. B. Lawrence. St. George's H., May 7, 1891 (amat.).

PRETENDED PURITAN, THE. F. T. Horde, jun. Pr. 1779.

PRETENDER, THE. P. Elderton. 1746. N.p.

PRETENDER, THE. Hist. P. 3 a. G. Duncan. Princess's, May 27, 1876.

PRETENDER'S FLIGHT; OR, A MOCK CORONATION, WITH THE HUMOURS OF THE FACETIOUS HARRY ST. JOHN, THE F. J. Phillips. Pr. 1716. See *The Earl of Mar.*

PRETENDERS; OR, THE TOWN UNMASKED, THE. C. T. Dilke. Pr. 1698. L.I.F., 1698.

PRETESTUS. P. Ac. at Court, 1574.

PRETTY BEQUEST, A. T. M. Watson. M. by H. Clarke. St. George's H, June 29, 1885.

PRETTY DRUIDESS; OR, THE MOTHER, THE MAID, AND THE MISTLETOE BOUGH, THE. Extrav. W. S. Gilbert. Charing Cross, June 19, 1869.

PRETTY ESMIRELDA AND CAPTAIN PHŒBUS OF OURS. Burl. H. J. Byron. Gaiety, April 2, 1879.

PRETTY FANNY'S WAY. F.C. 3 a. F. F. Forshaw. Kennington, August 5, 1906 (C.P.).

PRETTY GIRLS OF STILBERG, THE. Military V. Princess's, November 26, 1870.

PRETTY HOUSEBREAKER, THE. F. 1 a. A. Halliday and W. Brough. Adelphi, July 15, 1861.

PRETTY JANE. Burl. J. Smith. Publ. by S. French, Limited.

PRETTY MOLLIE BARRINGTON. P. 1 a. Josephine Rae and T. Sidney. St. Leonards, June 6, 1892.

PRETTY NATIVE PRINCE, A. Ladywell Parish H., May 31, 1906.

PRETTY PERFUMERS, THE. Op-bouffe. 3 a. H. J. Byron. Alhambra, May 18, 1874.

PRETTY PERSIAN, THE. W. Jones.

PRETTY PIECE OF BUSINESS, A. C. 1 a. T. Morton. Hay., November 20, 1853; rev. Criterion, October 5, 1899.

PRETTY POLL. Ca. R. Reece. St. James's, January 8, 1876

PRETTY POLLY. Duol. B. Hood. Colchester T.R., April 26, 1900; Savoy, May 19, 1900.

PRETTY PREDICAMENTS. F. 1 a. A. J. Phipps. Belfast T.R., November 27, 1876.

PRETTY PRINCESS AND PRICKLY PEAR. Ex. 1 a. S. J. Fitzgerald. Publ. by S. French, Ltd.

PRETTY SISTER OF JOSE, THE. Mrs. Hodgson Burnett. D. of York's, October 16, 1903 (C.P.).

PREVIOUS ENGAGEMENT, A. P. 1 a. Blanche Wills Chandler. Avenue, November 22, 1900.

PREVIOUS SICILIAN, THE. B. of Action. 1 a. and 3 tab. M. by F. A. Blasis, Senna, and Bajetti. D.L., February 4, 1847.

PRICE, THE. Duol. Agnes Platt. Bloomsbury H., November 15, 1906.

PRICE OF A GIRL, THE. Dom. D. 4 a. Tottenham Pal., February 22, 1909.

PRICE OF A HAT, THE. Sk. Alicia Ramsay and Rudolph Cordova. Shepherd's Bush Empire, August 26, 1907.

PRICE OF EMPIRE, THE. Ad. A. Hope, of his novel, "The God in the Car." St. James's, February 18, 1896 (C.P.).

PRICE OF EXISTENCE, THE. D. C. H. Hazlewood. Britannia, December 18, 1872.

PRICE OF HER SOUL, THE. D. 4 a. W. Hibbert. Hammersmith, Lyric, May 1, 1905.

PRICE OF PEACE, THE. D. 4 a. Cecil Raleigh. D.L., September 20, 1900.

PRICE OF PLEASURE, THE. D. 4 a. M. Wallerton and F. Gilbert. Macclesfield T.R., August 17, 1903; Camberwell Metropole, May 16, 1904.

PRICE OF SIN, THE. D. 5 a. E. Hill Mitchelson. Greenwich Carlton, May 19, 1902.

PRICE OF SIN, THE. D. Epis. Norman Harvey. Greenwich Barnard's, February 7, 1907.

PRIDE. C. 3 a. J. Albery. Vaudeville, April 22, 1874.

PRIDE; OR, THE USURER'S DAUGHTER. D. 4 a. E. Towers, Pavilion, May 20, 1872.

PRIDE AND POVERTY. See *The Streets of London.*

PRIDE AND VANITY. C. 1 a. E. H. Keating. Publ. by S. French, Ltd.

PRIDE OF BIRTH, THE. G. H. B. Rodwell. Circa 1831.

PRIDE OF THE BROOKES, THE. C. 3 a. T. Corbett. Dublin R., September 25, 1905.

PRIDE OF TAKAHARA, THE. M.C. 2 a. Geo. H. Thompson. Littlehampton Terminus H., February 19, 1908 (amat.).

PRIDE OF THE FAMILY, THE. D. 3 a. A. Parry. Cambridge T.R., September 9, 1878.

PRIDE OF THE MARKET, THE. C.D. 2 a. J. R. Planche. Lyceum, October 18, 1846.

PRIDE OF REGIMENT. P. 1 a. F. D. Bone. Hay., February 28, 1908; rev. Hay., April 18, 1908; Royal Victoria H., S.E., February 20, 1909.

PRIDE SHALL HAVE A FALL. C. Crowley. C.G., March 11, 1824.

PRIEST HUNTER, THE. Irish D. 4 a. H. O'Grady. Manchester Queen's, April 3, 1893; Grand, April 17, 1893.

PRIEST OF THE TEMPLE, THE. D. 4 a. C. March. Sunderland Avenue, June 30, 1902; Liverpool Lyric T., July 21, 1902.

PRIEST OR PAINTER. C.D. 3 a. Adap. W. D. Howell's novel, "A Foregone Conclusion." W. Poel. Olympic, July 11, 1884.

PRIEST'S DAUGHTER, THE. T. 5 a. T. J. Serle. Sadler's Wells.

PRIEST'S HONOUR, A. P. 1 a. H. N. Brailsford. Bayswater Bijou, October 2, 1901.

PRIESTESS, THE. Sargent, 1855.

PRIMA DONNA, LA. O.C. 3 a. Adap. fr. well-known story by H. R. Farnie and Alfred Murray. M. by Tito Mattei. Avenue, October 16, 1889.

PRIMA DONNA, THE. D. 2 a. Dion Boucicault. Princess's, September 18, 1852.

PRIMA DONNA, THE. Sk. Holborn Empire, September 1, 1908.

PRIMITIVE PUPPET SHOW, THE. See *Piety in Pattens.*

PRIMROSE FARM. D. H. A. Major. Grecian, July 12, 1871.

PRIMROSE FARM. Rustic D. Frank Harvey. Ipswich T.R., January 14, 1885.

PRIMROSE GREEN; OR, LOVE IN THE COUNTRY. C.O. C.G., May 18, 1791. N.p.

PRIMROSE PATH, THE. P. 4 a. W. W Lindon. Vaudeville, May 11, 1892.

PRIMROSE WAY, THE. Int. N. Monck. Yeovil O.H., January 26, 1903 Balham Empire, September 21, 1903.

PRINCE AMABEL; OR, THE FAIRY ROSES. Fairy Extrav. W. Brough. St. James's, May 5, 1862; Royalty, September, 1865.

PRINCE AND THE BEGGAR MAID, THE. Rom. D. 4 a. Walter Howard. Lyceum, June 6, 1908.

PRINCE AND THE PAUPER, THE. P. 4 a. Adap. fr. Mark Twain by Mrs. Oscar Beringer. Gaiety, April 12, 1890.

PRINCE AND THE PAUPER, THE. P. 4 a. Adap. fr. Mark Twain by J. Hatton. Vaudeville, October 12, 1891.

PRINCE ARTHUR. Sk. Walthamstow Pal., June 15, 1908.

PRINCE CAMARALZAMAN; OR, THE FAIRIES' REVENGE. Fairy Extrav. Messrs. Bellingham and Best. Olympic, August 12, 1865.

PRINCE CHAP, THE. P. 3 a. E W. People. Criterion, July 16, 1906.

PRINCE CHARLES EDWARD STUART; OR, THE RISING OF 1745. Melo.-d. Spec. J. Crawford. Paisley Exch. Rooms., October 12, 1868.

PRINCE CHARLIE; OR, KING OF THE HIGHLAND HEARTS. Rom. D. 4 a. D. Tovey and S. H. Sime. Great Queen St., March 23, 1905.

PRINCE CHERRYSTAR. Extrav. T. Saunders. M. by H. Richardson. Hereford T.R., October 25, 1893.

PRINCE CHODIS; OR, THE MARRIAGE BY PROXY. C.O. 2 a. F. A. R. Lead and S. Hartly. M. by W. H. Baker. Perth T.R., December 4, 1901.

PRINCE D'AMOUR, THE. Masque. Sir W. D'Avenant. Ac. by members of Middle Temple, 1635.

PRINCE DE NOISY, LE. O. F. Rebel and F. Francœur. 1760.

PRINCE DEUCALION. D. B. Taylor. 1879.

PRINCE DORUS; OR, THE ROMANCE OF THE NOSE. Fairy Tale by the author of "Diogenes and His Lantern." Olympic, December 26, 1850.

PRINCE FOR AN HOUR, A. C.D. 1 a. J. Maddison Morton. Princess's, March 24, 1856.

PRINCE IN CONCEIT, A. Droll out of Shirley's *Opportunity*. 1672.

PRINCE KARATOFF. See *The Silver Shell*. P. 4 a. H. J. W. Dam. Birmingham P.O.W., December 2, 1892.

PRINCE KARL. C. 4 a. A. C. Gunter. (Orig. prod. in America.) Lyceum, October 19, 1888.

PRINCE LE BOO. Melod. Rom. F. on tale of that name. D.L., October 30, 1833.

PRINCE LOVE; OR, THE FAYS OF THE FOREST. Burl. F. Vaudervell. Islington Philharmonic, December 26, 1870.

PRINCE METHUSALEM. C.O. 3 a. M. by Strauss. Lyrics by H. S. Leigh. Novelty, May 19, 1883.

PRINCE METHUSALEM. 1902. O. Berodin.

PRINCE NYSEE NOSEY. Fa. 1 a. E. H. Keating. Publ. by S. French, Limited.

PRINCE OF AGRA, THE. T. Alt. of Dryden's "Aurengzebe" by W. Addington. C.G., April 7, 1774. N.p.

PRINCE OF ANGOLIA, THE. T. Alt. fr. *Oroonoko* by Dr. J. Ferriar. Pr. 1788.

PRINCE OF BARATASIA. Ca. 1 a. Morris and Cox. MS. with Douglas Cox.

PRINCE OF BORNEO, THE. O.F. 2 a. J. W. Herbert. M. by E. Jones. Add. numbers by G. H. Broadhurst. Strand, October 5, 1899.

PRINCE OF DARKNESS, THE. D. Prol. and 3 a. Adap. fr. M. Corelli's "Sorrows of Satan" by S. C. Henry. See *Sorrows of Satan*. Plymouth T.R., December 14, 1896.

PRINCE OF EGYPT, A. D. C. Squier Richmond T.R., August 21, 1882.

PRINCE OF HOMBURG, THE. Kleist.

PRINCE OF MISCHANCE, A. P. 4 a. Southampton P.O.W., October 7, 1897. C.p.

PRINCE OF PARTHIA, THE. T. T. Godfrey. Pr. 1765. (First American D.)

PRINCE OF PILSEN, THE. M.C. 2 a. F. Pixley and G. Luders. St. George's H., May 5, 1902; Shaftesbury, May 14, 1904.

PRINCE OF PLEASURE, THE. D. 4 a. M. Wallerton and F. Gilbert. Macclesfield T.R., August 17, 1903.

PRINCE OF PRIGGS REVELS; OR, THE PRACTICES OF THAT GRAND THIEF, CAPTAIN JAMES HIND, THE. C. J. S. Pr. 1651.

PRINCE OF ROGUES. D. 4 a. J. Douglas and W. Benson. Worthing T.R., September 11, 1902; Stratford T.R., April 17, 1905.

PRINCE OF SAUER-KRAUTENBERG, THE. C.O. 2 a. Lib. W. Boyce. M. by A. C. Davies. St. George's H., March 7, 1896.

PRINCE OF THE PEOPLE, A. D. 5 a. Elwyn Baron. Oldham Empire, June 4, 1906.

PRINCE OF THE PEOPLE, A. R.D. 11 sc. F. Thorpe-Tracey. Dundee Gaiety, July 5, 1909.

PRINCE OF TUNIS, THE. T. H. Mackenzie. Edinburgh. Pr. 1773.

PRINCE OF U.S.A. M. Melford.

PRINCE OF WALES'S VISIT, THE. F. Scarborough T.R., October 22, 1869.

PRINCE OR PEASANT. F. 1 a. F. D. Adams. Publ. by S. French, Limited.

PRINCE OTTO. P. Prol. and 3 a. Dram. by T. B. Thalberg and G. Gurney fr. R. L. Stevenson's novel. Harrogate Spa Concert R., March 24, 1888; Glasgow T.R., June 4, 1900.

PRINCE PEDRILLO. M.Ca. Miss J. A. Saull. Nottingham Central H., November 21, 1893

PRINCE PIPPO. Alexandra, December 26, 1866.

PRINCE PRETENDER; OR, BORROWDENE. C.O. Patrick Bidwell. M., Evelyn Baker. Sheffield Lyceum, September 7, 1906 (C.P.).

PRINCE PRETTY PET AND THE BUTTERFLY. Extrav. R. Brough. Lyceum, December 26, 1854.

PRINCE SOHOBAZAR; OR, EIGHTEEN CARAT SONGS. Burl. Extrav. by E. W. Bowles. Kilburn Town H., December 11., 1885.

PRINCE TUTIN. See *Invisible Prince*.

PRINCE'S LOVE AFFAIR, THE. Sk. Canterbury, July 5, 1909.

PRINCE'S MASQUE, THE. Masque. Ac. at Court on Twelfth Night, 1618, and February 21, 1618.

PRINCELY PLEASURES OF KENILWORTH CASTLE, THE. Masque. George Gascoigne. Pr. 1587.

PRINCEPS RHETORIC. See *Combate of Capps.*

PRINCESS, THE. Burl. fr. Tennyson's poem by W. S. Gilbert. Olympic, January 8, 1870.

PRINCESS; OR, LOVE AT FIRST SIGHT, THE. T.C. T. Killigrew. Pr. 1664.

PRINCESS AND THE BUTTERFLY; OR, THE FANTASTICS, THE. C. 5 a. A. W. Pinero. St. James's, March 29, 1897.

PRINCESS AND THE PHILOSOPHER. M.C. 2 a. Chas. M. Heslop. M. by Mabel Goyder. Norwich Assembly R., February 2, 1905.

PRINCESS AND THE STRANGER, THE. Int. Alex. Egerton. Songs and incidental M. by E. Overbeck. Stafford House, July 5, 1906.

PRINCESS AND THE VAGABOND, THE. Ro. P. 7 sc. Olive Fulton. Dundee Gaiety, November 9, 1908 (C.P.).

PRINCESS AURORA. 16th century "grand opera tabloid." Arr. by Tom S. Jones. Comp. by R. M. Harvey. Tivoli, August 28, 1908 (mat.).

PRINCESS CARLO'S PLOT. 3 a. Adapt. fr. Ouida's "Afternoon" by Hilda Hilton. Novelty, January 31, 1887.

PRINCESS CHARMING; OR, THE BARD, THE BARON, THE BEAUTY, THE BUFFER, AND THE BOGEY. Extrav. H. T. Arden. Cremorne Gardens, April 29, 1867.

PRINCESS DIANA. Emotional D. 4 a. W. Jones. Hull T.R., February 4, 1889.

PRINCESS GEORGE. D. 3 a. Adapt. fr. *La Princesse Georges* of A. Dumas, fils. Prince's, January 20, 1885.

PRINCESS IDA. Operatic perversion of Tennyson's "Princess." Prol. and 2 a. W. S. Gilbert. M. by A. Sullivan. Savoy, January 5, 1884.

PRINCESS IN BOHEMIA, A. C. 4 a. Gilbert Dale. Bradford T.R., June 29, 1908.

PRINCESS 'LIZA'S FAIRY. Lib. by Josephine Wurm. M. by Marie Wurm. Southampton P.O.W., June 3, 1893.

PRINCESS LOINTAINE, LA. P. 4 a. By Eugène Rostand. M. by Gabriel Pierné. (Paris Renaissance, April 5, 1895.) Daly's, June 17, 1895.

PRINCESS LOLAH; OR, THE LOVE OF THE RAJAH OF TITTIPOMPOM. A. J. Morris. M. by W. Tilbury. Lon. Pavilion M.H., February 18, 1901; Court, October 21, 1901.

PRINCESS MARGUERITE'S CHOICE. F. 1 a. F. D. Adams. Publ. S. French, Ltd.

PRINCESS MARY JANE. M. Piece. 2 a. Eastbourne Devonshire Park, October 28, 1907.

PRINCESS OF BAGDAD, THE. Sk. Harry Lowther. Manchester Tivoli, July 19, 1909.

PRINCESS OF CLEVE, THE. T. C. Nathaniel Lee. F. on Mme. de la Fayette's French play of the same title. D.G., 1681.

PRINCESS OF ELIS; OR, THE PLEASURES OF THE ENCHANTED ISLAND, THE. Dr. piece, in 3 parts. Transl. fr. Molière by J. Ozell.

PRINCESS OF GEORGIA, THE. O. 2 a. Margravine of Anspach. C.G., April 19, 1799. N.p.

PRINCESS OF KENSINGTON, A. C.A. 2 a. B. Hood. M. by E. German. Savoy, January 22, 1903.

PRINCESS OF ORANGE, A. P. 1 a. F. James. Lyceum, December 2, 1896.

PRINCESS OF PAIN, THE. Epis. E. Nolan O'Connor. Brighton New Pal. Pier T., June 18, 1906.

PRINCESS OF PARMA, THE. T. H. Smith. Epil. Mr. Motteux. Pr. 1699. L.I.F., 1699.

PRINCESS OF PARMA, THE. T. R. Cumberland. Mr. Hanbury's Private T. at Kelmarsh, October 21, 1778.

PRINCESS OF PARMESAN, THE. O. 2 a. Lib. by W. H. Millais. M. by M. Lathom. Matinée T. (St. Geo. H.), February 21, 1898.

PRINCESS OF PERSIA, THE. See *Distressed Innocence.*

PRINCESS OF TARENTO, THE. C. A. Macdonald. Pr. 1791.

PRINCESS OF THE PEARL ISLAND. Britannia, December 26, 1866.

PRINCESS OF TREBIZONDE, THE. C.O.D. 3 a. Offenbach. Ad. by C. L. Kenney. Gaiety, April 16, 1870.

PRINCESS OF ZANFARA, THE. D. Poem. Pr. 1789.

PRINCESS OSRA, LA. O. 3 a. Maurice Bérenger and M. by H. Bunning. Lib. (in French) M. Bérenger. C.G., July 14, 1902.

PRINCESS PRIMROSE AND THE FOUR PRETTY PRINCES. Burl. Extrav. Bellingham and Best. Olympic, January 13, 1866.

PRINCESS SPRINGTIME; OR, THE ENVOY WHO STOLE THE KING'S DAUGHTER. Fairy Extrav. F. on story of Countess d'Anois. H. J. Byron. Hay., December 26, 1864.

PRINCESS TARAKANOFF; OR, THE NORTHERN NIGHT, THE. Rom. Hist. P. 5 a. C. Graves. P.O.W., July 29, 1897 (C.P.).

PRINCESS TOTO. C.O. 3 a. W. S. Gilbert. M. by F. Clay. Nottingham T.R., July 1, 1876; Strand, October 2, 1876.

PRINCESS VERITA. Children's Fairy Oa. T. Cockburn and F. J. Smith. Newcastle Art T., October 7, 1896.

PRINCESS WHO WAS CHANGED INTO A DEER, THE. Fairy Burl. Spec. M. by R. Hughes. D.L., November 3, 1845.

PRINCESS'S IDEA, THE. Burl. 2 a. Theo. Moore. Being a reversion in 2 a. after Tennyson and Gilbert. Westminster Town H., May 6, 1892 (amat.).

PRINCESS'S NOSE, THE. C. 4 a. H. A. Jones. Duke of York's, March 11, 1902.

PRINCESSE AMASWAZEE. Burl. Extrav. T. Paulton. Eastbourne Pier, April 15, 1895.

PRINCESSE AURELIE, LE. C. Delavigne. 1828.

PRINCESSE D'AUBERGE. O. 3 a. Block. Prod. at Antwerp, under the name of *Herberg Princes*, in 1896.

PRINCESSE D'ELIDE. C. Molière. 1664. See "French Classical Plays."

PRINCESSE DE NAVARRE. O. Voltaire. 1743.

PRINCESSE DE NAVARRE. O. Rameau. 1747.

PRINCESSE DE TREBIZONDE. O. Offenbach. 1870. See *Princess of*, etc.

PRINCESSE DES CANARIES, LA. See *Pepita.*

PRINCESSE GEORGES, LA. C. 3 a. Alexandre Dumas, fils. Coronet, June 22, 1906.

PRINCESSES IN THE TOWER; OR, A MATCH FOR LUCIFER, THE. Extrav. F. Talfourd. Olympic, September 2, 1850.

PRINCIPAL BOY, THE. M.C. 3 a. Guy D'Lunor. Liverpool Lyric T., June 5, 1899.

PRINCIPLE AND PRACTICE COMBINED; OR, THE WRONGS OF MAN. O. (Often perf. by Jacobins of France.) By "One Who Feels Himself a Patriot." M. selected fr. modern French airs. Pr. 1792.

PRINZ PAPILLON. C. 4 a. F. Von Schönthan, Gt. Queen St. T., January 24, 1904.

PRIOR CLAIM, A. C. H. J. Pye and S. J. Arnold. D.L., October 29, 1805. Pr. 1805.

PRIOR CLAIM. C. 1 a. F. Lancaster. Publ. by S. French, Ltd.

PRISCILLA AND THE PRESIDENT. F. Rom. 3 a. Chs. M. Heslop. Wakefield O.H., April 24, 1907.

PRISE DE IRVIC, LA. O. Berlioz. Carlsruhe, 1893.

PRISON BREAKER; OR, THE ADVENTURES OF JOHN SHEPPARD, THE. F. Anon. Pr. 1725.

PRISONER, THE. M. Rom. 3 a. J. Rose. D.L. Co. at O.H. in Haymarket. Pr. 1792.

PRISONER; OR, THE FAIR ANCHORESS, THE. T.C. P. Massinger. Ent. Stationers' Co., September 9, 1653. N.p.

PRISONER; OR, THE RESEMBLANCE, THE. Transl. fr. French by H. Heartwell. Adap. to English stage as *The Castle of Sorrento*. Hay., 1799.

PRISONER AT LARGE, THE. C. 2 a. J. O'Keeffe. Haymarket, 1806; C.G., January 4, 1819.

PRISONER OF LYONS, THE.

PRISONER OF STATE. D. Stirling. 1847.

PRISONER OF THE BASTILLE, THE. P. 4 a. Norman Forbes. (A rev. vers. of *The Man in the Iron Mask*. Orig. prod., Adelphi, March 11, 1899.) Lyceum, May 13, 1909.

PRISONER OF THE CZAR, A. Dr. Sk. 1 a. Dora Deane and F. Brooke. M. by E. T. De Banzie. Palace, Bow, May 30, 1904.

PRISONER OF TOULON; OR, THE PEASANTS' REVENGE, THE. D. 3 a. A. B. Richards. D.L., March 2, 1868.

PRISONER OF WAR, THE. C. 2 a. Douglas Jerrold. D.L., February 8, 1842.

PRISONER OF ZENDA, THE. Rom. P. Prol. and 4 a. Adap. fr. Anthony Hope's story by E. Rose. St. James's, January 7, 1896; July 1, 1897; rev. St. James's, January 7, 1900; rev. St. James's, February 18, 1909.

PRISONER'S OPERA, THE, with other entertainments. E. Ward. Sadler's Wells. Pr. 1730.

PRISONERS, THE. F. C. T. Killigrew. Phœnix. Pr. 1641.

PRISONERS AT THE BAR, THE. Oa. C. H. Ross. M. by Frank Musgrave. Liverpool R Alexandra, June 17, 1878.

PRISONNIER, LE. O. Comique. Dellamaria. 1796.

PRISONNIER ANGLAIS, LE. O. 3 a. Grétry. 1787. Rev. as *Clarice et Belton*, 1793.

PRIVATE AND CONFIDENTIAL. F. Messrs. Eldred and Paulton. Liverpool P.O.W., April 1, 1870.

PRIVATE DETECTIVE, A. F.C. 1 a. S. Leigh and M. Pemberton. St. Geo. H., April 1, 1886.

PRIVATE ENQUIRY. F.C. 3 a. Adap. fr. Valabrègue's *La Securité des Familles* (Paris Vaudeville, 1888) by F. C. Burnand. Adelphi, March 24, 1862; Leicester O.H., November 25, 1890; January 7, 1891.

PRIVATE LIFE. D. Ealing Lyric H., July 1, 1882.

PRIVATE NOBODY. P. 1 a. F. D. Bone. Court, November 2, 1908 (mat.); South London, February 22, 1909.

PRIVATE SECRETARY, THE. Farc. C. 4 a. Adap. fr. Von Moser's "Der Bibliotheker." C. H. Hawtry. Cambridge T.R., November 14, 1883; Prince's, March 29, 1884; Globe, 1884 (3 a.); Comedy, July 4, 1892; Avenue, September 3, 1895; Grand, July 7, 1900.

PRIVATE THEATRE; OR, HIGHLAND FUNERAL. D. M'Laren. 1809.

PRIVATE THEATRICALS. F. J. Powell. 1787. N.dr.

PRIVATE VIEW, A. C. 1 a. E. Ferrers. St. George's H., June 6, 1898 (amat.). Publ. by S. French, Limited.

PRIVATE WIRE, A. V. A. Felix and L. Desprez. M. by P. Reeve. Savoy, March 31, 1883.

PRIVATEER, THE. O. Alt. fr. Cumberland's C. of *The Brothers*. Bath, July 10, 1813; Lyceum playbill, September 1, 1815.

PRIVATEER'S VENTURE, THE. D. Prol. and 2 a. H. Hayman. Victoria, June 5, 1876.

PRIVY COUNCIL, A. Ca. Major W. P. Drury and R. Pryce. Hay., September 6, 1905; rev. Hay., March 24, 1906.

PRIZE; OR, 2, 5 3, 8, THE. M.F. 2 a. P. Hoare. O.H., 1793; Lyceum playbill, June 12, 1809; D.L., March 12, 1814. N.p.

PRIZES AND BLANKS. Oa. 1 a. M. O. Booth. Ladbroke H., June 29, 1885.

PRO TEM. P. 3 a. Cosmo Hamilton. Adap. fr. Alfred Arthi's F., *Boute en Train*. Playhouse, April 29, 1908.

PROBENKANDIDAT, DER. P. 4 a. Max Dreyer. April 2, 1901. (German season.)

PROBEPFEIL, DER. C. 4 a. Oscar Blumenthal. October 26, 1900.

PROCLAIMED. Irish D. 4 a. W. Manning. Stockton-on-Tees T.R., October 29, 1886.

PROCRASTINATION; OR, THE LATE MR. M. C. 3 a. Hay., September 21, 1829.

PROCUREUR ARBITRE, LE. C. R. Poisson.

PRODIGAL, THE. C. Transl. fr. Voltaire. Dr. Franklin.

PRODIGAL, THE. D.P. F. G. Waldron. Taken fr. "Fatal Extravagance." Hay., December 2, 1793. Pr. 1794.

PRODIGAL, THE. Melo-d. 3 a. D.L., April 29, 1816.

PRODIGAL; OR, MARRIAGE A LA MODE, THE. C. 5 a. Pr. 1794.

PRODIGAL; OR, RECRUITS FOR THE QUEEN OF HUNGARY, THE. C. Thomas Odell. Alt. fr. Shadwell's "Woman Captain." Little T. in Hay., October 10, 1744.

PRODIGAL CHILD, THE. P. Mentioned in Histriomastix, 1610.

PRODIGAL DAUGHTER, A. See *His Wife*.

PRODIGAL DAUGHTER, THE. D. 4 a. H. Pettitt and Sir A Harris. D.L., September 17, 1892.

PRODIGAL FATHER, THE. F. 3 a. G Macdonough. Oxford New T., January 25, 1897; Strand, February 1, 1897.

PRODIGAL PARSON; OR, FOR EVER AND EVER, THE. Dom. D. 4 a. F. L. Connyngham and C. A. Clarke. Salford P.O.W., March 24, 1898 (C.P.); Lincoln T.R., May 16, 1898; Standard, June 19, 1899.

PRODIGAL REFORMED, THE. Jacob. 1738. See *The Nest of Plays*.

PRODIGAL SCHOLAR, THE. C. T. Randall. Ent. Stationers' Co., June 29, 1660. N.p.

PRODIGAL SON. O. Auber. H.M., 1851.

PRODIGAL SON, A. O. 2 a. Lib. by E. N. Willett. M. by F. C. Nicholls. Mill St., Liverpool, Mission H., March 18, 1896.

PRODIGAL SON, THE. Orat. by Hull. Set by Dr. Arnold. C.G. Pr. 1773.

PRODIGAL SON, THE. Orat. A. Sullivan. Worcester M. Festival, September 8, 1869.

PRODIGAL SON, THE. D. 4 a. Hall Caine, fr. his novel. Douglas Grand T., November 2, 1904; D.L., September 7, 1905; Adelphi, February 25, 1907.

PRODIGAL WIFE, THE. Sk. 3 scenes. Fk. Maxwell. Cardiff Pal., November 18, 1907.

PRODIGAL'S RETURN, THE. Oratorio. Rev. H. F. Limpus. St. James's H., May 10, 1870.

PRODIGAL'S RETURN, THE. Rom. D. 4 a. E. G. Marshall. Leyland Parish H., January 29, 1906 (amat.).

PRODIGALITY. D. Ac. at Court, 1568.

PROFESSIONAL BEAUTY, A. C. 3 a. V. Ambrose. Imperial T., June 1, 1880.

PROFESSIONALS PUZZLED; OR, STRUGGLES AT STARTING. Burl. Strand, January 26, 1832.

PROFESSOR, THE. F. Norwich T.R., March 12, 1868.

PROFESSOR, THE. F.C. 3 a. Adap. by G. Maxwell fr. Von Schonthan's *Das Raub der Sabinerimen*. Cambridge T.R., May 31, 1894.

PROFESSOR, THE. Duol. R. Barrington. M. by E. Solomon. St. Geo. H., July 15, 1895.

PROFESSOR OF WHAT? St. James's, October 6, 1866.

PROFESSOR'S LOVE STORY, THE. C. 3 a. J. M. Barrie. (First prod, in America.) Comedy. June 25, 1894; tfd. Garrick, August 13, 1894; rev. St. James's, December 7, 1903.

PROFESSOR'S SECRET, THE. Sk. Louis Dagmar. Ealing Hipp., August 3, 1908.

PROFESSOR'S VISION, THE. M. Playlet. Theo. Wood. Eastbourne Hipp., January 11, 1908.

PROFESSOR'S WOOING, THE. C. Pas. 4 a. Orig. prod. in America. W. H. Gillette. Royalty, February 15, 1887.

PROFETA, IL. O. Meyerbeer. (Paris, 1849.)

PROFEZIA D'ELISEO, LA. O. A. Ariosti. Wr. for Vienna, 1705

PROFLIGATE, THE. C. G. W. Taylor. 1820.

PROFLIGATE, THE. P. 4 a. A. W. Pinero. Garrick, April 24, 1889.

PROFLIGATE KING, THE. Sk. Albert Ward. Queen's, Poplar, December 3, 1906.

PROGENITOR OF MAN. Sk. 3sc. "B. B. and C. R." Middlesex, November 20, 1905.

PROGNE. T. Calfhill, 1566. N.p.

PROGRESS. C. 3 a. Adap. fr. Sardou's *Les Gamaches* by T. W. Robertson. Globe T., September 18, 1869.

PROJECTOR, THE. Ent. Ac. by gentlemen at the Naval Academy, Cold Harbour, Gosport, 1803, with the tragedy of *Montfort*.

PROJECTOR LATELY DEAD, A. C. 1636 N.p.

PROJECTORS, THE. C. J. Wilson. Ac. 1665.

PROJECTORS, THE. C. W. H. Pr. 1737.

PROJECTS, THE. F. J. P. Kemble. 1786. N.p. See *The Female Officer*.

PROMESSI SPOSI, I. O. 4 a. F. on Manzoni's novel. Lib. by H. Hersee. M. by A. Ponchielli. Milan, August 30, 1856; Edinburgh T.R., March 23, 1881

PROMESSI SPOSI, I. O. Petrella. Lecco, 1869.

PROMETHEUS. Pant. Anon. C.G., 1776.

PROMETHEUS; OR, THE MAN ON THE ROCK. Orig. Extrav. R. Reece. New Royalty, December 23, 1865.

PROMETHEUS; OR, THE WORLD DESPLAY'D. MS. Sold as part of Murphy's library.

PROMETHEUS BOUND. Transl. fr. Æschylus's T. by Potter, 1777; Buckley, 1849; Webster, 1866; Plumtre, 1869; and Lang, 1870. See "Greek Plays."

PROMETHEUS BOUND. T. E. Browning. 1838. Recast in 1850.

PROMETHEUS CHAIN'D. T. Transl. fr. Æschylus by R. Potter. Pr. 1777.

PROMETHEUS IN CHAINS. T. Transl. fr. Æschylus by T. Morel. Pr. 1773.

PROMETHEUS UNBOUND. Lyrical D. Shelley, 1821.

PROMETHEUS UNBOUND. Cantata. Dr. C. H. Parry.

PROMISE, A. P. 1 a. S. B. Lawrence. Globe, October 29, 1889.

PROMISE OF MAY, THE. Rustic D. 3 a. Alfred Tennyson. Globe, November 11, 1882.

PROMISE OR STRATEGY. C. 1 a. B. Tweedale. M. by B. Vine. Sydenham Westbrook Public H., January 12, 1901.

PROMISED IN PIQUE. P. 3 a. Globe, April 16, 1885.

PROMISED LAND; OR, THE SEARCH FOR THE SOUTHERN STAR, THE. D. H. Pettitt. Grecian, September 13, 1875.

PROMISES OF GOD, THE. Int. manifesting the promises fr. the beginning of the world to the death of Jesus Christ. By J. Bale. Publ. 1537.

PROMISING PUPIL. O. 1 a. L. Diehl. Publ. by S. French, Ltd.

PROMISSORY NOTE, THE. C. Oa. Freely transl. fr. French. Lyceum playbill, June 29, 1820; Bath, March 18, 1825.

PROMOS AND CASSANDRA. C. 2 a. Fr. which Shakespeare took his "Measure for Measure." By G. Whetstone. Pr. 1578.

PROMOTION. Hum. Duol. Bedford St. Bijou, October 27, 1907.

PROMOTION; OR, A MORNING AT VERSAILLES. V. 1 a. J. R. Planché. Played at principal Eng. and Amer. theatres.

PROMPTER'S BOX: A STORY OF THE FOOTLIGHTS AND THE FIRESIDE, THE. D. 4 a. H. J. Byron. See *Two Stars*. Adelphi, March 23, 1870.

PROOF, THE. P. 1 a. Alice Clayton Greene. Southport O.H., September 7, 1908; King's, April 26, 1909.

PROOF; OR, A CELEBRATED CASE. D. Prol. and 3 a. Adap. fr. transl. of Adolphé d'Ennery and Eugène Cormon's "Une Cause Célèbre." F. C. Burnand Adelphi, April 20, 1878.

PROOF OF LOVE. Bal. int. Byrne. 1813.

PROOF POSITIVE. C. 3 a. F. C. Burnand. Op. C., October 16, 1875.

PROOF PRESUMPTIVE; OR, THE ABBEY OF SAN MARCO. C.G., October 20, 1818.

PROPHECY, THE. R.P. 4 a. R. Ganthony. Fulham Grand, December 1, 1902; Avenue, March 10, 1903.

PROPHET, THE. C.O. R. Bentley. C.G., December 13, 1788. N.p.

PROPHET, THE. T. B. Taylor. 1874.

PROPHET, THE. O. 5 a. Meyeberbeer. Words by Scribe (Paris, April 16, 1849). In Ital. in 4 a. C.G., July 24, 1849. First time in English. Liverpool R. Court, March 2, 1892 (Carl Rosa Co.).

PROPHET, THE. F.C. 3 a. E. E. Granville. Maidenhead Grand H., January 2, 1893.

PROPHETESS, THE. Tragical History. Beaumont and Fletcher. Pr. 1647.

PROPHETESS, THE. T. 3 a. J. Galt. Pr. 1814 ? N.ac.

PROPHETESS; OR, THE HISTORY OF DIOCLESIAN. T.C. An adap. of above as an O. by Betterton. M. by Purcell. Pr. 1690.

PROPOSALS. F.C. 3 a. J. F. Gilmore. Vaudeville, December 15, 1887.

PROSCRIBED ROYALIST; OR, WHO STOLE THE DUCKS? THE. Burl. F. Seymour. Leicester O.H., August 1, 1881.

PROSERPINA. O. Lulli. February 3, 1680.

PROSERPINA. O. Winter. 1804.

PROSERPINE. O. Paisiello. 1801.

PROSERPINE. O. Saint-Saëns. Modern France.

PROSPERO; OR, THE KING OF THE CALABAN ISLANDS. Burl. Imperial, December 26, 1883.

PROTECTOR ET PROTEGE. Royalty, March 29, 1888.

PROTEUS. M. Dr. Poem. Hickford's Room, 1741. N.p.

PROTEUS; OR, HARLEQUIN IN CHINA. Pant. Mr. Woodward. Drury Lane T.R., 1755.

PROUD MAID, THE. Another title of Beaumont and Fletcher's *Maid's Tragedy*.

PROUD PRINCE; A STORY OF ROBERT, KING OF SICILY, A. P. J. H. McCarthy. M. by H. Sullivan Brooke. Vaudeville, September 11, 1908 (C.P.); Lyceum, September 4, 1909.

PROUD PRINCESS, THE. Oa. 3 a. Chs. Knight. M., Clive Courtney. Peckham All Saints' H., December 6, 1906 (amat.).

PROUD WIVES' PATER NOSTER, THE. P. Ent. Stationers' Co., 1559.

PROUD WOMAN OF ANTWERP, THE. P. W. Haughton in conjunction with J. Day. 1601. N.p.

PROVA D'UN OPERA, SERIA LA (Principal Scene from). O. Buffa. by Guecco. D.L., July 27, 1835.

PROVOCATION. Bal. Pant. Haughton. 1790.

PROVED TRUE. D. 5 a. M. Murdoch. Sadler's Wells, May 7, 1883.

PROVOKED HUSBAND, THE; OR, A JOURNEY TO LONDON. C. 5 a. Sir J. Vanbrugh, and finished after his death by C. Cibber. Drury Lane T.R., 1727; D.L., February 3, 1815, and October 13, 1818; C.G., 1805, and December 14, 1809, and 1823; Hay., November, 1855.

PROVOKED WIFE, THE. C. Sir J. Vanbrugh. L.I.F. Pr. 1697. Rev. Hay., January 19, 1706, with alterations.

PROVOST OF BRUGES, THE. T. 5 a. G. W. Lovell. F. on story of "The Serf." D.L., February 10, 1836.

PROXE; OR, LOVE'S AFTERGAME, THE. Ent. Stationers' Co., November 29, 1653. N.p. Prod. at Salisbury Court T., November 24, 1634.

PROXY, THE. See *Love's Aftergame.*

PRUDE, THE. C. Transl. fr. Voltaire. Dr. Franklin.

PRUDE, THE. C.O. Eliz. Ryves. Pr. 1777.

PRUDE; OR, WIN HER AND WEAR HER, THE. C. J. A. Weeks. Pr. 1791.

PRUDE'S PROGRESS, THE. C. 3 a. J. K. Jerome and E. Phillpots. Cambridge T.R., May 16, 1895; Comedy, May 22, 1895; tr. to Terry's, July 29, 1895.

PRUDENCE FOSTER. "Mezzotint." Bertha Moore. Royalty, June 6, 1905.

PRUDES AND PROS. F.C. 2 a. Adelene Voteere. St. Geo. H., June 20, 1891.

PRUNELLA. Int. Rd. Estcourt. Pr. before 1713. Introduced into Duke of Buckingham's rehearsal. Act. D.L., February 12, 1708.

PRUNELLA; OR, LOVE IN A DUTCH GARDEN. P. 3 a. Laurence Houseman and Granville Barker. M. by J. Moorat. Court, December 23, 1904; rev. Court, April 24, 1906, and May 7, 1907.

PRUSSIAN FESTIVAL. Occa. Bal. Anon. 1791.

PRYING LITTLE GIRL. C. 1 a. E. H. Keating. Publ. by S. French, Ltd.

PSEUDOLUS; OR, THE CHEAT. C. Plautus. Transl. into bl. verse by Thornton, Rich, Warner, and Colman, 1769-74. See "Latin Plays."

PSEUDOMASIA. T.C. Mewe. MS.

PSYCHE. The first English O. M. Lock. 1673

PSYCHE. Corneille. See "French Classical Plays."

PSYCHE. T. T. Shadwell. D. of Y., 1675. Pr. 1675. D.L., June 10, 1704.

PSYCHE. O. 5 a. Lulli. April 19, 1678.

PSYCHE. O. J. Ozell. Literal transl. of Molière's *Psyche*.

PSYCHE. O. Thomas. (Paris, 1878.)

PSYCHE. Idyll. 3 scenes. Dramatic action and dances. Arr. by Alfredo Curti. M. by Alfred Moul. Alhambra, April 5, 1909.

PSYCHE, DEBAUCH'D. C. T. Duffet. T.R., 1678. Mock opera of Shadwell's *Psyche*.

PSYCHICAL RESEARCH. C. 1 a. I. Cassilis. Publ. by S. French, Ltd.

PTOLEME. P. Mentioned by Gosson in "The Schoole of Abuse." Said to have been ac. at Bel Savage.

PUBLIC, THE. T. J. Maclaurin, Lord Dreghorn. Pr. 1799.

PUBLIC DINNER IN AID OF A PHILANTHROPIC OBJECT, A. Sk. R. Reece. Gallery of Illus., April 13, 1868.

PUBLIC-HOUSE; OR, CONSEQUENTIAL LANDLORD AND HIS CUSTOMERS. F. Pr. 1787.

PUBLIC OPINION. F. 3 a. R. C. Carton. Wyndham's, May 6, 1905.

PUBLIC WOOING. C. Margaret, Duchess of Newcastle. Pr. 1662.

PUBLISHER, THE. C. "A. J. Nib." Cork O.H., July 18, 1900.

PUCK. Fairy Extrav. An after-dinner Version of *Midsummer Night's Dream.* Hammersmith Lyric O.H., November 17, 1890.

PUCK; OR, THE LASS OF MOORSIDE. D. Prol. and 3 a. Adap. fr. Ouida's novel, "Puck," by Marian Grace. Bournemouth T.R., August 13, 1883; Shepherd's Bush Athenæum, July 31, 1884.

PUCK. See *The Artist's Revenge.*

PUDDENHEAD WILSON. Dr. by Frank Mayo fr. Mark Twain's novel. Eleph. and C., April 5, 1895.

PUFF OF SMOKE, A. C. J. Rowe and Mme. Goetz. St. George's H., circa 1865.

PUIRMAN AND THE PARDONER, THE. One of eight Int. by Sir David Lindsay. Publ. by J. Pinkerton. Pr. 1792.

PULCHERIE. Corneille. See "French Classical Plays."

PULLET, THE. D. Anon. See "Theatrical Recorder."

PULVERFAAS, DAS. Piece. 1 a. G. Kadebury. Comedy, February 22, 1901 (German season).

PUMP, THE. Ca. W. L. Clowes. Toole's, March 27, 1886.

PUNCH. Dom. C. 3 a. H. J. Byron. Vaudeville, May 26, 1881.

PUNCH. Toy T. 1 a. J. M. Barrie. Comedy, April 5, 1906.

PUNCH AND FUN. Sadler's Wells, June 9, 1862.

PUNCH AND JUDY. C. 1 a. Rachel Penn and M. E. Jones. Stage business by Ch. Lauri and R. Gratton. Savoy, June 8, 1893.

PUNCH AND JUDY. R.M.C.D. 3 a. A. Law. M. by G. Byng and A. Meredyth. Croydon New T.R., June 25, 1900.

PUNCH BOWL, THE. Holloway Empire, April 1, 1907.

PUNCH TURN'D SCHOOLMASTER. F. Pro. by Sheridan Perf. in Ireland. Pr. 1724.

PUNCHBOWL, THE; OR, THE ROYAL BREW. C.O. 2 a. Lib. T. M. Lord. M. by J. Storer. Novelty, June 18, 1887.

PUNCHINELLO. P. 1 a. Dr. Dabbs. Avenue, June 24, 1890.

PUNCHINELLO. P. 1 a. Adap. fr. F. by H. Carter. Fulham Grand T., September 11, 1903.

PUNCHINELLO; OR, THE MASKED MARRIAGE. M.D. 1 a. G. H. Chester and F. Hodson. Prod. by Apollo Operatic Soc. Wellington H., London, N.W., June 10, 1903.

PUNCTURED. Ca. 1 a. T. G. Warren. Strand, August 28, 1900.

PUNISHMENT OF THE VICES, THE. One of eight int. of Sir D. Lindsay. Publ. by John Pinkerton. Pr. 1792.

PUPILLA, LA. C.O. Paisiello, 1741-1816.

PUPILLA E'L TUTORE, LA. O. G. Abos. Naples, 1708-1786.

PUPPETS. Whimsical Sk. J. F. M'Ardle. Criterion, July 20, 1893.

PURE AND SIMPLE. Sk. Metropolitan, July 12, 1909.

PURE AS DRIVEN SNOW; OR, TEMPTED IN VAIN. D. 3 a. C. H. Hazlewood. Britannia, November 17, 1869.

PURE AS GOLD. P. 4 a. W. Marston. Sadler's Wells, November 9, 1863.

PURE AS SNOW. D. 3 a. E. Berrie. Bradford T.R., April 2, 1873.

PURE GOLD. Sadler's Wells, November 9, 1863.

PURELY PLATONIC. P. 1 a. E. Bliss. Enniskillen P.H., May 6, 1905.

PURELY PLATONIC. C. 1 a. Mrs. de Smart. Publ. by S. French, Ltd.

PURITAN, THE. P. 4 a. D. C. Murry, H. Murry, and J. L. Shine. Trafalgar, July 26. 1894.

PURITAN; OR, THE WIDOW OF WATLING STREET, THE. C. "W. S." (probably Wentworth Smith and not William Shakespeare). Ac. by children of St. Paul's. Pr. 1607. D.L., June 25, 1714.

PURITAN GIRL, THE.

PURITAN MAID, MODEST WIFE, AND WANTON WIDOW, THE. C. T. Middleton. Ent. Stationers' Co. September 9, 1653. Amongst those destroyed by Mr. Warburton's servant.

PURITAN'S DAUGHTER, THE. O. 3 a. Balfe. Wds. by J. V. Bridgeman. C.G., November 30, 1860.

PURITAN'S DAUGHTER, THE. D. 4 a. W. F. Lavington. Bayswater Bijou, March 8, 1875.

PURITANICAL JUSTICE; OR, THE BEGGARS TURN'D THIEVES, THE. F. Pr. 1698.

PURITANI, I. O. 2 a. Bellini (his last). Wds. by Count Pepoli. Paris, January 25, 1835; King's, May 21, 1835.

PURPLE ISLAND, THE. Ph. Fletcher.

PURPLE LADY, THE. F.C. 3 a. S. Rosenfeld. Liverpool Shakespeare, November 8, 1901.

PURRAH, THE. African tale. 3 a. J. Moser. Pr. 1808.

PURSE; OR, THE BENEVOLENT TAR, THE. M.D. J. C. Cross. 1794. D.L., May 10, 1814; rev. Lyceum, September 2, 1817.

PURSE OF GOLD, THE. P. 1 a. J. Sackville Martin. Court, May 9, 1909.

PURSER, THE. Nautical F.C. 3 a. J. T. Day. Portsmouth T.R., July 12, 1897; Strand, September 13, 1897.

PUSHKIN. D. Pietro Cossa.

PUSS IN BOOTS. Pant. Margravine of Anspach. Brandenburgh H., 1799.

PUSS IN BOOTS. R. Reece.

PUSS IN BOOTS. F. 1 a. E. H. Keating. Publ. by S. French, Ltd.

PUSS IN BOOTS. Extrav. M. Byam and B. Wyke. Croydon T.R., July 25, 1892.

PUSS IN BOOTS. Sk. Canterbury, December 7, 1908.

PUT ASUNDER. D. 4 a. F. Wills. Gaiety, May 28, 1883.

PUT ASUNDER. P. 1 a. Lyric Club, June 2, 1901.

PUT TO THE TEST. D. 1 a. W. Marston. Olympic, February 24, 1873.

PUT YOURSELF IN HIS PLACE. D. C. Reade. Adelphi, 1870.

PUTTING THE BEST FACE UPON IT. Extrav. Prod. under the auspices of the Architectural Assoc., Gaiety Restaurant, February 28, 1907.

PUTTING THINGS RIGHT. F.C. 3 a. H. Zimmermann. New Public H., April 25. 1885.

PYGMALION. O. Rameau. 1748.

PYGMALION. Lyrical P. 1 a. Rousseau, October 30, 1775.

PYGMALION. Mono. D. Transl. fr. Rousseau. Pr. 1779.

PYGMALION. O. Cherubini. 1809.

PYGMALION. Scene Tr. W. Mason. 1811.

PYGMALION; OR, THE STATUE FAIR. Burl. W. Brough. Strand, April 20, 1867.

PYGMALION AND GALATEA. Mythological C. 3 a. W. S. Gilbert. Hay., December 9, 1871; Comedy, June 7, 1900.

PYJAMAS. Sk. H. C. Sargent. London Pavilion, August 12, 1907.

PYKE O'CALLAGHAN. C. 2 a. Publ. by S. French, Ltd.

PYRAMID, THE. Shirley Brooks. Gal. of Illus., February 7, 1864.

PYRAMIDS, LIMITED. M.C. 2 a. By C. D. Frecker. St. George's H., May 9, 1902.

PYRAME ET THISBE. O. F. Rebel and F. Francœur. Académie, 1726.

PYRAME ET THISBE. T. Pradon.

PYRAME ET THISBE. O. Lagrange.

PYRAMUS AND THISBE. C. Masque. Staged by R. Leveridge. L.I.F., October 29, 1716. Pr. 1716.

PYRAMUS AND THISBE. Taken fr. *Midsummer Night's Dream.* Mock Op. M. by Lampe. C.G. Pr. 1745.

PYRAMUS AND THISBE. Pant. W. C. Oulton. Birmingham. Pr. 1798.

PYRAMUS AND THISBE. C. Matthews, jun. Hay., August, 1833.

PYRAMUS AND THISBE; OR, THE MARGATE MILKMAID. F. C. H. Stephenson. Manchester Prince's, October 12, 1877.

PYRRHUS. T. W. Russel. MS. (before 1814).

PYRRHUS. Italian O. H.M.

PYRRHUS AND DEMETRIUS. O. MacSwiny. Transl. fr. Italian of Scarlatti. Queen's in Haymarket. Pr. 1709.

PYRRHUS, KING OF EPIRUS. T. C Hopkins. L.I.F., by His Majesty's servants. 1695.

PYRRUS AND DEMETRIUS. O. Scarlatti. 1659-1725.

PYTHAGORAS. P. M. Slaughter. 1598. N.p.

Q

Q.E.D.; OR, ALL A MISTAKE. F. 1 a. Frank Marshall. Court, January 25, 1871.

Q.Q. C. 4 a. H. F. Johnson. Bristol Princes, December 12, 1895; Terry's, March 28, 1898.

QUACKS, THE. C. 2 a. D.L., April 21, 1784. N.p.

QUACKS, THE. F.C. 3 a. Adap. fr. Germ. of Von Moser by L. Honig. Royalty, September 11, 1887.

QUACKS; OR, LOVE'S THE PHYSICIAN, THE. C. 3 a. Owen M'Swiny. Transl. fr. Molière's "L'Amour Medicin." D.L., March 18, 1705. Pr. 1705.

QUACKS; OR, LOVE'S THE PHYSICIAN, THE. Owen M'Swiny. Former reduced to 1 a. 1745.

QUADRILLE; OR, A QUARREL FOR WHAT? THE. Oa. M. Mr. Price. Lyceum playbill, June 14, 1819; Bath, March 22, 1820.

QUADROON SLAVE, THE.

QUADRUPEDS; OR, THE MANAGER'S LAST KICK. Extrav. Lyceum, July 18, 1811, and September 2, 1815; Adelphi, 1823; D.L., June 13, 1831.

QUADRUPEDS OF QUEDLINBURGH; OR, THE ROVERS OF WEIMAR. Attributed to Colman, jun. Hay., July 26, 1811.

QUAKER, THE. C.O. 2 a. C. Dibdin. D.L., April 3, 1775; C.G., 1805, and September 18, 1809; D.L., June 10, 1815.

QUAKER'S OPERA, THE. T. Walker. Lee and Harper's Booth in Bartholomew Fair. Pr. 1728.

QUAKER'S WEDDING, THE. C. R. Wilkinson. Same as *Vice Reclaim'd.* D.L., 1703; L.I.F., October 22, 1719.

QUAKERS AND SHAKERS. F. Mr. Doyle. Liverpool T.R., July 14, 1873.

QUALITY STREET. C. 4 a. J. M. Barrie. Vaudeville, September 17, 1902.

QUARANTINE. Ware.

QUARREL, A. Duo. T. S. Wolton. Brompton Hospital, March 14, 1893; Parkhurst, May 4, 1894.

QUARREL OF THE FLOWERS. C. 1 a. G. S. Hodges. Publ. by S. French, Ltd.

QUARRY DELL. D. J. H. Delafield. Liverpool Colosseum, July 6, 1868.

QUARTER DAY. Int. R. Sicklemore Jover. Prod. at Lewes, 1798.

QUARTER DAY; OR, HOW TO PAY RENT WITHOUT MONEY. M.F. Globe, August 28, 1876.

QUARTER OF A MILLION OF MONEY, A. D. 3 a. E. Towers. New E. London, February 17, 1868.

QUARTER OF AN HOUR BEFORE DINNER; OR, QUALITY BINDING. Dr. Ent. 1 a. Rev. J. Rose. Hay., August 5, 1788. Pr. 1788.

QUARTETTE, THE; OR, INTERRUPTED HARMONY. Oa. M. by Mr. Hawes. Lyceum playbill, September 18, 1828.

QUASIMODO. O. F. Pedrell. Barcelona. 1874.

QUASIMODO, THE DEFORMED; OR, THE MAN WITH THE HUMP AND THE BELLE OF NOTRE DAME. Burl. H. Spry. Grecian, April 18, 1870.

QUATRE FILS AYNON, LES. O.C. M. by Balfe. Wds. by MM. Leuven and Brunswick. Paris, July 15, 1844. As *The Castle of Aymon; or, The Four Brothers*, 3 a., at Princess's, November 20, 1844.

QUAVERS AND CAPERS. Int. Alt. fr. Fielding's *Virgin Unmask'd.* D.L., June 3, 1817.

QUEEN, THE. M.P. 3 a. J. W. Swarbeck. Duke's, March 15, 1879.

QUEEN; OR, EXCELLENCY OF HER SEX, THE. T.C. Anon. Pr. 1653. See *The Dumb Knight.*

QUEEN AND CARDINAL. Hist. P. 5 a. W. S. Raleigh. Hay., October 26, 1881.

QUEEN AND CONCUBINE, THE. C. R. Brome. Pr. 1659.

QUEEN AND THE YEOMAN. City of London, January 19, 1852.

QUEEN CATHARINE; OR, THE RUINS OF LOVE. T. Mary Rix. Epil. by Mrs. Trotter. L.I.F., 1698.

QUEEN DODO. Britannia, December 26, 1883.

QUEEN ELIZABETH. P. T. Heywood. 1637.

QUEEN ELIZABETH. T. Manchester T.R., November 29, 1869.

QUEEN ELIZABETH; OR, AT THE QUEEN'S COMMAND. P. 4 a. Frances M. Leightner. Vaudeville, September 9, 1901.

QUEEN HESTER. Int. Pr. 1561.

QUEEN, I LOVE YOUR FIVE O'CLOCK TEA. O. 1 a. Kate Osborn. Publ. by S. French, Ltd.

QUEEN JUTA OF DENMARK. T. Bojé.

QUEEN MAB. Pant. H. Woodward. D.L., December 26, 1750.

QUEEN MAB. O. Burney. 1760.

QUEEN MAB. C. 3 a. S. W. Godfrey. Hay., March 21, 1874.

QUEEN MARY. D. D. 5 a. A. Tennyson. Lyceum, April 18, 1876.

QUEEN MARY; OR, THE TOWER OF LONDON. D. 3 a. Adelphi, 1840.

QUEEN MARY'S BOWER. C. 3 a. J. R. Planche. Hay., October 10, 1846.

QUEEN MOTHER, THE. T. Swinburne, 1861.

QUEEN O' DIAMONDS, THE. Melod. 5 a. W. A. Brabner. Manchester St. James's, December 22, 1894.

QUEEN O' MAY. Rustic O. 2 a. F. W. Legg. M. by Sir Sterndale Bennett. Birkenhead Argyle, July 28, 1896.

QUEEN O' SCOTS. Poetical D. 4 a. E. Rose and J. Todhunter. Kennington Princess of Wales's, October 5, 1900.

QUEEN OF AN HOUR. D. 5 a. J. Douglass and F. Stainforth. Standard, October 1, 1877.

QUEEN OF ARRAGON, THE. T.C. W. Habington. Pr. 1640. Ac. at Court and Black Fryars. Rev. at Restoration, with Prol. and Epil. by author of "Hudibras."

QUEEN OF ARRAGON, THE. C. 1 a. H. Paul. Sadler's Wells. May 12, 1854.

QUEEN OF ARTS. Extrav. Preston T.R., August 4, 1884.

QUEEN OF BOHEMIA, THE. See *The Vicar*.

QUEEN OF BOHEMIA, THE. D. 3 a. E. L. Blanchard. Olympic, October 6, 1845.

QUEEN OF BRILLIANTS, THE. C.O. 3 a. Adap. by B. Thomas fr. the German of T. Taube and I. Tuchs. M. by E. Jakobowski. Lyceum, September 8, 1894.

QUEEN OF CARTHAGE, THE. T. Marloe and Nash. 1594. See *Dido*.

QUEEN OF CONNAUGHT, THE. C.D. 4 a. Olympic, January 15, 1877.

QUEEN OF CORINTH, THE. T.C. Beaumont and Fletcher. Pr. 1647. Prod. between 1616-1619.

QUEEN OF CORSICA, THE. T. F. Jaques. Wr. 1642. Marquess of Lansdowne has the MS.

QUEEN OF CYPRUSS, THE. French spec. Adelphi, February, 1842.

QUEEN OF DIAMONDS. C.D. Miss Anne Brunton. Coatbridge T.R., March 20, 1882.

QUEEN OF DIAMONDS, THE. P. 4 a. H. Green. Chesterfield T.R., April 4, 1902.

QUEEN OF DIAMONDS, THE. P. 4 a. H. Green. Hartlepool Empress T., May 10, 1901; Chesterfield R., April 4, 1902.

QUEEN OF DIAMONDS; OR, THE SHADOWS OF LIFE, THE. D. 5 a. A. Shirley. Barrow Alhambra (prod. as *The Hand of Fate*), March 3, 1884; Standard, November 26, 1894.

QUEEN OF ENGLAND, A. Rom. P., f. on Dumas' work. C. A. Clarke. Eastbourne T.R., May 2, 1898; Kilburn T.R., November 21, 1898.

QUEEN OF FASHION, THE. D. Pro. and 4 a. T. Cannam and J. T. Preston. (Originally prod. as prol. and 5 a), Oldham; Sadler's Wells, March 19, 1888; Vaudeville, June 21, 1888.

QUEEN OF HEARTS, A. M.P. 4 a. Lib. by C. Burnette, lyrics by H. R. Clyne, M. by R. E. Irving. Huddersfield Empire, July 2, 1900. Entirely re-written by H. C. Newte, new lyrics by J. W. Houghton, M. by Philip Henry, additional numbers by E. G. Dunstan. Rawtenstall Grand, June 6, 1902.

QUEEN OF HEARTS, THE. Oa. 1 a. Lib. by Ch. Thomas, M. by Miss Harriet Young. Brighton Royal Pavilion, November 7, 1877; February 9, 1878.

QUEEN OF HEARTS. Burl. Sanger's Amphitheatre, Ramsgate, July 14, 1884.

QUEEN OF LOVE, THE. C.O. 2 a. F. Harrison. M. by J. T. Klee. Leicester R.O.H., December 13, 1900.

QUEEN OF MANOA, THE. P. 4 a. C. H. Chambers and W. O. Tristram. Hay., September 15, 1892.

QUEEN OF MAY. Grecian, December 1, 1857.

QUEEN OF MUSIC, THE. Sk. S. and L. Gordon. Middlesex, August 3, 1908; Metropolitan, January 11, 1909.

QUEEN OF SCOTS. T. Banks. 1684.

QUEEN OF SHEBA, THE. P. 4 a. Wds. by Barbier and Carré. M. by Gounod. Opera, February 28, 1862. Adap. by H. B. Farnie as *Irene*. Crystal Pal., August 12. 1865.

QUEEN OF SHEBA, THE. Comedy Novelty. 1 sc. Wr. by Austin P. Rubens. Surrey, May 8, 1909.

QUEEN OF SOCIETY. D. 3 a. C. Raleigh. Adelphi, February 5, 1903.

QUEEN OF SPADES, THE. D. 2 a. Adap. fr. "La Dame de Pique" by D. Boucicault. D.L., April 29, 1851.

QUEEN OF SPADES, THE. D. 4 a. Nita Rae. Blackburn Prince's, February 14, 1905 (C.P.).

QUEEN OF SPADES, THE. Bal. in 3 sc. Action and dances by Alfredo Curti. M. by Mario Costa. Alhambra, February 25, 1907.

QUEEN OF SPAIN; OR, FARINELLI AT MADRID, THE. M. Ent. J. Worsdale. Hay., 1744. N.p.

QUEEN OF THE ADRIATIC, THE. C.O. 1 a. G. Sheldon. Manchester Hulmer Hippo., November 25, 1907.

QUEEN OF THE FAIRIES. P. 2 sc. Sydney Blow. Lyrics by Douglas Hoare. M. by Edward Jones. London Coll., February 15, 1909.

QUEEN OF THE FROGS, THE. Fairy Extrav. 2 a. J. R. Planché. Lyceum, April 21, 1851.

QUEEN OF THE MARKET, THE. English ver. of *La Dame de la Halle*. Adelphi, 1852.

QUEEN OF THE MOOR. D. Prol., 4 a. Stoke Town Hall, December 26, 1899.

QUEEN OF THE NIGHT. D. 4 a. F. T. Tracy and I. Berlin. W. Bromwich New T.R., July 12, 1897; Stratford T.R., May 26, 1902.

QUEEN OF THE ROSE OF SALENCY. C From the French of Mme. Genlis. Pr. 1781.

QUEEN OF THE ROSES. Princess's, April 1850.

QUEEN OF THE ROSES, THE. C. 3 a. A. C. Calmour. Court, January 31, 1900; Wyndham's, June 13, 1902.

QUEEN OF THE THAMES; OR, THE ANGLERS. Oa. J. L. Hatton. 1 a. D.L, February 25, 1843.

QUEEN OF VILLAINY, A. D. Ridgewood Barrie. Greenwich Carlton, March 19, 1906.

QUEEN STORK. F. F. Waller. P.O.W., September 17, 1870.

QUEEN TOPAZ. See *La Reine Topaze*.

QUEEN TRAGEDY RESTOR'D. Dr. ent. Mrs. Hoper. Little T., Hay. Pr. 1749.

QUEEN WITHOUT A CROWN, A. Rom. P. Pro., 3 a. Arthur Shirley and Ben Landeck. Nottingham T.R., April 23, 1906.

QUEEN'S ARCADIA, THE. Past. T.C. S. Daniel. Christchurch Coll., Oxford, 1605, by University. Orig. called *Arcadia Restored*.

QUEEN'S BENCH, THE. F. 2 a. W. L. Ride. Strand, November 9, 1848.

QUEEN'S CASTLE, THE. C. 3 a. Robt. Wilford. Manchester St. James's, January 22, 1903.

QUEEN'S COLOURS, THE. D. 4 a. G. Conquest and H. Pettitt. Grecian, May 31, 1879.

QUEEN'S COMMAND, THE. D. 4 sc. W. Shakespeare. Lyceum, July 14, 1838.

QUEEN'S COUNSEL. F. 3 a. Adap. fr. *Les Pommes du Voisin* (C. by V. Sardou, f. upon *L'Aventure d'un Magistrat*, a story by Ch. de Bernard). J. Mortimer. Comedy, May 24, 1890.

QUEEN'S DOUBLE, THE. P. 4 a. Garrick, April 27, 1901.

QUEEN'S EVIDENCE. D. 4 a. G. Conquest and H. Pettitt. Grecian, June 5, 1876.

QUEEN'S EXCHANGE, THE. C. R. Brome. Blackfriars. Pr. 1657, and in 1661 as *The Royal Exchange*.

QUEEN'S FAVOURITE, THE. C. 4 a. Adap. fr. Scribe's *Le Verre d'Eau* by S. Grundy. Olympic, June 2, 1883.

QUEEN'S HOUSE, THE. Short P. 1 a. Mrs. C. Sim (Costume, Charles II.). MS. with Douglas Cox.

QUEEN'S JESTER, THE. C.O. Geo. H. Chitsam. Newport Lyceum, March 29, 1905; Worcester T.R., May 22, 1905.

QUEEN'S JEWELS; OR, THE PURITAN'S BRIDE, THE. D. 3 a. R. Dodson. E. London, November 25, 1876.

QUEEN'S MASQUES OF BEAUTY AND BLACKNESS, THE. Ben Jonson. Ac. at Court on Twelfth Night and at Whitehall, Beauty, 1608; Blackness, 1605.

QUEEN'S MESSENGER, A. P. 1 a. J. H. Manners, Haymarket (mat.), June 26, 1899; Avenue, October 6, 1899.

QUEEN'S MUSKETEERS, THE. C.O. 3 a. M. de St. Georges. M. Halévy. Perf. in Paris. D.L., August 3, 1846.

QUEEN'S NECKLACE. D. 4 a. D. M. Ford. F. in part on Dumas's novel, "Le Collet de la Reine." Stockport T.R., August 5, 1899.

QUEEN'S PARDON, THE. P. 4 a. J. H. Darnley. Cardiff T.R., August 19, 1897 (C.P.).

QUEEN'S PRIZE, THE. Ca. F. Mackay. Strand, November 21, 1894.

QUEEN'S PROCTOR; OR, DECREE NISI, THE. .C 3 a. Adap. by Herman Merivale fr. "Divorçons" by V. Sardou and E. de Najac. Royalty, February 28, 1896 (C.P.), and June 2, 1896; Strand, April 17, 1897.

QUEEN'S ROMANCE, A. 3 a. Ver. by J. Davidson of Victor Hugo's "Ruy Blas." Imperial, December 7, 1903 (C.P.), and December 11, 1904.

QUEEN'S ROOM, THE. Poetical P. 1 a. F. Moore. Op. C., October 20, 1891.

QUEEN'S SECRET. Adelphi, September 8, 1851.

QUEEN'S SHILLING, THE. C.D. 3 a. G. W. Godfrey. New ver. of *Le Fils de Famille* (Bayard and Bieville), already known on the English stage as *The Lancers*, 1853. Manchester Princes, October 12, 1877; Court, April 19, 1879.

QUEEN'S TRAGEDY, THE. P. 2 a. M. A. Curtois. St. Geo. H., October 13, 1899.

QUEEN'S VENGEANCE, A. Hist. D. 4 a. B. Ellis. Britannia, July 18, 1898.

QUEEN'S WAKE, THE. Masque. Ac. at Court in June, 1610.

QUEENS. Jonson. 1616.

QUEER LODGERS. F. A. A. Wilmot. Battersea Park T.H., March 1, 1800.

QUEER STREET. Dom. D. 2 a. R. Henry. Gaiety, March 21, 1892.

QUEER SUBJECT, THE. F. J. S. Coyne. Adelphi, 1837.

QUELLA'S CURSE. R. Col.-Sergeant F. W. Hopkins. Plymouth Marine T., November 6, 1900.

QUENTIN DURWARD. Announced (D., 5 a.), Maclean, about October 31, 1832. ? N. ac.

QUERER PER SOLO QUERER; TO LOVE ONLY FOR LOVE'S SAKE. P. 3 a. Transl. fr. Spanish of Antonio de Mendoza by Sir R. Fanshawe. Annexed to it is *Fiestas de Aranjeuz* (Festivals at Aranjeuz) by same author. Pr. 1671.

QUEST OF THE HOLY GRAIL, THE. Ernest Rhys. M. by Vincent Thomas. Court, July 3, 1908.

QUEST OF THE STAR, THE. Rom. Pastor. P. 1 a. Royal Botanical Gdns., June 17, 1907.

QUESTION, THE. P. 3 a. B. B. Ashford and J. S. Winter. Court, January 9, 1904.

QUESTION OF AGE, A. C. 3 a. Rob. Vernon Harcourt. Court, February 6, 1906.

QUESTION OF IDENTITY, A. P. 1 a. Archie J. Matthew. Court, March 14, 1909.

QUESTION OF MEMORY, A. D. 4 a. M. Field. Op. Comique, October 27, 1893.

QUESTION OF PROPERTY, A. P. 1 a. J. Sackville Martin. Margate T.R., January 13, 1908.

QUESTION OF THE DAY, THE. S.F. 1 a. L. Montague. Crediton T.H., January 14, 1903 (amat.) (C.P.).

QUESTION OF TIME, A. C. 1 a. F. Matthias Alexander and Evelyn Glover (suggested by an old English recitation). Coronet, October 26, 1908.

QUICK MARCH. C.O. 1 a. F. Wallerstein. Queen's, February 5, 1870.

QUICKSANDS. C.D. 4 a. Adap. fr. Mr. Lovett Cameron's novel, "A Devout Lover," by Charlotte E. Morland. Comedy, February 18, 1890.

QUICKSANDS; OR, THE PILLARS OF SOCIETY. P. 4 a. Adap. fr. the Norwegian of H. Ibsen by W. Archer. Gaiety, December 15, 1880.

QUICKSANDS AND WHIRLPOOLS. D. 4 a. R. Soutar. Victoria, March 21, 1868.

QUID PRO QUO. Vaude. Messrs. W. Bendall and Bridgman. Dilettante Circle, March 10, 1881. Revived as Oa. by W. Bendall. St. Geo. H., December 11, 1886.

QUID PRO QUO; OR, THE DAY OF DIYSES. C. Mrs. Gore. Hay., June 18, 1844.

QUIDNUNCS, THE. Moral Int. Pr. 1779.

QUIET CHATEAU, A. Ent. R. Reece. Gallery of Illus., December 26, 1867.

QUIET EVENING, A. C. 1 a. R. Bottomley. Brixton, May 12, 1902.

QUIET FAMILY, A. Orig. F. W. Suter. Surrey T., 1857.

QUIET IN HARNESS. C. 2 a. L. Rae. Standard, October 30, 1876.

QUIET LODGINGS. C.D. F. J. Stein. Blyth Octagon, October 30, 1872.

QUIET PIPE, A. Dom. Sc. Miss Cowen and S. M. Samuel. Folly, March 17, 1880.

QUIET RUBBER, A. C. 1 a. Adap. fr. the French, *La Partie de Piquet*, by C. F. Coghlan. Court, January 8, 1876.

QUIET WEDDING, A. F. 1 a. Walter Frith. MS. with Douglas Cox.

QUILP; OR, THE WANDERINGS OF LITTLE NELL. D. T. S. Paulton. Wolverhampton P.O.W., April 10, 1871.

QUINTUS FABIUS. Ac. by the children of Windsor. 1574.

QUIP FOR AN UPSTART COURTIER, A. C. Greene. 1592.

QUIPROQUO, LE. O. 2 a. Philidor. 1760.

QUITE ALONE. D. Miss Rose Evans. Gt. Yarmouth T.R., May 25, 1874.

QUITE AN ADVENTURE. Oa. F. Desprez. M. by E. Solomon. Olympic, September 7, 1881.

QUITE AT HOME! C. Ent. 1 a. R. Ryan. Adap. fr. French of "Sans Gêne." Lyceum Playbill, November 5, 1835; English Op. H., 1836.

QUITE BY ACCIDENT. F. F. Walters. P.O.W., September 11, 1869.

QUITE CORRECT. C. 3 a. From French piece, *Slanderer*. Hay., July 29, 1825.

QUITE THE DON QUIXOTE. Burl. 2 a. G. D. Lynch. M., C. Young. Ladbroke H., June 12, 1893.

QUITS. Oa. M. by J. Crook. Lib., B. T. Hughes. Avenue, October 1, 1888. St. James's H., November 10, 1884.

QUITS. P. 1 a. Roland Bottomley. Bedford Pk. St. Alban's H., November 18, 1904 (C.P.).

QUITS; OR, THE LUCKY BAG OF LIFE. D. 3 a. C. H. Stephenson and J. Brougham. Belfast T.R., August 29, 1870.

QUO VADIS. Adap. fr. Sienkiewicz's novel by W. Barrett. Edinburgh Lyceum, May 29, 1900; Kennington Princess of Wales's T., June 18, 1900.

QUO VADIS? P. 6 a. fr. Henryk Sienkiewicz's novel by S. Strange. Adelphi, May 5, 1900.

QUONG HI. F.C. 3 a. F. Mackay. Bristol Prince's, April 1, 1895; Terry's, June 27, 1895; Avenue, July 27, 1895.

R

R.F. AND M.F. P. 1 a. Croydon New, June 25, 1900.

RABAGES. C. Sardou. 1872.

RABBI JOSELMANN. O. Goldfaden (in Yiddish), Novelty, March 31, 1896.

RABBI'S SON; OR, THE LAST LINK IN THE CHAIN, THE. D. 4 a. E. Manuel. Britannia, April 14, 1879.

RABENVATER, EIN. F.C. 3 a. H. Fischer and J. Jarno. Gt. Queen St., January 13, 1905.

RACE FOR A DINNER; OR, NO DINNER YET, A. F. 1 a. Adap. fr. French by T. G. Rodwell. C.G., April 15, 1828.

RACE FOR A WIDOW, A. F. 1 a. T. J. Williams. Strand, April 23, 1860.

RACE FOR A WIFE, A. Ca. F. Cooper. Adelphi, August 19, 1876.

RACE FOR A WIFE, A. M.C.D. 3 a. H. Darnley. Walsall Grand T., November 3, 1897 (C.P.); T.R., Stratford, April 11, 1898.

RACE FOR HONOUR, A. Sk. Prod. by C. H. Barker. Camberwell Empire, December 3, 1906.

RACE OF LIFE, THE. D. 4 a. J. W. Whitbread. Dublin Queen's T., November 21, 1887.

RACHEL. D. Prol. and 3 a. Partly fr. "La Voleuse d'Enfants" of E. Grange and L. Thiboust by S. Grundy. Olympic, April 14, 1883.

RACHEL. Dr. Sk. 1 a. Miss Clo Graves. Hay., May 7, 1890.

RACHEL AND LEAH. D. (in Hebrew). Standard, September 25, 1896.

RACHEL THE REAPER. D. 2 a. C. Reade. Queen's. March 9, 1874.

RACHEL'S MESSENGER. P. 1 a. M. Watson. Princess's, February 28, 1891.

RACHEL'S PENANCE; OR, A DAUGHTER OF ISRAEL. D. 4 a. E. Manuel. Britannia, April 22, 1878.

RACING. Melo-d. G. H. Macdermott. Wolverhampton Standard, April 5, 1886; Islington Grand, September 5, 1887.

RADAMISTO. O. Handel. 1720.

RADICAL; OR, THE HONOUR OF THE HOUSE, THE. C.D. 3 a. E. Genet. Walham Green Beaufort H., November 6, 1888.

RADICAL CANDIDATE. F.C. A. Fryers. Crystal Palace, October 30, 1899.

RADICAL CANDIDATE, THE. Ca. Hugo Aimes. Margate R.T., February 18, 1907.

RAFALE, LA. D. 3 a. Henri Bernstein. (Orig. prod. at Paris, October 20, 1905). London Royalty, January 12, 1906. Eng. vers. under title of *The Whirlwind* at Birmingham T.R., April 9, 1906, and Cri., May 23, 1906 (rev.); Shaftesbury, April 5, 1908.

RAFFAEL CIMARO. P. T. J. Serle. Publ. 1819.

RAFFAELLE THE REPROBATE; OR, THE SECRET MISSION AND THE SIGNET RING. D. 2 a. T. E. Wilks. R. Victoria, September 13, 1841.

RAFFLES, THE AMATEUR CRACKSMAN. P. 4 a. W. Hornung and E. W. Presberey. Comedy, May 12, 1906.

RAFT; OR, BOTH SIDES OF THE WATER, THE. M. Int. J. C. Cross. C.G., March 31, 1798. Songs only publ., 1798.

RAG FAIR. D. 5 a. H. Wigan. Victoria, May 20, 1872.

RAGE, THE. C. F. Reynolds. C.G., October 23, 1794.

RAGGED JACK. D. H. J. Stanley. Liverpool Rotunda, May 24, 1880.

RAGGED MESSENGER, THE. P. 4 a. W. B. Maxwell and Geo. Paston. Adap. fr. the novel. Broadway, September 15, 1905 (C.P.).

RAGGED ROBIN. P. 1 a. F. Bowyer and W. Sprange. Southampton P.O.W., March 17, 1893.

RAGGED ROBIN. P. 4 a. Adap. fr. J. Richepin's drama, *Le Chemine*. Odéon, Paris, February 16, 1897; H.M., June 23, 1898.

RAGGED UPROAR; OR, THE OXFORD RORATORY, THE. D. Satire. Many scenes and 1 long a. Joan Plotwell and others. N.d.

RAGING TURK; OR, BAJAZET II., THE. T. Rev. T. Goffe. Students of Christchurch, Oxford.

RAGPICKER OF PARIS AND THE DRESSMAKER OF S. ANTOINE, THE. D. 3 a. and pro. E. Stirling. Surrey, June 23, 1847.

RAGS. Western American Mus. Sk. Horwich Prince's, March 1, 1909; Stratford R., June 21, 1909.

RAGS AND BONES. D. F. A. Scudamore. Cardiff T.R., July 23, 1883. Surrey, July 30, 1883.

RAID IN THE TRANSVAAL; OR, THE KING OF DIAMONDS, THE. Revised ver. of *The King of Diamonds*. Surrey, April 12, 1884, and March 2, 1896.

RAIGNE OF KING EDWARD THE THIRD, THE. Anon. Pr. 1596.

RAILROAD OF LOVE. Adap. fr. F. von Schoentham and G. Kadelberg's "Goldfische" by Aug. Daly. Gaiety, May 3, 1888; Daly's, June 25, 1895.

RAILROAD OF LOVE, THE. See *The Clutterbucks*.

RAILROAD STATION, THE. F. 1 a. T. E. Wilks. Olympic. October 3, 1840.

RAILWAY ADVENTURE, A. C. 1 a. F. on Viremsin's dr. sk. *En Wagon* by C. Cheltman.

RAILWAY BELLE, THE. F. 1 a. M. Lemon. Adelphi, November 20, 1854.

RAILWAY OF LIFE. Effingham, September 26, 1859.

RAIN CLOUDS. Dr. Sk. 1 a. W. R. Walkes. Queen's H., Langham Place, May 21, 1894; Portman Rooms, Baker Street, June 28, 1895.

RAIN DEARS, THE. Sk. London Hipp., December 21, 1908.

RAINY DAY, A. Oa. Words by Miss A. Smith. M. by Miss Virginia Gabriel. Gallery of Illus., May 23, 1868 (amat.).

RAINY DAY, A. C. 1 a. Agnes Leigh. Publ. by S. French, Ltd.

RAISED FROM THE ASHES. D. F. Fuller. Eleph. and C., May 31, 1879.

RAISING OF LAZARUS, THE. Orat., J. F. Barnett. June, 1838.

RAISING THE WIND. F. 2 a. J. Kenney. C.G., November 5, 1803.

RAJAH DE MYSORE, LE, O. 1 a. C. Lecocq. Park T., 1875.

RAKE AND HIS PUPIL, THE. D. 3 a. J. B. Buckstone. Adelphi, 1833.

RAKE'S PROGRESS, THE. D. 3 a. W. L. Rede. City, February, 1832; Queen's, January 23, 1833.

RAKE'S WIFE, THE. P. 4 a. Helen Wade and F. Herbert. Kingston County, July 8, 1901; Peckham Crown, May 16, 1904.

RAKE'S WILL, THE. P. 1 a. H. P. Grattan. Terry's, July 16, 1889.

RALPH GASTON. Surrey, September 17, 1860.

RALPH ROISTER DOISTER. Nicholas Udall. Taken fr. *Miles Gloriousus* of Plautus (first English comedy). 1551, or earlier. Ent. Stationers' H., 1566.

RAM ALLEY; OR, MERRY TRICKS. C. L. Barry. "Children of the Revels" acted it. Pr. 1611.

RAMAH DROOG; OR, WINE DOES WONDERS. C.O. J. Cobb. M. by Massinghi and Reeve. D.L., 1798. Reduced to 2 a. and perf. as an after-piece, May, 1805. D.L., December 18, 1816.

RAMBLING JUSTICE; OR, THE JEALOUS HUSBANDS, WITH THE HUMOURS OF JOHN TWYFORD. Greater part taken fr. Middleton's *More Dissemblers Besides Women*. C. J. Leanard. D.L., Pr. 1678 and in 1680 as *The Jealous Husbands, with the Humours of John Twyford, and the Rambling Justice*. T.R., 1680.

RAMBLING LADY. C. Southerne.

RAMPANT ALDERMAN; OR, NEWS FROM THE EXCHANGE, THE. F. Anon. Pr. 1685.

RAMSBOTTOMS AT RHEIMS. P. 2 a. C.G., July 11, 1825.

RAMSHAKEL THE GREAT. C.O. 2 a. S. Lamprey. Maidstone Corn Exchange, December 9, 1902 (amat.).

RANCHMAN'S ROMANCE, THE. P. 3 a. Constance Bromley. Leeds Queen's, June 20, 1906.

RANDALL, EARL OF CHESTER. P. T. Middleton. Ac. by Lord Admiral's servants, 1602.

RANDALL'S THUMB. C. 3 a. W. S. Gilbert. Court (opening), January 25, 1871.

RANDOLPH THE RECKLESS. Op. extrav. 2 a. V. Stevens. Salford P.O.W., August 6, 1888; Eleph. and C., September 9, 1889; Cork O.H. (new ver.), June 1, 1894.

RANELAGH. C.D. 2 a. J. P. Simpson and C. Wray. Hay., February 11, 1851.

RANGER IN WEDLOCK; OR, THE AMIABLE MISTAKE. C. Mr. Silvester. Hay., 1788. N.p.

RANGER'S COMEDY, THE. Ac. by Queen's men and Lord Sussex together. 1593. N.p.

RANK. C. Newcastle Tyne T., November 20, 1871.

RANK AND FAME. D. 5 a. L. Rae and F. Stainforth. Standard, March 29, 1875.

RANK AND RICHES. P. 4 a. and 5 tab. W. Collins. Adelphi, June 9, 1883.

RANSOM, THE. Planché. Hay., 1836.

RANSOM OF MANILLA; OR, ENGLAND'S ALLY, THE. Hist. P. R. G. Lee. Pr. 1793.

RANSOM'S FOLLY. P. R. H. Davis. D. of York's, July 21, 1903 (C.P.).

RANTZAU, I. O. 4 a. Lib. by G. Targioni-Tozetti and G. Menasci. F. on Erckmann Chatrian's novel. M. by Pietro Mascagni. Florence, November 10, 1892; C.G., July 7, 1893.

RAPE, THE T. L.I.F. Brady's P. alt.

RAPE; OR, INNOCENT IMPOSTORS, THE. T. Dr. Brady. Epil. by Mr. Shadwell. D.L., 1682; rev. with alts. at L.I.F., March 25, 1729.

RAPE OF EUROPA BY JUPITER, THE. M. Anon. Queen's in Dorset Gardens, by Their Majesties' servants. Pr. 1694.

RAPE OF HELEN, THE. Mock O. J. Breval. C.G., May 19, 1733.

RAPE OF LUCRECE, THE. Rom. T. T. Heywood. Red Bull, 1638.

RAPE OF PROSPERINE, THE. Pant. L. Theobald. M., Mr. Gaillard. T.R. in L.I.F. Pr. 1725.

RAPE OF THE SECOND HELEN. 1578-9.

RAPE UPON RAPE; OR, THE JUSTICE CAUGHT IN HIS OWN TRAP. C. Title under which Fielding's "Coffee-House Politician" was pr. in 1730.

RAPHAEL'S DREAM: OR, THE EGYPTIAN IDOL AND ARTIST'S STUDY. Invented, prod., and perf. by Ducrow (studies of ancient statues). D.L., March 17, 1534.

RAPHAELE REPROBATE. D. 2 a. Publ. by S. French, Ltd.

RAPHELINA, THE GIPSY MOTHER. D. Prol. and 4 a. Dumfries T.R., October 13, 1879.

RAPID THAW, A. C. 2 a. Adap. by T. W. Robertson. St. James's, March 2, 1867.

RAPPACINI'S DAUGHTER. See *The Poison Flower*.

RAPPAREE; OR, THE TREATY OF LIMERICK, THE. Irish D. 3 a. D. Boucicault. Princess's, September 9, 1870.

RAPPINGS AND TABLE-MOVINGS. Orig. F. 1 a. Howard Paul. Haymarket, June 16, 1853.

RAPPRESENTAZIONE. Orat. Emilio del Cavaliere. Rome, 1600.

RARE CHANCE OF LOVE AND FORTUNE. Probably another name for following.

RARE TRIUMPHS OF LOVE AND FORTUNE, THE. C. ? E. White. Ac. between 1581 and February, 1582. Pr. 1589.

RAREE SHOW; OR, THE FOX TRAP'T, THE. O. J. Petersen. Pr. and ac. at York, 1739.

RASSELAS, PRINCE OF ABYSSINIA; OR, THE HAPPY VALLEY. Extrav. F. on Dr. Johnson's story by W. Brough. Hay., December 26, 1862.

RASELLE, THE BOY MUSICIAN. Melo.-d. Prol. 2 a. A. Millard. Manchester Queen's, April 19, 1909.

RATHBOYS, THE. Standard, May 17, 1862.

RATIONAL DRESS. C. 1 a. I. Cassilis. Publ. by S. French, Ltd.

RATS. Duo. 1 a. W. A. Mackersy.

RATS OF RATS' CASTLE. J. B. Johnstone.

RATTENFANGER VON HAMELN, DER. Nessler. O.

RATTLIN, THE REEFER; OR, THE TIGER OF THE SEA. Naut. D. 3 a. J. L. Haines. Victoria, August 22, 1836.

RAUB DER SUBINERINNEN, DER. F.C. Franz von Schoenthum (Prod. as *A Night Off*). Strand, March 27, 1886; Opera Comique, October 31, 1894; St. Geo. Hall, February 9, 1900.

RAUBER, DIE. D.L., June 6, 1881; Opera Comique, November 9, 1894.

RAUF RUSTER DUSTER. See *Ralph*, etc.

RAVEN'S OAK. Ca. N. Wheatcroft. Warrington Public H., September, 1882.

RAVENS; OR, FORCE OF CONSCIENCE. Rom. D. Attrib. to Pocock. C.G., January 28, 1817.

RAVENS OF ORLEANS, THE. D. Moncrieff. Victoria, 1822.

RAVENSWOOD. P. 4 a. Adap. by H. Merivale fr. Sir W. Scott's "The Bride of Lammermoor." Lyceum, September 20, 1890. See *Master of Ravenswood*.

RAW CAROTTE, LE. Burl. G. Thorne. Margate T.R., September 19, 1873.

RAW RECRUIT, A. Oa. 1 a. C. Bellamy. M., Popsie Rowe. Wolverhampton Star, 1889.

RAY OF LIGHT, THE. C.D. Park, October 14, 1876.

RAY OF SUNLIGHT, A. P. 1 a. H. W. C. Newte. Bayswater Bijou, April 27, 1896.

RAYMOND. T. Pr. 1793.

RAYMOND AND AGNES; OR, THE CASTLE OF LINDENBURGH. Bal. Farley. Taken fr. T. Lewis's "The Monk" and Dr. Smollett's "Count Fathom." C.G., March 16, 1797.

RAYMOND AND AGNES. Rom. Eng. O. 3 a. Words by E. Fitzball. M. by E. J. Loder. Manchester, 1855; St. James's T., June 11, 1859.

RAYMOND AND AGNES; OR, THE BLEEDING NUN OF LINDENBURGH. Melo-d. 2 a. H. W. Grosette. Pl. as Ballet of Action. C.G., June 1, 1797; Lyceum playbill, July 5, 1819.

RAYMOND AND AGNES; THE TRAVELLERS BENIGHTED; OR, THE BLEEDING NUN OF LINDENBURGH. D. 2 a. M. G. Lewis. C.G.

RAYMOND, DUKE OF LYONS. Anon. 1613. N.p. Ac. at Court.

RAYMOND REMMINGTON. D. 1 a. W. Ashdowne. St. Alban's County H., December 11, 1893.

RAYNER. T. Joanna Baylie. Pr. 1804.

RE DI LAHORE, IL. Ital. O. 5 a. Gillett and Massenet. C.G., June 28, 1879.

RE PASTORE, IL. O. Mozart. Salisbury, 1775. First prod. April 23, 1775.

RE TEODORO. O. Paisello. 1785.

REACTIO. Satyre IV. J. Marston. Circa 1598.

READ AND WONDER. Probably wr. by George Wither. 1641.

READING FOR THE BAR. F. S. Grundy. Strand, October 2, 1876.

READY AND WILLING. D. 3 a. E. Towers. Effingham, May 13, 1867.

READY MONEY MORTIBOY. D. 4 a. F. on Besant and Rice's novel. W. Maurice and J. Rice. Court, March 12, 1874; Belfast T.R., January 28, 1878.

REAL AND IDEAL. C. 1 a. H. Wigan. Olympic, September 8, 1862.

REAL CASE OF HYDE AND SEEKYLL, THE. M.F. G. Grossmith. Royalty, September 3, 1888.

REAL EAST LYNNE, THE. Ina Leon Cassilis. Woolwich Royal Artillery, May 26, 1902.

REAL JACK, THE. Sk. by the Lupinos. M. by Joseph Tabrar. Empress, November 11, 1907.

REAL LADY MACBETH, A. F. E. Copping. Royal Park H., Camden Town, April 1, 1889.

REAL LIFE. C.D. 4 a. E. C. Bleackley. Manchester Queen's, December 9, 1872.

REAL LIFE. Rom. D. 4 a. R. Dodson. Surrey, August 21, 1882.

REAL LITTLE LORD FAUNTLEROY, THE. P. 3 a. Adap. by Mrs. Frances Hodgson Burnett fr. her own novel, "Little Lord Fauntleroy." Terry's, May 14, 1888.

REAL MR. JONATHAN, THE. F.C. 3 a. Mr. C. Vernon Proctor. Paignton Pier Pav., June 15, 1908.

REAL PRINCE, A. P. 1 a. Mrs. W. Greet. Bayswater Bijou, November 27, 1894.

REAL TRUTH ABOUT IVANHOE; OR, SCOTT SCOTCHED, THE. Burl. E. C. Nugent. M. by E. Solomon. Chelsea Barracks, February 1, 1889.

REAL WOMAN, THE. P. 3 a. Robert Hichens. Criterion, February 25, 1909.

REALISM. Ca. 1 a. Madeleine Lucette Ryley. Garrick, October 4, 1900.

REALITY. D. 4 a. C. Rogers. Barnsley T.R., December 30, 1889.

REALMS OF JOY, THE. F. F. L. Tomline. Royalty, October 18, 1873.

REAPER, THE. D. 1 a. S. Pritchard. Chiswick Town H., April 15, 1902.

REAPERS, THE. D. 2 a. S. Pritt. Preston T.R., June 21, 1897.

REAPERS; OR, FORGET AND FORGIVE, THE. D. 2 a. E. Stirling. Strand, August 4, 1856.

REAPERS; OR, THE ENGLISHMAN OUT OF PARIS, THE. O. Transl. of *Les Moissonneurs*. Pr. 1770.

REAPING THE HARVEST. D. Prol. and 3 a. A. Stafford. Woolwich T.R., June 27, 1887 (prod. as *True Grit*); Eleph. and C., December 3, 1887.

REAPING THE WHIRLWIND. Ca. H. Lennard. Novelty, April 26, 1884.

REAPING THE WHIRLWIND. P. 1 a. Allan Monkhouse. Manchester Gaiety, September 28, 1908.

REASONABLE ANIMALS, THE. Sat. Sk. Hay. Pr. 1782.

REBECCA. Orat. Smith. 1761.

REBECCA. D. 4 a. A. Halliday. D.L., September 23, 1871.

REBEKAH. Cant. Lib. by A. Matthison. M. by J. Barnaby. St. James's H., May 11, 1870.

REBEL'S WIFE, THE. D. 3 a. F. Jarman. Consett New T., December 8, 1898; Britannia, June 5, 1899.

REBELLION, THE. T. T. Rawlins. Ac. by H.M. Company of Revels. Pr. 1640.

REBELLION DEFEATED; OR, THE FALL OF DESMOND. T. J. Cutts. Pr. 1745.

REBELLION OF NAPLES; OR, THE TRAGEDY OF MASSINELLO, THE. See *Eye Witness*.

REBELS, THE. P. 4 a. Jas. B. Fagan. Camberwell Metropole, September 4, 1899.

RECALLED. C. Parkstone St. Peter's H., December 26, 1901.

RECALLED TO LIFE. D. Prol. and 4 a. J. J. Hewson. West Bromwich T.R., October 10, 1885; Shoreham Swiss Gardens, July 28, 1888.

RECEIPT TAX, THE. F. J. Dent. Hay., August 13, 1783. Pr. 1783.

RECEIPTED. Dr. Sk. Ellen Wallis and Mrs. Kirkham. Coronet, April 14, 1908. (C.P.)

RECEPTION, THE. P. 3 a. Chaplain in the Navy. Pr. at Plymouth, 1799.

RECESS, THE. Miss Lea. 1785.

RECKONING, THE. P. 3 a. E. Genet. Chelsea T.H., May 4, 1891.

RECKONING, THE. P. 4 a. S. Dauncey. Globe, December 3, 1891 (mat.); Grand, May 13, 1895.

RECKONING, THE. P. 1 a. S. Houghton and F. G. Nasmith. Manchester Queen's, July 22, 1907.

RECKONING DAY, THE. C.D. Wolverhampton T.R. and O.H., January, 1885.

RECLAIMED. C. 4 a. Adap. by J. Mortimer fr. *Les Vieux Garçons* of V. Sardou. Hay., September 14, 1881.

RECLAIMED; OR, BARWISE'S BOOK. C. 2 a. H. T. Craven. MS. with Douglas Cox.

RECLUSE, THE. O.D. 2 a. M. by Caraffa. Arr. for English stage by Horn. D.L., June 14, 1825.

RECOLLECTION OF O'FLANNIGAN AND THE FAIRIES, A. Extrav. 1 a. J. Brougham. Broadway New York.

RECOMMENDED TO MERCY. D. Prol. and 4 a. Adap. fr. Miss Braddon's novel, "Joshua Haggard" by W. Jones. Harrogate T.H., May 6, 1882; Dewsbury T.R., October 12, 1882; Pavilion, July 2, 1883.

RECONCILED; OR, GOOD FOR EVIL. Dom. C. 1 a. P. Gwynne and C. Harrison. Lincoln T.R., November 3, 1888.

RECONCILIATION, THE. P. 1 a. D.L., April 26, 1813.

RECONCILIATION, THE. Ca. G. F. Neville. Olympic, February 21, 1876.

RECONCILIATION; OR, THE BIRTHDAY. C. 5 a. Transl. fr. Kotzebue by C. Ludger. Pr. 1799. *The Birthday*, by T. Dibdin, taken from this.

RECONCILIATION; OR, THE TWO BROTHERS. Mentioned by Brewer.

RECONCILIATION NORMANDE. C. Dufresny. 1719.

RECRIMINATION; OR, A CURTAIN LECTURE. C. Clarke, 1813. D.L., April 22, 1813. N.p.

RECRUIT, THE. M.Int. Dumfries T., 1704; Lyceum, September 9, 1829.

RECRUITING MANAGER, THE. Prel. W. C. Oulton. 1785. N.p.

RECRUITING OFFICER, THE. C. 5 a. G. Farquhar. D.L., April 8, 1706; rev., February 27, 1816.

RECRUITING PARTY, THE. Military Sk. 3 sc. Earl of Kilmorey, K.P. Shrewsbury T.R., January 14, 1895.

RECRUITING SERGEANT, THE. M. by Dibdin. 1769.

RECRUITING SERGEANT, THE. M.E. I. Bickerstaff. Pr. 1770. D.L., June 3, 1789.

RECTOR; A STORY OF FOUR FRIENDS, THE. P. 4 a. A. W. Pinero. Court, March 24, 1883.

RECTOR'S DAUGHTER, THE. Ca. 2 sc. J. D. C. Strettell. *Matinée*, May 20, 1898.

RED AND BLUE. F.C. 3 a. F. F. Forshaw. Wolverhampton T.R., December 19, 1892.

RED AND WHITE EARTH. P. 4 a E. C. Thurston. Cork O.H., October 20, 1902.

RED BARN, THE. D. 4 a. G. Cower and L. Ellis. Barrow Alhambra, June 10, 1892.

RED COAT, THE. C.D. 4 a. B. Williams. West London, June 21, 1900.

RED CARNATIONS. C. 1 a. I. Aitken. Bayswater Bijou, March 21, 1901.

RED CROSS, THE. Military D. 1 a. D. Moore. Consett T.R., December 16, 1901.

RED CROSS KNIGHTS. P. 5 a. J. G. Holman. Hay., August 21, 1799. F. on Schiller's *The Robbers.*

RED DECK. D. Bolton O.H., December 8, 1873.

RED DWARF; OR, MYSTERY AND VENGEANCE, THE. D. Eleph. and C., April 21, 1873.

RED HANDS. D. Prol. and 3 a. Gilbert à Beckett. St. James's. January 30, 1869.

RED HUSSAR, THE. C.O. 3 a. H. P. Stephens. Lyric, November 23, 1889, to May 24, 1890.

RED JOSEPHINE. D. Mrs. S. Lane. Britannia, November 5, 1880.

RED KNAVE, THE. P. 1 a. A. E. Drinkwater. Coronet, March 17, 1902.

RED LAMP, THE. D. 4 a. W. O. Tristram. Comedy, April 20, 1887; Her M., June 12, 1897; rev., H.M., March 16, 1907.

RED LETTER, THE. Sk. H. Leslie Bell. Rochdale Circus, March 11, 1907.

RED LIGHT; OR, THE SIGNAL OF DANGER, THE. D. H. J. Stanley. Longton T.R., September 28, 1874; Liverpool Adelphi, March 29, 1897.

RED MAN'S RIFLE, THE. D. C. H. Hazlewood. Britannia, December 26, 1874.

RED MARINE; OR, THE SPECTRE'S COMPACT, THE. Supernatural C. Oa. C. W. Cottingham. Brighton Preston Assembly R., May 28, 1896.

RED MASK; OR, THE COUNCIL OF THREE, THE. Op.D. 3 a. (Paris as *Il Bravo.*) Adap. by Cooke. D.L., November 15, 1834.

RED POTTAGE. 4 a. D. M. Cholmondeley and F. Kinsey Peile. St. James's, October 2, 1900 (C.P.).

RED RAG, A. Ca. Adap. fr. the French of G. Ohnet by J. H. McCarthy. Toole's, February 18, 1888.

RED REEF. D. Bannister and Woods. Walsall Alexandra, September 8, 1884.

RED RIDER, THE. O. 1 a. P. Davey and A. P. Poley. Composed by J. W. Ivimey. St. Geo. H., March 23, 1895.

RED RIDING HOOD. Burl. Adelpi. Circa 1850.

RED ROB, THE COINER. Marylebone, June 6, 1863.

RED ROSES. Ep. 1 a. Lottie Blair Parker. D. of Y., November 12, 1898.

RED ROVER, THE. D. E. Fitzball. Adap. fr. Cooper's novel. Adelphi, 1829.

RED ROVER, THE. Burl. F. C. Burnand. Strand, December 26, 1877.

RED ROY; OR, OSWYN AND HELEN. Hist. bal. Hay., August, 1803.

RED SCARF, THE. Sk. Metropolitan, July 5, 1909.

RED SHOES, THE. Ballet. 4 tab, 5 scs. M. R. Mader. Alhambra, January 30, 1899.

RED SIGNAL, THE. D. 4 a. E. J. Lampard. Pontypridd Clarence, June 17, 1892 (C.P.); Birkenhead T.R., October 17, 1892.

RED SNOW. D. H. Mandeville. Londonderry Queen's, January 13, 1873.

RED SPIDER, THE. C.O. 3 a. Lib. S. Baring-Gould. M. by L. Drysdale. Lowestoft Marina, July 25, 1898.

RED SQUADRON. D. 4 a. J. Harkins, jun., and J. Macmahon. Bayswater Bijou, August 9, 1894 (C.P.); Pavilion, February 18, 1895.

RED STAR, THE. D. 4 a. Ilkeston T.R., July 10, 1894.

RED TAPE. C.

RED TERROR, THE. D. 4a. H. Whyte. Londonderry O.H., August 6, 1900; Edmonton T.R., August 10, 1903.

RED VIAL, THE. D. W. Collins. Olympic, October 11, 1858.

RED, WHITE, AND BLUE. Oa. G. H. Bush and E. A. Stunt. Vaudeville Club, Carter Street, Walworth, February 3, 1875.

REDAMISTO. O. Handel.

REDEEMED. Dr. Story. 3 a. J. Coggan. Vaudeville, June 7, 1883.

REDEMPTION. Orat. Dr. Arnold. 1786.

REDEMPTION. Orat. Coxe. Before 1814.

REDEMPTION. Orat. Gounod. First perf. at Birmingham Festival, August 30, 1882.

REDEMPTION OF AGNES, THE. It. Mediæval Relig. P. 3 a. W. Poel. Brighton R.T., February 15, 1907.

REDOWALD. M. Hazard. 1767.

REDSKINS, THE. Spec. 5 sc. A. Ramsay and R. de Cordova. Situations invented by A. Hengler. M. by C. C. Corri. Rev. Hippodrome, July 2, 1903; April 18, 1905. See *The Last of His Race.*

REFEREE, THE. Rev. ver. of *The Undergraduates.* C. 3 a. W. O. Tristram. Op. Comique, October 6, 1886; Vaudeville, December 21, 1886.

REFFLEY SPRING. O. Dr. Arne. 1772.

REFLECTION. Int. D.L., December 13, 1834.

REFORM. F. S. Foote, jun. Pr. 1792.

REFORMATION, THE. C. Arrowsmith. Duke's, 1673.

REFORMATION, THE. F. C.G., June 28, 1815.

REFORMED COQUETTE, THE. F. Pr. in the "Lady's Magazine" for the years 1787-1788.

REFORMED IN TIME. C.O. 2 a. C.G., May 23, 1798.

REFORMED RAKE, A. C. 3 a. P. Hardwicke and W. E. Grogan. Edinburgh Lyceum, February 14, 1902; Coronet, November 13, 1908.

REFORMED WIFE, THE. C. C. Burnaby. D.L., 1700; and D.L., October 31, 1707.

REFORMER, THE. Light C. 3 a. Cyril Harcourt. Court, January 8, 1907.

REFORMING A BURGLAR. M.F. C. James and V. Matthews. Steinway H., May 26, 1904.

REFUGEES, THE. Ca. J. M. Campbell. Adelphi, July 19, 1888.

REFUSAL; OR, THE LADIES' PHILOSOPHY, THE. C. Bor. in part fr. *Female Virtuosis,* which was partly transl. fr. the French by C. Cibber. D.L., February 14, 1721; C.G., D.L., October 5, 1817. (See *No Fools Like,* etc.)

REFUSAL OF HARLEQUIN, THE. Pant. C. Dibdin. Act. at the Circus. N.p.

REGAN-NA-GLENNA. D. F. Addersley. Cambridge T.R., September 16, 1878.

REGENERATES, THE. Travesty of Mr. Grundy's p., *The Degenerates.* Comedy, October 30, 1899.

REGENERE. Mono. M. G. Nazim. Royalty; January 31, 1889.

REGENT, THE. T. B. Greatheed. D.L., April 14, 1788. Pr. 1788.

REGENT, LE. V. Ancelot. 1831.

REGENT, THE. C. 2 a. D.L., October, 1834.

REGENT, THE. D. 2 a. January 8, 1855.

REGICIDE; OR, JAMES I. OF SCOTLAND, THE. T. Dr. Smollett. Pr. 1749.

REGICIDUM. T.C. Braithwaite. 1665.

REGIMENT, THE. C.D. 3 a. S. Osborn. Eleph. and C., May 12, 1888.

REGIMENTAL KIDDY, THE. F.C. 3 a. Adap. fr. French by P. Montague and De Villiers. Newcastle-on-Tyne T.R., May 25, 1903; Fulham Grand, September 14, 1903.

REGINA, B.A. O. 2 a. A. Sturgess and J. M. Glover. Birmingham Grand, August 2, 1897.

REGINA DI CIPRO, LA. O. Piccini. Turin, 1846.

REGINA DIGALCONDA, LA. O. Ranzzini. 1784.

REGINA DI SCOZIA, LA. O. 3 a. Mrs. E. M. Stuart Stress. Novelty, July 14, 1883.

REGIO. O. Scarlatti. 1713.

REGIONS OF ACCOMPLISHMENT, THE. M. Ent. C. Dibdin. Ac. at the Circus. N.p.

REGISTER OFFICE, THE. Ent. 2 a. E. Morton. Pr. at Salop, 1758.

REGISTER OFFICE, THE. F. 2 a. J. Reed. D.L., April 25, 1761. Pr. 1761.

REGISTRAR, THE. P. 1 a. D. Shtitzer. Beaumont H., E., June 14, 1909 (amat.).

REGISTRY OFFICE, THE. C.O. Miss Eleanor Farjeon. M. by H. Farjeon. St. George's H., June 29, 1900.

REGULAR FIX, A. F. 1 a. J. M. Morton. Olympic, October 11, 1860.

REGULAR TURK, A. F. R. Soutar. Gaiety, February 3, 1877.

REGULATORS, THE. C. G. Lillo.

REGULUS. T. J. Crowne. Ac. by Their Majesties' servants, T.R., 1694.

REGULUS. T. Pradon.

REGULUS. T. C. J. Dorat.

REGULUS. T. Hannah More. 1774.

REGULUS. T. W. Havard. T.R., 1744.

REGULUS. O. Transl. fr. *Metastasio*. J. Hoole. Pr. 1800.

REHEARSAL, THE. C. George Villiers. D. of Buckingham. D.L., 1671. Pr. 1672.

REHEARSAL, THE. Afterpiece. 3 a. The foregoing P. alt. by R. Wilson. Edinburgh and London.

REHEARSAL, THE. J. Moser. Pr., 1809, in the "European Magazine."

REHEARSAL; OR, A SECOND PART OF MRS. CONFUSION'S TRAVAIL AND HARD LABOUR SHE ENDURED IN THE BIRTH OF HER FIRST MONSTROUS OFFSPRING, THE CHILD OF DEFORMITY, THE HOPEFUL FRUIT OF SEVEN YEARS' TEEMING, AND A PRECIOUS BABE OF GRACE, DELIVERED IN THE YEAR 1648 by MERCURIUS BRITANICUS, THE. Pr. in the year 1718.

REHEARSAL; OR, BAYES IN PETTICOATS, THE. C. 2 a. Mrs. Clive. D.L. Pr. 1753. March 15, 1750.

REHEARSAL AT GOTHAM, THE. F. by Gay. Pr. 1754.

REHEARSAL OF KINGS. F. Anon. 1692.

REIGN OF BLOOD, THE. D. 4 a. E. Newbound. Britannia, May 17, 1880.

REIGN OF HELLEBORE, KING OF RIEN DE TOUT. T.C. Anon. 1760.

REIGN OF TERROR, A. L.T. 3 a. M. Melford. Brighton T.R., March 2, 1885; Avenue, April 9, 1885.

REIGN OF TERROR. P. 5 a. C. Claypole. Longton Queen's, January 22, 1903.

REIGN OF TERROR; OR, THE HORRORS OF THE FRENCH REVOLUTION, THE. Victoria, 1825.

REIGN OF TWELVE HOURS, THE. M.Ent. 2 a. M. by G. B. Herbert. Lyceum playbill, August 5, 1824.

REIGNING FAVOURITE, THE. D. 3 a. J. Oxenford. Strand, October 9, 1849.

REINE DE CHYPRE, LA. O. 5 a. Halévy. Paris, 1841; D.L., July 7, 1845.

REINE DE LA GLACE, LA. Ballet Div. 3 tab. By F. Stanley Smith. Brighton T.R., November 18, 1897.

REINE DE SABA, LA. O. C. Gounod. 1818-1893. Paris, 1862.

REINE DES HALLES, LA. See *Gibraltar*.

REINE DES NAIDES, LA. Fairy M. Legend. E. Coles. King's Cr., April 30, 1870.

REINE JEANNE, LA. O. 3 a. F. C. H. Monro. October 12, 1840.

REINE TOPAZ, LA. O.C. 3 a. Wds. by Lockroy and Battes. M. by Victor Massé. Théâtre Lyrique, December 27, 1856. As *Queen Topaz* at Her M., December 24, 1860.

REJECTED ADDRESSES; OR, THE TRIUMPH OF THE ALE KING. F. 2 a. By Stanley. 1812.

REJECTION; OR, EVERYBODY'S BUSINESS. F. Anon. Lyceum, November 20, 1811. N.p.

REJUVENATION OF AUNT MARY, THE. Margate R.T., October 5, 1907.

RELAPSE; OR, VIRTUE IN DANGER, THE. Sequel of *The Fool in Fashion*. C. 5 a. Sir J. Vanbrugh. D.L., 1697; C.G., January 2, 1745. See *A Trip to Scarborough*, *Love's Last Shift*.

RELATION OF THE LATE ROYAL ENTERTAINMENT GIVEN BY THE RT. HONOURABLE THE LORD KNOWLES AT CAWSOME HOUSE, A. See *Entertainment*.

RELEASED. D. 1 a. C. H. Dickinson. Comedy, April 9, 1890.

RELIEF OF LUCKNOW, THE. Spec. D. by Boucicault. D.L., September 15, 1862. Westminster T.R., Dec. 22, 1862.

RELIEF OF WILLIAMSTADT; OR, THE RETURN FROM VICTORY, THE. Int. C.G., 1793. N.p.

RELIGIOUS, THE. T.C. Duchess of Newcastle. Pr. 1662.

RELIGIOUS REBEL; OR, THE PILGRIM PRINCE. T. Anon. Pr. 1671.

RELY ON MY DISCRETION. F. T. A. Palmer. Royalty, January 17, 1870.

REMARKABLE CURE, A. F. P. Heriot. Vaudeville, March 8, 1883.

REMEMBER THE WAITER. C. sk. Perf. by Messrs. Frank Ellison and Stanley's Co., Waterloo Road. Victoria H., November 13, 1905.

REMEMBRANCE. P. 1 a. M. Robertson. Adap fr. Miss Harraden's story of *The Clockmaker and his Wife*. Terry's, June 8, 1899.

REMORSE. T. Coleridge. D.L., January 23, 1813, and April 14, 1817.

REMORSE; OR, THE PERILS OF A NIGHT. D. 4 a. G. L. Whiting. Victoria, Nov. 1, 1873.

RENAISSANCE. C. 3 a. Franz von Schoenthan and F. Coppell-Ellfield. Daly's, July 5, 1897; Comedy, November 23, 1900; Shaftesbury, May 24, 1905.

RENATA DI FRANCIA. T.P. Prol. and 5 a. Sig. Paolo Giacometti. Op. C., October 11, 1873.

RENCOUNTRE; OR, LOVE WILL FIND OUT THE WAY. Op. C. 2 a. Hay., July 12, 1827.

RENDEZVOUS, THE. Oa. 1 a. Adap. fr. French by R. Ayrton. M. by Mr. Price. Lyceum playbill, September 21, 1818; D.L., October 31, 1822, and April 26, 1833.

RENDEZVOUS; OR, TARS REGALING, THE. Int. of Songs. C.G., 1800.

RENDEZVOUS BOURGEOIS, LES. Op. C. Hoffmann. M. by Méhul. 1794.

RENDEZVOUS NOCTURNE, LE. O. Martini. 1773.

RENEGADE. O. Alt. fr. Don Sebastian Reynolds. December, 1812.

RENEGADE, THE. T.C. P. Massinger. Cockpit, D.L., April 17, 1624; Private Theatre, by his Majesty's servants, 1630.

RENEGADE, THE. D. 4 a. F. J. O'Hare. Dublin Queen's, June 4, 1906.

RENEWAL, THE, C. 1 a. Ben Philips. Prod. by the Argonauts, Rehearsal, W.C., November 13, 1908 (mat.).

RENFORTH, THE PRIDE OF THE TYNE. D. W. Stevens. Darlington T.R., June 17, 1878.

RENT. Irish D. M. A. Manning. Waterford O.H., September 19, 1881.

RENT DAY, THE. Orig. Dom. D. 2 a. D. Jerrold. D.L., January 25, 1832.

RENT FREE. Sk. 1 sc. Mark Melford. Collins's, August 27, 1900.

RENT WARNER, THE. D. 5 a. T. O'Conner. Limerick T.R., December 1, 1882.

REPARATION. P. 5 a. Adap. fr. German of Mosenthal. Gaiety, May 16, 1882.

REPARATION. Piece. 1 a. J. T. Grein and C. W. Jarvis. Vaudeville, May 12, 1892.

REPARATION, THE. C. M. P. Andrews. D.L., February 14, 1784. Pr. 1784.

REPARATION; OR, A LOYAL LOVE. D. 3 a. A. Shirley. New Cr. P.H., May 6, 1882.

REPARATION; OR, THE SCHOOL FOR LIBERTINES. D. T. P. Lathy. Boston (America). 1800.

REPARATUS. T.C. Drury, 1628.

REPENTANCE, A. D. 1 a. J. O. Hobbes. St. James's, February 28, 1899.

REPENTANCE OF KING ETHELRED, THE UNREADY, THE. Oa. 3 tab. Mrs. Burton and W. Hay. Shrewsbury, January 31, 1887.

REPENTANT SINNER, A. Dom. P. 5 a. Stourbridge Alhambra, December 26, 1908.

REPLY PAID. Duol. L. N. Parker. Ladbroke H., June 22, 1894.

REPORTED MISSING. Melo-d. 4 a. F. Dawson. Bristol T.R., June 4, 1894.

REPRIEVE, A. P. 1 a. R. Horniman. Kingston R. County, May 18, 1898.

REPRISAL; OR, THE TARS OF OLD ENGLAND, THE. C. 2 a. Dr. Smollett. D.L., January 22, 1757; Edinburgh, 1780.

REPTILE'S DAUGHTER, THE. Sk. Robert Trebor. Battersea Pal., December 14, 1908.

REPTILE'S DEVOTION, THE. Cecil H. Taylor. Leeds Queen's, July 9, 1908; Gainsborough Empire Pal., October 19, 1908 (C.P.).

REPUBLICAN MARRIAGE, A. Mrs. Holford. Olympic, November 8, 1878.

REPUTATION. D. T. P. Simpson. Bournemouth T.R., August 13, 1883.

REQUIEM. Mozart. Miscellaneous Act. *Zauberflöte*. D.L., March 19, 1817.

REQUITAL, THE. Duol. 1 a. E. Sprange. Exeter T.R., April 1, 1887.

RESCUE OF OLIVER GOLDSMITH, THE. Dr. Portrait by H. P. P. Greenwood. D. of Y., February 12, 1898.

RESCUE OF THE ORPHANS. D. C. H. Hazlewood. New Britannia.

RESCUE ON THE RAFT, THE. D. G. Conquest. Grecian, May 20, 1867.

RESCUED; OR, A GIRL'S ROMANCE. D. 4 a. D. Boucicault. King's Cross, August 27, 1879.

RESCUED FROM DEATH. D. 4 a. H. Montgomery. Barrow Alhambra, April 25, 1890.

RESCUED HONOUR, A. C. 3 a. A. Fay. Avenue, June 4, 1896.

RESEMBLANCE. D. Pro. and 4 a. Mme. C. Scotte. Vaudeville, December 10, 1885.

RESEMBLANCE; OR, THE PRISONER AT LARGE. C. John Baylis. Transl. fr. the French. Pr. 1804.

REST. Play. 1 a. H. V. Esmond. Avenue, June 10, 1892.

REST AT LAST. C. 3 a. E. T. Carpenter. Dulwich Shawbury H., May 10, 1888.

RESTAURATION; OR, RIGHT WILL TAKE PLACE, THE. T.C. D. of Buckingham. ? an adap. of Beaumont and Fletcher's *Philaster*. Pr. 1714.

RESTLESS NIGHT, A. F. F. Hay. Holborn, March 3, 1873. Two songs imitated fr. the French by W. H. C. Nation. Rev., Terry's, October 26, 1906.

RESTORATION OF KING CHARLES II.; OR, THE LIFE AND DEATH OF OLIVER CROMWELL, THE. Hist. T.C. Ballad O. W. Aston. Pr. 1733.

RESTORED. C.D. 3 a. C. R. Byrne. Dublin Queen's, February 27, 1872; Dublin T.R., May 27, 1876.

RESURRECTION, THE. Mystery of the 15th cent. MS. preserved in the Bodleian Library.

RESURRECTION, THE. Orat. Handel. 1708.

RESURRECTION. Orat. Dr. Arnold. 1777.

RESURRECTION, THE. Orat. Sir Geo. Macfarren. 1813-88.

RESURRECTION. D. 4 a. H. Bataille and M. Morton. Adap. fr. Tolstoy's novel. Vaudeville, October 23, 1902; H.M., February 17, 1903; rev. Royalty, February 12, 1906.

RESURRECTION. See "Miracle Plays."

RESURRECTION OF OUR LORD, THE. Orat. Schutz (1585-1672).

RESURREXIO DOMINI. See "Miracle Plays."

RETAINED FOR THE DEFENCE. F. 1 a. J. Oxenford. Olympic, May 23, 1859.

RETAINED ON BOTH SIDES. Oa. C. Lecocq. Manchester Prince's, November 13, 1876.

RETALIATION. F. L. MacNally. C.G., May 7, 1782. Pr. 1782.

RETALIATION. Ca. 1 a. Adap. fr. German by R. Dircks. Whitley-by-the-Sea Pav., August 6, 1890; Grand, July 27, 1891.

RETIRING. C.P. 3 a. H. W. Williamson. Globe, May 1, 1878.

RETOUR DE JERUSALEM, LE. D. 4 a. Maurice Donnay. Coronet, June 18, 1906.

RETOUR DU ROI, LE. O. by F. Rebel and F. Francœur. 1744.

RETRIBUTION. P. 5 a. J. Bennett. Idea fr. Sir W. Scott's "Rokeby." Sadler's Wells, February 11, 1850.

RETRIBUTION. Dr. Sk. H. E. Terry. Islington Empire, May 3, 1905.

RETRIBUTION. Dom. D. 4 a. Tom Taylor. F. on C. de Bernard's novel, "La Loi du Talion." Olympic, May 12, 1856.

RETURN FROM PARNASSUS; OR, A SCOURGE FOR SIMONY, THE. C. Anon. Ac. by students of S. John's College, Cambridge. Pr. 1606.

RETURN OF THE DRUSES. T. R. Browning. 1865.

RETURN OF THE FAIRIES. O. 1 a. Comery and Richards. Publ. by S. French, Ltd.

RETURN OF THE PRODIGAL, THE. C. 4 a. St. J. Hankin. Court, September 26, 1905; Court, April 29, 1907.

RETURN OF THE WANDERER, THE. C. H. Hazlewood. Britannia.

RETURN OF TOBIAS, THE. Sacr. D. Transl. fr. Mme. Genlis by T. Holcroft. 1786.

RETURN TICKET, A. Orig. F. 1 a. G. Spencer and W. Jones. St. James's, August 11, 1862.

RETURNED. Ca. Hy. M. Pitt. Sheffield T.R., May 7, 1869.

RETURNED "KILLED." P. 2 a. Planché. Transl. fr. the French. October 31, 1826.

RETURNING THE COMPLIMENT. Oa. 1 a. Otto Waldan. Comp. by H. J. Wood. R. Park Hall, November 5, 1890.

REUNITED. P. 1 a. Athenæum H., Tottenham Ct. Rd., July 24, 1888.

REVANCHE DES CIGALES, LA. Panto. P. (Paris, Cercle Funambulesque). First time in Engl. at St. Geo. H., April 17, 1897.

REVE, LE. O. 7 tab. Adap. fr. Zola's novel. M. by A. Bruneau. Poem by L. Gallet. C.G., October 29, 1891, and Paris Op. C. same year.

REVE D'AMOUR, LE. O. Auber (1782-1871). His last work.

REVEIL, LE. C. 3 a. M. Paul Hervieu. Royalty, October 25, 1907.

REVELATIONS OF LONDON. D. (Another ver. of *Les Miserables.*) Mr. Stevenson. Grecian, July 6, 1868.

REVENGE. Epis. 1 a. Wr. L. Warren. Broughton T.H., April 23, 1909 (amat.).

REVENGE, THE. T. 5 a. E. Young. Outlines fr. Shakespeare's "Othello" and Mrs. Behn's "Abdelaza." D.L. Pr. 1721. Rev. D.L., June 21, 1814, 1817, November 21, 1832.

REVENGE, THE. Burl. Chatterton. Marylebone Gardens, 1770.

REVENGE; OR, A MATCH IN NEWGATE, THE. C. Betterton. Duke's. 1680. (Rev. of Marston's "Dutch Courtezan").

REVENGE; OR, THE NOVICE OF SAN MARTINO. T. by Major Parlby. 1818. N.ac.

REVENGE FOR HONOUR. T. G. Chapman. Pr. 1654.

REVENGE OF ATHRIDATES, THE. Eng. O. Anon. M. selected by Tenducci. Alt. of "Pharnaces." Dublin Smock Alley. Pr. 1765.

REVENGE OF BUSSY D'AMBOIS, THE. T. G. Chapman. Private playhouse. White Friars. Pr. 1613.

REVENGE OF CERES, THE. D. 1 a. Joseph Moser. Pr. 1810.

REVENGEFUL QUEEN, THE. T. W. Phillips. Taken fr. Machiavel's "Florentine History." D.L., 1698. Pr. 1698.

REVENGER'S TRAGEDY, THE. T. C. Tourneur. Ac. by King's servants. Pr. 1607.

REVERA, OR VERITY. C. G. Ruggles. N.p.

REVERS DE LA MEDAILLE, LE. C. De Molière. 1861.

REVERSES. D. 2 a. H. B. Farnie. Strand, July 13, 1867.

REVIEW; OR, THE WAGS OF WINDSOR, THE. M.F. 1 a. G. Colman, jun. Hay., September 2, 1808; D.L., May 14, 1814; Lyceum playbill, April 23, 1822.

REVIEW; OR, THE WAGS OF WINDSOR, THE. C.O. by H. Lee, fr. *Caleb Quotem and his Wife; or Paint, Poetry, and Putty.*

REVOLT OF THE GREEKS; OR, THE MAID OF ATHENS, THE. D. D.L., June 10, 1824.

REVOLT OF THE HAREM, WITH THE EVOLUTION OF THE FEMALE ARMY (LAST ACT), THE. Ballet. D.L., October 8, 1835. Rev. as Fairy Ballet. 3 a. M. by T. Labarre. D.L., May 8, 1844.

REVOLT OF THE WORKHOUSE, THE. Travesty of *Revolt of the Harem.* G. à Beckett. Queen's.

REVOLTE, LA. P. 1 a. Villiers de L'Isle Adam. Transl. by Lady Barclay. Bayswater Bijou, April 5, 1906.

REVOLTED DAUGHTER, THE. C. 3 a. Israel Zangwill. Comedy, March 22, 1901.

REVOLTER, THE. T.C. Ac. between *The Hind and Panther* and *Religio Laici.* Anon.

REVOLUTION, THE. T. Catherine Trotter. Queen's, Hay., 1707.

REVOLUTION, THE. Hist. P. Lieutenant Christian. Pr. 1790.

REVOLUTION; OR, THE HAPPY CHANGE, THE. T.C. Ac. throughout English dominions. 1688.

REVOLUTION OF SWEDEN. T. Mrs. Cockburne. 1706.

REVUE, THE. C as. Raymond and P. Yorke. Lyrics by Roland Carse, M. by Maurice Jacobi. Tivoli, June 23, 1902.

REWARD OF SIN. D. Tom Midgley. Todmorden Town H., December 18, 1905 (amat.).

REWARDS OF VIRTUE, THE. C. J. Fountain. Pr. 1661. Rev. as *The Royal Shepherdess,* 1669.

REX CANN, THE WHIPPER-IN. D. Orig. prod. in Australia. Miss Helen Thompson. Liverpool R. Sefton, October 20, 1884.

REX ET PONTIFEX. Pant. R. Dodsley. Pr. 1745.

RHAMPSIHITUS. C.O. M. by A. Cellini. Lib. by E. Hamilton. Dublin T.R., May 6, 1876.

RHEINGOLD, DAS. O. Wagner. 1813-1883. Given at Munich in 1869; Bayreuth, 1876; Her M., May 5, 1882; C.G., June 22, 1892.

RHEINNISCEN. O. 3 a. Offenbach. Vienna. 1864.

RHESUS. T. Fr. "Euripides," by M. Wodhull. Pr. 1782; by R. Potter, 1783. See "Greek Plays."

RHODA. C.O. 3 a. Lib. by W. Parker. M. by A. L. Mora. Croydon T.R., September 27, 1886; Grand, November 1, 1886.

RHODON AND IRIS. Past. Ralph Knevit. Florists' Feast at Norwich, May 3, 1631.

RHYME AND REASON. D.L., November 11, 1828.

RHYS LEWIS. D. T. Morgan Edwards. Adap. fr. Daniel Owen's novel. Court, July 4, 1908.

RIBSTON'S RIDE. F.C. 3 a. W. A. Chandler. Novelty, May 7, 1897 (C.P.).

RICARDUS TERTIUS. T. MS. Brit. Mus. Lacy. 1586.

RICCIARDO E ZORAIDE. O. Rossini. Naples, 1818; King's T., June 5, 1823.

RICH AND POOR. C.O. Lewis. Lyceum, August 11, 1815.

RICH AND POOR. D. E. Price. Huddersfield T.R., July 21, 1873.

RICH AND POOR OF LONDON, THE. P. M. Goldberg. Manchester Osborne, March 12, 1900.

RICH JEW OF MALTA. T. Marlowe. 1586.

RICH MRS. REPTON, THE. C. 3 a. R. C. Carton. Duke of York's, April 20, 1904.

RICHARD ARMSTRONG. D. 3 a. W. Poole. Stoke Newington Assembly R., December 19, 1876.

RICHARD BRINSLEY SHERIDAN. P. 4 a. Gladys Unger. Garrick, January 4, 1904 (C.P.).

RICHARD CŒUR DE LION. Hist. R. J. Burgoyne. D.L. Pr. 1786. (Taken fr. D. of *Mons. Sedaine*, prod. in Paris October 21, 1784.)

RICHARD CŒUR DE LION. O. L. MacNally. C.G. Pr. 1786. Also from *Sedaine*.

RICHARD CŒUR DE LION. O. Benedict. 1863.

RICHARD CŒUR DE LION. D. 4 a. A. Halliday. D.L., September 26, 1874.

RICHARD CORDELION. Was licensed by Tilney, 1598.

RICHARD CORDELION'S FUNERAL. P. Wr. by Wilson, Chettle, Munday, and Drayton. Prod. by Henslowe's company in 1598.

RICHARD CROOKBACK. P. Ben Jonson. 1602.

RICHARD DUKE OF YORK; OR, THE CONTENTION OF YORK AND LANCASTER. Hist. P. D.L., January 3, 1818. See *True Tragedy of*.

RICHARD IN CYPRUS. T. T. Teres. N.d.

RICHARD LOVELACE. Hist. D. L. Irving. Bath T.R., July 11, 1898; Worthing T.R., July 27, 1903; Kennington, June 13, 1904.

RICHARD PLANTAGENET. Hist. D. by Haines. Victoria, 1836.

RICHARD SAVAGE. P. 4 a. J. M. Barrie and H. B. M. Watson. Criterion, April 16, 1891.

RICHARD THE CONFESSOR. P. Ac. by Earl of Sussex's men, December 31, 1593. N.p.

RICHARD THE FIRST. T. G. Sewell. Pr. 1728.

RICHARD II. T. W. Shakespeare. Prod. 1593. Rev. 1597. Ent. at Stationers' Hall August 29, 1597. F. on Holinshed's *Chronicle*. Printed: 1st qto., 1597; publ. by A Wise Printer; 2nd qto., 1598; 3rd qto., 1608; 4th qto., 1615; 5th qto. fr. 2nd folio, 1634; 1st folio, 1623. Altered by L. Theobald, L.I.F. Pr. 1720. Altered by F. Gentleman, Bath, 1754 (n.p.). Altered by J. Goodhall. Pr. 1772. Princess's, March 12, 1857; Lyceum, March 2, 1900; Comedy, May 13, 1901; H.M., September 10, 1903; April 24, 1905; H.M. (arr. by Beerbohm Tree), November 19, 1906; rev. Coronet, February 24, 1908.

RICHARD II. Nahum Tate. Ac. at D.L. under title of *The Sicilian Usurper*. Pr. 1681.

RICHARD II. Alfresco perf. in celebration of the quintencentenary of Richard's surrender to Bolingbroke at Flint. In the grounds of Flint Castle, August 21, 1899.

RICHARD III. T. In Latin verse. Legge. 1579.

RICHARD III. T. W. Shakespeare. F. on Holinshed's *Chronicle* and a preceding play on the same subject produced by the Queen's Co. in 1594. Suggested that this play was originally wr. by G. Peele and left unfinished by him and corrected and completed by W. S. Entered Stationers' Hall October 20, 1597. Pr.. 1st qto., 1597; 2nd qto., 1598; 3rd qto., 1602; 4th qto., 1605; 5th qto., 1612; 6th qto., 1622; 7th qto., 1629; 8th qto., 1634. First folio, 1623. Alt. by Colley Cibber, D.L., 1700. Alt. by J. P. Kemble, 1810. D.L., February 24, 1868; Lyceum, January 29, 1877; arr. by R. Mansfield, Globe, March 16, 1889; Olympic, April 25, 1892; Lyceum, December 19, 1896; Kennington P.O.W. (Murray Carson), September 11, 1899; Manchester Queen's, February 9, 1904.

RICHARD TURPIN AND TOM KING. P. Morris Barnett. See *Dick Turpin*.

RICHARD WHITTINGTON: HIS LOW BIRTH, FORTUNE, ETC. P. Payver. Ent. Stationers' Company in February, 1604. N.p.

RICHARD WHITTINGTON, ESQ. Bury T.R., September 9, 1892.

RICHARD WYE. P. 1 a. Charles Hannan. Brighton West Pier Pav., March 1, 1902.

RICHARD YE THIRD. Burl. Publ. by S. French, Ltd.

RICHARD'S PLAY. Ca. 1 a. Mary C. Rowsell and J. J. Dilley. Ladbroke H., January 14, 1891 (C.P.); Terry's, February 20, 1891.

RICHELIEU. P. 5 a. Lord Lytton. C.G., March 7, 1839; D.L., October 2, 1852; D.L., April 14, 1857; Lyceum, September 27, 1873 (rev.), and May 7, 1892.

RICHELIEU IN LOVE. Hay., October 30, 1852.

RICHELIEU REDRESSED. Burl. R. Reece. Olympic, October 27, 1873.

RICHES; OR, THE WIFE AND BROTHER. P. (F. on Massinger's C. of *The City Madam*.) Sir J. B. Burges. Lyceum, February 3, 1810; D.L., May 25, 1814.

RICHMOND GARDENER, THE. M.P. Richmond, 1790. N.p.

RICHMOND GARLAND, THE. M.P. Anon. 1790. N.p.

RICHMOND HEIRESS, THE. C. Alt. fr. Tom Durfey by F. G. Waldron. T.R., 1693; Richmond, 1777. N.p.

RICHMOND WELLS; OR, GOOD LUCK AT LAST. C. by J. Williams. Richmond Pinkethman's. Pr. 1723.

RICONOSCENZA, LA. O. Rossini. 1821.

RIDE A COCKHORSE. C. Pant. Lyceum playbill, December 26, 1835.

RIDE TO WIN, A. Sk. Max Goldberg. Croydon Empire, September 14, 1908.

RIDER; OR, THE HUMOURS OF AN INN, THE. F. 2 a. Pr. 1768.

RIDERS TO THE SEA. P. 1 a. J. M. Synge (Irish National T. Society). Royalty, March 26, 1904; Gt. Queen St., June 11, 1907.

RIDICULOUS GUARDIAN, THE. C. Burl. Hay. Pr. 1761.

RIDING TO WIN. D. 4 a. F. Herbert (E. Leicester) and W. Howard. New Cr. Broadway T., July 23, 1900.

RIENZI. T. 5 a. F. on Gibbon's History of Nicholas Rienzi, in "The Decline and Fall of the Roman Empire," by Mary Russell Mitford. D.L., October 9, 1828.

RIENZI. O. 4 a. R. Wagner. F. on Bulwer's novel. Dresden, 1842. Adap. into Eng. by J. P. Jackson. H.M., January 27, 1879; rev. by Moody Manners' company, Lyric, August 27, 1909.

RIENZI; OR, THE LAST OF THE TRIBUNES. D. Buckstone. F. on Lord Lytton's novel. Adelphi, February, 1831.

RIENZI REINSTATED; OR, THE LAST OF THE COBBLER. Burl. W. A. Allen. Globe, December 21, 1874.

RIFLE AND HOW TO USE IT, THE. F. 1 a. J. V. Bridgeman. Hay., September 20, 1859.

RIFLE VOLUNTEER. Duol. 1 a. Publ. by S. French, Ltd.

RIFLE VOLUNTEERS: RIFLEMAN! RIFLEMAN! RIFLEMAN! FORM; THE. Sk. E. Stirling. Adelphi, June 13, 1859.

RIFT WITHIN THE LUTE, THE. P. 1 a. C. H. Dickinson and A. Griffiths. Duke of York's, November 10, 1898; Avenue, January 26, 1899; Terry's, July 5, 1899.

RIGHT. P. 3 a. J. M. Killick. St. Geo. H., February 10, 1881.

RIGHT AGAINST MIGHT. C.D. 3 a. M. White. Novelty, July 27, 1891.

RIGHT AND WRONG. C. Burton. 1812.

RIGHT AND WRONG. D. Adap. fr. the French by F. Harvey. Swansea O.H., October 22, 1883.

RIGHT AND WRONG; OR, THE DREAM OF LIFE. D. Liverpool R. Colosseum, July 2, 1868.

RIGHT FELLOW; OR, THE WRONG FELLOW AND THE FELO D'YE SEE, THE. Burl. W. F. Marshall. New Cr. R. Naval School (amat.), December 22, 1868.

RIGHT MAN, THE. Rom. D. 5 a. G. Corner and L. Ellis. Sanger's, May 7, 1887.

RIGHT OF THE LORD OF THE MANOR, THE. C. Anon. Before 1814.

RIGHT OR WRONG. Ca. 1 a. J. J. Bidford. Criterion, May 4, 1887.

RIGHT OR WRONG. D. 4 a. F. Jerman. Blackburn Prince's, November 9, 1896; Britannia, July 25, 1898.

RIGHT WOMAN, A. C. F. Beaumont and J. Fletcher. Ent. Stationers' Co., June 29, 1660. N.p.

RIGHT'S RIGHT. D. 5 a. C. A. Clarke. West Bromwich T.R., November 8, 1886.

RIGHTFUL HEIR, THE. D. 5 a. Lord Lytton. Lyceum, October 3, 1868.

RIGHTFUL HEIR, THE. "M. satire on conventional comic." A. Sturgess. M. by J. W. Glover. Hastings Public H., September 18, 1899.

RIGHTFUL HEIR; OR, THE DEAD HAND AND THE HOUR OF ONE, THE. D. Swansea T.R., September 25, 1871.

RIGHTFUL HEIRESS, THE. C. 1 a. H. J. Field. Guildhall School of M., July 17, 1895.

RIGHTS AND PRIVILEGES. P. 3 a. B. M'Donald. Bayswater Bijou, May 12, 1898.

RIGHTS AND WRONGS OF WOMEN. F. 1 a. J. M. Morton. Hay., May 24, 1856.

RIGHTS OF HECATE; OR, HARLEQUIN FROM THE MOON, THE. Panto. Ent. Mr. Love (Dance). D.L., 1764. N.p.

RIGHTS OF MAN, THE. F. W. F. Sullivan. Buxton, 1791.

RIGHTS OF THE SOUL, THE. P. 1 a. G. Giacosa. Trans. by Miss F. M. Rankin. Kingsway, February 21, 1909.

RIGHTS OF WOMAN, THE. Ca. Miss Emma Schiff. Globe, January 9, 1871.

RIGHTS OF WOMEN, THE. M.P. 1 a. Hay., August 9, 1792. N.p.

RIGOLETTO. Italian O. Verdi. Lib. by Piane. (Venice, March 11, 1851.) F. on V. Hugo's D. *Le Roi s'amuse.* (In Italian at C.G. May 14, 1853.) Paris, January 19, 1857.

RINALDO. Poem. Circa 1560. See "Italian Classical Plays."

RINALDO. O. A. Hill. M. by Handel. Queen's, Haymarket, 1714.

RINALDO. Cantata. J. Brahms (1833).

RINALDO AND ARMIDA. T. Adap. fr. Tasso. J. Dennis. L.I.F. Pr. 1699.

RINALDO RINALDINI; OR, THE BRIGAND AND THE BLACKSMITH. Rom. d. 2 a. J. E. Wilks. Sadler's Wells, January 4, 1835.

RINALDO RINALDINI; OR, THE SECRET AVENGERS. Burl. J. C. Cross. Royal Circus Pr. 1801.

RING; OR, LOVE ME FOR MYSELF, THE. M.E. W. Linley. Alt. fr. his *The Pavilion.* Pr. 1800. D.L., January 21, 1800.

RING AND THE KEEPER, THE. Oa. J. P. Wooler. New Royalty.

RING BETWEEN, THE. Dr. sk. 1 sc. W. Felton. Middlesex, July 22, 1907.

RING DES NIBELUNGEN, DER. O. Wagner. See *Nibelungen Ring.*

RING FENCE, A. Ca. J. Strange Winter. Portsmouth T.R., November 27, 1893.

RING MISTRESS, THE. F.C. 3 a. R. Ganthony. Eastbourne Devonshire Park T., December 17, 1900; Lyric, December 20, 1900.

RING OF IRON, A. Dom. d. 5 a. F. Harvey. Portsmouth New T.R., September 15, 1884; Grand, August 3, 1885.

RING OF POLYCRATES, THE. Piece. 1 a. J. H. M'Carthy. Strand, June 24, 1892.

RING THAT BINDS, THE. D. 4 a. H. C. Sargent. Wolverhampton P.O.W., March 25, 1903; Alexandra Pal. T., September 7, 1903; Hammersmith Lyric, November 30, 1903.

RING UP 735 EAST. Sk. E. S. France. Willesden Hipp., December 7, 1908.

RINGDOVES, THE. C.I. C. Mathews. D.L., July 12, 1852.

RINNEGATO, IL. O. M. Bodogorefy. H.M.T., July 9, 1881.

RIP VAN WINKLE. D. 2 a. W. B. Bernard. Adelphi, October, 1832.

RIP VAN WINKLE. P. 4 a. Dion Boucicault. Royalty, February 6, 1908 (rev.).

RIP VAN WINKLE. Orig. Amer. O. 3 a. Lib. by J. H. Wainwright. M. by G. Bristowe. Niblo's Gardens, New York, by Pyne and Harrison Co., September 27, 1855.

RIP VAN WINKLE. Op. C. 3 a. and 5 tab. H. Meilhac, P. Gide, and H. B. Farnie. M. by R. Planquette. Comedy, October 14, 1882.

RIP VAN WINKLE. Rom. O. W. A. Kerman and F. Leoni. H.M., September 4, 1897.

RIP VAN WINKLE. New ver. (3 a.) of Washington Irving's story by S. A. Fitzgerald. Kennington P.O.W., November 27, 1899.

RIP VAN WINKLE. New ver. 3 a. Her M., May 30, 1900.

RIP VAN WINKLE. Sk. Bedford M.H., September 22, 1902.

RIP VAN WINKLE: A LEGEND OF SLEEPY HOLLOW. Rom d. 2 a. Fr. Washington Irving's story. By J. Kerr. W. London T.

RIP VAN WINKLE; OR, A LITTLE GAME OF NAP. Burl. H. S. Clarke. Portsmouth T.R., March 29, 1880.

RIPE FRUIT; OR, THE MARRIAGE ACT. Int. C. Stuart. Hay., 1781. N.p.

RIPPLES. C.D. 3 a. W. Browne and H. Moss. York T.R., November 19, 1880.

RIPPLINGS. Ca. C. Balcour. Sadler's Wells, March 24, 1883.

RIQUET. Planché. 1836.

RISE AND FALL OF ARCHITECTURE, THE. Farc. M.C. Book by "Purple Patch." M. arr. and comp. by Claude Kelly. King's H., W.C., March 24, 1909 (amat.).

RISE AND FALL OF RICHARD THE THIRD; OR, A NEW FRONT TO AN OLD DICKEY, THE. Burl. F. C. Burnand. Royalty, September 24, 1868.

RISE OF DICK HALWARD, THE. P. 3 a. J. K. Jerome. Garrick, October 19, 1895.

RISE OF THE MOON, THE. An Irish problem. P. 1 a. Lady Gregory. Dublin Abbey, March 9, 1907; Gt. Queen St., June 12, 1907.

RISING OF CARDINAL WOLSEY, THE. P. A. Mundy, assisted by Drayton, Chettle, and Smith. Ac 1601. N.p.

RISIN' O' THE MOON. Melo.-d. 4 a. H. G. Ransley. Liverpool College H., April 18, 1907.

RISING SUN, THE. Ca. A. Law. Newcastle-on-Tyne T.R., August 1, 1904.

RITES OF HECATE; OR, HARLEQUIN FROM THE MOON. Pant. Love. 1764. N.p.

RIVAL ARTISTES, THE. F. M. Kinghorne. Surrey, May 14, 1873.

RIVAL BEAUTIES, THE. C.O. 2 a. Randegger. Leeds T.R., 1864.

RIVAL BROTHERS, THE. T. Anon. L.I.F. Pr. 1704.

RIVAL CANDIDATES, THE. C.O. 2 a. Rev. H. Bate Dudley. D.L., February 1, 1775; Edinburgh, 1783.

RIVAL CANDIDATES. C. 4 a. G. R. Douglas. Folly, March 17, 1880.

RIVAL CANDIDATES, THE. P. C. T. Dazey and J. N. Morris. Wolverhampton T.R., April 9, 1894 (C.P.).

RIVAL CAPTAINS; OR, THE IMPOSTOR UNMASKED, THE. B.Op. (Author probably Thomas Phillips.) Hay., 1736. N.p.

RIVAL CONFIDENT, LE. O. 2 a. Grétry. 1788.

RIVAL FATHER, THE. F. Mr. Preston. 1754.

RIVAL FATHERS; OR, THE DEATH OF ACHILLES, THE. T. W. Hatchett. New T. in Hay. Pr. 1730.

RIVAL FLUNKIES, THE. F. Mr. Quayle. Barnsley R. Queen's, March 14, 1873.

RIVAL FOOLS, THE. C. Adap. of Fletcher's *Wit at Several Weapons*, by Colley Cibber. D.L., March 11, 1709. Pr. N.d.

RIVAL FOUNTAIN. Britannia, October 7, 1859.

RIVAL FRIENDS, THE. C. P. Hansted. Students of Queen's Coll., Cambridge. Pr. 1632.

RIVAL GENERALS, THE. T. J. Stirling. Dublin. Pr. 1722.

RIVAL KINGS; OR, THE LOVES OF OROONDATES AND SATIRA. T. J. Banks. Fr. Calprenède's *Cassandre*. T.R., 1679.

RIVAL KNIGHTS, THE. Dr. Rom. C.G., October 9, 1783.

RIVAL LADIES, THE. T. C. J. Dryden. T.R., 1679.

RIVAL LOVERS, THE. F. 2 a. T. Warboys. Fr. Regnard's *La Serenade*. Pr. 1777.

RIVAL MILLINERS, THE. C. T. Drury. Little T. in Hay., 1735.

RIVAL MOTHER, THE. C. Anon. 1678.

RIVAL MOTHER; OR, THE SAILOR'S STRATAGEM. C. *Lady of Distinction*. Dublin, 1789.

RIVAL NYMPHS; OR, THE MERRY SWAIN, THE. Past C. D. Bellamy, sen. and jun. 1740.

RIVAL OTHELLOS. F. 1 a. H. J. Byron Publ. by S. French, Limited.

RIVAL PAGES, THE. C. 1 a. C. Selby. Queen's T., October 8, 1835.

RIVAL POETS, THE; OR, THE LOVE CHARM. Oa. 2 a. H. Scott. M. by E. German. St. George's H., March 7, 1901 (amat.).

RIVAL PRIESTS; OR, THE FEMALE POLITICIAN, THE. D. Bellamy, sen. and jun. Ptd. 1739.

RIVAL QUEENS, THE. Prelude. T. Holcroft. C.G., 1794-1795. N.p.

RIVAL QUEENS; OR, THE DEATH OF ALEXANDER THE GREAT, THE. T. N. Lee. (It was from this play that Handel took his lines, "See the Conquering Hero comes," and introduced them in his *Judas Maccabeus*.) Partly f. on Calprenédè's *Cassandre*. T.R., 1677, and rev. November 23, 1795.

RIVAL QUEENS, WITH THE HUMOURS OF ALEXANDER THE GREAT, THE. T. C. Cibber. D.L.,; rev. C.G., April 19, 1780.

RIVAL RASCALS; OR, VIRTUE REWARDED AND VICE-VERSA, THE. Burl. A. Greenland, jun. St. George's H., May 3, 1877.

RIVAL ROMEOS. F. H. B. Farnie. St. James's, April 8, 1871.

RIVAL ROSES, THE, D. Scene. Written and composed by A. Gilbert. St. George's H., July 14, 1887.

RIVAL SISTERS, THE. T. A. Murphy. Hay., March 18, 1793.

RIVAL SISTERS; OR, THE VIOLENCE OF LOVE, THE. T. R. Gould. Prol. and Epil. by D'Urfey. T.R., 1696.

RIVAL SOLDIERS, THE. M.F. 1 a. D.L., July 8, 1814, and June 1, 1815.

RIVAL SOLDIERS; OR, SPRIGS OF LAUREL, THE. M. Int. J. O'Keefe. D.L., June 11, 1817; Lyceum playbill (rev.), September 19, 1817.

RIVAL STATUES; OR, HARLEQUIN HUMOURIST, THE. Pant. J. C. Cross. Pr. 1803.

RIVAL THEATRES; OR, A PLAYHOUSE TO BE LET, THE. F., to which is added *The Chocolate Makers; or, Mimickry Exposed*. Int., G. Stayley, Dublin. Pr. 1759.

RIVAL VALETS, THE. F. 2 a. J. Ebsworth. Hay., 1825.

RIVAL WIDOWS; OR, THE FAIR LIBERTINE, THE. C. Mrs. E. Cooper. T.R. Pr. 1735.

RIVALES, THE. C In Latin. By Wm. Gager. June, 1583.

RIVALS, THE. An alt. of *The Two Noble Kinsmen*, by Shakespeare and Fletcher, by D'Avenant. T.C. D. of Y., 1668.

RIVALS, THE. C. 5 a. R. B. Sheridan. C.G., January 17, 1775; October 1, 1800; and 1824; D.L., September 20, 1814; Hay., July 4, 1821; Olympic, December 27, 1847 (revival); Sadler's Wells, 1866; (?) Vaudeville; Court, November 11, 1895; produced by Cyril Maude and F. Harrison. Hay., March 27, 1900.

RIVALS, THE. Sacr. D. Rev. H. Boyd. Pr. 1793.

RIVALS, THE. O. Balfe. 1830.

RIVALS, THE. Sk. "An Episode of Early Roman Life." Pimlico Standard, July 22, 1907.

RIVER OF LIFE, THE. D. 4 a. A. Shirley and B. Landeck. Hull Grand, February 24, 1894. (C.P.)

RIVERSIDE STORY, A. P. 2 a. Mrs. Bancroft. Hay., May 22, 1890.

RIZPAH MISERY. Duol. Mrs. Vere Campbell. Glasgow Grand, February 6, 1894; Garrick, November 19, 1896.

ROAD OF LIFE, THE. D. E. L. Blanchard. Olympic.

ROAD, THE RIVER, AND THE RAIL, THE. D. G. Spencer. E. London, September 7, 1868.

ROAD TO FAME, THE. C. 3 a. Adap. fr. Von Kneisel's P. *Der Kucknek*, by A. White and P. Grunfeld. Vaudeville, May 7, 1885.

ROAD TO FORTUNE, A. Military D. 5 a. C. E. Dering. Stonehouse Grand, March 27, 1893; Hammersmith Lyric, July 16, 1894.

ROAD TO RIDGELEY, THE. See *The Worm Turns*.

ROAD TO RUIN, THE. C. 5 a. T. Holcroft. C.G., February 18, 1792; D.L., May 31, 1815; Hay., 1825; D.L., December 31, 1849; St. James's, February, 9, 1867; Vaudeville, 1873; Op.C., December 9, 1891.

ROADSIDE INN. Lyceum, January 21, 1865.

ROARING GIRL; OR, MOLL CUTPURSE, THE. P. T. Middleton and Mr. Dekker. Pr. 1611. Fortune's Stage, by the Prince's Players.

ROARING GIRL; OR, THE CATCHPOLE, THE. C. Mentioned by Jordan.

ROB ROY. O. Flotow. 1832.

ROB ROY. Astley's, February 9, 1857.

ROB ROY. Burl. S. French. Marylebone, June 29, 1867.

ROB ROY. C.O. H. B. Smith. M. by R. de Koven. Greenwich Morton's, September 29, 1894.

ROB ROY. D. Rom. 3 sc. A. Shirley and C. C. Corri. Hippodrome, June 26, 1905.

ROB ROY. Ver. by J. K. Park. Wishaw T.H., September 6, 1905.

ROB ROY, THE GREGARACH. Rom. D. 3 a. G. Soane. Partly original and partly on "Rob Roy." D.L., March 25, 1818.

ROB ROY MACGREGOR; OR, AULD LANG SYNE. Op. D. 3 a. J. Pocock. M. by J. Davy. C.G., March 12, 1818; D.L., July 3, 1821.

ROBBER, THE. Dr. P. 2 a. R. Cumberland. Tunbridge Wells, October 15, 1809. N.p.

ROBBER, THE. O. 1 a. Ross and Kreymann. Publ. by S. French, Ltd.

ROBBER, THE. Sk. William Gillette. London Coliseum, August 9, 1909.

ROBBER OF THE RHINE, THE. Melo-d. 2 a. G. Almar. Sadler's Wells, April, 1833.

ROBBER'S BRIDE, THE. Serio C.O. Freely transl. fr. the German D. *Die Rauberbraut*. M. by F. Ries. Lyceum, July 15, 1829.

ROBBER'S WIFE, THE. Rom. Dom. D. 2 a. I. Pocock, author of "Hit or Miss." C.G., January 7, 1830.

ROBBERS, THE. T. Fr. Schiller. Anon. Pr. 1792.

ROBBERS, THE. T. Transl. and alt. fr. German, with a preface, pro. and epil., by Margravine of Anspach. Brandenburgh Ho., 1798.

ROBBERS, THE. Transl. fr. Schiller by B. Thompson. Pr. 1800.

ROBBERS, THE. P. 5 a. Fr. Schiller, by J. Anderson. D.L., April 21, 1851.

ROBBERS; OR, HARLEQUIN TRAPPED BY COLUMBINE, THE. Dr. Ent. L.I.F., 1724.

ROBBERS OF CALABRIA. D. Lane.

ROBBERS OF THE PYRENEES, THE. D. 2 a. and pro. Fr. the French. W. E. Suter. Effingham, September 22, 1862.

ROBBERY UNDER ARMS. D. 5 a. Adap. by A. Dampier and G. Walch fr. R. Boldrewood's Rom. Orig. prod. in Australia. Princess's, October 22, 1894.

ROBBING HOOD; OR, THE MAID OF THE MILL 'ARD BY. Sk. Herbert Shelley. M. by Ernest Ruccalossi. Tivoli, December 26, 1906.

ROBBING ROY; OR, SCOTCHED AND KILT. Burl. F. C. Burnand. Gaiety, November 11, 1879.

ROBE OF RIGHTEOUSNESS, THE. P. 4 a. Norman Fowers. Ilkeston T.R., March 13, 1907.

ROBERT. Ca. Mrs. Charles Collette. Queen's Gate H., June 22, 1900.

ROBERT AND BERTRAM. C. Ballet. 2 a and an episode. M. by Schmidt. D.L., March 24, 1845.

ROBERT AND BERTRAM, OR, THE VOLATILE VAGRANTS. F.C. Adap. fr. the German of G. Roeder. 4 a. Lieut. S. G. Orton, R.N. Woolwich R. Artillery, April 2, 1888.

ROBERT BRUCE. O. Rossini. Paris, December 30, 1846.

ROBERT BURNS. Rom. 3 a. M. arr. by E. T. de Bauzie. Edinburgh T.R., May 28, 1896.

ROBERT BURNS; OR, RANTIN', ROVIN' ROBIN. D. 4 a. J. Garrow. Kilmarnock Corn Exch., November 21, 1902.

ROBERT CYCYLL. Subject same as Fr. *Robert le Diable*. High Cross in Chester, 1529. N.p.

ROBERT DEVEREUX. O. 3 a. Text by Romani (fr. Corneille). M. by Mercadante. Milan, March 10, 1833.

ROBERT DEVEREUX. O. 3 a. Lib. by Camerano (fr. Corneille's *Comte d' Essex*. M. by Donizetti. Naples, 1837; Paris, December 27, 1838; Her Maj., June 24, 1841.

ROBERT EARL OF HUNTINGDON'S DEATH; OR, ROBIN HOOD OF MERRY SHERWOOD; WITH THE TRAGEDY OF CHASTE MATILDA. Hist. P. A. Mundy and H. Chettle. Pr. 1601.

ROBERT EARL OF HUNTINGDON'S DOWNFALL. Hist. P. T. Heywood. Pr. 1601.

ROBERT EMMETT. D. 3 a. W. Digges. Leicester T.R., May 2, 1881.

ROBERT EMMETT. P. 4 a. D. Boucicault. Greenwich New P. of W., November 4, 1884.

ROBERT EMMETT, THE IRISH PATRIOT OF 1803. D. Blyth Octagon, February 14, 1873.

ROBERT HOOD. See *Death of the Earl of Huntington*.

ROBERT LE DIABLE. O. Meyerbeer. Lib. by Scribe. (Paris, 1831.)

ROBERT MACAIRE; OR, THE ROADSIDE INN TURNED INSIDE OUT. Burl. Extrav. H. J. Byron. Globe, April 16, 1870.

ROBERT MACAIRE; OR, LES AUBERGES DES ADRITS. Melo-d. 2 a. C. Selby. Victoria, December 3, 1834.

ROBERT MACAIRE RENOVATED. Burl. L. Clarance. Barnsley T.R., March 3, 1884.

ROBERT RABAGAS. C. 3 a. Stephen Fiske. St. James's, February 25, 1873.

ROBERT RICHBORNE; OR, THE DISPUTED TITLE. D. Liverpool Colosseum, July 31, 1871.

ROBERT THE DEVIL. O. 4 a. Meyerbeer. D.L., April 8, 1833; completed March 1, 1845; new ver., Liverpool R. Court, February 8, 1888.

ROBERT THE DEVIL. O. Extrav. W. S. Gilbert. Gaiety, December 21, 1868.

ROBERT THE DEVIL. Dr. Ver. of the Opera. Adelphi, December, 1831.

ROBERT THE DEVIL. See *The Demon*.

ROBERT THE DEVIL; OR, THE FIEND FATHER. Rom. O. 3 a. Adap. to English stage by R. Lacy. C.G., February 21, 1832.

ROBERT THE DEVIL! DUKE OF NORMANDY. M. Rom. 2 a. R. J. Raymond. C.G.

ROBERT THE INVALID. C. C. Reade. 1870. A ver. of Molière's *Le Malade Imaginaire*.

ROBERT THE SECOND. Wr. by Decker, Jonson, and Chettle. 1599.

ROBESPIERRE. D. 2 a. Burnand. Adelphi, 1840.

ROBESPIERRE. Dr. episode. 1 a. D. Buchanan. Weston-super-Mare Vict. H., April 24, 1905.

ROBESPIERRE. Hist. P. H. S. Springate. Wolverhampton P. of W., August 25, 1879.

ROBESPIERRE. D. 5 a. V. Sardou. Rendered into English by L. B. Irving. Lyceum, April 15, 1899, and May 27, 1901.

ROBIN CONSCIENCE. Int. Anon. 1624.

ROBIN DES BOIS. O. Weber. 1824.

ROBIN GOODFELLOW. P. Wr. by Henry Chettle. 1602.

ROBIN GOODFELLOW. P. 3 a. R. C. Carton. Garrick, January 5, 1893.

ROBIN GOODFELLOW; OR, THE RIVAL SISTERS. Pant. D.L., 1738.

ROBIN HOOD. Part I. by A. Mundy; Part II. A. Mundy and H. Chettle. 1598 and 1599. N.p.

ROBIN HOOD. O. Lee's and Harper's Booth, Bartholomew Fair. Pr. 1730.

ROBIN HOOD. O. Dr. Arne and Burney. 1741.

ROBIN HOOD. M. Ent. M. Mendez. T.R. Pr. 1751.

ROBIN HOOD. O. O'Keefe. M. by Shield. 1787.

ROBIN HOOD. Cantata. J. L. Hatton. 1809-86.

ROBIN HOOD. O. 3 a. Words by John Oxenford. M. by Sir Geo. Macfarren. Her M.T., October 11, 1860.

ROBIN HOOD. P. 5 a. Dennis Cleugh and Cecil Jones. Crystal Pal., December 10, 1906.

ROBIN HOOD. P. 4 a. Clifford Rean. Liverpool Star, December 24, 1906.

ROBIN HOOD. Rom. 4 a. Henry Hamilton and Wm. Devereux. Lyrics by H. Hamilton. M. by Herbert Bunning. Lyric, October 17, 1906; Lyric, December 21, 1907.

ROBIN HOOD. B. 1 a. F. C. Burnand. Publ. by S. French, Ltd.

ROBIN HOOD. Dr. M. Episode. Bradford Empire, September 21, 1907.

ROBIN HOOD AND HIS CREW OF SOLDIERS. Int. Nottingham, 1661.

ROBYN HODE; VERY PROPER TO BE PLAYED IN MAYE GAMES, PLAYE OF. Pr. for Wm. Copland, 1634.

ROBIN HOOD; OR, SHERWOOD FOREST. C.O. 2 a. Leonard MacNalty. D.L., December 16, 1816.

ROBIN HOOD; OR, SHERWOOD FOREST. THAT'S WHERE THE FORESTERS LODGE. Burl. F. Hall. Philharmonic, July 7, 1880.

ROBIN HOOD; OR, THE FORESTER'S GATE. Extrav. F. C. Burnand. Olympic, December 26, 1862.

ROBIN HOOD; OR, THE MERRY OUTLAWS OF SHERWOOD. Dr. Equestr. Spec. 3 a. E. Fitzball. Astley's Amphitheatre, October 8, 1860.

ROBIN HOOD AND HIS MERRY LITTLE MEN. Adelphi, December 22, 1877.

ROBIN HOOD AND LITTLE JOHN. C. 1594. N.p.

ROBIN HOOD AND MAID MARIAN. Dr. ballad-cycle by B. Hood. M. by W. W. Hedgcock. Hastings Pub. H., September 18, 1899.

ROBIN HOOD, Esq. Op. Burl. 2 a. S. Rogers. M. by Henry May. Chester Royalty, August 6, 1894.

ROBIN HOOD'S PENN'ORTHS. P. W. Houghton. 1600.

ROBIN THE ROVER. Burl. T. C. McGuire. Brighton Aquarium, July 19, 1897.

ROBINSON CRUSOE. This panto. subject was from the pen of Daniel De Foe (1160-1731). Pr. 1719.

ROBINSON CRUSOE. Pant. Sheridan. 1797.

ROBINSON CRUSOE. O. 3 a. Offenbach. 1867.

ROBINSON CRUSOE. Extrav. H. J. Byron. Crystal Pal., April 6, 1874.

ROBINSON CRUSOE. Burl. H. B. Farnie. Manchester Prince's, October 7, 1876; Folly, November 11, 1876.

ROBINSON CRUSOE. Oa. W. S. North and J. McCullum. Dublin Mansion H., February 16, 1895.

ROBINSON CRUSOE. Bks. and lyrics by Mr. and Mrs. Ernest Carpenter. M. comp. and arr. by Herr Raimund Pechotsch. Lyceum, December 23, 1907.

ROBINSON CRUSOE. Pant. Ed. Morris and E. H. Bertram. Belfast T.R., April 18, 1908.

ROBINSON CRUSOE; OR, HARLEQUIN FRIDAY. Pant. D.L., 1781. Said to be written by Sheridan. Ballet rev. D.L., 1800.

ROBINSON CRUSOE; OR, HARLEQUIN FRIDAY AND THE KING OF THE CARIBEE ISLANDS. Grotesque Panto. Opening. H. J. Byron. Princess's, December 26, 1860.

ROBINSON CRUSOE; OR, THE BOLD BUCCANEERS. Rom. D. 2 a. I. Pocock. C.G., 1817.

ROBINSON CRUSOE; OR, THE INJUN BRIDE AND THE INJURED WIFE. Burl. Hay., July 6, 1867

ROBINSON CRUSOE; OR, THE PIRATE WILL, PRETTY POLL AND CAPTAIN BILL. Burl. Todmorden T.R., October 29, 1883.

ROBINSON CRUSOE, JUNIOR. Burl. Extrav. C. W. McCabe and Ernest Barrington. Battersea Park Town H., December 26, 1892.

ROBINSON CRUSOE REVIVED. Burl. E. E. Bertrand. Dumfries T.R., February 5, 1877.

ROBUR RAGABAS; OR, 1792. D. Eleph. and C., March 8, 1873.

ROBUST INVALID, THE. C. 3 a. C. Reade. Adap. fr. Molière's *Malade Imaginaire*. Adelphi, June 15, 1870.

ROCAMBOLE; OR, THE KNAVES OF HEARTS AND THE COMPANIONS IN CRIME. Rom. D. Prol. and 3 a. W. E. Suter. Sadler's Wells (under title *Baccarat*), March 4, 1865; Grecian, February 26, 1866.

ROCHESTER. D. Moncrieff. Olympic, 1814.

ROCHESTER; OR, KING CHARLES THE SECOND'S MERRY DAYS. C. 2 a. W. T. Moncrieff. Olympic, November 16, 1818.

ROCK OF AGES. Cantata. Dr. J. F. Bridge.

ROCK OF ROME. Hist. P. Knowles. 1849.

ROCKET, THE. C. 3 a. A. W. Pinero. Liverpool P. of W., July 30, 1883; Gaiety, December 10, 1883.

ROCKLEYS, THE. D. 4 a. A. A. Hoffmann. Kilburn T.H., December 10, 1887.

ROCKYLOT, THE. Mus. C. 3 a. J. Birkett, jun. Morecambe Royalty T., February 5, 1900.

RODERICK. P. Ac. at Rose T. in October, 1600.

RODERICK RANDOM. C.O. 3 a. S. W. Ryley. Manchester, 1793. See *Northern Heroes*.

RODERIGO. O. Handel. 1706.

RODOGUNE; OR, THE RIVAL BROTHERS. T. S. Aspinwall. Transl. fr. the French of *Corneille*. Pr. 1765. See "French Classical Plays."

RODOLPHE. "Petite Piece." Scribe before 1822.

ROGER AND JOAN; OR, THE COUNTRY WEDDING. C. Masque. Anon. T.R. in C.G., 1739.

ROGER LA HONTE; OR, JEAN THE DISGRACED. See *A Man's Shadow*.

ROGER O'HARE. Victoria, August 26, 1865.

ROGUE AND VAGABONDS. C. 4 a. H. W. Eldridge. Tottenham Pub. H., April 15, 1895. MS. with Douglas Cox.

ROGUE AT LARGE, A. D. 4 a. Lillian Clare Cassidy. Hammersmith Lyric, April 19, 1909.

ROGUE RILEY; OR, THE FOUR-LEAVED SHAMROCK. Irish D. 3 a. E. C. Matthews. Aberdeen H.M., February 26, 1894.

ROGUE'S COMEDY, THE. P. 3 a. H. A. Jones. Garrick, April 21, 1896.

ROGUE'S DAUGHTER, A. C.D. 4 a. M. Hall-Page. Macclesfield T.R., February 4, 1903; Sheffield Alexandra, March 7, 1904.

ROGUE'S DAUGHTER, A. D. 4 a. Marie Menzies. Greenwich Morton's, October 23, 1905.

ROGUERY. Sk. Leicester Pav., May 10, 1909.

ROGUES ALL; OR, THREE GENERATIONS. F. 2 a. D.L., February 5, 1814.

ROGUES AND VAGABONDS. D. 4 a. E. H. Mitchelson and F. Brenton. Scarborough T.R., June 12, 1897 (C.P.); Surrey, July 17, 1899.

ROGUES OF THE TURF. P. 4 a. M. Goldberg. Salford Regent T., June 1, 1903; Dalston, April 4, 1904.

ROI CAROTTE, LE. English ver. by H. S. Leigh. M. by Offenbach. Alhambra, June 3, 1872.

ROI DE LAHORE, LE. O. 5 a. Lib. by Louis Gallet. M. by Jules Massenet. Paris Grand Opera, April 27, 1877; C.G., Royal Italian Opera, June 28, 1879.

ROI D'YS, LE. O. 3 a. Words by Edouard Blau and M. by E. Lalo. (1823-1892.) Paris Opera Com., 1888; C.G., July 17, 1901.

ROI ET LE FERMIER, LE. O. 3 a. Monsigny, November 22, 1762.

ROI LA DIT, LE. C.O. 3 a. Words by Edm. Gondinet. M. by Leo Délibes. (Paris, May 24, 1873.) Prod. in England at P.O.W. (by the students Royal Co. of M.), December 13, 1894.

ROI MALGRE LUI, LE. C.O. 3 a. Words by Emile de Najac and Paul Burani. M. by E. Chabrier. Paris Opera Comique, May 18, 1887.

ROISTER DOISTER. See *Ralph Roister Doister*.

ROKEBY. D. Adap. fr. Sir W. Scott by W. C. Macready. Circa 1820.

ROLAND. O. 5 a. Lulli. January 18, 1685.

ROLAND. O. Piccini. 1778.

ROLAND FOR AN OLIVER, A. M. Ent. C.G., 1819; Lyceum playbill (rev.), July 9, 1823.

ROLAND FOR AN OLIVER, A. F. 2 a. T. Morton. F. on Scribe's *Visite à Bedlam* and *Une Heure de Mariage*. D.L., April 27, 1826.

ROLEY POLEY. Grecian, December 24, 1877.

ROLL OF THE DRUM, THE. (See *When Greek Meets Greek*.) Rom. D. 3 a. T. E. Wilks. Adelphi.

ROLLA. O. Simon. Moscow, 1892.

ROLLA; OR, THE PERUVIAN HERO. T. Transl. fr. Kotzebue by M. G. Lewis. Pr. 1799.

ROLLA; OR, THE VIRGIN OF THE SUN. P. 5 a. Fr. German of Kotzebue by B. Thompson. Pr. 1801.

ROLLICKING RORY. Irish P. Chalmers Mackey. Preston R.T., August 3, 1907.

ROLLING STONE SOMETIMES GATHERS MOSS, A. D. 4 a. F. Marchant. Victoria, October 15, 1870.

ROLLO, DUKE OF NORMANDY. T. J. Fletcher. His Maj. servants. Pr. 1640.

ROMA; OR, THE DEPUTY. D. 4 a. Adap. fr. Sardou's play, *Daniel Rochat*, by G. Lubinxoff. Eastbourne T.R., November 16, 1885; Adelphi, November 28, 1885.

ROMAN, THE. Dr. Pm. S. Dobell. 1850.

ROMAN ACTOR, THE. T. P. Massinger. Private house by King's servants, October 11, 1626; Black Fryars, 1629; L.I.F., June 13, 1722.

ROMAN BRIDE'S REVENGE, THE. T. C. Gildon. D.L., 1697.

ROMAN BROTHER, THE. T. Heraud, nineteenth cent.

ROMAN COMIQUE, LE. Op. bo. Offenbach. 1861.

ROMAN DAUGHTER, THE. T. (At the end of *The Rake and Country Girl.*) W. Harbach. 1780-90.

ROMAN EMPRESS, THE. T. W. Joyner. T.R., 1671.

ROMAN FATHER, THE. Adaptation of Betterton of *Appius and Virginia.* 1679.

ROMAN FATHER, THE. T. Alt. fr. W. Whitehead. D.L., February 24, 1750; C.G., November 18, 1767.

ROMAN FATHER, THE. T. 1 a. of Mrs. Letitia Pilkington's P.

ROMAN GENERALS; OR, THE DISTRESSED LADIES, THE. T. Wr. in rhyme J. Dover. Pr. 1697.

ROMAN MAID, THE. T. Capt. R. Hurst. L.I.F., August 11, 1724.

ROMAN PARISIEN, UN. Gaiety, June 13, 1883.

ROMAN REVENGE, THE. T. A. Hill. Bath. Pr. 1753.

ROMAN SACRIFICE, THE. T. W. Shirley. D.L., December 18, 1777. N.p.

ROMAN VICTIM, THE. T. W. Shirley.

ROMAN VIRGIN; OR, UNJUST JUDGE, THE. See *Appius and Virginia.* T. T. Betterton. Duke's. Pr. 1679.

ROMANCE. C.G., February 2, 1860.

ROMANCE AND REALITY. J. Brougham. Mentioned by Brewer.

ROMANCE AND REALITY; OR, THE POET'S HOME. Oa. Lib. by H. Foulkard. M. by J. W. Elliott. Royalty, June 30, 1870; Concert H., Store St., May 10. 1871.

ROMANCE DE LA ROSE, LA. Op. bo. 1 a. Offenbach. 1870.

ROMANCE OF AN HOUR, THE. C. 2 a. H. Kelly. C.G. Pr. 1774.

ROMANCE OF LOVE, A. C.D. 2 a. A. Steven. Berwick-on-Tweed Queen's Rooms, October 13, 1891.

ROMANCE OF THE HAREM, A. C.O. Lib. by A. Sketchley. M. by J. P. Cole. St. George's, June 19, 1872; Kilburn T.H., May 28, 1887.

ROMANCE OF THE SHOPWALKER, THE. C. 3 a. R. Buchanan and C. Marlowe (Harriet Jay). Colchester T.R. (orig. prod.), February 24, 1896; Vaudeville, February 26, 1896.

ROMANCE OF YE OLDEN TIME. A. M.C. H. Tweedie and D. Worsley. Victoria, Hampton Hill, February 25, 1901.

ROMANCE UNDER DIFFICULTIES. F. 1 a. F. C. Burnand. Cambridge, 1856.

ROMANTIC AMOREUX, THE. New Div. Mons. Simon. D.L., October 9, 1830.

ROMANTIC ATTACHMENT, A. Ca. P.A. A. Wood. Hay., February 15, 1866.

ROMANTIC BARBER, THE. P. 1 a. A. Sutro. Dublin T.R., March 2, 1908; Fulham Grand, March 23, 1908.

ROMANTIC IDEA, A. C.D. 1 a. J. R. Planché. Lyceum, March 2, 1849; (rev.), Olympic, January 30, 1867.

ROMANTIC LOVER; OR, LOST AND FOUND, THE. C. J. T. Allingham. C.G., January 11, 1806. N.p.

ROMANTIC RUY BLAS. Vaudeville, January 3, 1873.

ROMANTIC TALE, A. M.P. J. B. Johnstone. Alhambra, August 7, 1871.

ROMANUS. T. ? James Cook. MS. preserved in British Museum.

ROMANY LOVE, Oa. G. F. Vincent. St. George's Hall, April 2, 1889.

ROMANY RYE, THE. Rom. D. 5 a. G. R. Sims. Princess's, June 10, 1882.

ROMANY'S REVENGE, THE. D. 4 a. W. Clive. Gateshead T.R., August 12, 1891; (as *Zamet; or, Bonnie Bohemia*), Standard, November 21, 1891.

ROME EXCIS'D. Tragi-comic ballad O. Pr. 1733.

ROME PRESERV'D. T. Transl. fr. Voltaire. Pr. 1760.

ROME SAUVEE. T. Voltaire. 1752.

ROME'S FOLLIES; OR, THE AMOROUS FRYARS. C. by N.N. Pr. 1681. Ac. by Persons of Quality's House, 1681.

ROMEA DI MONTFORT. O. Pedrotti. Verona, 1845.

ROMEO AND JULIET. Wr. in Spanish by Lopez de Vega.

ROMEO AND JULIET. Brooke. 1562.

ROMEO AND JULIET. T. W. Shakespeare. 1596; finished 1597. Entd. Stationers' Hall, January 22, 1607, and November 19, 1607. Shakespeare's earliest T. Ac. at the Curtain. Luii da Porto's novel, "Hystoria di dui nobili Amanti" (Venice, 1535), followed by Bandello's novel (Lucca, 1554), was the origin of Boisteau's. Fr. Boisteau Painter took his "Rhomeo and Julietta" (Palace of Pleasure, 1567) and Arthur Brooke his poem of "The Tragical History of Romeus and Juliet, containing a Rare Example of True Constancie," etc. (1562; second edition, 1587.) Shakespeare borrowed from the poem, using the novel occasionally. Pr. 1st qto. (imperfect), 1596; 2nd qto., 1599; 3rd qto., 1609; 4th qto., 1611; 5th qto., 1637; 1st folio, 1623. Alt. by J. Howard, n.p., no date; alt. by T. Cibber, Hay., 1744, and D.L., November 29, 1748; alt. by Garrick, 1750; also alt. by T. Sheridan, Lee, and Marsh; alt. anon., 1770; alt. by J. P. Kemble, 1811; Lyceum, September 21, 1895; Court, February 17, 1904; Manchester Queen's, January 14, 1905; Imperial, April 22, 1905; rev. Royalty, May 5, 1905; Waldorf, May 2, 1907; rev. Royalty, February 13, 1908; rev. Lyceum, March 14, 1908; rev. Court, April 19, 1909.

ROMEO AND JULIET. See *Caius Marius.*

ROMEO AND JULIET UP TO DATE. Burl. S. C. Henry. Bayswater Bijou T., May 20, 1893.

ROMEO AND JULIET UP TO LARKS. Burl. 2 a. C. Cane. Lyrics by C. Cain and M. B. Lucas. M. by H. A. Douglas. Dublin Queen's R., August 21, 1893 (amat.).

ROMEO AND JULIET TRAVESTIE; OR, THE CUP OF COLD POISON. Burl. 1 a. A. Halliday. Strand T., November 3, 1859.

ROMEO AND JULIETTE. O. 3 a. Wds. by D. Segur. M. by Steibelt. Paris, September 10, 1793.

ROMEO AND JULIETTE. O. Dedicated to Paganini. Wds. by Berlioz and Emil Deschamps. Conservatoire, November 24, 1839; New Philharmonic, March 24 and April 28, 1852.

ROMEO E GIULIETTA. O. Bellini. (Venice, 1830.)

ROMEO E GIULIETTA. 3 a. Fr. Italian O. Vaccaj. D.L., June 26, 1833.

ROMEO E GIULIETTA. O. 5 a. Wds. by Barbier and Carre and M. by Gounod. (Paris, April 27, 1867.) C.G., July 11, 1867. Lib. H. B. Farnie. First time in English, Liverpool R. Court, January 15, 1890.

ROMEO THE RADICAL AND JULIET THE JINGO; OR, OBSTRUCTION AND EFFECT. C.O. C. P. Emery. Walsall Alexandra, August 14, 1882.

ROMILDARE CONSTANZA. O. Meyerbeer. 1819.

ROMINAGROBIS. Britannia, December 26, 1877.

ROMP, THE. M.E. 2 a. Alt. fr. Bickerstaff's *Love in the City*. D.L., May 22, 1817; Lyceum, June 21, 1821.

ROMULUS. T. H. Johnson. Fr. French of Mons. De La Motte. Pr. 1724.

ROMULUS AND HERSILIA. T. Dr. R. Schomberg. N.p.

ROMULUS AND HERSILIA. O. Transl. fr. Metastasio by J. Hoole. Pr. 1800.

ROMULUS AND HERSILIA; OR, THE SABINE WAR. T. Anon. Duke's, 1683. Epil. by Mrs. Behn.

ROMULUS AND REMUS; OR, THE TWO RUM 'UNS. Classical Burl. R. Reece. Vaudeville, December 23, 1872.

RONNIE BLAIR. Sk. C. Douglas Carlile. Surrey, August 2, 1909.

ROOF SCRAMBLER, THE. Parody on *La Somnambula*. By G. A'Beckett. Victoria, June 15, 1835.

ROOKWOOD. D. G. Roberts. Liverpool Shakespeare, April 15, 1895.

ROOM FOR THE LADIES. F. J. P. Woolner. Charing Cross, September 11, 1869.

ROOM 70. F. P. Fitzgerald. Hay., January 4, 1886.

ROOT OF ALL EVIL, THE. D. Guernsey T.R., June 12, 1876.

ROOT OF ALL EVIL, THE. P. 3 a. J. Douglass. Longton Queen's T., April 11, 1901.

ROPE MERCHANT, THE. F. M. Melford. York T.R., March 8, 1890.

RORY O'MORE. D. 3 a. Samuel Lover. Adap. fr. his own novel. Adelphi, October, 1837.

RORY O'MORE. Irish D. 4 a. J. W. Whitbread. Dublin Queen's Royal, April 16, 1900.

ROSABEL. T. G. Warren. See *Houp La!*

ROSALBA. O. 1 a. E. Pizzi. C.G., September 26, 1902.

ROSALIE. P. 1 a. M. Max-Maurey. Shaftesbury, March 21, 1908.

ROSALIE; OR, FATHER AND DAUGHTER. P. 2 a. Hay., October 7, 1823.

ROSALIE ET MYRZA. O. Boieldieu. Rouen, October 28, 1795.

ROSALINDA. M.D. J. Lockman. M. by J. C. Smith. Hickford's Gt. Room in Brewer's Street. Pr. 1740.

ROSALYNDE, EUPHNE'S GOLDEN LEGACIE FOUND IN HIS CELL AT SCLEVTRA. Prose Tale by T. Lodge. Afterwards suggested the story of Shakespeare's *As You Like It*. Pr. 1590.

ROSAMOND. O. J. Addison. M. by T. Clayton. D.L., March 4, 1707.

ROSAMOND. O. Alt. fr. Addison. M. by Mr. Arnold. L.I.F., March 17, 1733; C.G. Pr. 1767.

ROSAMOND. T. Transl. by F. Holcroft.

ROSAMOND. Swinburn.

ROSAMOND THE FAIR. Barnett, 1836. See *Fair Rosamond.*

ROSAMUNDE. D. 4 a. W. Christine von Chery. M. by Frantz Schubert. December 20, 1823.

ROSANIA; OR, LOVE'S VICTORY. C. J. Shirley. Circa 1666. See *The Doubtful Heir.* Lic. June 1, 1640.

ROSBERRY SHRUB, THE. C. 1 a. F. C. Drake. Pub. by S. French, Limited.

ROSE, THE. C.O. 2 a. M. by Dr. Arne. D.L., December 2, 1772. Pr. 1773.

ROSE; OR, LOVE'S RANSOM. C.G., November 26, 1864.

ROSE AMONG THORNS, A. Dr. Sk. S. Damerell. Islington Myddelton H., November 21, 1898.

ROSE AND COLIN. C.O. 1 a. C. Dibdin. C.G., September 18, 1778. Pr. 1778.

ROSE AND THE RING, THE. C.O. M. by Elena Norton. Lib. by Mary Hayne. Dublin T.R., March 23, 1878.

ROSE AND THE RING, THE. Fireside Pant. Dram. by S. Clarke fr. Thackeray's story. M. by W. Slaughter. P.O.W., December 20, 1890.

ROSE BERND. P. 5 a. G. Hauptmann. Great Queen Street, February 2, 1905.

ROSE DE ST. FLEUR, LA. O. Offenbach. 1856.

ROSE ET COLAS. Op. C. Sedaine. M. by Monsigny. March 8, 1764.

ROSE GARDEN, THE. P. 1 a. Adap. by W. Trant fr. Mme. De Girardin's *La Joie Fait Peur*. Royalty, February 9, 1904.

ROSE MAIDEN, THE. Cant. F. Cowen. St. James's H., November 23, 1870.

ROSE MICHEL. D. 5 a. C. Clarke. Gaiety, March 27, 1875.

ROSE MICHEL; OR, SINNING TO SAVE. D. 5 a. Adap. fr. French by C. Millward. Blyth T.R., September 13, 1886.

ROSE OF ARRAGON. J. S. Knowles. Hay., June 4, 1842.

ROSE OF AUVERGNE. O. Pub. by S. French, Limited.

ROSE OF CASTILE. O. 3 a. Messrs. Harris and Falconer. (Fr. *Le Muletier de Tolede.*) M. by M. W. Balfe. Lyceum, October 29, 1857; D.L., September 13, 1858.

ROSE OF CORBEIL; OR, THE FOREST OF SENART, THE. Melo-d. 2 a. E. Stirling. City of London, November, 1838.

ROSE OF DAWN, THE. P. 3 a. H. T. Rainger. Cheltenham Victoria Rooms, February 22, 1907.

ROSE OF DEVON; OR, THE SPANISH ARMADA, THE. Rom. D. 4 a. F. on Chas. Kingsley's *Westward Ho!* By J. Jourdain. Eleph. and C., February 18, 1889.

ROSE OF ETTRICK VALE; OR, THE BRIDAL OF THE BORDERS, THE. D. 2 a. T. J. Lynch. Glasgow Queen's Street; Lyceum (rev.), December 7, 1835.

ROSE OF PERSIA, THE. C.O. 2 a. By Capt. B. Hood. M. by Sir A. Sullivan. Savoy, November 29, 1899.

ROSE OF RATHBOY, THE. Irish D. 4 a. D. Fitzgerald. Kennington P.O.W., August 14, 1899.

ROSE OF ROMFORD, THE. Oa. M. by F. Robinson. Lib. J. R. Martin. Birmingham P.O.W., February 16, 1885.

ROSE OF THE ALHAMBRA. Burl. Extrav. in 3 spasms. C. S. Parker. Stratford T.R., June 6, 1891.

ROSE OF SHARON, THE. Cantata. Sir Alex. Mackenzie.

ROSE OF THE RIVIERA, THE. M. Extrav. 2 a. R. Bacchus. Lyrics by G. Sheldon. Brighton, May 25, 1903.

ROSE OF WINDSOR, THE. O. W. English. Legendary O. Lib. by W. Parker. M. by B. Andrews. Accrington Prince's, August 16, 1889.

ROSE POMPOM. P. 1 a. Metropole, April 6, 1900.

ROSE WITH A THORN, THE. Fant. P. B. N. Graham. Perf. by Amateurs, Ladbroke H., November 22, 1906.

ROSE-SCENTED HANDKERCHIEF, THE. C. Baron St. Eton. Amateurs. Bayswater Bijou, April 28, 1906.

ROSEBUD OF STINGINGNETTLE FARM. Burl. 1 a. H. J. Byron. Pub. by S. French, Limited.

ROSEBUDS. C. C. Bradley. Cheltenham T.R., June 22, 1885.

ROSEDALE. American C.D. Wolverhampton P.O.W., May 1, 1876.

ROSEDALE. 5 a. Rev. ver. of Lester Wallack's P., by C. Arnold. Parkhurst, February 6, 1893.

ROSELLANA. O. F. von Flotow. (Left unfinished at his death.)

ROSEMARY. P. 4 a. L. N. Parker and M. Carson. Criterion, May 16, 1896; New, March 12, 1903; Wyndham's, April 29, 1903.

ROSENCRANTZ AND GUILDENSTERN. Tragic Episode in 3 tab. F. on old Danish legend of Hamlet by W. S. Gilbert. Vaudeville, June 3, 1891 (mat.); Court, April 27, 1892; Garrick, July 19, 1904.

ROSENMONTAG. Mil. T. 5 a. O. E. Hartleben. St. George's H., January 14, 1902.

ROSES; OR, KING HENRY VI., THE. Hist. P. Compiled fr. Shakespeare by Dr. Valpy. Reading School, October 15, 1795.

ROSES AND THORNS; OR, TWO HOUSES UNDER ONE ROOF. C. 3 a. J. Lunn. Hay., 1825; D.L., May 3, 1828.

ROSES OF SHADOW. P. 1 a. A. Raffalovich. Athenæum, Tottenham Court Road, January 26, 1893.

ROSIERE, LA. C.O. 3 a. H. Monkhouse. M. by Jakobowski. F. on the F.C., 3 a., by W. T. Moncrieff, *Joconde; or, The Festival of the Rosière*. Transl. fr. the French. Shaftesbury, January 14, 1893.

ROSIERE, LA. C. 1 a. E. H. Keating. Publ. by S. French, Limited.

ROSIERE DE SALENCY, LA. O. Grétry. 1774.

ROSINA. C.O. 2 a. Mrs. Brooke. F. on the Scriptural story of Ruth and Boaz. M. written and arranged by Wm. Shield. C.G., 1783; O.H., September 26, 1808; D.L., April 20, 1815; February 10, 1816; Lyceum, September 22, 1818; D.L., October 13, 1831.

ROSMER OF ROSMERSHOLM. See *Beata*.

ROSMERSHOLM. D. 4 a. H. Ibsen. Transl. by C. Archer. Orig. prod. at Bergen, 1887. Eng. transl. at Vaudeville, February 23, 1891; rev. Terry's, February 10, 1908.

ROSMONDA. T. Rucelleri. 1525.

ROSMUNDA. T. Alfieri. F. on Bandello's novel. Transl. by C. Lloyd. 1815.

ROSMUNDA; OR, THE DAUGHTER'S REVENGE. T. Wm. Preston. 1793.

ROSSIGNOL. O. 1 a. D'Etienne. M. by Lebrun. D.L., July 18, 1846.

ROSSIGNOL; OR, THE BIRD IN THE BUSH, THE. Pastoral Ballet. D.L., April 29, 1825.

ROSY DAWN, A. D. 1 a. W. Wade. Manchester C.T., December 13, 1902.

ROTHERIC O'CONNOR, KING OF CONNAUGHT; OR, THE DISTRESS'D PRINCESS. T. C. Shadwell. Dublin. Pr. 1720.

ROTHORNAGO; OR, THE MAGIC WITCH. Fairy Spec. 3 a. H. B. Farnie. Alhambra, December 22, 1879.

ROUGE ET MIS, LE. P. 1 a. Johannes Gravier. Shaftesbury, March 21, 1908.

ROUGE ET NOIR; OR, WHIGS AND WIDOWS. F. 2 a. J. Ebsworth. Edinburgh Adelphi, August 7, 1841.

ROUGET DE L'ISLE. P. 1 a. F. Wills and F. King. Criterion T., December 10, 1896 (as *An Old Song*); P.O.W., May 15, 1900.

ROUGH AND READY. D. 3 a. P. Meritt. Brighton T.R., November 21, 1873; Adelphi, January 31, 1874; Globe, July 19, 1875.

ROUGH AND READY. D. Pro. and 4 a. Rev. fr. the foregoing by J. Glendenning. Clapham Shakespeare, October 4, 1897.

ROUGH DIAMOND, A. C.D. 1 a. J. B. Buckstone. Lyceum, November 8, 1847.

ROUGH HANDS AND HONEST HEARTS. D. S. Shields T.R., March 31, 1873.

ROUGH HONESTY. D. W. H. Pitt. Walsall Alexandra, June 25, 1897.

ROUGH JUSTICE. Dr. Sk. 1 sc. H. Hunter. Bedford, April 5, 1909.

ROUGHLY WOO'D AND GENTLY WON. D. Lynn T.R., June 27, 1878.

ROUND A TREE. P. 1 a. W. H. Risque. V., November 11, 1896.

ROUND OF WRONG, THE. W. B. Bernard. Hay., 1846.

ROUND ROBIN. M. E. 2 a. C. Dibdin. Hay., June, 1811. N.p.

ROUND THE CLOCK. Farcical absurdity 3 a. J. F. McArdle. Liverpool Alex., March 25, 1878; Surrey, June 2, 1879.

ROUND THE GLOBE. Spec. J. F. McArdle. Liverpool Alex., March 29, 1875.

ROUND THE GLOBE IN EIGHTY DAYS. Birmingham T.R., November 15, 1875.

ROUND THE GOLDEN FLEECE. Op. bo. 3 a. C. Laroche and P. Tillot. M. by J. Rogers. Plymouth T.R., June 13, 1902.

ROUND THE LINKS. C. Sk. West T., Albert H., May 9, 1895.

ROUND THE RING. P. J. Cobbe and P. Meritt. Hull T.R., July 14, 1889.

ROUND THE RING. D. 4 a. P. Meritt. Hull T.R., July 14, 1890; Surrey, November 2, 1891.

ROUND THE WORLD. New ver. by A. Murray of J. Verne and D'Ennery's *Round the World in Eighty Days*. Empire, March 3, 1886.

ROUND THE WORLD IN EIGHTY DAYS. MM. D'Ennery and Verne. Spec. D. Princess's, March 15, 1875; Birmingham T.R., November 15, 1875.

ROUND THE WORLD IN EIGHTY DAYS. Burl. Capt. FitzGeorge. Brighton T.R., March 13, 1877.

ROUND TOWER; OR, THE CHIEFTAINS OF IRELAND, THE. B.P. J. C. Cross. C.G. Pr. 1809.

ROUNDHEAD, THE. Orig. Rom. D. 3 a. B. F. Bussey and W. T. Blackmore. Crystal Pal., June 12, 1883; Terry's, February 20, 1891.

ROUNDHEADS; OR, THE GOOD OLD CAUSE, THE. C. Mrs. Aphra Behn. Duke's, 1682. Borr. fr. Tatham's "The Rump."

ROUSED LION, THE. C.D. Adap. fr. French *Le Réveil du Lion*, by Webster. Hay., November 15, 1847. See *Evergreens.*

ROUT, THE. F. 2 a. Sir J. Hill. D.L., December 20, 1758.

ROUT; OR, THE MODERN FINE LADY. 2 a. (MS., Murphy's Library.)

ROUT ROUTED. C. Anon. 1800.

ROVER; OR, HAPPINESS AT LAST, THE. Dr. Past. S. Boyce. Pr. 1752.

ROVER; OR, THE BANISHED CAVALIERS, THE. C. 2 a. Mrs. Aphra Behn. Duke's, 1677; C.G. (with alts.). Pr. 1757.

ROVER RECLAIMED, THE. C. Anon. 1691.

ROVER RECLAIMED; OR, THE MAN OF MODE A COXCOMB, THE. C. Cambell (Before 1814.)

ROVER'S BRIDE; OR, THE BITTERN'S SWAMP, THE. Rom. D. 2 a. G. Olmar. From "Letitia," in "The Tales of a Voyager." Surrey.

ROVERS; OR, A DOUBLE DISAPPOINTMENT, THE. D. In imitation of German. Pr. 1798.

ROVING, THE. C. Middleton. 17th cent.

ROVING COMMISSION, A. Ca. J. Daly. Royalty, April 7, 1869.

ROVING HUSBAND RECLAIMED. C. Wr. by a "Club of Ladies." Pr. 1706.

ROVING MEG; OR, THE BARGEMAN'S SECRET. D. 4 a. A. A. Clarke. Birmingham Coutts's, June 26, 1899.

ROW IN THE FAMILY, A. H. Paull.

ROW IN THE HOUSE, A. F. 1 a. T. W. Robertson. Toole's, August 30, 1883.

ROWLAND. See *Roland.*

ROWLEY AND CHATTERTON IN THE SHADES; OR, NUGÆ, ANTIQUÆ, ET NOVÆ. Elysian Int. Pr. 1782.

ROWS OF CASTILLE, THE. Burl. Conway Edwardes. Brighton T.R., March 4, 1872.

ROXANA. T. Alabaster. Pr. 1632.

ROXANA. T. Magnocavallo. Pr. 1772.

ROYAL ACADEMICIANS, THE. F. "Anthony Jasquin" (John Williams). His Majesty's servants at Stone House, in Eutopia, 1786.

ROYAL ARGIVES, THE. T. N.p. Anon. (Before 1814.)

ROYAL BERKSHIRE REGIMENT, THE. Dom. D. 1 a. H. T. Van Laun and F. Reino. Comedy, June 29, 1886.

ROYAL BETROTHAL, A. P. 1 a. E. Ferris and B. P. Matthews. St. James's, December 3, 1900.

ROYAL BLACKMAIL, A. Dr. Epis. Mrs. T. P. O'Connor. Holloway Empire, December 9, 1907.

ROYAL CAPTIVE, THE. T. J. Maxwell. Pr. 1745

ROYAL CAPTIVES, THE. T. Taken fr. Euripides. Hay. Pr. 1729.

ROYAL CHACE; OR, MERLIN'S CAVE, THE. Dr. Ent. introduced into panto. of *Jupiter and Europa*. Words by E. Phillips. C.G. Pr. 1736.

ROYAL CHOICE, THE. P. Sir R. Stapylton. Ent. Stationers' Co., November 29, 1653. N.p.

ROYAL COMBAT, THE. C. John Forde. Ent. Stationers' Co., June 29, 1660. N.p. Destroyed by Mr. Warburton's servant.

ROYAL CONVERT, THE. T. N. Rowe. Queen's, Hay., November 25, 1707; and C.G., June 4, 1739.

ROYAL CUCKOLD; OR, GREAT BASTARD, THE. T.C. Transl. fr. Ger. by P. Vergerius. Pr. 1693.

ROYAL DIVORCE, A. Rom. D. 5 a. W. G. Wills and G. G. Collingham. Sunderland Avenue, May 1, 1891 (4 a.); New Olympic, September 10, 1891; Princess's, July 25, 1892; rev. Scala, January 13, 1906.

ROYAL EXCHANGE, THE. C. R. Brome. 1661. See *The Queen's Exchange.*

ROYAL FAMILY, A. C. of romance. 3 a. Capt. R. Marshall. Court T., October 14, 1899; D. of York's, May 4, 1907.

ROYAL FLIGHT; OR, THE CONQUEST OF IRELAND, THE. F. Pr. 1690.

ROYAL FLOWER, THE. Adap. by "Pem" fr. L. Œillet Blanc. Alphonse Daudet. Coronet, August 28, 1906.

ROYAL FUGITIVES, THE. Burl. Pr. 1792.

ROYAL GARLAND, THE. Occ. Int. Isaac Bickerstaffe. C.G. Pr. 1768.

ROYAL HEART, A. Sk. A. Scott Craven and J. D. Beresford. Empress, April 27, 1908.

ROYAL KING AND THE LOYAL SUBJECT, THE. T.C. 5 a. T. Heywood. Pr. 1637. Borrowed fr. Fletcher's *Loyal Subject.*

ROYAL MAIL, THE. D. Pro. and 3 a. J. Douglass and another. Standard, August 18, 1887.

ROYAL MAIL, THE. Do. p. 4 a. Eva Elwes Durham. Goddard's, March 11, 1908.

ROYAL MARRIAGE, A. Ballad O. 3 a. Anon. Pr. 1736.

ROYAL MARRIAGE, A. F. J. Douglass. jun. Standard, April 20, 1868.

ROYAL MARTYR, THE. T. Dryden. 1669.

ROYAL MARTYR; OR, KING CHARLES THE FIRST, THE. T. Alexander Fyfe. Pr. 1709.

ROYAL MASQUE AT HAMPTON COURT, THE. Hampton Court, January 8, 1604, by Queen and ladies of honour.

ROYAL MASTER, THE. T.C. J. Shirley. Dublin New T., 1638.

ROYAL MERCHANT, THE. O. T. Hull. F. on Beaumont and Fletcher. C.G. Pr. 1768.

ROYAL MESSAGE, THE. Dr. Poem. Rev. H. Boyd. Pr. 1793.

ROYAL MISCHIEF, THE. T. Mrs. De La Riviere Manley. L.I.F., by His Majesty's servants, 1696.

ROYAL MISTRESS, THE. Mrs. Manley. 1696.

ROYAL NECKLACE, A. P. 4 a. P. and C. Berton. Imperial, April 22, 1901.

ROYAL NUPTIALS. Interlude. C.G., November, 1816.

ROYAL OAK, THE. Hist. P. W. Dimond. F. on *Charles the Second.* Hay., June 10, 1811.

ROYAL OAK, THE. Hist. D. 5 a. H. Hamilton and A. Harris. D.L., September 23, 1889.

ROYAL PARDON; OR, THE HOUSE ON THE CLIFF, A. D. 4 a. G. Conquest and H. Pettitt. Grecian, October 28, 1878.

ROYAL PENITENT, THE. Sac. D. J. Bentley. Pr. 1803.

ROYAL REVENGE, A. P., prol. and 3 a. A. O'Connell, J. Fox, and E. McCarthy. M. by La Rondelle. Windsor T.R., September --, 1904; Stratford R., July 10, 1905.

ROYAL RIDDLE, THE. Burl. H. Mills. M. by A. Mills. Woolwich T.R., February 16, 1887. (Touchstone Dr. C.)

ROYAL RIVAL, A. P. 3 a. G. du Maurier. F. on Dumanoir and D'Ennery's *Don César De Bazan*. Coronet, May 20, 1901; D. of York's, August 24, 1901.

ROYAL ROUNDHEAD, A. M. Ca. H. Seton. M. by D. Harrison. Blackburn T.R., September 11, 1893; St. George's H., April 17, 1897.

ROYAL SCOUT, THE. D. G. Comer. Wigan R. Court, October 10, 1892.

ROYAL SHEPHERD, THE. O. R. Rolt. Taken fr. Metastasio. M. by Rush. D.L. Pr. 1764.

ROYAL SHEPHERD AND ROYAL SHEPHERDESS. See *Amintas*.

ROYAL SHEPHERDESS, THE. T.C. T. Shadwell. Revision of a work by Fountain. D. of York's. Pr. 1669.

ROYAL SHEPHERDS. Past. 3 a. J. Cunningham. Pr. 1765.

ROYAL SLAVE, THE. T.C. W. Cartwright. Ac. before King and Queen at Ch. Ch., Oxford, August 30, 1636; also at Hampton Court.

ROYAL STAR, THE. C.O. 3 a. M. Ordonneau and F. Richardson. M. by J. Clerice. P. of W., September 16, 1898.

ROYAL SUPPLIANTS, THE. T. Dr. Delap. Taken fr. Euripides and Æschylus. D.L. Pr. 1781.

ROYAL VAGRANTS; A STORY OF CONSCIENTIOUS OBJECTION, THE. C.O. 1 a. C. Hurst. M. by H. Waldo-Warner. Earlham H., Forest Gate, October 27, 1899; Guildhall Sch. M., July 6, 1900.

ROYAL VOYAGE; OR, THE IRISH EXPEDITION, THE. T.C. Pr. 1690.

ROYAL WATCHMAN, THE. C.O. Lib. by W. Boosey. M. by F. L. Moir. Exeter T.R., April 11, 1887.

ROYAL WORD, THE. C.O. 1 a. M. by I. de Lara and H. Hersée. Gaiety, April 17, 1883.

ROYALIST, THE. C. T. Durfey. D. of York's, 1682.

ROYALIST, THE. Richmond T.R., April 4, 1879.

ROYALIST, THE. P. 1 a. R. Oswald. Swansea Grand T., September 5, 1907.

RUBBER OF LIFE; OR, THE BEST OF THREE GAMES, THE. C. Prol. and 4 a. A. G. and F. R. Bagot. Brighton T.R., October 1, 1885; Strand, November 3, 1885.

RUBE, THE SHOWMAN. D. Messrs. Colman and C. Calvert. Newcastle-on-Tyne T.R., September 5, 1870.

RUBEZAHL. O. 2 a. Wds. by J. G. Rhode. M. by C. M. von Weber (1805-1806). (1st a. contained 15 sc., 2nd a. 12 sc.)

RUBY. D. 5 a. E. France. Sadler's Wells, January 31, 1885.

RUBY HEART, THE. P. 1 a. Josephine Rae and T. Sidney. St. Leonards-on-Sea, June 6, 1892.

RUBY RING, THE. O. St. J. Hamund and A. S. Beaumont. Sydenham Pub. H., May 9, 1902.

RUBY RING, THE. D. 5 a. H. B. Maxwell and J. D. Hunter. Hastings Pier Pav., July 3, 1905.

RUDDY GEORGE; OR, ROBIN RED BREAST. M. Parody. 1 a. H. G. F. Taylor and P. Reeve. Toole's, March 19, 1887.

RUDDYGORE; OR, THE WITCH'S CURSE. Supernatural C.O. 2 a. W. S. Gilbert. M. by Sir A. Sullivan. The name was afterwards changed to *Ruddigore* (January 27, 1887). Savoy, January 22, 1887.

RUDEUS. C. Transl. fr. Plautus by Rev. L. Echard. 1694. Also transl. by Rich and others. See "Latin Plays," "Westminster Plays."

RUDOLPHO, THE HUNGARIAN; OR, THE THRONE, THE TOMB, AND THE COTTAGE. D. 4a T. Mead. Victoria, April 1, 1871.

RUGANTINO; OR, THE BRAVO VENICE. See *The Venetian Outlaw*. Rom. Melod. 2 a. M. G. Lewis. M. by Dr. Busby. D.L., October 18, 1805, and June 5, 1817; with M. by Cooke, D.L., May 26, 1832.

RUIN OF ATHENS. Cantata. Beethoven (1770-1827.)

RUINED BY DRINK. Temperance D. 4 a. Noble Adkisson. Pub. by S. French, Ltd.

RUINED LIFE, A. Prol. and 4 a. A. Goodrich and J. R. Crauford. Grand, September 15, 1884

RUINED LIFE, A. Dr. epis. F. Price. Empress, June 7, 1909.

RUINS OF ATHENS, THE. D.P. Wr. by Kotzebue. Comp. by Beethoven. (Prod. by the opening of a new T. in Pesth, February 9, 1812.)

RULE A WIFE AND HAVE A WIFE. C. 5 a. Beaumont and Fletcher. Pr. 1640. D.L., 1624, and C.G.; Hay., June 29, 1809. See *An Equal Match*.

RULE, BRITANNIA. Comp. by Dr. Arne for his Masque *Alfred*. (First prod. at Maidenhead, Cliefden House, August 1, 1740.) He afterwards alt. Masque into an O., and was prod. at Dublin, Smock Alley T., March 10, 1744.

RULE, BRITANNIA. Sk. 2 a. J. Roberts. Hay. Pr. 1794.

RULE, BRITANNIA. F. M. Becher. D.L., December 26, 1870.

RULE, BRITANNIA; OR, ENGLAND EXPECTS EVERY MAN TO DO HIS DUTY. Nautical D. Liverpool R. Colosseum, September 7, 1868.

RULE OF THREE, THE. Ca. 1 a. Francis Talfourd. Strand, December 20, 1858.

RULE OF THREE, THE. P. 4 a. P. Leclerq. Shaftesbury, June 30, 1891.

RULER OF THE SPIRITS. O. Weber.

RULING PASSION, THE. C.O. L. M'Nally. Dublin, 1779. N.p.

RULING PASSION, THE. D. Prol. and 5 a. J. Willing. Standard, November 6, 1882.

RUM ONES; OR, CLUB NIGHT, THE. M. Assembly. Lyceum playbill (?), April 9, 1822.

RUMAN AND LUDMILA. O. Glinka (second work) (1803-1857).

RUMFUSKIN, Burl. Hay., October 13, 1822.

RUMFUSTIAN INNAMORATO. Burl. T. 1 a. D.L., February 24, 1824.

RUMMIN'S RECEPTION. M. Eccentricity. C. M. Rae. Newark T., February 8, 1879.

RUMOUR. P. 3 a. J. Strange Winter. Vaudeville, April 2, 1889.

RUMP; OR, THE MIRROR OF LATE TIMES, THE. C. J. Tatham. Private house in Dorset Court, 1661. Rev. by Mrs. Behn. See *The Roundheads*.

RUMP.—THE FAMOUS TRAGEDIE OF THE LIFE AND DEATH OF MRS. RUMP, ETC. Westminster, May 29, 1660.

RUMPLESTILTSKIN; OR, THE WOMAN AT THE WHEEL. Extrav. F. C. Burnand. New Royalty, March 28, 1864.

RUMPLESTILTSKIN. Fairy P. Mrs. Hugh Bell. Adelphi, May 18, 1903; Royalty, December 26, 1905.

RUN DOWN TO BRIGHTON, A. M. Sk. Alice Maud Meadows. St. Martin's T.H., July 24, 1893.

RUN IN. Ca. Mrs. Penn Gaskell. Harlesden Constitutional H., January 12, 1899.

RUN OF LUCK, A. Sporting D. 4 a. H. Pettitt and Aug. Harris. D.L., August 28, 1886.

RUN TO EARTH. D. C. Saunders. Dublin Queen's, September 27, 1873.

RUN TO EARTH. D. G. F. Macdonogh. Sheffield Alexandra, March 2, 1874.

RUN TO EARTH. D. 4 a. F. on Miss M. E. Braddon's novel. Athenæum H., Tottenham Court Road, November 27, 1889.

RUN TO EARTH; OR, A GOLDEN FORTUNE. D. 4 a. G. Roberts. Eleph. and C., April 11, 1887.

RUN TO EARTH; OR, JUSTICE AT LAST. D. Prol. and 3 a. J. Stevenson, jun. Croydon R., March 8, 1905. C.P.

RUN WILD. Dom. C. 3 a. E. Coffin. Strand, June 30, 1888.

RUNAWAY, THE. C. Mrs. Cowley. Pr. 1776. D.L.

RUNAWAY GIRL, A. M.P. 2 a. S. Hicks and H. Nicholls. M. by I. Caryll and L. Monckton. Gaiety, May 21, 1898.

RUNAWAY HUSBANDS. F. W. H. Jackson. Kew Prince's H., February 14, 1893.

RUNAWAY MATCH, A. F. A. Mayne. Sunderland T.R., February 2, 1872.

RUNAWAY MILLIONAIRE, A. M. Farcical C. 3 a. J. Sugarman. Bridlington R.V.T., April 3, 1902. See *The Runaways*.

RUNAWAYS, THE. Ca. F. W. Broughton. Chester T.R., September 6, 1880.

RUNAWAYS, THE. Ca. Mrs. Aria. Criterion, May 11, 1898.

RUNAWAYS, THE. M.F.C. J. Gerant. Jarrow T.R., December 13, 1901; (by Jacob Sugarman), Woolwich R. Artillery, July 28, 1902. See *A Runaway Millionaire*.

RUNNAMEDE. T. Rev. J. Logan. Pr. 1784. N.a.

RUNNING MASQUE, THE. Masque. 1619-20. N.ac.

RUPERT DREADWRIGHT; OR, THE PRISONER AND THE SECRETS OF THE IRON CHEST. D. H. R. Beverley. Barnsley R. Queen's, February 13, 1871.

RUPERT OF HENTZAU. P. 1 a. Anthony Hope. Glasgow T.R., October 5, 1899; St. James's, February 1, 1900.

RUPERT THE RECKLESS. B. 1 a. Miss Fitpatrick. Publ. by S. French, Ltd.

RURAL FELICITY. O.C. Buckstone. Hay., June, 1834; revised as C.D. at Hay., December 7, 1868.

RURAL SPORTS, THE. With a few comic scenes called *The Stratagems of Harlequin*. D.L., 1740.

RURALISING. Ca. George Carlyle. Hanley T.R., April 15, 1872.

RUSHFORD'S LAST RUSE. C.D. 3 a. Woods and Lawrence. Greenwich, October 21, 1878.

RUSSIA; OR, THE EXILES OF SIBERIA. D. Prol. and 3 a. H. B. Farnie and R. Reece. Queen's, October 27, 1877.

RUSSIAN. Melo.-d. T. Sheridan. D.L., May 13, 1813.

RUSSIAN AMBASSADOR, THE. F. H. Shield. Newcastle-on-Tyne T.R., April 25, 1871.

RUSSIAN BRIDE, THE. D. C. H. Hazlewood. Britannia, March 9, 1874.

RUSSIAN IMPOSTOR; OR, THE SIEGE OF SMOLENSKO, THE. P. H. Siddons. With alt. by S. J. Arnold. Lyceum, July 22, 1809.

RUSSLDA. D. 1 a. V. Feiani. Shaftesbury, February 18, 1908.

RUSSLAN I LIOUDMILLA. Russian Rom. O. 5 a. Based on a poem by Pushkin. M. by Glinka. Prod. at St. Petersburg November 27, 1842. Overture played at Crystal Palace July 4, 1874.

RUSTIC, THE. C.O. 2 a. Lib. A. S. Siedle. M. by W. F. Halley. Swansea P. of W.'s Drill H., April 3, 1888; Neath Assembly R., May 31, 1888.

RUSTIC CHIVALRY. O. 1 a. Mascagni. Lib. transl. fr. *Cavalleria Rusticana*. Liverpool R. Court T., January 14, 1892.

RUSTIC MAIDEN, THE. Dom. and Mus. D. 2 a. Olympic, January 2, 1882.

RUSTIC PRIMA DONNA. D. 1 a. Publ. by S. French, Ltd.

RUSTIC ROSES, THE. Oa. Liverpool T.R., November 24, 1873.

RUSTICITY. O. Author of *A Marvellous Pleasant Love Story*. Before 1814.

RUTH. Anon. Pr. 1703; Brooke, 1778; Rev. C. Davy, 1787.

RUTH. Orat. Wr. by C. R. Pr. 1769.

RUTH. D. 3 a. (Another ver. of Mosenthal's "Deborah.") R. Moore. Princess's, July 7, 1868.

RUTH. Orat. Otto Goldschmidt. Exeter H., November 17, 1869.

RUTH. F.C. Sheffield Alexandra O.H., March 12, 1883.

RUTH; OR, A POOR GIRL'S LIFE IN LONDON. D. C. H. Ross and P. Richards. Surrey, February 18, 1871.

RUTH; OR, OUR VILLAGE HOME. O. Announced for March 7, 1846, but (?) n.ac.

RUTH; OR, THE LASS THAT LOVES A SAILOR. Nautical and Dom. D. 3 a. J. T. Haines. Victoria T., January 23, 1843.

RUTH AND BOAZ. See *Rosina*.

RUTH AND NAOMI. Sac. D. Transl. fr. Mme. Genlis by T. Holcroft. Pr. 1786.

RUTH LEE. D. Leeds Amphi., May 1, 1869.

RUTH OAKLEY. Dom. D. 3 a. T. Williams and A. Harris. Marylebone, January 15, 1857.

RUTH TUDOR. D. Adelphi, 1837.

RUTH UNDERWOOD. P. 1 a. L. E. Mitchell. Strand, May 26, 1892.

RUTH'S ROMANCE; OR, A SUMMER EVENING'S SKETCH. Ca. 1 a. F. W. Broughton. Bath T.R., March 6, 1876.

RUTHVEN. D. 4 a. A. Harris. Royal Grecian, 1859.

RUY BLAS. P. V. Hugo. Overture comp. by Mendelssohn, who brought MS. to London 1844, which was tried at a Philharmonic Rehearsal. First perf. March 11, 1839. Perf. in London at a concert May 25, 1849.

RUY BLAS. D. 3 a. Fr. French of V. Hugo. Princess's, October 27, 1860.

RUY BLAS. Italian O. 4 a. F. on V. Hugo's play (Milan, 1869). Signor Marchetti, 1835-1902. H.M., November 24, 1877.

RUY BLAS. Engl. ver. of above, by W. Grist. Liverpool R. Court, February 4, 1886.

RUY BLAS. D. 4 a. C. Webb. Publ. by S. French, Ltd.

RUY BLAS; OR, THE BLASE ROUE. Burl. 3 a. A. C. Torr (F. Leslie) and H. F. Clarke. Birmingham Grand, September 3, 1889; Gaiety, September 21, 1889.

RUY BLAS RIGHTED; OR, THE LOVE, THE LUGGER, AND THE LACKEY. Burl. Vaudeville, January 3, 1873.

S

SABOTS DE LA MARQUIS. O. Comique. Boulanger. 1854.

SACERDOTESSA D'IRMINSUL, LA. O. Pacini. Trieste, 1817.

SACK FULL OF NEWS, A. P. Announced for the Boar's Head, without Aldgate. September 5, 1557. Suppressed.

SACK OF ROME, THE. T. 5 a. M. Warren. Boston. Pr. 1790.

SACONTALA; OR, THE FATAL RING. Indian D. Calidas. Transl. fr. Sanscrit by Sir Wm. Jones. Pr. at Calcutta, 1790.

SACRAMENT, PLAY OF THE. See "Miracle Plays."

SACRAMENT OF JUDAS, THE. P. 3 a. L. N. Parker. Fr. the French of Louis Tiercelin. P. of W., October 9, 1899; (alt. ver.), Comedy, May 22, 1901.

SACRED DRAMAS. Miss Hannah More. Pr. 1782. Contain *Balshazzar, Daniel, David and Goliath, Moses in the Bulrushes.*

SACRED DRAMAS. Transl. fr. Mme. Genlis by T. Holcroft. Pr. 1786. See *The Sacrifice of Isaac.*

SACRED DRAMAS. Intended chiefly for young people. J. Collet. Pr. 1806. Contain *Ehud, Esther, Naboth.*

SACRIFICE, THE. T. Sir Francis Fane. Pr. 1686.

SACRIFICE, THE. Rom. P. 1 a. L. Alan and G. Stanley. Balham Assembly Rooms T., December 2, 1901.

SACRIFICE, THE. P. 4 a. J. Fritz Russell-Young. Bayswater Bijou, January 31, 1907.

SACRIFICE; OR, CUPID'S VAGARIES. M. B. Victor. Pr. 1776.

SACRIFICE; OR, DEATH OF ABEL, THE. Orat. Dr. Arne. C.G., Pr.

SACRIFICE OF IPHIGENIA, THE. Ent. of music. Dr. Arne. New Wells ver., London Spa, Clerkenwell. Songs for panto., *Harlequin Mountebank; or, The Squire Electrified,* added to it.

SACRIFICE OF ISAAC, THE. Sac. D. Transl. fr. Mme. Genlis by T. Holcroft, 1786. See "Miracle Plays."

SACRIFICE OF LOVE. P. Neuman. 1799.

SACRIFICED. D. 1 a. Mabel Freund Lloyd. Vaudeville, July 2, 1891.

SACRIFIZIO D' ABRAM. O. Morlacchi. 1817.

SAD MEMORIES. P. 1 a. F. Withers. Blackburn T.R., February 22, 1895.

SAD ONE, THE. T. 5 a. Sir J. Suckling. Pr. 1659. Left unfin. by Author.

SAD SHEPHERD; OR, A TALE OF ROBIN HOOD, THE. Dr. Past. 3 a. Ben Jonson. Pr. 1640. Fulham Palace Grounds, July 23, 1898, by Elizabethan Stage Society.

SADAK AND KALASRADE. Spect. D. E. Stirling.

SADAK AND KALASRADE; OR, THE WATERS OF OBLIVION. O. Wr. by Miss Mitford. M. by Mr. Packer. Lyceum, April 20, 1835.

SADDUCEE AND THE SINNER, THE. P. 4 a. C. Hallward. Manchester T.R., February 29, 1904; Kennington, June 6, 1904.

SADIE OF BRANTOME. C.O. 2 a. P. J. Barrow. M. by Paul de Loëtz. Porth Palace, March 19, 1907.

SAFE AND SOUND. O. T. E. Hook. Lyceum, Pr. 1809.

SAFE AND SOUND. F. S. Howlett. Liverpool Grand, June 8, 1896.

SAFFO. O. Pacini. 1796-1867 (1842).

SAGE AND HIS FATHER, THE. C. Transl. Anon. See "Theatrical Recorder."

SAGE AND ONIONS. Oa. M. by J. Crook. Lib. by A. Maltby. Manchester T.R., April 12, 1880.

SAIL AHOY. Nautical D. Newcastle Tyne T., September 29, 1874.

SAILOR AND HIS LASS, A. D. 5 a. and 17 tableaux. R. Buchanan and A. Harris. D.L., October 15, 1883.

SAILOR AND SOLDIER; OR, FASHIONABLE AMUSEMENT., THE. M.F. 2 a. — Knight, Hull, 1805.

SAILOR OF FRANCE; OR, THE REPUBLICANS OF BREST, THE. Orig. D. 2 a. J. B. Johnstone. Surrey, November 28, 1854.

SAILOR'S DAUGHTER, THE. C. R. Cumberland. D.L., April 7, 1804. Pr. 1804.

SAILOR'S DEVOTION, A. D. W. Rendall. Swansea Star T., June 19, 1874.

SAILOR'S FAREWELL; OR, THE GUINEA OUTFIT, THE. C. 3 a. T. Boulton, Pr. 1768.

SAILOR'S FORTUNE, A. D. 5 a. F. A. Barnes. Spennymoor, Cambridge, December 22, 1888.

SAILOR'S HONOUR, A. D. 5 a. Arthur Carlton and W. R. Waldron. Lincoln T.R., June 8, 1894.

SAILOR'S KNOT, A. D. 4 a. H. Pettitt. D.L., September 5, 1891.

SAILORS' MASQUE, A. Masque ac. Court circa A.D. 1620.

SAILOR'S OPERA, THE, T. Rhodes. Pr. 1789.

SAILOR'S OPERA; OR, A TRIP TO JAMAICA, THE. Ptd. 1745. D.L., May 12, 1731.

SAILOR'S PRIZE; OR, MAY DAY WEDDING, THE. Inter. of dancing and singing. C.G., May 1, 1795. N.p.

SAILOR'S RETURN, THE. C.O. A. Davidson. N.p. (before 1814).

SAILOR'S RETURN, THE. F. 1 a. *The Sailor and Soldier* compressed and under a new title. Leeds, 1805.

SAILOR'S SHEET ANCHOR, THE. Mk Ent. Hay., 1783. N.p.

SAILOR'S SWEETHEART, A. N. D. 4 a. F. A. Stanley and A. F. Henderson. Fulham Grand, September 29, 1902.

SAILOR'S WEDDING, THE. Rom. D. A. H. Brinsley Hill. Marlborough, September 7, 1908.

SAILOR'S WIFE, A. Mus. Duo. Alf. Shaw. M. by Bert Hunter. Blackpool, Victoria Pier, July, 1909.

SAILORS OF THE KING, THE. P. 4 a. F. Bateman. Cardiff King's, August 7, 1905; Terriss, August 21, 1905.

SAINT ALBONS. T. James Shirley. Ent. Stationers' Co., February 14, 1639. N.p.

SAINT AND THE WOMAN, THE. P. 4 a. C. March. Spennymoor Cambridge, June 10, 1907.

SAINT ANDREW'S FESTIVAL; OR, THE GAME AT GOLF. Dr. Satire. J. B. Roberdeau. D.L., May, 1795. N.p.

SAINT ANGELA. P. 1 a. Mrs. G. Thompson and Miss K. Sinclair. Kilburn T.H., January 18, 1892.

SAINT ANTHONY'S PIG. M.E. Brewer. N.p.

SAINT AUBERT. T. Weston. 1808.

ST. BARTHOLOMEW; OR, A QUEEN'S LOVE. D. Mrs. S. Lane. Britannia, May 21, 1877.

ST. BOTULF. See "Miracle Plays."

SAINT CATHERINE. Miracle P. About 1110. Geoffrey de Gorham, Abbott of St. Albans. See "Miracle Plays."

ST. CECILIA'S DAY. Ode. Blow. 1648-1708.

SAINT CICELY; OR, THE CONVERTED TWINS. Christian T. E. M. Pr. 1666.

SAINT CLEMENT'S EVE. D. Sir H. Taylor. 1862.

ST. CUPID; OR, DOROTHY'S FORTUNE. C. 3 a. D. Jerrold. Windsor Castle, January 12, 1853; Princess's, January 13, 1853.

SAINT DAVID'S DAY; OR, THE HONEST WELCHMAN. M.F. 2 a. T. Dibdin. C.G., March 31, 1800.

SAINT ELIZABETH. Orat. F. Liszt. 1811-86.

ST. FABYAN. See "Miracle Plays."

SAINT GEORGE. Miracle P. Bassingbourne, 1511. N.p. See "Miracle Plays."

ST. GEORGE AND THE DRAGON. Extrav. Wr. by Capt. R. L. Bayliff. Richmond T.R., December 16, 1891.

ST. GEORGE AND THE DRAGOON. Burl. Torquay O.H., August 6, 1883.

SAINT GEORGE AND THE DRAGON; OR, THE SEVEN CHAMPIONS OF CHRISTENDOM. Christmas Spec. St. George Ducrow. D.L., December 26, 1833.

ST. GEORGE AND THE DRAGON; OR, THE SEVEN CHAMPIONS OF CHRISTENDOM. Sk. Wr. by Fred Ginnett and Wal Pink. Empress, November 4, 1907.

ST. GEORGE FOR ENGLAND. P. W. Smith. Destroyed by Warburton's servant.

ST. GEORGE OF CAPPADOCIA. See "Miracle Plays."

SAINT GILES'S SCRUTINY; OR, THE CRIES OF LONDON IN A NEW STYLE. Short Int. Anon. D.L., 1785.

SAINT HELENA; OR, THE ISLE OF LOVE. M.E. Capt. Ed. Thompson. Richmond and D.L., 1776. N.p.

SAINT JAMES'S PARK. C. Anon. Pr. 1733.

ST. JOHN THE BAPTIST. Orat. Stradella. 1645-81.

ST. JOHN THE BAPTIST. Orat. Sir Geo. Macfarren. 1813-88.

SAINT JOHN THE EVANGELIST. D.P.

ST JOHN'S EVE. Fant. 2 a. Gabrielle Festing and Dorothy Hart. Royal Albert H., November 7, 1908.

SAINT KATHARINE. Miracle P. Geoffrey, afterwards Abbot of St. Albans. About 1110.

SAINT KILDA; OR, THE SONS OF THE GUN. After piece. Anthony Davidson. N.p.

SAINT KILDA IN EDINBURGH; OR, NEWS FROM CAMPERDOWN. M.F. R. Heron. Edinburgh, 1798.

SAINT LEGER; OR, SPORTING LIFE, ITS TRICKSTERS AND ITS TRIALS. D. 3 a. Mr. Fox. Liverpool T.R., March 12, 1877.

SAINT MARC; OR, A HUSBAND'S SACRIFICE. New Rom. P. D.L., June 6, 1853.

SAINT MARGARET'S CAVE. P. — Carr. Hull, 1805. N.p.

SAINT MARTIN'S SUMMER. P. 3 a. Miss Clo Graves and Lady Colin Campbell. Brighton T.R., February 7, 1902.

ST. MARY'S EVE; A STORY OF THE SOLWAY. Orig. Dom. D. 2 a. B. Bernard. Adelphi, December, 1837, and January 10, 1838.

ST. MERIASCK, LIFE OF. See "Miracle Plays."

SAINT OLAVE. Miracle P. Ac. in London, 1557.

SAINT OR SINNER. D. Pro. and 4 a. F. on Hugo's *Les Miserables* by A. Dampier. Surrey, March 26, 1881.

SAINT PATRICK FOR IRELAND. Hist. P. J. Shirley. Pr. 1640.

SAINT PATRICK'S EVE; OR, THE ORDER OF THE DAY. D. M. by Cooke. D.L., November 24, 1832.

SAINT PATRICK'S DAY; OR, THE SCHEMING LIEUTENANT. F. 1 a. R. B. Sheridan. C.G., May 2, 1775; March 17, 1831.

ST. PAUL. Orat. Mendelssohn. Wr. for Dusseldorf Festival, 1836.

SAINT PETER. Orat. Benedict. 1866.

SAINT POLYCARP. Orat. Ouseley. 1825-89.

SAINT RONAN'S WELL. D. A. D. M'Neill. Edinburgh Princess's, September 16, 1871.

SAINT RONAN'S WELL. D. D. Fisher. Belfast T.R., January 31, 1876.

SAINT RONAN'S WELL. D. 4 a. R. Davey and W. Herries Pollock. F. on Sir W. Scott's novel. Trafalgar, June 12, 1893.

ST. SEBASTIAN. See "Miracle Plays."

SAINT STEPHEN'S GREEN; OR, THE GENEROUS LOVERS. C. W. Phillips. Pr. 1700.

SAINT VALENTINE. C.O. Words by G. F. Sharpe. M. by H. H. Bowman. Halifax T.R., March 14, 1892.

SAINT VALENTINE'S. Oa. 1 a. J. E. M. Aitken. H. à Court Bergne. M. by R. Clarke. Albert H. West T., June 11, 1897.

ST. VALENTINE'S DAY. M.C. C. W. McCabe. M. by W. J. Jennings. Battersea Park Town T., May 16, 1891.

SAINT VALENTINE'S DAY; OR, THE FATAL CHOICE. D. 3 a. W. Travers. East London, July 17, 1869.

SAINT VALENTINE'S EVE. Sk. Wr. and invented by David Devant. Brighton Mollison's H., November 13, 1902.

SAINT VALENTINE'S TRAGEDY. Dr. P. Kingsley. 1846. F. on the story of "St. Elizabeth of Hungary."

SAINTS AND SINNERS. P. 5 a. H. A. Jones. Greenwich P.O.W., September 17, 1884; Vaudeville, September 25, 1884, and January 27, 1892.

SAIROKU. Jap. ver. of the Trial scene fr. *The Merchant of Venice*. Shaftesbury, July 15, 1901.

SAKEPS, THE. C.O. 2 a. Bk. by Lewis Champion. Lyrics by Claude Selfe. M. by Percy Bowles. Balham Assem. Rooms, May 1, 1908 (amat.).

SAKUNTALA. D. By Hindu poet Kálidása. Pl. for first time in English in the Conservatory, Botanic Gardens, Regent's Park, July 3, 1899.

SAL HAWKINS. Episode. Beatrice de Burgh. Criterion, July 13, 1905 (C.P.); Hammersmith Palace, September 25, 1905.

SALAMMBO. D. Adap. fr. novel of same name. Ladbroke H., November 11, 1885.

SALAMMBO. O. 3 a. Wds. by Du Locle. M. by E. Reyer. Brussels, February 9, 1890. A setting of Flaubert's "Rom."

SALAMMBO, THE LOVELY QUEEN OF CARTHAGE. Burl. Holborn, May 6, 1871.

SALEM'S SORROW. D. Stockport T., November 25, 1872.

SALISBURY PLAIN. C. Ent. Stationers' Co., November 29, 1653 N.p.

SALLY. M.P. E. Righton and A. Smith. Torquay T.R., November 5, 1903.

SALLY CAVANAGH; OR, A TALE OF TIPPERARY. D. J. S. Mansfield. Dewsbury T.R., November 18, 1871.

SALLY IN OUR ALLEY. P. 3 a. F. Lister and P. Heriot. Sadler's Wells, August 31, 1888 (C.P.).

SALLY IN OUR ALLEY. Dr. Episode. Middlesex, December 22, 1902.

SALMACIDA SPOLIA. Masque. Songs by Sir W. Davenant. Scenes by Inigo Jones. M. by Richards. Presented by K. and Q. at Whitehall, 1639.

SALMACIS AND HERMAPHRODITUS. Probably by Beaumont.

SALOME. O. 4 a. Massenet. Prod. in Paris under title of *Hérodiade*. C.G., July 6, 1904.

SALOME. P. O. Wilde. Bayswater Bijou, May 10, 1905 (rev.); King's, Covent Garden, June 10, 1906.

SALOME. D 1 a. F. on Oscar Wilde's Fr. P. M. by R. Strauss. Dresden, December 9, 1905; New York, 1907, where representation was forbidden after first performance.

SALOMY, JANE. P. 4 a. Paul Armstrong. Adelphi. January 18, 1907.

SALOON, THE. M.E. C. Dibdin. Circus. N.p.

SALOPIAN SQUIRE; OR, THE JOYOUS MILLER, THE. Dr. Tale. E. Dower. Pr. 1738.

SALT OF LIFE, THE. D. 1 a. Pub. by S. French, Limited.

SALT TEARS. Serio C.D. 1 a. T. W. Speight. Strand, March 12, 1895; Royalty, July 24, 1873.

SALTHELLO OVIM. Illegitimate T. Hay., July 26, 1875.

SALTINBANCO; OR, THE DISAGREEABLE SURPRISE. O. R. Sicklemore. M. by Mr. Prince. Brighton. Pr. 1798.

SALTIMBANQUES, LES; OR, THE BOHEMIANS. C.D. in Engl. by Maurice Ordonneau and A. Sturgess. Northampton O.H., March 24, 1902.

SALUTATION, THE. See "Miracle Plays."

SALVATION. D. 4 a. Arthur Shirley. Smethwick T.R., March 5, 1908 (C.P.).

SALVATION JACK. Sk. E. C. Matthews and C. S. Self. Walthamstow Palace, September 23, 1907.

SALVATOR ROSA. O. Gomes. (Genoa, 1874.)

SALVATORI. T. Herault. 19th century.

SALVATORI. Olympic, March 28, 1853.

SALVE. Dr. Fragment. 1 a. O. Beringer. Op. C., March 15, 1895.

SALVINIANA. F. G. L. Gordon. Op. C., June 2, 1877.

SAM. Sk. Joan Barnett. Adap. fr. *The Ticket-of-Leave Man*. Royal M.H., July 21, 1900.

SAM CARR, THE MAN IN POSSESSION. F. Darlington T.R., June 21, 1872.

SAM SINGS (THE WARRIORS); OR, THE MAIDEN AND THE MANDARIN, THE. Chinese O. 2 a. E. Woodhead. M. by F. V. Lawton. Huddersfield R., May 27, 1901.

SAM WELLER; OR, THE PICKWICKIANS. Dr. ver. of "Pickwick Papers," by Moncrieff. Strand, July, 1837.

SAM'S ARRIVAL. Absurdity. 1 a. John Oxenford. Strand, September 8, 1862.

SAME THING, NOT QUITE. C. Sk. 1 sc. Mark Melford. London Pav., December 24, 1900.

SAMOR. Milman. 1818.

SAMPLE VERSUS PATTERN. F. 1 a. W. Sapté, jun. Liverpool Alexandra, April 11, 1887; P.O.W., June 15, 1887.

SAMPSON. P. E. Jubye (assisted by Rowley). Ac. 1602. N.p.

SAMPSON. Orat. N. Hamilton. M. by Handel. C.G. Pr. 1743.

SAMPSON. Orat. Alt. fr. Milton's "Sampson Agonistes." 1758.

SAMPSON AGONISTES. Dr. Poem. John Milton. Pr. 1671. Greek transl. by George H. Glasse. Publ. in 1789. Kensington Victoria and Albert Museum, April 7, 1900.

SAMSON AND DALILA. Sacred O. 3 a. Wds. by Ferdinand Lemaire. M. by Camille Saint-Saëns. Weimar, December 2, 1877. Recited at Promenade Concerts, France and Rouen, 1890; C.G., September 25, 1893; C.G., April 26, 1909.

SAMPSON'S WEDDING. F. G. F. Rowe. T.R., Croydon, November 19, 1869; Lyceum, March 30, 1870.

SAMSON. Orat. Alt. fr. Milton. 1758. See *Sampson*, etc.

SAMSON. P. 4 a. Henry Bernstein. Prod. for the first time in Eng. Garrick, February 3, 1909; Swansea Grand, January 25, 1909; Garrick, February 3, 1909; Adelphi, July 2, 1909.

SAMUEL IN SEARCH OF HIMSELF. F. 1 a. J. Stirling Coyne. Princess's, April, 1858.

SAMUEL OF POSEN. C.D. 4 a. Geo. H. Jessop. Gaiety, July 4, 1895.

SAN SIN. Chinese O. 3 sc. Lib. by H. Blau. M. by V. Hollaender. Manchester T.R., May 11, 1899; Grand T., August 3, 1899.

SAN TOY; OR, THE EMPEROR'S OWN. M.P. Edward Morton. Lyrics by H. Greenbank and Adrian Ross. M. by Sidney Jones. Daly's, October 21, 1899.

SANCHO AT COURT; OR, THE MOCK GOVERNOR. Op. C. James Ayres. Pr. 1742.

SANCHO THE GREAT; OR, THE MOCK GOVERNOR. F.C. 5 a. Anon. 1799.

SANCTUARY; OR, ENGLAND IN 1415, THE. Rom. D. 2 a. J. E. Carpenter. Surrey, October 8, 1855.

SANCTUS EDVARDUS CONFESSOR. An Academic P. Probably presented before King James at one of the Universities.

SANDFORD AND MERTON. P. 1 a. F. C. Burnand. M. by Solomon. Comedy, December 20, 1893.

SANDFORD AND MERTON'S CHRISTMAS PARTY. M. Sk. Lib. by F. C. Burnand. M. by A. S. Gatty. St. Geo. H., December 27, 1880.

SANDOW GIRL, THE. M.C. Physical skit. Wr. by H. Darnley. M. by D. Powell. Putney Hipp., June 3, 1907.

SANDS OF DEE, THE. "A sensational aquatic Hippodrama." Alicia Ramsay and Rudolph de Cordova. M. by Carl Kiefert. Prod. by Frank Parker. London Hipp., August 31, 1908.

SANDS OF TIME, THE. D. of Welsh interest. 4 a. Dr. S. J. Pryce Jenkins. Neath Assembly R., May 24, 1894; Clapham Shakespeare, February 23, 1903.

SANG-AZURE. O. 1 a. Herman and Pascal. Publ. by S. French, Ltd.

SANG BLEU. C. 3 a. Major Yeedham. Ryde T.R., April 10, 1888.

SANTA CHIARA. Italian O. 3 a. Wds. by Mme. Birch Pleiffer. M. by H.R.H. Duke Ernest Saxe-Coburg-Gotha. Coburg, 1854; Fr. transl. by Oppel. Paris, September 27, 1855; C.G., June 30, 1877.

SANTA CLAUS. Fairy extrav. C. Daly. M. by H. Godfrey and I. Corsi. Crystal Palace, December 24, 1898.

SANTA LUCIA, A. P. 2 a. Adap. fr. the Italian of Goffredo Cognetti. Scala, May 3, 1908.

SAPHIR, LE. O. 3 a. Felicien C. David. Paris, 1865.

SAPHO. O. 3 a. Gounod. His first O. Paris, April 16, 1851. Prod. in 4 ac. with additional M., April 2, 1884.

SAPHO. O. 5 a. Wds. by Henry Cain and Arthur Bernede. M. by J. Messenet. Paris Opera Comique, November 27, 1897.

SAPHO. C. 5 a. Al Daudet and A. Belot. (Mme. Réjane's season.) Notting Hill Coronet, June 17, 1901; June 8, 1903; (Mme. Jane Hading), June 13, 1906.

SAPHO. An adap. (3 a.) of Daudet's novel by C. Fitch. Adelphi, May 1, 1902.

SAPHO. Ver. of Daudet's novel. 4 a. B. Espinasse. Manchester Grand Junction T., April 13, 1903.

SAPHO. Eng. ver. Douglas Knight. Douglas Grand, July 22, 1903.

SAPHO. Sk. Barnoldswick. Queen's H., March 9, 1907.

SAPHO AND PHAO. C. J. Lyly. Ac. at Court and afterwards Blackfriars. Pr. 1584.

SAPIENTIA SALOMONIS. Latin T.C. Wr. in the time of Qn. Elizabeth by an English hand. N.d.

SAPPHO. D. W. Mason. 1797.

SAPPHO. Serious O. 3 a. Words by Cammarano. M. by G. Pacini. Naples, November 27, 1840.

SAPPHO. O. Transl. and adapt. fr. Italian by T. J. Serle. D.L., April 1, 1843.

SAPPHO. Standard, June 11, 1866.

SAPPHO. T. 3 a. W. G. Wills. Dublin Gaiety, June 7, 1875.

SAPPHO. Lyrical Rom. 1 a. H. Lobb. M. by W. Slaughter. Op. Comique, Femruary 10, 1886.

SAPPHO AND THE PHAON. T. 3 a. P. McKaye. Manchester, T.R., April 30, 1907 (C.P.).

SARACEN'S HEAD. Com. Sk. Hay., September 10, 1814. N.p.

SARAH. F.C. 3 a. F. Jarman. Waterford T.R., December 27, 1892.

SARAH BLANGE. Ad. fr. the French *Sarah le Créole*. Olympic, October 27, 1852.

SARAH JANE IN THE HAREM. M. Extrav. W. M. Akhurst. Liverpool T.R., August 30, 1875.

SARAH THE CREOLE; OR, A SNAKE IN THE GRASS. D. 5 a. M. Barnett. Olympic.

SARAH, THE FAIR MAIDEN OF THE RHINE. Richardsonian T.D. R. J. Blyth. St. George's, July 10, 1879.

SARAH'S YOUNG MAN. F. 1 a. W. E. Suter. Surrey, April 21, 1856; P.O.W., April 6, 1867; Charing Cr., June 23, 1870.

SARATOGA. Marshall. 1874. (Produced in London under the title of *Brighton*.)

SARDANAPAL. O. 3 a. Otto Bach. 1860.

SARDANAPALAS. O. A. S. Famintsin. St. Petersburg. 1875.

SARDANAPALUS. Burl. H. S. Granville. Limerick T.R., May 15, 1868. St. Geo. H., December 23, 1868.

SARDANAPALUS. Burl. G. à Beckett.

SARDANAPALUS, KING OF ASSYRIA. Spec. T. 5 a. Lord Byron. M. by Cooke. D.L., June 10, 1834; Princess's, June 13, 1853; Preston T.R., December 6, 1897.

SARGINO OSSIA L'ALLIEVO-DELL AMORE. O. Paer. 1803.

SARSFIELD: A STORY OF THE SIEGE OF LIMERICK. Hist. Irish D. 4 a. J. W. Whitbread. Dublin Queen's, December 16, 1904.

SARRENNA. Eng. O. 1 a. M. by H. Löhr. Book by A. Marsh. Lyric, September 6, 1907.

SATAN. Sk. 3 Tab. H. Gratton and E. Jones. Bedford M.H., October 23, 1899.

SATAN'S ANGEL; OR, THE ADVENTURESS. Sk. Canterbury, April 8, 1907.

SATAN'S DAUGHTER. D. Pro. and 4 a. Adap. fr. Ouida's "Folle Farine" by W. Avondale. Wolverhampton P.O.W., November 4, 1882.

SATANAS AND THE SPIRIT OF BEAUTY. Rom. Legendary Spec. 2 a. J. S. Coyne. Adelphi, February 11, 1841.

SATANELLA; OR, THE POWER OF LOVE. New Orig. Rom. O. 4 a. Wds. by Harris and Falconer. M. by Bale. National English O. C.G., December 20, 1858.

SATIRO MASTIX: OR, THE UNTRUSSING OF THE HUMOROUS POET. Dekker. Ac. privately by children of St. Paul's and publicly by Lord Chamberlain's servants. Pr. 1602.

SATISFACTION. Ca. C. Bridgman. Bristol New T.R., August 20, 1880.

SATURDAY NIGHT IN LONDON. D. 4 a. M. Wilkinson. Bristol T.R., June 12, 1899; Greenwich Carlton, April 29, 1901.

SATURDAY TO MONDAY. M.P. 3 a. F. Karno. Grimsby P.O.W., November 14, 1903.

SATURDAY TO MONDAY. C. 3 a. F. Fenn and R. Pryce. St. James's, April 14, 1904.

SATYR, THE. Masque. Ben Jonson. In Lord Spencer's ent. for the Queen and Prince Henry at Althorpe, 1603.

SATYRE OF THE THREE ESTATES. Sir D. Lindsay. 1602.

SATYROMASTIX, ETC. See *Satiro-Mastix*.

SAUCY MAY; OR, LOVE'S STRATAGEM. C. South Shields T.R., March 10, 1884.

SAUCY SALLY. C. 3 a. F. C. Burnand's adap. fr. Maurice Hennequin's *La Flamboyante*, prod. at Vaudeville, Paris, February 22, 1884. Southport O.H., July 1, 1892; Comedy, March 10, 1897; July 26, 1897.

SAUCY SULTANA, THE. Burl. 2 a. By Victor Stevens and J. C. Shepherd. Cambridge T.R., December 26, 1894.

SAUCY VALETS, THE. King.

SAUL. Orat. Words attrib. to Jennens and Morell. M. by Handel. First perf. King's, January 16, 1739; Dublin, May 25, 1742; rev. by Sacred Harmonic Society, March 20, 1840.

SAUL. T. A. Hill. Pr. 1760.

SAUL. T. Alfieri. Transl. by C. Lloyd. 1815.

SAUL, KING. T. Countess of Huntingdon. Pr. 1703.

SAUL AND JONATHAN. T. E. Crane. Pr. 1761.

SAUNY. See *Sawney*.

SAUVONS LA CAISSE. O. 1 a. C. Lecocq. Brussels. 1872.

SAVAGE; OR, THE FORCE OF NATURE, THE. Adap. of M. De L'Isle's "Arlequin Sauvage," by Mr. Miller.

SAVAGE AS A BEAR. Olympic, September 17, 1870.

SAVAGE BENEATH, THE. D. 1 a. Godfrey Dean. Rehearsal, W.C., May 23, 1908.

SAVANAROLA. Grand O. Prol. and 3 a. Wds. by G. à Beckett, M. by C. Villiers Stanford (wds. transl. by E. Frank). Hamburg, April 18, 1884; C.G. (German O., under Richter), July 9, 1884.

SAVANNAH, THE. D.L., March 7, 1861.

SAVED. D. 3 a. H. S. Granville. St. Geo. H., December 23, 1868.

SAVED; OR, A WIFE'S PERIL. D. 4 a. Adap. fr. "La Maison du Mari," by A. Shirley. Windsor, April 20, 1869; Leicester T.R., October 8, 1883; Holborn, December 26, 1885.

SAVED BY A SONG. Oa. Lib. Col H. R. Addison. M. by E. J. Loder. Princess's, December 21, 1868.

SAVED BY A WORD. D. E. Newbound. Britannia, February 26, 1877.

SAVED FROM SIN; OR, A SOLDIER'S HONOUR. D. H. C. Selby. Neath Star, February 26, 1884.

SAVED FROM THE HAREM. Spectacle. Max Goldberg. Empress M.H., December 24, 1906.

SAVED FROM THE SCAFFOLD. D. 4 a. L. Carson. Peterhead Music H., N.B., October 20, 1897.

SAVED FROM THE SEA. D. 4 a. A. Shirley and B. Landeck. Pav., March 4, 1895; Princess's, August 3, 1895.

SAVED FROM THE STREETS; OR, WAIFS AND STRAYS. D. 4 a. G. Conquest and R. H. Eaton. Surrey, October 18, 1886.

SAVED FROM THE WRECK; OR, THE SMUGGLER'S FATE. D. Weymouth T.R., April 12, 1869.

SAVED ON THE POST. F. C. Fenton. Camberwell Surrey Masonic H., December 13, 1893.

SAVIOLO. P. 1 a. E. Castle and W. Pollock. Lyceum, March 14, 1902.

SAVONAROLA. P. 4 a. Max. Pireau and A. Grey. Northwich Central T., March 22, 1901 (C.P.).

SAVOYARD, THE. O. 3 a. Pr. 1815.

SAW YE BONY COMING? OR, THE FEMALE VOLUNTEERS. M.D. A. MacLaren. 1804.

SAWNEY. An East-End Epis. Sybil Noble. Court, March 14, 1909.

SAWNEY THE SCOT; OR, THE TAMING OF THE SHREW. C. J. Lacy. M. by Purcell. Altd. fr. Shakespeare. Pr. 1698.

SAXON PRINCESS, THE. Intended for D. only. Mr. Pye. N.p.

SAYINGS AND DOINGS. J. M. Morton. C.G.

SCALA DI SETA. O. Rossini. Venice. 1812.

SCALDED BACK; OR, COMING SCARS, THE. Travestie of H. Conway and C. Carr's D., *Called Back*, by W. Yardley. Novelty, July 12, 1884.

SCALES OF JUSTICE, THE. D. 4 a. W. R. Waldron. Standard, December 10, 1894.

SCAMPS OF LONDON; OR, THE CROSS ROADS OF LIFE, THE. D. Adap. fr. French of W. J. Moncrieff. Re-arranged by F. Marchant. Sadler's Wells, November 13, 1843; Grecian, October 26, 1868.

SCAMPS OF SOCIETY. P. 3 a. Mr. and Mrs. Charles Carte. Darwen T.R., February 3, 1896.

SCAN MAG. F. D.L., October 13, 1836.

SCANDAL. C. 2 a. Adap. fr. *Les Scandales d'Hier* by A. Matthison. Royalty, June 1, 1878.

SCANDAL MONGERS, THE. C. 4 a. R. Orme. Court, July 3, 1905.

SCANDERBEG. T. W. Havard. F. on Lillo's *Christian Hero*. T. in Goodman's Fields, March 15, 1733.

SCANDERBEG; OR, LOVE AND LIBERTY. T. T. Wincop. Pr. 1747.

SCANDERBERG. O. F. Rebel and F. Francœur. Academie, 1735.

SCAPEGOAT, THE. F. 1 a. J. Poole. C.G., November 25, 1825; D.L., November 4, 4, 1828.

SCAPEGOAT, THE. D. 4 a. W. Lawrence. Huddersfield T.R., January 27, 1890.

SCAPEGOAT, THE. P. 4 a. Adap. by W. Jones fr. a novel by Gertrude Warden. Globe, July 7, 1891.

SCAPEGRACE, THE. D. W. Miller. Ramsgate Amphit., January 19, 1893.

SCAPEGRACE, THE. Wordless P. Narr. by Albert Chevalier. D. of York's, September 3, 1906.

SCAPIN IN MASQUERADE. F. D.L., November 12, 1803. Transl. fr. French, *Crispine Duegne*, by Segur.

SCAR ON THE WRIST, THE. D. Pro. and 3 a. P. Simpson and C. Templar. St. James's, March 9, 1878.

SCARAMOUCH, A PHILOSOPHER; HARLEQUIN, A SCHOOLBOY; BRAVO, MERCHANT AND MAGICIAN. C. Edward Ravenscroft. F. on Molière's P., *Le Mariage Force*. T.R., 1677.

SCARBOROUGH LASS. Int. Francis Gentleman. Ac. at York. N.p.

SCARECROW, THE. C. 3 a. C. Thomas. Strand, May 29, 1889.

SCARLET BROTHERHOOD; OR, THE NIHILISTS' DOOM, THE. D. E. Darbey and W. Manning. Stalybridge Grand, October 2, 1893.

SCARLET CLUE, THE. D. 4 a. St. B. Wynton. Windsor R.T., March 30, 1905; Grand T., May 28, 1906.

SCARLET COAT, THE. Rom. C. 4 a. W. E. Grogan. Oxford New T., November 22, 1899.

SCARLET DICK, AND THE ROAD AND ITS RIDERS. D. 3 a. J. B. Howe. Brittannia, July 24, 1867.

SCARLET DICK, THE KING'S HIGHWAYMAN. D. 4 a. J. B. Howe. Britannia, October 24, 1878.

SCARLET DYE, THE. D. 3 a. Julia M. Masters. Brighton T.R., February 15, 1887; St. George's H., May 25, 1888.

SCARLET FEATHER. C.O 2 a. Fr. *La Petite Mariée*, by MM. Leterrier and Vanloo. Adap. by H. Greenbank. M. by C. Lecocq. Shaftesbury, November 17, 1897.

SCARLET FLOWER, THE. Spec. P. 4 a. E Fenn and R. Price. Worthing T.R., June 4, 1903.

SCARLET HIGHWAYMAN, THE. D. Max Malcolm. Hammersmith Lyric, May 28, 1908 (C.P.).

SCARLET LETTER, THE. Rom. D. 5 a. Adap. by N. Forbes and S. Coleridge fr. Nathaniel Hawthorne's story. Royalty, May 9, 1888 (C.P.); Royalty, June 4, 1888 (evening bill).

SCARLET LETTER, THE. P. Pro. and 4 a. F. on Nathaniel Hawthorne's novel. Pro. by C. Charrington. P. by Alec Nelson (E. B Aveling). Olympic, June 5, 1888.

SCARLET MARK; OR, THE WITCH, THE ROVER, AND THE MYSTERY, THE. D. 3 a. C. H. Hazlewood. Britannia, November 18, 1868.

SCARLET PATROL, THE. M.C. 3 a. O. Trevine and St. John Hamund. Kingston R. County, August 26, 1907; Fulham Grand, September 16, 1907.

SCARLET PIMPERNEL, THE. Rom. C. 4 a. O. Barstow and R. Rose. Nottingham T.R., October 15, 1903; New, January 5, 1905, and rev. December 26, 1905; New, January 12, 1907; New, December 30, 1907; New, April 20, 1908 (rev.).

SCARLET SHOE, THE. P. 1 a. L. Clarke. Brighton West Pier, May 19, 1905.

SCARLET SIN, THE D. 5 a. G. R. Sims and A. Shirley. Liverpool Shakespeare T., September 3, 1900; Peckham Crown, September 17, 1900.

SCARLET SINS. D. 4 a C. Crozier and P. Milton. Wakefield O.H., October, 4, 1888.

SCARLET WOMAN, THE. D. 4 a. C. S. Beaulieu. Maidenhead G.E.T., March 16, 1903.

SCARRED HAND, THE. D. 4 a. V. de Garno and L. Montague. Officers' Club H., Aldershot, November 8, 1901; St. George's H., January 13, 1902.

SCENE FROM OSSEAN. Sir John Sinclair. Before 1814.

SCENE OF CONFUSION, A. F. Wilks. Victoria, September 16, 1839.

SCENES DE LA VIE DE BOHEME. Murger. See *Mimi*.

SCENES ON THE MISSISSIPPI. Poplar Queen's, December 14, 1908.

SCEPTIC, THE. P. 1 a. H. Hill. Camberwell Metropole, June 22, 1896.

SCEPTRE AND THE CROSS, THE. D. 4 a. May Wright. Oswaldtwistle T.H., October 12, 1898.

SCHAMYL. Adap. by P. Simpson. Princess's, November, 1854.

SCHAWSPIEL DIRECTOR. O. Mozart. (Schoenbrunn, 1786.)

SCHEME. F. H. Clyne. Bristol Old T.R., June 29, 1880.

SCHEME THAT FAILED, A. P. 4 a. Fred Green. Accrington Prince's, July 16, 1908.

SCHEMER, THE. D. 4 a. W. Stanhope. Margate T.R., December 14, 1887 (amat.).

SCHEMER, THE. F.C. 3 a. Brighton Aquarium. May 14, 1894.

SCHEMERS, THE. F. 2 a. MS. sold with Mr. Reed's library.

SCHEMERS, THE. Sk. Leonard Mortimer. Canterbury M.H., May 5, 1902.

SCHEMERS; OR, THE CITY MATCH, THE. C. Alt. of Jasper Mayne's *City Match*, by W. Broomfield. D.L., April 15, 1755. Pr. 1755.

SCHEMES FOR MEN. Ca. 1 a. P. Sidney. MS. with Mrs. Douglas Cox.

SCHEMING VALET; OR, BROTHER AND SISTER. Int. Anon. Theat. Mus. 1776.

SCHMETTERLINGSSCHLACHT, DIE. C. 4 a. H. Sudermann. Comedy, February, 15, 1901; rev. Great Queen Street, April 21, 1906.

SCHNEIDER. M.P. 3 a. A. Shirley and R. Ripleby. Widnes New Alexandra, April 16, 1892.

SCHNEWITTCHEN UND DIE LIEBENZWERGE. Fairy P. A. Gorner. Scala, December 26, 1906.

SCHOLAR, THE. C. R. Lovelace. Ac. at Gloucester Hall and Salisbury Court. N.p.

SCHOLAR, THE. Adap. fr. French by J. B. Buckstone. Hay., July, 1835.

SCHOLAR'S MATE. Ca. 1 a. H. A. Kennedy. Chelsea T.H., April 25, 1893.

SCHOOL. C. 4 a. T. W. Robertson. P. O. W., January 16, 1869. Garrick, September 19, 1891; Globe, January 7, 1899; rev. Coronet, June 28, 1909.

SCHOOL BORED. Extrav. 1 a. H. Heighway. Publ. by S. French, Ltd.

SCHOOL BOY, THE. See *Woman's Wit*.

SCHOOL BOY; OR, THE COMICAL REVENGE, THE. C. 2 a. C. Cibber. T.R. in D.L. Pr. 1707.

SCHOOL BOY'S MASQUE, THE. Th. Spateman. Pr. 1742.

SCHOOL DRUDGE; OR, THE MODERN CINDERELLA, THE. D. Greenwich T.R., September 5, 1881.

SCHOOL FOR ARROGANCE. C. Holcroft. C.G., February 4, 1791.

SCHOOL FOR AUTHORS, THE. C. 3 a. J. Tobin. Hay., December 5, 1808.

SCHOOL FOR COOKERY, THE. F. W. M. Gattie. Belverede H., Belvedere, Kent, June 10, 1879.

SCHOOL FOR COQUETTES, THE. Ca. 1 a. J. P. Simpson. New Strand, July 4, 1859.

SCHOOL FOR COQUETTES. Prose C. Mrs. Gore.

SCHOOL FOR DAUGHTERS. C. 3 a. Lawler. 1808. Publ. by S. French, Ltd.

SCHOOL FOR DIFFIDENCE, THE. C. W. Nation, jun. Plymouth Old, 1789.

SCHOOL FOR ELOQUENCE, THE. Int. Mrs. Cowley. D.L., April 4, 1780. N.p.

SCHOOL FOR FATHERS, THE. C.O. Alt. of *Lionel and Clarissa*. Isaac Bickerstaffe. D.L. Pr. 1770.

SCHOOL FOR FRIENDS, THE. C. Miss Chambers. D.L., December 10, 1805. Pr. 1805.

SCHOOL FOR GALLANTRY, THE. C. 1 a. New scene by Stamfield. M. by Cooke. D.L., May 3, 1828.

SCHOOL FOR GREYBEARDS; OR, THE MOURNING BRIDE, THE. C. Mrs. Cowley. Alt. of Mrs. Behn's *The Lucky Chance; or, The Alderman's Bargain*. D.L., November 25, 1786. Pr. 1786.

SCHOOL FOR GROWN CHILDREN. C. Morton. C.G., January 9, 1827.

SCHOOL FOR GROWN GENTLEMEN. C. Morton, 1827.

SCHOOL FOR GUARDIANS, THE. C. A. Murphy. C.G., January 10, 1767. Pr. 1767.

SCHOOL FOR HONOUR; OR, THE CHANCE OF WAR, THE. C. Transl. fr. German of Lessing. Same as *The Disbanded Officer; or, The Baroness of Bruchsal*. Anon. 1799.

SCHOOL FOR HUSBANDS, A. Transl. fr. Molière by J. Ozell.

SCHOOL FOR HUSBANDS, THE. Sk. 3 scenes. Gertrude Binns and J. Halford, junr. Mount View H., December 20, 1897.

SCHOOL FOR HUSBANDS. C. 4 a. Stanislaus Strange. Scala, March 10, 1906.

SCHOOL FOR INDIFFERENCE, THE. C. Taken fr. Cibber's *Comical Lovers*. Announced for D.L. 1787, but n.ac.

SCHOOL FOR INGRATITUDE, THE. C. —. Fisher. N.D. 1798.

SCHOOL FOR INTRIGUE, THE. C. 4 a. J. Mortimer. Olympic, December 1, 1873.

SCHOOL FOR KINGS. D.L., March 7, 1853.

SCHOOL FOR LADIES; OR, THE LEVEL OF LOVERS, THE. C. Hay., 1780. N.p.

SCHOOL FOR LOVERS, THE. C. W. Whitehead. D.L. Pr. 1762. F. on Fontenelle's *Le Testament*.

SCHOOL FOR MUFFS, THE. Ca. R. Dodson. Surrey, February 21, 1876.

SCHOOL FOR ORATORS; OR, A PEEP INTO THE FORUM, THE. F. Pr. 1809.

SCHOOL FOR PREJUDICE, THE. C. 5 a. T. Dibdin. Enlargement of his *Liberal Opinions*. C.G., January 3, 1801.

SCHOOL FOR PREJUDICE; OR, THE JEW AND THE YORKSHIREMAN, THE. C. D.L., June 28, 1814.

SCHOOL FOR RAKES, THE. C. Mrs. Eliz. Griffiths. Taken fr. Beaumarchais's *Eugenie*. D.L., February 4, 1769. Pr. 1769.

SCHOOL FOR SAINTS, A. C. 3 a. J. O. Hobbes. Lyceum, March 30, 1896 (C.P.).

SCHOOL FOR SCANDAL, THE. C. 5 a. R. Brinsley Sheridan. D.L., May 8, 1777; rev., Sadler's Wells, 1866; rev. Vaudeville, July 18, 1872; Criterion, April 1, 1891 (arr. by Ch. Wyndham); Daly's, November 13, 1893; Lyceum, June 20, 1896; Terry's, July 4, 1898; rev. St. James's, September 14, 1907; rev. H.M., April 7, 1909.

SCHOOL FOR SCANDAL, THE. C. Political satire. Anon. 1778, 1784; Ireland, 1788.

SCHOOL FOR SCANDAL; OR, NEWSPAPERS, THE. C. Pr. 1792.

SCHOOL FOR SCANDAL REVERSED. C. ("Humorists' Magazine.") Anon. 1787.

SCHOOL FOR SCANDAL SCANDALISED, THE. Int. 1 a. C.G., March 18, 1780.

SCHOOL FOR SCHEMING, A. C. D. Boucicault. Hay., February 4, 1847.

SCHOOL FOR SNOBS. P. 1 a. Hilda Hatton. Dorking P.H., January 25, 1909.

SCHOOL FOR SOLDIERS; OR, THE DESERTER, A. P. 4 a. J. Henry. Ac. in Jamaica. Pr. 1783.

SCHOOL FOR STEPMOTHERS. D. Berquin. 1793.

SCHOOL FOR THE KINGS, THE. D. 3 a. D.L., March 7, 1853.

SCHOOL FOR TIGERS. Mark Lemon.

SCHOOL FOR VANITY. C. S. J. Pratt. D.L., January 29, 1783. Pr. in his "Miscellanies," 1785.

SCHOOL FOR WIDOWS, THE. C. R. Cumberland. C.G., May 8, 1789. (*The County Attorney*, with alt.)

SCHOOL FOR WIVES, THE. C.T. ("St. James's Magazine.") Lloyd. 1768.

SCHOOL FOR WIVES, THE. C. H. Kelly. D.L., December 11, 1773; D.L., May 17, 1814.

SCHOOL FOR WIVES. P. 3 a. A. Dubourg. Publ. by Douglas Cox.

SCHOOL FOR WOMEN, A. F. Anon. C.G., March 19, 1735. N.p.

SCHOOL FOR WOMEN, A. C. Transl. fr. French of M. de Moissy by R. Lloyd.

SCHOOL FOR WOMEN. C. Transl. fr Molière's *Ecole des Femmes*. Ozell.

SCHOOL FOR WOMEN CRITICISED, THE. C. Transl. fr. Molière's *Ecole des Femmes*. Ozell.

SCHOOL GIRL, THE. C.O. 3 a. G. Manchester. M. by A. Maurice. Cardiff Grand T., September 2, 1895; Standard, October 14, 1895.

SCHOOL GIRL, THE. M.P. 2 a. H. Hamilton and P. Potter. Lyrics by C. H. Taylor. M. by L. Stuart. P.O.W.'s, May 9, 1903.

SCHOOL MODERATOR, THE. P. 1648. Probably same as *Combat of Caps*.

SCHOOL OF ABUSE. T. Lodge. Publ. 1579.

SCHOOL OF ACTION, THE. C. Sir R. Steele. 1809. Unfinished.

SCHOOL OF COMPLIMENTS, THE. C. J. Shirley. Afterwards called *Love Tricks; or, The School of Compliments*. Private house in D.L. and D. of Y.'s in L.I.F. Pr. 1631. See *Jenkin's Love Course*.

SCHOOL OF (HE)ARTS. Ca. G. R. Walker. Park, March 27, 1880.

SCHOOL MODERATOR, THE. In Mr. Garrick's Collection.

SCHOOL OF REFORM; OR, HOW TO RULE A HUSBAND, THE. C. 5 a. T. Morton. C.G., January 15, 1805.

SCHOOL OF SHAKESPEARE. Dr. Kenrick. 1774.

SCHOOL OF SHAKESPEARE; OR, HUMOURS AND PASSIONS, THE. Ent. 5 a. Hay., July 17, 1781, and August 7, 1781. N.p.

SCHOOL OF THE WORLD, THE. C. 3 a. Transl. from French by T. Holcroft. Pr. 1789.

SCHOOL PLAY. Int. Anon. Pr. 1664.

SCHOOLBOY'S DREAM, A. Song-Scena. Harry Dacre. Holloway Empire, July 15, 1907.

SCHOOLFELLOWS. C. 2 a. D. Jerrold. Queen's, February 16, 1835.

SCHOOLMASTER AT HOME, THE. Farcetta. 1 a. M. by A. Wade. Lyceum (playbill), September 5, 1835.

SCHOOLMASTER OF LYNN, THE. D. 3 a. Marylebone, August 23, 1879.

SCHOOLMATES. Rom. D. Pro. and 3 a. E. France. Norwich T.R., September 12, 1884.

SCHOOLMISTRESS, THE. F. 3 a. A. W. Pinero. Court, March 27, 1886.

SCHRIFTEN, THE ONE-EYED PILOT. D. G. Conquest and H. Pettitt. Grecian, April 2, 1877.

SCHWABENSTREICHE. Royalty, November 28, 1894.

SCHWEIZERFAMILE, DIE. O. Weigh.

SCHWENK THE DREAMER. C.O. H. Starr. Gloucester T.R., November 23, 1900.

SCIATICA. Sk. Greenwich Barnard's Pal., February 14, 1908.

SCIENCE OF ADVERTISEMENT. C. 1 a. H. C. Pemberton. Publ. by S. French, Limited.

SCIENCE OF LOVE, THE. Oa. J. A. Harcourt. Norwich, Noverre's R., October 16, 1874.

SCILLY GIRL, THE. M.P. Book and lyrics A. Mayhew, and M. by Wm. Neale. Woolwich Grand, December 12, 1904.

SCILLY SEASON, A. C.O. I a. F. Graves, Perth, Murray, January 9, 1909 (amat.).

SCIPIO AFRICANUS. T. C. Beckingham. T. in L.I.F., February 18, 1718.

SCIPIONE IN CARBAGINE. O. Mercadante. (Rome, 1820.)

SCOGAN AND SKELTON. P. Wm. Rankins. Ac. 1600. N.p.

SCORNFUL LADY, THE. C. Beaumont and Fletcher. Black Friars. Pr. 1616. See *The Capricious Lady, The False Heir*.

SCORNFUL LADY. Adap. fr. foregoing by T. J. Serle.

SCORPION, THE. Oxford Town H., December 1, 1884. See *That Young Man*.

SCOTCH. F. 3 a. Forbes Dawson. Ealing Lyric Hall, September 12, 1895.

SCOTCH GHOST, THE. Ballet. D.L., 1796. N.p.

SCOTCH MARRIAGE, A. C. 1 a. Fergus Hume. Criterion, December 26, 1907.

SCOTCH MIST, A. F.C. 3 a. E. Shepherd. Vaudeville, November 10, 1886.

SCOTCH MIXED. Mus. Sk. F. Price. Hackney Empire, January 4, 1909.

SCOTS FIGARIES; OR, A KNOT OF KNAVES, THE. C. J. Tatham. 1652.

SCOTS WHA HAE WI' WALLACE BLED. D. 5 a. Ernest Stevens. Glasgow Grand, October 15, 1895.

SCOTS CHIEF, THE. D. J. R. Anderson. Surrey, between 1863 and 1865.

SCOTTISH BLUEBELLS, THE. N.C. David James. M. by Esmond Carr. Edinburgh Grand, March 21, 1906.

SCOTTISH CHIEF, THE. Britannia, March 26, 1866.

SCOTTISH CHIEFS, THE. D. Mr. Egan. Leith T.R., March 12, 1868.

SCOTTISH HISTORIE OF JAMES IV.; SLAINE AT FLODDEN, THE. D. Greene. Pr. 1598.

SCOTTISH POLITIC PRESBYTER SLAIN BY AN ENGLISH INDEPENDENT; OR, THE INDEPENDENTS' VICTORY OVER THE PRESBYTER PARTY, THE. T.C. Anon. Pr. 1647.

SCOURGE FOR SIMONY, A. Anon. 1606. See *The Return from Parnassus*.

SCOURGE OF VILLAINIE, THE. J. Marston. Pr. 1598.

SCOWERERS, THE. C. Thomas Shadwell. Ac. by Their Maj.'s servants. Pr. 1691. D.L., August 22, 1717.

SCRAP OF PAPER, A. C.D. 3 a. Adapt. fr. Sardou's *Les Pattes de Mouche* by J. P. Simpson. St. James's, April 22, 1861.

SCRAPE O' THE PEN, A. Scottish C.D. 2 a. Graham Moffat. Glasgow Athenæum, April 23, 1909.

SCREW LOOSE, A. F. 3 a. M. Melford. Vaudeville, November 1, 1893.

SCRIBBLER, THE. C. Pr. at Dublin 1751.

SCRIBE, THE. Rom. P. 4 a. Boscombe Grand, May 12, 1899.

SCRIBE, THE. C.O. 1 a. P. Hope. Sydenham Public H., November 3, 1899.

SCRIBE; OR, LOVE AND LETTERS, THE. Oa. 1 a. P. Hayman. Globe, October 5, 1891.

SCROOGE. P. 1 a. Adap. by J. C. Buckstone fr. Dickens's "Christmas Carol." October 3, 1901.

SCRUB'S TRIP TO THE JUBILEE. See *The Stratford Jubilee*.

SCRUPULOUS MAN, A. C. 1 a. Max Hecht. Adap. fr. O. Mirbeau's *Scrupules*. St. James's, March 23, 1905.

SCUFFIARA RAGGIRATRICE, LA. O. Paisiello. 1741-1815.

SCULPTOR, THE. C. 3 a. Adap fr. German by T. G. Warren and J. Croft. Dublin Leinster H., August 18, 1893.

SCUTTLED SHIP, THE. D. Prol. and 5 a. C. Reade. Olympic, April 2, 1877.

SCYROS. Past. Ms. Brookes. 1612.

SCYTHES, THE. T. Voltaire. 1761.

SCYTHIAN SHEPHERD; OR, TAMERLAIN THE GREAT, THE. Mentioned by Saunders. 1681.

SEA, THE. Nautical D. 2 a. C. A. Somerset. Queen's, 1834.

SEA AND LAND. D. M. Lemon. Adelphi, May, 1852.

SEA CAPTAIN; OR, THE BIRTHRIGHT, THE. P. Lord Lytton. Hay., 1839.

SEA FLOWER, THE. P. 4 a. A. Law. Comedy, March 5, 1898.

SEA FRUIT. D. 5 a. H. Moss. Swansea T.R., May 29, 1893.

SEA GULLS. Original F. C. A. Maltby and F. Stainforth. Royalty, August 10, 1869.

SEA IS ENGLAND'S GLORY, THE. D. F. Marchant. Britannia, September 20, 1875.

SEA KING'S VOW; OR, A STRUGGLE FOR LIBERTY, THE. Hist. D. 3 a. E. Stirling. Surrey, February 16, 1846.

SEA MAID, THE. C. 3 a. Ronald McDonald. Manchester Queen's, January 16, 1906 (C.P.).

SEA NYMPHS, THE. Mus. Rom. Lib. by R. Reece and H. B. Farnie. M. by Lecocq. Brighton T.R., September 3, 1877: Folly, September 15, 1877.

SEA OF ICE; OR, THE PRAYER OF THE WRECKED AND THE GOLD-SEEKERS OF MEXICO. Rom. D. 5 a. Fr. French of MM. Dennery and Dugué. (Ambigu-Comique, Paris, October 20, 1853.) Glasgow R. Colosseum and O.H., November 28, 1867; Bristol, March 29, 1875.

SEA URCHINS, THE. See *The Mousetrap.*

SEA VOYAGE, THE. C. Beaumont and Fletcher. Pr. 1647. See *Commonwealth of Women.*

SEA VOYAGE, THE. Adap. of above by D'Urfey. 1686.

SEAGULL ROCK. Oa. R. T. Gunton. M. by W. Williams. Hatfield, February 21, 1895.

SEAGULLS. F. 1 a. C. Maltby and F. Stainforth. Royalty, August 10, 1869.

SEAL OF CONFESSION, THE. Dram. Inci. in 1 a. Percy Ford. Camberwell Empire, March 9, 1908.

SEAL OF SILENCE, THE. D. 4 a. C. W. Mill. Croydon T.R., February 10, 1902; Stratford T.R., July 14, 1902.

SEALED TO SILENCE. D. 4 a. Adap. by F. Moir Bussy and H. M. Holles from a novel by F. Freeland and S. Norton. Strand, April 10, 1896.

SEALED TO SILENCE. D. 5 a. H. V. Rees and S. Norton. Novelty, September 28, 1896.

SEAMAN'S HONEST WIFE, THE. P. MS. preserved in private library in Ireland, dated 1632.

SEAMAN'S RETURN; OR, THE UNEXPECTED MARRIAGE, THE. Op. F. J. Price. Ac. at Worcester, Shrewsbury, etc. Pr. 1795.

SEARCH AFTER HAPPINESS, THE. Past D. Miss Hannah More. (Her first production. Aged 17.) 1773.

SEARCH AFTER PERFECTION, A. C. 5 a. Joanna Baillie. Pr. 1814.

SEARCH FOR MONEY, A. C. by Rowley, 1609.

SEASIDE. Ballet, one tab. M. by Leopold Wenzel. Empire, September 10, 1900.

SEASIDE HERO, THE. D. 3 a. J. Carr. Pr. 1804.

SEASIDE MANIA. M. and Satirical Sk. C Grain. St. Geo. H., September 29, 1890.

SEASIDE STORY, THE. Op. D. 2 a. Mr. Dimond, jun. C.G., May 12, 1801. Pr. 1801.

SEASIDE STUDIES. W. Brough. Gal. of Illus., June 20, 1859.

SEASONS, THE. Dr. Ent. H. Woodward. Rev. S. Bishop. (Intended for C.G., but author died before completion.)

SEASONS, THE. Cantata. J. Haydn. 1803. Selection fr. Haydn. D.L., February 26, 1817.

SEAWEED HALL; OR, JACK AND JILL. Ca. 2 a. J. B. Johnston. Hoxton New Variety, March 14, 1870.

SEATS OF THE MIGHTY, THE. Prol. and 3 a. Adap. by G. Parker of his novel. (First prod. in America.) His Majesty's, April 28, 1897.

SEBASTIAN. T. G. P. Toosey. Pr. 1772.

SEBASTIAN, KING OF PORTUGAL. P. H. Chettle and T. Dekker. 1601. N.p.

SECOND CALENDER. Hay. N.d.

SECOND FAVOURITE, THE. P. 1 a. Edith Leyland-Clinton. Westminster Caxton H., November 13, 1905.

SECOND FIDDLE. See *The Shadow of the Mill.*

SECOND IN COMMAND. C. 4 a. R. Marshall. Hay., November 27, 1900.

SECOND LOVE. Orig. C.D. 3 a. J. P. Simpson. Hay., July 23, 1856.

SECOND MAIDEN'S TRAGEDY, THE. P. in MS. in Marquis of Lansdown's library. Escaped destruction of Mr. Warburton's servant. Entered Stationers' Co. April 9, 1653.

SECOND MARRIAGE, THE. C. Joanna Baillie. Pr. 1802.

SECOND MRS. GRUNDY, THE. C. 1 a. Barton White. Royalty, July 23, 1907.

SECOND MRS. TANQUERAY, THE. P. 4 a. A. W. Pinero. St. James's, May 27, 1893: rev. St. James's, June 20, 1895; Royalty, September 7, 1901; New, July 11, 1903.

SECONDA MOGLIE, LA. 4 a. Italian ver. of *Second Mrs. Tanqueray.* Lyceum, May 12, 1900.

SECONDE MADAME TANQUERAY, LA. French transl. of above by Hading and Stroheker. Notting Hill Coronet, June 15, 1903.

SECOND THOUGHT IS BEST. C.O. J. Hough. D.L., March 30, 1778.

SECOND THOUGHTS. F. J. B. Buckstone. D.L., Hay.; October 29, 1832.

SECOND THOUGHTS. C. 1 a. H. Gardner. Publ. by S. French, Limited.

SECOND THOUGHTS. Ca. 1 a. J. C. Herbert. Court, April 6, 1874.

SECOND THOUGHTS ARE BEST. C. Mrs. Cowley. 1781. N.p. See *The World as it Goes.*

SECOND TO NONE. Standard, November 5, 1864.

SECOND TO NONE. Melo-d. 4 a. W. Howard. Manchester Junction, April 1, 1907; West London, August 19, 1907.

SECOND VOLUME, THE. Episode. 1 a. F. Orres. St. George's H., March 2, 1895. (Irving Dr. Co.)

SECRET, A. Ca. Adap. fr. French by Constance Beerbohm. St. George's H., June 26. 1888.

SECRET, LE. O.C. Haffmann. M. by Méhul. 1793.

SECRET, THE. C. E. Morris. D.L., March 2, 1799. Pr. 1799.

SECRET, THE. F. 1 a. Adapt. fr. French by W. Barrymore. Greenwich, April 11, 1868.

SECRET; OR, THE HOLE IN THE WALL, THE. C.P. 1 a. C.G.

SECRET AND CONFIDENTIAL. P. 3 a. V. Widnell. Comedy T., September 16, 1902. Orig prod. under the title of *A Woman of Impulse,* Liverpool Court, March 24, 1902.

SECRET AGENT, THE. C. 2 a. Partly fr. the German by J. S. Coyne. Hay., March 10, 1855.

SECRET AGREEMENT, A. C.D. Prol. and 4 a E. Gregory. Novelty, July 31, 1886.

SECRET AT LARGE. M.F. O'Keeffe. Dublin. N.p.

SECRET CASTLE; OR, HENRY AND EDWY. F. Manchester. Anon., 1799. N.p.*

SECRET CRIME, A. C.D. 3 a. M. S. Dobson. Birmingham Queen's, December 12, 1892.

SECRET DE POLICHINELLE, LE. C. 3 a. P. Wolff. Notting Hill Coronet, June 29, 1903. (Gymnase Comp.)

SECRET ENLARGED, THE. See *The Agreeable Surprise.*

SECRET EXPEDITION, THE. F. 2 a. Anon. Pr 1757.

SECRET FOE, A. D. 4 a. J. A. Stevens. Brighton T.R., August 25, 1887; Op. C., August 27, 1887.

SECRET LOVE; OR, THE MAIDEN QUEEN. T.C. J. Dryden. F. on *Le Grand Cyrus* of Mlle. de Scudéry. T.R., 1679.

SECRET MINE. Pant. Dibdin and Fawcett

SECRET OF A LIFE. D. 4 a. A. Williams and G. Roberts. Grand, November 18, 1886.

SECRET OF STATE, A. P. 1 a. Eva Anstruther. St. Cuthbert's H., Earl's Court, June 23, 1898.

SECRET OF THE KEEP, THE. Ca. C. Raleigh. Garrick, September 8, 1898.

SECRET OF THE SEA, A. D. W. Muskerry. Cheltenham T.R., January 17, 1870.

SECRET OR NOTHING; OR, NO MASON, NO WIFE, THE. Dr. P. Arnold. Hay., April 27, 1807. N.p.

SECRET ORCHARD. THE. P. 4 a. Newcastle Tyne. E. Castle. March 14, 1901; Fulham Grand, May 13, 1901.

SECRET PLOT, THE. T. 3 a. R. Green. December 30, 1776. (When 8 years 11 months old.)

SECRET SERVICE. Afterpiece, 2 a. J. B. Planché. D.L., April 29, 1834.

SECRET SERVICE. American D. 4 a. W. Gillette. Terry's, May 10, 1895 (C.P.); Adelphi, May 15, 1897; tr. to Comedy, June 14, 1897 (perf. by Eng. Co.); August 5, 1897; Adelphi, November 24, 1897.

SECRET SOCIETY, THE. D. 4 a. C. Hannan. Givan Calendonian, July 6, 1895 (C.P.).

SECRET SORROW, A. P. 1 a. G. J. Dowse. Hackney Manor R., December 12, 1890.

SECRET TRIBUNAL, THE. P. 5 a. J. Boaden. C.G., June 3, 1795.

SECRET WEDDING, A. D. Mansfield T.R., July 29, 1907; Stratford T.R., December 30, 1907.

SECRETARY, THE. P. Sheridan Knowles. F. on Grattan's novel, "Highways and Byeways." D.L., April 24, 1843.

SECRETARY'S SECRET, THE. P. 1 a. A. Leslie. Crouch End Assem. Rooms, April 22, 1909.

SECRETARY'S WEDDING PRESENT, THE. P. 1 a. Henry Allen Ashton. Rehearsal, W.C., May 23, 1908.

SECRETS — — —; OR, THE CROSS AND THE CRESCENT. Revised Ver., 4 a., of *The Secrets of the Harem*, by M. Goldberg. Northampton O.H., August 12, 1901; Hammersmith Lyric T., August 19, 1901.

SECRETS OF THE HAREM. D. M. Goldberg. Sheffield City, December 24, 1896.

SECRETS OF THE HEART. O. 1 a. Dobson and Lehmann. Publ. by S. French, Ltd.

SECRETS OF THE POLICE. D. 4 a. M. Melford. Surrey, November 29, 1886.

SECRETS WORTH KNOWING. P. 5 a. J. Morton. Halifax T.R. (4 a.), May 1, 1878.

SECRETS WORTH KNOWING, AND THE WAY TO GET MONEY. C. Morton. C.G., January 11, 1798; D.L., December 18, 1821.

SECULAR MASQUE, THE. By J. Dryden, M. by Boyce. Pr. 1745.

SECUNDA PASTORUM. See "Miracle Plays."

SEDGEMON. P. 4 a. W. G. Wills and F. C. Wills. Sadler's Wells, August 20, 1881.

SEDUCER. T. Masterton. 180—.

SEDUCTION. C. T. Holcroft. D.L., March 12, 1787. Pr. 1787.

SEE IF YOU LIKE IT; OR, 'TIS ALL A MISTAKE. F. 2 a. Taken from *Comedy of Errors.* C.G., October 9, 1734.

SEE ME AND SEE ME NOT. (?) T. Nash. 1618. Running title of *Hans Beer Pot.*

SEE SAW. Dom. C. 3 a. G. Capel and J. R. Phillips. Terry's, February 22, 1889.

SEE-SAW, MARGERY DAW. E. L. Blanchard. D.L., December 26, 1856.

SEE-SAW OF LIFE. D. Prol. and 4 a. H. Bedford and A. Shirley. Worcester R., July 3, 1905; West London, October 30, 1905.

SEE SEE. Chinese C.O. 2 a. Book, C. H. Brookfield. Lyrics by Adrian Ross. M., Sidney Jones. P.O.W.'s, June 20, 1906.

SEEING FROU-FROU. C. 1 a. Adap. fr. *Le Roi Candaule* by A. Murray. Globe, April 16, 1881

SEEING IS BELIEVING. Dr. Proverb. 1 a. P. Joddrell. Hay., August 22, 1783; D.L., May 17, 1814.

SEEING THE GRECIAN PANTOMIME. F. Grecian, July 5, 1875.

SEEING THE WORLD. C. 3 a. E. G. Goodman. Leeds T.R., December 5, 1873.

SEEING TOOLE. F. J. Hollingshead and R. Reece. Gaiety, September 3, 1873.

SEEING WRIGHT. F. T. Morton. Adelphi, 1845.

SEEKING NOTORIETY; OR, A WOMAN'S FOLLY. Harry Bruce.

SEELEWIG. O. Sigmund Stapden. Pr. Nuremberg 1644.

SEIGNEUR'S DAUGHTER; OR, THE WORD OF HONOUR, THE. D. P. Meritt. Jersey T.R., July 24, 1876.

SEJANUS. T. F. Gentleman. Alt. of Ben Jonson's P. 1751.

SEJANUS: HIS FALL. T. Ben Jonson. Ac. by His Majesty's servants. 1603.

SEJOUR MILITAIRE, LE. O. 1 a. Auber. Paris, 1813.

SELECT DRAMATIC PIECES. Ascr. to Joddrell. 1787.

SELEO AND OLEMPO. Anon. March 5, 1594.

SELF. D. 4 a. J. Oxenford and H. Wigan. Mirror, September 27, 1875.

SELF. P. 1 a. C. Hopkins. York De Grey Rooms (amat.), April 10, 1896.

SELF; OR, MAN'S INHUMANITY. C.D. 5 a. B. M'Cullough. Bolton T.R., June, 1883; Britannia, July 26, 1886.

SELF-ACCUSATION; OR, A BROTHER'S LOVE! D. 2 a. M. Lemon. Lyceum, September 10, 1838.

SELF-CONDEMNED. P. Tableaux and 3 a. A. J. Maunday-Gregory. Southport Philharmonic H., August 1, 1898.

SELF-ENAMOURED; OR, THE LADIES' DOCTOR. C. Hifferman. Dublin, 1750.

SELF-IMMOLATION; OR, THE SACRIFICE OF LOVE. P. 3 a. Transl. fr. German of Kotzebue by H. Neuman. Prod. anon. as *Family Distress* at Hay. Pr. 1798.

SELF-IMPORTANT, THE. C. Unfinished. Rev. Dr. Stratford. N.p. Before 1814.

SELF-MADE. St. James's, January 18, 1862.

SELF-MADE MAN, THE. C. 3 a. W. J. S. Dowie. Middlesbro' T.R., March 8, 1878.

SELF-SACRIFICE; OR, THE MAID OF THE COTTAGE, THE. Melo-d. M. by Mr. Reeve. Lyceum playbill, July 19, 1819.

SELF-TORMENTOR; OR, WHIMS AND FANCIES. F. 2 a. From Terence. D.L., February 16, 1832.

SELF AND LADY. F.C. 3 a. P. Decourcelle. Margate Grand T., September 13, 1900; Vaudeville, September 19, 1900.

SELF RIVAL, THE. C. Mrs. Mary Davys. Pr. 1725.

SELFISHNESS. City of London, February 11, 1856.

SELIM AND ZULEIKA. T. 3 a. Pr. 1815.

SELIMA AND AZOR. Persian Tale. Transl. fr. French by Sir G. Collier. D.L., 1776.

SELIMUS, EMPEROR OF THE TURKS. T. Rev. T. Goffe. Ac. by Queen's Players.

SELIMUS, TRAGICALL RAIGNE OF. etc. Anon. Pr. 1594.

SELINDRA. T.C. Sir W. Killigrew. Pr. 1665.

SELMANE. T. Rev. J. H. Pott. Pr. 1782.

SEMELE. O. W. Congreve. M. by Handel. C.G. Pr. 1710 Alt. Anon. Pr. 1743.

SEMI-DETACHED. C. 1 a. H. Swears. Publ. by S. French Limited.

SEMIRAMIDE. O. Metastasio. 1729.

SEMIRAMIDE. O. B. Aliprandi. Munich, 1740.

SEMIRAMIDE. O. Gluck. Vienna, May 14, 1748.

SEMIRAMIDE. O. Meyerbeer. 1819.

SEMIRAMIDE. O. Bianchi. King's T.

SEMIRAMIDE. Ser. O. Rossini. Lib. by Rossi. (Venice, February 3, 1823; King's T., July 15, 1824.) C.G., November 15, 1870.

SEMIRAMIS. T. Transl. fr. Voltaire. Dr. Franklin. Pr. 1760.

SEMIRAMIS. T. G. E. Asyscough. Transl. fr. Voltaire. D.L. Pr. 1776.

SEMIRAMIS. T. Keate. N.p.

SEMIRAMIS. O. Rossini. Paris, July 9, 1860.

SEMIRAMIS. T. 1 a. Suggested by Whyte Melville's novel "Sarchedon." H. Newte. Bayswater Bijou, October 13, 1894 (C.P.).

SEN YAMEN. C.O. 2 a. W. Dawe. M. by R. Roberts. Ealing Lyric H., October 2, 1886.

SENATOR, THE. C. 4 a. D. D. Lloyd and S. Rosenfeld. Eleph. and C., October 22, 1889 (C.P.).

SENATOR'S WIFE, THE. C.D. 4 a. D. Belasco and H. C. De Mille. Orig. prod. in America. Manchester T.R., September 30, 1892.

SEND HER VICTORIOUS. D. 4 a. Alt. and rev. by S. Vane from his D., *For England*. Pav., November 13, 1899.

SEND HIM VICTORIOUS. Rom. P. 4 a. Herbert Skardon. Horwich Prince's T., December 30, 1907; Stratford T.R., May 25, 1908.

SEND THIRTY STAMPS. F. J. K. Angus. Sadler's Wells, April 16, 1884.

SENILE ODIUM. C. Hausted. 1633. Perf. by the Queen's College Students, Cambridge.

SENILIS AMOR. Latin C. 1635.

SENIOR WRANGLERS. Duo. E. H. Whitmore. Criterion, July 3, 1884.

SENOBIA. Ac. March 9, 1591. (According to Henslowe.)

SENSATIONAL CASE. C. 1 a. I. Cassilis. Publ. by S. French, Limited.

SENSATIONAL NOVEL, A. F. Clay. Gall. of Illustrations, January 30, 1871.

SENSE AND SENSATION; OR, THE SEVEN SISTERS OF THURLE. Morality. Pro. and 7 sc. Tom Taylor. Olympic, May 16, 1864.

SENSE OF HUMOUR, A. P. 3 a. Beryl and Cosmo Hamilton. Comedy, January 7, 1906; Playhouse, August 31, 1909.

SENSIBLE CONSTANZA, THE. Ser. C. 3 a. Chs. E. O. Thornton. Kingsway, May 11, 1908.

SENSUALIST, THE. D. 3 a. M. Buena and F. A. Laidlow. Northampton O.H., December 18, 1891, and June 27, 1892 (C.P.).

SENT TO THE TOWER. F. 1 a. J. M. Morton. Princess's, November, 1850.

SENTENCE, THE. T. 1 a. Rowan Orme. Court, July 7, 1908 (mat.).

SENTENCED, BUT NOT GUILTY. D. Liverpool Colosseum, October 18, 1876.

SENTENCED FOR LIFE. C.D. V. Dardy. West Bromwich T.R., March 28, 1900 (C.P.).

SENTENCED FOR LIFE. D. 6 a. F. Bateman and C. W. Mill. Birmingham Q.T., December 17, 1900 (C.P.); Greenwich Carlton, February 11, 1901; Standard (in 4 a.), August 24, 1903.

SENTENCED TO DEATH. D. J. H. Stanley. Longton T., August 18, 1873.

SENTENCED TO DEATH. D. 4 a. G. Conquest and H. Pettitt. Grecian, October 14, 1875.

SENTIMENTAL BRAY, THE. P. 1 a. F. D. Bone. (Prod. by the Play Actors.) Court, November 8, 1908.

SENTIMENTAL CUSS, A. C. 1 a. Douglas Murray. Vaudeville, October 31, 1907.

SENTIMENTAL MOTHER, THE. C. 5 a. 1789.

SENTIMENTALIST, THE. P. Pro. and 4 a. H. V. Esmond. D. of York's, October 26, 1901.

SENTIMENTALIST, THE. P. 1 a. J. M. Cuthbertson. Glasgow Athenæum, December 4, 1908 (amat.).

SENTINEL, THE. M. Burla. 1 a. Olympic, January 19, 1837. Publ. by S. French, Limited.

SENTRY, THE. M.V. 1 a. F. Remo and M. Watson. M. by I. Caryll. Lyric, April 5, 1890.

SEPARATE MAINTENANCE, THE. C. Geo. Coleman. Hay., August 31, 1779. N.p.

SEPARATE MAINTENANCE, THE. F. 1 a. J. S. Coyne. Hay., May, 1849.

SEPARATION. Society D. 5 a. Sir R. Roberts. Ealing Lyric H., October 2, 1886.

SEPARATION, THE. Joanna Baillie. C.G., 1836.

SEPARATION AND REPARATION. Morton. D.L., February 26, 1833.

SEPULTURE AND RESURRECTION, OF THE. 2 Comedies. Bishop Bale. N.p.

SEQUEL, THE. P. 1 a. L. N. Parker. Vaudeville, July 15, 1891; Criterion, January 4, 1902.

SEQUEL OF HENRY THE FOURTH, THE. Alt. fr. Shakespeare by Mr. Betterton. 1719. D.L. N.d.

SEQUEL TO FLORA; OR, HOB'S WEDDING. Hippisley Ballad F. L.I.F., March 20, 1732.

SERAGLIO, THE. C.O. C. Dibdin and Dr. Arnold. C.G., November 14, 1776. Pr. 1776.

SERAGLIO, THE. O. Mozart. 1827.

SERAIL. O. Mozart. 1782.

SERAPHINA. P. Dr. Blacklock. N.p.

SERAPHINA THE FAIR. Burl. C. W. Laidlow. Southend Public H., December 26, 1874.

SERAPHINE. C. M. Victorien Sardou. Queen's, May 1, 1869.

SERENADE; OR, DISAPPOINTMENT, THE. Mentioned in Pepys's Diary, May 7, 1669.

SERENATA, LA. C.O. L. M'Hale. M. by J. Batchelder and O. Gaggs. Manchester Princess's, June 18, 1888.

SERF, THE. T. 5 a. Alt. fr. German of Ranpach and adapt. by A. Talbot. C.G., January 23, 1828.

SERF; OR, LOVE LEVELS ALL, THE. Orig. D. 3 a. T. Taylor. Olympic.

SERGE PANINE. P. 5 a. Fr. G. Ohnet's French D. of same name by J. H. Thorp. Gaiety, June 11, 1883; Ipswich T.R., August 18, 1884; Avenue, June 4, 1891. (English ver. of novel prod. at Adelphi, May 3, 1882. See *Love's Anguish*.)

SERGEANT BRUE. M.C. 3 a. O. Hall and Liza Lehmann. Strand, June 14, 1904; P.O.W.'s, July 11, 1904.

SERGEANT LEROUX. P. The Hon. Mrs. Walter Forbes. Sunderland Avenue, November 30, 1903 (C.P.).

SERGEANT LONGFELLOW. Egyptian M.C. Vashti Wynne. M. by Dudley Powell. Hackney Empire, September 6, 1000.

SERGEANT-MAJOR, THE. Sk. F. D. Bone. Middlesex M.H., May 20, 1908.

SERGEANT OF HUSSARS, THE. An incident of the Franco-German War in 1 a. Cicely Hamilton. Bedford Street Bijou, June 23, 1907; rev. Scala, June 25, 1908.

SERGEANT'S DAUGHTER, THE. D. 3 a. Adap. fr. French by G. Massinger. Cheltenham T.R., February 13, 1888.

SERGEANT'S WEDDING, THE. C.D. 1 a. T. E Wilks. Prince's, November 19, 1840.

SERGEANT'S WIFE, THE. D. 2 a. J. Banim. M. by Goss. Lyceum, July 24, 1827.

SERGEANT'S WIFE, THE. D. S. J. Arnold. D.L., June 8, 1835.

SERIES OF PLAYS. Joanna Baillie. 1798.

SERIOUS AFFAIR, A. F. 1 a. Publ. by S. French, Ltd.

SERIOUS FAMILY, THE. C. 3 a. M. Barnett. Adap. fr. French *Le Mari à la Campagne*. Hay., October 30, 1849; rev. January 14, 1867.

SERIOUS YOUTH, Surrey, March 16, 1857.

SERMON OF FOLLY, THE. Int. Sir D. Lindsay. Pr. 1792.

SERPEDON. Ac. by the servants of Lord Chamberlain. 1580.

SERPENT OF THE NILE, THE. Spec. D. Adelphi, 1840.

SERPENT ON THE HEARTH, THE. Rom. D. 3 a. J. P. Simpson. Adelphi, August 2, 1869.

SERPENT'S COIL, THE. D. 5 a. E. Hill-Mitchelson and C. H. Longden. West Hartlepool T.R., December 23, 1895; Surrey, June 15, 1896.

SERPENT'S TOOTH, THE. Melo-d. 4 a. J. Denton. Kingston County, April 25, 1904.

SERPENTS. T.C. Anon. 1607.

SERRAGLIO, IL. O. Mozart. (Vienna, 1782.)

SERSE. O. Cavalli. Paris, 1647.

SERTORIUS. T. Corneille. 1662. See "French Classical Plays."

SERTORIUS. T. J. Bancroft. D.L., 1679.

SERVA PADRONA, LA. O. 2 a. Wds. by Nelli. M. by Pergolesi. Naples, August 23, 1733; Paris, October 4, 1746.

SERVA PADRONA, LA. O. G. Abos. Naples, 1708-1786.

SERVA PADRONA, LA. M. Ent. S. Storace. Transl. fr. Italian. Marylebone Gardens, 1758.

SERVANT IN THE HOUSE, THE. C. 5 a. Chas. Rann Kennedy. Bayswater Bijou, June 19, 1907; Adelphi, October 25, 1909.

SERVANT MISTRESS, THE. Burl. Anon. Pr. 1770.

SERVANT OF THE PUBLIC, A. Ro. epil. 4 a. D. Kimball. Dramtised fr. Anthony Hope's novel. Margate R., April 10, 1909; Terry's, May 16, 1909.

SERVANT OR SUITOR. F. Royalty, May 20, 1872.

SERVING HIM RIGHT. C.D. 2 a. M. Barnett and C. Mathews. Lyceum, October, 1850.

SERVING THE QUEEN. D. 5 a. H. Leonard. Surrey, October 17, 1898.

SESOSTRIS. T. Amore. 1667.

SESOSTRIS; OR, ROYALTY IN DISGUISE. T. John Sturmy. L.I.F., January 1, 1728. Pr. 1728.

SET AT MAN, THE. P. Ac. in 1594-5.

SET AT TENNIS, THE. P. A. Mundy. 1602. N.p.

SET OF HORSES, THE. C. fr. German of Emdorff. Pr. 1792.

SETH GREEN; OR, STRUCK OIL AT LAST. Amer. D. Eleph. and C., October 25, 1884.

SETHONA. T. Alexander Dow. D.L., February 19, 1774. Pr. 1774.

SETTING OF THE SUN, THE. C. 1 a. C. Hannam. Liverpool Court, October 13, 1892; Camberwell Metropole, September 24, 1900; Royalty, November 10, 1906. See *Love Wisely*.

SETTLED OUT OF COURT. P. 4 a. E. Burney. Globe, June 3, 1897.

SETTLEMENT IN FULL, A. D. Inc. 1 a. H. Maxwell. St. Leonards Pier Pav., November 24, 1898.

SETTLING DAY. C. 5 a. T. Taylor. Olympic, March 4, 1865.

SETTLING DAY. P. 4 a. F. A. Scudamore. Northampton O.H., September 14, 1893; Surrey June 3, 1895.

SETTLING THE VERDICT. F. 1 a. Publ. by S. French, Limited.

SEVEN AGAINST THEBES, THE. T. Æschylus. Transl. by Potter, 1777; Buckley, 1849; Davies, 1864; Plumtre, 1869. See "Greek Plays."

SEVEN AGES OF WOMAN. E. L. Blanchard.

SEVEN CHAMPIONS OF CHRISTENDOM, THE. J. Kirke. Cockpit and the Bull, 1638.

SEVEN CHAMPIONS OF CHRISTENDOM, THE. Comic Fantastic Spec. 2 a. J. R. Planché. Lyceum, April 9, 1849.

SEVEN CHAMPIONS OF CHRISTENDOM; OR, GOOD LITTLE ST. GEORGE AND THE NAUGHTY SNAPDRAGON, THE. Burl. W. R. Osman. Alexandra, August 22, 1870.

SEVEN CHARMED SPUDS, THE. F. Mr. Quayle. Barnsley Queen's, April 29, 1872.

SEVEN CHIEFS AGAINST THEBES. T. Transl. fr. Æschylus by R. Potter. Pr. 1777.

SEVEN CLERKS; OR, THE THREE THIEVES AND THE DENOUNCER, THE. Rom. D. 2 a. T. E. Wilks. Surrey.

SEVEN DAYS OF THE WEEK, THE. Anon. June 3, 1595. N.p.

SEVEN DEADLY SINS, THE. P. R. Tarleton. N.p.

SEVEN LAST WORDS, THE. Orat. H. Schutz (1585-1672).

SEVEN LAST WORDS, THE. Orat. Haydn. 1803.

SEVEN POOR TRAVELLERS, THE. J. B. Johnstone.

SEVEN POOR TRAVELLERS, THE. D. C. Duval. Blackburn T.R., January 11, 1869.

SEVEN SINS; OR, PASSION'S PARADISE. D. 4 a. G. Conquest and P. Meritt. Grecian, August 27, 1874.

SEVEN SISTERS OF MUNICH. G. H. B. Rodwell. 1847.

SEVEN WISE MASTERS, THE. P. W. Haughton, assisted by Chettle, Dekker, and Day. 1600. N.p.

SEVEN YEARS' SECRET, THE. D. 2 a. C. H. Hazlewood. Britannia, October 31, 1870.

SEVEN YEARS AGO. D. H. P. Grattan. Grecian, March 18, 1879.

SEVENTEEN HUNDRED AND TWENTY; OR, THE HISTORIC, SATIRIC, TRAGI-COMIC HUMOURS OF EXCHANGE ALLEY. F. F. Hawling. D.L., 1723. N.p.

SEVENTEEN HUNDRED AND EIGHTY-ONE; OR, THE CARTEL AT PHILADELPHIA. Prel. C.G., April 28, 1781. N.p.

SEVENTEEN HUNDRED AND NINETY. P. 4 a. Henry Hunt. Fr. Dickens' *Tale of Two Cities*. Sheffield Bath Saloon T., October 30, 1894.

SEVERAL AFFAIRS. C. T. Meriton. N.p.

SEVERAL WITS. C. Duchess of Newcastle. Pr. 1662.

SEVERED; OR, THE WORLD BETWEEN THEM. D. 5 a. F. Jefferson. Grimsby P.O.W., January 26, 1885.

SEVERINE. P. Adap. fr. *La Princesse Georges* of A. Dumas fils. Gaiety, May 6, 1885.

SEWING MACHINE ON EASY TERMS, A. F. H. Hayman. Eleph. and C., September 30, 1876.

SEXES MIS-MATCHED, THE. See *Stroller's Packet*. Anon. Pr. 1741.

SEXTON; OR, THE MOCK TESTATOR, THE. Droll out of Beaumont and Fletcher's *Spanish Curate*. Pr. 1672.

SEXTON BLAKE. D. 3 a. C. Douglas Carlile. Surrey, January 21, 1907.

SEXTON BLAKE, DETECTIVE. Hammersmith King's T., January 18, 1908 (C.P.); Crown, February 24, 1908.

SEXTON OF COLOGNE, THE. G. H. B. Rodwell. 1836.

SGANARELLE. Molière. Transl. by Vanbrugh. See *Playhouse to Let*. See "French Classical Plays."

SHADES; OR, THE MYSTERY OF THE NORTH WING, THE. D. Orig. prod. in Australia. Miss Helen Thompson. Liverpool Sefton T., October 21, 1884

SHADES OF NIGHT, THE. Fantasy. 1 a. R. Marshall. Lyceum, March 14, 1896; rev Hay., July 20, 1903.

SHADOW AND SUNSHINE. D. 4 a. R. Palgrave. Edinburgh T.R., March 31, 1883.

SHADOW BETWEEN, THE. P. 5 a. Chas. Windermere and Lilford Arthur. Margate G.T., July 16, 1901.

SHADOW BETWEEN; OR, THE VULTURES OF KILDARE, THE. Melo-d. 4 a. H. Kingston, T. C. Denville, and Chas. Self. Hoxton King's, March 18, 1907.

SHADOW CHILD, THE. Sk. J. Willard and T. Gallon. Standard, February 15, 1909; Hammersmith Pal., June 15, 1909.

SHADOW DANCE, THE. Melod. 4 a. B. Landeck. F. on Victor Hugo's "Notre Dâme de Paris." M. by N. Lambelet. Grand, October 7, 1901; Princess's, November 12, 1901.

SHADOW HAND, THE. D. 4 a. C. A. Lee. Widnes Alexandra T., March 8, 1893; Macclesfield T.R., January 5, 1894; South Shields T.R., July 12, 1897.

SHADOW HUNT, A. C. 4 a. R. Davey and W. Pollock. Ladbroke H., April 25, 1891 (C.P.).

SHADOW OF A CRIME, THE. D. 3 a. C. S. Cheltnam. Belfast T.R., August 23, 1869.

SHADOW OF A CRIME, THE. D. 4 a. E. Ward. Manchester Queen's, December 19, 1887.

SHADOW OF A LIE, THE. D. 4 a. Lascelles Hasbrouck. Ladbroke H., January 10, 1907.

SHADOW OF CRIME. Dom. D. 4 a. Nita Rae. Reading County T., August 17, 1905. (C.P.); Hastings Pier Pav., May 28, 1906; Dalston, March 18, 1907.

SHADOW OF DEATH, THE. Rom. D. J. R. Walrond. Victoria, September 25, 1876.

SHADOW OF LIFE, THE. D. Liverpool Adelphi, October 14, 1872.

SHADOW OF NIGHT, THE. G. Chapman. Pr. 1594.

SHADOW OF SIN, THE. Melo-d. 4 a. F. Jarman. Hanley T.R., February 20, 1893.

SHADOW OF THE CROSS; OR, ANNO DOMINI 670. Hist. D. 4 a. A. H. Ward. Stratford T.R., September 26, 1904.

SHADOW OF THE MILL, THE. D. Prol. and 3 a. J. Burnley. F. on author's novel "Second Fiddle." Bradford Pullan's T., August 24, 1885.

SHADOW OF THE SCAFFOLD, THE; OR, A MODERN MAGDALEN. D. 4 a. W. Hibbert. (Produced as *A Modern Magdalen* at Southport O.H., January 20, 1902.) Greenwich Carlton, February 17, 1902.

SHADOW OF THE SURPLICE, THE. D. 3 a. Gabriel Trarieux. Orig. prod. at the Odéon, May 14, 1907; Scala, March 30, 1908.

SHADOW OF THE SURPLICE, THE. W. H. C. Nation. Adap. fr. Gabriel Trarieux's *L'Otage*. Royalty, November 21, 1908.

SHADOW OF THE SWORD. Rom. D. 5 a. R. Buchanan. Brighton T.R., May 9, 1881; Olympic, April 8, 1882.

SHADOW OF WRONG. D. T. Mead. Cardiff T.R., July 2, 1872.

SHADOW ON THE BLIND, THE. Sk. Stafford Smith. Standard, July 6, 1908.

SHADOW ON THE HEARTH, THE. D. C. H. Hazlewood. Britannia, June 8, 1874.

SHADOW ON THE HEARTH, THE. D. 3 a. W. Maynard (Willert Beale). Crystal Pal., February 21, 1887.

SHADOW ON THE WALL, THE. D. M. by J. Thomson. Lyceum playbill, April 20, 1835.

SHADOW ON THE WALL, THE. D. T. J. Serle. Lyceum, 1835.

SHADOW SCEPTRE, A. Hist. P. 4 a. H. Hamilton. Manchester Prince's, April 15, 1882.

SHADOW-TREE SHAFT. D. 3 a. T. W. Robertson. Princess's, February 6, 1867.

SHADOWED BY THREE. See *Sins of New York*.

SHADOWED LIVES. D. 4 a. H. Cottesmore and A. Harrison. Kennington T., February 9, 1903.

SHADOWS. Rom. D. Pro. and 4 a. Sir C. L. Young. Princess's, May 27, 1871.

SHADOWS OF A CRIME, THE. P. 4 a. 11 sc. Nita Rae. Hastings Pier Pav., May 28, 1906.

SHADOWS OF A GREAT CITY. D. 5 a. J. Jefferson and L. R. Shewell. First prod. in America. Glasgow Princess's, February 28, 1887; London Princess's, July 14, 1887.

SHADOWS OF CRIME. Surrey, February 4, 1856.

SHADOWS OF LIFE; OR, THE HAND OF FATE. D. 4 a. A. Shirley. Barrow Alhambra (as *The Hand of Fate*), March 3, 1884; Eleph. and C., September 10, 1887.

SHADOWS OF THE PAST. C.D. 2 a. J. P. Simpson. Brighton T.R., November 1, 1867.

SHADOWS ON THE BLIND. F.C. 3 a. J. H. Darnley and H. Bruce. Liverpool P.O.W., September 27, 1897; Terry's, April 29, 1898.

SHADOWY WATERS, THE. P. W. B. Yeats. In verse. Great Queen Street, June 11, 1907.

SHADRAGH, THE HUNCHBACK. Irish D. W. Williams. S. Shields T.R., April 8, 1878. Eleph. and C., July 26, 1880.

SHAFT No. 2. Electrical D. 4 a. Gateshead Metropole, April 19, 1897.

SHAH; OR, THE PEEPSHOWMAN'S VISIT, THE. F. K. E. Hall. Coatbridge Prince's, July 12, 1873.

SHAH'S NEW SUIT, THE. C.O. 2 a. Court, November 28, 1904 (amat.).

SHAKE HANDS. St. James's, April 25, 1864.

SHAKESPEARE'S PLAYS.

Besides the First Folio of 1623, which is the first collected edition of the plays, a number of them were published separately in quarto before and after that date. The following is a list of

EARLY QUARTO EDITIONS.

Merry Wives of Windsor, 1602, 1619, 1630.
Comedy of Errors, 1595.
Much Ado About Nothing, 1600.
Love's Labour's Lost, 1598, 1631.
Midsummer Night's Dream, 1600, 1600.
Merchant of Venice, 1600, 1600, 1637, 1652.
Taming of the Shrew, 1631.
Richard II., 1597, 1598, 1608, 1615, 1634.
1. *Henry IV.*, 1598, 1599, 1604, 1608, 1613, 1622, 1632, 1639.
2. *Henry IV.*, 1600, 1600.
Henry V., 1600, 1602, 1608.
2. *Henry VI.*, 1594 (?), 1600 } 1619.
3. *Henry VI.*, 1595 (?), 1600 }
Richard III., 1597, 1598, 1602, 1605, 1612, 1622, 1629, 1634.
Troilus and Cressida, 1609, 1609.
Titus Andronicus, 1593, 1600, 1611.
Romeo and Juliet, 1597, 1599, 1609, 1611 (?), 1637.
Hamlet, 1603, 1604, 1605, 1611, 1631 (?), 1637, 1695.
Lear, 1608, 1608, 1655.
Othello, 1622, second quarto (date unknown) 1630, 1655.
Pericles, 1609, 1609, 1611, 1619, 1630, 1635.

The order in which the 36 plays contained in the First Folio of 1623 (entered at Stationers' Hall, November 8, 1623) are presented is shown in the following list, which forms a leaf of that edition:—

A CATALOGUE OF THE SEVERAL COMEDIES HISTORIES, AND TRAGEDIES CONTAINED IN THIS VOLUME.

COMEDIES.

The Tempest.
The Two Gentlemen of Verona.
The Merry Wives of Windsor.
Measure for Measure.
The Comedy of Errors.
Much Ado About Nothing.
Love's Labour's Lost.
Midsummer Night's Dream.
The Merchant of Venice.
As You Like It.
The Taming of the Shrew.
All's Well that Ends Well.
Twelfth Night; or, What You Will.
The Winter's Tale.

HISTORIES.

The Life and Death of King John.
The Life and Death of Richard II.
The First Part of King Henry IV.
The Second Part of King Henry IV.
The Life of King Henry V.
The First Part of King Henry VI.
The Second Part of King Henry VI.
The Third Part of King Henry VI.
The Life and Death of Richard III.
The Life of King Henry VIII.

TRAGEDIES.

Troilus and Cressida.
The Tragedy of Coriolanus.
Titus Andronicus.
Romeo and Juliet.
Timon of Athens.
The Life and Death of Julius Cæsar.
The Tragedy of Macbeth.
The Tragedy of Hamlet.
King Lear.
Othello, the Moor of Venice.
Antony and Cleopatra.
Cymbeline, King of Britain.

Pericles was not included in this edition.

OTHER EARLY EDITIONS.

2nd Folio, 1632.
3rd Folio, 1664.
4th Folio, 1685.
8vo. 7 Vol.. by Nicholas Rowe, 1709.
4th 6 Vol., by Pope, 1723.
4th, "Shakespeare Restored," by Lewis Theobald, 1726.
12mo., 10 Vol., by Pope, 1728.
8mo., 7 Vol., by Theobald, 1733.
12mo., 8 Vol., by Theobald, 1740.
4to., 6 Vol., by Sir Thomas Hanmer, 1744.
8vo., 8 Vol., by Dr. Warburton, 1747.
8vo., 8 Vol., by Dr. Johnson, 1765.
8vo., 4 Vol., by Steevens, 1766.
8vo., 10 Vol., by Capel, 1768.
4to., 6 Vol., by Sir Thomas Hanmer, 1771.
8vo., 10 Vol., by Dr. Johnson and Steevens, 1773.
8vo., 10 Vol., by Dr. Johnson and Steevens, 1778.
8vo., 10 Vol., by Dr. Johnson and Steevens (revised by Reed), 1785.
8vo., 10 Vol., by Malone, 1790.

The following is an approximate chronological order of the plays:—

	Date.	Poet's age.	No. of lines.
Titus Andronicus	1590	26	2,525
Love's Labour's Lost	1591	27	2,789
1 *Henry VI.*			2,693
2 *Henry VI.*			3,032
3 *Henry VI.*			
Midsummer Night's	1592	28	2,904
Dream			2,251
Comedy of Errors			1,770
Richard II.	1593	29	2,644
Two Gentlemen of Verona	1593-5	29	2,060
Twelfth Night	1594-1601	30	2,684
Troilus and Cressida	1594-1607	30	3,423
King John	1595	31	2,553
Richard III.			3,599
Romeo and Juliet	1596	32	3,002
Merchant of Venice			2,705
1 *Henry IV.*	1597	33	3,170
2 *Henry IV.*	1598	34	3,437
Merry Wives of Windsor	1598-1605	34	3,018
Henry V.			3,320
Much Ado About Nothing	1599	35	2,823
Julius Cæsar	1600	36	2,440
As You Like It			2,904
Hamlet	1601-3	37	3,924
Taming of the Shrew (complete)	1602	38	2,671
Measure for Measure	1603	39	2,809
Othello			3,324
All's Well that Ends Well	1604	40	2,981
Lear	1605	41	3,298
Macbeth	1606	42	1,993
Timon of Athens			2.358
Pericles	1607	43	2,386
Antony and Cleopatra	1608	44	3,964
Cymbeline	1608-10	44	3,448
Coriolanus	1609	45	3,392
Tempest	1610-11	46	2,068
Winter's Tale	1611	47	2,750
Henry VIII.			2,754
Total Number of Lines			105,866

The following six plays were printed with *Pericles* in the third folio as additions to the collection in the first folio:—

The London Prodigal. Comedy. Wr. 1605. Pr. 1605. Acted at the Globe.

The Yorkshire Tragedy. Wr. 1608. Pr. 1608. Acted at the Globe. Very short and not divided into acts.

The History of Sir John Oldcastle, the Good Lord Cobham. Tragedy. Wr. 1598. Pr. 1600. Acted by the Admiral's company. Partly taken from Fuller's "Church History" and Fox's "Book of Martyrs."

These three had Shakespeare's name in full on the title-page:—

The Life and Death of Lord Cromwell. Hist. play. Wr. 1602. Pr. 1602. Acted by the Queen's company. Plot taken from Fox's "Martyrology," Dr. Burnet's "Hist. Reform.," Fuller's "Church History," Wanley's "History of Man," Hackwell's "Apology," and Lloyd's "English Worthies."

The Puritan; or, The Widow of Watling Street. Comedy. Wr. 1600. Pr. 1607. Acted by the children of St. Paul's.

The Tragedy of Locrine, the Eldest Son of Brutus. Wr. 1593. Pr. 1595. "Newly set forth, overseen, and corrected by W. S."

These last three have "W. S." on the title page.

Other plays have been attributed in part also to Shakespeare, notably:—

The Birth of Merlin; or, The Child has Lost a Father. Tragi-comedy. Pr. 1662 as by Shakespeare and Rowley. "Several times acted." Giles Jacob, 1719, states: "Shakespeare assisted in this play."

Mucedorus and Amadon, with the Merry Conceits of Mouse. Pr. 1598. Acted at the Globe 1668. Giles Jacobs states: "This play was supposed to be writ by Shakespeare."

The Troublesome Reign of King John (in two parts). Pr. 1591, 1611, 1622. Acted by the Queen's company. The title-page of 1611 states: "By W. Sh.," and that of 1622 as by Shakespeare, whose name appears in full. It was on this play *King John* was founded

SHAKESPEARE'S GENEALOGY.

The following genealogical notes will be of interest:—

Richard Shakespeare.

	Born.	Died.
John	? 1530	1601
Henry	—	1596

John Shakespeare, married in 1557 Mary Arden, died 1608, youngest daughter of Robert Arden, of Wellingcote.

	Born.	Died.
Joan	1558	In infancy.
Margaret	1562	1563
WILLIAM	1564	1616
Gilbert	1566	before 1612
Joan	1569	after 1600 married Mr. Hart.
Anne	1571	1579
Richard	1573	1612
Edmund	1580	1607

William Shakespeare. Born in Henley Street, Stratford-on-Avon, 23 April, 1564. Married Anne Hathaway (b. 1556 d. 6 Aug., 1623), daughter of Richard Hathaway, of Shottery, on 28 Nov., 1582. Died 23 April, 1616, aged 52 years. Buried 25 April, 1616, in Trinity Church, Stratford.

	Born	Died	
Susanna	1583	11.7.1649	Married on 5.6.1607 to Dr. John Hall (d. 25.11.1635, aged 60).
Hamnet } twins		1596	
Judith }	1585	1662	Married on 10.2.1616 to Thos. Quiney

John and Susanna Hall.
Elizabeth. Born 1608. Married 22.4.1626 to Thomas Nash (d. 4.4.1647) and on 5.6.1649 to John Barnard (b. 1605, d. 5.3.1674). She had no children and died in 1670; buried at Abington 17.2.1670.

Thomas and Judith Quiney.

	Baptised	Buried
Shakespeare Quiney	23.11.1616	8.5.1617
Richard ,, ...	9. 2.1618	26.2.1639
Thomas ,, ...	29. 8.1619	28.1.1639

(All died unmarried.)
Thus the race of William Shakespeare became extinct.

SHAKESPEARE. C. 4 a. E. E. Greville. Maidenhead Grand H., May 27, 1891; Globe, June 27, 1892.

SHAKESPEARE AND SHAW. Revue by J. B. Fagan. Hay., May 18, 1905.

SHAKESPEARE v. HARLEQUIN. Panto. D. 2 a. M. by Reeve and Cooke. D.L., April 8, 1820.

SHAKESPEARE'S EARLY DAYS. Hist. P. 2 a. C. A. Somerset. C.G., October 29, 1829.

SHAKESPEARE'S GARLAND. Collection of songs. Anon. Pr. 1769.

SHAKESPEARE'S HOUSE. Adelphi, April 27, 1864.

SHAKESPEARE'S JUBILEE. M. G. S. Carey. Pr 1769.

SHAKESPEAREAN LUNATIC, A. Sk. Camberwell Pal., July 6, 1908.

SHAKUNTALAH. Extract fr. Kaladisha's D. Gaiety, December 12, 1885. (Played by Parsee Co.)

SHALL WE FORGIVE HER? D. 5 a. F. Harvey. Sheffield Alexandra, April 2, 1894; Adelphi, June 20, 1894.

SHALL WE REMEMBER? D. 1 a. W. Turnbull and R. Castleton Ellis. Camberwell Surrey Masonic H., December 13, 1893; St. George's H., October 13, 1899.

SHAM BEGGAR, THE. C. 2 a. Extract fr. novel of "The Adventures of Jack Smart." Pr. 1756.

SHAM CONJUROR, THE. C. Masque. C.G., 1741. N.p.

SHAM COSTERS, THE. Sk. Standard, May 4, 1908.

SHAM FIGHT; OR, POLITICAL HUMBUG, THE. State F. 2 a. Ac. at M--d--n. Pr. 1756.

SHAM LAWYER; OR, THE LUCKY EXTRAVAGANT, THE. C. J. Drake. T.R., 1697.

SHAM PHILOSOPHER; OR, COUNTRY GAMBOL, THE. C. 2 a. Taken fr. Marmontel. (MS. in Mr. Reed's library.) Before 1814.

SHAM PRINCE; OR, NEWS FROM PASSAU, THE. C. C. Shadwell. Dublin. Pr. 1720.

SHAM SOLICITOR, THE. Oa. Wr. and composed by J. Tabrar. Imperial, October 1, 1883.

SHAM SQUIRE, THE. Irish D. 4 a. J. W. Whitbread. Dublin Queen's, December 26, 1903.

SHAME. P. C. Noble. Huddersfield T.R. and O.H., October 12, 1883.

SHAME. D. 1 a. Alice Chapin and E. H. C. Oliphant. Vaudeville, July 21, 1892.

SHAMEFUL BEHAVIOUR. Ca. 2 a. A. C. Troughton. Strand, November 28, 1859.

SHAMROCK; OR, THE ANNIVERSARY OF S. PATRICK, THE. F. J. O'Keeffe. C.G., April, 1783. Changed to *The Poor Soldier*.

SHAMROCK AND THE ROSE, THE. D. 4 a. W. Reynolds, Huddersfield T.R., October 7, 1891; Grand, Sept. 26, 1892.

SHAMROCK OF IRELAND, THE. D. 3 a. J. B. Howe. Britannia, May 20, 1867.

SHAMUS-NA-GLAUNA; OR, THE SPEIDHOIR. Irish D. B. Aylmer. Manchester Queen's, August 21, 1876.

SHAMUS-NA-LENA; OR, THE SPEIDHOR. D. 4 a. E. Towers. Liverpool T.R., March 6, 1876; Pavilion, October 7, 1876.

SHAMUS O'BRIEN. C.O. 2 a. Lib. by G. H. Jessop. (After J. Sheridan Le Fanu.) M. by C. V. Stanford. Op. Comique, March 2, 1896.

SHAMUS O'BRIEN; OR, THE BOULD BOY OF GLENGALL. Melo. D. 4 a. F. Malder and C. Vernon. West London, April 26, 1897.

SHANCKE'S ORDINARIE. C. Shanke. 1623. N.p.

SHANDY THE SPALPEEN. Irish D. A. Hayward. Barnsley Gaiety. June 24, 1879.

SHANE-NA-LAWN. Irish C.D. J. C. Roche and J. A. Knox. (Orig. prod. in Chicago, 1885.) Liverpool R. Alexandra, April 22, 1889.

SHANKS' MARE. F. W. A. Vicars. Duke's, February 9, 1878.

SHARES. C. 2 a. Glasgow T.R., February 7, 1873.

SHARP AND FLAT. Mus. F. Lawler, 1813. Lyceum playbill, August 7, 1815; Lyceum, August 29, 1821.

SHARP PRACTICE; OR, THE "LEAR" OF CRIPPLEGATE. Serio C.D. 1 a. J. Lunn. Brighton T.R., August 18, 1862.

SHARP SET; OR, THE VILLAGE HOTEL. C. Sk. Lyceum, May 15, 1809.

SHARP WAY TO CATCH A WIFE, A. F. R. Barrett. Dublin Queen's, January 13, 1869.

SHARPER, THE. C. M. Clancy. Smock Alley, Dublin. Pr. 1750.

SHARPERS, THE. Ballad O. M. Gardiner. Smock Alley, Dublin. Pr. 1740.

SHARPS AND FLATS. Duo. E. Wright. Westminster Town H., February 11, 1895.

SHARPS AND FLATS; OR, THE RACECOURSE OF LIFE. D. 3 a. F. Marchant. Britannia, August 15, 1870.

SHATTERED FETTERS. P. 1 a. H. Earlesmere. Sheffield Cambridge H., July 10, 1894.

SHATTERED IDOL, A. D. 4 a. Chevalier Cimino. Oxford T.R., January 6, 1877.

SHATTERED IDOL, A. Ca. Dudley Colosseum, October 18, 1895.

SHATTERED LIVES. D. Prol. and 4 a. A. W. Parry. Liverpool Granby H., December 12, 1890.

SHATTERED NERVES. Ca. 1 a. Childe Pemberton. Publ. S. French, Limited.

SHATTERED 'UN. Burl. Sk. on Chatterton. A. Chevalier. Vaudeville, June 3, 1891.

SHAUGHRAUN, THE. Irish D. 4 a. D. Boucicault. D.L., September 4, 1875; Adelphi, December, 1875.

SHE. Rom. D. Prol. and 5 a. Dr. by E. Rose by permission fr. Rider Haggard's novel. Hay., May 25, 1888 (C.P.). Re-wr. and arr. for Miss Sophie Eyre by W. Sidney and C. Graves. Novelty, May 10, 1888 (C.P.); May 25, 1888; and Gaiety, September 6, 1888.

SHE; OR, THE FIRE OF LIFE. Mystical P. 2 parts. Adapt. by J. F. Preston fr. Rider Haggard's novel. Woolwich T.R., September 24, 1888.

SHE DEVIL, A. D. 4 a. R. Barrie. Lancaster Athenæum, November 25, 1902. See *A Queen of Villainy.*

SHE GALLANT; OR, RECRUITS FOR THE KING OF PRUSSIA, THE. Afterpiece. C.G., March 20, 1759 N.p.

SHE GALLANT; OR, SQUARE TOES OUT-WITTED, THE. C. 2 a. O'Keeffe. Smock Alley, Dublin. Pr. 1767.

SHE GALLANTS, THE. C. Lord Landsdowne. L.I.F. Pr. 1696. See *Once a Lover*, etc.

SHE LIVES; OR, THE GENEROUS BROTHER. C. Mary Goldsmith. Hay., 1803. N.p.

SHE SAINT, THE. P. Robert Daborne. 1614.

SHE STANDS ALONE. D. 4 a. Wm. Hibbert. Hammersmith Lyric, June 18, 1906.

SHE STOOPS TO CONQUER; OR, THE MISTAKES OF A NIGHT. C. 3 a. Oliver Goldsmith. C.G., March 15, 1773; D.L., January 25, 1823; Hay., 1856; Vaudeville, April 15, 1890; re-arr. by Chas. Wyndham, Criterion, May 10, 1890; rev. Terry's, June 6, 1898; rev. Coronet, February 18, 1908.

SHE STOOPS TO CONQUER. An Eng. O. 3 a. Adap. by E. Fitzball fr. Goldsmith's C. M. by Macfarren. D.L., February 11, 1864; rev. Hay., February 20, 1909.

SHE VENTURES AND HE WINS. C. "By a lady." Epil. by Mr. Motteux. L.I.F. Pr. 1696.

SHE WOLF, THE. See *La Lupa.*

SHE WOU'D AND SHE WOU'D NOT; OR, THE KIND IMPOSTOR. C. 5 a. Colley Cibber. Taken fr. Spanish *The Trepanner Trepanned* and *Counterfeits.* D.L., November 26, 1702; January 28, 1814; Hay. July 16, 1868.

SHE WOULD AND HE WOULD NOT. C. 2 a. J. M. Morton. St. James's, September 6, 1862.

SHE WOULD IF SHE COULD. C. Sir G. Etheridge. Duke's, 1671.

SHE WOULD BE A DUCHESS. See *The Irishman in Spain.*

SHE'S ELOP'D. C. John O'Keeffe. D.L. May 19, 1798. N.p.

SHE'S MAD FOR A HUSBAND. Mus. Ent. C. Dibdin. Sadler's Wells. N.p.

SHE'S NOT HIM AND HE'S NOT HER. F. 3 a. A. Erskine. Pr. 1764.

SHEBEEN, THE. P. 1 a. F. Harvey. Folkestone Harvey Inst., May 5, 1896.

SHEEP, DUCK, AND THE COCK, THE. Dr. fable. Anon. Bath, 1783.

SHEEP IN WOLF'S CLOTHING, A. Dom. D. 1 a. T. Taylor. Adapt. fr. Mme. de Girardin's *Une Femme qui déteste son Mari.* Olympic, February 19, 1857.

SHEEP SHEARING, THE. Dram. Past. 3 a. Taken fr. Shakespeare by G. Colman. Hay. Pr. 1777.

SHEEP SHEARING; OR, FLORIZEL AND PERDITA, THE. Past. C. MacNamara Morgan. Taken fr. Shakespeare's *Winter's Tale.* Dublin. Pr. 1767. See *Florizel and Perdita.*

SHEERLUCK JONES. Dr. criticism in four paragraphs. Malcolm Watson and E. La Lerre. Terry's, October 29, 1901.

SHEET ANCHOR OF ALBION, THE. Brighton, August 12, 1806. N.p.

SHELL OF A MAN, THE. P. 1 a. Mrs. George Cran, Great Queen Street, June 25, 1907.

SHELTER. Ca. W. H. Goldsmith. Stockton-on-Tees T.R., July 21, 1890.

SHEPHERD BOY, THE. O.D. 2 a. M. Mr. Reeve. Lyceum playbill, September 7, 1825.

SHEPHERD OF COURNOUAILLES, THE. Oa. 1 a. G. March. M. by Virginia Gabriel. Liverpool St. Geo. H., April 28, 1879.

SHEPHERD OF DERWENT VALE; OR, THE INNOCENT CULPRIT, THE. Trachtimary Tale. (?) J. Lunn. M. by Horn. D.L., February 12, 1825.

SHEPHERD OF SNOWDON, THE. Mus. Afterpiece. A. Davidson. Salisbury.

SHEPHERD OF TOLOSA, THE. Mentioned by Brewer.

SHEPHERD'S ARTIFICE, THE. Dr. Past. C. Dibdin. C.G. Pr. 1765.

SHEPHERD'S COURTSHIP, THE. M. Past. 4 int. W. Shirley. N.p.

SHEPHERD'S HOLIDAY, THE. T. C. Past. J. Rutter. Ac. before their Majesties at Whitehall, 1635.

SHEPHERD'S LOTTERY, THE. M. Ent. M. Mendez. M. by Dr. Boyce. D.L. Pr. 1751.

SHEPHERD'S MASQUE, THE. Masque. Ac. at Court. Temp. James I.

SHEPHERD'S OPERA, THE. John Maxwell. Pr. 1739, at York.

SHEPHERD'S PARADISE, THE. Past. W. Montague. Ac. before Charles I. by the Queen and her Ladies of Honour. Pr. 1629.

SHEPHERD'S STAR. Britannia, December 26, 1819.

SHEPHERD'S WEDDING, THE. O. C. Dibdin. C.G., about 1761

SHEPHERD'S WEDDING, THE. Past. C. 1 a. A. Steele. Pr. 1789.

SHEPHERDESS OF CHEAPSIDE, THE. M.F. J. Cobb. D.L., February 20, 1796.

SHEPHERDESS OF THE ALPS, THE. C.O. C. Dibdin. C.G., January 18, 1780. Pr. 1780.

SHERIFF AND THE ROSEBUD, THE. Sk. 1 a. W. J. T. Collins, fr. story by H. A. Vachell. Newport Lyceum, July 10, 1905; Manchester Hipp., June 23, 1908; Shepherd's Bush Empire, July 27, 1908.

SHERLOCK HOLMES. Psychological D. 5 a. C. Rogers. Glasgow T.R., May 28, 1894.

SHERLOCK HOLMES. D. 4 a. Dr. A. Conan Doyle and W. Gillette. F. on Doyle's novel, "The Strange Case of Miss Faulkner." Orig. prod. in America. Liverpool Shakespeare, September 2, 1901; Lyceum, September 9, 1901; Duke of York, October 17, 1905. (See *Shirlock.*)

SHERLOCK HOLMES, PRIVATE DETECTIVE. P. 4 a. Hanley T.R., December 15, 1903 (C.P.).

SHERMAN, THE. See "Miracle Plays."

SHIELD OF DAVID, THE. By M.B. and B. B. West London, April 3, 1899.

SHILLING DAY AT THE EXHIBITION, A. F. 1 a. A. Halliday and W. Brough. Adelphi, June 9, 1862.

SHILLY-SHALLY. C. 3 a. C. Reade and A Trollope. Gaiety, April 1, 1872.

SHINDY IN A SHANTY, A. Irish F. H. O'Grady. West Hartlepool Gaiety, August 7, 1875.

SHINGAWN; OR, OLD IRELAND'S SHAMROCK HAS NOT WITHERED YET, THE. D. 4 a. E. Sterling. Portsmouth R. Albert, February 5, 1872.

SHIP, THE. P. Ac. before 1611.

SHIP AHOY. D. 3 a. G. Roberts. Surrey, October 3, 1874.

SHIP AND THE PLOUGH, THE. Petite P. Ac. between P. and F. at C.G., May 31, 1804. N.p.

SHIP LAUNCH, THE. F. 1 a. D.L., May 17, 1804. N.p.

SHIPMATES. C.D. 3 a. C. V. Bridgman. Sunderland Lyceum, March 3, 1873.

SHIPWRECK, THE. Transl. fr. Plautus by Bonnell Thornton. Pr. 1767.

SHIPWRECK, THE. O. Alt. fr. Shakespeare and Dryden. M. by Smith. Exeter Exchange Patagonian. Pr. 1780.

SHIPWRECK, THE. C.O. 2 a. S. J. Arnold. M. by Dr. Arnold. D.L., December 20, 1796. Pr. 1796. Lyceum, July 24, 1816 (? same piece).

SHIPWRECK; OR, FATAL CURIOSITY, THE. T. 5 a. Mackenzie. Alt. fr. Lillo's *Fatal Curiosity*. C.G., February 10, 1784. Pr. 1784.

SHIPWRECK; OR, FRENCH INGRATITUDE, THE. Panto. Ballet. Ac. C.G., 1793. N.p.

SHIPWRECK; OR, THE FARMER ON THE COAST, THE. Dr. Piece. Hyland. Pr. 1746.

SHIPWRECKED LOVERS, THE. T. J. Templeton. Pr 1801.

SHIRTMAKER OF TOXTETH PARK, THE. D. H. J. Stanley. Liverpool Sefton, June 26, 1880.

SHO GUN, THE. C.O. G. Ade. M. by G. Luders. Bayswater Bijou, November 24, 1904 (C.P.).

SHOCK-HEADED PETER. Children's F. 2 a. P. Carr and N. Playfair. Garrick, December 26, 1900, and December 14, 1901.

SHOCKING EVENTS. F. J. B. Buckstone (?). Olympic, January, 1838.

SHODDY. C.D. 3 a. A. Wood. Bristol Old T., November 6, 1876.

SHOEMAKER'S A GENTLEMAN, A. C. W. Rowley. Rell. Bull., 1638, Dorset Gardens (rev.).

SHOEMAKER'S HOLIDAY; OR, THE GENTLE CRAFT, THE. C. T. Dekker. Ac. before the Q. by Earl of Nottingham and Servants. January 1, 1599. Pr. b.l. 1600. (Ascr. by some to Holyday.)

SHOOTING STARS. Extrav. M. by Hervé. Folly, November 22, 1877.

SHOOTING THE MOON. Orig. F. 1 a. F. F. Cooper. Strand, October 29, 1850.

SHOP. C.D. 2 a. A. Morris. Harrow Public H., April 13, 1904.

SHOP BOY, THE. Absurdity. 3 a. Adap. by H. Pleon fr. Peck's *Bad Boy*. West Hartlepool Alhambra, October 10, 1895.

SHOP GIRL, THE. M.F. H. J. Dam. M. by I. Caryll. Additions by A. Ross and L. Monckton. Gaiety, November 24, 1894.

SHOP HOURS. Sk. Edgar Dereve. M. by Henry W. May. Richmond, May 25, 1908.

SHOP-WALKER, THE. F. 1 a. D.L., December 17, 1825.

SHOP-WALKER, THE. F.C. 3 a. R. Buchanan and Marlowe. MS. with Douglas Cox.

SHOP-WALKER, THE. F. D. Brooke. Islington Myddelton H., February 5, 1892.

SHORE ACRES. P. 4 a. J. A. Herne. Waldorf, May 21, 1906.

SHORE, AND JANE SHORE, HIS WIFE, LIFE AND DEATH OF. Second part of Heywood's *Edward the Fourth*. Ac. by Earl of Derby and his servants. Ent. Stationers' Co., August 28, 1599.

SHORT AND SWEET. D. 1 a. A. C. Troughton. Strand, October 10, 1861; Court, March 13, 1875.

SHORT EXPOSURE, A. F. J. Anstey. Criterion, June 3, 1901.

SHORT REIGN AND A MERRY ONE, A. J. Poole. C.G., November 19, 1819.

SHORT VIEW. Jeremy Collier.

SHORTHAND. F. A. J. Barclay. Hammersmith Lyric H., February 11, 1889.

SHOULD THIS MEET THE EYE. F. 1 a. A. Maltby. Lyceum, June 10, 1872.

SHOULDER TO SHOULDER. Irish D. 5 a. J. W. Whitbread. Limerick T.R., November 8, 1886.

SHOW GIRL, THE. Sk. C. Rae-Brown. Middlesex, April 19, 1909.

SHOW FOLKS. Marylebone, July 7, 1857.

SHOW OF HANDS, A. Dr. Sk. W. R. Walkes. Park Lane Grosvenor House, March 6, 1890.

SHOWER OF BLACKS, A. A. Shirley and E. Bucalossi. Terry's, December 26, 1887.

SHOWER OF HUSBANDS, A. F.C. 2 a. A. Morris. MS. with Douglas Cox.

SHOWER OF KISSES, A. P. 1 a. Charlotte Morland. Hammersmith Lyric, June 27, 1893.

SHOWING UP OF BLANCO POSNET, THE. P. 1 a. G. B. Shaw. Dublin Abbey, August 25, 1909.

SHOWMAN, THE. M.P. 3 a. J. Ward. Hyde T.R., January 31, 1901.

SHOWMAN, THE. R.M. 4 a. C. Darrell and G. Testo Sante. Radcliffe O.H., near Manchester, May 9, 1904.

SHOWMAN'S DAUGHTER, THE. Dom. C. 3 a. Frances Hodgson-Burnett. Worcester T.R., October 12, 1891; Royalty, January 6, 1892.

SHOWMAN'S SWEETHEART, THE. M.C. 3 a. A. Law, G. Byng. Lyrics by the author and G. Eden. Crouch End Queen's O.H., August 29, 1898.

SHOWS OF THE SEASON. M. Sk. C. Grain. St. Geo. H., June 18, 1884.

SHPIELLER, THE. Sk. 5 sc. J. Coherny. Inci. M. by Sam Aarons. Paragon, March 25, 1907.

SHRINE OF MAMMON. Mrs. George Corbett. Acton St. Alban's Parish H., December 6, 1900 (amat.).

SHRINE OF THE GOLDEN HAWK, THE. An Egyptian P. By Florence Farr and M. O. Shakespeare. Bayswater Bijou, January 20, 1902.

SHROVE TUESDAY IN ST. ALBANS, 1461. Hist. Wordless P. 4 parts. By C. H. Ashdown. M. by W. H. Bell. St. Albans County H., May 17, 1898.

SHUFFLING, CUTTING, AND DEALING WITH OLIVER PROTECTOR AND OTHERS. Neville. Ac. from 1653-1658. Pr. 1659.

SHULAMITE, THE. P. 3 a. Claude Askew and E. Knoblauch. Savoy, May 12, 1906.

SHUTTLECOCK, THE. F.D. 3 a. H. J. Byron, completed by J. Ashby Sterry. Toole's, May 16, 1885.

SHYLOCK. Burl. Publ. by S. French, Ltd.

SHYLOCK; OR, THE MERCHANT OF VENICE PRESERVED. F. Talfourd. Olympic, June 4, 1853.

SHYLOCK AND CO. F. 3 a. G. Canninge and A. Chevalier. Adap. fr. *L'Article 7 of Bataille and Fengère.* Camden Town Park H., December 5, 1890 (C.P.); (as "I.O.U."), Richmond T.R., January 17, 1891; Criterion, June 18, 1892.

SI SLOCUM. D. Clifton W. Tayleure. Olympic, December 18, 1876.

SIAMESE TWINS, THE. F. 1 a. G. A. à Beckett. Queen's, 1834.

SIBERIA. P. 5 a. B. Campbell (orig. prod. San Francisco, 1882). Princess's, December 14, 1887.

SIBERIA. D. Sk. 3 a. Surrey, March 13, 1905.

SICELIDES. Piscatory D. P. Fletcher. Cambridge King's Coll., 1614.

SICILIAN, THE. Operatic Melo-d. Surrey, July 1, 1816.

SICILIAN; OR, LOVE MAKES A PAINTER, THE. C. Transl. fr. Molière by J. Ozell. Pr. 1714.

SICILIAN BRIDE, THE. O. 4 a. Wds. by Bunn fr. St. George's. M. by Balfe. D.L., March 6, 1852.

SICILIAN CAPTIVE, THE. Symmons. 1800.

SICILIAN IDYLL, A. 2 sc. J. Todhunter. M.D. Bedford Park Club H.; St. Geo. H., July 1, 1890; Vaude., June 15, 1891.

SICILIAN LOVER, THE. T. Mary Robinson. Pr. 1796.

SICILIAN ROMANCE; OR, THE APPARITION OF THE CLIFFS, THE. O. H. Siddons. C.G., May 28, 1794. Pr. 1794.

SICILIAN SUMMER, A. C. H. Taylor. 1850.

SICILIAN USURPER, THE. T. N. Tate. Alt. of Shakespeare's "Richard II.," under which title it was published in 1681.

SICILIAN VESPERS. Kenney. 1840.

SICILIEN, LE. Molière. See "French Classical Plays."

SICILY AND NAPLES; OR, THE FATAL UNION. T. S. Harding. Pr. 1640.

SID. C.D. P. Meritt. Grecian, June 12, 1871.

SIDNEY CARTON. Adap. fr. "A Tale of Two Cities" by E. Pemberton. Norwich, January, 1893.

SIDONIE. D. 3 a. F. Lyster and P. Heriot. Orig. prod. in America. Novelty, December 14, 1887.

SIEBEN GASLEIN, DIE. O. Humperdinck.

SIEGE, THE. (Not to be confounded with *The Siege of Rhodes.*) T.C. Sir W. Davenant. Bye plot taken from *The Humorous Lieutenant.* Pr. 1673.

SIEGE; OR, LOVE'S CONVERT, THE. T.C. W. Cartwright. Pr. 1651.

SIEGE AND SURRENDER OF MONS, THE. T.C. Anon. Pr. 1691.

SIEGE OF ACRE, THE. Pant. Int. C.G., 1800. N.p.

SIEGE OF ALEPPO, THE. T. W. Hawkins. Pr. 1758.

SIEGE OF ANTWERP, THE. See *A Larum for London.*

SIEGE OF AQUILEIA, THE. T. J. Home. T.R. in D.L., February 21, 1760. Pr. 1760.

SIEGE OF BABYLON, THE. T.C. S. Pordage. Duke's, 1678.

SIEGE OF BELGRADE, THE. C.O. 3 a. J. Cobb. 1791. D.L., March 8, 1814; Lyceum, September 8, 1815.

SIEGE OF BERWICK, THE. T. 4 a. Jeringham. C.G. Pr. 1794.

SIEGE OF CALAIS, THE. T. C. Denis. Transl. fr. French of M. De Belloy. Pr. 1765.

SIEGE OF CONSTANTINOPLE, THE. T. N. Payne. Duke's, 1675.

SIEGE OF CORINTH, THE. O. 3 a. F. on Byron's poem. M. by Rossini. Adap. by Cooke. Paris, October 9, 1826; D.L., November 8, 1836.

SIEGE OF CURZOLA, THE. C.O. J. O'Keeffe. Hay., 1786. N.p.

SIEGE OF CUZCO, THE. T. W. Sotheby. Pr. 1800.

SIEGE OF DAMASCUS, THE. T. J. Hughes. (Plot suggested by Davenant's *The Siege.*) D.L., 1720.

SIEGE OF DERRY, THE. T.C. Anon. Pr 1692 See *Piety and Valour.*

SIEGE OF DUNKIRK, THE. P. C. Massey. Ac. in 1602. N.p.

SIEGE OF GIBRALTAR, THE. M.F. F. Pilon. C.G., April 25, 1780. Pr. 1780.

SIEGE OF GRENADA. T. Dryden.

SIEGE OF ISCA; OR, THE BATTLES OF THE WEST, THE. Hist. Operatic Melo-d. Dr. J. Kemp. New T., Tottenham Street. 1810.

SIEGE OF ISMAEL, THE. T. W. Preston. 1794.

SIEGE OF JERUSALEM, THE. T. Lady Strathmore. 1774.

SIEGE OF JERUSALEM, THE. T. G. Gregory, D.D. N.p.

SIEGE OF JERUSALEM BY TITUS VESPASIAN, THE. T. Mary Latter. Pr. 1763. Prefixed to it is *An Essay on the Mystery and Mischiefs of Stagecraft.*

SIEGE OF LONDON, THE. Ac. December 26, 1594. N.p.

SIEGE OF MARSEILLES, THE. T. W. J. Mickle. Pr. 1794.

SIEGE OF MEAUX, THE. T. 3 a. H. J. Pye. C.G., May 19, 1794. Pr. 1794.

SIEGE OF MEMPHIS; OR, THE AMBITIOUS QUEEN, THE. T. T. Durfey. T.R., 1676. Pr. 1676.

SIEGE OF NAMUR, THE. Droll ac. at Bartholomew Fair, 1698.

SIEGE OF PALMYRA, THE. T. W. Hilton. Pr. 1776.

SIEGE OF PERTH; OR, SIR WILLIAM WALLACE, THE SCOTS' CHAMPION, THE. Grand Martial Ent. A. Maclaren. Dumfries, 1792.

SIEGE OF QUEBEC; OR, HARLEQUIN ENGINEER, THE. Pant. C.G., 1760. N.p.

SIEGE OF RHODES, THE. P. Sir W. Davenant. Brought out as ent. in 1656. Elaborated and second part added in 1662. Ac. at L.I.F. Women perf. on the stage in this piece.

SIEGE OF ROCHELLE, THE. Orig. O. 2 a. F. on Mme. A'Genlis's novel. E. Fitzball. M. by Balfe. D.L., October 29, 1835.

SIEGE OF ST. QUENTIN; OR, SPANISH HEROISM, THE. D. 3 a. T. E. Hook. D.L., November 10, 1808. Pr. 1808.

SIEGE OF SERINGAPATAM. International Exhibition, 1863.

SIEGE OF SINOPE, THE. T. Mrs. Brooke. C.G., January 31, 1781. Pr. 1781.

SIEGE OF TAMOR, THE. T. G. E. Howard. Assisted in lyric parts by H. Brooke. Pr. 1773.

SIEGE OF THE CASTLE OF ÆSCULAPIUS, THE, Heroic C. Warwick Lane T, Pr, 1768,

SIEGE OF TROY, THE. D. E. Settle. D.L., 1701.

SIEGE OF TROY, THE. T.C. 3 a. Pr. 1718.

SIEGE OF TROY, THE. Burl. R. B. Brough.

SIEGE OF TROY, THE. Lyceum, December 27, 1858.

SIEGE OF URBAN, THE. T.C. Sir W. Killigrew. Pr. 1666.

SIEGFRIED. O. 3 a. R. Wagner. Her M., May 8, 1882; C.G., June 8, 1892.

SIFACE. O. J. C. Bach. Circa 1771.

SIGESMAR THE SWITZER. Melo. D. M. by Cooke. Action by Johnson. D.L., September 26, 1818.

SIGHS; OR, THE DAUGHTER. C. P. Hoare. Taken fr. Kotzebue, 1799. Hay., 1806.

SIGHT AND SEARCH. P. MS. preserved in private library in Ireland. Dated 1643.

SIGHT AND SOUND. Dom. D. Britannia, November 20, 1876.

SIGISMONDO. O. Rossini. (Venice, 1815.)

SIGN OF THE CROSS, THE. P. 4 a. Wilson Barrett. Orig. prod. in America. Leeds Grand, August 26, 1895; Lyric, January 4, 1896; (rev.) August 21, 1897; Lyceum, October 19, 1899.

SIGNA. Rom. O. 2 a. G. à Beckett, H. Rudall, and F. E. Weatherley. M. by F. H. Cowen. Italian vers. by G. Mazzucati. F. on Ouida's novel. Milan, November 12, 1893. C.G., June 30, 1894.

SIGNAL, THE. D. 3 a. J. S. Coyne. Olympic, April 8, 1844.

SIGNAL, THE. Sk. Manchester Tivoli, September 27, 1909.

SIGNAL LIGHTS. American D. 5 a. W. J. Thompson. Birkenhead Metropole, July 30, 1894; Pavilion, September 10, 1894.

SIGNOR APPIANI. P. 1 a. Plymouth T.R., October 22, 1897.

SIGNOR FAGOTTO. Op. bo. 1 a. Offenbach. 1868.

SIGURD. Grand O. M. by M. Reyer. Lib. by MM. Camille du Locle and Alfred Blau. Brussels, January 7, 1884; C.G., July 15, 1884; Paris, June 12, 1885.

SILAS BRUTON; OR, THE MURDER AT THE OLD CROOK FARM. D. H. Hayman. Victoria, April 12, 1877.

SILAS MARNER'S TREASURE. D. Liverpool T.R., May 1, 1876.

SILENCE. D. 4 a. C. H. Ross. Holborn, May 6, 1871.

SILENCE OF A CHATTERBOX, THE. P. 1 a. Constance Prevost. F. on a story by Miss Wilford. Terry's, October 30, 1899.

SILENCE OF DEAN MAITLAND, THE. P. 3 a. Taken fr. Maxwell Gray's novel by F. O. Chambers. Kidderminster T.R. and O.H., April 12, 1898.

SILENCE OF NIGHT, THE. D. 4 a. J. D. Saunders. Clapham Shakespeare, July 19, 1897.

. SILENT ACCUSER, THE. D. 4 a. B. Espinasse and Jas. Bell. Peckham Crown, July 24, 1905.

SILENT BATTLE, THE. Orig. called *Agatha*. P. 3 a. I. Henderson. Criterion, May 24, 1892, and December 8, 1892.

SILENT FOE, A. D. 4 a. E. V. Edwards. Stalybridge Grand, September 22, 1902.

SILENT HOUSE. D. 4 a. C. March. Greenwich Carlton, July 1, 1901.

SILENT PROTECTOR, A. Ca. 1 a. T. J. Williams. P.O.W., March 7, 1868.

SILENT SHORE, THE. Dramatised ver. Pro. and 4a. by J. Bloundelle-Burton of his rom. Olympic, May 8, 1888.

SILENT SYSTEM, THE. F. 1 a. T. J. Williams. Strand, July 3, 1862.

SILENT VENGEANCE, A. D. 4 a. H. Grattan. Leeds T.R., September 16, 1901; Camberwell Metropole, October 7, 1901.

SILENT WITNESS, A. Dr. rom. 4 a. J. Coleman. Olympic, May 18, 1889.

SILENT WITNESS, A; OR, A SISTER OF THE RED CROSS, THE. Sk. Hal Collier. Foresters' M.H., December 3, 1900.

SILENT WOMAN, A. F. 1 a. T. H. Lacy. August 17, 1835. Adap. fr. Burnand's *Dumb Belle*.

SILENT WOMAN, A. Ben Jonson. 1609. Great Queen Street T., May 8, 1905.

SILKEN FETTERS. C. 3 a. L. Buckingham. Hay., November 14, 1863.

SILLY SEASON, THE. F.C. 3 a. G. Lash-Gordon and B. Nash. Shepherd's Bush Athenæum, December 30, 1892.

SILLY SERVANT, THE. Sk. Prod. by Tom Kelso. Royal Standard, December 10, 1906.

SILVANA (*The Dumb Wood-Maiden*). Ro. O. 3 a. Wds. by F. K. Heimer. M. by Weber. (Frankfort, September 16, 1810.) Prod. in England as *Sylvana*. Surrey, September 2, 1828.

SILVANA. See *The Girl of the Wood*.

SILVANO. It. O. Mascagni. Italy, 1895.

SILVANUS. Latin C. Rollinson. Ac. at Cambridge 1596. Transcribed in 1600.

SILVER AGE, THE. Hist. P. T. Heywood. Pr. 1613.

SILVER ARROW, ETC., THE. Panto. D.L., January 6, 1819.

SILVER BOX, THE. P. 3 a. J. Galsworthy. Court, September 25, 1906; April 8, 1907.

SILVER BULLET, THE. D. W. Seaman. Britannia, August 16, 1875.

SILVER CAGE, THE. Oa. G. Bell. Op. C., July 31, 1874.

SILVER CRESCENT, THE. Melo-d. Lyceum, 1839.

SILVER CROSS, THE. M. and Dom. C. 4 a. D. Hender. Birkenhead T.R., April 25, 1898.

SILVER FALLS, THE. D. 4 a. G. R. Sims and H. Pettitt. Adelphi. December 29, 1888.

SILVER FORTUNE, THE. Mus. C.D. 3 a. W. Miller and P. Havard. M. by E. Lawson. Ramsgate Sanger's Amphi., October 15, 1888.

SILVER GUILT. Burl. W. Warham. Strand, June 9, 1883.

SILVER HONEYMOON, A. Dom. C. R. Hemy. Trafalgar, May 8, 1894.

SILVER HORSESHOE, THE. D. 4 a. St. A. Miller. Brighton Aquarium, February 4, 1895; Novelty, February 3, 1896.

SILVER KEEPSAKE, THE. C. 1 a. E. Norwood. York T.R., December 19, 1894.

SILVER KEY, THE. Ver. 4 a. of the Elder Dumas's *Mlle. de Belle Isle*, by S. Grundy. H.M., July 10, 1897, and November 1, 1897.

SILVER KING, THE. D. 5 a. H. A. Jones and H. Herman. Princess's, November 16, 1882; Olympic, January 3, 1891; rev. Lyceum, September 2, 1899; Adelphi, January 21, 1903.

SILVER LINE, THE. P. without words. 1 a. C. D. Marius. Gaiety, May 25, 1891.

SILVER LINING, THE. C. 3 a. L. Buckingham. St. James's, January 30, 1864.

SILVER LINK, THE. C. 3 a. H. and J. A. Bleackley. Comedy, May 13, 1902.

SILVER SHAFT, THE. D. Pro. and 3 a. C. A. Clarke. Warrington Public H., November 21, 1889.

SILVER SHELL, THE. P. 4 a. H. J. W. Dam. Prod. as *Prince Karatoff* at Birmingham P.O.W., December 2, 1892; Avenue, April 15, 1893.

SILVER SHIELD, THE. C. 3 a. S. Grundy. Strand, May 19, 1885.

SILVER SLIPPER, THE. Extrav. O. Hall. Lyrics by W. H. Risqué. M. by L. Stuart. Lyric, June 1, 1901.

SILVER SPOON, A. C.F. 3 a. A. Maltby and F. Lindo. Buxton Pav. T., June 22, 1900.

SILVER STICK, THE. M.P. 2 a. Alfred England. M. by Carl St. Amory. Northampton O.H., December 8, 1906 (C.P.); Northampton O.H., December 17, 1906.

SILVER TANKARD; OR, THE POINT AT PORTSMOUTH, THE. Mus. F. M. of Anspach and Lady Craven. Hay., July 18, 1781. N.p.

SILVER TANKARD, THE. P. 1 a. Cecil Egerton. Court, March 3, 1909.

SILVER TOWER. Standard, April 13, 1857.

SILVER VEIL, THE. D. 3 a. A. I. Smith. Battersea Park T.H., February 6, 1888.

SILVER WEDDING, A. C.D. 3 a. E. Ferris and P. Heriot. Fulham Grand, July 2, 1900.

SILVER WEDDING, THE. C. T. I. Warman. Coventry Co-operative Assembly R., February 2, 1885.

SILVESTER DAGGERWOOD. F. 1 a. G. Coleman, jun. Hay., 1795; D.L., February 19, 1814. See *New Hay at the Old Market.*

SILVIA. See *Sylvia.*

SIMO. C. Anon. 1652.

SIMON; OR, MORE WAYS THAN ONE. D. C. H. Hazlewood. Philharmonic, January 17, 1876.

SIMON; OR, THE LOST HEIR RESTORED. D. J. S. Spackman. Greenock T.R., May 10, 1875. Rev. 1881.

SIMON BOCCANEGRA. O. 3 a. and prol. Lib. by Piane. M. by Verdi. Venice, March 12, 1857. Fresh lib. by Boito. Milan, March 24, 1881.

SIMON IN LOVE; OR, THE INNOCENT THEFT. C. Transl. fr. French by J. Kelly. T.R. in D.L., 1733.

SIMON LEE; OR, THE MURDER OF THE 5 FIELDS COPSE. Dom. D. 3 a. G. D. Pitt. City of London, April 1, 1839.

SIMON MONEYPENNY. D. 4 a. J. Gower. Linlithgow Town H. May 3, 1888.

SIMON OF ATHENS; OR, THE MAN-HUNTER. T. T. Shadwell. D. of Y., 1678.

SIMON THE LEPER. C. Bishop Bale. N.p.

SIMON THE SMITH. C.O. Rom. By E. W. Bowles. M. by L. N. Parker and M. Clark. Bayswater Victoria H., April 18, 1890.

SIMON THE TANNER. Victoria, April 7, 1856.

SIMON THE THIEF. Victoria, January 6, 1866.

SIMOON. P. August Strinberg. Transl. and arr. by F. Castles and A. E. Browne. Bloomsbury H., November 29, 1906.

SIMPKIN, THE HUMOURS OF. Droll by Kirkman. 1672.

SIMPLE HEARTS. Dom. D. 6 a. C. H. Lorenzo. Wrexham Public H., December 24, 1888.

SIMPLE (?) LIFE, THE. P. 1 a. E. O. Brookes and R. C. Jenkins. Swansea G.T., April 29, 1907; Kingston Royal County, May 18, 1908.

SIMPLE SIMON. P. 4 a. Murray Carson and Nora Keith. Manchester Prince's, October 7, 1907; Garrick, November 13, 1907.

SIMPLE STORY, THE. Novel by Mrs. Inchbald. Circa 1790.

SIMPLE SWEEP, A. M. Sk. 1 a. Lib. by F. W. Broughton. M. by Rev. Father Downes. Leeds Grand, March 1, 1882; Princess's, April 26, 1882.

SIMPLETON THE SMITH. Int. Anon. 1662. See *The Wits.*

SIMPSON AND COMPANY. C. 2 a. J. Poole. D.L., January 4, 1823; D.L., June 11, 1824; Lyceum playbill (rev.), May 19, 1822; D.L., March 10, 1851.

SIMPSON AND DELILAH. Ca. 1 a. S. Edwards. Avenue, June 3, 1882.

SIMSON'S LITTLE HOLIDAY. H. Nicholls. D.L., September 13, 1884.

SIN AND ITS SHADOWS. D. 4 a. H. Lemmon. Oxford T.R., September 21, 1885.

SIN AND SORROW. Orig. D. Prol. and 3 a. H. Leslie. Grecian, September 17, 1866.

SIN AND THE SINNER. "Society D." H. Morton Baird. Richmond Castle, April 22, 1909.

SIN EATER, THE. P. 1 a. Jean Macpherson. Lyric, March 17, 1908 (C.P.).

SIN OF A LIFE, THE. D. 3 a. N. Lee. Victoria, September 28, 1867.

SIN OF A LIFE, THE. D. 4 a. W. Reynolds. Taken fr. Ouida's novel, "Wanda." Princess's, September 30, 1901.

SIN OF HER CHILDHOOD, THE. D. in prol. and 4 a. J. A. Campbell. Barrow Royalty T., April 24, 1903 (C.P.); Accrington Prince's, December 24, 1903; Hammersmith Lyric, October 31, 1904.

SIN OF ST. HULDA, THE. D. 4 a. G. S. Ogilvie. Shaftesbury, April 9, 1896.

SIN OF WILLIAM JACKSON, THE. P. 3 a. Baroness Orczy and M. Barstow. Lyric, August 28, 1906.

SIN'S ANGEL. D. 4 a. H. Moss. Ipswich Lyceum, November 16, 1893.

SINBAD. D.L., December 26, 1882.

SINBAD; OR, THE DRYLAND SAILOR. Burl. J. Horner. Coventry T.R., July 7, 1884.

SINBAD THE SAILOR; OR, THE TAR THAT WAS "PITCHED" INTO. Burl. F. W. Greene. Edinburgh Princess's, March 31, 1879.

SINFUL CITY, THE. P. in Pro. and 4 a. A. Shirley and W. Muskerry. Leeds Queen's, April 4, 1902.

SINGER'S VOLUNTARY. P. J. Singer. Ac. in 1602. N.p.

SINGING SERVANTS. Sk. Holborn Empire, February 17, 1908.

SINGLE HEART AND DOUBLE FACE. Dom. D. 5 a. C. Reade. Edinburgh Princess's, June 1, 1882.

SINGLE LIFE. C. 3 a. J. B. Buckstone. Hay., 1839.

SINK OR SWIM. C. 2 a. T. Morton. Olympic, August 2, 1852.

SINLESS SECRET, A. D. 5 a. F. Lindo. F. on Rita's novel. Comedy, January 7, 1890.

SINLESS SHAME, A. D. 4 a. G. Elliott. Rev. Cheltenham T.R., February 28, 1887.

SINLESS SINNER, A. Dom. D. 3 a. Marie Edward Saker. Ealing Lyric, April 15, 1896.

SINNER, THE. D. 4 a. C. Watson Mill. Sunderland R., July 26, 1909.

SINNER'S POINT. C.D. 4 a. Augusta Tullock. Manchester St. James's, January 22, 1903 (C.P.); Sunderland R., April 6, 1903.

SINS OF A CITY, THE. D. G. Conquest and P. Meritt. Surrey, September 29, 1884.

SINS OF A CITY, THE. D. in Pro. and 4 a. Nita Rae. Morriston O.H., May 1, 1902; Rotherhithe Terriss, December 14, 1903.

SINS OF NEW YORK. Sensational D. 5 a. F. on E. M. Murdoch's story, *Shadowed by Three*, by A. Horner. Birkenhead T.R., February 10, 1890.

SINS OF SOCIETY. D. Pro. and 3 a. Charles Darrell. Darlington T.R., November 26, 1906.

SINS OF SOCIETY, THE. D. (of modern life.) 4 a. C. Raleigh and H. Hamilton. D.L., September 12, 1907.

SINS OF THE FATHERS, THE. Ca. 1 a. W. Lestocq. Globe, January 30, 1886.

SINS OF THE FATHERS, THE. P. 1 a. H. Beatty and S. F. Harrison. Glasgow Royalty, April 24, 1896.

SINS OF THE FATHERS, THE. D. Pro. and 4 a. W. J. Mackay and W. Davidson. Bishop Auckland Eden, December 23, 1897; Stratford T.R., October 17, 1898.

SINS OF THE FATHERS; OR, THE UNNATURAL BROTHERS. D. 6 a. M. Melford. Pavilion, May 4, 1885.

SINS OF THE NIGHT. D. 5 a. F. Harvey. Barnsley T.R., March 30, 1893; Grand, May 22, 1893.

SIR ALAN'S WIFE. D. 4 a. S. Mackaye. Herne Bay T.H., August 17, 1888 (C.P.).

SIR ANTHONY. C. 3 a. C Haddon Chambers. Wyndham's, November 28, 1908.

SIR ANTHONY LOVE; OR, THE RAMBLING LADY. C. T. Southern. T.R., 1690.

SIR BARNABY WHIGG; OR, NO WIT LIKE A WOMAN'S. C. T. Durfey. T.R., 1681.

SIR CLYOMON, KNIGHT OF THE GOLDEN SHIELD, AND CLAMYDES, THE WHITE KNIGHT. Hist. P. Anon. Pr. 1599.

SIR COURTLY NICE; OR, IT CANNOT BE. C. F. on Moreto's *No Pued-eser*, by J. Crowne. T.R., 1685.

SIR FOPLING FLUTTER. C. Etherege. 1676. Second title of *The Man of Mode*.

SIR FRANCIS DRAKE. Hist. P., with instrumental and vocal music. Sir W. Davenant. Cockpit in D.L. Pr. 1659. See *Playhouse To Be Let*.

SIR FRANCIS DRAKE AND IRON ARM. Spec. J. C. Cross. Pr. 1800.

SIR GEORGE AND A DRAGON; OR, WE ARE SEVEN. Burl. F. C. Burnand. Strand, March 31, 1870.

SIR GEORGE OF ALMACK'S. C. 4 a. H. F. Malty. Dover R.T., February 28, 1907; Kingston Royal County, December 11, 1907.

SIR GEORGE'S FOLLY. C.O. 2 a. Bk. by W. Livingstone. M. by Dr. Koeller. Belfast T.R., January 27, 1908.

SIR GIDDY WHIM; OR, THE LUCKY ARMOUR. C. Anon. Pr. 1703.

SIR GILES GOOSE-CAPPE, KNIGHT. C. Anon. Ac. by Children of the Chapel and in a private house in Salisbury Court, 1636.

SIR GORGER THE GIANT AND LITTLE BOY BLUE. M. Fairy P. A. Giffard. Parkhurst, June 19, 1897.

SIR HARRY GAYLOVE; OR, COMEDY IN EMBRIO. Mrs. J. Marshall. Pro. by Blacklock and epil. Dr. Downmam. Pr. 1772.

SIR HARRY WILDAIR. Sequel to *The Constant Couple*. C. G. Farquhar. D.L., 1701.

SIR HERCULES BUFFOON; OR, THE POETICAL SQUIRE. C. J. Lacy. Duke's. Pr. 1684.

SIR JACK O' LANTERN, THE KNIGHT OF (K)NIGHTS; OR, A CURIOUS CURSE, CURIOUSLY CURED. C.O. 3 a. Lib. by A. H. Ward. M. by H. Vernon. Neath Bijou, August 31, 1892.

SIR JASPER'S TENANT. See *Mirabel*.

SIR JOHN BUTT. F. 2 a. Smith. Pr. 1798.

SIR JOHN COCKLE AT COURT. F. R. Dodsley. Sequel to *The King and the Miller of Mansfield*. T.R. in D.L., 1737.

SIR JOHN FALSTAFF IN MASQUERADE. F. S. Johnson. Hay., 1741. N.p.

SIR JOHN MANDEVILLE. P. Anon. February 24, 1591.

SIR JOHN MANDEVILLE, THE GOOD LORD COBHAM. Hist. P. Ac. by E. of Nottingham's servants. Pr. 1600.

SIR JOHN MANDEVILLE. Part I. Anon. Part II. Not to be found.

SIR JOHN MANDEVILLE; OR, LOVE AND ZEAL. T. Brereton. Since the Restoration.

SIR JOHN OLDCASTLE. Munday and Drayton. Ascr. W. Shakespeare. Pr. 1600 and 1601.

SIR JOHN OLDCASTLE. Part II. Lost. Anon.

SIR JOHN OLDCASTLE. T. Thos. Brereton.

SIR MARIGOLD THE DOTTIE; OR, THE MOONLIGHT KNIGHT. Burl. 1 a. C. F. Fuller. H.M.S. "Rainbow," April 16, 1885.

SIR MARMADUKE MAXWELL. C. Cunningham. 1827.

SIR MARTIN MAR-ALL; OR, FEIGNED INNOCENCE. C. J. Dryden. Partly f. on Quinault's *L'Amour Indiscret* and partly fr. Molière's *L'Etourdi*. Transl. by Duke of Newcastle. L.I.F., August 16, 1667; Hay., July 26, 1707.

SIR MARTIN MAR-ALL. C. Literal transl. of Molière's *L'Etourdi* by J. Ozell.

SIR MARTYN SKINK. Hist. P. R. Brome and T. Heywood. Ent. Stationers' Co., April 8, 1654. N.p.

SIR PATIENT FANCY. C. Mrs. Behn. Partly f. on Molière's plays, *La Malade Imaginaire* and *Mons. de Pourceaugnac*. Duke's, 1678.

SIR PLACIDAS. P. Circa 1600.

SIR REGINALD; OR, AN ANCESTRAL INCUBUS. Oa. 1 a. Lib. by J. M. Taylor and L. Ray. M. by V. Phillips. St. George's H., January 6, 1894.

SIR RICHARD GRINVILLE. Mentioned by Brewer.

SIR ROGER DE COVERLEY. C. J. Miller. N.p.

SIR ROGER DE COVERLEY. C. Dr. Dodd. N.p.

SIR ROGER DE COVERLEY. J. F. Smith. Adelphi, 1836.

SIR ROGER DE COVERLEY. C.D. 4 a. A. F. Cross. Nuneaton P.O.W., February 28, 1902.

SIR ROGER DE COVERLEY. Old English Bal. Div. in 3 tab. Story by Adrian Ross. M. by Osmond Carr. Dances and action by Mme. Katti Lanner. Empire, May 7, 1907.

SIR ROGER DE COVERLEY; OR, THE MERRY CHRISTMAS. Dr. Ent. 2 a. Mr. Dorman. D.L., December 30, 1746.

SIR ROGER DE COVERLEY; OR, THE WIDOW AND HER WOOERS. D. 3 a. Author of *Vicar of Wakefield*. Olympic, April 22, 1851.

SIR SOLOMAN; OR, THE CAUTIOUS COXCOMB. C. Transl. fr. Molière's *L'Ecole des Femmes* by L. Caryll. Ac. L.I.F., 1669-70. Pr. 1671.

SIR THOMAS CALLICO; OR, THE MOCK NABOB. F. Anon. Formed fr. *Sir Courtly Nice*. C.G., July 6, 1758. N.p.

SIR THOMAS MORE. T. Rev. James Hurdis. Pr. 1792.

SIR THOMAS MORE. MS. (British Museum).

SIR THOMAS OVERBURY. T. R. Savage. T.R. in D.L., June 12, 1723.

SIR THOMAS OVERBURY. T. Alt. fr. foregoing. Savage died before completion. Finished by W. Woodfall and Mr. Colman. C.G., February 1, 1777.

SIR THOMAS OVERBURY'S LIFE AND UNTIMELY DEATH. T. Ford. 1614.

SIR THOMAS WYATT. T. Webster and Dekker. 1607.

SIR WALTER RALEIGH. T. G. Sewell, M.D. L.I.F., January 16, 1719; D.L., December 14, 1789 (rev.). See *The Masquerade*.

SIR WILLIAM LONGSWOOD. P. M. Drayton. Ac. 1598. N.p.

SIR WILLIAM WALLACE OF ELLERSLIE; OR, THE SIEGE OF DUMBARTON CASTLE. T. J. Jackson. Edinburgh, 1780. N.p.

SIREN, THE. D. 3 a. J. P. Simpson. Lyceum, November 27, 1869.

SIRENE, LA. O. Comique. 3 a. Wds. by Scribe. M. by Auber. Opera Comique, March 26, 1844; (in Eng. as *The Syren*), Princess's, October 14, 1844.

SIROES. O. Transl. fr. Metastasio. J. Hoole. Pr. 1800.

SISSORS. See *Sithors*.

SISTER, THE. C. Mrs. Charlotte Lennox. Epil. by Dr. Goldsmith. Taken fr. dramatist's own novel, "Henrietta." C.G., February 18, 1769. Pr. 1769.

SISTER, THE. D. Transl. fr. Goethe. Pr. 1792.

SISTER BEATRICE. Miracle in 3 a. M. Maeterlinck. Court, March 28, 1909.

SISTER GRACE. C.D. Dr. J. Scott Buttams. Avenue, June 26, 1884.

SISTER MARY. P. 4 a. W. Barrett and C. Scott. Brighton T.R., March 8, 1886; Comedy, September 11, 1886.

SISTER MONICA. P. by Betty Brandon. Cambridge New, May 10, 1907.

SISTER OF CHARITY, THE. Rom. D. 2 a. Lyceum playbill, July 2, 1829.

SISTER'S EFFORT, A. Sk. W. Heron. Cambridge M.H., March 10, 1900.

SISTER'S HONOUR, A. Sk. Canterbury, July 12, 1907.

SISTER'S LOVE, A. D. H. F. Youle. New Holborn, July 24, 1867 (amat.).

SISTER'S PENANCE, A. D. 3 a. T. Taylor and A. W. Dubourg. Adelphi, November 26, 1866.

SISTER'S REVENGE, A. Dram. Duol. C. Martin. Rehearsal, W.C., January 29, 1909 (C.P.).

SISTER'S SACRIFICE. R.D. 4 a. S. A. Miller and M. Turner. June 3, 1901; Liverpool Rotunda, July 30, 1900; Surrey, June 3, 1901.

SISTER'S SIN, A. D. 4 a. Mrs. F. G. Kimberley. Accrington Prince's, November 28, 1900; Eleph. and Castle, August 5, 1901.

SISTER'S VOW, A. W. Stanhope. Liverpool P.O.W., May 19, 1888.

SISTERLY SERVICE. Ca. 1 a. J. P. Wooler. Strand, February 9, 1860.

SISTERS. C. H. Pettitt and F. W. Broughton. Liverpool P.O.W., March 31, 1883.

SISTERS. C.D. 4 a. Edith Courteney. Addlestone Jubilee H., December 28, 1893; Balham Assembly R., September 30, 1895.

SISTERS, THE. T. Foote. Pr. 1762.

SISTERS, THE. C. J. Shirley. Ac. in private house in Blackfryars, 1652. Rev., with alterations, L.I.F., November 28, 1723.

SISTERS, THE. D. 4 a. C. H. Hazlewood. Britannia, June 10, 1878.

SITHORS TO GRIND. D. 3 a. G. R. Walker. Edinburgh T.R., April 7, 1873.

SIX AND EIGHTPENCE. Ca. Prince's. March 17, 1884.

SIX AND SIX. Ca. 1 a. Lib. by T. B Hughes. M. by P. W. Hatton. Hull T.R., August 9, 1880.

SIX CLOTHIERS OF THE WEST, THE. P. W. Houghton (assisted by R. Hathwaye and W. Smith). Ac. 1601. Second part by same. Ac. in 1601. N.p.

SIX DAYS' ADVENTURE; OR, THE NEW UTOPIA. C. E. Howard. D. of Y., 1671.

SIX FOOLS. P. Ac. at Court, 1563.

SIX MONTHS AGO. Ca. 1 a. Adap. fr. French by Mr. Merivale, July 26, 1867. Bayswater Bijou, January 20, 1877.

SIX PERSONS. Duol. I. Zangwill. Hay., December 22, 1893, and January 18, 1894.

SIX PHYSICIANS. F. C.G., November 13, 1818.

SIX YEOMEN OF THE WEST, THE. P. W. Houghton, assisted by J. Day. Ac. 1601.

SIXES. Ca. A. Lindsay. Vaudeville, August 5, 1893.

SIXES. Ca. 1 a. Mrs. L. D'Orsay. Publ. by Douglas Cox.

SIXES AND SEVENS. Duol. E. H. Whitmore. Criterion, June 14, 1894; Garrick. December 29, 1894.

SIXPENNY TELEGRAM, A. Ca. 1 a. Florence Bell. Publ. by S. French, Ltd.

SIXPENNY WIRE, A. Dom. D. 1 "flash." C. Rae-Brown. So. Kensington, May Street Schoolroom, January 18, 1887.

SIXTEEN AND SIXTY. M.F. 2 a. Author of *The Gondolier; or, A Night in Venice*. Pr. 1815.

1643. Da. F. Stuart-Whyte. Empress, June 14, 1909.

SIXTEEN, NOT OUT. C. 2 sc. J. Blair. P.O.W., February 29, 1892.

1679. D. C. Webb. Glasgow T.R., September 23, 1872.

SIXTEEN-STRING JACK; OR, THE KNAVE OF KNAVE'S ACRE. Rom. Orig. D. 2 a. T. E. Wilks. City of London.

SIXTEEN YEARS AGO. D. J. Wolff. E. London, March 11, 1871.

SIXTH COMMANDMENT, THE. Rom. P. 5 a. R. Buchanan. Partly f. on suggestions contained in Doskoievsky's novel, "Crime et Châtiment." Shaftesbury, October 8, 1890.

SIXTH COMMANDMENT, THE. P. 1 a. C. Hamilton. Orig. called *The Traveller Returns*. Wyndham's, September 12, 1906.

SIXTUS THE FIFTH. Olympic, February 17, 1851.

SIXTY-THIRD LETTER. M.F. W. C. Oulton. M. by Dr. Arnold. Hay., July 28, 1802. Pr. 1803.

SIXTY YEARS AGO. Standard, December 27, 1852.

SKATING. Pant. Absurdity. J. Hickory Wood and Syd. Chaplin. Poplar Queen's, May 3, 1909.

SKELETON, THE. C. 3 a. F. on the German of Von Moser by A. Stannus and Y. Stephens. Vaudeville, May 27, 1887.

SKELETON IN A CUPBOARD, A. F.C. 3 a. C. Kelly. Kingston County, April 18, 1904.

SKELETON LOVER, THE. M.D. F. on a Black Letter Tract, *The Condign Punishment of a Transylvanian Necromancer.* M. by G. H. Rodwell. Lyceum playbill (fourteenth time), August 19, 1830.

SKELETON WITNESS; OR, THE MURDER OF THE MOUNT, THE. D. 3 a. W. L. Rede. Surrey T.

SKELETONS IN THE CUPBOARD; OR, THE CAPTAIN'S TROUBLES. M.Ca. 1 a. Julia Agnes Fraser. Publ. by J. Smith, Plymouth.

SKETCH OF A FINE LADY'S RETURN FROM A ROUT, THE. F. Catharine Clive. D.L., March 21, 1763. N.p.

SKETCH WITHOUT A NAME. Prod. by Geo. Gray. Camberwell Pal., January 21, 1907.

SKETCH WITHOUT A NAME, A. T. M. Paull. Holloway Empire, August 10, 1908.

SKETCHES FROM LIFE. C. 3 a. R. Sicklemore. Brighton T.R., 1802.

SKETCHES FROM LIFE; OR, THE WANDERING BARD. O. S. B. Frome. Songs pr. 1809.

SKIPPED BY THE LIGHT OF THE MOON. M.C. 2 a. G. R. Sims. Lyrics, P. Marshall. M. by G. Pack and H. W. May. Reading County T., August 24, 1896 (first time in England); Camberwell Metropole, April 5, 1807.

SKIPPER AND CO., WALL STREET. C. H. J. W. Dam. Adelphi, April 28, 1903 (C.P.).

SKIRT DANCER, THE. M.C. 2 a. By G. Ridgwell, E. Mansell, and F. Mackay. M. by H. Trotere. Woolwich Artillery T., March 28, 1898; Fulham Grand, June 27, 1898.

SKITTLES. C. 3 a. Paul Rubens and Lechmere Worrall. February 14, 1908 (amat.).

SKITTLES, LIMITED. F.C. 3 a. R. Blake. Richmond T.R., January 17, 1895. See *Limited.*

SKY HIGH. Sk. Wal Pink. M. by J. S. Baker Islington Empire, June 1, 1908 .

SKYWARD GUIDE, THE. D. 4 a. Mrs. Albert Bradshaw and M. Melford. Royalty, May 9, 1895.

SLACKSTER, THE. D. 3 sc. C. Douglas Carlile. Sadler's Wells, September 13, 1909.

SLANDER. D. Rev. ver. of *Jack* by E. Byam Wyke. York T.R., September 16, 1878.

SLANDER. C. F. Nirdlinger. Eng. ver. of José Echegaray's *El Gran Galeoto.* Birmingham T.R., December 9, 1908. See *The World and His Wife.*

SLANDERER, THE. C. Samuel Foote. (Unfinished.)

SLASHER AND CRASHER. Orig. F. 1 a. J. M. Morton. Adelphi, November 16, 1848.

SLATE PENCILLINGS; OUT OF SPIRITS. F. Fk. Hay. Globe, October 24, 1876.

SLATERSTEIN, LIMITED. Sk. Poplar Hipp., May 10, 1909.

SLAVE, THE. O. 3 a. T. Morton. M. by Bishop. C.G., November 12, 1816; D.L., May 31, 1825, and March 27, 1827; D.L., March 4, 1850 (rev.).

SLAVE GIRL, THE. D. 4 a. L. E. Mitchell (orig. called *Deborah,* and prod., Avenue, February 22, 1892). Bristol Princess's, September 26, 1893.

SLAVE HUNTER, THE. City of London, August 6, 1866.

SLAVE LIFE. Tom Taylor and others. Adelphi, November 29, 1852.

SLAVE OF DRINK, THE. D. 4 a. W. Reynolds. Workington Queen's O.H., August 4, 1890.

SLAVE OF SIN, THE. Melo-d. 4 a. E. Thane. Chorley Grand, January 30, 1901; Halifax T.R., July 29, 1901.

SLAVE'S RANSOM, A. D. 3 a. C. Osborne. Newcastle-upon-Tyne T.R., June 4, 1874.

SLAVEANA. Extrav. F. Hay and F. W. Green. Brighton T.R., October 11, 1875.

SLAVES. D. Maclaren. Pr. 1807. See *A Wife to be Sold.*

SLAVES OF PASSION. Anglo-Russian D. 4 a. R. Castleton. (Orig. prod. as *The Cross of Olga.*) Eleph. and C., July 25, 1904.

SLAVES OF THE RING. P. 3 a. S. Grundy. Garrick, December 29, 1894.

SLAVERY. See *Uncle Tom's Cabin.*

SLEDGE HAMMER, THE. D. 4 a. Nestor Le Thiers. Adap. to the English stage fr. the Flemish. Kilburn T.R., February 22, 1897. Adap. by the late Wilson Barrett. W. London, December 19, 1904.

SLEEP-WALKER, A. F. W. Ellis. Royalty, December 6, 1898.

SLEEP-WALKER, THE. 1 a. D.L., November 22, 1825; Strand, July 25, 1893.

SLEEP-WALKER, THE. C. See *The Somnambule.*

SLEEP-WALKER; OR, WHICH IS THE LADY? THE. F. 2 a. W. C. Oulton, C.G.

SLEEPERS AWAKENED. F.A. 1 a. F. D. Adams. Publ. by S. French, Ltd.

SLEEPING BEAUTY, THE. Melo-d. St. G. Skeffington. D.L., December 6, 1805.

SLEEPING BEAUTY, THE. Fa. 1 a. E. H. Keating. Publ. by S. French, Ltd.

SLEEPING BEAUTY; HER SEVEN FAIRY GODMOTHERS AND A WICKED FAIRY, THE. Burl. C. Daly and B. Chatterton. Aldershot T.R., August 3, 1885.

SLEEPING BEAUTY IN THE WOOD. Fairy extrav. 3 parts. J. R. Planché. D.L., April 20, 1840.

SLEEPING BEAUTY OF FLOWERLAND, THE. Fairy P. Regent's Park Botanic Gardens, July 11, 1905.

SLEEPING DOGS. F.C. 3 a. M. Melford. Cambridge New T., January 18, 1897; Imperial, May 2, 1898.

SLEEPING DRAUGHT, THE. F. 2 a. S. Penley. D.L., April 1, 1818; Lyceum (rev.), December 26, 1821; D.L., April 11, 1851.

SLEEPING DRAUGHT, THE. P. 1 a. Miss Keating. Publ. by S. French, Ltd.

SLEEPING HARE, THE. C. 2 a. J. J. Dilley. Cavendish Rooms, April 6, 1868 (amat.).

SLEEPING PARTNER, THE. C. 3 a. English ver. of Miss Martha Morton's C., *His Wife's Father.* F. on a German P. by L'Arrouge. Criterion, August 17, 1897.

SLEEPING POWDER, THE. F. Sk. Bert Danson. Pimlico Standard, April 2, 1904.

SLEEPING QUEEN MAZEPPA, THE. O. Balfe. See *Il Talismano.*

SLEEPWALKER, THE. (Rev. ver. of C. H. Abbott and Willie Edouin's *Fast Asleep*, adap. fr. a story by W. S. Gilbert and prod. at a mat. at the Criterion, March 1, 1892.) F.C. 3 a. C. H. Abbott. Liverpool P.O.W.'s, April 5, 1893.

SLEIGH BELLS, THE. D. G. F. Rowe. Liverpool P.O.W.'s, March 11, 1872.

SLEIGH BELLS, THE. Sk. A new ver. by E Hoggan-Armadale of *Le Juif Polonnais*. Camberwell Empire, January 6, 1908.

SLENDER THREAD, A. P. 1 a. "Alton Ignis." Rochdale Church Schools, April 18, 1896.

SLI SLOCUM; OR, LIFE ON THE WESTERN BORDER. American D. Clifton W. Tayleure. Liverpool Amphitheatre, June 8, 1876.

SLICE OF LUCK, A. F. 1 a. J. M. Morton. Adelphi, June 17, 1867.

SLICE OF LUCK, A. O. 1 a. Oxenford and Pascal. Publ. by S. French, Ltd.

SLIGHT HEADACHE, A. C. 1 a. P. J. Barrow. Southsea Portland H., January 25, 1898.

SLIGHT MISTAKE, A. F. E. Stirling. Folkestone T., August 4, 1869.

SLIGHT MISTAKE, A. F. Miss Julia Agnes Fraser. Strathaven Victoria, May 6, 1873.

SLIGHT MISTAKE, A. Ca. J. Wise. Matlock House, Matlock, June 7, 1897.

SLIGHT MISTAKE, A. C. 1 a. E. H. Keating. Publ. by S. French, Ltd.

SLIGHT MISTAKES. F. H. Herman. Folly, January 31, 1876.

SLIGHT MISTAKES. Orig. F. 1 a. J. M. Morton. C.G., revised for representation January 1, 1884.

SLIGHT MISUNDERSTANDING, A. 1 a. L. C. White. Bayswater Bijou, January 31, 1906 (amat.).

SLIGHTED MAID, THE. C. Sir R. Stapleton. L.I.F., 1663.

SLIGHTED TREASURES. C. 1 a. W. Suter. Publ. by S. French, Ltd.

SLIGHTLY SUSPICIOUS. F. J. Byron. Globe, October5, 1891.

SLIP, THE F. Christopher Bullock. Taken fr. Middleton's *Mad World, My Masters*. L.I.F., February 3, 1715. Pr. 1715.

SLIPPERY JIM. Sk. Luke Jellings and Geo. Bellamy. Holloway Empire, December 14, 1908.

SLOCUM'S PERPLEXITIES. Oa. Surrey Masonic H., November 22, 1898.

SLOW AND SURE. D. 3 a. W. H. Abel. Pavilion, August 28, 1876.

SLOW MAN, THE. F. 1 a. Mark Lemon. Adelphi, April, 1855.

SLOWTOP'S ENGAGEMENTS. F. 1 a. Fr. the French by C. Smith. Cheltenham Olympic, January 13, 1862; Limerick Athenæum, February 4, 1880.

SLUMS OF LONDON, THE. D. 4 a. C. A. Aldin. Newcastle-on-Tyne Grainger T., December 19, 1892; Britannia, April 24, 1893.

SLY AND SHY. F. F. Manby. Southampton T.R., November 4, 1870.

SLY AND SHY. Oa. M. by W. A. Slaughter. Lib. A. R. Phillips. Edinburgh Princess's, May 21, 1883.

SLY DOGS. F.C. 3 a. C. Daly. Torquay T.R. and O.H., April 11, 1887.

SMACK FOR SMACK. St. James's, November 26, 1860.

SMALL AND EARLY. M. Sk. C. Grain. St. Geo. H., June 5, 1882.

SMALL HOLDING, A. F. 1 a. F. Howell Evans. Manchester Prince's, April 10, 1909.

SMALL TALK; OR, THE WESTMINSTER BOY. F. E. Topham. C.G., May 11, 1786. N.p.

SMART SET, THE. M. "as you like it" by George Dance. M. by Ernest Vousden and others. Strand, December 13, 1901.

SMART SET, THE. M. Playlet. 1 a. Camberwell Empire, April 22, 1907.

SMILES AND KISSES. M.F. Manchester Comedy, February 23, 1885; Olympic, June 27, 1885.

SMILES AND TEARS; OR, THE WIDOW'S STRATAGEM. C. Mrs. C. Kemble. C.G., December 12, 1815.

SMITH. C. 4 a. W. Somerset Maugham. Comedy, September 30, 1909.

SMITH, BROWN, JONES, AND ROBINSON. F.C. 3 a. H. and E. Paulton and K. Lee. Coventry O.H., July 29, 1901; Clapham Shakespeare, August 5, 1901; Brixton T., April 9, 1903.

SMITH'S MIXTURE. F. J. R. Cranford. Philharmonic, April 19, 1879.

SMITHS OF NORWOOD. St. James's, January 19, 1863.

SMOCK ALLEY SECRETS; OR, THE MANAGER WORRIED. Occ. Prel. P. Lefanu. Dublin, 1778. N.p.

SMOKE. Ca. 1 a. B. Webster, jun. Adelphi, December 26, 1870; Op. C., November 6, 1890.

SMOKE AND THE FIRE, THE. C. 3 a. Cosmo Gordon-Lennox and Clyde Fitch. New T., September 17, 1907.

SMOKED MISER; OR, THE BENEFIT OF HANGING. F. 1 a. D. Jerrold. Sadler's Wells, June, 1823.

SMOULDERING FIRES. D. 4 a. W. Avondale, Walsall Alexandra, April 23, 1883.

SMUGGLERS, THE. F. 3 a. T. Odell. Little T. in Hay., 1729.

SMUGGLERS, THE. M.E. Birch. D.L., April 13, 1796.

SNAEFEL. D. 3 a. P. Meritt and H. Spry. Gaiety, June 30, 1873.

SNAKE, THE. Sk. 1 sc. Wal Pink. Middlesex M.H., January 25, 1903.

SNAKE IN THE GRASS, THE. D. Ent. Aaron Hill. Pr. 1760.

SNAKE IN THE GRASS, THE. City, November 8, 1858.

SNAKE IN THE GRASS, THE. Epis. L. S. Hughes. Cripplegate Inst., April 3, 1907.

SNAKES IN THE GRASS. F. 2 a. J. B. Buckstone. D.L., November 3. 1829.

SNAPPING TURTLES; OR, MATRIMONIAL MASQUERADING, THE. Duo. 1 a. J. B. Buckstone. Hay., October, 1845.

SNAPT GOLD RING, A. D. 1 a. Miss E. White and E. Wolstenholme. Ladbroke H., January 7, 1903.

SNARES OF LONDON. D. 4 a. W. Burnot, Marguerite Trevosper, and H. Bruce. Stratford Royal, April 16, 1900.

SNATCHED FROM DEATH. D. 1 a. Stephanie Baring and W. Beaumont. Novelty, October 12, 1896.

SNATCHED FROM THE GRAVE. D. G. Conquest and H. Pettitt. Grecian, March 13, 1876.

SNEAKING REGARD, A. F. Miss Ada Moore. Surrey, April 16, 1870.

SNEEWITTCHEN. Fairy O. Gwendolen J. Watson. Based on Grimm's "Forest Legend." Cavendish R., Mortimer Street, W., June 27, 1901.

SNIP, SNAP, SNORUM. Grecian, September 24, 1875.

SNIPED. Sk. C. Cane-Horton. Standard, September 23, 1907.

SNOW DRIFT; OR, THE CROSS ON THE BOOT, THE. D. 2 a. A. Coates. Britannia, February 15, 1869.

SNOW FLAKES. C.D. H. F. Hyde. Portsmouth Prince's, March 14, 1878.

SNOW MAN, THE. F.P. 2 a. and 6 tab. Adap. fr. the French of Chivot and Vanloo by A. Sturgess. M. by A. Banès and W. Slaughter. Lyceum, December 21, 1899.

SNOW WHITE. Fairy O. 2 a. Adap. fr. a German legend by Florence Hoare. M. by Mme. Mely (Countess Vanden Heuvel). St. Geo. H., May 3, 1899.

SNOWBALL, THE. F.C. 3 a. Sydney Grundy. Strand, February 2, 1879.

SNOWDROP. Mrs. Beringer. Ac. at Sir Spencer Wells' house.

SNOWDROP. P. 1 a. N. Doone and H. W. Newte. Bayswater Bijou, February 1, 1894.

SNOWDROP AND THE SEVEN LITTLE MEN. Fairy P. 2 a. P. Carr. Court, December 26, 1903; Royalty, December 24, 1904.

SNOWDROP; OR, THE SEVEN MANNIKINS AND THE MAGIC MIRROR. Burl. Extrav. F. C. Burnand. New Royalty, November 21, 1864.

SNOWSTORM, THE. P. 1 a. S. Bowkett. Gaiety, October 1, 1892.

SNOWWHITE. Fa. 1 a. F. D. Adams. Publ. by S. French, Limited.

SNUFF-BOX; OR, A TRIP TO BATH. C. 2 a. W. Heard. Hay. Pr. 1775.

SNUG LITTLE KINGDOM, A. C. 3 a. M. Ambient. Royalty, January 31, 1903.

SO RUNS THE WORLD AWAY. P. 1 a. G. Phillipson. St. Geo. H., January 22, 1889.

SOAP AT HOME. F. Nancy Yorke and G. H. Inglis. Victoria H., May 6, 1905.

SOCIABLE COMPANIONS; OR, THE FEMALE WITS, THE. C. Margaret Duchess of Newcastle. Pr. 1668.

SOCIAL DEBTS. F.C. 3 a. F. on a German P., B. White. Kingston R. County T., December 2, 1897.

SOCIAL GLASS, THE. D. 5 a. T. T. Woodward. Publ. by S. French, Ltd.

SOCIAL PEST, A. D. 4 a. F. Vanneck. Novelty, January 3, 1891.

SOCIAL SINNERS. F.C. Sunderland T.R., August 17, 1885.

SOCIALIST, A. F. Fr. the Swedish, by H. Bellingham. Royalty, April 16, 1887.

SOCIETY. C. 3 a. T. W. Robertson. P.O.W., November 11, 1865.

SOCIETY BEAUTY, A. F.C. Adap. fr. French. Sturton. Cambridge Town H., May 1, 1884.

SOCIETY BUTTERFLY, A. C. R. Buchanan and H. Murray. Op. C., May 10, 1894.

SOCIETY PEEPSHOW, THE. M. Sk. C. Grain. St. Geo. H., June 14, 1890.

SOCIETY SAINT, A. P. 3 a. J. R. Wallace. St. Geo. H., January 16, 1892.

SOCIETY SAINT, A. C. 1 a. Sir W. L. Young. (Played by the "Old Stagers.") Canterbury T.R., August 5, 1901.

SOCIETY SCANDAL, A. M.C. 2 a. Lib. by G. Logan. M. by A. Cooke. S. Shields T.R., August 31, 1896.

SOCIETY TAILOR, THE. C. 1 a. H. Percy. Guildford Town H., February 12, 1895.

SOCIETY WOMAN, A. D. Epis. By C. Watson Mill. London, January 14, 1907.

SOCIETY'S VERDICT. P. 4 a. By X. L. Shaftesbury, March 26, 1900.

SOCK AND BUSKIN. P. Ac. at private T. in Fishamble St., Dublin, January 27, 1809.

SOCK AND BUCKSKIN; OR, MUDDLED OR MIXED. Extrav. H. Pettitt. Surrey, June 19, 1880.

SOCRATES. Dr. Poem. Amyas Bushe. Pr. 1758.

SOCRATES. T. Transl. fr. the French of Voltaire. J. Thomson. Pr. 1760. Also transl. by Dr. Francklin.

SOCRATES. Dr. Poem. A. Becket. 1806.

SOCRATES TRIUMPHANT; OR, THE DANGER OF BEING WISE IN A COMMONWEALTH OF FOOLS. T. Anon. Pr. 1716.

SODOM. P. Fishbourne. See *Valentinian*.

SODOM'S ENDE. P. 5 a. H. Sudermann (Herr Junkermann's season). St. George's H., March 20, 1900; Great Queen Street, May 5, 1906.

SOFONISBA. O. Gluck. Milan. 1744.

SOFONISBE. O. Leo. 1718.

SOFT-SEX. Hay., August 31, 1861.

SOFT SOAP. F. Oa. 1 a. Lib. by J. Jourdain. M. by H. G. French. Eleph and C., September 29, 1888.

SOFTY OF MERRINGTON, THE. D. W. Stevens. Seaham Harbour T.R., February 11, 1878.

SOGGARTH AROON. D. 4 a. J. Colman. Birmingham G.T., November 29, 1897.

SOIREE CARNIVAL, UNE. Ballet. D.L., April 12, 1851.

SOIXANTE-SIXIEME, LE. Op. Bo. 1 a. Offenbach. 1856.

SOL GANDY. P. H. Bellingham and W. Best. Leicester R.O.H., April 1, 1887.

SOLD AGAIN. F. 1 a. R. Soutar. Brighton T.R., July 31, 1876; Gaiety, August 26, 1876.

SOLD FOR A SONG. Inter. M. by A. Lee. Lyceum (playbill), September 5, 1829.

SOLD UP. F.C. 3 a. M. Goldberg. Nottingham Grand, December 22, 1890 (amat.).

SOLDIER, THE. T. R. Lovelace. 1618-1658. N.p.

SOLDIER AND A MAN, A. Dom. and military D. 4 a. B. Landeck. Coventry R.O.H., August 29, 1898; Clapham Shakespeare, September 5, 1898.

SOLDIER AND SAILOR. M.F. M'Laren. 1805. See *The Old Roscius*.

SOLDIER OF FORTUNE, A. C.D. 2 a. F. W. Broughton. Jarrow T.R., March 16, 1889.

SOLDIER OF FORTUNE, THE. C. P. W. Dwyer. 1805. Pr. N.d.

SOLDIER OF FORTUNE, THE. P. 4 a. G. Holmes. Halifax R., September 22, 1905; Scarboro' Londesboro', November 9, 1905; Crouch End O.H., November 28, 1905; Poplar Prince's, March 11, 1907.

SOLDIER OF FRANCE, A. Mil. Ro. D. 4 a. Clarence Burnette and C. A. Clarke. Woolwich T.R., April 13, 1908.

SOLDIER OF JAPAN, A. D. 1 a. W. P. Sheen. South London M.H., July 19, 1904.

SOLDIER OF THE CZAR, A. P. 1 a. Kingston County, October 3, 1904.

SOLDIER OF THE CZAR, THE. D. 4 a. W. Hubert. Belfast T.R., September 26, 1902; Brixton, November 21, 1902.

SOLDIER'S COURTSHIP, A. C.P. 1 a. J. Poole. D.L., December 3, 1833.

SOLDIER'S DAUGHTER, A C. 1 a. E. M. Cobham. Gravesend P.H., May 11, 1897.

SOLDIER'S DAUGHTER, A. Episode. 1 a. Mrs. Charles Sim. Comedy, February 5, 1900.

SOLDIER'S DAUGHTER, THE. C. 5 a. A. Cherry. D.L., 1804; October 31, 1815; October 16, 1829.

SOLDIER'S DAUGHTERS, A. P. 1 a. Cosmo Hamilton. Kingsway, May 14, 1908; Playhouse, September 15, 1909.

SOLDIER'S DREAM, THE. Vent. Sk. 1 a. F. W. Millis. Plymouth Palace, February 24, 1902.

SOLDIER'S FORTUNE, A. D. Prol. and 2 a. G. Pearce. Hanley T.R., February 11, 1878.

SOLDIER'S FORTUNE, THE. C. T. Otway. Duke's T., 1681. Sequel to this play is *The Atheist; or, The Second Part of the Soldier's Fortune*. F. on Scarron's novel, "The Invisible Mistress."

SOLDIER'S FORTUNE, THE. F. Taken fr. foregoing. C.G. N.p.

SOLDIER'S HONOUR, A. Military D. E. F. Welch. Dudley Port Colosseum, December 17, 1902.

SOLDIER'S HONOUR, A. D. 4 a. Mrs. F. G. Kimberley. Longsight King's, August 8, 1906 (C.P.); Manchester Junction, February 25, 1907; Eleph. and C., April 6, 1908.

SOLDIER'S LAST STAKE, THE. C. G. Jacob. Pr. 1723.

SOLDIER'S LEGACY, THE. Oxenford and Macfarren. Circa 1862.

SOLDIER'S OPERA; OR, LIFE WITHOUT A MASK, THE. Capt. P. Ewing. 1792. Pr. N.d.

SOLDIER'S PROGRESS; OR, THE HORRORS OF WAR, THE. Pictorial D. in 4 parts. J. Courtnay. R. Vic. T., November 5, 1849.

SOLDIER'S RETURN; OR, WHAT CAN BEAUTY DO? THE. C.O. 2 a. T. E. Hook. D.L., April 23, 1805.

SOLDIER'S SON, A. Military and Dom. D. 5 a. C. Newton and W. Boyne. Kennington P.O.W., August 7, 1899.

SOLDIER'S STRATAGEMS. C. 3 a. C.G., November 5, 1828. N.p.

SOLDIER'S WEDDING, THE. P. 4 a. Walter Melville. Terriss, October 8, 1906.

SOLDIER'S WIDOW, THE. Tableaux Vivants, illustrating Schiffer's poem. D.L., June 7, 1831.

SOLDIER'S WIDOW; OR, THE HAPPY RELIEF, THE. M. Ent. A. MacLaren. Pr. 1800. Second title also *The Generous Tar*.

SOLDIER'S WIFE, A. C.D. 4 a. H. E. Whitmore. Margate G.T., May 29, 1899.

SOLDIER'S WIFE; OR, NOT ON THE STRENGTH, A. Oa. S. Dalgleish and W. Peacock. M. by Marie Brook. Grand H., Hotel Cecil, February 25, 1898.

SOLDIER'D CITIZEN, THE. See *The Crafty Merchant*. Ent. Stationers' Co., June 29, 1660. Destroyed by Mr. Warburton's servant.

SOLDIERS OF THE QUEEN; OR, BRITON AND BOER. P. 4 a. M. Goldberg. Leeds T.R., May 9, 1898.

SOLE SURVIVOR; OR, A TALE OF THE GOODWIN SANDS, THE. D. 4 a. G. Conquest and H. Pettitt. Grecian, October 5, 1876.

SOLICITOR, THE. F.C. 3 a. J. H. Darnley. Liverpool R. Court, May 5, 1890; Toole's, July 3, 1890.

SOLICITOUS CITIZEN; OR, THE DEVIL TO DO ABOUT DR. S—C—L. C. Anon. Pr. N.d. Before 1814.

SOLID SILVER. D. Darlington T.R., May 17, 1880.

SOLIMAN AND PERSEDA. See *Solyman*, etc.

SOLITARY KNIGHT, THE. Perf. by the servants of Lord Howard, 1576.

SOLNESS LE CONSTRUCTEUR. Opera Comique, March 27, 1895.

SOLOMON. Serenata. E. Moore. M. by Dr. Boyce. Pr. 1742.

SOLOMON. Orat. Handel. C.G. Pr. 1748.

SOLOMON. Orat. Caldara. 1678-1763.

SOLOMON. Sacred D. R. Huish. Transl. fr. German of Klopstock. Pr. 1809.

SOLOMON. See *Solyman*.

SOLOMON, THE SIBERIAN. Yiddish D. 4 a. John Jackson. M., F. Staul. Pavilion, September 6, 1906.

SOLOMON THE WISE. Pavilion (Jewish season), August 28, 1908.

SOLOMON'S SWORD. Oa. in Hindustani. Gaiety, December 12, 1885. Played by Parsee Company.

SOLOMON'S TEMPLE. Anon. Pr. 1797.

SOLOMON'S TEMPLE. Orat. Weekes. N.d. Before 1814.

SOLOMON'S TWINS. F.C. 3 a. F. K. Peile. Vaudeville, May 11, 1897.

SOLOMON'S WISDOM, KING. Int. R. Cox. Pr. N.d.

SOLON; OR, PHILOSOPHY NO DEFENCE AGAINST LOVE. T.C. M. Bladen. Pr. 1705. Third act contains a masque, *Orpheus and Eurydice*.

SOLON SHINGLE. New Adelphi, July 3, 1865.

SOLYMAN. Latin T. MS. dated March, 1581, in British Museum.

SOLYMAN. T. 5 a. Anon. Pr. 1807.

SOLYMAN AND PERSEDA. T. Introduced in the *Spanish Tragedy*. Probably also by Thos. Kyd. Circa 1599.

SOME BELLS THAT RING AN OLD YEAR OUT AND A NEW ONE IN. Britannia, December 15, 1862.

SOME DAY. P. 3 a. Mrs. Newton Phillips and John Tresahar. St. Geo. H., May 13, 1889.

SOME DAY. D. in prol. and 3 a. By V. Temple. Salford P.O.W., February 1, 1907.

SOMEBODY ELSE. See *Les Amourettes*. Petite D. D.L., December 12, 1856.

SOMEBODY ELSE. F. 1 a. J. R. Planché. Hay. T.R.

SOMEBODY'S COMEDY. M.S. sold as part of Mr. A. Murphy's library.

SOMEBODY'S SWEETHEART. M.C.D. 3 a. E. Marris. W. Hartlepool T.R., July 17, 1899; Stratford T.R., June 22, 1903.

SOMERSET MASQUE, THE. Thomas Campion. Pr. 1614.

SOMETHING LIKE A NUGGET. D. "Lyulph." Norwich T.R., January 25, 1869.

SOMETHING TO DO. C. Alt. fr. German. Mr. R. Hoare. D.L., January 22, 1808.

SOMETHING TO DO. F. 1 a. J. M. Morton. Hay., under title of *News from China*. Revised and adapted for representation, April 1, 1884.

SOMEWHAT, THE. Dr. P. Ed. Barnard. Pr. 1757.

SOMNABULA, LA. O. 2 a. Lib. by Romani. M. by Bellini. Adap. by Bishop. Wr. for Pasta and Rubini. Milan, March 6, 1831; King's, July 28, 1831; Paris, October 28, 1831; (under Italian title) D.L., May 1, 1833.

SOMNAMBULA, LA. Div. from Ballet of. Arr. by Mons. Anothole. D.L., February 18, 1833.

SOMNAMBULA, LA. See *The Female Sleepwalker, The Roof Scrambler.*

SOMNAMBULA; OR, THE SUPPER, THE SLEEPER, AND THE MERRY SWISS BOY, LA. Burl. Extrav. H. J. Byron. P.O.W., April 15, 1865.

SOMNAMBULE; OR, THE SLEEPWALKER, THE. O. Transl. fr. French of *Pont de Vile* by M. of Auspach. Lady Craven. Ac. at Newbury. Pr. 1778.

SOMNAMBULIST, THE. Taken fr. Ballet of *La Somnambule*. By MM. Scribe and Aumer.

SOMNAMBULIST, THE. F. 1 a. Lord Kilmarnock (MS. with Douglas Cox).

SOMNAMBULIST; OR, THE PHANTOM OF THE VILLAGE, THE. Dr. Ent. 2 a. W. T. Moncrieff. C.G., February 19, 1828.

SOMNAMBULO AND LIVELY LITTLE ALESSIO, IL. Burl. H. J. Byron. Gaiety, April 6, 1878.

SON AND STRANGER. Cant. Mendelssohn. Guildhall Sch. of M., December 23, 1896.

SON OF A KING, A. P. 4 a. Pierre Decourcelle and M. Morton. Vaudeville, October 16, 1902.

SON OF A SINNER. P. 1 a. F. Forshaw. Parkhurst, July 13, 1896.

SON OF NIGHT, THE. D. 4 a. Sadler's Wells, September 2, 1872.

SON OF SATAN. D. 4 a. C. Rean. Smethwick T.R., October 0, 1902; Aston T.R., July 27, 1903.

SON OF THE SOIL, A. Rom. P. 3 a. F. on *Lion Amoreux* of Pousard. H. C. Merivale. Court, September 4, 1872.

SON OF THE SUN; OR, THE FATE OF THE PHAETON, THE. Queen's.

SON'S DEVOTION, A. Sk. E. Ramier. Collins's, March 11, 1907.

SON-IN-LAW, THE. F. 2 a. J. O'Keefe. Hay., August 14, 1779; D.L., 1827.

SONATA MILITAIRE. O. Boccherini. 1743-1805.

SONG OF LOVE TRIUMPHANT, THE. Lib. by N. Wilde fr. Tourgeniev. Moscow, 1899.

SONG OF SOLOMON, THE. D. J. Bland. Pr. 1750.

SONG OF SOLOMON, THE. T. Francis. 1781.

SONG OF SONGS, WHICH IS SOLOMON'S, THE. Arr. for the stage by Nugent Monck. Prod. by the Engl. Drama Society. Queen's Gate H., S.W., March 8, 1908.

SONG OF THE PEOPLE, A. Dr. Epis. Tom Tindall. Camberwell Empire, April 15, 1907.

SONG OF THE RIVER, THE. Playlet, in two Tableaux. M'L. Loader and F. A. Ellis. Bath T.R., July 4, 1898.

SONG OF THE RIVER, THE. P. Pro. and 3 a. Mlle. Coquelicot. St. George's H., August 2, 1900.

SONG OF THE TORCH, THE. Cos. P. 4 a. Ian Hanford (Pendicaris). Margate R.T., May 13, 1907; King's, W., July 15, 1907.

SONG OF THE WILDERNESS, THE. P. 5 a. F. Hahn. Vienna, 1842.

SONGE D'UNE NUIT D'ETE. O. 3 a. Wds. by Rosier and de Leuven. M. by Ambroise Thomas. Paris, April 20, 1850.

SONIA. Dr. Sk. Miss E. Overbeck. West T., Albert H., May 9, 1895.

SONS; OR, FAMILY FEUDS, THE. T. P. T. Jones. Pr. 1809.

SONS OF ANACREON, THE. M. Prel. D.L., 1785, and June 12, 1821. N.p.

SONS OF BRITAIN. Harry Bruce.

SONS OF BRITANNIA, THE. Int. A. Sherreffs. Edinburgh, 1796.

SONS OF COLUMBIA. Britannia, March 10, 1862.

SONS OF ERIN. D. 4 a. W. J. Patmore. Surrey, September 11, 1893.

SONS OF ERIN; OR, MODERN SENTIMENT, THE. C. Mrs. Lefanu. D.L., April 11, 1812; December 6, 1814; Lyceum, May 11, 1825.

SONS OF FRANCE. D. L. Kean. Wolverhampton P.O.W., December 8, 1873.

SONS OF FREEDOM. D. A. Faucquez. City of London, June 27, 1868.

SONS OF THE EMPIRE, THE. Military D. 4 a. W. J. Mackay. Britannia, November 20, 1899.

SONS OF THE FORGE; OR, THE BLACKSMITH AND THE BARON, THE. D. C. H. Hazlewood. Britannia, August 29, 1870.

SONS OF THE SEA. D. 4 a. M. Wilkinson. Birmingham Queen's, April 8, 1895; West London, May 9, 1898.

SONS OF TOIL. Melo-d. Pro. and 3 a. L. Gilbert. Greenwich, Morton's, July 31, 1899.

SONS OF TOIL; OR, ENGLISH HEARTS AND HOMES, THE. D. 3 a. J. Levey. Marylebone, November 8, 1873.

SOOTHING SYSTEM, THE. Episode. A. Bourchier. Adap. fr. story by E. A. Poe. Garrick, July 30, 1903.

SOP IN THE PAN; OR, THE BEAU OUTWITTED, THE. F. 2 a. Taken fr. Cibber's *The Refusal* by R. Oliphant. Liverpool, 1790.

SOPHIA. C. 4 a. F. on incidents in Fielding's novel "Tom Jones" by R. Buchanan. Vaudeville, April 12, 1886; rev. June 2, 1892.

SOPHIA'S SUPPER. F. 1 a. H. R. Addison. Surrey, April 30, 1849.

SOPHISTER, THE. C. Anon. Dr. Zouch. Ac. at one of the Universities, 1638.

SOPHOMPANEAS; OR, JOSEPH. T. Transl. fr. the Latin of H. Grotius by F. Goldsmith. Pr. 1640.

SOPHONISBA. T. By J. Thompson. D.L., February 28, 1730.

SOPHONISBA. T. Alfieri. Transl. by C. Lloyd. 1815.

SOPHONISBA; OR, HANNIBAL'S OVERTHROW. D. in rhyme. N. Lee. T.R., 1676; Hay., August 1, 1707.

SOPHONISBA; OR, THE WONDER OF WOMEN. T. J. Marston. Blackfryars. 1606.

SOPHONISBE. T. Mairet. 1630. Imitated fr. the Fr. T. *Trissino.*

SOPHONISBE. T. Corneille. See "French Classical Plays."

SOPHONISBE. T. Legrange Chancel.

SOPHY, THE. T. Sir J. Denham. Same story as Baron's *Mirza*. Black Friars. Pr. 1641.

SOPHY MIRZA. T. Same subject as the foregoing. 2 a. Wr. by Mr. Hughes and finished by W. Muncombe. MS.

SORCERER, THE. C.O. 3 a. Lib. by W. S. Gilbert. M. by A. Sullivan. Op.C., November 17, 1877; Savoy, October 11, 1884, and September 22, 1898.

SORCERESS, THE. T. 3 a. Pr. 1814.

SORCERESS, THE. Hebrew Mus. P. 5 a. Holborn International T., January 15, 1884.

SORCERESS OF LOVE, A. Ver. of Sardou's *Patrie* (Paris, 1869.), by L. N. Parker. Liverpool Shakespeare, October 1, 1894.

SORCIER, LE. O. 2 a. F. A. D. Philidor. 1764.

SORCIERE, LA. P. V. Sardou. H.M., June 20, 1904; Royalty, October 27, 1907.

SORDELLO. R. Browning. 1839.

SORDELLO. D. Pietro Cossa.

SORROW OF A SECRET, THE. P. 3 a. W. Buckland. Ladbroke H., March 28, 1892.

SORROWFUL SATAN; OR, LUCIFER'S MATCH. Duol. Alice Chapin. M. by P. Rex. Kentish Town Stanley H., October 27, 1897.

SORROWS OF SATAN, THE. P. 4 a. F. on G. A. Sala's story "Margaret Forster" and Marie Corelli's "Sorrows of Satan." Nottingham T.R., March 1, 1897; Clapham Shakespeare, April 12, 1897; Court, July 29, 1901.

SORROWS OF SATAN, THE. P. 4 a. Adap. by H. Woodgate and P. M. Berton fr. M. Corelli's novel. See *Prince of Darkness*. Shaftesbury, January 9, 1897.

SORROWS OF SATAN, THE. P. 3 a. Adap. by S. C. Henry fr. Corelli's novel. Hammersmith Lyric, May 3, 1897.

SORROWS OF SATAN, THE. Dr. ver. of Marie Corelli's novel by H. S. Dacre. Britannia, July 5, 1897.

SORROWS OF WERTHER, THE. P. 1 a. C.G., May 6, 1818.

SOT, THE. Burl. Hay. Pr. 1775. See *Squire Badger*.

SOUL OF HONOUR, THE. Rom. D. Pro. and 5 a. Adap. fr. French by H. B. Farnie.

SOUL OF PRIVATE STEPHENS, THE. C. 1 a. H. Lloyd. Wolverhampton Tettenhall Drill H., January 13, 1902.

SOUL'S TRAGEDY, A. P. R. Browning. (Stage Society's mat.). Court, March 14, 1904.

SOUL'S WELFARE, THE. T.C. Richard Tuke. Pr. 1672. See *The Divine Comedian*.

SOUR GRAPES. C. 4 a. H. J. Byron. Olympic, November 4, 1873.

SOUR GRAPES. Masque. J. Gray. M. by Florence Gilbert and C. Dick. West T. Albert Hall, April 17, 1894

SOUSA GIRL, THE. C.O. 2 a. C. Vanderbilt. Bayswater Bijou, December 17, 1902.

SOUTH BRITON, THE. C. 5 a. Smock Alley, Dublin, and C.G., April 12, 1774. Pr. 1774.

SOUTH SEA; OR, THE BITERS BIT. F. W. R. Chetwood. Pr. 1720.

SOUTHDOWN, A.D. SOCIETY'S DRESS REHEARSAL OF "EAST LYNNE," THE. Burl. M. H. Hoffman. Stockport Mechanics' Inst., January 23, 1896.

SOUTHERN BELLE. M.C. 2 a. O. Carr. Southend Empire, March 7, 1901; Brixton T., May 20, 1901.

SOUTHERN CLIMES. D. P. Beyruth. Birkenhead T.R., April 29, 1876.

SOUTHERN CROSS, THE. D. Pro. and 2 a. G. Peel. Victoria, August 9, 1873.

SOUTHERNER, JUST ARRIVED, A. F. 1 a. Horace Wigan. Olympic, November 3, 1862.

SOUTHWARK FAIR; OR, THE SHEEP-SHEARERS. F. 3 sc. C. Coffey. 1729. Second title also *Sheepshearing*.

SOUVENT HOMME VARIE. D.L., June 28, 1893.

SOVEREIGN REMEDY. F. 1 a. Miss Woodruffe. Publ. by S. French, Ltd.

SOWER WENT FORTH, A. P. in prol. and 3 a. Walter Nixey. Llanelly T.R., April 27, 1908 (C.P.).

SOWING AND REAPING. C. 2 a. C. Vernon. Prod. at a mat., Criterion, July 5, 1890, and February 25, 1891.

SOWING THE STORM. D. 3 a. F. A. Palmer. MS. with Douglas Cox.

SOWING THE WIND. C. 4 a. S. Grundy. Comedy, September 30, 1893, and March 9, 1895.

SPADRA, THE SATIRIST. D. Sheffield T.R., November 18, 1869.

SPAE WIFE. D. 4 a. Adap. by D. Boucicault from Scott's *Guy Mannering*. Eleph. and C., March 30, 1886.

SPALPEEN, THE. D. H. Braham. Paignton Bijou T., October 11, 1875.

SPAN OF LIFE, THE. Melo. D. 4 a. S. Vane. Sheffield Alexandra, November 6, 1891 (C.P.); Islington Grand, June 6, 1892; Princess's, May 18, 1896.

SPANIARD and SIORLAMH. T., with other poems. P. Fitzgerald. Pr. 1810.

SPANIARDS; OR, THE EXPULSION OF THE MOORS, THE. Heroic D. 5 a. Pr. 1814. Not ac. before then.

SPANIARDS DISMAYED; OR, TRUE BLUE FOR EVER, THE. F. on inter. of *Nancy*. C.G. Pr. 1780.

SPANIARDS IN PERU. With instrumental and vocal music. Cockpit in D.L. Pr. 1648.

SPANIARDS IN PERU; OR, THE DEATH OF ROLLA. T. Transl. fr. Kotzebue. Annie Plumptree. Pr. 1799.

SPANISH BARBER; OR, THE FRUITLESS PRECAUTION, THE. C., with songs. G. Colman. Taken fr. *Barbier de Seville* by Mons. Beaumarchais. Hay., August 30, 1777, and 1806. N.p.

SPANISH BAWD, CELESTINA; OR, CALESTO AND MELIBEA, THE. T.C. 21 a. (Longest ever pr.). Orig. in Spanish. Transl. by J. Mabbe. 1638.

SPANISH BOND, A. G. à Beckett and German Reed. St. George's H., circa 1865.

SPANISH BONDS; OR, WARS IN WEDLOCK. Hay., August 2, 1823.

SPANISH BRIDAL, THE. Ro. O. 3 a. M. by F. Robinson. Lib. by A. S. Johnstone. Birmingham, Harborne and Edgbaston Inst., December 14, 1883.

SPANISH CURATE, THE. C. Beaumont and Fletcher. Ac. 1622. L.I.F., November 17, 1722. See *The Sexton*.

SPANISH CURATE, THE. F. Fr. Beaumont and Fletcher. 1647. N.p.

SPANISH CURATE, THE. F. Alt. fr. Beaumont and Fletcher. D.L., October 19, 1749; C.G., May 10, 1783. Another version n.p.

SPANISH DANCERS; OR, FANS AND FANDANGOES, THE. Burl. 1 a. C. Selby. St. James's, October 18, 1854.

SPANISH DIVERTISEMENT, A. D.L., May 6, 1817.

SPANISH DOLLARS; OR, THE PRIEST OF THE PARISH. Mus. Ent. A. Cherry. M. by Davy. C.G., May 9, 1805.

SPANISH DUKE OF LERMA, THE. P. Henry Shirley. Ent. on Stationers' Co.'s book, September 9, 1653. N.p.

SPANISH FATHER, THE. T. H. Mackenzie. 1808.

SPANISH FIG, THE. Ac. 1601-1602.

SPANISH FRYAR; OR, THE DOUBLE DISCOVERY, THE. T.C. John Dryden. Duke's and T.R., 1681.

SPANISH GALLANTRIES, THE. Ballet. 2 a. and 5 tab. M. by Mons. Blasis, père. D.L., March 4, 1847.

SPANISH GALLANTS, THE. Ballet. By Noble. M. by Cooke. D.L., March 18, 1824.

SPANISH GIPSY. C. Middleton and Rowley. 1653. See *Spanish Gypsies.*

SPANISH GIPSY. Dr. Pm. "G. Eliot" (Mrs. Lewes). Publ. 1868.

SPANISH, GIRL, THE. City of London, April 13, 1857.

SPANISH GYPSIES, THE. C. W. Rowley and T. Middleton. D.L. and Salisbury Court, 1661; Matinee T., April 5, 1898 (rev.). See *Spanish Gypsy.*

SPANISH HEROINE, THE. M.D. M'Laren. 1808.

SPANISH HUSBAND; OR, FIRST AND LAST LOVE, THE. New D. 3 a. D.L., May 25, 1830.

SPANISH LADY, THE. Mus. Ent. Thomas Hull. (Before 1765.) C.G., May 2, 1765. Pr. 1765.

SPANISH LOVERS, THE. T.C. Wm. Davenant. Licensed November 30, 1639. See *The Distresses.*

SPANISH MASQUERADO. C. Greene. 1589.

SPANISH MAZE, THE. T. Ac. at Court, 1605.

SPANISH MOOR'S TRAGEDY, THE. Haughton, Day, and Dekker. Probably the same as *Lust's Dominion.* Prod. 1600.

SPANISH MORRIS, THE. P. W. Haughton (assisted by Dekker and Day). Ac. 1599. N.p.

SPANISH PATRIOTS A THOUSAND YEARS AGO. Hist. D. Code. 1812.

SPANISH PURCHASE, THE. C. Amongst those destroyed by Warburton's servant.

SPANISH RIVALS, THE. Mus. F. M. Lonsdale. M. by Linley. D.L., Pr. 1784.

SPANISH ROGUE, THE. C. Thomas Duffet. T.R., 1674.

SPANISH SOLDIER, THE. T. Thomas Dekker. Ent. in Stationers' Co.'s book, May 16, 1631. N.p. (?). See *The Noble Spanish Souldier.*

SPANISH STUDENT, THE. Longfellow's T. See *Victorian.* Bayswater Bijou, November 13, 1895 (amat.).

SPANISH TRAGEDY. Anon. 1605. See *Jeronymo.*

SPANISH TRAGEDY; OR, HIERONIMO IS MAD AGAIN, THE. Thos. Kyd. Pr. 1603. Ac. about 1588.

SPANISH VICEROY; OR, THE HONOUR OF WOMAN, THE. C. Philip Massinger. Ac. 1624. Ent. in Stationers' Co.'s book, September 9, 1653. N.p. Amongst those destroyed by Warburton's servants.

SPANISH WIVES, THE. F. 3 a. Mrs. Mary Pix. T. in Dorset Gardens, 1696. D.L., July 14, 1703.

SPANKING LEGACY. F. 1 a. T. G. Blake. Publ. by S. French, Limited.

'SPARAGUS GARDEN, THE. C. Richard Brone. Salisbury Court, 1635. Pr. 1640.

SPARE BED, THE. F. F. Cooper. Victoria, July 1833.

SPARE ROOM, THE. Curtain raiser. Leopold A. D. Montague. Royalty, June 18, 1894.

SPARE ROOM, THE. P. 1 a. E. M. Bryant Cri., February 27, 1909.

SPARE THE ROD AND SPOIL THE CHILD. Marylebone, March 14, 1859.

SPARKLE'S LITTLE SYSTEM. Ca. N. Doone. Pier T., Folkestone, June 1, 1893; Camberwell Metropole, March 2, 1903.

SPARTACUS. T. Saurin. 1746.

SPARTAN DAME, THE. T. T. Southern. D.L., December 11, 1719.

SPARTAN LADIES, THE. C. L. Carlell. Ent. at Stationers' Company, September 4, 1646.

SPEAK OUT BOLDLY. C. 1 a. W. E. Suter. Publ. by S. French, Limited.

SPECIAL PERFORMANCES. F. 1 a. W. Harrison. Holborn, April 13, 1868.

SPECIALIST; OR, AN INITIAL BLUNDER, THE. M.C. 2 a. E. Richardson. M. by Geo. Richardson. Myddelton H., Islington, April 21, 1896.

SPECTRE; OR, THE LOVERS' STRATAGEM, THE. Ballet (new). Noble. M. by Cooke. D.L., November 11, 1826.

SPECTRE BRIDEGROOM; OR, A GHOST IN SPITE OF HIMSELF, THE. F. 2 a. W. T. Moncrieff. F. on tale in "Sketch Book." D.L., June 2, 1821.

SPECTRE KNIGHT, THE. Oa. 1 a. Lib. by J. Albery. M. by A. Cellier. Op. C., February 9, 1878.

SPECTRE OF SHOOTER'S HILL; OR, THE BROKEN HOT CROSS BUN, THE. O. Burl. W. Sallenger. M. by B. J. Hancock, A.C.O. R. Artillery T., Woolwich, October 20, 1888.

SPECTRE ON HORSEBACK; OR, DON GIOVANNI, A. Extrav. D.L., June 12, 1829.

SPECTRE'S BRIDE, THE. Cantata. A. Dvorak (b. 1841).

SPECTRES OF THE PAST. P. 4 a., consisting of D. and Burl. J. W. Whitbread. Queen's, Dublin, January 3, 1893.

SPECTRES OF THE SANCTUM. Theosophical and spiritualistic Sk, by Mr. J. N. Maskelyne. St. George's H., May 1, 1907.

SPECTRESHEIN. Extrav. Robert Reece. Alhambra, August 14, 1875.

SPECTRUM. Anon. About 1606.

SPECULATION. C. F. Reynolds. C.G., November 7, 1795. Pr. 1795.

SPECULATION. C. 3 a. Wm. Sapte, jun. P.O.W., January 23, 1886.

SPEECHES AT PRINCE HENRY'S BARRIERS. M. Ben Jonson. Pr. 1640.

SPEECHLESS WIFE, THE. M.D. C.G., May 22, 1794. F. on Prior's poem, "The Ladle." N.p.

SPEED THE PLOUGH. C. 5 a. Thomas Morton. (Said to be taken partly from Kotzebue.) C.G., 1796.; February 8, 1800; Hay., 1806; D.L., July 1, 1814; Lyceum, May 31, 1826.

SPELL, THE. T. Of truth in panels. Rosamund Langbridge. M. by Norman O'Neill. November 2, 1906. See *The Tragedy of Truth.*

SPELL BOUND. D. Henry Faucit Saville. Dundee T.R., February 3, 1871.

SPELLBOUND. D. 4 a. Lenton Mackay. Sheffield Stacey's, November 28, 1892.

SPELLBOUND GARDEN, THE. Masque. Louis N. Parker and Murray Carson. Glasgow Royalty, November 30, 1896; Brixton, December 7, 1896.

SPELLING BEE, A. An Absurdity. Robt. Reece. Gaiety, February 16, 1876.

SPENCERS, THE. P. Henry Porter. Ac. 1598. N.p.

SPENDTHRIFT, THE. C. Anon. 1680.

SPENDTHRIFT, THE. C. Matthew Draper. Hay. Pr. 1731. Taken fr. "London Prodigal."

SPENDTHRIFT, THE. C. Foote. Transl. fr. the French. Pr. 1762.

SPENDTHRIFT; OR, A CHRISTMAS GAMBOL, THE. F. Dr. Kenrick. C.G., 1778. N.p. Taken fr. Charles Johnson's "Country Lassies."

SPENDTHRIFT; OR, THE FEMALE CONSPIRACY, THE. C. Samuel Foote. Ac. with *The Romp* at Hay., 1781.

SPENDTHRIFT; OR, THE SCRIVENER'S DAUGHTER, THE. C. 5 a. James Albery. Olympic, May 24, 1875.

SPERLING AND SPERBER. Pancras Road, December 15, 1884.

SPHINX, LE. Fr. D. M. Octave Feuillet. Princess's, May 11, 1874.

SPHINX, THE. D. 4 a. Campbell Clarke. (English ver.) Edinburgh T.R., August 12, 1874; Hay., August 22, 1874.

SPHINX; A TOUCH FROM THE ANCIENTS, THE. New version of Bros. Brough's burl. by Walter Boult. Liverpool P.O.W., January 6, 1872.

SPIA, LA. O. Arditi. New York, 1856.

SPIDER AND THE FLIE, THE. A parable made by John Heywood. Pr. 1556.

SPIDER AND THE FLY, THE. Pant. Joseph Addison. Britannia, December 26, 1890.

SPIDER AND THE FLY, THE. P. 1 a. Aubrey Fitzgerald. Ryde T.R., July 25, 1900; Tivoli, February 18, 1907.

SPIDER AND THE FLY, THE. D. 4 a. A. Shirley and Sutton Vane. Brighton Grand, April 16, 1906; Kennington, August 6, 1906.

SPIDER'S WEB, THE. D. B. Henry. Liverpool T.R., July 17, 1876.

SPIDER'S WEB, THE. D. 4 a. Henry Pettitt. Glasgow Grand, May 28, 1883. Olympic, December 1, 1883.

SPIDER'S WEB, THE. C.D. 3 a. J. Cross. Manchester St. James's, September 8, 1905.

SPIDERS AND FLIES; OR, CAUGHT IN THE WEB. D. 4 a. Elliot Galer. Grecian, October 8, 1868.

SPIGHTFUL SISTER, THE. C. Abraham Bailey. Pr. 1667.

SPIN FOR LIFE, A. C.D. 5 a. Wm. Carriden. Edinburgh Queen's, October 16, 1897 (C.P.); T.R., West Bromwich, July 25, 1898.

SPINSTER, THE. F.C. 3 a. Percy Gwynne and Cyril Harrison. New Cross Public H., April 30, 1887.

SPINSTERS' CLUB, THE. C. 2 a. Miss H. Packer. Brixton H., February 16, 1905.

SPIRIT CHILD'S PRAYER. City of London, February 27, 1865.

SPIRIT OF AIR, THE. Fairy ballet. 2 a. M. by Eliason. D.L., November 17, 1838.

SPIRIT OF CONTRADICTION, THE. F. 2 a. "Gentleman of Cambridge." C.G., March 6, 1760. Pr. 1760.

SPIRIT OF POETRY, THE. Depicting in 3 sc. "The Spirit of Poetry," "A Day of Sunshine," "It is Not Always May" (by Longfellow), and "The Bandit's Death" (by Tennyson). Aldwych, June 22, 1909.

SPIRIT OF THE BELL, THE. C.O. 2 a. M. by G. H. Rodwell. Lyceum. June 8, 1835.

SPIRIT OF THE MOON; OR, THE INUNDATION OF THE NILE. Rom. tale. C.G., April 19, 1824.

SPIRIT OF THE TIMES, THE. Roberdeau. 1792. See *The Point of Honour*.

SPIRIT OF THE VALLEY, THE. Legend. 3 tab. M. Saint Leon. Transl. by H. Markwell. D.L., June 6, 1853.

SPIRIT WORLD, THE. Ca. Worcester T.R., April 6, 1888.

SPIRITISME. C. 3a. Victorien Sardou. Adelphi (Mme. Bernhardt's season), July 6, 1897.

SPIRITUAL MINOR, THE. C. Imitation of Foote's *Minor*. Pr. 1763.

SPIRITUALIST, THE. F.C. 3 a. H. Durez. Ladbroke Hall, August 1, 1891 (C.P.).

SPIRITUALIST, THE. Melo-d. 4 a. Fred Jarman. Surrey, July 14, 1902.

SPITALFIELDS WEAVER, THE. Bayly. Publ. by S. French, Ltd.

SPITE AND MALICE; OR, A LAUGHABLE ACCIDENT. Dr. sk. 2 a. M'Laren. 1811.

SPITEFUL. See *Spightful*.

SPITFIRE, THE. J. M. Morton. Lyceum.

SPITZ-SPITZE, THE SPIDER CRAB. Pant. Geo. Conquest and H. Spry. Grecian, December 27, 1875.

SPLEEN; OR, ISLINGTON SPA, THE. Comic piece. 2 a. George Colman. D.L., March 7, 1776. Pr. 1776.

SPLENDID INVESTMENT, A. Orig. F. 1 a. Bayle-Bernard. Olympic, February 11, 1857.

SPOILED CHILD, THE. C. Fr. the French of Mme. Genlis. Pr. 1781.

SPOILED CHILD, THE. F. 2 a. Mrs. Jordan. Probably D.L., March 22, 1790, and December 5, 1820; Lyceum, June 2, 1820.

SPOILT CHILD, THE. Bickerstaffe. Mentioned by Brewer.

SPOILING THE BROTH. C. 1 a. Bertha N. Graham. Court, March 3, 1909 (amat.).

SPOONS. C. 3 a. W. Lowe. West Hartlepool Gaiety, May 9, 1881.

SPORT. Ca. G. A. Nicholson. Park, February 5, 1876.

SPORT; OR, THE QUEEN'S BOUNTY. M.C. 2 a. Lib. and lyrics by Montague Turner and William Edwardes Sprange. M. by Thos. Hunter. Plymouth Prince's, June 6, 1895 (C.P.); Plymouth T.R., March 30, 1896; Parkhurst, May 19, 1896.

SPORT UPON SPORT. Collection of drolls by Kirkman, 1662. See *The Wits*.

SPORTING DUCHESS, THE. C. Int. A. Branscombe. Tivoli, February 27, 1905.

SPORTING GIRL, THE. Mus. P. 3 a. T. Gilbert Perry. M. by Alfred Sugden. Greenwich Carlton, May 30, 1904.

SPORTING INTELLIGENCE EXTRAORDINARY. Olympic, December 17, 1861.

SPORTING KING, THE. D. 3 a. C. Whitlock. Gateshead Metropole, May 27, 1907.

SPORTING LIFE. D. 4 a. Cecil Raleigh and Seymour Hicks. Clapham Shakespeare, October 18, 1897; Shaftesbury, January 22, 1898.

SPORTING LUCK Sk. Wr. and comp. by Towyn Trevone. Leeds Empire, January 15, 1909; Hammersmith and Ealing, January 18, 1909.

SPORTING NIGHT-MAJOR, A. New Sk. C. Clark and Murray King. M. by Walter Slaughter. Lyrics by Fred Bowyer. Bournemouth T.R., April 13, 1900.

SPORTING SIMPSON. F. Miss Martindale. Glasgow Royalty T., September 22, 1902; Royalty, October 4, 1902.

SPORTSMAN, THE. F.C. 3 a. Ad. by W. Lestocq fr. Georges Feydeau's *Monsieur Chasse*. Palais Royal, April 23, 1892; Comedy, October 3, 1892 (C.P.) and January 21, 1893.

SPOSA AND APPENZELLO, LA. O. Randegger. Circa 1852.

SPOSA D'ABIDO, LA. O. Poniatowski. Venice, 1847.

SPOSA IN LIVORNO, LA. O. Rossi. Rome, 1807.

SPOSO DELUSO, LO. O. Mozart. 1756-1791.

SPOTTED LION, THE. F. W. Sapte, jun. Gaiety, October 8, 1888.

SPOTTIE, THE TERROR OF WEARSIDE. D. H. A. Langlois. Sunderland Lyceum, August 20, 1877.

SPOUTER; OR, THE DOUBLE REVENGE, THE. C.F. 3 a. Henry Dell. Pr. 1756.

SPOUTER; OR, THE TRIPLE REVENGE, THE. C.F. 2 a. Mr. Murphy. Pr. 1756.

SPRAY OF LILAC; OR, AFTER LONG YEARS, A. P. 3 a. J. Y. F. Cooke. Croydon G.T., December 6, 1902.

SPREADING THE NEWS. C. 1 a. Lady Gregory. Irish Players, St. George's H., November 27, 1905.

SPREE IN PARIS, AND WHAT HAPPENED, A. M.C. Wr. by Rose Edouin. Comp. by G. Encyl Lewis. Belfast R.T., November 25, 1907.

SPRIG OF JASMINE, A. P.A. A. C. Travis and F. Bentz. Ripon Victoria H., October 5, 1906.

SPRIGHTLY ROMANCE OF MARSAC, THE. F.C. Miss Elliot Seawell. Orig. prod. in America. Ladbroke H., February 2, 1898 (C.P.).

SPRIGS OF LAUREL. M.F. 2 a. J. O'Keeffe. C.G., May 11, 1793.

SPRING, THE. Past. James Harris. D.L., October 22, 1762. Pr. 1762. See *Daphnis and Amaryllès.*

SPRING AND AUTUMN; OR, MARRIED FOR MONEY. C.D. 2 a. Adap. fr. French by James Kenny. Hay., September 6, 1827.

SPRING AND FALL OF LIFE. Grecian, May 21, 1866.

SPRING CHICKEN, THE. M.P. G. Grossmith. Adap. fr. Jaime and Duval's *Coquin de Printemps*. Addl. lyrics by A. Ross and P. Greenbank. M. by J. Caryll and L. Monckton. Gaiety, May 30, 1905.

SPRING CLEAN, A. Dom. D. A. Anderson. Brighton Aquarium, March 2, 1903.

SPRING CLEANING. Sk. Newport Empire, August 16, 1909.

SPRING LEAVES. Ca. Adap. fr. the Dutch by J. T. Grein and C. W. Jarvis. Court, March 14, 1891.

SPRING LEGEND, THE. P. C. P. Colnaghi and Cotsford Dick. M. by Cotsford Dick. O. Comique, December 17, 1891.

SPRING LOCK, THE. Mus. Ent. 3 a. M. by G. H. Rodwell. Lyceum playbill, August 18, 1829.

SPRING VALLEY; OR, THE DISGUISED LIEUTENANT. Int. 2 a., with songs. Pr. 1787.

SPRING'S DELIGHTS. Mus. Sk. Rewritten upon an old subject by Corney Grain. St. George's Hall., February 18, 1884.

SPRING'S GLORY, VINDICATING LOVE BY TEMPERANCE AGAINST THE TENET. Masq. Thomas Nabbes. Dedicated to Peter Ball, Esq. 1638.

SPRING-HEELED JACK. D. 4 a. W. Travers. Marylebone, June 1, 1868.

SPUR OF THE MOMENT, THE. Orig. whimsical D. 1 a. Henry J. Byron. Globe, May 4, 1872.

SPURIUS. T. Heylin. 1616. N.p.

SPY, THE. P. 1 a. H. M. Paull. Ealing Lyric, April 23, 1896.

SPY, THE. P. 1 a. Cecil Raleigh. Comedy, September 21, 1888; Coliseum, October 23, 1905.

SPY, THE. Sk. By Percy Ford. Camberwell Empire, July 8, 1907.

SPY; A STORY OF THE AMERICAN REBELLION, THE. Military D. 5 a. Geo. Turner. Jorrell (Novelty), November 30, 1889.

SQUABBLES. C. 1 a. T. Stanley Rogers. Liverpool Bijou O.H., December 17, 1881.

SQUARING THE CIRCLE. Ca. Francis Drake. Globe, May 8, 1876.

SQUATTER'S DAUGHTER, THE. M.C.D. 3 a. W. Carr. M. by Sparrow Harris. Coventry O.H., March 5, 1900.

SQUEEZE TO THE CORONATION, A. Loyal Sk. Lyceum playbill, July 19, 1821.

SQUIRE, THE. P. 3 a. A. W. Pinero. St. James's, December 29, 1881; Kennington P.O.W., February 26, 1900.

SQUIRE BADGER. Burla. 2 parts. M. by Dr. Arne. Hay. Pr. 1772. Afterwards produced as *The Sot.*

SQUIRE BASINGHALL; OR, THE CHEAPSIDE BEAU. C. N.p. C.G., July 23, 1735.

SQUIRE BRAINLESS; OR, TRICK UPON TRICK. C. Aaron Hill. D.L., April 27, 1710. N.p.

SQUIRE BURLESQUED; OR, THE SHARPERS OUTWITTED, THE. C. Bartholomew Bourgeois. Pr. 1765.

SQUIRE DICK. P. 1 a. Arthur Eckersley. Rugby Town Hall, January 28, 1904.

SQUIRE HUMPHREY. C. 1 a. Adap. by W. T. Blackmore fr. the Comédie Française piece, *L'Eté de St. Martin*. Oxford New T., June 20, 1887.

SQUIRE OF ALSATIA; OR, THE GENTLEMAN OF ALSATIA, THE. C. Thomas Shadwell. Ac. by their Majesties' servants, 1688. See *The Choleric Man.*

SQUIRE OF DAMES, THE. C. 4 a. Adap. by R. C. Carton fr. *L'Ami des Femmes* of Dumas fils. Criterion, November 5, 1895.

SQUIRE OF LITTLE CLODBURY. C. 4 a. Leonard C. White. Stanley Hall, South Norwood, May 7, 1904.

SQUIRE OF RINGWOOD CHASE, THE. New Royalty, May 2, 1865

SQUIRE OF UNDERCLIFFE, THE. D. 4 a. S. Theo James. Prince's T., Accrington, July 10, 1895.

SQUIRE OLD SAPP; OR, THE NIGHT ADVENTURERS. C. T. Durfey. Duke's, 1679.

SQUIRE TRELOOBY. C. Ascr. to Vanbrugh, Congreve, and Walsh. Hay., 1706. Transl. fr. "Monsieur de Porceaugnac."

SQUIRE'S DAUGHTER, THE. Oa. J. E. Bloomer. Sheffield Alexandra O.H., November 7, 1879.

SQUIRE'S MARIA; OR, TOO, TOO FAR FROM THE MADDING CROWD. Burl. Harry Adams. Hanley T.R., July 17, 1882.

SQUIRE'S MASQUE, THE. Masque. Ac. at Court, 1615.

SQUIRE'S WIFE, THE. D. 4 a. Fred Jarman. Huddersfield T.R. and O.H., July 15, 1889.

SQUIRE'S WILL, THE. Dr. Epis. By E. Haslingden Russell. Liverpool P.O.W., December 6, 1897.

STABAT MATER. (Tribulation.) Words by W. Ball. G. Rossini. (1792-1868.)

STADIUM, THE. Sk. East Ham Palace June 21, 1909.

STAFF OF DIAMONDS, THE. Nautical D. 2 a. C. H. Hazlewood. Surrey, January 21, 1861.

STAGE, THE. C. 1 a. West Digges. Duke's, May 21, 1877.

STAGE AND STATE. D. 3 a. J. Palgrave Simpson. T.R., Edinburgh. October 2, 1868.

STAGE BEAUX TOSS'D IN A BLANKET; OR, HYPOCRISY A LA MODE. C. Intended as satire against Collier. Sam Brown, 1704. Not intended to be acted.

STAGE COACH, A. Ca. 1 a. Frederic de Lara. Ladbroke Hall, May, 1887; Globe, May 7, 1892. See *Another Matinée*.

STAGE COACH, THE. F. Geo. Farquhar and Peter Motteux. Pr. 1705. D.L., February 2, 1704.

STAGE DORA; OR, WHO KILLED COCK ROBIN? Travestie of Sardou's "Fédora" by F. C. Burnand. Toole's, May 26, 1883.

STAGE LAND. C. 3 a. G. R. Douglas. Vaudeville, January 2, 1875.

STAGE MASK, A. Playlet. Talfourd Major. Brompton Hospital, November 25, 1902.

STAGE MUTINEERS; OR, A PLAYHOUSE TO BE LET, THE. T.C. F. Ballad O. Anon. C.G., October 31, 1733. Pr. 1733.

STAGE NAME, A. P. 1 a. Ino Rozant. Rehearsal, W.C., April 4, 1909.

STAGE PRETENDERS; OR, THE ACTOR TURNED POET, THE. F. To which is annexed "A Sessions of the Poets on the Death of Mr. Rowe." Pr. 1720.

STAGE STRUCK. Co. Cha. Stanley Rogers. Publ. by S. French, Ltd.

STAGE STRUCK; OR, THE LOVES OF AUGUSTUS PORTARLINGTON AND CELESTINA BEVERLEY. F. 1 a. Ad. from "Love in the East." Wm. Dimond. T.R., D.L.; Lyceum playbill, November 12, 1835.

STALKING-HORSE, THE. C. 2 a. L. Carr. Shanklin Inst., April 20, 1909 (amat.).

STALLION, THE. Droll. Pr. 1672.

STAND AND DELIVER; OR, THE PERILS OF THE ROAD. D. 3 a. J. Archer. Eleph. and Castle, November 23, 1885.

STAPLE OF NEWS. C. Ben Jonson. (Four persons are introduced on the stage who remain on the stage and criticise the chief incidents of the play.) Ac. by His Majesty's servants, 1625.

STAR OF HOPE, THE. D. 4 a. Wynn Miller and C. A. Clarke. Manchester St. James, January 14, 1901.

STAR OF INDIA, THE. D. 5 a. Geo. R. Sims and A. Shirley. Princess's, April 4, 1896.

STAR OF PARIS, THE. P. in Pro. and 3 a. R. H. Curtis. Dover R., December 2, 1905.

STAR OF SEVILLE. Mrs. Butler. 1837.

STAR OF THE NORTH. Adap. to the Engl. stage from Meyerbeer's *L'Etoile du Nord* by F. W. Pratt. Court, February 1, 1889.

STAR OF THE NORTH, THE. D. 3 a. Adap. fr. the French. T. W. Robertson.

STAR OF THE RHINE: OR, THE GENIUS OF DANCING, THE. Ballet Fantastique. M. Barrez. M. by M. Boisselot. D.L., February 24, 1852.

STAR OF THE WOODLANDS, THE. City of London, March 11, 1861.

STAR TURN, A. M.F. "Horthur Leuberts." M. by A. Maurice. Trafalgar Square, April 27, 1893.

STAR-SPANGLED BANNER, THE. Irish-American Military D. 4 a. W. J. Patmore. Parkhurst, February 11, 1892.

STAR-SPANGLED BANNER; OR, THE FAR WEST. Irish-American D. 5 a. Julia Agnes Fraser. Publ. by Frend and Co., Plymouth.

STARNO. P. F. Sayers. Pr. 1790.

STARR'S GIRL. R.P. 4 a. Alice E. Ives. Southend Empire, November 20, 1902.

STARS, THE. Bal. O. 5 a. Simon. Moscow, 1902.

STARS AND GARTERS. Burl. Robert Reece and H. B. Farnie. Folly, September 21, 1878.

STARTING PRICE. D. 4 a. C. A. Clarke. T.R., Runcorn, July 21, 1894.

STARVED TO DEATH; OR, HIGH CRIME AND LOW CRIME. D. 3 a. Adelphi, Liverpool, August 26, 1872.

STATE COURIER, THE. D. James Pitney Weston. Wigan T.R., November 20, 1871.

STATE FARCE; OR, THEY ARE ALL COME HOME, THE. Ridicule on the expedition to France under Sir Ed. Hawke and Sir J. Mordaunt. Pr. 1757.

STATE JUGGLER; OR, SIR POLITIC RIBBAND, THE. Excise O. Anon. Pr. 1733.

STATE OF INNOCENCE AND FALL OF MAN, THE. O. J. Dryden. Quasi-dram. Ver. of "Paradise Lost." Pr. 1678.

STATE OF PHYSIC, THE. C. Anon. Pr. 1742.

STATE PRISONER, THE. Stirling. 1847.

STATE PRISONER, THE. D. 1 a. Wm. Gowing. February 18, 1851.

STATE PUPPET SHOW, THE. Called also *The Humours of Punch's Resignation.* Old T., near Pall Mall. N.d. Circa 1741.

STATE SECRET. F.C. 3 a. Adap. fr. the German of Messrs. Cassell and Duckworth. Prince's T., Bradford, December 20, 1889.

STATE SECRET, A. Sk. Tottenham Pal., August 30, 1909.

STATE SECRETS; OR, PUBLIC MEN IN PRIVATE LIFE. Hist. D. 1 a. C.G., June 12, 1821.

STATE SECRETS; OR, THE TAILOR OF TAMWORTH. F. 1 a. T. Egerton Wilks. Surrey, September 12, 1836.

STATE TRIAL, A. Duol. L. Irving. Garrick, November 19, 1896.

STATESMAN, THE. F. J. Dent. Announced for perf. at D.L., 1781-1782, but not ac. or pr

STATESMAN FOILED, THE. M.C. 2 a. R. Dossie. M. by Mr. Rush. Hay., July 8, 1768. Pr. 1768.

STATIRA. T. Pradon. Circa 1690.

STATUE, LA. Op. C. 3 a. Text by Carré and Barbier. M. by E. Reyer. Paris Op. C., April 11, 1861; rev. as *Grando* in 1903.

STATUE, THE. Past Masque. Perf. privately. Pr. 1777.

STATUE, THE. M. Ent. C. Dibdin. Ac. at the Circus. N.d. Rev., Victoria, 1868.

STATUE BRIDE, THE. Oa. 2 tab. M. by E. Aspa. Words by V. Amcotts. Gallery of Illustration, June 19, 1868.

STATUE DU COMMANDEUR, LA. P. without words. P. Endel and E. Mangin, fr. Champfleury's book. M. by A. David. P.O.W., June 11, 1892.

STATUE FEAST, THE. P. 2 a. Alt. fr. Molière by Lady Craven. Ac. at Benham House by Lord Craven's children, 1782. N.p.

STATUE IN THE SQUARE, THE. Dr. scena. J. C. Worden. Blackpool Palace, March 16, 1905.

STATUE OF ALBEMARLE, THE. M.F.C. 1 a. Mrs. Bernard Whishaw. M. by Fred Whishaw. Trafalgar Sq., November 16, 1892.

STATUE OF MESSINA, THE. Sk. A. L. Hatzan. Shoreditch Empire, February 20, 1909.

STAY AT HOME. G. H. Lewes. Lyceum.

STEAM HAMMER, THE. Sk. W. H. Benson. Sadler's Wells, February 15, 1909.

STEEL HAND AND HIS NINE THIEVES. Britannia, May 11, 1857.

STEEPLE JACK. Dom. C. 1 a. T. Edgar Pemberton. Liverpool P.O.W., March 23, 1888.

STEEPLECHASE; OR, IN THE PIGSKIN, THE. Orig. F. 1 a. J. M. Morton. Adelphi, March 22, 1865; Hay.

STELLA. D. Transl. fr. German of Goethe. Pr. 1798. Another ver. by Shobert, 1804.

STELLA. D. 5 a. Transl. fr. German of Goethe by B. Thompson. Pr. 1804.

STELLA. C. 3 a. B. W. Lindon. St. Geo. H., November 21, 1889.

STELLA AND LEATHERLUNGS; OR, A STAR AND A STROLLER. C. Sk. D.L., October 2, 1823.

STEMMING THE STREAM. D. 3 a. Conducted by W. H. C. Nation. Adap. fr. a serial novel which appeared in the Covent Garden Magazine. Scala, October 26, 1907.

STEP-BROTHERS. C. 3 a. Rev. ver. of *The Actor* by T. Edgar Pemberton. Dundee H.M.T., February 6, 1891.

STEPHANIE. T. Story. 1877.

STEPHEN DIGGES. Adelphi, September 14, 1874.

STEPHEN, KING. P. Ascr. to Wm. Shakespeare. Ent. in book of Stationers' Co., June 29, 1660. N.p.

STEPMOTHER, THE. T.C. Sir Robt. Stapylton. L.I.F. by D. of York's servants. 1664.

STEPMOTHER, THE. T. Earl of Carlisle. Pr. 1800.

STEPMOTHER, THE. C. 1 a. C.G., October 22, 1828. N.p.

STEPMOTHER, THE. Oa. Lib. by Arthur Sketchley. M. by Walter Austen. St. Geo. Hall, May 5, 1880.

STEPMOTHER, THE. Sk. 3 sc. A. Shirley. Camberwell Empire, March 18, 1907; Crown, May 27, 1907.

STEPMOTHER'S TRAGEDY, THE. P. Henry Chettle. Ac. 1599. N.p.

STEPPING STONES. C. 3 a. Geo. Fox. Novelty, May 7, 1887 (amat.).

STEPSISTER, THE. Dom. C. 1 a. Wm. Sapte, jun. Comedy, June 4, 1887.

STEWARD, THE. Adap. of Holcroft's *Deserted Daughters.*

STEWARD; OR, FASHION AND FEELING, THE. C. 5 a. By author of "The Scapegrace." C.G., September 15, 1819.

STEWKLEY. Ac. December 11, 1596. Probably either *The Battle of Alcazar* or *The Life and Death of Captain Stukeley.*

STICHUS. C. Plautus. Adap. fr. a Greek P. by Menander, and transl. into blk. verse by Thornton, Rich. Warner, and Colman. 1769-74. See "Latin Plays."

STIFELLIO. D. Verdi. Trieste, November 16, 1850.

STIFTUNGEFEST. Op. C. October 17, 1893.

STIGMATA. T. with Prelude. 4 a. Sutherland-Dix and Eva Unsell. Court, July 31, 1909.

STILLICON. T. Thomas Corneille. 1660.

STILL ALARM, THE. Rom. C.D. 4 a. Joseph Arthur and A. C. Wheeler. Fourteenth St. T., New York, August 30, 1887; Princess's, August 2, 1888; Grand, December 1, 1888.

STILL WATERS RUN DEEP. C. 3 a. F. on De Bernard's "Le Gendre" by Tom Taylor. Olympic, May 14, 1855; Criterion, October 13, 1890; Wyndham's, March 14, 1902.

STINGAREE, THE BUSHRANGER. P. 4 a. E. W. Hornung. Queen's, February 1, 1908.

STIRRING OF EMBERS, THE. C. 4 a. H. Aymes. Albert H. T., November 18, 1904 (C.P.).

STIRRING TIMES. M.P. Frank H. Celli and Brian Daly. Southport O.H., August 2, 1897; Clapham Shakespeare, August 9, 1897.

STOCK EXCHANGE; OR, THE GREEN BUSINESS, THE. C.D. 1 a. Ch. Dance. Princess's T., April 5, 1858.

STOCK JOBBERS; OR, THE HUMOURS OF EXCHANGE ALLEY. C. 3 a. W. R. Chetwood. Pr. 1720.

STOICUS VAPULANS. O. Anon. Ac. at St. John's College, Cambridge, by the Students, 1648.

STOLEN; OR, THE STREET BALLAD SINGER. American D. Prol. and 3 a. Sadler's Wells, November 23, 1868.

STOLEN; OR, £20 REWARD. F. 1 a. Wm. Hancock. New Royalty, December 26, 1863.

STOLEN AWAY. D. 3 a. R. Dodson. Britannia, March 15, 1875.

STOLEN BIRTHRIGHT; OR, THE FATHER'S REVENGE, THE. Melo-d. 4 a. Sydney Spenser. Colne T.R., September 28, 1896.

STOLEN FORTUNE; OR, THE BLIND WIFE AND THE DETECTIVE, THE. D. F. Clarke. Birkenhead T.R., April 9, 1877.

STOLEN FROM HOME; OR, HUMAN HEARTS. D. 3 a. Sadler's Wells, October 12, 1891.

STOLEN HEIRESS; OR, THE SALAMANCA DOCTOR OUTPLOTTED, THE. T.C. Susanna Centlivre. L.I.F., December 31, 1702.

STOLEN JEWESS; OR, THE TWO ISRAELITES, THE. Orig. Rom. D. 3 a. C. H. Hazlewood. Britannia, April 1, 1872. Second title also *The Two Children of Israel.*

STOLEN KISSES; OR, THE LION AND THE MOUSE. C.D. 3 a. Paul Meritt. Liverpool Amphi., November 6, 1876; Globe, June 2, 1877; July 2, 1877.

STONE BROKE. Ca. R. Standish Sievier. Blackburn T.R., March 23, 1892; Grand, March 28, 1892.

STONE EATER, THE. Int. C. Stuart. D.L., May 14, 1788. Pr. 1788.

STONE GUEST, THE. O. A. S. Dargonijsky. (Sometimes called *The Gospel of the New School.*) 1872.

STONEHENGE. Past. John Speed. Ac. before Dr. Baylie. 1636. N.p.

STOP, THIEF! F.C. 3 a. Mark Melford. Halifax T.R., May 24, 1889 (C.P.); Strand, November 11, 1889.

STORES, THE. C.O. Lib. by Ed. Rose and Augustus Harris. M. by Bucalossi. D.L., March 14, 1881.

STORKS, THE See "Greek Plays."

STORM, THE. Orat. Haydn. March 26, 1791.

STORM, THE. D. 3 a. Mr. Holford. Pr. with *The Cave of Neptune*, 1799.

STORM, THE. Piece. 1 a and 2 tab. Ian Robertson. Royalty, October 24, 1896.

STORM, THE. D. Sk. P. Sykes. Collins's, April 15, 1907.

STORM, THE. P. 1 a. H. Barden. Dublin Abbey. April 22, 1909 (amat.).

STORM AND SUNSHINE. P. 2 a. Mrs. Newton Phillips. Crystal Palace, July 24, 1889.

STORM CLOUDS. Dr. Int. G. Henry Brumell. T.R., Bury, June 19, 1900.

STORM DEED; OR, BLACK GANG CHINE, THE. D. 3 a. W. Seaman. Eleph. and C., April 2, 1877.

STORM IN A TEACUP, A. Ca. 1 a. Bayle Bernard. Princess's, March 20, 1854.

STORM SIGNAL, THE. Grecian, October 29, 1866.

STORM-BEATEN. D. Pro. and 5 a. F. upon the same plot as the author's novel, "God and the Man," by Robert Buchanan. Adelphi, March 14, 1883.

STORMCOAST. D. 4 a. Fredk. Vanneck. Globe, December 11, 1888.

STORMING AND CAPTURE OF DELHI. Astley's, November 23, 1857.

STORMY PETREL, THE. C. 3 a. W. Strange Hall, Glasgow. King's, July 25, 1907.

STORMY TIMES. E. 1 a. C. Harrison. Hastings Pier Pavilion, February 24, 1902.

STORY OF A SIN, THE. D. 4 a. Adap. by Courtenay Thorpe fr. a novel by Miss Helen Mathers bearing the same title. Richmond T.R., August 1, 1895.

STORY OF ORESTES, THE. Ver. (3 a.) b Prof. Warr of the trilogy, "Agamemnon, Chœphori and Eumenides," of Æschylus. Prince's Hall, May 13, 1886.

STORY OF PROCIDA, A. D. 1 a. St. James's, November 4, 1867.

STORY OF THE FORTY-FIVE. A. D. Watts Philipps. Adelphi, November 12, 1860.

STORY OF WATERLOO, A. A. Conan Doyle. Bristol Prince's, September 21, 1894. Lyceum, May 4, 1895.

STORY OF WINIFRED. P. 4 a. Arthur Bertram and Gordon Holmes. Orig. ac. as *When Woman Strays.* Hammersmith King's T., March 16, 1903.

STOUT GENTLEMAN, THE. M.F. Lyceum playbill, September 8, 1825.

STOWAWAY, THE. D. 5 a. Tom Craven. Dewsbury T.R., September 29, 1884. Sadler's Wells, February 21, 1885. Entirely re-written ver. prod. Middlesbrough T.R., June 14, 1886.

STRADELLA. O. 5 a. Niedermeyer. M. by F. Flotow. Adap. to English stage by Benedict. Paris, March 3, 1837. Re-comp. as *Allesandro Stradella*, and prod. at Hamburg, December 30, 1844. Alt. by Bunn, and prod. at D.L., June 6, 1846.

STRAFFORD. Hist. T. Robert Browning. C.G., May 1, 1837.

STRAFFORD. Hist. T. Sterling. 1843.

STRAIGHT FROM THE HEART. D. 4 a. Sutton Vane and Arthur Shirley. Pavilion, August 3, 1896.

STRAIGHT FROM THE SHOULDER. D. 4 a. Broadway, August 10, 1908.

STRAIGHT TIP, THE. F. D.L., September 20, 1873.

STRANGE ADVENTURE OF A FRENCH PIANIST. Monol. Frederic Dardle. Steinway Hall, July 2, 1891.

STRANGE ADVENTURES OF MISS BROWN, THE. F.P. 3 a. Robert Buchanan and Charles Marlowe. Vaude., June 26, 1895; Terry's, October 14, 1895; Court, September 23, 1901.

STRANGE BUT TRUE. Grecian, July 2, 1866.

STRANGE DISCOVERY, THE. T.C. J. Gough. Pr. 1640 and 1717. ? by Charles Gildon.

STRANGE GENTLEMAN, THE. F. Charles Dickens. St. James's, September 29, 1836; rev. Charing Cross, 1873.

STRANGE GUEST, A. P. 1 a. Fr. the French by Frank Lange. Globe, April 16, 1892.

STRANGE HISTORY, A. Dr. tale (nine chapters). Slingsby Lawrence (G. H. Lewes) and Chas. Mathews. Lyceum, March 29, 1853.

STRANGE HOST; OR, A HAPPY NEW YEAR, A. V. Arthur Law. M. by King Hall. St. Geo. Hall, December 6, 1882.

STRANGE NEWS OUT OF POLAND. P. Wm. Houghton, assisted by Pett. Ac. 1600.

STRANGE RELATION, A. C. 3 a. E. Compton. Liverpool P.O.W., May 22, 1876.

STRANGE RELATION, A. C. 1 a. L. Montague. Publ. by S. French, Ltd.

STRANGE SEQUEL, A. P. 4 a. Fred Pemberton. Seaford Queen's H., July 15, 1903.

STRANGER, THE. C. Sheridan. 1797. Freely transl. fr. Kotzebue's German comedy by A. S. Pr. 1798.

STRANGER, THE. D. 5 a. Transl. fr. German of Kotzebue (*Misanthropy and Repentance*) by Benjamin Thompson. D.L., March 24, 1798, and March 25, 1819.

STRANGER, THE. P. fr. Kotzebue. Lyceum playbill, June 8, 1825.

STRANGER, THE. P. fr. Kotzebue. 5 a. Surrey, February 2, 1865.

STRANGER, THE. Arrangement in 3 a. of Kotzebue's P. Olympic, January 28, 1891 (rev.).

STRANGER. Burl. Reece.

STRANGER, THE. See *La Straniera.*

STRANGER; OR, MISANTHROPY AND REPENTANCE. D. 5 a. Transl. fr. German of Kotzebue by George Papendick. Pr. 1798.

STRANGER IN NEW YORK, A. M.C. 3 a. Charles Hayt. M. by Mr. Stahl. Gaiety (copy), February 11, 1897; D. of Y., June 21, 1898.

STRANGER, STRANGER THAN EVER, THE. Piece of Extravagance in 1 a. R. Reece. Queen's, November 4, 1868; Royalty, October 26, 1870.

STRANGER TO HIMSELF, A. Melo-d. 4 a. Gerald Holcroft. Birmingham Queen's T., June 17, 1889.

STRANGERS AT HOME, THE. C.O. James Cobb. M. by Linley. D.L., December 8, 1785. Pr. 1786. See *Algerine Slaves.*

STRANGERS WITHIN THE GATES. P. 3 a. H. C. M. Hardinge. Court, February 7, 1909.

STRANGERS YET. D. C. Oswald Allen. Grecian, May 20, 1872.

STRANGLERS OF PARIS, THE. D. 5 a. Adap. fr. Adolphe Belot's Porte St. Martin D., *Les Estrangleurs de Paris.* Arthur Shirley. Surrey, October 17, 1887.

STRANIERA, LA. *The Stranger.* Ital. O. 2 a. By Romani. M. by Bellini. Scala, Milan, February 14, 1829; King's, June 23, 1832.

STRATAGEM. T.C. Anon. N.D. (before 1814).

STRATAGEM, THE. Ca. Adap. fr. German of Emil Pohl by F. Kinsey Peile. Croydon G.T., February 12, 1906; Court, July 2, 1907.

STRATAGEMS OF HARLEQUIN, THE. See *Rural Sports.* 1740.

STRATFORD JUBILEE, THE (with *Scrub's Trip to the Jubilee*). C. 2 a. Francis Gentleman. Stratford-on-Avon. Pr. 1769.

STRATHLOGAN. Modern Irish D. 3 a. Charles Overton and Hugh Moss. Princess's, June 9, 1892.

STRATHMORE; OR, LOVE AND DUTY. T. 4 a. Westland Marston. Hay., June 20, 1849.

STRATHMORE. See *Wrath.*

STRATONICI. O. C. Hoffmann. M. by Méhul. Op. C., May 3, 1792.

STRAVAGANZA DEL CONTE, LE. O. D. Cimarosa (his first O.). Naples, 1772.

STRAW HAT, THE. F. Liverpool P.O.W., December 13, 1873.

STRAWBERRIES AND CREAM. F.P. 2 a. E. T. de Bauzie and James Grant. Glasgow Princess's, February 26, 1891.

STRAYED AWAY. D. 4 a. W. Travers. East London, August 15, 1870.

STRAYED FROM THE FOLD. D. 4 a. Mortimer Murdoch. Pavilion, June 8, 1878.

STREAK O' SUNSHINE. M.D. 3 a. Loftus Don. M. by Geo. le Brunn. Great Yarmouth R. Aquarium, March 12, 1888; Sadler's Wells, May 7, 1888.

STREAKS OF GOLD. C. Miss Maud Randford. Sunderland T.R., March 14, 1878.

STREANSHALL ABBEY; OR, THE DANISH INVASION. P. Francis Gibson. Ac. at Whitby. Pr. 1800.

STREET, THE. P. 3 a. A. R. Williams. Manchester Midland, November 5, 1907.

STREETS; OR, A TALE OF WICKED LONDON, THE. D. 4 a. Geo. Lash Gordon. Sadler's Wells, December 6, 1884.

STREETS OF LONDON, THE. D. Pro. and 4 a. Dion Boucicault. Substance of this D. used by W. Stirling Coyne at the Surrey, 1857, and Strand shortly after by R. Barrett, under the respective titles of *Fraud and its Victims* and *Pride and Poverty.* Origin of adaps. was a 7 a. French D., *Les Pauvres de Paris,* by MM. Brisebarre and Eugène Nus (Ambigu Comique, 1856). Princess's, August 5, 1864, January 14. 1867, and December 15, 1869; Adelphi, May 7, 1891; Princess's, June 16, 1900. See *Islington; or, Life in the Streets.*

STREETS TO THE HULKS; OR, THE OLD WORLD AND THE NEW, THE. D. 3 a. Geo. Conquest. Grecian, May 17, 1869.

STRICKEN DOWN. D. Charles Dillon. Glasgow T.R., June 13, 1870.

STRIFE. P. 3 a. J. Galsworthy. D. of Y., March 9, 1909; Hay., March 20, 1909; tfd. Adelphi, March 29, 1909.

STRIKE, THE. Dion Boucicault. Lyceum (orig. prod. as *The Lay Strike*), September 16, 1866; Novelty, August 24, 1896.

STRIKE, THE. D. Lester Herbert. Northampton T.R., June 23, 1873.

STRIKE, THE. Sk. Paragon, June 29, 1908.

STRIKE; OR, HEADS, HANDS, AND HEARTS, THE. Herbert J. Stanley. Albion, May 3, 1875.

STRIKE AT ARLINGFORD, THE. P. 3 a. Geo. Moore. Op. C., February 21, 1893.

STRIKING SIMILARITY, A. F. Frederick Hay. Liverpool P.O.W., May 30, 1870; Surrey, October 8, 1870.

STRIKING THE HOUR. D. W. H. Pitt. City of London, May 20, 1867.

STRING OF PEARLS, THE. Melo-d. C. A. Clarke and H. R. Silva. New ver. of *Sweeney Todd.* Birkenhead T.R., November 26, 1892.

STROKE OF BUSINESS, A. P. 1 a. Arthur Morrison and Horace Newte. Adap. fr. former's story, "Divers Vanities." Kingsway, November 18, 1907.

STROKE OF LUCK, A. P. Prol. and 4 a. Captain Bagot and J. K. Murray. Cardiff Grand T., August 7, 1899.

STROLLER, THE. Poetic Idyll. 1 a. Adap. fr. François Coppée's "Le Passant," and versified by Mrs. Olive Logan. Princess's, October 22, 1887. See *The Waif.*

STROLLER'S PACKET BROKE OPEN. Collection of seven drolls borrowed fr. different plays:—

(1) THE BILKER BILK'D; OR, THE BANQUET OF WILES, fr. "The Woman's Revenge," by C. Bullock.

(2) THE BRAGGADOCIO; OR, HIS WORSHIP THE CULLY. From "Old Bachelor," by Congreve.

(3) THE FEIGNED SHIPWRECK; OR, THE IMAGINARY HEIR, fr. "The Elder Brother," by Beaumont and Fletcher.

(4) THE GUARDIANS OVERREACH'D IN THEIR OWN HUMOUR; OR, THE LOVER METAMORPHOSED, fr. "Bold Stroke for a Wife," by Mrs. Centlivre.

(5) THE LITIGIOUS SUITOR DEFEATED; OR, A NEW TRICK TO GET A WIFE, fr. "Woman's a Riddle," by Bullock.

(6) THE SEXES MISMATCH'D: OR, A NEW WAY TO GET A HUSBAND, fr. "Oroonoka," by Southern, and "Monsieur Thomas," by Beaumont and Fletcher.

(7) THE WITCHCRAFT OF LOVE; OR, STRATAGEM UPON STRATAGEM, fr. "Man's Bewitch'd; or, The Devil to do About Here," by Mrs. Centlivre. Perf. at country fairs.

STROLLERS, THE. F. Extract fr. John Durant Breval's "The Play is the Plot." Ac. at D.L. Pr. 1727.

STROLLERS, THE. See *I Pagliacci.*

STROLLERS; OR, ON THE ROAD. D. 4 a. G. W. Glenny. Athenæum. Llanelly, August 27, 1888.

STROM DER. D. 3 a. Max Halbe. Gt. Queen St., February 27, 1905.

STRONG AS DEATH. D. Pr. and 4 a. Douglas M. Ford. Gloucester T.R., June 19, 1899.

STRONGBOW; OR, THE BRIDE OF THE BATTLEFIELD. C.O. 3 a. Lib. by Messrs. W. Percy French and L. H. Brindley. M. by W. Houston Collisson. Dublin Queen's Royal T., May 2, 1892.

STRONGER SEX, THE. P. 3 a. J. Valentine. Apollo, January 22, 1907.

STRONGER WOMAN, THE. P. August Strindberg. Transl. and arr. by F. Castle and E. A. Brown. Bloomsbury H., November 29, 1906.

STRONGHEART. Amer. C.D. 4 a. W. C. de Mille. Aldwych, April 8, 1907.

STRUCK. P. 1 a. The Hon. and Rev. James Adderley. Saltley Carlton, November 16, 1907.

STRUCK IN THE DARK. D. 4 a. Reginald Moore. Granville Hall T., Ramsgate. October 5, 1875.

STRUCK OFF THE ROLLS. Melo-d. 4 a. William B. Broadhead. Manchester Royal Osborne T., January 7, 1901.

STRUCK OIL; OR, THE PENNYSYLVANIAN DUTCHMAN. D. 3 a. Adelphi, April 17, 1876.

STRUENSEE. T. Beer. 1827.

STRUGGLE FOR LIFE, THE. D. 4 a. Adapt. by Robert Buchanan and Fredk. Horner fr. Alphonse Daudet's play, *La Lutte pour la Vie* (Gymnase Dramatique, October 30, 1889). Av., September 25, 1890.

STRUGGLE FOR LIFE; OR, A BURGLAR'S FATE, A. D. E. Drayton. Sadler's Wells, September 22, 1884.

STRUGGLING FOR WEALTH. C.D. Prol. and 3 a. W. A. Gosnay. Surrey, December 21, 1880.

STRYLIUS. Latin C. Nicholas Robinson. 1553.

STUDENT A LA MODE, THE. O. C.G. Pr. 1754. Transl. of *Lo Studenta alla Moda.*

STUDENT OF LYONS, THE. G. H. Redwell. Circa 1831.

STUDENTS' FROLIC. St. James's Hall, May 24, 1864.

STUDENT'S WHIM. See *Minerva's Triumph.*

STUDENTS, THE. C. Alt. fr. Shakespeare's *Love's Labour's Lost.* Pr. 1762.

STUDENTS, THE. C. 3 a. Pr. 1779.

STUDENTS; OR, THE HUMOURS OF ST. ANDREWS, THE. F. James Stewart. Hay. Pr. 1779.

STUDENTS OF BONN, THE. Oa. D.L., March 28, 1842.

STUDENTS OF JENNA; OR, THE FAMILY CONCERT, THE. Oa. M. by Mons. Chelard. D.L., June 4, 1833.

STUDENTS OF SALAMANCA, THE. C. Jameson. C.G., June 23, 1813.

STUDIO ROMANCE, A. Piece. 1 a. Chas. Colton. Bayswater Bijou, May 17, 1902.

STUDY IN "A" FLAT, A. C. 1 a. J. S. Martin. Leigh Assem. Rooms, March 16, 1903; Hammersmith King's T., June 8, 1903.

STUDY OF TWO WOMEN, A. Dr. Sk. 1 a. Mrs. Wilton. Brompton Hospital, February 15, 1898

STUFFED DOG, A. C. 2 barks and a bite. J. A. Knox and E. Atwell. Camden Town Park Hall, November 2, 1889 (C.P.).

STURDY BEGGARS, THE. New Ballad O. Pr. 1733.

STURGFLATTERY. P. N.p. 1598.

STURM, DIE. Weber. Orat. D.L., March 25, 1825.

STUTZEN DER GESELLSCHAFT. DIE. D. 4 a. Henrik Ibsen. Great Queen Street, February 3, 1906.

SUB-EDITOR, THE. F. 3 a. Edmund Payne and Cyril Harrison. Brixton, November 5, 1896.

SUBALTERNS. F.C. Capt. F. W Marshall. Aldershot R., April 29, 1901.

SUBJECTION OF KEZIA, THE. P. Mrs. Havelock Ellis. Court, January 7, 1908; rev. Garrick, March 10, 1908.

SUBJECTS' JOY FOR THE KING'S RESTORATION, The. Masque. Dr. Anthony Sadler. 1660.

SUBLIME AND BEAUTIFUL, THE. Mus. Ent. f. on *The Sultan.* C.G., December 5, 1828.

SUBSTANCE AND THE SHADOW, THE. D. 2 a. Frank Mullin and Thos. Atkinson. Newcastle-on-Tyne Art Gallery T., January 30, 1894.

SUBSTITUTE, A. Ca. James Payn. Court, September 9, 1876.

SUBSTITUTE, THE. Ca. Malcolm Bell. Steinway H., March 23, 1893.

SUBSTITUTES. Ca. 1 a. E. Kingsley. MS. with Douglas Cox.

SUCCESS. P. 1 a. F. Hamilton Knight. T. and O.H., Cheltenham, February 29, 1892; Eleph. and C., April 11, 1892.

SUCCESS; OR, A HIT IF YOU LIKE. J. R. Planché. Adelphi, December 12, 1825.

SUCCESS; OR, THE MODERN CINDERELLA. C. 2 a. H. F. Hyde. Great Grimsby T.R., April 30, 1879.

SUCCESS OF SENTIMENT, THE. P. 3 a. H. Cranmer Byng. (Prod. by the Play Actors.) Court, September 27, 1908.

SUCCESSFUL FAILURE, A. Episode, by F. Stanmore. Queen's Gate H., W., May 2, 1902.

SUCCESSFUL MISSION, A. Duol. 1 a. P.O.W., July 14, 1894.

SUCCESSFUL PIRATE, THE. C. C. Johnson. Taken fr. "Arviragus and Phelicia" by Lodowick Carlell. D.L., November 7, 1712. Pr. 1713.

SUCCESSFUL STRANGERS, THE. T.C. W. Mountfort. T.R., 1690.

SUCH A GOOD MAN. C.D. W. Besant and J. Rice. Olympic, December 18, 1879.

SUCH A FAME. Ca. 1 a. H. Swears. St. George's H., March 1, 1902. Publ. by S. French, Limited.

SUCH A GUY MANNERING. Burl. W. Strachan, jun. Newcastle-on-Tyne Tyne T., April 27, 1868.

SUCH A NICE GIRL. An irresponsible mus. absurdity in 2 a. Words and lyrics by F. Stanmore. M. by E. Paschal. Worthing R.T., July 1, 1907; Kingston R. County, August 8, 1907.

SUCH IS LIFE. D. By the author of "The Knapsack." Elephant and Castle, February 28, 1885.

SUCH IS LIFE. 4 a. H. H. Rignold. Langton Queen's, December 2, 1893; Liverpool Rotunda, July 8, 1901.

SUCH IS LOVE. C. 1 a. A. M. Mond. Avenue, July 5, 1894.

SUCH IS THE LAW. D. 3 a. Tom Tayler and Paul Meritt. St. James's, April 20, 1878.

SUCH STUFF AS DREAMS ARE MADE OF. D. 4 a. Taken from Calderon's *La Vida es Sueño* by Ed. Fitzgerald. St. George's H., May 15, 1899.

SUCH THINGS ARE. P. Eliz. Inchbald. C.G., February 10, 1787.

SUCH THINGS HAVE BEEN. Int. Probably written by Mr. Ryder. Taken fr. Jackman's F., *A Trip to London*. C.G., March 31, 1789. N.p.

SUCH THINGS WERE. T. Prince Hoare. Bath, January 11, 1788.

SUDDEN ARRIVAL. C. 1 a. F. Hay. Publ. by S. French, Ltd.

SUDDEN ARRIVALS; OR, TOO BUSY BY HALF. C. J. Cobb. Lyceum, December 9, 1809.

SUDDEN SQUALL. C. 1 a. Mrs. Lancaster Wallis. Publ. by S. French, Ltd.

SUDDEN THOUGHTS. F. 1 a. T. E. Wilks. City of London, October 21, 1837.

SUE. P. 3 a. Bret Harte and T. E. Pemberton. Adapt. fr. Bret Harte's Story, "The Judgment of Bolivas Plain. Garrick, June 10, 1898.

SUFFRAGETTE'S TRIUMPH, THE. Duo. H. M. Holles. Foresters' M.H., December 27, 1906.

SUFFRAGETTES, THE. Sk. Geo. Thorne. Middlesex, December 22, 1908.

SUFFRAGETTES IN POWER, THE. C. Oa. Collins's, September 13, 1909.

SUGAR AND CREAM. Ca. 1 a. J. P. Hurst. Windsor Royal T., January 13, 1883; Globe, March, 1884.

SUGAR AND SPICE; OR, A GORILLA WARFARE. F. Eccen. J. F. M'Ardle. West Hartlepool Gaiety T., September 11, 1882.

SUGAR BOWL, THE. C. 4 a. Madeleine Lucette Ryley. Queen's, October 8, 1907.

SUGGESTION; OR, THE HYPNOTIST. M. Collins and H. Brown. Hammersmith Lyric O.H., November 21, 1891.

SUGGS IN DANGER. F. T. Atkinson, jun. Sadler's Wells, October 10, 1882.

SUICIDE, THE. 4 a. G. Colman. Hay., July 11, 1778. N.p.

SUIT OF TWEEDS, A. F. 1 a. Frederick Hay. Strand T., January 14, 1867.

SUITE DU COMTE D'ALBERT, LE. O. 2 a. Gretry, 1786.

SUITED AT LAST. F. 1 a. Ed Bedford. M. by G. Burton, Staveley Inst., March 25, 1895.

SUITOR AND SERVANT. Dr. Adap. of a F. by Mcilhac and Halévy. Royalty, 1872.

SUIVANTE, LA. C. Corneille. See "French Classical Plays."

SULIEMAN. T. 5 a. Pr. 1814. ? N.ac.

SULLEN LOVERS; OR, THE IMPERTINENTS. THE. C. (fr. Molière). T. Shadwell. L.I.F., May 5, 1668, and October 5, 1703.

SULTAN, THE. O. Dr. Arne. 1759.

SULTAN, THE. C.F. 1 a. D.L., February 11, 1828.

SULTAN THE. Sk. Stoke Newington Pal., May 18, 1908.

SULTAN; OR, A PEEP INTO THE SERAGLIO, THE. F. Bickerstaffe. 2 a. D.L., December 12, 1775; Edinburgh, 1782, and June 2, 1817.

SULTAN; OR, LOVE AND FAME, THE. T. F. Gentleman. Hay., 1770. Frequently ac. at Bath, York, and Scarborough.

SULTAN OF MOCHA, THE. C.O. 3 a. A. Cellier. Manchester Prince's, November 16, 1874; St. James's, April 17, 1876; rev. by W. Lestocq, Strand, September 21, 1887.

SULTAN OF RANOGOO, THE. M.C. W. Summers. Liverpool R. Hipp., July 6. 1903.

SULTANA; OR, THE JEALOUS QUEEN, THE. T. W. Gardiner. Pr. at Gloucester 1806.

SULTANESS, THE. T. C. Johnson. D.L., February 25 1717.

SULTANITA; OR, THE DAUGHTER OF BETHLEHEM, LA. Hebrew O. 5 a. A. Goldfaden. Standard, November 30, 1895.

SUMACHAUM, THE. Irish D. 3 a. Barry Connor. Britannia, August 5, 1878.

SUMMER AMUSEMENT; OR, AN ADVENTURE AT MARGATE. C.O. Andrew and Miles. Hay., July 11, 1779. N.p.

SUMMER CLOUD, A. C. Strand, September 20, 1880.

SUMMER CLOUDS. 1 a. N. Doone. Toole's, February 16, 1891.

SUMMER CLOUDS. Sk. Ellen Lancaster Wallis. Wolverhampton Grand, April 15, 1899; Grand, April 17, 1899.

SUMMER FLIES; OR, THE WILL FOR THE DEED. Dibdin, Hay., June 16, 1823.

SUMMER GIRL, THE. M.C. C. M. G. Hislop. Norwich Agricultural H., January 21, 1904.

SUMMER LIGHTNING. C. 1. Publ. by S. French, Ltd.

SUMMER ROSES. Rom. Playlet. R. Wilford. Lancaster Athenæum, August 7, 1907.

SUMMER SALES, THE. Sk. St. James's, July 3, 1905.

SUMMER STORMS. D. 3 a. H. J. Jennings. Birmingham T.R., December 18, 1876.

SUMMER'S DREAM, A. 1 a. Rose Meller. Avenue, July 14, 1891.

SUMMER'S LAST WILL AND TESTAMENT. C. T. Nash. P. at the house of some nobleman, 1592. Pr. 1600.

SUMMER'S TALE, THE. M.C. 3 a. Richard Cumberland. C.G., December 6, 1765.

SUMMERLAND'S MISTAKE. F. Wolverhampton P.O.W., March 10, 1873.

SUMMONED TO COURT. F. J. J. Dillay and L. Clifton. Imperial, March 4, 1880; New Sadler's Wells, March 27, 1880.

SUN IN ARIES; OR, CONFIRMATION OF EDWARD BARKHAM, THE. C. Middleton. 1621. See Pageants (No. 25).

SUN'S DARLING. Ancient Masque. Ford and Dekker and Rowley. D.L. Cockpit, 1623-4 and 1657; Queen's Gate H., October 31, 1906. Pr. 1656.

SUNBEAM. F. 3 a. C. Hannan. MS. with Douglas Cox.

SUNBURY SCANDAL, THE. F. C. 3 a. F. Horner. Terry's, June 11, 1896.

SUNDAY. P. 4 a. "T. Raceward." Eastbourne Devonshire Park T., January 11, 1904; Comedy, April 2, 1904.

SUNDOWN TO DAWN. D. J. Mortimer. Brighton T.R., March 1, 1875; Britannia, July 15, 1876.

SUNDOWNER, THE. D. 1 a. Brian Daly and J. M. East. Hammersmith Lyric, October 13, 1900.

SUNDOWNER, THE. Sk. Fred Kitchen and Frank Lister. Granville, August 26, 1907.

SUNKEN BELL, THE. P. 5 a. Gerhart Hauptman's fairy P. in English v. by C. H. Meltzer. Waldorf, April 22, 1907.

SUNLIGHT AND SHADOW. C. 3 a. R. C. Carton. Avenue, November 1, 1890; St. James's, January 31, 1891.

SUNNY FLORIDA. Mus. 2 a. H. Marris. Warrington R. Court T., November 2, 1896.

SUNNY SEASIDE, THE. Sk. Wal Pink. Oxford, December 24, 1906.

SUNNY SIDE, THE. C. 1 a. C. M. Rae (from About's *Risette*). Strand T., May 18, 1885.

SUNNY SOUTH, THE. D. 5 a. G. Darrell. Islington Grand, October 27, 1884; Surrey, September 5, 1898.

SUNNY SOUTH; OR, THE PICCADILLY BRIGANDS AND THE HAPPY VALET, THE. Burl. 1 a. Charles Heslop. Grounds of Mr. E. F. Boardman, Norwich, June 30, 1904.

SUNSET. Ca. 1 a. J. K. Jerome. F. on Tennyson's poem, "The Sisters." Comedy, February 13, 1888.

SUNSHINE. Ca. 1 a. F. W. Broughton. Bristol Old T.R., January 5, 1880; Bradford T.R., May 5, 1880; Strand, June 2, 1884.

SUNSHINE AND RAIN. Fanciful C. 3 a. Mackinnon Walbrook. Brighton West Pier Pav., April 22, 1901.

SUNSHINE AND SHADOW. M.D. Adap. by Miss Augusta Thomson. Marylebone, March 25, 1867.

SUNSHINE AND SHADOW. Dr. Sk. J. A. T. Lloyd. Middlesex, October 14, 1907.

SUNSHINE AFTER RAIN. F. T. Dibdin. 1795. See *Mad Guardian*.

SUNSHINE THROUGH THE CLOUDS. D. 1 a. Slingsby Lawrence (*i.e.*, G. H. Lewes). Adap. fr. *La Joie fait Peur*. Lyceum, June 15, 1854.

SUPER, THE. 1 a. A. M. Heathcote. Criterion, May 24, 1894.

SUPERANNUATED GALLANT, THE. F. J. Reid. Pr. 1745.

SUPERIOR MISS PELLENDER, THE. C. 3 a. S. Bowkett. Waldorf, January 17, 1906.

SUPERIOR PERSON, A. Duol. 1 a. Ina Leon Cassilis.

SUPERIOR SEX, THE. C.O. 3 a. Wr. by H. D. Banning. Comp. by J. H. Maunder. Southend Empire, March 30, 1909 (amat.).

SUPERIOR SEX, THE. Sk. Leon M. Lion and Eliot S. Eliot. Empire M.H., September 13, 1909.

SUPERIORITY. C. Ant. Brewer. 1607.

SUPPER DANCES. C. 1 a. Sir W. L. Young. Publ. by S. French, Limited.

SUPPER FOR TWO; OR, THE WOLF AND THE LAMB. F. J. W. Gifford. Glasgow Princess's T., November 23, 1883.

SUPPER GRATIS. F. 1 a. W. Reeve. Publ. by S. French, Limited.

SUPPLIANTS, THE. T. Transl. fr. Euripides by M. Wodhull. 1782.

SUPPLICANTS, THE. T. Transl. fr. Euripides by R. Potter. 1777 and 1781. See "Greek Plays."

SUPPLICATION OF PIERCE PENNILESS, ETC. Nash. 1592.

SUPPLICE D'UN HOMME, LE. See *The Member for Slocum*.

SUPPOSED INCONSISTENCY. P. Anon. Entered Stationers' Co., November 29, 1653.

SUPPOSES, THE. C. Geo. Gascoigne. Fr. Ariosto. Gray's Inn, 1566. Pr. 1587.

SUPREMACY. Sk. Woolwich Hipp., July 26, 1909.

SUPREMACY. Sk. Chelsea Palace, August 2, 1909.

SURCOUF. See *Paul Jones*.

SURE TO WIN. D. Huddersfield Gymnasium T., May 2, 1876.

SURE TO WIN. Sporting P. 1 a. W. H. Goldsmith. Novelty, November 16, 1896.

SURENA. C. Corneille. 1674. See "French Classical Plays."

SURPRISAL, THE. T.C. Sir R. Howard. T.R., 1665; D.L., August 19, 1715. Pr. 1665.

SURPRISE, A. Protean Sk. C. W. Calvert. St Geo H., May 22, 1897.

SURPRISE, THE. Droll. (Fr. *The Maid in the Mill.*) Pr. 1672.

SURPRISES; OR, A DAY IN CONEY ISLAND. M.C. 3 a. C. Burnette. Workington T.R., October 3, 1890.

SURPRISES DE L'AMOUR, LES. O. 3 a. Rameau. July 12, 1757.

SURRENDER OF CALAIS. P. 3 a. G. Colman, jun. D.L., May 30, 1814, and May 14, 1817; rev., June 25, 1823.

SURRENDER OF CALAIS. Hist. D. Anon. Pr. York, 1801.

SURRENDER OF CALAIS, THE. Lib. by Planché. M. by H. Smart. N. comp.

SURRENDER OF TRINIDAD; OR, SAFE MOORED AT LAST. D. C.G., May 11, 1797. N.p.

SURRENDER OF VALENCIENNES, THE. Mus. Mil. Spec. Doncaster, November, 1793. N.p.

SUSAN HOPLEY. C. 1 a. Publ. by S. French, Ltd.

SUSAN HOPLEY; OR, THE VICISSITUDES OF A SERVANT GIRL. D. 3 a. G. Dibdin Pitt. Roy. Victoria T., May 31, 1841.

SUSAN IN SEARCH OF A HUSBAND. F. 4 a. J. K. Jerome. Scala, March 16, 1906 C.P.

SUSAN SMITH. Princess's, October 29, 1860.

SUSANNA. P. Thos. Garter. Entered by Thos. Colwell at Stationers' H., 1568 to 1569. Pr. 1578.

SUSANNA; OR, INNOCENCE PRESERVED. M.D. Elizabeth Tollett. 1755.

SUSANNA'S TEARS. Langbaine. Langbaine and Jacob mention a P. of this name.

SUSANNAH. Orat. Set by Handel. C.G. Pr. 1743.

SUSANNAH—AND SOME OTHERS. C. 4 a. Mme. Albanesi. Royalty, January 22, 1908.

SUSPECTED. Scena. Norwich R., January 7, 1905.

SUSPICION. D. Britannia, August 11, 1875.

SUSPICIOUS HUSBAND. C. 5 a. B. Hoadley. C.G., February 12, 1747; D.L., August 23, 1817.

SUSPICIOUS HUSBAND CRITICISED; OR, THE PLAGUE OF ENVY. F. Chas. Macklin. D.L., March 24, 1747.

SUZANNE. Petite D. M. by T. G. Reed. D.L., June 22, 1841.

SUZANNE. M.C. M. Paladilhe. Lib. by H. S. Leigh. Portsmouth T.R., March 1, 1884.

SUZERAINE. P. 4 a. Dario Nicodemi. F. on H. Harland's novel, "The Lady Paramount." Royalty, June 18, 1906.

SWADDLERS. C. Anon. Pr. N.d. Before 1814.

SWAGGERING DAMSEL, THE. C. R. Chamberlain. Pr. 1640.

SWALLOW'S NEST, THE. Marylebone, May 25, 1863.

SWANHITO. O. 1 a. Haeffer and Pascal. Publ. by S. French, Ltd.

SWASHBUCKLER, THE. C. 4 a. Louis N. Parker. Duke of York's, November 17, 1900.

SWATLANA. O. Y. Arnold. 1854.

SWAY BOAT, THE. P. 3 a. Wilfred T. Coleby. Kingsway, October 9, 1908.

SWEDISH PATRIOTISM. M.D. C.G., May, 1819.

SWEDLAND, KING OF. P. Anon. Destroyed by Warburton's servant.

SWEENEY TODD; THE BARBER OF FLEET STREET; OR, THE STRING OF PEARLS. D. 3 a. F. Hazleton. Bower T., 1862.

SWEEP FOR A KING. Mythical Ro. Harry Bruce. Hoxton T., April 2, 1888.

SWEEPSTAKES. M.C. 1 a. E. Lake. Terry's, May 21, 1891.

SWEET AND TWENTY. C. 3 a. Basil Hood. Vaudeville, April 24, 1901.

SWEET BELLS JANGLED. C.D. 3 a. Mr. Hastings. Olympic, June 28, 1879.

SWEET BRIAR. M.P. 3 a. H. Shelley. M. by Grabau. Bath T.R., June 6, 1898; Hammersmith Lyric, July 4, 1898.

SWEET CUPID'S NET. C. 3 a. J. Cross. Strand, April 21, 1892.

SWEET DECEPTION, A. 1 a. N. Doone. Brompton Hospital, November 24, 1898.

SWEET GIRL, THE. M.P. 2 a. Adap. fr. the German of Alexander Landesberg and Leo Stein by E. Demain Grange. M. by Rheinhardt, added M. by Ernest Irving. Kennington Princess of Wales's, July 26, 1902; rev., Nottingham T.R., August 27, 1906.

SWEET INNISFAIL. Irish D. 4 a. W. Reynolds. Manchester Queen's T., August 16, 1886.

SWEET INNISFAIL. Sk. Richmond Hipp., October 26, 1908.

SWEET KITTY BELLAIRS. C. 4 a. D. Belasco. F. on Egerton Castle's novel, "The Bath Comedy." Hay., October 5, 1907.

SWEET LAVENDER. C. 3 a. A. W. Pinero. Terry's, March 21, 1888 (ran for 683 perfs.)

SWEET MISTRESS DOROTHY. Sk. Roy Redgrave. Foresters', May 18, 1908.

SWEET NANCY. C. 3 a. Adap. fr. Rhoda Broughton by R. Buchanan. Lyric, July 12, 1890; Royalty, October 6, 1890; Court, February 8, 1897; Avenue, January 6, 1898.

SWEET NELL OF OLD DRURY. P. 4 a. P. Kester. Hay., August 30, 1900.

SWEET OLDEN DAYS. Ca. 1 a. H. C. Dalroy. Plymouth T.R., October 15, 1894.

SWEET OLIVIA. P. 3 a. F. by C. Hannan on Oliver Goldsmith's "Vicar of Wakefield." Leamington New T.R., March 27, 1903; W. London, March 29, 1905.

SWEET PRUE. D. 1 a. Claude Dickens Court, February 11, 1901.

SWEET REVENGE; OR, ALL IN HONOUR. D. 3 a. J. Fox and J. F. McArdle. Liverpool T.R., April 17, 1876; Pavilion, June 22, 1878.

SWEET SEVENTEEN. C. 3 a. F. De Lara. Brighton Aquarium, November 26, 1894.

SWEET SIMPLICITY. C. W. F. Field. Southall Public Rooms, February 23, 1891.

SWEET WILL. C. 1 a. H. A. Jones. (1st perf.), New Club, C.G., March 5, 1887; Shaftesbury, July 25, 1890.

SWEETHEART, GOOD-BYE. Ca. 1 a. Mrs. Fairbairn. Scarborough T.R., October 10, 1881.

SWEETHEART, GOOD-BYE. Ca. M. Holt. Strand, December 22, 1884.

SWEETHEARTS. D. Contrast. 2 a. W. S. Gilbert. P.O.W., November 7, 1874.

SWEETHEARTS AND WIVES. O.C. Kenney. Hay., July, 1823; Lyceum, 1823.

SWETNAM, THE WOMAN-HATER, ARRAIGNED BY WOMEN. C. Anon. Ac. by the Queen's servants at the Red Bull, 1620.

SWIFT AND VANESSA. D. 4 a. A. O'D. Bartholeyns. P. Royalty, January 11, 1904.

SWINDLER, THE. C. 2 a. Pr. 1785.

SWINDLER; OR, THE CAPTIVE MAID, THE. D. A. Campbell. Britannia, August 25, 1873.

SWINDLERS, THE. F. D.L., April 25, 1774. N.p.

SWINEHERD AND THE PRINCESS, THE. M.P. 3 a. F. on Hans Andersen's story. Royalty, December 19, 1901.

SWING BRIDGE, THE. M.D. 2 a. M. by Mr. Reeve. Lyceum play bill, July 1, 1823.

SWISS COTTAGE; OR, WHY DON'T SHE MARRY, THE. V. A. H. Bayley. D.L., January 15, 1852. Stamped at Birmingham, May 31, 1852.

SWISS EXPRESS, THE. Pan. F. A. H. Gilbert and C. Renad. Princess's, December 26, 1891.

SWISS GUIDE, THE. M.D. Sk. 3 sc. Albert M. Hall. April 22, 1901.

SWISS SWAINS. O. 1 a. B. Webster. Publ. by S. French, Ltd.

SWISS VILLAGERS, THE. Past. Ballet. By Noble. D.L., February 3, 1823.

SWITZER, THE. P. A. Wilson. Ent. Stationers' Co., September 4, 1646. N.p.

SWITZERLAND. T. 5 a. D.L., February 15, 1819.

SWOP, THE. F. Anon. Hay., June 22, 1789. N.p.

SWORD, THE. C. Berquin. 1793.

SWORD AND THE HAND. T. Beer. 1832.

SWORD OF DAMOCLES, THE. F. Fr. the German by Phillip Darwin. Middlesex Asylum T., November 14, 1880; St. George's H., January 11, 1890.

SWORD OF HONOUR, THE. P. 3 a. L. Montague. Liverpool Balfour Inst., January 19, 1907.

SWORD OF JUSTICE, THE. Sk. Percy Ford. Camberwell Empire, June 1, 1908.

SWORD OF PEACE; OR, A VOYAGE OF LOVE, THE. C. Mrs. Starke. Hay., August 9, 1789.

SWORD OF THE KING, THE. Rom. P. 4 a. Ronald Macdonald. Wyndham's, April 9, 1904.

SWORDS INTO ANCHORS. C. Blaneh. Pr. 1725.

SWORDSMAN'S DAUGHTER, THE. D. 5 a. Adap. by B. Thomas and C. Scott fr. *Le Maître d'Armes*. Adelphi, August 31, 1895.

SYBIL; OR, LOVE RULES. Idyl. Mr. Haxell. Terry's, September 25, 1889.

SYBIL; OR, THE ELDER BRUTUS. P. Mr. Cumberland. N.p.

SYBIL, THE HUNCHBACK. D. Prol. and 3 a. F. Ford. Huddersfield T.R., April 14, 1873; Marylebone, June 22, 1874.

SYBILLA; OR, STEP BY STEP. C.D. 3 a. J. P. Simpson. St. James's T., October 29, 1864.

SYBYLE; OR, WEARY OF BONDAGE. D. 4 a. Charing C., October 22, 1873.

SYDNEY CARTON. P. Prol. and 4 a. F. on Dickens's "Tale of Two Cities," by T. E. Pemberton. Norwich T.R., January 2, 1893.

SYDNEY CARTON'S SACRIFICE. Sk. Based on Dickens's "Tale of Two Cities." B. Soane Roby. Camberwell Palace, January 28, 1907.

SYLLA. D. Ent. Tr. Mr. Derrick. 1753.

SYLLA'S GHOST. D. Satirical Piece. Anon. 1689.

SYLPH, THE Dramatised R. C. Leftley. 1802.

SYLPHIDE, LA. Ballet. 2 a. Lib. by A. Nourrit. M. by Schneitzhoffer. Paris, March 12, 1832; C.G., July 26, 1832; D.L., July 27, 1835, and May 8, 1837.

SYLPHIDE, THE. Extrav. 1 a. W. Brough. Princess's T., April 9, 1860.

SYLPHS; OR, HARLEQUINS' GAMBOLS, THE. Pant. M. by Fisher. C.G., 1774.

SYLVAIN. Op. C. Marmontel. M. by Grétry. 1770.

SYLVAN STATUE; OR, THE FESTIVAL OF THE FAUNS, THE. Extrav. H. F. Arden. Surrey Zool. Gardens, May 13, 1872.

SYLVANA. O. Weber. 1810. Alt. fr. *The Wood Girl*. See *Silvana*.

SYLVIA. Bal. Pant. 2 a. and 3 tab. Lib. by Barbier. M. by Leo Delibes. Paris, January 14, 1876.

SYLVIA. Bal. Pant. 2 a. and 3 tab. Lib. SOPHER. C. Anon. 1800. N.ac.

SYLVIA. O. 3 a. Lib. by M. Parry. M. by Dr. J. Parry. Cardiff T.R., August 12, 1895.

SYLVIA; OR, THE BARON'S BRIDE. R.O. 3 a. M. J. Blatchford. M. by J. H. Sykes. Halifax Grand T., October 20, 1891.

SYLVIA; OR, THE COUNTY BURIAL. Ballad O. G. Lillo. T.R., L.I.F., November 10, 1730. Pr. 1731.

SYLVIA; OR, THE FOREST FLOWER. New Royalty, February 17, 1866.

SYLVIA OF THE LETTERS. P. 4 a. Jerome K. Jerome. Playhouse, October 15, 1907.

SYLVIA'S ROMANCE. Ca. L. Olde. Perf. by the Old Stagers at Canterbury, August 8, 1899.

SYMPATHETIC SOULS. P. 1 a. Adap. by Sydney Grundy fr. Eugène Scribe's *Les Inconsolables*. Kennington T., February 26, 1900.

SYMPATHY. Ca. 1 a. A. W. Dubourg. Manchester T.R., April 29, 1873.

SYNDICATE, THE. F.C. 2 a. Adelene Votieri. St. George's H., June 16, 1897 (mat.).

SYRACUSAN, THE. T. Dr. Dodd. 1750. N.p.

SYRACUSIAN GOSSIPS, THE. Int. 3 a. Mr. Polwhele. 1786.

SYREN, THE. O. Auber. D.L., October 14, 1844. See *La Sirene*.

SYREN OF PARIS, THE. Rom. D. 2 a. Adap. fr. the French by W. Suter. Queen's, April 1, 1861.

SYRENS, THE. Masque. 2 a. Captain E. Thompson. C.G., 1776.

SYSTEM OF LAVATER; OR, THE KNIGHTS OF THE PAST. M.F. Anon. 1797. Edinburgh. N.p.

SYSTEMATIC OR IMAGINARY PHILOSOPHER. C. Anon. 1800. N.ac.

T

TABITHA'S COURTSHIP. Comedy, February 18, 1890.

TABLE D'HOTE. C. 1 a. Hamilton Aidé. Publ. by S. French, Ltd.

TABLEAU PARLANT, LE. Grétry. 1769.

TABLES, THE. P. 1 a. Lady Bancroft. Criterion, June 3, 1901.

TABOO, THE. Leamington, May 22, 1894.

TACT. Avenue, March 14, 1885.

TAFFY'S TRIUMPH. Liverpool T.R., August 10, 1874.

TAG IN TRIBULATION. Int. 1 a. T. Dibdin. C.G., May 7, 1799. N.p.

TAILOR MAKES THE MAN. Globe, February 21, 1876.

TAILORS; OR, A TRAGEDY FOR WARM WEATHER, THE. Burl. 3 a. Colman. Hay., July 2, 1767.

TAKE BACK THE HEART. Eastbourne, June 1, 1886.

TAKE CARE OF DOWB. F. 1 a. J. M. Morton. Publ. by S. French, Ltd.

TAKE THAT GIRL AWAY. F. 2 a. L. S. Buckingham. Publ. by S. French, Ltd.

TAKEN BY FORCE. Novelty, March 8, 1897.

TAKEN BY STORM. F. 1 a. A. Maltby. Publ. by S. French, Ltd.

TAKEN FOR GRANTED. Ca. 1 a. Reg. W. Cusin. Publ. by S. French, Ltd.

TAKEN FROM LIFE. D. 5 a. H. Pettitt. Adelphi, December 31, 1881.

TAKEN FROM MEMORY. Brit., November 10, 1873.

TAKEN FROM THE FRENCH. C. 1 a. J. M. Morton. Publ. by S. French, Ltd.

TAKING BY STORM. Lyceum, May 31, 1852.

TAKING IT EASY. Toole's, November, 1882.

TAKING THE BULL BY THE HORNS. Hammersmith, June 6, 1889.

TAKING THE WATERS. St. Geo. H., November 1, 1886.

TAKING THE VEIL. D. 3 a. C. H. Hazlewood. Brit., July 30, 1870.

TALBOT'S TRUST. Globe, September 13, 1875.

TALE IN A TUB. Ladbroke H., January 23, 1893.

TALE OF A COAT. Hay., November 6, 1858.

TALE OF A COMET. C. 1 a. F. L. Horne. Publ. by S. French, Ltd.

TALE OF A TELEGRAM. F.C. M. C. Martyn. Barnes. Cleveland H., February 21, 1903.

TALE OF A TELEPHONE. D.L., January 12, 1879.

TALE OF A TIGRESS, THE. Sk. Mark Melford. Clapham G.T., April 22, 1907.

TALE OF A TUB, A. C. Ben Jonson. Pr. 1640.

TALE OF A TUB. Duke's, March 16, 1876.

TALE OF A MYSTERY. Melo-d. Thos. Holcroft. C.G., November 13, 1802.

TALE OF MANTUA. Knowles. 1830.

TALE OF OLD CHINA, A. F. C. Burnand and Molloy. St. Geo. H. circa 1865.

TALE OF TELL. Darwen T.R., February 26, 1883.

TALE OF TERROR, A. D. Rom. Henry Siddons. C.G., May 12, 1803.

TALE OF THE CASTLE, A; OR, WHO IS SHE LIKE? C. 5 a. Edinburgh, 1793. N.p.

TALE OF THE THAMES. Surrey, October 28, 1895.

TALE OF TROY. Prince's Hall, May 14, 1886.

TALE OF TWO CITIES. Lyceum, January 30, 1860.

TALE OF TWO CITIES. See *Sydney Carton*.

TALES OF HOFFMAN. O. Jacques Offenbach. Adelphi (German season), April 17, 1907.

TALES OF THE HALL. See *Love or Life*.

TALISMAN, THE. F. Anon. Hay., 1784. N.p.

TALISMAN, THE. Burl. J. F. McArdle. Liverpool T.R., August 10, 1874.

TALISMAN, THE. Burl. Philharmonic, March 29, 1875.

TALISMAN; OR, KING RICHARD CŒUR DE LION AND THE KNIGHT OF THE COUCHANT LEOPARD, THE. Burl. M. J. G. Reed. D.L., March 28, 1853.

TALISMANO, IL. O. 3 a. Adap. fr. Italian by Zaffira. M. by M. W. Balfe. D.L., June 11, 1874; Liverpool R. Court T., January 15, 1891.

TALK OF THE DEVIL. Olympic, 1831.

TALK OF THE TOWN, THE. C. 4 a. A. E. Drinkwater. Cork O.H., December 4, 1896.

TALK OF THE TOWN, THE. F. 3 a. Eille Norwood. A rev. ver. of *The Noble Art*, which see. Strand, August 10, 1901.

TALK OF THE TOWN, THE. M.C. Seymour Hicks. M. by H. E. Haines. Lyrics, C. Taylor.. Additions by H. M'Cunn and E. Baker. Lyric, January 5, 1905.

TALLOW CHANDLER BEWITCHED; OR, LOVE'S DISGUISES, THE. F. A. Rhodes. Greenwich, November 28, 1868.

TALLY HO! V. 1 a. T. M. Watson. M. A. Caldicott. St. George's H., November 9, 1887.

TALLY HO! C. 3 a. "Henry Whitestone." Bradford R.T., November 28, 1907.

TALPÆ. T. Singleton. February 7, 1688-9. N.p.

TAM O' SHANTER. F. 2 a. H. R. Addison. D.L., November 25, 1834.

TAM O' SHANTER. Burl. W. Lowe. Dundee O.H., February 10, 1873.

TAM O' SHANTER; OR, THE BRIG O' DOON. Extrav. Glasgow R. Colosseum T. and O.H., June 1, 1868.

TAMAR CAM. Plot only existing. Anon. Mentioned by Barker.

TAMAR, PRINCE OF NUBIA. T. Michael Clancy, M.D. Smock Alley, Dublin, 1739. N.p.

TAME CAT, A. Ca. L. N. Parker. Matinée T., June 21, 1898.

TAME CATS. C. 3 a. Edmund Yates P.O.W., December 12, 1868.

TAMER TAMED. P. Fletcher. See *Woman's Prize*. Pr. 1647.

TAMER TAM'D. Alt. fr. Beaumont and Fletcher's *Woman's Prize*. Margrairne of Anspach's private T., Brandenburg House, June 9, 1795. N.p.

TAMERLAN ET BAJAZET. Ballet. Bishop. King's, 1806.

TAMBERLANE. T. Nicholas Rowe. L.I.F., 1702; D.L., November 6, 1815; C.G., November 9, 1819.

TAMBERLANE. T. Part 11. Anon. MS. in possession of Mr. Stephen Jones.

TAMBERLANE THE GREAT. T. C. Saunders. T.R., 1681.

TAMBERLAINE THE GREAT; OR, THE SCYTHIAN SHEPHERD. T. 2 parts. 2 p. 5a. C. Marlowe. Ac. before 1587. Pr. fl., 1590; Lord Admiral's servants, 1593.

TAMERLANO. O. Pescetti (with Cocchi). Venice, 1754.

TAMING A TIGER. F. 1 a. Adap. fr. the French.

TAMING A TRUANT. C. 3 a. Publ. by S. French, Ltd.

TAMING OF A SHREW, THE. Pleasaunt Conceited Historie, by the Right Honourable the Earl of Pembroke. 1596.

TAMING OF THE SHREW. C. Wm. Shakespeare. F. on an old P., *The Taminge of a Shrewe* (possibly written by Marlowe in 1589), and on the *Supposes* of Gascoigne, transl. fr. Ariosto, 1566. Ent. Stationers' Co., May 2, 1594; January 22, 1607; November 19, 1607. Pr. 1st folio, 1623; 1st quarto from 1st folio, 1631. Ac. at Hounslows T., 1593. Recent rev. (ver. by A. Daly), Gaiety, May 29, 1888; Lyceum, July 8, 1890; Daly's, June 27, 1893; Comedy, January 2, 1901; Adelphi (in 4 a.), September 29, 1904; Adelphi, June 2, 1906; Oxford New T., by the O.U.D.S., February 6. 1907; Coronet, February 29, 1908; Aldwych, June 22, 1908.

TAMING OF THE SHREW. O. 4 a. Goetz. Transl. into Eng. by Rev. J. Troutbeck. D.L., October 12, 1878; Her M., January 20, 1880.

TAMING THE TRUANT. C. 3 a. H. Wigan. Olympic, March 19, 1863.

TAMLIN. An "auld sang." 1 a. Lady Archibald Campbell. Edinburgh T.R., November 27, 1899.

TAMWORTH IN A.D. 670; OR, THE PAGAN KING, THE CHRISTIAN BISHOP, AND THE PRINCELY MARTYRS OF EAGLE'S HALL. Hist. P. 5 a. Tamworth Pavilion, August 22, 1894.

TANCRED. T. Sir Henry Wotton. N.p.

TANCRED. O. Monteverde (1568-1643).

TANCRED AND GISMUND. T. Robert Wilmot. Acted before Her Majesty by the Gentlemen of the Inner Temple. 1592.

TANCRED AND SIGISMUNDA. F. Jas. Thomson. D.L., March 18, 1745.

TANCREDI. O. Rossini (Venice, February 6, 1813). King's T., 1818, and May 4, 1820.

TANGERINE TANGLE, A. C.O. 2 a. Norman D. Slee. M. by W. Slaughter and Marjorie Slaughter. Vaudeville, July 2, 1909.

TANGLE, A. P. 1 a. George Knight, Liverpool Shakespeare, July 26, 1894.

TANGLED CHAIN, A. Adap. fr. Mrs. Panton's novel by Miss H. Lindley. P.O.W., March 6, 1888.

TANGLED SKEIN, A. D. 3 a. O. Allen and D. Fleck. Grecian, August 19, 1872.

TANGLED SKEIN, A. P. 1 a. H. Tuite. Glasgow Royalty, February 24, 1905 (C.P.).; Nenagh H., January 10, 1908.

TANGLED SKEIN, THE. P. Baroness Orezy and Montagu Barstow. Coronet, March 30, 1908 (C.P.).

TANGLED WEB, A. C. 4 a. V. Chester. Criterion, July 3, 1884.

TANGLED WEB, A. D. 4 a. V. Fenn. Cardiff T.R., April 10, 1902.

TANNER OF DENMARKE, THE. Recorded in Henslowe's Register. May 28, 1591. N.p.

TANNHAUSER (Tannhäuser und der Sängerkrieg auf Wartburg). Rom. o. 3 a. R. Wagner. (Dresden, October 19, 1845.) C.G., May 6, 1876; Her M. T., February 14, 1882.

TANTALUS; OR, MANY A SLIP 'TWIXT CUP AND LIP. Burl. A. Matthison and C. Wyndham. Folly, October 14, 1878.

TANTALUS AT LAW. C. 1 a. Holcroft. 1789.

TANTARA RARA; OR, ROGUES ALL. F. Transl. fr. the French. John O'Keefe. C.G., March 1, 1788. Pr. 1798.

TARADIDDLES; OR, WHITE LIES. F. 1 a. T. W. Stones-Davidson, Shereham Swiss Gardens T., July 31, 1890 (C.P.).

TARANTULA. F. Dent. Lost. Mentioned by Barker.

TARANTULA, THE. Mary A. Scott. Hay., September 4, 1897.

TARANTULA; OR, THE SPIDER KING, THE. Extrav. A. Smith. Adelphi, December 26, 1850.

TARANTULE, LA. Ballet. 2 a. M. by Gide. D.L., March 18, 1846.

TARARA; OR, THE BRIGAND'S TRUST. C.O. R. T. Nicholson. Loughton, Lopping H., November 28, 1907.

TARARE. O. James and Beaumarchais. 1787.

TARES. 3 a. Mrs. Oscar Beringer. P.O.W., January 31, 1888; Op. C., January 21, 1889.

TARRARE, THE TARTAR CHIEF. O. M. by Solieri. Lyceum, August 15, 1825.

TARS AT TORBAY; OR, SAILORS ON SATURDAY NIGHT. Int. Anon. Hay., 1799.

TARS ON SHORE; OR, LOVE AND JOLLITY. M.P. D.L., June 26, 1818.

TARSIS ET ZELIE. O. F. Rebel and F. Francœur. Académie, 1728.

TARTAR WITCH; OR, THE PEDLAR BOY, THE.

TARTUFFE. Molière. See "French Classical Plays."

TARTUFFE; OR, THE FRENCH PURITAN. C. M. Medbourne. T.R., 1670, and L.I.F., June 20, 1718. Pr. 1670.

TARTUFFE; OR, THE HYPOCRITE. C. Transl. fr. Molière by John Ozell.

TARUGO'S WILES; OR, THE COFFEE HOUSE. C. Sir T. St. Serfe. Duke of York's T. 1668.

TASSO'S MELANCHOLY. P. Acted according to Henslowe. August 12, 1594. N.p.

TASTE. F. 2 a. S. Foote. D.L., January 11, 1752.

TASTE AND FEELING. D. caricature. Anon. Hay., August 13, 1790.

TATTERCOATS. M.P. in prologue and 3 sc. Adap. fr. an Old English fairy tale. M. by Alfred Scott-Gatty and Nicholas C. Gatty. Lyrics by Alfred Scott-Gatty, lib. by Robert Stewart. Savoy, February 22, 1900; February 5, 1902.

TATTERLEY. Rom. P. 4 a. Adap. fr. Tom Gallon's novel of the same name, by the author and Arthur Shirley. Southampton Grand, December 12, 1898.

TATTLER; OR, INDISCREET LOVER, THE. C. Transl. fr. Voltaire. Mentioned by Barker.

TATTLERS, THE. C. Dr. Benj. Hoadly. C.G., April 29, 1797.

TATTOOED MAN, THE. C.O. 2 a. Books and lyrics by H. B. Smith. M. by V. Herbert. Bayswater Bijou, February 11, 1907.

TAUNTON VALE. D. 3 a. L. N. Parker Manchester T.R., June 12, 1890.

TAVERN BILKERS. Pant. John Weaver. D.L., 1702.

TAVERNE DES TRABANS, LA. O. 3 a. C. Maréchal. Paris Op. Com., 1881.

TAWNO'S BRIDE. Burl. 2 a. E. W. Bowles and G. R. Phillips. M. by T. M. Clarke. St. Geo. H., February 16, 1892 (amat.).

TAXES, THE. D. Ent. Dr. Bacon. 1757.

TAXI, THE. Sk. Wal Pink. Clapham Grand, April 12, 1909.

TCHAO CHI COU ELL; OR, THE LITTLE ORPHAN OF THE FAMILY OF TOCHOO. T. R. Brooks, 1737.

TEA. F.C. 3 a. M. Noel. Torquay Bath Saloon, January 11, 1807; Criterion, May 4, 1887.

TEA AT FOUR O'CLOCK. C. Mrs. Burton Harrison. Madison Sq. T., January 13, 1887.

TEA SHOP STRIKE, THE. Sk. H. M. Vernon. Hackney Empire, June 1, 1908.

TEACHER TAUGHT. C. 1 a. Sir W. L. Young. Publ. by S. French, Ltd.

TEACHER TAUGHT, THE. F. 1 a. E. Stirling. Sadler's Wells T., October 17, 1850.

TEAGUE'S RAMBLE TO LONDON. Int. Hay., 1770. N.p.

TEAROOM; OR, FICTION AND REALITY. Anon. 1811.

TEARS. C. B. Rowe. Op. C., February 17, 1877.

TEARS AND TRIUMPHS OF PARNASSUS. Ode. R. Lloyd. 1760.

TEARS, IDLE TEARS. D. 1 a. C. Scott. Globe, December 4, 1872.

TEARS OF BRITAIN; OR, THE FUNERAL OF LORD NELSON. D. Sk. E. J. Eyre. N.ac. N.d.

TEASING MADE EASY. C. 3 a. Jameson. Hay., July 30, 1817; September 7, 1824.

TECALCO. O. 1 a. M. H. Spier. Terry's, May 24, 1889.

TECHNOGAMIA; OR, THE MARRIAGE OF THE ARTS. C., or Morality. B. Holiday. Ac. by the Students of Christ Church, Oxford, 1618 and 1630.

TEDDY. See *Teddy's Wives.*

TEDDY SMILES; THE SPORTSMAN. Sk. Camberwell Empire, June 10, 1907.

TEDDY THE TILER. F. 1 a. Taken fr. the French by G. H. Rodwell; C.G., February 8, 1830; D.L., September 24, 1832.

TEDDY TRAVERS. C. 3 a. O. P. Martin, Ladbroke H., April 16, 1907.

TEDDY'S WIVES. F.C. 3 a. F. Hume. Eastbourne T.R., April 4, 1896 (as *Teddy*); Kilburn T.R., August 1, 1896; Strand, September 24, 1896. See *Mormon.*

TEETOTAL FAMILY. F. A. Halliday. R. Alexandra T., Liverpool; April 7, 1869.

TEKELI. Melo-d. 3 a. T. E. Hook, 1806. D.L., June, 1808, and June 20, 1817; and March 17, 1835.

TELEGRAM, THE. Strand, November 23, 1857.

TELEGRAM, THE. P. by Sapte. Globe, November 12, 1888.

TELEGRAPH, THE; OR, A NEW WAY OF KNOWING THINGS. C. John Dent. C.G., April 8, 1795.

TELEMACHUS. Masque. Geo. Graham. 1763.

TELEMACHUS. O. Bishop, C.G., June, 1815.

TELEMACHUS; OR, THE ISLAND OF CALYPSO. Classical and mythological extrav. J. R. Planché and C. Dance. Olympic T., December 26, 1834.

TELEMACCO. Gnua. Munich, 1780.

TELEMACO. O. A. Scarlatti. 1718.

TELEMAQUE. O. Boieldieu. (1775-1834.)

TELEPHONE, THE. F. 1 a. Arthur Clements. Strand T., April 22, 1878.

TELEPHONE GIRL, THE. M.C. 2 a. Lib. by A. Harris, F. C. Burnand, and A. Sturgess. M. by G. Serpette and J. M. Glover. Wolverhampton Grand, May 25, 1896; Camberwell Metropole, July 27, 1896.

TELL, AND THE STRIKE OF THE CANTONS; OR, THE PAIR, THE MEDDLER, AND THE APPLE. Fairy Rom. F. Talfourd. Strand, December 26, 1859.

TELL RE-TOLD; OR, THE PLOT, THE PATRIOT, AND THE PIPPIN. Burl. 2 a. H. W. Capper and H. Walther. M. by C. Locknane. St. Geo. H., February 12, 1894.

TELL TRUTH AND SHAME THE DEVIL. A. 2 a. William Dunlap. Perf. by the Old American Company in New York, 1797. C.G., May 18, 1799.

TELL WITH A VENGEANCE. Burl. H. J. Byron. Publ. by S. French, Ltd.

TELLTALE, THE. C. Anon. 1661. N.p.

TEMISTOOLE. D. Metastasio, 1738.

TEMPER; OR, THE DOMESTIC TYRANT. F. 2 a. Lyceum, May 1, 1809.

TEMPERANCE DOCTOR, THE. D. 2 a. H. Seymour. Publ. by S. French, Ltd.

TEMPERANCE REFORMER, THE. Sk. Empress, July 12, 1909.

TEMPEST. C. William Shakespeare. 1610-11. A pamphlet describing the tempest of July, 1609, which dispersed the fleet of Sir George Somers and Sir Thomas Gates, in which the Admiral's ship was wrecked on the island of Bermuda, was published December, 1609. The narrative, in which the Bermudas is called the Island of Devils, is dated October 13, 1610. *The True Declaration of the Council of Virginia*, publ. 1610, was founded on above. Ac. at Blackfriars, 1611; vers. by Shadwell, (?) 1673; vers. by J. Dryden and Sir W. Davenant, with second title, *The Enchanted Island*, added. Dorset Gardens, 1670; Duke of York's, 1676; vers. by D. Garrick, D.L., 1756; vers. by R. B. Sheridan, 1777; vers. by J. C. Kemble, D.L., 1789; Lyceum, April 5, 1900; prod. by J. H. Leigh, Court, October 26, 1903; vers. by Beerbohm Tree, H.M., September 13, 1904; April 25, 1905.

TEMPEST, THE. O. Purcell (1658-95).

TEMPEST. O. Halévy. Her M., July 8, 1849.

TEMPEST, THE. See *Prospero*.

TEMPEST IN TEACUPS. O. 2 a. C. Pirkis and Adrian Ross. M., Florean Pascal. St. George's Parish Hall, Forest Hill, December 13, 1899.

TEMPEST OF THE HEART. D. 3 a. W. Travers. E. London, March 8, 1868.

TEMPEST TOSSED. D. 4 a. E. Darby. Marylebone, November 15, 1886.

TEMPLAR, THE. D. A. R. Slous. Princess's, November 9, 1850.

TEMPLAR AND THE JEWESS, THE. D. Marschner. D.L., May 26, 1841.

TEMPLE, THE. Masque. George Chapman. 1614.

TEMPLE BEAU, THE. C. H. Fielding. New T., Goodman's Fields, January 26, 1730.

TEMPLE DE LA GLOIRE. O. Voltaire. 1744.

TEMPLE DE LA GLOIRE, LE. Fête in 3 a. and pro. Rameau, November 27, 1745.

TEMPLE MASQUE, THE. Masque. 1618.

TEMPLE OF DEATH. D. Adap. fr. French by H. M. Milner. Victoria, December 26, 1821.

TEMPLE OF DULLNESS, THE. C.O. Colley Cibber. D.L., January 17, 1745.

TEMPLE OF HYMEN. M. Wignell. 1762.

TEMPLE OF LOVE. Masque. Sir Wm. Davenant and Inigo Jones. 1634. Ac. by the Queen and her Ladies on Shrove Tuesday, 1634.

TEMPLE OF LOVE. Past. O. Motteux and Signor J. Saggione. Haymarket, March 7, 1706.

TEMPLE OF PEACE, THE. Masque. 1 a Anon. Dublin, 1749.

TEMPLE OF VESTA, THE. D. Poem. Rev. H. Boyd. Pr. in Dublin, 1793.

TEMPLE RESTOR'D. Masque. A. Townshend. Presented at Whitehall by Q. and Ladies of Honour, 1631.

TEMPLER AND JUDIN. O. Marschner (1796-1861). F. on Sir W. Scott's *Ivanhoe*.

TEMPORAL POWER. P. 5 a. Marie Corelli. Morecambe, August 23, 1902.

TEMPTATION. M. Play. Chas. Carte. T.R., Scarborough, August 12, 1895.

TEMPTATION. D. 4 a. Russel Vaun. Hammersmith Lyric, June 21, 1909.

TEMPTATION, THE. D. Mrs. T. P. O'Connor. Liverpool Shakespeare, June 1, 1905.

TEMPTATION; OR, THE FATAL BRAND. D. 2 a. W. T. Townsend.

TEMPTATION OF CHRIST, OF THE. Bishop Bale. 1538. N.p.

TEMPTATION OF MAN, THE. Ac. at Norwich, 1565.

TEMPTATION OF SAMUEL BURGE, THE. F. W. W. Jacobs and Fredk. Fenn. Imperial, November 9, 1905.

TEMPTATIONS OF THE GREAT CITY. D. 4 a. E. Montefiore. Bath T.R., October 3, 1898.

TEMPTED. D. E. Reynolds. Longton T.R., December 2, 1872.

TEMPTED, THE. D. Lieut.-Colonel Addeson. Norwich T.R., November 24, 1871.

TEMPTED, FALLEN, AND SAVED. D. 5 a. Cheltenham T.R., October 24, 1871.

TEMPTED TO SIN. D. 5 a. A. Conquest and H. Whyte. Surrey, November 3, 1902.

TEMPTER, THE. Poet. P. 4 a. H. A. Jones. Hay., September 20, 1893.

TEMPTER OF WOMEN, THE. C.D. 4 a. Clifford Rean. T.R., Aston, July 25, 1904; Stratford T.R., September 12, 1904.

TEMPTING BAIT, A. F. W. J. Austin. Op. C., October 16, 1875.

TEMPTRESS, THE. M. 4 a. W. P. Sheen. Wigan T.R., May 10, 1900; P.T., Broughton, June 23, 1902; Pavilion, February 29, 1904.

TEN DANCING PRINCESSES. Fairy Extrav. 1 a. L. Debenham. Publ. by S. French, Ltd.

TEN MINUTES FOR REFRESHMENTS. M. Sk. Lib. by R. Mansfield. M. by J. M. Glover. Olympic, January 14, 1882.

TEN NIGHTS IN A BAR-ROOM. D. 5 a. W. Pratt. Publ. by S. French, Ltd.

TEN O'CLOCK SQUAD, THE. M. Sk. H. M. Vernon. Lyrics by C. Wilmot and M. by H. E. Darewski, jun. Shepherd's Bush Empire, April 1, 1908; Canterbury, February 8, 1909.

TEN OF 'EM. Op. bo. Adap. by A. Matthison. M. by F. von Suppé. D.L., December 2, 1874.

TEN POUNDS D. 2 a. Publ. by S. French, Ltd.

TEN-THIRTY (10.30) DOWN EXPRESS. THE. Melo-d. 5 a. Horace Stanley. Bootle, Muncaster T., June 19, 1899.

TEN THOUSAND A YEAR. Adap. of S. Warren's novel by Peake. Adelphi, November, 1841.

TEN TORTURED TUTORS. Extrav. 1 a. W. Heighway. Publ. by S. French, Ltd.

TEN YEARS HENCE. C. 2 a. Mary Seymour. Publ. by S. French, Ltd.

TENANT FOR LIFE. Sadler's Wells, November 1, 1858.

TENDER CHORD, THE. F. C. 2 a. J. Mortimer. Charing Cross, April 19, 1873.

TENDER CHORD, THE. Rom. Adap. from the French by Alfred Maltby. Terry's, June 27, 1899.

TENDER HUSBAND; OR, THE ACCOMPLISHED FOOLS, THE. C. by Sir R. Steele. F. on Moliére's "Le Sicilien ou l'Amour Paintre." T.R., 1703; D.L., April 23, 1705.

TENDER PRECAUTIONS; OR, THE ROMANCE OF MARRIAGE. C. 1 a. T. J. Serle. Royal Princess's November 24, 1851.

TENDER SISTERS, THE. C. Transl. by Gilbert. 1805.

TENDER WIFE, THE. C. A. MS. sold as part of the library of the late Mr. Arthur Murphy.

TENNIS. Ca. L. B. Eastwood. Swansea T.R., March 6, 1893.

TENTERHOOKS. F. C. 3 a. H. M. Paull. Comedy, May 1, 1889.

TENTH OF AUGUST, THE. P. 3 a. Alexandre von Herder. New., December 16, 1907.

TEODOSIO, IL. O. 3 a. Scarlatti. Naples, 1709.

TERAMINTA. O. Henry Carey. M. by J. C. Smith. L.I.F., 1732.

TERAPH, THE. C.D. 2 a. Mr. Hedworth Williamson. T.R., Darlington, January 26, 1900; Court, May 29, 1900.

TEREMENT, THE. See "Miracle Plays."

TERENCE. C. 4 a. Adap. by Mrs. B. M. Croker fr. her novel of same name. (Orig. prod. Margate R., February 18, 1907.) Dublin Gaiety, March 1, 1909.

TERESA. P. 3 a. G. P. Bancroft. Camberwell Metropole, May 16, 1898; Garrick, September 8, 1898.

TERM DAY; OR, THE UNJUST STEWARD. C. 5 a. T. Houston, of Newcastle. Pr. 1803.

TERMAGANT, THE. P. 4 a. Louis N. Parker and Murray Carson. H.M., September 1, 1898.

TERPISCHORE. New Div. D.L., June 5, 1855.

TERPSICHORE. P. 1 a. Justin H. McCarthy. Lyric, July 12, 1894.

TERPSICHORE'S RETURN. Ballet. D.L., November, 1805.

TERRIBLE FRIGHT, A. Vaude. Arthur Law. M. by Corney Grain. St. Geo. Hall, June 18, 1884.

TERRIBLE SECRET, A. F. 1 a. J. Stirling Coyne. D.L., October 28, 1861.

TERRIBLE SECRET, A. D. 3 a. W. R. Waldron. Colne Free Trade Hall, September 30, 1889.

TERRIBLE TINKER, A. F. 1 a. T. J. Williams. Astley's, December 27, 1869.

TERRIBLE TRILBY. Burl. Harry Pleon. Brighton Eden T., March 12, 1896.

TERRITORIALS. Sk. Bedford, January 11, 1909; Brixton Empress, February 22, 1909.

TERROR, THE. Dr. Epis. Bertha Moore. Royal Albert Hall, June 28, 1907.

TERROR OF LONDON, THE. D. W. James and Harold Whyte. Grecian, October 23, 1879.

TERROR OF PARIS, THE. D. 4 a. E. Hill Mitchelson and Charles Longden. Burnley Victoria O.H., July 2, 1894; Pav., June 24, 1895.

TERRORISTS, THE. Sk. Paragon, November 11, 1907.

TERRORS OF A GAY CITY, THE. Melo-d. 4 a. George Lyttleton. Cradley Heath T.R., January 21, 1897.

TERRY; OR, TRUE TO HIS TRUST. P. 1 a. Sutton Vane. Parkhurst, April 27, 1891.

TESS. P. 4 a. Adap. by H. Mountford fr. Thomas Hardy's novel "Tess of the D'Urbervilles." Blackpool Grand, January 5, 1900.

TESS. P. 4 a. Adap. by H. A. Kennedy from Thomas Hardy's novel, "Tess of the D'Urbervilles." Coronet, February 19, 1900; Comedy, April 14, 1900.

TESS. O. 4 a. In Italian. Frederic d'Erlanger (from "Tess of the D'Urbervilles," by Thomas Hardy). Lib. by Luigi Illics. C.G., July 14, 1909.

TESS OF THE D'URBERVILLES. Adap. of Thomas Hardy's novel by Lorimer Stoddart. St. James's, March 2, 1897 (C.P.).

TEST, A. D. 1 a. Alec Nelson and Philip Bourke Marston. Ladbroke Hall, December 15, 1885.

TEST, THE. P. 3 a. T. W. Eastwood. Court, January 3, 1909.

TEST MATCH, THE. M.S. Fred Burgoyne and Guy Jones. Camberwell Metropole, October 1, 1900.

TEST OF FRIENDSHIP, A. Sk. Percy Ford. Camberwell Empire, March 25, 1907.

TEST OF GUILT; OR, TRAITS OF ANCIENT SUPERSTITION, THE. Metrical Dr. Tale. Joseph Strutt. Pr. 1808.

TEST OF LOVE, THE. M.E. Transl. fr. the French by Robinson. Hay., August 17, 1787.

TEST OF TRUTH; OR, IT'S A LONG LANE THAT HAS NO TURNING, THE. C. 2 a. Wm. E. Suter. T. de la Porte Saint Martin, September 6, 1806. Ver. called *Bird in Hand Worth Two in Bush* played at Surrey, January 19, 1857.

TEST OF UNION AND LOYALTY, THE. Piece wr. and spoken by W. F. Sullivan. Pr. 1797.

TESTAMENT ORC LES BILLETS-DOUX, LE. O. Auber. O. Comique, 1819.

TESTIMONIAL, THE. P. 1 a. Adap. fr. Max Maurey's *La Recommendation*. Terry's, May 23, 1909.

TESTY LORD, THE. Title under which the comic scenes of *The Maid's Tragedy* were afterwards played.

TETHY'S FESTIVAL; OR, THE QUEEN'S WAKE. Masque. Samuel Daniel. Whitehall, June 5, 1610.

TEUZONE. O. A. Ariosti. 1727.

TEXAN, THE. P. 4 a. Tyrone Power. Princess's, June 21, 1894.

TEXAS WOOING, A. Sk. C. B. Middleton. Bedford M.H., May 3, 1909.

THAD; OR, LINKED BY LOVE. C. 3 a. Paul Meritt. Grecian, July 29, 1872.

THAIS. O. Massenet. Setting of Anatole France's Rom. 1894.

THALABA, THE DESTROYER. Spec. D. Fitzball. Victoria, August, 1822.

THALIA'S TEACUP; OR, THE DELIGHTS OF DECEIT. C. 3 a. Norreys Connell. Court, July 24, 1909.

THALIA'S TEARS. Poetical effusion. Andrew Cherry. D.L., December 12, 1806. N.p.

THAMES; OR, ADRIFT ON THE TIDE, THE. D. 4 a. R. Dodson. Surrey, September 29, 1879.

THANKS TO JACK. Ca. Evelyn Hardie. Eastbourne Devonshire Park, April 11, 1891.

THAT AFFAIR AT FINCHLEY. C. Sk. 1 a. J. Stirling Coyne. Strand, October 14, 1861.

THAT AWFUL BOY. F. W. F. Miller. Southampton P.O.W., January 15, 1891.

THAT AWFUL LEGACY. F. Percy Warlow. Stalybridge Grand, September 27, 1898.

THAT BEASTLY CHILD. Sk. Mark Melford. Middlesex, January 9, 1899.

THAT BEAUTIFUL BICEPS. F. H. Saville Clarke. D.L., September 23, 1876.

THAT BEAUTIFUL WRETCH. D. Adap. fr. the French. Liverpool Bijou O.H., December 26, 1881.

THAT BLESSED BABY. F. Moore. Adelphi, February 11, 1856.

THAT BRUTE SIMMONS. P. 1 a. Arthur Morrison and Herbert C. Sergeant. New, August 30, 1904.

THAT CHARMING MRS. SPENCER. C. 3 a. Adelene Votieri. Ipswich Lyceum, November 18, 1897.

THAT COUPLE FROM CUBA. F. H. T. Johnson. Edinburgh Lyceum, May 27, 1898.

THAT DID IT. "Tabloid M.C." Wr. by Eustace Burnaby and H. S. Browning. M. by E. Burnaby. Lyrics by G. Grossmith, jun., and Ralph Roberts. Crouch End Hipp., May 11, 1908.

THAT DOCTOR CUPID. Fantastic C. 3 a. Robert Buchanan. Partly suggested by Foote's farce, *The Devil Upon Two Sticks*. Vaudeville, January 14, 1889.

THAT DREADFUL BOY. V. Gilbert à Beckett. M. by Corney Grain. St. Geo. Hall, December 26, 1882.

THAT DREADFUL DOCTOR. Ca. 1 a. Sir C. L. Young.

THAT DREADFUL MENU. Dom. "Breeze." Corney Grain. St. Geo. Hall. October 29, 1894.

THAT EASTERN ANOMALY. Criterion, May 3, 1905.

THAT FATAL HOUR. Sk. Clive F. Curry. Shepherd's Bush Athenæum, October 8, 1895.

THAT FOREIGNER. "Tariff Reform P." Mr. Alan H Burgoyne. Bayswater Bijou, February 27, 1908 (amat.).

THAT FRENCHWOMAN. F. Mary Ellis Smith. Ladbroke Hall, January 7, 1903.

THAT GIRL. C. 3 a. F. on a story by Clementina Black, by Mrs. O. Beringer and Henry Hamilton. Hay., July 30, 1890.

THAT GIRL CARROTS. Sk. Standard, December 14, 1908.

THAT HAT. C. Sk. Wal Pink. The London, February 20, 1899.

THAT HORRID BIGGINS. New Royalty, January 29, 1866.

THAT HOUSE IN HIGH STREET. Strand, July 28, 1856.

THAT IDIOT CARLO. Ca. Philip Hayman. Blackburn T.R., February 12, 1891.

THAT IMPIOUS PIANO. P. 1 a. Lyddell Sawyer. Scala, December 17, 1906 (amat.).

THAT MAN AND I. P. Pro. and 4 a. Mrs. Frances Hodgson Burnett. New, October 24, 1903 (C.P.).

THAT MYSTERIOUS NOVEL. Oa. 1 a. M. by Lita Jarratt. Steinway Hall, April 2, 1897.

THAT NAUGHTY CAN-CAN. F. W. J. Sorrell. Edinburgh Princess's, November 24, 1873.

THAT ODIOUS CAPTAIN CUTTER. Ca. 1 a. J. Palgrave Simpson. Olympic, February 21, 1851.

THAT RASCAL PAT. F. 1 a. J. Holmes Grover. Publ. by S. French, Ltd.

THAT RASCAL RUDOLPH. Oa. Knight Summers. M. by Denham Harrison. Bayswater Bijou, March 29, 1807.

THAT RING. F. V. C. Rolfe. St. Geo. Hall, May 4, 1893.

THAT SISTER OF MINE. Ca. S. J. Adair-Fitzgerald. St. Geo. Hall, December 10, 1900.

THAT TELEGRAM. F. W. Sapte, jun. Globe, November 12, 1888.

THAT TERRIBLE GIRL. M.F.C. 3 a. J. Stephens. Royalty, March 9, 1895.

THAT TERRIBLE TOMBOY. M.C. 2 a. A Wood. M. by C. Legrand. Windsor T.R., March 9, 1903.

THAT TERRIBLE TURK AND HIS LOVING LEGACY. M.C. Wr. by F. W. Sidney. Lyrics by Eardley Turner. M. by Odoardo Barri. Lib. adap. from a *Loving Legacy*. Clapham Shakespeare, April 4, 1898.

THAT WILL BE SHALL BE. P. First ac. in December, 1596.

THAT WOMAN FROM FRANCE. D. 4 a. Frank M. Thorne Nottingham King's T., March 27, 1902; Manchester, August 25, 1902; Surrey, September 15, 1902.

THAT WOMAN IN PINK. M. Ca. Herbert Harraden, Terry's, April 30, 1891.

THAT WRETCH OF A WOMAN. D. 4 a. Walter Melville. Standard, November 4, 1901.

THAT YOUNG MAN. C. 3 a. F. upon *Der Elephant* of Von Moser. By Edwd. Rose. Oxford T.H., December 1, 1884.

THAT'S WHY SHE LOVED HIM. C. Preston T.R., May 8, 1876.

THAT'S WHY SHE LOVED HIM. D. 4 a. Such Granville. R. Aquarium T., August 3, 1878.

THEAGENE ET CHARICLEE. T. Racine. 1662.

THEATRE OF APOLLO, THE. Masque. Preserved in British Museum.

THEATRE OF EDUCATION, THE. Transl. fr. the Fr. of the Countess of Genlis. Collection of small dr. pieces in three volumes. Pr. 1781.

THEATRES, THE. F. Anon. Pr. 1733.

THEATRIC COUNT, THE. T.C. 5 a. Adap. of Bicchieri's *Orgoglio Cupitoso* and *Conte Teatrino*. Pr. 1809.

THEATRICAL CANDIDATES, THE. M.P. David Garrick. D.L., 1775. Ac. at opening of the theatre after alterations.

THEATRICAL MANAGERS, THE. Dr. Sat. Pr. 1751. Abuse on Mr. Garrick.

"THEATRICAL RECORDER, THE." A monthly publication, edited by Mr. Holcroft, 1744-1809, which contained a number of dr. transl. fr. French, Italian, Spanish, and German. 2 vols.

THEBAIDE, LA. T. Racine. 1664. See "French Classical Plays."

THEBAIS. T. Thos. Newton. 1581. Transl. fr. Seneca.

THEBAIS. T. Transl. fr. Seneca by Sir E. Sherburne, Bart.

THEFT FOR A LIFE, A. D. T. B. Bannister. Wolverhampton P.D.W., April 23, 1877; Gloucester T.R., August 16, 1882.

THEIR EXPERIMENT. P. Mrs. de Courcy Laffan. West T., Albert Hall, April 20, 1904.

THEIR NEW PAYING GUEST. F. 1 a. Publ. by S. French, Ltd.

THEIR REAL SELVES. Duol. Bertha Graham. 92, Victoria St., S.W., February 17, 1905.

THELYPTHORA; OR, MORE WIVES THAN ONE. F. F. Pilon. C.G., March 8, 1781. N.p.

THELYPTHORA; OR, THE BLESSINGS OF TWO WIVES AT ONCE. C. F. Whimsical colloquial piece. 1 a. Thomas Knight. C.G., March 8, 1781; Hull, 1783.

THEMIS. F.C. 3 a. and 4 sc. Adap. fr. the Fr. of Victirien Sardou by H. P. Stevens. Royalty, March 29, 1880.

THEMISTOCLE. O. 3 a. F. A. D. Philidor. May 25, 1786.

THEMISTOCLES. O. Transl. fr. *Metastasio*. John Hoole. Ptd. 1800.

THEMISTOCLES, THE LOVER OF HIS COUNTRY. T. Dr. Samuel Madden. L.I.F., February 10, 1729.

THEN! AND NOW! Mus. satirical Sk. Corney Grain. St. Geo. H., March 30, 1891.

THEN FLOWERS GREW FAIRER. Piece. 1 a. Sutton Vane. Ealing Lyric H., August 12, 1892; Terry's, August 30, 1894.

THEODORA. O. Dr. Morell. M. by Handel. Pr. 1749.

THEODORA. T. 5 a. Miss Baillie. Not ac. before 1814

THEODORA. P. 6 a. and 8 tab. Robert Buchanan. Adap. fr. Victorien Sardou's piece (originally prod. at the Porte St. Martin, December 26, 1884; Brighton T.R., November 11, 1889; Princess's, May 5, 1890; Olympic (new), August 1, 1891.

THEODORA. See *The O'Doro*.

THEODORA; OR, THE SPANISH DAUGHTER. T. Lady Burrell. Pr. 1800.

THEODORA, ACTRESS AND EMPRESS. Original His. D. 5 a. Watts Phillips. New Surrey, April 9, 1866.

THEODORE. O. J. H. Colls. Pr. 1805.

THEODORE. Corneille. See "French Classical Plays."

THEODORICK, KING OF DENMARK. T. "Young Gentlewoman." F. on "Ildegarte." Pr 1752.

THEODOSIUS: OR, THE FORCE OF LOVE. T. F. on Gomberville's "Pharamond." Nathaniel Lee. Duke's T. Pr. 1680.

THEODOSIUS; OR, THE FORCE OF LOVE. Lee's T. Set to m. by Purcell, and prod. as English opera.

THEOMACHIA. Latin C. Peter Heylin. 1618. N.p.

THEORY AND PRACTICE. Duol. 1 a. Arthur Benham. Terry's, April 28, 1893. Independent T. perf.

THERE AND BACK. F.C. 3 a. Geo. Arlis. Bath T.R., December 7, 1895 (C.P.); Bolton T.R., October 19, 1900; Prince of Wales's, May 22, 1902.

THERE'S MANY A SLIP 'TWIXT CUP AND LIFE. C. 3 a. Robt. W. Hall. St. Geo., January 4, 1877.

THERE'S MANY A SLIP 'TWIXT CUP AND LIP. Ver., 3 a., Robert Marshall, of Scribe and Legouvé's comedy, *Bataille de Dames*. Hay., August 23, 1902.

THERESE. Princess's, April 26, 1850.

THERESE, ORPHAN OF GENEVA. Kerr. Mentioned by Brewer.

THERESE RAQUIN. D. 4 a. Emile Zola. Transl. by A. Teixeira de Mattos. Royalty, October 9, 1891.

THERESE, THE ORPHAN OF GENEVA. D. 3 a. John H. Payne. M. by Horn. D.L., February 2, 1821.

THERMIDOR. P. 4 a. Victorien Sardou. Comedie Française. January 24, 1891.; Op. C., May 23, 1892. Fr. season conducted by Coquelin ainé.

THERMOPYLÆ; OR, REPULSED INVASION. T.D. 3 a. J. P. Roberdeau. An enlargement of Glover's poem, "Leonidas." Gosport Naval Academy, April, 1805.

THERSYTES, HIS HUMOURS AND CONCEITS. Int. Anon. 1598. See "Miracle Plays."

THESEE. O. 5 a. Lulli. Paris, January 11, 1675.

THESEE. O. J. C. Mondonville (his last O.). Paris, 1767.

THESEUS. O Handel. 1715.

THESEUS AND ARIADNE; OR, THE MARRIAGE OF BACCHUS. Classical extrav. 2 a. J. R. Planché. Lyceum, March 2, 1848.

THESMOPHORIAZUSÆ. C. (B.C. 410.) Aristophanes. Transl. fr. the Greek by Mitchell, 1820-22; Hickie, 1853; and Rudd, 1867. See "Greek Plays."

THESPIS; OR, THE GODS GROWN OLD. W. S. Gilbert.

THESPIS AMONG THE OLYMPIANS. Operatic extrav. W. S. Gilbert. Gaiety, December 26, 1871.

THETIS AND PELEUS; OR, THE CHAIN OF ROSES. Mythological love story. 1 a. Author of "Princesses in the Tower," etc. Punch's. New Strand T., October 27, 1851.

THEY ALL LOVE JACK. D. 4 a. C. A. Clarke. Bootle, Muncaster T., October 3, 1898.

THEY WERE MARRIED. C. 4 a. Adap. fr. W. Besant's story of that name by J. R. Cranford and Fredk. Hawley. Strand, June 17, 1892.

THEY'VE BIT THE OLD ONE; OR, THE SCHEMING BUTLER. Int. J. C. Cross. C.G., May 1, 1798. N.p.

THICKER THAN WATER. Sk. Brixton Empress, October 14, 1908.

THIEF, THE. P. 3 a. Cosmo Gordon Lennox. Adap. fr. the French of Henry Bernstein. (Orig. prod. St. James's, November 12, 1907). Rev. St. James's, May 8, 1909

THIEF IN THE NIGHT, A. P. 4 a. G. Carlton Wallace. Eleph. and Castle, August 2, 1909.

THIEF MAKER, THE. D. Pro. and 3 a. Edward Towers. E. London, February 1, 1878.

THIERNA-NA-OGO; OR, THE PRINCE OF THE LAKES. Melo. fairy tale. F. on traditions of S. of Ireland. M. by Cooke. D.L., April 20, 1829.

THIERRY AND THEODORET. T. Beaumont and Fletcher. Blackfriars. Ptd. 1621. Ac. before 1616.

THIEVES, THE. See *Die Biberpetz.*

THIEVES OF LONDON. D. R. S. Gresham. Hoxton King's, January 28, 1907.

THIEVES OF PARIS. D. Stirling. 1856.

THIEVES! THIEVES! Olympic, March 12, 1857.

THIEVES' COMEDY, THE. P. G. Hauptmann. Transl. by C. F. Moles. Court, March 21, 1905.

THIMBLE'S FLIGHT FROM HIS SHOP-BOARD. Comic piece. 1 a. Hay., August 25, 1789.

THIMBLERIG, THE. F. Buckstone.

THIN ICE. P. 1 a. Cyril Twyford. Garrick, January 19, 1909.

THIN RED LINE, THE. Sk. E. C. Matthews. Walthamstow Palace, July 12, 1907.

THING OF RAGS AND PATCHES, A. P. 1 a. Max Montesole and Corvus Rex. Swansea Grand, November 9, 1907.

THIRD CLASS AND FIRST CLASS. Britannia, August 1, 1859.

THIRD TIME, THE. Ca. Ch. H. Dickinson. St. Geo. H., February 22, 1896.

THIRD TIME OF ASKING, THE. C. 1 a. M. E. Francis. Garrick, May 30, 1906.

THIRST FOR GOLD, THE. D. Adap. fr. the Fr. Adelphi, December, 1853; Olympic, March 20, 1869.

"1313." C. 2 a. Frank Desprez. Folly, May 7, 1879.

THIRTIETH OF OCTOBER, THE. Play. Anon. N.p. Entered on Stationers' Company's book, 1560

THIRTY THIEVES, THE. M. extrav. 2 a. W. H. Risque. Terry's, January 1, 1901.

THIRTY THOUSAND; OR, WHO'S THE RICHEST? O. Thos. Dibdin. M. by Braham, Davy, and Reeve. Ptd. 1805. C.G., December 10, 1804.

£30,000; OR, THE DREAD SECRET. D. Pro. and 2 a. L. W. Harleigh. Elephant and Castle, October 11, 1875; Barnsley T. of V., May 8, 1876.

THIRTY-THREE NEXT BIRTHDAY. F. 1 a. J. M. Morton. Princess's, November 22, 1858.

THIRTY-THREE TO ONE CHANCE, A. Sk. R. Heaton Gray. Sadler's Wells, July 12, 1909.

THIRTY YEARS IN SIBERIA. D. in Hebrew. Standard, September 22, 1896.

THIRTY YEARS OF A GAMBLER'S LIFE. Adelphi, 1827.

THIRTY YEARS OF A WOMAN'S LIFE. D. J. B. Buckstone. Adelphi, January, 1834.

THIS HILL IS DANGEROUS TO CYCLISTS. Playlet. Alicia A. Leith. Kensington Queen's Gate H., December 4, 1900.

THIS HOUSE TO LET. D. Pro. and 3 a. E. Towers. East London, September 11, 1869.

THIS HOUSE TO LET. O. M. by Jacques Greebes. Lib. by Edward Oxenford. Brighton R. Aquarium, June 21, 1884.

THIS PLOT OF GROUND TO LET. F. Alexandra, January 26, 1874.

THIS WOMAN AND THAT. P. 3 a. Pierre Leclercq. Globe. August 2, 1890.

THIS WOMAN AND THIS MAN. P. 3 a. Avery Hopwood. Bayswater Bijou, January 18, 1909 (C.P.).

THIS WORLD OF OURS. D. 4 a. Seymour Hicks Brighton T.R., July 20, 1891; Pavilion, August 1, 1892.

THISTLE AND RAMPANT LION, THE. Extrav. Dundee O.H., March 11, 1872.

THOMAS A BECKET. T. Tennyson. 1780.

THOMAS AND SALLY. Mus. enter. Carey.

THOMAS AND SALLY; OR, THE SAILOR'S RETURN. Mus. enter. 2 a. Isaac Bickerstaff. M. by Dr. Arne. C.G., November 28, 1760; Edinburgh, 1782

THOMAS AND SUSAN; OR, THE FORTUNATE TAR. Mus. enter. Royalty, 1787.

THOMAS CHATTERTON. 1 a. Pl., 3 episodes. Mlle. Coquelicot. Ladbroke Hall, July 25, 1901.

THOMAS DOUGH. P. Wm. Haughton, in conjunction with John Day. Ac. 1601. N.p.

THOMAS LORD CROMWELL. See "Cromwell."

THOMAS MERRY. T. Wm. Haughton, in conjunction with John Day. Ac. 1599.

THOMAS STROWDE. Parts II. and III. (Part I. not mentioned.) Wm. Haughton and John Day. Ac. 1601. Probably the same as *The Blind Beggar of Bethnal Green.*

THOMAS, THE RHYMER. Fairy Oa. Evelyn L. Thomas. M. by John Farmer. Marlborough T.H., March 30, 1894.

THOMASO; OR, THE WANDERER. In two parts. Thomas Killigrew. Pr. 1664. Both parts acted.

THOMPSON'S VISIT. F. John T. Douglass. Standard, September 23, 1872.

THOMYRIS, QUEEN OF SCYTHIA. O. Peter Motteux T.R. in D.L.

THORGRIM. Rom. O. 4 a. M. by Dr. F. H. Cowen. Lib. by Joseph Bennett. F. on the Icelandic rom., "Viglund the Fair." D.L., April 22, 1890. Perf. by the Carl Rosa Op.

THORNEY ABBEY; OR, THE LONDON MAID. T. by "T. W." 1662.

THORNEYCROFT COUSINS, THE. O. 3 a. Lib. and part of the M. by Col. Thorneycroft; remainder of the M. by Ardrani. Wolverhampton, Tettenhall Towers, private T., April 17, 1888.

THOROUGH BASE. Oa. 1 a. Wds. by T. Edgar Pemberton. M. by T. Anderton. Birmingham Bijou T., April 7, 1884.

THOROUGHBRED. Comic P. 3 a. Ralph R Lumley. Toole's, February 13, 1895.

THORSTEIN ABBEY. C.O., in pro. and 2 a. Rev. H. D. Hinde. M. comp. by the Misses E. Wykes, R. E. Teague, and L. Stocks. Southgate Village H., January 6, 1909 (amat.).

THOSE FATAL FETTERS. Dr. Sk. Edith Lennin. Marlborough Rooms, Regent Street, W., November 8, 1901.

THOSE HORRID GAROTTERS. F. Olympic, February 3, 1873

THOSE LANDLADIES! Duol. 1 a. Ina Leon Cassilis.

THOSE MYSTERIOUS SHOTS. Oa. Cecil Deane. M. by Noel Coonyn. St. Geo. H., June 28, 1894.

THOSE PAPERS. Sk. Wal Pink. Middlesex, September, 1899.

THOSE TERRIBLE TWINS. F.C. 3 a. B. A. B. Cardiff T.R., June 25, 1900.

THOSE VOLUNTEERS. C. Brandon Ellis. Bath T.R., September 20, 1875.

THOSE ——— PUT ASUNDER. C.D. 1 a. Claude Trevelyan. Acton Central Hall, December 15, 1897.

THOU SHALT NOT KILL. D. 4 a. F. A. Scudamore. Shakespeare, July 31, 1899.

£1,000 REWARD. Pro. and 4 a. Messrs. Cordyce and Roberts. December 15, 1892. As pro. and 3 a. Charles Rogers. Cardiff G.T., March 6, 1893; Pavilion, July 16, 1894; Novelty, February 3, 1896.

THRACIAN WONDER, THE. C. Hist. John Webster and Wm. Rowley. Pr. 1661. Ac. with great success.

THREAD OF SILK, A. C. 3 a. Arthur Matthison. Crystal Palace, November 3, 1881.

THREATENING EYE, THE. D. 4 a. E. L. Knight and John Jourdain. Greenwich P.O.W., May 12, 1885.

THREE AND THE DEUCE; OR, WHICH IS WHICH? C.D. 3 a. Prince Hoare. Taken from Spanish comedy, *Los Tres Mellizos*. Hay., 1795; Lyceum playbill, April 22, 1809; D.L., March 14, 1814; Lyceum playbill, July 17, 1823.

THREE BARROWS, THE. P. 4 a. Chas. McEvoy. Manchester Gaiety, March 22, 1909; Coronet, June 10, 1909

THREE BEARS, THE. M.P. Wr. and comp. by A. S. Scott Gatty. Vaudeville, June 20, 1907.

THREE BEGGARS; OR, A NIGHT AT AN INN, THE. C.O. 2 a. Wds. by Sinclair Dunn. M. by Ed. Belville. R.A.M., July 28, 188[illegible].

THREE BLACK SEALS, THE. Hist. D. Stirling. 1864.

THREE BLIND MICE. C. 3 a. Arthur Law. Margate T.R., July 30, 1906; Criterion, February 14, 1907.

THREE BLIND MICE; OR, THE RIGHT MARIA. C. 3 a. Brandon Ellis. Grimsby T R., March 5, 1883.

THREE BROTHERS, THE. T. Wentworth Smith. Ac. by Lord Admiral's servants, 1602. N.p.

THREE CONJURORS, THE. Political Int. Pr. 1763.

THREE CONSPIRATORS, THE. M. Sk. Alfred Thompson. Belfast T.R., October 16, 1874.

THREE CRIMINALS, THE. See *Two Men*.

THREE CRUMPS; OR, THE CROOKED BROTHERS OF DAMASCUS, THE. The Sans Pareil, 1818.

THREE CUCKOOS, THE. F. 1 a. J. M. Morton. Hay., March 13, 1850.

THREE DAUGHTERS OF M. DUPONT, THE. C. 4 a. E. Brieux. Transl. by St. J. Hankin. C.G. King's Hall, March 12, 1905.

THREE DEEP. F. By Lunn. Partly taken fr. the Fr. C.G., May 2, 1826.

THREE DOCTORS, THE. F. R. T. Gammon. Hatfield, February 6, 1896.

THREE DOROTHIES; OR, JODELET BOX'D, THE. C. Transl. fr. Scarron in 1657 by Sir Wm Lower. N.p.

THREE FAIRY GIFTS. Fairy P. 1 a. Florence Davenport Adams. Worthing Assembly Rooms, April 7, 1896.

THREE FISHERS, THE. P. 1 a. Leopold Montague. Crediton T.H., November 15, 1905 (C.P.).

THREE FURIES, THE. Orig. Ca. 1 a. Geo. Roberts. St. James's, March 13, 1865.

THREE GRACES, THE. Burl. G. A'Beckett. Princess's, April, 1843.

THREE GRACES, THE. C. 4 a. H. Beale Collins. Kingston R. County, February 11, 1898.

THREE GRACES, THE. C. 3 a. W. R. Waldron. Norton Thespian T., May 31, 1904 (amat.).

THREE GREAT WORTHIES. Standard, October 1, 1866.

THREE HATS, THE. F.C. 3 a. Adap. fr. "Les Trois Chapeaux" of M. Alfred Hennequin by Owen Dove and Alfred Maltby. Bath T.R., June 22, 1883; Royalty, December 20, 1883.

THREE HATS, THE. New ver. of Alfred Hennequin's "Les Trois Chapeaux" by H. Cory Woodrow Ealing Lyric, June 11, 1896.

THREE HATS. F.C. 3 a. Hennequin. Adap. by Arthur Shirley. Reading T.R. Perf. in London, provinces, America, and Australia.

THREE HATS, THE. A. à Beckett and Edouard Marlois. St. Geo. H.

THREE HOURS AFTER MARRIAGE. C. 3 a. Messrs. Gay, Pope, and Arbuthnot. D.L., January 16, 1717.

THREE HUNCHBACKS, THE. F. Maurice de Frece. Liverpool T.R., April 15, 1872.

THREE IN A PICKLE. Sk. Paragon, September 7, 1907.

THREE KEYS. D. 4 a. Harry Croft Hillier. Manchester St. James's, June 7, 1888.

THREE KINGS OF COLEYN (Cologne). See "Miracle Plays."

THREE KISSES, THE. M.P. 2 a. Book by P. Greenbank and L. Bantock. Lyrics by P. Greenbank M. by H. Talbot. Apollo, August 21, 1907.

THREE LADIES OF LONDON, THE. C. By R. W. Pr. 1584.

THREE LAWS OF NATURE. Bishop Bale. 1538. See Int. concerning, etc.

THREE LINES A SHILLING. F. Sk. Malcolm Lisle. W. London, April 21, 1906.

THREE LITTLE BRITONS. Naval and military Spec. D. 4 a. A. Newman and E. Turney. Torquay T.R., July 30, 1908.

THREE LITTLE HEARTS OF GOLD. M.C. R. L. Cavendish and S. E. Blythe. Devonport Metropole, July 18, 1904.

THREE LITTLE MAIDS. M.P. 3 a. Wr. and comp. by Paul Rubens, and additional numbers by H. Talbot and Percy Greenbank. Apollo, May 10, 1902.

THREE LORDS AND THREE LADIES OF LONDON. R. W. Pr. 1590.

THREE MEN IN A BOAT. Sk. Euston, August 30, 1903.

THREE MERRY BOYS, THE. Taken fr. *The Bloody Brother*.

THREE MILES FROM PARIS. P. 1 a. C.G., January 15, 1818.

THREE MILLIONS OF MONEY. C. 4 a. F. Lyster and J. Mackay. St. James's, October 14, 1876.

THREE MUSKET-DEARS AND A LITTLE ONE IN, THE. Orig. military Burl. Joseph and Harry Paulton. Strand, October 5, 1871,

THREE MUSKETEERS, THE. Adap. fr. Dumas's novel. "Les Trois Mousquetaires," by C Dillon, C. Rice, and Aug. Harris. Lyceum, October 16, 1856.

THREE MUSKETEERS, THE. City of London, June 1, 1857.

THREE MUSKETEERS, THE. P. 5 a. Dramatised from Dumas's novel by Max Goldberg. Manchester St. James's, August 8, 1892; Manchester Royal Osborne, November 21, 1898.

THREE MUSKETEERS, THE. Rom. D. 4 a. Adap. fr. Dumas's novel of the same name. W. Heron-Brown. Imperial, June 25, 1898 (C.P.).

THREE MUSKETEERS, THE. D. Ver. of Dumas's novel. Pro. and 4 a. H. A. Saintsbury. Holloway Parkhurst, September 5, 1898.

THREE MUSKETEERS, THE. Ver. of Dumas's novel by Henry Hamilton. Camberwell Metropole, September 12, 1898; Globe, October 22, 1898; Lyceum. November 3, 1900; rev. Lyric, March 3, 1909.

THREE MUSKETEERS, THE. Adap. fr. Dumas's novel by Brian Daly and J. M. East. Hammersmith Lyric, November 7, 1898.

THREE MUSKETEERS, THE. P. 5 a. Adap. fr. Dumas's famous novel by F. Carl. St. Leonards Pier Pavilion T., January 16, 1899.

THREE MUSKETEERS, THE. O.D. 3 a. Herbert Whitney. M. by Reginald Somerville. Liverpool R. Court, March 24, 1899.

THREE MUSKETEERS, THE. P. 5 a. Adap. by Ernest Norris fr. Dumas's novel. Crouch End O.H., March 31, 1902.

THREE MUSKETEERS; OR, THE QUEEN, THE CARDINAL, AND THE ADVENTURER, THE. D. 3 a. Chas. Rice. F. on Dumas's novel. Manchester, August 2, 1850; Britannia, October 24, 1898; rev. Lyric, May 1, 1909.

THREE OF A KIND. American farcelet. Canterbury, January 4, 1904.

THREE OF A SUIT. C.D. 3 a. Forbes Dawson. Bournemouth T.R., June 10, 1901; New Cross Broadway, February 3, 1902.

THREE OF US, THE. P. 4 a. Rachel Crothers. Orig. prod. in America. Terry's, June 10, 1908.

THREE OLD WOMEN WEATHERWISE, THE. See *The Old Women.*

THREE OUTLAWS, THE. Adap. 1 a. Fr. the story of the same name by Sir Gilbert Parker. Worthing T.R., May 11, 1903; Fulham Grand, May 18, 1903.

THREE PER CENTS, THE. C. F. Reynolds. C G. November 12, 1903. N.p.

THREE PERILS; OR, WINE, WOMEN, AND GAMBLING, THE D. 3 a. Fred. Marchant. Britannia, October 5, 1870.

THREE PLAYS IN ONE. Ac. by Her Majesty's servants at Somerset Place. 1585.

THREE PRINCES, THE. Surrey, April 1, 1850.

THREE RED MEN; OR, THE BROTHERS OF BLUETHANPT, THE. Rom. D. 3 a. Thos. Archer. Ac. 1848.

THREE SELECT SCENES OF GUARINI'S PASTOR FIDO. Daniel Bellamy, jun. Pr. 1746.

THREE SISTERS OF MANTUA, THE. Ac. by the Earl of Warwick's servants, 1578.

THREE SOUND NAPS. O. Sir J. Carr. N.p. before 1814.

THREE STRANGERS, THE. C. Miss Lee. 1835.

THREE TENANTS. O. 1 a. A'Becket and Reed. Publ. by S. French, Ltd.

THREE THIEVES, THE. Sk. Hackney Empire, February 17, 1908.

THREE TURNS, THE. F.C. 3 a. Mrs. R. Pacheco and Chas. Dickson. Lyrics by Otto A. Hauerbact. M. by Karl Koschna. Bayswater Bijou, March 3, 1908.

THREE VICES OVERCOME TRUTH AND CHASTITY. Int. Sir David Lindsay. Pr. 1792.

THREE WARNINGS, THE. D. Alfred Rayner. New Pavilion. March 30, 1872.

THREE WARNINGS—RUIN, DEGRADATION AND DEATH, THE. D. A. Warner. Hanley T.R., October 20, 1873.

THREE WAYFARERS, THE. P. 1 a. Thomas Hardy. Terry's, June 3, 1893.

THREE WEEKS. P. Elinor Glynn. F. on her book of same name. Adelphi, July 23, 1908.

THREE WEEKS AFTER MARRIAGE; OR, WHAT WE MUST ALL COME TO. C. 2 a. Arthur Murphy. C.G., January, 1764; C.G., 1776; Edinburgh, 1782 and 1783; D.L., May 10, 1815; Lyceum playbill, April 20, 1809, and April 9, 1822.

THREE WISHES, THE D. 1 a. and 3 tab. Leslie Tomm. Sydenham Public H., March 6, 1903.

THREE WOMEN, THE. Pavilion, November 19, 1866.

THREE YEARS IN A MAN TRAP. D. 3 a. W. Stephens. Birkenhead T.R., April 29, 1874.

THREE YEARS IN A MAN TRAP. D. C. H. Morton. Liverpool R. Amphitheatre, January 20, 1879.

THREE YEARS' SYSTEM, THE. F. Walter Maynard (Willert Beale). Crystal Palace, February 21, 1887.

THREEPENNY BIT, A. C. 3 a. J. Maddison Morton and A. W. Young. Brighton T.R., August 18, 1870.

THREEPENNY BITS. T.F. Isaac Zangwill. F. on a chapter of the writer's, "Old Maids' Club." Chatham O.H., April 25, 1895; Garrick, May 6, 1895.

THRICE MARRIED. P. 1 a. Howard Paul. D.L., March 12, 1854.

THRILLBY. Burl. 1 a. W. Muskerry. M. by F. Osmond Carr. Richmond T.R., May 11, 1896.

THRONE OF TERROR, THE. D. 5 a. W. J. Miller. Greenwich, June 26, 1905.

THROUGH A GLASS DARKLY. D. 4 a. Edwin Martin Seymour. Olympic, April 28, 1896 (C.P.).

THROUGH DARK TO DAWN; OR, A WIFE'S HONOUR. Dom. P. 4 a. Chas. Riminton and Harry Furnival. Brighouse Albert, November 30, 1905.

THROUGH FIRE AND SNOW. C.D. Pro. and 3 a. Max Goldberg. Scarborough T.R., February 15, 1886.

THROUGH FIRE AND WATER. Orig. C.D. 3 a. Walter Gordon. Adelphi, June 26, 1865.

THROUGH MY HEART FIRST. Rom. D. 3 a. J. M. Campbell. Edinburgh T.R., 4 a., March 17, 1884; Grand, June 2, 1884.

THROUGH SEAS OF BLOOD. Melo-d. of real life in 4 a. Said to be wr. by three distinguished authors who wish to preserve their anonymity. Botanic Gdns. (A.O.F. Garden Party), June 22, 1909.

THROUGH THE BREAKERS. M. Owen Davis. (For the first time in England.) Bristol R.T., November 12, 1900.

THROUGH THE FIRE. Ca. 1 a. W Lestocq and Yorke Stephens. Strand, February 25, 1888.

THROUGH THE FIRE. D. Gilbert Hastings. Leeds T.R., September 8, 1879.

THROUGH THE FURNACE. D. 4 a. W. Howell-Poole. Called *Wronged* during its provincial tour. Olympic, July 29, 1885.

THROUGH THE LOOKING GLASS. M.F. Lib. by H. P. Stephens. M. by E. Solomon. Gaiety, July 17, 1882.

THROUGH THE WORLD. D. Cecil Wray. Brighton T.R., April 20, 1874.

THROUGH THE WORLD; OR, A BLIND CHILD'S PERIL. Rom. D. Pro. and 3 a. Brandon Ellis. Pavilion, July 1, 1901.

THROW OF THE DICE, A. P. 1 a. H. Arthur Kennedy. Strand, May 27, 1890.

THROW PHYSIC TO THE DOGS. F. 2 a. H. Lee. Known as *Caleb Quotem and His Wife*. Hay., July 6, 1798.

THROWN TOGETHER. Sk. Dora V. Greet.

THUGS OF PARIS, THE. D. Brandon Ellis. Goole T.R., April 11, 1887.

THUMBSCREW, THE. D. 5 a. Henry J. Byron. Holborn, April 4, 1874.

THUMPING LEGACY, THE. F. 1 a. John Maddison Morton. D.L., February 11, 1843.

THUNDER ODE, THE. Ode on the Hurricane in the West Indies. M. by Dr. Arne. C.G. Pr. 1773.

THUNDERBOLT, THE. D. 4 a. D. Belac and W. Hamilton. West Bromwich T.R., April 4, 1894 (C.P.).

THUNDERBOLT, THE. P. 3 a. Richd. Ganthony. (A sequel to *A Message from Mars.*) Dublin T.R., May 10, 1906.

THUNDERBOLT, THE. An episode in the history of a provincial family. 4 a. A. W. Pinero. St. James's, May 9, 1908.

THY NEIGHBOUR'S WIFE. D. Chas. H. Longden and Eric Hudson. Leeds Queen's, December 18, 1905.

THYESTES. T. Jasper Heywood. Transl. fr. Seneca's "Thyestes." Ptd. 1561.

THYESTES. T. John Wright. Transl. fr. Seneca. See *Mock Thyestes*. Ac. 1674.

THYESTES. T. John Crowne. Partly f. on Seneca's "Thyestes." T.R. in D.L., 1681.

THYRA. Oa. Lib. by Ernest Pertence. M. by Algernon Lindo. Bayswater Bijou, December 17, 1896 (amat.).

THYRSANDA. P.J. John Evelyn, 1663.

THYRSIS. Past. J. Oldmixon. 1697. Pr. n.d. See Motteux's *Novelty*.

THYRZA FLEMING. P. 4 a. Dorothy Leighton (Mrs. G. C. Ashton Jonson). Terry's, January 4, 1895. (Independent Theatre.)

TIBERIUS CLAUDIUS NERO. T.

TIBERIUS IN CAPREÆ. P. Mr. Cumberland. N.p.

TICKET OF LEAVE, A. F. 1 a. Watts Phillips. Adelphi, December 1, 1862.

TICKET-OF-LEAVE MAN, THE. D. 4 a. T. Taylor. F. on French dr. tale, "Le Retour de Melum," by Brisebarre and Nuz. Olympic, May 27, 1863; Holborn, 1873.

TICKET-OF-LEAVE MAN, THE. See *Sam*.

TICKET-OF-LEAVE MAN'S LEFT; OR, SIX YEARS AFTER, THE. Orig. D. 3 a. Chas. Smith Cheltnam (a continuation of above). Greenwich New T., April 2, 1866.

TICKET-OF-LEAVE MAN'S WIFE. D. 3 a. C. S. Cheltnam. Publ. by S. French, Ltd.

TICKLE AND SCRUBBS. F. W. S. Penley and Frank Wyatt. Trafalgar Square, May 31, 1893.

TICKLISH TIMES. F. 1 a. J. M. Morton Olympic, March 8. 1858.

TIDAL HOUR, THE. Dom. D. 1 a. Rex Watney. Bayswater Victoria Hall, February 1, 1890 (amat.).

TIDDLEWINK. F. Maurice de Frece. Liverpool T.R., May 4, 1874.

TIDE AND TIME. D. Pro. and 3 a. Henry Leslie. Surrey, March 9, 1867.

TIDE OF TIME, THE. Orig. C. 3 a. W. Bayle-Bernard. Hay., December 13, 1858.

TIDE TARRIETH FOR NO MAN. C. George Wapul. Ent. on book of Stationers' Co., October 26, 1576. Pr. b.l.

TIGER, THE. Oa. 1 a. F. C. Burnand and Edward Solomon. St. James's, May 3, 1890.

TIGER LILY. Dr. Inc. 1 a. Margaret Wallace. St. George's H., January 16, 1892.

TIGER LILY, THE. D. 4 a. Isabel and Robert Castleton. Hammersmith Lyric, July 31, 1905.

TIGER OF MEXICO; OR, A ROUGH ROAD TO A GOLDEN LAND, THE. Rom. D. 4 a. J. B. Johnston. Britannia, April 18, 1881.

TIGER'S DEN, THE. D. 4 a. Chas. Freeman. Stratford R T., May 6, 1907.

TIGER'S GRIP, THE. D. 4 a. Max Goldberg and George Comer. Ipswich Lyceum, March 23, 1898 (C.P.).

TIGHT CORNER, A. F. 3 a. Sidney Bowkett. Terry's, October 12, 1901.

TIGHT CORNER, A. C. 3 a. Herbert Swears. Portsmouth T.R., May 9, 1906; Coronet, April 29, 1907.

TIGRESS, THE. Pro. and 4 a. Adap. fr. the American novel, "Crucify Her." Ramsey Morris. Comedy, June 29, 1889.

'TILDA'S NEW HAT. P. 1 a. Geo. Paston (Prod. by the Play Actors). Court, November 8, 1908; H.M., January 26, 1909.

TILL DEATH DO US PART. D. Pro. and 4 a. Geo. Corner. Surrey, April 20, 1885.

TILL SUNDAY; OR, THE GIRL WHO TOOK THE WRONG TOWING PATH. Arthur Roberts. Tivoli, January 6, 1908.

TILL THE BELLS RING. Ca. 1 a. G. Moffat. Glasgow Athenæum, March 26, 1908.

TILL THE HALF-HOUR. Episode. Arthur M. Heathcote. Ladbroke H., January 31, 1891.

TILL WE MEET AGAIN. P. 1 a. Mrs. Edward Saker. Kingston R. County, November 21, 1898.

TILLI. Op. C. September 18, 1894.

TIMANTHES. T. John Hoole. C.G., Pr. 1770.

TIME, A PASSING PHANTASY. P. F. N. Connell. Bloomsbury H., November 29, 1907; Court, June 21, 1909.

TIME AND THE HOUR. Orig. Rom. D. 3 a. Palgrave Simpson and Felix Dale. Queen's, June 29, 1868.

TIME AND TIDE: A TALE OF THE THAMES. Orig. D. 3 a. Harry Leslie. Surrey, March 9, 1867.

TIME, HUNGER, AND THE LAW. P. of Russian peasant life. 1 a. Lawrence Irving. Criterion, May 24, 1894.

TIME IS MONEY. Ca. Mrs. Hugh Bell and Arthur Cecil. Newcastle-on-Tyne T.R., September 5, 1890; Comedy, April 21, 1892; P.O.W., June 25, 1903; rev. Hipp., August 2, 1909.

TIME MACHINE, THE. M.F. 2 a. Books and lyrics by A. Stigant. M. by M. Strong. Bradford T.R., November 13, 1903.

TIME, THE AVENGER. D. 4 a. Tom Craven. Surrey, October 10, 1892.

TIME TRIES ALL. D. 2 a. John Courtney. Olympic, September 4, 1848.

TIME VINDICATED TO HIMSELF AND TO HIS HONOURS. Masque. Ben Jonson. Presented at Court on Twelfth Night, 1623.

TIME WILL TELL. C. 3 a. Herbert Gardiner. Bridgwater House, May 8, 1882; Windsor T.R., November 30, 1882; Trafalgar Square, May 8, 1893.

TIME WORKS WONDERS. C. 5 a. Douglas Jerrold. Hay., April 26, 1845; Sadler's Wells, 1866.

TIME'S A TELL-TALE. C. Henry Siddons. D.L., October 27, 1807. Pr. 1807.

TIME'S REVENGE. D. Britannia, October 4, 1875.

TIME'S REVENGE. P. 1 a. W. Edwardes Sprange. Toole's, May 20, 1890.

TIME'S REVENGE. D. 5 a. S. Creagh Henry. Public H., Tonbridge, June 20, 1898; Eastbourne T.R., May 4, 1899.

TIME'S TRIUMPH. Registered by Henslowe as ac. April 13, 1597.

TIME'S TRIUMPH. D. 4 a. H. J. Byron. Dublin Gaiety, August 19, 1872; Charing Cross, May 12, 1873.

TIMELY AWAKENING, A. Sk. Tivoli, August 3, 1908.

TIMELY MOVEMENT, A. Dom. P. 1 a. E. Andrews. Public H., Harrow, February 9, 1888.

TIMES, THE. C. Mrs. Eliz. Griffiths. D.L. Pr. 1780.

TIMES, THE. Orig. D. 3 a. John Daly. Olympic, July 18, 1853.

TIMES, THE. C. 4 a. Arthur W. Pinero. Terry's, October 24, 1891.

TIMES; OR, A FIG FOR INVASION, THE. Mus. Ent. 2 a. By a British Officer. Pr. 1797.

TIMKINS, THE TROUBADOUR. F. 1 a. By ——. Queen's, August 31, 1868.

TIMMIN'S RIDE. C. 1 a. Edward Ferris and Arthur Stuart. Carlisle Her M., September 14, 1900.

TIMOCLEA. Perf. at Hampton before Her Majesty. 1573-4.

TIMOCRATE. O. Leo. 1723.

TIMOLEON. T. Benjamin Martin. D.L., 1729.

TIMOLEON. T. M.S. Pope.

TIMOLEON. T. George Butt. D.P. Pr. 1777.

TIMOLEON; OR, THE REVOLUTION. T.C. Anon. Pr. 1697.

TIMON. C. Anon. N.p. Before 1814.

TIMON IN LOVE; OR, THE INNOCENT THIEF. C. J. Kelly. D.L. Pr. 1733. Transl. of "Timon Misanthrope," by M. De L'Isle.

TIMON OF ATHENS. T. W. Shakespeare. This play was not completed by Shakespeare, but probably by Cyril Tourneur. F. on a passage in Plutarch's *Life of Antonius* and the 28th Novel in Vol. I. of Painter's *Palace of Pleasure* and on Lucien's *Dialogues*. Partly wr. in 1606. Pr. Folio, 1623. Alt. by J. Love, 1768; alt. by R. Cumberland. D.L. Pr. 1771. Alt. by Thos. Hull. C.G., May 13, 1786. N.p. Recent rev. at Court T., May 18, 1904.

TIMON OF ATHENS. O. Purcell (1658-95).

TIMON OF ATHENS, THE MAN-HATER, THE HISTORY OF. Alt. fr. Shakespeare by T. Shadwell. Duke's T. Pr. 1678.

TIMONE. The first It. C. Bajardo. Before 1494.

TIMOTHY TO THE RESCUE. Orig. F. 1 a. Hy. J. Byron. Strand, May 30, 1864.

TIMOUR, THE CREAM OF ALL THE TARTARS. Burl. Princess's, 1845

TIMOUR THE TARTAR. Rom. Melo-d. 2 a. M. G. Lewis. C.G., April 29, 1811; May 1, 1811; D.L., May 16, 1831.

TIMOTEA, IL. Cantata. Marcello (1686-1739).

TIMOUR THE TARTAR; OR, THE IRON MASTER OF SAMARKAND-BY-OXUS. Extrav. J. Oxenford and Shirley Brooks. Olympic, December 26, 1860.

TIMOUR THE TARTAR; OR, THE SWELL BELLE OF THE PERIOD. Burl. Edward Chamberlaine. Alexandra, December 27, 1869.

TIMSON'S LITTLE HOLIDAY. F. 1 a. H. Nicholls. Publ. by S. French, Limited.

TIN BOX, THE. F.C. 3 a. Geo. Manville Fenn. Globe, April 16, 1892.

TINKER OF TOTNESS, THE. P. Anon. Ac. July 18, 1596. N.p.

TINSEL QUEEN, A. D. Pro. and 3 a. W. E. Morton. Sadler's Wells, December 10, 1883.

TINTED VENUS, A. See *A Vision of Venus*. Ca. Adap. fr. Anstey's novel by Elizabeth Bessle. Bramblebury, Wandsworth Common, October 12, 1889.

TIP-TOP FLAT. F.Sk. Mark Melford. Charing Cross Gatti's, November 3, 1902.

TIPPERARY LEGACY. C. Coyne. 1847.

TIPPOO SAIB; OR, BRITISH VALOUR IN INDIA. Pant. Ballet. Lonsdale. C.G., June 6, 1791. N.p.

TIPSTER, THE. P. 1 a. Lewin Fitzhamon. Dunstable Corn Exchange, January 22, 1898.

'TIS A WISE CHILD KNOWS ITS OWN FATHER. C. 3 a. F. G. Waldron. Hay., September 21, 1795. N.p.

'TIS ALL A FARCE. F. John Till Allingham. Hay., June 17, 1800. Pr. 1800.

'TIS AN ILL WIND BLOWS NOBODY GOOD; OR, THE ROAD TO ODIHAM. F. Anon. D.L., April 14, 1788. N.p.

'TIS BETTER THAN IT WAS. C. George Digby, Earl of Bristol. F. on Calderon's "Mejor Esta que Estaba." Duke's T., 1662-1665. N.p.

'TIS GOOD SLEEPING IN A WHOLE SKIN. C. Wm. Wager. Destroyed by Mr. Warburton's servant.

'TIS NO DECEIT TO DECEIVE THE DECEIVER. P. Henry Chettle. Ac., 1598. N.p.

'TIS PITY SHE'S A WHORE. T. John Forde. Phœnix D.L., 1633.

'TIS WELL IF IT TAKES. C. Wm. Taverner. L.I.F., February 28, 1719.

'TIS WELL IT'S NO WORSE. C. Isaac Bickerstaff. D.L. Pr. 1770. See *The Pannel*.

'TIS WELL THEY ARE MARRIED. Dr. Piece. 1 a. Brandenburgh House T., June, 1804. N.p.

TIT FOR TAT. C. 3 a. (George Colman.) Hay., August 29, 1786. Alt. fr. *The Mutual Deception.*

TIT FOR TAT. Oa. 2 a. Francis Talfourd and Alfred Wigan. Olympic, January 22, 1855.

TIT FOR TAT. C. Audrey Anderson. Brighton Aquarium, March 2, 1903.

TIT FOR TAT; OR, A DISH OF THE AUCTIONEER'S OWN CHOCOLATE. Int. Henry Woodward. D.L., 1749. N.p.

TIT FOR TAT; OR, COMEDY AND TRAGEDY AT WAR. Charlotte Charke. Punch's T. in St. James's St., 1743. N.p.

TIT FOR TAT; OR, THE TABLES TURNED. Alt. and adap. fr. "Cose San Tutte." New C.O. M. by Mozart. Lyceum playbill, July 29, 1828.

TIT-BITS. Extrav. G. L. Gordon. Blackpool Winter Gardens, May 25, 1883.

TITA IN THIBET. C.O. 2 a. Lib. by Frank Desprez. Royalty, January 1, 1879.

TITE ET BERENICE. Corneille. See "French Classical Plays."

TITERUS AND GALATEA. C. Entered on Book of Stationers Co., April 1, 1585.

TITHONUS AND AURORA. Ent. M. by J. Dunn. Sadler's Wells. Pr. 1746.

TITLE. C. 3 a. Adap. fr. the French of Eugène. M. by T. Edgar Pemberton. Liverpool R. Alexandra, June 8, 1885.

TITLE MART, THE. C. 3 a. Winston Churchill. Shaftesbury, November 17, 1905 (C.P.).

TITO. O. Mozart, 1791.

TITO MANLIO. O. G. Abos. London, 1756.

TITTLE-TATTLE; OR, TASTE A LA MODE. F. Timothy Tribble. Pr. 1749.

TITUS. O. Transl. fr. Metatasio. John Hoole. Pr. 1767.

TITUS. O. Mozart. D.L., March 31, 1841.

TITUS AND ANDRONICUS. Anon. Ac. by Earl of Sussex's men, January 23, 1593.

TITUS ANDRONICUS; OR, THE RAPE OF LAVINIA. T. Ed. Ravenscroft. Alt. fr. Shakespeare. T.R. Pr. 1687.

TITUS AND BERENICE. T. Thos. Otway. F. on Jean Racine's "Berenice." Ac. at His Royal Highness's T., 1677.

TITUS AND GISSIPPUS. Ralph Radcliffe. 1576.

TITUS AND VESPASIAN. P. Ac. according to Henslowe. April 11, 1591.

TITUS ANDRONICUS. T. W. Shakespeare. Possibly *Titus and Andronicus* improved upon. ? Ac. at Rose, 1592. Not pr. with Shakespeare's name as author during his lifetime. The story was known by Painter, who alludes to it in his *Palace of Pleasure*. Halliwell thinks Shakespeare's play (? *Titus and Vespasian*) is lost, and was the one ent. by J. Danter in 1594. Ent. Stationers' Co., February 6, 1594; April 19, 1602. Pr. qto 1593, 1600, 1611. First folio, 1623. Ac. by servants of the Earls of Pembroke, Derby, and Essex.

TITUS VESPASIAN. T. John Cleland. 1755. Enlarged transl. of "Clemenza di Tito" of Metastasio.

TO ARMS; OR, THE BRITISH RECRUIT. Mus. Int. Thomas Hurlstone. May 3, 1793.

TO BE CONTINUED IN OUR NEXT. F. W. James. Marylebone, June 17, 1867.

TO BE OR NOT TO BE? Duol. Mrs. E. Argent Lonergan. Hornsey National Hall, November 24, 1894.

TO CALL HER MINE. Dr. Episode. Benjamin Landeck. Surrey, December 18, 1893.

TO LOVE ONLY FOR LOVE'S SAKE. See *Querer pro Solo Querer.*

TO MARRY OR NOT TO MARRY? C. Eliz. Inchbald. C.G., February 16, 1805. Pr. 1805.

TO OBLIGE BENSON. Ca. 1 a. Adap. fr. Fr. Vaude's "Un Service à Blanchard" by Tom Taylor. Olympic T., March 6, 1854.

TO PARENTS AND GUARDIANS. Orig. C.D. 1 a. By author of "Vicar of Wakefield." Royal Lyceum T., September 28, 1846; Westminster T.R., December 22, 1862.

TO PARIS AND BACK FOR FIVE POUNDS. F. 1 a. J. M. Morton. Hay., February 5, 1853.

TO THE DEATH. D. Pro. and 3 a. Adap. by Rutland Barrington fr. Arch. Clavering Gunter's novel, "Mr. Barnes of New York." Olympic, March 23, 1888, and May 16, 1888 (under title of *Mr. Barnes of New York*).

TO THE DEATH. Dr. Episode. Octavia Kenmore. Crouch End O.H., October 23, 1905.

TO THE GREEN ISLES DIRECT. Mus. Eccentricity. W. M. Akhurst. Britannia, May 25, 1874.

TO THE RESCUE. Ca. Dora V. Greet. P.O.W., June 13, 1889 (mat.); Court, December 9, 1889.

TO-DAY. C. 3 a. Adap. by C. H. E. Brookfield fr. "Divorçons," by Victorien Sardou. Comedy, December 5, 1892.

TO-DAY. C.D. 1 a. C. Vieson. London Avenue, August 7, 1895 (C.P.); Hull Grand T., August 26, 1895.

TO-DAY AND YESTERDAY. Duol. Mrs. George Corbett. St. Alban's Parish Hall, Acton, December 6, 1900.

TO-MORROW. Fantastic P. 3 a. Paisley T., January 12, 1904; Crouch End O.H., November 3, 1905.

TO-MORROW. Sk. Bolossy Kiralfy. London Hipp., December 24, 1908.

TO-NIGHT AT EIGHT. F. T. D. M'Cord and G. A. Topis. Camden Town Park Hall, April 18, 1887.

TO-NIGHT, UNCLE. H. J. Byron. 1878.

TO-NIGHT'S THE NIGHT. C.S. Wal Pink. M. by G. Le Brun. Tivoli, January 22, 1900.

TOAST OF THE TOWN, THE. Sk. Luke Jennings. Crouch End Hipp., June 22, 1908; Holborn Empire, August 10, 1908.

TOBACCO BOX; OR, SOLDIER'S PLEDGE OF LOVE, THE. M.I. Hay., August 13, 1782.

TOBACCO JARS. Oa. 1 a. Lady Monckton. M. by Harriet Young. St. Geo. Hall, June 12, 1889.

TOBACCONIST; OR, ALCHYMICAL SWINDLERS DETECTED, THE. Modernised fr. Ben Jonson's C. of *The Alchymist* by Francis Gentleman. F. 2 a. D.L., May 24, 1816; Lyceum playbill, April 9, 1822.

TOBIAS. P. H. Chettle. Ac. 1602. N.p.

TOBIT. An old English Mystery. Ac. at Lincoln in July, 1563.

TOCHTER DES HERRN FABRICUS, DIE. P. 4 a. Adolf Wilbrandt. St. Geo. Hall, November 19, 1901.

TOD JESU, DER. Orat. Grann. 1701-59.

TODDLES. F. 3 a. Clyde Fitch. Adap. fr. *Triplepatte* (by Tristan Bernard and Andre Godfernaux). D. of York's, September 3, 1906; Wyndham's, December 10, 1906; Playhouse, January 28, 1907; Playhouse, May 20, 1908.

TODOISKA. M. Rom. M. by Storage. D.L., March 22, 1814.

TOFF JIM. P. 1 a. F. Wright, jun. Apollo, May 11, 1901.

TOILERS ON THE THAMES; OR, THE DARK SIDE OF LONDON LIFE. D. 2 a. W. E. Waldron. Grecian, March 1, 1869.

TOISON D'OR, LA. Corneille. See "French Classical Plays."

TOLEDAD, LA. C.O. 2 a. F. Carré and A. Moore. M. by E. Audran. Windsor T.R., April 11, 1903; Kennington T., April 20, 1903.

TOLLCROSS; OR, THE MURDER AT THE TURNPIKE GATE 100 YEARS AGO. H. Campbell. Glasgow New Adelphi T., March 19, 1877.

TOLOMEO. O. G. Colla. Milan, 1774.

TOM. C. 1 a. H. E. Dalroy and A. Bearne. Derby Lecture H., December 28, 1893.

TOM AND JERRY; OR, LIFE IN LONDON IN 1820. D. 3 a. Fr. Pierce Egan's work, by W. J. Moncrieff. C.G.; Adelphi, November 26, 1821; Tottenham, July, 1830; Victoria, March 5, 1870.

TOM BEDLAM, THE TINKER. P. Ac. at Theobald's before James I., 1617-8.

TOM BOWLING. Nautical D. 2 a. A. L. V. Campbell. Sadler's Wells T., February 1, 1830.

TOM COBB. Orig. F.C. 3 a. W. S. Gilbert. St. James's, April 24, 1875.

TOM CRINGLE; OR, THE MAN OF THE IRON HAND. Nautical D. 2 a. E. Fitzball. Surrey, May 26, 1834.

TOM, DICK, AND HARRY. F.C. 3 a. Orig. prod. in America as *Incog.* Mrs. R. Pacheco. Manchester T.R., August 24, 1893; Trafalgar Square, November 2, 1893.

TOM DOUGH. P. In 2 parts. John Day. 2nd pt. mentioned by Henslowe under date of 1601.

TOM ESSENCE; OR, THE MODISH WIFE. C. Partly transl. fr. "Le Cocu Imaginaire" of Molière by Thomas Rawlins. Duke's T. Pr. 1677.

TOM FOOL. F. Stevens. 1760.

TOM HOYDEN O' TAUNTON DEAN. C. or F. By Richard Brome. Mentioned in the Epil. to the *Court Beggar.* 1653.

TOM JONES. C.O. J. Reed. C.G., January 14, 1769. Pr. 1769. F. on Fielding's novel of same title.

TOM JONES. O. Philidor. 1726-1797.

TOM JONES. C.O. 3 a. A. M. Thompson and R. Courtneidge. Lyrics by C. H. Taylor. M. by E. German. Manchester Prince's, March 30, 1907; Apollo, April 17, 1907.

TOM JONES. See *Sophia.*

TOM NODDY'S SECRET. F. 1 a. T. H. Bayly. Hay., 1838; D.L., June 7, 1839.

TOM PINCH. Dom. C. 3 a. J. J. Dilley and L. Clifton. Adap. fr. Dickens's "Martin Chuzzlewit." Vaudeville, March 10, 1881; rev. St. James's, September 5, 1903.

TOM SMART. C. 3 a. H. T. Craven.

TOM THRASHER. F. 1 a. A. Harris. Adelphi, July 6, 1868.

TOM THUMB. Burla. 1 a. Alt. fr. Fielding by Kane O'Hara. Pr. 1805. C.G., December 14, 1809; Adelphi, October 18, 1819; Lyceum playbill, June 6, 1824; C.G., 1829.

TOM THUMB. Adap. as Ballad O. by Mrs. E. Haywood and Mr. Hatcher fr. Fielding. Ac. at Little T. in Hay.

TOM THUMB. First time. D.L., June 9, 1824.

TOM THUMB. See *The Tragedy of Tragedies.*

TOM THUMB THE GREAT. F. 1 a. H. Fielding. Little T. in Hay., October 3, 1730; D.L., July 11, 1815.

TOM TIDDLER. Victoria, December 24, 1878.

TOM, TOM, THE PIPER'S SON. Elephant and C., December 27, 1875.

TOM TRUANT. D. 4 a. D. Stewart. Marylebone, March 7, 1874.

TOM TYLERE AND HIS WIFE. Mor. Int. Anon. Ascr. to W. Wayer. 1569. Publ. 1578.

TOM'S MOTHER-IN-LAW. Co. 2 a. C. Forrester-Jones and J. D. Clay. Swindon Corn Exchange, May 14, 1894.

TOM'S REVENGE. D. Herr Bandmann. Edinburgh T.R., March 25, 1874.

TOM'S SECOND MISSUS. P. 1 a. M. E. Francis (Mrs. F. Blundell). Playhouse, April 30, 1907.

TOM'S WIFE. C. 1 a. N. Parker. Worthing Assembly R., April 7, 1896.

TOMBO CHIQUI; OR, AMERICAN SAVAGE. C. 3 a. Cleland. Transl. fr. the French, 1758.

TOMKINS AND THE TROUBADOUR. F. 1 a. Queen's, August 31, 1868.

TOMKINS'S VENUS. C. 3 a. Roland Bottomley. St. Leonards Pav., July 27, 1907.

TOMMY. C. Mrs. Willard. Olympic, February 9, 1891.

TOMMY. P. 3 a. J. K. Jerome. Manchester Midland, November 27, 1907; London prod., Camden, December 3, 1907.

TOMMY AND HARRY. Britannia, December 26, 1872.

TOMMY AT COLLEGE. M. Sk. C. Grain. St. Geo. H., April 7, 1890.

TOMMY ATKINS. D. 4 a. A. Shirley and B. Landeck. Pav., September 16, 1895, and February 26, 1896; Duke of York's, December 23, 1895; rev. Princess's, July 31, 1897.

TOMMY DODD. F. 3 a. O. Shillingford. Cardiff T.R., December 13, 1897; Globe, August 30, 1898.

TOMMY'S TUTORS. F. E. B. Wyke. Rhyl Bijou, June 24, 1881.

TOMUMBEIUS. MS. of the 17th century belonging to Dr. N. Johnson in Bodleian Library.

TON; OR, FOLLIES OF FASHION, THE. C. Lady Wallace. C.G., April 8, 1788.

TON OF GOLD. Pavilion, October 21, 1866.

TONGUE OF SLANDER. D. 4 a. G. T. G. Warren and J. Douglass. Standard, October 17, 1887.

TONY LUMPKIN IN TOWN; OR, THE DILETTANTI. F. J. O'Keeffe. Hay., July 2, 1778. Pr. 1780, 1798.

TONY LUMPKIN'S RAMBLE TO TOWN. C.G., April 10, 1792.

TOO AGREEABLE TO BE TRUE. C. 2 a. W. Reeves. Newcastle Tyne T., December 9, 1870; Scarborough T.R., June 28, 1878.

TOO CIVIL BY HALF. F. Dent. D.L., November 5, 1782.

TOO CLEVER. C. Liverpool Alexandra, April 2, 1876.

TOO CURIOUS BY HALF; OR, MARPLOT IN SPAIN. O. 2 a. M. by W. Reeves. Skit on Mrs. Centliere's sequel to *The Busy Body.* Lyceum, August 27, 1823.

TOO FATIGUING. C. Scarborough T.R., August 24, 1885.

TOO FRIENDLY BY HALF. F. Anon. C.G., October 29, 1807. N.p.

TOO GOOD TO BE TRUE. P. Chettle. Assisted by R. Hathways and Wentworth Smith. 1601. N.p.

TOO HAPPY BY HALF. F. 1 a. James Field. St. James's, January 5, 1895.

TOO KIND. C. Paul Feinbond. Coventry T.R., July 3, 1876.

TOO LATE. P. 5 a. George F. Thompson. Globe, June 29, 1881.

TOO LATE. Sk. Metropolitan, August 23, 1909.

TOO LATE; OR, THE HANDS OF DESTINY. D. 3 a. Chas. Quayle. Barnsley Circus of Varieties, April 2, 1876; Albion, August 14, 1876; Imperial, September 21, 1885.

TOO LATE FOR DINNER. F. C.G., February 22, 1820; D.L., 1828.

TOO LATE FOR THE TRAIN. F. M. Morton. D.L., November 2, 1852.

TOO LATE TO CALL BACK YESTERDAY. C. R. Davenport. 1639.

TOO LATE TO SAVE; OR, DOOMED TO DIE. D. 4 a. T. A. Palmer. Exeter T.R., 1861.

TOO LEARNED BY HALF; OR, THE PHILOSOPHER OUTWITTED. F. 1 a. Sharpe. 1793.

TWO LOVELY BLACK-EYED SUSAN. Crystal Palace, April 2, 1888.

TOO LOVING BY HALF. Int. Horatio Robson. For the benefit of Mrs. Martyr. C.G., October 5, 1784.

TOO MANY; OR, DEMOCRACY. C. Alfieri. 1805.

TOO MANY BY ONE. F. C. Burnand and F. Cowan. St. Geo. H. Circa 1865.

TOO MANY COOKS. M.F. 1 a. J. Kenney. C.G., 1805.

TOO MANY COOKS. Offenbach. Circa 1862.

TOO MANY COOKS. C. 3 a. W. Lonnen. Southend Empire, April 20, 1903; Woolwich Royal Artillery, June 29, 1903.

TOO MUCH FOR GOOD NATURE. F. 1 a. Ed. Falenier. D.L., November 9, 1858.

TOO MUCH FOR JOHNSON. 3 a. F. on Maurice Ordonneau's *La Plantation Thomassin.* Garrick, April 18, 1898.

TOO MUCH MARRIED. Glasgow G.T., April 19, 1886.

TOO MUCH OF A GOOD THING. C.D. 1 a. A. Harris. L.T., December 2, 1855; D.L., December 1, 1857.

TOO MUCH THE WAY OF THE WORLD. C. Herbert. ? 1817.

TOO SOON. M.P. H. B. Maxwell. Liverpool Shakespeare, April 28, 1904 (C.P.).

TOO TRUE. D. 3 a. H. T. Craven. Duke's, January 12, 1876.

TOODLES, THE. F. City, 1832.

TOOLE AT HOME; A TOUCH AT THE TIMES.

TOOLE AT SEA. F. R. Reece. Gaiety, December 3, 1875.

TOOLEY. Ac. by Lord Howard's servants. 1576.

TOOTH FOR A WIFE, A. Sk. Middlesex, May 12, 1908; Bow Pal., November 12, 1908.

TOOTHACHE; OR, THE PRINCE AND THE CHIMNEY-SWEEPER. F. 1 a.

TOOTH-DRAWER. C. Anon. (Advert. in "Wit and Drollery.") 1661. N.p.

TOOTSIE. F. A. H. Townley. Camden Town Park H., May 16, 1888.

TOOTSIE'S LOVERS. Burl. W. T. Le Queux. Brentford T. of Varieties, April 19, 1886.

TOP OF THE BILL, THE. Sk. Standard, June 29, 1908.

TOPLITSKY. Sk. Palace, August 9, 1909.

TOPSIDE DOG, THE. P. 1 a. F. D. Bone. Court, November 3, 1908 (mat.).

TOPSY-TURVEY TIMES. M. Absurdity. 3 a. Leslie Hawkins. Widnes Alexandra, December 6, 1907.

TOPSY-TURVEY HOTEL, THE. M.F.C. 3 a. Fr. French of Maurice Ordonneau. Adap. by A. Sturgess. M. by V. Rogers and L. Monckton. Comedy, September 21, 1898.

TOPSY-TURVEYDOM. Extrav. W. S. Gilbert. Criterion, March 21, 1874.

TOPSY-TURVEYDOM. F.C. 3 a. R. Byford. Liverpool Court T., March 29, 1895.

TOREADOR, LE. Op. C. Adam. 1849.

TOREADOR, THE. M.P. James T. Tanner and Harry Nicholls. Lyrics by Adrian Ross and Percy Greenbank. M. by Ivan Caryll and Lionel Monckton. Gaiety, June 17, 1901.

TORETTA; A TALE OF SEVILLE. D. 3 a. M. Lavenu. D.L., November 9, 1846.

TORNADO, THE. "An American Scenic Production." 5 a. Lincoln J. Carter. (First time in England.) Northampton O.H., February 6, 1899; Brixton T., June 12, 1899.

TORPEDO, THE. F. 1 a. H. T. Johnson. N.p.

TORRENDAL. T. Cumberland. Adv. 1809.

TORRID ZONE, THE. D. 2 a. Stephen Clarke. 1809.

TORRENT, THE. Dr. Int. Sarga. Camden, April 17, 1908.

TORRIEMONDO, IL. See "Italian Classical Plays."

TORQUATO TASSO. O. Donizetti. (Rome, 1833.)

TORTESA, THE USURER. C. Willis. 1841.

TORTURE OF SHAME, THE. P. 4 a. J. Gannon. Liverpool Adelphi, May 25, 1896.

TORVALDO E DORLISKA. O. Rossini. Rome, December 26, 1815.

TOSCA, LA. P. F. C. Grove and H. Hamilton. Transl. fr. the French of Sardou. Garrick, November 28, 1889.

TOSCA, LA. D. 5 a. Victorien Sardou. R. Eng. O.H. (Sarah Bernhardt's season), June 13, 1892; Adelphi, July 8, 1897; Royalty, October 28, 1907.

TOSCA, LA. O. Illica and Giacoso. M. by Puccini. Rome, January 14, 1900; C.G., July 12, 1900.

TOSS UP. F. J. Addison. Woolwich Recreation Rooms, November 11, 1876.

TOT. D. 3 a. F. Hazleton. Grecian, April 14, 1879.

TOTO AND TATA. O. 3 a. M. by Banès P. Bilhand and A. Barré. (Orig. prod. as *Toto* at the Menies Plaisirs, Paris, June 10, 1892.) English ver. by A. M. Thompson. Lyrics by B. Jones and J. J. Wood. Leeds Grand, August 23, 1897; Camberwell Metropole, September 20, 1897.

TOTTENHAM COURT. C. T. Nabbes. Salisbury Court, 1638.

TOTTIE'S TELEGRAM. C.O. 1 a. W. Sapte, jun. Cheltenham T.R., April 29, 1886.

TOTTLES. C.D. 3 a. H. J. Byron. Gaiety, December 22, 1875.

TOUCH AND GO. Burl. W. Andrews. Liverpool P.O.W., March 8, 1886.

TOUCH AND TAKE; OR, SATURDAY NIGHT AND SUNDAY MORNING. F. D.L., January 6, 1855.

TOUCH AT THE TIMES, A. Prel. Hay., August 20, 1788.

TOUCH AT THE TIMES, A. M. Ent. Archibald M'Laren. 1804.

TOUCH AT THE TIMES, A. C. Jameson. 1812.

TOUCH OF NATURE, A. D. 4 a. M. Wilkinson. Bristol T.R., May 19, 1902.

TOUCHEE. Duol. Prod. by Amal. Players' Association, February 7, 1907.

TOUCHSTONE; OR, HARLEQUIN TRAVELLER, THE. Pant. Charles Dibdin. C.G., January 4, 1779.

TOUCHSTONE; OR, THE WORLD AS IT GOES, THE. C. 4 a. Kenney. D.L., April 3, 1817.

TOUGH YARN, A. D. 2 a. J. H. Avondale. Shoreham Swiss Gardens, September 24, 1877.

TOUR DE LONDRES. D. By Nus. 1855.

TOURIST, THE. F.C. 3 a. Barton White. Brighton Aquarium T., June 12, 1899.

TOURIST; OR, HERE, THERE, AND EVERYWHERE. M.C. 2 a. Lib., Montague. M., T. Hunter. Portsmouth Prince's, November 5, 1895.

TOURIST FRIEND, THE. M. by Chas. Smith. 1810.

TOURIST'S TICKET, A. F. T. J. Williams. Globe, April 1, 1872.

TOURNAMENT, THE. Int. T. Chatterton. 1778.

TOURNAMENT, THE. F. Mariana Starke. Imitation fr. a German D. called *Agnes Bernauer*. 1800.

TOWER, THE. J. Henderson. Adap. fr. Harrison Ainsworth's novel. Bayswater Bijou, May 22, 1896 (C.P.).

TOWER OF BABEL, THE. Soc. O. 1 a. M. by Rubinstein. 1870.

TOWER OF BABEL, THE. Dom. Pm. A. Austin. 1871.

TOWER OF LOCHLAIN; OR, THE IDIOT SON. Melo-d. 3 a. Adap. by D. Jerrold. London Theatres.

TOWER OF LONDON, THE. O. A. Cellin. Manchester Prince's, October 4, 1875.

TOWER OF LONDON, THE. Sk. Stratford Empire, May 10, 1909.

TOWER OF LONDON; OR, THE DEATH OMEN AND THE FATE OF LADY JANE GREY. D. 3 a. T. H. Higgie and T. H. Lacy. City of London T., December 26, 1840.

TOWER OF NESLE; OR, THE CHAMBER OF DEATH. D. 3 a. G. Almar. Fr. the French of Galliardet. Surrey, September 17, 1833.

TOWERS OF URBANDINE, THE. P. Carr. Hull.

TOWN AND COUNTRY; OR, WHICH IS BEST? C. T. Morton. C.G., March 10, 1807; D.L., February 13, 1815, and May 3, 1816.

TOWN BEFORE YOU, THE. C. Mrs. Cowley. C.G. 1795.

TOWN FOP; OR, SIR TIMOTHY TAWDEY, THE. C. Adap. fr. Wilkin's *The Miseries of Enforced Marriage*. Mrs. Aphra Behn. Duke's T., 1677.

TOWN SHIFTS; OR, SUBURB JUSTICE, THE. C. Edward Revet. Duke. 1671.

TOWN UNMASKED, THE. C. Enumerated in a list of publications at the beginning of The Ladies' Visiting Day. 1701.

TOWNELEY PLAYS. See "Miracle Plays."

TOY; OR, THE LIE OF THE DAY, THE. C. John O'Keeffe. C.G., February 3, 1789.

TOY SHOP, THE. D. Sat. Robert Dodsley. C.G., February 3, 1785.

TOY SHOP, THE. D. 1 a. For children. E. Weitzel. 1891 (C.P.).

TOY TO PLEASE MY LADY, A. P. Anon. N.p. December 11, 1595.

TOYSHOP OF THE HEART, THE. P. 1 a. Ella Hepworth-Dixon. Playhouse, November 26, 1908 (mat.).

TRA-LA-LA TOSCA. Burl. 2 a. F. C. Burnand. Royalty. January 9, 1890.

TRACHINIÆ. T. Transl. fr. Sophocles by Geo. Adams, 1729; D. Francklin, 1759; Dale, 1824; and Plumtre, 1865.

TRACHINIAN VIRGINS, THE. T. Transl. fr. Sophocles by R. Potter. 1788. See "Greek Plays."

TRACK OF BLOOD, THE. Burl. Melo-d. 2 a. and 6 sc. Captain Robert Marshall. Theatrical Fête, Botanical Gardens, Regent's Park, July 8, 1904.

TRADESMAN'S SON, THE. D. 2 a. Surrey T., October, 1862.

TRAFALGAR; OR, THE SAILOR'S PLAY. Pr. Uxbridge, 1807.

TRAFALGAR DAY. Naval Epis. C. A. Clark and W. S. Hartford. Paragon, May 10, 1909.

TRAGEDIAN'S SUPPER, A. T.C. 1 a. F. Williams and L. J. McQuilland. Belfast Bangor Ward H., July 24, 1905.

TRAGEDY, A. F.C. 3 a. C. S. Fawcett. Royalty, April 28, 1887.

TRAGEDY A-LA-MODE. F. S. Foote. Pr. 1795. See *Diversions of the Morning; Wandering Patentee.*

TRAGEDY OF LYNDHURST HALL, THE. Sk. Rotherhithe Hipp., June 7, 1909.

TRAGEDY OF TRAGEDIES; OR, THE FALL OF TOM THUMB. F. H. Fielding. See *Tom Thumb*.

TRAGEDY OF TRUTH, A. In two panels. Rosamund Langbridge. M. by Norman O'Neill. Adelphi, June 17, 1907; rev. Adelphi, September 28, 1908. (Orig. prod. as *The Spell* at Manchester R., November 2, 1906.)

TRAGICAL ACTORS; OR, THE MARTYRDOME OF THE LATE KING CHARLES, THE. Ptd. for Sir Arthur, 1600.

TRAGICAL AND LAMENTABLE MURDER OF MASTER G. SAUNDERS, THE.

TRAGOPODAGRA; OR, THE GOUT. T. Transl. fr. Lucian by Dr. Thomas Francklin. 1780.

TRAIL OF SIN, THE. H. Leslie. Victoria, September, 1863.

TRAIL OF THE SERPENT, THE. D. G. Lauder. Eleph. and C., August 4, 1879.

TRAIL OF THE SERPENT, THE. P. 3 a. W. Walker. Huddersfield, The Armoury, January 18, 1881.

TRAIL OF THE SERPENT, THE. D. F. M. Watson. Burnley Gaiety, July 6, 1896.

TRAIL OF THE SERPENT, THE. See *Dark Deeds*.

TRAIN DE LUXE. C. 1 a. H. C. Pemberton. Publ. by S. French, Ltd.

TRAINED TO CRIME. D. 4 a. E. Towers. Pavilion, September 28, 1878.

TRAINING A HUSBAND. Duol. Mrs. Christina. Dening. Somerville Club, 231, Oxford Street, February 21, 1893.

TRAITOR, THE. Rom. T. J. Shirley. Ac. by His Majesty's servants. Pr. 1635. Licensed 1631. L.I.F., November 10, 1718.

TRAITOR, THE. D. 4 a. E. Hill-Mitchelson. Wigan New T.R., July 27, 1903; Stratford T.R., November 23, 1903.

TRAITOR, THE. D. 4 a. Bert Haldane. Greenwich Carlton, July 27, 1903.

TRAITOR, THE. Sk. South London, May 17, 1909.

TRAITOR, THE. See *Traytor*.

TRAITOR PRINCE, A. D. 4 a. George A. De Grey. Widnes Alexandra, November 20, 1902; Smethwick T.R., August 3, 1903; Surrey, September 7, 1903.

TRAITOR TO THE CZAR, A. Russian D. Rotherham T.R., June 22, 1904 (C.P.).

TRAITOR'S GATE; OR, THE TOWER OF LONDON IN 1553. Hist. D. 3 a. W. J. Lucas. Pavilion, 1834.

TRAMPS, THE. Dom. D. 1 a. and 3 sc. W. Stephens and B. M'Cullough. West London, December 19, 1896.

TRAMPS; OR, BYGONE DAYS, THE. 3 a. C. Harrison. Warrington Public H., October 4, 1889.

TRAMP'S ADVENTURE; OR, TRUE TO THE LAST. D 2 a. F. Phillips. Surrey, 1862.

TRANSFERRED GHOST. Co. N. Lynn. M. by J. Crook. Garrick, November 19, 1896.

TRANSFORMATION. Prel. Hay., July 8, 1787.

TRANSFORMATION; OR, LOVE AND LAW. M.F. Ascr. to Mr. Allingham. Lyceum, November 30, 1810.

TRANSGRESSOR, THE. P. 4 a. A. W. Gattie. Court, January 27, 1894.

TRANSIT OF VENUS, THE. M.C. 2 a. J. T. Tanner. M. by N. Lambelet. Dublin T.R., April 9, 1898; Crouch End O.H., September 26, 1898.

TRANSPORTED FOR LIFE. D. 4 a. M. Murdoch. Eleph. and C., October 30, 1880.

TRAP, THE. P. 1 a. Arthur Eckersley and Arthur Curtis. New Brighton W.G., July 20, 1909.

TRAPPED. Sk. Stockport Mechanics' Inst., January 27, 1898.

TRAPPED AT LAST. C. 3 a. Geo. F. Neville. Royalty, March 25, 1882.

TRAPPER, THE. D. Geo. Roberts. Sadler's Wells, April 2, 1888.

TRAPPING A TARTAR. C.D. 1 a. E. Stirling. Astley's T., June 6, 1864.

TRAPPOLIN CREDUTO PRINCIPE; OR, TRAPPOLIN SUPPOSED A PRINCE. T.C. Sir A. Cokain. New ver. of the story of "Old Fortunatus." Pr. 1658. Another ver. by Allan Ramsay pr. 1733.

TRAUMULUS. P. 5 a. Arno Holz and Oskar Gerschke. Gt. Queen St., November 29, 1904.

TRAVELLER, THE. C. Fr. the French of Madam Genlis. 1781.

TRAVELLER; OR, THE MARRIAGE IN SICILY, THE. Anon. 1809. Never perf.

TRAVELLERS, THE. Com. 3 a. Lieut. N. B. Harrison. 1788.

TRAVELLER RETURNS, THE. Melo. 1 a. C. Hamilton. Brighton New Pal. T., May 11, 1906. See *The Sixth Commandment*.

TRAVELLERS, THE. O. Victoria, September, 1819.

TRAVELLERS; OR, MUSIC'S FASCINATION, THE. O.D. 5 a. A. Cherry. M. by Mr. Corri. D.L., 1806; May 15, 1823; and April 25, 1836.

TRAVELLERS BENIGHTED; OR, THE FOREST OF ROSENWALD, THE. Fr. "Raymond and Agnes." Grosette. Hay., September 30, 1811. N.p.

TRAVELLERS IN SWITZERLAND, THE. C. Op. Rev. Henry Bate Dudley. C.G., February 22, 1794.

TRAVELLING CARRIAGE, THE. D. 2 a. D.L., October 26, 1835.

TRAVELS OF THE THREE ENGLISH BROTHERS, SIR THOMAS, SIR ANTHONY, AND MR. ROBERT SHIRLEY, THE. Hist. P. John Day, assisted by W. Rowley and G. Wilkins. Curtain Theatre, 1607.

TRAVERS'S SECRET. D. 4 a. James E. Thorrington. Southend Pier Pav., February 21, 1899.

TRAVIATA, LA. O. Verdi. (Venice, March 6, 1853.) An op. ver. of Duma's *La Dame aux Camélias*.

TRAYTOR, THE. T. Rev. with alterations. Shirley or Rivers. Alt. by Christopher Bullock. 1718.

TRAYTOR, THE. See *Traitor*.

TRAYTOR TO HIMSELF; OR, MAN'S HEART HIS GREATEST ENEMY, THE. Moral Intl. Williams Johns. Perf. at the Public School of Evesham, 1678.

TREACHERIES OF THE PAPISTS, THE. D. Bishop Bale.

TREACHEROUS BARON; OR, ALBERT AND EMMA, THE. Bal. Anon. 1812.

TREACHEROUS BROTHERS, THE. T. George Powel. T.R., 1690. Pr. 1696.

TREACHEROUS HUSBAND, THE. T. Samuel Davey. Dublin, 1737.

TREACHEROUS SON-IN-LAW, THE. T. Thomas Pierson. Pr. Stockton, Stokesley, Yorkshire, 1786.

TREACHERY. Dr. Sk. Camberwell Empire, June 10, 1907.

TREADMILL OF SOCIETY, THE. C. 3 a. G. P. Wilson. Brighton R., June 19, 1905.

TREASURE, THE. C. Transl. fr. Plautus by Bonnell Thornton. 1767.

TREASURE, THE. F. 3 a. P. C. Carton and C. Raleigh. Strand, May 1, 1888.

TREASURE, THE. P. 1 a. Elizabeth Kirby. F. on a story by L. N. Becke in the "Smart Set." Kingsway, October 9, 1908.

TREASURE ISLAND. C.O. 3 a. P. Eland. M. by V. Exley and R. Illingworth. Additional numbers by C. Crabtree. Bradford R., August 7, 1905

TREASURE SHIP IN FAIRY SEAS, THE. Spec. by Frank Parker. M. by Carl Kiefert. London Hipp., December 24, 1906.

TREASURE TROVE. V. A. Law. M. by A. J. Caldicott. St. George's H., June 6, 1883.

TREATY OF PEACE, THE. D. 3 a. G. L. Gordon. Park, August 3, 1878; Plymouth T.R., April 30, 1883.

TREE DUMAS SKITEERS, THE. "D. in 6 tabloids." Introduced in act two of *Milord Sir Smith*. Comedy, January 25, 1899.

TREE OF KNOWLEDGE, THE. P. 5 a. R. C. Carton. St. James's, October 25, 1897.

TREIZE, LES. O. 3 a. Halévy. April 15, 1838.

TRELAWNEY OF THE WELLS. C. 4 a. A. W. Pinero. Court, January 20, 1898.

TREMENDOUS MYSTERY, A. F. C. Burnand and King Hall. St. Geo. H. Circa 1865.

TREPAN; OR, VIRTUE REWARDED, THE O. John Maxwell. Pr. by Thomas Gent, 1739.

TRESOR SUPPOSE, LE. O. Méhul (1763-1817). Recently rev. in Germany.

TRESPASSERS BEWARE. Co. 1 a. C. Thomas. Avenue, April 26, 1888.

TRESPASSERS BEWARE. Sk. Frank Gough and Wal Pink. M. by Kenneth Lyle. Canterbury M.H., December 24, 1906.

TRESPASSERS WILL BE PROSECUTED. Mod. P. 3 a. M. A. Arabian. Manchester Gaiety, April 26, 1906.

TRIAL (or Tryal). C. Joanna Baillie. 1798.

TRIAL. See *Tryal.*

TRIAL BY BATTLE, A. Victoria.

TRIAL BY JURY. C.O. 1 a. W. S. Gilbert. M. by A. Sullivan. Royalty, March 25, 1875; Savoy, September 22, 1898.

TRIAL BY JURY, THE. F. T. E. Hook. Hay., May 25, 1811.

TRIAL OF ABRAHAM. Dram. Poem. Ascr. to Mr. Farrar. Oundle, 1700.

TRIAL OF EFFIE DEANS, THE. Dion Boucicault. Westminster Astley's, January 26, 1863.

TRIAL OF LOVE, THE. C. 5 a. D.L., March 1, 1827.

TRIAL OF LOVE, THE. P. S. W. Lovell. Princess's, June 7, 1852.

TRIAL OF PLEASURE, THE. Skelton, 1567.

TRIALS OF TOMKINS, THE. F. 1 a. T. J. Williams. Adelphi T., April 6, 1863.

TRIBULATION; OR, UNWELCOME VISITORS. C. 2 a. J. Poole. Taken fr. French c., *Un Moment d'Imprudence.* Hay., May 3, 1825.

TRIBUT DE ZAMORA. O. Gounod. Paris, 1881.

TRICK; OR, THE VINTNER OUTWITTED. F. Yarrow. Pr. at York. 1742.

TRICK FOR TRICK. F. 2 a. T. Fabian. D.L., 1735.

TRICK FOR TRICK. D. H. J. Stanley. Barnsley Queen's. March 2, 1874.

TRICK FOR TRICK. Irish D. Mr. Gathercole. Dewsbury T.R., February 16, 1877.

TRICK FOR TRICK. D. 4 a. Amy Forrest. Stratford T.R., December 16, 1889.

TRICK FOR TRICK; OR, THE DEBAUCHED HYPOCRITE. C. T. D'Urfey. Revival of Beaumont and Fletcher's *Monsieur Thomas.* T.R., 1678.

TRICK FOR TRICK; OR, ADMIRAL'S DAUGHTER. F. Anon. 1812.

TRICK OF ESMERALDAY. W. E. Bailey and Edgar Ward. West London, February 13, 1897.

TRICK TO CATCH THE OLD ONE. C. T. Middleton. Ac. at Pauls and Black-Fryars, 1616. Pr. 1608. See *A New Way to Pay Old Debts.*

TRICK TO CHEAT THE DEVIL, A. Probably Davenport's *New Trick to Cheat the Devil.* 1639.

TRICK UPON TRICK; OR, SQUIRE BRAINLESS. C. Aaron Hill. D.L., December 22, 1789.

TRICK UPON TRICK; OR, THE VINTNER IN THE SUDS. Edinburgh, 1787.

TRICK YOUTH. Anon. See *Walks of Islington.*

TRICKED. C.O Miss Lena Dalrymple. Athlone Barracks T., September, 1884.

TRICKING A 'TEC. F. E. Drew. M. S. Howard. St. Geo. H., July 21, 1890.

TRICKS. D. E. B. Wyke. Huddersfield T.R., May 11, 1878.

TRICKS. F.C. 3 a. W. F. Field. Orig. pl. as *The Captain.* Barnsley T.R., May 9, 1889.

TRICKS AND HONOURS. Oa. L. Gray. West T., Albert H., May 7, 1897. Matinée T., (late St. Geo. H.), November 11, 1897.

TRICKS OF HARLEQUIN; OR, THE SPANIARD OUTWITTED. Pant. ent. Comic part of *Perseus and Andromeda.* Pr. at Derby. Thought to be compiled by Geo. Browning.

TRICKS OF THE TURF. D. Victoria, May 13, 1867.

TRICKS UPON TRAVELLERS. C.O. Ascribed to Sir J. B. Burgess. Lyceum playbill, August 29, 1810. N.p.

TRICKY ESMERALDA; OR, A WOMAN'S WIT. M.Sk. W. E. Binley and E. Ward. West London, February 13, 1897.

TRICKY TROUVILLE. M. Mélange. 1 a. F. Bowyer and M. by E. Woodville. Stratford Borough, June 1, 1905.

TRICOTRIN. See *A People's Hero* and *A Child of Chance.*

TRILBY. P. 4 a. Dr. by M. Salter fr. G. Du Maurier's novel. Manchester T.R., September 7, 1895; Hay., October 30, 1895; Her Maj., June 7, 1897; May 30, 1903 (and rev.); November 8, 1904.

TRILBY. Burl. H. Pleon. Crewe Lyceum T., November 9, 1895.

TRILBY; OU, LE LUTIN DU FOYER. V. 1 a. Pl. in Fr. by Fr. Co. Lyceum, June 11, 1828.

TRILBY. See *Thrillby.*

TRINUMMUS. C. (B.C. 254-184). Plautus. Adap. fr. the Greek P. by Philemon; trans. into bl. verse by Thornton, Rich. Warner, and Colman, 1769-74. See "Latin Plays," "Westminster Plays."

TRIOMPHE DE L'AMOUR, LE. B.O. Lulli. April 19, 1681.

TRIOMPHE DES ARTS, LE. O. Lamotte.

TRIP TO BENGAL, A. Mus. ent. 2 a. Charles Smith, 1802. Never perf.

TRIP TO BLACKPOOL, A. Farc. Frenzy. 3 a. J. Russell Bogue. Hereford T.R., April 9, 1900.

TRIP TO BRIGHTON, A. F. J. E. Soden. Globe, November 9, 1874.

TRIP TO BRIGHTON. Mus. farc. d. 3 a. Tom R. Seymour. Ly. by Arthur E. Burne. M. by Signor Perrini. Horwich Prince's T., August 7, 1899.

TRIP TO CALAIS, A. C. Samuel Foote. Intended for representation at the Hay. in 1776, but altered and acted under the title of *The Capuchin.*

TRIP TO CALAIS, A. Medley Maritime Sk. "Tim Timbertoe." Before 1812.

TRIP TO CHICAGO, A. Mus. F.C. 2 a. Prod. in America. Vaudeville, August 5, 1893.

TRIP TO CHINATOWN, A. M.C. 2 a. C. Hoyt. Toole's September 29, 1894; Strand, December 17, 1894.

TRIP TO GRETNA, A. C. 2 a. W. B. D'Almeida. Vaudeville, June 3, 1891.

TRIP TO INDIA, A. Dr. Sk. Mr. Bennett. Criterion, November 25, 1875.

TRIP TO KISSINGEN, A. T. Taylor. Lyceum, 1846.

TRIP TO MARGATE, A. F. 3 a. W. Stephens. Peckham Crown T., December 14, 1903.

TRIP TO MIDGET-TOWN, A. American Spectacular Musical B. 4 a. and 11 tab., by Robert Breitenbach. M. by Victor Hollaender. Olympic, September 1, 1899.

TRIP TO PARIS. Lecture by C. Matthews. Lyceum, March 8, 1819, and November 25, 1826.

TRIP TO PLYMOUTH DOCK; OR, THE LAUNCH OF THE "CÆSAR," A. F. Robinson. 1793.

TRIP TO PORTSMOUTH, A. O. Dr. Arne. 1772.

TRIP TO PORTSMOUTH, A. Sk. 1 a. George Alexander Stephens. M. by Didbin. Hay., August 11, 1773.

TRIP TO RUM TUM, A. F.C. 4 a. Russell Bogue. Prod. under title of *O'Hooligan's Holiday*. West Stanley Victoria, February 12, 1894.

TRIP TO SCARBOROUGH, A. C. 3 a. R. B. Sheridan. D.L., February 24, 1777, and December 6, 1815, and October 7, 1823; rev. Charing Cross, 1873.

TRIP TO SCARBOROUGH. F. J. E. Soden. Scarborough St. Geo. H., August 24, 1874.

TRIP TO SCARBOROUGH. See *Miss Hoyden's Husband.*

TRIP TO SCOTLAND, A. F. 1 a. W. Whitehead. D.L., January 6, 1776.

TRIP TO THE HIGHLANDS, A. M.P. 3 a. F. Locke. M. by Mrs. Maitland Malcolm, E. T. de Banzie, W. S. Phipp, and J. G. Aitken. Edinburgh Grand T., April 3, 1905; Marlborough, May 29, 1905.

TRIP TO THE ISLE OF MAN. M. Sk. 2 a. S. F. Bailey. Bootle County H., November 10, 1898.

TRIP TO THE NORE, A. M.E. 1 a. Andrew Franklin. D.L., November 9, 1797.

TRIP TO WALES, A. M.F. 2 a. J. Parry. D.L., November 10, 1826.

TRIPHALES, THE. See "Greek Plays."

TRIPLE ALLIANCE, THE. F.C. 3 a. Chatham O.H., April 26, 1897; Strand, December 6, 1897. See *Poor Tommy.*

TRIPLE BILL, THE. 1 a. Mrs. Adams-Acton, at her residence, St. John's Wood, March 2, 1894.

TRIPLE MARRIAGE, THE. C. Transl. fr. the French of Destouches. Pr. in Foote's Comic T. Vol. 1. 1766.

TRIPLE VENGEANCE. D. 4 a. H. Fuller. Buckie, N.B., Fisherman's H., January 20, 1900.

TRIPLICITY OF CUCKOLDS, THE. P. Thomas Dekker. Ac. 1598.

TRISTAM AND ISEULT. P. 4 a. J. Comyns Carr. Adelphi, September 4, 1907.

TRISTAM, DE LYONS. P. Wr. 1599.

TRISTAM SHANDY. F. 2 a. Leonard McNally. C.G., March 26, 1783.

TRISTAN. D. 5 a. B. H. Hilton. Liverpool Court T., September 7, 1882.

TRISTAN UND ISOLDE. O. R. Wagner. Munich, 1865; D.L., June 20, 1882; C.G., June 15, 1892; first time in English by Carl Rosa company, Liverpool R. Court., April 15, 1898; Lyceum, February 3, 1899; (Moody-Manners' Co.), Lyric, August 2, 1907.

TRISTERMAGH. D. 4 a. M. Ouseley. Walsall T.R., July 23, 1883.

TRISTIA OVID. See "Latin Plays."

TRIUMPH, THE. D. 1 a. Horace W. C. Newte. Folkestone Pleasure Gardens, March 26, 1900.

TRIUMPH OF A LOST CAUSE, THE. Rom. P. 4 a. H. M. Farrington. Kingston County T., June 26, 1905.

TRIUMPH OF ARMS, A. F. W. Foulton. Olympic, December 16, 1872.

TRIUMPH OF BEAUTY, THE. Masque. J. Shirley. Ac. privately. Pr. 1646.

TRIUMPH OF CONSCIENCE, THE. Dr. sk. 1 a. M. Boulton Lancaster Athenæum, May 10, 1905 (C.P.).

TRIUMPH OF CUPID, THE. Masque. Sir George Howard.

TRIUMPH OF DEATH, THE. One of Beaumont and Fletcher's *Four Plays in One*. (Langbaine says this is founded on a novel in the "Fortunate, Deceived, and Unfortunate Lovers.") 1691.

TRIUMPH OF FIDELITY. O. burl. Anon. Rice's Rooms, Brewer Street, Golden Square, 1790.

TRIUMPH OF FIDELITY. D. T. Harpley. Pr. at Liverpool 1790.

TRIUMPH OF GENIUS; OR, THE ACTOR'S JUBILEE. C. 3 a. James Cawdell. Ac. at Scarborough, 1785. N.p.

TRIUMPH OF HEALTH AND PROSPERITY. Middleton. Pr. 1626.

TRIUMPH OF HIBERNIA. M. Anon. C.G., 1752.

TRIUMPH OF HONOUR. T.C. 1 a. Taken fr. Beaumont and Fletcher's *Four Plays in One.* Hay., August 13, 1783. N.p.

TRIUMPH OF HYMEN. M. John Wignell Sheeter's Booth Fair, Bartholomew Fair, 1761.

TRIUMPH OF HYMEN. M. (With poems.) Ryves. Addressed to a nobleman on his marriage, 1777.

TRIUMPH OF HYMEN. Bal. Anon. D.L., 1796.

TRIUMPH OF LONDON, THE. T. Jordan. 1678.

TRIUMPH OF LOVE, THE. Italian O. Her M., April 9, 1705.

TRIUMPH OF LOVE AND BEAUTY. See Collier's "Annals of the Stage." 1515.

TRIUMPH OF MARS AND VENUS, THE. Dram. Perf. Ac. at Christmas, 1552-3.

TRIUMPH OF MIRTH; OR, HARLEQUIN'S WEDDING. Pant. D.L., 1782.

TRIUMPH OF ORIANA, THE. O. Morley. 1601.

TRIUMPH OF PEACE. M. J. Shirley. Whitehall, February 3, 1633. Pr. 1633.

TRIUMPH OF PEACE. M. Dodsley. M. by Dr. Arne. D.L., February 21, 1749.

TRIUMPH OF PRINCE D'AMOUR. M. Sir W. Davenant. 1635.

TRIUMPH OF THE PHILISTINES; AND HOW MR. JORDAN PRESERVED THE MORALS OF MARKET PEWBURY UNDER VERY TRYING CIRCUMSTANCES. C. 3 a. H. A. Jones. St James's, May 11, 1895.

TRIUMPH OF TIME, THE. Masque. One of the four pieces forming Beaumont and Fletcher's *Four Plays or Moral Representations in One.*

TRIUMPH OF TIME AND TRUTH. Orat. Handel. 1745.

TRIUMPH OF TRUTH. Orat. Jefferys. 1767.

TRIUMPH OF TRUTH. P. 4 a. A. Amard. Walsall Grand, January 11, 1904; Dalston, May 16, 1904.

TRIUMPHANT WIDOW; OR, THE MEDLEY OF HONOURS, THE. C. William Duke of Newcastle. Duke's T., 1677.

TRIUMPHS, THE. See *Four Plays in One.*

TRIUMPHS OF FAME AND HONOUR, THE. Compiled by John Taylor, the Water Poet 1634.

TRIUMPHS OF FRIENDSHIP. M. (Unfinished.) Pr. in the "Oxford Miscellany." 1752.

TRIUMPHS OF HEALTH AND PROSPERITY, THE. Middleton, 1625.

TRIUMPHS OF HONOUR AND INDUSTRY. THE. Middleton, 1617.

TRIUMPHS OF HONOUR AND VIRTUE, THE. Middleton. 1622.

TRIUMPHS OF INTEGRITY, THE. Middleton, 1623.

TRIUMPHS OF LONDON, THE. See "London's Annual Triumphs."

TRIUMPHS OF LOVE AND ANTIQUITY, THE. M. Middleton. Perf. at the confirmation of Sir Wm. Cockain, Lord Mayor of London. 1619.

TRIUMPHS OF LOVE AND FORTUNE. Anon. 1589.

TRIUMPHS OF LOVE AND HONOUR. Thos. Cooke. D.L., 1731.

TRIUMPHS OF RE-UNITED BRITANNIA. Pageant. A. Munday. Pr. 1605.

TRIUMPHS OF THE GOUT. Burl. Transl. fr the Greek of Lucian by Gilbert West. Pr. 1747.

TRIUMPHS OF THE SONS OF BALIOL; OR, LIBERTY VANQUISHED. 5 a. By the author of "The Acts of the Apostles." 1810.

TRIUMPHS OF TRUTH. Middleton. 1613.

TRIUMPHS OF VIRTUE. T.C. Anon. D.L., 1697.

TRIXIE. C. 3 a. J. Strange Winter. Scala, July 10, 1908.

TRIXIE IN SEARCH OF A TITLE. M.P. 2 a. D. Day. Lyrics by W. H. Phelan and F. Day. M. by F. Day. Cavendish Rooms, Mortimer St., May 3, 1905.

TRIXIE TRUST. Sk. Bedford M.H., April 3, 1899.

TROADES. T. Transl. fr. Seneca by S. Pordage. 1660.

TROADES. T. Transl. fr. Euripides. Mr. Jas. Banister. 1780.

TROADES; OR, THE ROYAL CAPTIVES. T. Transl. fr. Seneca Sir Edward Sherborne. 1649.

TROAS. T. Transl. fr. Seneca. J. Heywood. 1581.

TROAS. T. Transl. fr. Seneca by J. Talbot. 1686.

TROIA NOVA TRIUMPHANS. Pageant. T. Decker. Ac. 1612.

TROILUS AND CRESSIDA. T. W. Shakespeare. Wr. 1062. Pr. 1608 as never having been ac. F. on Chaucer's Troilus and Cresseide for love story. Caxton's "Troy Book" for story of Hector and Ajax. Chapman's Homer for Thersites, Patroclus, etc. Entered Stationers' Hall, February 7, 1603, and January 28, 1609. Pr. 4to 1609. Great Queen Street, June 1, 1907.

TROILUS AND CRESSIDA; OR, TRUTH FOUND TOO LATE. T. J. Dryden. Duke's T., 1679.

TROIS COUSINS. C. Dancourt. 1664.

TROIS MESSIEURS DE HAVRE, LES. D. 1 a. Leo Marches and C. Vautel. Shaftesbury, March 27, 1908.

TROIS RIVAUX, LES. C. Saurin. 1758.

TROIS SULTANES, LES. B. M. Simon. D.L., August 10, 1830.

TROJA DISTRUTTA. T. Andrea. 1663.

TROJAN CAPTIVES, THE. T. Transl. fr. Euripides by M. Wodhull. 1782. See "Greek Plays."

TROJAN DAMES, THE. T. Transl. fr. Euripides. R. Potter. 1783. See "Greek Plays."

TROJAN WOMAN, THE G. Murray. Transl. fr. Euripides. Court, April 11, 1905.

TROM-AL CAZAR. Op. bo. 1 a. Offenbach. 1856.

TROMB-AL-CA-ZAR; OR, THE ADVENTURES OF AN OPERATIC TROUPE. M. extrav. 1 a. Adap. fr. Offenbach by C. H. Stevenson. Gaiety, August 22, 1870.

TROMPETER VON SAKKINGER, DIE. O. Nessler. Probably the most popular opera in the repertory of German opera houses.

TROOPER BILL. Dr. mil. Sk. Ed. Mactyre. M. by A. Robey. Crouch End Hippo., May 27, 1907.

TROOPER BLAKE. P. 1 a. Margaret Young. Dublin Gaiety, August 12, 1896.

TROOPER CLAIRETTE. C.O. 3 a. Ch. Fawcett. M. by Victor Roger. Adap. fr. *Les Vingt-Nuit Jours de Clairette* of H. Raymond and Antony Mars Folies Dramatiques, May 3, 1892; Liverpool P.O.W., October 31, 1892; Op. C., December 22, 1892.

TROOPER HUGH. Dr. Sk. F. on story of that name by A Wilkinson. York T.R., May 8, 1891.

TROOPER'S OPERA, THE. Anon. Brit. Theatre, 1736.

TROPHEE, LE. O. F. Rebel and F. Francœur. 1745.

TROT'S TROUBLES. C. S. Shields T.R., October 25, 1875.

TROTTY VECK. D. 2 a. Mrs. Charles Calvert. Gaiety, December 26, 1872.

TROUBADOUR, DER. Alex. E. Fesca. (His best O.) Brunswick, 1854.

TROUBADOUR, THE. D. 4 a. Lib. by F. Hueffer. M. by Sir A. C. Mackenzie. D.L., June 8, 1886.

TROUBLED WATERS. F.C. 3 a. Fred Brock. Bayswater Bijou, December 2, 1899 (amat.).

TROUBLES. C. 1 a. B. W. Findon. St. Geo. H., November 22, 1888.

TROUBLES OF A TOURIST, THE. M. Sk. C. Grain. St. Geo. H., October 6, 1884.

TROUBLES OF TRUMBLE, THE. M.F.C. 3 a. Lib. by Fred A. Ellis. Stafford Lyceum T., September 15, 1904 (C.P.).

TROUBLESOME RAIGNE OF KING JOHN, THE. 2 parts. C. Marlowe. Pr. 1591.

TROVATORE, IL. O. Verdi. Rome, January 19, 1853.

TROVATORE, IL. Rom. D. W. E. Suter. Fr. Verdi's opera. C.G., May 10, 1855.

TROVATORE, IL. See *The Mad Mother and Her Lost Son.*

TROVATORE; OR, LARKS WITH A LIBRETTO. Burl. H. J. Byron. Olympic, April 26, 1880.

TROY. P. Ac. at the Rose T., 1596. See *Troye.*

TROY AGAIN. Burl. 1 a. E. A. Bowles. St. Geo. H., March 13, 1888.

TROY'S REVENGE. P. Henry Chettel. 1598.

TROYE. P. Ac. (according to Henslowe), June 22, 1596.

TROYENS, LES. O. Berlioz. (1803-1869.)

TRUANT TOMMY. M. Duol. Leopold Montague. Crediton Town H., October 2, 1901.

TRUANTS, THE. C. 3 a. Wilfred P. Coleby. Kingsway, February 11, 1909.

TRUCULENTUS (B.C. 254-184). Plautus. Transl. into bl. verse by Thornton, Rich, Warner, and Colman. 1769-74. See "Latin Plays."

TRUDGE AND WOWSKI. Prel. T. Knight. Bristol, 1790.

TRUE AS STEEL. D. E. Romaine. Darlington T.R., August 21, 1871; Alfred, September 25, 1871.

TRUE AS STEEL. C. 3 a. Wybert Reeve.

TRUE AS STEEL. W. Muskerry.

TRUE AS STEEL; OR, THE REGENT'S DAUGHTER. D. 2 a. C. H. Hazlewood. Britannia, December 6, 1869.

TRUE AS TRUTH. P. 1 a. A. E. Drinkwater. Glasgow R.T., December 4, 1891.

TRUE AT LAST. Marylebone, April 2, 1866. Stevens. 1771. N.p.

TRUE BLUE; OR, AFLOAT AND ASHORE. D. 5 a. S. Outram and S. Gordon. Olympic, March 19, 1896.

TRUE BLUE. See *The Press Gang*.

TRUE-BORN IRISHMAN, THE. F. Charles Macklin. Dublin, 1763. See *The Irish Fine Lady*.

TRUE-BORN IRISHMAN, THE. F. G. A. Stevens. Ac. at York. 1771. N.p.

TRUE-BORN SCOTCHMAN, THE. C. Charles Macklin. Dublin, July, 1764. See *The Man of the World*.

TRUE BRITISH TAR; OR, A FRIEND AT A PINCH, THE. Mus. 1 a. Hull, 1786.

TRUE BRITON, THE. F. Cranke. D.L., April 17, 1782.

TRUE COLOURS. C. 1 a. J. P. Hurst. Globe, June 11, 1888.

TRUE COLOURS. P. 4 a. C. Hartley. Vaudeville, June 4, 1889.

TRUE FRIENDS. M. Ent. T. Dibdin. M. Attwood. C.G., February 19, 1800.

TRUE GRIT. D. 5 a. H. Pettitt and A. Flaxman. Wigan T.R., March 29, 1895.

TRUE GRIT; OR, REAPING THE HARVEST. D. 4 a. A. Stafford. Woolwich T.R., June 27, 1887.

TRUE HEART. D. Prol. and 3 a. H. Byalt. Leamington T.R., November 23, 1868.

TRUE HEARTS. C. 3 a. F. Bell. St. George's H., May 28, 1874.

TRUE LOVE. C. 3 a. A. Goodrich. Brighton T.R., October 9, 1885.

TRUE LOVE CAN NE'ER FORGET. O. Lover. 1797.

TRUE LOVERS' KNOTS. C. 3 a. H. Pettitt. Gloucester T.R., January 8, 1874.

TRUE NOBILITY. C.D. 3 a. T. M. Ford. Tottenham Holcombe H., April 16, 1892 (amat.).

TRUE PATRIOTISM; OR, POVERTY ENOBLED BY VIRTUE. D. Holford. 1799.

TRUE STORY; TOLD IN TWO CITIES, A. D. 5 a. E. Galer. Leicester O.H., February 7, 1884; D.L., June 15, 1885.

TRUE TILL DEATH. D. 4 a. H. Marston. Adap. fr. the French. Standard, October 23, 1876.

TRUE TILL DEATH. D. 4 a. F. Dix. Bristol T.R., July 13, 1896.

TRUE TILL DEATH. Melo-d. 3 a. Enid Edoni. Brentford Castle, March 12, 1898 (C.P.).

TRUE TO HIS COLOURS. Military Sk. F. Bean. Sadler's Wells, August 15, 1892.

TRUE TO THE CORE. Dom. D. 4 a. W. Clare. Longton Queen's, May 30, 1902; Croydon T.R., June 29, 1903.

TRUE TO THE CORE: A STORY OF THE ARMADA. (T. P. Cook prize D.) D. A. R. Slous. Surrey, September 8, 1866; Princess's, June 15, 1867; rev. Novelty, April 5, 1897.

TRUE TO THE LAST. D. 4 a. J. W. Whitbread. Elephant and Castle, July 16, 1888.

TRUE TO THE QUEEN. Military D. 4 a. H. Whyte. Peckham Crown T., November 26, 1900; (rev. ver.) Grand, July 29, 1901. See *An Englishman's Honour*.

TRUE TRAGEDY OF RICHARD DUKE OF YORK. Ac. 1595. (This is the foundation play of the 3rd part of Shakespeare's *Henry the Sixth*.) Repr. 1600.

TRUE TROJANS; OR, FUIMUS TROES, THE. (Æneid II.) Hist. P. Dr. Fisher. 1633. See *Fuimus Troes*.

TRUE WIDOW, THE. C. T. Shadwell. Duke's, March 21, 1678.

TRUE WOMAN, A. D. 3 a. R. Dodson. Brighton T.R., April 13, 1878.

TRUE WOMAN, A. Dom. D. 4 a. W. J. Wild. Mechanics' Inst., Stockport, February 3, 1897.

TRULY WISE MAN, THE. Anon. See *Theatre of Education*. Pr. 1781.

TRUMP CARD, THE. D. Leicester T.R., February 25, 1878.

TRUMP CARD, THE. D. 5 a. F. W. Broughton and J. W. Jones. Leeds Grand T., April 3, 1882.

TRUMPET CALL, THE. D. 4 a. G. R. Sims and R. Buchanan. Adelphi, August 1, 1891.

TRUMPET MAJOR, THE. P. 4 a. A. H. Evans. Adap. fr. Thomas Hardy's novel. Dorchester Corn Exchange, November 18, 1908 (amat.).

TRUMPETER of SAKKINGEN, THE. O. in German. Nessler. D.L., July 8, 1892.

TRUMPETER'S WEDDING, THE. J. M Morton. Hay.

TRUST. D 4 a H. W. C. Newte. Ladbrook H., April 30, 1891.

TRUST AND TRIAL. D. 4 a. A. C. Calmour. Hull T.R., September 6, 1880; Gaiety, October 9, 1880.

TRUST TO LUCK. D. 3 a. C. A. Clarke. Newport, Mon., New T., April 27, 1891.

TRUTH. Charles Mathews. Olympic, October, 1837.

TRUTH. C. 3 a. B. Howard. Criterion, February 8, 1879, and September 11, 1890.

TRUTH. C. 4 a. Clyde Fitch. Comedy, April 6, 1907.

TRUTH; OR, A GLASS TOO MUCH. D. C. Mathews. Adelphi, March 10, 1834.

TRUTH; OR, THE SPELLS OF LOVE. Spec. 3 a. W. H. Pitt. Britannia, April 10, 1871.

TRUTH AGAINST THE WORLD. D. S. Spencer. East London, April 27, 1870.

TRUTH AND FICTION. Princess's, May 21, 1861.

TRUTH AND FILIAL LOVE. D. 3 a. 1797.

TRUTH, FAITHFULNESS, AND MERCY. Ac. at Whitehall, 1574.

TRUTH FOUND TOO LATE. A ver. of *Troilus and Cressida*, with the above as additional title. J. Dryden. (?) 1679.

TRUTH IN ABSENCE. Sk. Shepherd's Bush Empire, December 21, 1908.

TRUTH'S SUPPLICATION TO CANDLE-LIGHT. P. T. Dekker. 1599.

TRUTHFUL JAMES. C. 3 a. J. Mortimer and C. Klein. G. Yarmouth T.R., September 24, 1894; Royalty, October 2, 1894.

TRY AGAIN. F. Anon. Hay., June 26, 1790.

TRYAL OF CONJUGAL LOVE, THE. See *Nest of Plays*. Jacob. 1738.

TRYAL OF THE LADY ALLUREA LUXURY, THE. D. Anon. 1757.

TRYAL OF TREASURE, A. P.

TRYAL OF SAMUEL FOOTE, ESQ., FOR A LIBEL ON PETER PARAGRAPH, THE. Foote. Hay., 1763. See *The Orators*.

TRYAL OF THE TIME KILLERS, THE. C. 5 a. Dr. Bacon. 1745.

TRYAL OF TREASURE, THE. Ent. Thomas Purfoote. 1567.

TRYAL'S ALL. C. Believed to be the production of Mr. Herbert. Dublin Crow Street T., 1802.

TRYALL OF CHIVALRY, THE HISTORY OF. Ascr. to William Wayer. Ac. by the Right Hon. the Lord of Darby and his servants, 1605.

TRYALS OF THE HEART. P. 3 a. D.L., April 24, 1799.

TRYING A MAGISTRATE. F. Sk. J. L. Toole. Globe, December 17, 1877.

TRYING IT ON. F. 1 a. Wm. Brough. Lyceum, May 3, 1853.

TRYING SCENES OF LIFE. D. C. Gardner. Sunderland Lyceum, July 19, 1876.

TRYPHON. T. Roger Boyle. Earl of Orrery, Duke of York's, 1668; L.I.F., December 8, 1668.

TU QUOQUE. C. by Cook. By reason of Greene's fine acting often called *Greene's Tu Quoque*, q.v. 1599.

TU QUOQUE. See *The Bubble*.

TUBBY AND GAWKS. P. 1 a. F. K. Péile. Avenue, December 31, 1903.

TUFELHAUSER. Rom. D. 2 a. J. B. Johnstone. First perf. at Surrey T., March 24, 1856.

TUMBLE-DOWN DICK; OR, PHAETON IN THE SUDS. F. H. Fielding. Hay., 1737.

TUNBRIDGE WELLS; OR, A DAY'S COURTSHIP. C. Rawlins. D.L., 1678.

TUNBRIDGE WALKS; OR, THE YEOMAN OF KENT. C. T. Baker. D.L., January 27, 1703.

TUPPENNY TUBE; OR, THE FLYING MACHINE, THE. Sk. 2 sc. Wr. by Tom Terriss. Islington Empire, April 13, 1908.

TUPPINS AND CO. Malcolm Watson and Ed. Solomon. St. Geo. H., March 29, 1889.

TUPYSIUS AND CO. Ca. 1 a. M. Watson and E. Solomon. St. Geo. H., June 24, 1889.

TURCARET. C. Lesage. 1708.

TURCO IN INDIA. O. Rossini. 1814.

TURES IN ITALIA, IL. Rossini. Milan, August 14, 1814; King's T., May 19, 1821.

TURF, THE. Racing Sk. Lemon. Wigan T.R., February 29, 1884.

TURK AND NO TURK. M.C. G. Colman, jun. Hay., July 9, 1785. N.p.

TURKE, THE. T. John Mason called in another edition pr. in 1632, "An excellent Tragedy of Muleasses the Turk, and Borgias Governor of Florence. Ent. Stationer's H., October 3, 1608. Pr. qto 1610.

TURKINGTON'S TALISMAN. M.C. 3 a. B. Banks and C. Krall. Dublin Leinster H., December 11, 1893.

TURKISH BATH. F. 1 a. Montagu Williams and F. C. Burnand. Adelphi, April 29, 1861.

TURKISH BATH, A. Duol. A. Chapman and E. L. Furst. Bayswater Bijou, April 21, 1903.

TURKISH COURT; OR, THE LONDON 'PRENTICE, THE. Burl. Mrs. Letitia Pilkington. Dublin Little T., Capel Street. 1748. N.p.

TURKISH LOVERS, THE. O. Rossini. Adap. by R. Lacy. D.L., May 1, 1827.

TURKISH LOVERS; OR, THE PACHA'S REVENGE, THE. Oriental Spec. 2 a. Capt. W. H. Armstrong. M. by Harroway. D.L., March 7, 1853.

TURKISH MAHOMET AND HIREN, THE FAIRE GREEK, THE. P. G. Peele. 1594. N.p.

TURKO THE TERRIBLE; OR, THE FAIRY ROSES. Extrav. W. Brough. Holborn, December 26, 1868.

TURLUTUTU. Britannia, December 26, 1877.

TURN HIM OUT. F. 1 a. T. J. Williams. Strand, August 17, 1863.

TURN OF THE TIDE, THE. D. 4 a. F. C. Burnand. Long Acre Queen's T., May 29, 1869; Grecian, March 7, 1870.

TURN OUT. M.F. 2 a. J. Kenney. D.L., March 7, 1812, and February 12, 1814; Lyceum, June 26, 1816.

TURN ROUND. D. Newport, Mon., Victoria H., October 29, 1870 (amat.).

TURN TO THE RIGHT; OR, A PLEA FOR A SIMPLE LIFE. C. 4 a. W. F. Stanley. Sherwood Stanley H., May 23, 1905.

TURNCOAT. A parody of the Tragedy of *Athelstan*. 1756.

TURNED HEAD, THE. F. 1 a. G. A. à Beckett. Strand, November 24, 1834; Victoria, 1835.

TURNED OUT TO STARVE; OR, THE HAND THAT GOVERNS ALL. D. 2 a. T. Webb. Britannia, February 21, 1870.

TURNED UP. F.C. 3 a. M. Melford. Glasgow Grand T., April 19, 1886; Vaudeville, May 27, 1886; Strand, February 14, 1891.

TURNING THE TABLES. F. 1 a. J. Poole. D.L., November 11, 1830, and March 4, 1851.

TURNING THE TABLES. F. Sk. By Miss Louisa Peach. Britannia, October 15, 1902.

TURNING THE TABLES. Sk. Empress, May 3, 1900.

TURNIP-TOP VILLAGE. F. 1 a. B. R. Morton. Publ. by S. French, Ltd.

TURNO ARICINI. O. Leo and Vinci. Brussels Conservatoire. Naples, 1724.

TURNO ARICINO. O. Scarlatti. Rome. 1720.

TURNPIKE GATE, THE. M. Ent. 2 a. T. Knight. C.G., November 14, 1799; D.L., February 9, 1814; Lyceum, September 12, 1818.

TURPIN A LA MODE. M. Burl. 2 a. G. P. Huntley and G. Gray. M. by H. C. Barry. Add. lyrics by J. J. Wood. Chester Royalty, March 29, 1897.

TURPIN'S RIDE TO YORK. Sk. Oxford M.H., May 27, 1908.

TURPIN'S RIDE TO YORK; OR, THE DEATH OF BONNY BLACK BESS. Spec. Sk. 5 sc. Paragon M.H., August 14, 1905.

TURQUOISE RING, THE. G. W. Godfrey and Lionel Benson. Circa 1865.

TURRET CLOCK, THE. Melo-d. 2 a. M. by Lanza. D.L., January 28, 1818.

TURTLE DOVES. F.C. 3 a. Ashton-under-Lyne Booth's T., November 22, 1880.

TUSCAN TREATY; OR, TARQUIN'S OVERTHROW, THE. T. Revised and alt. by W. Bond. Prol. by A. Hill. C.G., 1733.

TUTOR, THE. Burl. Anon. D.L., December 14, 1759. N.p.

TUTOR, THE. F. Ascr. to Rev. J. Townley. D.L., 1765. Pr. 1765.

TUTOR FOR THE BEAUX; OR, LOVE IN A LABYRINTH, A. C. J. Hewitt. L.I.F., February 21, 1737.

TUTTY IN MASCHERA. C.O. Pedrotti. 1817-1893. Paris.

'TWAS ALL FOR LOVE. C. 3 a. S. Granville. King's Cr., November 12, 1877.

'TWAS DAWN AND DAYLIGHT. Sk. Stoke Newington Pal., July 6, 1908.

'TWAS EVER THUS. P. 3 a. D. Cooke. Hackney Manor T., April 22, 1901.

'TWAS I. F. 1 a. J. H. Payne. C.G., December, 1825; rev., Lyceum, November 20, 1828.

'TWAS IN TRAFALGAR'S BAY. Hist. Rom. D. 5 a. J. Henderson, Cardiff T.R., February 2, 1889; Marylebone, November 21, 1891.

TWEE DU. Welsh Light O. 2 a. G. Blackmore. S. Norwood Stanley Hall, November 28, 1907 (amat.).

TWEEDIE'S RIGHTS. C.D. 2 a. J. Albery. Vaudeville, May 27, 1871.

TWEEDLETON'S TAIL COAT. F. T. J. Williams. Lyceum, October 8, 1866.

TWELFTH NIGHT. O. C.G., November 8, 1820.

TWELFTH NIGHT. Kitchen Scene. Arr. as a Sk. Holborn Empire, September 27, 1909.

TWELFTH NIGHT; OR, WHAT YOU WILL. C. W. Shakespeare. Begun 1594, completed 1601. Source of plot probably Barnaby Rich's history of *Apolonius and Silla*. Pr. in 1581. Ac. at Middle Temple H., 1602. Marston took the second title for a play of his own in 1607. Pr. 1623. Hay., November 11, 1848; Princess's, 1850; Daly's, January 8, 1894; Lyceum, March 22, 1900; H.M., February 5, 1901; H.M., June 2, 1902; April 26, 1905; April 27, 1906; rev. Waldorf, April 26, 1907; rev. by Mr. Tree, H.M., April 22, 1908.

TWELFTH NIGHT'S REVELS. Masque. Ben Jonson. Ac. at Court in January, 1618. Also known as *The Masque of Blackness*.

TWELFTH OF AUGUST. D.F. Brighton, August 13, 1805. N.p.

TWELVE ANGELS. D. 3 a. E. Towers. East London, November 6, 1869.

TWELVE LABOURS OF HERCULES, THE. C. 2 a. R. B. Brough. Punch's Playhouse and Strand T., December 26, 1851.

TWELVE MONTHS. MS. of the 17th century. 1846.

TWELVE MONTHS, THE. Burl. G. A. à Beckett. Strand.

TWELVE, PRECISELY; OR, A NIGHT AT DOVER. P. 1 a. Milner. Olympic, January 1, 1821; Hay., October 11, 1822.

TWENTIETH-CENTURY GIRL; OR, THE WEAKER VESSEL. M.C. C. Trevelyan. Norwich T.R., December 26, 1895.

TWENTY DAYS IN THE SHADE. Farc. C. 3 a. Adap. by Paul M. Potter fr. the Fr. of Hennequin and Veber. Margate R., March 29, 1909.

TWENTY MINUTES' CONVERSATION UNDER AN UMBRELLA. Int. A. W. Dubourg, Hay., July 4, 1873.

TWENTY MINUTES WITH A TIGER. F. 1 a. Adap. fr. the French. D.L., October 29, 1855.

TWENTY PER CENT. F. 2 a. D.L., November 2, 1815.

£20 A YEAR, ALL FOUND. F. H. J. Byron. Folly, April 17, 1876.

TWENTY STRAWS. D. B. Henry. Blyth Octagon T., January 27, 1873.

TWENTY THOUSAND POUNDS A YEAR. D. E. Towers. New Pavilion, September 18, 1871.

TWENTY YEARS AGO. M.E. M. by T. Walsh. Lyceum playbill, July 31, 1816.

TWENTY YEARS AGO. Melo-d. J. Pocock. Lyceum, July, 1810; D.L.C., May 31, 1811.

TWENTY YEARS IN A DEBTORS' PRISON. City, September 20, 1858.

TWENTY-ONE. O. 1 a. J. Wild. Trans. fr. *Le Trente et Quarante*, 1804. N.ac.

TWENTY-ONE. Fairy Oa. 2 a. Lucy Wintle. Bayswater Bijou, June 22, 1905.

22A, CURZON STREET. P. 3 a. Brandon Thomas and J. Edwards. Garrick, March 2, 1898.

TWENTY-FOURTH OF GEORGE II., THE. New Royalty, May 2, 1866.

24 H.-P. ELOPEMENT, A. Ca. Mrs. Caleb Porter and J. Condurier. Fr. the French of Pierre Louÿs and Henri de Forge. New, July 1, 1904.

TWENTY-FIVE. P. 1 a. Lady Gregory. Queen's Gate Hall, May 2, 1903 (amat.).

TWICE FOOLED. Co. 1 a. "Lamda Ma." Gaiety, July 23, 1895.

TWICE KILLED. F. J. Oxenford. Olympic November 26, 1835. D.L., March 31, 1852.

TWICE MARRIED. C.D. 3 a. C. O'Neill and H. Sylvester. Gaiety, April 25, 1867.

TWICE MARRIED AND A MAID STILL. Droll. Pd. N.d.

TWICE-TOLD TALE, A. F. 1 a. J. P. Wooler. Olympic, September 27, 1858.

TWICE WEDDED. D. 3 a. J. Horn. Banbury Exchange H., August 9, 1882.

TWIDDLETON TWINS, THE. F. M. B. Spurr and J. R. Crauford. M. by G. Sardelli. Cripplegate Inst., March 3, 1900.

TWIG FOLLY. D. 4 a. R. Dodson. Pavilion, April 22, 1878.

TWILIGHT. D. 3 a. W. Barrett. Sunderland Lyceum, September 20, 1871.

TWILIGHT. M.C. 2 a. W. Geary. Gas Band Room, Brentford, March 24, 1887.

TWILIGHT. P. 1 a. H. E. Dalroy. Middlesbrough T.R., June 19, 1893; Parkhurst, May 7, 1894.

TWILIGHT. P. 1 a. H. Swears. Hammersmith Lyric, August 31, 1896.

TWILIGHT TO DAWN. D. 2 a. Stafford Lyceum T., October 8, 1885.

TWIN ADVENTURERS; OR, BLUNDERING BROTHERS. D.L., May 17, 1710.

TWIN BROTHERS, THE. C. Transl. fr Plautus by Richard Warner. 1772.

TWIN BROTHERS; OR, THE WARNING VISION, THE. D. W. Paul. Marylebone, February 16, 1874.

TWIN RIVALS, THE. C. G. Farquhar, C.G., December 14, 1702.

TWIN SISTER, THE. 4 a. Transl. by L. N. Parker fr. L. Fulda. Duke of York's, January 1, 1902.

TWIN SISTERS, THE. C. 3 a. Miss E. Schiff. Charing Cr., April 18, 1870.

TWIN SISTERS, THE. D. B Lemain. Tunstall T.R., October 8, 1877.

TWINS. F.C. 3 a. Joseph Derrick. Olympic, August 2, 1884.

TWINS, THE. T.C. W. Rider. Salisbury Court, 1655.

TWINS; OR, THE COMEDY OF ERRORS, THE. Alt. fr. Shakespeare by T. Hull. C.G., 1762. N.p.

TWINS; OR, WHICH IS IT, HE OR HIS BROTHER? THE. F. M. G. Lewis. D.L., April 8, 1799.

TWINS; OR, WHICH IS WHICH? THE. C. 3 a. An alt. fr. *The Comedy of Errors* by W. Woods. Edinburgh, 1780.

TWINS OF SKIRLAUGH HALL, THE. P. and pro. 4 a. Emma Brooke. Adap. fr. her novel of same name. Margate T.R., June 17, 1907.

TWINS' TRAGEDY, THE. See *The Twynnes*, etc.

TWINE THE PLAIDEN; OR, THE IMPROVISATORE. D. 4 a. G. R. Walker. Plymouth T.R., August 10, 1877; Globe, May 22, 1878.

TWINKLE, TWINKLE, LITTLE STAR. Aquarium, December 26, 1876.

TWISTING AND TWINING; OR, TEA'S THE TWADDLE. Int. Hay., 1785. N.p.

TWISTING OF THE ROPE. D. Hyde. Wr. in the Irish language. Dublin Gaiety, October 21, 1901 (amat.).

'TWIXT AXE AND CROWN; OR, THE LADY ELIZABETH. Hist. P. 5 a. Tom Taylor. Queen's, Long Acre, January 22, 1870; Princess's, 1873; Manchester T.R. (rev. ver.), October 12, 1889; Fulham Grand, February 19, 1906.

'TWIXT CRIME AND PRISON. Playlet. P. F. Parry. Woolwich Public H., November 11, 1897.

'TWIXT CUP AND LIP. C. 3 a. C. A. de la Plume. Olympic, June 14, 1873.

'TWIXT CUP AND LIP. Ca. 2 a. W. Sapte, jun. Ealing Lyric H., April 18, 1889; Strand, November 18, 1893.

'TWIXT CUP AND LIP. Ca. F. M. Douglas. F. on a story by Thackeray. Bayswater Bijou, October 2, 1901.

'TWIXT DAWN AND DAYLIGHT. Sk. V. L. Granville and Fred Russell. Stoke Newington Palace, July 6, 1908.

'TWIXT DUSK AND DAWN. Sk. 3 sc. W. H. Benson. Battersea Palace, January 4, 1909.

'TWIXT GOLD AND LOVE; OR, A TRUE WOMAN'S HEART. D. Scarborough T.R., November 5, 1883.

'TWIXT GOOD AND EVIL. D. 4 a. C. A. Clarke and T. Morton Powell. Farnworth Queen's, December 17, 1900.

'TWIXT HEART AND SOUL. D. 1 a. B. Copping. Newmarket Victoria H., September 8, 1902.

'TWIXT KITH AND KIN. D. 4 a. Adap. by J. J. Blood fr. Miss Braddon's *Cut by the County*. Birmingham P.O.W., August 25, 1887; Grand, October 10, 1887.

'TWIXT LOVE AND ART. C. 3 a. Adap. fr. Julian Hawthorne's story "Pauline" by H. B. Cooper. Wolverhampton T.R., December 18, 1882.

'TWIXT LOVE AND DUTY. 1 a. M. Harvey. Southampton P.O.W., July 11, 1889.

'TWIXT LOVE AND DUTY. C.D. Pro. and 4 a. J. Worden and R. Johnston. Preston T.R., December 9, 1889.

'TWIXT LOVE AND DUTY. D. J. Curtain. Lowestoft Public H., March 26, 1894.

'TWIXT LOVE AND DUTY. P. 1 a. C. Windermere. Dublin T.R., May 11, 1901.

'TWIXT LOVE AND WAR. Oa. R. Miles. Wells Town H., January 18, 1892.

'TWIXT NIGHT AND MORN. D. 2 episodes. E. M. Seymour. Avenue, May 28, 1896.

'TWIXT THE CUP AND THE LIP. J. Poole. Hay., June 12, 1826.

TWO ANGRIE WOMEN OF ABINGTON, THE. C. H. Porter. In 2 parts. Ac. by the Lord Admiral's servants. 1599. Pr. 1599. See *Two Merry Women*.

TWO APPRENTICES; OR, INDUSTRY AND IDLENESS REWARDED, THE. Pant. W. C. Oulton. F. on Hogarth's pant. Birmingham, 1798. N.p.

TWO BLINDS, THE. Oa. A. Clements. Gaiety T., August 31, 1874.

TWO BLINDS, THE. See *Blind Beggars*.

TWO BONNYCASTLES, THE. F. 1 a. J. M. Morton. Hay., November 11, 1851.

TWO BOYS, THE. Adap. fr. *Les Deux Gosses*. G. R. Sims and A. Shirley. Princess's T., May 21, 1896 (C.P.). See *Two Little Vagabonds*.

TWO BROTHERS. D. 1 a. Publ. by S. French, Ltd.

TWO BROTHERS, THE. T. by Smith. Ac. 1602.

TWO CAN PLAY AT THE GAME. C. 1 a. Publ. by S. French, Ltd.

TWO CHRISTMAS EVES. Dom. D. 4 a. A. E. Drinkwater. Liverpool Shakespeare, December 1, 1888; (5 a.) Ealing Victoria H., February 5, 1891.

TWO CHUMS. C. 1 a. L. Debenham. Publ. by S. French, Ltd.

TWO COMMON SAILORS, THE. Nautical D. 4 a. R. Overton. Colchester T.R., April 9, 1883.

TWO CONFESSIONS. Episode. 1 a. F. Fenn. St. Geo. H., April 11, 1899.

TWO CONNOISSEURS, THE. C. W. Hayley. Hay., September 2, 1784.

TWO COQUETTES, THE. C. 4 a. J. Albery. Liverpool P.O.W., October 29, 1870.

TWO DOCTOR HOBBS'S. F. C.G., July 1, 1815.

TWO DOORS IN A PASSAGE. Manchester Tivoli, April 26, 1909.

TWO DROVERS, THE. Legendary D. 2 a. H. Goff. Surrey.

TWO ENGLISH GENTLEMEN; OR, THE SHAM FUNERAL, THE. C. J. Stewart. Hay., 1774.

TWO FACES UNDER A HOOD. C.O. T. Dibdin. M. by Mr. Shield. C.G., November 17, 1807.

TWO FARMERS, THE. M. Afterpiece. 1800. ? N. ac.

TWO FLAGS, THE. Franco-British. Div. in 3 sc. Arr. and prod. by Alfrido Curti. M. comp. and arr. by Geo. W. Byng. Alhambra, May 25, 1908.

TWO FLATS AND A SHARP. F. 1 a. By A. Maltby. Globe, December 17, 1873.

TWO FOSCARI, THE. Byron, 1821.

TWO FRIENDS, THE. D. Proverb. Transl. fr. the French of Carmentel by Thos. Holcroft. 1804.

TWO FRIENDS, THE. D. 2 a. By R. Lacy. Hay., July 11, 1828.

TWO FRIENDS, THE. See *The Binbian Mine.*

TWO FRIENDS; OR, THE LIVERPOOL MERCHANT. D. By C. H. 1800.

TWO GALLEY SLAVES, THE. Melo-d. 2 a. Adap. fr. the French by J. H. Payne. M. by Cooke and Horn. C.G., November 6, 1822.

TWO GAY DECEIVERS; OR, BLACK, WHITE, AND GREY. F. 1 a. Robertson and T. H. Lacy. Strand.

TWO GENTLEMEN OF VERONA C. W. Shakespeare. Begun 1593, completed 1595. Greater part taken from the story of the Shepherdess Felismona in the *Diana* of Montemayor (1560). Transl. of *Diana* by Thomas Wilson in 1595-6. N.p. Another by Bartholomew Young, 1582-3. Pr. November, 1598. End of play taken fr. "Apollonius and Sylla," a novel by Bandello, extant in 1554. Mentioned by Meres in 1598. Alt. by B. Victor, D.L., December 22, 1762; J. P. Kemble, C.G., 1808; Court, April 8, 1904; Daly's, July 2, 1905.

TWO GENTLEMEN OF VERONA. O. C.G., 1821.

TWO GENTS IN A FIX. F. 1 a. W. E. Suter.

TWO GREGORIES; OR, WHERE DID THE MONEY COME FROM? T. Dibdin. Lyceum, August 31, 1821, and November 1, 1824; Surrey, 1821; D.L., June 14, 1826.

TWO HARLEQUINS. F. 3 a. Brown. M. by Noble. Ac. by the K.'s Italian comedians at Paris. Afterwards perf. at L.I.F., 1718.

TWO HARLEQUINS, THE. O. 1 a. M. E. Jonas. English words by G. à Beckett. Gaiety, December 21, 1868.

TWO HARPIES, THE. P. Michael Drayton, assisted by Dekker, Mundy, Middleton, and Webster. 1602. N.p.

TWO HEADS ARE BETTER THAN ONE. F. 1 a. L. Horne. Lyceum, December, 1854; D.L., December 8, 1856.

TWO HEARTS. P. 1 a. S. J. A. Fitzgerald. Royalty, February 6, 1894. (Soc. of Br. Dr. Art.)

TWO HEARTS, THE. P. 4 a. W. Ellis. Brunswick House, S.W., November 4, 1901.

TWO HEARTS OF GOLD. M.D. 4 a. R. P. Oglesby and C. H. Pierson. Bradford Prince's, February 11, 1903.

TWO HOUSES, THE. C. Dibdin. 1785. N.p. See *A Game at Commerce.*

TWO HOUSES OF GRENADA, THE. C.D. 3 a. M. by Wade. D.L., October 31, 1826.

TWO HUNDRED A YEAR. Ca. 1 a. A. W. Pinero. Globe, October 6, 1877; Liverpool P.O.W., September 8, 1882.

TWO HUNDRED YEARS AGO; OR, TWO LOVES AND TWO LIVES. D. 3 a. R. Dodson. Victoria, April 13, 1872.

TWO HUSSARS, THE. Military Scena. Harry Bruce. Sebright M.H., August 18, 1890.

TWO HUSSARS, THE. Military D. 4 a. W. Burnot and H. Bruce. Darwen T.R., August 4, 1894; Surrey, June 8, 1896; (second edition) York T.R., February 17, 1896.

TWO IN A FLAT. F. C. Epis. F. Monckton and Chas. Windermere. Battersea Palace, January 4, 1909.

TWO IN A TRAP. Duol. A. E. Drinkwater. Wyndham's, June 22, 1909.

TWO IN THE BUSH. F. M. Carson. Olympic, August 15, 1891.

TWO IN THE DARK. Ca. Mme. Paul Blouet fr. Croquet Poulle. Crouch End O.H., May 1, 1899.

TWO IN THE MORNING. C. Sc. C. Mathews. C.G., October 3, 1840.

TWO ITALIAN GENTLEMEN, THE. D. Munday. 1584. Afterwards called *Fidele and Fortunio.*

TWO JOHNNIES, THE. F.C. 3 a. Adap. fr. *Durand et Durand* by M. Ordonneau and A. Valabègne by F. Horner and F. Wyatt. Northampton O.H., April 27, 1888; Comedy, June 6, 1889; Trafalgar Square, October 5, 1893.

TWO JOLLY BACHELORS. P. 1 a. Ed Martin Seymour. Publ. by S. French, Ltd.

TWO KINGS IN A COTTAGE. Mentioned in Herbert's Diary under date of November 19, 1623.

TWO KLINGSBERGS, THE. D. One of Kotzebue's best plays, but not yet transl. into English.

TWO LAMENTABLE TRAGEDIES. Yarrington. Pr. 1661.

TWO LITTLE DRUMMER BOYS. D. 4 a. Walter Howard. Glasgow Grand, June 1, 1899; Loughborough New T., October 23, 1899.

TWO LITTLE HEROES. Surrey, May 20, 1901.

TWO LITTLE MAIDS FROM SCHOOL. Adap. by R. Buchanan and C. Marlowe (fr. Duma's "Leur Demoiselles de St. Cyr"). Camberwell Metropole, November 21, 1898.

TWO LITTLE SAILOR BOYS. D. 4 a. Walter Howard. Plymouth T.R., July 15, 1901; Stratford T.R., March 31, 1902; Rotherhithe Terriss, February 3, 1902.

TWO LITTLE VAGABONDS. Melo-d. 5 a. (Adap. by G. R. Sims and A. Shirley fr. *Les Deux Gosses*, by Pierre Decourcelle, Ambigu, Paris, February 19, 1896). Princess's, September 23, 1896, October 4, 1897, and October 21, 1901; Lyceum, July 24, 1909. See *The Two Boys.*

TWO LITTLE WOODEN SHOES. See *The Little Pilgrim.*

TWO LOVELY BLACK-EY'D SUSAN. Burl. Perversion of D. Jerrold's D. by Horace Lennard. M. by O. Barrett. Crystal Pal., April 2, 1888; Strand, April 11, 1888.

TWO LOVES AND A LIFE. D. T. Taylor and C. Reade. Adelphi, March 20, 1854; Sadler's Wells, October 31, 1868.

TWO MAIDS OF MORE CLACKE, WITH THE LIFE AND SIMPLE MANER OF JOHN IN THE HOSPITALL, THE HISTORY OF THE. R. Armin. 1609. Pl. by children of the King's Majestie's Revels.

TWO MAJORS, THE. Oa. Mr. Faning. Royal Acad., July 18, 1877.

TWO MAKE A PAIR, THE. C. Fr. the French. D.L., April 7, 1827.

TWO MARY ANNES, THE. Sk. F. Conti and R. M. Harvey. Shepherd's Bush Empire, March 27, 1907.

TWO MEN. Afterwards called *The Three Criminals.* D. 4 a. W. Bourne. Cardiff Grand, December 7, 1896; West London, December 14, 1896.

TWO MEN AND A MAID. D. 4 a. F. H. Purchase and J. Webster. Comedy, June 20, 1893 (Sch. Dr. Art perf.).

TWO MEN AND A MAID. P. 4 a. M. Watson. Northampton O.H., March 1, 1905 (C.P.).

TWO MEN AND A WOMAN. D. 4 a. C. Alan-Himeson. Mexborough P.O.W., September 4, 1901; Garston T.R., December 16, 1901.

TWO MEN AND A WOMAN. Dr. Episode. Madge Girdlestone. Palace, February 20, 1905.

TWO MERRY MILKMAIDS; OR, THE BEST WORDS WEAR THE GARLAND. C. By J. C. 1620. Ac. by the company of Revels before the King, 1661. See *The Invisible Smirk.*

TWO MERRY WOMEN OF ABINGTON, THE. P. Henry Porter. 1598. N.p. See *Two Angrie Women.*

TWO MISERS, THE. M.F. H. O'Hara. M. by Cooke. C.G., January 21, 1775; D.L., April 16, 1816.

TWO MISS PETTIFERS. 4 a. W. Sayer Mackay and R. Ord. Newcastle-on-Tyne, March 3, 1904.

TWO MISSES IBBETSON. P. 1 a. Ina Leon Cassilis. Pub. by French, Ltd.

TWO MR. BROWNS. F. Wr. by "a gentleman of Bath." Bath, May 6, 1825.

TWO MR. WETHERBYS. C. 3 a. St. John Hankin. Imperial, March 15, 1903.

TWO MRS. HOMESPUNS, THE. F.C. J. H. Darnley and H. A. Bruce. Camberwell Metropole, March 25, 1901.

TWO MOTHERS, THE. D. 5 a. Mayer and Child. Duke's T., March 31, 1877.

TWO MOTHERS, THE. D. 4 a. W. A. Brabner and J. M. Hardie, jun. Glasgow Metropole, March 5, 1900; Greenwich Morton's, June 18, 1900.

"TWO" MUCH ALIKE. Burl. Ca. Geo. Grossmith, jun., and A. R. Rogers. Gallery of Illustration. February 12, 1870.

TWO MURDERERS, THE. Adap. by Selby fr. the French. City T., 1835.

TWO NAUGHTY BOYS. M. Fairy P. 2 a. Geo. Grossmith, jun. F. on the picture-books of W. Busch and P. Cox. Comp. by Constance Tippett. Lyrics by P. Greenbank. Add. numbers by C. H. Bovill and P. Braham. Gaiety, January 8, 1907.

TWO NAUGHTY OLD LADIES. C. 1 a. A. Rose. Pub. by S. French, Ltd.

TWO NOBLE KINSMEN, THE. T.C. Possibly W. Shakespeare wrote part of this play in 1609, and Fletcher completed it in 1613. In the quarto of 1634 it is stated to have been written by Shakespeare and Fletcher. The play f. on "The Knight's Tale" of Chaucer. Blackfriars, 1634.

TWO NOBLE KINSMEN, THE. See *The Rivals.*

TWO NOBLE LADIES; OR, CONVERTED CONJUROR. MS. preserved in private library in Ireland.

TWO O'CLOCK IN THE MORNING. Comic scene. D.L., June 22, 1841.

TWO OLD BLOKES. C. 1 a. Portsmouth T.R., March 17, 1871.

TWO OLD MAIDS OF FLORENCE. F. Anon. 1608.

TWO ON A 'BUS. Duol. Sk. Herbert Swears. Cripplegate Institute, November 17, 1904.

TWO OR ONE? Avenue, March 3, 1891. See *Will He Come Home Again?*

TWO ORPHANS, THE. D. 6 a. Adap. fr. the French by J. Oxenford. Olympic T., September 14, 1874.

TWO ORPHANS, THE. See *The Blind Girl's Fortune.*

TWO PAGES OF FREDERICK THE GREAT. J. Poole. C.G., December 1, 1821.

TWO PATHS IN LIFE, THE. D. E. R. Callender. Plymouth T.R., April 9, 1875; Victoria, April 22, 1876.

TWO PENCE. F. 2 a. M. by G. Reeves and M. Pindar. Lyceum, July 14, 1821.

TWO PHOTOGRAPHS. F. 1 a. A. Clements. Strand, March 6, 1884.

TWO PICTURES. Dr. Epis. Arthur Shirley. Chelsea Palace, January 7, 1907.

TWO PINS, THE. C. of the middle ages in 4 a. Frank Stayton. Newcastle T.R., April 2, 1908; Aldwych, June 8, 1908.

TWO PLOTS DISCOVERED; A THIRD PAYS FOR ALL. C. By "G. P." Intended to be ac. at C.G. 1742.

TWO POETS, THE. F. 1 a. John Courtnay. Surrey T., November 25, 1850.

TWO POETS, THE. C.O. 2 a. J. E. Germain. St. Geo. H., December 21, 1886.

TWO PRINCESSES. C. 1 a. L. Debenham. Pub. by S. French, Ltd.

TWO PRO'S, THE. M.F. 1 a. F Bowyer and G. Jacobi. P.O.W., December 4, 1886.

TWO PUDDIFOOTS. F. 1 a. Adap. by J M. Morton. Olympic, October 14, 1867.

TWO Q.C.'S, THE. O. Captain F. Fox. M. by H. C. Banks. Alexandra Pal., July 25, 1881.

TWO QUEENS, THE. C. 1 a. J. B. Buckstone. May 5, 1836.

TWO QUEENS OF BRENTFORD; OR, BAYES NO POETASTER, THE. M.F. T Durfey. 1721.

TWO RECRUITS. C. 3 a. F. Wyatt. Toole's, November 8, 1890.

TWO RINGS, THE. O. I. Range. Hastings Public H., April 6, 1885.

TWO ROADS OF LIFE; OR, RIGHT AND WRONG, THE. D. Swansea T.R., August 14, 1871.

TWO ROSES, THE. C. 3 a. J. Albery. Vaudeville, June 4, 1870.

TWO RUBIES, THE. D. C. Kingsley. Liverpool Adelphi, January 12, 1894.

TWO RUNAWAY GIRLS. Sk. 1 scene. Brien M'Cullough. Clapham Junction Grand, August 8, 1904.

TWO SAMPLES. C. 3 a. H. T. Craven.

TWO SECONDS. C. M. Mr. Barnett. Lyceum, August 28, 1827.

TWO SINNES OF KING DAVID, THE. Int. Anon. 1561. N.p.

TWO SISTERS. C. 1 a. E. H. Keating. Pub. by S. French, Ltd.

TWO SISTERS. D. Warrington P.O.W., March 10, 1875.

TWO SONS. D. 4 a. E. Manuel. Britannia, November 12, 1877.

TWO SOSIAS, THE. 3 a. Taken fr. *Amphitryon.* Hay., August 31, 1792.

TWO STARS; OR, THE FOOTLIGHTS AND THE FIRESIDE. Strand T., October, 1872.

TWO STRINGS TO A BEAU. C. 1 a. Hamilton Aidé. Pub. by S. French, Ltd.

TWO STRINGS TO HER BOW. C. 2 a. Mrs. Burton Harrison. Sedgwick H., Lenox. September 27, 1884.

TWO STRINGS TO YOUR BOW. F. 1 a. R. Jephson Alt. of *The Hotel; or, Servant with Two Masters.* C.G., February 16, 1791.

TWO STRINGS TO YOUR BOW. F. By A. Cherry. D.L., March 10, 1814.

TWO STUDENTS, THE. Surrey, February 16, 1861.

TWO SUICIDES. Piece. 1 a. N. Doone. R. Soc. of British Artists, January 24, 1891.

TWO THORNES, THE. C. 4 a. J. Albery. St. James's T., March 4, 1871.

TWO TO ONE. M.C. 3 a. G. Colman, jun. M. by Dr. Arnold. Hay., 1784.

TWO TO ONE. C. 1 a. A. C. Baker. Pub. by S. French, Ltd.

TWO TO ONE; OR, THE IRISH FOOTMAN. F. 1 a. A. Clements. Sadler's Wells, October 17, 1872; and Strand.

TWO TO ONE BAR ONE. M.P. 1 a. Sidney Dark.

TWO TOREADORS. Sk. Marshall Moore. Empress, August 2, 1909.

TWO TRAGEDIES IN ONE. R. Yarrington. 1601.

TWO UP AND ONE TO PLAY. Ca. C. R. Hallward. Kennington T., August 24, 1903.

TWO VALIANT KNIGHTES, SIR CLYOMON AND CLAMYDES. Anon. 1599.

TWO WEDDING RINGS. Dom. D. 4 a. G. S. Bellamy and F. Romer. Britannia, February 27, 1882.

TWO WINTERS. Marylebone, March 7, 1859.

TWO WISE MEN AND ALL THE REST FOOLS. C. 7 a. G. Chapman. 1619.

TWO WIVES; OR, A HINT TO HUSBANDS. Int. 1 a. M. by Mr. Parry. Lyceum, August 9, 1821; D.L., July 2, 1824.

TWO WOMEN. D. 4 a. Adap. fr. Hugo's *Marie Tudor* by E. Rose. Standard, April 6, 1885.

TWO WOMEN. By One of Them. Dr. fragment. Terry's, June 17, 1895.

TWO WORDS; OR, SILENT, NOT DUMB. Melo-d. M. by M. Addison. Lyceum, September 7, 1816; rev. August 24, 1826.

TWO'S COMPANY. C. Percy Andreae. Bradford T.R., May 20, 1895; Parkhurst, December 12, 1895.

'TWOULD PUZZLE A CONJUROR. C.D. 2 a. J. Poole. Hay. T.R., September 11, 1824.

TWYNNE'S TRAGEDYE, THE. Niccols. Ent. Stationers' Co., February 15, 1611, by E. Blunt. N.p.

TYPEWRITER, THE. F. J. East. Battersea Park T.H., February 23, 1892 (C.P.).

TYPEWRITER, THE. Duol. A. Eldred. Ryde T.R., July 6, 1903 (C.P.).

TYPEWRITER GIRL, THE. M.C. G. H. Perrin and P. S. Burraston. Portishead Assembly R., April 27, 1905.

TYPHOON, THE. D. Spec. 4 sc. Alicia Ramsay and Rudolph de Cordova. M. by Carl Kiefert. London Hipp., April 1, 1907.

TYPIST, THE. P. 1 a. Ella Erskine. Olympia Garden T. (Women of All Nations Exhibition), September 15, 1909.

TYRANNIC LOVE; OR, THE ROYAL MARTYR. T. J. Dryden. Ent. at Stat. H., July 14, 1669. T.R., 1679. Pr. 1670.

TYRANNICAL GOVERNMENT ANATOMISED; OR, A DISCOURSE CONCERNING EVIL COUNSELLORS: BEING THE LIFE AND DEATH OF JOHN THE BAPTIST. Anon. 1642.

TYRANNY: A TALE OF THE PRESS GANG OF 1810. D. Scarborough T.R., January, 1884.

TYRANNY OF TEARS, THE. 4 a. H. Chambers. Criterion, April 6, 1899; Wyndham's, January 29, 1902.

TYRANNY TRIUMPHANT AND LIBERTY LOST; THE MUSES RUN MAD; APOLLO STRUCK DUMB, AND ALL COVENT GARDEN CONFOUNDED. Sat. F. Fitzcrambo. 1743.

TYRANT, THE. T. P. Massinger. Ent. Stationers' Co., June 29, 1660. N.p. Destroyed by Warburton's servant.

TYRANT, THE. Melo-d. 4 a. F. C. Somerfield and F. Ludovic. Adap. fr. Victor Hugo's *Angelo*. Manchester Osborne, December 17, 1906; Dalston, August 24, 1908.

TYRANT KING OF CRETE, THE. T. Sir C. Sedley. 1702. Alt. of Killigrew's *The Conspiracy*.

TYRANT SLAVE, THE VICTIM, AND THE TAR. Burl. Pub. by S. French, Ltd.

TYROLESE PEASANT, THE. Dom. D. 2 a. D.L., May 8, 1832.

TYRTEE. O. 3 a. J. F. Lesneur. Comp. 1794. N.ac.

TYTHE PIG, THE. Ballet. C.G., May 12, 1795.

TZIGANE, LA. O. Strauss. Paris, 1877.

TZIGANE, THE. C.O. R. de Koven and H. B. Smith. Balham Assembly R., May 16, 1895 (C.P.).

U

UADHACT, AN (*The Will*). P. Padraic O'Conaire. Court, July 4, 1908.

UGLIEST WOMAN ON EARTH, THE. P. 4 a. F. Melville. Rotherhithe Terriss, November 14, 1904.

UGLY BARRINGTON. See *The Honeymoon in Eclipse*.

UGLY CLUB, THE. D. Caricature. Edmund Spencer. D.L., June 6, 1798.

UGLY CUSTOMER, AN. F. 1 a. T. J. Williams. Adelphi, December 6, 1860,

UGLY DUCKLING, THE. M. Sk. C. Grain. St. Geo. H., December 20, 1893.

UGLY LOVER; OR, THE PLAINEST MAN IN FRANCE, THE. Adap. fr. the French by H. W. C. Newte. Ladbroke H., March 11, 1898.

UGONE. T. Armstrong. 1870.

UGONOTTI GL'. O. Meyerbeer. Paris, 1836.

UHLANS. C.O. Messrs. Morrison. Dublin Gaiety T., March 10, 1884.

ULF THE MINSTREL. Burl. R. Reece. New Royalty, March 31, 1866.

ULSTER HERO, HENRY JOY M'CRACKEN, THE. Irish D. 5 a. J. W. Whitbread. Dublin Queen's, January 12, 1903.

ULVENE, THE SYREN QUEEN. D. H. T. Munns. Birmingham T.R., March 31, 1874.

ULYSSES. T. N. Rowe. Hay., November 23, 1705.

ULYSSES. O. Humphreys. M. by J. C. Smith, jun. L.I.F., 1733.

ULYSSES. Poetic D. 3 a. S. Philips. Her M., February 1, 1902.

ULYSSES; OR, THE IRON CLAD WARRIORS AND THE LITTLE TUG OF WAR. Burl. F. C. Burnand. St. James's T., April 17, 1865.

ULYSSES REDUX. T. Gager. 1574-90. N.p. Ac. at Christ Church, Oxford.

UMBRELLA, THE. Ca. 1 a. A. W. Dubourg. See *Twenty Minutes*, etc.

UMBRELLA DUOLOGUE. C. 1 a. E. D. Battiscombe. Publ. by S. French, Ltd.

UMPIRE, THE. D. and Pro. 5 a. Burnley T.R., January 31, 1887.

UNA. Burl. Dublin Queen's, April 5, 1875.

UNANSWERED. P. 1 a. Cecilia Brookes. Court, July 4, 1909.

UNAVOIDABLE. P. 1 a. Violet Lewis and F. Kingston. Ladbroke H., November 26, 1905.

UNBIDDEN GUEST, THE. Dr. Episode. 1 a. G. W. Appleton. Dublin T.R., July 13, 1900.

UNBLUSHING IMPUDENCE. F. R. Moore. Dublin Gaiety, May 10, 1875.

UNCAS, THE LAST OF THE MOHICANS. Pavilion, March 3, 1866.

UNCLE. F.C. 3 a. H. J. Byron. Dublin Gaiety T., November 4, 1878; Gaiety, February 1, 1879.

UNCLE CROCHET. F. 1 a. Mrs. Alfred Phillips. Olympic T., April 18, 1853.

UNCLE DICK. M. Sk. C. Grain. St. Geo. H., December 20, 1894.

UNCLE DICK'S DARLING. D. 3 a. H. J. Byron. Gaiety, December 13, 1869.

UNCLE JACK. D. 1 a. Adap. by F. Monk and A. C. Fraser Wood fr. a story by W. Besant. Sutton Coldfield T.H., April 4, 1893.

UNCLE JACK. C. 3 a. R. Ganthony. Richmond Castle. October 30, 1907.

UNCLE JOE. D. 3 a. G. L. Gordon. Liverpool P.O.W., February 18, 1876.

UNCLE JOE AT OXBRIDGE. C.O. L. H. Outram. Cambridge T.R., June 12, 1885.

UNCLE JOHN. J. B. Buckstone. Hay., October, 1833.

UNCLE JOHN. C. G. R. Sims and C. Raleigh. Vaudeville, April 3, 1893.

UNCLE JOHNSON. Co. F. Willmer. Liverpool P.O.W., June 11, 1877.

UNCLE JONATHAN. American C. 1 a. H. Coveney. First time in England. St. Leonards Pier Pav., July 3, 1899.

UNCLE JOSH. C.D. 4 a. Prod. in America. Blackburn T.R., July 30, 1888.

UNCLE MIKE. P. 4 a. Florence Warden. Terry's, December 8, 1892.

UNCLE NED. M.F. O. Trevine. Liverpool P.O.W., May 11, 1903.

UNCLE RIP. F. 2 a. R. B. Peake. Lyceum T., June 13, 1842.

UNCLE SILAS. D. 4 a. F. upon S. Le Fanu's novel by S. Hicks and L. Irving. Shaftesbury, February 12, 1893.

UNCLE STARLIGHT'S WILL. F. M. De Frece. Liverpool T.R., July 8, 1872.

UNCLE THATCHER. 1 a. C. Brooke. Court, June 1, 1896.

UNCLE TOM. D. 4 a. By L. Rae. Adap. fr. the French ver. of Mrs. Stowe's story. Standard, September 30, 1878.

UNCLE TOM. C. G. R. Sims and C. Raleigh. Vaudeville, April 3, 1893.

UNCLE TOM'S CABIN. D. 3 a. By C. Hermann. Adap. fr. Mrs. Beecher Stowe's novel. Manchester Royal, February 1, 1853; Princess's, October 31, 1892.

UNCLE TOM'S CABIN. D. 5 a. G. F. Rowe. Manchester T.R., August 19, 1878; Princess's, August 31, 1878.

UNCLE TOM'S CABIN. New ver. of Mrs. Harriet Beecher Stowe's story. Kennington T., July 13, 1903.

UNCLE TOM'S CABIN. See *Slavery*.

UNCLE TOM'S CABIN; OR, THE HORRORS OF SLAVERY. Dom. D. 3 a. By E. Fitzball. M. by Harroway. D.L., December 27, 1852.

UNCLE TOO MANY. C. Thomson. 1828.

UNCLE TRUE; OR, LITTLE GERTY. D. 4 a. Portsmouth R. Albert, March 27, 1871.

UNCLE YANK'S MISHAPS. Absurdity. 3 a. C. Wilmott and C. H. Mannon. Liverpool Shakespeare, June 27, 1892.

UNCLE ZAC; OR, A WILD REVENGE. D. 4 a. G.R. Walker. Scarboro' T.R., February 2, 1880; Standard, June 4, 1883. (Also as *A Mad Revenge*.)

UNCLE ZACHARY. C.D. 2 a. J. Oxenford. Olympic, March 8, 1860.

UNCLE'S BLUNDER. M.Sk. Frank F. Silvester and M. Wellings. St. Alban's Town H., December 18, 1893.

UNCLE'S COURTSHIP. Sk. Beatrice Webb and Alfred Philips. Islington Empire, October 7, 1907.

UNCLE'S GHOST. F. 3 a. W. Sapte, Jun. P.O.W., June 15, 1887; Op. C., January 17, 1894.

UNCLE'S WILL. Ca. 1 a. T. Smith. Hay., October 24, 1870.

UNCLE'S WILL; OR, THE WIDOW'S CHOICE. F. Transl. fr. the French by Peter Berard, 1808. N.ac. See *Who Wins?*

UNCLES AND AUNTS. F.C. 3 a. W. Lestocq and W. Everard. Comedy, August 22, 1888; Great Queen St. T., November 4, 1901.

UNCONSCIOUS COUNTERFEIT, THE. Afterpiece. Anon. D.L., February 9, 1809. N.p.

UNDER A BAN. D. 3 a. W. Duckworth. Liverpool Alexandra, March 7, 1870.

UNDER A VEIL. Ca. Sir R. Roberts. Richmond T.R., January 7, 1876; Olympic, May 15, 1876.

UNDER COMPULSION. P. 3 a. Sutton Vane. Accrington Prince's T., January 17, 1897 (C.P.).

UNDER COVER. Ca. Adap. fr. La Céramique (known also as *Le Bibelot* and *La Soupière*) of Ernest d'Hervilly by C. Bridgman. Gaiety, January 9, 1886; Royalty, March 29, 1888 (French season). See also *Cups and Saucers* and *Bric-à-Brac*.

UNDER FALSE COLOURS. C. 3 a. F. C. Taylor. Cavendish R., June 15, 1870.

UNDER FALSE COLOURS. D. 3 a. Mrs. Steel. Langham Pl. St. Geo H., February 9, 1896.

UNDER FALSE COLOURS. D. 4 a. M. Wallerton and Frances Gilbert. West London, March 18, 1901.

UNDER FIRE. C. 4 a. Westland Marston. Vaudeville, April 1, 1885.

UNDER FIRE. F. Mary Street Schoolroom, Kensington, April 16, 1888.

UNDER PROOF; OR, VERY MUCH ABOVE PA. Burl. E. Rose. Edinburgh Princess's T., May 1, 1879.

UNDER REMAND. D. 4 a. Reginald R. Stockton and E. Hudson. Bolton T.R., July 23, 1894; Surrey, June 1, 1896.

UNDER SUSPICION. Sk. in 1 sc. H. Hunter. Bedford M.H., June 14, 1909.

UNDER THE BRITISH FLAG. P. 4 a. J. M. Curtin. Lowestoft Public H., December 26 1896 (amat.).

UNDER THE CANOPY. Russo-Jewish D. 4 a. J. James Hewson. Partly f. on Joseph Hatton's novel, "By Order of the Czar." Pavilion, November 2, 1903.

UNDER THE CLOCK. M. Extrav. 1 a. C. H. Brookfield and S. Hicks. M. by E. Jones. Court, November 25, 1893.

UNDER THE CZAR. D. 4 a. Fred Jarman. Oldham Colosseum, July 9, 1894; Eleph. and C., April 13, 1896.

UNDER THE EARTH; OR, SONS OF TOIL. D. Ver. of Dickens's "Hard Times." Astley's, April 22, 1867.

UNDER THE FLAG OF TRUCE. Sk. R. Redgrave. Britannia, November 6, 1900.

UNDER THE GASLIGHT; OR, LIFE AND LOVE IN THESE TIMES. D. of American life. 4 a. Aug. Daly. New York T., August, 1867; Newcastle Tyne T., April 20, 1868; Pavilion, July 20, 1868. See *London by Gaslight.*

UNDER THE GREENWOOD TREE. P. 4 a. Being the story of Mary Hamilton. H. V. Esmond. Lyric, September 10, 1907.

UNDER THE LINE; OR, THE LIFE OF A SLAVER, FROM HER FITTING-OUT TO HER DESTRUCTION. Christmas Annual. John Green. Wear Mus. H., December 17, 1881.

UNDER THE MASK OF TRUTH. D. 4 a. S. Vane and A. Shirley. Surrey (C.P. under the title *The Mask of Guilt*), June 21, 1894; Brighton Eden T., October 29, 1894; Camberwell Metropole, November 19, 1894.

UNDER THE MISTLETOE. C.D. Pro. and 5 tab. M. St. John and R. M. Jephson. Imperial, December 5, 1881.

UNDER THE OLD FLAG. C. 4 a. V. Sardou. Adap. by E. Gregory. Globe, April 19, 1900 (C.P.).

UNDER THE OLD NAME. P. 1 a. S. Pritt. Preston T.R., July 27, 1896.

UNDER THE POLAR STAR. Rom. D. 5 a. C. M. Green and D. Belasco. New York, August 20, 1896.

UNDER THE RED CROSS. D. 3 a. G. B. Nichols. Taunton London Hotel Assembly R., April 16, 1900; Stratford R., July 30, 1900.

UNDER THE RED ROBE. Rom. 4 a. Adap. by E. Rose fr. Stanley Weyman's novel. Hay., October 17, 1896.

UNDER THE ROSE. F. 1 a. E. Roberts. St. James's, March 24, 1862.

UNDER THE RUSSIAN FLAG. Rom. D. 4 a. W. Howard. Manchester Grand Junction, September 1, 1902.

UNDER THE SCREW; OR, A YOUNG WIFE'S TROUBLES. D. T. Mead. Eleph. and C., October 6, 1873.

UNDER THE SEA. Sk. Oxford, July 26, 1909.

UNDER THE SHADOW OF OLD ST. PAUL'S. D. F. Merchant. East London, October 12, 1872.

UNDER THE SNOW. D. Britannia, August 27, 1877.

UNDER THE STARS; OR, THE STOLEN HEIRESS. D. 4 a. W. Banks. Oldham T.R., September 1, 1879; Marylebone, August 2, 1880.

UNDER THE STARS AND STRIPES. Mil. M.D. 4 a. A. Cunningham. Tyldesley R.T., August 3, 1907.

UNDER TWO FLAGS. D. W. H. Abel. Norwich T.R., November 14, 1870.

UNDER TWO FLAGS. Pro. and 4 a. G. Daventry, fr. Ouida's novel. Dundee T.R., September 15, 1882; Pavilion, August 11, 1884.

UNDER TWO FLAGS. D. 4 a. E. Elsner. Adap. fr. Ouida's novel. Cork O.H., March 3, 1902; Coronet, September 1, 1902.

UNDER TWO FLAGS. New ver. of Ouida's novel. Stratford R., July 26, 1909.

UNDER TWO REIGNS. Dr. Pro. and 3 a. W. Percival and J. Willing. Park T., May 3, 1879.

UNDER WHICH KING? P. 4 a. James Burnard Fagan. Adelphi, June 5, 1905.

UNDERBARNET. 19th century. Ingemann.

UNDERCURRENT, THE. C. 4 a. R. C. Carton. Criterion, September 14, 1901.

UNDERCURRENT, THE. P. 4 a. Herbert Chorley. Dedham, Essex, Grammar School H., July 8, 1908 (C.P.).

UNDERGRADUATE, THE. D. 4 a. J. C. Freund. Queen's, June 22, 1872.

UNDERGRADUATES, THE. F. C. 3 a. W. O. Tristram. Op. Comique, October 6, 1886.

UNDERGRADUATES, THE. See *The Referee.*

UNDERGROUND JOURNEY, AN. Ca. Mrs. Hugh Bell and C. H. Brookfield. Comedy, February 9, 1893.

UNDERSTUDY, THE. Ca. G. H. R. Dabbs. Shanklin Lit. Inst., December 15, 1887.

UNDERSTUDY, THE. Duol. Miss E. Bessie. Op. Comique, July 30, 1892.

UNDERSTUDY, THE. Sk. M. Prel. Camberwell Empire, June 10, 1906.

UNDERTAKER, THE. Tobin.

UNDESIRED, THE. Sk. Wr. by L. Mortimer. Bedford M.H., December 1, 1902.

UNDINE. Hay., December 27, 1858.

UNDINE. Cantata. Sir Julius Benedict (1804-85).

UNDINE. Spec. Rom. R. Reece. Olympic, July 2, 1870.

UNDINE. Burl. Yarmouth T.R., August 13, 1883.

UNDINE. Dr. P. Pro., 3 a, and epil. W. L. Courtney. Liverpool Shakespeare T., September 23, 1903; Criterion (first act), May 23, 1907.

UNDINE; OR, THE SPIRIT OF THE WATERS. Melo-d. Rom. C.G., April 23, 1821.

UNDINE UNDONE. Burl. Halifax T.R., April 21, 1873.

UNEASY MAN, THE. C. Anon. Transl. fr. St. Foix, 1771. N.ac.

UNEASY MATCH, THE. T.C. Durfey. Alt. fr. Shakespeare's *Cymbeline.* 1682.

UNEMPLOYED. P. 1 a. Margaret M. Mack. Aldwych, March 28, 1909; Manchester Gaiety, August 30, 1909.

UNEQUAL MATCH, THE. C. 3 a. Tom Taylor. Hay., November 7, 1857. See *The Injured Princess.*

UNEQUAL RIVALS, THE. Pastoral. J. Learmont. 1791. Pr. at Edinburgh.

UNEQUALLY SENTENCED. D. 3 a. Ipswich T.R., March 27, 1876.

UNEXPECTED, THE. F. Dublin T.R., November 28, 1870.

UNEXPECTED VISIT, AN. Duol. D. Archer. Mat., June 21, 1898.

UNEXPECTED VISIT, AN. Duol. D. Milward. St. George's H., February 3, 1900.

UNFEELING PARENT, THE. Petite Piece. 1 a. By a gentleman of Dublin. Perf. in that city, 1793.

UNFINISHED GENTLEMAN, THE. F. 1 a. C. Selby. Adelphi T., December 2, 1834.

UNFINISHED STORY, THE. Duol. Ina Leon Cassilis. St. James's H., May 22, 1891.

UNFORESEEN, THE. P. 4 a. R. Marshall. Hay., December 2, 1902.

UNFORSEEN, THE. Sk. Brixton Empress, September 28, 1908.

UNFORESEEN EVENTS. C.O. Anon. Mentioned in the "Theatrical Recorder."

UNFORTUNATE BEAU, THE. C. J. Williams. An alt. fr. *Woman is a Riddle*. Dublin Capel Street, 1784. N.p.

UNFORTUNATE COUPLE, THE. T. Motteux. Pr. 1697. See *The Novelty*.

UNFORTUNATE DUTCHESS OF MALFY; OR, THE UNNATURAL BROTHERS. T. Anon. Dedicated by the publ., Hugh Newman to the Duke of Beaufort. Queen's T., Hay., 1708.

UNFORTUNATE FAVOURITE, THE. T. Wr. by a Person of Honour. 1664.

UNFORTUNATE FORTUNATE, THE. T.C. B. Garfield. Pr. 1650.

UNFORTUNATE GENERAL, THE. A French Historical P. By Hathway, Smith, and Day. Wr. early in 1603.

UNFORTUNATE LOVERS, THE. T. Sir W. Davenant. Blackfriars, 1643. Licensed 1635. Pr. 1643. See *All's Lost by Lust*.

UNFORTUNATE MISS BAILEY. G. A. Bechell.

UNFORTUNATE MOTHER, THE. T. T. Nabbes. 1640. P. of this name ac. L.I.F. 1698.

UNFORTUNATE PIETY, THE. T. Massinger. Ac. by King's Co., June 13, 1631. (Lost.)

UNFORTUNATE SHEPHERD, THE. Pastoral. J. Tutchin. Pr. 1685.

UNFORTUNATE USURPER, THE. T. Anon. 1663. Plot f. on *Andronicus Comnenus*.

UNGRATEFUL FAVOURITE. Anon. 1664.

UNGRATEFUL LOVERS, THE. Mentioned in Pepys's Diary, September 11, 1667.

UNHAPPY FAIR IRENE, THE. T. G. Swinhoe. 1658.

UNHAPPY FATHER, THE. T. Mary Leapor. Pr. 1751. N.ac.

UNHAPPY FAVOURITE; OR, THE EARL OF ESSEX. T. J. Banks. T.R., 1682; Hay., November 29, 1706.

UNHAPPY KINDNESS; OR, A FRUITLESS REVENGE, THE. T. T. Scott. An alt. of Fletcher's *Wife of a Month*. D.L., 1697.

UNHAPPY PENITENT. T. Mrs. Catherine Trotter, afterwards Cockburn. D.L., 1701.

UNHAPPY PRINCESS. Fa. 1 a. A. Levy. Publ. by S. French, Ltd.

UNICORN FROM THE STARS, THE. P. 3 a. W. B. Yeats and Lady Gregory. Dublin Abbey, November 21, 1907.

UNINHABITED ISLAND, THE. D. Transl. fr. Metastasio by Anna Williams. Pr. 1766.

UNINHABITED ISLAND, THE. O. Transl. fr. Metastasio by J. Hoole. 1800.

UNINVITED GUEST, AN. P. 1 a. Brian Daly and J. M. East. Hammersmith Lyric T., March 18, 1901.

UNINVITED GUEST, AN. Sk. Camberwell Palace, July 13, 1908.

UNION; OR, ST. ANDREW'S DAY, THE. Div. of dialogue, song, and dance. Anon. D.L., May 18, 1791. N.p.

UNION JACK, THE. D. 4 a. H. Pettit and S. Grundy. Adelphi, July 18, 1888.

UNION OF THE THREE SISTER ARTS, THE. M.E. Anon. L.I.F., 1723. N.p.

UNION WHEEL, THE. D. J. Fox. Sheffield T.R., April 16, 1870.

UNIONIST, THE. P. E. R. Cleaton. Liverpool P.O.W., September 8, 1890.

UNITED. D. 3 a. J. N. Harley and A. Creamer. Consett T.R., October 1, 1886.

UNITED. C.D. 1 a. A. Selwyn. Ealing Victoria H., December 18, 1890.

UNITED KINGDOMS, THE. T.C. Edward Howard. Cockpit in D.L. soon after the Restoration.

UNITED PAIR, A. V. Adap. fr. a story by the late Hugh Conway. By C. Carr. M. by A. J. Caldicott. St. Geo. H., April 5, 1886.

UNITED SERVICE; OR, LION OF ENGLAND AND THE EAGLE OF FRANCE. D.L., January 17, 1854.

UNITED STATES. F.C. 3 a. Chs. Hannan. Crouch End O.H., March 5, 1907.

UNITED WE STAND. 1 a. J. H. Dickson. 170, Belsize Road, Hampstead, February 28, 1892.

UNIVERSAL EQUALITY; OR, JONATHAN BAXTER'S PEEP INTO THE FUTURE. Political Sk. 1 sc. Julia Agnes Fraser. Publ. by Menzies and Co., Edinburgh.

UNIVERSAL GALLANT, THE; OR, THE DIFFERENT HUSBANDS. C. H. Fielding. C.G., 1734; D.L., February 10, 1735.

UNIVERSAL PASSION, THE. C. Rev. J. Miller. Alt. of Shakespeare's *All's Well that Ends Well*. D.L., February 28, 1737.

UNIVERSAL PRIG, THE. P. G. A. Riley and S. S. Waterhouse and H. Brookes. Blackpool Grand T., March 21, 1903 (C.P.)

UNJUST JUDGE; OR, APPIUS AND VIRGINIA, THE. T. T. Betterton. Orig. wr. by Webster. 1654. Ac. at L.I.F., 1670.

UNKNOWN; OR, A RIVER MYSTERY, THE. D. 5 a. J. A. Stevens. Surrey, July 31, 1882.

UNKNOWN GUEST, THE. Operatic D. 3 a. D.L., March 29, 1815.

UNKNOWN LOVER, THE. P. Gosse. 1878.

UNKNOWN PHILANTHROPIST, THE. P. 4 a. Coryton Day. Ladbroke H., March 7, 1907.

UNKNOWN QUANTITY, AN. M. Dial. Adelene Votieri. M. by D. Harrison. Bayswater Bijou, March 29, 1897.

UNLAWFUL PRESENT, THE. D. 1 a. C. H. Hazlewood. Britannia, June 3, 1872.

UNLIMITED CASH. C. 3 a. F. C. Burnand. Gaiety, October 27, 1879.

UNLIMITED CONFIDENCE. D. 1 a. A. C. Troughton. Strand, February 1, 1864.

UNLUCKY COINCIDENCE, AN. C. 1 a. C. Crozier. Ladbroke H., February 26, 1897.

UNLUCKY FRIDAY. D. 1 a. Transl. and adap. fr. the French by H. T. Craven. Sadler's Wells, November 17, 1858.

UNLUCKY MORTAL. Hay., June 4, 1863.

UNMASKED, THE. D. 4 a. C. Merton. Pavilion, November 13, 1875.

UNMASKED, THE. C. 3 a. C. Waddie. Glasgow Athenæum, October 23, 1899.

UNNAMED PLAY, THE. V. Biene and J. Post. Birmingham G.T., May 23, 1902.

UNNATURAL BROTHER, THE. T. Dr. E. Filmer. L.I.F., 1697.

UNNATURAL COMBAT, THE. T. P. Massinger. Ac. by H.M. servants. Globe, 1639.

UNNATURAL MOTHER, THE. T. By a Lady. L.I.F., 1698. Part of plot borrowed fr. Settle's *Distress'd Innocence*.

UNNATURAL TRAGEDY, THE. T. Duchess of Newcastle. Pr. 1662. 1674. The prol. and epil. wr. by the Duke, her husband.

UNPAID DEBT, AN. P. 4 a. C. H. Dickinson. St. Geo. H., December 19, 1893.

UNPROTECTED FEMALE, AN. F. 1 a. J. S. Coyne. Strand, February 4, 1850.

UNREAL RICHES. P. 1 a. C. Raleigh. Reading County T., September 22, 1890.

UNRECORDED TRIAL, AN. P. 1 a. W. Herbage. Adap. fr. the story of H. A. Herring. Albert Hall T., February 9, 1904.

UNRELATED TWINS, THE. F.P. 3 a. E. Marris. Swindon, May 13, 1905 (C.P.), as *The Double Event*); Torquay O.H., May 29, 1905.

UNRESERVED YOUNG LADY, THE. C. 3 a. Taken fr. the French and pr. in the *Lady's Magazine*. 1788.

UNSANCTIFIED GARMENT, AN. C. 3 a. Messrs. Gray and Martin. St. Geo. H., December 20, 1895.

UNSEEN HELMSMAN, THE. P. 1 a. L. Alma-Tadema. Comedy, June 17, 1901.

UNSEEN POWER, THE. M.D. 4 a. Harry Starr. Lancaster Athenæum, September 10, 1907.

UNSEEN WORLD, THE. D. 4 a. C. Henry. Gateshead Metropole, August 17, 1901.

UNSERE DON JUAN. F. 4 a. L. Treptow. Comedy, February 8, 1901.

UNTER VIER AUGEN. Ca. 1 a. M. Behrend. St. Geo. H., November 19, 1901.

UNTIL THE DAY BREAK. D. 5 a. Isabel Beresford. Bayswater Bijou, May 17, 1898.

UNTO THE THIRD AND FOURTH GENERATION. Mrs. Augustus Bright's novels. See *Dane's Dyke*.

UNTREO. Daly's, June 27, 1897.

UNTRUSSING THE HUMOROUS POET, THE. T. Decker. 1602. See *Satyromastix*.

UNWARRANTABLE INTRUSION. F. 1 a. J. M. Morton. Publ. by S. French, Ltd.

UNWEDDED WIFE, AN. D. 4 a. West London, September 10, 1906.

UNWELCOME MRS. HATCH, THE. P. 4 a. Glasgow Royalty, November 25, 1901.

UNWRITTEN LAW, THE. Sk. Prod. by John Lawson. Holborn Empire, May 6, 1907.

UP A TREE. F. 1 a. I. J. Williams. Adelphi, March 10, 1873.

UP ALL NIGHT; OR, THE SMUGGLERS' CAVE. C.O. King. M. by Arnold. Lyceum, June 26, 1809; rev. September 15, 1815.

UP AT THE HILLS. C. of Indian life. 2 a. T. Taylor. St. James's T., October 29, 1860.

UP FOR THE CATTLE SHOW. F. 1 a. H. Lemon. Adelphi, December 7, 1867.

UP FOR THE JUBILEE. F. J. Bracewell. Grand, May 30, 1887.

UP IN THE WORLD. F. 1 a. J. Worthington. Surrey, 1858.

UP IN THE WORLD. C. 3 a. A. Sketchley. Strand, February 9, 1871.

UP THE LADDER. C. 3 a. Miss Herbert. Limerick T.R., December 1, 1876.

UP THE RIVER. M. Sk. R. Reece and H. B. Farnie. M. by Hervé. Folly, September 15, 1877.

UP TO TOWN. O. T. Dibdin. C.G., November 11, 1811.

UP TO TOWN AND BACK AGAIN BY THE OLD HIGHFLYER. Mr. Rayner's entertainment.

UP TRAIN, THE. Ca. Adap. fr. the French by C. P. Colnaghi. Hay., May 22, 1890.

UP-RIVER GIRL; OR, MAIDEN AND MILLIONAIRE, THE. M.C. H. C. Newton. Hay., February 8, 1904 (C.P.).

UP-TO-DATE PHOTOGRAPHY. Sk. Askmore Russen and J. Bastian. Oxford M.H., August 3, 1896.

UPHOLSTERER; OR, WHAT NEWS? THE. F. 2 a. A. Murphy. D.L., March 30, 1758; Edinburgh, 1872. An additional scene to this F., wr. by Mr. Moser, was pr. in the "European Magazine," 1807.

UPON THE WATERS. Dom. D. 1 a. R. Courtneidge and A. M. Thompson. Manchester Prince's, June 13, 1898.

UPPER CLASSES, THE. C. 2 a. F. Willmer. Liverpool P.O.W.'s, October 2, 1876.

UPPER CRUST, THE. C. 3 a. H. J. Byron. Folly, March 31, 1880. Toole's, April 23, 1891.

UPPER HAND, THE. C. 3 a. C. Winthorp and W. Lisle. Terry's, May 29, 1899.

UPS AND DOWNS. C. 3 a. M. Melford. Jersey T.R., October 18, 1886.

UPS AND DOWNS. Sk. Miss C. F. Reynolds. St. Leonard's Pier Pav., June 4, 1897.

UPS AND DOWNS; OR, BLACKLEY'S MISTAKE. Ca. C. Arden. Athenæum, Tott. Ct. Rd., July 25, 1888.

UPS AND DOWNS; OR, THE LADDER OF LIFE. C. D.L., May 27, 1828.

UPS AND DOWNS OF DEAL AND BLACK-EYED SUSAN, THE. Burl. Marylebone, June 10, 1867.

UPS AND DOWNS OF LIFE. D. 4 a. F. A. Scudamore. Northampton O.H., August 1, 1892; Pav., August 8, 1892.

UPSIDE DOWN. F.M.C. 3 a. B. Wyke. Thirsk Pub. H., November 1, 1886.

UPSTAIRS AND DOWNSTAIRS; OR, THE GREAT PERCENTAGE QUESTION. F. 1 a. W. Brough and A. Halliday. Strand, May 15, 1865.

URANIA; OR, THE ILLUMINE. C. 2 a. W. R. Spencer, D.L., January 22, 1802.

URGENT PRIVATE AFFAIRS. F. 1 a. J. S. Coyne. Adelphi, January 7, 1856.

URIEL ACOSTA. O. A. S. Famitsin (Famintsin). N.ac.

URIEL ACOSTA. T. Carl Gutzkow. Great Queen St., November 21, 1905; Pavilion (Jewish season), August 21, 1908.

USE AND ABUSE OF DRINK, THE. New ver. of *L'Assommoir*. Ryde T.R., June 4, 1880.

USE OF POETS, THE. Ca. A. Tayler. Comedy, July 18, 1901.

USED UP. C. C. J. Mathews. Adap. fr. the French *L'homme Blasé*. 1845.

USED UP. C.D. 2 a. D. Boucicault. D.L., November 22, 1855.

USURER, THE. Sk. Sydney Mason. Middlesex, June 22, 1908.

USURPER, THE. T. E. Howard. T.R., 1668.

USURPER, THE. T. Rev. J. Delap. Pr. at Lewes, 1808. N.ac.

USURPER DETECTED; OR, RIGHT WILL PREVAIL. C.T.F. 2 a. Anon. 1718.

USURPERS; OR, THE COFFEE HOUSE POLITICIANS, THE. F. Anon. 1749.

UT PICTURA POESIO; OR, THE ENRAGED MUSICIAN. Mus. Ent. G. Colman. Hay., 1789.

UTER PENDRAGON. Anon. Recorded in Henderson's list as having been ac. April 29, 1597. N.p.

UTHAL. O. 1 a. Méhul Feydeau. May 17, 1806. Recently rev. in Germany.

UTOPIA; OR, THE FINGER OF FATE. C.O. M. by Dr. W. H. Hunt. Lib. J. J. Wood. Birkenhead Town H., April 4, 1891.

UTOPIA, LIMITED; OR, THE FLOWERS OF PROGRESS. C.O. W. S. Gilbert and A. Sullivan. Savoy, October 7, 1893.

UTRUM HORUM. C. 2 a. Anon. 1797.

UTTERMOST FARTHING, THE. P. 4 a. B. Cane. Coventry O.H., November 23, 1895; Southampton P.O.W., December 6, 1895.

V

V.C. D. 1 a. S. Vane Parkhurst. April 13, 1891.

V. DOCQ. Melo-d. 2 a. Publ. by S. French, Limited.

VACANCES, LES. C. Dancourt. 1659.

VACANT PLACE, A. Duol. Mrs. C. G. Compton. Terry's, June 23, 1899.

VAGABOND, THE. Victoria, October 1, 1866.

VAGABOND, THE. C. 3 a. W. S. Gilbert. Olympic, March 25, 1878. Prod. Olympic, February 25, 1878, as *The Ne'er-do-Weel.*

VAGABOND, THE. P. 4 a. M.C. Washburn Freund. Adap. fr. the German of Dr. Richard Fellinger. (Prod. by the Play Actors.) Court, November 29, 1908.

VAGABOND; OR, PARTED BY CRIME, THE. Sk. H. A. Lonsdell. Poplar Queen's, September 23, 1895.

VAGABOND KING, THE. P. 4 a. L. N. Parker. Camberwell Metropole, October 18, 1897; Court, November 4, 1897.

VAGARIES OF NICHOLAS; OR, THE ADVENTURES OF A VENTRILOQUIST, THE. D.L., June 14, 1822.

VAGRANT, THE. Dom. D. 5 a. G. De Lara. Scarborough Aquarium, December 7, 1891; Sadler's Wells, October 17, 1892.

VAIN SACRIFICE, A. C.D. 3 a. W. E. Grogan. Strand, November 14, 1893.

VAL D'ANDORRE, LE. O. Halévy. Paris, 1848.

VALE OF CONTENT, THE. D. 4 a. Dr. W. Hall. Southport O.H., December 19, 1903.

VALE OF CONTENT, THE. Transl. of Hermann Sudermann's *Das Glück im Winkel.* Coronet, June 8, 1909.

VALE OF PETRARCH, THE. Dr. Poem. 5 a. S. J. Pratt. N.p. N.ac. (before 1812).

VALE OF THE 25TH. P. 1 a. E. Ferris and P. Heriot. Fulham G.T., July 2, 1900. Afterwards called *The Yellow Peril.*

VALENTIA; OR, THE FATAL BIRTHDAY. T. T. Stewart. 1772.

VALENTINE. Guilbert de Pixérécourt. 1820.

VALENTINE, A. F. 1 a. W. Brough and A. Halliday. Adelphi, February 12, 1863.

VALENTINE AND ORSON. Int. by T. Gosson and R. Hancock. May 23, 1595. N.p.

VALENTINE AND ORSON. P. A. Munday and R. Hathways. 1598.

VALENTINE AND ORSON. W. White. Pl. by Her Majesty's Players. Ent. Stationers' H., March 31, 1600. N.p.

VALENTINE AND ORSON. Rom. Melo-d. 2 a. T. Dibdin. C.G., April 3, 1804, and July 25, 1804.

VALENTINE AND ORSON. C. Melo-d. 2 a. M. by Jouve. D.L., October 15, 1825; March 27, 1837; D.L. (scenes from), April 18, 1853.

VALENTINE AND ORSON. Burl. D. 2 a. R. Reece. Gaiety, December 23, 1882.

VALENTINE AND ORSON. Burl. 1 a. and 3 tab. J. Ellis. Brentford T.R., November 1, 1898.

VALENTINE AND PAULINE. Rom. P. 4 a. C. Hannan. Duke of York's, July 30, 1908 (C.P.).

VALENTINE'S DAY. M.D. W. Heard. D.L., March 22, 1776.

VALENTINE'S DAY. Hay., December 26, 1859.

VALENTINE'S DAY. See *Saint Valentine's Day.*

VALENTINE'S DAY; OR, THE AMOROUS KNIGHT AND THE BELLE WIDOW. C. 3a. Anon. N.ac. 1809.

VALENTIAN. T. Fletcher and Beaumont, 1647.

VALENTINIAN. T. John Wilmot (Earl of Rochester). Alt. fr. Fletcher. T.R., 1685.

VALERIE. F. Scribe. 1822.

VALET WITH TWO MASTERS, THE. F. J. Baylis. Transl. fr. the French. 1804. N.ac.

VALETUDINARIUM. Latin C. Wm. Johnson, a student of King's College, Cambridge. Ac. before the University, 1638. N.p.

VALIANT CID, THE. P. Transl. fr. Corneille. Ment. in Pepys's Diary, December 1, 1662.

VALIANT OF THE 9TH. Amer. Spec. Mil. Sk. H. C. Robinson. Southport Pav., January 28, 1905.

VALIANT SCHOLAR, THE. D. Ment. in Sir H. Herbert's Diary under date of June 3, 1622.

VALIANT SCOT, THE. P. J. W. 1637.

VALIANT WELCHMAN; OR, THE LIFE AND VALIANT DEEDS OF CARADOC OF CAMBRIA, THE. T.C. R.A. Ac. by Princess of Wales's Servants, 1663; L.I.F., May 19, 1727.

VALJEAN; OR, A LIFE'S SACRIFICE. D. 5 a. A. Willoughby. Glasgow P.O.W., August 5, 1878.

VALKYRIE, THE. O. Wagner. In English. Garrick, February 3, 1897 (Carl Rosa Co.).

VALLEY OF DIAMONDS; OR, HARLEQUIN SINBAD. Pant. D.L., December 26, 1814.

VALMONDI; OR, THE UNHALLOWED SEPULCHRE. Adelphi, March, 1825.

VALSE, LA. Duol. Royalty (French Plays), January 31, 1889.

VALSEI (*i.e.*, WALLACE); OR, THE HERO OF SCOTLAND. T. Perobo. 1772.

VALTEGER. Recorded by Henslowe as having been ac. December 4, 1590.

VALUE OF BEING EXTINCT, THE. F. 3 a. C. James and C. Goodhart. Kingston County T., October 3, 1904.

VALUE OF TRUTH. C. 1 a. E. H. Keating. Publ. by S. French, Ltd.

VAMPIRE, LE. Carmouche. 1820.

VAMPIRE, THE. Phantasm. 3 a. D. Boucicault. Princess's, June 14, 1852.

VAMPIRE, THE. Burl. R. Reece. Strand, August 15, 1872.

VAMPIRE, THE. Adap. fr. the French of C. C. Vylons and Pierre Souvestre by Jose G. Levy. Paragon, September 27, 1909.

VAMPIRE; OR, THE BRIDE OF THE ISLES, THE. Rom. Melo-d. Transl. of *Le Vampire*, by J. R. Planché.

VAMPYR, DER. R.O. 3 a. Freely transl. from the German of W. A. Wohlbrück. M. by Marschner. Lyceum, August 25, 1829.

VAN BIENE'S DILEMMA. Sk. Metropolitan, August 16, 1909.

VAN DYKE, THE. Dr. Epis. 1 a. Cosmo Gordon Lennox. Adap. fr. the Fr. of Eugène Fourrier's *Peringue*. H.M., March 16, 1907.

VAN THE VIRGINIAN. D. 5 a. St. Helens T.R., August 11, 1879.

VANDERDECKEN. D. W. G. Wills and Percy Fitzgerald. Based on *The Flying Dutchman*. Lyceum, June 8, 1878.

VANDERDECKEN; OR, THE FLYING ANGLO-DUTCHMAN'S PHANTOM PENNY STEAMER. Burl. W. Edgar. M. by Meyer Lutz. Novelty, December 9, 1886.

VANDYCK: A PLAY OF GENOA. P. Richards. 1850.

VANDYKE BROWN. F. 1 a. A. C. Troughton. Strand, March 24, 1859.

VANELIA; OR, THE AMOURS OF THE GREAT. O. Anon. 1732.

VANELLA, T. Anon. 1736. N.ac.

VANGUARD; OR, BRITISH TARS REGALING AFTER BATTLE, THE. Int. of Songs. Anon. C.G., April 3, 1799.

VANINA D'ORNANO. O. Halévy (left unfinished at author's death, and was completed by Bizet).

VANISHING HUSBAND, A. F. 3 a. Stockton-on-Tees. T.R., January 29, 1897 (C.P.).

VANITY. C. T. D. F. Micklethwaite. Adap. fr. Thackeray's "Vanity Fair." Leeds A.R., March 27, 1882.

VANITY. D. 4 a. J. H. McCarthy. Adap. fr. Sardou's "Maison Neuve." Plymouth R., August 11, 1886.

VANITY FAIR. Caricature. 3 a. G. W. Godfrey. Court, April 27, 1895. See *Vanity*.

VANITY OF VANITIES. Duol. J. H. McCarthy. Shaftesbury, July 4, 1890.

VANITY OF YOUTH, THE. C. 4 a. Wyndham's, November 11, 1902.

VANITY PUNISHED. D. Berquin. 1793.

VANQUISHED IN LOVE; OR, THE JEALOUS QUEEN. Dr. Ent. D. Bellamy, sen. and jun. Pr. 1739-1740. N.ac.

VARIATIONS. Duol. Margaret Young. F. on Ger. theme Garrick, May 18, 1899.

VARIETY. C. R. Griffiths. Pro. by Tickell. D.L., 1782.

VARIETY, THE. C. Wm. Duke of Newcastle. Blackfriars, 1649.

VARIETY GIRL, THE. M.C. 2 a. C. Davis. Lyrics by A. E. Ellis. Belfast Grand O.H., September 1, 1902.

VARINA. Dr. Sk. Roy Milton. Lancaster Athenæum, August 7, 1907.

VARNA'S REVENGE. Sk. 1 sc. Brixton Empress M.H., April 29, 1907.

'VARSITY BELLE, THE. F. Fred Jarman. M. by Edward Jones. Lyrics by Geo. Porrington. Dover T.R., February 20, 1905.

'VARSITY BOAT RACE, THE. F. C. H. Stephenson and F. Robson. Olympic, April 6, 1870.

VATHEK. C. Mentioned in the Theatre of Education, 1781.

VAUTOUR, MONS. Duval, 1805.

VAUXHALL IN MINIATURE. D.L., June 18, 1816.

VAYVOOD, THE. P. T. Downton. Ac. 1598. N.p.

VEILCHENFRESSER, DER. C. G. Von Moser. Royalty, January 4, 1904.

VEILED PICTURE, THE. C. 3 a. W. F. Lyon. Edinburgh Princess's, June 11, 1883.

VEILED PROPHET, THE. O. 3 a. Lib. by B. Squire. F. on Moore's *Lalla Rookh*. M. by Dr. C. V. Stanford. Court O.H., Hanover, February, 1881; C.G., July 26, 1893.

VEILED PROPHET OF KHORASSAN; OR, THE MANIAC, THE MYSTERY, AND THE MALEDICTION, THE. Burl. H. L. Walford. Gallery of Illus., November 24, 1870 (amat.).

VEINE, LA. C. 4 a. A. Capus. Paris Var., April 2, 1901; Garrick, July 14, 1902.

VELLEDA. O. Lenepveu. C. G., July 4, 1882.

VELVET AND RAGS. D. Pro. and 3 a. P. Meritt and G. Conquest. Grecian, April 6, 1873.

VELYA. P. Ac. at Rose T., 1595.

VENCESLAS. T. Rotrou. 1647.

VENDANGES DE SURESNES. C. Dancourt. 1657

VENDETTA. Victoria, May 11, 1863.

VENDETTA. D. 4 a. W. Stephens. St. Geo. H., April 17, 1868 (amat.).

VENDETTA. P. 5 a. N. Doone. Taken fr. Marie Corelli's novel. Kennington, March 28, 1904.

VENDETTA. Dr. M. Sk. By Jas. Howard. Lyrics by H. Lambert. Shepherd's Bush Empire, January 28, 1907.

VENDETTA; OR, LIFE'S CHANCES, THE. D. 5 a. Britannia, August 5, 1896.

VENDETTA; OR, THE BOOK WITH THE IRON CLASPS. D. Pro. 4 a. Croydon T.R., April 8, 1878.

VENDETTA; OR, THE CORSICAN BROTHERS, THE. New D. 5 a., 5 tab. F. on Dumas' romance. D.L., February 27, 1854.

VENDETTA; OR, THE CORSICAN'S REVENGE, THE. Play. 4 a. Adap. by W. Calvert. Fr. A C. Gunter's novel, "Mr. Barnes of New York." Sadler's Wells, September 7, 1888.

VENDOME EN ESPAGNE. O. Auber (with Hérold). 1823.

VENETIAN COMEDY. Recorded by Henslowe as having been ac. August 25, 1594.

VENETIAN NUPTIALS; OR, THE GUARDIAN OUTWITTED. Ballet by D'Egville. D.L., October 31, 1822.

VENETIAN OUTLAW, THE. D. 3 a. Transl. and adap. to the English stage by R. W. Elliston. D.L., 1805.

VENETIAN OUTLAW, HIS COUNTRY'S FRIEND, THE. D. J. Powell. 1805. N.ac.

VENETIAN SINGER, A. C.O. 1 a. B. C. Stephenson. M. by E. Jakobowski. Court, November 25, 1893.

VENGEANCE. M.D. 4 a. A. St. John. Macclesfield T.R., September 11, 1897.

VENGEANCE. D.E. 3 sc. Hammersmith Palace, January 21, 1907.

VENGEANCE. See *An April Folly*.

VENGEANCE IS MINE. Rom. D. 4 a. Sutton Vane. Cheltenham A.R., April 29, 1891 (C.P.); Pavilion, January 22, 1892.

VENGEANCE IS MINE. D. 1 a., 3 sc. W. G. Fortescue. Beverley, Somerville's T., January 28, 1897.

VENGEANCE IS MINE. C.D. in pro. and 4 a. By W. H. Dearlove. Maidenhead T.R., April 3, 1899.

VENGEANCE IS THINE. D. 5 a. J. Mill. Britannia, July 29, 1895.

VENGEANCE OF JIM, THE. Ca. S. Killby. Royal King's Lynn, February 25, 1909.

VENGEANCE OF MRS. VANSITTART, THE. C. 3 a. Arthur Hare and H. Eves. Garrick, July 16, 1901.

VENGEANCE OF WOMEN, THE. D. 4 a. F. A. Scudamore. West London, July 24, 1905.

VENICE. O. Extrav. C. Searle. Alhambra, May 5, 1879.

VENICE PRESERVED; OR, A PLOT DISCOVERED. T. 5 a. Thos. Otway. Occ. pro. and epil. Duke's T., 1682; rev. C.G., 1824 and 1836; rev. by the Otway Society at Royalty, June 13, 1904. See *Braganza*.

VENITIENNE, LA. D. Anicet Bourgeois. 1834.

VENONI; OR, THE NOVICE OF ST. MARK'S. D. 3 a. M. G. Lewis. Transl. fr. *Les Victimes Cloitrées*. D.L., 1809.

VENT DU SOIR. Op. bo. 1 a. Offenbach. 1857.

VENTAGLIO, IL. O. Raimondi. Naples, 1831.

VENUS. F. Sk. Jessie Robertson. Novelty, May 11, 1896.

VENUS; OR, THE GODS AS THEY WERE AND NOT AS THEY OUGHT TO HAVE BEEN. Burl. 5 a. E. Rose and Augustus Harris. Royalty, June 27, 1879. Re-written by W. Yardley. Liverpool P.O.W., March 26, 1890; Grand, September 22, 1890.

VENUS AND ADONIS. Masque. S. Holland. 1656.

VENUS AND ADONIS. Masque. C. Cibber. M. by Dr. Pepusch. D.L., 1715.

VENUS AND ADONIS. Ca. M. Melford. Wolverhampton T.R., August 13, 1885.

VENUS AND ADONIS; OR, A MAID'S PHILOSOPHY. Supposed to be wr. by Robert Cox. 1659.

VENUS AND ADONIS; OR, THE TRIUMPHS OF LOVE. Mock O. Punch's T.; C.G., 1713.

VENUS AND ADONIS; OR, THE TWO RIVALS AND THE SMALL BOAR. F. C. Burnand. Hay., March 28, 1864.

VENUS AND ANCHISES. A Pastoral. Wr. about 1660. MS. copy in Sion Coll. Library.

VENUS BEWILDERED. F.C. Cheltenham R. April 9, 1883.

VENUS OF VENICE, THE. O. Burl. 3 a. M. Turner. M. by H. C. Barry. Lincoln T.R., August 1, 1892.

VENUS VERSUS MARS. Ca. J. T. Douglass, jun. Standard, September 5, 1870.

VEPRES SICILIENNES, LES. T. Delavigne. 1819.

VEPRES SICILIENNES, LES. O. Verdi. Paris, 1855.

VERA. D. 4 a. M. E. Smith. Globe, July 1, 1890.

VERA, THE MEDIUM. P. 4 a. Richard Harding Davis. Garrick, November 2, 1908 (C.P.).

VERACITY. Whimsical C. 3 a. W. Parke. Gaiety, April 20, 1886.

VERBUM SAP. Ca. A. Maltby. Criterion, March 20, 1880.

VERDICT: SUICIDE OR MURDER? Sk. E. Gurney. West London, May 13, 1895.

VERDICT OF THE WORLD, THE. D. 3 a. G. Lauder. Britannia, August 5, 1872.

VERGER, THE. V. 1 a. W. Frith. M. by K. Hall. St. Geo. H., December 9, 1889.

VERKAUFTE BRAUT, DIE. C.O. 3 a. F. Smetana (1824-1884). Vienna, 1890; D.L., June 27, 1895.

VERONIQUE. C.O. 3 a. A. Vanloo and G. Duval. English ver. by H. Hamilton. M. by A. Messager. Notting Hill Coronet, May 5, 1903; Apollo, May 18, 1904.

VERRE D'EAU, LE. C. Scribe. 1842.

VERSIPELLIS. C. MS. Rev. T. Pestell. 1631.

VERSPRECHEN HINTER'M HERD, DAS. St. Geo. H., March 26, 1868.

VERSUNKENE GLOCKE, DIE. Fairy P. 5 a. G. Hauptmann. Gt. Queen Street T., February 11, 1903.

VERT VERT. O. 3 a. Offenbach. 1869.

VERT VERT. Op. bo. 3 a. H. and R. Mansell. St. James's, May 2, 1874.

VERT VERT; OR, THE PET PARROT. Parisian Ballet Panto. M. by Deldeveze and Tolbecque. D.L., February 6, 1852.

VERTUMNUS. T. Gwinne. Ac. at Oxford, 1605. 1607.

VERTUMNUS AND POMONA. Past. Matthew Field. C.G., February 21, 1782. Songs only pr.

VERVEN, LA. C. Spanish Ballet. M. by Hughes. D.L., December 2, 1846.

VERY CATCHING. Burnand and Molloy. November 18, 1872.

VERY GOOD WIFE, A. C. G. Powell. Pr. 1693. T.R., 1695.

VERY LAST DAYS OF POMPEII, THE. Burl. R. Reece. Vaudeville T., February 13, 1872.

VERY LATEST EDITION OF THE GATHERING OF THE CLANS, THE. Extrav. G. W. Hunt. East London, October 18, 1873.

VERY LITTLE FAUST AND MORE MEPHISTOPHELES. Burl. F. C. Burnand. Charing Cr., August 18, 1869.

VERY LITTLE HAMLET. Burl. Pro. and 3 a. W. Yardley. Gaiety, November 29, 1884.

VERY LOW SPIRITS. F. W. Bourne. Exeter T.R., November 27, 1876.

VERY MAN, THE. F.C. 3 a. W. H. Pollock and G. Pollock. Princess's, February 27, 1902.

VERY PLEASANT EVENING, A. F. 1 a. W. E. Luter.

VERY SERIOUS AFFAIR, A. F. 1 a. A. Harris. Lyceum, October, 1857.

VERY SUSPICIOUS. Ca. 1 a. J. P. Simpson. Lyceum, June 12, 1852.

VERY SUSPICIOUS. Duol. D.L., October 15, 1853.

VERY, VERY MUCH ENGAGED. Ca. 1 a. J. Haworth and R. C. Buchanan. Glasgow Ath., October 15, 1895 (C.P.); Coatbridge T., October 13, 1900.

VERY WOMAN; OR, THE PRINCE OF TARENT, A. T.C. New Version of (probably) *A Right Woman*. P. Massinger. King's Comp., June 6, 1634; Blackfriars, 1655.

VESPASIAN. O. A. Ariosti. 1724.

VESPERS OF PALERMO. T. Hemans. C.G., December 12, 1823.

VESPRI SICILIANI, I. O. Verdi. Paris, 1855.

VESTA. Burl. H. B. Farnie. St. James's, February 9, 1871.

VESTA'S TEMPLE. "Absurdity." Court, November 14, 1872.

VESTAL, THE. T. H. Glapthorne. Destroyed by Mr. Warburton's servant.

VESTAL VIRGIN, THE. H. Brooke. 1778. N.ac.

VESTAL VIRGIN; OR, THE ROMAN LADIES, THE. T. Sir R. Howard. T.R., 1665.

VESTALE, LA. O. Rauzzini. London, 1787.

VESTALE, LA. O. Spontini. Paris, 1807.

VESTALE, LA. O. Puccitta. 1810.

VESTALE, LA. O. Mercadante. Paris, 1841.

VETAH. Indian C.O. 3 a. Kate Santley. M. by Jacobi. Portsmouth T.R., August 30, 1886.

VETERAN, THE. P. 1 a. Ellerslie Pyne. Shotton T.R., November 6, 1905.

VETERAN; OR, THE FARMER'S SONS, THE. C.D. 3 a. M. by Whittaker, Parry, Rooke, Knight, and Cooke. D.L., February 23, 1822.

VETERAN DISMISSED WITH HONOUR. D. Berquin. 1793.

VETERAN OF 102 YEARS; OR, FIVE GENERATIONS, THE. D. 1 a. Adap. fr. the French. H. M. Miller. Royal Coburg T. Pub. by S. French, Ltd.

VETERAN TAR, THE. C.O. 2 a. S. J. Arnold. D.L., January 29, 1801. M. by Dr. Arnold.

VEUVE, LA. Corneille. See "French Classical Plays."

VEUVE, LA. P. 1 a. Eugene Heros and Leon Abric. Shaftesbury, March 27, 1908.

VEUVE DE MALABAR. O. Kalkbrenner. 1799.

VEVA. Rom. D. Pro. and 3 a. C. O'Neill. Strand, April 26, 1883.

VIAGGIO A REIMS, IL. O. Rossini. Paris, June 19, 1825.

VICAR, THE. P. 4 a. Adap. by J. Hatton and J. Albery fr. Hatton's novel, "The Queen of Bohemia." Windsor T.R., January 28, 1885 (C.P.); Sunderland T.R., November 11, 1886.

VICAR, THE. P. 3 a. C. W. Hannan. Adap. fr. *The Vicar of Wakefield*. Torquay T.R., April 22, 1893.

VICAR AND MOSES; OR, LINGO'S WEDDING, THE. Burl. W. C. Oulton. 1789.

VICAR OF BRAY, THE. C.O. 2 a. S. Grundy. M. by E. Solomon. Globe, July 22, 1882; Savoy, January 28, 1892.

VICAR OF WAKEFIELD, THE. Oliver Goldsmith. Dramatised in 1819 and played as an O. in 1823.

VICAR OF WAKEFIELD, THE. D. 3 a. J. S. Coyne. Strand, March 4, 1850.

VICAR OF WAKEFIELD, THE. D. 4 a. J. T. Douglass. Standard, October 31, 1870.

VICAR OF WAKEFIELD, THE. D. 3 a. W. Farren, jun. Ladbroke H., January 2, 1888.

VICAR OF WAKEFIELD, THE. 3 a. C. Hannan. West London, March 29, 1905.

VICAR OF WAKEFIELD, THE. Light O. 3 a. Lyrics by Laurence Housman. M. by Liza Lehmann. Manchester Prince's, November 12, 1907; P.O.W., December 12, 1907.

VICAR OF WAKEFIELD, THE. See *The Vicar*, *Betrayed*, *Olivia*.

VICAR OF WIDE-AWAKE-FIELD; OR, THE MISS TERRY-OUS UNCLE, THE. Burl. of *Olivia*. H. P. Stephens and W. Yardley. Gaiety, August 8, 1885.

VICAR'S DAUGHTER, THE. D. 1 a. E. Drew. Tottenham Court Road Athenæum, January 28, 1889.

VICAR'S DAUGHTER, THE. D. 4 a. M. Corney. Halifax T.R., August 20, 1896.

VICAR'S DILEMMA, THE. C. 3 a. "A. Vicarson." Watford Clarendon H., January 31, 1898; Terry's, July 11, 1898.

VICARAGE, A FIRESIDE STORY, THE. Saville Rowe. P.O.W., March 31, 1877.

VICE CHANCELLOR, THE. F. S. M. Fox. Camden T., February 26, 1900.

VICE RECLAIMED; OR, THE PASSIONATE MISTRESS. C. R. Wilkinson. T.R., June 23, 1703.

VICE V. VIRTUE. D. 5 a. J. Barker. Nelson Grand, August 22, 1891.

VICE VERSA; A LESSON TO FATHERS. Dr. Stk. 3 tab. E. Rose fr. story by F. Anstey. Gaiety, April 9, 1883.

VICEROY, THE. T. Hayley. Pr. at Chichester, 1811.

VICEROY, THE. Hist. Oa. (in Yiddish). 4 a. S. Feinmar. Pav., E., April 10, 1907.

VICISSITUDES OF SIR ROGER TICHBORNE, THE. D. Trowbridge Court H., June 21, 1872.

VICTIM, THE. T. C. Johnson. D.L., January 5, 1714. Epil. by Cibber.

VICTIM, THE. T. Boyer. See *Achilles and Iphigenia in Aulis*. 1714.

VICTIM OF ST. VINCENT. Transl. and adap. by T. J. Serle.

VICTIM OF VILLAINY, A. Dom. Melo-d. W. Howe. Bayswater Bijou, May 26, 1904. Stratford Borough, August 1, 1904.

VICTIMS, THE. C. 3 a. Tom Taylor. Hay., July 8, 1857.

VICTIMS OF CIRCUMSTANCES, THE. Sensational C.D. Louis H. Carlton. Northampton O.H., December 2, 1904 (C.P.).

VICTIMS OF LOVE AND PLEASURE. In the works of H. Brooke, author of *Gustavus Vasa*. 1778.

VICTIMS OF POWER. D. 5 a. E. Hill-Mitchelson and C. H. Longden. Keighley Queen's T., March 15, 1895.

VICTOIRE. D. Adelphi, December, 1837.

VICTOIRE. Military C.O. 2 a. Albert Smythe. M. by E. Little. Dublin Leinster H., April 17, 1893.

VICTOR AND HORTENSE. V.

VICTOR DURAND. D. 4 a. H. G. Carleton. Prince's, December 13, 1884.

VICTOR VANQUISHED, THE C. 1 a. C. Dance. Princess's T. March 25, 1845.

VICTORIA. "Story, with songs." 3 a. Geo. V. Hobart. M. by Victor Herbert. Bayswater Bijou, November 27, 1908 (mat.).

VICTORIA AND MERRIE ENGLAND. Ballet. Sir A. Sullivan. Alhambra, May 25, 1897.

VICTORIA CROSS, THE. Military D. 5 a. J. W. Whitbread. Brentford T. of V., March 22, 1886; Dublin Queen's T., September 7, 1896; Stratford T.R., October 19, 1896; Pavilion, July 26, 1897.

VICTORIA STAKES, THE. D.Sk. E. Skuse. Novelty, June 1, 1896.

VICTORIAN. O. 4 a. F. on Longfellow's *Spanish Student* by J. T. R. Anderson. M. by J. Edwards. Sheffield T.R., April 6, 1883; C.G., January 19, 1884.

VICTORINE. D. J. B. Buckstone. Adelphi, October, 1831.

VICTORIOUS LOVE. T. W. Walker. D.L., 1698. This is an imitation of Southern's *Oroonoko*.

VICTORY. D. 4 a. J. Hewetson-Porter. Warrington Royal, April 28, 1890.

VICTORY AND DEATH OF LORD NELSON. Melo.-d. R. Cumberland. D.L., November 11, 1805.

VIDA. D. 4 a. Ina Leon Cassilis and C. Lander. Ladbroke H., October 12, 1891 (C.P.); Scarborough Lond., November 17, 1891; P.O.W., March 1, 1892.

VIDENA. D. J. A. Heraud. Marylebone, 1854.

VIDOCQ; THE FRENCH POLICE SPY. Melo.-d. 2 a. Adapt. fr. Vidocq's Autobiography. Surrey T.

VIDULARIA. See "Latin Plays."

VIE, LA. Op. burl. 3 a. Offenbach and H. B. Farnie, from *La Vie Parisienne*. Brighton R., September 17, 1883; Avenue, October 3, 1883.

VIE DE CAFE. Dupenty. 1850.

VIE PARISIENNE, LA. Op. bo. fr. Offenbach by F. C. Burnand. Holborn, March 30, 1872.

VIEILLE, LA. O. F. J. Fetis. Paris, 1826.

VIELLE DE NOEL, UNE. P. Prol. and 3 a. Marguerite de St. Maude. Portman Rooms, W., July 20, 1905.

VIEILLE RENOMEE, UNE. P. 1 a. R. Athys. Royalty, July 23, 1907.

VIENNA BY NIGHT. Burl. Oa. Earl's Court Summer T., May 9, 1907.

VIENNA BESIEGED. Droll. Ac. at Bartholomew Fair. Ment. in the "Theatre of Compliments," 1688.

VIERTE GEBOT, DAS. D. 4 a. Ludwig Auzen Gruber. Comedy, April 9, 1901.

VIEUX CHATEAU. O. Dellamaria. 1799.

VIEUX FAT, LE. C. Andrieux. 1810.

VIEUX, GARCON, LE. Petite piece. Scribe (before 1822).

VIEUX GARCONS, LES. French C. 5 a. V. Sardou. Princess's, April 25, 1870; Royalty, November 9, 1885.

VIEUX PECHES, LES. D. Dumanois. 1833.

VIGILANT DETECTIVES, THE. C.O. W. T. Hawkins. M. by W. H. Cross. Huddersfield Industrial Exhibition, September 13, 1883.

VIGLUND THE FAIR. See *Thorgrim*.

VIGNE, LA. O. M. by Rousseau. 1882.

VIKINGS, THE. 4 a. Ver. of H. Ibsen's *Warriors of Helgeland*. Imperial, April 15, 1903.

VILIKINS AND HIS DINAH. T.C. Burl. 1 a. F. C. Burnand. A.D.C. Rooms, November 8 1855.

VILLAGE; OR, WORLD'S EPITOME, THE C. Cherry. 1805.

VILLAGE BLACKSMITH. Surrey, June 1, 1857.

VILLAGE BLACKSMITH, THE. D. 5 a. G. C. Wallace. Leeds Queen's, January 8, 1903 (C.P.); Bury T.R., February 20, 1903; Stratford T.R., August 1, 1904.

VILLAGE BLACKSMITH, THE. See *The Merry Blacksmith*.

VILLAGE BLACKSMITH; A CHRISTMAS STORY OF JOY AND SORROW, THE. D. F. Marchant. Oriental, January 31, 1868; Derby Lecture H., January 18, 1875.

VILLAGE BLACKSMITH; A STORY OF THREE CHRISTMAS EVES, THE D. 4 a. H. Leslie. Greenwich, February 10, 1868.

VILLAGE CONJUROR, THE. Intl. Transl. fr. J. J. Rousseau. Fontainebleu, October 18, 1753; Academy of M., March 1, 1753.

VILLAGE COQUETTE, THE. F. Simon. D.L., April 16, 1792. N.p.

VILLAGE COQUETTES, THE. O. C. Dickens. M. by J. Hullah. St. James's, December 6, 1836.

VILLAGE DANS LES MONTAGNES, LE. O. P. L. L. Benoit. 1857.

VILLAGE DOCTOR; OR, KILLING NO CURE, THE. Burl. J. C. Cross. Circa 1796.

VILLAGE FETE, THE. Past. Burla. F. on *Love in a Village*. C.G., May 19, 1797; New T., Tottenham Street, April 23, 1810.

VILLAGE FORGE, THE. D. 5 a. G. Conquest and T. Craven. Surrey, September 15, 1890.

VILLAGE LAWYER, THE. F. 1 a. Adap. fr. *L'Avocat Patelin* by Mr. Lyons. Hay., August 28, 1787.

VILLAGE LAWYER, THE. F. Mrs. Macready. Perf. at all London theatres, 1795. Hay., 1826.

VILLAGE MADCAP, THE. M.D. 3 a. E. Mervyn. Stourbridge Alhambra, December 5, 1898 (C.P.).

VILLAGE MAID, THE. O. 3 a. By a young lady. 1792.

VILLAGE NIGHTINGALE, THE. O. 1 a. H. T. Craven. M. by Nelson. Strand, June 12, 1851.

VILLAGE OF SHIFT 'EM, THE. Sk. Granville M.H., May 17, 1909.

VILLAGE OF YOUTH, THE. Past. P. Bessie Hatton. Radstock Rectory Grounds, July 12, 1899; St. James's, March 18, 1909 (mat.).

VILLAGE OPERA, THE. C. Johnson. D.L., February 6, 1729.

VILLAGE POLITICS. Anon. 1793.

VILLAGE POST OFFICE, THE. P. 2 a. Dr. G. H. R. Dabbs. Shanklin Inst., April 24, 1889 (amat.).

VILLAGE PRIEST, A. P. 5 a. S. Grundy. Adap. fr. MM. Wm. Busnach and Cauvius's *Le Secret de la Terreuse*. (Paris, October 12, 1889.) Hay., April 3, 1890.

VILLAGE STORY, A. Dom. D. 3 a. T. J. Serle. Surrey.

VILLAGE TALE. Sadler's Wells, April, 1850.

VILLAGE TO COURT. D. 2 a. Publ. by S. French, Ltd.

VILLAGE TRICKS. Ballet Div. Lyceum playbill, June 27, 1816.

VILLAGE VENUS. A. M.C. 2 a. V. Stevens and A. Birch. Nottingham Grand, August 5, 1895.

VILLAGE VIRTUES. D. Satr. M. G. Lewis. 1796. N.ac.

VILLAGE WEDDING; OR, THE FAITHFUL COUNTRY MAID, THE. Past. Ent. of M. J. Love. Ac. at Richmond, 1767.

VILLAGERS, THE. F. 2 a. Anon taken fr. *The Village Opera*. D.L., March 23, 1756. N.p.

VILLAGERS, THE. Petite P. W. Earle, jun. (Before 1814.)

VILLAGERS, THE. C.O. Worgan. 1808.

VILLAIN, THE. T. T. Porter. Epil. by Sir W. Davenant. Duke of York's, 1663.

VILLAIN AND VICTIM. Duol. W. R. Walkas. Hay., December 12, 1894.

VILLAINOUS SQUIRE AND THE VILLAGE ROSE. Past. 1 a. H. J. Byron. Toole's, June 5, 1882.

VILLANA CONTESSA, LA. O. L. Rossi. Naples.

VILLARIO. 5 a. Joanna Baillie. Pr. 1814. (?) N.ac.

VILLEKYNS AND HIS DINAH. Burl. F. Eyles. Shoreham Swiss Gdns., July 7, 1873.

VILLI; OR, THE WITCH DANCERS, LE. Lib. by Fontana. O. 2 a M. by Puccini. Milan, May 31, 1884; rev. Scala, January 24. 1885; Manchester Comedy, September 24, 1897

VILLIAM THE VICIOUS. Burl. 2 a. H, Hall. M. by E. Jonghmanns. Blackburn Prince's, February 25, 1895.

VILLIKINS AND HIS DINAH. Burl. F. C Burnand. University A.D.C., November 8, 1858.

VILLIKINS AND HIS DINAH. James Bruton, author of *Cut for Partners*.

VILLON, POET AND CUT-THROAT. T. 1 a. S. C. Courte. B'ham Grand, April 12, 1894; Royalty, June 28, 1894.

VILMA. P. 5 a. P. Berton. Fr. Henry Greville's novel, "Les Epreuves de Ruissa." Stoke Newington Alexandra, August 17, 1904: Manchester Queen's, October 3, 1904.

VIMONDA. T. A. McDonald. Hay., September 5, 1787.

VINCENT VERIPHLEET; OR, HE COULDN'T SAY NO. C. Mr. Wynne. Carlisle Bijou, August 5, 1869.

VINDICTIVE MAN, THE. C. T. Holcroft D.L., November 20, 1806.

VINDIMIATRICE, LE. O. Grétry.

VINELAND. Fans. Bal. 4 tab. Designed by Mr. Wilhelm; arr. and prod. by Mme. Katti Lanner. M. by L. Wenzel. Empire, September 26, 1903.

VINGT-ET-UN. O. 1 a. Virginia and Wintle. Publ. by S. French, Ltd.

VINTAGE, THE. Divertissement. Mrs. Barrymore. D.L., October 2, 1829.

VINTAGERS, THE. M.R. E. J. Eyre. Hay, August 1. 1809.

VINTNER IN THE SUDS. 1 a. Taken fr. *Match in Newgate*. D.L., April 25, 1740.

VINTNER TRICKED, THE. F. H. Ward. D.L., April 9, 1746. This is a ver. of *The Dutch Courtezan*.

VIOLA. D. M. Price, Halifax T.R., August 9, 1870.

VIOLET, THE. D. 3 a. J. M. Maddox. Princess's T., November 18, 1845.

VIOLET THE DANCER. D. 5 a. Walter Thurlstone. Goole T.R., February 1, 1907.

VIOLET'S PLAYTHINGS. M.F. Miss Augusta Thomson. Marylebone, April 1, 1867.

VIOLETS. P. 1 a. E. Bliss. Chesterfield Memorial H., April 8, 1901.

VIOLIN GIRL, THE. Sk. Edgar Dereve. M. by Henry W. May. Richmond Hipp., January 6, 1908.

VIOLIN MAKER OF CREMONA, THE. C. 1 a. Adap. fr. Coppée's *Le Luthier de Crèmone* by Henry Neville. Olympic, July 2, 1877 See *Fennel*.

VIOLIN PLAYERS, THE. P. 1 a. A. Berlyn. Adap. fr. F. Coppée's *Le Luthier de Crèmone* Shaftesbury, April 22, 1890.

VIPER ON THE HEARTH, THE. D. 1 a. J. M. Campbell. Criterion, May 15, 1888.

VIRATA. Flight of imagination. 3 a. F. Alford and Emil Hardy. M. by H. E. Warner. Richmond Castle, November 26, 1907.

VIRGIN GODDESS, THE. T. 3 a. Rudolph Besier. Adelphi, October 23, 1907.

VIRGIN MARTYR, THE. T. P. Massinger and T. Dekker. Ac. by the servants of His Maj. Revels, 1620. Pr. 1622.

VIRGIN OF THE SUN, THE. P. Transl. fr. the German of Kotzebue by Ann Plumptre. 1799. N.ac.

VIRGIN OF THE SUN, THE. Transl. fr. the German by J. Lawrence. 1799. N.ac.

VIRGIN OF THE SUN, THE. Reynolds. C.G., January 31, 1812.

VIRGIN OF THE SUN, THE. See *Rolla*.

VIRGIN PLAY, A. 1582.

VIRGIN PROPHETESS; OR, THE FATE OF TROY, THE. O. E. Settle. T.R., 1701.

VIRGIN QUEEN, THE. T. R. Barford. L.I.F., December 7, 1728.

VIRGIN QUEEN, THE. D. F. G. Waldron. 1797. N.ac.

VIRGIN UNMASKED, THE. F. Anon. D.L., January 6, 1735.

VIRGIN UNMASKED. M. Ent. H. Fielding, 1786. See *Old Man's Wisdom*.

VIRGIN VICTIM, THE. Anon. Pr. at Huntingdon, 1777.

VIRGIN WIDOW, THE. C. F. Quarles. Pr. 1649.

VIRGINIA T. H. Crisp. D.L., February 25, 1754.

VIRGINIA. T. Mrs. Frances Brooke. 1756.

VIRGINIA. Past. D. Anon. 1787.

VIRGINIA. C.O. Mrs. F. Plowden. D.L., October 30, 1800.

VIRGINIA. O. 3 a. Major Jones. M. by Joseph Parry. Swansea T.R., July 12, 1883 (C.P.).

VIRGINIA. O. Mercadante. Naples, 1866.

VIRGINIA. P. 4 a. Wr. by Mrs. Langtry and J. H. Manners. M'ch'r T.R., October 2, 1902.

VIRGINIA. See *The Crossways*.

VIRGINIA; OR, THE FALL OF THE DECEMVIRI. T. J. Bidlake. 1800. D.L., May 29, 1820.

VIRGINIA; OR, THE SOLDIER'S DAUGHTER. T. 5 a. E. F. Cole. Adap. fr. the French of Latour de Saint y Bars. Globe, June 28, 1889.

VIRGINIA AND PAUL. C.O. 2 a. E. Soloman and H. P. Stephens. Gaiety, July 16, 1883.

VIRGINIAN, THE. D. 5 a. B. Campbell. St. James's, November 20, 1876.

VIRGINIAN MUMMY. See *The Antiquarian.*

VIRGINIUS. T. 5 a. J. S. Knowles. C.G., May 17, 1820; Olympic, May 7, 1892; Lyric, May 8, 1897.

VIRGINIUS; OR, THE LIBERATION OF ROME. T. D.L., October 13, 1823.

VIRGINIUS; OR, THE TRIALS OF A FOND PAPA. Burl. 1 a. L. Buckingham. St. James's T., October 1, 1859.

VIRTUE. An Int. By Skelton. (Not now known.)

VIRTUE AND BEAUTY RECONCILED. M. Anon. In honour of the marriage of the K. and Q. N.d.

VIRTUE BETRAYED; OR, ANNE BULLEN. T. J. Banks. D.T., 1682.

VIRTUE TRIUMPHANT. T.P. Dublin Crow Street. Pr. 1783.

VIRTUOSI AMBUTANDI, LE. C.O. V. Fioravanti. 1807.

VIRTUOSO, THE. C. T. Shadwell. Duke of York's T., 1676.

VIRTUOUS OCTAVIA. T.C. S. Brandon. Pr. 1598. N.ac.

VIRTUOUS WIFE; OR, GOOD LUCK AT LAST. C. T. Durfey. Duke's T., 1680.

VISION, THE. "Morality." The Hon. Eleanor Norton. M. by R. Clarke. C.G. King's, March 11, 1907.

VISION OF DELIGHT, THE. Masque. Ben Jonson. Presented at Court, Christmas, 1617. Pr. 1641.

VISION OF JAPAN, A. Sk. London Coll., February 8, 1909.

VISION OF PURITY, THE. Poetical P. Eleanor Norton. H.M., April 21, 1904 (C.P.).

VISION OF THE BARD, THE. J. S. Knowles. C.G., 1832.

VISION OF THE NIGHT. See *Was It a Dream?*

VISION OF THE TWELVE GODDESSES. Masque. S. Daniel. (Orig. prod. Hampton Court, January 8, 1604.) Botanic Gardens, Regent's Park, July 6, 1908.

VISIONS OF THE PAST. M. Playlet. Brighton G.T., April 15, 1907.

VISION OF VENUS, A. Midsummer Night's Nightmare. 2 a. H. Pleon. Adap. fr. F. Anstey's novel, "A Tinted Venus." Britannia, March 20, 1893.

"VISIONS OF WAGNER." Prod. by Chas. Wilson. London Col., September 7, 1908.

VISIT, A. Piece. 2 a. W. Archer. Fr. the Danish of E. Brandès. Royalty, March 4, 1892.

VISITE A BEDLAM (UNE). "Petite Piece." Scribe before 1822.

VISITING CARD, THE. Ca. T. Craven. Britannia, May 30, 1887.

VISPE COMARI DI WINDSOR, LE. It. O. Otto Nicolai. C.G., July 14, 1877.

VITER PER LO CZAR, LA. Ital. ver. of Russian O. M. Glinka. St. Petersburg, November 27, 1836; C.G., July 12, 1887.

VITAL SPARK, THE. P. 1 a. Adap. by W. Trant fr. *L'Etincelle.* Royalty, February 9, 1904.

VITTORIA CONTARINI. Ro. P. Pro. and 4 a. A. W. Dubourg. Princess's, May 11, 1807.

VITTORIA COROMBONA; OR, THE WHITE DEVIL. T. by J. Webster. Ac. at T.R. by His Majesty's servants, 1672. Orig. pr. 1612.

VIVA. D. 4 a. M. Bode. Merthyr Levino's Circus, September 12, 1887.

VIVA; OR, A WOMAN OF WAR. Spec. D. S. F. Cody. Leicester O.H., December 21, 1900 (C.P.).

VIVANDIERE, LA. O. 3 a. Henri Cain. Eng. transl. by G. Whyte. M. by B. Godard. Paris O. Com., April, 1895; Liverpool Court, March 10, 1896; Garrick, January 20, 1897.

VIVANDIERE; OR, TRUE TO THE CORPS. O. Extrav. W. S. Gilbert. Queen's, January 22, 1868.

VIVANNE; OR, THE ROMANCE OF A FRENCH MARRIAGE. D. 3 a. By the author of *The Member for Paris* and G. Canninge. Olympic, July 6, 1878.

VIVIANE. Bal. 5 a. Pugno. 1886.

VOCAL RECITAL, A. M. Sk. Corney Grain. St. Geo. H., April 6, 1885.

VOCATION DE MARIUS, LA. O. 4 a. Pugno. Paris, 1890.

VOGELHANDLER, DER. C.O. 3 a. M. West and L. Held. D.L., June 17, 1895.

VOICE FROM THE BOTTLE, A. F. J. P. Webster. Princess's, March 17, 1888.

VOICE FROM THE GRAVE, A. D. 4 a. S. Planché and F. D. Wood. Maidenhead T.R., April 19, 1897; Walsall Grand, July 21, 1902; Surrey, March 30, 1903.

VOICE OF CONSCIENCE, THE. D. 5 a. S. C. Henry. Ladbroke H., February 1, 1898. C.p.

VOICE OF DUTY, THE. Duol. H. F. Battersby. Comedy, January 23, 1908 (mat.).

VOICE OF ISIS, THE. P. 1 a. R. M. Paul. St. John's Wood All Saints' H., January 28, 1909.

VOICES OF LONDON. D. 4 a. W. Bourne. Cardiff Grand, March 30, 1899; Stratford T.R., June 26, 1899.

VOICE OF NATURE, THE. P. 3 a. J. Boaden. Hay., July 31, 1802.

VOICE OF THE PEOPLE. P. 4 a. M. Goldberg. Liverpool Star T., May 2, 1904; Dalston, November 14, 1904.

VOKIN'S VENGEANCE. Oa. H. F. Du Terreaux. M. by J. P. Cole. St. George's T., June 19, 1872; Garrick, November 1, 1879.

VOL. III. C. W. Ellis. Ladbroke H., January 12, 1891. See *Volume III.*

VOLCANO, THE. M. by J. Moorehead, with Attwood. (? 1880.)

VOLCANO, THE. F. 3 a. R. R. Lumley. Court, March 14, 1891.

VOLCANO, THE. Sensational Spec. 1 sc. Wr. by Alicia Ramsey and Rudolph de Cordova. M. by Carl Kiefert. London Hipp., April 20, 1908.

VOLCANO; OR, THE RIVAL HARLEQUINS, THE. S.C. Pant. T. Dibdin. C.G. Songs only pr., 1799.

VOLOGESE. O. Nicola Sala. 1787.

VOLOGESE. O. Leo. 1744.

VOLPONE; OR, THE FOX. C. Ben Jonson. Ac. by King's servants, 1605.

VOLPONE; OR, THE FOX. C. Alt. fr. Ben Jonson. C.G.

VOLTAIRE'S WAGER; OR, DESPITE THE WORLD. Hon. L. Wingfield. Dundee T.R., May 17, 1875.

VOLTIGEURES, LES. O. C. 3 a. E. Gondinet and G. Duval and Planquette. Gaiety, July 23, 1881.

VOLUME III. C. 1 a. W. Lisle. Publ by S. French, Ltd. See *Vol. III.*

VOLUNTARY CONTRIBUTIONS. Occ. Int. W. Porter. C.G., May 12, 1798.

VOLUNTEER BALL. F. by F. C. Burnand and M. Williams. Strand.

VOLUNTEER RETURNED; OR, LOVE IN VARIOUS SHAPES, THE. D. Anon. 3 a. Pr. in *Lady's Magazine*, 1784.

VOLUNTEER REVIEW; OR, THE LITTLE MAN IN GREEN. F. Extrav. 1 a. T. J. Williams.

VOLUNTEERS; OR, ADVENTURES OF RODERICK RANDOM AND HIS FRIEND STRAP. Int. Anon. 1748. See *The Northern Heiress*.

VOLUNTEERS; OR, BRITONS, STRIKE HOME, THE. F. Woods. Hull, 1778.

VOLUNTEERS; OR, TAYLORS IN ARMS, THE. C. 1 a. G. Downing. C.G., 1780.

VOLUNTEERS; OR, THE STOCK JOBBERS. C. T. Shadwell. Prol. by Mr. Durfey. Ac. by Their Majesties' Servants, 1693.

VORTIGERN. T. W. H. Ireland. D.L., 1799.

VORTIGERN AND ROWENA. See *Vortigern*.

VORTIGERNE. P. Anon. Ac. at the Rose, 1593. N.p.

VORTIMER; OR, THE TRUE PATRIOT. T. Abraham Portal. 1796.

VOTARIES OF APOLLO, THE. D.L. June 13, 1822.

VOTARY OF WEALTH, THE. C. J. G. Holman. C.G., January 12, 1799.

VOTE FOR GIGGS. F.C. 3 a. Adap. fr. Albin Vallabrègues *L'Homme de Paille*. Paris, November, 1885; Vaudeville, May 12, 1892.

VOTES FOR WOMEN. Dr. Tract. 3 a. Eliz. Robins. Court, April 9, 1907.

VOW, THE. C.O. C. Macartney. Pr. at Sheffield (before 1814)

VOW, THE. P. 1 a. Lady Clerke Jervoise. New, June 28, 1904.

VOW AND A GOOD ONE, A. P. Ac. on Twelfth Night, 1623.

VOW BREAKER; OR, THE FAIR MAID OF CLIFTON IN NOTTINGHAM. T. W. Sampson. 1636.

VOW OF SILENCE. Victoria, April 31, 1854.

VOW OF VENGEANCE, THE. Victoria, June 11, 1821.

VOYAGE DANS LA LUNE, LE. O. Buffe. Adap. by H. S. Leigh fr. Offenbach. Alhambra, April 15, 1876.

VOYAGE DE MM. DUNANAN, LE. O. 3 a. Offenbach. 1862.

VOYAGE EN CHINE, LE. Bazin. See *A Cruise to China*.

VOYAGE EN SUISSE, LE. 3 a. and 5 tab. R. Reece. Adap, fr. the French. Gaiety, March 27, 1880.

VOYAGE TO NOOTKA. C.O. A. Davidson. Ac. at Wimborne in Dorsetshire (before 1814).

VOYSEY INHERITANCE, THE. P. 5 a. Granville Barker. Court, November 7, 1905.

VULCAN'S WEDDING; OR, THE LOVERS SURPRISED. Burl. O. Anon. N.p.; n.ac.

VULTURES OF LONDON; OR, IN TOILS OF TERROR. D. 4 a. J. Rochefort. Surrey, November 9, 1903.

W

WAGER, THE. M.E. Anon. 1808.

WAGER, THE. C.O. 2 a. J. A. Kappey. Chatham Roy. Marine T., June 20, 1871; Gaiety, November 23, 1872.

WAGER, THE. Ca. G. B. Halliday. Southampton T.R., October 13, 1879.

WAGER; OR, THE MIDNIGHT HOUR, THE. C.D. 3 a. Taken fr. Dumaniant's C., *Guerre Ouverte* and *Midnight Hour*. M. by Cooke. D.L., November 23, 1825.

WAGES OF SIN, THE. D. 4 a. F. Harvey. Coventry T.R., August 3, 1882; Standard, August 21, 1882.

WAGS OF WAPPING, THE. Ballet. M. by Ambroise Thomas. (In Paris as *Betty*.) D.L., November 16, 1846.

WAIF, THE. P. 1 a. Frank Dix. Kennington, October 27, 1908 (mat.).

WAIF; OR, SPRUNG FROM THE STREETS, THE. D. Adap. of *La Chiffonier de Paris* by Felix Pyat. Holborn, 1873.

WAIF OF THE STREETS, THE. D. Pavilion, April 19, 1877.

WAIFS. Sk. Prod. by Blanche Leroy. Rugby R.M.H., December 10, 1906.

WAIFS, THE. 1a. Transl. by Cotsford Dick fr. François Coppée's *Le Passant*. Ver. of piece prod. at Princess's in October, 1887, as *The Stroller*. Hay., May 11, 1892.

WAIFS; OR, WORKING IN THE DARK. D. Prol, and 4 a. M. Murdock. Edinburgh T.R., November 1, 1869.

WAIFS OF NEW YORK, THE. D. Miss Kate Raymond. Liverpool T.R., September 13, 1895.

WAIFS OF NEW YORK. D. O. B. Collins. Albion, May 18, 1878.

WAIT AND HOPE. D. 3 a. H. J. Byron. Gaiety, March 1, 1871.

WAIT AND HOPE; OR, THE STAIN UPON THE HAND. D. 3 a. L. Nanton. East London, May 14, 1869.

WAIT FOR A YEAR AND A DAY. C.D. 2 a. Liverpool P.O.W., January 22, 1876.

WAIT FOR AN ANSWER. F. H. Lemon. Holborn T., September 25, 1869.

WAIT TILL I'M A MAN; OR, THE PLAYGROUND AND THE BATTLEFIELD. D. 3 a. C. H. Hazlewood. Britannia, April 13, 1868.

WAITER, THE. C. 2 a. R. Henry. Ladbroke H., July 7, 1887.

WAITING. Dr. Epis. 1 a. Transl. fr. the Swedish by D. Bergandahl. Edinburgh T.R., April 29, 1877.

WAITING CONSENT. C. 1 a. Mrs. Fairbairn (May Holt). Folly, June 11, 1881.

WAITING FOR AN OMNIBUS IN THE LOWTHER ARCADE ON A RAINY DAY. F. 1 a. J. M. Morton. Adelphi, June 26, 1854.

WAITING FOR DEATH; OR, THE IRON GRAVE. D. 4 a. L. Robertson and M. Comerford. Eleph. and C., February 9, 1878.

WAITING FOR THE COACH. Oa. Lib. by F. A. Clement. M. by Oliver Notcutt. Ladbroke H., July 7, 1891.

WAITING FOR THE DAWN. D. 3 a. P. Moore. Sheffield T.R., June 6, 1870.

WAITING FOR THE TRAIN. Ca. A. A. Wilmot. Novelty, February 6, 1891. C.p.

WAITING FOR THE TRAIN. Duol. S. J. A. Fitzgerald. Salle Erard, June 3, 1899.

WAITING FOR THE UNDERGRAD. Strand, August 27, 1866.

WAITING FOR THE VERDICT; OR, FALSELY ACCUSED. Dom. D. 3 a. F. on E. Solomon's picture, by C. H. Hazlewood. City of London, January 29, 1859.

WAITING MAID; OR, THE FAMILY NOSE, A. Op. Lynn Royd. M. by P. A. Henry. Hackney Manor T., February 20, 1900.

WAKE UP, ENGLAND! Sk. N. Wrighton. Leeds Empire, February 22, 1909.

WAKE UP, ENGLAND! Sk. Madge Duckworth and Ridgewood Barrie. Tonypandy R., July 5, 1909.

WAKEFIELD PLAYS. See "Miracle Plays."

WALD, DER. O. 1 a. M. by Ethel M. Smith. Dresden, September, 1901; and C.G., July 18, 1902; New York, March, 1903; and C.G., June 26, 1903.

WALK, THE. Duol. Roy Horniman. Apollo, January 27, 1908

WALK FOR A WAGER; OR, A BAILIFF'S BET. M.F. M. by Mr. Pindar. Lyceum playbill, August 2, 1819.

WALKER, LONDON. C. 3 a. J. M. Barrie. Toole's, February 25, 1892.

WALKING STATUE; OR, THE DEVIL IN THE WINE CELLAR, THE. F. A. Hill. D.L., 1707, and January 9, 1710.

WALKS OF ISLINGTON AND HOGSDON, WITH THE HUMOURS OF WOOD STREET COMPTER, THE. C. T. Jordan. Ac. for nineteen nights, 1657.

WALKURE, DIE. O. 3 a. R. Wagner. H.M., May 6, 1882. See *The Nibelungen Ring*.

WALL OF CHINA, THE. F. AS. Matthison. Criterion, April 15, 1876.

WALLACE. T. Anon. Pr. at Edinburgh, 1799. N.ac.

WALLACE. Walker. C.G., November 14, 1820.

WALLACE; OR, THE BATTLE OF STIRLING BRIDGE. P. 5 a. C. Waddie. Stirling Town Hall T., September 10, 1898.

WALLACE AND BRUCE. D. Robe. Coatbridge Adelphi, November 27, 1869.

WALLACE, THE HERO OF SCOTLAND. Rom. Hist. D. 3 a. W. Barrymore. Astley's, January 3, 1820.

WALLENSTEIN'S. Transl. fr. the German of Schiller by S. T. Coleridge. 1800. N.a.

WALLENSTEIN'S LAGER. German P. by Schiller. D.L., July 19, 1881.

WALLET OF WHIMS AND WAGGERIES. B. Webster. Adelphi, 1836.

WALLOONS, THE. C. R. Cumberland. C.G., April 29, 1782. N.p.

WALLS HAVE EARS. M. Trifle. C. Grain. St. George's H., March 26, 1894.

WALLS OF JERICHO, THE. P. 4 a. A. Sutro. Garrick, October 31, 1904; Shaftesbury, October 2, 1905; rev. Garrick, June 4, 1907.

WALLY AND THE WIDOW. C. 1 a. Ethel L. Newman. Publ. by S. French, Limited.

WALPOLE. C. Lord Lytton. 1869.

WALTER TYRREL. Fitzball. C.G., circa 1838.

WALTHEOFF THE SAXON. 5 a. T. J. Serle. Exeter.

WALTZ, THE. C.O. Alt. fr. *The Gentleman Dancing Master*. Arnold. 1813.

WALTZ, THE. F.C. 1 a. G. K. W. Scarborough Spa, July 8, 1895.

WALTZ BY ARDITI, A. F. 1 a. J. Oxenford. Adelphi, March 7, 1874.

WALTZ DREAM, A. Oa. 3 a. M. by by Oscar Strauss. Bk. by Felix Doerman and Leopold Jacobson. Lyrics by Adrian Ross. Hicks, March 7, 1908.

WAND OF WEDLOCK, THE. 3 a. Ellen Lancaster Wallis and H. Macpherson. Cardiff Grand T., April 13, 1896.

WANDERER, THE. Dr. ver. of *Auld Robin Gray*. Dundee H.M., December 26, 1893.

WANDERER; OR, A GLEAM OF SUNSHINE, THE. D. W. Travers. Grecian, October 4, 1869.

WANDERER; OR, THE RIGHTS OF HOSPITALITY, THE. Hist. D. 3 a. C. Kemble. C.G., January 12, 1808.

WANDERER AND TRAVELLER. Religious D. J. Hunter. 1733.

WANDERER FROM VENUS, THE. F.C. 3 a. R. Buchanan and C. Marlowe. Croydon Grand T., June 8, 1896.

WANDERERS, THE. American D. Pemberton Alhambra T., July 6, 1885.

WANDERING BOYS; OR, THE CASTLE OF OLIVAL, THE. Melo-d. 2 a. Adap. fr. *Le Pelerin Blanc* of Pixerecourt by J. Kerr. M. by Bishop. C.G., February 24, 1814; D.L., May 30, 1825.

WANDERING HEIR, THE. D. 5 a. C. Reade. Liverpool Amphitheatre, September 10, 1873; Queen's, November 15, 1873.

WANDERING JANET; A STORY OF THE DEE. Aberdeen T.R., January 18, 1873.

WANDERING JEW, THE. D. 4 a. Leopold Lewis. Adelphi, April 14, 1873.

WANDERING JEW, THE. D. G. L. Whiting. Britannia, June 18, 1873.

WANDERING JEW, THE. D. 3 a. T. S. Paulton. New ver. Marylebone, July 7, 1873.

WANDERING JEW; OR, LOVE'S MASQUERADE, THE. C. 2 a. A. Franklin. D.L. 1797.

WANDERING LADIES, THE. P. Sir Chas. Sedley. Ment. by Pepys under the date of January 11, 1667-8; supposed to be a second title of *The Mulberry Garden*.

WANDERING LOVER, THE. T.C. T. Meriton. Ac. privately. 1658.

WANDERING LOVERS, THE. J. Fletcher. Blackfriars. 1623. Destroyed by Warburton's servant.

WANDERING LOVERS; OR, PAINTER. C. Massinger. Ent. Stationers' Co., September 9, 1653.

WANDERING MINSTREL, THE. F. H. Mayhew. Queen's, January, 1834; Royal Fitzroy, January 16, 1834; Windsor T., April 20, 1869.

WANDERING MINSTREL. M.F. 1 a. T. C. McQuire. Eastbourne T.R., February 8, 1904.

WANDERING OUTLAW; OR, THE HORN OF RETRIBUTION, THE. D.

WANDERING WHORES, THE. P. Anon. Pr. 1663.

WANTED. F. H. W. Williamson. Gaiety, April 1, 1884.

WANTED. Canadian Playlet. Herbert Terry. Bradford, September 16, 1907.

WANTED, A BABY. F.C. 3 a. H. Francks. Sydenham Public H., March 6, 1903.

WANTED, A COMPANION. F. P. M. Levey. Dublin T.R., February 10, 1873.

WANTED, A FRENCH MAID. M.F. 1 a. Mlle. Jane May. Kennington P.O.W., April 22, 1901.

WANTED, A GOVERNESS. F. 1 a. Lyceum playbill, September 15, 1817; D.L., June 3, 1818.

WANTED, A HUSBAND. Olympic, January 28, 1850.

WANTED, A KING. Japanese M.P. 2 a. G. Elmer. Hackney Manor H.T., April 7, 1900.

WANTED, A PARTNER. Burl. Adelphi, September 29, 1828.

WANTED, A PARTNER FOR THE STAGE. Sk. Middlesex M.H., December 2, 1907.

WANTED, A SHE-WOLF. G. H. Lewes. Lyceum.

WANTED, 1,000 SPIRITED YOUNG MILLINERS FOR THE GOLD DIGGINGS. F. 1 a. J. S. Coyne. Royal Olympic, October 2, 1852.

WANTED, A TYPEWRITER. F. J. B. Harris-Burland and A. Weatherley. Portishead Assembly R., July 16, 1896 (C.P.).

WANTED, A WIFE. O. E. Spencer. M. by R. Aspa. Leamington Music H., November 15, 1871.

WANTED, A WIFE. F.C. 3 a. J. H. Darnley. Edinburgh T.R., November 4, 1889; Terry's, May 28, 1890.

WANTED, A WIFE; OR, A CHEQUE ON MY BANKER. C. 5 a. D.L., May 3, 1819.

WANTED, A WIFE AND CHILD. F. J. E. Soden. Alfred, October 16, 1871.

WANTED, A YOUNG LADY. F. 1 a. W. E. Suter.

WANTED AN ENEMY. F. H. P. Grattan. Newcastle Tyne, December 10, 1886.

WANTED AN HEIR. M.C. 1 a. M. Watson. M. by Caldicolt. St. Geo. H., April 2, 1888.

WANTED AN HEIRESS. C. 3 a. C. W. McCabe. Greenwich Lecture H., November 13, 1897; Balham Assembly R., June 11, 1898.

WANTED BY THE POLICE. Melo-d. 4 a. C. Brooke. Chatham O.H., May 23, 1898.

WANTED BY THE POLICE. D. 4 a. Ronald Grahame. Cardiff R.T., July 29, 1907.

WANTED HUSBANDS FOR SIX. M. Sk. Adap. by C. Kenny. D.L., March 11, 1867.

WANTED: JAMES BURTON. Dr. Epis. 1 a. J. H. Jay. Ramsgate Victoria, July 8, 1907.

WANTED TO MARRY. F. W. Sawyer. Brighton.

WANTON COUNTESS; OR, TEN THOUSAND POUNDS FOR A PREGNANCY, THE. Ballad O. Dedicated to Sir T. Gaudy, of Gaudy Hall. 1733.

WANTON JESUIT; OR, INNOCENCE SEDUCED. Ballad O. Hay., 1731.

WANTON WIFE, THE. See *Barnsby Brittle*.

WAPPENHAUSE, DIE. P. 4 a. P. O. Hoecker. Royalty, December 1, 1903.

WAPPING OLD STAIRS. C.O. 2 a. S. Robertson and H. Talbot. King's Lynn T.R., January 4, 1894; Vaudeville, February 17, 1894.

WAR. D. 3 a. T. W. Robertson. St. James's T., January 16, 1871.

WAR. D. C. Daley. Portsmouth R. Albert, January 23, 1871.

WAR BALLOON; OR, THE NIGHTLY COURIER OF THE AIR, THE. D. W. Lovegrave. Barnsley R. Queen's, April 3, 1871; Victoria, May 6, 1871 (as *The War Balloon; or, The Crime in the Clouds*).

WAR CLOUD, THE. D. 5 a. H. Barrs. Castleford T.R., January 12, 1895; Wolverhampton Grand T., June 17, 1895; Stratford T.R., May 8, 1899.

WAR CORRESPONDENT. Surrey, November 28, 1898.

WAR IN ABYSSINIA, THE. D. Marylebone, May 11, 1868.

WAR IN TURKEY. Britannia, May 22, 1854.

WAR OF GRAMMAR, THE. T.C., 1666.

WAR OF WEALTH, THE. American D. 4 a. C. J. Dazey and S. Vane. Bolton T.R., February 8, 1895 (C.P.); Surrey, October 31, 1898.

WAR SPECIAL, THE. P. 1 a. Fred Wright, jun. Criterion, April 9, 1901; Metropole, February 23, 1903.

WAR—THE FUGITIVES; OR, SURROUNDED. D. W. H. Abel. Ipswich T.R., January 7, 1871.

WAR TIME; A TALE OF THE PRESS GANG. D. South Shields T.R., December 9, 1867.

WAR TO THE KNIFE. C. 3 a. H. J. Byron. P.O.W., June 10, 1865.

WAR VERSUS ART. M. Sk. M. Wilson. Free Library, Walworth Road, April 26, 1898.

WAR WITHOUT BLOWS, AND LOVE WITHOUT STRIFE. T. Heywood. 1598. N.p.

WARBURTON'S SERVANT. John Warburton, Somerset Herald-at-Arms, amassed a considerable collection of old plays in MS., presumed to be originals. By some strange negligence a servant of his, probably a cook, found easy access to them, and before a discovery was made had devoted from time to time nearly the whole collection to culinary purposes as waste paper. Mr. Warburton died May 12, 1759. The following plays were destroyed:—

ANTONIO AND VALLIA. Phill. Massinger.
BEAUTY IN A TRANCE. Jo. Forde.
BELIEVE AS YOU LIST. C. Phill. Massinger.
CITTY SHUFFLER.
CRAFTY MARSHALL, THE. C. Shack. Marmion.
DUKE HUMPHREY. Will. Shakespeare.
DUTCHESS OF FERNANDINA. T. Henry Glapthorne.
FAIR FAVOURITE, THE.
FAIRY QUEEN, THE.
FAST AND WELCOME. Phill. Massinger.
FLYING VOICE, THE. R. Wood.
FORCED LADY, THE. T. Phill. Massinger.
FOUR HONOURED LIVES. Possibly same as *The Honourable Loves*.
GOOD BEGINNING MAY HAVE A GOOD END, A. Jo. Forde.
GOVERNOR, THE. T. Sir Corn. Formido.
GREAT MAN, THE.
HENRY I. AND HENRY II. Will. Shakespeare and Robert Davenport.
HONOUR OF WOMEN, THE. C. P. Massinger.
HONOURABLE LOVES, THE. Will. Rowley.
INCONSTANT LADY, THE. Wm. Wilson.
INTERLUDE, AN. By Ra. Wood.
ITALIAN NIGHT PIECE, THE.
JOBE, THE HISTORY OF. Robt. Green.

JOBE, THE TRAGEDY OF.
JOCONDO AND ASTOLFO, THE TALE OF. Tho. Decker.
JUDGE, THE. C. Phill. Massinger.
KING AND THE SUBJECT, THE. (Title probably altered to *The Tyrant.*)
KING OF SWEDLAND. (? Dekker's *King of Swethland.*)
A PLAY BY WILL. SHAKESPEARE. possibly *The History of King Stephen.* Ent. at the Stationers' Co., June 29, 1660. N.p.
LONDON MERCHANT, THE. C. Jo. Forde.
LOVE HATH FOUND OUT HIS EYES. Tho. Jorden.
LOVERS OF LOODGATE.
MAIDEN'S HOLIDAY, THE. Christopher Marlowe.
MASQUE, A. R. Govell.
MINERVA'S SACRIFICE. Phill. Massinger.
NOBLE CHOICE, THE. T.C. P. Massinger.
NOBLE TRYAL, THE.
NOBLEMAN, THE. T.C. Cyrill Tourneur.
NONESUCH, THE. C. Wm. Rowley.
NOTHING IMPOSSIBLE TO LOVE. T.P. Sir Robert le Greece.
ORPHEUS. C.
PARLIAMENT OF LOVE, THE. Wm. Rowley.
PHILENZO AND HIPPOLITO. C. Phill. Massinger.
PURITAN MAID, THE MODEST WIFE, AND THE WANTON WIDOW, THE. Tho. Middleton.
ROYAL COMBAT, THE. C. Jo. Forde.
ST. GEORGE FOR ENGLAND. Will. Smithe.
SOLDIER'D CITIZEN, THE.
SPANISH PURCHASE, THE. C.
SPANISH VICEROY, THE.
'TIS GOOD SLEEPING IN A WHOLE SKIN. W. Wager.
TYRANT, THE. See *The King and the Subject.* T. Phill. Massinger.
VESTAL, THE. T. H. Glapthorne.
WANDERING LOVERS, THE.
WIDOW'S PRIZE, THE. C. Will. Sampson.
WOMAN'S PLOT, THE. Phill. Massinger.
YORKSHIRE GENTLEWOMAN AND HER SONS.
And some works by Sir John Suckling.

The plays which escaped were:
BUGBEARS. C. Jo. Geffrey.
QUEEN OF CORSICA, THE. T. F. Jaques.
SECOND MAIDEN'S TRAGEDY. George Chapman.

WARD, THE. T.C. T. Neale. September 16, 1637. MS. in the Bodleian Library.

WARD IN CHANCERY, THE. C. F. Pilon. See *The Toy.*

WARD OF THE CASTLE, THE. C.O. 2 a. Miss Burke. 1793.

WARLAM CHESTER. Anon. Ac. Nov. 30, 1594. N.p.

WARLOCK, THE. C.O. 3 a. A. Smythe. M. by E. Little. Dublin Queen's R.T. February 1, 1892.

WARLOCK OF THE GLEN, THE. Melo-d. 2 a. C. E. Walker. C.G., December 2, 1820.

WARM CORNER, A. Sk. Islington Morley H., April 30, 1904.

WARM MEMBER. A. C. 1 a. P. Seaton Terry's, April 9, 1898.

WARM MEMBERS. C. 3 a. Hackney Manor R., December 8, 1891.

WARM RECEPTION, A. F. G. S. Hodgson. Surrey, October 7, 1872.

WARNING FOR FAIRE WOMEN. T. J. Lyly. Ac. in the reign of Q. Elizabeth by Lord Chamberlain's servants, 1599.

WARNING TO BACHELORS, A. C. 1 a. J. Mortimer. Vaudeville, December 9, 1871.

WARNING TO PARENTS, A. F. G. Roberts. Albion, March 5, 1877.

WARNING TO WOMEN, A. Rom. D. 4 a. C. Watson Mill. Eccles Lyceum, May 26, 1907; Stratford T.R., July 23, 1907.

WARNING VOICE, A. City of London, April 9, 1864.

WARP AND WOOF. P. 4 a. Hon. Mrs. Alfred Lyttelton. Camden T., June 6, 1904; Vaudeville, June 27, 1904.

WARRANTED BURGLAR-PROOF. V. 1 a. Lib. by B. C. Stephenson. M. by I. Caryll and H. J. Leslie. P.O.W., March 31, 1888.

WARRANTED SOUND AND QUIET IN HARNESS. C. 3 a. J. T. Douglass. Greenwich, November 10, 1871.

WARRENS OF VIRGINIA, THE. D. 4 a. William C. de Mille. Grand, November 14, 1907 (C.P.).

WARRES OF POMPEY AND CÆSAR, THE. C. Chapman, 1607. See *Cæsar and Pompey.*

WARRIORS OF HELGELAND. See *The Vikings.*

WARS OF CYRUS, KING OF PERSIA, AGAINST ANTIOCHUS, KING OF ASSYRIA. T. Anon. 1594.

WARWICK PAGEANT, THE. Arr. by Louis N. Parker. Warwick Castle, July 2, 1906.

WARWICK. See *Earl of Warwick.*

WARY WIDOW; OR, SIR NOISY PARROT, THE. C. H. Higden. T.R., 1693.

WAS I TO BLAME? F. 1 a. G. H. Rodwell. Adelphi T.

WAS IT A DREAM? Ca. 1 a. Adap. fr. Richard Marsh's story, "A Vision of the Night," by Edith Blair Staples. Stockport Mechanics' Inst., January 23, 1896.

WAS IT MURDER? D. 4 a. F. Herbert and B. Daly. Surrey, June 23, 1902.

WAS SHE TO BLAME? C.D. 1 a. H. L. Bedford. Crouch End O.H., December 5, 1904.

WAS SHE TO BLAME? Melo-d. 4 a. Mrs. F. G. Kimberley. Manchester Junction, April 12, 1909.

WASHED ASHORE. T. 1 a. Fr. the German by G. Hein. Egremont Inst., near Birkenhead, October 6, 1894.

WASHINGTON WATTS. F.C. J. Schonberg. Margate T.R., August 15, 1879.

WASPS, THE. C. (B.C. 422.) Aristophanes, transl. by Mitchell, 1820-22; Hickie, 1853; Rudd, 1867; and Rogers, 1876. See *Greek Plays.*

WASPS. C. Muriel Carmel Goldsmid. Royalty, November 27, 1907.

WASTE. T. 4 a. Prod. by the Incorporated Stage Society. Granville Barker. Imperial, November 24, 1907; Savoy, January 28, 1908 (C.P.).

WASTE OF TIME, A. F. Brighton R.T., June 18, 1907; Coronet, July 2, 1907.

WASTED LIFE, A. D. 1 a. L. Osmond and F. Herbert. St. Alban's H., June 12, 1894.

WASTED LIVES. D. Bishop Auckland T.R., January 29, 1875.

WASTREL, THE. 4 a. H. Byalt and H Moss. Royalty, August 2, 1894 (C.P.).

WAT TYLER. P. Southey.

WAT TYLER. Burl. G. A. Sala. Gaiety, December 20, 1869.

WAT TYLER AND JACK STRAW; OR, THE MOB REFORMERS. D. Ent. Ac. at Pinkenthman and Giffard's Booth in Bartholomew Fair, 1730.

WATCH AND WAIT. D. 3 a. T. H. Higgie and R. Shepherd. Surrey, September 23, 1871.

WATCH AND WARD. A. Wigan.

WATCH BOY, THE. Lyceum, November 6, 1865.

WATCH DOG OF THE WALSINGHAMS, THE. Rom. D. 5 a. J. P. Simpson. Liverpool R. Amphi., August 28, 1869; Surrey, October 16, 1869.

WATCH HOUSE, THE. F. 2 a. J. Galt. Pr. 1814.

WATCHERS ON THE LAYSHIPS, THE. D. Adap. fr. Horace Butler's novel. Penzance Central H., November 13, 1885.

WATCHING AND WAITING. C. 3 a. Agatha and Archibald Hodgson. Southampton P.O.W., January 15, 1891 (Amateurs); Terry's, June 23, 1891.

WATCHMAN OF NEW YORK. Victoria, March 24, 1856.

WATCHWORD; OR, THE QUITO GATE, THE. Melo-d. Attributed to Bell. D.L., October 19, 1816.

WATER BABES, THE. Burl. E. W. Bowles. Novelty, February 9, 1887; St. Geo. H., March 12, 1889 (Folly D.C.); rev. (M. by M. Clark) Leamington T.R., August 6, 1894; Parkhurst, December 2, 1895.

WATER BABIES. R. Barrington. M. by F. Rosse; additional numbers by A. Fox and A. Cellier. An adap. of Kingsley's book. Garrick, December 18, 1902, and December 22, 1903.

WATER CARRIER, THE. O. 3 a. See *Deux Journées, Les*. Cherubini. Princess's, October 27, 1875.

WATER CURE, A. Vaudeville by Arnold Felix. M. by Geo. Gear. St. Geo. H., October 22, 1883.

WATCH CURE, THE. F. Sk. 1 a. L. Sterner. Brixton T., March 14, 1904; Comedy, March 14, 1905.

WATER LEADERS. See *Watter Leaders*.

WATER RAT, THE. Sk. Bedford, July 8, 1907.

WATER WITCHES. F. 1 a. J. S. Coyne. English O.H., June 7, 1842; Globe, May, 1871.

WATER'S WATER. F. Sergt. Young, of the Royal Lanarkshire Militia. N.ac. Pr. Dundee, 1801.

WATERCRESS GIRL, THE. City of London, October 14, 1865.

WATERLOO. Mil. Spec. W. M. Akherst. Sanger's Amphi., October 21, 1876.

WATERLOO. P. 1 a. A. Conan Doyle. (The late Sir Henry Irving's season.) Rev. D.L., June 5, 1905.

WATERLOO CUP, THE. D. Newcastle-on-Tyne Amphi., June 21, 1897.

WATERMAN. O. 1a. Young and Pascal. Publ. by S. French, Limited.

WATERMAN; OR, THE FIRST OF AUGUST, THE, Ballad O. C. Dibdin. Hay., August 17, 1774; D.L., June 3, 1822; Lyceum, July 22, 1837; Crystal Palace, December 16, 1869.

WATERMAN OF BANKSIDE; OR, THE ORIGIN OF DOGGETT'S COAT AND BADGE. Victoria, August 4, 1879.

WATERS OF BITTERNESS, THE. P. 1 a. S. M. Fox. Imperial (Stage Society), June 8, 1903.

WATERS OF STRIFE. Costume C. Pastoral. Max Pireau. Bedford Park, September 15, 1907.

WATTER LEADERS, THE. See "Miracle Plays."

WATTIE AND MEG. Burl. W. Lowe. Dundee O.H., January 20, 1873.

WAVE OF WAR, THE. 4 a. F. Chesterley and H. Piffard. Terry's, December 15, 1887.

WAVERLEY; OR, A REBEL FOR LOVE. D. Edinburgh T.R., September 11, 1871.

WAVERLEY; OR, SIXTY YEARS SINCE Adap. of Scott's novel by E. Fitzball. Victoria, March, 1824.

WAXWORK MAN, THE. D. 3 a. C. A. Clarke. Victoria, June 26, 1871.

WAXWORKS' REVELS. Xmas Extrav. W. Heighway. Pub. by S. French, Ltd.

WAY DOWN EAST. P. 4 a. Lottie Blair Parker and Joseph R. Grismer. Aldwych, April 23, 1908 (C.P.).

WAY OF THE WICKED; OR, THE KNIGHTS OF THE GREEN BAIZE. D. J. H. Grover. Liverpool Royal Colosseum, February 11, 1871.

WAY OF THE WIND, THE. F. W. Mackay. Brighton T.R., August 28, 1876; Globe, September 11, 1876.

WAY OF THE WORLD. C. W. Congreve. L.I.F., 1699; C.G., December 7, 1732. Ac. by J. P. Kemble D.L., 1800; Hay., 1844; Court, April 17, 1904; Royalty, November 7, 1904.

WAY OF THE WORLD, THE. D. 5 a. W. B. Payne. Dewsbury T.R., February 12, 1883; Britannia, September 13, 1886.

WAY OF THE WORLD, THE. Melo-d. 5 a. H. E. Fielding. West London, July 9, 1900.

WAY OF TRANSGRESSORS, THE. D. in a prol. and 3 a. Nita Rae. Glasgow Lyceum, November 15, 1901.

WAY OF WAR, THE. P. 1 a. F. Prevost (Prevost Battersby). Wyndham's, December 8, 1902.

WAY OUT, THE. P. 1 a. George Unwin. Newcastle R.T., August 3, 1908.

WAY OUT WEST. D. Junius Booth. Lincoln R., September 2, 1909.

WAY TO CONTENT ALL WOMEN; OR, HOW A MAN MAY PLEASE HIS WIFE, THE. Gunnel. Ment. in Herbert's Diary, April 17, 1624.

WAY TO GET MARRIED, THE. C. 5 a. T. Morton. C.G., January 23, 1796; D.L., 1815 and 1828; Lyceum playbill, June 4, 1829.

WAY TO GET UNMARRIED. D.S. J. C. Cross. C.G., 1796.

WAY TO KEEP HIM, THE. C. 3 a. A. Murphy. 1760. Enlarged edition, D.L., 1761.

WAY TO RIG HIM, THE. C. A. Murphy. D.L.; Hay., 1820.

WAY TO WIN HER, THE. C. 5 a. Pr. 1814.

WAY WOMEN LOVE, THE. D. 5 a. G. B. Nichols. Yeovil Assembly R., January 2, 1901; Surrey, May 5, 1902.

WAYFARERS. 1 a. Herbert Swears. Matinée T., May 20, 1898.

WAYS AND MEANS. C. Anon. Ac. Dublin Smock Alley, 1785.

WAYS AND MEANS; OR, A TRIP TO DOVER. C. G. Colman, jun. Hay., July 10, 1788, and 1806; D.L., April 11, 1818.

WAYS OF MEN, THE. P. 4 a. A. Ward. West Hartlepool Grand, March 11, 1909 (C.P.).

WAYS OF MEN, THE. P. 4 a. J. E. Vivian Edmonds. Rochdale R., April 19, 1909.

WAYSIDE COTTAGE, THE. Ca. 1 a. W. Poel. Adap. fr. Kotzebue's *Halfway House*. Aberdeen House, London.

WE ALL HAVE OUR LITTLE FAULTS. F. 1 a. W. E. Suter. Grecian, October 6, 1864.

WE ARE BUT HUMAN. D. 4 a. Nita Rae. Lowestoft Marina T., January 28, 1903.

WE FLY BY NIGHT; OR, LONG STORIES. F. with songs. G. Colman. C.G., January 28, 1806.

WE HAVE ALL OUR DESERTS. C. H. S. Woodfall. 1784. N.ac.

WE THREE. C. 1 a. Eric Scott. Ladbroke H., June 24, 1902.

WEAK POINTS. J. B. Buckstone. Hay.

WEAK WOMAN. C. 3 a. H. J. Byron. Strand, May 6, 1875.

WEAKER SEX, THE. C. 3 a. A. W. Pinero. Manchester T.R., September 28, 1888; Court, March 16, 1889.

WEAKEST GOETH TO THE WALL, THE. (?) Webster and Dekker. Pr. 1600.

WEAKEST GOETH TO THE WALL, THE. Anon. Ac. by the Earl of Oxford, Lord Great Chamberlain, his servants. 1618.

WEAL OR WOE. D. A. Vaughan. Rotherham T.R., April 10, 1878.

WEALTH. C.D. 2 a. R. Lacy. Royalty, October 8, 1870.

WEALTH. 4 a. H. A. Jones. Hay., April 27, 1889.

WEALTH; OR, A PITMAN'S SECRET. D. Fredk. Wright. Bradford T.R., April 16, 1877.

WEALTH AND HEALTH. C. Ent. at the Stationers' Co., 1557-8.

WEALTH AND WANT. D. E. Newton. Bradford Pullan's T., March 3, 1884.

WEALTH GOT AND LOST. D. 3 a. C. H. Hazlewood. Britannia, December 5, 1870.

WEALTH OF THE WORLD, THE. D. 4 a. E J. Lampard. Blyth T.R., June 29, 1891.

WEALTH, WOMEN, AND WICKEDNESS. D. 4 a. J. Denton. (Orig. prod. as *The Serpent's Tooth* at the Kingston County, April 25, 1904.) December 5, 1905.

WEALTHY WIDOW; OR, THEY ARE BOTH TO BLAME, THE. C. 3 a. J. Poole. Partly fr. the French. D.L., October 29, 1827.

WEARING O' THE GREEN, THE. Dom. Irish D. 3 a. E. C. Matthews. Dublin Queen's R.T., June 22, 1896.

WEARING O' THE GREEN. Irish O.C.D. 4 a. W. Howard. Workington T.R., August 1, 1896; Greenwich Morton's, April 10, 1899.

WEARING OF THE GREEN; OR, THE LOVER'S LEAP. D. 3 a. L. Downey. Victoria, October 1, 1877.

WEARING THE APRON. Sk. Greenwich Pal., January 31, 1908.

WEARY OF BONDAGE. D. An adap. of *Sybile* by Fredk. Soutiê. Charing Cross, 1873.

WEATHER, THE. P. J. Heywood. 1533.

WEATHER OR NO. M. Duol. A. Ross and W. Beach. M. by L. Selby. Savoy, August 15, 1896.

WEATHER PERMITTING Ca. W. R. Snow. Globe, November 27, 1872.

WEATHER-HEN, THE. C. 4 a. B. Thomas and G. Barker. Terry's T., June 29, 1899; Comedy, July 8, 1899.

WEATHERCOCK, THE. M. Ent. Forest. C.G., October 17, 1775.

WEATHERCOCK, THE. F. J. T. Allingham. D.L., November 18, 1805.

WEATHERWISE. Unreality. 1 a. H. C. Newton. M. by E. Ford. Lyric, December 27, 1893.

WEAVER OF LYONS; OR, THE THREE CONSCRIPTS. F. 1 a. J. Barber. Ashley's T., November 24, 1844.

WEAVER'S DAUGHTER, THE. D. W. Darlington. Sadler's Wells, March 10, 1863.

WEAVERS, THE. D. 5 a. Mary Morrison. Transl. fr. Gerhart Hauptmann. Crystal Pal., April 1, 1901; Scala, December 9, 1907.

WEB OF FATE, THE. D. 4 a. Augusta Tullock. Braintree Lecture H., October 9, 1899; Elephant and Castle, July 9, 1900.

WEBER, DIE. D. 5 a. G. Hauptmann. Great Queen St., January 5, 1905.

WEBSTERS, THE. P. 3 a. Frank Kingston. Terry's, December 11, 1907.

WEBSTER'S WALLET. Ent. B. Webster. Strand, 1837.

WEDDED AND LOST; OR, THE PERILS OF A BRIDE. D. W. Travers. Britannia, September 5, 1868.

WEDDED BLISS. Ca. G. L. Gordon. Cork T.R., October 3, 1871; Dublin T.R., April 2, 1873.

WEDDED BLISS. Ca. 1 a. Adap. fr. the French by H. Paulton. Avenue, October 16, 1882.

WEDDED, NOT WIVED. Rom. D. 5 a. J. Coleman. Hull T.R., April 5, 1886.

WEDDED TO CRIME. D. 4 a. F. Jarman and W. Selwyn. Sadler's Wells, May 25, 1891.

WEDDING. C. J. Shirley. Phœnix in D.L. Pr. 1629.

WEDDING, THE. E. Hawker. L.I.F., May 6, 1729.

WEDDING; OR, THE COUNTRY HOUSEWIFE, THE. B.O. 1734. N.ac.

WEDDING BELLS. D. 3 a. C. Merton. Britannia, October 2, 1876.

WEDDING BREAKFAST. J. M. Morton. Hay.

WEDDING DAY, THE. C. H. Fielding. T.R., 1742.

WEDDING DAY, THE. C. 2 a. Mrs. Eliz. Inchbald. D.L., November 4, 1794; D.L., 1826.

WEDDING DAY, THE. T. John Logan. N.p. N.ac.

WEDDING DRESS. Ca. 1 a. E. Rose.

WEDDING EVE, A. "An American transformation." Holborn Empire, September 16, 1907.

WEDDING EVE, THE. D. 3 a. J. B. Howe. Britannia, April 8, 1867.

WEDDING EVE, THE. C.O. 3 a. Adap. fr. the French of MM. Bisson and Bureau-Jattiot. Lyrics by Latimer. M. by F. Toulmouche. Trafalgar Sq., September 10, 1892.

WEDDING GOWN, THE. C. By author of *Rent Day*. D.L., January 2, 1834.

WEDDING GUEST. O. 1 a. Byron and Schubert. Pub. by S. French, Ltd.

WEDDING GUEST, THE. P. 3 a. J. M. Barrie. Garrick, September 27, 1900.

WEDDING MARCH, THE. W. S. Gilbert. See *Haste to the Wedding*.

WEDDING MARCH, THE. Eccentricity. 3 a. F. L. Tomline. Court, November 15, 1873.

WEDDING MORN, THE. P. 1 a. E. V. Edmonds. Salford Regent, August 25, 1903; Eccles Lyceum, September 7, 1903.

WEDDING NIGHT, THE. P. Lord Falkland. Ment. by Pepys, 1667. Probably same as *The Marriage Night*.

WEDDING NIGHT, THE. Mus.T. J. Cobb. Transl. fr. French. M. by Dr. Arnold. Hay, 1780.

WEDDING OF CAMACHO, THE. O. Mendelssohn. 1809-47.

WEDDING PRESENT, A. F. A. Arthur. St. Geo. H., November 10, 1868.

WEDDING PRESENT, THE. C.O. 2 a. M. by Horn. D.L., October 28, 1825.

WEDDING RING, THE. C.O. 2 a. C. Dibdin. D.L., February 1, 1773.

WEDDING RING, THE. M. 4 a. Ben Landeck. Reading Royal County T., March 19, 1903; Dalston T., February 15, 1904.

WEDLOCK. See *Ariane.*

WEE CURLY. D. Adap. fr. a local story. Greenock T.R., April 2, 1883.

WEE WILLIE WINKIE. Nursery rhyme Pant. 3 a. H. Weston Wells. M. by Fred Leeds. Brockley St. Peter's H., April 6, 1907.

WEEDING OF COVENT GARDEN; OR, THE MIDDLESEX JUSTICE OF PEACE. C. R. Brome. 1658.

WEEDS. C. 4 a. Miss Walford. Gallery of Illust., May 6, 1871 (amat.).

WEEDS. Ca. 1 a. T. E. Pemberton. Birmingham P.O.W., November 16, 1874.

WEEDS AND FLOWERS. D. W. R. Abel. Norwich T.R., January 27, 1875.

WEEDS AND FLOWERS; OR, THE GARDEN OF LIFE. D. 3 a. W. H. Abel. E. London, July 25, 1870.

WEEDS AND FLOWERS OF ERIN, THE. D. 3 a. G. H. Macdermott. Liverpool R. Colosseum, March 14, 1870; Grecian, August 1, 1870.

WEEPING OF THE THREE MARIES. A Mystery of the 15th century. MS. preserved in Bodleian Library

WEEPING WILLOW, THE. Burl. Messrs. P. Davey, H. Linford, and H. S. Ram. Staines Town H., May 5, 1886.

WEEPING WIVES. C. 1 a. Giraudin and Thibouot. Tuxedo Club T., October 25, 1886. March 30, 1857.

WEIGHED IN THE BALANCE. D. 4 a. W. H. Hoskins. Darlington T.R., February 2, 1882; Margate T.R., August 9, 1881.

WEIGHED IN THE BALANCE. P. 1 a. Fr. a story by W. H. C. Nation, with four songs imitated fr. the French. Terry's, February 6, 1907; Scala, October 25, 1907.

WEIRD DESTINY, A. P. Pro. and 3 a. W. Stanhope. Margate T.R., August 13, 1888.

WEIRD EXPERIENCE, A. Sk. G. M. Marriott. Sadler's Wells, December 9, 1895.

WELCH HEIRESS. C. Jerningham. D.L., April 17, 1795. See *Welsh*, etc.

WELCOME AND FAREWELL. D. Harness. 1837.

WELCOME LITTLE STRANGER. Adelphi, March 30, 1857.

WELCOME LITTLE STRANGER. C. 3 a. Adap. by J. Albery fr. the C., *Le Petit Ludovic*, of MM. Crisafulli and V. Bernard. (Arts T., Paris, March 17, 1879) Criterion, August 6, 1890.

WELCOME VISIT, A. Ca. E. Norwood. Harwich Pub. H., July 14, 1887.

WELL MATCHED. Ca. P. Harvard. Ealing Pub. H., March 26, 1887; Manchester Comedy T., September 24, 1888; St. James's, May 14, 1889.

WELL OF THE SAINTS, THE. P. 3 a. J. M. Synge. Dublin Abbey, February 4, 1905; Irish Players, St. George's H., November 27, 1905.

WELL OF WISHES, THE. O. 2 a. B. Brook. M. by J. E. Barkworth. Ladbroke H., May 10, 1889.

WELL PAIR'D. F.C. F. G. Morley. Bayswater Bijou T., June 7, 1879.

WELL PLAYED; OR, THE MAJOR'S DILEMMA. F. 1 a. A. F. Knight. Uxbridge Assem. R., January 28, 1888; Town H., January 28, 1893.

WELSH. See *Welch.*

WELSH; OR, GRUB STREET OPERA. Fielding. 1731. See *Grub*, etc.

WELSH AMBASSADOR, THE. P. Wr. about 1623.

WELSH HEIRESS. C. 1 a. T. Cullum. Comedy, January 21, 1893.

WELSH OPERA, THE; OR, THE GREY MARE THE BETTER HORSE. H. Fielding. Hay., 1731.

WELSH ORPHAN; OR, THE WORKGIRL OF CARDIFF, THE. D. P. Cavendish. Cardiff, March 12, 1894. C.P.

WELSH RABBITS. M. and D. Absurdity. K. Summers and R. Reece. Folly, May 21, 1881.

WELSH SUNSET, A. Oa. Fredk. Fenn. M. by P. Michael Faraday. Savoy, July 15, 1908.

WELSH TRAVELLER, THE. D. Ment. by Herbert. May 10, 1622.

WELSHMAN, THE. Drayton. According to Henslowe, a P. with this title was ac. November 29, 1595.

WELSHMAN'S PRICE (? PRIZE), THE. Mentioned by Henslowe as belonging to the stock of the Rose T., 1598.

WENCESLAUS. See *Venceslas.*

WEP-TON-NO-MAH, THE INDIAN MAIL-CARRIER. Melo-d. 5 a. Go-Won-Go-Mohawk. Orig. prod. in America. Liverpool Shakespeare T., April 10, 1893; Eleph. and C., September 11, 1893.

WERE WOLF, THE. 1 a. Lillian Mowbray and W. H. Pollock. Avenue, February 15, 1898. C.P.

WERNER; OR, THE INHERITANCE. T. 5 a. Lord Byron. Based on one of Miss Lee's Canterbury Tales.

WERTER. T. 3 a. F. Reynolds. Ac. at C.G., Bath, Bristol, and Dublin. Pr. Dublin, 1786, and London, 1796.

WERTHER. F. DUVAL, 1817.

WERTHER. O. 4 a. E. Blau, P. Milliet, and G. Hartsmann. M. by J. Massenet. (Op. Comique, Paris, January 16, 1893) C.G., June 11, 1894.

WEST END; OR, THE DOINGS OF THE SMART SET, THE. M.C. 3 a. G. Dance and G. Arliss. Norwich T.R., September 29, 1902.

WEST INDIAN, THE. C. R. Cumberland. 1771. D.L., July 8, 1814; rev. Lyceum, April 23, 1822.

WEST WIND; OR, OFF FOR LONDON. F. Wastell. 1812.

WESTMINSTER; OR, THE HOUSE OF COMMONS. F. Mackay. Dundee H. Maj., February 18, 1893 (C.P.).

WESTMINSTER FAYRE. Anon. 1647.

WESTMINSTER PLAYS, THE. Began in 1709. From that time the play was usually one of the following four of Terence:—*Eunuchus, Adelphi, Phormio*, and *Andria*, but there were occasional performances of *Amphitruo*, 1720 and 1792, *Aulularia*, 1796, and *Rudens*, 1798 (Plautus); and of *Ignoramus*, a Jacobean Latin play, in 1712, 1713, 1730, 1747, and 1793. The above-named four plays of Terence were regularly performed till 1860, when the *Trinummus* of Plautus was substituted for the *Eunuchus*. In 1907 an expurgated and abridged form of *Eunuchus* was given under the title of "Famulus." Fuller details will be found in *Lusus Alteri Westminasterienses*, in three parts (1863, 1867, 1907). See "Latin Plays."

WESTON THE WALKER. F. Birmingham P.O.W., April 17, 1876.

WESTON'S RETURN FROM THE UNIVERSITIES OF PARNASSUS. Int. Hay., 1775. N.p.

WESTWARD HO! C. T. Dekker and J. Webster. 1607.

WESTWARD HO! Rom. P. 5 a. F. by M. Goldberg on C. Kingsley's novel. Dewsbury T.R., July 18, 1892.

WESTWARD HO! See *The Rose of Devon.*

WET BLANKET, A. Ca. 1 a. M. S. Clarke.

WET DAY, A. F.C. 3 a. W. Browne. Vaudeville, August 1, 1884.

WET WEATHER. F. Hay., July 20, 1819.

WEXFORD. Irish Melo-d. 4 a. F. N. Conyers. Wolverhampton Star T., June 17, 1889.

WEXFORD WELLS. C. M. Concanen. 1712.

WHALERS, THE. Victoria, December 5, 1863.

WHANG FONG; OR, HOW REMARKABLE. F. 2 a. M. by Pindar. Lyceum Playbill, August 21, 1820.

WHAT A BLUNDER! C.O. 3 a. J. G. Holman. M. by J. Davy. Hay., August 14, 1800.

WHAT A MAN MADE HER. Soc. D. Ch. Darrell. Brighouse Albert, September 20, 1909.

WHAT A WOMAN DID. D. 4 a. F. M. Watson. Woolwich R. Artillery, October 5, 1903; West London, July 4, 1904.

WHAT AN ESCAPE. F. 1 a. W. Grossmith.

WHAT AN IDEA! O. Knight Summers. M. by H. M. H. Terry. Brighton Aquar., June 25, 1883.

WHAT! ANOTHER! F. C. A. East and B. Daley. West London, June 24, 1901.

WHAT BECAME OF MRS. RACKET. M.C. 3 a. C. Townsend and C. Dixon. Margate T.R., June 17, 1901; Woolwich Artillery, June 22, 1903.

WHAT BECAME OF TOTMAN. M.C. 2 a. A. Hammond. M. by A. Cooke. Deal Globe T., June 3, 1901.

WHAT DOES HE WANT? C.G., January 29, 1856.

WHAT D'YE CALL IT? THE. T.C.P.F. J. Gay. D.L., February 23, 1715; C.G., 1751, and at Edinburgh, 1786.

WHAT EVERY WOMAN KNOWS. C. 4 a. J. M. Barrie. Duke of York's, September 3, 1908.

WHAT GREATER LOVE. D. 1 a. S. Bowkett. Publ. by S. French, Ltd.

WHAT HAPPENED TO FLANNIGAN. Sk. Middlesex, June 1, 1908.

WHAT HAPPENED TO HOOLEY. F. F. L. Conynghame. Wolverhampton Star, March 11, 1899 (C.P.).

WHAT HAPPENED TO JONES. F. 3 a. G. H. Broadhurst. Vaudeville, August 24, 1897. (C.P.); Croydon Grand, May 30, 1898; Strand, July 12, 1898; Terry's, January 22, 1900.

WHAT IS SHE? C. By a Lady. C.G., April 27, 1799.

WHAT IS SHE? O. 4 a. Lib. by J. Palgrave Simpson. M. by W. Plumpton. Gallery of Illus., April 29, 1871; Manchester T.R., March 2, 1874.

WHAT MEN CALL LOVE; OR, A TALE OF THE REAL AND THE FALSE. M. 5 a. C. Du Gué. Huddersfield T.R., April 24, 1903. (C.P.); Birmingham Alexandra T., March 21, 1904.

WHAT MEN DARE. C.D. 5 a. C. R. Kennedy and M. Sherbrooke. Newcastle-on-Tyne R., August 7, 1905.

WHAT MIGHT HAVE BEEN. D. R. Vaun. Llandudno, Rivière's O.H., May 14, 1896; Bayswater Bijou, December 19, 1896; Wyndham's, December 13, 1900.

WHAT! MORE TROUBLE! F.C. 3 a. W. T. M'Clellan. P.O.W., July 20, 1899.

WHAT NEXT? F. Dibdin. D.L., February 29, 1816.

WHAT NEWS FROM BANTRY BAY? F. M'Laren. N.p. (Before 1814.)

WHAT PAMELA WANTED. C. 3 a. C. Brookfield. Adap. fr. the French of F. de Gresac and P. Veber. Criterion, April 22, 1905.

WHAT RAILING DID. Sk. E. J. Hart. Granville M.H., May 24, 1909.

WHAT SHALL I SING? M. Sk. R. Blunt. Ealing Lyric H., September 22, 1892.

WHAT THE BOOKSHELF HID. Ca. Miss B. M. Peyton. Jersey Oddfellows' H., November 26, 1903.

WHAT THE BUTLER DID; OR, THE MAN WITH TWO WIVES. Sk. A. Voyce. Richmond, March 18, 1907.

WHAT THE BUTLER SAW. F.C. 3 a. E. F. Parry and F. Mouillot. Wyndham's, August 2, 1905.

WHAT THE PUBLIC WANTS. P. 4 a. A. Bennett. Aldwych, May 2, 1909; Royalty, May 27, 1909.

WHAT THE WOMAN SAID. Playlet. Bertha Graham. 92, Victoria Street, S.W., March 22, 1909.

WHAT TRUE LOVE CAN DO. P. Prol. and 1 a. Basil Young. Croydon Public H., October 25, 1907 (amat.).

WHAT UNCLE'S LOST. "Musical Squall," by Syd. O'Malley. M. by H. Pether and C. Thornton. Brixton Empress, January 24, 1907.

WHAT WE HAVE BEEN AND WHAT WE MAY BE; OR, BRITAIN IN HER GLORY. F. H. Siddons. Newcastle, 1796. N.p.

WHAT WE MUST ALL COME TO. C. 2 a. C.G., 1764. See *Three Weeks After Marriage.*

WHAT WIFE? J. Poole. D.L.

WHAT WILL BE SHALL BE. According to Henslow. Ac. December 30, 1596. N.p.

WHAT WILL BECOME OF HIM? OR, LIFE IN LONDON AS IT WAS AND IS. D. Prol. and 3 a. F. Marchant. Britannia, May 20, 1872; Marylebone, September 28, 1874.

WHAT WILL HE DO WITH IT? F. Mr. Lightfoot. Vauxhall Br. Road Assembly R., July 11, 1871.

WHAT WILL THE NEIGHBOURS SAY? F. J. T. Douglass. Standard, September 1, 1873.

WHAT WILL THE WORLD SAY? F. W. Gillum. Pr. in a collection of poems, 1787. N.ac.

WHAT WILL THE WORLD SAY? C. 5 a. M. Lemon. C.G., October, 1841.

WHAT WILL THE WORLD SAY? C. 4 a. G. P. Bancroft. Terry's, January 26, 1899.

WHAT WILL THEY SAY AT BROMPTON? Ca. 1 a. J. S. Coyne. Olympic T., November 23, 1857.

WHAT WOMEN DO. Sk. Epis. of London life. By Fred Moule. Middlesex M.H., December 16, 1907.

WHAT WOMEN DO FOR MEN. Sk. Luke Jellings. Camberwell Empire, March 2, 1908.

WHAT WOMEN SUFFER. Dom. C.D. 4 a. H. G. Brandon. Greenwich, July 17, 1905.

WHAT WOMEN WILL DO. C.D. Pro. and 3 a. J. K. Jerome. Bristol (C.P.). Birmingham T.R., September 17, 1890.

WHAT WOMEN WORSHIP. D. 4 a. W. Bailey and C. Berte. M. by P. Kurtz. West London, May 8, 1905.

WHAT WOULD A GENTLEMAN DO? P. 3 a. G. Dayle. Apollo, September 20, 1902.

WHAT WOULD SHE NOT? OR, THE TEST OF AFFECTION. C. W. Ross. Portsmouth, 1790.

WHAT WOULD THE MAN BE AT? P. 1 a. C.G., April 8, 1801. N.p.

WHAT YOU WILL; OR, TWELFTH NIGHT. C. John Marston. 1607.

WHAT'LL SAY AT BROMPTON. Ca. 1 a. Publ. by S. French, Ltd.

WHAT'S A MAN OF FASHION? F. Reynolds. C.G., November 27, 1815.

WHAT'S CHARLES WORTH? Sk. C. Calvert. Camberwell Empire. February 15, 1909.

WHAT'S HIS NAME? F. 1 a. J. Strachan.

WHAT'S IN A NAME? Duol. Katherine Green. Queen's H., February 9, 1895.

WHAT'S IT ON? OR, SHAKESPEAREIENCE TEACHES. Burl. W. Routledge. Gallery of Illus., January 29, 1870 (amat.).

WHAT'S THE MATTER? Burl. W. C. Oulton. 1789.

WHAT'S THE ODDS. C. 3 a. J. W. Jones. Bolton T.R., May 1, 1882; Ashton People's O.H., May 14, 1883.

WHAT'S YOUR GAME? Surrey, September 27, 1858.

WHEAT KING, THE. D. 4 a. Dr. by Miss Elliot Page and Mrs. Ashton Jonson fr. F. Norris's novel. "The Pit." Apollo, April 16, 1904; Avenue, May 7, 1904.

WHEEL OF FORTUNE. C. R. Cumberland. D.L., 1795; C.G., December 15, 1809; D.L., April 29, 1815, and March 4, 1850.

WHEEL OF FORTUNE, THE. Melo-d. Pro. and 4 a. W. H. Poole. Sadler's Wells, January 12, 1891.

WHEEL OF FORTUNE, THE. D. 1 a. W. Melville. Rotherhithe Terriss, September 1, 1905.

WHEEL OF FORTUNE; OR, THE HAWK'S NEST, THE. D. H. Collier. Rotherham T.R., May 4, 1883.

WHEEL OF TIME. West Bromwich R., December 26, 1892.

WHEELS WITHIN WHEELS. C. 3 a. R. C. Carlton. Court, May 23, 1899; Criterion, May 14, 1901.

WHEN A LASS LOVE'S. Melo-d. 4 a. Tom Craven. Margate R., November 23, 1908; Dalston, April 5, 1909.

WHEN A MAN HATES. D. 4 a. C. Burnette. Ilkeston T.R., August 29, 1904; Stratford T.R., June 26, 1905.

WHEN A MAN MARRIES. C. 4 a. M. Carson and Norah Keith. Wyndham's, March 3, 1904.

WHEN A MAN'S IN LOVE. C. 3 a. A. Hope and E. Rose. Court, October 19, 1898.

WHEN A MAN'S MARRIED. F.C. G. Logan. Dover T.R., June 25, 1900.

WHEN A WOMAN IS MARRIED. D. 4 a. W. Melville. Standard, August 4, 1902.

WHEN DARKNESS FALLS; OR, THE CRY OF THE CHILDREN. P. 4 a. Surrey, May 18, 1903.

WHEN DENNY COMES MARCHING HOME. F. E. Selwyn. Princess's, April 28, 1902.

WHEN GEORGE WAS KING. Costume D. L. Hawkins. Stalybridge Grand (as *Master of Hope*), December 2, 1892; Batley T.R., December 26, 1899; Greenwich Morton's, July 2, 1900.

WHEN GEORGE III. WAS KING. C.O. 2 a. C. Riminton and R. Forsyth. Folkestone Pier T., December 26, 1895.

WHEN GEORGE THE FOURTH WAS KING. 1 a. F. W. Moore. Birmingham T.R., September 17, 1896; Grand, October 12, 1896.

WHEN GREEK MEETS GREEK. Rom. D. 4 a. Adap. by J. Hatton from his novel. St. Helens T.R., March 23, 1896 (as *The Roll of the Drum*); Surrey, June 29, 1896.

WHEN I'M A MAN. P. 1 a. S. J. Adair FitzGerald. Publ. by S. French, Ltd.

WHEN I'M GROWN UP. P. 1 a. S. J. A. FitzGerald. Publ. by S. French, Ltd.

WHEN IT TAKES PLACE, I SHALL KEEP MY SEAT AND GET A PEEP. C.G., July 7, 1820.

WHEN IT WAS DARK. P. 4 a. Frank Vernon and Walter Maxwell. Adap. fr. Guy Thorne's novel of same name. Cheltenham O.H., November 9, 1905 (C.P.); West London, April 8, 1907.

WHEN IT WAS DARK. P. Pro. and 4 a. F. on Guy Thorne's novel. Cradley Empire, February 9, 1907. See *Darkness*.

WHEN IT WAS DARK. P. Prol. and 4 a. Adap. by Rev. Forbes Phillips fr. Guy Thorne's novel. Kingston Royal County, February 12, 1907.

WHEN KNIGHTHOOD WAS IN FLOWER. P. 4 a. Paul Kester. Dram. fr. the novel of same name by Chs. Major. Waldorf, May 18, 1907.

WHEN KNIGHTS WERE BOLD. F. 3 a. Chs. Marlowe. Nottingham T.R., September 17, 1906; Wyndham's, January 29, 1907.

WHEN KNIGHTS WERE BOLDER. M.C. Fan. Messrs. Wimperis, Davenport, and L. Godfrey Turner. M. by Miss M. Slaughter. Eastbourne D.P., May 13, 1907.

WHEN LONDON SLEEPS. Melo-d. 4 a. C. Darrell. Crewe Lyceum, March 19, 1896; Darlington T.R., May 18, 1896; Clapham Shakespeare, June 23, 1897.

WHEN ONE DOOR SHUTS ANOTHER OPENS. O. Lib. by Charles Thomas. M. by Harriet Young. Hove T.H., October 29, 1885; Queen's Gate H., May 14, 1896.

WHEN OTHER LIPS. Melo-d. T. A. Jones. Oxford East Oxford, August 26, 1907; Terriss, October 21, 1907; Sheffield Alex., December 4, 1907.

WHEN THE CAT'S AWAY. O. 1 a. Dr. A. K. Matthews. M. by B. Andrew. Garrick, November 19, 1896.

WHEN THE CAT'S AWAY. Sk. Nita Rae. Manchester Tivoli, April 19, 1907.

WHEN THE CAT'S AWAY. Sk. Camberwell Empire, July 12, 1909.

WHEN THE CAT'S AWAY. F.C. 1 a. Ed. Irwin and Stanley Lathbury. Seacombe Irving, September 30, 1907.

WHEN THE CLOCK STRIKES NINE. D. 3 a. C. H. Hazlewood. Britannia, March 8, 1869.

WHEN THE DEVIL DRIVES. Melo-d. 4 a. "Thomas Raceward." Manchester Queen's T., June 24, 1901.

WHEN THE DEVIL WAS ILL. Orig. C. 4 a. Chas. McEvoy. Carlisle H.M.T., August 29, 1908; Coronet, June 14, 1909.

WHEN THE LAMPS ARE LIGHTED. D. 4 a. G. R. Sims and L. Merrick. Salford Regent T., October 11, 1897; Grand, November 22, 1897.

WHEN THE LIGHTS ARE LOW. D. 4 a. E. Hill-Mitchelsen. Bootle, Muncaster T., August 11, 1902; Woolwich Artillery, October 27, 1902

WHEN THE TIDE COMES IN. P. 1 a. Marie Neilson. Eastbourne Pier Pav., October 8, 1903.

WHEN THE WHEELS RUN DOWN. P. 1 a. Maud M. Rogers. St. Geo. H., April 29, 1899 (amat.).

WHEN THE WIFE'S AWAY. See *While the Cat's*, etc.

WHEN THERE'S LOVE AT HOME. D. Pro. and 4 a. Maud Hildyard and Russell Vaun. Northampton O.H., April 25, 1907 (C.P.).

WHEN TRUST IS ALL. D. 2 episodes. B. Tweedale. Sydenham P.H., January 12, 1901.

WHEN TWO PLAY ONE GAME. C. Duol. E. C. Matthews and J. Weaver. Richmond Hipp., February 3, 1908.

WHEN WE DEAD AWAKEN. Dr. epil. 3 a. H. Ibsen. Transl. by W. Archer. Imperial, January 26, 1903.

WHEN WE WERE TWENTY-ONE. P. 4 a. H. V. Esmond. Orig. prod. in America. Comedy, September 2, 1901.

WHEN WIDOWS WOOED. M. Sk. A. Chevalier. Ladbroke H., May 10, 1899.

WHEN WOMAN STRAYS. P. 4 a. A. Bertram and G. Holmes. Liverpool P.O.W., December 13, 1902.

WHEN WOMEN HATE. D. 4 a. W. Hibbert. Aston T.R., January 8, 1904; Pavilion, August 1, 1904.

WHEN WOMEN RULE. Athletic scena. Bradford Pal., May 15, 1908.

WHEN YOU SEE ME YOU KNOW ME; OR, THE FAMOUS CHRONICLE HISTORIE OF KING HENRY VIII., WITH THE BIRTH AND VIRTUOUS LIFE OF EDWARD PRINCE OF WALES. S. Rowley. Pr. 1605.

WHERE IS WILLIAM? C. 3 a. Chs. Windermere. Worthing T.R., June 21, 1907; Richmond Castle, September 9, 1909.

WHERE SHALL I DINE? F. 1 a. Rodwell. C.G., 1819, and Lyceum Playbill, July 29, 1823.

WHERE THE CROWS GATHERED. D. 1 a. S. Bond. Criterion, July 5, 1905.

WHERE THERE IS NOTHING. P. 5 a. W. B. Yeats. Court, June 26, 1904.

WHERE THERE IS SMOKE. C. 1 a. H. Heaton. Croydon Grand, August 29, 1903.

WHERE THERE'S A WILL THERE'S A WAY. C.D. 1 a. J. M. Morton. New Strand T., September 6, 1829.

WHERE TO FIND A FRIEND. C. 5 a. Leigh, author of *Grieving's a Folly*, Lyceum, May 20, 1811; D.L., November 23, 1815.

WHERE WOMAN LOVES. Sk. Longsight King's, June 25, 1908.

WHERE'S BABY? Sk. J. H. Wood and E. L. Furst. Bayswater Bijou, April 21, 1903; Hammersmith Palace, September 14, 1905.

WHERE'S BERTRAM? F.C. 3 a. C. H. Abbott. Kingston County T., December 1, 1902.

WHERE'S PRODGERS? F. 6 a. E. Hester. Maidenhead Grand H., August 27, 1896.

WHERE'S THE CAT? C. 3 a. J. Albery. Criterion, November 20, 1880.

WHERE'S UNCLE? M.C. 3 a. F. D. Foster. Sheffield Lyceum T., May 16, 1904; Stratford Borough, July 11, 1904.

WHERE'S YOUR WIFE? F. J. V. Bridgeman. Strand, September 21, 1863.

WHICH? F. 2 a. (? 1 a.). A. G. Bagot. Gaiety, February 18, 1886; Torquay T.R., May 1, 1886.

WHICH IS IT. Duol. Bertha Moore. Royal Albert H., June 28, 1907.

WHICH IS THE MAN? C. Mrs. Cowley. C.G., February 9, 1782.

WHICH IS THE MASTER? M. Ent. Anon. C.G., May 15, 1807. N.p.

WHICH IS WHICH? C. 1 a. S. T. Smith. Court, July 10, 1871; Gaiety, October 25, 1873.

WHICH OF THE TWO? C. 1 a. J. M. Morton. Strand.

WHICH SHALL I MARRY? F. 1 a. W. E. Suter. July 10, 1863.

WHICH WINS? C.D. 4 a. J. W. Pigott. Terry's, June 12, 1889.

WHIFF ON THE SLY, A. Duol. Leopold Montague. Hartley Wintney Jubilee Institute, February 14, 1901.

WHIG AND TORY. C. B. Griffin. L.I.F., January 26, 1720.

WHILE IT'S TO BE HAD. F. C. Collette. Mirror, December 17, 1874.

WHILE THE CAT'S AWAY (otherwise *When the Wife's Away*). F.C. 3 a. E. F. Parry and F. Mouillot. Dublin R., March 6, 1905.

WHILE THE SNOW IS FALLING. D. Rochdale P.O.W., March 10, 1873.

WHILE THERE'S LIFE THERE'S HOPE. Strand, July 2, 1863.

WHIM, THE. C. 3 a. Lady Wallace. Pr. at Margate, 1785. N.ac

WHIM; OR, THE MERRY CHEAT, THE F. C.G., 1741.

WHIM; OR, THE MISER'S RETREAT, THE. F. Alt. fr. the French of *La Maison Rustique*. Ac. at Goodman's Fields, 1734.

WHIMSICAL LOVERS; OR, THE DOUBLE INFIDELITY. C. Transl. fr. the French. Pr. 1762.

WHIMSICAL SERENADE, THE. F. T. Horde, jun., 1781. Pr. at Oxford. N.ac.

WHIMSICALITY; OR, GREAT NEWS FROM FRANCE. M.F. Maclaren. Pr. 1810.

WHIMSIES OF SIGNIOR HIDALGO; OR, THE MASCULINE BRIDGE. C. In Harleian MSS., No. 5,152.

WHIP, THE. Sporting D. 4 a. Cecil Raleigh and Henry Hamilton. D.L., September 9, 1909.

WHIP HAND, THE. C. 3 a. H. C. Merivale and C. Dale. Cambridge T.R., January 21, 1885.

WHIP HAND, THE. C. 4 a. Mrs. Kitcat and K. Snowden. Esher Village H., June 14, 1905; Kingston R.C., October 28, 1907.

WHIPPING POST; OR, LIFE IN THE RANKS. D. 4 a. E. France. Norwich T.R., March 10, 1884; Standard, August 18, 1884.

WHIPS OF STEEL. C.D. 4 a. J. J. Delley and Mary C. Rowsell. St. Geo. H., May 7, 1889.

WHIPS THAT SCOURGE. D. 4 a. Emily Beauchamp. Balham Duchess T., October 9, 1900.

WHIRL OF THE TOWN, THE. M. Absurdity. 2 a. and 6 sc. H. Morton. M. by G. Kerker. New Century (late Adelphi), September 11, 1901.

WHIRLIGIG, THE. P. 1 a. Eva Anstruther. Kingsway, May 19, 1908.

WHIRLPOOL, THE. P. 3 a. Herbert Swears, f. on a short story by Cyrus Townsend Brady. Cardiff New, February 22, 1908; Marlborough, September 21, 1908.

WHIRLWIND, THE. P. 3 a. Adap. fr. H. Bernstein's *La Rafale* by Henry Melvill. Birmingham T.R., April 9, 1906; Criterion, May 23, 1906. See *La Rafale*.

WHIRLWIND, THE. C. 4 a. S. Rosenfeld. Eleph. and C., September 27, 1890 (C.P.).

WHISKY DEMON; OR, THE DREAM OF THE REVELLER, THE. D. 5 a. Pavilion, November 9, 1867

WHISPERER; OR, WHAT YOU PLEASE. P. Anon. (Before 1814.)

WHIST. Ca. F. Wilson. Brighton St. James's H., August 20, 1897.

WHISTLE FOR IT. M.E. 2 a. Hon. G Lambe. M. by Fanza. C.G., April 10, 1807.

WHISTLER; OR, THE FATE OF THE LILY OF ST. LEONARD'S, THE. D. 3 a. G. D. Pitt. Victoria T., January 18, 1833.

WHITE BLACKBIRD, THE. M.C. F. Bowyer and W. E. Sprange. M. by J. W. Ivimey. Croydon Grand, August 1, 1898; Islington Grand, August 8, 1898.

WHITE BOY, THE. D. T. Taylor. Olympic, October, 1866.

WHITE BOYS. Surrey, January 20, 1862.

WHITE BOYS OF KERRY, THE. D. H. P Grattan. Bradford T.R., October 14, 1872.

WHITE BRIDE, THE. Dr. Sk. Pro. and Epis. Standard, March 16, 1908.

WHITE CAT, THE. Fairy Extrav. 2 a. J. R. Planché. C.G., March 28, 1842.

WHITE CAT, THE. Fairy Spec. Adap. by H. S. Leigh. Queen's, December 2, 1875.

WHITE CAT, THE. D.L., December 26, 1877.

WHITE CAT, THE. Pant. Wr. and invented by J. Hickory Wood and A. Collins. M. by J. Glover. D.L., December 26, 1904.

WHITE CAT; OR, HARLEQUIN IN FAIRYLAND, THE. Pant. Kirby. 1812.

WHITE CAT, THE; OR, PRINCE LARDIDARDI AND THE RADIANT ROSETTA. Fairy Burl. F. C. Burnand. Globe T., December 26, 1870.

WHITE CHATEAU. Grecian, October 14, 1861.

WHITE CHIEF, THE. Pavilion, November 5, 1866.

WHITE CHRYSANTHEMUM, THE. C. 3 a. L. Bantock and A. Anderson. M. by H. Talbot. Criterion, August 31, 1905.

WHITE CLIFFS, THE. D. 3 a. P. Meritt and H. Pettitt. Hull T.R., December 13, 1880.

WHITE COCKADE, THE. D. 4 a. Watts Phillips.

WHITE COCKADE, THE. D. 3 a. T. Taylor. Croydon, August 26, 1874.

WHITE COCKADE, THE. O. 1 a. Lib. David Cook. M. by Dr. Macmillian. St. Andrew's Hall, Glasgow, November 24, 1892.

WHITE COCKADE, THE. O. 3 a. R. W. Burnett and Charles Harris. Salle Erard, Regent Street, March 7, 1895.

WHITE CUIRASSIER, THE. Military C.O. 2 a. H. W. Simonton. M. by Julius Arscott T.R., Jersey, October 9, 1895.

WHITE DEMON, A. D. 4 a. Chs. Freeman. Stratford R.T., April 29, 1907.

WHITE DEVIL; OR, A MORPHIA MANIAC, A. D. 4 a. Chas. Freeman. Royal Willenhall, February 1, 1894.

WHITE DEVIL; OR, THE TRAGEDY OF PAULO GIORDANO URSINI, DUKE OF BRACHIANO; WITH THE LIFE AND DEATH OF VITTORIA COROMBONA, THE FAMOUS VENETIAN COURTEZAN, THE. T. John Webster. Ac. by the Queen's servants at the Phœnix, 1612.

WHITE DOVE, THE. P. 1 a. R. H. Powell. Glasgow Royalty, April 21, 1909.

WHITE EAGLE, THE; OR, LIONEL, PRINCE OF SAXONY. Spectacular D. Victoria, 1828.

WHITE ELEPHANT, THE. F. H. Hayman. Eleph. and C., November 27, 1875.

WHITE ELEPHANT, A. Ca. Arthur M. Heathcote. Brompton Hospital, February 6, 1894.

WHITE ELEPHANT, A. F. 3 a. R. C. Carton. Comedy, November 19, 1896.

WHITE ENSIGN, THE. D. 5 a. C. E. Dering. Aston T.R., August 2, 1900.

WHITE ETHIOPIAN, THE. T. In Harleian MSS., No. 7,313.

WHITE FARM; OR, THE WIDOW'S VISION, THE. Melo-d. 2 a. W. T. Lucas. Queen's T., 1856.

WHITE FAWN, THE. Materially different edition from the following. F. C. Burnand Liverpool.

WHITE FAWN; OR, THE LOVERS OF PRINCE BUTTERCUP AND THE PRINCESS DAISY, THE. Spec. Extrav. F. C. Burnand. Holborn T., April 13, 1868.

WHITE HAIR, THE. P. 1 a. Ella Erskine. Court, July 31, 1909.

WHITE HAND OF A WOMAN, THE. Sk. in 3 sc. George R. Sims. Sadler's Wells, September 28, 1908.

WHITE HAT, THE. F. Adelphi, April 14, 1873.

WHITE HAWK, THE. Rom. D. 4 a. H. C. Bailey and D. Kimball. Adap. fr. H. C. Bailey's novel *Beaujeu*. Aldwych, May 30, 1909.

WHITE HEATHER, THE. D. 4 a. Cecil Raleigh and Henry Hamilton. D.L., August 16, 1897; rev. May 7, 1898.

WHITE HORSE OF THE PEPPERS, THE. C.D. S. Lover.

WHITE HYPOCRITE, THE. C. Henry Mackenzie. N.p. (before 1814).

WHITE KNIGHT, THE. C. 3 a. Stuart Ogilvie. Terry's, February 26, 1898.

WHITE LADY, THE. Lever de Rideau. P.O.W., July 28, 1892.

WHITE LADY, THE. P. Isabel Alexander. Scala, July 10, 1908.

WHITE LADY OF BERLIN CASTLE. T. C. Winchester. 1875.

WHITE LADY; OR, THE SPIRIT OF AVENEL, THE. M. Rom. M. chiefly fr. Boildeau's D. *Dame Blanche*. Adap. by J. Cooke. D.L., October 9, 1826.

WHITE LIE, A. Ca. Adap. by Jas. Mortimer fr. Meilhac's *L'Eté de St. Martin*. Novelty, November 24, 1888.

WHITE LIE, A. 3 a. Sydney Grundy. T.R., Nottingham, February 8, 1889; Court, May 25, 1889; rev. ver. Avenue, January 7, 1893.

WHITE LIES. F. West T., Albert Hall, June 11, 1897.

WHITE LIES. See *A Double Marriage*

WHITE LIES; OR, THE MAJOR AND THE MINOR. D.L., December 2, 1826.

WHITE LILY, THE. American D. 4 a. T.R., Hanley, August 31, 1891.

WHITE MAGIC. O. M. by Sig. Biletta. D.L., April 17, 1852.

WHITE MAGIC. Fairy P. 1 a. Netta Syrett. M. by D. Young. St. James's, January 10, 1905.

WHITE MAID. O. 3 a. Transl. fr. a French O. C.G., January 2, 1827. N.p. See *La Dame Blanche*.

WHITE MAN, THE. A Rom. of the West, in 4 a. Edwin Milton Royle. Lyric, January 11, 1908.

WHITE MILLINER, THE. C. 2 a. Douglass Jerrold. C.G., February 9, 1841.

WHITE PALFREY. Astley's, May 24, 1858.

WHITE PASSION FLOWER, A. P. of Mn. life, in Pro. and 3 a. E. Willett. Kennington T., September 9, 1903.

WHITE PASSPORT, THE. D. 3 a. Pavilion, March 29, 1869.

WHITE PHANTOM, THE. D. 2 a. Cecil Pitt. Marylebone, October 19, 1867.

WHITE PILGRIM, THE. D. 3 a. Hermann C. Merivale. Court, February 14, 1874.

WHITE PLUME; OR, THE BORDER CHIEFTAIN, THE. M.R.D. T. Dibdin. C.G., April 10, 1806. Songs only. Pr. 1806.

WHITE PROPHET, THE. P. 4 a. Hall Caine. Garrick, November 27, 1908 (C.P.).

WHITE QUEEN, THE. Hist. D. J. W. Boulding. Sadler's Wells, October 12, 1883; new and rev. edition, Birmingham T.R., June 26, 1899; Grand, July 17, 1899.

WHITE ROSE, THE. Rom. D. 4 a. Geo. R. Sims and Robert Buchanan. F. on Sir Walter Scott's "Woodstock." Adelphi, April 23, 1892.

WHITE ROSES. C. 2 tab. Edwin Gilbert. Fr. Miss Mary C. Rowsell's story of Petronella. Ladbroke H., August 20, 1891; Parkhurst, December 14, 1891.

WHITE SCARF. Standard, January 30, 1864.

WHITE SERGEANTS. Adelphi, May 6, 1850.

WHITE SILK DRESS, THE. M.F. 2 a. M. by A. M'Lean, Reginald Somerville, and G. Byng. P.O.W., October 3, 1896.

WHITE SLAVE, THE. 5 a. Bartley Campbell. (Orig. prod. in America.) Bristol Prince's T., August 4, 1884; Grand, August 18, 1884.

WHITE SLAVE; OR, THE FLAG OF FREEDOM, THE. D. 2 a. Edward Stirling. Victoria T., August 10, 1849.

WHITE SLAVES OF LONDON, THE. D. 4 a. A. Shirley. Hammersmith Lyric, September 21, 1904.

WHITE STOCKING, A. C. 1 a. Edward Ferris and Arthur Stewart. Comedy, October 3, 1896.

WHITE STOCKINGS. C. G. W. Hannon. T.R., Stratford, E., August 31, 1888.

WHITE WOODS. Victoria, February 2, 1852.

WHITEBAIT AT GREENWICH. F. 1 a. John Maddison Morton. Adelphi, November 13, 1853, and Hay.

WHITECHAPEL GIRL, A. C.D. 5 a. T. W. Palrow. Norwich T.R., October 29, 1900.

WHITECHAPEL KING, THE (otherwise *The World's Way*, Pavilion, May 18, 1903). D. 5 a. C. Hannan. Hammersmith Lyric, May 8, 1905.

WHITEFRIARS; OR, THE DAYS OF CLAUDE DU VAL. D. 3 a. Fr. novel of same name. W. T. Townsend. Surrey T.

WHITER THAN SNOW. Dom. D. 5 a. Kenneth Lee. Opera Comique, June 25, 1885.

WHITEWASHING JULIA. C. 3 a. Henry Arthur Jones. Garrick, March 2, 1903.

WHITSUN PLAYS. R. Higden. 1328. See *Chester Whitsun Plays*.

WHITSUNTIDE; OR, THE CLOWN'S CONTENTION. Past. Anon. L.I.F., 1722.

WHITTINGTON. O. Lib. by H. B. Farnie. M. by Offenbach. Alhambra, December 26, 1874.

WHITTINGTON AND HIS CAT. O. Samuel Davey. Dublin Smock Alley, 1739.

WHITTINGTON AND HIS CAT. O. 3 a. Offenbach. Alhambra, 1874.

WHITTINGTON AND HIS CAT. Burl. D. 3 a. F. C. Burnand. Gaiety, October 15, 1881.

WHITTINGTON, JUNIOR, AND HIS SENSATIONAL CAT. Burl. Robert Reece. Royalty, November 23, 1870.

WHITTINGTON, OF HIS LOWE BIRTHE, HIS GREAT FORTUNE, THE HISTORY OF RICHARD. As it was plaied by the Prynce's Servants. Payver, February 8, 1604.

WHO DID IT; OR, THE MYSTERY OF ROSEDALE HOLLOW. D. W. Vollaire. T.R., Scarborough, May 11, 1875.

WHO DID IT; OR, THE TRACK OF CRIME. D. Britannia, December 18, 1867.

WHO IS SHE? Petit C. 19th cen. Stirling.

WHO IS SHE? P. 4 a. Mr. Hill-Mitchelson. Wigan Hipp., December 16, 1907; Hammersmith Lyric, March 15, 1909.

WHO IS SYLVESTER? C. Sk. F. A. Morgon. Richmond, May 13, 1907.

WHO IS SYLVIA? C. 1 a. Austin Fryers. Opera Comique, November 12, 1892.

WHO IS WHO; OR, ALL IN A FOG. F. 1 a. Thos. J. Williams. G.T., October 16, 1869.

WHO KILLED COCK ROBIN? F. 2 a. Chas Matthews. Hay., November 13, 1865.

WHO PAYS THE RECKONING? M. Ent. 2 a. S. J. Arnold. Hay., July, 1795. N.p.

WHO SPEAKS FIRST? C. 1 a. Chas. Dance. Lyceum, January 11, 1849; Charing Cross, June 23, 1870.

WHO STOLE THE CLOCK? F. 1 a. Publ. by S. French, Ltd.

WHO STOLE THE POCKET-BOOK? OR, A DINNER FOR SIX. F. 1 a. John Maddison Morton. Adelphi, March 29, 1852; Hay.

WHO STOLE THE TARTS? O. 2 a. Frank Silvester. Regent Street Polytechnic, June 2, 1894.

WHO WANTS A GUINEA? O. 5 a. Geo. Colman, jun. C.G., April 18, 1805; Lyceum, May 15, 1821; D.L., May 28, 1828.

WHO WANTS A WIFE? M.D. C.G., April, 1816.

WHO WAS THE WOMAN? D. Nita Rae. Liverpool T.R., October 28, 1907.

WHO WINS? OR, THE WIDOW'S CHOICE. M.F. John Till Allingham. C.G., February 25, 1808. See *Uncle's Will*.

WHO WON. C. 1 a. Kate Goddard. Publ. by S. French, Ltd.

WHO'D BE A MANAGER? F. Dublin Queen's T., December 15, 1876.

WHO'D HAVE THOUGHT IT? F. James Cobb. C.G., April 28, 1781. N.p.

WHO'LL LEND ME A WIFE? F. 2 a. J. G. Millengen. Victoria T., July 22, 1834.

WHO'S AFRAID? F. Dr. Jodrell. 1787. N.a.

WHO'S AFRAID? F. Henley Attwater. Bloomsbury H., October 18, 1907.

WHO'S AFRAID? AH! AH! AH! Int. Sir J. Carr. M. by Reeves. Hay., September 12, 1805. N.p.

WHO'S AT HOME? OR, MAN AND WIFE BEFORE MARRIAGE. C.O. 2 a. Lyceum playbill, August 1, 1825.

WHO'S BROWN? F.C. 3 a. Frank Wyatt. Sunderland Av., May 13, 1901, under the title of *A Naked Truth;* Kennington Princess of Wales's, September 15, 1902.

WHO'S HAMILTON? F.C. 3 a. Keith Lonsdale. Ealing T., May 25, 1903.

WHO'S MARRIED? F. Mrs. Adams Acton. Bayswater Bijou T., June 22, 1893; private residence of Mrs. A. A., December 21, 1895.

WHO'S MY FATHER? F. C.G., April 13, 1818.

WHO'S MY HUSBAND? F. 1 a. J. M. Morton. Hay., October 16, 1847.

WHO'S THE COMPOSER? C.D. 2 a. J. Maddison Morton. Hay., October 28, 1845.

WHO'S THE DUPE? F. Mrs. Cowley. D.L., May 10, 1779.

WHO'S THE HEIR? O. 1 a. Geo. Marsh. Gallery of Illus., March 5, 1869; Sunderland T.R., October 14, 1870.

WHO'S THE ROGUE? M.F. By an Oxford student. M. by Florio. C.G., April 15, 1801.

WHO'S THE VICTIM? F. C. H. Hazelwood. City of London T.

WHO'S TO BE MASTER? C. Stratford T.R., March 29, 1886.

WHO'S TO BLAME; OR, NO FOOL LIKE AN OLD ONE? F. T. Meadows. 1805.

WHO'S TO HAVE HER? M.F. T. Dibdin. 1813.

WHO'S TO INHERIT? C. 1 a. Publ. by S. French, Ltd.

WHO'S TO WIN? D. Weymouth T.R., May 24, 1871; Glasgow Adelphi, April 29, 1878.

WHO'S TO WIN; OR, THE POOL OF THE FOUR WILLOWS? Marylebone, June 18, 1877; Bradford Pullan's T. of Varieties, January 8, 1883.

WHO'S TO WIN HIM? C. 1 a. T. J. Williams. Lyceum, January 20, 1868.

WHO'S WHO? F. 1 a. Sydney Dark Adap. fr. French of Tristan Bernard. Savoy, May 28, 1904.

WHO'S WHO? Sk. Brighton Alhambra, May 25, 1908.

WHO'S WHO; OR, THE DOUBLE IMPOSTURE? F. 1 a. J. Poole. D.L., November 15, 1815.

WHO'S YOUR FRIEND? C.D. 2 a. Publ. by S. French, Ltd.

WHO'S ZOO. F. M.C. Abusrdity. Glasgow Pavilion, September 30, 1907. See *Whose Zoo.*

WHOLE CONTENTION BETWEEN TWO FAMOUS HOUSES, LANCASTER AND YORK. In 2 pts. Pr. 1619.

WHOM DO THEY TAKE ME FOR? J. M. Morton. Hay., June, 1847.

WHORE IN GRAIN, THE. P. Ment. in Sir Henry Herbert's Diary, January 26, 1624.

WHORE NEW VAMPED, THE. C. Ac. at the Red Bull, 1639. N.p.

WHORE OF BABYLON, THE. Hist. John Dekker. Pr. 1607.

WHORE OF BABYLON, THE. Said to be wr. by King Edward VI. N.p.

WHOSE ZOO? Fant. 1 a. R. Bankier. Glasgow Royalty, May 19, 1909.

WHOSE WIFE; OR, A CORONER'S HONEYMOON? F.C. 3 a. Frank Horridge. Bournemouth T.R., August 20, 1898.

WHOSOEVER SHALL OFFEND. See *Money and Man.*

WHY BROWN WENT TO BRIGHTON. F.C. 3 a. Fenton Mackay and W. Stephens. Kennington Princess of Wales, May 5, 1902.

WHY MEN LOVE WOMEN. Walter Howard. Manchester Osborne T., July 29, 1901.

WHY NOT? Epis. C.H. M. Hardinge. New T., November 2, 1905.

WHY SMITH LEFT HOME. F. 3 a. Geo. H. Broadhurst. First time in England, Margate G., April 27, 1899; Strand, May 1, 1899.

WHY THE THIRD FLOOR PASSED. Sk. J. J. Spencer. Metropolitan, December 28, 1908.

WHY WILLIAM LIED. F.C. 3 a. Phillip Clifford. Bristol Prince's, June 11, 1904; Lowestoft Marina, July 11, 1904.

WHY WOMAN SINS. D. W. P. Sheen and Fred S. Jennings. Wigan T.R., May 10, 1900; Terriss, January 28, 1901.

WHY WOMEN WEEP. C. 1 a. F. W. Broughton. Criterion, January 24, 1888; Wyndham's, May 14, 1902.

WICKED CITY, THE. D. 4 a. Ronald Grahame and Guy Logan. Bristol T.R., September 30, 1901; Elep. and C., April 21, 1902.

WICKED DUKE, THE. G. à Beckett and German Reed. St. Geo. H., circa 1865.

WICKED PARIS. D. 3 a. Wilford Stephens. Gloucester T.R., April 28, 1884.

WICKED UNCLE, THE. F. Fred Wright, jun. Gaiety. December 6, 1900.

WICKED WIFE, A. D. 1 a. John Courtney. Hay., February, 1857.

WICKED WORLD, THE. Fairy C. 4 a. W. S. Gilbert. Hay., January 4, 1873.

WICKERD, THE WITCHERER. D. Sheffield Alexandra O.H., April 14, 1873.

WICKLOW GOLD MINES, THE. M.E. Alt. fr. *The Lad of the Hills.* O'Keefe. 1798. Hay., 1810. N.p.

WICKLOW MOUNTAINS, THE. O. John O'Keeffe. C.G., October 10, 1796.

WICKLOW ROSE, THE. Irish C.O. R. Reece. M. by G. B. Allen. Manchester Prince's T., May 3, 1882.

WIDE AWAKE. Ca. Adap. fr. the German by Morris Dare. Portsmouth T.R., July 18, 1887.

WIDE AWAKE. See *Fast Asleep.*

WIDE WORLD, THE. D. 5 a. F. M. Watson. Blackburn Prince's, July 8, 1895.

WIDERSPAUSTIGEN ZAHMUNG DER. O. Goetz 1840-1876. F. on *The Taming of the Shrew.*

WIDOW, THE. O. Ben Jonson, John Fletcher, and Thos. Middleton. Blackfriars, 1634. Pr. 1652.

WIDOW, THE. C. Walter C. Rhodes. Battersea Park T.H., February 4, 1889.

WIDOW, THE. F.C. 3a. A. G. Bagot. Windsor T.R., November 18, 1890; Comedy, April 21, 1892.

WIDOW; OR, WHO WINS. The. F. 2 a. John Tell Allingham. C.G.

WIDOW AND NO WIDOW, A. D.F. Paul Jodrell. Hay., July 7, 1779. Pr. 1780.

WIDOW AND THE RIDING HORSE, THE. D. Trifle. Transl. fr. the German of Kotzebue by Anne Plumptre. 1799. N.ac.

WIDOW AND WIFE. D. 3 a. H. J. Byron. Bristol Old T.R., September 11, 1876.

WIDOW BEWITCHED, THE. C. John Mootley. Goodman's Fields, 1730.

WIDOW BEWITCHED, THE. F. 1 a. W. J Lucas. Princess's T., 1845.

WIDOW BEWITCHED. Gall. of Illus,, August 14, 1865.

WIDOW BUDD, THE. P. 1 a. A. Leslie. Crouch End Assem. R., April 22, 1909.

WIDOW CAPET, THE. Hist. Playlet. Louis Cohen. Coronet, November 24, 1907 (C.P.).

WIDOW HUNT A. C. Strand, November 6, 1868.

WIDOW HUNT, THE. See *Everybody's Friend.*

WIDOW MEAD, THE. D.D. 2 a. Arthur Hewson. Thornton Heath Baths, January 19, 1901.

WIDOW OF DELPHI; OR, THE DESCENT OF THE DEITIES. M.C. Richard Cumberland. M. by T. H. Butler. C.G., 1780. Songs only pr.

WIDOW OF MALABAR, THE. T. 3 a. Miss Mariana Starke. C.G., 1791.

WIDOW OF MALABAR; OR, THE TYRANNY OF CUSTOM, THE. F. 5 a. Col. Davies Humphreys. Philadelphia, May 7, 1790; Pr. at New York.

WIDOW OF SAREPTA, THE. Sacr. D. Thos. Holcroft. Transl. fr. Madam Genlis. 1786.

WIDOW OF WALLINGFORD, THE. C. 2 a. Anon. Said to have been perf. in the neighbourhood of Wallingford, 1775.

WIDOW QUEEN, THE. Hist. D. M. by E. J. Leder. Lyceum Playbill, October 9, 1834.

WIDOW QUEEN, THE. C. 2 a. T. J. Serle. Lyceum, 1835.

WIDOW RANTER; OR, THE HISTORY OF BACON IN VIRGINIA. T.C. Mrs. A. Behn. Ac. by His Majesty's Servants, 1690.

WIDOW WIGGINS, THE. Monol. Ent. Adelphi, 1836; D.L., April 28, 1836.

WIDOW WINSOME, THE. 3 parts. Alfred Colmore. Criterion, October 27, 1888.

WIDOW WOOS, THE. P. 1 a. M. E. Francis (Mrs. Francis) Blundell and Sydney Valentine. Hay., January 9, 1904.

WIDOW'D WIFE, THE. C. Dr. Kenrick. D.L., December 5, 1767.

WIDOWS BEWITCHED. Britannia, December 11, 1854.

WIDOW'S CAP, THE. Ca. Arthur Chapman. Ladbroke Hall, April 7, 1888.

WIDOW'S CHARMS, THE. Anthony Mundy. Ac. 1602.

WIDOW'S ONLY SON, THE. C. Richard Cumberland. C.G., June 7, 1810. N.p.

WIDOW'S PRIZE, THE. C. William Sampson. Entered on the books of the Stationers' Company, September 9, 1653. Destroyed by Warburton's servant.

WIDOW'S SON; OR, THE TWIN BROTHERS, THE. D. Beaumont Hughes. Paisley T.R., May 1, 1868.

WIDOW'S TEARS, THE. C. Geo. Chapman. Black and White Friars, 1612.

WIDOW'S VICTIM, THE. F. 1 a. Chas. Selby. Adelphi T., October 17, 1535.

WIDOW'S VOW, THE. F. 2 a. Eliz Inchbald. Hay., 1786.

WIDOW'S WEEDS. Ca. 1 a. John Oxenford and Horace Wigan. Strand, March 19, 1870.

WIDOW'S WISH; OR, THE EQUIPAGE OF LOVERS, THE. F. Henry Ward. Ac. at York 1746.

WIDOW'S WOOING, A. Ca. Edwin Oliver. St. Albans County H., October 23, 1893.

WIDOWER'S HOUSES. P. 3 a. G. Bernard Shaw. Royalty, December 9, 1892.

WIDOWER'S TEARS, THE. C. Geo. Chapman. Pr. 1612.

WIE DIE ALTEN SUNGEN. C. 4 a. Karl Niemann (German season). Royalty, January 29, 1904.

WIFE; A TALE OF MANTNA, THE. Burl. 5 a. Sheridan Knowles. C.G., 1833; D.L., February 12, 1835; Strand, July, 1837; D.L., February 21, 1870; Pavilion, November 9, 1892.

WIFE AND NO WIFE, A. F. C. Coffey. Pr. 1732. N.ac.

WIFE AND THE WOMAN, THE. P. 4 a. and 7 sc. Tom Craven. Gateshead King's, November 20, 1905.

WIFE FOR A DAY, A. F. A. Byron. Whitehaven T.R., June 20, 1873.

WIFE FOR A MONTH. T.C. Beaumont and Fletcher. 1647.

WIFE IN THE RIGHT, A. C. Mrs. Elizabeth Griffith. C.G., March 5, 1772.

WIFE OF A MILLION, THE. C. 5 a. Francis Latham. Ac. by His Majesty's Servants of the Theatres Royal, Norwich, Lincoln, and Canterbury. 1803.

WIFE OF BATH, THE. C. John Gay. D.L., May 12, 1713. Alt. and revived at Lincoln's Inn Fields January 19, 1730.

WIFE OF DIVES, THE. C.D. 3 a. S. X Courte. Birmingham T.R., August 27, 1894; Opera Comique, November 26, 1894; Brighton T.R., 1895. See *The Great Pearl Case.*

WIFE OF SCARLI, THE. 3 a. Adapt. fr. the "Tristi Amori" of Guiseppe Giacosa. Birmingham P.O.W., September 9, 1897.

WIFE OF SEVEN HUSBANDS; OR, A LEGEND OF PEDLARS ACRE, THE. Melo-d. 2 a. Geo. Almar. Surrey T., 1831.

WIFE OF TWO HUSBANDS, THE. M.D. 3 a. James Cobb. D.L., November 1, 1803.

WIFE OR NO WIFE. D. John A. Heraud. Hay.. July 23, 1855.

WIFE OR NO WIFE. D. Pro. and 4 chapters. Adap. fr. Wilkie Collins' novel "Man and Wife," by David S. James. Torquay T.R., May 21, 1883.

WIFE O.. WIDOW? D. 4 a. Clifton W. Tayleure. Grand, February 15, 1886.

WIFE OR WIDOW? P. Roland Oliver. Surrey, April 9, 1903 (C.P.).

WIFE TO BE LET, A. C. Mrs. Elizabeth Haywood. D.L., August 12, 1723.

WIFE TO BE LET, A. C. 2 a. Adap. of Mrs. Haywood's C. Ann Minton. 1802.

WIFE TO BE SOLD; OR, WHO BIDS MOST? A. To which is added *The Slaves.* M. F. Maclaren. 1807.

WIFE WELL MANAGED, A. F. Mrs. Centlivre. 1715.

WIFE WELL MANAGED, A. F. H. Carey. 1735-6.

WIFE WELL WON, A. D. 3 a. Edmund Falconer. Hay., December 30, 1867

WIFE WITH A SMILE, GO AWAY YOU BOYS, THE. Sk. A. Bond Sayers. Prod. by the Water Rats at the London Pav., November 21, 1904.

WIFE WITH TWO HUSBANDS, A. M.D 3 a. Cobb. Transl. fr. the French of Pixerécourt. 1803. N.ac.

WIFE WITH TWO HUSBANDS, THE. T.C. 3 a. Miss Gunning. 1803. N.ac.

WIFE WITHOUT A SMILE, A. C. in disguise. 3 a. Arthur W. Pinero. Wyndham's, October 12, 1904.

WIFE WOMAN OF HOGSDEN, THE. C. Thos. Heywood.

WIFE'S DEVOTION, A. D. prol. and 3 a. J. H. Darnley and Geo. Manville Fenn. Liverpool Shakespeare, May 6, 1889; West London, April 13, 1896.

WIFE'S EVIDENCE, THE. D. C. H. Hazlewood. Britannia, May 1, 1872.

WIFE'S EXCUSES; OR, CUCKOLDS MAKE THEMSELVES, THE. C. Richard Estcourt. 1706.

WIFE'S PORTRAIT, THE. Household Picture. Dr. Westland Marston. Fr. the German. Hay., March 10, 1862; Princess's, 1864.

WIFE'S RELIEF; OR, THE HUSBAND'S CURE, THE. C. Charles Johnson. D.L., November 12, 1711. See *The Gamester*.

WIFE'S REVENGE. Surrey, November 23, 1857.

WIFE'S SACRIFICE, A. 5 a. Adapt. of D'Ennery and Tarbe's "Martyre," by Sidney Grundy and Sutherland Edwards. St. James's, May 25, 1886.

WIFE'S SECOND FLOOR. J. M. Morton. Princess's.

WIFE'S SECRET, THE. 5 a. Geo. W. Lovell. Hay., January 17, 1848; Surrey, November 14, 1868.

WIFE'S STRATAGEM, THE. C. Alt. fr. Shirley by J. Poole. C.G., March 13, 1827.

WIFE'S TRAGEDY, THE. D. 5 a. Mrs. Edward Thomas. Standard, December 10, 1870.

WIFE'S VICTORY, A. C.D. 5 a. Liverpool R. Amphi., March 28, 1879.

WIFEY. C. 3 a. James Mortimer. Adapt. fr. the French. Strand, November 10, 1885.

WIG AND GOWN. D. 3 a. James Albery. Globe, April 6, 1874.

WIGGLES. Sk. Willie Atom. Empress, July 12, 1909.

WILD BOY OF BOHEMIA; OR, THE FORCE OF NATURE, THE. Melo-d. 2 a. John Walker. Ac. in London.

WILD CHARLEY. D. 2 a. C. H. Hazlewood. Britannia, October 28, 1867.

WILD CHERRY, A. O. R. Reece. Reigate, September 2, 1867.

WILD DUCK, THE. P. 5 a. H. Ibsen. Royalty, May 5, 1894; Globe, May 17, 1897; Court, October 17, 1905. See *Der Wildente*.

WILD DUCKS. F. 1 a. Edward Stirling. Marylebone, January 7, 1850.

WILD FLOWER, A. C.D. 3 a. Brighton T.R., March 5, 1900; Camberwell Metropole, March 19, 1900.

WILD FLOWER OF THE PRAIRIE; OR, A FATHER'S LEGACY. D. 2 a. F. Fuller and H. Richardson. Elephant and Castle, September 8, 1877.

WILD FLOWERS. D. 1 a. Edward Rose. T.R., October 4, 1880.

WILD GALLANT, THE. C. John Dryden. T.R., 1669.

WILD GOOSE, A. D. 5 a. John Lester Wallack. Hay., April 29, 1867.

WILD GOOSE CHASE. C. 5 a. Beaumont and Fletcher. Pr. 1652. D.L., October 21, 1820. Pastoral performance, R. Botanical Gardens, Regent's Park, July 18, 1904.

WILD ISLANDERS; OR, THE COURT OF PEKIN. Ballet. D.L., October 21, 1805.

WILD LOVE; OR, EAGLE WALLY, A. Rom. D. Miss Linda Dietz. Transl. fr. the German of W. von Hillern. T.R., Bristol, April 18, 1881.

WILD MAN, THE. D. 4 a. Pavilion (Jewish season), August 29, 1908.

WILD OATS; OR, THE STROLLING GENTLEMEN. C. John O'Keeffe. C.G., April 6, 1791; January 31, 1814; Criterion, May 18, 1891.

WILD PRIMROSE, THE. C.D. 4 a. Novelty, February 7, 1891.

WILD RABBIT, THE. F. C. 3 a. Geo. Arliss. Wolverhampton Grand T., January 23, 1899; Criterion, July 25, 1899.

WILD SWANS. O. 1 a. Gillington and Horrocks. Publ. by S. French, Ltd.

WILD VIOLET, THE. Parkhurst T., September 1, 1891; Colne T.R., September 13, 1894.

WILD WEST, THE. Rom. D. 3 a. Alfred Stafford. Woolwich T.R., June 6, 1887.

WILDERNESS, THE. C. 3 a. H. V. Esmond. St. James's, April 11, 1901.

WILDENTE, DER (*The Wild Duck*). P. 5 a. H. Ibsen. Great Queen Street, March 3, 1905.

WILDFIRE. Extrav. H. B. Farnie and Robert Reece. Alhambra, December 24, 1877.

WILDFIRE NED. Britannia, December 19, 1866.

WILDSCHUTZ, DER (*The Poacher*). O. Lortzing (1803-1852). D.L., July 3, 1895.

WILFRED'S CHOICE. Herbert H. Cullum. Maidstone, December 14, 1894.

WILFUL BEAUTY, THE. Extrav. A. E. Burton. St. Geo. Hall, November 14, 1885.

WILFUL MURDER. D. 4 a. John F. Preston. Woolwich T.R., April 2, 1888.

WILFUL MURDERS. F. 1 a. Thos. Higgie. Princess's T., July, 1847.

WILFUL WARD, THE. C. 1 a. J. P. Wooler. Strand, November 14, 1864.

WILHELM TELL. German play by Schiller. D.L., June 9, 1881.

WILIS, THE. See *The Night Dancers*.

WILL, THE. See *An Uadhact*.

WILL; OR, THE MAN OF STRAW, THE. C. 5 a. T. Reynolds. 1797. Lyceum, October 21, 1809; D.L., October 17, 1825; October 18, 1826.

WILL AND NO WILL; OR, WIT'S LAST STAKE. Petite pièce. King. D.L., April 24, 1799.

WILL AND THE WAY, THE. C. 1 a. Justin Huntley M'Carthy. Avenue, May 21, 1890.

WILL AND THE WAY, THE. Ca. B. N. Graham. Bayswater Bijou, March 21, 1901.

WILL AND THE WAY; OR, THE MYSTRIES OF CARROW ALLEY. Rom. D. 3 a. F. on work of the same name. W. R. Waldron. T.R., Leeds, April 19, 1860.

WILL FOR THE DEED, THE. C. 3 a. Thomas Dibdin. C.G., 1805.

WILL HE COME HOME AGAIN? Ca. Mrs. Bernhard Whislaw. Avenue, March 3, 1891; Princess's, May 28, 1892.

WILL O' THE WISP; OR, THE MYSTERY OF THE RUINED MILL. D. Hanley Royal Pottery T., September 27, 1869.

WILL OF A WOMAN, THE. P. George Chapman. 1598. N.p.

WILL OF THE WISE KING KINO, THE. Extrav. James Albery. Princess's, September 13, 1873.

WILL OR NO WILL; OR, A BONE FOR THE LAWYERS, A. F. Chas. Macklin. D.L., April 23, 1746. N.p.

WILL OR THE WIDOW; OR, PUNS IN PLENTY, THE. Dram. Trifle. Theodore Edward Hook. Orange Hall, near Windsor, January 31, 1810. N.p.

WILL PONTYPRIDD. Welsh D. Merthyr Tydfil Cambrian T., March 9, 1875.

WILL WITH A VENGEANCE, A. C.O. 1 a. Frederick Hay. M. by Edward Solomon. Globe, November 27, 1876.

WILLIAM. P. 1 sc. Transl. fr. the German of J. W. von Göethe by Louis N. Parker. Parkhurst, May 13, 1892.

WILLIAM AND LUCY. O. Mr. Paton. Pr. at Edinburgh. 1780.

WILLIAM AND NANNY. Ballad F. 2 a. R. J. Goodenough. C.G., November 12, 1779. See *The Cottagers*.

WILLIAM AND SUSAN. D.L., March 7, 1859.

WILLIAM AND SUSAN. D. 3 a. W. J. Wills. St. James's, October 9, 1880.

WILLIAM AND SUSAN; OR, THE SAILOR'S SHEET ANCHOR. Mus. Piece. Anon. Hay., 1875. N.p.

WILLIAM CARTWRIGHT. P. William Haughton. 1602. N.p.

WILLIAM LONGBEARD; OR, WILLIAM LONGSWORD. P. Drayton, 1598.

WILLIAM SIMPSON, THE. Ca. 1 a. Percy Fitzgerald. Olympic, December 16, 1872.

WILLIAM TELL. Tra. Eugenius Roche. 1808.

WILLIAM TELL. His. P. 3 a. Sheridan Knowles. M. by Bishop. D.L., May 11, 1825.

WILLIAM TELL. Burl. Arthur J. O'Neill. Sadler's Wells, October 19, 1867.

WILLIAM TELL; A TELLING VERSION OF AN OLD TELL TALE. Burl. Leicester Buckingham. Strand T., April 13, 1857.

WILLIAM TELL TOLD AGAIN. Burl. R. Reece. Gaiety, December 21, 1876.

WILLIAM TELL WITH A VENGEANCE; OR, THE PET, THE PARROT, AND THE PIPPIN. Burl. Henry J. Byron. Liverpool Alexandra T., September 4, 1867; Strand, October 5, 1867.

WILLIAM THE CONQUEROR. P. Ac. by Earl of Sussex's Men. January 4, 1593.

WILLIAM THOMPSON; OR, WHICH IS HE? F. 2 a. Caroline Boaden. Hay., September 11, 1829.

WILLIE THE WANDERER. Marylebone, August 6, 1866.

WILLIE REILLY AND HIS OWN DEAR COLLEEN BAWN. Marylebone, May 5, 1861.

WILLIKIND AND HYS DINAH. Pathetic T. 3 sc. J. Stirling Coyne. Hay., March 16, 1854.

WILLING SLAVE, A. T.C. Mark Melford. Bristol T., July 13, 1883.

WILLIS, MRS. F.C. 3 a. H. Malyon-Hesford. Strand, March 20, 1900.

WILLOW COPSE, THE. D. Dion Boucicault. Adelphi; Princess's, November 1, 1869.

WILLOW MARSH. Sadler's Wells, October 8, 1862.

WILLOW PATTERN, THE. Oa. Two episodes. Basil Hood. M. by Cecil Cook. Savoy, November 14, 1901.

WILLOW PATTERN PLATE, THE. C.O. 2 a. Sidney Bowkett and Geo. D. Day. Lyrics by G. D. Day. M. by Ed. Dean. Lowestoft Pub. H., August 24, 1897 (C.P.).

WILLOW PATTERN PLATE, THE. Sk. Eugene Magnus. Camberwell Empire, September 16, 1908; Terry's (as a Chinese Mus. Rom.), April 10, 1909.

WILLOW POOL; OR, THE SHADOW OF DEATH, THE. D. 2 a. Grecian, November 14, 1870.

WILLY REILLY. D. F. Brady. Glasgow New Adelphi, March 29, 1875.

WILLY REILLY; OR, THE FAIR LADY OF BOYLE. Irish D. 4 a. G. Coyne and J. W. Whitbread. Dublin Queen's, April 24, 1905.

WILMORE CASTLE. C.O. R. Houlton. D.L., 1800.

WILTSHIRE TOM. Ent. at Court. Ascr. to Robert Cox. Pr. n.d. (Before 1814.)

WILY BEGUILED. C. Anon. Pr. 1606.

WILY FALSE ONE. 1677.

WIN HER AND TAKE HER; OR, OLD FOOLS WILL BE MEDDLING. C. Dedicated to Lord Danby by Underhill. Epil. wr. by Durfey. T.R., 1691. Pr.

WIN HER AND WEAR HER. C.O. F. on Miss Century's *A Bold Stroke for a Wife*. M. by J. Barnett. D.L., October 18, 1832.

WIND AND WAVE; OR, THE FOYDTEN'S TRUST. D. Pro. and 3 a. Reginald Moore. Nottingham T.R., March 30, 1868.

WINDMILL, THE. F. 1 a. Edward Morton. D.L., January 25, 1842.

WINDMILLS. C. 3 a. W. Kingsley Tarpey. Comedy, June 17, 1901.

WINDOW CLEANER, THE. F. Absurdity. Henry Carlton. Canning Town Albert H., June 19, 1905.

WINDOW CLEANER, THE. Sk. by Herbert Sargent. Liverpool Tivoli, February 14, 1907.

WINDOW INTO YESTERDAY, A. P. 1 a. J. Edwards and J. H. Drummond. C.G. King's, May 16, 1907.

WINDSOR CASTLE. O. J. P. Salomon (one of his most important compositions), for the Prince of Wales's Wedding, April 8, 1795.

WINDSOR CASTLE. O. Burl. 1 a. F. C. Burnand and Montague Williams. Strand, June 5, 1865.

WINDSOR CASTLE. D. Prol. and 3 a. Frederick Marchant. East London, February 15, 1873.

WINE, BEER, ALE, AND TOBACCO CONTENDING FOR SUPERIORITY. Int. Pr. 1630.

WINE, BEER, AND ALE TOGETHER BY THE EARS. Anon. Pr. 1629.

WINE DOES WONDERS. C. 3 a. Taken fr. *Inconstant*. Hay., July 19, 1820.

WINGS OF MEMORY, THE. Duo. Albert Chevalier. Small Queen's Hall, Langham Place, W., April 8, 1901.

WINGS OF THE STORM. D. Pro. and 3 a. R. J. Barlow and Wm. North. Globe, October 5, 1891.

WINGS OF WEALTH; OR, A DISPUTED MARRIAGE. D. Albert H. Clarke. Willenhall Royal, October 25, 1894.

WINIFRED'S VOW. C. 3 a. John Douglas. M. by Henry Parks, jun. Novelty, March 19, 1892.

WINKHOPPER'S PLOT. F. V. C. Rolfe. Novelty, June 7, 1897.

WINNIE BROOKE, WIDOW. C. 3 a. M. Watson and H. Fordwych. Boscombe Grand T., April 2, 1904; Criterion, September 1, 1904.

WINNING A HUSBAND. C. Buckstone.

WINNING A WIFE. Ca. 1 a. By T. H. L. Gt. Yarmouth Aquarium, November 12, 1888.

WINNING CARD, THE. A. Wood. Adap. fr. the French. Hay., October 14, 1867.

WINNING DEFEAT. D. 4 a. Duncan Campbell and Marcus Quaire. Novelty, May 30, 1891.

WINNING HAND, THE. D. 5 a. Geo. Conquest and St. Aubyn Miller. Surrey, September 9, 1895.

WINNING HAZARD, A. Ca. 1 a. J. P. Wooler. P.O.W., April 15, 1865.

WINNING SUIT. Princess's, February 16, 1863.

WINONA, THE SIOUX QUEEN; OR, THE DEATH SHOT OF THE DOG OF THE PRAIRIE. American D. Pro. and 3 a. Park, February 2, 1881.

WINTER FEAST, THE. T. 5 a. C. Rann Kennedy. Bayswater Bijou, June 19, 1907.

WINTER IN HOLLAND. Sk. Empire, February 4, 1909

WINTER SPORT. P. 1 a. "D. Brandon." Court, November 18, 1908.

WINTER'S EVE, A. Sk. Fred Norburn and J. Campling. Cambridge M.H., February 14, 1907.

WINTER'S TALE, THE. T.C. Wm. Shakespeare. Wr. 1604. Plot taken fr. *Dorastus and Fawnia,* which was pr. 1588. Globe, 1613. Pr. 1st Fo., 1623 Alt. by Ch. Marsh, 1756. N.ac. Ac. by J. P. Kemble 1811. Princess's, April 28, 1856. Arr. in 3 a. by H. Beerbohm Tree. Rev. H.M., September 1, 1906; April 23, 1907.

WINTER'S TALE. See *Florizel and Perdita.*

WIRE ENTANGLEMENT, A. Ca. 1 a. Robt. Marshall. Comedy, September 22, 1907.

WISDOM OF DR. DODIPOLE. C. Lyly. 1600.

WIRELESS. D. 3 a. Paul Armstrong and Winchell Smith. York R.T., October 19, 1908 (C.P.).

WISDOM OF FOLLY. C. 3 a. Cosmo Hamilton. Comedy, October 9, 1902.

WISDOM OF LORD GLYNDE, THE. C. 1 a. Estelle Burney. Duke of York's, June 28, 1904.

WISDOM OF THE TWELVE GODDESSES. Daniel. 1604. See *The Vision of the Twelve Goddesses.*

WISDOM OF THE WISE, THE. C. 3 a. "John Oliver Hobbes" (Mrs. Craigie). St. James's, November 22, 1900.

WISE CHILD, A. C. 3 a. G. R. Sims. Liverpool P.O.W., July 31, 1882.

WISE ELEPHANTS OF THE EAST. Astley's, December 5, 1853.

WISE MAN, THE. Yiddish Epis. 4 a. N. Rokow. Pav., June 28, 1909.

WISE MEN OF CHESTER, THE. P. Ac. October 2, 1594. Not now known.

WISE MEN OF THE EAST, THE. P. Taken fr. Kotzebue and Elizabeth Inchbald. C.G., November 30, 1799.

WISE WOMAN OF HOGSDON, THE. C. Thos. Heywood. Pr. 1638.

WISHES; OR, HARLEQUIN'S MOUTH OPENED, THE. C. Thos. Bentley. Ac. 1761.

WISHES OF A FREE PEOPLE, THE. D. poem. Dr. Hiffernan. 1761.

WISHING GATE. Effingham, September 3, 1866.

WISHING GLEN. Britannia, June 22, 1863.

WISHING OAK, THE. O. 1 a. P. J. Barrow. M. by J. H. Nicholson. Portsmouth Prince's, January 27, 1898.

WIT AND FOLLY. Dialogue. John Heywood. Circa 1550.

WIT AND SCIENCE. Moral P. J. Redford. Ptd. for the Shakespeare Society, 1848.

WIT AND WILL. P. Ac. at Court in June, 1568.

WIT AT A PINCH; OR, THE LUCKY PRODIGAL. F. Anon. L.I.F., 1715.

WIT AT SEVERAL WEAPONS. C. Beaumont and Fletcher. 1647.

WIT FOR MONEY; OR, POET STUTTER. Dia. Anon. 1691.

WIT IN A CONSTABLE. C. Henry Glapthorne. Cockpit in D.L., 1640.

WIT IN A MADNESS. P. Brome. Ent. on books of Stationers' Co., March 19, 1639. N.P.

WIT OF A WOMAN, THE. C. Anon. 1604.

WIT OF A WOMAN, THE. C. 3 a. T. Walker, L.I.F., June 24, 1704. Pr. 1705.

WIT WITHOUT MONEY. C. Beaumont and Fletcher. D.L., 1639. With alt. and amendments by some persons of quality. Duke's Old T., February 26, 1678.

WIT'S CABAL. C. 2 a. Duchess of Newcastle. 1662.

WIT'S LAST STAKE. F. Thos. King. D.L., April 14, 1768.

WITCH, THE. T.C. Tho. Middleton. Ac. by His Majesty's Servants at Blackfriars. 1778.

WITCH, THE. D. 5 a. Adap. fr. *Die Hexe* of Herr Fitger by C. Marsham Rae. Princess's, April 26, 1887; alt. to 4 a., Princess's, October, 1887; St. James's, November 5, 1887

WITCH-FINDER, THE. D. 2 a. D.L., February 19, 1829.

WITCH OF DERNCLEUGH, THE. M.D. 3 a. New version of *Guy Mannering.* Lyceum Playbill, July 30, 1821.

WITCH OF EDMONTON, THE. T.C. Wm. Rowley. Ac. by the Prince's Servants, Cockpit, D.L., 1658.

WITCH OF ISLINGTON, THE. Anon. July 14, 1597. N.p.

WITCH OF PENDLE, THE. Tudor P. 4 a. J. D. Baxter. Blackburn Prince's, May 21, 1909 (C.P.).

WITCH OF THE WOOD; OR, THE NUTTING GIRLS, THE. M.F. C.G., May 19, 1796.

WITCH OF WINDERMERE, THE. C.D. 1 a. Chas. Selby. Marylebone, December 4, 1848.

WITCHCRAFT OF LOVE, THE. Anon. 1741. (See Strollers' Packet.)

WITCHES; OR, HARLEQUIN CHEROKEE, THE. Pant. Mr. Love. D.L., 1762.

WITCHES' BOON, THE. Pro. and 3 a. James W. Furrell. Ladbroke H., September 11, 1888. C.P.

WITCHES' REVELS; OR, THE BIRTH OF HARLEQUIN, THE. Pant. C.G., June 2, 1798.

WITCHES SON, THE. 2 a. T. J. Serle.

WITCHES' WEEDS; OR, PRIDE AND PATIENCE, THE. D. 3 a. Pavilion, September 26, 1868.

WITCHES OF MACBETH, THE. J. N. Maskelyne. Adap. fr. Shakespeare's *Macbeth.* St. Geo. H., November 13, 1908 (mat.).

WITH A VIEW TO MATRIMONY. Ca. C. R. Sawin. Stevenage Public H., December 4, 1907.

WITH EDGED TOOLS. P. 5 a. H. Armitage, fr. H. Seton Merriman's novel. Hull T.R., February 3, 1908; Ayr Gaiety, February 20, 1907 (C.P.); Hammersmith King's, April 6, 1908.

WITH FLYING COLOURS. D. 5 a. Seymour Hicks and Fred G. Latham. Adelphi, August 19, 1899.

WITH HAND AND HEART. C. 1 a. Benjamin Landeck and Ernest E. Norris. Fairseat, Highgate, July 21, 1888.

WITH THE COLOURS. Military D. 5 a. Elliot Galer and Jas. Mew. Leicester R.O.H., August 14, 1886; Grand, August 23, 1886.

WITHERED HAND, THE. C.D. 4 a. Charles Baldwin and Fred Kitchen. Eleph. and C., June 23, 1904. C.p.

WITHERED LEAVES. C. 1 a. Fred Broughton. Sheffield, T.R., May 2, 1875; Terry's, October 31, 1892.

WITHIN AND WITHOUT. Dr. Poem. McDonnell. 1856.

WITHOUT A HOUSE. C. Henry J. Byron. Cardiff T.R., May 24, 1880.

WITHOUT INCUMBRANCE. F. 1 a. J. Palgrave Simpson. Strand, August 12, 1850.

WITHOUT LOVE. D. 4 a. Edmund Yates and A. W. Dubourg. Olympic, December 16, 1872.

WITHOUT MONEY OR FRIENDS. C.D. 4 a. Brandon Ellis. Portsmouth Prince's, September 7, 1874.

WITLESS. P. Ent. at Stationers' Co., 1500-1. No copy is known to exist now.

WITNESS, THE. T.D. 3 a. John Galt. N.ac. before 1814. Pr. 1814.

WITNESS, THE. Melo-d. M. by A. Lee. Lyceum playbill, August 12, 1829.

WITNESS, THE. P. 3 a. Dr. G. H. R. Dabbs. Southampton P.O.W., December 24, 1889.

WITS, THE. C. Sir W. Davenant. Blackfriars, 1636.

WITS; OR, SPORT UPON SPORT, THE. Kirkman. A collection of various drolls and farces. 1662. See *Philetus and Constantia.*

WITS LED BY THE NOSE; OR, A POET'S REVENGE. C. Anon. T.R., 1678.

WITTIKIND AND HIS BROTHERS. Burl. Tom Taylor. Princess's.

WITTIKIND AND HIS BROTHERS; OR, THE SEVEN SWAN PRINCES AND THE MELUSINE. Orig. Fairy Tale. 2 a. By the author of the "Vicar of Wakefield." Princess's T., April 12, 1852.

WITTY COMBAT; OR, THE FEMALE VICTOR, THE. T.C. By "T. P." Ac. by persons of quality. 1663. See *The German Princess*

WITTY FAIR ONE, THE. C. James Shirley. D.L., 1633.

WIVES. 3 a. A. C. Calmour. Vaudeville, March 8, 1883.

WIVES. A SEQUEL TO MAIDS; OR, THE NUNS OF GLOSSENBURY. James Wild. Pr. 1804. N.ac

WIVES AS THEY WERE AND MAIDS AS THEY ARE C. Elizabeth Inchbald. C.G., March 4, 1797.

WIVES BY ADVERTISEMENT. F. D. Jerrold.

WIVES' EXCUSE; OR, CUCKHOLDS MAKE THEMSELVES. Thos. Southern. T.R., 1692.

WIVES IN PLENTY; OR, THE MORE THE MERRIER. C. 3 a. Anon. Hay., November 25, 1793.

WIVES PLEASED AND MAIDS HAPPY. C. Milns. 1788. N.p.

WIVES REVENGED, THE. C.O. Chas. Dibdin. T. fr. the French. C.G., September 18, 1778.

WIZARD, THE. C. 5 a. Wr. before 1640. MS. in British Museum, which formerly belonged to Cartwright.

WIZARD, THE. P. Simon Baylie. In MS., which is preserved in Durham Cathedral Library.

WIZARD, THE. See *The Black Dwarf.*

WIZARD; OR, THE BROWN MAN OF THE MOOR, THE. Melo-d. Rom. M. by Mrs. Horn. Lyceum playbill, July 26, 1817.

WIZARD OF THE MOOR, THE. Melo-d. 3 a. Hy. Gott. West London T.

WIZARD OF THE NILE; OR, THE EGYPTIAN BEAUTY, THE. Harry B. Smith. M. by Victor Herbert. Shaftesbury, September 6, 1897.

WIZARD OF THE WAVES; OR, THE SHIP OF THE AVENGER, THE. Legendary Nautical D. 3 a. J. T. Haines. Victoria T., September 2, 1840.

WIZARD OF THE WILDERNESS, THE. F. Gaiety, March 8, 1873

WOGGLE BUG, THE. M.C. Bayswater Bijou, June 16, 1905 (C.P.).

WOGGLES WAXWORKS. F. Geo. Cabal. Surrey, June 2, 1879

WOLF, THE. Sk. Star M.H., April 19, 1909.

WOLF, THE. Dr. Fant. Wr. and comp. by E. L. Lomax. Roy. A. of M., May 22, 1909.

WOLF AND THE LAMB, THE. C. C. Mathews, jun. Hay, 1832.

WOLF IN SHEEP'S CLOTHING, A. F. Conducted by W. H. C. Nation fr. a story which appeared in the "Covent Garden Magazine." Royalty, November 21, 1908.

WOLF OF THE PYRENEES, THE. D. 3 a. W. Travers. Britannia, April 13, 1868.

WOLF! WOLF! Ca. 1 a. T. E. Pemberton.

WOLFE TONE. Irish D. 4 a. J. W. Whitbread. Dublin Queen's R.T., December 26, 1898.

WOLVES. D. Blackburn T.R., March 16, 1870.

WOLVES. D. Gardiner Coyne. Whitehaven T.R., November 17, 1882.

WOLVES AND WAIFS. C.D. 5 a. Alfred Cox. Brighton Gaiety, July 20, 1891.

WOLVES OF LONDON. Rom. D. 4 a. Hugh Montgomery. Greenock T.R., August 13, 1904. C.P.

WOMAN. Rom. D. Dion Boucicault. C.G., October 2, 1843.

WOMAN; OR, LOVE AGAINST THE WORLD. C. E. Falconer. Lyceum, September 19, 1860.

WOMAN: HER RISE AND FALL IN LIFE. 3 a. W. H. Pitt. Britannia, November 13, 1871.

WOMAN ADRIFT, A. D. Pro. and 3 a. W. T. M'Clelland. Oldham Empire, February 18, 1901; Standard, July 15, 1901.

WOMAN AGAINST WOMAN. Rom. D. 5 a. Frank Harvey. Adap. fr. the French. Portsmouth T.R., March 9, 1883; Grand, March 22, 1886.

WOMAN AND THE APPLE. Dr. Sk. Holborn Empire, December 30, 1907.

WOMAN AND THE LAW. Hull T.R., Ju'y 28, 1884. See *Passion Flower*.

WOMAN AND WAR. Milit. and Rom. D. Harry Bruce. Islington Empire, November 7, 1904.

WOMAN AND WINE. D. 4 a. Ben Landeck and Arthur Shirley. Pavilion, October 11, 1897; Princess's, March 8, 1899.

WOMAN-CAPTAIN, THE. C. Thos. Shadwell. Duke's T., 1680. Rev. in 1744 under title *The Prodigal*.

WOMAN FIEND, A. P. 1 a. A. E. Halliwell. Liverpool R., February 4, 1905.

WOMAN FROM GAOL, THE. D. 4 a. Geo. R. Sims. Pavilion, September 7, 1903.

WOMAN FROM NOWHERE, THE. Ma. 4 a. Arthur Shirley. Islington Grand, May 16, 1904.

WOMAN FROM RUSSIA, THE. Dom. P. of "Passion, Virtue, and Humour." 4 a. F. G. Ingleby. Jarrow T.R., July 25, 1908 (C.P.); Sheffield Alexandra, September 22, 1908.

WOMAN FROM SCOTLAND YARD, THE. P. G. E. Clive and Alex. C. Grant. Sutton-in-Ashfield King's T., March 21, 1907; Manchester Osborne, May 20, 1907; Stratford R., August 5, 1907.

WOMAN FROM THE PEOPLE, THE. D. Hastings Music H., May 29, 1884.

WOMAN HARD TO PLEASE. Anon. 1597. N.p. Not now known.

WOMAN HATER, THE. C. Beaumont and Fletcher. Pr. 1607.

WOMAN HATER, THE. F.C. 3 a. David Lloyd. Adap. for English stage by Edw. Terry. Newcastle T.R., September 2, 1887; Terry's, December 1, 1887.

WOMEN HATER, THE. See *The Misogynist*. 1 a. G. W. Godfrey. Manchester T.R., October 25, 1895.

WOMAN HE LOVED AND THE WOMAN THAT LOVED HIM. D. 3 a. Charles Daly. Grecian, July 8, 1872.

WOMAN I ADORE, THE. F. 1 a. John Madison Morton, Hay., October 9, 1850.

WOMAN IN BLACK, THE. F.C. 2 sc. Mrs. Adam Acton. Private residence Mrs. A. A., St. John's Wood, December 21, 1895.

WOMAN IN BLACK; OR, HAUNTED LIVES, THE. Rev. ver. of Wilton Jones's *Haunted Lives*. Olympic, May 10, 1884; Standard, December 2, 1895.

WOMAN IN MAUVE, THE. Burl. D. 3 a. Watts Phillips. Liverpool P.O.W., December, 1864; Hay., March 18, 1865.

WOMAN IN RED, THE. Victoria, March 30, 1864.

WOMAN IN RED, THE. D. Pro. and 3 a. Adap. and alt. fr. the French by J. S. Coyne. St. James's, April 13, 1868; Standard, June 7, 1869.

WOMAN IN THE CASE, A. C. 3 a. Geo. R. Sims and Leonard Merrick. Court, May 2, 1901.

WOMAN IN THE CASE, THE. P. 4 a. Clyde Fitch. Garrick, June 2, 1909.

WOMAN IN THE MOON, THE C John Lily. Pr. 1597.

WOMAN IN WHITE, THE. Surrey, November 3, 1860.

WOMAN IN WHITE, THE. D. Pro. and 4 a. Wilkie Collins. Olympic, October 9, 1871.

WOMAN IN WHITE, THE. P. Pro. and 5 a. Ver. by C. W. Somerset. Kennington, September 11, 1905.

WOMAN KILLED WITH KINDNESS, A. T. Thos. Heywood. Ac. by the Queen's Servants, 1617.

WOMAN MADE A JUSTICE, THE. C. Thos. Betterton. N.p.

WOMAN NEVER VEXED; OR, THE WIDOW OF CORNHILL, A. C. 5 a. W. Rowley. 1632. (See *New Wonder.*) Alt. and add. by J. R. Planché. C.G., November 9, 1824.

WOMAN OF BUSINESS. Adelphi, August 29, 1864.

WOMAN OF COLOUR; OR, SLAVERY IN FREEDOM. Surrey, November, 1853.

WOMAN OF IMPULSE, A. C. D. 4 a. V. Widnell. Liverpool R.C.T., March 24, 1902; Kennington Princess of W.'s, April 7, 1902.

WOMAN OF KRONSTADT, THE. P. 3 a. Max Pemberton and Geo. Fleming. An adap. of the former's novel, "Kronstadt." Garrick, February 8, 1908.

WOMAN OF NO IMPORTANCE, A. D. 4 a. Oscar Wilde. Hay., April 19, 1893; rev. H.M., May 22, 1907.

WOMAN OF PARIS, A. Dr. Sk. Roy Milton. Manchester Tivoli, July 4, 1907.

WOMAN OF PARIS, A. Sk. (New ver.) Canterbury, August 17, 1908.

WOMAN OF PLEASURE, A. D. Pro. and 4 a. James Willard. Southampton P.O.W., November 22, 1900.

WOMAN OF SAMARIA, THE. Cant. Sterndale Bennett. Birmingham, February 1867; St. James's H., February 21, 1868.

WOMAN OF SHAME, A. D. 4 a. Frank Price. Rotherham T.R., November 25, 1903.

WOMAN OF SHUNAN, THE. Orat. ("Elisha"). Hull, 1801.

WOMAN OF SPIRIT. T. Burla. Thos. Chatterton. 1770.

WOMAN OF TASTE; OR, THE YORKSHIRE LADY, THE. Ballad O. 1739.

WOMAN OF THE NIGHT, A. Dr. Sk. F. G. Brooke and Dora Deane. Canning Town Albert, August 7, 1905; Bow Pal., June 14, 1909.

WOMAN OF THE PEOPLE, THE. D. 4 a. Benjamin Webster. Liverpool Amphitheatre, February 17, 1877; Olympic, August 5, 1878.

WOMAN OF THE WORLD, A. Surrey, November 22, 1858.

WOMAN OF THE WORLD, A. C. 3 a. J. Stirling Coyne. Olympic, February 17, 1868.

WOMAN OF THE WORLD, A. C. 3 a. Adap. by B. C. Stephenson from Oscar Blumenthal's "Der Probepfeil." Hay., February 4, 1886.

WOMAN OF THE WORLD. A. Melo-d. Launcelot Usher. Boscombe Grand, March 1, 1900 (C.P.).

WOMAN OF THE WORLD, A. D. 4 a. Tom Terris. Lyric, June 13, 1903 (C.P.).

WOMAN OF THE WORLD, THE. D. 2 a. Adap. fr. tale of that name by Lady Clara Cavendish. Queen's T., November 13, 1858.

WOMAN OUTWITTED, A. D. 3 a. D. M. Henry and Edwin Drew. Novelty, November 16, 1886.

WOMAN OUTWITTED, A Sk. Greenwich Palace, October 21, 1907.

WOMAN PAYS, THE. D. 4 a. Arthur Shirley and Sutton Vane. Brighton Eden T., August 4, 1902.

WOMAN PAYS, THE. P. 3 a. Harry A. Spurr. Hull T.R., May 20, 1904.

WOMAN PAYS, THE. P. Frank M. Thorne. Gateshead Metropole, July 18, 1907; Wakefield O.H., August 2, 1907.

WOMAN RULES. Advertised among a list of plays printed for Richard Bentley and M Magnes. (Before 1814.)

WOMAN RULES THE WORLD. P. 5 a. John Douglass. Macclesfield T.R., September 3, 1903 (C.P.).

WOMAN SCORNED, A. D. 4 a. Wallace Pringle. Workington T.R., October 10, 1898.

WOMAN TAMER: OR, HOW TO BE HAPPY THOUGH MARRIED, THE. T. Neville Doone. Brompton Hospital, March 10, 1896; Crystal Palace, April 6, 1903.

WOMAN THAT GAMBLES, THE. D. 4 a. S. Buchanan Rogerson. (Orig. prod. at Oldham Colosseum T., January 29, 1906.) Poplar Prince's, July 2, 1906.

WOMAN THAT WAS A CAT, THE. Metamorphosical Sk. 1 a. Princess's, October, 1859.

WOMAN TRIUMPHANT. C. 1 a. Publ. by S. French, Limited.

WOMAN TURN'D BULLY. C. Anon. Duke of York, 1675.

WOMAN WHO GAMBLES, THE. D. 4 a. S. B. Rogerson. Oldham Colosseum, January 29, 1907; Poplar Prince's, July 2, 1907.

WOMAN WHO NEVER COMES, THE. P. Mrs. M. Sheldon. Bayswater Bijou, November 7, 1901.

WOMAN WHO SINNED, THE. Dom. D. 4 a. Augusta Tullock. See *Judith.*

WOMAN WHO WAS BORED, THE. C. 1 a. Mrs. Chas. Sugden. Adap. fr. Paul Bilhaud's *Une Femme Qui s'Ennuie.* Bournemouth Winter Gardens, November 21, 1905.

WOMAN WHO WAS DEAD, THE. D. 4 a. J. W. Sabben Clare. Dundee Gaiety, March 16, 1908; Stratford T.R., May 29, 1908.

WOMAN WHO WOOED WHILE THE WEALTH WOBBLED, THE. F. Sk. Quenton Ashlyn. Queen's H., December 13, 1897.

WOMAN WILL HAVE HER WILL, A. C. Entered on the Stationers' Books by W. White. August 3, 1601.

WOMAN WILL HAVE HER WILL. P. Wm. Haughton. Ptd. 1616.

WOMAN WORTH WINNING, A. D. 4 a. A. B. Mackay. Llanelly R.T., September 24, 1906; Stratford R.T., October 28, 1907.

WOMAN'S A RIDDLE. C. C. Bullock. L.I.F., 1716. Pr. 1718.

WOMAN'S A WEATHERCOCK. C. Nath. Field. Ac. before the King at Whitehall and in the Whitefriars, 1612.

WOMAN'S CAPRICE. Ca. 1 a. Adap. by H. M. Lewis. P.O.W., April 13, 1895.

WOMAN'S CONQUEST, A. T. C. Edward Howard. Theatre in Dorset Gardens, 1677.

WOMAN'S DECEIT; OR, THE SHADOW OF A LIFE, A. P. 1 a. H. O. Aylmer. Glasgow R., February 26, 1903.

WOMAN'S DEVOTION; OR, A WOMAN WITH A PAST, A. M. 4 a. G. A. De Grey. Walsall T.R., November 4, 1903; Plymouth Grand, December 19, 1904; Islington Grand. April 17, 1905.

WOMAN'S ERROR, A. Mus. D. Miss Ida Glen. Shrewsbury T.R., May 1, 1876.

WOMAN'S ERROR, A. Melo-d. 4 a. J. K. Murray. Manchester St. James', February 28, 1898.

WOMAN'S FAITH, A. D. 3 a. By the author of *The Mummy.* Lyceum Playbill, November 2, 1855.

WOMAN'S FOLLY, A. P. 4 a. Percy Sandiford and Alfred Holles. Greenwich Carlton, March 21, 1904. See *Seeking Notoriety.*

WOMAN'S FREAK. C. Miss A. Thompson. Chester M.H., December 15, 1882.

WOMAN FRIEND, A. Playlet. A. E. Halliwell. Liverpool T.R., February 4, 1905 (C.P.).

WOMAN'S GUILT, A. D. 3 a. Bernard Copping. Novelty, October 12, 1896.

WOMAN'S HEART. C. Orig. prod. at Boston, U.S.A. Richmond T.R., July 11, 1881.

WOMAN'S HEART, A. Play. 1 a. R. S. Warren Bell. Surrey, December 17, 1897.

WOMAN'S HERITAGE, THE. D.E. 1 a. Ralph Roberts. Margate T.R., July 7, 1902.

WOMAN'S HONOUR, A. Epis. 1 a. Bert Danson. Middlesex M.H., February 11, 1907.

WOMAN'S IDOL. D. 4 a. Chas. Daly and Francis Raphael. Margate T.R., July 29, 1891.

WOMAN'S JUDGMENT, A. P. 2 a. Bernard Tweedale. Sydenham Public H., February 1, 1902.

WOMAN'S LAW, THE. P. Anon. Ent. on the books of the Stationers' Co., November 29, 1652. N.p.

WOMAN'S LOVE. G. H. B. Rodwell. 1831.

WOMAN'S LOVE. D. Adap. fr. *La Dame aux Camelias* by Miss Alleyn. Manchester Prince's T., August 22, 1881.

WOMAN'S LOVE. See *Art and Artifice.*

WOMAN'S LOVE, A. D. 4 a. F. W. Bird. Woolwich T.R., March 10, 1890.

WOMAN'S LOVE, A. D. 1 a. H. Woodville. Vaudeville, March 16, 1899.

WOMAN'S LOVE, A. Dom. D. 5 sc. Nita Rae. Muncaster Bootle, June 22, 1908.

WOMAN'S LOVE; OR, KATE WYNSLEY, THE COTTAGE GIRL. D. 2 a. Tho. Egerton Wilks. Royal Victoria T., April 12, 1841.

WOMAN'S LOVE; OR, THE GIPSY'S VENGEANCE. D. Henry Cleveland. Elephant and Castle, May 8, 1875.

WOMAN'S MASTERPIECE. P. Anon. Ent. on the books of the Stationers' Co. November 29, 1653. N.p.

WOMAN'S MISTAKEN, THE. C. Drew and Davenport. Ent. on the books of the Stationers' Co., September 9, 1653. N.p.

WOMAN'S PAST, A. D. 4 a. H. F. Housden. Devonport Metropole, January 19, 1905, Aldershot R., June 2, 1905; Greenwich Carlton, March 26, 1906.

WOMAN'S PERIL; OR, SAVED FROM DEATH, A. D. 3 a. W. E. Suter and A. Crofte. Victoria, July 23, 1877.

WOMAN'S PLACE, A. C. Beaumont and Fletcher. 1647.

WOMAN'S PLOT, THE. C. Philip Massinger. Ac. at Court, 1621. Destroyed by Warburton's servant. See *Very Woman.*

WOMAN'S POWER; OR, MORE SINNED AGAINST THAN SINNING, A. D. 4 a. Fewlass Llewellyn and Arthur Bawtree. Bayswater Bijou, February 24, 1902 (C.P.).

WOMAN'S PRIZE; OR, THE TAMER TAMED, THE. C. Beaumont and Fletcher. 1633.

WOMAN'S PROPER PLACE. Duol. Wilton Jones and Gertrude Warden. St. James's, June 29, 1896; Birmingham T.R., October 5, 1896.

WOMAN'S REASON, A. 3 a. Chas. H. E. Brookfield and F. E. Philips. Shaftesbury, December 27, 1895.

WOMAN'S REPUTATION, A. Sk. Middlesex, May 22, 1908.

WOMAN'S REVENGE, A. D. Leopold Jordan. Ladbroke Hall, March 18, 1882.

WOMAN'S REVENGE, A. D. 4 a. Henry Pettitt. Adelphi, July 1, 1893.

WOMAN'S REVENGE, A; OR, A MATCH IN NEWGATE. C. 3 a. C. Bullock. L.I.F., 1715.

WOMAN'S REVOLT, A. Sk. W. L. Courtney. Palace, July 7, 1909.

WOMAN'S RIGHTS. Bouffonerie. M. by F. Marchant. Britannia, April 3, 1876.

WOMAN'S RIGHTS. Ca. 1 a. T. A. Palmer. Douglas, Isle of Man, Grand, August, 1882.

WOMAN'S RIGHTS. C. 1 a. J. Sackville Martin. Rochdale T.R., March 23, 1908; Coronet, June 14, 1909.

WOMAN'S SACRIFICE, A. D. 4 a. Alice Chaplin. Adapt. fr. French of Victor Hugo. St. George's Hall, June 3, 1899.

WOMAN'S SECRET, A. C.D. 4 a. Mrs. E. Argent-Lonergan. Watford Clarendon H., May 9, 1894 (C.P.).

WOMAN'S SHAME, A. D. 4 a. Fred Jarman. Dublin Queen's T., January 18, 1907.

WOMAN'S SILENCE, A. Rom. M.D. 3 a. Connie Meadows. Leith New T.R., November 26, 1904 (C.P.).

WOMAN'S SIN; OR, ON THE VERGE, A. Dom. D. Prol. and 3 a. Edwin France and F. Dobell. Wolverhampton T.R., March 10, 1888; Sadler's Wells, July 21, 1888.

WOMAN'S TEARS, A. Arthur Bourchier. Adap. fr. the French. Comedy, June 27, 1890.

WOMAN'S TOO HARD FOR HIM, THE. C. Anon. Ac. at Court, 1621. N.p.

WOMAN'S TRAGEDY, A. P. H. Chettle. 1598.

WOMAN'S TRIALS. D. 3 a. D.L., November 27, 1839.

WOMAN'S TRUST. D. E. Towers. Pavilion, September 2, 1872.

WOMAN'S TRUTH, A. Dom. D. 5 a. Walter Reynolds. Nottingham Grand T., December 24, 1886; Standard, July 4, 1887.

WOMAN'S VENGEANCE, A. D. 5 a. Frank Harvey. Adapt. fr. the French. Standard, May 28, 1888.

WOMAN'S VENGEANCE, A. D. Prol. and 3 a. H. Swinerd. Woolwich R. Artillery. November 15, 1869.

WOMAN'S VENGEANCE, A. Duo. Miss Clara Saville Clarke. St. George's H., December 19, 1892.

WOMAN'S VICTORY, A. C.D. Robert Dodson. Comedy, July 8, 1885.

WOMAN'S VICTORY, A. Melo-d. 5 a. W. A. Brabner. Pavilion, August 19, 1895.

WOMAN'S WAR. Rom. P. 4 a. Gerald Holcroft. Adapt. fr. the French. Aldershot T. Royal, July 14, 1902.

WOMAN'S WAY, A. Ca. 1 a. Ernest Hider Godbold. Redditch Public H., February 14, 1901.

WOMAN'S WAY, A. Sk. Edith Wheeler. Belfast Wellington Minor H., December 4, 1903.

WOMAN'S WAY, A. Sk. Mollie Laney. Manchester Hipp., July 20, 1908.

WOMAN'S WAY, A. C. 3 a. T. Buchanan. Hay., April 16, 1909 (C.P.).

WOMAN'S WHIM, A. D. Prol. and 3 a. Walter Stephens. St. George's H., December 2, 1867.

WOMAN'S WILES. C. 1 a. Wm. Young. Metropolitan M.H., December 17, 1906; Broughton T.R., November 26, 1907.

WOMAN'S WILL—A RIDDLE. C.D. 3 a. M. by Davey. Pr. 1815. Lyceum playbill, July 20, 1820.

WOMAN'S WIT. 3 a. Mrs. Adams Acton. Sunnyside, Langford Place, Abbey Road, N.W., July 20, 1893.

WOMAN'S WIT; OR, LOVE'S DISGUISES D. J. Sheridan Knowles. C.G., May 23, 1838.

WOMAN'S WIT; OR, THE LADY IN FASHION. C. Colley Cibber. T.R., 1697.

WOMAN'S WORLD. C. 3 a. J. P. Hurst. Court, December 8, 1896.

WOMAN'S WRONGS. Ca. 1 sc. A. M. Heathcote. Toole's, September 12, 1887.

WOMEN AND MEN. C. 3 a. Augustus Dubourg. Manchester T.R., May 22, 1871.

WOMEN ARE SO SERIOUS. C. 3 a. Brandon Thomas. Adapt. fr. Pierre Wolff's P. *Celles qu'on Respecte.* Court, May 31, 1901.

WOMEN, BEWARE WOMEN. T. Thos. Middleton. Pr. 1657.

WOMEN OF LONDON. Melo-d. 4 a. Harold Whyte. Peckham Crown, April 1, 1901.

WOMEN PLEASED. T.C. Beaumont and Fletcher. Pr. 1647. D.L., November 8, 1743. Pr. 1778.

WOMEN'S CONQUEST, A. T.C. by E. Howard. Ac. at Duke of York's, 1671.

WON AT LAST. C.D. 3 a. Wybert Reeve. Scarborough T.R., September 13, 1869; Charing Cross, October 30, 1869.

WON BY A HEAD. C. 3 a. Tom Taylor. Queen's, March 29, 1869.

WON BY A HEAD. D. 5 a. C. A. Clarke. Woolwich T.R., September 5, 1887.

WON BY A NECK. D. Chas. Horsman. Exeter T.R., August 16, 1879.

WON BY HONOURS. D.C. 4 a. Miss Annie Brunton. Brighton T.R., April 21, 1882; Comedy, July 12, 1882.

WON BY WAITING. Ca. Miss Queenie Sichel. Bayswater Bijou, December 6, 1902.

WON BY WIT. O. 1 a. Florence Attenborough. M. by Arthur Roby. Islington Myddelton H., October 16, 1895.

WON NOT WOED. Poetical D. Adam Lodge. Bayswater Bijou, April 16, 1877.

WONDER, THE. C. Lyceum Playbill, October 19, 1809; Bath T.R., 1843; Princess's, May, 1868.

WONDER; A WOMAN KEEPS A SECRET, THE. C. 3 a. Mrs. Susanna Centlivre (probably fr. Spanish original). D.L., April 27, 1714.

WONDER, AN HONEST YORKSHIREMAN, THE. Bal. O. Henry Carey. D.L., 1735.

WONDER OF A KINGDOM, THE. T.C. Thos. Dekker. 1636.

WONDER OF A WOMAN, THE. P. Anon. Ac. October 15, 1595. N.p.

WONDER OF WOMEN; OR, THE TRAGEDIE OF SOPHONISBA. John Marston. Blackfriars. Pr. 1606; re-pr. 1856.

WONDERFUL COUSIN, THE. O. M. by Offenbach. Brighton T.R., August 18, 1874.

WONDERFUL CURE, A. F. 1 a. Publ. by S. French, Limited.

WONDERFUL DUCK, THE. O.-bo. 3 a. Transl. by Chas. Lamb. Kerney. Opera Com., May 31, 1873.

WONDERFUL VISIT, A. Dramatised by H. S. Wells from his novel of the same name. Hastings Gaiety, April 8, 1896.

WONDERFUL WOMAN, A. C.D. 2 a. Geo. Dance. Lyceum, May 24, 1849.

WONDERFUL WOMAN, A. Rom. costume C. 3 a. (F. on the orig. P. by George Dance as a plot.) Entirely rewr. by Sydney Spenser. Inc. M. arr. by Wilfred E. Cotterill. St. Leonards Pier Pavilion, June 15, 1908.

WONDERFUL YEAR. C. Dekker. 1603.

WONDER-WORKER, THE. 3 a. Stuart Cumberland. T.R., Margate, June 1, 1894.

WONDER-WORKER, THE. Comic O. E. Cadman. M. by A. W. Ketelby. Fulham Grand, October 8, 1900.

WONDERS IN THE SUN; OR, THE KINGDOM OF BIRDS. C.A. T. D'Urfey. Queen's T., Hay., April 5, 1706.

WONDERS OF DERBYSHIRE, THE. Pant. Anon. D.L., 1779.

WOOD DEMON, THE. Grecian, December 24, 1873.

WOOD DEMON; OR, THE CLOCK HAS STRUCK, THE. Rom. Melo-d. M. G. Lewis. D.L., April 1, 1807.

WOOD NYMPH, THE. Cantata. Sir W. Sterndale Bennett. (1816-75.)

WOODBARROW FARM. C. 3 a. Jerome K. Jerome. Comedy, June 18, 1888; Vaudeville, January 13, 1891.

WOODCOCK'S LITTLE GAME. C.F. 2 a. J. M. Morton. St. James's. October 6, 1864.

WOODEN SHOE, THE. M.P. 1 a. Rita Strauss. M. by Marjorie Slaughter. Criterion, March 15, 1907.

WOODEN SPOON, THE. Oa. Gilbert Burgess. M. by Hope Temple. Trafalgar, September 26, 1892.

WOODEN SPOONMAKER, THE. Dom. D. 1 a. A. Halliday and W. Brough.

WOODEN WEDDING, A. C. 1 a. Rupert Hughes. F. on story by Mathilde Serac. Eastbourne Devonshire Park, May 26, 1902. Shaftesbury, June 3, 1902.

WOODGIRL, THE. O. Weber, 1800. See *Sylvana.*

WOODLAND PICNIC. C. 1 a. W. Reeve.

WOODMAN, THE. C.O. 3 a. Rev. Henry Bate Dudley. Pr. 1791. C.G., September 23, 1809.

WOODMAN'S HUT, THE. Melo-d. Rom. 3 a. W. H. Arnold. M. by Horn. D.L., April 12, 1814; Lyceum playbill, September 22, 1817.

WOODMAN'S SPELL, THE. D. 1 a. Publ. by S. French, Ltd.

WOODSTOCK. Pocock. See *The White Rose.*

WOODVIL. T. Lamb. Pr. 1802. See *John Woodvil.*

WOOER, THE. Int. Geo. Puttenham. Before 1814. N.p.

WOOING A WIDOW. C.Oa. 1 a. Walter Parke. Ladbroke H., December 17, 1903.

WOOING A WIDOW; OR, LOVE UNDER A LAMP POST. C. B. Bernard. Strand, November 24, 1834.

WOOING AND WAITING. C.O. 1 a. E. Lawrence Levy. M. by Fred W. Beard. Birmingham Ballsall Heath Institute, October 10, 1895.

WOOING BY WIRE. C. 1 a. Ernest Bellamy. Brixton, October 24, 1904.

WOOING IN JEST AND LOVING IN EARNEST. D. 1 a. Adolphus C. Troughton. Strand, November 1, 1858.

WOOING OF DEATH, THE. P. Henry Chettle. 1599. N.p.

WOOING ONE'S WIFE. F. 1 a. J. M. Morton. Olympic, October 21, 1861.

WOOL. D. 5 a. Henry Linden. Liverpool T.R., September 9, 1878.

WOOL GATHERING. F. 2 a. D.L., January 6, 1826.

WOOL GATHERING. A. Longridge. Adapt. fr. Kotzebue's *Die Zerstreuten.* St. George's H., June 26, 1888.

WORCESTER FIGHT. D. Epis. Maurice Delton and Ernest Genet. St. George's H., January 11, 1890.

WORCESTER SAUCE; OR, A MAN AND A BROTHER. F. Worcester Amateur Dramatic Club, April 26, 1872.

WORD FOR NATURE, A. C. Richard Cumberland. D.L., October 5, 1798.

WORD OF HONOUR. C. Skeffington. 1802. N.p.

WORD OF HONOUR, THE. C. 3 a. John Galt. Pr. 1814.

WORD OF HONOUR; A JERSEY LOVE STORY, THE. D. 3 a. Paul Meritt. Grecian T., October 22, 1874.

WORD TO THE WISE, A. C. Hugh Kelly. C.G., D.L., 1770.

WORDS MADE VISIBLE; OR, GRAMMAR AND RHETORIC ACCOMMODATED TO THE LIVES AND MANNERS OF MEN. 2 parts. Samuel Shaw. 1679.

WORK AND WAGES. D. 5 a. Wm. Bourne. Hanley T.R., January 27, 1890; Pav., June 23, 1890.

WORKE FOR CUTLERS; OR, A MERRY DIALOGUE BETWEENE SWORD, RAPPIER, AND DAGGER. Int. Anon. Act. in a show-room in the University of Cambridge. 1615.

WORK GIRL, THE. D. Pro. and 4 a. Geo. Conquest and Arthur Shirley. Surrey, April 15, 1895.

WORK GIRL, THE. Sk. F. on the D. Euston, June 14, 1909.

WORK OF MERCY, A. C.D. 3 a. P. Racer. Ladbroke Hall, April 8, 1892.

WORKBOX, THE. Ca. 1 a. Tom Craven. Worcester T.R., October 31, 1890; Weymouth T.R., July 9, 1891.

WORKBOX, THE. P. 1 a. Royalty, November 8, 1902.

WORKHOUSE, THE. P. 1 a. D. Shlitzer-Beaumont H., E., June 14, 1909.

WORKHOUSE, THE PALACE, AND THE GRAVE. Britannia, December 6, 1858.

WORKHOUSE WARD, THE. P. 1 a. Lady Gregory. Dublin Abbey, April 20, 1908; Court, June 8, 1909.

WORKING MAN, THE. Story of factory life. 4 a. H. Hardy. Oldham Colosseum, July 10, 1890.

WORKMAN, THE. D. 3 a. Edward Towers. Pav., October 9, 1880.

WORKMAN; OR, THE SHADOW ON THE HEARTH, THE. D. 5 a. Frank Harvey. Sunderland T.R., May 10, 1880; Olympic, July 18, 1881.

WORKMAN OF PARIS, THE. Adelphi. December, 1864.

WORKMAN'S HONOUR, A. P. 3 a. Liverpool Star, May 5, 1905.

WORKMAN'S WIFE, THE. C.D. Liverpool T.R., April 26, 1875.

WORLD, THE. Formerly belonged to the Cockpit Theatre.

WORLD, THE. C. 4 a. James Kenny. D.L., March 31, 1808; D.L., June 1, 1815.

WORLD, THE. C. James Kenney. Ac. at D.L. Pr. 1808.

WORLD, THE. D. 5 a. P. Meritt, H. Pettitt, and Aug. Harris. D.L., July 31, 1880; Princess's February 24, 1894.

WORLD AGAINST HER, THE. D. 5 a. Frank Harvey. Preston T.R., January 11, 1887; Grand, August 1, 1887; Surrey, July 2, 1888.

WORLD AND HIS WIFE, THE. P. 3 a. Chas. Fredk. Nirdlinger. Adap. fr. *El Gran Galeito*, by José Echegary (orig. prod. Birmingham, December 9, 1908, under title of *Slander*). Adelphi, June 15, 1909.

WORLDE AND THE CHILDE, THE. Anon. 1522.

WORLD AND THE STAGE, THE. D. 3 a. J. Palgrave Simpson. Hay., March 12, 1859.

WORLD AND THE WOMAN, THE. Do. D. 4 a. Lillian Clare Cassidy. Newcastle Pal., May 11, 1908; Hammersmith Lyric, March 10, 1909.

WORLD AS IT GOES; OR, A PARTY AT MONTPELLIER, THE. C. Mrs. Cowley. C.G., 1781.

WORLD AS IT GOES; OR, HONESTY THE BEST POLICY. F. J. H. Colls. Norwich T., 1792; Wolverhampton T.

WORLD AS IT WAGS, THE. T. S. Moore. Chesterfield, December 1, 1792.

WORLD IN A VILLAGE, THE. C. John O'Keefe. C.G., 1793.

WORLD IN THE MOON, THE. Mask. B. Jonson. 1620.

WORLD IN THE MOON, THE. D. C. C. Elkanah Settle. Dorset Garden, 1698.

WORLD OF FASHION, THE. C. 3 a. John Oxenford. Olympic, April 17, 1862.

WORLD OF SILENCE, THE. Dr. Sk. L. Mortimer and P. Wilson. Sadler's Wells, June 13, 1898.

WORLD OF SIN, THE. D. 4 a. Walter Melville. Standard, November 5, 1900.

WORLD OF TROUBLE IN A LOCKET, A. Harry and Edward Paulton. C. 3 a. See *In a Locket*. Birmingham Grand, December 3, 1894.

WORLD OF WOMEN, A. C.P. 4 a. F. A. Scudamore, Fulham Grand, April 13, 1903.

WORLD RUNS ON WHEELS, THE. P. G. Chapman. 1599.

WORLD, THE FLESH, AND THE DEVIL, THE. D. 4 a. Arthur Shirley, Robert Castleton, and F. Vancrossan. Margate R., December 4, 1899; Surrey, June 10, 1901.

WORLD, THE FLESH, AND THE DEVIL, THE. D. 4 a. Lesser Columbus. Pav., February 1, 1909.

WORLD TOSS'D AT TENNIS, THE. Masque. Thos. Middelton and Wm. Rowley. Ac. by the Prince's Servants, 1620.

WORLD TURNED UPSIDE DOWN. Regent St., December 26, 1873.

WORLD UNDERGROUND; OR, THE GOLDEN FLEECE AND THE BRAZEN WATERS, THE. Burl. G. C. Becket. Hay., December, 1848.

WORLD'S DESIRE, THE. D. 4 a. Barry Williams. Woolwich Royal Artillery, April 14, 1902; West London, December 15, 1902.

WORLD'S IDOL; OR, PLUTUS, THE GOD OF WEALTH, THE. Transl. fr. Greek of Aristophanes by H. H. B. 1659.

WORLD'S OPINION, THE. Sk. F. G. Brooke and Dora Deane. Poplar Queen's, December 9, 1907.

WORLD'S OPINION, THE. Sk. Sadler's Wells, August 23, 1909.

WORLD'S TRAGEDY, THE. Anon. September 11, 1595. N.p.

WORLD'S VERDICT, THE. D. 5 a. Arthur Jefferson. Merthyr Tydfil Empire, July 10, 1890; North Shields T.R., December 4, 1890; Jarrow T.R., August 5, 1893.

WORLD'S WAR. Victoria, April 17, 1854.

WORLD'S WAY, THE. D. 5 a. Ch. Hannan. Pavilion, May 18, 1903. See *The Whitechapel King*.

WORLDHAM, M.P. P. 1 a. Imperial, March 2, 1902.

WORM TURNS, THE. P. 1 a. The scene taken fr. Fk. Burlingham Harris's *The Road to Ridgeby*. Terry's, May 23, 1909.

WORN-OUT SHOES. O. 1 a. Bartholeyns and Cooke. Publ. by S. French, Ltd.

WORRYBURY'S WHIMS. F. Chas. Ross and Dominic Murray. Alexandra, May 20, 1865.

WORSE AFEARD THAN HURT. Michael Drayton, assisted by Thos. Dekker. Act. 1598. N.p.

WORSE AND WORSE. C. George Digby, Earl of Bristol. Duke's T., between 1662 and 1665.

WORSHIP OF BACCHUS. D. 5 a. Paul Meritt and Henry Pettitt. Olympic, July 21, 1879.

WORSHIP OF PLUTUS; OR, POSES, THE. P. Alice Clevedon. Ladbroke Hall, July 6, 1888.

WORST OF ALL WOMEN, THE. Melo.-d. 4 a. West London, June 5, 1905.

WORST WOMAN IN LONDON, THE. D. 4 a. Walter Melville. Standard, October 23, 1899; Adelphi, March 7, 1903.

WORTH A STRUGGLE. C.D. 4 a. W. R. Waldron. King's Cross, February 8, 1871; Norwich T.R., February 5, 1877.

WORTIGERNE. Sat. Anon. Pr. in the *Monthly Magazine*, 1800.

WOUNDS OF CIVIL WAR, LIVELY SET FORTH IN THE TRAGEDIES OF MARIUS AND SYLLA, THE. Hist. P. Thos. Lodge. Ac. by Lord Admiral's Servants, 1594.

WRANGLES. Duol. Lita Smith. Cheltenham Corn Exchange, March 26, 1900.

WRANGLING LOVERS; OR, LIKE MASTER LIKE MAN. F. William Lyon. 1745. Afterwards called *Lovers' Quarrels*.

WRANGLING LOVERS; OR, THE INVISIBLE MISTRESS, THE. C. Edward Ravenscroft. Duke's T., 1677.

WRATH; OR, A MESSAGE OF THE DEAD. D. 3 a. C. H. Stephenson. F. upon "Ouida's" novel of "Strathmore." Huddersfield T.R., October 6, 1882; Standard, December 18, 1882.

WREATHED DAGGER, THE. D. 3 a. Margaret E. M. Young. St. James's, October 23, 1908 (C.P.).

WRECK ASHORE, THE. D. John Baldwin Buckstone. Adelphi, October 21, 1830; Hay., October, 1830.

WRECK AT NEW BRIGHTON, THE. D. Birkenhead T.R., May 15, 1882.

WRECK OF THE ARGOSY, THE. O. 3 a. W. H. Birch. Reading T.H., October 3, 1871.

WRECK OF THE GOLDEN MARY. Victoria, January 19, 1857.

WRECK OF THE PINAFORE, THE. C.O. G. Luscombe Searelle. Lib. by H. Lingard. Op.C., May 27, 1882.

WRECKAGE. D. 1 a. G. Hein. Publ. by S. French, Ltd.

WRECKED. Dom. D. 4 a. W. Edwards Sprange. Margate T.R., December 4, 1884.

WRECKED, BUT NOT LOST. D. C. Stephenson. City of London, November 9, 1867.

WRECKED IN LONDON. D. 4 a. Geo. Roberts. Elephant and Castle, August 1, 1887; Woolwich R. Artillery, April 18, 1892.

WRECKER, THE. Nautical D. Frederick Marchant and C. Pitt. Britannia, July 1, 1878.

WRECKER OF MEN, A. D. 4 a. C. Watson Mill. Birmingham (Saltley) Carlton T., December 10, 1903; Greenwich Carlton, April 18, 1904.

WRECKER'S DAUGHTER, THE. 5 a. J. Sheridan Knowles. D.L., November 29, 1836.

WRECKERS, THE. D. Borrowdale Lambert. 1747.

WRECKERS, THE. Sk. Geraldine Campbell. Richmond Hipp., January 27, 1908.

WRECKERS, THE. O. 3 a. Ethel Smyth. Wds. by H. B. Brewster. H.M., June 22, 1909.

WRECKERS; OR, NAUTICAL LAW, THE. D. 4 a. R. Dodson. Carlisle H. Majesty's, December 4, 1884.

WREN BOYS; OR, THE MOMENT OF PERIL. D. 2 a. T. Egerton Wilks. City of London, October 8, 1838.

WRINKLES: A TALE OF TIME. D. 3 a. Hy. J. Byron. P.O.W., April 13, 1876.

WRINKLES ON THE RINK. Mus. Skating Skit. Roy Redgrave, H. Roxburg. M. by Dudley Powell. Paisley Hipp., February 20, 1909 (C.P.).

WRITING ON THE SHUTTERS. F. D.L., February 12, 1855.

WRITING ON THE WALL, THE. Melo.-d. 3 a. Thos. and J. M. Morton. Hay., August 9, 1852.

WRITING ON THE WALL, THE. P. 4 a. F. W. Hurlbat. Terry's, January 11, 1909 (C.P.).

WRITING-DESK; OR, YOUTH IN DANGER, THE. 4 a. Transl. fr. Kotzebue. 1799. N.ac. See *Wise Men of the East.*

WRITTEN IN SAND. C. 1 a. F. W. Broughton. Olympic, August 30, 1884.

WRONG ADDRESS, THE. Duol. Trafalgar, October 5, 1895.

WRONG BOTTLE; OR, A JEALOUS WIFE'S REVENGE AND ITS SEQUEL. Dr. Epis. Louis H. Carlton. Northampton O.H., December 2, 1904 (C.P.).

WRONG DOOR, THE. F.C. 3 a. By Ina Leon Cassilis. Comedy, April 20, 1890.

WRONG ENVELOPE, THE. Ca. Edith E. Cuthell. Novelty, June 20, 1888.

WRONG ENVELOPES, THE Ca. Strand, July 19, 1887.

WRONG GIRL, THE. F.C. 3 a. H. A. Kennedy. Strand, November 21, 1894.

WRONG LEGS, THE. Ca. 1 a. Alice Chapin. Ilkeston T.R., September 14, 1896.

WRONG LETTER, THE. F. absurdity. Brian McCullough. Metropolitan M.H., April 8, 1907.

WRONG MAN IN THE RIGHT PLACE, THE. F. Morton. Princess's, April 10, 1871.

WRONG MISS GORDON, THE. F. Bert Danson. Canterbury T.R., April 25, 1904.

WRONG MR. WRIGHT, THE. F. 3 a. Geo. H. Broadhurst. Eastbourne Devonshire Park T., November 2, 1899; Strand, November 6, 1899.

WRONG ROOM, THE. Sk. O. Ashley. Ladbroke H., July 18, 1907.

WRONG SIDE OF THE ROAD, THE. Duol. F. Howell Evans. Hammersmith Lyric, November 29, 1905 (C.P.).

WRONGED. See *Through the Furnace.*

WRONGED RIGHTED, THE. P. 2 a. Winwood Jones.

WRONGS OF POLAND. Victoria, February 1865.

WUNDAHWATTE; OR, THE PRINCESS'S DREAM. C.O. 2 a. J. E. Gravelins. M by Ernest G. Scott. Stoke Newington St. Andrew's Parish R., February 8, 1901.

WYAT'S HISTORY. Thos. Dekker and M. Webster. Pr. 1607.

WYLLARD'S WEIRD. C.D. Pro. and 3 a. Dr. Harry Lobb. F. on Miss Braddon's novel. Criterion, December 29, 1887.

WYTLES. Anon. Entered on books of the Stationers' Co. 1560. N.p.

X

X.L.C.; OR, TOO BALLET AWFUL FOR WORDS. Sk. Arr. by Paul Martinetti. London Pavilion, November 13, 1905. (Water Rats' *Matinée.*)

X. Y. Z. F. 2 a. Geo. Colman, junr. 1810. C.G.; D.L., March 3, 1827.

XERXES. T. Colley Cibber. L.I.F. House, by His Maj. Servants, 1699.

XIMENA; OR, THE HEROIC DAUGHTER. T. Colley Cibber. Taken fr. Corneille. C.G.; Little T.; D.L., November 1, 1718.

XIMENES. T. Percival Stockdale. 1788.

Y

YACHTING CRUISE, THE. F. C. Burnand. Gal. of Illus., April 2, 1866.

YAID A NAIN. P. Richd. Williams. Hulme T.H., December 5, 1908.

YAMA YAMA LAND. P. Pro. and 4 a. Grace Duffie Boylan. Ladbroke H., September 15, 1909.

YANKEE HOUSEKEEPER, THE. F. D.L., April 25, 1856.

YANKEE PEDLAR; OR, OLD TIMES IN VIRGINIA, THE. Local characteristic sk. 1 a. By Author of *Nervous Man*. D.L., November 1, 1836.

YAP YAPS, THE. Sk. 3 sc. Fred Karno and J. Hickory Wood. Margate Hipp., November 30, 1908; Paragon, December 7, 1908.

YARD ARM AND YARD ARM. Petite pièce. 1 a. Hay., September 8, 1806. N.p.

YARICO. Past. D. Anon. Mentioned in Mr. Oulton's list.

YARN SPINNERS, THE. Duol. Tom Craven. Southend Pier Pav., June 29, 1908.

YASHMAK, THE. M.P. 2 a. Cecil Raleigh and Seymour Hicks. M. by Napoleon Lambelet. Shaftesbury, March 31, 1897.

YE FANCY FAYRE. M. Sk. Corney Grain. St. George's H., May 30, 1881.

YE GOOD OLD DAYS. V. 1 a. Edgar Raymond. M. by John Ansell. Surrey Masonic H., April 28, 1897.

YE LADYE OF LYONS. Burl. Alf. Lewis Clifton. Great Yarmouth Aquarium, April 10, 1882.

YE LEGENDE; OR, THE FOUR PHANTOMS. C. 3 a. H. P. Grattan. Imperial, September 22, 1883.

YE MERRIE ENGLAND; OR, THE DAYS OF THE SECOND CHARLES. D. Geo. Webb. Liverpool T.R., November 12, 1877.

YE PLAYHOUSE PLOT. C. 1 a. Maude Thompson. St. Leonards Pier, April 5, 1906 (C.P.).

YE WYN-WYN-WU. F. J. T. McArdle. Olympic, November 17, 1875.

YEAR DOT, THE. Prehistoric Pant. Sk. C. Baldwin. Wallsend R., August 31, 1905. (C.p.)

YELLOW BOY. Extrav. West Hartlepool, T.R., May 16, 1883.

YELLOW CAT, THE. D. Epis. 2 tab. "M. B." and "B. B." Metropole, September 14, 1903.

YELLOW DREAD, THE. Modern Chinese D. 4 a. Ilett Ray. Seacombe Irving T., February 29, 1904.

YELLOW DWARF, THE. Burl. G. à Beckett. Princess's, December 26, 1842.

YELLOW DWARF, THE Burl. Extrav. Robert Reece and Alfred Thompson. Her M., December 30, 1882.

YELLOW DWARF; OR, THE GOOD SOVEREIGN AND THE GOOD YELLOW BOY, THE. Burl. Frank Hall. Philharmonic, March 29, 1880.

YELLOW DWARF AND THE RING OF THE GOLD MINES, THE. Fairy Extrav. 1 a. J. R. Planche. Olympic, December 26, 1854.

YELLOW FOG ISLAND, THE. M. Extrav. Arthur Sturgess. M. arr. by Napoleon Lambelet, with seven songs imitated fr. the French by W. H. C. Nation. Terry's, September 29, 1906

YELLOW KIDS, THE. F. Barnett. Adelphi, October, 1835.

YELLOW PASSPORT, THE. D. Pro. and 4 a. Henry Neville. Olympic, November 7, 1868.

YELLOW PERIL, THE. P. 1 a. Edward Ferris and Paul Heriot. (Orig. prod. at the Grand T., Fulham, under the title of *Val of the 25th*, on July 2, 1900.) Margate Grand, September 13, 1900; Vaudeville, September 19, 1900.

YELLOW ROSES. Dr. Sk. 1 a. Sir Chas. L. Young, Bart. High Wycombe, January 14, 1878; Scarborough Royal Hotel, December 16, 1878.

YELLOW TERROR, THE. Melo-d. 4 a. C. A. Clarke and Harry H. Spiers. Barnsley, September, 1900; Manchester St. James's T., October 1, 1900.

YEOMAN OF THE GUARD; OR, THE MERRYMAN AND HIS MAID, THE. C.O. 2 a. W. S. Gilbert. M. by A. Sullivan. Savoy, October 3, 1888; May 5, 1897; rev. Savoy, December 8, 1907; Savoy, March 1, 1909.

YEOMAN'S DAUGHTER, THE. D. M. by Mr. Howes. Lyceum playbill, July 14, 1834.

YEOMAN'S DAUGHTER, THE. Dom. D. 2 a. T. J. Searle. Adelphi.

YEOMAN'S SERVICE. Dom. C. 1 a. T. Edgar Pemberton. Novelty, September 19, 1885.

YES OR NO. M.F. J. Pocock. M. by Chas. Smith. Hay., 1808.

YES OR NO. C. 3 a. Emily Beauchamp. Dublin T.R. May 2, 1877; King's Cross, December 7, 1878; Strand, December 8, 1897.

YES OR NO. Duol. Portman Rooms, Baker Street, June 16, 1892.

YEW TREE RUINS; OR, THE WRECK, THE MISER, AND THE MINES. Dom. D. 3 a. J. T. Haines. January 11, 1841.

YGRAINE. T. 4 a. Miss E. Hamilton Moore. Manchester Queen's T., May 14, 1904.

YIV AND THE BLUE WOLF. Rom. P. 1 a. Stephen Bond. Notting Hill Coronet, March 9, 1903.

Y'LANG Y'LANG, THE FAIR MAID OF TOO BLOO. Chinese Extrav. Lib. by G. Manchester Cohen. M. by John W. Ivimey. Normansfeld, Hampton Wick, January 5, 1893.

YNKLE AND YARIEO. T. See *Inkle*, etc.

YO, YEA; OR, THE FRIENDLY TARS. O. Dibdin.

YORICK, THE KING'S JESTER. P. C. A. Somerset. Victoria, September, 1836.

YORICK'S LOVE. T.D. 3 a. Adap. fr. the Spanish by W. D. Howells. (Prod. in America.) Lyceum, April 12, 1884.

YORK PLAYS. See "Miracle Plays."

YORKSHIRE GAMESTER, THE. Monol.

YORKSHIRE GENTLEWOMAN AND HER SON, THE. T. Geo. Chapman. Entered on the books of the Stationers' Co. January 29, 1660. Destroyed by Warburton's servant.

YORKSHIRE GHOST, THE. C. 5 a. By Margravine of Anspach. Brandenburgh House. 1794. N.p.

YORKSHIRE LASS, A. D. 4 a. J. Wilton Jones. Olympic, February 18, 1891.

YORKSHIRE TRAGEDY, A. Anon. 1604. At one time pr. with the name of William Shakespeare. Globe, 1608.

YOU AND I. M.F. Seymour Hicks. Lyrics by Aubrey Hopwood. M. by Walter Slaughter. Vaudeville, April 24, 1901.

YOU CAN'T MARRY YOUR GRANDMOTHER. F. 1 a. Publ. by S. French, Ltd.

YOU MAY LIKE IT OR LET IT ALONE. Afterpiece. Lord Delaval's private T. 1791.

YOU MUST BE BURIED. C. Extrav. 1 a. Hay., August 11, 1827.

YOU MUSTN'T LAUGH. F.C. 3 a. Fr. the Russian by Gospodin A. Lubimoff. Op. C., November 5, 1892.

YOU NEVER CAN TELL. P. 3 a. G. Bernard Shaw. Strand, May 2, 1900; Court, June 12, 1900; rev. Court, July 9, 1906; Savoy, September 16, 1907.

YOU NEVER KNOW. F. Absurdity. 3 a. G. Dayle. Gaiety, November 28, 1899 (C.P.); Birkenhead Metropole, September 26, 1902; Hammersmith King's, May 12, 1905.

YOUNG ACTRESS, THE. Dion Boucicault. D.L., May 30, 1856.

YOUNG ADMIRAL, THE. T.C. James Shirley. Private House in D.L., 1637.

YOUNG AND HANDSOME. Fairy Extrav. 1 a. F. on Countess of Murat's fairy tale, *Jeune et Belle*, by J. R. Planchi. Olympic, October 26, 1856.

YOUNG APPRENTICE; OR, THE WATCHWORDS OF OLD LONDON, THE. D. 3 a. C. H. Hazlewood. Britannia, March 9, 1868.

YOUNG BURGLAR, THE. P. 1 a. Kennington P.O.W., April 22, 1891.

YOUNG COUPLE, THE. F. Miss Pope. Taken fr. the C. *Discovery*. April 21, 1767. N.p. D.L., October 27, 1857.

YOUNG COUPLE, THE. C. French piece. M. Scribe.

YOUNG COUPLES. Ca. 2 a. J. H. Johnstone. Gaiety, February 20, 1864.

YOUNG DICK WHITTINGTON. Burl. Extrav. J. Wilton Jones. Leicester T.R., April 18, 1881.

YOUNG DICK WHITTINGTON. Burl. Sk. H. T. Hayes. Collins's, March 23, 1896.

YOUNG ENGLAND. J. M. Morton. Hay.

YOUNG ENGLAND. P. 3 a. Mary Woodifield and H. Courthope. West Kensington St. Andrew's Hall, June 27, 1903.

YOUNG FOLKS, THE. P. 1 a. Edward Rose. Wimbledon Baths, October 21, 1895.

YOUNG FOLKS' WAYS. C. 4 a. Mrs. Burnett and W. H. Gillette. Prod. in America as *Esmeralda*. St. James's, October 20, 1883.

YOUNG FRA DIAVOLO, THE TERROR OF TERRACINA. Burl. Henry J. Byron. Gaiety, November 18, 1878.

YOUNG HUSBANDS. C. 2 a. J. Daly. Sadler's Wells, August, 1852.

YOUNG HUSSAR; OR, LOVE AND MERCY, THE. Op. piece. W. Dimond. D.L., 1807.

YOUNG HYPOCRITE, THE. C. Transl. fr. the French by Samuel Foote. 1762.

YOUNG KING; OR, THE MISTAKE, THE. Mrs. Behn. F. on Gomberville's *Cleopatre*. Duke's T., 1683.

YOUNG LAD FROM THE COUNTRY, A. F. 1 a. J. Oxenford. D.L., November 26, 1864.

YOUNG LIEUTENANT, THE. C.O. H. Dawson and A. F. Allen Towers. Lyrics by H. Dawson. M. by R. A. Smith. Newcastle-on-Tyne T., May 28. 1906 (amat.); Woolwich Artillery, May 20, 1907.

YOUNG MAN IN GREEN; OR, THE VOLUNTEER REVIEW, THE. F. T. J. Williams. Lyceum, February 1, 1869.

YOUNG MAN OF THE PERIOD, THE. F. J. T. Douglass. Standard, July 5, 1869.

YOUNG MEN AND OLD WOMEN. F. 2 a. Mrs. Inchbald. Hay., June 30, 1792.

YOUNG MR. YARDE. F.C. 3 a. Harold Ellis and Paul Rubens. Buxton Pav. T., August 15, 1898; Richmond T.R., August 22, 1898; Royalty, November 2, 1898.

YOUNG MRS. WINTHROP. C. 4 a. Bronson Howard. Marylebone T.R., September 21, 1882 (C.P.); Court, November 6, 1884.

YOUNG MOTHER, THE. C.D. 1 a. Chas. Silby. Hay., February 28, 1859.

YOUNG PRETENDER, A. C. 3 a. Barton White. Ramsgate Amphitheatre, July 3, 1890; Op.C., December 10, 1891.

YOUNG PRETENDER, THE. Ca. James Belverstone. Dundee T.R., June 29, 1874; Blackburn T.R., September 30, 1878.

YOUNG QUAKER, THE. C. 5 a. John O'Keefe. 1783. Lyceum, June 26, 1820; Hay., 1824.

YOUNG RECRUIT, THE. Pavilion, November 28, 1860.

YOUNG RECRUIT, THE. Burl. O. 3 a. B. C. Stephenson and Sir Augustus Harris. M. by Leopold Wenzel. Newcastle Tyne T., March 14, 1892; Grand, June 13, 1892.

YOUNG RIP VAN WINKLE. Burl. Robert Reece. Folly, April 17, 1876.

YOUNG TRAMP, A. C.D. Pro. and 3 a. W. G. Wills. Bristol Prince's T., September 12, 1885.

YOUNG WIDOW, THE. F. 1 a. J. T. G. Rodwell. Adelphi T., November 1, 1824.

YOUNG WIFE, A. C. 4 a. A. Lubimoff. Vaudeville, July 1, 1884.

YOUNG WIVES AND OLD HUSBANDS. C. 3 a. Richard Harris. Op.C., December 16, 1876.

YOUNGER BROTHER. C. Anon. Ent. on books of Stationers' Co., November 29, 1653. N.p.

YOUNGER BROTHER; OR, THE AMOROUS JILT, THE. C. Mrs. Alfred Behn. Alt. by Chas. Gildon. T.R., 1696. See *The Amorous Jilt*.

YOUNGER BROTHER; OR, THE SHAM MARQUIS. C. Anon. 1719.

YOUNGER GENERATION, THE. P. 1 a. Netta Syrett. Terry's, February 3, 1907.

YOUNGER SON, THE. C. 4 a. R. S. Sievier. Gaiety, June 9, 1893.

YOUNGEST OF THE ANGELS, THE. P. 1 a. Adap. by Maurice Hewlett fr. one of his novels. Court, February 27, 1907.

YOUNGEST OF THREE, THE. Rom. P. 4 a. H. F. Maltby. Jersey O.H., July 28, 1905; Worthing T.R., March 8, 1907; Crystal Palace, March 18, 1907.

YOUNGSTER'S ADVENTURE, A. Sk. 1 a. John S. Clarke. Strand, August 19, 1895.

YOUR FIVE GALLANTS. C. Thos. Middleton. Pr. 1607. See *Five Witty Gallants*.

YOUR LIFE'S IN DANGER. F. 1 a. J. M. Morton. Hay. T., October 29, 1848.

YOUR LIKENESS ONE SHILLING. F. 1 a. Publ. by S. French, Ltd.

YOUR OBEDIENT SERVANT. Inc. Lewis Ransome. Cry. Pal., July 1, 1909.

YOUR ONLY SARAH. F. A. E. Siedle. Swansea Grand T., September 21, 1904. (C.P.)

YOUR PHOTO WHILE YOU WAIT. Sk. Rose D'Evelyn. Dulwich Imperial H., January 9, 1905.

YOUR VOTE AND INTEREST. F. Alfred Maltby. Court T., February 4, 1874.

YOUR WIFE. F.C. 3 a. Adap. by Justin Huntly M'Carthy fr. *Prête moi ta Femme.* Paris Palais Royal, September, 1883; St. James's, June 26, 1890.

YOURS, OR MINE? M.E. Tobin. C.G., September 23, 1816.

YOURS TILL DEATH. D. 4 a. Mortimer Murdock. Pav., November 2, 1878.

YOUTH. Morality. Anon. 1549.

YOUTH. D. 8 tab. Paul Meritt and Augustus Harris. D.L., August 6, 1881.

YOUTH, LOVE, AND FOLLY. F. 1 a D.L., March 1, 1855.

YOUTH, LOVE, AND FOLLY; OR, THE LITTLE JOCKEY. C.O. 2 a. W. Dimond. D.L., 1805.

YOUTH'S COMEDY; OR, THE SOUL'S TRYALS AND TRIUMPHS. By the author of *Youth's Tragedy.* 1680.

YOUTH'S GLORY AND DEATH'S BANQUET. T. 2 parts Duchess of Newcastle. 1662.

YOUTH'S TRAGEDY. Dr. Poem. T. S. 1671.

YOUTHFUL DAYS OF GIL BLAS, THE. O.D. 2 a. Condensed ver. of *Gil Blas.* Lyceum playbill, September 6, 1822.

YOUTHFUL MARTYRS OF ROME. Oakley. 1856.

YOUTHFUL QUEEN; OR, CHRISTINE OF SWEDEN, THE. C. 2 a. Chas. Shannon. D.L., October 24, 1828.

YULE LOG, THE. F. 1 a. Ben Webster, jun. Adelphi, February 17, 1873.

YVETTE. M.P. without words. 4 a. M. Carré and Rémond and Audré Gedalge. Avenue, September 12, 1891.

YVETTE. Ver. 5 a. Pierre Berton, of Guy Maupassant's novel (MM. Felix Riche and Louis Hillier's French season). Avenue, June 22, 1904.

YVONNE. D. Kyrle Bellew. Richmond H.M.T., March 5, 1881.

YZDRA. T. 3 a. Louis V. Ledoux. Wyndham's, March 26, 1908 (C.P.).

Z

ZAIRE. T. Voltaire. 1733. See *Zara.*

ZAIRE. O. Winter. 1815.

ZAIS. O. 4 a. and Pro. Rameau. February 29, 1748.

ZAMEO. M.D. Victoria, October, 1834.

ZAMET; OR, BONNIE BOHEMIA. D. 4 a. Wybert Clive. Gateshead Royal, August 12, 1891. See *The Roman's Revenge.*

ZAMPA. O. Hérold. 1791-1833 (Paris, 1831). Her M., May 9, 1844.

ZAMPA. English ver. of Hérold's opera. Gaiety, October 8, 1870.

ZAMPA; OR, THE BUCKANEER AND THE LITTLE DEAR. Burl. T. F. Plowman. Court, October 2, 1872.

ZAMPA; OR, THE CRUEL CORSAIR AND THE MARBLE MAID. Burl. J. F. M'Ardle. Liverpool P.O.W., October 9, 1876.

ZANA. D. 4 a. G. W. Appleton. Croydon T.R., March 16, 1885.

ZANA; OR, THE PRIDE OF THE ALHAMBRA. D. 3 a. Britannia, September 19, 1870.

ZANETTA. O. Auber. 1840.

ZANETTO. O. Mascagni. F. on François Coppée's duo *Le Passant.* 1896. Given publicly for the first time in costume in England, St. James's, December 8, 1908.

ZANGA. D. Victoria, August 22, 1877.

ZANGRIDE. Spec. D. Hull Queen's T., July 16, 1868.

ZANONE; OR, THE DEY AND THE KNIGHT. Fantastical O. 3 a. Sydney Cubitt and Thos. Hackwood. Stroud Subscription Rooms, November 8, 1899.

ZAPFENSTREICH. D. 4 a. F. A. Beyerlein. (German season.) Royalty, January 8, 1904; Great Queen Street, January 11, 1905.

ZAPHIRA. T. Francis Gentleman. Bath. 1754.

ZAPOLYA. T. Coleridge. 1817. Fd. on *The Winter's Tale.*

ZAPPHIRA. T. 3 a. Anon. 1792.

ZARA. T. Transl. fr. Voltaire's *Zaïre.* By Aaron Hill, D.L., 1734; Johnson, 1735; and Dr. Francklin.

ZARAH, THE GIPSY. Rom. D. 2 a. Geo. Soane, A.B. Queen's T., October, 1835.

ZARTLICHEN VERWANDTEN, DIE. C. Roderick Benedia. St. George's H., October 24, 1900; Great Queen Street T., December 11, 1903.

ZAUBERFLOTE, DIE. O. Mozart. September 30, 1791; D.L., March 25, 1814. Lib. by E. Schikaneder. Although actually wr. before *La Clemanza,* Mozart's last work.

ZAZA. P. 5 a. David Belasco. Fr. Pierre Barton and Chas. Simon's P. Paris Vaudeville, May 12, 1898; Garrick, April 16, 1900.

ZAZA. O. 4 a. Ruggiero Leoncavallo. F. on *Fifi.* (Milan Liric, November 10, 1900.) Coronet, April 30, 1909.

ZELICA. O. 2 a. S. R. Philpot. Fr. Moore's *Lalla Rookh.* Brixton Gresham Hall, December 17, 1890.

ZELIDA. T. T. Horde, jun. (Oxford.) 1772.

ZELIDA; OR, THE PIRATES. C.O. 3 a. Henry Siddons. 1799. N.p.

ZELINDA. C. Calini. 1772.

ZELINDOR. O. F. Rebel and F. Francœur. 1745.

ZELMA; OR, AN INDIAN'S LOVE. D. 1 a. E. Newbound. Britannia, December 13, 1876.

ZELMA; OR, WILL O' THE WISP. Dram. Rom. Meyers. C.G., April 17, 1792.

ZELMANE; OR, THE CORINTHIAN QUEEN. T. Mountfort. L.I.F., 1705.

ZELMIRA. O. Rossini. Naples, December, 1821; King's T., January 24, 1824.

ZELOTYPUS. Latin C. Anon. MS. preserved in library of Emmanuel College, Cambridge.

ZEMBUCA; OR, THE NET-MAKER AND HIS WIFE. Dram. Rom. 2 a. Pocock. C.G., March 27, 1815.

ZEMIRE ET AZOR. O. Marmontel. M. by Grétry. December 16, 1771.

ZEMIRE ET AZOR. O. Spohr. (1784-1859.) April 4, 1819.

ZENO. Latin P. Simon. Ac. at Cambridge, 1630-1.

ZENOBIA. O. Nicola. Sala, 1761.

ZENOBIA. P. Ac. at Rose T., 1591.

ZENOBIA. O. Piccini. San Carlos, 1758.

ZENOBIA. T. Arthur Murphy. D.L., 1768.

ZENOBIA. O. John Hoole. 1800.

ZENOBIA. T. William Russell (Before 1814.) N.p.

ZENOBIA IN PALMIRA. O. Leo. Naples, 1725.

ZEPHYR. C. 4 a. Mrs. Bernard Wishaw. Avenue, March 3, 1891.

ZERAGO; OR, THE WILD TRIBE OF THE MOUNTAIN TORRENT. D. 3 a. Tunbridge Wells T.R., May 24, 1869.

ZERLINE. O. Auber. 1851.

ZILLAH. D. 5 a. Palgrave Simpson and Claude Templar. Lyceum, August 2, 1879.

ZILPHA. Rom. D. 4 a. Walter H. Jackson. Brentford Beach's H., February 24, 1887.

ZIMMERADSKI. P. 3 a. James Creed Meredith. Dublin Coffee Palace Concert H., October 21, 1896.

ZIMRI. Orat. Hawkesworth. M. by Stanley. 1760.

ZINGARA; OR, THE GIPSY, LA. Burla. Marylebone Gardens, August 21, 1773.

ZINGARO. P. 1 a. Japanese ver. of *Pygmalion and Galatea*. Coronet (mat.), May 21, 1900.

ZINGIS. T. Alex. Dow. D.L., December 17, 1768.

ZION. Cantata. N. W. Gade. (June, 1817.)

ZOBEIDE. T. Joseph Cradock. M. by J. A. Fisher. C.G., December 11, 1771.

ZOLA THE TRUTH SEEKER. D. 4 a. in Yiddish. Nahum Racknow. M. by Ferdinand Staub. Standard, August 9, 1898.

ZOLFARA, LA. The first 2 a. of a Sicilian D. in 3 a. Giusli Senople. Shaftesbury, February 7, 1908.

ZOO, THE. M. Novelty. R. Rowe. M. by Arthur Sullivan. St. James's, June 5, 1875.

ZORAIDA. T. William Hodson. D.L., December 13, 1779.

ZORAIDE DI GRANATA. O. Donizetti. 1822.

ZORIADA. O. Lib. by W. E. Unwin. M. by R. Pickel. Sidcup P.H., January 9, 1891.

ZORINSKI. 3 a. Thos. Morton. Hay., June 20, 1795.

ZOROASHAR; OR, THE SPIRIT OF THE STAR. Egyptian tale of Enchantment. M. by Cooke. D.L., April 21, 1824.

ZOROASTRE. O. 5 a. Rameau. December 5, 1749.

ZOROASTRES, THE TRAGEDY OF. Wr. by the Right Hon. the late Earl of Orrery, 1676. An early copy in MS., Sloane, 1828.

ZULIEMAN; OR, LOVE AND PENITENCE. M.D. 3 a. Bath, March 12, 1814. N.p.

ZULMA, LA. P. 4 a. P. Kester. South Shields Royal, June 5, 1905.

ZULU WAR; OR, THE FIGHT FOR THE QUEEN'S COLOURS, THE. D. 4 a. Butler Stanhope. Birkenhead T.R., June 6, 1881.

ZUMA. T. Transl. fr. the French by Thos. Rodd. 1800.

ZUMA; OR, THE TREE OF HEALTH. P. 3 a. T. Dibdin. C.G., February 21, 1818.

ZWEI GLUCKLICHE TAGE. F.C. 4 a. F. von Schönthan and G. Kadelburg. Great Queen Street, January 24, 1905.

ZWEI WAPPEN. C. 4 a. O. Blumenthal and G. Kadelburg. Great Queen Street, March 17, 1905.

ZWILLINGSBRUDER, DIE. M.F. Schubert. 1797-1828.

ZWILLINGSSCHWESTER, DIE (orig. of *The Twin Sister*, Duke of York's). C. 4 a. L. Fulda. Royalty, November 16, 1903.

LIST OF SUBSCRIBERS.

ADDENBROOKE, DR. H. H.,
Rockingham, Sparkhill, Birmingham.

ALEXANDER, GEORGE,
St. James's Theatre, King Street, S.W.

APPLIN, ARTHUR,
3, Artillery Mansions, Westminster.

ASHWELL, MISS LENA,
36, Grosvenor Street, London, S.W.

ASKEW, CLAUDE,
2H, Portman Mansions, Gloucester Place, W.

BAKER, A. C.

BARNES, J. H.,
Green Room Club, London.

BARTLETT, GEORGE,
48, St. George's Road, S.W.

BARTLETT, J. J.,
12, Angel Road, Hammersmith, W.

BEECHAM, JOSEPH,
Royal Court Theatre, Warrington.

BELLEW, KYRLE.

BENSON, F. R.,
11, Henrietta Street, W.C.

BIRMINGHAM AMATEUR OPERA SOCIETY,
Birmingham and Midland Institute, Birmingham.

BLACKLIN, RICHARD JAMES, JUNR.,
West Hartlepool.

BLACKMORE, HERBERT,
11, Garrick Street, W.C.

BLANCHE, MISS ADA,
"High Borgue," Malwood Road, Balham Hill, London, S.W.

BODIE, WALFORD,
"The Manor House," Macduff.

BOOR, FRANK,
21, Shaftesbury Avenue, London, W.

BOWLES, BENJ,
1, Guildhall Chambers, London, E.C.

BOX, FREDERICK G ,
Basingstoke.

BOYDEN, GEORGE,
"Herald" Office, Stratford-on-Avon.

BRADFORD PUBLIC LIBRARY.

BRERETON, AUSTIN.

BROADHEAD, PERCY BAYNHAM,
The Hippodrome, Manchester.

BULLOCH, J. M.,
118, Pall Mall, S.W.

BULMER, FRED,
Managers' Club, Savoy Mansions, W.C.

BUTLER, RICHARD,
"The Referee," Victoria House, Tudor Street, E.C.

BUTT, ALFRED,
Palace Theatre, W.

CAINE, HALL,
2, Whitehall Court, S.W.

CARSON, LIONEL,
16, York Street, W.C.

CARTE, D'OYLY, MRS.,
Savoy Theatre, London.

CLARKE, HARRY CORSON,
Lamb's Club, New York City, U.S.A.

COFFIN, CHARLES HAYDEN.

COLLINGHAM, GEORGE GERVASE,
33, St. Mary-at-Hill, London, E.C.

COMPTON, EDWARD,
1, Nevern Square, S.W.

COOKE, J. Y. F.,
51, Pall Mall, S.W.

COULSON, JOHN,
Theatre Royal, South Shields.

COURTNEY, W. L., M.A., LL.D.,
53, Gordon Square, W.C.

COX, ROLAND DOUGLAS,
22, Tavistock Street, W.C.

CRAVEN, ARTHUR SCOTT,
6, Comeragh Road, West Kensington.

CUMMINGS, DR. WM. H.,
Guildhall School of Music, Victoria Embankment, E.C.

CURRY, JOSEPH H.,
Prince of Wales's Theatre, Grimsby.

CURZON, FRANK,
Prince of Wales's Theatre, London.

CUTLER, MAURICE H.,
10, Grafton Road, Acton, W.

DAVEY, PETER,
Royal County Theatre, Kingston-on-Thames.

DORRILL, C. C.,
The New Theatre, Oxford.

ELDRED, ARTHUR,
61, Brixton Hill, S.W.

ELDRIDGE, WATSON,
"Ainsdale," Southport.

EMERY, EDWARD,
329, East 145th Street, New York City, U.S.A.

ESMOND, H. V.

FAIRBROTHER, MISS SYDNEY,
10, Hilldrop Crescent, N.

FENN, FREDERICK,
1, Gray's Inn Square, W.C.

FERNALD, C. B.,
London.

FISKE, STEPHEN,
Lotos Club, New York City, U.S.A.

FLINN, MADAME KATE,
11, Henrietta Street, Cavendish Square, W.

FORBES, NORMAN (ROBERTSON),
Berkeley House, Hay Hill, London, W.

FREE REFERENCE LIBRARY,
King Street, Manchester.

FROHMAN, DANIEL,
Lyceum Theatre, New York City, U.S.A.

GALSWORTHY, JOHN,
14, Addison Road, W.

GARRICK CLUB,
Garrick Street, W.C.

GEORGE, MISS MARIE,
16, Ridgmount Gardens, W.C.

GILDARD, F. GRAHAM,
32, Queen's Gate, Dowanhill, Glasgow.

GRACE, ALFRED.

GRAHAM, GEORGE,
Playgoers' Club, Clement's Inn, Strand, W.C.

GRAY, GEORGE,
Savage Club.

GREGOR, ALEX., M D.,
Tregear, Falmouth.

GREIN, J. T.,
29, Mincing Lane, E.C.

GRINFIELD, CHARLES THEODORE,
10, Ellenborough Park, Weston-super-Mare.

GROSSMITH, WEEDON,
1, Bedford Square, W.C.

GWENN, EDMUND.

HADLEY, HOWARD J.,
The National Amateur Operatic and Dramatic Association, 33, Park Avenue, Worcester.

HALLARD, C. M.,
26A, North Audley Street, W.

HARVEY, J. MARTIN,
30, Avenue Road, Regent's Park.

HENWOOD, ROGER,
33, London Road, Horsham.

HEWSON, J. JAMES,
Liverpool.

HORNIMAN, ROY.

JONES, HENRY ARTHUR,
Reform Club, London.

KELLY, W. W.,
Kelly's Theatre, Liverpool.

KENNEDY, CHARLES RANN,
New York, U.S.A.

KIDDIE, J. GAR,
Widnes.

KING, T. A.,
Norwich.

KNAPE, JOHN,
Tennyson Avenue, King's Lynn.

LAWRENCE, BOYLE,
"The Standard" Office, Shoe Lane, E.C.

LAWRENCE, W. J.,
Dublin.

LESTER, ALFRED,
Shaftesbnry Theatre, W.

LESTOCQ, W.,
Globe Theatre, London.

LINDON, MARK H.,
Theatre Royal, Stanley, co. Durham.

LOCKE, W. J.,
2, Carlyle Mansions, Cheyne Walk, S.W.

LONNON, MISS ABE,
c/o Edwin N. Low's S.S. Agency, 1,123, Broadway, New York City, U.S.A.

LORAINE, ROBERT,
51A, Conduit Street, W.

LOWNE, C. M.

LUMSDEN, HARRY, LL.B.,
Glasgow.

LYNN, NEVILLE,
"Thornleigh," Wealdstone, Harrow.

MACKAY, A. B.,
No. 1, Higson Street, Blackburn.

MACKEY, CHALMERS,
"Ashdale," Poulton-le-Fylde, Lancs.

MANCHESTER PLAYGOERS' CLUB.

MANNERS, CHARLES,
Moody-Manners Opera Co.'s Stores, "The Hyde," Hendon, London, N.W.

MARSHALL, CAPTAIN ROBERT,
3, Park Place, St. James's, S.W.

MAUDE, CYRIL,
The Playhouse, London.

MAY, AKERMAN,
Green Room Club, London.

MAYNARD, HORACE W.,
Playgoers' Club, London.

McCARTHY, JUSTIN HUNTLY.

McKINNEL, NORMAN.

McRAE, BRUCE,
"The Players," 16, Gramercy Park, New York, U.S.A.

METCALFE, JAMES S.,
"Life" Office, 17, West Thirty-first Street, New York City, U.S.A.

MILL, C. WATSON,
"Rivington," Dragon Road, Harrogate.

MORLEY, VICTOR,
Green Room Club, New York, U.S.A.

MORRITT, MISS GRETA,
17, Southwell Gardens, S.W.

MORTON, MICHAEL.

MOSS, SIR H. EDWARD,
Middleton Hall, Gorebridge, Midlothian, N.B.

MOUILLOT, FREDK.,
1 & 2, King Street, Covent Garden, W.C.

MUDDOCK, J. E. PRESTON,
"Donovan House," Nightingale Lane, London, S.W.

MULHOLLAND, J. B.,
King's Theatre, W.

NEVILLE, HENRY,
"Crescent House," Queen's Crescent, N.W.

NICHOLLS, HARRY,
Rupert Cottage, Bedford Park, W.

NIGHTINGALE, J. W.,
Great Yarmouth.

NIXON-NIRDLINGER, FRED. G.,
Park Theatre, Philadelphia, Pa., U.S.A.

NORTHWAY, ALFRED,
109, Cambridge Gardens, W.

NORWOOD, EILLE,
Savage Club, London, W.C.

PAGET, F. M.,
39, Carlton Mansions, Maida Vale, London.

PARKER, LOUIS N.,
3, Pembroke Road, Kensington, W.

PATMORE, W. J.,
10, Wellington Road, St. John's Wood, N.W.

PAULL, H. M.,
Green Room Club, London.

PAUNCEFORT, MISS CLAIRE,
239, King's Road, Chelsea, London.

PEARCE, MR. AND MRS. WALTER,
7H, Hyde Park Mansions, W.

PENLEY, WILLIAM SYDNEY,
"The Firs," Godalming.

PHILLIPS, CECIL LAWRENCE,
The Leicester Galleries, Leicester Square, W

PINERO, SIR ARTHUR,
115A, Harley Street, W.

PARSONS, MRS. ALICE.

PLAYGOERS' CLUB, THE,
6, Clement's Inn, Strand, London, W.C.

POEL, WILLIAM,
London.

POUNDS, COURTICE.

PROWSE, R. O.,
47, St. Quintin's Avenue, W.

RALEIGH, CECIL,
2, Brunswick Place, Regent's Park, N.W.

REES, B. PERCY,
Llanelly.

REEVE, MISS ADA,
Chideock, Dorset.

RIGNOLD, LIONEL.

ROBBINS, ALFRED EDWARD,
109, Cambridge Gardens, W.

ROBBINS, ALFRED F.,
"Dunheved," Villa Road, S.W.

ROBERTS, R. A.

ROCK, CHARLES.

ROSS, ADRIAN.

ROSS, GILBERT B.,
Hollingworth, Cheshire.

RONAN, E. P.,
Theatre Royal, Wexford.

SAVAGE, EDWARD J.,
Aberdeen.

SAVAGE, HENRY W.,
New York, U.S.A.

SEEBOLD, CARL ADOLF,
Theatre Royal, Worthing.

SELWYN AND CO.,
1,451, Broadway, New York City, U.S.A.

SCUTT, CHARLES E.,
Gaiety Theatre, Hastings.

SHAW, G. BERNARD,
10, Adelphi Terrace, London, W.C.

SIMS, GEORGE R.,
12, Clarence Terrace, Regent's Park, N.W.

SMITH, WINCHELL,
New York, N.Y., U.S.A.

SPENCE, EDWARD F.,
75, Bedford Court Mansions, Bedford Square, W.C.

SPENCER, T. H.,
Camberwell, London.

STAFFORD, EUGENE C.,
Bishopsdale Farm, Biddenden, Kent.

ST. JOHN, MISS AMY,
10, Milton Chambers, Cheyne Walk, Chelsea, S.W.

STOLL, OSWALD.

SUTRO, ALFRED.

TALBOT, HOWARD,
2, Piccadilly Chambers, Coventry Street, W.

TREE, SIR HERBERT BEERBOHM.

TURNER, ALFRED,
The Playhouse, Charing Cross.

TWYFORD, J. HENRY,
22A, Craven Hill Gardens, Lancaster Gate, W.

URWICK, H.,
St. Quentin, Malvern.

VANBRUGH, MISS VIOLET,
26, Langham Street, Portland Place, W.

VEDRENNE, J. E.,
52, Shaftesbury Avenue, London, W.

WALLER, LEWIS,
Lyric Theatre, W.

WATERS, JAMES,
"Carmelite House," Carmelite Street, E.C.

WELCH, JAMES,
Green Room Club, London.

WELFORD, DALLAS,
549, Riverside Drive, New York City, U.S.A.

WELLER, BERNARD,
44, Abbey Road, N.W.

WHITE, J. FISHER,
8, Holly Terrace, Highgate, N.

WYATT, T. R.,
Jackdaw D.C.

ZANGWILL, ISRAEL.